Limited-Overs International Cricket
The Complete Record

Limited-Overs International Cricket
The Complete Record

Bill Frindall

HEADLINE

First published in 1997
by HEADLINE BOOK PUBLISHING

10 9 8 7 6 5 4 3 2 1

C.I.P data is available from the British Library

ISBN 0 7472 1173 6

Typeset by
Letterpart Limited, Reigate, Surrey

Printed and bound in Great Britain by
Mackays of Chatham plc, Chatham, Kent

HEADLINE BOOK PUBLISHING
A division of Hodder Headline PLC
338 Euston Road
London NW1 3BH

CONTENTS

PREFACE

The first limited-overs international was a hastily arranged affair, played on the final scheduled day of a rain-aborted Test match to appease a disappointed Melbourne public. By coincidence, it not only took place on the very ground where Test cricket had begun 94 years earlier, but it also resulted in an Australian victory against England. More significantly it attracted 46,000 spectators, produced receipts of $A33,000, and began a revolution in international cricket.

When Australia toured England the following year, three limited-overs internationals replaced the extra (sixth) Test previously agreed by the respective Boards. Four years later, by which time a mere 18 internationals had been played (in Australia, England, New Zealand and Wales), cricket's inaugural World Cup was staged. Compared with the five-week, 42-match, 12-nation extravaganza planned for 1999, this was a very modest affair involving just 15 matches and five playing days.

The most far-reaching innovation in professional cricket this century has been the limited-overs format of the game. Instant cricket was conceived in the late Fifties to arrest the financial decline of the English county game. Attendances at the only inter-county competition in Britain, the County Championship, had fallen dramatically since the halcyon days immediately after the Second World War. From two million in 1950, the total attendance at county matches fell to 700,000 in 1963, the season when the first one-day county competition, the Gillette Cup, was introduced. An MCC committee had been set up in 1956 to examine the decline in attendances and the general tempo of the game. It was this committee, under the chairmanship of H.S.Altham, which proposed a limited-overs knock-out tournament. This revolutionary concept was certainly not palatable to many administrators either at Lord's or around the counties, but the desperate financial position of the county game demanded urgent action.

The format of the Gillette Cup was fine-tuned in 1962, when a three-match pilot scheme, the Midlands Knock-Out Cup, sponsored by Leicestershire and featuring four counties, was held at Leicester and Trent Bridge in May. Each innings was restricted to 65 overs with no bowler allowed to deliver more than 15. In the final, no limit was placed on the number of overs permitted to each bowler. This led to slow bowlers having scant say in the proceedings and was swiftly remedied when the rules of the Gillette Cup were drafted.

Limited-overs cricket had been born. Traditionalists were alarmed and many still are. Sir Neville Cardus wanted it named ' "Snicket" or "Slogget" but don't call it Cricket'. In its infancy it was considered to be little more than a bit of fun at the end of the season. Nobody took it seriously except the county treasurers. It took an Australian television magnate, Kerry Packer, to develop and repackage the instant game and unleash a monster which seriously threatens traditional Test cricket. It was Packer and his associates who turned the staid English version of the abridged game into a colourful pageant to capture an Australian television audience schooled on fast, action-packed sports such as Australian Rules Football and American Baseball. The dramatic advent of floodlit cricket, with such attendant innovations as white balls, black sightscreens and coloured clothing, was instantly popular. Australia's climate was ideal for late evening illuminated sport and the sight of the sun setting behind the clock tower of Sydney Cricket Ground's only surviving Victorian stand is quite breathtaking.

After two seasons of rebel cricket, dubbed 'The Packer Circus', the Australian Cricket Board made their peace and the schism ended. Television had won the battle and dictated terms. On 27 November 1979, cricket's inaugural *World* Series (*The World* was an American boxing publication) was launched, with Sydney staging the first official floodlit cricket international. The tally of internationals accelerated from that day. At that point, nearly nine years after the inaugural game, it stood at a mere 74. Skilful marketing produced a headlong proliferation of tournaments so that nine years later the total had reached 534, a tally which was to double in just over eight years. In 1984-85 Australia hosted 31 internationals during a period of just nine weeks, an astonishing display of overkill which threatened the rarity value of the four-yearly World Cup. With South Africa returning to the ICC fold and full member status being bestowed upon Sri Lanka and Zimbabwe, the growth of series and tournaments has continued unabated. Over 100 internationals have been staged in the extraordinary desert setting of Sharjah, and other associate ICC members such as Bangladesh, Singapore and Canada have hosted tournaments in recent months. The average number of internationals has risen to over 100 per year and poses a serious threat not only to the balance of the two forms of international cricket but to the physical and mental welfare of the cricketers themselves.

In 1985, in partnership with Hampshire's scorer, Vic Isaacs, I produced the forerunner of this compendium. It covered 329 of the first 331 matches, two dubious games, the Bushfire Appeal (*LOI No. 192*) and the 'Portmanteau Affair' (*LOI No. 269*) being subsequently accepted as bone fide internationals. The logistical hazards of hauling more than 1000 scorecards, and their attendant records, in cases full of looseleaf binders, up to commentary box eyries convinced me that a new book was needed. So too did the growing poularity of this form of cricket, and the number of requests for an authoritative reference work.

The first problem involved finding a format to house 1116 scores in a binder that would not be so large as to require a handle. Headline's sports publisher, Ian Marshall, aided by his design team, eventually found a satisfactory format for fitting two scores on each page.

Vic Isaacs and his son Richard, statistician/scorers both, supplied the basic scores and records on disk. My task was to check them against many sources, including my own scoresheets in 133 instances, denote floodlit matches, add award winners, debutants, number of appearances for umpires and fine tune the overall presentation. In the early days, many of these internationals were scored on loose sheets or in reserve scorebooks and the original records have gone astray or been destroyed. In numerous cases, the two official records do not agree or contain obvious errors. Often specialist scorers are not available and players or occasional amateurs are drafted in. Even such a recent and high-profile tournament as the 1996 World Cup produced a host of scoring errors and differences. With the help of Philip Bailey, Rajesh Kumar, Mohandas Menon, Allan Miller, Mohammad Ali Jafri, Harriet Monkhouse, Francis Payne, Andrew Samson, Cheryl Styles, Sa'adi Thawfeeq and John Ward solutions, many pluralist ones, were found.

Limited-overs cricket is all about scoring rates and, with only one innings per side, the layout we adopted could easily house additional columns for balls faced and numbers of fours/sixes hit. Only in the past two or three years have publications included such data and I did not expect to complete these details for more than 70% of the matches, especially as the early ones were not scored in the linear method which accurately records the number of balls faced. Thanks to the efforts of many contributors, more than 90% have been found and, in addition to most of those named above, grateful thanks are due to Jack Cameron, Ross Dundas, Ric Finlay, Jo King, Laurel Kirton, Ben Lawrence, Mubashir Ali Zaidi, Shahzad Ali Khan, Tariq Ali, Warwick Torrens, Charlie Wat and Wendy Wimbush. Correspondence from readers who can fill any of the remaining blanks before the next edition will be most welcome. Many of the balls/boundaries details have come from sources other than the official scorebooks. Some of those involving matches played in the Antipodes may have included wides as balls received. Although I understand that an official of the ICC recently asserted in an e-mail response to a statistician in Australia that wides should be counted as balls received, that is a view which I vehemently oppose, as does the game's law-makers, the MCC. It is patently unfair to include wides as balls received by a batsman for the obvious reason that he cannot add to his individual score from them. If a batsman hits a 'wide' the umpire must revoke his call. The only purpose served in recording the number of balls faced is to measure accurately the length of a batsman's innings. Interruptions and variable over rates make measurement by time a lottery and I have not included minutes batted in my scores. For those who respond with the old chestnut involving a batsman being stumped first ball off a wide, my reply is that he has been out without facing a ball, a fate suffered by more than a score of batsmen run out in the matches in this volume. I have not included 'fives' scored by batsmen because these are the result of fielding misadventures and not usually the reward for substantial hits.

Clive Hitchcock, the ICC's Administration Officer, has been unfailingly helpful, even combing his files to identify the early match referees. And it is with no disrespect for him or the International Cricket Council that, in addition to the wides issue, I strongly oppose another of their recent edicts. This concerns void matches. During the span of this book three matches have begun but been abandoned, declared void and replaced by a new match played on the following (reserve) day. When this situation first arose in county limited-overs competitions, the Test and County Cricket Board consulted me in making their ruling which remains that such aborted contests should not be included in any records, team or individual. The ICC upheld that view when the three matches in question were played and the organisers publicly confirmed that action in each case. A recent ICC meeting apparently – it was not made public at the time – reversed their ruling and decided that they should be included. Such action is unacceptable to most chroniclers and it will be of no surprise that The Association of Cricket Statisticians and Historians, of which I am a member, has excluded these abandoned and void games from the records in their current year book. For the record, the recently formed English Cricket Board has confirmed that such games will continue to be excluded from our domestic limited-overs records. Scores of the games in question, which would involve the ludicrous addition of 66 international caps for abandoned matches involving 29.5 overs of play, are included as a grumbling appendix to this book.

An asterisk (*) denotes the team's captain in the scores, and a not out innings or unbroken partnership in the records. A dagger (†) signifies the appointed wicket-keeper. The matches are arranged chronologically by series or tournament, with each having a reference number to show its position in the general order and its place in the matches between the two teams involved: e.g. 1024/75 is the 1024th match listed and was the 75th contest between Australia and West Indies. In recent years, Sri Lanka has expanded its season to host countries out of their own summers and some matches have been played there during the English season. The order of these has been dealt with individually. The five matches staged in Toronto in September 1996 produced a new problem as the North American season coincides with Britain's and they were played in 1996 as opposed to 1996-97 as were those staged a few weeks earlier in Colombo under the banner of the Singer World Series. To avoid confusion, the Test match seniority of countries has been retained in arranging the order of match titles on neutral territory and in organising the Records section, Individual Career Records and Index of Cricketers.

Throughout, the term 'international' refers to a limited-overs international and not to a Test match. The erroneous appellation 'one-day international' will not appear again. All these matches have been limited-overs affairs, some more limited than others, not all have been completed on a single day. In fact, 17 have involved play on two days, another 11 have been played on the reserve day after the original one was washed out, and then there were those three void and replayed . . .

My thanks to Wendy Wimbush for compiling the invaluable Index of Cricketers, to my wife Debbie for inputting it on to disk and checking several editions of proofs, to Gordon Burling for expertly 'nit-picking' the entire work, to Chris Leggett and his typesetting team at Letterpart and to Ian Marshall and Headline for commissioning and masterminding the entire project.

BILL FRINDALL
Urchfont
26 June 1997

Limited-Overs Internationals
1970-71 to 1996

AUSTRALIA v ENGLAND 1970-71

At Melbourne Cricket Ground on 5 January 1971.   Result: **AUSTRALIA** won by 5 wickets.   Toss: Australia.
Award: J.H.Edrich.   LOI debuts: All.   40 eight-ball overs match.

See *Preface*. John Edrich, scorer of the first fifty in these internationals, was adjudged the first international Man of the Match by C.S. (Charles) Elliott, the Derbyshire batsman and Test umpire who was visiting Australia on a Churchill Fellowship. Cowdrey, Shuttleworth, Connolly, Lawry, McKenzie and Thomson (Alan) each made their only LOI appearance.

ENGLAND		Runs	Balls	4/6
G.Boycott	c Lawry b Thomson	8	37	–
J.H.Edrich	c Walters b Mallett	82	119	4
K.W.R.Fletcher	c G.S.Chappell b Mallett	24	47	1
B.L.D'Oliveira	run out	17	16	1
J.H.Hampshire	c McKenzie b Mallett	10	13	–
M.C.Cowdrey	c Marsh b Stackpole	1	5	–
* R.Illingworth	b Stackpole	1	7	–
† A.P.E.Knott	b McKenzie	24	31	1
J.A.Snow	b Stackpole	2	16	–
K.Shuttleworth	c Redpath b McKenzie	7	19	–
P.Lever	not out	4	6	–
Extras	(b 1, lb 9)	10		
Total	(39.4 overs)	**190**		

AUSTRALIA		Runs	Balls	4/6
* W.M.Lawry	c Knott b Illingworth	27	49	–
K.R.Stackpole	c and b Shuttleworth	13	15	2
I.M.Chappell	st Knott b Illingworth	60	103	5/1
K.D.Walters	c Knott b D'Oliveira	41	51	6
I.R.Redpath	b Illingworth	12	14	1
G.S.Chappell	not out	22	29	1
† R.W.Marsh	not out	10	18	2
A.A.Mallett				
G.D.McKenzie				
A.N.Connolly				
A.L.Thomson				
Extras	(lb 4, w 1, nb 1)	6		
Total	(34.6 overs; 5 wickets)	**191**		

AUSTRALIA	O	M	R	W
McKenzie	7.4	0	22	2
Thomson	8	2	22	1
Connolly	8	0	62	0
Mallett	8	1	34	3
Stackpole	8	0	40	3

ENGLAND	O	M	R	W
Snow	8	0	38	0
Shuttleworth	7	0	29	1
Lever	5.6	0	30	0
Illingworth	8	1	50	3
D'Oliveira	6	1	38	1

FALL OF WICKETS
1-21, 2-87, 3-124, 4-144, 5-148, 6-152, 7-156, 8-171, 9-183, 10-190

FALL OF WICKETS
1-19, 2-51, 3-117, 4-158, 5-165

Umpires: T.F.Brooks (1) and L.P.Rowan (1).

ENGLAND v AUSTRALIA 1972

At Old Trafford, Manchester, on 24 August 1972.   Result: **ENGLAND** won by 6 wickets.   Toss: Australia.
Award: D.L.Amiss.   LOI debuts: England – D.L.Amiss, G.G.Arnold, D.B.Close, A.W.Greig, R.A.Woolmer; Australia – R.Edwards, D.K.Lillee, R.A.L.Massie, A.P.Sheahan, G.D.Watson.   55-over match.

The first official limited-overs international in England attracted 11,000 spectators. They saw Dennis Amiss celebrate his debut with the first LOI hundred (off 130 balls in the 46th over) and share with Keith Fletcher the first hundred partnership, the pair adding 125 in 86 minutes off 160 balls. Adjudicator Cyril Washbrook was spared a testing task.

AUSTRALIA		Runs	Balls	4/6
K.R.Stackpole	c D'Oliveira b Greig	37	62	6
G.D.Watson	b Arnold	0	1	–
* I.M.Chappell	b Woolmer	53	75	5
G.S.Chappell	b Woolmer	40	66	3
R.Edwards	run out	57	84	6
A.P.Sheahan	b Arnold	6	9	–
K.D.Walters	lbw b Woolmer	2	7	–
† R.W.Marsh	c Close b Snow	11	17	1
A.A.Mallett	not out	6	15	–
D.K.Lillee				
R.A.L.Massie				
Extras	(b 2, lb 3, nb 5)	10		
Total	(55 overs; 8 wickets)	**222**		

ENGLAND		Runs	Balls	4/6
G.Boycott	c Marsh b Watson	25	38	3
D.L.Amiss	b Watson	103	134	9
K.W.R.Fletcher	b Massie	60	76	8
* D.B.Close	run out	1	1	–
J.H.Hampshire	not out	25	41	5
B.L.D'Oliveira	not out	5	5	1
A.W.Greig				
† A.P.E.Knott				
R.A.Woolmer				
J.A.Snow				
G.G.Arnold				
Extras	(b 1, lb 6)	7		
Total	(49.1 overs; 4 wickets)	**226**		

ENGLAND	O	M	R	W
Snow	11	1	33	1
Arnold	11	0	38	2
Greig	11	0	50	1
Woolmer	10	1	33	3
D'Oliveira	9	1	37	0
Close	3	0	21	0

AUSTRALIA	O	M	R	W
Lillee	11	2	49	0
Massie	11	1	49	1
Watson	8	1	28	2
Mallett	11	1	43	0
G.S.Chappell	3	0	20	0
Walters	3	1	16	0
Stackpole	2.1	0	14	0

FALL OF WICKETS
1-4, 2-66, 3-125, 4-156, 5-167, 6-170, 7-205, 8-222

Umpires: C.S.Elliott (1) and A.E.G.Rhodes (1).

FALL OF WICKETS
1-48, 2-173, 3-174, 4-215

ENGLAND v AUSTRALIA 1972

At Lord's, London on 26 August 1972.   Result: **AUSTRALIA** won by 5 wickets.   Toss: Australia.
Award: G.S.Chappell.   LOI debuts: Australia – D.J.Colley.   55-over match.

Australia overhauled the largest LOI total so far to level the series in front of a near-capacity crowd of 22,000. Alan Knott, improvising audaciously, reached his fifty off 47 balls. Australia's first hundred partnership in these internationals took 78 minutes (130 balls).

ENGLAND		Runs	Balls	4/6
G.Boycott	b Lillee	8	8	1
D.L.Amiss	b Mallett	25	65	2
* D.B.Close	run out	43	40	7/1
K.W.R.Fletcher	c Stackpole b G.S.Chappell	20	56	1
J.H.Hampshire	st Marsh b Mallett	13	32	2
B.L.D'Oliveira	c I.M.Chappell b Lillee	6	13	1
A.W.Greig	b Massie	31	43	2
† A.P.E.Knott	c Mallett b Massie	50	50	6
R.A.Woolmer	run out	9	10	–
J.A.Snow	not out	5	9	–
G.G.Arnold	not out	11	12	2
Extras	(b 1, lb 10, w 1, nb 3)	15		
Total	(55 overs; 9 wickets)	**236**		

AUSTRALIA		Runs	Balls	4/6
K.R.Stackpole	lbw b D'Oliveira	52	70	6
R.Edwards	c Knott b Snow	6	7	–
* I.M.Chappell	c Knott b Woolmer	31	58	4
G.S.Chappell	lbw b Snow	48	82	5
A.P.Sheahan	c Knott b Snow	50	71	5/1
G.D.Watson	not out	11	15	2
† R.W.Marsh	not out	6	12	1
D.J.Colley				
A.A.Mallett				
D.K.Lillee				
R.A.L.Massie				
Extras	(b 6, lb 14, w 12, nb 4)	36		
Total	(51.3 overs; 5 wickets)	**240**		

AUSTRALIA	O	M	R	W
Lillee	11	0	56	2
Massie	11	1	35	2
Colley	11	1	72	0
Mallett	11	2	24	2
G.S.Chappell	11	0	34	1

ENGLAND	O	M	R	W
Snow	11	2	35	3
Arnold	11	0	47	0
D'Oliveira	11	0	46	1
Greig	9	1	29	0
Woolmer	9.3	1	47	1

FALL OF WICKETS
1-11, 2-65, 3-87, 4-114, 5-121, 6-121, 7-198, 8-217, 9-218

1-44, 2-112, 3-116, 4-219, 5-224

Umpires: A.E.Fagg (1) and T.W.Spencer (1).

ENGLAND v AUSTRALIA 1972

At Edgbaston, Birmingham on 28 August 1972.   Result: **ENGLAND** won by 2 wickets.   Toss: England.
Award: B.Wood.   LOI debuts: England – B.Wood; Australia – J.R.Hammond.   55-over match.

England became the first holders of the Prudential Trophy. They were to compete for a separate one against each visiting country, World Cup seasons apart, until 1984, when Texaco took over the sponsorship. Geoff Arnold returned the first four-wicket analysis. Alan Oakman, a former first-class umpire and then Warwickshire's coach, deputised when Arthur Fagg was taken ill on the morning of the match.

AUSTRALIA		Runs	Balls	4/6
K.R.Stackpole	b Woolmer	61	144	5
R.Edwards	b Arnold	6	12	1
* I.M.Chappell	run out	3	7	–
G.S.Chappell	c Wood b D'Oliveira	13	18	2
A.P.Sheahan	c Woolmer b Wood	19	44	1
K.D.Walters	b Wood	15	19	2
† R.W.Marsh	lbw b Arnold	0	3	–
A.A.Mallett	b Arnold	8	20	1
J.R.Hammond	not out	15	28	1
D.K.Lillee	c Wood b Arnold	13	16	1
R.A.L.Massie	not out	16	24	2
Extras	(lb 6, nb 4)	10		
Total	(55 overs; 9 wickets)	**179**		

ENGLAND		Runs	Balls	4/6
G.Boycott	c Massie b Lillee	41	90	4
D.L.Amiss	c Marsh b G.S.Chappell	40	59	3
* D.B.Close	c Marsh b Lillee	5	9	–
K.W.R.Fletcher	c Marsh b Hammond	34	64	3
B.L.D'Oliveira	run out	2	9	–
B.Wood	lbw b Lillee	19	30	2
A.W.Greig	not out	24	33	4
† A.P.E.Knott	c Mallett b Walters	6	14	–
R.A.Woolmer	c Marsh b Walters	0	2	–
J.A.Snow	not out	0	2	–
G.G.Arnold				
Extras	(lb 5, w 4)	9		
Total	(51.3 overs; 8 wickets)	**180**		

ENGLAND	O	M	R	W
Snow	11	0	29	0
Arnold	11	3	27	4
Greig	10	3	24	0
D'Oliveira	6	1	19	1
Woolmer	11	1	50	0
Wood	6	0	20	2

AUSTRALIA	O	M	R	W
Lillee	11	2	25	3
Massie	8.3	3	45	0
Mallett	4	0	16	0
Hammond	9	1	41	1
G.S.Chappell	11	3	20	1
Walters	8	1	24	2

FALL OF WICKETS
1-8, 2-15, 3-40, 4-87, 5-111, 6-112, 7-127, 8-136, 9-158

1-76, 2-89, 3-94, 4-104, 5-143, 6-154, 7-172, 8-172

Umpires: D.J.Constant (1) and A.S.M.Oakman (1).

NEW ZEALAND v PAKISTAN 1972-73

At Lancaster Park, Christchurch on 11 February 1973.   Result: **NEW ZEALAND** won by 22 runs.   Toss: Pakistan.
Awards: batting – M.G.Burgess, Sadiq Mohammed; bowling – D.R.Hadlee, Sarfraz Nawaz; fielding – Asif Iqbal,
G.M.Turner.   LOI debuts: All.   40 eight-ball overs match.

New Zealand's inaugural limited-overs international was the first to be staged on a Sunday. Attended by 12,000, it began
at noon and ended in Stygian gloom and light rain at 6.30pm. Peter Coman, a 29-year-old right-hander from
Christchurch, was the first player to appear at this level who was destined not to play Test cricket.

NEW ZEALAND		Runs	Balls	4/6	PAKISTAN		Runs	Balls	4/6
P.G.Coman	b Salim	24			* Intikhab Alam	lbw b D.R.Hadlee	10		
G.M.Turner	c Majid b Sarfraz	10			Sadiq Mohammed	lbw b Howarth	37		7
* B.E.Congdon	c Wasim Bari b Sarfraz	3			Majid Khan	lbw b D.R.Hadlee	8		
B.F.Hastings	b Sarfraz	4			Mushtaq Mohammed	b D.R.Hadlee	27		4
M.G.Burgess	c Asif Masood b Intikhab	47		2/1	Asif Iqbal	c Coman b D.R.Hadlee	3		
G.E.Vivian	c Wasim Bari b Asif Iqbal	14			Wasim Raja	run out	4		
† K.J.Wadsworth	b Majid	30			Nasim-ul-Ghani	c and b Howarth	1		
D.R.Hadlee	run out	0			† Wasim Bari	b Congdon	21		
R.J.Hadlee	not out	21	23	4	Salim Altaf	c Hastings b Congdon	21		–/1
H.J.Howarth	c Wasim Bari b Salim	1			Sarfraz Nawaz	run out	17		3
R.O.Collinge	c Salim b Sarfraz	9			Asif Masood	not out	4		
Extras	(b 5, lb 11, nb 8)	24			Extras	(b 7, lb 1, nb 4)	12		
Total	(38.3 overs)	**187**			**Total**	(33.3 overs)	**165**		

PAKISTAN	O	M	R	W	NEW ZEALAND	O	M	R	W
Asif Masood	8	1	28	0	Collinge	8	1	35	0
Salim Altaf	7	0	22	2	R.J.Hadlee	5	0	37	0
Sarfraz Nawaz	7.3	0	46	4	D.R.Hadlee	8	0	34	4
Asif Iqbal	5	0	32	1	Howarth	8	0	30	2
Majid Khan	8	0	23	1	Congdon	4.3	1	17	2
Intikhab Alam	3	1	12	1					

FALL OF WICKETS
1-35, 2-43, 3-45, 4-62, 5-98, 6-143, 7-152, 8-160, 9-176, 10-187

FALL OF WICKETS
1-43, 2-52, 3-60, 4-71, 5-93, 6-99, 7-103, 8-136, 9-145, 10-165

Umpires: F.R.Goodall (1) and E.G.Wainscott (1).

PRUDENTIAL TROPHY (1st Match)   LOI No: 6/1

ENGLAND v NEW ZEALAND 1973

At St Helen's, Swansea on 18 July 1973.   Result: **ENGLAND** won by 7 wickets.   Toss: New Zealand.
Award: D.L.Amiss.   LOI debuts: England – F.C.Hayes, G.R.J.Roope, D.L.Underwood; New Zealand – V.Pollard,
R.E.Redmond, B.R.Taylor.   55-over match.

New Zealand were dismissed for the lowest LOI total so far. Dominating the only Prudential Trophy match to be played
outside England, Dennis Amiss continued his monopoly of LOI hundreds, reaching his second one off 116 balls in the
39th over.

NEW ZEALAND		Runs	Balls	4/6	ENGLAND		Runs	Balls	4/6
R.E.Redmond	lbw b Arnold	3	11	–	G.Boycott	c Turner b Congdon	20	88	1
G.M.Turner	c and b Illingworth	26	69	2	D.L.Amiss	c Pollard b Taylor	100	121	14/1
* B.E.Congdon	c Knott b Snow	2	6	–	G.R.J.Roope	b Howarth	0	4	–
B.F.Hastings	c Roope b Snow	0	12	–	F.C.Hayes	not out	20	47	3
M.G.Burgess	c Knott b Arnold	1	4	–	K.W.R.Fletcher	not out	16	13	3
V.Pollard	c Knott b Arnold	55	112	8/1	A.W.Greig				
† K.J.Wadsworth	lbw b Underwood	3	19	–	* R.Illingworth				
B.R.Taylor	c Fletcher b Snow	22	42	4	† A.P.E.Knott				
R.J.Hadlee	c Snow b Greig	28	30	1/2	J.A.Snow				
R.O.Collinge	c Knott b Snow	4	8	–	G.G.Arnold				
H.J.Howarth	not out	5	4	1	D.L.Underwood				
Extras	(lb 2, w 7)	9			Extras	(b 1, lb 1, w 1)	3		
Total	(52.5 overs)	**158**			**Total**	(45.3 overs; 3 wickets)	**159**		

ENGLAND	O	M	R	W	NEW ZEALAND	O	M	R	W
Snow	10	0	32	4	Collinge	6	2	18	0
Arnold	11	2	28	3	Hadlee	11	1	35	0
Greig	9.5	2	26	1	Taylor	8.3	1	37	1
Underwood	11	3	29	1	Howarth	11	3	34	1
Illingworth	11	1	34	1	Congdon	9	2	32	1

FALL OF WICKETS
1-4, 2-9, 3-14, 4-15, 5-70, 6-81, 7-108, 8-133, 9-144, 10-158

FALL OF WICKETS
1-96, 2-97, 3-135

Umpires: D.J.Constant (2) and C.S.Elliott (2).

4

ENGLAND v NEW ZEALAND 1973

At Old Trafford, Manchester on 20 July 1973.   No result.   Toss: New Zealand.
Award: None.   LOI debuts: None.   55-over match.

Old Trafford, venue of the only two Test matches in England to be abandoned without a ball bowled, staged the first limited-overs international to enter the 'no result' category. With no rest day available to offset the effect of two heavy storms, the Trophy was awarded to England.

ENGLAND		Runs	Balls	4/6	NEW ZEALAND
G.Boycott	lbw b Taylor	15	26	3	G.M.Turner
D.L.Amiss	c Wadsworth b Congdon	34	64	4	R.E.Redmond
G.R.J.Roope	c Wadsworth b Hadlee	44	103	2	* B.E.Congdon
F.C.Hayes	b Congdon	9	25	1	B.F.Hastings
K.W.R.Fletcher	c Hadlee b Taylor	25	39	–/1	M.G.Burgess
A.W.Greig	c Taylor b Collinge	14	13	–/2	V.Pollard
* R.Illingworth	c Turner b Hadlee	4	11	–	† K.J.Wadsworth
† A.P.E.Knott	c Wadsworth b Taylor	12	10	1	B.R.Taylor
G.G.Arnold	not out	0	–	–	R.J.Hadlee
J.A.Snow					R.O.Collinge
P.Lever					H.J.Howarth
Extras	(lb 6, w 4)	10			
Total	(48.3 overs; 8 wickets)	**167**			

NEW ZEALAND	O	M	R	W
Collinge	11	0	52	1
Taylor	10.3	3	25	3
Hadlee	8	1	23	2
Congdon	8	1	24	2
Howarth	11	1	33	0

FALL OF WICKETS
1-23, 2-57, 3-75, 4-112, 5-150, 6-153, 7-160, 8-167

Umpires: H.D.Bird (1) and A.E.G.Rhodes (2).

ENGLAND v WEST INDIES 1973

At Headingley, Leeds on 5 September 1973.   Result: **ENGLAND** won by 1 wicket.   Toss: West Indies.
Award: M.H.Denness   LOI debuts: England – M.H.Denness, M.Hendrick, C.M.Old, M.J.Smith, R.W.Taylor, R.G.D.Willis; West Indies – All.   55-over match.

Mike Denness celebrated his debut as England's captain by contributing the highest score of the first LOI to be won by the final pair of batsmen. Garfield Sobers failed to score on his only appearance in these internationals.

WEST INDIES		Runs	Balls	4/6	ENGLAND		Runs	Balls	4/6
R.C.Fredericks	c Greig b Willis	4	12	1	G.Boycott	c Kanhai b Holder	0	13	–
M.L.C.Foster	c Greig b Old	25	62	4	M.J.Smith	lbw b Julien	31	71	2
* R.B.Kanhai	c Greig b Underwood	55	75	5/1	* M.H.Denness	b Gibbs	66	117	6
C.H.Lloyd	b Willis	31	32	2/1	F.C.Hayes	c Murray b Julien	9	27	2
A.I.Kallicharran	st Taylor b Underwood	26	68	3	K.W.R.Fletcher	lbw b Holder	2	10	–
G.St A.Sobers	c Taylor b Old	0	6	–	A.W.Greig	c Sobers b Boyce	48	54	4
B.D.Julien	c Taylor b Old	0	2	–	C.M.Old	b Sobers	4	15	–
K.D.Boyce	b Underwood	7	17	1	† R.W.Taylor	run out	8	18	1
† D.L.Murray	run out	11	29	–	M.Hendrick	b Boyce	1	2	–
V.A.Holder	c Old b Hendrick	10	21	–	R.G.D.Willis	not out	5	4	–
L.R.Gibbs	not out	0	–	–	D.L.Underwood	not out	1	2	–
Extras	(lb 12)	12			Extras	(b 1, lb 3, nb 3)	7		
Total	(54 overs)	**181**			**Total**	(54.3 overs; 9 wickets)	**182**		

ENGLAND	O	M	R	W	WEST INDIES	O	M	R	W
Willis	10	2	29	2	Sobers	10.3	3	31	1
Hendrick	11	4	27	1	Holder	11	1	34	2
Old	11	1	43	3	Boyce	11	1	40	2
Underwood	11	2	30	3	Julien	11	1	40	2
Greig	11	0	40	0	Gibbs	11	0	30	1

FALL OF WICKETS
1-4, 2-65, 3-115, 4-132, 5-133, 6-133, 7-158, 8-159, 9-181, 10-181

FALL OF WICKETS
1-3, 2-74, 3-93, 4-95, 5-143, 6-157, 7-171, 8-176, 9-176

Umpires: C.S.Elliott (3) and A.E.Fagg (2).

ENGLAND v WEST INDIES 1973

At Kennington Oval, London on 7 September 1973.   Result: **WEST INDIES** won by 8 wickets.   Toss: England.
Award: R.C.Fredericks.   LOI debuts: England – J.A.Jameson, D.Lloyd; West Indies – R.G.A.Headley, D.A.Murray.
55-over match.

West Indies won the Prudential Trophy on faster scoring rate over the two matches. Roy Fredericks completed his
nation's first LOI hundred off 113 balls in the 36th over, his partnership of 143 off 182 balls with Alvin Kallicharran
being then the LOI record for any wicket.

ENGLAND		Runs	Balls	4/6	WEST INDIES		Runs	Balls	4/6
M.J.Smith	b Lloyd	19	36	1	R.C.Fredericks	b Arnold	105	122	10/1
J.A.Jameson	c Holder b Gibbs	28	85	1	R.G.A.Headley	c Taylor b Arnold	19	41	2
*M.H.Denness	lbw b Lloyd	0	4	–	A.I.Kallicharran	not out	53	94	4
D.Lloyd	run out	8	43	–	†D.A.Murray	not out	1	4	–
K.W.R.Fletcher	b Julien	63	80	6	*R.B.Kanhai				
A.W.Greig	c Lloyd b Foster	17	29	–	C.H.Lloyd				
C.M.Old	c Murray b Holder	21	22	3	M.L.C.Foster				
†R.W.Taylor	run out	3	7	–	B.D.Julien				
G.G.Arnold	c Julien b Foster	17	20	–	K.D.Boyce				
R.G.D.Willis	not out	4	4	–	V.A.Holder				
D.L.Underwood	not out	1	4	–	L.R.Gibbs				
Extras	(b 2, lb 3, nb 3)	8			Extras	(b 1, lb 6, nb 5)	12		
Total	(55 overs; 9 wickets)	**189**			**Total**	(42.2 overs; 2 wickets)	**190**		

WEST INDIES	O	M	R	W	ENGLAND	O	M	R	W
Holder	11	0	40	1	Willis	10.2	0	55	0
Julien	11	2	35	1	Arnold	9	1	24	2
Lloyd	11	2	25	2	Old	10	0	52	0
Gibbs	11	4	12	1	Underwood	7	0	26	0
Boyce	6	0	47	0	Greig	6	2	21	0
Foster	5	0	22	2					

FALL OF WICKETS   FALL OF WICKETS
1-38, 2-39, 3-59, 4-59, 5-100, 6-135, 7-142, 8-177, 9-184   1-43, 2-186

Umpires: A.E.G.Rhodes (3) and T.W.Spencer (2).

NEW ZEALAND v AUSTRALIA 1973-74

At Carisbrook, Dunedin on 30 March 1974.   Result: **AUSTRALIA** won by 7 wickets.   Toss: New Zealand.
Awards: batting – I.M.Chappell, B.E.Congdon; bowling – G.J.Gilmour, D.R.O'Sullivan; fielding – K.J.Wadsworth,
K.D.Walters.   LOI debuts: New Zealand – B.L.Cairns, D.R.O'Sullivan; Australia – R.J.Bright, I.C.Davis, G.Dymock,
G.J.Gilmour, M.H.N.Walker.   35 eight-ball overs match.

Ian Chappell scored 50 from 40 balls as Australia sped to victory with 85 balls to spare.

NEW ZEALAND		Runs	Balls	4/6	AUSTRALIA		Runs	Balls	4/6
P.G.Coman	b Gilmour	0	7	–	I.R.Redpath	run out	0	2	–
G.M.Turner	c I.M.Chappell b Walker	5	14	–	K.R.Stackpole	c Wadsworth b D.R.Hadlee	50	73	8
*B.E.Congdon	c Marsh b G.S.Chappell	82	112	10	*I.M.Chappell	b O'Sullivan	83	68	12/2
B.F.Hastings	b Walker	27	40	4	G.S.Chappell	not out	42	32	6/1
M.G.Burgess	c Dymock b G.S.Chappell	3	18	–	I.C.Davis	not out	11	28	–
V.Pollard	c Walters b Gilmour	12	33	1	K.D.Walters				
†K.J.Wadsworth	c Walters b Dymock	7	21	1	†R.W.Marsh				
R.J.Hadlee	c Marsh b G.S.Chappell	3	6	–	M.H.N.Walker				
D.R.Hadlee	c Walters b Dymock	8	17	1	G.J.Gilmour				
B.L.Cairns	not out	30	18	6	R.J.Bright				
D.R.O'Sullivan	not out	1	2	–	G.Dymock				
Extras	(lb 9, nb 7)	16			Extras	(lb 3, nb 6)	9		
Total	(35 overs; 9 wickets)	**194**			**Total**	(24.3 overs; 3 wickets)	**195**		

AUSTRALIA	O	M	R	W	NEW ZEALAND	O	M	R	W
Walker	7	0	36	2	R.J.Hadlee	6	0	35	0
Gilmour	7	1	19	2	Cairns	4.3	0	38	0
Dymock	7	0	28	2	Congdon	2	0	30	0
Bright	7	0	44	0	O'Sullivan	7	2	38	1
G.S.Chappell	7	0	51	3	D.R.Hadlee	5	0	45	1

FALL OF WICKETS   FALL OF WICKETS
1-0, 2-12, 3-61, 4-94, 5-140, 6-145, 7-153, 8-153, 9-186   1-0, 2-136, 3-160

Umpires: E.W.Dempster (1) and L.H.G.Harmer (1).

NEW ZEALAND v AUSTRALIA 1973-74

At Lancaster Park, Christchurch on 31 March 1974.   Result: **AUSTRALIA** won by 31 runs.   Toss: Australia.
Awards: batting – K.J.Wadsworth, A.J.Woodcock; bowling – R.O.Collinge, A.A.Mallett; fielding – P.G.Coman, I.R.Redpath.
LOI debuts: New Zealand – J.M.Parker; Australia – A.J.Woodcock.   35 eight-ball overs match.

Confronted by the (then) highest LOI total and with half his side dismissed for 83, Ken Wadsworth responded with New Zealand's first hundred (off 98 balls) in these matches. It was also the first LOI hundred by a wicket-keeper and he shared with Bev Congdon his country's first hundred partnership.

AUSTRALIA		Runs	Balls	4/6
A.J.Woodcock	b Hadlee	53	67	5/1
K.R.Stackpole	c Wadsworth b Collinge	11	23	1
* I.M.Chappell	c Wadsworth b Cairns	86	67	10/2
G.S.Chappell	not out	75	83	5/2
K.D.Walters	b Collinge	19	34	1
I.R.Redpath	c Coman b Congdon	8	10	–
† R.W.Marsh	not out	1	1	–
M.H.N.Walker				
G.J.Gilmour				
A.A.Mallett				
G.Dymock				
Extras	(b 2, lb 6, nb 4)	12		
Total	(35 overs; 5 wickets)	**265**		

NEW ZEALAND		Runs	Balls	4/6
G.M.Turner	c I.M.Chappell b Gilmour	6	19	–
P.G.Coman	b Walker	38	39	3/2
J.M.Parker	c Gilmour b Mallett	14	35	1
B.F.Hastings	c G.S.Chappell b Mallett	7	14	1
M.G.Burgess	c Walters b Mallett	3	6	–
† K.J.Wadsworth	c I.M.Chappell b Walters	104	98	16
* B.E.Congdon	not out	49	72	4
D.R.Hadlee	not out	4	5	–
R.O.Collinge				
B.L.Cairns				
D.R.O'Sullivan				
Extras	(b 1, lb 1, nb 7)	9		
Total	(35 overs; 6 wickets)	**234**		

NEW ZEALAND	O	M	R	W
Collinge	7	1	38	2
Cairns	7	0	58	1
Congdon	7	0	77	1
O'Sullivan	7	0	43	0
Hadlee	7	1	37	1

AUSTRALIA	O	M	R	W
Gilmour	7	0	36	1
Walker	7	1	35	1
Mallett	7	0	47	3
Dymock	7	1	49	0
Walters	7	0	58	1

FALL OF WICKETS
1-39, 2-102, 3-176, 4-232, 5-261

FALL OF WICKETS
1-19, 2-58, 3-64, 4-70, 5-83, 6-213

Umpires: F.R.Goodall (2) and E.G.Wainscott (2).

ENGLAND v INDIA 1974

At Headingley, Leeds on 13 July 1974.   Result: **ENGLAND** won by 4 wickets.   Toss: England.
Award: J.H.Edrich.   LOI debuts: England – R.D.Jackman; India – All.   55-over match.

India first excursion into limited-overs internationals produced the highest match aggregate so far (531) when they were unable to defend the equal-highest total so far. The last four balls were bowled in heavy rain.

INDIA		Runs	Balls	4/6
S.M.Gavaskar	b Arnold	28	35	3/1
S.S.Naik	lbw b Jackman	18	29	2
* A.L.Wadekar	b Jackman	67	82	10
G.R.Viswanath	b Woolmer	4	4	1
† F.M.Engineer	lbw b Old	32	51	3
B.P.Patel	c Fletcher b Greig	82	78	8/2
E.D.Solkar	lbw b Arnold	3	9	–
S.Abid Ali	c and b Woolmer	17	24	1
Madan Lal	b Old	2	10	–
S.Venkataraghavan	not out	1	2	–
B.S.Bedi	c Lloyd b Old	0	2	–
Extras	(lb 8, nb 3)	11		
Total	(53.5 overs)	**265**		

ENGLAND		Runs	Balls	4/6
D.L.Amiss	lbw b Solkar	20	35	3
D.Lloyd	st Engineer b Solkar	34	63	3
J.H.Edrich	c Bedi b Venkataraghavan	90	97	6/1
* M.H.Denness	c Venkataraghavan b Madan Lal	8	13	1
K.W.R.Fletcher	c and b Bedi	39	59	2
A.W.Greig	c and b Bedi	40	28	2/1
† A.P.E.Knott	not out	15	13	1
C.M.Old	not out	5	3	1
R.A.Woolmer				
R.D.Jackman				
G.G.Arnold				
Extras	(lb 12, nb 3)	15		
Total	(51.1 overs; 6 wickets)	**266**		

ENGLAND	O	M	R	W
Arnold	10	1	42	2
Old	10.5	0	43	3
Jackman	11	0	44	2
Woolmer	11	0	62	2
Greig	11	0	63	1

INDIA	O	M	R	W
Abid Ali	9	0	51	0
Solkar	11	1	31	2
Madan Lal	9.1	0	43	1
Venkataraghavan	11	0	58	1
Bedi	11	0	68	2

FALL OF WICKETS
1-44, 2-50, 3-60, 4-130, 5-181, 6-194, 7-246, 8-264, 9-265, 10-265

FALL OF WICKETS
1-37, 2-84, 3-96, 4-178, 5-212, 6-254

Umpires: W.E.Alley (1) and H.D.Bird (2).

ENGLAND v INDIA 1974

At Kennington Oval, London on 15, 16 July 1974.　　Result: **ENGLAND** won by 6 wickets.　　Toss: India.
Award: K.W.R.Fletcher.　　LOI debuts: India – G.Bose, A.V.Mankad.　　55-over match.

This was the first international to involve play on a second day. Rain delayed the start until 1.30pm and brought about a premature close at 5.49pm with England 19 for 1 after 7 overs.

INDIA		Runs	Balls	4/6
S.M.Gavaskar	c Arnold b Jackman	20	23	3
S.S.Naik	c Greig b Old	20	39	1
G.Bose	c Denness b Jackman	13	18	1
* A.L.Wadekar	c Lloyd b Underwood	6	8	1
G.R.Viswanath	c Knott b Old	32	59	1
† F.M.Engineer	lbw b Jackman	4	15	–
B.P.Patel	run out	12	23	–
A.V.Mankad	b Old	44	61	3
E.D.Solkar	c Knott b Greig	0	17	–
S.Abid Ali	c Smith b Greig	6	10	–
Madan Lal	not out	3	13	–
Extras	(lb 9, w 1, nb 1)	11		
Total	(47.3 overs)	**171**		

ENGLAND	O	M	R	W
Arnold	7	0	20	0
Old	9.3	0	36	3
Jackman	11	1	41	3
Underwood	11	0	36	1
Greig	9	0	27	2

FALL OF WICKETS
1-40, 2-48, 3-60, 4-64, 5-75, 6-94, 7-139, 8-142, 9-156, 10-171

ENGLAND		Runs	Balls	4/6
M.J.Smith	c Engineer b Abid Ali	6	19	–
D.Lloyd	c sub (S.M.H.Kirmani) b Bose	39	81	4
J.H.Edrich	c Patel b Madan Lal	19	48	1
* M.H.Denness	c Wadekar b Mankad	24	37	2
K.W.R.Fletcher	not out	55	79	7
A.W.Greig	not out	24	29	3
† A.P.E.Knott				
C.M.Old				
R.D.Jackman				
G.G.Arnold				
D.L.Underwood				
Extras	(lb 4, w 1)	5		
Total	(48.5 overs; 4 wickets)	**172**		

INDIA	O	M	R	W
Abid Ali	11	3	21	1
Solkar	11	3	37	0
Madan Lal	10	0	23	1
Bose	11	2	39	1
Mankad	5.5	0	47	1

FALL OF WICKETS
1-19, 2-65, 3-71, 4-113

Umpires: C.S.Elliott (4) and A.Jepson (1).

ENGLAND v PAKISTAN 1974

At Trent Bridge, Nottingham on 31 August 1974.　　Result: **PAKISTAN** won by 7 wickets.　　Toss: England.
Award: Majid Khan.　　LOI debuts: Pakistan – Imran Khan, Zaheer Abbas.　　50-over match.

Rain caused the start to be delayed by 90 minutes and the match to be reduced to 50 overs per innings. David Lloyd became the first to bat throughout an LOI innings. This was also the first limited-overs international in which two hundreds were scored, Majid completing his off only 88 balls.

ENGLAND		Runs	Balls	4/6
D.Lloyd	not out	116	159	8/1
M.J.Smith	c Sadiq b Sarfraz	14	31	1
J.H.Edrich	c Wasim Bari b Asif Iqbal	18	30	2
* M.H.Denness	st Wasim Bari b Intikhab	32	49	2
C.M.Old	st Wasim Bari b Majid	39	31	2/1
A.W.Greig	not out	7	5	–
K.W.R.Fletcher				
† A.P.E.Knott				
P.Lever				
D.L.Underwood				
R.G.D.Willis				
Extras	(b 5, lb 11, nb 2)	18		
Total	(50 overs; 4 wickets)	**244**		

PAKISTAN	O	M	R	W
Asif Masood	10	2	31	0
Sarfraz Nawaz	10	0	46	1
Asif Iqbal	10	1	40	1
Imran Khan	10	0	36	0
Intikhab Alam	7	0	58	1
Majid Khan	3	0	15	1

FALL OF WICKETS
1-27, 2-59, 3-162, 4-226

PAKISTAN		Runs	Balls	4/6
Sadiq Mohammed	b Lever	41	52	6
Majid Khan	c Old b Underwood	109	93	16/1
Zaheer Abbas	c and b Willis	31	51	3
Asif Iqbal	not out	24	38	3
Mushtaq Mohammed	not out	24	30	2
Wasim Raja				
* Intikhab Alam				
Imran Khan				
Sarfraz Nawaz				
† Wasim Bari				
Asif Masood				
Extras	(b 1, lb 11, nb 5)	17		
Total	(42.5 overs; 3 wickets)	**246**		

ENGLAND	O	M	R	W
Willis	10	2	34	1
Lever	10	0	58	1
Old	10	0	65	0
Underwood	8	1	32	1
Greig	4.5	0	40	0

FALL OF WICKETS
1-113, 2-187, 3-199

Umpires: W.L.Budd (1) and D.J.Constant (3).

ENGLAND v PAKISTAN 1974

At Edgbaston, Birmingham on 3 September 1974.　　Result: **PAKISTAN** won by 8 wickets.　Toss: Pakistan.
Award: Asif Masood.　　LOI debuts: None.　　35-over match.

England recorded their lowest total in these matches, albeit in an innings reduced to 35 overs because of rain, as
Pakistan became the first visiting side to win the Prudential Trophy two-nil.

ENGLAND		Runs	Balls	4/6	PAKISTAN		Runs	Balls	4/6
D.Lloyd	b Sarfraz	4	16	–	Sadiq Mohammed	c Lloyd b Underwood	12	39	1
M.J.Smith	lbw b Asif Masood	0	2	–	Majid Khan	lbw b Arnold	0	1	–
J.H.Edrich	b Sarfraz	6	16	–	Zaheer Abbas	not out	57	61	7
* M.H.Denness	b Imran	9	24	–	Mushtaq Mohammed	not out	1	13	–
K.W.R.Fletcher	c Wasim Bari b Asif Masood	2	6	–	Asif Iqbal				
A.W.Greig	run out	1	5	–	Wasim Raja				
C.M.Old	c Wasim Raja b Asif Iqbal	0	10	–	* Intikhab Alam				
† R.W.Taylor	not out	26	67	–	Imran Khan				
G.G.Arnold	b Imran	2	11	–	Sarfraz Nawaz				
D.L.Underwood	b Asif Iqbal	17	49	2	† Wasim Bari				
P.Lever	not out	8	5	–	Asif Masood				
Extras	(lb 6)	6			Extras	(b 1, lb 7, nb 6)	14		
Total	(35 overs; 9 wickets)	81			Total	(18 overs; 2 wickets)	84		

PAKISTAN	O	M	R	W	ENGLAND	O	M	R	W
Asif Masood	7	2	9	2	Arnold	6	3	7	1
Sarfraz Nawaz	7	0	15	2	Lever	4	0	22	0
Imran Khan	7	2	16	2	Old	5	0	25	0
Asif Iqbal	7	1	17	2	Underwood	3	0	16	1
Intikhab Alam	6	1	12	0					
Majid Khan	1	0	6	0	FALL OF WICKETS				
					1-1, 2-60				

FALL OF WICKETS
1-1, 2-12, 3-13, 4-20, 5-24, 6-25, 7-25, 8-28, 9-68

Umpires: H.D.Bird (3) and C.S.Elliott (5).

AUSTRALIA v ENGLAND 1974-75

At Melbourne Cricket Ground on 1 January 1975.　　Result: **ENGLAND** won by 3 wickets.　　Toss: England.
Awards: D.L.Amiss and I.M.Chappell.　　LOI debuts: Australia – W.J.Edwards, A.G.Hurst, T.J.Jenner, J.R.Thomson;
England – B.W.Luckhurst.　　40 eight-ball overs match.

Staged immediately after the tense drama of the drawn third Test, this match was contested by tired players in great
heat and before a meagre audience by Melbourne's standards (18,977).

AUSTRALIA		Runs	Balls	4/6	ENGLAND		Runs	Balls	4/6
W.J.Edwards	b Arnold	2	14	–	D.L.Amiss	b Walker	47	54	6
I.R.Redpath	c Greig b Lever	2	9	–	D.Lloyd	run out	49	95	5
* I.M.Chappell	c Lever b Old	42	49	6	B.W.Luckhurst	run out	14	58	1
G.S.Chappell	b Old	44	50	3	K.W.R.Fletcher	c Redpath b Thomson	31	48	4
R.Edwards	b Old	20	38	1	C.M.Old	b Hurst	12	10	–/1
K.D.Walters	b Old	18	20	1	A.W.Greig	run out	3	1	–
† R.W.Marsh	run out	14	22	–	* M.H.Denness	c Walker b Hurst	12	24	1
T.J.Jenner	c Fletcher b Greig	12	25	1	† A.P.E.Knott	not out	2	9	–
M.H.N.Walker	b Greig	20	35	1	D.L.Underwood	not out	1	2	–
J.R.Thomson	b Arnold	4	16	–	G.G.Arnold				
A.G.Hurst	not out	1	3	–	P.Lever				
Extras	(b 7, w 1, nb 3)	11			Extras	(b 5, lb 11, nb 4)	20		
Total	(34.5 overs)	190			Total	(37.1 overs; 7 wickets)	191		

ENGLAND	O	M	R	W	AUSTRALIA	O	M	R	W
Lever	5	0	24	1	Thomson	7	1	33	1
Arnold	8	2	30	2	Hurst	8	0	27	2
Greig	7.5	0	48	2	Jenner	8	1	24	1
Old	8	0	57	4	Walters	3	0	32	0
Underwood	6	0	20	0	Walker	8	0	27	1
					G.S.Chappell	3	0	24	0
					W.J.Edwards	0.1	0	0	0

FALL OF WICKETS
1-5, 2-11, 3-65, 4-105, 5-122, 6-139, 7-159, 8-173, 9-183, 10-190

Umpires: R.C.Bailhache (1) and T.F.Brooks (2).

FALL OF WICKETS
1-70, 2-117, 3-124, 4-154, 5-157, 6-182, 7-182

NEW ZEALAND v ENGLAND 1974-75

At Carisbrook, Dunedin on 8 March 1975.   No result.   Toss: New Zealand.
Award: None.   LOI debuts: New Zealand – B.G.Hadlee, G.P.Howarth; England – F.J.Titmus.   35 eight-ball overs match.

Rain caused this match to be abandoned at 3.20pm.

ENGLAND		Runs	Balls	4/6
D.L.Amiss	c Wadsworth b R.J.Hadlee	3		
B.Wood	b H.J.Howarth	33		
B.W.Luckhurst	c G.P.Howarth b Collinge	0		
K.W.R.Fletcher	c Turner b Congdon	11		
* J.H.Edrich	c R.J.Hadlee b H.J.Howarth	8		
C.M.Old	c Parker b H.J.Howarth	27		–/1
† R.W.Taylor	not out	23		
F.J.Titmus	b D.R.Hadlee	11		
G.G.Arnold	b D.R.Hadlee	0		
D.L.Underwood	c Parker b R.J.Hadlee	2		
M.Hendrick	b Collinge	1		
Extras	(lb 12, nb 5)	17		
Total	**(34.1 overs)**	**136**		

NEW ZEALAND		Runs	Balls	4/6
G.M.Turner	not out	8		
B.G.Hadlee	not out	7		
J.M.Parker				
G.P.Howarth				
* B.E.Congdon				
† K.J.Wadsworth				
B.F.Hastings				
R.J.Hadlee				
D.R.Hadlee				
R.O.Collinge				
H.J.Howarth				
Extras				
Total	**(4 overs; 0 wickets)**	**15**		

NEW ZEALAND	O	M	R	W
Collinge	6.1	0	17	2
R.J.Hadlee	7	0	21	2
H.J.Howarth	7	0	35	3
Congdon	7	0	25	1
D.R.Hadlee	7	1	21	2

ENGLAND	O	M	R	W
Arnold	2	0	6	0
Hendrick	2	0	9	0

FALL OF WICKETS
1-14, 2-17, 3-36, 4-51, 5-90, 6-90, 7-122, 8-122, 9-132, 10-136

Umpires: E.W.Dempster (2) and E.G.Wainscott (3).

NEW ZEALAND v ENGLAND 1974-75

At Basin Reserve, Wellington on 9 March 1975.   No result.   Toss: New Zealand.
Award: None.   LOI debuts: New Zealand – J.F.M.Morrison.   35 eight-ball overs match.

Rain again prevented a likely New Zealand victory. Bev Congdon, unavailable because of business commitments for the imminent World Cup tournament, handed the captaincy to Glenn Turner and proceeded to score his only LOI hundred.

NEW ZEALAND		Runs	Balls	4/6
* G.M.Turner	b Hendrick	18		
J.F.M.Morrison	c Taylor b Lever	5		
B.E.Congdon	lbw b Lever	101		7/1
B.F.Hastings	c Greig b Titmus	37		
† K.J.Wadsworth	lbw b Titmus	0		
J.M.Parker	c Wood b Titmus	25		
G.P.Howarth	c sub (D.L.Amiss) b Old	13		
R.J.Hadlee	not out	6		
D.R.Hadlee	run out	0		
R.O.Collinge	c Titmus b Lever	0		
H.J.Howarth	b Lever	11		
Extras	(b 6, lb 2, nb 3)	11		
Total	**(34.6 overs)**	**227**		

ENGLAND		Runs	Balls	4/6
B.Wood	not out	14		
B.W.Luckhurst	c Wadsworth b Collinge	1		
K.W.R.Fletcher	not out	18		
J.H.Edrich				
* M.H.Denness				
A.W.Greig				
C.M.Old				
† R.W.Taylor				
F.J.Titmus				
P.Lever				
M.Hendrick				
Extras	(b 1, lb 1)	2		
Total	**(10 overs; 1 wicket)**	**35**		

ENGLAND	O	M	R	W
Lever	6.6	0	35	4
Old	6	0	32	1
Hendrick	4	0	21	1
Greig	5	0	34	0
Titmus	7	0	53	3
Wood	6	0	41	0

NEW ZEALAND	O	M	R	W
Collinge	4	1	9	1
D.R.Hadlee	3	0	6	0
Congdon	2	0	14	0
R.J.Hadlee	1	0	4	0

FALL OF WICKETS
1-3

FALL OF WICKETS
1-13, 2-46, 3-130, 4-130, 5-178, 6-206, 7-209, 8-209, 9-210, 10-227

Umpires: J.B.R.Hastie (1) and R.L.Monteith (1).

10

ENGLAND v INDIA 1975

At Lord's, London on 7 June 1975.   Result: **ENGLAND** won by 202 runs.   Toss: England.
Award: D.L.Amiss.   LOI debuts: India – M.Amarnath, A.D.Gaekwad, K.D.Ghavri.

The inaugural World Cup tournament involved eight teams playing 15 matches according to 60-over Gillette Cup rules. With Dennis Amiss contributing his third hundred, England achieved the first score of 300 in these internationals. Their margin of victory, the largest until 1984-85 (*LOI No. 297*), owed much to Sunil Gavaskar's extraordinarily defensive display. Chris Old reached his fifty off 30 balls – still the fastest for England.

ENGLAND		Runs	Balls	4/6
J.A.Jameson	c Venkataraghavan b Amarnath	21	42	2
D.L.Amiss	b Madan Lal	137	147	18
K.W.R.Fletcher	b Abid Ali	68	107	4/1
A.W.Greig	lbw b Abid Ali	4	8	–
* M.H.Denness	not out	37	31	2/1
C.M.Old	not out	51	30	4/2
B.Wood				
† A.P.E.Knott				
J.A.Snow				
P.Lever				
G.G.Arnold				
Extras	(lb 12, w 2, nb 2)	16		
Total	(60 overs; 4 wickets)	334		

INDIA		Runs	Balls	4/6
S.M.Gavaskar	not out	36	174	1
E.D.Solkar	c Lever b Arnold	8	34	–
A.D.Gaekwad	c Knott b Lever	22	46	2
G.R.Viswanath	c Fletcher b Old	37	59	5
B.P.Patel	not out	16	57	–
M.Amarnath				
† F.M.Engineer				
S.Abid Ali				
Madan Lal				
* S.Venkataraghavan				
K.D.Ghavri				
Extras	(lb 3, w 1, nb 9)	13		
Total	(60 overs; 3 wickets)	132		

INDIA	O	M	R	W
Madan Lal	12	1	64	1
Amarnath	12	2	60	1
Abid Ali	12	0	58	2
Ghavri	11	1	83	0
Venkataraghavan	12	0	41	0
Solkar	1	0	12	0

ENGLAND	O	M	R	W
Snow	12	2	24	0
Arnold	10	2	20	1
Old	12	4	26	1
Greig	9	1	26	0
Wood	5	2	4	0
Lever	10	0	16	1
Jameson	2	1	3	0

FALL OF WICKETS
1-54, 2-230, 3-237, 4-245

FALL OF WICKETS
1-21, 2-50, 3-108

Umpires: D.J.Constant (4) and J.G.Langridge (1).

NEW ZEALAND v EAST AFRICA 1975

At Edgbaston, Birmingham on 7 June 1975.   Result: **NEW ZEALAND** won by 181 runs.   Toss: New Zealand.
Award: G.M.Turner.   LOI debuts: New Zealand – B.J.McKechnie; East Africa – All.

Glenn Turner's innings, the first of 150 or more, remained the highest in these internationals until 1983 (*LOI No. 216*).

NEW ZEALAND		Runs	Balls	4/6
* G.M.Turner	not out	171		16/2
J.F.M.Morrison	c and b Nana	14		–
G.P.Howarth	b Mehmood	20		2
J.M.Parker	c Zulfiqar b Sethi	66		7
B.F.Hastings	c Sethi b Zulfiqar	8		1
† K.J.Wadsworth	b Nagenda	10		–/1
R.J.Hadlee	not out	6		–
B.J.McKechnie				
D.R.Hadlee				
H.J.Howarth				
R.O.Collinge				
Extras	(b 1, lb 8, w 5)	14		
Total	(60 overs; 5 wickets)	309		

EAST AFRICA		Runs	Balls	4/6
Frasat Ali	st Wadsworth b H.J.Howarth	45		1/1
S.Walusimba	b D.R.Hadlee	15		1
R.K.Sethi	run out	1		–
S.Sumar	b D.R.Hadlee	4		–
Jawahir Shah	c and b H.J.Howarth	5		–
* Harilal Shah	lbw b H.J.Howarth	0		–
Mehmood Quaraishy	not out	16		–
Zulfiqar Ali	b D.R.Hadlee	30		4
† H.McLeod	b Collinge	5		–
P.G.Nana	not out	1		–
J.Nagenda				
Extras	(lb 5, nb 1)	6		
Total	(60 overs; 8 wickets)	128		

EAST AFRICA	O	M	R	W
Nagenda	9	1	50	1
Frasat Ali	9	0	50	0
Nana	12	2	34	1
Sethi	10	1	51	1
Zulfiqar Ali	12	0	71	1
Mehmood Quaraishy	8	0	39	1

NEW ZEALAND	O	M	R	W
Collinge	12	5	23	1
R.J.Hadlee	12	6	10	0
McKechnie	12	2	39	0
D.R.Hadlee	12	1	21	3
H.J.Howarth	12	3	29	3

FALL OF WICKETS
1-51, 2-103, 3-252, 4-278, 5-292

FALL OF WICKETS
1-30, 2-32, 3-36, 4-59, 5-59, 6-84, 7-121, 8-126

Umpires: H.D.Bird (4) and A.E.Fagg (3).

11

AUSTRALIA v PAKISTAN 1975

At Headingley, Leeds on 7 June 1975.   Result: **AUSTRALIA** won by 73 runs.   Toss: Australia.
Award: D.K.Lillee.   LOI debuts: Australia – R.B.McCosker, A.Turner; Pakistan – Naseer Malik.

Headingley's gates were closed on a capacity crowd (22,000) for the first time since 1966. Dennis Lillee achieved the first five-wicket analysis in these internationals. Jeff Thomson bowled 12 no-balls, including five in his first over.

AUSTRALIA		Runs	Balls	4/6
A.Turner	c Mushtaq b Asif Iqbal	46	54	4
R.B.McCosker	c Wasim Bari b Naseer	25	76	2
* I.M.Chappell	c Wasim Raja b Sarfraz	28	30	5
G.S.Chappell	c Asif Iqbal b Imran	45	56	5
K.D.Walters	c Sarfraz b Naseer	2	13	–
R.Edwards	not out	80	94	6
† R.W.Marsh	c Wasim Bari b Imran	1	5	–
M.H.N.Walker	b Asif Masood	18	28	2
J.R.Thomson	not out	20	14	2/1
A.A.Mallett				
D.K.Lillee				
Extras	(lb 7, nb 6)	13		
Total	(60 overs; 7 wickets)	**278**		

PAKISTAN	O	M	R	W
Naseer Malik	12	2	37	2
Asif Masood	12	0	50	1
Sarfraz Nawaz	12	0	63	1
Asif Iqbal	12	0	58	1
Imran Khan	10	0	44	2
Wasim Raja	2	0	13	0

FALL OF WICKETS
1-63, 2-99, 3-110, 4-124, 5-184, 6-195, 7-243

Umpires: W.E.Alley (2) and T.W.Spencer (3).

PAKISTAN		Runs	Balls	4/6
Sadiq Mohammed	b Lillee	4	12	–
Majid Khan	c Marsh b Mallett	65	76	11
Zaheer Abbas	c Turner b Thomson	8	10	2
Mushtaq Mohammed	c G.S.Chappell b Walters	8	32	–
* Asif Iqbal	b Lillee	53	95	8
Wasim Raja	c Thomson b Walker	31	57	4
Imran Khan	c Turner b Walker	9	19	1
Sarfraz Nawaz	c Marsh b Lillee	0	2	–
† Wasim Bari	c Marsh b Lillee	2	18	–
Asif Masood	c Walker b Lillee	6	7	1
Naseer Malik	not out	0	13	–
Extras	(lb 4, w 3, nb 12)	19		
Total	(53 overs)	**205**		

AUSTRALIA	O	M	R	W
Lillee	12	2	34	5
Thomson	8	2	25	1
Walker	12	3	32	2
Mallett	12	1	49	1
Walters	6	0	29	1
G.S.Chappell	3	0	17	0

FALL OF WICKETS
1-15, 2-27, 3-68, 4-104, 5-181, 6-189, 7-189, 8-195, 9-203, 10-205

WEST INDIES v SRI LANKA 1975

At Old Trafford, Manchester on 7 June 1975.   Result: **WEST INDIES** won by 9 wickets.   Toss: West Indies.
Award: B.D.Julien.   LOI debuts: West Indies – I.V.A.Richards, A.M.E.Roberts; Sri Lanka – All.

Sri Lanka were dismissed for their lowest LOI total until 1986-87 (*LOI No. 405*). As the match was completed before 3.30pm, the teams staged an exhibition match for the crowd of 5,000.

SRI LANKA		Runs	Balls	4/6
† E.R.Fernando	c Murray b Julien	4	–	
B.Warnapura	c Murray b Boyce	8	2	
* A.P.B.Tennekoon	c Murray b Julien	0	–	
P.D.Heyn	c Lloyd b Roberts	2	–	
M.H.Tissera	c Kallicharran b Julien	14	1	
L.R.D.Mendis	c Murray b Boyce	8	1	
A.N.Ranasinghe	b Boyce	0	–	
H.S.M.Pieris	c Lloyd b Julien	3	–	
A.R.M.Opatha	b Roberts	11	1	
D.S.de Silva	c Lloyd b Holder	21	2	
L.W.S.Kaluperuma	not out	6	–	
Extras	(b 3, lb 3, nb 3)	9		
Total	(37.2 overs)	**86**		

WEST INDIES	O	M	R	W
Roberts	12	5	16	2
Boyce	8	1	22	3
Julien	12	3	20	4
Gibbs	4	0	17	0
Holder	1.2	0	2	1

FALL OF WICKETS
1-5, 2-5, 3-16, 4-21, 5-41, 6-41, 7-42, 8-48, 9-58, 10-86

Umpires: W.L.Budd (2) and A.Jepson (2).

WEST INDIES		Runs	Balls	4/6
R.C.Fredericks	c Warnapura b De Silva	33	4	
† D.L.Murray	not out	30	2/1	
A.I.Kallicharran	not out	19	–	
R.B.Kanhai				
* C.H.Lloyd				
I.V.A.Richards				
B.D.Julien				
K.D.Boyce				
V.A.Holder				
A.M.E.Roberts				
L.R.Gibbs				
Extras	(b 2, lb 1, w 1, nb 1)	5		
Total	(20.4 overs; 1 wicket)	**87**		

SRI LANKA	O	M	R	W
Opatha	4	0	19	0
De Silva	8	1	33	1
Pieris	2	0	13	0
Kaluperuma	6.4	1	17	0

FALL OF WICKETS
1-52

FIRST (PRUDENTIAL) WORLD CUP (5th Match)   LOI No: 23/5

ENGLAND v NEW ZEALAND 1975

At Trent Bridge, Nottingham on 11 June 1975.   Result: **ENGLAND** won by 80 runs.   Toss: New Zealand.
Award: K.W.R.Fletcher.   LOI debuts: None.

Keith Fletcher, who completed his only LOI hundred from 126 balls, was run out off the final ball of the innings.

ENGLAND		Runs	Balls	4/6
J.A.Jameson	c Wadsworth b Collinge	11	31	–
D.L.Amiss	b Collinge	16	18	3
K.W.R.Fletcher	run out	131	147	13
F.C.Hayes	lbw b R.J.Hadlee	34	80	5
* M.H.Denness	c Morrison b D.R.Hadlee	37	52	1/1
A.W.Greig	b D.R.Hadlee	9	19	–
C.M.Old	not out	20	16	–/1
† A.P.E.Knott				
D.L.Underwood				
G.G.Arnold				
P.Lever				
Extras	(lb 6, w 1, nb 1)	8		
Total	(60 overs; 6 wickets)	266		

NEW ZEALAND		Runs	Balls	4/6
J.F.M.Morrison	c Old b Underwood	55	85	6/1
* G.M.Turner	b Lever	12	34	1
B.G.Hadlee	b Greig	19	77	1
J.M.Parker	b Greig	1	8	–
B.F.Hastings	c Underwood b Old	10	26	1
† K.J.Wadsworth	b Arnold	25	24	3
R.J.Hadlee	b Old	0	6	–
B.J.McKechnie	c Underwood b Greig	27	50	4
D.R.Hadlee	c Arnold b Greig	20	42	2
H.J.Howarth	not out	1	7	–
R.O.Collinge	b Underwood	6	6	–/1
Extras	(b 1, lb 4, w 1, nb 4)	10		
Total	(60 overs)	186		

NEW ZEALAND	O	M	R	W
Collinge	12	2	43	2
R.J.Hadlee	12	2	66	1
D.R.Hadlee	12	1	55	2
McKechnie	12	2	38	0
Howarth	12	2	56	0

ENGLAND	O	M	R	W
Arnold	12	3	35	1
Lever	12	0	37	1
Old	12	2	29	2
Greig	12	0	45	4
Underwood	12	2	30	2

FALL OF WICKETS
1-27, 2-28, 3-111, 4-177, 5-200, 6-266

FALL OF WICKETS
1-30, 2-83, 3-91, 4-95, 5-129, 6-129, 7-129, 8-177, 9-180, 10-186

Umpires: W.E.Alley (3) and T.W.Spencer (4).

FIRST (PRUDENTIAL) WORLD CUP (6th Match)   LOI No: 24/1

INDIA v EAST AFRICA 1975

At Headingley, Leeds on 11 June 1975.   Result: **INDIA** won by 10 wickets.   Toss: East Africa.
Award: F.M.Engineer.   LOI debuts: East Africa – P.S.Mehta, D.J.Pringle, Yunus Badat.

India gained the first ten-wicket victory in these internationals. Bishan Bedi's analysis remains the most economical from 12 overs. The paying attendance was 720.

EAST AFRICA		Runs	Balls	4/6
Frasat Ali	b Abid Ali	12		1
S.Walusimba	lbw b Abid Ali	16		1
† P.S.Mehta	run out	12		–
Yunus Badat	b Bedi	1		–
Jawahir Shah	b Amarnath	37		5
* Harilal Shah	c Engineer b Amarnath	0		–
R.K.Sethi	c Gaekwad b Madan Lal	23		2
Mehmood Quaraishy	run out	6		–
Zulfiqar Ali	not out	2		–
P.G.Nana	lbw b Madan Lal	0		–
D.J.Pringle	b Madan Lal	2		–
Extras	(lb 8, nb 1)	9		
Total	(55.3 overs)	120		

INDIA		Runs	Balls	4/6
S.M.Gavaskar	not out	65		9
† F.M.Engineer	not out	54		7
A.D.Gaekwad				
G.R.Viswanath				
B.P.Patel				
E.D.Solkar				
S.Abid Ali				
Madan Lal				
M.Amarnath				
* S.Venkataraghavan				
B.S.Bedi				
Extras	(b 4)	4		
Total	(29.5 overs; 0 wickets)	123		

INDIA	O	M	R	W
Abid Ali	12	5	22	2
Madan Lal	9.3	2	15	3
Bedi	12	8	6	1
Venkataraghavan	12	4	29	0
Amarnath	10	0	39	2

EAST AFRICA	O	M	R	W
Frasat Ali	6	1	17	0
Pringle	3	0	14	0
Zulfiqar Ali	11	3	32	0
Nana	4.5	0	36	0
Sethi	5	0	20	0

FALL OF WICKETS
1-26, 2-36, 3-37, 4-56, 5-56, 6-98, 7-116, 8-116, 9-116, 10-120

Umpires: H.D.Bird (5) and A.Jepson (3).

13

AUSTRALIA v SRI LANKA 1975

At Kennington Oval, London on 11 June 1975.   Result: **AUSTRALIA** won by 52 runs.   Toss: Sri Lanka.
Award: A.Turner.   LOI debuts: Sri Lanka – S.R.de S.Wettimuny.

Alan Turner reached the first pre-lunch LOI hundred out of 178 during the 34th over. His partnership of 182 with Rick McCosker remained the World Cup first-wicket record until 1995-96 (*LOI No. 1071*). Duleep Mendis (concussion) and Sunil Wettimuny (bruised foot) were injured by balls from Jeff Thomson and required treatment at St Thomas' Hospital.

AUSTRALIA		Runs	Balls	4/6
R.B.McCosker	b De Silva	73	111	2
A.Turner	c Mendis b De Silva	101	113	9/1
* I.M.Chappell	b Kaluperuma	4	7	1
G.S.Chappell	c Opatha b Pieris	50	50	5/1
K.D.Walters	c Tennekoon b Pieris	59	66	5
J.R.Thomson	not out	9	7	–
† R.W.Marsh	not out	9	7	–
R.Edwards				
M.H.N.Walker				
D.K.Lillee				
A.A.Mallett				
Extras	(b 1, lb 20, w 1, nb 1)	23		
Total	(60 overs; 5 wickets)	**328**		

SRI LANKA		Runs	Balls	4/6
S.R.de S.Wettimuny	retired hurt	53	102	7
† E.R.Fernando	b Thomson	22	18	4
B.Warnapura	st Marsh b Mallett	31	39	5
L.R.D.Mendis	retired hurt	32	45	5
* A.P.B.Tennekoon	b I.M.Chappell	48	71	6
M.H.Tissera	c Turner b I.M.Chappell	52	72	7
A.N.Ranasinghe	not out	14	18	3
H.S.M.Pieris	not out	0	3	–
A.R.M.Opatha				
D.S.de Silva				
L.W.S.Kaluperuma				
Extras	(b 6, lb 8, w 8, nb 2)	24		
Total	(60 overs; 4 wickets)	**276**		

SRI LANKA	O	M	R	W
Opatha	9	0	32	0
Pieris	11	0	68	2
Warnapura	9	0	40	0
Ranasinghe	7	0	55	0
De Silva	12	3	60	2
Kaluperuma	12	0	50	1

AUSTRALIA	O	M	R	W
Lillee	10	0	42	0
Thomson	12	5	22	1
Mallett	12	0	72	1
Walters	6	1	33	0
Walker	12	1	44	0
G.S.Chappell	4	0	25	0
I.M.Chappell	4	0	14	2

FALL OF WICKETS
1-182, 2-187, 3-191, 4-308, 5-308

FALL OF WICKETS
1-30, 2-84, 3-246, 4-268

Umpires: W.L.Budd (3) and A.E.Fagg (4).

WEST INDIES v PAKISTAN 1975

At Edgbaston, Birmingham on 11 June 1975.   Result: **WEST INDIES** won by 1 wicket.   Toss: Pakistan.
Award: Sarfraz Nawaz.   LOI debuts: Pakistan – Javed Miandad, Parvez Mir; West Indies – C.G.Greenidge.

Joining forces at 203 for 9 in the 46th over, Deryck Murray and Andy Roberts added 64 to snatch an epic victory with two balls to spare.

PAKISTAN		Runs	Balls	4/6
* Majid Khan	c Murray b Lloyd	60		6
Sadiq Mohammed	c Kanhai b Julien	7		1
Zaheer Abbas	lbw b Richards	31		4
Mushtaq Mohammed	b Boyce	55		3
Wasim Raja	b Roberts	58		6
Javed Miandad	run out	24		2
Parvez Mir	run out	4		–
† Wasim Bari	not out	1		–
Sarfraz Nawaz	not out	0		–
Asif Masood				
Naseer Malik				
Extras	(b 1, lb 15, w 4, nb 6)	26		
Total	(60 overs; 7 wickets)	**266**		

WEST INDIES		Runs	Balls	4/6
R.C.Fredericks	lbw b Sarfraz	12		2
C.G.Greenidge	c Wasim Bari b Sarfraz	4		1
A.I.Kallicharran	c Wasim Bari b Sarfraz	16		1
R.B.Kanhai	b Naseer	24		3
* C.H.Lloyd	c Wasim Bari b Miandad	53		8
I.V.A.Richards	c Zaheer b Parvez	13		2
B.D.Julien	c Miandad b Asif	18		2
† D.L.Murray	not out	61		6
K.D.Boyce	b Naseer	7		–
V.A.Holder	c Parvez b Sarfraz	16		1
A.M.E.Roberts	not out	24		3
Extras	(lb 10, w 1, nb 8)	19		
Total	(59.4 overs; 9 wickets)	**267**		

WEST INDIES	O	M	R	W
Roberts	12	1	47	1
Boyce	12	2	44	1
Julien	12	1	41	1
Holder	12	3	56	0
Richards	4	0	21	1
Lloyd	8	1	31	1

PAKISTAN	O	M	R	W
Asif Masood	12	1	64	1
Sarfraz Nawaz	12	1	44	4
Naseer Malik	12	2	42	2
Parvez Mir	9	1	42	1
Javed Miandad	12	0	46	1
Mushtaq Mohammed	2	0	7	0
Wasim Raja	0.4	0	3	0

FALL OF WICKETS
1-21, 2-83, 3-140, 4-202, 5-249, 6-263, 7-265

FALL OF WICKETS
1-6, 2-31, 3-36, 4-84, 5-99, 6-145, 7-151, 8-166, 9-203

Umpires: D.J.Constant (5) and J.G.Langridge (2).

ENGLAND v EAST AFRICA 1975

At Edgbaston, Birmingham on 14 June 1975.   Result: **ENGLAND** won by 196 runs.   Toss: East Africa.
Award: J.A.Snow.   LOI debuts: None.

The last of East Africa's three excursions at this level. John Snow claimed 4 for 5 in an opening spell of six overs. Don Pringle, father of Derek (Cambridge, Essex and England) was fatally injured in a car accident four months later.

ENGLAND		Runs	Balls	4/6
B.Wood	b Mehmood	77		6
D.L.Amiss	c Nana b Zulfiqar	88		7
F.C.Hayes	b Zulfiqar	52		6/2
A.W.Greig	lbw b Zulfiqar	9		–
† A.P.E.Knott	not out	18		–
C.M.Old	b Mehmood	18		3
* M.H.Denness	not out	12		1
K.W.R.Fletcher				
J.A.Snow				
P.Lever				
D.L.Underwood				
Extras	(b 7, lb 7, w 1, nb 1)	16		
Total	(60 overs; 5 wickets)	**290**		

EAST AFRICA		Runs	Balls	4/6
Frasat Ali	b Snow	0		–
S.Walusimba	lbw b Snow	7		–
Yunus Badat	b Snow	0		–
Jawahir Shah	lbw b Snow	4		–
R.K.Sethi	b Lever	30		3
* Harilal Shah	b Greig	6		–
Mehmood Quaraishy	c Amiss b Greig	19		2
Zulfiqar Ali	b Lever	7		–
† H.McLeod	b Lever	0		–
P.G.Nana	not out	8		–
D.J.Pringle	b Old	3		–
Extras	(lb 6, w 1, nb 3)	10		
Total	(52.3 overs)	**94**		

EAST AFRICA	O	M	R	W
Frasat Ali	9	0	40	0
Pringle	12	0	41	0
Nana	12	2	46	0
Sethi	5	0	29	0
Zulfiqar Ali	12	0	63	3
Mehmood Quaraishy	10	0	55	2

ENGLAND	O	M	R	W
Snow	12	6	11	4
Lever	12	3	32	3
Underwood	10	5	11	0
Wood	7	3	10	0
Greig	10	1	18	2
Old	1.3	0	2	1

FALL OF WICKETS
1-158, 2-192, 3-234, 4-244, 5-277

FALL OF WICKETS
1-7, 2-7, 3-15, 4-21, 5-42, 6-72, 7-76, 8-79, 9-88, 10-94

Umpires: W.E.Alley (4) and J.G.Langridge (3).

NEW ZEALAND v INDIA 1975

At Old Trafford, Manchester on 14 June 1975.   Result: **NEW ZEALAND** won by 4 wickets.   Toss: India.
Award: G.M.Turner.   LOI debuts: None.

New Zealand qualified for the semi-finals as Glenn Turner's second hundred of the tournament elevated his World Cup average to 297.

INDIA		Runs	Balls	4/6
S.M.Gavaskar	c R.J.Hadlee b D.R.Hadlee	12		2
† F.M.Engineer	lbw b R.J.Hadlee	24		3
A.D.Gaekwad	c Hastings b R.J.Hadlee	37		3
G.R.Viswanath	lbw b McKechnie	2		–
B.P.Patel	c Wadsworth b H.J.Howarth	9		1
E.D.Solkar	c Wadsworth b H.J.Howarth	13		2
S.Abid Ali	c H.J.Howarth b McKechnie	70		5/1
Madan Lal	c and b McKechnie	20		4
M.Amarnath	c Morrison b D.R.Hadlee	1		–
* S.Venkataraghavan	not out	26		3
B.S.Bedi	run out	6		
Extras	(b 5, w 1, nb 4)	10		
Total	(60 overs)	**230**		

NEW ZEALAND		Runs	Balls	4/6
* G.M.Turner	not out	114		13
J.F.M.Morrison	c Engineer b Bedi	17		2
G.P.Howarth	run out	9		–
J.M.Parker	lbw b Abid Ali	1		–
B.F.Hastings	c Solkar b Amarnath	34		3
† K.J.Wadsworth	lbw b Madan Lal	22		3
R.J.Hadlee	b Abid Ali	15		2
D.R.Hadlee	not out	8		2
B.J.McKechnie				
H.J.Howarth				
R.O.Collinge				
Extras	(b 8, lb 5)	13		
Total	(58.5 overs; 6 wickets)	**233**		

NEW ZEALAND	O	M	R	W
Collinge	12	2	43	0
R.J.Hadlee	12	2	48	2
D.R.Hadlee	12	3	32	2
McKechnie	12	1	49	3
H.J.Howarth	12	0	48	2

INDIA	O	M	R	W
Madan Lal	11.5	1	62	1
Amarnath	8	1	40	1
Bedi	12	6	28	1
Abid Ali	12	2	35	2
Venkataraghavan	12	0	39	0
Solkar	3	0	16	0

FALL OF WICKETS
1-17, 2-48, 3-59, 4-81, 5-94, 6-101, 7-156, 8-157, 9-217, 10-230

FALL OF WICKETS
1-45, 2-62, 3-70, 4-135, 5-185, 6-224

Umpires: W.L.Budd (4) and A.E.Fagg (5).

AUSTRALIA v WEST INDIES 1975

At Kennington Oval, London on 14 June 1975.   Result: **WEST INDIES** won by 7 wickets.   Toss: West Indies.
Award: A.I.Kallicharran.   LOI debuts: None.

Immediately before his dismissal, Alvin Kallicharran scored 35 off ten successive balls from Dennis Lillee, five of them bouncers: 4444414604.

AUSTRALIA		Runs	Balls	4/6
R.B.McCosker	c Fredericks b Julien	0	3	–
A.Turner	lbw b Roberts	7	18	–
* I.M.Chappell	c Murray b Boyce	25	63	–
G.S.Chappell	c Murray b Boyce	15	33	–
K.D.Walters	run out	7	18	–
R.Edwards	b Richards	58	74	6
† R.W.Marsh	not out	52	84	4
M.H.N.Walker	lbw b Holder	8	22	1
J.R.Thomson	c Holder b Richards	1	3	–
D.K.Lillee	b Roberts	3	12	–
A.A.Mallett	c Murray b Roberts	0	1	–
Extras	(lb 9, w 1, nb 6)	16		
Total	(53.4 overs)	**192**		

WEST INDIES		Runs	Balls	4/6
R.C.Fredericks	c Marsh b Mallett	58	105	5
C.G.Greenidge	lbw b Walker	16	18	2
A.I.Kallicharran	c Mallett b Lillee	78	83	14/1
I.V.A.Richards	not out	15	38	2
R.B.Kanhai	not out	18	33	1
* C.H.Lloyd				
B.D.Julien				
† D.L.Murray				
K.D.Boyce				
V.A.Holder				
A.M.E.Roberts				
Extras	(b 4, lb 2, w 3, nb 1)	10		
Total	(46 overs; 3 wickets)	**195**		

WEST INDIES	O	M	R	W
Julien	12	2	31	1
Roberts	10.4	1	39	3
Boyce	11	0	38	2
Holder	10	0	31	1
Lloyd	4	1	19	0
Richards	6	0	18	2

AUSTRALIA	O	M	R	W
Lillee	10	0	66	1
Thomson	6	1	21	0
Walker	12	2	41	1
G.S.Chappell	4	0	13	0
Mallett	11	2	35	1
I.M.Chappell	3	1	9	0

FALL OF WICKETS
1-0, 2-21, 3-49, 4-56, 5-61, 6-160, 7-173, 8-174, 9-192, 10-192

FALL OF WICKETS
1-29, 2-153, 3-159

Umpires: H.D.Bird (6) and D.J.Constant (6).

PAKISTAN v SRI LANKA 1975

At Trent Bridge, Nottingham on 14 June 1975.   Result: **PAKISTAN** won by 192 runs.   Toss: Sri Lanka.
Award: Zaheer Abbas.   LOI debuts: Sri Lanka – G.R.A.de Silva.

Put in to bat, Pakistan responded with their highest LOI total until 1983 (*LOI No. 198*).

PAKISTAN		Runs	Balls	4/6
Sadiq Mohammed	c Opatha b Warnapura	74		12/1
* Majid Khan	c Tennekoon b D.S.de Silva	84		9/1
Zaheer Abbas	b Opatha	97		10/1
Mushtaq Mohammed	c Heyn b Warnapura	26		2
Wasim Raja	c Opatha b Warnapura	2		–
Javed Miandad	not out	28		1
Imran Khan	b Opatha	0		–
Parvez Mir	not out	4		–
† Wasim Bari				
Asif Masood				
Naseer Malik				
Extras	(b 4, lb 4, w 2, nb 5)	15		
Total	(60 overs; 6 wickets)	**330**		

SRI LANKA		Runs	Balls	4/6
† E.R.Fernando	c and b Miandad	21		3
B.Warnapura	b Imran	2		–
* A.P.B.Tennekoon	lbw b Naseer	30		4
M.H.Tissera	c Wasim Bari b Sadiq	12		2
P.D.Heyn	c Zaheer b Miandad	1		–
A.N.Ranasinghe	b Wasim Raja	9		–
H.S.M.Pieris	lbw b Parvez	16		2
A.R.M.Opatha	c Zaheer b Sadiq	0		–
D.S.de Silva	b Imran	26		4
L.W.S.Kaluperuma	not out	13		1
G.R.A.de Silva	c Wasim Raja b Imran	0		–
Extras	(lb 1, w 3, nb 4)	8		
Total	(50.1 overs)	**138**		

SRI LANKA	O	M	R	W
Opatha	12	0	67	2
Pieris	9	0	54	0
G.R.A.de Silva	7	1	46	0
D.S.de Silva	12	1	61	1
Kaluperuma	9	1	35	0
Warnapura	8	0	42	3
Ranasinghe	3	0	10	0

PAKISTAN	O	M	R	W
Asif Masood	6	2	14	0
Imran Khan	7.1	3	15	3
Javed Miandad	7	2	22	2
Naseer Malik	6	1	19	1
Sadiq Mohammed	6	1	20	2
Wasim Raja	7	4	7	1
Mushtaq Mohammed	5	0	16	0
Parvez Mir	6	1	17	1

FALL OF WICKETS
1-159, 2-168, 3-256, 4-268, 5-318, 6-318

FALL OF WICKETS
1-5, 2-44, 3-60, 4-61, 5-75, 6-79, 7-90, 8-113, 9-135, 10-138

Umpires: A.Jepson (4) and T.W.Spencer (5).

ENGLAND v AUSTRALIA 1975

At Headingley, Leeds on 18 June 1975. Result: **AUSTRALIA** won by 4 wickets. Toss: Australia.
Award: G.J.Gilmour. LOI debuts: None.

This semi-final lasted just 65 overs. The left-handed Gary Gilmour took full advantage of conditions ideal for swing and seam bowling, a damp pitch and heavy atmosphere, to return the first six-wicket analysis in limited-overs internationals. It remained the record until the 1983 World Cup when Winston Davis took 7 for 51 on the same ground (*LOI No. 203*).

ENGLAND		Runs	Balls	4/6
D.L.Amiss	lbw b Gilmour	2	7	–
B.Wood	b Gilmour	6	19	1
K.W.R.Fletcher	lbw b Gilmour	8	45	–
A.W.Greig	c Marsh b Gilmour	7	25	1
F.C.Hayes	lbw b Gilmour	4	6	1
* M.H.Denness	b Walker	27	60	1
† A.P.E.Knott	lbw b Gilmour	0	5	–
C.M.Old	c G.S.Chappell b Walker	0	3	–
J.A.Snow	c Marsh b Lillee	2	14	–
G.G.Arnold	not out	18	30	2
P.Lever	lbw b Walker	5	13	–
Extras	(lb 5, w 7, nb 2)	14		
Total	(36.2 overs)	**93**		

AUSTRALIA		Runs	Balls	4/6
A.Turner	lbw b Arnold	7	20	–
R.B.McCosker	b Old	15	50	–
* I.M.Chappell	lbw b Snow	2	19	–
G.S.Chappell	lbw b Snow	4	9	1
K.D.Walters	not out	20	43	2
R.Edwards	b Old	0	3	–
† R.W.Marsh	b Old	5	8	–
G.J.Gilmour	not out	28	28	5
M.H.N.Walker				
D.K.Lillee				
J.R.Thomson				
Extras	(b 1, lb 6, nb 6)	13		
Total	(28.4 overs; 6 wickets)	**94**		

AUSTRALIA	O	M	R	W
Lillee	9	3	26	1
Gilmour	12	6	14	6
Walker	9.2	3	22	3
Thomson	6	0	17	0

ENGLAND	O	M	R	W
Arnold	7.4	2	15	1
Snow	12	0	30	2
Old	7	2	29	3
Lever	2	0	7	0

FALL OF WICKETS
1-2, 2-11, 3-26, 4-33, 5-35, 6-36, 7-37, 8-52, 9-73, 10-93

FALL OF WICKETS
1-17, 2-24, 3-32, 4-32, 5-32, 6-39

Umpires: W.E.Alley (5) and D.J.Constant (7).

WEST INDIES v NEW ZEALAND 1975

At Kennington Oval, London on 18 June 1975. Result: **WEST INDIES** won by 5 wickets. Toss: West Indies.
Award: A.I.Kallicharran. LOI debuts: None.

Glenn Turner's dismissal, after adding 90 off 141 balls with Geoff Howarth, began a collapse in which nine wickets fell for 60 runs in 22.2 overs.

NEW ZEALAND		Runs	Balls	4/6
* G.M.Turner	c Kanhai b Roberts	36	74	3
J.F.M.Morrison	lbw b Julien	5	26	–
G.P.Howarth	c Murray b Roberts	51	93	3
J.M.Parker	b Lloyd	3	12	–
B.F.Hastings	not out	24	57	4
† K.J.Wadsworth	c Lloyd b Julien	11	21	1
B.J.McKechnie	lbw b Julien	1	9	–
D.R.Hadlee	c Holder b Julien	0	10	–
B.L.Cairns	b Holder	10	14	1
H.J.Howarth	b Holder	0	1	–
R.O.Collinge	b Holder	2	4	–
Extras	(b 1, lb 5, w 2, nb 7)	15		
Total	(52.2 overs)	**158**		

WEST INDIES		Runs	Balls	4/6
R.C.Fredericks	c Hastings b Hadlee	6	14	–
C.G.Greenidge	lbw b Collinge	55	95	9/1
A.I.Kallicharran	c and b Collinge	72	92	7/1
I.V.A.Richards	lbw b Collinge	5	10	1
R.B.Kanhai	not out	12	18	2
* C.H.Lloyd	c Hastings b McKechnie	3	8	–
B.D.Julien	not out	4	5	1
† D.L.Murray				
K.D.Boyce				
V.A.Holder				
A.M.E.Roberts				
Extras	(lb 1, nb 1)	2		
Total	(40.1 overs; 5 wickets)	**159**		

WEST INDIES	O	M	R	W
Julien	12	5	27	4
Roberts	11	3	18	2
Holder	8.2	0	30	3
Boyce	9	0	31	0
Lloyd	12	1	37	1

NEW ZEALAND	O	M	R	W
Collinge	12	4	28	3
Hadlee	10	0	54	1
Cairns	6.1	2	23	0
McKechnie	8	0	37	0
H.J.Howarth	4	0	15	0

FALL OF WICKETS
1-8, 2-98, 3-106, 4-106, 5-125, 6-133, 7-139, 8-155, 9-155, 10-158

FALL OF WICKETS
1-8, 2-133, 3-139, 4-142, 5-151

Umpires: W.L.Budd (5) and A.E.Fagg (6).

AUSTRALIA v WEST INDIES 1975

At Lord's, London on 21 June 1975.　Result: **WEST INDIES** won by 17 runs.　Toss: Australia.
Award: C.H.Lloyd.　LOI debuts: None.

At 8.42pm on the longest day of the year, West Indies became the first holders of the World Cup. Their leader, Clive Lloyd, contributed an 82-ball hundred to their highest LOI total so far. Viv Richards was responsible for the first three of five run outs in Australia's reply. Jeff Thomson was no-balled 13 times.

WEST INDIES		Runs	Balls	4/6
R.C.Fredericks	hit wicket b Lillee	7	13	–
C.G.Greenidge	c Marsh b Thomson	13	61	1
A.I.Kallicharran	c Marsh b Gilmour	12	18	2
R.B.Kanhai	b Gilmour	55	105	8
* C.H.Lloyd	c Marsh b Gilmour	102	85	12/2
I.V.A.Richards	b Gilmour	5	11	1
K.D.Boyce	c G.S.Chappell b Thomson	34	37	3
B.D.Julien	not out	26	37	1
† D.L.Murray	c and b Gilmour	14	10	1/1
V.A.Holder	not out	6	2	1
A.M.E.Roberts				
Extras	(lb 6, nb 11)	17		
Total	(60 overs; 8 wickets)	**291**		

AUSTRALIA		O	M	R	W
Lillee		12	1	55	1
Gilmour		12	2	48	5
Thomson		12	1	44	2
Walker		12	1	71	0
G.S.Chappell		7	0	33	0
Walters		5	0	23	0

FALL OF WICKETS
1-12, 2-27, 3-50, 4-199, 5-206, 6-209, 7-261, 8-285

AUSTRALIA		Runs	Balls	4/6
A.Turner	run out	40	24	1
R.B.McCosker	c Kallicharran b Boyce	7	54	1
* I.M.Chappell	run out	62	93	6
G.S.Chappell	run out	15	23	2
K.D.Walters	b Lloyd	35	51	5
† R.W.Marsh	b Boyce	11	24	–
R.Edwards	c Fredericks b Boyce	28	37	2
G.J.Gilmour	c Kanhai b Boyce	14	11	2
M.H.N.Walker	run out	7	9	1
J.R.Thomson	run out	21	21	2
D.K.Lillee	not out	16	19	1
Extras	(b 2, lb 9, nb 7)	18		
Total	(58.4 overs)	**274**		

WEST INDIES		O	M	R	W
Julien		12	0	58	0
Roberts		11	1	45	0
Boyce		12	0	50	4
Holder		11.4	1	65	0
Lloyd		12	1	38	1

FALL OF WICKETS
1-25, 2-81, 3-115, 4-162, 5-170, 6-195, 7-221, 8-231, 9-233, 10-274

Umpires: H.D.Bird (7) and T.W.Spencer (6).

AUSTRALIA v WEST INDIES 1975-76

At Adelaide Oval on 20 December 1975.　Result: **AUSTRALIA** won by 5 wickets.　Toss: Australia.
Award: I.M.Chappell.　LOI debuts: Australia – G.J.Cosier; West Indies – L.G.Rowe.　40 eight-ball overs match.

This initial meeting on Australian soil of the first World Cup finalists was staged four days after West Indies had gained an innings victory in the Perth Test.

WEST INDIES		Runs	Balls	4/6
R.C.Fredericks	b Lillee	21	21	3
C.G.Greenidge	c and b Cosier	41	63	1/2
L.G.Rowe	c Marsh b Gilmour	5	21	–
I.V.A.Richards	c Cosier b Gilmour	74	87	7/1
* C.H.Lloyd	c Marsh b Walker	1	11	–
A.I.Kallicharran	c Mallett b G.S.Chappell	37	55	2
B.D.Julien	b G.S.Chappell	9	16	1
† D.L.Murray	b Walker	8	19	–
K.D.Boyce	c and b Walker	9	17	1
V.A.Holder	lbw b Walker	0	1	–
A.M.E.Roberts	not out	3	4	–
Extras	(b 1, lb 4, nb 11)	16		
Total	(37.6 overs)	**224**		

AUSTRALIA		O	M	R	W
Lillee		8	1	44	1
Gilmour		8	0	48	2
Cosier		6	1	33	1
Walker		6.6	1	19	4
Mallett		2	0	21	0
G.S.Chappell		7	0	43	2

FALL OF WICKETS
1-39, 2-48, 3-86, 4-96, 5-188, 6-189, 7-201, 8-220, 9-220, 10-224

AUSTRALIA		Runs	Balls	4/6
A.Turner	c Murray b Holder	46	50	8
R.B.McCosker	c Murray b Roberts	0	2	–
I.M.Chappell	c Greenidge b Boyce	63	105	8/2
* G.S.Chappell	c and b Holder	59	82	6
I.R.Redpath	run out	24	32	3
G.J.Cosier	not out	25	32	1
M.H.N.Walker	not out	3	5	–
† R.W.Marsh				
G.J.Gilmour				
D.K.Lillee				
A.A.Mallett				
Extras	(lb 3, nb 2)	5		
Total	(31.5 overs; 5 wickets)	**225**		

WEST INDIES		O	M	R	W
Roberts		4	0	22	1
Julien		8	0	66	0
Holder		7.5	1	53	2
Boyce		7	0	41	1
Lloyd		3	0	28	0
Richards		2	0	10	0

FALL OF WICKETS
1-1, 2-86, 3-119, 4-179, 5-214

Umpires: R.C.Bailhache (2) and M.G.O'Connell (1).

NEW ZEALAND v INDIA 1975-76

At Lancaster Park, Christchurch on 21 February 1976.   Result: **NEW ZEALAND** won by 9 wickets.   Toss: India.
Award: R.O.Collinge.   LOI debuts: New Zealand – G.N.Edwards; India – S.M.H.Kirmani, P.Sharma, D.B.Vengsarkar.

These two 35 eight-ball overs internationals followed a drawn three-match Test rubber. On a true surface India managed to score only 36 runs from their first 120 balls. Richard Collinge achieved New Zealand's first five-wicket analysis at this level.

INDIA		Runs	Balls	4/6
P.Sharma	b Collinge	6		
D.B.Vengsarkar	run out	16		
A.D.Gaekwad	c R.J.Hadlee b Cairns	3		
G.R.Viswanath	c Turner b Cairns	56		5
B.P.Patel	c Wadsworth b D.R.Hadlee	17		
M.Amarnath	b Collinge	26		
E.D.Solkar	c Cairns b D.R.Hadlee	1		
† S.M.H.Kirmani	c D.R.Hadlee b Collinge	8		
Madan Lal	c Wadsworth b Collinge	8		
S.Venkataraghavan	b Collinge	0		
* B.S.Bedi	not out	4		
Extras	(b 2, lb 6, nb 1)	9		
Total	(35 overs)	**154**		

NEW ZEALAND		Runs	Balls	4/6
* G.M.Turner	not out	63		5
G.N.Edwards	lbw b Bedi	41		4/1
B.E.Congdon	not out	45		2/1
J.M.Parker				
M.G.Burgess				
† K.J.Wadsworth				
B.L.Cairns				
R.J.Hadlee				
B.J.McKechnie				
R.O.Collinge				
D.R.Hadlee				
Extras	(lb 6)	6		
Total	(30.3 overs; 1 wicket)	**155**		

NEW ZEALAND	O	M	R	W
Collinge	7	1	23	5
Cairns	7	1	20	2
R.J.Hadlee	6	0	28	0
McKechnie	5	0	16	0
D.R.Hadlee	7	0	41	2
Congdon	3	0	17	0

INDIA	O	M	R	W
Madan Lal	4.3	1	22	0
Solkar	5	0	27	0
Bedi	7	0	24	1
Amarnath	7	0	37	0
Venkataraghavan	7	0	39	0

FALL OF WICKETS
1-7, 2-16, 3-30, 4-87, 5-113, 6-117, 7-138, 8-149, 9-149, 10-154

FALL OF WICKETS
1-73

Umpires: E.W.Dempster (3) and A.M.Rangi (1).

NEW ZEALAND v INDIA 1975-76

At Eden Park, Auckland on 22 February 1976.   Result: **NEW ZEALAND** won by 80 runs.   Toss: New Zealand.
Award: K.J.Wadsworth.   LOI debuts: India – B.S.Chandrasekhar, P.Krishnamurthy, Sudhakar Rao.

In his final appearance for New Zealand, Ken Wadsworth added 52 in just 25 minutes with Mark Burgess. Six months later he died of cancer at the age of 29.

NEW ZEALAND		Runs	Balls	4/6
* G.M.Turner	st Krishnamurthy b Venkataraghavan	52		6
G.N.Edwards	c Madan Lal b Chandrasekhar	32		4
B.L.Cairns	run out	31		–/2
B.E.Congdon	c and b Solkar	2		–
J.M.Parker	c Venkataraghavan b Solkar	14		–
M.G.Burgess	b Chandrasekhar	38		4/1
† K.J.Wadsworth	not out	46	32	4/2
R.J.Hadlee	c Krishnamurthy b Chandrasekhar	0		–
B.J.McKechnie	c Rao b Amarnath	8		–
R.O.Collinge	not out	0		–
D.R.Hadlee				
Extras	(b 2, lb 11)	13		
Total	(35 overs; 8 wickets)	**236**		

INDIA		Runs	Balls	4/6
P.Sharma	b Cairns	14		
D.B.Vengsarkar	c Turner b D.R.Hadlee	43		8
A.D.Gaekwad	st Wadsworth b McKechnie	13		
B.P.Patel	c Turner b R.J.Hadlee	44		5/1
M.Amarnath	b D.R.Hadlee	3		
E.D.Solkar	run out	2		
Sudhakar Rao	run out	4		
Madan Lal	c D.R.Hadlee b Parker	13		
* S.Venkataraghavan	c Parker b Burgess	1		
† P.Krishnamurthy	c and b Edwards	6		
B.S.Chandrasekhar	not out	11		
Extras	(lb 2)	2		
Total	(31.6 overs)	**156**		

INDIA	O	M	R	W
Madan Lal	7	0	37	0
Solkar	7	0	46	2
Amarnath	7	0	59	1
Chandrasekhar	7	0	36	3
Venkataraghavan	7	0	45	1

NEW ZEALAND	O	M	R	W
Collinge	3	0	19	0
R.J.Hadlee	7	0	35	1
Cairns	7	1	33	1
D.R.Hadlee	7	0	18	2
McKechnie	4	0	24	1
Parker	2	0	10	1
Burgess	1	0	10	1
Edwards	0.6	0	5	1

FALL OF WICKETS
1-71, 2-106, 3-109, 4-142, 5-142, 6-194, 7-194, 8-230

FALL OF WICKETS
1-40, 2-66, 3-78, 4-97, 5-103, 6-120, 7-128, 8-139, 9-139, 10-156

Umpires: W.R.C.Gardiner (1) and J.B.R.Hastie (2).

ENGLAND v WEST INDIES 1976

At North Marine Road, Scarborough on 26 August 1976.　Result: **WEST INDIES** won by 6 wickets.　Toss: West Indies.
Award: I.V.A.Richards　LOI debuts: England – G.D.Barlow, I.T.Botham, G.A.Gooch, J.K.Lever, D.S.Steele; West Indies –
M.A.Holding, C.L.King.　55-over match.

Barry Wood was bowled by the first ball of the match. Michael Holding's return from long-leg deflected off the nearer
wicket to break the far one with Graham Barlow and Alan Knott (on his only appearance as England's captain) by then
in mid pitch. The dumbfounded umpires rejected the run out appeal. Viv Richards's first LOI hundred took 118 balls.

ENGLAND		Runs	Balls	4/6	WEST INDIES		Runs	Balls	4/6
B.Wood	b Roberts	0	1	–	R.C.Fredericks	b Hendrick	1	4	–
D.L.Amiss	b Julien	34	55	3	C.G.Greenidge	b Wood	27	36	3/1
D.S.Steele	c King b Roberts	8	12	1	I.V.A.Richards	not out	119	133	20/1
R.A.Woolmer	c Murray b Holding	3	14	–	* C.H.Lloyd	b Underwood	20	27	3/1
G.D.Barlow	not out	80	139	8	L.G.Rowe	c Hendrick b Botham	10	37	1
G.A.Gooch	c Holder b Roberts	32	69	4	C.L.King	not out	14	9	1/1
I.T.Botham	c Fredericks b Holding	1	7	–	† D.L.Murray				
*†A.P.E.Knott	run out	16	20	1	B.D.Julien				
D.L.Underwood	c Julien b Roberts	14	16	2	V.A.Holder				
J.K.Lever					M.A.Holding				
M.Hendrick					A.M.E.Roberts				
Extras	(lb 11, w 1, nb 2)	14			Extras	(b 8, lb 8)	16		
Total	(55 overs; 8 wickets)	202			Total	(41 overs; 4 wickets)	207		

WEST INDIES	O	M	R	W	ENGLAND	O	M	R	W
Roberts	11	0	32	4	Lever	9	1	38	0
Holding	11	1	38	2	Hendrick	9	3	38	1
Holder	11	3	30	0	Wood	8	2	29	1
Julien	11	2	37	1	Underwood	9	1	35	1
King	6	0	25	0	Botham	3	0	26	1
Lloyd	5	1	26	0	Woolmer	2	0	16	0
					Steele	1	0	9	0

FALL OF WICKETS
1-0, 2-18, 3-23, 4-72, 5-136, 6-145, 7-181, 8-202

Umpires: D.J.Constant (8) and A.Jepson (5).

FALL OF WICKETS
1-3, 2-77, 3-116, 4-176

ENGLAND v WEST INDIES 1976

At Lord's, London on 28, 29 August 1976.　Result: **WEST INDIES** won by 36 runs.　Toss: England.
Award: I.V.A.Richards.　LOI debuts: England – D.W.Randall.　50-over match.

Reduced by five overs an innings when rain delayed the start by 90 minutes, this match was taken into the reserve day
by a subsequent 75-minute stoppage. Richards reached his fifty off 42 balls. England were 47 for 4 after 14 overs
overnight.

WEST INDIES		Runs	Balls	4/6	ENGLAND		Runs	Balls	4/6
R.C.Fredericks	c Randall b Hendrick	19	42	2	B.Wood	c and b Roberts	4	4	1
C.G.Greenidge	b Hendrick	29	32	3/1	D.L.Amiss	c Murray b Roberts	12	21	2
I.V.A.Richards	c Woolmer b Greig	97	96	10	R.A.Woolmer	b Roberts	9	20	1
* C.H.Lloyd	c Barlow b Woolmer	27	34	2/1	G.D.Barlow	c Holder b Roberts	0	7	–
C.L.King	c Wood b Woolmer	1	11	–	G.A.Gooch	c Murray b Holder	5	21	–
L.G.Rowe	b Underwood	4	12	–	D.W.Randall	c King b Lloyd	88	133	10/1
† D.L.Murray	c and b Underwood	1	6	–	* A.W.Greig	c Richards b Julien	3	8	–
B.D.Julien	c Randall b Underwood	4	15	–	†A.P.E.Knott	run out	22	39	1/1
M.A.Holding	c Barlow b Wood	16	25	2	R.D.Jackman	b Holder	14	25	–
V.A.Holder	b Greig	2	3	–	D.L.Underwood	c Greenidge b Lloyd	2	4	–
A.M.E.Roberts	not out	7	17	–	M.Hendrick	not out	0	–	–
Extras	(b 5, lb 5, w 1, nb 3)	14			Extras	(lb 14, w 4, nb 8)	26		
Total	(47.5 overs)	221			Total	(45.3 overs)	185		

ENGLAND	O	M	R	W	WEST INDIES	O	M	R	W
Hendrick	9	2	34	2	Roberts	8	1	27	4
Jackman	10	1	50	0	Holding	8	0	26	0
Woolmer	10	0	52	2	Julien	10	4	22	1
Underwood	10	0	27	3	Holder	10	0	35	2
Greig	5.5	0	31	2	King	8	0	45	0
Wood	3	0	13	1	Lloyd	1.3	0	4	2

FALL OF WICKETS
1-51, 2-53, 3-121, 4-124, 5-135, 6-143, 7-154, 8-193, 9-201, 10-221

FALL OF WICKETS
1-4, 2-25, 3-30, 4-31, 5-48, 6-62, 7-125, 8-180, 9-185, 10-185

Umpires: W.E.Alley (6) and A.E.Fagg (7).

ENGLAND v WEST INDIES 1976

At Edgbaston, Birmingham on 30 (*no play*), 31 August 1976.   Result: **WEST INDIES** won by 50 runs.   Toss: England.
Award: C.H.Lloyd.   LOI debuts: None.

Rain delayed the start until 1.50pm on the reserve day and reduced the match to 32 overs per innings. Clive Lloyd required 42 balls for his fifty. Vanburn Holder returned the first five-wicket analysis for West Indies in these matches.

WEST INDIES		Runs	Balls	4/6
R.C.Fredericks	c Barlow b Lever	1	4	–
C.G.Greenidge	c Hendrick b Underwood	42	41	4/1
I.V.A.Richards	c Wood b Lever	0	2	–
* C.H.Lloyd	b Greig	79	59	3/7
L.G.Rowe	run out	45	42	5
C.L.King	lbw b Hendrick	7	9	–
B.D.Julien	b Hendrick	5	7	1
† D.L.Murray	run out	27	24	1
M.A.Holding	b Botham	3	7	–
A.M.E.Roberts	not out	0	1	–
V.A.Holder				
Extras	(lb 12, nb 2)	14		
Total	(32 overs; 9 wickets)	**223**		

ENGLAND	O	M	R	W
Hendrick	10	0	45	2
Lever	10	1	57	2
Botham	3	0	31	1
Underwood	3	0	28	1
Greig	6	0	48	1

FALL OF WICKETS
1-7, 2-7, 3-95, 4-145, 5-162, 6-174, 7-209, 8-223, 9-223

Umpires: H.D.Bird (8) and W.L.Budd (6).

ENGLAND		Runs	Balls	4/6
B.Wood	b Julien	34	49	5
D.L.Amiss	b Julien	47	54	7
G.D.Barlow	lbw b Holder	0	3	–
G.A.Gooch	c Murray b Holder	3	12	–
D.W.Randall	c Murray b Holder	39	29	8
* A.W.Greig	b Holder	2	6	–
I.T.Botham	c Julien b Fredericks	20	21	1
† A.P.E.Knott	c Greenidge b Holder	10	8	2
D.L.Underwood	st Murray b Richards	6	8	–
J.K.Lever	b Fredericks	1	2	–
M.Hendrick	not out	1	1	–
Extras	(b 2, lb 6, nb 2)	10		
Total	(31.4 overs)	**173**		

WEST INDIES	O	M	R	W
Roberts	5	1	9	0
Holding	7	1	34	0
Holder	10	0	50	5
Julien	7	0	56	2
Fredericks	1.4	0	10	2
Richards	1	0	4	1

FALL OF WICKETS
1-54, 2-59, 3-73, 4-89, 5-111, 6-138, 7-151, 8-171, 9-171, 10-173

PAKISTAN v NEW ZEALAND 1976-77

At Jinnah Park, Sialkot on 16 October 1976.   Result: **NEW ZEALAND** won by 1 run.   Toss: New Zealand.
No award.   LOI debuts: New Zealand – R.W.Anderson, N.M.Parker, A.D.G.Roberts, G.B.Troup.   35 eight-ball overs match.

The inaugural limited-overs international in Pakistan resulted in the first instance of victory by a single run. Requiring four runs from Richard Collinge's final ball, Wasim Bari was restricted to a two.

NEW ZEALAND		Runs	Balls	4/6
J.F.M.Morrison	b Intikhab	15		2
* G.M.Turner	b Asif Masood	67		6
N.M.Parker	lbw b Intikhab	0	3	–
G.P.Howarth	b Miandad	43		5
A.D.G.Roberts	c Wasim Bari b Sarfraz	16		
† J.M.Parker	c Mushtaq b Miandad	2		
R.W.Anderson	not out	4		
B.L.Cairns	c Zaheer b Imran	24		–/1
D.R.O'Sullivan	run out	1		
R.O.Collinge	not out	5		
G.B.Troup				
Extras	(b 3, lb 11, nb 7)	21		
Total	(35 overs; 8 wickets)	**198**		

PAKISTAN	O	M	R	W
Sarfraz Nawaz	7	0	35	1
Imran Khan	7	0	36	1
Asif Masood	7	0	38	1
Intikhab Alam	7	0	36	2
Javed Miandad	6	0	31	2
Wasim Raja	1	0	1	0

FALL OF WICKETS
1-48, 2-48, 3-135, 4-143, 5-160, 6-161, 7-188, 8-189

Umpires: Javed Akhtar (1) and Mahboob Shah (1).

PAKISTAN		Runs	Balls	4/6
Majid Khan	b Roberts	20		3
Sadiq Mohammed	run out	17		
Zaheer Abbas	st J.M.Parker b O'Sullivan	23		2/1
* Mushtaq Mohammed	c Roberts b Troup	46		1
Javed Miandad	b Cairns	47		1
Intikhab Alam	c N.M.Parker b Collinge	7		
Wasim Raja	b Cairns	8		
Imran Khan	not out	4		
Sarfraz Nawaz	run out	0		
Asif Masood	run out	0		
† Wasim Bari	not out	2		
Extras	(b 18, lb 5)	23		
Total	(35 overs; 9 wickets)	**197**		

NEW ZEALAND	O	M	R	W
Collinge	7	0	37	1
Cairns	7	0	36	2
Roberts	7	0	30	1
Troup	7	1	29	1
O'Sullivan	7	0	42	1

FALL OF WICKETS
1-38, 2-43, 3-89, 4-139, 5-166, 6-188, 7-191, 8-192, 9-195

WEST INDIES v PAKISTAN 1976-77

At Albion Sports Complex, Berbice, Guyana on 16 March 1977.   Result: **WEST INDIES** won by 4 wickets.   Toss: West Indies.
Award: Asif Iqbal.   LOI debuts: West Indies – C.E.H.Croft, J.Garner; Pakistan – Mohsin Khan.   45-over match.

A new sporting complex, 75 miles south-east of Georgetown, attracted nearly 15,000 spectators for the Caribbean's first limited-overs international. Rain seepage through the covers delayed the start and reduced the contest from 50 to 45 overs per innings.

PAKISTAN		Runs	Balls	4/6
Majid Khan	c Lloyd b Garner	23		
Sadiq Mohammed	c Murray b Croft	6		
Zaheer Abbas	c Julien b Garner	10		
Mohsin Khan	lbw b Julien	15		
Wasim Raja	c Fredericks b Croft	0		
* Asif Iqbal	not out	59		4/1
Javed Miandad	c Greenidge b Croft	15		
Imran Khan	b Garner	39		
Sarfraz Nawaz	not out	2		
† Wasim Bari				
Salim Altaf				
Extras	(b 1, lb 4, w 1, nb 1)	7		
Total	(45 overs; 7 wickets)	176		

WEST INDIES		Runs	Balls	4/6
R.C.Fredericks	c Asif Iqbal b Majid	44		
C.G.Greenidge	b Imran	8		–/1
I.V.A.Richards	c Mohsin b Sarfraz	20		
A.I.Kallicharran	c Asif Iqbal b Sarfraz	24		
* C.H.Lloyd	not out	45		–/1
C.L.King	c Wasim Bari b Asif Iqbal	0		
B.D.Julien	c Wasim Bari b Sarfraz	20		
† D.L.Murray	not out	11		
J.Garner				
A.M.E.Roberts				
C.E.H.Croft				
Extras	(b 4, lb 4, w 1, nb 1)	10		
Total	(43.2 overs; 6 wickets)	182		

WEST INDIES	O	M	R	W
Roberts	9	3	27	0
Julien	9	1	30	1
Croft	9	2	50	3
Garner	9	3	27	3
King	9	0	35	0

PAKISTAN	O	M	R	W
Sarfraz Nawaz	9	1	42	3
Imran Khan	9	1	41	1
Salim Altaf	8	0	27	0
Asif Iqbal	8	0	30	1
Majid Khan	9	1	26	1
Sadiq Mohammed	0.2	0	6	0

FALL OF WICKETS
1-32, 2-36, 3-46, 4-47, 5-67, 6-104, 7-171

Umpires: C.Paynter (1) and C.F.Vyfhuis (1).

FALL OF WICKETS
1-27, 2-59, 3-96, 4-121, 5-122, 6-151

ENGLAND v AUSTRALIA 1977

At Old Trafford, Manchester on 2 June 1977.   Result: **ENGLAND** won by 2 wickets.   Toss: Australia.
Award: R.W.Marsh.   LOI debuts: England – J.M.Brearley, P.Willey; Australia – D.W.Hookes, M.F.Malone, K.J.O'Keeffe, L.S.Pascoe, C.S.Serjeant.   55-over match.

Tony Greig having been relieved of England's captaincy because of his involvement with World Series cricket, his successor, Mike Brearley, began his reign with a hard-fought victory. The pitch was underprepared following the head groundsman's unheralded departure three days earlier.

AUSTRALIA		Runs	Balls	4/6
R.B.McCosker	c Knott b Willis	1	8	–
I.C.Davis	c Greig b Lever	1	5	–
* G.S.Chappell	lbw b Underwood	30	63	3
C.S.Serjeant	c Randall b Greig	46	109	4/1
K.D.Walters	c Amiss b Old	0	6	–
D.W.Hookes	c Knott b Greig	11	48	–
† R.W.Marsh	b Lever	42	29	5/2
K.J.O'Keeffe	not out	16	37	1
M.H.N.Walker	c Barlow b Underwood	5	11	1
M.F.Malone	c Brearley b Underwood	4	4	1
L.S.Pascoe	not out	4	12	–
Extras	(b 4, lb 4, nb 1)	9		
Total	(55 overs; 9 wickets)	169		

ENGLAND		Runs	Balls	4/6
D.L.Amiss	c Serjeant b Walker	8	23	1
* J.M.Brearley	lbw b Malone	29	70	5
D.W.Randall	c McCosker b Malone	19	28	4
G.D.Barlow	run out	42	66	7
P.Willey	c Walker b O'Keeffe	1	4	–
A.W.Greig	run out	22	29	3
† A.P.E.Knott	not out	21	21	3
C.M.Old	c Hookes b Walker	25	23	4
J.K.Lever	c Walters b Walker	1	4	–
D.L.Underwood	not out	0	5	–
R.G.D.Willis				
Extras	(b 1, lb 3, w 1)	5		
Total	(45.2 overs; 8 wickets)	173		

ENGLAND	O	M	R	W
Willis	8	2	16	1
Lever	10	1	45	2
Underwood	11	1	29	3
Old	11	3	30	1
Willey	11	1	29	0
Greig	4	0	11	2

AUSTRALIA	O	M	R	W
Pascoe	10.2	1	44	0
Walker	7	3	20	3
Malone	11	1	37	2
O'Keeffe	11	3	36	1
Chappell	6	1	31	0

FALL OF WICKETS
1-2, 2-2, 3-55, 4-62, 5-93, 6-94, 7-145, 8-152, 9-156

Umpires: D.J.Constant (9) and B.J.Meyer (1).

FALL OF WICKETS
1-17, 2-51, 3-70, 4-71, 5-123, 6-125, 7-160, 8-168

ENGLAND v AUSTRALIA 1977

At Edgbaston, Birmingham on 4 June 1977.   Result: **ENGLAND** won by 101 runs.   Toss: Australia.
Award: J.K.Lever.   LOI debuts: Australia – K.J.Hughes, R.D.Robinson.   55-over match.

Greg Chappell and Gary Cosier achieved the only instance of two bowlers taking five wickets in the same LOI innings. Australia's total remained their lowest (subsequently equalled) in all internationals and the lowest by any side in Prudential or Texaco Trophy matches.

ENGLAND		Runs	Balls	4/6
D.L.Amiss	c Marsh b Chappell	35	52	5
* J.M.Brearley	lbw b Chappell	10	38	1
D.W.Randall	c Marsh b Chappell	0	1	–
G.D.Barlow	c Hughes b Chappell	25	29	3
P.Willey	c Marsh b Cosier	6	18	1
A.W.Greig	c Chappell b Cosier	0	15	–
† A.P.E.Knott	lbw b Cosier	0	4	–
C.M.Old	c Hughes b Chappell	35	59	6
J.K.Lever	not out	27	85	2
D.L.Underwood	b Cosier	0	18	–
R.G.D.Willis	c Marsh b Cosier	7	17	1
Extras	(lb 15, w 4, nb 7)	26		
Total	**(53.5 overs)**	**171**		

AUSTRALIA		Runs	Balls	4/6
I.C.Davis	c Old b Willis	0	2	–
C.S.Serjeant	b Willis	2	17	–
* G.S.Chappell	b Lever	19	21	4
G.J.Cosier	lbw b Lever	3	11	–
K.J.Hughes	c Knott b Lever	2	11	–
R.D.Robinson	b Old	12	32	2
† R.W.Marsh	c Old b Lever	1	4	–
R.J.Bright	not out	17	37	1/1
M.H.N.Walker	run out	0	2	–
M.F.Malone	run out	1	5	–
J.R.Thomson	b Greig	3	12	–
Extras	(b 4, lb 5, nb 1)	10		
Total	**(25.2 overs)**	**70**		

AUSTRALIA	O	M	R	W
Thomson	9	0	46	0
Malone	11	2	27	0
Chappell	11	5	20	5
Walker	11	3	29	0
Cosier	8.5	3	18	5
Bright	3	0	5	0

ENGLAND	O	M	R	W
Willis	6	1	14	2
Lever	11	2	29	4
Old	7	2	15	1
Greig	1.2	0	2	1

FALL OF WICKETS
1-0, 2-27, 3-31, 4-34, 5-35, 6-38, 7-58, 8-58, 9-60, 10-70

FALL OF WICKETS
1-19, 2-19, 3-67, 4-84, 5-84, 6-84, 7-90, 8-145, 9-160, 10-171

Umpires: W.E.Alley (7) and W.L.Budd (7).

ENGLAND v AUSTRALIA 1977

At Kennington Oval, London on 6 June 1977.   Result: **AUSTRALIA** won by 2 wickets.   Toss: Australia.
Award: G.S.Chappell.   LOI debuts: England – G.Miller.   55-over match.

Dennis Amiss became the first batsman to score four hundreds in these matches. Greg Chappell's score remained the record in Prudential Trophy matches. To avoid having to return on Jubilee Day, the match was completed in torrential rain.

ENGLAND		Runs	Balls	4/6
D.L.Amiss	b Pascoe	108	146	7
* J.M.Brearley	st Robinson b O'Keeffe	78	113	11
D.W.Randall	c and b Bright	6	4	1
G.D.Barlow	run out	2	11	–
A.W.Greig	c Robinson b Thomson	4	11	–
† A.P.E.Knott	c Robinson b Pascoe	4	4	1
G.Miller	c Robinson b Pascoe	4	4	1
C.M.Old	c Thomson b Chappell	20	25	2
J.K.Lever	b Thomson	2	11	–
D.L.Underwood	c Pascoe b Dymock	5	9	1
R.G.D.Willis	not out	0	–	–
Extras	(lb 1, w 2, nb 6)	9		
Total	**(54.2 overs)**	**242**		

AUSTRALIA		Runs	Balls	4/6
† R.D.Robinson	c Brearley b Willis	70	111	5/1
R.B.McCosker	lbw b Old	11	36	–
* G.S.Chappell	not out	125	137	11
K.J.Hughes	lbw b Willis	3	6	–
K.D.Walters	c Brearley b Underwood	12	18	2
D.W.Hookes	b Lever	3	8	–
R.J.Bright	c Randall b Old	0	2	–
K.J.O'Keeffe	run out	0	1	–
J.R.Thomson	run out	3	3	–
G.Dymock	not out	2	2	–
L.S.Pascoe				
Extras	(b 1, lb 14, w 1, nb 1)	17		
Total	**(53.2 overs; 8 wickets)**	**246**		

AUSTRALIA	O	M	R	W
Thomson	11	2	51	2
Dymock	10	0	39	1
Pascoe	11	0	44	3
O'Keeffe	11	0	43	1
Bright	11	1	56	1
Chappell	0.2	0	0	1

ENGLAND	O	M	R	W
Willis	11	0	49	2
Lever	10	0	43	1
Old	10.2	0	56	2
Underwood	11	2	21	1
Miller	5	0	24	0
Greig	6	0	36	0

FALL OF WICKETS
1-161, 2-168, 3-179, 4-196, 5-203, 6-207, 7-217, 8-227, 9-241, 10-242

FALL OF WICKETS
1-33, 2-181, 3-186, 4-209, 5-225, 6-228, 7-228, 8-237

Umpires: H.D.Bird (9) and K.E.Palmer (1).

PAKISTAN v ENGLAND 1977-78

At Zafar Ali Stadium, Sahiwal on 23 December 1977.　Result: **ENGLAND** won by 3 wickets.　Toss: Pakistan.
Awards: batting – Javed Miandad; bowling and fielding – I.T.Botham.　LOI debuts: Pakistan – Aamer Hameed, Hasan Jamil, Liaqat Ali, Mudassar Nazar, Shafiq Ahmed; England – P.R.Downton, P.H.Edmonds, M.W.Gatting, B.C.Rose.

England's first limited-overs excursion in Pakistan involved a three-match tournament of 35 eight-ball overs per innings. This initial encounter produced a dramatic climax when, with the scores level, Ian Botham drove the final ball to the cover boundary.

PAKISTAN		Runs	Balls	4/6
Mudassar Nazar	run out	20	51	3
Sadiq Mohammed	b Botham	2	5	–
Shafiq Ahmed	b Miller	29	43	2
Javed Miandad	not out	77	109	3/2
Wasim Raja	c Randall b Botham	36	38	4/1
Parvez Mir	lbw b Hendrick	18	28	2
Hasan Jamil	c Downton b Botham	20	11	1
*†Wasim Bari	not out	1	1	–
Salim Altaf				
Aamer Hameed				
Liaqat Ali				
Extras	(lb 3, nb 2)	5		
Total	(35 overs; 6 wickets)	**208**		

ENGLAND		Runs	Balls	4/6
* J.M.Brearley	c Parvez b Aamer	30	56	4
B.C.Rose	c and b Wasim Raja	54	104	6
M.W.Gatting	run out	17	40	2
D.W.Randall	c Wasim Bari b Salim	35	41	2/2
C.M.Old	lbw b Parvez	1	3	–
G.R.J.Roope	b Liaqat Ali	29	27	1/2
I.T.Botham	not out	15	12	1
P.H.Edmonds	run out	5	5	–
G.Miller	not out	0	1	–
† P.R.Downton				
M.Hendrick				
Extras	(b 5, lb 14, nb 7)	26		
Total	(35 overs; 7 wickets)	**212**		

ENGLAND	O	M	R	W
Hendrick	7	0	50	1
Botham	7	0	39	3
Old	7	0	49	0
Edmonds	7	0	19	0
Miller	7	0	46	1

PAKISTAN	O	M	R	W
Salim Altaf	7	0	34	1
Liaqat Ali	7	0	50	1
Aamer Hameed	7	1	32	1
Parvez Mir	4	0	18	1
Javed Miandad	7	1	29	0
Wasim Raja	2	0	11	1
Mudassar Nazar	1	0	12	0

FALL OF WICKETS
1-4, 2-46, 3-63, 4-114, 5-167, 6-201

Umpires: Azhar Hussain (1) and Shakoor Rana (1).

FALL OF WICKETS
1-66, 2-111, 3-127, 4-134, 5-181, 6-193, 7-205

PAKISTAN v ENGLAND 1977-78

At Jinnah Park, Sialkot on 30 December 1977.　Result: **ENGLAND** won by 6 wickets.　Toss: England.
Awards: batting – Wasim Raja; bowling – J.K.Lever; fielding – D.W.Randall.　LOI debuts: Pakistan – Haroon Rashid, Iqbal Qasim, Sikander Bakht; England – G.A.Cope.

With Mike Brearley resting himself, Geoffrey Boycott made his first appearance as England's captain and won an important toss. His place in the batting order was determined by strategy and not malady. Ian Botham again made the winning hit but this time with 17 balls to spare. One of Wasim Raja's sixes narrowly missed a browsing water buffalo.

PAKISTAN		Runs	Balls	4/6
Sadiq Mohammed	c Taylor b Lever	13	32	2
Mudassar Nazar	c Randall b Cope	33	55	3
Shafiq Ahmed	c and b Edmonds	9	33	–
Haroon Rashid	c Rose b Miller	5	27	–
Javed Miandad	run out	8	9	–/1
Wasim Raja	b Botham	43	54	2/2
*†Wasim Bari	b Edmonds	1	6	–
Hasan Jamil	c Taylor b Lever	28	42	1/1
Salim Altaf	not out	4	8	–
Iqbal Qasim	c and b Lever	0	3	–
Sikander Bakht	run out	0	5	–
Extras	(b 4, lb 2, nb 1)	7		
Total	(33.7 overs)	**151**		

ENGLAND		Runs	Balls	4/6
B.C.Rose	b Qasim	45	106	1
G.R.J.Roope	c Haroon b Sikander	7	21	–
G.Miller	c Sikander b Qasim	16	34	1
D.W.Randall	not out	51	81	2
M.W.Gatting	run out	5	6	–
I.T.Botham	not out	17	22	–
* G.Boycott				
† R.W.Taylor				
P.H.Edmonds				
J.K.Lever				
G.A.Cope				
Extras	(lb 4, w 1, nb 6)	11		
Total	(32.7 overs; 4 wickets)	**152**		

ENGLAND	O	M	R	W
Lever	6	1	18	3
Botham	6.7	0	21	1
Cope	7	0	19	1
Miller	6	1	43	1
Edmonds	7	0	28	2
Gatting	1	0	15	0

PAKISTAN	O	M	R	W
Salim Altaf	5.7	0	20	0
Sikander Bakht	6	0	25	1
Javed Miandad	7	0	32	0
Iqbal Qasim	7	2	16	2
Hasan Jamil	6	0	39	0
Wasim Raja	1	0	9	0

FALL OF WICKETS
1-20, 2-55, 3-57, 4-65, 5-74, 6-76, 7-140, 8-150, 9-150, 10-151

FALL OF WICKETS
1-17, 2-43, 3-104, 4-112

Umpires: Javed Akhtar (2) and Khalid Aziz (1).

PAKISTAN v ENGLAND 1977-78

At Gaddafi Stadium, Lahore on 13 January 1978.   Result: **PAKISTAN** won by 36 runs.   Toss: England.
Award: Wasim Raja.   LOI debuts: Pakistan – Arshad Pervez.

General Zia-ul-Haq and Prime Minister James Callaghan watched 70 minutes of play but departed before England suffered their first defeat of the tour in their tenth match.

PAKISTAN		Runs	Balls	4/6
Mudassar Nazar	b Edmonds	30	66	1
Arshad Pervez	b Lever	8	29	–
Shafiq Ahmed	st Taylor b Edmonds	3	15	–
Javed Miandad	c Boycott b Lever	31	75	1
Wasim Raja	c Boycott b Cope	0	4	–
Mohsin Khan	not out	51	75	4
Hasan Jamil	c Boycott b Old	21	15	1/1
Sarfraz Nawaz	not out	1	4	–
*†Wasim Bari				
Aamer Hameed				
Iqbal Qasim				
Extras	(lb 11, nb 2)	13		
Total	(35 overs; 6 wickets)	**158**		

ENGLAND		Runs	Balls	4/6
G.Boycott	lbw b Sarfraz	6	21	–
*J.M.Brearley	c Shafiq b Sarfraz	1	8	–
D.W.Randall	c Mudassar b Wasim Raja	32	77	2
M.W.Gatting	c and b Jamil	3	32	–
I.T.Botham	c Wasim Bari b Qasim	11	10	2
C.M.Old	c Wasim Raja b Jamil	4	8	–
G.R.J.Roope	run out	37	73	1
†R.W.Taylor	b Wasim Raja	12	25	1
P.H.Edmonds	run out	0	2	–
J.K.Lever	c Aamer b Wasim Raja	0	4	–
G.A.Cope	not out	1	1	–
Extras	(b 2, lb 6, w 1, nb 6)	15		
Total	(31.6 overs)	**122**		

ENGLAND	O	M	R	W
Old	7	0	35	1
Lever	7	1	25	2
Botham	7	0	41	0
Edmonds	7	1	28	2
Cope	7	0	16	1

PAKISTAN	O	M	R	W
Sarfraz Nawaz	5	2	7	2
Aamer Hameed	4	1	6	0
Hasan Jamil	5	0	20	2
Iqbal Qasim	7	2	25	1
Javed Miandad	6	0	26	0
Wasim Raja	4.6	0	23	3

FALL OF WICKETS
1-22, 2-41, 3-52, 4-53, 5-112, 6-148

FALL OF WICKETS
1-11, 2-15, 3-25, 4-42, 5-49, 6-97, 7-118, 8-119, 9-121, 10-122

Umpires: Khalid Aziz (2) and Shakoor Rana (2).

WEST INDIES v AUSTRALIA 1977-78

At Recreation Ground, St John's, Antigua on 22 February 1978.   Result: **WEST INDIES** won on faster scoring rate.   Toss: Australia.
Award: D.L.Haynes.   LOI debuts: West Indies – R.A.Austin, S.F.A.F.Bacchus, W.W.Daniel, D.L.Haynes, I.T.Shillingford; Australia – I.W.Callen, W.M.Clark, W.M.Darling, T.J.Laughlin, S.J.Rixon, R.B.Simpson, P.M.Toohey, G.M.Wood, G.N.Yallop.   50-over match.

The World Series schism was responsible for the appearance of 14 debutants in this match. Desmond Haynes emulated Dennis Amiss (*LOI No. 2*) by scoring a hundred on debut. He was to wait more than five years before registering the next of his record 17 centuries. West Indies had secured the match long before fading light caused its premature end.

WEST INDIES		Runs	Balls	4/6
R.A.Austin	c Simpson b Clark	8	–	
D.L.Haynes	b Thomson	148	136	16/2
I.V.A.Richards	c sub (B.Yardley) b Callen	9	2	
A.I.Kallicharran	c Rixon b Laughlin	7	1	
S.F.A.F.Bacchus	hit wicket b Laughlin	0	–	
I.T.Shillingford	b Thomson	24	4	
*†D.L.Murray	c Simpson b Laughlin	51	3	
J.Garner	c Rixon b Thomson	13	1	
A.M.E.Roberts	c Callen b Thomson	3	–	
W.W.Daniel	not out	14	2	
C.E.H.Croft	not out	5	–	
Extras	(b 3, lb 10, nb 18)	31		
Total	(50 overs; 9 wickets)	**313**		

AUSTRALIA		Runs	Balls	4/6
G.M.Wood	c Shillingford b Croft	24	4	
W.M.Darling	c Kallicharran b Croft	8	1	
G.N.Yallop	c and b Garner	12	1	
P.M.Toohey	lbw b Garner	5	-1	
G.J.Cosier	c Daniel b Croft	84	11/1	
*R.B.Simpson	b Garner	13	2	
T.J.Laughlin	c Richards b Daniel	2	–	
†S.J.Rixon	not out	20	1	
I.W.Callen	not out	3	–	
J.R.Thomson				
W.M.Clark				
Extras	(nb 10)	10		
Total	(36 overs; 7 wickets)	**181**		

AUSTRALIA	O	M	R	W
Thomson	10	0	67	4
Clark	10	3	22	1
Callen	7	1	42	1
Laughlin	9	2	54	3
Simpson	10	0	65	0
Cosier	4	0	32	0

WEST INDIES	O	M	R	W
Roberts	7	0	38	0
Croft	10	1	44	3
Garner	8	0	29	3
Daniel	9	1	35	1
Austin	1	0	13	0
Richards	1	0	12	0

FALL OF WICKETS
1-27, 2-56, 3-78, 4-78, 5-121, 6-247, 7-282, 8-288, 9-303

FALL OF WICKETS
1-20, 2-38, 3-48, 4-56, 5-94, 6-99, 7-172

Umpires: R.Gosein (1) and W.Malcolm (1).

WEST INDIES v AUSTRALIA 1977-78

At Mindoo Phillip Park, Castries, St Lucia on 12 April 1978.   Result: **AUSTRALIA** won by 2 wickets.   Toss: West Indies.
Award: R.B.Simpson.   LOI debuts: West Indies – S.T.Clarke, H.A.Gomes, A.E.Greenidge, D.R.Parry, N.Phillip, S.Shivnarine; Australia – B.Yardley.   35-over match.

Rain reduced the match by 15 overs per innings. Ian Callen's driven single to mid-off gave Australia a last-ball victory.

WEST INDIES		Runs	Balls	4/6
A.E.Greenidge	run out	23	33	4
* A.I.Kallicharran	c Simpson b Yardley	34	52	4/1
H.A.Gomes	c Darling b Simpson	7	15	–
S.F.A.F.Bacchus	c and b Simpson	0	4	–
I.T.Shillingford	c Wood b Callen	6	17	–
† D.A.Murray	b Yardley	2	12	–
S.Shivnarine	not out	20	43	I
N.Phillip	c Rixon b Callen	0	5	–
D.R.Parry	c and b Callen	5	7	I
V.A.Holder	b Clark	30	30	2/2
S.T.Clarke	b Clark	0	I	–
Extras	(lb 4, nb 8)	12		
Total	(34.4 overs)	**139**		

AUSTRALIA		Runs	Balls	4/6
W.M.Darling	c Parry b Holder	21	57	I
G.M.Wood	c Murray b Clarke	9	22	I
P.M.Toohey	c Clarke b Parry	30	44	2
C.S.Serjeant	run out	25	32	3
G.N.Yallop	c Shillingford b Parry	7	13	–
* R.B.Simpson	c Parry b Phillip	23	29	1/1
† S.J.Rixon	c Murray b Holder	0	I	–
B.Yardley	run out	7	12	–
I.W.Callen	not out	3	4	–
J.R.Thomson	not out	I	I	–
W.M.Clark				
Extras	(b 5, lb 6, nb 3)	14		
Total	(35 overs; 8 wickets)	**140**		

AUSTRALIA	O	M	R	W
Thomson	7	I	20	0
Callen	7	0	24	3
Clark	6.4	0	39	2
Simpson	7	0	30	2
Yardley	7	3	14	2

WEST INDIES	O	M	R	W
Clarke	7	I	15	I
Phillip	7	0	22	I
Gomes	4	0	18	0
Holder	7	0	28	2
Parry	7	I	27	2
Shivnarine	3	0	16	0

FALL OF WICKETS
1-48, 2-69, 3-69, 4-69, 5-74, 6-80, 7-85, 8-92, 9-139, 10-139

Umpires: P.Alleyne (I) and R.Gosein (2).

FALL OF WICKETS
1-25, 2-61, 3-80, 4-95, 5-119, 6-120, 7-133, 8-138

ENGLAND v PAKISTAN 1978

At Old Trafford, Manchester on 24, 25 May 1978.   Result: **ENGLAND** won by 132 runs.   Toss: England.
Award: R.G.D.Willis.   LOI debuts: England – D.I.Gower, C.T.Radley.   55-over match.

Pakistan, 12 for 2 after 11 overs overnight, were dismissed for their lowest LOI total until 1991-92 (*LOI No. 726*).

ENGLAND		Runs	Balls	4/6
B.Wood	c Miandad b Wasim Raja	26	90	2
* G.Boycott	c Wasim Bari b Sarfraz	3	8	–
C.T.Radley	c and b Mudassar	79	129	8
D.I.Gower	c Miandad b Mudassar	33	41	4
G.R.J.Roope	c Wasim Bari b Sikander	10	26	I
I.T.Botham	c Haroon b Sikander	31	24	3/1
G.Miller	b Sikander	0	4	–
C.M.Old	not out	6	12	–
P.H.Edmonds	not out	4	3	–
† R.W.Taylor				
R.G.D.Willis				
Extras	(b 2, lb 15, w 3, nb 5)	25		
Total	(55 overs; 7 wickets)	**217**		

PAKISTAN		Runs	Balls	4/6
Mudassar Nazar	c Wood b Botham	8	38	–
Sadiq Mohammed	b Willis	3	6	–
Haroon Rashid	b Old	I	9	–
Javed Miandad	lbw b Willis	9	39	I
Mohsin Khan	c Roope b Willis	I	6	–
Wasim Raja	lbw b Willis	0	I	–
Sarfraz Nawaz	c Taylor b Botham	7	24	I
*† Wasim Bari	b Wood	19	49	3
Iqbal Qasim	b Wood	9	34	I
Sikander Bakht	not out	16	46	3
Liaqat Ali	b Old	7	31	–
Extras	(lb 3, w I, nb I)	5		
Total	(47 overs)	**85**		

PAKISTAN	O	M	R	W
Sarfraz Nawaz	11	6	13	I
Liaqat Ali	11	3	20	0
Sikander Bakht	11	0	56	3
Mudassar Nazar	11	I	52	2
Iqbal Qasim	4	I	24	0
Wasim Raja	7	I	27	I

ENGLAND	O	M	R	W
Willis	11	5	15	4
Old	7	4	6	2
Botham	8	I	17	2
Wood	11	3	25	2
Edmonds	10	4	17	0

FALL OF WICKETS
1-3, 2-86, 3-157, 4-158, 5-176, 6-185, 7-209

Umpires: D.J.Constant (10) and K.E.Palmer (2).

FALL OF WICKETS
1-3, 2-7, 3-20, 4-21, 5-21, 6-31, 7-31, 8-60, 9-61, 10-85

ENGLAND v PAKISTAN 1978

At Kennington Oval, London on 26 May 1978.   Result: **ENGLAND** won by 94 runs.   Toss: Pakistan.
Award: D.I.Gower.   LOI debuts: Pakistan – Naeem Ahmed.   55-over match.

Bob Willis made his debut as England's captain when Geoff Boycott was sidelined with a thumb injury. Making his second international appearance, David Gower delighted a crowd of 17,450 with his maiden hundred off 116 balls.

ENGLAND		Runs	Balls	4/6
D.Lloyd	b Wasim Raja	34	61	5
B.Wood	b Sarfraz	8	20	1
C.T.Radley	b Liaqat Ali	13	34	1
D.I.Gower	not out	114	122	6
G.R.J.Roope	c Naeem b Mudassar	35	71	1
I.T.Botham	b Mudassar	1	3	–
G.Miller	lbw b Sikander	0	3	–
C.M.Old	not out	25	24	2
† R.W.Taylor				
J.K.Lever				
* R.G.D.Willis				
Extras	(b 5, lb 9, nb 4)	18		
Total	(55 overs; 6 wickets)	**248**		

PAKISTAN	O	M	R	W
Sarfraz Nawaz	11	2	48	1
Liaqat Ali	11	1	41	1
Sikander Bakht	11	0	53	1
Wasim Raja	6	0	14	1
Naeem Ahmed	10	0	43	0
Mudassar Nazar	6	0	31	2

FALL OF WICKETS
1-27, 2-60, 3-83, 4-188, 5-194, 6-195

PAKISTAN		Runs	Balls	4/6
Mudassar Nazar	c Willis b Botham	56	136	4
Sadiq Mohammed	c and b Old	9	25	1
Arshad Pervez	lbw b Miller	3	18	–
Javed Miandad	b Old	0	3	–
Haroon Rashid	st Taylor b Miller	20	53	1
Wasim Raja	c sub (P.H.Edmonds) b Lloyd	44	60	2/1
*†Wasim Bari	c Taylor b Wood	1	5	–
Sarfraz Nawaz	c Gower b Wood	12	23	1
Naeem Ahmed	not out	0	8	–
Sikander Bakht	not out	0	–	–
Liaqat Ali				
Extras	(b 1, lb 7, w 1)	9		
Total	(55 overs; 8 wickets)	**154**		

ENGLAND	O	M	R	W
Willis	9	1	25	0
Old	11	1	26	2
Miller	11	3	24	2
Botham	11	2	36	1
Lever	7	1	17	0
Wood	4	0	14	2
Lloyd	2	1	3	1

FALL OF WICKETS
1-27, 2-38, 3-39, 4-80, 5-117, 6-130, 7-154, 8-154

Umpires: H.D.Bird (10) and W.L.Budd (8).

ENGLAND v NEW ZEALAND 1978

At North Marine Road, Scarborough on 15 July 1978.   Result: **ENGLAND** won by 19 runs.   Toss: New Zealand.
Award: G.A.Gooch.   LOI debuts: New Zealand – S.L.Boock, J.G.Wright.   55-over match.

Lance Cairns took 4 for 5 in nine balls as England's last nine wickets fell for 28 runs in exactly ten overs. Bad light stopped play for 44 minutes when New Zealand had reached 101 for 6 after 34 overs, the match eventually being completed at 7.32pm.

ENGLAND		Runs	Balls	4/6
* J.M.Brearley	c Burgess b Boock	31	79	2
G.A.Gooch	c Parker b Cairns	94	129	9/2
C.T.Radley	c Parker b Cairns	41	64	5
D.I.Gower	c Burgess b Cairns	4	5	–
I.T.Botham	c Anderson b Cairns	3	8	–
G.R.J.Roope	b Cairns	11	17	1
G.Miller	c Edwards b Hadlee	2	15	–
† R.W.Taylor	lbw b Hadlee	0	1	–
J.K.Lever	not out	5	8	–
M.Hendrick	not out	2	4	–
R.G.D.Willis				
Extras	(b 2, lb 10, w 1)	13		
Total	(55 overs; 8 wickets)	**206**		

NEW ZEALAND	O	M	R	W
Hadlee	11	3	22	2
Collinge	11	0	46	0
Cairns	11	3	28	5
Congdon	11	2	25	0
Boock	9	1	57	1
Howarth	2	0	15	0

FALL OF WICKETS
1-67, 2-178, 3-181, 4-185, 5-185, 6-198, 7-198, 8-198

NEW ZEALAND		Runs	Balls	4/6
J.G.Wright	run out	18	42	1
R.W.Anderson	c Taylor b Hendrick	12	24	1
G.P.Howarth	c Taylor b Hendrick	42	88	3
* M.G.Burgess	b Botham	1	7	–
J.M.Parker	b Willis	7	16	1
† G.N.Edwards	c Gower b Gooch	12	14	1
R.J.Hadlee	st Taylor b Gooch	1	11	–
B.E.Congdon	not out	52	76	6
B.L.Cairns	run out	23	44	1
R.O.Collinge	not out	5	8	–
S.L.Boock				
Extras	(lb 13, w 1)	14		
Total	(55 overs; 8 wickets)	**187**		

ENGLAND	O	M	R	W
Willis	11	1	35	1
Hendrick	11	1	35	2
Lever	11	2	25	0
Botham	11	1	43	1
Miller	1	0	6	0
Gooch	10	1	29	2

FALL OF WICKETS
1-28, 2-43, 3-51, 4-62, 5-91, 6-97, 7-105, 8-173

Umpires: D.J.Constant (11) and J.G.Langridge (4).

ENGLAND v NEW ZEALAND 1978

At Old Trafford, Manchester on 17 July 1978.   Result: **ENGLAND** won by 126 runs.   Toss: England.
Award: C.T.Radley.   LOI debuts: New Zealand – B.P.Bracewell, B.A.Edgar.   55-over match.

Clive Radley scored his only hundred in these matches off 129 balls. Having returned the most expensive LOI analysis until 1983 (*LOI No. 197*), Lance Cairns struck 50 off 37 balls.

ENGLAND		Runs	Balls	4/6
*J.M.Brearley	c Edwards b Bracewell	27	58	3
G.A.Gooch	run out	0	2	–
C.T.Radley	not out	117	140	11
D.I.Gower	run out	50	80	7
D.W.Randall	run out	41	40	4/1
I.T.Botham	c Edgar b Hadlee	34	13	3/1
G.Miller				
†R.W.Taylor				
P.H.Edmonds				
J.K.Lever				
R.G.D.Willis				
Extras	(lb 6, w 1, nb 2)	9		
Total	(55 overs; 5 wickets)	**278**		

NEW ZEALAND	O	M	R	W
Hadlee	11	1	70	1
Collinge	11	0	48	0
Bracewell	11	0	41	1
Congdon	11	2	26	0
Cairns	11	0	84	0

FALL OF WICKETS
1-0, 2-44, 3-149, 4-238, 5-278

NEW ZEALAND		Runs	Balls	4/6
J.G.Wright	b Botham	30	58	3
B.A.Edgar	run out	31	75	3
G.P.Howarth	st Taylor b Edmonds	12	29	2
†G.N.Edwards	c Randall b Miller	0	3	–
*M.G.Burgess	c Taylor b Willis	0	2	–
B.E.Congdon	c Randall b Edmonds	2	21	–
R.J.Hadlee	c Gower b Miller	1	6	–
B.L.Cairns	c Botham b Edmonds	60	43	4/4
R.O.Collinge	c Gooch b Lever	3	7	–
B.P.Bracewell	not out	0	4	–
J.M.Parker	absent hurt	–		
Extras	(b 7, lb 6)	13		
Total	(41.2 overs)	**152**		

ENGLAND	O	M	R	W
Willis	9	5	21	1
Lever	7	0	28	1
Miller	11	4	27	2
Botham	7	0	24	1
Edmonds	7.2	1	39	3

FALL OF WICKETS
1-44, 2-80, 3-80, 4-84, 5-84, 6-85, 7-88, 8-133, 9-152

Umpires: H.D.Bird (11) and B.J.Meyer (2).

PAKISTAN v INDIA 1978-79

At Ayub National Stadium, Quetta on 1 October 1978.   Result: **INDIA** won by 4 runs.   Toss: India.
Award: M.Amarnath.   LOI debuts: India – S.Amarnath, C.P.S.Chauhan, Kapil Dev.

This three-match tournament involving innings of 40 six-ball overs marked the first engagement between these countries since 13 February 1961. It resulted in India's first LOI victory against a Test-playing country. Sarfraz Nawaz needed a six from the final ball to reverse that result.

INDIA		Runs	Balls	4/6
C.P.S.Chauhan	lbw b Sarfraz	2	11	–
A.D.Gaekwad	c Imran b Jamil	16	35	1
S.Amarnath	c Zaheer b Jamil	37	41	4
G.R.Viswanath	run out	9	20	1
D.B.Vengsarkar	run out	34	57	3/1
M.Amarnath	c and b Sarfraz	51	61	5
Kapil Dev	not out	13	12	2
†S.M.H.Kirmani	b Sarfraz	0	1	–
K.D.Ghavri	not out	1	2	–
S.Venkataraghavan				
*B.S.Bedi				
Extras	(b 1, lb 5, nb 1)	7		
Total	(40 overs; 7 wickets)	**170**		

PAKISTAN	O	M	R	W
Imran Khan	8	1	38	0
Sarfraz Nawaz	8	1	34	3
Hasan Jamil	8	1	29	2
Mudassar Nazar	8	0	32	0
Iqbal Qasim	8	1	30	0

FALL OF WICKETS
1-7, 2-60, 3-60, 4-72, 5-148, 6-163, 7-163

PAKISTAN		Runs	Balls	4/6
Majid Khan	b M.Amarnath	50	64	2
Mudassar Nazar	lbw b Ghavri	10	21	1
Zaheer Abbas	b M.Amarnath	26	39	1
Javed Miandad	lbw b Bedi	6	19	–
*Mushtaq Mohammed	run out	6	7	–
Hasan Jamil	c Gaekwad b Bedi	16	19	–
Mohsin Khan	run out	17	33	1
Imran Khan	b Kapil Dev	2	12	–
†Wasim Bari	not out	11	13	–
Sarfraz Nawaz	not out	14	13	–
Iqbal Qasim				
Extras	(lb 6, w 1, nb 1)	8		
Total	(40 overs; 8 wickets)	**166**		

INDIA	O	M	R	W
Kapil Dev	8	0	27	1
Ghavri	8	0	35	1
M.Amarnath	8	0	38	2
Bedi	8	0	44	2
Venkataraghavan	8	0	14	0

FALL OF WICKETS
1-22, 2-82, 3-89, 4-100, 5-100, 6-119, 7-134, 8-139

Umpires: Mahboob Shah (2) and Shujauddin (1).

PAKISTAN v INDIA 1978-79

At Jinnah Park, Sialkot on 13 October 1978.   Result: **PAKISTAN** won by 8 wickets.   Toss: Pakistan.
Award: Hasan Jamil.   LOI debuts: Pakistan – Azmat Rana; India – Yashpal Sharma.

India's total remains the lowest in any limited-overs international in Pakistan.

INDIA		Runs	Balls	4/6	PAKISTAN		Runs	Balls	4/6
S.M.Gavaskar	b Salim	4			Sadiq Mohammed	c Yashpal b Kapil Dev	1		
D.B.Vengsarkar	c Wasim Raja b Sikander	3			Azmat Rana	not out	22		
S.Amarnath	run out	1			Zaheer Abbas	c Kapil Dev b Gavaskar	48		
G.R.Viswanath	c Wasim Bari b Salim	0			Javed Miandad	not out	4		
M.Amarnath	not out	34			Wasim Raja				
Yashpal Sharma	b Jamil	11			* Mushtaq Mohammed				
Kapil Dev	c Mushtaq b Jamil	5			Hasan Jamil				
† S.M.H.Kirmani	lbw b Jamil	5			Sarfraz Nawaz				
K.D.Ghavri	run out	5			† Wasim Bari				
S.Venkataraghavan	b Sikander	0			Salim Altaf				
* B.S.Bedi	c Miandad b Sarfraz	2			Sikander Bakht				
Extras	(b 2, lb 4, nb 3)	9			Extras	(lb 7, w 1)	8		
Total	(34.2 overs)	**79**			**Total**	(16.5 overs; 2 wickets)	**83**		

PAKISTAN	O	M	R	W	INDIA	O	M	R	W
Sarfraz Nawaz	5.2	2	6	1	Kapil Dev	6	0	31	1
Salim Altaf	5	2	7	2	Ghavri	6	0	18	0
Sikander Bakht	8	2	11	2	M.Amarnath	2	0	4	0
Hasan Jamil	8	2	18	3	Bedi	2	0	12	0
Wasim Raja	8	0	28	0	Gavaskar	0.5	0	10	1

FALL OF WICKETS
1-7, 2-9, 3-11, 4-16, 5-36, 6-48, 7-60, 8-71, 9-71, 10-79

FALL OF WICKETS
1-2, 2-79

Umpires: Agha Saadat (1) and Shakoor Rana (3).

PAKISTAN v INDIA 1978-79

At Zafar Ali Stadium, Sahiwal on 3 November 1978.   Result: **PAKISTAN** won (conceded by India).   Toss: Pakistan.
Award: Asif Iqbal.   LOI debuts: India – B.Reddy.

Bishan Bedi called his batsmen from the field (when 23 runs were wanted from 14 balls with eight wickets in hand) in
protest against the persistent short-pitched bowling of Sarfraz Nawaz. The latter's last four deliveries were all bouncers
which had not been called wide.

PAKISTAN		Runs	Balls	4/6	INDIA		Runs	Balls	4/6
Majid Khan	b Venkataraghavan	37			C.P.S.Chauhan	c Wasim Bari b Jamil	23		
Azmat Rana	b M.Amarnath	20			A.D.Gaekwad	not out	78		
Zaheer Abbas	c Ghavri b Venkataraghavan	17			S.Amarnath	c Imran b Asif	62		
Asif Iqbal	c Bedi b Ghavri	62			G.R.Viswanath	not out	8		
Javed Miandad	lbw b M.Amarnath	7			M.Amarnath				
Hasan Jamil	b Kapil Dev	26			Kapil Dev				
* Mushtaq Mohammed	not out	16			Yashpal Sharma				
Imran Khan	c S.Amarnath b Kapil Dev	10			K.D.Ghavri				
Sarfraz Nawaz	not out	0			† B.Reddy				
† Wasim Bari					S.Venkataraghavan				
Salim Altaf					* B.S.Bedi				
Extras	(lb 7, nb 3)	10			Extras	(b 2, lb 5, nb 5)	12		
Total	(40 overs; 7 wickets)	**205**			**Total**	(37.4 overs; 2 wickets)	**183**		

INDIA	O	M	R	W	PAKISTAN	O	M	R	W
Kapil Dev	8	0	49	2	Imran Khan	7	0	22	0
Ghavri	8	0	33	1	Sarfraz Nawaz	6.4	0	16	0
Venkataraghavan	8	0	34	2	Salim Altaf	8	0	41	0
M.Amarnath	8	0	35	2	Hasan Jamil	8	0	48	1
Bedi	8	0	44	0	Asif Iqbal	8	0	44	1

FALL OF WICKETS
1-38, 2-66, 3-93, 4-111, 5-167, 6-187, 7-201

FALL OF WICKETS
1-44, 2-163

Umpires: Javed Akhtar (3) and Khizer Hayat (1).

29

AUSTRALIA v ENGLAND 1978-79

At Sydney Cricket Ground on 13 January 1979.   No result.   Toss: England.
LOI debuts: Australia – A.R.Border, P.H.Carlson, J.A.Maclean; England – R.W.Tolchard.

The first encounter of a scheduled three-match series involving innings of 40 eight-ball overs, at Melbourne on 26 December, had been abandoned without a ball bowled. When this second match was ended by rain after 40 minutes, the tour itinerary was revised to incorporate additional internationals on 4 and 7 February in place of England's three-day fixture against Geelong and Districts XI. Allan Border made the first of his record 273 appearances.

AUSTRALIA		Runs	Balls	4/6	ENGLAND				
G.M.Wood	c Tolchard b Old	6	24	–	* J.M.Brearley				
W.M.Darling	not out	7	32	–	G.Boycott				
K.J.Hughes	not out	0	2	–	D.W.Randall				
* G.N.Yallop					D.I.Gower				
G.J.Cosier					G.A.Gooch				
P.M.Toohey					I.T.Botham				
A.R.Border					† R.W.Tolchard				
P.H.Carlson					P.H.Edmonds				
† J.A.Maclean					C.M.Old				
G.Dymock					M.Hendrick				
A.G.Hurst					J.K.Lever				
Extras	(lb 4)		4						
Total	(7.2 overs; 1 wicket)		17						

ENGLAND	O	M	R	W
Lever	3	0	8	0
Old	3.2	1	5	1
Hendrick	1	1	0	0

FALL OF WICKETS
1-17

Umpires: A.R.Crafter (1) and C.E.Harvey (1).

AUSTRALIA v ENGLAND 1978-79

At Melbourne Cricket Ground on 24 January 1979.   Result: **ENGLAND** won by 7 wickets.   Toss: Australia.
Award: M.Hendrick.   LOI debuts: Australia – A.M.J.Hilditch, R.M.Hogg; England – D.L.Bairstow.

England's bowlers took full advantage of a pitch with uneven bounce. Geoffrey Boycott painstakingly saw the touring team to their modest target.

AUSTRALIA		Runs	Balls	4/6	ENGLAND		Runs	Balls	4/6
G.M.Wood	c Gower b Edmonds	28	66	4	G.Boycott	not out	39	107	3
A.M.J.Hilditch	c Bairstow b Botham	10	39	1	* J.M.Brearley	b Hogg	0	12	–
A.R.Border	c Willis b Hendrick	11	18	2	D.W.Randall	c Yallop b Dymock	12	37	–
* G.N.Yallop	run out	9	36	–	G.A.Gooch	b Carlson	23	45	2
K.J.Hughes	lbw b Hendrick	0	5	–	D.I.Gower	not out	19	29	3
P.H.Carlson	c Randall b Willis	11	27	2	I.T.Botham				
T.J.Laughlin	c Willis b Hendrick	6	26	1	P.H.Edmonds				
† J.A.Maclean	c Edmonds b Botham	11	33	2	† D.L.Bairstow				
R.M.Hogg	c Botham b Hendrick	4	6	–	J.K.Lever				
G.Dymock	c and b Botham	1	14	–	R.G.D.Willis				
A.G.Hurst	not out	0	4	–	M.Hendrick				
Extras	(b 4, lb 2, nb 4)	10			Extras	(lb 5, nb 4)	9		
Total	(33.5 overs)	101			**Total**	(28.2 overs; 3 wickets)	102		

ENGLAND	O	M	R	W	AUSTRALIA	O	M	R	W
Willis	8	4	15	1	Hogg	6	1	20	1
Lever	5	2	7	0	Dymock	6	1	16	1
Hendrick	8	1	25	4	Laughlin	5	1	13	0
Botham	4.5	2	16	3	Carlson	5	0	21	1
Edmonds	7	0	26	1	Hurst	5.2	1	14	0
Gooch	1	0	2	0	Border	1	0	9	0

FALL OF WICKETS
1-27, 2-52, 3-54, 4-55, 5-76, 6-78, 7-94, 8-99, 9-101, 10-101

FALL OF WICKETS
1-7, 2-29, 3-69

Umpires: A.R.Crafter (2) and C.E.Harvey (2).

AUSTRALIA v ENGLAND 1978-79

At Melbourne Cricket Ground on 4 February 1979.   Result: **AUSTRALIA** won by 4 wickets.   Toss: Australia.
Award: D.I.Gower.   LOI debuts: Australia – K.J.Wright.

David Gower counteracted a damp pitch of variable bounce and overcast conditions, piercing a circle of boundary fielders to reach his hundred with an off-drive off the final ball of the innings.

ENGLAND		Runs	Balls	4/6
G.Boycott	lbw b Laughlin	33	86	1
* J.M.Brearley	c Wright b Dymock	0	2	–
D.W.Randall	lbw b Dymock	4	14	–
G.A.Gooch	c Hurst b Carlson	19	50	2
D.I.Gower	not out	101	100	9
I.T.Botham	c Wood b Hurst	31	41	3
† D.L.Bairstow	run out	1	4	–
C.M.Old	not out	16	24	–
R.G.D.Willis				
M.Hendrick				
J.K.Lever				
Extras	(b 3, lb 3, nb 1)	7		
Total	(40 overs; 6 wickets)	212		

AUSTRALIA		Runs	Balls	4/6
G.M.Wood	b Old	23	54	2
W.M.Darling	c Old b Willis	7	12	1
K.J.Hughes	c Boycott b Lever	50	99	4
* G.N.Yallop	c Gower b Hendrick	31	66	1
P.M.Toohey	not out	54	55	2
G.J.Cosier	b Lever	28	14	2/1
P.H.Carlson	c Boycott b Lever	0	3	–
T.J.Laughlin	not out	15	11	1/1
† K.J.Wright				
G.Dymock				
A.G.Hurst				
Extras	(lb 6, nb 1)	7		
Total	(38.6 overs; 6 wickets)	215		

AUSTRALIA	O	M	R	W
Hurst	8	1	36	1
Dymock	8	1	31	2
Carlson	8	1	27	1
Cosier	8	0	48	0
Laughlin	8	0	63	1

ENGLAND	O	M	R	W
Willis	8	1	21	1
Lever	7	1	51	3
Hendrick	8	0	47	1
Old	8	1	31	1
Botham	7.6	0	58	0

FALL OF WICKETS
1-0, 2-7, 3-50, 4-89, 5-153, 6-158

FALL OF WICKETS
1-7, 2-55, 3-90, 4-145, 5-185, 6-185

Umpires: R.C.Bailhache (3) and D.G.Weser (1).

AUSTRALIA v ENGLAND 1978-79

At Melbourne Cricket Ground on 7 February 1979.   Result: **AUSTRALIA** won by 6 wickets.   Toss: Australia.
Award: G.Dymock.   LOI debuts: None

David Bairstow was run out while attempting a sixth run from an on-drive by Mike Brearley.

ENGLAND		Runs	Balls	4/6
G.Boycott	c Cosier b Dymock	2	11	–
* J.M.Brearley	c Wright b Cosier	46	112	3
D.W.Randall	c Hughes b Dymock	0	1	–
G.A.Gooch	c Hughes b Hurst	4	13	1
D.I.Gower	c Wood b Hurst	3	10	–
I.T.Botham	b Cosier	13	19	3
† D.L.Bairstow	run out	3	28	–
P.H.Edmonds	lbw b Laughlin	15	42	1
J.K.Lever	b Laughlin	1	14	–
R.G.D.Willis	c Wright b Cosier	2	8	–
M.Hendrick	not out	0	1	–
Extras	(lb 2, nb 3)	5		
Total	(31.7 overs)	94		

AUSTRALIA		Runs	Balls	4/6
G.M.Wood	c Bairstow b Botham	30	38	2
W.M.Darling	c Brearley b Willis	14	21	3
K.J.Hughes	c Brearley b Willis	0	9	–
* G.N.Yallop	b Lever	25	69	1
P.M.Toohey	not out	16	28	–
G.J.Cosier	not out	8	10	1
P.H.Carlson				
T.J.Laughlin				
† K.J.Wright				
G.Dymock				
A.G.Hurst				
Extras	(nb 2)	2		
Total	(21.5 overs; 4 wickets)	95		

AUSTRALIA	O	M	R	W
Hurst	5	3	7	2
Dymock	6	1	21	2
Carlson	8	2	22	0
Cosier	7	1	22	3
Laughlin	5.7	0	17	2

ENGLAND	O	M	R	W
Willis	5	2	16	2
Hendrick	6	0	32	0
Botham	5.5	0	30	1
Lever	5	0	15	1

FALL OF WICKETS
1-29, 2-37, 3-54, 4-87

FALL OF WICKETS
1-10, 2-10, 3-17, 4-22, 5-42, 6-56, 7-91, 8-91, 9-94, 10-94

Umpires: R.C.Bailhache (4) and D.G.Weser (2).

WEST INDIES v INDIA 1979

At Edgbaston, Birmingham, on 9 June 1979.   Result: **WEST INDIES** won by 9 wickets.   Toss: West Indies.
Award: C.G.Greenidge.   LOI debuts: India – S.C.Khanna.

Like its predecessor, this second World Cup tournament involved eight teams playing 15 matches spread over as many
days and according to 60-overs Gillette Cup rules. Gordon Greenidge and Desmond Haynes registered the first of their
15 three-figure opening partnerships in these internationals.

INDIA		Runs	Balls	4/6
S.M.Gavaskar	c Holding b Roberts	8		
A.D.Gaekwad	c King b Holding	11		
D.B.Vengsarkar	c Kallicharran b Holding	7		
G.R.Viswanath	b Holding	75		
B.P.Patel	run out	15		
M.Amarnath	c Murray b Croft	8		
Kapil Dev	b King	12		
† S.C.Khanna	c Haynes b Holding	0		
K.D.Ghavri	c Murray b Garner	12		
* S.Venkataraghavan	not out	13		
B.S.Bedi	c Lloyd b Roberts	13		
Extras	(b 6, lb 3, w 3, nb 4)	16		
Total	**(53.1 overs)**	**190**		

WEST INDIES		Runs	Balls	4/6
C.G.Greenidge	not out	106		
D.L.Haynes	lbw b Kapil Dev	47		
I.V.A.Richards	not out	28		
A.I.Kallicharran				
* C.H.Lloyd				
C.L.King				
† D.L.Murray				
A.M.E.Roberts				
J.Garner				
M.A.Holding				
C.E.H.Croft				
Extras	(lb 6, nb 7)	13		
Total	**(51.3 overs; 1 wicket)**	**194**		

WEST INDIES	O	M	R	W
Roberts	9.1	0	32	2
Holding	12	2	33	4
Garner	12	1	42	1
Croft	10	1	31	1
King	10	1	36	1

INDIA	O	M	R	W
Kapil Dev	10	1	46	1
Ghavri	10	2	25	0
Venkataraghavan	12	3	30	0
Bedi	12	0	45	0
Amarnath	7.3	0	35	0

FALL OF WICKETS
1-10, 2-24, 3-29, 4-56, 5-77, 6-112, 7-119, 8-155, 9-163, 10-190

FALL OF WICKETS
1-138

Umpires: D.G.L.Evans (1) and J.G.Langridge (5).

NEW ZEALAND v SRI LANKA 1979

At Trent Bridge, Nottingham, on 9 June 1979.   Result: **NEW ZEALAND** won by 9 wickets.   Toss: New Zealand.
Award: G.P.Howarth.   LOI debuts: New Zealand – J.V.Coney, W.K.Lees, L.W.Stott; Sri Lanka – D.L.S.de Silva, R.L.Dias,
S.A.Jayasinghe, S.P.Pasqual.

Glenn Turner and Geoff Howarth, the latter batting with a runner because of a hamstring injury, took New Zealand to
an emphatic win.

SRI LANKA		Runs	Balls	4/6
B.Warnapura	c and b McKechnie	20		
S.R.de S.Wettimuny	b Cairns	16		
* A.P.B.Tennekoon	b Stott	59		6
R.L.Dias	c and b Stott	25		
L.R.D.Mendis	c Turner b Troup	14		
D.S.de Silva	c Burgess b Stott	6		
† S.A.Jayasinghe	run out	1		
S.P.Pasqual	b Hadlee	1		
A.R.M.Opatha	b McKechnie	18		
D.L.S.de Silva	c Wright b McKechnie	10		
G.R.A.de Silva	not out	2		
Extras	(lb 13, w 2, nb 2)	17		
Total	**(56.5 overs)**	**189**		

NEW ZEALAND		Runs	Balls	4/6
G.M.Turner	not out	83		4
J.G.Wright	c Tennekoon b G.R.A.de Silva	34		6
G.P.Howarth	not out	63		8/1
J.V.Coney				
* M.G.Burgess				
† W.K.Lees				
B.J.McKechnie				
B.L.Cairns				
R.J.Hadlee				
L.W.Stott				
G.B.Troup				
Extras	(lb 7, w 2, nb 1)	10		
Total	**(47.4 overs; 1 wicket)**	**190**		

NEW ZEALAND	O	M	R	W
Hadlee	12	3	24	1
Troup	10	0	30	1
Cairns	12	1	45	1
McKechnie	10.5	2	25	3
Stott	12	1	48	3

SRI LANKA	O	M	R	W
Opatha	7	1	31	0
D.L.S.de Silva	8	2	18	0
Warnapura	7	0	30	0
D.S.de Silva	9	0	42	0
G.R.A.de Silva	12	1	39	1
Pasqual	4.4	0	20	0

FALL OF WICKETS
1-26, 2-57, 3-107, 4-137, 5-149, 6-150, 7-150, 8-154, 9-178, 10-189

FALL OF WICKETS
1-64

Umpires: W.L.Budd (9) and K.E.Palmer (3).

ENGLAND v AUSTRALIA 1979

At Lord's, London, on 9 June 1979.　Result: **ENGLAND** won by 6 wickets.　Toss: England.
Award: G.A.Gooch.　LOI debuts: None.

A full house of 25,000 witnessed a comfortable home victory and the unusual spectacle of Geoffrey Boycott taking twice as many wickets as he had scored runs.

AUSTRALIA		Runs	Balls	4/6
A.M.J.Hilditch	b Boycott	47	108	2
W.M.Darling	lbw b Willis	25	61	3
A.R.Border	c Taylor b Edmonds	34	74	4
* K.J.Hughes	c Hendrick b Boycott	6	13	1
G.N.Yallop	run out	10	20	1
G.J.Cosier	run out	6	20	–
T.J.Laughlin	run out	8	22	–
† K.J.Wright	lbw b Old	6	15	–
G.Dymock	not out	4	12	–
R.M.Hogg	run out	0	5	–
A.G.Hurst	not out	3	10	–
Extras	(b 4, lb 5, w 1)	10		
Total	(60 overs; 9 wickets)	**159**		

ENGLAND		Runs	Balls	4/6
* J.M.Brearley	c Wright b Laughlin	44	147	2
G.Boycott	lbw b Hogg	1	5	–
D.W.Randall	c Wright b Hurst	1	3	–
G.A.Gooch	lbw b Laughlin	53	96	6
D.I.Gower	not out	22	30	2
I.T.Botham	not out	18	14	2
P.H.Edmonds				
† R.W.Taylor				
C.M.Old				
M.Hendrick				
R.G.D.Willis				
Extras	(lb 10, nb 11)	21		
Total	(47.1 overs; 4 wickets)	**160**		

ENGLAND	O	M	R	W
Willis	11	2	20	1
Hendrick	12	2	24	0
Old	12	2	33	1
Botham	8	0	32	0
Edmonds	11	1	25	1
Boycott	6	0	15	2

AUSTRALIA	O	M	R	W
Hogg	9	1	25	1
Hurst	10	3	33	1
Dymock	11	2	19	0
Cosier	8	1	24	0
Laughlin	9.1	0	38	2

FALL OF WICKETS
1-56, 2-97, 3-111, 4-131, 5-132, 6-137, 7-150, 8-153, 9-153

FALL OF WICKETS
1-4, 2-5, 3-113, 4-124

Umpires: D.J.Constant (12) and B.J.Meyer (3).

PAKISTAN v CANADA 1979

At Headingley, Leeds, on 9 June 1979.　Result: **PAKISTAN** won by 8 wickets.　Toss: Canada.
Award: Sadiq Mohammed.　LOI debuts: Canada – all.

Glenroy Sealy, one of their six West Indian-born players, hit the opening ball of Canada's first major international for four.

CANADA		Runs	Balls	4/6
G.R.Sealy	c and b Asif	45		
C.J.D.Chappell	c and b Sikander	14		
F.A.Dennis	c Wasim b Sarfraz	25		
M.P.Stead	c Zaheer b Asif	10		
C.A.Marshall	b Imran	8		
J.C.B.Vaughan	c and b Asif	0		
*† B.M.Mauricette	c Zaheer b Sarfraz	15		
Tariq Javed	st Wasim b Majid	3		
J.M.Patel	b Sarfraz	0		
C.C.Henry	not out	1		
J.N.Valentine				
Extras	(lb 10, w 5, nb 3)	18		
Total	(60 overs; 9 wickets)	**139**		

PAKISTAN		Runs	Balls	4/6
Majid Khan	b Valentine	1		
Sadiq Mohammed	not out	57		
Zaheer Abbas	run out	36		
Haroon Rashid	not out	37		
Javed Miandad				
* Asif Iqbal				
Mudassar Nazar				
Imran Khan				
† Wasim Bari				
Sarfraz Nawaz				
Sikander Bakht				
Extras	(b 1, lb 3, w 1, nb 4)	9		
Total	(40.1 overs; 2 wickets)	**140**		

PAKISTAN	O	M	R	W
Imran Khan	11	1	27	1
Sarfraz Nawaz	10	1	26	3
Mudassar Nazar	4	1	11	0
Sikander Bakht	12	5	18	1
Majid Khan	11	4	11	1
Asif Iqbal	12	2	28	3

CANADA	O	M	R	W
Valentine	9	3	18	1
Vaughan	5	1	21	0
Henry	5	0	26	0
Patel	11.1	0	27	0
Sealy	6	0	21	0
Stead	4	0	18	0

FALL OF WICKETS
1-54, 2-85, 3-103, 4-110, 5-110, 6-129, 7-134, 8-138, 9-139

FALL OF WICKETS
1-4, 2-61

Umpires: H.D.Bird (12) and A.G.T.Whitehead (1).

SECOND (PRUDENTIAL) WORLD CUP (5th Match): WEST INDIES v SRI LANKA
At Kennington Oval, London, on 13, 14, 15 June 1979. No result – match abandoned without a ball bowled.

NEW ZEALAND v INDIA 1979

At Headingley, Leeds, on 13 June 1979.   Result: **NEW ZEALAND** won by 8 wickets.   Toss: New Zealand.
Award: B.A.Edgar.   LOI debuts: None.

Mark Burgess won an important toss on a morning ideal for seam and swing bowling.

INDIA		Runs	Balls	4/6	NEW ZEALAND		Runs	Balls	4/6
S.M.Gavaskar	c Lees b Hadlee	55		5	J.G.Wright	c and b Amarnath	48		1
A.D.Gaekwad	b Hadlee	10			B.A.Edgar	not out	84		8
D.B.Vengsarkar	c Lees b McKechnie	1			B.L.Cairns	run out	2		–
G.R.Viswanath	c Turner b Cairns	9			G.M.Turner	not out	43		6
B.P.Patel	b Troup	38		5	J.V.Coney				
M.Amarnath	b Troup	1			* M.G.Burgess				
Kapil Dev	c and b Cairns	25		3	J.F.M.Morrison				
K.D.Ghavri	c Coney b McKechnie	20			B.J.McKechnie				
† S.C.Khanna	c Morrison b McKechnie	7			† W.K.Lees				
* S.Venkataraghavan	c Lees b Cairns	1			R.J.Hadlee				
B.S.Bedi	not out	1			G.B.Troup				
Extras	(lb 8, w 5, nb 1)	14			Extras	(lb 3, nb 3)	6		
Total	(55.5 overs)	**182**			**Total**	(57 overs; 2 wickets)	**183**		

NEW ZEALAND	O	M	R	W	INDIA	O	M	R	W
Hadlee	10	2	20	2	Amarnath	12	1	39	1
Troup	10	2	36	2	Bedi	12	1	32	0
Cairns	11.5	0	36	3	Venkataraghavan	12	0	34	0
McKechnie	12	1	24	3	Ghavri	10	1	34	0
Coney	7	0	33	0	Kapil Dev	11	3	38	0
Morrison	5	0	19	0					

FALL OF WICKETS
1-27, 2-38, 3-53, 4-104, 5-107, 6-147, 7-153, 8-180, 9-180, 10-182

FALL OF WICKETS
1-100, 2-103

Umpires: W.L.Budd (10) and A.G.T.Whitehead (2).

AUSTRALIA v PAKISTAN 1979

At Trent Bridge, Nottingham, on 13, 14 June 1979.   Result: **PAKISTAN** won by 89 runs.   Toss: Australia.
Award: Asif Iqbal.   LOI debuts: Australia – J.K.Moss, G.D.Porter.

At the close of an interrupted first day, Australia were 17 for 0 after 5 overs.

PAKISTAN		Runs	Balls	4/6	AUSTRALIA		Runs	Balls	4/6
Sadiq Mohammed	c Moss b Porter	27	73	2	W.M.Darling	c Wasim Bari b Imran	13	25	1
Majid Khan	b Dymock	61	100	7/1	A.M.J.Hilditch	c Sadiq b Mudassar	72	129	4
Zaheer Abbas	c and b Cosier	16	32	1	A.R.Border	b Sikander	0	5	–
Haroon Rashid	c Wright b Cosier	16	42	2	* K.J.Hughes	lbw b Sikander	15	37	2
Javed Miandad	c Border b Cosier	46	46	4	G.N.Yallop	b Majid	37	64	2
* Asif Iqbal	c sub (D.F.Whatmore) b Hurst	61	57	7	J.K.Moss	run out	7	16	–
Wasim Raja	c Moss b Border	18	12	2/1	G.J.Cosier	c and b Majid	0	1	–
Imran Khan	not out	15	9	–	† K.J.Wright	c Wasim Bari b Imran	23	37	–
Mudassar Nazar	not out	1	1	–	G.D.Porter	c Sadiq b Majid	3	9	–
† Wasim Bari					G.Dymock	lbw b Sikander	10	18	–
Sikander Bakht					A.G.Hurst	not out	3	2	–
Extras	(b 6, lb 4, w 5, nb 10)	25			Extras	(b 1, lb 5, w 8)	14		
Total	(60 overs; 7 wickets)	**286**			**Total**	(57.1 overs)	**197**		

AUSTRALIA	O	M	R	W	PAKISTAN	O	M	R	W
Porter	12	3	20	1	Asif Iqbal	12	0	36	0
Dymock	12	3	28	1	Majid Khan	12	0	53	3
Cosier	12	1	54	3	Mudassar Nazar	12	0	31	1
Hurst	12	0	65	1	Imran Khan	10.1	2	29	2
Yallop	8	0	56	0	Sikander Bakht	11	1	34	3
Border	4	0	38	1					

FALL OF WICKETS
1-99, 2-99, 3-133, 4-152, 5-239, 6-268, 7-274

FALL OF WICKETS
1-22, 2-24, 3-46, 4-117, 5-136, 6-137, 7-172, 8-175, 9-193, 10-197

Umpires: H.D.Bird (13) and K.E.Palmer (4).

ENGLAND v CANADA 1979

At Old Trafford, Manchester, on 13 *(no play)*, 14 June 1979.　Result: **ENGLAND** won by 8 wickets.　Toss: Canada.
Award: C.M.Old.　LOI debuts: Canada – R.G.Callender.

Electing to bat in reasonable conditions, Canada were dismissed in 157 minutes for the first LOI total under 70. Their total and the match aggregate of 91 runs remained the lowest at this level until 1992-93 (*LOI No. 812*). At 3 hours 35 minutes, this remains the shortest completed international match in England.

CANADA		Runs	Balls	4/6
G.R.Sealy	c Botham b Hendrick	3	9	–
C.J.D.Chappell	lbw b Botham	5	31	–
F.A.Dennis	hit wicket b Willis	21	99	2
Tariq Javed	lbw b Old	4	40	–
J.C.B.Vaughan	b Old	1	10	–
C.A.Marshall	b Old	2	7	–
†B.M.Mauricette	b Willis	0	8	–
M.P.Stead	b Old	0	12	–
J.M.Patel	b Willis	1	14	–
R.G.Callender	b Willis	0	3	–
J.N.Valentine	not out	3	11	–
Extras	(lb 4, nb 1)	5		
Total	(40.3 overs)	**45**		

ENGLAND		Runs	Balls	4/6
* J.M.Brearley	lbw b Valentine	0	10	–
G.Boycott	not out	14	36	–
D.W.Randall	b Callender	5	11	1
G.A.Gooch	not out	21	31	2/1
D.I.Gower				
I.T.Botham				
G.Miller				
† R.W.Taylor				
C.M.Old				
R.G.D.Willis				
M.Hendrick				
Extras	(w 3, nb 3)	6		
Total	(13.5 overs; 2 wickets)	**46**		

ENGLAND	O	M	R	W
Willis	10.3	3	11	4
Hendrick	8	4	5	1
Botham	9	5	12	1
Miller	2	1	1	0
Boycott	1	0	3	0
Old	10	5	8	4

CANADA	O	M	R	W
Valentine	7	2	20	1
Callender	6	1	14	1
Stead	0.5	0	6	0

FALL OF WICKETS
1-3, 2-11

FALL OF WICKETS
1-5, 2-13, 3-25, 4-29, 5-37, 6-38, 7-41, 8-41, 9-42, 10-45

Umpires: J.G.Langridge (6) and B.J.Meyer (4).

INDIA v SRI LANKA 1979

At Old Trafford, Manchester, on 16, 18 June 1979.　Result: **SRI LANKA** won by 47 runs.　Toss: India.
Award: L.R.D.Mendis.　LOI debuts: Sri Lanka – F.R.M.de S.Goonatilleke, R.S.Madugalle.

Sri Lanka gained the first limited-overs international victory by an associate ICC member. Saturday's delayed start meant that India's reply was delayed until the Monday.

SRI LANKA		Runs	Balls	4/6
* B.Warnapura	c Gaekwad b Amarnath	18		2
S.R.de S.Wettimuny	c Vengsarkar b Kapil Dev	67		8
R.L.Dias	c and b Amarnath	50		2
L.R.D.Mendis	run out	64		1/3
R.S.Madugalle	c Khanna b Amarnath	4		–
S.P.Pasqual	not out	23		1
D.S.de Silva	not out	1		–
† S.A.Jayasinghe				
A.R.M.Opatha				
D.L.S.de Silva				
F.R.M.de S.Goonatilleke				
Extras	(lb 8, w 2, nb 1)	11		
Total	(60 overs; 5 wickets)	**238**		

INDIA		Runs	Balls	4/6
S.M.Gavaskar	c Dias b Warnapura	26		2
A.D.Gaekwad	c sub‡ b D.L.S.de Silva	33		2
D.B.Vengsarkar	c D.L.S.de Silva b D.S.de Silva	36		3
G.R.Viswanath	run out	22		–
B.P.Patel	b D.S.de Silva	10		1
Kapil Dev	c Warnapura b D.L.S.de Silva	16		2
M.Amarnath	b D.S.de Silva	7		–
K.D.Ghavri	c Warnapura b Opatha	3		–
† S.C.Khanna	c Dias b Opatha	10		1
* S.Venkataraghavan	not out	9		–
B.S.Bedi	c Jayasinghe b Opatha	5		–
Extras	(lb 10, w 3, nb 1)	14		
Total	(54.1 overs)	**191**		

INDIA	O	M	R	W
Kapil Dev	12	2	53	1
Ghavri	12	0	53	0
Amarnath	12	3	40	3
Bedi	12	2	37	0
Venkataraghavan	12	0	44	0

SRI LANKA	O	M	R	W
Opatha	10.1	0	31	3
Goonatilleke	9	1	34	0
Warnapura	12	0	47	1
D.L.S.de Silva	12	0	36	2
D.S.de Silva	11	1	29	3

FALL OF WICKETS
1-31, 2-127, 3-147, 4-175, 5-227

FALL OF WICKETS
1-60, 2-76, 3-119, 4-132, 5-147, 6-160, 7-162, 8-170, 9-185, 10-191

Umpires: K.E.Palmer (5) and A.G.T.Whitehead (3).

‡(G.R.A.de Silva)

WEST INDIES v NEW ZEALAND 1979

At Trent Bridge, Nottingham, on 16 June 1979.   Result: **WEST INDIES** won by 32 runs.   Toss: New Zealand.
Award: C.H.Lloyd.   LOI debuts: New Zealand – E.J.Chatfield.

For the only time in this 1979 tournament West Indies failed to bowl out their opposition.

WEST INDIES		Runs	Balls	4/6	NEW ZEALAND		Runs	Balls	4/6
C.G.Greenidge	c Edgar b Coney	65		3/1	B.A.Edgar	run out	12		
D.L.Haynes	lbw b Hadlee	12			J.G.Wright	c Lloyd b Garner	15		
I.V.A.Richards	c Burgess b Coney	9			J.V.Coney	c Garner b King	36		3
A.I.Kallicharran	b McKechnie	39		2	G.M.Turner	c Lloyd b Roberts	20		
* C.H.Lloyd	not out	73		4	J.F.M.Morrison	c Murray b Garner	11		
C.L.King	lbw b Cairns	12			* M.G.Burgess	c Richards b Roberts	35		3
† D.L.Murray	c Coney b Chatfield	12			† W.K.Lees	b Croft	5		
A.M.E.Roberts	c Lees b Cairns	1			R.J.Hadlee	b Roberts	42		4
J.Garner	not out	9			B.J.McKechnie	not out	13		
M.A.Holding					B.L.Cairns	b Holding	1		
C.E.H.Croft					E.J.Chatfield	not out	3		
Extras	(b 5, lb 7)	12			Extras	(lb 14, w 4, nb 1)	19		
Total	(60 overs; 7 wickets)	244			Total	(60 overs; 9 wickets)	212		

NEW ZEALAND	O	M	R	W	WEST INDIES	O	M	R	W
Hadlee	11	2	41	1	Roberts	12	2	43	3
Chatfield	11	0	45	1	Holding	12	1	29	1
Cairns	12	1	48	2	Croft	12	1	38	1
Coney	12	0	40	2	Garner	12	0	45	2
McKechnie	11	0	46	1	King	12	1	38	1
Morrison	3	0	12	0					

FALL OF WICKETS
1-23, 2-61, 3-117, 4-152, 5-175, 6-202, 7-204

FALL OF WICKETS
1-27, 2-38, 3-90, 4-91, 5-138, 6-143, 7-160, 8-199, 9-202

Umpires: H.D.Bird (14) and B.J.Meyer (5).

AUSTRALIA v CANADA 1979

At Edgbaston, Birmingham, on 16 June 1979.   Result: **AUSTRALIA** won by 7 wickets.   Toss: Australia.
Award: A.G.Hurst.   LOI debuts: Canada – S.Baksh.

Alan Hurst returned the best analysis of this World Cup after Glenroy Sealy had struck four boundaries in Rodney
Hogg's opening over.

CANADA		Runs	Balls	4/6	AUSTRALIA		Runs	Balls	4/6
G.R.Sealy	c Porter b Dymock	25	30	4	A.M.J.Hilditch	c Valentine b Henry	24	30	3
C.J.D.Chappell	lbw b Hurst	19	42	2	W.M.Darling	lbw b Valentine	13	16	2
F.A.Dennis	lbw b Hurst	1	8	–	A.R.Border	b Henry	25	53	4
Tariq Javed	c Wright b Porter	8	30	1	* K.J.Hughes	not out	27	40	2
S.Baksh	b Hurst	0	6	–	G.N.Yallop	not out	13	20	–
J.C.B.Vaughan	b Porter	29	43	4	G.J.Cosier				
*†B.M.Mauricette	c Hilditch b Cosier	5	22	–	† K.J.Wright				
J.M.Patel	b Cosier	2	4	–	G.D.Porter				
R.G.Callender	c Wright b Hurst	0	2	–	R.M.Hogg				
C.C.Henry	c Hughes b Hurst	5	11	1	G.Dymock				
J.N.Valentine	not out	0	6	–	A.G.Hurst				
Extras	(b 4, lb 5, w 1, nb 1)	11			Extras	(lb 1, nb 3)	4		
Total	(33.2 overs)	105			Total	(26 overs; 3 wickets)	106		

AUSTRALIA	O	M	R	W	CANADA	O	M	R	W
Hogg	2	0	26	0	Valentine	3	0	28	1
Hurst	10	3	21	5	Callender	3	0	12	0
Dymock	8	2	17	1	Henry	10	0	27	2
Porter	6	2	13	2	Vaughan	6	0	15	0
Cosier	7.2	2	17	2	Patel	4	0	20	0

FALL OF WICKETS
1-44, 2-50, 3-51, 4-51, 5-78, 6-97, 7-97, 8-98, 9-104, 10-105

FALL OF WICKETS
1-23, 2-53, 3-72

Umpires: D.J.Constant (13) and J.G.Langridge (7).

ENGLAND v PAKISTAN 1979

At Headingley, Leeds, on 16 June 1979.   Result: **ENGLAND** won by 14 runs.   Toss: Pakistan.
Award: M.Hendrick.   LOI debuts: None.

Bowlers dominated this enthralling match, Mike Hendrick commanding great control of length and seam movement in the best spell of his international career. Having dismissed four of Pakistan's first five batsmen in eight balls at a cost of three runs, he held a leaping catch at deep mid-off to end the contest.

ENGLAND		Runs	Balls	4/6
* J.M.Brearley	c Wasim Bari b Imran	0	2	–
G.Boycott	lbw b Majid	18	54	2
D.W.Randall	c Wasim Bari b Sikander	1	5	–
G.A.Gooch	c Sadiq b Sikander	33	90	5
D.I.Gower	b Majid	27	40	3
I.T.Botham	b Majid	22	48	1/1
P.H.Edmonds	c Wasim Raja b Asif	2	23	–
† R.W.Taylor	not out	20	59	1
C.M.Old	c and b Asif	2	7	–
R.G.D.Willis	b Sikander	24	37	3
M.Hendrick	not out	1	1	–
Extras	(lb 3, w 7, nb 5)	15		
Total	(60 overs; 9 wickets)	**165**		

PAKISTAN		Runs	Balls	4/6
Majid Khan	c Botham b Hendrick	7	20	1
Sadiq Mohammed	b Hendrick	18	27	4
Mudassar Nazar	lbw b Hendrick	0	2	–
Zaheer Abbas	c Taylor b Botham	3	19	–
Haroon Rashid	c Brearley b Hendrick	1	2	–
Javed Miandad	lbw b Botham	0	4	–
* Asif Iqbal	c Brearley b Willis	51	104	5
Wasim Raja	lbw b Old	21	25	4
Imran Khan	not out	21	82	1
† Wasim Bari	c Taylor b Boycott	17	33	2
Sikander Bakht	c Hendrick b Boycott	2	19	–
Extras	(lb 8, w 1, nb 1)	10		
Total	(56 overs)	**151**		

PAKISTAN	O	M	R	W
Imran Khan	12	3	24	1
Sikander Bakht	12	3	32	3
Mudassar Nazar	12	4	30	0
Asif Iqbal	12	3	37	2
Majid Khan	12	2	27	3

ENGLAND	O	M	R	W
Willis	11	2	37	1
Hendrick	12	6	15	4
Botham	12	3	38	2
Old	12	2	28	1
Edmonds	3	0	8	0
Boycott	5	0	14	2
Gooch	1	0	1	0

FALL OF WICKETS
1-0, 2-4, 3-51, 4-70, 5-99, 6-115, 7-115, 8-118, 9-161

FALL OF WICKETS
1-27, 2-27, 3-28, 4-30, 5-31, 6-34, 7-86, 8-115, 9-145, 10-151

Umpires: W.L.Budd (11) and D.G.L.Evans (2).

ENGLAND v NEW ZEALAND 1979

At Old Trafford, Manchester, on 20 June 1979.   Result: **ENGLAND** won by 9 runs.   Toss: New Zealand.
Award: G.A.Gooch.   LOI debuts: England – W.Larkins.

A sun-drenched crowd of 22,000 saw England win a fluctuating match by the slenderest runs margin in World Cup matches so far. New Zealand's last pair required 14 runs from the final over, bowled by Ian Botham.

ENGLAND		Runs	Balls	4/6
* J.M.Brearley	c Lees b Coney	53	115	3
G.Boycott	c Howarth b Hadlee	2	14	–
W.Larkins	c Coney b McKechnie	7	37	–
G.A.Gooch	b McKechnie	71	84	1/3
D.I.Gower	run out	1	1	–
I.T.Botham	lbw b Cairns	21	30	2
D.W.Randall	not out	42	50	1/1
C.M.Old	c Lees b Troup	0	2	–
† R.W.Taylor	run out	12	25	1
R.G.D.Willis	not out	1	2	–
M.Hendrick				
Extras	(lb 8, w 3)	11		
Total	(60 overs; 8 wickets)	**221**		

NEW ZEALAND		Runs	Balls	4/6
J.G.Wright	run out	69	137	9
B.A.Edgar	lbw b Old	17	38	1
G.P.Howarth	lbw b Boycott	7	12	1
J.V.Coney	lbw b Hendrick	11	39	–
G.M.Turner	lbw b Willis	30	51	2
* M.G.Burgess	run out	10	13	–
R.J.Hadlee	b Botham	15	32	–
† W.K.Lees	b Hendrick	23	20	–/1
B.L.Cairns	c Brearley b Hendrick	14	6	1/1
B.J.McKechnie	not out	4	9	–
G.B.Troup	not out	3	3	–
Extras	(b 5, w 4)	9		
Total	(60 overs; 9 wickets)	**212**		

NEW ZEALAND	O	M	R	W
Hadlee	12	4	32	1
Troup	12	1	38	1
Cairns	12	2	47	1
Coney	12	0	47	1
McKechnie	12	1	46	2

ENGLAND	O	M	R	W
Botham	12	3	42	1
Hendrick	12	0	55	3
Old	12	1	33	1
Boycott	9	1	24	1
Gooch	3	1	8	0
Willis	12	1	41	1

FALL OF WICKETS
1-13, 2-38, 3-96, 4-98, 5-145, 6-177, 7-178, 8-219

FALL OF WICKETS
1-47, 2-58, 3-104, 4-112, 5-132, 6-162, 7-180, 8-195, 9-208

Umpires: J.G.Langridge (8) and K.E.Palmer (6).

WEST INDIES v PAKISTAN 1979

At Kennington Oval, London, on 20 June 1979. Result: **WEST INDIES** won by 43 runs. Toss: Pakistan.
Award: C.G.Greenidge. LOI debuts: None.

In similar conditions, 20,000 spectators saw West Indies amass their highest total of the tournament and withstand a second-wicket stand of 166 from 36 overs by Majid Khan and Zaheer Abbas. Colin Croft's decisive 12-ball spell accounted for both partners plus Javed Miandad for just four runs.

WEST INDIES		Runs	Balls	4/6
C.G.Greenidge	c Wasim b Asif	73	107	5/1
D.L.Haynes	c and b Asif	65	115	4
I.V.A.Richards	b Asif	42	62	1
* C.H.Lloyd	c Mudassar b Asif	37	38	3
C.L.King	c sub (Wasim Raja) b Sarfraz	34	25	3
A.I.Kallicharran	b Imran	11	14	–
A.M.E.Roberts	not out	7	4	–
J.Garner	not out	1	1	–
† D.L.Murray				
M.A.Holding				
C.E.H.Croft				
Extras	(b 1, lb 17, w 1, nb 4)	23		
Total	(60 overs; 6 wickets)	**293**		

PAKISTAN		Runs	Balls	4/6
Majid Khan	c Kallicharran b Croft	81	124	7
Sadiq Mohammed	c Murray b Holding	2	7	–
Zaheer Abbas	c Murray b Croft	93	122	8/1
Haroon Rashid	run out	15	22	1
Javed Miandad	lbw b Croft	0	1	–
* Asif Iqbal	c Holding b Richards	17	20	1
Mudassar Nazar	c Kallicharran b Richards	2	9	–
Imran Khan	c and b Richards	6	4	1
Sarfraz Nawaz	c Haynes b Roberts	12	15	–
† Wasim Bari	c Murray b Roberts	9	12	–
Sikander Bakht	not out	1	4	–
Extras	(lb 9, w 2, nb 1)	12		
Total	(56.2 overs)	**250**		

PAKISTAN	O	M	R	W
Imran Khan	9	1	43	1
Sarfraz Nawaz	12	1	71	1
Sikander Bakht	6	1	24	0
Mudassar Nazar	10	0	50	0
Majid Khan	12	2	26	0
Asif Iqbal	11	0	56	4

WEST INDIES	O	M	R	W
Roberts	9.2	2	41	2
Holding	9	1	28	1
Croft	11	0	29	3
Garner	12	1	47	0
King	7	0	41	0
Richards	8	0	52	3

FALL OF WICKETS
1-132, 2-165, 3-233, 4-236, 5-285, 6-285

FALL OF WICKETS
1-10, 2-176, 3-187, 4-187, 5-208, 6-220, 7-221, 8-228, 9-246, 10-250

Umpires: W.L.Budd (12) and D.J.Constant (14).

ENGLAND v WEST INDIES 1979

At Lord's, London, on 23 June 1979. Result: **WEST INDIES** won by 92 runs. Toss: England.
Award: I.V.A.Richards. LOI debuts: None.

Viv Richards delighted a capacity all-ticket crowd of 25,000 with what remains the highest score in a World Cup final, his partnership of 139 with Collis King coming from 126 balls in 77 minutes. England's last eight wickets fell in 26 balls as Joel Garner, twice on a hat-trick, terminated the match with a spell of 5 for 4 in 11 balls.

WEST INDIES		Runs	Balls	4/6
C.G.Greenidge	run out	9	31	–
D.L.Haynes	c Hendrick b Old	20	27	3
I.V.A.Richards	not out	138	157	11/3
A.I.Kallicharran	b Hendrick	4	17	–
* C.H.Lloyd	c and b Old	13	33	2
C.L.King	c Randall b Edmonds	86	66	10/3
† D.L.Murray	c Gower b Edmonds	5	9	1
A.M.E.Roberts	c Brearley b Hendrick	0	7	–
J.Garner	c Taylor b Botham	0	5	–
M.A.Holding	b Botham	0	6	–
C.E.H.Croft	not out	0	2	–
Extras	(b 1, lb 10)	11		
Total	(60 overs; 9 wickets)	**286**		

ENGLAND		Runs	Balls	4/6
* J.M.Brearley	c King b Holding	64	130	7
G.Boycott	c Kallicharran b Holding	57	105	3
D.W.Randall	b Croft	15	22	–
G.A.Gooch	b Garner	32	28	4
D.I.Gower	b Garner	0	4	–
I.T.Botham	c Richards b Croft	4	3	–
W.Larkins	b Garner	0	1	–
P.H.Edmonds	not out	5	8	–
C.M.Old	b Garner	0	2	–
† R.W.Taylor	c Murray b Garner	0	1	–
M.Hendrick	b Croft	0	5	–
Extras	(lb 12, w 2, nb 3)	17		
Total	(51 overs)	**194**		

ENGLAND	O	M	R	W
Botham	12	2	44	2
Hendrick	12	2	50	2
Old	12	0	55	2
Boycott	6	0	38	0
Edmonds	12	2	40	2
Gooch	4	0	27	0
Larkins	2	0	21	0

WEST INDIES	O	M	R	W
Roberts	9	2	33	0
Holding	8	1	16	2
Croft	10	1	42	3
Garner	11	0	38	5
Richards	10	0	35	0
King	3	0	13	0

FALL OF WICKETS
1-22, 2-36, 3-55, 4-99, 5-238, 6-252, 7-258, 8-260, 9-272

FALL OF WICKETS
1-129, 2-135, 3-183, 4-183, 5-186, 6-186, 7-192, 8-192, 9-194, 10-194

Umpires: H.D.Bird (15) and B.J.Meyer (6).

AUSTRALIA v WEST INDIES 1979-80

At Sydney Cricket Ground on 27 November 1979.   Result: **AUSTRALIA** won by 5 wickets.   Toss: Australia.
Award: G.S.Chappell.   LOI debuts: Australia – B.M.Laird.

Cricket's inaugural *World* Series celebrated the end of the Packer schism and began with the first official (Australian Cricket Board) limited-overs international to be staged under floodlights. This triangular tournament of 50-over (six-balls) matches involved 12 qualifying games followed by a best-of-three set of finals for the two leaders.

WEST INDIES		Runs	Balls	4/6
C.G.Greenidge	b Lillee	5	19	–
D.L.Haynes	b Border	29	51	2
I.V.A.Richards	lbw b Lillee	9	8	1
A.I.Kallicharran	c and b Border	49	94	4
* C.H.Lloyd	c Marsh b Border	16	24	–
C.L.King	b Pascoe	29	32	2
† D.L.Murray	b Pascoe	27	52	1
A.M.E.Roberts	b Pascoe	16	16	1
J.Garner	run out	5	4	–
M.A.Holding	c McCosker b Pascoe	2	2	–
C.E.H.Croft	not out	0	–	–
Extras	(lb 3, nb 3)	6		
Total	(49.3 overs)	**193**		

AUSTRALIA		Runs	Balls	4/6
R.B.McCosker	lbw b Holding	1	7	–
B.M.Laird	b Croft	20	38	2
A.R.Border	c Murray b Croft	17	59	–
* G.S.Chappell	not out	74	100	6
K.J.Hughes	b Richards	52	60	3/1
D.W.Hookes	b Richards	0	2	–
† R.W.Marsh	not out	18	22	–
R.J.Bright				
D.K.Lillee				
R.M.Hogg				
L.S.Pascoe				
Extras	(lb 14)	14		
Total	(47.1 overs; 5 wickets)	**196**		

AUSTRALIA	O	M	R	W
Lillee	6	2	10	2
Pascoe	9.3	1	29	4
Bright	5	0	26	0
Hogg	10	0	49	0
Border	10	0	36	3
Chappell	9	0	37	0

WEST INDIES	O	M	R	W
Roberts	9	1	35	0
Holding	8.1	2	28	1
Croft	10	0	30	2
Garner	10	2	42	0
Richards	10	0	47	2

FALL OF WICKETS
1-1, 2-37, 3-52, 4-144, 5-144

FALL OF WICKETS
1-6, 2-18, 3-89, 4-112, 5-117, 6-164, 7-177, 8-187, 9-193, 10-193

Umpires: R.G.Harris (1) and C.E.Harvey (3).

ENGLAND v WEST INDIES 1979-80

At Sydney Cricket Ground on 28 November 1979.   Result: **ENGLAND** won by 2 runs (revised target).
Toss: West Indies.   Award: P.Willey.   LOI debuts: England – G.R.Dilley.

Rain reduced West Indies' innings to 47 overs and revised their target to 199. With Colin Croft needing three runs from Ian Botham's final ball, Mike Brearley positioned all his fielders, including his wicket-keeper, around the boundary.

ENGLAND		Runs	Balls	4/6
D.W.Randall	c Parry b Garner	49		
* J.M.Brearley	c Greenidge b Parry	25		
D.I.Gower	b Croft	44		
G.A.Gooch	c and b Parry	2		
P.Willey	not out	58		
I.T.Botham	b Garner	11		
† D.L.Bairstow	c Murray b Garner	0		
G.Miller	b Roberts	4		
G.R.Dilley	run out	1		
D.L.Underwood				
R.G.D.Willis				
Extras	(b 4, lb 13)	17		
Total	(50 overs; 8 wickets)	**211**		

WEST INDIES		Runs	Balls	4/6
C.G.Greenidge	c Willis b Miller	42		
D.L.Haynes	b Dilley	4		
L.G.Rowe	lbw b Willis	60		
A.I.Kallicharran	run out	44		
* C.H.Lloyd	c Brearley b Willis	4		
† D.L.Murray	c Gower b Underwood	3		
D.R.Parry	b Underwood	4		
A.M.E.Roberts	c Randall b Underwood	16		
J.Garner	not out	8		
M.A.Holding	c Gower b Underwood	0		
C.E.H.Croft	b Botham	3		
Extras	(b 1, lb 7)	8		
Total	(47 overs)	**196**		

WEST INDIES	O	M	R	W
Roberts	9	0	37	1
Holding	9	0	47	0
Croft	10	0	34	1
Garner	10	0	31	3
Parry	10	0	35	2
Kallicharran	2	0	10	0

ENGLAND	O	M	R	W
Dilley	6	2	21	1
Botham	7	1	26	1
Underwood	10	0	44	4
Miller	10	0	33	1
Willey	8	0	29	0
Willis	6	0	35	2

FALL OF WICKETS
1-79, 2-88, 3-91, 4-160, 5-195, 6-195, 7-210, 8-211

FALL OF WICKETS
1-19, 2-68, 3-132, 4-143, 5-144, 6-155, 7-177, 8-185, 9-186, 10-196

Umpires: C.E.Harvey (4) and A.G.Watson (1).

AUSTRALIA v ENGLAND 1979-80

At Melbourne Cricket Ground on 8 December 1979.　　Result: **ENGLAND** won by 3 wickets.　　Toss: England.
Award: G.S.Chappell.　　LOI debuts: Australia – J.M.Wiener.

Belatedly included when Geoff Miller withdrew through lumbago, Geoffrey Boycott played one of his most aggressive innings.

AUSTRALIA		Runs	Balls	4/6	ENGLAND		Runs	Balls	4/6
J.M.Wiener	b Botham	7	22	1	D.W.Randall	lbw b Bright	28	69	2
B.M.Laird	lbw b Dilley	7	24	1	G.Boycott	c Lillee b Hogg	68	85	7
A.R.Border	c Willey b Dilley	29	54	1/1	P.Willey	c Marsh b Hogg	37	54	2
*G.S.Chappell	c Gooch b Willey	92	115	10	D.I.Gower	c Marsh b Lillee	17	24	–/1
K.J.Hughes	st Bairstow b Gooch	23	24	3	G.A.Gooch	run out	1	2	–
K.D.Walters	c Randall b Gooch	12	22	1	I.T.Botham	c Walters b Hogg	10	10	1
†R.W.Marsh	c Bairstow b Willey	14	23	–	*J.M.Brearley	c Marsh b Lillee	27	39	2
R.J.Bright	c Gooch b Willey	1	6	–	†D.L.Bairstow	not out	15	15	2
D.K.Lillee	not out	13	7	2	G.R.Dilley	not out	0	–	–
R.M.Hogg	c Brearley b Underwood	1	3	–	D.L.Underwood				
J.R.Thomson					R.G.D.Willis				
Extras	(b 1, lb 5, nb 2)	8			Extras	(lb 3, nb 3)	6		
Total	(50 overs; 9 wickets)	**207**			**Total**	(49 overs; 7 wickets)	**209**		

ENGLAND	O	M	R	W	AUSTRALIA	O	M	R	W
Dilley	10	1	30	2	Lillee	10	1	36	2
Botham	9	2	27	1	Hogg	10	2	26	3
Willis	7	0	28	0	Thomson	10	1	49	0
Gooch	6	0	32	2	Chappell	8	0	40	0
Underwood	10	0	49	1	Bright	9	1	40	1
Willey	8	0	33	3	Walters	2	0	12	0

FALL OF WICKETS
1-15, 2-15, 3-73, 4-114, 5-145, 6-184, 7-193, 8-193, 9-207

FALL OF WICKETS
1-71, 2-134, 3-137, 4-138, 5-148, 6-183, 7-205

Umpires: W.J.Copeland (1) and R.A.French (1).

AUSTRALIA v WEST INDIES 1979-80

At Melbourne Cricket Ground on 9 December 1979.　　Result: **WEST INDIES** won by 80 runs.　　Toss: Australia.
Award: I.V.A.Richards.　　LOI debuts: None.

Match reduced to 48 overs by Australia's sluggish over-rate (3½-hour deadline). Viv Richards ignored a back injury to score the first 150 outside England in these matches. His partnership of 205 with Desmond Haynes was the first of 200 or more and remained the record until 1983-84 (*LOI No. 229*).

WEST INDIES		Runs	Balls	4/6	AUSTRALIA		Runs	Balls	4/6
C.G.Greenidge	c Marsh b Lillee	11	20	1	J.M.Wiener	c and b Parry	27	64	2
D.L.Haynes	c Marsh b Thomson	80	122	5	B.M.Laird	b Holding	7	15	1
I.V.A.Richards	not out	153	130	16/1	A.R.Border	run out	44	58	2
A.I.Kallicharran	not out	16	17	2	*G.S.Chappell	c Richards b King	31	21	3
L.G.Rowe					K.J.Hughes	b Holding	12	16	1
C.L.King					D.W.Hookes	c Murray b Roberts	9	27	–
*†D.L.Murray					†R.W.Marsh	c Rowe b Roberts	13	11	–/1
D.R.Parry					R.J.Bright	not out	19	43	1
A.M.E.Roberts					D.K.Lillee	b King	19	24	1
J.Garner					R.M.Hogg	not out	3	9	–
M.A.Holding					J.R.Thomson				
Extras	(b 1, lb 10)	11			Extras	(b 1, lb 6)	7		
Total	(48 overs; 2 wickets)	**271**			**Total**	(48 overs; 8 wickets)	**191**		

AUSTRALIA	O	M	R	W	WEST INDIES	O	M	R	W
Lillee	10	1	48	1	Roberts	8	1	33	2
Hogg	10	1	50	0	Holding	10	2	29	2
Chappell	4	0	24	0	Garner	10	1	26	0
Thomson	8	0	43	1	King	10	0	40	2
Bright	6	0	29	0	Parry	10	0	56	1
Hookes	1	0	10	0					
Border	7	0	40	0					
Wiener	2	0	16	0					

FALL OF WICKETS
1-28, 2-233

FALL OF WICKETS
1-16, 2-54, 3-102, 4-119, 5-128, 6-147, 7-151, 8-185

Umpires: K.J.Carmody (1) and R.V.Whitehead (1).

AUSTRALIA v ENGLAND 1979-80

At Sydney Cricket Ground on 11 December 1979.   Result: **ENGLAND** won by 72 runs.   Toss: England.
Award: G.Boycott.   LOI debuts: None.

Match reduced to 49 overs by slow over rate. Geoffrey Boycott continued to astonish with another dashing, cavalier display which included his rare lofted on-drive. During his only hundred in these matches he even managed to fox the umpires by taking strike at the wrong end after a drinks break.

ENGLAND		Runs	Balls	4/6
G.Boycott	b Lillee	105	124	7
D.W.Randall	run out	42	76	5
P.Willey	c Walker b Chappell	64	58	8
D.I.Gower	c Wiener b Lillee	7	16	–
G.A.Gooch	b Thomson	11	9	1
I.T.Botham	c Walters b Lillee	5	4	1
† D.L.Bairstow	c sub (D.W.Hookes) b Lillee	18	10	1/1
* J.M.Brearley	not out	2	2	–
G.R.Dilley				
D.L.Underwood				
R.G.D.Willis				
Extras	(lb 6, w 1, nb 3)	10		
Total	(49 overs; 7 wickets)	**264**		

AUSTRALIA		Runs	Balls	4/6
J.M.Wiener	st Bairstow b Willey	14	38	1
W.M.Darling	c Randall b Willis	20	34	2
A.R.Border	b Willey	1	4	–
* G.S.Chappell	run out	0	6	–
K.J.Hughes	c Bairstow b Willis	1	5	–
K.D.Walters	c Bairstow b Botham	34	40	1
† R.W.Marsh	b Dilley	12	20	–
T.J.Laughlin	c Gooch b Randall	74	97	4
D.K.Lillee	b Botham	14	14	2
J.R.Thomson	run out	0	1	–
M.H.N.Walker	not out	9	29	–
Extras	(lb 10, w 2, nb 1)	13		
Total	(47.2 overs)	**192**		

AUSTRALIA	O	M	R	W
Lillee	10	0	56	4
Thomson	9	0	53	1
Walker	10	1	30	0
Laughlin	8	0	39	0
Border	4	0	24	0
Chappell	5	0	28	1
Walters	3	0	24	0

ENGLAND	O	M	R	W
Dilley	9	0	29	1
Botham	10	1	36	2
Willis	10	1	32	2
Willey	5	0	18	2
Underwood	6	1	29	0
Gooch	7	0	33	0
Randall	0.2	0	2	1

FALL OF WICKETS
1-78, 2-196, 3-220, 4-236, 5-242, 6-245, 7-264

FALL OF WICKETS
1-33, 2-36, 3-36, 4-38, 5-39, 6-63, 7-115, 8-146, 9-147, 10-192

Umpires: J.R.Collins (1) and L.J.Stevens (1).

AUSTRALIA v WEST INDIES 1979-80

At Sydney Cricket Ground on 21 December 1979.   Result: **AUSTRALIA** won by 7 runs.   Toss: West Indies.
Award: I.M.Chappell.   LOI debuts: None.

Recalled after a four-year absence, Ian Chappell's 65-ball innings of 63 not out deservedly earned him the match award. West Indies lost their last seven wickets for 45 runs.

AUSTRALIA		Runs	Balls	4/6
J.M.Wiener	c Lloyd b Holding	7	22	1
B.M.Laird	c Rowe b Roberts	1	9	–
A.R.Border	c Murray b Garner	17	40	–
* G.S.Chappell	c Lloyd b Richards	24	83	–
K.J.Hughes	c Roberts b King	13	19	1
I.M.Chappell	not out	63	65	6
† R.W.Marsh	run out	33	54	1
D.K.Lillee	not out	12	9	2
L.S.Pascoe				
R.M.Hogg				
G.Dymock				
Extras	(lb 4, nb 2)	6		
Total	(50 overs; 6 wickets)	**176**		

WEST INDIES		Runs	Balls	4/6
C.G.Greenidge	c Marsh b Lillee	33	53	5
D.L.Haynes	c I.M.Chappell b Lillee	0	5	–
I.V.A.Richards	c Hogg b Dymock	62	79	5
A.I.Kallicharran	b Pascoe	19	38	2
L.G.Rowe	c Border b G.S.Chappell	5	18	–
* C.H.Lloyd	c Wiener b Dymock	0	1	–
C.L.King	c Marsh b G.S.Chappell	9	17	2
† D.L.Murray	not out	17	25	3
A.M.E.Roberts	lbw b Pascoe	8	20	1
J.Garner	c G.S.Chappell b Lillee	2	7	–
M.A.Holding	b Lillee	0	2	–
Extras	(lb 8, nb 6)	14		
Total	(42.5 overs)	**169**		

WEST INDIES	O	M	R	W
Roberts	10	1	28	1
Holding	10	1	33	1
King	10	0	38	1
Garner	10	2	34	1
Richards	8	0	35	1
Lloyd	2	0	2	0

AUSTRALIA	O	M	R	W
Lillee	8.5	0	28	4
Pascoe	10	1	38	2
Hogg	10	3	47	0
Dymock	10	1	28	2
G.S.Chappell	4	0	14	2

FALL OF WICKETS
1-1, 2-11, 3-28, 4-44, 5-94, 6-160

FALL OF WICKETS
1-7, 2-74, 3-112, 4-124, 5-124, 6-139, 7-144, 8-158, 9-169, 10-169

Umpires: R.A.French (2) and A.G.Watson (2).

ENGLAND v WEST INDIES 1979-80

At Woolloongabba, Brisbane on 23 December 1979.   Result: **WEST INDIES** won by 9 wickets.   Toss: West Indies.
Award: C.G.Greenidge.   LOI debuts: None.

Derek Randall was dismissed by the first ball bowled in a limited-overs international at 'The Gabba'. Viv Richards
contributed 85 to an unbroken second-wicket partnership of 109 with Gordon Greenidge.

ENGLAND		Runs	Balls	4/6	WEST INDIES		Runs	Balls	4/6
D.W.Randall	c Lloyd b Roberts	0	1	–	C.G.Greenidge	not out	85	122	9/1
G.Boycott	c sub (M.D.Marshall) b Holding	68	114	3	D.L.Haynes	c Underwood b Gooch	41	86	4
P.Willey	run out	34	51	4	I.V.A.Richards	not out	85	77	10/2
D.I.Gower	c Holding b Roberts	59	74	7	A.I.Kallicharran				
G.A.Gooch	b Garner	17	23	–/1	L.G.Rowe				
I.T.Botham	lbw b Holding	4	9	–	* C.H.Lloyd				
† D.L.Bairstow	c Lloyd b Roberts	12	18	–	C.L.King				
* J.M.Brearley	not out	9	9	1	† D.L.Murray				
G.R.Dilley	b Garner	0	3	–	A.M.E.Roberts				
D.L.Underwood					J.Garner				
R.G.D.Willis					M.A.Holding				
Extras	(lb 8, w 5, nb 1)	14			Extras	(lb 4, nb 3)	7		
Total	(50 overs; 8 wickets)	**217**			**Total**	(46.5 overs; 1 wicket)	**218**		

WEST INDIES	O	M	R	W	ENGLAND	O	M	R	W
Roberts	10	3	26	3	Botham	10	1	39	0
Holding	10	1	44	2	Dilley	8	1	25	0
Garner	10	0	37	2	Willis	10	2	27	0
Richards	10	0	44	0	Underwood	9	0	43	0
King	10	0	52	0	Willey	6	0	39	0
					Gooch	3.5	0	38	1

FALL OF WICKETS
1-0, 2-70, 3-167, 4-174, 5-191, 6-205, 7-209, 8-217

FALL OF WICKETS
1-109

Umpires: C.E.Harvey (5) and M.W.Johnson (1).

AUSTRALIA v ENGLAND 1979-80

At Sydney Cricket Ground on 26 December 1979.   Result: **ENGLAND** won by 4 wickets.   Toss: Australia.
Award: G.Boycott.   LOI debuts: None.

Match reduced to 47 overs by afternoon rain. Another exceptional innings by Geoffrey Boycott was played against the
deafening background of a Speedway and Fireworks Spectacular at the adjoining Showground.

AUSTRALIA		Runs	Balls	4/6	ENGLAND		Runs	Balls	4/6
B.M.Laird	b Botham	6	27	–	G.A.Gooch	lbw b Hogg	29	35	4
J.M.Wiener	c Bairstow b Botham	2	14	–	G.Boycott	not out	86	134	6
A.R.Border	c Gower b Gooch	22	53	2	P.Willey	b Pascoe	51	77	5
* G.S.Chappell	run out	52	82	3	D.I.Gower	c Marsh b Hogg	2	12	–
K.J.Hughes	b Willis	23	39	–/1	D.W.Randall	c G.S.Chappell b Pascoe	1	5	–
I.M.Chappell	not out	60	50	6	I.T.Botham	lbw b Hogg	6	10	–/1
† R.W.Marsh	c Bairstow b Dilley	10	13	–/1	* J.M.Brearley	c Marsh b Hogg	0	3	–
D.K.Lillee	not out	2	4	–	† D.L.Bairstow	not out	7	8	–
R.M.Hogg					G.R.Dilley				
G.Dymock					D.L.Underwood				
L.S.Pascoe					R.G.D.Willis				
Extras	(b 3, lb 10, nb 4)	17			Extras	(lb 1, w 1, nb 11)	13		
Total	(47 overs; 6 wickets)	**194**			**Total**	(45.1 overs; 6 wickets)	**195**		

ENGLAND	O	M	R	W	AUSTRALIA	O	M	R	W
Dilley	10	1	32	1	Lillee	10	0	47	0
Botham	9	1	33	2	Pascoe	10	2	28	2
Willis	10	1	38	1	Hogg	10	0	46	4
Underwood	10	2	36	0	Dymock	10	1	38	0
Gooch	8	0	38	1	G.S.Chappell	5.1	0	23	0

FALL OF WICKETS
1-5, 2-21, 3-50, 4-109, 5-135, 6-179

FALL OF WICKETS
1-41, 2-152, 3-157, 4-170, 5-179, 6-179

Umpires: P.M.Cronin (1) and R.C.Isherwood (1).

AUSTRALIA v ENGLAND 1979-80

At Sydney Cricket Ground on 14 January 1980.   Result: **ENGLAND** won by 2 wickets.   Toss: England.
Award: D.K.Lillee.   LOI debuts: England – J.E.Emburey, G.B.Stevenson.

The ninth match, between England and West Indies, due to take place on 12 January in Melbourne, was abandoned without a ball bowled. Graham Stevenson celebrated his international debut by taking 4 for 7 in 20 balls before leading England to a thrilling victory with seven balls to spare, thus ensuring that Australia would not qualify for the finals, a catastrophe which was not to occur again until 1996-97.

AUSTRALIA		Runs	Balls	4/6
J.M.Wiener	st Bairstow b Emburey	33	80	3
R.B.McCosker	c Brearley b Willey	41	67	2
I.M.Chappell	c Randall b Emburey	8	15	–
* G.S.Chappell	c Randall b Stevenson	34	55	2
K.J.Hughes	c Larkins b Lever	34	42	I
A.R.Border	c Bairstow b Lever	0	3	–
† R.W.Marsh	c Bairstow b Stevenson	0	2	–
D.K.Lillee	lbw b Stevenson	0	I	–
G.Dymock	run out	0	9	–
J.R.Thomson	not out	3	12	–
L.S.Pascoe	b Stevenson	5	II	I
Extras	(lb I, w 3, nb I)	5		
Total	(48.4 overs)	**163**		

ENGLAND	O	M	R	W
Lever	9	I	II	2
Botham	7	0	33	0
Gooch	3	0	13	0
Stevenson	9.4	0	33	4
Emburey	10	I	33	2
Willey	10	0	35	I

FALL OF WICKETS
1-74, 2-82, 3-89, 4-148, 5-149, 6-150, 7-150, 8-152, 9-155, 10-163

Umpires: R.C.Isherwood (2) and R.V.Whitehead (2).

ENGLAND		Runs	Balls	4/6
G.A.Gooch	c McCosker b Pascoe	69	123	5
W.Larkins	c Thomson b Lillee	5	31	–
P.Willey	lbw b Lillee	0	2	–
D.I.Gower	c Marsh b Lillee	3	7	–
* J.M.Brearley	b G.S.Chappell	5	19	–
D.W.Randall	c Pascoe b G.S.Chappell	0	II	–
I.T.Botham	b Lillee	0	3	–
† D.L.Bairstow	not out	21	68	–
J.E.Emburey	c G.S.Chappell b Dymock	18	22	2
G.B.Stevenson	not out	28	18	3
J.K.Lever				
Extras	(lb 5, w I, nb 9)	15		
Total	(48.5 overs; 8 wickets)	**164**		

AUSTRALIA	O	M	R	W
Thomson	9.5	0	46	0
Dymock	9	I	30	I
Lillee	10	6	12	4
Pascoe	10	0	38	I
G.S.Chappell	10	3	23	2

FALL OF WICKETS
1-31, 2-31, 3-40, 4-51, 5-56, 6-61, 7-105, 8-129

ENGLAND v WEST INDIES 1979-80

At Adelaide Oval on 16 January 1980.   Result: **WEST INDIES** won by 107 runs.   Toss: England.
Award: A.M.E.Roberts.   LOI debuts: None.

Witnessed by a capacity crowd of 24,986, Andy Roberts returned the first five-wicket World Series analysis.

WEST INDIES		Runs	Balls	4/6
C.G.Greenidge	c Emburey b Willey	50		
D.L.Haynes	c Gooch b Stevenson	26		
I.V.A.Richards	b Botham	88		
A.I.Kallicharran	c and b Botham	57		
C.L.King	run out	12		
J.Garner	not out	7		
A.M.E.Roberts	not out	0		
* C.H.Lloyd				
L.G.Rowe				
† D.L.Murray				
M.A.Holding				
Extras	(b I, lb 4, nb I)	6		
Total	(50 overs; 5 wickets)	**246**		

ENGLAND	O	M	R	W
Lever	10	I	54	0
Botham	10	0	35	2
Gooch	2	0	22	0
Stevenson	8	I	53	I
Emburey	10	0	39	0
Willey	10	I	37	I

FALL OF WICKETS
1-58, 2-115, 3-224, 4-227, 5-245

Umpires: P.M.Cronin (2) and G.Duperouzel (I).

ENGLAND		Runs	Balls	4/6
G.A.Gooch	b King	20		
* J.M.Brearley	c Murray b Roberts	0		
P.Willey	c Lloyd b King	5		
W.Larkins	c Lloyd b King	24		
D.I.Gower	c sub (D.R.Parry) b King	12		
D.W.Randall	b Roberts	16		
I.T.Botham	c Haynes b Roberts	22		
† D.L.Bairstow	not out	23		
G.B.Stevenson	b Roberts	I		
J.E.Emburey	c Murray b Roberts	I		
J.K.Lever	b Garner	II		
Extras	(lb 2, w I, nb I)	4		
Total	(42.5 overs)	**139**		

WEST INDIES	O	M	R	W
Roberts	10	5	22	5
Holding	7	0	16	0
King	9	3	23	4
Garner	7.5	3	9	I
Richards	7	0	46	0
Kallicharran	2	0	19	0

FALL OF WICKETS
1-5, 2-24, 3-31, 4-52, 5-68, 6-98, 7-100, 8-105, 9-109, 10-139

AUSTRALIA v WEST INDIES 1979-80

At Sydney Cricket Ground on 18 January 1980.　Result: **AUSTRALIA** won by 9 runs.　Toss: Australia.
Award: R.B.McCosker.　LOI debuts: Australia – D.F.Whatmore.

Defeated in each of their four encounters with England, Australia gained their third win against West Indies. Rick McCosker and Julien Wiener shared Australia's first three-figure opening partnership in World Series matches. Final points: England 11, West Indies 7, Australia 6.

AUSTRALIA		Runs	Balls	4/6
R.B.McCosker	c Lloyd b Holding	95	135	4
J.M.Wiener	c Gomes b Parry	50	84	4
K.J.Hughes	b Parry	4	10	–
* G.S.Chappell	c and b Parry	2	4	–
G.N.Yallop	b Roberts	11	19	1
D.F.Whatmore	c Murray b Holding	2	6	–
† R.W.Marsh	c Lloyd b Roberts	5	9	–
D.K.Lillee	c Murray b Holding	0	5	–
G.Dymock	not out	4	11	–
M.H.N.Walker	run out	5	8	–
L.S.Pascoe	b Holding	0	1	–
Extras	(b 1, lb 10, w 1)	12		
Total	(48.3 overs)	**190**		

WEST INDIES	O	M	R	W
Holding	9.3	2	17	4
Croft	10	0	22	0
King	9	0	40	0
Roberts	10	0	38	2
Parry	10	0	61	3

FALL OF WICKETS
1-103, 2-124, 3-134, 4-161, 5-166, 6-177, 7-177, 8-177, 9-190, 10-190

WEST INDIES		Runs	Balls	4/6
L.G.Rowe	lbw b Dymock	3	15	–
D.L.Haynes	c Marsh b Lillee	1	7	–
A.I.Kallicharran	lbw b Chappell	66	74	3
† D.A.Murray	c Chappell b Pascoe	35	98	6
* C.H.Lloyd	not out	34	52	3
C.L.King	lbw b Walker	0	1	–
H.A.Gomes	lbw b Lillee	4	7	–
D.R.Parry	b Pascoe	9	12	2
A.M.E.Roberts	c Marsh b Lillee	2	5	–
M.A.Holding	c and b Pascoe	8	14	–
C.E.H.Croft	c Lillee b Chappell	8	20	1
Extras	(b 3, nb 8)	11		
Total	(49.1 overs)	**181**		

AUSTRALIA	O	M	R	W
Lillee	10	3	17	3
Dymock	10	2	18	1
Walker	10	2	46	1
Pascoe	10	0	34	3
Chappell	7.1	0	37	2
Wiener	2	0	18	0

FALL OF WICKETS
1-4, 2-8, 3-91, 4-134, 5-135, 6-140, 7-152, 8-157, 9-166, 10-181

Umpires: K.J.Carmody (2) and A.G.Watson (3).

ENGLAND v WEST INDIES 1979-80

At Melbourne Cricket Ground on 20 January 1980.　Result: **WEST INDIES** won by 2 runs.　Toss: England.
LOI debuts: None.

Beset by three dropped catches and two vital run outs, England came within a whisker of snatching an unlikely victory against the favourites. The task of scoring 15 from Michael Holding's final over was reduced to four off the last ball. Attendance: 29,000.

WEST INDIES		Runs	Balls	4/6
C.G.Greenidge	c Larkins b Botham	80	132	6
D.L.Haynes	c Bairstow b Willis	9	20	–
I.V.A.Richards	c Bairstow b Dilley	23	34	2
A.I.Kallicharran	b Botham	42	61	3
* C.H.Lloyd	b Botham	4	7	–
C.L.King	not out	31	27	1/1
† D.L.Murray	c Bairstow b Dilley	4	10	–
A.M.E.Roberts	run out	1	3	–
J.Garner	run out	3	4	–
M.A.Holding	not out	5	5	–
C.E.H.Croft				
Extras	(lb 11, w 1, nb 1)	13		
Total	(50 overs; 8 wickets)	**215**		

ENGLAND	O	M	R	W
Willis	10	1	51	1
Botham	10	2	33	3
Emburey	10	0	31	0
Dilley	10	0	39	2
Willey	10	0	48	0

FALL OF WICKETS
1-17, 2-66, 3-161, 4-168, 5-168, 6-181, 7-183, 8-197

Umpires: R.C.Bailhache (5) and C.E.Harvey (6).

ENGLAND		Runs	Balls	4/6
G.A.Gooch	c King b Holding	9	22	–
G.Boycott	c Greenidge b Roberts	35	66	1
P.Willey	run out	51	91	3
D.I.Gower	c Holding b Roberts	10	17	–
W.Larkins	run out	34	42	2
I.T.Botham	c Lloyd b Roberts	19	31	–
* J.M.Brearley	not out	25	25	1
† D.L.Bairstow	run out	4	8	–
J.E.Emburey				
G.R.Dilley				
R.G.D.Willis				
Extras	(b 12, lb 12, w 1, nb 1)	26		
Total	(50 overs; 7 wickets)	**213**		

WEST INDIES	O	M	R	W
Roberts	10	1	30	3
Holding	10	1	43	1
Garner	10	1	27	0
Croft	10	1	23	0
King	4	0	30	0
Richards	6	1	34	0

FALL OF WICKETS
1-13, 2-74, 3-96, 4-152, 5-164, 6-190, 7-213

ENGLAND v WEST INDIES 1979-80

At Sydney Cricket Ground on 22 January 1980.   Result: **WEST INDIES** won by 8 wickets.   Toss: England.
Finals Award: C.G.Greenidge.   LOI debuts: None.

This emphatic second victory, by eight wickets and with 15 balls in hand, rendered a third final (scheduled for Sydney two days later) unnecessary.

ENGLAND		Runs	Balls	4/6
G.A.Gooch	lbw b Garner	23		
G.Boycott	c Greenidge b Roberts	63		
P.Willey	b Garner	3		
D.I.Gower	c Murray b Holding	27		
W.Larkins	b Croft	14		
I.T.Botham	c King b Roberts	37		
† D.L.Bairstow	not out	18		
* J.M.Brearley	run out	4		
J.E.Emburey	run out	6		
G.R.Dilley				
R.G.D.Willis				
Extras	(b 1, lb 11, nb 1)	13		
Total	(50 overs; 8 wickets)	**208**		

WEST INDIES		Runs	Balls	4/6
C.G.Greenidge	not out	98		
D.L.Haynes	lbw b Botham	17		
I.V.A.Richards	c Botham b Willey	65		
A.I.Kallicharran	not out	8		
* C.H.Lloyd				
C.L.King				
† D.L.Murray				
A.M.E.Roberts				
J.Garner				
M.A.Holding				
C.E.H.Croft				
Extras	(b 5, lb 10, w 5, nb 1)	21		
Total	(47.3 overs; 2 wickets)	**209**		

WEST INDIES	O	M	R	W
Roberts	10	3	31	2
Holding	10	1	34	1
Croft	10	3	29	1
Garner	10	0	44	2
Richards	3	0	19	0
King	7	1	38	0

ENGLAND	O	M	R	W
Willis	10	0	35	0
Dilley	7	0	37	0
Botham	10	1	28	1
Emburey	9.3	0	48	0
Willey	10	2	35	1
Gooch	1	0	5	0

FALL OF WICKETS
1-40, 2-54, 3-118, 4-126, 5-155, 6-188, 7-194, 8-208

FALL OF WICKETS
1-61, 2-180

Umpires: A.R.Crafter (3) and M.G.O'Connell (2).

NEW ZEALAND v WEST INDIES 1979-80

At Lancaster Park, Christchurch on 6 February 1980.   Result: **NEW ZEALAND** won by 1 wicket.
Toss: New Zealand.   Award: R.J.Hadlee.   LOI debuts: New Zealand – P.E.McEwan, J.F.Reid.   50-over match.

Gordon Greenidge contributed 103, out of 175 for 5, in 172 minutes, his second LOI hundred. Much to the delight of a New Zealand Day crowd of 14,000, Jeremy Coney's fourth boundary completed a one-wicket victory and his own fifty with just two balls to spare.

WEST INDIES		Runs	Balls	4/6
D.L.Haynes	lbw b Coney	27	3	
C.G.Greenidge	b Cairns	103	135	10/2
L.G.Rowe	run out	4		
A.I.Kallicharran	run out	6		
* C.H.Lloyd	b Hadlee	14		
C.L.King	c Lees b Cairns	12		
D.R.Parry	not out	11		
J.Garner	c Coney b Hadlee	5		
† D.L.Murray	not out	3		
M.A.Holding				
C.E.H.Croft				
Extras	(b 4, lb 10, nb 4)	18		
Total	(50 overs; 7 wickets)	**203**		

NEW ZEALAND		Runs	Balls	4/6
J.G.Wright	c Lloyd b King	20		4
B.A.Edgar	c Murray b Garner	18		3
J.F.Reid	c Murray b Parry	5		
J.M.Parker	c Lloyd b Garner	0		
* G.P.Howarth	c Parry b King	18		
P.E.McEwan	c and b Parry	12		
J.V.Coney	not out	53		4
† W.K.Lees	b Parry	25		–/2
R.J.Hadlee	c Garner b Holding	41		6
B.L.Cairns	run out	1		
G.B.Troup	not out	0		
Extras	(b 1, lb 10, w 1, nb 2)	14		
Total	(49.4 overs; 9 wickets)	**207**		

NEW ZEALAND	O	M	R	W
Hadlee	10	3	28	2
Troup	10	0	30	0
Cairns	10	1	37	2
McEwan	10	0	40	0
Coney	8	0	41	1
Howarth	2	0	9	0

WEST INDIES	O	M	R	W
Holding	9.4	1	23	1
Croft	10	2	46	0
Garner	10	2	42	2
King	10	1	35	2
Parry	10	0	47	3

FALL OF WICKETS
1-81, 2-94, 3-126, 4-165, 5-175, 6-185, 7-196

FALL OF WICKETS
1-28, 2-40, 3-41, 4-56, 5-78, 6-80, 7-134, 8-194, 9-203

Umpires: F.R.Goodall (3) and R.L.Monteith (2).

ENGLAND v WEST INDIES 1980

At Headingley, Leeds on 28, 29 May 1980.   Result: **WEST INDIES** won by 24 runs.   Toss: England.
Award: C.J.Tavaré.   LOI debuts: England – C.J.Tavaré; West Indies – M.D.Marshall.   55-over match.

Rain interruptions on both days extended this encounter until 2.36 on the second afternoon. Ian Botham made his debut as England's captain. Chris Old's analysis of 11-4-12-2 remains the most economical by an England bowler completing his maximum bowling allowance. England were 35 for 3 after 23 overs overnight.

WEST INDIES		Runs	Balls	4/6
C.G.Greenidge	b Botham	78	147	11/1
D.L.Haynes	c Tavaré b Old	19	48	2
I.V.A.Richards	c Gower b Gooch	7	13	1
S.F.A.F.Bacchus	c Lever b Gooch	2	6	–
A.I.Kallicharran	c Botham b Old	10	48	1
* C.H.Lloyd	c and b Lever	21	23	–/1
M.D.Marshall	b Botham	6	10	1
† D.L.Murray	run out	9	12	–
A.M.E.Roberts	c Botham b Dilley	10	13	1
J.Garner	run out	14	10	2
M.A.Holding	not out	0		
Extras	(b 5, lb 15, w 2)	22		
Total	(55 overs)	**198**		

ENGLAND		Runs	Balls	4/6
G.Boycott	c Kallicharran b Garner	5	40	–
P.Willey	c Richards b Marshall	7	38	1
C.J.Tavaré	not out	82	129	5
G.A.Gooch	c Murray b Richards	2	7	–
D.I.Gower	c Murray b Holding	12	16	2
* I.T.Botham	c Murray b Marshall	30	22	5
D.Lloyd	b Greenidge	1	8	–
† D.L.Bairstow	c Garner b Holding	16	23	–
C.M.Old	b Marshall	4	11	–
G.R.Dilley	c Haynes b Roberts	0	5	–
J.K.Lever	run out	6	10	–
Extras	(b 3, lb 4, w 2)	9		
Total	(51.2 overs)	**174**		

ENGLAND	O	M	R	W
Dilley	11	3	41	1
Lever	11	3	36	1
Botham	11	1	45	2
Old	11	4	12	2
Gooch	7	2	30	2
Willey	4	0	12	0

WEST INDIES	O	M	R	W
Holding	9	3	16	2
Roberts	11	4	30	1
Garner	9.2	0	20	1
Marshall	11	2	28	3
Richards	7	0	50	1
Greenidge	4	0	21	1

FALL OF WICKETS
1-36, 2-49, 3-51, 4-110, 5-151, 6-161, 7-163, 8-178, 9-197, 10-198

FALL OF WICKETS
1-11, 2-15, 3-23, 4-38, 5-81, 6-86, 7-130, 8-149, 9-150, 10-174

Umpires: B.J.Meyer (7) and K.E.Palmer (7).

ENGLAND v WEST INDIES 1980

At Lord's, London on 30 May 1980.   Result: **ENGLAND** won by 3 wickets.   Toss: England.
Award: G.Boycott.   LOI debuts: England – V.J.Marks.   55-over match.

A capacity crowd saw Ian Botham on-drive the winning pair of runs with three balls to spare. The final over of the touring team's innings, bowled by Bob Willis, had produced four wickets and four runs. West Indies won the Prudential Trophy by superior scoring rate in the two matches.

WEST INDIES		Runs	Balls	4/6
C.G.Greenidge	c Lever b Marks	39	85	5/1
D.L.Haynes	c Willis b Marks	50	86	3/2
S.F.A.F.Bacchus	run out	40	53	5
* I.V.A.Richards	c Lever b Botham	26	33	–
A.I.Kallicharran	c Willis b Old	11	24	1
C.L.King	run out	33	27	1/2
A.M.E.Roberts	not out	25	20	–/2
J.Garner	run out	0	–	–
M.D.Marshall	b Willis	0	1	–
M.A.Holding	b Willis	0	2	–
† D.A.Murray				
Extras	(lb 9, nb 2)	11		
Total	(55 overs; 9 wickets)	**235**		

ENGLAND		Runs	Balls	4/6
P.Willey	c and b Holding	56	93	5
G.Boycott	run out	70	115	4
C.J.Tavaré	c Murray b Holding	5	14	–
G.A.Gooch	c Bacchus b Marshall	12	14	2
D.I.Gower	c Bacchus b Roberts	12	17	2
* I.T.Botham	not out	42	49	3/1
V.J.Marks	b Holding	9	20	–
† D.L.Bairstow	run out	2	7	–
J.K.Lever	not out	0	–	–
C.M.Old				
R.G.D.Willis				
Extras	(lb 22, w 4, nb 2)	28		
Total	(54.3 overs; 7 wickets)	**236**		

ENGLAND	O	M	R	W
Willis	10	1	25	2
Lever	7	1	23	0
Botham	11	2	71	1
Old	11	1	43	1
Marks	11	1	44	2
Willey	5	0	18	0

WEST INDIES	O	M	R	W
Roberts	11	3	42	1
Holding	11	0	28	3
Garner	10.3	0	41	0
Marshall	11	1	45	1
Richards	5	0	28	0
Greenidge	6	0	24	0

FALL OF WICKETS
1-86, 2-113, 3-147, 4-169, 5-186, 6-231, 7-233, 8-233, 9-235

FALL OF WICKETS
1-135, 2-143, 3-156, 4-160, 5-176, 6-212, 7-231

Umpires: D.J.Constant (15) and D.G.L.Evans (3).

ENGLAND v AUSTRALIA 1980

At Kennington Oval, London on 20 August 1980.　　Result: **ENGLAND** won by 23 runs.　　Toss: Australia.
Award: M.Hendrick.　　LOI debuts: England – C.W.J.Athey, A.R.Butcher.　　55-over match.

Mike Hendrick claimed his only five-wicket analysis at international level, his best return from 30 Test matches being 4 for 28.

ENGLAND		Runs	Balls	4/6		AUSTRALIA		Runs	Balls	4/6
G.A.Gooch	b Border	54	83	6		B.M.Laird	lbw b Gooch	15	33	–
G.Boycott	c Hughes b Lillee	99	159	10		G.M.Wood	c Athey b Jackman	4	10	–
A.R.Butcher	lbw b Dymock	14	26	1		* G.S.Chappell	c Bairstow b Hendrick	36	63	2
C.W.J.Athey	c Chappell b Lillee	32	40	2		A.R.Border	b Hendrick	13	31	1
M.W.Gatting	not out	17	18	1		K.J.Hughes	not out	73	102	2
* I.T.Botham	c Yallop b Lillee	4	2	1		G.N.Yallop	b Hendrick	0	9	–
P.Willey	c Yallop b Lillee	2	3	–		† R.W.Marsh	c Bairstow b Hendrick	41	48	3
† D.L.Bairstow	not out	9	5	1		D.K.Lillee	c Willey b Hendrick	0	1	–
R.D.Jackman						J.R.Thomson	run out	15	20	–
C.M.Old						G.Dymock	not out	14	16	1
M.Hendrick						L.S.Pascoe				
Extras	(b 2, lb 8, w 3, nb 4)	17				Extras	(b 3, lb 10, w 1)	14		
Total	(55 overs; 6 wickets)	248				Total	(55 overs; 8 wickets)	225		

AUSTRALIA	O	M	R	W		ENGLAND	O	M	R	W
Lillee	11	1	35	4		Old	9	0	43	0
Thomson	11	3	25	0		Jackman	11	0	46	1
Dymock	9	0	50	1		Botham	9	1	28	0
Pascoe	11	1	50	0		Gooch	7	0	29	1
Border	11	2	61	1		Hendrick	11	3	31	5
Chappell	2	0	10	0		Willey	8	0	34	0

FALL OF WICKETS
1-108, 2-140, 3-212, 4-221, 5-225, 6-232

FALL OF WICKETS
1-11, 2-36, 3-68, 4-71, 5-75, 6-161, 7-161, 8-192

Umpires: W.E.Alley (8) and D.G.L.Evans (4).

ENGLAND v AUSTRALIA 1980

At Edgbaston, Birmingham on 22 August 1980.　　Result: **ENGLAND** won by 47 runs.　　Toss: Australia.
Award: G.A.Gooch　　LOI debuts: England – R.O.Butcher; Australia – J.Dyson.　　55-over match.

The first of Graham Gooch's eight hundreds in these matches was completed off 107 balls. Roland Butcher's 35-ball fifty was the fastest and England's total the highest in Prudential Trophy games.

ENGLAND		Runs	Balls	4/6		AUSTRALIA		Runs	Balls	4/6
G.A.Gooch	b Thomson	108	113	11		B.M.Laird	c Emburey b Hendrick	36	71	2
G.Boycott	c Marsh b Border	78	98	11		J.Dyson	b Hendrick	24	55	1
C.W.J.Athey	b Pascoe	51	67	3/1		K.J.Hughes	c and b Gooch	98	84	10
R.O.Butcher	c Dyson b Pascoe	52	38	5		A.R.Border	run out	26	24	1
M.W.Gatting	run out	2	5	–		G.N.Yallop	not out	52	66	3
* I.T.Botham	b Pascoe	2	2	–		D.K.Lillee	b Hendrick	21	25	1
† D.L.Bairstow	b Lillee	6	7	–		R.J.Bright	not out	5	5	–
R.D.Jackman	c Marsh b Pascoe	6	4	1		* G.S.Chappell				
J.E.Emburey	not out	1	1	–		† R.W.Marsh				
C.M.Old	not out	2	1	–		J.R.Thomson				
M.Hendrick						L.S.Pascoe				
Extras	(b 4, lb 3, w 1, nb 4)	12				Extras	(b 1, lb 9, w 1)	11		
Total	(55 overs; 8 wickets)	320				Total	(55 overs; 5 wickets)	273		

AUSTRALIA	O	M	R	W		ENGLAND	O	M	R	W
Thomson	11	1	69	1		Old	11	2	44	0
Lillee	11	0	43	1		Jackman	11	1	45	0
Pascoe	11	0	69	4		Botham	11	1	41	0
Bright	8	0	48	0		Hendrick	10	0	54	3
Chappell	11	0	65	0		Emburey	8	0	51	0
Border	3	0	14	1		Gooch	3	0	16	1
						Boycott	1	0	11	0

FALL OF WICKETS
1-154, 2-215, 3-292, 4-298, 5-302, 6-311, 7-313, 8-318

FALL OF WICKETS
1-53, 2-80, 3-119, 4-222, 5-229

Umpires: H.D.Bird (16) and D.O.Oslear (1).

PAKISTAN v WEST INDIES 1980-81

At National Stadium, Karachi on 21 November 1980.   Result: **WEST INDIES** won by 4 wickets.   Toss: West Indies.
Award: I.V.A.Richards   LOI debuts: Pakistan – Mansoor Akhtar, Mohammad Nazir, Taslim Arif; West Indies –
M.R.Pydanna.

A series of three 40-over matches began with a low-scoring game on an unreliable pitch. Michael Holding seriously
injured his shoulder taking a brilliant return catch. Gordon Greenidge, dropping down the order because of back
problems, slipped a disc as he cover-drove the winning three runs off Imran Khan's final ball.

PAKISTAN		Runs	Balls	4/6
† Taslim Arif	c Marshall b Croft	4		
Sadiq Mohammed	c Holding b Richards	40		
Mansoor Akhtar	b Garner	24		
* Javed Miandad	c Pydanna b Croft	8		
Wasim Raja	c Holding b Richards	2		
Majid Khan	c Lloyd b Kallicharran	16		
Mudassar Nazar	c and b Holding	4		
Imran Khan	c Bacchus b Kallicharran	2		
Sarfraz Nawaz	run out	8		
Iqbal Qasim	not out	6		
Mohammad Nazir	not out	2		
Extras	(b 1, lb 5, w 4, nb 1)	11		
Total	(40 overs; 9 wickets)	**127**		

WEST INDIES		Runs	Balls	4/6
D.L.Haynes	b Qasim	4		
S.F.A.F.Bacchus	hit wicket b Mudassar	36		
I.V.A.Richards	st Taslim b Majid	36		
* C.H.Lloyd	c Sadiq b Mudassar	9		
A.I.Kallicharran	lbw b Imran	14		
C.G.Greenidge	not out	21		
M.D.Marshall	run out	0		
J.Garner	not out	0		
† M.R.Pydanna				
M.A.Holding				
C.E.H.Croft				
Extras	(b 2, lb 4, w 1, nb 1)	8		
Total	(40 overs; 6 wickets)	**128**		

WEST INDIES	O	M	R	W
Holding	5.3	3	5	1
Croft	7	1	17	2
Marshall	8	0	34	0
Garner	8	0	26	1
Richards	8	0	24	2
Kallicharran	3.3	0	10	2

PAKISTAN	O	M	R	W
Imran Khan	7	3	14	1
Sarfraz Nawaz	6	0	25	0
Iqbal Qasim	8	2	21	0
Mohammad Nazir	8	1	25	0
Mudassar Nazar	4	0	13	2
Majid Khan	7	1	22	1

FALL OF WICKETS
1-5, 2-59, 3-74, 4-81, 5-83, 6-97, 7-102, 8-114, 9-119

FALL OF WICKETS
1-18, 2-69, 3-85, 4-93, 5-124, 6-124

Umpires: Javed Akhtar (4) and Khalid Aziz (3).

PAKISTAN v WEST INDIES 1980-81

At Jinnah Park, Sialkot on 5 December 1980.   Result: **WEST INDIES** won by 7 wickets.   Toss: West Indies.
Award: I.V.A.Richards.   LOI debuts: Pakistan – Ashraf Ali.

As 30,000 tickets had been sold for 12,000 seats, the crowd's behaviour rather upstaged the cricket.

PAKISTAN		Runs	Balls	4/6
Mudassar Nazar	c Marshall b Croft	3		
Sadiq Mohammed	c Lloyd b Garner	13		
Zaheer Abbas	not out	95		12
* Javed Miandad	st Pydanna b Richards	16		
Majid Khan	c Clarke b Richards	34		1/3
Wasim Raja	not out	22		
Imran Khan				
† Ashraf Ali				
Sarfraz Nawaz				
Iqbal Qasim				
Sikander Bakht				
Extras	(lb 12, w 3, nb 2)	17		
Total	(40 overs; 4 wickets)	**200**		

WEST INDIES		Runs	Balls	4/6
D.L.Haynes	c Qasim b Imran	16		
S.F.A.F.Bacchus	lbw b Sarfraz	79		9
I.V.A.Richards	lbw b Sikander	83		8/2
† M.R.Pydanna	not out	2		
* C.H.Lloyd	not out	1		
A.I.Kallicharran				
H.A.Gomes				
S.T.Clarke				
M.D.Marshall				
J.Garner				
C.E.H.Croft				
Extras	(b 20)	20		
Total	(35.3 overs; 3 wickets)	**201**		

WEST INDIES	O	M	R	W
Clarke	8	1	28	0
Croft	8	2	28	1
Garner	8	2	36	1
Marshall	8	1	38	0
Richards	8	0	53	2

PAKISTAN	O	M	R	W
Imran Khan	8	1	30	1
Sarfraz Nawaz	7.3	0	29	1
Sikander Bakht	4	0	22	1
Iqbal Qasim	8	0	37	0
Majid Khan	2	0	20	0
Wasim Raja	4	0	27	0
Mudassar Nazar	2	0	16	0

FALL OF WICKETS
1-5, 2-35, 3-80, 4-138

FALL OF WICKETS
1-22, 2-198, 3-198

Umpires: Amanullah Khan (1) and Shakoor Rana (4).

PAKISTAN v WEST INDIES 1980-81

At Gaddafi Stadium, Lahore on 19 December 1980.   Result: **WEST INDIES** won by 7 runs.   Toss: Pakistan.
Award: S.T.Clarke.   LOI debuts: Pakistan – Ijaz Faqih, Rashid Khan, Salim Pervez, Tahir Naqqash.

West Indies gained their sixth win against Pakistan in as many of these internationals. Three different wicket-keepers represented Pakistan in the series.

WEST INDIES		Runs	Balls	4/6
A.I.Kallicharran	lbw b Wasim Raja	50		
D.L.Haynes	b Rashid	2		
I.V.A.Richards	c Taslim b Rashid	0		
* C.H.Lloyd	c Wasim Bari b Wasim Raja	13		
H.A.Gomes	c and b Majid	32		
D.R.Parry	run out	32		
S.T.Clarke	b Majid	20		–/3
M.D.Marshall	run out	12		
J.Garner	not out	3		
† D.A.Murray				
C.E.H.Croft				
Extras	(lb 3, w 3)	6		
Total	(40 overs; 8 wickets)	**170**		

PAKISTAN		Runs	Balls	4/6
Salim Pervez	c Murray b Garner	18		
Taslim Arif	run out	24		
Zaheer Abbas	b Clarke	42		
* Javed Miandad	b Clarke	23		
Wasim Raja	not out	22		
Majid Khan	run out	16		
Ijaz Faqih	run out	0		
Rashid Khan	not out	4		
† Wasim Bari				
Tahir Naqqash				
Sikander Bakht				
Extras	(b 1, lb 8, nb 5)	14		
Total	(40 overs; 6 wickets)	**163**		

PAKISTAN	O	M	R	W
Sikander Bakht	1	0	3	0
Rashid Khan	8	2	31	2
Tahir Naqqash	8	1	37	0
Ijaz Faqih	8	1	30	0
Wasim Raja	8	0	28	2
Majid Khan	7	0	35	2

WEST INDIES	O	M	R	W
Clarke	8	0	25	2
Croft	7	0	28	0
Garner	8	2	18	1
Marshall	6	0	27	0
Parry	8	1	33	0
Richards	3	0	18	0

FALL OF WICKETS
1-10, 2-10, 3-36, 4-92, 5-110, 6-134, 7-164, 8-170

FALL OF WICKETS
1-44, 2-63, 3-116, 4-123, 5-155, 6-157

Umpires: Khizer Hayat (2) and Mahboob Shah (3).

AUSTRALIA v NEW ZEALAND 1980-81

At Adelaide Oval on 23 November 1980.   Result: **NEW ZEALAND** won by 3 wickets.   Toss: New Zealand.
Award: E.J.Chatfield.   LOI Debuts: Australia – T.M.Chappell, S.F.Graf, G.F.Lawson; New Zealand – M.C.Snedden.

This second World Series triangular tournament of 50-over games was extended to 15 qualifying matches with a best-of-five set of finals. Substitute John Bracewell became the first non-wicket-keeper to hold four catches in a limited-overs international.

AUSTRALIA		Runs	Balls	4/6
J.Dyson	c sub (J.G.Bracewell) b Chatfield	69	120	4
G.M.Wood	c sub (J.G.Bracewell) b Chatfield	19	41	1
* G.S.Chappell	c Lees b Chatfield	25	34	2
K.J.Hughes	c Wright b McEwan	20	28	1/1
A.R.Border	c Lees b Chatfield	5	8	–
† R.W.Marsh	c sub (J.G.Bracewell) b Cairns	44	30	3/3
S.F.Graf	c sub (J.G.Bracewell) b Chatfield	0	3	–
T.M.Chappell	c Hadlee b Cairns	12	17	1
D.K.Lillee	c Wright b Cairns	3	8	–
G.F.Lawson	not out	4	12	–
L.S.Pascoe				
Extras	(lb 1, nb 15)	16		
Total	(50 overs; 9 wickets)	**217**		

NEW ZEALAND		Runs	Balls	4/6
J.G.Wright	c Dyson b G.S.Chappell	60	128	4
B.A.Edgar	c T.M.Chappell b Graf	25	57	2
P.E.McEwan	run out	3	5	–
* G.P.Howarth	run out	37	41	4
R.J.Hadlee	lbw b Lillee	39	29	5
J.M.Parker	c and b Lillee	16	25	1
J.V.Coney	not out	10	11	1
† W.K.Lees	c Lawson b Lillee	2	7	–
B.L.Cairns	not out	4	1	1
E.J.Chatfield				
M.C.Snedden				
Extras	(lb 15, nb 8)	23		
Total	(49.1 overs; 7 wickets)	**219**		

NEW ZEALAND	O	M	R	W
Hadlee	10	1	25	0
Snedden	10	1	34	0
Coney	4	0	14	0
Cairns	10	0	58	3
Chatfield	10	1	34	5
McEwan	6	0	36	1

AUSTRALIA	O	M	R	W
Lillee	10	2	40	3
Pascoe	10	3	30	0
Lawson	9.1	1	42	0
T.M.Chappell	5	0	21	0
Graf	10	1	40	1
G.S.Chappell	5	0	23	1

FALL OF WICKETS
1-37, 2-92, 3-142, 4-147, 5-150, 6-150, 7-167, 8-171, 9-217

FALL OF WICKETS
1-61, 2-67, 3-140, 4-151, 5-198, 6-203, 7-211

Umpires: A.R.Crafter (4) and P.M.Cronin (3).

AUSTRALIA v NEW ZEALAND 1980-81

At Sydney Cricket Ground on 25 November 1980.   Result: **AUSTRALIA** won by 94 runs.   Toss: Australia.
Award: G.S.Chappell.   LOI debuts: New Zealand – I.D.S.Smith.

Greg Chappell's score was the Australian record in limited-overs internationals until 1990-91 (*LOI No. 650*).

AUSTRALIA		Runs	Balls	4/6
J.Dyson	b Hadlee	79	126	8
K.J.Hughes	c Smith b McEwan	19	26	1
* G.S.Chappell	not out	138	109	10/1
A.R.Border	c Snedden b Chatfield	9	12	–
K.D.Walters	not out	26	26	1
T.M.Chappell				
† R.W.Marsh				
D.K.Lillee				
S.F.Graf				
G.F.Lawson				
L.S.Pascoe				
Extras	(b 6, lb 12)	18		
Total	(50 overs; 3 wickets)	**289**		

NEW ZEALAND		Runs	Balls	4/6
J.M.Parker	c Dyson b Pascoe	6	15	–
B.A.Edgar	lbw b G.S.Chappell	34	52	4
P.E.McEwan	c G.S.Chappell b Lawson	23	24	2
* G.P.Howarth	c Marsh b Pascoe	46	76	1
M.G.Burgess	b Lillee	29	35	2
R.J.Hadlee	c Dyson b Graf	10	10	–/1
B.L.Cairns	c Border b Pascoe	16	15	–
I.D.S.Smith	c Marsh b Graf	1	2	–
† W.K.Lees	c Dyson b Pascoe	8	13	1
M.C.Snedden	b Pascoe	3	8	–
E.J.Chatfield	not out	4	10	–
Extras	(lb 11, w 1, nb 3)	15		
Total	(42.5 overs)	**195**		

NEW ZEALAND	O	M	R	W
Hadlee	10	1	66	1
Snedden	10	1	58	0
Cairns	10	0	41	0
Chatfield	10	1	55	1
McEwan	10	0	51	1

AUSTRALIA	O	M	R	W
Lillee	7	0	26	1
Pascoe	7.5	1	30	5
Lawson	10	0	43	1
G.S.Chappell	10	1	41	1
Graf	8	0	40	2

FALL OF WICKETS
1-29, 2-180, 3-207

FALL OF WICKETS
1-14, 2-63, 3-73, 4-138, 5-155, 6-173, 7-176, 8-181, 9-190, 10-195

Umpires: R.C.Bailhache (6) and M.W.Johnson (2).

AUSTRALIA v INDIA 1980-81

At Melbourne Cricket Ground on 6 December 1980.   Result: **INDIA** won by 66 runs.   Toss: Australia.
Award: S.M.Patil.   LOI debuts: India – K.Azad, R.M.H.Binny, D.R.Doshi, S.M.Patil, T.E.Srinivasan.

Match reduced to 49 overs by slow over rate. Australia were unable to combat the accuracy of India's attack on a slow
pitch of uneven bounce. Sandeep Patil's rapid 64 proved to be the decisive innings.

INDIA		Runs	Balls	4/6
* S.M.Gavaskar	c Lawson b Lillee	4	11	–
T.E.Srinivasan	c G.S.Chappell b Lillee	6	12	–
D.B.Vengsarkar	b G.S.Chappell	22	72	–
G.R.Viswanath	b T.M.Chappell	22	44	1
K.Azad	c Lawson b Pascoe	4	22	–
S.M.Patil	b G.S.Chappell	64	70	4
Kapil Dev	b Lawson	6	16	–
† S.M.H.Kirmani	not out	48	52	4
R.M.H.Binny	run out	0	1	–
K.D.Ghavri	run out	0	–	–
D.R.Doshi				
Extras	(b 11, lb 15, nb 6)	32		
Total	(49 overs; 9 wickets)	**208**		

AUSTRALIA		Runs	Balls	4/6
J.Dyson	run out	23	66	–
K.J.Hughes	b Patil	35	53	4
* G.S.Chappell	c Gavaskar b Doshi	11	19	1
A.R.Border	c Azad b Doshi	6	19	–
K.D.Walters	st Kirmani b Doshi	27	31	1
T.M.Chappell	run out	14	41	–
† R.W.Marsh	b Ghavri	7	7	–
S.F.Graf	b Binny	5	11	1
D.K.Lillee	run out	5	3	–
G.F.Lawson	c Doshi b Binny	0	1	–
L.S.Pascoe	not out	0	3	–
Extras	(lb 2, nb 7)	9		
Total	(42.1 overs)	**142**		

AUSTRALIA	O	M	R	W
Lillee	7	1	22	2
Pascoe	10	0	32	1
Graf	10	0	30	0
Lawson	9	0	46	1
T.M.Chappell	5	0	14	1
G.S.Chappell	8	1	32	2

INDIA	O	M	R	W
Ghavri	9.1	1	32	1
Binny	6	0	23	2
Kapil Dev	7	2	15	0
Doshi	10	1	32	3
Patil	10	1	31	1

FALL OF WICKETS
1-12, 2-22, 3-58, 4-66, 5-73, 6-111, 7-203, 8-208, 9-208

FALL OF WICKETS
1-60, 2-62, 3-73, 4-80, 5-118, 6-129, 7-137, 8-139, 9-139, 10-142

Umpires: M.G.O'Connell (3) and R.V.Whitehead (3).

AUSTRALIA v NEW ZEALAND 1980-81

At Melbourne Cricket Ground on 7 December 1980.　Result: **AUSTRALIA** won by 4 wickets.　Toss: New Zealand.
Award: A.R.Border.　LOI debuts: None.

Mark Burgess regained the New Zealand captaincy temporarily after Geoff Howarth had damaged his hand in a match against Southern New South Wales two days earlier.

NEW ZEALAND		Runs	Balls	4/6
J.G.Wright	b Pascoe	57	119	3
B.A.Edgar	run out	33	67	2
J.V.Coney	run out	9	26	–
P.E.McEwan	b Lillee	17	31	–
R.J.Hadlee	c T.M.Chappell b Pascoe	1	8	–
* M.G.Burgess	c Border b Pascoe	14	14	2
J.M.Parker	lbw b G.S.Chappell	3	7	–
† W.K.Lees	c G.S.Chappell b Lillee	0	3	–
G.B.Troup	not out	7	16	–
S.L.Boock	lbw b Lillee	2	3	–
E.J.Chatfield	lbw b Pascoe	0	6	–
Extras	(b 2, lb 10, w 1)	13		
Total	(49.5 overs)	**156**		

AUSTRALIA		Runs	Balls	4/6
J.Dyson	lbw b Hadlee	3	17	–
A.R.Border	c Edgar b Chatfield	55	111	3
* G.S.Chappell	st Lees b Boock	48	70	3
K.J.Hughes	run out	19	35	1
K.D.Walters	lbw b Boock	7	11	1
T.M.Chappell	b Hadlee	6	13	–
G.M.Wood	not out	1	14	–
† R.W.Marsh	not out	10	13	1
D.K.Lillee				
S.F.Graf				
L.S.Pascoe				
Extras	(b 2, lb 8)	10		
Total	(47.2 overs; 6 wickets)	**159**		

AUSTRALIA	O	M	R	W
Lillee	10	3	19	3
Pascoe	9.5	3	37	4
Graf	4	0	15	0
G.S.Chappell	10	1	23	1
T.M.Chappell	10	2	27	0
Walters	6	0	22	0

NEW ZEALAND	O	M	R	W
Troup	9	3	15	0
Hadlee	10	0	34	2
Chatfield	9.2	1	34	1
McEwan	5	0	18	0
Boock	10	1	30	2
Coney	4	0	18	0

FALL OF WICKETS
1-74, 2-95, 3-112, 4-116, 5-138, 6-141, 7-142, 8-147, 9-153, 10-156

FALL OF WICKETS
1-15, 2-107, 3-116, 4-124, 5-143, 6-145

Umpires: R.C.Bailhache (7) and R.A.French (3).

NEW ZEALAND v INDIA 1980-81

At WACA Ground, Perth on 9 December 1980.　Result: **INDIA** won by 5 runs.　Toss: India.
Award: R.J.Hadlee.　LOI debuts: None.

Richard Hadlee dismissed Sunil Gavaskar with the opening ball of Perth's first international. Although New Zealand's last-wicket pair contributed 21 runs to a low-scoring game, an exceptional catch at mid-wicket off the penultimate ball found them six runs short of their target.

INDIA		Runs	Balls	4/6
* S.M.Gavaskar	c Lees b Hadlee	0	1	–
R.M.H.Binny	c Parker b Chatfield	14		
D.B.Vengsarkar	c Coney b Troup	12		
G.R.Viswanath	c Coney b Hadlee	10		
Yashpal Sharma	b Cairns	23		1
S.M.Patil	c Parker b Hadlee	39		3
Kapil Dev	c Lees b Hadlee	0		–
† S.M.H.Kirmani	c Parker b Cairns	1		–
K.Azad	c and b Chatfield	29		3
K.D.Ghavri	b Hadlee	14		
D.R.Doshi	not out	2		–
Extras	(b 9, lb 6, w 2, nb 1)	18		
Total	(47.4 overs)	**162**		

NEW ZEALAND		Runs	Balls	4/6
J.G.Wright	c Vengsarkar b Kapil Dev	4		
B.A.Edgar	b Binny	16		
P.E.McEwan	c Yashpal b Doshi	41		2
J.M.Parker	c Kapil Dev b Binny	1		–
J.V.Coney	c Kirmani b Patil	5		
* M.G.Burgess	c sub (N.S.Yadav) b Doshi	10		
R.J.Hadlee	c Kirmani b Binny	20		
B.L.Cairns	c Vengsarkar b Ghavri	26		1
† W.K.Lees	c Vengsarkar b Binny	16		1
G.B.Troup	run out	5		
E.J.Chatfield	not out	6		
Extras	(lb 4, w 1, nb 2)	7		
Total	(49.5 overs)	**157**		

NEW ZEALAND	O	M	R	W
Hadlee	9	1	32	5
Chatfield	8.4	0	33	2
Troup	10	2	36	1
Coney	10	1	25	0
Cairns	10	2	18	2

INDIA	O	M	R	W
Kapil Dev	10	2	33	1
Ghavri	10	0	30	1
Binny	9.5	1	41	4
Patil	10	3	24	1
Doshi	10	4	22	2

FALL OF WICKETS
1-0, 2-27, 3-35, 4-46, 5-116, 6-116, 7-116, 8-119, 9-157, 10-162

FALL OF WICKETS
1-13, 2-22, 3-28, 4-50, 5-80, 6-80, 7-130, 8-130, 9-136, 10-157

Umpires: A.R.Crafter (5) and D.G.Weser (3).

AUSTRALIA v INDIA 1980-81

At Sydney Cricket Ground on 18 December 1980.   Result: **AUSTRALIA** won by 9 wickets.   Toss: Australia.
Award: A.R.Border.   LOI debuts: None.

Match reduced to 49 overs by slow over rate. In a faultless display, Allan Border scored the first of only three hundreds in 252 LOI innings.

INDIA		Runs	Balls	4/6
* S.M.Gavaskar	b Pascoe	22	26	2
R.M.H.Binny	c Marsh b Graf	31	53	4
D.B.Vengsarkar	c Marsh b Pascoe	4	17	–
G.R.Viswanath	b Graf	43	80	2
Yashpal Sharma	b Lillee	34	61	2
S.M.Patil	b T.M.Chappell	0	7	–
K.Azad	lbw b Lillee	1	4	–
Kapil Dev	c Dyson b Hogg	4	5	–
† S.M.H.Kirmani	run out	24	26	1
K.D.Ghavri	not out	11	19	1
D.R.Doshi				
Extras	(b 1, lb 3, nb 2)	6		
Total	(49 overs; 9 wickets)	**180**		

AUSTRALIA		Runs	Balls	4/6
J.Dyson	c Kirmani b Kapil Dev	20	37	2
A.R.Border	not out	105	122	12
* G.S.Chappell	not out	52	99	3
K.J.Hughes				
K.D.Walters				
T.M.Chappell				
† R.W.Marsh				
S.F.Graf				
D.K.Lillee				
R.M.Hogg				
L.S.Pascoe				
Extras	(lb 4, nb 2)	6		
Total	(42.2 overs; 1 wicket)	**183**		

AUSTRALIA	O	M	R	W
Lillee	10	1	29	2
Hogg	10	1	48	1
Pascoe	9	2	34	2
Graf	10	1	23	2
T.M.Chappell	10	0	40	1

INDIA	O	M	R	W
Ghavri	8	0	25	0
Binny	7	0	29	0
Kapil Dev	8	1	27	1
Patil	8	0	49	0
Doshi	10	0	40	0
Gavaskar	1.2	0	7	0

FALL OF WICKETS
1-31, 2-42, 3-64, 4-129, 5-130, 6-133, 7-139, 8-151, 9-180

FALL OF WICKETS
1-56

Umpires: R.A.French (4) and R.V.Whitehead (4).

NEW ZEALAND v INDIA 1980-81

At Woolloongabba, Brisbane on 21 December 1980.   Result: **NEW ZEALAND** won by 3 wickets.   Toss: India.
Award: Kapil Dev.   LOI debuts: India – Yograj Singh.

Match reduced to 49 overs by slow over rate. An unbroken eighth-wicket stand of 39 from 31 balls between Jeremy Coney and Lance Cairns took New Zealand to victory with two balls to spare. Earlier, Coney's last three overs had conceded 43 runs during Kapil Dev's onslaught.

INDIA		Runs	Balls	4/6
* S.M.Gavaskar	c Coney b Troup	1	14	–
C.P.S.Chauhan	c Hadlee b Snedden	46	69	4
D.B.Vengsarkar	c Lees b Cairns	13	51	2
G.R.Viswanath	b Snedden	2	12	–
Yashpal Sharma	c Wright b Snedden	16	29	2
S.M.Patil	c Wright b Cairns	16	31	1
Kapil Dev	c Cairns b Troup	75	51	9/3
† S.M.H.Kirmani	c Edgar b Troup	18	20	2
K.D.Ghavri	not out	9	10	1
Yograj Singh	c Burgess b Troup	0	1	–
D.R.Doshi	run out	0	5	–
Extras	(b 2, lb 6)	8		
Total	(48.5 overs)	**204**		

NEW ZEALAND		Runs	Balls	4/6
J.G.Wright	c sub (K.Azad) b Kapil Dev	42	70	3
B.A.Edgar	b Doshi	28	75	1
† W.K.Lees	c Yograj Singh b Doshi	20	29	1
* G.P.Howarth	c Kapil Dev b Doshi	0	5	–
J.M.Parker	c Kirmani b Doshi	11	24	–
J.V.Coney	not out	47	52	4
M.G.Burgess	b Yograj Singh	13	14	1
R.J.Hadlee	c Vengsarkar b Yograj Singh	0	5	–
B.L.Cairns	not out	27	19	3
M.C.Snedden				
G.B.Troup				
Extras	(b 6, lb 9, w 1, nb 1)	17		
Total	(48.4 overs; 7 wickets)	**205**		

NEW ZEALAND	O	M	R	W
Hadlee	9.5	1	21	0
Troup	9	2	19	4
Snedden	10	0	33	3
Cairns	10	1	53	2
Coney	10	0	70	0

INDIA	O	M	R	W
Yograj Singh	8.4	0	44	2
Ghavri	10	1	38	0
Kapil Dev	10	0	37	1
Patil	10	1	39	0
Doshi	10	0	30	4

FALL OF WICKETS
1-3, 2-45, 3-52, 4-79, 5-84, 6-136, 7-190, 8-203, 9-204, 10-204

FALL OF WICKETS
1-67, 2-93, 3-97, 4-103, 5-130, 6-158, 7-166

Umpires: R.A.French (5) and M.W.Johnson (3).

NEW ZEALAND v INDIA 1980-81

At Adelaide Oval on 23 December 1980.   Result: **INDIA** won by 6 runs.   Toss: India.
Award: Yashpal Sharma.   LOI debuts: None.

India just managed to defend their highest total of this series when Kapil Dev claimed New Zealand's last two wickets with the first and third balls of the final over.

INDIA		Runs	Balls	4/6
* S.M.Gavaskar	c Lees b Troup	17		
C.P.S.Chauhan	c Coney b Snedden	43		1
D.B.Vengsarkar	b Snedden	3		
Yashpal Sharma	c Cairns b Troup	72		3/4
S.M.Patil	c Coney b Chatfield	6		
Kapil Dev	c Lees b Snedden	27		5
† S.M.H.Kirmani	not out	39		4
R.M.H.Binny	c Wright b Troup	4		
K.D.Ghavri	not out	10		
Yograj Singh				
D.R.Doshi				
Extras	(lb 8, nb 1)	9		
Total	(50 overs; 7 wickets)	**230**		

NEW ZEALAND		Runs	Balls	4/6
J.G.Wright	b Patil	18		1/1
J.M.Parker	c Chauhan b Yograj Singh	13		
* G.P.Howarth	st Kirmani b Doshi	26		1
J.V.Coney	run out	49		3
† W.K.Lees	lbw b Ghavri	6		
M.G.Burgess	run out	42		2
R.J.Hadlee	c Gavaskar b Doshi	4		
B.L.Cairns	b Ghavri	39	38	3/2
M.C.Snedden	c Ghavri b Kapil Dev	4		
G.B.Troup	b Kapil Dev	5		
E.J.Chatfield	not out	0		
Extras	(b 2, lb 12, nb 4)	18		
Total	(49.3 overs)	**224**		

NEW ZEALAND	O	M	R	W
Hadlee	10	2	42	0
Troup	10	0	65	3
Snedden	10	2	30	3
Cairns	10	3	30	0
Chatfield	10	0	54	1

INDIA	O	M	R	W
Yograj Singh	9	1	39	1
Binny	10	0	47	0
Ghavri	10	1	49	2
Kapil Dev	9.3	1	34	2
Patil	1	0	3	1
Doshi	10	1	34	2

FALL OF WICKETS
1-23, 2-30, 3-95, 4-102, 5-153, 6-192, 7-209

FALL OF WICKETS
1-36, 2-36, 3-105, 4-123, 5-125, 6-134, 7-213, 8-213, 9-224, 10-224

Umpires: A.R.Crafter (6) and M.G.O'Connell (4).

AUSTRALIA v INDIA 1980-81

At Sydney Cricket Ground on 8 January 1981.   Result: **AUSTRALIA** won by 9 wickets   Toss: Australia.
Award: G.S.Chappell   LOI debuts: None.

Put in on a pitch affected by the previous day's torrential rain, India were dismissed in 113 minutes for their lowest total in these matches. This remains the shortest completed LOI, the actual playing time totalling 3 hours 26 minutes. This match was switched from Perth because of an industrial dispute at airports.

INDIA		Runs	Balls	4/6
C.P.S.Chauhan	b Lillee	2	16	–
R.M.H.Binny	c Marsh b G.S.Chappell	16	44	2
D.B.Vengsarkar	c Marsh b Pascoe	3	20	–
G.R.Viswanath	c Marsh b Hogg	23	22	3
* S.M.Gavaskar	b G.S.Chappell	1	6	–
Yashpal Sharma	lbw b G.S.Chappell	6	16	1
Kapil Dev	lbw b Hogg	0	1	–
† S.M.H.Kirmani	run out	4	13	–
K.D.Ghavri	c Marsh b G.S.Chappell	1	8	–
Yograj Singh	not out	0	7	–
D.R.Doshi	b G.S.Chappell	2	4	–
Extras	(lb 3, w 1, nb 1)	5		
Total	(25.5 overs)	**63**		

AUSTRALIA		Runs	Balls	4/6
J.Dyson	not out	13	59	–
G.M.Wood	c Binny b Kapil Dev	11	24	1
* G.S.Chappell	not out	33	48	3
K.J.Hughes				
A.R.Border				
K.D.Walters				
T.M.Chappell				
† R.W.Marsh				
D.K.Lillee				
R.M.Hogg				
L.S.Pascoe				
Extras	(lb 3, w 1, nb 3)	7		
Total	(21 overs; 1 wicket)	**64**		

AUSTRALIA	O	M	R	W
Lillee	5	2	3	1
Hogg	7	2	14	2
G.S.Chappell	9.5	5	15	5
Pascoe	4	0	26	1

INDIA	O	M	R	W
Kapil Dev	9	5	15	1
Ghavri	4	0	14	0
Yograj Singh	4	1	9	0
Doshi	1	0	6	0
Binny	3	1	13	0

FALL OF WICKETS
1-2, 2-24, 3-26, 4-32, 5-50, 6-54, 7-55, 8-60, 9-61, 10-63

FALL OF WICKETS
1-18

Umpires: M.G.O'Connell (5) and D.G.Weser (4).

NEW ZEALAND v INDIA 1980-81

At Melbourne Cricket Ground on 10 January 1981.   Result: **NEW ZEALAND** won by 10 wickets.   Toss: New Zealand.
Award: B.A.Edgar   LOI debuts: None.

Rain delayed the start by 50 minutes. A subsequent 80-minute break when India were 34 for 3 in the 18th over further reduced the contest to 34 overs.

INDIA		Runs	Balls	4/6
* S.M.Gavaskar	lbw b Chatfield	8	31	–
T.E.Srinivasan	b Coney	4	23	–
D.B.Vengsarkar	c Parker b Coney	0	2	–
G.R.Viswanath	run out	33	52	3
S.M.Patil	c Coney b Snedden	8	22	1
Yashpal Sharma	b Cairns	5	17	–
Kapil Dev	run out	21	19	–
† S.M.H.Kirmani	run out	7	8	–
K.D.Ghavri	c Howarth b Snedden	6	11	–
R.M.H.Binny	not out	5	14	–
D.R.Doshi	not out	5	5	–
Extras	(lb 10)	10		
Total	(34 overs; 9 wickets)	**112**		

NEW ZEALAND		Runs	Balls	4/6
J.G.Wright	not out	39	87	1
B.A.Edgar	not out	65	89	4
J.M.Parker				
* G.P.Howarth				
J.V.Coney				
† W.K.Lees				
M.G.Burgess				
R.J.Hadlee				
B.L.Cairns				
M.C.Snedden				
E.J.Chatfield				
Extras	(lb 8, nb 1)	9		
Total	(29 overs; 0 wickets)	**113**		

NEW ZEALAND	O	M	R	W
Hadlee	8	3	15	0
Chatfield	8	2	14	1
Coney	6	3	18	2
Cairns	7	0	39	1
Snedden	5	0	16	2

INDIA	O	M	R	W
Kapil Dev	8	0	29	0
Ghavri	7	2	15	0
Binny	4	0	23	0
Patil	2	0	10	0
Doshi	8	0	27	0

FALL OF WICKETS
1-13, 2-13, 3-13, 4-46, 5-60, 6-66, 7-82, 8-98, 9-100

Umpires: R.C.Bailhache (8) and R.V.Whitehead (5).

AUSTRALIA v INDIA 1980-81

At Melbourne Cricket Ground on 11 January 1981.   Result: **AUSTRALIA** won by 7 wickets.   Toss: Australia.
Award: G.M.Wood   LOI debuts: None.

Poor fielding resulted in India suffering their third defeat in four days.

INDIA		Runs	Balls	4/6
* S.M.Gavaskar	b T.M.Chappell	80	142	5
R.M.H.Binny	c G.S.Chappell b T.M.Chappell	21	66	3
D.B.Vengsarkar	c Hughes b Lillee	46	60	3
Kapil Dev	c T.M.Chappell b G.S.Chappell	4	4	1
S.M.Patil	b G.S.Chappell	3	3	–
Yashpal Sharma	not out	21	15	1
† S.M.H.Kirmani	not out	3	11	–
G.R.Viswanath				
K.D.Ghavri				
Yograj Singh				
D.R.Doshi				
Extras	(b 2, lb 11, nb 1)	14		
Total	(50 overs; 5 wickets)	**192**		

AUSTRALIA		Runs	Balls	4/6
A.R.Border	b Patil	39	52	4
G.M.Wood	not out	98	155	8
* G.S.Chappell	c Viswanath b Doshi	7	12	1
K.J.Hughes	run out	0	–	–
K.D.Walters	not out	43	67	3
J.Dyson				
T.M.Chappell				
† R.W.Marsh				
S.F.Graf				
D.K.Lillee				
L.S.Pascoe				
Extras	(b 1, lb 5)	6		
Total	(47.2 overs; 3 wickets)	**193**		

AUSTRALIA	O	M	R	W
Lillee	10	1	29	1
Pascoe	9	1	33	0
Graf	6	0	31	0
G.S.Chappell	10	4	23	2
T.M.Chappell	9	0	41	2
Border	6	0	21	0

INDIA	O	M	R	W
Binny	9.2	1	42	0
Ghavri	9	1	37	0
Kapil Dev	9	1	27	0
Patil	10	0	43	1
Doshi	10	0	38	1

FALL OF WICKETS
1-57, 2-158, 3-165, 4-165, 5-169

FALL OF WICKETS
1-69, 2-96, 3-97

Umpires: P.M.Cronin (4) and R.A.French (6).

AUSTRALIA v NEW ZEALAND 1980-81

At Sydney Cricket Ground on 13 January 1981.   Result: **NEW ZEALAND** won by 1 run.   Toss: New Zealand.
Award: J.G.Wright.   LOI debuts: None.

With three needed from the last ball, Richard Hadlee dived to intercept a strong drive by Doug Walters and flicked the ball back to run out his partner.

NEW ZEALAND		Runs	Balls	4/6
J.G.Wright	c T.M.Chappell b G.S.Chappell	78	135	9
B.A.Edgar	b Hogg	0	4	–
* G.P.Howarth	lbw b Pascoe	20	22	2
J.M.Parker	c Pascoe b T.M.Chappell	23	45	3
M.G.Burgess	c Walters b Graf	14	18	1
J.V.Coney	c Marsh b Pascoe	18	22	2
R.J.Hadlee	c Hogg b Graf	9	19	–
B.L.Cairns	b Pascoe	7	8	–
† I.D.S.Smith	not out	23	19	1/1
M.C.Snedden	not out	8	15	–
E.J.Chatfield				
Extras	(lb 16, w 1, nb 3)	20		
Total	(50 overs; 8 wickets)	**220**		

AUSTRALIA	O	M	R	W
Lillee	10	2	27	0
Hogg	8	0	40	1
Pascoe	10	0	37	3
G.S.Chappell	9	2	35	1
Graf	10	0	40	2
T.M.Chappell	3	0	21	1

FALL OF WICKETS
1-2, 2-30, 3-75, 4-105, 5-134, 6-176, 7-181, 8-191

AUSTRALIA		Runs	Balls	4/6
A.R.Border	b Chatfield	8	21	1
G.M.Wood	c Smith b Coney	37	67	3
* G.S.Chappell	c Coney b Cairns	30	44	1
K.J.Hughes	c Smith b Snedden	21	35	–
K.D.Walters	not out	50	72	4
T.M.Chappell	run out	0	5	–
† R.W.Marsh	c Smith b Hadlee	49	48	4
S.F.Graf	run out	7	10	–
D.K.Lillee				
R.M.Hogg				
L.S.Pascoe				
Extras	(b 3, lb 12, w 1, nb 1)	17		
Total	(50 overs; 7 wickets)	**219**		

NEW ZEALAND	O	M	R	W
Hadlee	10	1	46	1
Chatfield	10	2	26	1
Coney	10	0	41	1
Cairns	10	1	48	1
Snedden	10	0	41	1

FALL OF WICKETS
1-18, 2-74, 3-90, 4-122, 5-123, 6-201, 7-219

Umpires: M.W.Johnson (4) and D.G.Weser (5).

AUSTRALIA v INDIA 1980-81

At Sydney Cricket Ground on 15 January 1981.   Result: **AUSTRALIA** won by 27 runs.   Toss: India.
Award: A.R.Border.   LOI debuts: None.

Another outstanding innings by Allan Border ensured that Australia would make their first appearance in the World Series finals.

AUSTRALIA		Runs	Balls	4/6
A.R.Border	c Azad b Doshi	85	131	6
G.M.Wood	c Binny b Patil	26	28	2
* G.S.Chappell	c Yashpal b Patil	2	5	–
K.J.Hughes	c Kapil Dev b Binny	39	50	3
K.D.Walters	b Ghavri	38	53	1
T.M.Chappell	c Vengsarkar b Kapil Dev	14	21	–
† R.W.Marsh	c Reddy b Ghavri	12	7	1
S.F.Graf	c Azad b Kapil Dev	2	4	–
D.K.Lillee	not out	4	4	1
R.M.Hogg	not out	1	1	–
L.S.Pascoe				
Extras	(b 1, lb 16, nb 2)	19		
Total	(50 overs; 8 wickets)	**242**		

INDIA	O	M	R	W
Kapil Dev	10	1	46	2
Ghavri	10	0	39	2
Binny	10	0	45	1
Patil	10	2	34	2
Doshi	10	0	59	1

FALL OF WICKETS
1-48, 2-55, 3-155, 4-181, 5-216, 6-230, 7-233, 8-240

INDIA		Runs	Balls	4/6
* S.M.Gavaskar	lbw b Lillee	1	8	–
R.M.H.Binny	lbw b Graf	34	45	4
D.B.Vengsarkar	c Marsh b Hogg	52	74	5
G.R.Viswanath	c and b G.S.Chappell	7	19	–
Yashpal Sharma	c and b G.S.Chappell	25	34	2
S.M.Patil	b Lillee	27	42	2
Kapil Dev	c Marsh b Lillee	20	35	1
K.Azad	b Lillee	19	24	2
K.D.Ghavri	not out	11	10	2
† B.Reddy	not out	8	11	1
D.R.Doshi				
Extras	(lb 10, nb 1)	11		
Total	(50 overs; 8 wickets)	**215**		

AUSTRALIA	O	M	R	W
Lillee	10	1	32	4
Hogg	10	1	34	1
Pascoe	10	0	64	0
Graf	10	2	36	1
G.S.Chappell	10	0	38	2

FALL OF WICKETS
1-2, 2-59, 3-78, 4-112, 5-135, 6-161, 7-196, 8-197

Umpires: D.G.Weser (6) and R.V.Whitehead (6).

NEW ZEALAND v INDIA 1980-81

At Woolloongabba, Brisbane on 18 January 1981.　　Result: **NEW ZEALAND** won by 22 runs.　　Toss: India.
Award: J.V.Coney.　　LOI debuts: None.

This result guaranteed New Zealand's place in the best-of-five finals.

NEW ZEALAND		Runs	Balls	4/6	INDIA		Runs	Balls	4/6
J.G.Wright	b Ghavri	14	29	1	* S.M.Gavaskar	run out	9	26	–
B.A.Edgar	b Doshi	34	52	1	R.M.H.Binny	c Cairns b Coney	35	52	5
* G.P.Howarth	c Patil b Doshi	45	55	5	D.B.Vengsarkar	run out	66	77	6
J.M.Parker	c Reddy b Kapil Dev	6	12	1	G.R.Viswanath	b Coney	9	22	–
M.G.Burgess	c Viswanath b Azad	26	49	1	Kapil Dev	b Coney	0	2	–
J.V.Coney	run out	49	58	1/3	S.M.Patil	run out	48	53	3/2
† I.D.S.Smith	c sub (N.S.Yadav) b Kapil Dev	12	10	2	Yashpal Sharma	c Smith b Snedden	13	20	1
R.J.Hadlee	b Ghavri	32	24	2/2	K.Azad	c Parker b Snedden	19	21	3
B.L.Cairns	b Kapil Dev	0	1		K.D.Ghavri	b Snedden	2	7	–
M.C.Snedden	not out	6	15	–	† B.Reddy	not out	3	9	–
E.J.Chatfield	not out	0	2	–	D.R.Doshi	lbw b Hadlee	0	1	–
Extras	(b 1, lb 13, w 1, nb 3)	18			Extras	(b 4, lb 11, nb 1)	16		
Total	(50 overs; 9 wickets)	242			Total	(48.1 overs)	220		

INDIA	O	M	R	W	NEW ZEALAND	O	M	R	W
Kapil Dev	10	3	37	3	Hadlee	9.1	2	15	1
Ghavri	10	0	61	2	Chatfield	10	1	42	0
Binny	4	0	25	0	Coney	10	1	28	3
Patil	10	0	38	0	Cairns	10	0	54	0
Doshi	10	0	25	2	Snedden	8	0	57	3
Azad	3	1	26	1	Burgess	1	0	8	0
Yashpal Sharma	3	0	12	0					

FALL OF WICKETS
1-28, 2-95, 3-108, 4-108, 5-166, 6-199, 7-207, 8-207, 9-241

FALL OF WICKETS
1-32, 2-73, 3-86, 4-86, 5-178, 6-179, 7-197, 8-213, 9-220, 10-220

Umpires: P.M.Cronin (5) and M.W.Johnson (5).

AUSTRALIA v NEW ZEALAND 1980-81

At Sydney Cricket Ground on 21 January 1981.　　No result.　　Toss: Australia.
LOI debuts: None.

A thunderstorm during the dinner interval terminated this obligatory 'qualifying' match. Final points: Australia 13, New Zealand 11, India 6.

AUSTRALIA		Runs	Balls	4/6	NEW ZEALAND		Runs	Balls	4/6
A.R.Border	c Hadlee b McKechnie	40	69	3	J.G.Wright	c Marsh b G.S.Chappell	8	33	–
G.M.Wood	c Smith b Chatfield	5	20	–	B.A.Edgar	not out	2	15	–
* G.S.Chappell	c Burgess b McEwan	74	80	8	* G.P.Howarth	not out	0	1	–
K.J.Hughes	c Coney b McEwan	14	12	1	M.G.Burgess				
K.D.Walters	run out	16	25	–	P.E.McEwan				
T.M.Chappell	lbw b Cairns	14	25	–	J.V.Coney				
† R.W.Marsh	c Hadlee b McKechnie	0	3	–	† I.D.S.Smith				
S.F.Graf	lbw b Hadlee	2	10	–	B.J.McKechnie				
D.K.Lillee	c Coney b Cairns	0	2	–	R.J.Hadlee				
R.M.Hogg	run out	1	9	–	B.L.Cairns				
M.H.N.Walker	not out	0	6	–	E.J.Chatfield				
Extras	(lb 12, w 2)	14			Extras	(b 8, lb 4, nb 1)	13		
Total	(43.1 overs)	180			Total	(8 overs; 1 wicket)	23		

NEW ZEALAND	O	M	R	W	AUSTRALIA	O	M	R	W
Hadlee	8	4	13	1	Lillee	3	1	6	0
Chatfield	8.1	2	15	1	Walker	4	3	3	0
Coney	4	0	19	0	G.S.Chappell	1	0	1	1
Cairns	8	2	37	2					
McKechnie	10	0	53	2	FALL OF WICKETS				
McEwan	5	0	29	2	1-22				

FALL OF WICKETS
1-10, 2-98, 3-125, 4-149, 5-173, 6-175, 7-179, 8-179, 9-179, 10-180

Umpires: R.A.French (7) and M.G.O'Connell (6).

AUSTRALIA v NEW ZEALAND 1980-81

At Sydney Cricket Ground on 29 January 1981.   Result: **NEW ZEALAND** won by 78 runs.   Toss: Australia.
LOI debuts: Australia – M.F.Kent.

With rain forecast, Australia had to at least match New Zealand's run rate of 4.66 per over. Brian McKechnie wrecked their attempt by taking three key wickets in eight balls. Richard Hadlee overcame a strained shoulder to return his best LOI figures in Australia.

NEW ZEALAND		Runs	Balls	4/6
J.G.Wright	b Chappell	81	111	3
B.A.Edgar	c Walters b Lillee	21	55	3
* G.P.Howarth	c Border b Walker	47	68	4
J.V.Coney	c and b Pascoe	0	3	–
M.G.Burgess	lbw b Lillee	15	23	–
R.J.Hadlee	not out	23	28	–
B.L.Cairns	c Walker b Pascoe	18	20	1/1
B.J.McKechnie	not out	1	1	
† I.D.S.Smith				
M.C.Snedden				
E.J.Chatfield				
Extras	(b 18, w 7, nb 2)	27		
Total	**(50 overs; 6 wickets)**	**233**		

AUSTRALIA		Runs	Balls	4/6
G.M.Wood	c Burgess b Hadlee	13	24	1
M.F.Kent	c Howarth b Hadlee	12	18	1
† R.W.Marsh	c Coney b Chatfield	0	4	–
* G.S.Chappell	c Wright b Chatfield	31	50	3
K.J.Hughes	lbw b Hadlee	0	3	–
A.R.Border	c Coney b McKechnie	55	74	6/2
K.D.Walters	b McKechnie	20	30	–
D.K.Lillee	c Cairns b McKechnie	7	5	–
M.H.N.Walker	c Smith b Hadlee	4	15	–
R.M.Hogg	c Smith b Hadlee	1	5	–
L.S.Pascoe	not out	3	10	–
Extras	(b 2, lb 6, w 1)	9		
Total	**(39.3 overs)**	**155**		

AUSTRALIA	O	M	R	W
Hogg	10	1	37	0
Walker	10	1	31	1
Lillee	10	0	47	2
Pascoe	10	0	48	2
Chappell	10	0	43	1

NEW ZEALAND	O	M	R	W
Chatfield	10	3	38	2
Hadlee	8.3	4	26	5
McKechnie	9	1	23	3
Snedden	6	1	25	0
Cairns	6	0	34	0

FALL OF WICKETS
1-45, 2-148, 3-152, 4-172, 5-198, 6-231

FALL OF WICKETS
1-28, 2-28, 3-28, 4-28, 5-93, 6-135, 7-145, 8-147, 9-148, 10-155

Umpires: R.C.Bailhache (9) and M.W.Johnson (6).

AUSTRALIA v NEW ZEALAND 1980-81

At Melbourne Cricket Ground on 31 January 1981.   Result: **AUSTRALIA** won by 7 wickets   Toss: Australia.
LOI debuts: Australia – G.R.Beard.

An authoritative innings by Greg Chappell on a low-bouncing pitch enabled Australia to draw level in this record-breaking number of 'finals'.

NEW ZEALAND		Runs	Balls	4/6
J.G.Wright	c Marsh b Lillee	11	16	1
B.A.Edgar	c Border b T.M.Chappell	28	56	2
* G.P.Howarth	b Walker	7	14	–
J.V.Coney	lbw b Lillee	4	8	1
M.G.Burgess	run out	13	44	1
P.E.McEwan	run out	12	32	–
B.J.McKechnie	lbw b T.M.Chappell	0	10	–
† I.D.S.Smith	b G.S.Chappell	13	27	1
R.J.Hadlee	c G.S.Chappell b Beard	16	43	1
B.L.Cairns	c T.M.Chappell b Beard	14	21	1
E.J.Chatfield	not out	2	11	–
Extras	(lb 4, w 1, nb 1)	6		
Total	**(46.4 overs)**	**126**		

AUSTRALIA		Runs	Balls	4/6
G.M.Wood	c Smith b Chatfield	32	87	4
A.R.Border	c Burgess b Howarth	19	27	1
* G.S.Chappell	not out	58	87	4
K.J.Hughes	st Smith b Cairns	12	33	–
K.D.Walters	not out	4	4	–
G.R.Beard				
T.M.Chappell				
† R.W.Marsh				
D.K.Lillee				
M.H.N.Walker				
L.S.Pascoe				
Extras	(b 2, lb 2, w 1)	5		
Total	**(39.3 overs; 3 wickets)**	**130**		

AUSTRALIA	O	M	R	W
Lillee	8	0	25	2
Walker	10	0	25	1
Beard	8.4	3	20	2
G.S.Chappell	10	2	22	1
T.M.Chappell	10	1	28	2

NEW ZEALAND	O	M	R	W
Hadlee	10	2	29	0
Chatfield	6	1	21	1
McEwan	4	0	18	0
Howarth	4	0	13	1
Cairns	10	1	23	1
McKechnie	5.3	1	21	0

FALL OF WICKETS
1-14, 2-21, 3-30, 4-62, 5-70, 6-71, 7-92, 8-95, 9-113, 10-126

FALL OF WICKETS
1-30, 2-85, 3-118

Umpires: R.A.French (8) and D.G.Weser (7).

57

AUSTRALIA v NEW ZEALAND 1980-81

At Melbourne Cricket Ground on 1 February 1981.   Result: **AUSTRALIA** won by 6 runs.   Toss: Australia.
LOI debuts: None.

With six runs needed to tie the match, Greg Chappell ordered his younger brother, Trevor, to bowl the final ball underarm along the ground. Such tactics, condemned by New Zealand's Prime Minister, were subsequently banned.

AUSTRALIA		Runs	Balls	4/6
A.R.Border	c Parker b Hadlee	5	8	–
G.M.Wood	b McEwan	72	114	4
* G.S.Chappell	c Edgar b Snedden	90	122	7
M.F.Kent	c Edgar b Snedden	33	38	2
† R.W.Marsh	not out	18	13	1
K.D.Walters	not out	6	5	–
K.J.Hughes				
G.R.Beard				
T.M.Chappell				
D.K.Lillee				
M.H.N.Walker				
Extras	(b 8, lb 3)	11		
Total	(50 overs; 4 wickets)	**235**		

NEW ZEALAND		Runs	Balls	4/6
J.G.Wright	c Kent b G.S.Chappell	42	81	4
B.A.Edgar	not out	102	141	7
* G.P.Howarth	c Marsh b G.S.Chappell	18	20	2
B.L.Cairns	b Beard	12	10	2
M.G.Burgess	c T.M.Chappell b G.S.Chappell	2	5	–
P.E.McEwan	c Wood b Beard	11	18	–
J.M.Parker	c T.M.Chappell b Lillee	24	19	1
R.J.Hadlee	lbw b T.M.Chappell	4	2	1
† I.D.S.Smith	b T.M.Chappell	4	3	–
B.J.McKechnie	not out	0	1	–
M.C.Snedden				
Extras	(lb 10)	10		
Total	(50 overs; 8 wickets)	**229**		

NEW ZEALAND	O	M	R	W
Hadlee	10	0	41	1
Snedden	10	0	52	2
Cairns	10	0	34	0
McKechnie	10	0	54	0
McEwan	7	1	31	1
Howarth	3	0	12	0

AUSTRALIA	O	M	R	W
Lillee	10	1	34	1
Walker	10	0	35	0
Beard	10	0	50	2
G.S.Chappell	10	0	43	3
T.M.Chappell	10	0	57	2

FALL OF WICKETS
1-8, 2-153, 3-199, 4-215

FALL OF WICKETS
1-85, 2-117, 3-136, 4-139, 5-172, 6-221, 7-225, 8-229

Umpires: P.M.Cronin (6) and D.G.Weser (8).

AUSTRALIA v NEW ZEALAND 1980-81

At Sydney Cricket Ground on 3 February 1981.   Result: **AUSTRALIA** won by 6 wickets.   Toss: New Zealand.
Finals award: G.S.Chappell.   LOI debuts: None.

New Zealand, although outraged by Australia's conduct in the previous match, failed to exploit another dream start by their opening batsmen. This result at least rendered a fifth final unnecessary.

NEW ZEALAND		Runs	Balls	4/6
J.G.Wright	c Border b T.M.Chappell	57	88	2
B.A.Edgar	run out	38	76	–
* G.P.Howarth	c Kent b Hogg	46	55	3
M.G.Burgess	b G.S.Chappell	20	34	–
R.J.Hadlee	c Border b Lillee	15	20	–
J.M.Parker	c Marsh b Lillee	12	13	1
P.E.McEwan	c Hogg b Lillee	4	7	–
B.L.Cairns	b Pascoe	7	11	–
† I.D.S.Smith	not out	2	3	–
M.C.Snedden				
E.J.Chatfield				
Extras	(lb 9, nb 5)	14		
Total	(50 overs; 8 wickets)	**215**		

AUSTRALIA		Runs	Balls	4/6
G.M.Wood	run out	34	78	2
A.R.Border	b Snedden	19	30	2
* G.S.Chappell	b Snedden	87	102	5
K.J.Hughes	b Snedden	47	57	3
† R.W.Marsh	not out	18	17	–/1
M.F.Kent	not out	4	3	1
K.D.Walters				
T.M.Chappell				
D.K.Lillee				
R.M.Hogg				
L.S.Pascoe				
Extras	(lb 8, w 1)	9		
Total	(47.4 overs; 4 wickets)	**218**		

AUSTRALIA	O	M	R	W
Lillee	10	2	27	3
Hogg	10	0	46	1
Pascoe	10	0	51	1
G.S.Chappell	10	1	36	1
T.M.Chappell	10	0	41	1

NEW ZEALAND	O	M	R	W
Chatfield	10	1	30	0
Hadlee	8.4	1	43	0
Snedden	9	0	27	3
McEwan	10	1	58	0
Burgess	10	0	51	0

FALL OF WICKETS
1-90, 2-119, 3-171, 4-177, 5-200, 6-201, 7-210, 8-215

FALL OF WICKETS
1-37, 2-90, 3-188, 4-209

Umpires: R.C.Bailhache (10) and A.R.Crafter (7).

WEST INDIES v ENGLAND 1980-81

At Arnos Vale, Kingstown, St Vincent on 4 February 1981.   Result: **WEST INDIES** won by 2 runs.   Toss: England.
Award: C.E.H.Croft.   LOI debuts: West Indies – E.H.Mattis.   50-over match.

St Vincent's first international attracted an estimated crowd of 10,000. Colin Croft took full advantage of an uneven pitch to become the second bowler after Gary Gilmour (*LOI No. 31*) to record a six-wicket analysis. Ten of the 15 runs he conceded came off one over.

WEST INDIES		Runs	Balls	4/6
D.L.Haynes	c Emburey b Stevenson	34		8
S.F.A.F.Bacchus	c Stevenson b Old	1		
E.H.Mattis	run out	62		
A.I.Kallicharran	b Emburey	2		
* C.H.Lloyd	c Willey b Stevenson	2		
H.A.Gomes	b Willey	8		
† D.A.Murray	b Gooch	1		
A.M.E.Roberts	st Bairstow b Gooch	2		
J.Garner	run out	4		
M.A.Holding	b Botham	1		
C.E.H.Croft	not out	2		
Extras	(lb 4, w 1, nb 3)	8		
Total	(47.2 overs)	**127**		

ENGLAND		Runs	Balls	4/6
G.Boycott	c Mattis b Croft	2		
G.A.Gooch	c Lloyd b Roberts	11		
P.Willey	c Murray b Croft	0		
D.I.Gower	c Haynes b Kallicharran	23		
R.O.Butcher	c Murray b Croft	1		
* I.T.Botham	c Murray b Croft	60		
M.W.Gatting	b Croft	3		
† D.L.Bairstow	b Croft	5		
J.E.Emburey	b Holding	5		
G.B.Stevenson	not out	6		
C.M.Old	b Holding	1		
Extras	(lb 8)	8		
Total	(48.2 overs)	**125**		

ENGLAND	O	M	R	W
Old	5	4	8	1
Botham	8	1	32	1
Stevenson	8.2	2	18	2
Emburey	10	4	20	1
Willey	10	1	29	1
Gooch	6	1	12	2

WEST INDIES	O	M	R	W
Roberts	10	1	30	1
Holding	9.2	2	30	2
Croft	9	4	15	6
Garner	10	2	17	0
Kallicharran	10	3	25	1

FALL OF WICKETS
1-14, 2-14, 3-14, 4-15, 5-80, 6-88, 7-111, 8-114, 9-123, 10-125

FALL OF WICKETS
1-5, 2-48, 3-51, 4-58, 5-89, 6-90, 7-102, 8-110, 9-120, 10-127

Umpires: D.M.Archer (1) and S.Mohammed (1).

WEST INDIES v ENGLAND 1980-81

At Albion Sports Complex, Berbice on 26 February 1981.   Result: **WEST INDIES** won by 6 wickets.   Toss: West Indies.
Award: H.A.Gomes.   LOI debuts: None.   50-over match.

This uneven contest was overshadowed by uncertainty regarding the Guyanese government's impending revocation of Robin Jackman's visitor's permit and the possible abandonment of the remainder of the tour.

ENGLAND		Runs	Balls	4/6
G.Boycott	b Richards	7		
G.A.Gooch	c Murray b Roberts	11		
M.W.Gatting	c Mattis b Gomes	29		
D.I.Gower	b Gomes	3		
R.O.Butcher	c Haynes b Gomes	5		
* I.T.Botham	b Roberts	27		
P.Willey	b Croft	21		
† D.L.Bairstow	b Croft	16		
J.E.Emburey	c Croft b Holding	0		
G.B.Stevenson	not out	8		
G.R.Dilley	b Croft	3		
Extras	(b 4, lb 2, nb 1)	7		
Total	(47.2 overs)	**137**		

WEST INDIES		Runs	Balls	4/6
C.G.Greenidge	run out	2		
D.L.Haynes	c Gooch b Emburey	48		
I.V.A.Richards	c Stevenson b Dilley	3		
E.H.Mattis	b Emburey	24		
H.A.Gomes	not out	22		
* C.H.Lloyd	not out	25		
† D.A.Murray				
A.M.E.Roberts				
M.A.Holding				
J.Garner				
C.E.H.Croft				
Extras	(b 4, lb 8, nb 2)	14		
Total	(39.3 overs; 4 wickets)	**138**		

WEST INDIES	O	M	R	W
Roberts	7	0	17	2
Holding	7	1	13	1
Richards	10	0	26	1
Croft	6.2	1	9	3
Gomes	10	2	30	3
Garner	7	2	35	0

ENGLAND	O	M	R	W
Dilley	5	0	21	1
Botham	7	1	24	0
Stevenson	6	0	21	0
Emburey	10	4	22	2
Gooch	2	0	8	0
Willey	9	0	23	0
Gower	0.3	0	5	0

FALL OF WICKETS
1-16, 2-27, 3-34, 4-59, 5-62, 6-108, 7-112, 8-119, 9-132, 10-137

FALL OF WICKETS
1-6, 2-11, 3-85, 4-90

Umpires: D.J.Narine (1) and C.F.Vyfhuis (2).

NEW ZEALAND v INDIA 1980-81

At Eden Park, Auckland on 14 February 1981.　Result: **NEW ZEALAND** won by 78 runs.　Toss: India.
Award: B.A.Edgar.　LOI debuts: None.

Reduced from 50 to 45 overs by India's extremely slow over rate, this match introduced coloured 'pyjamas', white balls and black sightscreens to New Zealand and attracted a crowd of 25,000.

NEW ZEALAND		Runs	Balls	4/6
J.G.Wright	c Binny b Ghavri	10		
B.A.Edgar	not out	99		
G.N.Edwards	c Chauhan b Ghavri	36		3
* G.P.Howarth	c Yograj Singh b Patil	11		
J.V.Coney	c and b Kapil Dev	2		
† I.D.S.Smith	lbw b Patil	10		
R.J.Hadlee	c Vengsarkar b Ghavri	22		
B.L.Cairns	not out	12		
M.C.Snedden				
G.B.Troup				
E.J.Chatfield				
Extras	(lb 11, w 1, nb 4)	16		
Total	(45 overs; 6 wickets)	**218**		

INDIA		Runs	Balls	4/6
C.P.S.Chauhan	b Hadlee	6		
* S.M.Gavaskar	c Smith b Snedden	14		
D.B.Vengsarkar	run out	0		
G.R.Viswanath	b Chatfield	14		
S.M.Patil	b Chatfield	4		
Yashpal Sharma	c Edwards b Cairns	17		
Kapil Dev	run out	50		4/1
R.M.H.Binny	c Edwards b Cairns	12		
K.D.Ghavri	not out	6		
Yograj Singh	c Hadlee b Troup	1		
† S.M.H.Kirmani	not out	10		
Extras	(lb 5, nb 1)	6		
Total	(45 overs; 9 wickets)	**140**		

INDIA	O	M	R	W
Kapil Dev	10	1	40	1
Ghavri	10	1	40	3
Binny	6	2	26	0
Yograj Singh	9	0	57	0
Patil	10	1	39	2

NEW ZEALAND	O	M	R	W
Hadlee	6	3	6	1
Troup	10	3	21	1
Chatfield	10	2	36	2
Snedden	8	2	26	1
Coney	3	0	7	0
Cairns	7	2	33	2
Howarth	1	0	5	0

FALL OF WICKETS
1-24, 2-112, 3-127, 4-132, 5-156, 6-196

Umpires: B.A.Bricknell (1) and F.R.Goodall (4).

FALL OF WICKETS
1-9, 2-10, 3-31, 4-40, 5-41, 6-86, 7-122, 8-122, 9-124

NEW ZEALAND v INDIA 1980-81

At Seddon Park, Hamilton on 15 February 1981.　Result: **NEW ZEALAND** won by 57 runs.　Toss: India.
Award: J.V.Coney.　LOI debuts: New Zealand – G.K.Robertson.　50-over match.

New Zealand gained a comprehensive win in spite of dropping three catches in the first four overs of India's reply.

NEW ZEALAND		Runs	Balls	4/6
J.G.Wright	c Kirmani b Binny	38		2
B.A.Edgar	b Kapil Dev	1		–
G.N.Edwards	c Vengsarkar b Yograj Singh	17		
* G.P.Howarth	c Chauhan b Patil	17		
J.V.Coney	c Vengsarkar b Ghavri	46		3/2
† I.D.S.Smith	c Vengsarkar b Patil	0		–
R.J.Hadlee	c Azad b Ghavri	23		
G.K.Robertson	c Patil b Kapil Dev	17		
M.C.Snedden	not out	11		
G.B.Troup	not out	14		1/1
E.J.Chatfield				
Extras	(b 1, lb 10, w 10, nb 5)	26		
Total	(50 overs; 8 wickets)	**210**		

INDIA		Runs	Balls	4/6
C.P.S.Chauhan	b Snedden	31		1
R.M.H.Binny	c Howarth b Chatfield	18		3
D.B.Vengsarkar	b Hadlee	41		3
K.Azad	b Robertson	10		
* G.R.Viswanath	b Snedden	5		
S.M.Patil	b Robertson	20		2
Yashpal Sharma	b Hadlee	9		
Kapil Dev	lbw b Troup	1		
† S.M.H.Kirmani	c Smith b Troup	2		–
K.D.Ghavri	c Wright b Troup	3		–
Yograj Singh	not out	0		–
Extras	(b 6, lb 4, w 2, nb 1)	13		
Total	(45.2 overs)	**153**		

INDIA	O	M	R	W
Kapil Dev	10	1	34	2
Yograj Singh	10	2	37	1
Ghavri	10	1	47	2
Binny	10	2	38	1
Patil	10	1	28	2

NEW ZEALAND	O	M	R	W
Hadlee	8	1	27	2
Troup	9.2	2	18	3
Chatfield	10	1	31	1
Robertson	10	1	29	2
Snedden	8	1	35	2

FALL OF WICKETS
1-13, 2-43, 3-89, 4-91, 5-92, 6-165, 7-166, 8-185

Umpires: J.B.R.Hastie (3) and R.L.Monteith (3).

FALL OF WICKETS
1-34, 2-82, 3-104, 4-111, 5-127, 6-140, 7-141, 8-149, 9-153, 10-153

ENGLAND v AUSTRALIA 1981

At Lord's, London on 4 June 1981.   Result: **ENGLAND** won by 6 wickets.   Toss: England.
Award: G.Boycott.   LOI debuts: England – G.W.Humpage, J.D.Love.   55-over match.

A steadfast effort by Geoffrey Boycott, far removed from his Australian mode of strokeplay, guided England to a comfortable win.

AUSTRALIA		Runs	Balls	4/6
J.Dyson	lbw b Willis	2	2	–
G.M.Wood	run out	22	29	2
T.M.Chappell	run out	16	40	–
* K.J.Hughes	lbw b Jackman	12	26	1
A.R.Border	not out	73	115	6/1
M.F.Kent	c Gooch b Botham	28	71	2
† R.W.Marsh	b Botham	18	18	2
R.J.Bright	b Willis	18	20	1
G.F.Lawson	not out	12	9	2
D.K.Lillee				
R.M.Hogg				
Extras	(b 1, lb 8)	9		
Total	(55 overs; 7 wickets)	**210**		

ENGLAND		Runs	Balls	4/6
G.A.Gooch	c Kent b Lillee	53	89	6/1
G.Boycott	not out	75	135	3
M.W.Gatting	lbw b Lillee	0	3	–
D.I.Gower	c Kent b Chappell	47	50	7
J.D.Love	c Bright b Lawson	15	26	1
* I.T.Botham	not out	13	8	2
P.Willey				
† G.W.Humpage				
R.D.Jackman				
R.G.D.Willis				
M.Hendrick				
Extras	(b 5, lb 4)	9		
Total	(51.4 overs; 4 wickets)	**212**		

ENGLAND	O	M	R	W
Willis	11	0	56	2
Botham	11	1	39	2
Hendrick	11	2	32	0
Jackman	11	1	27	1
Willey	6	1	26	0
Gooch	5	1	21	0

AUSTRALIA	O	M	R	W
Hogg	11	1	36	0
Lillee	11	3	23	2
Lawson	9	0	51	1
Chappell	11	1	50	1
Bright	9.4	0	43	0

FALL OF WICKETS
1-86, 2-86, 3-172, 4-199

FALL OF WICKETS
1-2, 2-36, 3-48, 4-60, 5-134, 6-162, 7-189

Umpires: W.E.Alley (9) and H.D.Bird (17).

ENGLAND v AUSTRALIA 1981

At Edgbaston, Birmingham on 6 June 1981.   Result: **AUSTRALIA** won by 2 runs.   Toss: England.
Award: M.W.Gatting.   LOI debuts: Australia – T.M.Alderman.   55-over match.

Edgbaston's revolutionary 11½-ton 'Brumbrella' cover ensured that this match would be completed on its appointed day. Its Scandinavian polythene easily protected the square and most of the outfield from the effects of an hour's rain, so allowing a prompt restart.

AUSTRALIA		Runs	Balls	4/6
G.M.Wood	c Willis b Jackman	55	80	1
T.M.Chappell	c Humpage b Botham	0	1	–
G.N.Yallop	b Hendrick	63	132	4
* K.J.Hughes	run out	34	41	2/1
A.R.Border	run out	17	17	1/1
† R.W.Marsh	c Love b Botham	20	18	1
M.F.Kent	lbw b Willis	1	3	–
G.F.Lawson	not out	29	26	–/2
D.K.Lillee	run out	8	12	–
R.M.Hogg	not out	0	2	–
T.M.Alderman				
Extras	(b 1, lb 18, w 1, nb 2)	22		
Total	(55 overs; 8 wickets)	**249**		

ENGLAND		Runs	Balls	4/6
G.A.Gooch	b Hogg	11	25	1
G.Boycott	b Lawson	14	40	2
M.W.Gatting	c Lawson b Lillee	96	131	14/1
D.I.Gower	b Alderman	2	10	–
J.D.Love	b Lawson	43	53	6
P.Willey	c Wood b Chappell	37	33	4
* I.T.Botham	c Hughes b Lawson	24	21	3
† G.W.Humpage	b Lillee	5	10	–
R.D.Jackman	run out	2	3	–
R.G.D.Willis	not out	1	1	–
M.Hendrick	c Marsh b Lillee	0	2	–
Extras	(lb 12)	12		
Total	(54.5 overs)	**247**		

ENGLAND	O	M	R	W
Willis	11	3	41	1
Botham	11	1	44	2
Hendrick	11	2	21	1
Jackman	11	0	47	1
Willey	6	0	36	0
Gooch	5	0	38	0

AUSTRALIA	O	M	R	W
Hogg	11	2	42	1
Lillee	10.5	2	36	3
Alderman	11	1	46	1
Lawson	11	2	42	3
Chappell	11	0	69	1

FALL OF WICKETS
1-20, 2-27, 3-36, 4-111, 5-177, 6-224, 7-232, 8-244, 9-244, 10-247

FALL OF WICKETS
1-10, 2-96, 3-160, 4-171, 5-183, 6-193, 7-213, 8-248

Umpires: D.J.Constant (16) and A.G.T.Whitehead (4).

ENGLAND v AUSTRALIA 1981

At Headingley, Leeds on 8 June 1981.   Result: **AUSTRALIA** won by 71 runs.   Toss: England.
Award: G.M.Wood.   LOI debuts: None.   55-over match.

Rodney Marsh became the first to hold five catches in a limited-overs international as Australia won the Prudential Trophy for the first time in four attempts.

AUSTRALIA		Runs	Balls	4/6
G.M.Wood	run out	108	150	8
J.Dyson	c Gooch b Hendrick	22	48	3
G.N.Yallop	run out	48	90	2
* K.J.Hughes	c Gatting b Jackman	0	1	–
A.R.Border	c Jackman b Willis	5	9	1
† R.W.Marsh	c Humpage b Botham	1	2	–
T.M.Chappell	c Gooch b Willis	14	23	1
G.F.Lawson	run out	8	9	–
D.K.Lillee	not out	0	–	–
R.M.Hogg				
T.M.Alderman				
Extras	(lb 27, w 1, nb 2)	30		
Total	(55 overs; 8 wickets)	**236**		

ENGLAND	O	M	R	W
Willis	11	1	35	2
Botham	11	2	42	1
Hendrick	11	3	31	1
Gooch	11	0	50	0
Jackman	11	1	48	1

FALL OF WICKETS
1-43, 2-173, 3-173, 4-187, 5-189, 6-216, 7-236, 8-236

ENGLAND		Runs	Balls	4/6
G.A.Gooch	c Marsh b Lawson	37	67	5
G.Boycott	c Marsh b Hogg	4	21	1
M.W.Gatting	c Marsh b Hogg	32	55	6
D.I.Gower	b Alderman	5	17	–
J.D.Love	b Chappell	3	21	–
P.Willey	c Marsh b Hogg	42	66	4
* I.T.Botham	c Hughes b Chappell	5	13	1
† G.W.Humpage	c Border b Alderman	6	14	–
R.D.Jackman	b Chappell	14	22	1
R.G.D.Willis	not out	2	7	–
M.Hendrick	c Marsh b Hogg	0	2	–
Extras	(b 10, w 1, nb 4)	15		
Total	(46.5 overs)	**165**		

AUSTRALIA	O	M	R	W
Hogg	8.5	1	29	4
Lillee	7	0	37	0
Lawson	11	3	34	1
Alderman	11	3	19	2
Chappell	9	0	31	3

FALL OF WICKETS
1-5, 2-71, 3-80, 4-89, 5-95, 6-106, 7-133, 8-160, 9-164, 10-165

Umpires: B.J.Meyer (8) and K.E.Palmer (8).

WEST INDIES v PAKISTAN 1981-82

At Melbourne Cricket Ground on 21 November 1981.   Result: **WEST INDIES** won by 18 runs.   Toss: Pakistan.
Award: C.G.Greenidge.   LOI debuts: Pakistan – Rizwan-uz-Zaman.

The third World Series again involved 15 qualifying 50-over matches and a best-of-five sequence of finals. Gordon Greenidge and Desmond Haynes equalled the (then) LOI first-wicket partnership record of 182 set by Australia in 1975 (*LOI No. 25*).

WEST INDIES		Runs	Balls	4/6
C.G.Greenidge	c Rizwan b Sarfraz	103	161	5/1
D.L.Haynes	b Mudassar	84	94	6
I.V.A.Richards	b Imran	17	12	2
S.F.A.F.Bacchus	c Rizwan b Sarfraz	8	9	1
* C.H.Lloyd	b Sarfraz	10	11	1
A.M.E.Roberts	c Mansoor b Imran	0	1	–
J.Garner	c Ashraf b Imran	0	3	–
M.D.Marshall	not out	9	9	1
H.A.Gomes	c and b Sarfraz	0	1	–
† D.A.Murray	not out	1	1	–
C.E.H.Croft				
Extras	(lb 13)	13		
Total	(50 overs; 8 wickets)	**245**		

PAKISTAN	O	M	R	W
Sarfraz Nawaz	9	2	37	4
Imran Khan	10	2	23	3
Sikander Bakht	9	0	46	0
Iqbal Qasim	10	0	49	0
Majid Khan	5	0	34	0
Mudassar Nazar	7	0	43	1

FALL OF WICKETS
1-182, 2-203, 3-222, 4-223, 5-223, 6-224, 7-244, 8-244

PAKISTAN		Runs	Balls	4/6
Mudassar Nazar	b Marshall	51	86	1
Rizwan-uz-Zaman	c Roberts b Garner	14	52	1
* Javed Miandad	c Murray b Roberts	74	81	8
Mansoor Akhtar	b Marshall	2	4	–
Majid Khan	c Bacchus b Roberts	56	69	1
Imran Khan	c Murray b Roberts	0	1	–
Wasim Raja	not out	10	10	–
† Ashraf Ali	not out	1	4	–
Sarfraz Nawaz				
Iqbal Qasim				
Sikander Bakht				
Extras	(b 2, lb 7, w 4, nb 6)	19		
Total	(50 overs; 6 wickets)	**227**		

WEST INDIES	O	M	R	W
Roberts	10	1	42	3
Marshall	10	1	27	2
Garner	10	0	30	1
Croft	10	1	57	0
Richards	10	0	52	0

FALL OF WICKETS
1-53, 2-120, 3-124, 4-212, 5-212, 6-221

Umpires: R.C.Bailhache (11) and R.A.French (9).

AUSTRALIA v PAKISTAN 1981-82

At Melbourne Cricket Ground on 22 November 1981.　　Result: **PAKISTAN** won by 4 wickets.　　Toss: Pakistan.
Award: Javed Miandad.　　LOI debuts: None.

Mudassar Nazar and Javed Miandad shared Pakistan's first three-figure partnership for the third wicket in these matches.

AUSTRALIA		Runs	Balls	4/6
G.M.Wood	run out	23	34	3/1
W.M.Darling	c Sarfraz b Sikander	41	70	3
* G.S.Chappell	c Wasim b Sikander	3	10	–
A.R.Border	b Sikander	6	18	–
K.J.Hughes	c Mudassar b Sikander	67	83	4
† R.W.Marsh	b Sarfraz	15	14	2
B.Yardley	b Imran	28	58	–
S.F.Graf	run out	8	12	–
G.F.Lawson	not out	4	5	–
J.R.Thomson	run out	3	4	–
T.M.Alderman				
Extras	(b 2, lb 3, w 3, nb 3)	11		
Total	(50 overs; 9 wickets)	209		

PAKISTAN		Runs	Balls	4/6
Mudassar Nazar	c Marsh b Chappell	44	106	4
Mansoor Akhtar	c Yardley b Alderman	12	22	2
Zaheer Abbas	c Marsh b Alderman	2	5	–
* Javed Miandad	c Lawson b Chappell	72	82	7
Wasim Raja	c Darling b Chappell	8	10	1
Imran Khan	not out	28	38	1
Ijaz Faqih	b Thomson	17	22	2
† Ashraf Ali	not out	15	17	1
Sarfraz Nawaz				
Tahir Naqqash				
Sikander Bakht				
Extras	(lb 7, w 3, nb 2)	12		
Total	(49.2 overs; 6 wickets)	210		

PAKISTAN	O	M	R	W
Imran Khan	10	1	42	1
Sarfraz Nawaz	10	0	44	1
Tahir Naqqash	10	0	46	0
Sikander Bakht	10	1	34	4
Ijaz Faqih	10	1	32	0

AUSTRALIA	O	M	R	W
Thomson	9.2	0	47	1
Alderman	10	0	20	2
Graf	10	0	34	0
Lawson	8	1	43	0
Yardley	3	0	21	0
Chappell	9	1	33	3

FALL OF WICKETS
1-48, 2-51, 3-71, 4-80, 5-102, 6-188, 7-197, 8-204, 9-209

FALL OF WICKETS
1-19, 2-21, 3-126, 4-139, 5-151, 6-184

Umpires: B.E.Martin (1) and R.V.Whitehead (7).

AUSTRALIA v WEST INDIES 1981-82

At Sydney Cricket Ground on 24 November 1981.　　Result: **AUSTRALIA** won by 7 wickets.　　Toss: West Indies.
Award: B.M.Laird.　　LOI debuts: None.

Match reduced to 49 overs by slow over rate (Australia were fined $600). Initially omitted from Australia's 'instant' team because of his slow scoring, Bruce Laird breezed to his only hundred in 23 LOI innings to ensure a comfortable win.

WEST INDIES		Runs	Balls	4/6
C.G.Greenidge	b Thomson	39	74	6
D.L.Haynes	c and b Thomson	30	51	2
I.V.A.Richards	run out	47	58	2
S.F.A.F.Bacchus	c Hughes b Thomson	4	9	–
* C.H.Lloyd	c Thomson b Lawson	63	59	7
† D.A.Murray	c Graf b Lawson	5	14	–
M.D.Marshall	not out	16	22	1
A.M.E.Roberts	run out	15	11	2
J.Garner	lbw b Alderman	1	3	–
M.A.Holding	not out	2	2	–
C.E.H.Croft				
Extras	(lb 7, w 5, nb 2)	14		
Total	(49 overs; 8 wickets)	236		

AUSTRALIA		Runs	Balls	4/6
W.M.Darling	c Murray b Holding	5	9	–
B.M.Laird	not out	117	159	10
* G.S.Chappell	lbw b Roberts	1	5	–
A.R.Border	run out	29	45	2/1
K.J.Hughes	not out	62	74	6
G.M.Wood				
† R.W.Marsh				
S.F.Graf				
G.F.Lawson				
J.R.Thomson				
T.M.Alderman				
Extras	(b 1, lb 13, w 4, nb 5)	23		
Total	(47 overs; 3 wickets)	237		

AUSTRALIA	O	M	R	W
Lawson	10	2	28	2
Alderman	10	0	35	1
Thomson	10	0	55	3
Graf	9	0	56	0
Chappell	10	0	48	0

WEST INDIES	O	M	R	W
Holding	10	0	34	1
Roberts	9	0	44	1
Marshall	10	0	45	0
Garner	9	0	43	0
Croft	9	0	48	0

FALL OF WICKETS
1-64, 2-89, 3-98, 4-170, 5-197, 6-197, 7-229, 8-232

FALL OF WICKETS
1-7, 2-8, 3-90

Umpires: A.R.Crafter (8) and M.W.Johnson (7).

WEST INDIES v PAKISTAN 1981-82

At Adelaide Oval on 5 December 1981.   Result: **PAKISTAN** won by 8 runs.   Toss: West Indies.
Award: Wasim Raja.   LOI debuts: West Indies – P.J.L.Dujon.

Match reduced to 49 overs by slow over rate. Pakistan gained their first win in eight LOI matches against West Indies. Wasim Raja, an occasional bowler, became the first leg-spinner to return a four-wicket analysis in these games.

PAKISTAN		Runs	Balls	4/6
Mudassar Nazar	c Greenidge b Holding	11	23	2
Mohsin Khan	run out	11	30	1
Zaheer Abbas	c Murray b Roberts	46	114	2
* Javed Miandad	lbw b Marshall	1	10	–
Wasim Raja	b Garner	1	3	–
Imran Khan	c Murray b Marshall	1	4	–
Ijaz Faqih	c Lloyd b Holding	20	47	1
† Ashraf Ali	c Bacchus b Richards	3	11	–
Sarfraz Nawaz	not out	34	42	2
Tahir Naqqash	run out	1	4	–
Sikander Bakht	run out	3	9	–
Extras	(b 1, lb 4, w 2, nb 1)	8		
Total	(49 overs)	**140**		

WEST INDIES		Runs	Balls	4/6
C.G.Greenidge	b Sarfraz	4	8	1
D.L.Haynes	c Ashraf b Tahir	7	34	–
I.V.A.Richards	c Ashraf b Sarfraz	9	17	–
S.F.A.F.Bacchus	b Wasim	37	67	2
* C.H.Lloyd	c Tahir b Ijaz	28	44	2
P.J.L.Dujon	b Wasim	0	7	–
M.D.Marshall	b Wasim	20	29	3
† D.A.Murray	lbw b Wasim	0	2	–
A.M.E.Roberts	b Imran	4	17	–
M.A.Holding	c Wasim b Imran	8	9	–/1
J.Garner	not out	1	8	–
Extras	(lb 7, w 2, nb 5)	14		
Total	(38.5 overs)	**132**		

WEST INDIES	O	M	R	W
Roberts	10	3	19	1
Holding	10	1	28	2
Garner	10	3	32	1
Marshall	9	0	18	2
Richards	10	1	35	1

PAKISTAN	O	M	R	W
Imran Khan	9.5	0	13	2
Sarfraz Nawaz	6	0	24	2
Sikander Bakht	4	0	11	0
Tahir Naqqash	6	0	25	1
Ijaz Faqih	6	0	20	1
Wasim Raja	7	0	25	4

FALL OF WICKETS
1-16, 2-27, 3-31, 4-34, 5-35, 6-63, 7-68, 8-125, 9-127, 10-140

FALL OF WICKETS
1-7, 2-19, 3-38, 4-85, 5-88, 6-107, 7-107, 8-120, 9-120, 10-132

Umpires: A.R.Crafter (9) and B.E.Martin (2).

AUSTRALIA v PAKISTAN 1981-82

At Adelaide Oval on 6 December 1981.   Result: **AUSTRALIA** won by 38 runs.   Toss: Australia.
Award: G.S.Chappell.   LOI debuts: None.

Surprisingly, Pakistan's chief destroyer of the previous day was not called upon to bowl.

AUSTRALIA		Runs	Balls	4/6
W.M.Darling	run out	35	74	–
B.M.Laird	lbw b Sikander	20	31	2
* G.S.Chappell	c Wasim b Ijaz	38	38	4
A.R.Border	c Wasim b Mudassar	25	29	2/1
K.J.Hughes	c Mudassar b Sarfraz	14	18	1
G.M.Wood	not out	43	54	3
† R.W.Marsh	c Ashraf b Mudassar	10	16	–
G.F.Lawson	b Sarfraz	2	7	–
D.K.Lillee	c Sarfraz b Imran	7	9	–
J.R.Thomson	b Imran	6	11	–
T.M.Alderman	c Ashraf b Imran	1	11	–
Extras	(lb 2, w 3, nb 2)	7		
Total	(48.3 overs)	**208**		

PAKISTAN		Runs	Balls	4/6
Mudassar Nazar	run out	14	45	–
Mohsin Khan	c Marsh b Chappell	27	62	1
Zaheer Abbas	c Alderman b Lawson	38	48	3
* Javed Miandad	c Alderman b Chappell	4	9	–
Wasim Raja	c Darling b Lawson	2	15	–
Imran Khan	c Darling b Alderman	18	34	–
Ijaz Faqih	c Marsh b Thomson	18	26	2
Sarfraz Nawaz	c Darling b Chappell	5	12	–
Tahir Naqqash	not out	21	39	–
† Ashraf Ali	not out	11	16	–
Sikander Bakht				
Extras	(lb 8, w 1, nb 3)	12		
Total	(50 overs; 8 wickets)	**170**		

PAKISTAN	O	M	R	W
Imran Khan	9.3	3	19	3
Sarfraz Nawaz	10	0	44	2
Sikander Bakht	9	0	29	1
Ijaz Faqih	7	0	43	1
Tahir Naqqash	6	0	41	0
Mudassar Nazar	7	0	25	2

AUSTRALIA	O	M	R	W
Alderman	10	1	26	1
Lawson	10	1	33	2
Chappell	10	1	31	3
Lillee	10	0	23	0
Thomson	10	0	45	1

FALL OF WICKETS
1-43, 2-84, 3-103, 4-136, 5-136, 6-169, 7-176, 8-187, 9-199, 10-208

FALL OF WICKETS
1-41, 2-57, 3-79, 4-84, 5-91, 6-121, 7-134, 8-138

Umpires: R.C.Bailhache (12) and R.A.French (10).

AUSTRALIA v PAKISTAN 1981-82

At Sydney Cricket Ground on 17 December 1981.   Result: **PAKISTAN** won by 6 wickets.   Toss: Pakistan.
Award: Mudassar Nazar.   LOI debuts: Australia – D.M.Wellham.

Postponed from 8 December because of a strike by power workers, this match featured the first of seven memorable LOI hundreds from Zaheer Abbas and an excellent all-round performance by Mudassar Nazar.

AUSTRALIA		Runs	Balls	4/6
W.M.Darling	run out	74	100	6
B.M.Laird	b Sikander	12	27	–
G.M.Wood	b Mudassar	25	48	3
A.R.Border	c Ashraf b Mudassar	2	8	–
D.M.Wellham	run out	42	69	–
* G.S.Chappell	c Miandad b Mudassar	0	4	–
† R.W.Marsh	not out	54	49	5/1
D.K.Lillee				
G.F.Lawson				
J.R.Thomson				
T.M.Alderman				
Extras	(b 2, lb 7, w 1, nb 3)	13		
Total	(50 overs; 6 wickets)	**222**		

PAKISTAN		Runs	Balls	4/6
Mudassar Nazar	c Alderman b Thomson	50	67	6
Mohsin Khan	b Lawson	2	13	–
Zaheer Abbas	b Chappell	108	110	12
* Javed Miandad	lbw b Chappell	22	32	2
Majid Khan	not out	20	34	2
Wasim Raja	not out	9	9	–
Imran Khan				
† Ashraf Ali				
Sarfraz Nawaz				
Tahir Naqqash				
Sikander Bakht				
Extras	(b 2, lb 5, w 4, nb 1)	12		
Total	(43.2 overs; 4 wickets)	**223**		

PAKISTAN	O	M	R	W
Imran Khan	10	0	47	0
Sikander Bakht	8	0	48	1
Sarfraz Nawaz	9	0	38	0
Tahir Naqqash	3	0	21	0
Majid Khan	10	0	35	0
Mudassar Nazar	10	4	20	3

AUSTRALIA	O	M	R	W
Lawson	9	0	43	1
Alderman	10	1	41	0
Lillee	8	1	38	0
Thomson	7	0	27	1
Border	3	0	24	0
Chappell	6.2	0	38	2

FALL OF WICKETS
1-40, 2-106, 3-110, 4-132, 5-132, 6-222

FALL OF WICKETS
1-15, 2-120, 3-174, 4-205

Umpires: R.A.French (11) and M.W.Johnson (8).

WEST INDIES v PAKISTAN 1981-82

At WACA Ground, Perth on 19 December 1981.   Result: **WEST INDIES** won by 7 wickets.   Toss: Pakistan.
Award: D.L.Haynes.   LOI debuts: West Indies – A.L.Logie.

Following two successive defeats and some strong words from their captain, West Indies recovered their true form. Jeff Dujon kept wicket at international level for the first time.

PAKISTAN		Runs	Balls	4/6
Mudassar Nazar	c Richards b Marshall	30	53	2
Mohsin Khan	c Lloyd b Garner	6	30	1
Zaheer Abbas	c Dujon b Richards	35	61	3
* Javed Miandad	c Bacchus b Richards	21	41	1
Wasim Raja	c Haynes b Richards	17	34	1
Imran Khan	not out	29	44	1
Ijaz Faqih	c Haynes b Garner	2	5	–
Sarfraz Nawaz	c Roberts b Garner	0	1	–
† Wasim Bari	run out	4	4	–
Sikander Bakht	c Dujon b Marshall	0	4	–
Majid Khan	absent hurt	–	–	–
Extras	(b 4, lb 3, w 2, nb 7)	16		
Total	(44.4 overs)	**160**		

WEST INDIES		Runs	Balls	4/6
D.L.Haynes	not out	82	135	12
S.F.A.F.Bacchus	c Wasim Bari b Imran	4	7	–
I.V.A.Richards	c Wasim Bari b Sarfraz	8	14	1
* C.H.Lloyd	c and b Wasim Raja	32	50	4
H.A.Gomes	not out	26	54	2
† P.J.L.Dujon				
A.L.Logie				
M.D.Marshall				
M.A.Holding				
J.Garner				
A.M.E.Roberts				
Extras	(b 1, lb 3, w 2, nb 3)	9		
Total	(42.2 overs; 3 wickets)	**161**		

WEST INDIES	O	M	R	W
Holding	8	1	15	0
Roberts	8	1	21	0
Garner	9	1	23	3
Marshall	9.4	0	33	2
Richards	10	0	52	3

PAKISTAN	O	M	R	W
Imran Khan	8.2	0	38	1
Sarfraz Nawaz	10	1	29	1
Sikander Bakht	6	0	27	0
Mudassar Nazar	1	0	1	0
Ijaz Faqih	6	0	30	0
Wasim Raja	10	1	26	1
Javed Miandad	1	0	1	0

FALL OF WICKETS
1-29, 2-61, 3-106, 4-107, 5-148, 6-151, 7-152, 8-156, 9-160

FALL OF WICKETS
1-5, 2-21, 3-95

Umpires: B.E.Martin (3) and R.V.Whitehead (8).

AUSTRALIA v WEST INDIES 1981-82

At WACA Ground, Perth on 20 December 1981.   Result: **WEST INDIES** won by 8 wickets.   Toss: West Indies.
Award: C.H.Lloyd.   LOI debuts: None.

Blitzed by the West Indies pace quartet on a fast pitch, Australia were then subjected to a (then) record LOI third-wicket partnership of 153 (unbroken) between Viv Richards and Clive Lloyd in peak form.

AUSTRALIA		Runs	Balls	4/6
W.M.Darling	b Holding	7	12	–
B.M.Laird	lbw b Marshall	7	29	–
* G.S.Chappell	c Haynes b Holding	0	1	–
A.R.Border	c Bacchus b Marshall	27	67	–
K.J.Hughes	c Holding b Marshall	18	27	2
G.M.Wood	run out	54	83	6
† R.W.Marsh	c Logie b Richards	0	5	–
D.K.Lillee	not out	42	61	3
G.F.Lawson	b Garner	0	3	–
J.R.Thomson	run out	5	13	1
T.M.Alderman	not out	9	7	1
Extras	(lb 12, w 5, nb 2)	19		
Total	(50 overs; 9 wickets)	**188**		

WEST INDIES		Runs	Balls	4/6
D.L.Haynes	c Chappell b Lillee	9	15	1
S.F.A.F.Bacchus	c Thomson b Alderman	21	29	4
I.V.A.Richards	not out	72	62	8/3
* C.H.Lloyd	not out	80	82	11
H.A.Gomes				
† P.J.L.Dujon				
A.L.Logie				
M.D.Marshall				
A.M.E.Roberts				
M.A.Holding				
J.Garner				
Extras	(w 4, nb 4)	8		
Total	(30 overs; 2 wickets)	**190**		

WEST INDIES	O	M	R	W
Holding	10	0	37	2
Roberts	10	1	26	0
Garner	10	1	32	1
Marshall	10	0	31	3
Richards	10	0	43	1

AUSTRALIA	O	M	R	W
Lillee	6	1	36	1
Alderman	8	1	41	1
Thomson	5	0	24	0
Lawson	6	0	46	0
Chappell	5	0	35	0

FALL OF WICKETS
1-10, 2-10, 3-30, 4-62, 5-78, 6-80, 7-150, 8-150, 9-166

FALL OF WICKETS
1-23, 2-37

Umpires: R.C.Bailhache (13) and A.R.Crafter (10).

AUSTRALIA v PAKISTAN 1981-82

At Melbourne Cricket Ground on 9 January 1982.   Result: **PAKISTAN** won by 25 runs.   Toss: Australia.
Award: Zaheer Abbas.   LOI debuts: None.

Four run outs contributed heavily to Australia's failure to achieve a modest target.

PAKISTAN		Runs	Balls	4/6
Mudassar Nazar	lbw b Thomson	40	80	4
Mansoor Akhtar	c Marsh b Alderman	5	4	–
Zaheer Abbas	c Laird b Thomson	84	113	–
* Javed Miandad	c Darling b Lillee	37	62	1
Imran Khan	run out	3	5	–
Wasim Raja	not out	19	23	2
Ijaz Faqih	run out	1	2	–
Sarfraz Nawaz	not out	14	16	1
† Wasim Bari				
Tahir Naqqash				
Sikander Bakht				
Extras	(lb 10, w 1, nb 4)	15		
Total	(50 overs; 6 wickets)	**218**		

AUSTRALIA		Runs	Balls	4/6
G.M.Wood	c Wasim Raja b Mudassar	38	77	2
B.M.Laird	run out	4	6	–
J.Dyson	lbw b Sikander	11	33	–
* G.S.Chappell	b Ijaz	35	50	1
A.R.Border	not out	75	85	5
W.M.Darling	run out	5	12	–
† R.W.Marsh	c Miandad b Ijaz	2	6	–
D.K.Lillee	run out	8	15	–
G.F.Lawson	run out	1	3	–
J.R.Thomson	b Imran	2	4	–
T.M.Alderman	b Sikander	0	4	–
Extras	(b 4, lb 8)	12		
Total	(49 overs)	**193**		

AUSTRALIA	O	M	R	W
Lawson	10	0	36	0
Alderman	10	0	37	1
Lillee	10	1	37	1
Thomson	10	0	55	2
Chappell	10	0	38	0

PAKISTAN	O	M	R	W
Imran Khan	9	2	21	1
Sarfraz Nawaz	8	0	34	0
Tahir Naqqash	8	0	35	0
Sikander Bakht	8	0	33	2
Mudassar Nazar	6	0	24	1
Ijaz Faqih	10	0	34	2

FALL OF WICKETS
1-10, 2-79, 3-169, 4-172, 5-193, 6-199

FALL OF WICKETS
1-5, 2-41, 3-74, 4-135, 5-147, 6-153, 7-175, 8-182, 9-190, 10-193

Umpires: A.R.Crafter (11) and R.V.Whitehead (9).

AUSTRALIA v WEST INDIES 1981-82

At Melbourne Cricket Ground on 10 January 1982.   Result: **WEST INDIES** won by 5 wickets.   Toss: Australia.
Award: P.J.L.Dujon.   LOI debuts: None.

The attendance of 78,142 was the world record for a limited-overs match until *LOI No. 174* was played on the same ground a year later.

AUSTRALIA		Runs	Balls	4/6
B.M.Laird	hit wicket b Holding	4	13	–
G.M.Wood	c Greenidge b Holding	3	7	–
R.B.McCosker	run out	20	31	2
* G.S.Chappell	c Logie b Roberts	59	96	2
A.R.Border	b Marshall	6	12	–
W.M.Darling	c Holding b Gomes	20	51	–
† R.W.Marsh	c Logie b Gomes	0	8	–
B.Yardley	c Logie b Holding	23	27	1
D.K.Lillee	c Holding b Roberts	1	9	–
G.F.Lawson	not out	0	2	–
M.F.Malone	b Holding	1	6	–
Extras	(lb 4, w 1, nb 4)	9		
Total	(42.5 overs)	**146**		

WEST INDIES		Runs	Balls	4/6
C.G.Greenidge	c Border b Malone	9	27	–
D.L.Haynes	lbw b Lawson	1	13	–
I.V.A.Richards	c Lawson b Yardley	32	64	2
H.A.Gomes	c Laird b Malone	7	41	–
* C.H.Lloyd	lbw b Lawson	37	57	2/1
† P.J.L.Dujon	not out	51	80	5
M.D.Marshall	not out	5	4	–
A.L.Logie				
A.M.E.Roberts				
M.A.Holding				
J.Garner				
Extras	(lb 3, w 1, nb 1)	5		
Total	(47.1 overs; 5 wickets)	**147**		

WEST INDIES	O	M	R	W
Holding	7.5	1	32	4
Roberts	7	0	23	2
Garner	6	0	13	0
Marshall	5	0	12	1
Richards	10	1	31	0
Gomes	7	1	26	2

AUSTRALIA	O	M	R	W
Lillee	10	0	34	0
Lawson	9.1	0	31	2
Malone	10	5	9	2
Chappell	9	1	33	0
Yardley	6	0	25	1
Border	3	0	10	0

FALL OF WICKETS
1-7, 2-16, 3-33, 4-41, 5-99, 6-101, 7-140, 8-144, 9-145, 10-146

FALL OF WICKETS
1-7, 2-18, 3-48, 4-52, 5-137

Umpires: R.C.Bailhache (14) and B.E.Martin (4).

WEST INDIES v PAKISTAN 1981-82

At Sydney Cricket Ground on 12 January 1982.   Result: **WEST INDIES** won by 7 wickets.   Toss: Pakistan.
Award: C.G.Greenidge.   LOI debuts: Pakistan – Salim Malik.

Sarfraz Nawaz declined to play in Pakistan's first day/night game as he felt unable to see properly when wearing glasses under floodlights. West Indies qualified for the finals with this emphatic win. Gus Logie appeared in four games without batting or bowling.

PAKISTAN		Runs	Balls	4/6
Mohsin Khan	b Marshall	12	31	2
Mansoor Akhtar	run out	13	32	–
Zaheer Abbas	run out	1	5	–
* Javed Miandad	c Dujon b Garner	26	61	1
Wasim Raja	c Logie b Roberts	33	61	1/1
Salim Malik	b Garner	0	2	–
Imran Khan	not out	62	79	5
Ijaz Faqih	b Garner	5	13	–
Tahir Naqqash	not out	23	20	2
† Wasim Bari				
Sikander Bakht				
Extras	(b 1, lb 5, w 7, nb 3)	16		
Total	(50 overs; 7 wickets)	**191**		

WEST INDIES		Runs	Balls	4/6
C.G.Greenidge	lbw b Imran	84	122	9/3
D.L.Haynes	b Imran	2	14	–
I.V.A.Richards	b Tahir	41	49	7
* C.H.Lloyd	not out	35	53	2
H.A.Gomes	not out	15	25	–
† P.J.L.Dujon				
A.L.Logie				
M.D.Marshall				
A.M.E.Roberts				
M.A.Holding				
J.Garner				
Extras	(lb 5, w 5, nb 5)	15		
Total	(42.1 overs; 3 wickets)	**192**		

WEST INDIES	O	M	R	W
Holding	10	1	37	0
Roberts	10	0	47	1
Marshall	10	1	33	1
Garner	10	1	17	3
Richards	10	0	41	0

PAKISTAN	O	M	R	W
Imran Khan	10	0	42	2
Sikander Bakht	7	1	40	0
Wasim Raja	9.1	0	37	0
Tahir Naqqash	10	0	31	1
Ijaz Faqih	6	0	27	0

FALL OF WICKETS
1-26, 2-32, 3-32, 4-75, 5-75, 6-122, 7-144

FALL OF WICKETS
1-37, 2-107, 3-155

Umpires: M.W.Johnson (9) and B.E.Martin (5).

AUSTRALIA v PAKISTAN 1981-82

At Sydney Cricket Ground on 14 January 1982.   Result: **AUSTRALIA** won by 76 runs.   Toss: Pakistan.
Award: K.J.Hughes.   LOI debuts: None.

Australia posted their highest total of this season's tournament when batting first and defended it with ease.

AUSTRALIA		Runs	Balls	4/6
G.M.Wood	b Mudassar	42	73	3
B.M.Laird	c Wasim Bari b Mudassar	45	83	3
R.B.McCosker	lbw b Mudassar	13	29	–
* G.S.Chappell	c Wasim Raja b Sikander	36	38	3
K.J.Hughes	not out	63	73	4/1
† R.W.Marsh	c Zaheer b Imran	3	5	
A.R.Border	not out	11	6	2
D.K.Lillee				
G.F.Lawson				
J.R.Thomson				
M.F.Malone				
Extras	(b 3, lb 8, w 3, nb 3)	17		
Total	(50 overs; 5 wickets)	**230**		

PAKISTAN		Runs	Balls	4/6
Mudassar Nazar	b Lillee	5	13	1
Mansoor Akhtar	c Lawson b Chappell	40	55	4
Zaheer Abbas	c Border b Lawson	12	18	1
* Javed Miandad	lbw b Chappell	8	29	–
Wasim Raja	b Malone	16	23	1
Imran Khan	b Thomson	39	59	1
Ijaz Faqih	c Marsh b Malone	0	2	–
Sarfraz Nawaz	c Hughes b Lillee	5	15	–
Tahir Naqqash	c Lillee b Lawson	13	19	–
† Wasim Bari	retired hurt	9	11	–
Sikander Bakht	not out	0	1	–
Extras	(lb 6, w 1)	7		
Total	(40.3 overs)	**154**		

PAKISTAN	O	M	R	W
Imran Khan	10	0	37	1
Sarfraz Nawaz	9	0	45	0
Tahir Naqqash	5	2	20	0
Sikander Bakht	9	0	43	1
Mudassar Nazar	10	1	36	3
Ijaz Faqih	7	0	32	0

AUSTRALIA	O	M	R	W
Lillee	7.3	1	23	2
Thomson	7	1	19	2
Lawson	8	0	45	2
Malone	10	2	36	2
Chappell	8	0	24	2

FALL OF WICKETS
1-80, 2-108, 3-111, 4-198, 5-206

FALL OF WICKETS
1-8, 2-30, 3-66, 4-71, 5-89, 6-89, 7-99, 8-129, 9-150

Umpires: R.A.French (12) and R.V.Whitehead (10).

WEST INDIES v PAKISTAN 1981-82

At Woolloongabba, Brisbane on 16 January 1982.   Result: **WEST INDIES** won by 1 wicket (revised target).
Toss: West Indies.   Award: S.F.A.F.Bacchus.   LOI debuts: None.

An hour's delay, following a storm after Pakistan's innings, reduced West Indies' allotment to 30 overs and their target to 107 runs. Pakistan would have reached the finals at Australia's expense had they not allowed the last-wicket pair to scramble two singles.

PAKISTAN		Runs	Balls	4/6
Mudassar Nazar	run out	40	90	2
Mansoor Akhtar	c Greenidge b Holding	4	29	–
Zaheer Abbas	c Lloyd b Richards	17	49	–/1
* Javed Miandad	c Lloyd b Roberts	25	32	2
Imran Khan	c Dujon b Garner	31	28	4/1
Wasim Raja	retired hurt	12	29	–
Majid Khan	c Dujon b Holding	10	13	1
† Ashraf Ali	run out	3	22	–
Sarfraz Nawaz	c Clarke b Garner	10	10	1
Iqbal Qasim	c Greenidge b Garner	2	5	–
Sikander Bakht	not out	1	1	–
Extras	(b 2, lb 12, w 6, nb 2)	22		
Total	(50 overs)	**177**		

WEST INDIES		Runs	Balls	4/6
C.G.Greenidge	b Sarfraz	7	14	–
D.L.Haynes	c sub (Mohsin Khan) b Sarfraz	13	44	1
I.V.A.Richards	c Imran b Sarfraz	0	3	–
H.A.Gomes	b Sikander	13	35	–
* C.H.Lloyd	c Mudassar b Sikander	1	2	–
S.F.A.F.Bacchus	not out	36	42	3
A.M.E.Roberts	c Sarfraz b Mudassar	1	2	–
† P.J.L.Dujon	c and b Sikander	13	14	2
S.T.Clarke	c Ashraf b Imran	1	8	–
M.A.Holding	c Ashraf b Mudassar	8	14	–/1
J.Garner	not out	1	3	–
Extras	(b 4, lb 4, w 5)	13		
Total	(28.5 overs; 9 wickets)	**107**		

WEST INDIES	O	M	R	W
Holding	10	3	23	2
Clarke	10	2	28	0
Roberts	10	1	33	1
Garner	10	1	19	3
Richards	10	0	52	1

PAKISTAN	O	M	R	W
Imran Khan	10	1	23	1
Sarfraz Nawaz	10	1	31	3
Sikander Bakht	6.5	0	29	3
Mudassar Nazar	2	0	11	2

FALL OF WICKETS
1-16, 2-57, 3-101, 4-111, 5-115, 6-161, 7-165, 8-175, 9-177

FALL OF WICKETS
1-12, 2-12, 3-36, 4-38, 5-61, 6-69, 7-83, 8-90, 9-105

Umpires: R.A.French (13) and R.V.Whitehead (11).

AUSTRALIA v WEST INDIES 1981-82

At Woolloongabba, Brisbane on 17 January 1982.　　Result: **WEST INDIES** won by 5 wickets.　Toss: West Indies.
Award: H.A.Gomes.　　LOI debuts: None.

A storm mid-way through Australia's innings caused the match to be reduced to 40 overs. Viv Richards captained as Clive Lloyd was unwell. West Indies' sixth consecutive win was watched by a capacity crowd of 22,610.

AUSTRALIA		Runs	Balls	4/6
B.M.Laird	b Garner	26	51	3
G.M.Wood	c Lloyd b Richards	15	66	–
R.B.McCosker	c Bacchus b Clarke	18	44	1
* G.S.Chappell	c Greenidge b Garner	61	43	8
K.J.Hughes	st Dujon b Richards	2	11	–
A.R.Border	c Garner b Holding	20	17	2
† R.W.Marsh	c Greenidge b Garner	7	7	–
J.R.Thomson	b Holding	0	4	–
D.K.Lillee	c Holding b Garner	11	6	1/1
G.F.Lawson	not out	4	1	1
M.F.Malone	not out	0	–	–
Extras	(b 2, lb 9, w 9, nb 1)	21		
Total	(40 overs; 9 wickets)	**185**		

WEST INDIES		Runs	Balls	4/6
C.G.Greenidge	c Wood b Chappell	16	33	2
D.L.Haynes	c Marsh b Lillee	11	28	1
* I.V.A.Richards	c Lillee b Thomson	34	47	2
H.A.Gomes	not out	56	84	2
S.F.A.F.Bacchus	run out	20	12	2
C.H.Lloyd	c Border b Thomson	30	28	4
† P.J.L.Dujon	not out	6	7	1
A.M.E.Roberts				
S.T.Clarke				
M.A.Holding				
J.Garner				
Extras	(lb 7, w 4, nb 2)	13		
Total	(38.4 overs; 5 wickets)	**186**		

WEST INDIES	O	M	R	W
Holding	8	1	38	2
Clarke	9	1	22	1
Garner	9	0	45	4
Roberts	5	1	11	0
Richards	7	0	36	2
Gomes	2	0	12	0

AUSTRALIA	O	M	R	W
Lillee	9	2	32	1
Thomson	10	2	40	2
Malone	10	1	34	0
Chappell	4	0	22	1
Lawson	5.4	0	45	0

FALL OF WICKETS
1-51, 2-58, 3-97, 4-113, 5-159, 6-161, 7-165, 8-181, 9-181

FALL OF WICKETS
1-27, 2-32, 3-94, 4-116, 5-174

Umpires: A.R.Crafter (12) and M.W.Johnson (10).

AUSTRALIA v WEST INDIES 1981-82

At Sydney Cricket Ground on 19 January 1982.　　Result: **AUSTRALIA** won on faster scoring rate.　Toss: Australia.
Award: A.M.E.Roberts.　　LOI debuts: None.

A boundary by Allan Border off the final ball before rain ended play gave Australia victory by 0.11 of a run per over. They qualified for the finals by virtue of a faster scoring rate in the preliminary matches (West Indies 14 points, Australia and Pakistan 8 each). The attendance of 52,053 was then a record for a day/night match.

WEST INDIES		Runs	Balls	4/6
C.G.Greenidge	b Lillee	1	2	–
D.L.Haynes	b Malone	5	29	–
* I.V.A.Richards	b Thomson	64	94	6
H.A.Gomes	c Marsh b Pascoe	3	14	–
S.F.A.F.Bacchus	c Hughes b Malone	20	39	1
† P.J.L.Dujon	b Thomson	30	56	2
M.D.Marshall	not out	32	43	1
A.M.E.Roberts	c Wood b Pascoe	9	13	1
M.A.Holding	c Marsh b Pascoe	0	1	–
S.T.Clarke	b Lillee	16	10	2
J.Garner	run out	2	3	–
Extras	(lb 5, w 1, nb 1)	7		
Total	(50 overs)	**189**		

AUSTRALIA		Runs	Balls	4/6
G.M.Wood	c Roberts b Holding	1	7	–
W.M.Darling	c Clarke b Roberts	34	61	3
J.Dyson	b Garner	37	75	2
* G.S.Chappell	lbw b Roberts	0	2	–
K.J.Hughes	b Roberts	25	56	–
A.R.Border	not out	30	46	3
† R.W.Marsh	c Greenidge b Marshall	12	16	1
D.K.Lillee	b Holding	6	4	1
L.S.Pascoe	not out	0	1	–
J.R.Thomson				
M.F.Malone				
Extras	(lb 16, w 5, nb 2)	23		
Total	(43.1 overs; 7 wickets)	**168**		

AUSTRALIA	O	M	R	W
Lillee	10	0	47	2
Thomson	10	1	36	2
Pascoe	10	0	44	3
Malone	10	1	27	2
Chappell	10	0	28	0

WEST INDIES	O	M	R	W
Holding	6.1	0	34	2
Clarke	10	1	20	0
Marshall	10	0	43	1
Roberts	10	3	15	3
Garner	7	0	33	1

FALL OF WICKETS
1-2, 2-23, 3-40, 4-79, 5-103, 6-137, 7-155, 8-156, 9-182, 10-189

FALL OF WICKETS
1-6, 2-57, 3-61, 4-97, 5-125, 6-144, 7-157

Umpires: R.C.Bailhache (15) and M.W.Johnson (11).

69

AUSTRALIA v WEST INDIES 1981-82

At Melbourne Cricket Ground on 23 January 1982.   Result: **WEST INDIES** won by 86 runs.   Toss: Australia.
LOI debuts: None.

Match reduced to 49 overs by slow over rate. West Indies cruised to victory on the back of exceptional innings by Gordon Greenidge and Viv Richards on an extremely slow pitch of uneven bounce.

WEST INDIES		Runs	Balls	4/6
C.G.Greenidge	b Lillee	59	112	4
D.L.Haynes	c Marsh b Pascoe	13	27	2
I.V.A.Richards	c Wood b Chappell	78	97	6/1
* C.H.Lloyd	c Pascoe b Thomson	20	24	1
S.F.A.F.Bacchus	c Marsh b Thomson	2	6	–
† P.J.L.Dujon	c Hughes b Pascoe	6	13	–
H.A.Gomes	run out	6	13	–
A.M.E.Roberts	run out	5	5	–
M.A.Holding	not out	7	8	–
S.T.Clarke	not out	0	–	–
J.Garner				
Extras	(lb 5, w 12, nb 3)	20		
Total	(49 overs; 8 wickets)	**216**		

AUSTRALIA		O	M	R	W
Lillee		10	3	35	1
Thomson		10	1	44	2
Malone		10	2	25	0
Pascoe		9	1	33	2
Chappell		10	0	59	1

FALL OF WICKETS
1-26, 2-138, 3-179, 4-184, 5-197, 6-198, 7-204, 8-210

AUSTRALIA		Runs	Balls	4/6
W.M.Darling	c Bacchus b Garner	14	20	–
G.M.Wood	run out	19	57	4
J.Dyson	b Clarke	0	2	–
* G.S.Chappell	lbw b Garner	4	12	–
K.J.Hughes	b Richards	4	18	–
A.R.Border	c and b Gomes	16	23	1
† R.W.Marsh	c Bacchus b Clarke	32	31	3/1
D.K.Lillee	b Clarke	11	18	1
J.R.Thomson	b Holding	5	9	–
L.S.Pascoe	not out	3	21	–
M.F.Malone	st Dujon b Gomes	10	18	1
Extras	(b 4, lb 5, w 2, nb 1)	12		
Total	(37.4 overs)	**130**		

WEST INDIES		O	M	R	W
Holding		8	1	19	1
Roberts		5	1	16	0
Clarke		9	1	22	3
Garner		6	3	7	2
Richards		5	1	29	1
Gomes		4.4	0	25	2

FALL OF WICKETS
1-30, 2-30, 3-43, 4-43, 5-56, 6-64, 7-107, 8-110, 9-117, 10-130

Umpires: M.W.Johnson (12) and R.V.Whitehead (12).

AUSTRALIA v WEST INDIES 1981-82

At Melbourne Cricket Ground on 24 January 1982.   Result: **WEST INDIES** won by 128 runs.   Toss: West Indies.
LOI debuts: None.

More of the same, again in intense heat and before a disappointing crowd, by MCG standards, of around 25,000.

WEST INDIES		Runs	Balls	4/6
C.G.Greenidge	c Marsh b Malone	47	62	7
D.L.Haynes	c Dyson b Pascoe	52	85	3
I.V.A.Richards	c Dyson b Chappell	60	83	3/1
S.F.A.F.Bacchus	c Malone b Thomson	31	25	5
* C.H.Lloyd	not out	22	23	2
† P.J.L.Dujon	b Lillee	5	11	–
A.M.E.Roberts	b Pascoe	0	4	–
S.T.Clarke	b Pascoe	5	8	–
M.A.Holding	b Pascoe	0	3	–
J.Garner	run out	0	1	–
H.A.Gomes				
Extras	(b 2, lb 9, w 2)	13		
Total	(50 overs; 9 wickets)	**235**		

AUSTRALIA		O	M	R	W
Lillee		10	0	53	1
Pascoe		10	1	39	4
Thomson		10	1	31	1
Malone		10	0	37	1
Chappell		10	0	62	1

FALL OF WICKETS
1-65, 2-150, 3-200, 4-204, 5-220, 6-225, 7-235, 8-235, 9-235

AUSTRALIA		Runs	Balls	4/6
G.M.Wood	c Haynes b Clarke	7	21	1
B.M.Laird	c Haynes b Roberts	13	44	2
A.R.Border	c Dujon b Roberts	13	13	1
* G.S.Chappell	b Garner	1	8	–
K.J.Hughes	lbw b Garner	0	1	–
J.Dyson	b Clarke	18	35	1
† R.W.Marsh	b Gomes	15	34	1
D.K.Lillee	c Dujon b Gomes	0	3	–
J.R.Thomson	b Gomes	15	15	1/1
L.S.Pascoe	lbw b Gomes	0	1	–
M.F.Malone	not out	15	24	3
Extras	(b 2, lb 3, w 4, nb 1)	10		
Total	(32.2 overs)	**107**		

WEST INDIES		O	M	R	W
Holding		10	3	25	0
Clarke		6.2	1	15	2
Garner		5	2	10	2
Roberts		5	1	16	2
Gomes		6	1	31	4

FALL OF WICKETS
1-14, 2-42, 3-43, 4-43, 5-43, 6-65, 7-65, 8-81, 9-81, 10-107

Umpires: R.C.Bailhache (16) and R.A.French (14).

AUSTRALIA v WEST INDIES 1981-82

At Sydney Cricket Ground on 26 January 1982.   Result: **AUSTRALIA** won by 46 runs.   Toss: West Indies.
LOI debuts: None.

Australia avoided a finals whitewash by maintaining their total supremacy over West Indies in day/night contests.

AUSTRALIA		Runs	Balls	4/6
B.M.Laird	c Richards b Clarke	14	37	1
G.M.Wood	c and b Gomes	45	77	5
G.S.Chappell	b Garner	0	5	–
K.J.Hughes	b Holding	28	50	4
A.R.Border	not out	69	67	7
D.W.Hookes	c Dujon b Holding	1	5	–
R.W.Marsh	b Clarke	20	23	2
D.K.Lillee	b Clarke	1	2	–
J.R.Thomson	c Dujon b Roberts	7	14	–
L.S.Pascoe	not out	15	21	1
M.F.Malone				
Extras	(lb 13, nb 1)	14		
Total	(50 overs; 8 wickets)	**214**		

WEST INDIES		Runs	Balls	4/6
C.G.Greenidge	lbw b Lillee	5	22	–
D.L.Haynes	c Chappell b Pascoe	26	45	3
I.V.A.Richards	lbw b Lillee	4	10	1
H.A.Gomes	c Marsh b Thomson	0	9	–
* C.H.Lloyd	not out	63	87	4
S.F.A.F.Bacchus	run out	19	22	3
† P.J.L.Dujon	c sub (J.Dyson) b Malone	10	20	1
A.M.E.Roberts	lbw b Chappell	1	5	–
M.A.Holding	c Thomson b Chappell	6	18	–
S.T.Clarke	run out	16	20	1
J.Garner	c sub (J.Dyson) b Pascoe	3	8	–
Extras	(b 1, lb 3, w 9, nb 2)	15		
Total	(42.5 overs)	**168**		

WEST INDIES	O	M	R	W
Holding	10	2	32	2
Clarke	10	2	30	3
Garner	10	0	42	1
Roberts	10	1	50	1
Gomes	10	0	46	1

AUSTRALIA	O	M	R	W
Lillee	10	4	18	2
Thomson	6	0	38	1
Pascoe	6.5	1	21	2
Malone	10	1	33	1
Chappell	10	1	43	2

FALL OF WICKETS
1-19, 2-20, 3-94, 4-100, 5-103, 6-145, 7-147, 8-167

FALL OF WICKETS
1-20, 2-34, 3-41, 4-41, 5-68, 6-88, 7-95, 8-113, 9-164, 10-168

Umpires: A.R.Crafter (13) and B.E.Martin (6).

AUSTRALIA v WEST INDIES 1981-82

At Sydney Cricket Ground on 27 January 1982.   Result: **WEST INDIES** won by 18 runs.   Toss: West Indies.
Finals award: I.V.A.Richards.   LOI debuts: None.

After six defeats, West Indies gained their first victory against Australia in a match involving floodlit play to win the Benson and Hedges Cup for the second time.

WEST INDIES		Runs	Balls	4/6
C.G.Greenidge	b Malone	64	124	1/1
D.L.Haynes	lbw b Lillee	8	25	1
I.V.A.Richards	run out	70	88	4/1
S.F.A.F.Bacchus	b Thomson	17	17	1
* C.H.Lloyd	not out	41	30	6
† P.J.L.Dujon	b Pascoe	13	13	1
A.M.E.Roberts	b Thomson	5	3	1
S.T.Clarke	not out	2	2	–
H.A.Gomes				
M.A.Holding				
J.Garner				
Extras	(lb 14)	14		
Total	(50 overs; 6 wickets)	**234**		

AUSTRALIA		Runs	Balls	4/6
G.M.Wood	c Lloyd b Holding	69	107	2
B.M.Laird	lbw b Garner	13	32	2
* G.S.Chappell	c Richards b Clarke	10	18	1
K.J.Hughes	c Lloyd b Richards	27	39	2/1
A.R.Border	b Richards	23	33	1
D.W.Hookes	c Greenidge b Garner	17	28	–
† R.W.Marsh	c Gomes b Roberts	5	6	–
L.S.Pascoe	b Roberts	7	15	–
J.R.Thomson	not out	19	18	–
D.K.Lillee	b Roberts	4	2	1
M.F.Malone	not out	5	6	–
Extras	(b 4, lb 10, w 2, nb 1)	17		
Total	(50 overs; 9 wickets)	**216**		

AUSTRALIA	O	M	R	W
Lillee	10	4	30	1
Thomson	10	0	60	2
Pascoe	10	1	46	1
Malone	10	1	50	1
Chappell	10	2	34	0

WEST INDIES	O	M	R	W
Holding	10	1	36	1
Clarke	10	3	40	1
Garner	10	1	27	2
Roberts	10	0	48	3
Richards	10	0	48	2

FALL OF WICKETS
1-13, 2-151, 3-155, 4-198, 5-224, 6-229

FALL OF WICKETS
1-37, 2-57, 3-102, 4-135, 5-163, 6-173, 7-176, 8-194, 9-198,

Umpires: A.R.Crafter (14) and B.E.Martin (7).

INDIA v ENGLAND 1981-82

At Sardar Patel Stadium, Ahmedabad on 25 November 1981.   Result: **ENGLAND** won by 5 wickets.   Toss: England.
Award: M.W.Gatting.   LOI debuts: India – Randhir Singh, R.J.Shastri, K.Srikkanth; England – G.Cook, C.J.Richards.
46-over match.

India staged its first home limited-overs international more than a decade after the inaugural match. Intended to be 50-over affairs, the duration of these three Wills Series games was decided by the number of overs completed by the cut-off point of the lunch interval. Ian Botham completed proceedings by sweeping and pulling successive sixes.

INDIA		Runs	Balls	4/6
* S.M.Gavaskar	c Gooch b Willis	0		
K.Srikkanth	b Botham	0		
D.B.Vengsarkar	c and b Underwood	46	89	8
G.R.Viswanath	c Cook b Gooch	8		
K.Azad	b Botham	30	61	2/1
Madan Lal	c Lever b Underwood	6		
† S.M.H.Kirmani	not out	18		
R.J.Shastri	run out	19		
R.M.H.Binny	not out	2		
D.R.Doshi				
Randhir Singh				
Extras	(b 4, lb 13, w 7, nb 3)	27		
Total	(46 overs; 7 wickets)	**156**		

ENGLAND		Runs	Balls	4/6
G.A.Gooch	c Kirmani b Binny	23		4
G.Boycott	lbw b Madan Lal	5		
G.Cook	c Viswanath b Binny	13		1
D.I.Gower	c and b Binny	8		1
* K.W.R.Fletcher	b Doshi	26	65	2
M.W.Gatting	not out	47		5
I.T.Botham	not out	25		1/2
† C.J.Richards				
J.K.Lever				
D.L.Underwood				
R.G.D.Willis				
Extras	(lb 7, w 2, nb 4)	13		
Total	(43.5 overs; 5 wickets)	**160**		

ENGLAND	O	M	R	W
Willis	9	3	17	1
Botham	10	4	20	2
Lever	10	0	46	0
Gooch	7	0	28	1
Underwood	10	3	18	2

INDIA	O	M	R	W
Madan Lal	10	2	30	1
Randhir Singh	6	0	18	0
Binny	7.5	3	35	3
Shastri	10	1	24	0
Doshi	10	1	40	0

FALL OF WICKETS
1-2, 2-8, 3-39, 4-91, 5-113, 6-119, 7-154

FALL OF WICKETS
1-5, 2-43, 3-46, 4-61, 5-126,

Umpires: M.V.Gothoskar (1) and S.N.Hanumantha Rao (1).

INDIA v ENGLAND 1981-82

At Burlton Park, Jullundur on 20 December 1981.   Result: **INDIA** won by 6 wickets.   Toss: India.
Award: D.B.Vengsarkar.   LOI debuts: India – S.V.Nayak. 36-over match.

India gained their first limited-overs victory against England in five attempts, the contest being drastically reduced by early-morning mist. Mike Gatting struck 26 runs, including four sixes off five balls, during an over from Ravi Shastri.

ENGLAND		Runs	Balls	4/6
G.A.Gooch	b Madan Lal	12		
G.Boycott	run out	6		
I.T.Botham	lbw b Madan Lal	5		
* K.W.R.Fletcher	c Azad b Patil	5		
D.I.Gower	run out	53		
M.W.Gatting	not out	71	58	4/4
G.Cook	b Kapil Dev	1		
† C.J.Richards	lbw b Kapil Dev	0		
J.K.Lever				
D.L.Underwood				
R.G.D.Willis				
Extras	(b 2, lb 4, w 1, nb 1)	8		
Total	(36 overs; 7 wickets)	**161**		

INDIA		Runs	Balls	4/6
K.Srikkanth	lbw b Botham	17		3
D.B.Vengsarkar	not out	88		9
K.Azad	c Gower b Gooch	14		1
S.M.Patil	b Gooch	3		–
Kapil Dev	c Willis b Underwood	6		1
Yashpal Sharma	not out	28		1/1
* S.M.Gavaskar				
S.V.Nayak				
Madan Lal				
† S.M.H.Kirmani				
R.J.Shastri				
Extras	(b 3, lb 3, nb 2)	8		
Total	(35.3 overs; 4 wickets)	**164**		

INDIA	O	M	R	W
Kapil Dev	8	1	26	2
Madan Lal	7	0	33	2
Nayak	7	2	25	0
Patil	7	0	16	1
Shastri	7	0	53	0

ENGLAND	O	M	R	W
Willis	7.3	2	41	0
Lever	7	0	31	0
Gooch	7	0	25	2
Botham	7	0	33	1
Underwood	7	1	26	1

FALL OF WICKETS
1-18, 2-22, 3-25, 4-48, 5-158, 6-161, 7-161

FALL OF WICKETS
1-41, 2-69, 3-78, 4-89,

Umpires: J.D.Ghosh (1) and Swaroop Kishen (1).

INDIA v ENGLAND 1981-82

At Barabati Stadium, Cuttack on 27 January 1982.   Result: **INDIA** won by 5 wickets.   Toss: India.
Award: S.M.Gavaskar.   LOI debuts: India – Arun Lal, A.Malhotra.   46-over match.

For the third time in this rubber, the side winning the toss elected to bowl during the misty morning, enjoy choice batting conditions after lunch and duly win the match. This victory gave India their first limited-overs trophy.

ENGLAND		Runs	Balls	4/6	INDIA		Runs	Balls	4/6
G.A.Gooch	c Arun Lal b Madan Lal	3			* S.M.Gavaskar	st Taylor b Underwood	71		
G.Cook	c Nayak b Patil	30			Arun Lal	c Gooch b Botham	9		
C.J.Tavaré	c Madan Lal b Shastri	11			D.B.Vengsarkar	c Willis b Gooch	13		
D.I.Gower	c and b Patil	42			S.M.Patil	b Underwood	64		
I.T.Botham	b Nayak	52		/2	Yashpal Sharma	not out	34		
* K.W.R.Fletcher	b Madan Lal	69		/4	Kapil Dev	c Gooch b Underwood	0		
M.W.Gatting	not out	8			A.Malhotra	not out	28		
† R.W.Taylor	not out	2			† S.M.H.Kirmani				
J.K.Lever					S.V.Nayak				
D.L.Underwood					Madan Lal				
R.G.D.Willis					R.J.Shastri				
Extras	(lb 9, w 1, nb 3)	13			Extras	(lb 7, w 2, nb 3)	12		
Total	(46 overs; 6 wickets)	230			Total	(42 overs; 5 wickets)	231		

INDIA	O	M	R	W	ENGLAND	O	M	R	W
Kapil Dev	8	3	23	0	Willis	6	1	29	0
Madan Lal	8	0	56	2	Botham	8	0	48	1
Nayak	10	1	51	1	Lever	10	0	55	0
Shastri	10	1	34	1	Gooch	8	0	39	1
Patil	10	0	53	2	Underwood	10	0	48	3

FALL OF WICKETS
1-13, 2-33, 3-86, 4-101, 5-181, 6-228

FALL OF WICKETS
1-16, 2-59, 3-135, 4-184, 5-184

Umpires: P.R.Punjabi (1) and K.B.Ramaswami (1).

SRI LANKA v ENGLAND 1981-82

At Sinhalese Sports Club, Colombo on 13 February 1982.   Result: **ENGLAND** won by 5 runs.   Toss: Sri Lanka.
Award: I.T.Botham.   LOI debuts: Sri Lanka – A.L.F.de Mel, R.S.A.Jayasekera, S.Wettimuny; England – P.J.W.Allott.
45-over match.

Sri Lanka, having been granted full membership of the ICC on 21 July 1981, staged its first home international four days before its inaugural Test.

ENGLAND		Runs	Balls	4/6	SRI LANKA		Runs	Balls	4/6
G.A.Gooch	b G.R.A.de Silva	64			* B.Warnapura	c Gower b Allott	10		
G.Cook	c G.R.A.de Silva b Kaluperuma	28			S.Wettimuny	c Richards b Allott	46		
D.I.Gower	run out	15			† R.S.A.Jayasekera	c Gooch b Willis	17		
I.T.Botham	b De Mel	60	50	7/2	R.L.Dias	c and b Underwood	4		
* K.W.R.Fletcher	b D.S.de Silva	12			L.R.D.Mendis	c Gower b Underwood	2		
M.W.Gatting	c Mendis b De Mel	3			R.S.Madugalle	b Willis	22		
† C.J.Richards	b G.R.A.de Silva	3			A.N.Ranasinghe	c Cook b Botham	51		
J.E.Emburey	lbw b De Mel	0			D.S.de Silva	b Botham	8		
P.J.W.Allott	run out	0			A.L.F.de Mel	not out	13		
D.L.Underwood	b De Mel	4			L.W.S.Kaluperuma	not out	14		
R.G.D.Willis	not out	2			G.R.A.de Silva				
Extras	(b 6, lb 2, w 2, nb 10)	20			Extras	(b 5, lb 10, w 2, nb 2)	19		
Total	(44.4 overs)	211			Total	(45 overs; 8 wickets)	206		

SRI LANKA	O	M	R	W	ENGLAND	O	M	R	W
De Mel	8.4	1	34	4	Willis	9	1	32	2
Ranasinghe	8	2	20	0	Botham	9	0	45	2
Kaluperuma	7	0	35	1	Emburey	5	0	18	0
D.S.de Silva	9	0	31	1	Allott	9	0	40	2
G.R.A.de Silva	9	0	56	2	Gooch	6	1	18	0
Wettimuny	3	0	15	0	Underwood	7	0	34	2

FALL OF WICKETS
1-55, 2-83, 3-152, 4-191, 5-197, 6-202, 7-205, 8-205, 9-205, 10-211

FALL OF WICKETS
1-34, 2-75, 3-84, 4-92, 5-92, 6-160, 7-175, 8-187

Umpires: C.E.B.Anthony (1) and H.C.Felsinger (1).

SRI LANKA v ENGLAND 1981-82

At Sinhalese Sports Club, Colombo on 14 February 1982.   Result: **SRI LANKA** won by 3 runs.   Toss: England.
Award: S.Wettimuny.   LOI debuts: Sri Lanka – H.M.Goonatilleke, A.Ranatunga.   45-over match.

Sri Lanka gained a notable victory after England lost their last five wickets for nine runs, four of them to run outs in the space of nine balls.

SRI LANKA		Runs	Balls	4/6		ENGLAND		Runs	Balls	4/6
* B.Warnapura	c Taylor b Botham	4				G.A.Gooch	st Goonatilleke b G.R.A.de Silva	74		
S.Wettimuny	not out	86	109			G.Cook	st Goonatilleke b G.R.A.de Silva	32		
L.R.D.Mendis	c and b Botham	0		–		D.I.Gower	lbw b De Mel	6		
R.L.Dias	hit wicket b Lever	26				I.T.Botham	c and b Warnapura	13		
A.Ranatunga	run out	42				* K.W.R.Fletcher	run out	38		
A.N.Ranasinghe	c Gooch b Underwood	0		–		C.J.Tavaré	b D.S.de Silva	5		
R.S.Madugalle	c Taylor b Lever	12				M.W.Gatting	run out	18		
A.L.F.de Mel	run out	14				† R.W.Taylor	run out	3		–
D.S.de Silva	not out	9				J.K.Lever	not out	2		–
† H.M.Goonatilleke						D.L.Underwood	run out	0	1	–
G.R.A.de Silva						R.G.D.Willis	c Madugalle b De Mel	0	1	–
Extras	(b 2, lb 18, w 1, nb 1)	22				Extras	(lb 19, w 1, nb 1)	21		
Total	(45 overs; 7 wickets)	**215**				**Total**	(44.5 overs)	**212**		

ENGLAND	O	M	R	W		SRI LANKA	O	M	R	W
Willis	9	1	26	0		De Mel	8.5	0	14	2
Botham	9	4	29	2		Ranasinghe	9	0	37	0
Lever	9	0	51	2		Warnapura	9	0	42	1
Gooch	9	0	50	0		D.S.de Silva	9	0	54	1
Underwood	9	0	37	1		G.R.A.de Silva	9	1	44	2

FALL OF WICKETS
1-5, 2-5, 3-43, 4-130, 5-130, 6-138, 7-186

FALL OF WICKETS
1-109, 2-122, 3-122, 4-147, 5-170, 6-203, 7-206, 8-211, 9-211, 10-212

Umpires: K.T.Francis (1) and P.W.Vidanagamage (1).

NEW ZEALAND v AUSTRALIA 1981-82

At Eden Park, Auckland on 13 February 1982.   Result: **NEW ZEALAND** won by 46 runs.   Toss: Australia.
Award: G.S.Chappell.   LOI debuts: New Zealand – M.D.Crowe.   50-over match.

Greg Chappell's 82-ball hundred was an effective retort to a hostile, boisterous crowd of 43,000, one of whom recalled the notorious underarm delivery (*LOI No. 113*) by rolling a bowls wood across the outfield. This being prior to the era of spare umpires armed with replays, Bruce Edgar was allowed a second chance after being bowled leg bail when 7.

NEW ZEALAND		Runs	Balls	4/6		AUSTRALIA		Runs	Balls	4/6
J.G.Wright	run out	18	48	3		G.M.Wood	run out	1	9	–
B.A.Edgar	b Pascoe	79	119	7/1		B.M.Laird	c Crowe b Cairns	11	35	2
J.F.Reid	c Alderman b Chappell	20	32	1		J.Dyson	c Crowe b Troup	32	71	4
* G.P.Howarth	c Marsh b Lillee	34	48	3		* G.S.Chappell	c Howarth b Troup	108	92	15
J.V.Coney	run out	45	33	4/1		K.J.Hughes	c Crowe b Coney	16	24	1
R.J.Hadlee	b Alderman	11	13	1		A.R.Border	b Crowe	6	16	–
B.L.Cairns	not out	18	9	1/1		† R.W.Marsh	b Troup	1	3	–
M.D.Crowe						J.R.Thomson	c Snedden b Troup	0	9	–
† I.D.S.Smith						D.K.Lillee	c Wright b Crowe	1	5	–
M.C.Snedden						L.S.Pascoe	not out	2	6	–
G.B.Troup						T.M.Alderman	b Snedden	1	2	–
Extras	(lb 13, w 1, nb 1)	15				Extras	(b 4, lb 9, nb 2)	15		
Total	(50 overs; 6 wickets)	**240**				**Total**	(44.5 overs)	**194**		

AUSTRALIA	O	M	R	W		NEW ZEALAND	O	M	R	W
Thomson	10	2	36	0		Cairns	10	1	31	1
Alderman	10	3	41	1		Hadlee	8	3	15	0
Pascoe	10	0	35	1		Snedden	7.5	1	35	1
Chappell	10	0	57	1		Coney	7	0	45	1
Lillee	10	0	56	1		Troup	10	1	44	4
						Crowe	2	0	9	2

FALL OF WICKETS
1-28, 2-89, 3-148, 4-184, 5-210, 6-240

FALL OF WICKETS
1-1, 2-21, 3-109, 4-144, 5-182, 6-187, 7-189, 8-190, 9-192, 10-194

Umpires: B.A.Bricknell (2) and J.B.R.Hastie (4).

NEW ZEALAND v AUSTRALIA 1981-82

At Carisbrook, Dunedin on 17 February 1982.　Result: **AUSTRALIA** won by 6 wickets.　Toss: Australia.
Award: A.R.Border.　LOI debuts: New Zealand – B.R.Blair.　49-over match.

An attendance of 15,000, a record for Carisbrook, saw Australia exploit a seaming, bouncy pitch to draw level in the three-match rubber.

NEW ZEALAND		Runs	Balls	4/6
B.A.Edgar	lbw b Alderman	3	24	–
J.G.Wright	b Lillee	5	33	–
M.D.Crowe	c Hughes b Alderman	3	13	–
G.P.Howarth	c Chappell b Thomson	12	29	1
J.V.Coney	b Alderman	54	88	3/1
B.R.Blair	c Laird b Lillee	29	67	2
R.J.Hadlee	b Lillee	7	4	1
I.D.S.Smith	not out	14	29	–
B.L.Cairns	c Dyson b Pascoe	3	9	–
M.C.Snedden	run out	3	3	–
E.J.Chatfield	not out	2	12	–
Extras	(lb 11, w 1, nb 12)	24		
Total	(49 overs; 9 wickets)	**159**		

AUSTRALIA		Runs	Balls	4/6
G.M.Wood	b Chatfield	4	22	–
B.M.Laird	not out	71	125	8
J.Dyson	c Smith b Cairns	18	47	1/1
* G.S.Chappell	c Howarth b Hadlee	0	3	–
K.J.Hughes	b Hadlee	5	9	–
A.R.Border	not out	53	68	4
† R.W.Marsh				
D.K.Lillee				
J.R.Thomson				
L.S.Pascoe				
T.M.Alderman				
Extras	(lb 8, nb 1)	9		
Total	(45 overs; 4 wickets)	**160**		

AUSTRALIA	O	M	R	W
Thomson	10	1	30	1
Alderman	10	3	22	3
Lillee	10	3	24	3
Chappell	10	1	30	0
Pascoe	9	0	29	1

NEW ZEALAND	O	M	R	W
Chatfield	10	1	30	1
Hadlee	9	3	24	2
Snedden	9	1	41	0
Coney	9	1	32	0
Cairns	8	1	24	1

FALL OF WICKETS
1-14, 2-26, 3-27, 4-39, 5-124, 6-132, 7-136, 8-143, 9-150

FALL OF WICKETS
1-12, 2-37, 3-39, 4-45

Umpires: F.R.Goodall (5) and D.A.Kinsella (1).

NEW ZEALAND v AUSTRALIA 1981-82

At Basin Reserve, Wellington on 20 February 1982.　Result: **AUSTRALIA** won by 8 wickets.　Toss: Australia.
Award: T.M.Alderman.　LOI debuts: None.　50-over match.

To the immense disappointment of New Zealand's first all-ticket crowd (18,000), Terry Alderman capitalised on a fast-seaming pitch of variable bounce to dismiss the home side for their lowest total until 1985-86 (*LOI No.* 384).

NEW ZEALAND		Runs	Balls	4/6
J.G.Wright	c Alderman b Thomson	0	1	–
B.A.Edgar	b Alderman	11	35	–
M.D.Crowe	c Laird b Alderman	7	17	–
* G.P.Howarth	b Alderman	7	16	1
J.V.Coney	c Hughes b Lillee	3	22	–
B.R.Blair	lbw b Alderman	2	3	–
† I.D.Smith	c Border b Alderman	0	12	–
R.J.Hadlee	c Hughes b Lillee	18	31	3
B.L.Cairns	c Alderman b Pascoe	14	24	1
M.C.Snedden	b Lillee	1	10	–
G.B.Troup	not out	2	6	–
Extras	(lb 6, w 1, nb 2)	9		
Total	(29 overs)	**74**		

AUSTRALIA		Runs	Balls	4/6
B.M.Laird	lbw b Hadlee	10	53	–
† R.W.Marsh	b Cairns	3	9	–
J.Dyson	not out	26	122	3
* G.S.Chappell	not out	24	78	4
K.J.Hughes				
G.M.Wood				
A.R.Border				
D.K.Lillee				
J.R.Thomson				
L.S.Pascoe				
T.M.Alderman				
Extras	(lb 5, w 2, nb 5)	12		
Total	(20.3 overs; 2 wickets)	**75**		

AUSTRALIA	O	M	R	W
Thomson	5	1	11	1
Alderman	10	2	17	5
Lillee	10	3	14	3
Pascoe	4	1	23	1

NEW ZEALAND	O	M	R	W
Hadlee	8.3	2	25	1
Cairns	4	1	12	1
Troup	6	1	23	0
Snedden	2	1	3	0

FALL OF WICKETS
1-0, 2-20, 3-23, 4-30, 5-32, 6-35, 7-37, 8-71, 9-71, 10-74

FALL OF WICKETS
1-4, 2-28

Umpires: F.R.Goodall (6) and S.J.Woodward (1).

PAKISTAN v SRI LANKA 1981-82

At National Stadium, Karachi on 12 March 1982.   Result: **PAKISTAN** won by 8 wickets.   Toss: Pakistan.
Award: Mohsin Khan.   LOI debuts: Pakistan – Jalaluddin, Salim Yousuf; Sri Lanka – J.R.Ratnayeke, R.G.C.E.Wijesuriya

The first of a three-match 40-over Wills Series was ruined by crowd invasions. Suspended when Sri Lanka were 147 for 2 after 29 overs as police quelled the rioters with tear gas, it was resheduled for 35 overs. When further disturbances forced the players off after 33 overs, that innings was closed.

SRI LANKA		Runs	Balls	4/6
* B.Warnapura	b Qasim	77	98	10
S.Wettimuny	b Jalaluddin	2	7	–
R.L.Dias	c and b Tahir	57	71	4
L.R.D.Mendis	not out	5	12	–
A.Ranatunga	not out	15	13	1
R.S.Madugalle				
D.S.de Silva				
A.L.F.de Mel				
† R.S.A.Jayasekera				
J.R.Ratnayeke				
R.G.C.E.Wijesuriya				
Extras	(b 10, lb 1, w 1, nb 3)	15		
Total	(33 overs; 3 wickets)	171		

PAKISTAN		Runs	Balls	4/6
Mansoor Akhtar	b Wijesuriya	20	33	9
Mohsin Khan	c Mendis b Ratnayeke	85	91	9
* Javed Miandad	not out	56	54	4/
Wasim Raja	not out	0	4	–
Salim Malik				
Haroon Rashid				
Tahir Naqqash				
Rashid Khan				
Iqbal Qasim				
† Salim Yousuf				
Jalaluddin				
Extras	(b 3, lb 5, w 3, nb 2)	13		
Total	(29.2 overs; 2 wickets)	174		

PAKISTAN	O	M	R	W
Tahir Naqqash	6	0	19	1
Rashid Khan	8	0	40	0
Iqbal Qasim	5	0	32	1
Jalaluddin	5	1	14	1
Wasim Raja	5	0	29	0
Javed Miandad	4	0	22	0

SRI LANKA	O	M	R	W
De Mel	6	2	28	
Ratnayeke	6.2	0	40	
Wijesuriya	8	0	48	
De Silva	6	0	30	
Ranatunga	3	0	15	

FALL OF WICKETS
1-5, 2-144, 3-151

FALL OF WICKETS
1-52, 2-157

Umpires: Shakil Khan (1) and Tariq Ata (1).

PAKISTAN v SRI LANKA 1981-82

At Gaddafi Stadium, Lahore on 29 March 1982.   Result: **SRI LANKA** won on faster scoring rate.   Toss: Sri Lanka.
Award: R.L.Dias.   LOI debuts: None.

Before bad light terminated play, Sri Lanka scored 21 runs off the last two overs to win by 6.87 runs per over against Pakistan's 5.97. Zaheer Abbas took only 80 balls to reach his hundred, the fastest on record in these matches until he himself surpassed it in *LOI No. 163*.

PAKISTAN		Runs	Balls	4/6
Mudassar Nazar	b De Silva	27		
Mohsin Khan	run out	6		
Zaheer Abbas	c Madugalle b Ratnayeke	123		15/3
* Javed Miandad	run out	1		
Haroon Rashid	not out	63		
Imran Khan	not out	9		
Mansoor Akhtar				
† Ashraf Ali				
Tahir Naqqash				
Rashid Khan				
Sikander Bakht				
Extras	(lb 2, w 8)	10		
Total	(40 overs; 4 wickets)	239		

SRI LANKA		Runs	Balls	4/6
* B.Warnapura	c Miandad b Sikander	5		
S.Wettimuny	c Ashraf b Mudassar	32		5
R.L.Dias	c Imran b Mudassar	81	59	12
L.R.D.Mendis	b Tahir	52		6/
R.S.Madugalle	not out	36		
A.Ranatunga	not out	5		
D.S.de Silva				
† H.M.Goonatilleke				
A.L.F.de Mel				
J.R.Ratnayeke				
A.N.Ranasinghe				
Extras	(lb 7, w 7, nb 2)	16		
Total	(33 overs; 4 wickets)	227		

SRI LANKA	O	M	R	W
De Mel	8	1	31	0
Ratnayeke	8	1	42	1
Ranasinghe	6	0	33	0
Warnapura	2	0	21	0
De Silva	8	0	49	1
Ranatunga	8	0	53	0

PAKISTAN	O	M	R	W
Imran Khan	5	1	20	
Sikander Bakht	5	1	15	
Tahir Naqqash	8	0	65	
Mudassar Nazar	8	0	56	
Rashid Khan	7	0	55	

FALL OF WICKETS
1-14, 2-86, 3-92, 4-215

FALL OF WICKETS
1-10, 2-87, 3-160, 4-185

Umpires: Mian Mohammad Aslam (1) and Rab Nawaz (1).

PAKISTAN v SRI LANKA 1981-82

At National Stadium, Karachi on 31 March 1982.   Result: **PAKISTAN** won by 5 wickets.   Toss: Pakistan.
Award: Mudassar Nazar.   LOI debuts: Pakistan – Tausif Ahmed.

With both appointed captains injured, Zaheer Abbas and Duleep Mendis deputised. Pakistan convincingly won the only uninterrupted game of the series.

SRI LANKA		Runs	Balls	4/6	PAKISTAN		Runs	Balls	4/6
S.Wettimuny	c Mansoor b Mudassar	27	37	2/1	Mudassar Nazar	c sub (J.B.M.Perera) b Ranatunga	79	82	9
† H.M.Goonatilleke	c Imran b Sikander	5	8	–	Mohsin Khan	c Madugalle b Ranasinghe	36	49	4
R.L.Dias	b Mudassar	49	59	5	* Zaheer Abbas	b G.R.A.de Silva	1	4	–
* L.R.D.Mendis	b Tausif Ahmed	44	47	5	Mansoor Akhtar	st Goonatilleke b G.R.A.de Silva	31	36	2
R.S.Madugalle	st Salim b Wasim	46	41	3/2	Haroon Rashid	c and b G.R.A.de Silva	4	6	–
A.Ranatunga	b Imran	6	10	1	Wasim Raja	not out	41	33	5/1
A.N.Ranasinghe	c and b Imran	24	15	2/2	Imran Khan	not out	15	22	1
A.L.F.de Mel	run out	5	6	–	† Salim Yousuf				
D.S.de Silva	run out	2	2	–	Rashid Khan				
J.R.Ratnayeke	not out	0	2	–	Tausif Ahmed				
G.R.A.de Silva	b Sikander	1	5	–	Sikander Bakht				
Extras	(lb 4, w 5)	9			Extras	(lb 10, w 2, nb 3)	15		
Total	(38.3 overs)	**218**			**Total**	(38.1 overs; 5 wickets)	**222**		

PAKISTAN	O	M	R	W	SRI LANKA	O	M	R	W
Imran Khan	7	1	10	2	De Mel	7	0	35	0
Sikander Bakht	5.3	0	34	2	Ratnayeke	4.1	0	34	0
Rashid Khan	4	0	37	0	Ranasinghe	8	1	27	1
Mudassar Nazar	8	0	42	2	D.S.de Silva	4	0	34	0
Tausif Ahmed	8	0	41	1	Ranatunga	7	0	36	1
Wasim Raja	6	0	45	1	G.R.A.de Silva	8	0	41	3

FALL OF WICKETS
1-7, 2-54, 3-113, 4-147, 5-170, 6-198, 7-211, 8-213, 9-214, 10-218

FALL OF WICKETS
1-90, 2-91, 3-154, 4-162, 5-170

Umpires: Ghafoor Butt (1) and Shakil Khan (2).

ENGLAND v INDIA 1982

At Headingley, Leeds on 2 June 1982.   Result: **ENGLAND** won by 9 wickets.   Toss: England.
Award: B.Wood.   LOI debuts: England – A.J.Lamb; India – G.A.Parkar.   55-over match.

The toss proved vital after Headingley's covers were unable to prevent a freak hailstorm from wetting the pitch in two patches. Allied to a steamy morning, conditions were ideal for seam and swing bowling. Kapil Dev's heroic effort included a 35-ball fifty and sixes off successive balls from Ian Botham.

INDIA		Runs	Balls	4/6	ENGLAND		Runs	Balls	4/6
* S.M.Gavaskar	c Botham b Allott	38	61	4	B.Wood	not out	78	137	4
G.A.Parkar	c Tavaré b Willis	10	33	1	C.J.Tavaré	lbw b Madan Lal	66	120	5
D.B.Vengsarkar	c Taylor b Botham	5	26	–	A.J.Lamb	not out	35	50	4
G.R.Viswanath	b Botham	9	14	2	D.I.Gower				
S.M.Patil	c Taylor b Botham	0	6	–	I.T.Botham				
Yashpal Sharma	c Taylor b Allott	20	59	1/1	D.W.Randall				
R.J.Shastri	run out	18	56	1	G.Miller				
Kapil Dev	run out	60	37	5/3	G.R.Dilley				
† S.M.H.Kirmani	c Taylor b Botham	11	24	–	† R.W.Taylor				
S.V.Nayak	c Tavaré b Willis	3	19	–	P.J.W.Allott				
Madan Lal	not out	1	1	–	* R.G.D.Willis				
Extras	(b 4, lb 9, w 1, nb 4)	18			Extras	(b 1, lb 7, w 3, nb 4)	15		
Total	(55 overs)	**193**			**Total**	(50.1 overs; 1 wicket)	**194**		

ENGLAND	O	M	R	W	INDIA	O	M	R	W
Willis	11	0	32	2	Kapil Dev	9	2	21	0
Dilley	5	1	20	0	Madan Lal	9	3	21	1
Allott	11	4	21	2	Nayak	9	0	37	0
Botham	11	0	56	4	Shastri	11	0	37	0
Wood	7	2	17	0	Patil	7	0	29	0
Miller	10	0	29	0	Yashpal Sharma	5.1	0	34	0

FALL OF WICKETS
1-30, 2-54, 3-58, 4-59, 5-68, 6-113, 7-114, 8-154, 9-192, 10-193

FALL OF WICKETS
1-133

Umpires: D.J.Constant (17) and D.O.Oslear (2).

ENGLAND v INDIA 1982

At Kennington Oval, London on 4 June 1982.   Result: **ENGLAND** won by 114 runs.   Toss: India.
Award: A.J.Lamb.   LOI debuts: None.   55-over match.

Overcoming a slow outfield, Allan Lamb and David Gower added 159 off 172 balls, then England's highest LOI partnership for the third wicket.

ENGLAND		Runs	Balls	4/6
B.Wood	b Patil	15	39	–
C.J.Tavaré	b Patil	27	53	1
A.J.Lamb	c and b Madan Lal	99	109	5
D.I.Gower	c Vengsarkar b Yashpal	76	90	2/1
I.T.Botham	run out	4	7	1
D.W.Randall	run out	24	25	–
G.Miller	run out	0	–	–
G.R.Dilley	c Yashpal b Madan Lal	1	3	–
† R.W.Taylor	not out	3	8	–
P.J.W.Allott	run out	5	4	1
* R.G.D.Willis				
Extras	(b 3, lb 10, w 6, nb 3)	22		
Total	(55 overs; 9 wickets)	**276**		

INDIA		Runs	Balls	4/6
* S.M.Gavaskar	c Willis b Miller	15	54	–
G.A.Parkar	c Botham b Willis	2	14	–
D.B.Vengsarkar	c Taylor b Dilley	15	27	1
Yashpal Sharma	lbw b Allott	2	21	–
A.Malhotra	b Botham	4	14	–
S.M.Patil	b Miller	1	5	–
Kapil Dev	c Gower b Wood	47	62	4/1
† S.M.H.Kirmani	c Botham b Miller	8	29	1
Madan Lal	not out	53	75	4/1
R.J.Shastri	not out	9	30	–
S.V.Nayak				
Extras	(b 1, lb 3, w 2)	6		
Total	(55 overs; 8 wickets)	**162**		

INDIA	O	M	R	W
Kapil Dev	11	1	39	0
Madan Lal	11	0	50	2
Nayak	11	1	48	0
Patil	11	0	37	2
Yashpal Sharma	3	0	27	1
Shastri	8	0	53	0

ENGLAND	O	M	R	W
Willis	7	2	10	1
Dilley	7	1	19	1
Botham	9	2	22	1
Allott	8	3	24	1
Miller	11	3	27	3
Wood	11	0	51	1
Tavaré	2	0	3	0

FALL OF WICKETS
1-43, 2-53, 3-212, 4-218, 5-260, 6-260, 7-267, 8-268, 9-276

FALL OF WICKETS
1-5, 2-28, 3-36, 4-42, 5-42, 6-43, 7-66, 8-131

Umpires: D.G.L.Evans (5) and B.J.Meyer (9).

ENGLAND v PAKISTAN 1982

At Trent Bridge, Nottingham on 17 July 1982.   Result: **ENGLAND** won by 7 wickets.   Toss: Pakistan.
Award: A.J.Lamb.   LOI debuts: England – E.E.Hemmings, D.R.Pringle.   55-over match.

Derek Pringle, son of Donald who represented East Africa in the 1975 Prudential World Cup, provided the first instance of two generations of a family appearing in limited-overs internationals.

PAKISTAN		Runs	Balls	4/6
Mudassar Nazar	run out	51	86	5
Mohsin Khan	b Botham	47	74	4/1
Zaheer Abbas	lbw b Pringle	53	72	5
Javed Miandad	c Willis b Pringle	28	49	1
Majid Khan	c Willis b Botham	23	20	2
Wasim Raja	c Hemmings b Botham	14	19	1
* Imran Khan	not out	16	10	1
Sarfraz Nawaz	not out	2	3	–
† Wasim Bari				
Iqbal Qasim				
Sikander Bakht				
Extras	(b 4, lb 4, w 6, nb 2)	16		
Total	(55 overs; 6 wickets)	**250**		

ENGLAND		Runs	Balls	4/6
D.I.Gower	c Wasim Bari b Sikander	17	32	2
C.J.Tavaré	b Imran	48	83	4
A.J.Lamb	c Wasim Bari b Imran	118	121	14
M.W.Gatting	not out	37	46	4
I.T.Botham	not out	10	9	1
D.W.Randall				
G.Miller				
D.R.Pringle				
E.E.Hemmings				
† R.W.Taylor				
* R.G.D.Willis				
Extras	(lb 12, w 5, nb 5)	22		
Total	(47.1 overs; 3 wickets)	**252**		

ENGLAND	O	M	R	W
Willis	11	1	46	0
Botham	11	0	57	3
Pringle	11	1	50	2
Miller	11	1	36	0
Hemmings	11	1	45	0

PAKISTAN	O	M	R	W
Imran Khan	11	2	35	2
Sarfraz Nawaz	11	3	43	0
Sikander Bakht	7	0	34	1
Iqbal Qasim	7	0	49	0
Mudassar Nazar	5.1	0	26	0
Majid Khan	4	0	25	0
Wasim Raja	2	0	18	0

FALL OF WICKETS
1-102, 2-103, 3-175, 4-208, 5-222, 6-238

FALL OF WICKETS
1-25, 2-132, 3-234

Umpires: D.G.L.Evans (6) and A.G.T.Whitehead (5).

ENGLAND v PAKISTAN 1982

At Old Trafford, Manchester on 19 July 1982.   Result: **ENGLAND** won by 73 runs.   Toss: Pakistan.
Award: M.W.Gatting.   LOI debuts: None.   55-over match.

Ian Botham, who hit four sixes off Iqbal Qasim, added 84 off 64 balls in 27 minutes with Mike Gatting.

ENGLAND		Runs	Balls	4/6
D.I.Gower	c Wasim Bari b Mudassar	33	50	4
C.J.Tavaré	run out	16	31	1
A.J.Lamb	c Wasim Bari b Qasim	27	41	4
M.W.Gatting	run out	76	81	8/1
I.T.Botham	c Wasim Raja b Imran	49	28	2/4
D.W.Randall	run out	6	11	–
G.Miller	b Imran	26	33	3
D.R.Pringle	not out	34	45	3
E.E.Hemmings	c Qasim b Tahir	1	7	–
R.W.Taylor	not out	1	3	–
R.G.D.Willis				
Extras	(lb 16, w 10)	26		
Total	(55 overs; 8 wickets)	**295**		

PAKISTAN	O	M	R	W
Imran Khan	11	1	48	2
Tahir Naqqash	10	0	37	1
Sikander Bakht	11	0	42	0
Mudassar Nazar	11	0	50	1
Iqbal Qasim	8	0	76	1
Majid Khan	4	1	16	0

FALL OF WICKETS
1-32, 2-54, 3-101, 4-185, 5-217, 6-226, 7-280, 8-284

PAKISTAN		Runs	Balls	4/6
Mudassar Nazar	run out	31	50	3
Mohsin Khan	b Pringle	17	40	–
Zaheer Abbas	c Randall b Pringle	13	14	1
Mansoor Akhtar	run out	28	37	3
Majid Khan	b Miller	5	19	–
Wasim Raja	c Botham b Willis	60	61	6/2
* Imran Khan	c Gower b Miller	31	45	5
Tahir Naqqash	run out	1	3	–
† Wasim Bari	b Hemmings	4	10	–
Iqbal Qasim	lbw b Botham	13	18	2
Sikander Bakht	not out	2	3	–
Extras	(lb 14, w 2, nb 1)	17		
Total	(49.4 overs)	**222**		

ENGLAND	O	M	R	W
Willis	8	0	36	1
Botham	8.4	0	40	1
Miller	11	1	56	2
Pringle	11	0	43	2
Hemmings	11	3	30	1

FALL OF WICKETS
1-52, 2-55, 3-82, 4-97, 5-123, 6-183, 7-200, 8-201, 9-213, 10-222

Umpires: H.D.Bird (18) and D.J.Constant (18).

INDIA v SRI LANKA 1982-83

At Gandhi Sports Complex, Amritsar on 12 September 1982.   Result: **INDIA** won by 78 runs.   Toss: Sri Lanka.
Award: D.R.Doshi.   LOI debuts: Sri Lanka – V.B.John.   46-over match.

This three-match rubber was sandwiched around the inaugural Indo-Sri Lankan Test in which the tourists achieved an honourable draw. Gavaskar was unavailable because of a foot injury.

INDIA		Runs	Balls	4/6
R.M.H.Binny	lbw b De Mel	16	29	
K.Srikkanth	c John b Warnapura	57	43	10/1
D.B.Vengsarkar	c Ratnayeke b De Silva	23	37	
A.Malhotra	b Warnapura	40	60	
S.M.Patil	lbw b Ranasinghe	15	21	
Kapil Dev	st Goonatilleke b De Silva	49	31	3/1
Yashpal Sharma	not out	37	37	
M.Amarnath	c Wettimuny b John	13	12	
S.M.H.Kirmani				
Madan Lal				
D.R.Doshi				
Extras	(lb 4, w 11, nb 4)	19		
Total	(46 overs; 7 wickets)	**269**		

SRI LANKA		Runs	Balls	4/6
* B.Warnapura	b Madan Lal	0	15	–
S.Wettimuny	b Amarnath	43	60	
R.L.Dias	c Yashpal b Doshi	39	49	
L.R.D.Mendis	c Kapil Dev b Doshi	33	39	
R.S.Madugalle	c Madan Lal b Doshi	1	9	–
A.N.Ranasinghe	c Binny b Amarnath	35	27	
A.L.F.de Mel	c Madan Lal b Doshi	1	2	–
D.S.de Silva	b Kapil Dev	9	19	
† H.M.Goonatilleke	not out	14	31	
J.R.Ratnayeke	not out	6	25	
V.B.John				
Extras	(b 1, lb 5, w 2, nb 2)	10		
Total	(46 overs; 8 wickets)	**191**		

SRI LANKA	O	M	R	W
De Mel	7	0	58	1
John	9	1	44	1
Ratnayeke	7	1	37	0
Warnapura	10	1	41	2
De Silva	10	0	49	2
Ranasinghe	3	0	21	1

FALL OF WICKETS
1-62, 2-95, 3-129, 4-162, 5-173, 6-241, 7-269

INDIA	O	M	R	W
Kapil Dev	8	6	9	1
Madan Lal	8	2	24	1
Binny	6	0	33	0
Doshi	10	0	44	4
Amarnath	9	0	50	2
Patil	3	0	17	0
Vengsarkar	1	0	4	0
Malhotra	1	0	0	0

FALL OF WICKETS
1-8, 2-67, 3-95, 4-98, 5-155, 6-158, 7-166, 8-175

Umpires: R.Mehra (1) and P.R.Punjabi (2).

INDIA v SRI LANKA 1982-83

At Feroz Shah Kotla, Delhi on 15 September 1982.　　Result: **INDIA** won by 6 wickets.　　Toss: Sri Lanka.
Award: K.Srikkanth.　　LOI debuts: None.　　50-over match.

Roy Dias scored Sri Lanka's first hundred at this level. His partnership of 170 with Sidath Wettimuny was the national record for any wicket until 1995-96 and remains their highest for the second wicket.

SRI LANKA		Runs	Balls	4/6
* B.Warnapura	lbw b Kapil Dev	4	7	
S.Wettimuny	c Srikkanth b Binny	74	107	
R.L.Dias	c Doshi b Binny	102	114	8
L.R.D.Mendis	c Srikkanth b Binny	10	11	
A.N.Ranasinghe	b Kapil Dev	20	17	
J.R.Ratnayeke	st Kirmani b Madan Lal	2	6	
R.S.Madugalle	c Kirmani b Madan Lal	7	8	
A.L.F.de Mel	run out	28	21	
† H.M.Goonatilleke	not out	4	8	
G.R.A.de Silva	not out	6	5	
V.B.John				
Extras	(b 2, lb 18)	20		
Total	(50 overs; 8 wickets)	**277**		

INDIA		Runs	Balls	4/6
R.M.H.Binny	lbw b John	10	13	
K.Srikkanth	c Mendis b Warnapura	95	66	13/1
D.B.Vengsarkar	c Warnapura b Ratnayeke	53	66	
A.Malhotra	not out	44	56	
S.M.Patil	c Dias b De Silva	64	48	
* Kapil Dev	not out	1	3	
M.Amarnath				
Yashpal Sharma				
Madan Lal				
† S.M.H.Kirmani				
D.R.Doshi				
Extras	(b 5, lb 8, nb 1)	14		
Total	(40.5 overs; 4 wickets)	**281**		

INDIA	O	M	R	W
Kapil Dev	10	0	41	2
Madan Lal	10	0	51	2
Binny	7	0	39	3
Patil	4	0	24	0
Amarnath	10	0	52	0
Doshi	5	0	34	0
Yashpal Sharma	4	0	16	0

SRI LANKA	O	M	R	W
De Mel	2	0	23	0
John	5	0	44	1
Ratnayeke	8	0	48	1
De Silva	5.5	0	36	1
Ranasinghe	10	0	78	0
Warnapura	10	1	38	1

FALL OF WICKETS
1-10, 2-180, 3-198, 4-218, 5-229, 6-229, 7-240, 8-269

FALL OF WICKETS
1-26, 2-160, 3-168, 4-278

Umpires: B.Ganguli (1) and S.N.Hanumantha Rao (2).

INDIA v SRI LANKA 1982-83

At Karnataka State CA Stadium, Bangalore on 26 September 1982.　　Result: **INDIA** won by 6 wickets.　　Toss: Sri Lanka.
Award: K.Srikkanth.　　LOI debuts: Sri Lanka – R.J.Ratnayake.　　50-over match.

Roy Dias became the first batsman to score hundreds in successive limited-overs internationals. Sri Lanka's batsmen did not register another hundred in these matches until 1990-91 (*LOI No. 656*). Srikkanth achieved a scoring rate of 125 runs per 100 balls in this rubber.

SRI LANKA		Runs	Balls	4/6
* B.Warnapura	lbw b Kapil Dev	1	6	
S.Wettimuny	lbw b Binny	18	34	
R.L.Dias	c Doshi b Kapil Dev	121	144	11
L.R.D.Mendis	b Doshi	23	38	
R.S.Madugalle	run out	18	37	
A.L.F.de Mel	b Doshi	25	16	
J.R.Ratnayeke	b Madan Lal	1	3	
D.S.de Silva	lbw b Madan Lal	3	7	
† H.M.Goonatilleke	not out	8	11	
R.J.Ratnayake	not out	6	9	
V.B.John				
Extras	(b 1, lb 3, nb 5)	9		
Total	(50 overs; 8 wickets)	**233**		

INDIA		Runs	Balls	4/6
R.M.H.Binny	run out	15	17	
K.Srikkanth	b De Silva	92	83	
D.B.Vengsarkar	c Dias b De Mel	42	61	
A.Malhotra	not out	27	44	
* Kapil Dev	c Ratnayeke b De Mel	15	14	
Yashpal Sharma	not out	30	27	
S.M.Patil				
M.Amarnath				
Madan Lal				
† S.M.H.Kirmani				
D.R.Doshi				
Extras	(b 7, lb 1, w 3, nb 2)	13		
Total	(39.2 overs; 4 wickets)	**234**		

INDIA	O	M	R	W
Kapil Dev	10	2	41	2
Madan Lal	10	0	41	2
Amarnath	10	0	53	0
Binny	10	0	54	1
Doshi	10	0	35	2

SRI LANKA	O	M	R	W
De Mel	8	1	58	2
John	9	0	33	0
Warnapura	2	0	15	0
Ratnayake	7	0	38	0
Ratnayeke	3	0	25	0
De Silva	10	1	51	1
Dias	0.2	0	1	0

FALL OF WICKETS
1-2, 2-48, 3-106, 4-157, 5-193, 6-198, 7-208, 8-222

FALL OF WICKETS
1-34, 2-153, 3-160, 4-177

Umpires: D.N.Dotiwalla (1) and K.B.Ramaswami (2).

PAKISTAN v AUSTRALIA 1982-83

At Niaz Stadium, Hyderabad on 20 September 1982.   Result: **PAKISTAN** won by 59 runs.   Toss: Australia.
Award: Mohsin Khan.   LOI debuts: None.

The first of this three-match Wills Series of 40-over matches featured the first hat-trick in international limited-overs cricket when Jalaluddin dismissed Marsh, Yardley and Lawson with the last three balls of his seventh over.

PAKISTAN		Runs	Balls	4/6
Mudassar Nazar	c Marsh b Alderman	28	56	2
Mohsin Khan	c Dyson b Lawson	104	101	15
* Zaheer Abbas	c Wood b Yardley	26	26	3
Javed Miandad	not out	31	35	4
Mansoor Akhtar	c Laird b Thomson	8	6	–
Haroon Rashid	b Callen	4	14	1
Tahir Naqqash	c and b Alderman	8	5	2
† Wasim Bari	not out	5	7	–
Jalaluddin				
Tausif Ahmed				
Sikander Bakht				
Extras	(b 1, lb 6, nb 8)	15		
Total	(40 overs; 6 wickets)	**229**		

AUSTRALIA		Runs	Balls	4/6
B.M.Laird	b Tausif	44	69	5
G.M.Wood	c Jalaluddin b Tausif	52	74	5
* K.J.Hughes	c Haroon b Tausif	2	7	–
A.R.Border	c Wasim b Jalaluddin	24	31	2
J.Dyson	not out	30	43	1
† R.W.Marsh	b Jalaluddin	1	7	–
B.Yardley	c Wasim b Jalaluddin	0	1	–
G.F.Lawson	b Jalaluddin	0	1	–
I.W.Callen	b Sikander	0	4	–
J.R.Thomson	c Zaheer b Mohsin	1	2	–
T.M.Alderman	not out	1	2	–
Extras	(lb 6, w 8, nb 1)	15		
Total	(40 overs; 9 wickets)	**170**		

AUSTRALIA	O	M	R	W
Lawson	8	0	29	1
Alderman	8	0	63	2
Callen	8	0	32	1
Thomson	8	0	48	1
Yardley	8	1	42	1

PAKISTAN	O	M	R	W
Sikander Bakht	7	0	24	1
Tahir Naqqash	7	0	20	0
Jalaluddin	8	1	32	4
Mudassar Nazar	8	0	38	0
Tausif Ahmed	8	0	38	3
Mohsin Khan	1	0	2	1
Mansoor Akhtar	1	0	1	0

FALL OF WICKETS
1-82, 2-160, 3-169, 4-180, 5-191, 6-202

Umpires: Khizer Hayat (3) and Mahboob Shah (4).

FALL OF WICKETS
1-104, 2-106, 3-109, 4-157, 5-162, 6-162, 7-162, 8-164, 9-169

PAKISTAN v AUSTRALIA 1982-83

At Gaddafi Stadium, Lahore on 8 October 1982.   Result: **PAKISTAN** won by 28 runs.   Toss: Australia.
Award: Zaheer Abbas.   LOI debuts: Australia – G.M.Ritchie.

A three-hour innings by Bruce Laird provided welcome respite to an antiquated scoreboard but left Australia short of the required rate.

PAKISTAN		Runs	Balls	4/6
Mohsin Khan	run out	17		–
Mudassar Nazar	lbw b Thomson	7		1
Zaheer Abbas	st Marsh b Border	109		12/2
Javed Miandad	not out	61		4
* Imran Khan	not out	29		–
Mansoor Akhtar				
Haroon Rashid				
Tahir Naqqash				
† Wasim Bari				
Jalaluddin				
Tausif Ahmed				
Extras	(b 1, lb 6, w 1, nb 3)	11		
Total	(40 overs; 3 wickets)	**234**		

AUSTRALIA		Runs	Balls	4/6
B.M.Laird	not out	91		8
G.M.Wood	b Jalaluddin	21		3
J.Dyson	c Imran b Jalaluddin	11		1
A.R.Border	b Tausif	0		–
* K.J.Hughes	c Mudassar b Imran	64		7
G.M.Ritchie	not out	4		–
† R.W.Marsh				
G.F.Lawson				
I.W.Callen				
J.R.Thomson				
T.M.Alderman				
Extras	(lb 10, w 4, nb 1)	15		
Total	(40 overs; 4 wickets)	**206**		

AUSTRALIA	O	M	R	W
Thomson	8	0	41	1
Lawson	8	0	47	0
Alderman	8	1	29	0
Callen	8	1	50	0
Border	8	1	56	1

PAKISTAN	O	M	R	W
Imran Khan	8	1	38	1
Tahir Naqqash	8	0	28	0
Jalaluddin	8	1	33	2
Tausif Ahmed	8	0	40	1
Mudassar Nazar	6	0	40	0
Zaheer Abbas	2	0	12	0

FALL OF WICKETS
1-17, 2-52, 3-171

Umpires: Amanullah Khan (2) and Shakoor Rana (5).

FALL OF WICKETS
1-37, 2-73, 3-73, 4-190

PAKISTAN v AUSTRALIA 1982-83

At National Stadium, Karachi on 22 October 1982.   No result.   Toss: Australia.
LOI debuts: Australia – W.B.Phillips.

This final match of the Australians' tour was abandoned after three of the tourists had been struck by missiles thrown by spectators.

PAKISTAN		Runs	Balls	4/6	AUSTRALIA
Mohsin Khan	not out	25	39	3	W.B.Phillips
Mudassar Nazar	b Alderman	8	22	1	G.M.Wood
Zaheer Abbas	not out	5	12	1	J.Dyson
Javed Miandad					A.R.Border
* Imran Khan					* K.J.Hughes
Mansoor Akhtar					G.M.Ritchie
Wasim Raja					† R.W.Marsh
Tahir Naqqash					G.F.Lawson
† Wasim Bari					I.W.Callen
Jalaluddin					J.R.Thomson
Tausif Ahmed					T.M.Alderman
Extras	(b 1, lb 2, w 2, nb 1)	6			
Total	(12 overs; 1 wicket)	44			

AUSTRALIA	O	M	R	W
Thomson	4	2	9	0
Lawson	2	0	7	0
Alderman	6	2	22	1

FALL OF WICKETS
1-23

Umpires: Amanullah Khan (3) and Shakoor Rana (6).

PAKISTAN v INDIA 1982-83

At Municipal Stadium, Gujranwala on 3 December 1982.   Result: **PAKISTAN** won by 14 runs.   Toss: India.
Award: Javed Miandad.   LOI debuts: India – B.S.Sandhu.

Javed Miandad dominated the first of this four-match 40-over rubber, batting for 114 minutes and scoring the first of his eight hundreds at this level.

PAKISTAN		Runs	Balls	4/6	INDIA		Runs	Balls	4/6
Mohsin Khan	b Madan Lal	5		1	* S.M.Gavaskar	lbw b Imran	1	2	–
Mudassar Nazar	run out	20		2	K.Srikkanth	c Wasim Bari b Imran	6		1
Zaheer Abbas	c Kapil Dev b Madan Lal	10		1	D.B.Vengsarkar	run out	39		5
Javed Miandad	not out	106		12/1	M.Amarnath	c Tahir b Jalaluddin	51		–
* Imran Khan	b Kapil Dev	49		3/1	S.M.Patil	c Mohsin b Mudassar	4		–
Mansoor Akhtar	not out	21		2	Kapil Dev	c Mansoor b Jalaluddin	15		–/1
Wasim Raja					Yashpal Sharma	not out	56		4/2
Ijaz Faqih					† S.M.H.Kirmani	not out	27		1
Tahir Naqqash					Madan Lal				
† Wasim Bari					R.J.Shastri				
Jalaluddin					B.S.Sandhu				
Extras	(b 1, lb 6, w 6)	13			Extras	(b 1, lb 3, w 5, nb 2)	11		
Total	(40 overs; 4 wickets)	224			Total	(40 overs; 6 wickets)	210		

INDIA	O	M	R	W	PAKISTAN	O	M	R	W
Kapil Dev	8	1	42	1	Imran Khan	8	0	38	2
Madan Lal	8	0	39	2	Jalaluddin	8	2	36	2
Amarnath	8	1	20	0	Tahir Naqqash	8	0	31	0
Sandhu	8	0	55	0	Ijaz Faqih	8	0	38	0
Shastri	6	0	41	0	Mudassar Nazar	7	0	50	0
Patil	2	0	14	0	Zaheer Abbas	1	0	6	0

FALL OF WICKETS
1-5, 2-25, 3-49, 4-160

FALL OF WICKETS
1-2, 2-13, 3-84, 4-100, 5-120, 6-121

Umpires: Amanullah Khan (4) and Shakil Khan (3).

PAKISTAN v INDIA 1982-83

At Ibn-e-Qasim Bagh Stadium, Multan on 17 December 1982.   Result: **PAKISTAN** won by 37 runs.   Toss: Pakistan.
Award: Zaheer Abbas.   LOI debuts: None.

Zaheer Abbas (72 balls) scored the fastest recorded hundred in limited-overs internationals until 1988-89 (*LOI No. 538*);
it remains the third-fastest. His second-wicket stand of 205 with Mohsin Khan equalled the (then) LOI record for any
wicket (*LOI No. 78*). For the first time, two hundreds were scored in the same LOI innings.

PAKISTAN		Runs	Balls	4/6	INDIA		Runs	Balls	4/6
Mohsin Khan	not out	117	118	9/1	K.Srikkanth	b Jalaluddin	8	21	1
Mudassar Nazar	run out	12	29	–	Arun Lal	b Jalaluddin	6	10	–
Zaheer Abbas	b Kapil Dev	118	86	10/4	D.B.Vengsarkar	c Sikander b Zaheer	37	50	1
Javed Miandad	not out	3	7		M.Amarnath	c Mansoor b Ijaz	6	25	–
Mansoor Akhtar					S.M.Patil	c Miandad b Zaheer	84	60	7/3
Imran Khan					* Kapil Dev	b Mudassar	35	21	2/2
Wasim Raja					Yashpal Sharma	c and b Mudassar	16	13	2
Ijaz Faqih					† S.M.H.Kirmani	not out	16	26	1
Wasim Bari					R.J.Shastri	not out	3	16	–
Jalaluddin					B.S.Sandhu				
Sikander Bakht					D.R.Doshi				
Extras	(b 1, lb 10, w 2)	13			Extras	(lb 10, w 3, nb 2)	15		
Total	(40 overs; 2 wickets)	**263**			**Total**	(40 overs; 7 wickets)	**226**		

INDIA	O	M	R	W	PAKISTAN	O	M	R	W
Kapil Dev	8	0	42	1	Imran Khan	8	4	14	0
Sandhu	8	0	28	0	Jalaluddin	4	0	21	2
Amarnath	6	0	46	0	Ijaz Faqih	8	0	50	1
Doshi	8	1	58	0	Mudassar Nazar	7	0	40	2
Yashpal Sharma	6	0	45	0	Sikander Bakht	8	1	50	0
Shastri	4	0	31	0	Zaheer Abbas	4	0	33	2
					Mansoor Akhtar	1	0	3	0

FALL OF WICKETS
1-41, 2-246

FALL OF WICKETS
1-14, 2-17, 3-34, 4-143, 5-162, 6-190, 7-205

Umpires: Khizer Hayat (4) and Shakoor Rana (7).

PAKISTAN v INDIA 1982-83

At Gaddafi Stadium, Lahore on 31 December 1982.   Result: **INDIA** won on faster scoring rate.   Toss: Pakistan.
Award: Javed Miandad.   LOI debuts: Pakistan – Shahid Mahboob.

Zaheer Abbas, who became the first to score five LOI hundreds, and Javed Miandad scored hundreds off 79 and 73
balls respectively. Rain reduced the match to 33 overs and bad light brought a premature end, India being awarded the
match on scoring rate over the first 27 overs (7.14 compared with Pakistan's 6.48). Shahid Mahboob was the first to take
a wicket with his first ball in LOIs.

PAKISTAN		Runs	Balls	4/6	INDIA		Runs	Balls	4/6
Mohsin Khan	c and b Kapil Dev	0	2	–	* S.M.Gavaskar	c Mansoor b Tahir	69	76	7/1
Mudassar Nazar	c and b Shastri	24	32	–	K.Srikkanth	c Zaheer b Shahid	39	29	3/3
Zaheer Abbas	c Srikkanth b Amarnath	105	82	8/1	S.M.Patil	c Wasim Raja b Mudassar	51	51	3/2
Javed Miandad	not out	119	77	6/5	Kapil Dev	lbw b Mudassar	8	5	–
Wasim Raja	not out	1	2		Yashpal Sharma	not out	4	4	–
Mansoor Akhtar					M.Amarnath	not out	1	2	–
* Imran Khan					D.B.Vengsarkar				
Ijaz Faqih					† S.M.H.Kirmani				
Tahir Naqqash					R.J.Shastri				
† Wasim Bari					Madan Lal				
Shahid Mahboob					B.S.Sandhu				
Extras	(lb 1, w 2)	3			Extras	(lb 8, w 11, nb 2)	21		
Total	(33 overs; 3 wickets)	**252**			**Total**	(27 overs; 4 wickets)	**193**		

INDIA	O	M	R	W	PAKISTAN	O	M	R	W
Kapil Dev	7	0	73	1	Imran Khan	5	2	23	0
Madan Lal	7	0	35	0	Tahir Naqqash	6	0	42	1
Sandhu	7	0	52	0	Shahid Mahboob	7	0	55	1
Shastri	7	0	39	1	Ijaz Faqih	7	0	39	0
Amarnath	5	0	50	1	Mudassar Nazar	2	0	13	2

FALL OF WICKETS
1-1, 2-70, 3-228

FALL OF WICKETS
1-57, 2-172, 3-185, 4-192

Umpires: Khizer Hayat (5) and Shakoor Rana (8).

PAKISTAN v INDIA 1982-83

At National Stadium, Karachi on 21 January 1983.   Result: **PAKISTAN** won by 8 wickets.   Toss: India.
Award: Zaheer Abbas.   LOI debuts: India – Maninder Singh, T.A.P.Sekar.

Zaheer extended his record to six hundreds and became the first to score three in successive innings as Pakistan won the series 3-1.

INDIA		Runs	Balls	4/6
K.Srikkanth	c Tahir b Ijaz	48	76	5
Arun Lal	b Sarfraz	16	34	–/1
M.Amarnath	b Sarfraz	8	22	1
Yashpal Sharma	c Imran b Sarfraz	27	42	1
Kapil Dev	c Mansoor b Imran	20	18	1/1
* S.M.Gavaskar	c Wasim Raja b Imran	23	26	1/1
D.B.Vengsarkar	not out	22	22	–
† S.M.H.Kirmani	not out	1	8	–
B.S.Sandhu				
Maninder Singh				
T.A.P.Sekar				
Extras	(lb 12, w 16, nb 4)	32		
Total	(40 overs; 6 wickets)	**197**		

PAKISTAN		Runs	Balls	4/6
Mohsin Khan	lbw b Sandhu	5	10	1
Mudassar Nazar	not out	61	89	3
Zaheer Abbas	c Amarnath b Sandhu	113	99	11/3
Javed Miandad	not out	6	12	–
Mansoor Akhtar				
Wasim Raja				
* Imran Khan				
Ijaz Faqih				
Tahir Naqqash				
† Wasim Bari				
Sarfraz Nawaz				
Extras	(lb 10, w 3)	13		
Total	(35 overs; 2 wickets)	**198**		

PAKISTAN	O	M	R	W
Imran Khan	8	3	15	2
Tahir Naqqash	8	1	38	0
Mudassar Nazar	8	1	30	0
Sarfraz Nawaz	8	1	31	3
Ijaz Faqih	8	0	51	1

INDIA	O	M	R	W
Kapil Dev	5	1	11	0
Sandhu	7	0	38	2
Sekar	4	0	19	0
Srikkanth	2	0	27	0
Yashpal Sharma	8	0	39	0
Maninder Singh	8	0	47	0
Gavaskar	1	0	4	0

FALL OF WICKETS
1-41, 2-54, 3-120, 4-124, 5-162, 6-192

FALL OF WICKETS
1-9, 2-179

Umpires: Khizer Hayat (6) and Mahboob Shah (5).

AUSTRALIA v NEW ZEALAND 1982-83

At Melbourne Cricket Ground on 9 January 1983.   Result: **AUSTRALIA** won by 8 wickets.   Toss: Australia.
Award: J.Dyson.   LOI debuts: Australia – C.G.Rackemann, K.C.Wessels; New Zealand – J.J.Crowe, P.N.Webb.

This World Series still involved 15 preliminary games but the number of finals was reduced back to three. Kim Hughes captained Australia for the first time at home.

NEW ZEALAND		Runs	Balls	4/6
J.G.Wright	c Dyson b Rackemann	54	64	9
B.A.Edgar	lbw b Rackemann	38	74	–
* G.P.Howarth	c and b Rackemann	5	10	–
J.J.Crowe	c Lawson b Chappell	7	15	1
J.V.Coney	c Marsh b Rackemann	4	14	–
J.F.M.Morrison	c Marsh b Thomson	10	24	1
† P.N.Webb	b Lawson	9	32	1
R.J.Hadlee	run out	24	27	2/1
B.L.Cairns	c Hookes b Lawson	7	16	–
M.C.Snedden	c Marsh b Hogg	2	6	–
E.J.Chatfield	not out	0	–	–
Extras	(lb 9, w 7, nb 5)	21		
Total	(44.5 overs)	**181**		

AUSTRALIA		Runs	Balls	4/6
K.C.Wessels	b Snedden	79	118	10
J.Dyson	not out	78	146	6/1
G.S.Chappell	c and b Snedden	3	9	–
* K.J.Hughes	not out	7	11	1
D.W.Hookes				
A.R.Border				
† R.W.Marsh				
G.F.Lawson				
R.M.Hogg				
J.R.Thomson				
C.G.Rackemann				
Extras	(b 1, lb 11, w 3)	15		
Total	(46.4 overs; 2 wickets)	**182**		

AUSTRALIA	O	M	R	W
Lawson	7.5	1	28	2
Thomson	9	1	39	1
Hogg	8	0	32	1
Rackemann	10	1	39	4
Chappell	10	1	22	1

NEW ZEALAND	O	M	R	W
Hadlee	9.4	2	36	0
Chatfield	10	4	18	0
Snedden	10	1	47	2
Cairns	8	1	30	0
Coney	9	1	36	0

FALL OF WICKETS
1-84, 2-89, 3-98, 4-114, 5-128, 6-134, 7-167, 8-173, 9-181, 10-181

FALL OF WICKETS
1-154, 2-168

Umpires: A.R.Crafter (15) and R.V.Whitehead (13).

AUSTRALIA v ENGLAND 1982-83

At Sydney Cricket Ground on 11 January 1983.   Result: **AUSTRALIA** won by 31 runs.   Toss: England.
Award: C.G.Rackemann.   LOI debuts: England – N.G.Cowans, T.E.Jesty.

England's last six wickets fell for 18 runs, Greg Chappell taking three in five balls.

AUSTRALIA		Runs	Balls	4/6
J.Dyson	c Randall b Marks	49	96	3
K.C.Wessels	b Cowans	18	40	1
G.S.Chappell	c Marks b Botham	3	10	–
* K.J.Hughes	c Taylor b Jesty	0	3	–
D.W.Hookes	b Marks	11	22	1
A.R.Border	b Miller	22	33	4
† R.W.Marsh	c Taylor b Miller	7	19	–
G.F.Lawson	not out	33	37	3
J.R.Thomson	b Miller	8	19	–
R.M.Hogg	c and b Cowans	8	4	2
C.G.Rackemann	b Willis	0	4	–
Extras	(lb 13, w 8)	21		
Total	(46.4 overs)	**180**		

ENGLAND	O	M	R	W
Willis	6.4	1	20	1
Cowans	7	0	20	2
Botham	7	1	41	1
Jesty	6	0	23	1
Marks	10	1	27	2
Miller	10	0	28	3

FALL OF WICKETS
1-26, 2-33, 3-36, 4-77, 5-118, 6-124, 7-132, 8-158, 9-175, 10-180

ENGLAND		Runs	Balls	4/6
D.I.Gower	c Hookes b Thomson	9	9	1
C.J.Tavaré	c Border b Rackemann	6	34	–
A.J.Lamb	b Thomson	49	92	6
D.W.Randall	b Rackemann	5	10	–
I.T.Botham	b Rackemann	18	30	1
T.E.Jesty	run out	12	19	2
G.Miller	lbw b Hogg	2	15	–
V.J.Marks	not out	7	36	–
† R.W.Taylor	lbw b Chappell	2	11	–
* R.G.D.Willis	c Marsh b Chappell	0	1	–
N.G.Cowans	b Chappell	4	7	–
Extras	(lb 12, w 17, nb 6)	35		
Total	(41.1 overs)	**149**		

AUSTRALIA	O	M	R	W
Lawson	8	1	33	0
Thomson	10	4	21	2
Hogg	10	1	15	1
Rackemann	8	1	28	3
Chappell	5.1	0	17	3

FALL OF WICKETS
1-11, 2-44, 3-53, 4-95, 5-131, 6-131, 7-135, 8-142, 9-142, 10-149

Umpires: R.A.French (15) and M.W.Johnson (13).

ENGLAND v NEW ZEALAND 1982-83

At Melbourne Cricket Ground on 13 January 1983.   Result: **NEW ZEALAND** won by 2 runs.   Toss: England.
Award: D.I.Gower.   LOI debuts: None.

Vic Marks was bowled with three needed from the final ball. David Gower's third LOI hundred was completed off 112 balls.

NEW ZEALAND		Runs	Balls	4/6
J.G.Wright	run out	55	85	7
B.A.Edgar	c Randall b Marks	30	77	3
B.L.Cairns	c Miller b Botham	36	26	3/2
G.M.Turner	b Willis	38	51	2
* G.P.Howarth	c Willis b Botham	13	16	2
J.F.M.Morrison	c Randall b Botham	11	14	1
R.J.Hadlee	c Botham b Willis	24	18	2/1
J.V.Coney	not out	13	14	–
† W.K.Lees	run out	3	2	–
M.C.Snedden				
E.J.Chatfield				
Extras	(b 1, lb 10, w 5)	16		
Total	(50 overs; 8 wickets)	**239**		

ENGLAND	O	M	R	W
Willis	8	1	29	2
Cowans	10	0	50	0
Jesty	3	0	11	0
Botham	10	0	40	3
Marks	9	0	47	1
Miller	10	0	46	0

FALL OF WICKETS
1-87, 2-100, 3-137, 4-164, 5-188, 6-205, 7-231, 8-239

ENGLAND		Runs	Balls	4/6
D.I.Gower	c Turner b Hadlee	122	134	8
C.J.Tavaré	run out	16	40	1
A.J.Lamb	st Lees b Coney	15	29	3
T.E.Jesty	c Wright b Coney	5	16	–
I.T.Botham	c Chatfield b Snedden	41	47	2/2
D.W.Randall	c Snedden b Coney	8	12	–
G.Miller	c Turner b Chatfield	2	8	–
V.J.Marks	b Snedden	5	11	–
† R.W.Taylor	not out	5	10	–
* R.G.D.Willis				
N.G.Cowans				
Extras	(lb 14, w 3, nb 1)	18		
Total	(50 overs; 8 wickets)	**237**		

NEW ZEALAND	O	M	R	W
Snedden	10	0	34	2
Chatfield	10	0	38	1
Cairns	10	1	64	0
Hadlee	10	1	37	1
Coney	10	0	46	3

FALL OF WICKETS
1-42, 2-80, 3-92, 4-190, 5-205, 6-221, 7-223, 8-237

Umpires: M.W.Johnson (14) and B.E.Martin (8).

ENGLAND v NEW ZEALAND 1982-83

At Woolloongabba, Brisbane on 15 January 1983.   Result: **ENGLAND** won by 54 runs.   Toss: New Zealand.
Award: D.I.Gower.   LOI debuts: England – I.J.Gould.

David Gower's 158, his second successive hundred, was England's highest LOI score until 1993 (*LOI No. 831*) and remains the record for World Series matches. He reached 50 off 49 balls, 100 off 85 balls and 150 off 114 balls, the latter being the fewest until 1987-88 (*LOI No. 457*).

ENGLAND		Runs	Balls	4/6
† I.J.Gould	c Howarth b Troup	15	26	1
C.J.Tavaré	b Cairns	24	60	3
D.I.Gower	c sub (J.J.Crowe) b Snedden	158	118	18/4
A.J.Lamb	c Cairns b Hadlee	13	16	2
I.T.Botham	c Webb b Hadlee	0	13	–
D.W.Randall	run out	34	67	2
T.E.Jesty	not out	4	7	–
G.Miller				
V.J.Marks				
* R.G.D.Willis				
N.G.Cowans				
Extras	(lb 9, w 9, nb 1)	19		
Total	(50 overs; 6 wickets)	**267**		

NEW ZEALAND		Runs	Balls	4/6
J.G.Wright	c Randall b Cowans	30	33	4
B.A.Edgar	c Gould b Botham	40	78	3
* G.P.Howarth	c Jesty b Marks	13	19	2
B.L.Cairns	c Gould b Marks	12	9	1/1
G.M.Turner	c Jesty b Botham	29	42	1
J.V.Coney	st Gould b Marks	13	23	1
† P.N.Webb	c Cowans b Botham	4	18	–
R.J.Hadlee	b Willis	21	32	3
M.C.Snedden	run out	0	1	–
G.B.Troup	c Botham b Willis	39	41	4/1
E.J.Chatfield	not out	0	–	
Extras	(lb 6, w 6)	12		
Total	(48.2 overs)	**213**		

NEW ZEALAND	O	M	R	W
Hadlee	10	1	44	2
Chatfield	10	3	44	0
Snedden	10	0	76	1
Troup	7	1	38	1
Cairns	10	0	29	1
Coney	3	0	17	0

ENGLAND	O	M	R	W
Willis	9.2	1	30	2
Cowans	10	0	52	1
Botham	9	2	47	3
Marks	10	2	30	3
Miller	10	1	42	0

FALL OF WICKETS
1-26, 2-89, 3-114, 4-116, 5-229, 6-267

FALL OF WICKETS
1-43, 2-75, 3-100, 4-100, 5-148, 6-148, 7-150, 8-150, 9-213, 10-213

Umpires: R.A.French (16) and B.E.Martin (9).

AUSTRALIA v ENGLAND 1982-83

At Woolloongabba, Brisbane on 16 January 1983.   Result: **AUSTRALIA** won by 7 wickets.   Toss: Australia.
Award: D.W.Hookes.   LOI debuts: None.

One member of a capacity all-ticket crowd of 22,174 released on to the outfield a piglet with flanks labelled 'Botham' and 'Eddie'. It was arrested before David Hookes completed Australia's victory with 22 runs from a Bob Willis over.

ENGLAND		Runs	Balls	4/6
† I.J.Gould	run out	2	8	–
G.Cook	c Hookes b Lawson	2	9	–
D.I.Gower	b Hogg	22	44	3
A.J.Lamb	c Marsh b Thomson	19	46	1
I.T.Botham	c Hookes b Rackemann	29	40	4
D.W.Randall	b Lawson	57	97	4/1
T.E.Jesty	c Marsh b Rackemann	0	12	–
G.Miller	run out	4	5	–
V.J.Marks	b Thomson	3	5	–
* R.G.D.Willis	not out	7	29	–
N.G.Cowans	c Lawson b Rackemann	0	8	–
Extras	(b 4, lb 12, w 13, nb 8)	37		
Total	(46.4 overs)	**182**		

AUSTRALIA		Runs	Balls	4/6
K.C.Wessels	c Gould b Botham	19	51	2
J.Dyson	c Marks b Botham	40	73	6
G.S.Chappell	c Jesty b Botham	30	31	2/1
D.W.Hookes	not out	54	56	8/1
A.R.Border	not out	30	36	2
* K.J.Hughes				
† R.W.Marsh				
G.F.Lawson				
J.R.Thomson				
R.M.Hogg				
C.G.Rackemann				
Extras	(lb 9, w 2)	11		
Total	(41 overs; 3 wickets)	**184**		

AUSTRALIA	O	M	R	W
Lawson	10	2	23	2
Thomson	10	0	32	2
Hogg	9	1	29	1
Rackemann	8.4	1	28	3
Chappell	9	1	33	0

ENGLAND	O	M	R	W
Willis	7	1	31	0
Cowans	9	1	35	0
Botham	8	1	29	3
Miller	6	0	25	0
Marks	10	0	46	0
Jesty	1	0	7	0

FALL OF WICKETS
1-2, 2-10, 3-54, 4-71, 5-128, 6-138, 7-143, 8-165, 9-178, 10-182

FALL OF WICKETS
1-41, 2-95, 3-98

Umpires: M.W.Johnson (15) and P.J.McConnell (1).

AUSTRALIA v NEW ZEALAND 1982-83

At Sydney Cricket Ground on 18 January 1983.   Result: **NEW ZEALAND** won by 47 runs.   Toss: Australia.
Award: D.W.Hookes.   LOI debuts: None.

New Zealand, relieved at being asked to bat in their first outing under lights for two seasons, scored 63 off their last six overs.

NEW ZEALAND		Runs	Balls	4/6	AUSTRALIA		Runs	Balls	4/6
J.G.Wright	c Marsh b Hogg	1	21	–	J.Dyson	run out	11	35	1
B.A.Edgar	b Chappell	32	82	–	K.C.Wessels	c Cairns b Snedden	58	105	2
* G.P.Howarth	c Marsh b Chappell	29	45	3	G.S.Chappell	c Webb b Snedden	1	5	–
G.M.Turner	b Thomson	55	64	4	* K.J.Hughes	c and b Cairns	1	4	–
J.J.Crowe	run out	56	73	1	D.W.Hookes	run out	68	91	4/3
R.J.Hadlee	c Chappell b Thomson	5	6	1	A.R.Border	c Hadlee b Cairns	11	14	–
J.V.Coney	c Marsh b Lawson	13	10	–/1	† R.W.Marsh	b Cairns	6	10	1
B.L.Cairns	c Border b Hogg	2	3	–	G.F.Lawson	run out	0	3	–
† P.N.Webb	not out	10	7	1	J.R.Thomson	b Cairns	0	1	–
M.C.Snedden					R.M.Hogg	not out	3	6	–
E.J.Chatfield					C.G.Rackemann	lbw b Hadlee	2	2	–
Extras	(b 7, lb 10, w 6)	23			Extras	(b 4, lb 9, w 5)	18		
Total	(50 overs; 8 wickets)	**226**			**Total**	(45.3 overs)	**179**		

AUSTRALIA	O	M	R	W	NEW ZEALAND	O	M	R	W
Lawson	10	3	33	1	Chatfield	10	1	47	0
Hogg	10	2	32	2	Hadlee	8.3	2	19	1
Thomson	10	0	42	2	Snedden	8	2	24	2
Rackemann	10	0	59	0	Cairns	10	4	16	4
Chappell	10	0	37	2	Coney	9	0	55	0

FALL OF WICKETS
1-7, 2-65, 3-93, 4-159, 5-167, 6-191, 7-194, 8-226

FALL OF WICKETS
1-27, 2-28, 3-29, 4-145, 5-163, 6-169, 7-169, 8-169, 9-176, 10-179

Umpires: M.W.Johnson (16) and P.J.McConnell (2).

ENGLAND v NEW ZEALAND 1982-83

At Sydney Cricket Ground on 20 January 1983.   Result: **ENGLAND** won by 8 wickets.   Toss: New Zealand.
Award: A.J.Lamb.   LOI debuts: England – G.Fowler.

Chris Tavaré, who made his highest LOI score, and Allan Lamb, who reached his only international hundred in Australia off 104 balls, shared an unbroken third-wicket partnership of 190 off 212 balls.

NEW ZEALAND		Runs	Balls	4/6	ENGLAND		Runs	Balls	4/6
J.G.Wright	c Randall b Willis	9	20	1	C.J.Tavaré	not out	83	127	8/1
B.A.Edgar	c Willis b Cowans	74	134	7/1	G.Fowler	c sub (P.N.Webb) b Chatfield	0	21	–
* G.P.Howarth	c Miller b Willis	1	9	–	D.I.Gower	b Hadlee	0	6	–
G.M.Turner	c Gower b Marks	37	54	2	A.J.Lamb	not out	108	106	9/1
B.L.Cairns	c Gower b Miller	11	11	1	I.T.Botham				
† W.K.Lees	b Botham	12	14	–/1	D.W.Randall				
J.J.Crowe	run out	12	20	–	G.Miller				
R.J.Hadlee	c Lamb b Willis	15	13	1	† I.J.Gould				
J.V.Coney	c Miller b Willis	6	8	–	V.J.Marks				
M.C.Snedden	not out	2	2	–	* R.G.D.Willis				
E.J.Chatfield	lbw b Botham	0	2	–	N.G.Cowans				
Extras	(lb 17, w 3)	20			Extras	(b 1, lb 5, w 3)	9		
Total	(47.2 overs)	**199**			**Total**	(42.4 overs; 2 wickets)	**200**		

ENGLAND	O	M	R	W	NEW ZEALAND	O	M	R	W
Willis	9	0	23	4	Hadlee	9	2	37	1
Cowans	10	1	26	1	Chatfield	10	2	25	1
Botham	8.2	0	30	2	Cairns	8	2	31	0
Marks	10	0	49	1	Snedden	8.4	0	61	0
Miller	10	0	51	1	Coney	7	0	37	0

FALL OF WICKETS
1-14, 2-20, 3-101, 4-118, 5-152, 6-171, 7-178, 8-197, 9-197, 10-199

FALL OF WICKETS
1-9, 2-10

Umpires: A.R.Crafter (16) and R.A.French (17).

AUSTRALIA v NEW ZEALAND 1982-83

At Melbourne Cricket Ground on 22 January 1983.　Result: **NEW ZEALAND** won by 58 runs.　Toss: Australia.
Award: J.G.Wright.　LOI debuts: None.

John Wright deputised as captain for Geoff Howarth who retired (pinched nerve in back) early in Australia's innings.
Struck by a lifting ball from Richard Hadlee, Rodney Hogg's left ear required 11 stitches.

NEW ZEALAND		Runs	Balls	4/6
J.G.Wright	c Dyson b Rackemann	84	138	9
B.A.Edgar	c Marsh b Rackemann	32	61	3
G.M.Turner	lbw b Thomson	31	45	3
R.J.Hadlee	c Wessels b Rackemann	21	17	3
* G.P.Howarth	run out	30	19	4
J.J.Crowe	not out	20	20	–
B.L.Cairns	c Border b Lawson	0	1	–
† W.K.Lees	not out	5	5	1
M.C.Snedden				
G.B.Troup				
E.J.Chatfield				
Extras	(b 4, lb 13, w 4, nb 2)	23		
Total	(50 overs; 6 wickets)	**246**		

AUSTRALIA		O	M	R	W
Lawson		10	2	27	1
Hogg		10	1	40	0
Rackemann		10	0	52	3
Thomson		10	0	52	1
Chappell		10	0	52	0

FALL OF WICKETS
1-83, 2-151, 3-184, 4-198, 5-236, 6-236

AUSTRALIA		Runs	Balls	4/6
K.C.Wessels	c sub (J.V.Coney) b Troup	62	116	6
J.Dyson	c Wright b Snedden	21	44	2
D.W.Hookes	c Hadlee b Cairns	1	4	–
* K.J.Hughes	c Hadlee b Troup	12	12	1
G.S.Chappell	c Snedden b Troup	37	40	2
A.R.Border	c and b Troup	5	6	1
† R.W.Marsh	c sub (P.N.Webb) b Snedden	32	28	3
G.F.Lawson	lbw b Hadlee	0	2	–
R.M.Hogg	retired hurt	0	3	–
J.R.Thomson	c Crowe b Chatfield	4	12	–
C.G.Rackemann	not out	0	1	–
Extras	(lb 11, w 1, nb 2)	14		
Total	(44.1 overs)	**188**		

NEW ZEALAND	O	M	R	W
Hadlee	8	2	21	1
Chatfield	9	1	38	1
Snedden	7.1	1	12	2
Troup	10	0	54	4
Cairns	10	0	49	1

FALL OF WICKETS
1-41, 2-43, 3-66, 4-129, 5-142, 6-151, 7-155, 8-155, 9-188

Umpires: R.A.French (18) and R.V.Whitehead (14).

AUSTRALIA v ENGLAND 1982-83

At Melbourne Cricket Ground on 23 January 1983.　Result: **AUSTRALIA** won by 5 wickets.　Toss: Australia.
Award: A.J.Lamb.　LOI debuts: Australia – J.N.Maguire.

Match reduced to 37 overs by morning rain. The attendance of 84,153 was the international limited-overs record until
LOI No. 239 was played at this venue a year later.

ENGLAND		Runs	Balls	4/6
C.J.Tavaré	c Lillee b Rackemann	20	51	2
I.T.Botham	b Lillee	19	22	4
D.I.Gower	c Marsh b Rackemann	6	22	–
A.J.Lamb	c sub (K.H.MacLeay) b Lillee	94	76	9/1
D.W.Randall	not out	51	54	2
† I.J.Gould	b Hogg	3	3	–
T.E.Jesty	not out	1	2	–
D.R.Pringle				
G.Miller				
* R.G.D.Willis				
N.G.Cowans				
Extras	(lb 10, w 4, nb 5)	19		
Total	(37 overs; 5 wickets)	**213**		

AUSTRALIA	O	M	R	W
Hogg	7	0	36	1
Lillee	8	2	50	2
Rackemann	8	0	41	2
Chappell	7	0	33	0
Maguire	7	0	34	0

FALL OF WICKETS
1-32, 2-50, 3-66, 4-205, 5-209

AUSTRALIA		Runs	Balls	4/6
J.Dyson	run out	54	84	4
A.R.Border	run out	54	48	9
D.W.Hookes	c Gower b Cowans	50	42	6/1
* K.J.Hughes	c Miller b Cowans	6	8	–
G.S.Chappell	not out	32	24	4
† R.W.Marsh	run out	8	3	2
K.C.Wessels	not out	5	6	1
R.M.Hogg				
D.K.Lillee				
J.N.Maguire				
C.G.Rackemann				
Extras	(lb 5, w 2, nb 1)	8		
Total	(34.4 overs; 5 wickets)	**217**		

ENGLAND	O	M	R	W
Willis	6.4	1	29	0
Cowans	6	0	46	2
Botham	7	1	45	0
Pringle	7	0	47	0
Miller	8	0	42	0

FALL OF WICKETS
1-85, 2-157, 3-167, 4-176, 5-190

Umpires: A.R.Crafter (17) and P.J.McConnell (3).

AUSTRALIA v ENGLAND 1982-83

At Sydney Cricket Ground on 26 January 1983.   Result: **ENGLAND** won by 98 runs.   Toss: England.
Award: R.D.Jackman.   LOI debuts: None.

Match reduced to 41 overs by afternoon rain. England chose Australia Day to gain their first victory against the hosts in this tournament. Robin Jackman took three prime wickets in seven balls.

ENGLAND		Runs	Balls	4/6
C.J.Tavaré	c Marsh b Thomson	14	47	1
I.T.Botham	c Wessels b Hogg	0	2	–
D.I.Gower	b Lillee	25	31	4
A.J.Lamb	lbw b Lillee	0	5	–
D.W.Randall	run out	47	64	4
T.E.Jesty	b Maguire	30	51	2
† I.J.Gould	c Wessels b Hogg	42	42	–
V.J.Marks	c and b Lillee	22	13	4
E.E.Hemmings	run out	3	4	–
R.D.Jackman	b Hogg	0	2	–
* R.G.D.Willis	not out	5	2	1
Extras	(b 2, lb 4, w 9, nb 4)	19		
Total	(41 overs)	**207**		

AUSTRALIA		Runs	Balls	4/6
J.Dyson	c Randall b Botham	23	47	1
A.R.Border	c and b Willis	31	22	4
D.W.Hookes	b Marks	32	52	3/1
* K.J.Hughes	c Gould b Jackman	0	2	–
G.S.Chappell	b Jackman	0	3	–
K.C.Wessels	b Jackman	1	3	–
† R.W.Marsh	b Hemmings	1	15	–
D.K.Lillee	b Hemmings	3	7	–
J.R.Thomson	b Marks	7	11	1
R.M.Hogg	not out	0	3	–
J.N.Maguire	c Lamb b Hemmings	2	6	–
Extras	(b 2, lb 2, w 3, nb 2)	9		
Total	(27.3 overs)	**109**		

AUSTRALIA	O	M	R	W
Hogg	10	1	44	3
Maguire	8	0	42	1
Lillee	8	0	34	3
Thomson	8	0	40	1
Chappell	7	0	28	0

ENGLAND	O	M	R	W
Willis	6	1	23	1
Jackman	10	1	41	3
Botham	2	0	13	1
Marks	6	0	12	2
Hemmings	3.3	0	11	3

FALL OF WICKETS
1-8, 2-45, 3-47, 4-47, 5-101, 6-157, 7-197, 8-201, 9-201, 10-207

FALL OF WICKETS
1-40, 2-72, 3-73, 4-73, 5-77, 6-96, 7-99, 8-106, 9-106, 10-109

Umpires: R.A.French (19) and B.E.Martin (10).

ENGLAND v NEW ZEALAND 1982-83

At Adelaide Oval on 29 January 1983.   Result: **NEW ZEALAND** won by 4 wickets.   Toss: England.
Award: R.J.Hadlee.   LOI debuts: None.

David Gower completed his epic fifth LOI hundred off 82 balls; it remains the fastest for England. New Zealand took full advantage of perfect batting conditions to record the highest second innings total in limited-overs internationals until 1990 (*LOI No. 632*). Trevor Jesty completed 50 off 35 balls, while Ian Botham and Richard Hadlee each took 44 balls.

ENGLAND		Runs	Balls	4/6
C.J.Tavaré	c Crowe b Chatfield	16	54	1
I.T.Botham	b Chatfield	65	54	7/4
D.I.Gower	c Coney b Troup	109	85	12/1
A.J.Lamb	run out	19	23	3
D.W.Randall	c Wright b Snedden	31	49	5
T.E.Jesty	not out	52	35	4/2
† I.J.Gould	not out	1	1	–
V.J.Marks				
E.E.Hemmings				
R.D.Jackman				
* R.G.D.Willis				
Extras	(lb 1, w 1, nb 1)	3		
Total	(50 overs; 5 wickets)	**296**		

NEW ZEALAND		Runs	Balls	4/6
G.M.Turner	b Willis	23	22	4
J.G.Wright	run out	30	58	2
* G.P.Howarth	b Jackman	3	12	–
J.J.Crowe	c Willis b Botham	50	66	4/1
B.L.Cairns	c Gower b Botham	49	24	4/3
J.V.Coney	not out	47	51	1
R.J.Hadlee	c Jesty b Jackman	79	64	5/1
† W.K.Lees	not out	1	1	–
M.C.Snedden				
G.B.Troup				
E.J.Chatfield				
Extras	(b 2, lb 7, nb 6)	15		
Total	(48.5 overs; 6 wickets)	**297**		

NEW ZEALAND	O	M	R	W
Hadlee	10	1	36	0
Cairns	10	1	45	0
Snedden	10	0	72	1
Chatfield	10	2	64	2
Troup	10	0	76	1

ENGLAND	O	M	R	W
Willis	9.5	2	43	1
Jackman	10	1	49	2
Jesty	8	0	52	0
Hemmings	6	0	49	0
Botham	8	0	61	2
Marks	7	1	28	0

FALL OF WICKETS
1-75, 2-86, 3-121, 4-204, 5-278

FALL OF WICKETS
1-26, 2-33, 3-96, 4-166, 5-166, 6-287

Umpires: A.R.Crafter (18) and R.A.French (20).

AUSTRALIA v ENGLAND 1982-83

At Adelaide Oval on 30 January 1983.   Result: **ENGLAND** won by 14 runs.   Toss: England.
Award: D.I.Gower.   LOI debuts: None.

Match reduced to 47 overs by Australia's slow over rate (in severe heat). Attendance: 34,897.

ENGLAND		Runs	Balls	4/6
C.J.Tavaré	b Hogg	18	50	1
I.T.Botham	b Lawson	14	16	3
D.I.Gower	c Lillee b Thomson	77	98	4
A.J.Lamb	b Hogg	2	15	–
D.W.Randall	c and b Lawson	49	56	1
T.E.Jesty	not out	22	28	2
†I.J.Gould	c Lillee b Lawson	9	20	–
V.J.Marks	not out	10	13	–
E.E.Hemmings				
R.D.Jackman				
*R.G.D.Willis				
Extras	(b 1, lb 14, w 6, nb 6)	27		
Total	(47 overs; 6 wickets)	228		

AUSTRALIA		Runs	Balls	4/6
J.Dyson	c Lamb b Hemmings	17	60	1
A.R.Border	c Randall b Willis	19	31	2
D.W.Hookes	c Jesty b Jackman	76	95	8/1
*K.J.Hughes	c Gower b Marks	4	10	–
G.S.Chappell	c Gower b Jackman	33	36	1
†R.W.Marsh	c Jackman b Botham	7	6	1
K.C.Wessels	b Botham	7	11	–
G.F.Lawson	not out	28	24	–/1
J.R.Thomson	not out	12	10	2
D.K.Lillee				
R.M.Hogg				
Extras	(b 6, lb 5)	11		
Total	(47 overs; 7 wickets)	214		

AUSTRALIA	O	M	R	W
Lawson	10	0	27	3
Lillee	10	0	50	0
Hogg	9	1	25	2
Thomson	9	0	38	1
Chappell	7	0	45	0
Hookes	2	0	16	0

ENGLAND	O	M	R	W
Willis	10	1	40	1
Jackman	10	3	36	2
Botham	7	0	49	2
Hemmings	10	0	40	1
Marks	10	1	38	1

FALL OF WICKETS
1-25, 2-62, 3-70, 4-176, 5-178, 6-200

FALL OF WICKETS
1-27, 2-89, 3-97, 4-149, 5-161, 6-167, 7-189

Umpires: M.W.Johnson (17) and P.J.McConnell (4).

AUSTRALIA v NEW ZEALAND 1982-83

At Adelaide Oval on 31 January 1983.   Result: **NEW ZEALAND** won by 47 runs.   Toss: New Zealand.
Award: G.M.Turner.   LOI debuts: Australia – T.G.Hogan, K.H.MacLeay.

Australia's fifth defeat in six matches, in temperatures that rose to obscene levels, guaranteed New Zealand a place in the finals for the second time.

NEW ZEALAND		Runs	Balls	4/6
J.G.Wright	c Border b Thomson	15	41	2
B.A.Edgar	b MacLeay	18	50	1
G.M.Turner	c Hookes b Thomson	84	109	8
J.J.Crowe	c and b Hogan	14	24	–
B.L.Cairns	c MacLeay b Hogan	0	3	–
*G.P.Howarth	c Hughes b Chappell	15	27	–
R.J.Hadlee	run out	8	8	1
J.V.Coney	c Marsh b Thomson	5	12	–
†W.K.Lees	b Hogg	10	11	–
M.C.Snedden	not out	16	17	1
E.J.Chatfield	not out	2	2	–
Extras	(lb 8, w 2, nb 3)	13		
Total	(50 overs; 9 wickets)	200		

AUSTRALIA		Runs	Balls	4/6
J.Dyson	c Coney b Chatfield	24	58	–
A.R.Border	c Snedden b Chatfield	41	72	3
D.W.Hookes	c Lees b Hadlee	27	35	1/1
*K.J.Hughes	c Wright b Coney	6	25	–
G.S.Chappell	c Lees b Cairns	7	14	–
K.H.MacLeay	lbw b Hadlee	3	8	–
†R.W.Marsh	c Hadlee b Coney	15	23	2
G.F.Lawson	b Coney	7	14	–
T.G.Hogan	run out	4	11	–
J.R.Thomson	b Cairns	3	5	–
R.M.Hogg	not out	1	1	–
Extras	(lb 13, w 2)	15		
Total	(44 overs)	153		

AUSTRALIA	O	M	R	W
Lawson	10	3	20	0
Hogg	9	0	32	1
Thomson	5	0	27	3
MacLeay	10	0	39	1
Hogan	10	0	42	2
Chappell	6	0	27	1

NEW ZEALAND	O	M	R	W
Hadlee	7	1	15	2
Cairns	10	0	41	2
Snedden	7	1	16	0
Chatfield	10	1	26	2
Coney	10	0	40	3

FALL OF WICKETS
1-23, 2-64, 3-95, 4-95, 5-144, 6-156, 7-170, 8-171, 9-195

FALL OF WICKETS
1-64, 2-76, 3-103, 4-112, 5-116, 6-116, 7-141, 8-148, 9-149, 10-153

Umpires: A.R.Crafter (19) and R.A.French (21).

BENSON AND HEDGES WORLD SERIES (14th Match)

ENGLAND v NEW ZEALAND 1982-83

At WACA Ground, Perth on 5 February 1983.   Result: **NEW ZEALAND** won by 7 wickets.   Toss: New Zealand.
Award: R.J.Hadlee.   LOI debuts: None.

Having scored 45 for 3 after 17.3 overs, England found their innings reduced to 23 overs after heavy rain. A helicopter was used to dry the flooded outfield.

ENGLAND		Runs	Balls	4/6
C.J.Tavaré	c Lees b Hadlee	0	11	–
I.T.Botham	c Lees b Hadlee	19	21	2/1
D.I.Gower	not out	35	60	3
A.J.Lamb	c Crowe b Snedden	7	25	1
D.W.Randall	c Howarth b Snedden	12	12	1
T.E.Jesty	run out	0	3	–
† I.J.Gould	b Snedden	0	1	–
V.J.Marks	b Hadlee	2	4	–
R.D.Jackman	not out	0	1	–
* R.G.D.Willis				
N.G.Cowans				
Extras	(b 3, lb 10)	13		
Total	(23 overs; 7 wickets)	**88**		

NEW ZEALAND		Runs	Balls	4/6
J.G.Wright	c Tavaré b Willis	12	24	1
G.M.Turner	c Jackman b Willis	0	1	–
J.J.Crowe	c Botham b Cowans	18	29	1
J.V.Coney	not out	29	43	3
* G.P.Howarth	not out	26	29	2
J.F.M.Morrison				
R.J.Hadlee				
B.L.Cairns				
† W.K.Lees				
M.C.Snedden				
E.J.Chatfield				
Extras	(lb 1, w 3)	4		
Total	(20.3 overs; 3 wickets)	**89**		

NEW ZEALAND	O	M	R	W
Hadlee	8	2	15	3
Cairns	5	0	21	0
Snedden	6	1	25	3
Chatfield	4	1	14	0

ENGLAND	O	M	R	W
Willis	8.3	1	28	2
Cowans	8	0	32	1
Jackman	2	0	16	0
Botham	2	0	9	0

FALL OF WICKETS
1-18, 2-23, 3-37, 4-66, 5-66, 6-82, 7-87

FALL OF WICKETS
1-5, 2-20, 3-47

Umpires: R.A.French (22) and P.J.McConnell (5).

BENSON AND HEDGES WORLD SERIES (15th Match)

AUSTRALIA v NEW ZEALAND 1982-83

At WACA Ground, Perth on 6 February 1983.   Result: **AUSTRALIA** won by 27 runs.   Toss: New Zealand.
Award: R.W.Marsh.   LOI debuts: Australia – S.B.Smith.

After conceding only seven runs from five overs, Richard Hadlee retired with a hamstring injury which ended his tournament. This win gave the hosts a place in the finals – qualifying points: New Zealand 12, Australia 10, England 8.

AUSTRALIA		Runs	Balls	4/6
G.M.Wood	c Wright b Chatfield	25	49	3
S.B.Smith	c Webb b Chatfield	28	56	1
* K.J.Hughes	b Morrison	21	51	–
A.R.Border	c and b Coney	2	6	–
D.W.Hookes	b Hadlee	12	32	1
G.S.Chappell	b Snedden	24	43	–
† R.W.Marsh	c Snedden b Morrison	31	50	2
G.F.Lawson	b Snedden	8	14	–
J.R.Thomson	b Morrison	4	4	–
R.M.Hogg	not out	1	1	–
D.K.Lillee	not out	0	1	–
Extras	(b 9, lb 19, w 7)	35		
Total	(50 overs; 9 wickets)	**191**		

NEW ZEALAND		Runs	Balls	4/6
* G.P.Howarth	b Hogg	8	16	–
J.G.Wright	c Marsh b Chappell	33	66	1
G.M.Turner	c Marsh b Lillee	30	47	4
J.J.Crowe	c Marsh b Lillee	0	1	–
J.V.Coney	c Thomson b Chappell	10	16	–/1
† P.N.Webb	c Border b Chappell	7	32	–
J.F.M.Morrison	not out	25	53	2
R.J.Hadlee	c Marsh b Hogg	5	12	1
B.L.Cairns	run out	1	2	–
M.C.Snedden	c Thomson b Lawson	25	31	2
E.J.Chatfield	b Lawson	0	2	–
Extras	(b 2, lb 6, w 8, nb 4)	20		
Total	(44.5 overs)	**164**		

NEW ZEALAND	O	M	R	W
Hadlee	5	2	7	1
Cairns	6	0	20	0
Snedden	10	1	41	2
Chatfield	10	2	30	2
Coney	10	0	22	1
Morrison	9	0	36	3

AUSTRALIA	O	M	R	W
Lawson	9.5	0	24	2
Hogg	9	0	37	2
Lillee	10	2	24	2
Thomson	8	0	24	0
Chappell	8	0	35	3

FALL OF WICKETS
1-9, 2-61, 3-61, 4-81, 5-92, 6-108, 7-123, 8-125, 9-162, 10-164

FALL OF WICKETS
1-65, 2-74, 3-77, 4-110, 5-118, 6-159, 7-183, 8-188, 9-191

Umpires: A.R.Crafter (20) and M.W.Johnson (18).

AUSTRALIA v NEW ZEALAND 1982-83

At Sydney Cricket Ground on 9 February 1983.   Result: **AUSTRALIA** won by 6 wickets (revised target).
Toss: New Zealand.   LOI debuts: None.

Match initially reduced to 49 overs by slow over-rate before a 25-minute stoppage for rain revised Australia's target to 150 runs within 38 overs. Attendance: 30,527.

NEW ZEALAND		Runs	Balls	4/6
J.G.Wright	c Chappell b Lawson	36	86	2
B.A.Edgar	b Thomson	12	41	1
G.M.Turner	lbw b Lillee	4	20	–
* G.P.Howarth	c Marsh b Chappell	9	24	–
J.V.Coney	not out	58	70	4/1
J.F.M.Morrison	b Lillee	35	49	5
† W.K.Lees	c Marsh b Lawson	1	4	–
B.L.Cairns	c Lillee b Hogg	9	8	–/1
M.C.Snedden	not out	2	3	–
G.B.Troup				
E.J.Chatfield				
Extras	(lb 15, w 11, nb 1)	27		
Total	(49 overs; 7 wickets)	**193**		

AUSTRALIA		Runs	Balls	4/6
G.M.Wood	b Chatfield	12	42	–
S.B.Smith	b Cairns	10	10	1
* K.J.Hughes	c Coney b Chatfield	63	74	7
A.R.Border	c sub (J.J.Crowe) b Chatfield	9	21	–
D.W.Hookes	not out	20	31	2
G.S.Chappell	not out	21	21	2/1
† R.W.Marsh				
G.F.Lawson				
J.R.Thomson				
R.M.Hogg				
D.K.Lillee				
Extras	(b 4, lb 16)	20		
Total	(33.1 overs; 4 wickets)	**155**		

AUSTRALIA	O	M	R	W
Lawson	10	4	28	2
Hogg	10	2	24	1
Lillee	10	1	35	2
Thomson	10	0	42	1
Chappell	9	0	37	1

NEW ZEALAND	O	M	R	W
Troup	5	0	30	0
Cairns	8.1	0	27	1
Snedden	9	0	45	0
Chatfield	10	1	27	3
Coney	1	0	6	0

FALL OF WICKETS
1-44, 2-57, 3-77, 4-81, 5-166, 6-171, 7-190

FALL OF WICKETS
1-14, 2-59, 3-83, 4-119

Umpires: R.A.French (23) and M.W.Johnson (19).

AUSTRALIA v NEW ZEALAND 1982-83

At Melbourne Cricket Ground on 13 February 1983.   Result: **AUSTRALIA** won by 149 runs.   Toss: Australia.
Finals award: K.J.Hughes.   LOI debuts: New Zealand – R.J.Webb.

Braced by a partisan audience of 71,393 and an opening partnership of 140 in 25 overs, Australia amassed the highest World Series total until 1984-85. Lance Cairns set LOI records, subsequently beaten, for the fastest fifty (21 balls) and most sixes (6).

AUSTRALIA		Runs	Balls	4/6
G.M.Wood	b Coney	91	84	9
S.B.Smith	b Webb	117	130	10
* K.J.Hughes	c Lees b Chatfield	12	13	–
A.R.Border	c and b Chatfield	11	15	1
D.W.Hookes	c Wright b Webb	40	39	3
G.S.Chappell	c Wright b Cairns	7	9	–
† R.W.Marsh	not out	3	2	–
K.H.MacLeay	run out	10	6	–/1
G.F.Lawson	run out	3	2	–
R.M.Hogg				
D.K.Lillee				
Extras	(b 1, lb 7)	8		
Total	(50 overs; 8 wickets)	**302**		

NEW ZEALAND		Runs	Balls	4/6
G.M.Turner	c Marsh b Lawson	1	11	–
J.G.Wright	c Marsh b Hogg	3	12	–
* G.P.Howarth	b Lawson	3	13	–
J.J.Crowe	lbw b MacLeay	27	48	3
J.V.Coney	b Lillee	2	23	–
J.F.M.Morrison	b Lillee	2	6	–
† W.K.Lees	run out	3	9	–
B.L.Cairns	c Smith b Lawson	52	25	1/6
M.C.Snedden	c Marsh b Hookes	35	49	4/1
E.J.Chatfield	lbw b Chappell	10	36	–
R.J.Webb	not out	6	10	1
Extras	(lb 6, w 2, nb 1)	9		
Total	(39.5 overs)	**153**		

NEW ZEALAND	O	M	R	W
Webb	9	1	47	2
Cairns	8	0	56	1
Chatfield	10	0	54	2
Snedden	7	0	47	0
Morrison	7	0	39	0
Coney	9	0	51	1

AUSTRALIA	O	M	R	W
Lawson	8	3	11	3
Hogg	10	1	31	1
Lillee	7	3	29	2
MacLeay	8	0	56	1
Chappell	5	0	15	1
Hookes	1.5	0	2	1

FALL OF WICKETS
1-140, 2-167, 3-205, 4-261, 5-280, 6-285, 7-289, 8-302

FALL OF WICKETS
1-8, 2-8, 3-13, 4-23, 5-42, 6-44, 7-92, 8-103, 9-144, 10-153

Umpires: A.R.Crafter (21) and P.J.McConnell (6).

NEW ZEALAND v ENGLAND 1982-83

At Eden Park, Auckland on 19 February 1983.   Result: **NEW ZEALAND** won by 6 wickets.   Toss: England.
Award: G.M.Turner.   LOI debuts: None.

Glenn Turner, representing his country at home for the first time in six years, began his international opening partnership with Bruce Edgar with a stand of 101 off 133 balls. The attendance of 41,000 was then a record for any day of cricket in New Zealand.

ENGLAND		Runs	Balls	4/6
C.J.Tavaré	b Cairns	11	30	–
I.T.Botham	c Morrison b Chatfield	12	38	1
D.I.Gower	c Morrison b Snedden	84	110	6/1
A.J.Lamb	run out	0	1	–
D.W.Randall	b Chatfield	30	44	4
T.E.Jesty	c Coney b Chatfield	1	9	–
† I.J.Gould	lbw b Cairns	3	11	–
G.Miller	lbw b Morrison	3	17	–
V.J.Marks	not out	23	30	–
R.D.Jackman	b Cairns	4	11	–
* R.G.D.Willis	not out	1	1	–
Extras	(lb 10, w 2)	12		
Total	**(50 overs; 9 wickets)**	**184**		

NEW ZEALAND		Runs	Balls	4/6
G.M.Turner	c sub (N.G.Cowans) b Willis	88	129	11
B.A.Edgar	c Jackman b Miller	35	73	6
B.L.Cairns	c Lamb b Botham	19	11	1/2
J.J.Crowe	lbw b Botham	15	40	1
J.V.Coney	not out	9	18	1
* G.P.Howarth	not out	14	11	1/1
J.F.M.Morrison				
† W.K.Lees				
M.C.Snedden				
E.J.Chatfield				
R.J.Webb				
Extras	(b 1, lb 4, nb 2)	7		
Total	**(46.3 overs; 4 wickets)**	**187**		

NEW ZEALAND	O	M	R	W
Webb	10	0	30	0
Cairns	10	2	28	3
Snedden	8	1	35	1
Chatfield	10	0	27	3
Coney	2	0	17	0
Morrison	10	1	35	1

ENGLAND	O	M	R	W
Willis	10	1	39	1
Jackman	8.3	0	38	0
Botham	8	0	40	2
Marks	10	1	30	0
Miller	10	0	33	1

FALL OF WICKETS
1-17, 2-40, 3-40, 4-104, 5-106, 6-110, 7-115, 8-168, 9-176

FALL OF WICKETS
1-101, 2-129, 3-164, 4-166

Umpires: F.R.Goodall (7) and D.A.Kinsella (2).

NEW ZEALAND v ENGLAND 1982-83

At Basin Reserve, Wellington on 23 February 1983.   Result: **NEW ZEALAND** won by 103 runs.   Toss: England.
Award: G.M.Turner.   LOI debuts: None.

Put in to bat, the hosts' new opening pair produced a stand of 152 from 176 balls as New Zealand posted their highest LOI total at home (until the following month).

NEW ZEALAND		Runs	Balls	4/6
G.M.Turner	b Willis	94	94	12/1
B.A.Edgar	run out	60	94	5
B.L.Cairns	b Willis	44	31	5/2
J.G.Wright	b Miller	30	28	5
J.V.Coney	not out	31	36	1
* G.P.Howarth	c Botham b Jackman	10	14	1
J.F.M.Morrison	b Botham	8	9	–
† W.K.Lees	not out	3	2	–
M.C.Snedden				
E.J.Chatfield				
R.J.Webb				
Extras	(lb 9, w 4, nb 2)	15		
Total	**(50 overs; 6 wickets)**	**295**		

ENGLAND		Runs	Balls	4/6
C.J.Tavaré	c Howarth b Chatfield	32	58	4
I.T.Botham	c Lees b Cairns	15	18	2
D.I.Gower	c and b Chatfield	2	12	–
A.J.Lamb	b Coney	7	22	1
D.W.Randall	c Howarth b Morrison	16	36	1
† I.J.Gould	c Wright b Coney	14	27	1
G.Miller	b Cairns	46	48	6
V.J.Marks	c Snedden b Webb	27	26	3
D.R.Pringle	b Webb	11	11	1
R.D.Jackman	b Cairns	9	14	1
* R.G.D.Willis	not out	2	3	–
Extras	(lb 6, w 5)	11		
Total	**(44.5 overs)**	**192**		

ENGLAND	O	M	R	W
Willis	9	0	54	2
Jackman	10	2	38	1
Pringle	7	0	57	0
Miller	10	0	51	1
Marks	7	0	34	0
Botham	7	0	46	1

NEW ZEALAND	O	M	R	W
Snedden	10	1	39	0
Cairns	10	0	38	3
Webb	7.5	0	28	2
Chatfield	7	1	26	2
Coney	5	0	16	2
Morrison	5	0	34	1

FALL OF WICKETS
1-152, 2-192, 3-214, 4-250, 5-275, 6-287

FALL OF WICKETS
1-20, 2-37, 3-52, 4-60, 5-83, 6-106, 7-162, 8-170, 9-182, 10-192

Umpires: S.C.Cowman (1) and S.J.Woodward (2).

NEW ZEALAND v ENGLAND 1982-83

At Lancaster Park, Christchurch on 26 February 1983.   Result: **NEW ZEALAND** won by 84 runs.   Toss: New Zealand.
Award: M.C.Snedden.   LOI debuts: None.

A record Lancaster Park crowd of 31,750 saw New Zealand gain a clean sweep in this tournament with their third emphatic win without the injured Richard Hadlee. Lance Cairns hit two sixes over the number four stand.

NEW ZEALAND		Runs	Balls	4/6
G.M.Turner	lbw b Botham	34	45	4/1
B.A.Edgar	b Marks	32	58	4
J.G.Wright	st Gould b Marks	2	16	–
B.L.Cairns	c Marks b Jackman	21	17	1/2
J.J.Crowe	lbw b Jackman	18	28	1
J.V.Coney	run out	30	45	3
* G.P.Howarth	lbw b Miller	8	21	1
J.F.M.Morrison	not out	24	30	2
† W.K.Lees	c Botham b Cowans	2	12	–
M.C.Snedden	not out	31	30	3
E.J.Chatfield				
Extras	(lb 5, w 3, nb 1)	9		
Total	(50 overs; 8 wickets)	**211**		

ENGLAND		Runs	Balls	4/6
† I.J.Gould	c Turner b Snedden	0	2	–
C.J.Tavaré	b Snedden	4	7	–
D.I.Gower	c Wright b Chatfield	53	75	6
A.J.Lamb	c Chatfield b Morrison	37	76	4
I.T.Botham	c and b Morrison	3	18	–
D.W.Randall	b Coney	2	6	–
G.Miller	c and b Chatfield	7	15	1
V.J.Marks	b Cairns	1	11	–
R.D.Jackman	b Cairns	5	11	–
* R.G.D.Willis	c Coney b Morrison	6	14	–
N.G.Cowans	not out	1	4	–
Extras	(lb 6, w 1, nb 1)	8		
Total	(40.1 overs)	**127**		

ENGLAND	O	M	R	W
Cowans	10	3	55	1
Willis	10	1	35	0
Botham	5	1	17	1
Marks	10	2	31	2
Miller	7	1	32	1
Jackman	8	1	32	2

NEW ZEALAND	O	M	R	W
Snedden	7	3	14	2
Cairns	7	0	13	2
Chatfield	8	2	26	2
Coney	10	0	42	1
Morrison	8.1	0	24	3

FALL OF WICKETS
1-64, 2-70, 3-93, 4-103, 5-126, 6-152, 7-153, 8-156

FALL OF WICKETS
1-0, 2-8, 3-94, 4-103, 5-105, 6-114, 7-114, 8-116, 9-125, 10-127

Umpires: F.R.Goodall (8) and I.C.Higginson (1).

NEW ZEALAND v SRI LANKA 1982-83

At Carisbrook, Dunedin on 2 March 1983.   Result: **NEW ZEALAND** won by 65 runs.   Toss: Sri Lanka.
Award: J.G.Wright.   LOI debuts: Sri Lanka – R.G.de Alwis, E.R.N.S.Fernando, Y.Goonasekera, M.de S.Wettimuny.

Sri Lanka's first tour of New Zealand involved two Test matches sandwiched between a three-match 50-over Rothmans Cup series. Ewan Chatfield fully utilised a pitch of variable bounce to return New Zealand's most frugal analysis involving a full allowance of overs.

NEW ZEALAND		Runs	Balls	4/6
G.M.Turner	b John	18	20	2
B.A.Edgar	c De Alwis b De Mel	3	26	–
J.G.Wright	lbw b Ratnayake	45	82	4/1
J.J.Crowe	lbw b Ratnayeke	5	26	–
J.V.Coney	b Ratnayake	15	62	1
* G.P.Howarth	b Ratnayake	11	21	–
B.L.Cairns	b John	37	33	5
R.J.Hadlee	b John	11	19	–
M.C.Snedden	not out	13	13	–
† W.K.Lees	not out	7	7	1
E.J.Chatfield				
Extras	(lb 10, w 4, nb 4)	18		
Total	(50 overs; 8 wickets)	**183**		

SRI LANKA		Runs	Balls	4/6
S.Wettimuny	run out	15	52	1
E.R.N.S.Fernando	c Turner b Hadlee	0	3	–
M.de S.Wettimuny	b Hadlee	2	11	–
Y.Goonasekera	run out	23	60	1
R.S.Madugalle	run out	3	10	–
* D.S.de Silva	b Chatfield	18	52	3
A.L.F.de Mel	lbw b Hadlee	1	12	–
J.R.Ratnayeke	c Snedden b Coney	14	24	2
† R.G.de Alwis	not out	13	43	2
R.J.Ratnayake	c Coney b Howarth	15	35	2
V.B.John				
Extras	(b 2, lb 10, w 2)	14		
Total	(50 overs; 9 wickets)	**118**		

SRI LANKA	O	M	R	W
De Mel	9.3	2	36	1
John	10	4	28	3
Ratnayake	10	0	30	3
Ratnayeke	10	0	45	1
De Silva	10	1	20	0
S.Wettimuny	0.3	0	6	0

NEW ZEALAND	O	M	R	W
Hadlee	8	3	9	3
Cairns	10	6	10	0
Snedden	9	1	25	0
Chatfield	10	4	8	1
Coney	10	1	42	1
Howarth	2	0	10	1
Wright	1	1	0	0

FALL OF WICKETS
1-26, 2-26, 3-50, 4-99, 5-113, 6-124, 7-150, 8-165

FALL OF WICKETS
1-1, 2-7, 3-39, 4-46, 5-62, 6-65, 7-85, 8-85, 9-118

Umpires: S.C.Cowman (2) and I.C.Higginson (2).

NEW ZEALAND v SRI LANKA 1982-83

At McLean Park, Napier on 19 March 1983.   Result: **NEW ZEALAND** won by 7 wickets.   Toss: New Zealand.
Award: M.D.Crowe.   LOI debuts: None.

Napier's first limited-overs international celebrated the centenary of the Hawke's Bay Cricket Association and attracted a crowd of over 10,000.

SRI LANKA		Runs	Balls	4/6
S.Wettimuny	b M.D.Crowe	20	65	3
E.R.N.S.Fernando	run out	0	7	
† R.G.de Alwis	b Cairns	12	40	1
Y.Goonasekera	c Turner b M.D.Crowe	11	18	1
* L.R.D.Mendis	c Hadlee b Chatfield	11	33	
R.S.Madugalle	b Cairns	7	11	–/1
A.L.F.de Mel	c Coney b Chatfield	19	68	2
J.R.Ratnayeke	c M.D.Crowe b Snedden	27	30	2
D.S.de Silva	not out	37	29	3
R.J.Ratnayake	not out	1	2	–
V.B.John				
Extras	(b 10, lb 11, nb 1)	22		
Total	(50 overs; 8 wickets)	**167**		

NEW ZEALAND		Runs	Balls	4/6
G.M.Turner	c Ratnayake b John	25	28	5
B.A.Edgar	c Madugalle b Ratnayeke	8	32	
* J.G.Wright	hit wicket b De Silva	31	36	4
J.J.Crowe	not out	46	89	6
M.D.Crowe	not out	43	48	6
B.L.Cairns				
R.J.Hadlee				
J.V.Coney				
M.C.Snedden				
† W.K.Lees				
E.J.Chatfield				
Extras	(b 1, lb 4, w 3, nb 7)	15		
Total	(36.4 overs; 3 wickets)	**168**		

NEW ZEALAND	O	M	R	W
Hadlee	10	3	22	0
Snedden	10	2	25	1
Cairns	10	2	25	2
Chatfield	10	2	43	2
M.D.Crowe	10	2	30	2

SRI LANKA	O	M	R	W
De Mel	4	0	27	0
John	10	4	31	1
Ratnayake	6.4	0	17	1
Ratnayeke	7	0	39	1
De Silva	6	1	28	1
Goonasekera	3	0	11	0

FALL OF WICKETS
1-5, 2-35, 3-51, 4-51, 5-63, 6-76, 7-105, 8-161

FALL OF WICKETS
1-32, 2-56, 3-81

Umpires: F.R.Goodall (9) and D.A.Kinsella (3).

NEW ZEALAND v SRI LANKA 1982-83

At Eden Park, Auckland on 20 March 1983.   Result: **NEW ZEALAND** won by 116 runs.   Toss: New Zealand.
Award: G.M.Turner.   LOI debuts: Sri Lanka – S.Jeganathan.

New Zealand's highest total in a home international secured their seventh successive LOI victory (including the Bushfire Appeal match, *LOI No. 192*, played on 17 March).

NEW ZEALAND		Runs	Balls	4/6
G.M.Turner	c Ratnayeke b Ratnayake	140	130	13/3
B.A.Edgar	c De Mel b Goonasekera	52	99	7
B.L.Cairns	b Ratnayake	18	13	1/2
J.G.Wright	b Wettimuny	45	34	4/1
R.J.Hadlee	c Ratnayeke b De Mel	9	9	1
J.J.Crowe	not out	17	11	1/1
M.D.Crowe	not out	7	5	–
* G.P.Howarth				
M.C.Snedden				
† W.K.Lees				
E.J.Chatfield				
Extras	(b 3, lb 10, w 3)	16		
Total	(50 overs; 5 wickets)	**304**		

SRI LANKA		Runs	Balls	4/6
S.Wettimuny	run out	31	64	3
E.R.N.S.Fernando	b Cairns	36	72	5
Y.Goonasekera	c Edgar b Cairns	35	26	6
* L.R.D.Mendis	c Wright b Cairns	7	11	1
R.S.Madugalle	not out	30	54	5
D.S.de Silva	b Cairns	1	3	–
A.L.F.de Mel	c Hadlee b M.D.Crowe	16	23	2
J.R.Ratnayeke	not out	13	40	–
† R.G.de Alwis				
S.Jeganathan				
R.J.Ratnayake				
Extras	(b 4, lb 9, w 5, nb 1)	19		
Total	(50 overs; 6 wickets)	**188**		

SRI LANKA	O	M	R	W
De Mel	10	1	65	1
Ratnayake	10	0	50	2
Ratnayeke	5	0	41	0
De Silva	10	0	46	0
Jeganathan	10	0	49	0
Goonasekera	3	0	24	1
Wettimuny	2	0	13	1

NEW ZEALAND	O	M	R	W
Hadlee	7	2	18	0
Snedden	7	0	22	0
Cairns	10	2	23	4
M.D.Crowe	10	1	51	1
Chatfield	10	0	47	0
Wright	2	0	2	0
Edgar	2	0	5	0
J.J.Crowe	1	0	1	0
Turner	1	1	0	0

FALL OF WICKETS
1-132, 2-158, 3-230, 4-267, 5-279

FALL OF WICKETS
1-55, 2-110, 3-111, 4-118, 5-123, 6-165

Umpires: I.C.Higginson (3) and S.J.Woodward (3).

WEST INDIES v INDIA 1982-83

At Queen's Park Oval, Port-of-Spain, Trinidad on 9 March 1983.   Result: **WEST INDIES** won by 52 runs.   Toss: India.
Award: D.L.Haynes.   LOI debuts: None.

Match reduced initially to 45 overs because the pitch had been dampened by excessive sweating from the covers and
then to 39 overs through India's slow over-rate. An earth tremor in mid-afternoon caused a few minor injuries among
the 30,000 crowd.

WEST INDIES		Runs	Balls	4/6
C.G.Greenidge	c Madan Lal b Maninder	66	75	4/4
D.L.Haynes	c Yashpal b Kapil Dev	97	104	12
I.V.A.Richards	c Gaekwad b Amarnath	32	38	4
A.L.Logie	not out	6	12	–
* C.H.Lloyd	c Kirmani b Kapil Dev	3	7	–
H.A.Gomes				
† P.J.L.Dujon				
M.D.Marshall				
A.M.E.Roberts				
M.A.Holding				
J.Garner				
Extras	(b 4, lb 5, w 1, nb 1)	11		
Total	**(38.5 overs; 4 wickets)**	**215**		

INDIA		Runs	Balls	4/6
S.M.Gavaskar	c Roberts b Garner	25	59	3
A.D.Gaekwad	b Gomes	22	52	2
M.Amarnath	run out	27	33	1
D.B.Vengsarkar	c Logie b Roberts	27	26	1/1
* Kapil Dev	lbw b Roberts	0	1	–
Yashpal Sharma	c Haynes b Gomes	2	6	–
A.Malhotra	c Holding b Gomes	21	14	3
† S.M.H.Kirmani	not out	13	16	–
Madan Lal	not out	13	30	1
Maninder Singh				
S.Venkataraghavan				
Extras	(b 1, lb 3, w 5, nb 4)	13		
Total	**(39 overs; 7 wickets)**	**163**		

INDIA	O	M	R	W
Kapil Dev	6.5	0	21	2
Madan Lal	7	0	34	0
Venkataraghavan	9	0	48	0
Amarnath	7	0	39	1
Maninder Singh	9	0	62	1

WEST INDIES	O	M	R	W
Holding	5	1	8	0
Roberts	7	2	27	2
Marshall	8	0	25	0
Garner	9	1	39	1
Gomes	9	0	50	3
Logie	1	0	1	0

FALL OF WICKETS
1-125, 2-198, 3-207, 4-215

FALL OF WICKETS
1-56, 2-58, 3-110, 4-110, 5-115, 6-117, 7-140

Umpires: D.J.Narine (2) and A.E.Weekes (1).

WEST INDIES v INDIA 1982-83

At Albion Sports Complex, Berbice on 29 March 1983.   Result: **INDIA** won by 27 runs.   Toss: West Indies.
Award: Kapil Dev.   LOI debuts: West Indies – W.W.Davis.

In an innings reduced to 47 overs by their hosts' slow over-rate, India amassed the (then) highest LOI total against West
Indies. Kapil Dev's astonishing assault included India's fastest recorded fifty in these matches (22 balls).

INDIA		Runs	Balls	4/6
S.M.Gavaskar	run out	90	117	8
R.J.Shastri	c Dujon b Marshall	30	56	1
M.Amarnath	b Richards	30	34	2
* Kapil Dev	b Roberts	72	38	7/3
Yashpal Sharma	c Greenidge b Davis	23	26	3
D.B.Vengsarkar	not out	18	19	1/1
A.Malhotra	not out	1	3	–
Madan Lal				
† S.M.H.Kirmani				
B.S.Sandhu				
S.Venkataraghavan				
Extras	(b 1, lb 9, w 4, nb 4)	18		
Total	**(47 overs; 5 wickets)**	**282**		

WEST INDIES		Runs	Balls	4/6
C.G.Greenidge	c and b Kapil Dev	16	28	–/1
D.L.Haynes	lbw b Sandhu	2	7	–
I.V.A.Richards	b Madan Lal	64	51	11/1
* C.H.Lloyd	c Amarnath b Madan Lal	8	4	–/1
S.F.A.F.Bacchus	c Yashpal b Shastri	52	65	3/1
H.A.Gomes	c Kapil Dev b Shastri	26	28	–/1
† P.J.L.Dujon	not out	53	64	3/1
M.D.Marshall	c Sandhu b Shastri	5	6	–
A.M.E.Roberts	b Kapil Dev	12	10	1/1
M.A.Holding	c Malhotra b Sandhu	2	8	–
W.W.Davis	not out	7	12	–
Extras	(lb 6, w 1, nb 1)	8		
Total	**(47 overs; 9 wickets)**	**255**		

WEST INDIES	O	M	R	W
Holding	7	0	49	0
Roberts	9	0	44	1
Davis	8	0	40	1
Marshall	7	0	23	1
Gomes	10	0	64	0
Richards	6	0	44	1

INDIA	O	M	R	W
Kapil Dev	10	0	33	2
Sandhu	10	0	38	2
Madan Lal	9	0	65	2
Venkataraghavan	10	0	63	0
Shastri	8	0	48	3

FALL OF WICKETS
1-93, 2-152, 3-224, 4-246, 5-277

FALL OF WICKETS
1-6, 2-22, 3-62, 4-98, 5-154, 6-181, 7-192, 8-228, 9-232

Umpires: D.M.Archer (2) and M.Baksh (1).

WEST INDIES v INDIA 1982-83

At Queen's Park, St George's, Grenada on 7 April 1983.   Result: **WEST INDIES** won by 7 wickets.   Toss: West Indies.
Award: H.A.Gomes.   LOI debuts: None.   50-over match.

A public holiday was declared for Grenada's first international match.

INDIA		Runs	Balls	4/6
S.M.Gavaskar	c Richards b Roberts	3		
R.J.Shastri	c Dujon b Marshall	17		
M.Amarnath	b Gomes	11		
D.B.Vengsarkar	c Richards b Gomes	54		-/2
A.Malhotra	c Richards b Gomes	7		
Yashpal Sharma	b Holding	25		
* Kapil Dev	lbw b Roberts	1		
Madan Lal	b Gomes	6		
† S.M.H.Kirmani	run out	3		
B.S.Sandhu	not out	16		
S.Venkataraghavan	b Holding	3		
Extras	(b 5, lb 7, w 5, nb 3)	20		
Total	(44.4 overs)	**166**		

WEST INDIES		Runs	Balls	4/6
C.G.Greenidge	c Sandhu b Shastri	64		5/2
D.L.Haynes	c Venkataraghavan b Amarnath	19		
I.V.A.Richards	c Shastri b Venkataraghavan	28		
S.F.A.F.Bacchus	not out	26		
† P.J.L.Dujon	not out	20		
* C.H.Lloyd				
H.A.Gomes				
M.D.Marshall				
A.M.E.Roberts				
M.A.Holding				
J.Garner				
Extras	(lb 7, w 3)	10		
Total	(40.2 overs; 3 wickets)	**167**		

WEST INDIES	O	M	R	W
Holding	8.4	2	15	2
Roberts	9	0	38	2
Garner	10	1	30	0
Marshall	7	2	25	1
Gomes	10	0	38	4

INDIA	O	M	R	W
Kapil Dev	6	2	21	0
Sandhu	8	2	30	0
Madan Lal	7	1	37	0
Amarnath	4	0	23	1
Venkataraghavan	8	0	24	1
Shastri	5	1	10	1
Yashpal Sharma	2.2	0	12	0

FALL OF WICKETS
1-9, 2-36, 3-47, 4-74, 5-109, 6-114, 7-127, 8-138, 9-153, 10-166

FALL OF WICKETS
1-61, 2-106, 3-132

Umpires: S.E.Parris (1) and P.C.White (1).

AUSTRALIA v NEW ZEALAND 1982-83

At Sydney Cricket Ground on 17 March 1983.   Result: **NEW ZEALAND** won by 14 runs.   Toss: Australia.
Award: M.D.Crowe.   LOI debuts: Australia – M.R.Whitney; New Zealand – T.J.Franklin.

During their Rothmans Series with Sri Lanka, New Zealand flew across the Tasman Sea for a one-off game in aid of the
Australian Bushfire Appeal fund, Trevor Franklin joining the team from the NZ Emerging Players tour already there.
This match was not originally included as an official LOI.

NEW ZEALAND		Runs	Balls	4/6
T.J.Franklin	b Maguire	0	13	–
B.A.Edgar	c Hookes b Maguire	5	34	–
* G.P.Howarth	b Whitney	6	14	–
M.D.Crowe	c Hughes b Chappell	66	67	2/1
J.V.Coney	c Marsh b MacLeay	27	47	–
B.L.Cairns	b Rackemann	1	2	–
R.J.Hadlee	c Smith b Rackemann	0	10	–
J.F.M.Morrison	not out	15	18	1
† W.K.Lees	b Whitney	3	8	–
M.C.Snedden	not out	0	2	–
E.J.Chatfield				
Extras	(b 1, lb 5, w 9)	15		
Total	(35 overs; 8 wickets)	**138**		

AUSTRALIA		Runs	Balls	4/6
G.M.Wood	not out	11	33	–
S.B.Smith	c Lees b Snedden	8	7	1
* K.J.Hughes	c Lees b Crowe	13	35	1
D.W.Hookes	c Crowe b Hadlee	18	27	–/1
A.R.Border	c Cairns b Chatfield	17	45	–
G.S.Chappell	c Lees b Chatfield	2	3	–
† R.W.Marsh	c Howarth b Chatfield	5	12	1
K.H.MacLeay	c Lees b Snedden	41	37	4/1
J.N.Maguire	c Snedden b Chatfield	1	5	–
C.G.Rackemann	b Crowe	0	3	–
M.R.Whitney	run out	1	2	–
Extras	(lb 3, w 4)	7		
Total	(34 overs)	**124**		

AUSTRALIA	O	M	R	W
Rackemann	7	2	17	2
Maguire	7	4	9	2
Whitney	7	3	19	2
Chappell	7	0	36	1
MacLeay	7	0	42	1

NEW ZEALAND	O	M	R	W
Hadlee	7	1	15	1
Snedden	7	1	24	2
Cairns	6	1	28	0
Chatfield	7	0	20	4
Crowe	7	2	30	2

FALL OF WICKETS
1-10, 2-22, 3-25, 4-118, 5-119, 6-119, 7-122, 8-137

FALL OF WICKETS
1-10, 2-40, 3-49, 4-55, 5-64, 6-72, 7-89, 8-91, 9-122, 10-124

Umpires: R.A.French (24) and M.W.Johnson (20).

SRI LANKA v AUSTRALIA 1982-83

At P.Saravanamuttu Stadium, Colombo on 13 April 1983.　　Result: **SRI LANKA** won by 2 wickets.　　Toss: Australia.
Award: R.G.de Alwis.　　LOI debuts: Australia – R.D.Woolley.

Australia began this series of four 45-over matches the day after their arrival. Guy de Alwis equalled the LOI record by holding five catches, one of them an outstanding effort, diving wide on the leg side.

AUSTRALIA		Runs	Balls	4/6
G.M.Wood	b De Silva	50	71	5
S.B.Smith	c De Alwis b John	1	15	–
G.N.Yallop	c De Alwis b Ranatunga	39	70	4
* G.S.Chappell	c De Alwis b John	11	38	1
D.W.Hookes	c De Alwis b Ranatunga	0	4	–
A.R.Border	b De Silva	10	21	–
† R.D.Woolley	c De Alwis b De Mel	16	24	1
T.G.Hogan	c Ratnayake b De Mel	27	25	4/1
D.K.Lillee	run out	5	5	–
R.M.Hogg	not out	0	–	–
J.N.Maguire				
Extras	(lb 7, w 2)	9		
Total	**(45 overs; 9 wickets)**	**168**		

SRI LANKA		Runs	Balls	4/6
S.Wettimuny	b Hogan	37	79	–
E.R.N.S.Fernando	st Woolley b Hogan	31	53	–
R.L.Dias	lbw b Chappell	5	5	–
* L.R.D.Mendis	b Hogan	16	28	1
R.S.Madugalle	c Smith b Maguire	9	40	–
A.Ranatunga	c Hogan b Hogg	10	22	–
A.L.F.de Mel	c Woolley b Maguire	27	27	–
D.S.de Silva	not out	15	13	–
† R.G.de Alwis	b Hogg	6	6	–
R.J.Ratnayake	not out	0	–	–
V.B.John				
Extras	(lb 5, w 5, nb 3)	13		
Total	**(44.1 overs; 8 wickets)**	**169**		

SRI LANKA	O	M	R	W
De Mel	9	2	35	2
John	9	1	33	2
Ratnayake	9	1	44	0
Ranatunga	9	1	26	2
De Silva	9	0	21	2

AUSTRALIA	O	M	R	W
Hogg	9	1	40	2
Maguire	8.1	0	43	2
Lillee	9	0	25	0
Chappell	9	2	21	1
Hogan	9	1	27	3

FALL OF WICKETS
1-15, 2-87, 3-103, 4-107, 5-109, 6-118, 7-144, 8-167, 9-168

FALL OF WICKETS
1-71, 2-82, 3-82, 4-102, 5-112, 6-139, 7-157, 8-168

Umpires: C.E.B.Anthony (2) and P.W.Vidanagamage (2).

SRI LANKA v AUSTRALIA 1982-83

At P.Saravanamuttu Stadium, Colombo on 16 April 1983.　　Result: **SRI LANKA** won by 4 wickets.　　Toss: Sri Lanka.
Award: A.Ranatunga.　　LOI debuts: None.

A superb innings by the 19-year-old Arjuna Ranatunga took Sri Lanka to victory with ten balls to spare after 90 runs had been required from the last 12 overs.

AUSTRALIA		Runs	Balls	4/6
G.M.Wood	lbw b Ratnayake	9	36	–
K.C.Wessels	b Ratnayake	39	63	4
G.N.Yallop	c Mendis b Ranatunga	59	63	6/1
* G.S.Chappell	not out	54	76	5
D.W.Hookes	run out	27	26	2
A.R.Border	c Dias b John	6	5	1
† R.D.Woolley	not out	3	3	–
B.Yardley				
T.G.Hogan				
D.K.Lillee				
R.M.Hogg				
Extras	(lb 8, nb 2)	10		
Total	**(45 overs; 5 wickets)**	**207**		

SRI LANKA		Runs	Balls	4/6
S.Wettimuny	b Yardley	56	92	4
E.R.N.S.Fernando	run out	34	21	2
R.L.Dias	c Wood b Yardley	2	7	–
* L.R.D.Mendis	b Yardley	2	7	–
A.Ranatunga	not out	55	39	3/3
R.S.Madugalle	b Hogan	37	23	3/1
A.L.F.de Mel	c Wood b Border	1	3	–
D.S.de Silva	not out	7	11	–
† R.G.de Alwis				
R.J.Ratnayake				
V.B.John				
Extras	(b 2, lb 14, nb 3)	19		
Total	**(43.2 overs; 6 wickets)**	**213**		

SRI LANKA	O	M	R	W
De Mel	9	1	29	0
John	9	0	33	1
Ratnayake	9	0	38	2
Ranatunga	9	0	45	1
De Silva	9	0	52	0

AUSTRALIA	O	M	R	W
Hogg	7	1	18	0
Lillee	9	0	30	0
Chappell	6.2	0	37	0
Hogan	9	0	62	1
Yardley	9	0	28	3
Border	2	0	10	1
Yallop	1	0	9	0

FALL OF WICKETS
1-34, 2-77, 3-136, 4-195, 5-201

FALL OF WICKETS
1-101, 2-101, 3-107, 4-108, 5-177, 6-178.

Umpires: D.P.Buultjens (1) and H.C.Felsinger (2).

SRI LANKA v AUSTRALIA 1982-83

At Sinhalese Sports Club, Colombo on 29 April 1983.   No result.   Toss: Sri Lanka.
LOI debuts: None.

Sri Lanka won their first one-day series when this match was abandoned after a storm ending a four-month drought flooded the ground.

AUSTRALIA		Runs	Balls	4/6	SRI LANKA
G.M.Wood	b Ranatunga	35	44	6	S.Wettimuny
K.C.Wessels	c Dias b De Silva	43	64	5	E.R.N.S.Fernando
G.N.Yallop	c De Alwis b De Silva	51	55	6	R.L.Dias
D.W.Hookes	c De Alwis b John	23	33	3	* L.R.D.Mendis
A.R.Border	b De Mel	10	18	–	A.Ranatunga
* G.S.Chappell	not out	9	14	1	R.S.Madugalle
† R.D.Woolley	not out	12	11	1	A.L.F.de Mel
T.G.Hogan					D.S.de Silva
B.Yardley					† R.G.de Alwis
R.M.Hogg					R.J.Ratnayake
J.N.Maguire					V.B.John
Extras	(lb 8, w 1, nb 2)	11			
Total	(39.2 overs; 5 wickets)	194			

SRI LANKA	O	M	R	W
De Mel	9	0	44	1
John	6.2	1	23	1
Ranatunga	9	0	42	1
Ratnayake	6	0	23	0
De Silva	9	0	51	2

FALL OF WICKETS
1-60, 2-105, 3-151, 4-172, 5-172

Umpires: K.T.Francis (2) and P.W.Vidanagamage (3).

SRI LANKA v AUSTRALIA 1982-83

At Sinhalese Sports Club, Colombo on 30 April 1983.   No result.   Toss: Australia.
LOI debuts: Sri Lanka – G.N.de Silva, D.S.B.P.Kuruppu.

A match, reduced to 30 overs when overnight rain delayed the start, was abandoned after a subsequent downpour. Later the drenched teams staged an exhibition match.

AUSTRALIA		Runs	Balls	4/6	SRI LANKA
K.C.Wessels	b De Mel	6	18	–	S.Wettimuny
G.M.Wood	b De Mel	2	8	–	E.R.N.S.Fernando
G.N.Yallop	not out	60	81	7/2	R.L.Dias
D.W.Hookes	b Ratnayeke	49	40	6/2	* L.R.D.Mendis
S.B.Smith	not out	0	–	–	A.Ranatunga
* G.S.Chappell					R.S.Madugalle
A.R.Border					A.L.F.de Mel
† R.D.Woolley					G.N.de Silva
B.Yardley					† D.S.B.P.Kuruppu
R.M.Hogg					J.R.Ratnayeke
J.N.Maguire					V.B.John
Extras	(b 2, lb 4, w 1)	7			
Total	(19.2 overs; 3 wickets)	124			

SRI LANKA	O	M	R	W
De Mel	4	0	9	2
John	5	0	15	0
De Silva	4	0	21	0
Ranatunga	3	0	35	0
Ratnayeke	2.2	0	16	1
Wettimuny	1	0	21	0

FALL OF WICKETS
1-3, 2-12, 3-124

Umpires: D.P.Buultjens (2) and S.Ponnadurai (1).

ENGLAND v NEW ZEALAND 1983

At Kennington Oval, London, on 9 June 1983.   Result: **ENGLAND** won by 106 runs.   Toss: England.
Award: A.J.Lamb.   LOI debuts: None.

This third world tournament involved 27 matches instead of its predecessors' 15, each team playing its three opponents twice in the expanded group stage. Martin Snedden remains the only bowler to have conceded 100 runs in any limited-overs international.

ENGLAND		Runs	Balls	4/6
G.Fowler	c Coney b Cairns	8	19	1
C.J.Tavaré	c Edgar b Chatfield	45	91	4
D.I.Gower	c Edgar b Coney	39	62	6
A.J.Lamb	b Snedden	102	105	12/2
M.W.Gatting	b Snedden	43	47	3
I.T.Botham	c Lees b Hadlee	22	16	–/1
† I.J.Gould	not out	14	12	1
G.R.Dilley	not out	31	14	4
V.J.Marks				
P.J.W.Allott				
* R.G.D.Willis				
Extras	(lb 12, w 1, nb 5)	18		
Total	(60 overs; 6 wickets)	322		

NEW ZEALAND	O	M	R	W
Hadlee	12	4	26	1
Cairns	12	4	57	1
Snedden	12	1	105	2
Chatfield	12	1	45	1
Coney	6	1	20	1
Crowe	6	0	51	0

FALL OF WICKETS
1-13, 2-79, 3-117, 4-232, 5-271, 6-278

NEW ZEALAND		Runs	Balls	4/6
G.M.Turner	lbw b Willis	14	28	2
B.A.Edgar	c Gould b Willis	3	6	–
J.G.Wright	c Botham b Dilley	10	17	1
* G.P.Howarth	c Lamb b Marks	18	44	1
J.V.Coney	run out	23	52	2
M.D.Crowe	run out	97	118	8
† W.K.Lees	b Botham	8	23	–
R.J.Hadlee	c Lamb b Marks	1	9	–
B.L.Cairns	lbw b Botham	1	2	–
M.C.Snedden	c Gould b Gatting	21	34	1
E.J.Chatfield	not out	9	24	1
Extras	(b 2, lb 4, w 4, nb 1)	11		
Total	(59 overs)	216		

ENGLAND	O	M	R	W
Willis	7	2	9	2
Dilley	8	0	33	1
Botham	12	0	42	2
Allott	12	1	47	0
Marks	12	1	39	2
Gatting	8	1	35	1

FALL OF WICKETS
1-3, 2-28, 3-31, 4-62, 5-85, 6-123, 7-136, 8-138, 9-190, 10-216

Umpires: B.J.Meyer (10) and D.O.Oslear (3).

PAKISTAN v SRI LANKA 1983

At St Helen's, Swansea, on 9 June 1983.   Result: **PAKISTAN** won by 50 runs.   Toss: Sri Lanka.
Award: Mohsin Khan.   LOI debuts: Sri Lanka – M.A.R.Samarasekera.

This contest, the first World Cup match to be staged outside the Test match arenas, produced three major LOI records, all subsequently beaten: the highest total, the highest total by a team batting second and losing, and the highest match aggregate. Imran Khan's 30-ball fifty was Pakistan's fastest until 1986-87 (LOI No. 434).

PAKISTAN		Runs	Balls	4/6
Mohsin Khan	b John	82	121	5/1
Mudassar Nazar	c De Silva b Ratnayake	36	72	2
Zaheer Abbas	c Kuruppu b De Mel	82	81	10
Javed Miandad	lbw b De Mel	72	52	4/3
* Imran Khan	not out	56	33	6/2
Ijaz Faqih	run out	2	3	–
Tahir Naqqash	not out	0	–	–
† Wasim Bari				
Rashid Khan				
Shahid Mahboob				
Sarfraz Nawaz				
Extras	(b 4, lb 4)	8		
Total	(60 overs; 5 wickets)	338		

SRI LANKA	O	M	R	W
De Mel	12	2	69	2
John	12	2	58	1
Ratnayake	12	0	65	1
Ranatunga	9	0	53	0
De Silva	10	0	52	0
Samarasekera	5	0	33	0

FALL OF WICKETS
1-88, 2-156, 3-229, 4-325, 5-332

SRI LANKA		Runs	Balls	4/6
S.Wettimuny	c Rashid b Sarfraz	12	26	1
D.S.B.P.Kuruppu	run out	72	101	7/2
R.L.Dias	b Rashid	5	21	–
* L.R.D.Mendis	b Tahir	16	17	3
A.Ranatunga	c and b Mudassar	31	42	5
M.A.R.Samarasekera	run out	0	2	–
D.S.de Silva	c Wasim Bari b Sarfraz	35	51	1
A.L.F.de Mel	c Tahir b Shahid	11	22	–
† R.G.de Alwis	not out	59	56	5/1
R.J.Ratnayake	c Mudassar b Sarfraz	13	13	–/1
V.B.John	not out	12	11	2
Extras	(lb 8, w 10, nb 4)	22		
Total	(60 overs; 9 wickets)	288		

PAKISTAN	O	M	R	W
Sarfraz Nawaz	12	1	40	3
Shahid Mahboob	11	0	48	1
Tahir Naqqash	8	0	49	1
Rashid Khan	12	1	55	1
Ijaz Faqih	12	0	52	0
Mudassar Nazar	4	0	18	1
Zaheer Abbas	1	0	4	0

FALL OF WICKETS
1-34, 2-58, 3-85, 4-142, 5-143, 6-157, 7-180, 8-234, 9-262

Umpires: K.E.Palmer (9) and D.R.Shepherd (1).

AUSTRALIA v ZIMBABWE 1983

At Trent Bridge, Nottingham, on 9 June 1983.   Result: **ZIMBABWE** won by 13 runs.   Toss: Australia.
Award: D.A.G.Fletcher.   LOI debuts: Zimbabwe – All.

Duncan Fletcher, the first player to score a fifty and take four wickets in a limited-overs international, led Zimbabwe to victory in their first official match at this level. Dennis Lillee became the first bowler to take 100 LOI wickets and Rodney Marsh the first wicket-keeper to make 100 dismissals.

ZIMBABWE		Runs	Balls	4/6
A.H.Shah	c Marsh b Lillee	16		
G.A.Paterson	c Hookes b Lillee	27		2
J.G.Heron	c Marsh b Yallop	14		1
A.J.Pycroft	b Border	21		1
†D.L.Houghton	c Marsh b Yallop	0		–
*D.A.G.Fletcher	not out	69		5
K.M.Curran	c Hookes b Hogg	27		2
I.P.Butchart	not out	34		2
P.W.E.Rawson				
A.J.Traicos				
V.R.Hogg				
Extras	(lb 18, w 7, nb 6)	31		
Total	(60 overs; 6 wickets)	**239**		

AUSTRALIA		O	M	R	W
Lawson		11	2	33	0
Hogg		12	3	43	1
Lillee		12	1	47	2
Thomson		11	1	46	0
Yallop		9	0	28	2
Border		5	0	11	1

FALL OF WICKETS
1-55, 2-55, 3-86, 4-86, 5-94, 6-164

AUSTRALIA		Runs	Balls	4/6
G.M.Wood	c Houghton b Fletcher	31		3
K.C.Wessels	run out	76		5
*K.J.Hughes	c Shah b Fletcher	0		–
D.W.Hookes	c Traicos b Fletcher	20		1
G.N.Yallop	c Pycroft b Fletcher	2		–
A.R.Border	c Pycroft b Curran	17		–
†R.W.Marsh	not out	50		3/2
G.F.Lawson	b Butchart	0		–
R.M.Hogg	not out	19		1
D.K.Lillee				
J.R.Thomson				
Extras	(b 2, lb 7, w 2)	11		
Total	(60 overs; 7 wickets)	**226**		

ZIMBABWE	O	M	R	W
Hogg	6	2	15	0
Rawson	12	1	54	0
Butchart	10	0	39	1
Fletcher	11	1	42	4
Traicos	12	2	27	0
Curran	9	0	38	1

FALL OF WICKETS
1-61, 2-63, 3-114, 4-133, 5-138, 6-168, 7-176

Umpires: D.J.Constant (19) and M.J.Kitchen (1).

WEST INDIES v INDIA 1983

At Old Trafford, Manchester, on 9, 10 June 1983.   Result: **INDIA** won by 34 runs.   Toss: West Indies.
Award: Yashpal Sharma.   LOI debuts: None.

West Indies, who suffered their first defeat in a World Cup match, were 67 for 2 after 22 overs at stumps on the first day, rain having delayed the start until 1.35pm. India's only previous World Cup win had been against East Africa in 1975.

INDIA		Runs	Balls	4/6
S.M.Gavaskar	c Dujon b Marshall	19		
K.Srikkanth	c Dujon b Holding	14		
M.Amarnath	c Dujon b Garner	21		
S.M.Patil	b Gomes	36		
Yashpal Sharma	b Holding	89	127	9
*Kapil Dev	c Richards b Gomes	6		
R.M.H.Binny	lbw b Marshall	27		
Madan Lal	not out	21		
†S.M.H.Kirmani	run out	1		
R.J.Shastri	not out	5		
B.S.Sandhu				
Extras	(b 4, lb 10, w 1, nb 8)	23		
Total	(60 overs; 8 wickets)	**262**		

WEST INDIES	O	M	R	W
Holding	12	3	32	2
Roberts	12	1	51	0
Marshall	12	1	48	2
Garner	12	1	49	1
Richards	2	0	13	0
Gomes	10	0	46	2

FALL OF WICKETS
1-21, 2-46, 3-76, 4-125, 5-141, 6-214, 7-243, 8-246

WEST INDIES		Runs	Balls	4/6
C.G.Greenidge	b Sandhu	24		
D.L.Haynes	run out	24		
I.V.A.Richards	c Kirmani b Binny	17		
S.F.A.F.Bacchus	b Madan Lal	14		
*C.H.Lloyd	b Binny	25		
†P.J.L.Dujon	c Sandhu b Binny	7		
H.A.Gomes	run out	8		
M.D.Marshall	st Kirmani b Shastri	2		
A.M.E.Roberts	not out	37		
M.A.Holding	b Shastri	8		
J.Garner	st Kirmani b Shastri	37		–/1
Extras	(b 4, lb 17, w 4)	25		
Total	(54.1 overs)	**228**		

INDIA	O	M	R	W
Kapil Dev	10	0	34	0
Sandhu	12	1	36	1
Madan Lal	12	1	34	1
Binny	12	1	48	3
Shastri	5.1	0	26	3
Patil	3	0	25	0

FALL OF WICKETS
1-49, 2-56, 3-76, 4-96, 5-107, 6-124, 7-126, 8-130, 9-157, 10-228

Umpires: B.Leadbeater (1) and A.G.T.Whitehead (6).

ENGLAND v SRI LANKA 1983

At County Ground, Taunton, on 11 June 1983.   Result: **ENGLAND** won by 47 runs.   Toss: England.
Award: D.I.Gower.   LOI debuts: None.

David Gower's sixth hundred equalled the record currently held by Zaheer Abbas. Vic Marks returned England's first five-wicket analysis in limited-overs internationals and the only one in six World Cup tournaments.

ENGLAND		Runs	Balls	4/6
G. Fowler	b John	22	59	1
C.J.Tavaré	c De Alwis b Ranatunga	32	61	4
D.I.Gower	b De Mel	130	120	12/5
A.J.Lamb	b Ratnayake	53	51	4/2
M.W.Gatting	run out	7	8	–
I.T.Botham	run out	0	1	–
† I.J.Gould	c Ranatunga b Ratnayake	35	40	2
G.R.Dilley	b De Mel	29	16	5
V.J.Marks	run out	5	5	–
P.J.W.Allott	not out	0	–	–
* R.G.D.Willis				
Extras	(lb 11, w 9)	20		
Total	(60 overs; 9 wickets)	**333**		

SRI LANKA	O	M	R	W
De Mel	12	3	62	2
John	12	0	55	1
Ratnayake	12	0	66	2
Ranatunga	12	0	65	1
De Silva	12	0	65	0

FALL OF WICKETS
1-49, 2-78, 3-174, 4-193, 5-194, 6-292, 7-298, 8-333, 9-333

SRI LANKA		Runs	Balls	4/6
S.Wettimuny	lbw b Marks	33	66	3/1
D.S.B.P.Kuruppu	c Gatting b Dilley	4	3	1
R.L.Dias	c Botham b Dilley	2	15	–
* L.R.D.Mendis	c Willis b Marks	56	64	5/1
R.S.Madugalle	c Tavaré b Marks	12	26	1
A.Ranatunga	c Lamb b Marks	34	45	4
D.S.de Silva	st Gould b Marks	28	37	2
† R.G.de Alwis	not out	58	51	6/1
A.L.F.de Mel	c Dilley b Allott	27	26	2
R.J.Ratnayake	c Lamb b Dilley	15	18	1
V.B.John	b Dilley	0	1	–
Extras	(lb 12, w 2, nb 3)	17		
Total	(58 overs)	**286**		

ENGLAND	O	M	R	W
Willis	11	3	43	0
Dilley	11	0	45	4
Allott	12	1	82	1
Botham	12	0	60	0
Marks	12	3	39	5

FALL OF WICKETS
1-11, 2-17, 3-92, 4-108, 5-117, 6-168, 7-192, 8-246, 9-281, 10-286

Umpires: M.J.Kitchen (2) and K.E.Palmer (10).

NEW ZEALAND v PAKISTAN 1983

At Edgbaston, Birmingham, on 11, 12 June 1983.   Result: **NEW ZEALAND** won by 52 runs.   Toss: Pakistan.
Award: Abdul Qadir.   LOI debuts: New Zealand – J.G.Bracewell; Pakistan – Abdul Qadir.

New Zealand were 211 for 8 after 56 overs at stumps, the start having been delayed until 1.45pm. Pakistan lost their first three batsmen for no runs to the first eight balls of their innings.

NEW ZEALAND		Runs	Balls	4/6
G.M.Turner	c Wasim b Rashid	27	37	5
B.A.Edgar	c Imran b Qadir	44	107	3
J.G.Wright	c Wasim b Qadir	9	14	1
B.L.Cairns	b Qadir	4	6	1
* G.P.Howarth	st Wasim b Qadir	16	35	1
J.V.Coney	c Ijaz b Shahid	33	65	3
M.D.Crowe	c Mohsin b Rashid	34	53	2
R.J.Hadlee	c Wasim b Sarfraz	13	11	1
J.G.Bracewell	lbw b Rashid	3	6	–
† W.K.Lees	not out	24	21	2
E.J.Chatfield	not out	6	8	–
Extras	(lb 20, w 4, nb 1)	25		
Total	(60 overs; 9 wickets)	**238**		

PAKISTAN	O	M	R	W
Sarfraz Nawaz	11	1	49	1
Shahid Mahboob	10	2	38	1
Rashid Khan	11	0	47	3
Mudassar Nazar	12	1	40	0
Abdul Qadir	12	4	21	4
Ijaz Faqih	1	0	6	0
Zaheer Abbas	3	0	12	0

FALL OF WICKETS
1-57, 2-68, 3-80, 4-109, 5-120, 6-166, 7-197, 8-202, 9-223

PAKISTAN		Runs	Balls	4/6
Mohsin Khan	lbw b Hadlee	0	3	–
Mudassar Nazar	c Lees b Cairns	0	2	–
Zaheer Abbas	b Hadlee	0	3	–
Javed Miandad	lbw b Chatfield	35	61	3
* Imran Khan	c Chatfield b Hadlee	9	26	1
Ijaz Faqih	c Edgar b Coney	12	37	1
Shahid Mahboob	c Wright b Coney	17	31	2
† Wasim Bari	c Edgar b Coney	34	71	2
Abdul Qadir	not out	41	68	2/1
Sarfraz Nawaz	c Crowe b Chatfield	13	14	2
Rashid Khan	c and b Cairns	9	21	–
Extras	(b 5, lb 6, w 3, nb 2)	16		
Total	(55.2 overs)	**186**		

NEW ZEALAND	O	M	R	W
Hadlee	9	2	20	3
Cairns	9.2	3	21	2
Chatfield	12	0	50	2
Crowe	2	0	12	0
Coney	12	3	28	3
Bracewell	11	2	39	0

FALL OF WICKETS
1-0, 2-0, 3-0, 4-22, 5-54, 6-60, 7-102, 8-131, 9-158, 10-186

Umpires: H.D.Bird (19) and B.Leadbeater (2).

102

AUSTRALIA v WEST INDIES 1983

At Headingley, Leeds, on 11, 12 June 1983.   Result: **WEST INDIES** won by 101 runs.   Toss: Australia.
Award: W.W.Davis.   LOI debuts: None.

Rain and poor light prevented play until 3.30pm, West Indies being 160 for 5 after 42 overs at the close. Winston Davis returned the first seven-wicket LOI analysis, concluding it with a spell of 6 for 14 in 33 balls. It was the LOI record until 1991-92 (*LOI No. 685*) and remains the only seven-wicket haul in World Cup matches.

WEST INDIES		Runs	Balls	4/6
C.G.Greenidge	c Wood b Hogg	4	1	
D.L.Haynes	c Marsh b Lawson	13	1	
I.V.A.Richards	b Lawson	7	1	
H.A.Gomes	c Marsh b Lillee	78	4	
C.H.Lloyd	lbw b MacLeay	19	1/1	
S.F.A.F.Bacchus	c Wessels b Yallop	47	5	
†P.J.L.Dujon	lbw b Lawson	12	–	
A.M.E.Roberts	c Marsh b Lillee	5	–	
M.A.Holding	run out	20	2	
W.W.Daniel	not out	16	2	
W.W.Davis				
Extras	(b 1, lb 9, w 10, nb 11)	31		
Total	(60 overs; 9 wickets)	**252**		

AUSTRALIA	O	M	R	W
Lawson	12	3	29	3
Hogg	12	1	49	1
MacLeay	12	1	31	1
Lillee	12	0	55	2
Yallop	5	0	26	1
Border	7	0	31	0

FALL OF WICKETS
1-7, 2-25, 3-32, 4-78, 5-154, 6-192, 7-208, 8-211, 9-252

AUSTRALIA		Runs	Balls	4/6
G.M.Wood	retired hurt	2	–	
K.C.Wessels	b Roberts	11	2	
*K.J.Hughes	c Lloyd b Davis	18	–/2	
D.W.Hookes	c Dujon b Davis	45	5	
G.N.Yallop	c Holding b Davis	29	4	
A.R.Border	c Lloyd b Davis	17	2	
K.H.MacLeay	c Haynes b Davis	1	–	
†R.W.Marsh	c Haynes b Holding	8	1	
G.F.Lawson	c Dujon b Davis	2	–	
R.M.Hogg	not out	0	–	
D.K.Lillee	b Davis	0	–	
Extras	(b 1, lb 4, w 5, nb 8)	18		
Total	(30.3 overs)	**151**		

WEST INDIES	O	M	R	W
Roberts	7	0	14	1
Holding	8	2	23	1
Davis	10.3	0	51	7
Daniel	3	0	35	0
Gomes	2	0	10	0

FALL OF WICKETS
1-18, 2-55, 3-114, 4-116, 5-126, 6-137, 7-141, 8-150, 9-151

Umpires: D.J.Constant (20) and D.G.L.Evans (7).

INDIA v ZIMBABWE 1983

At Grace Road, Leicester, on 11 June 1983.   Result: **INDIA** won by 5 wickets.   Toss: India.
Award: Madan Lal.   LOI debuts: Zimbabwe – R.D.Brown.

Syed Kirmani became the first to hold five catches in a World Cup match and established the Indian record in limited-overs internationals.

ZIMBABWE		Runs	Balls	4/6
A.H.Shah	c Kirmani b Sandhu	8	32	1
G.A.Paterson	lbw b Madan Lal	22	51	2
J.G.Heron	c Kirmani b Madan Lal	18	30	2
A.J.Pycroft	c Shastri b Binny	14	21	1
D.L.Houghton	c Kirmani b Madan Lal	21	47	1
*D.A.G.Fletcher	b Kapil Dev	13	32	–
K.M.Curran	run out	8	16	–
I.P.Butchart	not out	22	35	2
R.D.Brown	c Kirmani b Shastri	6	27	–
P.W.E.Rawson	c Kirmani b Binny	3	6	–
A.J.Traicos	run out	2	13	–
Extras	(lb 9, w 9)	18		
Total	(51.4 overs)	**155**		

INDIA	O	M	R	W
Kapil Dev	9	3	18	1
Sandhu	9	1	29	1
Madan Lal	10.4	0	27	3
Binny	11	2	25	2
Shastri	12	1	38	1

FALL OF WICKETS
1-13, 2-55, 3-56, 4-71, 5-106, 6-114, 7-115, 8-139, 9-148, 10-155

INDIA		Runs	Balls	4/6
K.Srikkanth	c Butchart b Rawson	20	27	–
S.M.Gavaskar	c Heron b Rawson	4	11	–
M.Amarnath	c sub (G.E.Peckover) b Traicos	44	79	4
S.M.Patil	b Fletcher	50	54	7/1
R.J.Shastri	c Brown b Shah	17	27	1
Yashpal Sharma	not out	18	19	2
*Kapil Dev	not out	2	8	–
R.M.H.Binny				
Madan Lal				
†S.M.H.Kirmani				
B.S.Sandhu				
Extras	(w 2)	2		
Total	(37.3 overs; 5 wickets)	**157**		

ZIMBABWE	O	M	R	W
Rawson	5.1	1	11	2
Curran	6.5	1	33	0
Butchart	5	1	21	0
Traicos	11	1	41	1
Fletcher	6	1	32	1
Shah	3.3	0	17	1

FALL OF WICKETS
1-13, 2-32, 3-101, 4-128, 5-148

Umpires: J.Birkenshaw (1) and R.Palmer (1).

ENGLAND v PAKISTAN 1983

At Lord's, London, on 13 June 1983.　Result: **ENGLAND** won by 8 wickets.　Toss: Pakistan.
Award: Zaheer Abbas.　LOI debuts: None.

Zaheer Abbas led Pakistan after Imran had injured his left ankle.

PAKISTAN		Runs	Balls	4/6	ENGLAND		Runs	Balls	4/6
Mohsin Khan	c Tavaré b Willis	3	29	–	G.Fowler	not out	78	151	5
Mudassar Nazar	c Gould b Allott	26	98	2	C.J.Tavaré	lbw b Rashid	8	21	–
Mansoor Akhtar	c Gould b Willis	3	15	–	D.I.Gower	c Sarfraz b Mansoor	48	72	6
Javed Miandad	c Gould b Botham	14	26	2	A.J.Lamb	not out	48	62	5/1
Zaheer Abbas	not out	83	104	7/1	M.W.Gatting				
* Imran Khan	run out	7	35	1	I.T.Botham				
Wasim Raja	c Botham b Marks	9	19	2	† I.J.Gould				
Abdul Qadir	run out	0	2	–	V.J.Marks				
Sarfraz Nawaz	c and b Botham	11	15	2	G.R.Dilley				
† Wasim Bari	not out	18	21	1	P.J.W.Allott				
Rashid Khan					* R.G.D.Willis				
Extras	(b 5, lb 8, w 3, nb 3)	19			Extras	(b 1, lb 12, w 2, nb 2)	17		
Total	(60 overs; 8 wickets)	193			Total	(50.4 overs; 2 wickets)	199		

ENGLAND	O	M	R	W	PAKISTAN	O	M	R	W
Willis	12	4	24	2	Rashid Khan	7	2	19	1
Dilley	12	1	33	0	Sarfraz Nawaz	11	5	22	0
Allott	12	2	48	1	Wasim Raja	3	0	14	0
Botham	12	3	36	2	Mudassar Nazar	8	0	30	0
Marks	12	1	33	1	Abdul Qadir	9.4	0	53	0
					Mansoor Akhtar	12	2	44	1

FALL OF WICKETS
1-29, 2-33, 3-49, 4-67, 5-96, 6-112, 7-118, 8-154

FALL OF WICKETS
1-15, 2-93

Umpires: B.J.Meyer (11) and A.G.T.Whitehead (7).

NEW ZEALAND v SRI LANKA 1983

At County Ground, Bristol, on 13 June 1983.　Result: **NEW ZEALAND** won by 5 wickets.　Toss: New Zealand.
Award: R.J.Hadlee.　LOI debuts: None.

Richard Hadlee's analysis of 5 for 25 remains the best for New Zealand in World Cup matches.

SRI LANKA		Runs	Balls	4/6	NEW ZEALAND		Runs	Balls	4/6
S.Wettimuny	lbw b Hadlee	7	19	1	G.M.Turner	c Mendis b De Silva	50	60	8
D.S.B.P.Kuruppu	c Hadlee b Chatfield	26	60	5	J.G.Wright	lbw b De Mel	45	52	8
R.L.Dias	b Chatfield	25	43	4	* G.P.Howarth	c Madugalle b Ratnayake	76	79	14
* L.R.D.Mendis	b Hadlee	43	70	2	M.D.Crowe	c De Alwis b De Mel	0	11	–
R.S.Madugalle	c Snedden b Coney	60	87	3/1	J.J.Crowe	lbw b John	23	26	4
A.Ranatunga	lbw b Hadlee	0	3	–	J.V.Coney	not out	2	10	–
D.S.de Silva	b Coney	13	20	–	† I.D.S.Smith	not out	4	1	1
† R.G.de Alwis	c Howarth b Snedden	16	17	2	R.J.Hadlee				
A.L.F.de Mel	c and b Hadlee	1	6	–	B.L.Cairns				
R.J.Ratnayake	b Hadlee	5	9	–	M.C.Snedden				
V.B.John	not out	2	5	–	E.J.Chatfield				
Extras	(lb 6, w 1, nb 1)	8			Extras	(lb 6, w 3)	9		
Total	(56.1 overs)	206			Total	(39.2 overs; 5 wickets)	209		

NEW ZEALAND	O	M	R	W	SRI LANKA	O	M	R	W
Hadlee	10.1	4	25	5	De Mel	8	2	30	2
Snedden	10	1	38	1	John	8.2	0	49	1
Chatfield	12	4	24	2	Ratnayake	12	0	60	1
Cairns	7	0	35	0	De Silva	9	0	39	1
Coney	12	0	44	2	Ranatunga	2	0	22	0
M.D.Crowe	5	0	32	0					

FALL OF WICKETS
1-16, 2-56, 3-73, 4-144, 5-144, 6-171, 7-196, 8-199, 9-199, 10-206

FALL OF WICKETS
1-89, 2-99, 3-110, 4-176, 5-205

Umpires: H.D.Bird (20) and D.R.Shepherd (2).

AUSTRALIA v INDIA 1983

At Trent Bridge, Nottingham, on 13 June 1983.   Result: **AUSTRALIA** won by 162 runs.   Toss: Australia.
Award: T.M.Chappell.   LOI debuts: None.

Ken MacLeay, Wiltshire born, remains the only bowler after Gary Gilmour (*LOI No. 31*) to take six wickets for Australia in a World Cup match.

AUSTRALIA		Runs	Balls	4/6
K.C.Wessels	b Kapil Dev	5	11	1
T.M.Chappell	c Srikkanth b Amarnath	110	131	11
* K.J.Hughes	b Madan Lal	52	86	3
D.W.Hookes	c Kapil Dev b Madan Lal	1	4	–
G.N.Yallop	not out	66	73	5
A.R.Border	c Yashpal b Binny	26	23	1
† R.W.Marsh	c Sandhu b Kapil Dev	12	15	1
K.H.MacLeay	c and b Kapil Dev	4	5	–
T.G.Hogan	b Kapil Dev	11	9	–/1
G.F.Lawson	c Srikkanth b Kapil Dev	6	3	1
R.M.Hogg	not out	2	2	–
Extras	(b 1, lb 14, w 8, nb 2)	25		
Total	**(60 overs; 9 wickets)**	**320**		

INDIA		Runs	Balls	4/6
R.J.Shastri	lbw b Lawson	11	18	1
K.Srikkanth	c Border b Hogan	39	63	6
M.Amarnath	run out	2	17	–
D.B.Vengsarkar	lbw b MacLeay	5	14	1
S.M.Patil	b MacLeay	0	7	–
Yashpal Sharma	c and b MacLeay	3	11	–
* Kapil Dev	b Hogan	40	27	2/1
Madan Lal	c Hogan b MacLeay	27	39	2
R.M.H.Binny	lbw b MacLeay	0	6	–
† S.M.H.Kirmani	b MacLeay	12	23	2
B.S.Sandhu	not out	9	12	–/1
Extras	(b 1, lb 4, w 3, nb 2)	10		
Total	**(37.5 overs)**	**158**		

INDIA	O	M	R	W
Kapil Dev	12	2	43	5
Sandhu	12	1	52	0
Binny	12	0	52	1
Shastri	2	0	16	0
Madan Lal	12	0	69	2
Patil	6	0	36	0
Amarnath	4	0	27	1

AUSTRALIA	O	M	R	W
Lawson	5	1	25	1
Hogg	7	2	23	0
Hogan	12	1	48	2
MacLeay	11.5	3	39	6
Border	2	0	13	0

FALL OF WICKETS
1-11, 2-155, 3-159, 4-206, 5-254, 6-277, 7-289, 8-301, 9-307

FALL OF WICKETS
1-38, 2-43, 3-57, 4-57, 5-64, 6-66, 7-124, 8-126, 9-136, 10-158

Umpires: D.O.Oslear (4) and R.Palmer (2).

WEST INDIES v ZIMBABWE 1983

At New Road, Worcester, on 13 June 1983.   Result: **WEST INDIES** won by 8 wickets.   Toss: West Indies.
Award: C.G.Greenidge.   LOI debuts: Zimbabwe – G.E.Peckover.

An unbroken partnership of 195 between Gordon Greenidge and Larry Gomes, still the West Indies LOI record for the third wicket and then the World Cup record for any wicket, ensured that Zimbabwe would not repeat their giant-killing act.

ZIMBABWE		Runs	Balls	4/6
A.H.Shah	b Roberts	2		–
G.A.Paterson	c Dujon b Holding	4		–
J.G.Heron	st Dujon b Gomes	12	73	–
A.J.Pycroft	run out	13		1
† D.L.Houghton	c Dujon b Roberts	54		5/1
* D.A.G.Fletcher	not out	71		7
K.M.Curran	b Roberts	7		1
I.P.Butchart	lbw b Holding	0		–
G.E.Peckover	not out	16		3
P.W.E.Rawson				
A.J.Traicos				
Extras	(b 1, lb 23, w 7, nb 7)	38		
Total	**(60 overs; 7 wickets)**	**217**		

WEST INDIES		Runs	Balls	4/6
C.G.Greenidge	not out	105		5/1
D.L.Haynes	c Houghton b Rawson	2		2
I.V.A.Richards	lbw b Rawson	16		2
H.A.Gomes	not out	75		5
S.F.A.F.Bacchus				
* C.H.Lloyd				
† P.J.L.Dujon				
A.M.E.Roberts				
M.A.Holding				
W.W.Daniel				
W.W.Davis				
Extras	(b 1, lb 8, w 9, nb 2)	20		
Total	**(48.3 overs; 2 wickets)**	**218**		

WEST INDIES	O	M	R	W
Roberts	12	4	36	3
Holding	12	2	33	2
Daniel	12	4	21	0
Davis	12	2	34	0
Gomes	8	0	42	1
Richards	4	1	13	0

ZIMBABWE	O	M	R	W
Rawson	12	1	39	2
Curran	10.3	1	37	0
Butchart	9	1	40	0
Fletcher	4	0	22	0
Traicos	9	0	37	0
Shah	4	0	23	0

FALL OF WICKETS
1-7, 2-7, 3-35, 4-65, 5-157, 6-181, 7-183

FALL OF WICKETS
1-3, 2-23

Umpires: J.Birkenshaw (2) and D.G.L.Evans (8).

ENGLAND v NEW ZEALAND 1983

At Edgbaston, Birmingham, on 15 June 1983.   Result: **NEW ZEALAND** won by 2 wickets.   Toss: England.
Award: J.V.Coney.   LOI debuts: None.

John Bracewell completed New Zealand's first limited-overs victory against England with a boundary off the penultimate ball.

ENGLAND		Runs	Balls	4/6
G.Fowler	c J.J.Crowe b Chatfield	69	112	9
C.J.Tavaré	c Cairns b Coney	18	44	1
I.T.Botham	c and b Bracewell	12	9	1/1
D.I.Gower	not out	92	96	6/4
A.J.Lamb	c J.J.Crowe b Cairns	8	14	1
M.W.Gatting	b Cairns	1	5	–
† I.J.Gould	lbw b Cairns	4	14	–
V.J.Marks	b Hadlee	5	15	–
G.R.Dilley	b Hadlee	10	19	–
P.J.W.Allott	c Smith b Hadlee	0	1	–
* R.G.D.Willis	lbw b Chatfield	0	3	–
Extras	(b 4, lb 10, w 1)	15		
Total	(55.2 overs)	234		

NEW ZEALAND		Runs	Balls	4/6
G.M.Turner	lbw b Willis	2	5	–
B.A.Edgar	c Gould b Willis	1	6	–
* G.P.Howarth	run out	60	104	5/1
J.J.Crowe	b Allott	17	46	1
M.D.Crowe	b Marks	20	40	2
J.V.Coney	not out	66	97	9
† I.D.S.Smith	b Botham	4	6	1
R.J.Hadlee	b Willis	31	45	3
B.L.Cairns	lbw b Willis	5	6	–
J.G.Bracewell	not out	4	7	1
E.J.Chatfield				
Extras	(b 2, lb 22, w 1, nb 3)	28		
Total	(59.5 overs; 8 wickets)	238		

NEW ZEALAND	O	M	R	W
Hadlee	10	3	32	3
Cairns	11	0	44	3
Coney	12	2	27	1
Bracewell	12	0	66	1
Chatfield	10.2	0	50	2

ENGLAND	O	M	R	W
Willis	12	1	42	4
Dilley	12	1	43	0
Botham	12	1	47	1
Allott	11.5	2	44	1
Marks	12	1	34	1

FALL OF WICKETS
1-63, 2-77, 3-117, 4-143, 5-154, 6-162, 7-203, 8-233, 9-233, 10-234

FALL OF WICKETS
1-2, 2-3, 3-47, 4-75, 5-146, 6-151, 7-221, 8-231

Umpires: J.Birkenshaw (3) and K.E.Palmer (11).

WEST INDIES v INDIA 1983

At Kennington Oval, London, on 15 June 1983.   Result: **WEST INDIES** won by 66 runs.   Toss: West Indies.
Award: I.V.A.Richards.   LOI debuts: None.

Dilip Vengsarkar retired at 90 for 2 after being struck in the mouth by a lifting ball from Malcolm Marshall.

WEST INDIES		Runs	Balls	4/6
C.G.Greenidge	c Vengsarkar b Kapil Dev	9		
D.L.Haynes	c Kapil Dev b Amarnath	38		
I.V.A.Richards	c Kirmani b Sandhu	119	146	6/1
* C.H.Lloyd	run out	41		
S.F.A.F.Bacchus	b Binny	8		
† P.J.L.Dujon	c Shastri b Binny	9		
H.A.Gomes	not out	27		
A.M.E.Roberts	c Patil b Binny	7		
M.D.Marshall	run out	4		
M.A.Holding	c sub (K.Azad) b Madan Lal	2		
W.W.Davis	not out	0		
Extras	(lb 13, w 5)	18		
Total	(60 overs; 9 wickets)	282		

INDIA		Runs	Balls	4/6
K.Srikkanth	c Dujon b Roberts	2		
R.J.Shastri	c Dujon b Roberts	6		
M.Amarnath	c Lloyd b Holding	80		
D.B.Vengsarkar	retired hurt	32		
S.M.Patil	c and b Gomes	21		
Yashpal Sharma	run out	9		
* Kapil Dev	c Haynes b Holding	36		
R.M.H.Binny	lbw b Holding	1		
Madan Lal	not out	8		
† S.M.H.Kirmani	b Marshall	0		
B.S.Sandhu	run out	0		
Extras	(b 3, lb 13, nb 5)	21		
Total	(53.1 overs)	216		

INDIA	O	M	R	W
Kapil Dev	12	0	46	1
Sandhu	12	2	42	1
Binny	12	0	71	3
Amarnath	12	0	58	1
Madan Lal	12	0	47	1

WEST INDIES	O	M	R	W
Roberts	9	1	29	2
Holding	9.1	0	40	3
Marshall	11	3	20	1
Davis	12	2	51	0
Gomes	12	1	55	1

FALL OF WICKETS
1-17, 2-118, 3-198, 4-213, 5-239, 6-240, 7-257, 8-270, 9-280

FALL OF WICKETS
1-2, 2-21, 3-130, 4-143, 5-193, 6-195, 7-212, 8-214, 9-216

Umpires: B.J.Meyer (12) and D.R.Shepherd (3).

PAKISTAN v SRI LANKA 1983

At Headingley, Leeds, on 16 June 1983.   Result: **PAKISTAN** won by 11 runs.   Toss: Sri Lanka.
Award: Abdul Qadir.   LOI debuts: None.

Imran Khan scored Pakistan's first hundred in World Cup matches. Abdul Qadir and Ashanta de Mel, who repeated his feat two days later, remain the only bowlers to return five-wicket World Cup analyses for their respective countries.

PAKISTAN		Runs	Balls	4/6
Mohsin Khan	c Ranatunga b De Mel	3	14	–
Mansoor Akhtar	c De Alwis b De Mel	6	32	–
Zaheer Abbas	c Dias b De Mel	15	28	2
Javed Miandad	lbw b Ratnayake	7	14	1
Imran Khan	not out	102	133	11
Ijaz Faqih	lbw b Ratnayake	0	1	–
Shahid Mahboob	c De Silva b De Mel	77	126	6
Sarfraz Nawaz	c Madugalle b De Mel	9	10	1
Abdul Qadir	not out	5	7	–
Wasim Bari				
Rashid Khan				
Extras	(b 1, lb 4, w 4, nb 2)	11		
Total	(60 overs; 7 wickets)	**235**		

SRI LANKA		Runs	Balls	4/6
S.Wettimuny	c Shahid b Rashid	50	127	4
D.S.B.P.Kuruppu	b Rashid	12	36	1
R.L.Dias	st Wasim b Qadir	47	73	7
* L.R.D.Mendis	c Wasim b Qadir	33	49	5
R.J.Ratnayake	st Wasim b Qadir	1	6	–
R.S.Madugalle	c Qadir b Shahid	26	20	1/1
A.Ranatunga	c Zaheer b Qadir	0	1	–
D.S.de Silva	run out	1	3	–
† R.G.de Alwis	c Miandad b Qadir	4	5	1
A.L.F.de Mel	c Imran b Sarfraz	17	19	1
V.B.John	not out	6	15	–
Extras	(lb 8, w 17, nb 2)	27		
Total	(58.3 overs)	**224**		

SRI LANKA	O	M	R	W
De Mel	12	1	39	5
John	12	1	48	0
Ratnayake	12	2	42	2
Ranatunga	11	0	49	0
De Silva	12	1	42	0
Wettimuny	1	0	4	0

PAKISTAN	O	M	R	W
Rashid Khan	12	4	31	2
Sarfraz Nawaz	11.3	2	25	1
Shahid Mahboob	10	1	62	1
Mansoor Akhtar	1	0	8	0
Ijaz Faqih	12	0	27	0
Abdul Qadir	12	1	44	5

FALL OF WICKETS
1-6, 2-25, 3-30, 4-43, 5-43, 6-187, 7-204

FALL OF WICKETS
1-22, 2-101, 3-162, 4-162, 5-166, 6-166, 7-171, 8-193, 9-199, 10-224

Umpires: D.O.Oslear (5) and A.G.T.Whitehead (8).

AUSTRALIA v ZIMBABWE 1983

At County Ground, Southampton, on 16 June 1983.   Result: **AUSTRALIA** won by 32 runs.   Toss: Australia.
Award: D.L.Houghton.   LOI debuts: None.

Zimbabwe's highest total and individual score (so far) proved insufficient to upstage Australia a second time.

AUSTRALIA		Runs	Balls	4/6
G.M.Wood	c Rawson b Traicos	73		5
T.M.Chappell	c Traicos b Rawson	22		4
K.J.Hughes	b Traicos	31		2
D.W.Hookes	c Brown b Fletcher	10	14	–
G.N.Yallop	c Houghton b Curran	20		3
A.R.Border	b Butchart	43	61	2
R.W.Marsh	not out	35		1/2
K.H.MacLeay	c Rawson b Butchart	9		–/1
T.G.Hogan	not out	5		–
D.K.Lillee				
R.M.Hogg				
Extras	(lb 16, w 2, nb 6)	24		
Total	(60 overs; 7 wickets)	**272**		

ZIMBABWE		Runs	Balls	4/6
R.D.Brown	c Marsh b Hogan	38		4
G.A.Paterson	lbw b Hogg	17		1
J.G.Heron	run out	3		–
A.J.Pycroft	run out	13	24	1
† D.L.Houghton	c Hughes b Chappell	84	65	9/1
* D.A.G.Fletcher	b Hogan	2		–
K.M.Curran	lbw b Chappell	35		2
I.P.Butchart	lbw b Hogg	0		–
P.W.E.Rawson	lbw b Hogg	0		–
A.J.Traicos	b Chappell	19	37	2
V.R.Hogg	not out	7		–
Extras	(b 1, lb 10, w 1, nb 10)	22		
Total	(59.5 overs)	**240**		

ZIMBABWE	O	M	R	W
Hogg	9	2	34	0
Rawson	9	0	50	1
Fletcher	9	1	27	1
Butchart	10	0	52	2
Traicos	12	1	28	2
Curran	11	0	57	1

AUSTRALIA	O	M	R	W
Hogg	12	0	40	3
Lillee	9	1	23	0
Hogan	12	0	33	2
MacLeay	9	0	45	0
Border	9	1	30	0
Chappell	8.5	0	47	3

FALL OF WICKETS
1-46, 2-124, 3-150, 4-150, 5-219, 6-231, 7-249

FALL OF WICKETS
1-48, 2-53, 3-79, 4-97, 5-109, 6-212, 7-213, 8-213, 9-213, 10-240

Umpires: D.G.L.Evans (9) and R.Palmer (3).

ENGLAND v PAKISTAN 1983

At Old Trafford, Manchester, on 18 June 1983.　Result: **ENGLAND** won by 7 wickets.　Toss: Pakistan.
Award: G.Fowler.　LOI debuts: None.

A capacity Old Trafford crowd saw England qualify for the semi-finals.

PAKISTAN		Runs	Balls	4/6	ENGLAND		Runs	Balls	4/6
Mohsin Khan	c Marks b Allott	32	98	3	G.Fowler	c Miandad b Mudassar	69	96	7
Mudassar Nazar	c Gould b Dilley	18	23	2	C.J.Tavaré	c Wasim Raja b Zaheer	58	116	5
Zaheer Abbas	c Gould b Dilley	0	8	–	D.I.Gower	c Zaheer b Mudassar	31	48	3
Javed Miandad	run out	67	100	6	A.J.Lamb	not out	38	57	4
* Imran Khan	c Willis b Marks	13	28	2	M.W.Gatting	not out	14	27	1
Wasim Raja	c Willis b Marks	15	24	3	I.T.Botham				
Ijaz Faqih	not out	42	52	5	† I.J.Gould				
Sarfraz Nawaz	b Willis	17	20	1/1	V.J.Marks				
Abdul Qadir	run out	6	7	–	G.R.Dilley				
† Wasim Bari	not out	2	3	–	P.J.W.Allott				
Rashid Khan					* R.G.D.Willis				
Extras	(b 3, lb 14, w 2, nb 1)	20			Extras	(b 1, lb 15, w 7)	23		
Total	(60 overs; 8 wickets)	232			Total	(57.2 overs; 3 wickets)	233		

ENGLAND	O	M	R	W	PAKISTAN	O	M	R	W
Willis	12	3	37	1	Rashid Khan	11	1	58	0
Dilley	12	2	46	2	Sarfraz Nawaz	10.2	2	22	0
Allott	12	1	33	1	Abdul Qadir	11	0	51	0
Botham	12	1	51	0	Ijaz Faqih	6	0	19	0
Marks	12	0	45	2	Mudassar Nazar	12	2	34	2
					Zaheer Abbas	7	0	26	0

FALL OF WICKETS
1-33, 2-34, 3-87, 4-116, 5-144, 6-169, 7-204, 8-221

FALL OF WICKETS
1-115, 2-165, 3-181

Umpires: H.D.Bird (21) and D.O.Oslear (6).

NEW ZEALAND v SRI LANKA 1983

At County Ground, Derby, on 18 June 1983.　Result: **SRI LANKA** won by 3 wickets.　Toss: Sri Lanka.
Award: A.L.F.de Mel.　LOI debuts: None.

Sri Lanka gained their second victory in three world tournaments, Ashanta de Mel emulating Gary Gilmour's 1975 feat by taking five or more wickets in an innings in two consecutive World Cup matches.

NEW ZEALAND		Runs	Balls	4/6	SRI LANKA		Runs	Balls	4/6
G.M.Turner	c Dias b De Mel	6	10	1	S.Wettimuny	b Cairns	4	30	–
J.G.Wright	c De Alwis b De Mel	0	7	–	D.S.B.P.Kuruppu	c and b Snedden	62	120	10
* G.P.Howarth	b Ratnayake	15	23	2	A.Ranatunga	b Crowe	15	22	2
M.D.Crowe	lbw b Ratnayake	8	32	–	R.L.Dias	not out	64	101	9
B.A.Edgar	c Samarasekera b De Silva	27	77	3	* L.R.D.Mendis	lbw b Chatfield	0	2	–
J.V.Coney	c sub (E.R.N.S.Fernando) b De Silva	22	50	2	R.S.Madugalle	c Lees b Snedden	6	18	–
R.J.Hadlee	c Madugalle b De Mel	15	39	3	M.A.R.Samarasekera	c Lees b Hadlee	5	11	–
† W.K.Lees	c Ranatunga b De Mel	2	16	–	D.S.de Silva	run out	2	10	–
B.L.Cairns	c Dias b De Mel	6	7	1	† R.G.de Alwis	not out	11	11	–
M.C.Snedden	run out	40	55	5	A.L.F.de Mel				
E.J.Chatfield	not out	19	48	2	R.J.Ratnayake				
Extras	(b 4, lb 5, w 11, nb 1)	21			Extras	(b 1, lb 4, w 10)	15		
Total	(58.2 overs)	181			Total	(52.5 overs; 7 wickets)	184		

SRI LANKA	O	M	R	W	NEW ZEALAND	O	M	R	W
De Mel	12	4	32	5	Hadlee	12	3	16	1
Ratnayake	11	4	18	2	Cairns	10	2	35	1
Ranatunga	10	2	50	0	Snedden	10.5	1	58	2
De Silva	12	5	11	2	Chatfield	12	3	23	1
Samarasekera	11.2	2	38	0	Crowe	4	2	15	1
Wettimuny	2	0	11	0	Coney	4	1	22	0

FALL OF WICKETS
1-8, 2-8, 3-32, 4-47, 5-88, 6-91, 7-105, 8-115, 9-116, 10-181

FALL OF WICKETS
1-15, 2-49, 3-129, 4-130, 5-139, 6-151, 7-161

Umpires: D.J.Constant (21) and B.Leadbeater (3).

AUSTRALIA v WEST INDIES 1983

At Lord's, London, on 18 June 1983.   Result: **WEST INDIES** won by 7 wickets.   Toss: Australia.
Award: I.V.A.Richards.   LOI debuts: None.

Australia's highest total (so far) batting first against West Indies proved insufficient to avenge the result of their classic 1975 final.

AUSTRALIA		Runs	Balls	4/6
G.M.Wood	b Marshall	17	24	–
T.M.Chappell	c Dujon b Marshall	5	14	1
* K.J.Hughes	b Gomes	69	124	8
D.W.Hookes	c Greenidge b Davis	56	74	4/2
G.N.Yallop	not out	52	74	3
A.R.Border	c and b Gomes	11	24	1
† R.W.Marsh	c Haynes b Holding	37	26	4/2
T.G.Hogan	not out	0	1	–
J.R.Thomson				
D.K.Lillee				
R.M.Hogg				
Extras	(b 1, lb 18, w 6, nb 1)	26		
Total	(60 overs; 6 wickets)	**273**		

WEST INDIES		Runs	Balls	4/6
C.G.Greenidge	c Hughes b Hogg	90	140	8
D.L.Haynes	b Hogan	33	46	3
I.V.A.Richards	not out	95	117	9/3
H.A.Gomes	b Chappell	15	26	1
* C.H.Lloyd	not out	19	22	3
S.F.A.F.Bacchus				
† P.J.L.Dujon				
M.D.Marshall				
A.M.E.Roberts				
M.A.Holding				
W.W.Davis				
Extras	(b 3, lb 18, w 1, nb 2)	24		
Total	(57.5 overs; 3 wickets)	**276**		

WEST INDIES	O	M	R	W
Roberts	12	0	51	0
Marshall	12	0	36	2
Davis	12	0	57	1
Holding	12	1	56	1
Gomes	12	0	47	2

AUSTRALIA	O	M	R	W
Hogg	12	0	25	1
Thomson	11	0	64	0
Hogan	12	0	60	1
Lillee	12	0	52	0
Chappell	10.5	0	51	1

FALL OF WICKETS
1-10, 2-37, 3-138, 4-176, 5-202, 6-266

FALL OF WICKETS
1-79, 2-203, 3-228

Umpires: K.E.Palmer (12) and A.G.T.Whitehead (9).

INDIA v ZIMBABWE 1983

At Nevill Ground, Tunbridge Wells, on 18 June 1983.   Result: **INDIA** won by 31 runs.   Toss: India.
Award: Kapil Dev.   LOI debuts: None.

Taking strike when his side was 17 for 5, Kapil Dev batted for 181 minutes to record the highest score in World Cup matches until 1987-88 (*LOI No. 457*), completing his hundred off 72 balls. It was India's first hundred in limited-overs internationals and remains easily their highest innings. His unbroken stand of 126 with Syed Kirmani remains the LOI ninth-wicket world record.

INDIA		Runs	Balls	4/6
S.M.Gavaskar	lbw b Rawson	0	6	–
K.Srikkanth	c Butchart b Curran	0		–
M.Amarnath	c Houghton b Rawson	5		1
S.M.Patil	c Houghton b Curran	1		–
Yashpal Sharma	c Houghton b Rawson	9		1
Kapil Dev	not out	175		16/6
* R.M.H.Binny	lbw b Traicos	22		2
R.J.Shastri	c Pycroft b Fletcher	1		–
Madan Lal	c Houghton b Curran	17		1
† S.M.H.Kirmani	not out	24		2
B.S.Sandhu				
Extras	(lb 9, w 3)	12		
Total	(60 overs; 8 wickets)	**266**		

ZIMBABWE		Runs	Balls	4/6
R.D.Brown	run out	35		2
G.A.Paterson	lbw b Binny	23		4
J.G.Heron	run out	3		–
A.J.Pycroft	c Kirmani b Sandhu	6		1
† D.L.Houghton	lbw b Madan Lal	17		2
* D.A.G.Fletcher	c Kapil Dev b Amarnath	13		–
K.M.Curran	c Shastri b Madan Lal	73		8
I.P.Butchart	b Binny	18		1
G.E.Peckover	c Yashpal b Madan Lal	14		–
P.W.E.Rawson	not out	2		–
A.J.Traicos	c and b Kapil Dev	3		–
Extras	(lb 17, w 7, nb 4)	28		
Total	(57 overs)	**235**		

ZIMBABWE	O	M	R	W
Rawson	12	4	47	3
Curran	12	1	65	3
Butchart	12	2	38	0
Fletcher	12	2	59	1
Traicos	12	0	45	1

INDIA	O	M	R	W
Kapil Dev	11	1	32	1
Sandhu	11	2	44	1
Binny	11	2	45	2
Madan Lal	11	2	42	3
Amarnath	12	1	37	1
Shastri	1	0	7	0

FALL OF WICKETS
1-0, 2-6, 3-6, 4-9, 5-17, 6-77, 7-78, 8-140

FALL OF WICKETS
1-44, 2-48, 3-61, 4-86, 5-103, 6-113, 7-168, 8-189, 9-230, 10-235

Umpires: M.J.Kitchen (3) and B.J.Meyer (13).

ENGLAND v SRI LANKA 1983

At Headingley, Leeds, on 20 June 1983.   Result: **ENGLAND** won by 9 wickets.   Toss: England.
Award: R.G.D.Willis.   LOI debuts: None.

Graeme Fowler, who compiled his fourth successive fifty of this tournament, completed England's comprehensive victory with a single at 4.43pm.

SRI LANKA		Runs	Balls	4/6
S.Wettimuny	lbw b Botham	22	49	3
D.S.B.P.Kuruppu	c Gatting b Willis	6	36	1
A.Ranatunga	c Lamb b Botham	0	16	–
R.L.Dias	c Gould b Cowans	7	24	1
* L.R.D.Mendis	b Allott	10	38	–
R.S.Madugalle	c Gould b Allott	0	6	–
D.S.de Silva	c Gower b Marks	15	36	1
† R.G.de Alwis	c Marks b Cowans	19	20	2/1
A.L.F.de Mel	c Lamb b Marks	10	23	2
R.J.Ratnayake	not out	20	32	1/1
V.B.John	c Cowans b Allott	15	27	1
Extras	(b 5, lb 2, w 3, nb 2)	12		
Total	(50.4 overs)	**136**		

ENGLAND	O	M	R	W
Willis	9	4	9	1
Cowans	12	3	31	2
Botham	9	4	12	2
Allott	10.4	0	41	3
Gatting	4	2	13	0
Marks	6	2	18	2

FALL OF WICKETS
1-25, 2-30, 3-32, 4-40, 5-43, 6-54, 7-81, 8-97, 9-103, 10-136

ENGLAND		Runs	Balls	4/6
G.Fowler	not out	81	77	11
C.J.Tavaré	c De Alwis b De Mel	19	48	1/1
D.I.Gower	not out	27	24	3
A.J.Lamb				
M.W.Gatting				
I.T.Botham				
† I.J.Gould				
V.J.Marks				
P.J.W.Allott				
* R.G.D.Willis				
N.G.Cowans				
Extras	(b 1, lb 3, w 3, nb 3)	10		
Total	(24.1 overs; 1 wicket)	**137**		

SRI LANKA	O	M	R	W
De Mel	10	1	33	1
Ratnayake	5	0	23	0
John	6	0	41	0
De Silva	3	0	29	0
Ranatunga	0.1	0	1	0

FALL OF WICKETS
1-68

Umpires: B.Leadbeater (4) and R.Palmer (4).

NEW ZEALAND v PAKISTAN 1983

At Trent Bridge, Nottingham, on 20 June 1983.   Result: **PAKISTAN** won by 11 runs.   Toss: Pakistan.
Award: Imran Khan.   LOI debuts: None.

Pakistan's victory enabled them to finish equal second with New Zealand in Group A. They qualified for the semi-finals on superior overall scoring rate (4.01 to New Zealand's 3.94), the unbroken fourth-wicket stand of 147 off 132 balls between Zaheer Abbas, who scored his seventh LOI hundred, and Imran Khan proving decisive.

PAKISTAN		Runs	Balls	4/6
Mohsin Khan	c Cairns b Coney	33	64	3
Mudassar Nazar	b Coney	15	60	–
Javed Miandad	b Hadlee	25	45	1
Zaheer Abbas	not out	103	121	6
* Imran Khan	not out	79	74	7/1
Ijaz Faqih				
Shahid Mahboob				
Sarfraz Nawaz				
Abdul Qadir				
† Wasim Bari				
Rashid Khan				
Extras	(b 1, lb 2, w 2, nb 1)	6		
Total	(60 overs; 3 wickets)	**261**		

NEW ZEALAND	O	M	R	W
Hadlee	12	1	61	1
Cairns	12	1	45	0
Chatfield	12	0	57	0
Coney	12	0	42	2
Bracewell	12	0	50	0

FALL OF WICKETS
1-48, 2-54, 3-114

NEW ZEALAND		Runs	Balls	4/6
G.M.Turner	c Wasim b Sarfraz	4	16	–
J.G.Wright	c Imran b Qadir	19	57	1
* G.P.Howarth	c Miandad b Zaheer	39	51	3
M.D.Crowe	b Mudassar	43	62	4
B.A.Edgar	lbw b Shahid	6	22	–
J.V.Coney	run out	51	78	3
R.J.Hadlee	c Mohsin b Mudassar	11	20	1
B.L.Cairns	c Imran b Qadir	0	3	–
† W.K.Lees	c sub (Mansoor Akhtar) b Mudassar	26	25	4
J.G.Bracewell	c Mohsin b Sarfraz	34	24	7
E.J.Chatfield	not out	3	6	–
Extras	(lb 8, w 5, nb 1)	14		
Total	(59.1 overs)	**250**		

PAKISTAN	O	M	R	W
Rashid Khan	6	1	24	0
Sarfraz Nawaz	9.1	1	50	2
Abdul Qadir	12	0	53	2
Ijaz Faqih	6	1	21	0
Shahid Mahboob	10	0	37	1
Mudassar Nazar	12	0	43	3
Zaheer Abbas	4	1	8	1

FALL OF WICKETS
1-13, 2-44, 3-85, 4-102, 5-130, 6-150, 7-152, 8-187, 9-246, 10-250

Umpires: D.G.L.Evans (10) and M.J.Kitchen (4).

AUSTRALIA v INDIA 1983

At County Ground, Chelmsford, on 20 June 1983.   Result: **INDIA** won by 118 runs.   Toss: India.
Award: R.M.H.Binny.   LOI debuts: None.

Australia, led by David Hookes in the absence of the injured Kim Hughes, would have qualified at the expense of the eventual champions had they not collapsed dramatically, losing six wickets for 32 runs to the swing bowling of Roger Binny and Madan Lal.

INDIA		Runs	Balls	4/6		AUSTRALIA		Runs	Balls	4/6
S.M.Gavaskar	c Chappell b Hogg	9	10	1		T.M.Chappell	c Madan Lal b Sandhu	2	5	–
K.Srikkanth	c Border b Thomson	24	22	3		G.M.Wood	c Kirmani b Binny	21	32	2
M.Amarnath	c Marsh b Thomson	13	20	2		G.N.Yallop	c and b Binny	18	30	2
Yashpal Sharma	c Hogg b Hogan	40	40	1		* D.W.Hookes	b Binny	1	2	–
S.M.Patil	c Hogan b MacLeay	30	25	4		A.R.Border	b Madan Lal	36	49	5
Kapil Dev	c Hookes b Hogg	28	32	3		† R.W.Marsh	lbw b Madan Lal	0	2	–
K.Azad	c Border b Lawson	15	18	1		K.H.MacLeay	c Gavaskar b Madan Lal	5	6	1
R.M.H.Binny	run out	21	32	2		T.G.Hogan	c Srikkanth b Binny	8	10	2
Madan Lal	not out	12	15	–		G.F.Lawson	b Sandhu	16	20	1
S.M.H.Kirmani	lbw b Hogg	10	20	1		R.M.Hogg	not out	8	12	1
B.S.Sandhu	b Thomson	8	18	1		J.R.Thomson	b Madan Lal	0	5	–
Extras	(lb 13, w 9, nb 15)	37				Extras	(lb 5, w 5, nb 4)	14		
Total	(55.5 overs)	**247**				**Total**	(38.2 overs)	**129**		

AUSTRALIA	O	M	R	W		INDIA	O	M	R	W
Lawson	10	1	40	1		Kapil Dev	8	2	16	0
Hogg	12	2	40	3		Sandhu	10	1	26	2
Hogan	11	1	31	1		Madan Lal	8.2	3	20	4
Thomson	10.5	0	51	3		Binny	8	2	29	4
MacLeay	12	2	48	1		Amarnath	2	0	17	0
						Azad	2	0	7	0

FALL OF WICKETS
1-27, 2-54, 3-65, 4-118, 5-157, 6-174, 7-207, 8-215, 9-232, 10-247

FALL OF WICKETS
1-3, 2-46, 3-48, 4-52, 5-52, 6-69, 7-78, 8-115, 9-129, 10-129

Umpires: J.Birkenshaw (4) and D.R.Shepherd (4).

WEST INDIES v ZIMBABWE 1983

At Edgbaston, Birmingham, on 20 June 1983.   Result: **WEST INDIES** won by 10 wickets.   Toss: Zimbabwe.
Award: S.F.A.F.Bacchus.   LOI debuts: None.

West Indies achieved their first ten-wicket win in World Cup matches, the unbroken stand of 172 remaining their highest opening LOI partnership in England.

ZIMBABWE		Runs	Balls	4/6		WEST INDIES		Runs	Balls	4/6
R.D.Brown	c Lloyd b Marshall	14		–		D.L.Haynes	not out	88		9
S.A.Paterson	c Richards b Garner	6		1		S.F.A.F.Bacchus	not out	80		8
G.Heron	c Dujon b Garner	0		–		A.L.Logie				
A.J.Pycroft	c Dujon b Marshall	4		–		I.V.A.Richards				
D.L.Houghton	c Lloyd b Daniel	0		–		H.A.Gomes				
A.G.Fletcher	b Richards	23		2		* C.H.Lloyd				
K.M.Curran	b Daniel	62		4/1		† P.J.L.Dujon				
P.Butchart	c Haynes b Richards	8		–		M.D.Marshall				
G.E.Peckover	c and b Richards	3		–		J.Garner				
I.W.E.Rawson	b Daniel	19		1		W.W.Daniel				
A.J.Traicos	not out	1		–		W.W.Davis				
Extras	(b 4, lb 13, w 7, nb 7)	31				Extras	(lb 1, w 3)	4		
Total	(60 overs)	**171**				**Total**	(45.1 overs; 0 wickets)	**172**		

WEST INDIES	O	M	R	W		ZIMBABWE	O	M	R	W
Marshall	12	3	19	2		Rawson	12	3	38	0
Garner	7	4	13	2		Butchart	4	0	23	0
Davis	8	2	13	0		Traicos	12	2	24	0
Daniel	9	2	28	3		Curran	9	0	44	0
Gomes	12	2	26	0		Fletcher	8.1	0	39	0
Richards	12	1	41	3						

FALL OF WICKETS
1-17, 2-17, 3-41, 4-42, 5-42, 6-79, 7-104, 8-115, 9-170, 10-171

Umpires: H.D.Bird (22) and D.J.Constant (22).

ENGLAND v INDIA 1983

At Old Trafford, Manchester, on 22 June 1983.   Result: **INDIA** won by 6 wickets.   Toss: England.
Award: M.Amarnath.   LOI debuts: None.

India gained their first limited-overs victory against England in England, Sandeep Patil completing his fifty off 32 balls with the winning hit.

ENGLAND		Runs	Balls	4/6	INDIA		Runs	Balls	4/6
G.Fowler	b Binny	33	59	3	S.M.Gavaskar	c Gould b Allott	25	41	3
C.J.Tavaré	c Kirmani b Binny	32	51	4	K.Srikkanth	c Willis b Botham	19	44	3
D.I.Gower	c Kirmani b Amarnath	17	30	1	M.Amarnath	run out	46	92	4/
A.J.Lamb	run out	29	58	1	Yashpal Sharma	c Allott b Willis	61	115	4
M.W.Gatting	b Amarnath	18	46	1	S.M.Patil	not out	51	32	8
I.T.Botham	b Azad	6	26	–	* Kapil Dev	not out	1	6	–
† I.J.Gould	run out	13	36	–	K.Azad				
V.J.Marks	b Kapil Dev	8	18	–	R.M.H.Binny				
G.R.Dilley	not out	20	26	2	Madan Lal				
P.J.W.Allott	c Patil b Kapil Dev	8	14	–	† S.M.H.Kirmani				
* R.G.D.Willis	b Kapil Dev	0	2	–	B.S.Sandhu				
Extras	(b 1, lb 17, w 7, nb 4)	29			Extras	(b 5, lb 6, w 1, nb 2)	14		
Total	(60 overs)	213			Total	(54.4 overs; 4 wickets)	217		

INDIA	O	M	R	W	ENGLAND	O	M	R	W
Kapil Dev	11	1	35	3	Willis	10.4	2	42	
Sandhu	8	1	36	0	Dilley	11	0	43	0
Binny	12	1	43	2	Allott	10	3	40	
Madan Lal	5	0	15	0	Botham	11	4	40	
Azad	12	1	28	1	Marks	12	1	38	
Amarnath	12	1	27	2					

FALL OF WICKETS
1-69, 2-84, 3-107, 4-141, 5-150, 6-160, 7-175, 8-177, 9-202, 10-213

FALL OF WICKETS
1-46, 2-50, 3-142, 4-205

Umpires: D.G.L.Evans (11) and D.O.Oslear (7).

PAKISTAN v WEST INDIES 1983

At Kennington Oval, London, on 22 June 1983.   Result: **WEST INDIES** won by 8 wickets.   Toss: West Indies.
Award: I.V.A.Richards.   LOI debuts: None.

West Indies, who won a crucial toss in conditions ideal for seam and swing bowling, restricted Pakistan to just two boundaries, one of them edged. Mohsin Khan's 237-minute innings included 43 singles.

PAKISTAN		Runs	Balls	4/6	WEST INDIES		Runs	Balls	4/
Mohsin Khan	b Roberts	70	176	1	C.G.Greenidge	lbw b Rashid	17		
Mudassar Nazar	c and b Garner	11	39	–	D.L.Haynes	b Qadir	29		
Ijaz Faqih	c Dujon b Holding	5	19	–	I.V.A.Richards	not out	80		11/
Zaheer Abbas	b Gomes	30	38	1	H.A.Gomes	not out	50		3
* Imran Khan	c Dujon b Marshall	17	41	–	* C.H.Lloyd				
Wasim Raja	lbw b Marshall	0	3	–	S.F.A.F.Bacchus				
Shahid Mahboob	c Richards b Marshall	6	10	–	† P.J.L.Dujon				
Sarfraz Nawaz	c Holding b Roberts	3	12	–	M.D.Marshall				
Abdul Qadir	not out	10	21	–	A.M.E.Roberts				
† Wasim Bari	not out	4	7	–	J.Garner				
Rashid Khan					M.A.Holding				
Extras	(b 6, lb 13, w 4, nb 5)	28			Extras	(b 2, lb 6, w 4)	12		
Total	(60 overs; 8 wickets)	184			Total	(48.4 overs; 2 wickets)	188		

WEST INDIES	O	M	R	W	PAKISTAN	O	M	R	W
Roberts	12	3	25	2	Rashid Khan	12	2	32	
Garner	12	1	31	1	Sarfraz Nawaz	8	0	23	
Marshall	12	2	28	3	Abdul Qadir	11	1	42	
Holding	12	1	25	1	Shahid Mahboob	11	1	43	
Gomes	7	0	29	1	Wasim Raja	1	0	9	
Richards	5	0	18	0	Zaheer Abbas	4.4	1	24	
					Mohsin Khan	1	0	3	

FALL OF WICKETS
1-23, 2-34, 3-88, 4-139, 5-139, 6-159, 7-164, 8-171

FALL OF WICKETS
1-34, 2-56

Umpires: D.J.Constant (23) and A.G.T.Whitehead (10).

112

WEST INDIES v INDIA 1983

At Lord's, London, on 25 June 1983.   Result: **INDIA** won by 43 runs.   Toss: West Indies.
Award: M.Amarnath.   LOI debuts: None.

India achieved one of cricket's major upsets when they dismissed West Indies for their lowest World Cup total so far and ruined their hopes of a hat-trick of Prudential Cup triumphs. They were most worthy champions having defeated the holders, Australia, and England en route to the final.

INDIA		Runs	Balls	4/6
S.M.Gavaskar	c Dujon b Roberts	2	12	–
K.Srikkanth	lbw b Marshall	38	57	7/1
M.Amarnath	b Holding	26	80	3
Yashpal Sharma	c sub (A.L.Logie) b Gomes	11	32	1
S.M.Patil	c Gomes b Garner	27	29	–/1
* Kapil Dev	c Holding b Gomes	15	8	3
K.Azad	c Garner b Roberts	0	3	–
R.M.H.Binny	c Garner b Roberts	2	8	–
Madan Lal	b Marshall	17	27	–/1
† S.M.H.Kirmani	b Holding	14	43	–
B.S.Sandhu	not out	11	30	1
Extras	(b 5, lb 5, w 9, nb 1)	20		
Total	(54.4 overs)	**183**		

WEST INDIES		Runs	Balls	4/6
C.G.Greenidge	b Sandhu	1	12	–
D.L.Haynes	c Binny b Madan Lal	13	33	2
I.V.A.Richards	c Kapil Dev b Madan Lal	33	28	7
* C.H.Lloyd	c Kapil Dev b Binny	8	17	1
H.A.Gomes	c Gavaskar b Madan Lal	5	16	–
S.F.A.F.Bacchus	c Kirmani b Sandhu	8	25	–
† P.J.L.Dujon	b Amarnath	25	73	–/1
M.D.Marshall	c Gavaskar b Amarnath	18	51	–
A.M.E.Roberts	lbw b Kapil Dev	4	14	–
J.Garner	not out	5	19	–
M.A.Holding	lbw b Amarnath	6	24	–
Extras	(lb 4, w 10)	14		
Total	(52 overs)	**140**		

WEST INDIES	O	M	R	W
Roberts	10	3	32	3
Garner	12	4	24	1
Marshall	11	1	24	2
Holding	9.4	2	26	2
Gomes	11	1	49	2
Richards	1	0	8	0

INDIA	O	M	R	W
Kapil Dev	11	4	21	1
Sandhu	9	1	32	2
Madan Lal	12	2	31	3
Binny	10	1	23	1
Amarnath	7	0	12	3
Azad	3	0	7	0

FALL OF WICKETS
1-2, 2-59, 3-90, 4-92, 5-110, 6-111, 7-130, 8-153, 9-161, 10-183

FALL OF WICKETS
1-5, 2-50, 3-57, 4-66, 5-66, 6-76, 7-119, 8-124, 9-126, 10-140

Umpires: H.D.Bird (23) and B.J.Meyer (14).

INDIA v PAKISTAN 1983-84

At Lal Bahadur Stadium, Hyderabad on 11 September 1983.   Result: **INDIA** won by 4 wickets.   Toss: India.
Award: M.Amarnath.   LOI debuts: Pakistan – Azeem Hafeez, Qasim Omar.

India's World Cup-winning eleven continued their successful run in two matches against Pakistan, both of which were reduced from 50 to 46 overs, presumably because of slow over-rates.

PAKISTAN		Runs	Balls	4/6
Mohsin Khan	b Sandhu	6	42	–
Mudassar Nazar	c Kirmani b Kapil Dev	0	1	–
* Zaheer Abbas	c Kirmani b Sandhu	20	35	3
Javed Miandad	not out	66	110	4
Wasim Raja	c Kapil Dev b Sandhu	0	4	–
Qasim Omar	c Kirmani b Binny	5	26	1
† Wasim Bari	run out	18	55	–
Tahir Naqqash	c Amarnath b Binny	1	6	–
Jalaluddin	run out	5	4	1
Azeem Hafeez	not out	5	5	1
Mohammad Nazir				
Extras	(lb 4, w 18, nb 3)	25		
Total	(46 overs; 8 wickets)	**151**		

INDIA		Runs	Balls	4/6
S.M.Gavaskar	c Wasim Bari b Mudassar	33	60	4
K.Srikkanth	lbw b Jalaluddin	16	26	2
M.Amarnath	not out	60	118	5
Yashpal Sharma	b Mudassar	2	15	–
S.M.Patil	c Miandad b Mudassar	1	14	–
K.Azad	c Wasim Raja b Nazir	7	13	–
* Kapil Dev	c Mohsin b Azeem	18	23	2/1
R.M.H.Binny	not out	0	–	–
Madan Lal				
† S.M.H.Kirmani				
B.S.Sandhu				
Extras	(b 1, lb 3, w 10, nb 1)	15		
Total	(43 overs; 6 wickets)	**152**		

INDIA	O	M	R	W
Kapil Dev	9	3	16	1
Sandhu	9	2	27	3
Madan Lal	10	2	22	0
Binny	8	2	34	2
Amarnath	10	0	27	1

PAKISTAN	O	M	R	W
Jalaluddin	8	0	34	1
Tahir Naqqash	5	1	16	0
Mudassar Nazar	10	3	17	3
Azeem Hafeez	10	0	43	1
Mohammad Nazir	10	1	27	1

FALL OF WICKETS
1-1, 2-23, 3-35, 4-36, 5-62, 6-123, 7-129, 8-136

FALL OF WICKETS
1-30, 2-69, 3-77, 4-81, 5-113, 6-151

Umpires: P.G.Pandit (1) and M.G.Subramaniam (1).

INDIA v PAKISTAN 1983-84

At Sawai Mansingh Stadium, Jaipur on 2 October 1983.   Result: **INDIA** won by 4 wickets.   Toss: India.
Award: S.M.Patil.   LOI debuts: None.   46-over match.

The first LOI match in which no-balls and wides were debited to bowlers' analyses. Sandeep Patil's 28-ball fifty remains the third-fastest on record for India. A third match, played under lights in New Delhi on 21 September was ruled as an unofficial 'festival tie' for the Prime Minister's Relief Fund.

PAKISTAN		Runs	Balls	4/6
Mudassar Nazar	b Binny	27	66	–
Mohsin Khan	c Patil b Madan Lal	22	55	2
* Zaheer Abbas	lbw b Kapil Dev	48	59	1
Javed Miandad	lbw b Madan Lal	1	3	–
Wasim Raja	run out	17	27	–
Salim Malik	c Azad b Kapil Dev	27	37	2
† Wasim Bari	not out	5	18	–
Tahir Naqqash	run out	0	6	–
Jalaluddin	c and b Madan Lal	0	1	–
Azeem Hafeez	run out	7	7	1
Mohammad Nazir	not out	0	–	–
Extras	(lb 6, w 4, nb 2)	12		
Total	(46 overs; 9 wickets)	**166**		

INDIA		Runs	Balls	4/6
S.M.Gavaskar	b Nazir	41	82	5
K.Srikkanth	b Jalaluddin	17	24	3
M.Amarnath	b Tahir	1	19	–
S.M.Patil	c Mohsin b Nazir	51	28	7/2
* Kapil Dev	c Wasim Bari b Jalaluddin	9	20	–
K.Azad	b Mudassar	4	15	1
Yashpal Sharma	not out	23	32	2
R.M.H.Binny	not out	11	20	2
Madan Lal				
† S.M.H.Kirmani				
B.S.Sandhu				
Extras	(b 4, lb 3, w 4, nb 1)	12		
Total	(40.4 overs; 6 wickets)	**169**		

INDIA	O	M	R	W
Kapil Dev	10	2	33	2
Sandhu	10	1	36	0
Madan Lal	10	1	27	3
Binny	10	0	38	1
Amarnath	6	0	26	0

PAKISTAN	O	M	R	W
Azeem Hafeez	6.4	1	24	0
Jalaluddin	10	2	41	2
Tahir Naqqash	4	0	19	1
Mudassar Nazar	10	0	41	1
Mohammad Nazir	10	1	37	2

FALL OF WICKETS
1-55, 2-57, 3-60, 4-100, 5-153, 6-155, 7-155, 8-155, 9-165

FALL OF WICKETS
1-30, 2-52, 3-108, 4-120, 5-129, 6-135

Umpires: S.R.Bose (1) and R.Mehra (2).

INDIA v WEST INDIES 1983-84

At Sher-i-Kashmir Stadium, Srinagar on 13 October 1983.   Result: **WEST INDIES** won on faster scoring rate.
Toss: West Indies.   Award: D.L.Haynes.   LOI debuts: West Indies – E.A.E.Baptiste, R.A.Harper.   45-over match.

When a dust storm and failing light ended play one ball after the halfway mark in the West Indies innings, scores were compared after 22 overs. At that point India had totalled 80.

INDIA		Runs	Balls	4/6
S.M.Gavaskar	c Richards b Marshall	11		
K.Srikkanth	c Greenidge b Harper	40		
D.B.Vengsarkar	c Marshall b Baptiste	28		
Yashpal Sharma	c Haynes b Harper	7		
S.M.Patil	b Baptiste	0		
* Kapil Dev	c Dujon b Holding	17		
K.Azad	c and b Harper	21		–/2
R.M.H.Binny	c Dujon b Roberts	10		
Madan Lal	run out	13		
† S.M.H.Kirmani	not out	8		
B.S.Sandhu	c Richards b Marshall	0		
Extras	(b 2, lb 5, w 3, nb 11)	21		
Total	(41.2 overs)	**176**		

WEST INDIES		Runs	Balls	4/6
C.G.Greenidge	not out	44		
D.L.Haynes	not out	55		
I.V.A.Richards				
H.A.Gomes				
* C.H.Lloyd				
† P.J.L.Dujon				
E.A.E.Baptiste				
R.A.Harper				
M.D.Marshall				
A.M.E.Roberts				
M.A.Holding				
Extras	(lb 4, w 2, nb 3)	9		
Total	(22.4 overs; 0 wickets)	**108**		

WEST INDIES	O	M	R	W
Roberts	9	0	26	1
Marshall	7.2	2	13	2
Holding	7	0	32	1
Baptiste	9	1	50	2
Harper	9	1	34	3

INDIA	O	M	R	W
Kapil Dev	5	1	12	0
Sandhu	7	0	10	0
Madan Lal	6.4	0	51	0
Binny	4	0	26	0

FALL OF WICKETS
1-19, 2-65, 3-80, 4-90, 5-114, 6-143, 7-151, 8-155, 9-176, 10-176

Umpires: J.D.Ghosh (2) and Mohammad Ghouse (1).

INDIA v WEST INDIES 1983-84

At Moti Bagh Stadium, Baroda on 9 November 1983.   Result: **WEST INDIES** won by 4 wickets.   Toss: India.
Award: C.G.Greenidge.   LOI debuts: None.   49-over match.

Krish Srikkanth's uncharacteristic 20-over innings of 19 was in stark contrast to Clive Lloyd's decisive 17-ball cameo.

INDIA		Runs	Balls	4/6
A.D.Gaekwad	c Dujon b Daniel	0		
K.Srikkanth	b Harper	19		
R.J.Shastri	c Richards b Gomes	65	125	5
S.M.Patil	c Gomes b Baptiste	31	49	
A.Malhotra	c Haynes b Gomes	29		
R.M.H.Binny	not out	22		
Kapil Dev	b Marshall	15		
K.Azad	not out	9		
Madan Lal				
‡S.M.H.Kirmani				
B.S.Sandhu				
Extras	(b 5, lb 12, w 3, nb 4)	24		
Total	(49 overs; 6 wickets)	**214**		

WEST INDIES		Runs	Balls	4/6
C.G.Greenidge	st Kirmani b Azad	63		
D.L.Haynes	b Madan Lal	38		
I.V.A.Richards	c Gaekwad b Shastri	18		
H.A.Gomes	lbw b Kapil Dev	26		
* C.H.Lloyd	c Sandhu b Kapil Dev	31	17	4/1
† P.J.L.Dujon	not out	15		
M.D.Marshall	b Madan Lal	3		
E.A.E.Baptiste	not out	4		
R.A.Harper				
A.M.E.Roberts				
W.W.Daniel				
Extras	(b 7, lb 8, w 4)	19		
Total	(47.5 overs; 6 wickets)	**217**		

WEST INDIES	O	M	R	W
Roberts	9	2	30	0
Daniel	8	1	23	1
Marshall	9	0	34	1
Baptiste	10	2	39	1
Harper	10	0	47	1
Gomes	3	0	17	2

INDIA	O	M	R	W
Kapil Dev	8.5	1	38	2
Sandhu	8	0	53	0
Madan Lal	9	0	39	2
Binny	2	0	16	0
Shastri	10	2	23	1
Azad	10	1	29	1

FALL OF WICKETS
1-7, 2-47, 3-116, 4-157, 5-167, 6-189

FALL OF WICKETS
1-69, 2-101, 3-156, 4-180, 5-203, 6-212

Umpires: S.Banerjee (1) and V.K.Ramaswamy (1).

INDIA v WEST INDIES 1983-84

At Nehru Stadium, Indore on 1 December 1983.   Result: **WEST INDIES** won by 8 wickets.   Toss: India.
Award: C.G.Greenidge.   LOI debuts: None.   47-over match.

Capitalising on an opening stand of 149, West Indies stunned a crowd estimated at 28,000 by winning the Charminar
Challenge Cup with two matches in hand.

INDIA		Runs	Balls	4/6
S.M.Gavaskar	c Dujon b Roberts	15		
K.Srikkanth	run out	0		
M.Amarnath	run out	55	122	4
Arun Lal	c Haynes b Holding	0		
A.Malhotra	c Harper b Baptiste	40	44	7
* Kapil Dev	c Holding b Harper	28	25	3/1
R.M.H.Binny	c and b Harper	12		
R.J.Shastri	not out	41	36	2/2
Madan Lal	not out	19		
† S.M.H.Kirmani				
B.S.Sandhu				
Extras	(b 6, lb 8, w 11, nb 5)	30		
Total	(47 overs; 7 wickets)	**240**		

WEST INDIES		Runs	Balls	4/6
C.G.Greenidge	lbw b Kapil Dev	96	127	10/1
D.L.Haynes	st Kirmani b Shastri	54	77	
I.V.A.Richards	not out	49	50	3/1
* C.H.Lloyd	not out	27	23	3/1
H.A.Gomes				
† P.J.L.Dujon				
E.A.E.Baptiste				
R.A.Harper				
M.D.Marshall				
A.M.E.Roberts				
M.A.Holding				
Extras	(b 1, lb 12, nb 2)	15		
Total	(45.2 overs; 2 wickets)	**241**		

WEST INDIES	O	M	R	W
Marshall	9	1	27	0
Roberts	8	0	35	1
Holding	7	2	19	1
Baptiste	10	4	44	1
Harper	10	0	55	2
Gomes	3	0	30	0

INDIA	O	M	R	W
Kapil Dev	9.2	1	41	1
Sandhu	7	0	26	0
Madan Lal	9	0	36	0
Binny	3	0	26	0
Shastri	8	1	53	1
Amarnath	9	0	44	0

FALL OF WICKETS
1-3, 2-32, 3-39, 4-123, 5-155, 6-172, 7-180

FALL OF WICKETS
1-149, 2-193

Umpires: M.Y.Gupte (1) and R.V.Ramani (1).

INDIA v WEST INDIES 1983-84

At Keenan Stadium, Jamshedpur on 7 December 1983.   Result: **WEST INDIES** won by 104 runs.   Toss: India.
Award: I.V.A.Richards.   LOI debuts: India – C.Sharma.   45-over match.

A second-wicket partnership of 221 off only 26 overs between Gordon Greenidge and Viv Richards, still the national record and the world LOI record until 1993-94, enabled West Indies to amass their (then) highest total. Richards reached 50 off 31 balls and 100 off 72, the latter remaining the West Indies record.

WEST INDIES		Runs	Balls	4/6	INDIA		Runs	Balls	4/6
C.G.Greenidge	b Shastri	115	94	10/5	S.M.Gavaskar	c Dujon b Roberts	83	96	6/3
D.L.Haynes	b Sharma	1			K.Srikkanth	c Dujon b Roberts	3		
I.V.A.Richards	c Amarnath b Kapil Dev	149	99	20/3	M.Amarnath	b Holding	16		
† P.J.L.Dujon	lbw b Sharma	49			A.Malhotra	st Dujon b Harper	65	70	7
* C.H.Lloyd	c Amarnath b Kapil Dev	3			* Kapil Dev	not out	44		4/2
E.A.E.Baptiste	st Kirmani b Madan Lal	1			Arun Lal	lbw b Roberts	0		
M.D.Marshall	b Kapil Dev	5			R.M.H.Binny	not out	12		
A.M.E.Roberts	not out	1			R.J.Shastri				
R.A.Harper	b Sharma	0			Madan Lal				
M.A.Holding	not out	0			† S.M.H.Kirmani				
H.A.Gomes					C.Sharma				
Extras	(lb 4, w 4, nb 1)	9			Extras	(lb 3, w 2, nb 1)	6		
Total	(45 overs; 8 wickets)	333			Total	(45 overs; 5 wickets)	229		

INDIA	O	M	R	W	WEST INDIES	O	M	R	W
Kapil Dev	9	1	44	3	Marshall	6	0	18	0
Sharma	9	0	60	3	Roberts	10	1	54	3
Binny	1.5	0	17	0	Holding	6	1	15	1
Madan Lal	9	0	47	1	Baptiste	10	0	51	0
Amarnath	9.1	0	79	0	Harper	10	0	52	1
Shastri	7	0	77	1	Gomes	2	0	25	0
					Richards	1	0	8	0

FALL OF WICKETS
1-27, 2-248, 3-304, 4-320, 5-324, 6-331, 7-332, 8-332

FALL OF WICKETS
1-23, 2-50, 3-155, 4-181, 5-181

Umpires: P.G.Pandit (2) and S.R.Ramchandra Rao (1).

INDIA v WEST INDIES 1983-84

At Nehru Stadium, Gauhati on 17 December 1983.   Result: **WEST INDIES** won by 6 wickets.   Toss: West Indies.
Award: G.A.Parkar.   LOI debuts: India – R.R.Kulkarni; West Indies – R.B.Richardson.   44-over match.

A clean sweep of this five-match rubber gave West Indies some measure of revenge for their defeat in the World Cup final. Both captains stood down to rest before the imminent fifth Test. Desmond Haynes (12) retired at 37 and resumed at 157.

INDIA		Runs	Balls	4/6	WEST INDIES		Runs	Balls	4/6
K.Srikkanth	b Daniel	11			C.G.Greenidge	c Parkar b Randhir Singh	35		
G.A.Parkar	c Daniel b Baptiste	42			D.L.Haynes	run out	14		
D.B.Vengsarkar	c Pydanna b Baptiste	2			R.B.Richardson	st Kirmani b Shastri	46		
A.Malhotra	run out	26			* I.V.A.Richards	c Kirmani b Shastri	23		
M.Amarnath	c Holding b Richards	23			H.A.Gomes	not out	33		
R.M.H.Binny	c Haynes b Richards	33			M.D.Marshall	not out	10		–/1
R.J.Shastri	run out	18			E.A.E.Baptiste				
*†S.M.H.Kirmani	not out	6			R.A.Harper				
R.R.Kulkarni	not out	1			† M.R.Pydanna				
C.Sharma					M.A.Holding				
Randhir Singh					W.W.Daniel				
Extras	(b 4, lb 7, w 1, nb 4)	16			Extras	(b 4, lb 8, w 4, nb 5)	21		
Total	(44 overs; 7 wickets)	178			Total	(41.4 overs; 4 wickets)	182		

WEST INDIES	O	M	R	W	INDIA	O	M	R	W
Marshall	5	2	8	0	Sharma	9	0	31	0
Holding	7	1	28	0	Binny	6	0	35	0
Baptiste	9	0	31	2	Randhir Singh	6	0	30	1
Daniel	4	1	9	1	Kulkarni	9	1	26	0
Harper	9	0	39	0	Shastri	9	2	19	2
Richards	8	0	33	2	Amarnath	2.4	0	20	0
Gomes	2	0	14	0					

FALL OF WICKETS
1-99, 2-119, 3-157, 4-163

FALL OF WICKETS
1-54, 2-62, 3-67, 4-113, 5-117, 6-167, 7-172

Umpires: R.Mrithyunjayan (1) and A.L.Narasimhan (1).

AUSTRALIA v WEST INDIES 1983-84

At Melbourne Cricket Ground on 8 January 1984.　　Result: **WEST INDIES** won by 27 runs.　　Toss: West Indies.
Award: I.V.A.Richards.　　LOI debuts: Australia – G.R.J.Matthews; West Indies – R.S.Gabriel.

The second LOI match in which no-balls and wides were debited to bowlers' analyses. Unless otherwise noted, this was the *modus operandi* for all future matches. This 15-match tournament of 50-over matches again culminated in a best-of-three sequence of finals. Attendance at this opening fixture was 72,610.

WEST INDIES		Runs	Balls	4/6
D.L.Haynes	c Hughes b Hogg	17	61	2
R.S.Gabriel	c Marsh b Hogg	13	30	1
I.V.A.Richards	c Marsh b Maguire	53	62	6
* C.H.Lloyd	c Rackemann b Matthews	65	78	8
† P.J.L.Dujon	c Wessels b Hogg	5	12	1
M.D.Marshall	run out	9	7	1
E.A.E.Baptiste	not out	28	27	1
H.A.Gomes	b Rackemann	21	24	2
M.A.Holding	not out	1	1	–
J.Garner				
W.W.Daniel				
Extras	(b 1, lb 6, w 1, nb 1)	9		
Total	(50 overs; 7 wickets)	**221**		

AUSTRALIA		Runs	Balls	4/6
K.C.Wessels	b Garner	7	24	1
W.B.Phillips	c and b Marshall	10	26	1
* K.J.Hughes	run out	5	10	–
A.R.Border	not out	84	109	3
G.R.J.Matthews	c Dujon b Daniel	2	5	–
† R.W.Marsh	run out	31	56	2
G.F.Lawson	b Baptiste	2	4	–
J.N.Maguire	b Richards	0	3	–
R.M.Hogg	lbw b Holding	21	18	2
G.N.Yallop	c Lloyd b Marshall	13	28	–
C.G.Rackemann	run out	2	3	–
Extras	(lb 10, w 1, nb 6)	17		
Total	(46 overs)	**194**		

AUSTRALIA	O	M	R	W
Lawson	10	1	34	0
Rackemann	10	2	39	1
Hogg	10	1	29	3
Maguire	10	1	47	1
Matthews	10	0	65	1

WEST INDIES	O	M	R	W
Garner	8	2	28	1
Marshall	9	2	25	2
Daniel	6	1	24	1
Holding	10	0	42	1
Baptiste	7	0	41	1
Richards	6	1	24	1

FALL OF WICKETS
1-28, 2-34, 3-137, 4-153, 5-167, 6-173, 7-220

FALL OF WICKETS
1-12, 2-28, 3-31, 4-44, 5-108, 6-114, 7-115, 8-153, 9-191,10-194

Umpires: A.R.Crafter (22) and R.C.Isherwood (3).

AUSTRALIA v PAKISTAN 1983-84

At Sydney Cricket Ground on 10 January 1984.　　Result: **AUSTRALIA** won by 34 runs.　　Toss: Pakistan.
Award: K.C.Wessels.　　LOI debuts: None.

Rodney Marsh became the first wicket-keeper to complete the double of 1,000 runs and 100 dismissals when he had scored 26.

AUSTRALIA		Runs	Balls	4/6
K.C.Wessels	b Sarfraz	92	123	9
W.B.Phillips	c Wasim b Sarfraz	2	4	–
* K.J.Hughes	c Imran b Sarfraz	5	13	–
A.R.Border	c Wasim b Sarfraz	54	73	5
D.W.Hookes	b Azeem	25	33	1
† R.W.Marsh	b Rashid	66	48	7/1
G.R.J.Matthews	run out	0	1	–
G.F.Lawson	not out	3	4	–
J.N.Maguire	c Wasim b Azeem	2	6	–
R.M.Hogg	not out	2	2	–
C.G.Rackemann				
Extras	(lb 9, w 2, nb 2)	13		
Total	(50 overs; 8 wickets)	**264**		

PAKISTAN		Runs	Balls	4/6
Mohsin Khan	lbw b Rackemann	9	23	–
Mudassar Nazar	c Marsh b Lawson	17	21	1
Qasim Omar	lbw b Rackemann	1	7	–
Javed Miandad	run out	67	93	5
* Imran Khan	run out	39	64	5
Mansoor Akhtar	c Lawson b Matthews	33	38	1/1
Sarfraz Nawaz	b Hogg	6	14	–
† Wasim Bari	b Matthews	13	17	2
Rashid Khan	c Marsh b Rackemann	10	9	1
Mohammad Nazir	not out	2	8	–
Azeem Hafeez	not out	7	11	1
Extras	(b 5, lb 16, w 2, nb 3)	26		
Total	(50 overs; 9 wickets)	**230**		

PAKISTAN	O	M	R	W
Sarfraz Nawaz	10	2	27	4
Rashid Khan	10	1	42	1
Mohammad Nazir	9	0	67	0
Azeem Hafeez	10	0	60	2
Mudassar Nazar	9	0	44	0
Mansoor Akhtar	2	0	15	0

AUSTRALIA	O	M	R	W
Lawson	10	3	26	1
Rackemann	10	2	35	3
Maguire	10	0	49	0
Hogg	10	0	38	1
Matthews	10	0	61	2

FALL OF WICKETS
1-3, 2-17, 3-157, 4-167, 5-248, 6-249, 7-256, 8-261

FALL OF WICKETS
1-30, 2-32, 3-33, 4-119, 5-175, 6-193, 7-201, 8-217, 9-221

Umpires: P.J.McConnell (7) and S.G.Randell (1).

WEST INDIES v PAKISTAN 1983-84

At Melbourne Cricket Ground on 12 January 1984.   Result: **PAKISTAN** won by 97 runs.   Toss: Pakistan.
Award: Qasim Omar.   LOI debuts: None.

Pakistan dismissed West Indies for their lowest total in any limited-overs international until 1992-93, fast-medium bowler Azeem Hafeez producing the only four-wicket return of his 15-match career.

PAKISTAN		Runs	Balls	4/6
Mudassar Nazar	c Dujon b Holding	31	45	1
Mohsin Khan	lbw b Garner	16	27	2
Mansoor Akhtar	run out	19	56	2
Javed Miandad	b Marshall	41	79	–
* Imran Khan	c and b Baptiste	7	12	–
Qasim Omar	b Daniel	69	78	4
Sarfraz Nawaz	c Richards b Holding	7	8	1
Abdul Qadir	not out	6	4	–
Rashid Khan	run out	2	1	–
† Wasim Bari				
Azeem Hafeez				
Extras	(lb 3, w 5, nb 2)	10		
Total	(50 overs; 8 wickets)	**208**		

WEST INDIES		Runs	Balls	4/6
D.L.Haynes	b Rashid	2	24	–
R.S.Gabriel	run out	0	5	–
I.V.A.Richards	c Qadir b Sarfraz	7	11	–
H.A.Gomes	c Qadir b Rashid	1	12	–
* C.H.Lloyd	c Mansoor b Azeem	12	43	–
† P.J.L.Dujon	c Imran b Azeem	30	65	3
M.D.Marshall	c Azeem b Sarfraz	20	40	1
E.A.E.Baptiste	c Mansoor b Azeem	3	4	–
M.A.Holding	c and b Azeem	1	3	–
J.Garner	not out	21	29	–
W.W.Daniel	c Sarfraz b Mudassar	12	15	–
Extras	(lb 1, nb 1)	2		
Total	(41.4 overs)	**111**		

WEST INDIES	O	M	R	W
Garner	10	2	21	1
Marshall	6	0	27	1
Holding	10	0	56	2
Daniel	10	0	46	1
Richards	6	0	26	0
Baptiste	8	0	29	1

PAKISTAN	O	M	R	W
Sarfraz Nawaz	9	2	24	2
Rashid Khan	6	3	10	2
Azeem Hafeez	10	1	22	4
Abdul Qadir	10	0	29	0
Mudassar Nazar	6.4	0	25	1

FALL OF WICKETS
1-27, 2-70, 3-77, 4-87, 5-182, 6-196, 7-206, 8-208

FALL OF WICKETS
1-1, 2-9, 3-9, 4-10, 5-45, 6-56, 7-63, 8-65, 9-94, 10-111

Umpires: M.W.Johnson (21) and S.G.Randell (2).

WEST INDIES v PAKISTAN 1983-84

At Woolloongabba, Brisbane on 14 January 1984.   Result: **WEST INDIES** won by 5 wickets.   Toss: Pakistan.
Award: Mudassar Nazar.   LOI debuts: None.

West Indies exacted swift retribution for their crushing defeat two days earlier, Viv Richards contributing another batting cameo.

PAKISTAN		Runs	Balls	4/6
Mudassar Nazar	c and b Richards	68	114	7
Mohsin Khan	b Daniel	4	7	–
Mansoor Akhtar	b Richards	32	75	1/1
Javed Miandad	run out	9	19	–
Qasim Omar	c Logie b Daniel	18	36	2
* Imran Khan	c Dujon b Holding	9	7	–
Sarfraz Nawaz	c Haynes b Holding	0	4	–
Abdul Qadir	c Lloyd b Daniel	2	17	–
Rashid Khan	c Dujon b Holding	2	6	–
† Wasim Bari	not out	10	14	1
Azeem Hafeez	not out	3	12	–
Extras	(b 1, lb 6, w 3, nb 7)	17		
Total	(50 overs; 9 wickets)	**174**		

WEST INDIES		Runs	Balls	4/6
D.L.Haynes	c Wasim b Mudassar	53	100	6
R.S.Gabriel	b Qadir	20	52	1/1
R.B.Richardson	c Wasim b Rashid	25	59	2
I.V.A.Richards	b Azeem	37	17	6/1
* C.H.Lloyd	c Wasim b Mudassar	11	7	–/1
† P.J.L.Dujon	not out	10	13	2
A.L.Logie	not out	1	3	–
E.A.E.Baptiste				
M.A.Holding				
W.W.Daniel				
W.W.Davis				
Extras	(lb 9, w 8, nb 1)	18		
Total	(40.2 overs; 5 wickets)	**175**		

WEST INDIES	O	M	R	W
Holding	10	1	46	3
Daniel	10	1	27	3
Davis	10	2	29	0
Baptiste	10	2	28	0
Richards	10	0	37	2

PAKISTAN	O	M	R	W
Sarfraz Nawaz	6	2	28	0
Rashid Khan	8	3	18	1
Azeem Hafeez	9.2	0	58	1
Abdul Qadir	7	4	16	1
Mudassar Nazar	10	0	46	2

FALL OF WICKETS
1-10, 2-97, 3-121, 4-128, 5-144, 6-144, 7-157, 8-159, 9-160

FALL OF WICKETS
1-47, 2-102, 3-143, 4-161, 5-161

Umpires: A.R.Crafter (23) and R.C.Isherwood (4).

AUSTRALIA v PAKISTAN 1983-84

At Woolloongabba, Brisbane on 15 January 1984.　　No result.　Toss: Australia.
LOI debuts: None.

Rain interrupted this match when Pakistan were 108 for 3 in the 31st over, reducing it to a 42-over contest. The arrival of another tempest early in Australia's innings closed the scorebooks.

PAKISTAN		Runs	Balls	4/6
Mudassar Nazar	c Hookes b Lawson	2	6	–
Mohsin Khan	c Wessels b Hogg	14	33	3
Mansoor Akhtar	b Hogg	47	106	3
Javed Miandad	c Wessels b Maguire	1	6	–
Qasim Omar	run out	40	65	5
* Imran Khan	c Marsh b Hogg	26	22	–/2
Tahir Naqqash	not out	13	12	1
Rashid Khan	not out	11	10	1
Sarfraz Nawaz				
† Wasim Bari				
Azeem Hafeez				
Extras	(lb 23, w 7)	30		
Total	(42 overs; 6 wickets)	184		

AUSTRALIA		Runs	Balls	4/6
G.M.Ritchie	not out	6	17	1
K.C.Wessels	not out	5	9	–
* K.J.Hughes				
A.R.Border				
D.W.Hookes				
† R.W.Marsh				
K.H.MacLeay				
G.F.Lawson				
J.N.Maguire				
R.M.Hogg				
C.G.Rackemann				
Extras	(lb 1, w 3)	4		
Total	(3.5 overs; 0 wickets)	15		

AUSTRALIA	O	M	R	W
Lawson	9	3	12	1
Rackemann	9	3	45	0
Hogg	8	0	34	3
Maguire	10	0	31	1
MacLeay	6	0	39	0

PAKISTAN	O	M	R	W
Sarfraz Nawaz	2	1	8	0
Rashid Khan	1.5	0	6	0

FALL OF WICKETS
1-2, 2-29, 3-30, 4-116, 5-159, 6-160

Umpires: R.A.French (25) and M.W.Johnson (22).

AUSTRALIA v WEST INDIES 1983-84

At Sydney Cricket Ground on 17 January 1984.　Result: **WEST INDIES** won by 28 runs.　Toss: West Indies.
Award: D.L.Haynes.　LOI debuts: None.

Australia were fined $600 for reducing this match to 49 overs through their tardy bowling rate. Desmond Haynes recorded his first LOI hundred since his debut in February 1978 (*LOI No. 48*). Seventy of the 42,323 crowd were arrested for inebriated misbehaviour, mostly involving cardboard drink-trays.

WEST INDIES		Runs	Balls	4/6
D.L.Haynes	not out	108	130	8
R.S.Gabriel	lbw b Lawson	0	3	–
R.B.Richardson	c Hughes b Rackemann	11	33	1
I.V.A.Richards	c Wessels b Hogg	19	26	3
* C.H.Lloyd	lbw b Hogg	40	60	3/2
† P.J.L.Dujon	c Wessels b Rackemann	8	14	–
A.L.Logie	b Lawson	9	17	–
E.A.E.Baptiste	b Lawson	5	7	–
M.A.Holding	not out	6	5	–
W.W.Daniel				
W.W.Davis				
Extras	(lb 16, w 1)	17		
Total	(49 overs; 7 wickets)	223		

AUSTRALIA		Runs	Balls	4/6
G.M.Ritchie	run out	30	54	1
K.C.Wessels	lbw b Richards	27	77	–
* K.J.Hughes	b Baptiste	19	27	1
A.R.Border	c Richards b Baptiste	1	3	–
D.W.Hookes	c Logie b Daniel	35	60	2
† R.W.Marsh	b Daniel	27	33	1
K.H.MacLeay	b Holding	15	23	–
G.F.Lawson	run out	3	6	–
R.M.Hogg	b Holding	1	4	–
C.G.Rackemann	not out	9	11	–
J.N.Maguire	not out	2	4	–
Extras	(lb 19, w 4, nb 3)	26		
Total	(49 overs; 9 wickets)	195		

AUSTRALIA	O	M	R	W
Lawson	10	1	30	3
Rackemann	10	0	33	2
MacLeay	10	0	47	0
Hogg	10	1	59	2
Maguire	9	1	38	0

WEST INDIES	O	M	R	W
Holding	10	0	35	2
Daniel	10	0	29	2
Davis	9	1	39	0
Baptiste	10	1	32	2
Richards	10	0	41	1

FALL OF WICKETS
1-1, 2-24, 3-55, 4-135, 5-168, 6-195, 7-207

FALL OF WICKETS
1-68, 2-75, 3-76, 4-100, 5-155, 6-164, 7-171, 8-175, 9-192

Umpires: A.R.Crafter (24) and M.W.Johnson (23).

119

WEST INDIES v PAKISTAN 1983-84

At Sydney Cricket Ground on 19 January 1984.　　Result: **WEST INDIES** won by 5 wickets.　　Toss: Pakistan.
Award: R.B.Richardson.　　LOI debuts: None.

West Indies overcame the temporary loss of their captain after he had injured the third finger on his right hand attempting a slip catch in the previous match.

PAKISTAN		Runs	Balls	4/6
Mudassar Nazar	lbw b Holding	7	10	–
Mohsin Khan	c Dujon b Marshall	13	34	–
Mansoor Akhtar	c Dujon b Daniel	4	20	–
Javed Miandad	b Baptiste	31	78	1
Qasim Omar	not out	67	120	3
* Imran Khan	lbw b Holding	17	33	1
Rashid Khan	b Holding	1	4	–
Abdul Qadir	b Holding	7	10	–
Sarfraz Nawaz	b Daniel	0	2	–
† Wasim Bari	not out	6	10	–
Azeem Hafeez				
Extras	(b 1, lb 13, w 7, nb 10)	31		
Total	(50 overs; 8 wickets)	**184**		

WEST INDIES		Runs	Balls	4/6
D.L.Haynes	c Mudassar b Qadir	37	95	–
R.S.Gabriel	b Azeem	15	40	2
R.B.Richardson	st Wasim b Qadir	53	94	6
* I.V.A.Richards	c Rashid b Qadir	2	4	–
† P.J.L.Dujon	run out	13	18	–
A.L.Logie	not out	28	31	3
M.D.Marshall	not out	16	19	–
E.A.E.Baptiste				
M.A.Holding				
W.W.Daniel				
W.W.Davis				
Extras	(b 4, lb 10, w 7)	21		
Total	(48.3 overs; 5 wickets)	**185**		

WEST INDIES	O	M	R	W
Holding	10	2	26	4
Daniel	10	2	60	2
Davis	10	3	30	0
Marshall	6	4	5	1
Richards	5	0	24	0
Baptiste	9	2	25	1

PAKISTAN	O	M	R	W
Sarfraz Nawaz	9	1	31	0
Rashid Khan	9.3	3	26	0
Azeem Hafeez	10	0	53	1
Mudassar Nazar	10	1	34	0
Abdul Qadir	10	1	27	3

FALL OF WICKETS
1-16, 2-28, 3-35, 4-96, 5-137, 6-143, 7-157, 8-161

FALL OF WICKETS
1-30, 2-109, 3-120, 4-138, 5-141

Umpires: P.J.McConnell (8) and B.E.Martin (11).

AUSTRALIA v PAKISTAN 1983-84

At Melbourne Cricket Ground on 21 January 1984.　　Result: **AUSTRALIA** won by 43 runs.　　Toss: Australia.
Award: K.C.Wessels.　　LOI debuts: None.

The second five-wicket analysis of Abdul Qadir's LOI career was the first by a Pakistan bowler in Australia.

AUSTRALIA		Runs	Balls	4/6
G.M.Ritchie	c and b Ijaz	27	44	3
K.C.Wessels	c Imran b Qadir	86	118	10
* K.J.Hughes	lbw b Mudassar	0	1	–
A.R.Border	b Azeem	12	36	–
D.W.Hookes	st Wasim b Qadir	37	40	3
S.B.Smith	b Qadir	0	10	–
† R.W.Marsh	c Imran b Qadir	11	17	–/1
G.F.Lawson	not out	14	12	1
R.M.Hogg	c and b Qadir	0	1	–
J.N.Maguire	not out	14	21	–
C.G.Rackemann				
Extras	(lb 8)	8		
Total	(50 overs; 8 wickets)	**209**		

PAKISTAN		Runs	Balls	4/6
Mudassar Nazar	c Wessels b Hogg	12	54	1
Mohsin Khan	c Marsh b Border	22	48	2
Mansoor Akhtar	run out	1	3	–
Javed Miandad	b Hogg	56	68	4
Qasim Omar	c and b Border	2	9	–
* Imran Khan	c Marsh b Maguire	17	35	–
Ijaz Faqih	b Hogg	17	19	2
Abdul Qadir	b Hogg	23	29	3
Rashid Khan	not out	2	4	–
† Wasim Bari	run out	2	3	–
Azeem Hafeez	b Lawson	0	3	–
Extras	(b 1, lb 6, w 4, nb 1)	12		
Total	(45 overs)	**166**		

PAKISTAN	O	M	R	W
Azeem Hafeez	10	0	44	1
Rashid Khan	10	1	32	0
Mudassar Nazar	10	2	31	1
Ijaz Faqih	10	1	41	1
Abdul Qadir	10	1	53	5

AUSTRALIA	O	M	R	W
Lawson	8	2	19	1
Rackemann	7	0	23	0
Hogg	10	2	33	4
Wessels	7	0	28	0
Border	7	0	24	2
Maguire	6	0	32	1

FALL OF WICKETS
1-57, 2-58, 3-123, 4-138, 5-140, 6-172, 7-178, 8-178

FALL OF WICKETS
1-33, 2-35, 3-56, 4-61, 5-89, 6-124, 7-161, 8-162, 9-164, 10-166

Umpires: P.J.McConnell (9) and B.E.Martin (12).

AUSTRALIA v WEST INDIES 1983-84

At Melbourne Cricket Ground on 22 January 1984.   Result: **WEST INDIES** won by 26 runs.   Toss: West Indies.
Award: I.V.A.Richards.   LOI debuts: None.

Watched by a world record limited-overs international crowd of 86,133, Viv Richards played a remarkable innings on a dead pitch.

WEST INDIES		Runs	Balls	4/6
D.L.Haynes	b Hogg	64	108	3
R.S.Gabriel	c Maguire b Rackemann	8	28	–
H.A.Gomes	lbw b Wessels	7	18	–
I.V.A.Richards	c Smith b Rackemann	106	95	12/1
* C.H.Lloyd	b Maguire	27	27	2
† P.J.L.Dujon	not out	21	20	2
M.D.Marshall	b Lawson	1	3	–
A.L.Logie	not out	9	4	1
E.A.E.Baptiste				
M.A.Holding				
W.W.Daniel				
Extras	(lb 7, w 2)	9		
Total	(50 overs; 6 wickets)	**252**		

AUSTRALIA		Runs	Balls	4/6
G.M.Ritchie	c Holding b Baptiste	28	61	1
K.C.Wessels	b Richards	60	98	2
A.R.Border	b Baptiste	0	1	–
* K.J.Hughes	b Daniel	71	73	3
D.W.Hookes	c Logie b Richards	6	13	–
S.B.Smith	c Gomes b Daniel	26	28	1
† W.B.Phillips	not out	18	17	2
G.F.Lawson	b Holding	0	3	–
J.N.Maguire	b Marshall	3	4	–
C.G.Rackemann	b Holding	0	2	–
R.M.Hogg	b Holding	2	2	–
Extras	(b 3, lb 6, w 3)	12		
Total	(49.5 overs)	**226**		

AUSTRALIA	O	M	R	W
Lawson	10	2	28	1
Rackemann	9	3	43	2
Hogg	10	0	56	1
Wessels	8	0	32	1
Border	5	0	35	0
Maguire	8	0	51	1

WEST INDIES	O	M	R	W
Holding	9.5	0	35	3
Daniel	10	0	38	2
Baptiste	7	0	24	2
Marshall	10	0	49	1
Richards	10	0	51	2
Gomes	3	0	20	0

FALL OF WICKETS
1-24, 2-50, 3-140, 4-199, 5-230, 6-238

FALL OF WICKETS
1-62, 2-63, 3-119, 4-146, 5-186, 6-203, 7-216, 8-223, 9-224, 10-226

Umpires: R.A.French (26) and R.C.Isherwood (5).

AUSTRALIA v PAKISTAN 1983-84

At Sydney Cricket Ground on 25 January 1984.   Result: **AUSTRALIA** won by 87 runs.   Toss: Australia.
Award: S.B.Smith.   LOI debuts: None.

Returning to his customary berth of opener, Steve Smith scored his second World Series hundred.

AUSTRALIA		Runs	Balls	4/6
S.B.Smith	c Qadir b Rashid	106	129	12
K.C.Wessels	c Imran b Tahir	7	22	1
G.M.Ritchie	st Ashraf b Qadir	31	47	2
* K.J.Hughes	b Qadir	3	7	–
A.R.Border	b Mudassar	11	22	1
W.B.Phillips	run out	25	45	–
† R.W.Marsh	c Ashraf b Tahir	20	18	3
G.F.Lawson	st Ashraf b Qadir	2	6	1
J.N.Maguire	not out	7	8	1
R.M.Hogg	not out	8	9	–
C.G.Rackemann				
Extras	(b 8, lb 3, w 10, nb 3)	24		
Total	(50 overs; 8 wickets)	**244**		

PAKISTAN		Runs	Balls	4/6
Mudassar Nazar	run out	0	3	–
Mohsin Khan	b Lawson	1	5	–
* Imran Khan	run out	41	83	3
Javed Miandad	c Marsh b Maguire	26	65	3
Qasim Omar	c Marsh b Hogg	0	8	–
Wasim Raja	st Marsh b Wessels	32	32	2/1
Ijaz Faqih	b Hogg	14	15	2
Tahir Naqqash	b Hogg	0	5	–
Abdul Qadir	c Marsh b Hogg	9	14	–
Rashid Khan	b Border	17	30	–
† Ashraf Ali	not out	11	25	–
Extras	(b 2, lb 3, w 1)	6		
Total	(47.2 overs)	**157**		

PAKISTAN	O	M	R	W
Rashid Khan	9	0	36	1
Tahir Naqqash	10	3	56	2
Abdul Qadir	9	1	42	3
Mudassar Nazar	10	1	33	1
Ijaz Faqih	7	0	36	0
Wasim Raja	5	0	30	0

AUSTRALIA	O	M	R	W
Lawson	6	3	15	1
Rackemann	10	2	16	0
Maguire	9	1	19	1
Hogg	10	0	37	4
Wessels	9	0	50	1
Border	3.2	0	15	1

FALL OF WICKETS
1-18, 2-85, 3-97, 4-122, 5-196, 6-216, 7-221, 8-234

FALL OF WICKETS
1-0, 2-1, 3-45, 4-46, 5-103, 6-103, 7-104, 8-120, 9-129, 10-157

Umpires: R.A.French (27) and R.C.Isherwood (6).

WEST INDIES v PAKISTAN 1983-84

At Adelaide Oval on 28 January 1984.   Result: **WEST INDIES** won by 1 wicket.   Toss: Pakistan.
Award: M.D.Marshall.   LOI debuts: None.

A fine all-round display by Malcolm Marshall piloted West Indies to a one-wicket victory with five balls to spare. This was the first single-wicket win in limited-overs internationals in Australia.

PAKISTAN		Runs	Balls	4/6
Mudassar Nazar	c Dujon b Baptiste	18	39	—
Mansoor Akhtar	c Dujon b Marshall	20	44	2
Qasim Omar	run out	26	71	—
* Javed Miandad	c Dujon b Marshall	4	16	—
Salim Malik	b Marshall	1	5	—
Wasim Raja	c Richards b Gomes	46	40	2/1
Ijaz Faqih	not out	23	41	—
Abdul Qadir	c Baptiste b Gomes	4	11	—
Tahir Naqqash	run out	0	5	—
Rashid Khan	not out	16	30	—
† Wasim Bari				
Extras	(lb 14, w 2, nb 3)	19		
Total	(50 overs; 8 wickets)	**177**		

WEST INDIES		Runs	Balls	4/6
D.L.Haynes	c Wasim Bari b Wasim Raja	3	16	—
R.S.Gabriel	b Qadir	10	51	1
A.L.Logie	c Miandad b Rashid	19	15	4
I.V.A.Richards	c Mansoor b Qadir	18	21	3
H.A.Gomes	c Wasim Bari b Mudassar	3	13	—
* C.H.Lloyd	run out	10	22	—
† P.J.L.Dujon	st Wasim Bari b Qadir	10	14	2
M.D.Marshall	not out	56	84	4
E.A.E.Baptiste	c Rashid b Wasim Raja	24	35	2
M.A.Holding	lbw b Wasim Raja	10	18	—
W.W.Daniel	not out	7	13	—
Extras	(b 1, lb 4, w 4, nb 1)	10		
Total	(49.1 overs; 9 wickets)	**180**		

WEST INDIES	O	M	R	W
Holding	8	1	21	0
Daniel	10	3	25	0
Marshall	9	1	28	3
Baptiste	10	0	33	1
Richards	6	0	30	0
Gomes	7	0	26	2

PAKISTAN	O	M	R	W
Rashid Khan	8.1	3	29	1
Tahir Naqqash	7	1	35	0
Wasim Raja	10	1	33	3
Abdul Qadir	10	1	34	3
Mudassar Nazar	10	0	32	1
Ijaz Faqih	4	0	12	0

FALL OF WICKETS
1-40, 2-42, 3-54, 4-59, 5-127, 6-127, 7-135, 8-136

FALL OF WICKETS
1-9, 2-28, 3-52, 4-59, 5-61, 6-75, 7-92, 8-145, 9-159

Umpires: R.A.French (28) and B.E.Martin (13).

AUSTRALIA v WEST INDIES 1983-84

At Adelaide Oval on 29 January 1984.   Result: **WEST INDIES** won by 6 wickets.   Toss: Australia.
Award: A.L.Logie.   LOI debuts: None.

West Indies defeated their hosts for the fourth successive time in spite of Viv Richards being bowled off his pads first ball by Allan Border's occasional left-arm spin.

AUSTRALIA		Runs	Balls	4/6
S.B.Smith	b Marshall	55	111	2
K.C.Wessels	c Dujon b Daniel	4	8	—
G.M.Ritchie	run out	0	2	—
* K.J.Hughes	c Dujon b Baptiste	10	34	2
A.R.Border	b Richards	17	40	—
W.B.Phillips	st Dujon b Richards	2	14	—
† R.W.Marsh	not out	34	59	1
G.F.Lawson	c and b Daniel	18	28	1
J.N.Maguire	not out	9	9	—
R.M.Hogg				
C.G.Rackemann				
Extras	(b 7, lb 3, w 2, nb 4)	16		
Total	(50 overs; 7 wickets)	**165**		

WEST INDIES		Runs	Balls	4/6
D.L.Haynes	c Marsh b Rackemann	4	17	1
R.S.Gabriel	c Lawson b Border	41	72	1/2
H.A.Gomes	run out	27	69	—
I.V.A.Richards	b Border	0	1	—
* C.H.Lloyd	not out	38	53	1/1
A.L.Logie	not out	49	62	—
† P.J.L.Dujon				
M.D.Marshall				
E.A.E.Baptiste				
M.A.Holding				
W.W.Daniel				
Extras	(lb 7, w 1, nb 2)	10		
Total	(45.1 overs; 4 wickets)	**169**		

WEST INDIES	O	M	R	W
Holding	7	2	20	0
Daniel	8	0	35	2
Marshall	10	3	21	1
Baptiste	5	2	9	1
Gomes	10	1	42	0
Richards	10	0	28	2

AUSTRALIA	O	M	R	W
Lawson	6	1	10	0
Rackemann	10	0	35	0
Hogg	10	0	31	0
Maguire	8	1	44	0
Wessels	3	0	9	0
Border	7	0	25	2
Smith	1	0	4	0
Hughes	0.1	0	4	0

FALL OF WICKETS
1-14, 2-14, 3-34, 4-71, 5-85, 6-115, 7-149

FALL OF WICKETS
1-14, 2-67, 3-68, 4-89

Umpires: A.R.Crafter (25) and M.W.Johnson (24).

AUSTRALIA v PAKISTAN 1983-84

At Adelaide Oval on 30 January 1984.　Result: **AUSTRALIA** won by 70 runs.　Toss: Australia.
Award: K.C.Wessels.　LOI debuts: Australia – D.M.Jones.

Mohsin Khan was so distressed by this defeat, which eliminated Pakistan from the finals, that he announced his retirement from international cricket with immediate effect. His revelation was to prove slightly exaggerated as he appeared in another 18 Tests and 37 internationals.

AUSTRALIA		Runs	Balls	4/6
S.B.Smith	b Ijaz	36	81	3
K.C.Wessels	b Ijaz	61	96	4
G.M.Ritchie	b Ijaz	12	30	–
* K.J.Hughes	st Wasim Bari b Ijaz	11	13	1
A.R.Border	run out	10	12	–
†W.B.Phillips	b Mudassar	17	21	–
D.M.Jones	not out	40	33	4
T.G.Hogan	c Wasim Raja b Mudassar	3	8	–
J.N.Maguire	c Mansoor b Rashid	1	3	–
R.M.Hogg	not out	6	6	–
C.G.Rackemann				
Extras	(lb 9, w 2, nb 2)	13		
Total	(50 overs; 8 wickets)	**210**		

PAKISTAN		Runs	Balls	4/6
Mansoor Akhtar	b Hogg	22	24	3
* Javed Miandad	c Hogan b Rackemann	34	29	7
Qasim Omar	c Ritchie b Rackemann	2	8	–
Wasim Raja	c Hughes b Wessels	17	66	1
Mudassar Nazar	c Phillips b Rackemann	1	10	–
Mohsin Khan	lbw b Wessels	19	61	–
Salim Malik	lbw b Hogan	14	16	–
Ijaz Faqih	c Phillips b Rackemann	13	31	–
Abdul Qadir	b Hogg	3	12	–
Rashid Khan	c Hogan b Rackemann	1	10	–
†Wasim Bari	not out	2	6	–
Extras	(b 6, lb 5, w 1)	12		
Total	(45.2 overs)	**140**		

PAKISTAN	O	M	R	W
Rashid Khan	10	1	33	1
Mudassar Nazar	10	0	50	2
Ijaz Faqih	10	1	43	4
Wasim Raja	10	2	23	0
Abdul Qadir	10	0	52	0

AUSTRALIA	O	M	R	W
Hogg	8	2	26	2
Rackemann	8.2	2	16	5
Maguire	10	1	33	0
Hogan	10	2	22	1
Wessels	9	0	32	2

FALL OF WICKETS
1-70, 2-115, 3-126, 4-135, 5-145, 6-163, 7-169, 8-179

FALL OF WICKETS
1-56, 2-56, 3-58, 4-60, 5-98, 6-115, 7-123, 8-137, 9-137, 10-140

Umpires: P.J.McConnell (10) and S.G.Randell (3).

WEST INDIES v PAKISTAN 1983-84

At WACA Ground, Perth on 4 February 1984.　Result: **WEST INDIES** won by 7 wickets.　Toss: Pakistan.
Award: I.V.A.Richards.　LOI debuts: None.

West Indies gained their seventh successive victory in this competition.

PAKISTAN		Runs	Balls	4/6
Mudassar Nazar	c Marshall b Baptiste	54	117	3
Mansoor Akhtar	c Garner b Davis	3	23	–
Mohsin Khan	b Harper	32	74	3/1
* Javed Miandad	b Harper	26	23	3
Qasim Omar	c Richards b Davis	16	30	–
Salim Malik	b Garner	14	17	–
Ijaz Faqih	b Garner	0	1	–
Abdul Qadir	not out	6	9	–
Rashid Khan	not out	10	14	–
Azeem Hafeez				
†Ashraf Ali				
Extras	(b 7, lb 7, w 6, nb 1)	21		
Total	(50 overs; 7 wickets)	**182**		

WEST INDIES		Runs	Balls	4/6
D.L.Haynes	not out	78	140	8
R.S.Gabriel	c Ashraf b Mudassar	29	32	5
R.B.Richardson	c and b Mudassar	7	42	1
* I.V.A.Richards	c Salim b Ijaz	40	47	5
A.L.Logie	not out	14	14	2
†P.J.L.Dujon				
M.D.Marshall				
E.A.E.Baptiste				
R.A.Harper				
W.W.Davis				
J.Garner				
Extras	(lb 10, w 5)	15		
Total	(45 overs; 3 wickets)	**183**		

WEST INDIES	O	M	R	W
Garner	9	3	12	2
Davis	10	0	34	2
Baptiste	10	0	36	1
Marshall	6	0	20	0
Harper	10	0	42	2
Richards	5	0	24	0

PAKISTAN	O	M	R	W
Rashid Khan	10	1	25	0
Azeem Hafeez	6	0	51	0
Mudassar Nazar	10	1	33	2
Abdul Qadir	10	3	19	0
Ijaz Faqih	9	0	44	1
Mansoor Akhtar	0	0	1	0

FALL OF WICKETS
1-13, 2-88, 3-129, 4-135, 5-159, 6-163, 7-164

FALL OF WICKETS
1-38, 2-58, 3-153

Umpires: R.A.French (29) and S.G.Randell (4).

AUSTRALIA v WEST INDIES 1983-84

At WACA Ground, Perth on 5 February 1984.   Result: **AUSTRALIA** won by 14 runs.   Toss: Australia.
Award: M.A.Holding.   LOI debuts: None.

Unfashionably, Rodney Marsh chose the aftermath of a comprehensive victory before a (then) record Perth crowd of 27,027 to announce the imminent end of his playing career. Terry Alderman made a successful return to international cricket 14 months after severely dislocating his right shoulder. Final points: West Indies 16, Australia 11, Pakistan 3.

AUSTRALIA		Runs	Balls	4/6
S.B.Smith	c Dujon b Daniel	12	31	1
K.C.Wessels	c Daniel b Marshall	50	103	–
G.M.Ritchie	c Gabriel b Holding	3	7	–
* K.J.Hughes	c Richardson b Marshall	67	95	5/2
A.R.Border	b Richards	1	2	–
D.M.Jones	b Holding	23	28	–
† R.W.Marsh	not out	27	32	2
G.F.Lawson	run out	3	4	–
R.M.Hogg	run out	2	4	–
T.M.Alderman	not out	0	4	–
C.G.Rackemann				
Extras	(b 3, lb 14, w 3, nb 3)	23		
Total	(50 overs; 8 wickets)	**211**		

WEST INDIES		Runs	Balls	4/6
D.L.Haynes	c Marsh b Wessels	52	105	4/1
R.B.Richardson	c Wessels b Lawson	2	16	–
A.L.Logie	c Hughes b Alderman	3	9	–
I.V.A.Richards	b Alderman	7	11	1
* C.H.Lloyd	b Hogg	31	60	3
† P.J.L.Dujon	b Rackemann	0	1	–
M.D.Marshall	c Marsh b Rackemann	2	8	–
E.A.E.Baptiste	c Marsh b Lawson	1	3	–
M.A.Holding	lbw b Wessels	64	39	10/1
R.S.Gabriel	b Rackemann	12	12	1
W.W.Daniel	not out	0	4	–
Extras	(b 3, lb 11, w 8, nb 1)	23		
Total	(43.3 overs)	**197**		

WEST INDIES	O	M	R	W
Holding	10	1	31	2
Daniel	10	1	43	1
Marshall	10	2	27	2
Baptiste	10	0	46	0
Richards	10	0	47	1

AUSTRALIA	O	M	R	W
Lawson	8	1	32	2
Alderman	10	3	19	2
Hogg	9	2	36	1
Wessels	8	2	50	2
Rackemann	8.3	0	46	3

FALL OF WICKETS
1-15, 2-21, 3-140, 4-142, 5-157, 6-185, 7-192, 8-201

FALL OF WICKETS
1-17, 2-23, 3-37, 4-92, 5-93, 6-101, 7-102, 8-156, 9-188, 10-197

Umpires: R.C.Isherwood (7) and P.J.McConnell (11).

AUSTRALIA v WEST INDIES 1983-84

At Sydney Cricket Ground on 8 February 1984.   Result: **WEST INDIES** won by 9 wickets.   Toss: West Indies.
LOI debuts: None.

Rain delayed the start and reduced this match to a 46-over contest. The Australians blamed their poor performance on a contractual dispute with their Board concerning the forthcoming tour of the Caribbean.

AUSTRALIA		Runs	Balls	4/6
S.B.Smith	c and b Daniel	50	80	4
K.C.Wessels	c Richards b Holding	2	4	–
G.M.Ritchie	lbw b Garner	10	25	–
* K.J.Hughes	b Marshall	0	11	–
A.R.Border	b Daniel	18	48	–
D.M.Jones	b Marshall	17	20	1
† R.W.Marsh	c Lloyd b Baptiste	15	27	–
G.F.Lawson	b Garner	22	25	1
R.M.Hogg	c Gomes b Baptiste	2	3	–
T.M.Alderman	b Holding	7	20	–
C.G.Rackemann	not out	4	12	–
Extras	(lb 9, w 1, nb 3)	13		
Total	(44.4 overs)	**160**		

WEST INDIES		Runs	Balls	4/6
D.L.Haynes	lbw b Rackemann	13	46	1
R.B.Richardson	not out	80	137	6/1
H.A.Gomes	not out	46	81	1
I.V.A.Richards				
* C.H.Lloyd				
† P.J.L.Dujon				
M.D.Marshall				
E.A.E.Baptiste				
M.A.Holding				
J.Garner				
W.W.Daniel				
Extras	(b 3, lb 14, w 1, nb 4)	22		
Total	(43.1 overs; 1 wicket)	**161**		

WEST INDIES	O	M	R	W
Holding	8.4	0	27	2
Garner	9	2	19	2
Marshall	9	1	24	2
Daniel	9	0	42	2
Richards	5	0	29	0
Baptiste	4	0	10	2

AUSTRALIA	O	M	R	W
Lawson	9	1	21	0
Alderman	9	2	19	0
Rackemann	9	0	31	1
Hogg	7	0	40	0
Wessels	4	0	15	0
Border	5	0	17	0
Smith	0.1	0	1	0

FALL OF WICKETS
1-5, 2-23, 3-38, 4-82, 5-93, 6-119, 7-127, 8-133, 9-152, 10-160

FALL OF WICKETS
1-29

Umpires: A.R.Crafter (26) and R.A.French (30).

AUSTRALIA v WEST INDIES 1983-84

At Melbourne Cricket Ground on 11 February 1984.   Result: **MATCH TIED.**   Toss: West Indies.
LOI debuts: None.

Limited-overs international cricket produced its first tied match when Carl Rackemann, attempting a bye to the wicket-keeper, was run out off the ultimate ball with the scores level. Steve Smith was unable to bat having dislocated and torn ligaments in his left shoulder after diving in the field.

WEST INDIES		Runs	Balls	4/6
D.L.Haynes	c Hogan b Border	18	53	2
R.S.Gabriel	c Smith b Rackemann	19	35	4
R.B.Richardson	c Marsh b Lawson	43	70	5
I.V.A.Richards	c Hogan b Wessels	59	70	5
* C.H.Lloyd	c Hogg b Wessels	11	19	1
H.A.Gomes	not out	25	34	1
† P.J.L.Dujon	not out	33	24	3
M.D.Marshall				
E.A.E.Baptiste				
M.A.Holding				
J.Garner				
Extras	(lb 10, w 3, nb 1)	14		
Total	(50 overs; 5 wickets)	**222**		

AUSTRALIA		Runs	Balls	4/6
K.C.Wessels	c Marshall b Holding	77	109	6
D.M.Jones	c Dujon b Holding	12	29	1
* K.J.Hughes	lbw b Marshall	53	89	2
A.R.Border	c Dujon b Garner	14	31	–
G.M.Ritchie	c Dujon b Garner	4	6	–
† R.W.Marsh	b Garner	16	13	1
G.F.Lawson	not out	21	19	2
T.G.Hogan	c sub (A.L.Logie) b Holding	6	8	–
R.M.Hogg	run out	3	3	–
C.G.Rackemann	run out	1	1	–
S.B.Smith				
Extras	(b 2, lb 8, w 1, nb 4)	15		
Total	(50 overs; 9 wickets)	**222**		

AUSTRALIA	O	M	R	W
Lawson	10	4	26	1
Rackemann	10	4	52	1
Hogg	9	1	40	0
Hogan	10	2	31	0
Border	6	0	34	1
Wessels	5	0	29	2

WEST INDIES	O	M	R	W
Holding	10	0	39	3
Garner	10	1	39	3
Baptiste	10	0	44	0
Marshall	10	1	27	1
Richards	3	0	26	0
Gomes	7	0	37	0

FALL OF WICKETS
1-33, 2-54, 3-116, 4-137, 5-173

FALL OF WICKETS
1-23, 2-132, 3-161, 4-169, 5-176, 6-192, 7-209, 8-218, 9-222

Umpires: R.A.French (31) and M.W.Johnson (25).

AUSTRALIA v WEST INDIES 1983-84

At Melbourne Cricket Ground on 12 February 1984.   Result: **WEST INDIES** won by 6 wickets.   Toss: Australia.
Finals Award: J.Garner.   LOI debuts: Australia – D.C.Boon.

Incensed at having to play a third final after gaining a win and a tie in the previous two, West Indies were only partially appeased by the ACB's substantially increasing the prize-money. Even had Australia won this match, West Indies, by virtue of their superior rate in the preliminary matches, would still have gained their third trophy in three attempts.

AUSTRALIA		Runs	Balls	4/6
K.C.Wessels	b Garner	17	33	–
A.R.Border	b Garner	4	15	–
D.C.Boon	b Davis	39	71	–
* K.J.Hughes	c and b Baptiste	65	88	4
D.M.Jones	c Garner b Holding	3	9	–
W.B.Phillips	c Holding b Garner	22	38	–
† R.W.Marsh	c Dujon b Garner	35	40	2
G.F.Lawson	b Garner	7	11	–
T.G.Hogan	not out	1	2	–
R.M.Hogg				
C.G.Rackemann				
Extras	(b 1, lb 14, w 2, nb 2)	19		
Total	(50 overs; 8 wickets)	**212**		

WEST INDIES		Runs	Balls	4/6
D.L.Haynes	b Lawson	1	7	–
R.B.Richardson	lbw b Hogg	27	44	4
H.A.Gomes	lbw b Lawson	0	1	–
A.L.Logie	c Rackemann b Wessels	88	103	7
† P.J.L.Dujon	not out	82	109	9
M.D.Marshall	not out	6	11	–
R.A.Harper				
E.A.E.Baptiste				
* M.A.Holding				
J.Garner				
W.W.Davis				
Extras	(b 4, lb 3, w 2)	9		
Total	(45.3 overs; 4 wickets)	**213**		

WEST INDIES	O	M	R	W
Holding	10	1	33	1
Garner	10	1	31	5
Marshall	10	0	44	0
Davis	10	0	45	1
Baptiste	10	0	44	1

AUSTRALIA	O	M	R	W
Lawson	9	1	45	2
Rackemann	9.3	2	40	0
Hogg	8	1	22	0
Hogan	10	0	39	0
Border	3	0	13	0
Wessels	6	0	47	1

FALL OF WICKETS
1-14, 2-25, 3-125, 4-140, 5-140, 6-185, 7-210, 8-212

FALL OF WICKETS
1-3, 2-3, 3-52, 4-176

Umpires: M.W.Johnson (26) and P.J.McConnell (12).

NEW ZEALAND v ENGLAND 1983-84

At Lancaster Park, Christchurch on 18 February 1984.   Result: **ENGLAND** won by 54 runs.   Toss: New Zealand.
Award: D.W.Randall.   LOI debuts: England – N.A.Foster, C.L.Smith.

No-balls and wides were not debited to bowlers' analyses in this 50-over series. England gained some revenge for their innings defeat in the second Test a fortnight previously on a similar sub-standard surface of mobile plate-sized mosaics.

ENGLAND		Runs	Balls	4/6
D.I.Gower	c J.J.Crowe b Hadlee	3	11	–
C.L.Smith	run out	17	68	1/1
A.J.Lamb	c Robertson b Hadlee	43	83	3
D.W.Randall	c Cairns b Hadlee	70	85	8
I.T.Botham	c Smith b Hadlee	1	6	–
M.W.Gatting	b Hadlee	0	1	–
V.J.Marks	lbw b Cairns	28	40	3
† R.W.Taylor	run out	2	3	–
N.A.Foster	c Wright b Cairns	0	1	–
N.G.Cowans	not out	4	2	–
* R.G.D.Willis				
Extras	(b 8, lb 4, nb 8)	20		
Total	(50 overs; 9 wickets)	**188**		

NEW ZEALAND		Runs	Balls	4/6
J.G.Wright	c Taylor b Willis	4	21	–
B.A.Edgar	c Taylor b Botham	10	34	–
* G.P.Howarth	run out	18	47	–
M.D.Crowe	run out	0	2	–
J.J.Crowe	b Botham	0	10	–
J.V.Coney	c Botham b Foster	19	50	2
B.L.Cairns	lbw b Marks	23	26	2/1
R.J.Hadlee	c Gower b Marks	23	31	2/2
† I.D.S.Smith	c Gower b Foster	7	15	–
G.K.Robertson	lbw b Willis	10	10	–
E.J.Chatfield	not out	0	13	–
Extras	(lb 9, w 6, nb 5)	20		
Total	(42.1 overs)	**134**		

NEW ZEALAND	O	M	R	W
Hadlee	10	2	32	5
Chatfield	10	4	20	0
Cairns	10	2	41	2
Coney	10	1	30	0
Robertson	10	0	45	0

ENGLAND	O	M	R	W
Willis	6.1	1	18	2
Cowans	10	2	37	0
Botham	6	3	7	2
Foster	10	4	19	2
Marks	10	1	33	2

FALL OF WICKETS
1-9, 2-59, 3-107, 4-109, 5-109, 6-177, 7-184, 8-184, 9-188

FALL OF WICKETS
1-7, 2-38, 3-38, 4-38, 5-44, 6-76, 7-112, 8-120, 9-124, 10-134

Umpires: F.R.Goodall (10) and I.C.Higginson (4).

NEW ZEALAND v ENGLAND 1983-84

At Basin Reserve, Wellington on 22 February 1984.   Result: **ENGLAND** won by 6 wickets.   Toss: New Zealand.
Award: V.J.Marks.   LOI debuts: None.

Vic Marks recorded England's best limited-overs analysis and became the first England bowler to take five wickets twice. Chris Smith scored 60 of his 70 runs in boundaries.

NEW ZEALAND		Runs	Balls	4/6
B.A.Edgar	b Marks	12	52	–
T.J.Franklin	c and b Marks	6	35	–
* G.P.Howarth	lbw b Marks	21	44	2
M.D.Crowe	c Foster b Marks	8	15	1
J.J.Crowe	c Foster b Marks	1	6	–
J.V.Coney	b Botham	44	73	3/1
R.J.Hadlee	c Randall b Foster	21	35	2
B.L.Cairns	c Gower b Foster	0	1	–
† I.D.S.Smith	lbw b Botham	0	4	–
G.K.Robertson	run out	11	13	1
E.J.Chatfield	not out	0	5	–
Extras	(lb 9, w 2)	11		
Total	(47.1 overs)	**135**		

ENGLAND		Runs	Balls	4/6
D.I.Gower	c J.J.Crowe b Chatfield	21	39	3
C.L.Smith	b Hadlee	70	118	15
A.J.Lamb	c and b Chatfield	6	22	1
D.W.Randall	not out	25	77	1
I.T.Botham	b Hadlee	15	14	2
M.W.Gatting	not out	0	1	–
V.J.Marks				
† R.W.Taylor				
N.A.Foster				
N.G.Cowans				
* R.G.D.Willis				
Extras	(lb 2)	2		
Total	(45.1 overs; 4 wickets)	**139**		

ENGLAND	O	M	R	W
Willis	9	4	17	0
Cowans	10	1	33	0
Marks	10	3	20	5
Botham	8.1	1	25	2
Foster	10	3	29	2

NEW ZEALAND	O	M	R	W
Hadlee	10	2	31	2
Robertson	6	0	28	0
Coney	10	1	29	0
Chatfield	10	5	16	2
Cairns	9.1	1	33	0

FALL OF WICKETS
1-23, 2-34, 3-50, 4-52, 5-63, 6-104, 7-104, 8-104, 9-135, 10-135

FALL OF WICKETS
1-36, 2-54, 3-117, 4-135

Umpires: G.C.Morris (1) and S.J.Woodward (4).

NEW ZEALAND v ENGLAND 1983-84

At Eden Park, Auckland on 25 February 1984.   Result: **NEW ZEALAND** won by 7 wickets.   Toss: England.
Award: M.D.Crowe.   LOI debuts: None.

The partnership of 160 off 190 balls between Geoff Howarth and Martin Crowe was New Zealand's highest for the third wicket in limited-overs internationals until 1994-95. The first of Crowe's four LOI hundreds came from 103 balls.

ENGLAND		Runs	Balls	4/6
D.I.Gower	lbw b Chatfield	35	56	1/1
C.L.Smith	b Hadlee	5	11	1
A.J.Lamb	not out	97	140	7/1
D.W.Randall	b Boock	11	21	2
I.T.Botham	c Wright b Coney	18	32	1
M.W.Gatting	c Smith b Chatfield	4	12	–
V.J.Marks	b Chatfield	3	6	–
† R.W.Taylor	run out	8	19	–
N.A.Foster	run out	1	5	–
N.G.Cowans	run out	0	–	–
* R.G.D.Willis	not out	7	3	1
Extras	(b 4, lb 11, w 1, nb 4)	20		
Total	(50 overs; 9 wickets)	**209**		

NEW ZEALAND		Runs	Balls	4/6
P.N.Webb	b Willis	8	12	2
J.G.Wright	c and b Marks	14	29	1
* G.P.Howarth	lbw b Botham	72	120	7
M.D.Crowe	not out	105	105	11/1
J.V.Coney	not out	2	7	–
J.J.Crowe				
R.J.Hadlee				
B.L.Cairns				
† I.D.S.Smith				
S.L.Boock				
E.J.Chatfield				
Extras	(lb 7, w 2)	9		
Total	(45.3 overs; 3 wickets)	**210**		

NEW ZEALAND	O	M	R	W
Cairns	10	2	31	0
Hadlee	10	2	51	1
Boock	10	0	40	1
Coney	10	0	38	1
Chatfield	10	2	29	3

ENGLAND	O	M	R	W
Willis	10	1	36	1
Cowans	9.3	0	59	0
Marks	10	1	27	1
Botham	7	1	22	1
Foster	6	0	37	0
Smith	3	0	20	0

FALL OF WICKETS
1-6, 2-73, 3-86, 4-130, 5-140, 6-148, 7-185, 8-192, 9-192

FALL OF WICKETS
1-22, 2-34, 3-194

Umpires: D.A.Kinsella (4) and G.C.Morris (2).

WEST INDIES v AUSTRALIA 1983-84

At Albion Sports Complex, Berbice on 29 February 1984.   Result: **WEST INDIES** won by 8 wickets.   Toss: Australia.
Award: D.L.Haynes.   LOI debuts: West Indies – M.A.Small.   50-over match.

The touring team's late arrival by helicopter from Georgetown delayed the start by 30 minutes. Fortunately there were only minor casualties when the wooden scoreboard, a key vantage point, collapsed under the weight of its perching spectators.

AUSTRALIA		Runs	Balls	4/6
K.C.Wessels	c Small b Richards	44	77	4
S.B.Smith	b Gomes	60	110	2
G.M.Ritchie	run out	46	61	–
* K.J.Hughes	b Gomes	2	6	–
A.R.Border	b Gomes	2	12	–
D.M.Jones	not out	43	43	–
† W.B.Phillips	not out	0	1	–
G.F.Lawson				
R.M.Hogg				
C.G.Rackemann				
T.M.Alderman				
Extras	(b 7, lb 18, nb 9)	34		
Total	(50 overs; 5 wickets)	**231**		

WEST INDIES		Runs	Balls	4/6
C.G.Greenidge	c Phillips b Rackemann	23	44	1
D.L.Haynes	not out	133	147	14
R.B.Richardson	c Jones b Alderman	61	103	8
* I.V.A.Richards	not out	4	1	1
A.L.Logie				
† P.J.L.Dujon				
H.A.Gomes				
J.Garner				
W.W.Daniel				
M.A.Small				
W.W.Davis				
Extras	(lb 5, nb 7)	12		
Total	(48 overs; 2 wickets)	**233**		

WEST INDIES	O	M	R	W
Garner	10	1	35	0
Daniel	5	0	19	0
Davis	10	1	66	0
Small	5	0	14	0
Richards	10	0	38	1
Gomes	10	0	34	3

AUSTRALIA	O	M	R	W
Lawson	10	3	26	0
Alderman	10	0	62	1
Hogg	8	0	40	0
Rackemann	10	1	54	1
Border	6	1	22	0
Wessels	4	0	24	0

FALL OF WICKETS
1-106, 2-137, 3-143, 4-159, 5-222

FALL OF WICKETS
1-62, 2-229

Umpires: C.E.Cumberbatch (1) and D.J.Narine (3).

WEST INDIES v AUSTRALIA 1983-84

At Queen's Park Oval, Port-of-Spain, Trinidad on 14 March 1984.　　Result: **AUSTRALIA** won by 4 wickets.　　Toss: Australia.
Award: K.C.Wessels.　　LOI debuts: None.　　37-over match.

A start delayed by the pitch sweating under its covers allied to Australia's slow over-rate reduced the match to 37 overs.
Boundary overthrows ended the contest with two balls to spare.

WEST INDIES		Runs	Balls	4/6
C.G.Greenidge	c Lawson b Wessels	63	79	8/1
D.L.Haynes	b Lawson	1	14	–
R.B.Richardson	c Phillips b Lawson	0	5	–
I.V.A.Richards	c Alderman b Maguire	67	73	7/1
* C.H.Lloyd	not out	31	28	4
† P.J.L.Dujon	c Maguire b Alderman	16	26	–
M.D.Marshall	run out	0	1	–
J.Garner	not out	0	–	–
H.A.Gomes				
W.W.Daniel				
M.A.Small				
Extras	(b 1, lb 8, w 3)	12		
Total	(37 overs; 6 wickets)	**190**		

AUSTRALIA		Runs	Balls	4/6
K.C.Wessels	c Richards b Daniel	67	95	6/1
D.W.Hookes	b Garner	14	15	2
S.B.Smith	c Richards b Small	27	46	1
* K.J.Hughes	run out	18	22	2
D.M.Jones	run out	26	5	–
A.R.Border	not out	3	23	2
† W.B.Phillips	run out	10	12	–
G.F.Lawson	not out	0	2	–
J.N.Maguire				
R.M.Hogg				
T.M.Alderman				
Extras	(b 7, lb 15, w 2, nb 5)	29		
Total	(36.4 overs; 6 wickets)	**194**		

AUSTRALIA	O	M	R	W
Lawson	9	1	40	2
Alderman	9	2	39	1
Hogg	6	0	49	0
Maguire	9	1	28	1
Wessels	4	0	25	1

WEST INDIES	O	M	R	W
Garner	9.4	2	24	1
Daniel	9	0	56	1
Small	9	0	40	1
Marshall	9	0	52	0

FALL OF WICKETS
1-25, 2-25, 3-135, 4-145, 5-173, 6-178

FALL OF WICKETS
1-30, 2-98, 3-143, 4-157, 5-162, 6-188

Umpires: L.H.Barker (1) and S.Mohammed (2).

WEST INDIES v AUSTRALIA 1983-84

At Mindoo Phillip Park, Castries, St Lucia on 19 April 1984.　　Result: **WEST INDIES** won by 7 wickets.　　Toss: West Indies.
Award: D.L.Haynes.　　LOI debuts: West Indies – T.R.O.Payne.　　45-over match.

The partnership of 150 between Allan Border and Kim Hughes was then Australia's fourth-wicket LOI record and
remains their best against West Indies.

AUSTRALIA		Runs	Balls	4/6
S.B.Smith	b Garner	6	10	1
† W.B.Phillips	b Marshall	0	6	–
G.M.Ritchie	c Dujon b Garner	0	3	–
A.R.Border	c Dujon b Garner	90	141	7/1
* K.J.Hughes	b Holding	78	76	8/2
D.W.Hookes	c Dujon b Marshall	22	26	3
D.M.Jones	c and b Marshall	0	4	–
T.G.Hogan	c and b Marshall	0	1	–
G.F.Lawson	run out	2	2	–
J.N.Maguire	not out	1	2	–
C.G.Rackemann	not out	0	5	–
Extras	(b 1, lb 2, w 2, nb 2)	7		
Total	(45 overs; 9 wickets)	**206**		

WEST INDIES		Runs	Balls	4/6
C.G.Greenidge	c Lawson b Hogan	42	54	3/2
D.L.Haynes	not out	102	142	11/3
R.B.Richardson	c Hogan b Maguire	6	25	1
A.L.Logie	c Phillips b Maguire	28	21	4
† P.J.L.Dujon	not out	13	10	2
T.R.O.Payne				
M.D.Marshall				
E.A.E.Baptiste				
R.A.Harper				
J.Garner				
* M.A.Holding				
Extras	(b 4, lb 10, w 2, nb 1)	17		
Total	(41.4 overs; 3 wickets)	**208**		

WEST INDIES	O	M	R	W
Garner	10	0	33	3
Marshall	10	2	34	4
Holding	10	0	57	1
Baptiste	8	0	42	0
Harper	7	0	37	0

AUSTRALIA	O	M	R	W
Lawson	10	1	43	0
Rackemann	10	0	56	0
Maguire	10	0	57	2
Hogan	10	0	31	1
Border	1	0	3	0
Jones	0.4	0	4	0

FALL OF WICKETS
1-2, 2-6, 3-8, 4-158, 5-198, 6-199, 7-202, 8-205, 9-205

FALL OF WICKETS
1-96, 2-119, 3-180

Umpires: S.Mohammed (3) and P.C.White (2).

WEST INDIES v AUSTRALIA 1983-84

At Sabina Park, Kingston, Jamaica on 26 April 1984.　Result: **WEST INDIES** won by 9 wickets.　Toss: West Indies.
Award: D.L.Haynes.　LOI debuts: None.　50-over match.

The first limited-overs international to be played in Jamaica. Desmond Haynes carried West Indies to a 3-1 win in the series with his third undefeated hundred in four innings.

AUSTRALIA		Runs	Balls	4/6
S.B.Smith	b Harper	50	83	3
† W.B.Phillips	c Logie b Garner	13	11	2
G.M.Ritchie	c Haynes b Garner	84	129	4
A.R.Border	b Harper	28	38	1/1
* K.J.Hughes	c Greenidge b Garner	8	16	–
D.W.Hookes	b Marshall	0	2	–
G.R.J.Matthews	b Marshall	10	14	1
T.G.Hogan	not out	1	2	–
G.F.Lawson				
R.M.Hogg				
J.N.Maguire				
Extras	(b 5, lb 2, w 4, nb 4)	15		
Total	(50 overs; 7 wickets)	**209**		

WEST INDIES		Runs	Balls	4/6
C.G.Greenidge	b Maguire	34	70	4
D.L.Haynes	not out	104	102	10/1
R.B.Richardson	not out	51	100	6
* I.V.A.Richards				
A.L.Logie				
† P.J.L.Dujon				
M.D.Marshall				
E.A.E.Baptiste				
R.A.Harper				
J.Garner				
M.A.Holding				
Extras	(b 5, lb 8, w 4, nb 5)	22		
Total	(47.4 overs; 1 wicket)	**211**		

WEST INDIES	O	M	R	W
Garner	10	0	47	3
Marshall	10	1	26	2
Baptiste	5	0	19	0
Holding	8	0	44	0
Harper	10	1	41	2
Richards	7	0	25	0

AUSTRALIA	O	M	R	W
Lawson	8	1	39	0
Hogg	8.4	0	51	0
Maguire	6	1	16	1
Hogan	10	2	31	0
Matthews	10	1	42	0
Border	5	0	19	0

FALL OF WICKETS
1-22, 2-111, 3-161, 4-185, 5-187, 6-205, 7-209

FALL OF WICKETS
1-80

Umpires: L.H.Barker (2) and J.R.Gayle (1).

SRI LANKA v NEW ZEALAND 1983-84

At Sinhalese Sports Club, Colombo on 3 March 1984.　Result: **NEW ZEALAND** won by 104 runs.　Toss: Sri Lanka.
Award: J.F.Reid.　LOI debuts: None.　42-over match.

No-balls and wides were not debited to bowlers' analyses in this series. John Reid was treated for heat exhaustion after his rapid innings of 80. Sri Lanka's last seven wickets produced only 32 runs.

NEW ZEALAND		Runs	Balls	4/6
* G.P.Howarth	c Kuruppu b Ranatunga	33	53	2
J.G.Wright	c and b De Mel	20	43	1
J.F.Reid	c John b Ratnayeke	80	76	2/2
M.D.Crowe	c De Mel b De Silva	29	27	3
J.J.Crowe	not out	39	50	1/1
R.J.Hadlee	c Ranatunga b Ratnayeke	6	9	–
B.L.Cairns	b John	1	3	–
J.V.Coney	not out	4	4	–
† I.D.S.Smith				
S.L.Boock				
E.J.Chatfield				
Extras	(b 1, lb 8, w 3, nb 10)	22		
Total	(42 overs; 6 wickets)	**234**		

SRI LANKA		Runs	Balls	4/6
S.Wettimuny	c Coney b Chatfield	16	33	2
D.S.B.P.Kuruppu	c Hadlee b Coney	38	55	4
R.L.Dias	c and b Boock	9	26	–
* L.R.D.Mendis	b Boock	15	33	–
A.Ranatunga	c Coney b Boock	16	14	1
J.R.Ratnayeke	run out	1	4	–
D.S.de Silva	c J.J.Crowe b Hadlee	8	22	–
R.S.Madugalle	b Cairns	5	13	1
† R.G.de Alwis	c Smith b Hadlee	8	15	–
A.L.F.de Mel	b Hadlee	2	7	–
V.B.John	not out	6	4	1
Extras	(b 1, lb 4, w 1)	6		
Total	(37.3 overs)	**130**		

SRI LANKA	O	M	R	W
De Mel	7	1	40	1
John	9	1	39	1
Ratnayeke	8	0	37	2
De Silva	9	0	42	1
Ranatunga	9	0	54	1

NEW ZEALAND	O	M	R	W
Cairns	9	0	35	1
Hadlee	8.3	0	22	3
Chatfield	4	0	24	1
Boock	9	0	28	3
Coney	7	2	15	1

FALL OF WICKETS
1-58, 2-76, 3-123, 4-220, 5-227, 6-229

FALL OF WICKETS
1-54, 2-60, 3-73, 4-98, 5-100, 6-102, 7-111, 8-122, 9-123, 10-130

Umpires: D.P.Buultjens (3) and H.C.Felsinger (3).

SRI LANKA v NEW ZEALAND 1983-84

At Tyronne Fernando Stadium, Moratuwa on 31 March 1984.　Result: **SRI LANKA** won by 41 runs.　Toss: New Zealand.
Award: S.H.U.Karnain.　LOI debuts: Sri Lanka – P.A.de Silva, S.H.U.Karnain; New Zealand – D.A.Stirling.　40-over match.

Uvais Karnain, a 21-year-old medium-pace bowler, celebrated his international debut by scoring 28 off 24 balls before producing Sri Lanka's best bowling analysis until 1992-93. Rain delayed the start of Moratuwa's first international by 75 minutes and bad light interrupted a New Zealand innings which ended in semi-darkness.

SRI LANKA		Runs	Balls	4/6
S.Wettimuny	b Chatfield	6	33	–
D.S.B.P.Kuruppu	c Wright b Stirling	4	19	1
R.S.Madugalle	c Coney b Chatfield	10	27	–/1
A.Ranatunga	not out	50	60	4
* L.R.D.Mendis	c Smith b Cairns	4	13	–
P.A.de Silva	b Hadlee	8	23	–
J.R.Ratnayeke	run out	12	27	–
S.H.U.Karnain	c Cairns b M.D.Crowe	28	24	3/1
† R.G.de Alwis	run out	1	3	–
D.S.de Silva	not out	18	16	2
V.B.John				
Extras	(b 1, lb 10, w 1, nb 4)	16		
Total	(40 overs; 8 wickets)	**157**		

NEW ZEALAND		Runs	Balls	4/6
J.G.Wright	c Wettimuny b John	3	16	–
B.A.Edgar	c De Alwis b Karnain	12	37	1
* G.P.Howarth	b Karnain	12	20	1
B.L.Cairns	b Karnain	5	12	–
M.D.Crowe	c De Alwis b Karnain	9	13	1
J.J.Crowe	lbw b Karnain	9	8	–/1
J.V.Coney	b Ranatunga	11	15	1
R.J.Hadlee	c P.A.de Silva b Ranatunga	13	20	1
† I.D.S.Smith	c P.A.de Silva b D.S.de Silva	11	18	–
D.A.Stirling	not out	13	21	1
E.J.Chatfield	lbw b Ranatunga	5	18	–
Extras	(b 1, lb 11, nb 1)	13		
Total	(34 overs)	**116**		

NEW ZEALAND	O	M	R	W
Cairns	8	1	11	1
Hadlee	8	2	27	1
Stirling	5	1	34	1
Chatfield	8	0	29	2
Coney	6	0	21	0
M.D.Crowe	5	0	19	1

SRI LANKA	O	M	R	W
John	7	0	12	1
Ratnayeke	6	0	14	0
Karnain	8	1	26	5
D.S.de Silva	5	0	28	1
Ranatunga	8	1	23	3

FALL OF WICKETS
1-11, 2-22, 3-37, 4-48, 5-69, 6-110, 7-110, 8-112

FALL OF WICKETS
1-4, 2-31, 3-34, 4-39, 5-49, 6-66, 7-76, 8-88, 9-96, 10-116

Umpires: K.T.Francis (3) and P.W.Vidanagamage (4).

SRI LANKA v NEW ZEALAND 1983-84

At P.Saravanamuttu Stadium, Colombo on 1 April 1984.　Result: **NEW ZEALAND** won by 86 runs.　Toss: Sri Lanka.
Award: B.L.Cairns.　LOI debuts: None.　44-over match.

Lance Cairns hit 26 (three sixes over mid-wicket and two fours) off the final over of New Zealand's innings, bowled by Vinothen John.

NEW ZEALAND		Runs	Balls	4/6
* J.G.Wright	c De Alwis b Ratnayeke	10	20	1
B.A.Edgar	b D.S.de Silva	24	50	2
M.D.Crowe	run out	68	84	4
J.F.Reid	c D.S.de Silva b John	9	15	1
J.J.Crowe	b Ranatunga	5	11	–
J.V.Coney	c and b Ranatunga	13	26	1
R.J.Hadlee	c Madugalle b Ranatunga	9	5	1
† I.D.S.Smith	run out	13	13	1
B.L.Cairns	not out	40	26	4/3
S.L.Boock	not out	8	8	1
E.J.Chatfield				
Extras	(lb 1, w 1)	2		
Total	(44 overs; 8 wickets)	**201**		

SRI LANKA		Runs	Balls	4/6
S.Wettimuny	c Smith b Hadlee	33	62	2
D.S.B.P.Kuruppu	c Smith b Hadlee	3	7	–
R.S.Madugalle	c sub (J.G.Bracewell) b Boock	10	34	1
P.A.de Silva	run out	7	17	1
A.Ranatunga	c J.J.Crowe b Cairns	13	26	–/1
* L.R.D.Mendis	c Hadlee b Chatfield	7	15	–
S.H.U.Karnain	c Boock b Cairns	1	3	–
J.R.Ratnayeke	c Reid b Chatfield	7	14	–
† R.G.de Alwis	lbw b Hadlee	9	30	–
D.S.de Silva	not out	14	21	2
V.B.John	c sub (J.G.Bracewell) b Coney	1	3	–
Extras	(b 6, lb 4)	10		
Total	(38.1 overs)	**115**		

SRI LANKA	O	M	R	W
John	9	1	43	1
Ratnayeke	8	0	32	1
Karnain	9	0	41	0
D.S.de Silva	9	0	34	1
Ranatunga	9	0	49	3

NEW ZEALAND	O	M	R	W
Cairns	7	2	14	2
Hadlee	6	0	19	3
Chatfield	9	2	13	2
Boock	9	1	22	1
Coney	6.1	1	24	1
M.D.Crowe	1	0	13	0

FALL OF WICKETS
1-16, 2-45, 3-63, 4-77, 5-114, 6-124, 7-153, 8-154

FALL OF WICKETS
1-6, 2-29, 3-39, 4-73, 5-76, 6-79, 7-85, 8-94, 9-114, 10-115

Umpires: H.C.Felsinger (4) and K.T.Francis (4).

PAKISTAN v ENGLAND 1983-84

At Gaddafi Stadium, Lahore on 9 March 1984.   Result: **PAKISTAN** won by 6 wickets.   Toss: Pakistan.
Award: Zaheer Abbas.   LOI debuts: Pakistan – Saadat Ali.

No-balls and wides were not debited to bowlers' analyses in this 40-over series. Ian Botham aggravated a knee injury and departed for home the following day.

ENGLAND		Runs	Balls	4/6
† G.Fowler	b Sarfraz	43		
C.J.Tavaré	c Ashraf b Rashid	4		
D.I.Gower	c Omar b Shahid	7		
A.J.Lamb	run out	57		
D.W.Randall	run out	16		
I.T.Botham	not out	18		
M.W.Gatting	b Sarfraz	9		
G.R.Dilley	lbw b Sarfraz	1		
V.J.Marks	b Rashid	2		
N.A.Foster	not out	6		
* R.G.D.Willis				
Extras	(lb 13, w 6, nb 2)	21		
Total	(40 overs; 8 wickets)	**184**		

PAKISTAN		Runs	Balls	4/6
Mohsin Khan	b Dilley	39		
Saadat Ali	run out	44		
Qasim Omar	c Fowler b Marks	11		
* Zaheer Abbas	not out	59		
Salim Malik	c Tavaré b Willis	11		
Mudassar Nazar	not out	8		
Wasim Raja				
Shahid Mahboob				
† Ashraf Ali				
Sarfraz Nawaz				
Rashid Khan				
Extras	(b 1, lb 5, w 1, nb 8)	15		
Total	(38.4 overs; 4 wickets)	**187**		

PAKISTAN	O	M	R	W
Rashid Khan	8	1	28	2
Shahid Mahboob	8	2	28	1
Mudassar Nazar	8	1	34	0
Sarfraz Nawaz	8	0	33	3
Wasim Raja	8	0	40	0

ENGLAND	O	M	R	W
Willis	7.4	1	25	1
Dilley	8	0	38	1
Botham	7	0	43	0
Marks	8	1	32	1
Foster	8	0	34	0

FALL OF WICKETS
1-11, 2-24, 3-94, 4-134, 5-147, 6-160, 7-164, 8-173

FALL OF WICKETS
1-79, 2-96, 3-120, 4-156

Umpires: Amanullah Khan (5) and Shakil Khan (4).

PAKISTAN v ENGLAND 1983-84

At National Stadium, Karachi on 26 March 1984.   Result: **ENGLAND** won by 6 wickets.   Toss: England.
Award: M.W.Gatting.   LOI debuts: Pakistan – Anil Dalpat, Naved Anjum; England – N.G.B.Cook.

Chris Smith's leg-breaks claimed their only victims in limited-overs internationals.

PAKISTAN		Runs	Balls	4/6
Mohsin Khan	st Fowler b Cook	37	56	5
Saadat Ali	not out	78	119	4
Wasim Raja	c Fowler b Gatting	14	17	2
Salim Malik	c Foster b Gatting	2	8	–
Qasim Omar	c and b Gatting	7	15	–
Naved Anjum	st Fowler b Smith	2	7	–
Mudassar Nazar	run out	6	7	1
Abdul Qadir	c Cook b Smith	3	5	–
* Sarfraz Nawaz	c Gower b Cowans	3	7	–
† Anil Dalpat	not out	0	–	–
Rashid Khan				
Extras	(b 4, lb 4, nb 3)	11		
Total	(40 overs; 8 wickets)	**163**		

ENGLAND		Runs	Balls	4/6
† G.Fowler	c Anil b Mudassar	25	54	4
C.L.Smith	lbw b Qadir	17	43	2
* D.I.Gower	b Mudassar	31	33	3
A.J.Lamb	c Salim b Naved	19	28	–
M.W.Gatting	not out	38	49	2
D.W.Randall	not out	19	29	1
C.J.Tavaré				
V.J.Marks				
N.A.Foster				
N.G.B.Cook				
N.G.Cowans				
Extras	(b 1, lb 8, w 3, nb 3)	15		
Total	(38.4 overs; 4 wickets)	**164**		

ENGLAND	O	M	R	W
Foster	8	0	36	0
Cowans	5	0	20	1
Gatting	8	1	32	3
Marks	8	1	22	0
Cook	8	0	34	1
Smith	3	0	8	2

PAKISTAN	O	M	R	W
Rashid Khan	8	0	31	0
Sarfraz Nawaz	7.4	1	24	0
Mudassar Nazar	8	1	22	2
Abdul Qadir	8	0	33	1
Wasim Raja	5	0	30	0
Naved Anjum	2	0	9	1

FALL OF WICKETS
1-76, 2-102, 3-107, 4-123, 5-135, 6-146, 7-155, 8-160

FALL OF WICKETS
1-37, 2-79, 3-88, 4-119

Umpires: Mahboob Shah (6) and Shakil Khan (5).

PAKISTAN v SRI LANKA 1983-84

At Sharjah CA Stadium, UAE on 6 April 1984.   Result: **SRI LANKA** won by 5 wickets.   Toss: Sri Lanka.
Award: R.L.Dias.   LOI debuts: None.   46-over match.

No-balls and wides were not debited to bowlers' analyses in this series, the first to be staged outside the Test-playing countries. Entrepreneur A.R.Bukhatir brought international cricket to the Middle East; his oasis of a stadium with its turf pitch was to be the first venue to stage a hundred of these matches. It also provided limited-overs cricket's first independent umpires.

PAKISTAN		Runs	Balls	4/6
Mohsin Khan	c Dias b D.S.de Silva	27		2
Saadat Ali	c Kuruppu b Ranatunga	30		2
Mudassar Nazar	c Kuruppu b Karnain	1		–
* Zaheer Abbas	c Ratnayeke b Ranatunga	47		2/2
Javed Miandad	b John	9		1
Salim Malik	run out	17		1
Abdul Qadir	b D.S.de Silva	7		–/1
Shahid Mahboob	not out	18		1
Sarfraz Nawaz	c John b Ranatunga	5		–
† Anil Dalpat	c Ranatunga b Ratnayeke	5		–
Rashid Khan	not out	0		–
Extras	(b 4, lb 8, w 8, nb 1)	21		
Total	(46 overs; 9 wickets)	**187**		

SRI LANKA		Runs	Balls	4/6
S.Wettimuny	run out	18		1
† D.S.B.P.Kuruppu	c Anil b Mudassar	25		3
R.L.Dias	not out	57		1
* L.R.D.Mendis	b Qadir	20		2
A.Ranatunga	st Anil b Qadir	26		1/1
R.S.Madugalle	c Zaheer b Sarfraz	4		1
P.A.de Silva	not out	14		2
S.H.U.Karnain				
D.S.de Silva				
J.R.Ratnayeke				
V.B.John				
Extras	(b 4, lb 14, w 6, nb 2)	26		
Total	(43.3 overs; 5 wickets)	**190**		

SRI LANKA	O	M	R	W
John	10	3	26	1
Ratnayeke	9	0	33	1
Karnain	7	1	19	1
D.S.de Silva	10	0	50	2
Ranatunga	10	0	38	3

PAKISTAN	O	M	R	W
Shahid Mahboob	9	1	30	0
Rashid Khan	8	2	26	0
Mudassar Nazar	7	0	25	1
Sarfraz Nawaz	10	1	36	1
Abdul Qadir	9	0	42	2
Saadat Ali	0.3	0	5	0

FALL OF WICKETS
1-59, 2-60, 3-84, 4-110, 5-142, 6-154, 7-157, 8-165, 9-185

Umpires: H.D.Bird (*England*) (24) and Swaroop Kishen (*Pakistan*) (2).

FALL OF WICKETS
1-52, 2-67, 3-105, 4-163, 5-170

INDIA v SRI LANKA 1983-84

At Sharjah CA Stadium, UAE on 8 April 1984.   Result: **INDIA** won by 10 wickets.   Toss: India.
Award: S.C.Khanna.   LOI debuts: India – M.Prabhakar.   41-over match.

Sri Lanka, surprise winners of the inaugural match, were dismissed for what remains their lowest LOI total against India.

SRI LANKA		Runs	Balls	4/6
S.Wettimuny	c Madan Lal b Prabhakar	12	32	–
† D.S.B.P.Kuruppu	c Khanna b Sharma	0	1	–
R.L.Dias	c Vengsarkar b Prabhakar	5	27	–
* L.R.D.Mendis	c Patil b Sharma	1	5	–
R.S.Madugalle	b Madan Lal	38	76	5
A.Ranatunga	run out	9	20	1
P.A.de Silva	lbw b Madan Lal	11	27	1
S.H.U.Karnain	lbw b Madan Lal	0	7	–
J.R.Ratnayeke	b Shastri	2	7	–
D.S.de Silva	not out	8	28	–
V.B.John	c Gavaskar b Sharma	2	14	–
Extras	(lb 4, w 3, nb 1)	8		
Total	(41 overs)	**96**		

INDIA		Runs	Balls	4/6
† S.C.Khanna	not out	51	69	6
G.A.Parkar	not out	32	68	3
D.B.Vengsarkar				
* S.M.Gavaskar				
S.M.Patil				
R.J.Shastri				
K.Azad				
R.M.H.Binny				
Madan Lal				
M.Prabhakar				
C.Sharma				
Extras	(b 1, w 12, nb 1)	14		
Total	(21.4 overs; 0 wickets)	**97**		

INDIA	O	M	R	W
Sharma	8	1	22	3
Prabhakar	10	3	16	2
Binny	7	0	25	0
Madan Lal	8	2	11	3
Shastri	7	1	13	1
Azad	1	0	1	0

SRI LANKA	O	M	R	W
John	9	1	30	0
Ratnayeke	4	0	27	0
Karnain	2	0	4	0
D.S.de Silva	6	0	21	0
Madugalle	0.4	0	1	0

FALL OF WICKETS
1-1, 2-17, 3-20, 4-26, 5-53, 6-79, 7-81, 8-82, 9-86, 10-96

Umpires: H.D.Bird (*England*) (25) and Shakoor Rana (*Pakistan*) (9).

INDIA v PAKISTAN 1983-84

At Sharjah CA Stadium, UAE on 13 April 1984.   Result: **INDIA** won by 54 runs.   Toss: India.
Award: S.C.Khanna.   LOI debuts: None.   46-over match.

An impressive all-round bowling performance gained India a comprehensive victory, the Rothmans Asia Cup and a purse of $50,000.

INDIA		Runs	Balls	4/6	PAKISTAN		Runs	Balls	4/6
†S.C.Khanna	c Anil b Mudassar	56	72	3/2	Mohsin Khan	c Parkar b Shastri	35	65	1
G.A.Parkar	run out	22	55	2	Saadat Ali	run out	13	21	1
D.B.Vengsarkar	b Shahid	14	44	1	Mudassar Nazar	st Khanna b Shastri	18	50	–
S.M.Patil	c Salim b Sarfraz	43	50	5/1	* Zaheer Abbas	c Madan Lal b Binny	27	45	1
* S.M.Gavaskar	not out	36	55	2	Salim Malik	run out	15	17	–
R.J.Shastri					Qasim Omar	c Prabhakar b Binny	16	30	2
K.Azad					Shahid Mahboob	run out	0	1	–
R.M.H.Binny					Abdul Qadir	run out	0	1	–
Madan Lal					Sarfraz Nawaz	c Patil b Binny	4	13	–
M.Prabhakar					†Anil Dalpat	st Khanna b Shastri	1	2	–
C.Sharma					Azeem Hafeez	not out	0	5	–
Extras	(b 1, lb 12, w 1, nb 3)	17			Extras	(lb 5)	5		
Total	(46 overs; 4 wickets)	**188**			**Total**	(39.4 overs)	**134**		

PAKISTAN	O	M	R	W	INDIA	O	M	R	W
Azeem Hafeez	7	0	41	0	Sharma	7	0	18	0
Sarfraz Nawaz	10	1	37	1	Prabhakar	7	0	17	0
Shahid Mahboob	10	1	23	1	Binny	9.4	0	33	3
Abdul Qadir	10	3	36	0	Madan Lal	6	1	21	0
Mudassar Nazar	9	3	34	1	Shastri	10	0	40	3

FALL OF WICKETS
1-54, 2-88, 3-110, 4-188

FALL OF WICKETS
1-23, 2-69, 3-70, 4-92, 5-125, 6-125, 7-125, 8-128, 9-133, 10-134

Umpires: H.D.Bird (*England*) (26) and H.C.Felsinger (*Sri Lanka*) (5).

ENGLAND v WEST INDIES 1984

At Old Trafford, Manchester on 31 May 1984.   Result: **WEST INDIES** won by 104 runs.   Toss: West Indies.
Award: I.V.A.Richards.   LOI debuts: England – T.A.Lloyd.

No-balls and wides were not debited to bowlers in this 55-over Texaco Trophy series. The inaugural match was dominated by the highest innings in limited-overs international cricket. Viv Richards (50 off 59 balls, 100 off 112 balls, 150 off 147 balls) became the first to score 3,000 LOI runs, contributing 93 to the only century last-wicket stand at this level.

WEST INDIES		Runs	Balls	4/6	ENGLAND		Runs	Balls	4/6
C.G.Greenidge	c Bairstow b Botham	9	11	1	G.Fowler	c Lloyd b Garner	1	5	–
D.L.Haynes	run out	1	5	–	T.A.Lloyd	c Dujon b Holding	15	42	2
R.B.Richardson	c and b Willis	6	24	–	M.W.Gatting	lbw b Garner	0	5	–
I.V.A.Richards	not out	189	170	21/5	* D.I.Gower	c Greenidge b Marshall	15	38	–
H.A.Gomes	b Miller	4	17	1	A.J.Lamb	c Richardson b Gomes	75	89	8
* C.H.Lloyd	c Pringle b Miller	8	21	1	I.T.Botham	c Richardson b Baptiste	2	6	–
†P.J.L.Dujon	c Gatting b Miller	0	1	–	†D.L.Bairstow	c Garner b Richards	13	34	2
M.D.Marshall	run out	4	3	–	G.Miller	b Richards	7	24	–
E.A.E.Baptiste	c Bairstow b Botham	26	49	2	D.R.Pringle	c Garner b Holding	6	21	–
J.Garner	c and b Foster	3	5	–	N.A.Foster	b Garner	24	38	2
M.A.Holding	not out	12	27	2	R.G.D.Willis	not out	1	2	–
Extras	(b 4, lb 2, w 1, nb 3)	10			Extras	(lb 6, nb 3)	9		
Total	(55 overs; 9 wickets)	**272**			**Total**	(50 overs)	**168**		

ENGLAND	O	M	R	W	WEST INDIES	O	M	R	W
Willis	11	2	38	1	Garner	8	1	18	3
Botham	11	0	67	2	Holding	11	2	23	2
Foster	11	0	61	1	Baptiste	11	0	38	1
Miller	11	1	32	3	Marshall	6	1	20	1
Pringle	11	0	64	0	Richards	11	1	45	2
					Gomes	3	0	15	1

FALL OF WICKETS
1-5, 2-11, 3-43, 4-63, 5-89, 6-98, 7-102, 8-161, 9-166

FALL OF WICKETS
1-7, 2-8, 3-33, 4-48, 5-51, 6-80, 7-100, 8-115, 9-162, 10-168

Umpires: D.J.Constant (24) and D.R.Shepherd (5).

ENGLAND v WEST INDIES 1984

At Trent Bridge, Nottingham on 2 June 1984.   Result: **ENGLAND** won by 3 wickets.   Toss: England.
Award: D.R.Pringle.   LOI debuts: None.

Overnight rain delayed the start by 30 minutes and reduced the match to 50 overs. By dismissing Viv Richards for 186 fewer runs than he had amassed at Old Trafford, England were able to notch their fourth win in 17 matches against West Indies.

WEST INDIES		Runs	Balls	4/6	ENGLAND		Runs	Balls	4/6
C.G.Greenidge	c Botham b Pringle	20	38	2	G.Fowler	b Baptiste	25	62	2
D.L.Haynes	lbw b Willis	4	23	–	T.A.Lloyd	c Dujon b Baptiste	49	103	1
R.B.Richardson	c Gower b Pringle	10	30	1	* D.I.Gower	lbw b Marshall	36	42	3
I.V.A.Richards	c Pringle b Miller	3	12	–	A.J.Lamb	b Gomes	11	24	–
H.A.Gomes	b Pringle	15	39	–	I.T.Botham	c Gomes b Holding	15	23	1
* C.H.Lloyd	c Pringle b Miller	52	66	3/3	M.W.Gatting	b Garner	6	14	–
† P.J.L.Dujon	run out	21	36	1	† D.L.Bairstow	b Holding	9	16	–
M.D.Marshall	run out	20	22	1	G.Miller	not out	3	6	–
E.A.E.Baptiste	lbw b Willis	19	16	1	D.R.Pringle	not out	2	3	–
M.A.Holding	b Botham	0	2	–	N.A.Foster				
J.Garner	not out	6	11	–	R.G.D.Willis				
Extras	(lb 7, nb 2)	9			Extras	(b 4, lb 14, nb 6)	24		
Total	(48.3 overs)	179			Total	(47.5 overs; 7 wickets)	180		

ENGLAND	O	M	R	W	WEST INDIES	O	M	R	W
Willis	9.3	0	26	2	Garner	9	1	22	1
Botham	9	1	33	1	Holding	8.5	1	29	2
Pringle	10	3	21	3	Marshall	10	1	30	1
Miller	10	2	44	2	Baptiste	10	2	31	2
Foster	10	0	46	0	Richards	5	0	23	0
					Gomes	5	0	21	1

FALL OF WICKETS
1-24, 2-38, 3-39, 4-43, 5-75, 6-128, 7-148, 8-160, 9-161, 10-179

FALL OF WICKETS
1-75, 2-103, 3-131, 4-145, 5-157, 6-173, 7-177

Umpires: H.D.Bird (27) and D.O.Oslear (8).

ENGLAND v WEST INDIES 1984

At Lord's, London on 4 June 1984.   Result: **WEST INDIES** won by 8 wickets.   Toss: West Indies.
Award: R.A.Harper.   LOI debuts: None.

Another withering display by Viv Richards, whose fifty took 45 balls, ensured that West Indies would become the first holders of the Texaco Trophy.

ENGLAND		Runs	Balls	4/6	WEST INDIES		Runs	Balls	4/6
G.Fowler	b Holding	34	72	1	C.G.Greenidge	c Bairstow b Pringle	32	81	3
T.A.Lloyd	b Harper	37	83	–	D.L.Haynes	c Randall b Miller	18	51	2
* D.I.Gower	b Marshall	29	57	–	H.A.Gomes	not out	56	90	4
A.J.Lamb	run out	0	1	–	I.V.A.Richards	not out	84	65	10/4
I.T.Botham	c Harper b Baptiste	22	27	1/1	* C.H.Lloyd				
D.W.Randall	c Dujon b Marshall	8	13	–	† P.J.L.Dujon				
† D.L.Bairstow	b Marshall	8	22	–	M.D.Marshall				
G.Miller	b Holding	10	27	–	E.A.E.Baptiste				
D.R.Pringle	lbw b Garner	8	22	–	R.A.Harper				
N.A.Foster	not out	4	8	–	J.Garner				
R.G.D.Willis	not out	6	9	–	M.A.Holding				
Extras	(b 1, lb 17, w 4, nb 8)	30			Extras	(b 1, w 1, nb 5)	7		
Total	(55 overs; 9 wickets)	196			Total	(46.5 overs; 2 wickets)	197		

WEST INDIES	O	M	R	W	ENGLAND	O	M	R	W
Garner	11	4	17	1	Willis	10.5	2	52	0
Holding	11	0	33	2	Botham	8	0	25	0
Marshall	11	0	38	3	Miller	9	1	35	1
Baptiste	11	1	40	1	Pringle	8	0	38	1
Harper	11	0	38	1	Foster	11	1	40	0

FALL OF WICKETS
1-60, 2-91, 3-91, 4-128, 5-144, 6-151, 7-167, 8-177, 9-182

FALL OF WICKETS
1-50, 2-63

Umpires: D.G.L.Evans (12) and B.J.Meyer (15).

INDIA v AUSTRALIA 1984-85

At Jawaharlal Nehru Stadium, New Delhi on 28 September 1984. Result: **AUSTRALIA** won by 48 runs. Toss: Australia.
Award: K.C.Wessels. LOI debuts: India – A.K.Patel. 48-over match.

A crowd of 35,000 attended the new international venue for the first floodlit official international in India. Australia's win was remarkable considering they had only an hour's practice since arriving and lost seven wickets for 20 runs at the end of their innings. Kepler Wessels scored his only hundred in 105 LOI innings for two countries.

AUSTRALIA		Runs	Balls	4/6
K.C.Wessels	c Parkar b Madan Lal	107	133	13
G.M.Wood	c Khanna b Sharma	0	4	–
K.J.Hughes	c Parkar b Patel	72	93	10
G.N.Yallop	st Khanna b Azad	22	27	2
A.R.Border	st Khanna b Azad	0	3	–
W.B.Phillips	run out	1	3	–
T.G.Hogan	lbw b Madan Lal	6	8	1
G.F.Lawson	c Vengsarkar b Kapil Dev	2	10	–
R.M.Hogg	not out	0	8	–
C.G.Rackemann	run out	2	8	–
J.N.Maguire				
Extras	(b 3, lb 4, nb 1)	8		
Total	(48 overs; 9 wickets)	**220**		

INDIA		Runs	Balls	4/6
† S.C.Khanna	c Phillips b Rackemann	13	20	2
G.A.Parkar	c Lawson b Rackemann	16	25	3
D.B.Vengsarkar	c Yallop b Maguire	33	86	3
S.M.Patil	lbw b Hogg	22	18	4
* S.M.Gavaskar	c Wood b Rackemann	25	54	–
K.Azad	c Phillips b Maguire	0	2	–
Kapil Dev	b Hogan	39	47	6
R.J.Shastri	st Phillips b Hogan	5	17	–
Madan Lal	c Lawson b Rackemann	1	8	–
C.Sharma	not out	9	8	1
A.K.Patel	c Phillips b Hogan	0	3	–
Extras	(lb 2, nb 7)	9		
Total	(40.5 overs)	**172**		

INDIA	O	M	R	W
Kapil Dev	9	1	43	1
Sharma	9	0	49	1
Madan Lal	7	2	23	2
Patel	10	2	27	1
Shastri	3	0	23	0
Azad	10	1	48	2

AUSTRALIA	O	M	R	W
Lawson	5	0	23	0
Rackemann	10	1	41	4
Hogg	6	1	21	1
Maguire	10	1	41	2
Hogan	9.5	1	44	3

FALL OF WICKETS
1-14, 2-142, 3-200, 4-200, 5-204, 6-213, 7-216, 8-220, 9-220

FALL OF WICKETS
1-17, 2-44, 3-76, 4-96, 5-97, 6-148, 7-160, 8-161, 9-172, 10-172

Umpires: B.Ganguli (2) and P.D.Reporter (1).

INDIA v AUSTRALIA 1984-85

At University Stadium, Trivandrum on 1 October 1984. No result. Toss: Australia.
LOI debuts: None. 37-over match.

Torrential rain ruined the first international to be staged at India's most Christianised state, Kerala. The match was initially reduced to 37 overs by a delayed start and further rain left Australia to score 146 in 32 overs. Dilip Vengsarkar overcame a poor pitch at the most southerly of India's many international venues to complete 1,000 LOI runs.

INDIA		Runs	Balls	4/6
† S.C.Khanna	c Phillips b Rackemann	4	14	–
G.A.Parkar	c Phillips b Rackemann	3	14	–
D.B.Vengsarkar	b Hogan	77	79	7/3
S.M.Patil	c Yallop b Rackemann	16	36	3
Kapil Dev	b Wessels	12	16	2
K.Azad	c and b Hogan	6	13	–
* S.M.Gavaskar	c Wood b Hogan	14	12	1
R.J.Shastri	c Rackemann b Hogan	2	7	–
Madan Lal	b Border	9	9	1
C.Sharma	not out	13	16	–
A.K.Patel	c Hughes b Border	6	8	–
Extras	(b 5, lb 6, nb 2)	13		
Total	(37 overs)	**175**		

AUSTRALIA		Runs	Balls	4/6
G.M.Wood	not out	7	22	1
K.C.Wessels	lbw b Kapil Dev	12	18	1
A.R.Border	not out	4	7	1
* K.J.Hughes				
G.N.Yallop				
S.B.Smith				
† W.B.Phillips				
T.G.Hogan				
G.F.Lawson				
C.G.Rackemann				
J.N.Maguire				
Extras	(b 1, lb 4, w 1)	6		
Total	(7.4 overs; 1 wicket)	**29**		

AUSTRALIA	O	M	R	W
Lawson	7	0	29	0
Rackemann	8	4	7	3
Maguire	5	0	38	0
Wessels	7	0	44	1
Hogan	8	0	33	4
Border	2	0	13	2

INDIA	O	M	R	W
Kapil Dev	4	1	14	1
Sharma	3.4	1	10	0

FALL OF WICKETS
1-24

FALL OF WICKETS
1-7, 2-10, 3-53, 4-80, 5-103, 6-136, 7-146, 8-146, 9-166, 10-175

Umpires: V.K.Ramaswamy (2) and Swaroop Kishen (3).

INDIA v AUSTRALIA 1984-85

At Keenan Stadium, Jamshedpur on 3 October 1984.   No result.   Toss: Australia.
LOI debuts: None.   24-over match.

Known as 'the portmanteau affair' because it started three hours late when the truck conveying the players' kit some 150 kms from Calcutta went missing. Reduced to a 24-over contest, it was terminated by rain after 25 minutes and was originally excluded from the list of official internationals.

INDIA		Runs	Balls	4/6	AUSTRALIA
† S.C.Khanna	c Border b Rackemann	3	6	–	G.M.Wood
G.A.Parkar	b Rackemann	12	18	1	K.C.Wessels
D.B.Vengsarkar	not out	1	10	–	A.R.Border
Kapil Dev	not out	0	2	–	* K.J.Hughes
* S.M.Gavaskar					G.N.Yallop
R.J.Shastri					S.B.Smith
K.Azad					† W.B.Phillips
Madan Lal					R.M.Hogg
R.M.H.Binny					G.F.Lawson
C.Sharma					J.N.Maguire
A.K.Patel					C.G.Rackemann
Extras	(lb 4, nb 1)	5			
Total	(5.1 overs; 2 wickets)	21			

AUSTRALIA	O	M	R	W
Lawson	3	0	14	0
Rackemann	2.1	0	3	2

FALL OF WICKETS
1-6, 2-21

Umpires: V.K.Ramaswamy (3) and Swaroop Kishen (4).

INDIA v AUSTRALIA 1984-85

At Sardar Patel Stadium, Ahmedabad on 5 October 1984.   Result: **AUSTRALIA** won by 7 wickets.   Toss: Australia.
Award: G.F.Lawson.   LOI debuts: None.   46-over match.

Australia overcame India's first century opening partnership in 11 matches between these countries to clinch this five-match series.

INDIA		Runs	Balls	4/6	AUSTRALIA		Runs	Balls	4/6
R.J.Shastri	st Phillips b Hogan	45	73	4	K.C.Wessels	c Kirmani b Patel	42	70	6
R.M.H.Binny	st Phillips b Hogan	57		8	G.M.Wood	run out	32		4
D.B.Vengsarkar	b Lawson	14	23	–	A.R.Border	not out	62	88	5
S.M.Patil	c Hughes b Wessels	3		–	* K.J.Hughes	lbw b Kapil Dev	29		1
Kapil Dev	b Lawson	28	30	2/1	G.N.Yallop	not out	32		3
* S.M.Gavaskar	b Lawson	4	5	–	S.B.Smith				
K.Azad	not out	39		2/4	† W.B.Phillips				
Madan Lal	not out	6		–	T.G.Hogan				
† S.M.H.Kirmani					J.N.Maguire				
C.Sharma					G.F.Lawson				
A.K.Patel					C.G.Rackemann				
Extras	(b 1, lb 5, nb 4)	10			Extras	(b 1, lb 10, nb 2)	13		
Total	(46 overs; 6 wickets)	206			Total	(43.5 overs; 3 wickets)	210		

AUSTRALIA	O	M	R	W	INDIA	O	M	R	W
Lawson	10	2	25	3	Kapil Dev	8	1	27	1
Rackemann	8	0	50	0	Sharma	7	1	21	0
Maguire	8	0	56	0	Binny	2	0	21	0
Wessels	10	0	29	1	Madan Lal	7.5	0	35	0
Hogan	10	2	40	2	Patel	10	0	44	1
					Azad	9	0	51	0

FALL OF WICKETS
1-104, 2-111, 3-122, 4-133, 5-145, 6-161

FALL OF WICKETS
1-67, 2-89, 3-162

Umpires: D.N.Dotiwala (2) and V.Vikramraju (1).

INDIA v AUSTRALIA 1984-85

At Nehru Stadium, Indore on 6 October 1984.   Result: **AUSTRALIA** won by 6 wickets.   Toss: Australia.
Award: R.J.Shastri.   LOI debuts: Australia – M.J.Bennett.   44-over match.

Although Ravi Shastri contributed India's second LOI hundred to their highest total of this series, it was insufficient to prevent a third Australian victory.

INDIA		Runs	Balls	4/6	AUSTRALIA		Runs	Balls	4/6
G.A.Parkar	b Rackemann	6	24	1	S.B.Smith	c Kapil Dev b Patel	56	54	7
R.J.Shastri	b Maguire	102	141	11/1	† W.B.Phillips	c Patel b Kapil Dev	33	23	6/1
R.M.H.Binny	c Ritchie b Maguire	37	33	6/1	G.N.Yallop	b Patel	42	57	4
S.M.Gavaskar	b Maguire	40	46	3	G.M.Ritchie	not out	59	64	3/1
K.Azad	c Smith b Rackemann	11	10	1	* K.J.Hughes	c Prabhakar b Patel	6	7	1
Kapil Dev	not out	22	11	1/1	K.C.Wessels	not out	35	37	3
S.C.Khanna	not out	1	2		G.M.Wood				
Madan Lal					G.F.Lawson				
M.Prabhakar					M.J.Bennett				
B.S.Sandhu					J.N.Maguire				
A.K.Patel					C.G.Rackemann				
Extras	(b 5, lb 3, w 4, nb 4)	16			Extras	(lb 4, nb 1)	5		
Total	(44 overs; 5 wickets)	235			Total	(40.1 overs; 4 wickets)	236		

AUSTRALIA	O	M	R	W	INDIA	O	M	R	W
Lawson	10	2	48	0	Kapil Dev	8	0	62	1
Rackemann	8	1	37	2	Prabhakar	2	0	15	0
Maguire	10	0	61	3	Sandhu	6	0	38	0
Bennett	10	0	37	0	Madan Lal	6	0	19	0
Wessels	6	0	44	0	Patel	10	0	43	3
					Azad	2	0	16	0
					Shastri	6	0	35	0
					Gavaskar	0.1	0	4	0

FALL OF WICKETS
1-23, 2-83, 3-198, 4-207, 5-217

FALL OF WICKETS
1-53, 2-122, 3-153, 4-163

Umpires: S.R.Bose (2) and P.G.Pandit (3).

PAKISTAN v INDIA 1984-85

At Ayub National Stadium, Quetta on 12 October 1984.   Result: **PAKISTAN** won by 46 runs.   Toss: India.
Award: Manzoor Elahi.   LOI debuts: Pakistan – Manzoor Elahi.

Manzoor Elahi enjoyed a notable introduction to the international arena at the start of this 40-over Wills Series.

PAKISTAN		Runs	Balls	4/6	INDIA		Runs	Balls	4/6
Mohsin Khan	lbw b Sharma	13	27	1	R.J.Shastri	lbw b Tahir	6	22	–
Saadat Ali	c Khanna b Sandhu	12	27	1	† S.C.Khanna	lbw b Tahir	31	37	4
Zaheer Abbas	c and b Maninder	55	56	3	R.M.H.Binny	c Miandad b Mudassar	19	57	–
Javed Miandad	run out	25	51	1	* S.M.Gavaskar	st Ashraf b Tausif	25	38	1
Naved Anjum	c Amarnath b Kapil Dev	30	27	2/1	S.M.Patil	c Ashraf b Naved	11	17	1
Manzoor Elahi	b Kapil Dev	36	39	5	Kapil Dev	b Manzoor	0	1	–
Ashraf Ali	c Maninder b Kapil Dev	6	7	1	M.Amarnath	b Manzoor	5	16	–
Mudassar Nazar	not out	7	6	–	C.Sharma	not out	20	16	2
Tahir Naqqash	not out	0	–	–	Madan Lal	run out	6	9	–
Rashid Khan					B.S.Sandhu	b Naved	7	10	–
Tausif Ahmed					Maninder Singh	b Rashid	4	7	–
Extras	(lb 12, w 3)	15			Extras	(b 2, lb 10, w 5, nb 2)	19		
Total	(40 overs; 7 wickets)	199			Total	(37.1 overs)	153		

INDIA	O	M	R	W	PAKISTAN	O	M	R	W
Kapil Dev	8	0	36	3	Tahir Naqqash	6	0	35	2
Sharma	7	0	42	1	Rashid Khan	6.1	1	20	1
Sandhu	7	0	35	1	Mudassar Nazar	8	2	14	1
Madan Lal	5	1	20	0	Tausif Ahmed	8	0	27	1
Maninder Singh	5	0	24	1	Manzoor Elahi	4	0	18	2
Shastri	8	0	30	0	Naved Anjum	5	0	27	2

FALL OF WICKETS
1-27, 2-39, 3-113, 4-122, 5-165, 6-174, 7-199

FALL OF WICKETS
1-33, 2-42, 3-83, 4-91, 5-92, 6-110, 7-114, 8-123, 9-136, 10-153

Umpires: Javed Akhtar (5) and Khizer Hayat (7).

PAKISTAN v INDIA 1984-85

At Jinnah Park, Sialkot on 31 October 1984.   No result.   Toss: Pakistan.
LOI debuts: Pakistan – Sajid Ali.

This match and the remainder of the tour were cancelled immediately that news of the assassination of Mrs Indira Gandhi was received from Delhi.

INDIA		Runs	Balls	4/6	PAKISTAN	
A.D.Gaekwad	b Mudassar	12			Saadat Ali	
G.A.Parkar	b Mudassar	20			Sajid Ali	
D.B.Vengsarkar	not out	94			* Zaheer Abbas	
S.M.Patil	b Tausif	59			Javed Miandad	
R.J.Shastri	not out	6			Naved Anjum	
* M.Amarnath					Manzoor Elahi	
R.M.H.Binny					Mudassar Nazar	
† S.M.H.Kirmani					† Ashraf Ali	
Madan Lal					Tahir Naqqash	
B.S.Sandhu					Rashid Khan	
Maninder Singh					Tausif Ahmed	
Extras	(lb 9, w 6, nb 4)	19				
Total	(40 overs; 3 wickets)	**210**				

PAKISTAN	O	M	R	W
Rashid Khan	8	0	43	0
Tahir Naqqash	8	0	55	0
Mudassar Nazar	8	1	27	2
Manzoor Elahi	8	3	24	0
Naved Anjum	1	0	10	0
Tausif Ahmed	7	0	42	1

FALL OF WICKETS
1-35, 2-53, 3-196

Umpires: Mian Mohammad Aslam (2) and Shakoor Rana (10).

SRI LANKA v NEW ZEALAND (1st Match)   LOI No: 274/10

SRI LANKA v NEW ZEALAND 1984-85

At P.Saravanamuttu Stadium, Colombo on 3 November 1984.   Result: **SRI LANKA** won by 4 wickets.   Toss: New Zealand.
Award: P.A.de Silva.   LOI debuts: Sri Lanka – S.A.R.Silva.   45-over match.

This two-day 45-over series was played by New Zealand en route to a tour of Pakistan. An undefeated fifty by the 19-year-old Aravinda de Silva took Sri Lanka to a comprehensive win with 5.2 overs in hand.

NEW ZEALAND		Runs	Balls	4/6	SRI LANKA		Runs	Balls	4/6
J.G.Wright	c Silva b John	11	25	2	S.Wettimuny	c Edgar b Cairns	1	27	–
B.A.Edgar	c Silva b Ratnayeke	6	50	–	† S.A.R.Silva	c Boock b Chatfield	21	34	4
M.D.Crowe	b Ranatunga	23	44	1	R.S.Madugalle	c Wright b Chatfield	31	38	5
J.F.Reid	c Ratnayeke b De Mel	21	46	–	A.Ranatunga	c Reid b Coney	9	15	–
J.J.Crowe	not out	57	66	5/1	R.L.Dias	c Wright b Boock	34	48	1
* J.V.Coney	c P.A.de Silva b John	24	24	1/1	* L.R.D.Mendis	c J.J.Crowe b Coney	3	6	–
B.L.Cairns	c P.A.de Silva b John	4	7	–	P.A.de Silva	not out	50	54	4
† I.D.S.Smith	not out	5	5	–	A.L.F.de Mel	not out	15	23	1
M.C.Snedden					D.S.de Silva				
S.L.Boock					J.R.Ratnayeke				
E.J.Chatfield					V.B.John				
Extras	(b 1, lb 14, w 3, nb 2)	20			Extras	(b 3, lb 5, nb 2)	10		
Total	(45 overs; 6 wickets)	**171**			**Total**	(39.4 overs; 6 wickets)	**174**		

SRI LANKA	O	M	R	W	NEW ZEALAND	O	M	R	W
De Mel	9	3	29	1	Snedden	6	1	30	0
John	9	2	39	3	Cairns	6.4	2	37	1
Ratnayeke	9	0	40	1	Chatfield	9	0	36	2
Ranatunga	9	0	23	1	Boock	9	0	29	1
D.S.de Silva	9	1	25	0	Coney	4	0	16	2
					M.D.Crowe	5	0	18	0

FALL OF WICKETS
1-20, 2-36, 3-58, 4-84, 5-124, 6-133

FALL OF WICKETS
1-13, 2-43, 3-62, 4-75, 5-79, 6-144

Umpires: D.P.Buultjens (4) and H.C.Felsinger (6).

SRI LANKA v NEW ZEALAND 1984-85

At Tyronne Fernando Stadium, Moratuwa on 4 November 1984.   Result: **NEW ZEALAND** won by 7 wickets.
Toss: New Zealand.   Award: M.D.Crowe.   LOI debuts: New Zealand – E.J.Gray.   39-over match.

A flawless innings by Martin Crowe enabled New Zealand to square this brief series.

SRI LANKA		Runs	Balls	4/6
S.Wettimuny	b M.D.Crowe	3	30	–
S.A.R.Silva	c Smith b M.D.Crowe	9	50	–
R.S.Madugalle	run out	0	2	–
R.L.Dias	st Smith b Coney	10	27	–
L.R.D.Mendis	c Snedden b Stirling	13	35	–
A.Ranatunga	run out	15	33	–
P.A.de Silva	run out	15	19	–
A.L.F.de Mel	c M.D.Crowe b Stirling	15	11	–/1
D.S.de Silva	b Chatfield	13	22	–
J.R.Ratnayeke	not out	7	19	–
V.B.John	not out	0	3	–
Extras	(b 3, lb 7, w 1, nb 3)	14		
Total	(39 overs; 9 wickets)	**114**		

NEW ZEALAND		Runs	Balls	4/6
J.G.Wright	b De Mel	6	18	–
P.E.McEwan	c P.A.de Silva b De Mel	9	22	–
J.F.Reid	c Dias b Ranatunga	34	94	3
M.D.Crowe	not out	52	57	7/1
J.J.Crowe	not out	7	6	1
* J.V.Coney				
E.J.Gray				
† I.D.S.Smith				
D.A.Stirling				
M.C.Snedden				
E.J.Chatfield				
Extras	(lb 3, w 5, nb 2)	10		
Total	(31.4 overs; 3 wickets)	**118**		

NEW ZEALAND	O	M	R	W
Chatfield	9	2	16	1
Snedden	7	2	14	0
M.D.Crowe	9	3	20	2
Stirling	7	2	29	2
Coney	4	0	7	1
McEwan	3	0	18	0

SRI LANKA	O	M	R	W
De Mel	7	3	26	2
John	9	2	40	0
Ratnayeke	6	0	10	0
D.S.de Silva	4	1	14	0
Ranatunga	5.4	1	25	1

FALL OF WICKETS
1-15, 2-19, 3-98

FALL OF WICKETS
1-12, 2-12, 3-22, 4-35, 5-47, 6-66, 7-91, 8-91, 9-114

Umpires: K.T.Francis (5) and P.W.Vidanagamage (5).

PAKISTAN v NEW ZEALAND 1984-85

At Shahi Bagh Stadium, Peshawar on 12 November 1984.   Result: **PAKISTAN** won by 46 runs.   Toss: New Zealand.
Award: Zakir Khan.   LOI debuts: Pakistan – Zakir Khan.   39-over match.

Zakir Khan wrecked New Zealand's innings with his lone four-wicket haul in 17 limited-overs internationals.

PAKISTAN		Runs	Balls	4/6
Sajid Ali	c J.J.Crowe b Cairns	16	44	1
Saadat Ali	c Cairns b Chatfield	1	13	–
* Zaheer Abbas	lbw b Cairns	13	16	1
Javed Miandad	not out	80	86	4/2
Naved Anjum	c M.D.Crowe b Stirling	29	36	2
Manzoor Elahi	c Stirling b Snedden	15	22	1
Mudassar Nazar	not out	17	21	–
Sarfraz Nawaz				
† Anil Dalpat				
Tausif Ahmed				
Zakir Khan				
Extras	(b 2, lb 8, w 8, nb 2)	20		
Total	(39 overs; 5 wickets)	**191**		

NEW ZEALAND		Runs	Balls	4/6
J.J.Crowe	c Anil b Zakir	8	26	1
J.G.Wright	lbw b Manzoor	8	16	1
M.D.Crowe	c Anil b Zakir	8	10	1
P.E.McEwan	lbw b Zakir	3	6	–
J.F.Reid	c Miandad b Zakir	14	22	1
* J.V.Coney	c and b Mudassar	23	36	1
† I.D.S.Smith	c Sajid b Mudassar	59	60	5
M.C.Snedden	c Anil b Mudassar	1	5	–
B.L.Cairns	c Zaheer b Tausif	7	11	1
D.A.Stirling	run out	2	7	–
E.J.Chatfield	not out	1	4	–
Extras	(lb 4, w 7)	11		
Total	(36.2 overs)	**145**		

NEW ZEALAND	O	M	R	W
Stirling	8	0	32	1
Cairns	8	0	38	2
Chatfield	7	0	38	1
M.D.Crowe	8	0	37	0
Snedden	8	0	36	1

PAKISTAN	O	M	R	W
Manzoor Elahi	8	1	27	1
Zakir Khan	8	2	19	4
Sarfraz Nawaz	4	1	18	0
Naved Anjum	3	0	13	0
Tausif Ahmed	7	0	30	1
Mudassar Nazar	6.2	0	34	3

FALL OF WICKETS
1-14, 2-27, 3-38, 4-87, 5-123

FALL OF WICKETS
1-19, 2-19, 3-22, 4-39, 5-44, 6-99, 7-103, 8-113, 9-142, 10-145

Umpires: Athar Zaidi (1) and Javed Akhtar (6).

PAKISTAN v NEW ZEALAND 1984-85

At Iqbal Stadium, Faisalabad on 23 November 1984. Result: **PAKISTAN** won by 5 runs. Toss: New Zealand.
Award: Salim Malik. LOI debuts: Pakistan – Shoaib Mohammed, Wasim Akram. 20-over match.

Rain reduced this contest to a farcical 20-over slog, each bowler being restricted to four overs.

PAKISTAN		Runs	Balls	4/6
Mohsin Khan	b M.D.Crowe	0	3	–
Salim Malik	b Snedden	41	34	1
* Zaheer Abbas	c Stirling b Snedden	25	34	4/1
Javed Miandad	run out	20	15	2
Manzoor Elahi	not out	39	29	2/2
Mudassar Nazar	lbw b M.D.Crowe	10	11	1
Shoaib Mohammed	not out	10	9	1
† Anil Dalpat				
Zakir Khan				
Wasim Akram				
Tausif Ahmed				
Extras	(lb 7, w 4, nb 1)	12		
Total	(20 overs; 5 wickets)	**157**		

NEW ZEALAND		Runs	Balls	4/6
J.G.Wright	b Mudassar	55	47	5
J.J.Crowe	lbw b Zakir	7	14	–
M.D.Crowe	c Zaheer b Mudassar	19	17	3
P.E.McEwan	lbw b Mudassar	7	8	–
B.L.Cairns	c Salim b Mudassar	10	14	–/1
J.G.Bracewell	not out	17	14	1
† I.D.S.Smith	run out	3	4	–
D.A.Stirling	run out	1	1	–
* J.V.Coney	not out	17	7	4
M.C.Snedden				
E.J.Chatfield				
Extras	(b 2, lb 7, w 7)	16		
Total	(20 overs; 7 wickets)	**152**		

NEW ZEALAND	O	M	R	W
M.D.Crowe	4	0	17	2
Coney	2	0	10	0
Cairns	4	0	25	0
Chatfield	2	0	25	0
Snedden	4	0	41	2
Stirling	4	0	32	0

PAKISTAN	O	M	R	W
Wasim Akram	4	0	31	0
Zakir Khan	4	0	28	1
Manzoor Elahi	4	0	31	0
Mudassar Nazar	4	0	27	4
Tausif Ahmed	4	0	26	0

FALL OF WICKETS
1-3, 2-67, 3-81, 4-105, 5-128

FALL OF WICKETS
1-20, 2-61, 3-78, 4-106, 5-112, 6-127, 7-132

Umpires: Amanullah Khan (6) and Ikram Rabbani (1).

PAKISTAN v NEW ZEALAND 1984-85

At Jinnah Park, Sialkot on 2 December 1984. Result: **NEW ZEALAND** won by 34 runs. Toss: Pakistan.
Award: M.D.Crowe. LOI debuts: Pakistan – Mohsin Kamal. 36-over match.

Salim Malik became the first non-substitute fielder to hold four catches in a limited-overs international. New Zealand's first win of the Pakistan section of their tour, following four defeats and a draw, kept this four-match series alive.

NEW ZEALAND		Runs	Balls	4/6
J.G.Wright	c Salim Malik b Kamal	24	46	3
J.G.Bracewell	c Salim Malik b Kamal	1	7	–
J.F.Reid	run out	34	66	3
M.D.Crowe	b Kamal	67	61	8/1
J.J.Crowe	not out	15	18	2
P.E.McEwan	st Salim Yousuf b Tausif	4	5	1
B.L.Cairns	b Tausif	0	2	–
* J.V.Coney	run out	1	1	–
† I.D.S.Smith	c Salim Malik b Tausif	9	5	1
D.A.Stirling	c Salim Malik b Tausif	4	7	–
M.C.Snedden	not out	0	–	–
Extras	(lb 6, w 21, nb 1)	28		
Total	(36 overs; 9 wickets)	**187**		

PAKISTAN		Runs	Balls	4/6
Mohsin Khan	lbw b Stirling	2	2	–
Shoaib Mohammed	lbw b M.D.Crowe	22	27	1/1
Salim Malik	b M.D.Crowe	6	11	1
Javed Miandad	c Wright b Cairns	14	26	1
* Zaheer Abbas	c J.J.Crowe b Bracewell	42	51	2
Manzoor Elahi	b Cairns	16	30	1
Mudassar Nazar	c Stirling b Snedden	3	7	–
† Salim Yousuf	lbw b Bracewell	1	6	–
Tausif Ahmed	not out	27	34	1
Zakir Khan	not out	8	25	–
Mohsin Kamal				
Extras	(lb 6, w 3, nb 3)	12		
Total	(36 overs; 8 wickets)	**153**		

PAKISTAN	O	M	R	W
Mohsin Kamal	8	0	46	3
Zakir Khan	8	0	22	0
Mudassar Nazar	8	0	58	0
Manzoor Elahi	6	0	17	0
Tausif Ahmed	6	0	38	4

NEW ZEALAND	O	M	R	W
Stirling	8	0	36	1
M.D.Crowe	5	0	21	2
Cairns	6	0	30	2
Snedden	8	0	29	1
Bracewell	8	0	23	2
Coney	1	0	8	0

FALL OF WICKETS
1-14, 2-47, 3-128, 4-156, 5-162, 6-166, 7-168, 8-178, 9-187

FALL OF WICKETS
1-2, 2-14, 3-42, 4-52, 5-90, 6-97, 7-100, 8-133

Umpires: Rab Nawaz (2) and Shakoor Rana (11).

PAKISTAN v NEW ZEALAND 1984-85

At Ibn-e-Qasim Bagh Stadium, Multan on 7 December 1984.   Result: **PAKISTAN** won by 1 wicket.   Toss: New Zealand.
Award: Zaheer Abbas.   LOI debuts: Pakistan – Masood Iqbal.   35-over match.

This series was decided off the final ball when last man Mohsin Kamal scored the winning run. Crowd disturbances involving police and tear gas delayed the start and reduced the match to 35 overs. Zaheer Abbas's fifty came from 45 balls.

NEW ZEALAND		Runs	Balls	4/6	PAKISTAN		Runs	Balls	4/6
J.G.Wright	b Tausif	11	26	1	Saadat Ali	c Bracewell b Stirling	6	9	–
P.E.McEwan	c Saadat b Kamal	22	35	2	Shoaib Mohammed	c Bracewell b Coney	35	44	5
J.F.Reid	run out	10	13	2	* Zaheer Abbas	b Bracewell	73	62	9
M.D.Crowe	run out	28	26	3	Javed Miandad	c Smith b Snedden	32	39	1
J.J.Crowe	run out	13	23	1	Salim Malik	c Cairns b Snedden	28	22	2
J.V.Coney	c Salim b Zaheer	34	37	3	Manzoor Elahi	c Bracewell b Snedden	8	9	–
I.D.S.Smith	c Miandad b Saadat	41	40	4	Mudassar Nazar	run out	1	2	–
B.L.Cairns	c Salim b Saadat	2	4	–	Tausif Ahmed	not out	15	17	–
J.G.Bracewell	not out	14	13	–	Shahid Mahboob	lbw b M.D.Crowe	1	3	–
D.A.Stirling	not out	1	3	–	† Masood Iqbal	run out	2	2	–
M.C.Snedden					Mohsin Kamal	not out	5	5	–
Extras	(b 18, lb 8, w 10, nb 1)	37			Extras	(lb 5, w 1, nb 2)	8		
Total	(35 overs; 8 wickets)	**213**			**Total**	(35 overs; 9 wickets)	**214**		

PAKISTAN	O	M	R	W	NEW ZEALAND	O	M	R	W
Mohsin Kamal	5	0	21	1	M.D.Crowe	5	0	22	1
Shahid Mahboob	4	0	18	0	Stirling	7	0	44	1
Tausif Ahmed	7	0	30	1	Snedden	7	0	38	3
Mudassar Nazar	7	0	40	0	Cairns	5	0	42	0
Zaheer Abbas	6	0	35	1	Coney	4	0	27	1
Manzoor Elahi	2	0	19	0	Bracewell	7	0	36	1
Saadat Ali	4	0	24	2					

FALL OF WICKETS
1-40, 2-47, 3-64, 4-110, 5-114, 6-179, 7-183, 8-211

FALL OF WICKETS
1-8, 2-80, 3-148, 4-154, 5-164, 6-169, 7-199, 8-203, 9-206

Umpires: Said Ahmed Shah (1) and B.K.Tahir (1).

INDIA v ENGLAND 1984-85

At Nehru Stadium, Poona on 5 December 1984.   Result: **ENGLAND** won by 4 wickets.   Toss: England.
Awards: D.B.Vengsarkar and M.W.Gatting.   LOI debuts: India – R.S.Ghai, K.S.More; England – R.M.Ellison, R.T.Robinson.   45-over match.

Mike Gatting's only hundred in 88 limited-overs international innings carried England to victory, his unbroken seventh-wicket partnership of 86 with Paul Downton being scored off 85 balls.

INDIA		Runs	Balls	4/6	ENGLAND		Runs	Balls	4/6
K.Srikkanth	b Edmonds	50	83	6	G.Fowler	c Yashpal b Sharma	5		1
* S.M.Gavaskar	b Foster	0			R.T.Robinson	lbw b Ghai	15		2
D.B.Vengsarkar	b Ellison	105	131	10/1	M.W.Gatting	not out	115	134	12
S.M.Patil	run out	2		–	A.J.Lamb	c and b Prabhakar	3		–
Yashpal Sharma	c Ellison b Foster	37		4	V.J.Marks	run out	31		–
R.J.Shastri	c Ellison b Foster	11		1	* D.I.Gower	c Shastri b Binny	3		–
R.M.H.Binny	not out	0		–	R.M.Ellison	run out	4		–
† K.S.More					† P.R.Downton	not out	27		1
M.Prabhakar					P.H.Edmonds				
C.Sharma					N.A.Foster				
R.S.Ghai					N.G.Cowans				
Extras	(lb 2, w 7)	9			Extras	(lb 8, nb 4)	12		
Total	(45 overs; 6 wickets)	**214**			**Total**	(43.2 overs; 6 wickets)	**215**		

ENGLAND	O	M	R	W	INDIA	O	M	R	W
Cowans	8	0	32	0	Sharma	8.2	0	50	1
Foster	10	0	44	3	Prabhakar	10	1	27	1
Ellison	7	0	45	1	Ghai	9	0	38	1
Marks	10	0	48	0	Shastri	8	0	49	0
Edmonds	10	0	43	1	Binny	8	0	43	1

FALL OF WICKETS
1-1, 2-119, 3-126, 4-189, 5-212, 6-214

FALL OF WICKETS
1-14, 2-43, 3-47, 4-114, 5-117, 6-129

Umpires: S.Banerjee (2) and Mohammad Ghouse (2).

INDIA v ENGLAND 1984-85

At Barabati Stadium, Cuttack on 27 December 1984.　　Result: **ENGLAND** won on faster scoring rate.　Toss: England.
Award: R.J.Shastri.　　LOI debuts: None.　49-over match.

After conceding India's record opening partnership in all limited-overs internationals, England opted to continue batting in appalling light until 20 runs from two overs put them ahead on scoring rate for the first time, by 0.08 of a run.

INDIA		Runs	Balls	4/6	ENGLAND		Runs	Balls	4/6
K.Srikkanth	lbw b Gatting	99	112	4/3	G.Fowler	c Shastri b Binny	15		–
R.J.Shastri	b Gatting	102	145	6/1	R.T.Robinson	b Prabhakar	1		–
D.B.Vengsarkar	c Gower b Marks	23		3	M.W.Gatting	b Patel	59		4
Yashpal Sharma	lbw b Marks	4		–	* D.I.Gower	c Prabhakar b Binny	21		2
M.Amarnath	not out	1		–	A.J.Lamb	run out	28		2
R.M.H.Binny	b Marks	2		–	V.J.Marks	run out	44		4
* S.M.Gavaskar	not out	6		–	† P.R.Downton	not out	44		3
† K.S.More					R.M.Ellison	not out	14		–
M.Prabhakar					P.H.Edmonds				
R.S.Ghai					N.A.Foster				
A.K.Patel					N.G.Cowans				
Extras	(b 5, lb 5, w 3, nb 2)	15			Extras	(lb 9, w 1, nb 5)	15		
Total	(49 overs; 5 wickets)	252			Total	(46 overs; 6 wickets)	241		

ENGLAND	O	M	R	W	INDIA	O	M	R	W
Foster	5	0	26	0	Ghai	8	0	40	0
Cowans	10	0	39	0	Prabhakar	10	1	34	1
Ellison	6	0	31	0	Binny	7	0	48	2
Edmonds	10	0	47	0	Patel	10	0	53	1
Marks	8	0	50	3	Shastri	10	0	48	0
Gatting	10	0	49	2	Amarnath	1	0	9	0

FALL OF WICKETS
1-188, 2-235, 3-243, 4-243, 5-246

FALL OF WICKETS
1-3, 2-50, 3-93, 4-128, 5-145, 6-203

Umpires: J.D.Ghosh (3) and P.G.Pandit (4).

INDIA v ENGLAND 1984-85

At Chinnaswamy Stadium, Bangalore on 20 January 1985.　　Result: **ENGLAND** won by 3 wickets.　Toss: England.
Award: A.J.Lamb.　　LOI debuts: India – M.Azharuddin, S.Viswanath.　46-over match.

A disappointed home crowd reacted by throwing bottles on to the field when five overs of England's innings remained. Sunil Gavaskar led his players off and there was a 25-minute delay before Allan Lamb took England to an unassailable 3-0 series lead.

INDIA		Runs	Balls	4/6	ENGLAND		Runs	Balls	4/6
* S.M.Gavaskar	c Gatting b Marks	40		3	G.Fowler	run out	45		4
K.Srikkanth	b Cowans	29		2/1	R.T.Robinson	c Viswanath b Kapil Dev	2		–
D.B.Vengsarkar	st Downton b Marks	23		2	M.W.Gatting	run out	3		–
Kapil Dev	c Gower b Marks	8		–	* D.I.Gower	b Shastri	38		4
Yashpal Sharma	run out	8		–	A.J.Lamb	not out	59	87	4/1
R.J.Shastri	b Edmonds	33		1	V.J.Marks	c Gavaskar b Patel	17		1
M.Azharuddin	not out	47		6	† P.R.Downton	c Shastri b Kapil Dev	12		2
† S.Viswanath	not out	6		–	P.H.Edmonds	c Viswanath b Kapil Dev	7		1
A.K.Patel					R.M.Ellison	not out	1		–
R.S.Ghai					N.A.Foster				
T.A.P.Sekhar					N.G.Cowans				
Extras	(b 4, lb 6, w 1)	11			Extras	(lb 10, w 7, nb 5)	22		
Total	(46 overs; 6 wickets)	205			Total	(45 overs; 7 wickets)	206		

ENGLAND	O	M	R	W	INDIA	O	M	R	W
Cowans	10	1	31	1	Kapil Dev	10	0	38	3
Foster	6	0	33	0	Sekhar	9	0	36	0
Ellison	6	0	25	0	Patel	10	1	42	1
Marks	10	1	35	3	Ghai	4	0	37	0
Edmonds	10	0	44	1	Shastri	10	2	29	1
Gatting	4	0	27	0	Yashpal Sharma	2	0	14	0

FALL OF WICKETS
1-70, 2-70, 3-90, 4-108, 5-119, 6-185

FALL OF WICKETS
1-15, 2-21, 3-91, 4-103, 5-144, 6-186, 7-204

Umpires: S.K.Das (1) and R.V.Ramani (2).

INDIA v ENGLAND 1984-85

At Vidarbha CA Ground, Nagpur on 23 January 1985.   Result: INDIA won by 3 wickets.   Toss: India.
Award: Kapil Dev.   LOI debuts: India – L.S.Rajput; England – J.P.Agnew, C.S.Cowdrey, M.D.Moxon.   50-over match.

Two spectators were killed and more than 20 injured when a temporary stand collapsed during Nagpur's first international.

ENGLAND		Runs	Balls	4/6
G.Fowler	b Shastri	37		3
M.D.Moxon	c Srikkanth b Kapil Dev	70	126	7
M.W.Gatting	b Shastri	1		–
D.I.Gower	c and b Shastri	11		1
A.J.Lamb	st Viswanath b Shastri	30	26	1/2
C.S.Cowdrey	not out	46	41	4/1
V.J.Marks	b Sekhar	4		–
R.Downton	c Rajput b Sekhar	13		1
P.H.Edmonds	not out	8		1
P.Agnew				
N.G.Cowans				
Extras	(b 3, lb 15, w 1, nb 1)	20		
Total	(50 overs; 7 wickets)	240		

INDIA		Runs	Balls	4/6
K.Srikkanth	b Cowans	6		1
L.S.Rajput	c Downton b Cowans	0		–
D.B.Vengsarkar	c Downton b Agnew	11		1
M.Azharuddin	b Cowdrey	47	66	2/2
* S.M.Gavaskar	b Agnew	52		4
Kapil Dev	c Gatting b Cowans	54	44	3/4
R.J.Shastri	not out	24		–
M.Prabhakar	b Agnew	4		–
† S.Viswanath	not out	23		3
T.A.P.Sekhar				
A.K.Patel				
Extras	(b 3, lb 14, w 1, nb 2)	20		
Total	(47.4 overs; 7 wickets)	241		

INDIA	O	M	R	W
Kapil Dev	10	1	42	1
Prabhakar	10	1	36	0
Sekhar	10	0	50	2
Patel	10	1	54	0
Shastri	10	1	40	4

ENGLAND	O	M	R	W
Cowans	10	0	44	3
Agnew	10	0	38	3
Marks	6	0	32	0
Edmonds	10	0	44	0
Cowdrey	7.4	0	52	1
Gatting	4	0	14	0

FALL OF WICKETS
1-70, 2-78, 3-100, 4-154, 5-176, 6-199, 7-221

FALL OF WICKETS
1-5, 2-11, 3-31, 4-90, 5-166, 6-197, 7-204

Umpires: R.Mrithyunjayan (2) and A.L.Narasimhan (2).

INDIA v ENGLAND 1984-85

At Sector 16 Stadium, Chandigarh on 27 January 1985.   Result: ENGLAND won by 7 runs.   Toss: India.
Award: R.J.Shastri.   LOI debuts: England – B.N.French.   15-over match.

Kapil Dev's home city enjoyed a modest international baptism. After a freak overnight storm had flooded the ground, the teams played a 15-over affair in slippery conditions to appease a crowd of 25,000.

ENGLAND		Runs	Balls	4/6
G.Fowler	run out	17	15	1
M.W.Gatting	c Azharuddin b Sekhar	31	29	2
D.I.Gower	b Sekhar	19	13	1/1
A.J.Lamb	not out	33	19	2/2
C.S.Cowdrey	c Rajput b Shastri	5	3	1
P.H.Edmonds	c Azharuddin b Sekhar	5	3	–
V.J.Marks	run out	2	3	–
R.M.Ellison	not out	4	5	–
P.Agnew				
N.A.Foster				
B.N.French				
Extras	(lb 5)	5		
Total	(15 overs; 6 wickets)	121		

INDIA		Runs	Balls	4/6
R.J.Shastri	run out	53	45	5
K.Srikkanth	run out	9	9	1
Kapil Dev	c Agnew b Edmonds	17	15	–
M.Azharuddin	c Gatting b Edmonds	10	11	1
Yashpal Sharma	b Cowdrey	6	6	1
* S.M.Gavaskar	not out	2	4	–
L.S.Rajput	not out	1	1	–
† S.Viswanath				
T.A.P.Sekhar				
M.Prabhakar				
C.Sharma				
Extras	(lb 4, w 12)	16		
Total	(15 overs; 5 wickets)	114		

INDIA	O	M	R	W
Kapil Dev	3	0	17	0
Prabhakar	3	0	26	0
Sharma	3	0	20	0
Sekhar	3	0	23	3
Shastri	3	0	30	1

ENGLAND	O	M	R	W
Agnew	3	0	23	0
Foster	3	0	17	0
Ellison	3	0	20	0
Edmonds	3	0	20	2
Gatting	2	0	27	0
Cowdrey	1	0	3	1

FALL OF WICKETS
1-31, 2-71, 3-74, 4-86, 5-93, 6-104

FALL OF WICKETS
1-22, 2-49, 3-83, 4-111, 5-112

Umpires: R.B.Gupta (1) and B.Nagaraja Rao (1).

AUSTRALIA v WEST INDIES 1984-85

At Melbourne Cricket Ground on 6 January 1985.   Result: **WEST INDIES** won by 7 wickets.   Toss: West Indies.
Award: D.L.Haynes.   LOI debuts: Australia – C.J.McDermott, S.P.O'Donnell.

Graeme Wood was out to the first ball of the match. Desmond Haynes's sixth LOI hundred was his third in consecutive innings against Australia, all undefeated.

AUSTRALIA		Runs	Balls	4/6
G.M.Wood	c Holding b Garner	0	1	–
A.M.J.Hilditch	c Holding b Baptiste	27	53	3
K.C.Wessels	run out	33	57	2
* A.R.Border	c Baptiste b Garner	73	101	5
D.C.Boon	b Marshall	55	62	2
† W.B.Phillips	c Greenidge b Garner	23	16	1/1
S.P.O'Donnell	not out	7	6	–
G.F.Lawson	not out	8	8	–
M.J.Bennett				
C.J.McDermott				
R.M.Hogg				
Extras	(lb 7, w 4, nb 3)	14		
Total	(50 overs; 6 wickets)	240		

WEST INDIES		Runs	Balls	4/6
C.G.Greenidge	b Bennett	12	46	1
D.L.Haynes	not out	123	130	15
R.B.Richardson	c Boon b Lawson	34	48	4
I.V.A.Richards	c Phillips b McDermott	47	43	4/1
H.A.Gomes	not out	2	2	–
* C.H.Lloyd				
† P.J.L.Dujon				
M.D.Marshall				
E.A.E.Baptiste				
M.A.Holding				
J.Garner				
Extras	(b 1, lb 17, w 5)	23		
Total	(44.5 overs; 3 wickets)	241		

WEST INDIES	O	M	R	W
Garner	10	2	41	3
Marshall	10	0	32	1
Baptiste	9	0	73	1
Holding	10	1	41	0
Richards	10	1	37	0
Gomes	1	0	9	0

AUSTRALIA	O	M	R	W
Lawson	10	0	45	1
McDermott	9.5	0	52	1
Hogg	8	0	43	0
O'Donnell	3	0	24	0
Bennett	10	2	23	1
Wessels	2	0	18	0
Border	2	0	18	0

FALL OF WICKETS
1-0, 2-48, 3-78, 4-193, 5-220, 6-224

FALL OF WICKETS
1-69, 2-140, 3-234

Umpires: A.R.Crafter (27) and P.J.McConnell (13).

AUSTRALIA v SRI LANKA 1984-85

At Sydney Cricket Ground on 8 January 1985.   Result: **AUSTRALIA** won by 6 wickets.   Toss: Sri Lanka.
Award: A.R.Border.   LOI debuts: None.

Sri Lanka's concession of 2½ overs to no-balls and wides proved crucial in a tight finish to their first experience of floodlit cricket. Graeme Wood retired because of cramp. Australia were fined $600 for an over-rate which reduced the match to 49 overs.

SRI LANKA		Runs	Balls	4/6
S.Wettimuny	c Phillips b Rackemann	20	64	2
† S.A.R.Silva	c Bennett b Hogg	68	109	7
D.S.B.P.Kuruppu	c Wood b Bennett	22	31	2
R.L.Dias	c Border b O'Donnell	60	60	2
* L.R.D.Mendis	b Hogg	16	11	3
P.A.de Silva	b Hogg	17	15	1
A.L.F.de Mel	b Hogg	0	1	–
J.R.Ratnayeke	not out	8	10	–
R.J.Ratnayake	not out	4	2	1
D.S.de Silva				
V.B.John				
Extras	(b 5, lb 5, w 13, nb 1)	24		
Total	(49 overs; 7 wickets)	239		

AUSTRALIA		Runs	Balls	4/6
A.M.J.Hilditch	run out	23	58	–
G.M.Wood	retired hurt	52	75	5
K.C.Wessels	c Silva b Ratnayeke	1	6	–
* A.R.Border	not out	79	82	7
D.C.Boon	c sub (S.H.U.Karnain) b De Mel	44	57	3
† W.B.Phillips	c Silva b De Mel	3	2	–
S.P.O'Donnell	not out	20	18	1
M.J.Bennett				
C.J.McDermott				
R.M.Hogg				
C.G.Rackemann				
Extras	(b 4, lb 4, w 4, nb 6)	18		
Total	(46.2 overs; 4 wickets)	240		

AUSTRALIA	O	M	R	W
Hogg	10	0	47	4
O'Donnell	9	2	39	1
McDermott	10	1	49	0
Bennett	10	1	44	1
Rackemann	10	0	50	1

SRI LANKA	O	M	R	W
De Mel	9.3	0	59	2
John	9	1	40	0
Ratnayake	8.5	0	32	0
Ratnayeke	9	0	69	1
D.S.de Silva	10	1	32	0

FALL OF WICKETS
1-66, 2-104, 3-160, 4-181, 5-214, 6-214, 7-229

FALL OF WICKETS
1-68, 2-70, 3-171, 4-176

Umpires: R.A.French (32) and P.J.McConnell (14).

WEST INDIES v SRI LANKA 1984-85

At Tasmanian CA Ground, Hobart on 10 January 1985.   Result: **WEST INDIES** won by 8 wickets.   Toss: West Indies.
Award: L.R.D.Mendis.   LOI debuts: West Indies – C.A.Walsh.

This was the first international to be played in Tasmania. Having courageously resisted the West Indies pace attack on a lively pitch, Duleep Mendis savaged 29 runs off his last nine balls, all off-breaks from Viv Richards, who captained throughout the remaining preliminary matches.

SRI LANKA		Runs	Balls	4/6
S.Wettimuny	c Richards b Garner	8	32	1
S.A.R.Silva	c Dujon b Garner	4	24	–
D.S.B.P.Kuruppu	c Richardson b Holding	8	29	1
R.L.Dias	c Dujon b Walsh	27	56	2
L.R.D.Mendis	run out	56	48	8
P.A.de Silva	c sub (R.A.Harper) b Richards	8	26	–
J.R.Ratnayeke	b Richards	8	22	1
S.H.U.Karnain	not out	20	28	–/2
R.J.Ratnayake	not out	23	48	1
D.S.de Silva				
V.B.John				
Extras	(b 12, lb 10, w 12, nb 1)	35		
Total	(50 overs; 7 wickets)	**197**		

WEST INDIES		Runs	Balls	4/6
C.G.Greenidge	c Kuruppu b D.S.de Silva	61	107	5
D.L.Haynes	c Silva b Ratnayake	32	32	7
R.B.Richardson	not out	52	85	4/1
A.L.Logie	not out	34	30	2/2
* I.V.A.Richards				
H.A.Gomes				
† P.J.L.Dujon				
M.D.Marshall				
M.A.Holding				
J.Garner				
C.A.Walsh				
Extras	(lb 11, w 5, nb 3)	19		
Total	(40.4 overs; 2 wickets)	**198**		

WEST INDIES	O	M	R	W
Marshall	10	3	37	0
Garner	10	1	19	2
Holding	10	1	25	1
Walsh	10	1	47	1
Richards	10	2	47	2

SRI LANKA	O	M	R	W
John	6.4	2	30	0
Ratnayeke	7	0	41	0
Ratnayake	7	0	31	1
D.S.de Silva	10	3	29	1
Karnain	8	0	41	0
P.A.de Silva	2	0	15	0

FALL OF WICKETS
1-19, 2-24, 3-39, 4-115, 5-127, 6-142, 7-145

FALL OF WICKETS
1-50, 2-144

Umpires: R.C.Isherwood (8) and S.G.Randell (5).

WEST INDIES v SRI LANKA 1984-85

At Woolloongabba, Brisbane on 12 January 1985.   Result: **WEST INDIES** won by 90 runs.   Toss: Sri Lanka.
Award: I.V.A.Richards.   LOI debuts: None.

West Indies overcame the absence of their injured star openers to record the highest World Series total at The Gabba so far. The fifth-wicket stand of 152 between Viv Richards and Clive Lloyd remains the West Indies record and was the world LOI record until 1995-96. Michael Holding became the first to take 100 LOI wickets for West Indies.

WEST INDIES		Runs	Balls	4/6
R.B.Richardson	c Silva b John	1	4	–
T.R.O.Payne	c John b Karnain	20	48	2
H.A.Gomes	c Silva b Karnain	28	61	4
* I.V.A.Richards	c Silva b John	98	98	6/3
A.L.Logie	c P.A.de Silva b D.S.de Silva	10	10	2
C.H.Lloyd	not out	89	76	7/3
† P.J.L.Dujon	c Mendis b Ratnayake	11	10	2
M.D.Marshall	not out	1	1	–
M.A.Holding				
W.W.Davis				
J.Garner				
Extras	(b 1, lb 5, w 4, nb 2)	12		
Total	(50 overs; 6 wickets)	**270**		

SRI LANKA		Runs	Balls	4/6
S.Wettimuny	c Dujon b Garner	2	23	–
† S.A.R.Silva	b Davis	20	33	2
D.S.B.P.Kuruppu	c Payne b Holding	4	30	–
R.L.Dias	c Dujon b Holding	80	109	9
* L.R.D.Mendis	b Holding	14	13	2
P.A.de Silva	c Richards b Davis	13	19	–/1
S.H.U.Karnain	st Dujon b Richards	9	24	–
R.J.Ratnayake	st Dujon b Richards	19	17	–/2
D.S.de Silva	b Lloyd	9	20	1
V.B.John	c Logie b Gomes	0	1	–
G.N.de Silva	not out	2	6	–
Extras	(lb 3, w 3, nb 2)	8		
Total	(48.1 overs)	**180**		

SRI LANKA	O	M	R	W
G.N.de Silva	10	0	42	0
John	10	2	52	2
Ratnayake	10	0	39	1
Karnain	10	0	55	2
D.S.de Silva	8	0	57	1
Dias	2	0	19	0

WEST INDIES	O	M	R	W
Marshall	5	2	9	0
Garner	5	2	14	1
Holding	10	0	38	3
Davis	10	0	29	2
Richards	10	0	45	2
Gomes	8	0	42	1
Lloyd	0.1	0	0	1

FALL OF WICKETS
1-7, 2-45, 3-73, 4-92, 5-244, 6-269

FALL OF WICKETS
1-4, 2-29, 3-35, 4-59, 5-88, 6-114, 7-144, 8-176, 9-177, 10-180

Umpires: R.A.French (33) and M.W.Johnson (27).

AUSTRALIA v WEST INDIES 1984-85

At Woolloongabba, Brisbane on 13 January 1985.　Result: **WEST INDIES** won by 5 wickets.　Toss: West Indies.
Award: C.H.Lloyd.　LOI debuts: None.

Ponderous batting by Kepler Wessels, who spent 25 overs making 47, led to panic in the lower order and four run outs, three of them victims of the 40-year-old Clive Lloyd.

AUSTRALIA		Runs	Balls	4/6
G.M.Wood	c Dujon b Richards	38	70	2
A.M.J.Hilditch	c Garner b Davis	19	51	1
K.C.Wessels	c Logie b Richards	47	75	2
* A.R.Border	run out	7	15	–
D.C.Boon	lbw b Richards	4	8	–
S.P.O'Donnell	run out	25	37	–
† S.J.Rixon	run out	3	11	–
M.J.Bennett	c Logie b Marshall	3	12	–
G.F.Lawson	c Dujon b Garner	7	7	1
C.J.McDermott	run out	13	13	1
R.M.Hogg	not out	6	11	–
Extras	(lb 10, w 4, nb 5)	19		
Total	(50 overs)	**191**		

WEST INDIES		Runs	Balls	4/6
D.L.Haynes	c Hogg b O'Donnell	46	67	6
R.B.Richardson	b McDermott	16	23	3
H.A.Gomes	b McDermott	0	2	–
I.V.A.Richards	c Border b Hogg	49	62	6/1
* C.H.Lloyd	not out	52	61	6/1
A.L.Logie	c Rixon b O'Donnell	7	14	1
† P.J.L.Dujon	not out	6	3	1
M.D.Marshall				
M.A.Holding				
W.W.Davis				
J.Garner				
Extras	(b 5, lb 8, w 5, nb 1)	19		
Total	(37.4 overs; 5 wickets)	**195**		

WEST INDIES	O	M	R	W
Marshall	10	2	42	1
Garner	10	1	33	1
Holding	10	0	31	0
Davis	10	0	37	1
Richards	10	0	38	3

AUSTRALIA	O	M	R	W
Lawson	10	1	35	0
Hogg	8	1	41	1
O'Donnell	9	0	47	2
McDermott	7	1	33	2
Bennett	3	0	21	0
Boon	0.4	0	5	0

FALL OF WICKETS
1-49, 2-77, 3-97, 4-107, 5-153, 6-160, 7-162, 8-171, 9-173, 10-191

FALL OF WICKETS
1-50, 2-50, 3-74, 4-172, 5-188

Umpires: M.W.Johnson (28) and S.G.Randell (6).

AUSTRALIA v WEST INDIES 1984-85

At Sydney Cricket Ground on 15 January 1985.　Result: **WEST INDIES** won by 5 wickets.　Toss: Australia.
Award: I.V.A.Richards.　LOI debuts: Australia – R.G.Holland.

Slow scoring by Kepler Wessels (63 in 39 overs) again led to suicidal running. Viv Richards became the first to score eight hundreds in limited-overs internationals, reaching the landmark off 122 balls.

AUSTRALIA		Runs	Balls	4/6
G.M.Wood	c Holding b Davis	21	33	–
K.C.Wessels	st Dujon b Richards	63	133	3
D.C.Boon	run out	20	41	–
* A.R.Border	run out	24	51	2
G.M.Ritchie	not out	30	40	2
S.P.O'Donnell	b Marshall	17	15	1/1
† S.J.Rixon	not out	2	2	–
G.F.Lawson				
M.J.Bennett				
C.J.McDermott				
R.G.Holland				
Extras	(lb 10, w 3, nb 10)	23		
Total	(50 overs; 5 wickets)	**200**		

WEST INDIES		Runs	Balls	4/6
D.L.Haynes	c O'Donnell b McDermott	13	19	–
R.B.Richardson	lbw b Lawson	9	25	–
H.A.Gomes	c Wessels b McDermott	0	4	–
I.V.A.Richards	not out	103	122	7/1
* C.H.Lloyd	c Rixon b McDermott	38	49	2/1
A.L.Logie	c Rixon b Lawson	12	15	1/1
† P.J.L.Dujon	not out	15	34	–
M.D.Marshall				
M.A.Holding				
W.W.Davis				
J.Garner				
Extras	(b 1, lb 5, w 2, nb 3)	11		
Total	(43.3 overs; 5 wickets)	**201**		

WEST INDIES	O	M	R	W
Marshall	10	0	38	1
Garner	10	1	44	0
Holding	10	1	36	0
Davis	10	2	31	1
Richards	10	0	41	1

AUSTRALIA	O	M	R	W
Lawson	10	1	32	2
McDermott	10	0	30	3
Bennett	6	0	40	0
O'Donnell	7.3	0	43	0
Holland	10	0	50	0

FALL OF WICKETS
1-42, 2-103, 3-137, 4-161, 5-197

FALL OF WICKETS
1-23, 2-23, 3-25, 4-115, 5-138

Umpires: R.C.Isherwood (9) and S.G.Randell (7).

WEST INDIES v SRI LANKA 1984-85

At Sydney Cricket Ground on 17 January 1985.   Result: **WEST INDIES** won by 65 runs.   Toss: West Indies.
Award: C.G.Greenidge.   LOI debuts: None.

The opening stand of 128 by Gordon Greenidge and Desmond Haynes was their best effort against Sri Lanka until their next encounter nine days later. Roy Dias became the first Sri Lankan to score 1,000 LOI runs.

WEST INDIES		Runs	Balls	4/6	SRI LANKA		Runs	Balls	4/6
C.G.Greenidge	b D.S.de Silva	67			† S.A.R.Silva	c Greenidge b Marshall	5		
D.L.Haynes	run out	54			J.R.Ratnayeke	c Dujon b Davis	17		
R.B.Richardson	not out	57			P.A.de Silva	c Dujon b Holding	21		
I.V.A.Richards	b De Mel	30			* L.R.D.Mendis	c Dujon b Holding	2		
A.L.Logie	not out	47			R.L.Dias	not out	65		
P.J.L.Dujon					R.S.Madugalle	b Harper	25		
M.D.Marshall					S.H.U.Karnain	not out	41		
R.A.Harper					R.J.Ratnayake				
M.A.Holding					A.L.F.de Mel				
W.W.Davis					D.S.de Silva				
C.A.Walsh					V.B.John				
Extras	(lb 5, w 5, nb 2)	12			Extras	(b 2, lb 7, w 4, nb 13)	26		
Total	(50 overs; 3 wickets)	267			Total	(50 overs; 5 wickets)	202		

SRI LANKA	O	M	R	W	WEST INDIES	O	M	R	W
De Mel	10	1	50	1	Marshall	10	1	33	1
John	10	0	53	0	Walsh	10	1	45	0
Ratnayeke	3	0	19	0	Davis	10	0	52	1
Ratnayake	10	0	58	0	Holding	10	2	32	2
D.S.de Silva	10	1	48	1	Harper	10	0	31	1
Karnain	7	1	34	0					

FALL OF WICKETS
1-12, 2-54, 3-54, 4-64, 5-124

FALL OF WICKETS
1-128, 2-128, 3-186

Umpires: M.W.Johnson (29) and B.E.Martin (14).

AUSTRALIA v SRI LANKA 1984-85

At Melbourne Cricket Ground on 19 January 1985.   Result: **SRI LANKA** won by 4 wickets   Toss: Sri Lanka.
Award: R.J.Ratnayake   LOI debuts: None.

Sri Lanka gained their first win of the tournament when Aravinda de Silva top-edged a six over the wicket-keeper's head with four balls left.

AUSTRALIA		Runs	Balls	4/6	SRI LANKA		Runs	Balls	4/6
G.M.Wood	b Ratnayake	42	52	6	S.Wettimuny	lbw b Hogg	17	45	–
K.C.Wessels	b Ratnayake	28	53	1	† S.A.R.Silva	c Hogg b O'Donnell	23	50	1
G.M.Ritchie	c Madugalle b Karnain	13	26	1	R.S.Madugalle	c Border b O'Donnell	24	37	1
* A.R.Border	st Silva b D.S.de Silva	1	3	–	R.L.Dias	run out	48	64	1
D.C.Boon	c Wettimuny b Dias	34	66	1	* L.R.D.Mendis	c Wessels b Hogg	35	34	3
† W.B.Phillips	c De Mel b Dias	67	75	5	P.A.de Silva	not out	46	37	2/2
S.P.O'Donnell	b Ratnayake	7	9	–	S.H.U.Karnain	b Lawson	16	19	1
G.F.Lawson	c Madugalle b Dias	11	8	2	R.J.Ratnayake	not out	5	12	–
M.J.Bennett	not out	6	7	–	A.L.F.de Mel				
C.J.McDermott	b Ratnayake	0	2	–	D.S.de Silva				
R.M.Hogg	not out	5	3	–	V.B.John				
Extras	(lb 9, w 3)	12			Extras	(b 1, lb 14, nb 1)	16		
Total	(50 overs; 9 wickets)	226			Total	(49.2 overs; 6 wickets)	230		

SRI LANKA	O	M	R	W	AUSTRALIA	O	M	R	W
De Mel	7	1	45	0	Lawson	10	0	51	1
John	10	1	32	0	McDermott	9.2	1	36	0
Ratnayake	10	3	37	4	Hogg	10	1	31	2
D.S.de Silva	10	0	33	1	O'Donnell	10	1	43	2
Karnain	9	0	45	1	Bennett	9	1	48	0
Dias	4	0	25	3	Wessels	1	0	6	0

FALL OF WICKETS
1-68, 2-73, 3-74, 4-88, 5-160, 6-191, 7-204, 8-220, 9-220

FALL OF WICKETS
1-38, 2-52, 3-86, 4-150, 5-161, 6-196

Umpires: R.A.French (34) and M.W.Johnson (30).

AUSTRALIA v WEST INDIES 1984-85

At Melbourne Cricket Ground on 20 January 1985.   Result: **WEST INDIES** won by 65 runs.   Toss: Australia.
Award: I.V.A.Richards.   LOI debuts: None.

Australia's fifth defeat from six outings in this tournament prompted stern criticism of the team by its captain.

WEST INDIES		Runs	Balls	4/6	AUSTRALIA		Runs	Balls	4/6
C.G.Greenidge	c Phillips b Hogg	33	48	6	G.M.Wood	c Dujon b Marshall	9	22	1
D.L.Haynes	c and b O'Donnell	23	38	2	† W.B.Phillips	c Greenidge b Garner	4	10	–
R.B.Richardson	c Phillips b O'Donnell	21	38	2	D.M.Jones	c Haynes b Marshall	0	6	–
I.V.A.Richards	c Boon b McDermott	74	61	7	S.P.O'Donnell	run out	11	24	1
* C.H.Lloyd	run out	16	19	1	* A.R.Border	c Richards b Holding	61	80	4
A.L.Logie	c Border b Wessels	72	64	3/2	D.C.Boon	b Richards	34	59	4
† P.J.L.Dujon	c Phillips b Hogg	23	38	–	G.M.Ritchie	b Davis	6	13	–
M.A.Holding	not out	2	3	–	K.C.Wessels	b Richards	21	22	1
M.D.Marshall	not out	2	1	–	G.F.Lawson	not out	18	37	–
J.Garner					C.J.McDermott	run out	19	33	2
W.W.Davis					R.M.Hogg				
Extras	(b 1, lb 3, w 1)	5			Extras	(b 6, lb 12, w 1, nb 4)	23		
Total	(50 overs; 7 wickets)	271			Total	(50 overs; 9 wickets)	206		

AUSTRALIA	O	M	R	W	WEST INDIES	O	M	R	W
Lawson	10	0	47	0	Marshall	9	1	29	1
McDermott	10	0	50	1	Garner	9	2	17	1
Hogg	10	1	56	2	Holding	10	1	36	1
O'Donnell	10	0	40	2	Davis	10	1	52	1
Wessels	8	0	58	1	Richards	10	0	43	2
Border	2	0	16	0	Logie	1	0	10	0
					Richardson	1	0	1	0

FALL OF WICKETS
1-56, 2-58, 3-103, 4-138, 5-201, 6-252, 7-268

FALL OF WICKETS
1-14, 2-15, 3-21, 4-34, 5-115, 6-126, 7-163, 8-169, 9-206

Umpires: R.C.Isherwood (10) and P.J.McConnell (15).

AUSTRALIA v SRI LANKA 1984-85

At Sydney Cricket Ground on 23 January 1985.   Result: **AUSTRALIA** won by 3 wickets.   Toss: Australia.
Award: K.C.Wessels.   LOI debuts: None.

With both teams having won only one match, this was an important victory for the embattled hosts.

SRI LANKA		Runs	Balls	4/6	AUSTRALIA		Runs	Balls	4/6
S.Wettimuny	b Wessels	21	60	1	G.M.Wood	c Ratnayake b De Mel	0	2	–
† S.A.R.Silva	run out	2	5	–	S.B.Smith	c Silva b John	4	17	–
R.S.Madugalle	c Phillips b Hogg	7	16	–	K.C.Wessels	c Mendis b Karnain	82	97	4
R.L.Dias	c Phillips b Wessels	19	42	1	* A.R.Border	st Silva b D.S.de Silva	57	67	7
* L.R.D.Mendis	c Phillips b Lawson	80	79	8	D.M.Jones	not out	62	70	4
P.A.de Silva	not out	81	87	7	D.C.Boon	lbw b John	3	6	–
R.J.Ratnayake	b McDermott	7	5	1	† W.B.Phillips	b Ratnayake	19	20	2
S.H.U.Karnain	not out	10	12	–	S.P.O'Donnell	c Karnain b De Mel	2	7	–
A.L.F.de Mel					G.F.Lawson	not out	0	–	–
D.S.de Silva					C.J.McDermott				
V.B.John					R.M.Hogg				
Extras	(lb 9, w 1, nb 3)	13			Extras	(lb 10, w 3)	13		
Total	(50 overs; 6 wickets)	240			Total	(47.1 overs; 7 wickets)	242		

AUSTRALIA	O	M	R	W	SRI LANKA	O	M	R	W
Lawson	10	2	32	1	De Mel	8	0	53	2
McDermott	10	1	59	1	John	10	1	35	2
Hogg	10	2	33	1	D.S.de Silva	10	0	62	1
O'Donnell	10	0	46	0	Karnain	10	0	38	1
Wessels	10	0	61	2	Ratnayake	8.1	0	37	1
					Dias	1	0	7	0

FALL OF WICKETS
1-3, 2-23, 3-54, 4-55, 5-194, 6-204

FALL OF WICKETS
1-0, 2-29, 3-119, 4-187, 5-195, 6-231, 7-238

Umpires: A.R.Crafter (28) and S.G.Randell (8).

WEST INDIES v SRI LANKA 1984-85

At Adelaide Oval on 26 January 1985.   Result: **WEST INDIES** won by 8 wickets.   Toss: West Indies.
Award: C.G.Greenidge.   LOI debuts: None.

Gordon Greenidge contributed his sixth hundred to his team's eighth successive win in this tournament, sharing an opening partnership of 133 with Desmond Haynes.

SRI LANKA		Runs	Balls	4/6
† S.A.R.Silva	c Garner b Davis	5		
D.S.B.P.Kuruppu	c Dujon b Walsh	7		
R.S.Madugalle	b Davis	1		
R.L.Dias	b Holding	66		
* L.R.D.Mendis	c Richards b Davis	45		
A.Ranatunga	c sub (R.B.Richardson) b Holding	31		
S.H.U.Karnain	not out	20		
R.J.Ratnayake	not out	12		
A.L.F.de Mel				
D.S.de Silva				
G.N.de Silva				
Extras	(b 2, lb 9, w 2, nb 4)	17		
Total	(50 overs; 6 wickets)	**204**		

WEST INDIES		Runs	Balls	4/6
C.G.Greenidge	not out	110	128	15
D.L.Haynes	b D.S.de Silva	51	53	
H.A.Gomes	c and b Ranatunga	24		
A.L.Logie	not out	7		
I.V.A.Richards				
* C.H.Lloyd				
† P.J.L.Dujon				
M.A.Holding				
J.Garner				
W.W.Davis				
C.A.Walsh				
Extras	(lb 4, w 1, nb 8)	13		
Total	(37.2 overs; 2 wickets)	**205**		

WEST INDIES	O	M	R	W
Garner	10	2	27	0
Davis	10	5	21	3
Walsh	10	0	54	1
Holding	10	0	46	2
Richards	10	0	45	0

SRI LANKA	O	M	R	W
De Mel	4	0	34	0
G.N.de Silva	8.2	1	56	0
Ratnayake	10	0	41	0
D.S.de Silva	7	0	36	1
Ranatunga	8	1	34	1

FALL OF WICKETS
1-5, 2-13, 3-22, 4-115, 5-164, 6-181

FALL OF WICKETS
1-133, 2-178

Umpires: R.A.French (35) and B.E.Martin (15).

AUSTRALIA v WEST INDIES 1984-85

At Adelaide Oval on 27 January 1985.   Result: **WEST INDIES** won by 6 wickets.   Toss: West Indies.
Award: J.Garner.   LOI debuts: Australia – R.J.McCurdy.

Graeme Wood batted through the innings for his second LOI hundred but he was given a hostile reception by the crowd for his poor calling which caused two run outs, one of them the local favourite, Rod McCurdy.

AUSTRALIA		Runs	Balls	4/6
K.C.Wessels	run out	1	20	
G.M.Wood	not out	104	142	
* A.R.Border	lbw b Marshall	0	1	
D.M.Jones	b Garner	11	21	
S.B.Smith	c Dujon b Davis	21	37	
† W.B.Phillips	run out	36	37	
S.P.O'Donnell	c Dujon b Garner	9	21	
G.F.Lawson	hit wicket b Marshall	4	13	
C.J.McDermott	c Logie b Garner	2	5	
R.J.McCurdy	run out	1	2	
R.M.Hogg	not out	3	4	
Extras	(lb 5, nb 3)	8		
Total	(50 overs; 9 wickets)	**200**		

WEST INDIES		Runs	Balls	4/6
C.G.Greenidge	lbw b McDermott	39	59	
D.L.Haynes	b McCurdy	14	26	
R.B.Richardson	c Smith b McDermott	34	40	
I.V.A.Richards	c Border b McCurdy	51	74	
* C.H.Lloyd	not out	47	66	
A.L.Logie	not out	2	1	
† P.J.L.Dujon				
M.D.Marshall				
W.W.Davis				
M.A.Holding				
J.Garner				
Extras	(b 2, lb 8, w 1, nb 3)	14		
Total	(43.4 overs; 4 wickets)	**201**		

WEST INDIES	O	M	R	W
Garner	10	3	17	3
Marshall	10	1	35	2
Davis	10	0	53	1
Holding	10	0	51	0
Richards	10	0	39	0

AUSTRALIA	O	M	R	W
Lawson	9	0	32	0
McCurdy	9.4	2	38	2
McDermott	7	0	37	2
Hogg	8	0	46	0
O'Donnell	10	1	38	0

FALL OF WICKETS
1-4, 2-4, 3-19, 4-72, 5-154, 6-167, 7-178, 8-181, 9-184

FALL OF WICKETS
1-31, 2-93, 3-103, 4-199

Umpires: A.R.Crafter (29) and M.W.Johnson (31).

AUSTRALIA v SRI LANKA 1984-85

At Adelaide Oval on 28 January 1985.　　Result: **AUSTRALIA** won by 232 runs.　　Toss: Sri Lanka.
Award: A.R.Border.　　LOI debuts: None.

An unbroken partnership of 224 between Dean Jones and Allan Border, the record for any wicket until 1993-94 and still the world record for the third-wicket and Australia's highest for any wicket, carried the hosts to the highest LOI total in Australia. Their margin of victory remains the LOI world record. Border's 78-ball hundred is the fastest for Australia.

AUSTRALIA		Runs	Balls	4/6
G.M.Wood	c D.S.de Silva b Karnain	30	55	
S.B.Smith	c Silva b Karnain	55	88	
D.M.Jones	not out	99	77	4/3
* A.R.Border	not out	118	88	10/3
D.C.Boon				
K.C.Wessels				
† W.B.Phillips				
S.P.O'Donnell				
G.F.Lawson				
R.J.McCurdy				
R.M.Hogg				
Extras	(b 6, lb 8, w 4, nb 3)	21		
Total	(50 overs; 2 wickets)	323		

SRI LANKA		Runs	Balls	4/6
† S.A.R.Silva	lbw b McCurdy	0	2	
A.Ranatunga	c Phillips b McCurdy	5	15	
P.A.de Silva	lbw b Lawson	6	7	
R.L.Dias	c Smith b Lawson	3	11	
* L.R.D.Mendis	c Boon b McCurdy	7	9	
R.S.Madugalle	lbw b O'Donnell	8	35	
S.H.U.Karnain	c Wessels b O'Donnell	21	67	
R.J.Ratnayake	c Jones b Hogg	2	6	
D.S.de Silva	not out	15	48	
V.B.John	c Hogg b Wessels	8	7	
G.N.de Silva	st Phillips b Wessels	7	12	
Extras	(b 1, lb 5, w 3)	9		
Total	(35.5 overs)	91		

SRI LANKA	O	M	R	W
Ratnayake	10	1	51	0
John	10	1	64	0
G.N.de Silva	10	0	50	0
D.S.de Silva	5	0	42	0
Karnain	8	0	56	2
Ranatunga	6	0	36	0
Dias	1	0	10	0

AUSTRALIA	O	M	R	W
Lawson	7	5	5	2
McCurdy	5	1	19	3
Hogg	8	1	18	1
O'Donnell	9	1	19	2
Wessels	4.5	0	16	2
Boon	2	0	8	0

FALL OF WICKETS
1-94, 2-99

FALL OF WICKETS
1-3, 2-12, 3-14, 4-23, 5-25, 6-45, 7-52, 8-66, 9-75, 10-91

Umpires: R.C.Isherwood (11) and B.E.Martin (16).

WEST INDIES v SRI LANKA 1984-85

At WACA Ground, Perth on 2 February 1985.　　Result: **WEST INDIES** won by 82 runs.　　Toss: Sri Lanka.
Award: H.A.Gomes.　　LOI debuts: None.

Larry Gomes contributed his lone hundred, and his first three sixes, in a career involving 64 LOI innings as West Indies reached their highest LOI total in Australia and became the first team to complete a clean sweep of their ten preliminary matches in this competition. This result eliminated Sri Lanka from the finals.

WEST INDIES		Runs	Balls	4/6
C.G.Greenidge	b Ratnayake	42		
D.L.Haynes	c Silva b John	27		
H.A.Gomes	c Dias b De Mel	101	89	6/3
I.V.A.Richards	b John	46		
A.L.Logie	run out	6		
* C.H.Lloyd	not out	54	29	
† P.J.L.Dujon	c De Silva b De Mel	13		
M.D.Marshall	not out	2		
W.W.Davis				
J.Garner				
C.A.Walsh				
Extras	(lb 10, w 6, nb 2)	18		
Total	(50 overs; 6 wickets)	309		

SRI LANKA		Runs	Balls	4/6
S.Wettimuny	run out	0		
† S.A.R.Silva	c Dujon b Walsh	85	96	
J.R.Ratnayeke	b Richards	24		
R.L.Dias	run out	1		
* L.R.D.Mendis	c Dujon b Walsh	8		
P.A.de Silva	c Dujon b Richards	5		
A.Ranatunga	not out	63		
S.H.U.Karnain	not out	28		
R.J.Ratnayake				
A.L.F.de Mel				
V.B.John				
Extras	(lb 6, w 5, nb 2)	13		
Total	(50 overs; 6 wickets)	227		

SRI LANKA	O	M	R	W
De Mel	10	0	67	2
John	10	0	44	2
Ratnayake	10	0	58	1
Ratnayeke	10	0	48	0
Karnain	6	0	35	0
Ranatunga	3	0	39	0
Dias	1	0	8	0

WEST INDIES	O	M	R	W
Garner	6	3	6	0
Davis	6	1	34	0
Marshall	6	0	17	0
Walsh	10	0	52	2
Richards	10	0	47	2
Gomes	7	0	41	0
Haynes	5	0	24	0

FALL OF WICKETS
1-47, 2-99, 3-216, 4-223, 5-241, 6-280

FALL OF WICKETS
1-0, 2-100, 3-102, 4-120, 5-133, 6-137

Umpires: A.R.Crafter (30) and S.G.Randell (9).

AUSTRALIA v SRI LANKA 1984-85

At WACA Ground, Perth on 3 February 1985.   Result: **AUSTRALIA** won by 9 wickets.   Toss: Sri Lanka.
Award: S.B.Smith.   LOI debuts: Sri Lanka – D.M.Vonhagt.

The unbroken stand of 157 in 93 minutes between Steve Smith and Wayne Phillips was the Australian second-wicket
record until 1986-87 and remains their best for that wicket against Sri Lanka. Final points: West Indies 20, Australia 6,
Sri Lanka 2.

SRI LANKA		Runs	Balls	4/6		AUSTRALIA		Runs	Balls	4/6
S.A.R.Silva	c Phillips b O'Donnell	51	86	2		S.B.Smith	not out	73	73	9
D.M.Vonhagt	c Wessels b Alderman	8	17	1		K.C.Wessels	c Silva b John	8	12	1
L.R.D.Mendis	c Wood b Lawson	2	3	–		† W.B.Phillips	not out	75	68	8
R.L.Dias	c Alderman b Lawson	4	4	1		* A.R.Border				
P.A.de Silva	st Phillips b Wessels	52	97	3		G.M.Wood				
A.Ranatunga	c Phillips b Hogg	10	11	2		D.M.Jones				
S.H.U.Karnain	c Border b Hogg	8	13	–		S.P.O'Donnell				
J.R.Ratnayeke	run out	1	7			G.F.Lawson				
R.J.Ratnayake	c Phillips b O'Donnell	16	15	3		R.J.McCurdy				
A.L.F.de Mel	not out	11	16	–		R.M.Hogg				
V.B.John	b McCurdy	0	3	–		T.M.Alderman				
Extras	(lb 2, w 5, nb 1)	8				Extras	(lb 8, w 6, nb 2)	16		
Total	(44.3 overs)	171				Total	(23.5 overs; 1 wicket)	172		

AUSTRALIA	O	M	R	W		SRI LANKA	O	M	R	W
Lawson	7	1	24	2		De Mel	8	0	45	0
Alderman	10	0	41	1		John	6.5	0	43	1
McCurdy	5.3	0	15	1		Ratnayake	5	0	40	0
O'Donnell	10	0	42	2		Ratnayeke	4	0	36	0
Hogg	10	1	40	2						
Wessels	2	0	7	1		FALL OF WICKETS				
						1-15				

FALL OF WICKETS
1-16, 2-19, 3-26, 4-94, 5-110, 6-123, 7-126, 8-147, 9-166, 10-171

Umpires: P.J.McConnell (16) and B.E.Martin (17).

AUSTRALIA v WEST INDIES 1984-85

At Sydney Cricket Ground on 6 February 1985.   Result: **AUSTRALIA** won by 26 runs.   Toss: West Indies.
LOI debuts: None.

The last of Allan Border's three hundreds – he was to play a record 252 innings in these internationals – supported by
spirited fast bowling, brought about the West Indies' only defeat of this tournament.

AUSTRALIA		Runs	Balls	4/6		WEST INDIES		Runs	Balls	4/6
S.B.Smith	c Richardson b Garner	6	12	–		D.L.Haynes	b Lawson	11	13	2
G.M.Wood	c Richards b Garner	0	2	–		R.B.Richardson	lbw b McCurdy	0	3	–
K.C.Wessels	c Dujon b Marshall	11	51	–		H.A.Gomes	lbw b McCurdy	9	14	1
* A.R.Border	not out	127	140	13		I.V.A.Richards	b McDermott	68	88	4
D.M.Jones	b Davis	3	6	–		* C.H.Lloyd	c Wessels b McDermott	20	39	2/1
† W.B.Phillips	c Garner b Holding	50	71	3		A.L.Logie	c Wood b Hogg	12	20	–
S.P.O'Donnell	lbw b Garner	17	22	–		† P.J.L.Dujon	b McDermott	14	22	–
G.F.Lawson	not out	14	15	–/1		M.D.Marshall	b McCurdy	43	46	3/1
C.J.McDermott						M.A.Holding	b O'Donnell	1	2	
R.J.McCurdy						J.Garner	run out	27	31	1
R.M.Hogg						W.W.Davis	not out	8	8	1
Extras	(b 2, lb 6, nb 11)	19				Extras	(lb 7, nb 1)	8		
Total	(50 overs; 6 wickets)	247				Total	(47.3 overs)	221		

WEST INDIES	O	M	R	W		AUSTRALIA	O	M	R	W
Garner	10	3	29	3		Lawson	9	1	41	1
Holding	10	0	40	1		McCurdy	9.3	1	40	3
Marshall	10	0	55	1		Hogg	10	0	35	1
Davis	10	0	57	1		McDermott	10	0	44	3
Richards	10	0	58	0		O'Donnell	9	0	54	1

FALL OF WICKETS
1-3, 2-7, 3-58, 4-64, 5-169, 6-205

FALL OF WICKETS
1-10, 2-20, 3-20, 4-82, 5-107, 6-137, 7-140, 8-147, 9-210, 10-221

Umpires: A.R.Crafter (31) and M.W.Johnson (32).

AUSTRALIA v WEST INDIES 1984-85

At Melbourne Cricket Ground on 10 February 1985.   Result: **WEST INDIES** won by 4 wickets.   Toss: West Indies.
LOI debuts: None.

A dazzling 56-ball innings of 60 by Gus Logie enabled West Indies to draw level in the best-of-three finals, Jeff Dujon sealing the match with cover-driven boundaries off the first two balls of the final over.

AUSTRALIA		Runs	Balls	4/6
S.B.Smith	b Davis	54	101	2
G.M.Wood	c Richards b Holding	81	119	6
* A.R.Border	c Dujon b Marshall	39	48	1/1
† W.B.Phillips	not out	56	37	6
D.M.Jones	not out	13	15	1
K.C.Wessels				
S.P.O'Donnell				
G.F.Lawson				
C.J.McDermott				
R.J.McCurdy				
R.M.Hogg				
Extras	(b 2, lb 10, w 7, nb 9)	28		
Total	(50 overs; 3 wickets)	**271**		

WEST INDIES		Runs	Balls	4/6
D.L.Haynes	c Wessels b Hogg	44	39	4
R.B.Richardson	c Wessels b O'Donnell	50	90	4
H.A.Gomes	b O'Donnell	47	50	5
I.V.A.Richards	lbw b Lawson	9	17	–
* C.H.Lloyd	c O'Donnell b Lawson	13	11	1
A.L.Logie	hit wicket b McCurdy	60	56	5
† P.J.L.Dujon	not out	39	34	4
M.D.Marshall	not out	0	2	–
M.A.Holding				
W.W.Davis				
J.Garner				
Extras	(b 2, lb 8, nb 1)	11		
Total	(49.2 overs; 6 wickets)	**273**		

WEST INDIES	O	M	R	W
Garner	10	0	60	0
Marshall	10	0	64	1
Holding	10	1	41	1
Davis	10	0	43	1
Richards	10	0	51	0

AUSTRALIA	O	M	R	W
Lawson	10	0	34	2
McCurdy	10	0	69	1
McDermott	10	0	56	0
Hogg	9.2	0	58	1
O'Donnell	10	0	46	2

FALL OF WICKETS
1-135, 2-186, 3-203

FALL OF WICKETS
1-78, 2-137, 3-154, 4-158, 5-179, 6-265

Umpires: R.C.Isherwood (12) and P.J.McConnell (17).

AUSTRALIA v WEST INDIES 1984-85

At Sydney Cricket Ground on 12 February 1985.   Result: **WEST INDIES** won by 7 wickets.   Toss: West Indies.
Finals Awards: A.R.Border and M.A.Holding.   LOI debuts: Australia – R.B.Kerr.

West Indies' fourth World Series Cup triumph maintained their 100% success rate in this competition. Michael Holding achieved his only five-wicket analysis in 102 limited-overs internationals. Graeme Wood retired when his left index finger was fractured by a ball from Winston Davis but he returned when the eighth wicket fell and added a record 52 with Simon O'Donnell for Australia's ninth wicket.

AUSTRALIA		Runs	Balls	4/6
G.M.Wood	not out	36	60	1
K.C.Wessels	c Richards b Holding	17	48	–/1
R.B.Kerr	c Logie b Davis	4	18	–
* A.R.Border	c Garner b Holding	4	22	–
D.M.Jones	b Richards	16	28	–/1
† W.B.Phillips	c Dujon b Holding	3	7	–
S.P.O'Donnell	c and b Garner	69	80	3/2
G.F.Lawson	c Richards b Holding	4	12	–
C.J.McDermott	c Dujon b Holding	0	3	–
R.J.McCurdy	run out	12	27	1
R.M.Hogg	c Richards b Garner	1	4	–
Extras	(b 2, lb 4, w 4, nb 2)	12		
Total	(50 overs)	**178**		

WEST INDIES		Runs	Balls	4/6
D.L.Haynes	not out	76	133	–
R.B.Richardson	run out	3	12	–
H.A.Gomes	c Border b McDermott	3	23	–
I.V.A.Richards	c sub (P.H.Marks) b McDermott	76	104	4
A.L.Logie	not out	11	15	1
* C.H.Lloyd				
† P.J.L.Dujon				
M.D.Marshall				
M.A.Holding				
W.W.Davis				
J.Garner				
Extras	(b 4, lb 2, nb 4)	10		
Total	(47 overs; 3 wickets)	**179**		

WEST INDIES	O	M	R	W
Garner	10	4	34	2
Marshall	10	0	37	0
Davis	10	1	23	1
Holding	10	1	26	5
Richards	10	0	52	1

AUSTRALIA	O	M	R	W
Lawson	10	1	22	0
McCurdy	10	2	31	0
McDermott	10	2	36	2
Hogg	9	0	42	0
O'Donnell	8	0	42	0

FALL OF WICKETS
1-47, 2-51, 3-57, 4-64, 5-80, 6-89, 7-89, 8-124, 9-176, 10-178

FALL OF WICKETS
1-14, 2-34, 3-162

Umpires: R.A.French (36) and P.J.McConnell (18).

NEW ZEALAND v PAKISTAN 1984-85

At McLean Park, Napier on 12 January 1985.   Result: **NEW ZEALAND** won by 110 runs.   Toss: New Zealand.
Award: R.J.Hadlee.   LOI debuts: None.

Geoff Howarth survived a chance off the first ball of this series of four 50-over matches to score the only fifty of the match off 77 balls.

NEW ZEALAND		Runs	Balls	4/6	PAKISTAN		Runs	Balls	4/6
* G.P.Howarth	st Anil b Iqbal Qasim	68	94	4	Mudassar Nazar	c Smith b Hadlee	17	13	3
J.G.Wright	c Kamal b Tahir	24	50	3	Mohsin Khan	b Cairns	4	13	I
J.F.Reid	b Mudassar	II	26	–	Qasim Omar	c Smith b Hadlee	0	6	–
M.D.Crowe	c Qasim Omar b Tahir	32	36	2/1	* Javed Miandad	run out	38	69	I
* I.D.S.Smith	run out	14	19	I	Salim Malik	run out	II	19	I
J.J.Crowe	run out	35	35	1/1	Wasim Raja	c Smith b Chatfield	30	68	I
J.V.Coney	not out	24	25	2	Tahir Naqqash	lbw b Cairns	II	18	I
R.J.Hadlee	not out	34	26	3/1	Iqbal Qasim	b Chatfield	9	18	–
B.L.Cairns					† Anil Dalpat	not out	21	46	3
J.G.Bracewell					Azeem Hafeez	c Hadlee b Howarth	15	31	2
E.J.Chatfield					Mohsin Kamal	not out	0	6	–
Extras	(b 4, lb 17, w 14)	35			Extras	(b 4, lb 3, w 4)	II		
Total	(50 overs; 6 wickets)	277			Total	(50 overs; 9 wickets)	167		

PAKISTAN	O	M	R	W	NEW ZEALAND	O	M	R	W
Azeem Hafeez	10	0	47	0	Hadlee	8	0	30	2
Mohsin Kamal	10	0	61	0	Cairns	10	0	27	2
Tahir Naqqash	10	0	60	2	Chatfield	10	2	20	2
Mudassar Nazar	10	0	51	I	Coney	10	0	45	0
Iqbal Qasim	10	I	37	I	Bracewell	10	I	28	0
					Howarth	I	0	4	I
					Wright	I	0	6	0

FALL OF WICKETS
1-62, 2-103, 3-157, 4-160, 5-189, 6-225

Umpires: D.A.Kinsella (5) and S.J.Woodward (5).

FALL OF WICKETS
1-24, 2-24, 3-26, 4-46, 5-91, 6-106, 7-125, 8-132, 9-161

NEW ZEALAND v PAKISTAN 1984-85

At Seddon Park, Hamilton on 15 January 1985.   Result: **NEW ZEALAND** won by 4 wickets.   Toss: Pakistan.
Award: Javed Miandad.   LOI debuts: None.

Javed Miandad and Martin Crowe played exceptional innings on a slow pitch, their fifties coming from 63 and 67 balls respectively.

PAKISTAN		Runs	Balls	4/6	NEW ZEALAND		Runs	Balls	4/6
Mohsin Khan	c Smith b Chatfield	49	96	5/1	* G.P.Howarth	c Anil b Wasim	5	6	I
Wasim Raja	c Reid b Coney	15	56	I	J.G.Wright	c Miandad b Salim	39	73	–
Qasim Omar	b Coney	15	26	1/1	J.F.Reid	b Wasim	17	39	I
* Javed Miandad	not out	90	92	9/1	M.D.Crowe	c Tahir b Iqbal Qasim	59	72	3/2
Salim Malik	run out	14	10	2	J.J.Crowe	b Iqbal Qasim	35	51	3/1
Mudassar Nazar	not out	22	25	2	J.V.Coney	not out	31	29	2
Shoaib Mohammed					† I.D.S.Smith	c Azeem b Tahir	13	12	I
Tahir Naqqash					R.J.Hadlee	not out	13	16	I
† Anil Dalpat					B.L.Cairns				
Iqbal Qasim					J.G.Bracewell				
Azeem Hafeez					E.J.Chatfield				
Extras	(b 1, lb 10, w 3, nb 2)	16			Extras	(lb 5, w 5)	10		
Total	(50 overs; 4 wickets)	221			Total	(48.5 overs; 6 wickets)	222		

NEW ZEALAND	O	M	R	W	PAKISTAN	O	M	R	W
Cairns	10	2	58	0	Wasim Raja	10	0	29	2
Hadlee	10	3	46	0	Salim Malik	10	I	34	I
Coney	10	I	16	2	Iqbal Qasim	10	0	58	2
Bracewell	10	0	51	0	Azeem Hafeez	7.5	0	36	0
Chatfield	10	0	39	I	Mudassar Nazar	7	0	41	0
					Tahir Naqqash	4	0	19	I

FALL OF WICKETS
1-32, 2-62, 3-131, 4-160

Umpires: D.A.Kinsella (6) and T.A.McCall (1).

FALL OF WICKETS
1-9, 2-36, 3-90, 4-154, 5-164, 6-191

NEW ZEALAND v PAKISTAN 1984-85

At Lancaster Park, Christchurch on 6 February 1985.   Result: **NEW ZEALAND** won by 13 runs.   Toss: New Zealand.
Award: J.F.Reid.   LOI debuts: Pakistan – Ramiz Raja.

Pakistan required 15 runs off the last over but Richard Hadlee sealed the fate of the Rothmans Cup by taking three wickets with the first four balls.

NEW ZEALAND		Runs	Balls	4/6
* G.P.Howarth	c Anil b Azeem	12	32	1
J.G.Wright	c Salim b Tahir	65	86	5/1
J.F.Reid	c Salim b Azeem	88	101	5
M.D.Crowe	run out	20	17	2
B.L.Cairns	c and b Mudassar	8	8	1
R.J.Hadlee	c Anil b Tahir	9	13	1
J.J.Crowe	c Wasim b Tahir	13	21	1
J.V.Coney	c Iqbal Qasim b Azeem	12	15	1
† I.D.S.Smith	not out	5	5	–
J.G.Bracewell	not out	20	8	4
E.J.Chatfield				
Extras	(b 3, lb 5, w 4)	12		
Total	(50 overs; 8 wickets)	**264**		

PAKISTAN		Runs	Balls	4/6
Mudassar Nazar	c J.J.Crowe b Cairns	8	21	–
Qasim Omar	run out	1	1	–
Salim Malik	b Cairns	0	5	–
Zaheer Abbas	st Smith b Bracewell	58	79	7
* Javed Miandad	c M.D.Crowe b Cairns	30	50	2
Ramiz Raja	run out	75	76	7/1
Wasim Raja	c Howarth b Chatfield	12	22	2
† Anil Dalpat	c M.D.Crowe b Hadlee	37	35	4
Tahir Naqqash	c Howarth b Hadlee	11	12	–
Azeem Hafeez	not out	1	1	–
Iqbal Qasim	b Hadlee	0	1	–
Extras	(b 4, lb 6, w 4, nb 4)	18		
Total	(49.4 overs)	**251**		

PAKISTAN	O	M	R	W
Wasim Raja	10	1	34	0
Azeem Hafeez	10	0	56	3
Iqbal Qasim	5	0	33	0
Mudassar Nazar	10	0	56	1
Tahir Naqqash	8	0	40	3
Salim Malik	3	0	16	0
Zaheer Abbas	4	0	21	0

NEW ZEALAND	O	M	R	W
Cairns	10	4	39	3
Hadlee	9.4	1	32	3
Chatfield	10	0	75	1
Coney	10	0	44	0
Bracewell	10	1	51	1

FALL OF WICKETS
1-29, 2-121, 3-166, 4-177, 5-192, 6-216, 7-237, 8-241

FALL OF WICKETS
1-1, 2-1, 3-22, 4-105, 5-105, 6-129, 7-237, 8-250, 9-250, 10-251

Umpires: F.R.Goodall (11) and G.C.Morris (3).

NEW ZEALAND v PAKISTAN 1984-85

At Eden Park, Auckland on 16 (*no play*), 17 February 1985.   No result.   Toss: Pakistan.
LOI debuts: None.

Rain, which postponed this final match until the reserve day, returned during the interval between innings.

PAKISTAN		Runs	Balls	4/6
Mudassar Nazar	c Crowe b Chatfield	10	29	1
Qasim Omar	c Smith b Snedden	6	26	–
Zaheer Abbas	c Smith b Chatfield	4	14	–
* Javed Miandad	run out	9	42	–
Ramiz Raja	st Smith b Bracewell	59	83	2/1
Salim Malik	lbw b Chatfield	7	13	–
Wasim Raja	c Howarth b Bracewell	0	12	–
† Anil Dalpat	c Bracewell b McEwan	3	17	–
Tahir Naqqash	c Wright b Snedden	61	49	4/3
Rashid Khan	not out	8	13	–
Wasim Akram	b Hadlee	2	3	–
Extras	(b 3, lb 9, w 8)	20		
Total	(49.1 overs)	**189**		

NEW ZEALAND
* G.P.Howarth
J.G.Wright
J.F.Reid
J.J.Crowe
P.E.McEwan
J.V.Coney
R.J.Hadlee
† I.D.S.Smith
M.C.Snedden
J.G.Bracewell
E.J.Chatfield

NEW ZEALAND	O	M	R	W
Chatfield	10	2	20	3
Hadlee	9.1	3	24	1
Snedden	10	3	36	2
McEwan	10	0	54	1
Bracewell	10	1	43	2

FALL OF WICKETS
1-17, 2-25, 3-25, 4-61, 5-70, 6-73, 7-92, 8-156, 9-182, 10-189

Umpires: T.A.McCall (2) and S.J.Woodward (6).

AUSTRALIA v ENGLAND 1984-85

At Melbourne Cricket Ground on 17 February 1985.   Result: **AUSTRALIA** won by 7 wickets.   Toss: England.
Award: R.B.Kerr.   LOI debuts: None.   49-over match.

Australia celebrated the 150th anniversary of the founding of the state of Victoria by hosting a 13-match 50-over tournament featuring all seven Test-playing nations divided into two groups. A crowd of 82,494 attended the first game to be staged beneath the MCG's new floodlights. Australia were fined $550 for failing to bowl their overs in the allotted 3½ hours.

ENGLAND		Runs	Balls	4/6
G.Fowler	c and b McDermott	26	48	2
† P.R.Downton	c McCurdy b McDermott	27	64	2
* D.I.Gower	c Alderman b McCurdy	6	13	–
A.J.Lamb	c Kerr b Lawson	53	53	3
M.W.Gatting	c Alderman b O'Donnell	34	54	–
C.S.Cowdrey	lbw b McDermott	0	1	–
V.J.Marks	b Lawson	24	38	1
P.H.Edmonds	b Lawson	20	22	2
R.M.Ellison	not out	2	4	–
J.P.Agnew	not out	2	3	–
N.G.Cowans				
Extras	(b 3, lb 12, nb 5)	20		
Total	(49 overs; 8 wickets)	214		

AUSTRALIA		Runs	Balls	4/6
K.C.Wessels	c Gatting b Ellison	39	50	5
R.B.Kerr	not out	87	126	5
K.J.Hughes	run out	0	3	–
* A.R.Border	c Cowans b Marks	1	6	–
D.M.Jones	not out	78	94	8
† W.B.Phillips				
S.P.O'Donnell				
G.F.Lawson				
C.J.McDermott				
R.J.McCurdy				
T.M.Alderman				
Extras	(b 1, lb 3, nb 6)	10		
Total	(45.2 overs; 3 wickets)	215		

AUSTRALIA	O	M	R	W
Lawson	10	3	31	3
Alderman	10	0	48	0
McDermott	10	0	39	3
McCurdy	10	1	42	1
O'Donnell	9	0	39	1

ENGLAND	O	M	R	W
Cowans	10	0	52	0
Ellison	10	4	34	1
Agnew	8	0	59	0
Marks	7.2	0	33	1
Edmonds	10	0	33	0

FALL OF WICKETS
1-61, 2-66, 3-76, 4-159, 5-159, 6-166, 7-200, 8-211

FALL OF WICKETS
1-57, 2-57, 3-58

Umpires: A.R.Crafter (32) and R.C.Isherwood (13).

INDIA v PAKISTAN 1984-85

At Melbourne Cricket Ground on 20 February 1985.   Result: **INDIA** won by 6 wickets.   Toss: Pakistan.
Award: M.Azharuddin.   LOI debuts: India – L.Sivaramakrishnan.

Imran Khan returned to international cricket after more than a year's absence. Mohammed Azharuddin enjoyed a notable first appearance in Australia.

PAKISTAN		Runs	Balls	4/6
Mohsin Khan	c Viswanath b Binny	3	13	–
Qasim Omar	c and b Sivaramakrishnan	57	102	4
Zaheer Abbas	c and b Sivaramakrishnan	25	56	1
* Javed Miandad	c Sivaramakrishnan b Binny	17	35	–
Ramiz Raja	c Shastri b Kapil Dev	29	37	–
Imran Khan	c Madan Lal b Kapil Dev	14	23	1
Mudassar Nazar	run out	6	8	–
Tahir Naqqash	c Amarnath b Madan Lal	0	3	–
Rashid Khan	c Shastri b Binny	17	16	–
† Anil Dalpat	c Kapil Dev b Binny	9	8	–
Wasim Akram	not out	0	–	–
Extras	(lb 3, w 2, nb 1)	6		
Total	(49.2 overs)	183		

INDIA		Runs	Balls	4/6
R.J.Shastri	c Miandad b Imran	2	5	–
K.Srikkanth	c Mohsin b Imran	12	26	2
M.Azharuddin	not out	93	135	4
D.B.Vengsarkar	c Mudassar b Imran	0	1	–
* S.M.Gavaskar	lbw b Mudassar	54	92	1
M.Amarnath	not out	11	16	–
Kapil Dev				
R.M.H.Binny				
Madan Lal				
† S.Viswanath				
L.Sivaramakrishnan				
Extras	(lb 9, w 3)	12		
Total	(45.5 overs; 4 wickets)	184		

INDIA	O	M	R	W
Kapil Dev	9	1	31	2
Binny	8.2	3	35	4
Madan Lal	9	2	27	1
Amarnath	3	0	11	0
Sivaramakrishnan	10	0	49	2
Shastri	10	1	27	0

PAKISTAN	O	M	R	W
Imran Khan	10	1	27	3
Wasim Akram	8.5	0	38	0
Rashid Khan	7	0	38	0
Tahir Naqqash	10	0	34	0
Mudassar Nazar	10	0	38	1

FALL OF WICKETS
1-8, 2-73, 3-98, 4-119, 5-144, 6-151, 7-155, 8-156, 9-183, 10-183

FALL OF WICKETS
1-2, 2-27, 3-27, 4-159

Umpires: R.A.French (37) and P.J.McConnell (19).

WEST INDIES v NEW ZEALAND 1984-85

At Sydney Cricket Ground on 19 (*no play*), 21 February 1985.　No result.　Toss: New Zealand.
LOI debuts: None.

This floodlit match was the only rain-affected contest in the tournament. Rained off on its original date, it endured a day's hiatus to avoid a clash of television scheduling before eventually being aborted after another heavy shower.

NEW ZEALAND		Runs	Balls	4/6
* G.P.Howarth	c Dujon b Garner	8	31	1
J.G.Wright	c Logie b Davis	22	55	1
J.F.Reid	not out	22	30	–
M.D.Crowe	not out	0	–	–
J.J.Crowe				
J.V.Coney				
R.J.Hadlee				
† I.D.S.Smith				
B.L.Cairns				
M.C.Snedden				
E.J.Chatfield				
Extras	(lb 1, nb 4)	5		
Total	(18.4 overs; 2 wickets)	57		

WEST INDIES
R.B.Richardson
D.L.Haynes
H.A.Gomes
I.V.A.Richards
* C.H.Lloyd
A.L.Logie
† P.J.L.Dujon
M.D.Marshall
M.A.Holding
W.W.Davis
J.Garner

WEST INDIES	O	M	R	W
Garner	6	3	11	1
Marshall	6	1	13	0
Davis	3.4	0	23	1
Holding	3	0	9	0

FALL OF WICKETS
1-21, 2-57

Umpires: M.W.Johnson (33) and S.G.Randell (10).

NEW ZEALAND v SRI LANKA 1984-85

At Melbourne Cricket Ground on 23 February 1985.　Result: **NEW ZEALAND** won by 51 runs.　Toss: Sri Lanka.
Award: J.F.Reid.　LOI debuts: None.

New Zealand became the first team to qualify for the semi-finals.

NEW ZEALAND		Runs	Balls	4/6	SRI LANKA		Runs	Balls	4/6
* G.P.Howarth	c Madugalle b John	11	27	1	† S.A.R.Silva	c Crowe b Chatfield	33	55	4
J.G.Wright	b John	4	9	1	J.R.Ratnayeke	run out	8	33	1
J.F.Reid	c Dias b Karnain	62	108	4	R.S.Madugalle	lbw b Coney	8	24	–
M.D.Crowe	run out	22	31	2	R.L.Dias	c Smith b Coney	9	15	1
P.E.McEwan	b John	27	38	3	* L.R.D.Mendis	c and b Hadlee	7	10	1
J.V.Coney	c De Silva b Karnain	21	31	–	A.Ranatunga	c Wright b Coney	34	40	–
R.J.Hadlee	c De Mel b Ratnatunga	9	8	–	S.H.U.Karnain	lbw b Hadlee	0	2	–
† I.D.S.Smith	b Ratnayake	22	16	2	A.L.F.de Mel	run out	27	26	–
B.L.Cairns	c De Mel b Ratnayake	25	21	2	R.J.Ratnayake	c Hadlee b Coney	1	4	–
M.C.Snedden	b Ratnayake	7	6	–	D.S.de Silva	not out	24	32	1
E.J.Chatfield	not out	2	8	–	V.B.John	c Chatfield b Cairns	11	17	1
Extras	(lb 6, w 5)	11			Extras	(lb 9, nb 1)	10		
Total	(49.4 overs)	223			**Total**	(42.4 overs)	172		

SRI LANKA	O	M	R	W	NEW ZEALAND	O	M	R	W
John	10	1	29	3	Cairns	8.4	1	25	1
De Mel	10	0	48	0	Hadlee	6	1	23	2
Ratnayake	8.5	1	40	3	Chatfield	10	3	25	1
De Silva	5	0	25	0	Snedden	8	0	44	0
Karnain	9.5	0	50	2	Coney	10	0	46	4
Ranatunga	6	0	25	1					

FALL OF WICKETS
1-11, 2-21, 3-64, 4-100, 5-145, 6-161, 7-170, 8-213, 9-216, 10-223

FALL OF WICKETS
1-26, 2-48, 3-60, 4-67, 5-75, 6-75, 7-118, 8-125, 9-143,10-172

Umpires: P.J.McConnell (20) and B.E.Martin (18).

AUSTRALIA v PAKISTAN 1984-85

At Melbourne Cricket Ground on 24 February 1985.   Result: **PAKISTAN** won by 62 runs.   Toss: Australia.
Award: Wasim Akram.   LOI debuts: None.

An unknown 18-year-old left-arm swing bowler called Wasim Akram achieved the first of many remarkable performances at international level by taking Australia's first five wickets for 13 runs in 28 balls.

PAKISTAN		Runs	Balls	4/6
Mudassar Nazar	c McDermott b O'Donnell	69	86	7
Mohsin Khan	b Alderman	81	109	5
Qasim Omar	b O'Donnell	31	40	3
Javed Miandad	b McCurdy	19	27	1
* Zaheer Abbas	b Lawson	3	6	–
Imran Khan	not out	32	27	1/1
Ramiz Raja	c Alderman b Lawson	3	6	–
Tahir Naqqash	not out	5	3	–
† Anil Dalpat				
Rashid Khan				
Wasim Akram				
Extras	(lb 8, w 9, nb 2)	19		
Total	(50 overs; 6 wickets)	262		

AUSTRALIA	O	M	R	W
Lawson	10	2	45	2
Alderman	10	0	42	1
McDermott	8	0	51	0
McCurdy	10	0	58	1
O'Donnell	10	1	42	2
Wessels	2	0	16	0

FALL OF WICKETS
1-141, 2-190, 3-190, 4-196, 5-224, 6-229

AUSTRALIA		Runs	Balls	4/6
K.C.Wessels	b Wasim	10	11	1
R.B.Kerr	b Wasim	2	7	1
D.M.Jones	b Wasim	11	11	1
* A.R.Border	hit wicket b Wasim	11	17	1
K.J.Hughes	c Tahir b Wasim	1	14	–
† W.B.Phillips	c Miandad b Tahir	44	50	6
S.P.O'Donnell	not out	74	101	4
G.F.Lawson	c Ramiz b Mudassar	27	26	2
C.J.McDermott	run out	4	7	–
R.J.McCurdy	run out	1	5	–
T.M.Alderman	b Imran	2	9	–
Extras	(b 2, lb 9, w 2)	13		
Total	(42.3 overs)	200		

PAKISTAN	O	M	R	W
Imran Khan	6.3	0	24	1
Wasim Akram	8	1	21	5
Rashid Khan	10	0	51	0
Zaheer Abbas	3	0	16	0
Tahir Naqqash	7	0	37	0
Mudassar Nazar	8	0	40	1

FALL OF WICKETS
1-4, 2-15, 3-30, 4-37, 5-42, 6-121, 7-128, 8-184, 9-187, 10-200

Umpires: R.C.Isherwood (14) and M.W.Johnson (34).

ENGLAND v INDIA 1984-85

At Sydney Cricket Ground on 26 February 1985.   Result: **INDIA** won by 86 runs.   Toss: England.
Award: K.Srikkanth.   LOI debuts: None.

India qualified for the semi-finals as England lost their last eight wickets for 36 runs on a turning pitch, Sadanand Viswanath becoming the fourth wicket-keeper, and second Indian, to make five dismissals in an innings.

INDIA		Runs	Balls	4/6
R.J.Shastri	c Fowler b Ellison	13	38	–
K.Srikkanth	run out	57	53	10
M.Azharuddin	c and b Cowans	45	67	1
D.B.Vengsarkar	run out	43	62	1
Kapil Dev	c Downton b Cowans	29	23	–/1
* S.M.Gavaskar	not out	30	31	2
M.Amarnath	c Lamb b Cowans	6	11	–
R.M.H.Binny	c Marks b Foster	2	3	–
Madan Lal	c Downton b Foster	0	1	–
† S.Viswanath	run out	8	11	–
L.Sivaramakrishnan				
Extras	(lb 2)	2		
Total	(50 overs; 9 wickets)	235		

ENGLAND	O	M	R	W
Cowans	10	0	59	3
Ellison	10	1	46	1
Foster	10	0	33	2
Edmonds	10	1	38	0
Marks	10	0	57	0

FALL OF WICKETS
1-67, 2-74, 3-147, 4-183, 5-197, 6-216, 7-220, 8-220, 9-235

ENGLAND		Runs	Balls	4/6
G.Fowler	c Viswanath b Binny	26	40	1
M.D.Moxon	c and b Sivaramakrishnan	48	86	1
* D.I.Gower	c Vengsarkar b Sivaramakrishnan	25	34	–
A.J.Lamb	b Sivaramakrishnan	13	20	–
M.W.Gatting	c Viswanath b Shastri	7	15	–
† P.R.Downton	c Shastri b Kapil Dev	9	17	–
V.J.Marks	st Viswanath b Shastri	2	7	–
P.H.Edmonds	st Viswanath b Shastri	5	10	–
R.M.Ellison	c Viswanath b Madan Lal	1	5	–
N.A.Foster	c Srikkanth b Madan Lal	1	13	–
N.G.Cowans	not out	3	5	–
Extras	(b 3, lb 4, w 1, nb 1)	9		
Total	(41.4 overs)	149		

INDIA	O	M	R	W
Kapil Dev	7	0	21	1
Binny	8	0	33	1
Madan Lal	6.4	0	19	2
Sivaramakrishnan	10	0	39	3
Shastri	10	2	30	3

FALL OF WICKETS
1-41, 2-94, 3-113, 4-126, 5-126, 6-130, 7-142, 8-144, 9-146, 10-149

Umpires: R.A.French (38) and B.E.Martin (19).

WEST INDIES v SRI LANKA 1984-85

At Melbourne Cricket Ground on 27 February 1985.   Result: **WEST INDIES** won by 8 wickets.   Toss: Sri Lanka.
Award: J.R.Ratnayeke.   LOI debuts: None.

Morning rain delayed the start by 30 minutes and reduced this match to 47 overs. West Indies qualified for the semi-finals at some cost, the pitch's extravagant bounce causing injuries to Richie Richardson (bruised cheek) and Larry Gomes (broken nose and two lost teeth).

SRI LANKA		Runs	Balls	4/6
†S.A.R.Silva	c Haynes b Garner	4	33	–
J.R.Ratnayeke	c Haynes b Holding	50	101	3
R.L.Dias	c Dujon b Davis	16	26	3
A.Ranatunga	b Richards	1	2	–
*L.R.D.Mendis	run out	1	5	–
R.S.Madugalle	not out	36	58	–
D.S.de Silva	c and b Richards	5	19	–
S.H.U.Karnain	c and b Richards	1	9	–
A.L.F.de Mel	not out	15	30	–
R.J.Ratnayake				
V.B.John				
Extras	(b 1, lb 4, w 1)	6		
Total	(47 overs; 7 wickets)	**135**		

WEST INDIES		Runs	Balls	4/6
D.L.Haynes	b De Mel	36	50	3
R.B.Richardson	retired hurt	11	13	1
H.A.Gomes	retired hurt	20	24	2
I.V.A.Richards	c De Mel b Ratnayake	12	10	2
*C.H.Lloyd	not out	14	24	2
A.L.Logie	not out	29	27	3
†P.J.L.Dujon				
M.D.Marshall				
M.A.Holding				
W.W.Davis				
J.Garner				
Extras	(b 1, lb 7, w 2, nb 4)	14		
Total	(23.1 overs; 2 wickets)	**136**		

WEST INDIES	O	M	R	W
Marshall	10	1	26	0
Garner	10	3	16	1
Davis	9	0	35	1
Holding	9	1	26	1
Richards	9	0	27	3

SRI LANKA	O	M	R	W
De Mel	8	0	47	1
John	7	0	39	0
Ratnayake	7	0	29	1
Ranatunga	1.1	0	13	0

FALL OF WICKETS
1-7, 2-52, 3-53, 4-57, 5-86, 6-102, 7-106

FALL OF WICKETS
1-86, 2-90

Umpires: A.R.Crafter (33) and S.G.Randell (11).

ENGLAND v PAKISTAN 1984-85

At Melbourne Cricket Ground on 2 March 1985.   Result: **PAKISTAN** won by 67 runs.   Toss: Pakistan.
Award: A.J.Lamb.   LOI debuts: None.

Having lost both their previous games, England's only chance of qualifying was to beat Pakistan and score at an exceptional rate. Needing 214 within 33 overs, they were on course only during Allan Lamb's superb innings.

PAKISTAN		Runs	Balls	4/6
Mudassar Nazar	c Foster b Edmonds	77	102	7
Mohsin Khan	c Moxon b Ellison	9	26	–
Ramiz Raja	c Moxon b Marks	21	35	2
*Javed Miandad	c Downton b Foster	11	31	–
Imran Khan	b Ellison	35	58	3
Salim Malik	c Gatting b Foster	8	9	–
Qasim Omar	b Cowans	12	16	–
Tahir Naqqash	not out	21	15	–
†Anil Dalpat	b Ellison	8	8	–
Azeem Hafeez	not out	0	1	–
Wasim Akram				
Extras	(b 5, lb 4, w 2)	11		
Total	(50 overs; 8 wickets)	**213**		

ENGLAND		Runs	Balls	4/6
G.Fowler	c Anil b Imran	0	2	–
*D.I.Gower	c Tahir b Imran	27	33	3
A.J.Lamb	c Wasim b Azeem	81	69	12/1
M.W.Gatting	c Mudassar b Tahir	11	15	2
†P.R.Downton	run out	6	7	–
R.M.Ellison	c Anil b Tahir	6	9	–
V.J.Marks	run out	1	3	–
M.D.Moxon	c Imran b Azeem	3	6	–
P.H.Edmonds	not out	0	1	–
N.A.Foster	run out	1	1	–
N.G.Cowans	b Tahir	0	1	–
Extras	(b 1, lb 7, w 1, nb 1)	10		
Total	(24.2 overs)	**146**		

ENGLAND	O	M	R	W
Cowans	10	0	52	1
Ellison	10	0	42	3
Foster	10	0	56	2
Marks	10	2	25	1
Edmonds	10	1	29	1

PAKISTAN	O	M	R	W
Imran Khan	7	0	33	2
Wasim Akram	10	0	59	0
Azeem Hafeez	3	0	22	2
Tahir Naqqash	4.2	0	24	3

FALL OF WICKETS
1-37, 2-93, 3-114, 4-126, 5-144, 6-181, 7-183, 8-212

FALL OF WICKETS
1-0, 2-56, 3-102, 4-125, 5-138, 6-139, 7-141, 8-145, 9-146, 10-146

Umpires: R.C.Isherwood (15) and M.W.Johnson (35).

AUSTRALIA v INDIA 1984-85

At Melbourne Cricket Ground on 3 March 1985.   Result: **INDIA** won by 8 wickets.   Toss: India.
Award: R.J.Shastri.   LOI debuts: None.

India easily maintained their unbeaten record, the hosts' demise clinching Pakistan's place in the semi-finals. Final points: Group A – India 6, Pakistan 4, Australia 2, England 0; Group B – West Indies 3 (run rate 5.87), New Zealand 3 (4.07), Sri Lanka 0.

AUSTRALIA		Runs	Balls	4/6
G.M.Wood	b Binny	1	12	–
R.B.Kerr	b Kapil Dev	4	8	–
K.C.Wessels	c Madan Lal b Kapil Dev	6	15	–
* A.R.Border	b Binny	4	16	–
D.M.Jones	c Viswanath b Amarnath	12	21	1
† W.B.Phillips	c Amarnath b Sivaramakrishnan	60	92	2
S.P.O'Donnell	c Amarnath b Shastri	17	51	1
G.F.Lawson	c and b Sivaramakrishnan	0	2	–
R.M.Hogg	run out	22	39	2
R.J.McCurdy	not out	13	25	–
T.M.Alderman	b Binny	6	19	–
Extras	(b 2, lb 9, w 5, nb 2)	18		
Total	**(49.3 overs)**	**163**		

INDIA		Runs	Balls	4/6
R.J.Shastri	c Phillips b O'Donnell	51	94	4
K.Srikkanth	not out	93	115	12
M.Azharuddin	lbw b Alderman	0	2	–
D.B.Vengsarkar	not out	11	16	–
* S.M.Gavaskar				
M.Amarnath				
Kapil Dev				
Madan Lal				
R.M.H.Binny				
† S.Viswanath				
L.Sivaramakrishnan				
Extras	(lb 1, w 3, nb 6)	10		
Total	**(36.1 overs; 2 wickets)**	**165**		

INDIA	O	M	R	W
Kapil Dev	10	2	25	2
Binny	7.3	0	27	3
Madan Lal	5	0	18	0
Amarnath	7	1	16	1
Sivaramakrishnan	10	0	32	2
Shastri	10	1	34	1

AUSTRALIA	O	M	R	W
Lawson	8	1	35	0
Hogg	6	2	16	0
McCurdy	7.1	0	30	0
Alderman	8	0	38	1
O'Donnell	7	0	45	1

FALL OF WICKETS
1-5, 2-5, 3-17, 4-17, 5-37, 6-85, 7-85, 8-134, 9-147, 10-163

FALL OF WICKETS
1-124, 2-125

Umpires: A.R.Crafter (34) and P.J.McConnell (21).

NEW ZEALAND v INDIA 1984-85

At Sydney Cricket Ground on 5 March 1985.   Result: **INDIA** won by 7 wickets.   Toss: India.
Award: R.J.Shastri.   LOI debuts: None.

India galloped through to the final on the back of an outstanding unbroken fourth-wicket partnership between Dilip Vengsarkar, who hit 50 off 48 balls, and Kapil Dev. Overcoming accurate bowling on a slow pitch with low bounce, they scored 105 off 74 balls.

NEW ZEALAND		Runs	Balls	4/6
J.G.Wright	c Viswanath b Kapil Dev	0	3	–
P.E.McEwan	c Viswanath b Binny	9	15	1
J.F.Reid	c Kapil Dev b Shastri	55	101	2
M.D.Crowe	c Azharuddin b Madan Lal	9	25	1
* G.P.Howarth	run out	7	15	–
J.V.Coney	b Shastri	33	67	1
† I.D.S.Smith	c Amarnath b Madan Lal	19	35	1
R.J.Hadlee	c Madan Lal b Shastri	3	10	–
B.L.Cairns	c Srikkanth b Madan Lal	39	29	4
M.C.Snedden	c Azharuddin b Madan Lal	7	5	1
E.J.Chatfield	not out	0	–	–
Extras	(lb 21, w 1, nb 3)	25		
Total	**(50 overs)**	**206**		

INDIA		Runs	Balls	4/6
R.J.Shastri	c McEwan b Hadlee	53	84	2
K.Srikkanth	c Reid b Chatfield	9	28	–
M.Azharuddin	c Coney b Cairns	24	54	2
D.B.Vengsarkar	not out	63	59	4
Kapil Dev	not out	54	37	5
* S.M.Gavaskar				
M.Amarnath				
R.M.H.Binny				
Madan Lal				
† S.Viswanath				
L.Sivaramakrishnan				
Extras	(b 1, lb 2, nb 1)	4		
Total	**(43.3 overs; 3 wickets)**	**207**		

INDIA	O	M	R	W
Kapil Dev	10	1	34	1
Binny	6	0	28	0
Madan Lal	8	1	37	4
Amarnath	7	0	24	0
Sivaramakrishnan	9	1	31	0
Shastri	10	1	31	3

NEW ZEALAND	O	M	R	W
Cairns	9	0	35	1
Hadlee	8.3	3	50	1
Chatfield	10	0	38	1
Snedden	8	1	37	0
Coney	8	0	44	0

FALL OF WICKETS
1-0, 2-14, 3-52, 4-69, 5-119, 6-145, 7-151, 8-188, 9-206, 10-206

FALL OF WICKETS
1-28, 2-73, 3-102

Umpires: R.A.French (39) and P.J.McConnell (22).

WEST INDIES v PAKISTAN 1984-85

At Melbourne Cricket Ground on 6 March 1985.   Result: **PAKISTAN** won by 7 wickets.   Toss: West Indies.
Award: Ramiz Raja.   LOI debuts: None.

Mudassar Nazar's best LOI return and some courageous batting gained Pakistan only their third win in 18 internationals against West Indies, who were led by Clive Lloyd for the last time.

WEST INDIES		Runs	Balls	4/6
D.L.Haynes	c Mudassar b Tahir	18	55	2
R.B.Richardson	b Tahir	13	29	2
† P.J.L.Dujon	c Anil b Wasim Raja	22	31	3
I.V.A.Richards	c Anil b Tahir	1	7	–
* C.H.Lloyd	c Miandad b Mudassar	25	41	2
A.L.Logie	c Omar b Mudassar	8	17	–
M.D.Marshall	c Miandad b Mudassar	10	15	–
R.A.Harper	not out	25	33	1
M.A.Holding	b Wasim Akram	5	12	–
J.Garner	c Wasim Raja b Mudassar	13	26	–
W.W.Davis	c Miandad b Mudassar	3	8	–
Extras	(b 4, lb 7, w 4, nb 1)	16		
Total	(44.3 overs)	**159**		

PAKISTAN		Runs	Balls	4/6
Mudassar Nazar	c Logie b Marshall	6	21	1
Mohsin Khan	c Dujon b Garner	23	93	–
Ramiz Raja	c and b Harper	60	88	7
Qasim Omar	not out	42	57	3/1
* Javed Miandad	not out	10	26	–
Salim Malik				
Imran Khan				
Wasim Raja				
Tahir Naqqash				
† Anil Dalpat				
Wasim Akram				
Extras	(b 3, lb 7, w 6, nb 3)	19		
Total	(46 overs; 3 wickets)	**160**		

PAKISTAN	O	M	R	W
Imran Khan	9	1	39	0
Wasim Akram	10	2	26	1
Tahir Naqqash	8	3	23	3
Wasim Raja	10	0	32	1
Mudassar Nazar	7.3	0	28	5

WEST INDIES	O	M	R	W
Marshall	9	2	25	1
Garner	8	3	19	1
Holding	8	3	19	0
Davis	7	0	35	0
Harper	10	1	38	1
Richards	4	0	14	0

FALL OF WICKETS
1-29, 2-44, 3-45, 4-61, 5-75, 6-96, 7-103, 8-122, 9-152, 10-159

FALL OF WICKETS
1-8, 2-97, 3-116

Umpires: R.C.Isherwood (16) and S.G.Randell (12).

WEST INDIES v NEW ZEALAND 1984-85

At Sydney Cricket Ground on 9 March 1985.   Result: **WEST INDIES** won by 6 wickets.   Toss: West Indies.
Award: I.V.A.Richards.   LOI debuts: None.

West Indies gained some consolation by winning this losing semi-finalists' play-off. A Viv Richards straight drive removed the copper bracelet from the arm of Lance Cairns.

NEW ZEALAND		Runs	Balls	4/6
* G.P.Howarth	lbw b Garner	11	38	1
J.G.Wright	c Logie b Garner	5	16	–
J.F.Reid	c Dujon b Davis	18	43	–
M.D.Crowe	c Harper b Holding	8	34	–
J.J.Crowe	b Harper	1	13	–
J.V.Coney	c Payne b Garner	35	76	1
† I.D.S.Smith	c Payne b Harper	15	29	–
B.L.Cairns	b Holding	5	13	–
R.J.Hadlee	b Marshall	11	25	–
J.G.Bracewell	not out	11	15	–
E.J.Chatfield	not out	2	4	–
Extras	(b 1, lb 8, w 2, nb 5)	16		
Total	(50 overs; 9 wickets)	**138**		

WEST INDIES		Runs	Balls	4/6
D.L.Haynes	c Coney b Hadlee	1	6	–
R.B.Richardson	c Smith b Hadlee	8	38	–
T.R.O.Payne	b Chatfield	28	54	3
A.L.Logie	not out	34	51	3
* I.V.A.Richards	b Hadlee	51	61	4/1
† P.J.L.Dujon	not out	9	19	1
M.D.Marshall				
R.A.Harper				
M.A.Holding				
J.Garner				
W.W.Davis				
Extras	(lb 3, w 2, nb 3)	8		
Total	(37.2 overs; 4 wickets)	**139**		

WEST INDIES	O	M	R	W
Garner	10	2	29	3
Marshall	10	1	32	1
Davis	10	0	23	1
Holding	10	1	23	2
Harper	10	2	22	2

NEW ZEALAND	O	M	R	W
Hadlee	10	4	23	3
Bracewell	8	2	42	0
Chatfield	9	0	25	1
Cairns	8	0	39	0
Coney	2.2	0	7	0

FALL OF WICKETS
1-14, 2-24, 3-45, 4-51, 5-52, 6-78, 7-83, 8-116, 9-127

FALL OF WICKETS
1-4, 2-24, 3-54, 4-126

Umpires: R.A.French (40) and M.W.Johnson (36).

INDIA v PAKISTAN 1984-85

At Melbourne Cricket Ground on 10 March 1985.   Result: **INDIA** won by 8 wickets.   Toss: Pakistan.
Award: K.Srikkanth.   LOI debuts: None.

India confirmed their domination of the abbreviated game with this confident victory against their arch rivals. Ravi Shastri contributed his third successive fifty and won the series award (a car). The attendance of 35,296 was the highest in Australia at a match in which the home side was not involved.

PAKISTAN		Runs	Balls	4/6
Mudassar Nazar	c Viswanath b Kapil Dev	14	39	–
Mohsin Khan	c Azharuddin b Kapil Dev	5	17	–
Ramiz Raja	c Srikkanth b Sharma	4	12	–
Qasim Omar	b Kapil Dev	0	1	–
* Javed Miandad	st Viswanath b Sivaramakrishnan	48	92	2
Imran Khan	run out	35	67	2
Salim Malik	c Sharma b Sivaramakrishnan	14	14	–
Wasim Raja	not out	21	26	1
Tahir Naqqash	c Viswanath b Shastri	10	8	1
† Anil Dalpat	c Shastri b Sivaramakrishnan	0	2	–
Azeem Hafeez	not out	7	28	–
Extras	(b 7, lb 8, w 1, nb 2)	18		
Total	(50 overs; 9 wickets)	**176**		

INDIA		Runs	Balls	4/6
R.J.Shastri	not out	63	148	3
K.Srikkanth	c Wasim Raja b Imran	67	77	6/2
M.Azharuddin	b Tahir	25	26	3
D.B.Vengsarkar	not out	18	32	–
* S.M.Gavaskar				
M.Amarnath				
Kapil Dev				
Madan Lal				
C.Sharma				
† S.Viswanath				
L.Sivaramakrishnan				
Extras	(lb 2, w 2)	4		
Total	(47.1 overs; 2 wickets)	**177**		

INDIA	O	M	R	W
Kapil Dev	9	1	23	3
Sharma	7	1	17	1
Madan Lal	6	1	15	0
Amarnath	9	0	27	0
Shastri	10	0	44	1
Sivaramakrishnan	9	0	35	3

PAKISTAN	O	M	R	W
Imran Khan	10	3	28	1
Azeem Hafeez	10	1	29	0
Tahir Naqqash	10	2	35	1
Wasim Raja	7.1	0	42	0
Mudassar Nazar	8	0	26	0
Salim Malik	2	0	15	0

FALL OF WICKETS
1-17, 2-29, 3-29, 4-33, 5-101, 6-131, 7-131, 8-142, 9-145

FALL OF WICKETS
1-103, 2-142

Umpires: A.R.Crafter (35) and R.C.Isherwood (17).

WEST INDIES v NEW ZEALAND 1984-85

At Recreation Ground, St John's, Antigua on 20 March 1985.   Result: **WEST INDIES** won by 23 runs.   Toss: New Zealand.
Award: R.A.Harper.   LOI debuts: New Zealand – R.T.Hart.   46-over match.

A capacity crowd of 11,000, enjoying a national holiday proclaimed to celebrate the appointment of Viv Richards as West Indies captain, was treated to a brilliant batting and fielding display by their local hero. Roger Harper's 29-ball 45 proved to be a crucial innings.

WEST INDIES		Runs	Balls	4/6
C.G.Greenidge	c Smith b Troup	3	10	–
D.L.Haynes	b Troup	54	100	5
R.B.Richardson	b Hadlee	3	5	–
* I.V.A.Richards	b Coney	70	85	7/1
A.L.Logie	c Cairns b Coney	11	17	–
† P.J.L.Dujon	st Smith b Coney	14	17	1
R.A.Harper	not out	45	29	3/3
E.A.E.Baptiste	b Cairns	8	12	–
M.A.Holding	b Hadlee	9	9	1
J.Garner	not out	1	1	–
W.W.Davis				
Extras	(b 1, lb 6, w 3, nb 3)	13		
Total	(46 overs; 8 wickets)	**231**		

NEW ZEALAND		Runs	Balls	4/6
J.G.Wright	b Holding	0	14	–
R.T.Hart	c Dujon b Garner	3	29	–
J.J.Crowe	b Harper	52	85	5/2
M.D.Crowe	lbw b Harper	41	56	3
B.L.Cairns	c Richards b Holding	20	27	2
J.V.Coney	run out	18	31	1
R.J.Hadlee	c Harper b Holding	2	5	–
† I.D.S.Smith	c Holding b Garner	13	13	4
* G.P.Howarth	not out	12	16	–
G.B.Troup	not out	16	15	2
E.J.Chatfield				
Extras	(b 2, lb 18, w 5, nb 6)	31		
Total	(46 overs; 8 wickets)	**208**		

NEW ZEALAND	O	M	R	W
Troup	10	0	52	2
Hadlee	10	0	29	2
Chatfield	8	0	38	0
Cairns	8	0	42	1
Coney	10	0	63	3

WEST INDIES	O	M	R	W
Garner	10	4	26	2
Holding	10	2	33	3
Baptiste	10	1	49	0
Davis	8	0	46	0
Harper	8	0	34	2

FALL OF WICKETS
1-4, 2-7, 3-134, 4-141, 5-160, 6-191, 7-208, 8-226

FALL OF WICKETS
1-5, 2-20, 3-111, 4-124, 5-151, 6-158, 7-173, 8-180

Umpires: A.E.Weekes (2) and P.C.White (3).

WEST INDIES v NEW ZEALAND 1984-85

At Queen's Park Oval, Port-of-Spain, Trinidad on 27 March 1985.   Result: **WEST INDIES** won by 6 wickets.
Toss: West Indies.   Award: W.W.Davis.   LOI debuts: New Zealand – K.R.Rutherford.   22-over match.

Heavy rain halted play at 11.32am with 22 of the 50 overs bowled. The umpires eventually closed New Zealand's innings and relegated the match to a 22-overs frolic which restarted at 4.10pm. The run-ups were still so wet that Richard Hadlee could not be bowled in case he slipped and was injured.

NEW ZEALAND		Runs	Balls	4/6	WEST INDIES		Runs	Balls	4/6
J.G.Wright	c Dujon b Davis	5	8	1	D.L.Haynes	b Chatfield	4	5	1
K.R.Rutherford	c Dujon b Davis	2	13	–	R.B.Richardson	c Smith b Troup	3	18	–
J.J.Crowe	c Richards b Davis	0	8	–	H.A.Gomes	c Smith b Troup	4	14	–
M.D.Crowe	not out	20	65	2	* I.V.A.Richards	c Cairns b Rutherford	27	40	2
J.V.Coney	not out	19	41	2	A.L.Logie	not out	8	27	1
* G.P.Howarth					† P.J.L.Dujon	not out	4	1	1
† I.D.S.Smith					R.A.Harper				
R.J.Hadlee					E.A.E.Baptiste				
B.L.Cairns					M.A.Holding				
G.B.Troup					J.Garner				
E.J.Chatfield					W.W.Davis				
Extras	(lb 1, w 1, nb 3)	5			Extras	(lb 2, w 1, nb 2)	5		
Total	(22 overs; 3 wickets)	51			Total	(17 overs; 4 wickets)	55		

WEST INDIES	O	M	R	W	NEW ZEALAND	O	M	R	W
Garner	6	2	6	0	Chatfield	6	0	15	1
Davis	6	2	7	3	Troup	5	1	22	2
Holding	5	0	16	0	Coney	3	1	4	0
Baptiste	5	0	21	0	Rutherford	3	0	12	1

FALL OF WICKETS
1-6, 2-9, 3-9

FALL OF WICKETS
1-4, 2-11, 3-21, 4-51

Umpires: C.E.Cumberbatch (2) and S.Mohammed (4).

WEST INDIES v NEW ZEALAND 1984-85

At Albion Sports Complex, Berbice on 14 April 1985.   Result: **WEST INDIES** won by 130 runs.   Toss: New Zealand.
Award: D.L.Haynes.   LOI debuts: None.   50-over match.

Desmond Haynes scored his seventh LOI hundred and his second in successive visits to Berbice. Viv Richards became the first batsman to score 4,000 runs. Another capacity crowd (15,000) had to evade both a swarm of bees and the smoke from a fire lit in an adjacent field to evict them.

WEST INDIES		Runs	Balls	4/6	NEW ZEALAND		Runs	Balls	4/6
D.L.Haynes	not out	145	157	16	* G.P.Howarth	b Garner	3	11	–
R.B.Richardson	c Smith b Hadlee	7	26	1	J.G.Wright	b Garner	0	7	–
H.A.Gomes	c Smith b Chatfield	13	19	2	J.J.Crowe	b Davis	9	33	–
* I.V.A.Richards	c Wright b Bracewell	51	78	4	M.D.Crowe	b Holding	20	33	2
A.L.Logie	c Troup b Cairns	26	23	2	J.V.Coney	b Baptiste	11	31	1
R.A.Harper	c Smith b Troup	1	2	–	† I.D.S.Smith	b Baptiste	1	4	–
† P.J.L.Dujon	not out	4	3	–	R.J.Hadlee	b Harper	16	63	2
E.A.E.Baptiste					J.G.Bracewell	c Richards b Gomes	15	62	–
M.A.Holding					B.L.Cairns	c Davis b Harper	33	28	1/3
J.Garner					G.B.Troup	not out	6	14	–
W.W.Davis					E.J.Chatfield	b Gomes	6	6	1
Extras	(lb 6, w 1, nb 5)	12			Extras	(b 2, lb 4, w 1, nb 2)	9		
Total	(50 overs; 5 wickets)	259			Total	(48.1 overs)	129		

NEW ZEALAND	O	M	R	W	WEST INDIES	O	M	R	W
Troup	7	0	28	1	Garner	6	1	16	2
Hadlee	10	1	46	1	Davis	6	3	7	1
Chatfield	10	1	35	1	Holding	6	0	12	1
Bracewell	9	0	50	1	Baptiste	7	2	18	2
Cairns	10	0	69	1	Harper	10	1	35	2
Coney	4	0	25	0	Richards	10	4	23	0
					Gomes	2.1	0	6	2
					Logie	1	0	6	0

FALL OF WICKETS
1-18, 2-47, 3-172, 4-252, 5-253

FALL OF WICKETS
1-4, 2-8, 3-24, 4-41, 5-48, 6-55, 7-75, 8-115, 9-121, 10-129

Umpires: L.H.Barker (3) and D.J.Narine (4).

WEST INDIES v NEW ZEALAND 1984-85

At Queen's Park Oval, Port-of-Spain, Trinidad on 17 April 1985.　　Result: **WEST INDIES** won by 10 wickets.
Toss: West Indies.　　Award: J.Garner.　　LOI debuts: None.　　50-over match.

New Zealand were dismissed well before lunch; Joel Garner, with his vast bounce and movement, was virtually unplayable on a well-grassed pitch. West Indies gained the first ten-wicket win on home soil by any country.

NEW ZEALAND		Runs	Balls	4/6	WEST INDIES		Runs	Balls	4/6
* G.P.Howarth	c Dujon b Garner	6	31	–	D.L.Haynes	not out	85	86	12/2
J.G.Wright	c Dujon b Garner	1	12	–	R.B.Richardson	not out	28	62	3
J.J.Crowe	c Richardson b Garner	4	4	1	H.A.Gomes				
M.D.Crowe	b Garner	1	13	–	* I.V.A.Richards				
J.V.Coney	c Dujon b Richards	33	51	5	A.L.Logie				
† I.D.S.Smith	c and b Holding	3	14	–	† P.J.L.Dujon				
R.J.Hadlee	c Richards b Davis	41	102	4	R.A.Harper				
B.L.Cairns	b Harper	12	12	1	E.A.E.Baptiste				
J.G.Bracewell	run out	1	6	–	M.A.Holding				
G.B.Troup	run out	4	13	–	J.Garner				
E.J.Chatfield	not out	1	2	–	W.W.Davis				
Extras	(lb 3, w 2, nb 4)	9			Extras	(lb 2, nb 2)	4		
Total	(42.2 overs)	**116**			**Total**	(24.2 overs; 0 wickets)	**117**		

WEST INDIES	O	M	R	W	NEW ZEALAND	O	M	R	W
Garner	6	1	10	4	Hadlee	6	1	18	0
Davis	6.2	1	10	1	Troup	8	2	30	0
Baptiste	5	0	31	0	Cairns	6	0	50	0
Holding	7	1	24	1	Chatfield	4	0	14	0
Harper	10	2	18	1	Bracewell	0.2	0	3	0
Richards	8	1	20	1					

FALL OF WICKETS
1-6, 2-10, 3-14, 4-18, 5-25, 6-83, 7-100, 8-104, 9-114, 10-116

Umpires: C.E.Cumberbatch (3) and S.Mohammed (5).

WEST INDIES v NEW ZEALAND 1984-85

At Kensington Oval, Bridgetown, Barbados on 23 April 1985.　　Result: **WEST INDIES** won by 112 runs.
Toss: New Zealand.　　Award: D.L.Haynes.　　LOI debuts: None.　　49-over match.

Barbados belatedly staged its first limited-overs international. Desmond Haynes emulated Viv Richards by scoring his eighth LOI hundred and shared with Larry Gomes a partnership of 184 which remains a national second-wicket record against New Zealand.

WEST INDIES		Runs	Balls	4/6	NEW ZEALAND		Runs	Balls	4/6
D.L.Haynes	c Coney b Chatfield	116	138	9/2	* G.P.Howarth	c Dujon b Davis	6	34	–
R.B.Richardson	c Coney b Chatfield	21	30	2/1	J.G.Wright	c Richards b Garner	22	31	5
H.A.Gomes	c J.J.Crowe b Cairns	78	91	9	K.R.Rutherford	c Holding b Harper	18	68	2
* I.V.A.Richards	not out	33	24	4/1	M.D.Crowe	c Logie b Davis	6	5	1
A.L.Logie	not out	11	12	1	J.V.Coney	b Baptiste	5	18	–
† P.J.L.Dujon					J.J.Crowe	c Logie b Harper	30	63	1/1
R.A.Harper					B.L.Cairns	c Logie b Harper	5	8	1
E.A.E.Baptiste					† I.D.S.Smith	c Garner b Davis	37	28	7
M.A.Holding					R.J.Hadlee	not out	16	38	1
J.Garner					G.B.Troup	not out	0	5	–
W.W.Davis					E.J.Chatfield				
Extras	(lb 5, w 1)	6			Extras	(b 2, lb 2, w 1, nb 3)	8		
Total	(49 overs; 3 wickets)	**265**			**Total**	(49 overs; 8 wickets)	**153**		

NEW ZEALAND	O	M	R	W	WEST INDIES	O	M	R	W
Troup	10	0	57	0	Garner	6	2	10	1
Hadlee	9	1	26	0	Davis	8	0	32	3
Chatfield	10	1	61	2	Baptiste	7	1	11	1
Cairns	10	1	63	1	Holding	6	1	10	0
Coney	10	0	53	0	Harper	10	0	38	3
					Richards	8	0	31	0
					Gomes	3	1	16	0
					Logie	1	0	1	0

FALL OF WICKETS
1-31, 2-215, 3-223

FALL OF WICKETS
1-30, 2-30, 3-36, 4-47, 5-83, 6-91, 7-103, 8-152

Umpires: D.M.Archer (3) and L.H.Barker (4).

163

INDIA v PAKISTAN 1984-85

At Sharjah CA Stadium, UAE on 22 March 1985.   Result: **INDIA** won by 38 runs.   Toss: Pakistan.
Award: Imran Khan.   LOI debuts: None.

50-over tournament. Imran Khan exploited a damp pitch to claim Pakistan's first six-wicket analysis. Sunil Gavaskar equalled the record for most catches in the field as Pakistan were dismissed on a dried, turning surface for their (then) second-lowest total.

INDIA		Runs	Balls	4/6
R.J.Shastri	lbw b Imran	0	1	–
K.Srikkanth	c Salim b Imran	6	5	1
M.Azharuddin	b Tausif	47	93	3
D.B.Vengsarkar	c Ashraf b Imran	1	4	–
* S.M.Gavaskar	c Ashraf b Imran	2	9	–
M.Amarnath	b Imran	5	10	1
Kapil Dev	b Tausif	30	44	4
R.M.H.Binny	c Miandad b Mudassar	8	19	1
Madan Lal	c Ashraf b Imran	11	39	1
† S.Viswanath	not out	3	28	–
L.Sivaramakrishnan	c Salim b Wasim	1	6	–
Extras	(b 5, lb 4, w 2)	11		
Total	(42.4 overs)	**125**		

PAKISTAN		Runs	Balls	4/6
Mudassar Nazar	c Gavaskar b Binny	18	18	2
Mohsin Khan	run out	10	9	1
Ramiz Raja	c Gavaskar b Kapil Dev	29	71	1
* Javed Miandad	c Gavaskar b Shastri	0	15	–
† Ashraf Ali	c Vengsarkar b Sivaramakrishnan	0	11	–
Imran Khan	st Viswanath b Sivaramakrishnan	0	4	–
Salim Malik	c Gavaskar b Shastri	17	39	1
Manzoor Elahi	c and b Madan Lal	9	24	–
Tahir Naqqash	c Viswanath b Kapil Dev	1	2	–
Tausif Ahmed	b Kapil Dev	0	7	–
Wasim Akram	not out	0	–	–
Extras	(lb 1, w 1, nb 1)	3		
Total	(32.5 overs)	**87**		

PAKISTAN	O	M	R	W
Imran Khan	10	2	14	6
Wasim Akram	7.4	0	27	1
Tahir Naqqash	5	0	12	0
Mudassar Nazar	10	1	36	1
Tausif Ahmed	10	0	27	2

INDIA	O	M	R	W
Kapil Dev	6.5	1	17	3
Binny	3	0	24	1
Sivaramakrishnan	7	2	16	2
Shastri	10	5	17	2
Madan Lal	6	2	12	1

FALL OF WICKETS
1-0, 2-12, 3-20, 4-28, 5-34, 6-80, 7-95, 8-113, 9-121, 10-125

FALL OF WICKETS
1-13, 2-35, 3-40, 4-41, 5-41, 6-74, 7-85, 8-87, 9-87, 10-87

Umpires: H.D.Bird (*England*) (27) and M.W.Johnson (*Australia*) (37).

ENGLAND v AUSTRALIA 1984-85

At Sharjah CA Stadium, UAE on 24 March 1985.   Result: **AUSTRALIA** won by 2 wickets.   Toss: Australia.
Award: G.R.J.Matthews.   LOI debuts: England – N.Gifford, C.M.Wells.

Captained by 44-year-old Norman Gifford on his LOI debut, England, the only country not to enter their strongest team in the first Sharjah competition to involve teams selected by national Boards of Control, were narrowly defeated off the final ball.

ENGLAND		Runs	Balls	4/6
G.Fowler	c Hughes b Alderman	26	33	3
R.T.Robinson	c Rixon b Matthews	37	73	5
M.D.Moxon	lbw b O'Donnell	0	1	–
D.W.Randall	st Rixon b Bennett	19	46	2
C.M.Wells	lbw b Bennett	17	29	2
D.R.Pringle	st Rixon b Border	4	41	–
P.H.Edmonds	not out	15	42	2
† B.N.French	c Rixon b Border	4	10	–
R.M.Ellison	c Wessels b Border	24	26	3
N.A.Foster	not out	5	5	–
* N.Gifford				
Extras	(b 9, lb 5, w 6, nb 6)	26		
Total	(50 overs; 8 wickets)	**177**		

AUSTRALIA		Runs	Balls	4/6
K.C.Wessels	b Edmonds	16	36	1
G.M.Wood	c French b Pringle	35	50	2/2
D.M.Jones	c Moxon b Edmonds	27	45	3
* A.R.Border	c and b Pringle	9	21	1
K.J.Hughes	c French b Foster	14	33	–
G.R.J.Matthews	c Foster b Ellison	24	50	1
S.P.O'Donnell	c Moxon b Ellison	19	39	1
† S.J.Rixon	not out	11	19	–
M.J.Bennett	run out	0	–	–
R.J.McCurdy	not out	6	7	–
T.M.Alderman				
Extras	(lb 9, w 8)	17		
Total	(50 overs; 8 wickets)	**178**		

AUSTRALIA	O	M	R	W
Alderman	7	1	36	1
McCurdy	5	0	23	0
O'Donnell	8	2	26	1
Bennett	10	2	27	2
Matthews	10	3	15	1
Border	7	0	21	3
Wessels	3	0	15	0

ENGLAND	O	M	R	W
Foster	10	1	34	1
Ellison	10	1	28	2
Pringle	10	0	49	2
Edmonds	10	2	31	2
Gifford	10	1	27	0

FALL OF WICKETS
1-47, 2-53, 3-95, 4-109, 5-123, 6-128, 7-134, 8-169

FALL OF WICKETS
1-54, 2-64, 3-82, 4-100, 5-120, 6-151, 7-168, 8-168

Umpires: Khizer Hayat (*Pakistan*) (8) and Swaroop Kishen (*India*) (5).

164

ENGLAND v PAKISTAN 1984-85

At Sharjah CA Stadium, UAE on 26 March 1985.   Result: **PAKISTAN** won by 43 runs.   Toss: England.
Award: Javed Miandad.   LOI debuts: England – R.J.Bailey, P.I.Pocock.

Only Javed Miandad and debutant Rob Bailey adapted to a sharply turning pitch in this play-off between the losing semi-finalists.

PAKISTAN		Runs	Balls	4/6
Mudassar Nazar	c French b Gifford	36	85	2
Mohsin Khan	c Robinson b Pringle	13	30	1
Ramiz Raja	c Robinson b Pringle	16	21	3
*Javed Miandad	c Gifford b Edmonds	71	117	3
Salim Malik	lbw b Gifford	2	9	–
Imran Khan	c Pringle b Gifford	0	1	–
Shoaib Mohammed	st French b Gifford	3	13	–
†Ashraf Ali	not out	19	22	1
Tahir Naqqash	not out	2	4	–
Tausif Ahmed				
Wasim Akram				
Extras	(b 1, lb 9, w 2, nb 1)	13		
Total	(50 overs; 7 wickets)	**175**		

ENGLAND	O	M	R	W
Ellison	7	1	18	0
Pringle	7	1	32	2
Edmonds	10	0	47	1
Pocock	10	1	20	0
Gifford	10	0	23	4
Bailey	6	0	25	0

FALL OF WICKETS
1-24, 2-43, 3-107, 4-113, 5-113, 6-125, 7-172

ENGLAND		Runs	Balls	4/6
G.Fowler	c Miandad b Tausif	19	56	1
R.T.Robinson	b Tahir	9	18	1
M.D.Moxon	b Shoaib	11	30	–
C.M.Wells	b Shoaib	5	15	–
R.J.Bailey	not out	41	83	–
D.R.Pringle	b Wasim	13	31	1
P.H.Edmonds	c and b Shoaib	3	17	–
R.M.Ellison	b Wasim	3	6	–
†B.N.French	c Shoaib b Tahir	7	18	1
*N.Gifford	c Miandad b Imran	0	8	–
P.I.Pocock	run out	4	9	–
Extras	(b 1, lb 12, nb 4)	17		
Total	(48.2 overs)	**132**		

PAKISTAN	O	M	R	W
Imran Khan	9	2	26	1
Wasim Akram	10	0	28	2
Tahir Naqqash	9.2	1	20	2
Tausif Ahmed	10	1	25	1
Shoaib Mohammed	10	1	20	3

FALL OF WICKETS
1-19, 2-35, 3-48, 4-49, 5-76, 6-89, 7-98, 8-117, 9-121, 10-132

Umpires: M.W.Johnson (*Australia*) (38) and Swaroop Kishen (*India*) (6).

AUSTRALIA v INDIA 1984-85

At Sharjah CA Stadium, UAE on 29 March 1985.   Result: **INDIA** won by 3 wickets.   Toss: India.
Award: M.Amarnath.   LOI debuts: None.

India added the Rothmans Trophy and $45,000 to their burgeoning one-day coffers in a match broadcast live on Dubai television for the first time.

AUSTRALIA		Runs	Balls	4/6
G.M.Wood	run out	27	37	4
K.C.Wessels	c Gavaskar b Madan Lal	30	68	2
D.M.Jones	c Viswanath b Madan Lal	8	10	2
*A.R.Border	c and b Amarnath	27	38	3
K.J.Hughes	c and b Amarnath	11	24	–
G.R.J.Matthews	lbw b Kapil Dev	11	31	–
S.P.O'Donnell	run out	3	25	–
†S.J.Rixon	run out	4	14	–
M.J.Bennett	lbw b Shastri	0	2	–
R.J.McCurdy	c Vengsarkar b Shastri	0	5	–
C.J.McDermott	not out	0	–	–
Extras	(lb 13, w 5)	18		
Total	(42.3 overs)	**139**		

INDIA	O	M	R	W
Kapil Dev	6	3	9	1
Binny	5	0	25	0
Madan Lal	7	0	30	2
Sivaramakrishnan	8	1	29	0
Shastri	9.3	1	14	2
Amarnath	7	1	19	2

FALL OF WICKETS
1-60, 2-71, 3-78, 4-114, 5-115, 6-131, 7-138, 8-139, 9-139, 10-139

INDIA		Runs	Balls	4/6
R.J.Shastri	c Rixon b O'Donnell	9	26	1
K.Srikkanth	lbw b McDermott	0	1	–
M.Azharuddin	c Jones b McDermott	22	44	3
D.B.Vengsarkar	b McDermott	35	43	6
S.M.Gavaskar	run out	20	50	2
M.Amarnath	not out	24	44	3
*Kapil Dev	b Matthews	1	14	–
R.M.H.Binny	b Matthews	2	5	–
Madan Lal	not out	7	14	1
†S.Viswanath				
L.Sivaramakrishnan				
Extras	(lb 9, w 7, nb 4)	20		
Total	(39.2 overs; 7 wickets)	**140**		

AUSTRALIA	O	M	R	W
McDermott	10	0	36	3
McCurdy	4	1	10	0
O'Donnell	4	1	11	1
Bennett	10	0	35	0
Matthews	10	1	33	2
Border	1.2	0	6	0

FALL OF WICKETS
1-2, 2-37, 3-41, 4-98, 5-103, 6-117, 7-120

Umpires: H.D.Bird (*England*) (28) and Khizer Hayat (*Pakistan*) (9).

ENGLAND v AUSTRALIA 1985

At Old Trafford, Manchester on 30 May 1985.   Result: **AUSTRALIA** won by 3 wickets.   Toss: England.
Award: I.T.Botham.   LOI debuts: None.

55-over tournament. Geoff Lawson dismissed Gower and Lamb with successive balls, returning his only four-wicket analysis in 79 internationals.

ENGLAND		Runs	Balls	4/6
G.A.Gooch	c O'Donnell b Holland	57	123	5
G.Fowler	c Phillips b McDermott	10	17	2
*D.I.Gower	b Lawson	3	11	–
A.J.Lamb	c Phillips b Lawson	0	1	–
I.T.Botham	b Matthews	72	82	2/5
M.W.Gatting	not out	31	54	1
P.Willey	b Holland	12	18	2
†P.R.Downton	c Matthews b Lawson	11	18	–
P.H.Edmonds	c Border b Lawson	0	2	–
P.J.W.Allott	b McDermott	2	5	–
N.G.Cowans	c and b McDermott	1	2	–
Extras	(b 2, lb 7, w 2, nb 9)	20		
Total	**(54 overs)**	**219**		

AUSTRALIA		Runs	Balls	4/6
K.C.Wessels	c Botham b Willey	39	88	5
G.M.Wood	c Downton b Cowans	8	12	1
D.M.Wellham	c and b Edmonds	12	39	–
*A.R.Border	c and b Allott	59	76	4/1
D.C.Boon	c Botham b Gooch	12	24	–
†W.B.Phillips	c Gatting b Cowans	28	37	3
S.P.O'Donnell	b Botham	1	3	–
G.R.J.Matthews	not out	29	31	1
G.F.Lawson	not out	14	15	1
C.J.McDermott				
R.G.Holland				
Extras	(b 2, lb 12, w 4)	18		
Total	**(54.1 overs; 7 wickets)**	**220**		

AUSTRALIA	O	M	R	W
Lawson	10	1	26	4
McDermott	11	0	46	3
O'Donnell	11	0	44	0
Matthews	11	1	45	1
Holland	11	2	49	2

ENGLAND	O	M	R	W
Cowans	10.1	1	44	2
Botham	11	2	41	1
Allott	11	0	47	1
Edmonds	11	2	33	1
Willey	9	1	31	1
Gooch	2	0	10	1

FALL OF WICKETS
1-21, 2-27, 3-27, 4-143, 5-160, 6-181, 7-203, 8-203, 9-213, 10-219

FALL OF WICKETS
1-15, 2-52, 3-74, 4-118, 5-156, 6-157, 7-186

Umpires: D.G.L.Evans (13) and K.E.Palmer (13).

ENGLAND v AUSTRALIA 1985

At Edgbaston, Birmingham on 1 June 1985.   Result: **AUSTRALIA** won by 4 wickets.   Toss: Australia.
Award: A.R.Border.   LOI debuts: None.

England suffered their eighth defeat in a sequence of nine internationals.

ENGLAND		Runs	Balls	4/6
G.A.Gooch	b McDermott	115	159	9/1
R.T.Robinson	c and b O'Donnell	26	48	4
*D.I.Gower	c Phillips b O'Donnell	0	7	–
A.J.Lamb	b Thomson	25	56	1
I.T.Botham	c Wellham b Lawson	29	36	2
M.W.Gatting	c Lawson b McDermott	6	13	–
P.Willey	c Phillips b Lawson	0	2	–
†P.R.Downton	not out	16		1
P.H.Edmonds	not out	6	6	–
P.J.W.Allott				
N.G.Cowans				
Extras	(lb 2, w 2, nb 4)	8		
Total	**(55 overs; 7 wickets)**	**231**		

AUSTRALIA		Runs	Balls	4/6
K.C.Wessels	c and b Willey	57	100	6
G.M.Wood	lbw b Cowans	5	14	1
D.M.Wellham	lbw b Botham	7	19	1
*A.R.Border	not out	85	123	5
D.C.Boon	b Allott	13	12	1/1
†W.B.Phillips	c Gatting b Cowans	14	16	2
S.P.O'Donnell	b Botham	28	34	4
G.R.J.Matthews	not out	8	7	1
G.F.Lawson				
C.J.McDermott				
J.R.Thomson				
Extras	(lb 13, w 2, nb 1)	16		
Total	**(54 overs; 6 wickets)**	**233**		

AUSTRALIA	O	M	R	W
Lawson	11	0	53	2
McDermott	11	0	56	2
O'Donnell	11	2	32	2
Thomson	11	0	47	1
Matthews	10	1	38	0
Border	1	0	3	0

ENGLAND	O	M	R	W
Botham	10	2	38	2
Cowans	11	2	42	2
Allott	10	1	40	1
Willey	11	1	38	1
Edmonds	10	0	48	0
Gooch	2	0	14	0

FALL OF WICKETS
1-63, 2-69, 3-134, 4-193, 5-206, 6-208, 7-216

FALL OF WICKETS
1-10, 2-19, 3-116, 4-137, 5-157, 6-222

Umpires: D.J.Constant (25) and D.R.Shepherd (6).

ENGLAND v AUSTRALIA 1985

At Lord's, London on 3 June 1985.　　Result: **ENGLAND** won by 8 wickets.　　Toss: England.
Award: D.I.Gower.　　LOI debuts: None.

Ian Botham was the first to complete the LOI double of 1,000 runs and 100 wickets. The partnership of 202 between Graham Gooch, who hit his second hundred in succession, and David Gower remains England's second-wicket record. For the first time three hundreds were scored in a limited-overs international.

AUSTRALIA		Runs	Balls	4/6
G.M.Wood	not out	114	165	10/1
A.M.J.Hilditch	lbw b Foster	4	8	I
G.M.Ritchie	c Gooch b Botham	15	46	2
A.R.Border	b Gooch	44	60	5
D.C.Boon	c Gower b Willey	45	47	3/1
W.B.Phillips	run out	10	5	2
S.P.O'Donnell	not out	0	1	–
G.R.J.Matthews				
G.F.Lawson				
C.J.McDermott				
J.R.Thomson				
Extras	(b 2, lb 13, w 6, nb 1)	22		
Total	(55 overs; 5 wickets)	254		

ENGLAND		Runs	Balls	4/6
G.A.Gooch	not out	117	164	13/1
R.T.Robinson	lbw b McDermott	7	18	I
* D.I.Gower	c Border b McDermott	102	118	14/1
A.J.Lamb	not out	9	8	I
I.T.Botham				
M.W.Gatting				
P.Willey				
† P.R.Downton				
N.A.Foster				
P.J.W.Allott				
N.G.Cowans				
Extras	(b 2, lb 9, w 2, nb 9)	22		
Total	(49 overs; 2 wickets)	257		

ENGLAND	O	M	R	W
Cowans	8	2	22	0
Foster	11	0	55	I
Botham	8	I	27	I
Allott	7	I	45	0
Gooch	11	0	46	I
Willey	10	I	44	I

AUSTRALIA	O	M	R	W
Lawson	9	0	37	0
McDermott	10	0	51	2
Thomson	8	I	50	0
O'Donnell	11	0	54	0
Matthews	10	0	49	0
Border	I	0	5	0

FALL OF WICKETS
1-6, 2-47, 3-143, 4-228, 5-252

FALL OF WICKETS
1-25, 2-227

Umpires: H.D.Bird (29) and B.J.Meyer (16).

SRI LANKA v INDIA 1985-86

At Sinhalese Sports Club, Colombo on 25 August 1985.　　Result: **INDIA** won by 2 wickets.　　Toss: India.
Award: R.L.Dias.　　LOI debuts: India – G.Sharma.

Dilip Vengsarkar played the decisive innings as India narrowly won their inaugural limited-overs international in Sri Lanka.

SRI LANKA		Runs	Balls	4/6
† S.A.R.Silva	c C.Sharma b Shastri	36	75	I
J.R.Ratnayeke	c Shastri b Amarnath	13	47	I
R.S.Madugalle	c and b G.Sharma	3	13	–
R.L.Dias	b C.Sharma	80	67	8/1
A.Ranatunga	b C.Sharma	64	48	5/1
* L.R.D.Mendis	not out	29	17	3
P.A.de Silva	b C.Sharma	4	2	I
A.L.F.de Mel	not out	2	3	–
R.J.Ratnayake				
R.G.C.E.Wijesuriya				
V.B.John				
Extras	(lb 10)	10		
Total	(45 overs; 6 wickets)	241		

INDIA		Runs	Balls	4/6
R.J.Shastri	c Ratnayeke b Ranatunga	67	102	5
K.Srikkanth	c De Mel b Wijesuriya	29	37	2/1
M.Azharuddin	b Wijesuriya	7	9	–
D.B.Vengsarkar	c Ratnayeke b Ratnayake	89	82	11/1
* Kapil Dev	c Silva b Ratnayeke	24	19	I
S.M.Gavaskar	run out	0	1	–
M.Amarnath	c Silva b Ratnayeke	2	3	–
C.Sharma	run out	8	5	I
† S.Viswanath	not out	7	5	I
L.Sivaramakrishnan	not out	I	4	–
G.Sharma				
Extras	(lb 6, w 1, nb 1)	8		
Total	(44.3 overs; 8 wickets)	242		

INDIA	O	M	R	W
Kapil Dev	9	I	47	0
C.Sharma	9	2	50	3
G.Sharma	9	0	21	I
Amarnath	8	0	40	I
Shastri	5	0	35	I
Sivaramakrishnan	5	0	38	0

SRI LANKA	O	M	R	W
De Mel	8.3	I	54	0
John	9	0	32	0
Ratnayake	9	0	35	2
Wijesuriya	8	0	56	2
Ratnayeke	6	0	32	2
Ranatunga	4	0	27	I

FALL OF WICKETS
1-34, 2-40, 3-82, 4-192, 5-227, 6-231

FALL OF WICKETS
1-61, 2-81, 3-135, 4-185, 5-196, 6-200, 7-221, 8-234

Umpires: H.C.Felsinger (7) and P.W.Vidanagamage (6).

SRI LANKA v INDIA 1985-86

At P.Saravanamuttu Stadium, Colombo on 21 September 1985.　　Result: **SRI LANKA** won by 14 runs.　　Toss: India.
Award: R.S.Madugalle.　　LOI debuts: None.

A polished and powerful 39-ball fifty by Ranjan Madugalle inflicted a surprise defeat on the world limited-overs champions in a truncated match.

SRI LANKA		Runs	Balls	4/6
† S.A.R.Silva	b Kapil Dev	11	15	4
P.A.de Silva	c Kapil Dev b Shastri	24	25	1/1
R.L.Dias	b G.Sharma	27	23	3
* L.R.D.Mendis	run out	20	22	-/1
A.Ranatunga	b Binny	7	10	–
R.S.Madugalle	not out	50	39	2/3
J.R.Ratnayake	not out	26	35	1
A.L.F.de Mel				
R.J.Ratnayake				
R.G.C.E.Wijesuriya				
V.B.John				
Extras	(lb 4, w 1, nb 1)	6		
Total	(28 overs; 5 wickets)	**171**		

INDIA		Runs	Balls	4/6
R.J.Shastri	st Silva b Wijesuriya	25	32	2
K.Srikkanth	b John	10	16	1/1
M.Azharuddin	c Mendis b John	26	30	2
D.B.Vengsarkar	run out	50	46	5
S.M.Gavaskar	not out	36	34	3
* Kapil Dev	not out	6	10	–
M.Amarnath				
R.M.H.Binny				
C.Sharma				
† S.Viswanath				
G.Sharma				
Extras	(lb 2, w 2)	4		
Total	(28 overs; 4 wickets)	**157**		

INDIA	O	M	R	W
Kapil Dev	5	0	26	1
C.Sharma	6	0	49	0
Shastri	6	0	22	1
Binny	5	0	42	1
G.Sharma	6	1	28	1

SRI LANKA	O	M	R	W
De Mel	3	0	20	0
John	6	0	26	2
Ratnayake	6	0	33	0
Ratnayeke	6	0	34	0
Wijesuriya	5	0	31	1
Ranatunga	2	0	11	0

FALL OF WICKETS
1-21, 2-54, 3-86, 4-86, 5-98

FALL OF WICKETS
1-12, 2-60, 3-75, 4-143

Umpires: B.C.Cooray (1) and K.T.Francis (6).

SRI LANKA v INDIA 1985-86

At P.Saravanamuttu Stadium, Colombo on 22 September 1985.　　No result.　　Toss: Sri Lanka.
Award: D.B.Vengsarkar.　　LOI debuts: None.

Fading light enabled Sri Lanka to draw this series after Dilip Vengsarkar's third fifty of the series had boosted India's run rate. Sri Lanka were attempting a revised target of 72 in 15 overs when play was abandoned.

INDIA		Runs	Balls	4/6
R.J.Shastri	lbw b Ratnayeke	45	69	2
K.Srikkanth	b De Mel	8	25	–
M.Azharuddin	run out	13	10	–
D.B.Vengsarkar	b Ratnayake	55	55	3
M.Amarnath	c Silva b Ratnayake	5	10	–
* Kapil Dev	c Wijesuriya b Ranatunga	12	15	1
S.M.Gavaskar	not out	39	44	3
R.M.H.Binny	not out	8	12	1
C.Sharma				
† S.Viswanath				
G.Sharma				
Extras	(b 3, lb 5, w 1)	9		
Total	(40 overs; 6 wickets)	**194**		

SRI LANKA		Runs	Balls	4/6
† S.A.R.Silva	b Kapil Dev	1	4	–
P.A.de Silva	c Vengsarkar b C.Sharma	2	6	–
R.L.Dias	c Kapil Dev b C.Sharma	12	20	1
* L.R.D.Mendis	not out	14	22	1
R.S.Madugalle	c Viswanath b Kapil Dev	1	3	–
A.Ranatunga	not out	0	1	–
J.R.Ratnayeke				
A.L.F.de Mel				
R.J.Ratnayake				
R.G.C.E.Wijesuriya				
V.B.John				
Extras	(lb 1, w 1)	2		
Total	(9.2 overs; 4 wickets)	**32**		

SRI LANKA	O	M	R	W
De Mel	8	0	39	1
John	8	2	22	0
Ratnayake	7	0	41	2
Ranatunga	6	0	23	1
Ratnayeke	7	0	38	1
Wijesuriya	4	0	23	0

INDIA	O	M	R	W
Kapil Dev	5	0	20	2
C.Sharma	4.2	0	11	2

FALL OF WICKETS
1-4, 2-4, 3-26, 4-32

FALL OF WICKETS
1-25, 2-55, 3-84, 4-102, 5-135, 6-173

Umpires: D.C.C.Perera (1) and K.T.Ponnambalam (1).

PAKISTAN v SRI LANKA 1985-86

At Shahi Bagh Stadium, Peshawar on 13 October 1985.   Result: **PAKISTAN** won by 8 wickets.   Toss: Pakistan.
Award: Mudassar Nazar.   LOI debuts: None.

Pakistan dominated this four-match 40-over series from the outset.

SRI LANKA		Runs	Balls	4/6
S.A.R.Silva	b Tahir	25	62	2
P.A.de Silva	c Ashraf b Imran	0	1	–
R.S.Madugalle	b Zakir	0	14	–
R.L.Dias	b Mudassar	5	14	–
L.R.D.Mendis	b Qadir	23	33	1
A.Ranatunga	lbw b Qadir	11	16	2
J.R.Ratnayeke	b Mudassar	0	3	–
A.L.F.de Mel	run out	36	34	3/1
R.J.Ratnayake	b Tahir	19	28	2
R.G.C.E.Wijesuriya	lbw b Imran	0	9	–
V.B.John	not out	3	6	–
Extras	(b 4, lb 3, w 9, nb 7)	23		
Total	(39.2 overs)	**145**		

PAKISTAN		Runs	Balls	4/6
Mudassar Nazar	lbw b De Mel	40	59	4
Shoaib Mohammed	not out	72		11
Ramiz Raja	b Wijesuriya	7		1
* Javed Miandad	not out	8		2
Zaheer Abbas				
Salim Malik				
Imran Khan				
† Ashraf Ali				
Tahir Naqqash				
Abdul Qadir				
Zakir Khan				
Extras	(b 4, lb 3, w 7, nb 6)	20		
Total	(32.5 overs; 2 wickets)	**147**		

PAKISTAN	O	M	R	W
Imran Khan	8	0	22	2
Zakir Khan	8	2	21	1
Mudassar Nazar	8	0	32	2
Tahir Naqqash	7.2	0	29	2
Abdul Qadir	8	0	34	2

SRI LANKA	O	M	R	W
De Mel	8	2	27	1
John	5	0	28	0
Ratnayake	5	1	22	0
Wijesuriya	6	1	18	1
Ratnayeke	4.5	0	33	0
Ranatunga	4	0	12	0

FALL OF WICKETS
1-2, 2-11, 3-35, 4-50, 5-66, 6-69, 7-90, 8-126, 9-133, 10-145

FALL OF WICKETS
1-113, 2-138

Umpires: Javed Akhtar (7) and Khizer Hayat (10).

PAKISTAN v SRI LANKA 1985-86

At Municipal Stadium, Gujranwala on 23 October 1985.   Result: **PAKISTAN** won by 15 runs.   Toss: Sri Lanka.
Award: P.A.de Silva.   LOI debuts: None.

The estimated attendance of 20,000 exceeded the stadium's capacity by 5,000. One man was killed and nine injured
when their vantage point, a tree branch outside the ground, broke under their weight.

PAKISTAN		Runs	Balls	4/6
Mudassar Nazar	c Silva b Ratnayake	11	31	1
Shoaib Mohammed	c Madugalle b De Mel	4	3	1
Ramiz Raja	b Wijesuriya	45	57	5
* Javed Miandad	c Silva b Ratnayake	10	25	1
Zaheer Abbas	c De Silva b Ratnayake	61	67	3
Salim Malik	not out	72	60	6/1
Imran Khan	not out	1	2	–
† Salim Yousuf				
Tahir Naqqash				
Abdul Qadir				
Zakir Khan				
Extras	(lb 7, w 11, nb 2)	20		
Total	(40 overs; 5 wickets)	**224**		

SRI LANKA		Runs	Balls	4/6
† S.A.R.Silva	c Salim Yousuf b Qadir	19	34	1
P.A.de Silva	run out	86	92	2/4
R.S.Madugalle	c Miandad b Qadir	7	14	–
R.L.Dias	c Tahir b Imran	43	54	2
* L.R.D.Mendis	run out	4	3	–
A.Ranatunga	not out	17	17	–
A.L.F.de Mel	b Tahir	7	12	–
R.J.Ratnayake	run out	9	7	1
J.R.Ratnayeke	not out	0	1	–
R.G.C.E.Wijesuriya				
V.B.John				
Extras	(lb 10, w 4, nb 3)	17		
Total	(40 overs; 7 wickets)	**209**		

SRI LANKA	O	M	R	W
De Mel	6	0	41	1
John	8	1	17	0
Ratnayake	8	0	51	3
Ratnayeke	6	0	44	0
Wijesuriya	8	0	40	1
Ranatunga	4	0	24	0

PAKISTAN	O	M	R	W
Imran Khan	8	0	47	1
Zakir Khan	3	0	23	0
Abdul Qadir	8	0	25	2
Mudassar Nazar	8	0	39	0
Shoaib Mohammed	6	0	30	0
Tahir Naqqash	7	0	35	1

FALL OF WICKETS
1-6, 2-49, 3-68, 4-106, 5-222

FALL OF WICKETS
1-53, 2-65, 3-161, 4-163, 5-169, 6-195, 7-209

Umpires: Mian Mohammad Aslam (3) and Shakoor Rana (12).

PAKISTAN v SRI LANKA 1985-86

At Gaddafi Stadium, Lahore on 25 October 1985.　　Result: **PAKISTAN** won by 5 wickets.　　Toss: Pakistan.
Award: Javed Miandad.　　LOI debuts: Sri Lanka – F.S.Ahangama.

The match was reduced to ensure the first innings would end in time for Juma prayers at 12.45pm. Another capacity crowd – 40,000 – were entertained by a run rate in excess of one per ball.

SRI LANKA		Runs	Balls	4/6
† S.A.R.Silva	lbw b Tahir	19	46	1
P.A.de Silva	lbw b Imran	0	4	–
R.S.Madugalle	c Imran b Mudassar	73	77	3/4
A.Ranatunga	b Tahir	39	39	4
R.L.Dias	c Salim Malik b Mudassar	9	12	–
* L.R.D.Mendis	not out	27	25	3
A.L.F.de Mel	c Salim Yousuf b Tahir	2	3	–
R.J.Ratnayake	c Zaheer b Mohsin	26	14	4/1
R.G.C.E.Wijesuriya	not out	6	7	
V.B.John				
F.S.Ahangama				
Extras	(b 4, lb 15, w 8)	27		
Total	(38 overs; 7 wickets)	**228**		

PAKISTAN	O	M	R	W
Imran Khan	7	1	33	1
Mohsin Kamal	6	1	18	1
Abdul Qadir	8	0	26	0
Tahir Naqqash	8	0	59	3
Mudassar Nazar	6	0	41	2
Salim Malik	2	0	22	0
Shoaib Mohammed	1	0	10	0

FALL OF WICKETS
1-2, 2-42, 3-135, 4-151, 5-165, 6-174, 7-211

PAKISTAN		Runs	Balls	4/6
Mudassar Nazar	run out	16	30	1
Shoaib Mohammed	lbw b De Mel	14	17	1
Ramiz Raja	c De Mel b Ratnayake	56	56	6
* Javed Miandad	not out	91	75	8
Zaheer Abbas	b Ranatunga	21	28	–
Salim Malik	c De Mel b Ratnayake	13	8	2
Imran Khan	not out	2	3	–
† Salim Yousuf				
Tahir Naqqash				
Abdul Qadir				
Mohsin Kamal				
Extras	(b 1, lb 5, w 6, nb 6)	18		
Total	(36.3 overs; 5 wickets)	**231**		

SRI LANKA	O	M	R	W
De Mel	7	0	38	1
John	8	0	45	0
Ratnayake	6.3	0	50	2
Ahangama	3	0	23	0
Wijesuriya	8	0	46	0
Ranatunga	4	0	23	1

FALL OF WICKETS
1-27, 2-53, 3-130, 4-188, 5-206

Umpires: Amanullah Khan (7) and Shakoor Rana (13).

PAKISTAN v SRI LANKA 1985-86

At Niaz Stadium, Hyderabad on 3 November 1985.　　Result: **PAKISTAN** won by 89 runs.　　Toss: Sri Lanka.
Award: Javed Miandad.　　LOI debuts: Sri Lanka – A.P.Gurusinha.

Pakistan completed their series whitewash on a pitch relaid only four weeks previously. Aravinda de Silva hooked the first ball of Sri Lanka's innings for six.

PAKISTAN		Runs	Balls	4/6
Mudassar Nazar	c and b Wijesuriya	29	55	–
Mohsin Khan	lbw b John	6	18	–
Ramiz Raja	lbw b Ratnayeke	45	43	4
* Javed Miandad	c sub (S.Warnakulasuriya) b Ratnayeke	56	49	5
Zaheer Abbas	c Gurusinha b Ratnayeke	26	27	2
Salim Malik	c Mendis b Wijesuriya	16	21	–
† Salim Yousuf	b Ratnayeke	0	4	–
Abdul Qadir	not out	20	15	1/1
Tahir Naqqash	not out	7	4	–
Tausif Ahmed				
Mohsin Kamal				
Extras	(b 4, lb 7)	11		
Total	(39 overs; 7 wickets)	**216**		

SRI LANKA	O	M	R	W
De Mel	8	1	42	0
John	8	1	34	1
Ratnayake	8	0	45	1
Wijesuriya	5	0	25	2
Ratnayeke	6	0	34	3
Ranatunga	4	0	25	0

FALL OF WICKETS
1-12, 2-81, 3-91, 4-127, 5-163, 6-168, 7-195

Umpires: Feroz Butt (1) and Shakil Khan (6).

SRI LANKA		Runs	Balls	4/6
P.A.de Silva	c Mohsin Khan b Mohsin Kamal	19	22	–/1
J.R.Ratnayeke	c Salim Yousuf b Mohsin Kamal	8	14	1
R.S.Madugalle	c Tahir b Mudassar	9	16	–
R.L.Dias	b Mudassar	13	31	–
* L.R.D.Mendis	st Salim Yousuf b Qadir	46	74	3
A.Ranatunga	c Tahir b Tausif	1	8	–
† A.P.Gurusinha	run out	0	3	–
A.L.F.de Mel	c sub (Shoaib Mohammed) b Zaheer	0	16	–
R.J.Ratnayake	c Mohsin Kamal b Zaheer	2	6	–
R.G.C.E.Wijesuriya	not out	12	32	–
V.B.John	c Salim Malik b Qadir	7	9	1
Extras	(lb 7, w 1, nb 2)	10		
Total	(37.2 overs)	**127**		

PAKISTAN	O	M	R	W
Mohsin Kamal	4	0	26	2
Tahir Naqqash	3	0	12	0
Mudassar Nazar	8	0	23	2
Tausif Ahmed	8	2	20	1
Abdul Qadir	7.2	2	13	2
Zaheer Abbas	7	0	26	2

FALL OF WICKETS
1-20, 2-34, 3-41, 4-69, 5-80, 6-83, 7-87, 8-91, 9-112, 10-127

WEST INDIES v PAKISTAN 1985-86

At Sharjah CA Stadium, UAE on 15 November 1985.   Result: **WEST INDIES** won by 7 wickets.   Toss: Pakistan.
Award: R.B.Richardson.   LOI debuts: West Indies – A.H.Gray.

45-over tournament. Imran Khan hit three sixes in an over from Joel Garner having mistakenly batted first in the belief that West Indies were more vulnerable when chasing a target.

PAKISTAN		Runs	Balls	4/6
Mudassar Nazar	c Logie b Holding	18	58	–
Mohsin Khan	not out	86	126	5/1
Qasim Omar	c Richards b Gray	2	18	–
Ramiz Raja	c and b Garner	35	54	2
Javed Miandad	b Marshall	16	8	3
Imran Khan	not out	25	9	–/3
Salim Malik				
Salim Yousuf				
Wasim Akram				
Abdul Qadir				
Tausif Ahmed				
Extras	(b 1, lb 6, w 4, nb 3)	14		
Total	(45 overs; 4 wickets)	196		

WEST INDIES		Runs	Balls	4/6
D.L.Haynes	b Wasim	0	4	–
R.B.Richardson	not out	99	141	11/1
H.A.Gomes	c Salim Yousuf b Mudassar	32	68	3
* I.V.A.Richards	c Salim Yousuf b Imran	51	50	5/1
A.L.Logie	not out	6	6	1
† P.J.L.Dujon				
M.D.Marshall				
R.A.Harper				
J.Garner				
M.A.Holding				
A.H.Gray				
Extras	(lb 8, nb 3)	11		
Total	(44.1 overs; 3 wickets)	199		

WEST INDIES	O	M	R	W
Garner	9	1	59	1
Gray	8	1	32	1
Holding	5	0	17	1
Marshall	8	1	30	1
Harper	9	2	26	0
Richards	6	0	25	0

PAKISTAN	O	M	R	W
Wasim Akram	8.1	1	40	1
Imran Khan	9	0	41	1
Mudassar Nazar	9	0	32	1
Tausif Ahmed	9	1	38	0
Abdul Qadir	9	0	40	0

FALL OF WICKETS
1-50, 2-58, 3-142, 4-161

FALL OF WICKETS
1-0, 2-72, 3-177

Umpires: H.D.Bird (*England*) (30) and D.R.Shepherd (*England*) (7).

INDIA v PAKISTAN 1985-86

At Sharjah CA Stadium, UAE on 17 November 1985.   Result: **PAKISTAN** won by 48 runs.   Toss: India.
Award: Mudassar Nazar.   LOI debuts: None.

Pakistan inflicted a rare defeat on the current limited-overs kings.

PAKISTAN		Runs	Balls	4/6
Mudassar Nazar	c Vengsarkar b Sivaramakrishnan	67	117	4/1
Mohsin Khan	run out	2	15	–
Ramiz Raja	c Gavaskar b Binny	66	91	4
Javed Miandad	not out	37	34	3
* Imran Khan	run out	9	6	1
Salim Malik	not out	12	8	1
† Salim Yousuf				
Mohsin Kamal				
Wasim Akram				
Abdul Qadir				
Tausif Ahmed				
Extras	(lb 8, w 1, nb 1)	10		
Total	(45 overs; 4 wickets)	203		

INDIA		Runs	Balls	4/6
S.M.Gavaskar	st Salim Yousuf b Tausif	63	105	3
K.Srikkanth	c Salim Yousuf b Mohsin Kamal	4	12	–
M.Azharuddin	lbw b Wasim	3	13	–
D.B.Vengsarkar	c Salim Malik b Tausif	27	53	2
R.J.Shastri	run out	12	12	1
* Kapil Dev	lbw b Tausif	0	3	–
M.Amarnath	b Mudassar	11	21	2
R.M.H.Binny	c Tausif b Mohsin Kamal	11	12	1
C.Sharma	b Mudassar	1	7	–
† S.M.H.Kirmani	not out	5	8	–
L.Sivaramakrishnan	run out	1	1	–
Extras	(b 2, lb 9, w 4, nb 2)	17		
Total	(40.4 overs)	155		

INDIA	O	M	R	W
Kapil Dev	7	1	26	0
Binny	9	1	36	1
Sharma	7	1	40	0
Shastri	9	1	26	0
Sivaramakrishnan	9	0	40	1
Amarnath	4	0	27	0

PAKISTAN	O	M	R	W
Wasim Akram	7.4	2	15	1
Mohsin Kamal	7	0	27	2
Mudassar Nazar	9	0	43	2
Imran Khan	1.1	0	3	0
Abdul Qadir	6.5	0	26	0
Tausif Ahmed	9	2	30	3

FALL OF WICKETS
1-18, 2-118, 3-169, 4-185

FALL OF WICKETS
1-9, 2-28, 3-84, 4-115, 5-118, 6-129, 7-135, 8-139, 9-151, 10-155

Umpires: H.D.Bird (*England*) (31) and D.R.Shepherd (*England*) (8).

INDIA v WEST INDIES 1985-86

At Sharjah CA Stadium, UAE on 22 November 1985.   Result: **WEST INDIES** won by 8 wickets.   Toss: India.
Award: J.Garner.   LOI debuts: None.

Joel Garner followed his most expensive analysis with his most economical one as West Indies won the Rothmans Cup and $50,000. Voted 'Player of the Series', Richie Richardson was presented with $3,000 and a car.

INDIA		Runs	Balls	4/6
* S.M.Gavaskar	not out	76	128	4/3
K.Srikkanth	b Garner	6	18	1
M.Amarnath	c Richards b Garner	0	7	–
D.B.Vengsarkar	c Garner b Holding	6	33	–
M.Azharuddin	run out	35	72	2
Kapil Dev	not out	28	25	2
R.J.Shastri				
R.M.H.Binny				
† S.M.H.Kirmani				
R.S.Ghai				
L.Sivaramakrishnan				
Extras	(lb 17, w 4, nb 8)	29		
Total	(45 overs; 4 wickets)	**180**		

WEST INDIES		O	M	R	W
Marshall		9	2	35	0
Garner		9	4	11	2
Walsh		9	1	37	0
Holding		9	3	28	1
Harper		9	0	52	0

FALL OF WICKETS
1-10, 2-11, 3-25, 4-125

WEST INDIES		Runs	Balls	4/6
D.L.Haynes	not out	72	105	6
R.B.Richardson	b Ghai	72	103	7
H.A.Gomes	b Kapil Dev	10	28	–
* I.V.A.Richards	not out	24	13	2/2
A.L.Logie				
† P.J.L.Dujon				
M.D.Marshall				
R.A.Harper				
J.Garner				
M.A.Holding				
C.A.Walsh				
Extras	(lb 8)	8		
Total	(41.3 overs; 2 wickets)	**186**		

INDIA	O	M	R	W
Kapil Dev	8	1	29	1
Binny	7	0	36	0
Ghai	8.3	0	54	1
Shastri	9	1	27	0
Sivaramakrishnan	9	0	32	0

FALL OF WICKETS
1-114, 2-147

Umpires: H.D.Bird (*England*) (32) and D.R.Shepherd (*England*) (9).

PAKISTAN v WEST INDIES 1985-86

At Municipal Stadium, Gujranwala on 27 November 1985.   Result: **WEST INDIES** won by 8 wickets.   Toss: West Indies.
Award: I.V.A.Richards.   LOI debuts: None.

Thanks to an extraordinary piece of mayhem by their captain, West Indies drew first blood in this five-match 40-over tournament. Abdul Qadir conceded 24 runs from one over.

PAKISTAN		Runs	Balls	4/6
Mudassar Nazar	c Walsh b Holding	77	118	6/1
Mohsin Khan	c Dujon b Walsh	17		3
Ramiz Raja	b Harper	17		2
Javed Miandad	lbw b Harper	22		1
* Imran Khan	c Harper b Holding	45	42	6/1
Salim Malik	not out	11		1
† Salim Yousuf	not out	0		–
Wasim Akram				
Abdul Qadir				
Tausif Ahmed				
Mohsin Kamal				
Extras	(b 3, lb 13, w 8, nb 5)	29		
Total	(40 overs; 5 wickets)	**218**		

WEST INDIES	O	M	R	W
Marshall	8	0	47	0
Garner	6	1	24	0
Walsh	8	0	39	1
Holding	8	1	39	2
Harper	8	2	37	2
Richards	2	0	16	0

FALL OF WICKETS
1-29, 2-74, 3-113, 4-169, 5-218

WEST INDIES		Runs	Balls	4/6
D.L.Haynes	c sub (Shoaib Mohd) b Wasim	39	59	4
R.B.Richardson	lbw b Mohsin Kamal	5	8	1
A.L.Logie	not out	78	107	11
* I.V.A.Richards	not out	80	39	10/4
† P.J.L.Dujon				
M.D.Marshall				
R.A.Harper				
M.A.Holding				
J.Garner				
A.H.Gray				
C.A.Walsh				
Extras	(b 1, lb 8, w 13)	22		
Total	(35.3 overs; 2 wickets)	**224**		

PAKISTAN	O	M	R	W
Wasim Akram	6	1	31	1
Mohsin Kamal	5.3	1	34	1
Abdul Qadir	6	1	39	0
Mudassar Nazar	5	0	31	0
Tausif Ahmed	5	1	46	0
Imran Khan	8	0	34	0

FALL OF WICKETS
1-8, 2-105

Umpires: Athar Zaidi (2) and Khizer Hayat (11).

PAKISTAN v WEST INDIES 1985-86

At Gaddafi Stadium, Lahore on 29 November 1985.   Result: **PAKISTAN** won by 6 wickets.   Toss: Pakistan.
Award: Abdul Qadir.   LOI debuts: None.

A crowd of 30,000 exhorted Pakistan to their first LOI home win against West Indies as Abdul Qadir made amends.

WEST INDIES		Runs	Balls	4/6
D.L.Haynes	b Zakir	26		3
R.B.Richardson	c Ramiz b Wasim	22		2
A.L.Logie	b Zakir	9		1
I.V.A.Richards	b Mudassar	53		2/1
H.A.Gomes	b Qadir	23		–
P.J.L.Dujon	b Qadir	4		–
R.A.Harper	c Salim Malik b Mudassar	5		–
M.D.Marshall	b Wasim	1		–
M.A.Holding	st Salim Yousuf b Qadir	0		–
A.H.Gray	not out	7		1
C.A.Walsh	c Wasim b Qadir	7		–/1
Extras	(b 3, lb 7, w 4, nb 2)	16		
Total	(36.2 overs)	**173**		

PAKISTAN		Runs	Balls	4/6
Mudassar Nazar	c Walsh b Gray	15		2
Mohsin Khan	lbw b Gray	43	78	3
Ramiz Raja	c and b Holding	12		1
Javed Miandad	b Harper	41		3
*Imran Khan	not out	22		–
Salim Malik	not out	26		3
†Salim Yousuf				
Abdul Qadir				
Wasim Akram				
Mohsin Kamal				
Zakir Khan				
Extras	(b 1, lb 8, w 2, nb 5)	16		
Total	(38.3 overs; 4 wickets)	**175**		

PAKISTAN	O	M	R	W
Imran Khan	5	1	25	0
Wasim Akram	5	0	24	2
Zakir Khan	8	0	31	2
Mohsin Kamal	8	0	40	0
Abdul Qadir	5.2	0	17	4
Mudassar Nazar	5	0	26	2

WEST INDIES	O	M	R	W
Marshall	7.3	0	38	0
Gray	8	0	36	2
Walsh	8	0	32	0
Holding	7	1	33	1
Harper	8	0	27	1

FALL OF WICKETS
1-23, 2-47, 3-124, 4-126

FALL OF WICKETS
1-45, 2-61, 3-70, 4-129, 5-143, 6-151, 7-156, 8-156, 9-164, 10-173

Umpires: Amanullah Khan (8) and Shakoor Rana (14).

PAKISTAN v WEST INDIES 1985-86

At Shahi Bagh Stadium, Peshawar on 2 December 1985.   Result: **WEST INDIES** won by 40 runs.   Toss: West Indies.
Award: I.V.A.Richards.   LOI debuts: None.

Another Viv Richards epic put the scoreboard operators under pressure.

WEST INDIES		Runs	Balls	4/6
D.L.Haynes	c Mohsin Kamal b Imran	60	97	2
R.B.Richardson	st Salim Yousuf b Tausif	27	52	3
H.A.Gomes	run out	15	26	–
*I.V.A.Richards	c Mohsin Khan b Imran	66	39	5/4
A.L.Logie	lbw b Imran	0	1	–
†P.J.L.Dujon	not out	9	15	–
R.A.Harper	not out	0	3	–
M.D.Marshall				
M.A.Holding				
J.Garner				
C.A.Walsh				
Extras	(b 4, lb 13, w 3, nb 4)	24		
Total	(40 overs; 5 wickets)	**201**		

PAKISTAN		Runs	Balls	4/6
Mudassar Nazar	c and b Holding	19	43	1
Mohsin Khan	c Harper b Marshall	6	10	–
Ramiz Raja	run out	38	61	1
Javed Miandad	c Gomes b Holding	2	5	–
*Imran Khan	b Harper	8	12	–
Salim Malik	b Walsh	7	8	–
Abdul Qadir	b Marshall	37	33	2
†Salim Yousuf	b Holding	8	19	–
Wasim Akram	b Holding	9	13	1
Mohsin Kamal	b Marshall	5	7	–
Tausif Ahmed	not out	3	4	–
Extras	(b 3, lb 9, w 3, nb 4)	19		
Total	(39.3 overs)	**161**		

PAKISTAN	O	M	R	W
Imran Khan	7	0	39	3
Wasim Akram	6	0	24	0
Tausif Ahmed	8	1	24	1
Mohsin Kamal	8	0	31	0
Abdul Qadir	6	1	42	0
Mudassar Nazar	5	0	24	0

WEST INDIES	O	M	R	W
Marshall	8	1	36	3
Garner	8	1	22	0
Walsh	8	0	36	1
Holding	7.3	0	17	4
Harper	8	1	38	1

FALL OF WICKETS
1-15, 2-37, 3-47, 4-65, 5-80, 6-106, 7-138, 8-142, 9-149, 10-161

FALL OF WICKETS
1-70, 2-100, 3-169, 4-170, 5-192

Umpires: Ikram Rabbani (2) and Mian Mohammad Aslam (4).

PAKISTAN v WEST INDIES 1985-86

At Pindi Club Ground, Rawalpindi on 4 December 1985.   Result: **PAKISTAN** won by 5 wickets.   Toss: Pakistan.
Award: Shoaib Mohammed.   LOI debuts: Pakistan – Zulqarnain.

Shoaib Mohammed's dismissal of Viv Richards and sheet-anchor innings were major factors in Pakistan's drawing level in the series.

WEST INDIES		Runs	Balls	4/6
D.L.Haynes	run out	23	39	3
R.B.Richardson	not out	92	118	10/2
A.L.Logie	c sub (Tahir Naqqash) b Tausif	0	5	–
* I.V.A.Richards	c Zulqarnain b Shoaib	21	16	4
H.A.Gomes	run out	1	1	–
† P.J.L.Dujon	run out	12	29	–
R.A.Harper	lbw b Qadir	10	8	–/1
M.D.Marshall	c Zulqarnain b Wasim	20	18	1/1
M.A.Holding	c Imran b Wasim	2	4	–
J.Garner	not out	1	1	–
C.A.Walsh				
Extras	(b 4, lb 10, w 1, nb 2)	17		
Total	(40 overs; 8 wickets)	**199**		

PAKISTAN		O	M	R	W
Imran Khan		6	0	33	0
Wasim Akram		6	0	41	2
Tausif Ahmed		6	2	12	1
Mohsin Kamal		6	0	44	0
Shoaib Mohammed		8	0	30	1
Abdul Qadir		8	2	25	1

PAKISTAN		Runs	Balls	4/6
Shoaib Mohammed	c Walsh b Garner	53	80	3/1
Qasim Omar	lbw b Walsh	27	48	2
Javed Miandad	not out	67	82	2/1
Salim Malik	c Haynes b Harper	14	12	2
* Imran Khan	run out	8	11	1
Ramiz Raja	c and b Richards	3	6	–
Abdul Qadir	not out	0	1	–
Wasim Akram				
Mohsin Kamal				
Tausif Ahmed				
† Zulqarnain				
Extras	(b 9, lb 15, nb 7)	31		
Total	(39.1 overs; 5 wickets)	**203**		

WEST INDIES		O	M	R	W
Marshall		8	2	27	0
Garner		8	1	33	1
Walsh		8	0	43	1
Harper		8	0	41	1
Richards		2	0	6	1
Holding		5.1	0	29	0

FALL OF WICKETS
1-57, 2-57, 3-99, 4-100, 5-124, 6-136, 7-166, 8-198

FALL OF WICKETS
1-57, 2-141, 3-171, 4-184, 5-195

Umpires: Shakoor Rana (15) and Tariq Ata (2).

PAKISTAN v WEST INDIES 1985-86

At National Stadium, Karachi on 6 December 1985.   Result: **WEST INDIES** won by 8 wickets.   Toss: West Indies.
Award: M.D.Marshall.   LOI debuts: None.

Pakistan's collapse in this deciding match triggered the traditional crowd invasions. Pakistan's innings was halted at 87 for 4 and reduced by two overs when a stand was set alight. The police exchanged tear gas for assorted missiles.

PAKISTAN		Runs	Balls	4/6
Mohsin Khan	c Richardson b Marshall	54	106	2
Shoaib Mohammed	c Richardson b Gray	1	6	–
Ramiz Raja	c Dujon b Marshall	0	4	–
Salim Malik	run out	7	15	1
* Imran Khan	run out	19	40	1
Javed Miandad	b Holding	28	36	1
Abdul Qadir	not out	5	9	–
Wasim Akram	b Holding	0	2	–
† Zulqarnain	not out	4	11	–
Mohsin Kamal				
Tausif Ahmed				
Extras	(lb 4, w 4, nb 1)	9		
Total	(38 overs; 7 wickets)	**127**		

WEST INDIES		O	M	R	W
Marshall		8	1	25	2
Gray		6	4	14	1
Walsh		8	0	20	0
Holding		8	0	35	2
Harper		6	0	20	3
Richards		2	0	9	0

WEST INDIES		Runs	Balls	4/6
D.L.Haynes	c Mohsin Khan b Mohsin Kamal	39	73	4
R.B.Richardson	lbw b Wasim	13	32	2
H.A.Gomes	not out	20	67	1
* I.V.A.Richards	not out	40	36	4
A.L.Logie				
† P.J.L.Dujon				
R.A.Harper				
M.D.Marshall				
M.A.Holding				
C.A.Walsh				
A.H.Gray				
Extras	(b 1, lb 5, w 7, nb 3)	16		
Total	(34.1 overs; 2 wickets)	**128**		

PAKISTAN		O	M	R	W
Wasim Akram		8	0	25	1
Mohsin Kamal		7	1	47	1
Abdul Qadir		8	2	19	0
Imran Khan		8	2	19	0
Tausif Ahmed		3.1	0	12	0

FALL OF WICKETS
1-2, 2-3, 3-14, 4-45, 5-116, 6-117, 7-119

FALL OF WICKETS
1-26, 2-77

Umpires: Mahboob Shah (7) and Shakil Khan (7).

AUSTRALIA v NEW ZEALAND 1985-86

At Melbourne Cricket Ground on 9 January 1986.   No result.   Toss: Australia.
LOI debuts: Australia – S.P.Davis, D.R.Gilbert, B.A. Reid, S.R.Waugh; New Zealand – E.B.McSweeney.

The seventh World Series 50-over tournament again involved 15 qualifying games before the best-of-three finals.
Interrupted by rain after 35 minutes and reduced to 31 overs (which Australia failed to bowl), this match was abandoned
when further rain fell in the interval.

NEW ZEALAND		Runs	Balls	4/6	AUSTRALIA
J.G.Wright	run out	5	16	–	† W.B.Phillips
B.A.Edgar	b Davis	17	25	1	D.C.Boon
M.D.Crowe	b Gilbert	71	57	4	* A.R.Border
J.F.Reid	c Phillips b Davis	7	13	–	G.M.Ritchie
J.V.Coney	c Phillips b Waugh	24	32	1	D.W.Hookes
R.J.Hadlee	b Gilbert	5	8	–	S.R.Waugh
J.G.Bracewell	c Waugh b McDermott	13	15	–	G.R.J.Matthews
B.R.Blair	not out	7	8	–	C.J.McDermott
E.B.McSweeney	not out	2	3	–	B.A.Reid
S.L.Boock					D.R.Gilbert
E.J.Chatfield					S.P.Davis
Extras	(lb 5, w 3, nb 2)	10			
Total	(29 overs; 7 wickets)	**161**			

AUSTRALIA	O	M	R	W
McDermott	6	1	20	1
Davis	6	1	30	2
Reid	6	0	36	0
Matthews	4	0	24	0
Gilbert	5	0	33	2
Waugh	2	0	13	1

FALL OF WICKETS
1-10, 2-30, 3-50, 4-127, 5-137, 6-146, 7-152

Umpires: A.R.Crafter (36) and R.C.Isherwood (18).

NEW ZEALAND v INDIA 1985-86

At Woolloongabba, Brisbane on 11 January 1986.   Result: **INDIA** won by 5 wickets.   Toss: India.
Award: Kapil Dev.   LOI debuts: New Zealand – S.R.Gillespie; India – N.S.Yadav.

Kapil Dev and Ravi Shastri carried India to their highest total batting second with an unbroken stand of 87 from 86
balls.

NEW ZEALAND		Runs	Balls	4/6	INDIA		Runs	Balls	4/6
B.A.Edgar	b Kapil Dev	75	118	3	K.Srikkanth	run out	50	69	7
J.G.Wright	c Kirmani b Binny	2	9	–	S.M.Gavaskar	b Chatfield	27	17	4/1
M.D.Crowe	c and b Amarnath	76	83	8	M.Amarnath	b Boock	61	73	9/1
J.F.Reid	b Shastri	11	13	1	M.Azharuddin	run out	13	12	2
R.J.Hadlee	c Amarnath b Yadav	22	16	1/2	D.B.Vengsarkar	c Coney b Gillespie	9	29	–
* J.V.Coney	c Azharuddin b Yadav	11	11	1	* Kapil Dev	not out	54	53	5
B.R.Blair	not out	29	34	2/1	R.J.Shastri	not out	36	41	–
† E.B.McSweeney	b Sharma	6	7	–	R.M.H.Binny				
S.R.Gillespie	b Sharma	7	13	–	C.Sharma				
S.L.Boock	run out	0	1	–	† S.M.H.Kirmani				
E.J.Chatfield	not out	1	1	–	N.S.Yadav				
Extras	(lb 15, w 1, nb 3)	19			Extras	(lb 8, w 4, nb 1)	13		
Total	(50 overs; 9 wickets)	**259**			**Total**	(48 overs; 5 wickets)	**263**		

INDIA	O	M	R	W
Kapil Dev	10	0	28	1
Binny	6	1	29	1
Sharma	7	0	43	2
Amarnath	10	1	40	1
Yadav	8	0	51	2
Shastri	9	0	53	1

NEW ZEALAND	O	M	R	W
Chatfield	9	2	51	1
Hadlee	10	3	42	0
Blair	3	0	27	0
Gillespie	9	1	39	1
Coney	6	0	36	0
Boock	10	0	55	1
Crowe	1	0	5	0

FALL OF WICKETS
1-12, 2-142, 3-171, 4-196, 5-209, 6-223, 7-238, 8-254, 9-256

FALL OF WICKETS
1-40, 2-137, 3-154, 4-162, 5-176

Umpires: M.W.Johnson (39) and B.E.Martin (20).

AUSTRALIA v INDIA 1985-86

At Woolloongabba, Brisbane on 12 January 1986.   Result: **AUSTRALIA** won by 4 wickets.   Toss: Australia.
Award: G.R.J.Matthews.   LOI debuts: None.

This match was played on the pitch which had produced 522 runs the previous day.

INDIA		Runs	Balls	4/6
S.M.Gavaskar	b Davis	5	8	–
K.Srikkanth	c Matthews b McDermott	6	9	1
M.Amarnath	c Phillips b Gilbert	13	27	1
D.B.Vengsarkar	run out	19	63	1
M.Azharuddin	b Waugh	35	57	3
* Kapil Dev	run out	16	19	–/1
R.J.Shastri	b Reid	0	6	–
R.M.H.Binny	lbw b Waugh	8	12	–
C.Sharma	run out	22	28	1
† S.M.H.Kirmani	c Matthews b McDermott	27	33	4
N.S.Yadav	not out	0	2	–
Extras	(lb 6, w 2, nb 2)	10		
Total	(43 overs)	**161**		

AUSTRALIA		Runs	Balls	4/6
† W.B.Phillips	c Amarnath b Binny	8	9	2
D.C.Boon	c Gavaskar b Binny	14	22	2
* A.R.Border	c Kirmani b Sharma	16	25	3
D.W.Hookes	c Azharuddin b Binny	5	16	1
G.M.Ritchie	c and b Sharma	1	8	–
S.R.Waugh	b Yadav	40	95	2
G.R.J.Matthews	not out	46	77	1
C.J.McDermott	not out	24	21	4
D.R.Gilbert				
B.A.Reid				
S.P.Davis				
Extras	(lb 9, w 1)	10		
Total	(45.2 overs; 6 wickets)	**164**		

AUSTRALIA	O	M	R	W
McDermott	9	1	32	2
Davis	7	2	11	1
Gilbert	9	1	42	1
Waugh	10	0	46	2
Reid	8	1	24	1

INDIA	O	M	R	W
Kapil Dev	9.2	1	31	0
Binny	10	2	38	3
Sharma	6	0	28	2
Shastri	10	1	23	0
Amarnath	3	0	11	0
Yadav	7	1	24	1

FALL OF WICKETS
1-5, 2-13, 3-29, 4-69, 5-100, 6-100, 7-102, 8-113, 9-160, 10-161

FALL OF WICKETS
1-20, 2-27, 3-45, 4-45, 5-48, 6-127

Umpires: R.A.French (41) and S.G.Randell (13).

AUSTRALIA v NEW ZEALAND 1985-86

At Sydney Cricket Ground on 14 January 1986.   Result: **AUSTRALIA** won by 4 wickets.   Toss: Australia.
Award: D.R.Gilbert.   LOI debuts: Australia – G.R.Marsh.

Dave Gilbert's best LOI analysis dominated a low-scoring match on a seaming pitch far from ideal for instant cricket.
Playing in his 79th international, Richard Hadlee completed the double of 1,000 runs and 100 wickets.

NEW ZEALAND		Runs	Balls	4/6
J.G.Wright	st Phillips b Matthews	22	66	1
B.A.Edgar	c Ritchie b Davis	0	5	–
M.D.Crowe	c Phillips b Gilbert	9	24	–
J.F.Reid	c Phillips b Waugh	9	28	–
J.J.Crowe	c Marsh b Reid	12	37	–
* J.V.Coney	c Boon b Gilbert	58	86	2
J.G.Bracewell	c and b Gilbert	5	16	–
R.J.Hadlee	c Phillips b Gilbert	21	24	1
† E.B.McSweeney	b Gilbert	3	4	–
S.R.Gillespie	c Matthews b Davis	1	13	–
E.J.Chatfield	not out	4	5	–
Extras	(lb 2, w 3, nb 3)	8		
Total	(49.2 overs)	**152**		

AUSTRALIA		Runs	Balls	4/6
D.C.Boon	lbw b Gillespie	21	36	2
G.R.Marsh	c McSweeney b Chatfield	13	43	–
* A.R.Border	st McSweeney b Bracewell	16	31	1
G.M.Ritchie	c McSweeney b Hadlee	68	92	5
† W.B.Phillips	c Coney b Hadlee	3	20	–
S.R.Waugh	not out	19	48	1
G.R.J.Matthews	c M.D.Crowe b Chatfield	1	7	–
C.J.McDermott	not out	1	1	–
B.A.Reid				
D.R.Gilbert				
S.P.Davis				
Extras	(lb 5, w 4, nb 2)	11		
Total	(45.1 overs; 6 wickets)	**153**		

AUSTRALIA	O	M	R	W
McDermott	9	3	21	0
Davis	8.2	3	17	2
Gilbert	10	0	46	5
Matthews	10	1	17	1
Waugh	3	0	12	1
Reid	9	0	37	1

NEW ZEALAND	O	M	R	W
Hadlee	10	0	42	2
Chatfield	10	3	21	2
Gillespie	7.1	0	30	1
Bracewell	10	2	29	1
Coney	5	0	15	0
M.D.Crowe	3	1	11	0

FALL OF WICKETS
1-1, 2-19, 3-42, 4-44, 5-68, 6-84, 7-140, 8-144, 9-147, 10-152

FALL OF WICKETS
1-34, 2-41, 3-72, 4-87, 5-151, 6-152

Umpires: B.E.Martin (21) and S.G.Randell (14).

AUSTRALIA v INDIA 1985-86

At Melbourne Cricket Ground on 16 January 1986.　Result: **INDIA** won by 8 wickets.　Toss: India.
Award: S.R.Waugh.　LOI debuts: None.

Two interruptions for rain reduced this match by five overs. Australia's emphatic defeat was watched by a crowd of 52,612.

AUSTRALIA		Runs	Balls	4/6
G.R.Marsh	b Kapil Dev	5	28	–
D.C.Boon	run out	23	33	3
G.R.J.Matthews	run out	11	10	–
* A.R.Border	b Binny	0	1	–
G.M.Ritchie	c More b Shastri	3	13	–
S.R.Waugh	not out	73	104	2
† W.B.Phillips	b Sivaramakrishnan	7	25	–
C.J.McDermott	c Azharuddin b Sharma	12	20	1
D.R.Gilbert	c Sivaramakrishnan b Sharma	7	17	–
B.A.Reid	c Srikkanth b Binny	4	8	–
S.P.Davis	run out	6	10	–
Extras	(lb 8, w 1, nb 1)	10		
Total	**(44.2 overs)**	**161**		

INDIA		Runs	Balls	4/6
K.Srikkanth	run out	22	51	2
S.M.Gavaskar	c Phillips b Reid	59	99	2
M.Amarnath	not out	58	77	6
M.Azharuddin	not out	11	20	–
A.Malhotra				
* Kapil Dev				
R.M.H.Binny				
R.J.Shastri				
† K.S.More				
C.Sharma				
L.Sivaramakrishnan				
Extras	(lb 5, w 2, nb 5)	12		
Total	**(40.2 overs; 2 wickets)**	**162**		

INDIA	O	M	R	W
Kapil Dev	8.2	2	25	1
Binny	9	1	39	2
Shastri	9	1	23	1
Sharma	9	0	29	2
Sivaramakrishnan	9	1	37	1

AUSTRALIA	O	M	R	W
McDermott	8.2	1	29	0
Davis	9	3	16	0
Reid	9	0	39	1
Gilbert	7	0	41	0
Waugh	3	0	16	0
Matthews	4	0	16	0

FALL OF WICKETS
1-18, 2-31, 3-31, 4-40, 5-50, 6-80, 7-100, 8-128, 9-141, 10-161

FALL OF WICKETS
1-37, 2-126

Umpires: M.W.Johnson (40) and S.G.Randell (15).

NEW ZEALAND v INDIA 1985-86

At WACA Ground, Perth on 18 January 1986.　Result: **NEW ZEALAND** won by 3 wickets.　Toss: New Zealand.
Award: M.D.Crowe.　LOI debuts: None.

India were dismissed on an erratic newly laid pitch for the lowest LOI total against New Zealand at that time.

INDIA		Runs	Balls	4/6
K.Srikkanth	run out	0	4	–
S.M.Gavaskar	c M.D.Crowe b Gillespie	9	30	1
M.Amarnath	c M.D.Crowe b Snedden	30	71	2
M.Azharuddin	b M.D.Crowe	11	38	1
A.Malhotra	c Wright b Hadlee	15	26	2
R.J.Shastri	c McSweeney b Chatfield	23	47	2
* Kapil Dev	c J.J.Crowe b Hadlee	0	1	–
C.Sharma	c McSweeney b Snedden	6	16	1
R.M.H.Binny	c Wright b Snedden	1	9	–
† K.S.More	c Snedden b Chatfield	2	18	–
L.Sivaramakrishnan	not out	2	13	–
Extras	(lb 6, w 6, nb 2)	14		
Total	**(44.2 overs)**	**113**		

NEW ZEALAND		Runs	Balls	4/6
B.A.Edgar	c Gavaskar b Binny	13	42	–
J.G.Wright	c Kapil Dev b Sharma	13	27	2
M.D.Crowe	c Azharuddin b Kapil Dev	33	58	2
J.F.Reid	c Gavaskar b Kapil Dev	14	42	–
J.J.Crowe	c Gavaskar b Kapil Dev	0	12	–
* J.V.Coney	not out	19	40	2
R.J.Hadlee	b Sharma	5	19	1
† E.B.McSweeney	c Kapil Dev b Sharma	5	9	–
M.C.Snedden	not out	0	3	–
S.R.Gillespie				
E.J.Chatfield				
Extras	(lb 3, w 2, nb 8)	13		
Total	**(40.1 overs; 7 wickets)**	**115**		

NEW ZEALAND	O	M	R	W
Chatfield	9.2	4	9	2
Hadlee	8	1	16	2
Gillespie	10	2	20	1
Snedden	8	2	23	3
M.D.Crowe	4	0	20	1
Coney	5	0	19	0

INDIA	O	M	R	W
Kapil Dev	10	4	26	3
Binny	8.1	0	25	1
Sharma	8	0	26	3
Amarnath	2	0	8	0
Shastri	10	2	17	0
Sivaramakrishnan	2	0	10	0

FALL OF WICKETS
1-0, 2-23, 3-58, 4-60, 5-93, 6-93, 7-104, 8-106, 9-108, 10-113

FALL OF WICKETS
1-28, 2-31, 3-77, 4-83, 5-86, 6-95, 7-111

Umpires: R.C.Isherwood (19) and P.J.McConnell (23).

AUSTRALIA v NEW ZEALAND 1985-86

At WACA Ground, Perth on 19 January 1986.   Result: **AUSTRALIA** won by 4 wickets.   Toss: Australia.
Award: A.R.Border.   LOI debuts: Australia – G.S.Trimble.

Much to the delight of the seam bowlers, the previous day's pitch was used for this game.

NEW ZEALAND		Runs	Balls	4/6
B.A.Edgar	c Border b Waugh	10	50	1
J.G.Wright	b Davis	9	27	–
M.D.Crowe	c Boon b Waugh	1	6	–
J.F.Reid	b Reid	11	33	–
J.J.Crowe	run out	63	99	4
* J.V.Coney	c Marsh b Matthews	33	77	1
R.J.Hadlee	not out	15	16	1
† E.B.McSweeney	not out	0	–	–
M.C.Snedden				
S.R.Gillespie				
E.J.Chatfield				
Extras	(b 2, lb 10, w 2, nb 3)	17		
Total	(50 overs; 6 wickets)	159		

AUSTRALIA		Runs	Balls	4/6
D.C.Boon	c Coney b Hadlee	6	12	1
G.R.Marsh	c McSweeney b M.D.Crowe	20	64	1
* A.R.Border	run out	58	104	7
G.M.Ritchie	c M.D.Crowe b Coney	5	18	–
S.R.Waugh	c J.J.Crowe b Chatfield	23	40	3
G.R.J.Matthews	c M.D.Crowe b Hadlee	7	18	1
† W.B.Phillips	not out	28	14	3/2
G.S.Trimble	not out	0	3	
C.J.McDermott				
B.A.Reid				
S.P.Davis				
Extras	(lb 10, w 3, nb 1)	14		
Total	(45.1 overs; 6 wickets)	161		

AUSTRALIA	O	M	R	W
McDermott	10	1	20	0
Davis	10	3	13	1
Waugh	10	3	28	2
Reid	10	1	36	1
Trimble	4	0	32	0
Matthews	6	0	18	1

NEW ZEALAND	O	M	R	W
Chatfield	10	0	39	1
Hadlee	9.1	1	35	2
Gillespie	8	2	23	0
Snedden	6	0	20	0
M.D.Crowe	8	1	16	1
Coney	4	1	18	1

FALL OF WICKETS
1-12, 2-13, 3-32, 4-36, 5-118, 6-156

FALL OF WICKETS
1-9, 2-61, 3-78, 4-117, 5-131, 6-144

Umpires: R.A.French (42) and S.G.Randell (16).

AUSTRALIA v INDIA 1985-86

At Sydney Cricket Ground on 21 January 1986.   Result: **AUSTRALIA** won by 100 runs.   Toss: India.
Award: G.R.Marsh.   LOI debuts: None.

This match attracted a crowd of 31,241. Geoff Marsh scored the first of nine hundreds and Sunil Gavaskar made his
highest so far in limited-overs internationals.

AUSTRALIA		Runs	Balls	4/6
G.R.Marsh	c Azharuddin b Sharma	125	145	11
D.C.Boon	c Amarnath b Shastri	83	104	5
* A.R.Border	c Srikkanth b Sharma	52	42	1
† W.B.Phillips	c Kapil Dev b Sharma	7	6	1
G.M.Ritchie	run out	1	2	–
S.R.Waugh	not out	6	4	–
C.J.McDermott	run out	2	2	–
G.R.J.Matthews	not out	1	1	–
D.R.Gilbert				
B.A.Reid				
S.P.Davis				
Extras	(lb 9, w 2, nb 4)	15		
Total	(50 overs; 6 wickets)	292		

INDIA		Runs	Balls	4/6
K.Srikkanth	c Border b Davis	20	16	–/1
S.M.Gavaskar	not out	92	144	4
M.Amarnath	c Matthews b Gilbert	16	54	–
A.Malhotra	c Matthews b Gilbert	5	17	–
* Kapil Dev	c McDermott b Matthews	28	39	–
M.Azharuddin	not out	17	40	–
R.J.Shastri				
C.Sharma				
R.M.H.Binny				
† K.S.More				
L.Sivaramakrishnan				
Extras	(lb 8, w 2, nb 4)	14		
Total	(50 overs; 4 wickets)	192		

INDIA	O	M	R	W
Kapil Dev	10	0	68	0
Binny	7	0	48	0
Sharma	9	0	61	3
Amarnath	10	0	36	0
Shastri	10	0	42	1
Sivaramakrishnan	4	0	28	0

AUSTRALIA	O	M	R	W
McDermott	9	0	27	0
Davis	7	0	30	1
Reid	10	0	28	0
Gilbert	10	0	36	2
Matthews	10	0	49	1
Waugh	3	0	10	0
Marsh	1	0	4	0

FALL OF WICKETS
1-152, 2-273, 3-282, 4-283, 5-283, 6-286

FALL OF WICKETS
1-31, 2-74, 3-93, 4-158

Umpires: M.W.Johnson (41) and P.J.McConnell (24).

NEW ZEALAND v INDIA 1985-86

At Melbourne Cricket Ground on 23 January 1986.   Result: **NEW ZEALAND** won by 5 wickets.   Toss: New Zealand.
Award: M.D.Crowe.   LOI debuts: None.

In the closest finish of the tournament, New Zealand won off the penultimate ball.

INDIA		Runs	Balls	4/6
R.J.Shastri	lbw b Hadlee	6	31	–
K.Srikkanth	c and b Chatfield	9	24	1
M.Amarnath	c and b Bracewell	74	101	3
D.B.Vengsarkar	b Bracewell	43	60	2
M.Azharuddin	run out	12	17	–
Kapil Dev	c Bracewell b Chatfield	47	39	–
A.Malhotra	c Wright b Chatfield	7	12	–
C.Sharma	not out	20	11	2
R.M.H.Binny	b Chatfield	11	7	–
† K.S.More	not out	1	1	–
N.S.Yadav				
Extras	(b 2, lb 3, w 3)	8		
Total	(50 overs; 8 wickets)	**238**		

NEW ZEALAND		Runs	Balls	4/6
J.G.Wright	st More b Amarnath	39	52	4
B.A.Edgar	c Vengsarkar b Shastri	30	74	–
M.D.Crowe	c Shastri b Kapil Dev	67	93	2
J.F.Reid	run out	35	36	1
J.J.Crowe	b Kapil Dev	30	21	3
* J.V.Coney	not out	27	22	1
R.J.Hadlee	not out	1	4	–
† E.B.McSweeney				
S.L.Boock				
J.G.Bracewell				
E.J.Chatfield				
Extras	(b 1, lb 7, w 2)	10		
Total	(49.5 overs; 5 wickets)	**239**		

NEW ZEALAND	O	M	R	W
Chatfield	10	2	28	4
Hadlee	10	1	52	1
M.D.Crowe	5	0	13	0
Boock	8	0	51	0
Coney	7	0	36	0
Bracewell	10	0	53	2

INDIA	O	M	R	W
Kapil Dev	10	1	36	2
Binny	5.5	1	31	0
Sharma	10	0	57	0
Amarnath	5	0	26	1
Shastri	10	0	30	1
Yadav	9	0	51	0

FALL OF WICKETS
1-15, 2-16, 3-98, 4-115, 5-182, 6-205, 7-205, 8-220

FALL OF WICKETS
1-49, 2-112, 3-176, 4-185, 5-235

Umpires: B.E.Martin (22) and P.J.McConnell (25).

NEW ZEALAND v INDIA 1985-86

At Adelaide Oval on 25 January 1986.   Result: **INDIA** won by 5 wickets.   Toss: India.
Award: M.Azharuddin.   LOI debuts: None.

A lusty innings by Richard Hadlee, followed by Stuart Gillespie's career-best bowling return, could not prevent India from ending a run of three defeats.

NEW ZEALAND		Runs	Balls	4/6
J.G.Wright	c More b Binny	7	21	–
B.A.Edgar	c Vengsarkar b Binny	2	22	–
M.D.Crowe	c More b Shastri	28	52	2
J.F.Reid	c Vengsarkar b Kulkarni	9	31	–
J.J.Crowe	c Malhotra b Kulkarni	7	33	–
* J.V.Coney	c and b Shastri	4	16	–
R.J.Hadlee	b Kapil Dev	71	68	5/2
J.G.Bracewell	c Kapil Dev b Amarnath	20	31	–
† E.B.McSweeney	b Sharma	5	7	–
S.R.Gillespie	b Kapil Dev	4	11	–
E.J.Chatfield	not out	4	13	–
Extras	(lb 4, w 5, nb 2)	11		
Total	(49.2 overs)	**172**		

INDIA		Runs	Balls	4/6
R.J.Shastri	lbw b Hadlee	2	8	–
K.Srikkanth	c Coney b Gillespie	16	36	2
M.Amarnath	c McSweeney b Gillespie	5	32	–
D.B.Vengsarkar	c M.D.Crowe b Gillespie	32	57	4
M.Azharuddin	not out	69	90	8
A.Malhotra	c Reid b Gillespie	33	54	3
* Kapil Dev	not out	6	5	1
C.Sharma				
R.M.H.Binny				
R.R.Kulkarni				
† K.S.More				
Extras	(b 1, lb 4, w 6)	11		
Total	(46 overs; 5 wickets)	**174**		

INDIA	O	M	R	W
Kapil Dev	9.2	3	24	2
Binny	7	1	13	2
Sharma	10	0	46	1
Kulkarni	9	1	28	2
Shastri	10	1	36	2
Amarnath	4	0	21	1

NEW ZEALAND	O	M	R	W
Hadlee	10	3	28	1
Chatfield	10	5	13	0
Gillespie	10	3	30	4
M.D.Crowe	4	0	25	0
Coney	5	0	29	0
Bracewell	7	0	44	0

FALL OF WICKETS
1-12, 2-13, 3-37, 4-57, 5-58, 6-65, 7-119, 8-130, 9-144, 10-172

FALL OF WICKETS
1-2, 2-25, 3-26, 4-85, 5-158

Umpires: A.R.Crafter (37) and R.A.French (43).

AUSTRALIA v INDIA 1985-86

At Adelaide Oval on 26 January 1986.   Result: **AUSTRALIA** won by 36 runs.   Toss: India.
Award: B.A.Reid.   LOI debuts: None.

Bruce Reid's best bowling performance in 61 internationals ensured that Australia would compete in the finals.

AUSTRALIA		Runs	Balls	4/6	INDIA		Runs	Balls	4/6
D.C.Boon	c Kulkarni b Ghai	27	50	4	K.Srikkanth	lbw b McDermott	10	23	–
G.R.Marsh	c Vengsarkar b Sharma	25	64	1	S.M.Gavaskar	c Phillips b Reid	77	110	4/1
* A.R.Border	c Kapil Dev b Shastri	9	20	–	M.Amarnath	c Phillips b McDermott	0	1	–
G.M.Ritchie	run out	28	50	–	D.B.Vengsarkar	c Border b Reid	17	33	1
S.R.Waugh	c Kapil Dev b Sharma	81	75	4/2	M.Azharuddin	c Border b Reid	2	13	–
G.R.J.Matthews	c More b Sharma	44	40	1	R.J.Shastri	c Border b McDermott	55	62	4/1
† W.B.Phillips	not out	23	8	3/1	* Kapil Dev	c Phillips b Reid	25	24	2
C.J.McDermott	b Kapil Dev	1	3	–	C.Sharma	c McDermott b Reid	13	11	–
D.R.Gilbert	run out	1	1	–	R.R.Kulkarni	not out	5	4	–
B.A.Reid	not out	1	2	–	R.S.Ghai	run out	1	3	–
S.P.Davis					† K.S.More	run out	0	3	–
Extras	(lb 12, w 7, nb 3)	22			Extras	(b 6, lb 7, w 3, nb 5)	21		
Total	(50 overs; 8 wickets)	262			Total	(45.3 overs)	226		

INDIA	O	M	R	W	AUSTRALIA	O	M	R	W
Kapil Dev	10	2	50	1	McDermott	8	1	20	3
Kulkarni	10	1	53	0	Davis	7.3	0	38	0
Ghai	10	1	54	1	Gilbert	10	1	50	0
Shastri	10	1	33	1	Reid	10	0	53	5
Sharma	10	0	60	3	Waugh	5	0	26	0
					Matthews	5	0	26	0

FALL OF WICKETS
1-50, 2-60, 3-79, 4-134, 5-226, 6-250, 7-255, 8-257

FALL OF WICKETS
1-26, 2-26, 3-60, 4-75, 5-172, 6-182, 7-218, 8-218, 9-220, 10-226

Umpires: R.C.Isherwood (20) and P.J.McConnell (26).

AUSTRALIA v NEW ZEALAND 1985-86

At Adelaide Oval on 27 January 1986.   Result: **NEW ZEALAND** won by 206 runs.   Toss: New Zealand.
Award: R.J.Hadlee.   LOI debuts: None.

Australia were dismissed for their equal-lowest score (also *LOI No. 43*) and suffered their heaviest defeat by a runs margin.

NEW ZEALAND		Runs	Balls	4/6	AUSTRALIA		Runs	Balls	4/6
J.G.Bracewell	c Border b McDermott	0	1	–	G.R.Marsh	c Coney b Hadlee	0	2	–
B.A.Edgar	c Border b Reid	61	84	3	D.C.Boon	c McSweeney b Hadlee	10	29	1
M.D.Crowe	c Border b Reid	26	45	3	S.R.Waugh	c Coney b Chatfield	3	12	–
J.G.Wright	c Gilbert b McDermott	61	85	4/2	G.S.Trimble	c Coney b Hadlee	4	2	1
R.J.Hadlee	c McDermott b Davis	24	21	1	G.R.J.Matthews	lbw b Gillespie	4	28	–
* J.V.Coney	c Phillips b Reid	40	34	4	* A.R.Border	c Gillespie b Chatfield	9	11	2
J.J.Crowe	not out	24	19	2	† W.B.Phillips	c Chatfield b Bracewell	22	38	2
B.R.Blair	b Davis	21	15	3	C.J.McDermott	c Wright b Gillespie	1	6	–
† E.B.McSweeney	not out	4	2	–	D.R.Gilbert	c and b Bracewell	8	31	1
S.R.Gillespie					B.A.Reid	lbw b Blair	1	3	–
E.J.Chatfield					S.P.Davis	not out	0	2	–
Extras	(lb 9, w 5, nb 1)	15			Extras	(lb 3, w 1, nb 4)	8		
Total	(50 overs; 7 wickets)	276			Total	(26.3 overs)	70		

AUSTRALIA	O	M	R	W	NEW ZEALAND	O	M	R	W
McDermott	10	1	70	2	Hadlee	5	1	14	3
Davis	10	0	46	2	Chatfield	7	2	9	2
Reid	10	1	41	3	Gillespie	5	0	21	2
Matthews	10	0	49	0	M.D.Crowe	4	0	13	0
Gilbert	10	0	61	0	Bracewell	3.3	1	3	2
					Blair	2	0	7	1

FALL OF WICKETS
1-0, 2-37, 3-157, 4-160, 5-224, 6-226, 7-272

FALL OF WICKETS
1-0, 2-10, 3-15, 4-20, 5-31, 6-47, 7-55, 8-68, 9-70, 10-70

Umpires: A.R.Crafter (38) and B.E.Martin (23).

AUSTRALIA v NEW ZEALAND 1985-86

At Sydney Cricket Ground on 29 January 1986.　　Result: **AUSTRALIA** won by 99 runs.　　Toss: Australia.
Award: D.C.Boon.　　LOI debuts: None.

Bruce Reid achieved the second hat-trick in limited-overs internationals, dismissing Blair with the last ball of his eighth over before disposing of McSweeney and Gillespie with the first two balls of his ninth.

AUSTRALIA		Runs	Balls	4/6
D.C.Boon	b Gillespie	64	95	3
G.R.Marsh	b Bracewell	37	66	1
* A.R.Border	run out	29	39	1
D.M.Jones	lbw b Hadlee	53	58	1
S.R.Waugh	run out	17	22	1
G.R.J.Matthews	c Wright b Chatfield	10	13	–
† W.B.Phillips	b Hadlee	3	3	–
C.J.McDermott	not out	6	4	–
D.R.Gilbert	not out	6	7	–
B.A.Reid				
S.P.Davis				
Extras	(b 1, lb 8, nb 5)	14		
Total	(50 overs; 7 wickets)	**239**		

NEW ZEALAND		Runs	Balls	4/6
J.G.Bracewell	b McDermott	0	2	–
B.A.Edgar	c Phillips b Davis	18	36	–
M.D.Crowe	b McDermott	9	15	–
J.G.Wright	c Waugh b Matthews	24	65	2
* J.V.Coney	b Gilbert	25	43	–
J.J.Crowe	b Davis	19	49	–
R.J.Hadlee	not out	30	37	1/1
B.R.Blair	c Marsh b Reid	3	4	–
† E.B.McSweeney	c Border b Reid	1	2	–
S.R.Gillespie	b Reid	0	1	–
E.J.Chatfield	b Davis	0	6	–
Extras	(lb 7, w 2, nb 2)	11		
Total	(42.4 overs)	**140**		

NEW ZEALAND	O	M	R	W
Hadlee	10	1	36	2
Chatfield	10	1	48	1
Gillespie	10	0	48	1
Bracewell	10	1	43	1
M.D.Crowe	1	0	11	0
Coney	9	0	44	0

AUSTRALIA	O	M	R	W
McDermott	7	1	28	2
Davis	9.4	2	25	3
Reid	9	2	29	3
Matthews	10	0	27	1
Gilbert	7	0	24	1

FALL OF WICKETS
1-98, 2-124, 3-147, 4-185, 5-217, 6-224, 7-225

FALL OF WICKETS
1-0, 2-14, 3-39, 4-77, 5-91, 6-122, 7-133, 8-137, 9-137, 10-140

Umpires: R.A.French (44) and R.C.Isherwood (21).

AUSTRALIA v INDIA 1985-86

At Melbourne Cricket Ground on 31 January 1986.　　Result: **INDIA** won by 6 wickets.　　Toss: Australia.
Award: D.B.Vengsarkar.　　LOI debuts: None.

Kapil Dev's fine all-round display brought about a vital Indian victory.

AUSTRALIA		Runs	Balls	4/6
G.R.Marsh	c Gavaskar b Shastri	74	106	4
D.C.Boon	c Kapil Dev b Shastri	76	102	5
* A.R.Border	c Malhotra b Kapil Dev	18	32	–
D.M.Jones	b Kapil Dev	33	36	1
† W.B.Phillips	run out	8	4	1
S.R.Waugh	b Kapil Dev	3	5	–
D.M.Wellham	not out	12	7	1
C.J.McDermott	lbw b Kapil Dev	0	1	–
D.R.Gilbert	not out	7	8	–
B.A.Reid				
S.P.Davis				
Extras	(lb 3, w 1)	4		
Total	(50 overs; 7 wickets)	**235**		

INDIA		Runs	Balls	4/6
S.M.Gavaskar	b Gilbert	72	123	3
K.Srikkanth	c Jones b Davis	27	34	5
A.Malhotra	c Davis b Gilbert	14	32	–
D.B.Vengsarkar	not out	77	88	5
* Kapil Dev	c Wellham b Davis	23	18	2
C.Sharma	not out	6	3	1
M.Azharuddin				
R.M.H.Binny				
R.J.Shastri				
† K.S.More				
L.Sivaramakrishnan				
Extras	(lb 14, w 3, nb 2)	19		
Total	(48.5 overs; 4 wickets)	**238**		

INDIA	O	M	R	W
Kapil Dev	9	0	30	4
Binny	6	1	24	0
Sharma	7	0	29	0
Sivaramakrishnan	8	0	52	0
Shastri	10	0	43	2
Azharuddin	10	0	54	0

AUSTRALIA	O	M	R	W
McDermott	9.5	0	55	0
Davis	10	2	40	2
Reid	9	0	34	0
Gilbert	10	0	43	2
Waugh	6	0	34	0
Border	4	0	18	0

FALL OF WICKETS
1-146, 2-161, 3-194, 4-212, 5-212, 6-224, 7-224

FALL OF WICKETS
1-46, 2-79, 3-181, 4-230

Umpires: A.R.Crafter (39) and M.W.Johnson (42).

NEW ZEALAND v INDIA 1985-86

At North Tasmania CA Ground, Launceston on 2 February 1986.   Result: **INDIA** won by 21 runs (revised target).
Toss: New Zealand.   Award: C.Sharma.   LOI debuts: None.

Launceston's first international decided who would oppose the hosts in the finals. By taking three wickets in six balls, after rain had reduced New Zealand's target to 190 from 45 overs, Kapil Dev ensured it would be India. Final points: Australia 13, India 10, New Zealand 7.

INDIA		Runs	Balls	4/6
K.Srikkanth	lbw b Snedden	22	44	2
S.M.Gavaskar	c McSweeney b Hadlee	1	3	–
M.Amarnath	c McSweeney b Gillespie	24	50	3
A.Malhotra	c Snedden b Gillespie	39	72	4/1
M.Azharuddin	c McSweeney b M.D.Crowe	3	4	–
R.J.Shastri	b Snedden	23	46	4
* Kapil Dev	lbw b Gillespie	2	4	–
C.Sharma	not out	38	37	3/1
R.M.H.Binny	lbw b Hadlee	24	25	3
R.R.Kulkarni	c Gillespie b Chatfield	9	11	1
† K.S.More	not out	1	2	–
Extras	(lb 7, w 7, nb 2)	16		
Total	(48 overs; 9 wickets)	**202**		

NEW ZEALAND		Runs	Balls	4/6
J.J.Crowe	c Kulkarni b Binny	3	17	–
B.A.Edgar	c More b Shastri	26	54	3
M.D.Crowe	c and b Binny	10	21	1
J.F.Reid	b Kulkarni	37	63	2
* J.V.Coney	c Shastri b Kapil Dev	37	61	1
R.J.Hadlee	c Azharuddin b Sharma	5	9	–
B.R.Blair	c Srikkanth b Binny	19	24	2
† E.B.McSweeney	b Kapil Dev	0	1	–
M.C.Snedden	c Binny b Kapil Dev	1	4	–
S.R.Gillespie	not out	15	21	2
E.J.Chatfield	not out	0	2	–
Extras	(lb 8, w 7)	15		
Total	(45 overs; 9 wickets)	**168**		

NEW ZEALAND	O	M	R	W
Hadlee	10	5	17	2
Chatfield	9	0	43	1
Gillespie	9	0	54	3
Snedden	10	0	46	2
M.D.Crowe	10	2	35	1

INDIA	O	M	R	W
Kapil Dev	9	1	26	3
Binny	9	1	26	3
Sharma	9	1	35	1
Shastri	9	0	33	1
Kulkarni	9	0	40	1

FALL OF WICKETS
1-1, 2-52, 3-56, 4-64, 5-119, 6-127, 7-127, 8-180, 9-199

FALL OF WICKETS
1-7, 2-27, 3-48, 4-102, 5-113, 6-135, 7-135, 8-147, 9-163

Umpires: A.R.Crafter (40) and S.G.Randell (17).

AUSTRALIA v INDIA 1985-86

At Sydney Cricket Ground on 5 February 1986.   Result: **AUSTRALIA** won by 11 runs.   Toss: India.
LOI debuts: Australia – T.J.Zoehrer.

Australia were 69 for 0 when a storm reduced the contest to 44 overs. Sunil Gavaskar damaged a finger dropping David Boon at slip in the first over and was unable to open the innings.

AUSTRALIA		Runs	Balls	4/6
D.C.Boon	c Malhotra b Shastri	50	92	1
G.R.Marsh	c Sharma b Azharuddin	36	66	4
D.M.Wellham	b Amarnath	6	7	–
* A.R.Border	c Azharuddin b Shastri	12	21	–
D.M.Jones	not out	30	44	1
S.R.Waugh	b Azharuddin	1	4	–
G.R.J.Matthews	run out	7	11	–
† T.J.Zoehrer	b Kapil Dev	11	19	–
C.J.McDermott	run out	0	1	–
B.A.Reid	not out	4	3	–
S.P.Davis				
Extras	(b 1, lb 6, w 2, nb 4)	13		
Total	(44 overs; 8 wickets)	**170**		

INDIA		Runs	Balls	4/6
R.J.Shastri	c Zoehrer b Davis	8	12	–
K.Srikkanth	b Davis	0	5	–
M.Amarnath	c Marsh b Matthews	13	36	–
D.B.Vengsarkar	c Jones b Waugh	45	81	–/1
M.Azharuddin	b Matthews	1	14	–
S.M.Gavaskar	c Jones b Border	32	58	1
* Kapil Dev	b Matthews	0	1	–
A.Malhotra	c and b Border	12	20	–
C.Sharma	not out	19	19	1
R.M.H.Binny	b Border	16	15	1
† K.S.More	b Davis	2	5	–
Extras	(b 2, lb 6, w 2, nb 1)	11		
Total	(43.4 overs)	**159**		

INDIA	O	M	R	W
Kapil Dev	9	2	21	1
Binny	7	0	30	0
Sharma	5	0	34	0
Amarnath	5	0	21	1
Shastri	9	0	31	2
Azharuddin	9	0	26	2

AUSTRALIA	O	M	R	W
McDermott	5	0	26	0
Davis	7.4	3	10	3
Reid	9	2	34	0
Matthews	9	0	27	3
Waugh	8	1	31	1
Border	5	0	23	3

FALL OF WICKETS
1-69, 2-86, 3-110, 4-118, 5-122, 6-135, 7-164, 8-164

FALL OF WICKETS
1-4, 2-11, 3-40, 4-52, 5-82, 6-82, 7-112, 8-126, 9-149, 10-159

Umpires: R.A.French (45) and M.W.Johnson (43).

AUSTRALIA v INDIA 1985-86

At Melbourne Cricket Ground on 9 February 1986.   Result: **AUSTRALIA** won by 7 wickets.   Toss: Australia.
Finals Award: G.R.J.Matthews.   LOI debuts: None.

Australia won the World Series Cup for the third time. Mohinder Amarnath became the first batsman to be dismissed 'handled the ball' in limited-overs internationals when he pushed away a turning ball from Greg Matthews that spun back towards his wicket.

INDIA		Runs	Balls	4/6
S.M.Gavaskar	c Border b Davis	11	26	1
K.Srikkanth	c and b Matthews	37	71	2
M.Amarnath	handled the ball	15	32	1
D.B.Vengsarkar	b Matthews	41	66	4
* Kapil Dev	c Zoehrer b Reid	1	5	–
M.Azharuddin	run out	14	26	1
R.J.Shastri	run out	49	52	–
C.Sharma	run out	0	–	–
R.M.H.Binny	c and b Reid	4	10	–
† K.S.More	run out	1	6	~
N.S.Yadav	not out	1	14	–
Extras	(lb 7, w 4, nb 2)	13		
Total	(50 overs)	**187**		

AUSTRALIA		Runs	Balls	4/6
D.C.Boon	run out	44	78	4
G.R.Marsh	lbw b Kapil Dev	9	24	–
D.M.Wellham	c Azharuddin b Kapil Dev	43	97	1
* A.R.Border	not out	65	67	5
D.M.Jones	not out	19	23	–
S.R.Waugh				
G.R.J.Matthews				
† T.J.Zoehrer				
C.J.McDermott				
B.A.Reid				
S.P.Davis				
Extras	(b 1, lb 2, w 5)	8		
Total	(47.2 overs; 3 wickets)	**188**		

AUSTRALIA	O	M	R	W
McDermott	10	0	35	0
Davis	10	1	23	1
Reid	10	0	37	2
Waugh	3	0	15	0
Matthews	10	1	37	2
Border	7	0	33	0

INDIA	O	M	R	W
Kapil Dev	9	1	26	2
Binny	2	0	13	0
Sharma	8.2	0	42	0
Azharuddin	8	0	37	0
Yadav	10	0	27	0
Shastri	10	1	40	0

FALL OF WICKETS
1-34, 2-66, 3-70, 4-71, 5-108, 6-151, 7-151, 8-163, 9-168, 10-187

FALL OF WICKETS
1-31, 2-77, 3-144

Umpires: A.R.Crafter (41) and P.J.McConnell (27).

WEST INDIES v ENGLAND (1st Match)   LOI No: 364/19

WEST INDIES v ENGLAND 1985-86

At Sabina Park, Kingston, Jamaica on 18 February 1986.   Result: **WEST INDIES** won by 6 wickets.   Toss: West Indies.
Award: M.D.Marshall.   LOI debuts: West Indies – B.P.Patterson; England – L.B.Taylor, J.G.Thomas.

Patrick Patterson dismissed Robinson and Gower with his fourth and eighth balls in international cricket. Mike Gatting returned to London for surgery after his nose was fractured and flattened when he missed an attempted hook at a bouncer from Malcolm Marshall, the ball dislodging a bail.

ENGLAND		Runs	Balls	4/6
G.A.Gooch	b Marshall	36		
R.T.Robinson	b Patterson	0	4	–
* D.I.Gower	c Richards b Patterson	0	4	–
M.W.Gatting	b Marshall	10		
A.J.Lamb	c Greenidge b Marshall	30		
P.Willey	c Richardson b Marshall	26		
† P.R.Downton	lbw b Garner	8		
J.E.Emburey	b Garner	5		
N.A.Foster	not out	5		
J.G.Thomas	not out	0		
L.B.Taylor				
Extras	(b 8, lb 2, w 4, nb 11)	25		
Total	(46 overs; 8 wickets)	**145**		

WEST INDIES		Runs	Balls	4/6
C.G.Greenidge	c Downton b Thomas	45		
D.L.Haynes	c Downton b Foster	35		
R.B.Richardson	lbw b Gooch	32		
H.A.Gomes	st Downton b Willey	19		
† P.J.L.Dujon	not out	3		
R.A.Harper	not out	1		
* I.V.A.Richards				
M.D.Marshall				
J.Garner				
B.P.Patterson				
C.A.Walsh				
Extras	(b 4, lb 2, nb 5)	11		
Total	(43.5 overs; 4 wickets)	**146**		

WEST INDIES	O	M	R	W
Garner	10	0	18	2
Patterson	7	0	17	2
Walsh	9	0	42	0
Marshall	10	1	23	4
Harper	10	0	35	0

ENGLAND	O	M	R	W
Taylor	7	2	17	0
Thomas	8	1	35	1
Foster	10	1	44	1
Emburey	10	3	19	0
Willey	6.5	0	25	1
Gooch	2	2	0	1

FALL OF WICKETS
1-2, 2-10, 3-47, 4-63, 5-125, 6-125, 7-137, 8-143

FALL OF WICKETS
1-84, 2-89, 3-142, 4-142

Umpires: D.M.Archer (4) and A.J.Gaynor (1).

WEST INDIES v ENGLAND 1985-86

At Queen's Park Oval, Port-of-Spain, Trinidad on 4 March 1986.   Result: **ENGLAND** won by 5 wickets.   Toss: England.
Award: G.A.Gooch.   LOI debuts: West Indies – C.A.Best; England – W.N.Slack, D.M.Smith.

England gained their first limited-overs victory in the Caribbean with a leg-bye off the final ball. Viv Richards scored the fastest fifty (25 balls) on record for West Indies. Graham Gooch scored England's only LOI hundred in the West Indies.

WEST INDIES		Runs	Balls	4/6
D.L.Haynes	b Foster	53		
C.A.Best	run out	10		
R.B.Richardson	not out	79	70	7/3
*I.V.A.Richards	c Foster b Botham	82	39	6/4
R.A.Harper	not out	0		
H.A.Gomes				
†T.R.O.Payne				
M.D.Marshall				
J.Garner				
C.A.Walsh				
B.P.Patterson				
Extras	(lb 4, nb 1)	5		
Total	(37 overs; 3 wickets)	**229**		

ENGLAND		Runs	Balls	4/6
G.A.Gooch	not out	129	126	17/1
I.T.Botham	c Richards b Garner	8		
W.N.Slack	c Payne b Walsh	34		
A.J.Lamb	b Garner	16		
*D.I.Gower	run out	9		
P.Willey	c Richards b Garner	10		
D.M.Smith	not out	10		
†P.R.Downton				
R.M.Ellison				
J.E.Emburey				
N.A.Foster				
Extras	(b 1, lb 7, nb 6)	14		
Total	(37 overs; 5 wickets)	**230**		

ENGLAND	O	M	R	W
Botham	8	1	59	1
Foster	10	1	42	1
Ellison	8	0	57	0
Emburey	8	2	48	0
Willey	3	0	19	0

WEST INDIES	O	M	R	W
Garner	9	1	62	3
Patterson	6	0	30	0
Walsh	9	0	49	1
Marshall	10	1	59	0
Harper	3	0	22	0

FALL OF WICKETS
1-37, 2-106, 3-223

FALL OF WICKETS
1-9, 2-98, 3-143, 4-170, 5-183

Umpires: C.E.Cumberbatch (4) and S.Mohammed (6).

WEST INDIES v ENGLAND 1985-86

At Kensington Oval, Bridgetown, Barbados on 19 March 1986.   Result: **WEST INDIES** won by 135 runs.   Toss: England.
Award: I.V.A.Richards.   LOI debuts: None.

England's total remains their lowest in 51 internationals against West Indies.

WEST INDIES		Runs	Balls	4/6
C.G.Greenidge	c Downton b Foster	31		
D.L.Haynes	b Foster	28		
R.B.Richardson	b Botham	62	74	8/1
*I.V.A.Richards	c Foster b Emburey	62	56	7/2
†P.J.L.Dujon	c Lamb b Foster	23		
R.A.Harper	not out	24		
J.Garner	b Emburey	3		
M.D.Marshall	c and b Botham	9		
M.A.Holding	not out	0		
H.A.Gomes				
B.P.Patterson				
Extras	(b 4, w 2, nb 1)	7		
Total	(46 overs; 7 wickets)	**249**		

ENGLAND		Runs	Balls	4/6
G.A.Gooch	c Dujon b Garner	6		
R.T.Robinson	c Richardson b Marshall	23		
W.N.Slack	c Dujon b Marshall	9		
*D.I.Gower	lbw b Holding	0		
A.J.Lamb	c Marshall b Holding	18		
I.T.Botham	c Garner b Marshall	14		
P.Willey	c Greenidge b Harper	9		
†P.R.Downton	b Harper	0		
J.E.Emburey	c Dujon b Patterson	15		
N.A.Foster	not out	9		
J.G.Thomas	c Richards b Patterson	0		
Extras	(lb 3, w 3, nb 5)	11		
Total	(39 overs)	**114**		

ENGLAND	O	M	R	W
Botham	9	2	39	2
Thomas	7	1	50	0
Foster	9	0	39	3
Willey	6	0	21	0
Gooch	6	1	41	0
Emburey	9	0	55	2

WEST INDIES	O	M	R	W
Garner	6	2	6	1
Patterson	9	1	38	2
Marshall	6	2	14	3
Holding	10	1	29	2
Harper	8	1	24	2

FALL OF WICKETS
1-61, 2-64, 3-181, 4-195, 5-225, 6-239, 7-248

FALL OF WICKETS
1-18, 2-42, 3-42, 4-46, 5-69, 6-81, 7-82, 8-85, 9-113, 10-114

Umpires: D.M.Archer (5) and L.H.Barker (5).

WEST INDIES v ENGLAND 1985-86

At Queen's Park Oval, Port-of-Spain, Trinidad on 31 March 1986.   Result: **WEST INDIES** won by 8 wickets.
Toss: West Indies.   Award: J.Garner.   LOI debuts: None.

West Indies gained their third comfortable victory of their first home series of internationals to be staged entirely on
Test match grounds.

ENGLAND		Runs	Balls	4/6
G.A.Gooch	c Richards b Marshall	10		
R.T.Robinson	b Marshall	55	107	
* D.I.Gower	b Walsh	20		
A.J.Lamb	c Dujon b Walsh	16		
I.T.Botham	c Harper b Garner	29		
P.Willey	c Greenidge b Marshall	6		
† P.R.Downton	c Greenidge b Marshall	12		
R.M.Ellison	b Garner	5		
J.E.Emburey	not out	2		
P.H.Edmonds	b Garner	0		
N.A.Foster				
Extras	(b 1, lb 4, w 2, nb 3)	10		
Total	(47 overs; 9 wickets)	**165**		

WEST INDIES		Runs	Balls	4/6
C.G.Greenidge	b Foster	0	2	
D.L.Haynes	not out	77		
R.B.Richardson	c Gooch b Emburey	31		
* I.V.A.Richards	not out	50		–/2
H.A.Gomes				
† P.J.L.Dujon				
R.A.Harper				
M.D.Marshall				
M.A.Holding				
J.Garner				
C.A.Walsh				
Extras	(lb 7, w 1)	8		
Total	(38.2 overs; 2 wickets)	**166**		

WEST INDIES	O	M	R	W
Marshall	9	0	37	4
Garner	9	1	22	3
Holding	9	1	32	0
Walsh	10	0	25	2
Harper	10	0	44	0

ENGLAND	O	M	R	W
Foster	6	1	27	1
Ellison	7	0	30	0
Botham	5	0	24	0
Edmonds	10	1	38	0
Emburey	10	2	31	1
Gower	0.2	0	9	0

FALL OF WICKETS
1-15, 2-49, 3-88, 4-126, 5-138, 6-154, 7-161, 8-165, 9-165

FALL OF WICKETS
1-0, 2-75

Umpires: C.E.Cumberbatch (5) and S.Mohammed (7).

SRI LANKA v PAKISTAN 1985-86

At Asgiriya Stadium, Kandy on 2 March 1986.   Result: **PAKISTAN** won by 8 wickets.   Toss: Pakistan.
Award: Mohsin Khan.   LOI debuts: Sri Lanka – S.D.Anurasiri, A.M.de Silva, R.S.Mahanama, K.G.Perera,
S.K.Ranasinghe.

A wet pitch and light rain reduced Kandy's first limited-overs international from 45 to 25 overs per side. Wasim
conceded 16 off his last over as Pakistan's bowlers fell two short of that meagre ration.

SRI LANKA		Runs	Balls	4/6
S.K.Ranasinghe	c Qadir b Tausif	41	49	3
† A.M.de Silva	b Zakir	8		–
P.A.de Silva	b Imran	21		–
A.Ranatunga	c Ramiz b Qadir	2		–
* L.R.D.Mendis	c Wasim b Qadir	5		–
R.L.Dias	c Miandad b Qadir	12		–
R.S.Mahanama	not out	15		–
A.L.F.de Mel	not out	16		–
R.J.Ratnayake				
S.D.Anurasiri				
K.G.Perera				
Extras	(lb 3, nb 1)	4		
Total	(23 overs; 6 wickets)	**124**		

PAKISTAN		Runs	Balls	4/6
Mudassar Nazar	c A.M.de Silva b Ranasinghe	41	50	–
Mohsin Khan	c A.M.de Silva b Ratnayake	59	57	7/1
Javed Miandad	not out	18		1
Ramiz Raja	not out	0		–
Salim Malik				
* Imran Khan				
Abdul Qadir				
Tausif Ahmed				
Wasim Akram				
Zakir Khan				
† Zulqarnain				
Extras	(lb 6, nb 1)	7		
Total	(21.3 overs; 2 wickets)	**125**		

PAKISTAN	O	M	R	W
Imran Khan	4	0	15	1
Wasim Akram	4	0	34	0
Zakir Khan	5	0	22	1
Tausif Ahmed	5	0	27	1
Abdul Qadir	5	0	23	3

SRI LANKA	O	M	R	W
De Mel	4.3	1	25	0
Ratnayake	4	0	17	1
Ranasinghe	5	0	31	1
Ranatunga	2	0	12	0
Anurasiri	4	0	19	0
Perera	2	0	15	0

FALL OF WICKETS
1-30, 2-68, 3-71, 4-78, 5-83, 6-101

FALL OF WICKETS
1-66, 2-124

Umpires: K.T.Francis (7) and S.Ponnadurai (2).

SRI LANKA v PAKISTAN 1985-86

At Tyronne Fernando Stadium, Moratuwa on 8 March 1986.   No result.   Toss: Sri Lanka.
LOI debuts: Sri Lanka – K.N. Amalean, C.P.H.Ramanayake.

Rain continued to plague this series, terminating this second contest after Pakistan had completed their innings and causing the third match, the inaugural international at Colombo's Khettarama Stadium, to be abandoned on 9 March without a ball bowled.

PAKISTAN		Runs	Balls	4/6	SRI LANKA
Mudassar Nazar	c Kuruppu b Ramanayake	29			† D.S.B.P.Kuruppu
Mohsin Khan	c Mahanama b De Mel	16			S.K.Ranasinghe
Ramiz Raja	c Kuruppu b Ramanayake	6			P.A.de Silva
Javed Miandad	c Kuruppu b Ranasinghe	30			R.L.Dias
Salim Malik	c Mahanama b Ramanayake	1			* L.R.D.Mendis
* Imran Khan	c De Silva b Amalean	20			A.Ranatunga
Abdul Qadir	run out	1			R.S.Mahanama
Wasim Akram	c Ranasinghe b Anurasiri	7			A.L.F.de Mel
Tausif Ahmed	not out	0			C.P.H.Ramanayake
Zakir Khan	not out	5			S.D.Anurasiri
† Zulqarnain					K.N.Amalean
Extras	(lb 8, w 1, nb 1)	10			
Total	(38 overs; 8 wickets)	125			

SRI LANKA	O	M	R	W
De Mel	8	1	25	1
Amalean	7	1	15	1
Ramanayake	6	0	25	3
Ranasinghe	9	0	30	1
Anurasiri	8	2	22	1

FALL OF WICKETS
1-34, 2-55, 3-72, 4-76, 5-108, 6-112, 7-120, 8-120

Umpires: H.C.Felsinger (8) and K.T.Ponambalam (2).

SRI LANKA v PAKISTAN 1985-86

At Sinhalese Sports Club, Colombo on 11 March 1986.   Result: **PAKISTAN** won by 8 wickets (revised target).
Toss: Pakistan.   Award: A.Ranatunga.   LOI debuts: None.

The elements completed a full sweep of this series, a 90-minute minor monsoon halting Pakistan's response at 45 for 0 after 13.5 overs. The visitors easily achieved their revised target of 102 from 24 overs.

SRI LANKA		Runs	Balls	4/6	PAKISTAN		Runs	Balls	4/6
† D.S.B.P.Kuruppu	c Zulqarnain b Zakir	4			Mudassar Nazar	c Kuruppu b Ranasinghe	35	64	3
S.K.Ranasinghe	c Imran b Wasim	14			Mohsin Khan	b Amalean	30	45	3
R.L.Dias	c Miandad b Wasim	1		–	Javed Miandad	not out	22		
* L.R.D.Mendis	c Zulqarnain b Zakir	0		–	Ramiz Raja	not out	13		
R.S.Mahanama	c Zulqarnain b Qadir	22			Salim Malik				
A.Ranatunga	not out	74	89	4/1	* Imran Khan				
P.A.de Silva	c Salim b Qadir	11			Abdul Qadir				
A.L.F.de Mel	b Wasim	13			Wasim Akram				
C.P.H.Ramanayake	b Wasim	0		–	Tausif Ahmed				
S.D.Anurasiri	not out	4			Zakir Khan				
K.N.Amalean					† Zulqarnain				
Extras	(b 1, lb 4, w 8, nb 4)	17			Extras	(lb 2, nb 1)	3		
Total	(38 overs; 8 wickets)	160			Total	(23 overs; 2 wickets)	103		

PAKISTAN	O	M	R	W
Imran Khan	8	2	22	0
Wasim Akram	9	1	28	4
Zakir Khan	9	0	42	2
Tausif Ahmed	2	0	10	0
Abdul Qadir	9	0	47	2
Mudassar Nazar	1	0	6	0

SRI LANKA	O	M	R	W
De Mel	8	1	22	0
Amalean	7	1	31	1
Ramanayake	3	0	20	0
Ranasinghe	5	0	28	1

FALL OF WICKETS
1-65, 2-71

FALL OF WICKETS
1-13, 2-23, 3-24, 4-25, 5-86, 6-122, 7-149, 8-149

Umpires: H.C.Felsinger (9) and P.W.Vidanagamage (7).

NEW ZEALAND v AUSTRALIA 1985-86

At Carisbrook, Dunedin on 19 March 1986.   Result: **NEW ZEALAND** won by 30 runs.   Toss: Australia.
Award: M.D.Crowe.   LOI debuts: New Zealand – T.E.Blain.

Favoured by a seaming pitch and sluggish outfield, Simon Davis began this four-match 50-over series by returning the most economical 10-over analysis in matches between these two countries.

NEW ZEALAND		Runs	Balls	4/6
K.R.Rutherford	b Gilbert	23	77	1
B.A.Edgar	c Phillips b Gilbert	35	58	2
M.D.Crowe	b Reid	47	77	4
* J.V.Coney	c Marsh b Waugh	5	8	1
J.G.Wright	run out	6	11	–
B.R.Blair	c Waugh b McDermott	12	35	–
R.J.Hadlee	not out	21	17	2
† T.E.Blain	not out	24	18	4
J.G.Bracewell				
S.R.Gillespie				
E.J.Chatfield				
Extras	(lb 10, w 2, nb 1)	13		
Total	(50 overs; 6 wickets)	186		

AUSTRALIA		Runs	Balls	4/6
D.C.Boon	c Rutherford b Chatfield	13	30	1
G.R.Marsh	b Hadlee	35	96	1
† W.B.Phillips	c Blain b Gillespie	23	47	3
* A.R.Border	c Blain b Crowe	3	4	–
G.M.Ritchie	c and b Bracewell	9	30	1
G.R.J.Matthews	c Wright b Bracewell	25	26	1/1
S.R.Waugh	c Crowe b Hadlee	29	24	2/1
C.J.McDermott	lbw b Hadlee	0	2	–
D.R.Gilbert	b Crowe	2	14	–
B.A.Reid	c Crowe b Hadlee	2	9	–
S.P.Davis	not out	0	–	–
Extras	(lb 12, w 3)	15		
Total	(47 overs)	156		

AUSTRALIA	O	M	R	W
McDermott	10	0	40	1
Davis	10	2	12	0
Reid	10	1	53	1
Gilbert	10	2	35	2
Waugh	10	0	36	1

NEW ZEALAND	O	M	R	W
Hadlee	9	5	15	4
Chatfield	8	2	19	1
Gillespie	10	2	39	1
Crowe	10	4	23	2
Bracewell	7	0	30	2
Coney	3	0	18	0

FALL OF WICKETS
1-65, 2-72, 3-80, 4-87, 5-117, 6-146

FALL OF WICKETS
1-13, 2-52, 3-55, 4-82, 5-122, 6-124, 7-126, 8-142, 9-156, 10-156

Umpires: B.L.Aldridge (1) and G.C.Morris (4).

NEW ZEALAND v AUSTRALIA 1985-86

At Lancaster Park, Christchurch on 22 March 1986.   Result: **NEW ZEALAND** won by 53 runs.   Toss: Australia.
Award: J.V.Coney.   LOI debuts: None.

Ken Rutherford and Bruce Edgar took full advantage of a pacier pitch and outfield to post New Zealand's record opening stand against Australia.

NEW ZEALAND		Runs	Balls	4/6
K.R.Rutherford	c Waugh b Reid	64	89	5/1
B.A.Edgar	b Reid	74	105	7
M.D.Crowe	c Ritchie b Waugh	12	14	–
* J.V.Coney	run out	64	55	8
J.G.Wright	c Matthews b McDermott	6	16	–
R.J.Hadlee	c Ritchie b Davis	11	6	2
B.R.Blair	c McDermott b Davis	13	12	1
† T.E.Blain	not out	0	2	–
J.G.Bracewell	not out	2	1	–
S.R.Gillespie				
E.J.Chatfield				
Extras	(lb 8, w 2, nb 2)	12		
Total	(49 overs; 7 wickets)	258		

AUSTRALIA		Runs	Balls	4/6
G.R.Marsh	run out	9	16	2
D.C.Boon	c and b Gillespie	47	58	9
* A.R.Border	c Blair b Crowe	27	45	3
G.M.Ritchie	c Crowe b Hadlee	31	55	2
G.R.J.Matthews	c Wright b Bracewell	13	20	1
† W.B.Phillips	run out	12	13	1
S.R.Waugh	b Hadlee	10	18	–
C.J.McDermott	b Chatfield	37	29	3/2
D.R.Gilbert	run out	5	15	–
B.A.Reid	c Crowe b Chatfield	3	4	–
S.P.Davis	not out	1	1	–
Extras	(lb 8, w 2)	10		
Total	(45.4 overs)	205		

AUSTRALIA	O	M	R	W
McDermott	10	1	50	1
Davis	10	1	51	2
Reid	10	0	44	2
Gilbert	5	0	29	0
Matthews	5	0	29	0
Waugh	9	0	47	1

NEW ZEALAND	O	M	R	W
Hadlee	10	2	36	2
Chatfield	8.4	3	38	2
Gillespie	8	0	51	1
Crowe	7	0	27	1
Bracewell	10	2	37	1
Coney	2	0	8	0

FALL OF WICKETS
1-125, 2-150, 3-170, 4-191, 5-212, 6-246, 7-256

FALL OF WICKETS
1-27, 2-67, 3-99, 4-132, 5-137, 6-150, 7-160, 8-189, 9-204, 10-205

Umpires: F.R.Goodall (12) and R.L.McHarg (1).

NEW ZEALAND v AUSTRALIA 1985-86

At Basin Reserve, Wellington on 26 March 1986.   Result: **AUSTRALIA** won by 3 wickets.   Toss: New Zealand.
Award: W.B.Phillips.   LOI debuts: None.

Australia reduced a daunting target of 88 from 11 overs to two runs from the last. In a dramatic finale, Wayne Phillips, who had contributed a 26-ball fifty, and Waugh fell to the first two balls.

NEW ZEALAND		Runs	Balls	4/6
K.R.Rutherford	c Davis b Matthews	79	105	3
B.A.Edgar	st Phillips b Matthews	29	62	2
M.D.Crowe	b McDermott	28	38	1
*J.V.Coney	run out	24	27	1
J.J.Crowe	b Waugh	16	25	–
B.R.Blair	run out	19	23	–
R.J.Hadlee	run out	7	10	–
†T.E.Blain	c Phillips b Davis	11	10	1
J.G.Bracewell	c Marsh b Davis	0	2	–
S.R.Gillespie	not out	0	–	–
E.J.Chatfield				
Extras	(b 7, lb 8, nb 1)	16		
Total	(50 overs; 9 wickets)	**229**		

AUSTRALIA		Runs	Balls	4/6
D.C.Boon	b Chatfield	1	17	–
G.R.Marsh	c Coney b M.D.Crowe	53	96	5
*A.R.Border	c Blain b M.D.Crowe	21	43	3
G.M.Ritchie	run out	1	6	–
S.R.Waugh	run out	71	94	5
G.R.J.Matthews	b Gillespie	9	14	–
†W.B.Phillips	lbw b Hadlee	53	32	9
R.J.Bright	not out	0	1	–
C.J.McDermott	not out	4	1	1
B.A.Reid				
S.P.Davis				
Extras	(b 2, lb 10, w 1, nb 6)	19		
Total	(49.3 overs; 7 wickets)	**232**		

AUSTRALIA	O	M	R	W
McDermott	10	1	41	1
Davis	10	1	37	2
Reid	7	0	32	0
Waugh	7	0	31	1
Matthews	10	0	42	2
Bright	6	0	31	0

NEW ZEALAND	O	M	R	W
Hadlee	9.3	3	26	1
Chatfield	10	3	48	1
Gillespie	10	0	45	1
M.D.Crowe	8	1	44	2
Bracewell	10	0	46	0
Coney	2	0	11	0

FALL OF WICKETS
1-86, 2-145, 3-146, 4-184, 5-190, 6-205, 7-224, 8-228, 9-229

FALL OF WICKETS
1-12, 2-54, 3-56, 4-108, 5-142, 6-228, 7-228

Umpires: B.L.Aldridge (2) and G.C.Morris (5).

NEW ZEALAND v AUSTRALIA 1985-86

At Eden Park, Auckland on 29 March 1986.   Result: **AUSTRALIA** won by 44 runs.   Toss: Australia.
Award: G.R.J.Matthews.   LOI debuts: None.

Australia levelled the series 2-2 after rain had delayed the start and reduced the contest by five overs an innings.

AUSTRALIA		Runs	Balls	4/6
G.R.Marsh	run out	19	18	2
D.C.Boon	b Bracewell	40	66	6/1
*A.R.Border	run out	21	35	3
G.M.Ritchie	b Gray	53	63	5
S.R.Waugh	run out	1	6	–
G.R.J.Matthews	b Chatfield	54	50	3/1
†W.B.Phillips	c Blain b Chatfield	10	11	–
R.J.Bright	b Hadlee	6	8	–
C.J.McDermott	not out	12	10	1
B.A.Reid	b Hadlee	1	2	–
S.P.Davis	run out	0	1	–
Extras	(b 1, lb 12, nb 1)	14		
Total	(44.5 overs)	**231**		

NEW ZEALAND		Runs	Balls	4/6
K.R.Rutherford	run out	12	32	1
B.A.Edgar	c Boon b Reid	22	47	–
M.D.Crowe	c Border b Matthews	14	25	2
*J.V.Coney	run out	11	18	1
B.R.Blair	c Boon b Matthews	11	21	1
†T.E.Blain	c and b Matthews	7	19	–
R.J.Hadlee	c Matthews b Davis	40	43	2/2
E.J.Gray	c Phillips b Reid	7	19	–
J.G.Bracewell	c Matthews b Waugh	20	17	3
S.R.Gillespie	not out	18	21	1/1
E.J.Chatfield	not out	7	14	1
Extras	(b 1, lb 16, nb 1)	18		
Total	(45 overs; 9 wickets)	**187**		

NEW ZEALAND	O	M	R	W
Hadlee	8.5	0	35	2
Chatfield	9	0	37	2
Gillespie	8	1	55	0
Crowe	2	0	15	0
Bracewell	9	0	31	1
Gray	8	0	45	1

AUSTRALIA	O	M	R	W
McDermott	9	1	23	0
Davis	8	2	28	1
Reid	9	1	30	2
Matthews	9	1	33	3
Waugh	9	1	45	1
Boon	1	0	11	0

FALL OF WICKETS
1-25, 2-86, 3-87, 4-96, 5-196, 6-209, 7-209, 8-229, 9-231, 10-231

FALL OF WICKETS
1-32, 2-53, 3-59, 4-77, 5-78, 6-100, 7-112, 8-149, 9-161

Umpires: R.L.McHarg (2) and S.J.Woodward (7).

SRI LANKA v PAKISTAN 1985-86

At P.Saravanamuttu Stadium, Colombo on 30 March 1986.　　Result: **PAKISTAN** won by 81 runs.　　Toss: Sri Lanka.
Award: Mohsin Khan.　　LOI debuts: None.

This second (45-over) Asia Cup tournament was staged without the 1983-84 winners, India. For the first time, independent umpires stood in internationals hosted by a full ICC member.

PAKISTAN		Runs	Balls	4/6
Mudassar Nazar	c De Silva b De Mel	15		
Mohsin Khan	c and b Anurasiri	39		
Ramiz Raja	c Kuruppu b Ratnayeke	26		
Javed Miandad	c Dias b Anurasiri	9		
Qasim Omar	st Kuruppu b Ranatunga	16		
Manzoor Elahi	c Kuruppu b Ranatunga	6		
* Imran Khan	c De Silva b De Mel	21		
Abdul Qadir	c Anurasiri b Amalean	14		
Wasim Akram	c sub b Ratnayeke	24		
† Zulqarnain	not out	11		
Zakir Khan	b Ratnayeke	1		
Extras	(b 5, lb 7, w 2, nb 1)	15		
Total	**(45 overs)**	**197**		

SRI LANKA		Runs	Balls	4/6
† D.S.B.P.Kuruppu	c and b Qadir	34		
M.A.R.Samarasekera	c Imran b Zakir	5		
A.P.Gurusinha	c Zulqarnain b Zakir	8		
R.L.Dias	c Miandad b Zakir	0		
A.Ranatunga	c Zulqarnain b Manzoor	7		
* L.R.D.Mendis	c Zulqarnain b Imran	0		
P.A.de Silva	c Miandad b Manzoor	12		
J.R.Ratnayeke	not out	22		
A.L.F.de Mel	c Zulqarnain b Manzoor	0		
S.D.Anurasiri	c Imran b Qadir	5		
K.N.Amalean	c Imran b Qadir	9		
Extras	(b 4, lb 3, w 7)	14		
Total	**(33.5 overs)**	**116**		

SRI LANKA	O	M	R	W
De Mel	9	1	40	2
Amalean	7	1	30	1
Ratnayeke	9	1	32	3
Samarasekera	2	0	19	0
Anurasiri	9	1	27	2
Ranatunga	9	1	37	2

PAKISTAN	O	M	R	W
Wasim Akram	6	1	17	0
Zakir Khan	6	0	34	3
Manzoor Elahi	9	1	22	3
Imran Khan	5	0	12	1
Abdul Qadir	7.5	1	24	3

FALL OF WICKETS
1-18, 2-87, 3-87, 4-108, 5-118, 6-119, 7-141, 8-179, 9-187, 10-197

FALL OF WICKETS
1-24, 2-32, 3-32, 4-52, 5-53, 6-67, 7-83, 8-94, 9-105, 10-116

Umpires: H.D.Bird (*England*) (33) and D.R.Shepherd (*England*) (10).

PAKISTAN v BANGLADESH 1985-86

At Tyronne Fernando Stadium, Moratuwa on 31 March 1986.　　Result: **PAKISTAN** won by 7 wickets.　　Toss: Pakistan.
Award: Wasim Akram.　　LOI debuts: Bangladesh – All.

Bangladesh, who qualified by winning the South-East Asia Cricket Conference Tournament at Dacca in February 1984, became the first associate ICC member to contest an official LOI outside World Cup tournaments.

BANGLADESH		Runs	Balls	4/6
Raquib-ul-Hassan	c Zulqarnain b Zakir	5		
Nur-ul-Abedin	c Zulqarnain b Imran	0		
* Gazi Ashraf	b Wasim	0		
Shahid-ur-Rehman	c and b Qadir	37		
Minhaz-ul-Abedin	c Manzoor b Wasim	6		
Rafiq Alam	c Ramiz b Wasim	14		
Farooq Chowdhury	c Zulqarnain b Qadir	14		
Jahangir Shah	b Wasim	0		
† Hafiz-ur-Rehman	b Imran	8		
Ghulam Nousher	not out	1		
Sami-ur-Rehman	st Zulqarnain b Qadir	0		
Extras	(lb 4, w 4, nb 1)	9		
Total	**(35.3 overs)**	**94**		

PAKISTAN		Runs	Balls	4/6
Mudassar Nazar	not out	47	86	4
Mohsin Khan	lbw b Jahangir	28		
Ramiz Raja	lbw b Jahangir	0		
Javed Miandad	c Hafiz b Ashraf	15		
Qasim Omar	not out	3		
Manzoor Elahi				
* Imran Khan				
Abdul Qadir				
Wasim Akram				
† Zulqarnain				
Zakir Khan				
Extras	(lb 4, w 1)	5		
Total	**(32.1 overs; 3 wickets)**	**98**		

PAKISTAN	O	M	R	W
Imran Khan	7	3	11	2
Wasim Akram	9	2	19	4
Zakir Khan	7	0	27	1
Manzoor Elahi	5	1	18	0
Abdul Qadir	7.3	1	15	3

BANGLADESH	O	M	R	W
Ghulam Nousher	7	1	32	0
Sami-ur-Rehman	7	1	15	0
Farooq Chowdhury	6	0	13	0
Jahangir Shah	9	1	23	2
Gazi Ashraf	3	0	7	1
Raquib-ul-Hassan	0.1	0	4	0

FALL OF WICKETS
1-3, 2-4, 3-15, 4-27, 5-68, 6-70, 7-79, 8-93, 9-93, 10-94

FALL OF WICKETS
1-45, 2-55, 3-85

Umpires: H.C.Felsinger (10) and P.W.Vidanagamage (8).

SRI LANKA v BANGLADESH 1985-86

At Asgiriya Stadium, Kandy on 2 April 1986.   Result: **SRI LANKA** won by 7 wickets.   Toss: Sri Lanka.
Award: A.P.Gurusinha.   LOI debuts: None.

Their total of 131 and Minhaz-ul-Abedin's contribution of 40 were to remain Bangladesh records for another three
matches, until April 1990 (*LOI No. 626*).

BANGLADESH		Runs	Balls	4/6
Raquib-ul-Hassan	lbw b Ranatunga	12		
Nur-ul-Abedin	c Mahanama b Ratnayeke	13		
* Gazi Ashraf	c Kuruppu b Ranatunga	10		
Minhaz-ul-Abedin	run out	40		
Shahid-ur-Rehman	c Mendis b Ratnayeke	25		
Rafiq Alam	b Amalean	10		
Farooq Chowdhury	not out	3		
Jahangir Shah	run out	1		
Sami-ur-Rehman	c Dias b Amalean	4		
Ghulam Nousher	not out	3		
† Hafiz-ur-Rehman				
Extras	(b 1, lb 4, w 3, nb 2)	10		
Total	(45 overs; 8 wickets)	**131**		

SRI LANKA		Runs	Balls	4/6
† D.S.B.P.Kuruppu	c Sami b Nousher	3		
R.S.Mahanama	c Hafiz b Chowdhury	25		
A.P.Gurusinha	not out	44		
R.L.Dias	c Raquib b Ashraf	0		
A.Ranatunga	not out	41		
* L.R.D.Mendis				
P.A.de Silva				
J.R.Ratnayeke				
A.L.F.de Mel				
S.D.Anurasiri				
K.N.Amalean				
Extras	(b 3, lb 7, w 9)	19		
Total	(31.3 overs; 3 wickets)	**132**		

SRI LANKA	O	M	R	W
De Mel	9	1	30	0
Amalean	9	2	15	2
Ratnayeke	9	1	41	2
Ranatunga	9	1	17	2
Anurasiri	9	2	23	0

BANGLADESH	O	M	R	W
Ghulam Nousher	9	0	45	1
Sami-ur-Rehman	3	0	15	0
Jahangir Shah	6	0	18	0
Farooq Chowdhury	8.3	2	22	1
Gazi Ashraf	5	0	22	1

FALL OF WICKETS
1-26, 2-29, 3-49, 4-92, 5-119, 6-119, 7-120, 8-126

FALL OF WICKETS
1-8, 2-63, 3-64

Umpires: Mahboob Shah (*Pakistan*) (8) and D.R.Shepherd (*England*) (11).

SRI LANKA v NEW ZEALAND 1985-86

At Khettarama Stadium, Colombo on 5 April 1986.   Result: **NEW ZEALAND** won by 6 wickets.   Toss: New Zealand.
Award: M.C.Snedden.   LOI debuts: New Zealand – W.Watson.

Although debarred from the Asia Cup itself, New Zealand competed in this concurrent triangular tournament, also
sponsored by John Player. The Khettarama Stadium, later renamed after R.Premadasa, made its delayed debut as the
72nd ground to stage an international.

SRI LANKA		Runs	Balls	4/6
† D.S.B.P.Kuruppu	c McSweeney b Snedden	23	58	3
R.S.Mahanama	lbw b Snedden	12	53	–
A.P.Gurusinha	c J.J.Crowe b Watson	14	47	–
A.Ranatunga	c McSweeney b Snedden	23	37	2
* L.R.D.Mendis	c Gray b Bracewell	24	31	–
P.A.de Silva	c J.J.Crowe b Watson	4	4	1
S.K.Ranasinghe	c Gray b Watson	0	1	–
J.R.Ratnayeke	not out	22	30	–
C.P.H.Ramanayake	run out	0	–	–
S.D.Anurasiri	run out	0	–	–
K.N.Amalean				
Extras	(b 8, lb 5, nb 2)	15		
Total	(43 overs; 9 wickets)	**137**		

NEW ZEALAND		Runs	Balls	4/6
K.R.Rutherford	c Mahanama b Ratnayeke	34	50	4
* J.G.Wright	c and b Ranatunga	24	50	4
M.D.Crowe	c Mahanama b Ranatunga	4	19	–
J.J.Crowe	run out	20	49	1
T.E.Blain	not out	26	42	2
J.G.Bracewell	not out	16	15	3
E.J.Gray				
G.K.Robertson				
† E.B.McSweeney				
M.C.Snedden				
W.Watson				
Extras	(b 4, lb 8, w 3, nb 1)	16		
Total	(36.2 overs; 4 wickets)	**140**		

NEW ZEALAND	O	M	R	W
Robertson	8	2	26	0
Watson	9	2	15	3
Gray	9	0	15	0
Snedden	9	1	26	3
Bracewell	8	0	42	1

SRI LANKA	O	M	R	W
Amalean	7	0	29	0
Ramanayake	3	0	20	0
Ratnayeke	7	1	24	1
Anurasiri	9	1	19	0
Ranatunga	6	0	17	2
Ranasinghe	2	0	7	0
De Silva	2.2	0	12	0

FALL OF WICKETS
1-39, 2-40, 3-79, 4-88, 5-96, 6-96, 7-130, 8-136, 9-137

FALL OF WICKETS
1-62, 2-71, 3-72, 4-110

Umpires: H.D.Bird (*England*) (34) and Mahboob Shah (*Pakistan*) (9).

SRI LANKA v PAKISTAN 1985-86

At Sinhalese Sports Club, Colombo on 6 April 1986.   Result: **SRI LANKA** won by 5 wickets.   Toss: Sri Lanka.
Award: Javed Miandad.   LOI debuts: None.

Sri Lanka won the John Player Gold Leaf Trophy, a notable victory despite the absence of Pakistan's key bowler, Imran Khan (calf strain), which was commemorated by President Jayawardene granting a public holiday. This game also counted in the triangular tournament.

PAKISTAN		Runs	Balls	4/6
Mudassar Nazar	b De Mel	2		
Mohsin Khan	run out	7		
Ramiz Raja	c Mahanama b Amalean	2		
Javed Miandad	c Ratnayeke b Amalean	67	100	4
* Imran Khan	lbw b Ratnayeke	2		
Salim Malik	c and b Anurasiri	23		
Manzoor Elahi	b Amalean	37		
Abdul Qadir	c De Mel b Ratnayeke	30		
Wasim Akram	c Gurusinha b Amalean	6		
† Zulqarnain	not out	1		
Zakir Khan				
Extras	(lb 4, w 8, nb 2)	14		
Total	(45 overs; 9 wickets)	**191**		

SRI LANKA		Runs	Balls	4/6
† D.S.B.P.Kuruppu	c Salim b Qadir	30		
R.S.Mahanama	c Qadir b Manzoor	21		
A.P.Gurusinha	c Zulqarnain b Qadir	4		
P.A.de Silva	c sub‡ b Mudassar	52	66	2
A.Ranatunga	c Mohsin b Qadir	57		6/1
* L.R.D.Mendis	not out	22		
R.L.Dias	not out	0		
J.R.Ratnayeke				
A.L.F.de Mel				
S.D.Anurasiri				
K.N.Amalean				
Extras	(b 1, lb 6, w 2)	9		
Total	(42.2 overs; 5 wickets)	**195**		

SRI LANKA	O	M	R	W
De Mel	9	2	21	1
Amalean	9	1	46	4
Ratnayeke	8	0	50	2
Ranatunga	9	1	27	0
Anurasiri	9	0	24	1
De Silva	1	0	19	0

PAKISTAN	O	M	R	W
Wasim Akram	7.2	2	22	0
Zakir Khan	6	0	36	0
Abdul Qadir	9	0	32	3
Manzoor Elahi	9	0	30	1
Salim Malik	3	0	19	0
Mudassar Nazar	8	0	49	1

FALL OF WICKETS
1-6, 2-10, 3-24, 4-32, 5-72, 6-137, 7-179, 8-185, 9-191

FALL OF WICKETS   ‡ (Tausif Ahmed)
1-40, 2-59, 3-64, 4-161, 5-191

Umpires: H.D.Bird (*England*) (35) and D.R.Shepherd (*England*) (12).

NEW ZEALAND v PAKISTAN 1985-86

At Sinhalese Sports Club, Colombo on 7 April 1986.   Result: **PAKISTAN** won by 4 wickets.   Toss: Pakistan.
Award: M.D.Crowe.   LOI debuts: None.

With each country winning one match, Pakistan were awarded the Triangular Trophy on run rate, Javed Miandad being adjudged 'Man of the Tournament'. John Wright sustained a fractured arm while fielding.

NEW ZEALAND		Runs	Balls	4/6
K.R.Rutherford	c Tausif b Wasim	9	27	1
* J.G.Wright	st Zulqarnain b Tausif	42	78	5
M.D.Crowe	c Manzoor b Kamal	75	85	6
J.J.Crowe	run out	42	48	3
B.R.Blair	c Zulqarnain b Kamal	0	1	-
G.K.Robertson	c Zulqarnain b Kamal	7	5	-
J.G.Bracewell	not out	15	10	1/1
† T.E.Blain	b Kamal	0	1	
E.J.Gray	b Wasim	1	2	
M.C.Snedden	not out	2	2	
E.J.Chatfield				
Extras	(b 1, lb 14, w 6)	21		
Total	(42 overs; 8 wickets)	**214**		

PAKISTAN		Runs	Balls	4/6
Mudassar Nazar	run out	19	44	3
Mohsin Khan	c Gray b Chatfield	16	20	3
Ramiz Raja	c Blair b Gray	25	47	1
* Javed Miandad	b Snedden	68	81	5
Salim Malik	run out	32	25	4
Manzoor Elahi	c Blair b Snedden	27	15	1/2
Abdul Qadir	not out	11	12	1
Wasim Akram	not out	8	2	-/1
Mohsin Kamal				
† Zulqarnain				
Tausif Ahmed				
Extras	(lb 11)	11		
Total	(40.4 overs; 6 wickets)	**217**		

PAKISTAN	O	M	R	W
Wasim Akram	9	2	19	2
Mohsin Kamal	8	0	47	4
Manzoor Elahi	9	0	33	0
Abdul Qadir	9	1	51	0
Tausif Ahmed	6	0	38	1
Mudassar Nazar	1	0	11	0

NEW ZEALAND	O	M	R	W
Chatfield	9	4	18	1
Robertson	6	0	40	0
Snedden	8.4	0	55	2
M.D.Crowe	3	0	20	0
Bracewell	9	0	41	0
Gray	5	0	32	1

FALL OF WICKETS
1-16, 2-102, 3-181, 4-182, 5-194, 6-202, 7-202, 8-211

FALL OF WICKETS
1-31, 2-42, 3-140, 4-162, 5-173, 6-206

Umpires: H.C.Felsinger (11) and P.W.Vidanagamage (9).

NEW ZEALAND v INDIA 1985-86

At Sharjah CA Stadium, UAE on 10 April 1986.   Result: **INDIA** won by 3 wickets.   Toss: India.
Award: E.J.Chatfield.   LOI debuts: India – C.S.Pandit.

The inaugural Austral-Asia Cup (50-over) tournament was staged for the joint benefit of Vijay Hazare, Dilip Vengsarkar (India), Javed Miandad and Wazir Mohammed (Pakistan). New Zealand, bereft of half their regular team, made their first appearance at Sharjah.

NEW ZEALAND		Runs	Balls	4/6
K.R.Rutherford	b Maninder	12	53	–
M.C.Snedden	c Patil b Maninder	26	75	1
M.D.Crowe	lbw b Madan Lal	1	9	–
* J.J.Crowe	not out	36	56	3
T.E.Blain	c Patil b Maninder	0	1	–
B.R.Blair	run out	0	2	–
J.G.Bracewell	b Shastri	25	35	1/1
E.J.Gray	b Shastri	2	14	–
G.K.Robertson	b Azad	0	2	–
† E.B.McSweeney	not out	18	17	1/2
E.J.Chatfield				
Extras	(lb 12)	12		
Total	(44 overs; 8 wickets)	**132**		

INDIA		Runs	Balls	4/6
S.M.Gavaskar	c McSweeney b Chatfield	0	6	–
K.Srikkanth	c Blair b Chatfield	11	14	2
M.Azharuddin	c and b Chatfield	6	18	–
S.M.Patil	b M.D.Crowe	7	12	1
K.Azad	b Bracewell	30	61	–/2
R.J.Shastri	st McSweeney b Gray	25	59	–
* Kapil Dev	c Blair b Snedden	9	29	–
† C.S.Pandit	not out	33	34	4
Madan Lal	not out	8	12	1
R.M.H.Binny				
Maninder Singh				
Extras	(lb 5)	5		
Total	(41.4 overs; 7 wickets)	**134**		

INDIA	O	M	R	W
Kapil Dev	6	3	7	0
Binny	5	0	12	0
Madan Lal	7	1	12	1
Maninder Singh	9	0	23	3
Shastri	9	0	25	2
Azad	8	0	41	1

NEW ZEALAND	O	M	R	W
Chatfield	9	5	14	3
Robertson	4	0	13	0
M.D.Crowe	5	1	16	1
Snedden	7	1	24	1
Bracewell	9	1	34	1
Gray	7.4	1	28	1

FALL OF WICKETS
1-37, 2-42, 3-48, 4-48, 5-48, 6-81, 7-95, 8-96

FALL OF WICKETS
1-0, 2-8, 3-19, 4-25, 5-81, 6-81, 7-116

Umpires: D.M.Archer (*West Indies*) (6) and A.J.Gaynor (*West Indies*) (2).

AUSTRALIA v PAKISTAN 1985-86

At Sharjah CA Stadium, UAE on 11 April 1986.   Result: **PAKISTAN** won by 8 wickets.   Toss: Australia.
Award: Mudassar Nazar.   LOI debuts: None.

In the absence of Allan Border, Australia were captained by Ray Bright for the only time. Mudassar Nazar completed 2000 runs in his 88th international.

AUSTRALIA		Runs	Balls	4/6
D.C.Boon	c Mohsin Khan b Tausif	44	81	4
G.R.Marsh	c Mudassar b Qadir	26	62	3
D.M.Jones	lbw b Tausif	8	17	–
G.M.Ritchie	not out	60	72	2
S.R.Waugh	c Zulqarnain b Wasim	26	37	1
G.R.J.Matthews	c Miandad b Mohsin Kamal	20	20	1
C.J.McDermott	run out	1	2	
† T.J.Zoehrer	run out	5	2	
* R.J.Bright				
S.P.Davis				
B.A.Reid				
Extras	(lb 10, w 1, nb 1)	12		
Total	(50 overs; 7 wickets)	**202**		

PAKISTAN		Runs	Balls	4/6
Mudassar Nazar	b Reid	95	140	5
Mohsin Khan	lbw b Bright	46	79	6
Ramiz Raja	not out	56	76	2
Manzoor Elahi	not out	2	3	
* Javed Miandad				
Salim Malik				
Wasim Akram				
Abdul Qadir				
Mohsin Kamal				
Tausif Ahmed				
† Zulqarnain				
Extras	(lb 5, w 2)	7		
Total	(49.1 overs; 2 wickets)	**206**		

PAKISTAN	O	M	R	W
Wasim Akram	10	0	38	1
Mohsin Kamal	10	0	51	1
Manzoor Elahi	10	0	58	0
Tausif Ahmed	10	1	19	2
Abdul Qadir	10	0	26	1

AUSTRALIA	O	M	R	W
McDermott	10	2	29	0
Davis	8	2	28	0
Reid	9.1	0	51	1
Waugh	6	1	25	0
Bright	10	1	28	1
Matthews	6	0	40	0

FALL OF WICKETS
1-63, 2-79, 3-90, 4-140, 5-195, 6-197, 7-202

FALL OF WICKETS
1-80, 2-195

Umpires: D.M.Archer (*West Indies*) (7) and A.J.Gaynor (*West Indies*) (3).

INDIA v SRI LANKA 1985-86

At Sharjah CA Stadium, UAE on 13 April 1986.   Result: **INDIA** won by 3 wickets.   Toss: India.
Award: S.M.Gavaskar.   LOI debuts: None.

As winners of the Asia Cup, Sri Lanka had enjoyed a bye in the preliminary round.

SRI LANKA		Runs	Balls	4/6	INDIA		Runs	Balls	4/6
R.S.Mahanama	c Patil b Sharma	9	30	–	K.Srikkanth	st De Alwis b Anurasiri	59	63	5/1
P.A.de Silva	c Maninder b Sharma	5	9	–	S.M.Gavaskar	c De Silva b De Mel	71	109	6/1
A.P.Gurusinha	b Azad	68	113	–/1	M.Azharuddin	b De Mel	30	65	1
R.L.Dias	b Maninder	9	30	–	S.M.Patil	b De Mel	10	20	–
* L.R.D.Mendis	c Azharuddin b Madan Lal	32	50	–	K.Azad	c Gurusinha b Anurasiri	1	2	–
A.Ranatunga	run out	28	25	2	* Kapil Dev	c Dias b Anurasiri	3	3	–
† R.G.de Alwis	run out	19	13	1/1	R.J.Shastri	not out	21	28	2
A.L.F.de Mel	not out	15	19	1	† C.S.Pandit	run out	2	5	–
R.J.Ratnayake	c Azad b Sharma	1	3	–	Madan Lal	not out	1	3	–
J.R.Ratnayeke	run out	3	6	–	Maninder Singh				
S.D.Anurasiri	not out	2	3	–	C.Sharma				
Extras	(b 1, lb 12, nb 1)	14			Extras	(lb 6, w 1, nb 1)	8		
Total	(50 overs; 9 wickets)	**205**			**Total**	(49.1 overs; 7 wickets)	**206**		

INDIA	O	M	R	W	SRI LANKA	O	M	R	W
Kapil Dev	10	1	39	0	De Mel	10	0	40	3
Sharma	9	1	35	3	Ratnayake	9.1	1	36	0
Madan Lal	8	0	40	1	Anurasiri	10	0	40	3
Maninder Singh	10	2	19	1	Ratnayeke	10	0	39	0
Shastri	8	0	40	0	De Silva	3	0	9	0
Azad	5	0	19	1	Ranatunga	7	0	36	0

FALL OF WICKETS
1-8, 2-20, 3-58, 4-129, 5-135, 6-165, 7-188, 8-195, 9-201

FALL OF WICKETS
1-93, 2-165, 3-170, 4-171, 5-175, 6-191, 7-194

Umpires: D.M.Archer (*West Indies*) (8) and A.J.Gaynor (*West Indies*) (4).

NEW ZEALAND v PAKISTAN 1985-86

At Sharjah CA Stadium, UAE on 15 April 1986.   Result: **PAKISTAN** won by 10 wickets.   Toss: Pakistan.
Award: Abdul Qadir.   LOI debuts: None.

New Zealand, who qualified for the semi-finals by being the preliminary round's 'closest loser', were dismissed for what remains their lowest total in any limited-overs international. Abdul Qadir returned Pakistan's (and Sharjah's) most economical 10-over analysis.

NEW ZEALAND		Runs	Balls	4/6	PAKISTAN		Runs	Balls	4/6
K.R.Rutherford	c Miandad b Imran	2	31	–	Mudassar Nazar	not out	32	67	4
M.C.Snedden	b Wasim	0	5	–	Mohsin Khan	not out	34	69	3
M.D.Crowe	c Qadir b Wasim	9	13	–/1	Ramiz Raja				
* J.J.Crowe	c Zulqarnain b Wasim	1	5	–	Javed Miandad				
E.J.Gray	b Manzoor	17	75	1	Salim Malik				
B.R.Blair	b Qadir	9	42	1	* Imran Khan				
T.E.Blain	b Qadir	0	2	–	Abdul Qadir				
J.G.Bracewell	b Qadir	0	2	–	Wasim Akram				
† E.B.McSweeney	c Wasim b Qadir	7	26	–	Manzoor Elahi				
E.J.Chatfield	c sub (Qasim Omar) b Manzoor	2	14	–	Tausif Ahmed				
W.Watson	not out	1	10	–	† Zulqarnain				
Extras	(b 1, lb 5, w 8, nb 2)	16			Extras		0		
Total	(35.5 overs)	**64**			**Total**	(22.4 overs; 0 wickets)	**66**		

PAKISTAN	O	M	R	W	NEW ZEALAND	O	M	R	W
Imran Khan	7	2	11	1	Chatfield	3	2	3	0
Wasim Akram	7	3	10	3	Watson	7	0	15	0
Abdul Qadir	10	4	9	4	Gray	8.4	3	22	0
Tausif Ahmed	10	2	20	0	Bracewell	4	0	26	0
Manzoor Elahi	1.5	0	8	2					

FALL OF WICKETS
1-4, 2-15, 3-18, 4-18, 5-32, 6-32, 7-32, 8-48, 9-55, 10-64

Umpires: D.M.Archer (*West Indies*) (9) and A.J.Gaynor (*West Indies*) (5).

INDIA v PAKISTAN 1985-86

At Sharjah CA Stadium, UAE on 18 April 1986.   Result: **PAKISTAN** won by 1 wicket.   Toss: Pakistan.
Award: Javed Miandad.   LOI debuts: None.

Watched by a capacity crowd of 20,000, Javed Miandad reached his third LOI hundred off 107 balls before completing an epic victory by hitting the ultimate ball (from Chetan Sharma) for six. Pakistan's first success in a major tournament was worth $40,000 in prize money.

INDIA		Runs	Balls	4/6
K.Srikkanth	c Wasim b Qadir	75	80	8/2
S.M.Gavaskar	b Imran	92	134	6
D.B.Vengsarkar	b Wasim	50	64	–/1
K.Azad	b Wasim	0	3	–
* Kapil Dev	b Imran	8	8	1
C.Sharma	run out	10	10	1
R.J.Shastri	b Wasim	1	2	–
† C.S.Pandit	not out	0	2	–
M.Azharuddin				
Madan Lal				
Maninder Singh				
Extras	(lb 6, w 2, nb 1)	9		
Total	(50 overs; 7 wickets)	245		

PAKISTAN		Runs	Balls	4/6
Mudassar Nazar	lbw b Sharma	5	22	1
Mohsin Khan	b Madan Lal	36	53	4
Ramiz Raja	b Maninder	10	15	–
Javed Miandad	not out	116	114	3/3
Salim Malik	run out	21	37	–
Abdul Qadir	c sub (R.Lamba) b Kapil Dev	34	39	1/1
* Imran Khan	b Madan Lal	7	10	–
Manzoor Elahi	c Shastri b Sharma	4	5	–
Wasim Akram	run out	3	4	–
† Zulqarnain	b Sharma	0	1	–
Tausif Ahmed	not out	1	1	–
Extras	(lb 11)	11		
Total	(50 overs; 9 wickets)	248		

PAKISTAN	O	M	R	W
Imran Khan	10	2	40	2
Wasim Akram	10	1	42	3
Manzoor Elahi	5	0	33	0
Mudassar Nazar	5	0	32	0
Abdul Qadir	10	2	49	1
Tausif Ahmed	10	1	43	0

INDIA	O	M	R	W
Kapil Dev	10	1	45	1
Sharma	9	0	51	3
Madan Lal	10	0	53	2
Maninder Singh	10	0	36	1
Shastri	9	0	38	0
Azharuddin	2	0	14	0

FALL OF WICKETS
1-117, 2-216, 3-216, 4-229, 5-242, 6-245, 7-245

FALL OF WICKETS
1-9, 2-39, 3-61, 4-110, 5-181, 6-209, 7-215, 8-236, 9-241

Umpires: D.M.Archer (*West Indies*) (10) and A.J.Gaynor (*West Indies*) (6).

ENGLAND v INDIA 1986

At Kennington Oval, London on 24 May 1986.   Result: **INDIA** won by 9 wickets.   Toss: India.
Award: M.Azharuddin.   LOI debuts: None.

India inflicted England's largest defeat by a wickets margin in 55-over home internationals. The unbroken stand of 163 between Sunil Gavaskar and Mohammed Azharuddin remains India's highest for the second wicket against England.

ENGLAND		Runs	Balls	4/6
G.A.Gooch	c Azharuddin b Sharma	30	52	1/1
G.Fowler	run out	20	77	1
M.W.Gatting	c Kapil Dev b Shastri	27	58	1
* D.I.Gower	c Kapil Dev b Shastri	0	1	–
A.J.Lamb	c Kapil Dev b Maninder	0	7	–
D.R.Pringle	c Azharuddin b Sharma	28	66	1
† P.R.Downton	c Azharuddin b Binny	4	17	–
R.M.Ellison	c and b Binny	10	15	–
J.E.Emburey	run out	20	22	2
G.R.Dilley	c Pandit b Sharma	6	12	–
L.B.Taylor	not out	1	6	–
Extras	(b 1, lb 10, w 3, nb 2)	16		
Total	(55 overs)	162		

INDIA		Runs	Balls	4/6
K.Srikkanth	c Downton b Dilley	0	1	–
S.M.Gavaskar	not out	65	132	5
M.Azharuddin	not out	83	154	8
D.B.Vengsarkar				
S.M.Patil				
R.J.Shastri				
* Kapil Dev				
† C.S.Pandit				
C.Sharma				
R.M.H.Binny				
Maninder Singh				
Extras	(lb 9, w 4, nb 2)	15		
Total	(47.2 overs; 1 wicket)	163		

INDIA	O	M	R	W
Kapil Dev	11	1	32	0
Binny	11	2	38	2
Sharma	11	2	25	3
Maninder Singh	11	1	31	1
Shastri	11	0	25	2

ENGLAND	O	M	R	W
Dilley	11	0	53	1
Taylor	7	1	30	0
Pringle	8.2	4	20	0
Ellison	10	1	36	0
Emburey	11	2	15	0

FALL OF WICKETS
1-54, 2-67, 3-67, 4-70, 5-102, 6-115, 7-131, 8-138, 9-151, 10-162

FALL OF WICKETS
1-0

Umpires: D.R.Shepherd (13) and A.G.T.Whitehead (11).

ENGLAND v INDIA 1986

At Old Trafford, Manchester on 26 May 1986.   Result: **ENGLAND** won by 5 wickets.   Toss: England.
Award: D.I.Gower.   LOI debuts: None.

England's victory came too slowly by 40 balls to prevent India from winning the Texaco Trophy on overall run rate.
Kapil Dev completed 50 off 43 balls and with Ravi Shastri shared India's highest sixth-wicket partnership against
England (104).

INDIA		Runs	Balls	4/6	ENGLAND		Runs	Balls	4/6
K.Srikkanth	c Fowler b Emburey	67	93	5	G.A.Gooch	lbw b Kapil Dev	10	17	1
S.M.Gavaskar	c Gooch b Ellison	4	6	1	G.Fowler	c and b Binny	10	33	1
M.Azharuddin	c Gower b Edmonds	7	39	–	* D.I.Gower	b Binny	81	94	4
D.B.Vengsarkar	b Emburey	29	46	2	A.J.Lamb	run out	45	71	3
S.M.Patil	b Dilley	12	27	1	M.W.Gatting	run out	39	53	2
R.J.Shastri	not out	62	72	4	D.R.Pringle	not out	49	52	3
* Kapil Dev	c Downton b Dilley	51	45	5	† P.R.Downton	not out	4	4	–
C.Sharma	not out	8	6	–	P.H.Edmonds				
† C.S.Pandit					J.E.Emburey				
R.M.H.Binny					R.M.Ellison				
Maninder Singh					G.R.Dilley				
Extras	(b 5, lb 4, w 2, nb 3)	14			Extras	(lb 13, w 5)	18		
Total	(55 overs; 6 wickets)	254			Total	(53.5 overs; 5 wickets)	256		

ENGLAND	O	M	R	W	INDIA	O	M	R	W
Dilley	11	2	46	2	Kapil Dev	10	0	41	1
Ellison	11	0	55	1	Binny	10	1	47	2
Pringle	11	0	49	0	Sharma	9.5	0	49	0
Edmonds	11	1	49	1	Shastri	11	0	37	0
Emburey	11	1	46	2	Maninder Singh	11	0	55	0
					Azharuddin	2	0	14	0

FALL OF WICKETS
1-4, 2-49, 3-109, 4-117, 5-130, 6-234

FALL OF WICKETS
1-18, 2-27, 3-142, 4-157, 5-242

Umpires: H.D.Bird (36) and D.J.Constant (26).

ENGLAND v NEW ZEALAND 1986

At Headingley, Leeds on 16 July 1986.   Result: **NEW ZEALAND** won by 47 runs.   Toss: New Zealand.
Award: J.J.Crowe.   LOI debuts: England – M.R.Benson.

New Zealand gained their first victory in Prudential/Texaco Trophy matches.

NEW ZEALAND		Runs	Balls	4/6	ENGLAND		Runs	Balls	4/6
B.A.Edgar	lbw b Foster	0	11	–	G.A.Gooch	b Hadlee	18	37	4
J.G.Wright	c Richards b Ellison	21	55	2	M.R.Benson	c Chatfield b Bracewell	24	58	3
K.R.Rutherford	b Ellison	11	32	–	D.I.Gower	b Coney	18	38	1
M.D.Crowe	b Ellison	9	16	2	A.J.Lamb	run out	33	45	5
* J.V.Coney	run out	27	54	3	* M.W.Gatting	b Gray	19	27	1/1
J.J.Crowe	c and b Foster	66	94	7	D.R.Pringle	c Rutherford b Gray	28	42	2
R.J.Hadlee	lbw b Dilley	11	15	1	† C.J.Richards	run out	8	11	1
E.J.Gray	not out	30	34	2	J.E.Emburey	lbw b Bracewell	0	2	–
† I.D.S.Smith	run out	4	9	–	R.M.Ellison	run out	12	12	–/1
J.G.Bracewell	not out	10	13	–	N.A.Foster	b Hadlee	5	11	–
E.J.Chatfield					G.R.Dilley	not out	2	8	–
Extras	(lb 18, w 7, nb 3)	28			Extras	(lb 1, w 2)	3		
Total	(55 overs; 8 wickets)	217			Total	(48.2 overs)	170		

ENGLAND	O	M	R	W	NEW ZEALAND	O	M	R	W
Dilley	11	1	37	1	Hadlee	9.2	0	29	2
Foster	9	1	27	2	Chatfield	8	2	24	0
Pringle	9	0	42	0	Bracewell	11	2	27	2
Ellison	11	1	43	3	M.D.Crowe	4	0	15	0
Emburey	11	0	30	0	Gray	11	1	55	2
Gooch	4	0	20	0	Coney	5	0	19	1

FALL OF WICKETS
1-9, 2-36, 3-48, 4-54, 5-112, 6-138, 7-165, 8-187

FALL OF WICKETS
1-38, 2-48, 3-83, 4-103, 5-131, 6-143, 7-144, 8-162, 9-165, 10-170

Umpires: J.Birkenshaw (5) and B.J.Meyer (17).

ENGLAND v NEW ZEALAND 1986

At Old Trafford, Manchester on 18 July 1986.   Result: **ENGLAND** won by 6 wickets.   Toss: England.
Award: C.W.J.Athey.   LOI debuts: None.

New Zealand, who won the Texaco Trophy on overall run rate, scored 88 off their last five overs, including 26 from the 55th bowled by Graham Gooch. The latter gained some revenge by sharing an opening stand of 193 with Bill Athey which remains England's LOI record.

NEW ZEALAND		Runs	Balls	4/6
J.G.Wright	c Pringle b Embury	39	71	3
B.A.Edgar	lbw b Dilley	5	10	–
K.R.Rutherford	b Edmonds	63	111	5
M.D.Crowe	not out	93	74	11/2
* J.V.Coney	run out	1	5	–
J.J.Crowe	b Pringle	48	55	4
R.J.Hadlee	not out	18	6	2/1
E.J.Gray				
† I.D.S.Smith				
J.G.Bracewell				
W.Watson				
Extras	(lb 2, w 14, nb 1)	17		
Total	(55 overs; 5 wickets)	284		

ENGLAND		Runs	Balls	4/6
G.A.Gooch	c and b Coney	91	102	9
C.W.J.Athey	not out	142	172	14
D.I.Gower	c Wright b Coney	9	18	1
A.J.Lamb	b Bracewell	28	27	3
* M.W.Gatting	b M.D.Crowe	7	4	1
D.R.Pringle	not out	0	–	–
† C.J.Richards				
J.E.Emburey				
P.H.Edmonds				
N.A.Foster				
G.R.Dilley				
Extras	(lb 5, w 3, nb 1)	9		
Total	(53.4 overs; 4 wickets)	286		

ENGLAND	O	M	R	W
Dilley	9	0	55	1
Foster	7	0	40	0
Pringle	10	2	63	1
Gooch	7	0	48	0
Edmonds	11	1	42	1
Emburey	11	1	34	1

NEW ZEALAND	O	M	R	W
Hadlee	11	1	34	0
Watson	11	1	46	0
M.D.Crowe	6	0	36	1
Bracewell	10.4	0	67	1
Gray	4	0	39	0
Coney	11	0	59	2

FALL OF WICKETS
1-16, 2-89, 3-133, 4-136, 5-249

FALL OF WICKETS
1-193, 2-219, 3-265, 4-274

Umpires: K.E.Palmer (14) and N.T.Plews (1).

INDIA v AUSTRALIA 1986-87

At Sawai Mansingh Stadium, Jaipur on 7 September 1986.   Result: **INDIA** won by 7 wickets.   Toss: India.
Award: K.Srikkanth.   LOI debuts: India – R.Lamba.

Even a world record opening partnership of 212 by Geoff Marsh and David Boon failed to produce a target capable of extending Krish Srikkanth. Playing conditions imposed no penalty on India for strategically bowling fewer than the stipulated 50 overs in the given time.

AUSTRALIA		Runs	Balls	4/6
G.R.Marsh	run out	104	139	9/1
D.C.Boon	c Shastri b Azharuddin	111	118	10/2
D.M.Jones	not out	17	12	2
* A.R.Border	run out	3	3	–
G.M.Ritchie	not out	7	7	–
S.R.Waugh				
G.R.J.Matthews				
† T.J.Zoehrer				
C.J.McDermott				
B.A.Reid				
S.P.Davis				
Extras	(b 1, lb 3, w 1, nb 3)	8		
Total	(47 overs; 3 wickets)	250		

INDIA		Runs	Balls	4/6
K.Srikkanth	c Jones b Reid	102	104	10/1
S.M.Gavaskar	run out	26	56	3
R.Lamba	c Border b Matthews	64	53	8/1
D.B.Vengsarkar	not out	18	24	–
* Kapil Dev	not out	26	13	3/2
M.Azharuddin				
R.M.H.Binny				
† C.S.Pandit				
R.J.Shastri				
C.Sharma				
Maninder Singh				
Extras	(b 1, lb 11, w 1, nb 2)	15		
Total	(41 overs; 3 wickets)	251		

INDIA	O	M	R	W
Kapil Dev	9	0	48	0
Binny	7	1	41	0
Shastri	10	1	31	0
Sharma	4	0	31	0
Maninder Singh	10	0	42	0
Azharuddin	7	0	53	1

AUSTRALIA	O	M	R	W
McDermott	10	0	75	0
Davis	7	0	48	0
Reid	8	1	27	1
Waugh	7	0	42	0
Matthews	9	0	47	1

FALL OF WICKETS
1-212, 2-225, 3-228

FALL OF WICKETS
1-86, 2-188, 3-210

Umpires: S.Banerjee (3) and B.Nagaraja Rao (2).

INDIA v AUSTRALIA 1986-87

At Sher-i-Kashmir Stadium, Srinagar on 9 September 1986.   Result: **AUSTRALIA** won by 3 wickets.   Toss: Australia.
Award: A.R.Border.   LOI debuts: None.

Australia emulated India's tactic and deliberately slowed their bowling rate to produce a 47-over match. Dilip Vengsarkar retired with back spasms.

INDIA		Runs	Balls	4/6
K.Srikkanth	c Zoehrer b Matthews	24	35	3
S.M.Gavaskar	run out	52	56	5/2
R.Lamba	c Zoehrer b Davis	1	7	–
D.B.Vengsarkar	retired hurt	12	21	1
M.Azharuddin	c Marsh b Waugh	16	44	–
R.J.Shastri	b Reid	37	52	3
†C.S.Pandit	b Reid	24	26	2
*Kapil Dev	c Marsh b Davis	16	11	2/1
C.Sharma	b Waugh	17	14	1
R.M.H.Binny	not out	11	17	–
Maninder Singh	not out	2	4	–
Extras	(lb 5, w 3, nb 2)	10		
Total	**(47 overs; 8 wickets)**	**222**		

AUSTRALIA		Runs	Balls	4/6
D.C.Boon	c Lamba b Kapil Dev	0	5	–
G.R.Marsh	c Pandit b Binny	17	34	3
D.M.Jones	c Pandit b Binny	12	26	2
*A.R.Border	not out	90	106	6/1
G.M.Ritchie	st Pandit b Shastri	28	41	1/1
G.R.J.Matthews	run out	31	43	1
S.R.Waugh	st Pandit b Shastri	20	19	4
†T.J.Zoehrer	c and b Kapil Dev	1	5	–
C.J.McDermott	not out	7	5	1
B.A.Reid				
S.P.Davis				
Extras	(b 1, lb 12, w 1, nb 6)	20		
Total	**(46 overs; 7 wickets)**	**226**		

AUSTRALIA	O	M	R	W
McDermott	9	1	37	0
Davis	10	1	51	2
Matthews	9	0	52	1
Reid	10	2	37	2
Waugh	9	0	40	2

INDIA	O	M	R	W
Kapil Dev	9	2	37	2
Binny	8	0	25	2
Sharma	9	0	41	0
Shastri	10	0	60	2
Maninder Singh	10	0	50	0

FALL OF WICKETS
1-50, 2-51, 3-108, 4-123, 5-161, 6-192, 7-192, 8-216

FALL OF WICKETS
1-0, 2-19, 3-39, 4-102, 5-172, 6-213, 7-216

Umpires: S.B.Kulkarni (1) and R.S.Rathore (1).

INDIA v AUSTRALIA 1986-87

At Lal Bahadur Stadium, Hyderabad on 24 September 1986.   No result.   Toss: India.
LOI debuts: India – R.P.Singh; Australia – G.C.Dyer.

India again chose to bowl and perpetuated the 'go-slow' ploy only for a thunderstorm to intervene. Greg Ritchie's thunderous innings included 22 runs off Madan Lal's last over.

AUSTRALIA		Runs	Balls	4/6
D.C.Boon	c Kapil Dev b Madan Lal	26	40	2
G.R.Marsh	run out	30	52	1/1
D.M.Jones	c Madan Lal b Shastri	48	63	3/1
*A.R.Border	c Lamba b Shastri	7	10	–
G.M.Ritchie	st Pandit b Kapil Dev	75	53	7/3
G.R.J.Matthews	c Maninder b Sharma	20	32	1/1
S.R.Waugh	not out	25	34	4
†G.C.Dyer				
D.R.Gilbert				
B.A.Reid				
S.P.Davis				
Extras	(b 2, lb 5, w 3, nb 1)	11		
Total	**(47 overs; 6 wickets)**	**242**		

INDIA		Runs	Balls	4/6
K.Srikkanth	b Reid	9	14	2
R.Lamba	not out	20	36	2
M.Azharuddin	not out	9	14	1
D.B.Vengsarkar				
R.J.Shastri				
*Kapil Dev				
†C.S.Pandit				
Madan Lal				
R.P.Singh				
G.Sharma				
Maninder Singh				
Extras	(lb 1, w 2)	3		
Total	**(10.4 overs; 1 wicket)**	**41**		

INDIA	O	M	R	W
Kapil Dev	10	1	40	1
Singh	4	1	19	0
Madan Lal	9	0	60	1
Shastri	10	0	36	2
Maninder Singh	7	0	42	0
Sharma	7	0	38	1

AUSTRALIA	O	M	R	W
Davis	5.4	0	19	0
Reid	4	0	20	1
Gilbert	1	0	1	0

FALL OF WICKETS
1-18

FALL OF WICKETS
1-55, 2-78, 3-111, 4-126, 5-159, 6-242

Umpires: R.R.Kadam (1) and R.V.Ramani (3).

INDIA v AUSTRALIA 1986-87

At Feroz Shah Kotla, Delhi on 2 October 1986.   Result: **INDIA** won by 3 wickets.   Toss: India.
Award: R.Lamba.   LOI debuts: None.

The hosts honed their delaying tactics to a fine art, bowling a pathetic 45 overs in the allotted 3½ hours. The unbroken stand of 102 between Steve Waugh and Greg Dyer remains Australia's record for the seventh wicket.

AUSTRALIA		Runs	Balls	4/6
D.C.Boon	c Srikkanth b Binny	24	26	4
G.R.Marsh	lbw b Binny	5	14	1
D.M.Jones	run out	43	48	3/2
* A.R.Border	c Lamba b Maninder	5	17	–
G.M.Ritchie	lbw b Shastri	35	39	2/2
G.R.J.Matthews	st Pandit b Maninder	15	34	1
S.R.Waugh	not out	57	53	4/1
† G.C.Dyer	not out	45	43	4/1
D.R.Gilbert				
B.A.Reid				
S.P.Davis				
Extras	(b 3, lb 4, w 1, nb 1)	9		
Total	(45 overs; 6 wickets)	238		

INDIA		Runs	Balls	4/6
K.Srikkanth	c Ritchie b Reid	9	26	–
S.M.Gavaskar	c Border b Davis	6	10	1
R.Lamba	c sub (M.R.J.Veletta) b Waugh	74	68	8/1
D.B.Vengsarkar	c Matthews b Waugh	37	53	2/1
* Kapil Dev	c Dyer b Gilbert	36	37	2
† C.S.Pandit	b Reid	13	16	–
R.J.Shastri	not out	29	26	3/1
M.Azharuddin	c Ritchie b Reid	15	18	1
Madan Lal	not out	9	7	1
R.M.H.Binny				
Maninder Singh				
Extras	(b 4, lb 6, w 4)	14		
Total	(43.3 overs; 7 wickets)	242		

INDIA	O	M	R	W
Kapil Dev	10	1	35	0
Binny	8	0	75	2
Madan Lal	8	0	45	0
Maninder Singh	10	0	30	2
Shastri	9	2	46	1

AUSTRALIA	O	M	R	W
Davis	9.3	1	28	1
Reid	9	0	43	3
Gilbert	10	0	59	1
Waugh	10	0	48	2
Matthews	5	0	54	0

FALL OF WICKETS
1-8, 2-42, 3-73, 4-85, 5-118, 6-136

FALL OF WICKETS
1-7, 2-24, 3-126, 4-141, 5-168, 6-193, 7-232

Umpires: A.L.Narasimhan (3) and J.D.Roy (1).

INDIA v AUSTRALIA 1986-87

At Gujarat Stadium, Motera, Ahmedabad on 5 October 1986.   Result: **INDIA** won by 52 runs.   Toss: India.
Award: R.J.Shastri.   LOI debuts: None.

A severely overcrowded Gujarat Stadium became Ahmedabad's second LOI venue, with at least 60,000 exhorting India to clinch the series. They duly obliged through exceptional fielding despite Australia needing only 108 from the last 25 overs with eight wickets in hand.

INDIA		Runs	Balls	4/6
K.Srikkanth	c Dyer b Gilbert	26	51	4
S.M.Gavaskar	b Davis	12	21	2
R.Lamba	run out	17	43	–
M.Azharuddin	c and b Gilbert	10	15	1
* Kapil Dev	c Boon b Waugh	6	8	–
† C.S.Pandit	c Border b Matthews	8	18	–
R.J.Shastri	c Jones b Davis	53	54	6
Madan Lal	run out	30	54	3
R.M.H.Binny	c Boon b McDermott	1	5	–
G.Sharma	b Davis	7	20	–
Maninder Singh	not out	8	7	1
Extras	(lb 3, w 11, nb 1)	15		
Total	(47.4 overs)	193		

AUSTRALIA		Runs	Balls	4/6
G.R.Marsh	run out	43	96	2
D.C.Boon	c Madan Lal b Kapil Dev	5	12	–
D.M.Jones	c Lamba b Kapil Dev	2	7	–
* A.R.Border	run out	43	64	5
G.M.Ritchie	run out	22	39	2
G.R.J.Matthews	c Srikkanth b Sharma	0	4	–
S.R.Waugh	c Pandit b Shastri	9	23	–
† G.C.Dyer	run out	6	7	1
C.J.McDermott	st Pandit b Shastri	4	3	1
D.R.Gilbert	not out	3	9	–
S.P.Davis	b Madan Lal	1	6	–
Extras	(w 3)	3		
Total	(43.3 overs)	141		

AUSTRALIA	O	M	R	W
Davis	9.4	0	35	3
McDermott	8	1	24	1
Gilbert	10	0	52	2
Waugh	10	0	46	1
Matthews	10	1	33	1

INDIA	O	M	R	W
Kapil Dev	8	1	17	2
Binny	6	0	27	0
Shastri	9	2	23	2
Sharma	10	0	42	1
Maninder Singh	10	2	29	0
Madan Lal	0.3	0	3	1

FALL OF WICKETS
1-33, 2-59, 3-77, 4-81, 5-86, 6-98, 7-165, 8-166, 9-181, 10-193

FALL OF WICKETS
1-9, 2-17, 3-86, 4-104, 5-105, 6-126, 7-126, 8-130, 9-138, 10-141

Umpires: B.R.Keshavamurthy (1) and M.G.Mukherjee (1).

INDIA v AUSTRALIA 1986-87

At Racecourse Ground, Rajkot on 7 October 1986.   Result: **AUSTRALIA** won by 7 wickets.   Toss: Australia.
Award: A.R.Border.   LOI debuts: None.

Having celebrated Rajkot's admission to the international arena by smiting a fifty off 26 balls, including 24 off an over from Craig McDermott, Kapil Dev took no further part in the match. Raman Lamba scored his only hundred in 32 internationals.

INDIA		Runs	Balls	4/6	AUSTRALIA		Runs	Balls	4/6
K.Srikkanth	c McDermott b Matthews	23	36	2	G.R.Marsh	run out	39	44	5
R.Lamba	b Reid	102	120	8/2	D.C.Boon	st Pandit b Shastri	39	45	3
M.Azharuddin	run out	28	56	2	D.M.Jones	c Lamba b Singh	55	42	3/1
D.B.Vengsarkar	c Marsh b Waugh	25	29	1	* A.R.Border	not out	91	88	9
Kapil Dev	lbw b Waugh	58	31	5/2	G.M.Ritchie	not out	35	62	4
R.J.Shastri	run out	2	2	–	G.R.J.Matthews				
C.S.Pandit	not out	14	15	–	S.R.Waugh				
Madan Lal	not out	1	1	–	† G.C.Dyer				
R.S.Ghai					C.J.McDermott				
R.P.Singh					B.A.Reid				
Maninder Singh					S.P.Davis				
Extras	(b 1, lb 5, w 1)	7			Extras	(lb 4)	4		
Total	(48 overs; 6 wickets)	260			Total	(46.3 overs; 3 wickets)	263		

AUSTRALIA	O	M	R	W	INDIA	O	M	R	W
Davis	9	0	34	0	Madan Lal	8	0	50	0
McDermott	9	1	61	0	Singh	9.4	0	58	1
Waugh	10	1	50	2	Ghai	6.2	0	37	0
Matthews	8	0	51	1	Shastri	10	0	50	1
Reid	10	0	48	1	Maninder Singh	10	0	49	0
Border	2	0	10	0	Srikkanth	2	0	11	0
					Azharuddin	0.3	0	4	0

FALL OF WICKETS
1-59, 2-143, 3-179, 4-181, 5-200, 6-259

FALL OF WICKETS
1-68, 2-85, 3-176

Umpires: K.R.Karimaniokan (1) and R.Ravindram (1).

PAKISTAN v WEST INDIES 1986-87

At Shahi Bagh Stadium, Peshawar on 17 October 1986.   Result: **WEST INDIES** won by 4 wickets.   Toss: Pakistan.
Award: C.G.Greenidge.   LOI debuts: Pakistan – Salim Jaffer; West Indies – W.K.M.Benjamin.

Five-match 50-over series. Javed Miandad deputised as wicket-keeper when Anil Dalpat retired ill in the third over and held an outstanding catch to dismiss Viv Richards. Gordon Greenidge completed 3000 runs in his 72nd international.

PAKISTAN		Runs	Balls	4/6	WEST INDIES		Runs	Balls	4/6
Mudassar Nazar	lbw b Gray	15	32	2	C.G.Greenidge	c Tausif b Wasim	67	104	8
Mohsin Khan	lbw b Marshall	4	23	–	R.B.Richardson	b Imran	10	22	2
Ramiz Raja	b Gray	31	71	1	H.A.Gomes	b Tausif	18	51	2
Javed Miandad	c Dujon b Benjamin	2	12	–	A.L.Logie	run out	0	2	–
Salim Malik	c Dujon b Gray	30	64	2	* I.V.A.Richards	c Miandad b Salim Jaffer	7	23	–
Imran Khan	not out	23	36	–/1	† P.J.L.Dujon	st Miandad b Qadir	5	27	–
Abdul Qadir	b Patterson	34	45	4/2	R.A.Harper	not out	34	48	2
Wasim Akram	run out	5	10	–	M.D.Marshall	not out	0	1	–
Anil Dalpat	not out	3	4	–	W.K.M.Benjamin				
Tausif Ahmed					A.H.Gray				
Salim Jaffer					B.P.Patterson				
Extras	(b 2, lb 11, w 2, nb 2)	17			Extras	(b 8, lb 11, w 3, nb 2)	24		
Total	(49 overs; 7 wickets)	164			Total	(45.3 overs; 6 wickets)	165		

WEST INDIES	O	M	R	W	PAKISTAN	O	M	R	W
Patterson	10	0	38	1	Imran Khan	7.3	2	22	1
Gray	10	1	20	3	Wasim Akram	10	2	28	1
Marshall	9	1	21	1	Tausif Ahmed	10	2	29	1
Benjamin	10	2	29	1	Salim Jaffer	8	0	24	1
Harper	10	0	43	0	Abdul Qadir	10	0	43	1

FALL OF WICKETS
1-20, 2-24, 3-27, 4-84, 5-93, 6-141, 7-158

FALL OF WICKETS
1-24, 2-89, 3-96, 4-117, 5-118, 6-150

Umpires: Athar Zaidi (3) and Shakoor Rana (16).

PAKISTAN v WEST INDIES 1986-87

At Municipal Stadium, Gujranwala on 4 November 1986.　　Result: **WEST INDIES** won on faster scoring rate.
Toss: Pakistan.　　Award: M.D.Marshall.　　LOI debuts: Pakistan – Asif Mujtaba.

By bowling a mere 12 overs per hour, West Indies extended play into dusk and prompted the crowd to bombard the field with bottles and firecrackers. When play was abandoned, regulations decreed that maiden overs be discarded when calculating the run rate! The Jeff Dujon/Malcolm Marshall stand of 115 remains the LOI seventh-wicket world record.

WEST INDIES		Runs	Balls	4/6
C.G.Greenidge	c Salim Yousuf b Salim Jaffer	10	14	1/1
D.L.Haynes	c Salim Yousuf b Salim Jaffer	9	32	–
R.B.Richardson	lbw b Manzoor	23	56	3
A.L.Logie	b Salim Jaffer	0	2	–
* I.V.A.Richards	c Tausif b Qadir	17	27	–/1
† P.J.L.Dujon	not out	57	73	5/2
R.A.Harper	lbw b Qadir	1	20	–
M.D.Marshall	run out	66	78	10
W.K.M.Benjamin	not out	2	1	–
C.A.Walsh				
B.P.Patterson				
Extras	(b 1, lb 4, w 2, nb 4)	11		
Total	(50 overs; 7 wickets)	**196**		

PAKISTAN		Runs	Balls	4/6
Mohsin Khan	b Marshall	4	10	1
Shoaib Mohammed	run out	3	34	–
Ramiz Raja	c Richards b Benjamin	30	58	2/
Asif Mujtaba	c Richardson b Marshall	0	10	–
* Javed Miandad	not out	74	109	6
Manzoor Elahi	c Dujon b Benjamin	4	8	–
Abdul Qadir	c Dujon b Benjamin	0	1	–
† Salim Yousuf	not out	23	38	1
Wasim Akram				
Tausif Ahmed				
Salim Jaffer				
Extras	(b 1, lb 9, w 7)	17		
Total	(43.5 overs; 6 wickets)	**155**		

PAKISTAN	O	M	R	W
Wasim Akram	10	2	41	0
Salim Jaffer	10	0	49	3
Manzoor Elahi	10	2	25	1
Abdul Qadir	10	1	45	2
Tausif Ahmed	5	1	17	0
Asif Mujtaba	5	1	14	0

WEST INDIES	O	M	R	W
Marshall	8	2	18	
Patterson	7.5	2	33	
Benjamin	10	1	21	
Walsh	10	1	31	
Harper	8	0	42	

FALL OF WICKETS
1-19, 2-22, 3-22, 4-67, 5-67, 6-79, 7-194

FALL OF WICKETS
1-5, 2-22, 3-23, 4-65, 5-75, 6-75

Umpires: Khizer Hayat (12) and Tariq Ata (3).

PAKISTAN v WEST INDIES 1986-87

At Jinnah Park, Sialkot on 14 November 1986.　　Result: **WEST INDIES** won by 4 wickets.　　Toss: Pakistan.
Award: P.J.L.Dujon.　　LOI debuts: Pakistan – Ijaz Ahmed.

West Indies took a winning lead in the series after dew on the pitch had delayed the start. Police used tear gas to disperse an estimated 5000 trying to join a capacity attendance of 25,000. Five tree perchers sustained fractured limbs when a branch snapped.

PAKISTAN		Runs	Balls	4/6
Rizwan-uz-Zaman	c Greenidge b Walsh	4	62	–
Shoaib Mohammed	c Dujon b Walsh	7	36	1
Ramiz Raja	lbw b Benjamin	13	40	–
Javed Miandad	b Marshall	34	76	2
Abdul Qadir	b Harper	2	9	–
* Imran Khan	c and b Walsh	9	26	–
Ijaz Ahmed	b Marshall	19	23	2
Manzoor Elahi	not out	24	17	2/1
† Salim Yousuf	not out	3	4	–
Tausif Ahmed				
Salim Jaffer				
Extras	(b 1, lb 8, w 22, nb 2)	33		
Total	(45 overs; 7 wickets)	**148**		

WEST INDIES		Runs	Balls	4/
C.G.Greenidge	lbw b Salim Jaffer	1	5	–
D.L.Haynes	run out	38	89	4
R.B.Richardson	run out	36	86	4
A.L.Logie	not out	25	83	2
* I.V.A.Richards	b Shoaib	0	1	–
† P.J.L.Dujon	b Salim Jaffer	38	39	4/
R.A.Harper	c Manzoor b Imran	1	3	–
M.D.Marshall	not out	1	1	–
W.K.M.Benjamin				
A.H.Gray				
C.A.Walsh				
Extras	(lb 7, w 3, nb 1)	11		
Total	(44.3 overs; 6 wickets)	**151**		

WEST INDIES	O	M	R	W
Marshall	9	2	29	2
Gray	9	1	28	0
Walsh	9	1	38	3
Benjamin	9	1	19	1
Harper	9	0	25	1

PAKISTAN	O	M	R	W
Imran Khan	9	2	25	
Salim Jaffer	8	1	29	
Tausif Ahmed	8.3	1	20	0
Abdul Qadir	9	0	30	4/
Shoaib Mohammed	7	0	31	
Manzoor Elahi	3	0	9	0

FALL OF WICKETS
1-25, 2-29, 3-70, 4-77, 5-101, 6-104, 7-140

FALL OF WICKETS
1-1, 2-79, 3-86, 4-87, 5-145, 6-146

Umpires: Amanullah Khan (9) and Shakil Khan (8).

PAKISTAN v WEST INDIES 1986-87

At Ibn-e-Qasim Bagh Stadium, Multan on 17 November 1986.   Result: **WEST INDIES** won by 89 runs.
Toss: Pakistan.   Award: A.H.Gray.   LOI debuts: None.

To avoid playing in fading light the last two matches were reduced to 45 overs per innings. Javed Miandad celebrated his 100th LOI appearance by completing 3000 runs.

WEST INDIES		Runs	Balls	4/6
D.L.Haynes	b Tausif	21	55	2
R.B.Richardson	c Tausif b Salim Jaffer	26	53	4
A.L.Logie	lbw b Imran	46	63	5
I.V.A.Richards	b Tausif	4	8	–
H.A.Gomes	run out	38	48	4
P.J.L.Dujon	not out	10	18	–
R.A.Harper	not out	34	19	4/2
M.D.Marshall				
W.K.M.Benjamin				
A.H.Gray				
C.A.Walsh				
Extras	(b 16, lb 6, w 1)	23		
Total	(44 overs; 5 wickets)	**202**		

PAKISTAN	O	M	R	W
Imran Khan	9	1	46	1
Salim Jaffer	9	1	22	1
Tausif Ahmed	9	1	29	2
Abdul Qadir	9	1	32	0
Shoaib Mohammed	4	0	25	0
Wasim Akram	4	0	26	0

FALL OF WICKETS
1-50, 2-51, 3-61, 4-153, 5-153

PAKISTAN		Runs	Balls	4/6
Shoaib Mohammed	c Richards b Benjamin	11	35	–
Sajid Ali	lbw b Marshall	7	13	1
Ramiz Raja	c Dujon b Walsh	7	17	1
Javed Miandad	c Gomes b Gray	30	76	3
Ijaz Ahmed	c Dujon b Walsh	1	17	–
* Imran Khan	c Logie b Gray	24	44	1
Abdul Qadir	run out	1	1	–
† Salim Yousuf	st Dujon b Gomes	9	17	1
Wasim Akram	c Richards b Gray	4	3	1
Tausif Ahmed	c Dujon b Gray	1	6	–
Salim Jaffer	not out	2	7	–
Extras	(b 5, lb 5, w 5, nb 1)	16		
Total	(38.2 overs)	**113**		

WEST INDIES	O	M	R	W
Marshall	5	1	7	1
Gray	9	0	36	4
Walsh	5	4	7	2
Benjamin	9	3	27	1
Harper	9	1	22	0
Richards	1	0	3	0
Gomes	0.2	0	1	1

FALL OF WICKETS
1-15, 2-27, 3-27, 4-30, 5-94, 6-95, 7-96, 8-100, 9-108, 10-113

Umpires: Mahboob Shah (10) and Shakoor Rana (17).

PAKISTAN v WEST INDIES 1986-87

At Niaz Stadium, Hyderabad on 18 November 1986.   Result: **PAKISTAN** won by 11 runs.   Toss: West Indies.
Award: Imran Khan.   LOI debuts: None.

Abdul Qadir fractured a finger on his left hand attempting a return catch from Desmond Haynes but continued his spell and dismissed Viv Richards first ball.

PAKISTAN		Runs	Balls	4/6
Sajid Ali	c Harper b Richards	10	42	–
Shoaib Mohammed	c Richards b Patterson	3	32	–
Ramiz Raja	st Dujon b Harper	32	67	–
Javed Miandad	b Benjamin	30	47	3
Manzoor Elahi	c Patterson b Richardson	31	31	3/1
Ijaz Ahmed	run out	18	16	1
* Imran Khan	not out	27	21	–/2
† Salim Yousuf	not out	23	23	1
Abdul Qadir				
Tausif Ahmed				
Salim Jaffer				
Extras	(b 3, lb 15, w 7, nb 3)	28		
Total	(45 overs; 6 wickets)	**202**		

WEST INDIES	O	M	R	W
Patterson	9	3	46	1
Walsh	8	2	25	0
Richards	9	1	24	1
Benjamin	9	0	36	1
Harper	9	0	49	1
Richardson	1	0	4	1

FALL OF WICKETS
1-13, 2-24, 3-85, 4-85, 5-139, 6-150

WEST INDIES		Runs	Balls	4/6
C.G.Greenidge	c Qadir b Manzoor	13	26	2
D.L.Haynes	c Miandad b Shoaib	59	87	4/1
R.B.Richardson	c Shoaib b Imran	70	116	6/1
* I.V.A.Richards	lbw b Qadir	0	1	–
A.L.Logie	c Manzoor b Salim Jaffer	16	25	1
R.A.Harper	b Imran	0	1	–
† P.J.L.Dujon	not out	6	10	–
W.K.M.Benjamin	c Shoaib b Salim Jaffer	0	1	–
H.A.Gomes	not out	8	10	1
C.A.Walsh				
B.P.Patterson				
Extras	(lb 16, w 2, nb 1)	19		
Total	(45 overs; 7 wickets)	**191**		

PAKISTAN	O	M	R	W
Imran Khan	9	1	37	2
Salim Jaffer	9	1	37	2
Manzoor Elahi	7	1	38	1
Tausif Ahmed	9	1	30	0
Abdul Qadir	9	0	21	1
Shoaib Mohammed	2	0	12	1

FALL OF WICKETS
1-31, 2-122, 3-122, 4-172, 5-172, 6-175, 7-175

Umpires: Masroor Ali (1) and Shakil Khan (9).

INDIA v SRI LANKA 1986-87

At Sharjah CA Stadium, UAE on 27 November 1986.   Result: **INDIA** won by 7 wickets.   Toss: India.
Award: K.Srikkanth.   LOI debuts: Sri Lanka – G.F.Labrooy, H.P.Tillekeratne.

Immediately after contesting six internationals and three Tests, Pakistan and West Indies flew to the Gulf to compete with India and Sri Lanka in a 45-over six-match tournament worth £60,000 in prize money.

SRI LANKA		Runs	Balls	4/6	INDIA		Runs	Balls	4/6
R.S.Mahanama	b Sharma	26	65	–	K.Srikkanth	b Gurusinha	92	89	10/2
P.A.de Silva	c Azharuddin b Sharma	33	40	3/1	S.M.Gavaskar	c De Alwis b Labrooy	27	43	2
A.Ranatunga	b Madan Lal	39	44	1/2	R.Lamba	b Labrooy	0	3	–
* L.R.D.Mendis	b Binny	35	46	2	M.Azharuddin	not out	50	79	–
A.P.Gurusinha	b Binny	4	12	–	* Kapil Dev	not out	34	36	3
H.P.Tillekeratne	b Sharma	18	30	–	R.J.Shastri				
† R.G.de Alwis	b Kapil Dev	17	13	1/1	† C.S.Pandit				
A.L.F.de Mel	c Maninder b Kapil Dev	11	9	1	R.M.H.Binny				
R.J.Ratnayake	not out	8	8	–	C.Sharma				
G.F.Labrooy	run out	3	4	–	Madan Lal				
S.D.Anurasiri	not out	0	–	–	Maninder Singh				
Extras	(lb 19, nb 1)	20			Extras	(b 1, lb 3, w 8)	12		
Total	(45 overs; 9 wickets)	**214**			**Total**	(41.3 overs; 3 wickets)	**215**		

INDIA	O	M	R	W	SRI LANKA	O	M	R	W
Kapil Dev	9	2	28	2	De Mel	9	0	32	0
Binny	9	0	42	2	Ratnayake	7	1	44	0
Sharma	8	0	40	3	Labrooy	8	1	32	2
Maninder Singh	2	0	8	0	Anurasiri	5	0	30	0
Madan Lal	9	0	37	1	Ranatunga	4	0	28	0
Shastri	8	0	40	0	Gurusinha	8.3	1	45	1

FALL OF WICKETS
1-61, 2-84, 3-125, 4-138, 5-159, 6-185, 7-199, 8-204, 9-213

FALL OF WICKETS
1-42, 2-42, 3-153

Umpires: H.D.Bird (*England*) (37) and D.R.Shepherd (*England*) (14).

WEST INDIES v PAKISTAN 1986-87

At Sharjah CA Stadium, UAE on 28 November 1986.   Result: **WEST INDIES** won by 9 wickets.   Toss: Pakistan.
Award: A.L.Logie.   LOI debuts: None.

An epic umpiring oversight allowed Courtney Walsh an illegal tenth over during which he terminated the Pakistan innings. Gus Logie deservedly won the match award for an exceptional display of fielding, holding three catches and effecting two run-outs.

PAKISTAN		Runs	Balls	4/6	WEST INDIES		Runs	Balls	4/6
Mudassar Nazar	c Logie b Benjamin	14	57	–	C.G.Greenidge	c Salim Yousuf b Manzoor	74	102	7/1
† Salim Yousuf	c Logie b Gray	1	5	–	D.L.Haynes	not out	59	88	5/1
Ramiz Raja	c and b Walsh	44	93	–	R.B.Richardson	not out	5	9	1
Javed Miandad	run out	32	34	3	* I.V.A.Richards				
Manzoor Elahi	b Gray	14	15	1/1	A.L.Logie				
Ijaz Ahmed	c Logie b Harper	4	10	–	† P.J.L.Dujon				
* Imran Khan	b Walsh	15	21	1	R.A.Harper				
Asif Mujtaba	run out	0	3	–	M.D.Marshall				
Wasim Akram	c Benjamin b Walsh	2	9	–	W.K.M.Benjamin				
Tausif Ahmed	not out	4	9	–	A.H.Gray				
Salim Jaffer	b Walsh	0	7	–	C.A.Walsh				
Extras	(lb 7, w 6)	13			Extras	(lb 3, w 4)	7		
Total	(43.4 overs)	**143**			**Total**	(33.2 overs; 1 wicket)	**145**		

WEST INDIES	O	M	R	W	PAKISTAN	O	M	R	W
Marshall	8	1	16	0	Imran Khan	6	0	33	0
Gray	8	2	18	2	Wasim Akram	9	0	26	0
Benjamin	9	1	37	1	Salim Jaffer	5	1	18	0
Walsh	9.4	1	31	4	Tausif Ahmed	6	0	35	0
Harper	9	1	34	1	Mudassar Nazar	4	0	10	0
					Manzoor Elahi	3.2	0	20	1

FALL OF WICKETS
1-5, 2-31, 3-87, 4-106, 5-119, 6-121, 7-123, 8-130, 9-141, 10-143

FALL OF WICKETS
1-126

Umpires: H.D.Bird (*England*) (38) and D.R.Shepherd (*England*) (15).

WEST INDIES v INDIA 1986-87

At Sharjah CA Stadium, UAE on 30 November 1986. Result: **WEST INDIES** won by 33 runs. Toss: India.
Award: I.V.A.Richards. LOI debuts: None.

Malcolm Marshall bowled the decisive ball of this contest; having been savaged for 10 runs off two balls, he removed the dangerous Krish Srikkanth with a fast breakback.

WEST INDIES		Runs	Balls	4/6
C.G.Greenidge	lbw b Kapil Dev	0	5	–
D.L.Haynes	c Srikkanth b Madan Lal	12	48	–
R.B.Richardson	run out	18	28	–
I.V.A.Richards	c Binny b Maninder	62	58	5/3
A.L.Logie	not out	58	93	1
P.J.L.Dujon	c Pandit b Azharuddin	9	9	1
R.A.Harper	lbw b Azharuddin	1	8	–
M.D.Marshall	run out	10	9	1
W.K.M.Benjamin	run out	5	4	1
A.H.Gray	not out	10	9	1
C.A.Walsh				
Extras	(b 1, lb 9, w 2, nb 1)	13		
Total	(45 overs; 8 wickets)	198		

INDIA		Runs	Balls	4/6
K.Srikkanth	b Marshall	12	8	1/1
S.M.Gavaskar	b Gray	63	107	2
R.Lamba	c Dujon b Gray	0	13	–
D.B.Vengsarkar	c Dujon b Benjamin	2	18	–
M.Azharuddin	b Gray	38	67	1
* Kapil Dev	not out	23	29	2
R.J.Shastri	b Benjamin	0	1	–
† C.S.Pandit	c Greenidge b Walsh	3	4	–
Madan Lal	b Marshall	8	16	–
R.M.H.Binny	not out	1	7	–
Maninder Singh				
Extras	(b 4, lb 9, w 2)	15		
Total	(45 overs; 8 wickets)	165		

INDIA	O	M	R	W
Kapil Dev	9	2	33	1
Binny	9	0	41	0
Madan Lal	6	2	11	1
Shastri	4	0	32	0
Maninder Singh	8	0	30	1
Azharuddin	9	1	41	2

WEST INDIES	O	M	R	W
Marshall	9	2	25	2
Gray	9	0	32	3
Benjamin	9	0	33	2
Harper	9	0	31	0
Walsh	9	0	31	1

FALL OF WICKETS
1-17, 2-22, 3-31, 4-123, 5-130, 6-131, 7-136, 8-161

FALL OF WICKETS
1-0, 2-33, 3-43, 4-124, 5-141, 6-143, 7-166, 8-174

Umpires: H.D.Bird (*England*) (39) and D.R.Shepherd (*England*) (16).

PAKISTAN v SRI LANKA 1986-87

At Sharjah CA Stadium, UAE on 2 December 1986. Result: **PAKISTAN** won by 4 wickets. Toss: Pakistan.
Award: A.P.Gurusinha. LOI debuts: None.

Ijaz Ahmed eased Pakistan home in a low-scoring match by taking 10 runs off Graeme Labrooy's last over.

SRI LANKA		Runs	Balls	4/6
R.S.Mahanama	lbw b Wasim	0	9	–
P.A.de Silva	c Miandad b Manzoor	3	24	–
A.P.Gurusinha	run out	60	97	3
A.Ranatunga	c Salim Yousuf b Salim Jaffer	14	29	1
L.R.D.Mendis	b Mudassar	12	18	1
H.P.Tillekeratne	run out	19	49	1
R.G.de Alwis	lbw b Imran	0	11	–
A.L.F.de Mel	not out	21	16	3
J.R.Ratnayeke	not out	17	17	2
R.J.Ratnayake				
G.F.Labrooy				
Ext. as	(b 2, lb 8, w 8)	18		
Total	(45 overs; 7 wickets)	164		

PAKISTAN		Runs	Balls	4/6
Mohsin Khan	b Labrooy	7	27	–
Shoaib Mohammed	c and b Gurusinha	19	63	1
Ramiz Raja	c Labrooy b De Mel	39	70	2
Javed Miandad	c De Alwis b Ranatunga	32	46	2
* Imran Khan	c Mendis b Ratnayake	22	32	1
Manzoor Elahi	run out	7	11	–
Mudassar Nazar	not out	6	7	–
Ijaz Ahmed	not out	13	12	1
Wasim Akram				
† Salim Yousuf				
Salim Jaffer				
Extras	(b 2, lb 12, w 4, nb 2)	20		
Total	(44 overs; 6 wickets)	165		

PAKISTAN	O	M	R	W
Imran Khan	9	0	34	1
Wasim Akram	9	0	25	1
Manzoor Elahi	7	0	21	1
Salim Jaffer	9	0	40	1
Mudassar Nazar	6	0	16	1
Shoaib Mohammed	5	1	18	0

SRI LANKA	O	M	R	W
De Mel	9	1	29	1
Ratnayake	9	0	27	1
Labrooy	8	1	29	1
Gurusinha	9	0	27	1
Ratnayeke	6	0	25	0
Ranatunga	3	0	14	1

FALL OF WICKETS
1-2, 2-15, 3-50, 4-71, 5-119, 6-125, 7-128

FALL OF WICKETS
1-21, 2-49, 3-95, 4-124, 5-137, 6-142

Umpires: H.D.Bird (*England*) (40) and D.R.Shepherd (*England*) (17).

WEST INDIES v SRI LANKA 1986-87

At Sharjah CA Stadium, UAE. on 3 December 1986.   Result: **WEST INDIES** won by 193 runs.   Toss: Sri Lanka.
Award: C.A.Walsh.   LOI debuts: None.

West Indies won the Champions Trophy and £22,000 when Courtney Walsh took five wickets in 19 balls for just one run. Sri Lanka's total was the lowest by any Test-playing country until 1992-93 (*LOI No. 812*) and remains the least for them and the record for Sharjah.

WEST INDIES		Runs	Balls	4/6	SRI LANKA		Runs	Balls	4/
C.G.Greenidge	lbw b De Mel	67	83	7	R.S.Mahanama	c Dujon b Marshall	13	26	
R.B.Richardson	c Tillekeratne b Ratnayeke	109	120	8/1	D.S.B.P.Kuruppu	run out	9	14	1
* I.V.A.Richards	b Ratnayeke	39	42	3/1	A.P.Gurusinha	b Harper	15	35	1
R.A.Harper	lbw b Ratnayeke	15	14	–/1	A.Ranatunga	c Walsh b Harper	8	31	–
A.L.Logie	not out	9	9	–	P.A.de Silva	run out	3	3	–
W.K.M.Benjamin	b Ratnayeke	0	1	–	* L.R.D.Mendis	c Dujon b Walsh	2	15	–
M.D.Marshall	not out	3	2	–	† H.P.Tillekeratne	not out	2	29	–
H.A.Gomes					A.L.F.de Mel	b Walsh	0	2	–
† P.J.L.Dujon					J.R.Ratnayeke	b Walsh	0	4	–
A.H.Gray					R.J.Ratnayeke	b Walsh	0	4	–
C.A.Walsh					G.F.Labrooy	b Walsh	1	8	–
Extras	(b 1, lb 5)	6			Extras	(lb 2)	2		
Total	(45 overs; 5 wickets)	248			Total	(28.3 overs)	55		

SRI LANKA	O	M	R	W	WEST INDIES	O	M	R	W
De Mel	9	1	48	1	Marshall	5	1	16	
Ratnayake	9	2	30	1	Gray	5	0	15	
Labrooy	7	0	36	0	Benjamin	5	0	13	
Ratnayeke	9	0	59	3	Harper	9	4	8	2
Gurusinha	9	0	51	0	Walsh	4.3	3	1	5
Ranatunga	2	0	18	0					

FALL OF WICKETS (West Indies)
1-132, 2-220, 3-221, 4-242, 5-245

FALL OF WICKETS (Sri Lanka)
1-22, 2-22, 3-45, 4-45, 5-50, 6-51, 7-51, 8-51, 9-51, 10-55

Umpires: H.D.Bird (*England*) (41) and D.R.Shepherd (*England*) (18).

INDIA v PAKISTAN 1986-87

At Sharjah CA Stadium, UAE on 5 December 1986.   Result: **PAKISTAN** won by 3 wickets.   Toss: Pakistan.
Award: Manzoor Elahi.   LOI debuts: None.

Manzoor Elahi played a match-winning innings after six wickets had fallen for 14 runs. Maninder Singh's left-arm spin claimed its only four-wicket return in 59 matches, including Javed Miandad first ball.

INDIA		Runs	Balls	4/6	PAKISTAN		Runs	Balls	4/
K.Srikkanth	c Salim Yousuf b Imran	3	5	–	Ramiz Raja	c and b Shastri	21	71	2
S.M.Gavaskar	b Imran	0	3	–	Shoaib Mohammed	c Gavaskar b Maninder	28	66	2
R.Lamba	c Shoaib b Imran	6	43	–	Asif Mujtaba	c Gavaskar b Shastri	11	12	2
D.B.Vengsarkar	b Salim Jaffer	6	27	–	Javed Miandad	c and b Maninder	0	1	–
M.Azharuddin	c Miandad b Manzoor	49	86	4	* Imran Khan	c Vengsarkar b Maninder	0	2	–
R.J.Shastri	b Mudassar	1	12	–	Mudassar Nazar	c Srikkanth b Maninder	1	6	–
* Kapil Dev	b Shoaib	36	30	4	Ijaz Ahmed	c Maninder b Madan Lal	10	25	–
† C.S.Pandit	b Wasim	18	23	–	Manzoor Elahi	not out	50	54	3/1
Madan Lal	run out	5	8	–	† Salim Yousuf	not out	15	26	1
R.M.H.Binny	b Wasim	0	1	–	Wasim Akram				
Maninder Singh	not out	1	5	–	Salim Jaffer				
Extras	(b 1, lb 8, w 9, nb 1)	19			Extras	(lb 4, w 2, nb 3)	9		
Total	(40.2 overs)	144			Total	(43.3 overs; 7 wickets)	145		

PAKISTAN	O	M	R	W	INDIA	O	M	R	W
Imran Khan	8	0	27	3	Kapil Dev	8	2	31	0
Wasim Akram	7.2	4	4	2	Binny	8.3	0	32	0
Salim Jaffer	7	0	22	1	Maninder Singh	9	2	22	4
Mudassar Nazar	9	2	34	1	Madan Lal	9	0	25	1
Manzoor Elahi	5	0	32	1	Shastri	9	1	31	2
Shoaib Mohammed	4	0	16	1					

FALL OF WICKETS (India)
1-2, 2-8, 3-16, 4-39, 5-42, 6-110, 7-128, 8-136, 9-136, 10-144

FALL OF WICKETS (Pakistan)
1-51, 2-53, 3-53, 4-53, 5-65, 6-65, 7-108

Umpires: H.D.Bird (*England*) (42) and D.R.Shepherd (*England*) (19).

INDIA v SRI LANKA 1986-87

At Green Park, Kanpur on 24 December 1986. Result: **SRI LANKA** won by 117 runs. Toss: India.
Award: A.Ranatunga. LOI debuts: India – B.Arun; Sri Lanka – E.A.R.de Silva.

Kanpur's first limited-overs international attracted 55,000 fans but the eight-day-old Test pitch produced the lowest total in India and the lowest by any opponent against Sri Lanka. Arjuna Ranatunga returned his only four-wicket analysis.

SRI LANKA		Runs	Balls	4/6
R.S.Mahanama	c Vengsarkar b Kapil Dev	13	35	–
J.R.Ratnayeke	lbw b Kapil Dev	7	9	1
A.P.Gurusinha	c Madan Lal b Maninder	35	58	4
P.A.de Silva	c Maninder b Sharma	3	18	–
A.Ranatunga	lbw b Arun	31	49	2
R.L.Dias	c and b Maninder	11	27	–
L.R.D.Mendis	b Sharma	26	45	2
R.G.de Alwis	b Maninder	15	20	1/1
A.L.F.de Mel	not out	23	13	2/1
R.J.Ratnayake	not out	19	10	3/1
E.A.R.de Silva				
Extras	(lb 7, w 2, nb 3)	12		
Total	(46 overs; 8 wickets)	**195**		

INDIA		Runs	Balls	4/6
S.M.Gavaskar	c De Alwis b Ratnayake	2	8	–
K.Srikkanth	c De Alwis b Ranatunga	17	42	1
R.Lamba	lbw b Ratnayake	5	11	–
D.B.Vengsarkar	run out	15	20	1
R.J.Shastri	b Ranatunga	8	22	2
* Kapil Dev	c and b Ratnayeke	9	13	–/1
† C.S.Pandit	c and b Ranatunga	0	3	–
B.Arun	c E.A.R.de Silva b Ratnayeke	8	12	1
Madan Lal	c Mahanama b Ratnayeke	1	9	–
C.Sharma	c Gurusinha b Ranatunga	8	9	1
Maninder Singh	not out	0	~	–
Extras	(lb 1, w 3, nb 1)	5		
Total	(24.1 overs)	**78**		

INDIA	O	M	R	W
Kapil Dev	7	3	10	2
Arun	8	0	43	1
Sharma	8	0	50	2
Madan Lal	8	1	36	0
Maninder Singh	10	2	24	3
Shastri	5	0	25	0

SRI LANKA	O	M	R	W
De Mel	7	1	22	0
Ratnayake	6	1	16	2
Ratnayeke	3.1	0	12	3
E.A.R.de Silva	2	0	13	0
Ranatunga	6	1	14	4

FALL OF WICKETS
1-15, 2-33, 3-43, 4-95, 5-101, 6-117, 7-150, 8-155

FALL OF WICKETS
1-6, 2-18, 3-37, 4-47, 5-56, 6-59, 7-59, 8-65, 9-78, 10-78

Umpires: D.N.Dotiwala (3) and S.R.Phookan (1).

INDIA v SRI LANKA 1986-87

At Nehru Stadium, Gauhati on 11 January 1987. Result: **INDIA** won by 8 wickets. Toss: India.
Award: S.M.Gavaskar. LOI debuts: None.

Aided by an over-watered pitch and a masterly innings from Sunil Gavaskar, India drew level in the series of five matches intended to feature 50-over innings.

SRI LANKA		Runs	Balls	4/6
J.R.Ratnayeke	c Shastri b Yadav	11	43	–
P.A.de Silva	c Azharuddin b Madan Lal	3	13	–
A.P.Gurusinha	b Yadav	6	39	1
R.L.Dias	lbw b Shastri	26	69	2
A.Ranatunga	c Srikkanth b Maninder	0	7	–
* L.R.D.Mendis	lbw b Kapil Dev	31	48	2
R.S.Madugalle	not out	22	31	1
R.J.Ratnayake	run out	17	21	2
A.L.F.de Mel	c Azharuddin b Shastri	7	7	1
† R.G.de Alwis	not out	6	5	–
E.A.R.de Silva				
Extras	(b 4, lb 8, w 3, nb 1)	16		
Total	(46 overs; 8 wickets)	**145**		

INDIA		Runs	Balls	4/6
K.Srikkanth	lbw b Ratnayake	19	20	2
S.M.Gavaskar	not out	70	83	6/1
R.Lamba	lbw b Ratnayeke	2	2	–
D.B.Vengsarkar	not out	43	62	4
M.Azharuddin				
R.J.Shastri				
* Kapil Dev				
† C.S.Pandit				
Madan Lal				
N.S.Yadav				
Maninder Singh				
Extras	(lb 1, w 9, nb 2)	12		
Total	(27.3 overs; 2 wickets)	**146**		

INDIA	O	M	R	W
Kapil Dev	9	1	32	1
Madan Lal	9	1	25	1
Yadav	9	2	18	2
Maninder Singh	10	1	30	1
Shastri	9	0	28	2

SRI LANKA	O	M	R	W
De Mel	7	0	43	0
Ratnayake	6	0	26	1
Ratnayeke	6.3	0	38	1
Ranatunga	5	0	24	0
E.A.R.de Silva	3	1	14	0

FALL OF WICKETS
1-7, 2-27, 3-33, 4-33, 5-91, 6-93, 7-120, 8-135

FALL OF WICKETS
1-44, 2-50

Umpires: R.B.Gupta (2) and P.G.Pandit (5).

INDIA v SRI LANKA 1986-87

At Feroz Shah Kotla, Delhi on 13 January 1987.　Result: **INDIA** won by 6 wickets.　Toss: India.
Award: A.Ranatunga.　LOI debuts: None.

India counteracted some spirited batting by Asanka Gurusinha and Arjuna Ranatunga by deliberately bowling only 44 overs in the allotted time.

SRI LANKA		Runs	Balls	4/6
J.R.Ratnayeke	c Pandit b Kulkarni	22	56	
P.A.de Silva	b Kulkarni	51	108	
A.P.Gurusinha	c Madan Lal b Azharuddin	54	64	3/2
A.Ranatunga	c Pandit b Kapil Dev	41	30	2/3
R.J.Ratnayake	c Maninder b Kulkarni	2	3	–
A.L.F.de Mel	b Kapil Dev	5	8	
* L.R.D.Mendis	not out	9	6	
R.L.Dias	not out	1	1	–
R.S.Madugalle				
† R.G.de Alwis				
G.F.Labrooy				
Extras	(b 2, lb 11, w 9, nb 1)	23		
Total	(44 overs; 6 wickets)	**208**		

INDIA		Runs	Balls	4/6
K.Srikkanth	c Ranatunga b Ratnayake	28	41	
S.M.Gavaskar	c sub (R.S.Mahanama) b Ranatunga	36	67	
M.Azharuddin	c Ranatunga b Labrooy	6	8	
D.B.Vengsarkar	b Ranatunga	56	68	6
R.Lamba	not out	57	56	
* Kapil Dev	not out	16	16	
R.J.Shastri				
† C.S.Pandit				
Madan Lal				
R.R.Kulkarni				
Maninder Singh				
Extras	(b 1, lb 1, w 8)	10		
Total	(41.3 overs; 4 wickets)	**209**		

INDIA	O	M	R	W
Kapil Dev	8	0	48	2
Madan Lal	7	1	21	0
Kulkarni	10	0	42	3
Maninder Singh	10	2	30	0
Shastri	7	0	40	0
Azharuddin	2	0	14	1

SRI LANKA	O	M	R	W
Ratnayake	8.3	0	48	1
Labrooy	10	0	48	1
De Mel	7	0	36	0
Ranatunga	10	0	42	2
Ratnayeke	6	0	33	0

FALL OF WICKETS
1-54, 2-132, 3-158, 4-162, 5-179, 6-201

FALL OF WICKETS
1-50, 2-60, 3-97, 4-163

Umpires: S.K.Ghosh (1) and R.R.Kadam (2).

INDIA v SRI LANKA 1986-87

At Moti Bagh Stadium, Baroda on 15 January 1987.　Result: **INDIA** won by 94 runs.　Toss: Sri Lanka.
Award: S.M.Gavaskar.　LOI debuts: None.

A runaway start by their opening pair put India firmly in control from the start and Sri Lanka's batsmen were unable to cope with a spin-friendly surface.

INDIA		Runs	Balls	4/6
K.Srikkanth	c Mahanama b Anurasiri	63	63	
S.M.Gavaskar	c Mendis b Labrooy	69	94	
R.Lamba	st De Alwis b Anurasiri	22	28	
* Kapil Dev	b Ratnayake	5	8	
D.B.Vengsarkar	c sub (A.L.F.de Mel) b Labrooy	22	23	
R.J.Shastri	c Mendis b Labrooy	20	14	
† C.S.Pandit	c sub (B.R.Jurangpathy) b Labrooy	12	14	
M.Azharuddin	lbw b Labrooy	5	8	
R.R.Kulkarni	not out	3	5	
Maninder Singh	not out	1	3	
N.S.Yadav				
Extras	(b 2, lb 7, w 2, nb 2)	13		
Total	(43 overs; 8 wickets)	**235**		

SRI LANKA		Runs	Balls	4/6
R.S.Mahanama	b Kulkarni	25	38	
J.R.Ratnayeke	st Pandit b Yadav	14	27	
A.P.Gurusinha	st Pandit b Yadav	26	62	
R.L.Dias	run out	0	2	
A.Ranatunga	b Maninder	20	24	
* L.R.D.Mendis	c Azharuddin b Shastri	21	19	
R.J.Ratnayake	c Lamba b Shastri	2	6	
† R.G.de Alwis	c Srikkanth b Shastri	10	24	
G.F.Labrooy	lbw b Srikkanth	12	6	
S.D.Anurasiri	not out	0	11	
R.S.Madugalle	absent hurt	–		
Extras	(lb 7, w 2, nb 2)	11		
Total	(36.3 overs)	**141**		

SRI LANKA	O	M	R	W
Ratnayake	10	0	34	0
Labrooy	10	0	57	5
Ratnayeke	8	0	52	1
Anurasiri	10	0	45	2
Ranatunga	4	0	30	0
Gurusinha	1	0	8	0

INDIA	O	M	R	W
Kulkarni	8	1	31	1
Kapil Dev	6	1	15	0
Yadav	7	0	20	2
Maninder Singh	10	1	38	1
Shastri	5	1	24	3
Srikkanth	0.3	0	6	1

FALL OF WICKETS
1-96, 2-161, 3-167, 4-169, 5-199, 6-224, 7-228, 8-232

FALL OF WICKETS
1-45, 2-49, 3-49, 4-94, 5-96, 6-101, 7-126, 8-128, 9-141

Umpires: P.G.Pandit (6) and S.R.Ramchandra Rao (2).

INDIA v SRI LANKA 1986-87

At Wankhede Stadium, Bombay on 17 January 1987. Result: **INDIA** won by 10 runs. Toss: Sri Lanka.
Award: R.S.Mahanama. LOI debuts: None.

The Wankhede Stadium's first limited-overs international produced 588 runs at the blistering rate of 7.35 per over. India withstood a brilliant assault by Asanka Gurusinha, only narrowly defending their highest total until 1995-96 (*LOI No. 1094*) to win the series 4-1.

INDIA		Runs	Balls	4/6
K.Srikkanth	c Mahanama b Ranatunga	46		8
S.M.Gavaskar	c De Mel b Ranatunga	25		3
M.Azharuddin	not out	108		8
D.B.Vengsarkar	c De Mel b Ratnayeke	52		3/1
R.Lamba	c sub (B.R.Jurangpathy) b Labrooy	39		4/1
Kapil Dev	not out	4		1
C.S.Pandit				
Madan Lal				
N.S.Yadav				
R.R.Kulkarni				
Maninder Singh				
Extras	(b 5, lb 9, w 8, nb 3)	25		
Total	(40 overs; 4 wickets)	**299**		

SRI LANKA		Runs	Balls	4/6
S.Wettimuny	b Kulkarni	14		1
R.S.Mahanama	run out	98	91	7
A.Ranatunga	c Yadav b Madan Lal	29		2
* L.R.D.Mendis	run out	30		3
R.L.Dias	st Pandit b Yadav	15		2
† A.P.Gurusinha	c Kapil Dev b Kulkarni	52	34	5/2
R.J.Ratnayake	not out	28		2/1
A.L.F.de Mel	b Kapil Dev	7		–
J.R.Ratnayeke	not out	5		–
S.D.Anurasiri				
G.F.Labrooy				
Extras	(lb 7, w 4)	11		
Total	(40 overs; 7 wickets)	**289**		

SRI LANKA	O	M	R	W
Ratnayake	10	1	63	0
Ratnayeke	6	0	50	1
De Mel	4	0	45	0
Ranatunga	10	0	59	2
Labrooy	10	0	68	1

INDIA	O	M	R	W
Kapil Dev	9	0	68	1
Kulkarni	9	0	57	2
Madan Lal	7	0	51	1
Maninder Singh	10	0	69	0
Yadav	5	0	37	1

FALL OF WICKETS
1-67, 2-88, 3-203, 4-287

FALL OF WICKETS
1-36, 2-84, 3-147, 4-174, 5-244, 6-256, 7-266

Umpires: D.N.Dotiwala (4) and R.R.Kadam (3).

WEST INDIES v PAKISTAN 1986-87

At WACA Ground, Perth on 30 December 1986. Result: **PAKISTAN** won by 34 runs. Toss: West Indies.
Award: Mudassar Nazar. LOI debuts: None.

This four-nation 50-over tournament was staged as part of a sports festival coinciding with Australia's defence of yachting's America's Cup outside Fremantle. The WACA's first floodlit match attracted only 11,900.

PAKISTAN		Runs	Balls	4/6
Qasim Omar	run out	30	49	3/1
Shoaib Mohammed	c Richards b Benjamin	34	83	1
Ramiz Raja	c Richardson b Gray	42	70	1
Javed Miandad	c Richards b Walsh	53	69	5
* Imran Khan	c Benjamin b Gray	16	17	–
Manzoor Elahi	c Richardson b Gray	4	5	–
Ijaz Ahmed	c sub (H.A.Gomes) b Gray	2	5	–
Wasim Akram	c Harper b Walsh	9	8	1
† Salim Yousuf	not out	2	2	–
Mudassar Nazar				
Salim Jaffer				
Extras	(lb 3, w 3, nb 1)	7		
Total	(50 overs; 8 wickets)	**199**		

WEST INDIES		Runs	Balls	4/6
C.G.Greenidge	b Wasim	22	42	2/1
D.L.Haynes	c Salim Yousuf b Mudassar	25	61	2
R.B.Richardson	run out	38	48	3/1
* I.V.A.Richards	lbw b Mudassar	10	28	–
A.L.Logie	c Salim Yousuf b Mudassar	7	16	–
† P.J.L.Dujon	c Shoaib b Salim Jaffer	13	28	–
R.A.Harper	not out	20	31	1/1
W.K.M.Benjamin	c Salim Jaffer b Shoaib	3	8	–
M.A.Holding	b Shoaib	5	9	–
A.H.Gray	c Imran b Salim Jaffer	3	4	–
C.A.Walsh	b Wasim	2	6	–
Extras	(lb 16, nb 1)	17		
Total	(46.2 overs)	**165**		

WEST INDIES	O	M	R	W
Gray	10	1	45	4
Walsh	10	0	48	2
Holding	10	0	30	0
Benjamin	10	2	35	1
Harper	10	0	38	0

PAKISTAN	O	M	R	W
Imran Khan	7	2	18	0
Salim Jaffer	10	2	29	2
Wasim Akram	7.2	2	13	2
Manzoor Elahi	2	0	10	0
Mudassar Nazar	10	0	36	3
Shoaib Mohammed	10	0	43	2

FALL OF WICKETS
1-51, 2-72, 3-163, 4-166, 5-177, 6-188, 7-188, 8-199

FALL OF WICKETS
1-40, 2-71, 3-105, 4-106, 5-123, 6-128, 7-139, 8-150, 9-155, 10-165

Umpires: P.J.McConnell (28) and S.G.Randell (18).

AUSTRALIA v ENGLAND 1986-87

At WACA Ground, Perth on 1 January 1987.   Result: **ENGLAND** won by 37 runs.   Toss: England.
Award: I.T.Botham.   LOI debuts: Australia – M.R.Whitney; England – B.C.Broad, P.A.J.DeFreitas, G.C.Small.

Australia's first appearance under the new Perth lights attracted a record WACA crowd of 27,125. Ian Botham completed England's fastest individual fifty against Australia off 32 balls during an over from Simon Davis in which he scored 26 (442466).

ENGLAND		Runs	Balls	4/6
B.C.Broad	run out	76	113	7
C.W.J.Athey	c Zoehrer b O'Donnell	34	60	3/1
D.I.Gower	c Zoehrer b Whitney	6	6	1
A.J.Lamb	c Zoehrer b Reid	66	72	5
I.T.Botham	c Zoehrer b Waugh	68	39	7/3
* M.W.Gatting	not out	5	6	–
† C.J.Richards	c Border b Reid	4	5	–
P.A.J.DeFreitas	not out	0	–	–
J.E.Emburey				
G.C.Small				
G.R.Dilley				
Extras	(b 2, lb 6, w 4, nb 1)	13		
Total	(49 overs; 6 wickets)	**272**		

AUSTRALIA		Runs	Balls	4/6
G.R.Marsh	b Botham	28	42	3
D.C.Boon	c Emburey b DeFreitas	1	9	–
D.M.Jones	c Gower b Dilley	104	125	9/2
* A.R.Border	b Emburey	26	38	2
S.R.Waugh	c Richards b Small	16	24	1
S.P.O'Donnell	run out	0	10	–
K.H.MacLeay	c Emburey b Dilley	21	31	1
† T.J.Zoehrer	c Botham b DeFreitas	1	2	–
M.R.Whitney	run out	6	10	–
B.A.Reid	b DeFreitas	10	13	1
S.P.Davis	not out	1	3	–
Extras	(lb 7, w 10, nb 4)	21		
Total	(48.2 overs)	**235**		

AUSTRALIA	O	M	R	W
Davis	8	1	48	0
Whitney	10	0	56	1
MacLeay	9	0	51	0
Reid	10	1	46	2
O'Donnell	7	0	39	1
Waugh	5	0	24	1

ENGLAND	O	M	R	W
DeFreitas	9.2	0	42	3
Dilley	10	1	31	2
Botham	10	0	52	1
Small	9	0	62	1
Emburey	10	0	41	1

FALL OF WICKETS
1-86, 2-95, 3-150, 4-256, 5-262, 6-271

FALL OF WICKETS
1-7, 2-50, 3-125, 4-149, 5-158, 6-210, 7-214, 8-217, 9-233, 10-235

Umpires: R.A.French (46) and P.J.McConnell (29).

AUSTRALIA v PAKISTAN 1986-87

At WACA Ground, Perth on 2 January 1987.   Result: **PAKISTAN** won by 1 wicket.   Toss: Australia.
Award: D.M.Jones.   LOI debuts: Australia – G.A.Bishop.

Dean Jones scored his second hundred on successive days, sharing a partnership of 173 with Steve Waugh which remains the world record for the fourth wicket in limited-overs internationals.

AUSTRALIA		Runs	Balls	4/6
G.R.Marsh	run out	28	46	4
G.A.Bishop	c Salim Jaffer b Imran	6	20	–
D.M.Jones	b Wasim	121	113	9/2
* A.R.Border	b Mudassar	14	17	2
S.R.Waugh	b Imran	82	102	5/1
G.R.J.Matthews	b Wasim	3	5	–
S.P.O'Donnell	not out	9	6	–/1
K.H.MacLeay	not out	1	3	–
† T.J.Zoehrer				
M.R.Whitney				
B.A.Reid				
Extras	(b 2, lb 1, w 5, nb 1)	9		
Total	(50 overs; 6 wickets)	**273**		

PAKISTAN		Runs	Balls	4/6
Qasim Omar	c Border b Waugh	67	80	10
Shoaib Mohammed	lbw b MacLeay	9	14	1
Ramiz Raja	c Bishop b MacLeay	0	3	–
Javed Miandad	b Reid	7	15	1
Mudassar Nazar	lbw b Waugh	7	25	–
* Imran Khan	c Zoehrer b Waugh	20	23	1/1
Manzoor Elahi	c and b Whitney	48	44	5/1
Asif Mujtaba	not out	60	56	5
† Salim Yousuf	c O'Donnell b Whitney	31	27	4
Wasim Akram	c Whitney b Waugh	5	10	–
Salim Jaffer	not out	3	2	–
Extras	(lb 15, w 1, nb 1)	17		
Total	(49.5 overs; 9 wickets)	**274**		

PAKISTAN	O	M	R	W
Imran Khan	10	0	43	2
Wasim Akram	10	1	58	2
Salim Jaffer	10	2	43	0
Mudassar Nazar	10	0	56	1
Asif Mujtaba	5	0	32	0
Shoaib Mohammed	3	0	22	0
Manzoor Elahi	2	0	16	0

AUSTRALIA	O	M	R	W
MacLeay	10	0	36	2
Whitney	10	0	58	2
Reid	10	0	61	1
Waugh	9.5	0	48	4
O'Donnell	10	0	56	0

FALL OF WICKETS
1-26, 2-49, 3-70, 4-243, 5-254, 6-271

FALL OF WICKETS
1-34, 2-40, 3-73, 4-93, 5-96, 6-129, 7-181, 8-224, 9-267

Umpires: A.R.Crafter (42) and S.G.Randell (19).

ENGLAND v WEST INDIES 1986-87

At WACA Ground, Perth on 3 January 1987.   Result: **ENGLAND** won by 19 runs.   Toss: West Indies.
Award: G.R.Dilley.   LOI debuts: None.

Graham Dilley combined pace and late swing to take 4 for 7 in 19 balls as West Indies lost consecutive internationals for the first time since the 1981-82 World Series.

ENGLAND		Runs	Balls	4/6
B.C.Broad	c Garner b Marshall	0		
C.W.J.Athey	c Richardson b Garner	1		
D.I.Gower	c Dujon b Garner	11		
A.J.Lamb	c Harper b Marshall	71	108	
* M.W.Gatting	c Garner b Walsh	15		
I.T.Botham	c Greenidge b Harper	11		
† C.J.Richards	c Dujon b Garner	50	63	
J.E.Emburey	c Harper b Garner	18		
P.H.Edmonds	not out	16		
G.R.Dilley	c and b Garner	1		
G.C.Small	not out	8		
Extras	(lb 10, w 8, nb 8)	26		
Total	(50 overs; 9 wickets)	**228**		

WEST INDIES	O	M	R	W
Marshall	10	1	30	2
Garner	10	0	47	5
Holding	10	0	33	0
Walsh	9	0	40	1
Harper	10	0	63	1
Richards	1	0	5	0

FALL OF WICKETS
1-3, 2-10, 3-35, 4-67, 5-96, 6-156, 7-194, 8-209, 9-211

WEST INDIES		Runs	Balls	4/6
C.G.Greenidge	b Small	20		
D.L.Haynes	lbw b Small	4		
R.B.Richardson	c Gatting b Botham	12		
* I.V.A.Richards	c Broad b Emburey	45		
A.L.Logie	c Richards b Dilley	51		
† P.J.L.Dujon	b Dilley	36		
R.A.Harper	run out	4		
M.D.Marshall	b Dilley	7		
M.A.Holding	c Edmonds b Dilley	7		
J.Garner	not out	4		
C.A.Walsh	lbw b Emburey	0		
Extras	(b 4, lb 9, w 4, nb 2)	19		
Total	(48.2 overs)	**209**		

ENGLAND	O	M	R	W
Dilley	10	0	46	4
Small	10	1	37	2
Botham	10	1	29	1
Edmonds	9	1	53	0
Emburey	9.2	0	31	2

FALL OF WICKETS
1-9, 2-39, 3-51, 4-104, 5-178, 6-187, 7-187, 8-201, 9-208, 10-209

Umpires: R.A.French (47) and P.J.McConnell (30).

AUSTRALIA v WEST INDIES 1986-87

At WACA Ground, Perth on 4 January 1987.   Result: **WEST INDIES** won by 164 runs.   Toss: Australia.
Award: C.G.Greenidge.   LOI debuts: None.

A combination of Gordon Greenidge's only LOI hundred against Australia and a bouncy pitch (Geoff Marsh was hit in the throat by one of many short-pitched balls) ensured that West Indies easily avoided losing an unprecedented third successive international.

WEST INDIES		Runs	Balls	4/6
C.G.Greenidge	b Waugh	100	119	12
D.L.Haynes	c Zoehrer b MacLeay	18	41	2
H.A.Gomes	b O'Donnell	18	42	1
* I.V.A.Richards	lbw b O'Donnell	13	18	1
A.L.Logie	b Reid	13	19	–
† P.J.L.Dujon	c Zoehrer b O'Donnell	9	16	–
R.A.Harper	c Zoehrer b O'Donnell	2	6	–
M.A.Holding	not out	53	35	5/1
J.Garner	lbw b McDermott	1	4	–
A.H.Gray	not out	10	7	1
C.A.Walsh				
Extras	(lb 13, w 3, nb 2)	18		
Total	(50 overs; 8 wickets)	**255**		

AUSTRALIA	O	M	R	W
Reid	10	2	40	1
MacLeay	10	1	29	1
McDermott	10	0	67	1
Waugh	10	0	41	1
O'Donnell	10	0	65	4

FALL OF WICKETS
1-46, 2-95, 3-127, 4-176, 5-176, 6-180, 7-203, 8-210

AUSTRALIA		Runs	Balls	4/6
D.C.Boon	b Garner	2	8	–
G.R.Marsh	c Richards b Gray	5	20	–
D.M.Jones	c Harper b Garner	2	22	–
* A.R.Border	c Greenidge b Holding	9	37	1
G.A.Bishop	c Dujon b Holding	7	24	1
S.R.Waugh	b Harper	29	47	2/1
S.P.O'Donnell	lbw b Harper	8	18	1
K.H.MacLeay	c Logie b Holding	5	16	–
† T.J.Zoehrer	lbw b Gray	4	13	–
C.J.McDermott	c Gomes b Gray	7	10	1
B.A.Reid	not out	1	4	–
Extras	(lb 5, w 2, nb 5)	12		
Total	(35.4 overs)	**91**		

WEST INDIES	O	M	R	W
Garner	6	2	10	2
Gray	7.4	0	9	3
Walsh	6	1	11	0
Holding	10	1	32	3
Harper	6	1	24	2

FALL OF WICKETS
1-4, 2-12, 3-16, 4-25, 5-36, 6-66, 7-78, 8-78, 9-89, 10-91

Umpires: A.R.Crafter (43) and S.G.Randell (20).

ENGLAND v PAKISTAN 1986-87

At WACA Ground, Perth on 5 January 1987.　　Result: **ENGLAND** won by 3 wickets.　　Toss: Pakistan.
Award: B.C.Broad.　　LOI debuts: None.

Ramiz Raja was erroneously given run out by French at square-leg when, not hearing Crafter's 'no-ball' call, he left his wicket after being 'caught' at wide mid-on. Under Law 38 (2), a batsman can only be given out in such circumstances if 'he attempts to run'.

PAKISTAN		Runs	Balls	4/6
Qasim Omar	b Botham	32	53	4
Shoaib Mohammed	c DeFreitas b Emburey	66	117	4
Ramiz Raja	run out	15	40	–
Javed Miandad	c Athey b Emburey	59	65	2/2
*Imran Khan	c Gower b DeFreitas	23	28	2
Manzoor Elahi	not out	9	7	1
Wasim Akram	not out	1	1	–
Asif Mujtaba				
†Salim Yousuf				
Mudassar Nazar				
Salim Jaffer				
Extras	(lb 15, w 1, nb 8)	24		
Total	(50 overs; 5 wickets)	229		

ENGLAND	O	M	R	W
DeFreitas	9	1	24	1
Small	10	0	41	0
Foster	4	0	23	0
Botham	10	1	37	1
Gatting	7	0	24	0
Emburey	10	0	65	2

FALL OF WICKETS
1-61, 2-98, 3-156, 4-198, 5-225

Umpires: A.R.Crafter (44) and R.A.French (48).

ENGLAND		Runs	Balls	4/6
B.C.Broad	c Salim Yousuf b Imran	97	130	7
C.W.J.Athey	b Manzoor	42	90	4
D.I.Gower	c Shoaib b Mudassar	2	3	–
A.J.Lamb	c Miandad b Shoaib	32	31	4
I.T.Botham	c Ramiz b Wasim	10	16	–
*M.W.Gatting	run out	7	8	–
†C.J.Richards	run out	0	3	–
P.A.J.DeFreitas	not out	13	11	1
J.E.Emburey	not out	11	8	1
N.A.Foster				
G.C.Small				
Extras	(b 1, lb 13, w 3, nb 1)	18		
Total	(49.4 overs; 7 wickets)	232		

PAKISTAN	O	M	R	W
Wasim Akram	9.4	1	28	1
Salim Jaffer	10	2	43	0
Imran Khan	9	0	41	1
Mudassar Nazar	10	0	39	1
Asif Mujtaba	3	0	19	0
Manzoor Elahi	3	0	24	1
Shoaib Mohammed	5	0	24	1

FALL OF WICKETS
1-104, 2-108, 3-156, 4-184, 5-199, 6-204, 7-208

ENGLAND v PAKISTAN 1986-87

At WACA Ground, Perth on 7 January 1987.　　Result: **ENGLAND** won by 5 wickets.　　Toss: England.
Award: Javed Miandad.　　LOI debuts: None.

Saluted by a spectacular firework display, England comfortably won the Benson and Hedges Challenge, their first success in a tournament involving three or more teams.

PAKISTAN		Runs	Balls	4/6
Qasim Omar	c Broad b Botham	21	47	2
Shoaib Mohammed	b Dilley	0	2	–
Ramiz Raja	c Athey b Botham	22	57	3
Javed Miandad	not out	77	127	6
Asif Mujtaba	c Gower b Botham	7	17	1
*Imran Khan	c Richards b Gatting	5	18	–
Manzoor Elahi	c Gower b Small	20	21	2
†Salim Yousuf	c Athey b Small	0	1	–
Mudassar Nazar	c Gower b Emburey	0	3	–
Wasim Akram	c Gatting b Small	2	6	–
Salim Jaffer	not out	3	5	–
Extras	(lb 5, w 1, nb 3)	9		
Total	(50 overs; 9 wickets)	166		

ENGLAND	O	M	R	W
DeFreitas	10	1	33	0
Dilley	10	0	23	1
Botham	10	2	29	3
Small	10	0	28	3
Emburey	8	0	34	1
Gatting	2	0	14	1

FALL OF WICKETS
1-2, 2-36, 3-58, 4-76, 5-89, 6-127, 7-127, 8-128, 9-131

Umpires: A.R.Crafter (45) and R.A.French (49).

ENGLAND		Runs	Balls	4/6
B.C.Broad	c Salim Yousuf b Wasim	0	10	–
C.W.J.Athey	c Salim Yousuf b Imran	1	7	–
D.I.Gower	c Shoaib b Imran	31	39	4
A.J.Lamb	c Salim Yousuf b Wasim	47	79	4
*M.W.Gatting	b Wasim	49	72	4
I.T.Botham	not out	23	22	3
†C.J.Richards	not out	7	14	–
P.A.J.DeFreitas				
J.E.Emburey				
G.R.Dilley				
G.C.Small				
Extras	(lb 8, w 1)	9		
Total	(40.1 overs; 5 wickets)	167		

PAKISTAN	O	M	R	W
Imran Khan	8	2	30	2
Wasim Akram	10	2	27	3
Salim Jaffer	10	1	43	0
Mudassar Nazar	5.1	0	22	0
Shoaib Mohammed	2	0	11	0
Manzoor Elahi	5	0	26	0

FALL OF WICKETS
1-1, 2-7, 3-47, 4-136, 5-145

ENGLAND v WEST INDIES 1986-87

At Woolloongabba, Brisbane on 17 January 1987.　Result: **ENGLAND** won by 6 wickets.　Toss: England.
Award: G.R.Dilley.　LOI debuts: None.

This eighth World Series saw the number of qualifying games reduced to 12. Early moisture within the pitch gave the toss added value and England duly won their sixth international in succession as temperatures reached 100 degrees and batting conditions improved.

WEST INDIES		Runs	Balls	4/6
C.G.Greenidge	lbw b DeFreitas	0	9	–
D.L.Haynes	c DeFreitas b Emburey	48	75	3/1
R.B.Richardson	c Botham b Dilley	15	31	–
* I.V.A.Richards	b Dilley	0	2	–
A.L.Logie	c Lamb b Emburey	46	78	4
† P.J.L.Dujon	b DeFreitas	22	36	3
R.A.Harper	lbw b Small	2	4	–
M.D.Marshall	b Dilley	13	24	1
M.A.Holding	c Richards b Emburey	0	4	–
J.Garner	c Richards b Dilley	1	13	–
C.A.Walsh	not out	3	3	–
Extras	(lb 4)	4		
Total	(46.3 overs)	**154**		

ENGLAND		Runs	Balls	4/6
B.C.Broad	b Richards	49	113	3/1
C.W.J.Athey	c Dujon b Holding	14	45	–
D.I.Gower	c Garner b Harper	42	42	6
A.J.Lamb	c sub (W.K.M.Benjamin) b Harper	22	36	–/1
* M.W.Gatting	not out	3	16	–
I.T.Botham	not out	14	18	2
† C.J.Richards				
P.A.J.DeFreitas				
J.E.Emburey				
G.C.Small				
G.R.Dilley				
Extras	(lb 2, w 2, nb 8)	12		
Total	(43.1 overs; 4 wickets)	**156**		

ENGLAND	O	M	R	W
Dilley	8.3	1	23	4
DeFreitas	9	2	17	2
Botham	10	1	46	0
Small	10	1	29	1
Emburey	9	0	35	3

WEST INDIES	O	M	R	W
Marshall	5	1	11	0
Garner	4	0	17	0
Holding	6	0	33	1
Walsh	7.1	0	19	0
Harper	10	0	43	2
Richards	10	1	27	1
Richardson	1	0	4	0

FALL OF WICKETS
1-1, 2-26, 3-26, 4-112, 5-120, 6-122, 7-147, 8-148, 9-151, 10-154

FALL OF WICKETS
1-30, 2-91, 3-134, 4-140

Umpires: M.W.Johnson (44) and P.J.McConnell (31).

AUSTRALIA v ENGLAND 1986-87

At Woolloongabba, Brisbane on 18 January 1987.　Result: **AUSTRALIA** won by 11 runs.　Toss: Australia.
Award: D.M.Jones.　LOI debuts: Australia – P.L.Taylor.

Dean Jones scored his third hundred in successive innings against England and, with Geoff Marsh, added 178 to record Australia's highest second-wicket LOI partnership until 1990-91.

AUSTRALIA		Runs	Balls	4/6
G.R.Marsh	lbw b Dilley	93	121	4
D.M.Wellham	c Emburey b Small	26	58	4
D.M.Jones	b Emburey	101	101	6/2
* A.R.Border	b Dilley	11	10	1
S.R.Waugh	not out	14	12	1
S.P.O'Donnell	not out	3	3	–
G.R.J.Matthews				
K.H.MacLeay				
† T.J.Zoehrer				
P.L.Taylor				
B.A.Reid				
Extras	(lb 9, w 3, nb 1)	13		
Total	(50 overs; 4 wickets)	**261**		

ENGLAND		Runs	Balls	4/6
B.C.Broad	c Matthews b O'Donnell	15	30	–
C.W.J.Athey	c O'Donnell b Reid	111	152	10
D.I.Gower	b Waugh	15	23	–
A.J.Lamb	c Marsh b Matthews	6	15	–
I.T.Botham	b O'Donnell	22	26	1
* M.W.Gatting	b Taylor	30	25	3/1
† C.J.Richards	c O'Donnell b Reid	7	9	1
P.A.J.DeFreitas	c Border b Waugh	6	3	1
J.E.Emburey	not out	24	14	4
G.C.Small	run out	2	4	–
G.R.Dilley	not out	0	–	–
Extras	(b 1, lb 10, nb 1)	12		
Total	(50 overs; 9 wickets)	**250**		

ENGLAND	O	M	R	W
Dilley	10	2	40	2
DeFreitas	10	2	41	0
Small	10	0	57	1
Botham	10	0	54	0
Emburey	10	0	60	1

AUSTRALIA	O	M	R	W
MacLeay	8	0	39	0
Reid	10	1	34	2
O'Donnell	10	0	59	2
Waugh	9	0	56	2
Matthews	10	0	34	1
Taylor	3	0	17	1

FALL OF WICKETS
1-48, 2-226, 3-234, 4-246

FALL OF WICKETS
1-48, 2-73, 3-92, 4-149, 5-197, 6-210, 7-218, 8-225, 9-250

Umpires: M.W.Johnson (45) and P.J.McConnell (32).

AUSTRALIA v WEST INDIES 1986-87

At Melbourne Cricket Ground on 20 January 1987.   Result: **WEST INDIES** won by 7 wickets.   Toss: West Indies.
Award: D.L.Haynes.   LOI debuts: None.

A crowd of 63,164 saw West Indies gain their 100th win in 131 internationals. Malcolm Marshall took his 100th LOI wicket in 81 matches. The MCG became the first ground to stage 50 internationals.

AUSTRALIA		Runs	Balls	4/6
G.R.Marsh	c Dujon b Garner	1	7	–
D.M.Wellham	run out	7	32	1
D.M.Jones	lbw b Marshall	11	24	1
* A.R.Border	not out	64	120	4
S.R.Waugh	hit wicket b Holding	15	56	–
G.R.J.Matthews	run out	0	–	–
S.P.O'Donnell	c Holding b Marshall	52	64	2/1
K.H.MacLeay	not out	12	6	1
† T.J.Zoehrer				
P.L.Taylor				
B.A.Reid				
Extras	(b 5, lb 4, w 1, nb 9)	19		
Total	(50 overs; 6 wickets)	**181**		

WEST INDIES		Runs	Balls	4/6
C.G.Greenidge	c Border b Waugh	35	53	4
D.L.Haynes	lbw b Matthews	67	121	6
R.B.Richardson	b Taylor	20	35	2
A.L.Logie	not out	44	71	2
† P.J.L.Dujon	not out	2	14	–
* I.V.A.Richards				
R.A.Harper				
M.D.Marshall				
M.A.Holding				
J.Garner				
C.A.Walsh				
Extras	(b 7, lb 3, w 1, nb 3)	14		
Total	(48.2 overs; 3 wickets)	**182**		

WEST INDIES	O	M	R	W
Marshall	9	0	40	2
Garner	9	1	47	1
Holding	10	1	15	1
Walsh	10	2	37	0
Harper	10	0	26	0
Richards	2	0	7	0

AUSTRALIA	O	M	R	W
MacLeay	6	0	20	0
Reid	8.2	2	33	0
O'Donnell	7	0	27	0
Waugh	7	0	30	1
Matthews	10	2	27	1
Taylor	10	1	35	1

FALL OF WICKETS
1-2, 2-23, 3-30, 4-74, 5-74, 6-165

FALL OF WICKETS
1-54, 2-92, 3-171

Umpires: A.R.Crafter (46) and R.A.French (50).

AUSTRALIA v ENGLAND 1986-87

At Sydney Cricket Ground on 22 January 1987.   Result: **ENGLAND** won by 3 wickets.   Toss: Australia.
Award: A.J.Lamb.   LOI debuts: None.

Allan Lamb, who had failed to register a boundary in his previous 97 balls, hit Bruce Reid for 18 (24624) in the final over to complete a sensational win with a ball to spare. The SCG became the second ground to stage 50 internationals.

AUSTRALIA		Runs	Balls	4/6
G.R.Marsh	c Richards b Edmonds	47	67	2
D.M.Wellham	c Athey b Emburey	97	144	5
D.M.Jones	c Athey b DeFreitas	34	23	2/1
* A.R.Border	c Dilley b Edmonds	13	19	1
S.R.Waugh	c Athey b Dilley	10	18	–
G.R.J.Matthews	c DeFreitas b Emburey	2	3	–
K.H.MacLeay	b Dilley	12	12	–
† T.J.Zoehrer	not out	9	14	–
P.L.Taylor	st Richards b Emburey	0	2	–
S.P.O'Donnell				
B.A.Reid				
Extras	(b 2, lb 5, nb 2)	9		
Total	(50 overs; 8 wickets)	**233**		

ENGLAND		Runs	Balls	4/6
B.C.Broad	c Matthews b Taylor	45	58	4
C.W.J.Athey	c Zoehrer b Reid	2	22	–
D.I.Gower	c Wellham b O'Donnell	50	66	2
A.J.Lamb	not out	77	102	2/1
* M.W.Gatting	b O'Donnell	1	8	–
I.T.Botham	b Waugh	27	30	2
J.E.Emburey	run out	4	5	–
† C.J.Richards	c Waugh b O'Donnell	3	5	–
P.A.J.DeFreitas	not out	6	6	–
P.H.Edmonds				
G.R.Dilley				
Extras	(lb 16, w 2, nb 1)	19		
Total	(49.5 overs; 7 wickets)	**234**		

ENGLAND	O	M	R	W
Dilley	9	2	28	2
DeFreitas	10	0	46	1
Gatting	2	0	11	0
Botham	10	0	51	0
Emburey	9	0	42	3
Edmonds	10	0	48	2

AUSTRALIA	O	M	R	W
MacLeay	4	0	22	0
Reid	9.5	3	44	1
Taylor	10	0	42	1
Waugh	5	0	22	1
Matthews	10	1	36	0
Border	3	0	13	0
O'Donnell	8	0	39	3

FALL OF WICKETS
1-109, 2-156, 3-189, 4-205, 5-208, 6-208, 7-230, 8-233

FALL OF WICKETS
1-33, 2-51, 3-137, 4-143, 5-186, 6-191, 7-202

Umpires: A.R.Crafter (47) and R.A.French (51).

ENGLAND v WEST INDIES 1986-87

At Adelaide Oval on 24 January 1987.   Result: **ENGLAND** won by 89 runs.   Toss: West Indies.
Award: B.C.Broad.   LOI debuts: None.

England gained an unprecedented third consecutive victory against West Indies, the match turning on Chris Broad's 20-yard sprint at wide long-on to end a threatening innings by Viv Richards.

ENGLAND		Runs	Balls	4/6
B.C.Broad	st Dujon b Richards	55	96	
C.W.J.Athey	c Marshall b Harper	64	110	
D.I.Gower	c Haynes b Gray	29		
I.T.Botham	c Logie b Walsh	7		
A.J.Lamb	not out	33		
* M.W.Gatting	c Dujon b Walsh	3		
† C.J.Richards	b Marshall	18		
J.E.Emburey	not out	16		
P.A.J.DeFreitas				
G.C.Small				
G.R.Dilley				
Extras	(b 4, lb 13, w 5, nb 5)	27		
Total	(50 overs; 6 wickets)	**252**		

WEST INDIES		O	M	R	W
Marshall		9	1	39	1
Gray		10	0	43	1
Garner		9	1	31	0
Walsh		10	0	55	2
Harper		9	0	46	1
Richards		3	0	21	1

FALL OF WICKETS
1-121, 2-148, 3-161, 4-177, 5-182, 6-220

WEST INDIES		Runs	Balls	4/6
C.G.Greenidge	lbw b DeFreitas	3		
D.L.Haynes	b Small	22		
R.B.Richardson	c Lamb b DeFreitas	3		
* I.V.A.Richards	c Broad b Botham	43		
A.L.Logie	c Gower b Dilley	43		
† P.J.L.Dujon	c Dilley b Emburey	25		
R.A.Harper	c Dilley b Emburey	4		
M.D.Marshall	c Athey b Emburey	3		
J.Garner	c DeFreitas b Emburey	0		
A.H.Gray	not out	7		
C.A.Walsh	b DeFreitas	3		
Extras	(w 2, nb 5)	7		
Total	(45.5 overs)	**163**		

ENGLAND		O	M	R	W
Dilley		8	1	19	1
DeFreitas		7.5	1	15	3
Botham		10	0	46	1
Small		10	1	46	1
Emburey		10	0	37	4

FALL OF WICKETS
1-3, 2-15, 3-60, 4-92, 5-136, 6-141, 7-150, 8-150, 9-157, 10-163

Umpires: B.E.Martin (24) and S.G.Randell (21).

AUSTRALIA v WEST INDIES 1986-87

At Adelaide Oval on 25 January 1987.   Result: **WEST INDIES** won by 16 runs.   Toss: Australia.
Award: G.R.Marsh.   LOI debuts: None.

West Indies beat Australia for the fifth successive time, a run extending back to February 1985.

WEST INDIES		Runs	Balls	4/6
D.L.Haynes	c Zoehrer b Davis	3	8	–
R.B.Richardson	b Waugh	72	134	3
H.A.Gomes	b Matthews	43	72	–
* I.V.A.Richards	c Davis b Waugh	69	64	7/2
A.L.Logie	run out	0	–	–
† P.J.L.Dujon	not out	12	25	–
R.A.Harper	not out	13	4	1/1
M.D.Marshall				
J.Garner				
A.H.Gray				
C.A.Walsh				
Extras	(b 3, lb 15, w 7)	25		
Total	(50 overs; 5 wickets)	**237**		

AUSTRALIA		O	M	R	W
Davis		8	1	21	1
Reid		10	0	43	0
Waugh		7	0	41	2
Matthews		10	0	34	1
O'Donnell		7	0	31	0
Taylor		8	0	49	0

FALL OF WICKETS
1-18, 2-110, 3-184, 4-184, 5-221

AUSTRALIA		Runs	Balls	4/6
G.R.Marsh	c Harper b Walsh	94	137	3/1
D.M.Wellham	c Dujon b Marshall	3	11	–
D.M.Jones	lbw b Garner	40	79	3
* A.R.Border	b Harper	1	6	–
S.R.Waugh	c Richards b Harper	24	38	1
G.R.J.Matthews	c and b Harper	3	8	–
S.P.O'Donnell	c Dujon b Marshall	0	1	–
P.L.Taylor	b Walsh	4	11	–
† T.J.Zoehrer	not out	22	20	3
B.A.Reid	b Walsh	1	2	–
S.P.Davis	not out	3	2	–
Extras	(b 1, lb 11, w 10, nb 4)	26		
Total	(50 overs; 9 wickets)	**221**		

WEST INDIES		O	M	R	W
Marshall		10	2	34	2
Gray		10	1	44	0
Garner		10	0	36	1
Walsh		10	0	46	3
Harper		10	0	49	3

FALL OF WICKETS
1-4, 2-85, 3-86, 4-158, 5-171, 6-172, 7-183, 8-199, 9-217

Umpires: R.C.Bailhache (17) and A.R.Crafter (48).

AUSTRALIA v ENGLAND 1986-87

At Adelaide Oval on 26 January 1987.   Result: **AUSTRALIA** won by 33 runs.   Toss: Australia.
Award: S.R.Waugh.   LOI debuts: None.

Allan Border and Steve Waugh celebrated Australia Day with a partnership of 164 which remains the fourth-wicket record in World Series matches.

AUSTRALIA		Runs	Balls	4/6
G.R.Marsh	c Emburey b DeFreitas	8	15	1
D.M.Wellham	c Richards b DeFreitas	9	21	1
D.M.Jones	c Richards b DeFreitas	8	15	–
* A.R.Border	c Broad b DeFreitas	91	122	5/1
S.R.Waugh	not out	83	120	8
S.P.O'Donnell	run out	6	6	–
G.R.J.Matthews	c Lamb b Dilley	0	5	–
† T.J.Zoehrer	not out	5	3	–
K.H.MacLeay				
P.L.Taylor				
S.P.Davis				
Extras	(b 1, lb 8, w 4, nb 2)	15		
Total	(50 overs; 6 wickets)	225		

ENGLAND		Runs	Balls	4/6
B.C.Broad	c Border b Waugh	46	95	2
C.W.J.Athey	lbw b Davis	12	24	–
D.I.Gower	c Waugh b O'Donnell	21	25	3
* M.W.Gatting	b Taylor	46	54	3
A.J.Lamb	run out	8	17	–
I.T.Botham	st Zoehrer b Taylor	18	28	–
† C.J.Richards	b Waugh	2	13	–
J.E.Emburey	run out	17	21	–
P.A.J.DeFreitas	c Jones b Taylor	8	8	–
G.C.Small	b MacLeay	2	3	–
G.R.Dilley	not out	3	2	–
Extras	(lb 8, w 1)	9		
Total	(48.1 overs)	192		

ENGLAND	O	M	R	W
Dilley	10	1	41	1
DeFreitas	10	1	35	4
Botham	10	0	42	0
Small	10	0	42	0
Emburey	10	0	56	0

AUSTRALIA	O	M	R	W
Davis	8	0	18	1
MacLeay	10	1	43	1
Matthews	4	0	21	0
O'Donnell	9	0	43	1
Waugh	10	1	30	2
Taylor	7.1	0	29	3

FALL OF WICKETS
1-21, 2-24, 3-37, 4-201, 5-211, 6-219

FALL OF WICKETS
1-23, 2-55, 3-125, 4-138, 5-144, 6-152, 7-168, 8-184, 9-188, 10-192

Umpires: A.R.Crafter (49) and S.G.Randell (22).

AUSTRALIA v WEST INDIES 1986-87

At Sydney Cricket Ground on 28 January 1987.   Result: **AUSTRALIA** won by 36 runs.   Toss: Australia.
Award: S.P.O'Donnell.   LOI debuts: None.

Australia gained their first victory against West Indies in any form of cricket for almost two years.

AUSTRALIA		Runs	Balls	4/6
G.R.Marsh	c Garner b Walsh	20	49	1
* A.R.Border	hit wicket b Walsh	19	52	2
D.M.Jones	c Richards b Benjamin	22	38	1
G.M.Ritchie	c Haynes b Garner	35	51	3
D.M.Wellham	c Dujon b Marshall	39	60	–
S.R.Waugh	run out	16	24	1
S.P.O'Donnell	run out	6	7	–
† T.J.Zoehrer	run out	1	1	–
G.R.J.Matthews	not out	13	12	–
P.L.Taylor	c Dujon b Marshall	2	7	–
S.P.Davis	run out	3	5	–
Extras	(b 3, lb 10, w 3, nb 2)	18		
Total	(50 overs)	194		

WEST INDIES		Runs	Balls	4/6
D.L.Haynes	b Matthews	17	45	–
R.B.Richardson	c Zoehrer b O'Donnell	0	15	–
H.A.Gomes	c and b O'Donnell	1	8	–
* I.V.A.Richards	c Zoehrer b Matthews	70	96	9
A.L.Logie	c Wellham b Waugh	2	13	–
† P.J.L.Dujon	c Wellham b Waugh	14	21	1
R.A.Harper	not out	20	49	–
M.D.Marshall	c Waugh b O'Donnell	2	14	–
W.K.M.Benjamin	c Zoehrer b O'Donnell	5	5	1
J.Garner	c and b Taylor	18	8	1
C.A.Walsh	c Border b Matthews	3	5	–
Extras	(b 2, lb 2, w 2)	6		
Total	(46.1 overs)	158		

WEST INDIES	O	M	R	W
Marshall	10	1	29	2
Garner	10	1	32	1
Walsh	10	1	41	2
Benjamin	10	0	45	1
Harper	10	0	34	0

AUSTRALIA	O	M	R	W
Davis	8	0	29	0
O'Donnell	10	2	19	4
Waugh	10	1	21	2
Matthews	8.1	2	32	3
Taylor	10	0	53	1

FALL OF WICKETS
1-33, 2-58, 3-69, 4-112, 5-158, 6-170, 7-173, 8-179, 9-187, 10-194

FALL OF WICKETS
1-12, 2-14, 3-40, 4-59, 5-89, 6-114, 7-126, 8-133, 9-152, 10-158

Umpires: R.A.French (52) and M.A.Johnson (46).

ENGLAND v WEST INDIES 1986-87

At Melbourne Cricket Ground on 30 January 1987.　　Result: **WEST INDIES** won by 6 wickets.　　Toss: England.
Award: I.V.A.Richards.　　LOI debuts: None.

Viv Richards became the first to score 5000 runs in limited-overs internationals. Michael Holding sustained a torn hamstring in darting forward to catch Ian Botham. With two matches to play each, all three sides were level with six points.

ENGLAND		Runs	Balls	4/6
B.C.Broad	c Garner b Holding	33	95	2
C.W.J.Athey	lbw b Garner	2	15	–
D.I.Gower	b Marshall	8	15	1
A.J.Lamb	run out	0	1	–
* M.W.Gatting	b Harper	13	32	1
I.T.Botham	c and b Holding	15	27	2
J.E.Emburey	c Harper b Garner	34	53	–/1
‡ C.J.Richards	b Marshall	8	41	–
P.A.J.DeFreitas	c Haynes b Garner	13	18	–
N.A.Foster	b Marshall	5	7	–
G.C.Small	not out	1	1	–
Extras	(lb 3, w 4, nb 8)	15		
Total	(48.2 overs)	147		

WEST INDIES		Runs	Balls	4/6
D.L.Haynes	lbw b Foster	13	64	1
R.B.Richardson	c Richards b DeFreitas	0	12	–
H.A.Gomes	run out	36	96	2
* I.V.A.Richards	b Foster	58	84	5/2
A.L.Logie	not out	19	44	–
† P.J.L.Dujon	not out	1	3	–
R.A.Harper				
M.D.Marshall				
M.A.Holding				
J.Garner				
C.A.Walsh				
Extras	(lb 10, w 8, nb 3)	21		
Total	(48.3 overs; 4 wickets)	148		

WEST INDIES	O	M	R	W
Marshall	9.2	2	30	3
Garner	9	1	37	3
Holding	8.3	2	19	2
Walsh	5	1	16	0
Harper	10	0	26	1
Richards	6.3	1	16	0

ENGLAND	O	M	R	W
DeFreitas	10	2	15	1
Small	10	3	16	0
Botham	10	3	28	0
Foster	9	1	25	2
Emburey	9.3	1	54	0

FALL OF WICKETS
1-11, 2-27, 3-37, 4-61, 5-77, 6-84, 7-111, 8-136, 9-144, 10-147

FALL OF WICKETS
1-7, 2-49, 3-98, 4-146

Umpires: R.C.Bailhache (18) and S.G.Randell (23).

AUSTRALIA v ENGLAND 1986-87

At Melbourne Cricket Ground on 1 February 1987.　　Result: **AUSTRALIA** won by 109 runs.　　Toss: England.
Award: S.R.Waugh　　LOI debuts: None.

A crowd of 58,580, plus a piglet labelled 'Gatting', attended England's third successive defeat.

AUSTRALIA		Runs	Balls	4/6
G.R.Marsh	c Emburey b Foster	28	44	5
* A.R.Border	c Athey b Small	45	95	1
D.M.Jones	c Athey b Gatting	93	100	7
G.M.Ritchie	st French b Gatting	9	11	1
D.M.Wellham	c Lamb b Gatting	3	7	–
S.R.Waugh	not out	49	36	7
S.P.O'Donnell	not out	4	8	–
† T.J.Zoehrer				
G.R.J.Matthews				
P.L.Taylor				
S.P.Davis				
Extras	(lb 7, w 9, nb 1)	17		
Total	(50 overs; 5 wickets)	248		

ENGLAND		Runs	Balls	4/6
B.C.Broad	b O'Donnell	2	10	–
I.T.Botham	c and b Matthews	45	87	4/1
D.I.Gower	c Taylor b Davis	11	10	2
A.J.Lamb	run out	11	27	–
* M.W.Gatting	c Davis b Waugh	6	15	–
C.W.J.Athey	lbw b O'Donnell	29	72	1
J.E.Emburey	b Matthews	1	11	–
P.A.J.DeFreitas	b Waugh	11	16	1
N.A.Foster	b Waugh	4	14	–
† B.N.French	not out	5	12	–
G.C.Small	c Matthews b Jones	4	11	–
Extras	(b 2, lb 7, w 1)	10		
Total	(47.3 overs)	139		

ENGLAND	O	M	R	W
DeFreitas	8	2	37	0
Small	10	0	49	1
Botham	10	0	35	0
Foster	7	1	20	1
Emburey	6	0	41	0
Gatting	9	0	59	3

AUSTRALIA	O	M	R	W
Davis	8	1	20	1
O'Donnell	9	2	33	2
Matthews	10	1	24	2
Waugh	10	0	26	3
Taylor	9	1	23	0
Jones	1.3	0	4	1

FALL OF WICKETS
1-61, 2-127, 3-144, 4-154, 5-223

FALL OF WICKETS
1-4, 2-25, 3-52, 4-65, 5-87, 6-90, 7-117, 8-129, 9-130, 10-139

Umpires: R.A.French (53) and B.E.Martin (25).

ENGLAND v WEST INDIES 1986-87

At Devonport Oval on 3 February 1987.　　Result: **ENGLAND** won by 29 runs.　　Toss: West Indies.
Award: B.C.Broad.　　LOI debuts: None.

Devonport provided the 77th venue for a limited-overs international and the second within Tasmania. By taking three wickets in an over, John Emburey completed the victory which virtually assured England of a place in the finals.

ENGLAND		Runs	Balls	4/6
B.C.Broad	c Dujon b Walsh	76	143	6
I.T.Botham	c Richardson b Gray	8	16	1
D.I.Gower	c Payne b Marshall	3	18	–
A.J.Lamb	c Logie b Harper	36	71	1/1
* M.W.Gatting	c Richardson b Gray	6	10	–
C.W.J.Athey	lbw b Marshall	3	8	–
J.E.Emburey	c Garner b Walsh	2	8	–
P.A.J.DeFreitas	not out	15	26	–
N.A.Foster	run out	0	4	–
† B.N.French	b Marshall	0	1	–
G.C.Small	not out	6	5	–
Extras	(lb 14, w 3, nb 5)	22		
Total	(50 overs; 9 wickets)	**177**		

WEST INDIES		Runs	Balls	4/6
R.B.Richardson	c French b DeFreitas	2	2	–
T.R.O.Payne	c French b Botham	18	19	–
A.L.Logie	b Foster	31	65	–
H.A.Gomes	c Emburey b Botham	19	47	1
* I.V.A.Richards	b Botham	1	7	–
† P.J.L.Dujon	c Gatting b Emburey	34	57	3
R.A.Harper	c French b Small	4	14	–
M.D.Marshall	c Athey b DeFreitas	27	26	–
J.Garner	b Emburey	4	10	–
A.H.Gray	c and b Emburey	0	1	–
C.A.Walsh	not out	1	3	–
Extras	(lb 5, w 2)	7		
Total	(48 overs)	**148**		

WEST INDIES	O	M	R	W
Marshall	10	0	31	3
Gray	10	2	29	2
Garner	10	0	30	0
Walsh	10	1	31	2
Harper	10	0	42	1

ENGLAND	O	M	R	W
DeFreitas	9	1	20	2
Small	10	0	35	1
Foster	10	0	29	1
Botham	10	1	33	3
Emburey	9	0	26	3

FALL OF WICKETS
1-23, 2-29, 3-103, 4-129, 5-133, 6-143, 7-158, 8-159, 9-160

FALL OF WICKETS
1-10, 2-25, 3-71, 4-73, 5-90, 6-95, 7-132, 8-147, 9-147, 10-148

Umpires: A.R.Crafter (50) and S.G.Randell (24).

AUSTRALIA v WEST INDIES 1986-87

At Sydney Cricket Ground on 6 February 1987.　　Result: **AUSTRALIA** won by 2 wickets.　　Toss: West Indies.
Award: T.J.Zoehrer.　　LOI debuts: None.

Needing to win and score 374 to exceed England's run rate, West Indies failed to reach the finals for the first time in five World Series tournaments. Final points: Australia (after four successive wins) 10, England 8, West Indies 6.

WEST INDIES		Runs	Balls	4/6
R.B.Richardson	c Ritchie b Davis	11	21	2
T.R.O.Payne	c and b Taylor	60	119	4
A.L.Logie	c Zoehrer b Waugh	14	32	2
* I.V.A.Richards	c and b Matthews	25	26	2/1
H.A.Gomes	run out	38	61	–
† P.J.L.Dujon	lbw b Taylor	2	9	–
R.A.Harper	c Wellham b Davis	20	10	1/1
W.K.M.Benjamin	c Wellham b Taylor	8	8	1
J.Garner	run out	6	4	–
A.H.Gray	run out	1	3	–
C.A.Walsh	not out	1	3	–
Extras	(b 1, lb 3, w 2)	6		
Total	(49 overs)	**192**		

AUSTRALIA		Runs	Balls	4/6
G.R.Marsh	c Richardson b Harper	33	76	–
† T.J.Zoehrer	c Richards b Walsh	50	59	5
D.M.Jones	c and b Harper	7	29	–
G.M.Ritchie	c and b Garner	25	45	–
D.M.Wellham	c Garner b Gray	24	40	1
S.R.Waugh	st Dujon b Richards	11	17	1
* A.R.Border	b Richards	8	17	–
S.P.O'Donnell	not out	23	15	3
G.R.J.Matthews	b Richards	0	2	–
P.L.Taylor	not out	0	1	–
S.P.Davis				
Extras	(b 8, lb 3, w 2, nb 1)	14		
Total	(49.1 overs; 8 wickets)	**195**		

AUSTRALIA	O	M	R	W
Davis	10	3	31	2
O'Donnell	10	1	33	0
Waugh	9	1	41	1
Matthews	10	0	47	1
Taylor	10	0	36	3

WEST INDIES	O	M	R	W
Garner	10	1	37	1
Gray	8	0	48	1
Benjamin	3.1	1	15	0
Walsh	10	2	16	1
Harper	10	1	34	2
Richards	7	0	29	3
Gomes	1	0	5	0

FALL OF WICKETS
1-20, 2-35, 3-70, 4-148, 5-152, 6-174, 7-177, 8-187, 9-190, 10-192

FALL OF WICKETS
1-74, 2-87, 3-106, 4-131, 5-155, 6-163, 7-191, 8-191

Umpires: R.A.French (54) and P.J.McConnell (33).

AUSTRALIA v ENGLAND 1986-87

At Melbourne Cricket Ground on 8 February 1987.   Result: **ENGLAND** won by 6 wickets.   Toss: England.
LOI debuts: None.

Drizzle delayed the start by an hour, reducing each innings by six overs. The toss proved decisive on an overcast morning which cleared to a sunny afternoon ideal for batting. For the first time the BBC televised live cricket from overseas throughout the night.

AUSTRALIA		Runs	Balls	4/6
G.R.Marsh	c Gatting b DeFreitas	2	5	–
† T.J.Zoehrer	c Gatting b Dilley	0	3	–
D.M.Jones	b DeFreitas	67	107	6/1
* A.R.Border	c French b Foster	42	85	1
G.M.Ritchie	run out	13	21	–
S.R.Waugh	c DeFreitas b Emburey	1	4	–
S.P.O'Donnell	b Dilley	10	17	–
G.R.J.Matthews	b Dilley	8	19	–
P.L.Taylor	not out	3	6	–
B.A.Reid	not out	5	6	1
S.P.Davis				
Extras	(lb 10, w 3, nb 7)	20		
Total	(44 overs; 8 wickets)	**171**		

ENGLAND		Runs	Balls	4/6
B.C.Broad	c Jones b Matthews	12	41	1
I.T.Botham	c Marsh b Matthews	71	52	11/1
C.W.J.Athey	c and b Matthews	12	51	–
D.I.Gower	c Taylor b Reid	45	47	6
A.J.Lamb	not out	15	21	2
* M.W.Gatting	not out	3	8	–
J.E.Emburey				
P.A.J.DeFreitas				
N.A.Foster				
† B.N.French				
G.R.Dilley				
Extras	(b 5, lb 3, w 4, nb 2)	14		
Total	(36 overs; 4 wickets)	**172**		

ENGLAND	O	M	R	W
Dilley	9	2	32	3
DeFreitas	9	0	32	2
Botham	9	0	26	0
Foster	9	0	42	1
Emburey	8	0	29	1

AUSTRALIA	O	M	R	W
Davis	4	0	17	0
O'Donnell	4	0	25	0
Reid	5	0	31	1
Waugh	8	1	36	0
Matthews	9	1	27	3
Taylor	5	0	24	0
Jones	1	0	4	0

FALL OF WICKETS
1-3, 2-3, 3-106, 4-134, 5-137, 6-146, 7-161, 8-164

FALL OF WICKETS
1-91, 2-93, 3-147, 4-159

Umpires: P.J.McConnell (34) and S.G.Randell (25).

AUSTRALIA v ENGLAND 1986-87

At Sydney Cricket Ground on 11 February 1987.   Result: **ENGLAND** won by 8 runs.   Toss: England.
Finals Award: I.T.Botham.   LOI debuts: None.

Ian Botham turned a low-scoring match on a sub-standard pitch by dismissing three of Australia's first four batsmen for 7 runs in 27 balls. Combined with The Ashes and the Perth Challenge, England's first World Series title completed a unique treble.

ENGLAND		Runs	Balls	4/6
B.C.Broad	c O'Donnell b Matthews	53	87	3
I.T.Botham	c Ritchie b O'Donnell	25	31	4
C.W.J.Athey	b Matthews	16	39	1
D.I.Gower	c Wellham b Taylor	17	23	2
* M.W.Gatting	run out	7	13	–
A.J.Lamb	c Zoehrer b O'Donnell	35	39	1
J.E.Emburey	c Zoehrer b Waugh	6	24	–
P.A.J.DeFreitas	c Jones b Taylor	1	6	–
N.A.Foster	c Taylor b Davis	7	16	–
† B.N.French	not out	9	12	–
G.R.Dilley	not out	6	11	–
Extras	(lb 4, w 1)	5		
Total	(50 overs; 9 wickets)	**187**		

AUSTRALIA		Runs	Balls	4/6
G.R.Marsh	lbw b Botham	28	64	1
* A.R.Border	c French b Botham	27	63	2
D.M.Jones	c and b Emburey	13	19	1
G.M.Ritchie	c DeFreitas b Botham	4	14	–
D.M.Wellham	c Gower b DeFreitas	30	51	1
S.R.Waugh	run out	22	48	–
S.P.O'Donnell	not out	40	27	1/1
† T.J.Zoehrer	lbw b DeFreitas	0	1	–
G.R.J.Matthews	run out	3	9	–
P.L.Taylor	not out	3	6	–
S.P.Davis				
Extras	(b 1, lb 6, w 2)	9		
Total	(50 overs; 8 wickets)	**179**		

AUSTRALIA	O	M	R	W
Davis	10	0	44	1
O'Donnell	10	1	37	2
Waugh	10	0	42	1
Matthews	10	1	31	2
Taylor	10	2	29	2

ENGLAND	O	M	R	W
Dilley	10	1	34	0
DeFreitas	10	1	34	2
Botham	10	1	26	3
Foster	10	0	51	0
Emburey	10	2	27	1

FALL OF WICKETS
1-36, 2-73, 3-102, 4-120, 5-121, 6-143, 7-146, 8-170, 9-170

FALL OF WICKETS
1-55, 2-70, 3-72, 4-80, 5-124, 6-135, 7-135, 8-151

Umpires: A.R.Crafter (51) and R.A.French (55).

INDIA v PAKISTAN 1986-87

At Nehru Stadium, Indore on 27 January 1987.   Result: **PAKISTAN** won by 3 wickets.   Toss: Pakistan.
Award: Abdul Qadir.   LOI debuts: None.

Intertwined with their five-Test tour of India, Pakistan played a series of six 45-over internationals. In the absence of Kapil Dev (strained thigh muscle), Ravi Shastri led India for the first time.

INDIA		Runs	Balls	4/6	PAKISTAN		Runs	Balls	4/6
K.Srikkanth	b Imran	2	14	–	Mudassar Nazar	c and b Shastri	43	80	4
S.M.Gavaskar	c Salim Yousuf b Imran	10	22	1	Rizwan-uz-Zaman	c Maninder b Sharma	2	15	–
M.Azharuddin	st Salim Yousuf b Qadir	17	53	1	Ijaz Ahmed	c and b Shastri	17	34	1
D.B.Vengsarkar	c Ijaz b Salim Jaffer	5	25	–	Javed Miandad	b Maninder	13	24	–
* R.J.Shastri	b Manzoor	50	68	5/1	Abdul Qadir	c Lamba b Shastri	39	46	3/1
R.Lamba	b Qadir	5	22	1	Salim Malik	run out	23	24	2
† C.S.Pandit	not out	33	40	2	* Imran Khan	not out	22	26	2
Madan Lal	c Imran b Mudassar	38	26	4/1	Manzoor Elahi	c Sharma b Srikkanth	27	19	2/2
C.Sharma	not out	7	2	–/1	† Salim Yousuf	not out	0	–	–
R.R.Kulkarni					Wasim Akram				
Maninder Singh					Salim Jaffer				
Extras	(b 4, lb 8, w 15, nb 2)	29			Extras	(b 4, lb 5, w 1, nb 4)	14		
Total	(45 overs; 7 wickets)	196			Total	(44 overs; 7 wickets)	200		

PAKISTAN	O	M	R	W	INDIA	O	M	R	W
Imran Khan	10	1	41	2	Sharma	7	1	25	1
Wasim Akram	10	1	35	0	Madan Lal	10	1	37	0
Salim Jaffer	10	2	28	1	Kulkarni	3	0	31	0
Mudassar Nazar	5	0	29	1	Maninder Singh	10	1	31	1
Abdul Qadir	8	1	42	2	Shastri	10	1	37	3
Manzoor Elahi	2	0	9	1	Azharuddin	3	0	20	0
					Srikkanth	1	0	10	1

FALL OF WICKETS
1-10, 2-19, 3-29, 4-62, 5-85, 6-123, 7-188

Umpires: S.Banerjee (4) and R.B.Gupta (3).

INDIA v PAKISTAN 1986-87

At Eden Gardens, Calcutta on 18 February 1987.   Result: **PAKISTAN** won by 2 wickets.   Toss: Pakistan.
Award: Salim Malik.   LOI debuts: Pakistan – Younis Ahmed.

Calcutta's first limited-overs international attracted a crowd estimated at 90,000 and featured epic displays of aggressive batting by Krish Srikkanth, with an 89-ball hundred, and Salim Malik, who transformed the match by scoring Pakistan's fastest fifty off 23 balls.

INDIA		Runs	Balls	4/6	PAKISTAN		Runs	Balls	4/6
K.Srikkanth	c Salim Yousuf b Wasim	123	103	14/1	Ramiz Raja	c Maninder b Shastri	58	67	6
L.S.Rajput	b Imran	0	3	–	Younis Ahmed	c and b Shastri	58	82	5
R.Lamba	lbw b Imran	4	13	–	Javed Miandad	lbw b Maninder	13	19	–
D.B.Vengsarkar	c Salim Yousuf b Salim Jaffer	12	36	1	Abdul Qadir	b Shastri	9	9	1
M.Azharuddin	c Younis b Wasim	49	62	4	Manzoor Elahi	lbw b Shastri	14	16	2
* Kapil Dev	c and b Wasim	6	9	–	* Imran Khan	b Kapil Dev	2	7	–
R.J.Shastri	not out	21	13	1	Salim Malik	not out	72	36	11/1
† C.S.Pandit	not out	6	5	1	Wasim Akram	c Azharuddin b Kapil Dev	3	3	–
R.M.H.Binny					† Salim Yousuf	run out	0	2	–
Madan Lal					Mudassar Nazar	not out	1	1	–
Maninder Singh					Salim Jaffer				
Extras	(b 1, lb 6, w 7, nb 3)	17			Extras	(b 1, lb 7, w 1, nb 2)	11		
Total	(40 overs; 6 wickets)	238			Total	(39.3 overs; 8 wickets)	241		

PAKISTAN	O	M	R	W	INDIA	O	M	R	W
Imran Khan	10	0	59	2	Kapil Dev	9.3	0	53	2
Wasim Akram	10	0	49	3	Binny	2	0	21	0
Mudassar Nazar	4	0	30	0	Madan Lal	5	0	33	0
Salim Jaffer	10	0	49	1	Maninder Singh	10	0	70	1
Manzoor Elahi	6	0	44	0	Shastri	10	0	38	4
					Rajput	3	0	18	0

FALL OF WICKETS
1-3, 2-13, 3-58, 4-203, 5-204, 6-216

Umpires: D.N.Dotiwala (5) and R.V.Ramani (4).

FALL OF WICKETS
1-106, 2-132, 3-142, 4-150, 5-161, 6-174, 7-224, 8-232

INDIA v PAKISTAN 1986-87

At Lal Bahadur Stadium, Hyderabad on 20 March 1987. Result: (TIED) INDIA won by losing fewer wickets.
Toss: Pakistan. LOI debuts: None.

Had Abdul Qadir not attempted a futile second run off the final ball, Pakistan would have won a match tied on runs and wickets by having the higher score after 25 overs. Ravi Shastri and Kapil Dev shared India's only hundred partnership for the fifth wicket. Krish Srikkanth retired after edging a ball from Wasim Akram, his left eyebrow requiring 14 stitches.

INDIA		Runs	Balls	4/6
K.Srikkanth	retired hurt	2	13	–
S.M.Gavaskar	c Manzoor b Wasim	1	10	–
R.Lamba	c Miandad b Ijaz	41	73	4
M.Azharuddin	c Manzoor b Salim Jaffer	18	33	1
† S.Viswanath	c Wasim b Qadir	1	11	–
R.J.Shastri	not out	69	74	5/2
* Kapil Dev	lbw b Imran	59	52	6/1
Madan Lal	run out	1	5	–
M.Prabhakar	not out	0	–	–
G.Sharma				
Maninder Singh				
Extras	(lb 5, w 11, nb 4)	20		
Total	(44 overs; 6 wickets)	212		

PAKISTAN		Runs	Balls	4/6
Ramiz Raja	c Azharuddin b Kapil Dev	23	31	3
Younis Ahmed	st Viswanath b Sharma	26	69	1
Salim Malik	c Shastri b Sharma	84	89	3/1
Javed Miandad	lbw b Shastri	25	37	–
Manzoor Elahi	not out	27	24	1/1
* Imran Khan	c Maninder b Sharma	7	10	1
Wasim Akram	run out	8	4	–/1
Abdul Qadir	run out	1	1	–
† Salim Yousuf				
Ijaz Faqih				
Salim Jaffer				
Extras	(b 2, lb 2, w 7)	11		
Total	(44 overs; 7 wickets)	212		

PAKISTAN	O	M	R	W	INDIA	O	M	R	W
Imran Khan	9	2	27	1	Kapil Dev	10	0	44	1
Wasim Akram	9	0	45	1	Prabhakar	8	1	32	0
Salim Jaffer	9	0	51	1	Madan Lal	4	0	22	0
Abdul Qadir	9.2	0	44	1	Maninder Singh	10	0	41	0
Ijaz Faqih	6	0	31	1	Sharma	6	0	29	3
Manzoor Elahi	1.4	0	9	0	Shastri	6	0	40	1

FALL OF WICKETS
1-6, 2-53, 3-59, 4-95, 5-207, 6-212

FALL OF WICKETS
1-39, 2-82, 3-146, 4-187, 5-197, 6-209, 7-212

Umpires: S.K.Ghosh (2) and V.Vikramraju (2).

INDIA v PAKISTAN 1986-87

At Nehru Stadium, Poona on 22 March 1987. Result: PAKISTAN won by 6 wickets. Toss: India.
Award: Salim Jaffer. LOI debuts: None.

Pakistan's fourth consecutive success with the toss proved crucial after a delay to dry the pitch had reduced the overs from 50 to 47. Pakistan bowled only 42 in the time allowed and, as batting conditions improved under a strong sun, took a decisive 3-1 lead in the rubber.

INDIA		Runs	Balls	4/6
S.M.Gavaskar	run out	7	24	1
R.Lamba	c Qadir b Salim Jaffer	27	62	3
M.Azharuddin	b Tausif	0	2	–
D.B.Vengsarkar	lbw b Salim Jaffer	2	22	–
† S.Viswanath	b Salim Jaffer	5	6	1
R.J.Shastri	c Salim Yousuf b Wasim	21	43	1
* Kapil Dev	lbw b Tausif	6	5	1
M.Prabhakar	not out	17	58	–
R.R.Kulkarni	c Tausif b Qadir	15	15	2
G.Sharma	run out	4	4	–
Maninder Singh	not out	2	12	–
Extras	(b 1, lb 6, w 6, nb 1)	14		
Total	(42 overs; 9 wickets)	120		

PAKISTAN		Runs	Balls	4/6
Ramiz Raja	run out	33	74	2
† Salim Yousuf	lbw b Kapil Dev	15	29	2
Salim Malik	c Vengsarkar b Maninder	17	28	1
Javed Miandad	c sub (C.S.Pandit) b Kapil Dev	22	55	1
* Imran Khan	not out	17	36	1
Manzoor Elahi	not out	7	4	1
Ijaz Faqih				
Wasim Akram				
Abdul Qadir				
Tausif Ahmed				
Salim Jaffer				
Extras	(b 4, lb 3, w 1, nb 2)	10		
Total	(37.2 overs; 4 wickets)	121		

PAKISTAN	O	M	R	W	INDIA	O	M	R	W
Imran Khan	7	2	20	0	Kapil Dev	7	0	32	2
Wasim Akram	10	3	37	1	Kulkarni	2	0	10	0
Tausif Ahmed	10	2	18	2	Maninder Singh	10	1	21	1
Salim Jaffer	9	0	25	3	Sharma	10	0	28	0
Abdul Qadir	6	0	13	1	Shastri	8.2	0	23	0

FALL OF WICKETS
1-21, 2-21, 3-36, 4-44, 5-48, 6-63, 7-88, 8-109, 9-114

FALL OF WICKETS
1-33, 2-65, 3-77, 4-114

Umpires: R.R.Kadam (4) and S.R.Ramchandra Rao (3).

INDIA v PAKISTAN 1986-87

At Vidarbha CA Ground, Nagpur on 24 March 1987.   Result: **PAKISTAN** won by 41 runs.   Toss: India.
Award: Wasim Akram.   LOI debuts: None.

Javed Miandad and Imran Khan shared Pakistan's only three-figure partnership for the fourth wicket against India. For the first time in 23 Indo-Pakistan internationals the match aggregate exceeded 500 runs. Ravi Shastri scored 50 off 33 balls.

PAKISTAN		Runs	Balls	4/6
Ramiz Raja	run out	8	13	–
Ijaz Ahmed	b Maninder	34	48	4
Salim Malik	c Azharuddin b Maninder	17	25	2
Javed Miandad	c Shastri b Kapil Dev	78	88	5/1
Manzoor Elahi	lbw b Sharma	4	8	–
* Imran Khan	run out	73	65	7/2
Wasim Akram	not out	48	21	4/4
† Salim Yousuf	not out	3	3	
Abdul Qadir				
Tausif Ahmed				
Salim Jaffer				
Extras	(b 3, lb 10, w 4, nb 4)	21		
Total	(44 overs; 6 wickets)	**286**		

INDIA		Runs	Balls	4/6
S.M.Gavaskar	c Salim Jaffer b Wasim	70	96	5/1
L.S.Rajput	b Salim Jaffer	8	26	–
R.Lamba	c Manzoor b Qadir	10	13	1
D.B.Vengsarkar	b Qadir	34	35	2/1
* Kapil Dev	b Qadir	6	5	1
R.J.Shastri	c Manzoor b Imran	52	39	3/4
C.Sharma	run out	5	6	–
M.Azharuddin	b Wasim	12	18	–
† S.Viswanath	b Wasim	6	8	–
M.Prabhakar	not out	9	12	–
Maninder Singh	not out	5	8	–
Extras	(lb 8, w 18, nb 2)	28		
Total	(44 overs; 9 wickets)	**245**		

INDIA	O	M	R	W
Kapil Dev	10	0	57	1
Prabhakar	4	0	24	0
Sharma	9	0	70	1
Maninder Singh	10	1	43	2
Shastri	7	0	55	0
Rajput	4	0	24	0

PAKISTAN	O	M	R	W
Imran Khan	10	0	48	1
Wasim Akram	10	1	26	3
Salim Jaffer	6	0	31	1
Abdul Qadir	10	0	75	3
Tausif Ahmed	7	0	49	0
Manzoor Elahi	1	0	8	0

FALL OF WICKETS
1-19, 2-68, 3-73, 4-83, 5-225, 6-245

FALL OF WICKETS
1-25, 2-40, 3-105, 4-115, 5-191, 6-202, 7-203, 8-216, 9-227

Umpires: S.B.Kulkarni (2) and R.S.Rathore (2).

INDIA v PAKISTAN 1986-87

At Keenan Stadium, Jamshedpur on 26 March 1987.   Result: **PAKISTAN** won by 5 wickets.   Toss: Pakistan.
Award: M.Prabhakar.   LOI debuts: None.

The opening partnership of 154 between Sunil Gavaskar and Manoj Prabhakar, who completed his first LOI hundred from 115 balls, remains India's highest against Pakistan. Although Dilip Vengsarkar added a 39-ball fifty, Pakistan won the rubber 5-1.

INDIA		Runs	Balls	4/6
S.M.Gavaskar	c Manzoor b Qadir	69	86	5
M.Prabhakar	b Wasim	106	121	13
R.Lamba	b Tausif	9	13	–
D.B.Vengsarkar	not out	54	42	6
R.J.Shastri	not out	10	8	–
M.Azharuddin				
* Kapil Dev				
† S.Viswanath				
R.R.Kulkarni				
G.Sharma				
Maninder Singh				
Extras	(b 5, lb 3, w 7, nb 2)	17		
Total	(44 overs; 3 wickets)	**265**		

PAKISTAN		Runs	Balls	4/6
Ramiz Raja	c Viswanath b Kapil Dev	28	32	3
Ijaz Ahmed	lbw b Maninder	72	83	6/2
Salim Malik	lbw b Kulkarni	13	28	1
Javed Miandad	not out	78	71	4/1
* Imran Khan	c Azharuddin b Sharma	23	28	–
Manzoor Elahi	b Kapil Dev	18	18	2
Wasim Akram	not out	12	7	1/1
† Salim Yousuf				
Abdul Qadir				
Tausif Ahmed				
Salim Jaffer				
Extras	(b 3, lb 10, w 3, nb 6)	22		
Total	(43.2 overs; 5 wickets)	**266**		

PAKISTAN	O	M	R	W
Imran Khan	10	1	55	0
Salim Jaffer	7	0	45	0
Abdul Qadir	10	0	52	1
Wasim Akram	10	0	63	1
Tausif Ahmed	5	0	31	1
Manzoor Elahi	2	0	11	0

INDIA	O	M	R	W
Kapil Dev	9.2	0	42	2
Prabhakar	6	0	36	0
Kulkarni	5	0	27	1
Maninder Singh	10	0	45	1
Shastri	7	0	48	0
Sharma	6	0	55	1

FALL OF WICKETS
1-154, 2-171, 3-247

FALL OF WICKETS
1-52, 2-81, 3-140, 4-195, 5-247

Umpires: S.Banerjee (5) and V.Vikramraju (3).

NEW ZEALAND v WEST INDIES 1986-87

At Carisbrook, Dunedin on 18 March 1987.   Result: **WEST INDIES** won by 95 runs.   Toss: New Zealand.
Award: I.V.A.Richards.   LOI debuts: New Zealand – P.A.Horne, D.N.Patel; West Indies – C.L.Hooper.

Viv Richards became the first to score nine LOI hundreds when he struck a six off his 95th ball. His all-round feat of
scoring a hundred and taking five wickets in one of these matches remains unique. His stand of 120 with Carl Hooper
(on his international debut) is the West Indies fourth-wicket record against New Zealand.

WEST INDIES		Runs	Balls	4/6
C.G.Greenidge	lbw b Snedden	15	41	1
D.L.Haynes	lbw b Hadlee	0	2	–
R.B.Richardson	run out	17	23	2
C.L.Hooper	c McSweeney b Snedden	48	79	2/1
* I.V.A.Richards	c Hadlee b M.D.Crowe	119	113	10/4
A.L.Logie	st McSweeney b Coney	6	11	–
† P.J.L.Dujon	c J.J.Crowe b Coney	1	9	–
J.Garner	run out	6	9	1
A.H.Gray	c Snedden b Hadlee	5	6	–
C.A.Walsh	not out	7	7	1
B.P.Patterson	not out	0	–	–
Extras	(b 3, lb 10)	13		
Total	(50 overs; 9 wickets)	**237**		

NEW ZEALAND		Runs	Balls	4/6
J.G.Wright	st Dujon b Richards	34	68	3
† E.B.McSweeney	run out	9	20	1
M.D.Crowe	c Richardson b Garner	7	29	–
P.A.Horne	c Greenidge b Gray	17	40	1
J.J.Crowe	c Dujon b Richards	7	18	–
D.N.Patel	c Dujon b Richards	15	11	2
* J.V.Coney	c Patterson b Richards	7	14	1
J.G.Bracewell	b Gray	9	23	–
R.J.Hadlee	b Richards	11	17	1
M.C.Snedden	c Hooper b Walsh	7	9	1
E.J.Chatfield	not out	2	7	–
Extras	(b 4, lb 10, w 1, nb 2)	17		
Total	(42.1 overs)	**142**		

NEW ZEALAND	O	M	R	W
Hadlee	10	1	46	2
Chatfield	10	2	35	0
Snedden	10	1	38	2
Coney	9	1	34	2
M.D.Crowe	7	0	26	1
Patel	2	0	19	0
Bracewell	2	0	26	0

WEST INDIES	O	M	R	W
Garner	10	3	18	1
Patterson	6	0	15	0
Walsh	6.1	1	28	1
Gray	10	1	26	2
Richards	10	0	41	5

FALL OF WICKETS
1-15, 2-44, 3-72, 4-78, 5-100, 6-105, 7-118, 8-130, 9-134, 10-142

FALL OF WICKETS
1-0, 2-34, 3-50, 4-170, 5-201, 6-205, 7-215, 8-227, 9-233

Umpires: F.R.Goodall (13) and G.C.Morris (6).

NEW ZEALAND v WEST INDIES 1986-87

At Eden Park, Auckland on 21 March 1987.   Result: **WEST INDIES** won by 6 wickets.   Toss: West Indies.
Award: C.G.Greenidge.   LOI debuts: None.

John Wright, who tore a hamstring when 33 and used a runner, and Martin Crowe shared New Zealand's first hundred
partnership against West Indies. The third match, scheduled for 25, 26 March, was abandoned without a ball bowled
when Wellington's Basin Reserve remained waterlogged after three days of heavy rain.

NEW ZEALAND		Runs	Balls	4/6
† E.B.McSweeney	c Richardson b Garner	0	3	–
J.G.Wright	c Logie b Richards	45	81	3
M.D.Crowe	c Dujon b Gray	53	86	6
P.A.Horne	lbw b Richards	0	1	–
D.N.Patel	c Hooper b Richards	15	26	1
* J.V.Coney	c Richardson b Patterson	52	63	3
J.G.Bracewell	c Logie b Patterson	14	25	–
R.J.Hadlee	c Dujon b Walsh	18	15	1
M.C.Snedden	c Logie b Walsh	2	3	–
S.L.Boock	not out	1	3	–
E.J.Chatfield	run out	1	1	–
Extras	(lb 6, w 2, nb 4)	12		
Total	(50 overs)	**213**		

WEST INDIES		Runs	Balls	4/6
C.G.Greenidge	c Hadlee b Boock	104	100	9/4
D.L.Haynes	lbw b Bracewell	61	109	2
R.B.Richardson	c Bracewell b Patel	12	42	–
C.L.Hooper	b Bracewell	10	11	1
A.L.Logie	not out	15	24	–
* I.V.A.Richards	not out	14	14	2
† P.J.L.Dujon				
J.Garner				
A.H.Gray				
C.A.Walsh				
B.P.Patterson				
Extras	(lb 1)	1		
Total	(49 overs; 4 wickets)	**217**		

WEST INDIES	O	M	R	W
Garner	10	4	18	1
Patterson	9	2	52	2
Walsh	9	0	45	2
Gray	7	0	35	1
Richards	10	0	34	3
Hooper	5	0	23	0

NEW ZEALAND	O	M	R	W
Hadlee	6	0	17	0
Chatfield	6	0	27	0
Snedden	4	0	27	0
Crowe	7	0	26	0
Boock	10	0	45	1
Coney	2	0	11	0
Bracewell	10	1	40	2
Patel	4	0	23	1

FALL OF WICKETS
1-0, 2-105, 3-106, 4-106, 5-134, 6-172, 7-204, 8-211, 9-211, 10-213

FALL OF WICKETS
1-134, 2-176, 3-186, 4-196

Umpires: B.L.Aldridge (3) and R.L.McHarg (3).

NEW ZEALAND v WEST INDIES 1986-87

At Lancaster Park, Christchurch on 28 March 1987.   Result: **WEST INDIES** won by 10 wickets.   Toss: New Zealand.
Award: C.G.Greenidge.   LOI debuts: None.

Gordon Greenidge, whose ninth LOI hundred emulated the tally of Viv Richards, and Desmond Haynes shared the record West Indies opening partnership of 192 and achieved the highest total to gain a ten-wicket victory in these matches.

NEW ZEALAND		Runs	Balls	4/6
K.R.Rutherford	b Garner	2	12	–
P.A.Horne	run out	15	46	1
M.D.Crowe	lbw b Walsh	42	71	5
J.J.Crowe	c Richardson b Gray	2	12	–
D.N.Patel	b Hooper	36	62	3
*J.V.Coney	b Hooper	21	42	2
J.G.Bracewell	b Hooper	0	3	–
R.J.Hadlee	c Payne b Walsh	24	28	2
†E.B.McSweeney	not out	13	18	1
M.C.Snedden	c Gray b Patterson	4	7	–
E.J.Chatfield	not out	3	5	–
Extras	(b 3, lb 9, w 12, nb 5)	29		
Total	(50 overs; 9 wickets)	**191**		

WEST INDIES		Runs	Balls	4/6
C.G.Greenidge	not out	133	140	16/4
D.L.Haynes	not out	53	100	6
R.B.Richardson				
C.L.Hooper				
*I.V.A.Richards				
A.L.Logie				
†T.R.O.Payne				
J.Garner				
A.H.Gray				
C.A.Walsh				
B.P.Patterson				
Extras	(lb 3, w 2, nb 1)	6		
Total	(39.2 overs; 0 wickets)	**192**		

WEST INDIES	O	M	R	W
Garner	10	1	33	1
Patterson	9	0	34	1
Walsh	7	0	18	2
Gray	10	2	30	1
Richards	8	0	37	0
Hooper	6	0	27	3

NEW ZEALAND	O	M	R	W
Chatfield	9	1	19	0
Hadlee	7	0	33	0
Snedden	7	0	37	0
Bracewell	5	0	26	0
M.D.Crowe	3	0	19	0
Coney	3	0	22	0
Patel	5	0	31	0
Rutherford	0.2	0	2	0

FALL OF WICKETS
1-3, 2-63, 3-74, 4-77, 5-138, 6-138, 7-145, 8-174, 9-180

Umpires: B.L.Aldridge (4) and F.R.Goodall (14).

ENGLAND v INDIA 1986-87

At Sharjah CA Stadium, UAE on 2 April 1987.   Result: **INDIA** won by 3 wickets.   Toss: India.
Award: Kapil Dev.   LOI debuts: England – D.J.Capel, N.H.Fairbrother, J.J.Whitaker.

Captained for the first time by John Emburey and bereft of Gatting, Gower, Lamb and Botham from their triumphant tour of Australia, England paid their second and most recent visit to the Emirates. Sri Lanka provided the umpires for this six-match 50-over tournament.

ENGLAND		Runs	Balls	4/6
G.A.Gooch	b Maninder	31	53	5
B.C.Broad	st Viswanath b Shastri	57	94	3
R.T.Robinson	c Srikkanth b Shastri	34	45	–
N.H.Fairbrother	c Azharuddin b Shastri	14	22	1
J.J.Whitaker	b Sharma	4	12	–
D.J.Capel	run out	8	15	–
*J.E.Emburey	b Kapil Dev	25	27	–/1
P.A.J.DeFreitas	not out	18	22	1
†C.J.Richards	not out	14	13	–
N.A.Foster				
P.H.Edmonds				
Extras	(lb 4, w 2)	6		
Total	(50 overs; 7 wickets)	**211**		

INDIA		Runs	Balls	4/6
M.Prabhakar	c Edmonds b Foster	4	25	–
K.Srikkanth	c Fairbrother b Capel	56	73	5/1
R.Lamba	c Whitaker b Edmonds	4	14	1
D.B.Vengsarkar	c Robinson b Edmonds	40	66	2
R.J.Shastri	c Edmonds b Emburey	7	21	–
*Kapil Dev	c Capel b Emburey	64	54	5/1
M.Azharuddin	not out	24	33	–
†S.Viswanath	b Emburey	3	3	–
B.Arun	not out	7	6	1
G.Sharma				
Maninder Singh				
Extras	(b 2, lb 2, w 1)	5		
Total	(48.5 overs; 7 wickets)	**214**		

INDIA	O	M	R	W
Kapil Dev	8	1	30	1
Prabhakar	8	2	17	0
Arun	4	0	32	0
Sharma	10	0	38	1
Shastri	10	1	47	3
Maninder Singh	10	0	43	1

ENGLAND	O	M	R	W
DeFreitas	10	3	33	0
Foster	9	1	46	1
Capel	10	0	45	1
Edmonds	10	0	48	2
Emburey	9.5	0	38	3

FALL OF WICKETS
1-60, 2-106, 3-134, 4-143, 5-145, 6-167, 7-184

FALL OF WICKETS
1-22, 2-33, 3-86, 4-97, 5-146, 6-194, 7-200

Umpires: D.P.Buultjens (SL) (5) and P.W.Vidanagamage (SL) (10).

AUSTRALIA v PAKISTAN 1986-87

At Sharjah CA Stadium, UAE on 3 April 1987.　　Result: **PAKISTAN** won by 6 wickets.　　Toss: Pakistan.
Award: Mudassar Nazar.　　LOI debuts: Australia – M.R.J.Veletta.

Australia lost their first three wickets for eight and their last three for one.

AUSTRALIA		Runs	Balls	4/6
G.R.Marsh	c Salim Yousuf b Manzoor	1	9	–
M.R.J.Veletta	b Wasim	0	3	–
D.C.Boon	c Miandad b Mudassar	71	132	6/1
* A.R.Border	c Salim Yousuf b Manzoor	5	15	1
S.P.O'Donnell	run out	54	69	2/2
S.R.Waugh	c Manzoor b Mudassar	8	19	1
G.R.J.Matthews	not out	9	30	–
† T.J.Zoehrer	b Mudassar	11	20	–
P.L.Taylor	run out	0	2	–
B.A.Reid	b Wasim	0	3	–
S.P.Davis	not out	2	1	–
Extras	(lb 11, w 3, nb 1)	15		
Total	(50 overs; 9 wickets)	**176**		

PAKISTAN		Runs	Balls	4/6
Mudassar Nazar	run out	64	135	4
Ramiz Raja	b Davis	3	7	–
Salim Malik	c Waugh b Reid	9	22	1
* Javed Miandad	not out	74	97	8
Ijaz Ahmed	c O'Donnell b Matthews	2	7	–
Manzoor Elahi	not out	12	15	1
Abdul Qadir				
Wasim Akram				
† Salim Yousuf				
Ijaz Faqih				
Tausif Ahmed				
Extras	(b 4, lb 7, w 2, nb 3)	16		
Total	(46.4 overs; 4 wickets)	**180**		

PAKISTAN	O	M	R	W
Wasim Akram	10	2	23	2
Manzoor Elahi	7	3	20	2
Abdul Qadir	10	1	26	0
Tausif Ahmed	8	2	19	0
Ijaz Faqih	5	0	33	0
Mudassar Nazar	10	1	44	3

AUSTRALIA	O	M	R	W
Davis	10	2	26	1
Reid	8.4	3	26	1
O'Donnell	7	1	21	0
Waugh	6	0	34	0
Matthews	10	1	31	1
Taylor	5	1	31	0

FALL OF WICKETS
1-1, 2-1, 3-8, 4-122, 5-148, 6-152, 7-171, 8-171, 9-172

FALL OF WICKETS
1-13, 2-28, 3-144, 4-147

Umpires: D.P.Buultjens (SL) (6) and P.W.Vidanagamage (SL) (11).

AUSTRALIA v INDIA 1986-87

At Sharjah CA Stadium, UAE on 5 April 1987.　　Result: **INDIA** won by 7 wickets.　　Toss: India.
Award: M.Azharuddin.　　LOI debuts: None.

Geoff Marsh led Australia for the first time in the absence of Allan Border with a finger injury. The partnership of 165 between Sunil Gavaskar and Mohammed Azharuddin was then India's record for the second wicket and remains so against Australia.

AUSTRALIA		Runs	Balls	4/6
M.R.J.Veletta	c Gavaskar b Prabhakar	5	10	–
* G.R.Marsh	c Vengsarkar b Sharma	39	89	2
D.C.Boon	c Vengsarkar b Kapil Dev	62	113	3
S.R.Waugh	c Sharma b Maninder	20	43	–
S.P.O'Donnell	c Viswanath b Maninder	5	11	–
G.M.Ritchie	lbw b Kapil Dev	3	5	–
D.M.Wellham	not out	17	17	–
G.R.J.Matthews	not out	17	16	1
† T.J.Zoehrer				
B.A.Reid				
S.P.Davis				
Extras	(b 1, lb 4, w 1, nb 2)	8		
Total	(50 overs; 6 wickets)	**176**		

INDIA		Runs	Balls	4/6
K.Srikkanth	c Matthews b Reid	0	3	–
S.M.Gavaskar	not out	78	109	6/1
M.Azharuddin	c Marsh b O'Donnell	84	129	4/1
* Kapil Dev	b Waugh	2	4	–
R.J.Shastri	not out	2	10	–
D.B.Vengsarkar				
M.Prabhakar				
B.Arun				
† S.Viswanath				
G.Sharma				
Maninder Singh				
Extras	(b 3, lb 5, w 1, nb 2)	11		
Total	(42 overs; 3 wickets)	**177**		

INDIA	O	M	R	W
Kapil Dev	8	0	36	2
Prabhakar	10	2	18	1
Maninder Singh	9	0	26	2
Arun	3	0	17	0
Sharma	10	0	46	1
Shastri	10	0	28	0

AUSTRALIA	O	M	R	W
Reid	10	1	35	1
Davis	7	2	22	0
O'Donnell	8	0	36	0
Matthews	9	0	43	0
Waugh	8	0	33	1

FALL OF WICKETS
1-0, 2-165, 3-169

FALL OF WICKETS
1-20, 2-82, 3-129, 4-136, 5-141, 6-142

Umpires: D.P.Buultjens (SL) (7) and P.W.Vidanagamage (SL) (12).

ENGLAND v PAKISTAN 1986-87

At Sharjah CA Stadium, UAE on 7 April 1987.   Result: **ENGLAND** won by 5 wickets.   Toss: England.
Award: R.T.Robinson.   LOI debuts: None.

England, who fielded outstandingly, inflicted their third defeat of the season on Pakistan. The all-Nottinghamshire partnership of 140 between Chris Broad and Tim Robinson remains England's highest for the second wicket against Pakistan.

PAKISTAN		Runs	Balls	4/6		ENGLAND		Runs	Balls	4/6
Mudassar Nazar	c Richards b DeFreitas	3	4	–		G.A.Gooch	c Salim Malik b Imran	1	9	–
Ramiz Raja	run out	44	77	3		B.C.Broad	c Ijaz b Mudassar	65	86	4
Ijaz Ahmed	run out	1	4	–		R.T.Robinson	c Manzoor b Qadir	83	104	10
Javed Miandad	run out	60	101	4		J.J.Whitaker	not out	44	53	2/1
Salim Malik	c Richards b Capel	1	10	–		N.H.Fairbrother	c Ramiz b Qadir	6	15	–
*Imran Khan	c Richards b Foster	46	65	4		D.J.Capel	st Salim Yousuf b Qadir	2	7	–
Manzoor Elahi	c and b Capel	3	7	–		*J.E.Emburey	not out	5	10	–
Wasim Akram	c Fairbrother b Capel	10	13	–/1		†C.J.Richards				
†Salim Yousuf	b Emburey	8	8	1		P.A.J.DeFreitas				
Abdul Qadir	not out	13	16	1		N.A.Foster				
Tausif Ahmed	not out	3	2	–		G.C.Small				
Extras	(b 8, lb 8, w 4, nb 5)	25				Extras	(b 2, lb 9, w 3)	14		
Total	(50 overs; 9 wickets)	**217**				**Total**	(47.2 overs; 5 wickets)	**220**		

ENGLAND	O	M	R	W		PAKISTAN	O	M	R	W
DeFreitas	10	0	47	1		Imran Khan	9	2	24	1
Small	10	2	25	0		Wasim Akram	9.2	0	38	0
Foster	10	0	47	1		Abdul Qadir	10	0	47	3
Emburey	10	1	44	1		Mudassar Nazar	10	0	41	1
Capel	10	0	38	3		Manzoor Elahi	6	0	39	0
						Tausif Ahmed	3	0	20	0

FALL OF WICKETS
1-10, 2-11, 3-77, 4-83, 5-175, 6-175, 7-188, 8-190, 9-211

FALL OF WICKETS
1-3, 2-143, 3-166, 4-182, 5-188

Umpires: D.P.Buultjens (SL) (8) and P.W.Vidanagamage (SL) (13).

ENGLAND v AUSTRALIA 1986-87

At Sharjah CA Stadium, UAE on 9 April 1987.   Result: **ENGLAND** won by 11 runs.   Toss: Australia.
Award: G.A.Gooch.   LOI debuts: None.

England recorded the highest total of this tournament and were the only side to win after batting first. The stand of 159 between David Boon and Allan Border remains Australia's highest for the third wicket against England.

ENGLAND		Runs	Balls	4/6		AUSTRALIA		Runs	Balls	4/6
G.A.Gooch	lbw b Waugh	86	119	7/1		G.R.Marsh	lbw b DeFreitas	0	1	–
B.C.Broad	b Taylor	44	86	2		D.C.Boon	c Broad b Emburey	73	108	4
R.T.Robinson	lbw b O'Donnell	5	4	1		D.M.Wellham	c Robinson b Small	2	20	–
N.H.Fairbrother	run out	32	40	2/1		*A.R.Border	c Bailey b Emburey	84	104	5
R.J.Bailey	c O'Donnell b Reid	11	25	–		S.P.O'Donnell	run out	6	8	–
D.J.Capel	run out	17	19	2		S.R.Waugh	b Foster	14	27	–
*J.E.Emburey	not out	18	10	3		G.R.J.Matthews	c Gooch b DeFreitas	13	10	–
P.A.J.DeFreitas	not out	1	1	–		†T.J.Zoehrer	run out	1	3	–
†C.J.Richards						P.L.Taylor	not out	14	12	2
N.A.Foster						B.A.Reid	run out	2	3	–
G.C.Small						S.P.Davis	not out	3	3	–
Extras	(b 1, lb 7, w 6, nb 2)	16				Extras	(lb 6, nb 1)	7		
Total	(50 overs; 6 wickets)	**230**				**Total**	(50 overs; 9 wickets)	**219**		

AUSTRALIA	O	M	R	W		ENGLAND	O	M	R	W
Reid	10	0	50	1		DeFreitas	10	1	40	2
Davis	8	3	24	0		Small	9	1	23	1
Matthews	7	0	31	0		Capel	5	0	28	0
Waugh	10	1	49	1		Gooch	6	0	34	0
Taylor	7	0	41	1		Emburey	10	1	38	2
O'Donnell	8	0	27	1		Foster	10	0	50	1

FALL OF WICKETS
1-118, 2-125, 3-167, 4-188, 5-193, 6-229

FALL OF WICKETS
1-0, 2-7, 3-166, 4-166, 5-177, 6-195, 7-200, 8-200, 9-204

Umpires: D.P.Buultjens (SL) (9) and P.W.Vidanagamage (SL) (14).

INDIA v PAKISTAN 1986-87

At Sharjah CA Stadium, UAE on 10 April 1987.   Result: **PAKISTAN** won by 8 wickets.   Toss: Pakistan.
Award: D.B.Vengsarkar.   LOI debuts: None.

To win the tournament, Pakistan needed to reach their target of 184 in 32.4 overs. Determined not to risk losing to their arch rivals, they eschewed all risks and were content to allow England to win the Sharjah Cup and £18,750 prize-money on superior run rate.

INDIA		Runs	Balls	4/6
K.Srikkanth	c Salim Yousuf b Wasim	5	15	–
S.M.Gavaskar	b Imran	0	8	–
M.Azharuddin	lbw b Imran	1	5	–
D.B.Vengsarkar	not out	95	151	7
M.Prabhakar	run out	33	51	2
R.J.Shastri	c Miandad b Qadir	8	23	1
*Kapil Dev	c Salim Yousuf b Imran	19	27	1
†S.Viswanath	run out	2	6	–
B.Arun	c Ramiz b Imran	6	14	–
Maninder Singh	not out	2	3	–
G.Sharma				
Extras	(b 1, lb 6, w 3, nb 2)	12		
Total	(50 overs; 8 wickets)	**183**		

PAKISTAN		Runs	Balls	4/6
Ramiz Raja	c sub (C.S.Pandit) b Shastri	53	72	4
Ijaz Ahmed	b Maninder	9	13	1
Salim Malik	not out	61	98	2
Javed Miandad	not out	52	67	5
*Imran Khan				
Manzoor Elahi				
Mudassar Nazar				
†Salim Yousuf				
Wasim Akram				
Abdul Qadir				
Salim Jaffer				
Extras	(b 3, lb 6)	9		
Total	(41.4 overs; 2 wickets)	**184**		

PAKISTAN	O	M	R	W
Imran Khan	10	1	27	4
Wasim Akram	10	2	21	1
Manzoor Elahi	5	0	29	0
Mudassar Nazar	10	0	39	0
Salim Jaffer	5	0	21	0
Abdul Qadir	10	1	39	1

INDIA	O	M	R	W
Kapil Dev	8	1	27	0
Prabhakar	4	0	30	0
Maninder Singh	10	2	28	1
Shastri	10	0	37	1
Sharma	7	0	36	0
Arun	2	0	11	0
Azharuddin	0.4	0	6	0

FALL OF WICKETS
1-5, 2-5, 3-7, 4-82, 5-116, 6-151, 7-160, 8-179

FALL OF WICKETS
1-22, 2-91

Umpires: D.P.Buultjens (SL) (10) and P.W.Vidanagamage (SL) (15).

ENGLAND v PAKISTAN 1987

At Kennington Oval, London on 21 May 1987.   Result: **ENGLAND** won by 7 wickets.   Toss: England.
Award: B.C.Broad.   LOI debuts: None.

The fourth of Javed Miandad's eight LOI hundreds was his only one against England. David Gower became the first to appear in 100 limited-overs internationals for England. Mike Gatting retired at tea (83 for 1) because of an infected toe.

PAKISTAN		Runs	Balls	4/6
Mudassar Nazar	c DeFreitas b Foster	45	129	3
Ramiz Raja	run out	0	–	–
Mansoor Akhtar	c Gatting b Dilley	12	17	1
Javed Miandad	c Lamb b Dilley	113	145	11
*Imran Khan	c Broad b Foster	7	18	–
Wasim Akram	b Emburey	12	11	–/1
Manzoor Elahi	not out	18	11	1
Salim Malik	not out	8	6	–
Ijaz Ahmed				
†Salim Yousuf				
Tausif Ahmed				
Extras	(b 1, lb 8, w 4, nb 4)	17		
Total	(55 overs; 6 wickets)	**232**		

ENGLAND		Runs	Balls	4/6
B.C.Broad	c sub (Asif Mujtaba) b Wasim	99	168	4
C.W.J.Athey	c Salim Malik b Mudassar	33	61	3
*M.W.Gatting	retired hurt	2	3	–
A.J.Lamb	c sub (Asif Mujtaba) b Tausif	61	71	3/1
D.I.Gower	not out	15	15	1
I.T.Botham	not out	6	10	1
†C.J.Richards				
J.E.Emburey				
P.A.J.DeFreitas				
N.A.Foster				
G.R.Dilley				
Extras	(lb 9, w 2, nb 6)	17		
Total	(53.1 overs; 3 wickets)	**233**		

ENGLAND	O	M	R	W
Dilley	11	1	63	2
DeFreitas	11	3	50	0
Botham	11	2	38	0
Foster	11	0	36	2
Emburey	11	1	36	1

PAKISTAN	O	M	R	W
Imran Khan	8	0	30	0
Manzoor Elahi	11	1	31	0
Wasim Akram	11	0	60	1
Mudassar Nazar	11	1	41	1
Tausif Ahmed	10.1	0	47	1
Mansoor Akhtar	2	0	15	0

FALL OF WICKETS
1-0, 2-18, 3-128, 4-169, 5-206, 6-208

FALL OF WICKETS
1-76, 2-199, 3-218

Umpires: D.R.Shepherd (20) and A.G.T.Whitehead (12).

ENGLAND v PAKISTAN 1987

At Trent Bridge, Nottingham on 23 May 1987.   Result: **PAKISTAN** won by 6 wickets.   Toss: Pakistan.
Award: Javed Miandad.   LOI debuts: None.

In Mike Gatting's absence John Emburey led England at home for the first time. Pakistan ended a run of four defeats against England.

ENGLAND		Runs	Balls	4/6
B.C.Broad	c Salim Yousuf b Wasim	52	84	3
C.W.J.Athey	lbw b Imran	1	10	–
G.A.Gooch	lbw b Mohsin	9	30	1
A.J.Lamb	c Salim Yousuf b Tausif	26	57	–
D.I.Gower	b Mudassar	24	43	1
I.T.Botham	c Mohsin b Tausif	0	8	–
† C.J.Richards	c Manzoor b Mohsin	0	9	–
* J.E.Emburey	b Wasim	25	44	3
P.A.J.DeFreitas	c Manzoor b Imran	3	9	–
N.A.Foster	run out	5	13	–
G.R.Dilley	not out	0	–	–
Extras	(lb 8, w 4)	12		
Total	**(51.1 overs)**	**157**		

PAKISTAN		Runs	Balls	4/6
Mudassar Nazar	lbw b Foster	12	39	1
Ramiz Raja	c Gooch b DeFreitas	13	30	1
Mansoor Akhtar	b Foster	21	52	3
Javed Miandad	not out	71	129	3
Salim Malik	run out	9	19	1
* Imran Khan	not out	21	46	–/1
Manzoor Elahi				
Wasim Akram				
† Salim Yousuf				
Tausif Ahmed				
Mohsin Kamal				
Extras	(lb 8, w 2, nb 1)	11		
Total	**(52 overs; 4 wickets)**	**158**		

PAKISTAN	O	M	R	W
Imran Khan	9	1	31	2
Mohsin Kamal	11	1	31	2
Wasim Akram	9.1	1	18	2
Mudassar Nazar	11	1	36	1
Tausif Ahmed	11	1	33	2

ENGLAND	O	M	R	W
Dilley	9	4	16	0
DeFreitas	11	2	30	1
Foster	11	1	25	2
Botham	7	0	34	0
Emburey	11	2	33	0
Gooch	3	0	12	0

FALL OF WICKETS
1-15, 2-45, 3-75, 4-117, 5-117, 6-117, 7-121, 8-144, 9-157, 10-157

FALL OF WICKETS
1-23, 2-29, 3-64, 4-81

Umpires: D.J.Constant (27) and B.J.Meyer (18).

ENGLAND v PAKISTAN 1987

At Edgbaston, Birmingham on 25 May 1987.   Result: **ENGLAND** won by 1 wicket.   Toss: England.
Award: P.A.J.DeFreitas.   LOI debuts: None.

Javed Miandad extended his sequence of successive fifties to eight. Mudassar Nazar, dismissed by the first ball of the match, took his 100th wicket and completed the career double of 1000 runs and 100 wickets in his 106th international.

PAKISTAN		Runs	Balls	4/6
Mudassar Nazar	lbw b Thomas	0	1	–
Ramiz Raja	run out	46	72	6
Mansoor Akhtar	c Richards b Thomas	0	3	–
Javed Miandad	c Gower b Foster	68	128	3
Salim Malik	b Emburey	45	61	3
* Imran Khan	not out	24	41	–/2
Manzoor Elahi	b Emburey	0	2	–
† Salim Yousuf	run out	0	3	–
Wasim Akram	c Richards b Foster	0	5	–
Tausif Ahmed	b Foster	0	5	–
Mohsin Kamal	not out	11	12	2
Extras	(b 2, lb 13, w 1, nb 3)	19		
Total	**(55 overs; 9 wickets)**	**213**		

ENGLAND		Runs	Balls	4/6
B.C.Broad	c Miandad b Mohsin	15	38	–
C.W.J.Athey	c Salim Yousuf b Imran	5	26	–
D.I.Gower	b Mudassar	11	20	–
A.J.Lamb	c Mansoor b Mudassar	14	48	–
* M.W.Gatting	c Miandad b Mohsin	41	56	6
I.T.Botham	c sub (Asif Mujtaba) b Tausif	24	39	2
† C.J.Richards	run out	16	37	–
J.E.Emburey	run out	16	19	–/1
N.A.Foster	not out	14	21	1
P.A.J.DeFreitas	b Imran	33	22	4/1
J.G.Thomas	not out	1	3	–
Extras	(lb 14, w 12, nb 1)	27		
Total	**(54.3 overs; 9 wickets)**	**217**		

ENGLAND	O	M	R	W
Thomas	11	0	59	2
DeFreitas	11	1	30	0
Botham	11	1	31	0
Foster	11	1	29	3
Emburey	11	1	49	2

PAKISTAN	O	M	R	W
Imran Khan	11	0	43	2
Mohsin Kamal	11	0	47	2
Wasim Akram	10.3	2	34	0
Mudassar Nazar	11	2	17	2
Tausif Ahmed	11	0	62	1

FALL OF WICKETS
1-0, 2-0, 3-73, 4-168, 5-170, 6-170, 7-170, 8-170, 9-178

FALL OF WICKETS
1-18, 2-31, 3-34, 4-75, 5-105, 6-140, 7-155, 8-167, 9-209

Umpires: H.D.Bird (43) and K.E.Palmer (15).

PAKISTAN v SRI LANKA 1987-88

At Niaz Stadium, Hyderabad, Pakistan, on 8 October 1987.   Result: **PAKISTAN** won by 15 runs.   Toss: Pakistan.
Award: Javed Miandad.   LOI debuts: None.

Sponsored by Reliance Industrial of Bombay, the first oriental World Cup lasted more than five weeks involving 27 matches and 21 venues in India and Pakistan. Fewer daylight hours compelled 9am starts and 50-over innings. Javed Miandad extended his record run of fifties to nine and completed 4000 runs. Imran Khan's 100th wicket completed his career double.

PAKISTAN		Runs	Balls	4/6
Ramiz Raja	c Ratnayake b Anurasiri	76	115	3
Ijaz Ahmed	c Kuruppu b Ratnayake	16	34	2
Mansoor Akhtar	c Ratnayake b Ratnayeke	12	23	–
Javed Miandad	b Ratnayeke	103	100	6
Wasim Akram	run out	14	14	–
Salim Malik	not out	18	12	1
* Imran Khan	b Ratnayake	2	4	–
† Salim Yousuf	not out	1	1	–
Mudassar Nazar				
Abdul Qadir				
Tausif Ahmed				
Extras	(lb 15, w 9, nb 1)	25		
Total	(50 overs; 6 wickets)	**267**		

SRI LANKA		Runs	Balls	4/6
R.S.Mahanama	c Miandad b Mansoor	89	117	7/1
† D.S.B.P.Kuruppu	c Salim Yousuf b Imran	9	24	1
R.L.Dias	b Qadir	5	21	–
A.Ranatunga	b Tausif	24	29	3
* L.R.D.Mendis	run out	1	6	–
A.P.Gurusinha	b Qadir	37	39	2/1
P.A.de Silva	b Imran	42	32	3/1
J.R.Ratnayeke	c Salim Yousuf b Wasim	7	13	–
R.J.Ratnayake	c Mudassar b Wasim	8	9	–
V.B.John	not out	1	4	–
S.D.Anurasiri	run out	0	3	–
Extras	(b 7, lb 14, w 7, nb 1)	29		
Total	(49.2 overs)	**252**		

SRI LANKA	O	M	R	W
John	10	2	37	0
Ratnayake	10	0	64	2
Ratnayeke	9	0	47	2
De Silva	10	0	44	0
Anurasiri	10	0	52	1
Gurusinha	1	0	8	0

PAKISTAN	O	M	R	W
Imran Khan	10	2	42	2
Wasim Akram	9.2	1	41	2
Mudassar Nazar	9	0	63	0
Abdul Qadir	10	1	30	2
Tausif Ahmed	10	0	48	1
Mansoor Akhtar	1	0	7	1

FALL OF WICKETS
1-48, 2-67, 3-180, 4-226, 5-259, 6-266

FALL OF WICKETS
1-29, 2-57, 3-100, 4-103, 5-182, 6-190, 7-209, 8-223, 9-251, 10-252

Umpires: V.K.Ramaswamy (India) (4) and S.J.Woodward (New Zealand) (8).

ENGLAND v WEST INDIES 1987-88

At Municipal Stadium, Gujranwala, Pakistan, on 9 October 1987.   Result: **ENGLAND** won by 2 wickets.   Toss: England.
Award: A.J.Lamb.   LOI debuts: None.

Derek Pringle's concession of 22 runs from the 49th over was counterbalanced when 31 runs were scored (22 by Allan Lamb) off Courtney Walsh's last two overs, the final one producing 15: (Lamb) 2, 4, 4 wides, 1 off a no-ball; (Neil Foster) 4.

WEST INDIES		Runs	Balls	4/6
D.L.Haynes	run out	19	45	1
C.A.Best	b DeFreitas	5	15	–
R.B.Richardson	b Foster	53	80	8
* I.V.A.Richards	b Foster	27	36	3
† P.J.L.Dujon	run out	46	76	3
A.L.Logie	b Foster	49	41	3/1
R.A.Harper	b Small	24	10	3/1
C.L.Hooper	not out	1	2	–
W.K.M.Benjamin	not out	7	2	1
C.A.Walsh				
B.P.Patterson				
Extras	(lb 9, nb 3)	12		
Total	(50 overs; 7 wickets)	**243**		

ENGLAND		Runs	Balls	4/6
G.A.Gooch	c Dujon b Hooper	47	93	3
B.C.Broad	c Dujon b Walsh	3	12	–
R.T.Robinson	run out	12	35	1
* M.W.Gatting	b Hooper	25	23	3
A.J.Lamb	not out	67	68	5/1
D.R.Pringle	c Best b Hooper	12	23	–
† P.R.Downton	run out	3	4	–
J.E.Emburey	b Patterson	22	15	2/1
P.A.J.DeFreitas	b Patterson	23	21	2
N.A.Foster	not out	9	6	1
G.C.Small				
Extras	(lb 14, w 6, nb 3)	23		
Total	(49.3 overs; 8 wickets)	**246**		

ENGLAND	O	M	R	W
DeFreitas	10	2	31	1
Foster	10	0	53	3
Emburey	10	1	22	0
Small	10	0	45	1
Pringle	10	0	83	0

WEST INDIES	O	M	R	W
Patterson	10	0	49	2
Walsh	9.3	0	65	1
Harper	10	0	44	0
Benjamin	10	2	32	0
Hooper	10	0	42	3

FALL OF WICKETS
1-8, 2-53, 3-105, 4-122, 5-205, 6-235, 7-235

FALL OF WICKETS
1-14, 2-40, 3-98, 4-99, 5-123, 6-131, 7-162, 8-209,

Umpires: A.R.Crafter (Australia) (52) and R.B.Gupta (India) (4).

INDIA v AUSTRALIA 1987-88

At M.A.Chidambaram Stadium, Madras, India, on 9 October 1987.　Result: **AUSTRALIA** won by 1 run.　Toss: India.
Award: G.R.Marsh.　LOI debuts: India – N.S.Sidhu; Australia – T.M.Moody.

Almost six years after India had staged its inaugural international, its third-oldest Test ground provided the 79th LOI
venue. Australia's victory remains the narrowest by a runs margin in all World Cup tournaments.

AUSTRALIA		Runs	Balls	4/6
D.C.Boon	lbw b Shastri	49	68	5
G.R.Marsh	c Azharuddin b Prabhakar	110	141	7/1
D.M.Jones	c Sidhu b Maninder	39	35	2/2
* A.R.Border	b Binny	16	22	–
T.M.Moody	c Kapil Dev b Prabhakar	8	13	1
S.R.Waugh	not out	19	17	–
S.P.O'Donnell	run out	7	10	–
† G.C.Dyer				
P.L.Taylor				
C.J.McDermott				
B.A.Reid				
Extras	(lb 18, w 2, nb 2)	22		
Total	(50 overs; 6 wickets)	**270**		

INDIA	O	M	R	W
Kapil Dev	10	0	41	0
Prabhakar	10	0	47	2
Binny	7	0	46	1
Maninder	10	0	48	1
Shastri	10	0	50	1
Azharuddin	3	0	20	0

INDIA		Runs	Balls	4/6
K.Srikkanth	lbw b Waugh	70	83	7
S.M.Gavaskar	c Reid b Taylor	37	32	6/1
N.S.Sidhu	b McDermott	73	79	4/5
D.B.Vengsarkar	c Jones b McDermott	29	45	2
M.Azharuddin	b McDermott	10	14	1
* Kapil Dev	c Boon b O'Donnell	6	10	–
R.J.Shastri	c and b McDermott	12	11	1
† K.S.More	not out	12	14	2
R.M.H.Binny	run out	0	3	–
M.Prabhakar	run out	5	7	–
Maninder Singh	b Waugh	4	5	–
Extras	(b 2, lb 7, w 2)	11		
Total	(49.5 overs)	**269**		

AUSTRALIA	O	M	R	W
McDermott	10	0	56	4
Reid	10	2	35	0
O'Donnell	9	1	32	1
Taylor	5	0	46	1
Waugh	9.5	0	52	2
Border	6	0	39	0

FALL OF WICKETS
1-110, 2-174, 3-228, 4-237, 5-251, 6-270

FALL OF WICKETS
1-69, 2-131, 3-207, 4-229, 5-232, 6-246, 7-256, 8-256, 9-265, 10-269

Umpires: D.M.Archer (*West Indies*) (11) and H.D.Bird (*England*) (44).

NEW ZEALAND v ZIMBABWE 1987-88

At Lal Bahadur Stadium, Hyderabad, India, on 10 October 1987.　Result: **NEW ZEALAND** won by 3 runs.　Toss: Zimbabwe.
Award: D.L.Houghton.　LOI debuts: New Zealand – A.H.Jones; Zimbabwe – E.A.Brandes, A.C.Waller.

David Houghton's 142, Zimbabwe's first hundred in limited-overs internationals, remains the national record in these
matches. His partnership of 117 with Iain Butchart is the eighth-wicket record in World Cup matches.

NEW ZEALAND		Runs	Balls	4/6
M.C.Snedden	c Waller b Rawson	64	96	3
J.G.Wright	c Houghton b Traicos	18	40	1
M.D.Crowe	c and b Rawson	72	88	5/1
A.H.Jones	c Brandes b Shah	0	6	–
* J.J.Crowe	c Brown b Curran	31	35	2
D.N.Patel	lbw b Shah	0	2	–
J.G.Bracewell	not out	13	20	–
† I.D.S.Smith	c Brown b Curran	29	20	2/1
S.L.Boock	not out	0	–	–
W.Watson				
E.J.Chatfield				
Extras	(b 4, lb 4, w 4, nb 3)	15		
Total	(50 overs; 7 wickets)	**242**		

ZIMBABWE	O	M	R	W
Curran	10	0	51	2
Rawson	10	0	62	2
Brandes	7	2	24	0
Traicos	10	2	28	1
Butchart	4	0	27	0
Shah	9	0	42	2

ZIMBABWE		Runs	Balls	4/6
R.D.Brown	c J.J.Crowe b Chatfield	1	10	–
A.H.Shah	lbw b Snedden	5	13	–
† D.L.Houghton	c M.D.Crowe b Snedden	142	137	13/6
A.J.Pycroft	run out	12	22	2
K.M.Curran	c Boock b Watson	4	8	–
A.C.Waller	c Smith b Watson	5	14	–
G.A.Paterson	c Smith b Boock	2	11	–
P.W.E.Rawson	lbw b Boock	1	10	–
I.P.Butchart	run out	54	70	2/1
E.A.Brandes	run out	0	–	–
* A.J.Traicos	not out	4	6	–
Extras	(lb 7, w 1, nb 1)	9		
Total	(49.4 overs)	**239**		

NEW ZEALAND	O	M	R	W
Chatfield	10	2	26	1
Snedden	9	0	53	2
Watson	10	2	36	2
Bracewell	7	0	48	0
Patel	5	0	27	0
Boock	8.4	0	42	2

FALL OF WICKETS
1-59, 2-143, 3-145, 4-166, 5-169, 6-205, 7-240

FALL OF WICKETS
1-8, 2-10, 3-61, 4-67, 5-86, 6-94, 7-104, 8-221, 9-221, 10-239

Umpires: Mahboob Shah (*Pakistan*) (11) and P.W.Vidanagamage (*Sri Lanka*) (16).

PAKISTAN v ENGLAND 1987-88

At Pindi Club Ground, Rawalpindi, Pakistan, on 12 (*no play*), 13 October 1987.   Result: **PAKISTAN** won by 18 runs.
Toss: England.   Award: Abdul Qadir.   LOI debuts: None.

A saturated outfield precluded play on the first day. England lost their last six wickets for 15 runs in 16 balls. Pakistan set a record (until *LOI 547*) by conceding 40 extras. Imran Khan achieved the first instance of a denizen being unable to take the field in an international in Pakistan because of food poisoning.

PAKISTAN		Runs	Balls	4/6
Mansoor Akhtar	c Downton b Foster	6	24	1
Ramiz Raja	run out	15	40	1
Salim Malik	c Downton b DeFreitas	65	80	8
Javed Miandad	lbw b DeFreitas	23	50	3
Ijaz Ahmed	c Robinson b Small	59	59	4/1
* Imran Khan	b Small	22	32	2
Wasim Akram	b DeFreitas	5	3	1
† Salim Yousuf	not out	16	10	–
Abdul Qadir	not out	12	7	1/1
Tausif Ahmed				
Salim Jaffer				
Extras	(lb 10, w 3, nb 3)	16		
Total	(50 overs; 7 wickets)	**239**		

ENGLAND		Runs	Balls	4/6
G.A.Gooch	b Qadir	21	41	3
B.C.Broad	b Tausif	36	78	2
R.T.Robinson	b Qadir	33	62	1
* M.W.Gatting	b Salim Jaffer	43	47	4
A.J.Lamb	lbw b Qadir	30	38	3
D.R.Pringle	run out	8	14	–
J.E.Emburey	run out	1	1	–
† P.R.Downton	c Salim Yousuf b Qadir	0	2	–
P.A.J.DeFreitas	not out	3	3	–
N.A.Foster	run out	6	5	–
G.C.Small	lbw b Salim Jaffer	0	1	–
Extras	(b 6, lb 26, w 8)	40		
Total	(48.4 overs)	**221**		

ENGLAND	O	M	R	W
DeFreitas	10	1	42	3
Foster	10	1	35	1
Small	10	1	47	2
Pringle	10	0	54	0
Emburey	10	0	51	0

PAKISTAN	O	M	R	W
Wasim Akram	9	0	32	0
Salim Jaffer	9.4	0	42	2
Tausif Ahmed	10	0	39	1
Abdul Qadir	10	0	31	4
Salim Malik	7	0	29	0
Mansoor Akhtar	3	0	16	0

FALL OF WICKETS
1-13, 2-51, 3-112, 4-123, 5-202, 6-210, 7-210

FALL OF WICKETS
1-52, 2-92, 3-141, 4-186, 5-206, 6-207, 7-207, 8-213, 9-221, 10-221

Umpires: A.R.Crafter (*Australia*) (53) and R.B.Gupta (*India*) (5).

AUSTRALIA v ZIMBABWE 1987-88

At M.A.Chidambaram Stadium, Madras, India, on 13 October 1987.   Result: **AUSTRALIA** won by 96 runs.
Toss: Zimbabwe.   Award: S.R.Waugh.   LOI debuts: Australia – T.B.A.May; Zimbabwe – M.P.Jarvis.

Allan Border completed 4000 runs in his 155th match.

AUSTRALIA		Runs	Balls	4/6
G.R.Marsh	c Curran b Shah	62	101	8
D.C.Boon	c Houghton b Curran	2	15	–
D.M.Jones	run out	2	12	–
* A.R.Border	c Shah b Butchart	67	88	8
S.R.Waugh	run out	45	41	3/2
S.P.O'Donnell	run out	3	11	–
† G.C.Dyer	c Paterson b Butchart	27	20	1/2
P.L.Taylor	not out	17	13	1
C.J.McDermott	c Brown b Curran	1	3	–
T.B.A.May	run out	1	1	–
B.A.Reid				
Extras	(w 8)	8		
Total	(50 overs; 9 wickets)	**235**		

ZIMBABWE		Runs	Balls	4/6
R.D.Brown	b O'Donnell	3	30	–
G.A.Paterson	run out	16	53	1
† D.L.Houghton	c O'Donnell b May	11	22	1
A.J.Pycroft	run out	9	29	1
K.M.Curran	b O'Donnell	30	38	1/3
A.C.Waller	c and b May	19	22	1/1
A.H.Shah	b McDermott	2	9	–
P.W.E.Rawson	b Reid	15	14	2
I.P.Butchart	c Jones b O'Donnell	18	32	2
* A.J.Traicos	c and b O'Donnell	6	5	1
M.P.Jarvis	not out	1	1	–
Extras	(b 2, lb 3, w 3, nb 1)	9		
Total	(42.4 overs)	**139**		

ZIMBABWE	O	M	R	W
Curran	8	0	29	2
Jarvis	10	0	40	0
Rawson	6	0	39	0
Butchart	10	1	59	2
Traicos	10	0	36	0
Shah	6	0	32	1

AUSTRALIA	O	M	R	W
McDermott	7	1	13	1
Reid	7	1	21	1
O'Donnell	9.4	1	39	4
Waugh	6	3	7	0
May	8	0	29	2
Taylor	5	0	25	0

FALL OF WICKETS
1-10, 2-20, 3-133, 4-143, 5-155, 6-202, 7-228, 8-230, 9-235

FALL OF WICKETS
1-13, 2-27, 3-41, 4-44, 5-79, 6-97, 7-97, 8-124, 9-137, 10-139

Umpires: Khizer Hayat (*Pakistan*) (13) and D.R.Shepherd (*England*) (21).

WEST INDIES v SRI LANKA 1987-88

At National Stadium, Karachi, Pakistan, on 13 October 1987.   Result: **WEST INDIES** won by 191 runs.   Toss: Sri Lanka.
Award: I.V.A.Richards.   LOI debuts: None.

West Indies amassed their highest total and the record in all LOIs until 1992. Viv Richards, who began his tenth
hundred on a hat-trick, reached 50 off 62 balls, 100 off 97 and 150 off a record (until *LOI No. 1009*) 112. His score and
the West Indies total remained World Cup records until 1995-96.

WEST INDIES		Runs	Balls	4/6
D.L.Haynes	b Gurusinha	105	124	10/1
C.A.Best	b Ratnayeke	18	30	1
R.B.Richardson	c Kuruppu b Ratnayeke	0	1	–
* I.V.A.Richards	c Mahanama b De Mel	181	125	16/7
A.L.Logie	not out	31	25	–
R.A.Harper	not out	5	2	–
C.L.Hooper				
† P.J.L.Dujon				
W.K.M.Benjamin				
C.A.Walsh				
B.P.Patterson				
Extras	(b 4, lb 8, w 4, nb 4)	20		
Total	(50 overs; 4 wickets)	360		

SRI LANKA		Runs	Balls	4/6
R.S.Mahanama	c Dujon b Walsh	12	4	3
† D.S.B.P.Kuruppu	lbw b Patterson	14	14	–
A.P.Gurusinha	b Hooper	36	108	1/1
P.A.de Silva	c Dujon b Hooper	9	27	–
A.Ranatunga	not out	52	93	5
* L.R.D.Mendis	not out	37	45	5
R.S.Madugalle				
J.R.Ratnayeke				
A.L.F.de Mel				
V.B.John				
S.D.Anurasiri				
Extras	(b 1, lb 2, w 6)	9		
Total	(50 overs; 4 wickets)	169		

SRI LANKA	O	M	R	W
John	10	1	48	0
Ratnayeke	8	0	68	2
Anurasiri	10	0	39	0
De Mel	10	0	97	1
De Silva	6	0	35	0
Ranatunga	2	0	18	0
Gurusinha	4	0	43	1

WEST INDIES	O	M	R	W
Patterson	7	0	32	1
Walsh	7	2	23	1
Harper	10	2	15	0
Benjamin	4	0	11	0
Hooper	10	0	39	2
Richards	8	0	22	0
Richardson	4	0	24	0

FALL OF WICKETS
1-45, 2-45, 3-227, 4-343

FALL OF WICKETS
1-24, 2-31, 3-57, 4-112

Umpires: V.K.Ramaswamy (*India*) (5) and S.J.Woodward (*New Zealand*) (9).

INDIA v NEW ZEALAND 1987-88

At Chinnaswamy Stadium, Bangalore, India, on 14 October 1987.   Result: **INDIA** won by 16 runs.
Toss: New Zealand.   Award: Kapil Dev.   LOI debuts: None.

Kapil Dev, whose 50 took 43 balls, added 82 off the last 52 balls with Kiran More.

INDIA		Runs	Balls	4/6
K.Srikkanth	run out	9	19	1
S.M.Gavaskar	run out	2	14	–
N.S.Sidhu	c Jones b Patel	75	71	4/4
D.B.Vengsarkar	c and b Watson	0	8	–
M.Azharuddin	c Boock b Patel	21	57	1
R.J.Shastri	c and b Patel	22	44	–/1
* Kapil Dev	not out	72	58	4/1
M.Prabhakar	c and b Chatfield	3	5	–
† K.S.More	not out	42	26	5
L.Sivaramakrishnan				
Maninder Singh				
Extras	(lb 4, w 2)	6		
Total	(50 overs; 7 wickets)	252		

NEW ZEALAND		Runs	Balls	4/6
M.C.Snedden	c Shastri b Azharuddin	33	63	2
K.R.Rutherford	c Srikkanth b Shastri	75	95	6/2
M.D.Crowe	st More b Maninder	9	12	1
A.H.Jones	run out	64	86	2
* J.J.Crowe	c Vengsarkar b Maninder	7	11	–
D.N.Patel	run out	1	3	–
J.G.Bracewell	c Maninder b Shastri	8	14	–
† I.D.S.Smith	b Prabhakar	10	5	–
S.L.Boock	not out	7	8	–
W.Watson	not out	2	3	–
E.J.Chatfield				
Extras	(b 5, lb 9, w 5, nb 1)	20		
Total	(50 overs; 8 wickets)	236		

NEW ZEALAND	O	M	R	W
Chatfield	10	1	39	1
Snedden	10	1	56	0
Watson	9	0	59	1
Boock	4	0	26	0
Bracewell	7	0	32	0
Patel	10	0	36	3

INDIA	O	M	R	W
Kapil Dev	10	1	54	0
Prabhakar	8	0	38	1
Azharuddin	4	0	11	1
Sivaramakrishnan	8	0	34	0
Maninder	10	0	40	2
Shastri	10	0	45	2

FALL OF WICKETS
1-11, 2-16, 3-21, 4-86, 5-114, 6-165, 7-170

FALL OF WICKETS
1-67, 2-86, 3-146, 4-168, 5-170, 6-189, 7-206, 8-225

Umpires: D.M.Archer (*West Indies*) (12) and H.D.Bird (*England*) (45).

PAKISTAN v WEST INDIES 1987-88

At Gaddafi Stadium, Lahore, Pakistan, on 16 October 1987.   Result: **PAKISTAN** won by 1 wicket.   Toss: West Indies.
Award: Salim Yousuf.   LOI debuts: West Indies – P.V.Simmons.

With Pakistan's last pair requiring 14 from the final over bowled by Courtney Walsh, Salim Jaffer (1) and Abdul Qadir (12622) delighted the 50,000 crowd. Walsh declined to run out Jaffer off the last ball for backing up too eagerly.

WEST INDIES		Runs	Balls	4/6
D.L.Haynes	b Salim Jaffer	37	81	3
P.V.Simmons	c and b Tausif	50	57	8
R.B.Richardson	c Ijaz b Salim Jaffer	11	22	1
I.V.A.Richards	c Salim Malik b Imran	51	52	4/1
A.L.Logie	c Mansoor b Salim Jaffer	2	4	–
C.L.Hooper	lbw b Wasim	22	37	2
P.J.L.Dujon	lbw b Wasim	5	12	–
R.A.Harper	c Mansoor b Imran	0	1	–
E.A.E.Baptiste	b Imran	14	20	1
C.A.Walsh	lbw b Imran	7	6	1
B.P.Patterson	not out	0	4	–
Extras	(b 1, lb 14, w 2)	17		
Total	**(49.3 overs)**	**216**		

PAKISTAN		Runs	Balls	4/6
Ramiz Raja	c Richards b Harper	42	87	1
Mansoor Akhtar	b Patterson	10	24	2
Salim Malik	c Baptiste b Walsh	4	7	1
Javed Miandad	c and b Hooper	33	72	1
Ijaz Ahmed	b Walsh	6	14	–
* Imran Khan	c Logie b Walsh	18	26	1
† Salim Yousuf	c Hooper b Walsh	56	49	7
Wasim Akram	c Richardson b Patterson	7	8	–
Abdul Qadir	not out	16	9	–/1
Tausif Ahmed	run out	0	1	–
Salim Jaffer	not out	1	3	–
Extras	(b 5, lb 12, w 7)	24		
Total	**(50 overs; 9 wickets)**	**217**		

PAKISTAN	O	M	R	W
Imran Khan	8.3	2	37	4
Wasim Akram	10	0	45	2
Abdul Qadir	8	0	42	0
Tausif Ahmed	10	2	35	1
Salim Jaffer	10	0	30	3
Salim Malik	3	0	12	0

WEST INDIES	O	M	R	W
Patterson	10	1	51	2
Walsh	10	1	40	4
Baptiste	8	1	33	0
Harper	10	0	28	1
Hooper	10	0	38	1
Richards	2	0	10	0

FALL OF WICKETS
1-91, 2-97, 3-118, 4-121, 5-169, 6-184, 7-184, 8-196, 9-207, 10-216

FALL OF WICKETS
1-23, 2-28, 3-92, 4-104, 5-110, 6-183, 7-200, 8-202, 9-203

Umpires: A.R.Crafter (*Australia*) (54) and S.J.Woodward (*New Zealand*) (10).

ENGLAND v SRI LANKA 1987-88

At Shahi Bagh Stadium, Peshawar, Pakistan, on 17 October 1987.   Result: **ENGLAND** won by 109 runs (revised target).
Toss: England.   Award: A.J.Lamb.   LOI debuts: None.

A storm from the Khyber interrupted Sri Lanka's innings, reducing their target to 267 from 45 overs.

ENGLAND		Runs	Balls	4/6
G.A.Gooch	c and b Anurasiri	84	100	8
B.C.Broad	c De Silva b Ratnayeke	28	60	1
M.W.Gatting	b Ratnayake	58	63	3
A.J.Lamb	c De Silva b Ratnayeke	76	58	3/2
J.E.Emburey	not out	30	19	3/1
C.W.J.Athey	not out	2	2	–
† P.R.Downton				
P.A.J.DeFreitas				
D.R.Pringle				
E.E.Hemmings				
G.C.Small				
Extras	(lb 13, w 5)	18		
Total	**(50 overs; 4 wickets)**	**296**		

SRI LANKA		Runs	Balls	4/6
R.S.Mahanama	c Gooch b Pringle	11	39	2
† D.S.B.P.Kuruppu	c Hemmings b Emburey	13	26	1
A.P.Gurusinha	run out	1	12	–
R.S.Madugalle	b Hemmings	30	49	3
A.Ranatunga	lbw b DeFreitas	40	67	4
* L.R.D.Mendis	run out	14	33	1
P.A.de Silva	c Emburey b Hemmings	6	14	–
J.R.Ratnayeke	c Broad b Emburey	1	5	–
R.J.Ratnayake	not out	14	22	1
V.B.John	not out	8	7	1
S.D.Anurasiri				
Extras	(b 2, lb 9, w 6, nb 3)	20		
Total	**(45 overs; 8 wickets)**	**158**		

SRI LANKA	O	M	R	W
Ratnayeke	9	0	62	2
John	10	0	44	0
De Silva	7	0	33	0
Ratnayake	10	0	60	1
Anurasiri	8	0	44	1
Ranatunga	6	0	40	0

ENGLAND	O	M	R	W
DeFreitas	9	2	24	1
Small	7	0	27	0
Pringle	4	0	11	1
Emburey	10	1	26	2
Hemmings	10	1	31	2
Gooch	2	0	9	0
Athey	1	0	10	0
Broad	1	0	6	0
Lamb	1	0	3	0

FALL OF WICKETS
1-89, 2-142, 3-218, 4-287

FALL OF WICKETS
1-31, 2-32, 3-37, 4-99, 5-105, 6-113, 7-119, 8-137

Umpires: R.B.Gupta (*India*) (6) and V.K.Ramaswamy (*India*) (6).

INDIA v ZIMBABWE 1987-88

At Wankhede Stadium, Bombay, India, on 17 October 1987.   Result: **INDIA** won by 8 wickets.   Toss: Zimbabwe.
Award: M.Prabhakar.   LOI debuts: Zimbabwe – K.J.Arnott, M.A.Meman.

Manoj Prabhakar's late swing claimed four wickets in 17 balls. Sunil Gavaskar scored his first 36 runs in boundaries.

ZIMBABWE		Runs	Balls	4/6	INDIA		Runs	Balls	4/6
G.A.Paterson	b Prabhakar	6	21	–	K.Srikkanth	c Paterson b Traicos	31	38	4
K.J.Arnott	lbw b Prabhakar	1	6	–	S.M.Gavaskar	st Houghton b Traicos	43	52	9
† D.L.Houghton	b Prabhakar	0	12	–	M.Prabhakar	not out	11	41	1
A.J.Pycroft	st More b Shastri	61	102	2	D.B.Vengsarkar	not out	46	37	4/3
K.M.Curran	c More b Prabhakar	0	1	–	N.S.Sidhu				
A.C.Waller	st More b Maninder	16	42	1	M.Azharuddin				
I.P.Butchart	c Sivaramakrishnan b Maninder	10	23	1	* Kapil Dev				
A.H.Shah	c More b Maninder	0	1	–	R.J.Shastri				
M.A.Meman	run out	19	22	2	† K.S.More				
* A.J.Traicos	c Gavaskar b Sivaramakrishnan	0	1	–	L.Sivaramakrishnan				
M.P.Jarvis	not out	8	35	–	Maninder Singh				
Extras	(b 2, lb 6, w 6)	14			Extras	(lb 1, w 4)	5		
Total	**(44.2 overs)**	**135**			**Total**	**(27.5 overs; 2 wickets)**	**136**		

INDIA	O	M	R	W	ZIMBABWE	O	M	R	W
Kapil Dev	8	1	17	0	Curran	6	0	32	0
Prabhakar	8	1	19	4	Jarvis	4	0	22	0
Maninder	10	0	21	3	Butchart	3	0	20	0
Azharuddin	1	0	6	0	Traicos	8	0	27	2
Sivaramakrishnan	9	0	36	1	Meman	6.5	0	34	0
Shastri	8.2	0	28	1					

FALL OF WICKETS
1-3, 2-12, 3-13, 4-13, 5-47, 6-67, 7-67, 8-98, 9-99, 10-135

FALL OF WICKETS
1-76, 2-80

Umpires: Mahboob Shah (*Pakistan*) (12) and D.R.Shepherd (*England*) (22).

AUSTRALIA v NEW ZEALAND 1987-88

At Nehru Stadium, Indore, India, on 18 (*no play*), 19 October 1987.   Result: **AUSTRALIA** won by 3 runs.
Toss: New Zealand.   Award: D.C.Boon.   LOI debuts: None.

The captains opted for a 30-over match rather than shared points after heavy rain had prevented play on the first day.
Needing seven to win off Steve Waugh's last over, New Zealand scored three singles and lost as many wickets.

AUSTRALIA		Runs	Balls	4/6	NEW ZEALAND		Runs	Balls	4/6
D.C.Boon	c Wright b Snedden	87	96	5/2	K.R.Rutherford	b O'Donnell	37	38	2/2
G.R.Marsh	c J.J.Crowe b Snedden	5	9	–	J.G.Wright	c Dyer b O'Donnell	47	44	1/2
D.M.Jones	c Rutherford b Patel	52	48	1/3	M.D.Crowe	c Marsh b Waugh	58	48	5
* A.R.Border	c M.D.Crowe b Chatfield	34	28	3	A.H.Jones	c Marsh b McDermott	15	23	–
S.R.Waugh	not out	13	8	1/1	* J.J.Crowe	c and b Reid	3	10	–
T.M.Moody	not out	0	3	–	D.N.Patel	run out	13	9	1
S.P.O'Donnell					J.G.Bracewell	c and b Reid	6	4	1
† G.C.Dyer					† I.D.S.Smith	b Waugh	1	2	–
T.B.A.May					M.C.Snedden	run out	1	1	–
C.J.McDermott					W.Watson	not out	2	3	–
B.A.Reid					E.J.Chatfield	not out	0	–	–
Extras	(b 1, lb 5, w 2)	8			Extras	(b 4, lb 5, w 4)	13		
Total	**(30 overs; 4 wickets)**	**199**			**Total**	**(30 overs; 9 wickets)**	**196**		

NEW ZEALAND	O	M	R	W	AUSTRALIA	O	M	R	W
Snedden	6	0	36	2	McDermott	6	0	30	1
Chatfield	6	0	27	1	Reid	6	0	38	2
Watson	6	0	34	0	May	6	0	39	0
Patel	6	0	45	1	O'Donnell	6	0	44	2
Bracewell	6	0	51	0	Waugh	6	0	36	2

FALL OF WICKETS
1-17, 2-134, 3-171, 4-196

FALL OF WICKETS
1-83, 2-94, 3-133, 4-140, 5-165, 6-183, 7-193, 8-193, 9-195

Umpires: D.M.Archer (*West Indies*) (13) and Khizer Hayat (*Pakistan*) (14).

PAKISTAN v ENGLAND 1987-88

At National Stadium, Karachi, Pakistan, on 20 October 1987.   Result: **PAKISTAN** won by 7 wickets.   Toss: Pakistan.
Award: Imran Khan.   LOI debuts: None.

The partnerships of 135 for the third wicket between Bill Athey and Mike Gatting and 167 for the second wicket
between Ramiz Raja and Salim Malik remain national LOI records.

ENGLAND		Runs	Balls	4/6
G.A.Gooch	c Wasim b Imran	16	27	2
R.T.Robinson	b Qadir	16	26	1
C.W.J.Athey	b Tausif	86	104	6/2
M.W.Gatting	c Salim Yousuf b Qadir	60	65	3/1
A.J.Lamb	b Imran	9	15	–
J.E.Emburey	lbw b Qadir	3	11	–
P.R.Downton	c Salim Yousuf b Imran	6	13	–
P.A.J.DeFreitas	c Salim Yousuf b Imran	13	15	1
N.A.Foster	not out	20	20	2
G.C.Small	run out	0	1	–
E.E.Hemmings	not out	4	3	–
Extras	(lb 7, w 4)	11		
Total	(50 overs; 9 wickets)	**244**		

PAKISTAN		Runs	Balls	4/6
Ramiz Raja	c Gooch b DeFreitas	113	148	5
Mansoor Akhtar	run out	29	49	3
Salim Malik	c Athey b Emburey	88	92	7
Javed Miandad	not out	6	3	1
Ijaz Ahmed	not out	4	2	1
* Imran Khan				
† Salim Yousuf				
Wasim Akram				
Abdul Qadir				
Tausif Ahmed				
Salim Jaffer				
Extras	(lb 6, w 1)	7		
Total	(49 overs; 3 wickets)	**247**		

PAKISTAN	O	M	R	W
Imran Khan	9	0	37	4
Wasim Akram	8	0	44	0
Tausif Ahmed	10	0	46	1
Abdul Qadir	10	0	31	3
Salim Jaffer	8	0	44	0
Salim Malik	5	0	35	0

ENGLAND	O	M	R	W
DeFreitas	8	2	41	1
Foster	10	0	51	0
Hemmings	10	1	40	0
Emburey	10	0	34	1
Small	9	0	63	0
Gooch	2	0	12	0

FALL OF WICKETS
1-26, 2-52, 3-187, 4-187, 5-192, 6-203, 7-206, 8-230, 9-230

FALL OF WICKETS
1-61, 2-228, 3-243

Umpires: A.R.Crafter (*Australia*) (55) and V.K.Ramaswamy (*India*) (7).

WEST INDIES v SRI LANKA 1987-88

At Green Park, Kanpur, India, on 21 October 1987.   Result: **WEST INDIES** won by 25 runs.   Toss: Sri Lanka.
Award: P.V.Simmons.   LOI debuts: None.

Gus Logie and Arjuna Ranatunga each improvised superbly to score at almost a run a ball on an extremely sluggish
pitch.

WEST INDIES		Runs	Balls	4/6
D.L.Haynes	b Anurasiri	24	36	3
P.V.Simmons	c Madugalle b Ratnayeke	89	126	11
R.B.Richardson	c Mahanama b Jeganathan	4	12	–
* I.V.A.Richards	c Ratnayeke b De Silva	14	25	–
A.L.Logie	not out	65	66	7
C.L.Hooper	st Kuruppu b De Silva	6	8	1
† P.J.L.Dujon	c Kuruppu b Ratnayeke	6	14	–
R.A.Harper	b Ratnayeke	3	6	–
W.K.M.Benjamin	b Ratnayeke	0	3	–
C.A.Walsh	not out	9	8	1
B.P.Patterson				
Extras	(b 2, lb 7, w 7)	16		
Total	(50 overs; 8 wickets)	**236**		

SRI LANKA		Runs	Balls	4/6
R.S.Mahanama	b Patterson	0	3	–
† D.S.B.P.Kuruppu	c and b Hooper	33	82	1
J.R.Ratnayeke	lbw b Benjamin	15	22	1
R.S.Madugalle	c Haynes b Harper	18	42	–
A.Ranatunga	not out	86	100	7/2
* L.R.D.Mendis	b Walsh	19	34	1
P.A.de Silva	b Patterson	8	9	–
R.J.Ratnayake	c Walsh b Patterson	5	7	–
S.Jeganathan	run out	3	9	–
V.B.John	not out	1	3	–
S.D.Anurasiri				
Extras	(b 2, lb 11, nb 10)	23		
Total	(50 overs; 8 wickets)	**211**		

SRI LANKA	O	M	R	W
Ratnayeke	10	1	41	3
John	5	1	25	0
Ratnayake	5	0	39	1
Jeganathan	10	1	33	1
Anurasiri	10	1	46	1
De Silva	10	0	43	2

WEST INDIES	O	M	R	W
Patterson	10	0	31	3
Walsh	9	2	43	1
Benjamin	10	0	43	1
Harper	10	1	29	1
Hooper	8	0	35	1
Richards	3	0	17	0

FALL OF WICKETS
1-62, 2-80, 3-115, 4-155, 5-168, 6-199, 7-213, 8-214

FALL OF WICKETS
1-2, 2-28, 3-66, 4-86, 5-156, 6-184, 7-200, 8-209

Umpires: Amanullah Khan (*Pakistan*) (10) and Mahboob Shah (*Pakistan*) (13).

INDIA v AUSTRALIA 1987-88

At Feroz Shah Kotla, Delhi, India, on 22 October 1987.   Result: INDIA won by 56 runs.   Toss: Australia.
Award: M.Azharuddin.   LOI debuts: Australia – A.K.Zesers.

Kapil Dev took his first wicket of the tournament in India's fourth match. Mohammed Azharuddin concluded the match with his best LOI analysis.

INDIA		Runs	Balls	4/6
K.Srikkanth	c Dyer b McDermott	26	37	3
S.M.Gavaskar	b O'Donnell	61	72	7
N.S.Sidhu	c Moody b McDermott	51	70	2
D.B.Vengsarkar	c O'Donnell b Reid	63	60	3/2
* Kapil Dev	c Dyer b McDermott	3	5	–
M.Azharuddin	not out	54	45	5/1
R.J.Shastri	c and b Waugh	8	7	1
† K.S.More	not out	5	4	–
M.Prabhakar				
C.Sharma				
Maninder Singh				
Extras	(b 1, lb 6, w11)	18		
Total	(50 overs; 6 wickets)	289		

AUSTRALIA		Runs	Balls	4/6
G.R.Marsh	st More b Maninder	33	56	2
D.C.Boon	c More b Shastri	62	59	7
D.M.Jones	c Kapil Dev b Maninder	36	55	–
* A.R.Border	c Prabhakar b Maninder	12	24	–
S.R.Waugh	c Sidhu b Kapil Dev	42	52	3
T.M.Moody	run out	2	6	–
S.P.O'Donnell	b Azharuddin	5	10	–
† G.C.Dyer	c Kapil Dev b Prabhakar	15	12	–/1
C.J.McDermott	c and b Azharuddin	4	5	–
A.K.Zesers	not out	2	11	–
B.A.Reid	c Sidhu b Azharuddin	1	6	–
Extras	(lb 11, w 8)	19		
Total	(49 overs)	233		

AUSTRALIA	O	M	R	W
O'Donnell	9	1	45	1
Reid	10	0	65	1
Waugh	10	0	59	1
McDermott	10	0	61	3
Moody	2	0	15	0
Zesers	9	1	37	0

INDIA	O	M	R	W
Kapil Dev	8	1	41	1
Prabhakar	10	0	56	1
Maninder	10	0	34	3
Shastri	10	0	35	1
Sharma	7.1	0	37	0
Azharuddin	3.5	0	19	3

FALL OF WICKETS
1-50, 2-125, 3-167, 4-178, 5-243, 6-274

FALL OF WICKETS
1-88, 2-104, 3-135, 4-164, 5-167, 6-182, 7-214, 8-227, 9-231, 10-233

Umpires: Khalid Aziz (Pakistan) (4) and D.R.Shepherd (England) (23).

NEW ZEALAND v ZIMBABWE 1987-88

At Eden Gardens, Calcutta, India, on 23 October 1987.   Result: NEW ZEALAND won by 4 wickets.   Toss: New Zealand.
Award: J.J.Crowe.   LOI debuts: None.

The highest score of Jeff Crowe's 75-match limited-overs international career carried his team to victory in their second close encounter with Zimbabwe.

ZIMBABWE		Runs	Balls	4/6
G.A.Paterson	run out	0	8	–
A.H.Shah	c M.D.Crowe b Watson	41	90	2
K.J.Arnott	run out	51	83	5
† D.L.Houghton	c M.D.Crowe b Boock	50	57	5
A.J.Pycroft	not out	52	46	2/1
K.M.Curran	b Boock	12	11	–
A.C.Waller	not out	8	5	1
I.P.Butchart				
E.A.Brandes				
* A.J.Traicos				
M.P.Jarvis				
Extras	(lb 7, w 6)	13		
Total	(50 overs; 5 wickets)	227		

NEW ZEALAND		Runs	Balls	4/6
K.R.Rutherford	b Brandes	22	32	2
J.G.Wright	b Shah	12	32	1
M.D.Crowe	c Butchart b Shah	58	58	8
D.N.Patel	c Arnott b Brandes	1	4	–
* J.J.Crowe	not out	88	105	8
A.H.Jones	c Jarvis b Traicos	15	35	1
M.C.Snedden	b Jarvis	4	13	–
† I.D.S.Smith	not out	17	10	2
S.L.Boock				
E.J.Chatfield				
W.Watson				
Extras	(b 1, lb 5, w 4, nb 1)	11		
Total	(47.4 overs; 6 wickets)	228		

NEW ZEALAND	O	M	R	W
Chatfield	10	2	47	0
Snedden	10	2	32	0
Watson	10	1	45	1
Boock	10	1	43	2
Patel	10	1	53	0

ZIMBABWE	O	M	R	W
Curran	2	0	12	0
Jarvis	7.4	0	39	1
Brandes	10	1	44	2
Shah	10	0	34	2
Traicos	10	0	43	1
Butchart	8	0	50	0

FALL OF WICKETS
1-1, 2-82, 3-121, 4-180, 5-216

FALL OF WICKETS
1-37, 2-53, 3-56, 4-125, 5-158, 6-182

Umpires: Khizer Hayat (Pakistan) (15) and P.W.Vidanagamage (Sri Lanka) (17).

PAKISTAN v SRI LANKA 1987-88

At Iqbal Stadium, Faisalabad, Pakistan, on 25 October 1987.   Result: **PAKISTAN** won by 113 runs.   Toss: Pakistan.
Award: Salim Malik.   LOI debuts: None.

By adding 154 from their last 15 overs, Pakistan clinched first place in their group and a home semi-final.

PAKISTAN		Runs	Balls	4/6
Ramiz Raja	c and b Anurasiri	32	49	2
Mansoor Akhtar	b Jeganathan	33	61	2
Salim Malik	b Ratnayeke	100	95	10
Javed Miandad	run out	1	8	–
Wasim Akram	c Ranatunga b De Silva	39	40	2/2
Ijaz Ahmed	c and b John	30	18	5
Imran Khan	run out	39	20	5/1
Manzoor Elahi	not out	4	6	–
Salim Yousuf	not out	11	6	–/1
Abdul Qadir				
Tausif Ahmed				
Extras	(lb 6, w 2)	8		
Total	(50 overs; 7 wickets)	**297**		

SRI LANKA		Runs	Balls	4/6
R.S.Mahanama	run out	8	13	1
† D.S.B.P.Kuruppu	c Salim Yousuf b Imran	0	1	–
J.R.Ratnayeke	run out	22	60	2
R.S.Madugalle	c Salim Yousuf b Manzoor	15	38	2
A.Ranatunga	c and b Qadir	50	66	4
* L.R.D.Mendis	b Qadir	58	65	6
P.A.de Silva	not out	13	35	–
A.L.F.de Mel	b Qadir	0	3	–
S.Jeganathan	c Salim Yousuf b Miandad	1	11	–
V.B.John	not out	1	12	–
S.D.Anurasiri				
Extras	(b 4, lb 4, w 6, nb 2)	16		
Total	(50 overs; 8 wickets)	**184**		

SRI LANKA	O	M	R	W
Ratnayeke	10	0	58	1
John	8	1	53	1
De Mel	10	0	53	0
Jeganathan	9	1	45	1
Anurasiri	7	0	45	1
De Silva	6	0	37	1

PAKISTAN	O	M	R	W
Imran Khan	3.2	1	13	1
Wasim Akram	7	0	34	0
Manzoor Elahi	9.4	0	32	1
Tausif Ahmed	10	1	23	0
Abdul Qadir	10	0	40	3
Salim Malik	7	1	29	0
Javed Miandad	3	0	5	1

FALL OF WICKETS
1-64, 2-72, 3-77, 4-137, 5-197, 6-264, 7-285

FALL OF WICKETS
1-4, 2-11, 3-41, 4-70, 5-150, 6-173, 7-173, 8-179

Umpires: R.B.Gupta (*India*) (7) and S.J.Woodward (*New Zealand*) (11).

ENGLAND v WEST INDIES 1987-88

At Sawai Mansingh Stadium, Jaipur, India, on 26 October 1987.   Result: **ENGLAND** won by 34 runs.   Toss: West Indies.
Award: G.A.Gooch.   LOI debuts: None.

This match and England's hopes of reaching the semi-final turned when Eddie Hemmings, having twice been hit for six by a rampant Viv Richards, bowled his tormentor off stump. West Indies lost their last six wickets for 27 runs.

ENGLAND		Runs	Balls	4/6
G.A.Gooch	c Harper b Patterson	92	137	7
R.T.Robinson	b Patterson	13	19	2
C.W.J.Athey	c Patterson b Harper	21	44	3
* M.W.Gatting	lbw b Richards	25	24	1
A.J.Lamb	c Richardson b Patterson	40	52	3
J.E.Emburey	not out	24	16	4
P.A.J.DeFreitas	not out	16	9	3
† P.R.Downton				
N.A.Foster				
G.C.Small				
E.E.Hemmings				
Extras	(b 5, lb 10, w 22, nb 1)	38		
Total	(50 overs; 5 wickets)	**269**		

WEST INDIES		Runs	Balls	4/6
D.L.Haynes	c Athey b DeFreitas	9	14	2
P.V.Simmons	b Emburey	25	28	5
R.B.Richardson	c Downton b Small	93	130	8/1
* I.V.A.Richards	b Hemmings	51	51	4/3
A.L.Logie	c Hemmings b Emburey	22	21	3
C.L.Hooper	c Downton b DeFreitas	8	11	1
† P.J.L.Dujon	c Downton b Foster	1	4	–
R.A.Harper	run out	3	4	–
W.K.M.Benjamin	c Foster b DeFreitas	8	16	–
C.A.Walsh	b Hemmings	2	3	–
B.P.Patterson	not out	4	8	–
Extras	(lb 7, w 1, nb 1)	9		
Total	(48.1 overs)	**235**		

WEST INDIES	O	M	R	W
Patterson	9	0	56	3
Walsh	10	0	24	0
Benjamin	10	0	63	0
Harper	10	1	52	1
Hooper	3	0	27	0
Richards	8	0	32	1

ENGLAND	O	M	R	W
DeFreitas	9.1	2	28	3
Foster	10	0	52	1
Emburey	9	0	41	2
Small	10	0	61	1
Hemmings	10	0	46	2

FALL OF WICKETS
1-35, 2-90, 3-154, 4-209, 5-250

FALL OF WICKETS
1-18, 2-65, 3-147, 4-182, 5-208, 6-211, 7-219, 8-221, 9-224, 10-235

Umpires: Mahboob Shah (*Pak*) (14) and P.W.Vidanagamage (*SL*) (18).

INDIA v ZIMBABWE 1987-88

At Gujarat Stadium, Motera, Ahmedabad, India, on 26 October 1987.   Result: **INDIA** won by 7 wickets.   Toss: India.
Award: Kapil Dev.   LOI debuts: None.

Navjot Sidhu extended the remarkable start to his limited-overs international career (nearly four years after making his Test match debut) by scoring his fourth fifty in successive innings.

ZIMBABWE		Runs	Balls	4/6	INDIA		Runs	Balls	4/6
R.D.Brown	c More b Sharma	13	52	2	K.Srikkanth	lbw b Jarvis	6	9	1
A.H.Shah	run out	0	3	–	S.M.Gavaskar	c Butchart b Rawson	50	114	3
K.J.Arnott	b Kapil Dev	60	126	1	N.S.Sidhu	c Brandes b Rawson	55	61	5/1
A.J.Pycroft	c More b Sharma	2	9	–	D.B.Vengsarkar	not out	33	43	1
† D.L.Houghton	c Kapil Dev b Shastri	22	35	–	* Kapil Dev	not out	41	25	2/3
A.C.Waller	c Shastri b Maninder	39	44	4/1	M.Azharuddin				
I.P.Butchart	b Kapil Dev	13	14	1	R.J.Shastri				
P.W.E.Rawson	not out	16	17	–	† K.S.More				
E.A.Brandes	not out	3	4	–	M.Prabhakar				
M.P.Jarvis					C.Sharma				
* A.J.Traicos					Maninder Singh				
Extras	(b 1, lb 12, w 9, nb 1)	23			Extras	(lb 6, w3)	9		
Total	(50 overs; 7 wickets)	**191**			**Total**	(42 overs; 3 wickets)	**194**		

INDIA	O	M	R	W	ZIMBABWE	O	M	R	W
Kapil Dev	10	2	44	2	Brandes	6	0	28	0
Prabhakar	7	2	12	0	Jarvis	8	1	21	1
Sharma	10	0	41	2	Shah	8	0	40	0
Maninder	10	1	32	1	Traicos	10	0	39	0
Shastri	10	0	35	1	Rawson	8	0	46	2
Azharuddin	3	0	14	0	Butchart	2	0	14	0

FALL OF WICKETS
1-4, 2-36, 3-40, 4-83, 5-150, 6-155, 7-184

FALL OF WICKETS
1-11, 2-105, 3-132

Umpires: D.M.Archer (*West Indies*) (14) and H.D.Bird (*England*) (46).

AUSTRALIA v NEW ZEALAND 1987-88

At Sector 16 Stadium, Chandigarh, India, on 27 October 1987.   Result: **AUSTRALIA** won by 17 runs.   Toss: Australia.
Award: G.R.Marsh.   LOI debuts: None.

Geoff Marsh emulated the 1975 feats of Sunil Gavaskar and Glenn Turner by batting throughout a World Cup innings.

AUSTRALIA		Runs	Balls	4/6	NEW ZEALAND		Runs	Balls	4/6
G.R.Marsh	not out	126	149	12/3	M.C.Snedden	b Waugh	32	56	3
D.C.Boon	run out	14	28	1	J.G.Wright	c and b Zesers	61	82	4
D.M.Jones	c Smith b Watson	56	80	1/2	M.D.Crowe	run out	4	5	–
* A.R.Border	b Snedden	1	4	–	K.R.Rutherford	c Jones b McDermott	44	57	4
M.R.J.Veletta	run out	0	1	–	* J.J.Crowe	c and b Border	27	28	3
S.R.Waugh	b Watson	1	7	–	D.N.Patel	st Dyer b Border	3	10	–
† G.C.Dyer	b Chatfield	8	10	–	J.G.Bracewell	run out	12	20	–
C.J.McDermott	lbw b Chatfield	5	7	–	† I.D.S.Smith	c Boon b Waugh	12	15	–
T.B.A.May	run out	15	10	1	S.L.Boock	run out	12	8	1
A.K.Zesers	not out	8	3	1	W.Watson	run out	8	8	–/1
B.A.Reid					E.J.Chatfield	not out	5	6	–
Extras	(lb 10, w 7)	17			Extras	(b 1, lb 7, w 4, nb 2)	14		
Total	(50 overs; 8 wickets)	**251**			**Total**	(48.4 overs)	**234**		

NEW ZEALAND	O	M	R	W	AUSTRALIA	O	M	R	W
Snedden	10	0	48	1	McDermott	10	1	43	1
Chatfield	10	2	52	2	Reid	6	0	30	0
Boock	10	1	45	0	Waugh	9.4	0	37	2
Bracewell	4	0	24	0	Zesers	6	0	37	1
Watson	8	0	46	2	May	10	0	52	0
Patel	8	0	26	0	Border	7	0	27	2

FALL OF WICKETS
1-25, 2-151, 3-158, 4-158, 5-175, 6-193, 7-201, 8-228

FALL OF WICKETS
1-72, 2-82, 3-127, 4-173, 5-179, 6-186, 7-206, 8-208, 9-221, 10-234

Umpires: Khizer Hayat (*Pakistan*) (16) and D.R.Shepherd (*England*) (24).

AUSTRALIA v ZIMBABWE 1987-88

At Barabati Stadium, Cuttack, India, on 30 October 1987.　Result: **AUSTRALIA** won by 70 runs.　Toss: Zimbabwe.
Award: D.C.Boon.　LOI debuts: None.

Andy Waller, a victim of the well-grassed pitch's uneven bounce, retired after being struck on the bridge of his nose by a sharply lifting ball from Bruce Reid but subsequently resumed his innings.

AUSTRALIA		Runs	Balls	4/6
D.C.Boon	c Houghton b Butchart	93	101	9/1
G.R.Marsh	run out	37	65	1
D.M.Jones	not out	58	72	1/1
C.J.McDermott	c Rawson b Traicos	9	10	–/1
A.R.Border	st Houghton b Traicos	4	6	–
M.R.J.Veletta	run out	43	39	3
S.R.Waugh	not out	10	14	1
S.P.O'Donnell				
G.C.Dyer				
T.B.A.May				
B.A.Reid				
Extras	(b 3, lb 3, w 6)	12		
Total	(50 overs; 5 wickets)	266		

ZIMBABWE		Runs	Balls	4/6
A.H.Shah	b Waugh	32	90	4
A.C.Waller	c Waugh b McDermott	38	83	2
K.M.Curran	c Waugh b May	29	57	2
A.J.Pycroft	c Dyer b McDermott	38	46	2
† D.L.Houghton	lbw b May	1	11	–
I.P.Butchart	st Dyer b Border	3	5	–
P.W.E.Rawson	not out	24	29	2/1
E.A.Brandes	not out	18	11	1/2
K.J.Arnott				
M.P.Jarvis				
* A.J.Traicos				
Extras	(lb 5, w 6, nb 2)	13		
Total	(50 overs; 6 wickets)	196		

ZIMBABWE	O	M	R	W
Rawson	9	0	41	0
Jarvis	6	0	33	0
Shah	7	0	31	0
Brandes	10	1	58	0
Traicos	10	0	45	2
Butchart	8	0	52	1

FALL OF WICKETS
1-90, 2-148, 3-159, 4-170, 5-248

AUSTRALIA	O	M	R	W
McDermott	10	0	43	2
Reid	9	2	30	0
Waugh	4	0	9	1
O'Donnell	7	1	21	0
May	10	1	30	2
Border	8	0	36	1
Jones	1	0	5	0
Boon	1	0	17	0

FALL OF WICKETS
1-55, 2-89, 3-92, 4-97, 5-139, 6-156

Umpires: Mahboob Shah (*Pak*) (15) and P.W.Vidanagamage (*SL*) (19).

ENGLAND v SRI LANKA 1987-88

At Nehru Stadium, Poona, India, on 30 October 1987.　Result: **ENGLAND** won by 8 wickets.　Toss: Sri Lanka.
Award: G.A.Gooch.　LOI debuts: None.

England qualified for the semi-finals despite missing four catches, one of which caused Graham Gooch to retire with a dislocated finger. When he returned it was to share with Tim Robinson England's highest opening stand against Sri Lanka.

SRI LANKA		Runs	Balls	4/6
R.S.Mahanama	c Emburey b DeFreitas	14	28	1
J.R.Ratnayeke	lbw b Small	7	26	–
A.P.Gurusinha	run out	34	63	3
R.L.Dias	st Downton b Hemmings	80	105	6/3
* L.R.D.Mendis	b DeFreitas	7	11	1
R.S.Madugalle	c sub (P.W.Jarvis) b Hemmings	22	38	–/1
P.A.de Silva	not out	23	18	2
A.L.F.de Mel	c Lamb b Hemmings	0	2	–
S.Jeganathan	not out	20	15	2/1
V.B.John				
S.D.Anurasiri				
Extras	(lb 3, w 3, nb 5)	11		
Total	(50 overs; 7 wickets)	218		

ENGLAND		Runs	Balls	4/6
G.A.Gooch	c and b Jeganathan	61	79	7
R.T.Robinson	b Jeganathan	55	75	7
C.W.J.Athey	not out	40	55	–
* M.W.Gatting	not out	46	40	4
A.J.Lamb				
† P.R.Downton				
J.E.Emburey				
P.A.J.DeFreitas				
N.A.Foster				
G.C.Small				
E.E.Hemmings				
Extras	(b 1, lb 13, w 3)	17		
Total	(41.2 overs; 2 wickets)	219		

ENGLAND	O	M	R	W
DeFreitas	10	2	46	2
Small	10	1	33	1
Foster	10	0	37	0
Emburey	10	1	42	0
Hemmings	10	0	57	3

FALL OF WICKETS
1-23, 2-25, 3-113, 4-125, 5-170, 6-177, 7-180

SRI LANKA	O	M	R	W
Ratnayeke	8	1	37	0
John	6	2	19	0
De Mel	4.2	0	34	0
Jeganathan	10	0	45	2
Anurasiri	10	0	45	0
De Silva	3	0	25	0

FALL OF WICKETS
1-123, 2-132

Umpires: D.M.Archer (*West Indies*) (15) and Khizer Hayat (*Pakistan*) (17).

PAKISTAN v WEST INDIES 1987-88

At National Stadium, Karachi, Pakistan, on 30 October 1987.　　Result: **WEST INDIES** won by 28 runs.
Toss: West Indies.　　Award: R.B.Richardson.　　LOI debuts: None.

A match meaningless in terms of influencing the semi-final draw was upstaged by a more entertaining traditional clash between students protesting at the confiscation of their leader and riot police armed with steel-tipped batons and tear gas.

WEST INDIES		Runs	Balls	4/6
D.L.Haynes	c Imran b Mudassar	25	52	1
P.V.Simmons	b Wasim	6	9	1
R.B.Richardson	c Qadir b Imran	110	135	8/2
* I.V.A.Richards	b Wasim	67	75	2/2
A.L.Logie	c Mudassar b Imran	12	17	–
R.A.Harper	b Wasim	2	7	–
C.L.Hooper	not out	5	7	–
W.K.M.Benjamin	c Mudassar b Imran	0	1	–
† P.J.L.Dujon	not out	1	1	–
C.A.Walsh				
B.P.Patterson				
Extras	(b 3, lb 10, w 16, nb 1)	30		
Total	(50 overs; 7 wickets)	258		

PAKISTAN	O	M	R	W
Imran Khan	9	0	57	3
Wasim Akram	10	0	45	3
Abdul Qadir	10	1	29	0
Mudassar Nazar	10	0	47	1
Salim Jaffer	6	0	37	0
Salim Malik	5	0	30	0

FALL OF WICKETS
1-19, 2-84, 3-221, 4-242, 5-248, 6-255, 7-255

PAKISTAN		Runs	Balls	4/6
Mudassar Nazar	b Harper	40	55	3
Ramiz Raja	c Hooper b Patterson	70	111	3
Salim Malik	c Richards b Walsh	23	37	–
Javed Miandad	b Benjamin	38	38	3
Ijaz Ahmed	b Benjamin	6	10	–
* Imran Khan	c Harper b Walsh	8	11	–
† Salim Yousuf	b Patterson	7	11	–
Wasim Akram	lbw b Patterson	0	2	–
Abdul Qadir	not out	8	11	–
Shoaib Mohammed	b Benjamin	0	1	–
Salim Jaffer	not out	8	16	–
Extras	(b 4, lb 6, w 10, nb 2)	22		
Total	(50 overs; 9 wickets)	230		

WEST INDIES	O	M	R	W
Patterson	10	1	34	3
Walsh	10	1	34	2
Harper	10	0	38	1
Benjamin	10	0	69	3
Richards	10	0	45	0

FALL OF WICKETS
1-78, 2-128, 3-147, 4-167, 5-186, 6-202, 7-202, 8-208, 9-208

Umpires: R.B.Gupta (*India*) (8) and V.K.Ramaswamy (*India*) (8).

INDIA v NEW ZEALAND 1987-88

At Vidarbha CA Ground, Nagpur, India, on 31 October 1987.　　Result: **INDIA** won by 9 wickets.　　Toss: New Zealand.
Awards: S.M.Gavaskar and C.Sharma.　　LOI debuts: New Zealand – D.K.Morrison.

Chetan Sharma bowled Rutherford, Smith and Chatfield with the last three balls of his sixth over to record the only World Cup hat-trick. Sunil Gavaskar completed his only hundred in 108 internationals off 85 balls, the third-fastest in World Cup matches, his partnership of 136 in 17 overs with Krish Srikkanth securing a home semi-final for India on run rate.

NEW ZEALAND		Runs	Balls	4/6
J.G.Wright	run out	35	59	4
P.A.Horne	b Prabhakar	18	35	1
M.D.Crowe	c Pandit b Azharuddin	21	24	2
K.R.Rutherford	b Sharma	26	54	1
* J.J.Crowe	b Maninder	24	24	3
D.N.Patel	c Kapil Dev b Shastri	40	51	3
M.C.Snedden	run out	23	28	2
† I.D.S.Smith	b Sharma	0	1	–
E.J.Chatfield	b Sharma	0	1	–
W.Watson	not out	12	25	1
D.K.Morrison				
Extras	(lb 14, w 7, nb 1)	22		
Total	(50 overs; 9 wickets)	221		

INDIA	O	M	R	W
Kapil Dev	6	0	24	0
Prabhakar	7	0	23	1
Sharma	10	2	51	3
Maninder	10	0	51	1
Shastri	10	1	32	1
Azharuddin	7	0	26	1

FALL OF WICKETS
1-46, 2-84, 3-90, 4-122, 5-181, 6-182, 7-182, 8-182, 9-221

INDIA		Runs	Balls	4/6
K.Srikkanth	c Rutherford b Watson	75	58	9/3
S.M.Gavaskar	not out	103	88	10/3
M.Azharuddin	not out	41	51	5
N.S.Sidhu				
D.B.Vengsarkar				
* Kapil Dev				
R.J.Shastri				
† C.S.Pandit				
M.Prabhakar				
C.Sharma				
Maninder Singh				
Extras	(lb 1, w 2, nb 2)	5		
Total	(32.1 overs; 1 wicket)	224		

NEW ZEALAND	O	M	R	W
Morrison	10	0	69	0
Chatfield	4.1	1	39	0
Snedden	4	0	29	0
Watson	10	0	50	1
Patel	4	0	36	0

FALL OF WICKETS
1-136

Umpires: H.D.Bird (*England*) (47) and D.R.Shepherd (*England*) (25).

PAKISTAN v AUSTRALIA 1987-88

At Gaddafi Stadium, Lahore, Pakistan, on 4 November 1987.   Result: **AUSTRALIA** won by 18 runs.   Toss: Australia.
Award: C.J.McDermott.   LOI debuts: None.

Craig McDermott completed Pakistan's third successive World Cup semi-final defeat when he returned the only five-wicket analysis of this tournament. Javed Miandad deputised as wicket-keeper when the ball deflected off a pad into Salim Yousuf's mouth.

AUSTRALIA		Runs	Balls	4/6
G.R.Marsh	run out	31	57	2
D.C.Boon	st Miandad b Salim Malik	65	91	4
D.M.Jones	b Tausif	38	45	3
A.R.Border	run out	18	22	2
M.R.J.Veletta	b Imran	48	50	2
S.R.Waugh	not out	32	28	4/1
S.P.O'Donnell	run out	0	2	–
G.C.Dyer	b Imran	0	1	–
C.J.McDermott	b Imran	1	3	–
T.B.A.May	not out	0	2	–
B.A.Reid				
Extras	(b 1, lb 19, w 13, nb 1)	34		
Total	(50 overs; 8 wickets)	**267**		

PAKISTAN		Runs	Balls	4/6
Ramiz Raja	run out	1	1	–
Mansoor Akhtar	b McDermott	9	19	–
Salim Malik	c McDermott b Waugh	25	31	3
Javed Miandad	b Reid	70	103	4
* Imran Khan	c Dyer b Border	58	84	4
Wasim Akram	b McDermott	20	13	–/2
Ijaz Ahmed	c Jones b Reid	8	7	1
† Salim Yousuf	c Dyer b McDermott	21	15	2
Abdul Qadir	not out	20	16	2
Salim Jaffer	c Dyer b McDermott	0	2	–
Tausif Ahmed	c Dyer b McDermott	1	3	–
Extras	(lb 6, w 10)	16		
Total	(49 overs)	**249**		

PAKISTAN	O	M	R	W
Imran Khan	10	1	36	3
Salim Jaffer	6	0	57	0
Wasim Akram	10	0	54	0
Abdul Qadir	10	0	39	0
Tausif Ahmed	10	1	39	1
Salim Malik	4	0	22	1

AUSTRALIA	O	M	R	W
McDermott	10	0	44	5
Reid	10	2	41	2
Waugh	9	1	51	1
O'Donnell	10	1	45	0
May	6	0	36	0
Border	4	0	26	1

FALL OF WICKETS
1-73, 2-155, 3-155, 4-215, 5-236, 6-236, 7-241, 8-249

FALL OF WICKETS
1-2, 2-37, 3-38, 4-150, 5-177, 6-192, 7-212, 8-236, 9-247, 10-249

Umpires: H.D.Bird (*England*) (48) and D.R.Shepherd (*England*) (26).

INDIA v ENGLAND 1987-88

At Wankhede Stadium, Bombay, India, on 5 November 1987.   Result: **ENGLAND** won by 35 runs.   Toss: India.
Award: G.A.Gooch.   LOI debuts: None.

Adeptly utilising the sweep and pull against India's left-arm spinners, Graham Gooch scored the only hundred of his (eventual) 21 World Cup appearances. Eddie Hemmings captured four key wickets for 21 runs in 34 balls to take England into their second World Cup final.

ENGLAND		Runs	Balls	4/6
G.A.Gooch	c Srikkanth b Maninder	115	136	11
R.T.Robinson	st More b Maninder	13	36	2
C.W.J.Athey	c More b Sharma	4	17	–
* M.W.Gatting	b Maninder	56	62	5
A.J.Lamb	not out	32	29	2
J.E.Emburey	lbw b Kapil Dev	6	10	–
P.A.J.DeFreitas	b Kapil Dev	7	8	1
† P.R.Downton	not out	1	5	–
N.A.Foster				
G.C.Small				
E.E.Hemmings				
Extras	(b 1, lb 18, w 1)	20		
Total	(50 overs; 6 wickets)	**254**		

INDIA		Runs	Balls	4/6
K.Srikkanth	b Foster	31	55	4
S.M.Gavaskar	b DeFreitas	4	7	1
N.S.Sidhu	c Athey b Foster	22	40	–
M.Azharuddin	lbw b Hemmings	64	74	7
C.S.Pandit	lbw b Foster	24	30	3
* Kapil Dev	c Gatting b Hemmings	30	22	3
R.J.Shastri	c Downton b Hemmings	21	32	2
† K.S.More	c and b Emburey	0	5	–
M.Prabhakar	c Downton b Small	4	11	–
C.Sharma	c Lamb b Hemmings	0	1	–
Maninder Singh	not out	0	–	–
Extras	(b 1, lb 9, w 6, nb 3)	19		
Total	(45.3 overs)	**219**		

INDIA	O	M	R	W
Kapil Dev	10	1	38	2
Prabhakar	9	1	40	0
Maninder	10	0	54	3
Sharma	9	0	41	1
Shastri	10	0	49	0
Azharuddin	2	0	13	0

ENGLAND	O	M	R	W
DeFreitas	7	0	37	1
Small	6	0	22	1
Emburey	10	1	35	1
Foster	10	0	47	3
Hemmings	9.3	1	52	4
Gooch	3	0	16	0

FALL OF WICKETS
1-40, 2-79, 3-196, 4-203, 5-219, 6-231

FALL OF WICKETS
1-7, 2-58, 3-73, 4-121, 5-168, 6-204, 7-205, 8-218, 9-219, 10-219

Umpires: A.R.Crafter (*Australia*) (56) and S.J.Woodward (*New Zealand*) (12).

ENGLAND v AUSTRALIA 1987-88

At Eden Gardens, Calcutta, India, on 8 November 1987.   Result: **AUSTRALIA** won by 7 runs.   Toss: Australia.
Award: D.C.Boon.   LOI debuts: None.

Australia gained their first World Cup title when England's ninth-wicket pair failed to score 17 off the 50th over, bowled by Craig McDermott. Their margin of victory remains the narrowest in these finals. David Boon scored his fifth fifty in six innings.

AUSTRALIA		Runs	Balls	4/6
D.C.Boon	c Downton b Hemmings	75	125	7
G.R.Marsh	b Foster	24	49	3
D.M.Jones	c Athey b Hemmings	33	57	1/1
C.J.McDermott	b Gooch	14	8	2
* A.R.Border	run out	31	31	3
M.R.J.Veletta	not out	45	31	6
S.R.Waugh	not out	5	4	–
S.P.O'Donnell				
† G.C.Dyer				
T.B.A.May				
B.A.Reid				
Extras	(b 1, lb 13, w 5, nb 7)	26		
Total	(50 overs; 5 wickets)	**253**		

ENGLAND		Runs	Balls	4/6
G.A.Gooch	lbw b O'Donnell	35	57	4
R.T.Robinson	lbw b McDermott	0	1	–
C.W.J.Athey	run out	58	103	2
* M.W.Gatting	c Dyer b Border	41	45	3/1
A.J.Lamb	b Waugh	45	45	4
† P.R.Downton	c O'Donnell b Border	9	8	1
J.E.Emburey	run out	10	16	–
P.A.J.DeFreitas	c Reid b Waugh	17	10	2/1
N.A.Foster	not out	7	6	–
G.C.Small	not out	3	3	–
E.E.Hemmings				
Extras	(b 1, lb 14, w 2, nb 4)	21		
Total	(50 overs; 8 wickets)	**246**		

ENGLAND	O	M	R	W
DeFreitas	6	1	34	0
Small	6	0	33	0
Foster	10	0	38	1
Hemmings	10	1	48	2
Emburey	10	0	44	0
Gooch	8	1	42	1

AUSTRALIA	O	M	R	W
McDermott	10	1	51	1
Reid	10	0	43	0
Waugh	9	0	37	2
O'Donnell	10	1	35	1
May	4	0	27	0
Border	7	0	38	1

FALL OF WICKETS
1-75, 2-151, 3-166, 4-168, 5-241

FALL OF WICKETS
1-1, 2-66, 3-135, 4-170, 5-188, 6-218, 7-220, 8-235

Umpires: R.B.Gupta (*India*) (9) and Mahboob Shah (*Pakistan*) (16).

PAKISTAN v ENGLAND 1987-88

At Gaddafi Stadium, Lahore on 18 November 1987.   Result: **ENGLAND** won by 2 wickets.   Toss: Pakistan.
Award: J.E.Emburey.   LOI debuts: Pakistan – Zahid Ahmed.

For the second international in succession Salim Yousuf (dislocated thumb) was injured while keeping wicket, Salim Malik deputising from the third over. Abdul Qadir led Pakistan in this three-match 45-over series which followed the World Cup, Javed Miandad being indisposed.

PAKISTAN		Runs	Balls	4/6
Ramiz Raja	c Gatting b Capel	38	54	3
Shoaib Mohammed	c French b Foster	11	22	2
Salim Malik	run out	30	54	4
Ijaz Ahmed	c Gooch b Hemmings	17	33	1
Mudassar Nazar	c Fairbrother b Foster	10	23	–
† Salim Yousuf	c French b Hemmings	22	23	2
Manzoor Elahi	b Emburey	14	16	2
Wasim Akram	b Emburey	5	8	–
* Abdul Qadir	run out	7	4	–/1
Zahid Ahmed	c and b Emburey	0	5	–
Salim Jaffer	not out	2	7	–
Extras	(b 1, lb 5, w 2, nb 2)	10		
Total	(41.3 overs)	**166**		

ENGLAND		Runs	Balls	4/6
G.A.Gooch	b Qadir	43	59	6
B.C.Broad	c Manzoor b Wasim	1	3	–
* M.W.Gatting	lbw b Qadir	16	45	–
C.W.J.Athey	lbw b Wasim	20	67	–
D.J.Capel	run out	8	19	1
N.H.Fairbrother	b Zahid	25	36	2
J.E.Emburey	c Ijaz b Zahid	4	9	–
P.A.J.DeFreitas	not out	14	18	–/1
N.A.Foster	lbw b Wasim	0	6	–
† B.N.French	not out	7	8	–
E.E.Hemmings				
Extras	(b 13, lb 10, w 4, nb 2)	29		
Total	(44.3 overs; 8 wickets)	**167**		

ENGLAND	O	M	R	W
DeFreitas	7	1	19	0
Foster	8	1	37	2
Capel	9	0	43	1
Emburey	8.3	2	17	3
Hemmings	9	1	44	2

PAKISTAN	O	M	R	W
Wasim Akram	9	0	25	3
Salim Jaffer	3	0	18	0
Mudassar Nazar	9	1	19	0
Manzoor Elahi	2	0	12	0
Abdul Qadir	8.3	2	32	2
Zahid Ahmed	9	1	24	2
Shoaib Mohammed	4	0	14	0

FALL OF WICKETS
1-25, 2-62, 3-96, 4-102, 5-132, 6-138, 7-154, 8-163, 9-163, 10-166

FALL OF WICKETS
1-5, 2-61, 3-74, 4-89, 5-120, 6-127, 7-137, 8-140

Umpires: Shakil Khan (10) and Shakoor Rana (18).

PAKISTAN v ENGLAND 1987-88

At National Stadium, Karachi on 20 November 1987.　Result: **ENGLAND** won by 23 runs.　Toss: England.
Award: G.A.Gooch.　LOI debuts: None.

Graham Gooch registered the highest of his eight LOI hundreds. David Capel's 37-ball fifty included three sixes off successive balls (from Shoaib Mohammed). Ramiz Raja, the first to be dismissed for obstruction in these matches, intercepted the ball with his bat to avoid being run out while taking a second run off the final ball to complete his hundred.

ENGLAND		Runs	Balls	4/6	PAKISTAN		Runs	Balls	4/6
G.A.Gooch	st Zulqarnain b Qadir	142	134	14	Ramiz Raja	obstructed the field	99	122	6
B.C.Broad	c Manzoor b Qadir	22	54	1	Shoaib Mohammed	run out	37	62	3
* M.W.Gatting	run out	21	27	1	Salim Malik	c Fairbrother b Foster	35	33	4
N.H.Fairbrother	b Zahid	2	7	–	Manzoor Elahi	run out	17	12	1/1
D.J.Capel	not out	50	40	3/3	* Abdul Qadir	c Broad b Foster	0	1	–
J.E.Emburey	c Manzoor b Qadir	1	2	–	Ijaz Ahmed	c Athey b Emburey	26	17	4
P.A.J.DeFreitas	b Mohsin	0	1	–	Wasim Akram	c Foster b Emburey	9	7	1
N.A.Foster	not out	5	2	1	Asif Mujtaba	b Capel	0	2	–
C.W.J.Athey					Zahid Ahmed	not out	3	8	–
† B.N.French					† Zulqarnain				
E.E.Hemmings					Mohsin Kamal				
Extras	(b 3, lb 9, w 6, nb 2)	20			Extras	(lb 7, w 7)	14		
Total	(44 overs; 6 wickets)	263			Total	(44 overs; 8 wickets)	240		

PAKISTAN	O	M	R	W	ENGLAND	O	M	R	W
Wasim Akram	4	1	9	0	DeFreitas	9	1	35	0
Mohsin Kamal	9	0	57	1	Foster	9	0	47	2
Manzoor Elahi	3	0	19	0	Capel	8	1	41	1
Zahid Ahmed	7	0	37	1	Hemmings	9	0	45	0
Asif Mujtaba	3	0	25	0	Emburey	9	0	65	2
Abdul Qadir	8	0	30	3					
Salim Malik	5	0	32	0	**FALL OF WICKETS**				
Shoaib Mohammed	5	0	42	0	1-77, 2-138, 3-172, 4-172, 5-214, 6-228, 7-230, 8-240				

FALL OF WICKETS
1-70, 2-135, 3-140, 4-249, 5-251, 6-251

Umpires: Khizer Hayat (18) and Mahboob Shah (17).

PAKISTAN v ENGLAND 1987-88

At Shahi Bagh Stadium, Peshawar on 22 November 1987.　Result: **ENGLAND** won by 98 runs.　Toss: England.
Award: N.A.Foster.　LOI debuts: Pakistan – Shakil Khan; England – R.C.Russell.

England completed a clean sweep of this rubber, Pakistan being further weakened by the absence of Wasim Akram (strained groin) and Shoaib Mohammed's retirement at 11 for 1 for stitches to his left eyebrow after missing a hook.

ENGLAND		Runs	Balls	4/6	PAKISTAN		Runs	Balls	4/6
G.A.Gooch	c Zulqarnain b Mudassar	57	78	5	Ramiz Raja	lbw b Foster	5	9	–
B.C.Broad	b Shakil	66	110	6	Shoaib Mohammed	retired hurt	6	16	–
* M.W.Gatting	c Manzoor b Qadir	53	51	4	Salim Malik	b Cook	52	78	1
D.J.Capel	st Zulqarnain b Tausif	25	17	1/1	Ijaz Ahmed	c Russell b Cook	15	23	1
J.E.Emburey	run out	3	3	–	Mudassar Nazar	b Capel	1	10	–
P.A.J.DeFreitas	c Shoaib b Qadir	3	3	–	Manzoor Elahi	c Gooch b Emburey	21	23	1/1
C.W.J.Athey	st Zulqarnain b Qadir	6	9	–	* Abdul Qadir	c Russell b DeFreitas	21	22	1/1
N.H.Fairbrother	run out	1	1	–	† Zulqarnain	c Russell b DeFreitas	0	2	–
N.A.Foster	not out	2	1	–	Mohsin Kamal	b Foster	5	7	–
† R.C.Russell	not out	2	2	–	Tausif Ahmed	not out	0	0	–
N.G.B.Cook					Shakil Khan	b Foster	0	4	–
Extras	(b 1, lb 7, w 5, nb 5)	18			Extras	(lb 3, w 3, nb 6)	12		
Total	(45 overs; 8 wickets)	236			Total	(31.5 overs)	138		

PAKISTAN	O	M	R	W	ENGLAND	O	M	R	W
Mohsin Kamal	9	0	37	0	DeFreitas	7	0	31	2
Shakil Khan	9	0	50	1	Foster	6.5	0	20	3
Mudassar Nazar	9	0	33	1	Cook	6	1	18	2
Tausif Ahmed	9	0	59	1	Capel	9	0	44	1
Abdul Qadir	9	0	49	3	Emburey	3	0	22	1

FALL OF WICKETS　　　　　　　　　　　　　　　**FALL OF WICKETS**
1-101, 2-168, 3-214, 4-221, 5-221, 6-231, 7-232, 8-234　　1-11, 2-34, 3-43, 4-78, 5-122, 6-126, 7-138, 8-138, 9-138

Umpires: Amanullah Khan (11) and Javed Akhtar (8).

INDIA v WEST INDIES 1987-88

At Vidarbha CA Ground, Nagpur on 8 December 1987.　　Result: **WEST INDIES** won by 10 runs.　　Toss: West Indies.
Award: B.P.Patterson.　　LOI debuts: India – Arshad Ayub.

Patrick Patterson was the first bowler to take six wickets in a limited-overs international in India. A one-man demo by Viv Richards persuaded umpire Mehra to reverse his decision concerning the former's appeal against Dilip Vengsarkar for a low slip catch.

WEST INDIES		Runs	Balls	4/6
C.G.Greenidge	b Maninder	36	40	1
D.L.Haynes	run out	20	46	–
R.B.Richardson	c Gaekwad b Maninder	11	29	1
* I.V.A.Richards	st More b Maninder	1	6	–
A.L.Logie	lbw b Shastri	13	46	1
C.L.Hooper	not out	57	84	3/1
† P.J.L.Dujon	c Vengsarkar b Shastri	4	7	
R.A.Harper	st More b Gaekwad	7	17	
W.K.M.Benjamin	b Kapil Dev	31	29	3/3
C.A.Walsh	not out	3	4	–
B.P.Patterson				
Extras	(lb 12, w 2, nb 6)	20		
Total	(50 overs; 8 wickets)	**203**		

INDIA		Runs	Balls	4/6
K.Srikkanth	c Richards b Patterson	5	24	1
Arun Lal	b Patterson	7	20	
A.D.Gaekwad	lbw b Patterson	0	1	–
* D.B.Vengsarkar	c Richards b Benjamin	8	26	1
C.S.Pandit	lbw b Richards	6	8	1
R.J.Shastri	b Patterson	20	57	1
Kapil Dev	c Haynes b Patterson	87	64	9/2
† K.S.More	c Haynes b Patterson	33	36	6
Arshad Ayub	b Hooper	4	5	1
C.Sharma	lbw b Walsh	2	20	–
Maninder Singh	not out	4	13	–
Extras	(b 2, lb 7, w 3, nb 5)	17		
Total	(44.4 overs)	**193**		

INDIA	O	M	R	W
Kapil Dev	7	0	13	1
Sharma	7	0	49	0
Maninder Singh	8	0	40	3
Arshad Ayub	10	0	26	0
Shastri	10	1	24	2
Gaekwad	8	0	39	1

WEST INDIES	O	M	R	W
Patterson	9.4	0	29	6
Walsh	9	0	21	1
Richards	9	1	39	1
Benjamin	10	1	53	1
Hooper	7	0	42	1

FALL OF WICKETS
1-51, 2-71, 3-73, 4-81, 5-101, 6-107, 7-128, 8-193

FALL OF WICKETS
1-13, 2-13, 3-18, 4-31, 5-31, 6-144, 7-145, 8-150, 9-155, 10-193

Umpires: R.Mehra (3) and V.Vikramraju (4).

INDIA v WEST INDIES 1987-88

At Nehru Stadium, Gauhati on 23 December 1987.　　Result: **WEST INDIES** won by 52 runs.　　Toss: India.
Award: I.V.A.Richards.　　LOI debuts: None.

Although this seven-match series was scheduled to involve 50-over innings, this contest was reduced to 45 to combat the earlier twilight in Assam.

WEST INDIES		Runs	Balls	4/6
D.L.Haynes	b Maninder	17	42	3
P.V.Simmons	c Srikkanth b Amarnath	34	48	3/1
R.B.Richardson	c More b Amarnath	10	45	–
* I.V.A.Richards	st More b Shastri	41	52	1/1
A.L.Logie	lbw b Kapil Dev	34	40	1
C.L.Hooper	c Kapil Dev b Shastri	2	11	–
R.A.Harper	not out	18	17	1/1
W.K.M.Benjamin	st More b Shastri	4	8	–
† P.J.L.Dujon	not out	13	8	2
C.A.Walsh				
B.P.Patterson				
Extras	(lb 12, w 2)	14		
Total	(45 overs; 7 wickets)	**187**		

INDIA		Runs	Balls	4/6
K.Srikkanth	b Walsh	1	13	–
A.D.Gaekwad	b Benjamin	12	30	2
M.Amarnath	c Richards b Hooper	33		2
* D.B.Vengsarkar	c Harper b Richards	24		–
M.Azharuddin	c and b Hooper	3	8	–
Kapil Dev	not out	22	29	1
R.J.Shastri	b Walsh	12	26	1
† K.S.More	c Dujon b Patterson	1	6	–
M.Prabhakar	lbw b Walsh	1	4	–
Arshad Ayub	run out	6	12	–
Maninder Singh	b Walsh	0	1	–
Extras	(b 8, lb 8, w 4)	20		
Total	(41.3 overs)	**135**		

INDIA	O	M	R	W
Kapil Dev	9	1	47	1
Prabhakar	4	0	22	0
Maninder Singh	9	3	19	1
Amarnath	9	1	21	2
Shastri	9	0	30	3
Arshad Ayub	5	0	36	0

WEST INDIES	O	M	R	W
Patterson	8	2	20	1
Walsh	7.3	2	16	4
Benjamin	5	1	15	1
Harper	9	0	21	0
Richards	8	0	37	1
Hooper	4	1	10	2

FALL OF WICKETS
1-40, 2-62, 3-74, 4-143, 5-145, 6-163, 7-170

FALL OF WICKETS
1-9, 2-25, 3-83, 4-89, 5-89, 6-117, 7-118, 8-122, 9-134, 10-135

Umpires: S.K.Ghosh (3) and R.V.Ramani (5).

INDIA v WEST INDIES 1987-88

At Eden Gardens, Calcutta on 2 January 1988.   Result: **INDIA** won by 56 runs.   Toss: India.
Award: M.Amarnath.   LOI debuts: India – W.V.Raman, A.K.Sharma, S.K.Sharma.

Led for the first time by Ravi Shastri and spurred on by a crowd estimated at 85,000, India ended a sequence of nine defeats by West Indies since the 1983 World Cup final.

INDIA		Runs	Balls	4/6	WEST INDIES		Runs	Balls	4/6
K.Srikkanth	c Dujon b Walsh	1	8	–	C.G.Greenidge	c Amarnath b Maninder	44	70	3/1
Arun Lal	c Greenidge b Hooper	51	67	5	D.L.Haynes	lbw b Kapil Dev	3	10	–
M.Amarnath	run out	70	83	9	R.B.Richardson	run out	28	38	3
S.K.Sharma	c Richardson b Richards	0	4	–	* I.V.A.Richards	c Arun Lal b Maninder	3	13	–
M.Azharuddin	run out	44	57	2/1	A.L.Logie	c Azharuddin b Shastri	38	55	2
Kapil Dev	c Benjamin b Richards	1	2	–	C.L.Hooper	lbw b Kapil Dev	27	40	2
* R.J.Shastri	lbw b Patterson	25	29	1	W.K.M.Benjamin	c and b Shastri	1	5	–
W.V.Raman	not out	8	15	–	† P.J.L.Dujon	run out	2	5	–
† K.S.More	not out	9	6	1	E.A.E.Baptiste	lbw b Amarnath	6	8	–
A.K.Sharma					C.A.Walsh	c sub (S.V.Manjrekar) b S.K.Sharma	2	5	–
Maninder Singh					B.P.Patterson	not out	3	7	–
Extras	(lb 10, w 2, nb 1)	13			Extras	(lb 6, w 2, nb 1)	9		
Total	(45 overs; 7 wickets)	**222**			**Total**	(41.5 overs)	**166**		

WEST INDIES	O	M	R	W	INDIA	O	M	R	W
Patterson	9	0	36	1	Kapil Dev	7	1	20	2
Walsh	9	2	26	1	S.K.Sharma	5.5	0	29	1
Baptiste	5	0	23	0	Amarnath	9	0	46	1
Benjamin	5	0	29	0	Maninder Singh	9	0	19	2
Richards	9	0	48	2	Shastri	9	1	31	2
Hooper	8	0	50	1	A.K.Sharma	2	0	15	0

FALL OF WICKETS
1-2, 2-130, 3-131, 4-138, 5-140, 6-194, 7-210

FALL OF WICKETS
1-12, 2-53, 3-65, 4-92, 5-152, 6-153, 7-153, 8-158, 9-162, 10-166

Umpires: R.B.Gupta (10) and P.D.Reporter (2).

INDIA v WEST INDIES 1987-88

At Racecourse Ground, Rajkot on 5 January 1988.   Result: **WEST INDIES** won by 6 wickets.   Toss: India.
Award: I.V.A.Richards.   LOI debuts: India – S.V.Manjrekar; West Indies – D.Williams.

Viv Richards completed the last of his (then) record 11 hundreds off 75 balls with his seventh six, three of which had come off successive balls from Ravi Shastri. India were fined 15,000 rupees for failing to bowl their scheduled 46 overs in the allotted time.

INDIA		Runs	Balls	4/6	WEST INDIES		Runs	Balls	4/6
K.Srikkanth	c Williams b Benjamin	32	55	4	D.L.Haynes	b Raman	49	90	2
Arun Lal	c Greenidge b Patterson	10	14	1	R.B.Richardson	c Kapil Dev b S.K.Sharma	27	24	3
W.V.Raman	c Baptiste b Patterson	95	123	6	A.L.Logie	c Viswanath b Arshad Ayub	12	26	–
M.Azharuddin	c and b Richards	24	26	1/1	* I.V.A.Richards	not out	110	77	7/7
Kapil Dev	c Logie b Richards	22	12	3	C.L.Hooper	c Manjrekar b Kapil Dev	12	15	–
* R.J.Shastri	c and b Hooper	7	9	–	E.A.E.Baptiste	not out	7	9	–
† S.Viswanath	c Baptiste b Richards	1	5	–	C.G.Greenidge				
S.V.Manjrekar	not out	19	19	3	W.K.M.Benjamin				
A.K.Sharma	not out	2	2	–	† D.Williams				
Arshad Ayub					C.A.Walsh				
S.K.Sharma					B.P.Patterson				
Extras	(lb 8, nb 1)	9			Extras	(lb 7, w 1)	8		
Total	(43 overs; 7 wickets)	**221**			**Total**	(40.1 overs; 4 wickets)	**225**		

WEST INDIES	O	M	R	W	INDIA	O	M	R	W
Patterson	8	1	49	2	Kapil Dev	8	1	22	1
Walsh	8	0	39	0	S.K.Sharma	6	0	31	1
Benjamin	9	0	35	1	A.K.Sharma	3	0	12	0
Baptiste	9	1	40	0	Arshad Ayub	10	1	55	0
Richards	8	0	42	3	Shastri	9	1	50	0
Hooper	1	0	8	1	Raman	4	0	44	1
					Srikkanth	0.1	0	4	0

FALL OF WICKETS
1-34, 2-69, 3-119, 4-151, 5-173, 6-176, 7-214

FALL OF WICKETS
1-38, 2-77, 3-147, 4-191

Umpires: D.N.Dotiwala (6) and S.B.Kulkarni (3).

INDIA v WEST INDIES 1987-88

At Gujarat Stadium, Motera, Ahmedabad on 7 January 1988.   Result: **WEST INDIES** won by 2 runs.   Toss: India.
Award: K.Srikkanth.   LOI debuts: None.

After much confusion and argument between the touring administration and the Indian Board this charity match was designated an official limited-overs international but was excluded from the Charminar Challenge series.

WEST INDIES		Runs	Balls	4/6
R.B.Richardson	b C.Sharma	4	9	I
P.V.Simmons	lbw b Kapil Dev	20	35	2
P.J.L.Dujon	c and b C.Sharma	II	I4	I
* I.V.A.Richards	b Amarnath	I7	24	3
A.L.Logie	c Srikkanth b Arshad Ayub	30	56	3
C.L.Hooper	c Arun Lal b Srikkanth	33	69	2
E.A.E.Baptiste	run out	31	34	2
W.K.M.Benjamin	b Arshad Ayub	5	9	–
† D.Williams	run out	I	I	–
W.W.Davis	b Kapil Dev	10	23	–
B.P.Patterson	not out	I3	I6	I/I
Extras	(b 7, lb 10, w 3, nb I)	21		
Total	(48.3 overs)	**196**		

INDIA		Runs	Balls	4/6
K.Srikkanth	c Baptiste b Richards	53	71	5/I
Arun Lal	c Williams b Patterson	I6	36	2
M.Amarnath	c Simmons b Baptiste	21	46	I
W.V.Raman	c Williams b Benjamin	I4	26	I
Kapil Dev	run out	21	26	–/2
S.V.Manjrekar	c Richards b Benjamin	0	2	–
* R.J.Shastri	b Davis	I9	39	–
† S.Viswanath	b Patterson	7	22	–
C.Sharma	not out	I6	I5	2
Arshad Ayub	c Simmons b Patterson	I4	24	I
S.K.Sharma	not out	I	4	–
Extras	(b I, lb 8, w 3)	12		
Total	(50 overs; 9 wickets)	**194**		

INDIA	O	M	R	W
C.Sharma	7	0	31	2
S.K.Sharma	5	I	24	0
Amarnath	10	I	28	I
Kapil Dev	8.3	0	21	2
Arshad Ayub	10	I	37	2
Shastri	3	0	23	0
Srikkanth	5	I	15	I

WEST INDIES	O	M	R	W
Patterson	9	2	26	3
Davis	10	2	35	I
Benjamin	10	0	30	2
Baptiste	10	0	49	I
Richards	10	I	43	I
Hooper	I	0	2	0

FALL OF WICKETS
1-6, 2-28, 3-55, 4-65, 5-111, 6-163, 7-166, 8-168, 9-173, 10-196

FALL OF WICKETS
1-26, 2-69, 3-98, 4-127, 5-127, 6-136, 7-160, 8-162, 9-191

Umpires: P.G.Pandit (7) and R.V.Ramani (6).

INDIA v WEST INDIES 1987-88

At Nahar Singh Stadium, Faridabad on 19 January 1988.   Result: **WEST INDIES** won by 4 wickets.   Toss: West Indies.
Award: M.Amarnath.   LOI debuts: None.

Faridabad provided India with its 25th LOI venue, Mohinder Amarnath with his first hundred in these matches, and West Indies with a decisive 4-1 lead in the series.

INDIA		Runs	Balls	4/6
K.Srikkanth	b Baptiste	28	41	2
Arun Lal	c Dujon b Walsh	0	I	–
M.Amarnath	not out	100	148	4/I
W.V.Raman	b Benjamin	I3	23	2
M.Azharuddin	b Baptiste	2	8	–
Kapil Dev	c Hooper b Benjamin	45	44	4
* R.J.Shastri	c Baptiste b Davis	28	30	3
† K.S.More	not out	9	7	–
C.Sharma				
Arshad Ayub				
Maninder Singh				
Extras	(lb 4, nb I)	5		
Total	(50 overs; 6 wickets)	**230**		

WEST INDIES		Runs	Balls	4/6
D.L.Haynes	b Kapil Dev	12	22	I
P.V.Simmons	c and b Srikkanth	67	96	4
R.B.Richardson	lbw b Srikkanth	49	90	5
* I.V.A.Richards	c Arun Lal b Srikkanth	9	8	I
A.L.Logie	run out	29	32	2
C.L.Hooper	not out	39	26	3/I
† P.J.L.Dujon	st More b Shastri	9	18	I
E.A.E.Baptiste	not out	3	3	–
W.K.M.Benjamin				
W.W.Davis				
C.A.Walsh				
Extras	(b I, lb 13)	14		
Total	(49.1 overs; 6 wickets)	**231**		

WEST INDIES	O	M	R	W
Walsh	10	I	42	I
Davis	10	0	69	I
Benjamin	10	2	38	2
Baptiste	10	2	41	2
Richards	8	I	31	0
Hooper	2	0	5	0

INDIA	O	M	R	W
Kapil Dev	9	I	37	I
Sharma	5	0	25	0
Amarnath	6	0	I4	0
Maninder Singh	9.1	0	55	0
Arshad Ayub	10	0	37	0
Shastri	4	0	24	I
Srikkanth	6	0	25	3

FALL OF WICKETS
1-3, 2-50, 3-73, 4-76, 5-142, 6-213

FALL OF WICKETS
1-18, 2-126, 3-144, 4-155, 5-192, 6-223

Umpires: S.K.Ghosh (4) and V.K.Ramaswamy (9).

244

INDIA v WEST INDIES 1987-88

At Roop Singh Stadium, Gwalior on 22 January 1988.　　Result: **WEST INDIES** won by 73 runs.　　Toss: India.
Award: C.L.Hooper.　　LOI debuts: India – N.D.Hirwani.

Carl Hooper dominated the inaugural international in Gwalior with his first LOI hundred, scoring 57 of the last 67 runs added by West Indies from just 33 balls. His partnership of 108 with Gus Logie remains a national fifth-wicket record against India.

WEST INDIES		Runs	Balls	4/6
D.L.Haynes	b Sharma	5	15	–
P.V.Simmons	lbw b Arshad Ayub	21	22	2
R.B.Richardson	c Arshad Ayub b Shastri	30	39	4
* I.V.A.Richards	c Sharma b Amarnath	33	35	2/1
A.L.Logie	c Sharma b Arshad Ayub	54	84	1
C.L.Hooper	not out	113	97	12/2
E.A.E.Baptiste	run out	4	9	–
W.K.M.Benjamin	not out	0	–	–
† P.J.L.Dujon				
C.A.Walsh				
B.P.Patterson				
Extras	(b 2, lb 14, w 2)	18		
Total	(50 overs; 6 wickets)	**278**		

INDIA		Runs	Balls	4/6
K.Srikkanth	c Baptiste b Patterson	9	24	2
Arun Lal	b Patterson	0	3	–
M.Amarnath	c Dujon b Patterson	3	15	–
W.V.Raman	c Dujon b Walsh	1	4	–
M.Azharuddin	c Dujon b Benjamin	23	33	3
Kapil Dev	b Baptiste	52	42	8/1
* R.J.Shastri	not out	73	72	11/1
† K.S.More	run out	10	16	1
Arshad Ayub	st Dujon b Richards	12	14	2
S.K.Sharma	c Haynes b Richards	1	11	–
N.D.Hirwani	b Patterson	2	16	–
Extras	(b 4, lb 8, w 4, nb 3)	19		
Total	(41 overs)	**205**		

INDIA	O	M	R	W
Sharma	6	0	42	1
Amarnath	10	0	43	1
Arshad Ayub	9	1	36	2
Shastri	9	0	48	1
Hirwani	10	0	34	0
Raman	3	0	23	0
Kapil Dev	3	0	36	0

WEST INDIES	O	M	R	W
Patterson	8	0	29	4
Walsh	6	1	23	1
Benjamin	10	1	34	1
Baptiste	5	0	37	1
Richards	9	0	34	2
Hooper	2	0	27	0
Simmons	1	0	9	0

FALL OF WICKETS
1-8, 2-55, 3-65, 4-103, 5-211, 6-268

FALL OF WICKETS
1-1, 2-14, 3-15, 4-15, 5-88, 6-94, 7-117, 8-134, 9-152, 10-205

Umpires: D.N.Dotiwala (7) and S.B.Kulkarni (4).

INDIA v WEST INDIES 1987-88

At University Stadium, Trivandrum on 25 January 1988.　　Result: **WEST INDIES** won by 9 wickets.　　Toss: West Indies.
Award: P.V.Simmons.　　LOI debuts: None.

Krish Srikkanth's fourth LOI hundred failed to prevent West Indies from winning the series 6-1. The opening stand of 164 between Gordon Greenidge and Phil Simmons remains the highest for West Indies in India.

INDIA		Runs	Balls	4/6
K.Srikkanth	b Baptiste	101	106	10/3
R.Lamba	lbw b Patterson	8	18	1
M.Amarnath	b Patterson	56	87	3/1
Kapil Dev	lbw b Richards	1	4	–
* R.J.Shastri	st Williams b Richards	3	6	–
M.Azharuddin	c Baptiste b Davis	36	33	4
† K.S.More	c Richards b Patterson	3	3	–
S.V.Manjrekar	not out	14	16	1
S.K.Sharma	run out	2	2	–
Maninder Singh	not out	1	2	–
N.D.Hirwani				
Extras	(b 2, lb 7, w 1, nb 4)	14		
Total	(45 overs; 8 wickets)	**239**		

WEST INDIES		Runs	Balls	4/6
C.G.Greenidge	st More b Maninder	84	76	4/5
P.V.Simmons	not out	104	129	4/4
R.B.Richardson	not out	37	55	4
* I.V.A.Richards				
A.L.Logie				
C.L.Hooper				
E.A.E.Baptiste				
W.K.M.Benjamin				
W.W.Davis				
† D.Williams				
B.P.Patterson				
Extras	(b 1, lb 12, w 1, nb 2)	16		
Total	(42.5 overs; 1 wicket)	**241**		

WEST INDIES	O	M	R	W
Patterson	9	0	34	3
Davis	9	0	59	1
Benjamin	9	0	41	0
Baptiste	9	0	51	1
Richards	8	0	40	2
Hooper	1	0	5	0

INDIA	O	M	R	W
Kapil Dev	4	0	28	0
Sharma	6.5	0	47	0
Amarnath	5	0	21	0
Maninder Singh	9	0	42	0
Hirwani	9	0	40	0
Shastri	2	0	24	0
Srikkanth	7	0	26	0

FALL OF WICKETS
1-33, 2-160, 3-161, 4-167, 5-200, 6-203, 7-231, 8-234

FALL OF WICKETS
1-164

Umpires: P.G.Pandit (8) and V.Vikramraju (5).

AUSTRALIA v SRI LANKA 1987-88

At WACA Ground, Perth on 2 January 1988.　　Result: **AUSTRALIA** won by 81 runs.　　Toss: Sri Lanka.
Award: S.R.Waugh.　　LOI debuts: Australia – A.I.C.Dodemaide.

The ninth World Series followed the now established format of 12 qualifying games and a best-of-three set of finals. Tony Dodemaide emulated Uvais Karnain of Sri Lanka (*LOI No. 257*) by taking five wickets on his first appearance in limited-overs internationals.

AUSTRALIA		Runs	Balls	4/6	SRI LANKA		Runs	Balls	4/6
D.C.Boon	c and b De Silva	56	81	6	R.S.Mahanama	c Dodemaide b Waugh	19	49	1
G.R.Marsh	c De Alwis b Ramanayake	14	53	–	A.P.Gurusinha	c Dyer b Dodemaide	0	2	–
D.M.Jones	c Gurusinha b De Silva	55	63	3	P.A.de Silva	b Dodemaide	11	22	1
* A.R.Border	c Mahanama b De Silva	31	24	3	A.Ranatunga	c Border b Dodemaide	7	16	–
M.R.J.Veletta	run out	27	33	2	* R.S.Madugalle	c Border b Waugh	7	24	–
S.R.Waugh	not out	35	32	2	H.P.Tillekeratne	c Dyer b May	9	29	–
† G.C.Dyer	run out	9	12	–	J.R.Ratnayeke	b Whitney	19	38	–
A.I.C.Dodemaide	c Mahanama b Ratnayeke	4	6	–	† R.G.de Alwis	c Marsh b Dodemaide	44	42	4/1
C.J.McDermott	not out	0	–	–	C.P.H.Ramanayake	c Jones b Waugh	6	14	1
T.B.A.May					G.F.Labrooy	lbw b Dodemaide	33	39	4/1
M.R.Whitney					K.N.Amalean	not out	0	–	–
Extras	(b 4, lb 7, w 4, nb 3)	18			Extras	(b 4, lb 3, w 2, nb 4)	13		
Total	(50 overs; 7 wickets)	249			Total	(44.2 overs)	168		

SRI LANKA	O	M	R	W	AUSTRALIA	O	M	R	W
Ratnayeke	9	0	35	1	Dodemaide	7.2	0	21	5
Labrooy	9	0	38	0	McDermott	5	1	15	0
Amalean	6	1	27	0	Whitney	10	0	26	1
Ramanayake	7	1	33	1	Waugh	10	2	34	3
De Silva	10	0	58	3	May	10	3	49	1
Ranatunga	9	0	47	0	Jones	2	0	16	0

FALL OF WICKETS
1-57, 2-84, 3-143, 4-189, 5-199, 6-224, 7-238

FALL OF WICKETS
1-2, 2-20, 3-33, 4-49, 5-50, 6-78, 7-82, 8-118, 9-168, 10-168

Umpires: P.J.McConnell (35) and T.A.Prue (1).

AUSTRALIA v NEW ZEALAND 1987-88

At WACA Ground, Perth on 3 January 1988.　　Result: **NEW ZEALAND** won by 1 run.　　Toss: New Zealand.
Award: A.H.Jones.　　LOI debuts: None.

With Australia needing eight to win off Martin Snedden's final over, New Zealand again kept calm under pressure to gain their third LOI victory by a single run. The only previous instance in World Series matches had involved the same teams (*LOI No. 107*).

NEW ZEALAND		Runs	Balls	4/6	AUSTRALIA		Runs	Balls	4/6
J.G.Wright	c and b McDermott	13	27	1	G.R.Marsh	c sub (P.A.Horne) b Bracewell	24	69	2
A.H.Jones	c Boon b Waugh	87	107	9	D.C.Boon	c Patel b Bracewell	44	63	7
M.D.Crowe	c Dyer b Taylor	45	65	4	D.M.Jones	run out	92	91	5/1
* J.J.Crowe	c Taylor b Whitney	0	3	–	* A.R.Border	lbw b Hadlee	3	5	–
D.N.Patel	c Dyer b Taylor	3	15	–	M.R.J.Veletta	b Hadlee	7	14	–
† T.E.Blain	c Border b McDermott	16	27	2	S.R.Waugh	c Blain b Hadlee	0	6	–
R.J.Hadlee	c Taylor b Dodemaide	23	29	–	† G.C.Dyer	c sub (P.A.Horne) b Snedden	4	22	–
J.G.Bracewell	run out	4	17	–	P.L.Taylor	c J.J.Crowe b Chatfield	16	22	1
M.C.Snedden	not out	11	12	–	C.J.McDermott	c Patel b Chatfield	7	5	–/1
S.R.Gillespie	run out	6	6	1	A.I.C.Dodemaide	not out	9	7	–
E.J.Chatfield	not out	1	2	–	M.R.Whitney	c Bracewell b Snedden	3	8	–
Extras	(lb 16, w 5, nb 2)	23			Extras	(lb 11, w 6, nb 5)	22		
Total	(50 overs; 9 wickets)	232			Total	(49.4 overs)	231		

AUSTRALIA	O	M	R	W	NEW ZEALAND	O	M	R	W
Dodemaide	10	1	43	1	Chatfield	10	1	39	2
McDermott	10	0	37	2	Hadlee	10	0	35	3
Waugh	10	0	49	1	Gillespie	7	1	48	0
Whitney	10	0	46	1	Snedden	9.4	0	51	2
Taylor	10	0	41	2	Bracewell	10	0	27	2
					Patel	3	0	20	0

FALL OF WICKETS
1-27, 2-133, 3-134, 4-145, 5-177, 6-189, 7-203, 8-219, 9-228

FALL OF WICKETS
1-78, 2-81, 3-84, 4-102, 5-105, 6-132, 7-183, 8-198, 9-221, 10-231

Umpires: R.C.Bailhache (19) and P.J.McConnell (36).

NEW ZEALAND v SRI LANKA 1987-88

At Sydney Cricket Ground on 5 January 1988.   Result: **NEW ZEALAND** won by 6 wickets.   Toss: Sri Lanka.
Award: E.J.Chatfield.   LOI debuts: None.

Martin Crowe scored his 2000th run in 67 limited-overs internationals. Asoka de Silva was recalled by the New Zealand captain when he walked without an appeal after being run out via umpire Crafter's leg.

SRI LANKA		Runs	Balls	4/6
R.S.Mahanama	b Morrison	0	4	–
A.P.Gurusinha	run out	23	50	I
P.A.de Silva	c Blain b Chatfield	5	35	–
A.Ranatunga	c Blain b Snedden	35	51	5
* R.S.Madugalle	c M.D.Crowe b Morrison	13	39	I
H.P.Tillekeratne	lbw b Snedden	0	3	–
† R.G.de Alwis	c Patel b Bracewell	32	37	4
J.R.Ratnayeke	c Wright b Chatfield	41	41	2/1
G.F.Labrooy	c Patel b Chatfield	3	5	–
E.A.R.de Silva	b Chatfield	6	13	–
C.P.H.Ramanayake	not out	II	14	–
Extras	(lb 3, w 2)	5		
Total	**(48.2 overs)**	**174**		

NEW ZEALAND		Runs	Balls	4/6
J.G.Wright	c Mahanama b Ramanayake	41	75	3/1
A.H.Jones	c and b Ramanayake	34	82	2
M.D.Crowe	c P.A.de Silva b Labrooy	52	68	5
D.N.Patel	c De Alwis b Ratnayeke	29	55	I
† T.E.Blain	not out	5	10	I
* J.J.Crowe	not out	6	7	–
R.J.Hadlee				
J.G.Bracewell				
M.C.Snedden				
D.K.Morrison				
E.J.Chatfield				
Extras	(b I, lb 6, w 4)	II		
Total	**(48.4 overs; 4 wickets)**	**178**		

NEW ZEALAND	O	M	R	W
Morrison	10	2	43	2
Hadlee	9	4	12	0
Chatfield	9.2	I	32	4
Bracewell	10	0	41	I
Snedden	10	I	43	2

SRI LANKA	O	M	R	W
Ratnayeke	9.4	0	40	I
Labrooy	10	I	37	I
Ramanayake	10	2	28	2
E.A.R.de Silva	10	I	17	0
Ranatunga	5	0	27	0
P.A.de Silva	4	0	22	0

FALL OF WICKETS
1-0, 2-14, 3-40, 4-76, 5-76, 6-82, 7-134, 8-147, 9-159, 10-174

FALL OF WICKETS
1-80, 2-82, 3-167, 4-167

Umpires: A.R.Crafter (57) and R.A.French (56).

AUSTRALIA v NEW ZEALAND 1987-88

At Melbourne Cricket Ground on 7 January 1988.   Result: **AUSTRALIA** won by 6 runs.   Toss: Australia.
Award: S.R.Waugh.   LOI debuts: None.

Steve Waugh played an exceptional innings in extreme heat which demanded unofficial drinks breaks after every two overs.

AUSTRALIA		Runs	Balls	4/6
D.C.Boon	b Chatfield	9	24	I
G.R.Marsh	c Patel b Gillespie	12	28	I
D.M.Jones	b Snedden	48	77	4
* A.R.Border	c Wright b Gillespie	0	I	–
M.R.J.Veletta	c Blain b Snedden	4	12	–
S.R.Waugh	b Snedden	68	91	3
† G.C.Dyer	c Jones b Chatfield	38	46	2
P.L.Taylor	run out	2	2	–
A.I.C.Dodemaide	c Gillespie b Hadlee	8	9	–
C.J.McDermott	c M.D.Crowe b Chatfield	9	II	–
M.R.Whitney	not out	2	2	–
Extras	(lb 12, nb 4)	16		
Total	**(49.4 overs)**	**216**		

NEW ZEALAND		Runs	Balls	4/6
J.G.Wright	run out	20	27	2
A.H.Jones	c Dodemaide b McDermott	59	106	4
D.N.Patel	b Whitney	12	24	I
M.D.Crowe	b Dodemaide	37	62	I
* J.J.Crowe	c and b Taylor	9	21	–
† T.E.Blain	b Dodemaide	7	13	–
R.J.Hadlee	c Taylor b Waugh	23	24	I
J.G.Bracewell	c Boon b McDermott	9	II	I
M.C.Snedden	c Waugh b McDermott	3	5	–
S.R.Gillespie	not out	8	10	–
E.J.Chatfield	not out	0	–	–
Extras	(b 4, lb 10, w 6, nb 3)	23		
Total	**(50 overs; 9 wickets)**	**210**		

NEW ZEALAND	O	M	R	W
Chatfield	10	2	31	3
Hadlee	8.4	I	42	I
Snedden	10	I	36	3
Gillespie	9	0	41	2
Bracewell	8	0	32	0
Patel	4	0	22	0

AUSTRALIA	O	M	R	W
Dodemaide	10	I	25	2
McDermott	10	0	50	3
Whitney	10	0	46	I
Waugh	10	0	41	I
Taylor	10	0	34	I

FALL OF WICKETS
1-47, 2-79, 3-121, 4-138, 5-157, 6-168, 7-180, 8-188, 9-209

FALL OF WICKETS
1-17, 2-31, 3-31, 4-39, 5-127, 6-192, 7-195, 8-197, 9-211, 10-216

Umpires: R.C.Bailhache (20) and P.J.McConnell (37).

NEW ZEALAND v SRI LANKA 1987-88

At Adelaide Oval on 9 January 1988.　　Result: **NEW ZEALAND** won by 4 wickets.　　Toss: Sri Lanka.
Award: R.J.Hadlee.　　LOI debuts: None.

John Wright deputised as captain when Jeff Crowe dropped himself through lack of form. With New Zealand needing six off the last three balls, Terry Blain obliged with a two and a boundary.

SRI LANKA		Runs	Balls	4/6		NEW ZEALAND		Runs	Balls	4/6
R.S.Mahanama	c Blain b Snedden	51	84	5		K.R.Rutherford	c Kuruppu b Ratnayeke	1	5	–
† D.S.B.P.Kuruppu	c Hadlee b Morrison	23	22	4		* J.G.Wright	run out	61	76	3
A.P.Gurusinha	c and b Gillespie	7	32	1		A.H.Jones	b Ramanayake	63	116	2/1
P.A.de Silva	c Jones b Chatfield	51	56	4		M.D.Crowe	c Gurusinha b Ramanayake	39	42	4
A.Ranatunga	c Gillespie b Hadlee	42	53	3/1		D.N.Patel	st Kuruppu b P.A.de Silva	9	12	–
* R.S.Madugalle	c Crowe b Gillespie	3	8	–		R.J.Hadlee	c Gurusinha b Ratnayeke	25	33	–
M.A.R.Samarasekera	b Gillespie	3	5	–		† T.E.Blain	not out	25	22	1
J.R.Ratnayeke	c Rutherford b Hadlee	23	25	1		M.C.Snedden	not out	0	–	–
G.F.Labrooy	b Hadlee	0	1	–		S.R.Gillespie				
E.A.R.de Silva	c Chatfield b Morrison	15	16	–		D.K.Morrison				
C.P.H.Ramanayake	not out	3	3	–		E.J.Chatfield				
Extras	(lb 12, w 2, nb 6)	20				Extras	(b 2, lb 3, w 8, nb 6)	19		
Total	(49.5 overs)	**241**				**Total**	(49.5 overs; 6 wickets)	**242**		

NEW ZEALAND	O	M	R	W		SRI LANKA	O	M	R	W
Morrison	5.5	1	39	2		Labrooy	10	2	39	0
Hadlee	10	1	35	3		Ratnayeke	9.5	0	44	2
Chatfield	10	1	43	1		Ramanayake	7	0	47	2
Gillespie	10	0	40	3		E.A.R.de Silva	10	2	40	0
Snedden	10	0	47	1		P.A.de Silva	9	0	41	1
Patel	4	0	25	0		Samarasekera	4	0	26	0

FALL OF WICKETS
1-35, 2-66, 3-121, 4-160, 5-187, 6-192, 7-206, 8-207, 9-234, 10-241

FALL OF WICKETS
1-1, 2-103, 3-164, 4-180, 5-204, 6-236

Umpires: L.J.King (1) and P.J.McConnell (38).

AUSTRALIA v SRI LANKA 1987-88

At Adelaide Oval on 10 January 1988.　　Result: **AUSTRALIA** won by 81 runs.　　Toss: Australia.
Award: D.C.Boon.　　LOI debuts: None.

During the highest of his five LOI hundreds David Boon equalled Greg Chappell's Australian record (*LOI No. 146*) by hitting 15 boundaries in an innings.

AUSTRALIA		Runs	Balls	4/6		SRI LANKA		Runs	Balls	4/6
G.R.Marsh	run out	37	63			R.S.Mahanama	c Veletta b Whitney	50	77	7
D.C.Boon	c Madugalle b P.A.de Silva	122	130	15		D.S.B.P.Kuruppu	b McDermott	5	13	–
D.M.Jones	c Gurusinha b Labrooy	69	68			A.P.Gurusinha	run out	43	79	3
* A.R.Border	c E.A.R.de Silva b Ratnayeke	13	18			P.A.de Silva	run out	43	36	1/2
M.R.J.Veletta	run out	5	9			A.Ranatunga	c Veletta b Dodemaide	23	23	–
S.R.Waugh	not out	8	6			* R.S.Madugalle	lbw b Dodemaide	7	10	–
C.J.McDermott	run out	8	4			J.R.Ratnayeke	b Dodemaide	1	4	–
† G.C.Dyer	not out	3	2			† R.G.de Alwis	not out	11	14	–
A.I.C.Dodemaide						E.A.R.de Silva	c Veletta b McDermott	3	17	–
P.L.Taylor						G.F.Labrooy	not out	3	18	–
M.R.Whitney						C.P.H.Ramanayake				
Extras	(b 4, lb 16, w 4)	24				Extras	(b 1, lb 11, w 6, nb 1)	19		
Total	(50 overs; 6 wickets)	**289**				**Total**	(50 overs; 8 wickets)	**208**		

SRI LANKA	O	M	R	W		AUSTRALIA	O	M	R	W
Ratnayeke	10	0	49	1		Dodemaide	10	1	27	3
Labrooy	10	0	44	1		McDermott	10	0	31	2
Ramanayake	8	0	46	0		Whitney	10	0	53	1
E.A.R.de Silva	4	0	27	0		Waugh	10	0	37	0
Ranatunga	8	0	50	0		Taylor	10	1	48	0
P.A.de Silva	10	0	53	1						

FALL OF WICKETS
1-115, 2-199, 3-244, 4-268, 5-274, 6-282

FALL OF WICKETS
1-9, 2-106, 3-132, 4-172, 5-187, 6-189, 7-190, 8-197

Umpires: A.R.Crafter (58) and M.W.Johnson (47).

NEW ZEALAND v SRI LANKA 1987-88

At Bellerive Oval, Hobart on 12 January 1988.   Result: **SRI LANKA** won by 4 wickets.   Toss: Sri Lanka.
Award: R.S.Mahanama.   LOI debuts: None.

The first international staged at the new headquarters of the Tasmanian Cricket Association saw Sri Lanka end a run of 14 successive defeats since their last win on 24 December 1986. Richard Hadlee became the first to appear in 100 LOIs for New Zealand.

NEW ZEALAND		Runs	Balls	4/6
K.R.Rutherford	b Ranatunga	24	59	1
J.G.Wright	c Madugalle b Ratnayeke	8	39	1
* J.J.Crowe	run out	0	2	–
M.D.Crowe	c De Alwis b Ramanayake	25	33	3
D.N.Patel	c P.A.de Silva b Ranatunga	0	2	–
T.E.Blain	not out	49	96	4
R.J.Hadlee	c sub‡ b Ratnayeke	52	68	2
† I.D.S.Smith	c Mahanama b Ratnayeke	9	7	1
S.R.Gillespie	not out	9	5	–
D.K.Morrison				
E.J.Chatfield				
Extras	(lb 9, w 11, nb 3)	23		
Total	(50 overs; 7 wickets)	**199**		

SRI LANKA		Runs	Balls	4/6
D.S.B.P.Kuruppu	c M.D.Crowe b Morrison	12	25	1
R.S.Mahanama	run out	58	83	4/1
A.P.Gurusinha	c Smith b Hadlee	5	12	–
P.A.de Silva	c Chatfield b Gillespie	55	102	5/1
A.Ranatunga	c Morrison b Hadlee	11	13	2
* R.S.Madugalle	c Wright b Rutherford	10	25	–
J.R.Ratnayeke	not out	21	25	2
† R.G.de Alwis	not out	7	5	–
G.F.Labrooy				
E.A.R.de Silva				
C.P.H.Ramanayake				
Extras	(b 1, lb 10, w 5, nb 5)	21		
Total	(46.3 overs; 6 wickets)	**200**		

SRI LANKA	O	M	R	W
Ratnayeke	9	1	33	3
Labrooy	10	0	43	0
Ranatunga	10	1	34	2
Ramanayake	10	2	30	1
Gurusinha	2	0	15	0
E.A.R.de Silva	5	1	16	0
P.A.de Silva	4	0	19	0

NEW ZEALAND	O	M	R	W
Chatfield	10	1	30	0
Hadlee	10	1	22	2
Morrison	8.3	1	36	1
Gillespie	10	0	51	1
Patel	3	0	25	0
Rutherford	5	0	25	1

FALL OF WICKETS
1-28, 2-32, 3-67, 4-67, 5-70, 6-165, 7-179

FALL OF WICKETS
1-24, 2-33, 3-136, 4-151, 5-167, 6-185

Umpires: M.W.Johnson (48) and S.G.Randell (26).

‡(H.P.Tillekeratne)

AUSTRALIA v SRI LANKA 1987-88

At Melbourne Cricket Ground on 14 January 1988.   Result: **AUSTRALIA** won by 38 runs.   Toss: Australia.
Award: P.L.Taylor.   LOI debuts: None.

Peter Taylor followed up a handy innings with his only four-wicket analysis in 83 limited-overs internationals.

AUSTRALIA		Runs	Balls	4/6
D.C.Boon	c Ranatunga b Ratnayeke	1	7	–
G.R.Marsh	c De Alwis b Labrooy	0	4	–
D.M.Jones	c Mahanama b Ranatunga	31	57	1
M.R.J.Veletta	b Jeganathan	46	68	3
S.R.Waugh	c De Alwis b Labrooy	27	40	2
A.R.Border	c Labrooy b De Silva	61	60	5
† G.C.Dyer	c Madugalle b Labrooy	4	18	–
P.L.Taylor	not out	27	29	1
C.J.McDermott	c Gurusinha b Labrooy	19	14	3
A.I.C.Dodemaide	not out	10	7	–
T.B.A.May				
Extras	(lb 11, w 6)	17		
Total	(50 overs; 8 wickets)	**243**		

SRI LANKA		Runs	Balls	4/6
R.S.Mahanama	b Dodemaide	7	6	–
D.S.B.P.Kuruppu	lbw b Waugh	22	42	2
A.P.Gurusinha	c Border b McDermott	7	12	1
P.A.de Silva	c Boon b McDermott	10	10	1
A.Ranatunga	run out	67	86	6
* R.S.Madugalle	c and b Taylor	44	61	2/1
† R.G.de Alwis	c Veletta b Taylor	0	3	–
J.R.Ratnayeke	c Dyer b Dodemaide	16	23	2
G.F.Labrooy	c McDermott b Taylor	13	18	2
S.Jeganathan	c Border b Taylor	1	4	–
C.P.H.Ramanayake	not out	6	7	1
Extras	(lb 8, w 3, nb 1)	12		
Total	(44.5 overs)	**205**		

SRI LANKA	O	M	R	W
Ratnayeke	8	0	24	1
Labrooy	10	1	39	4
Ramanayake	5	0	32	0
Ranatunga	10	0	47	1
Jeganathan	7	0	36	1
De Silva	10	0	54	1

AUSTRALIA	O	M	R	W
Dodemaide	7.5	2	36	2
McDermott	10	2	42	2
Waugh	7	0	33	1
May	10	0	48	0
Taylor	10	1	38	4

FALL OF WICKETS
1-2, 2-6, 3-66, 4-90, 5-158, 6-172, 7-190, 8-220

FALL OF WICKETS
1-14, 2-27, 3-38, 4-66, 5-163, 6-163, 7-164, 8-183, 9-189, 10-205

Umpires: R.C.Bailhache (21) and R.A.French (57).

NEW ZEALAND v SRI LANKA 1987-88

At Woolloongabba, Brisbane on 16 January 1988.   Result: **NEW ZEALAND** won by 4 wickets.   Toss: New Zealand.
Award: M.D.Crowe.   LOI debuts: None.

The match was reduced first by a rain-delayed start (to 43 overs) and further by a tardy bowling rate which earned New Zealand a fine of $A1600. Jeff Crowe again stood down.

SRI LANKA		Runs	Balls	4/6
R.S.Mahanama	c Blain b Chatfield	12	55	–
D.S.B.P.Kuruppu	c Patel b Morrison	47	71	5
A.P.Gurusinha	run out	0	10	–
P.A.de Silva	run out	25	25	4
A.Ranatunga	run out	25	27	2
* R.S.Madugalle	c Blain b Morrison	5	10	–
M.A.R.Samarasekera	c Snedden b Chatfield	8	18	–
J.R.Ratnayeke	not out	15	18	2
† R.G.de Alwis	c Rutherford b Chatfield	2	4	–
G.F.Labrooy	not out	2	11	–
C.P.H.Ramanayake				
Extras	(lb 9, w 12, nb 2)	23		
Total	(39 overs; 8 wickets)	**164**		

NEW ZEALAND	O	M	R	W
Hadlee	9	1	25	0
Morrison	6	0	39	2
Chatfield	9	2	27	3
Gillespie	8	0	39	0
Snedden	7	0	25	0

FALL OF WICKETS
1-52, 2-54, 3-97, 4-103, 5-111, 6-139, 7-142, 8-145

Umpires: R.C.Bailhache (22) and C.D.Timmins (1).

NEW ZEALAND		Runs	Balls	4/6
K.R.Rutherford	b Labrooy	1	7	–
* J.G.Wright	c Ranatunga b Ramanayake	22	30	3
A.H.Jones	c De Alwis b Ranatunga	29	61	2
M.D.Crowe	run out	43	60	4
D.N.Patel	c Ranatunga b Ramanayake	1	9	–
† T.E.Blain	b Ranatunga	17	20	2
R.J.Hadlee	not out	21	30	2
M.C.Snedden	not out	15	19	2
S.R.Gillespie				
E.J.Chatfield				
D.K.Morrison				
Extras	(b 2, lb 5, w 10, nb 1)	18		
Total	(37.1 overs; 6 wickets)	**167**		

SRI LANKA	O	M	R	W
Ratnayeke	7.1	0	40	0
Labrooy	8	1	32	1
Ramanayake	8	2	28	2
Samarasekera	3	0	18	0
Ranatunga	8	0	35	2
De Silva	3	1	7	0

FALL OF WICKETS
1-1, 2-43, 3-78, 4-90, 5-122, 6-139

AUSTRALIA v NEW ZEALAND 1987-88

At Woolloongabba, Brisbane on 17 January 1988   Result: **AUSTRALIA** won by 5 wickets.   Toss: Australia.
Award: S.R.Waugh.   LOI debuts: New Zealand – V.R.Brown.

The brave initiative of curator Kevin Mitchell, who astonished the umpires by covering the pitch when New Zealand were 137 for 3 after 40.3 overs, seconds before a heavy deluge, ensured that only 37 minutes were lost. Allan Border and John Wright made their 100th appearances in the World Series and all LOIs respectively.

NEW ZEALAND		Runs	Balls	4/6
J.G.Wright	c Dyer b Waugh	19	46	1
A.H.Jones	b Waugh	65	131	4
* J.J.Crowe	c McDermott b Taylor	41	72	3
M.D.Crowe	c Davis b Taylor	1	4	–
R.J.Hadlee	not out	9	12	–
V.R.Brown	c Dyer b McDermott	10	7	2
† T.E.Blain	not out	8	2	–/1
K.R.Rutherford				
M.C.Snedden				
S.R.Gillespie				
E.J.Chatfield				
Extras	(lb 13, w 8, nb 2)	23		
Total	(44 overs; 5 wickets)	**176**		

AUSTRALIA	O	M	R	W
Dodemaide	9	1	26	0
McDermott	10	0	49	1
Davis	10	0	33	0
Waugh	8	1	23	2
Taylor	7	0	32	2

FALL OF WICKETS
1-42, 2-128, 3-131, 4-156, 5-168

Umpires: A.R.Crafter (59) and M.W.Johnson (49).

AUSTRALIA		Runs	Balls	4/6
G.R.Marsh	c Blain b Chatfield	1	4	–
D.C.Boon	lbw b Snedden	48	47	7
C.J.McDermott	c Blain b Chatfield	0	1	–
D.M.Jones	c Brown b Snedden	31	45	2/1
M.R.J.Veletta	not out	32	55	2
S.R.Waugh	c Blain b Snedden	45	38	5
* A.R.Border	not out	9	14	–/1
† G.C.Dyer				
P.L.Taylor				
A.I.C.Dodemaide				
S.P.Davis				
Extras	(lb 8, w 2, nb 1)	11		
Total	(33.2 overs; 5 wickets)	**177**		

NEW ZEALAND	O	M	R	W
Chatfield	5	2	19	2
Hadlee	7	0	28	0
Snedden	8	2	40	3
Gillespie	6.2	0	31	0
Brown	7	0	51	0

FALL OF WICKETS
1-2, 2-2, 3-79, 4-90, 5-154

AUSTRALIA v SRI LANKA 1987-88

At Sydney Cricket Ground on 19 January 1988.   Result: **AUSTRALIA** won by 3 wickets.   Toss: Australia.
Award: M.R.J.Veletta.   LOI debuts: Sri Lanka – S.M.S.Kaluperuma.

Mike Whitney and Steve Waugh each returned their best analyses in limited-overs internationals.

SRI LANKA		Runs	Balls	4/6
R.S.Mahanama	c Border b Whitney	12	27	1
D.S.B.P.Kuruppu	b Whitney	2	12	–
A.P.Gurusinha	c Jones b Whitney	37	101	1/1
S.M.S.Kaluperuma	b Waugh	4	24	–
P.A.de Silva	c Dyer b Waugh	79	100	7
A.Ranatunga	c Marsh b Waugh	16	21	2
* R.S.Madugalle	lbw b Waugh	0	4	–
J.R.Ratnayeke	c Boon b Whitney	1	2	–
† R.G.de Alwis	c Marsh b Dodemaide	4	2	1
G.F.Labrooy	not out	6	8	–
C.P.H.Ramanayake	not out	5	3	1
Extras	(b 2, lb 16, w 3, nb 1)	22		
Total	(50 overs; 9 wickets)	**188**		

AUSTRALIA		O	M	R	W
Whitney		10	2	34	4
Dodemaide		10	1	34	1
Waugh		10	0	33	4
May		10	0	22	0
Taylor		10	1	47	0

FALL OF WICKETS
1-16, 2-27, 3-39, 4-113, 5-140, 6-148, 7-162, 8-172, 9-179

AUSTRALIA		Runs	Balls	4/6
D.C.Boon	c Mahanama b Ratnayeke	15	30	2
G.R.Marsh	c Gurusinha b Ramanayake	8	33	1
D.M.Jones	c De Alwis b Ramanayake	9	27	1
M.R.J.Veletta	not out	68	91	1
S.R.Waugh	c Mahanama b Ramanayake	16	22	2
* A.R.Border	c and b De Silva	12	30	–
† G.C.Dyer	b Waugh	4	16	–
A.I.C.Dodemaide	c Kaluperuma b Labrooy	30	46	2
P.L.Taylor	not out	10	8	–
T.B.A.May				
M.R.Whitney				
Extras	(lb 10, w 3, nb 4)	17		
Total	(49.3 overs; 7 wickets)	**189**		

SRI LANKA	O	M	R	W
Ratnayeke	10	1	32	1
Labrooy	9.3	1	43	1
Ramanayake	10	0	35	3
Ranatunga	9	0	35	1
De Silva	10	0	31	1
Kaluperuma	1	0	3	0

FALL OF WICKETS
1-25, 2-30, 3-49, 4-72, 5-91, 6-100, 7-173

Umpires: T.A.Prue (2) and S.G.Randell (27).

AUSTRALIA v NEW ZEALAND 1987-88

At Sydney Cricket Ground on 20 January 1988.   Result: **AUSTRALIA** won by 78 runs.   Toss: Australia.
Award: G.R.Marsh.   LOI debuts: None.

An all-ticket crowd of 41,813 witnessed a dead match, both sides having qualified for the finals. New Zealand rested Hadlee, Wright and Martin Crowe. Final points: Australia 14, New Zealand 8, Sri Lanka 2.

AUSTRALIA		Runs	Balls	4/6
G.R.Marsh	c Brown b Chatfield	101	148	5
D.C.Boon	c Blain b Snedden	8	16	1
D.M.Jones	c Bracewell b Gillespie	15	24	3
M.R.J.Veletta	c Gillespie b Bracewell	19	33	1
S.R.Waugh	c Crowe b Watson	0	4	–
* A.R.Border	run out	22	34	2/1
† G.C.Dyer	c Crowe b Brown	11	18	–
C.J.McDermott	c Jones b Chatfield	18	14	1/1
A.I.C.Dodemaide	not out	11	13	–
P.L.Taylor	not out	3	2	–
S.P.Davis				
Extras	(b 2, lb 6, w 4, nb 1)	13		
Total	(50 overs; 8 wickets)	**221**		

NEW ZEALAND		O	M	R	W
Snedden		10	1	36	1
Chatfield		10	3	26	2
Watson		10	1	49	1
Gillespie		6	0	31	1
Bracewell		10	1	47	1
Brown		4	0	24	1

FALL OF WICKETS
1-17, 2-50, 3-88, 4-88, 5-145, 6-162, 7-194, 8-217

Umpires: A.R.Crafter (60) and L.J.King (2).

NEW ZEALAND		Runs	Balls	4/6
† T.E.Blain	c Jones b McDermott	1	11	–
A.H.Jones	c Dyer b Davis	19	38	2
* J.J.Crowe	c Veletta b Dodemaide	6	31	–
K.R.Rutherford	c McDermott b Davis	10	24	1
D.N.Patel	b Davis	13	26	–
V.R.Brown	st Dyer b Taylor	32	71	1
J.G.Bracewell	b Waugh	38	52	2
M.C.Snedden	c Veletta b Taylor	6	8	–
S.R.Gillespie	lbw b Taylor	2	5	–
W.Watson	c Boon b Waugh	1	11	–
E.J.Chatfield	not out	1	1	–
Extras	(lb 7, w 5, nb 2)	14		
Total	(44.5 overs)	**143**		

AUSTRALIA		O	M	R	W
Dodemaide		9	1	21	1
McDermott		8	1	31	1
Davis		10	1	27	3
Waugh		7.5	0	33	2
Taylor		10	2	24	3

FALL OF WICKETS
1-3, 2-30, 3-34, 4-48, 5-73, 6-119, 7-131, 8-138, 9-141, 10-143

AUSTRALIA v NEW ZEALAND 1987-88

At Melbourne Cricket Ground on 22 January 1988.　　Result: **AUSTRALIA** won by 8 wickets.　　Toss: Australia.
LOI debuts: None.

Ewen Chatfield was playing his 100th international. Surprisingly, the unbroken partnership of 107 between Dean Jones and Mike Veletta remains Australia's highest for the third wicket against New Zealand.

NEW ZEALAND		Runs	Balls	4/6
J.G.Wright	c Dyer b Davis	16	53	1
A.H.Jones	c Dyer b Dodemaide	4	16	–
M.D.Crowe	c Dyer b Dodemaide	48	72	4
* J.J.Crowe	run out	33	56	2
R.J.Hadlee	c Boon b McDermott	34	48	3
† T.E.Blain	run out	1	4	–
V.R.Brown	c Waugh b Davis	2	7	–
J.G.Bracewell	c Border b Waugh	17	18	2
M.C.Snedden	c Taylor b McDermott	15	19	–
W.Watson	c Border b Waugh	1	5	–
E.J.Chatfield	not out	3	3	–
Extras	(lb 2, w 1)	3		
Total	(49.5 overs)	**177**		

AUSTRALIA		Runs	Balls	4/6
D.C.Boon	c Bracewell b Watson	47	74	6
G.R.Marsh	b Watson	9	44	–
D.M.Jones	not out	58	75	4
M.R.J.Veletta	not out	57	80	7
* A.R.Border				
S.R.Waugh				
† G.C.Dyer				
A.I.C.Dodemaide				
P.L.Taylor				
C.J.McDermott				
S.P.Davis				
Extras	(b 2, lb 3, w 2, nb 2)	9		
Total	(44.5 overs; 2 wickets)	**180**		

AUSTRALIA	O	M	R	W
Dodemaide	10	2	29	2
McDermott	9.5	0	37	2
Davis	10	1	27	2
Waugh	10	0	47	2
Taylor	10	0	35	0

NEW ZEALAND	O	M	R	W
Chatfield	7.5	2	19	0
Hadlee	9	0	36	0
Snedden	10	3	39	0
Watson	10	3	36	2
Bracewell	8	0	45	0

FALL OF WICKETS
1-11, 2-47, 3-91, 4-126, 5-129, 6-132, 7-143, 8-161, 9-169, 10-177

FALL OF WICKETS
1-33, 2-73

Umpires: R.C.Bailhache (23) and P.J.McConnell (39).

AUSTRALIA v NEW ZEALAND 1987-88

At Sydney Cricket Ground on 24 January 1988.　　Result: **AUSTRALIA** won by 6 wickets.　　Toss: Australia.
Finals Award: D.M.Jones.　　LOI debuts: None.

A rain break of 117 minutes reduced this match by 12 overs an innings and the floodlights were used briefly to counteract the overcast conditions.

NEW ZEALAND		Runs	Balls	4/6
† T.E.Blain	c Veletta b McDermott	9	24	–
J.G.Wright	c Waugh b Dodemaide	8	23	–
M.D.Crowe	b Davis	8	16	–
A.H.Jones	not out	56	82	3
R.J.Hadlee	c Border b Waugh	19	35	–
* J.J.Crowe	c Jones b McDermott	42	40	4/1
D.N.Patel	not out	11	12	
J.G.Bracewell				
M.C.Snedden				
E.J.Chatfield				
W.Watson				
Extras	(b 11, w 4)	15		
Total	(38 overs; 5 wickets)	**168**		

AUSTRALIA		Runs	Balls	4/6
G.R.Marsh	c Wright b Hadlee	5	16	1
D.C.Boon	c Snedden b Watson	43	56	3
C.J.McDermott	c M.D.Crowe b Snedden	24	16	4
D.M.Jones	not out	53	70	2
M.R.J.Veletta	c sub (K.R.Rutherford) b Snedden	30	35	1
* A.R.Border	not out	11	10	2
S.R.Waugh				
† G.C.Dyer				
A.I.C.Dodemaide				
P.L.Taylor				
S.P.Davis				
Extras	(lb 3)	3		
Total	(34.1 overs; 4 wickets)	**169**		

AUSTRALIA	O	M	R	W
Dodemaide	8	0	27	1
McDermott	8	0	29	2
Davis	8	1	23	1
Taylor	7	0	27	0
Waugh	7	0	51	1

NEW ZEALAND	O	M	R	W
Hadlee	8	2	22	1
Chatfield	6	2	34	0
Snedden	8	0	45	2
Bracewell	7	0	37	0
Watson	5.1	0	28	1

FALL OF WICKETS
1-20, 2-21, 3-31, 4-79, 5-139

FALL OF WICKETS
1-12, 2-48, 3-91, 4-145

Umpires: A.R.Crafter (61) and P.J.McConnell (40).

252

AUSTRALIA v ENGLAND 1987-88

At Melbourne Cricket Ground on 4 February 1988.   Result: **AUSTRALIA** won by 22 runs.   Toss: Australia.
Award: G.R.Marsh.   LOI debuts: England – P.W.Jarvis, N.V.Radford.

Australia took this celebration of 200 years of white settlement rather more seriously than the touring team. Conceding the equivalent of three overs of no-balls and wides, the latter failed to bowl the required 50 overs and forfeited the equivalent of their appearance money.

AUSTRALIA		Runs	Balls	4/6
D.C.Boon	c and b Capel	33	63	3
G.R.Marsh	run out	87	122	5
D.M.Jones	c sub (M.D.Moxon) b Emburey	30	47	2
M.R.J.Veletta	c Capel b Emburey	13	20	–
S.R.Waugh	run out	27	25	2
* A.R.Border	c Gatting b DeFreitas	19	21	1
A.I.C.Dodemaide	not out	7	7	–
P.L.Taylor	not out	1	1	–
† G.C.Dyer				
S.P.Davis				
M.R.Whitney				
Extras	(lb 6, w 5, nb 7)	18		
Total	(48 overs; 6 wickets)	235		

ENGLAND		Runs	Balls	4/6
B.C.Broad	c Dyer b Waugh	25	43	–
R.T.Robinson	c Dodemaide b Whitney	35	51	5
P.A.J.DeFreitas	run out	21	27	1
C.W.J.Athey	c Border b Davis	4	10	–
N.H.Fairbrother	st Dyer b Taylor	22	38	1
* M.W.Gatting	c Border b Whitney	37	47	2
D.J.Capel	c Taylor b Davis	18	28	1
J.E.Emburey	b Dodemaide	26	25	–
† C.J.Richards	not out	14	18	–
N.V.Radford	not out	0	4	–
P.W.Jarvis				
Extras	(lb 9, w 1, nb 1)	11		
Total	(48 overs; 8 wickets)	213		

ENGLAND	O	M	R	W
DeFreitas	10	1	43	1
Radford	10	0	61	0
Capel	8	1	30	1
Jarvis	10	0	42	0
Emburey	10	0	53	2

AUSTRALIA	O	M	R	W
Whitney	10	1	37	2
Dodemaide	10	1	35	1
Davis	10	0	55	2
Waugh	10	0	42	1
Taylor	8	0	35	1

FALL OF WICKETS
1-70, 2-133, 3-169, 4-184, 5-222, 6-233

FALL OF WICKETS
1-58, 2-65, 3-82, 4-96, 5-123, 6-172, 7-175, 8-213

Umpires: R.C.Bailhache (24) and A.R.Crafter (62).

NEW ZEALAND v ENGLAND 1987-88

At Carisbrook, Dunedin on 9 March 1988.   Result: **ENGLAND** won by 5 wickets.   Toss: New Zealand.
Award: J.G.Wright.   LOI debuts: New Zealand – M.J.Greatbatch, C.M.Kuggeleijn.

John Emburey's four-wicket return exceeded his reward from the three-match Test series which preceded this 50-over rubber.

NEW ZEALAND		Runs	Balls	4/6
R.B.Reid	c Broad b DeFreitas	8	29	1
* J.G.Wright	c Moxon b Radford	70	92	8/1
M.D.Crowe	b Jarvis	18	19	3
M.J.Greatbatch	c Capel b Emburey	28	48	4
K.R.Rutherford	c French b Capel	13	26	1
C.M.Kuggeleijn	c Gatting b DeFreitas	34	53	2
J.G.Bracewell	run out	7	18	–
† I.D.S.Smith	b Emburey	0	2	–
M.C.Snedden	b Emburey	7	11	–
W.Watson	not out	0	–	–
E.J.Chatfield	st French b Emburey	0	1	–
Extras	(lb 13, w 5, nb 1)	19		
Total	(49.4 overs)	204		

ENGLAND		Runs	Balls	4/6
B.C.Broad	run out	33	57	3
M.D.Moxon	c Smith b Chatfield	6	23	1
R.T.Robinson	lbw b Snedden	17	30	3
* M.W.Gatting	c Kuggeleijn b Rutherford	42	43	5
N.H.Fairbrother	not out	50	75	7
D.J.Capel	c Smith b Chatfield	48	65	4
J.E.Emburey	not out	2	4	–
P.A.J.DeFreitas				
† B.N.French				
P.W.Jarvis				
N.V.Radford				
Extras	(lb 6, w 2, nb 1)	9		
Total	(49.2 overs; 5 wickets)	207		

ENGLAND	O	M	R	W
DeFreitas	10	1	26	2
Radford	10	0	47	1
Capel	10	1	45	1
Jarvis	10	2	34	1
Emburey	9.4	0	39	4

NEW ZEALAND	O	M	R	W
Watson	10	2	46	0
Chatfield	10	2	15	2
Kuggeleijn	7	0	31	0
Snedden	10	1	46	1
Bracewell	7.2	0	42	0
Rutherford	5	0	21	1

FALL OF WICKETS
1-24, 2-50, 3-127, 4-140, 5-157, 6-188, 7-190, 8-204, 9-204, 10-204

FALL OF WICKETS
1-28, 2-53, 3-69, 4-114, 5-192

Umpires: R.L.McHarg (4) and G.C.Morris (7).

NEW ZEALAND v ENGLAND 1987-88

At Lancaster Park, Christchurch on 12 March 1988.   Result: **ENGLAND** won by 6 wickets.   Toss: England.
Award: B.C.Broad.   LOI debuts: None.

Rain delayed the start by 45 minutes and reduced the overs by five per innings.

NEW ZEALAND		Runs	Balls	4/6
R.B.Reid	c Broad b Capel	8	25	1
* J.G.Wright	c DeFreitas b Embury	43	73	3/1
M.D.Crowe	c French b DeFreitas	2	5	–
M.J.Greatbatch	run out	15	30	1
K.R.Rutherford	run out	5	14	–
C.M.Kuggeleijn	b Embury	40	64	2/1
J.G.Bracewell	run out	43	49	4
† I.D.S.Smith	c Fairbrother b Embury	19	11	3
M.C.Snedden	not out	1	1	–
W.Watson	not out	2	1	–
E.J.Chatfield				
Extras	(lb 5, w 3)	8		
Total	(45 overs; 8 wickets)	**186**		

ENGLAND	O	M	R	W
DeFreitas	9	0	53	1
Capel	9	3	27	1
Jarvis	9	0	33	0
Radford	9	0	30	0
Embury	9	1	38	3

FALL OF WICKETS
1-24, 2-26, 3-53, 4-68, 5-86, 6-149, 7-183, 8-183

Umpires: B.L.Aldridge (5) and G.C.Morris (8).

ENGLAND		Runs	Balls	4/6
B.C.Broad	c Rutherford b Snedden	56	78	3/1
M.D.Moxon	c Kuggeleijn b Watson	17	20	1
R.T.Robinson	c Chatfield b Rutherford	44	68	4
* M.W.Gatting	b Watson	33	40	3
N.H.Fairbrother	not out	25	31	3
D.J.Capel	not out	6	20	–
J.E.Emburey				
P.A.J.DeFreitas				
† B.N.French				
P.W.Jarvis				
N.V.Radford				
Extras	(lb 4, w 3)	7		
Total	(42.5 overs; 4 wickets)	**188**		

NEW ZEALAND	O	M	R	W
Watson	9	1	31	2
Chatfield	7	0	32	0
Bracewell	5	0	28	0
Snedden	9	0	33	1
Kuggeleijn	6	0	31	0
Rutherford	6.5	0	29	1

FALL OF WICKETS
1-37, 2-112, 3-151, 4-167

NEW ZEALAND v ENGLAND 1987-88

At McLean Park, Napier on 16 March 1988.   Result: **NEW ZEALAND** won by 7 wickets.   Toss: New Zealand.
Award: J.G.Wright.   LOI debuts: New Zealand – R.H.Vance.

Chris Broad and John Wright registered their only LOI hundreds in 34 and 149 matches respectively. New Zealand's last
century had been scored four years previously (*LOI No. 251*).

ENGLAND		Runs	Balls	4/6
B.C.Broad	b Snedden	106	140	9/1
C.W.J.Athey	run out	0	–	–
R.T.Robinson	c Smith b Snedden	36	48	6
P.A.J.DeFreitas	c Kuggeleijn b Rutherford	23	11	2/2
* M.W.Gatting	b Rutherford	6	18	1
N.H.Fairbrother	c and b Kuggeleijn	1	5	–
D.J.Capel	c Morrison b Kuggeleijn	14	34	1
J.E.Emburey	c and b Snedden	15	15	1/1
P.W.Jarvis	not out	5	11	–
† B.N.French	b Chatfield	0	3	–
N.V.Radford	c Rutherford b Snedden	0	3	–
Extras	(lb 10, w 2, nb 1)	13		
Total	(47.3 overs)	**219**		

NEW ZEALAND	O	M	R	W
Morrison	7	0	32	0
Watson	5	0	24	0
Chatfield	9	0	40	1
Snedden	8.3	0	34	4
Rutherford	10	0	39	2
Kuggeleijn	8	0	40	2

FALL OF WICKETS
1-1, 2-80, 3-114, 4-137, 5-142, 6-186, 7-205, 8-216, 9-218, 10-219

Umpires: F.R.Goodall (15) and S.J.Woodward (13).

NEW ZEALAND		Runs	Balls	4/6
* J.G.Wright	c Robinson b Emburey	101	120	15
R.H.Vance	b DeFreitas	5	16	1
A.H.Jones	b Jarvis	16	42	1
M.J.Greatbatch	not out	64	74	7/1
K.R.Rutherford	not out	27	31	4
C.M.Kuggeleijn				
† I.D.S.Smith				
M.C.Snedden				
D.K.Morrison				
W.Watson				
E.J.Chatfield				
Extras	(lb 6, w 4)	10		
Total	(46.3 overs; 3 wickets)	**223**		

ENGLAND	O	M	R	W
DeFreitas	10	2	30	1
Capel	9	0	50	0
Radford	8	0	31	0
Jarvis	9.3	1	45	1
Emburey	7	0	47	1
Gatting	3	0	14	0

FALL OF WICKETS
1-24, 2-62, 3-172

NEW ZEALAND v ENGLAND 1987-88

At Eden Park, Auckland on 19 March 1988.   Result: **NEW ZEALAND** won by 4 wickets.   Toss: New Zealand.
Award: A.H.Jones.   LOI debuts: None.

The largest crowd of England's New Zealand tour, estimated at 20,000, saw the home team square the series with four balls to spare.

ENGLAND		Runs	Balls	4/6
B.C.Broad	b Snedden	12	30	–
M.D.Moxon	b Watson	19	35	2
P.A.J.DeFreitas	c Crowe b Watson	6	11	1
R.T.Robinson	c Kuggeleijn b Rutherford	13	37	–
* M.W.Gatting	c Wright b Watson	48	87	1
N.H.Fairbrother	b Kuggeleijn	54	65	4/1
D.J.Capel	b Chatfield	25	25	3
J.E.Emburey	b Chatfield	11	9	–
P.W.Jarvis	run out	0	1	–
† B.N.French	c Greatbatch b Chatfield	2	7	–
N.V.Radford	not out	0	–	–
Extras	(lb 12, w 5, nb 1)	18		
Total	(50 overs)	208		

NEW ZEALAND		Runs	Balls	4/6
* J.G.Wright	b Radford	47	86	7
A.H.Jones	c Radford b Jarvis	90	126	9
M.D.Crowe	c French b Jarvis	13	22	–
M.J.Greatbatch	c Radford b Jarvis	5	14	–
K.R.Rutherford	lbw b Jarvis	0	1	–
C.M.Kuggeleijn	b Capel	2	11	–
R.J.Hadlee	not out	33	38	2/1
† I.D.S.Smith	not out	1	3	–
M.C.Snedden				
W.Watson				
E.J.Chatfield				
Extras	(b 3, lb 12, w 5)	20		
Total	(49.2 overs; 6 wickets)	211		

NEW ZEALAND	O	M	R	W
Hadlee	10	0	43	0
Watson	10	0	36	3
Snedden	10	2	30	1
Chatfield	10	2	31	3
Kuggeleijn	5	0	28	1
Rutherford	5	0	28	1

ENGLAND	O	M	R	W
DeFreitas	10	0	45	0
Capel	10	0	42	1
Radford	10	2	32	1
Jarvis	9.2	1	33	4
Emburey	10	0	44	0

FALL OF WICKETS
1-33, 2-33, 3-41, 4-71, 5-146, 6-179, 7-197, 8-197, 9-208, 10-208

FALL OF WICKETS
1-86, 2-115, 3-129, 4-129, 5-138, 6-199

Umpires: R.L.McHarg (5) and S.J.Woodward (14).

WEST INDIES v PAKISTAN 1987-88

At Sabina Park, Kingston, Jamaica on 12 March 1988.   Result: **WEST INDIES** won by 47 runs.   Toss: Pakistan.
Award: A.L.Logie   LOI debuts: West Indies – C.E.L.Ambrose.

Gus Logie, who completed his only hundred in 133 LOI innings from 113 balls, with Richie Richardson shared a partnership of 187 which remains the West Indies third-wicket record against Test-playing countries. Curtly Ambrose took four wickets on his international debut.

WEST INDIES		Runs	Balls	4/6
D.L.Haynes	b Imran	0	2	–
P.V.Simmons	c Ramiz b Imran	15	11	3
R.B.Richardson	b Salim Jaffer	84	124	6
A.L.Logie	not out	109	119	10
* I.V.A.Richards	b Imran	15	20	1
C.L.Hooper	not out	1	4	–
† P.J.L.Dujon				
W.K.M.Benjamin				
C.E.L.Ambrose				
C.A.Walsh				
B.P.Patterson				
Extras	(b 3, lb 10, w 1, nb 3)	17		
Total	(46 overs; 4 wickets)	241		

PAKISTAN		Runs	Balls	4/6
Ramiz Raja	b Ambrose	5	5	–
Shoaib Mohammed	b Ambrose	3	11	–
Salim Malik	b Walsh	20	52	3
Javed Miandad	c Richards b Ambrose	47	83	3/1
Ijaz Ahmed	run out	39	46	4
* Imran Khan	b Ambrose	7	11	1
† Salim Yousuf	c Logie b Patterson	10	21	–
Naved Anjum	not out	17	35	1
Zakir Khan	not out	11	22	–
Tausif Ahmed				
Salim Jaffer				
Extras	(b 10, lb 12, w 9, nb 4)	35		
Total	(46 overs; 7 wickets)	194		

PAKISTAN	O	M	R	W
Imran Khan	8	1	36	3
Salim Jaffer	10	1	55	1
Naved Anjum	10	1	37	0
Zakir Khan	10	0	54	0
Tausif Ahmed	5	0	28	0
Shoaib Mohammed	3	0	18	0

WEST INDIES	O	M	R	W
Patterson	10	2	21	1
Ambrose	10	1	39	4
Walsh	10	1	37	1
Benjamin	10	1	34	0
Richards	5	1	30	0
Hooper	1	0	11	0

FALL OF WICKETS
1-0, 2-25, 3-212, 4-236

FALL OF WICKETS
1-7, 2-8, 3-55, 4-131, 5-145, 6-146, 7-163

Umpires: D.Sang Hue (1) and J.R.Gayle (2).

WEST INDIES v PAKISTAN 1987-88

At Recreation Ground, St John's, Antigua on 15 March 1988.　Result: **WEST INDIES** won by 5 wickets.　Toss: West Indies.
Award: W.K.M.Benjamin.　LOI debuts: Pakistan – Haafiz Shahid.

Gordon Greenidge deputised as West Indies captain for the first time. Curtly Ambrose remains the only bowler to take four wickets in each of his first two limited-overs internationals.

PAKISTAN		Runs	Balls	4/6
Mudassar Nazar	b Ambrose	4	24	–
Ramiz Raja	c Hooper b Patterson	14	21	3
Salim Malik	c Greenidge b Ambrose	0	4	–
Javed Miandad	c Dujon b Benjamin	24	60	2
Ijaz Ahmed	c Simmons b Benjamin	6	14	–
* Imran Khan	c and b Ambrose	53	82	3
Naved Anjum	b Benjamin	2	8	–
† Salim Yousuf	run out	24	38	2
Wasim Akram	c Simmons b Ambrose	18	25	1
Haafiz Shahid	not out	7	6	–
Salim Jaffer	not out	2	5	–
Extras	(lb 2, w 7, nb 3)	12		
Total	(46 overs; 9 wickets)	**166**		

WEST INDIES		Runs	Balls	4/6
* C.G.Greenidge	c Imran b Haafiz	35	64	5
P.V.Simmons	b Mudassar	54	60	9
R.B.Richardson	c Miandad b Mudassar	12	12	1
C.A.Best	lbw b Imran	17	30	3
A.L.Logie	c Ijaz b Imran	9	15	1
C.L.Hooper	not out	21	26	3
† P.J.L.Dujon	not out	11	18	2
W.K.M.Benjamin				
C.E.L.Ambrose				
C.A.Walsh				
B.P.Patterson				
Extras	(b 2, w 2, nb 4)	8		
Total	(37.1 overs; 5 wickets)	**167**		

WEST INDIES	O	M	R	W
Patterson	8	0	37	1
Ambrose	10	2	35	4
Benjamin	10	1	27	3
Walsh	10	1	25	0
Hooper	8	0	40	0

PAKISTAN	O	M	R	W
Imran Khan	7	1	38	2
Wasim Akram	6	1	22	0
Salim Jaffer	8.1	0	36	0
Haafiz Shahid	9	0	39	1
Mudassar Nazar	7	1	30	2

FALL OF WICKETS
1-20, 2-23, 3-24, 4-40, 5-72, 6-78, 7-118, 8-156, 9-163

FALL OF WICKETS
1-88, 2-104, 3-106, 4-123, 5-144

Umpires: L.H.Barker (6) and P.C.White (4).

WEST INDIES v PAKISTAN 1987-88

At Queen's Park Oval, Port-of-Spain, Trinidad on 18 March 1988.　Result: **WEST INDIES** won by 50 runs.　Toss: Pakistan.
Award: D.L.Haynes.　LOI debuts: Pakistan – Aamer Malik.

Desmond Haynes, who scored his tenth hundred (off 104 balls) in these internationals, was adjudged lbw to Salim Jaffer by debutant umpire Mohammed Hosein when 85, but was recalled when Pakistan withdrew the appeal after he indicated the ball had first hit his bat.

WEST INDIES		Runs	Balls	4/6
D.L.Haynes	not out	142	132	13/1
P.V.Simmons	c Salim Malik b Naved	12	15	2
R.B.Richardson	c Qadir b Jaffer	78	76	12
* C.G.Greenidge	c and b Salim Malik	27	37	4
A.L.Logie	c Salim Yousuf b Imran	9	10	1
C.L.Hooper	not out	27	15	3
† P.J.L.Dujon				
W.K.M.Benjamin				
C.E.L.Ambrose				
C.A.Walsh				
B.P.Patterson				
Extras	(b 4, lb 12, w 4)	20		
Total	(47 overs; 4 wickets)	**315**		

PAKISTAN		Runs	Balls	4/6
Ramiz Raja	b Benjamin	47	53	7
Mudassar Nazar	c Dujon b Benjamin	33	48	4
† Salim Yousuf	c Ambrose b Walsh	8	7	–/1
Aamer Malik	run out	12	23	1
Javed Miandad	c Ambrose b Hooper	17	22	–
Salim Malik	c and b Ambrose	85	55	10
* Imran Khan	c Hooper b Patterson	20	20	1
Ijaz Ahmed	c sub (A.H.Gray) b Patterson	9	11	–
Naved Anjum	c Walsh b Patterson	7	7	–
Abdul Qadir	c Dujon b Ambrose	2	5	–
Salim Jaffer	not out	2	6	–
Extras	(b 4, lb 5, w 11, nb 3)	23		
Total	(43.3 overs)	**265**		

PAKISTAN	O	M	R	W
Imran Khan	8	0	48	1
Naved Anjum	9	0	56	1
Salim Jaffer	9	0	58	1
Abdul Qadir	10	0	64	0
Mudassar Nazar	4	0	32	0
Salim Malik	7	0	41	1

WEST INDIES	O	M	R	W
Patterson	10	0	78	3
Ambrose	8.3	0	29	2
Walsh	8	1	43	1
Benjamin	10	0	65	2
Hooper	7	0	41	1

FALL OF WICKETS
1-28, 2-180, 3-236, 4-270

FALL OF WICKETS
1-70, 2-80, 3-107, 4-111, 5-188, 6-242, 7-248, 8-260, 9-260, 10-265

Umpires: C.E.Cumberbatch (6) and Mohammed Hosein (1).

WEST INDIES v PAKISTAN 1987-88

At Queen's Park Oval, Port-of-Spain, Trinidad on 20 March 1988.   Result: **WEST INDIES** won by 7 wickets.   Toss: Pakistan.
Award: C.G.Greenidge.   LOI debuts: Pakistan – Moin-ul-Atiq.

Played on the same pitch as its predecessor, this match produced 11 sixes and 42 fours. Imran Khan allowed David
Williams, a specialist wicket-keeper, to deputise when Jeff Dujon was injured and was subsequently caught by him.

PAKISTAN		Runs	Balls	4/6
Ramiz Raja	c Greenidge b Patterson	71	72	10/1
Moin-ul-Atiq	c Greenidge b Gray	46	56	4
Salim Malik	b Gray	26	33	4
Javed Miandad	c Richardson b Patterson	59	49	2/3
*Imran Khan	c sub (D.Williams) b Benjamin	16	22	–
Ijaz Ahmed	c Gray b Patterson	19	14	1/1
†Salim Yousuf	not out	8	7	–
Haafiz Shahid	not out	2	5	–
Shoaib Mohammed				
Abdul Qadir				
Zakir Khan				
Extras	(b 3, lb 15, w 1, nb 5)	24		
Total	(43 overs; 6 wickets)	**271**		

WEST INDIES		Runs	Balls	4/6
*C.G.Greenidge	b Haafiz	66	51	7/3
P.V.Simmons	c Salim Yousuf b Haafiz	49	55	4/1
R.B.Richardson	not out	79	87	6/1
A.L.Logie	c and b Salim Malik	29	26	2
C.A.Best	not out	32	31	2/1
C.L.Hooper				
†P.J.L.Dujon				
W.K.M.Benjamin				
A.H.Gray				
C.A.Walsh				
B.P.Patterson				
Extras	(b 4, lb 7, w 3, nb 3)	17		
Total	(40.1 overs; 3 wickets)	**272**		

WEST INDIES	O	M	R	W
Patterson	9	0	77	3
Walsh	9	0	43	0
Gray	10	0	45	2
Benjamin	8	0	58	1
Hooper	7	0	30	0

PAKISTAN	O	M	R	W
Imran Khan	8	0	76	0
Zakir Khan	6	0	49	0
Abdul Qadir	10	0	42	0
Haafiz Shahid	9.1	1	56	2
Salim Malik	4	0	23	1
Shoaib Mohammed	3	0	15	0

FALL OF WICKETS
1-109, 2-139, 3-160, 4-194, 5-256, 6-256

FALL OF WICKETS
1-112, 2-149, 3-207

Umpires: G.T.Browne (1) and C.E.Cumberbatch (7).

WEST INDIES v PAKISTAN 1987-88

At Bourda, Georgetown, Guyana on 30 March 1988.   Result: **WEST INDIES** won by 7 wickets.   Toss: West Indies.
Award: Javed Miandad.   LOI debuts: None.

Eleven years after the inaugural international in the Caribbean, Bourda became the 83rd ground to stage one. Javed
Miandad completed Pakistan's first LOI hundred against West Indies off the final ball of the innings. This clean sweep
extended the West Indies sequence of international wins to ten.

PAKISTAN		Runs	Balls	4/6
Ramiz Raja	b Gray	67	79	12
Shoaib Mohammed	c Dujon b Marshall	0	7	–
†Aamer Malik	run out	6	25	1
Javed Miandad	not out	100	99	10
Salim Malik	c Benjamin b Gray	0	1	–
*Imran Khan	run out	17	25	1
Ijaz Ahmed	b Walsh	10	10	1
Wasim Akram	c Haynes b Gray	0	4	–
Ijaz Faqih	not out	6	14	–
Abdul Qadir				
Salim Jaffer				
Extras	(b 3, lb 6, nb 6)	15		
Total	(43 overs; 7 wickets)	**221**		

WEST INDIES		Runs	Balls	4/6
D.L.Haynes	c Salim Malik b Wasim	9	8	2
P.V.Simmons	b Imran	79	73	11/2
R.B.Richardson	c Ijaz Ahmed b Imran	68	94	10
†P.J.L.Dujon	not out	18	27	2
*C.G.Greenidge	not out	26	23	4
A.L.Logie				
C.L.Hooper				
M.D.Marshall				
W.K.M.Benjamin				
A.H.Gray				
C.A.Walsh				
Extras	(b 9, lb 13, w 1, nb 2)	25		
Total	(37 overs; 3 wickets)	**225**		

WEST INDIES	O	M	R	W
Marshall	10	2	42	1
Walsh	10	2	50	1
Gray	10	0	44	3
Benjamin	7	0	31	0
Hooper	6	0	45	0

PAKISTAN	O	M	R	W
Imran Khan	8	0	59	2
Wasim Akram	10	0	62	1
Abdul Qadir	7	1	23	0
Salim Jaffer	5	1	31	0
Ijaz Faqih	7	0	28	0

FALL OF WICKETS
1-1, 2-42, 3-94, 4-94, 5-160, 6-183, 7-184

FALL OF WICKETS
1-15, 2-172, 3-182

Umpires: D.M.Archer (16) and C.R.Duncan (1).

INDIA v SRI LANKA 1987-88

At Sharjah CA Stadium, UAE on 25 March 1988.   Result: **INDIA** won by 18 runs.   Toss: Sri Lanka.
Award: P.A.de Silva.   LOI debuts: None.

Former Indian captain Lala Amarnath was the major beneficiary of this triangular 50-over tournament. Ravi Shastri, leading India in the enforced absence of Dilip Vengsarkar, took his 100th LOI wicket, so completing the double, in 100 matches.

INDIA		Runs	Balls	4/6	SRI LANKA		Runs	Balls	4/6
K.Srikkanth	c Mahanama b Ramanayake	32	38	3/1	R.S.Mahanama	b Hirwani	51	124	1
N.S.Sidhu	b Ratnayeke	17	45	2	D.S.B.P.Kuruppu	c Shastri b Sharma	6	14	1
M.Amarnath	run out	1	3	–	A.P.Gurusinha	run out	0	1	–
W.V.Raman	c Madugalle b De Silva	21	60	1	P.A.de Silva	b Hirwani	88	100	3
M.Azharuddin	b Ramanayake	7	10	–	A.Ranatunga	c Azharuddin b Shastri	8	11	–
Kapil Dev	c Madugalle b De Silva	48	43	3/2	* R.S.Madugalle	st More b Shastri	11	19	–
* R.J.Shastri	c Mahanama b Ratnayeke	26	40	–/1	† R.G.de Alwis	c Srikkanth b Kapil Dev	2	4	–
† K.S.More	run out	9	13	–/1	J.R.Ratnayeke	run out	4	8	–
Arshad Ayub	not out	31	43	2	G.F.Labrooy	run out	0	–	–
C.Sharma	not out	12	10	2	C.P.H.Ramanayake	run out	11	13	–
N.D.Hirwani					S.D.Anurasiri	not out	3	3	–
Extras	(b 1, lb 7, w 5, nb 2)	15			Extras	(b 3, lb 10, w 3, nb 1)	17		
Total	(50 overs; 8 wickets)	**219**			**Total**	(49.2 overs)	**201**		

SRI LANKA	O	M	R	W	INDIA	O	M	R	W
Ratnayeke	10	0	34	2	Kapil Dev	9.2	2	26	1
Labrooy	9	0	41	0	Sharma	6	3	19	1
Ramanayake	7	0	37	2	Amarnath	6	0	26	0
Anurasiri	10	0	44	0	Shastri	8	0	40	2
De Silva	9	2	28	1	Hirwani	10	1	40	2
Ranatunga	5	0	27	0	Arshad Ayub	10	0	37	0

FALL OF WICKETS
1-31, 2-32, 3-63, 4-71, 5-125, 6-140, 7-152, 8-198

FALL OF WICKETS
1-14, 2-14, 3-151, 4-158, 5-177, 6-180, 7-181, 8-182, 9-190, 10-201

Umpires: Khizer Hayat (*Pakistan*) (19) and Mahboob Shah (*Pakistan*) (18).

NEW ZEALAND v INDIA 1987-88

At Sharjah CA Stadium, UAE on 27 March 1988.   Result: **INDIA** won by 73 runs.   Toss: New Zealand.
Award: M.Amarnath.   LOI debuts: None.

India's total was the record for any Sharjah international to date, while the partnership of 158 between Navjot Sidhu and Mohinder Amarnath remains their highest for any wicket against New Zealand. Kiran More was the fifth wicket-keeper, and third Indian, to make five dismissals in a match.

INDIA		Runs	Balls	4/6	NEW ZEALAND		Runs	Balls	4/6
K.Srikkanth	b Watson	1	7	–	* J.G.Wright	c More b Kapil Dev	19	31	2
N.S.Sidhu	c Rutherford b Watson	88	98	6/3	R.H.Vance	c More b Arshad Ayub	42	95	1
W.V.Raman	c Greatbatch b Hadlee	1	10	–	A.H.Jones	c and b Azharuddin	6	20	–
M.Amarnath	not out	102	139	6	M.J.Greatbatch	c More b Hirwani	45	67	3
Kapil Dev	c Kuggeleijn b Hadlee	5	8	–	K.R.Rutherford	c sub b Hirwani	3	3	–
M.Azharuddin	run out	29	22	2	† I.D.S.Smith	b Hirwani	17	14	–/1
* R.J.Shastri	c Smith b Hadlee	29	18	1/1	C.M.Kuggeleijn	st More b Hirwani	3	7	–
† K.S.More	not out	3	3	–	R.J.Hadlee	not out	35	45	1/2
C.Sharma					D.K.Morrison	st More b Arshad Ayub	6	17	–
Arshad Ayub					W.Watson	not out	4	14	–
N.D.Hirwani					E.J.Chatfield				
Extras	(lb 4, w 4, nb 1)	9			Extras	(b 1, lb 6, w 6, nb 1)	14		
Total	(50 overs; 6 wickets)	**267**			**Total**	(50 overs; 8 wickets)	**194**		

NEW ZEALAND	O	M	R	W	INDIA	O	M	R	W
Hadlee	10	0	54	3	Kapil Dev	10	2	30	1
Watson	10	2	36	2	Sharma	7	0	28	0
Morrison	10	0	45	0	Azharuddin	4	0	15	1
Chatfield	10	0	57	0	Shastri	8	1	29	0
Rutherford	5	0	38	0	Hirwani	10	0	43	4
Kuggeleijn	5	0	33	0	Arshad Ayub	10	1	41	2
					Raman	1	0	1	0

FALL OF WICKETS
1-1, 2-4, 3-162, 4-167, 5-212, 6-260

FALL OF WICKETS
1-32, 2-46, 3-118, 4-120, 5-124, 6-139, 7-144, 8-175

Umpires: Khizer Hayat (*Pakistan*) (20) and Mahboob Shah (*Pakistan*) (19).

NEW ZEALAND v SRI LANKA 1987-88

At Sharjah CA Stadium, UAE on 29 March 1988.   Result: **NEW ZEALAND** won by 99 runs.   Toss: Sri Lanka.
Award: A.H.Jones.   LOI debuts: None.

New Zealand's tally of five run outs equalled the LOI record set in Australia's innings in the inaugural World Cup final at Lord's in 1975 (*LOI No. 33*).

NEW ZEALAND		Runs	Balls	4/6
* J.G.Wright	c Kuruppu b Ratnayeke	0	2	–
R.H.Vance	run out	45	78	3/1
A.H.Jones	run out	85	98	4/2
K.R.Rutherford	st Kuruppu b E.A.R.de Silva	65	62	8
D.N.Patel	run out	27	31	3
M.J.Greatbatch	c Kaluperuma b Ratnayeke	15	11	2
† T.E.Blain	run out	6	9	1
C.M.Kuggeleijn	not out	7	7	1
D.K.Morrison	run out	0	2	–
W.Watson	not out	2	2	–
E.J.Chatfield				
Extras	(lb 4, w 2)	6		
Total	(50 overs; 8 wickets)	**258**		

SRI LANKA		Runs	Balls	4/6
† D.S.B.P.Kuruppu	run out	46	70	1/1
A.P.Gurusinha	c Vance b Watson	27	49	2
* R.S.Madugalle	c Jones b Kuggeleijn	15	30	–
P.A.de Silva	c Blain b Rutherford	1	3	–
A.Ranatunga	b Kuggeleijn	6	12	–
J.R.Ratnayeke	c Blain b Patel	25	46	1
S.M.S.Kaluperuma	lbw b Patel	7	17	1
E.A.R.de Silva	c Jones b Patel	4	15	–
G.F.Labrooy	b Morrison	5	6	1
S.D.Anurasiri	not out	5	11	–
K.N.Amalean	run out	6	7	–
Extras	(lb 3, w 8, nb 1)	12		
Total	(42.5 overs)	**159**		

SRI LANKA	O	M	R	W
Ratnayeke	10	0	33	2
Labrooy	7	0	41	0
Anurasiri	10	0	49	0
E.A.R.de Silva	10	0	42	1
Ranatunga	8	0	44	0
P.A.de Silva	4	0	31	0
Amalean	1	0	14	0

NEW ZEALAND	O	M	R	W
Morrison	8	0	36	1
Chatfield	8	0	24	0
Watson	5	0	19	1
Kuggeleijn	10	2	32	2
Rutherford	5	0	23	1
Patel	6.5	0	22	3

FALL OF WICKETS
1-0, 2-94, 3-197, 4-201, 5-223, 6-248, 7-248, 8-249

FALL OF WICKETS
1-50, 2-93, 3-96, 4-96, 5-111, 6-124, 7-140, 8-142, 9-150, 10-159

Umpires: Khizer Hayat (*Pakistan*) (21) and Mahboob Shah (*Pakistan*) (20).

NEW ZEALAND v SRI LANKA 1987-88

At Sharjah CA Stadium, UAE on 31 March 1988.   Result: **NEW ZEALAND** won by 43 runs.   Toss: New Zealand.
Award: R.H.Vance.   LOI debuts: None.

By winning this match New Zealand went through to the final against India.

NEW ZEALAND		Runs	Balls	4/6
R.H.Vance	run out	96	125	3/2
* J.G.Wright	st De Alwis b P.A.de Silva	45	61	5
A.H.Jones	b Ranatunga	33	45	–/1
M.J.Greatbatch	run out	12	18	–
K.R.Rutherford	c Gurusinha b E.A.R.de Silva	9	13	–
R.J.Hadlee	c Ratnayeke b E.A.R.de Silva	14	13	–/1
D.N.Patel	lbw b E.A.R.de Silva	0	1	–
C.M.Kuggeleijn	not out	24	22	2
† T.E.Blain	not out	6	6	–
W.Watson				
E.J.Chatfield				
Extras	(b 1, lb 5, w 4)	10		
Total	(50 overs; 7 wickets)	**249**		

SRI LANKA		Runs	Balls	4/6
R.S.Mahanama	c Rutherford b Patel	43	71	1
D.S.B.P.Kuruppu	c Vance b Watson	0	7	–
A.P.Gurusinha	lbw b Hadlee	60	92	4
P.A.de Silva	c and b Kuggeleijn	1	4	–
A.Ranatunga	b Patel	2	4	–
* R.S.Madugalle	run out	25	42	1
J.R.Ratnayeke	c Kuggeleijn b Watson	31	35	2
† R.G.de Alwis	not out	16	19	1
E.A.R.de Silva	b Chatfield	10	13	1
G.F.Labrooy	b Watson	1	9	–
S.D.Anurasiri	not out	3	6	–
Extras	(lb 12, w 1, nb 1)	14		
Total	(50 overs; 9 wickets)	**206**		

SRI LANKA	O	M	R	W
Ratnayeke	8	0	27	0
Labrooy	10	0	65	0
P.A.de Silva	10	1	41	1
Ranatunga	10	0	43	1
Anurasiri	4	0	29	0
E.A.R.de Silva	8	0	38	3

NEW ZEALAND	O	M	R	W
Hadlee	10	1	25	1
Watson	9	1	37	3
Chatfield	10	0	48	1
Kuggeleijn	10	0	37	1
Patel	10	0	45	2
Jones	1	0	2	0

FALL OF WICKETS
1-76, 2-146, 3-180, 4-199, 5-204, 6-204, 7-230

FALL OF WICKETS
1-0, 2-90, 3-92, 4-95, 5-115, 6-158, 7-174, 8-192, 9-196

Umpires: Khizer Hayat (*Pakistan*) (22) and Mahboob Shah (*Pakistan*) (21).

NEW ZEALAND v INDIA 1987-88

At Sharjah CA Stadium, UAE on 1 April 1988.   Result: **INDIA** won by 52 runs.   Toss: India.
Award: R.J.Shastri.   LOI debuts: None.

Ravi Shastri, who completed 2000 LOI runs, and Kapil Dev added 73 off 26 balls as Ewen Chatfield's last five overs cost 51 runs, his first five having conceded just six.

INDIA		Runs	Balls	4/6
K.Srikkanth	b Chatfield	14	32	2
N.S.Sidhu	c Hadlee b Patel	33	53	3
W.V.Raman	b Kuggeleijn	7	34	–
M.Amarnath	c Greatbatch b Morrison	58	75	3/1
M.Azharuddin	run out	6	13	–
* R.J.Shastri	b Hadlee	72	66	3/3
Kapil Dev	not out	49	26	3/2
† K.S.More	c Morrison b Chatfield	5	3	1
Arshad Ayub	not out	0	–	–
S.K.Sharma				
N.D.Hirwani				
Extras	(b 1, lb 3, w 2)	6		
Total	(50 overs; 7 wickets)	**250**		

NEW ZEALAND	O	M	R	W
Hadlee	10	0	49	1
Watson	7	2	37	0
Chatfield	10	0	57	2
Kuggeleijn	10	0	38	1
Patel	9	0	32	1
Morrison	4	0	33	1

FALL OF WICKETS
1-28, 2-49, 3-70, 4-82, 5-154, 6-227, 7-232

Umpires: Khizer Hayat (*Pakistan*) (23) and Mahboob Shah (*Pakistan*) (22).

NEW ZEALAND		Runs	Balls	4/6
R.H.Vance	c More b Sharma	3	11	–
* J.G.Wright	run out	55	65	7
A.H.Jones	lbw b Amarnath	15	33	–
M.J.Greatbatch	c Kapil Dev b Hirwani	47	64	1/1
D.N.Patel	c Shastri b Hirwani	1	3	–
R.J.Hadlee	c Arshad Ayub b Hirwani	3	8	–
C.M.Kuggeleijn	c Srikkanth b Hirwani	7	13	–
† I.D.S.Smith	c Sharma b Raman	40	28	1/2
D.K.Morrison	b Kapil Dev	7	23	–
W.Watson	b Shastri	10	14	–/1
E.J.Chatfield	not out	1	13	–
Extras	(lb 7, w 2)	9		
Total	(45.3 overs)	**198**		

INDIA	O	M	R	W
Kapil Dev	7.3	2	14	1
Sharma	6	0	21	1
Shastri	9	0	25	1
Amarnath	2	0	14	1
Hirwani	10	0	46	4
Arshad Ayub	9	0	48	0
Raman	2	0	23	1

FALL OF WICKETS
1-15, 2-60, 3-92, 4-94, 5-94, 6-113, 7-160, 8-182, 9-196, 10-198

ENGLAND v WEST INDIES 1988

At Edgbaston, Birmingham on 19 May 1988.   Result: **ENGLAND** won by 6 wickets.   Toss: England.
Award: G.C.Small.   LOI debuts: England – M.A.Lynch.

Gladstone Small returned his only four-wicket analysis in 53 limited-overs internationals.

WEST INDIES		Runs	Balls	4/6
C.G.Greenidge	b Small	18	39	2
P.V.Simmons	c Lamb b Dilley	22	16	3
R.B.Richardson	lbw b Pringle	11	22	–
* I.V.A.Richards	c Emburey b Small	13	7	3
A.L.Logie	c Downton b Small	51	96	3
C.L.Hooper	c Emburey b Small	51	96	5
† P.J.L.Dujon	run out	27	39	–
R.A.Harper	b Emburey	4	10	–
M.D.Marshall	c Lamb b DeFreitas	6	10	–
C.E.L.Ambrose	b Emburey	1	2	–
C.A.Walsh	not out	2	2	–
Extras	(lb 2, w 3, nb 6)	11		
Total	(55 overs)	**217**		

ENGLAND	O	M	R	W
DeFreitas	11	2	45	1
Dilley	11	0	64	1
Small	11	0	31	4
Pringle	11	5	26	1
Emburey	11	1	49	2

FALL OF WICKETS
1-34, 2-50, 3-66, 4-72, 5-169, 6-180, 7-195, 8-209, 9-212, 10-217

Umpires: J.Birkenshaw (6) and B.J.Meyer (19).

ENGLAND		Runs	Balls	4/6
G.A.Gooch	c Harper b Ambrose	43	93	3
B.C.Broad	c Greenidge b Marshall	35	55	3
* M.W.Gatting	not out	82	125	7
M.A.Lynch	run out	0	2	–
A.J.Lamb	b Hooper	11	22	–
D.R.Pringle	not out	23	31	–
† P.R.Downton				
J.E.Emburey				
P.A.J.DeFreitas				
G.C.Small				
G.R.Dilley				
Extras	(b 2, lb 10, w 7, nb 6)	25		
Total	(53 overs; 4 wickets)	**219**		

WEST INDIES	O	M	R	W
Ambrose	11	1	39	1
Walsh	11	1	50	0
Richards	7	1	29	0
Marshall	11	1	32	1
Harper	7	0	33	0
Hooper	6	0	24	1

FALL OF WICKETS
1-70, 2-119, 3-121, 4-153

ENGLAND v WEST INDIES 1988

At Headingley, Leeds on 21 May 1988.   Result: **ENGLAND** won by 47 runs.   Toss: West Indies.
Award: D.R.Pringle.   LOI debuts: West Indies – I.R.Bishop.

England's second decisive victory clinched the Texaco Trophy and their first home LOI series win against West Indies.
Gordon Greenidge completed 4000 runs in 97 internationals.

ENGLAND		Runs	Balls	4/6
G.A.Gooch	c Greenidge b Simmons	32	95	3
B.C.Broad	c Dujon b Ambrose	13	27	2
* M.W.Gatting	c Richards b Marshall	18	42	2
M.A.Lynch	lbw b Marshall	2	9	–
A.J.Lamb	c Dujon b Simmons	2	12	–
D.R.Pringle	c Dujon b Walsh	39	55	2/1
† P.R.Downton	c Dujon b Bishop	30	47	2
J.E.Emburey	c Ambrose b Bishop	8	20	1
P.A.J.DeFreitas	not out	15	27	1
G.C.Small	not out	7	10	–
G.R.Dilley				
Extras	(b 3, lb 1, w 3, nb 13)	20		
Total	(55 overs; 8 wickets)	**186**		

WEST INDIES		Runs	Balls	4/6
C.G.Greenidge	c Downton b Small	21	54	3
P.V.Simmons	b DeFreitas	1	6	–
R.B.Richardson	c Downton b Dilley	1	4	–
* I.V.A.Richards	b Small	31	29	6
A.L.Logie	c Lynch b Dilley	8	18	–
C.L.Hooper	lbw b Pringle	12	32	2
† P.J.L.Dujon	b Pringle	12	18	2
M.D.Marshall	c Downton b Gooch	1	6	–
C.E.L.Ambrose	c Downton b Pringle	23	67	1
C.A.Walsh	b Emburey	18	42	1
I.R.Bishop	not out	2	7	–
Extras	(lb 3, w 3, nb 3)	9		
Total	(46.3 overs)	**139**		

WEST INDIES	O	M	R	W
Walsh	11	0	39	1
Ambrose	7	2	19	1
Marshall	9	1	29	2
Bishop	11	1	32	2
Simmons	9	2	30	2
Richards	8	0	33	0

ENGLAND	O	M	R	W
Dilley	11	0	45	2
DeFreitas	9	2	29	1
Small	9	2	11	2
Pringle	11	0	30	3
Gooch	3	0	12	1
Emburey	3.3	0	9	1

FALL OF WICKETS
1-29, 2-64, 3-72, 4-80, 5-83, 6-149, 7-154, 8-169

FALL OF WICKETS
1-2, 2-11, 3-38, 4-67, 5-67, 6-83, 7-84, 8-104, 9-132, 10-139

Umpires: D.J.Constant (28) and D.R.Shepherd (27).

ENGLAND v WEST INDIES 1988

At Lord's, London on 23, 24 May 1988.   Result: **ENGLAND** won by 7 wickets.   Toss: England.
Award: P.A.J.DeFreitas.   LOI debuts: None.

England extended their sequence of limited-overs wins against West Indies to nine out of ten, the tourists having ended
a thrice-interrupted first day at 125 for 6 after 50 overs. Courtney Walsh achieved the most economical analysis in
Prudential/Texaco Trophy matches.

WEST INDIES		Runs	Balls	4/6
C.G.Greenidge	c DeFreitas b Emburey	39	94	5/1
D.L.Haynes	run out	10	50	1
R.B.Richardson	c Downton b Pringle	13	46	1
* I.V.A.Richards	c Emburey b DeFreitas	9	16	1
A.L.Logie	run out	0	4	–
C.L.Hooper	run out	12	46	1
† P.J.L.Dujon	not out	30	44	1
M.D.Marshall	b Emburey	41	30	2/2
W.K.M.Benjamin				
C.A.Walsh				
I.R.Bishop				
Extras	(b 2, lb 10, w 12)	24		
Total	(55 overs; 7 wickets)	**178**		

ENGLAND		Runs	Balls	4/6
G.A.Gooch	st Dujon b Hooper	28	100	1
B.C.Broad	b Bishop	34	114	1
* M.W.Gatting	not out	40	58	4
M.A.Lynch	b Bishop	6	21	1
A.J.Lamb	not out	30	23	5
D.R.Pringle				
† P.R.Downton				
J.E.Emburey				
P.A.J.DeFreitas				
G.C.Small				
N.V.Radford				
Extras	(b 6, lb 17, w 5, nb 14)	42		
Total	(50 overs; 3 wickets)	**180**		

ENGLAND	O	M	R	W
DeFreitas	11	5	20	1
Radford	11	2	29	0
Small	10	1	34	0
Pringle	11	4	27	1
Emburey	10	1	53	2
Gooch	2	1	3	0

WEST INDIES	O	M	R	W
Marshall	9	2	21	0
Walsh	11	5	11	0
Bishop	11	1	33	2
Benjamin	9	0	38	0
Hooper	10	0	54	1

FALL OF WICKETS
1-71, 2-108, 3-124

FALL OF WICKETS
1-40, 2-75, 3-79, 4-79, 5-95, 6-111, 7-178

Umpires: H.D.Bird (49) and N.T.Plews (2).

ENGLAND v SRI LANKA 1988

At Kennington Oval, London on 4 September 1988.   Result: **ENGLAND** won by 5 wickets.   Toss: England.
Award: K.J.Barnett.   LOI debuts: England – K.J.Barnett, R.A.Smith; Sri Lanka – M.A.W.R.Madurasinghe.

Having struck a 52-ball fifty, Dilip Mendis sustained a damaged leg muscle, faced his final two balls with a runner and did not field. Vic Marks was recalled for a final international appearance after an absence of more than three years and Graham Gooch captained his first international.

SRI LANKA		Runs	Balls	4/6
† D.S.B.P.Kuruppu	lbw b Gooch	38	66	5
M.A.R.Samarasekera	b Small	10	29	1
P.A.de Silva	b Gooch	16	28	1
A.Ranatunga	run out	37	62	3
L.R.D.Mendis	b Small	60	65	6/1
* R.S.Madugalle	c Foster b Pringle	17	26	–
J.R.Ratnayeke	c Pringle b Small	19	19	3
H.P.Tillekeratne	not out	15	27	–
G.F.Labrooy	not out	10	11	–
M.A.W.R.Madurasinghe				
S.D.Anurasiri				
Extras	(b 1, lb 10, w 8, nb 1)	20		
Total	(55 overs; 7 wickets)	**242**		

ENGLAND		Runs	Balls	4/6
* G.A.Gooch	c De Silva b Labrooy	7	10	1
R.T.Robinson	lbw b Ratnayeke	13	33	–
K.J.Barnett	run out	84	146	5
A.J.Lamb	c sub (B.Rajadurai) b Labrooy	66	70	3/1
R.A.Smith	c Kuruppu b Labrooy	9	13	1
R.J.Bailey	not out	43	34	3/1
D.R.Pringle	not out	19	11	1/1
† R.C.Russell				
V.J.Marks				
N.A.Foster				
G.C.Small				
Extras	(w 3, nb 1)	4		
Total	(52.4 overs; 5 wickets)	**245**		

ENGLAND	O	M	R	W
Foster	11	0	47	0
Small	11	1	44	3
Gooch	11	1	35	2
Pringle	11	0	46	1
Marks	11	0	59	0

SRI LANKA	O	M	R	W
Ratnayeke	9.4	3	37	1
Labrooy	10	0	40	3
Samarasekera	11	0	52	0
Ranatunga	11	0	42	0
Anurasiri	6	0	31	0
De Silva	2	0	19	0
Madurasinghe	3	0	24	0

FALL OF WICKETS
1-21, 2-54, 3-75, 4-144, 5-190, 6-193, 7-224

FALL OF WICKETS
1-9, 2-22, 3-140, 4-154, 5-213

Umpires: J.W.Holder (1) and K.E.Palmer (16).

PAKISTAN v AUSTRALIA 1988-89

At Gaddafi Stadium, Lahore on 14 October 1988.   Result: **(TIED) PAKISTAN** won by losing fewer wickets.
Toss: Pakistan.   Award: Mudassar Nazar.   LOI debuts: Australia – J.D.Siddons, I.A.Healy.

45-over match. Internationals scheduled for Gujranwala (30 September) and Karachi (14 October) were cancelled due to floods and riots. Further rioting compelled this game to be moved from Hyderabad and to be played a day early. Pakistan needed five runs off the last two overs.

AUSTRALIA		Runs	Balls	4/6
D.C.Boon	lbw b Mudassar	38	41	4
G.R.Marsh	b Wasim	89	126	2/1
* A.R.Border	b Mudassar	11	24	–
M.R.J.Veletta	c Miandad b Qadir	18	27	–
J.D.Siddons	c Shoaib b Wasim	32	37	3
S.R.Waugh	run out	7	4	1
P.L.Taylor	not out	12	8	1
C.J.McDermott	lbw b Wasim	6	4	1
† I.A.Healy	run out	1	1	–
A.I.C.Dodemaide	not out	5	3	–
T.B.A.May				
Extras	(lb 3, w 6, nb 1)	10		
Total	(45 overs; 8 wickets)	**229**		

PAKISTAN		Runs	Balls	4/6
Mudassar Nazar	run out	76	108	9
Ramiz Raja	c Dodemaide b May	24	45	3
Salim Malik	c Border b McDermott	44	43	7/1
* Javed Miandad	lbw b Taylor	10	12	–
Ijaz Ahmed	b Waugh	39	36	3/1
Manzoor Elahi	run out	13	14	1
† Salim Yousuf	not out	4	8	–
Wasim Akram	c Border b Dodemaide	1	7	–
Abdul Qadir	not out	0	1	–
Shoaib Mohammed				
Mohsin Kamal				
Extras	(b 4, lb 9, nb 5)	18		
Total	(45 overs; 7 wickets)	**229**		

PAKISTAN	O	M	R	W
Wasim Akram	9	0	38	3
Mohsin Kamal	5	0	39	0
Manzoor Elahi	7	0	23	0
Mudassar Nazar	9	0	40	2
Abdul Qadir	7	0	36	1
Shoaib Mohammed	1	0	6	0
Javed Miandad	7	0	44	0

AUSTRALIA	O	M	R	W
McDermott	9	0	43	1
Dodemaide	8	0	36	1
May	9	1	31	1
Waugh	8	0	42	1
Taylor	9	0	48	1
Border	2	0	16	0

FALL OF WICKETS
1-71, 2-94, 3-146, 4-196, 5-199, 6-208, 7-216, 8-217

FALL OF WICKETS
1-53, 2-141, 3-168, 4-170, 5-204, 6-226, 7-229

Umpires: Ikram Rabbani (3) and Mian Mohammad Aslam (5).

WEST INDIES v INDIA 1988-89

At Sharjah CA Stadium, UAE on 16 October 1988.   Result: **INDIA** won by 23 runs.   Toss: West Indies.
Award: K.Srikkanth.   LOI debuts: None.

50-over tournament. West Indies sustained their first defeat in the Gulf. Krish Srikkanth hit sixes off three successive balls from Roger Harper as he shared India's record third-wicket stand against West Indies with his captain. Kapil Dev became the leading LOI wicket-taker, surpassing Joel Garner's 146. Sanjeev Sharma recorded India's (then) best analysis.

INDIA		Runs	Balls	4/6
K.Srikkanth	b Hooper	112	113	10/5
N.S.Sidhu	c Dujon b Patterson	3	25	–
M.Amarnath	run out	7	31	–
D.B.Vengsarkar	not out	76	100	6/1
Kapil Dev	c Logie b Hooper	3	7	–
R.J.Shastri	c Greenidge b Hooper	17	21	–/1
M.Azharuddin	not out	5	7	–
K.S.More				
S.K.Sharma				
Maninder Singh				
N.D.Hirwani				
Extras	(b 4, lb 5, w 5, nb 1)	15		
Total	(50 overs; 5 wickets)	**238**		

WEST INDIES		Runs	Balls	4/6
* C.G.Greenidge	c Kapil Dev b Sharma	27	51	4
D.L.Haynes	b Kapil Dev	87	121	6/1
R.B.Richardson	c Vengsarkar b Hirwani	38	48	2
C.L.Hooper	c More b Hirwani	25	20	1/2
A.L.Logie	c Kapil Dev b Hirwani	3	6	–
† P.J.L.Dujon	b Hirwani	10	13	–
R.A.Harper	b Sharma	4	15	–
C.E.L.Ambrose	not out	2	6	–
W.K.M.Benjamin	lbw b Sharma	0	2	–
C.A.Walsh	c Sidhu b Sharma	2	3	–
B.P.Patterson	b Sharma	2	6	–
Extras	(b 1, lb 12, w 2)	15		
Total	(48.3 overs)	**215**		

WEST INDIES	O	M	R	W
Patterson	9	2	37	1
Ambrose	9	1	38	0
Walsh	10	1	35	0
Benjamin	10	0	49	0
Harper	5	0	38	0
Hooper	7	0	32	3

INDIA	O	M	R	W
Kapil Dev	9	2	24	1
Sharma	7.3	0	26	5
Shastri	10	0	41	0
Maninder Singh	10	0	50	0
Hirwani	10	1	50	4
Srikkanth	2	0	11	0

FALL OF WICKETS
1-12, 2-42, 3-162, 4-170, 5-218

FALL OF WICKETS
1-42, 2-134, 3-142, 4-178, 5-192, 6-208, 7-210, 8-210, 9-212, 10-215

Umpires: H.D.Bird (*England*) (50) and D.R.Shepherd (*England*) (28).

WEST INDIES v PAKISTAN 1988-89

At Sharjah CA Stadium, UAE on 18 October 1988.   Result: **PAKISTAN** won by 84 runs.   Toss: West Indies.
Award: Wasim Akram.   LOI debuts: None.

Pakistan achieved their highest total and record opening partnership in internationals against West Indies. Gordon Greenidge celebrated his 100th international by batting throughout the innings, completing his tenth hundred in the final over.

PAKISTAN		Runs	Balls	4/6
Mudassar Nazar	st Dujon b Hooper	64	99	6
Ramiz Raja	st Dujon b Harper	64	85	4
Javed Miandad	c Hooper b Walsh	79	67	4/3
Salim Malik	c Dujon b Patterson	42	35	4/1
Ijaz Ahmed	c Patterson b Ambrose	16	11	2
Manzoor Elahi	c Bishop b Ambrose	12	8	1
Wasim Akram	not out	2	3	–
* Salim Yousuf	not out	0	–	–
Shoaib Mohammed				
Abdul Qadir				
Tausif Ahmed				
Extras	(b 2, lb 8, w 3, nb 2)	15		
Total	(50 overs; 6 wickets)	**294**		

WEST INDIES		Runs	Balls	4/6
* C.G.Greenidge	not out	102	154	5
D.L.Haynes	c and b Wasim	1	5	–
R.B.Richardson	c Miandad b Wasim	6	13	–
C.L.Hooper	c Salim Yousuf b Wasim	0	4	–
A.L.Logie	run out	12	38	1
† P.J.L.Dujon	c Wasim b Mudassar	37	55	1
R.A.Harper	not out	22	45	1
C.E.L.Ambrose				
C.A.Walsh				
B.P.Patterson				
I.R.Bishop				
Extras	(b 1, lb 17, w 2, nb 10)	30		
Total	(50 overs; 5 wickets)	**210**		

WEST INDIES	O	M	R	W
Patterson	8	0	72	1
Ambrose	9	3	41	2
Walsh	7	0	36	1
Bishop	6	0	47	0
Harper	10	0	40	1
Hooper	10	0	48	1

PAKISTAN	O	M	R	W
Wasim Akram	9	0	37	3
Manzoor Elahi	10	0	40	0
Tausif Ahmed	10	0	21	0
Mudassar Nazar	10	0	48	1
Abdul Qadir	10	0	35	0
Javed Miandad	1	0	11	0

FALL OF WICKETS
1-113, 2-153, 3-252, 4-278, 5-281, 6-294

FALL OF WICKETS
1-12, 2-24, 3-24, 4-74, 5-146

Umpires: H.D.Bird (*England*) (51) and D.R.Shepherd (*England*) (29).

INDIA v PAKISTAN 1988-89

At Sharjah CA Stadium, UAE on 19 October 1988.   Result: **PAKISTAN** won by 34 runs.   Toss: India.
Award: Salim Malik.   LOI debuts: None.

Under the unusual playing conditions, this victory, which completed a clean sweep of the preliminary round-robin, gave
Pakistan a bye to the final.

PAKISTAN		Runs	Balls	4/6	INDIA		Runs	Balls	4/
Mudassar Nazar	run out	11	31	–	K.Srikkanth	lbw b Wasim	19	24	2
Ramiz Raja	c Maninder b Sharma	2	2	–	N.S.Sidhu	run out	38	58	3
Salim Malik	c More b Maninder	101	124	5/1	M.Amarnath	run out	15	21	–
* Javed Miandad	run out	52	75	4	* D.B.Vengsarkar	c Miandad b Wasim	51	71	1
Abdul Qadir	c Kapil Dev b Maninder	1	3	–	M.Azharuddin	c Salim Malik b Qadir	26	50	–
Wasim Akram	b Maninder	2	4	–	R.J.Shastri	c sub ‡ b Salim Jaffer	33	40	2
Ijaz Ahmed	c Azharuddin b Kapil Dev	26	24	2	Kapil Dev	c Manzoor b Salim Jaffer	3	5	–
Manzoor Elahi	run out	9	18	1	† K.S.More	c sub ‡ b Salim Jaffer	2	4	–
† Salim Yousuf	c Hirwani b Kapil Dev	25	18	1/1	S.K.Sharma	not out	8	17	–
Tausif Ahmed	run out	2	3	–	Maninder Singh	not out	6	10	–
Salim Jaffer	not out	0	–	–	N.D.Hirwani				
Extras	(lb 11, w 1, nb 3)	15			Extras	(lb 5, w 4, nb 2)	11		
Total	(49.1 overs)	**246**			**Total**	(50 overs; 8 wickets)	**212**		

INDIA	O	M	R	W	PAKISTAN	O	M	R	W
Kapil Dev	9.1	2	31	2	Wasim Akram	10	1	39	2
Sharma	8	0	51	1	Salim Jaffer	9	0	37	
Amarnath	5	0	20	0	Manzoor Elahi	3	0	22	
Maninder Singh	10	0	47	3	Mudassar Nazar	10	0	38	
Shastri	10	0	45	0	Tausif Ahmed	10	0	37	
Hirwani	7	0	41	0	Abdul Qadir	8	0	34	

FALL OF WICKETS
1-3, 2-41, 3-167, 4-171, 5-179, 6-180, 7-200, 8-229, 9-239, 10-246

FALL OF WICKETS
1-40, 2-70, 3-75, 4-132, 5-183, 6-196, 7-196, 8-201

Umpires: H.D.Bird (*England*) (52) and D.R.Shepherd (*England*) (30).   ‡ (Shoaib Mohammed)

WEST INDIES v INDIA 1988-89

At Sharjah CA Stadium, UAE on 21 October 1988.   Result: **WEST INDIES** won by 8 wickets.   Toss: India.
Award: D.L.Haynes.   LOI debuts: None.

West Indies rediscovered their form, equalled the (then) record partnership of 165 for any wicket in a Sharjah
tournament, and emphatically won this 'semi-final'.

INDIA		Runs	Balls	4/6	WEST INDIES		Runs	Balls	4/
K.Srikkanth	c Dujon b Ambrose	6	12	–	* C.G.Greenidge	not out	77	118	4/
R.J.Shastri	c Logie b Harper	35	90	2	D.L.Haynes	b Sharma	85	121	9/
M.Amarnath	c Dujon b Walsh	20	25	2	R.B.Richardson	c More b Sharma	0	1	–
* D.B.Vengsarkar	b Walsh	3	7	–	C.L.Hooper	not out	2	5	–
M.Azharuddin	c Harper b Hooper	25	39	1	A.L.Logie				
Kapil Dev	c Greenidge b Hooper	0	4	–	† P.J.L.Dujon				
C.S.Pandit	not out	31	52	–	R.A.Harper				
† K.S.More	c Logie b Ambrose	30	56	1	C.E.L.Ambrose				
S.K.Sharma	not out	13	15	1	C.A.Walsh				
Maninder Singh					B.P.Patterson				
N.D.Hirwani					I.R.Bishop				
Extras	(b 2, lb 4)	6			Extras	(lb 6, w 1, nb 4)	11		
Total	(50 overs; 7 wickets)	**169**			**Total**	(40 overs; 2 wickets)	**175**		

WEST INDIES	O	M	R	W	INDIA	O	M	R	W
Patterson	9	0	39	0	Kapil Dev	4	0	14	0
Ambrose	9	2	31	2	Sharma	6	0	25	2
Walsh	6	0	19	2	Maninder Singh	10	0	32	0
Bishop	6	0	13	0	Shastri	6	0	31	0
Harper	10	0	28	1	Hirwani	10	0	49	0
Hooper	10	1	33	2	Srikkanth	4	0	18	0

FALL OF WICKETS
1-16, 2-41, 3-45, 4-85, 5-86, 6-93, 7-144

FALL OF WICKETS
1-165, 2-165

Umpires: H.D.Bird (*England*) (53) and D.R.Shepherd (*England*) (31).

WEST INDIES v PAKISTAN 1988-89

At Sharjah CA Stadium, UAE on 22 October 1988.   Result: **WEST INDIES** won by 11 runs.   Toss: Pakistan.
Award: C.E.L.Ambrose.   LOI debuts: West Indies – K.L.T.Arthurton.

West Indies won their third trophy in successive visits to the Gulf. Desmond Haynes became the second after Viv Richards to score 5000 LOI runs. Abdul Qadir took his 100th wicket in 69 internationals. Local umpire Fareed Malik deputised at square-leg throughout Pakistan's innings for a dehydrated Harold Bird.

WEST INDIES		Runs	Balls	4/6
C.G.Greenidge	c Manzoor b Mudassar	37	48	3
D.L.Haynes	c Salim Malik b Shoaib	45	87	2
R.B.Richardson	b Qadir	2	13	–
C.L.Hooper	c Ijaz b Qadir	62	71	4
K.L.T.Arthurton	c Salim Yousuf b Wasim	27	44	–/1
P.J.L.Dujon	not out	21	26	1
R.A.Harper	c Qadir b Tausif	16	17	–/1
C.E.L.Ambrose	not out	3	3	–
C.A.Walsh				
B.P.Patterson				
I.R.Bishop				
Extras	(b 3, lb 10, w 3, nb 6)	22		
Total	(50 overs; 6 wickets)	**235**		

PAKISTAN		Runs	Balls	4/6
Mudassar Nazar	b Ambrose	9	12	–
Ramiz Raja	b Ambrose	4	6	1
Shoaib Mohammed	c Bishop b Walsh	15	33	1
* Javed Miandad	b Ambrose	76	120	1
Salim Malik	c Harper b Hooper	38	49	1
Ijaz Ahmed	lbw b Bishop	17	27	1
Manzoor Elahi	b Patterson	33	34	3
† Salim Yousuf	run out	0	1	–
Wasim Akram	b Ambrose	1	4	–
Abdul Qadir	b Bishop	10	14	1
Tausif Ahmed	not out	0	1	–
Extras	(b 1, lb 13, w 5, nb 2)	21		
Total	(49.4 overs)	**224**		

PAKISTAN	O	M	R	W
Wasim Akram	10	0	45	1
Manzoor Elahi	3	0	20	0
Mudassar Nazar	10	0	41	1
Abdul Qadir	10	0	41	2
Tausif Ahmed	10	0	49	1
Shoaib Mohammed	7	0	26	1

WEST INDIES	O	M	R	W
Patterson	8	0	40	1
Ambrose	10	0	29	4
Walsh	10	0	42	1
Bishop	8.4	0	38	2
Harper	6	0	26	0
Hooper	7	0	35	1

FALL OF WICKETS
1-74, 2-79, 3-118, 4-185, 5-190, 6-228

FALL OF WICKETS
1-8, 2-20, 3-49, 4-128, 5-159, 6-192, 7-192, 8-202, 9-218, 10-224

Umpires: H.D.Bird (*England*) (54) and D.R.Shepherd (*England*) (32).

PAKISTAN v SRI LANKA 1988-89

At National Stadium, Dacca on 27 October 1988.   Result: **SRI LANKA** won by 5 wickets.   Toss: Sri Lanka.
Award: R.S.Mahanama.   LOI debuts: Sri Lanka – K.I.W.Wijegunawardene.

Bangladesh staged its inaugural internationals, extending the number of venues to 85 by simultaneously introducing its capital, Dacca (now spelt 'Dhaka' locally), and the southern port of Chittagong.

PAKISTAN		Runs	Balls	4/6
Ramiz Raja	b Labrooy	3		
Aamer Malik	c Mahanama b Wijegunawardene	11		
Shoaib Mohammed	b Wijegunawardene	10		
Javed Miandad	retired hurt	25		
Salim Malik	c Mahanama b Labrooy	30	36	1
Ijaz Ahmed	c Kuruppu b Labrooy	54	58	4
* Salim Yousuf	c sub ‡ b Ratnayeke	31	24	
Manzoor Elahi	c Mahanama b Ratnayeke	12		
Wasim Akram	not out	9		
Abdul Qadir	not out	2		
Tausif Ahmed				
Extras	(lb 5, w 1, nb 1)	7		
Total	(44 overs; 7 wickets)	**194**		

SRI LANKA		Runs	Balls	4/6
R.S.Mahanama	c Salim Yousuf b Wasim	55	92	3
† D.S.B.P.Kuruppu	c and b Qadir	35		
M.A.R.Samarasekera	c Salim Yousuf b Manzoor	10		
P.A.de Silva	c Manzoor b Wasim	48	38	7
A.Ranatunga	run out	7		
L.R.D.Mendis	not out	20		
J.R.Ratnayeke	not out	2		
* R.S.Madugalle				
G.F.Labrooy				
K.I.W.Wijegunawardene				
S.D.Anurasiri				
Extras	(b 1, lb 9, w 3, nb 5)	18		
Total	(38.5 overs; 5 wickets)	**195**		

SRI LANKA	O	M	R	W
Ratnayeke	9	1	27	2
Labrooy	8	1	36	3
Wijegunawardene	8	1	29	2
Samarasekera	9	1	34	0
Anurasiri	4	0	22	0
Ranatunga	3	0	27	0
De Silva	3	0	14	0

PAKISTAN	O	M	R	W
Wasim Akram	7.5	0	34	2
Manzoor Elahi	8	0	43	1
Aamer Malik	2	0	10	0
Abdul Qadir	8	0	48	1
Tausif Ahmed	9	0	26	0
Shoaib Mohammed	4	0	24	0

FALL OF WICKETS
1-3, 2-24, 3-35, 4-98, 5-155, 6-180, 7-187

FALL OF WICKETS
1-72, 2-100, 3-116, 4-138, 5-192

‡ (H.P.Tillekeratne)

Umpires: R.B.Gupta (*India*) (11) and V.K.Ramaswamy (*India*) (10).

BANGLADESH v INDIA 1988-89

At Chittagong Stadium on 27 October 1988.   Result: **INDIA** won by 9 wickets.   Toss: India.
Award: N.S.Sidhu.   LOI debuts: Bangladesh – Amin-ul-Islam, Athar Ali Khan, Azhar Hussain, Ghulam Farooq, Harun-ur-Rashid, Nasir Ahmed, Zahid Razzak.

At the time they were played, matches involving Bangladesh were not classified as official limited-overs internationals. At their AGM in July 1989, ICC retrospectively granted Bangladesh official status for its Asia Cup matches.

BANGLADESH		Runs	Balls	4/6	INDIA		Runs	Balls	4/6
Azhar Hussain	lbw b Sharma	1	7	–	K.Srikkanth	c Athar b Hussain	24	45	3
Harun-ur-Rashid	b Kapil Dev	0	14	–	N.S.Sidhu	not out	50	71	4/1
* Gazi Ashraf	b Maninder	11	70	–	M.Amarnath	not out	19	41	–
Athar Ali Khan	c Kapil Dev b Amarnath	16	34	1	* D.B.Vengsarkar				
Minhaz-ul-Abedin	b Arshad Ayub	22	67	2	M.Azharuddin				
Amin-ul-Islam	lbw b Arshad Ayub	10	26	1	Kapil Dev				
Zahid Razzak	b Arshad Ayub	6	21	–	† K.S.More				
Ghulam Farooq	c Sidhu b Hirwani	4	9	–	S.K.Sharma				
Jahangir Shah	not out	7	14	–	Arshad Ayub				
† Nasir Ahmed	not out	9	10	1	Maninder Singh				
Ghulam Nousher					N.D.Hirwani				
Extras	(b 1, lb 6, w 5, nb 1)	13			Extras	(lb 4, w 3)	7		
Total	(45 overs; 8 wickets)	99			Total	(26 overs; 1 wicket)	100		

INDIA	O	M	R	W	BANGLADESH	O	M	R	W
Kapil Dev	6	2	14	1	Ghulam Nousher	6	2	15	0
Sharma	9	2	22	1	Ghulam Farooq	4	0	19	0
Amarnath	6	1	8	1	Jahangir Shah	6	1	16	0
Maninder Singh	9	6	9	1	Azhar Hussain	7	0	30	0
Arshad Ayub	9	2	20	3	Athar Ali Khan	2	0	12	0
Hirwani	6	0	19	1	Minhaz-ul-Abedin	1	0	4	0

FALL OF WICKETS
1-1, 2-2, 3-33, 4-40, 5-65, 6-72, 7-79, 8-79

FALL OF WICKETS
1-47

Umpires: K.T.Francis (*Sri Lanka*) (8) and Tariq Ata (*Pakistan*) (4).

INDIA v SRI LANKA 1988-89

At National Stadium, Dacca on 29 October 1988.   Result: **SRI LANKA** won by 17 runs.   Toss: India.
Award: P.A.de Silva.   LOI debuts: None.

Arjuna Ranatunga made his first appearance as Sri Lanka's captain. In his 129th match, Kapil Dev became the first bowler to take 150 LOI wickets.

SRI LANKA		Runs	Balls	4/6	INDIA		Runs	Balls	4/6
R.S.Mahanama	lbw b Amarnath	21	35	1	K.Srikkanth	c Mahanama b Ranatunga	42	54	4
† D.S.B.P.Kuruppu	b Sharma	16	35	1	N.S.Sidhu	c Kuruppu b Ranatunga	50	55	3
M.A.R.Samarasekera	b Srikkanth	66	69	2/1	M.Amarnath	run out	31	34	2/1
P.A.de Silva	lbw b Arshad Ayub	69	63	3/3	* D.B.Vengsarkar	c Wijegunawardene b De Silva	34	24	2/1
* A.Ranatunga	not out	49	32	5	Kapil Dev	lbw b Wijegunawardene	7	13	–
L.R.D.Mendis	c Amarnath b Kapil Dev	19	19	–/1	M.Azharuddin	c Madurasinghe b Ratnayeke	34	38	1/2
J.R.Ratnayeke	b Kapil Dev	16	18	1	† K.S.More	c Ratnayeke b Wijegunawardene	6	8	–
H.P.Tillekeratne	not out	2	1	–	Arshad Ayub	run out	9	7	–
K.I.W.Wijegunawardene					S.K.Sharma	c Tillekeratne b Wijegunawardene	28	26	2
M.A.W.R.Madurasinghe					Maninder Singh	c De Silva b Wijegunawardene	7	6	–
C.P.H.Ramanayake					N.D.Hirwani	not out	1	1	–
Extras	(lb 9, w 1, nb 3)	13			Extras	(lb 1, w 3, nb 1)	5		
Total	(45 overs; 6 wickets)	271			Total	(44 overs)	254		

INDIA	O	M	R	W	SRI LANKA	O	M	R	W
Kapil Dev	9	0	39	2	Ratnayeke	8	0	47	1
Sharma	8	1	44	1	Ramanayake	8	0	36	0
Amarnath	4	0	27	1	Wijegunawardene	9	0	49	4
Maninder Singh	5	0	26	0	Samarasekera	2	0	17	0
Hirwani	4	0	38	0	Ranatunga	5	0	27	2
Arshad Ayub	9	0	55	0	Madurasinghe	6	0	41	0
Srikkanth	6	0	33	1	De Silva	6	0	36	1

FALL OF WICKETS
1-35, 2-52, 3-178, 4-184, 5-216, 6-269

FALL OF WICKETS
1-89, 2-96, 3-146, 4-166, 5-167, 6-182, 7-195, 8-224, 9-252, 10-254

Umpires: Salim Badar (*Pakistan*) (1) and Tariq Ata (*Pakistan*) (5).

BANGLADESH v PAKISTAN 1988-89

At Chittagong Stadium on 29 October 1988.   Result: **PAKISTAN** won by 173 runs.   Toss: Pakistan.
Award: Moin-ul-Atiq.   LOI debuts: Bangladesh – Akram Khan, Farooq Ahmed, Wahid-ul-Ghani.

The partnership of 205 between Moin-ul-Atiq and Ijaz Ahmed was then Pakistan's highest for any wicket and remains their third-wicket record. The number of balls in which Ijaz Ahmed completed his rapid hundred is awaited.

PAKISTAN		Runs	Balls	4/6	BANGLADESH		Runs	Balls	4/6
Ramiz Raja	c Nasir b Nousher	10			Azhar Hussain	c Salim Yousuf b Iqbal	10		
Moin-ul-Atiq	lbw b Athar	105	117		Farooq Ahmed	lbw b Iqbal	14		
Salim Malik	c and b Hussain	15			* Gazi Ashraf	b Iqbal	10		
Ijaz Ahmed	not out	124	87	9/4	Athar Ali Khan	c Ramiz b Qadir	22		
Manzoor Elahi	not out	7			Minhaz-ul-Abedin	lbw b Shoaib	11		
Shoaib Mohammed					Amin-ul-Islam	b Qadir	0		
Salim Yousuf					Jahangir Shah	not out	8		
Wasim Akram					Akram Khan	not out	21		
Abdul Qadir					Wahid-ul-Ghani				
Tausif Ahmed					† Nasir Ahmed				
Iqbal Qasim					Ghulam Nousher				
Extras	(b 3, lb 6, w 14)	23			Extras	(b 4, lb 5, w 5, nb 1)	15		
Total	(45 overs; 3 wickets)	284			Total	(45 overs; 6 wickets)	111		

BANGLADESH	O	M	R	W	PAKISTAN	O	M	R	W
Ghulam Nousher	8	0	55	1	Wasim Akram	6	3	10	0
Jahangir Shah	9	1	53	0	Manzoor Elahi	4	1	9	0
Athar Ali Khan	9	0	54	1	Tausif Ahmed	8	2	12	0
Azhar Hussain	4	0	24	1	Iqbal Qasim	9	3	13	3
Wahid-ul-Ghani	6	0	32	0	Shoaib Mohammed	8	0	21	1
Akram Khan	5	0	28	0	Abdul Qadir	9	0	27	2
Minhaz-ul-Abedin	2	0	17	0	Ramiz Raja	1	0	10	0
Amin-ul-Islam	2	0	12	0					

FALL OF WICKETS
1-43, 2-72, 3-277

FALL OF WICKETS
1-30, 2-39, 3-54, 4-82, 5-82, 6-82

Umpires: R.B.Gupta (*India*) (12) and S.Ponnadurai (*Sri Lanka*) (3).

INDIA v PAKISTAN 1988-89

At National Stadium, Dacca on 31 October 1988.   Result: **INDIA** won by 4 wickets.   Toss: India.
Award: Arshad Ayub.   LOI debuts: None.

India gained only their second LOI success against Pakistan in the last dozen encounters. Arshad Ayub returned India's (then) best analysis in internationals, capturing the last four wickets for five runs off 15 balls.

PAKISTAN		Runs	Balls	4/6	INDIA		Runs	Balls	4/6
Ramiz Raja	lbw b Arshad Ayub	33	53	3	K.Srikkanth	b Qadir	23	44	2
Moin-ul-Atiq	b Maninder	38	64	2	N.S.Sidhu	b Naved	3	17	–
Salim Malik	lbw b Maninder	19	30	1	M.Amarnath	not out	74	122	6
Ijaz Ahmed	b Kapil Dev	14	40	–	* D.B.Vengsarkar	lbw b Qadir	0	2	–
† Aamer Malik	lbw b Arshad Ayub	2	18	–	M.Azharuddin	lbw b Wasim	15	28	–
Shoaib Mohammed	b Arshad Ayub	2	5	–	Kapil Dev	st Aamer b Qadir	2	12	–
Naved Anjum	lbw b Arshad Ayub	1	7	–	A.K.Sharma	b Wasim	2	4	–
Wasim Akram	b Arshad Ayub	4	7	–	† C.S.Pandit	not out	5	9	–
* Abdul Qadir	run out	3	4	–	S.K.Sharma				
Haafiz Shahid	b Kapil Dev	2	12	–	Arshad Ayub				
Tausif Ahmed	not out	7	8	1	Maninder Singh				
Extras	(b 1, lb 7, w 8, nb 1)	17			Extras	(b 1, lb 6, w 5, nb 7)	19		
Total	(42.2 overs)	142			Total	(40.4 overs; 6 wickets)	143		

INDIA	O	M	R	W	PAKISTAN	O	M	R	W
Kapil Dev	6.2	1	16	2	Wasim Akram	9	0	29	2
S.K.Sharma	7	0	26	0	Naved Anjum	8.4	0	30	1
Amarnath	5	0	29	0	Abdul Qadir	9	3	27	3
Maninder Singh	9	1	25	2	Haafiz Shahid	3	0	17	0
Arshad Ayub	9	0	21	5	Tausif Ahmed	9	0	22	0
A.K.Sharma	5	0	15	0	Shoaib Mohammed	1	0	6	0
Srikkanth	1	0	2	0	Salim Malik	1	0	5	0

FALL OF WICKETS
1-62, 2-91, 3-97, 4-107, 5-112, 6-116, 7-124, 8-128, 9-133, 10-142

FALL OF WICKETS
1-13, 2-76, 3-76, 4-110, 5-113, 6-116

Umpires: K.T.Francis (*Sri Lanka*) (9) and S.Ponnadurai (*Sri Lanka*) (4).

BANGLADESH v SRI LANKA 1988-89

At National Stadium, Dacca on 2 November 1988.　　Result: **SRI LANKA** won by 9 wickets.　　Toss: Sri Lanka.
Award: D.S.B.P.Kuruppu.　　LOI debuts: None.

Sri Lanka completed their unbeaten run in the preliminary matches. Final points: Sri Lanka 12, India 8, Pakistan 4, Bangladesh 0.

BANGLADESH		Runs	Balls	4/6
Farooq Ahmed	c Ramanayake b Ratnayeke	0		
Harun-ur-Rashid	c Kuruppu b Ratnayeke	0		
Azhar Hussain	lbw b Ratnayeke	3		
* Gazi Ashraf	c Kuruppu b Ramanayake	2		
Athar Ali Khan	st Kuruppu b De Silva	30		
Minhaz-ul-Abedin	c Anurasiri b Madurasinghe	10		
Akram Khan	c Kuruppu b Anurasiri	9		
Amin-ul-Islam	c Anurasiri b Ratnayeke	27		
Ghulam Farooq	not out	23		
† Nasir Ahmed	not out	2		
Ghulam Nousher				
Extras	(b 1, lb 2, w 5, nb 4)	12		
Total	(45 overs; 8 wickets)	**118**		

SRI LANKA		Runs	Balls	4/6
† D.S.B.P.Kuruppu	not out	58		
* J.R.Ratnayeke	lbw b Hussain	17		
M.A.R.Samarasekera	not out	38		
P.A.de Silva				
L.R.D.Mendis				
H.P.Tillekeratne				
S.H.U.Karnain				
K.I.W.Wijegunawardene				
M.A.W.R.Madurasinghe				
C.P.H.Ramanayake				
S.D.Anurasiri				
Extras	(b 1, lb 4, w 1, nb 1)	7		
Total	(30.5 overs; 1 wicket)	**120**		

SRI LANKA	O	M	R	W
Ratnayeke	8	1	23	4
Ramanayake	6	2	6	1
Wijegunawardene	6	1	21	0
Samarasekera	2	0	11	0
Anurasiri	9	2	18	1
Madurasinghe	9	0	11	1
De Silva	5	1	25	1

BANGLADESH	O	M	R	W
Ghulam Nousher	4	1	15	0
Ghulam Farooq	8	1	34	0
Athar Ali Khan	4	0	17	0
Azhar Hussain	6.5	0	20	1
Amin-ul-Islam	6	0	23	0
Akram Khan	2	0	6	0

FALL OF WICKETS
1-1, 2-2, 3-8, 4-8, 5-42, 6-62, 7-68, 8-114

FALL OF WICKETS
1-57

Umpires: V.K.Ramaswamy (*India*) (11) and Salim Badar (*Pakistan*) (2).

INDIA v SRI LANKA 1988-89

At National Stadium, Dacca on 4 November 1988.　　Result: **INDIA** won by 6 wickets.　　Toss: India.
Award: N.S.Sidhu.　　LOI debuts: None.

Sri Lanka failed to post a challenging total after losing four prime wickets to run outs. India, who won the first tournament (Sharjah 1983-84) and withdrew from the second (Sri Lanka 1985-86), thus won this third (Wills) Asia Cup and a winner's cheque for $US30,000 (£17,340).

SRI LANKA		Runs	Balls	4/6
R.S.Mahanama	lbw b Amarnath	23	47	1
† D.S.B.P.Kuruppu	st Pandit b Maninder	21	41	1
M.A.R.Samarasekera	run out	26	36	2
P.A.de Silva	run out	18	25	–
* A.Ranatunga	run out	5	24	–
L.R.D.Mendis	c Amarnath b Srikkanth	36	36	3/1
J.R.Ratnayeke	run out	7	19	–
S.H.U.Karnain	c Pandit b Srikkanth	11	18	1
G.F.Labrooy	b Kapil Dev	1	4	–
K.I.W.Wijegunawardene	not out	8	9	–
M.A.W.R.Madurasinghe	b Srikkanth	2	9	–
Extras	(lb 5, w 7, nb 6)	18		
Total	(43.2 overs)	**176**		

INDIA		Runs	Balls	4/6
K.Srikkanth	run out	23	28	3
N.S.Sidhu	b Wijegunawardene	76	87	4/1
M.Amarnath	c Kuruppu b Madurasinghe	7	17	1
* D.B.Vengsarkar	not out	50	81	–
M.Azharuddin	c Kuruppu b Wijegunawardene	0	2	–
Kapil Dev	not out	12	12	2
A.K.Sharma				
† C.S.Pandit				
S.K.Sharma				
Arshad Ayub				
Maninder Singh				
Extras	(b 1, lb 5, w 2, nb 4)	12		
Total	(37.1 overs; 4 wickets)	**180**		

INDIA	O	M	R	W
Kapil Dev	7	0	30	1
S.K.Sharma	5	0	20	0
Amarnath	6	0	21	1
Maninder Singh	9	0	35	1
Arshad Ayub	9	0	24	0
A.K.Sharma	4	0	29	0
Srikkanth	3.2	0	12	3

SRI LANKA	O	M	R	W
Ratnayeke	9	1	35	0
Labrooy	5	0	30	0
Ranatunga	1	0	12	0
Madurasinghe	9	1	30	1
De Silva	4	0	30	0
Wijegunawardene	9	0	33	2
Mahanama	0.1	0	4	0

FALL OF WICKETS
1-53, 2-57, 3-97, 4-105, 5-113, 6-130, 7-164, 8-165, 9-166, 10-176

FALL OF WICKETS
1-45, 2-69, 3-155, 4-155

Umpires: Salim Badar (*Pakistan*) (3) and Tariq Ata (*Pakistan*) (6).

INDIA v NEW ZEALAND 1988-89

At Indira Priyadarshani Stadium, Vishakhapatnam on 10 December 1988.   Result: **INDIA** won by 4 wickets.   Toss: India.
Award: K.Srikkanth.   LOI debuts: India – V.B.Chandrasekhar.

India's 27th international venue saw Krish Srikkanth complete 3000 runs in 104 matches, return India's best analysis against New Zealand and become the second player after Viv Richards to score 50 and take five wickets in an international.

NEW ZEALAND		Runs	Balls	4/6
J.G.Wright	c Vengsarkar b Kapil Dev	2	–	
A.H.Jones	c S.K.Sharma b Maninder	66		3/1
K.R.Rutherford	b Srikkanth	67		4
M.J.Greatbatch	run out	0	–	
T.J.Franklin	c S.K.Sharma b Srikkanth	21	–	
I.D.S.Smith	b Srikkanth	6	–	
J.G.Bracewell	c Pandit b Srikkanth	12		1
C.M.Kuggeleijn	c and b Srikkanth	4	–	
M.C.Snedden	not out	6	–	
W.Watson	b Kapil Dev	1	–	
E.J.Chatfield	not out	0	–	
Extras	(lb 4, w 5, nb 2)	11		
Total	(50 overs; 9 wickets)	**196**		

INDIA		Runs	Balls	4/6
K.Srikkanth	c Chatfield b Bracewell	70	87	8
V.B.Chandrasekhar	lbw b Watson	10	20	2
N.S.Sidhu	run out	24	49	4
* D.B.Vengsarkar	run out	0	2	–
M.Azharuddin	not out	48	74	3
Kapil Dev	c Greatbatch b Watson	22	25	3
† C.S.Pandit	c Rutherford b Snedden	2	13	–
A.K.Sharma	not out	3	3	–
Arshad Ayub				
S.K.Sharma				
Maninder Singh				
Extras	(lb 15, w 1, nb 2)	18		
Total	(46.2 overs; 6 wickets)	**197**		

INDIA	O	M	R	W
Kapil Dev	7	0	16	2
S.K.Sharma	6	0	13	0
Azharuddin	2	0	11	0
Maninder Singh	10	0	49	1
Arshad Ayub	10	0	45	0
A.K.Sharma	8	0	31	0
Srikkanth	7	0	27	5

NEW ZEALAND	O	M	R	W
Chatfield	8	0	38	0
Watson	10	0	37	2
Snedden	4.2	0	20	1
Rutherford	4	0	25	0
Bracewell	10	1	36	1
Kuggeleijn	10	1	26	0

FALL OF WICKETS
1-2, 2-116, 3-116, 4-163, 5-168, 6-176, 7-182, 8-191, 9-194

FALL OF WICKETS
1-16, 2-79, 3-79, 4-129, 5-180, 6-188

Umpires: S.Banerjee (6) and R.V.Ramani (7).

INDIA v NEW ZEALAND 1988-89

At Barabati Stadium, Cuttack on 12 December 1988.   Result: **INDIA** won by 5 wickets.   Toss: New Zealand.
Award: N.S.Sidhu.   LOI debuts: None.

Because of the early twilight in this region, the overs were reduced from the standard 50 per innings.

NEW ZEALAND		Runs	Balls	4/6
J.G.Wright	b Maninder	39	59	4
A.H.Jones	c Srikkanth b Maninder	16	45	1
K.R.Rutherford	lbw b Arshad Ayub	4	15	–
M.J.Greatbatch	run out	1	2	–
E.J.Gray	b Kapil Dev	38	80	3
I.D.S.Smith	lbw b A.K.Sharma	9	28	–
C.M.Kuggeleijn	c S.K.Sharma b Srikkanth	9	17	–
J.G.Bracewell	not out	24	28	2
M.C.Snedden	not out	2	3	–
W.Watson				
E.J.Chatfield				
Extras	(b 4, lb 9, w 4, nb 1)	18		
Total	(45 overs; 7 wickets)	**160**		

INDIA		Runs	Balls	4/6
K.Srikkanth	lbw b Watson	5	9	1
V.B.Chandrasekhar	b Kuggeleijn	9	29	1
N.S.Sidhu	c Smith b Watson	67	108	2/1
* D.B.Vengsarkar	c Smith b Bracewell	15	36	–
M.Azharuddin	c Bracewell b Gray	32	28	1/2
Kapil Dev	not out	27	41	1/1
A.K.Sharma	not out	2	1	–
† C.S.Pandit				
S.K.Sharma				
Arshad Ayub				
Maninder Singh				
Extras	(lb 4)	4		
Total	(41.3 overs; 5 wickets)	**161**		

INDIA	O	M	R	W
Kapil Dev	7	0	29	1
S.K.Sharma	5	0	19	0
Maninder Singh	9	2	23	2
Arshad Ayub	9	0	23	1
A.K.Sharma	7	0	25	1
Srikkanth	8	0	28	1

NEW ZEALAND	O	M	R	W
Chatfield	9	2	23	0
Watson	7.3	0	33	2
Kuggeleijn	9	0	29	1
Snedden	5	0	11	0
Bracewell	5	0	37	1
Gray	6	0	24	1

FALL OF WICKETS
1-52, 2-64, 3-65, 4-67, 5-90, 6-109, 7-156

FALL OF WICKETS
1-5, 2-30, 3-69, 4-117, 5-159

Umpires: D.N.Dotiwala (8) and S.B.Kulkarni (5).

INDIA v NEW ZEALAND 1988-89

At Nehru Stadium, Indore on 15 December 1988.　　Result: **INDIA** won by 53 runs.　　Toss: New Zealand.
Award: A.K.Sharma.　　LOI debuts: None.

The start was delayed and the number of overs reduced when both teams objected to the state of the pitch and outfield. John Wright became the first New Zealander to score 3000 runs (113 matches). Krish Srikkanth's part-time bowling snared its second five-wicket haul in three matches.

INDIA		Runs	Balls	4/6
K.Srikkanth	b Snedden	23	49	2/1
V.B.Chandrasekhar	b Kuggeleijn	53	77	7
N.S.Sidhu	c Rutherford b Kuggeleijn	14	22	–
* D.B.Vengsarkar	c Jones b Gray	14	25	–
M.Azharuddin	c Bracewell b Gray	17	33	–
Kapil Dev	c Blain b Snedden	11	14	1
A.K.Sharma	not out	52	47	3/3
† C.S.Pandit	not out	19	24	–
S.K.Sharma				
Arshad Ayub				
Maninder Singh				
Extras	(b 1, lb 12, w 6)	19		
Total	(45 overs; 6 wickets)	**222**		

NEW ZEALAND		Runs	Balls	4/6
* J.G.Wright	c Arshad Ayub b Maninder	43	74	4
A.H.Jones	c Pandit b S.K.Sharma	6	19	1
K.R.Rutherford	c Kapil Dev b S.K.Sharma	6	17	–
M.J.Greatbatch	c Kapil Dev b Srikkanth	64	97	5
† T.E.Blain	c Maninder b Srikkanth	17	20	1
C.M.Kuggeleijn	run out	0	–	–
J.G.Bracewell	b Srikkanth	7	5	–
E.J.Gray	st Pandit b Srikkanth	3	6	–
M.C.Snedden	c Pandit b Srikkanth	6	13	–
W.Watson	not out	3	14	–
E.J.Chatfield	not out	0	1	–
Extras	(lb 10, w 2, nb 2)	14		
Total	(45 overs; 9 wickets)	**169**		

NEW ZEALAND	O	M	R	W
Chatfield	7	2	23	0
Watson	5	1	30	0
Snedden	8	0	43	2
Kuggeleijn	9	2	31	2
Rutherford	3	0	16	0
Bracewell	8	0	40	0
Gray	5	0	26	2

INDIA	O	M	R	W
Kapil Dev	9	2	18	0
S.K.Sharma	7	0	22	2
Maninder Singh	9	1	28	1
Arshad Ayub	9	0	27	0
A.K.Sharma	5	0	32	0
Srikkanth	6	0	32	5

FALL OF WICKETS
1-59, 2-91, 3-105, 4-125, 5-141, 6-168

FALL OF WICKETS
1-12, 2-24, 3-75, 4-125, 5-129, 6-144, 7-154, 8-161, 9-168

Umpires: R.B.Gupta (13) and R.S.Rathore (3).

INDIA v NEW ZEALAND 1988-89

At Moti Bagh Stadium, Baroda on 17 December 1988.　　Result: **INDIA** won by 2 wickets.　　Toss: New Zealand.
Award: M.Azharuddin.　　LOI debuts: India – R.Patel, M.Venkataramana.

Mohammad Azharuddin's 62-ball hundred was the fastest in internationals until 1995-96, while his stand of 127 with Ajay Sharma (50 off 36 balls) remains India's highest for the sixth wicket. Martin Snedden took his 100th wicket in 80 matches. A fifth match, at the Molana Azad Stadium in Jammu (new venue) on 19 December, was abandoned without a ball bowled.

NEW ZEALAND		Runs	Balls	4/6
* J.G.Wright	st Pandit b Venkataramana	70	96	7/1
A.H.Jones	c Pandit b Venkataramana	57	85	3
K.R.Rutherford	c Manjrekar b C.Sharma	32	43	1
M.J.Greatbatch	not out	84	67	8/2
T.E.Blain	not out	11	16	–
† I.D.S.Smith				
C.M.Kuggeleijn				
J.G.Bracewell				
M.C.Snedden				
D.K.Morrison				
E.J.Chatfield				
Extras	(b 1, lb 13, w 6, nb 4)	24		
Total	(50 overs; 3 wickets)	**278**		

INDIA		Runs	Balls	4/6
† C.S.Pandit	b Snedden	30	44	3
V.B.Chandrasekhar	c Bracewell b Morrison	1	4	–
W.V.Raman	run out	5	10	–
S.V.Manjrekar	c Chatfield b Morrison	52	69	2
* D.B.Vengsarkar	b Kuggeleijn	28	46	1
M.Azharuddin	not out	108	65	10/3
A.K.Sharma	c Jones b Morrison	50	36	5
S.K.Sharma	run out	0	–	–
C.Sharma	c Smith b Snedden	0	2	–
M.Venkataramana	not out	0	–	–
R.Patel				
Extras	(b 2, lb 5, w 1)	8		
Total	(47.1 overs; 8 wickets)	**282**		

INDIA	O	M	R	W
C.Sharma	10	0	54	1
Patel	10	1	58	0
S.K.Sharma	10	0	74	0
Venkataramana	10	0	36	2
A.K.Sharma	9	1	31	0
Raman	1	0	11	0

NEW ZEALAND	O	M	R	W
Morrison	10	0	50	3
Chatfield	10	0	61	0
Snedden	9	0	51	2
Bracewell	10	0	49	0
Kuggeleijn	8.1	0	64	0

FALL OF WICKETS
1-140, 2-155, 3-211

FALL OF WICKETS
1-3, 2-12, 3-50, 4-118, 5-133, 6-260, 7-263, 8-278

Umpires: P.G.Pandit (9) and V.K.Ramaswamy (12).

WEST INDIES v PAKISTAN 1988-89

At Adelaide Oval on 10 December 1988.   Result: **WEST INDIES** won by 89 runs.   Toss: Pakistan.
Award: D.L.Haynes.   LOI debuts: Pakistan – Aqib Javed.

The tenth World Series was the first to feature shirts bearing players' names. Early rain reduced the match by three overs per side. Desmond Haynes scored his 11th hundred to equal the record tally of Viv Richards. Abdul Qadir arrived in Australia four hours before the game began.

WEST INDIES		Runs	Balls	4/6
C.G.Greenidge	b Qadir	70	83	8/1
D.L.Haynes	c Miandad b Imran	111	107	8/4
R.B.Richardson	c Salim Yousuf b Aqib	1	6	–
I.V.A.Richards	lbw b Qadir	1	7	–
C.L.Hooper	c Wasim b Tausif	15	21	1
A.L.Logie	c Salim Yousuf b Tausif	14	13	–
M.D.Marshall	b Imran	20	35	–
W.K.M.Benjamin	lbw b Wasim	0	2	–
D.Williams	c Salim Yousuf b Qadir	5	8	1
C.E.L.Ambrose	not out	0	3	–
C.A.Walsh	not out	1	3	–
Extras	(b 7, lb 15, w 2, nb 7)	31		
Total	(47 overs; 9 wickets)	**269**		

PAKISTAN		Runs	Balls	4/6
Ramiz Raja	not out	69	127	1
Sajid Ali	c Greenidge b Marshall	2	8	–
Salim Malik	b Marshall	7	13	–
Javed Miandad	c Williams b Walsh	38	63	3
Ijaz Ahmed	c Williams b Marshall	26	33	1
Wasim Akram	b Marshall	9	10	–
* Imran Khan	c Richards b Benjamin	8	15	–
† Salim Yousuf	c Richards b Ambrose	6	8	–
Abdul Qadir	not out	4	10	–
Tausif Ahmed				
Aqib Javed				
Extras	(lb 5, w 2, nb 4)	11		
Total	(47 overs; 7 wickets)	**180**		

PAKISTAN	O	M	R	W
Imran Khan	10	0	47	2
Wasim Akram	10	0	45	1
Aqib Javed	9	0	49	1
Tausif Ahmed	9	0	72	2
Abdul Qadir	9	0	34	3

WEST INDIES	O	M	R	W
Marshall	10	1	34	4
Ambrose	8	2	22	1
Benjamin	9	0	30	1
Walsh	10	0	41	1
Richards	9	0	43	0
Hooper	1	0	5	0

FALL OF WICKETS
1-169, 2-174, 3-181, 4-217, 5-218, 6-240, 7-241, 8-262, 9-263

FALL OF WICKETS
1-3, 2-17, 3-81, 4-129, 5-141, 6-152, 7-166

Umpires: A.R.Crafter (63) and R.J.Evans (1).

AUSTRALIA v PAKISTAN 1988-89

At Adelaide Oval on 11 December 1988.   Result: **AUSTRALIA** won by 9 wickets.   Toss: Pakistan.
Award: M.G.Hughes.   LOI debuts: Australia – M.G.Hughes, M.E.Waugh.

Mark Waugh's first appearance, alongside his brother Steve, provided international cricket with its first twins. A 20-minute rain interruption in Pakistan's innings reduced the match to a 48-over contest. For the first time in any completed LOI innings, none of the ten dismissals featured a catch.

PAKISTAN		Runs	Balls	4/6
Ramiz Raja	b Hughes	3	18	–
Sajid Ali	b McDermott	15	40	–
† Salim Yousuf	run out	12	13	1/1
Javed Miandad	b McDermott	18	27	2
Salim Malik	run out	44	41	5
Ijaz Ahmed	b Hughes	37	41	2
* Imran Khan	not out	23	59	1
Wasim Akram	b Taylor	7	7	–
Abdul Qadir	lbw b Hughes	10	15	1
Tausif Ahmed	b Alderman	1	9	–
Aqib Javed	lbw b S.R.Waugh	0	8	–
Extras	(lb 2, w 2, nb 3)	7		
Total	(45.4 overs)	**177**		

AUSTRALIA		Runs	Balls	4/6
G.R.Marsh	not out	86	135	7
D.C.Boon	run out	27	29	4
D.M.Jones	not out	55	95	1/1
S.R.Waugh				
M.E.Waugh				
* A.R.Border				
† I.A.Healy				
P.L.Taylor				
C.J.McDermott				
M.G.Hughes				
T.M.Alderman				
Extras	(b 4, lb 3, w 1, nb 2)	10		
Total	(42.2 overs; 1 wicket)	**178**		

AUSTRALIA	O	M	R	W
Alderman	9	3	15	1
Hughes	10	1	30	3
McDermott	10	0	51	2
S.R.Waugh	7.4	0	27	1
Taylor	9	0	52	1

PAKISTAN	O	M	R	W
Imran Khan	10	3	33	0
Aqib Javed	9	0	45	0
Wasim Akram	7	0	22	0
Abdul Qadir	7	0	36	0
Tausif Ahmed	9	0	31	0
Salim Malik	0.2	0	4	0

FALL OF WICKETS
1-5, 2-30, 3-42, 4-71, 5-114, 6-146, 7-155, 8-174, 9-175, 10-177

FALL OF WICKETS
1-52

Umpires: L.J.King (3) and T.A.Prue (3).

AUSTRALIA v WEST INDIES 1988-89

At Sydney Cricket Ground on 13 December 1988.　　Result: **WEST INDIES** won by 1 run.　　Toss: West Indies.
Award: D.L.Haynes.　　LOI debuts: None.

West Indies gained their first victory in Sydney since February 1985 when Craig McDermott, needing two off the last ball, hit a full toss from Curtly Ambrose directly to mid-wicket. Australia's first partnership featuring the Waugh twins ended in a run out.

WEST INDIES		Runs	Balls	4/6
C.G.Greenidge	c M.E.Waugh b Taylor	52	65	4/1
D.L.Haynes	c and b Hughes	78	116	5
R.B.Richardson	b Taylor	12	10	1
* I.V.A.Richards	st Healy b Taylor	12	23	–
C.L.Hooper	c Healy b Hughes	20	29	–
† P.J.L.Dujon	c and b Border	8	11	–
M.D.Marshall	c sub (G.M.Wood) b McDermott	17	15	2
W.K.M.Benjamin	b Hughes	6	12	1
C.E.L.Ambrose	not out	1	4	–
C.A.Walsh	b McDermott	2	2	–
Extras	(lb 8, nb 4)	12		
Total	**(48 overs)**	**220**		

AUSTRALIA		Runs	Balls	4/6
D.C.Boon	b Marshall	71	120	6
G.R.Marsh	c Ambrose b Walsh	19	49	1
D.M.Jones	lbw b Walsh	1	5	–
S.R.Waugh	run out	40	57	2
M.E.Waugh	b Benjamin	18	19	1
* A.R.Border	run out	8	10	–
† I.A.Healy	not out	23	20	1
P.L.Taylor	c Hooper b Benjamin	16	16	–
C.J.McDermott	c Richards b Ambrose	6	7	1
M.G.Hughes				
T.M.Alderman				
Extras	(b 6, lb 6, w 4, nb 1)	17		
Total	**(50 overs; 8 wickets)**	**219**		

AUSTRALIA	O	M	R	W
Alderman	7	0	30	0
Hughes	10	0	48	3
S.R.Waugh	4	0	15	0
McDermott	7	0	37	2
Taylor	10	0	50	3
Border	10	0	32	2

WEST INDIES	O	M	R	W
Marshall	10	0	40	1
Ambrose	10	1	41	1
Benjamin	10	1	44	2
Walsh	10	0	36	2
Richards	10	0	46	0

FALL OF WICKETS
1-90, 2-114, 3-144, 4-182, 5-189, 6-190, 7-199, 8-217, 9-217, 10-220

FALL OF WICKETS
1-50, 2-54, 3-141, 4-144, 5-158, 6-177, 7-207, 8-219

Umpires: R.J.Evans (2) and P.J.McConnell (41).

AUSTRALIA v WEST INDIES 1988-89

At Melbourne Cricket Ground on 15 December 1988.　　Result: **WEST INDIES** won by 34 runs.　　Toss: West Indies.
Award: C.E.L.Ambrose.　　LOI debuts: None.

Gordon Greenidge scored his fifth fifty in six successive innings. Australia's second partnership featuring the Waugh twins also ended in a run out. Curtly Ambrose took the last four wickets in ten balls to return his best LOI analysis.

WEST INDIES		Runs	Balls	4/6
C.G.Greenidge	c Boon b Taylor	57	69	9
D.L.Haynes	c Alderman b McDermott	8	28	1
R.B.Richardson	b McDermott	5	7	1
A.L.Logie	c and b Border	44	67	4
* I.V.A.Richards	c Healy b S.R.Waugh	58	74	4
C.L.Hooper	c Boon b S.R.Waugh	17	22	–
† P.J.L.Dujon	c Healy b S.R.Waugh	3	7	–
M.D.Marshall	c Healy b McDermott	19	19	3
W.K.M.Benjamin	lbw b McDermott	0	1	–
C.E.L.Ambrose	not out	12	9	1
C.A.Walsh	run out	1	1	–
Extras	(lb 5, w 5, nb 2)	12		
Total	**(49.2 overs)**	**236**		

AUSTRALIA		Runs	Balls	4/6
G.R.Marsh	c Hooper b Ambrose	6	39	1
D.C.Boon	c Dujon b Benjamin	20	43	2
D.M.Jones	lbw b Richards	43	68	3
S.R.Waugh	run out	54	67	2
M.E.Waugh	b Ambrose	32	37	–
* A.R.Border	run out	12	11	2
† I.A.Healy	c Ambrose b Benjamin	3	3	–
P.L.Taylor	b Ambrose	4	14	–
C.J.McDermott	c Dujon b Ambrose	2	6	–
M.G.Hughes	not out	4	6	–
T.M.Alderman	b Ambrose	0	1	–
Extras	(b 4, lb 7, w 10, nb 1)	22		
Total	**(47.2 overs)**	**202**		

AUSTRALIA	O	M	R	W
Alderman	7	1	22	0
Hughes	8	0	39	0
McDermott	9.2	2	38	4
S.R.Waugh	10	0	57	3
Taylor	10	0	52	1
Border	5	0	23	1

WEST INDIES	O	M	R	W
Marshall	10	0	39	0
Ambrose	8.2	1	17	5
Walsh	10	0	45	0
Benjamin	9	0	35	2
Richards	10	0	55	1

FALL OF WICKETS
1-33, 2-45, 3-89, 4-162, 5-194, 6-202, 7-203, 8-203, 9-235, 10-236

FALL OF WICKETS
1-25, 2-53, 3-110, 4-168, 5-184, 6-190, 7-192, 8-197, 9-202, 10-202

Umpires: R.C.Bailhache (25) and C.D.Timmins (2).

WEST INDIES v PAKISTAN 1988-89

At Bellerive Oval, Hobart on 17 December 1988.　Result: **WEST INDIES** won by 17 runs.　Toss: Pakistan.
Award: D.L.Haynes.　LOI debuts: None.

A 64-minute rain delay reduced the match to 43 overs each. Desmond Haynes became the first to score 12 hundreds in limited-overs internationals. Umpire Timmins was struck between the shoulder blades by a return from substitute Sajid Ali.

WEST INDIES		Runs	Balls	4/6
D.L.Haynes	lbw b Imran	101	112	8/1
R.B.Richardson	c Wasim b Mudassar	8	38	–
† P.J.L.Dujon	c and b Wasim	63	71	4
A.L.Logie	not out	40	31	3
* I.V.A.Richards	c Tausif b Imran	10	8	2
R.A.Harper	not out	0	–	–
C.L.Hooper				
M.D.Marshall				
W.K.M.Benjamin				
C.E.L.Ambrose				
C.A.Walsh				
Extras	(lb 12, w 8, nb 2)	22		
Total	(43 overs; 4 wickets)	**244**		

PAKISTAN		Runs	Balls	4/6
Mudassar Nazar	lbw b Walsh	12	32	–
Ramiz Raja	c Logie b Marshall	3	22	–
† Salim Yousuf	c sub (K.L.T.Arthurton) b Walsh	9	20	1
Javed Miandad	c Hooper b Ambrose	62	78	3
Salim Malik	c Logie b Richards	68	63	4/2
Ijaz Ahmed	c Harper b Richards	12	8	1/1
* Imran Khan	c Walsh b Benjamin	37	19	5/1
Wasim Akram	c Hooper b Benjamin	17	14	–/1
Abdul Qadir	not out	2	2	–
Tausif Ahmed	not out	0	–	–
Aqib Javed				
Extras	(lb 4, w 1)	5		
Total	(43 overs; 8 wickets)	**227**		

PAKISTAN	O	M	R	W
Imran Khan	9	1	49	2
Wasim Akram	9	0	35	1
Mudassar Nazar	7	0	36	1
Aqib Javed	8	0	48	0
Abdul Qadir	6	0	36	0
Tausif Ahmed	4	0	28	0

WEST INDIES	O	M	R	W
Marshall	9	1	31	1
Ambrose	9	3	46	1
Walsh	8	1	23	2
Benjamin	9	1	52	2
Richards	6	0	48	2
Harper	2	0	23	0

FALL OF WICKETS
1-28, 2-173, 3-219, 4-238

FALL OF WICKETS
1-9, 2-23, 3-26, 4-147, 5-170, 6-170, 7-225, 8-226

Umpires: S.G.Randell (28) and C.D.Timmins (3).

WEST INDIES v PAKISTAN 1988-89

At WACA Ground, Perth on 1 January 1989.　Result: **WEST INDIES** won by 7 wickets.　Toss: West Indies.
Award: I.R.Bishop.　LOI debuts: Pakistan – Saeed Anwar.

West Indies gained their seventh consecutive win after Ian Bishop had taken the first four wickets for 15 runs in 5.3 overs on a fast, bouncy pitch. Javed Miandad's 167-ball marathon included 47 singles and the only boundary of the innings.

PAKISTAN		Runs	Balls	4/6
Ramiz Raja	lbw b Bishop	6	11	–
† Salim Yousuf	b Bishop	2	16	–
Saeed Anwar	c Hooper b Marshall	3	13	–
Javed Miandad	not out	63	167	1
Salim Malik	c Richards b Bishop	1	13	–
Ijaz Ahmed	c Greenidge b Bishop	1	13	–
* Imran Khan	c Dujon b Walsh	7	32	–
Wasim Akram	c Dujon b Hooper	13	23	–
Tausif Ahmed	run out	12	27	–
Mohsin Kamal	b Bishop	1	3	–
Aqib Javed	not out	0	1	–
Extras	(b 1, lb 8, w 13, nb 9)	31		
Total	(50 overs; 9 wickets)	**140**		

WEST INDIES		Runs	Balls	4/6
C.G.Greenidge	c Tausif b Aqib	13	38	–
D.L.Haynes	c Salim Yousuf b Wasim	23	43	1
R.B.Richardson	not out	50	79	5
† P.J.L.Dujon	c Wasim b Aqib	10	18	–
C.L.Hooper	not out	33	60	3
* I.V.A.Richards				
R.A.Harper				
M.D.Marshall				
W.K.M.Benjamin				
C.A.Walsh				
I.R.Bishop				
Extras	(lb 3, w 3, nb 7)	13		
Total	(38.2 overs; 3 wickets)	**142**		

WEST INDIES	O	M	R	W
Marshall	7	0	17	1
Bishop	10	1	27	5
Walsh	10	2	21	1
Benjamin	10	3	17	0
Hooper	8	0	28	1
Richards	5	0	21	0

PAKISTAN	O	M	R	W
Imran Khan	9	2	23	0
Mohsin Kamal	9.2	0	56	0
Wasim Akram	10	0	27	1
Aqib Javed	10	0	33	2

FALL OF WICKETS
1-30, 2-44, 3-61

FALL OF WICKETS
1-12, 2-20, 3-21, 4-22, 5-32, 6-59, 7-94, 8-135, 9-139

Umpires: R.C.Bailhache (26) and T.A.Prue (4).

AUSTRALIA v PAKISTAN 1988-89

At WACA Ground, Perth on 2 January 1989.   Result: **PAKISTAN** won by 38 runs.   Toss: Pakistan.
Award: Aamer Malik.   LOI debuts: None.

Australia were fined $600 for failing to complete their overs in the allotted 3½ hours. Simon O'Donnell, having recovered from lymphatic cancer, was cheered to the wicket by a record crowd of 27,472 and top-scored on his first international appearance since the 1987-88 World Cup final.

PAKISTAN		Runs	Balls	4/6
Moin-ul-Atiq	c Healy b McDermott	8	24	–
Saeed Anwar	c Border b Alderman	15	39	1
Aamer Malik	c O'Donnell b McDermott	90	135	8
Javed Miandad	c Alderman b O'Donnell	31	64	1
Salim Malik	c Healy b Waugh	0	3	–
Ijaz Ahmed	c Border b Hughes	17	22	2
* Imran Khan	c Healy b Waugh	23	23	2
Wasim Akram	not out	5	4	–
† Salim Yousuf	not out	1	1	–
Tausif Ahmed				
Aqib Javed				
Extras	(b 1, lb 3, w 16, nb 6)	26		
Total	(49 overs; 7 wickets)	216		

AUSTRALIA		Runs	Balls	4/6
D.C.Boon	c Ijaz b Aqib	24	47	3
G.R.Marsh	c Salim Yousuf b Aqib	24	54	1
D.M.Jones	run out	13	29	1
G.M.Wood	c and b Aamer	2	7	–
* A.R.Border	c Miandad b Aamer	11	32	–
S.R.Waugh	b Aqib	12	20	1
S.P.O'Donnell	b Wasim	46	55	3
† I.A.Healy	c Salim Yousuf b Wasim	16	29	1
C.J.McDermott	c Ijaz b Wasim	0	3	–
M.G.Hughes	c Ijaz b Wasim	8	11	1
T.M.Alderman	not out	0	4	–
Extras	(lb 10, w 4, nb 8)	22		
Total	(46.1 overs)	178		

AUSTRALIA	O	M	R	W
Alderman	10	1	32	1
Hughes	10	1	49	1
McDermott	10	2	38	2
O'Donnell	10	0	45	1
Waugh	9	0	48	2

PAKISTAN	O	M	R	W
Imran Khan	8	0	30	0
Wasim Akram	8.1	0	25	4
Aqib Javed	10	1	28	3
Aamer Malik	10	1	35	2
Tausif Ahmed	6	0	29	0
Salim Malik	4	0	21	0

FALL OF WICKETS
1-30, 2-30, 3-113, 4-118, 5-154, 6-200, 7-209

FALL OF WICKETS
1-46, 2-67, 3-73, 4-79, 5-98, 6-102, 7-152, 8-152, 9-174, 10-178

Umpires: R.J.Evans (3) and P.J.McConnell (42).

AUSTRALIA v WEST INDIES 1988-89

At Melbourne Cricket Ground on 5 January 1989.   Result: **AUSTRALIA** won by 8 runs.   Toss: West Indies.
Award: S.R.Waugh.   LOI debuts: None.

Australia gained their first win in 14 internationals against West Indies at the MCG. The match was reduced by one over after a 21-minute shower, when Australia were 81 for 1 after 21.1 overs, and by another because of West Indies' slow over rate.

AUSTRALIA		Runs	Balls	4/6
G.R.Marsh	run out	52	82	3
D.C.Boon	b Ambrose	8	18	–
D.M.Jones	lbw b Richards	43	89	1
G.M.Wood	c Hooper b Bishop	39	54	–
S.R.Waugh	b Ambrose	34	24	4
* A.R.Border	run out	13	13	–
S.P.O'Donnell	run out	1	7	–
† I.A.Healy	b Ambrose	1	2	–
P.L.Taylor	c Dujon b Bishop	7	4	1
C.J.McDermott	not out	2	2	–
T.M.Alderman	b Bishop	0	1	–
Extras	(b 3, lb 11, w 6, nb 6)	26		
Total	(47.4 overs)	226		

WEST INDIES		Runs	Balls	4/6
C.G.Greenidge	b McDermott	11	27	1
D.L.Haynes	c Border b Alderman	0	1	–
R.B.Richardson	c and b Taylor	63	81	4
† P.J.L.Dujon	c and b Border	39	61	2
* I.V.A.Richards	c Marsh b Alderman	48	55	3
C.L.Hooper	c McDermott b Taylor	14	31	1
R.A.Harper	c Waugh b McDermott	15	15	1
C.E.L.Ambrose	not out	7	7	–
W.K.M.Benjamin	b Alderman	7	7	1
I.R.Bishop	not out	4	3	–
C.A.Walsh				
Extras	(lb 9, w 1)	10		
Total	(48 overs; 8 wickets)	218		

WEST INDIES	O	M	R	W
Ambrose	9	2	26	3
Bishop	9.4	0	50	3
Walsh	10	0	30	0
Benjamin	6	0	35	0
Harper	8	0	42	0
Richards	5	0	29	0

AUSTRALIA	O	M	R	W
Alderman	9	1	30	3
McDermott	8	0	54	2
O'Donnell	8	0	35	0
Waugh	10	0	36	0
Taylor	10	0	36	2
Border	3	0	18	1

FALL OF WICKETS
1-26, 2-106, 3-144, 4-202, 5-202, 6-207, 7-217, 8-220, 9-225, 10-226

FALL OF WICKETS
1-9, 2-21, 3-113, 4-127, 5-160, 6-189, 7-202, 8-213

Umpires: A.R.Crafter (64) and L.J.King (4).

WEST INDIES v PAKISTAN 1988-89

At Woolloongabba, Brisbane on 7 January 1989.　　Result: **PAKISTAN** won by 55 runs.　　Toss: West Indies.
Award: Imran Khan.　　LOI debuts: None.

The umpires' zealous interpretation of the playing conditions led to record LOI totals of wides (37) and extras (59).
Viv Richards (156 matches) became the first to complete 6000 runs, Richie Richardson made his 100th appearance and
Imran Khan completed 2000 runs.

PAKISTAN		Runs	Balls	4/6
Ramiz Raja	c Dujon b Ambrose	5	33	1
Moin-ul-Atiq	c Richards b Marshall	2	18	–
Aamer Malik	c Richards b Ambrose	75	119	5
Javed Miandad	c Benjamin b Bishop	38	78	2
Salim Malik	c Hooper b Bishop	3	6	–
* Imran Khan	not out	67	41	7/2
Ijaz Ahmed	c Bishop b Ambrose	3	5	–
Wasim Akram	run out	2	2	–
† Salim Yousuf	not out	4	4	–
Abdul Qadir				
Aqib Javed				
Extras	(b 8, lb 10, w 37, nb 4)	59		
Total	(50 overs; 7 wickets)	**258**		

WEST INDIES		Runs	Balls	4/6
C.G.Greenidge	b Aqib	46	79	4
D.L.Haynes	b Aqib	26	28	5
R.B.Richardson	c Aqib b Wasim	17	19	2
† P.J.L.Dujon	c and b Aamer	0	6	–
* I.V.A.Richards	run out	18	36	1
C.L.Hooper	b Wasim	18	27	1
R.A.Harper	b Salim Malik	6	7	1
M.D.Marshall	b Wasim	39	33	2/2
W.K.M.Benjamin	c Miandad b Imran	0	5	–
C.E.L.Ambrose	b Imran	2	8	–
I.R.Bishop	not out	0	–	–
Extras	(lb 15, w 13, nb 3)	31		
Total	(40.4 overs)	**203**		

WEST INDIES	O	M	R	W
Marshall	10	0	34	1
Ambrose	10	0	39	3
Benjamin	9	1	64	0
Bishop	10	0	51	2
Harper	6	1	31	0
Richards	5	0	21	0

PAKISTAN	O	M	R	W
Imran Khan	9.4	0	42	2
Aqib Javed	10	1	49	2
Wasim Akram	7	0	27	3
Aamer Malik	4	0	20	1
Abdul Qadir	7	0	28	0
Salim Malik	3	0	22	1

FALL OF WICKETS
1-9, 2-20, 3-127, 4-137, 5-197, 6-220, 7-225

FALL OF WICKETS
1-34, 2-63, 3-64, 4-131, 5-131, 6-150, 7-196, 8-199, 9-202, 10-203

Umpires: R.C.Bailhache (27) and C.D.Timmins (4).

AUSTRALIA v PAKISTAN 1988-89

At Woolloongabba, Brisbane on 8 January 1989.　　Result: **AUSTRALIA** won by 5 wickets.　　Toss: Pakistan.
Award: T.M.Alderman.　　LOI debuts: None.

Terry Alderman bowled Ramiz Raja and Aamer Malik with the first two balls of the match. Javed Miandad completed
5000 runs in his 144th international.

PAKISTAN		Runs	Balls	4/6
Ramiz Raja	b Alderman	0	1	–
Shoaib Mohammed	c Marsh b O'Donnell	29	58	3
Aamer Malik	b Alderman	0	1	–
Javed Miandad	run out	54	107	2
Ijaz Ahmed	c Boon b Taylor	41	50	3
Salim Malik	c and b O'Donnell	22	24	2
* Imran Khan	c Border b Alderman	28	30	1/1
† Salim Yousuf	c McDermott b O'Donnell	2	6	–
Wasim Akram	c and b Taylor	4	7	–
Abdul Qadir	not out	9	18	–
Aqib Javed				
Extras	(b 1, lb 4, w 7, nb 2)	14		
Total	(50 overs; 9 wickets)	**203**		

AUSTRALIA		Runs	Balls	4/6
D.C.Boon	c Ijaz b Aqib	45	64	5
G.R.Marsh	b Aqib	41	72	–
C.J.McDermott	b Qadir	32	36	4/1
D.M.Jones	b Wasim	16	24	1
G.M.Wood	run out	8	21	–
* A.R.Border	not out	18	26	1
S.R.Waugh	not out	22	30	3
S.P.O'Donnell				
† I.A.Healy				
P.L.Taylor				
T.M.Alderman				
Extras	(b 4, lb 6, w 12)	22		
Total	(44.5 overs; 5 wickets)	**204**		

AUSTRALIA	O	M	R	W
Alderman	9	2	27	3
McDermott	10	0	45	0
O'Donnell	10	1	31	3
Waugh	9	0	35	0
Taylor	10	0	48	2
Border	2	0	12	0

PAKISTAN	O	M	R	W
Imran Khan	10	0	33	0
Aqib Javed	10	1	38	2
Aamer Malik	1	0	9	0
Wasim Akram	8.5	0	70	1
Abdul Qadir	10	1	26	1
Shoaib Mohammed	5	0	18	0

FALL OF WICKETS
1-0, 2-0, 3-64, 4-124, 5-152, 6-158, 7-167, 8-173, 9-203

FALL OF WICKETS
1-100, 2-100, 3-128, 4-164, 5-168

Umpires: L.J.King (5) and S.G.Randell (29).

AUSTRALIA v PAKISTAN 1988-89

At Melbourne Cricket Ground on 10 January 1989.　　Result: **AUSTRALIA** won by 6 runs (revised target).
Toss: Pakistan.　　Award: G.R.Marsh.　　LOI debuts: None.

Two stoppages for rain reduced Australia's innings by seven overs. A break of 110 minutes when Pakistan were 4 for 1 after 2.1 overs resulted in a revised target of 115 runs from 19 overs. In extremely slippery conditions the odds strongly favoured the batting side.

AUSTRALIA		Runs	Balls	4/6
G.R.Marsh	not out	125	121	9
D.C.Boon	c Wasim b Imran	11	27	1
* A.R.Border	c Aamer b Miandad	60	83	8
M.E.Waugh	b Tausif	12	13	–
S.R.Waugh	lbw b Tausif	0	2	–
G.M.Wood	not out	24	19	1
S.P.O'Donnell				
† I.A.Healy				
P.L.Taylor				
M.G.Hughes				
T.M.Alderman				
Extras	(b 5, lb 12, w 5, nb 4)	26		
Total	(43 overs; 4 wickets)	**258**		

PAKISTAN		Runs	Balls	4/6
Javed Miandad	c Taylor b Hughes	16	25	2
Saeed Anwar	run out	0	–	–
Ijaz Ahmed	c S.R.Waugh b O'Donnell	7	11	–
* Imran Khan	run out	42	40	–
Salim Malik	c and b Taylor	11	14	–
† Aamer Malik	c and b Border	5	7	–
Wasim Akram	b Alderman	17	14	1
Shoaib Mohammed	not out	2	2	–
Abdul Qadir	not out	1	1	–
Tausif Ahmed				
Aqib Javed				
Extras	(b 2, lb 4, w 1)	7		
Total	(19 overs; 7 wickets)	**108**		

PAKISTAN	O	M	R	W
Imran Khan	7	0	36	1
Aqib Javed	10	3	40	0
Wasim Akram	9	0	59	0
Tausif Ahmed	7	0	43	2
Abdul Qadir	7	0	35	0
Javed Miandad	3	0	28	1

AUSTRALIA	O	M	R	W
Alderman	4	0	22	1
O'Donnell	4	0	15	1
S.R.Waugh	4	0	27	0
Hughes	4	0	18	1
Taylor	2	0	16	1
Border	1	0	4	1

FALL OF WICKETS
1-22, 2-136, 3-178, 4-178

FALL OF WICKETS
1-0, 2-13, 3-37, 4-59, 5-68, 6-105, 7-106

Umpires: A.R.Crafter (65) and S.G.Randell (30).

AUSTRALIA v WEST INDIES 1988-89

At Sydney Cricket Ground on 12 January 1989.　　Result: **AUSTRALIA** won by 61 runs.　　Toss: Australia.
Award: P.L.Taylor.　　LOI debuts: None.

Although, with the finalists decided, this game had no relevance, it attracted a crowd of 45,620. Final points: West Indies 10 (run rate 4.50), Australia 10 (4.48), Pakistan 4 (4.24). A Fijian-born NSWCA administrative assistant fielded substitute for one over of the West Indies innings.

AUSTRALIA		Runs	Balls	4/6
D.C.Boon	c Arthurton b Marshall	6	11	–/1
G.R.Marsh	c Arthurton b Bishop	24	59	2
D.M.Jones	b Ambrose	77	132	4
M.E.Waugh	c Haynes b Marshall	42	53	1
S.R.Waugh	not out	40	40	3
* A.R.Border	b Ambrose	3	6	–
S.P.O'Donnell	not out	3	2	–
† I.A.Healy				
P.L.Taylor				
C.J.McDermott				
M.G.Hughes				
Extras	(lb 7, w 4, nb 9)	20		
Total	(48 overs; 5 wickets)	**215**		

WEST INDIES		Runs	Balls	4/6
D.L.Haynes	st Healy b Border	58	80	2/1
† P.J.L.Dujon	c Taylor b S.R.Waugh	17	38	1
R.B.Richardson	c Border b McDermott	8	13	–
K.L.T.Arthurton	b Border	22	40	1
* I.V.A.Richards	c Marsh b Taylor	3	12	–
A.L.Logie	not out	29	50	–
R.A.Harper	lbw b Border	1	6	–
M.D.Marshall	lbw b Taylor	1	3	–
C.E.L.Ambrose	c Border b Taylor	6	18	–
I.R.Bishop	not out	4	28	–
B.P.Patterson				
Extras	(lb 4, nb 1)	5		
Total	(48 overs; 8 wickets)	**154**		

WEST INDIES	O	M	R	W
Marshall	10	3	25	2
Patterson	9	0	50	0
Bishop	10	1	34	1
Ambrose	9	0	42	2
Harper	9	0	51	0
Richards	1	0	6	0

AUSTRALIA	O	M	R	W
O'Donnell	7	0	22	0
Hughes	7	1	26	0
McDermott	7	0	26	1
S.R.Waugh	3	0	13	1
Taylor	10	2	22	3
Border	10	1	33	3
Jones	4	0	8	0

FALL OF WICKETS
1-9, 2-59, 3-137, 4-191, 5-211

FALL OF WICKETS
1-49, 2-63, 3-107, 4-110, 5-124, 6-125, 7-126, 8-134

Umpires: P.J.McConnell (43) and T.A.Prue (5).

AUSTRALIA v WEST INDIES 1988-89

At Melbourne Cricket Ground on 14 January 1989.　Result: **AUSTRALIA** won by 2 runs.　Toss: Australia.
LOI debuts: None.

Courtney Walsh needed four from Merv Hughes's final ball for West Indies to have avoided their fourth successive defeat. Curtly Ambrose captured his second five-wicket haul of the tournament. Allan Border set a new LOI fielding record when he held his 79th catch.

AUSTRALIA		Runs	Balls	4/6	WEST INDIES		Runs	Balls	4/6
G.R.Marsh	lbw b Ambrose	18	46	2	C.G.Greenidge	c Healy b Hughes	5	17	1
D.C.Boon	c Dujon b Ambrose	0	9	–	D.L.Haynes	lbw b Hughes	6	19	–
G.M.Wood	c Logie b Marshall	6	11	–	R.B.Richardson	c Healy b O'Donnell	24	49	2
* A.R.Border	c Greenidge b Ambrose	78	103	6/1	A.L.Logie	lbw b Alderman	4	8	1
D.M.Jones	c Logie b Walsh	36	75	4	* I.V.A.Richards	c Border b Alderman	14	20	2
S.R.Waugh	c and b Ambrose	33	38	3	C.L.Hooper	c Jones b Taylor	33	44	2/1
S.P.O'Donnell	b Marshall	10	16	–	† P.J.L.Dujon	c Jones b Taylor	27	43	1
† I.A.Healy	not out	3	3	–	M.D.Marshall	run out	18	21	2
P.L.Taylor	run out	0	2	–	C.E.L.Ambrose	b O'Donnell	23	36	2
M.G.Hughes	lbw b Ambrose	0	5	–	I.R.Bishop	not out	33	40	2
T.M.Alderman					C.A.Walsh	not out	3	3	–
Extras	(lb 9, w 6, nb 5)	20			Extras	(b 3, lb 6, w 3)	12		
Total	(50 overs; 9 wickets)	**204**			**Total**	(50 overs; 9 wickets)	**202**		

WEST INDIES	O	M	R	W	AUSTRALIA	O	M	R	W
Marshall	9	1	31	2	Alderman	10	2	29	2
Ambrose	10	2	26	5	Hughes	10	1	34	2
Bishop	10	0	37	0	O'Donnell	7	0	36	2
Walsh	10	0	45	1	Waugh	10	0	43	0
Richards	10	0	48	0	Taylor	10	2	35	2
Hooper	1	0	8	0	Border	3	0	16	0

FALL OF WICKETS
1-15, 2-26, 3-34, 4-133, 5-176, 6-200, 7-202, 8-202, 9-204

FALL OF WICKETS
1-14, 2-16, 3-23, 4-41, 5-76, 6-108, 7-129, 8-148, 9-196

Umpires: L.J.King (6) and S.G.Randell (31).

AUSTRALIA v WEST INDIES 1988-89

At Sydney Cricket Ground on 16 January 1989.　Result: **WEST INDIES** won by 92 runs.　Toss: West Indies.
LOI debuts: None.

Australia conceded their highest total in 116 World Series matches so far. Viv Richards, the first to score 2000 runs, and Gordon Greenidge, 1000, achieved notable milestones against Australia. Richie Richardson attracted the first international dismissal by a combination of twins.

WEST INDIES		Runs	Balls	4/6	AUSTRALIA		Runs	Balls	4/6
C.G.Greenidge	c Jones b Taylor	46	56	7/1	D.C.Boon	c Richardson b Bishop	36	37	4/1
D.L.Haynes	c S.R.Waugh b Border	62	68	7	G.R.Marsh	run out	22	39	2
R.B.Richardson	c M.E.Waugh b S.R.Waugh	55	77	1	D.M.Jones	c sub (R.A.Harper) b Bishop	27	26	3/1
A.L.Logie	c and b Border	18	34	–	* A.R.Border	c Richardson b Bishop	10	24	–
* I.V.A.Richards	b Hughes	53	40	3/3	M.E.Waugh	c and b Bishop	22	25	2
C.L.Hooper	c M.E.Waugh b Hughes	12	12	1	S.R.Waugh	st Dujon b Hooper	8	17	–
M.D.Marshall	b Hughes	4	5	–	G.R.J.Matthews	run out	4	12	–
† P.J.L.Dujon	b Hughes	5	5	–	† I.A.Healy	run out	7	9	1
C.E.L.Ambrose	not out	7	3	–/1	P.L.Taylor	not out	13	27	1
I.R.Bishop	run out	0	1	–	M.G.Hughes	b Hooper	13	34	1
C.A.Walsh					T.M.Alderman	b Hooper	0	2	–
Extras	(b 5, lb 9, w 1)	15			Extras	(b 1, lb 10, w 9, nb 3)	23		
Total	(50 overs; 9 wickets)	**277**			**Total**	(40 overs)	**185**		

AUSTRALIA	O	M	R	W	WEST INDIES	O	M	R	W
Alderman	8	0	42	0	Marshall	5	1	30	0
Hughes	7	0	44	4	Ambrose	6	1	30	0
Matthews	7	0	62	0	Bishop	10	0	52	4
S.R.Waugh	8	0	45	1	Walsh	9	1	40	0
Taylor	10	0	31	1	Hooper	10	2	22	3
Border	10	0	39	2					

FALL OF WICKETS
1-57, 2-94, 3-100, 4-133, 5-137, 6-149, 7-149, 8-162, 9-185, 10-185

FALL OF WICKETS
1-99, 2-120, 3-166, 4-246, 5-258, 6-263, 7-270, 8-277, 9-277

Umpires: P.J.McConnell (44) and T.A.Prue (6).

AUSTRALIA v WEST INDIES 1988-89

At Sydney Cricket Ground on 18 January 1989.   Result: **WEST INDIES** won by 8 wickets (revised target).
Toss: Australia.   Finals Awards: A.R.Border and D.L.Haynes.   LOI debuts: None.

Two rain breaks, 123 minutes with Australia 83 for 2 after 23.1 overs and 83 minutes when West Indies were 47 for 2 after 6.4 overs, first reduced the match to 38 overs and finally revised the target to 108 from 18. West Indies comfortably gained their fifth World Series title in six attempts.

AUSTRALIA		Runs	Balls	4/6	WEST INDIES		Runs	Balls	4/6
G.R.Marsh	run out	31	72	4	C.G.Greenidge	c S.R.Waugh b Alderman	4	3	–
D.C.Boon	b Walsh	16	36	1	D.L.Haynes	not out	40	36	3/1
D.M.Jones	not out	93	82	8/2	R.B.Richardson	c Healy b Alderman	0	2	–
* A.R.Border	c Richardson b Richards	32	25	4	* I.V.A.Richards	not out	60	40	6/3
M.E.Waugh	b Hooper	5	6	–	A.L.Logie				
S.R.Waugh	not out	27	17	1/1	C.L.Hooper				
S.P.O'Donnell					M.D.Marshall				
† I.A.Healy					† D.Williams				
P.L.Taylor					C.E.L.Ambrose				
M.G.Hughes					I.R.Bishop				
T.M.Alderman					C.A.Walsh				
Extras	(b 6, lb 9, w 4, nb 3)	22			Extras	(lb 6, w 1)	7		
Total	(38 overs; 4 wickets)	226			Total	(13.2 overs; 2 wickets)	111		

WEST INDIES	O	M	R	W	AUSTRALIA	O	M	R	W
Marshall	8	0	45	0	Alderman	4	0	22	2
Ambrose	8	1	45	0	Hughes	3	0	21	0
Bishop	7	0	32	0	S.R.Waugh	3.2	0	27	0
Walsh	7	0	39	1	Taylor	2	0	23	0
Hooper	5	0	38	1	O'Donnell	1	0	12	0
Richards	3	0	12	1					

FALL OF WICKETS
1-40, 2-70, 3-137, 4-152

FALL OF WICKETS
1-4, 2-4

Umpires: P.J.McConnell (45) and T.A.Prue (7).

NEW ZEALAND v PAKISTAN 1988-89

At Carisbrook, Dunedin on 6 February 1989.   Result: **NEW ZEALAND** won by 8 wickets.   Toss: New Zealand.
Award: R.J.Hadlee.   LOI debuts: None.

This match, surplus to the later Rothmans Cup series, was played on the scheduled fourth day of the rain-aborted first Test. On a wicket of variable bounce, Richard Hadlee was at times unplayable as he became the first to take five wickets in an LOI innings on five occasions.

PAKISTAN		Runs	Balls	4/6	NEW ZEALAND		Runs	Balls	4/6
Mudassar Nazar	c J.J.Crowe b Snedden	14	52	–	* J.G.Wright	c Ijaz b Sikander	35	62	3
Shoaib Mohammed	c Smith b Hadlee	0	4	–	R.H.Vance	b Imran	46	109	2
Aamer Malik	run out	1	15	–	A.H.Jones	not out	55	79	5
Javed Miandad	c Smith b Watson	16	53	1	M.D.Crowe	not out	17	29	–
Salim Malik	c sub (J.G.Bracewell) b Hadlee	83	98	9/2	J.J.Crowe				
* Imran Khan	c J.J.Crowe b Hadlee	22	31	1	D.N.Patel				
Ijaz Ahmed	b Hadlee	9	16	–	R.J.Hadlee				
† Salim Yousuf	c Smith b Hadlee	2	5	–	† I.D.S.Smith				
Abdul Qadir	run out	9	10	–/1	M.C.Snedden				
Sikander Bakht	not out	6	5	–	E.J.Chatfield				
Aqib Javed	not out	1	2	–	W.Watson				
Extras	(lb 5, w 1, nb 1)	7			Extras	(lb 11, w 9, nb 1)	21		
Total	(48 overs; 9 wickets)	170			Total	(46.3 overs; 2 wickets)	174		

NEW ZEALAND	O	M	R	W	PAKISTAN	O	M	R	W
Hadlee	10	0	38	5	Imran Khan	10	0	42	1
Watson	10	1	31	1	Sikander Bakht	8.3	0	43	1
Snedden	9	2	18	1	Aqib Javed	8	1	26	0
Chatfield	10	2	36	0	Mudassar Nazar	10	1	23	0
Patel	9	1	42	0	Abdul Qadir	10	0	29	0

FALL OF WICKETS
1-2, 2-14, 3-21, 4-75, 5-119, 6-129, 7-139, 8-160, 9-165

FALL OF WICKETS
1-73, 2-113

Umpires: R.S.Dunne (1) and S.J.Woodward (15).

NEW ZEALAND v PAKISTAN 1988-89

At Lancaster Park, Christchurch on 4 March 1989.   Result: **NEW ZEALAND** won by 7 wickets.   Toss: New Zealand.
Award: A.H.Jones.   LOI debuts: None.

Pakistan were unlucky to lose both Javed Miandad (back problems) and the toss before a delayed start of a match reduced by three overs each and begun in heavy, overcast conditions ideal for seam and swing bowling.

PAKISTAN		Runs	Balls	4/6	NEW ZEALAND		Runs	Balls	4/6
Mudassar Nazar	b Morrison	8	21	1	*J.G.Wright	c Tausif b Imran	7	9	1
Shoaib Mohammed	c Greatbatch b Morrison	2	5	–	R.H.Vance	c Aamer b Salim Jaffer	3	10	–
†Aamer Malik	b Morrison	7	31	–	A.H.Jones	not out	62	129	4
Salim Malik	lbw b Robertson	6	22	–	M.D.Crowe	c Salim Malik b Salim Jaffer	45	81	2
*Imran Khan	c Crowe b Snedden	38	78	2	M.J.Greatbatch	not out	35	33	5
Ramiz Raja	run out	51	92	3	C.M.Kuggeleijn				
Ijaz Ahmed	not out	42	30	3/2	†I.D.S.Smith				
Abdul Qadir	run out	0	1	–	G.K.Robertson				
Tausif Ahmed	not out	8	6	–	M.C.Snedden				
Salim Jaffer					D.K.Morrison				
Aqib Javed					W.Watson				
Extras	(lb 2, w 2, nb 4)	8			Extras	(b 5, lb 4, w 1, nb 9)	19		
Total	(47 overs; 7 wickets)	170			Total	(40.5 overs; 3 wickets)	171		

NEW ZEALAND	O	M	R	W	PAKISTAN	O	M	R	W
Morrison	10	2	44	3	Imran Khan	5	0	17	1
Watson	10	1	47	0	Salim Jaffer	10	0	35	2
Robertson	9	2	21	1	Aqib Javed	9.5	1	33	0
Snedden	9	1	17	1	Mudassar Nazar	8	0	35	0
Kuggeleijn	9	0	39	0	Tausif Ahmed	6	0	32	0
					Abdul Qadir	2	0	10	0

FALL OF WICKETS
1-7, 2-14, 3-23, 4-23, 5-101, 6-148, 7-151

FALL OF WICKETS
1-10, 2-12, 3-115

Umpires: B.L.Aldridge (6) and R.L.McHarg (6).

NEW ZEALAND v PAKISTAN 1988-89

At Basin Reserve, Wellington on 8 March 1989.   Result: **NEW ZEALAND** won by 6 wickets.   Toss: New Zealand.
Award: Shoaib Mohammed.   LOI debuts: None.

Shoaib Mohammed compiled Pakistan's (then) highest score and, with Ramiz Raja, shared a partnership of 152, a national record for any wicket against New Zealand until 1993-94. Ian Smith's highest LOI score included a 37-ball fifty. Salim Malik completed 2000 runs.

PAKISTAN		Runs	Balls	4/6	NEW ZEALAND		Runs	Balls	4/6
Mudassar Nazar	c Smith b Watson	3	28	–	R.H.Vance	b Mudassar	8	37	–
Shoaib Mohammed	not out	126	155	13	*J.G.Wright	c Aamer b Salim Jaffer	0	7	–
†Aamer Malik	run out	3	7	–	A.H.Jones	run out	67	84	6
Ramiz Raja	c Vance b Robertson	72	85	6	M.D.Crowe	not out	87	95	5
Salim Malik	c Vance b Robertson	9	8	1	M.J.Greatbatch	c Salim Malik b Tausif	9	10	1
*Imran Khan	b Morrison	17	13	–	†I.D.S.Smith	not out	62	51	5
Ijaz Ahmed	c Robertson b Morrison	2	5	–	C.M.Kuggeleijn				
Abdul Qadir	not out	8	4	1	G.K.Robertson				
Salim Jaffer					M.C.Snedden				
Tausif Ahmed					D.K.Morrison				
Aqib Javed					W.Watson				
Extras	(lb 4, w 7, nb 2)	13			Extras	(b 9, lb 10, w 2)	21		
Total	(50 overs; 6 wickets)	253			Total	(46.5 overs; 4 wickets)	254		

NEW ZEALAND	O	M	R	W	PAKISTAN	O	M	R	W
Morrison	10	0	62	2	Imran Khan	9	1	33	0
Watson	10	0	48	1	Salim Jaffer	9	1	48	1
Snedden	10	0	31	0	Aqib Javed	8	0	44	0
Robertson	10	0	56	2	Mudassar Nazar	9	1	45	1
Kuggeleijn	10	0	52	0	Abdul Qadir	3.5	0	30	0
					Tausif Ahmed	8	0	35	1

FALL OF WICKETS
1-15, 2-24, 3-176, 4-192, 5-225, 6-242

FALL OF WICKETS
1-3, 2-56, 3-133, 4-146

Umpires: B.L.Aldridge (7) and S.J.Woodward (16).

NEW ZEALAND v PAKISTAN 1988-89

At Eden Park, Auckland on 11 March 1989.　　Result: **PAKISTAN** won by 7 wickets.　　Toss: Pakistan.
Award: Ramiz Raja.　　LOI debuts: None.

Pakistan won their first international in New Zealand. Salim Malik reached his fifty off 33 balls.

NEW ZEALAND		Runs	Balls	4/6
*J.G.Wright	c Aamer b Aqib	59	79	6/1
A.H.Jones	c Aamer b Qadir	82	93	4
M.D.Crowe	b Qadir	32	32	3
M.J.Greatbatch	c Ijaz b Tausif	1	3	–
J.J.Crowe	b Aqib	27	42	–/1
†I.D.S.Smith	lbw b Aqib	8	10	–
C.M.Kuggeleijn	c Salim Malik b Imran	12	23	–
G.K.Robertson	b Salim Jaffer	4	8	–
M.C.Snedden	b Salim Jaffer	7	6	–
D.K.Morrison	run out	2	2	–
W.Watson	not out	4	3	1
Extras	(b 2, lb 4, w 5)	11		
Total	(49.5 overs)	**249**		

PAKISTAN		Runs	Balls	4/6
Ramiz Raja	c J.J.Crowe b Morrison	101	114	9/1
Shoaib Mohammed	c Kuggeleijn b Snedden	15	37	1
†Aamer Malik	run out	23	46	1
*Imran Khan	not out	51	62	1/2
Salim Malik	not out	56	34	9
Ijaz Ahmed				
Mudassar Nazar				
Abdul Qadir				
Tausif Ahmed				
Salim Jaffer				
Aqib Javed				
Extras	(lb 4, nb 1)	5		
Total	(48.3 overs; 3 wickets)	**251**		

PAKISTAN	O	M	R	W
Imran Khan	10	1	41	1
Salim Jaffer	6.5	1	38	2
Aqib Javed	10	0	48	3
Tausif Ahmed	10	0	49	1
Abdul Qadir	10	0	49	2
Mudassar Nazar	3	0	18	0

NEW ZEALAND	O	M	R	W
Morrison	10	1	63	1
Watson	9	1	37	0
Snedden	9.3	1	57	1
Robertson	10	1	42	0
Kuggeleijn	10	0	48	0

FALL OF WICKETS
1-94, 2-178, 3-181, 4-182, 5-194, 6-224, 7-236, 8-238, 9-245, 10-249

FALL OF WICKETS
1-45, 2-106, 3-168

Umpires: R.S.Dunne (2) and R.L.McHarg (7).

NEW ZEALAND v PAKISTAN 1988-89

At Seddon Park, Hamilton on 14 March 1989.　　Result: **NEW ZEALAND** won by 7 wickets.　　Toss: New Zealand.
Award: D.K.Morrison.　　LOI debuts: None.

On a pitch tailor-made for seam bowling, Pakistan were dismissed for their lowest total against New Zealand. Andrew Jones registered his sixth successive fifty as New Zealand won their first home series for four years.

PAKISTAN		Runs	Balls	4/6
Ramiz Raja	c Watson b Morrison	0	3	–
Shoaib Mohammed	c and b Morrison	3	13	–
†Aamer Malik	lbw b Snedden	11	35	1
*Imran Khan	c Smith b Morrison	2	18	–
Mudassar Nazar	b Morrison	48	115	1
Salim Malik	lbw b Snedden	1	15	–
Ijaz Ahmed	c Smith b Robertson	5	27	–
Abdul Qadir	c Morrison b Kuggeleijn	41	58	3/1
Tausif Ahmed	c Smith b Watson	13	16	1
Salim Jaffer	not out	3	3	–
Aqib Javed	not out	1	2	–
Extras	(b 4, lb 1, w 3, nb 2)	10		
Total	(50 overs; 9 wickets)	**138**		

NEW ZEALAND		Runs	Balls	4/6
*J.G.Wright	c Salim Malik b Imran	1	10	–
A.H.Jones	not out	63	120	6
M.D.Crowe	c Ijaz b Imran	15	26	2
M.J.Greatbatch	b Tausif	6	16	–
J.J.Crowe	not out	39	70	5
C.M.Kuggeleijn				
†I.D.S.Smith				
G.K.Robertson				
M.C.Snedden				
D.K.Morrison				
W.Watson				
Extras	(b 4, lb 7, w 4)	15		
Total	(39.4 overs; 3 wickets)	**139**		

NEW ZEALAND	O	M	R	W
Morrison	10	1	33	4
Watson	10	3	20	1
Snedden	10	3	14	2
Robertson	10	2	21	1
Kuggeleijn	10	0	45	1

PAKISTAN	O	M	R	W
Imran Khan	10	1	24	2
Salim Jaffer	8	1	26	0
Aqib Javed	6.4	1	23	0
Tausif Ahmed	9	1	29	1
Abdul Qadir	6	0	26	0

FALL OF WICKETS
1-0, 2-3, 3-17, 4-19, 5-25, 6-40, 7-103, 8-133, 9-137

FALL OF WICKETS
1-6, 2-28, 3-43

Umpires: G.I.J.Cowan (1) and R.S.Dunne (3).

WEST INDIES v INDIA 1988-89

At Kensington Oval, Bridgetown, Barbados on 7 March 1989.　Result: **WEST INDIES** won by 50 runs.　Toss: India.
Award: D.L.Haynes.　LOI debuts: None.

Desmond Haynes extended his record tally of hundreds to 13 while Viv Richards celebrated his 37th birthday by scoring a 38-ball 40, taking three wickets and holding three catches.

WEST INDIES		Runs	Balls	4/6
C.G.Greenidge	b Kapil Dev	4	10	–
D.L.Haynes	not out	117	132	8/5
R.B.Richardson	c Sidhu b Kapil Dev	18	20	2
K.L.T.Arthurton	c Srikkanth b Shastri	25	60	2
* I.V.A.Richards	b A.K.Sharma	40	38	3
A.L.Logie	not out	19	14	2
† P.J.L.Dujon				
E.A.E.Baptiste				
C.E.L.Ambrose				
I.R.Bishop				
C.A.Walsh				
Extras	(b 5, lb 11, w 3, nb 6)	25		
Total	(48 overs; 4 wickets)	**248**		

INDIA		Runs	Balls	4/6
R.J.Shastri	b Walsh	23	55	1
K.Srikkanth	c Richards b Bishop	18	40	3
N.S.Sidhu	c Baptiste b Richards	21	32	3
* D.B.Vengsarkar	b Richards	23	23	2
M.Azharuddin	c and b Baptiste	10	20	–
Kapil Dev	c and b Richards	0	3	–
A.K.Sharma	not out	43	48	2/2
† K.S.More	c Richards b Baptiste	32	32	4
S.K.Sharma	b Bishop	6	11	1
Arshad Ayub	not out	4	5	–
C.Sharma				
Extras	(lb 7, w 3, nb 8)	18		
Total	(48 overs; 8 wickets)	**198**		

INDIA	O	M	R	W
Kapil Dev	9	0	30	2
S.K.Sharma	8	0	55	0
C.Sharma	6	0	32	0
Shastri	10	0	43	1
Arshad Ayub	10	2	46	0
A.K.Sharma	5	0	26	1

WEST INDIES	O	M	R	W
Ambrose	10	0	42	0
Bishop	9	0	30	2
Walsh	10	1	30	1
Baptiste	9	0	42	2
Richards	10	0	47	3

FALL OF WICKETS
1-26, 2-51, 3-116, 4-195

FALL OF WICKETS
1-40, 2-60, 3-91, 4-100, 5-106, 6-107, 7-179, 8-186

Umpires: D.M.Archer (17) and L.H.Barker (7).

WEST INDIES v INDIA 1988-89

At Queen's Park Oval, Port-of-Spain, Trinidad on 9 March 1989.　Result: **WEST INDIES** won by 6 wickets.
Toss: West Indies.　Award: C.G.Greenidge.　LOI debuts: None.

Kapil Dev provided India's only resistance, scoring 44 off 47 balls and conceding only three singles plus a no-ball in his seven overs.

INDIA		Runs	Balls	4/6
R.J.Shastri	c Richardson b Baptiste	10	36	1
K.Srikkanth	c Dujon b Ambrose	5	17	–
N.S.Sidhu	run out	12	34	1
* D.B.Vengsarkar	c and b Richards	7	24	–
M.Azharuddin	c Richardson b Baptiste	19	28	1
Kapil Dev	c Logie b Richards	44	47	4
A.K.Sharma	b Richards	5	6	–
† K.S.More	c and b Richards	7	22	–
S.K.Sharma	c Dujon b Bishop	14	22	–
C.Sharma	run out	15	32	–
N.D.Hirwani	not out	0	1	–
Extras	(b 1, lb 7, w 1, nb 1)	10		
Total	(48 overs)	**148**		

WEST INDIES		Runs	Balls	4/6
C.G.Greenidge	lbw b Srikkanth	70	106	6/2
D.L.Haynes	c More b Shastri	8	36	–
R.B.Richardson	not out	35	58	1/1
A.L.Logie	c and b Srikkanth	0	1	–
K.L.T.Arthurton	c S.K.Sharma b Srikkanth	15	20	3
* I.V.A.Richards	not out	11	6	1/1
† P.J.L.Dujon				
E.A.E.Baptiste				
C.E.L.Ambrose				
I.R.Bishop				
C.A.Walsh				
Extras	(lb 8, w 1, nb 3)	12		
Total	(38.4 overs; 4 wickets)	**151**		

WEST INDIES	O	M	R	W
Ambrose	9	2	24	1
Bishop	9	1	22	1
Walsh	10	1	31	0
Baptiste	10	1	21	2
Richards	10	0	42	4

INDIA	O	M	R	W
Kapil Dev	7	4	4	0
C.Sharma	7	0	27	0
A.K.Sharma	2	0	5	0
Shastri	8	0	39	1
Hirwani	10	0	42	0
Srikkanth	4.4	1	26	3

FALL OF WICKETS
1-13, 2-22, 3-32, 4-43, 5-69, 6-81, 7-107, 8-118, 9-144, 10-148

FALL OF WICKETS
1-38, 2-110, 3-110, 4-139

Umpires: C.E.Cumberbatch (8) and Mohammed Hosein (2).

WEST INDIES v INDIA 1988-89

At Queen's Park Oval, Port-of-Spain, Trinidad on 11 March 1989.   Result: **WEST INDIES** won by 6 wickets.
Toss: India.   Award: K.L.T.Arthurton.   LOI debuts: India – R.R.Singh.

West Indies would have clinched this five-match series less easily had Keith Arthurton not survived a simple stumping chance before he had scored.

INDIA		Runs	Balls	4/6
K.Srikkanth	c Ambrose b Walsh	17	64	–
N.S.Sidhu	c Ambrose b Richards	50	92	2/1
M.Azharuddin	run out	36	32	5
* D.B.Vengsarkar	c Richards b Ambrose	38	43	3
Kapil Dev	c Arthurton b Ambrose	12	21	1
R.R.Singh	b Richards	3	5	–
R.J.Shastri	c Richardson b Bishop	3	4	–
A.K.Sharma	c Richards b Bishop	9	10	1
† K.S.More	c and b Bishop	4	8	–
C.Sharma	not out	2	5	–
N.D.Hirwani	b Bishop	0	2	–
Extras	(b 2, lb 10, w 5, nb 1)	18		
Total	(49.5 overs)	**192**		

WEST INDIES		Runs	Balls	4/6
C.G.Greenidge	lbw b Kapil Dev	3	10	–
D.L.Haynes	c Srikkanth b C.Sharma	18	36	3
R.B.Richardson	run out	30	61	2
K.L.T.Arthurton	not out	76	114	5
* I.V.A.Richards	c and b Hirwani	3	5	–
A.L.Logie	not out	45	57	2
† P.J.L.Dujon				
E.A.E.Baptiste				
C.E.L.Ambrose				
I.R.Bishop				
C.A.Walsh				
Extras	(b 2, lb 7, w 2, nb 7)	18		
Total	(47.2 overs; 4 wickets)	**193**		

WEST INDIES	O	M	R	W
Ambrose	10	1	29	2
Bishop	9.5	1	33	4
Walsh	10	0	22	1
Baptiste	10	0	49	0
Richards	10	1	47	2

INDIA	O	M	R	W
Kapil Dev	9	0	35	1
C.Sharma	8	0	23	1
A.K.Sharma	5	0	24	0
Shastri	10	2	31	0
Hirwani	10	0	45	1
Srikkanth	4	0	19	0
Singh	1.2	0	7	0

FALL OF WICKETS
1-47, 2-113, 3-115, 4-147, 5-156, 6-175, 7-177, 8-186, 9-190, 10-192

FALL OF WICKETS
1-11, 2-34, 3-83, 4-101

Umpires: C.E.Cumberbatch (9) and G.T.Johnson (1).

WEST INDIES v INDIA 1988-89

At Recreation Ground, St. John's, Antigua on 18 March 1989.   Result: **WEST INDIES** won by 8 wickets.   Toss: India.
Award: C.G.Greenidge.   LOI debuts: None.

Gordon Greenidge's tally of eight sixes remained the LOI record until 1995-96; it was the last of his 11 hundreds.

INDIA		Runs	Balls	4/6
K.Srikkanth	c Dujon b Bishop	7		
Arun Lal	c Arthurton b Bishop	1		
M.Azharuddin	run out	27		
* D.B.Vengsarkar	c Arthurton b Bishop	88		
R.J.Shastri	c and b Richards	44		
Kapil Dev	c Greenidge b Ambrose	12		
A.K.Sharma	c Richardson b Ambrose	29		
R.R.Singh	not out	10		
† K.S.More	c sub (W.K.M.Benjamin) b Bishop	0		
Arshad Ayub	not out	1		
C.Sharma				
Extras	(lb 11, w 3, nb 4)	18		
Total	(50 overs; 8 wickets)	**237**		

WEST INDIES		Runs	Balls	4/6
C.G.Greenidge	c Kapil Dev b A.K.Sharma	117	123	7/8
D.L.Haynes	run out	42	68	
R.B.Richardson	not out	58	93	
† P.J.L.Dujon	not out	11		
* I.V.A.Richards				
K.L.T.Arthurton				
A.L.Logie				
E.A.E.Baptiste				
C.E.L.Ambrose				
I.R.Bishop				
C.A.Walsh				
Extras	(lb 6, w 1, nb 5)	12		
Total	(43.2 overs; 2 wickets)	**240**		

WEST INDIES	O	M	R	W
Ambrose	10	1	42	2
Bishop	10	1	46	4
Walsh	10	0	54	0
Baptiste	10	0	36	0
Richards	10	0	48	1

INDIA	O	M	R	W
Kapil Dev	6	0	26	0
C.Sharma	7.2	0	52	0
Azharuddin	2	0	10	0
A.K.Sharma	10	0	47	1
Shastri	5	0	36	0
Arshad Ayub	10	0	36	0
Srikkanth	3	0	27	0

FALL OF WICKETS
1-9, 2-11, 3-62, 4-169, 5-185, 6-201, 7-229, 8-231

FALL OF WICKETS
1-86, 2-216

Umpires: S.A.Bucknor (1) and A.E.Weekes (3).

WEST INDIES v INDIA 1988-89

At Bourda, Georgetown, Guyana on 21 March 1989.　　Result: **WEST INDIES** won by 101 runs.　　Toss: India.
Award: D.L.Haynes.　　LOI debuts: None.

Desmond Haynes, whose highest score extended his world record haul of hundreds to 14, shared the last of his 15 century opening partnerships with Gordon Greenidge. West Indies completed their third clean-sweep of a five-match home series. Krish Srikkanth missed the ensuing Test series when his left wrist was fractured by a lifting ball from Ian Bishop.

WEST INDIES		Runs	Balls	4/6
C.G.Greenidge	c C.Sharma b A.K.Sharma	80	114	9/1
D.L.Haynes	not out	152	126	12/6
R.B.Richardson	c Sidhu b C.Sharma	42	52	5
K.L.T.Arthurton	not out	0	–	–
* I.V.A.Richards				
A.L.Logie				
† P.J.L.Dujon				
E.A.E.Baptiste				
C.E.L.Ambrose				
I.R.Bishop				
C.A.Walsh				
Extras	(lb 7, w 2, nb 6)	15		
Total	(43.5 overs; 2 wickets)	**289**		

INDIA		Runs	Balls	4/6
K.Srikkanth	retired hurt	17	26	2
Arun Lal	c Logie b Bishop	6	12	1
N.S.Sidhu	c Dujon b Ambrose	4	13	–
* D.B.Vengsarkar	c Baptiste b Walsh	22	33	3
M.Azharuddin	b Walsh	19	21	4
Kapil Dev	b Richards	38	48	3
R.J.Shastri	run out	3	6	–
A.K.Sharma	c Walsh b Richards	30	35	2/1
† K.S.More	not out	20	35	2
Arshad Ayub	lbw b Richards	2	3	–
C.Sharma	not out	6	6	1
Extras	(b 2, lb 16, w 1, nb 2)	21		
Total	(44 overs; 8 wickets)	**188**		

INDIA	O	M	R	W
Kapil Dev	8	2	39	0
C.Sharma	7.5	1	38	1
A.K.Sharma	7	0	42	1
Azharuddin	2	0	23	0
Shastri	7	0	52	0
Arshad Ayub	8	0	55	0
Srikkanth	4	0	33	0

WEST INDIES	O	M	R	W
Ambrose	5	0	18	1
Bishop	5	1	15	1
Richards	10	1	41	3
Walsh	9	0	27	2
Arthurton	3	0	10	0
Baptiste	10	0	48	0
Richardson	2	0	11	0

FALL OF WICKETS
1-185, 2-280

FALL OF WICKETS
1-10, 2-33, 3-61, 4-84, 5-96, 6-141, 7-162, 8-166

Umpires: L.H.Barker (8) and C.R.Duncan (2).

PAKISTAN v SRI LANKA 1988-89

At Sharjah CA Stadium, UAE on 23 March 1989.　　Result: **PAKISTAN** won by 30 runs.　　Toss: Sri Lanka.
Award: Shoaib Mohammed.　　LOI debuts: Pakistan – Mushtaq Ahmed.

Only two countries contested this Cricketers' Benefit Fund Series. The main recipient, Abdul Qadir, injured his left hand attempting a return catch and missed the second match.

PAKISTAN		Runs	Balls	4/6
Ramiz Raja	b Ratnayeke	13	35	2
Shoaib Mohammed	st Kuruppu b Ranatunga	76	94	8
Salim Malik	st Kuruppu b E.A.R.de Silva	71	80	4
* Imran Khan	b E.A.R.de Silva	16	19	1
Ijaz Ahmed	b Ranatunga	18	16	3
† Aamer Malik	run out	14	27	1
Abdul Qadir	b Labrooy	7	12	1
Mushtaq Ahmed	c Kuruppu b Ratnayeke	0	3	–
Tausif Ahmed	not out	6	4	–
Salim Jaffer	not out	10	10	–
Aqib Javed				
Extras	(lb 3, w 2, nb 1)	6		
Total	(50 overs; 8 wickets)	**237**		

SRI LANKA		Runs	Balls	4/6
R.S.Mahanama	c Mushtaq b Aqib	14	20	1
† D.S.B.P.Kuruppu	b Mushtaq	22	58	1
M.A.R.Samarasekera	lbw b Imran	7	14	1
P.A.de Silva	c and b Mushtaq	48	58	4
* A.Ranatunga	c Aamer b Salim Jaffer	23	33	1
L.R.D.Mendis	c sub ‡ b Salim Jaffer	17	34	2
H.P.Tillekeratne	b Imran	26	29	–
J.R.Ratnayeke	run out	8	15	–
G.F.Labrooy	b Tausif	7	7	1
E.A.R.de Silva	not out	19	21	2
K.I.W.Wijegunawardene	b Aqib	0	4	
Extras	(b 4, lb 8, w 3, nb 1)	16		
Total	(48.4 overs)	**207**		

SRI LANKA	O	M	R	W
Ratnayeke	10	0	31	2
Labrooy	8	0	41	1
E.A.R.de Silva	10	0	47	2
Wijegunawardene	4	0	21	0
P.A.de Silva	3	0	19	0
Samarasekera	5	0	28	0
Ranatunga	10	0	47	2

PAKISTAN	O	M	R	W
Imran Khan	8	0	31	2
Aqib Javed	6.4	0	15	2
Abdul Qadir	4.3	0	15	0
Salim Jaffer	10	0	50	2
Tausif Ahmed	10	0	51	1
Mushtaq Ahmed	9.3	1	33	2

FALL OF WICKETS
1-31, 2-158, 3-174, 4-183, 5-201, 6-221, 7-221, 8-221

FALL OF WICKETS
1-18, 2-29, 3-82, 4-109, 5-141, 6-148, 7-162, 8-175, 9-206, 10-207

‡ (Shahid Mahboob)

Umpires: R.B.Gupta (*India*) (14) and V.K.Ramaswamy (*India*) (13).

PAKISTAN v SRI LANKA 1988-89

At Sharjah CA Stadium, UAE on 24 March 1989. Result: **PAKISTAN** won by 7 wickets. Toss: Sri Lanka.
Award: Salim Malik. LOI debuts: Sri Lanka – N.L.K.Ratnayake.

Salim Malik scored his third hundred and shared in two three-figure partnerships in the same innings.

SRI LANKA		Runs	Balls	4/6
R.S.Mahanama	b Shoaib	35	56	2
† D.S.B.P.Kuruppu	st Salim Yousuf b Shoaib	63	98	4/1
P.A.de Silva	run out	60	62	6
M.A.R.Samarasekera	c Aamer b Salim Jaffer	15	19	1/1
* A.Ranatunga	c Aqib b Imran	20	33	1
L.R.D.Mendis	run out	10	13	–
G.F.Labrooy	b Imran	0	1	–
H.P.Tillekeratne	not out	10	9	1
J.R.Ratnayeke	c Mushtaq b Imran	18	12	2/1
E.A.R.de Silva				
N.L.K.Ratnayake				
Extras	(lb 11, w 2)	13		
Total	(50 overs; 8 wickets)	**244**		

PAKISTAN		Runs	Balls	4/6
Ramiz Raja	b Ratnayeke	5	15	–
Shoaib Mohammed	c Tillekeratne b Ratnayeke	65	84	3
Aamer Malik	b P.A.de Silva	20	24	3
Salim Malik	not out	100	112	4
* Imran Khan	not out	50	53	3/1
Ijaz Ahmed				
† Salim Yousuf				
Mushtaq Ahmed				
Tausif Ahmed				
Salim Jaffer				
Aqib Javed				
Extras	(b 1, lb 5, w 1, nb 1)	8		
Total	(47.5 overs; 3 wickets)	**248**		

PAKISTAN	O	M	R	W
Imran Khan	10	0	49	3
Aqib Javed	9	0	32	0
Salim Jaffer	7	0	36	1
Tausif Ahmed	8	0	39	0
Shoaib Mohammed	10	0	42	2
Mushtaq Ahmed	6	0	35	0

SRI LANKA	O	M	R	W
Ratnayeke	9	0	35	1
Ratnayake	9.5	0	59	1
P.A.de Silva	10	0	38	1
Labrooy	6	0	42	0
Samarasekera	2	0	15	0
Ranatunga	9	0	42	0
E.A.R.de Silva	2	0	11	0

FALL OF WICKETS
1-74, 2-127, 3-157, 4-197, 5-211, 6-211, 7-219, 8-244

FALL OF WICKETS
1-18, 2-46, 3-148

Umpires: R.B.Gupta (*India*) (15) and V.K.Ramaswamy (*India*) (14).

ENGLAND v AUSTRALIA 1989

At Old Trafford, Manchester on 25 May 1989. Result: **ENGLAND** won by 95 runs. Toss: England.
Award: P.A.J.DeFreitas. LOI debuts: England – S.J.Rhodes.

David Gower, restored to England's captaincy after a three-year hiatus, opened the batting and celebrated his 100th LOI
innings with a 33-ball cameo which included six boundaries. Ian Botham made his first international appearance since
The Oval Test of August 1987.

ENGLAND		Runs	Balls	4/6
G.A.Gooch	c Jones b Border	52	111	4
* D.I.Gower	c Healy b Rackemann	36	33	5/1
M.W.Gatting	c Boon b Waugh	3	12	–
A.J.Lamb	b Lawson	35	59	–
R.A.Smith	c and b Alderman	35	40	4
I.T.Botham	c Boon b Lawson	4	12	–
D.R.Pringle	lbw b Waugh	9	18	–
† S.J.Rhodes	b Lawson	8	16	–
P.A.J.DeFreitas	not out	17	20	–
J.E.Emburey	b Rackemann	10	11	–
N.A.Foster	not out	5	3	–
Extras	(lb 12, w 3, nb 2)	17		
Total	(55 overs; 9 wickets)	**231**		

AUSTRALIA		Runs	Balls	4/6
G.R.Marsh	c Rhodes b Emburey	17	78	1
D.C.Boon	b DeFreitas	5	9	–
D.M.Jones	c Rhodes b Foster	4	15	1
* A.R.Border	b Foster	4	6	1
S.R.Waugh	c Smith b DeFreitas	35	74	2
T.M.Moody	b Emburey	24	38	–
M.R.J.Veletta	lbw b Pringle	17	31	1
† I.A.Healy	c Emburey b Foster	10	20	1
G.F.Lawson	c DeFreitas b Emburey	0	1	–
C.G.Rackemann	b Botham	6	9	–
T.M.Alderman	not out	0	2	–
Extras	(b 1, lb 9, w 4)	14		
Total	(47.1 overs)	**136**		

AUSTRALIA	O	M	R	W
Alderman	11	2	38	1
Lawson	11	1	48	3
Rackemann	10	1	33	2
Waugh	11	1	45	2
Moody	8	0	37	0
Border	4	0	18	1

ENGLAND	O	M	R	W
Foster	10	3	29	3
DeFreitas	8	1	19	2
Pringle	8	2	19	1
Botham	10.1	1	28	1
Emburey	11	0	31	3

FALL OF WICKETS
1-55, 2-70, 3-125, 4-161, 5-167, 6-179, 7-190, 8-203, 9-220

FALL OF WICKETS
1-8, 2-13, 3-17, 4-64, 5-85, 6-115, 7-119, 8-120, 9-136, 10-136

Umpires: J.W.Holder (2) and N.T.Plews (3).

ENGLAND v AUSTRALIA 1989

At Trent Bridge, Nottingham on 27 May 1989.   Result: **MATCH TIED.**   Toss: England.
Award: A.J.Lamb.   LOI debuts: None.

When Carl Rackemann missed the final ball (his first) from Phillip DeFreitas, Ian Healy scampered a bye. Earlier, Healy's runner, Dean Jones, had been expelled from the field after the batsman himself had run a rapid two runs in tandem. Allan Lamb completed the last of his four LOI hundreds off the final ball of the innings.

ENGLAND		Runs	Balls	4/6
G.A.Gooch	c Jones b Alderman	10	35	–
* D.I.Gower	b Waugh	28	59	3
M.W.Gatting	b May	37	76	3
A.J.Lamb	not out	100	105	9
R.A.Smith	st Healy b May	3	9	–
I.T.Botham	run out	8	15	–
D.R.Pringle	not out	25	32	2
† S.J.Rhodes				
P.A.J.DeFreitas				
J.E.Emburey				
N.A.Foster				
Extras	(lb 14, w 1)	15		
Total	(55 overs; 5 wickets)	226		

AUSTRALIA		Runs	Balls	4/6
D.C.Boon	b Botham	28	35	2
G.R.Marsh	lbw b Emburey	34	87	3
D.M.Jones	b Emburey	29	47	3
* A.R.Border	c Rhodes b Pringle	39	58	3
S.R.Waugh	run out	43	61	5
T.M.Moody	run out	10	7	–/1
† I.A.Healy	not out	26	28	–
G.F.Lawson	c Gooch b Foster	1	5	–
T.B.A.May	b DeFreitas	2	3	–
C.G.Rackemann	not out	0	1	–
T.M.Alderman				
Extras	(b 1, lb 6, w 7)	14		
Total	(55 overs; 8 wickets)	226		

AUSTRALIA	O	M	R	W
Alderman	9	2	38	1
Lawson	11	0	47	0
Rackemann	11	1	37	0
Waugh	11	1	47	1
May	11	1	35	2
Moody	2	0	8	0

ENGLAND	O	M	R	W
Foster	11	2	44	1
DeFreitas	11	0	48	1
Pringle	11	1	38	1
Botham	11	0	42	1
Emburey	11	0	47	2

FALL OF WICKETS
1-59, 2-81, 3-116, 4-153, 5-174, 6-205, 7-218, 8-225

FALL OF WICKETS
1-30, 2-57, 3-119, 4-123, 5-138

Umpires: H.D.Bird (55) and J.H.Hampshire (1).

ENGLAND v AUSTRALIA 1989

At Lord's, London on 29 May 1989.   Result: **AUSTRALIA** won by 6 wickets.   Toss: England.
Award: G.R.Marsh.   LOI debuts: None.

By scoring their seventh LOI hundreds, Graham Gooch equalled England's record and Geoff Marsh extended his for Australia. England won the Texaco Trophy by having lost fewer wickets in the tied game. Sheila Nicholls, a 19-year-old student from Essex, celebrated the most nubile streak in Lord's history with a notable cartwheel.

ENGLAND		Runs	Balls	4/6
G.A.Gooch	b Alderman	136	162	11
* D.I.Gower	c Veletta b Moody	61	100	6
M.W.Gatting	run out	18	31	2
A.J.Lamb	lbw b Alderman	0	1	–
R.A.Smith	b Rackemann	21	22	1
I.T.Botham	not out	25	11	3/1
P.A.J.DeFreitas	c Rackemann b Alderman	0	2	–
D.R.Pringle	run out	0	1	–
† S.J.Rhodes	not out	1	1	–
J.E.Emburey				
N.A.Foster				
Extras	(lb 14, w 2)	16		
Total	(55 overs; 7 wickets)	278		

AUSTRALIA		Runs	Balls	4/6
G.R.Marsh	not out	111	162	7/1
D.C.Boon	lbw b Foster	19	17	3
D.M.Jones	c Gower b Emburey	27	67	2
* A.R.Border	b Pringle	53	46	5
S.R.Waugh	c Gooch b Foster	35	32	–/2
T.M.Moody	not out	6	4	–
† M.R.J.Veletta				
G.F.Lawson				
T.B.A.May				
C.G.Rackemann				
T.M.Alderman				
Extras	(lb 18, w 8, nb 2)	28		
Total	(54.3 overs; 4 wickets)	279		

AUSTRALIA	O	M	R	W
Alderman	11	2	36	3
Rackemann	11	0	56	1
Lawson	11	0	48	0
Waugh	11	0	70	0
May	6	0	33	0
Moody	5	0	21	1

ENGLAND	O	M	R	W
DeFreitas	11	1	50	0
Foster	11	0	57	2
Pringle	10.3	0	50	1
Botham	11	0	43	0
Emburey	11	0	61	1

FALL OF WICKETS
1-24, 2-84, 3-197, 4-268

FALL OF WICKETS
1-123, 2-180, 3-182, 4-239, 5-266, 6-266, 7-268

Umpires: B.J.Meyer (20) and D.R.Shepherd (33).

WEST INDIES v INDIA 1989-90

At Sharjah CA Stadium, UAE on 13 October 1989.   Result: **WEST INDIES** won by 5 wickets.   Toss: India.
Award: I.V.A.Richards.   LOI debuts: None.

This match was postponed from the previous day because of the death of the UAE deputy prime minister. Beneficiaries from this triangular 50-over tournament were Krish Srikkanth, who made his first appearance as captain in his 112th international, and 'Polly' Umrigar (India), Fazal Mahmood and Iqbal Qasim (Pakistan), and the West Indies captain.

INDIA		Runs	Balls	4/6	WEST INDIES		Runs	Balls	4/6
* K.Srikkanth	c Dujon b Walsh	11	39		D.L.Haynes	c More b Arshad Ayub	12	36	1
N.S.Sidhu	c and b Walsh	28	51	4	P.V.Simmons	c Srikkanth b Prabhakar	6	26	1
M.Amarnath	b Richards	20	38	3	R.B.Richardson	c Vengsarkar b Prabhakar	5	9	–
D.B.Vengsarkar	run out	14	23	1	K.L.T.Arthurton	c Amarnath b Sharma	48	118	2
M.Azharuddin	run out	14	18	–	* I.V.A.Richards	c Sidhu b Arshad Ayub	34	33	4/1
R.J.Shastri	c Richardson b Richards	5	18	–	A.L.Logie	not out	59	65	6
Kapil Dev	c Dujon b Walsh	16	27	1	† P.J.L.Dujon	not out	3	2	–
A.K.Sharma	b Ambrose	17	28	2	M.D.Marshall				
M.Prabhakar	c Dujon b Walsh	0	2	–	C.E.L.Ambrose				
† K.S.More	b Ambrose	17	35	1	I.R.Bishop				
Arshad Ayub	not out	7	10	–	C.A.Walsh				
Extras	(b 1, lb 9, w 10)	20			Extras	(lb 3, w 1, nb 2)	6		
Total	(48.1 overs)	**169**			**Total**	(47.5 overs; 5 wickets)	**173**		

WEST INDIES	O	M	R	W	INDIA	O	M	R	W
Ambrose	9.1	1	22	2	Kapil Dev	8	4	16	0
Bishop	9	0	45	0	Prabhakar	10	2	45	2
Marshall	10	1	23	0	Arshad Ayub	10	2	27	2
Walsh	10	1	25	4	Shastri	10	1	41	0
Richards	10	0	44	2	Sharma	5	1	14	1
					Srikkanth	4.5	0	27	0

FALL OF WICKETS
1-43, 2-46, 3-72, 4-91, 5-97, 6-106, 7-126, 8-126, 9-146, 10-169

FALL OF WICKETS
1-18, 2-23, 3-31, 4-80, 5-165

Umpires: H.D.Bird (*England*) (56) and D.R.Shepherd (*England*) (34).

WEST INDIES v PAKISTAN 1989-90

At Sharjah CA Stadium, UAE on 14 October 1989.   Result: **PAKISTAN** won by 11 runs.   Toss: West Indies.
Award: Wasim Akram.   LOI debuts: Pakistan – Shahid Saeed, Waqar Younis.

Wasim Akram achieved the fourth hat-trick in internationals when he bowled Jeff Dujon, Malcolm Marshall and Curtly Ambrose with the last three balls of his eighth over, the latter dismissal being his 100th in 74 matches. Imran Khan scored 20 off Ambrose's final over.

PAKISTAN		Runs	Balls	4/6	WEST INDIES		Runs	Balls	4/6
Ramiz Raja	c Richardson b Walsh	17	37	2	D.L.Haynes	c Wasim b Imran	59	94	8
Shoaib Mohammed	b Richards	45	87	2	P.V.Simmons	lbw b Wasim	16	24	3
Shahid Saeed	b Bishop	22	43	1	R.B.Richardson	b Imran	31	45	1
Salim Malik	c Richards b Bishop	74	81	4	K.L.T.Arthurton	st Salim Yousuf b Mushtaq	0	1	–
Ijaz Ahmed	run out	6	12	–	* I.V.A.Richards	c sub (Sohail Fazal) b Shoaib	46	45	5/1
* Imran Khan	b Ambrose	45	41	2/2	C.A.Best	not out	53	68	2
Wasim Akram	lbw b Ambrose	0	1	–	† P.J.L.Dujon	b Wasim	6	9	–
† Salim Yousuf	c and b Bishop	4	4	–	M.D.Marshall	b Wasim	0	1	–
Abdul Qadir	not out	2	3	–	C.E.L.Ambrose	b Wasim	0	1	–
Mushtaq Ahmed					I.R.Bishop	b Qadir	0	3	–
Waqar Younis					C.A.Walsh	b Wasim	10	12	–
Extras	(b 4, lb 14, w 11, nb 6)	35			Extras	(lb 8, w 4, nb 6)	18		
Total	(50 overs; 8 wickets)	**250**			**Total**	(48.4 overs)	**239**		

WEST INDIES	O	M	R	W	PAKISTAN	O	M	R	W
Ambrose	10	1	58	2	Wasim Akram	9.4	1	38	5
Bishop	10	0	49	3	Waqar Younis	4	0	14	0
Walsh	10	0	36	1	Abdul Qadir	9	0	45	1
Marshall	10	0	41	0	Shahid Saeed	3	0	19	0
Richards	10	0	48	1	Imran Khan	10	0	51	2
					Mushtaq Ahmed	10	0	47	1
					Shoaib Mohammed	3	0	17	1

FALL OF WICKETS
1-31, 2-86, 3-139, 4-159, 5-214, 6-221, 7-226, 8-250

FALL OF WICKETS
1-32, 2-117, 3-118, 4-124, 5-195, 6-209, 7-209, 8-209, 9-210, 10-239

Umpires: D.P.Buultjens (*Sri Lanka*) (11) and S.Ponnadurai (*Sri Lanka*) (5).

INDIA v PAKISTAN 1989-90

At Sharjah CA Stadium, UAE on 15 October 1989.　　Result: **PAKISTAN** won by 6 wickets.　　Toss: India.
Award: N.S.Sidhu.　　LOI debuts: None.

India's total was their highest against Pakistan and at Sharjah, while the match aggregate of 547 runs was an Indo-Pakistan record. Navjot Sidhu hit his first LOI hundred and, with Mohinder Amarnath, shared India's (then) highest second-wicket stand against Pakistan.

INDIA		Runs	Balls	4/6
* K.Srikkanth	st Salim Yousuf b Mushtaq	51	70	4
N.S.Sidhu	b Wasim	108	121	8/1
M.Amarnath	c Salim Malik b Wasim	88	80	7/2
Kapil Dev	c Shahid b Wasim	13	7	2
R.J.Shastri	not out	0	1	–
M.Azharuddin	not out	2	1	–
D.B.Vengsarkar				
† K.S.More				
C.Sharma				
M.Prabhakar				
Arshad Ayub				
Extras	(lb 6, w 3, nb 2)	11		
Total	(46 overs; 4 wickets)	**273**		

PAKISTAN		Runs	Balls	4/6
Shahid Saeed	b Shastri	50	65	1/1
Shoaib Mohammed	run out	65	78	2
Wasim Akram	c More b Arshad Ayub	37	23	1/4
Salim Malik	not out	68	58	7
Javed Miandad	st More b Shastri	31	35	2
* Imran Khan	not out	17	12	1
Ijaz Ahmed				
† Salim Yousuf				
Abdul Qadir				
Mushtaq Ahmed				
Aqib Javed				
Extras	(lb 4, w 1, nb 1)	6		
Total	(44.4 overs; 4 wickets)	**274**		

PAKISTAN	O	M	R	W
Wasim Akram	9	0	30	3
Aqib Javed	8	0	46	0
Shahid Saeed	3	0	24	0
Shoaib Mohammed	2	0	18	0
Mushtaq Ahmed	10	0	47	1
Abdul Qadir	7	0	44	0
Imran Khan	7	0	58	0

INDIA	O	M	R	W
Kapil Dev	8	0	47	0
Prabhakar	10	0	46	0
Sharma	5.4	0	35	0
Amarnath	2	0	15	0
Arshad Ayub	10	0	67	1
Shastri	9	0	60	2

FALL OF WICKETS
1-92, 2-253, 3-271, 4-271

FALL OF WICKETS
1-99, 2-152, 3-169, 4-234

Umpires: H.D.Bird (*England*) (57) and D.R.Shepherd (*England*) (35).

WEST INDIES v INDIA 1989-90

At Sharjah CA Stadium, UAE on 16 October 1989.　　Result: **INDIA** won by 37 runs.　　Toss: West Indies.
Award: Kapil Dev.　　LOI debuts: None.

India's victory ended a sequence of seven defeats at the hands of West Indies. Having injured a finger fielding, Viv Richards batted at no. 9.

INDIA		Runs	Balls	4/6
* K.Srikkanth	b Walsh	40	56	4
R.Lamba	c Walsh b Ambrose	18	21	2
M.Amarnath	c Richards b Benjamin	29	63	2
D.B.Vengsarkar	run out	6	4	1
M.Azharuddin	b Walsh	28	57	–
A.K.Sharma	c Richardson b Ambrose	2	5	–
Kapil Dev	b Benjamin	41	50	2/1
R.J.Shastri	run out	6	17	–
M.Prabhakar	lbw b Marshall	8	17	–
† K.S.More	not out	2	9	–
Arshad Ayub	not out	7	5	–
Extras	(lb 10, w 11, nb 3)	24		
Total	(50 overs; 9 wickets)	**211**		

WEST INDIES		Runs	Balls	4/6
D.L.Haynes	b Kapil Dev	3	10	–
P.V.Simmons	c Vengsarkar b Prabhakar	3	23	–
R.B.Richardson	run out	39	55	–/1
K.L.T.Arthurton	b Arshad Ayub	16	46	–
C.A.Best	c Vengsarkar b Arshad Ayub	5	10	–
† P.J.L.Dujon	not out	37	61	1
M.D.Marshall	b Sharma	40	47	2/2
C.E.L.Ambrose	st More b Shastri	3	11	–
* I.V.A.Richards	run out	5	5	–
W.K.M.Benjamin	st More b Sharma	10	13	1
C.A.Walsh	b Kapil Dev	1	2	–
Extras	(lb 9, w 1, nb 2)	12		
Total	(46.4 overs)	**174**		

WEST INDIES	O	M	R	W
Ambrose	10	1	43	2
Benjamin	10	1	36	2
Walsh	10	1	32	2
Marshall	10	0	50	1
Richards	10	0	40	0

INDIA	O	M	R	W
Kapil Dev	7.4	1	19	2
Prabhakar	7	1	18	1
Arshad Ayub	10	0	29	2
Shastri	10	0	40	1
Sharma	10	0	44	2
Srikkanth	2	0	15	0

FALL OF WICKETS
1-37, 2-76, 3-82, 4-115, 5-123, 6-149, 7-164, 8-179, 9-201

FALL OF WICKETS
1-5, 2-24, 3-59, 4-71, 5-78, 6-129, 7-146, 8-157, 9-171, 10-174

Umpires: D.P.Buultjens (*Sri Lanka*) (12) and S.Ponnadurai (*Sri Lanka*) (6).

WEST INDIES v PAKISTAN 1989-90

At Sharjah CA Stadium, UAE on 17 October 1989.   Result: **PAKISTAN** won by 57 runs.   Toss: Pakistan.
Award: Imran Khan.   LOI debuts: West Indies – R.C.Haynes.

Pakistan secured the Champions Trophy with a match in hand, the defending holders being bereft of the services of Richards, Marshall and Logie through injury. Desmond Haynes, playing his 162nd match, captained for the first time. His unrelated namesake, Robert, took a wicket with his second ball.

PAKISTAN		Runs	Balls	4/6
Shoaib Mohammed	c Benjamin b Walsh	21	48	2
Ramiz Raja	c R.C.Haynes b Ambrose	33	62	2
Shahid Saeed	b R.C.Haynes	7	18	1
Salim Malik	c Dujon b Ambrose	16	19	1
Ijaz Ahmed	b Benjamin	50	53	8
* Imran Khan	not out	60	56	3
Sohail Fazal	c R.C.Haynes b Walsh	24	34	1
† Salim Yousuf	b Bishop	4	7	–
Mushtaq Ahmed	not out	3	3	–
Abdul Qadir				
Waqar Younis				
Extras	(b 8, lb 8, w 3)	19		
Total	**(50 overs; 7 wickets)**	**237**		

WEST INDIES		Runs	Balls	4/6
* D.L.Haynes	c Salim Yousuf b Waqar	15	29	2
P.V.Simmons	c Sohail b Waqar	27	32	4/1
R.B.Richardson	b Mushtaq	6	15	–
C.A.Best	b Qadir	44	74	4
K.L.T.Arthurton	b Qadir	1	3	–
R.C.Haynes	lbw b Qadir	4	10	–
† P.J.L.Dujon	c Salim Yousuf b Shoaib	26	39	2
C.E.L.Ambrose	not out	26	31	1/1
W.K.M.Benjamin	b Waqar	3	14	–
I.R.Bishop	run out	3	10	–
C.A.Walsh	b Imran	14	10	1/1
Extras	(lb 10, w 1)	11		
Total	**(44.4 overs)**	**180**		

WEST INDIES	O	M	R	W
Ambrose	10	0	43	2
Bishop	10	0	31	1
Benjamin	10	0	58	1
R.C.Haynes	10	1	44	1
Walsh	10	1	45	2

PAKISTAN	O	M	R	W
Imran Khan	5.4	0	21	1
Waqar Younis	9	2	28	3
Abdul Qadir	10	1	31	3
Mushtaq Ahmed	10	0	38	1
Sohail Fazal	1	0	4	0
Shahid Saeed	3	0	19	0
Shoaib Mohammed	6	0	29	1

FALL OF WICKETS
1-40, 2-55, 3-85, 4-86, 5-154, 6-207, 7-221

FALL OF WICKETS
1-43, 2-50, 3-52, 4-53, 5-65, 6-127, 7-135, 8-149, 9-155, 10-180

Umpires: H.D.Bird (*England*) (58) and D.R.Shepherd (*England*) (36).

INDIA v PAKISTAN 1989-90

At Sharjah CA Stadium, UAE on 20 October 1989.   Result: **PAKISTAN** won by 38 runs.   Toss: India.
Award: Salim Malik.   LOI debuts: None.

Salim Malik's fourth hundred was his third at Sharjah. Pakistan gained their seventh successive win against India in the Gulf.

PAKISTAN		Runs	Balls	4/6
Shahid Saeed	lbw b Prabhakar	16	35	1
Shoaib Mohammed	st More b A.K.Sharma	51	85	–
Salim Malik	c Azharuddin b Prabhakar	102	115	5
Sohail Fazal	c Azharuddin b Arshad Ayub	32	25	1/3
* Javed Miandad	not out	28	23	2
Ijaz Ahmed	not out	2	2	–
† Salim Yousuf				
Abdul Qadir				
Mushtaq Ahmed				
Waqar Younis				
Aqib Javed				
Extras	(b 3, lb 11, w 5, nb 2)	21		
Total	**(47 overs; 4 wickets)**	**252**		

INDIA		Runs	Balls	4/6
* K.Srikkanth	c Salim Yousuf b Aqib	8	12	–
N.S.Sidhu	c Ijaz b Mushtaq	28	40	2
M.Azharuddin	c Salim Yousuf b Aqib	12	31	–
D.B.Vengsarkar	lbw b Shoaib	35	75	1
R.J.Shastri	c Salim Malik b Mushtaq	22	22	2/1
A.K.Sharma	c Ijaz b Shahid	6	7	–
M.Prabhakar	run out	25	31	1
M.Amarnath	not out	30	35	2/1
† K.S.More	st Salim Yousuf b Shoaib	21	16	2
C.Sharma	c and b Aqib	7	5	–
Arshad Ayub	not out	5	6	–
Extras	(b 1, lb 9, w 5)	15		
Total	**(47 overs; 9 wickets)**	**214**		

INDIA	O	M	R	W
C.Sharma	9	0	42	0
Prabhakar	10	0	45	2
Amarnath	8	1	27	0
Arshad Ayub	9	0	51	1
Shastri	4	0	35	0
A.K.Sharma	7	0	38	1

PAKISTAN	O	M	R	W
Waqar Younis	6	0	18	0
Aqib Javed	10	0	49	3
Shahid Saeed	10	1	27	1
Mushtaq Ahmed	6	0	33	2
Abdul Qadir	7	0	35	0
Shoaib Mohammed	8	0	42	2

FALL OF WICKETS
1-33, 2-125, 3-195, 4-248

FALL OF WICKETS
1-17, 2-42, 3-53, 4-88, 5-100, 6-145, 7-146, 8-187, 9-202

Umpires: H.D.Bird (*England*) (59) and D.R.Shepherd (*England*) (37).

ENGLAND v SRI LANKA 1989-90

At Feroz Shah Kotla, Delhi on 15 October 1989.   Result: **ENGLAND** won by 5 wickets.   Toss: England.
Award: R.A.Smith.   LOI debuts: England – A.R.C.Fraser, A.J.Stewart.

Sponsored by the Madras Rubber Foundry and staged to celebrate the centenary of the birth of India's first post-Independence prime minister, Jawaharlal Nehru, this 50-over tournament involved all the current Test-playing countries except New Zealand. Wayne Larkins set LOI records by reappearing after an interlude of 9 years 267 days and 110 matches.

SRI LANKA		Runs	Balls	4/6	ENGLAND		Runs	Balls	4/6
R.S.Mahanama	run out	1	2	–	* G.A.Gooch	c P.A.de Silva b Labrooy	5		
† D.S.B.P.Kuruppu	c Russell b Fraser	5			W.Larkins	c P.A.de Silva b Ranatunga	19		
A.P.Gurusinha	c Lamb b Capel	19			R.A.Smith	not out	81	119	7
P.A.de Silva	lbw b Hemmings	80	89	10	A.J.Lamb	c P.A.de Silva b Wijegunawardene	52	66	2/3
* A.Ranatunga	b Gooch	7			A.J.Stewart	c Kuruppu b Ranatunga	4		
M.A.R.Samarasekera	c Stewart b Gooch	24			D.J.Capel	lbw b Wijegunawardene	4		
J.R.Ratnayeke	c Gooch b DeFreitas	6			† R.C.Russell	not out	10		
G.F.Labrooy	lbw b DeFreitas	0			P.A.J.DeFreitas				
E.A.R.de Silva	b DeFreitas	2			G.C.Small				
S.D.Anurasiri	not out	5			E.E.Hemmings				
K.I.W.Wijegunawardene	b Fraser	3			A.R.C.Fraser				
Extras	(b 6, lb 22, w 10, nb 3)	41			Extras	(b 1, lb 8, w 10, nb 2)	21		
Total	(48.3 overs)	**193**			**Total**	(48.4 overs; 5 wickets)	**196**		

ENGLAND	O	M	R	W	SRI LANKA	O	M	R	W
DeFreitas	10	3	38	3	Ratnayeke	7	1	10	0
Fraser	8.3	1	25	2	Labrooy	7	1	34	1
Small	6	0	26	0	Ranatunga	10	0	39	2
Capel	4	0	16	1	E.A.R.de Silva	10	0	29	0
Gooch	10	2	26	2	Anurasiri	3	0	22	0
Hemmings	10	1	34	1	P.A.de Silva	3	0	16	0
					Wijegunawardene	8.4	1	37	2

FALL OF WICKETS
1-1, 2-17, 3-42, 4-82, 5-154, 6-174, 7-180, 8-180, 9-186, 10-193

FALL OF WICKETS
1-18, 2-34, 3-137, 4-157, 5-170

Umpires: R.B.Gupta (16) and P.J.McConnell (*Australia*) (46).

ENGLAND v AUSTRALIA 1989-90

At Lal Bahadur Stadium, Hyderabad on 19 October 1989.   Result: **ENGLAND** won by 7 wickets.   Toss: Australia.
Award: W.Larkins.   LOI debuts: None.

Allan Border scored 50 off 31 balls and hit three successive balls of a Gladstone Small over for six. Graham Gooch and Wayne Larkins (100 off 108 balls) shared England's highest opening stand against Australia.

AUSTRALIA		Runs	Balls	4/6	ENGLAND		Runs	Balls	4/6
D.C.Boon	c Gooch b Fraser	0	6	–	* G.A.Gooch	lbw b Border	56	89	6
G.R.Marsh	c Lamb b Small	54	131	4	W.Larkins	c Border b May	124	126	18/2
D.M.Jones	run out	50	90	6	R.A.Smith	not out	24	35	3
P.L.Taylor	not out	36	41	3	A.J.Lamb	b Lawson	23	30	4
* A.R.Border	not out	84	44	8/5	A.J.Stewart	not out	4	8	–
S.R.Waugh					D.J.Capel				
S.P.O'Donnell					† R.C.Russell				
† I.A.Healy					D.R.Pringle				
T.B.A.May					G.C.Small				
G.F.Lawson					E.E.Hemmings				
T.M.Alderman					A.R.C.Fraser				
Extras	(lb 6, w 4, nb 8)	18			Extras	(b 1, lb 9, nb 2)	12		
Total	(50 overs; 3 wickets)	**242**			**Total**	(47.3 overs; 3 wickets)	**243**		

ENGLAND	O	M	R	W	AUSTRALIA	O	M	R	W
Fraser	10	2	48	1	Alderman	7	1	28	0
Pringle	10	3	42	0	Lawson	10	1	51	1
Small	10	0	55	1	May	10	0	55	1
Capel	8	0	39	0	O'Donnell	7.3	0	27	0
Gooch	10	3	35	0	Border	10	0	43	1
Hemmings	2	0	17	0	Taylor	3	0	29	0

FALL OF WICKETS
1-0, 2-108, 3-122

FALL OF WICKETS
1-185, 2-191, 3-234

Umpires: L.H.Barker (*West Indies*) (9) and Khizer Hayat (*Pakistan*) (24).

WEST INDIES v SRI LANKA 1989-90

At Racecourse Ground, Rajkot on 19 October 1989.   Result: **SRI LANKA** won by 4 wickets.   Toss: Sri Lanka.
Award: A.P.Gurusinha.   LOI debuts: None.

West Indies, who, along with India and Pakistan, were still contesting the Champions Trophy in Sharjah when this tournament began, lost to Sri Lanka for the first time. Desmond Haynes became the second after Viv Richards to score 6000 LOI runs.

WEST INDIES		Runs	Balls	4/6
D.L.Haynes	c Labrooy b P.A.de Silva	42	92	2
P.V.Simmons	c E.A.R.de Silva b Ratnayeke	7		
R.B.Richardson	c Ranatunga b Ratnayeke	5		
* I.V.A.Richards	b Wijegunawardene	24		/1
A.L.Logie	not out	54	73	2
C.A.Best	b E.A.R.de Silva	6		
† P.J.L.Dujon	c Ratnayeke b E.A.R.de Silva	4		
W.K.M.Benjamin	b Wijegunawardene	7		
C.E.L.Ambrose	c Gurusinha b P.A.de Silva	2		
I.R.Bishop	run out	3		
C.A.Walsh	not out	13		
Extras	(lb 2, w 7)	9		
Total	(50 overs; 9 wickets)	**176**		

SRI LANKA		Runs	Balls	4/6
R.S.Mahanama	c Dujon b Benjamin	12		
† D.S.B.P.Kuruppu	c Richards b Bishop	1		
A.P.Gurusinha	b Benjamin	66	90	6
P.A.de Silva	c Dujon b Benjamin	1		
J.R.Ratnayeke	c and b Richards	18		
* A.Ranatunga	c Richards b Ambrose	34		
M.A.R.Samarasekera	not out	12		
H.P.Tillekeratne	not out	10		
G.F.Labrooy				
E.A.R.de Silva				
K.I.W.Wijegunawardene				
Extras	(lb 14, w 7, nb 5)	26		
Total	(47.1 overs; 6 wickets)	**180**		

SRI LANKA	O	M	R	W
Ratnayeke	10	1	36	2
Labrooy	7	0	27	0
Ranatunga	3	0	14	0
Wijegunawardene	10	0	30	2
E.A.R.de Silva	10	0	30	2
P.A.de Silva	10	0	37	2

WEST INDIES	O	M	R	W
Ambrose	10	2	27	1
Bishop	10	1	44	1
Walsh	10	0	35	0
Benjamin	9	0	22	3
Richards	6	0	23	1
Simmons	2	0	11	0
Best	0.1	0	4	0

FALL OF WICKETS
1-12, 2-20, 3-83, 4-86, 5-96, 6-108, 7-141, 8-144, 9-157

FALL OF WICKETS
1-6, 2-43, 3-45, 4-80, 5-146, 6-156

Umpires: P.J.McConnell (*Australia*) (47) and P.D.Reporter (3).

AUSTRALIA v WEST INDIES 1989-90

At M.A.Chidambaram Stadium, Madras on 21 October 1989.   Result: **AUSTRALIA** won by 99 runs.   Toss: Australia.
Award: A.R.Border.   LOI debuts: None.

West Indies sustained their fifth consecutive defeat, equalling their worst LOI sequence, and their largest one by a runs margin. Tim May injured his knee fielding and was flown home after being stretchered off.

AUSTRALIA		Runs	Balls	4/6
G.R.Marsh	c D.L.Haynes b R.C.Haynes	74	129	5/2
D.C.Boon	b Benjamin	1	7	–
D.M.Jones	c Best b Walsh	20	29	2
* A.R.Border	c Ambrose b R.C.Haynes	46	79	4
S.R.Waugh	not out	53	44	4/2
S.P.O'Donnell	c R.C.Haynes b Benjamin	17	17	2
† I.A.Healy	b Benjamin	2	4	–
M.G.Hughes	not out	3	4	–
G.F.Lawson				
T.B.A.May				
T.M.Alderman				
Extras	(b 1, lb 12, w 7, nb 5)	25		
Total	(50 overs; 6 wickets)	**241**		

WEST INDIES		Runs	Balls	4/6
D.L.Haynes	run out	5	14	–
C.A.Best	b Alderman	0	1	–
R.B.Richardson	c and b Border	61	101	6
A.L.Logie	b O'Donnell	8	16	–
* I.V.A.Richards	b Hughes	5	10	–
† P.J.L.Dujon	b Border	13	26	2
R.C.Haynes	c Jones b Hughes	18	48	1
M.D.Marshall	c Alderman b Border	12	11	1/1
W.K.M.Benjamin	lbw b Jones	2	11	–
C.E.L.Ambrose	not out	0	1	–
C.A.Walsh	b Jones	6	8	–/1
Extras	(b 2, lb 3, w 4, nb 3)	12		
Total	(40.3 overs)	**142**		

WEST INDIES	O	M	R	W
Ambrose	9	1	37	0
Benjamin	9	2	38	3
Walsh	10	0	50	1
Marshall	10	0	31	0
Richards	6	0	36	0
R.C.Haynes	6	0	36	2

AUSTRALIA	O	M	R	W
Alderman	5	0	19	1
Lawson	7	0	18	0
Hughes	6	0	27	2
O'Donnell	6	0	19	1
Border	10	2	20	3
Jones	6.3	0	34	2

FALL OF WICKETS
1-2, 2-35, 3-147, 4-169, 5-230, 6-237

FALL OF WICKETS
1-2, 2-11, 3-36, 4-59, 5-86, 6-110, 7-122, 8-134, 9-134, 10-142

Umpires: S.K.Ghosh (5) and J.W.Holder (*England*) (3).

ENGLAND v PAKISTAN 1989-90

At Barabati Stadium, Cuttack on 22 October 1989.   Result: **ENGLAND** won by 4 wickets.   Toss: Pakistan.
Award: G.A.Gooch.   LOI debuts: None.

Salim Malik, having bowled, kept wicket after Salim Yousuf damaged a finger. Graham Gooch returned his best analysis for England.

PAKISTAN		Runs	Balls	4/6
Shahid Saeed	b Capel	5	28	–
Shoaib Mohammed	c Cook b Capel	3	34	–
Ijaz Ahmed	b Cook	15	29	2
Javed Miandad	b Gooch	14	51	–
Salim Malik	b Small	42	59	8
* Imran Khan	st Russell b Hemmings	19	30	2/1
† Salim Yousuf	c Lamb b Gooch	6	21	–
Abdul Qadir	c Russell b Cook	13	25	1
Wasim Akram	lbw b Gooch	0	1	–
Mushtaq Ahmed	not out	9	15	–
Waqar Younis	not out	4	13	–
Extras	(b 5, lb 8, w 2, nb 3)	18		
Total	(50 overs; 9 wickets)	**148**		

ENGLAND		Runs	Balls	4/6
* G.A.Gooch	b Wasim	7	20	1
W.Larkins	c Miandad b Wasim	0	1	–
R.A.Smith	c Miandad b Mushtaq	19	37	2
A.J.Lamb	b Salim Malik	42	62	5
A.J.Stewart	c Miandad b Qadir	31	58	3
D.J.Capel	run out	23	60	2
† R.C.Russell	not out	7	29	–
G.C.Small	not out	0	2	–
E.E.Hemmings				
A.R.C.Fraser				
N.G.B.Cook				
Extras	(b 8, lb 4, w 8)	20		
Total	(43.2 overs; 6 wickets)	**149**		

ENGLAND	O	M	R	W
Fraser	10	3	15	0
Capel	8	2	16	2
Small	8	2	29	1
Gooch	10	4	19	3
Cook	10	0	43	2
Hemmings	4	0	13	1

PAKISTAN	O	M	R	W
Wasim Akram	10	1	32	2
Waqar Younis	10	1	30	0
Abdul Qadir	9.2	2	29	1
Mushtaq Ahmed	6	2	25	1
Salim Malik	2	0	9	1
Imran Khan	6	1	12	0

FALL OF WICKETS
1-8, 2-16, 3-37, 4-53, 5-107, 6-111, 7-128, 8-128, 9-132

FALL OF WICKETS
1-1, 2-21, 3-68, 4-92, 5-139, 6-148

Umpires: R.B.Gupta (17) and V.K.Ramaswamy (15).

INDIA v SRI LANKA 1989-90

At Gujarat Stadium, Motera, Ahmedabad on 22 October 1989.   Result: **INDIA** won by 6 runs.   Toss: India.
Award: N.S.Sidhu.   LOI debuts: None.

Mohinder Amarnath, the first to be given out for handling the ball (*LOI No. 363*), was the second after Ramiz Raja (*LOI No. 479*) to obstruct the field when he kicked a ball out of the bowler's reach to avoid being run out.

INDIA		Runs	Balls	4/6
* K.Srikkanth	c Ranatunga b Wijegunawardene	16	38	
R.Lamba	c Ranatunga b Ratnayeke	11	36	
N.S.Sidhu	run out	80	88	5/1
M.Amarnath	obstructed the field	28	39	
M.Azharuddin	b Ratnayeke	26	43	
Kapil Dev	run out	6	10	
R.J.Shastri	c Tillekeratne b Labrooy	22	21	
A.K.Sharma	c Gurusinha b Ratnayeke	6	5	
† K.S.More	not out	7	7	
M.Prabhakar	not out	11	10	
Arshad Ayub				
Extras	(b 4, lb 5, w 5)	14		
Total	(50 overs; 8 wickets)	**227**		

SRI LANKA		Runs	Balls	4/6
R.S.Mahanama	c Sidhu b Prabhakar	12	31	
† D.S.B.P.Kuruppu	lbw b Kapil Dev	9	24	
A.P.Gurusinha	b Prabhakar	83	106	6
P.A.de Silva	c and b Arshad Ayub	20	29	
* A.Ranatunga	c Kapil Dev b Shastri	7	16	
M.A.R.Samarasekera	c and b Shastri	22	35	
H.P.Tillekeratne	run out	11	18	
G.F.Labrooy	b Prabhakar	25	19	
J.R.Ratnayeke	c Lamba b Kapil Dev	20	15	
E.A.R.de Silva	not out	1	1	
K.I.W.Wijegunawardene	b Kapil Dev	0	1	
Extras	(lb 7, w 4)	11		
Total	(49.4 overs)	**221**		

SRI LANKA	O	M	R	W
Ratnayeke	10	1	35	3
Labrooy	10	1	35	1
Wijegunawardene	10	0	60	1
Ranatunga	10	0	49	0
E.A.R.de Silva	10	0	39	0

INDIA	O	M	R	W
Kapil Dev	8.4	2	26	3
Prabhakar	9	2	34	3
Amarnath	4	0	20	0
Sharma	4	0	30	0
Shastri	10	0	47	2
Arshad Ayub	10	2	31	1
Srikkanth	4	0	26	0

FALL OF WICKETS
1-24, 2-34, 3-95, 4-168, 5-176, 6-199, 7-208, 8-209

FALL OF WICKETS
1-22, 2-24, 3-72, 4-87, 5-137, 6-161, 7-186, 8-220, 9-220, 10-221

Umpires: Khizer Hayat (*Pakistan*) (25) and P.J.McConnell (*Australia*) (48).

AUSTRALIA v PAKISTAN 1989-90

At Brabourne Stadium, Bombay on 23 October 1989.   Result: **PAKISTAN** won by 66 runs.   Toss: Australia.
Award: Imran Khan.   LOI debuts: Pakistan – Akram Raza.

The Brabourne Stadium, which staged its final Test match in 1972-73, became the 87th ground (India's 28th) to host an international. Terry Alderman took three wickets in seven balls. Australia's total remains their lowest against Pakistan.

PAKISTAN		Runs	Balls	4/6
Shoaib Mohammed	c Waugh b Alderman	73	121	7
Ramiz Raja	c Jones b Lawson	2	15	–
Shahid Saeed	c and b Alderman	6	31	–
† Javed Miandad	c Lawson b Border	34	44	2/1
Salim Malik	c Boon b Alderman	15	23	2
Ijaz Ahmed	c Border b Alderman	1	3	–
* Imran Khan	c Healy b Hughes	8	14	–
Wasim Akram	run out	28	24	2/2
Akram Raza	not out	12	27	–
Abdul Qadir	not out	5	3	1
Waqar Younis				
Extras	(b 2, lb 11, w 3, nb 5)	21		
Total	(50 overs; 8 wickets)	**205**		

AUSTRALIA		Runs	Balls	4/6
D.C.Boon	run out	0	4	–
G.R.Marsh	c Salim Malik b Waqar	8	35	1
D.M.Jones	lbw b Qadir	58	94	5
* A.R.Border	c Miandad b Imran	4	21	–
S.R.Waugh	b Imran	0	2	–
S.P.O'Donnell	lbw b Imran	3	10	–
P.L.Taylor	not out	31	71	1
† I.A.Healy	c Ijaz b Shoaib	7	14	1
M.G.Hughes	lbw b Qadir	0	3	–
G.F.Lawson	b Qadir	1	2	–
T.M.Alderman	lbw b Wasim	0	2	–
Extras	(b 4, lb 11, w 9, nb 3)	27		
Total	(43.2 overs)	**139**		

AUSTRALIA	O	M	R	W
Alderman	10	3	22	4
Lawson	10	1	34	1
Hughes	9	1	29	1
O'Donnell	10	1	38	0
Taylor	6	0	37	0
Border	5	0	32	1

PAKISTAN	O	M	R	W
Wasim Akram	6.2	0	21	1
Waqar Younis	7	2	27	1
Imran Khan	8	2	13	3
Akram Raza	10	0	26	0
Abdul Qadir	9	0	27	3
Shoaib Mohammed	3	0	10	1

FALL OF WICKETS
1-10, 2-29, 3-101, 4-138, 5-140, 6-153, 7-154, 8-197

FALL OF WICKETS
1-2, 2-46, 3-58, 4-58, 5-70, 6-104, 7-126, 8-134, 9-136, 10-139

Umpires: L.H.Barker (*West Indies*) (10) and P.D.Reporter (4).

INDIA v WEST INDIES 1989-90

At Feroz Shah Kotla, Delhi on 23 October 1989.   Result: **WEST INDIES** won by 20 runs.   Toss: India.
Award: I.V.A.Richards.   LOI debuts: None.

Mist delayed the start by 50 minutes and reduced each innings by four overs. India were fined $1250 for being an over short. Having savaged 44 runs from 42 balls, Viv Richards took three wickets in four balls and returned his best international analysis.

WEST INDIES		Runs	Balls	4/6
D.L.Haynes	c More b Prabhakar	6	15	1
C.A.Best	c Lamba b Sharma	13	44	–
R.B.Richardson	c and b Arshad Ayub	57	110	4
A.L.Logie	b Amarnath	8	10	–
* I.V.A.Richards	run out	44	42	3/1
† P.J.L.Dujon	st More b Arshad Ayub	3	7	–
M.D.Marshall	c Amarnath b Sharma	27	23	–/2
R.C.Haynes	b Sharma	4	5	–
W.K.M.Benjamin	b Kapil Dev	4	5	–
C.E.L.Ambrose	not out	6	5	1
C.A.Walsh	not out	6	3	1
Extras	(lb 12, w 5, nb 1)	18		
Total	(45 overs; 9 wickets)	**196**		

INDIA		Runs	Balls	4/6
* K.Srikkanth	c Dujon b Marshall	10	30	–
R.Lamba	c Dujon b Walsh	61	86	8
N.S.Sidhu	c D.L.Haynes b Walsh	9	22	–
M.Amarnath	c Logie b Richards	23	42	1
M.Azharuddin	c and b Richards	18	18	1
R.J.Shastri	c R.C.Haynes b Richards	20	25	–/1
Kapil Dev	c D.L.Haynes b Richards	7	7	1
M.Prabhakar	run out	1	8	–
† K.S.More	lbw b Richards	0	1	–
C.Sharma	not out	7	9	–
Arshad Ayub	b Richards	5	6	–
Extras	(b 1, lb 7, w 4, nb 3)	15		
Total	(41.4 overs)	**176**		

INDIA	O	M	R	W
Kapil Dev	8	1	23	1
Prabhakar	9	1	26	1
Sharma	9	0	46	3
Amarnath	10	0	34	1
Arshad Ayub	9	0	55	2

WEST INDIES	O	M	R	W
Ambrose	7	1	19	0
Benjamin	7	0	31	0
Walsh	9	1	37	2
Marshall	9	0	40	1
Richards	9.4	0	41	6

FALL OF WICKETS
1-11, 2-44, 3-65, 4-131, 5-139, 6-168, 7-177, 8-183, 9-185

FALL OF WICKETS
1-29, 2-74, 3-91, 4-115, 5-143, 6-158, 7-160, 8-160, 9-165, 10-176

Umpires: K.T.Francis (*Sri Lanka*) (10) and J.W.Holder (*England*) (4).

INDIA v ENGLAND 1989-90

At Green Park, Kanpur on 25 October 1989.　Result: **INDIA** won by 6 wickets.　Toss: India.
Award: C.Sharma.　LOI debuts: None.

Chetan Sharma completed his first hundred in any class of cricket with a boundary to win the match. Allan Lamb, who completed 3000 runs, added 130 with Alec Stewart to set England's highest fourth-wicket partnership against India.

ENGLAND		Runs	Balls	4/6
*G.A.Gooch	c Azharuddin b C.Sharma	21	33	2
W.Larkins	lbw b A.K.Sharma	42	68	3
R.A.Smith	c Azharuddin b Prabhakar	0	5	–
A.J.Lamb	c Srikkanth b C.Sharma	91	109	6
A.J.Stewart	run out	61	80	5/1
D.J.Capel	b Kapil Dev	2	3	–
P.A.J.DeFreitas	c Azharuddin b Kapil Dev	11	7	2
†R.C.Russell	not out	10	6	2
G.C.Small	not out	0	–	–
E.E.Hemmings				
A.R.C.Fraser				
Extras	(lb 7, w 7, nb 3)	17		
Total	(50 overs; 7 wickets)	**255**		

INDIA		Runs	Balls	4/6
*K.Srikkanth	st Russell b Hemmings	32	48	5
R.Lamba	c Russell b Small	16	38	–
N.S.Sidhu	run out	61	67	2/1
C.Sharma	not out	101	96	8/1
D.B.Vengsarkar	c Larkins b DeFreitas	31	45	4
Kapil Dev	not out	4	1	1
M.Azharuddin				
A.K.Sharma				
†K.S.More				
M.Prabhakar				
Arshad Ayub				
Extras	(lb 6, w 6, nb 2)	14		
Total	(48.1 overs; 4 wickets)	**259**		

INDIA	O	M	R	W
Kapil Dev	10	0	56	2
Prabhakar	10	0	50	1
C.Sharma	10	0	78	2
Arshad Ayub	10	0	27	0
A.K.Sharma	10	1	37	1

ENGLAND	O	M	R	W
Fraser	10	2	31	0
DeFreitas	10	0	66	1
Hemmings	10	0	51	1
Small	10	0	44	1
Capel	3	0	24	0
Gooch	5.1	0	37	0

FALL OF WICKETS
1-43, 2-48, 3-80, 4-210, 5-219, 6-239, 7-251

FALL OF WICKETS
1-41, 2-65, 3-170, 4-251

Umpires: K.T.Francis (*Sri Lanka*) (11) and Khizer Hayat (*Pakistan*) (26).

WEST INDIES v PAKISTAN 1989-90

At Burlton Park, Jullundur on 25 October 1989.　Result: **WEST INDIES** won by 6 wickets.　Toss: Pakistan.
Award: R.B.Richardson.　LOI debuts: None.

Originally scheduled for Chandigarh, this match was moved at late notice to an area in which the political instability constituted a serious security risk. Aamer Malik enjoyed a fine all-round match the day after arriving as replacement for the damaged Salim Yousuf.

PAKISTAN		Runs	Balls	4/6
Ramiz Raja	b Ambrose	14		1
Shoaib Mohammed	c Richards b Marshall	12		1
†Aamer Malik	run out	77	106	7
Javed Miandad	c Haynes b Ambrose	39		–/1
Salim Malik	not out	44	29	6
*Imran Khan	c Richards b Benjamin	24		2
Ijaz Ahmed				
Wasim Akram				
Abdul Qadir				
Mushtaq Ahmed				
Waqar Younis				
Extras	(b 5, lb 5, w 3)	13		
Total	(50 overs; 5 wickets)	**223**		

WEST INDIES		Runs	Balls	4/6
D.L.Haynes	b Wasim	4		–
P.V.Simmons	lbw b Wasim	16		2
R.B.Richardson	st Aamer b Qadir	80	116	4
†P.J.L.Dujon	st Aamer b Qadir	46		4
*I.V.A.Richards	not out	47	48	4
A.L.Logie	not out	12		2
K.L.T.Arthurton				
M.D.Marshall				
W.K.M.Benjamin				
C.E.L.Ambrose				
C.A.Walsh				
Extras	(b 2, lb 15, w 3, nb 1)	21		
Total	(48.3 overs; 4 wickets)	**226**		

WEST INDIES	O	M	R	W
Ambrose	10	0	45	2
Benjamin	10	0	45	1
Walsh	10	2	17	0
Marshall	10	1	51	1
Richards	7	0	38	0
Simmons	3	0	17	0

PAKISTAN	O	M	R	W
Wasim Akram	9.3	1	38	2
Waqar Younis	10	0	48	0
Mushtaq Ahmed	10	2	33	0
Imran Khan	5	1	22	0
Abdul Qadir	10	0	48	2
Shoaib Mohammed	4	0	20	0

FALL OF WICKETS
1-23, 2-27, 3-148, 4-164, 5-223

FALL OF WICKETS
1-21, 2-33, 3-127, 4-191

Umpires: J.W.Holder (*England*) (5) and V.K.Ramaswamy (16).

AUSTRALIA v SRI LANKA 1989-90

At Fatorda Stadium, Margao on 25 October 1989.   Result: **AUSTRALIA** won by 28 runs.   Toss: Australia.
Award: P.A.de Silva.   LOI debuts: Sri Lanka – T.L.Fernando.

A football stadium, which had never staged a first-class match, situated in the former Portuguese colony of Goa, became the 88th LOI venue and India's 29th. Built in under seven months, it boasted floodlights, a seating capacity of 40,000 and the best outfield in India.

AUSTRALIA		Runs	Balls	4/6
G.R.Marsh	run out	38	81	2
D.C.Boon	lbw b Fernando	19	43	2
D.M.Jones	lbw b Labrooy	85	101	7/2
* A.R.Border	b Labrooy	26	25	1/1
S.R.Waugh	run out	2	4	–
T.M.Moody	b Labrooy	12	25	–
S.P.O'Donnell	not out	6	11	–
† I.A.Healy	run out	3	7	–
M.G.Hughes	not out	8	6	1
G.F.Lawson				
T.M.Alderman				
Extras	(b 4, lb 10, w 8, nb 1)	23		
Total	(50 overs; 7 wickets)	**222**		

SRI LANKA		Runs	Balls	4/6
R.S.Mahanama	lbw b Alderman	5	9	–
† D.S.B.P.Kuruppu	b Hughes	13	47	1
A.P.Gurusinha	c Boon b Lawson	13	30	3
P.A.de Silva	b O'Donnell	96	107	7/3
J.R.Ratnayeke	run out	2	9	–
* A.Ranatunga	c Waugh b Border	15	29	–
H.P.Tillekeratne	c Boon b O'Donnell	24	40	2
T.L.Fernando	c Alderman b O'Donnell	8	6	–
G.F.Labrooy	run out	1	2	–
E.A.R.de Silva	not out	7	7	–
K.I.W.Wijegunawardene	b Lawson	0	1	–
Extras	(b 2, lb 2, w 4, nb 2)	10		
Total	(47.1 overs)	**194**		

SRI LANKA	O	M	R	W
Ratnayeke	9	1	34	0
Labrooy	10	1	38	3
Wijegunawardene	10	0	40	0
Fernando	3	0	16	1
E.A.R.de Silva	7	0	30	0
P.A.de Silva	9	0	36	0
Ranatunga	2	0	14	0

AUSTRALIA	O	M	R	W
Alderman	9	1	41	1
Lawson	8.1	2	23	2
Hughes	10	0	39	1
O'Donnell	10	1	48	3
Border	10	0	39	1

FALL OF WICKETS
1-40, 2-105, 3-160, 4-165, 5-190, 6-205, 7-210

FALL OF WICKETS
1-7, 2-21, 3-54, 4-74, 5-103, 6-166, 7-179, 8-182, 9-191, 10-194

Umpires: L.H.Barker (West Indies) (11) and P.D.Reporter (5).

ENGLAND v WEST INDIES 1989-90

At Roop Singh Stadium, Gwalior on 27 October 1989.   Result: **WEST INDIES** won by 26 runs.   Toss: West Indies.
Award: D.L.Haynes.   LOI debuts: None.

Desmond Haynes extended his record number of LOI hundreds to 15 and batted through a complete complement of overs for the sixth time. Malcolm Marshall's fifth four-wicket haul carried West Indies into the semi-finals.

WEST INDIES		Runs	Balls	4/6
D.L.Haynes	not out	138	164	12/2
P.V.Simmons	run out	13	30	1
R.B.Richardson	run out	44	56	4
* I.V.A.Richards	c Hemmings b Small	16	13	3
A.L.Logie	c Stewart b Small	17	23	3
M.D.Marshall	c Smith b Small	16	15	1
R.C.Haynes	not out	0	–	–
† P.J.L.Dujon				
W.K.M.Benjamin				
C.E.L.Ambrose				
C.A.Walsh				
Extras	(lb 10, w 9, nb 2)	21		
Total	(50 overs; 5 wickets)	**265**		

ENGLAND		Runs	Balls	4/6
* G.A.Gooch	c Dujon b Marshall	59	106	4
W.Larkins	c sub ‡ b Marshall	29	48	2
R.A.Smith	c Dujon b Marshall	65	74	7/1
A.J.Lamb	b Marshall	0	1	–
A.J.Stewart	c Logie b Simmons	20	21	1/1
D.J.Capel	b Benjamin	21	23	2
P.A.J.DeFreitas	c sub ‡ b Walsh	7	13	–
† R.C.Russell	not out	8	9	–
G.C.Small	b Benjamin	4	8	–
E.E.Hemmings	not out	1	1	–
A.R.C.Fraser				
Extras	(b 1, lb 13, w 11)	25		
Total	(50 overs; 8 wickets)	**239**		

ENGLAND	O	M	R	W
Fraser	10	1	47	0
DeFreitas	10	1	42	0
Capel	8	0	49	0
Small	10	0	39	3
Hemmings	7	0	44	0
Gooch	5	0	34	0

WEST INDIES	O	M	R	W
Ambrose	10	0	33	0
Benjamin	10	1	46	2
Walsh	10	0	41	1
Marshall	10	0	33	4
R.C.Haynes	4	0	25	0
Richards	5	0	44	0
Simmons	1	0	3	1

FALL OF WICKETS
1-31, 2-155, 3-188, 4-236, 5-264

FALL OF WICKETS
1-58, 2-150, 3-150, 4-189, 5-191, 6-209, 7-229, 8-238

Umpires: S.K.Ghosh (6) and V.K.Ramaswamy (17).

‡ (K.L.T.Arthurton)

AUSTRALIA v INDIA 1989-90

At Chinnaswamy Stadium, Bangalore on 27 October 1989.   Result: **INDIA** won by 3 wickets.   Toss: Australia.
Award: A.K.Sharma.   LOI debuts: None.

Buoyed by a crowd in excess of 50,000 and their highest opening stand in a home international against Australia, the hosts gained their place in the semi-finals. Greg Matthews had arrived in India as Tim May's replacement the previous afternoon.

AUSTRALIA		Runs	Balls	4/6
D.C.Boon	c Srikkanth b Amarnath	49	60	6
G.R.Marsh	st More b A.K.Sharma	27	48	I
D.M.Jones	c More b A.K.Sharma	53	77	1/1
* A.R.Border	b A.K.Sharma	41	46	4
S.R.Waugh	c A.K.Sharma b Kapil Dev	28	24	3
G.R.J.Matthews	lbw b Kapil Dev	5	8	–
S.P.O'Donnell	c sub (R.J.Shastri) b Prabhakar	17	19	1/1
† I.A.Healy	not out	14	13	–
M.G.Hughes	run out	I	2	–
G.F.Lawson	not out	3	3	–
T.M.Alderman				
Extras	(b 1, lb 7, w 1)	9		
Total	(50 overs; 8 wickets)	**247**		

INDIA		Runs	Balls	4/6
* K.Srikkanth	c O'Donnell b Matthews	58	65	6/1
R.Lamba	lbw b Matthews	57	92	5
M.Amarnath	b Matthews	5	5	I
D.B.Vengsarkar	c Boon b Lawson	25	43	2
M.Azharuddin	c and b Border	8	4	I
A.K.Sharma	c Waugh b Border	32	26	1/3
Kapil Dev	c Healy b Lawson	9	11	–
C.Sharma	not out	20	23	1/1
M.Prabhakar	not out	16	25	2
† K.S.More				
Arshad Ayub				
Extras	(lb 11, w 7, nb 1)	19		
Total	(47.1 overs; 7 wickets)	**249**		

INDIA	O	M	R	W
Prabhakar	7	I	35	I
Kapil Dev	10	0	49	2
C.Sharma	3	0	22	0
Amarnath	10	0	43	I
Arshad Ayub	10	0	49	0
A.K.Sharma	10	0	41	3

AUSTRALIA	O	M	R	W
Alderman	6	2	23	0
Lawson	10	I	39	2
Hughes	6	0	27	0
O'Donnell	5.1	0	42	0
Matthews	10	0	56	3
Border	10	0	51	2

FALL OF WICKETS
1-59, 2-109, 3-165, 4-188, 5-203, 6-214, 7-233, 8-236

FALL OF WICKETS
1-115, 2-122, 3-132, 4-141, 5-191, 6-199, 7-209

Umpires: L.H.Barker (*West Indies*) (12) and Khizer Hayat (*Pakistan*) (27).

PAKISTAN v SRI LANKA 1989-90

At K.D.'Babu' Singh Stadium, Lucknow on 27 October 1989.   Result: **PAKISTAN** won by 6 runs.   Toss: Pakistan.
Award: Imran Khan.   LOI debuts: None.

Lucknow provided the 89th LOI venue and 30th in India. After a (then) national record third-wicket partnership of 150 between Hashan Tillekeratne and Aravinda de Silva, Sri Lanka lost their last six wickets for 11 runs, the final four in the space of eight balls.

PAKISTAN		Runs	Balls	4/6
Ramiz Raja	run out	17	36	3
Shoaib Mohammed	b E.A.R.de Silva	11	42	I
Ijaz Ahmed	c Kuruppu b Wijegunawardene	0	I	–
Salim Malik	c Ranatunga b P.A.de Silva	27	37	–
* Imran Khan	not out	84	110	3
Abdul Qadir	c and b P.A.de Silva	18	28	–
Wasim Akram	b Labrooy	29	29	–
† Aamer Malik	not out	19	17	I
Akram Raza				
Mushtaq Ahmed				
Waqar Younis				
Extras	(b 3, lb 6, w 5)	14		
Total	(50 overs; 6 wickets)	**219**		

SRI LANKA		Runs	Balls	4/6
† D.S.B.P.Kuruppu	b Waqar	8	26	–
H.P.Tillekeratne	run out	71	131	1/1
A.P.Gurusinha	c and b Akram Raza	8	30	I
P.A.de Silva	c Salim Malik b Akram Raza	83	90	5/2
M.A.R.Samarasekera	b Qadir	3	6	–
* A.Ranatunga	run out	5	3	–
R.S.Mahanama	b Qadir	11	7	–/1
J.R.Ratnayeke	b Wasim	0	I	–
G.F.Labrooy	b Wasim	0	I	–
E.A.R.de Silva	run out	0	I	–
K.I.W.Wijegunawardene	not out	0	–	–
Extras	(b 3, lb 17, w 4)	24		
Total	(49.2 overs)	**213**		

SRI LANKA	O	M	R	W
Ratnayeke	10	2	48	0
Labrooy	10	0	52	I
Wijegunawardene	10	I	36	I
E.A.R.de Silva	10	2	31	I
P.A.de Silva	10	0	43	2

PAKISTAN	O	M	R	W
Waqar Younis	6	2	14	I
Wasim Akram	10	I	30	2
Akram Raza	10	0	34	2
Mushtaq Ahmed	8	I	39	0
Abdul Qadir	7.2	0	36	2
Imran Khan	7	0	29	0
Shoaib Mohammed	I	0	11	0

FALL OF WICKETS
1-30, 2-30, 3-32, 4-70, 5-115, 6-172

FALL OF WICKETS
1-18, 2-37, 3-187, 4-194, 5-202, 6-202, 7-212, 8-212, 9-213, 10-213

Umpires: R.B.Gupta (18) and P.J.McConnell (*Australia*) (49).

INDIA v PAKISTAN 1989-90

At Eden Gardens, Calcutta on 28 October 1989.   Result: **PAKISTAN** won by 77 runs.   Toss: India.
Award: Imran Khan.   LOI debuts: None.

Pakistan defended the highest total of the tournament to gain the last semi-final place at the expense of Australia. India, England, Pakistan and West Indies headed the qualifying table with 12 points apiece, their precedence decided by run-rate.

PAKISTAN		Runs	Balls	4/6
Ramiz Raja	c Kapil Dev b Srikkanth	77	90	4/1
† Aamer Malik	c A.K.Sharma b Amarnath	51	83	5
Salim Malik	c Srikkanth b A.K.Sharma	14	13	1
Javed Miandad	lbw b Arshad Ayub	13	23	–
Ijaz Ahmed	c Lamba b Kapil Dev	29	33	2/1
Abdul Qadir	c Vengsarkar b Arshad Ayub	17	14	2/1
* Imran Khan	not out	47	39	2/2
Wasim Akram	lbw b Prabhakar	1	3	–
Akram Raza	not out	9	9	1
Mushtaq Ahmed				
Aqib Javed				
Extras	(b 4, lb 11, w 5, nb 1)	21		
Total	(50 overs; 7 wickets)	279		

INDIA		Runs	Balls	4/6
* K.Srikkanth	run out	65	75	6
R.Lamba	c Aqib b Qadir	57	63	4/3
M.Amarnath	c Qadir b Mushtaq	20	36	1
D.B.Vengsarkar	c Imran b Akram Raza	10	19	–
C.Sharma	c sub ‡ b Mushtaq	10	16	–
A.K.Sharma	b Mushtaq	1	5	–
Kapil Dev	b Wasim	17	17	1/1
S.V.Manjrekar	run out	1	6	–
M.Prabhakar	not out	7	15	–
† K.S.More	b Aqib	2	3	–
Arshad Ayub	lbw b Wasim	0	1	–
Extras	(b 1, lb 8, w 3)	12		
Total	(42.3 overs)	202		

INDIA	O	M	R	W
Kapil Dev	10	0	60	1
Prabhakar	9	0	41	1
C.Sharma	5	0	23	0
Amarnath	10	0	45	1
A.K.Sharma	5	0	38	1
Arshad Ayub	7	1	31	2
Srikkanth	4	0	26	1

PAKISTAN	O	M	R	W
Wasim Akram	7.3	0	21	2
Aqib Javed	7	1	32	1
Akram Raza	10	1	47	1
Mushtaq Ahmed	10	0	51	3
Abdul Qadir	8	0	42	1

FALL OF WICKETS
1-97, 2-125, 3-165, 4-165, 5-196, 6-242, 7-243

FALL OF WICKETS
1-120, 2-132, 3-155, 4-166, 5-171, 6-176, 7-189, 8-196, 9-201, 10-202

‡ (Shoaib Mohammed)

Umpires: K.T.Francis (*Sri Lanka*) (12) and J.W.Holder (*England*) (6).

ENGLAND v PAKISTAN 1989-90

At Vidarbha CA Ground, Nagpur on 30 October 1989.   Result: **PAKISTAN** won by 6 wickets.   Toss: Pakistan.
Award: Ramiz Raja.   LOI debuts: England – N.Hussain.

Overnight rain delayed the start by 220 minutes and reduced the overs to 30 each. Ramiz Raja and Salim Malik, the latter batting throughout with a runner and reaching 50 off 36 balls, added 122 from only 78 balls in a national record fourth-wicket stand against England.

ENGLAND		Runs	Balls	4/6
* G.A.Gooch	c sub ‡ b Waqar	35	43	3
W.Larkins	c and b Akram Raza	25	31	2
R.A.Smith	b Qadir	55	57	4/2
† A.J.Stewart	b Waqar	0	2	–
N.Hussain	lbw b Qadir	2	12	–
A.J.Lamb	c Aamer b Qadir	6	7	–
D.J.Capel	run out	20	21	3
D.R.Pringle	not out	21	17	–/1
P.A.J.DeFreitas	not out	4	2	
G.C.Small				
A.R.C.Fraser				
Extras	(b 3, lb 20, w 3)	26		
Total	(30 overs; 7 wickets)	194		

PAKISTAN		Runs	Balls	4/6
Ramiz Raja	not out	85	82	8
Javed Miandad	b DeFreitas	17	14	3
Ijaz Ahmed	c Smith b DeFreitas	2	5	–
* Imran Khan	lbw b Small	15	32	–
Salim Malik	c Lamb b Fraser	66	41	6/3
Wasim Akram	not out	0	1	–
† Aamer Malik				
Abdul Qadir				
Akram Raza				
Mushtaq Ahmed				
Waqar Younis				
Extras	(lb 10)	10		
Total	(28.3 overs; 4 wickets)	195		

PAKISTAN	O	M	R	W
Imran Khan	4	0	26	0
Wasim Akram	6	0	28	0
Akram Raza	5	0	28	1
Waqar Younis	6	1	40	2
Mushtaq Ahmed	3	0	19	0
Abdul Qadir	6	0	30	3

ENGLAND	O	M	R	W
Fraser	6	0	58	1
DeFreitas	6	0	40	2
Capel	6	0	24	0
Pringle	5	0	33	0
Small	5.3	0	30	1

FALL OF WICKETS
1-44, 2-102, 3-103, 4-136, 5-144, 6-145, 7-184

FALL OF WICKETS
1-26, 2-32, 3-69, 4-191

‡ (Shoaib Mohammed)

Umpires: R.B.Gupta (19) and V.K.Ramaswamy (18).

INDIA v WEST INDIES 1989-90

At Wankhede Stadium, Bombay on 30 October 1989.   Result: **WEST INDIES** won by 8 wickets.   Toss: India.
Award: I.V.A.Richards.   LOI debuts: None.

To the immense disappointment of their vast population, the host nation failed to take advantage of an excellent batting surface, Courtney Walsh taking three key wickets on his 27th birthday. Adjudicator Asif Iqbal confounded all with his choice of match award.

INDIA		Runs	Balls	4/6
* K.Srikkanth	run out	1	10	–
R.Lamba	c Richardson b Walsh	29	45	4
M.Amarnath	b Walsh	15	47	2
D.B.Vengsarkar	c Richards b Walsh	8	28	–
M.Azharuddin	c Haynes b Simmons	38	56	3
Kapil Dev	lbw b Ambrose	19	35	4
A.K.Sharma	b Benjamin	15	23	–/1
M.Prabhakar	c Richards b Marshall	4	12	–
C.Sharma	c Richards b Benjamin	12	21	1
† K.S.More	not out	5	18	–
Arshad Ayub	c Marshall b Ambrose	3	12	–
Extras	(b 3, w 11, nb 2)	16		
Total	**(48.5 overs)**	**165**		

WEST INDIES		Runs	Balls	4/6
D.L.Haynes	lbw b Kapil Dev	64	100	7
P.V.Simmons	lbw b Kapil Dev	11	26	1
R.B.Richardson	not out	58	110	5
† P.J.L.Dujon	not out	20	25	3
* I.V.A.Richards				
K.L.T.Arthurton				
A.L.Logie				
M.D.Marshall				
W.K.M.Benjamin				
C.E.L.Ambrose				
C.A.Walsh				
Extras	(b 2, lb 4, w 3, nb 4)	13		
Total	**(42.1 overs; 2 wickets)**	**166**		

WEST INDIES	O	M	R	W
Ambrose	8.5	0	13	2
Benjamin	9	2	34	2
Walsh	10	0	39	3
Marshall	10	2	19	1
Richards	4	0	21	0
Simmons	7	0	36	1

INDIA	O	M	R	W
Kapil Dev	8	0	31	2
Prabhakar	4	0	21	0
Arshad Ayub	10	2	29	0
A.K.Sharma	10	2	30	0
Srikkanth	7	1	30	0
Azharuddin	3	0	17	0
Lamba	0.1	0	2	0

FALL OF WICKETS
1-3, 2-50, 3-55, 4-76, 5-107, 6-131, 7-141, 8-151, 9-159, 10-165

FALL OF WICKETS
1-22, 2-139

Umpires: J.W.Holder (*England*) (7) and P.J.McConnell (*Australia*) (50).

WEST INDIES v PAKISTAN 1989-90

At Eden Gardens, Calcutta on 1 November 1989.   Result: **PAKISTAN** won by 4 wickets.   Toss: West Indies.
Award: Imran Khan.   LOI debuts: None.

A crowd in excess of 70,000 saw Pakistan win the Nehru Cup and $US40,000 when Wasim Akram struck the penultimate ball for six. Desmond Haynes batted throughout an LOI innings for the seventh time and extended his record tally of hundreds to 16.

WEST INDIES		Runs	Balls	4/6
D.L.Haynes	not out	107	137	12
P.V.Simmons	c Ijaz b Mushtaq	40	69	3/1
R.B.Richardson	b Akram Raza	27	41	3
* I.V.A.Richards	c Mushtaq b Imran	21	12	2/1
† P.J.L.Dujon	c Qadir b Imran	28	25	4
A.L.Logie	c sub ‡ b Imran	14	8	2
M.D.Marshall	not out	10	9	2
R.C.Haynes				
W.K.M.Benjamin				
C.E.L.Ambrose				
C.A.Walsh				
Extras	(b 11, lb 14, w 1)	26		
Total	**(50 overs; 5 wickets)**	**273**		

PAKISTAN		Runs	Balls	4/6
† Aamer Malik	c Dujon b Benjamin	3	4	–
Ramiz Raja	c Logie b Walsh	35	31	6
Ijaz Ahmed	run out	56	66	7
Javed Miandad	c Richards b Benjamin	17	36	–
Salim Malik	c Dujon b Ambrose	71	62	6/1
* Imran Khan	not out	55	75	4
Akram Raza	run out	19	30	1
Wasim Akram	not out	6	1	–/1
Abdul Qadir				
Mushtaq Ahmed				
Aqib Javed				
Extras	(lb 4, w 10, nb 1)	15		
Total	**(49.5 overs; 6 wickets)**	**277**		

PAKISTAN	O	M	R	W
Aqib Javed	10	2	25	0
Wasim Akram	10	1	46	0
Akram Raza	5	0	26	1
Mushtaq Ahmed	9	0	55	1
Abdul Qadir	7	0	49	0
Imran Khan	9	0	47	3

WEST INDIES	O	M	R	W
Ambrose	10	0	41	1
Benjamin	10	0	71	2
Marshall	10	0	43	0
Walsh	10	0	55	1
R.C.Haynes	3	0	21	0
Richards	6.5	0	42	0

FALL OF WICKETS
1-83, 2-144, 3-175, 4-221, 5-244

FALL OF WICKETS
1-4, 2-64, 3-110, 4-133, 5-226, 6-270

Umpires: S.K.Ghosh (7) and P.D.Reporter (6).

‡ (Shoaib Mohammed)

PAKISTAN v INDIA 1989-90

At Municipal Stadium, Gujranwala on 18 December 1989.   Result: **PAKISTAN** won by 7 runs.   Toss: India.
Award: Saeed Anwar.   LOI debuts: India – S.A.Ankola, V.Razdan, S.R.Tendulkar.

Rain and bad light caused the first match, at Peshawar on 16 December, to be abandoned without a ball bowled. Similar conditions delayed this start by three hours, India failing to bowl their 20 overs in the allotted 85 minutes. Of the debutants, Salil Ankola hit his first ball for six but Sachin Tendulkar, 16 years 237 days, was out second ball.

PAKISTAN		Runs	Balls	4/6	INDIA		Runs	Balls	4/6
Mansoor Akhtar	run out	18	27	2	* K.Srikkanth	b Waqar	18	20	2
Ramiz Raja	c Sidhu b Maninder	10	17	–	R.Lamba	run out	9	19	1
Salim Malik	c Azharuddin b Maninder	0	3	–	N.S.Sidhu	c Mansoor b Aqib	2	6	–
Wasim Akram	run out	2	3	–	M.Azharuddin	c Salim b Aqib	21	19	2
Saeed Anwar	not out	42	32	4/2	S.R.Tendulkar	c Wasim b Waqar	0	2	–
Javed Miandad	run out	1	2	–	R.J.Shastri	b Waqar	1	6	–
* Imran Khan	c Srikkanth b Ankola	1	6	–	M.Prabhakar	lbw b Imran	10	11	1
Abdul Qadir	lbw b Lamba	0	1	–	† K.S.More	c Qadir b Imran	2	6	–
† Zulqarnain	c Prabhakar b Ankola	2	4	–	V.Razdan	b Imran	1	4	–
Waqar Younis	run out	3	3	–	S.A.Ankola	not out	7	3	–/1
Aqib Javed					Maninder Singh	not out	0	1	–
Extras	(lb 4, w 2, nb 2)	8			Extras	(b 2, lb 5, w 2)	9		
Total	(16 overs; 9 wickets)	**87**			**Total**	(16 overs; 9 wickets)	**80**		

INDIA	O	M	R	W	PAKISTAN	O	M	R	W
Prabhakar	3	0	8	0	Wasim Akram	4	0	16	0
Razdan	2	0	9	0	Imran Khan	4	0	18	3
Ankola	4	0	26	2	Waqar Younis	4	0	21	3
Maninder Singh	4	0	17	2	Aqib Javed	4	0	18	2
Lamba	2	0	9	1					
Shastri	1	0	14	0					

FALL OF WICKETS (PAKISTAN side)

FALL OF WICKETS
1-26, 2-32, 3-34, 4-36, 5-51, 6-59, 7-68, 8-73, 9-80

FALL OF WICKETS
1-20, 2-22, 3-29, 4-52, 5-59, 6-65, 7-68, 8-75, 9-87

Umpires: Mian Mohammad Aslam (6) and Feroz Butt (2).

PAKISTAN v INDIA 1989-90

At National Stadium, Karachi on 20 December 1989.   No result.   Toss: India.
LOI debuts: None.

By resorting to tear gas and a baton charge, Karachi's police converted crowd disturbances into a full-scale riot which, for the second time (also *LOI No. 161*), compelled an abandonment. Manoj Prabhakar took wickets with the last two balls of his opening over.

PAKISTAN		Runs	Balls	4/6	INDIA	
Ramiz Raja	lbw b Prabhakar	0	5	–	* K.Srikkanth	
Shoaib Mohammed	not out	13	32	–	R.Lamba	
Salim Malik	b Prabhakar	0	1	–	N.S.Sidhu	
Javed Miandad	lbw b Prabhakar	2	20	–	M.Azharuddin	
* Imran Khan	not out	9	28	–	S.V.Manjrekar	
Saeed Anwar					R.J.Shastri	
Wasim Akram					Kapil Dev	
Abdul Qadir					M.Prabhakar	
† Zulqarnain					† K.S.More	
Waqar Younis					S.A.Ankola	
Aqib Javed					Maninder Singh	
Extras	(lb 2, w 2)	4				
Total	(14.3 overs; 3 wickets)	**28**				

INDIA	O	M	R	W
Prabhakar	5	2	5	3
Kapil Dev	7	1	14	0
Ankola	2.3	0	7	0

FALL OF WICKETS
1-0, 2-0, 3-11

Umpires: Salim Badar (4) and Mahboob Shah (23).

PAKISTAN v INDIA 1989-90

At Gaddafi Stadium, Lahore on 22 December 1989.　　Result: **PAKISTAN** won by 38 runs.　　Toss: India.
Award: Aqib Javed.　　LOI debuts: None.

Pakistan again demonstrated their superiority over their arch-rivals in a match shortened by overnight rain. Krish Srikkanth was surprisingly recalled by the Pakistan captain after being adjudged lbw, only to be caught off the very next ball.

PAKISTAN		Runs	Balls	4/6
Shoaib Mohammed	run out	26	63	–
Ramiz Raja	c Maninder b Shastri	24	32	3
Saeed Anwar	run out	7	11	–
Salim Malik	c Razdan b Ankola	30	43	–
Wasim Akram	b Maninder	1	2	–
Javed Miandad	c Sidhu b Razdan	30	52	2
* Imran Khan	c Sidhu b Prabhakar	14	12	1
† Salim Yousuf	c Razdan b Prabhakar	3	4	–
Abdul Qadir	not out	0	4	–
Waqar Younis	not out	2	2	–
Aqib Javed				
Extras	(lb 6, w 5, nb 2)	13		
Total	(37 overs; 8 wickets)	**150**		

INDIA		Runs	Balls	4/6
* K.Srikkanth	c Salim Yousuf b Waqar	31	63	2
R.Lamba	lbw b Imran	7	24	1
N.S.Sidhu	c and b Imran	2	7	–
S.V.Manjrekar	c Salim Yousuf b Aqib	13	24	1
M.Azharuddin	c Saeed b Aqib	4	9	–
R.J.Shastri	run out	12	22	1
M.Prabhakar	b Aqib	0	1	–
† K.S.More	c Qadir b Wasim	6	10	–
S.A.Ankola	c Salim Yousuf b Wasim	0	1	–
V.Razdan	st Salim Yousuf b Qadir	18	19	3
Maninder Singh	not out	2	3	–
Extras	(b 4, lb 4, w 9)	17		
Total	(30.2 overs)	**112**		

INDIA	O	M	R	W
Prabhakar	8	0	24	2
Razdan	8	0	37	1
Ankola	4	1	20	1
Lamba	1	0	9	0
Maninder Singh	8	1	25	1
Shastri	8	0	29	1

PAKISTAN	O	M	R	W
Imran Khan	5	1	11	2
Wasim Akram	7	1	26	2
Aqib Javed	8	1	28	3
Waqar Younis	7	0	27	1
Abdul Qadir	3.2	0	12	1

FALL OF WICKETS
1-45, 2-57, 3-68, 4-72, 5-106, 6-131, 7-144, 8-145

FALL OF WICKETS
1-15, 2-18, 3-49, 4-66, 5-70, 6-70, 7-82, 8-82, 9-90, 10-112

Umpires: Khalid Aziz (5) and Shakoor Rana (19).

AUSTRALIA v SRI LANKA 1989-90

At Melbourne Cricket Ground on 26 December 1989.　　Result: **AUSTRALIA** won by 30 runs.　　Toss: Sri Lanka.
Award: S.P.O'Donnell.　　LOI debuts: Australia – G.D.Campbell, M.A.Taylor; Sri Lanka – S.T.Jayasuriya.

Dean Jones and Simon O'Donnell added an unbroken 108 off 98 balls to post Australia's first three-figure partnership for the sixth wicket. O'Donnell's 57 runs, four wickets, a catch and a run out left the adjudicator with a sinecure.

AUSTRALIA		Runs	Balls	4/6
M.A.Taylor	c and b Ratnayeke	11	25	–/1
G.R.Marsh	c P.A.de Silva b Ranatunga	38	82	2
D.C.Boon	c Jayasuriya b Ratnayake	11	19	–
D.M.Jones	not out	85	89	4/1
* A.R.Border	c Samarasekera b Ranatunga	11	15	1
S.R.Waugh	c Tillekeratne b Ranatunga	5	7	–
S.P.O'Donnell	not out	57	60	3/1
† I.A.Healy				
P.L.Taylor				
M.G.Hughes				
G.D.Campbell				
Extras	(lb 6, w 2, nb 2)	10		
Total	(48.5 overs; 5 wickets)	**228**		

SRI LANKA		Runs	Balls	4/6
R.S.Mahanama	c Border b Waugh	36	67	3
M.A.R.Samarasekera	c Hughes b O'Donnell	30	50	2
* A.Ranatunga	c Healy b O'Donnell	55	70	3
P.A.de Silva	c Border b P.L.Taylor	9	10	1
S.T.Jayasuriya	c Campbell b Hughes	3	5	–
A.P.Gurusinha	c O'Donnell b P.L.Taylor	22	40	–
† H.P.Tillekeratne	c Healy b O'Donnell	11	23	–
J.R.Ratnayeke	run out	0	2	–
E.A.R.de Silva	not out	13	17	–
G.F.Labrooy	b O'Donnell	6	2	–/1
R.J.Ratnayake	c Healy b Hughes	0	1	–
Extras	(lb 6, w 4, nb 3)	13		
Total	(47.2 overs)	**198**		

SRI LANKA	O	M	R	W
Labrooy	9	0	40	0
Ratnayeke	9	1	47	1
Ratnayake	9.5	0	43	1
Ranatunga	10	2	41	3
E.A.R.de Silva	10	0	42	0
Gurusinha	1	0	9	0

AUSTRALIA	O	M	R	W
Hughes	9.2	0	41	2
Campbell	10	2	36	0
O'Donnell	9	1	36	4
Waugh	6	0	26	1
P.L.Taylor	10	1	36	2
Border	3	0	17	0

FALL OF WICKETS
1-17, 2-42, 3-88, 4-106, 5-120

FALL OF WICKETS
1-59, 2-85, 3-101, 4-109, 5-161, 6-169, 7-169, 8-190, 9-197, 10-198

Umpires: L.J.King (7) and C.D.Timmins (5).

AUSTRALIA v SRI LANKA 1989-90

At WACA Ground, Perth on 30 December 1989.   Result: **AUSTRALIA** won by 9 wickets.   Toss: Sri Lanka.
Award: G.R.Marsh.   LOI debuts: None.

Two overs were deducted from each innings when the groundstaff forgot to mark out the fielding circles and there were further delays for repairs to a sound effects microphone in a stump, and more entertainingly, for a bouncy female wearing a tattoo.

SRI LANKA		Runs	Balls	4/6
R.S.Mahanama	lbw b Alderman	27	45	5
M.A.R.Samarasekera	c Alderman b Hughes	5	8	1
A.P.Gurusinha	c Healy b Alderman	0	3	–
† H.P.Tillekeratne	c Jones b O'Donnell	13	44	1
P.A.de Silva	c Border b Campbell	4	5	1
* A.Ranatunga	not out	71	106	7
S.T.Jayasuriya	c Healy b O'Donnell	13	16	–
J.R.Ratnayeke	lbw b Alderman	25	50	2
G.F.Labrooy	b Waugh	1	5	–
R.J.Ratnayake	c Waugh b O'Donnell	19	21	1/1
K.I.W.Wijegunawardene				
Extras	(lb 8, w 15, nb 2)	25		
Total	(48 overs; 9 wickets)	**203**		

AUSTRALIA		Runs	Balls	4/6
G.R.Marsh	not out	80	136	5
M.A.Taylor	c Tillekeratne b Wijegunawardene	37	50	6
D.C.Boon	not out	49	73	5
* A.R.Border				
D.M.Jones				
S.R.Waugh				
S.P.O'Donnell				
† I.A.Healy				
M.G.Hughes				
G.D.Campbell				
T.M.Alderman				
Extras	(lb 16, w 11, nb 11)	38		
Total	(38.5 overs; 1 wicket)	**204**		

AUSTRALIA	O	M	R	W
Hughes	10	0	35	1
Alderman	10	2	25	3
Campbell	10	2	54	1
O'Donnell	9	1	36	3
Waugh	9	0	45	1

SRI LANKA	O	M	R	W
Labrooy	10	1	46	0
Ratnayeke	7.5	0	51	0
Ratnayake	10	0	37	0
Wijegunawardene	7	0	33	1
Ranatunga	4	0	21	0

FALL OF WICKETS
1-8, 2-9, 3-50, 4-56, 5-60, 6-100, 7-162, 8-167, 9-203

FALL OF WICKETS
1-87

Umpires: A.R.Crafter (66) and R.J.Evans (4).

PAKISTAN v SRI LANKA 1989-90

At WACA Ground, Perth on 31 December 1989.   Result: **SRI LANKA** won by 3 wickets.   Toss: Pakistan.
Award: M.A.R.Samarasekera.   LOI debuts: None.

Both teams were fined for failing to bowl their overs at the required rate. Roshan Mahanama retired when 0 (at 1 for 0) after being hit amidships by Wasim Akram's fifth ball. He resumed at 179 for 5 and saw Sri Lanka to their only win of the tournament.

PAKISTAN		Runs	Balls	4/6
† Aamer Malik	b Ratnayeke	69	116	3
Shoaib Mohammed	b Ratnayeke	9	29	2
Mansoor Akhtar	run out	13	33	–
Saeed Anwar	run out	33	34	3
Javed Miandad	c Samarasekera b Labrooy	43	44	1
* Imran Khan	c and b Labrooy	32	27	2
Ijaz Ahmed	not out	3	4	–
Wasim Akram	run out	0	–	–
Abdul Qadir	not out	0	–	–
Waqar Younis				
Aqib Javed				
Extras	(b 1, lb 5, w 11, nb 3)	20		
Total	(47 overs; 7 wickets)	**222**		

SRI LANKA		Runs	Balls	4/6
R.S.Mahanama	not out	19	32	–
M.A.R.Samarasekera	c Aqib b Qadir	60	86	8
† H.P.Tillekeratne	c Aamer b Wasim	1	11	–
A.P.Gurusinha	b Waqar	37	49	5
P.A.de Silva	c Imran b Wasim	40	54	3
* A.Ranatunga	run out	0	–	–
S.T.Jayasuriya	c Aamer b Imran	24	40	–
J.R.Ratnayeke	c Saeed b Imran	2	5	–
R.J.Ratnayake	not out	1	2	–
G.F.Labrooy				
K.I.W.Wijegunawardene				
Extras	(b 1, lb 22, w 10, nb 6)	39		
Total	(45.3 overs; 7 wickets)	**223**		

SRI LANKA	O	M	R	W
Labrooy	10	1	43	2
Ratnayeke	10	2	33	2
Wijegunawardene	7	0	27	0
Ratnayake	9	0	54	0
Ranatunga	4	0	18	0
Gurusinha	7	0	41	0

PAKISTAN	O	M	R	W
Wasim Akram	10	1	37	2
Aqib Javed	10	0	45	0
Waqar Younis	8	1	44	1
Imran Khan	9.3	1	40	2
Abdul Qadir	8	0	34	1

FALL OF WICKETS
1-27, 2-51, 3-118, 4-151, 5-206, 6-220, 7-221

FALL OF WICKETS
1-8, 2-103, 3-120, 4-124, 5-179, 6-205, 7-211

Umpires: A.R.Crafter (67) and P.J.McConnell (51).

AUSTRALIA v PAKISTAN 1989-90

At Melbourne Cricket Ground on 3 January 1990.   Result: **AUSTRALIA** won by 7 wickets.   Toss: Pakistan.
Award: A.R.Border.   LOI debuts: Pakistan – Maqsood Rana, Nadeem Ghauri.

Imran Khan and Allan Border captained their countries for the 100th time in limited-overs internationals.

PAKISTAN		Runs	Balls	4/6
† Aamer Malik	c Healy b Rackemann	23	65	1
Shoaib Mohammed	c Healy b Rackemann	22	58	2
Mansoor Akhtar	b Taylor	32	42	–
Saeed Anwar	c Marsh b Taylor	3	11	–
* Imran Khan	c Hughes b O'Donnell	39	62	–
Ijaz Ahmed	run out	3	11	–
Wasim Akram	c Taylor b Rackemann	8	17	–
Abdul Qadir	c Border b Alderman	1	5	–
Maqsood Rana	run out	5	13	–
Nadeem Ghauri	not out	7	13	–
Aqib Javed	run out	1	5	–
Extras	(lb 8, w 8, nb 1)	17		
Total	(50 overs)	**161**		

AUSTRALIA		Runs	Balls	4/6
D.C.Boon	b Nadeem	39	66	1
G.R.Marsh	c Aamer b Wasim	3	8	–
D.M.Jones	b Aqib	2	15	–
* A.R.Border	not out	69	103	8
S.R.Waugh	not out	31	56	3
S.P.O'Donnell				
† I.A.Healy				
P.L.Taylor				
M.G.Hughes				
C.G.Rackemann				
T.M.Alderman				
Extras	(b 7, lb 8, w 2, nb 1)	18		
Total	(41 overs; 3 wickets)	**162**		

AUSTRALIA	O	M	R	W
Hughes	10	3	16	0
Alderman	10	2	31	1
Rackemann	10	2	21	3
O'Donnell	9	0	43	1
Taylor	10	0	36	2
Waugh	1	0	6	0

PAKISTAN	O	M	R	W
Wasim Akram	10	1	24	1
Aqib Javed	8	0	30	1
Maqsood Rana	2	0	11	0
Imran Khan	7	0	29	0
Nadeem Ghauri	10	3	30	1
Abdul Qadir	4	0	23	0

FALL OF WICKETS
1-56, 2-59, 3-67, 4-107, 5-115, 6-136, 7-138, 8-148, 9-156, 10-161

FALL OF WICKETS
1-6, 2-17, 3-81

Umpires: L.J.King (8) and S.G.Randell (32).

AUSTRALIA v SRI LANKA 1989-90

At Melbourne Cricket Ground on 4 January 1990.   Result: **AUSTRALIA** won by 73 runs.   Toss: Australia.
Award: D.M.Jones.   LOI debuts: None.

On a pitch where cracks developed and lifted the surface, causing balls either to bounce awkwardly or to shoot along
the ground, Sri Lanka lost their last six wickets for 8 runs off 31 balls.

AUSTRALIA		Runs	Balls	4/6
M.A.Taylor	c Tillekeratne b Ratnayeke	16	30	1
G.R.Marsh	c Tillekeratne b Labrooy	9	25	1
D.M.Jones	run out	69	98	2
* A.R.Border	c Jayasuriya b Ratnayake	10	16	–
S.R.Waugh	c Tillekeratne b Labrooy	0	5	–
S.P.O'Donnell	c Ranatunga b Ratnayeke	36	78	1
† I.A.Healy	c and b Labrooy	33	32	1
P.L.Taylor	not out	16	15	1
M.G.Hughes	not out	0	1	–
C.G.Rackemann				
T.M.Alderman				
Extras	(b 5, lb 5, w 3)	13		
Total	(50 overs; 7 wickets)	**202**		

SRI LANKA		Runs	Balls	4/6
R.S.Mahanama	lbw b Rackemann	27	44	2
M.A.R.Samarasekera	lbw b Alderman	6	17	–
† H.P.Tillekeratne	c Healy b Hughes	38	72	2
P.A.de Silva	lbw b O'Donnell	4	12	–
* A.Ranatunga	b P.L.Taylor	39	62	2
A.P.Gurusinha	st Healy b P.L.Taylor	8	20	–
R.J.Ratnayake	c Hughes b P.L.Taylor	1	3	–
S.T.Jayasuriya	c Healy b Alderman	0	3	–
J.R.Ratnayeke	c O'Donnell b Alderman	2	7	–
E.A.R.de Silva	run out	1	2	–
G.F.Labrooy	not out	1	5	–
Extras	(lb 1, w 1)	2		
Total	(41 overs)	**129**		

SRI LANKA	O	M	R	W
Labrooy	10	0	46	2
Ratnayeke	8	1	24	1
Ratnayake	10	2	44	3
E.A.R.de Silva	10	0	29	0
Ranatunga	2	0	13	0
P.A.de Silva	10	0	36	0

AUSTRALIA	O	M	R	W
Hughes	8	1	20	1
Alderman	9	1	29	3
Rackemann	8	0	19	1
O'Donnell	7	1	24	1
P.L.Taylor	9	0	36	3

FALL OF WICKETS
1-28, 2-28, 3-42, 4-46, 5-128, 6-163, 7-201

FALL OF WICKETS
1-8, 2-49, 3-58, 4-101, 5-121, 6-125, 7-125, 8-125, 9-127, 10-129

Umpires: S.G.Randell (33) and C.D.Timmins (6).

PAKISTAN v SRI LANKA 1989-90

At Woolloongabba, Brisbane on 10 February 1990.　Result: **PAKISTAN** won by 5 wickets.　Toss: Pakistan.
Award: Ijaz Ahmed.　LOI debuts: None.

Aravinda de Silva required six stitches in his jaw when he edged a reverse sweep. Champaka Ramanayake (side strain) was unable to complete his sixth over. Ijaz Ahmed reached his second LOI hundred off 97 balls. This first win of Pakistan's tour came in their tenth match.

SRI LANKA		Runs	Balls	4/6
M.A.R.Samarasekera	c Ijaz b Aqib	10	24	–
† H.P.Tillekeratne	c Ijaz b Mushtaq	61	121	3
A.P.Gurusinha	st Salim Yousuf b Mushtaq	88	108	5/2
R.J.Ratnayake	b Tausif	31	27	2/1
P.A.de Silva	c Waqar b Tausif	32	21	–/2
R.S.Mahanama	not out	4	4	–
* A.Ranatunga	not out	1	1	–
S.T.Jayasuriya				
E.A.R.de Silva				
C.P.H.Ramanayake				
N.L.K.Ratnayake				
Extras	(b 1, lb 14, w 7, nb 4)	26		
Total	(50 overs; 5 wickets)	253		

PAKISTAN		Runs	Balls	4/6
Ramiz Raja	c Gurusinha b Ramanayake	12	25	–
† Salim Yousuf	b E.A.R.de Silva	52	69	6
Ijaz Ahmed	not out	102	100	9/1
Javed Miandad	c Jayasuriya b P.A.de Silva	39	62	1
Salim Malik	st Tillekeratne b Gurusinha	14	13	–
* Imran Khan	c Mahanama b N.L.K.Ratnayake	15	13	2
Wasim Akram	not out	3	3	–
Tausif Ahmed				
Mushtaq Ahmed				
Waqar Younis				
Aqib Javed				
Extras	(lb 7, w 9, nb 1)	17		
Total	(47 overs; 5 wickets)	254		

PAKISTAN	O	M	R	W
Wasim Akram	10	1	39	0
Waqar Younis	5	0	27	0
Aqib Javed	10	1	39	1
Imran Khan	7	0	30	0
Tausif Ahmed	10	0	48	2
Mushtaq Ahmed	8	0	55	2

SRI LANKA	O	M	R	W
R.J.Ratnayake	9	1	39	0
N.L.K.Ratnayake	7	0	39	1
Ramanayake	5.2	0	25	1
Ranatunga	3	0	22	0
E.A.R.de Silva	10	0	47	1
Gurusinha	6.4	0	40	1
P.A.de Silva	6	0	35	1

FALL OF WICKETS
1-25, 2-163, 3-191, 4-236, 5-251

FALL OF WICKETS
1-45, 2-114, 3-193, 4-228, 5-251

Umpires: R.J.Evans (5) and C.D.Timmins (7).

AUSTRALIA v PAKISTAN 1989-90

At Woolloongabba, Brisbane on 11 February 1990.　Result: **AUSTRALIA** won by 67 runs.　Toss: Pakistan.
Award: T.M.Moody.　LOI debuts: None.

Australia registered their highest opening partnership and record total in internationals against Pakistan. Allan Border, playing his 197th match, became the first Australian to score 5000 LOI runs.

AUSTRALIA		Runs	Balls	4/6
M.A.Taylor	b Tausif	66	88	5
T.M.Moody	lbw b Mushtaq	89	82	4/4
D.M.Jones	run out	32	41	1/1
* A.R.Border	c Salim Yousuf b Wasim	26	30	1
S.R.Waugh	c Salim Malik b Mushtaq	13	16	2
S.P.O'Donnell	not out	31	28	2
† I.A.Healy	not out	22	20	1
P.L.Taylor				
M.G.Hughes				
C.G.Rackemann				
T.M.Alderman				
Extras	(b 3, lb 13, w 4, nb 1)	21		
Total	(50 overs; 5 wickets)	300		

PAKISTAN		Runs	Balls	4/6
Javed Miandad	c Waugh b Alderman	18	18	2
† Salim Yousuf	c M.A.Taylor b Hughes	7	6	1
Saeed Anwar	c Jones b Rackemann	37	24	4
Ramiz Raja	c P.L.Taylor b O'Donnell	9	17	1
Ijaz Ahmed	run out	27	32	2
* Imran Khan	c Border b Rackemann	82	89	4
Salim Malik	run out	27	26	1
Wasim Akram	b Rackemann	8	7	1
Mushtaq Ahmed	c M.A.Taylor b Rackemann	11	14	1
Tausif Ahmed	run out	1	3	–
Aqib Javed	not out	0	2	–
Extras	(b 2, lb 2, w 1, nb 1)	6		
Total	(39.1 overs)	233		

PAKISTAN	O	M	R	W
Wasim Akram	10	1	43	1
Imran Khan	10	0	54	0
Aqib Javed	10	0	54	0
Tausif Ahmed	10	0	57	1
Mushtaq Ahmed	10	0	76	2

AUSTRALIA	O	M	R	W
Alderman	5	0	39	1
Hughes	7	0	39	1
Rackemann	8.1	0	44	4
O'Donnell	8	0	43	1
P.L.Taylor	7	0	41	0
Border	4	0	23	0

FALL OF WICKETS
1-154, 2-176, 3-222, 4-241, 5-246

FALL OF WICKETS
1-20, 2-37, 3-66, 4-77, 5-132, 6-192, 7-206, 8-228, 9-233, 10-233

Umpires: R.J.Evans (6) and T.A.Prue (8).

AUSTRALIA v PAKISTAN 1989-90

At Sydney Cricket Ground on 13 February 1990.　Result: **PAKISTAN** won by 5 wickets.　Toss: Pakistan.
Award: Imran Khan.　LOI debuts: None.

Played on an underprepared pitch following 25 inches of rain in the previous 12 days, this game featured an exceptional innings by Dean Jones and an unexceptionally slow one by Shoaib Mohammed.

AUSTRALIA		Runs	Balls	4/6
M.A.Taylor	b Imran	23	76	1
T.M.Moody	b Wasim	3	13	–
D.M.Jones	run out	54	88	3
S.R.Waugh	c Miandad b Shoaib	28	63	–
S.P.O'Donnell	b Imran	3	7	–
* A.R.Border	run out	22	31	–
† I.A.Healy	b Wasim	11	16	–
P.L.Taylor	not out	3	6	–
C.J.McDermott	run out	0	1	–
C.G.Rackemann				
T.M.Alderman				
Extras	(lb 13, w 3, nb 2)	18		
Total	(50 overs; 8 wickets)	165		

PAKISTAN		Runs	Balls	4/6
Saeed Anwar	b McDermott	27	30	3/1
Shoaib Mohammed	c McDermott b O'Donnell	9	57	–
Ijaz Ahmed	b O'Donnell	3	13	–
Javed Miandad	lbw b Alderman	29	54	1
* Imran Khan	not out	56	106	4
Salim Malik	c Border b P.L.Taylor	0	4	–
Wasim Akram	not out	34	30	3/1
† Salim Yousuf				
Waqar Younis				
Aqib Javed				
Nadeem Ghauri				
Extras	(b 3, lb 4, nb 2)	9		
Total	(48.3 overs; 5 wickets)	167		

PAKISTAN	O	M	R	W
Wasim Akram	10	2	21	2
Waqar Younis	10	1	36	0
Aqib Javed	7	0	28	0
Nadeem Ghauri	10	1	23	0
Imran Khan	10	1	30	2
Shoaib Mohammed	3	0	14	1

AUSTRALIA	O	M	R	W
Alderman	10	2	29	1
McDermott	8	1	35	1
O'Donnell	9.3	1	32	2
Rackemann	8	1	24	0
P.L.Taylor	9	1	26	1
Border	4	0	14	0

FALL OF WICKETS
1-8, 2-68, 3-110, 4-123, 5-125, 6-153, 7-164, 8-165

FALL OF WICKETS
1-32, 2-38, 3-43, 4-102, 5-111

Umpires: R.J.Evans (7) and T.A.Prue (9).

PAKISTAN v SRI LANKA 1989-90

At Bellerive Oval, Hobart on 15 February 1990.　Result: **PAKISTAN** won by 6 wickets.　Toss: Pakistan.
Award: Ramiz Raja.　LOI debuts: None.

Ramiz Raja took full advantage of perfect playing conditions to register his third hundred in 101 internationals. Dropped three times in the nineties, it was his first hundred in four tours of Australia.

SRI LANKA		Runs	Balls	4/6
M.A.R.Samarasekera	lbw b Waqar	7	20	1
D.S.B.P.Kuruppu	c Salim Yousuf b Waqar	1	10	–
A.P.Gurusinha	b Waqar	59	84	5
† H.P.Tillekeratne	b Imran	19	43	2
P.A.de Silva	c and b Aqib	5	9	–
* A.Ranatunga	c Wasim b Nadeem	42	49	1/2
R.S.Mahanama	c Salim Yousuf b Nadeem	24	28	1
E.A.R.de Silva	b Waqar	1	9	–
R.J.Ratnayake	c Salim Yousuf b Wasim	14	26	1
G.F.Labrooy	c Ramiz b Aqib	2	8	–
K.I.W.Wijegunawardene	not out	0	4	–
Extras	(lb 10, w 9, nb 2)	21		
Total	(47.5 overs)	195		

PAKISTAN		Runs	Balls	4/6
Ramiz Raja	not out	116	148	8
Saeed Anwar	b Ratnayake	17	29	–
Ijaz Ahmed	lbw b Wijegunawardene	1	3	–
Javed Miandad	c E.A.R.de Silva b Wijegunawardene	42	90	–
Salim Malik	run out	3	5	–
† Salim Yousuf	not out	10	16	1
* Imran Khan				
Wasim Akram				
Waqar Younis				
Aqib Javed				
Nadeem Ghauri				
Extras	(b 1, lb 4, w 4)	9		
Total	(48.3 overs; 4 wickets)	198		

PAKISTAN	O	M	R	W
Wasim Akram	9	2	23	1
Imran Khan	10	0	28	1
Waqar Younis	10	2	39	4
Aqib Javed	8.5	0	44	2
Nadeem Ghauri	10	0	51	2

SRI LANKA	O	M	R	W
Labrooy	9	0	41	0
Ratnayake	9.3	0	47	1
Wijegunawardene	10	1	34	2
Ranatunga	10	0	37	0
E.A.R.de Silva	10	0	34	0

FALL OF WICKETS
1-6, 2-25, 3-62, 4-79, 5-151, 6-152, 7-158, 8-188, 9-193, 10-195

FALL OF WICKETS
1-46, 2-53, 3-158, 4-166

Umpires: L.J.King (9) and S.G.Randell (34).

PAKISTAN v SRI LANKA 1989-90

At Adelaide Oval on 17 February 1990.   Result: **PAKISTAN** won by 27 runs.   Toss: Sri Lanka.
Award: Saeed Anwar.   LOI debuts: None.

A pluperfect pitch yielded the (then) highest match aggregate for any 50-over international. The stand of 202 between Ramiz Raja, who completed 3000 runs, and Saeed Anwar, whose 100 took 87 balls, remains the first-wicket record for internationals in Australia.

PAKISTAN		Runs	Balls	4/6
Ramiz Raja	not out	107	154	3
Saeed Anwar	b E.A.R.de Silva	126	99	8/6
Salim Malik	c Ratnayake b E.A.R.de Silva	25	25	I
Wasim Akram	b Ratnayake	34	23	I/2
* Imran Khan	not out	I	I	–
Javed Miandad				
Ijaz Ahmed				
† Salim Yousuf				
Waqar Younis				
Aqib Javed				
Nadeem Ghauri				
Extras	(b 5, lb 10, w 4, nb 3)	22		
Total	(50 overs; 3 wickets)	**315**		

SRI LANKA		Runs	Balls	4/6
† D.S.B.P.Kuruppu	run out	37	58	2
M.A.R.Samarasekera	c Wasim b Aqib	24	34	4
P.A.de Silva	run out	22	17	I/I
* A.Ranatunga	c Salim Malik b Aqib	64	70	–/2
A.P.Gurusinha	c Miandad b Nadeem	16	17	2
R.S.Mahanama	run out	72	79	2
R.J.Ratnayake	b Waqar	3	5	–
G.F.Labrooy	b Waqar	12	12	–
E.A.R.de Silva	not out	3	6	–
H.P.Tillekeratne	not out	5	6	–
K.I.W.Wijegunawardene				
Extras	(b I, lb 21, w 6, nb 2)	30		
Total	(50 overs; 8 wickets)	**288**		

SRI LANKA	O	M	R	W
Labrooy	10	0	56	0
Ratnayake	10	I	38	I
Wijegunawardene	4	0	38	0
Ranatunga	10	0	50	0
P.A.de Silva	4	0	30	0
E.A.R.de Silva	9	0	57	2
Gurusinha	3	0	31	0

PAKISTAN	O	M	R	W
Wasim Akram	10	0	49	0
Waqar Younis	10	I	35	2
Aqib Javed	10	0	57	2
Nadeem Ghauri	8	0	54	I
Imran Khan	10	0	60	0
Ijaz Ahmed	2	0	11	0

FALL OF WICKETS
1-202, 2-252, 3-314

FALL OF WICKETS
1-55, 2-90, 3-94, 4-123, 5-251, 6-258, 7-271, 8-280

Umpires: A.R.Crafter (68) and S.G.Randell (35).

AUSTRALIA v SRI LANKA 1989-90

At Adelaide Oval on 18 February 1990.   Result: **AUSTRALIA** won by 7 wickets.   Toss: Sri Lanka.
Award: D.M.Jones.   LOI debuts: None.

Allan Border took his 50th wicket and became the second, after Viv Richards, to achieve the double of 5000 runs and 50 wickets in limited-overs internationals.

SRI LANKA		Runs	Balls	4/6
D.S.B.P.Kuruppu	c Alderman b Rackemann	12	17	–
M.A.R.Samarasekera	c Healy b Rackemann	I	13	–
A.P.Gurusinha	c Healy b Campbell	20	34	–
P.A.de Silva	b Alderman	39	29	3/3
* A.Ranatunga	c Healy b Campbell	I	7	–
† H.P.Tillekeratne	b Campbell	3	13	–
S.T.Jayasuriya	c M.A.Taylor b Border	31	66	I
E.A.R.de Silva	b O'Donnell	7	18	–
R.J.Ratnayake	run out	31	39	3
M.A.W.R.Madurasinghe	c P.L.Taylor b Border	I	8	–
K.I.W.Wijegunawardene	not out	I	5	–
Extras	(b I, lb 5, w I, nb 4)	11		
Total	(40.4 overs)	**158**		

AUSTRALIA		Runs	Balls	4/6
M.A.Taylor	c Madurasinghe b E.A.R.de Silva	23	54	3
D.M.Jones	not out	80	120	5
T.M.Moody	c Kuruppu b Gurusinha	5	19	–
* A.R.Border	b Madurasinghe	29	35	2
S.R.Waugh	not out	11	14	I
S.P.O'Donnell				
† I.A.Healy				
P.L.Taylor				
G.D.Campbell				
C.G.Rackemann				
T.M.Alderman				
Extras	(b 7, lb 2, w 2)	11		
Total	(40 overs; 3 wickets)	**159**		

AUSTRALIA	O	M	R	W
Alderman	7	0	30	I
Rackemann	9	0	48	2
Campbell	7	I	31	3
O'Donnell	7	0	19	I
P.L.Taylor	8	I	22	0
Border	2.4	I	2	2

SRI LANKA	O	M	R	W
Ratnayake	7	I	20	I
Wijegunawardene	7	0	34	0
Gurusinha	7	0	16	I
E.A.R.de Silva	10	0	37	I
Madurasinghe	6	0	27	I
Jayasuriya	3	0	16	0

FALL OF WICKETS
1-10, 2-21, 3-68, 4-70, 5-81, 6-88, 7-106, 8-150, 9-155, 10-158

FALL OF WICKETS
1-67, 2-78, 3-134

Umpires: A.R.Crafter (69) and P.J.McConnell (52).

AUSTRALIA v PAKISTAN 1989-90

At Sydney Cricket Ground on 20 February 1990.   Result: **PAKISTAN** won by 2 runs.   Toss: Pakistan.
Award: S.P.O'Donnell.   LOI debuts: None.

Allan Border was the first to appear in 200 limited-overs internationals. Imran Khan completed 3000 runs and, bowling the final over with Australia needing four to win, took two wickets and conceded a leg-bye. Final points: Australia 12, Pakistan 10, Sri Lanka 2.

PAKISTAN		Runs	Balls	4/6
Ramiz Raja	c Moody b Alderman	3	13	–
Saeed Anwar	c Waugh b Campbell	43	36	6/1
Salim Malik	c Moody b Rackemann	67	85	4
* Imran Khan	c M.A.Taylor b Alderman	56	98	3/1
Ijaz Ahmed	c Waugh b O'Donnell	9	18	–
† Salim Yousuf	lbw b O'Donnell	5	8	–
Aamer Malik	b Campbell	14	22	1
Mushtaq Ahmed	not out	17	17	–
Waqar Younis	run out	0	2	–
Tausif Ahmed	not out	1	2	–
Aqib Javed				
Extras	(w 2, nb 3)	5		
Total	(49 overs; 8 wickets)	**220**		

AUSTRALIA		Runs	Balls	4/6
M.A.Taylor	c Salim Yousuf b Waqar	29	25	4
T.M.Moody	st Salim Yousuf b Saeed	74	109	5
D.M.Jones	c Ijaz b Aqib	10	13	1
* A.R.Border	b Tausif	26	50	3
S.R.Waugh	st Salim Yousuf b Mushtaq	3	10	–
P.L.Taylor	c Imran b Mushtaq	14	28	–
S.P.O'Donnell	lbw b Imran	39	36	2/1
† I.A.Healy	run out	8	9	–
G.D.Campbell	not out	4	12	–
C.G.Rackemann	b Imran	0	2	–
T.M.Alderman	not out	0	1	–
Extras	(lb 5, w 6)	11		
Total	(49 overs; 9 wickets)	**218**		

AUSTRALIA	O	M	R	W
Alderman	9	2	46	2
Rackemann	10	0	45	1
Campbell	9	0	46	2
O'Donnell	10	0	32	2
P.L.Taylor	7	0	28	0
Border	4	0	23	0

PAKISTAN	O	M	R	W
Imran Khan	7	1	28	2
Waqar Younis	7	0	40	1
Aqib Javed	9	0	39	1
Aamer Malik	3	0	12	0
Tausif Ahmed	10	0	33	1
Mushtaq Ahmed	10	1	46	2
Saeed Anwar	3	0	15	1

FALL OF WICKETS
1-4, 2-74, 3-161, 4-176, 5-184, 6-196, 7-207, 8-218

FALL OF WICKETS
1-44, 2-58, 3-122, 4-127, 5-159, 6-169, 7-192, 8-218, 9-218

Umpires: L.J.King (10) and P.J.McConnell (53).

AUSTRALIA v PAKISTAN 1989-90

At Melbourne Cricket Ground on 23 February 1990.   Result: **AUSTRALIA** won by 7 wickets.   Toss: Australia.
LOI debuts: None.

A faulty weather forecast had led to the pitch being unprotected from overnight rain and, with it still moist, the toss proved crucial. In those conditions, Wasim Akram's innings was quite outstanding.

PAKISTAN		Runs	Balls	4/6
Saeed Anwar	c and b Alderman	2	5	–
Ramiz Raja	c Healy b O'Donnell	1	7	–
Salim Malik	c Alderman b Campbell	39	47	6
Javed Miandad	c Healy b Rackemann	2	26	–
* Imran Khan	c Healy b Rackemann	1	24	–
Ijaz Ahmed	lbw b O'Donnell	7	34	–
Wasim Akram	c P.L.Taylor b Campbell	86	76	5/3
† Salim Yousuf	c Alderman b P.L.Taylor	4	22	–
Tausif Ahmed	c P.L.Taylor b Campbell	10	43	–
Waqar Younis	b Alderman	0	1	–
Nadeem Ghauri	not out	3	4	–
Extras	(lb 3, w 3, nb 1)	7		
Total	(47.5 overs)	**162**		

AUSTRALIA		Runs	Balls	4/6
M.A.Taylor	c Salim Yousuf b Waqar	13	38	–
T.M.Moody	c Salim Yousuf b Wasim	4	13	–
D.M.Jones	not out	83	135	3/1
S.R.Waugh	b Wasim	13	32	1
* A.R.Border	not out	44	61	2
S.P.O'Donnell				
† I.A.Healy				
P.L.Taylor				
G.D.Campbell				
C.G.Rackemann				
T.M.Alderman				
Extras	(lb 3, w 1, nb 2)	6		
Total	(45.5 overs; 3 wickets)	**163**		

AUSTRALIA	O	M	R	W
Alderman	8.5	2	26	2
O'Donnell	10	2	29	2
Rackemann	10	5	32	2
Campbell	9	1	39	3
P.L.Taylor	10	0	33	1

PAKISTAN	O	M	R	W
Wasim Akram	10	0	30	2
Imran Khan	9	0	32	0
Waqar Younis	9	0	26	1
Nadeem Ghauri	9	0	27	0
Tausif Ahmed	8.5	0	45	0

FALL OF WICKETS
1-2, 2-8, 3-46, 4-50, 5-50, 6-77, 7-96, 8-153, 9-159, 10-162

FALL OF WICKETS
1-9, 2-23, 3-54

Umpires: A.R.Crafter (70) and P.J.McConnell (54).

AUSTRALIA v PAKISTAN 1989-90

At Sydney Cricket Ground on 25 February 1990.   Result: **AUSTRALIA** won by 69 runs.   Toss: Australia.
Finals Award: D.M.Jones.   LOI debuts: None.

Australia won the World Series for the fifth time in 11 seasons. Steve Waugh was dropped for the first time since his first appearance, ending a sequence of 87 internationals, and replaced by his twin.

AUSTRALIA		Runs	Balls	4/6
M.A.Taylor	c Waqar b Mushtaq	76	116	4
T.M.Moody	st Salim Yousuf b Nadeem	44	62	4
D.M.Jones	run out	46	52	1
*A.R.Border	not out	34	35	1
M.E.Waugh	run out	14	14	1
S.P.O'Donnell	c Salim Yousuf b Imran	3	9	–
†I.A.Healy	c Saeed b Mushtaq	15	13	–
P.L.Taylor	not out	3	3	–
G.D.Campbell				
C.G.Rackemann				
T.M.Alderman				
Extras	(b 1, lb 11, w 6, nb 2)	20		
Total	(50 overs; 6 wickets)	255		

PAKISTAN		Runs	Balls	4/6
Saeed Anwar	c Healy b O'Donnell	5	10	–
Ramiz Raja	lbw b Alderman	0	1	–
Wasim Akram	st Healy b P.L.Taylor	36	30	6/1
Salim Malik	b Alderman	15	22	2
Javed Miandad	run out	11	35	–
*Imran Khan	c M.A.Taylor b Campbell	1	15	–
Ijaz Ahmed	b P.L.Taylor	29	45	1
†Salim Yousuf	c Moody b O'Donnell	59	75	6
Mushtaq Ahmed	c Healy b P.L.Taylor	0	2	–
Waqar Younis	not out	20	29	–/1
Nadeem Ghauri	c Campbell b O'Donnell	4	8	–
Extras	(lb 2, w 2, nb 2)	6		
Total	(45 overs)	186		

PAKISTAN	O	M	R	W
Wasim Akram	10	0	42	0
Imran Khan	10	0	43	1
Waqar Younis	10	0	48	0
Nadeem Ghauri	10	0	45	1
Mushtaq Ahmed	10	0	65	2

AUSTRALIA	O	M	R	W
Alderman	7	1	28	2
O'Donnell	6	1	38	3
P.L.Taylor	10	1	43	3
Rackemann	8	1	20	0
Campbell	7	0	21	1
Border	7	0	34	0

FALL OF WICKETS
1-84, 2-179, 3-183, 4-207, 5-214, 6-231

FALL OF WICKETS
1-6, 2-6, 3-52, 4-62, 5-72, 6-76, 7-132, 8-132, 9-176, 10-186

Umpires: A.R.Crafter (71) and P.J.McConnell (55).

WEST INDIES v ENGLAND 1989-90

At Queen's Park Oval, Port-of-Spain, Trinidad on 14 February 1990.   No result.   Toss: England.
LOI debuts: None.

A five-match 50-over series for the Buckle Trophy. The Caribbean's first limited-overs international to be terminated by rain was also their first match of any sort to be televised live to Britain.

WEST INDIES		Runs	Balls	4/6
C.G.Greenidge	c Stewart b Capel	21	45	4
D.L.Haynes	c Russell b Lewis	25	51	2
R.B.Richardson	c Stewart b Fraser	51	81	3
C.L.Hooper	c Smith b Hemmings	17	26	2
C.A.Best	c and b Gooch	6	5	1
*I.V.A.Richards	b Small	32	42	1/2
E.A.Moseley	c Lewis b Fraser	2	4	–
M.D.Marshall	b Small	9	9	1
†P.J.L.Dujon	not out	15	16	–
I.R.Bishop	not out	18	21	–/1
C.A.Walsh				
Extras	(b 4, lb 4, w 3, nb 1)	12		
Total	(50 overs; 8 wickets)	208		

ENGLAND		Runs	Balls	4/6
*G.A.Gooch	not out	13	40	1
W.Larkins	c Best b Marshall	2	21	–
R.A.Smith	not out	6	20	–
A.J.Lamb				
A.J.Stewart				
D.J.Capel				
†R.C.Russell				
C.C.Lewis				
G.C.Small				
E.E.Hemmings				
A.R.C.Fraser				
Extras	(lb 1, nb 4)	5		
Total	(13 overs; 1 wicket)	26		

ENGLAND	O	M	R	W
Small	10	1	41	2
Fraser	10	1	37	2
Capel	6	0	25	1
Lewis	7	1	30	1
Hemmings	9	0	41	1
Gooch	8	0	26	1

WEST INDIES	O	M	R	W
Marshall	6	1	12	1
Bishop	5	2	6	0
Walsh	1	0	1	0
Moseley	1	0	6	0

FALL OF WICKETS
1-9

FALL OF WICKETS
1-49, 2-49, 3-89, 4-100, 5-155, 6-162, 7-172, 8-180

Umpires: D.M.Archer (18) and C.E.Cumberbatch (10).

WEST INDIES v ENGLAND 1989-90

At Queen's Park Oval, Port-of-Spain, Trinidad on 17 February 1990.   No result.   Toss: England.
LOI debuts: None.

With the outfield already damp when play started on time, a succession of showers ensured that there could be no resumption after the initial stoppage.

WEST INDIES		Runs	Balls	4/6	ENGLAND				
C.G.Greenidge	not out	8	21	1	* G.A.Gooch				
D.L.Haynes	not out	4	15	–	W.Larkins				
R.B.Richardson					R.A.Smith				
C.L.Hooper					A.J.Lamb				
C.A.Best					A.J.Stewart				
* I.V.A.Richards					D.J.Capel				
† P.J.L.Dujon					† R.C.Russell				
M.D.Marshall					C.C.Lewis				
E.A.Moseley					G.C.Small				
I.R.Bishop					E.E.Hemmings				
C.A.Walsh					A.R.C.Fraser				
Extras	(lb 1)			1					
Total	(5.5 overs; 0 wickets)			**13**					

ENGLAND	O	M	R	W
Small	3	1	7	0
Fraser	2.5	0	5	0

Umpires: D.M.Archer (19) and C.E.Cumberbatch (11).

WEST INDIES v ENGLAND 1989-90

At Sabina Park, Kingston, Jamaica on 3 March 1990.   Result: **WEST INDIES** won by 3 wickets.   Toss: England.
Award: R.B.Richardson.   LOI debuts: None.

With only two required off Angus Fraser's final ball for West Indies to win a tied match by having lost fewer wickets, Ian Bishop drove a boundary over extra-cover. Richie Richardson scored his only hundred in a home international.

ENGLAND		Runs	Balls	4/6	WEST INDIES		Runs	Balls	4/6
* G.A.Gooch	b Bishop	2	20	–	D.L.Haynes	c Smith b DeFreitas	8	21	–
W.Larkins	b Walsh	33	51	7	C.A.Best	b Small	4	4	–
R.A.Smith	c Marshall b Hooper	43	76	6	R.B.Richardson	not out	108	132	11/3
A.J.Lamb	b Bishop	66	97	4/1	C.L.Hooper	b Hemmings	20	57	1
A.J.Stewart	c Dujon b Hooper	0	1	–	* I.V.A.Richards	c Small b Hemmings	25	45	3
D.J.Capel	c Dujon b Bishop	28	48	1	K.L.T.Arthurton	c Russell b Hemmings	0	1	–
† R.C.Russell	b Marshall	2	9	–	† P.J.L.Dujon	c Smith b Small	27	37	4
P.A.J.DeFreitas	not out	3	4	–	E.A.Moseley	c Gooch b Fraser	0	1	–
G.C.Small	b Bishop	0	2	–	I.R.Bishop	not out	6	4	1
E.E.Hemmings					M.D.Marshall				
A.R.C.Fraser					C.A.Walsh				
Extras	(b 3, lb 25, w 6, nb 3)	37			Extras	(b 12, lb 4, w 1, nb 1)	18		
Total	(50 overs; 8 wickets)	**214**			**Total**	(50 overs; 7 wickets)	**216**		

WEST INDIES	O	M	R	W	ENGLAND	O	M	R	W
Marshall	10	1	39	1	Small	9	1	37	2
Bishop	10	1	28	4	DeFreitas	10	2	29	1
Walsh	6	0	38	1	Capel	9	1	47	0
Moseley	6	1	15	0	Fraser	10	0	41	0
Richards	9	0	32	0	Hemmings	10	0	31	3
Hooper	9	0	34	2	Gooch	2	0	15	0

FALL OF WICKETS
1-20, 2-71, 3-117, 4-117, 5-185, 6-206, 7-212, 8-214

FALL OF WICKETS
1-11, 2-23, 3-74, 4-158, 5-158, 6-204, 7-210

Umpires: L.H.Barker (13) and S.A.Bucknor (2).

WEST INDIES v ENGLAND 1989-90

At Bourda, Georgetown, Guyana on 7 March 1990.　Result: **WEST INDIES** won by 6 wickets.　Toss: West Indies.
Award: C.A.Best.　LOI debuts: None.

West Indies took a winning two-nil lead in the series. Desmond Haynes and Carlisle Best, who was run out attempting a second run off the stroke which completed his only LOI hundred, shared the (then) highest West Indies opening stand against England.

ENGLAND		Runs	Balls	4/6	WEST INDIES		Runs	Balls	4/6
* G.A.Gooch	b Moseley	33	57	5	D.L.Haynes	c DeFreitas b Hemmings	50	93	10
W.Larkins	c Richards b Moseley	34	62	4/1	C.A.Best	run out	100	119	12/1
R.A.Smith	c Richardson b Walsh	18	46	1	R.B.Richardson	c Russell b Capel	19	35	1
A.J.Lamb	c Dujon b Bishop	22	45	1	C.L.Hooper	not out	16	25	2
A.J.Stewart	c Dujon b Walsh	0	3	–	* I.V.A.Richards	c DeFreitas b Fraser	2	2	–
D.J.Capel	b Hooper	1	5	–	K.L.T.Arthurton	not out	0	–	–
† R.C.Russell	b Bishop	28	40	2	† P.J.L.Dujon				
P.A.J.DeFreitas	run out	11	18	–	E.A.E.Baptiste				
G.C.Small	not out	18	21	2	E.A.Moseley				
E.E.Hemmings	not out	0	–	–	I.R.Bishop				
A.R.C.Fraser					C.A.Walsh				
Extras	(b 1, lb 8, w 6, nb 8)	23			Extras	(lb 2, w 1, nb 1)	4		
Total	(48 overs; 8 wickets)	**188**			**Total**	(45.2 overs; 4 wickets)	**191**		

WEST INDIES	O	M	R	W	ENGLAND	O	M	R	W
Bishop	10	1	41	2	DeFreitas	7	1	32	0
Walsh	10	1	33	2	Small	9.2	1	43	0
Baptiste	8	3	21	0	Capel	9	2	39	1
Moseley	10	0	52	2	Fraser	10	1	42	1
Hooper	10	0	32	1	Hemmings	10	1	33	1

FALL OF WICKETS
1-71, 2-88, 3-109, 4-109, 5-112, 6-132, 7-156, 8-181

FALL OF WICKETS
1-113, 2-155, 3-179, 4-182

Umpires: D.M.Archer (20) and C.R.Duncan (3).

WEST INDIES v ENGLAND 1989-90

At Bourda, Georgetown, Guyana on 15 March 1990.　Result: **WEST INDIES** won by 7 wickets.　Toss: West Indies.
Award: C.G.Greenidge.　LOI debuts: West Indies – C.B.Lambert.

Played on the scheduled final day of the rain-aborted second Test, this match was given official LOI status but was not part of the Cable and Wireless Series.

ENGLAND		Runs	Balls	4/6	WEST INDIES		Runs	Balls	4/6
* G.A.Gooch	b Hooper	42	102	1	C.G.Greenidge	lbw b Fraser	77	122	8/2
W.Larkins	c and b Bishop	1	13	–	C.B.Lambert	b Hemmings	48	66	4/1
R.A.Smith	c Dujon b Bishop	1	5	–	R.B.Richardson	c Capel b Small	7	16	1
A.J.Lamb	c Best b Moseley	9	36	1	C.L.Hooper	not out	19	37	1
A.J.Stewart	b Hooper	13	39	1	C.A.Best	not out	7	14	–
R.J.Bailey	c and b Ambrose	42	54	3/1	K.L.T.Arthurton				
D.J.Capel	c Dujon b Ambrose	7	20	–	*†P.J.L.Dujon				
† R.C.Russell	c Best b Ambrose	19	18	3	E.A.E.Baptiste				
G.C.Small	c Dujon b Ambrose	0	2	–	E.A.Moseley				
E.E.Hemmings	not out	3	10	–	I.R.Bishop				
A.R.C.Fraser	not out	3	4	–	C.E.L.Ambrose				
Extras	(b 2, lb 9, w 13, nb 2)	26			Extras	(lb 2, w 4, nb 3)	9		
Total	(49 overs; 9 wickets)	**166**			**Total**	(40.2 overs; 3 wickets)	**167**		

WEST INDIES	O	M	R	W	ENGLAND	O	M	R	W
Bishop	7	2	22	2	Capel	9	1	41	0
Ambrose	9	1	18	4	Small	7	0	32	1
Moseley	10	1	48	1	Fraser	9.2	1	33	1
Baptiste	10	1	31	0	Gooch	5	1	22	0
Hooper	10	0	28	2	Hemmings	10	1	37	1
Best	3	0	8	0					

FALL OF WICKETS
1-13, 2-18, 3-46, 4-86, 5-88, 6-102, 7-149, 8-150, 9-160

FALL OF WICKETS
1-88, 2-105, 3-152

Umpires: D.M.Archer (21) and C.R.Duncan (4).

WEST INDIES v ENGLAND 1989-90

At Kensington Oval, Bridgetown, Barbados on 3 April 1990. Result: **WEST INDIES** won by 4 wickets. Toss: West Indies.
Award: R.B.Richardson. LOI debuts: None.

Light drizzle delayed the start by 85 minutes and reduced the match to 45 overs each. West Indies managed only 38 in the time allowed. David Smith, who had arrived two days earlier, was hit on the helmet (first ball) and thumb (fracture), his tour lasting 31 balls.

ENGLAND		Runs	Balls	4/6
D.M.Smith	b Moseley	5	31	–
W.Larkins	b Walsh	34	73	4
R.A.Smith	run out	69	84	7
* A.J.Lamb	not out	55	39	7
N.Hussain	not out	15	13	1
D.J.Capel				
† R.C.Russell				
P.A.J.DeFreitas				
C.C.Lewis				
G.C.Small				
E.E.Hemmings				
Extras	(b 2, lb 8, w 14, nb 12)	36		
Total	(38 overs; 3 wickets)	**214**		

WEST INDIES		Runs	Balls	4/6
C.G.Greenidge	c Russell b Small	6	19	1
* D.L.Haynes	c Hussain b Hemmings	45	54	7/1
R.B.Richardson	b Small	80	84	8/1
C.A.Best	c sub (A.J.Stewart) b Capel	51	43	6/1
A.L.Logie	c R.A.Smith b DeFreitas	2	8	–
C.L.Hooper	c Larkins b Small	12	13	2
† P.J.L.Dujon	not out	11	9	2
E.A.Moseley	not out	1	1	–
M.D.Marshall				
C.E.L.Ambrose				
C.A.Walsh				
Extras	(lb 6, w 1, nb 2)	9		
Total	(37.3 overs; 6 wickets)	**217**		

WEST INDIES	O	M	R	W
Ambrose	9	2	31	0
Walsh	8	0	49	1
Moseley	7	0	43	1
Marshall	8	0	50	0
Hooper	6	0	31	0

ENGLAND	O	M	R	W
Small	9	1	29	3
DeFreitas	8.3	0	63	1
Lewis	5	0	35	0
Capel	6	0	52	1
Hemmings	9	0	32	1

FALL OF WICKETS
1-47, 2-98, 3-161

FALL OF WICKETS
1-39, 2-78, 3-190, 4-193, 5-199, 6-212

Umpires: D.M.Archer (22) and L.H.Barker (14).

NEW ZEALAND v INDIA 1989-90

At Carisbrook, Dunedin on 1 March 1990. Result: **NEW ZEALAND** won by 108 runs. Toss: India.
Award: M.D.Crowe. LOI debuts: New Zealand – G.R.Larsen, S.J.Roberts, S.A.Thomson; India – S.L.V.Raju, A.S.Wassan.

New Zealand began their first home series involving three teams by ending a run of 11 successive defeats against India. Martin Crowe and Ken Rutherford shared a (then) national record fourth-wicket stand of 152. Shane Thomson took wickets with his first and third balls in LOIs, while Gavin Larsen did so with his second.

NEW ZEALAND		Runs	Balls	4/6
* J.G.Wright	c Kapil Dev b Wassan	23	44	3
M.D.Crowe	b Prabhakar	104	135	6/1
A.H.Jones	lbw b Wassan	0	1	–
M.J.Greatbatch	c Sharma b Wassan	13	22	–
K.R.Rutherford	not out	78	75	5/1
† I.D.S.Smith	b Kapil Dev	4	4	–
S.A.Thomson	b Prabhakar	3	4	–
G.R.Larsen				
M.C.Snedden				
D.K.Morrison				
S.J.Roberts				
Extras	(b 5, lb 10, w 5, nb 1)	21		
Total	(47 overs; 6 wickets)	**246**		

INDIA		Runs	Balls	4/6
W.V.Raman	c Wright b Snedden	32	38	5
V.B.Chandrasekhar	c Smith b Morrison	4	3	1
D.B.Vengsarkar	lbw b Morrison	2	5	–
* M.Azharuddin	c Greatbatch b Thomson	12	17	1
S.R.Tendulkar	c and b Thomson	0	2	–
A.K.Sharma	b Thomson	3	9	–
Kapil Dev	c Smith b Larsen	12	28	1
M.Prabhakar	run out	14	21	2
† K.S.More	not out	23	38	1/1
A.S.Wassan	b Morrison	16	24	1
S.L.V.Raju	run out	4	9	–
Extras	(b 4, lb 4, w 7, nb 1)	16		
Total	(32.1 overs)	**138**		

INDIA	O	M	R	W
Kapil Dev	9	0	49	1
Prabhakar	10	1	49	2
Wassan	10	0	45	3
Raju	9	0	38	0
Sharma	9	0	50	0

NEW ZEALAND	O	M	R	W
Morrison	8.1	2	43	3
Roberts	4	0	26	0
Thomson	6	1	19	3
Snedden	8	1	28	1
Larsen	6	1	14	1

FALL OF WICKETS
1-38, 2-38, 3-66, 4-218, 5-233, 6-246

FALL OF WICKETS
1-19, 2-33, 3-57, 4-57, 5-65, 6-65, 7-91, 8-97, 9-128, 10-138

Umpires: B.L.Aldridge (8) and R.S.Dunne (4).

AUSTRALIA v INDIA 1989-90

At Lancaster Park, Christchurch on 3 March 1990.   Result: **AUSTRALIA** won by 18 runs.   Toss: Australia.
Award: T.M.Alderman.   LOI debuts: None.

Mohammed Azharuddin, who led India for the first time in the previous match, appeared in his 100th international.
Terry Alderman became the third Australian after Gary Gilmour and Greg Chappell to return two five-wicket analyses.

AUSTRALIA		Runs	Balls	4/6	INDIA		Runs	Balls	4/6
M.A.Taylor	st More b Hirwani	10	48	1	V.B.Chandrasekhar	c Waugh b Alderman	8	19	–
D.C.Boon	run out	22	52	1	W.V.Raman	c M.A.Taylor b Alderman	2	6	–
D.M.Jones	c Manjrekar b Hirwani	32	42	1	S.V.Manjrekar	c Healy b Rackemann	6	24	–
* A.R.Border	run out	37	50	1/1	D.B.Vengsarkar	c Jones b Campbell	35	56	6
S.R.Waugh	c Manjrekar b Kapil Dev	10	28	–	* M.Azharuddin	c Alderman b P.L.Taylor	26	61	2
S.P.O'Donnell	lbw b Sharma	12	17	1	A.K.Sharma	lbw b O'Donnell	15	27	2
† I.A.Healy	run out	25	27	1/1	Kapil Dev	c Jones b Alderman	27	31	2
P.L.Taylor	not out	18	28	1	M.Prabhakar	c Waugh b Rackemann	21	34	3
G.D.Campbell	c More b Kapil Dev	0	3	–	† K.S.More	c Campbell b Alderman	8	8	1
C.G.Rackemann	c Kapil Dev b Prabhakar	6	9	–	A.S.Wassan	b Alderman	4	11	–
T.M.Alderman					N.D.Hirwani	not out	1	1	–
Extras	(lb 8, w 4, nb 3)	15			Extras	(b 4, lb 2, w 3, nb 7)	16		
Total	(50 overs; 9 wickets)	**187**			**Total**	(45 overs)	**169**		

INDIA	O	M	R	W	AUSTRALIA	O	M	R	W
Kapil Dev	10	0	29	2	Alderman	10	2	32	5
Prabhakar	10	3	35	1	Rackemann	9	0	27	2
Wassan	10	0	36	0	Campbell	8	0	29	1
Hirwani	10	2	39	2	O'Donnell	8	0	36	1
Sharma	10	0	40	1	P.L.Taylor	10	2	39	1

FALL OF WICKETS
1-31, 2-51, 3-92, 4-119, 5-123, 6-140, 7-170, 8-172, 9-187

FALL OF WICKETS
1-5, 2-14, 3-23, 4-75, 5-98, 6-110, 7-154, 8-155, 9-167, 10-169

Umpires: B.L.Aldridge (9) and R.L.McHarg (8).

NEW ZEALAND v AUSTRALIA 1989-90

At Lancaster Park, Christchurch on 4 March 1990.   Result: **AUSTRALIA** won by 150 runs.   Toss: Australia.
Award: D.M.Jones.   LOI debuts: None.

New Zealand, led by Martin Crowe for the first time after John Wright withdrew shortly before the toss with influenza,
lost their last eight wickets for 15 runs off 52 balls and sustained their largest defeat by a runs margin. Simon O'Donnell
took 5 for 5 in 28 balls.

AUSTRALIA		Runs	Balls	4/6	NEW ZEALAND		Runs	Balls	4/6
D.C.Boon	c Crowe b Larsen	67	90	5	* M.D.Crowe	c Waugh b Rackemann	17	26	4
G.R.Marsh	c Smith b Hadlee	2	5	–	A.H.Jones	c Border b Campbell	43	69	5
D.M.Jones	b Hadlee	107	143	8	M.J.Greatbatch	c Healy b Rackemann	0	4	–
S.R.Waugh	run out	3	11	–	K.R.Rutherford	lbw b O'Donnell	20	15	2
* A.R.Border	c Bracewell b Snedden	6	22	–	S.A.Thomson	b O'Donnell	1	9	–
S.P.O'Donnell	c Jones b Snedden	20	19	–/2	G.R.Larsen	b O'Donnell	1	7	–
† I.A.Healy	b Snedden	6	5	1	† I.D.S.Smith	c Border b Campbell	3	5	–
P.L.Taylor	not out	6	4	1	R.J.Hadlee	b Campbell	2	13	–
G.D.Campbell	b Morrison	2	4	–	J.G.Bracewell	b O'Donnell	0	1	–
C.G.Rackemann	not out	2	2	–	M.C.Snedden	c Jones b O'Donnell	0	6	–
T.M.Alderman					D.K.Morrison	not out	0	–	–
Extras	(lb 17, w 3, nb 3)	23			Extras	(lb 3, w 3, nb 1)	7		
Total	(50 overs; 8 wickets)	**244**			**Total**	(25.2 overs)	**94**		

NEW ZEALAND	O	M	R	W	AUSTRALIA	O	M	R	W
Hadlee	10	1	43	2	Alderman	7	1	34	0
Morrison	9	0	51	1	Rackemann	6	2	27	2
Snedden	10	2	32	3	Campbell	6.2	2	17	3
Thomson	8	0	49	0	O'Donnell	6	0	13	5
Larsen	10	0	32	1					
Bracewell	3	0	20	0					

FALL OF WICKETS
1-39, 2-39, 3-79, 4-81, 5-87, 6-91, 7-92, 8-93, 9-94, 10-94

FALL OF WICKETS
1-3, 2-148, 3-153, 4-190, 5-214, 6-229, 7-233, 8-240

Umpires: B.L.Aldridge (10) and R.L.McHarg (9).

NEW ZEALAND v INDIA 1989-90

At Basin Reserve, Wellington on 6 March 1990. Result: **INDIA** won by 1 run. Toss: India.
Award: Kapil Dev. LOI debuts: None.

Reduced by a six-minute shower during India's innings, this 49-over match produced a pulsating finish. Needing 11 from the last over, Richard Hadlee hit Kapil Dev for 4, 2, 2 and 1 (losing his partner to a run out), before being yorked by the fifth ball.

INDIA		Runs	Balls	4/6
W.V.Raman	run out	0	8	–
M.Prabhakar	c M.D.Crowe b Morrison	36	59	4
S.V.Manjrekar	run out	36	82	2
D.B.Vengsarkar	lbw b Morrison	0	1	–
* M.Azharuddin	run out	29	36	2
S.R.Tendulkar	c Smith b Thomson	36	39	5
Kapil Dev	c Rutherford b Morrison	46	38	4/1
† K.S.More	c Rutherford b Thomson	2	6	–
A.K.Sharma	c Smith b Hadlee	12	16	–
A.S.Wassan	not out	4	6	–
N.D.Hirwani	c M.D.Crowe b Hadlee	0	1	–
Extras	(lb 13, w 7)	20		
Total	**(48.2 overs)**	**221**		

NEW ZEALAND		Runs	Balls	4/6
* M.D.Crowe	c More b Kapil Dev	18	24	2
J.J.Crowe	c More b Hirwani	26	76	1
A.H.Jones	run out	9	23	–
M.J.Greatbatch	c Prabhakar b Wassan	53	70	3
K.R.Rutherford	b Prabhakar	44	50	–/1
R.J.Hadlee	b Kapil Dev	46	37	3
† I.D.S.Smith	c sub b Wassan	5	7	–
S.A.Thomson	c Wassan b Prabhakar	2	4	–
G.R.Larsen	b Prabhakar	0	2	–
M.C.Snedden	run out	0	–	–
D.K.Morrison	not out	0	–	–
Extras	(lb 11, w 6)	17		
Total	**(48.5 overs)**	**220**		

NEW ZEALAND	O	M	R	W
Hadlee	9.2	2	27	2
Snedden	10	0	50	0
Morrison	9	0	33	3
Thomson	10	0	47	2
Larsen	10	0	51	0

INDIA	O	M	R	W
Prabhakar	10	1	37	3
Kapil Dev	9.5	1	45	2
Wassan	10	0	46	2
Hirwani	10	0	46	1
Sharma	9	0	35	0

FALL OF WICKETS
1-8, 2-66, 3-66, 4-93, 5-122, 6-163, 7-173, 8-207, 9-219, 10-221

FALL OF WICKETS
1-33, 2-55, 3-68, 4-148, 5-174, 6-195, 7-210, 8-211, 9-220, 10-220

Umpires: G.I.J.Cowan (2) and S.J.Woodward (17).

AUSTRALIA v INDIA 1989-90

At Seddon Park, Hamilton on 8 March 1990. Result: **AUSTRALIA** won by 7 wickets. Toss: India.
Award: G.R.Marsh. LOI debuts: India – Gursharan Singh.

Australia's highest opening partnership in New Zealand, 112 from 184 balls, paved the way for a comfortable win. Geoff Marsh emulated Kapil Dev in the previous match by completing 3000 runs in internationals.

INDIA		Runs	Balls	4/6
W.V.Raman	c Healy b P.L.Taylor	58	86	7/1
M.Prabhakar	c M.A.Taylor b Hughes	7	13	1
S.V.Manjrekar	run out	33	70	1
* M.Azharuddin	lbw b Hughes	37	47	2/1
V.B.Chandrasekhar	c Border b P.L.Taylor	3	10	–
Gursharan Singh	lbw b P.L.Taylor	4	10	–
Kapil Dev	not out	48	53	4/1
A.K.Sharma	c Campbell b Hughes	7	6	–
† K.S.More	run out	1	2	–
A.S.Wassan	not out	8	4	1
N.D.Hirwani				
Extras	(lb 4, nb 1)	5		
Total	**(50 overs; 8 wickets)**	**211**		

AUSTRALIA		Runs	Balls	4/6
G.R.Marsh	c Gursharan Singh b Kapil Dev	86	144	10/1
M.A.Taylor	st More b Sharma	56	90	8
S.R.Waugh	c Prabhakar b Hirwani	23	32	2
D.C.Boon	not out	24	24	4
* A.R.Border	not out	9	6	–/1
S.P.O'Donnell				
† I.A.Healy				
P.L.Taylor				
M.G.Hughes				
G.D.Campbell				
T.M.Alderman				
Extras	(b 4, lb 5, w 4, nb 1)	14		
Total	**(48 overs; 3 wickets)**	**212**		

AUSTRALIA	O	M	R	W
Alderman	7	0	13	0
Hughes	7	0	36	3
Campbell	8	0	25	0
O'Donnell	9	1	62	0
P.L.Taylor	10	2	31	3
Border	9	0	40	0

INDIA	O	M	R	W
Kapil Dev	8	0	37	1
Prabhakar	8	1	29	0
Wassan	2	0	12	0
Hirwani	10	2	25	0
Raman	10	1	43	0
Sharma	10	0	57	1

FALL OF WICKETS
1-12, 2-92, 3-108, 4-114, 5-123, 6-174, 7-194, 8-200

FALL OF WICKETS
1-112, 2-158, 3-203

Umpires: G.I.J.Cowan (3) and R.L.McHarg (10).

NEW ZEALAND v AUSTRALIA 1989-90

At Eden Park, Auckland on 10 March 1990.　　Result: **AUSTRALIA** won on faster scoring rate.　　Toss: New Zealand.
Award: D.M.Jones.　　LOI debuts: None.

Dean Jones scored 50 off 37 balls. A 21-minute shower reduced the match by three overs, a further 26-minute break remodelled the hosts' target to 204 from 40 overs (Martin Crowe retiring with a groin strain at 115 for 1), and a final burst gave Australia victory on run rate.

AUSTRALIA		Runs	Balls	4/6
M.A.Taylor	c Larsen b Thomson	17	60	2
* G.R.Marsh	c Jones b Snedden	6	17	1
D.M.Jones	c and b Hadlee	59	42	8/1
D.C.Boon	c Rutherford b Morrison	9	10	1
S.R.Waugh	c Smith b Snedden	36	63	2
S.P.O'Donnell	run out	52	51	2/2
† I.A.Healy	not out	36	31	2
P.L.Taylor	not out	11	16	–
M.G.Hughes				
G.D.Campbell				
C.G.Rackemann				
Extras	(b 1, lb 4, w 7, nb 1)	13		
Total	(47 overs; 6 wickets)	**239**		

NEW ZEALAND		Runs	Balls	4/6
* J.G.Wright	b P.L.Taylor	48	53	9
M.D.Crowe	retired hurt	51	81	3
A.H.Jones	not out	26	46	–
M.J.Greatbatch	c Healy b Rackemann	0	3	–
K.R.Rutherford	not out	29	37	2
R.J.Hadlee				
† I.D.S.Smith				
G.R.Larsen				
S.A.Thomson				
M.C.Snedden				
D.K.Morrison				
Extras	(lb 3, w 9, nb 1)	13		
Total	(34.5 overs; 2 wickets)	**167**		

NEW ZEALAND	O	M	R	W
Hadlee	10	1	40	1
Snedden	9	1	45	2
Morrison	9	1	39	1
Thomson	8	0	60	1
Larsen	10	0	45	0
Rutherford	1	0	5	0

AUSTRALIA	O	M	R	W
Hughes	4	0	28	0
Campbell	7.5	0	37	0
O'Donnell	6	0	35	0
Rackemann	10	0	37	1
P.L.Taylor	7	0	27	1

FALL OF WICKETS
1-12, 2-61, 3-85, 4-118, 5-184, 6-194

FALL OF WICKETS
1-99, 2-115

Umpires: R.S.Dunne (5) and S.J.Woodward (18).

NEW ZEALAND v AUSTRALIA 1989-90

At Eden Park, Auckland on 11 March 1990.　　Result: **AUSTRALIA** won by 8 wickets.　　Toss: New Zealand.
Award: D.M.Jones.　　LOI debuts: None.

New Zealand qualified for the final on a run-rate quotient calculated by dividing runs scored by overs faced and multiplying the result by overs bowled divided by runs conceded. Allan Border blocked so that Dean Jones could complete a 91-ball hundred and 1000 LOI runs in 1989-90.

NEW ZEALAND		Runs	Balls	4/6
* J.G.Wright	c Healy b Rackemann	4	15	–
A.H.Jones	c Boon b Alderman	7	25	1
M.J.Greatbatch	c Jones b Campbell	11	31	1
K.R.Rutherford	c Healy b Rackemann	2	9	–
J.J.Crowe	c and b Alderman	28	61	2
G.R.Larsen	c Healy b O'Donnell	1	7	–
R.J.Hadlee	c Boon b Rackemann	79	92	5/2
† I.D.S.Smith	c Jones b Campbell	9	9	1
J.G.Bracewell	c Healy b Campbell	3	10	–
M.C.Snedden	c Marsh b Taylor	5	17	–
D.K.Morrison	not out	9	23	–
Extras	(lb 2, w 2)	4		
Total	(49.2 overs)	**162**		

AUSTRALIA		Runs	Balls	4/6
G.R.Marsh	b Bracewell	24	71	–
D.C.Boon	lbw b Morrison	9	15	–
D.M.Jones	not out	102	91	7/5
* A.R.Border	not out	19	66	2/1
S.R.Waugh				
S.P.O'Donnell				
† I.A.Healy				
P.L.Taylor				
G.D.Campbell				
C.G.Rackemann				
T.M.Alderman				
Extras	(lb 2, w 4, nb 4)	10		
Total	(39.1 overs; 2 wickets)	**164**		

AUSTRALIA	O	M	R	W
Alderman	10	2	34	2
Rackemann	10	2	22	3
O'Donnell	8	3	12	1
Campbell	10	0	37	3
Taylor	9.2	0	50	1
Border	2	0	5	0

NEW ZEALAND	O	M	R	W
Hadlee	9	3	34	0
Morrison	8	0	46	1
Snedden	5	0	13	0
Larsen	7.1	0	27	0
Bracewell	10	0	42	1

FALL OF WICKETS
1-12, 2-15, 3-26, 4-32, 5-33, 6-113, 7-134, 8-147, 9-147, 10-162

FALL OF WICKETS
1-13, 2-81

Umpires: R.S.Dunne (6) and S.J.Woodward (19).

AUSTRAL-ASIA CUP (1st Match)

INDIA v SRI LANKA 1989-90

At Sharjah CA Stadium, UAE on 25 April 1990.   Result: **SRI LANKA** won by 3 wickets.   Toss: Sri Lanka.
Award: A.Ranatunga.   LOI debuts: India – A.Kumble.

Sponsored by Sanyo (electronics), the second Austral-Asia Cup involved six teams divided into two groups. A spectacular innings by their captain enabled Sri Lanka to score 55 off the final five overs, 44 coming from the last 20 balls.

INDIA		Runs	Balls	4/6
K.Srikkanth	c Samarasekera b Karnain	19	34	–
W.V.Raman	c Tillekeratne b Ratnayeke	7	29	–
N.S.Sidhu	c Ratnayake b Gurusinha	64	73	4
* M.Azharuddin	c Madurasinghe b Ratnayeke	108	116	7
S.R.Tendulkar	run out	10	12	–
R.J.Shastri	c P.A.de Silva b Karnain	9	13	–
Kapil Dev	run out	8	11	1
† K.S.More	c Samarasekera b Ratnayeke	2	5	–
M.Prabhakar	not out	2	4	–
S.K.Sharma	not out	2	4	–
A.Kumble				
Extras	(lb 3, w 6, nb 1)	10		
Total	(50 overs; 8 wickets)	241		

SRI LANKA		Runs	Balls	4/6
M.A.R.Samarasekera	c More b Kapil Dev	14	32	1
† H.P.Tillekeratne	b Sharma	24	44	3
A.P.Gurusinha	run out	21	32	–
P.A.de Silva	b Sharma	34	47	2
* A.Ranatunga	not out	85	77	4/3
S.T.Jayasuriya	c Tendulkar b Shastri	4	15	–
S.H.U.Karnain	c More b Kumble	1	9	–
J.R.Ratnayeke	b Prabhakar	22	35	1
R.J.Ratnayake	not out	15	8	2
E.A.R.de Silva				
M.A.W.R.Madurasinghe				
Extras	(lb 12, w 7, nb 3)	22		
Total	(49.2 overs; 7 wickets)	242		

SRI LANKA	O	M	R	W
Ratnayeke	10	0	31	3
Ratnayake	10	0	52	0
Karnain	10	1	43	2
Ranatunga	8	0	40	0
E.A.R.de Silva	6	0	38	0
Gurusinha	6	0	34	1

INDIA	O	M	R	W
Kapil Dev	9.2	1	44	1
Prabhakar	10	1	51	1
Kumble	10	0	42	1
Sharma	10	1	63	2
Shastri	10	1	30	1

FALL OF WICKETS
1-30, 2-35, 3-149, 4-168, 5-190, 6-223, 7-236, 8-238

FALL OF WICKETS
1-29, 2-41, 3-97, 4-111, 5-128, 6-134, 7-203

Umpires: B.L.Aldridge (NZ) (11) and A.R.Crafter (*Australia*) (72).

AUSTRAL-ASIA CUP (2nd Match)

AUSTRALIA v NEW ZEALAND 1989-90

At Sharjah CA Stadium, UAE on 26 April 1990.   Result: **AUSTRALIA** won by 63 runs.   Toss: New Zealand.
Award: D.C.Boon.   LOI debuts: New Zealand – J.P.Millmow, M.W.Priest.

Steve Waugh completed 2000 runs in 83 LOI innings. Allan Border took 3 for 1 in 14 balls but conceded a six off the last ball of the match.

AUSTRALIA		Runs	Balls	4/6
G.R.Marsh	c Smith b Snedden	26	47	2
M.A.Taylor	run out	60	83	5
D.M.Jones	c Morrison b Snedden	1	5	–
D.C.Boon	not out	92	93	8
S.R.Waugh	run out	34	48	2
* A.R.Border	c Bracewell b Morrison	34	24	3/1
S.P.O'Donnell	not out	3	3	–
† I.A.Healy				
P.L.Taylor				
C.G.Rackemann				
T.M.Alderman				
Extras	(b 2, lb 4, w 2)	8		
Total	(50 overs; 5 wickets)	258		

NEW ZEALAND		Runs	Balls	4/6
* J.G.Wright	c Marsh b Alderman	0	2	–
M.D.Crowe	b P.L.Taylor	41	74	4
A.H.Jones	b O'Donnell	15	26	–
M.J.Greatbatch	b Border	37	76	2
K.R.Rutherford	c and b Border	20	26	1
† I.D.S.Smith	c Marsh b Border	2	8	–
J.G.Bracewell	not out	36	39	2/1
M.W.Priest	b Alderman	15	40	–
M.C.Snedden	not out	13	14	1
J.P.Millmow				
D.K.Morrison				
Extras	(lb 11, w 4, nb 1)	16		
Total	(50 overs; 7 wickets)	195		

NEW ZEALAND	O	M	R	W
Morrison	10	1	51	1
Millmow	10	0	57	0
Bracewell	10	0	47	0
Snedden	10	1	31	2
Priest	7	0	43	0
Rutherford	3	0	23	0

AUSTRALIA	O	M	R	W
Alderman	10	0	46	2
Rackemann	7	0	27	0
O'Donnell	10	3	27	1
Waugh	7	0	32	0
P.L.Taylor	10	0	27	1
Border	6	0	25	3

FALL OF WICKETS
1-67, 2-73, 3-115, 4-196, 5-247

FALL OF WICKETS
1-10, 2-26, 3-97, 4-121, 5-127, 6-129, 7-166

Umpires: R.B.Gupta (*India*) (20) and Khizer Hayat (*Pakistan*) (28).

INDIA v PAKISTAN 1989-90

At Sharjah CA Stadium, UAE on 27 April 1990.   Result: **PAKISTAN** won by 26 runs.   Toss: India.
Award: Waqar Younis.   LOI debuts: Pakistan – Sajjad Akbar.

Promoted to open the batting, Salim Yousuf responded with his highest LOI score. Salim Malik survived just long enough to complete 3000 runs in 105 innings.

PAKISTAN		Runs	Balls	4/6
Saeed Anwar	c Kapil Dev b Shastri	37	32	6
† Salim Yousuf	st More b Kumble	62	90	3/1
Salim Malik	b Shastri	7	17	–
Javed Miandad	run out	37	74	–
* Imran Khan	c More b Prabhakar	18	29	1
Wasim Akram	lbw b Sharma	11	12	–/1
Ijaz Ahmed	c Shastri b Prabhakar	32	27	3/1
Abdul Qadir	run out	1	4	–
Sajjad Akbar	run out	5	9	–
Waqar Younis	not out	7	6	–
Aqib Javed	not out	0	–	–
Extras	(b 4, lb 6, w 8)	18		
Total	(50 overs; 9 wickets)	**235**		

INDIA		Runs	Balls	4/6
K.Srikkanth	st Salim Yousuf b Sajjad	35	51	1
M.Prabhakar	run out	27	54	2
N.S.Sidhu	b Waqar	0	1	–
* M.Azharuddin	not out	78	95	2/2
Kapil Dev	b Waqar	1	2	–
S.V.Manjrekar	c Ijaz b Sajjad	10	24	–
S.R.Tendulkar	c Saeed b Imran	20	25	1
R.J.Shastri	c Salim Yousuf b Waqar	3	8	–
† K.S.More	c Miandad b Wasim	4	5	1
S.K.Sharma	c Salim Yousuf b Waqar	5	9	–
A.Kumble	run out	0	6	–
Extras	(b 2, lb 6, w 17, nb 1)	26		
Total	(46.3 overs)	**209**		

INDIA	O	M	R	W
Kapil Dev	5	0	30	0
Prabhakar	10	0	55	2
Sharma	10	0	52	1
Shastri	10	0	36	2
Kumble	10	0	33	1
Srikkanth	5	0	19	0

PAKISTAN	O	M	R	W
Wasim Akram	8.3	0	28	1
Aqib Javed	8	0	25	0
Waqar Younis	10	0	42	4
Abdul Qadir	7	0	44	0
Sajjad Akbar	10	1	45	2
Imran Khan	3	0	17	1

FALL OF WICKETS
1-73, 2-90, 3-130, 4-166, 5-178, 6-193, 7-195, 8-216, 9-235

FALL OF WICKETS
1-61, 2-61, 3-88, 4-91, 5-129, 6-165, 7-190, 8-197, 9-208, 10-209

Umpires: B.L.Aldridge (NZ) (12) and A.R.Crafter (Australia) (73).

NEW ZEALAND v BANGLADESH 1989-90

At Sharjah CA Stadium, UAE on 28 April 1990.   Result: **NEW ZEALAND** won by 161 runs.   Toss: New Zealand.
Award: A.H.Jones.   LOI debuts: Bangladesh – Inam-ul-Haq.

New Zealand converted their record opening partnership into the (then) second-highest LOI total; it remains the highest at Sharjah. Azhar Hussain was the first to score a fifty for Bangladesh.

NEW ZEALAND		Runs	Balls	4/6
M.D.Crowe	b Minhaz	69	71	2/1
* J.G.Wright	c and b Minhaz	93	98	8
A.H.Jones	c Jahangir b Nousher	93	72	4/3
M.J.Greatbatch	c Akram b Farooq	32	42	2/1
K.R.Rutherford	not out	30	22	2
S.A.Thomson	not out	8	8	–
† I.D.S.Smith				
J.G.Bracewell				
M.C.Snedden				
J.P.Millmow				
D.K.Morrison				
Extras	(lb 6, w 5, nb 2)	13		
Total	(50 overs; 4 wickets)	**338**		

BANGLADESH		Runs	Balls	4/6
Azhar Hussain	b Rutherford	54	126	4
Zahid Razzak	lbw b Millmow	4	10	–
* Gazi Ashraf	b Snedden	8	31	1
Akram Khan	c and b Bracewell	33	48	3
Minhaz-ul-Abedin	c Wright b Millmow	18	22	2
Amin-ul-Islam	not out	30	41	4
Inam-ul-Haq	not out	13	29	1
Jahangir Shah				
† Nasir Ahmed				
Ghulam Farooq				
Ghulam Nousher				
Extras	(b 1, lb 10, w 6)	17		
Total	(50 overs; 5 wickets)	**177**		

BANGLADESH	O	M	R	W
Ghulam Nousher	10	0	55	1
Ghulam Farooq	4.3	0	28	1
Jahangir Shah	9	0	62	0
Inam-ul-Haq	10	0	72	0
Azhar Hussain	7	0	51	0
Minhaz-ul-Abedin	7	0	39	2
Amin-ul-Islam	2	0	21	0
Gazi Ashraf	0.3	0	4	0

NEW ZEALAND	O	M	R	W
Morrison	6	0	19	0
Millmow	10	0	41	2
Thomson	10	1	32	0
Snedden	7	2	18	1
Bracewell	10	0	32	1
Jones	4	1	12	0
Rutherford	3	0	12	1

FALL OF WICKETS
1-158, 2-178, 3-269, 4-321

FALL OF WICKETS
1-11, 2-37, 3-39, 4-115, 5-137

Umpires: R.B.Gupta (India) (21) and Khizer Hayat (Pakistan) (29).

PAKISTAN v SRI LANKA 1989-90

At Sharjah CA Stadium, UAE on 29 April 1990.   Result: **PAKISTAN** won by 90 runs.   Toss: Sri Lanka.
Award: Ijaz Ahmed.   LOI debuts: Pakistan – Mansoor Rana.

Sharjah's 50th international saw Waqar Younis return his best LOI analysis and become the second Pakistan bowler after Imran Khan to take six wickets in an innings. Incredibly, Waqar's remarkable figures failed to win the match award.

PAKISTAN		Runs	Balls	4/6
Saeed Anwar	b Madurasinghe	40	48	1/2
† Salim Yousuf	run out	46	60	2/1
Javed Miandad	c Gurusinha b Ratnayeke	75	85	5
Salim Malik	b P.A.de Silva	26	30	–
Ijaz Ahmed	c Ranatunga b Ratnayeke	89	64	8/3
* Imran Khan	c Tillekeratne b Ratnayeke	8	7	–
Mansoor Rana	lbw b Ratnayeke	5	3	1
Mushtaq Ahmed	not out	4	4	–
Waqar Younis	b Ratnayeke	2	2	–
Zakir Khan	not out	2	1	–
Aqib Javed				
Extras	(b 2, lb 3, w 7, nb 2)	14		
Total	(50 overs; 8 wickets)	311		

SRI LANKA		Runs	Balls	4/6
M.A.R.Samarasekera	run out	29	30	3
H.P.Tillekeratne	lbw b Waqar	19	40	2
A.P.Gurusinha	c Salim Yousuf b Aqib	9	13	1
P.A.de Silva	b Waqar	0	1	–
† D.S.B.P.Kuruppu	b Waqar	41	61	3
* A.Ranatunga	c Saeed b Mushtaq	38	53	3
R.J.Ratnayake	b Waqar	26	19	–/3
S.H.U.Karnain	b Waqar	14	18	1
J.R.Ratnayeke	c Salim Yousuf b Zakir	9	46	–
E.A.R.de Silva	lbw b Waqar	0	7	–
M.A.W.R.Madurasinghe	not out	1	3	–
Extras	(b 2, lb 13, w 16, nb 4)	35		
Total	(47.4 overs)	221		

SRI LANKA	O	M	R	W
Ratnayeke	10	0	65	3
Ratnayake	9	0	44	2
Karnain	2	0	18	0
Madurasinghe	10	0	40	1
E.A.R.de Silva	8	0	57	0
P.A.de Silva	10	0	63	1
Ranatunga	1	0	19	0

PAKISTAN	O	M	R	W
Zakir Khan	9.4	0	41	1
Aqib Javed	9	2	34	1
Waqar Younis	10	1	26	6
Mushtaq Ahmed	8	0	49	1
Saeed Anwar	10	0	49	0
Mansoor Rana	1	0	7	0

FALL OF WICKETS
1-82, 2-110, 3-163, 4-246, 5-294, 6-301, 7-302, 8-307

FALL OF WICKETS
1-43, 2-60, 3-64, 4-64, 5-132, 6-184, 7-185, 8-214, 9-217, 10-221

Umpires: B.L.Aldridge (NZ) (13) and A.R.Crafter (*Australia*) (74).

AUSTRALIA v BANGLADESH 1989-90

At Sharjah CA Stadium, UAE on 30 April 1990.   Result: **AUSTRALIA** won by 7 wickets.   Toss: Bangladesh.
Award: P.L.Taylor.   LOI debuts: Bangladesh – Alam Talukdar.

Although Bangladesh survived their full allotment of overs, they were unable to restrain an Australian innings that featured only one specialist batsman.

BANGLADESH		Runs	Balls	4/6
Azhar Hussain	c Healy b Hughes	5	15	–
Zahid Razzak	c Healy b Campbell	4	13	–
* Gazi Ashraf	b P.L.Taylor	18	75	–
Akram Khan	c Marsh b O'Donnell	13	44	1
Farooq Ahmed	lbw b Waugh	6	19	1
Minhaz-ul-Abedin	c Healy b P.L.Taylor	0	3	–
Amin-ul-Islam	not out	41	76	3
Inam-ul-Haq	c Jones b Waugh	18	36	3
† Nasir Ahmed	b O'Donnell	3	13	–
Alam Talukdar	not out	7	16	1
Ghulam Nousher				
Extras	(b 2, lb 7, w 8, nb 2)	19		
Total	(50 overs; 8 wickets)	134		

AUSTRALIA		Runs	Balls	4/6
† I.A.Healy	c Hussain b Nousher	34	35	1
S.P.O'Donnell	c Ashraf b Minhaz	20	37	4
D.M.Jones	c Farooq b Minhaz	19	28	2
P.L.Taylor	not out	54	47	3
M.G.Hughes	not out	10	11	–/1
M.A.Taylor				
G.R.Marsh				
D.C.Boon				
* A.R.Border				
S.R.Waugh				
G.D.Campbell				
Extras	(lb 1, w 1, nb 1)	3		
Total	(25.4 overs; 3 wickets)	140		

AUSTRALIA	O	M	R	W
Hughes	10	3	15	1
Campbell	10	1	32	1
Waugh	10	2	22	2
O'Donnell	10	1	34	2
P.L.Taylor	10	2	22	2

BANGLADESH	O	M	R	W
Ghulam Nousher	6	0	27	1
Alam Talukdar	4	0	20	0
Azhar Hussain	7	0	26	0
Minhaz-ul-Abedin	6	0	43	2
Amin-ul-Islam	1.4	0	16	0
Inam-ul-Haq	1	0	7	0

FALL OF WICKETS
1-10, 2-12, 3-33, 4-47, 5-50, 6-59, 7-107, 8-121

FALL OF WICKETS
1-50, 2-58, 3-102

Umpires: R.B.Gupta (*India*) (22) and Khizer Hayat (*Pakistan*) (30).

315

NEW ZEALAND v PAKISTAN 1989-90

At Sharjah CA Stadium, UAE on 1 May 1990.   Result: **PAKISTAN** won by 8 wickets.   Toss: New Zealand.
Award: Waqar Younis.   LOI debuts: None.

Andrew Jones contributed 63.5% of the third-lowest total at Sharjah. Waqar Younis remains the only bowler to take four or more wickets in three successive LOI innings, a feat he subsequently twice repeated. He took 17 wickets at 7.41 in this tournament.

NEW ZEALAND		Runs	Balls	4/6
M.D.Crowe	c Salim Yousuf b Wasim	5	10	–
*J.G.Wright	b Aqib	1	10	–
A.H.Jones	c Imran b Mushtaq	47	85	4
M.J.Greatbatch	c sub (Mansoor Rana) b Wasim	4	15	–
K.R.Rutherford	c Salim Yousuf b Waqar	0	16	–
S.A.Thomson	b Waqar	4	16	1
J.G.Bracewell	c Aqib b Mushtaq	4	21	–
†I.D.S.Smith	c Salim Yousuf b Waqar	0	4	–
M.C.Snedden	lbw b Waqar	1	4	–
D.K.Morrison	lbw b Waqar	0	3	–
J.P.Millmow	not out	0	3	–
Extras	(lb 4, w 3, nb 1)	8		
Total	(31.1 overs)	**74**		

PAKISTAN		Runs	Balls	4/6
Saeed Anwar	c Thomson b Millmow	3	7	–
†Salim Yousuf	c Crowe b Millmow	25	19	4
Salim Malik	not out	31	46	4
*Imran Khan	not out	13	23	2
Javed Miandad				
Ijaz Ahmed				
Wasim Akram				
Mushtaq Ahmed				
Sajjad Akbar				
Waqar Younis				
Aqib Javed				
Extras	(lb 1, w 3, nb 1)	5		
Total	(15.4 overs; 2 wickets)	**77**		

PAKISTAN	O	M	R	W
Wasim Akram	6	1	16	2
Aqib Javed	6	0	23	1
Waqar Younis	9	2	20	5
Imran Khan	6	2	7	0
Mushtaq Ahmed	4.1	2	4	2

NEW ZEALAND	O	M	R	W
Morrison	4	0	32	0
Millmow	5	0	22	2
Thomson	4	1	9	0
Jones	2	0	8	0
Crowe	0.4	0	5	0

FALL OF WICKETS
1-7, 2-21, 3-37, 4-44, 5-56, 6-65, 7-70, 8-74, 9-74, 10-74

FALL OF WICKETS
1-19, 2-33

Umpires: A.R.Crafter (*Australia*) (75) and R.B.Gupta (*India*) (23).

AUSTRALIA v SRI LANKA 1989-90

At Sharjah CA Stadium, UAE on 2 May 1990.   Result: **AUSTRALIA** won by 114 runs.   Toss: Australia.
Award: S.P.O'Donnell.   LOI debuts: None.

Australia amassed their highest limited-overs score. Dean Jones surpassed Javed Miandad's record LOI tally for a season – 1098 runs in 1986-87. Simon O'Donnell's 18-ball fifty was the fastest until 1995-96 (*LOI No. 1087*) and his tally of sixes is the Australian record.

AUSTRALIA		Runs	Balls	4/6
M.A.Taylor	st Kuruppu b Madurasinghe	27	30	3
G.R.Marsh	c Kuruppu b Ratnayeke	68	104	3/1
D.M.Jones	not out	117	123	7/1
S.P.O'Donnell	b Ramanayake	74	29	4/6
D.C.Boon	not out	30	18	1/1
*A.R.Border				
S.R.Waugh				
†I.A.Healy				
P.L.Taylor				
C.G.Rackemann				
T.M.Alderman				
Extras	(b 5, lb 6, w 5)	16		
Total	(50 overs; 3 wickets)	**332**		

SRI LANKA		Runs	Balls	4/6
†D.S.B.P.Kuruppu	c Marsh b Alderman	14	21	1
M.A.R.Samarasekera	lbw b Alderman	25	26	4
H.P.Tillekeratne	st Healy b Border	76	109	5
P.A.de Silva	c Marsh b P.L.Taylor	19	21	2
*A.Ranatunga	c Rackemann b Waugh	26	32	1
J.R.Ratnayeke	run out	4	20	–
R.J.Ratnayake	c Border b P.L.Taylor	8	8	–/1
E.A.R.de Silva	c Healy b Border	9	6	–/1
C.P.H.Ramanayake	c Waugh b O'Donnell	19	28	–/1
M.A.W.R.Madurasinghe	not out	8	8	1
A.P.Gurusinha	absent hurt	–		
Extras	(b 1, lb 6, w 3)	10		
Total	(45.4 overs)	**218**		

SRI LANKA	O	M	R	W
Ratnayeke	10	0	70	1
Ratnayake	10	0	55	0
Madurasinghe	10	0	32	1
Ramanayake	10	0	82	1
E.A.R.de Silva	5	0	34	0
Gurusinha	5	0	48	0

AUSTRALIA	O	M	R	W
Alderman	7	0	35	2
Rackemann	10	0	51	0
O'Donnell	5.4	0	19	1
P.L.Taylor	10	1	28	2
Waugh	7	0	36	1
Border	6	0	42	2

FALL OF WICKETS
1-35, 2-172, 3-278

FALL OF WICKETS
1-25, 2-43, 3-77, 4-124, 5-135, 6-150, 7-174, 8-208, 9-218

Umpires: B.L.Aldridge (NZ) (14) and Khizer Hayat (*Pakistan*) (31).

AUSTRALIA v PAKISTAN 1989-90

At Sharjah CA Stadium, UAE on 4 May 1990.　　Result: **PAKISTAN** won by 36 runs.　　Toss: Pakistan.
Award: Wasim Akram.　　LOI debuts: None.

Wasim Akram ended Australia's sequence of ten wins when he bowled Hughes, Rackemann and Alderman with the last three balls of the tournament. He remains alone in taking two LOI hat-tricks. Dismissed for nought in his 100th international, Dean Jones scored 1164 from 22 innings in 1989-90.

PAKISTAN		Runs	Balls	4/6	AUSTRALIA		Runs	Balls	4/6
Saeed Anwar	c Healy b Rackemann	40	36	5	D.C.Boon	run out	37	58	3
† Salim Yousuf	lbw b Alderman	5	22	–	M.A.Taylor	run out	52	81	1
Javed Miandad	c Healy b Waugh	14	31	1	D.M.Jones	b Waqar	0	2	–
Salim Malik	c Border b P.L.Taylor	87	104	9/1	* A.R.Border	lbw b Waqar	1	5	–
Ijaz Ahmed	c Healy b Rackemann	20	30	1	S.R.Waugh	c Aqib b Mushtaq	64	83	6
* Imran Khan	c Healy b Rackemann	2	8	–	S.P.O'Donnell	c Ijaz b Mushtaq	33	28	4
Mansoor Rana	run out	10	21	–	P.L.Taylor	c Saeed b Mushtaq	9	6	–
Wasim Akram	not out	49	35	1/3	† I.A.Healy	not out	12	8	1
Mushtaq Ahmed	not out	17	15	2	M.G.Hughes	b Wasim	9	9	1
Waqar Younis					C.G.Rackemann	b Wasim	0	1	–
Aqib Javed					T.M.Alderman	b Wasim	0	1	–
Extras	(b 3, lb 10, w 9)	22			Extras	(lb 10, w 3)	13		
Total	(50 overs; 7 wickets)	266			Total	(46.5 overs)	230		

AUSTRALIA	O	M	R	W	PAKISTAN	O	M	R	W
Alderman	5	1	22	1	Wasim Akram	8.5	0	45	3
Hughes	10	0	55	0	Aqib Javed	7	0	27	0
Rackemann	10	0	49	3	Waqar Younis	8	0	38	2
O'Donnell	10	0	66	0	Mushtaq Ahmed	10	1	48	3
Waugh	5	0	22	1	Imran Khan	7	0	28	0
P.L.Taylor	10	0	39	1	Saeed Anwar	6	0	34	0

FALL OF WICKETS
1-40, 2-54, 3-80, 4-109, 5-154, 6-179, 7-207

FALL OF WICKETS
1-62, 2-62, 3-64, 4-133, 5-187, 6-207, 7-207, 8-230, 9-230, 10-230

Umpires: B.L.Aldridge (*New Zealand*) (15) and R.B.Gupta (*India*) (24).

ENGLAND v NEW ZEALAND 1990

At Headingley, Leeds on 23 May 1990.　　Result: **NEW ZEALAND** won by 4 wickets.　　Toss: New Zealand.
Award: M.J.Greatbatch.　　LOI debuts: New Zealand – C.Pringle.

Injuries to two bowlers prompted New Zealand to recruit Auckland-born Chris Pringle from his duties with Pudsey St Lawrence in the Bradford League. New Zealand's total was the highest by any side batting second until 1991-92 (*LOI No. 716*).

ENGLAND		Runs	Balls	4/6	NEW ZEALAND		Runs	Balls	4/6
* G.A.Gooch	c Millmow b Pringle	55	88	4/1	* J.G.Wright	c Stewart b Gooch	52	77	8
D.I.Gower	c Priest b Hadlee	1	8	–	A.H.Jones	st Russell b Gooch	51	66	4
R.A.Smith	c Crowe b Hadlee	128	168	16	M.D.Crowe	c Russell b Lewis	46	48	3
A.J.Lamb	run out	18	25	2	M.J.Greatbatch	not out	102	104	9/2
A.J.Stewart	lbw b Morrison	33	25	3/1	K.R.Rutherford	lbw b Lewis	0	2	–
D.R.Pringle	not out	30	17	5	R.J.Hadlee	c Lamb b Lewis	12	18	1
† R.C.Russell	c Crowe b Pringle	13	5	3	M.W.Priest	c Gower b Small	2	4	–
P.A.J.DeFreitas	not out	1	1	–	† I.D.S.Smith	not out	17	11	2
C.C.Lewis					C.Pringle				
G.C.Small					D.K.Morrison				
E.E.Hemmings					J.P.Millmow				
Extras	(lb 10, w 1, nb 5)	16			Extras	(b 5, lb 7, w 3, nb 1)	16		
Total	(55 overs; 6 wickets)	295			Total	(54.5 overs; 6 wickets)	298		

NEW ZEALAND	O	M	R	W	ENGLAND	O	M	R	W
Hadlee	11	4	46	2	Small	11	1	43	1
Pringle	11	2	45	2	DeFreitas	10.5	0	70	0
Morrison	11	0	70	1	Pringle	7	0	45	0
Millmow	11	0	65	0	Lewis	11	0	54	3
Priest	11	0	59	0	Hemmings	11	0	51	0
					Gooch	4	0	23	2

FALL OF WICKETS
1-5, 2-118, 3-168, 4-225, 5-261, 6-274

FALL OF WICKETS
1-97, 2-106, 3-224, 4-224, 5-254, 6-259

Umpires: B.J.Meyer (21) and N.T.Plews (4).

ENGLAND v NEW ZEALAND 1990

At Kennington Oval, London on 25 May 1990.   Result: **ENGLAND** won by 6 wickets.   Toss: England.
Award: D.E.Malcolm.   LOI debuts: England – D.E.Malcolm.

England won the Texaco Trophy on run rate. Mark Greatbatch became the first to score LOI hundreds in successive innings for New Zealand. Struck by balls from Chris Lewis, Ken Rutherford (left eyebrow) and Richard Hadlee (right hand) retired at 53 and 93 respectively.

NEW ZEALAND		Runs	Balls	4/6	ENGLAND		Runs	Balls	4/6
* J.G.Wright	c Small b Malcolm	15	41	2	* G.A.Gooch	not out	112	152	15
A.H.Jones	run out	15	31	1	D.I.Gower	b Hadlee	4	3	1
M.D.Crowe	c Russell b Lewis	7	31	–	R.A.Smith	c Smith b Hadlee	5	12	1
M.J.Greatbatch	c Smith b Malcolm	111	130	10/1	A.J.Lamb	lbw b Pringle	4	4	1
K.R.Rutherford	retired hurt	0	3	–	A.J.Stewart	c Morrison b Priest	28	57	3
R.J.Hadlee	retired hurt	9	24	–	† R.C.Russell	not out	47	71	5
M.W.Priest	c Smith b DeFreitas	24	51	–	C.C.Lewis				
† I.D.S.Smith	not out	25	17	2/1	P.A.J.DeFreitas				
C.Pringle	b Small	1	2	–	G.C.Small				
D.K.Morrison					E.E.Hemmings				
J.P.Millmow					D.E.Malcolm				
Extras	(lb 2, w 3)	5			Extras	(lb 7, w 5, nb 1)	13		
Total	(55 overs; 6 wickets)	**212**			**Total**	(49.3 overs; 4 wickets)	**213**		

ENGLAND	O	M	R	W	NEW ZEALAND	O	M	R	W
DeFreitas	11	1	47	1	Hadlee	11	2	34	2
Malcolm	11	5	19	2	Pringle	9.3	0	53	1
Lewis	11	1	51	1	Millmow	9	1	47	0
Small	11	0	59	1	Morrison	9	0	38	0
Hemmings	11	2	34	0	Priest	11	2	34	1

FALL OF WICKETS
1-25, 2-34, 3-53, 4-174, 5-202, 6-212

Umpires: D.J.Constant (29) and J.H.Hampshire (2).

ENGLAND v INDIA 1990

At Headingley, Leeds on 18 July 1990.   Result: **INDIA** won by 6 wickets.   Toss: India.
Award: A.Kumble.   LOI debuts: England – M.A.Atherton.

Shrewd adjudicator Geoffrey Boycott rewarded Anil Kumble for an outstanding spell of bowling in which he dismissed David Gower and Robin Smith without conceding a boundary.

ENGLAND		Runs	Balls	4/6	INDIA		Runs	Balls	4/6
* G.A.Gooch	c and b Shastri	45	75	7	W.V.Raman	c Atherton b DeFreitas	0	2	–
M.A.Atherton	lbw b Prabhakar	7	18	–	N.S.Sidhu	lbw b Lewis	39	70	5
D.I.Gower	b Kumble	50	95	3	S.V.Manjrekar	c Gower b Lewis	82	133	7
A.J.Lamb	c Prabhakar b Kapil Dev	56	77	3	S.R.Tendulkar	b Malcolm	19	35	1/1
R.A.Smith	c More b Kumble	6	5	1	* M.Azharuddin	not out	55	50	5
† R.C.Russell	c Manjrekar b Kapil Dev	14	20	–	R.J.Shastri	not out	23	29	4
P.A.J.DeFreitas	b Sharma	11	21	–	Kapil Dev				
C.C.Lewis	lbw b Prabhakar	6	7	1	M.Prabhakar				
E.E.Hemmings	b Sharma	3	3	–	† K.S.More				
A.R.C.Fraser	not out	4	4	–	S.K.Sharma				
D.E.Malcolm	c Kapil Dev b Prabhakar	4	3	1	A.Kumble				
Extras	(b 6, lb 8, w 9)	23			Extras	(lb 5, w 9, nb 1)	15		
Total	(54.3 overs)	**229**			**Total**	(53 overs; 4 wickets)	**233**		

INDIA	O	M	R	W	ENGLAND	O	M	R	W
Kapil Dev	11	1	49	2	DeFreitas	10	1	40	1
Prabhakar	10.3	1	40	3	Malcolm	11	0	57	1
Sharma	11	1	57	2	Fraser	11	3	37	0
Shastri	11	0	40	1	Lewis	10	0	58	2
Kumble	11	2	29	2	Hemmings	11	0	36	0

FALL OF WICKETS
1-22, 2-86, 3-134, 4-142, 5-186, 6-196, 7-211, 8-221, 9-224, 10-229

1-1, 2-76, 3-115, 4-183

Umpires: J.H.Hampshire (3) and J.W.Holder (8).

ENGLAND v INDIA 1990

At Trent Bridge, Nottingham on 20 July 1990.   Result: **INDIA** won by 5 wickets.   Toss: India.
Award: R.A.Smith.   LOI debuts: None.

India's second successive victory gained with 12 balls to spare secured them the Texaco Trophy for the first time. Robin Smith reached his second LOI hundred off 101 balls.

ENGLAND		Runs	Balls	4/6
* G.A.Gooch	b Prabhakar	7	15	1
M.A.Atherton	c More b Prabhakar	59	95	5
D.I.Gower	run out	25	30	6
A.J.Lamb	run out	3	18	–
R.A.Smith	b Shastri	103	105	11
† R.C.Russell	c Azharuddin b Kapil Dev	50	50	4
P.A.J.DeFreitas	c Vengsarkar b Sharma	1	4	–
C.C.Lewis	lbw b Prabhakar	7	10	–
G.C.Small	c Azharuddin b Kapil Dev	4	4	1
E.E.Hemmings	run out	0	–	–
A.R.C.Fraser	not out	0	–	–
Extras	(b 1, lb 12, w 8, nb 1)	22		
Total	(55 overs)	281		

INDIA		Runs	Balls	4/6
R.J.Shastri	c Atherton b Hemmings	33	57	3
N.S.Sidhu	b Small	23	27	3
S.V.Manjrekar	st Russell b Hemmings	59	94	4
D.B.Vengsarkar	b Lewis	54	62	3/2
* M.Azharuddin	not out	63	44	7
S.R.Tendulkar	b Fraser	31	26	3
Kapil Dev	not out	5	8	1
M.Prabhakar				
† K.S.More				
S.K.Sharma				
A.Kumble				
Extras	(lb 5, w 9)	14		
Total	(53 overs; 5 wickets)	282		

INDIA	O	M	R	W
Kapil Dev	11	2	40	2
Prabhakar	11	0	58	3
Sharma	10	0	50	1
Shastri	11	0	52	1
Kumble	11	1	58	0
Tendulkar	1	0	10	0

ENGLAND	O	M	R	W
Small	10	0	73	1
DeFreitas	11	0	59	0
Fraser	11	1	38	1
Hemmings	11	1	53	2
Lewis	10	0	54	1

FALL OF WICKETS
1-12, 2-47, 3-62, 4-173, 5-246, 6-254, 7-275, 8-280, 9-281, 10-281

FALL OF WICKETS
1-42, 2-69, 3-166, 4-186, 5-249

Umpires: M.J.Kitchen (5) and D.R.Shepherd (38).

PAKISTAN v NEW ZEALAND 1990-91

At Gaddafi Stadium, Lahore on 2 November 1990.   Result: **PAKISTAN** won by 19 runs.   Toss: New Zealand.
Award: Saeed Anwar.   LOI debuts: New Zealand – D.J.White.

A series of three 40-over matches. Saeed Anwar's hundred (off 114 balls) and Salim Malik's career-best analysis were both national records against New Zealand in Pakistan.

PAKISTAN		Runs	Balls	4/6
Saeed Anwar	c Smith b Morrison	101	115	11
Shoaib Mohammed	c Smith b Morrison	12	27	1
Salim Malik	c Morrison b Crowe	17	26	1
Manzoor Elahi	c and b Watson	17	27	2
Ijaz Ahmed	run out	5	8	–
* Javed Miandad	run out	11	18	–
† Salim Yousuf	c Smith b Morrison	1	4	–
Akram Raza	not out	13	12	1/1
Mushtaq Ahmed	run out	7	3	1
Waqar Younis				
Salim Jaffer				
Extras	(lb 7, w 5)	12		
Total	(40 overs; 8 wickets)	196		

NEW ZEALAND		Runs	Balls	4/6
D.J.White	c Saeed b Manzoor	13	40	–
* M.D.Crowe	b Manzoor	20	34	3
K.R.Rutherford	run out	12	32	–
M.J.Greatbatch	c Saeed b Akram Raza	36	43	2
D.N.Patel	b Salim Malik	16	18	1
† I.D.S.Smith	st Salim Yousuf b Salim Malik	47	31	4/1
M.W.Priest	st Salim Yousuf b Salim Malik	9	19	–
C.Pringle	st Salim Yousuf b Salim Malik	2	6	–
D.K.Morrison	lbw b Salim Malik	0	3	–
W.Watson	b Waqar	5	9	1
S.J.Roberts	not out	1	2	–
Extras	(b 1, lb 8, w 4, nb 3)	16		
Total	(39.2 overs)	177		

NEW ZEALAND	O	M	R	W
Pringle	6	0	22	0
Roberts	3	0	21	0
Watson	7	0	34	1
Morrison	8	0	28	3
Patel	8	0	36	0
Priest	4	0	24	0
Crowe	4	1	24	1

PAKISTAN	O	M	R	W
Salim Jaffer	5	0	16	0
Manzoor Elahi	8	1	32	2
Waqar Younis	7.2	0	26	1
Akram Raza	8	0	40	0
Mushtaq Ahmed	4	0	19	0
Salim Malik	7	2	35	5

FALL OF WICKETS
1-59, 2-114, 3-152, 4-161, 5-164, 6-168, 7-189, 8-196

FALL OF WICKETS
1-27, 2-40, 3-79, 4-104, 5-117, 6-149, 7-164, 8-164, 9-175, 10-177

Umpires: Khizer Hayat (32) and Mian Mohammad Aslam (7).

PAKISTAN v NEW ZEALAND 1990-91

At Shahi Bagh Stadium, Peshawar on 4 November 1990.   Result: **PAKISTAN** won by 8 wickets.   Toss: New Zealand.
Award: Saeed Anwar.   LOI debuts: New Zealand – G.E.Bradburn.

Waqar Younis recorded the best analysis against New Zealand until he himself improved upon it in 1993-94 (*LOI No. 898*). New Zealand lost all ten wickets for 77 runs.

NEW ZEALAND		Runs	Balls	4/6
D.J.White	c Salim Malik b Waqar	15	32	–
* M.D.Crowe	lbw b Waqar	46	55	4
K.R.Rutherford	lbw b Waqar	0	1	–
M.J.Greatbatch	run out	5	5	1
D.N.Patel	b Waqar	2	11	–
G.E.Bradburn	c Saeed b Akram Raza	30	61	1
† I.D.S.Smith	b Mushtaq	6	18	–
M.W.Priest	c Ramiz b Salim Malik	10	31	–
C.Pringle	c Miandad b Salim Malik	3	8	–
D.K.Morrison	lbw b Waqar	0	4	–
W.Watson	not out	0	1	–
Extras	(lb 7, w 2, nb 1)	10		
Total	(37.4 overs)	**127**		

PAKISTAN		Runs	Balls	4/6
Ramiz Raja	not out	50	65	7/2
Saeed Anwar	c Smith b Bradburn	67	75	5
Salim Malik	c Smith b Bradburn	1	6	–
Ijaz Ahmed	not out	7	29	–
* Javed Miandad				
Manzoor Elahi				
† Salim Yousuf				
Akram Raza				
Mushtaq Ahmed				
Waqar Younis				
Zakir Khan				
Extras	(lb 1, w 2)	3		
Total	(29.1 overs; 2 wickets)	**128**		

PAKISTAN	O	M	R	W
Manzoor Elahi	8	0	35	0
Zakir Khan	5	0	19	0
Waqar Younis	6.4	2	11	5
Mushtaq Ahmed	8	1	26	1
Akram Raza	7	0	22	1
Salim Malik	3	0	7	2

NEW ZEALAND	O	M	R	W
Pringle	4	0	15	0
Watson	3	0	16	0
Morrison	2	0	11	0
Patel	8	0	35	0
Priest	3	0	23	0
Bradburn	6	2	18	2
Crowe	3.1	0	9	0

FALL OF WICKETS
1-50, 2-50, 3-58, 4-65, 5-82, 6-95, 7-117, 8-127, 9-127, 10-127

FALL OF WICKETS
1-96, 2-98

Umpires: Javed Akhtar (9) and Said Ahmed Shah (2).

PAKISTAN v NEW ZEALAND 1990-91

At Jinnah Park, Sialkot on 6 November 1990.   Result: **PAKISTAN** won by 105 runs.   Toss: New Zealand.
Award: Ramiz Raja.   LOI debuts: Pakistan – Zahid Fazal.

Pakistan completed a clean sweep of victories in Test matches (three) and internationals. Ramiz Raja contributed a 111-ball hundred and Waqar Younis returned his second five-wicket haul in successive games.

PAKISTAN		Runs	Balls	4/6
Saeed Anwar	c White b Patel	35	48	2
Ramiz Raja	run out	114	123	14
Salim Malik	not out	65	68	5
Zahid Fazal	not out	5	2	1
Ijaz Ahmed				
* Javed Miandad				
Manzoor Elahi				
† Salim Yousuf				
Akram Raza				
Waqar Younis				
Zakir Khan				
Extras	(b 2, w 1, nb 1)	4		
Total	(40 overs; 2 wickets)	**223**		

NEW ZEALAND		Runs	Balls	4/6
D.J.White	b Manzoor	9	25	1
* M.D.Crowe	lbw b Manzoor	22	21	3
K.R.Rutherford	c and b Ijaz	24	24	3
M.J.Greatbatch	c Salim Yousuf b Manzoor	3	9	–
D.N.Patel	b Waqar	23	36	1/1
† I.D.S.Smith	c sub (Mushtaq Ahmed) b Ijaz	11	9	2
G.E.Bradburn	c Salim Yousuf b Waqar	0	2	–
M.W.Priest	c Salim Yousuf b Waqar	0	2	–
C.Pringle	lbw b Waqar	0	14	–
D.K.Morrison	not out	4	7	–
W.Watson	lbw b Waqar	0	3	–
Extras	(b 4, lb 5, w 10, nb 3)	22		
Total	(25 overs)	**118**		

NEW ZEALAND	O	M	R	W
Pringle	8	0	46	0
Watson	8	1	32	0
Morrison	3	0	17	0
Patel	7	0	44	1
Bradburn	4	0	24	0
Priest	5	0	27	0
Crowe	5	0	31	0

PAKISTAN	O	M	R	W
Manzoor Elahi	7	0	36	3
Zakir Khan	5	0	26	0
Ijaz Ahmed	7	0	31	2
Waqar Younis	6	1	16	5

FALL OF WICKETS
1-36, 2-47, 3-60, 4-74, 5-94, 6-97, 7-97, 8-107, 9-118, 10-118

FALL OF WICKETS
1-78, 2-217

Umpires: Khalid Aziz (6) and Shakil Khan (11).

PAKISTAN v WEST INDIES 1990-91

At National Stadium, Karachi on 9 November 1990.   Result: **PAKISTAN** won by 6 runs.   Toss: Pakistan.
Award: Waqar Younis.   LOI debuts: West Indies – B.C.Lara.

A capacity crowd of 25,000 saw Pakistan narrowly prevent West Indies from celebrating their 200th international with a victory. Waqar Younis achieved the unique feat of taking five wickets in an innings in three consecutive internationals.

PAKISTAN		Runs	Balls	4/6
Saeed Anwar	c and b Ambrose	20	24	3
Ramiz Raja	b Ambrose	10	30	1
Zahid Fazal	c Dujon b Hooper	22	31	3
Javed Miandad	hit wicket b Bishop	5	16	–
Salim Malik	c Haynes b Bishop	58	64	7
* Imran Khan	not out	53	51	5/1
† Salim Yousuf	not out	27	26	2/1
Akram Raza				
Mushtaq Ahmed				
Waqar Younis				
Salim Jaffer				
Extras	(lb 8, w 4, nb 4)	16		
Total	(40 overs; 5 wickets)	**211**		

WEST INDIES		Runs	Balls	4/6
* D.L.Haynes	b Waqar	67	92	10
C.A.Best	c Akram Raza b Imran	0	2	–
R.B.Richardson	c sub (Ijaz Ahmed) b Waqar	69	85	6/2
A.L.Logie	b Waqar	0	1	–
B.C.Lara	lbw b Waqar	11	20	2
C.L.Hooper	lbw b Waqar	15	21	1
† P.J.L.Dujon	c Salim Yousuf b Mushtaq	3	6	–
M.D.Marshall	not out	26	15	5
C.E.L.Ambrose	not out	1	3	–
I.R.Bishop				
C.A.Walsh				
Extras	(b 1, lb 5, w 3, nb 4)	13		
Total	(40 overs; 7 wickets)	**205**		

WEST INDIES	O	M	R	W
Bishop	8	1	45	2
Ambrose	8	0	40	2
Marshall	8	0	30	0
Walsh	8	0	51	0
Hooper	8	0	37	1

PAKISTAN	O	M	R	W
Imran Khan	7	0	53	1
Salim Jaffer	8	0	19	0
Akram Raza	8	0	37	0
Waqar Younis	8	0	52	5
Mushtaq Ahmed	8	0	32	1
Salim Malik	1	0	6	0

FALL OF WICKETS
1-32, 2-35, 3-49, 4-91, 5-166

FALL OF WICKETS
1-1, 2-139, 3-139, 4-149, 5-158, 6-171, 7-181

Umpires: Khizer Hayat (33) and Mahboob Shah (24).

PAKISTAN v WEST INDIES 1990-91

At Gaddafi Stadium, Lahore on 11 November 1990.   Result: **PAKISTAN** won by 5 wickets.   Toss: West Indies.
Award: Salim Malik.   LOI debuts: None.

Salim Malik rescued Pakistan's innings from a worrying start and carried them to victory in their 200th international.

WEST INDIES		Runs	Balls	4/6
C.G.Greenidge	c Salim Yousuf b Jaffer	9	27	1
* D.L.Haynes	c Waqar b Saeed	66	92	2
R.B.Richardson	c Salim Yousuf b Jaffer	0	3	–
C.A.Best	c and b Akram Raza	19	49	1
A.L.Logie	b Mushtaq	18	19	1
M.D.Marshall	b Mushtaq	4	7	–
C.L.Hooper	not out	27	21	2
† P.J.L.Dujon	run out	14	14	–
E.A.Moseley	not out	2	2	–
C.E.L.Ambrose				
I.R.Bishop				
Extras	(b 1, lb 10, w 2, nb 4)	17		
Total	(39 overs; 7 wickets)	**176**		

PAKISTAN		Runs	Balls	4/6
Saeed Anwar	c Dujon b Bishop	5	11	–
Ramiz Raja	b Ambrose	1	8	–
Zahid Fazal	c Richardson b Bishop	5	23	–
Javed Miandad	c Dujon b Marshall	23	30	1
Salim Malik	not out	91	98	8
* Imran Khan	c Richardson b Moseley	32	66	2
† Salim Yousuf	not out	0	–	–
Akram Raza				
Mushtaq Ahmed				
Waqar Younis				
Salim Jaffer				
Extras	(lb 5, w 7, nb 8)	20		
Total	(37.1 overs; 5 wickets)	**177**		

PAKISTAN	O	M	R	W
Imran Khan	5	2	13	0
Salim Jaffer	8	0	20	2
Akram Raza	8	0	32	1
Waqar Younis	8	1	33	0
Mushtaq Ahmed	7	0	48	2
Saeed Anwar	3	0	19	1

WEST INDIES	O	M	R	W
Bishop	7	0	36	2
Ambrose	8	2	20	1
Marshall	8	1	36	1
Moseley	8	0	47	1
Hooper	6.1	0	33	0

FALL OF WICKETS
1-4, 2-6, 3-23, 4-52, 5-175

FALL OF WICKETS
1-29, 2-29, 3-79, 4-113, 5-124, 6-134, 7-170

Umpires: Ikram Rabbani (4) and Javed Akhtar (10).

PAKISTAN v WEST INDIES 1990-91

At Ibn-e-Qasim Bagh Stadium, Multan on 13 November 1990.   Result: **PAKISTAN** won by 31 runs.   Toss: Pakistan.
Award: Imran Khan.   LOI debuts: Pakistan – Moin Khan.

Pakistan won their first series of internationals against West Indies. Gordon Greenidge completed 5000 runs in his 122nd match, while Imran Khan scored his 1000th run against West Indies.

PAKISTAN		Runs	Balls	4/6
Saeed Anwar	b Hooper	31	59	1
Shoaib Mohammed	c Richardson b Bishop	0	3	–
Zahid Fazal	c Williams b Moseley	1	3	–
Salim Malik	c Williams b Walsh	30	32	3
Ijaz Ahmed	b R.C.Haynes	22	38	2
* Imran Khan	not out	46	59	2
† Moin Khan	b Bishop	23	36	–
Akram Raza	b Walsh	0	8	–
Mushtaq Ahmed	b Walsh	0	1	–
Abdul Qadir	run out	1	4	–
Waqar Younis				
Extras	(lb 5, nb 9)	14		
Total	(40 overs; 9 wickets)	**168**		

WEST INDIES		Runs	Balls	4/6
C.G.Greenidge	b Waqar	35	110	2
* D.L.Haynes	b Akram Raza	18	22	2
R.B.Richardson	c Akram Raza b Imran	7	15	1
C.A.Best	b Mushtaq	10	19	1
A.L.Logie	b Mushtaq	7	11	–
C.L.Hooper	not out	32	48	1
R.C.Haynes	b Waqar	0	1	–
E.A.Moseley	c Saeed b Mushtaq	0	3	–
† D.Williams	not out	10	11	–
I.R.Bishop				
C.A.Walsh				
Extras	(b 2, lb 11, w 5)	18		
Total	(40 overs; 7 wickets)	**137**		

WEST INDIES	O	M	R	W
Bishop	8	0	35	2
Moseley	8	0	45	1
Walsh	8	0	28	3
Hooper	8	0	26	1
R.C.Haynes	8	0	29	1

PAKISTAN	O	M	R	W
Waqar Younis	7	0	19	2
Akram Raza	8	0	20	1
Mushtaq Ahmed	8	0	31	3
Imran Khan	8	1	26	1
Abdul Qadir	8	0	24	0
Saeed Anwar	1	0	4	–

FALL OF WICKETS
1-2, 2-3, 3-54, 4-88, 5-99, 6-157, 7-161, 8-161, 9-168

FALL OF WICKETS
1-35, 2-44, 3-67, 4-79, 5-107, 6-107, 7-110

Umpires: Riazuddin (1) and Siddiq Khan (1).

BENSON AND HEDGES WORLD SERIES (1st Match – floodlit)   LOI No: 642/44

AUSTRALIA v NEW ZEALAND 1990-91

At Sydney Cricket Ground on 29 November 1990.   Result: **AUSTRALIA** won by 61 runs (revised target).
Toss: New Zealand.   Award: A.R.Border.   LOI debuts: New Zealand – C.Z.Harris, R.G.Petrie.

Rain, which terminated Australia's innings, robbed Willie Watson of the chance of a hat-trick. A new regulation assessed New Zealand's target at 236 from 40 overs by taking into account Australia's 40 highest scoring overs and ignoring the three maidens. Based on run rate it would have been 216.

AUSTRALIA		Runs	Balls	4/6
D.C.Boon	c Smith b Pringle	0	3	–
G.R.Marsh	c Rutherford b Harris	46	78	2/1
D.M.Jones	c Harris b Morrison	36	58	5
* A.R.Border	b Morrison	39	51	4
M.E.Waugh	b Pringle	40	32	2/1
S.R.Waugh	c Watson b Petrie	7	16	–
S.P.O'Donnell	c Smith b Pringle	35	24	3/2
P.L.Taylor	c Crowe b Watson	8	5	1
† I.A.Healy	not out	8	6	–
C.G.Rackemann	c Petrie b Watson	0	1	–
B.A.Reid				
Extras	(b 4, lb 3, w 9, nb 1)	17		
Total	(43.5 overs; 9 wickets)	**236**		

NEW ZEALAND		Runs	Balls	4/6
J.G.Wright	run out	2	6	–
A.H.Jones	c M.E.Waugh b Rackemann	23	55	2
* M.D.Crowe	run out	21	48	2
M.J.Greatbatch	run out	20	25	2
K.R.Rutherford	lbw b Reid	33	37	2
† I.D.S.Smith	c M.E.Waugh b Reid	33	26	5
C.Z.Harris	not out	17	23	3
R.G.Petrie	c Jones b Taylor	1	7	–
C.Pringle	not out	4	9	–
D.K.Morrison				
W.Watson				
Extras	(b 3, lb 11, w 4, nb 2)	20		
Total	(40 overs; 7 wickets)	**174**		

NEW ZEALAND	O	M	R	W
Pringle	9	2	39	3
Petrie	9	0	43	1
Watson	8.5	1	51	2
Morrison	9	0	49	2
Harris	6	0	36	1
Crowe	2	0	11	0

AUSTRALIA	O	M	R	W
O'Donnell	8	2	18	0
Reid	8	4	18	2
Rackemann	7	1	23	1
S.R.Waugh	8	1	49	0
M.E.Waugh	3	0	20	0
Taylor	6	0	32	1

FALL OF WICKETS
1-0, 2-54, 3-134, 4-138, 5-163, 6-205, 7-226, 8-236, 9-236

FALL OF WICKETS
1-2, 2-49, 3-55, 4-80, 5-141, 6-153, 7-168

Umpires: L.J.King (11) and P.J.McConnell (56).

ENGLAND v NEW ZEALAND 1990-91

At Adelaide Oval on 1 December 1990.　　Result: **NEW ZEALAND** won by 7 runs.　　Toss: England.
Award: J.G.Wright.　　LOI debuts: England – J.E.Morris; New Zealand – R.T.Latham.

Allan Lamb, playing his 100th international, deputised as captain for Graham Gooch (poisoned hand). A rain break of 101 minutes, when New Zealand were 22 for 1 after 11 overs, reduced the match to 41 overs apiece, a ration which England failed to deliver. John Morris scored 50 off 35 balls on debut.

NEW ZEALAND		Runs	Balls	4/6
J.G.Wright	c Russell b Malcolm	67	88	6
A.H.Jones	c Russell b Malcolm	6	28	–
* M.D.Crowe	c Gower b Hemmings	16	32	–
K.R.Rutherford	b Small	50	53	2
R.T.Latham	b Small	27	31	2
† I.D.S.Smith	not out	10	7	1
C.Z.Harris	b Fraser	4	3	–
R.G.Petrie				
C.Pringle				
D.K.Morrison				
W.Watson				
Extras	(lb 12, w 5, nb 2)	19		
Total	(40 overs; 6 wickets)	199		

ENGLAND		Runs	Balls	4/6
D.I.Gower	c Crowe b Pringle	6	4	–/1
M.A.Atherton	c Smith b Morrison	33	73	1
R.A.Smith	c Crowe b Pringle	8	22	1
* A.J.Lamb	b Watson	49	62	4
J.E.Morris	not out	63	45	6
† R.C.Russell	b Petrie	7	10	–
C.C.Lewis	c Morrison b Petrie	6	11	–
G.C.Small	c Wright b Morrison	5	6	–
E.E.Hemmings	b Pringle	3	5	–
A.R.C.Fraser	run out	0	–	–
D.E.Malcolm	not out	3	2	–
Extras	(lb 5, w 4)	9		
Total	(40 overs; 9 wickets)	192		

ENGLAND	O	M	R	W
Fraser	8	1	33	1
Malcolm	9	0	39	2
Small	7	1	25	2
Lewis	8	0	39	0
Hemmings	8	0	51	1

NEW ZEALAND	O	M	R	W
Pringle	8	1	36	3
Petrie	8	0	26	2
Morrison	8	0	38	2
Watson	8	1	29	1
Harris	8	0	58	0

FALL OF WICKETS
1-16, 2-62, 3-114, 4-185, 5-188, 6-199

FALL OF WICKETS
1-6, 2-20, 3-91, 4-106, 5-126, 6-158, 7-173, 8-182, 9-188

Umpires: A.R.Crafter (76) and I.S.Thomas (1).

AUSTRALIA v NEW ZEALAND 1990-91

At Adelaide Oval on 2 December 1990.　　Result: **AUSTRALIA** won by 6 wickets.　　Toss: New Zealand.
Award: A.R.Border.　　LOI debuts: None.

The highlight of this unremarkable encounter, played on the previous day's pitch, came when David Boon pulled a ball for four and split his bat clean in two, the lower half flying 25 yards towards a cowering mid-wicket.

NEW ZEALAND		Runs	Balls	4/6
J.G.Wright	run out	16	39	–
A.H.Jones	lbw b Alderman	4	18	–
* M.D.Crowe	c Jones b M.E.Waugh	50	94	3
K.R.Rutherford	b Rackemann	40	71	1
R.T.Latham	not out	36	51	1
† I.D.S.Smith	c Healy b Rackemann	6	6	1
C.Z.Harris	c Healy b M.E.Waugh	1	11	–
R.G.Petrie	b S.R.Waugh	21	18	1
C.Pringle	not out	12	9	–/1
D.K.Morrison				
W.Watson				
Extras	(lb 4, w 11, nb 7)	22		
Total	(50 overs; 7 wickets)	208		

AUSTRALIA		Runs	Balls	4/6
G.R.Marsh	c Wright b Harris	45	78	4
D.C.Boon	c Harris b Morrison	33	50	6
D.M.Jones	c Jones b Watson	38	91	1
* A.R.Border	b Pringle	55	62	8
M.E.Waugh	not out	7	12	1
S.R.Waugh	not out	4	6	–
S.P.O'Donnell				
P.L.Taylor				
† I.A.Healy				
C.G.Rackemann				
T.M.Alderman				
Extras	(lb 9, w 17, nb 2)	28		
Total	(47 overs; 4 wickets)	210		

AUSTRALIA	O	M	R	W
Alderman	10	2	25	1
Rackemann	10	0	38	2
O'Donnell	10	1	45	0
S.R.Waugh	10	0	49	1
Taylor	5	0	22	0
M.E.Waugh	5	0	25	2

NEW ZEALAND	O	M	R	W
Pringle	10	0	42	1
Morrison	9	0	53	1
Petrie	10	0	32	0
Watson	10	1	38	1
Harris	7	0	26	1
Crowe	1	0	10	0

FALL OF WICKETS
1-8, 2-38, 3-122, 4-123, 5-131, 6-143, 7-185

FALL OF WICKETS
1-64, 2-115, 3-187, 4-200

Umpires: R.J.Evans (8) and T.A.Prue (10).

ENGLAND v NEW ZEALAND 1990-91

At WACA Ground, Perth on 7 December 1990.   Result: **ENGLAND** won by 4 wickets.   Toss: New Zealand.
Award: A.J.Stewart.   LOI debuts: England – M.P.Bicknell, P.C.R.Tufnell.

Martin Crowe completed 3000 runs in his 98th international. Ian Smith's right forefinger was fractured by a ball from
Chris Lewis. He took no further part in the tournament and Mark Greatbatch deputised as wicket-keeper throughout
England's innings.

NEW ZEALAND		Runs	Balls	4/6
J.G.Wright	c Lewis b Bicknell	6	21	1
A.H.Jones	run out	26	36	4
* M.D.Crowe	c Russell b Lewis	37	67	2
M.J.Greatbatch	c Larkins b Small	19	30	1
K.R.Rutherford	b Fraser	11	32	–
† I.D.S.Smith	c Lamb b Bicknell	15	21	1
C.Z.Harris	c Russell b Tufnell	0	9	–
R.G.Petrie	not out	14	35	–
C.Pringle	c and b Small	2	7	–
D.K.Morrison	c Russell b Lewis	7	34	–
W.Watson	b Lewis	1	8	–
Extras	(b 4, lb 8, w 4, nb 4)	20		
Total	**(49.2 overs)**	**158**		

ENGLAND		Runs	Balls	4/6
J.E.Morris	c Rutherford b Morrison	31	50	5
W.Larkins	c Crowe b Morrison	44	72	9
R.A.Smith	c sub (R.T. Latham) b Watson	0	3	–
* A.J.Lamb	lbw b Watson	20	30	2
A.J.Stewart	not out	29	43	4
† R.C.Russell	c Crowe b Pringle	5	24	–
C.C.Lewis	c Greatbatch b Pringle	0	10	–
G.C.Small	not out	9	33	1
M.P.Bicknell				
A.R.C.Fraser				
P.C.R.Tufnell				
Extras	(b 4, lb 8, w 10, nb 1)	23		
Total	**(43.5 overs; 6 wickets)**	**161**		

ENGLAND	O	M	R	W
Fraser	10	3	23	1
Bicknell	10	1	36	2
Lewis	9.2	1	26	3
Small	10	1	30	2
Tufnell	10	1	31	1

NEW ZEALAND	O	M	R	W
Pringle	10	1	45	2
Petrie	10	0	39	0
Morrison	10	1	27	2
Watson	10	1	26	2
Harris	3.5	0	12	0

FALL OF WICKETS
1-16, 2-52, 3-94, 4-99, 5-126, 6-126, 7-126, 8-128, 9-154, 10-158

FALL OF WICKETS
1-72, 2-73, 3-100, 4-101, 5-115, 6-129

Umpires: R.J.Evans (9) and T.A.Prue (11).

AUSTRALIA v ENGLAND 1990-91

At WACA Ground, Perth on 9 December 1990.   Result: **AUSTRALIA** won by 6 wickets.   Toss: England.
Award: D.M.Jones.   LOI debuts: None.

Playing his 94th international, David Boon emulated the three batsmen immediately below him in the order by scoring
his 3000th run. Dean Jones was the first to smite a six into the middle tier of the Prindiville Stand, a vast straight hit.

ENGLAND		Runs	Balls	4/6
J.E.Morris	b S.R.Waugh	7	29	1
W.Larkins	b O'Donnell	38	61	6
R.A.Smith	c Healy b Rackemann	37	60	3
* A.J.Lamb	c Alderman b O'Donnell	3	3	–
A.J.Stewart	c Alderman b Matthews	41	74	2
C.C.Lewis	lbw b Matthews	2	12	–
† R.C.Russell	c O'Donnell b Alderman	13	18	1
G.C.Small	c Border b O'Donnell	5	12	1
M.P.Bicknell	not out	31	24	3
A.R.C.Fraser	c M.E.Waugh b O'Donnell	4	13	–
P.C.R.Tufnell				
Extras	(b 3, lb 3, w 2, nb 3)	11		
Total	**(50 overs; 9 wickets)**	**192**		

AUSTRALIA		Runs	Balls	4/6
D.C.Boon	b Small	38	47	6
G.R.Marsh	c Lewis b Tufnell	37	79	6
D.M.Jones	not out	63	74	8/1
* A.R.Border	c Russell b Bicknell	24	47	2/1
M.E.Waugh	c Lewis b Bicknell	0	3	–
S.R.Waugh	not out	12	8	2
G.R.J.Matthews				
S.P.O'Donnell				
† I.A.Healy				
C.G.Rackemann				
T.M.Alderman				
Extras	(lb 8, w 10, nb 1)	19		
Total	**(41 overs; 4 wickets)**	**193**		

AUSTRALIA	O	M	R	W
Alderman	10	0	34	1
Rackemann	10	2	19	1
S.R.Waugh	10	1	52	1
O'Donnell	10	0	45	4
Matthews	10	0	36	2

ENGLAND	O	M	R	W
Fraser	9	2	30	0
Bicknell	9	0	55	2
Small	4.3	1	14	1
Lewis	8	1	36	0
Larkins	0.3	0	1	0
Tufnell	10	1	49	1

FALL OF WICKETS
1-31, 2-58, 3-62, 4-128, 5-136, 6-139, 7-154, 8-156, 9-192

FALL OF WICKETS
1-56, 2-110, 3-155, 4-155

Umpires: R.J.Evans (10) and P.J.McConnell (57).

AUSTRALIA v NEW ZEALAND 1990-91

At Melbourne Cricket Ground on 11 December 1990.   Result: **AUSTRALIA** won by 39 runs.   Toss: New Zealand.
Award: S.P.O'Donnell.   LOI debuts: New Zealand – B.A.Young.

Demolition work on the Southern Stand revealed the Yarra Park trees for the first time since 1936. Steve Waugh appeared in his 100th international. Dean Jones passed 4000 runs in his 104th international. Simon O'Donnell scored 50 off 36 balls.

AUSTRALIA		Runs	Balls	4/6
G.R.Marsh	b Bradburn	51	86	2/1
D.C.Boon	c Crowe b Petrie	5	23	–
D.M.Jones	run out	54	60	3
S.P.O'Donnell	b Morrison	66	43	7/2
* A.R.Border	c Latham b Pringle	40	42	1
M.E.Waugh	c Crowe b Pringle	9	18	–
S.R.Waugh	c Crowe b Morrison	4	11	–
G.R.J.Matthews	not out	16	13	1
† I.A.Healy	not out	6	4	–
M.G.Hughes				
T.M.Alderman				
Extras	(lb 7, w 5)	12		
Total	(50 overs; 7 wickets)	263		

NEW ZEALAND		Runs	Balls	4/6
* M.D.Crowe	c Matthews b M.E.Waugh	81	116	5
J.G.Wright	c M.E.Waugh b Alderman	24	37	2
M.J.Greatbatch	c Matthews b O'Donnell	7	5	1
K.R.Rutherford	c Alderman b S.R.Waugh	37	51	–
R.T.Latham	run out	4	11	–
G.E.Bradburn	c Healy b S.R.Waugh	6	14	–
† B.A.Young	not out	26	36	1
R.G.Petrie	b M.E.Waugh	10	16	–
C.Pringle	b M.E.Waugh	6	7	–
D.K.Morrison	not out	9	9	1
W.Watson				
Extras	(lb 8, w 4, nb 2)	14		
Total	(50 overs; 8 wickets)	224		

NEW ZEALAND	O	M	R	W
Pringle	10	1	40	2
Petrie	8	2	38	1
Morrison	10	0	45	2
Bradburn	9	1	56	1
Watson	10	0	59	0
Latham	3	0	18	0

AUSTRALIA	O	M	R	W
Alderman	8	1	24	1
Hughes	8	0	40	0
O'Donnell	10	1	42	1
S.R.Waugh	10	0	39	2
Matthews	8	0	51	0
M.E.Waugh	6	0	20	3

FALL OF WICKETS
1-16, 2-102, 3-122, 4-202, 5-232, 6-237, 7-244

FALL OF WICKETS
1-52, 2-59, 3-142, 4-146, 5-167, 6-181, 7-195, 8-205

Umpires: L.J.King (12) and S.G.Randell (36).

ENGLAND v NEW ZEALAND 1990-91

At Sydney Cricket Ground on 13 December 1990.   Result: **ENGLAND** won by 33 runs.   Toss: New Zealand.
Award: A.J.Lamb.   LOI debuts: None.

Graham Gooch returned from surgery on his hand to lead England for the first time in Australia. Martin Crowe, victim of an imaginative decision, top scored in his 100th international. Brawls on the infamous Hill scored 16 arrests and one policeman hospitalised.

ENGLAND		Runs	Balls	4/6
* G.A.Gooch	c Young b Petrie	3	13	–
W.Larkins	c Watson b Pringle	8	18	1
R.A.Smith	c Latham b Petrie	4	13	–
A.J.Lamb	b Morrison	72	110	7
J.E.Morris	run out	19	28	3
† A.J.Stewart	run out	42	59	3
C.C.Lewis	c and b Bradburn	4	4	1
M.P.Bicknell	b Pringle	8	17	–
E.E.Hemmings	not out	8	10	1
A.R.C.Fraser	lbw b Pringle	5	4	1
P.C.R.Tufnell	b Pringle	2	7	–
Extras	(lb 7, w 10, nb 2)	19		
Total	(46.4 overs)	194		

NEW ZEALAND		Runs	Balls	4/6
* M.D.Crowe	lbw b Fraser	76	107	4
J.G.Wright	c Lamb b Lewis	23	50	4
G.E.Bradburn	b Lewis	2	12	–
K.R.Rutherford	b Hemmings	1	12	–
R.T.Latham	c Smith b Hemmings	10	35	–
† B.A.Young	c Morris b Bicknell	25	36	1
C.Z.Harris	c Stewart b Lewis	12	20	–
R.G.Petrie	c Stewart b Lewis	2	7	–
C.Pringle	c Hemmings b Fraser	1	4	–
D.K.Morrison	not out	2	6	–
W.Watson	run out	0	–	–
Extras	(lb 5, w 2)	7		
Total	(48.1 overs)	161		

NEW ZEALAND	O	M	R	W
Pringle	8.4	0	35	4
Petrie	8	2	25	2
Watson	10	0	38	0
Morrison	10	0	45	1
Bradburn	10	0	44	1

ENGLAND	O	M	R	W
Bicknell	10	0	39	1
Fraser	9	1	21	2
Lewis	9.1	0	35	4
Tufnell	10	1	27	0
Hemmings	10	1	34	2

FALL OF WICKETS
1-7, 2-16, 2-23, 4-66, 5-143, 6-156, 7-179, 8-179, 9-188, 10-194

FALL OF WICKETS
1-56, 2-64, 3-66, 4-84, 5-138, 6-151, 7-158, 8-159, 9-160, 10-161

Umpires: A.R.Crafter (77) and I.S.Thomas (2).

ENGLAND v NEW ZEALAND 1990-91

At Woolloongabba, Brisbane on 15 December 1990.　Result: **NEW ZEALAND** won by 8 wickets.　Toss: New Zealand.
Award: M.D.Crowe.　LOI debuts: None.

Martin Crowe and John Wright shared New Zealand's highest LOI opening partnership in Australia: 109 off 139 balls.

ENGLAND		Runs	Balls	4/6
* G.A.Gooch	b Harris	48	87	3
W.Larkins	c Young b Petrie	15	32	3
R.A.Smith	b Morrison	41	72	3
A.J.Lamb	run out	10	12	–
J.E.Morris	c Young b Petrie	16	22	–
† A.J.Stewart	not out	30	44	2
C.C.Lewis	run out	3	6	–
P.A.J.DeFreitas	not out	27	26	3
A.R.C.Fraser				
D.E.Malcolm				
P.C.R.Tufnell				
Extras	(lb 8, w 5)	13		
Total	(50 overs; 6 wickets)	**203**		

NEW ZEALAND		Runs	Balls	4/6
* M.D.Crowe	c Gooch b Malcolm	78	102	8
J.G.Wright	c Stewart b Tufnell	54	80	7
A.H.Jones	not out	41	73	3
R.T.Latham	not out	17	17	3
K.R.Rutherford				
† B.A.Young				
C.Z.Harris				
R.G.Petrie				
C.Pringle				
D.K.Morrison				
W.Watson				
Extras	(b 1, lb 4, w 4, nb 5)	14		
Total	(44.3 overs; 2 wickets)	**204**		

NEW ZEALAND	O	M	R	W
Pringle	10	1	36	0
Petrie	10	1	32	2
Morrison	10	2	41	1
Watson	10	0	40	0
Harris	8	0	36	1
Latham	2	0	10	0

ENGLAND	O	M	R	W
Fraser	9	2	38	0
Malcolm	8	0	56	1
DeFreitas	8	0	31	0
Lewis	9.3	1	31	0
Tufnell	10	0	43	1

FALL OF WICKETS
1-27, 2-99, 3-115, 4-122, 5-143, 6-149

FALL OF WICKETS
1-109, 2-178

Umpires: S.G.Randell (37) and C.D.Timmins (8).

AUSTRALIA v ENGLAND 1990-91

At Woolloongabba, Brisbane on 16 December 1990.　Result: **AUSTRALIA** won by 37 runs.　Toss: Australia.
Award: D.M.Jones.　LOI debuts: None.

A sell-out crowd of 20,542 saw Dean Jones (50 off 66 balls, 100 off 118) record Australia's highest score in internationals. With Geoff Marsh he shared a national record second-wicket stand of 185 from 218 balls. Simon O'Donnell took his 100th wicket in 80 matches and Allan Border was the first to play 200 innings.

AUSTRALIA		Runs	Balls	4/6
D.C.Boon	lbw b Fraser	10	17	1
G.R.Marsh	c Larkins b Bicknell	82	124	5/1
D.M.Jones	c Tufnell b DeFreitas	145	136	12/4
S.R.Waugh	not out	14	19	–
M.E.Waugh	c Tufnell b DeFreitas	5	5	1
S.P.O'Donnell	c Morris b DeFreitas	0	1	–
* A.R.Border	not out	4	4	–
G.R.J.Matthews				
† I.A.Healy				
C.G.Rackemann				
B.A.Reid				
Extras	(b 3, lb 12, w 7, nb 1)	23		
Total	(50 overs; 5 wickets)	**283**		

ENGLAND		Runs	Balls	4/6
* G.A.Gooch	b Matthews	41	79	4
W.Larkins	b O'Donnell	19	28	2
A.J.Lamb	c Border b Matthews	35	43	2
† A.J.Stewart	run out	40	35	2/2
R.A.Smith	run out	6	9	–
J.E.Morris	c S.R.Waugh b Matthews	13	17	2
P.A.J.DeFreitas	not out	49	57	4/1
M.P.Bicknell	b Rackemann	25	25	1/1
E.E.Hemmings	not out	3	15	–
A.R.C.Fraser				
P.C.R.Tufnell				
Extras	(b 1, lb 8, w 5, nb 1)	15		
Total	(50 overs; 7 wickets)	**246**		

ENGLAND	O	M	R	W
Fraser	10	1	47	1
Bicknell	10	0	64	1
DeFreitas	10	0	57	3
Hemmings	10	0	57	0
Tufnell	10	0	43	0

AUSTRALIA	O	M	R	W
Reid	10	1	41	0
O'Donnell	10	2	43	1
Rackemann	10	0	41	1
S.R.Waugh	4	0	20	0
Matthews	10	0	54	3
M.E.Waugh	4	0	23	0
Border	1	0	9	0
Jones	1	0	6	0

FALL OF WICKETS
1-24, 2-209, 3-261, 4-272, 5-272

FALL OF WICKETS
1-26, 2-104, 3-121, 4-141, 5-151, 6-174, 7-213

Umpires: A.R.Crafter (78) and L.J.King (13).

AUSTRALIA v NEW ZEALAND 1990-91

At Bellerive Oval, Hobart on 18 December 1990.　　Result: **NEW ZEALAND** won by 1 run.　　Toss: Australia.
Award: B.A.Young.　　LOI debuts: None.

A record Hobart crowd of 11,056 saw Australia, playing their first international in Tasmania, snatch defeat from the jaws of victory to end a run of 12 consecutive wins against New Zealand. Requiring two runs, Bruce Reid failed to make any contact with Chris Pringle's final over.

NEW ZEALAND		Runs	Balls	4/6
M.D.Crowe	lbw b Alderman	5	16	–
J.G.Wright	c S.R.Waugh b O'Donnell	37	56	2/1
A.H.Jones	c Reid b S.R.Waugh	12	45	–
K.R.Rutherford	run out	26	48	2
C.Z.Harris	c Healy b Reid	17	55	–
R.T.Latham	c Jones b O'Donnell	38	44	2
B.A.Young	not out	41	37	1/1
R.G.Petrie	not out	6	6	–
C.Pringle				
D.K.Morrison				
W.Watson				
Extras	(lb 3, w 2, nb 7)	12		
Total	(50 overs; 6 wickets)	**194**		

AUSTRALIA		Runs	Balls	4/6
G.R.Marsh	c Latham b Harris	61	94	7
D.C.Boon	c Crowe b Pringle	2	7	–
S.R.Waugh	c Young b Morrison	16	27	3
M.E.Waugh	c Young b Petrie	14	33	–
† I.A.Healy	lbw b Watson	24	32	2
D.M.Jones	run out	25	32	3
S.P.O'Donnell	lbw b Harris	0	5	–
* A.R.Border	run out	12	26	–
G.R.J.Matthews	not out	24	32	3
T.M.Alderman	run out	5	5	1
B.A.Reid	run out	1	9	–
Extras	(lb 2, w 5, nb 2)	9		
Total	(50 overs)	**193**		

AUSTRALIA	O	M	R	W
Alderman	10	1	52	1
Reid	10	1	25	1
O'Donnell	10	0	50	2
S.R.Waugh	5	1	18	1
Matthews	10	1	33	0
M.E.Waugh	5	0	13	0

NEW ZEALAND	O	M	R	W
Pringle	10	1	34	1
Petrie	10	1	30	1
Morrison	10	1	56	1
Watson	10	0	29	1
Harris	10	0	42	2

FALL OF WICKETS
1-17, 2-40, 3-71, 4-110, 5-112, 6-169

FALL OF WICKETS
1-7, 2-52, 3-93, 4-111, 5-136, 6-137, 7-153, 8-177, 9-188, 10-193

Umpires: S.G.Randell (38) and C.D.Timmins (9).

AUSTRALIA v ENGLAND 1990-91

At Sydney Cricket Ground on 1 January 1991.　　Result: **AUSTRALIA** won by 68 runs.　　Toss: England.
Award: P.L.Taylor.　　LOI debuts: None.

Watched by a New Year's Day audience of 36,838, Mark Waugh and Simon O'Donnell shared a national record sixth-wicket partnership of 112 from 140 balls. Phil Tufnell muffed a simple return with both Waughs stranded at the far end.

AUSTRALIA		Runs	Balls	4/6
G.R.Marsh	lbw b Tufnell	29	55	3
D.C.Boon	lbw b Fraser	4	23	–
D.M.Jones	c Small b Tufnell	25	38	5
A.R.Border	c Small b Hemmings	4	9	–
M.E.Waugh	c Larkins b Fraser	62	69	5
S.R.Waugh	c Stewart b Tufnell	3	9	–
S.P.O'Donnell	not out	71	92	5/2
· I.A.Healy	c Atherton b Fraser	4	5	–
P.L.Taylor	not out	2	7	–
C.G.Rackemann				
T.M.Alderman				
Extras	(lb 5, w 11, nb 1)	17		
Total	(50 overs; 7 wickets)	**221**		

ENGLAND		Runs	Balls	4/6
* G.A.Gooch	b O'Donnell	37	44	2
W.Larkins	b Taylor	40	84	3
M.A.Atherton	c Healy b S.R.Waugh	8	20	1
† A.J.Stewart	c S.R.Waugh b Border	18	35	2
R.A.Smith	b Taylor	1	5	–
J.E.Morris	c M.E.Waugh b Taylor	8	20	–
P.A.J.DeFreitas	st Healy b Border	9	18	–
G.C.Small	st Healy b Border	15	31	2
E.E.Hemmings	run out	1	3	–
A.R.C.Fraser	c Boon b Rackemann	4	17	–
P.C.R.Tufnell	not out	0	2	–
Extras	(b 2, lb 7, w 1, nb 2)	12		
Total	(45.5 overs)	**153**		

ENGLAND	O	M	R	W
Fraser	10	2	28	3
Small	10	1	43	0
DeFreitas	10	0	48	0
Tufnell	10	2	40	3
Hemmings	10	0	57	1

AUSTRALIA	O	M	R	W
Alderman	8	0	28	0
Rackemann	7.5	1	25	1
O'Donnell	5	0	15	1
S.R.Waugh	6	0	25	1
Taylor	10	2	27	3
Border	9	1	24	3

FALL OF WICKETS
1-15, 2-55, 3-72, 4-82, 5-93, 6-205, 7-218

FALL OF WICKETS
1-65, 2-81, 3-103, 4-109, 5-117, 6-125, 7-135, 8-136, 9-153, 10-153

Umpires: L.J.King (14) and S.G.Randell (39).

AUSTRALIA v ENGLAND 1990-91

At Melbourne Cricket Ground on 10 January 1991.   Result: **AUSTRALIA** won by 3 runs.   Toss: Australia.
Award: I.A.Healy.   LOI debuts: None.

For England to reach the finals, Phil Tufnell needed four from Terry Alderman's final ball. His air shot condemned England to an alternative four-day match in Albury and defeat by NSW. Final points: Australia 14, New Zealand 6, England 4.

AUSTRALIA		Runs	Balls	4/6	ENGLAND		Runs	Balls	4/
D.C.Boon	c Small b DeFreitas	42	64	2	* G.A.Gooch	c Healy b M.E.Waugh	37	76	1
G.R.Marsh	c Stewart b Bicknell	7	22	–	D.I.Gower	lbw b Alderman	26	29	3
D.M.Jones	c Stewart b Bicknell	2	7	–	W.Larkins	b Alderman	0	2	–
* A.R.Border	c Larkins b Small	10	30	1	† A.J.Stewart	b Taylor	55	65	3
M.E.Waugh	run out	36	46	–/1	R.A.Smith	b M.E.Waugh	7	19	–
S.R.Waugh	not out	65	82	4	J.E.Morris	c Healy b M.E.Waugh	10	14	1
S.P.O'Donnell	c Bicknell b Gooch	7	13	–	P.A.J.DeFreitas	c Border b M.E.Waugh	6	13	1
† I.A.Healy	not out	50	37	2	G.C.Small	b Taylor	0	1	–
P.L.Taylor					M.P.Bicknell	c Alderman b S.R.Waugh	23	31	2
C.G.Rackemann					A.R.C.Fraser	not out	38	46	4/
T.M.Alderman					P.C.R.Tufnell	not out	5	8	–
Extras	(lb 1, w 1, nb 1)	3			Extras	(lb 6, w 5, nb 1)	12		
Total	(50 overs; 6 wickets)	222			Total	(50 overs; 9 wickets)	219		

ENGLAND	O	M	R	W	AUSTRALIA	O	M	R	W
Fraser	10	2	39	0	Alderman	9	2	31	2
Bicknell	9.5	0	33	2	Rackemann	7	0	52	2
Small	10	2	50	1	O'Donnell	7	0	28	0
Tufnell	3	0	23	0	S.R.Waugh	7	1	25	1
DeFreitas	7.1	0	37	1	M.E.Waugh	10	0	37	4
Gooch	10	0	39	1	Taylor	10	1	40	1

FALL OF WICKETS
1-14, 2-16, 3-30, 4-81, 5-112, 6-127

FALL OF WICKETS
1-39, 2-39, 3-93, 4-119, 5-139, 6-142, 7-142, 8-146, 9-176

Umpires: R.J.Evans (11) and L.J.King (15).

AUSTRALIA v NEW ZEALAND 1990-91

At Sydney Cricket Ground on 13 January 1991.   Result: **AUSTRALIA** won by 6 wickets.   Toss: New Zealand.
LOI debuts: None.

A groin strain ended Allan Border's record sequence of 127 consecutive World Series matches since 1979-80. Simon O'Donnell surpassed Dennis Lillee's Australian record of 103 LOI wickets and David Boon appeared in his 100th international.

NEW ZEALAND		Runs	Balls	4/6	AUSTRALIA		Runs	Balls	4/
* M.D.Crowe	c M.E.Waugh b P.L.Taylor	35	66	2	* G.R.Marsh	b Pringle	70	126	5
R.B.Reid	c M.A.Taylor b Alderman	17	39	2/1	M.A.Taylor	run out	41	40	5
J.G.Wright	b O'Donnell	10	20	1	D.M.Jones	b Morrison	49	72	2
A.H.Jones	c S.R.Waugh b M.E.Waugh	43	72	5	D.C.Boon	not out	14	33	1
K.R.Rutherford	c and b P.L.Taylor	7	13	–	M.E.Waugh	lbw b Morrison	0	3	–
† B.A.Young	b M.E.Waugh	19	30	–	S.R.Waugh	not out	16	28	2
R.T.Latham	not out	26	48	1	S.P.O'Donnell				
G.R.Larsen	lbw b M.E.Waugh	6	14	–	† I.A.Healy				
R.G.Petrie	not out	11	12	1	P.L.Taylor				
C.Pringle					T.M.Alderman				
D.K.Morrison					B.A.Reid				
Extras	(lb 10, w 11, nb 4)	25			Extras	(lb 5, w 2, nb 5)	12		
Total	(50 overs; 7 wickets)	199			Total	(49.1 overs; 4 wickets)	202		

AUSTRALIA	O	M	R	W	NEW ZEALAND	O	M	R	W
Alderman	8	1	23	1	Pringle	10	1	32	1
Reid	9	0	44	0	Petrie	10	1	41	0
O'Donnell	6	0	26	1	Morrison	10	1	43	0
S.R.Waugh	7	0	32	0	Larsen	8	1	36	0
P.L.Taylor	10	0	35	2	Jones	7	0	27	0
M.E.Waugh	10	2	29	3	Crowe	4.1	0	18	0

FALL OF WICKETS
1-55, 2-69, 3-101, 4-126, 5-136, 6-159, 7-170

FALL OF WICKETS
1-70, 2-170, 3-174, 4-176

Umpires: R.J.Evans (12) and L.J.King (16).

AUSTRALIA v NEW ZEALAND 1990-91

At Melbourne Cricket Ground on 15 January 1991.   Result: **AUSTRALIA** won by 7 wickets.   Toss: New Zealand.
Finals Award: M.A.Taylor.   LOI debuts: None.

Australia retained the World Series Cup to gain their sixth title in 12 seasons.

NEW ZEALAND		Runs	Balls	4/6
* M.D.Crowe	b Reid	6	21	–
R.B.Reid	c Jones b P.L.Taylor	64	94	5
J.G.Wright	c P.L.Taylor b O'Donnell	8	34	1
A.H.Jones	lbw b Reid	51	89	1
K.R.Rutherford	c P.L.Taylor b O'Donnell	37	43	1
R.T.Latham	not out	20	14	1
B.A.Young	c Jones b O'Donnell	11	6	2
C.Pringle	not out	1	1	–
G.R.Larsen				
R.G.Petrie				
D.K.Morrison				
Extras	(lb 8, w 1, nb 1)	10		
Total	(50 overs; 6 wickets)	**208**		

AUSTRALIA		Runs	Balls	4/6
M.A.Taylor	c Rutherford b Jones	71	93	8
* G.R.Marsh	c Young b Petrie	0	1	–
D.M.Jones	b Pringle	76	105	6/1
D.C.Boon	not out	40	64	3
M.E.Waugh	not out	3	14	–
S.R.Waugh				
S.P.O'Donnell				
† I.A.Healy				
P.L.Taylor				
T.M.Alderman				
B.A.Reid				
Extras	(b 1, lb 12, w 2, nb 4)	19		
Total	(45.3 overs; 3 wickets)	**209**		

AUSTRALIA	O	M	R	W
Alderman	7	1	21	0
Reid	10	3	35	2
O'Donnell	9	0	43	3
S.R.Waugh	9	1	37	0
P.L.Taylor	9	0	40	1
M.E.Waugh	6	0	24	0

NEW ZEALAND	O	M	R	W
Pringle	9.3	1	30	1
Petrie	9	0	51	1
Morrison	9	0	40	0
Larsen	10	2	32	0
Crowe	2	0	15	0
Jones	6	0	28	1

FALL OF WICKETS
1-14, 2-51, 3-102, 4-171, 5-177, 6-194

FALL OF WICKETS
1-2, 2-120, 3-199

Umpires: A.R.Crafter (79) and P.J.McConnell (58).

INDIA v SRI LANKA 1990-91

At Vidarbha CA Ground, Nagpur on 1 December 1990.   Result: **INDIA** won by 19 runs.   Toss: Sri Lanka.
Award: R.J.Shastri.   LOI debuts: Sri Lanka – M.S.Atapattu.

Aravinda de Silva's maiden hundred (off 118 balls) in his 74th match was the first century for Sri Lanka since 1982-83
(*LOI No. 158*). He also completed 2000 runs.

INDIA		Runs	Balls	4/6
R.J.Shastri	not out	101	147	12/1
N.S.Sidhu	lbw b Ratnayake	52	80	6
S.V.Manjrekar	c Tillekeratne b Wijegunawardene	14	23	1
* M.Azharuddin	b Gurusinha	2	4	–
S.R.Tendulkar	b Ratnayake	36	22	3/2
Kapil Dev	c Mahanama b Labrooy	7	7	1
V.Razdan	not out	4	4	–
M.Prabhakar				
† K.S.More				
Arshad Ayub				
A.Kumble				
Extras	(lb 9, w 6, nb 14)	29		
Total	(45 overs; 5 wickets)	**245**		

SRI LANKA		Runs	Balls	4/6
R.S.Mahanama	c More b Prabhakar	4	23	–
M.A.R.Samarasekera	lbw b Kapil Dev	0	1	–
A.P.Gurusinha	b Prabhakar	6	25	–
P.A.de Silva	c Razdan b Kapil Dev	104	124	6/1
* A.Ranatunga	run out	14	19	–
† H.P.Tillekeratne	c Razdan b Shastri	39	46	2
R.J.Ratnayake	not out	33	30	2/1
G.F.Labrooy	c More b Prabhakar	0	1	–
M.S.Atapattu	not out	8	4	1
M.A.W.R.Madurasinghe				
K.I.W.Wijegunawardene				
Extras	(lb 11, w 4, nb 3)	18		
Total	(45 overs; 7 wickets)	**226**		

SRI LANKA	O	M	R	W
Ratnayake	10	0	36	2
Labrooy	10	1	58	1
Wijegunawardene	8	0	49	1
Ranatunga	8	0	36	0
Madurasinghe	3	0	29	0
Gurusinha	6	0	28	1

INDIA	O	M	R	W
Kapil Dev	10	1	46	2
Prabhakar	10	1	47	3
Kumble	10	0	35	0
Razdan	4	0	31	0
Arshad Ayub	8	0	43	0
Shastri	3	0	13	1

FALL OF WICKETS
1-133, 2-164, 3-177, 4-224, 5-235

FALL OF WICKETS
1-1, 2-11, 3-12, 4-61, 5-155, 6-204, 7-208

Umpires: S.Banerjee (7) and S.K.Bansal (1).

INDIA v SRI LANKA 1990-91

At Nehru Stadium, Poona on 5 December 1990.　　Result: **INDIA** won by 6 wickets.　　Toss: India.
Award: S.R.Tendulkar.　　LOI debuts: Sri Lanka – D.Ranatunga.

Sachin Tendulkar's maiden fifty in limited-overs internationals arrived from 40 balls. It followed the wickets of both opening batsmen, a brace of catches and a run out.

SRI LANKA		Runs	Balls	4/6
R.S.Mahanama	c More b Tendulkar	24	57	3
D.Ranatunga	b Tendulkar	25	76	1
A.P.Gurusinha	c Tendulkar b Prabhakar	44	76	2
P.A.de Silva	c Shastri b Wassan	1	4	–
* A.Ranatunga	run out	58	27	5/1
R.J.Ratnayake	c Tendulkar b Arshad Ayub	1	4	–
M.S.Atapattu	run out	0	2	–
† H.P.Tillekeratne	not out	13	14	1
G.F.Labrooy	c Kumble b Arshad Ayub	21	12	2/1
S.D.Anurasiri	not out	6	10	–
K.I.W.Wijegunawardene				
Extras	(lb 10, w 16, nb 8)	34		
Total	(49 overs; 8 wickets)	**227**		

INDIA		Runs	Balls	4/6
R.J.Shastri	c Labrooy b Anurasiri	53	88	4
N.S.Sidhu	b Anurasiri	38	63	4/1
S.V.Manjrekar	c Wijegunawardene b Labrooy	23	38	–
* M.Azharuddin	not out	52	49	5
S.R.Tendulkar	b Labrooy	53	41	7/1
Kapil Dev	not out	0	–	–
M.Prabhakar				
† K.S.More				
A.S.Wassan				
Arshad Ayub				
A.Kumble				
Extras	(lb 1, w 6, nb 4)	11		
Total	(45.3 overs; 4 wickets)	**230**		

INDIA	O	M	R	W
Kapil Dev	7	1	15	0
Prabhakar	9	0	45	1
Tendulkar	9	0	39	2
Wassan	10	0	29	1
Kumble	6	0	51	0
Arshad Ayub	8	1	38	2

SRI LANKA	O	M	R	W
Ratnayake	9	1	43	0
Labrooy	9	0	50	2
Wijegunawardene	10	1	56	0
Anurasiri	10	0	44	2
A.Ranatunga	7	0	32	0
Atapattu	0.3	0	4	0

FALL OF WICKETS
1-52, 2-77, 3-80, 4-177, 5-178, 6-179, 7-180, 8-214

FALL OF WICKETS
1-76, 2-108, 3-146, 4-226

Umpires: N. Dutta (1) and S.T.Sambandam (1).

INDIA v SRI LANKA 1990-91

At Fatorda Stadium, Margao on 8 December 1990.　　Result: **SRI LANKA** won by 7 wickets.　　Toss: India.
Award: P.A.de Silva.　　LOI debuts: Sri Lanka – R.S.Kaluwitharana, K.P.J.Warnaweera.

Sri Lanka gained their sixth victory in 23 encounters with India and only their second against them on their own soil (also *LOI No. 407*).

INDIA		Runs	Balls	4/6
R.J.Shastri	c Gurusinha b Ramanayake	12	37	2
N.S.Sidhu	b Ramanayake	0	4	–
S.V.Manjrekar	c Mahanama b Ramanayake	14	15	2
* M.Azharuddin	c Mahanama b Anurasiri	20	47	2
S.R.Tendulkar	c and b Anurasiri	30	29	1/2
Kapil Dev	c Tillekeratne b Warnaweera	6	21	–
M.Prabhakar	not out	23	51	2
† K.S.More	c Kaluwitharana b Warnaweera	6	16	–
Arshad Ayub	c D.Ranatunga b De Silva	6	7	–
A.Kumble	lbw b Ratnayake	0	4	–
A.S.Wassan	b Ratnayake	0	8	–
Extras	(b 5, lb 5, w 6, nb 3)	19		
Total	(40.3 overs)	**136**		

SRI LANKA		Runs	Balls	4/6
R.S.Mahanama	lbw b Kumble	8	27	–
D.Ranatunga	c and b Kapil Dev	5	18	–
A.P.Gurusinha	c Azharuddin b Arshad Ayub	19	38	3
P.A.de Silva	not out	63	70	11
* A.Ranatunga	not out	30	42	3
R.S.Kaluwitharana				
† H.P.Tillekeratne				
R.J.Ratnayake				
C.P.H.Ramanayake				
S.D.Anurasiri				
K.P.J.Warnaweera				
Extras	(lb 5, w 4, nb 3)	12		
Total	(32.5 overs; 3 wickets)	**137**		

SRI LANKA	O	M	R	W
Ratnayake	6.3	3	17	2
Ramanayake	7	4	15	3
A.Ranatunga	4	0	22	0
Anurasiri	10	1	39	2
Warnaweera	10	1	24	2
De Silva	3	0	9	1

INDIA	O	M	R	W
Kapil Dev	4	0	16	1
Prabhakar	5	1	16	0
Kumble	10	1	40	1
Arshad Ayub	8.5	3	34	1
Shastri	3	0	15	0
Wassan	2	0	11	0

FALL OF WICKETS
1-0, 2-26, 3-39, 4-69, 5-93, 6-105, 7-118, 8-131, 9-133, 10-136

FALL OF WICKETS
1-10, 2-24, 3-55

Umpires: B.A.Jamula (1) and C.R.Vijayaraghavan (1).

PAKISTAN v SRI LANKA 1990-91

At Sharjah CA Stadium, UAE on 20 December 1990.   Result: **SRI LANKA** won by 6 wickets.   Toss: Sri Lanka.
Award: R.J.Ratnayake.   LOI debuts: None.

When India and West Indies withdrew because of the Gulf crisis, the scheduled four-nation Sharjah Champions Trophy
was transformed into a two-match Sharjah Cup series sponsored by Instaphone. The beneficiaries were Tausif Ahmed
and Wallis Mathias of Pakistan.

PAKISTAN		Runs	Balls	4/6	SRI LANKA		Runs	Balls	4/6
Saeed Anwar	c Tillekeratne b Ratnayake	32	47	5	D.Ranatunga	lbw b Wasim	0	7	–
Zahid Fazal	c Mahanama b Ratnayake	11	25	1	† H.P.Tillekeratne	lbw b Wasim	3	11	–
Javed Miandad	run out	4	7	–	A.P.Gurusinha	b Waqar	33	66	1/1
Salim Malik	c Tillekeratne b Ratnayake	0	1	–	P.A.de Silva	lbw b Aqib	23	24	2/1
Imran Khan	c Tillekeratne b Warnaweera	43	54	1/1	* A.Ranatunga	not out	45	86	1
Ijaz Ahmed	c Warnaweera b Ramanayake	38	70	1	R.S.Mahanama	not out	24	62	–
Wasim Akram	b Ramanayake	9	21	1	S.T.Jayasuriya				
Salim Yousuf	c Tillekeratne b Ratnayake	10	17	–	R.J.Ratnayake				
Mushtaq Ahmed	lbw b Ramanayake	4	5	–	G.F.Labrooy				
Waqar Younis	not out	2	9	–	C.P.H.Ramanayake				
Aqib Javed	c Tillekeratne b Ratnayake	0	5	–	K.P.J.Warnaweera				
Extras	(b 1, lb 7, w 6, nb 3)	17			Extras	(lb 6, w 26, nb 12)	44		
Total	(43 overs)	**170**			**Total**	(39.5 overs; 4 wickets)	**172**		

SRI LANKA	O	M	R	W	PAKISTAN	O	M	R	W
Labrooy	6	0	31	0	Imran Khan	8	2	33	0
Ramanayake	9	0	29	3	Wasim Akram	9	0	40	2
Ratnayake	9	1	32	5	Waqar Younis	9	1	35	1
A.Ranatunga	9	0	27	0	Aqib Javed	6	0	27	1
Warnaweera	9	0	36	1	Mushtaq Ahmed	5.5	0	24	0
Gurusinha	1	0	7	0	Ijaz Ahmed	2	0	7	0

FALL OF WICKETS
1-46, 2-56, 3-57, 4-57, 5-133, 6-147, 7-152, 8-157, 9-170, 10-170

FALL OF WICKETS
1-2, 2-27, 3-63, 4-95

Umpires: V.K.Ramaswamy (*India*) (19) and P.D.Reporter (*India*) (7).

PAKISTAN v SRI LANKA 1990-91

At Sharjah CA Stadium, UAE on 21 December 1990.   Result: **PAKISTAN** won by 50 runs.   Toss: Sri Lanka.
Award: Ijaz Ahmed.   LOI debuts: Pakistan – Aamir Sohail; Sri Lanka – C.P.Senanayake.

Pakistan squared the series and were awarded the Sharjah Cup on overall run rate, 4.08 compared with Sri Lanka's 3.65.
Intriguingly, Waqar Younis was the sixth bowler called upon.

PAKISTAN		Runs	Balls	4/6	SRI LANKA		Runs	Balls	4/6
Saeed Anwar	c Warnaweera b Labrooy	2	6	–	D.Ranatunga	c Salim Yousuf b Akram Raza	19	55	1
Aamir Sohail	run out	32	65	4	C.P.Senanayake	c Miandad b Mushtaq	24	49	2
Javed Miandad	lbw b Ramanayake	1	9	–	P.A.de Silva	b Waqar	24	31	–/1
Salim Malik	c Jayasuriya b Labrooy	0	2	–	* A.Ranatunga	c Salim Yousuf b Mushtaq	5	9	–
* Imran Khan	c Senanayake b Warnaweera	30	54	4	A.P.Gurusinha	run out	1	10	–
Ijaz Ahmed	not out	54	78	1/1	† H.P.Tillekeratne	c Ijaz b Wasim	27	67	–
Wasim Akram	b Warnaweera	4	13	–	S.T.Jayasuriya	lbw b Waqar	1	10	–
† Salim Yousuf	run out	14	24	–	R.J.Ratnayake	b Waqar	5	9	1
Akram Raza	run out	1	1	–	G.F.Labrooy	st Salim Yousuf b Mushtaq	2	8	–
Mushtaq Ahmed	run out	10	7	–	C.P.H.Ramanayake	not out	6	8	–
Waqar Younis	not out	0	–	–	K.P.J.Warnaweera	not out	1	2	–
Extras	(b 4, lb 10, w 18, nb 1)	33			Extras	(b 1, lb 8, w 7)	16		
Total	(43 overs; 9 wickets)	**181**			**Total**	(43 overs; 9 wickets)	**131**		

SRI LANKA	O	M	R	W	PAKISTAN	O	M	R	W
Labrooy	9	1	40	2	Imran Khan	8	1	21	0
Ramanayake	9	1	20	1	Wasim Akram	9	2	19	1
A.Ranatunga	7	1	24	0	Ijaz Ahmed	3	0	10	0
Ratnayake	9	0	57	0	Akram Raza	9	0	33	1
Warnaweera	9	2	26	2	Mushtaq Ahmed	6	0	14	3
					Waqar Younis	8	0	25	3

FALL OF WICKETS
1-9, 2-13, 3-15, 4-70, 5-82, 6-94, 7-134, 8-137, 9-165

FALL OF WICKETS
1-46, 2-47, 3-66, 4-68, 5-92, 6-100, 7-102, 8-122, 9-129

Umpires: V.K.Ramaswamy (*India*) (20) and P.D.Reporter (*India*) (8).

INDIA v BANGLADESH 1990-91

At Sector 16 Stadium, Chandigarh on 25 December 1990.   Result: **INDIA** won by 9 wickets.   Toss: Bangladesh.
Award: N.S.Sidhu.   LOI debuts: India – S.P.Mukherjee.

Pakistan withdrew from the fourth Asia Cup, sponsored by Videocon, because of intercommunal violence in India where
it was to be staged for the first time. Farooq Ahmed notched the highest score for Bangladesh to date and shared in
their only hundred partnership.

BANGLADESH		Runs	Balls	4/6	INDIA		Runs	Balls	4/
Azhar Hussain	c Azharuddin b Wassan	13	50	1	W.V.Raman	lbw b Athar	44	101	2
Nur-ul-Abedin	c Raju b Prabhakar	2	21	–	N.S.Sidhu	not out	104	109	10/
Farooq Ahmed	c Wassan b Raju	57	126	3	S.V.Manjrekar	not out	11	21	–
Athar Ali Khan	b Raju	44	76	6	* M.Azharuddin				
* Minhaz-ul-Abedin	b Kapil Dev	9	18	–	S.R.Tendulkar				
Akram Khan	lbw b Kapil Dev	10	14	1	Kapil Dev				
Inam-ul-Haq	not out	3	6	–	M.Prabhakar				
Amin-ul-Islam	not out	3	5	–	† K.S.More				
Ghulam Nousher					S.L.V.Raju				
† Nasir Ahmed					S.P.Mukherjee				
Alam Talukdar					A.S.Wassan				
Extras	(b 4, lb 9, w 9, nb 7)	29			Extras	(lb 3, w 7, nb 2)	12		
Total	(50 overs; 6 wickets)	170			Total	(36.5 overs; 1 wicket)	171		

INDIA	O	M	R	W	BANGLADESH	O	M	R	W
Kapil Dev	8	1	17	2	Ghulam Nousher	9	1	24	
Prabhakar	10	2	28	1	Alam Talukdar	3	0	16	
Wassan	10	0	41	1	Azhar Hussain	3	0	25	
Mukherjee	10	2	29	0	Inam-ul-Haq	5	0	26	
Raju	10	0	27	2	Minhaz-ul-Abedin	9	0	43	
Tendulkar	2	0	15	0	Athar Ali Khan	6	1	23	
					Amin-ul-Islam	1.5	0	11	

FALL OF WICKETS
1-8, 2-28, 3-136, 4-150, 5-159, 6-164

FALL OF WICKETS
1-121

Umpires: V.K.Ramaswamy (21) and P.D.Reporter (9).

INDIA v SRI LANKA 1990-91

At Barabati Stadium, Cuttack on 28 December 1990.   Result: **SRI LANKA** won by 36 runs.   Toss: Sri Lanka.
Award: A.Ranatunga.   LOI debuts: None.

For the first time in 24 meetings, India sustained successive defeats against Sri Lanka.

SRI LANKA		Runs	Balls	4/6	INDIA		Runs	Balls	4/
† H.P.Tillekeratne	c Raju b Wassan	26	57		R.J.Shastri	run out	4	25	
C.P.Senanayake	b Wassan	27	32		N.S.Sidhu	c Mahanama b Anurasiri	25	37	
A.P.Gurusinha	b Wassan	34	26		S.V.Manjrekar	run out	26	54	
P.A.de Silva	c More b Mukherjee	11	17		* M.Azharuddin	st Tillekeratne b Jayasuriya	40	61	
* A.Ranatunga	c and b Prabhakar	53	105		S.R.Tendulkar	lbw b Ranatunga	4	11	
R.S.Mahanama	run out	0	1		Kapil Dev	b Ratnayake	32	35	
S.T.Jayasuriya	lbw b Kapil Dev	23	24		M.Prabhakar	c De Silva b Warnaweera	4	15	
R.J.Ratnayake	b Kapil Dev	0	6		† K.S.More	b Ratnayake	27	34	
C.P.H.Ramanayake	b Kapil Dev	0	3		S.L.V.Raju	run out	0	6	
S.D.Anurasiri	run out	8	18		A.S.Wassan	b Ratnayake	1	3	
K.P.J.Warnaweera	not out	0	8		S.P.Mukherjee	not out	2	2	
Extras	(b 8, lb 19, w 4, nb 1)	32			Extras	(lb 6, w 2, nb 5)	13		
Total	(49.2 overs)	214			Total	(45.5 overs)	178		

INDIA	O	M	R	W	SRI LANKA	O	M	R	W
Kapil Dev	9.2	1	48	3	Ratnayake	6.5	1	24	3
Prabhakar	10	2	39	1	Ramanayake	5	0	12	0
Mukherjee	10	0	30	1	Anurasiri	10	0	44	
Wassan	10	0	28	3	Ranatunga	10	0	36	
Raju	10	0	42	0	Jayasuriya	6	0	22	
					Warnaweera	8	0	34	

FALL OF WICKETS
1-51, 2-62, 3-86, 4-159, 5-162, 6-190, 7-191, 8-191, 9-214, 10-214

FALL OF WICKETS
1-24, 2-37, 3-81, 4-95, 5-111, 6-123, 7-165, 8-166, 9-173, 10-178

Umpires: S.Banerjee (8) and V.K.Ramaswamy (22).

SRI LANKA v BANGLADESH 1990-91

At Eden Gardens, Calcutta on 31 December 1990.   Result: **SRI LANKA** won by 71 runs.   Toss: Sri Lanka.
Award: Athar Ali Khan.   LOI debuts: Sri Lanka – G.P.Wickremasinghe; Bangladesh – Saif-ul-Islam.

Fog delayed the start and reduced the match to 45 overs each. Bangladesh achieved their highest total, with Athar Ali
Khan contributing their record individual score. The stand of 139 from 108 balls by Aravinda de Silva and Arjuna
Ranatunga was Sri Lanka's fourth-wicket record until 1994-95.

SRI LANKA		Runs	Balls	4/6	BANGLADESH		Runs	Balls	4/6
† H.P.Tillekeratne	st Nasir b Hussain	39			Nur-ul-Abedin	lbw b Ramanayake	0		
C.P.Senanayake	c Akram b Nousher	0			Azhar Hussain	run out	10		
A.P.Gurusinha	lbw b Minhaz	38			Farooq Ahmed	c Tillekeratne b Wickremasinghe	12		
P.A.de Silva	run out	89			Athar Ali Khan	not out	78		
* A.Ranatunga	not out	64			* Minhaz-ul-Abedin	c De Silva b Anurasiri	33		
G.F.Labrooy	not out	4			Amin-ul-Islam	c Tillekeratne b Jayasuriya	1		
R.S.Mahanama					Akram Khan	run out	4		
S.T.Jayasuriya					Inam-ul-Haq	c and b Jayasuriya	5		
C.P.H.Ramanayake					† Nasir Ahmed	c and b De Silva	11		
S.D.Anurasiri					Ghulam Nousher	c Jayasuriya b Gurusinha	4		
G.P.Wickremasinghe					Saif-ul-Islam				
Extras	(lb 11, w 4)	15			Extras	(b 1, lb 2, w 13, nb 4)	20		
Total	(45 overs; 4 wickets)	**249**			**Total**	(45 overs; 9 wickets)	**178**		

BANGLADESH	O	M	R	W	SRI LANKA	O	M	R	W
Ghulam Nousher	9	0	46	1	Labrooy	5	0	19	0
Saif-ul-Islam	9	1	42	0	Ramanayake	5	0	13	1
Athar Ali Khan	4	0	24	0	Wickremasinghe	6	1	23	1
Akram Khan	4	0	25	0	Anurasiri	9	0	31	1
Azhar Hussain	9	0	33	1	Jayasuriya	9	1	39	2
Minhaz-ul-Abedin	6	1	37	1	De Silva	8	1	37	1
Inam-ul-Haq	2	0	15	0	Gurusinha	3	0	13	1
Amin-ul-Islam	2	0	16	0					

FALL OF WICKETS

SRI LANKA: 1-1, 2-23, 3-46, 4-96, 5-99, 6-108, 7-123, 8-167, 9-178

BANGLADESH: 1-0, 2-85, 3-87, 4-226

Umpires: S.Banerjee (9) and P.D.Reporter (10).

INDIA v SRI LANKA 1990-91

At Eden Gardens, Calcutta on 3 (*no play*), 4 January 1991.   Result: **INDIA** won by 7 wickets.   Toss: India.
Award: M.Azharuddin.   LOI debuts: None.

Kapil Dev's hat-trick was the highlight of a final, postponed and then reduced by rain, which secured India's third Asia
Cup title in three appearances. Watched by a crowd in excess of 75,000, he dismissed Mahanama with the last ball of his
sixth over, before despatching Jayasuriya and Ratnayake with the first two of his next.

SRI LANKA		Runs	Balls	4/6	INDIA		Runs	Balls	4/6
† H.P.Tillekeratne	c More b Wassan	15	52		R.J.Shastri	c Tillekeratne b Labrooy	6	22	
C.P.Senanayake	run out	25	39		N.S.Sidhu	c and b Ranatunga	15	31	
A.P.Gurusinha	run out	39	54		S.V.Manjrekar	not out	75	95	
P.A.de Silva	c and b Mukherjee	26	28		S.R.Tendulkar	lbw b Ratnayake	53	70	
* A.Ranatunga	run out	49	57		* M.Azharuddin	not out	54	39	
R.S.Mahanama	c More b Kapil Dev	5	10		Kapil Dev				
S.T.Jayasuriya	c Manjrekar b Kapil Dev	5	7		M.Prabhakar				
R.J.Ratnayake	lbw b Kapil Dev	0	3		† K.S.More				
G.F.Labrooy	c Prabhakar b Kapil Dev	10	12		S.L.V.Raju				
C.P.H.Ramanayake	not out	9	14		A.S.Wassan				
K.P.J.Warnaweera	not out	0	1		S.P.Mukherjee				
Extras	(b 1, lb 13, w 7)	21			Extras	(lb 1, w 1)	2		
Total	(45 overs; 9 wickets)	**204**			**Total**	(42.1 overs; 3 wickets)	**205**		

INDIA	O	M	R	W	SRI LANKA	O	M	R	W
Kapil Dev	9	0	31	4	Labrooy	8.1	1	29	1
Prabhakar	9	1	36	0	Ramanayake	7	2	32	1
Mukherjee	9	0	39	1	Ratnayake	8	0	34	1
Wassan	7	0	35	1	Ranatunga	2	0	12	1
Raju	8	0	34	0	Warnaweera	6	0	41	0
Shastri	3	0	15	0	Gurusinha	6	0	26	0
					Jayasuriya	5	0	30	0

FALL OF WICKETS

SRI LANKA: 1-48, 2-50, 3-92, 4-150, 5-175, 6-176, 7-181, 8-181, 9-202

INDIA: 1-14, 2-30, 3-121

Umpires: V.K.Ramaswamy (23) and P.D.Reporter (11).

NEW ZEALAND v SRI LANKA 1990-91

At McLean Park, Napier on 26 January 1991.   Result: **NEW ZEALAND** won by 5 wickets.   Toss: New Zealand.
Award: J.G.Wright.   LOI debuts: None.

After preparing a sound base of 87 for 1, Sri Lanka lost five key wickets for 27 runs and no batsman scored 30.

SRI LANKA		Runs	Balls	4/6
C.P.Senanayake	c Smith b Watson	26	44	2
† H.P.Tillekeratne	b Larsen	26	75	2
A.P.Gurusinha	run out	28	47	–
P.A.de Silva	b Larsen	6	9	–
* A.Ranatunga	b Pringle	29	59	1
R.S.Mahanama	b Harris	8	17	–
S.T.Jayasuriya	run out	0	2	–
E.A.R.de Silva	c Reid b Pringle	11	22	–
G.F.Labrooy	not out	22	29	1
R.J.Ratnayake	not out	3	3	–
C.P.H.Ramanayake				
Extras	(b 1, lb 10, w 7)	18		
Total	(50 overs; 8 wickets)	**177**		

NEW ZEALAND		Runs	Balls	4/6
R.B.Reid	c Gurusinha b Ratnayake	19	31	2
J.G.Wright	c Ratnayake b E.A.R.de Silva	64	113	6
* M.D.Crowe	c Tillekeratne b Ramanayake	3	14	–
A.H.Jones	c Tillekeratne b E.A.R.de Silva	29	60	1
† I.D.S.Smith	c Tillekeratne b Ratnayake	0	1	–
M.J.Greatbatch	not out	29	37	2
C.Z.Harris	not out	11	18	–
G.R.Larsen				
C.Pringle				
D.K.Morrison				
W.Watson				
Extras	(lb 4, w 16, nb 3)	23		
Total	(42.3 overs; 5 wickets)	**178**		

NEW ZEALAND	O	M	R	W
Pringle	10	0	44	2
Watson	10	0	31	1
Morrison	10	0	30	0
Larsen	10	3	25	2
Harris	10	0	36	1

SRI LANKA	O	M	R	W
Labrooy	9	0	38	0
Ramanayake	10	1	38	1
Ratnayake	8.3	1	27	2
E.A.R.de Silva	10	1	36	2
Ranatunga	4	0	21	0
Gurusinha	1	0	14	0

FALL OF WICKETS
1-41, 2-87, 3-96, 4-99, 5-114, 6-114, 7-131, 8-171

Umpires: G.I.J.Cowan (4) and S.J.Woodward (20).

NEW ZEALAND v SRI LANKA 1990-91

At Eden Park, Auckland on 28 January 1991.   Result: **NEW ZEALAND** won by 41 runs.   Toss: Sri Lanka.
Award: C.Pringle.   LOI debuts: None.

Sri Lanka's batting failed again, Asanka Gurusinha alone exceeding 25. His 61-ball fifty was the fastest of the match.

NEW ZEALAND		Runs	Balls	4/6
R.B.Reid	run out	44	79	4
J.G.Wright	c E.A.R.de Silva b Labrooy	4	8	1
* M.D.Crowe	c Gurusinha b E.A.R.de Silva	64	93	6
A.H.Jones	not out	64	76	4
† I.D.S.Smith	c E.A.R.de Silva b Ratnayake	21	14	4
M.J.Greatbatch	c P.A.de Silva b Ramanayake	14	18	1
C.Z.Harris	not out	18	21	1
G.R.Larsen				
R.G.Petrie				
C.Pringle				
W.Watson				
Extras	(b 2, lb 4, w 4, nb 3)	13		
Total	(50 overs; 5 wickets)	**242**		

SRI LANKA		Runs	Balls	4/6
C.P.Senanayake	c Wright b Watson	12	31	1
† H.P.Tillekeratne	run out	25	58	2
A.P.Gurusinha	c Larsen b Harris	81	90	6/2
P.A.de Silva	c Smith b Larsen	0	1	–
* A.Ranatunga	b Harris	24	34	2
R.S.Mahanama	c Reid b Jones	10	11	–
R.J.Ratnayake	c Petrie b Pringle	22	19	1/1
S.T.Jayasuriya	b Pringle	4	9	–
E.A.R.de Silva	not out	10	15	–
G.F.Labrooy	b Watson	3	4	–
C.P.H.Ramanayake	run out	0	1	–
Extras	(lb 6, w 4)	10		
Total	(44.4 overs)	**201**		

SRI LANKA	O	M	R	W
Labrooy	10	0	57	1
Ramanayake	10	0	49	1
Ratnayake	10	1	45	1
E.A.R.de Silva	10	0	41	1
Ranatunga	10	0	44	0

NEW ZEALAND	O	M	R	W
Watson	7.4	0	25	2
Petrie	8	0	41	0
Pringle	9	1	27	2
Larsen	10	1	37	1
Harris	6	0	38	2
Jones	4	0	27	1

FALL OF WICKETS
1-16, 2-99, 3-134, 4-164, 5-200

FALL OF WICKETS
1-25, 2-63, 3-64, 4-110, 5-123, 6-169, 7-185, 8-191, 9-201, 10-201

Umpires: B.L.Aldridge (16) and R.S.Dunne (7).

NEW ZEALAND v SRI LANKA 1990-91

At Carisbrook, Dunedin on 6 February 1991.   Result: **NEW ZEALAND** won by 107 runs.   Toss: Sri Lanka.
Award: K.R.Rutherford.   LOI debuts: None.

This match was played two days after the Wellington Test match in which Aravinda de Silva (267) and Martin Crowe (299) registered national record scores. New Zealand's clean sweep of the series was marred by Danny Morrison sustaining an ankle injury.

NEW ZEALAND		Runs	Balls	4/6
M.D.Crowe	lbw b Wijegunawardene	31	50	2/1
R.B.Reid	c Wijegunawardene b Ranatunga	53	68	6
A.H.Jones	c Ratnayake b Ranatunga	35	41	1
K.R.Rutherford	b Ramanayake	65	78	5
M.J.Greatbatch	c Senanayake b Gurusinha	26	39	2
I.D.S.Smith	not out	42	21	5/1
C.Z.Harris	c Gurusinha b Ramanayake	5	4	1
C.Pringle	not out	1	1	–
G.R.Larsen				
D.K.Morrison				
W.Watson				
Extras	(lb 10, w 4)	14		
Total	(50 overs; 6 wickets)	**272**		

SRI LANKA		Runs	Balls	4/6
C.P.Senanayake	c Crowe b Watson	12	14	2
R.S.Kaluwitharana	c Reid b Pringle	14	19	2
A.P.Gurusinha	b Watson	15	12	1/1
P.A.de Silva	c Rutherford b Watson	21	22	3
* A.Ranatunga	run out	50	59	4
† H.P.Tillekeratne	c Crowe b Harris	8	17	1
S.T.Jayasuriya	c Smith b Larsen	1	8	–
E.A.R.de Silva	c sub (J.G.Wright) b Crowe	16	24	1
R.J.Ratnayake	c sub (J.G.Wright) b Reid	19	23	2
C.P.H.Ramanayake	b Rutherford	0	2	–
K.I.W.Wijegunawardene	not out	0	3	–
Extras	(lb 1, w 7, nb 1)	9		
Total	(33.1 overs)	**165**		

SRI LANKA	O	M	R	W
Ratnayake	10	0	52	0
Ramanayake	9	0	60	2
Wijegunawardene	5	0	33	1
E.A.R.de Silva	10	0	44	0
Ranatunga	10	0	39	2
Gurusinha	6	0	34	1

NEW ZEALAND	O	M	R	W
Pringle	5	0	29	1
Watson	7	0	39	3
Larsen	10	0	36	1
Harris	5	0	30	1
Crowe	3	0	12	1
Rutherford	2	0	5	1
Reid	1.1	0	13	1

FALL OF WICKETS
1-78, 2-110, 3-133, 4-203, 5-243, 6-260

FALL OF WICKETS
1-15, 2-41, 3-43, 4-74, 5-102, 6-105, 7-139, 8-151, 9-151, 10-165

Umpires: R.S.Dunne (8) and R.L.McHarg (11).

NEW ZEALAND v ENGLAND 1990-91

At Lancaster Park, Christchurch on 9 February 1991.   Result: **ENGLAND** won by 14 runs.   Toss: England.
Award: K.R.Rutherford.   LOI debuts: None.

In preparation for the 1991-92 World Cup, two new (white) balls were used per innings. After a national record sixth-wicket partnership against England of 122 between Ken Rutherford and Chris Harris, New Zealand's tail was unable to score 19 from the last three overs.

ENGLAND		Runs	Balls	4/6
* G.A.Gooch	b Pringle	17	66	2
D.I.Gower	b Petrie	4	11	–
M.A.Atherton	b Watson	0	7	–
A.J.Lamb	run out	61	62	6
R.A.Smith	c Jones b Pringle	65	95	6/1
A.J.Stewart	c Wright b Pringle	40	40	5
† R.C.Russell	c sub (R.T.Latham) b Petrie	10	13	2
P.A.J.DeFreitas	not out	10	9	1
M.P.Bicknell	not out	0	–	–
E.E.Hemmings				
A.R.C.Fraser				
Extras	(lb 8, w 12, nb 3)	23		
Total	(50 overs; 7 wickets)	**230**		

NEW ZEALAND		Runs	Balls	4/6
* M.D.Crowe	c and b Bicknell	13	33	2
J.G.Wright	c Smith b DeFreitas	27	28	5
A.H.Jones	run out	17	30	2
K.R.Rutherford	c Gooch b Bicknell	77	111	5
M.J.Greatbatch	c Russell b Hemmings	0	6	–
† I.D.S.Smith	run out	4	3	1
C.Z.Harris	c Russell b Bicknell	56	77	4
G.R.Larsen	not out	1	9	–
R.G.Petrie	c Gower b Fraser	0	3	–
C.Pringle	not out	0	1	–
W.Watson				
Extras	(b 2, lb 14, w 5)	21		
Total	(50 overs; 8 wickets)	**216**		

NEW ZEALAND	O	M	R	W
Petrie	10	0	51	2
Watson	10	2	15	1
Pringle	10	0	54	3
Larsen	10	0	47	0
Harris	8	0	46	0
Rutherford	2	0	9	0

ENGLAND	O	M	R	W
Fraser	10	0	28	1
Bicknell	10	2	55	3
DeFreitas	10	3	36	1
Gooch	10	0	31	0
Hemmings	10	0	50	1

FALL OF WICKETS
1-6, 2-9, 3-46, 4-129, 5-192, 6-217, 7-220

FALL OF WICKETS
1-38, 2-50, 3-82, 4-86, 5-90, 6-212, 7-213, 8-215

Umpires: B.L.Aldridge (17) and R.S.Dunne (9).

NEW ZEALAND v ENGLAND 1990-91

At Basin Reserve, Wellington on 13 February 1991.   Result: **NEW ZEALAND** won by 9 runs.   Toss: England.
Award: A.H.Jones.   LOI debuts: New Zealand – C.L.Cairns.

At 147 for 3 in the 37th over, England were coasting to a series victory. Then, as panic and confusion reigned, they contrived to lose their remaining seven wickets for 40 runs in 11 overs.

NEW ZEALAND		Runs	Balls	4/6	ENGLAND		Runs	Balls	4/6
R.B.Reid	c Russell b Fraser	9	18	1	* G.A.Gooch	c Wright b Cairns	41	60	4
J.G.Wright	b Fraser	9	16	2	M.A.Atherton	c Cairns b Harris	26	61	4
* M.D.Crowe	c Russell b Bicknell	5	28	–	D.I.Gower	run out	11	26	4
A.H.Jones	b Fraser	64	91	3	A.J.Lamb	b Cairns	33	36	4
K.R.Rutherford	c and b Tufnell	19	39	–	R.A.Smith	b Pringle	38	65	4
C.Z.Harris	st Russell b Tufnell	9	23	–	A.J.Stewart	c Watson b Harris	5	10	–
† I.D.S.Smith	b Bicknell	28	40	1	† R.C.Russell	c Cairns b Harris	2	12	–
C.L.Cairns	c Smith b DeFreitas	5	8	–	P.A.J.DeFreitas	run out	2	3	–
G.R.Larsen	not out	10	16	–	M.P.Bicknell	c Jones b Pringle	9	7	1
C.Pringle	not out	18	15	1/1	A.R.C.Fraser	c Crowe b Pringle	5	8	–
W.Watson					P.C.R.Tufnell	not out	0	–	–
Extras	(lb 9, w 11)	20			Extras	(lb 8, w 7)	15		
Total	(49 overs; 8 wickets)	**196**			**Total**	(48 overs)	**187**		

ENGLAND	O	M	R	W	NEW ZEALAND	O	M	R	W
Fraser	9	1	22	3	Pringle	10	1	43	3
Bicknell	10	0	65	2	Watson	10	1	34	0
DeFreitas	10	2	22	1	Cairns	9	1	41	2
Gooch	10	2	33	0	Larsen	9	1	28	0
Tufnell	10	0	45	2	Harris	10	0	33	3

FALL OF WICKETS
1-20, 2-25, 3-43, 4-91, 5-109, 6-150, 7-158, 8-171

FALL OF WICKETS
1-73, 2-81, 3-93, 4-147, 5-160, 6-170, 7-173, 8-174, 9-179, 10-187

Umpires: G.I.J.Cowan (5) and S.J.Woodward (21).

NEW ZEALAND v ENGLAND 1990-91

At Eden Park, Auckland on 16 February 1991.   Result: **NEW ZEALAND** won by 7 runs.   Toss: England.
Award: C.Z.Harris.   LOI debuts: None.

Another spectacular England collapse, in which seven wickets were surrendered for 46 runs in 9.2 overs, extended their sequence of losing series against New Zealand since 1983-84. Andrew Jones scored his 2000th run in 52 internationals and Ian Smith hit 50 off 29 balls.

NEW ZEALAND		Runs	Balls	4/6	ENGLAND		Runs	Balls	4/6
* M.D.Crowe	b DeFreitas	6	16	–	* G.A.Gooch	b Larsen	47	74	6
R.B.Reid	c Lamb b Tufnell	26	65	4	M.A.Atherton	c Crowe b Harris	34	63	3
A.H.Jones	run out	64	84	6	D.I.Gower	c Jones b Harris	13	26	2
K.R.Rutherford	lbw b Gooch	12	31	–	A.J.Lamb	c Smith b Cairns	42	53	4/1
M.J.Greatbatch	c Lamb b DeFreitas	12	26	–	R.A.Smith	b Cairns	35	43	2
C.Z.Harris	b Fraser	39	44	2/1	A.J.Stewart	c Smith b Cairns	3	14	–
† I.D.S.Smith	not out	51	30	6/1	P.A.J.DeFreitas	c Crowe b Pringle	7	9	1
C.L.Cairns	run out	6	4	1	† R.C.Russell	b Cairns	13	7	2
C.Pringle	not out	0	–	–	G.C.Small	b Pringle	0	2	–
G.R.Larsen					A.R.C.Fraser	b Pringle	6	6	1
W.Watson					P.C.R.Tufnell	not out	3	3	–
Extras	(lb 5, w 3)	8			Extras	(lb 10, w 4)	14		
Total	(50 overs; 7 wickets)	**224**			**Total**	(49.5 overs)	**217**		

ENGLAND	O	M	R	W	NEW ZEALAND	O	M	R	W
Fraser	10	3	31	1	Pringle	9.5	0	43	3
DeFreitas	10	0	51	2	Watson	10	1	38	0
Small	10	2	51	0	Cairns	10	0	55	4
Gooch	10	0	40	1	Larsen	10	0	35	1
Tufnell	10	1	46	1	Harris	10	1	36	2

FALL OF WICKETS
1-7, 2-66, 3-98, 4-120, 5-135, 6-209, 7-215

FALL OF WICKETS
1-83, 2-91, 3-118, 4-171, 5-185, 6-194, 7-200, 8-203, 9-209, 10-217

Umpires: R.L.McHarg (12) and S.J.Woodward (22).

WEST INDIES v AUSTRALIA 1990-91

At Sabina Park, Kingston, Jamaica on 26 February 1991.　Result: **AUSTRALIA** won by 35 runs.　Toss: Australia.
Award: D.M.Jones.　LOI debuts: None.

West Indies, who sustained their first defeat in 19 home internationals since March 1986 (*LOI No. 365*), lost their last six wickets for 19 runs. Allan Border became the first non-wicket-keeper to hold 100 LOI catches.

AUSTRALIA		Runs	Balls	4/6	WEST INDIES		Runs	Balls	4/6
D.C.Boon	b Walsh	34	68	2	C.G.Greenidge	b S.R.Waugh	19	75	2
G.R.Marsh	run out	26	54	3	D.L.Haynes	c Healy b McDermott	17	20	3
D.M.Jones	not out	88	105	6	R.B.Richardson	c Jones b McDermott	64	66	5/1
* A.R.Border	b Hooper	8	10	1	C.L.Hooper	lbw b S.R.Waugh	6	12	–
M.E.Waugh	b Ambrose	67	67	6	* I.V.A.Richards	b Taylor	18	18	3
S.R.Waugh	not out	6	7	–	A.L.Logie	c S.R.Waugh b M.E.Waugh	65	65	7
† I.A.Healy					M.D.Marshall	run out	1	1	–
P.L.Taylor					† P.J.L.Dujon	c Border b McDermott	1	3	–
C.J.McDermott					A.H.Gray	c Healy b McDermott	2	6	–
M.R.Whitney					C.E.L.Ambrose	lbw b Taylor	0	4	–
B.A.Reid					C.A.Walsh	not out	1	3	–
Extras	(lb 7, w 3, nb 5)	15			Extras	(b 2, lb 6, w 3, nb 4)	15		
Total	(50 overs; 4 wickets)	244			Total	(46 overs)	209		

WEST INDIES	O	M	R	W	AUSTRALIA	O	M	R	W
Ambrose	9	1	46	1	Reid	7	2	33	0
Gray	10	0	53	0	McDermott	9	0	34	4
Marshall	6	0	27	0	Whitney	7	1	16	0
Walsh	7	1	30	1	S.R.Waugh	7	1	32	2
Hooper	10	0	44	1	Taylor	9	1	48	2
Richards	8	0	37	0	M.E.Waugh	7	0	38	1

FALL OF WICKETS
1-59, 2-73, 3-98, 4-234

FALL OF WICKETS
1-33, 2-48, 3-68, 4-95, 5-190, 6-191, 7-206, 8-206, 9-207, 10-209

Umpires: D.M.Archer (23) and S.A.Bucknor (3).

WEST INDIES v AUSTRALIA 1990-91

At Queen's Park Oval, Port-of-Spain, Trinidad on 9 March 1991.　Result: **AUSTRALIA** won by 45 runs.　Toss: West Indies.
Award: A.H.Gray.　LOI debuts: None.

West Indies fell eight overs short of the 42 to which each innings had been reduced after rain delayed the start by almost two hours. Tony Gray returned only the second six-wicket LOI analysis by any bowler in the Caribbean or against Australia anywhere.

AUSTRALIA		Runs	Balls	4/6	WEST INDIES		Runs	Balls	4/6
D.C.Boon	c Hooper b Moseley	5	9	1	P.V.Simmons	c Healy b Reid	13	16	1/1
G.R.Marsh	c Hooper b Gray	23	45	1	D.L.Haynes	c Healy b Whitney	45	62	7
D.M.Jones	b Gray	64	85	9	R.B.Richardson	c S.R.Waugh b McDermott	5	17	1
* A.R.Border	c Dujon b Gray	0	1	–	C.L.Hooper	c Healy b Whitney	3	9	–
M.E.Waugh	b Simmons	16	17	1/1	* I.V.A.Richards	c Marsh b Whitney	27	37	1/1
S.R.Waugh	b Gray	26	30	3	A.L.Logie	run out	7	12	–
† I.A.Healy	not out	13	18	1	† P.J.L.Dujon	b McDermott	7	13	–
P.L.Taylor	c and b Gray	1	8	–	M.D.Marshall	c Boon b McDermott	5	17	–
C.J.McDermott	b Ambrose	1	2	–	E.A.Moseley	c Taylor b M.E.Waugh	2	4	–
M.R.Whitney	c Hooper b Gray	0	7	–	C.E.L.Ambrose	c Taylor b M.E.Waugh	7	6	–
B.A.Reid					A.H.Gray	not out	0	2	–
Extras	(b 2, lb 7, w 7, nb 7)	23			Extras	(lb 2, nb 4)	6		
Total	(34 overs; 9 wickets)	172			Total	(31.1 overs)	127		

WEST INDIES	O	M	R	W	AUSTRALIA	O	M	R	W
Ambrose	8	2	17	1	Reid	5	0	25	1
Moseley	5	0	22	1	McDermott	7.1	0	29	3
Marshall	6	0	37	0	Whitney	9	0	41	3
Gray	9	0	50	6	S.R.Waugh	8	0	24	0
Hooper	3	0	18	0	M.E.Waugh	2	0	6	2
Richards	1	0	4	0					
Simmons	2	0	15	1					

FALL OF WICKETS
1-14, 2-47, 3-52, 4-78, 5-90, 6-112, 7-113, 8-115, 9-126, 10-127

FALL OF WICKETS
1-9, 2-84, 3-84, 4-106, 5-141, 6-161, 7-167, 8-168, 9-172

Umpires: L.H.Barker (15) and C.E.Cumberbatch (12).

WEST INDIES v AUSTRALIA 1990-91

At Queen's Park Oval, Port-of-Spain, Trinidad on 10 March 1991.   Result: **WEST INDIES** won by 7 wickets (revised target).
Toss: Australia.   Award: R.B.Richardson.   LOI debuts: None.

Rain between the innings reduced the hosts' target to 181 off 36 overs. Curtly Ambrose began the match with an 11-ball over (four wides and a no-ball). Geoff Marsh (100 appearances), Viv Richards (100 catches) and Richie Richardson (4000 runs) achieved notable milestones.

AUSTRALIA		Runs	Balls	4/6		WEST INDIES		Runs	Balls	4/6
G.R.Marsh	b Gray	81	118	8		P.V.Simmons	c Healy b Reid	0	3	–
M.A.Taylor	c Haynes b Ambrose	3	11	–		D.L.Haynes	b S.R.Waugh	16	38	–
D.M.Jones	c Richards b Gray	36	49	4/1		R.B.Richardson	c Border b M.E.Waugh	90	98	14
M.E.Waugh	b Simmons	17	23	–		C.G.Greenidge	not out	40	50	5/1
* A.R.Border	c Dujon b Patterson	22	33	2		A.L.Logie	not out	24	21	3
S.R.Waugh	b Ambrose	23	30	–		* I.V.A.Richards				
† I.A.Healy	not out	33	23	3		C.L.Hooper				
P.L.Taylor	b Ambrose	2	7	–		† P.J.L.Dujon				
C.J.McDermott	not out	3	3	–		C.E.L.Ambrose				
M.R.Whitney						A.H.Gray				
B.A.Reid						B.P.Patterson				
Extras	(b 2, lb 10, w 9, nb 4)	25				Extras	(b 1, lb 5, w 3, nb 2)	11		
Total	(49 overs; 7 wickets)	245				Total	(33.3 overs; 3 wickets)	181		

WEST INDIES	O	M	R	W		AUSTRALIA	O	M	R	W
Ambrose	10	1	37	3		Reid	7	0	28	1
Patterson	9	0	52	1		McDermott	5	0	21	0
Gray	10	0	59	2		S.R.Waugh	7	0	39	1
Simmons	10	0	35	1		P.L.Taylor	2	0	17	0
Hooper	10	0	50	0		Whitney	7	0	38	0
						M.E.Waugh	5.3	0	32	1

FALL OF WICKETS
1-13, 2-82, 3-116, 4-165, 5-191, 6-225, 7-239

FALL OF WICKETS
1-3, 2-72, 3-132

Umpires: L.H.Barker (16) and C.E.Cumberbatch (13).

WEST INDIES v AUSTRALIA 1990-91

At Kensington Oval, Bridgetown, Barbados on 13 March 1991.   Result: **AUSTRALIA** won by 37 runs.   Toss: Australia.
Award: G.R.Marsh.   LOI debuts: None.

West Indies sustained their first defeat in a home LOI series. Australia's victory was the first at international level by any touring team in Bridgetown since England won a rain-affected first Test in January 1935. Steve Waugh and Craig McDermott took their 100th wickets.

AUSTRALIA		Runs	Balls	4/6		WEST INDIES		Runs	Balls	4/6
M.A.Taylor	c Dujon b Ambrose	5	24	–		P.V.Simmons	b McDermott	23	24	2
G.R.Marsh	b Ambrose	113	136	8/3		D.L.Haynes	b Reid	22	25	3
D.M.Jones	c Walsh b Marshall	7	8	1		R.B.Richardson	c McDermott b Whitney	25	23	3
* A.R.Border	c Ambrose b Hooper	79	87	7/2		C.G.Greenidge	lbw b S.R.Waugh	17	25	1/1
M.E.Waugh	run out	49	35	4/1		* I.V.A.Richards	c and b S.R.Waugh	20	27	2
S.R.Waugh	lbw b Ambrose	5	3	–		A.L.Logie	c M.A.Taylor b M.E.Waugh	37	51	2
† I.A.Healy	not out	6	6	–		C.L.Hooper	c M.E.Waugh b P.L.Taylor	18	23	–
C.J.McDermott	not out	1	1	–		† P.J.L.Dujon	c P.L.Taylor b M.E.Waugh	39	41	4
P.L.Taylor						M.D.Marshall	c Whitney b McDermott	19	19	2
M.R.Whitney						C.E.L.Ambrose	not out	12	11	2
B.A.Reid						C.A.Walsh	c and b M.E.Waugh	4	3	1
Extras	(b 2, lb 7, w 4, nb 5)	18				Extras	(lb 6, w 1, nb 3)	10		
Total	(50 overs; 6 wickets)	283				Total	(47 overs)	246		

WEST INDIES	O	M	R	W		AUSTRALIA	O	M	R	W
Ambrose	10	1	38	3		Reid	7	0	52	1
Marshall	10	1	67	1		McDermott	8	0	40	2
Walsh	10	0	46	0		S.R.Waugh	7	0	25	2
Simmons	6	0	37	0		Whitney	10	1	39	1
Richards	4	0	29	0		P.L.Taylor	8	0	50	1
Hooper	10	0	57	1		M.E.Waugh	7	0	34	3

FALL OF WICKETS
1-19, 2-27, 3-173, 4-260, 5-271, 6-276

FALL OF WICKETS
1-39, 2-49, 3-89, 4-95, 5-118, 6-158, 7-177, 8-225, 9-241, 10-246

Umpires: D.M.Archer (24) and L.H.Barker (17).

WEST INDIES v AUSTRALIA 1990-91

At Bourda, Georgetown, Guyana on 20 March 1991.　　Result: **AUSTRALIA** won by 6 wickets.　　Toss: West Indies.
Award: G.R.Marsh.　　LOI debuts: None.

Australia completed an unprecedented 4-1 series win. Geoff Marsh's second successive hundred extended his Australian record to nine.

WEST INDIES		Runs	Balls	4/6
P.V.Simmons	c Hughes b Taylor	34	51	7
D.L.Haynes	lbw b Taylor	58	67	11
R.B.Richardson	c Healy b Hughes	94	88	11/1
C.G.Greenidge	run out	6	13	–
* I.V.A.Richards	c Whitney b M.E.Waugh	10	12	1
A.L.Logie	b McDermott	17	33	2
C.L.Hooper	c Taylor b McDermott	10	15	1
† P.J.L.Dujon	b Hughes	2	10	–
A.H.Gray	c Border b McDermott	6	6	1
C.A.Walsh	b Hughes	2	6	–
B.P.Patterson	not out	1	3	–
Extras	(lb 8, w 1, nb 2)	11		
Total	(49.5 overs)	**251**		

AUSTRALIA	O	M	R	W
McDermott	10	0	29	3
Hughes	9.5	0	33	3
S.R.Waugh	3	0	33	0
Whitney	9	0	46	0
Taylor	10	0	45	2
M.E.Waugh	6	0	36	1
Border	2	0	21	0

FALL OF WICKETS
1-85, 2-115, 3-136, 4-155, 5-217, 6-237, 7-239, 8-246, 9-248, 10-251

AUSTRALIA		Runs	Balls	4/6
G.R.Marsh	not out	106	158	8
D.C.Boon	b Patterson	9	20	–
D.M.Jones	run out	11	15	1
* A.R.Border	c Dujon b Walsh	60	61	5/2
M.E.Waugh	st Dujon b Hooper	7	13	–
S.R.Waugh	not out	26	38	1
† I.A.Healy				
P.L.Taylor				
C.J.McDermott				
M.G.Hughes				
M.R.Whitney				
Extras	(b 4, lb 4, w 11, nb 14)	33		
Total	(48.3 overs; 4 wickets)	**252**		

WEST INDIES	O	M	R	W
Patterson	6.3	0	34	1
Gray	8	0	44	0
Walsh	10	0	54	1
Simmons	10	0	53	0
Hooper	10	0	45	1
Richards	4	0	14	0

FALL OF WICKETS
1-12, 2-38, 3-161, 4-182

Umpires: C.E.Cumberbatch (14) and C.R.Duncan (5).

ENGLAND v WEST INDIES 1991

At Edgbaston, Birmingham on 23, 24 May 1991.　　Result: **ENGLAND** won by 1 wicket.　　Toss: England.
Award: M.A.Atherton.　　LOI debuts: England – G.A.Hick, R.K.Illingworth.

Three breaks for bad light took this match into the reserve day, England being 98 for 4 after 27 overs at stumps. A last-wicket partnership of 23 from 51 balls between Michael Atherton and Richard Illingworth, who faced 34 and missed nine, saw the hosts home by a whisker.

WEST INDIES		Runs	Balls	4/6
C.G.Greenidge	c Russell b Botham	23	56	3
P.V.Simmons	c Gooch b Lewis	4	25	1
R.B.Richardson	c Illingworth b Botham	3	21	–
* I.V.A.Richards	c Fairbrother b Gooch	30	45	4
C.L.Hooper	c Russell b Botham	10	28	1/1
A.L.Logie	c DeFreitas b Botham	18	11	2
† P.J.L.Dujon	c Lewis b Illingworth	5	18	–
M.D.Marshall	c Lewis b DeFreitas	17	42	1
C.E.L.Ambrose	not out	21	59	–
C.A.Walsh	not out	29	26	3/1
B.P.Patterson				
Extras	(b 1, lb 5, w 6, nb 1)	13		
Total	(55 overs; 8 wickets)	**173**		

ENGLAND	O	M	R	W
DeFreitas	11	3	22	1
Lewis	11	3	41	1
Pringle	7	0	22	0
Botham	11	2	45	4
Gooch	5	0	17	1
Illingworth	10	1	20	1

FALL OF WICKETS
1-8, 2-16, 3-48, 4-78, 5-84, 6-98, 7-103, 8-121

ENGLAND		Runs	Balls	4/6
* G.A.Gooch	lbw b Ambrose	0	2	–
M.A.Atherton	not out	69	147	4
G.A.Hick	c Richardson b Marshall	14	49	1
A.J.Lamb	b Hooper	18	26	2
N.H.Fairbrother	c Dujon b Hooper	4	6	–
I.T.Botham	lbw b Walsh	8	30	–
D.R.Pringle	c Richardson b Walsh	1	3	–
† R.C.Russell	c Dujon b Patterson	1	8	–
P.A.J.DeFreitas	c Richardson b Marshall	8	10	–
C.C.Lewis	c Richardson b Patterson	0	4	–
R.K.Illingworth	not out	9	34	1
Extras	(lb 9, w 18, nb 16)	43		
Total	(49.4 overs; 9 wickets)	**175**		

WEST INDIES	O	M	R	W
Ambrose	11	2	34	1
Patterson	11	2	38	2
Marshall	11	1	32	2
Walsh	11	0	34	2
Simmons	3	0	10	0
Hooper	2.4	0	18	2

FALL OF WICKETS
1-1, 2-41, 3-80, 4-87, 5-123, 6-126, 7-134, 8-147, 9-152

Umpires: J.H.Hampshire (4) and M.J.Kitchen (6).

ENGLAND v WEST INDIES 1991

At Old Trafford, Manchester on 25 May 1991.   Result: **ENGLAND** won by 9 runs.   Toss: West Indies.
Award: A.J.Lamb.   LOI debuts: England – M.R.Ramprakash.

The stand of 156 from 232 balls between Graham Gooch and Michael Atherton remains England's best start against West Indies. Gordon Greenidge injured his knee fielding and took no further part in the tour.

ENGLAND		Runs	Balls	4/6
* G.A.Gooch	b Hooper	54	110	4
M.A.Atherton	c sub (B.C.Lara) b Ambrose	74	123	6
G.A.Hick	b Ambrose	29	44	2
A.J.Lamb	c Dujon b Patterson	62	50	10
N.H.Fairbrother	not out	5	6	–
M.R.Ramprakash	not out	6	6	–
D.R.Pringle				
† R.C.Russell				
C.C.Lewis				
P.A.J.DeFreitas				
R.K.Illingworth				
Extras	(b 4, lb 16, w 14, nb 6)	40		
Total	(55 overs; 4 wickets)	**270**		

WEST INDIES		Runs	Balls	4/6
P.V.Simmons	run out	28	52	1
† P.J.L.Dujon	c DeFreitas b Lewis	21	29	3
R.B.Richardson	c Russell b Gooch	13	34	–
C.L.Hooper	c sub (D.A.Reeve) b Lewis	48	89	3
* I.V.A.Richards	lbw b Lewis	78	84	6/2
A.L.Logie	c Illingworth b Pringle	24	21	–
M.D.Marshall	c and b Pringle	22	15	1/1
C.G.Greenidge	run out	4	4	–
C.E.L.Ambrose	not out	5	4	1
C.A.Walsh	not out	1	1	–
B.P.Patterson				
Extras	(lb 4, w 10, nb 3)	17		
Total	(55 overs; 8 wickets)	**261**		

WEST INDIES	O	M	R	W
Ambrose	11	3	36	2
Patterson	10	1	39	1
Walsh	11	0	56	0
Marshall	10	0	45	0
Simmons	4	0	30	0
Hooper	9	0	44	1

ENGLAND	O	M	R	W
DeFreitas	11	3	50	0
Lewis	11	0	62	3
Pringle	11	2	52	2
Illingworth	11	1	42	0
Gooch	11	1	51	1

FALL OF WICKETS
1-156, 2-156, 3-258, 4-260

FALL OF WICKETS
1-34, 2-61, 3-69, 4-190, 5-208, 6-250, 7-250, 8-256

Umpires: H.D.Bird (60) and D.R.Shepherd (39).

ENGLAND v WEST INDIES 1991

At Lord's, London on 27 May 1991.   Result: **ENGLAND** won by 7 wickets.   Toss: England.
Award: N.H.Fairbrother.   LOI debuts: England – D.V.Lawrence, D.A.Reeve.

England celebrated Denis Compton's official opening of the Compton and Edrich stands by completing a clean sweep of this series. The partnership of 213 from 192 balls between Graeme Hick and Neil Fairbrother remains the highest by an England pair anywhere and the LOI record in England.

WEST INDIES		Runs	Balls	4/6
P.V.Simmons	c Russell b DeFreitas	5	16	1
† P.J.L.Dujon	b Lawrence	0	1	–
R.B.Richardson	c DeFreitas b Illingworth	41	56	7
B.C.Lara	c and b Illingworth	23	40	2
* I.V.A.Richards	c Illingworth b DeFreitas	37	57	4/1
A.L.Logie	c and b Gooch	82	99	10
C.L.Hooper	c Fairbrother b Lawrence	26	29	2
M.D.Marshall	c DeFreitas b Lawrence	13	16	–/1
C.E.L.Ambrose	not out	6	12	–
C.A.Walsh	lbw b Lawrence	0	2	–
B.P.Patterson	not out	2	10	–
Extras	(b 1, lb 9, w 14, nb 5)	29		
Total	(55 overs; 9 wickets)	**264**		

ENGLAND		Runs	Balls	4/6
* G.A.Gooch	run out	11	29	1
M.A.Atherton	c Dujon b Marshall	25	46	3
G.A.Hick	not out	86	102	8
N.H.Fairbrother	c Richards b Patterson	113	109	10/2
M.R.Ramprakash	not out	0	–	–
D.A.Reeve				
D.R.Pringle				
† R.C.Russell				
P.A.J.DeFreitas				
R.K.Illingworth				
D.V.Lawrence				
Extras	(b 4, lb 12, w 10, nb 4)	30		
Total	(46.1 overs; 3 wickets)	**265**		

ENGLAND	O	M	R	W
Lawrence	11	1	67	4
DeFreitas	11	1	26	2
Reeve	11	1	43	0
Illingworth	11	1	53	2
Pringle	9	0	56	0
Gooch	2	0	9	1

WEST INDIES	O	M	R	W
Ambrose	8	0	31	0
Patterson	10	0	62	1
Marshall	11	1	49	1
Walsh	11	1	50	0
Hooper	4.1	0	36	0
Simmons	2	0	21	0

FALL OF WICKETS
1-8, 2-8, 3-71, 4-91, 5-164, 6-227, 7-241, 8-258, 9-258

FALL OF WICKETS
1-28, 2-48, 3-261

Umpires: M.J.Kitchen (7) and D.R.Shepherd (40).

WEST INDIES v PAKISTAN 1991-92

At Sharjah CA Stadium, UAE on 17 October 1991.   Result: **WEST INDIES** won by 1 wicket.   Toss: West Indies.
Award: R.B.Richardson.   LOI debuts: None.

This tournament was played for the joint benefit of Wasim Raja, Mahmood Hussain (Pakistan), C.K.Nayudu, E.A.S.Prasanna (India) and Gordon Greenidge (West Indies). Despite developing cramp and requiring a runner, Richie Richardson scored a decisive hundred in his first match as captain.

PAKISTAN		Runs	Balls	4/6
Ramiz Raja	c Logie b Patterson	49	101	4
Sajid Ali	c Dujon b Ambrose	11	22	1
Ijaz Ahmed	lbw b Hooper	9	26	–
Salim Malik	b Hooper	1	2	–
Javed Miandad	b Simmons	47	78	1
* Imran Khan	c Logie b Patterson	11	17	–
Wasim Akram	run out	16	18	–
† Moin Khan	c Hooper b Bishop	18	14	3
Mushtaq Ahmed	lbw b Ambrose	4	6	–
Waqar Younis	b Bishop	9	11	–
Aqib Javed	not out	1	6	–
Extras	(lb 15, w 17, nb 7)	39		
Total	(48.3 overs)	**215**		

WEST INDIES		Runs	Balls	4/6
P.V.Simmons	run out	14	25	2
C.B.Lambert	c Moin b Wasim	0	6	–
* R.B.Richardson	not out	106	142	10
B.C.Lara	c Moin b Waqar	5	14	1
A.L.Logie	c Moin b Waqar	11	7	2
C.L.Hooper	run out	23	30	1
† P.J.L.Dujon	c Moin b Imran	15	25	–
W.K.M.Benjamin	lbw b Waqar	1	3	–
C.E.L.Ambrose	lbw b Imran	1	2	–
I.R.Bishop	lbw b Waqar	19	34	1
B.P.Patterson	not out	1	3	–
Extras	(b 4, lb 4, w 8, nb 5)	21		
Total	(47.3 overs; 9 wickets)	**217**		

WEST INDIES	O	M	R	W
Ambrose	9	1	33	2
Bishop	9.3	0	40	2
Patterson	10	0	48	2
Hooper	10	0	33	2
Benjamin	9	0	38	0
Simmons	1	0	8	1

PAKISTAN	O	M	R	W
Wasim Akram	8.3	1	37	1
Aqib Javed	10	2	32	0
Waqar Younis	9	0	48	4
Mushtaq Ahmed	10	0	54	0
Imran Khan	10	0	38	2

FALL OF WICKETS
1-6, 2-38, 3-49, 4-70, 5-121, 6-152, 7-157, 8-158, 9-203

FALL OF WICKETS
1-25, 2-53, 3-58, 4-132, 5-150, 6-171, 7-185, 8-199, 9-212, 10-215

Umpires: B.C.Cooray (SL) (2) and P.W.Vidanagamage (SL) (20).

INDIA v PAKISTAN 1991-92

At Sharjah CA Stadium, UAE. on 18 October 1991.   Result: **INDIA** won by 60 runs.   Toss: India.
Award: S.V.Manjrekar.   LOI debuts: India – V.G.Kambli, J.Srinath.

The tournament's eventual winners suffered their second successive defeat. Sachin Tendulkar's 40-ball fifty included 14 from the final over bowled by Waqar Younis.

INDIA		Runs	Balls	4/6
R.J.Shastri	run out	22	63	1
N.S.Sidhu	b Wasim	38	66	2
S.V.Manjrekar	lbw b Waqar	72	93	3
* M.Azharuddin	b Waqar	32	36	1
S.R.Tendulkar	not out	52	40	5
Kapil Dev	not out	10	9	–
V.G.Kambli				
† K.S.More				
M.Prabhakar				
J.Srinath				
S.L.V.Raju				
Extras	(lb 4, w 3, nb 5)	12		
Total	(50 overs; 4 wickets)	**238**		

PAKISTAN		Runs	Balls	4/6
Ramiz Raja	run out	35	74	4
Sajid Ali	c More b Prabhakar	5	9	1
Javed Miandad	lbw b Raju	61	94	2
Salim Malik	lbw b Shastri	19	26	1
* Imran Khan	b Prabhakar	1	6	–
Ijaz Ahmed	c and b Raju	4	7	–
Wasim Akram	b Srinath	14	21	–
† Moin Khan	not out	17	26	–
Akram Raza	c Azharuddin b Kapil Dev	0	3	–
Waqar Younis	b Prabhakar	6	6	1
Aqib Javed	b Prabhakar	4	10	–
Extras	(w 2, nb 10)	12		
Total	(44.4 overs)	**178**		

PAKISTAN	O	M	R	W
Imran Khan	10	0	44	0
Aqib Javed	10	3	38	0
Waqar Younis	10	0	65	2
Wasim Akram	10	0	42	1
Akram Raza	10	0	45	0

INDIA	O	M	R	W
Prabhakar	7.4	1	25	4
Kapil Dev	8	0	30	1
Srinath	9	1	31	1
Shastri	10	1	53	1
Raju	10	0	39	2

FALL OF WICKETS
1-44, 2-93, 3-149, 4-193

FALL OF WICKETS
1-8, 2-84, 3-124, 4-129, 5-129, 6-139, 7-155, 8-156, 9-166, 10-178

Umpires: P.W.Vidanagamage (SL) (21) and W.A.U.Wickremasinghe (SL) (1).

WEST INDIES v INDIA 1991-92

At Sharjah CA Stadium, UAE on 19 October 1991.   Result: **INDIA** won by 19 runs.   Toss: West Indies.
Award: M.Prabhakar.   LOI debuts: None.

The partnership of 128 in 24.5 overs between Navjot Sidhu and Sanjay Manjrekar equalled India's second-wicket record against West Indies.

INDIA		Runs	Balls	4/6
R.J.Shastri	st Dujon b Hooper	6	38	–
N.S.Sidhu	st Dujon b Hooper	98	113	6/1
S.V.Manjrekar	c Hooper b Bishop	56	81	2
* M.Azharuddin	c and b Simmons	12	14	–
S.R.Tendulkar	run out	22	27	3
V.G.Kambli	not out	23	29	–
Kapil Dev	c Simmons b Bishop	7	7	–
M.Prabhakar	not out	2	2	–
† K.S.More				
S.L.V.Raju				
A.Kumble				
Extras	(lb 2, w 7, nb 5)	14		
Total	**(50 overs; 6 wickets)**	**240**		

WEST INDIES		Runs	Balls	4/6
P.V.Simmons	lbw b Shastri	20	44	–
C.B.Lambert	c and b Kumble	66	89	4/1
* R.B.Richardson	c Azharuddin b Shastri	28	45	1
B.C.Lara	b Prabhakar	45	44	3
A.L.Logie	lbw b Kumble	4	9	1
C.L.Hooper	lbw b Kumble	17	24	–
K.L.T.Arthurton	st More b Kumble	2	6	–
† P.J.L.Dujon	lbw b Prabhakar	0	1	–
C.E.L.Ambrose	lbw b Prabhakar	0	1	–
I.R.Bishop	c Shastri b Prabhakar	23	29	1
B.P.Patterson	not out	3	8	–
Extras	(b 2, lb 7, nb 4)	13		
Total	**(48.5 overs)**	**221**		

WEST INDIES	O	M	R	W
Ambrose	10	2	32	0
Bishop	10	0	49	2
Patterson	10	0	47	0
Hooper	10	0	46	2
Simmons	8	0	49	1
Arthurton	2	0	15	0

INDIA	O	M	R	W
Prabhakar	9.5	0	30	4
Kapil Dev	9	0	50	0
Shastri	10	0	38	2
Raju	10	0	44	0
Kumble	10	0	50	4

FALL OF WICKETS
1-33, 2-161, 3-181, 4-184, 5-216, 6-232

FALL OF WICKETS
1-54, 2-116, 3-123, 4-133, 5-171, 6-175, 7-186, 8-186, 9-194, 10-221

Umpires: B.C.Cooray (SL) (3) and W.A.U.Wickremasinghe (SL) (2).

WEST INDIES v PAKISTAN 1991-92

At Sharjah CA Stadium, UAE on 21 October 1991.   Result: **PAKISTAN** won by 1 run.   Toss: Pakistan.
Award: R.B.Richardson.   LOI debuts: None.

West Indies required ten from Waqar Younis's final over. Richie Richardson and Jeff Dujon shared a world record sixth-wicket stand of 154. Javed Miandad, when 2, retired hurt at 38 and resumed at 229 for 6.

PAKISTAN		Runs	Balls	4/6
Ramiz Raja	c Logie b Ambrose	90	129	4
Sajid Ali	c Dujon b Ambrose	7	19	1
Javed Miandad	b Ambrose	2	13	–
Salim Malik	c Logie b Hooper	10	16	1
* Imran Khan	c Hooper b Ambrose	77	100	3/2
Ijaz Ahmed	not out	14	13	–
Wasim Akram	c Patterson b Bishop	19	10	2/1
† Moin Khan	b Ambrose	0	1	–
Akram Raza	not out	1	1	–
Waqar Younis				
Aqib Javed				
Extras	(lb 8, w 7, nb 1)	16		
Total	**(50 overs; 7 wickets)**	**236**		

WEST INDIES		Runs	Balls	4/6
P.V.Simmons	b Aqib	8	19	1
C.B.Lambert	b Aqib	7	15	1
* R.B.Richardson	c Ijaz b Waqar	122	121	7/3
B.C.Lara	lbw b Aqib	0	2	–
C.L.Hooper	lbw b Waqar	13	20	1
A.L.Logie	run out	0	6	–
† P.J.L.Dujon	run out	53	88	2
I.R.Bishop	b Waqar	16	19	1/1
C.E.L.Ambrose	lbw b Waqar	0	3	–
C.A.Walsh	b Wasim	0	6	–
B.P.Patterson	not out	1	1	–
Extras	(lb 6, w 9)	15		
Total	**(50 overs)**	**235**		

WEST INDIES	O	M	R	W
Ambrose	10	1	53	5
Bishop	10	1	44	1
Walsh	10	0	48	0
Patterson	10	1	53	0
Hooper	10	0	30	1

PAKISTAN	O	M	R	W
Wasim Akram	10	0	59	1
Aqib Javed	10	2	54	3
Akram Raza	10	0	40	0
Waqar Younis	10	1	39	4
Ijaz Ahmed	7	0	24	0
Imran Khan	3	0	13	0

FALL OF WICKETS
1-17, 2-63, 3-200, 4-202, 5-229, 6-229, 7-229

FALL OF WICKETS
1-16, 2-32, 3-32, 4-56, 5-57, 6-211, 7-217, 8-220, 9-227, 10-235

Umpires: B.C.Cooray (SL) (4) and P.W.Vidanagamage (SL) (22).

WEST INDIES v INDIA 1991-92

At Sharjah CA Stadium, UAE on 22 October 1991.   Result: **INDIA** won by 7 wickets.   Toss: India.
Award: S.R.Tendulkar.   LOI debuts: None.

India qualified for the final with their first LOI victory gained when batting second against West Indies. Kapil Dev
became the first to take 200 wickets (in 166 matches) when he dismissed Winston Benjamin.

WEST INDIES		Runs	Balls	4/6
P.V.Simmons	c Prabhakar b Kapil Dev	14	26	3
C.B.Lambert	lbw b Tendulkar	11	31	–
R.B.Richardson	c Azharuddin b Tendulkar	16	48	1
C.L.Hooper	run out	8	14	–
A.L.Logie	c More b Tendulkar	0	1	–
K.L.T.Arthurton	c and b Prabhakar	59	83	5/1
* P.J.L.Dujon	c More b Tendulkar	0	2	–
I.R.Bishop	c and b Prabhakar	14	49	–
W.K.M.Benjamin	lbw b Kapil Dev	9	15	–
C.E.L.Ambrose	not out	4	7	–
B.P.Patterson	run out	1	2	–
Extras	(lb 3, w 4, nb 2)	9		
Total	(46.2 overs)	**145**		

INDIA		Runs	Balls	4/6
W.V.Raman	lbw b Bishop	0	2	–
N.S.Sidhu	c Logie b Benjamin	44	99	3
S.V.Manjrekar	lbw b Bishop	43	80	4
* M.Azharuddin	not out	19	17	1
S.R.Tendulkar	not out	11	27	1
Kapil Dev				
V.G.Kambli				
M.Prabhakar				
† K.S.More				
S.L.V.Raju				
A.Kumble				
Extras	(b 8, lb 4, w 18)	30		
Total	(37.3 overs; 3 wickets)	**147**		

INDIA	O	M	R	W
Kapil Dev	8	1	23	2
Prabhakar	8.2	0	32	2
Tendulkar	10	1	34	4
Kumble	10	2	24	0
Raju	10	1	29	0

WEST INDIES	O	M	R	W
Bishop	7	2	28	2
Ambrose	8	1	22	0
Patterson	6.3	0	16	0
Hooper	6	0	24	0
Benjamin	9	0	34	1
Arthurton	1	0	11	0

FALL OF WICKETS
1-24, 2-39, 3-47, 4-47, 5-78, 6-78, 7-129, 8-130, 9-143, 10-145

FALL OF WICKETS
1-0, 2-108, 3-108

Umpires: P.W.Vidanagamage (SL) (23) and W.A.U.Wickremasinghe (SL) (3).

INDIA v PAKISTAN 1991-92

At Sharjah CA Stadium, UAE on 23 October 1991.   Result: **PAKISTAN** won by 4 runs.   Toss: Pakistan.
Award: Aamir Sohail.   LOI debuts: None.

When, in fading light, India failed to score 12 off the final over, bowled inevitably by Waqar Younis, Pakistan qualified
for the final (points: India 6, Pakistan 4, West Indies 2) despite their first three batsmen being newly arrived
replacements for injured players.

PAKISTAN		Runs	Balls	4/6
Aamir Sohail	c Tendulkar b Kapil Dev	91	133	4/1
Saeed Anwar	run out	1	3	–
Zahid Fazal	b Raju	39	72	2/1
Salim Malik	c Azharuddin b Srinath	42	61	1
* Imran Khan	b Prabhakar	43	24	4/2
Wasim Akram	b Srinath	2	7	–
Ijaz Ahmed	run out	9	9	–
† Moin Khan	not out	1	3	–
Akram Raza	not out	0	–	–
Waqar Younis				
Aqib Javed				
Extras	(b 1, lb 5, w 16, nb 7)	29		
Total	(50 overs; 7 wickets)	**257**		

INDIA		Runs	Balls	4/6
R.J.Shastri	b Waqar	77	99	8/1
V.G.Kambli	c Moin b Aqib	40	75	4
S.V.Manjrekar	c Ijaz b Wasim	49	67	1
* M.Azharuddin	b Akram Raza	0	1	–
S.R.Tendulkar	c sub (Mushtaq Ahmed) b Salim	49	38	3/2
Kapil Dev	lbw b Wasim	0	1	–
M.Prabhakar	not out	19	18	1
† K.S.More	not out	1	4	–
J.Srinath				
S.L.V.Raju				
A.Kumble				
Extras	(b 1, lb 3, w 12, nb 2)	18		
Total	(50 overs; 6 wickets)	**253**		

INDIA	O	M	R	W
Kapil Dev	10	2	31	1
Prabhakar	9	0	62	1
Tendulkar	6	0	20	0
Srinath	8	0	55	2
Kumble	7	0	35	0
Raju	10	0	48	1

PAKISTAN	O	M	R	W
Wasim Akram	9	0	44	2
Aqib Javed	10	1	36	1
Imran Khan	2	0	17	0
Akram Raza	10	0	43	1
Waqar Younis	10	0	59	1
Aamir Sohail	6	0	34	0
Salim Malik	3	0	16	1

FALL OF WICKETS
1-4, 2-90, 3-181, 4-202, 5-214, 6-255, 7-257

FALL OF WICKETS
1-124, 2-133, 3-134, 4-219, 5-219, 6-240

Umpires: B.C.Cooray (SL) (5) and W.A.U.Wickremasinghe (SL) (4).

INDIA v PAKISTAN 1991-92

At Sharjah CA Stadium, UAE on 25 October 1991.   Result: **PAKISTAN** won by 72 runs.   Toss: India.
Award: Aqib Javed.   LOI debuts: None.

Aqib Javed's late outswing produced the world record LOI analysis, including a hat-trick of lbws with the third, fourth
and fifth balls of his third over. Zahid Fazal retired with cramp at 194, his unbroken stand of 171 with Salim Malik being
Pakistan's third-wicket record against full member countries.

PAKISTAN		Runs	Balls	4/6
Aamir Sohail	c Kapil Dev b Prabhakar	1	24	–
Sajid Ali	c More b Kapil Dev	10	20	1
Zahid Fazal	retired hurt	98	119	8/1
Salim Malik	c Azharuddin b Prabhakar	87	95	6/1
* Imran Khan	c Manjrekar b Kapil Dev	13	22	1
Ijaz Ahmed	not out	16	13	1
Wasim Akram	b Kapil Dev	3	6	–
† Moin Khan	c More b Prabhakar	5	5	–
Akram Raza				
Waqar Younis				
Aqib Javed				
Extras	(lb 15, w 10, nb 4)	29		
Total	(50 overs; 6 wickets)	**262**		

INDIA		Runs	Balls	4/6
R.J.Shastri	lbw b Aqib	15	34	1
N.S.Sidhu	c Moin b Aqib	21	32	3
S.V.Manjrekar	c Waqar b Aqib	52	69	3/2
* M.Azharuddin	lbw b Aqib	0	1	–
S.R.Tendulkar	lbw b Aqib	0	1	–
V.G.Kambli	run out	30	45	2
Kapil Dev	b Aqib	8	11	–
M.Prabhakar	c Aamir b Aqib	7	12	–
† K.S.More	not out	26	35	4
J.Srinath	c Wasim b Akram Raza	14	34	1/1
S.L.V.Raju	run out	2	4	–
Extras	(lb 5, w 8, nb 2)	15		
Total	(46 overs)	**190**		

INDIA	O	M	R	W
Prabhakar	10	2	54	3
Kapil Dev	10	0	36	3
Tendulkar	5	0	24	0
Srinath	10	0	49	0
Shastri	8	0	39	0
Raju	7	0	45	0

PAKISTAN	O	M	R	W
Wasim Akram	10	3	21	0
Imran Khan	4	0	24	0
Aqib Javed	10	1	37	7
Waqar Younis	9	2	28	0
Akram Raza	9	0	56	1
Ijaz Ahmed	2	0	11	0
Salim Malik	2	0	8	0

FALL OF WICKETS
1-6, 2-23, 3-223, 4-230, 5-247, 6-262

FALL OF WICKETS
1-32, 2-47, 3-47, 4-47, 5-100, 6-129, 7-132, 8-143, 9-177, 10-190

Umpires: B.C.Cooray (SL) (6) and W.A.U.Wickremasinghe (SL) (5).

INDIA v SOUTH AFRICA 1991-92

At Eden Gardens, Calcutta on 10 November 1991.   Result: **INDIA** won by 3 wickets.   Toss: India.
Awards: A.A.Donald and S.R.Tendulkar.   LOI debuts: India – P.K.Amre; South Africa – All except K.C.Wessels who had
previously appeared for Australia.

South Africa's emergence from more than 21 years of political exile attracted a crowd of at least 90,452 (the number of
seats at Eden Gardens), most of them armed with fireworks. South Africa's inaugural limited-overs international was
also their first encounter at any level with India.

SOUTH AFRICA		Runs	Balls	4/6
S.J.Cook	lbw b Srinath	17	48	–
A.C.Hudson	c More b Kapil Dev	0	3	–
K.C.Wessels	b Tendulkar	50	95	3
P.N.Kirsten	b Raju	7	29	–
A.P.Kuiper	c Amre b Prabhakar	43	64	3/1
* C.E.B.Rice	b Prabhakar	14	23	1
R.P.Snell	c Amre b Kapil Dev	16	13	–
B.M.McMillan	run out	2	4	–
† D.J.Richardson	not out	4	4	–
T.G.Shaw	not out	0	–	–
A.A.Donald				
Extras	(lb 13, w 11)	24		
Total	(47 overs; 8 wickets)	**177**		

INDIA		Runs	Balls	4/6
R.J.Shastri	c Richardson b Donald	0	5	–
N.S.Sidhu	c McMillan b Donald	6	14	–
S.V.Manjrekar	b Donald	1	10	–
S.R.Tendulkar	c Snell b Donald	62	73	8/1
* M.Azharuddin	st Richardson b Shaw	16	21	1
P.K.Amre	lbw b Donald	55	74	8/1
Kapil Dev	b Kuiper	11	30	–
M.Prabhakar	not out	12	18	–
† K.S.More	not out	0	3	–
S.L.V.Raju				
J.Srinath				
Extras	(lb 2, w 11, nb 2)	15		
Total	(40.4 overs; 7 wickets)	**178**		

INDIA	O	M	R	W
Kapil Dev	9	2	23	2
Prabhakar	10	1	26	2
Srinath	10	0	39	1
Raju	10	0	32	1
Shastri	3	0	17	0
Tendulkar	5	0	27	1

SOUTH AFRICA	O	M	R	W
Donald	8.4	0	29	5
Snell	6	0	35	0
McMillan	6	0	30	0
Shaw	10	0	46	1
Rice	5	0	14	0
Kuiper	5	0	22	1

FALL OF WICKETS
1-3, 2-28, 3-49, 4-109, 5-151, 6-156, 7-167, 8-176

FALL OF WICKETS
1-1, 2-3, 3-20, 4-60, 5-116, 6-148, 7-177

Umpires: V.K.Ramaswamy (24) and R.S.Rathore (4).

INDIA v SOUTH AFRICA 1991-92

At Roop Singh Stadium, Gwalior on 12 November 1991.   Result: **INDIA** won by 38 runs.   Toss: South Africa.
Award: K.C.Wessels.   LOI debuts: South Africa – C.E.Eksteen, C.R.Matthews, M.Yachad.

The cramped crowd of 25,000 included some adroit rock throwers who, shunning parochial bias, scored direct hits on two Indian fielders. One of the victims, Navjot Sidhu, had shared a partnership of 130 with Krish Srikkanth; it remains India's only three-figure start against South Africa.

INDIA		Runs	Balls	4/6
K.Srikkanth	c Yachad b Snell	68	86	9
N.S.Sidhu	c Eksteen b Rice	61	91	4/1
S.V.Manjrekar	not out	52	52	4
S.R.Tendulkar	c Richardson b Matthews	4	8	–
* M.Azharuddin	c Kirsten b Donald	19	24	1
Kapil Dev	b Donald	3	7	–
P.K.Amre	b Donald	4	3	1
M.Prabhakar				
† K.S.More				
S.L.V.Raju				
J.Srinath				
Extras	(b 1, w 10, nb 1)	12		
Total	(45 overs; 6 wickets)	**223**		

SOUTH AFRICA		Runs	Balls	4/6
S.J.Cook	c More b Kapil Dev	0	4	–
M.Yachad	lbw b Raju	31	77	1
K.C.Wessels	c More b Srinath	71	96	6
P.N.Kirsten	lbw b Prabhakar	2	6	–
A.P.Kuiper	c Azharuddin b Kapil Dev	21	28	1/1
* C.E.B.Rice	c sub b Raju	12	14	–/1
† D.J.Richardson	c Kapil Dev b Raju	5	6	–
R.P.Snell	c Manjrekar b Srinath	2	4	–
C.R.Matthews	not out	10	16	–
C.E.Eksteen	not out	6	23	–
A.A.Donald				
Extras	(b 3, lb 14, w 5, nb 3)	25		
Total	(45 overs; 8 wickets)	**185**		

SOUTH AFRICA	O	M	R	W
Donald	9	1	36	3
Snell	9	0	43	1
Matthews	9	0	41	1
Eksteen	2	0	18	0
Rice	9	0	46	1
Kuiper	7	0	38	0

INDIA	O	M	R	W
Kapil Dev	9	3	27	2
Prabhakar	9	1	19	1
Tendulkar	7	0	31	0
Srinath	9	0	34	2
Raju	9	0	43	3
Srikkanth	2	0	14	0

FALL OF WICKETS
1-130, 2-144, 3-159, 4-202, 5-218, 6-223

FALL OF WICKETS
1-0, 2-94, 3-97, 4-143, 5-145, 6-164, 7-164, 8-167

Umpires: S.K.Bansal (2) and S.V.Ramani (8).

INDIA v SOUTH AFRICA 1991-92

At Jawaharlal Nehru Stadium, New Delhi on 14 November 1991.   Result: **SOUTH AFRICA** won by 8 wickets.
Toss: India.   Award: P.N.Kirsten.   LOI debuts: None.

This multi-surfaced athletics stadium produced a match aggregate of 575 runs for six wickets, one a run out, at 95.8 runs/wicket and 5.9 runs/over. Ravi Shastri and Sanjay Manjrekar shared India's highest second-wicket partnership in a home international.

INDIA		Runs	Balls	4/6
* R.J.Shastri	run out	109	149	11
K.Srikkanth	st Richardson b Kirsten	53	61	8
S.V.Manjrekar	c McMillan b Rice	105	82	8/2
S.R.Tendulkar	c Cook b Donald	1	3	–
Kapil Dev	not out	3	6	–
D.B.Vengsarkar				
P.K.Amre				
M.Prabhakar				
† C.S.Pandit				
S.L.V.Raju				
J.Srinath				
Extras	(b 4, lb 5, w 6, nb 1)	16		
Total	(50 overs; 4 wickets)	**287**		

SOUTH AFRICA		Runs	Balls	4/6
S.J.Cook	c Prabhakar b Srinath	35	46	3
K.C.Wessels	lbw b Raju	90	105	10
P.N.Kirsten	not out	86	92	6/1
A.P.Kuiper	not out	63	41	7/1
A.C.Hudson				
* C.E.B.Rice				
B.M.McMillan				
† D.J.Richardson				
R.P.Snell				
C.R.Matthews				
A.A.Donald				
Extras	(b 2, lb 5, w 4, nb 3)	14		
Total	(46.4 overs; 2 wickets)	**288**		

SOUTH AFRICA	O	M	R	W
Donald	10	0	55	1
Snell	10	1	56	0
Matthews	10	1	50	0
McMillan	8	0	40	0
Rice	9	0	54	1
Kirsten	3	0	23	1

INDIA	O	M	R	W
Kapil Dev	8	0	37	0
Prabhakar	8.4	0	64	0
Srinath	10	0	69	1
Tendulkar	6	0	38	0
Raju	10	0	48	1
Srikkanth	4	0	25	0

FALL OF WICKETS
1-86, 2-261, 3-264, 4-287

FALL OF WICKETS
1-72, 2-183

Umpires: S.Banerjee (10) and P.D.Reporter (12).

PAKISTAN v WEST INDIES 1991-92

At National Stadium, Karachi on 20 November 1991.   Result: **WEST INDIES** won by 24 runs.   Toss: West Indies.
Award: B.C.Lara.   LOI debuts: West Indies – A.C.Cummins, P.A.Wallace.

West Indies played this three-match series en route to Australia. Brian Lara's first international fifty took 59 balls. As
defeat loomed, some of the 50,000 crowd invaded the field and hurled missiles, one causing debutant Philo Wallace to
retire with a bruised shoulder.

WEST INDIES		Runs	Balls	4/6
D.L.Haynes	lbw b Mushtaq	45	76	4
P.A.Wallace	b Mushtaq	22	39	3
* R.B.Richardson	b Aqib	2	5	–
B.C.Lara	c Miandad b Wasim	54	59	2
C.L.Hooper	c Mushtaq b Wasim	17	17	1
K.L.T.Arthurton	b Wasim	4	3	1
† D.Williams	not out	5	7	–
I.R.Bishop	not out	3	2	–
C.E.L.Ambrose				
A.C.Cummins				
B.P.Patterson				
Extras	(lb 10, w 5, nb 3)	18		
Total	(34 overs; 6 wickets)	170		

PAKISTAN		Runs	Balls	4/6
Aamir Sohail	run out	1	4	–
Ramiz Raja	c Williams b Patterson	11	27	1
Zahid Fazal	c Lara b Patterson	17	39	2
Salim Malik	run out	16	27	–
Javed Miandad	c Richardson b Ambrose	31	37	1
* Imran Khan	c Arthurton b Hooper	15	31	1
Wasim Akram	st Williams b Hooper	0	1	–
† Moin Khan	c Richardson b Ambrose	18	20	2
Mushtaq Ahmed	c Bishop b Hooper	6	9	–
Waqar Younis	not out	11	13	1
Aqib Javed	b Hooper	2	4	–
Extras	(lb 5, w 8, nb 5)	18		
Total	(33.5 overs)	146		

PAKISTAN	O	M	R	W
Imran Khan	8	1	30	0
Wasim Akram	6	0	27	3
Aqib Javed	7	0	38	1
Mushtaq Ahmed	8	0	43	2
Waqar Younis	5	0	22	0

WEST INDIES	O	M	R	W
Bishop	6	2	23	0
Ambrose	7	0	28	2
Patterson	8	0	29	2
Cummins	5	0	27	0
Hooper	7.5	0	34	4

FALL OF WICKETS
1-55, 2-58, 3-126, 4-152, 5-156, 6-167

FALL OF WICKETS
1-8, 2-25, 3-45, 4-57, 5-82, 6-82, 7-119, 8-129, 9-134, 10-146

Umpires: Khizer Hayat (34) and Riazuddin (2).

PAKISTAN v WEST INDIES 1991-92

At Gaddafi Stadium, Lahore on 22 November 1991.   Result: **MATCH TIED**.   Toss: Pakistan.
Award: D.L.Haynes.   LOI debuts: Pakistan – Inzamam-ul-Haq

As this match was played under World Cup regulations, the tie stood even though West Indies lost fewer wickets.
Mushtaq Ahmed was run out attempting a second run from the last ball, ten having been needed off Curtly Ambrose's
final over.

WEST INDIES		Runs	Balls	4/6
D.L.Haynes	b Aqib	69	110	6
P.A.Wallace	lbw b Imran	32	37	4
* R.B.Richardson	c Aamir b Aqib	14	23	1
B.C.Lara	b Wasim	18	42	–
C.L.Hooper	c Inzamam b Wasim	22	18	1
K.L.T.Arthurton	not out	5	4	–
M.D.Marshall	not out	2	2	–
† D.Williams				
I.R.Bishop				
C.E.L.Ambrose				
B.P.Patterson				
Extras	(b 2, lb 11, w 9, nb 2)	24		
Total	(39 overs; 5 wickets)	186		

PAKISTAN		Runs	Balls	4/6
Aamir Sohail	c and b Patterson	13	21	–
Ramiz Raja	c Williams b Marshall	26	49	2
Inzamam-ul-Haq	b Marshall	20	29	2
Salim Malik	run out	0	2	–
* Imran Khan	c Richardson b Patterson	51	67	3
Ijaz Ahmed	c Williams b Ambrose	27	42	1
Wasim Akram	b Marshall	12	10	2
† Moin Khan	c and b Ambrose	7	9	–
Waqar Younis	not out	12	6	2
Mushtaq Ahmed	run out	1	1	–
Aqib Javed				
Extras	(lb 6, w 9, nb 2)	17		
Total	(39 overs; 9 wickets)	186		

PAKISTAN	O	M	R	W
Imran Khan	8	0	19	1
Wasim Akram	7	0	36	2
Aqib Javed	8	0	49	2
Mushtaq Ahmed	8	0	22	0
Waqar Younis	8	0	47	0

WEST INDIES	O	M	R	W
Bishop	7	0	41	0
Ambrose	8	1	28	2
Patterson	8	0	44	2
Marshall	8	0	39	3
Hooper	8	1	28	0

FALL OF WICKETS
1-53, 2-85, 3-134, 4-178, 5-183

FALL OF WICKETS
1-27, 2-69, 3-69, 4-70, 5-117, 6-136, 7-171, 8-180, 9-186

Umpires: Khizer Hayat (35) and Riazuddin (3).

PAKISTAN v WEST INDIES 1991-92

At Iqbal Stadium, Faisalabad on 24 November 1991.   Result: **WEST INDIES** won by 17 runs.   Toss: Pakistan.
Award: C.L.Hooper.   LOI debuts: None.

West Indies completed their theoretical clean sweep of the series when Curtly Ambrose and Malcolm Marshall snuffed out Pakistan's innings with four wickets in successive balls. Inzamam-ul-Haq took a wicket with his first ball at international level.

WEST INDIES		Runs	Balls	4/6
D.L.Haynes	c Moin b Aqib	8	27	–
P.A.Wallace	b Aqib	36	41	3/2
* R.B.Richardson	c Wasim b Aqib	5	10	1
B.C.Lara	c Moin b Inzamam	45	65	4
C.L.Hooper	c Zahid b Aqib	57	64	5/1
K.L.T.Arthurton	not out	29	26	2
M.D.Marshall	not out	7	7	–
† D.Williams				
R.C.Haynes				
C.E.L.Ambrose				
A.C.Cummins				
Extras	(lb 7, w 10)	17		
Total	(40 overs; 5 wickets)	204		

PAKISTAN		Runs	Balls	4/6
Ramiz Raja	c and b R.C.Haynes	29	61	2
Inzamam-ul-Haq	c Lara b Cummins	60	91	4
Zahid Fazal	c Cummins b Ambrose	53	50	2/1
Salim Malik	b Hooper	10	11	–
* Imran Khan	c Lara b Cummins	14	16	1
Ijaz Ahmed	c Richardson b Ambrose	4	5	–
Wasim Akram	b Marshall	0	1	–
† Moin Khan	not out	7	3	–
Waqar Younis	c and b Marshall	0	1	–
Mushtaq Ahmed	not out	5	2	–
Aqib Javed				
Extras	(lb 3, w 2)	5		
Total	(40 overs; 8 wickets)	187		

PAKISTAN	O	M	R	W
Imran Khan	8	0	36	0
Wasim Akram	8	1	43	0
Mushtaq Ahmed	8	0	33	0
Aqib Javed	8	1	31	4
Waqar Younis	5	0	30	0
Inzamam-ul-Haq	3	0	24	1

WEST INDIES	O	M	R	W
Ambrose	8	0	35	2
Cummins	8	1	27	2
Marshall	8	0	44	2
R.C.Haynes	8	0	34	1
Hooper	8	0	44	1

FALL OF WICKETS
1-65, 2-106, 3-126, 4-161, 5-175, 6-175, 7-175, 8-175

FALL OF WICKETS
1-43, 2-52, 3-52, 4-145, 5-186

Umpires: Athar Zaidi (4) and Khizer Hayat (36).

WEST INDIES v INDIA 1991-92

At WACA Ground, Perth on 6 December 1991.   Result: **MATCH TIED.**   Toss: West Indies.
Award: C.E.L.Ambrose.   LOI debuts: India – S.T.Banerjee.

For the second time in three internationals West Indies were involved in a tie, this time a genuine one with both sides bowled out (the first such instance). In dream conditions for swing and seam bowlers both teams made their (then) lowest totals against each other.

INDIA		Runs	Balls	4/6
R.J.Shastri	c Lara b Marshall	33	110	2
K.Srikkanth	c Hooper b Patterson	3	8	–
S.V.Manjrekar	c Williams b Cummins	15	39	–
S.R.Tendulkar	c Richardson b Cummins	1	9	–
* M.Azharuddin	c Lara b Ambrose	6	24	–
P.K.Amre	run out	20	50	–
Kapil Dev	c Richardson b Marshall	5	10	–
M.Prabhakar	run out	13	22	–
† K.S.More	c Richardson b Ambrose	4	10	–
S.T.Banerjee	not out	2	4	–
J.Srinath	run out	0	1	–
Extras	(lb 13, w 10, nb 1)	24		
Total	(47.4 overs)	126		

WEST INDIES		Runs	Balls	4/6
D.L.Haynes	c More b Kapil Dev	0	1	–
P.A.Wallace	b Prabhakar	11	33	–
* R.B.Richardson	c More b Kapil Dev	12	28	–
B.C.Lara	c More b Banerjee	14	38	1
C.L.Hooper	b Srinath	12	27	1
K.L.T.Arthurton	b Srinath	0	1	–
M.D.Marshall	c More b Banerjee	7	36	–
† D.Williams	c Srikkanth b Banerjee	5	7	–
C.E.L.Ambrose	run out	17	25	1/1
A.C.Cummins	c Azharuddin b Tendulkar	24	43	2
B.P.Patterson	not out	8	12	–
Extras	(lb 4, w 9, nb 3)	16		
Total	(41 overs)	126		

WEST INDIES	O	M	R	W
Patterson	10	1	28	1
Ambrose	8.4	3	9	2
Marshall	10	2	23	2
Cummins	9	1	21	2
Hooper	10	1	32	0

INDIA	O	M	R	W
Kapil Dev	10	3	30	2
Prabhakar	10	1	30	1
Srinath	10	2	27	2
Banerjee	10	2	30	3
Tendulkar	1	0	5	1

FALL OF WICKETS
1-8, 2-35, 3-41, 4-58, 5-74, 6-88, 7-111, 8-122, 9-125, 10-126

FALL OF WICKETS
1-0, 2-23, 3-25, 4-55, 5-55, 6-61, 7-69, 8-76, 9-113, 10-126

Umpires: R.J.Evans (13) and P.J.McConnell (59).

AUSTRALIA v INDIA 1991-92

At WACA Ground, Perth on 8 December 1991.　　Result: **INDIA** won by 107 runs.　　Toss: India.
Award: K.Srikkanth.　　LOI debuts: None.

Australia's total remains their lowest against India. Ravi Shastri captured the last five wickets in 32 balls to establish India's record LOI analysis until 1993-94.

INDIA		Runs	Balls	4/6	AUSTRALIA		Runs	Balls	4/6
R.J.Shastri	c Jones b Waugh	10	68	1	G.R.Marsh	c More b Banerjee	15	60	2
K.Srikkanth	c Moody b Waugh	60	60	8	D.C.Boon	c Kapil Dev b Prabhakar	1	16	–
S.V.Manjrekar	run out	2	6	–	D.M.Jones	b Kapil Dev	1	8	–
S.R.Tendulkar	c Taylor b Moody	36	65	3	* A.R.Border	c More b Srinath	32	45	5
* M.Azharuddin	c Healy b Moody	6	9	–	T.M.Moody	c More b Srinath	7	15	1
P.K.Amre	c Jones b McDermott	33	53	1	S.R.Waugh	c and b Shastri	5	30	–
Kapil Dev	not out	25	37	1	S.P.O'Donnell	c Kapil Dev b Shastri	10	27	–
M.Prabhakar	lbw b Waugh	2	10	–	† I.A.Healy	st More b Shastri	3	9	–
S.T.Banerjee	not out	6	5	–	P.L.Taylor	c Amre b Shastri	6	21	–
† K.S.More					C.J.McDermott	c Tendulkar b Shastri	5	9	1
J.Srinath					B.A.Reid	not out	1	2	–
Extras	(b 1, lb 10, w 16, nb 1)	28			Extras	(lb 4, w 6, nb 5)	15		
Total	(50 overs; 7 wickets)	208			Total	(37.5 overs)	101		

AUSTRALIA	O	M	R	W	INDIA	O	M	R	W
McDermott	10	1	40	1	Kapil Dev	6	2	5	1
Reid	10	2	16	0	Prabhakar	6	2	19	1
O'Donnell	7	0	39	0	Srinath	7	0	24	2
Waugh	10	1	46	3	Banerjee	8	1	26	1
Taylor	4	0	18	0	Shastri	6.5	1	15	5
Moody	9	0	38	2	Tendulkar	4	0	8	0

FALL OF WICKETS
1-49, 2-64, 3-95, 4-112, 5-115, 6-183, 7-193

FALL OF WICKETS
1-3, 2-6, 3-52, 4-65, 5-68, 6-75, 7-84, 8-93, 9-99, 10-101

Umpires: R.J.Evans (14) and T.A.Prue (12).

AUSTRALIA v INDIA 1991-92

At Bellerive Oval, Hobart on 10 December 1991.　　Result: **AUSTRALIA** won by 8 wickets.　　Toss: India.
Award: D.C.Boon.　　LOI debuts: None.

David Boon scored the first hundred by a Tasmanian on his home ground as Australia won their first LOI victory there.

INDIA		Runs	Balls	4/6	AUSTRALIA		Runs	Balls	4/6
R.J.Shastri	lbw b McDermott	0	6	–	D.C.Boon	not out	102	168	8
K.Srikkanth	c Healy b McDermott	7	36	1	G.R.Marsh	b Srinath	8	35	1
S.V.Manjrekar	c Healy b Reid	57	99	1	D.M.Jones	c Tendulkar b Manjrekar	48	99	2
S.R.Tendulkar	c Waugh b Taylor	57	107	3	* A.R.Border	not out	0	–	–
Kapil Dev	c and b Taylor	3	7	–	T.M.Moody				
P.K.Amre	b O'Donnell	8	13	–	S.R.Waugh				
* M.Azharuddin	not out	21	23	–	S.P.O'Donnell				
S.T.Banerjee	c Jones b McDermott	5	8	–	† I.A.Healy				
M.Prabhakar	run out	1	5	–	P.L.Taylor				
J.Srinath	not out	2	2	–	C.J.McDermott				
† K.S.More					B.A.Reid				
Extras	(b 1, lb 7, w 4, nb 2)	14			Extras	(b 3, lb 4, w 7, nb 4)	18		
Total	(50 overs; 8 wickets)	175			Total	(48.3 overs; 2 wickets)	176		

AUSTRALIA	O	M	R	W	INDIA	O	M	R	W
Reid	10	1	24	1	Kapil Dev	10	3	21	0
McDermott	10	3	19	3	Prabhakar	10	0	32	0
O'Donnell	10	1	35	0	Srinath	10	1	37	1
Waugh	7	0	31	0	Banerjee	6	0	41	0
Taylor	10	0	43	2	Shastri	10	0	29	0
Moody	3	0	15	0	Srikkanth	2	0	7	0
					Manjrekar	0.3	0	2	1

FALL OF WICKETS
1-2, 2-18, 3-120, 4-134, 5-137, 6-151, 7-162, 8-168

FALL OF WICKETS
1-45, 2-174

Umpires: S.G.Randell (40) and C.D.Timmins (10).

AUSTRALIA v WEST INDIES 1991-92

At Melbourne Cricket Ground on 12 December 1991.   Result: **AUSTRALIA** won by 9 runs.   Toss: Australia.
Award: S.R.Waugh.   LOI debuts: None.

Tom Moody hit the first six into the $150 million Great Southern Stand. Malcolm Marshall's analysis was the best of his 136-match career. The fielding of Steve Waugh and Allan Border was exceptional and accounted for the three run outs.

AUSTRALIA		Runs	Balls	4/6
G.R.Marsh	c Richardson b Marshall	43	111	3
D.C.Boon	b Marshall	8	33	–
D.M.Jones	c Williams b Marshall	0	9	–
* A.R.Border	st Williams b Hooper	37	71	–
T.M.Moody	run out	51	45	2/2
S.R.Waugh	c Williams b Cummins	8	15	–
† I.A.Healy	b Patterson	5	7	–
P.L.Taylor	c Lara b Ambrose	3	5	–
C.J.McDermott	lbw b Marshall	0	1	–
M.R.Whitney	not out	2	5	–
B.A.Reid	not out	2	3	–
Extras	(lb 9, w 2, nb 3)	14		
Total	(50 overs; 9 wickets)	**173**		

WEST INDIES		Runs	Balls	4/6
D.L.Haynes	c and b Taylor	62	107	5
C.A.Best	c Border b McDermott	5	6	–
* R.B.Richardson	c Waugh b McDermott	10	25	1
B.C.Lara	c and b Waugh	11	36	–
C.L.Hooper	lbw b Waugh	0	3	–
K.L.T.Arthurton	run out	28	62	2
M.D.Marshall	run out	3	5	–
† D.Williams	run out	10	19	–
C.E.L.Ambrose	b Taylor	18	23	1/1
A.C.Cummins	b McDermott	6	12	–
B.P.Patterson	not out	1	1	–
Extras	(b 1, lb 5, w 2, nb 2)	10		
Total	(49.1 overs)	**164**		

WEST INDIES	O	M	R	W
Ambrose	10	2	31	1
Patterson	10	0	49	1
Marshall	10	4	18	4
Cummins	10	1	35	1
Hooper	10	0	31	1

AUSTRALIA	O	M	R	W
Reid	9	1	33	0
McDermott	9.1	2	23	3
Whitney	10	3	29	0
Waugh	6	0	16	2
Moody	5	0	21	0
Taylor	10	1	36	2

FALL OF WICKETS
1-21, 2-29, 3-97, 4-103, 5-141, 6-154, 7-159, 8-165, 9-170

FALL OF WICKETS
1-9, 2-34, 3-64, 4-64, 5-119, 6-124, 7-129, 8-145, 9-162, 10-164

Umpires: A.R.Crafter (80) and P.J.McConnell (60).

WEST INDIES v INDIA 1991-92

At Adelaide Oval on 14 December 1991.   Result: **INDIA** won by 10 runs.   Toss: India.
Award: K.Srikkanth.   LOI debuts: None.

India took advantage of the first reliable batting surface of this tournament to amass its highest total. Desmond Haynes struck a six off Narendra Hirwani to become the first to score 7000 runs in limited-overs internationals.

INDIA		Runs	Balls	4/6
R.J.Shastri	c Williams b Ambrose	4	22	–
K.Srikkanth	st Williams b Hooper	82	84	10/1
S.V.Manjrekar	c Wallace b Arthurton	55	98	1
S.R.Tendulkar	c and b Arthurton	48	57	2
* M.Azharuddin	not out	31	28	–
Kapil Dev	not out	21	19	1
P.K.Amre				
M.Prabhakar				
† K.S.More				
J.Srinath				
N.D.Hirwani				
Extras	(lb 5, w 11, nb 5)	21		
Total	(50 overs; 4 wickets)	**262**		

WEST INDIES		Runs	Balls	4/6
D.L.Haynes	c Shastri b Srinath	89	116	6/1
P.A.Wallace	c Srinath b Hirwani	52	96	4/1
* R.B.Richardson	run out	2	7	–
B.C.Lara	lbw b Shastri	29	29	1
C.L.Hooper	c Manjrekar b Kapil Dev	12	19	–
K.L.T.Arthurton	c Amre b Kapil Dev	5	6	–
M.D.Marshall	lbw b Srinath	17	13	2
† D.Williams	c and b Prabhakar	3	4	–
C.E.L.Ambrose	b Kapil Dev	10	11	–
A.C.Cummins	b Kapil Dev	7	5	1
B.P.Patterson	not out	1	1	–
Extras	(b 1, lb 11, w 9, nb 4)	25		
Total	(50 overs)	**252**		

WEST INDIES	O	M	R	W
Ambrose	10	1	35	1
Patterson	6	0	47	0
Marshall	10	0	59	0
Cummins	10	0	41	0
Hooper	10	0	52	1
Arthurton	4	0	23	2

INDIA	O	M	R	W
Kapil Dev	10	1	54	4
Prabhakar	9	1	42	1
Srinath	10	0	35	2
Tendulkar	2	0	10	0
Hirwani	9	0	54	1
Shastri	10	0	45	1

FALL OF WICKETS
1-27, 2-123, 3-198, 4-220

FALL OF WICKETS
1-124, 2-127, 3-184, 4-205, 5-206, 6-212, 7-220, 8-243, 9-251, 10-252

Umpires: D.B.Hair (1) and L.J.King (17).

AUSTRALIA v INDIA 1991-92

At Adelaide Oval on 15 December 1991.   Result: **AUSTRALIA** won by 6 wickets.   Toss: India.
Award: A.R.Border.   LOI debuts: None.

Batting on the same pitch, India scored 105 runs fewer than on the previous day. Mohammed Azharuddin took his LOI tally to 3000 runs from 124 matches.

INDIA		Runs	Balls	4/6
R.J.Shastri	lbw b Reid	1	2	–
K.Srikkanth	c and b McDermott	3	4	–
S.V.Manjrekar	run out	12	32	–
S.R.Tendulkar	c Jones b Waugh	21	35	3
* M.Azharuddin	c Healy b Whitney	13	53	–
P.K.Amre	c Healy b Whitney	10	22	–
Kapil Dev	c Moody b Taylor	39	56	1
M.Prabhakar	run out	17	39	1
† K.S.More	lbw b McDermott	20	27	2
J.Srinath	run out	8	19	–
S.L.V.Raju	not out	3	7	–
Extras	(lb 6, w 4)	10		
Total	(48.4 overs)	**157**		

AUSTRALIA	O	M	R	W
Reid	10	1	32	1
McDermott	8.4	0	29	2
Waugh	10	1	27	1
Whitney	10	3	22	2
Taylor	10	1	41	1

FALL OF WICKETS
1-2, 2-4, 3-37, 4-41, 5-64, 6-69, 7-119, 8-133, 9-149, 10-157

Umpires: A.R.Crafter (81) and I.S.Thomas (3).

AUSTRALIA		Runs	Balls	4/6
D.C.Boon	b Kapil Dev	6	10	–
G.R.Marsh	b Prabhakar	3	14	–
D.M.Jones	not out	63	119	3/1
* A.R.Border	c sub (S.C.Ganguly) b Raju	76	102	5/2
T.M.Moody	c Tendulkar b Raju	0	6	–
S.R.Waugh	not out	0	–	–
† I.A.Healy				
P.L.Taylor				
C.J.McDermott				
M.R.Whitney				
B.A.Reid				
Extras	(lb 3, w 4, nb 3)	10		
Total	(40.5 overs; 4 wickets)	**158**		

INDIA	O	M	R	W
Kapil Dev	6	2	12	1
Prabhakar	6	0	20	1
Shastri	10	0	34	0
Srinath	6	0	30	0
Raju	9	1	32	2
Srikkanth	2	0	24	0
Tendulkar	1.5	0	3	0

FALL OF WICKETS
1-10, 2-17, 3-154, 4-156

AUSTRALIA v WEST INDIES 1991-92

At Sydney Cricket Ground on 18 December 1991.   Result: **AUSTRALIA** won by 51 runs.   Toss: Australia.
Award: G.R.Marsh.   LOI debuts: None.

Australia gained their fourth successive LOI victory against West Indies. Geoff Marsh scored his 4000th run in 107 internationals but later sustained concussion and a severely bruised neck when he collided with Dean Jones while attempting a catch.

AUSTRALIA		Runs	Balls	4/6
G.R.Marsh	c D.L.Haynes b Cummins	82	146	4/2
D.C.Boon	b Arthurton	61	91	7
D.M.Jones	b Ambrose	2	11	–
S.R.Waugh	b Ambrose	34	37	3
T.M.Moody	run out	8	9	–
* A.R.Border	b Hooper	1	4	–
† I.A.Healy	not out	17	10	2
P.L.Taylor	not out	2	3	–
C.J.McDermott				
M.R.Whitney				
B.A.Reid				
Extras	(b 2, lb 15, w 4, nb 6)	27		
Total	(50 overs; 6 wickets)	**234**		

WEST INDIES	O	M	R	W
Ambrose	10	3	26	2
Cummins	10	0	53	1
Marshall	9	2	39	0
R.C.Haynes	6	0	35	0
Hooper	10	0	42	1
Arthurton	5	1	22	1

FALL OF WICKETS
1-128, 2-137, 3-190, 4-204, 5-211, 6-214

Umpires: L.J.King (18) and S.G.Randell (41).

WEST INDIES		Runs	Balls	4/6
D.L.Haynes	c Healy b McDermott	9	18	–
P.A.Wallace	lbw b Reid	2	15	–
* R.B.Richardson	c Healy b Reid	6	30	–
B.C.Lara	c Waugh b Whitney	19	54	1
C.L.Hooper	c Waugh b Moody	77	87	5/1
K.L.T.Arthurton	b Waugh	38	63	2
M.D.Marshall	b Whitney	7	14	–
† D.Williams	b Whitney	0	1	–
R.C.Haynes	c Moody b McDermott	0	3	–
C.E.L.Ambrose	b Waugh	2	4	–
A.C.Cummins	not out	1	2	–
Extras	(lb 13, w 4, nb 5)	22		
Total	(46.5 overs)	**183**		

AUSTRALIA	O	M	R	W
Reid	10	2	29	2
McDermott	8	1	29	2
Waugh	6.5	0	33	2
Whitney	10	1	25	3
Taylor	5	0	32	0
Moody	7	0	22	1

FALL OF WICKETS
1-13, 2-17, 3-36, 4-70, 5-146, 6-177, 7-177, 8-178, 9-181, 10-183

AUSTRALIA v WEST INDIES 1991-92

At Melbourne Cricket Ground on 9 January 1992.   No result.   Toss: West Indies.
LOI debuts: None.

Persistent rain curtailed the West Indies innings and prevented a restart.

WEST INDIES		Runs	Balls	4/6
D.L.Haynes	c S.R.Waugh b Taylor	56	107	3/1
P.A.Wallace	c S.R.Waugh b McDermott	22	36	3
B.C.Lara	run out	22	46	1
* R.B.Richardson	run out	13	31	1
C.L.Hooper	b Taylor	7	16	–
K.L.T.Arthurton	not out	12	26	–
M.D.Marshall	c Healy b Whitney	4	8	–
C.E.L.Ambrose	b McDermott	7	11	–
A.C.Cummins	not out	1	2	–
† D.Williams				
B.P.Patterson				
Extras	(b 5, lb 9, w 1, nb 1)	16		
Total	(47 overs; 7 wickets)	**160**		

AUSTRALIA
G.R.Marsh
D.C.Boon
D.M.Jones
* A.R.Border
T.M.Moody
M.E.Waugh
S.R.Waugh
† I.A.Healy
P.L.Taylor
C.J.McDermott
M.R.Whitney

AUSTRALIA	O	M	R	W
McDermott	9	0	25	2
Whitney	10	0	28	1
Moody	5	0	28	0
S.R.Waugh	8	0	19	0
Taylor	10	1	28	2
M.E.Waugh	5	0	18	0

FALL OF WICKETS
1-33, 2-97, 3-113, 4-128, 5-137, 6-144, 7-159

Umpires: A.R.Crafter (82) and L.J.King (19).

WEST INDIES v INDIA 1991-92

At Woolloongabba, Brisbane on 11 January 1992.   Result: **WEST INDIES** won by 6 wickets.   Toss: India.
Award: A.C.Cummins.   LOI debuts: India – S.C.Ganguly.

West Indies gained their first win in six matches. Sachin Tendulkar, aged 18 but playing in his 27th international, made his highest score so far. Andy Cummins returned the first five-wicket LOI analysis at The Gabba.

INDIA		Runs	Balls	4/6
K.Srikkanth	c Marshall b Cummins	4	33	–
N.S.Sidhu	c Hooper b Marshall	1	19	–
S.V.Manjrekar	run out	1	4	–
S.R.Tendulkar	c sub b Cummins	77	127	5
* M.Azharuddin	lbw b Marshall	8	9	1
S.C.Ganguly	lbw b Cummins	3	13	–
M.Prabhakar	c and b Patterson	14	21	2
Kapil Dev	c Marshall b Patterson	28	58	2
† K.S.More	not out	11	10	–/1
S.L.V.Raju	c Williams b Cummins	8	8	–
J.Srinath	c Williams b Cummins	0	1	–
Extras	(b 4, lb 9, w 15, nb 8)	36		
Total	(48.3 overs)	**191**		

WEST INDIES		Runs	Balls	4/6
D.L.Haynes	c sub (P.K.Amre) b Raju	52	105	5
P.A.Wallace	c Srinath b Prabhakar	4	17	1
B.C.Lara	c Manjrekar b Srinath	4	27	–
* R.B.Richardson	lbw b Prabhakar	72	117	8
C.L.Hooper	not out	19	29	1
C.A.Best	not out	9	10	1
M.D.Marshall				
† D.Williams				
C.E.L.Ambrose				
A.C.Cummins				
B.P.Patterson				
Extras	(b 2, lb 8, w 13, nb 9)	32		
Total	(48.3 overs; 4 wickets)	**192**		

WEST INDIES	O	M	R	W
Ambrose	10	0	41	0
Marshall	10	0	30	2
Cummins	9.3	1	31	5
Patterson	9	0	52	2
Hooper	10	0	24	0

FALL OF WICKETS
1-14, 2-20, 3-21, 4-35, 5-62, 6-85, 7-161, 8-178, 9-191, 10-191

Umpires: D.B.Hair (2) and S.G.Randell (42).

INDIA	O	M	R	W
Kapil Dev	10	3	33	0
Prabhakar	9	1	39	2
Srinath	9	3	27	1
Tendulkar	7	0	27	0
Raju	10	0	33	1
Srikkanth	3	0	21	0
Sidhu	0.3	0	2	0

FALL OF WICKETS
1-13, 2-24, 3-133, 4-170

AUSTRALIA v WEST INDIES 1991-92

At Woolloongabba, Brisbane on 12 January 1992.   Result: **WEST INDIES** won by 12 runs.   Toss: Australia.
Award: B.C.Lara.   LOI debuts: None.

West Indies gained their only victory of the season against Australia shortly before the advance scouts of Tropical
Cyclone Betsi visited the ground.

WEST INDIES		Runs	Balls	4/6
D.L.Haynes	c Marsh b Whitney	11	39	–
P.A.Wallace	c Whitney b Moody	31	64	3/1
B.C.Lara	run out	69	85	5/1
* R.B.Richardson	c Moody b Taylor	50	65	3/1
C.L.Hooper	c and b S.R.Waugh	6	11	–
C.A.Best	b McDermott	30	21	1/1
M.D.Marshall	c Border b S.R.Waugh	4	6	–
C.E.L.Ambrose	b McDermott	2	3	–
A.C.Cummins	c Boon b S.R.Waugh	2	4	–
† D.Williams	not out	0	–	–
B.P.Patterson	lbw b McDermott	0	2	–
Extras	(lb 8, w 2)	10		
Total	(49.3 overs)	215		

AUSTRALIA		Runs	Balls	4/6
D.C.Boon	run out	77	115	7
G.R.Marsh	lbw b Patterson	29	50	2
D.M.Jones	b Patterson	0	10	–
* A.R.Border	run out	8	15	1
M.E.Waugh	b Cummins	17	25	1
T.M.Moody	b Ambrose	3	10	–
S.R.Waugh	b Patterson	3	7	–
† I.A.Healy	run out	11	16	–
P.L.Taylor	b Hooper	33	32	3
C.J.McDermott	c Haynes b Hooper	10	19	–
M.R.Whitney	not out	1	1	–
Extras	(b 1, lb 4, w 2, nb 4)	11		
Total	(49 overs)	203		

AUSTRALIA	O	M	R	W
McDermott	9.3	2	36	3
Whitney	10	2	39	1
S.R.Waugh	10	2	31	3
Moody	6	0	29	1
Taylor	10	0	44	1
M.E.Waugh	4	0	28	0

WEST INDIES	O	M	R	W
Marshall	9	1	39	0
Ambrose	10	1	37	1
Cummins	10	0	49	1
Patterson	10	1	37	3
Hooper	10	0	36	2

FALL OF WICKETS
1-27, 2-58, 3-168, 4-173, 5-185, 6-193, 7-210, 8-215, 9-215, 10-215

FALL OF WICKETS
1-70, 2-73, 3-84, 4-120, 5-135, 6-141, 7-152, 8-164, 9-200, 10-203

Umpires: I.S.Thomas (4) and C.D.Timmins (11).

AUSTRALIA v INDIA 1991-92

At Sydney Cricket Ground on 14 January 1992.   Result: **AUSTRALIA** won by 9 wickets.   Toss: India.
Award: C.J.McDermott.   LOI debuts: Australia – P.R.Reiffel.

The unbroken partnership of 167 between David Boon and Tom Moody remains Australia's second-wicket record
against India.

INDIA		Runs	Balls	4/6
R.J.Shastri	b Reiffel	22	67	1
K.Srikkanth	b Reiffel	42	59	5
N.S.Sidhu	c Boon b S.R.Waugh	1	6	–
S.V.Manjrekar	c Marsh b Moody	16	51	–
S.R.Tendulkar	run out	31	44	1
* M.Azharuddin	c Border b McDermott	22	29	1
Kapil Dev	run out	7	13	–
M.Prabhakar	c and b Whitney	8	12	–
† C.S.Pandit	c Healy b McDermott	2	5	–
S.L.V.Raju	not out	6	12	1
J.Srinath	b S.R.Waugh	5	6	1
Extras	(b 3, lb 5, w 4, nb 1)	13		
Total	(49.4 overs)	175		

AUSTRALIA		Runs	Balls	4/6
G.R.Marsh	b Prabhakar	3	17	–
D.C.Boon	not out	79	100	6
T.M.Moody	not out	87	123	5
* A.R.Border				
M.E.Waugh				
S.R.Waugh				
† I.A.Healy				
P.L.Taylor				
C.J.McDermott				
P.R.Reiffel				
M.R.Whitney				
Extras	(lb 5, w 2, nb 1)	8		
Total	(39.2 overs; 1 wicket)	177		

AUSTRALIA	O	M	R	W
McDermott	10	2	17	2
Whitney	10	1	36	1
Reiffel	10	1	27	2
S.R.Waugh	5.4	0	29	2
Taylor	9	0	40	0
Moody	5	0	18	1

INDIA	O	M	R	W
Kapil Dev	6	0	11	0
Prabhakar	8	0	29	1
Tendulkar	2	0	14	0
Srinath	8	1	28	0
Shastri	8	0	40	0
Raju	7	0	46	0
Manjrekar	0.2	0	4	0

FALL OF WICKETS
1-52, 2-57, 3-69, 4-111, 5-129, 6-150, 7-156, 8-161, 9-163, 10-175

FALL OF WICKETS
1-10

Umpires: D.B.Hair (3) and T.A.Prue (13).

WEST INDIES v INDIA 1991-92

At Melbourne Cricket Ground on 16 January 1992.　　Result: **INDIA** won by 5 wickets.　　Toss: West Indies.
Award: S.R.Tendulkar.　　LOI debuts: None.

India withstood an opening spell of 6-4-3-1 by Curtly Ambrose to qualify for the finals for the second time in three attempts. Final points: Australia 11, India 7, West Indies 6.

WEST INDIES		Runs	Balls	4/6
D.L.Haynes	c Pandit b Srinath	14	51	–
P.A.Wallace	run out	2	32	–
B.C.Lara	st Pandit b Hirwani	11	26	–
* R.B.Richardson	lbw b Hirwani	20	64	2
C.L.Hooper	c Manjrekar b Prabhakar	45	45	2/1
C.A.Best	b Srinath	29	42	3
M.D.Marshall	run out	0	–	–
† D.Williams	run out	3	10	–
C.E.L.Ambrose	not out	24	21	2
A.C.Cummins	not out	10	11	–
B.P.Patterson				
Extras	(b 1, lb 8, w 6, nb 2)	17		
Total	(50 overs; 8 wickets)	**175**		

INDIA		O	M	R	W
Prabhakar		9	1	20	1
Kapil Dev		10	2	27	0
Srinath		10	1	39	2
Hirwani		10	0	34	2
Tendulkar		10	1	38	0
Shastri		1	0	8	0

INDIA		Runs	Balls	4/6
R.J.Shastri	c Hooper b Ambrose	11	35	–
K.Srikkanth	c Williams b Ambrose	60	84	6/1
S.V.Manjrekar	c Williams b Patterson	2	24	–
S.R.Tendulkar	not out	57	88	2
* M.Azharuddin	c Lara b Hooper	5	12	–
P.K.Amre	c sub ‡ b Hooper	18	43	–
Kapil Dev	not out	1	3	–
M.Prabhakar				
† C.S.Pandit				
J.Srinath				
N.D.Hirwani				
Extras	(lb 11, w 2, nb 9)	22		
Total	(46.4 overs; 5 wickets)	**176**		

WEST INDIES	O	M	R	W
Marshall	10	1	33	0
Ambrose	10	4	17	2
Cummins	10	0	47	0
Patterson	8	1	31	1
Hooper	8	0	35	2
Richardson	0.4	0	2	0

FALL OF WICKETS
1-21, 2-24, 3-45, 4-84, 5-127, 6-128, 7-138, 8-147

FALL OF WICKETS
1-20, 2-38, 3-100, 4-115, 5-169

Umpires: P.J.McConnell (61) and C.D.Timmins (12).　　　　‡ (H.A.G.Anthony)

AUSTRALIA v INDIA 1991-92

At Melbourne Cricket Ground on 18 January 1992.　　Result: **AUSTRALIA** won by 88 runs.　　Toss: Australia.
LOI debuts: None.

Australia captured India's last five wickets for 15 runs to clinch a comfortable victory. David Boon scored his fourth fifty in successive innings and Mohammed Azharuddin took his 50th catch in 128 internationals.

AUSTRALIA		Runs	Balls	4/6
D.C.Boon	c Pandit b Prabhakar	78	107	9
G.R.Marsh	c Azharuddin b Tendulkar	21	46	2
D.M.Jones	c sub (N.S.Sidhu) b Kapil Dev	73	96	3
T.M.Moody	c Amre b Shastri	13	18	–
M.E.Waugh	c Amre b Shastri	3	7	–
* A.R.Border	not out	28	24	1
S.R.Waugh	not out	5	5	–
† I.A.Healy				
P.L.Taylor				
C.J.McDermott				
M.R.Whitney				
Extras	(lb 7, w 4, nb 1)	12		
Total	(50 overs; 5 wickets)	**233**		

INDIA	O	M	R	W
Kapil Dev	10	0	40	1
Prabhakar	10	2	53	1
Srinath	9	2	32	0
Tendulkar	6	0	29	1
Hirwani	5	0	34	0
Shastri	10	0	38	2

INDIA		Runs	Balls	4/6
R.J.Shastri	run out	17	50	1
K.Srikkanth	c Taylor b S.R.Waugh	41	49	4
S.V.Manjrekar	c Healy b S.R.Waugh	18	28	1
S.R.Tendulkar	c Whitney b Moody	4	10	–
* M.Azharuddin	c Healy b Moody	13	22	1
P.K.Amre	c Border b Taylor	20	41	–
Kapil Dev	not out	20	40	1
M.Prabhakar	run out	0	1	–
† C.S.Pandit	c S.R.Waugh b Taylor	0	2	–
J.Srinath	run out	0	4	–
N.D.Hirwani	c Marsh b McDermott	4	7	–
Extras	(lb 6, w 1, nb 1)	8		
Total	(42 overs)	**145**		

AUSTRALIA	O	M	R	W
McDermott	8	0	27	1
Whitney	8	2	19	0
S.R.Waugh	7	0	32	2
Moody	10	0	34	2
Taylor	9	0	27	2

FALL OF WICKETS
1-37, 2-72, 3-79, 4-84, 5-114, 6-130, 7-135, 8-136, 9-136, 10-145

FALL OF WICKETS
1-54, 2-142, 3-169, 4-176, 5-216

Umpires: A.R.Crafter (83) and T.A.Prue (14).

AUSTRALIA v INDIA 1991-92

At Sydney Cricket Ground on 20 January 1992.   Result: **AUSTRALIA** won by 6 runs.   Toss: Australia.
Finals Awards: D.C.Boon and G.R.Marsh.   LOI debuts: None.

When India notched only six of the 13 runs required from Mike Whitney's final over, Australia gained their seventh title in 13 seasons of the World Series circus.

AUSTRALIA		Runs	Balls	4/6
G.R.Marsh	c Amre b Srinath	78	138	3
D.C.Boon	b Prabhakar	20	42	3
D.M.Jones	st Pandit b Raju	9	23	–
T.M.Moody	c Tendulkar b Raju	15	32	–
M.E.Waugh	st Pandit b Raju	0	3	–
* A.R.Border	run out	38	39	3
S.R.Waugh	b Prabhakar	5	10	–
† I.A.Healy	run out	11	12	1
P.L.Taylor	not out	8	6	1
C.J.McDermott	b Prabhakar	5	5	–
M.R.Whitney	not out	0	1	–
Extras	(lb 9, w 3, nb 7)	19		
Total	(50 overs; 9 wickets)	**208**		

INDIA	O	M	R	W
Kapil Dev	10	1	42	0
Prabhakar	9	0	31	3
Srinath	7	1	30	1
Tendulkar	4	0	18	0
Shastri	10	1	46	0
Raju	10	1	32	3

FALL OF WICKETS
1-47, 2-74, 3-114, 4-117, 5-168, 6-175, 7-192, 8-200, 9-208

INDIA		Runs	Balls	4/6
R.J.Shastri	c Whitney b Moody	61	116	3
K.Srikkanth	c M.E.Waugh b Whitney	11	15	1
S.V.Manjrekar	run out	10	30	1
S.R.Tendulkar	c Whitney b S.R.Waugh	69	100	3
* M.Azharuddin	c Whitney b Border	11	9	1
Kapil Dev	lbw b McDermott	2	4	–
P.K.Amre	c Jones b McDermott	22	17	2
† C.S.Pandit	not out	5	8	–
M.Prabhakar	not out	4	6	–
S.L.V.Raju				
J.Srinath				
Extras	(lb 3, w 1, nb 3)	7		
Total	(50 overs; 7 wickets)	**202**		

AUSTRALIA	O	M	R	W
McDermott	9	1	37	2
Whitney	10	0	32	1
S.R.Waugh	10	1	40	1
Moody	10	1	31	1
Taylor	9	0	44	0
Border	2	0	15	1

FALL OF WICKETS
1-19, 2-45, 3-121, 4-146, 5-154, 6-190, 7-195

Umpires: P.J.McConnell (62) and S.G.Randell (43).

PAKISTAN v SRI LANKA (1st Match)

PAKISTAN v SRI LANKA 1991-92

At Sargodha Stadium on 10 January 1992.   Result: **PAKISTAN** won by 8 wickets.   Toss: Pakistan.
Award: Ramiz Raja.   LOI debuts: Sri Lanka – U.C.Hathurusinghe, R.S.Kalpage.

Sargodha Stadium housed the 90th ground to stage limited-overs internationals. The initial encounter of this five-match 40-over series saw Sri Lanka outplayed in overcast conditions on a pitch of uneven bounce.

SRI LANKA		Runs	Balls	4/6
R.S.Mahanama	lbw b Waqar	5	17	–
U.C.Hathurusinghe	c Moin b Imran	6	46	–
A.P.Gurusinha	c Imran b Akram Raza	37	56	3
* P.A.de Silva	c Wasim b Waqar	19	37	–
S.T.Jayasuriya	run out	26	37	1
† H.P.Tillekeratne	not out	37	34	–/1
M.S.Atapattu	b Aqib	4	11	–
R.S.Kalpage	not out	5	5	–
C.P.H.Ramanayake				
K.I.W.Wijegunawardene				
G.P.Wickremasinghe				
Extras	(b 1, lb 5, w 7, nb 3)	16		
Total	(40 overs; 6 wickets)	**155**		

PAKISTAN	O	M	R	W
Wasim Akram	8	0	33	0
Waqar Younis	8	2	13	2
Aqib Javed	8	1	26	1
Imran Khan	8	0	35	1
Akram Raza	8	0	42	1

FALL OF WICKETS
1-11, 2-27, 3-69, 4-79, 5-118, 6-138

Umpires: Amanullah Khan (12) and Khizer Hayat (37).

PAKISTAN		Runs	Balls	4/6
Ramiz Raja	c Mahanama b Wijegunawardene	74	83	10
Zahid Fazal	b Ramanayake	9	21	–
Javed Miandad	not out	60	105	7
Salim Malik	not out	9	14	1
* Imran Khan				
Inzamam-ul-Haq				
Wasim Akram				
† Moin Khan				
Akram Raza				
Waqar Younis				
Aqib Javed				
Extras	(lb 1, w 2, nb 2)	5		
Total	(36.5 overs; 2 wickets)	**157**		

SRI LANKA	O	M	R	W
Ramanayake	6	1	19	1
Wijegunawardene	8	0	41	1
Wickremasinghe	5	0	14	0
Gurusinha	4	0	21	0
Kalpage	7	1	32	0
Jayasuriya	6.5	0	29	0

FALL OF WICKETS
1-19, 2-131

PAKISTAN v SRI LANKA 1991-92

At National Stadium, Karachi on 13 January 1992.   Result: **PAKISTAN** won by 29 runs.   Toss: Sri Lanka.
Award: Imran Khan.   LOI debuts: None.

On course with a score of 100 for 2 in the 20th over, Sri Lanka capsized after Roshan Mahanama retired with cramp.

PAKISTAN		Runs	Balls	4/6	SRI LANKA		Runs	Balls	4/6
Ramiz Raja	c Labrooy b Jayasuriya	35	70	1	R.S.Mahanama	retired hurt	60	79	3
Inzamam-ul-Haq	run out	48	70	2	U.C.Hathurusinghe	b Wasim	14	19	2
Javed Miandad	b Wijegunawardene	29	33	2	A.P.Gurusinha	c Wasim b Waqar	13	15	2
Salim Malik	b Labrooy	36	42	2	* P.A.de Silva	c sub (Akram Raza) b Mushtaq	24	33	2
* Imran Khan	not out	44	27	5	S.T.Jayasuriya	lbw b Waqar	0	2	–
Wasim Akram	c Kalpage b Wijegunawardene	7	6	–	† H.P.Tillekeratne	not out	29	37	1
Ijaz Ahmed	not out	1	1	–	R.S.Kalpage	b Mushtaq	3	5	–
† Moin Khan					G.F.Labrooy	b Imran	13	11	–
Mushtaq Ahmed					C.P.H.Ramanayake	b Wasim	4	6	–
Waqar Younis					K.I.W.Wijegunawardene	run out	7	9	–
Aqib Javed					G.P.Wickremasinghe	b Wasim	0	3	–
Extras	(lb 4, w 1, nb 5)	10			Extras	(lb 10, w 3, nb 1)	14		
Total	(40 overs; 5 wickets)	210			Total	(36.1 overs)	181		

SRI LANKA	O	M	R	W	PAKISTAN	O	M	R	W
Ramanayake	6	2	17	0	Wasim Akram	6.1	0	31	3
Labrooy	8	0	56	1	Waqar Younis	8	1	38	2
Wickremasinghe	5	1	26	0	Aqib Javed	6	0	19	0
Wijegunawardene	8	0	43	2	Imran Khan	8	0	44	1
Kalpage	8	0	37	0	Mushtaq Ahmed	8	0	39	2
Jayasuriya	5	0	27	1					

FALL OF WICKETS
1-46, 2-66, 3-109, 4-111, 5-134, 6-155, 7-167, 8-178, 9-181

FALL OF WICKETS
1-89, 2-89, 3-150, 4-160, 5-194

Umpires: Mahboob Shah (25) and Riazuddin (4).

PAKISTAN v SRI LANKA 1991-92

At Niaz Stadium, Hyderabad on 15 January 1992.   Result: **PAKISTAN** won by 59 runs.   Toss: Sri Lanka.
Award: Javed Miandad.   LOI debuts: None.

Pakistan settled this series with their third emphatic victory, Javed Miandad scoring the last of his four hundreds in home internationals.

PAKISTAN		Runs	Balls	4/6	SRI LANKA		Runs	Balls	4/6
Ramiz Raja	c Labrooy b Ramanayake	12	24	2	U.C.Hathurusinghe	c Ijaz b Imran	19	41	2
Inzamam-ul-Haq	c Atapattu b Labrooy	60	78	6	M.A.R.Samarasekera	c Moin b Aqib	43	36	7
Javed Miandad	not out	115	103	12/2	* P.A.de Silva	c Moin b Aqib	2	5	–
Salim Malik	c De Silva b Wijegunawardene	40	38	3	† H.P.Tillekeratne	b Wasim	44	52	2/1
Wasim Akram	not out	7	2	–/1	S.T.Jayasuriya	lbw b Imran	0	1	–
* Imran Khan					A.P.Gurusinha	c Salim b Mushtaq	15	42	–
Ijaz Ahmed					G.F.Labrooy	lbw b Imran	7	6	1
† Moin Khan					M.S.Atapattu	not out	19	42	1
Mushtaq Ahmed					C.P.H.Ramanayake	b Wasim	1	12	–
Waqar Younis					K.I.W.Wijegunawardene	c Imran b Aqib	1	5	–
Aqib Javed					M.A.W.R.Madurasinghe	not out	3	7	–
Extras	(lb 2, w 2, nb 3)	7			Extras	(lb 14, w 8, nb 6)	28		
Total	(40 overs; 3 wickets)	241			Total	(40 overs; 9 wickets)	182		

SRI LANKA	O	M	R	W	PAKISTAN	O	M	R	W
Ramanayake	8	2	26	1	Wasim Akram	8	0	34	2
Wijegunawardene	8	0	49	1	Waqar Younis	8	0	42	0
Labrooy	6	0	51	1	Aqib Javed	8	0	30	3
Madurasinghe	8	2	34	0	Imran Khan	8	3	15	3
Gurusinha	2	0	13	0	Mushtaq Ahmed	8	0	47	1
Jayasuriya	8	0	66	0					

FALL OF WICKETS
1-70, 2-72, 3-80, 4-80, 5-119, 6-127, 7-167, 8-174, 9-177

FALL OF WICKETS
1-25, 2-134, 3-220

Umpires: Shakil Khan (12) and Taufiq Khan (1).

PAKISTAN v SRI LANKA 1991-92

At Ibn-e-Qasim Bagh Stadium, Multan on 17 January 1992.   Result: **SRI LANKA** won by 4 wickets.   Toss: Sri Lanka.
Award: Inzamam-ul-Haq.   LOI debuts: None.

Sri Lanka's record second-wicket partnership against Pakistan, 157 between 'Big Sam' Samarasekera and Asanka Gurusinha, enabled them to avert a series whitewash. The stand of 149 between Ramiz Raja and Inzamam-ul-Haq, who scored his first LOI hundred, was Pakistan's best start in any home international until 1995-96.

PAKISTAN		Runs	Balls	4/6
Ramiz Raja	st Tillekeratne b Jayasuriya	52	83	3
Inzamam-ul-Haq	c sub (R.S.Kalpage) b Jayasuriya	101	121	9/3
Ijaz Ahmed	c De Silva b Ramanayake	31	31	1/1
Wasim Akram	c Hathurusinghe b Wijegunawardene	6	5	1
† Moin Khan	not out	2	2	–
Mushtaq Ahmed	b Ramanayake	1	2	–
* Imran Khan				
Salim Malik				
Javed Miandad				
Waqar Younis				
Aqib Javed				
Extras	(lb 5, w 5, nb 2)	12		
Total	(40 overs; 5 wickets)	**205**		

SRI LANKA		Runs	Balls	4/6
U.C.Hathurusinghe	c Moin b Mushtaq	2	7	–
M.A.R.Samarasekera	c Inzamam b Mushtaq	76	88	5/1
A.P.Gurusinha	st Moin b Waqar	74	86	7/1
* P.A.de Silva	c Inzamam b Aqib	18	26	1
† H.P.Tillekeratne	run out	10	23	–
S.T.Jayasuriya	lbw b Aqib	5	6	–
M.S.Atapattu	not out	5	4	1
C.P.H.Ramanayake	not out	0	1	–
S.D.Anurasiri				
K.I.W.Wijegunawardene				
M.A.W.R.Madurasinghe				
Extras	(b 1, lb 7, w 5, nb 3)	16		
Total	(39.4 overs; 6 wickets)	**206**		

SRI LANKA	O	M	R	W
Ramanayake	8	1	30	2
Wijegunawardene	6	1	37	1
Gurusinha	2	0	14	0
Madurasinghe	8	1	36	0
Anurasiri	8	0	42	0
Jayasuriya	8	0	41	2

PAKISTAN	O	M	R	W
Wasim Akram	8	0	31	0
Waqar Younis	8	1	36	1
Aqib Javed	7.4	0	40	2
Imran Khan	6	0	40	0
Mushtaq Ahmed	8	0	37	2
Inzamam-ul-Haq	2	0	14	0

FALL OF WICKETS
1-149, 2-180, 3-196, 4-201, 5-205

FALL OF WICKETS
1-4, 2-161, 3-161, 4-183, 5-192, 6-203

Umpires: Mian Mohammad Aslam (8) and Shakoor Rana (20).

PAKISTAN v SRI LANKA 1991-92

At Rawalpindi Cricket Stadium on 19 January 1992.   Result: **PAKISTAN** won by 117 runs.   Toss: Sri Lanka.
Award: Inzamam-ul-Haq.   LOI debuts: None.

Rawalpindi's new stadium, the 91st LOI venue, saw Inzamam-ul-Haq's second successive hundred and a national record second-wicket partnership of 204. Javed Miandad scored his 6000th run in 185 internationals. Using tear gas and batons, police provided a 30-minute interlude demonstrating crowd control.

PAKISTAN		Runs	Balls	4/6
Ramiz Raja	b Wijegunawardene	5	11	1
Inzamam-ul-Haq	c Wickremasinghe b Ramanayake	117	103	13
Salim Malik	c Jayasuriya b Ramanayake	102	108	5
Javed Miandad	run out	19	13	–/2
Wasim Akram	not out	16	6	1/1
Ijaz Ahmed	not out	4	1	–
* Imran Khan				
† Moin Khan				
Mushtaq Ahmed				
Waqar Younis				
Aqib Javed				
Extras	(b 1, lb 2, w 5)	8		
Total	(40 overs; 4 wickets)	**271**		

SRI LANKA		Runs	Balls	4/6
R.S.Mahanama	lbw b Aqib	18	28	2
M.A.R.Samarasekera	b Waqar	13	13	2
A.P.Gurusinha	c Ramiz b Aqib	16	30	2
* P.A.de Silva	run out	17	17	2
† H.P.Tillekeratne	c Ramiz b Mushtaq	36	46	4
S.T.Jayasuriya	run out	3	5	–
M.S.Atapattu	run out	3	12	–
C.P.H.Ramanayake	b Waqar	26	45	3
K.I.W.Wijegunawardene	c Imran b Wasim	0	5	–
M.A.W.R.Madurasinghe	not out	6	27	–
G.P.Wickremasinghe	st Moin b Inzamam	5	6	1
Extras	(lb 4, w 6, nb 1)	11		
Total	(38.4 overs)	**154**		

SRI LANKA	O	M	R	W
Ramanayake	8	1	48	2
Wijegunawardene	8	0	68	1
Wickremasinghe	6	0	32	0
Madurasinghe	8	0	54	0
Gurusinha	3	0	23	0
Jayasuriya	7	0	43	0

PAKISTAN	O	M	R	W
Wasim Akram	8	2	20	1
Waqar Younis	8	0	42	2
Aqib Javed	6	0	25	2
Mushtaq Ahmed	8	0	29	1
Imran Khan	8	0	30	0
Inzamam-ul-Haq	0.4	0	4	1

FALL OF WICKETS
1-5, 2-209, 3-251, 4-251

FALL OF WICKETS
1-31, 2-37, 3-63, 4-75, 5-84, 6-91, 7-117, 8-130, 9-149, 10-154

Umpires: Javed Akhtar (11) and Siddiq Khan (2).

BANK OF NEW ZEALAND SERIES (1st Match)

NEW ZEALAND v ENGLAND 1991-92

At Eden Park, Auckland on 11 January 1992.   Result: **ENGLAND** won by 7 wickets.   Toss: New Zealand.
Award: D.A.Reeve.   LOI debuts: None.

Playing their first international for almost 11 months, New Zealand were defeated with 16.1 overs to spare. When Philip Tufnell returned England's most economical LOI analysis against New Zealand, a section of the crowd rewarded him with an assortment of fast-moving unfresh fruit.

NEW ZEALAND		Runs	Balls	4/6
J.G.Wright	c Stewart b Lewis	6	30	–
R.T.Latham	lbw b Pringle	25	43	–
* M.D.Crowe	b Reeve	31	71	2
A.H.Jones	c Stewart b Reeve	1	13	–
M.J.Greatbatch	c Hick b Reeve	4	9	–
C.Z.Harris	not out	38	73	1
C.L.Cairns	c Hick b Pringle	42	59	2/1
†I.D.S.Smith	c Gooch b Lewis	2	2	–
C.Pringle	not out	9	9	–
G.R.Larsen				
D.K.Morrison				
Extras	(lb 13, w 4, nb 3)	20		
Total	(50 overs; 7 wickets)	178		

ENGLAND		Runs	Balls	4/6
* G.A.Gooch	c Greatbatch b Harris	47	65	6
G.A.Hick	b Cairns	23	22	4
R.A.Smith	not out	61	71	11/1
A.J.Lamb	c Crowe b Harris	12	19	2
N.H.Fairbrother	not out	23	31	4
†A.J.Stewart				
D.A.Reeve				
C.C.Lewis				
D.R.Pringle				
P.A.J.DeFreitas				
P.C.R.Tufnell				
Extras	(lb 6, w 3, nb 4)	13		
Total	(33.5 overs; 3 wickets)	179		

ENGLAND	O	M	R	W
DeFreitas	10	1	34	0
Lewis	8	0	33	2
Pringle	6	1	32	2
Reeve	10	3	20	3
Tufnell	10	3	17	0
Hick	6	0	29	0

NEW ZEALAND	O	M	R	W
Morrison	5.5	0	35	0
Pringle	5	0	26	0
Cairns	5	0	32	1
Larsen	9	3	36	0
Harris	8	0	40	2
Latham	1	0	4	0

FALL OF WICKETS
1-21, 2-45, 3-51, 4-61, 5-81, 6-165, 7-167

FALL OF WICKETS
1-64, 2-109, 3-123

Umpires: D.B.Cowie (1) and S.J.Woodward (23).

BANK OF NEW ZEALAND SERIES (2nd Match)

NEW ZEALAND v ENGLAND 1991-92

At Carisbrook, Dunedin on 12 February 1992.   Result: **ENGLAND** won by 3 wickets.   Toss: New Zealand.
Award: K.R.Rutherford.   LOI debuts: New Zealand – M.L.Su'a.

On the slowest pitch of England's entire tour, New Zealand employed their fastest bowlers when the tourists needed 45 off the last seven overs.

NEW ZEALAND		Runs	Balls	4/6
R.T.Latham	run out	12	25	2
A.H.Jones	b Botham	20	54	2
M.J.Greatbatch	c Stewart b Reeve	10	16	1
* M.D.Crowe	c sub ‡ b Illingworth	29	55	3
K.R.Rutherford	run out	52	86	3
C.Z.Harris	b Pringle	32	52	3
C.L.Cairns	b Lewis	3	5	–
†I.D.S.Smith	not out	5	7	–
M.L.Su'a	not out	4	4	–
D.K.Morrison				
G.R.Larsen				
Extras	(b 1, lb 12, w 3, nb 3)	19		
Total	(50 overs; 7 wickets)	186		

ENGLAND		Runs	Balls	4/6
* G.A.Gooch	c Smith b Larsen	24	50	2
G.A.Hick	lbw b Morrison	7	11	1
R.A.Smith	b Larsen	17	37	3
A.J.Lamb	lbw b Latham	40	61	4
I.T.Botham	c Rutherford b Latham	28	43	2/1
†A.J.Stewart	b Latham	0	2	–
D.A.Reeve	not out	31	48	3
C.C.Lewis	c Greatbatch b Morrison	18	34	1/1
D.R.Pringle	not out	14	9	2
R.K.Illingworth				
P.C.R.Tufnell				
Extras	(lb 2, w 7)	9		
Total	(49.1 overs; 7 wickets)	188		

ENGLAND	O	M	R	W
Pringle	10	2	31	1
Lewis	9	0	32	1
Reeve	8	1	19	1
Botham	6	1	27	1
Illingworth	9	1	33	1
Tufnell	8	0	31	0

NEW ZEALAND	O	M	R	W
Morrison	7	0	27	2
Su'a	8	1	35	0
Larsen	10	1	24	2
Cairns	6.1	0	36	0
Harris	10	1	39	0
Latham	8	1	25	3

FALL OF WICKETS
1-14, 2-35, 3-54, 4-89, 5-163, 6-170, 7-180

FALL OF WICKETS
1-21, 2-54, 3-63, 4-108, 5-108, 6-131, 7-165

Umpires: B.L.Aldridge (18) and R.S.Dunne (10).

‡ (M.R.Ramprakash)

NEW ZEALAND v ENGLAND 1991-92

At Lancaster Park, Christchurch on 15 February 1992.　Result: **ENGLAND** won by 71 runs.　Toss: New Zealand.
Award: I.T.Botham.　LOI debuts: None.

Alec Stewart led England to a clean sweep of the series in his first international as captain, the match being reduced by ten overs apiece when overnight rain-water on the covers was spilt on to the pitch. Ian Botham's opening assault produced his highest LOI score.

ENGLAND		Runs	Balls	4/6
I.T.Botham	c Greatbatch b Latham	79	73	11/2
G.A.Hick	c Greatbatch b Larsen	18	29	1
R.A.Smith	c Smith b Cairns	85	71	13
*†A.J.Stewart	c Crowe b Su'a	13	32	–
A.J.Lamb	c Harris b Watson	25	16	2/2
G.A.Gooch	not out	22	13	2
C.C.Lewis	c Latham b Watson	0	2	–
D.R.Pringle	c Watson b Cairns	5	3	1
D.A.Reeve	not out	2	2	–
R.K.Illingworth				
G.C.Small				
Extras	(lb 2, w 4)	6		
Total	(40 overs; 7 wickets)	**255**		

NEW ZEALAND		Runs	Balls	4/6
R.T.Latham	c Reeve b Lewis	0	2	–
J.G.Wright	c Hick b Reeve	36	44	3/1
M.J.Greatbatch	b Pringle	5	18	1
* M.D.Crowe	c Stewart b Pringle	6	22	–
K.R.Rutherford	c sub ‡ b Botham	37	49	2
C.Z.Harris	run out	37	62	3
C.L.Cairns	c Smith b Illingworth	6	12	–
† I.D.S.Smith	c sub (P.A.J.DeFreitas) b Small	27	16	3/1
M.L.Su'a	not out	12	13	1
G.R.Larsen	not out	3	5	–
W.Watson				
Extras	(lb 6, w 6, nb 3)	15		
Total	(40 overs; 8 wickets)	**184**		

NEW ZEALAND	O	M	R	W
Cairns	6	0	37	2
Watson	8	1	64	2
Larsen	6	2	34	1
Su'a	5	0	35	1
Harris	8	0	35	0
Latham	7	0	48	1

ENGLAND	O	M	R	W
Lewis	6	1	21	1
Pringle	6	2	11	2
Small	8	0	46	1
Reeve	5	0	26	1
Botham	7	1	36	1
Illingworth	8	0	38	1

FALL OF WICKETS
1-60, 2-125, 3-166, 4-220, 5-228, 6-231, 7-248

FALL OF WICKETS
1-4, 2-20, 3-23, 4-92, 5-100, 6-112, 7-148, 8-171

Umpires: R.L.McHarg (13) and S.J.Woodward (24).　　　　‡ (M.R.Ramprakash)

NEW ZEALAND v AUSTRALIA 1991-92

At Eden Park, Auckland, New Zealand, on 22 February 1992.　Result: **NEW ZEALAND** won by 37 runs.
Toss: New Zealand.　Award: M.D.Crowe.　LOI debuts: None.

Pandering to the demands of television, this was the first World Cup to involve floodlit matches with its full panoply of coloured clothing, white balls and dark sightscreens. It remains the largest ever with 39 matches. The holders lost their last five wickets for 12 runs in 17 balls.

NEW ZEALAND		Runs	Balls	4/6
J.G.Wright	b McDermott	0	1	–
R.T.Latham	c Healy b Moody	26	44	4
A.H.Jones	lbw b Reid	4	14	1
* M.D.Crowe	not out	100	134	11
K.R.Rutherford	run out	57	71	6
C.Z.Harris	run out	14	15	2
† I.D.S.Smith	c Healy b McDermott	14	14	1
C.L.Cairns	not out	16	11	2
D.N.Patel				
G.R.Larsen				
W.Watson				
Extras	(lb 6, w 7, nb 4)	17		
Total	(50 overs; 6 wickets)	**248**		

AUSTRALIA		Runs	Balls	4/6
D.C.Boon	run out	100	131	11
G.R.Marsh	c Latham b Larsen	19	56	2
D.M.Jones	run out	21	27	3
* A.R.Border	c Cairns b Patel	3	11	–
T.M.Moody	c and b Latham	7	11	–
M.E.Waugh	lbw b Larsen	2	5	–
S.R.Waugh	c and b Larsen	38	34	3/1
† I.A.Healy	not out	7	9	–
C.J.McDermott	run out	1	1	–
P.L.Taylor	c Rutherford b Watson	1	2	–
B.A.Reid	c Jones b Harris	3	4	–
Extras	(lb 6, w 2, nb 1)	9		
Total	(48.1 overs)	**211**		

AUSTRALIA	O	M	R	W
McDermott	10	1	43	2
Reid	10	0	39	1
Moody	9	1	37	1
S.R.Waugh	10	0	60	0
Taylor	7	0	36	0
M.E.Waugh	4	0	27	0

NEW ZEALAND	O	M	R	W
Cairns	4	0	30	0
Patel	10	1	36	1
Watson	9	1	39	1
Larsen	10	1	30	3
Harris	7.1	0	35	1
Latham	8	1	35	1

FALL OF WICKETS
1-2, 2-13, 3-53, 4-171, 5-191, 6-215

FALL OF WICKETS
1-62, 2-92, 3-104, 4-120, 5-125, 6-199, 7-200, 8-205, 9-206, 10-211

Umpires: Khizer Hayat (*Pakistan*) (38) and D.R.Shepherd (*England*) (41).

ENGLAND v INDIA 1991-92

At WACA Ground, Perth, Australia, on 22 February 1992.   Result: **ENGLAND** won by 9 runs.   Toss: England.
Award: I.T.Botham.   LOI debuts: None.

Playing in his 100th international, Graham Gooch continued his innings with a runner after clobbering his leg with his bat. Krish Srikkanth became the first Indian to score 4000 LOI runs, while Ravi Shastri completed 3000.

ENGLAND		Runs	Balls	4/6
* G.A.Gooch	c Tendulkar b Shastri	51	89	I
I.T.Botham	c More b Kapil Dev	9	21	I
R.A.Smith	c Azharuddin b Prabhakar	91	108	8/2
G.A.Hick	c More b Banerjee	5	6	I
N.H.Fairbrother	c Srikkanth b Srinath	24	34	I
† A.J.Stewart	b Prabhakar	13	15	I
C.C.Lewis	c Banerjee b Kapil Dev	10	6	I
D.R.Pringle	c Srikkanth b Srinath	I	3	–
D.A.Reeve	not out	8	8	–
P.A.J.DeFreitas	run out	I	5	–
P.C.R.Tufnell	not out	3	5	–
Extras	(b I, lb 6, w 13)	20		
Total	(50 overs; 9 wickets)	**236**		

INDIA		Runs	Balls	4/6
R.J.Shastri	run out	57	112	2
K.Srikkanth	c Botham b DeFreitas	39	50	7
* M.Azharuddin	c Stewart b Reeve	0	I	–
S.R.Tendulkar	c Stewart b Botham	35	44	5
V.G.Kambli	c Hick b Botham	3	II	–
P.K.Amre	run out	22	31	–
Kapil Dev	c DeFreitas b Reeve	17	18	2
S.T.Banerjee	not out	25	16	1/1
† K.S.More	run out	I	4	–
M.Prabhakar	b Reeve	0	2	–
J.Srinath	run out	II	8	–
Extras	(lb 9, w 7, nb I)	17		
Total	(49.2 overs)	**227**		

INDIA	O	M	R	W
Kapil Dev	10	0	38	2
Prabhakar	10	3	34	2
Srinath	9	I	47	2
Banerjee	7	0	45	I
Tendulkar	10	0	37	0
Shastri	4	0	28	I

ENGLAND	O	M	R	W
Pringle	10	0	53	0
Lewis	9.2	0	36	0
DeFreitas	10	0	39	I
Reeve	6	0	38	3
Botham	10	0	27	2
Tufnell	4	0	25	0

FALL OF WICKETS
1-21, 2-131, 3-137, 4-197, 5-198, 6-214, 7-222, 8-223, 9-224

FALL OF WICKETS
1-63, 2-63, 3-126, 4-140, 5-149, 6-187, 7-194, 8-200, 9-201, 10-227

Umpires: J.D.Buultjens (*Sri Lanka*) (13) and P.J.McConnell (63).

SRI LANKA v ZIMBABWE 1991-92

At Pukekura Park, New Plymouth, New Zealand, on 23 February 1992.   Result: **SRI LANKA** won by 3 wickets.
Toss: Sri Lanka.   Award: A.Flower.   LOI debuts: Zimbabwe – K.G.Duers, A.Flower, W.R.James.

Surrounded on three sides by steeply banked grass terracing surmounted by a framework of exotic trees, Pukekura Park provided the 92nd LOI venue. Andy Flower was the third batsman to score a hundred on debut as Sri Lanka registered the highest total (until 1995-96) by a side batting second.

ZIMBABWE		Runs	Balls	4/6
† A.Flower	not out	115	152	8/1
W.R.James	c Tillekeratne b Wickremasinghe	17	21	3
A.J.Pycroft	c Ramanayake b Gurusinha	5	22	–
* D.L.Houghton	c Tillekeratne b Gurusinha	10	19	I
K.J.Arnott	c Tillekeratne b Wickremasinghe	52	56	4/1
A.C.Waller	not out	83	45	9/3
I.P.Butchart				
E.A.Brandes				
K.G.Duers				
M.P.Jarvis				
A.J.Traicos				
Extras	(b 2, lb 6, w 13, nb 9)	30		
Total	(50 overs; 4 wickets)	**312**		

SRI LANKA		Runs	Balls	4/6
R.S.Mahanama	c Arnott b Brandes	59	89	4
M.A.R.Samarasekera	c Duers b Traicos	75	61	11/1
* P.A.de Silva	c Houghton b Brandes	14	28	I
A.P.Gurusinha	run out	5	6	–
A.Ranatunga	not out	88	61	9/1
S.T.Jayasuriya	c Flower b Houghton	32	23	2/2
† H.P.Tillekeratne	b Jarvis	18	12	1/1
R.S.Kalpage	c Houghton b Brandes	II	14	I
C.P.H.Ramanayake	not out	I	I	–
K.I.W.Wijegunawardene				
G.P.Wickremasinghe				
Extras	(lb 5, w 5)	10		
Total	(49.2 overs; 7 wickets)	**313**		

SRI LANKA	O	M	R	W
Ramanayake	10	0	59	0
Wijegunawardene	7	0	54	0
Wickremasinghe	10	I	50	2
Gurusinha	10	0	72	2
Kalpage	10	0	51	0
Jayasuriya	3	0	18	0

ZIMBABWE	O	M	R	W
Jarvis	9.2	0	51	I
Brandes	10	0	70	3
Duers	10	0	72	0
Butchart	8	0	63	0
Traicos	10	I	33	I
Houghton	2	0	19	I

FALL OF WICKETS
1-30, 2-57, 3-82, 4-167

FALL OF WICKETS
1-128, 2-144, 3-155, 4-167, 5-212, 6-273, 7-308

Umpires: P.D.Reporter (*India*) (13) and S.J.Woodward (25).

WEST INDIES v PAKISTAN 1991-92

At Melbourne Cricket Ground, Australia, on 23 February 1992.　Result: **WEST INDIES** won by 10 wickets.
Toss: West Indies.　　Award: B.C.Lara.　　LOI debuts: Pakistan – Iqbal Sikander, Wasim Haider.

For the first time in limited-overs internationals only two wickets fell in a completed match, the last 344 being scored without a dismissal. Brian Lara retired at 175 after being yorked on the toe by Wasim Akram.

PAKISTAN		Runs	Balls	4/6
Ramiz Raja	not out	102	158	4
Aamir Sohail	c Logie b Benjamin	23	44	3
Inzamam-ul-Haq	c Hooper b Harper	27	39	–
* Javed Miandad	not out	57	61	5
Salim Malik				
Ijaz Ahmed				
Wasim Akram				
Iqbal Sikander				
Wasim Haider				
† Moin Khan				
Aqib Javed				
Extras	(b 1, lb 3, w 5, nb 2)	11		
Total	(50 overs; 2 wickets)	**220**		

WEST INDIES		Runs	Balls	4/6
D.L.Haynes	not out	93	144	7
B.C.Lara	retired hurt	88	101	11
* R.B.Richardson	not out	20	40	1
C.L.Hooper				
A.L.Logie				
K.L.T.Arthurton				
R.A.Harper				
M.D.Marshall				
W.K.M.Benjamin				
† D.Williams				
C.E.L.Ambrose				
Extras	(b 2, lb 8, w 7, nb 3)	20		
Total	(46.5 overs; 0 wickets)	**221**		

WEST INDIES	O	M	R	W
Marshall	10	1	53	0
Ambrose	10	0	40	0
Benjamin	10	0	49	1
Hooper	10	0	41	0
Harper	10	0	33	1

PAKISTAN	O	M	R	W
Wasim Akram	10	0	37	0
Aqib Javed	8.5	0	42	0
Wasim Haider	8	0	42	0
Ijaz Ahmed	6	1	29	0
Iqbal Sikander	8	1	26	0
Aamir Sohail	6	0	35	0

FALL OF WICKETS
1-45, 2-97

Umpires: S.G.Randell (44) and I.D.Robinson (*Zimbabwe*) (1).

NEW ZEALAND v SRI LANKA 1991-92

At Seddon (Trust Bank) Park, Hamilton, New Zealand, on 25 February 1992.　Result: **NEW ZEALAND** won by 6 wickets.
Toss: New Zealand.　　Award: K.R.Rutherford.　　LOI debuts: None.

John Wright overcame a shoulder injury sustained while fielding to score a vital fifty. He was forced to miss the next four matches.

SRI LANKA		Runs	Balls	4/6
R.S.Mahanama	c and b Harris	80	131	6
M.A.R.Samarasekera	c Wright b Watson	9	20	1
A.P.Gurusinha	c Smith b Harris	9	33	1
* P.A.de Silva	run out	31	45	2
A.Ranatunga	c Rutherford b Harris	20	26	2
S.T.Jayasuriya	run out	5	7	–
† H.P.Tillekeratne	c Crowe b Watson	8	19	–
R.S.Kalpage	c Larsen b Watson	11	17	–
C.P.H.Ramanayake	run out	2	1	–
S.D.Anurasiri	not out	3	2	–
G.P.Wickremasinghe	not out	3	4	–
Extras	(b 1, lb 15, w 4, nb 5)	25		
Total	(50 overs; 9 wickets)	**206**		

NEW ZEALAND		Runs	Balls	4/6
J.G.Wright	c and b Kalpage	57	76	9
R.T.Latham	b Kalpage	20	41	3
A.H.Jones	c Jayasuriya b Gurusinha	49	77	4
* M.D.Crowe	c Ramanayake b Wickremasinghe	5	23	–
K.R.Rutherford	not out	65	71	6/1
C.Z.Harris	not out	5	5	–
† I.D.S.Smith				
D.N.Patel				
D.K.Morrison				
G.R.Larsen				
W.Watson				
Extras	(lb 3, w 3, nb 3)	9		
Total	(48.2 overs; 4 wickets)	**210**		

NEW ZEALAND	O	M	R	W
Morrison	8	0	36	0
Watson	10	0	37	3
Larsen	10	1	29	0
Harris	10	0	43	3
Latham	3	0	13	0
Patel	9	0	32	0

SRI LANKA	O	M	R	W
Ramanayake	9.2	0	46	0
Wickremasinghe	8	1	40	1
Anurasiri	10	1	27	0
Kalpage	10	0	33	2
Gurusinha	4	0	19	1
Ranatunga	4	0	22	0
Jayasuriya	2	0	14	0
De Silva	1	0	6	0

FALL OF WICKETS
1-18, 2-50, 3-120, 4-172, 5-172, 6-181, 7-195, 8-199, 9-202

Umpires: P.D.Reporter (*India*) (14) and D.R.Shepherd (*England*) (42).

FALL OF WICKETS
1-77, 2-90, 3-105, 4-186

AUSTRALIA v SOUTH AFRICA 1991-92

At Sydney Cricket Ground, Australia, on 26 February 1992.   Result: **SOUTH AFRICA** won by 9 wickets.
Toss: Australia.   Award: K.C.Wessels.   LOI debuts: South Africa – W.J.Cronje, M.W.Pringle, J.N.Rhodes.

South Africa, late admissions to this tournament, met Australia for the first time since their isolation almost 22 years earlier. Kepler Wessels scored his fourth fifty in as many internationals for his native South Africa and completed 2000 runs in his dual-country career.

AUSTRALIA		Runs	Balls	4/6	SOUTH AFRICA		Runs	Balls	4/6
G.R.Marsh	c Richardson b Kuiper	25	72	1	* K.C.Wessels	not out	81	148	9
D.C.Boon	run out	27	32	4	A.C.Hudson	b Taylor	28	52	3
D.M.Jones	c Richardson b McMillan	24	51	1	P.N.Kirsten	not out	49	88	1
* A.R.Border	b Kuiper	0	1	–	A.P.Kuiper				
T.M.Moody	lbw b Donald	10	33	–	J.N.Rhodes				
S.R.Waugh	c Cronje b McMillan	27	51	1	W.J.Cronje				
† I.A.Healy	c McMillan b Donald	16	24	2	B.M.McMillan				
P.L.Taylor	b Donald	4	9	–	† D.J.Richardson				
C.J.McDermott	run out	6	12	–	R.P.Snell				
M.R.Whitney	not out	9	15	1	M.W.Pringle				
B.A.Reid	not out	5	10	–	A.A.Donald				
Extras	(lb 2, w 11, nb 4)	17			Extras	(lb 5, w 6, nb 2)	13		
Total	**(49 overs; 9 wickets)**	**170**			**Total**	**(46.5 overs; 1 wicket)**	**171**		

SOUTH AFRICA	O	M	R	W	AUSTRALIA	O	M	R	W
Donald	10	0	34	3	McDermott	10	1	23	0
Pringle	10	0	52	0	Reid	8.5	0	41	0
Snell	9	1	15	0	Whitney	6	0	26	0
McMillan	10	0	35	2	Waugh	4	1	16	0
Kuiper	5	0	15	2	Taylor	10	1	32	1
Cronje	5	1	17	0	Border	4	0	13	0
					Moody	4	0	15	0

FALL OF WICKETS
1-42, 2-76, 3-76, 4-97, 5-108, 6-143, 7-146, 8-156, 9-161

FALL OF WICKETS
1-74

Umpires: B.L.Aldridge (*New Zealand*) (19) and S.A.Bucknor (*West Indies*) (4).

PAKISTAN v ZIMBABWE 1991-92

At Bellerive Oval, Hobart, Australia, on 27 February 1992.   Result: **PAKISTAN** won by 53 runs.   Toss: Zimbabwe.
Award: Aamir Sohail.   LOI debuts: None.

Aamir Sohail's maiden international hundred was briefly Pakistan's highest World Cup score.

PAKISTAN		Runs	Balls	4/6	ZIMBABWE		Runs	Balls	4/6
Ramiz Raja	c Flower b Jarvis	9	16	1	K.J.Arnott	c Wasim b Iqbal	7	61	–
Aamir Sohail	c Pycroft b Butchart	114	136	12	† A.Flower	c Inzamam b Wasim	6	21	–
Inzamam-ul-Haq	c Brandes b Butchart	14	43	–	A.J.Pycroft	b Wasim	0	4	–
Javed Miandad	lbw b Butchart	89	94	5	* D.L.Houghton	c Ramiz b Aamir	44	82	3
Salim Malik	not out	14	12	–	A.H.Shah	b Aamir	33	58	2
Wasim Akram	not out	1	1	–	A.C.Waller	b Wasim	44	36	3/1
* Imran Khan					I.P.Butchart	c Miandad b Aqib	33	27	4
Mushtaq Ahmed					E.A.Brandes	not out	2	3	–
Iqbal Sikander					A.J.Traicos	not out	8	7	–
† Moin Khan					W.R.James				
Aqib Javed					M.P.Jarvis				
Extras	(lb 9, nb 4)	13			Extras	(b 3, lb 15, w 6)	24		
Total	**(50 overs; 4 wickets)**	**254**			**Total**	**(50 overs; 7 wickets)**	**201**		

ZIMBABWE	O	M	R	W	PAKISTAN	O	M	R	W
Brandes	10	1	49	0	Wasim Akram	10	2	21	3
Jarvis	10	1	52	1	Aqib Javed	10	1	49	1
Shah	10	1	24	0	Iqbal Sikander	10	1	35	1
Butchart	10	0	57	3	Mushtaq Ahmed	10	1	34	0
Traicos	10	0	63	0	Aamir Sohail	6	1	26	2
					Salim Malik	4	0	18	0

FALL OF WICKETS
1-29, 2-63, 3-208, 4-253

FALL OF WICKETS
1-14, 2-14, 3-33, 4-103, 5-108, 6-187, 7-190

Umpires: J.D.Buultjens (*Sri Lanka*) (14) and S.G.Randell (45).

ENGLAND v WEST INDIES 1991-92

At Melbourne Cricket Ground, Australia, on 27 February 1992.　Result: ENGLAND won by 6 wickets.　Toss: England. Award: C.C.Lewis.　LOI debuts: None.

With 10.1 overs in hand, England completed their fourth consecutive victory over West Indies and their eighth in succession against all opponents.

WEST INDIES		Runs	Balls	4/6
D.L.Haynes	c Fairbrother b DeFreitas	38	68	5
B.C.Lara	c Stewart b Lewis	0	2	–
* R.B.Richardson	c Botham b Lewis	5	17	I
C.L.Hooper	c Reeve b Botham	5	20	–
K.L.T.Arthurton	c Fairbrother b DeFreitas	54	101	2/2
A.L.Logie	run out	20	27	–/I
R.A.Harper	c Hick b Reeve	3	14	–
M.D.Marshall	run out	3	8	–
† D.Williams	c Pringle b DeFreitas	6	19	–
C.E.L.Ambrose	c DeFreitas b Lewis	4	6	–
W.K.M.Benjamin	not out	11	15	I
Extras	(lb 4, w 3, nb I)	8		
Total	(49.2 overs)	157		

ENGLAND		Runs	Balls	4/6
* G.A.Gooch	st Williams b Hooper	65	101	7
I.T.Botham	c Williams b Benjamin	8	28	I
R.A.Smith	c Logie b Benjamin	8	28	–
G.A.Hick	c and b Harper	54	55	3/I
N.H.Fairbrother	not out	13	28	I
† A.J.Stewart	not out	0	I	–
D.A.Reeve				
C.C.Lewis				
D.R.Pringle				
P.A.J.DeFreitas				
P.C.R.Tufnell				
Extras	(lb 7, w 4, nb I)	12		
Total	(39.5 overs; 4 wickets)	160		

ENGLAND	O	M	R	W
Pringle	7	3	16	0
Lewis	8.2	I	30	3
DeFreitas	9	2	34	3
Botham	10	0	30	I
Reeve	10	I	23	I
Tufnell	5	0	20	0

WEST INDIES	O	M	R	W
Ambrose	8	I	26	0
Marshall	8	0	37	0
Benjamin	9.5	2	22	2
Hooper	10	I	38	I
Harper	4	0	30	I

FALL OF WICKETS
1-0, 2-22, 3-36, 4-55, 5-91, 6-102, 7-116, 8-131, 9-145, 10-157

FALL OF WICKETS
1-50, 2-71, 3-126, 4-156

Umpires: K.E.Liebenberg (SA) (I) and S.J.Woodward (NZ) (26).

INDIA v SRI LANKA 1991-92

At Harrup Park, Mackay, Queensland, Australia, on 28 February 1992.　NO RESULT.　Toss: Sri Lanka. No award.　LOI debuts: India - A.Jadeja.

The sugar-growing centre of Mackay on the north Queensland coast provided the 93rd LOI venue. Although the first rain for two months briefly ceased, allowing a 20-over match to start at 2.45pm, its swift and torrential return condemned this encounter to being the shortest international ever.

INDIA		Runs	Balls	4/6
K.Srikkanth	not out	I	2	–
Kapil Dev	not out	0	–	–
* M.Azharuddin				
S.R.Tendulkar				
V.G.Kambli				
P.K.Amre				
A.Jadeja				
† K.S.More				
M.Prabhakar				
J.Srinath				
S.L.V.Raju				
Extras		–		
Total	(0.2 overs; 0 wickets)	I		

SRI LANKA	
R.S.Mahanama	
U.C.Hathurusinghe	
A.P.Gurusinha	
* P.A.de Silva	
A.Ranatunga	
S.T.Jayasuriya	
† H.P.Tillekeratne	
R.S.Kalpage	
C.P.H.Ramanayake	
K.I.W.Wijegunawardene	
G.P.Wickremasinghe	
Extras	
Total	

SRI LANKA	O	M	R	W
Ramanayake	0.2	0	I	0

Umpires: I.D.Robinson (Zimbabwe) (2) and D.R.Shepherd (England) (43).

NEW ZEALAND v SOUTH AFRICA 1991-92

At Eden Park, Auckland, New Zealand, on 29 February 1992.   Result: **NEW ZEALAND** won by 7 wickets.
Toss: South Africa.   Award: M.J.Greatbatch.   LOI debuts: South Africa – T.Bosch.

On their first visit to New Zealand for almost 28 years, South Africa were hijacked on a pitch of rolled mud by the host's containment policy centred around their frugal off-spinner, Dipak Patel. One of Mark Greatbatch's vast sixes struck the roof of the North Stand.

SOUTH AFRICA		Runs	Balls	4/6
* K.C.Wessels	c Smith b Watson	3	18	–
A.C.Hudson	b Patel	1	16	–
P.N.Kirsten	c Cairns b Watson	90	129	10
W.J.Cronje	c Smith b Harris	7	22	–
† D.J.Richardson	c Larsen b Cairns	28	53	1
A.P.Kuiper	run out	2	2	–
J.N.Rhodes	c Crowe b Cairns	6	13	–
B.M.McMillan	not out	33	40	1
R.P.Snell	not out	11	8	1
A.A.Donald				
T.Bosch				
Extras	(lb 8, nb 1)	9		
Total	(50 overs; 7 wickets)	190		

NEW ZEALAND		O	M	R	W
Watson		10	2	30	2
Patel		10	1	28	1
Larsen		10	1	29	0
Harris		10	2	33	1
Latham		2	0	19	0
Cairns		8	0	43	2

FALL OF WICKETS
1-8, 2-10, 3-29, 4-108, 5-111, 6-121, 7-162

Umpires: Khizer Hayat (*Pakistan*) (39) and P.D.Reporter (*India*) (15).

NEW ZEALAND		Runs	Balls	4/6
M.J.Greatbatch	b Kirsten	68	60	9/3
R.T.Latham	c Wessels b Snell	60	69	7
A.H.Jones	not out	34	63	4
† I.D.S.Smith	c Kirsten b Donald	19	8	4
* M.D.Crowe	not out	3	9	–
K.R.Rutherford				
C.Z.Harris				
C.L.Cairns				
D.N.Patel				
G.R.Larsen				
W.Watson				
Extras	(b 1, w 5, nb 1)	7		
Total	(34.3 overs; 3 wickets)	191		

SOUTH AFRICA		O	M	R	W
Donald		10	0	38	1
McMillan		5	1	23	0
Snell		7	0	56	1
Bosch		2.3	0	19	0
Cronje		2	0	14	0
Kuiper		1	0	18	0
Kirsten		7	0	22	1

FALL OF WICKETS
1-114, 2-155, 3-179

WEST INDIES v ZIMBABWE 1991-92

At Woolloongabba, Brisbane, Australia, on 29 February 1992.   Result: **WEST INDIES** won by 75 runs.
Toss: Zimbabwe.   Award: B.C.Lara.   LOI debuts: Zimbabwe – A.D.R.Campbell.

Kevin Arnott retired at 43 for 2 in the 14th over after sustaining a broken finger. Andy Pycroft (bruised cheekbone) and David Houghton (fractured toe) batted on gamely after their injuries.

WEST INDIES		Runs	Balls	4/6
P.V.Simmons	b Brandes	21	45	3
B.C.Lara	c Houghton b Shah	72	71	12
* R.B.Richardson	c Brandes b Jarvis	56	76	2/2
C.L.Hooper	c Pycroft b Traicos	63	67	5/1
K.L.T.Arthurton	b Duers	26	18	2/2
A.L.Logie	run out	5	6	–
M.D.Marshall	c Houghton b Brandes	2	10	–
† D.Williams	not out	8	6	1
W.K.M.Benjamin	b Brandes	1	4	–
A.C.Cummins				
B.P.Patterson				
Extras	(b 1, lb 6, w 2, nb 1)	10		
Total	(50 overs; 8 wickets)	264		

ZIMBABWE		O	M	R	W
Brandes		10	1	45	3
Jarvis		10	1	71	1
Duers		10	0	52	1
Shah		10	2	39	1
Traicos		10	0	50	1

FALL OF WICKETS
1-78, 2-103, 3-220, 4-221, 5-239, 6-254, 7-255, 8-264

Umpires: K.E.Liebenberg (*SA*) (2) and S.J.Woodward (*NZ*) (27).

ZIMBABWE		Runs	Balls	4/6
K.J.Arnott	retired hurt	16	36	1
† A.Flower	b Patterson	6	20	–
A.J.Pycroft	c Williams b Benjamin	10	24	–
* D.L.Houghton	c Patterson b Hooper	55	88	3
A.C.Waller	c Simmons b Benjamin	0	9	–
A.D.R.Campbell	c Richardson b Hooper	1	18	–
A.H.Shah	not out	60	87	4
E.A.Brandes	c and b Benjamin	6	9	–
A.J.Traicos	run out	8	19	–
M.P.Jarvis	not out	5	4	1
K.G.Duers				
Extras	(lb 9, w 5, nb 8)	22		
Total	(50 overs; 7 wickets)	189		

WEST INDIES		O	M	R	W
Patterson		10	0	25	1
Marshall		6	0	23	0
Benjamin		10	2	27	3
Cummins		10	0	33	0
Hooper		10	0	47	2
Arthurton		4	0	25	0

FALL OF WICKETS
1-21, 2-43, 3-48, 4-63, 5-132, 6-161, 7-181

AUSTRALIA v INDIA 1991-92

At Woolloongabba, Brisbane, Australia, on 1 March 1992.　Result: **AUSTRALIA** won by 1 run (*revised target*).
Toss: Australia.　Award: D.M.Jones.　LOI debuts: None.

When rain halted play for 21 minutes with India 45 for 1 after 16.2 overs, their target (under the 'highest scoring overs' formula) became 236 runs off 47 overs. Raju was run out attempting a third run off Moody's final ball by Waugh's return from long-on to Boon.

AUSTRALIA		Runs	Balls	4/6
M.A.Taylor	c More b Kapil Dev	13	22	–
G.R.Marsh	b Kapil Dev	8	29	1
† D.C.Boon	c Shastri b Raju	43	61	4
D.M.Jones	c and b Prabhakar	90	109	6/2
S.R.Waugh	b Srinath	29	48	1
T.M.Moody	b Prabhakar	25	23	3
* A.R.Border	b Jadeja b Kapil Dev	10	10	–
C.J.McDermott	c Jadeja b Prabhakar	2	5	–
P.L.Taylor	run out	1	1	–
M.G.Hughes	not out	0	4	–
M.R.Whitney				
Extras	(lb 7, w 5, nb 4)	16		
Total	(50 overs; 9 wickets)	**237**		

INDIA	O	M	R	W
Kapil Dev	10	2	41	3
Prabhakar	10	0	41	3
Srinath	8	0	48	1
Tendulkar	5	0	29	0
Raju	10	0	37	1
Jadeja	7	0	34	0

FALL OF WICKETS
1-18, 2-31, 3-102, 4-156, 5-198, 6-230, 7-235, 8-236, 9-237

INDIA		Runs	Balls	4/6
R.J.Shastri	c Waugh b Moody	25	70	1
K.Srikkanth	b McDermott	0	11	–
* M.Azharuddin	run out	93	103	10
S.R.Tendulkar	c Waugh b Moody	11	19	1
Kapil Dev	lbw b Waugh	21	21	3
S.V.Manjrekar	run out	47	42	3/1
A.Jadeja	b Hughes	1	4	–
† K.S.More	b Moody	14	8	2
J.Srinath	not out	8	8	–
M.Prabhakar	run out	1	1	–
S.L.V.Raju	run out	0	–	–
Extras	(lb 8, w 5)	13		
Total	(47 overs)	**234**		

AUSTRALIA	O	M	R	W
McDermott	9	1	35	1
Whitney	10	2	36	0
Hughes	9	1	49	1
Moody	9	0	56	3
Waugh	10	0	50	1

FALL OF WICKETS
1-6, 2-53, 3-86, 4-128, 5-194, 6-199, 7-216, 8-231, 9-232, 10-234

Umpires: B.L.Aldridge (*New Zealand*) (20) and I.D.Robinson (*Zimbabwe*) (3).

ENGLAND v PAKISTAN 1991-92

At Adelaide Oval, Australia, on 1 March 1992.　**NO RESULT.**　Toss: England.
No award.　LOI debuts: None.

England, having dismissed Pakistan for the lowest total by a Test-playing country in World Cup matches, were denied victory by the tournament's controversial rain regulation which revised England's target to 64 from 16 overs.

PAKISTAN		Runs	Balls	4/6
Ramiz Raja	c Reeve b DeFreitas	1	10	–
Aamir Sohail	c and b Pringle	9	39	–
Inzamam-ul-Haq	c Stewart b DeFreitas	0	1	–
* Javed Miandad	b Pringle	3	22	–
Salim Malik	c Reeve b Botham	17	20	3
Ijaz Ahmed	c Stewart b Small	0	15	–
Wasim Akram	b Botham	1	13	–
† Moin Khan	c Hick b Small	2	14	–
Wasim Haider	c Stewart b Reeve	13	46	1
Mushtaq Ahmed	c Reeve b Pringle	17	42	1
Aqib Javed	not out	1	21	–
Extras	(lb 1, w 8, nb 1)	10		
Total	(40.2 overs)	**74**		

ENGLAND	O	M	R	W
Pringle	8.2	5	8	3
DeFreitas	7	1	22	2
Small	10	1	29	2
Botham	10	4	12	2
Reeve	5	3	2	1

FALL OF WICKETS
1-5, 2-5, 3-14, 4-20, 5-32, 6-35, 7-42, 8-47, 9-62, 10-74

ENGLAND		Runs	Balls	4/6
* G.A.Gooch	c Moin b Wasim Akram	3	14	–
I.T.Botham	not out	6	22	–
R.A.Smith	not out	5	13	1
G.A.Hick				
N.H.Fairbrother				
† A.J.Stewart				
C.C.Lewis				
D.A.Reeve				
D.R.Pringle				
P.A.J.DeFreitas				
G.C.Small				
Extras	(b 1, lb 3, w 5, nb 1)	10		
Total	(8 overs; 1 wicket)	**24**		

PAKISTAN	O	M	R	W
Wasim Akram	3	0	7	1
Aqib Javed	3	1	7	0
Wasim Haider	1	0	1	0
Ijaz Ahmed	1	0	5	0

FALL OF WICKETS
1-14

Umpires: S.A.Bucknor (*West Indies*) (5) and P.J.McConnell (64).

SOUTH AFRICA v SRI LANKA 1991-92

At Basin Reserve, Wellington, New Zealand, on 2 March 1992.　　Result: **SRI LANKA** won by 3 wickets.
Toss: Sri Lanka.　　Award: A.Ranatunga.　　LOI debuts: South Africa – O.Henry, M.W.Rushmere.

Sri Lanka won their initial encounter with South Africa when Champaka Ramanayake cover-drove the penultimate ball to the boundary, seven runs having been required from Allan Donald's final over.

SOUTH AFRICA		Runs	Balls	4/6
* K.C.Wessels	c and b Ranatunga	40	94	–
A.P.Kuiper	b Anurasiri	18	44	3
P.N.Kirsten	c Hathurusinghe b Kalpage	47	81	5/1
J.N.Rhodes	c Jayasuriya b Wickremasinghe	28	21	2
M.W.Rushmere	c Jayasuriya b Ranatunga	4	9	–
W.J.Cronje	st Tillekeratne b Anurasiri	3	6	–
B.M.McMillan	not out	18	22	–
R.P.Snell	b Anurasiri	9	5	2
† D.J.Richardson	run out	0	–	–
O.Henry	c Kalpage b Ramanayake	11	13	1
A.A.Donald	run out	3	6	–
Extras	(lb 9, w 4, nb 1)	14		
Total	(50 overs)	**195**		

SRI LANKA		Runs	Balls	4/6
R.S.Mahanama	c Richardson b McMillan	68	121	6
U.C.Hathurusinghe	c Wessels b Donald	5	9	1
A.P.Gurusinha	lbw b Donald	0	4	–
* P.A.de Silva	b Donald	7	16	1
† H.P.Tillekeratne	c Rushmere b Henry	17	63	–
A.Ranatunga	not out	64	73	6
S.T.Jayasuriya	st Richardson b Kirsten	3	7	–
R.S.Kalpage	run out	5	11	–
C.P.H.Ramanayake	not out	4	2	1
S.D.Anurasiri				
G.P.Wickremasinghe				
Extras	(b 1, lb 7, w 13, nb 4)	25		
Total	(49.5 overs; 7 wickets)	**198**		

SRI LANKA	O	M	R	W
Ramanayake	9	2	19	1
Wickremasinghe	7	0	32	1
Anurasiri	10	1	41	3
Gurusinha	8	0	30	0
Kalpage	10	0	38	1
Ranatunga	6	0	26	2

SOUTH AFRICA	O	M	R	W
McMillan	10	2	34	1
Donald	9.5	0	42	3
Snell	10	1	33	0
Henry	10	0	31	1
Kuiper	5	0	25	0
Kirsten	5	0	25	1

FALL OF WICKETS
1-27, 2-114, 3-114, 4-128, 5-149, 6-153, 7-165, 8-165, 9-186, 10-195

FALL OF WICKETS
1-11, 2-12, 3-35, 4-87, 5-154, 6-168, 7-189

Umpires: Khizer Hayat (*Pakistan*) (40) and S.J.Woodward (28).

NEW ZEALAND v ZIMBABWE 1991-92

At McLean Park, Napier, New Zealand, on 3 March 1992.　　Result: **NEW ZEALAND** won by 48 runs (*revised target*).
Toss: Zimbabwe.　　Award: M.D.Crowe.　　LOI debuts: Zimbabwe – M.G.Burmester.

A fourth interruption by rain caused Zimbabwe's target to be revised finally to 154 from 18 overs. Martin Crowe's 30-ball fifty equalled the World Cup record shared by England's Chris Old (1975) and Pakistan's Imran Khan (1983).

NEW ZEALAND		Runs	Balls	4/6
M.J.Greatbatch	b Duers	15	16	2
R.T.Latham	b Brandes	2	6	–
A.H.Jones	c Waller b Butchart	57	58	9
* M.D.Crowe	not out	74	44	8/2
C.L.Cairns	not out	1	2	–
K.R.Rutherford				
C.Z.Harris				
† I.D.S.Smith				
D.N.Patel				
D.K.Morrison				
G.R.Larsen				
Extras	(b 6, lb 7)	13		
Total	(20.5 overs; 3 wickets)	**162**		

ZIMBABWE		Runs	Balls	4/6
† A.Flower	b Larsen	30	27	5
A.C.Waller	b Morrison	11	11	1/1
* D.L.Houghton	b Larsen	10	14	2
I.P.Butchart	c Cairns b Larsen	3	7	–
E.A.Brandes	b Harris	6	8	–
A.J.Pycroft	not out	13	20	–
A.D.R.Campbell	c Crowe b Harris	8	9	1
A.H.Shah	b Harris	7	8	1
M.G.Burmester	not out	4	8	–
A.J.Traicos				
K.G.Duers				
Extras	(lb 9, w 3, nb 1)	13		
Total	(18 overs; 7 wickets)	**105**		

ZIMBABWE	O	M	R	W
Brandes	5	1	28	1
Duers	6	0	17	1
Shah	4	0	34	0
Butchart	4	0	53	1
Burmester	1.5	0	17	0

NEW ZEALAND	O	M	R	W
Morrison	4	0	14	1
Cairns	2	0	27	0
Larsen	4	0	16	3
Harris	4	0	15	3
Latham	3	0	18	0
Crowe	1	0	6	0

FALL OF WICKETS
1-9, 2-25, 3-154

FALL OF WICKETS
1-22, 2-40, 3-63, 4-63, 5-75, 6-86, 7-97

Umpires: J.D.Buultjens (*Sri Lanka*) (15) and K.E.Liebenberg (*South Africa*) (3).

INDIA v PAKISTAN 1991-92

At Sydney Cricket Ground, Australia, on 4 March 1992.　Result: **INDIA** won by 43 runs.　Toss: India.
Award: S.R.Tendulkar.　LOI debuts: None.

Although the first meeting between India and Pakistan in five World Cup tournaments was preceded by several days of rain, it was free of interruption. Batsman Javed Miandad mockingly mimicked 'keeper Kiran More's frivolous appealing by leaping up and down.

INDIA		Runs	Balls	4/6
A.Jadeja	c Zahid b Wasim Haider	46	81	2
K.Srikkanth	c Moin b Aqib	5	40	–
* M.Azharuddin	c Moin b Mushtaq	32	51	4
V.G.Kambli	c Inzamam b Mushtaq	24	42	–
S.R.Tendulkar	not out	54	62	3
S.V.Manjrekar	b Mushtaq	0	1	–
Kapil Dev	c Imran b Aqib	35	26	2/1
† K.S.More	run out	4	4	–
M.Prabhakar	not out	2	1	–
J.Srinath				
S.L.V.Raju				
Extras	(lb 3, w 9, nb 2)	14		
Total	(49 overs; 7 wickets)	216		

PAKISTAN	O	M	R	W
Wasim Akram	10	0	45	0
Aqib Javed	8	2	28	2
Imran Khan	8	0	25	0
Wasim Haider	10	1	36	1
Mushtaq Ahmed	10	0	59	3
Aamir Sohail	3	0	20	0

FALL OF WICKETS
1-25, 2-86, 3-101, 4-147, 5-148, 6-208, 7-213

PAKISTAN		Runs	Balls	4/6
Aamir Sohail	c Srikkanth b Tendulkar	62	103	6
Inzamam-ul-Haq	lbw b Kapil Dev	2	7	–
Zahid Fazal	c More b Prabhakar	2	10	–
Javed Miandad	b Srinath	40	113	2
Salim Malik	c More b Prabhakar	12	9	2
* Imran Khan	run out	0	5	–
Wasim Akram	st More b Raju	4	8	–
Wasim Haider	b Srinath	13	25	–
† Moin Khan	c Manjrekar b Kapil Dev	12	12	1
Mushtaq Ahmed	run out	3	4	–
Aqib Javed	not out	1	12	–
Extras	(lb 6, w 15, nb 1)	22		
Total	(48.1 overs)	173		

INDIA	O	M	R	W
Kapil Dev	10	0	30	2
Prabhakar	10	1	22	2
Srinath	8.1	0	37	2
Tendulkar	10	0	37	1
Raju	10	1	41	1

FALL OF WICKETS
1-8, 2-17, 3-105, 4-127, 5-130, 6-141, 7-141, 8-161, 9-166, 10-173

Umpires: P.J.McConnell (65) and D.R.Shepherd (*England*) (44).

SOUTH AFRICA v WEST INDIES 1991-92

At Lancaster Park, Christchurch, New Zealand, on 5 March 1992.　Result: **SOUTH AFRICA** won by 64 runs.
Toss: West Indies.　Award: M.W.Pringle.　LOI debuts: None.

South Africa celebrated the 100th World Cup match actually played and their first match against West Indies by dismissing the latter for their lowest World Cup total to date. Meyrick Pringle took the first four wickets in 11 balls without conceding a run.

SOUTH AFRICA		Runs	Balls	4/6
* K.C.Wessels	c Haynes b Marshall	1	9	–
A.C.Hudson	c Lara b Cummins	22	60	3
P.N.Kirsten	c Williams b Marshall	56	91	2
M.W.Rushmere	st Williams b Hooper	10	24	–
A.P.Kuiper	b Ambrose	23	29	–/1
J.N.Rhodes	c Williams b Cummins	22	27	–
B.M.McMillan	c Lara b Benjamin	20	29	2
† D.J.Richardson	not out	20	26	1
R.P.Snell	c Haynes b Ambrose	3	6	–
M.W.Pringle	not out	5	6	–
A.A.Donald				
Extras	(lb 8, w 3, nb 7)	18		
Total	(50 overs; 8 wickets)	200		

WEST INDIES	O	M	R	W
Ambrose	10	1	34	2
Marshall	10	1	26	2
Hooper	10	0	45	1
Cummins	10	0	40	2
Benjamin	10	0	47	1

FALL OF WICKETS
1-8, 2-51, 3-73, 4-119, 5-127, 6-159, 7-181, 8-187

WEST INDIES		Runs	Balls	4/6
D.L.Haynes	c Richardson b Kuiper	30	83	3
B.C.Lara	c Rhodes b Pringle	9	13	2
* R.B.Richardson	lbw b Pringle	1	3	–
C.L.Hooper	c Wessels b Pringle	0	4	–
K.L.T.Arthurton	c Wessels b Pringle	0	4	–
A.L.Logie	c Pringle b Kuiper	61	69	9/1
M.D.Marshall	c Rhodes b Snell	6	10	1
† D.Williams	c Richardson b Snell	0	3	–
C.E.L.Ambrose	run out	12	15	2
A.C.Cummins	c McMillan b Donald	6	24	–
W.K.M.Benjamin	not out	1	4	–
Extras	(lb 9, w 1)	10		
Total	(38.4 overs)	136		

SOUTH AFRICA	O	M	R	W
Donald	6.4	2	13	1
Pringle	8	4	11	4
Snell	7	2	16	2
McMillan	8	2	36	0
Kuiper	9	0	51	2

FALL OF WICKETS
1-10, 2-19, 3-19, 4-19, 5-70, 6-70, 7-116, 8-117, 9-132, 10-136

Umpires: B.L.Aldridge (21) and S.G.Randell (*Australia*) (46).

AUSTRALIA v ENGLAND 1991-92

At Sydney Cricket Ground, Australia, on 5 March 1992.   Result: ENGLAND won by 8 wickets.   Toss: Australia.
Award: I.T.Botham.   LOI debuts: None.

Ian Botham reminded Australia of his 1981 deeds by following up his best LOI analysis, including 4 for 0 off seven balls,
with his only World Cup fifty in 18 innings.

AUSTRALIA		Runs	Balls	4/6
T.M.Moody	b Tufnell	51	91	3
M.A.Taylor	lbw b Pringle	0	11	–
D.C.Boon	run out	18	27	2
D.M.Jones	c Lewis b DeFreitas	22	50	2
S.R.Waugh	run out	27	43	2
* A.R.Border	b Botham	16	22	1
† I.A.Healy	c Fairbrother b Botham	9	7	–/1
P.L.Taylor	lbw b Botham	0	2	–
C.J.McDermott	c DeFreitas b Botham	0	2	–
M.R.Whitney	not out	8	27	1
B.A.Reid	b Reeve	1	22	–
Extras	(b 2, lb 8, w 5, nb 4)	19		
Total	**(49 overs)**	**171**		

ENGLAND		Runs	Balls	4/6
* G.A.Gooch	b Waugh	58	115	7
I.T.Botham	c Healy b Whitney	53	79	6
R.A.Smith	not out	30	60	5
G.A.Hick	not out	7	5	1
N.H.Fairbrother				
† A.J.Stewart				
C.C.Lewis				
D.A.Reeve				
D.R.Pringle				
P.A.J.DeFreitas				
P.C.R.Tufnell				
Extras	(lb 13, w 8, nb 4)	25		
Total	**(40.5 overs; 2 wickets)**	**173**		

ENGLAND	O	M	R	W
Pringle	9	1	24	1
Lewis	10	2	28	0
DeFreitas	10	3	23	1
Botham	10	1	31	4
Tufnell	9	0	52	1
Reeve	1	0	3	1

AUSTRALIA	O	M	R	W
McDermott	10	1	29	0
Reid	7.5	0	49	0
Whitney	10	2	28	1
Waugh	6	0	29	1
P.L.Taylor	3	0	7	0
Moody	4	0	18	0

FALL OF WICKETS
1-5, 2-35, 3-106, 4-114, 5-145, 6-155, 7-155, 8-155, 9-164, 10-171

FALL OF WICKETS
1-107, 2-153

Umpires: S.A.Bucknor (*West Indies*) (6) and Khizer Hayat (*Pakistan*) (41).

INDIA v ZIMBABWE 1991-92

At Seddon (Trust Bank) Park, Hamilton, New Zealand, on 7 March 1992.   Result: INDIA won by 55 runs (*revised total*).
Toss: India.   Award: S.R.Tendulkar.   LOI debuts: None.

A rain-delayed start reduced this match to 32 overs apiece. When Zimbabwe's innings was terminated by another
downpour, India's total was revised to 158 after 19 overs, Zimbabwe's being 103. India had actually scored 106 for 3 at
that point.

INDIA		Runs	Balls	4/6
K.Srikkanth	b Burmester	32	32	5
Kapil Dev	lbw b Brandes	10	14	–/1
* M.Azharuddin	c Flower b Burmester	12	15	2
S.R.Tendulkar	c Campbell b Burmester	81	77	8/1
S.V.Manjrekar	c Duers b Traicos	34	34	2
V.G.Kambli	b Traicos	1	2	–
A.Jadeja	c Shah b Traicos	6	6	–
† K.S.More	not out	15	8	–/1
J.Srinath	not out	6	4	1
M.Prabhakar				
S.L.V.Raju				
Extras	(lb 3, w 3)	6		
Total	**(32 overs; 7 wickets)**	**203**		

ZIMBABWE		Runs	Balls	4/6
A.H.Shah	b Tendulkar	31	51	3
† A.Flower	not out	43	56	3
A.C.Waller	not out	13	7	2
A.J.Pycroft				
* D.L.Houghton				
A.D.R.Campbell				
I.P.Butchart				
E.A.Brandes				
M.G.Burmester				
A.J.Traicos				
K.G.Duers				
Extras	(b 1, lb 11, w 5)	17		
Total	**(19.1 overs; 1 wicket)**	**104**		

ZIMBABWE	O	M	R	W
Brandes	7	0	43	1
Duers	7	0	48	0
Burmester	6	0	36	3
Shah	6	1	38	0
Traicos	6	0	35	3

INDIA	O	M	R	W
Kapil Dev	4	0	6	0
Prabhakar	3	0	14	0
Srinath	4	0	20	0
Tendulkar	6	0	35	1
Raju	2.1	0	17	0

FALL OF WICKETS
1-23, 2-43, 3-69, 4-168, 5-170, 6-182, 7-184

FALL OF WICKETS
1-79

Umpires: J.D.Buultjens (*Sri Lanka*) (16) and S.G.Randell (*Australia*) (47).

AUSTRALIA v SRI LANKA 1991-92

At Adelaide Oval, Australia, on 7 March 1992.   Result: **AUSTRALIA** won by 7 wickets.   Toss: Australia.
Award: T.M.Moody.   LOI debuts: None.

Aravinda de Silva's fifty was his first as Sri Lanka's captain and his only one in this tournament. Allan Border allowed himself a rare ten-over spell.

SRI LANKA		Runs	Balls	4/6
R.S.Mahanama	run out	7	10	1
M.A.R.Samarasekera	c Healy b Taylor	34	63	3
A.P.Gurusinha	lbw b Whitney	5	23	1
* P.A.de Silva	c Moody b McDermott	62	83	2
A.Ranatunga	c Jones b Taylor	23	52	–
S.T.Jayasuriya	lbw b Border	15	29	1
† H.P.Tillekeratne	run out	5	13	–
R.S.Kalpage	run out	14	15	1
C.P.H.Ramanayake	run out	5	10	–
S.D.Anurasiri	not out	4	4	–
G.P.Wickremasinghe				
Extras	(b 3, lb 6, w 5, nb 1)	15		
Total	(50 overs; 9 wickets)	**189**		

AUSTRALIA		Runs	Balls	4/6
T.M.Moody	c Mahanama b Wickremasinghe	57	86	4
G.R.Marsh	c Anurasiri b Kalpage	60	113	3/1
M.E.Waugh	c Mahanama b Wickremasinghe	26	26	–/2
D.C.Boon	not out	27	37	1
D.M.Jones	not out	12	8	–/1
S.R.Waugh				
* A.R.Border				
† I.A.Healy				
P.L.Taylor				
C.J.McDermott				
M.R.Whitney				
Extras	(lb 2, w 3, nb 3)	8		
Total	(44 overs; 3 wickets)	**190**		

AUSTRALIA	O	M	R	W
McDermott	10	0	28	1
S.R.Waugh	7	0	34	0
Whitney	10	3	26	1
Moody	3	0	18	0
Taylor	10	0	34	2
Border	10	0	40	1

SRI LANKA	O	M	R	W
Wickremasinghe	10	3	29	2
Ramanayake	9	1	44	0
Anurasiri	10	0	43	0
Gurusinha	6	0	20	0
Kalpage	8	0	41	1
Ranatunga	1	0	11	0

FALL OF WICKETS
1-8, 2-28, 3-72, 4-123, 5-151, 6-163, 7-166, 8-182, 9-189

FALL OF WICKETS
1-120, 2-130, 3-165

Umpires: P.D.Reporter (*India*) (16) and I.D.Robinson (*Zimbabwe*) (4).

NEW ZEALAND v WEST INDIES 1991-92

At Eden Park, Auckland, New Zealand, on 8 March 1992.   Result: **NEW ZEALAND** won by 5 wickets.
Toss: New Zealand.   Award: M.D.Crowe.   LOI debuts: None.

New Zealand reached the semi-finals with this fifth successive win, their first LOI victory against West Indies since 1979-80. Oddly, it was their first match of any kind against West Indies for five years. Martin Crowe took his tournament aggregate to 263 for once out.

WEST INDIES		Runs	Balls	4/6
D.L.Haynes	c and b Harris	22	61	–/1
B.C.Lara	c Rutherford b Larsen	52	81	7
* R.B.Richardson	c Smith b Watson	29	54	1
C.L.Hooper	c Greatbatch b Patel	2	9	–
K.L.T.Arthurton	b Morrison	40	54	3
A.L.Logie	b Harris	3	4	–
M.D.Marshall	b Larsen	5	14	–
† D.Williams	not out	32	24	5
W.K.M.Benjamin	not out	2	1	–
C.E.L.Ambrose				
A.C.Cummins				
Extras	(lb 8, w 7, nb 1)	16		
Total	(50 overs; 7 wickets)	**203**		

NEW ZEALAND		Runs	Balls	4/6
M.J.Greatbatch	c Haynes b Benjamin	63	77	7/3
R.T.Latham	c Williams b Cummins	14	27	1
A.H.Jones	c Williams b Benjamin	10	35	–
* M.D.Crowe	not out	81	81	12
K.R.Rutherford	c Williams b Ambrose	8	32	1
C.Z.Harris	c Williams b Cummins	7	23	–
D.N.Patel	not out	10	18	–
† I.D.S.Smith				
D.K.Morrison				
G.R.Larsen				
W.Watson				
Extras	(lb 7, w 5, nb 1)	13		
Total	(48.3 overs; 5 wickets)	**206**		

NEW ZEALAND	O	M	R	W
Morrison	9	1	33	1
Patel	10	2	19	1
Watson	10	2	56	1
Larsen	10	0	41	2
Harris	10	2	32	2
Latham	1	0	14	0

WEST INDIES	O	M	R	W
Ambrose	10	1	41	1
Marshall	9	1	35	0
Cummins	10	0	53	2
Hooper	10	0	36	0
Benjamin	9.3	3	34	2

FALL OF WICKETS
1-65, 2-95, 3-100, 4-136, 5-142, 6-156, 7-201

FALL OF WICKETS
1-67, 2-97, 3-100, 4-135, 5-174

Umpires: K.E.Liebenberg (*South Africa*) (4) and P.J.McConnell (*Australia*) (66).

SOUTH AFRICA v PAKISTAN 1991-92

At Woolloongabba, Brisbane, Australia, on 8 March 1992.　Result: **SOUTH AFRICA** won by 20 runs (*revised target*).
Toss: Pakistan.　Award: A.C.Hudson.　LOI debuts: None.

When rain halted play with Pakistan 74 for 2 after 21.3 overs, the farcical rain rule was again exposed, their target being revised to 193 from 36 overs (i.e the target was reduced by 14 overs but only by 18 runs).

SOUTH AFRICA		Runs	Balls	4/6
A.C.Hudson	c Ijaz b Imran	54	81	8
* K.C.Wessels	c Moin b Aqib	7	26	–
M.W.Rushmere	c Aamir b Mushtaq	35	70	2
A.P.Kuiper	c Moin b Imran	5	12	–
J.N.Rhodes	lbw b Iqbal	5	17	–
W.J.Cronje	not out	47	53	4
B.M.McMillan	b Wasim	33	44	1
† D.J.Richardson	b Wasim	5	10	–
R.P.Snell	not out	1	1	–
M.W.Pringle				
A.A.Donald				
Extras	(lb 8, w 9, nb 2)	19		
Total	(50 overs; 7 wickets)	211		

PAKISTAN		Runs	Balls	4/6
Aamir Sohail	b Snell	23	53	2
Zahid Fazal	c Richardson b McMillan	11	46	1
Inzamam-ul-Haq	run out	48	45	5
* Imran Khan	c Richardson b McMillan	34	53	5
Salim Malik	c Donald b Kuiper	12	11	–
Wasim Akram	c Snell b Kuiper	9	8	1
Ijaz Ahmed	c Rhodes b Kuiper	6	3	1
† Moin Khan	not out	5	5	–
Mushtaq Ahmed	run out	4	4	–
Iqbal Sikander	not out	1	3	–
Aqib Javed				
Extras	(lb 2, w 17, nb 1)	20		
Total	(36 overs; 8 wickets)	173		

PAKISTAN	O	M	R	W
Wasim Akram	10	0	42	2
Aqib Javed	7	1	36	1
Imran Khan	10	0	34	2
Iqbal Sikander	8	0	30	1
Ijaz Ahmed	7	0	26	0
Mushtaq Ahmed	8	1	35	1

SOUTH AFRICA	O	M	R	W
Donald	7	1	31	0
Pringle	7	0	31	0
Snell	8	2	26	1
McMillan	7	0	34	2
Kuiper	6	0	40	3
Cronje	1	0	9	0

FALL OF WICKETS
1-31, 2-98, 3-110, 4-111, 5-127, 6-198, 7-207

FALL OF WICKETS
1-50, 2-50, 3-135, 4-136, 5-156, 6-157, 7-163, 8-171

Umpires: B.L.Aldridge (*New Zealand*) (22) and S.A.Bucknor (*West Indies*) (7).

ENGLAND v SRI LANKA 1991-92

At Eastern Oval, Ballarat, Australia, on 9 March 1992.　Result: **ENGLAND** won by 106 runs.　Toss: England.
Award: C.C.Lewis.　LOI debuts: None.

The 94th LOI venue saw England add 106 off their last ten overs, Alec Stewart contributing a 32-ball fifty. Chris Lewis produced a spectacular all-round performance.

ENGLAND		Runs	Balls	4/6
* G.A.Gooch	b Labrooy	8	28	1
I.T.Botham	b Anurasiri	47	63	5/2
R.A.Smith	run out	19	39	2
G.A.Hick	b Ramanayake	41	62	3
N.H.Fairbrother	c Ramanayake b Gurusinha	63	70	2/2
† A.J.Stewart	c Jayasuriya b Gurusinha	59	36	7/1
C.C.Lewis	not out	20	6	1/2
D.R.Pringle	not out	0	–	–
D.A.Reeve				
P.A.J.DeFreitas				
R.K.Illingworth				
Extras	(b 1, lb 9, w 9, nb 4)	23		
Total	(50 overs; 6 wickets)	280		

SRI LANKA		Runs	Balls	4/6
R.S.Mahanama	c Botham b Lewis	9	19	1
M.A.R.Samarasekera	c Illingworth b Lewis	23	29	4
A.P.Gurusinha	c and b Lewis	7	9	–
* P.A.de Silva	c Fairbrother b Lewis	7	10	1
A.Ranatunga	c Stewart b Botham	36	51	6
† H.P.Tillekeratne	run out	4	30	–
S.T.Jayasuriya	c DeFreitas b Illingworth	19	16	2
G.F.Labrooy	c Smith b Illingworth	19	34	1
C.P.H.Ramanayake	c and b Reeve	12	38	–
S.D.Anurasiri	lbw b Reeve	11	19	–
G.P.Wickremasinghe	not out	6	16	–
Extras	(lb 7, w 8, nb 6)	21		
Total	(44 overs)	174		

SRI LANKA	O	M	R	W
Wickremasinghe	9	0	54	0
Ramanayake	10	1	42	1
Labrooy	10	1	68	1
Anurasiri	10	1	27	1
Gurusinha	10	0	67	2
Jayasuriya	1	0	12	0

ENGLAND	O	M	R	W
Pringle	7	1	27	0
Lewis	8	0	30	4
DeFreitas	5	0	31	0
Botham	10	0	33	1
Illingworth	10	0	32	2
Reeve	4	0	14	2

FALL OF WICKETS
1-44, 2-80, 3-105, 4-164, 5-244, 6-268

FALL OF WICKETS
1-33, 2-46, 3-56, 4-60, 5-91, 6-119, 7-123, 8-156, 9-158, 10-174

Umpires: Khizer Hayat (*Pakistan*) (42) and P.D.Reporter (*India*) (17).

WEST INDIES v INDIA 1991-92

At Basin Reserve, Wellington, New Zealand, on 10 March 1992.   Result: **WEST INDIES** won by 5 wickets (*revised target*).
Toss: India.   Award: A.C.Cummins.   LOI debuts: None.

West Indies became the first side to attain a rain-adjusted target when a 20-minute shower revised India's total to 194
from 46 overs.

INDIA		Runs	Balls	4/6
A.Jadeja	c Benjamin b Simmons	27	61	2
K.Srikkanth	c Logie b Hooper	40	70	2
* M.Azharuddin	c Ambrose b Cummins	61	84	4
S.R.Tendulkar	c Williams b Ambrose	4	11	–
S.V.Manjrekar	run out	27	40	–
Kapil Dev	c Haynes b Cummins	3	4	–
P.K.Amre	c Hooper b Ambrose	4	8	–
† K.S.More	c Hooper b Cummins	5	5	1
M.Prabhakar	c Richardson b Cummins	8	10	1
J.Srinath	not out	5	5	–
S.L.V.Raju	run out	1	1	–
Extras	(lb 6, w 5, nb 1)	12		
Total	(49.4 overs)	**197**		

WEST INDIES		Runs	Balls	4/6
D.L.Haynes	c Manjrekar b Kapil Dev	16	16	3
B.C.Lara	c Manjrekar b Srinath	41	37	6/1
P.V.Simmons	c Tendulkar b Prabhakar	22	20	2/1
* R.B.Richardson	c Srikkanth b Srinath	3	8	–
K.L.T.Arthurton	not out	58	99	3
A.L.Logie	c More b Raju	7	10	1
C.L.Hooper	not out	34	57	3
† D.Williams				
W.K.M.Benjamin				
C.E.L.Ambrose				
A.C.Cummins				
Extras	(lb 8, w 2, nb 4)	14		
Total	(40.2 overs; 5 wickets)	**195**		

WEST INDIES	O	M	R	W
Ambrose	10	1	24	2
Benjamin	9.4	0	35	0
Cummins	10	0	33	4
Simmons	9	0	48	1
Hooper	10	0	46	1
Arthurton	1	0	5	0

INDIA	O	M	R	W
Kapil Dev	8	0	45	1
Prabhakar	9	0	55	1
Raju	10	2	32	1
Srinath	9	2	23	2
Tendulkar	3	0	20	0
Srikkanth	1	0	7	0
Jadeja	0.2	0	5	0

FALL OF WICKETS
1-56, 2-102, 3-115, 4-166, 5-171, 6-172, 7-180, 8-186, 9-193, 10-197

FALL OF WICKETS
1-57, 2-82, 3-88, 4-98, 5-112

Umpires: S.G.Randell (*Australia*) (48) and S.J.Woodward (29).

SOUTH AFRICA v ZIMBABWE 1991-92

At Manuka Oval, Canberra, Australia, on 10 March 1992.   Result: **SOUTH AFRICA** won by 7 wickets.
Toss: South Africa.   Award: P.N.Kirsten.   LOI debuts: None.

The Manuka Oval, scene of Sir Donald Bradman's final innings (v MCC in 1962-63), provided the Australian Capital
Territory with its first international venue, the 95th on the LOI circuit. Andy Flower (6) retired with a damaged finger
and resumed at 80 for 5; David Houghton kept wicket.

ZIMBABWE		Runs	Balls	4/6
W.R.James	lbw b Pringle	5	12	1
† A.Flower	c Richardson b Cronje	19	44	–
A.J.Pycroft	c Wessels b McMillan	19	47	–
* D.L.Houghton	c Cronje b Kirsten	15	53	–
A.C.Waller	c Cronje b Kirsten	15	28	1
A.H.Shah	c Wessels b Kirsten	3	4	–
E.A.Brandes	c Richardson b McMillan	20	28	1/1
M.G.Burmester	c Kuiper b Cronje	1	10	–
A.J.Traicos	not out	16	40	1
M.P.Jarvis	c and b McMillan	17	21	1/1
K.G.Duers	b Donald	5	10	–
Extras	(lb 11, w 13, nb 4)	28		
Total	(48.3 overs)	**163**		

SOUTH AFRICA		Runs	Balls	4/6
* K.C.Wessels	b Shah	70	137	6
A.C.Hudson	b Jarvis	13	22	1
P.N.Kirsten	not out	62	103	3
A.P.Kuiper	c Burmester b Brandes	7	9	–
J.N.Rhodes	not out	3	3	–
W.J.Cronje				
B.M.McMillan				
† D.J.Richardson				
R.P.Snell				
M.W.Pringle				
A.A.Donald				
Extras	(lb 4, w 2, nb 3)	9		
Total	(45.1 overs; 3 wickets)	**164**		

SOUTH AFRICA	O	M	R	W
Donald	9.3	1	25	1
Pringle	9	0	25	1
Snell	10	3	24	0
Cronje	5	0	17	2
Kirsten	5	0	31	3
McMillan	10	1	30	3

ZIMBABWE	O	M	R	W
Brandes	9.1	0	40	1
Jarvis	9	2	23	1
Burmester	5	0	20	0
Shah	8	2	32	1
Duers	8	1	19	0
Traicos	6	0	26	0

FALL OF WICKETS
1-7, 2-51, 3-72, 4-80, 5-80, 6-115, 7-117, 8-123, 9-151, 10-163

FALL OF WICKETS
1-27, 2-139, 3-151

Umpires: S.A.Bucknor (*West Indies*) (8) and D.R.Shepherd (*England*) (45).

AUSTRALIA v PAKISTAN 1991-92

At WACA Ground, Perth, Australia, on 11 March 1992. Result: **PAKISTAN** won by 48 runs. Toss: Pakistan.
Award: Aamir Sohail. LOI debuts: None.

A rock-hard pitch produced some lively cricket and frayed tempers, Aamir Sohail, Moin Khan and Mike Whitney each
being fined $250 for misbehaviour during Australia's innings as the last eight wickets fell for 56.

PAKISTAN		Runs	Balls	4/6
Aamir Sohail	c Healy b Moody	76	106	8
Ramiz Raja	c Border b Whitney	34	61	4
Salim Malik	b Moody	0	6	–
Javed Miandad	c Healy b S.R.Waugh	46	75	3
* Imran Khan	c Moody b S.R.Waugh	13	22	–/1
Inzamam-ul-Haq	run out	16	16	–
Ijaz Ahmed	run out	0	2	–
Wasim Akram	c M.E.Waugh b S.R.Waugh	0	1	–
† Moin Khan	c Healy b McDermott	5	8	–
Mushtaq Ahmed	not out	3	5	–
Aqib Javed				
Extras	(lb 9, w 16, nb 2)	27		
Total	(50 overs; 9 wickets)	220		

AUSTRALIA	O	M	R	W
McDermott	10	0	33	1
Reid	9	0	37	0
S.R.Waugh	10	0	36	3
Whitney	10	1	50	1
Moody	10	0	42	2
M.E.Waugh	1	0	13	0

FALL OF WICKETS
1-78, 2-80, 3-157, 4-193, 5-194, 6-205, 7-205, 8-214, 9-220

AUSTRALIA		Runs	Balls	4/6
T.M.Moody	c Salim b Aqib	4	18	–
G.R.Marsh	c Moin b Imran	39	91	1
D.C.Boon	c Mushtaq b Aqib	5	15	1
D.M.Jones	c Aqib b Mushtaq	47	79	2
M.E.Waugh	c Ijaz b Mushtaq	30	42	2
* A.R.Border	c Ijaz b Mushtaq	1	4	–
S.R.Waugh	c Moin b Imran	5	6	1
† I.A.Healy	c Ijaz b Aqib	8	15	–
C.J.McDermott	lbw b Wasim	0	2	–
M.R.Whitney	b Wasim	5	9	–
B.A.Reid	not out	0	–	–
Extras	(lb 7, w 14, nb 7)	28		
Total	(45.2 overs)	172		

PAKISTAN	O	M	R	W
Wasim Akram	7.2	0	28	2
Aqib Javed	8	1	21	3
Imran Khan	10	1	32	2
Ijaz Ahmed	10	0	43	0
Mushtaq Ahmed	10	0	41	3

FALL OF WICKETS
1-13, 2-31, 3-116, 4-122, 5-123, 6-130, 7-156, 8-162, 9-167, 10-172

Umpires: K.E.Liebenberg (*South Africa*) (5) and P.D.Reporter (*India*) (18).

NEW ZEALAND v INDIA 1991-92

At Carisbrook, Dunedin, New Zealand, on 12 March 1992. Result: **NEW ZEALAND** won by 4 wickets. Toss: India.
Award: M.J.Greatbatch. LOI debuts: None.

New Zealand's sixth successive win equalled the record World Cup sequence achieved by West Indies in 1983. Martin
Crowe's dismissal, only his second of the tournament, was brought about by Kiran More scoring a direct hit with a back
flick from gully while facing the opposite direction.

INDIA		Runs	Balls	4/6
A.Jadeja	retired hurt	13	32	1
K.Srikkanth	c Latham b Patel	0	3	–
* M.Azharuddin	c Greatbatch b Patel	55	98	3/1
S.R.Tendulkar	c Smith b Harris	84	107	6
S.V.Manjrekar	c and b Harris	18	25	–
Kapil Dev	c Larsen b Harris	33	16	5
S.T.Banerjee	c Greatbatch b Watson	11	9	1
† K.S.More	not out	2	8	–
J.Srinath	not out	4	3	–
M.Prabhakar				
S.L.V.Raju				
Extras	(b 1, lb 4, w 4, nb 1)	10		
Total	(50 overs; 6 wickets)	230		

NEW ZEALAND	O	M	R	W
Cairns	8	1	40	0
Patel	10	0	29	2
Watson	10	1	34	1
Larsen	9	0	43	0
Harris	9	0	55	3
Latham	4	0	24	0

FALL OF WICKETS
1-4, 2-149, 3-166, 4-201, 5-222, 6-223

NEW ZEALAND		Runs	Balls	4/6
M.J.Greatbatch	c Banerjee b Raju	73	77	5/4
R.T.Latham	b Prabhakar	8	22	1
A.H.Jones	not out	67	107	8
* M.D.Crowe	run out	26	28	3/1
† I.D.S.Smith	c sub b Prabhakar	9	8	1
K.R.Rutherford	lbw b Raju	21	22	3/1
C.Z.Harris	b Prabhakar	4	17	–
C.L.Cairns	not out	4	5	1
D.N.Patel				
G.R.Larsen				
W.Watson				
Extras	(b 4, lb 3, w 4, nb 8)	19		
Total	(47.1 overs; 6 wickets)	231		

INDIA	O	M	R	W
Kapil Dev	10	0	55	0
Prabhakar	10	0	46	3
Banerjee	6	1	40	0
Srinath	9	0	35	0
Raju	10	0	38	2
Tendulkar	1	0	2	0
Srikkanth	1.1	0	8	0

FALL OF WICKETS
1-36, 2-118, 3-162, 4-172, 5-206, 6-225

Umpires: P.J.McConnell (*Australia*) (67) and I.D.Robinson (*Zimbabwe*) (5).

371

ENGLAND v SOUTH AFRICA 1991-92

At Melbourne Cricket Ground, Australia, on 12 March 1992. Result: **ENGLAND** won by 3 wickets (*revised target*).
Toss: England. Award: A.J.Stewart. LOI debuts: None.

Rain halted play for 43 minutes with England 62 for 0 from 12 overs and reduced their target to 226 off 41 overs. They completed a notable victory at 10.45pm, probably the latest finish to any international. South Africa's opening partnership was their highest until 1994-95.

SOUTH AFRICA		Runs	Balls	4/6
* K.C.Wessels	c Smith b Hick	85	126	6
A.C.Hudson	c and b Hick	79	115	7
P.N.Kirsten	c Smith b DeFreitas	11	12	–/1
J.N.Rhodes	run out	18	23	–
A.P.Kuiper	not out	15	12	1
W.J.Cronje	not out	13	15	–
B.M.McMillan				
† D.J.Richardson				
R.P.Snell				
M.W.Pringle				
A.A.Donald				
Extras	(b 4, lb 4, w 4, nb 3)	15		
Total	(50 overs; 4 wickets)	236		

ENGLAND	O	M	R	W
Pringle	9	2	34	0
DeFreitas	10	1	41	1
Botham	8	0	37	0
Small	2	0	14	0
Illingworth	10	0	43	0
Reeve	2.4	0	15	0
Hick	8.2	0	44	2

FALL OF WICKETS
1-151, 2-170, 3-201, 4-205

ENGLAND		Runs	Balls	4/6
*†A.J.Stewart	run out	77	88	7
I.T.Botham	b McMillan	22	30	1
R.A.Smith	c Richardson b McMillan	0	2	–
G.A.Hick	c Richardson b Snell	1	4	–
N.H.Fairbrother	not out	75	83	6
D.A.Reeve	c McMillan b Snell	10	15	–
C.C.Lewis	run out	33	22	4
D.R.Pringle	c Kuiper b Snell	1	3	–
P.A.J.DeFreitas	not out	1	1	–
R.K.Illingworth				
G.C.Small				
Extras	(lb 3, w 1, nb 2)	6		
Total	(40.5 overs; 7 wickets)	226		

SOUTH AFRICA	O	M	R	W
Donald	9	1	43	0
Pringle	8	0	44	0
Snell	7.5	0	42	3
McMillan	8	1	39	2
Kuiper	4	0	32	0
Cronje	3	0	14	0
Kirsten	1	0	9	0

FALL OF WICKETS
1-63, 2-63, 3-64, 4-132, 5-166, 6-216, 7-225

Umpires: B.L.Aldridge (*New Zealand*) (23) and J.D.Buultjens (*Sri Lanka*) (17).

WEST INDIES v SRI LANKA 1991-92

At Berri Oval, South Australia, on 13 March 1992. Result: **WEST INDIES** won by 91 runs.
Toss: Sri Lanka. Award: P.V.Simmons. LOI debuts: None.

Situated 200km east of Adelaide on a bend of the Murray River, the South Australian town of Berri sited the 96th ground to stage a limited-overs international. Phil Simmons reached his only World Cup hundred off 119 balls.

WEST INDIES		Runs	Balls	4/6
D.L.Haynes	c Tillekeratne b Ranatunga	38	47	3/1
B.C.Lara	c and b Ramanayake	1	6	–
P.V.Simmons	c Wickremasinghe b Hathurusinghe	110	125	8/2
* R.B.Richardson	run out	8	23	–
K.L.T.Arthurton	c Tillekeratne b Hathurusinghe	40	54	1
A.L.Logie	b Anurasiri	0	2	–
C.L.Hooper	c Gurusinha b Hathurusinghe	12	12	1
† D.Williams	c Tillekeratne b Hathurusinghe	2	3	–
C.E.L.Ambrose	not out	15	14	–/1
W.K.M.Benjamin	not out	24	20	1
A.C.Cummins				
Extras	(lb 9, w 3, nb 6)	18		
Total	(50 overs; 8 wickets)	268		

SRI LANKA	O	M	R	W
Wickremasinghe	7	0	30	0
Ramanayake	7	1	17	1
Anurasiri	10	0	46	1
Gurusinha	1	0	10	0
Ranatunga	7	0	35	1
Kalpage	10	0	64	0
Hathurusinghe	8	0	57	4

FALL OF WICKETS
1-6, 2-72, 3-103, 4-194, 5-195, 6-217, 7-223, 8-228

SRI LANKA		Runs	Balls	4/6
R.S.Mahanama	c Arthurton b Cummins	11	50	–
M.A.R.Samarasekera	lbw b Hooper	40	41	4/1
U.C.Hathurusinghe	run out	16	25	–
* P.A.de Silva	c and b Hooper	11	19	–
A.Ranatunga	c Benjamin b Arthurton	24	40	–/1
A.P.Gurusinha	c Richardson b Ambrose	10	30	–
† H.P.Tillekeratne	b Ambrose	3	9	–
R.S.Kalpage	not out	13	40	–
C.P.H.Ramanayake	b Arthurton	1	13	–
S.D.Anurasiri	b Benjamin	3	11	–
G.P.Wickremasinghe	not out	21	21	1
Extras	(lb 8, w 14, nb 2)	24		
Total	(50 overs; 9 wickets)	177		

WEST INDIES	O	M	R	W
Ambrose	10	2	24	2
Benjamin	10	0	34	1
Cummins	9	0	49	1
Hooper	10	1	19	2
Arthurton	10	0	40	2
Simmons	1	0	3	0

FALL OF WICKETS
1-56, 2-80, 3-86, 4-99, 5-130, 6-135, 7-137, 8-139, 9-149

Umpires: D.R.Shepherd (*England*) (46) and S.J.Woodward (*New Zealand*) (30).

AUSTRALIA v ZIMBABWE 1991-92

At Bellerive Oval, Hobart, Australia, on 14 March 1992.   Result: **AUSTRALIA** won by 128 runs.   Toss: Zimbabwe.
Award: S.R.Waugh.   LOI debuts: None.

This emphatic win left the holders with a chance of qualifying on run rate. Mark and Steve Waugh added 113 off 69
balls in 48 minutes for the fifth wicket, reaching their fifties from 32 and 39 balls respectively. Dean Jones completed
5000 runs in 131 internationals.

AUSTRALIA		Runs	Balls	4/6	ZIMBABWE		Runs	Balls	4/6
T.M.Moody	run out	6	8	–	A.H.Shah	run out	23	47	2
D.C.Boon	b Shah	48	84	4	† A.Flower	c Border b S.R.Waugh	20	49	1
D.M.Jones	b Burmester	54	71	4	A.D.R.Campbell	c M.E.Waugh b Whitney	4	20	1
* A.R.Border	st Flower b Traicos	22	29	2	A.J.Pycroft	c M.E.Waugh b S.R.Waugh	0	1	–
M.E.Waugh	not out	66	39	5/2	* D.L.Houghton	b McDermott	2	10	–
S.R.Waugh	b Brandes	55	43	4	A.C.Waller	c Taylor b Moody	18	39	2
† I.A.Healy	lbw b Duers	0	2	–	K.J.Arnott	b Whitney	8	15	–
P.L.Taylor	not out	1	1	–	E.A.Brandes	c McDermott b Taylor	23	28	3
C.J.McDermott					M.G.Burmester	c Border b Reid	12	24	–
M.R.Whitney					A.J.Traicos	c Border b Taylor	3	9	–
B.A.Reid					K.G.Duers	not out	2	10	–
Extras	(b 2, lb 8, w 2, nb 1)	13			Extras	(lb 12, w 8, nb 2)	22		
Total	(46 overs; 6 wickets)	265			Total	(41.4 overs)	137		

ZIMBABWE	O	M	R	W	AUSTRALIA	O	M	R	W
Brandes	9	0	59	1	McDermott	8	0	26	1
Duers	9	1	48	1	Reid	9	2	17	1
Burmester	9	0	65	1	S.R.Waugh	7	0	28	2
Shah	9	0	53	1	Whitney	10	3	15	2
Traicos	10	0	30	1	Moody	4	0	25	1
					Taylor	3.4	0	14	2

FALL OF WICKETS
1-8, 2-102, 3-134, 4-144, 5-257, 6-258

FALL OF WICKETS
1-47, 2-51, 3-51, 4-57, 5-69, 6-88, 7-97, 8-117, 9-132, 10-137

Umpires: B.L.Aldridge (*New Zealand*) (24) and S.A.Bucknor (*West Indies*) (9).

NEW ZEALAND v ENGLAND 1991-92

At Basin Reserve, Wellington, New Zealand, on 15 March 1992.   Result: **NEW ZEALAND** won by 7 wickets.
Toss: New Zealand.   Award: A.H.Jones.   LOI debuts: None.

A capacity crowd of 13,612 saw New Zealand achieve a record seventh successive World Cup victory to end England's
unbeaten sequence of 17 matches on tour in Australasia. Mark Greatbatch donned the gloves when Ian Smith
(migraine) retired after 15 overs.

ENGLAND		Runs	Balls	4/6	NEW ZEALAND		Runs	Balls	4/6
*†A.J.Stewart	c Harris b Patel	41	59	7	M.J.Greatbatch	c DeFreitas b Botham	35	37	4/1
I.T.Botham	b Patel	8	25	1	J.G.Wright	b DeFreitas	1	5	–
G.A.Hick	c Greatbatch b Harris	56	70	6/1	A.H.Jones	run out	78	113	13
R.A.Smith	c Patel b Jones	38	72	3	* M.D.Crowe	not out	73	81	6
A.J.Lamb	c Cairns b Watson	12	29	–	K.R.Rutherford	not out	3	12	–
C.C.Lewis	c and b Watson	0	1	–	C.Z.Harris				
D.A.Reeve	not out	21	27	1	C.L.Cairns				
D.R.Pringle	c sub (R.T.Latham) b Jones	10	16	–	† I.D.S.Smith				
P.A.J.DeFreitas	c Cairns b Harris	0	1	–	D.N.Patel				
R.K.Illingworth	not out	2	2	–	G.R.Larsen				
G.C.Small					W.Watson				
Extras	(b 1, lb 7, w 4)	12			Extras	(lb 9, w 1, nb 1)	11		
Total	(50 overs; 8 wickets)	200			Total	(40.5 overs; 3 wickets)	201		

NEW ZEALAND	O	M	R	W	ENGLAND	O	M	R	W
Patel	10	1	26	2	Pringle	6.2	1	34	0
Harris	8	0	39	2	DeFreitas	8.3	1	45	1
Watson	10	0	40	2	Botham	4	0	19	1
Cairns	3	0	21	0	Illingworth	9	1	46	0
Larsen	10	3	24	0	Hick	6	0	26	0
Jones	9	0	42	2	Reeve	3	0	9	0
					Small	4	0	13	0

FALL OF WICKETS
1-25, 2-95, 3-135, 4-162, 5-162, 6-169, 7-189, 8-195

FALL OF WICKETS
1-5, 2-62, 3-171

Umpires: S.G.Randell (*Australia*) (49) and I.D.Robinson (*Zimbabwe*) (6).

SOUTH AFRICA v INDIA 1991-92

At Adelaide Oval, Australia, on 15 March 1992.   Result: **SOUTH AFRICA** won by 6 wickets.   Toss: South Africa.
Award: P.N.Kirsten.   LOI debuts: None.

Morning drizzle reduced the match to 30 overs each. South Africa were now assured of a semi-final place unless an imminent all-white referendum rejected constitutional reform and their Board felt obliged to withdraw from the tournament. The poll was to receive a decisive vote of approval.

INDIA		Runs	Balls	4/6
K.Srikkanth	c Kirsten b Donald	0	5	–
S.V.Manjrekar	b Kuiper	28	53	–
*M.Azharuddin	c Kuiper b Pringle	79	77	6
S.R.Tendulkar	c Wessels b Kuiper	14	14	1
Kapil Dev	b Donald	42	29	3/1
V.G.Kambli	run out	1	3	–
P.K.Amre	not out	1	1	–
J.Srinath	not out	0	–	–
†K.S.More				
M.Prabhakar				
S.L.V.Raju				
Extras	(lb 7, w 6, nb 2)	15		
Total	(30 overs; 6 wickets)	**180**		

SOUTH AFRICA		Runs	Balls	4/6
A.C.Hudson	b Srinath	53	73	4
P.N.Kirsten	b Kapil Dev	84	86	7
A.P.Kuiper	run out	7	6	–
J.N.Rhodes	c Raju b Prabhakar	7	3	–/1
*K.C.Wessels	not out	9	6	1
W.J.Cronje	not out	8	6	1
B.M.McMillan				
†D.J.Richardson				
R.P.Snell				
M.W.Pringle				
A.A.Donald				
Extras	(lb 10, nb 3)	13		
Total	(29.1 overs; 4 wickets)	**181**		

SOUTH AFRICA	O	M	R	W
Donald	6	0	34	2
Pringle	6	0	37	1
Snell	6	1	46	0
McMillan	6	0	28	0
Kuiper	6	0	28	2

INDIA	O	M	R	W
Kapil Dev	6	0	36	1
Prabhakar	5.1	1	33	1
Tendulkar	6	0	20	0
Srinath	6	0	39	1
Raju	6	0	43	0

FALL OF WICKETS
1-1, 2-79, 3-103, 4-174, 5-177, 6-179

FALL OF WICKETS
1-128, 2-149, 3-157, 4-163

Umpires: J.D.Buultjens (*Sri Lanka*) (18) and Khizer Hayat (*Pakistan*) (43).

PAKISTAN v SRI LANKA 1991-92

At WACA Ground, Perth, Australia, on 15 March 1992.   Result: **PAKISTAN** won by 4 wickets.   Toss: Sri Lanka.
Award: Javed Miandad.   LOI debuts: None.

Sri Lanka's last-over defeat relegated them to bottom place among the Test-playing countries.

SRI LANKA		Runs	Balls	4/6
R.S.Mahanama	b Wasim	12	36	1
M.A.R.Samarasekera	st Moin b Mushtaq	38	59	1
U.C.Hathurusinghe	b Mushtaq	5	29	–
*P.A.de Silva	c Aamir b Ijaz	43	56	2
A.P.Gurusinha	c Salim b Imran	37	54	2
A.Ranatunga	c sub (Zahid Fazal) b Aamir	7	19	–
†H.P.Tillekeratne	not out	25	34	3
R.S.Kalpage	not out	13	14	–
C.P.H.Ramanayake				
K.I.W.Wijegunawardene				
G.P.Wickremasinghe				
Extras	(lb 15, w 11, nb 6)	32		
Total	(50 overs; 6 wickets)	**212**		

PAKISTAN		Runs	Balls	4/6
Aamir Sohail	c Mahanama b Ramanayake	1	10	–
Ramiz Raja	c Gurusinha b Wickremasinghe	32	56	3
*Imran Khan	c De Silva b Hathurusinghe	22	69	2
Javed Miandad	c Wickremasinghe b Gurusinha	57	84	3
Salim Malik	c Kalpage b Ramanayake	51	66	2
Inzamam-ul-Haq	run out	11	11	–
Ijaz Ahmed	not out	8	6	1
Wasim Akram	not out	5	5	1
†Moin Khan				
Mushtaq Ahmed				
Aqib Javed				
Extras	(lb 12, w 9, nb 8)	29		
Total	(49.1 overs; 6 wickets)	**216**		

PAKISTAN	O	M	R	W
Wasim Akram	10	0	37	1
Aqib Javed	10	0	39	0
Imran Khan	8	1	36	1
Mushtaq Ahmed	10	0	43	2
Ijaz Ahmed	8	0	28	1
Aamir Sohail	4	0	14	1

SRI LANKA	O	M	R	W
Wijegunawardene	10	1	34	0
Ramanayake	10	1	37	2
Wickremasinghe	9.1	0	41	1
Gurusinha	9	0	38	1
Hathurusinghe	9	0	40	1
Kalpage	2	0	14	0

FALL OF WICKETS
1-20, 2-48, 3-99, 4-132, 5-158, 6-187

FALL OF WICKETS
1-7, 2-68, 3-84, 4-185, 5-201, 6-205

Umpires: K.E.Liebenberg (*South Africa*) (6) and P.J.McConnell (68).

NEW ZEALAND v PAKISTAN 1991-92

At Lancaster Park, Christchurch, New Zealand, on 18 March 1992. Result: **PAKISTAN** won by 7 wickets. Toss: Pakistan.
Award: Mushtaq Ahmed. LOI debuts: None.

Pakistan's victory ended New Zealand's unbeaten run, despatched the holders, Australia, and, when West Indies lost later the same day, gained them a semi-final place. Ramiz Raja registered the highest score of the tournament and regained the national World Cup record.

NEW ZEALAND		Runs	Balls	4/6
M.J.Greatbatch	c Salim b Mushtaq	42	67	5/1
R.T.Latham	c Inzamam b Aqib	6	9	1
A.H.Jones	lbw b Wasim	2	3	–
*M.D.Crowe	c Aamir b Wasim	3	20	–
K.R.Rutherford	run out	8	35	–
C.Z.Harris	st Moin b Mushtaq	1	6	–
D.N.Patel	c Mushtaq b Aamir	7	13	–
†I.D.S.Smith	b Imran	1	4	–
G.R.Larsen	b Wasim	37	80	3
D.K.Morrison	c Inzamam b Wasim	12	45	1
W.Watson	not out	5	13	–
Extras	(b 3, lb 23, w 12, nb 4)	42		
Total	(48.2 overs)	166		

PAKISTAN		Runs	Balls	4/6
Aamir Sohail	c Patel b Morrison	0	1	–
Ramiz Raja	not out	119	155	16
Inzamam-ul-Haq	b Morrison	5	8	1
Javed Miandad	lbw b Morrison	30	85	1
Salim Malik	not out	9	23	1
*Imran Khan				
Wasim Akram				
Ijaz Ahmed				
†Moin Khan				
Mushtaq Ahmed				
Aqib Javed				
Extras	(lb 1, w 1, nb 2)	4		
Total	(44.4 overs; 3 wickets)	167		

PAKISTAN	O	M	R	W
Wasim Akram	9.2	0	32	4
Aqib Javed	10	1	34	1
Mushtaq Ahmed	10	0	18	2
Imran Khan	8	0	22	1
Aamir Sohail	10	1	29	1
Ijaz Ahmed	1	0	5	0

NEW ZEALAND	O	M	R	W
Morrison	10	0	42	3
Patel	10	2	25	0
Watson	10	3	26	0
Harris	4	0	18	0
Larsen	3	0	16	0
Jones	3	0	10	0
Latham	2	0	13	0
Rutherford	1.4	0	11	0
Greatbatch	1	0	5	0

FALL OF WICKETS
1-23, 2-26, 3-39, 4-85, 5-88, 6-93, 7-96, 8-106, 9-150, 10-166

FALL OF WICKETS
1-0, 2-9, 3-124

Umpires: S.A.Bucknor (*West Indies*) (10) and S.G.Randell (*Australia*) (50).

ENGLAND v ZIMBABWE 1991-92

At Lavington Sports Ground, Albury, Australia, on 18 March 1992. Result: **ZIMBABWE** won by 9 runs.
Toss: England. Award: E.A.Brandes. LOI debuts: None.

The NSW-Victoria border city of Albury provided the 97th LOI venue (the sixth new ground of this tournament) and the shock result of the season. Zimbabwe ended a World Cup and LOI record sequence of 18 defeats when they narrowly defended their lowest total to date.

ZIMBABWE		Runs	Balls	4/6
W.R.James	c and b Illingworth	13	46	1
†A.Flower	b DeFreitas	7	16	1
A.J.Pycroft	c Gooch b Botham	3	13	–
K.J.Arnott	lbw b Botham	11	33	–
*D.L.Houghton	c Fairbrother b Small	29	74	2
A.C.Waller	b Tufnell	8	16	1
A.H.Shah	c Lamb b Tufnell	3	16	–
I.P.Butchart	c Fairbrother b Botham	24	36	2
E.A.Brandes	st Stewart b Illingworth	14	24	1
A.J.Traicos	not out	0	6	–
M.P.Jarvis	lbw b Illingworth	6	6	–
Extras	(lb 8, w 8)	16		
Total	(46.1 overs)	134		

ENGLAND		Runs	Balls	4/6
*G.A.Gooch	lbw b Brandes	0	1	–
I.T.Botham	c Flower b Shah	18	34	4
A.J.Lamb	c James b Brandes	17	26	2
R.A.Smith	b Brandes	2	13	–
G.A.Hick	b Brandes	0	6	–
N.H.Fairbrother	c Flower b Butchart	20	77	–
†A.J.Stewart	c Waller b Shah	29	96	3
P.A.J.DeFreitas	c Flower b Butchart	4	17	–
R.K.Illingworth	run out	11	20	–
G.C.Small	c Pycroft b Jarvis	5	18	–
P.C.R.Tufnell	not out	0		–
Extras	(b 4, lb 3, w 11, nb1)	19		
Total	(49.1 overs)	125		

ENGLAND	O	M	R	W
DeFreitas	8	1	14	1
Small	9	1	20	1
Botham	10	2	23	3
Illingworth	9.1	0	33	3
Tufnell	10	2	36	2

ZIMBABWE	O	M	R	W
Brandes	10	4	21	4
Jarvis	9.1	0	32	1
Shah	10	3	17	2
Traicos	10	4	16	0
Butchart	10	1	32	2

FALL OF WICKETS
1-12, 2-19, 3-30, 4-52, 5-65, 6-77, 7-96, 8-127, 9-127, 10-134

FALL OF WICKETS
1-0, 2-32, 3-42, 4-42, 5-43, 6-95, 7-101, 8-108, 9-124, 10-125

Umpires: B.L.Aldridge (*New Zealand*) (25) and Khizer Hayat (*Pakistan*) (44).

AUSTRALIA v WEST INDIES 1991-92

At Melbourne Cricket Ground, Australia, on 18 March 1992. Result: **AUSTRALIA** won by 57 runs. Toss: Australia.
Award: D.C.Boon. LOI debuts: None.

Australia's win enabled the holders to finish fifth in the qualifying table (final order: New Zealand, England, South Africa, Pakistan, Australia, West Indies, India, Sri Lanka, Zimbabwe). Desmond Haynes became the second after Allan Border to appear in 200 internationals. The last of David Boon's five hundreds took him beyond 4000 runs.

AUSTRALIA		Runs	Balls	4/6
T.M.Moody	c Benjamin b Simmons	42	70	3
D.C.Boon	c Williams b Cummins	100	147	8
D.M.Jones	c Williams b Cummins	6	14	–
* A.R.Border	lbw b Simmons	8	10	1
M.E.Waugh	st Williams b Hooper	21	31	–
S.R.Waugh	b Cummins	6	14	–
† I.A.Healy	not out	11	11	–
P.L.Taylor	not out	10	6	1
C.J.McDermott				
M.R.Whitney				
B.A.Reid				
Extras	(lb 3, w 3, nb 6)	12		
Total	(50 overs; 6 wickets)	**216**		

WEST INDIES		Runs	Balls	4/6
D.L.Haynes	c Jones b McDermott	14	24	2
B.C.Lara	run out	70	97	3
P.V.Simmons	lbw b McDermott	0	1	–
* R.B.Richardson	c Healy b Whitney	10	44	–
K.L.T.Arthurton	c McDermott b Whitney	15	15	2
A.L.Logie	c Healy b Whitney	5	15	–
C.L.Hooper	c M.E.Waugh b Whitney	4	11	–
† D.Williams	c Border b Reid	4	15	–
W.K.M.Benjamin	lbw b S.R.Waugh	15	21	1
C.E.L.Ambrose	run out	2	7	–
A.C.Cummins	not out	5	10	–
Extras	(b 3, lb 5, w 3, nb 4)	15		
Total	(42.4 overs)	**159**		

WEST INDIES	O	M	R	W
Ambrose	10	0	46	0
Benjamin	10	1	49	0
Cummins	10	1	38	3
Hooper	10	0	40	1
Simmons	10	1	40	2

AUSTRALIA	O	M	R	W
McDermott	6	1	29	2
Reid	10	1	26	1
Whitney	10	1	34	4
S.R.Waugh	6.4	0	24	1
Taylor	4	0	24	1
Moody	6	1	14	0

FALL OF WICKETS
1-107, 2-128, 3-141, 4-185, 5-189, 6-200

FALL OF WICKETS
1-27, 2-27, 3-59, 4-83, 5-99, 6-117, 7-128, 8-137, 9-150, 10-159

Umpires: P.D.Reporter (*India*) (19) and D.R.Shepherd (*England*) (47).

NEW ZEALAND v PAKISTAN 1991-92

At Eden Park, Auckland, New Zealand, on 21 March 1992. Result: **PAKISTAN** won by 4 wickets. Toss: New Zealand.
Award: Inzamam-ul-Haq. LOI debuts: None.

A devastating display of hitting by Inzamam-ul-Haq, which included a 31-ball fifty, helped Pakistan to their highest World Cup total batting second. Martin Crowe, whose hamstring strain (when 82) required a runner, took his tournament aggregate to 456 runs (avge 114.00). Ramiz Raja scored his 4000th LOI run.

NEW ZEALAND		Runs	Balls	4/6
M.J.Greatbatch	b Aqib	17	22	–/2
J.G.Wright	c Ramiz b Mushtaq	13	44	1
A.H.Jones	lbw b Mushtaq	21	53	2
* M.D.Crowe	run out	91	83	7/3
K.R.Rutherford	c Moin b Wasim	50	68	5/1
C.Z.Harris	st Moin b Iqbal	13	12	1
† I.D.S.Smith	not out	18	10	3
D.N.Patel	lbw b Wasim	8	6	1
G.R.Larsen	not out	8	6	1
D.K.Morrison				
W.Watson				
Extras	(lb 11, w 8, nb 4)	23		
Total	(50 overs; 7 wickets)	**262**		

PAKISTAN		Runs	Balls	4/6
Aamir Sohail	c Jones b Patel	14	20	1
Ramiz Raja	c Morrison b Watson	44	55	6
* Imran Khan	c Larsen b Harris	44	93	1/2
Javed Miandad	not out	57	69	4
Salim Malik	c sub (R.T.Latham) b Larsen	1	2	–
Inzamam-ul-Haq	run out	60	37	7/1
Wasim Akram	b Watson	9	8	1
† Moin Khan	not out	20	11	2/1
Mushtaq Ahmed				
Iqbal Sikander				
Aqib Javed				
Extras	(b 4, lb 10, w 1)	15		
Total	(49 overs; 6 wickets)	**264**		

PAKISTAN	O	M	R	W
Wasim Akram	10	1	40	2
Aqib Javed	10	2	45	1
Mushtaq Ahmed	10	0	40	2
Imran Khan	10	0	59	0
Iqbal Sikander	9	0	56	1
Aamir Sohail	1	0	11	0

NEW ZEALAND	O	M	R	W
Patel	10	1	50	1
Morrison	9	0	55	0
Watson	10	2	39	2
Larsen	10	1	34	1
Harris	10	0	72	1

FALL OF WICKETS
1-35, 2-39, 3-87, 4-194, 5-214, 6-221, 7-244

FALL OF WICKETS
1-30, 2-84, 3-134, 4-140, 5-227, 6-238

Umpires: S.A.Bucknor (*West Indies*) (11) and D.R.Shepherd (*England*) (48).

ENGLAND v SOUTH AFRICA 1991-92

At Sydney Cricket Ground, Australia, on 22 March 1992.   Result: **ENGLAND** won by 19 runs (*revised target*).
Toss: South Africa.   Award: G.A.Hick.   LOI debuts: None.

The 'highest scoring overs' rain regulation produced its most farcical and unjust revision of the tournament when South Africa, 231 for 6 off 42.5 overs when rain halted play for 17 minutes, were required to score 252 runs from 43 overs – effectively 21 runs off one ball. The losers were fined 20% of their match fees for their sluggish over rate.

ENGLAND		Runs	Balls	4/6
* G.A.Gooch	c Richardson b Donald	2	8	–
I.T.Botham	b Pringle	21	27	3
† A.J.Stewart	c Richardson b McMillan	33	58	4
G.A.Hick	c Rhodes b Snell	83	90	9
N.H.Fairbrother	b Pringle	28	50	1
A.J.Lamb	c Richardson b Donald	19	22	1
C.C.Lewis	not out	18	17	2
D.A.Reeve	not out	25	14	4
P.A.J.DeFreitas				
G.C.Small				
R.K.Illingworth				
Extras	(b 1, lb 7, w 9, nb 6)	23		
Total	(45 overs; 6 wickets)	252		

SOUTH AFRICA		Runs	Balls	4/6
* K.C.Wessels	c Lewis b Botham	17	23	1
A.C.Hudson	lbw b Illingworth	46	53	6
P.N.Kirsten	b DeFreitas	11	26	–
A.P.Kuiper	b Illingworth	36	44	5
W.J.Cronje	c Hick b Small	24	46	1
J.N.Rhodes	c Lewis b Small	43	39	3
B.M.McMillan	not out	21	21	–
† D.J.Richardson	not out	13	10	1
R.P.Snell				
M.W.Pringle				
A.A.Donald				
Extras	(lb 17, w 4)	21		
Total	(43 overs; 6 wickets)	232		

SOUTH AFRICA	O	M	R	W
Donald	10	0	69	2
Pringle	9	2	36	2
Snell	8	0	52	1
McMillan	9	0	47	1
Kuiper	5	0	26	0
Cronje	4	0	14	0

ENGLAND	O	M	R	W
Botham	10	0	52	1
Lewis	5	0	38	0
DeFreitas	8	1	28	1
Illingworth	10	1	46	2
Small	10	1	51	2

FALL OF WICKETS
1-20, 2-39, 3-110, 4-183, 5-187, 6-221

FALL OF WICKETS
1-26, 2-61, 3-90, 4-131, 5-176, 6-206

Umpires: B.L.Aldridge (*New Zealand*) (26) and S.G.Randell (51).

ENGLAND v PAKISTAN 1991-92

At Melbourne Cricket Ground, Australia, on 25 March 1992.   Result: **PAKISTAN** won by 22 runs.   Toss: Pakistan.
Award: Wasim Akram.   LOI debuts: None.

An Australian record LOI crowd of 87,182 saw Sir Colin Cowdrey, president of ICC, present Imran Khan with the new World Cup, a Waterford crystal globe, after Pakistan had won their first title and relegated England to runners-up for the third time. Javed Miandad surpassed Vivian Richards's career record of 1013 World Cup runs.

PAKISTAN		Runs	Balls	4/6
Aamir Sohail	c Stewart b Pringle	4	19	–
Ramiz Raja	lbw b Pringle	8	26	1
* Imran Khan	c Illingworth b Botham	72	110	5/1
Javed Miandad	c Botham b Illingworth	58	98	4
Inzamam-ul-Haq	b Pringle	42	35	4
Wasim Akram	run out	33	19	4
Salim Malik	not out	0	1	–
Ijaz Ahmed				
† Moin Khan				
Mushtaq Ahmed				
Aqib Javed				
Extras	(lb 19, w 6, nb 7)	32		
Total	(50 overs; 6 wickets)	249		

ENGLAND		Runs	Balls	4/6
* G.A.Gooch	c Aqib b Mushtaq	29	66	1
I.T.Botham	c Moin b Wasim	0	6	–
† A.J.Stewart	c Moin b Aqib	7	16	1
G.A.Hick	lbw b Mushtaq	17	36	1
N.H.Fairbrother	c Moin b Aqib	62	70	3
A.J.Lamb	b Wasim	31	41	2
C.C.Lewis	b Wasim	0	1	–
D.A.Reeve	c Ramiz b Mushtaq	15	32	1
D.R.Pringle	not out	18	16	1
P.A.J.DeFreitas	run out	10	8	–
R.K.Illingworth	c Ramiz b Imran	14	11	2
Extras	(lb 5, w 13, nb 6)	24		
Total	(49.2 overs)	227		

ENGLAND	O	M	R	W
Pringle	10	2	22	3
Lewis	10	2	52	0
Botham	7	0	42	1
DeFreitas	10	1	42	0
Illingworth	10	0	50	1
Reeve	3	0	22	0

PAKISTAN	O	M	R	W
Wasim Akram	10	0	49	3
Aqib Javed	10	2	27	2
Mushtaq Ahmed	10	1	41	3
Ijaz Ahmed	3	0	13	0
Imran Khan	6.2	0	43	1
Aamir Sohail	10	0	49	0

FALL OF WICKETS
1-20, 2-24, 3-163, 4-197, 5-249, 6-249

FALL OF WICKETS
1-6, 2-21, 3-59, 4-69, 5-141, 6-141, 7-180, 8-183, 9-208, 10-227

Umpires: B.L.Aldridge (*New Zealand*) (27) and S.A.Bucknor (*West Indies*) (12).

WEST INDIES v SOUTH AFRICA 1991-92

At Sabina Park, Kingston, Jamaica on 7 April 1992.   Result: **WEST INDIES** won by 107 runs.   Toss: South Africa.
Award: P.V.Simmons.   LOI debuts: South Africa – C.J.P.G. van Zyl.

The five sixes struck between long-on and extra-cover by Phil Simmons (100 off 102 balls) remain the most conceded
by South Africa in an individual innings. One caused a five-minute delay when it was stolen from a neighbouring garden
and had to be retrieved by police.

WEST INDIES		Runs	Balls	4/6
D.L.Haynes	c Henry b Donald	9	27	–
B.C.Lara	c Wessels b Henry	50	68	4
P.V.Simmons	c Wessels b Kuiper	122	113	12/5
* R.B.Richardson	lbw b Kuiper	30	47	–
K.L.T.Arthurton	c Wessels b Donald	27	27	1
C.L.Hooper	not out	19	18	–
W.K.M.Benjamin	c Wessels b Kuiper	8	5	1
C.E.L.Ambrose	not out	0	–	–
† D.Williams				
A.C.Cummins				
B.P.Patterson				
Extras	(b 1, lb 5, w 12, nb 4)	22		
Total	(50 overs; 6 wickets)	**287**		

SOUTH AFRICA		Runs	Balls	4/6
A.C.Hudson	c and b Patterson	50	70	5
* K.C.Wessels	run out	8	17	1
P.N.Kirsten	c Lara b Patterson	15	39	2
A.P.Kuiper	st Williams b Hooper	15	35	–
W.J.Cronje	b Cummins	42	56	–/1
J.N.Rhodes	b Cummins	17	17	1
R.P.Snell	run out	1	2	–
† D.J.Richardson	c Arthurton b Benjamin	5	8	–
C.J.P.G.van Zyl	c Ambrose b Benjamin	0	9	–
O.Henry	b Benjamin	1	3	–
A.A.Donald	not out	5	3	1
Extras	(lb 8, w 10, nb 3)	21		
Total	(42.2 overs)	**180**		

SOUTH AFRICA	O	M	R	W
Donald	10	1	47	2
Snell	10	1	56	0
Van Zyl	8	2	53	0
Henry	10	0	53	1
Cronje	3	0	18	0
Kirsten	4	0	21	0
Kuiper	5	0	33	3

WEST INDIES	O	M	R	W
Ambrose	7	1	20	0
Patterson	7	2	17	2
Benjamin	9.2	0	45	3
Cummins	9	0	34	2
Hooper	8	0	44	1
Simmons	2	0	12	0

FALL OF WICKETS
1-32, 2-104, 3-209, 4-238, 5-277, 6-286

FALL OF WICKETS
1-10, 2-79, 3-82, 4-121, 5-153, 6-155, 7-161, 8-168, 9-174, 10-180

Umpires: S.A.Bucknor (13) and G.T.Johnson (2).

WEST INDIES v SOUTH AFRICA 1991-92

At Queen's Park Oval, Port-of-Spain, Trinidad on 11 April 1992.   Result: **WEST INDIES** won by 10 wickets.
Toss: West Indies.   Award: B.C.Lara.   LOI debuts: None.

This was the ninth and last instance of victory by a ten-wicket margin prior to 1997 and the fifth by West Indies. The
unbroken 154 shared by Desmond Haynes and Brian Lara remains the best LOI opening stand achieved by any side
against South Africa.

SOUTH AFRICA		Runs	Balls	4/6
A.C.Hudson	run out	6	26	1
* K.C.Wessels	c Williams b Ambrose	1	9	–
P.N.Kirsten	c Benjamin b Cummins	9	23	1
A.P.Kuiper	c Lara b Harper	19	64	–
W.J.Cronje	run out	22	30	4
J.N.Rhodes	run out	45	71	5
† D.J.Richardson	c Arthurton b Cummins	6	15	–
R.P.Snell	c Arthurton b Cummins	8	10	–
O.Henry	not out	8	10	1
M.W.Pringle	b Ambrose	1	4	–
A.A.Donald	b Ambrose	0	2	–
Extras	(lb 10, w 15, nb 2)	27		
Total	(43.4 overs)	**152**		

WEST INDIES		Runs	Balls	4/6
D.L.Haynes	not out	59	71	7/1
B.C.Lara	not out	86	91	13/2
P.V.Simmons				
* R.B.Richardson				
K.L.T.Arthurton				
R.A.Harper				
W.K.M.Benjamin				
C.E.L.Ambrose				
† D.Williams				
A.C.Cummins				
B.P.Patterson				
Extras	(b 1, lb 1, w 2, nb 5)	9		
Total	(25.5 overs; 0 wickets)	**154**		

WEST INDIES	O	M	R	W
Ambrose	7.4	0	24	3
Patterson	9	2	30	0
Cummins	9	0	40	3
Benjamin	8	0	21	0
Harper	10	0	27	1

SOUTH AFRICA	O	M	R	W
Donald	8	1	49	0
Pringle	7	0	32	0
Henry	4.5	0	41	0
Snell	6	0	30	0

FALL OF WICKETS
1-17, 2-24, 3-36, 4-67, 5-98, 6-118, 7-138, 8-146, 9-152, 10-152

Umpires: L.H.Barker (18) and C.E.Cumberbatch (15).

WEST INDIES v SOUTH AFRICA 1991-92

At Queen's Park Oval, Port-of-Spain, Trinidad on 12 April 1992.   Result: **WEST INDIES** won by 7 wickets.
Toss: West Indies.   Award: P.V.Simmons.   LOI debuts: None.

With his third hundred in four innings, Phil Simmons carried West Indies to a clean sweep in this inaugural series against South Africa.

SOUTH AFRICA		Runs	Balls	4/6
A.C.Hudson	c Williams b Harper	30	54	4
M.W.Rushmere	c and b Harper	29	71	2
* K.C.Wessels	b Benjamin	45	77	3
P.N.Kirsten	c Harper b Benjamin	28	50	2
A.P.Kuiper	c Richardson b Patterson	2	6	–
W.J.Cronje	run out	23	23	–/1
† D.J.Richardson	not out	17	18	–
C.J.P.G.van Zyl	not out	3	2	–
R.P.Snell				
M.W.Pringle				
T.Bosch				
Extras	(lb 8, w 3, nb 1)	12		
Total	(50 overs; 6 wickets)	189		

WEST INDIES		Runs	Balls	4/6
D.L.Haynes	b Pringle	0	1	–
B.C.Lara	c Pringle b Kuiper	35	73	4
P.V.Simmons	c Cronje b Snell	104	139	10/2
* R.B.Richardson	not out	37	44	2
K.L.T.Arthurton	not out	1	4	–
R.A.Harper				
W.K.M.Benjamin				
C.E.L.Ambrose				
† D.Williams				
A.C.Cummins				
B.P.Patterson				
Extras	(lb 7, w 4, nb 2)	13		
Total	(43 overs; 3 wickets)	190		

WEST INDIES	O	M	R	W
Ambrose	10	1	39	0
Patterson	10	2	35	1
Benjamin	10	1	37	2
Cummins	10	0	39	0
Harper	10	0	31	2

SOUTH AFRICA	O	M	R	W
Pringle	5	3	6	1
Bosch	6	0	47	0
Snell	10	2	45	1
Van Zyl	10	0	40	0
Kuiper	7	0	28	1
Kirsten	5	0	17	0

FALL OF WICKETS
1-54, 2-67, 3-135, 4-139, 5-142, 6-185

FALL OF WICKETS
1-0, 2-78, 3-182

Umpires: L.H.Barker (19) and C.E.Cumberbatch (16).

ENGLAND v PAKISTAN 1992

At Lord's, London on 20 May 1992.   Result: **ENGLAND** won by 79 runs.   Toss: Pakistan.
Award: R.A.Smith.   LOI debuts: None.

An attendance of 26,654 produced record gate receipts for a day's cricket in England: £707,584. England gained a small measure of atonement for losing the World Cup final exactly eight weeks earlier.

ENGLAND		Runs	Balls	4/6
* G.A.Gooch	c Moin b Aqib	9	24	1
† A.J.Stewart	c Asif b Naved	50	69	4
R.A.Smith	c Moin b Aqib	85	117	7
A.J.Lamb	c Miandad b Naved	60	70	5
N.H.Fairbrother	c Asif b Aqib	25	28	2
G.A.Hick	b Wasim	3	9	–
I.T.Botham	not out	10	15	–
C.C.Lewis	not out	6	6	–
D.R.Pringle				
P.A.J.DeFreitas				
R.K.Illingworth				
Extras	(lb 14, w 9, nb 7)	30		
Total	(55 overs; 6 wickets)	278		

PAKISTAN		Runs	Balls	4/6
Aamir Sohail	run out	36	68	3
Ramiz Raja	c and b Pringle	0	2	–
Salim Malik	c Stewart b Botham	24	38	4
* Javed Miandad	c Hick b Pringle	7	18	–
Inzamam-ul-Haq	c and b Botham	2	3	–
Asif Mujtaba	c Smith b Hick	52	81	2
Wasim Akram	st Stewart b Illingworth	34	61	2
Naved Anjum	c Hick b Pringle	3	6	–
† Moin Khan	c Stewart b Pringle	11	21	–
Mushtaq Ahmed	not out	7	21	–
Aqib Javed	b Hick	8	9	1
Extras	(lb 8, w 5, nb 2)	15		
Total	(54.2 overs)	199		

PAKISTAN	O	M	R	W
Wasim Akram	11	0	39	1
Aqib Javed	11	0	54	3
Naved Anjum	11	0	48	2
Mushtaq Ahmed	11	0	56	0
Asif Mujtaba	11	0	67	0

ENGLAND	O	M	R	W
DeFreitas	9	2	17	0
Pringle	11	1	42	4
Lewis	8	0	35	0
Botham	11	0	45	2
Illingworth	11	0	36	1
Hick	3.2	0	7	2
Fairbrother	1	0	9	0

FALL OF WICKETS
1-20, 2-115, 3-213, 4-238, 5-250, 6-268

FALL OF WICKETS
1-0, 2-49, 3-74, 4-78, 5-78, 6-161, 7-164, 8-181, 9-184, 10-199

Umpires: B.J.Meyer (22) and D.R.Shepherd (49).

ENGLAND v PAKISTAN 1992

At Kennington Oval, London on 22 May 1992.   Result: ENGLAND won by 39 runs.   Toss: England.
Award: A.J.Stewart.   LOI debuts: Pakistan – Tanvir Mehdi.

England's total was the highest in Texaco Trophy internationals until the next match. Neil Fairbrother and Graeme Hick added 93 off 66 balls, their fifties taking 55 and 44 balls respectively.

ENGLAND		Runs	Balls	4/6
* G.A.Gooch	run out	25	48	3
† A.J.Stewart	b Aqib	103	145	10
R.A.Smith	b Mushtaq	7	13	1
A.J.Lamb	st Moin Khan b Aamir	11	10	1
N.H.Fairbrother	b Tanvir	63	65	3
G.A.Hick	not out	71	51	8/1
I.T.Botham	not out	2	3	–
C.C.Lewis				
D.R.Pringle				
P.A.J.DeFreitas				
R.K.Illingworth				
Extras	(lb 8, w 9, nb 3)	20		
Total	(55 overs; 5 wickets)	302		

PAKISTAN		Runs	Balls	4/6
Aamir Sohail	b Illingworth	32	33	3
Ramiz Raja	c sub ‡ b DeFreitas	86	96	11
Salim Malik	b Pringle	26	40	1
Inzamam-ul-Haq	lbw b Pringle	15	15	3
* Javed Miandad	lbw b Botham	38	50	4
Asif Mujtaba	lbw b Illingworth	29	37	2
Naved Anjum	run out	6	8	–
† Moin Khan	c and b Lewis	15	16	1
Mushtaq Ahmed	c Illingworth b Lewis	8	7	1
Tanvir Mehdi	b DeFreitas	0	5	–
Aqib Javed	not out	0	–	–
Extras	(lb 4, w 3, nb 1)	8		
Total	(50.5 overs)	263		

PAKISTAN	O	M	R	W
Aqib Javed	10	0	70	1
Naved Anjum	9	0	37	0
Tanvir Mehdi	11	0	72	1
Mushtaq Ahmed	11	0	47	1
Aamir Sohail	11	0	52	1
Asif Mujtaba	3	0	16	0

ENGLAND	O	M	R	W
DeFreitas	10.5	0	59	2
Lewis	8	0	47	2
Botham	11	0	52	1
Illingworth	11	0	58	2
Pringle	9	1	35	2
Hick	1	0	8	0

FALL OF WICKETS
1-71, 2-81, 3-108, 4-202, 5-295

FALL OF WICKETS
1-81, 2-144, 3-148, 4-174, 5-220, 6-232, 7-249, 8-263, 9-263, 10-263

Umpires: M.J.Kitchen (8) and R.Palmer (5).

‡ (M.R.Ramprakash)

ENGLAND v PAKISTAN 1992

At Trent Bridge, Nottingham on 20 August 1992.   Result: ENGLAND won by 198 runs.   Toss: Pakistan.
Award: R.A.Smith.   LOI debuts: Pakistan – Rashid Latif.

England's total was the highest in all limited-overs internationals until 1995-96 (LOI No. 1073). Graeme Hick's 34-ball fifty remains the fastest in Texaco Trophy matches. England's victory is the fourth-largest by a runs margin.

ENGLAND		Runs	Balls	4/6
* G.A.Gooch	b Waqar	42	62	5
† A.J.Stewart	c Wasim b Waqar	34	52	4
R.A.Smith	c Ramiz b Aqib	77	72	6/2
N.H.Fairbrother	b Aqib	62	63	4/2
A.J.Lamb	lbw b Waqar	16	22	1
G.A.Hick	b Wasim	63	42	7/2
I.T.Botham	c Ramiz b Waqar	24	17	1/1
C.C.Lewis	not out	1	1	–
P.A.J.DeFreitas	not out	5	3	–
R.K.Illingworth				
G.C.Small				
Extras	(b 4, lb 12, w 18, nb 5)	39		
Total	(55 overs; 7 wickets)	363		

PAKISTAN		Runs	Balls	4/6
Aamir Sohail	c Botham b Lewis	17	20	3
Ramiz Raja	c Gooch b DeFreitas	0	1	–
* Salim Malik	c Small b Illingworth	45	57	4
Asif Mujtaba	c Lewis b DeFreitas	1	3	–
Inzamam-ul-Haq	run out	10	29	–
Ijaz Ahmed	c Gooch b Botham	23	33	3
Wasim Akram	lbw b Illingworth	1	2	–
† Rashid Latif	st Stewart b Illingworth	29	57	3
Waqar Younis	c Hick b DeFreitas	13	33	1
Mushtaq Ahmed	not out	14	31	2
Aqib Javed	c Stewart b Small	2	11	–
Extras	(lb 5, w 5)	10		
Total	(46.1 overs)	165		

PAKISTAN	O	M	R	W
Wasim Akram	11	0	55	1
Aqib Javed	11	0	55	2
Waqar Younis	11	0	73	4
Mushtaq Ahmed	11	1	58	0
Ijaz Ahmed	4	0	29	0
Aamir Sohail	3	0	34	0
Asif Mujtaba	4	0	43	0

ENGLAND	O	M	R	W
DeFreitas	11	1	33	3
Lewis	8	2	24	1
Botham	11	1	41	1
Small	5.1	0	28	1
Illingworth	11	1	34	3

FALL OF WICKETS
1-2, 2-22, 3-27, 4-60, 5-87, 6-98, 7-103, 8-129, 9-153, 10-165

FALL OF WICKETS
1-84, 2-95, 3-224, 4-250, 5-269, 6-353, 7-357

Umpires: B.Dudleston (1) and D.R.Shepherd (50).

ENGLAND v PAKISTAN 1992

At Lord's, London on 22, 23 August 1992.　　Result: **PAKISTAN** won by 3 runs.　Toss: Pakistan.
Award: Javed Miandad.　　LOI debuts: England – R.J.Blakey.

The enthralling finish to this match, a contest spread over two days and reduced to 50 overs each by a delayed start, was swiftly forgotten when it was revealed that Allan Lamb, during the innings in which he passed 4000 runs, had asked the umpires to change the ball because (allegedly) it had been tampered with.

PAKISTAN		Runs	Balls	4/6
Aamir Sohail	c Stewart b DeFreitas	20	35	3
Ramiz Raja	c Stewart b Botham	23	74	–
Salim Malik	st Blakey b Illingworth	48	76	3
* Javed Miandad	not out	50	60	5
Inzamam-ul-Haq	c Blakey b Reeve	16	25	2
Wasim Akram	b DeFreitas	23	26	2
Naved Anjum	not out	4	4	–
† Moin Khan				
Waqar Younis				
Mushtaq Ahmed				
Aqib Javed				
Extras	(b 2, lb 7, w 11)	20		
Total	(50 overs; 5 wickets)	**204**		

ENGLAND		Runs	Balls	4/6
I.T.Botham	st Moin b Aamir	40	69	5
* A.J.Stewart	lbw b Waqar	0	5	–
R.A.Smith	c Moin b Aqib	4	22	–
N.H.Fairbrother	b Aqib	33	30	5
A.J.Lamb	c Moin b Mushtaq	55	78	3
G.A.Hick	b Aamir	8	16	–
† R.J.Blakey	b Waqar	25	49	3
D.A.Reeve	not out	6	16	–
C.C.Lewis	c sub (Asif Mujtaba) b Wasim	1	5	–
P.A.J.DeFreitas	c Mushtaq b Wasim	0	2	–
R.K.Illingworth	b Waqar	4	11	–
Extras	(lb 8, w 11, nb 6)	25		
Total	(49.2 overs)	**201**		

ENGLAND	O	M	R	W
DeFreitas	10	2	39	2
Lewis	10	0	49	0
Botham	10	1	33	1
Reeve	10	1	31	1
Illingworth	10	0	43	1

PAKISTAN	O	M	R	W
Wasim Akram	10	2	41	2
Waqar Younis	9.2	0	36	3
Mushtaq Ahmed	10	1	34	1
Aqib Javed	9	0	39	2
Aamir Sohail	5	0	22	2
Naved Anjum	6	0	21	0

FALL OF WICKETS
1-32, 2-91, 3-102, 4-137, 5-189

FALL OF WICKETS
1-15, 2-30, 3-72, 4-111, 5-139, 6-172, 7-191, 8-193, 9-193, 10-201

Umpires: J.H.Hampshire (5) and K.E.Palmer (17).

ENGLAND v PAKISTAN 1992

At Old Trafford, Manchester on 24 August 1992.　　Result: **ENGLAND** won by 6 wickets.　Toss: Pakistan.
Award: R.A.Smith.　　LOI debuts: England – D.G.Cork.

England completed a 4-1 win in their longest series of home internationals. Alec Stewart and Wasim Akram scored their 1000th LOI runs, the latter completing the career double in his 126th match.

PAKISTAN		Runs	Balls	4/6
Aamir Sohail	run out	87	140	6
* Ramiz Raja	run out	37	53	4
Shoaib Mohammed	b Reeve	9	19	–
Inzamam-ul-Haq	lbw b Cork	75	86	6/1
Asif Mujtaba	c Smith b DeFreitas	10	13	1
Wasim Akram	not out	15	13	1
Naved Anjum	not out	12	8	2
† Moin Khan				
Waqar Younis				
Mushtaq Ahmed				
Aqib Javed				
Extras	(lb 6, w 2, nb 1)	9		
Total	(55 overs; 5 wickets)	**254**		

ENGLAND		Runs	Balls	4/6
* G.A.Gooch	b Aamir	45	42	6
† A.J.Stewart	st Moin Khan b Aamir	51	55	6
R.A.Smith	not out	85	91	9/1
N.H.Fairbrother	b Waqar	15	31	–
A.J.Lamb	c Moin b Waqar	2	4	–
G.A.Hick	not out	42	46	2/2
I.T.Botham				
D.A.Reeve				
D.G.Cork				
P.A.J.DeFreitas				
R.K.Illingworth				
Extras	(lb 7, w 3, nb 5)	15		
Total	(43.4 overs; 4 wickets)	**255**		

ENGLAND	O	M	R	W
DeFreitas	11	1	52	1
Cork	11	1	37	1
Botham	11	0	43	0
Reeve	11	1	57	1
Illingworth	11	0	59	0

PAKISTAN	O	M	R	W
Wasim Akram	9.4	1	45	0
Waqar Younis	8	0	58	2
Aqib Javed	6	0	42	0
Mushtaq Ahmed	9	0	48	0
Aamir Sohail	7	0	29	2
Naved Anjum	4	0	26	0

FALL OF WICKETS
1-69, 2-90, 3-189, 4-210, 5-240

FALL OF WICKETS
1-98, 2-101, 3-149, 4-159

Umpires: H.D.Bird (61) and M.J.Kitchen (9).

SRI LANKA v AUSTRALIA 1992-93

At P.Saravanamuttu Stadium, Colombo on 15 August 1992.   Result: **SRI LANKA** won by 4 wickets.   Toss: Sri Lanka.
Award: P.A.de Silva.   LOI debuts: None.

Restored to the captaincy for his country's first home international since April 1987, Arjuna Ranatunga infuriated his opposite number by demanding a runner because of 'stomach cramps' for the last two crucial overs. Asanka Gurusinha and Aravinda de Silva (100 off 99 balls) shared Sri Lanka's highest third-wicket stand against Australia.

AUSTRALIA		Runs	Balls	4/6
T.M.Moody	c and b Kalpage	54	90	6
M.A.Taylor	c Tillekeratne b Kalpage	94	129	7
D.M.Jones	st Kaluwitharana b Anurasiri	30	38	2
D.C.Boon	lbw b Ramanayake	0	3	–
M.E.Waugh	b Wickremasinghe	31	30	1
* A.R.Border	not out	19	12	2/1
G.R.J.Matthews	not out	1	2	–
† I.A.Healy				
C.J.McDermott				
A.I.C.Dodemaide				
M.R.Whitney				
Extras	(b 2, lb 8, w 4, nb 4)	18		
Total	(50 overs; 5 wickets)	**247**		

SRI LANKA		Runs	Balls	4/6
R.S.Mahanama	b Whitney	0	8	–
H.P.Tillekeratne	c Healy b McDermott	7	21	1
A.P.Gurusinha	c Waugh b Matthews	53	101	4/1
P.A.de Silva	run out	105	105	12/2
* A.Ranatunga	not out	45	46	2/2
M.S.Atapattu	c Waugh b Whitney	4	8	–
† R.S.Kaluwitharana	b Dodemaide	1	3	–
R.S.Kalpage	not out	11	7	1
C.P.H.Ramanayake				
S.D.Anurasiri				
G.P.Wickremasinghe				
Extras	(b 4, lb 10, w 8, nb 3)	25		
Total	(49.2 overs; 6 wickets)	**251**		

SRI LANKA	O	M	R	W
Wickremasinghe	9	1	35	1
Ramanayake	10	0	54	1
Gurusinha	8	0	30	0
Ranatunga	3	0	22	0
Anurasiri	10	0	44	1
Kalpage	10	0	52	2

AUSTRALIA	O	M	R	W
McDermott	9.2	1	64	1
Whitney	10	1	33	2
Dodemaide	10	0	50	1
Moody	7	1	36	0
Matthews	10	0	34	1
Border	3	0	20	0

FALL OF WICKETS
1-109, 2-175, 3-176, 4-216, 5-244

FALL OF WICKETS
1-3, 2-12, 3-159, 4-202, 5-212, 6-214

Umpires: B.C.Cooray (7) and W.A.U.Wickremasinghe (6).

SRI LANKA v AUSTRALIA 1992-93

At Khettarama Stadium, Colombo on 4 September 1992.   Result: **SRI LANKA** won by 5 wickets (revised target).
Toss: Sri Lanka.   Award: U.C.Hathurusinghe.   LOI debuts: None.

A 22-minute rain break reduced Sri Lanka's target, calculated on the old runs/over formula, to 191 off 44 overs. Chandika Hathurusinghe (48) retired with leg cramp at 122 and resumed at 190 to complete his fifty with the winning boundary.

AUSTRALIA		Runs	Balls	4/6
T.M.Moody	c Tillekeratne b Gurusinha	17	43	1/1
M.A.Taylor	run out	30	64	3/1
D.M.Jones	not out	59	89	1/1
D.C.Boon	run out	35	58	3
M.E.Waugh	lbw b Ramanayake	10	19	–
* A.R.Border	c Kalpage b Ramanayake	30	23	1/1
G.R.J.Matthews	c Tillekeratne b Wickremasinghe	1	2	–
† I.A.Healy	run out	6	6	–
C.J.McDermott	not out	1	3	–
A.I.C.Dodemaide				
M.R.Whitney				
Extras	(b 1, lb 15, w 3, nb 8)	27		
Total	(50 overs; 7 wickets)	**216**		

SRI LANKA		Runs	Balls	4/6
R.S.Mahanama	run out	33	55	2
U.C.Hathurusinghe	not out	52	92	6
A.P.Gurusinha	lbw b Dodemaide	4	3	1
P.A.de Silva	c Whitney b Matthews	63	61	4
* A.Ranatunga	c Dodemaide b Matthews	22	35	2
S.T.Jayasuriya	b McDermott	2	5	–
† H.P.Tillekeratne	not out	2	10	–
R.S.Kalpage				
C.P.H.Ramanayake				
S.D.Anurasiri				
G.P.Wickremasinghe				
Extras	(b 2, lb 7, w 4, nb 3)	16		
Total	(42.5 overs; 5 wickets)	**194**		

SRI LANKA	O	M	R	W
Ramanayake	10	2	43	2
Wickremasinghe	10	0	40	1
Hathurusinghe	10	1	34	0
Gurusinha	4	1	21	1
Ranatunga	3	1	11	0
Anurasiri	5	0	20	0
Kalpage	8	0	31	0

AUSTRALIA	O	M	R	W
McDermott	9	0	44	1
Whitney	7	0	27	0
Dodemaide	10	1	39	1
Moody	9	0	35	0
Matthews	6.5	0	34	2
Waugh	1	0	6	0

FALL OF WICKETS
1-56, 2-65, 3-127, 4-149, 5-194, 6-197, 7-207

FALL OF WICKETS
1-71, 2-77, 3-172, 4-176, 5-190

Umpires: B.C.Cooray (8) and T.M.Samarasinghe (1).

SRI LANKA v AUSTRALIA 1992-93

At Khettarama Stadium, Colombo on 5 September 1992.   Result: **AUSTRALIA** won by 5 wickets.   Toss: Australia.
Award: D.C.Boon.   LOI debuts: None.

Witnessed by a full house estimated at 35,000, Craig McDermott dismissed Roshan Mahanama with the opening ball of the first illuminated match to be staged in Sri Lanka. The home team appeared in turquoise and the Australians in unfamiliar salmon pink.

SRI LANKA		Runs	Balls	4/6
R.S.Mahanama	c Taylor b McDermott	0	1	–
U.C.Hathurusinghe	c Boon b Matthews	46	17	6
A.P.Gurusinha	lbw b Matthews	49	90	5/1
P.A.de Silva	c Matthews b Dodemaide	39	50	2
* A.Ranatunga	b Whitney	15	29	1
S.T.Jayasuriya	b Whitney	7	12	1
† H.P.Tillekeratne	not out	35	38	3
R.S.Kalpage	not out	1	5	–
C.P.H.Ramanayake				
E.A.R.de Silva				
G.P.Wickremasinghe				
Extras	(b 1, lb 5, w 9)	15		
Total	(50 overs; 6 wickets)	**207**		

AUSTRALIA		Runs	Balls	4/6
M.A.Taylor	c Gurusinha b Hathurusinghe	14	38	1
T.M.Moody	c Mahanama b Ramanayake	13	25	–
D.M.Jones	st Tillekeratne b E.A.R.de Silva	17	27	2
D.C.Boon	not out	69	96	3
M.E.Waugh	run out	52	63	4
* A.R.Border	c Gurusinha b Ramanayake	14	26	–
G.R.J.Matthews	not out	10	16	1
† I.A.Healy				
C.J.McDermott				
A.I.C.Dodemaide				
M.R.Whitney				
Extras	(b 4, lb 7, w 4, nb 4)	19		
Total	(47.5 overs; 5 wickets)	**208**		

AUSTRALIA	O	M	R	W
McDermott	10	1	30	1
Dodemaide	10	1	44	1
Whitney	10	1	40	2
Matthews	10	1	33	2
Moody	7	0	38	0
Border	3	0	16	0

SRI LANKA	O	M	R	W
Ramanayake	8.5	0	34	2
Wickremasinghe	9	0	32	0
Gurusinha	2	0	8	0
Hathurusinghe	10	0	38	1
E.A.R.de Silva	10	0	47	1
Kalpage	6	0	28	0
Jayasuriya	2	0	10	0

FALL OF WICKETS
1-0, 2-101, 3-112, 4-137, 5-145, 6-197

FALL OF WICKETS
1-28, 2-39, 3-58, 4-142, 5-186

Umpires: I.Anandappa (1) and W.A.U.Wickremasinghe (7).

ZIMBABWE v INDIA 1992-93

At Harare Sports Club on 25 October 1992.   Result: **INDIA** won by 30 runs.   Toss: Zimbabwe.
Award: S.V.Manjrekar.   LOI debuts: Zimbabwe – D.H.Brain, G.J.Crocker, C.N.Evans, G.W.Flower.

Zimbabwe's first home international was inaugurated by President Robert Mugabe, Harare's Sports Club becoming the 98th LOI ground. David Brain took a wicket with his second ball. Fellow debutant Gary Crocker was surprisingly not given the match award for his four wickets and 50 runs.

INDIA		Runs	Balls	4/6
R.J.Shastri	c G.W.Flower b Burmester	1	4	–
A.Jadeja	b Brain	0	1	–
* M.Azharuddin	c Brain b Crocker	29	58	3
S.R.Tendulkar	c Brain b Crocker	39	56	7
S.V.Manjrekar	c A.Flower b Crocker	70	70	4
P.K.Amre	lbw b Traicos	36	55	–/1
Kapil Dev	c Evans b G.W.Flower	5	9	–
M.Prabhakar	c sub (S.G.Peall) b Crocker	19	24	1
† K.S.More	run out	22	19	2
J.Srinath	not out	1	1	–
A.Kumble	run out	1	1	–
Extras	(b 5, lb 4, w 7)	16		
Total	(49.4 overs)	**239**		

ZIMBABWE		Runs	Balls	4/6
† A.Flower	run out	62	104	3
G.W.Flower	b Srinath	34	67	4
A.H.Shah	run out	16	30	–
* D.L.Houghton	c Amre b Jadeja	4	8	–
A.C.Waller	c Kumble b Prabhakar	9	13	–/1
C.N.Evans	c Azharuddin b Kumble	1	6	–
G.J.Crocker	b Kapil Dev	50	55	2/2
D.H.Brain	b Srinath	8	9	1
A.D.R.Campbell	b Srinath	0	1	–
M.G.Burmester	b Prabhakar	11	7	2
A.J.Traicos	not out	0	–	–
Extras	(b 1, lb 6, w 4, nb 3)	14		
Total	(49.1 overs)	**209**		

ZIMBABWE	O	M	R	W
Brain	10	0	52	1
Burmester	6	0	38	1
Shah	10	1	23	0
Crocker	7.4	0	26	4
Traicos	10	0	48	1
G.W.Flower	6	0	43	1

INDIA	O	M	R	W
Kapil Dev	8.1	1	27	1
Prabhakar	10	0	43	2
Tendulkar	3	0	16	0
Srinath	10	1	35	3
Shastri	5	0	22	0
Jadeja	5	0	24	1
Kumble	8	0	35	1

FALL OF WICKETS
1-1, 2-1, 3-75, 4-78, 5-151, 6-168, 7-211, 8-223, 9-238, 10-239

FALL OF WICKETS
1-63, 2-88, 3-98, 4-120, 5-123, 6-181, 7-196, 8-196, 9-209, 10-209

Umpires: I.D.Robinson (2) and R.B.Tiffin (1).

ZIMBABWE v NEW ZEALAND 1992-93

At Bulawayo Athletic Club on 31 October 1992.　Result: NEW ZEALAND won by 22 runs.　Toss: Zimbabwe.
Award: D.N.Patel.　LOI debuts: Zimbabwe – M.H.Dekker, S.G.Peall; New Zealand – S.B.Doull, D.J.Nash, A.C.Parore.

The 99th LOI venue provided Andrew Jones with his 25th fifty in 64 internationals; he failed to add to that tally in his final 23 matches and, although he scored seven hundreds in Test cricket, he made none at this level.

NEW ZEALAND		Runs	Balls	4/6
M.J.Greatbatch	c A.Flower b Brain	21	11	3/1
R.T.Latham	run out	45	59	2/1
A.H.Jones	st A.Flower b G.W.Flower	68	106	4
* M.D.Crowe	c Dekker b G.W.Flower	40	56	1/1
K.R.Rutherford	not out	35	47	1
D.N.Patel	c Crocker b G.W.Flower	4	8	–
† A.C.Parore	c Houghton b Shah	11	10	1
D.J.Nash	run out	3	3	–
S.B.Doull	not out	2	2	–
G.R.Larsen				
W.Watson				
Extras	(b 5, lb 4, w 4, nb 2)	15		
Total	(50 overs; 7 wickets)	244		

ZIMBABWE		Runs	Balls	4/6
† A.Flower	b Patel	10	19	1
G.W.Flower	c Greatbatch b Watson	0	3	–
* D.L.Houghton	c Watson b Patel	19	28	1
M.H.Dekker	lbw b Doull	79	118	4/1
A.C.Waller	st Parore b Patel	23	24	3
C.N.Evans	st Parore b Latham	22	42	1/1
A.H.Shah	run out	25	23	2
G.J.Crocker	c Crowe b Doull	9	12	–
S.G.Peall	b Watson	1	3	–
D.H.Brain	not out	16	17	1
A.J.Traicos	not out	7	13	–
Extras	(lb 8, w 3)	11		
Total	(50 overs; 9 wickets)	222		

ZIMBABWE	O	M	R	W
Brain	8	1	46	1
Peall	10	1	32	0
Crocker	3	0	17	0
Shah	9	0	57	1
Traicos	10	0	44	0
G.W.Flower	10	1	39	3

NEW ZEALAND	O	M	R	W
Doull	10	2	42	2
Watson	8	0	45	2
Patel	10	2	26	3
Larsen	6	0	33	0
Jones	10	0	36	0
Latham	5	0	27	1
Nash	1	0	5	0

FALL OF WICKETS
1-23, 2-110, 3-175, 4-192, 5-200, 6-233, 7-236

FALL OF WICKETS
1-4, 2-29, 3-34, 4-75, 5-126, 6-162, 7-195, 8-198, 9-200

Umpires: K.Kanjee (1) and I.D.Robinson (8).

ZIMBABWE v NEW ZEALAND 1992-93

At Harare Sports Club on 8 November 1992.　Result: NEW ZEALAND won by 4 wickets.　Toss: Zimbabwe.
Award: M.D.Crowe.　LOI debuts: Zimbabwe – E.A.Essop-Adam, U.Ranchod; New Zealand – B.R.Hartland.

This match was uniquely sandwiched between the first and second days of a Test match. After several warnings, Zimbabwe's record opening partnership ended when Grant Flower was run out by the bowler (Dipak Patel) for backing up illegally. Having scored 140 the previous day, Martin Crowe's 46-ball fifty took him beyond 4000 LOI runs.

ZIMBABWE		Runs	Balls	4/6
† A.Flower	c Parore b Patel	56	70	4
G.W.Flower	run out	63	93	1/1
* D.L.Houghton	c Greatbatch b Harris	50	42	2/2
M.H.Dekker	c Parore b Su'a	55	63	1/1
C.N.Evans	c Latham b Watson	12	18	–
E.A.Brandes	b Harris	2	3	–
E.A.Essop-Adam	not out	14	15	1
A.H.Shah	not out	4	2	1
D.H.Brain				
A.J.Traicos				
U.Ranchod				
Extras	(lb 7, w 3, nb 5)	15		
Total	(50 overs; 6 wickets)	271		

NEW ZEALAND		Runs	Balls	4/6
M.J.Greatbatch	c A.Flower b Brandes	55	62	3/3
R.T.Latham	c Essop-Adam b Ranchod	40	41	4
B.R.Hartland	c A.Flower b Brandes	5	9	–
* M.D.Crowe	b Brandes	94	87	8/1
K.R.Rutherford	c Essop-Adam b G.W.Flower	37	62	1
C.Z.Harris	b Brain	16	16	2
D.N.Patel	not out	1	3	–
† A.C.Parore	not out	3	3	–
M.L.Su'a				
G.R.Larsen				
W.Watson				
Extras	(lb 8, w 10, nb 3)	21		
Total	(46.5 overs; 6 wickets)	272		

NEW ZEALAND	O	M	R	W
Su'a	10	0	36	1
Patel	10	0	48	1
Watson	9	0	61	1
Larsen	10	0	45	0
Harris	10	0	60	2
Latham	1	0	14	0

ZIMBABWE	O	M	R	W
Brain	5	1	27	1
Ranchod	10	1	44	1
Shah	6	0	31	0
Brandes	8.5	0	74	3
Traicos	10	1	50	0
G.W.Flower	7	0	38	1

FALL OF WICKETS
1-124, 2-130, 3-199, 4-221, 5-232, 6-261

FALL OF WICKETS
1-98, 2-113, 3-114, 4-244, 5-266, 6-267

Umpires: K.Kanjee (2) and I.D.Robinson (9).

SRI LANKA v NEW ZEALAND 1992-93

At Khettarama Stadium, Colombo on 4 December 1992.   No result.   Toss: Sri Lanka.
LOI debuts: Sri Lanka – D.K.Liyanage, A.G.D.Wickremasinghe; New Zealand – J.T.C.Vaughan.

A downpour reduced Sri Lanka's target to 67 from 20 overs but the umpires controversially abandoned the match because of the wet outfield with the home side needing a cosy 26 from 58 balls.

NEW ZEALAND		Runs	Balls	4/6
† A.C.Parore	run out	20	34	1
J.G.Wright	b G.Wickremasinghe	7	17	1
A.H.Jones	st A.Wickremasinghe b Gurusinha	24	68	1/1
* M.D.Crowe	c A.Wickremasinghe b G.Wickremasinghe	1	5	–
K.R.Rutherford	c Liyanage b Kalpage	36	69	–
C.Z.Harris	not out	32	53	–
J.T.C.Vaughan	b Kalpage	6	21	–
G.E.Bradburn	b Kalpage	6	16	–
D.J.Nash	run out	9	8	–
M.L.Su'a	lbw b Gurusinha	1	7	–
C.Pringle	not out	3	8	–
Extras	(lb 8, w 13)	21		
Total	(50 overs; 9 wickets)	166		

SRI LANKA		Runs	Balls	4/6
R.S.Mahanama	not out	11	34	–
U.C.Hathurusinghe	c Parore b Pringle	5	24	–
A.P.Gurusinha	c Harris b Pringle	0	2	–
P.A.de Silva	not out	13	12	1
* A.Ranatunga				
H.P.Tillekeratne				
† A.G.D.Wickremasinghe				
D.K.Liyanage				
R.S.Kalpage				
S.D.Anurasiri				
G.P.Wickremasinghe				
Extras	(lb 2, w 10)	12		
Total	(10.2 overs; 2 wickets)	41		

SRI LANKA	O	M	R	W
G.P.Wickremasinghe	10	0	39	2
Liyanage	6	0	24	0
Hathurusinghe	10	2	20	0
Anurasiri	5	0	21	0
Kalpage	10	0	29	3
Gurusinha	9	1	25	2

NEW ZEALAND	O	M	R	W
Pringle	5.2	0	15	2
Su'a	4	0	13	0
Nash	1	0	11	0

FALL OF WICKETS
1-20, 2-20

FALL OF WICKETS
1-23, 2-37, 3-39, 4-99, 5-108, 6-124, 7-136, 8-148, 9-155

Umpires: K.T.Francis (13) and P. Manuel (1).

SRI LANKA v NEW ZEALAND 1992-93

At P.Saravanamuttu Stadium, Colombo on 12 December 1992.   Result: **SRI LANKA** won by 8 wickets.
Toss: Sri Lanka.   Award: R.S.Mahanama.   LOI debuts: None.

In the absence of Martin Crowe (hamstring strain), Andrew Jones led New Zealand for the first time.

NEW ZEALAND		Runs	Balls	4/6
B.R.Hartland	st A.Wickremasinghe b Jayasuriya	54	108	4
J.G.Wright	run out	1	8	–
* A.H.Jones	c Kalpage b Anurasiri	37	62	2
K.R.Rutherford	c Mahanama b Kalpage	2	5	–
C.Z.Harris	c Mahanama b Kalpage	2	16	–
† A.C.Parore	c Gurusinha b Jayasuriya	17	29	–
D.J.Nash	not out	40	46	1/2
J.T.C.Vaughan	c Hathurusinghe b Jayasuriya	12	15	1
G.E.Bradburn	not out	11	12	–
M.L.Su'a				
C.Pringle				
Extras	(b 4, lb 9, nb 1)	14		
Total	(50 overs; 7 wickets)	190		

SRI LANKA		Runs	Balls	4/6
R.S.Mahanama	not out	84	109	7/1
U.C.Hathurusinghe	c Rutherford b Su'a	14	44	2
A.P.Gurusinha	c Nash b Harris	37	45	4/1
P.A.de Silva	not out	43	30	5/2
* A.Ranatunga				
H.P.Tillekeratne				
S.T.Jayasuriya				
† A.G.D.Wickremasinghe				
R.S.Kalpage				
S.D.Anurasiri				
G.P.Wickremasinghe				
Extras	(b 5, lb 3, w 4, nb 2)	14		
Total	(37.4 overs; 2 wickets)	192		

SRI LANKA	O	M	R	W
G.P.Wickremasinghe	7	1	29	0
Gurusinha	7	1	11	0
Hathurusinghe	3	0	16	0
Anurasiri	10	0	34	1
Ranatunga	5	0	20	0
Kalpage	10	2	34	2
Jayasuriya	8	0	33	3

NEW ZEALAND	O	M	R	W
Pringle	9.4	1	45	0
Nash	6	2	15	0
Su'a	5	0	28	1
Vaughan	4	0	26	0
Harris	5	0	34	1
Bradburn	8	0	36	0

FALL OF WICKETS
1-46, 2-120

FALL OF WICKETS
1-17, 2-96, 3-100, 4-100, 5-108, 6-134, 7-150

Umpires: I.Anandappa (2) and S.Ponnadurai (7).

SRI LANKA v NEW ZEALAND 1992-93

At Khettarama Stadium, Colombo on 13 December 1992.   Result: **SRI LANKA** won by 31 runs.   Toss: New Zealand.
Award: R.S.Mahanama.   LOI debuts: New Zealand – M.J.Haslam, M.B.Owens.

Roshan Mahanama contributed a maiden LOI hundred to Sri Lanka's highest second-wicket partnership in a home international and to a convincing 2-0 series win.

SRI LANKA		Runs	Balls	4/6
R.S.Mahanama	c Jones b Harris	107	132	7
U.C.Hathurusinghe	b Pringle	5	11	1
A.P.Gurusinha	b Haslam	76	105	6
P.A.de Silva	c and b Pringle	20	15	2
* A.Ranatunga	c Jones b Pringle	16	14	2
S.T.Jayasuriya	run out	26	15	3
R.S.Kalpage	not out	3	3	–
H.P.Tillekeratne				
† A.G.D.Wickremasinghe				
S.D.Anurasiri				
G.P.Wickremasinghe				
Extras	(lb 2, w 5, nb 2)	9		
Total	(49 overs; 6 wickets)	262		

NEW ZEALAND		O	M	R	W
Owens		8	0	37	0
Pringle		8	0	59	3
Nash		6	0	44	0
Vaughan		10	1	27	0
Harris		10	0	48	1
Bradburn		2	0	17	0
Haslam		5	0	28	1

FALL OF WICKETS
1-9, 2-175, 3-203, 4-218, 5-246, 6-262

Umpires: K.T.Francis (14) and P.Manuel (2).

NEW ZEALAND		Runs	Balls	4/6
B.R.Hartland	c A.Wickremasinghe b Gurusinha	14	36	2
† A.C.Parore	b Gurusinha	13	29	–
* A.H.Jones	c Jayasuriya b Kalpage	32	50	1
K.R.Rutherford	c and b Kalpage	30	27	3
J.T.C.Vaughan	st A.Wickremasinghe b Kalpage	33	35	2
C.Z.Harris	not out	68	68	4/1
D.J.Nash	run out	8	19	–
C.Pringle	c Gurusinha b Anurasiri	3	5	–
G.E.Bradburn	run out	2	3	–
M.B.Owens	st A.Wickremasinghe b Anurasiri	0	3	–
M.J.Haslam	c Ranatunga b Tillekeratne	9	18	–
Extras	(lb 14, w 4, nb 1)	19		
Total	(48.5 overs)	231		

SRI LANKA	O	M	R	W
G.P.Wickremasinghe	6	2	13	0
Gurusinha	7	1	29	2
Hathurusinghe	2	0	16	0
Anurasiri	10	0	45	2
Kalpage	10	0	46	3
Ranatunga	5	1	26	0
De Silva	6	0	31	0
Jayasuriya	2	1	8	0
Tillekeratne	0.5	0	3	1

FALL OF WICKETS
1-29, 2-35, 3-88, 4-108, 5-165, 6-187, 7-194, 8-199, 9-203, 10-231

WEST INDIES v PAKISTAN 1992-93

At WACA Ground, Perth on 4 December 1992.   Result: **PAKISTAN** won by 5 wickets.   Toss: Pakistan.
Award: Wasim Akram.   LOI debuts: West Indies – K.C.G.Benjamin, J.R.Murray; Pakistan – Ata-ur-Rehman.

The World Cup holders gained a notable victory on their return to Australia; it was to be their only success in the 14th World Series tournament. Javed Miandad's 82-ball innings included 45 singles.

WEST INDIES		Runs	Balls	4/6
D.L.Haynes	c Rashid b Waqar	1	8	–
P.V.Simmons	c Rashid b Wasim	6	15	1
* R.B.Richardson	c Wasim b Aamir	23	49	2
B.C.Lara	c sub (Naved Anjum) b Mushtaq	59	104	5
C.L.Hooper	c Inzamam b Mushtaq	24	36	2
K.L.T.Arthurton	c Rashid b Wasim	9	13	1
† J.R.Murray	b Waqar	22	49	2
I.R.Bishop	c Rashid b Wasim	6	17	1
C.E.L.Ambrose	not out	15	18	1
A.C.Cummins	c Miandad b Wasim	0	1	–
K.C.G.Benjamin	not out	13	7	1
Extras	(b 4, lb 3, w 4, nb 8)	19		
Total	(50 overs; 9 wickets)	197		

PAKISTAN		O	M	R	W
Wasim Akram		9	1	46	4
Waqar Younis		7	2	26	2
Ata-ur-Rehman		10	0	29	0
Aamir Sohail		8	0	36	1
Mushtaq Ahmed		10	1	22	2
Asif Mujtaba		6	0	31	0

FALL OF WICKETS
1-1, 2-12, 3-64, 4-119, 5-138, 6-140, 7-153, 8-176, 9-177

Umpires: R.J.Evans (15) and L.J.King (20).

PAKISTAN		Runs	Balls	4/6
Aamir Sohail	c Haynes b Bishop	2	3	–
Ramiz Raja	c Murray b Benjamin	34	86	2
Salim Malik	c Murray b Benjamin	35	82	1
* Javed Miandad	not out	59	82	–
Inzamam-ul-Haq	c Lara b Hooper	28	37	3
Asif Mujtaba	run out	3	9	–
Wasim Akram	not out	21	17	1
† Rashid Latif				
Waqar Younis				
Mushtaq Ahmed				
Ata-ur-Rehman				
Extras	(lb 4, w 3, nb 10)	17		
Total	(49.2 overs; 5 wickets)	199		

WEST INDIES	O	M	R	W
Ambrose	9.2	2	30	0
Bishop	10	1	34	1
Cummins	10	0	41	0
Benjamin	10	0	46	2
Hooper	10	0	44	1

FALL OF WICKETS
1-6, 2-62, 3-102, 4-157, 5-163

Referee: R.Subba Row (*England*).

AUSTRALIA v WEST INDIES 1992-93

At WACA Ground, Perth on 6 December 1992.　　Result: **WEST INDIES** won by 9 wickets.　　Toss: Australia.
Award: P.V.Simmons.　　LOI debuts: None.

Spectators reacted to the exclusion of Western Australian players from the team by pelting some Australian fielders with fruit and cans.

AUSTRALIA		Runs	Balls	4/6
M.A.Taylor	run out	0	6	–
D.C.Boon	c Murray b Bishop	6	14	–
D.M.Jones	c Cummins b Simmons	14	61	–
S.R.Waugh	c Hooper b Simmons	4	33	–
M.E.Waugh	st Murray b Hooper	36	80	1
* A.R.Border	run out	15	35	2
G.R.J.Matthews	c Richardson b Hooper	32	51	1
† I.A.Healy	not out	21	23	–
P.R.Reiffel	not out	9	11	–
C.J.McDermott				
M.R.Whitney				
Extras	(lb 9, w 11, nb 3)	23		
Total	(50 overs; 7 wickets)	160		

WEST INDIES		Runs	Balls	4/6
D.L.Haynes	not out	81	121	11
B.C.Lara	c Border b Reiffel	29	43	4
P.V.Simmons	not out	43	74	6
* R.B.Richardson				
C.L.Hooper				
K.L.T.Arthurton				
A.L.Logie				
† J.R.Murray				
I.R.Bishop				
C.E.L.Ambrose				
A.C.Cummins				
Extras	(lb 6, w 1, nb 4)	11		
Total	(38.3 overs; 1 wicket)	164		

WEST INDIES	O	M	R	W
Bishop	10	1	20	1
Cummins	10	1	35	0
Simmons	10	2	22	2
Ambrose	10	1	37	0
Hooper	10	0	37	2

AUSTRALIA	O	M	R	W
McDermott	7	2	32	0
Whitney	5	0	30	0
Reiffel	6	1	12	1
S.R.Waugh	8	2	31	0
Matthews	9	0	32	0
M.E.Waugh	3.3	0	21	0

FALL OF WICKETS
1-4, 2-15, 3-32, 4-35, 5-64, 6-122, 7-137

FALL OF WICKETS
1-53

Umpires: R.J.Evans (16) and T.A.Prue (15).

Referee: R.Subba Row (*England*).

AUSTRALIA v WEST INDIES 1992-93

At Sydney Cricket Ground on 8 December 1992.　　Result: **AUSTRALIA** won by 14 runs.　　Toss: West Indies.
Award: M.A.Taylor.　　LOI debuts: Australia – D.R.Martyn.

A truncated match on a pitch still damp from three days of rain produced a fascinating tussle, West Indies being dismissed for their lowest total. Deputising as captain for the first time, Mark Taylor gained the match award for his leadership and exceptional catching.

AUSTRALIA		Runs	Balls	4/6
D.C.Boon	c Lara b Simmons	8	22	1
* M.A.Taylor	b Simmons	9	31	1
D.M.Jones	c Murray b Ambrose	21	54	1
S.R.Waugh	c Murray b Simmons	1	6	–
M.E.Waugh	st Murray b Hooper	17	25	1
D.R.Martyn	b Ambrose	0	3	–
G.R.J.Matthews	c Ambrose b Cummins	11	19	–
† I.A.Healy	c Cummins b Ambrose	3	10	–
P.R.Reiffel	not out	9	11	–
C.J.McDermott	lbw b Hooper	2	3	–
M.R.Whitney	not out	1	1	–
Extras	(lb 11, w 8)	19		
Total	(30 overs; 9 wickets)	101		

WEST INDIES		Runs	Balls	4/6
D.L.Haynes	c S.R.Waugh b Reiffel	5	30	–
B.C.Lara	b Whitney	4	12	–
P.V.Simmons	lbw b McDermott	0	3	–
* R.B.Richardson	c Healy b Whitney	6	16	–
A.L.Logie	c Taylor b Reiffel	20	31	2
K.L.T.Arthurton	c Taylor b S.R.Waugh	3	8	–
C.L.Hooper	c Taylor b Reiffel	6	21	–
† J.R.Murray	c Taylor b S.R.Waugh	2	13	–
I.R.Bishop	c Healy b M.E.Waugh	11	24	1
C.E.L.Ambrose	not out	13	18	1
A.C.Cummins	run out	2	4	–
Extras	(lb 13, w 2)	15		
Total	(29.3 overs)	87		

WEST INDIES	O	M	R	W
Bishop	6	0	20	0
Simmons	6	2	11	3
Ambrose	6	0	18	3
Cummins	6	1	16	1
Hooper	6	0	25	2

AUSTRALIA	O	M	R	W
McDermott	6	1	11	1
Whitney	6	1	11	2
Reiffel	6	1	14	3
S.R.Waugh	5.3	0	25	2
M.E.Waugh	6	0	13	1

FALL OF WICKETS
1-31, 2-32, 3-34, 4-61, 5-62, 6-79, 7-85, 8-90, 9-98

FALL OF WICKETS
1-6, 2-7, 3-18, 4-22, 5-31, 6-49, 7-55, 8-65, 9-75, 10-87

Umpires: D.B.Hair (4) and S.G.Randell (52).

Referee: R.Subba Row (*England*).

AUSTRALIA v PAKISTAN 1992-93

At Bellerive Oval, Hobart on 10 December 1992.   Result: **MATCH TIED.**   Toss: Australia.
Award: Asif Mujtaba.   LOI debuts: None.

Pakistan achieved the third tie in World Series matches by scoring 16 off the final over bowled by Steve Waugh (W410416), the left-handed Asif Mujtaba striking the decisive blow, off a slower ball, over mid-wicket. During the lunch interval media scorers had reinstated a crucial run missed by their official brethren.

AUSTRALIA		Runs	Balls	4/6
* M.A.Taylor	c Rashid b Aqib	46	107	1
D.C.Boon	lbw b Aqib	14	22	1
D.M.Jones	run out	53	73	–/1
S.R.Waugh	run out	26	29	1
M.E.Waugh	b Mushtaq	13	14	–
D.R.Martyn	run out	5	10	–
† I.A.Healy	c Miandad b Waqar	24	23	1
P.R.Reiffel	not out	23	25	1
C.J.McDermott	not out	2	2	–
T.B.A.May				
M.R.Whitney				
Extras	(b 3, lb 15, w 1, nb 3)	22		
Total	(50 overs; 7 wickets)	228		

PAKISTAN		Runs	Balls	4/6
Aamir Sohail	c Martyn b McDermott	6	6	1
Ramiz Raja	c S.R.Waugh b Whitney	4	11	1
Salim Malik	c Healy b McDermott	64	99	3
* Javed Miandad	lbw b Reiffel	14	50	1
Inzamam-ul-Haq	c Martyn b M.E.Waugh	22	34	1/1
Asif Mujtaba	not out	56	51	3/1
Wasim Akram	c Healy b McDermott	3	6	–
† Rashid Latif	run out	39	35	3
Waqar Younis	b McDermott	8	5	1
Mushtaq Ahmed	c Reiffel b S.R.Waugh	0	2	–
Aqib Javed	not out	5	2	1
Extras	(lb 6, w 1)	7		
Total	(50 overs; 9 wickets)	228		

PAKISTAN	O	M	R	W
Wasim Akram	10	3	34	0
Waqar Younis	9	1	43	1
Aqib Javed	10	0	35	2
Aamir Sohail	10	0	37	0
Mushtaq Ahmed	10	0	52	1
Asif Mujtaba	1	0	9	0

AUSTRALIA	O	M	R	W
McDermott	10	2	42	4
Whitney	10	3	29	1
Reiffel	8	2	29	1
S.R.Waugh	10	0	56	1
May	5	0	29	0
M.E.Waugh	7	0	37	1

FALL OF WICKETS
1-32, 2-124, 3-138, 4-164, 5-172, 6-179, 7-218

FALL OF WICKETS
1-6, 2-10, 3-41, 4-91, 5-123, 6-129, 7-197, 8-207, 9-212

Umpires: S.G.Randell (53) and C.D.Timmins (13).

Referee: R.Subba Row (*England*).

WEST INDIES v PAKISTAN 1992-93

At Adelaide Oval on 12 December 1992.   Result: **WEST INDIES** won by 4 runs.   Toss: Pakistan.
Award: C.L.Hooper.   LOI debuts: None.

An 86-minute rain interlude in the middle of the West Indies innings reduced the match to 42 overs each. The dismissal of Javed Miandad, the third batsman to appear in 200 internationals, triggered a spectacular collapse in which seven wickets fell for 25 runs in 37 balls. Pakistan's five run outs equalled the LOI record.

WEST INDIES		Runs	Balls	4/6
D.L.Haynes	b Wasim	6	19	–
B.C.Lara	b Aqib	15	52	–
P.V.Simmons	c Aamir b Wasim	5	8	–
* R.B.Richardson	not out	76	112	6/1
A.L.Logie	c Ramiz b Aamir	1	4	–
K.L.T.Arthurton	c Inzamam b Aamir	3	14	–
C.L.Hooper	c Rashid b Wasim	24	38	1
I.R.Bishop	c Asif b Mushtaq	17	20	1
A.C.Cummins	not out	4	5	–
† J.R.Murray				
C.E.L.Ambrose				
Extras	(b 1, lb 13, w 8, nb 4)	26		
Total	(42 overs; 7 wickets)	177		

PAKISTAN		Runs	Balls	4/6
Aamir Sohail	c Bishop b Simmons	41	49	4
Ramiz Raja	run out	52	80	3
Salim Malik	c Simmons b Ambrose	22	51	–
* Javed Miandad	c Simmons b Hooper	11	20	1
Inzamam-ul-Haq	run out	18	30	–
Asif Mujtaba	run out	0	2	–
Wasim Akram	b Hooper	2	7	–
† Rashid Latif	run out	1	2	–
Waqar Younis	b Hooper	5	5	–
Mushtaq Ahmed	run out	3	6	–
Aqib Javed	not out	7	8	–
Extras	(lb 3, w 4, nb 4)	11		
Total	(41.5 overs)	173		

PAKISTAN	O	M	R	W
Wasim Akram	9	1	38	3
Waqar Younis	8	0	38	0
Aamir Sohail	10	1	26	2
Aqib Javed	5	2	30	1
Mushtaq Ahmed	8	1	23	1
Asif Mujtaba	2	0	8	0

WEST INDIES	O	M	R	W
Bishop	8	0	38	0
Ambrose	9	0	41	1
Cummins	9	1	31	0
Simmons	8	0	29	1
Hooper	7.5	0	31	3

FALL OF WICKETS
1-16, 2-27, 3-56, 4-61, 5-81, 6-133, 7-172

FALL OF WICKETS
1-63, 2-117, 3-128, 4-148, 5-148, 6-151, 7-153, 8-162, 9-162, 10-173

Umpires: S.J.Davis (1) and T.A.Prue (16).

Referee: R.Subba Row (*England*).

AUSTRALIA v PAKISTAN 1992-93

At Adelaide Oval on 13 December 1992.   Result: **AUSTRALIA** won by 8 wickets.   Toss: Australia.
Award: M.A.Taylor.   LOI debuts: None.

Rain delayed the start by 35 minutes, reducing each innings by three overs. There was a bizarre finish when the first ball of the 46th over, Aamir Sohail's 10th, was called wide.

PAKISTAN		Runs	Balls	4/6
Aamir Sohail	run out	8	9	1
Ramiz Raja	b May	28	67	1
Asif Mujtaba	b S.R.Waugh	45	100	1
* Javed Miandad	b May	6	14	–
Inzamam-ul-Haq	not out	60	71	3/1
Saeed Anwar	run out	6	8	–
Wasim Akram	c Taylor b McDermott	36	15	3/2
† Rashid Latif	not out	0	–	–
Waqar Younis				
Mushtaq Ahmed				
Aqib Javed				
Extras	(lb 4, w 1, nb 1)	6		
Total	(47 overs; 6 wickets)	195		

AUSTRALIA		Runs	Balls	4/6
D.C.Boon	b Aamir	40	75	4
* M.A.Taylor	run out	78	109	1
D.M.Jones	not out	48	73	1
S.R.Waugh	not out	15	23	1
M.E.Waugh				
D.R.Martyn				
† I.A.Healy				
P.R.Reiffel				
C.J.McDermott				
T.B.A.May				
M.R.Whitney				
Extras	(lb 6, w 5, nb 4)	15		
Total	(45 overs; 2 wickets)	196		

AUSTRALIA	O	M	R	W
McDermott	9	0	56	1
Whitney	10	3	22	0
Reiffel	9	0	36	0
May	10	0	27	2
S.R.Waugh	9	0	50	1

PAKISTAN	O	M	R	W
Wasim Akram	9	0	39	0
Waqar Younis	10	2	32	0
Aqib Javed	9	0	36	0
Aamir Sohail	9	0	36	1
Mushtaq Ahmed	7	0	36	0
Asif Mujtaba	1	0	11	0

FALL OF WICKETS
1-10, 2-60, 3-68, 4-120, 5-137, 6-194

FALL OF WICKETS
1-70, 2-171

Umpires: I.S.Thomas (5) and C.D.Timmins (14).

Referee: R.Subba Row (*England*).

AUSTRALIA v WEST INDIES 1992-93

At Melbourne Cricket Ground on 15 December 1992.   Result: **AUSTRALIA** won by 4 runs.   Toss: Australia.
Award: M.E.Waugh.   LOI debuts: None.

A crowd of 74,450 saw a sensational twist to a mundane contest when West Indies, needing 26 to win with seven wickets in hand, collapsed to defeat in the space of 31 balls. Mark Waugh became the third player to score 50 and take five wickets in an international.

AUSTRALIA		Runs	Balls	4/6
* M.A.Taylor	c Hooper b Simmons	10	27	1
D.C.Boon	c Haynes b Ambrose	4	15	–
D.M.Jones	c Arthurton b Cummins	22	58	1
S.R.Waugh	run out	34	69	–
M.E.Waugh	c Hooper b Ambrose	57	70	5
D.R.Martyn	c Murray b Ambrose	40	49	–
† I.A.Healy	c Haynes b Hooper	13	14	–
G.R.J.Matthews	not out	6	4	–
P.R.Reiffel	run out	0	1	–
C.J.McDermott	not out	0	–	–
M.R.Whitney				
Extras	(lb 5, w 6, nb 1)	12		
Total	(50 overs; 8 wickets)	198		

WEST INDIES		Runs	Balls	4/6
B.C.Lara	b M.E.Waugh	74	123	2
D.L.Haynes	c Taylor b Whitney	4	13	–
P.V.Simmons	c Healy b Reiffel	24	49	–
* R.B.Richardson	c Taylor b M.E.Waugh	61	73	6/2
C.L.Hooper	c Martyn b S.R.Waugh	6	14	–
A.L.Logie	run out	0	–	–
K.L.T.Arthurton	c Jones b M.E.Waugh	9	16	–
† J.R.Murray	c and b M.E.Waugh	5	5	–
C.E.L.Ambrose	run out	0	4	–
A.C.Cummins	c McDermott b M.E.Waugh	2	3	–
C.A.Walsh	not out	0	–	–
Extras	(lb 9)	9		
Total	(50 overs)	194		

WEST INDIES	O	M	R	W
Ambrose	10	3	25	3
Simmons	10	3	31	1
Walsh	10	1	42	0
Cummins	10	0	45	1
Hooper	10	0	50	1

AUSTRALIA	O	M	R	W
McDermott	7	1	27	0
Whitney	10	1	27	1
Reiffel	10	1	45	1
Matthews	7	0	24	0
S.R.Waugh	10	0	38	1
M.E.Waugh	6	0	24	5

FALL OF WICKETS
1-13, 2-17, 3-63, 4-86, 5-160, 6-186, 7-192, 8-197

FALL OF WICKETS
1-18, 2-66, 3-158, 4-173, 5-178, 6-178, 7-187, 8-192, 9-192, 10-194

Umpires: L.J.King (21) and T.A.Prue (17).

Referee: R.Subba Row (*England*).

WEST INDIES v PAKISTAN 1992-93

At Sydney Cricket Ground on 17 December 1992.　　Result: **WEST INDIES** won by 133 runs.　　Toss: West Indies.
Award: P.V.Simmons.　　LOI debuts: West Indies – J.C.Adams.

Pakistan were dismissed for their second-lowest LOI total (until their next innings in Australia), the medium-paced swing of Phil Simmons returning the most economical ten-over analysis at this level: 10-8-3-4. Rashid Latif scored 8 off 72 balls.

WEST INDIES		Runs	Balls	4/6	PAKISTAN		Runs	Balls	4/6
B.C.Lara	run out	3	15	–	Aamir Sohail	c Benjamin b Simmons	6	19	I
D.L.Haynes	b Wasim	96	152	6	Ramiz Raja	c Lara b Patterson	0	I	–
P.V.Simmons	c Salim b Aamir	10	20	I	Asif Mujtaba	b Simmons	I	10	–
* R.B.Richardson	c Wasim b Mushtaq	33	58	4	Salim Malik	c Hooper b Simmons	0	7	–
C.L.Hooper	run out	17	31	–	* Javed Miandad	c Murray b Simmons	2	20	–
A.L.Logie	b Wasim	0	3	–	Inzamam-ul-Haq	c Hooper b Benjamin	17	47	I
J.C.Adams	lbw b Waqar	17	27	I	Wasim Akram	c Richardson b Benjamin	7	37	–
K.C.G.Benjamin	not out	9	7	–	† Rashid Latif	c Murray b Patterson	8	72	–
† J.R.Murray	run out	0	I	–	Waqar Younis	lbw b Hooper	17	35	I
C.E.L.Ambrose	b Waqar	0	I	–	Mushtaq Ahmed	c Benjamin b Adams	15	40	–
B.P.Patterson	not out	0	I	–	Ata-ur-Rehman	not out	0	9	–
Extras	(b 4, lb 9, w 12, nb 4)	29			Extras	(w I, nb 7)	8		
Total	(50 overs; 9 wickets)	**214**			**Total**	(48 overs)	**81**		

PAKISTAN	O	M	R	W	WEST INDIES	O	M	R	W
Wasim Akram	10	0	37	I	Patterson	9	2	19	2
Waqar Younis	10	I	29	3	Simmons	10	8	3	4
Aamir Sohail	10	I	38	I	Ambrose	10	4	19	0
Ata-ur-Rehman	10	0	47	0	Benjamin	9	I	28	2
Mushtaq Ahmed	10	0	50	I	Hooper	6	2	10	I
					Adams	4	2	2	I

FALL OF WICKETS
1-10, 2-40, 3-107, 4-151, 5-156, 6-195, 7-209, 8-210, 9-213

Umpires: D.B.Hair (5) and I.S.Thomas (6).

FALL OF WICKETS
1-2, 2-4, 3-9, 4-9, 5-14, 6-35, 7-35, 8-54, 9-78, 10-81

Referee: R.Subba Row (*England*).

WEST INDIES v PAKISTAN 1992-93

At Woolloongabba, Brisbane on 9 January 1993.　　Result: **WEST INDIES** won by 9 wickets.　　Toss: Pakistan.
Award: I.R.Bishop.　　LOI debuts: None.

The tournament resumed after a three-week hiatus during which Pakistan lost a three-match LOI series on the low, slow pitches of New Zealand. Returning to a fast, bouncy surface, they were despatched for their lowest score and in the fewest overs until the following month (*LOI No. 812*).

PAKISTAN		Runs	Balls	4/6	WEST INDIES		Runs	Balls	4/6
Saeed Anwar	c Lara b Bishop	2	4	–	B.C.Lara	c Waqar b Wasim	10	33	I
Shahid Saeed	c Lara b Bishop	I	17	–	D.L.Haynes	not out	25	62	2
Inzamam-ul-Haq	c Simmons b Benjamin	0	6	–	* R.B.Richardson	not out	22	36	2
* Javed Miandad	c Murray b Bishop	0	10	–	P.V.Simmons				
Salim Malik	b Ambrose	8	25	–	K.L.T.Arthurton				
Asif Mujtaba	b Benjamin	I	5	–	C.L.Hooper				
Wasim Akram	c Simmons b Ambrose	19	38	2	J.C.Adams				
† Rashid Latif	not out	22	27	2	† J.R.Murray				
Waqar Younis	c Lara b Ambrose	0	3	–	I.R.Bishop				
Mushtaq Ahmed	c Richardson b Bishop	2	9	–	C.E.L.Ambrose				
Aqib Javed	c Benjamin b Bishop	4	7	I	K.C.G.Benjamin				
Extras	(lb 3, w 8, nb I)	12			Extras	(w 6, nb 9)	15		
Total	(23.4 overs)	**71**			**Total**	(19.2 overs; I wicket)	**72**		

WEST INDIES	O	M	R	W	PAKISTAN	O	M	R	W
Bishop	8.4	0	25	5	Wasim Akram	9	0	33	I
Benjamin	6	2	16	2	Waqar Younis	7	3	13	0
Ambrose	6	I	13	3	Aqib Javed	2	0	16	0
Hooper	3	0	14	0	Mushtaq Ahmed	1.2	0	10	0

FALL OF WICKETS
1-2, 2-7, 3-7, 4-11, 5-12, 6-31, 7-54, 8-55, 9-58, 10-71

Umpires: S.J.Davis (2) and L.J.King (22).

FALL OF WICKETS
1-22

Referee: D.B.Carr (*England*).

AUSTRALIA v WEST INDIES 1992-93

At Woolloongabba, Brisbane on 10 January 1993.　　Result: **WEST INDIES** won by 7 runs.　　Toss: Australia.
Award: C.L.Hooper.　　LOI debuts: None.

Having qualified for the finals, West Indies made five changes to their side. Australia lost their last five wickets for 32, four of them to run outs.

WEST INDIES		Runs	Balls	4/6
D.L.Haynes	c Healy b Reiffel	36	50	5
B.C.Lara	c Healy b Whitney	10	28	1
* R.B.Richardson	c S.R.Waugh b Reiffel	1	7	–
C.L.Hooper	c Reiffel b M.E.Waugh	56	65	5/1
K.L.T.Arthurton	c Taylor b Reiffel	2	12	–
A.L.Logie	c Reiffel b McDermott	26	51	1
† D.Williams	not out	25	49	3
A.C.Cummins	run out	1	3	–
K.C.G.Benjamin	c S.R.Waugh b May	17	20	–/1
C.A.Walsh	b S.R.Waugh	12	16	1
B.P.Patterson	not out	1	1	–
Extras	(lb 8, w 2)	10		
Total	(50 overs; 9 wickets)	**197**		

AUSTRALIA		Runs	Balls	4/6
D.C.Boon	c Williams b Patterson	3	9	–
M.A.Taylor	c Richardson b Cummins	20	69	1
D.M.Jones	c Williams b Patterson	0	2	–
S.R.Waugh	c Logie b Walsh	24	42	4
M.E.Waugh	run out	54	72	1/1
* A.R.Border	b Hooper	11	19	1
† I.A.Healy	lbw b Walsh	41	63	2
P.R.Reiffel	run out	4	11	–
C.J.McDermott	run out	7	13	–
T.B.A.May	not out	3	6	–
M.R.Whitney	run out	2	2	–
Extras	(b 2, lb 6, w 9, nb 4)	21		
Total	(49 overs)	**190**		

AUSTRALIA	O	M	R	W
McDermott	10	2	25	1
Whitney	10	1	30	1
Reiffel	10	1	33	3
S.R.Waugh	7	1	30	1
May	8	0	48	1
M.E.Waugh	5	0	23	1

WEST INDIES	O	M	R	W
Patterson	10	0	31	2
Benjamin	10	1	32	0
Cummins	10	1	27	1
Walsh	10	0	49	2
Hooper	9	0	43	1

FALL OF WICKETS
1-26, 2-38, 3-65, 4-72, 5-129, 6-149, 7-152, 8-175, 9-196

FALL OF WICKETS
1-5, 2-10, 3-51, 4-61, 5-81, 6-158, 7-173, 8-176, 9-187, 10-190

Referee: D.B.Carr (*England*).

Umpires: I.S.Thomas (7) and C.D.Timmins (15).

AUSTRALIA v PAKISTAN 1992-93

At Melbourne Cricket Ground on 12 January 1993.　　Result: **AUSTRALIA** won by 32 runs.　　Toss: Australia.
Award: D.M.Jones.　　LOI debuts: None.

Australia's victory clinched their place in the finals, their captain becoming the fourth batsman after Desmond Haynes, Viv Richards and Javed Miandad to score 6000 runs. For the first time video cameras were used to aid crowd control.

AUSTRALIA		Runs	Balls	4/6
M.A.Taylor	c Rashid b Aqib	4	12	–
D.C.Boon	c Shahid b Asif	64	98	4
D.M.Jones	b Waqar	84	127	3/1
S.R.Waugh	c and b Asif	5	11	–
M.E.Waugh	b Waqar	12	19	–
* A.R.Border	not out	14	20	1
† I.A.Healy	run out	3	7	–
A.I.C.Dodemaide	not out	15	12	2
P.R.Reiffel				
C.J.McDermott				
T.B.A.May				
Extras	(b 3, lb 2, w 3, nb 3)	11		
Total	(50 overs; 6 wickets)	**212**		

PAKISTAN		Runs	Balls	4/6
Aamir Sohail	c Healy b McDermott	3	18	–
Ramiz Raja	c Healy b S.R.Waugh	40	79	3
Shahid Saeed	b Dodemaide	3	12	–
Salim Malik	b McDermott	37	67	1
* Javed Miandad	c Border b M.E.Waugh	40	59	2
Inzamam-ul-Haq	not out	39	47	–
Wasim Akram	c M.E.Waugh b Reiffel	3	7	–
† Rashid Latif	c Healy b Reiffel	5	6	–
Asif Mujtaba	not out	5	5	–
Waqar Younis				
Aqib Javed				
Extras	(b 1, lb 4)	5		
Total	(50 overs; 7 wickets)	**180**		

PAKISTAN	O	M	R	W
Wasim Akram	10	1	28	0
Aqib Javed	8	0	39	1
Waqar Younis	10	0	39	2
Aamir Sohail	5	0	27	0
Shahid Saeed	8	0	36	0
Asif Mujtaba	9	0	38	2

AUSTRALIA	O	M	R	W
McDermott	10	2	26	2
Dodemaide	8	0	25	1
Reiffel	10	1	37	2
S.R.Waugh	8	0	22	1
May	10	0	41	0
M.E.Waugh	4	0	24	1

FALL OF WICKETS
1-9, 2-133, 3-153, 4-180, 5-181, 6-187

FALL OF WICKETS
1-10, 2-28, 3-69, 4-97, 5-142, 6-154, 7-171

Umpires: D.B.Hair (6) and C.D.Timmins (16).

Referee: D.B.Carr (*England*).

AUSTRALIA v PAKISTAN 1992-93

At Sydney Cricket Ground on 14 January 1993. Result: **AUSTRALIA** won by 23 runs. Toss: Australia.
Award: S.R.Waugh. LOI debuts: None.

Dean Jones played despite fracturing his right thumb in the previous match. Australia's win enabled them to lead the qualifying table. Final points: Australia 11, West Indies 10, Pakistan 3.

AUSTRALIA		Runs	Balls	4/6	PAKISTAN		Runs	Balls	4/6
D.C.Boon	c sub (Saeed Anwar) b Asif	50	82	5	Aamir Sohail	b Dodemaide	7	34	1
M.A.Taylor	b Asif	58	78	5	Ramiz Raja	c Border b Matthews	67	85	9
D.M.Jones	b Mushtaq	13	17	1	Salim Malik	c Healy b Dodemaide	6	15	1
S.R.Waugh	c Asif b Waqar	64	65	6	* Javed Miandad	c M.E.Waugh b Border	41	59	3
M.E.Waugh	run out	11	16	–	Inzamam-ul-Haq	b McDermott	40	46	1/1
* A.R.Border	b Waqar	28	35	3	Wasim Akram	b Matthews	0	2	–
† I.A.Healy	lbw b Waqar	0	1	–	Asif Mujtaba	not out	47	44	4
G.R.J.Matthews	not out	10	12	1	Waqar Younis	not out	18	19	2
A.I.C.Dodemaide	run out	5	2	–	† Rashid Latif				
P.R.Reiffel	not out	2	2	–	Mushtaq Ahmed				
C.J.McDermott					Aqib Javed				
Extras	(b 6, lb 5, w 4, nb 4)	19			Extras	(b 1, lb 6, w 4)	11		
Total	(50 overs; 8 wickets)	260			Total	(50 overs; 6 wickets)	237		

PAKISTAN	O	M	R	W	AUSTRALIA	O	M	R	W
Wasim Akram	10	0	39	0	McDermott	9	3	27	1
Aqib Javed	9	0	52	0	Dodemaide	8	2	30	2
Waqar Younis	9	1	55	3	Reiffel	10	0	53	0
Mushtaq Ahmed	10	0	39	1	S.R.Waugh	5	0	26	0
Asif Mujtaba	9	0	47	2	Matthews	10	0	54	2
Aamir Sohail	3	0	17	0	Border	8	0	40	1

FALL OF WICKETS
1-112, 2-124, 3-144, 4-167, 5-230, 6-230, 7-245, 8-257

FALL OF WICKETS
1-24, 2-46, 3-130, 4-132, 5-133, 6-204

Umpires: T.A.Prue (18) and S.G.Randell (54).

Referee: D.B.Carr (*England*).

AUSTRALIA v WEST INDIES 1992-93

At Sydney Cricket Ground on 16 January 1993. Result: **WEST INDIES** won by 25 runs. Toss: West Indies.
LOI debuts: None.

In an attempt to add prestige to the event, the teams paraded for the national anthem prior to throwing souvenir yellow rubber balls into the crowd. Curtly Ambrose, enraged by Dean Jones requesting that he remove his white wristbands, took five wickets for the fourth time.

WEST INDIES		Runs	Balls	4/6	AUSTRALIA		Runs	Balls	4/6
B.C.Lara	c Dodemaide b Border	67	81	7	M.A.Taylor	c Simmons b Ambrose	28	49	3
D.L.Haynes	c and b Matthews	38	60	6	D.C.Boon	c Murray b Ambrose	16	37	2
P.V.Simmons	c M.E.Waugh b Matthews	5	4	1	D.M.Jones	c Simmons b Benjamin	13	22	3
* R.B.Richardson	c Dodemaide b Border	28	52	1	S.R.Waugh	c and b Hooper	15	29	–
C.L.Hooper	b S.R.Waugh	45	56	2	M.E.Waugh	run out	51	70	2
A.L.Logie	b S.R.Waugh	38	36	3	* A.R.Border	c Ambrose b Hooper	27	39	1
K.C.G.Benjamin	run out	0	4	–	† I.A.Healy	b Ambrose	33	30	1
I.R.Bishop	b McDermott	1	6	–	G.R.J.Matthews	c Lara b Benjamin	11	9	–
C.E.L.Ambrose	not out	5	3	–	A.I.C.Dodemaide	c Lara b Ambrose	3	3	–
† J.R.Murray					P.R.Reiffel	not out	12	12	–
A.C.Cummins					C.J.McDermott	c Simmons b Ambrose	0	1	–
Extras	(b 2, lb 8, nb 2)	12			Extras	(lb 3, nb 2)	5		
Total	(50 overs; 8 wickets)	239			Total	(49.3 overs)	214		

AUSTRALIA	O	M	R	W	WEST INDIES	O	M	R	W
McDermott	8	0	40	1	Bishop	10	0	45	0
Dodemaide	7	0	23	0	Simmons	2	0	14	0
Reiffel	5	1	30	0	Ambrose	9.3	2	32	5
Matthews	10	0	45	2	Benjamin	10	0	35	2
Border	10	0	46	2	Cummins	8	0	39	0
S.R.Waugh	10	0	45	2	Hooper	10	0	46	2

FALL OF WICKETS
1-90, 2-96, 3-128, 4-159, 5-216, 6-217, 7-220, 8-239

FALL OF WICKETS
1-41, 2-48, 3-69, 4-91, 5-147, 6-160, 7-179, 8-187, 9-214, 10-214

Umpires: T.A.Prue (19) and S.G.Randell (55).

Referee: D.B.Carr (*England*).

AUSTRALIA v WEST INDIES 1992-93

At Melbourne Cricket Ground on 18 January 1993.   Result: **WEST INDIES** won by 4 wickets.   Toss: Australia.
Finals Award: C.E.L.Ambrose.   LOI debuts: None.

West Indies gained their sixth World Series title in eight attempts, and their fifth in five play-offs against the hosts. For the first time in 14 WS tournaments no batsman scored a hundred. Allan Border was the first to appear in 250 internationals. Mark Waugh was run out for the fourth time in five innings.

AUSTRALIA		Runs	Balls	4/6	WEST INDIES		Runs	Balls	4/6
D.C.Boon	run out	19	50	1	B.C.Lara	c M.E.Waugh b McDermott	60	100	5
M.A.Taylor	c Ambrose b Bishop	33	73	2	D.L.Haynes	run out	0	3	–
D.M.Jones	c Murray b Bishop	5	14	–	P.V.Simmons	c M.E.Waugh b Dodemaide	0	1	–
S.R.Waugh	run out	25	50	–	* R.B.Richardson	c Reiffel b McDermott	5	8	1
M.E.Waugh	run out	8	26	–	C.L.Hooper	not out	59	132	3
* A.R.Border	c and b Hooper	8	13	–	A.L.Logie	c Healy b Reiffel	7	7	–
† I.A.Healy	c and b Ambrose	16	26	–	† J.R.Murray	c Healy b Dodemaide	1	12	–
G.R.J.Matthews	c Logie b Ambrose	15	25	–	I.R.Bishop	not out	4	25	–
A.I.C.Dodemaide	c Murray b Ambrose	1	5	–	K.C.G.Benjamin				
P.R.Reiffel	not out	7	7	1	C.E.L.Ambrose				
C.J.McDermott	b Hooper	0	3	–	A.C.Cummins				
Extras	(lb 3, nb 7)	10			Extras	(lb 7, w 2, nb 3)	12		
Total	(47.3 overs)	147			Total	(47 overs; 6 wickets)	148		

WEST INDIES	O	M	R	W	AUSTRALIA	O	M	R	W
Bishop	9	2	33	2	McDermott	10	0	35	2
Benjamin	10	0	33	0	Dodemaide	10	4	19	2
Ambrose	10	0	26	3	S.R.Waugh	10	1	30	0
Cummins	10	1	24	0	M.E.Waugh	4	0	17	0
Hooper	8.3	1	28	2	Reiffel	10	1	21	1
					Matthews	3	0	19	0

FALL OF WICKETS
1-54, 2-63, 3-65, 4-74, 5-94, 6-113, 7-133, 8-137, 9-146, 10-147

FALL OF WICKETS
1-7, 2-8, 3-23, 4-109, 5-125, 6-126

Umpires: D.B.Hair (7) and C.D.Timmins (17).

Referee: D.B.Carr (*England*).

SOUTH AFRICA v INDIA 1992-93

At Newlands, Cape Town on 7 December 1992.   Result: **SOUTH AFRICA** won by 6 wickets.   Toss: India.
Award: W.J.Cronje.   LOI debuts: South Africa – D.J.Callaghan, P.S.de Villiers.

The first limited-overs international played in South Africa introduced the 100th venue and an off-field third umpire using video evidence. Kepler Wessels was the first to be adjudged run out by this method, the process taking three minutes. 'Hansie' Cronje claimed his country's only five-wicket haul in a home match and won the game with a six.

INDIA		Runs	Balls	4/6	SOUTH AFRICA		Runs	Balls	4/6
A.Jadeja	c Kirsten b Cronje	48	103	3	* K.C.Wessels	run out	43	100	2
W.V.Raman	b Cronje	47	69	3	A.C.Hudson	c Prabhakar b Tendulkar	33	56	5
* M.Azharuddin	c Richardson b Donald	9	20	–	P.N.Kirsten	c Raman b Prabhakar	56	90	4
S.R.Tendulkar	b McMillan	15	27	1	J.N.Rhodes	c Tendulkar b Srinath	13	28	–
S.V.Manjrekar	c Matthews b Cronje	13	25	–	D.J.Callaghan	not out	17	19	2
P.K.Amre	c Hudson b Cronje	4	8	–	W.J.Cronje	not out	12	5	–/1
Kapil Dev	c Cronje b McMillan	27	27	2/1	B.M.McMillan				
M.Prabhakar	c Wessels b Cronje	8	14	1	† D.J.Richardson				
† K.S.More	c Kirsten b Donald	4	3	1	C.R.Matthews				
A.Kumble	not out	3	5	–	A.A.Donald				
J.Srinath	run out	0	–	–	P.S.de Villiers				
Extras	(lb 5, nb 1)	6			Extras	(b 4, lb 5, w 1, nb 1)	11		
Total	(50 overs)	184			Total	(49.3 overs; 4 wickets)	185		

SOUTH AFRICA	O	M	R	W	INDIA	O	M	R	W
Donald	10	2	32	2	Kapil Dev	10	1	43	0
De Villiers	7	2	24	0	Prabhakar	9.3	1	36	1
Matthews	10	0	38	0	Tendulkar	10	1	25	1
McMillan	10	0	42	2	Srinath	10	2	34	1
Callaghan	3	0	11	0	Kumble	10	0	38	0
Cronje	10	0	32	5					

FALL OF WICKETS
1-92, 2-103, 3-109, 4-133, 5-140, 6-140, 7-153, 8-158, 9-184, 10-184

FALL OF WICKETS
1-56, 2-108, 3-140, 4-168

Umpires: S.B.Lambson (1) and K.E.Liebenberg (7).

SOUTH AFRICA v INDIA 1992-93

At St George's Park, Port Elizabeth on 9 December 1992.   Result: **SOUTH AFRICA** won by 6 wickets.   Toss: India.
Award: B.M.McMillan.   LOI debuts: South Africa – B.N.Schultz.

India were dismissed for their lowest total against South Africa. Kapil Dev ran out Peter Kirsten for backing up illegally, having warned him previously on the tour. Kirsten was fined half his match fees for his reaction but his captain escaped censure for 'accidentally' engaging Kapil's shins with his bat.

INDIA		Runs	Balls	4/6
A.Jadeja	c McMillan b Schultz	5	19	1
W.V.Raman	b Matthews	33	60	5
* M.Azharuddin	run out	5	31	–
S.R.Tendulkar	c Richardson b Callaghan	10	33	–
S.V.Manjrekar	run out	17	38	–
P.K.Amre	run out	30	49	1
Kapil Dev	c Rhodes b McMillan	1	2	–
M.Prabhakar	c Richardson b McMillan	1	15	–
† K.S.More	b McMillan	32	39	3
A.Kumble	b McMillan	7	13	–
J.Srinath	not out	1	1	–
Extras	(lb 3, nb 2)	5		
Total	**(49.4 overs)**	**147**		

SOUTH AFRICA		Runs	Balls	4/6
A.C.Hudson	b Kapil Dev	5	13	1
* K.C.Wessels	c Jadeja b Prabhakar	30	83	1
P.N.Kirsten	run out	5	20	1
J.N.Rhodes	lbw b Srinath	13	27	2
D.J.Callaghan	not out	45	82	4
W.J.Cronje	not out	38	59	5
B.M.McMillan				
† D.J.Richardson				
C.R.Matthews				
A.A.Donald				
B.N.Schultz				
Extras	(b 2, lb 4, w 3, nb 3)	12		
Total	**(46.4 overs; 4 wickets)**	**148**		

SOUTH AFRICA	O	M	R	W
Donald	10	4	26	0
Schultz	9	1	35	1
Matthews	10	4	20	1
McMillan	9.4	0	32	4
Cronje	6	0	18	0
Callaghan	5	0	13	1

INDIA	O	M	R	W
Kapil Dev	9	2	19	1
Prabhakar	8	0	30	1
Kumble	10	1	22	0
Srinath	10	1	31	1
Tendulkar	5	1	18	0
Jadeja	4.4	1	22	0

FALL OF WICKETS
1-8, 2-40, 3-48, 4-65, 5-81, 6-82, 7-84, 8-112, 9-144, 10-147

FALL OF WICKETS
1-8, 2-20, 3-46, 4-70

Umpires: R.E.Koertzen (1) and C.J.Mitchley (1).

SOUTH AFRICA v INDIA 1992-93

At Centurion Park, Verwoerdburg, Pretoria on 11 December 1992.   Result: **INDIA** won by 4 wickets.   Toss: India.
Award: W.V.Raman.   LOI debuts: None.

Verwoerdburg, a town about ten miles south of the centre of Pretoria, was named after Hendrik Frencsh Verwoerd (1901-66), the Amsterdam-born, assassinated prime minister who was prime exponent of the apartheid policy. It was renamed 'Centurion' in 1995 shortly before staging its first Test match.

SOUTH AFRICA		Runs	Balls	4/6
* K.C.Wessels	b Kumble	34	75	4
A.C.Hudson	run out	87	130	7
P.N.Kirsten	b Shastri	19	32	1
J.N.Rhodes	run out	18	29	–/1
D.J.Callaghan	not out	32	26	1/1
W.J.Cronje	b Kumble	0	5	–
B.M.McMillan	not out	10	14	–
† D.J.Richardson				
C.R.Matthews				
A.A.Donald				
P.S.de Villiers				
Extras	(lb 7, w 1, nb 6)	14		
Total	**(50 overs; 5 wickets)**	**214**		

INDIA		Runs	Balls	4/6
A.Jadeja	c Richardson b Matthews	20	55	2
W.V.Raman	c McMillan b Donald	114	148	6/1
P.K.Amre	c Donald b Cronje	1	10	–
* M.Azharuddin	b Matthews	18	35	–
S.R.Tendulkar	c Richardson b Matthews	22	24	2
Kapil Dev	b De Villiers	1	5	–
R.J.Shastri	not out	27	16	4
† K.S.More	not out	4	6	–
M.Prabhakar				
A.Kumble				
J.Srinath				
Extras	(lb 1, w 4, nb 3)	8		
Total	**(49.1 overs; 6 wickets)**	**215**		

INDIA	O	M	R	W
Kapil Dev	5	1	19	0
Prabhakar	9	1	31	0
Srinath	9	0	38	0
Tendulkar	2	0	16	0
Jadeja	8	0	38	0
Kumble	10	0	29	2
Shastri	7	1	36	1

SOUTH AFRICA	O	M	R	W
Donald	10	1	45	1
De Villiers	10	1	33	1
Matthews	10	0	56	3
McMillan	9.1	0	36	0
Callaghan	3	0	13	0
Cronje	7	0	31	1

FALL OF WICKETS
1-92, 2-124, 3-163, 4-180, 5-181

FALL OF WICKETS
1-56, 2-72, 3-123, 4-168, 5-171, 6-194

Umpires: W.A.Diedricks (1) and S.B.Lambson (2).

SOUTH AFRICA v INDIA 1992-93

At The Wanderers, Johannesburg on 12 (*no play*), 13 December 1992.　Result: **SOUTH AFRICA** won by 6 wickets.
Toss: South Africa.　Award: J.N.Rhodes.　LOI debuts: None.

When a waterlogged ground caused this match to be rescheduled to the following day, it became the first day/night game to be played in South Africa on a Sunday.

INDIA		Runs	Balls	4/6
A.Jadeja	lbw b Callaghan	18	60	2
W.V.Raman	b Donald	0	16	–
P.K.Amre	lbw b Donald	2	9	–
* M.Azharuddin	c Richardson b Matthews	49	84	3
S.R.Tendulkar	c McMillan b Donald	21	44	1
R.J.Shastri	c McMillan b De Villiers	17	32	–
Kapil Dev	c Richardson b Matthews	18	25	–
J.Srinath	c Rhodes b McMillan	3	5	–
‡ K.S.More	run out	2	7	–
M.Prabhakar	not out	5	11	–
A.Kumble	not out	7	9	1
Extras	(b 1, lb 5, w 11, nb 2)	19		
Total	(50 overs; 9 wickets)	**161**		

SOUTH AFRICA		Runs	Balls	4/6
A.C.Hudson	c Azharuddin b Kumble	22	56	2
* K.C.Wessels	c Jadeja b Srinath	45	97	3
P.N.Kirsten	lbw b Srinath	21	47	1
J.N.Rhodes	not out	42	56	2/1
D.J.Callaghan	run out	12	27	–
W.J.Cronje	not out	11	8	1
B.M.McMillan				
† D.J.Richardson				
C.R.Matthews				
A.A.Donald				
P.S.de Villiers				
Extras	(lb 9, w 2, nb 1)	12		
Total	(48.3 overs; 4 wickets)	**165**		

SOUTH AFRICA	O	M	R	W
Donald	10	0	27	3
De Villiers	10	2	24	1
McMillan	10	0	39	1
Matthews	10	1	33	2
Callaghan	5	0	17	1
Cronje	5	0	15	0

INDIA	O	M	R	W
Kapil Dev	9	0	23	0
Prabhakar	8	1	24	0
Tendulkar	3	0	4	0
Kumble	9	1	33	1
Shastri	10	1	33	0
Srinath	9.3	1	39	2

FALL OF WICKETS
1-9, 2-12, 3-61, 4-107, 5-108, 6-136, 7-143, 8-149, 9-149

FALL OF WICKETS
1-47, 2-88, 3-95, 4-133

Umpires: K.E.Liebenberg (8) and C.J.Mitchley (2).

SOUTH AFRICA v INDIA 1992-93

At Springbok Park, Bloemfontein on 15 December 1992.　Result: **SOUTH AFRICA** won by 8 wickets.　Toss: South Africa.
Award: A.C.Hudson.　LOI debuts: India – V.Yadav.

Andrew Hudson scored South Africa's first hundred in limited-overs internationals as the hosts took an unbeatable 4-1 lead in the series. The game was marred by frequent crowd invasions and a 15-minute power failure.

INDIA		Runs	Balls	4/6
A.Jadeja	c McMillan b Donald	9	25	2
W.V.Raman	c McMillan b Matthews	16	46	–
M.Prabhakar	run out	36	57	3
* M.Azharuddin	not out	86	105	5/1
S.R.Tendulkar	b De Villiers	32	52	1
R.J.Shastri	not out	21	18	2
P.K.Amre				
Kapil Dev				
† V.Yadav				
A.Kumble				
J.Srinath				
Extras	(b 1, lb 3, w 1, nb 2)	7		
Total	(50 overs; 4 wickets)	**207**		

SOUTH AFRICA		Runs	Balls	4/6
* K.C.Wessels	c and b Kumble	55	95	3
A.C.Hudson	c Azharuddin b Srinath	108	147	8/1
P.N.Kirsten	not out	35	46	4
J.N.Rhodes	not out	0	1	–
D.J.Callaghan				
W.J.Cronje				
B.M.McMillan				
† D.J.Richardson				
C.R.Matthews				
A.A.Donald				
P.S.de Villiers				
Extras	(lb 5, w 2, nb 3)	10		
Total	(47.2 overs; 2 wickets)	**208**		

SOUTH AFRICA	O	M	R	W
Donald	10	2	36	1
De Villiers	10	0	29	1
Matthews	10	1	37	1
McMillan	10	0	59	0
Cronje	6	0	20	0
Callaghan	4	0	22	0

INDIA	O	M	R	W
Kapil Dev	9	1	35	0
Prabhakar	10	0	35	0
Srinath	9	0	43	1
Kumble	10	0	34	1
Shastri	5	0	25	0
Tendulkar	4	0	27	0
Amre	0.2	0	4	0

FALL OF WICKETS
1-17, 2-47, 3-88, 4-156

FALL OF WICKETS
1-125, 2-204

Umpires: R.E.Koertzen (2) and S.B.Lambson (3).

SOUTH AFRICA v INDIA 1992-93

At Kingsmead, Durban on 17 December 1992.   Result: **SOUTH AFRICA** won by 39 runs.   Toss: India.
Award: Kapil Dev.   LOI debuts: None.

The only match in this series lost by the side electing to bat second.

SOUTH AFRICA		Runs	Balls	4/6	INDIA		Runs	Balls	4/6
A.C.Hudson	c Yadav b Kapil Dev	15	29	1	M.Prabhakar	c Richardson b Matthews	21	48	–
* K.C.Wessels	c Manjrekar b Prabhakar	78	120	6	A.Jadeja	c Richardson b Pringle	12	45	1
P.N.Kirsten	c Manjrekar b Shastri	44	68	–/2	S.V.Manjrekar	run out	10	27	–
J.N.Rhodes	c Shastri b Kapil Dev	16	25	–/1	* M.Azharuddin	c De Villiers b Cronje	41	73	3/1
D.J.Callaghan	st Yadav b Kumble	8	12	1	S.R.Tendulkar	c Cronje b Pringle	23	39	–
W.J.Cronje	b Kapil Dev	25	29	2	Kapil Dev	c Richardson b Donald	30	37	5
† D.J.Richardson	run out	12	11	–	R.J.Shastri	c Kirsten b Pringle	5	6	–
M.W.Pringle	run out	9	8	–	† V.Yadav	b Matthews	3	3	–
C.R.Matthews	not out	1	1	–	C.Sharma	c Rhodes b De Villiers	15	12	1
A.A.Donald					A.Kumble	run out	0	1	–
P.S.de Villiers					S.L.V.Raju	not out	3	4	–
Extras	(b 2, lb 5, nb 1)	8			Extras	(b 1, lb 4, w 2, nb 7)	14		
Total	(50 overs; 8 wickets)	216			Total	(47.5 overs)	177		

INDIA	O	M	R	W	SOUTH AFRICA	O	M	R	W
Prabhakar	10	1	54	1	Donald	9	3	18	1
Kapil Dev	10	4	23	3	De Villiers	8.5	2	22	1
Raju	10	1	45	0	Matthews	10	0	40	2
Sharma	4	0	18	0	Pringle	10	0	51	3
Shastri	6	0	36	1	Callaghan	4	0	21	0
Kumble	10	1	33	1	Cronje	6	1	20	1

FALL OF WICKETS
1-28, 2-121, 3-157, 4-162, 5-173, 6-198, 7-215, 8-216

FALL OF WICKETS
1-40, 2-42, 3-65, 4-110, 5-127, 6-144, 7-153, 8-172, 9-173, 10-177

Umpires: W.A.Diedricks (2) and K.E.Liebenberg (9).

SOUTH AFRICA v INDIA 1992-93

At Buffalo Park, East London on 19 December 1992.   Result: **INDIA** won by 5 wickets.   Toss: India.
Award: P.K.Amre.   LOI debuts: None.

South Africa's seventh different venue in as many matches took the tally of LOI grounds to 106. They won this inaugural home series 5-2, their captain, Kepler Wessels, gaining the series award for scoring 342 runs, average 48.85.

SOUTH AFRICA		Runs	Balls	4/6	INDIA		Runs	Balls	4/6
* K.C.Wessels	c Tendulkar b Raju	57	100	7	M.Prabhakar	b Donald	12	19	1
A.C.Hudson	lbw b Prabhakar	8	14	2	S.V.Manjrekar	lbw b McMillan	6	34	–
P.N.Kirsten	c Banerjee b Raju	30	62	4	S.R.Tendulkar	c Richardson b Matthews	21	38	3
J.N.Rhodes	c Kumble b Prabhakar	37	59	–	* M.Azharuddin	run out	24	41	4
D.J.Callaghan	c Yadav b Raju	0	3	–	P.K.Amre	not out	84	98	5
W.J.Cronje	c Manjrekar b Kapil Dev	55	56	4	Kapil Dev	lbw b Matthews	17	33	–/1
B.M.McMillan	not out	3	7	–	† V.Yadav	not out	34	22	3
† D.J.Richardson	b Prabhakar	0	2	–	C.Sharma				
C.R.Matthews	run out	1	1	–	S.T.Banerjee				
A.A.Donald					S.L.V.Raju				
P.S.de Villiers					A.Kumble				
Extras	(lb 9, w 1, nb 2)	12			Extras	(lb 4, w 1, nb 1)	6		
Total	(50 overs; 8 wickets)	203			Total	(47.2 overs; 5 wickets)	204		

INDIA	O	M	R	W	SOUTH AFRICA	O	M	R	W
Prabhakar	10	1	43	3	Donald	10	0	49	1
Kapil Dev	10	4	27	1	De Villiers	8.2	3	26	0
Sharma	8	0	34	0	McMillan	10	1	38	1
Banerjee	3	0	20	0	Matthews	10	2	44	2
Raju	10	0	37	3	Callaghan	5	0	21	0
Kumble	9	0	33	0	Cronje	4	0	22	0

FALL OF WICKETS
1-21, 2-86, 3-108, 4-108, 5-199, 6-200, 7-201, 8-203

FALL OF WICKETS
1-16, 2-39, 3-43, 4-80, 5-130

Umpires: R.E.Koertzen (3) and C.J.Mitchley (3).

NEW ZEALAND v PAKISTAN 1992-93

At Basin Reserve, Wellington on 26 December 1992.   Result: **PAKISTAN** won by 50 runs.   Toss: New Zealand.
Award: Wasim Akram.   LOI debuts: None.

This three-match series took place during a three-week mid-term gap in Australia's World Series tournament, thus rendering the Pakistanis' appearances out of chronological order. The third umpire appeared for the first time in New Zealand. Pakistan gained their sixth successive win against their hosts.

PAKISTAN		Runs	Balls	4/6
Aamir Sohail	b Morrison	8	21	2
Ramiz Raja	b Harris	50	102	3
Salim Malik	run out	25	40	2
* Javed Miandad	c and b Morrison	46	91	–
Inzamam-ul-Haq	c Jones b Watson	0	7	–
Asif Mujtaba	c Patel b Harris	0	3	–
Wasim Akram	c Morrison b Harris	1	8	–
† Rashid Latif	c Latham b Watson	12	16	–
Waqar Younis	not out	4	3	–
Mushtaq Ahmed	not out	1	2	–
Aqib Javed				
Extras	(b 4, lb 3, w 3, nb 1)	11		
Total	(49 overs; 8 wickets)	158		

NEW ZEALAND		Runs	Balls	4/6
M.J.Greatbatch	c Waqar b Wasim	7	34	–
R.T.Latham	b Wasim	1	14	–
A.H.Jones	c Rashid b Wasim	0	3	–
* M.D.Crowe	c Aamir b Aqib	28	48	3
K.R.Rutherford	b Aqib	18	45	1
C.Z.Harris	b Aqib	7	23	–
D.N.Patel	c Inzamam b Mushtaq	1	15	–
† A.C.Parore	c Salim b Wasim	14	33	–
G.R.Larsen	c Rashid b Wasim	11	17	–/1
D.K.Morrison	run out	3	10	–
W.Watson	not out	1	1	–
Extras	(lb 8, w 6, nb 3)	17		
Total	(39.3 overs)	108		

NEW ZEALAND	O	M	R	W
Morrison	7	1	19	2
Watson	10	0	37	2
Patel	10	0	37	0
Larsen	10	0	30	0
Harris	10	1	24	3
Latham	2	0	4	0

PAKISTAN	O	M	R	W
Wasim Akram	9	1	19	5
Waqar Younis	8	2	14	0
Aqib Javed	10	1	27	3
Mushtaq Ahmed	8	1	20	1
Aamir Sohail	4.3	0	20	0

FALL OF WICKETS
1-14, 2-57, 3-116, 4-117, 5-119, 6-123, 7-152, 8-153

FALL OF WICKETS
1-10, 2-11, 3-19, 4-60, 5-73, 6-74, 7-77, 8-97, 9-106, 10-108

Umpires: R.S.Dunne (11) and C.E.King (1).

NEW ZEALAND v PAKISTAN 1992-93

At McLean Park, Napier on 28 December 1992.   Result: **NEW ZEALAND** won by 6 wickets.   Toss: New Zealand.
Award: M.D.Crowe.   LOI debuts: None.

Aqib Javed became the first player to be suspended (one international) for breaching the ICC Code of Conduct (he called umpire Aldridge an 'effing cheat'). Third umpire Steve Dunne gave the first two decisions on video evidence in New Zealand off successive balls. Rain reduced the match to 42 overs each.

PAKISTAN		Runs	Balls	4/6
Aamir Sohail	b Patel	9	12	–
Ramiz Raja	c Parore b Patel	1	6	–
Salim Malik	c Parore b Watson	39	87	4
* Javed Miandad	b Larsen	19	64	1
Inzamam-ul-Haq	c Parore b Larsen	2	13	–
Shahid Saeed	run out	14	30	–
† Rashid Latif	c Jones b Morrison	20	27	–
Wasim Akram	c Parore b Watson	12	7	1/1
Waqar Younis	not out	0	4	–
Mushtaq Ahmed	not out	0	–	–
Aqib Javed				
Extras	(b 3, lb 9, w 8)	20		
Total	(42 overs; 8 wickets)	136		

NEW ZEALAND		Runs	Balls	4/6
M.J.Greatbatch	c Rashid b Wasim	0	4	–
R.T.Latham	b Shahid	21	37	3
A.H.Jones	c Rashid b Waqar	17	65	1
* M.D.Crowe	not out	47	74	3
K.R.Rutherford	c Inzamam b Shahid	34	50	4
C.Z.Harris	not out	3	4	–
D.N.Patel				
† A.C.Parore				
G.R.Larsen				
D.K.Morrison				
W.Watson				
Extras	(b 1, lb 1, w 5, nb 8)	15		
Total	(37.4 overs; 4 wickets)	137		

NEW ZEALAND	O	M	R	W
Morrison	8	1	30	1
Patel	9	2	16	2
Watson	8	0	39	2
Larsen	9	2	15	2
Harris	8	1	24	0

PAKISTAN	O	M	R	W
Wasim Akram	9	2	22	1
Waqar Younis	9	0	36	0
Aqib Javed	8	1	39	1
Shahid Saeed	7	0	20	2
Mushtaq Ahmed	4	0	16	0
Salim Malik	0.4	0	2	0

FALL OF WICKETS
1-9, 2-14, 3-67, 4-69, 5-92, 6-113, 7-128, 8-135

FALL OF WICKETS
1-0, 2-30, 3-71, 4-133

Umpires: B.L.Aldridge (28) and D.M.Quested (1).

NEW ZEALAND v PAKISTAN 1992-93

At Eden Park, Auckland on 30 December 1992.   Result: **NEW ZEALAND** won by 6 wickets.   Toss: New Zealand.
Award: M.D.Crowe.   LOI debuts: None.

New Zealand won a low-scoring game on a slow pitch to take the series 2-1. Mark Greatbatch pulled the first ball of the hosts' innings into the South Stand for six.

PAKISTAN		Runs	Balls	4/6
Ramiz Raja	b Watson	23	50	2
Shahid Saeed	run out	17	37	3
Salim Malik	c Crowe b Larsen	23	43	2
Saeed Anwar	c Parore b Watson	0	1	–
* Javed Miandad	c Parore b Watson	30	72	1
Inzamam-ul-Haq	run out	2	6	–
Wasim Akram	c Harris b Morrison	21	48	1
Naved Anjum	st Parore b Harris	0	1	–
† Rashid Latif	not out	9	13	1
Waqar Younis	c Crowe b Morrison	0	7	–
Mushtaq Ahmed	c Greatbatch b Watson	6	11	–
Extras	(lb 5, nb 3)	8		
Total	(47.4 overs)	**139**		

NEW ZEALAND		Runs	Balls	4/6
M.J.Greatbatch	c Mushtaq b Wasim	24	37	2/2
R.T.Latham	c Inzamam b Waqar	0	5	–
A.H.Jones	lbw b Naved	9	47	–
* M.D.Crowe	not out	57	98	5
K.R.Rutherford	b Mushtaq	28	57	2
C.Z.Harris	not out	11	21	–
D.N.Patel				
† A.C.Parore				
G.R.Larsen				
D.K.Morrison				
W.Watson				
Extras	(lb 3, w 5, nb 3)	11		
Total	(42.4 overs; 4 wickets)	**140**		

NEW ZEALAND	O	M	R	W
Morrison	10	1	27	2
Patel	10	2	25	0
Watson	8.4	1	27	4
Larsen	10	2	20	1
Harris	6	1	22	1
Jones	2	0	6	0
Latham	1	0	7	0

PAKISTAN	O	M	R	W
Wasim Akram	9	2	28	1
Waqar Younis	10	2	27	1
Naved Anjum	10	1	30	1
Mushtaq Ahmed	9.4	1	34	1
Salim Malik	1	0	4	0
Shahid Saeed	3	0	14	0

FALL OF WICKETS
1-35, 2-43, 3-47, 4-75, 5-77, 6-123, 7-123, 8-127, 9-128, 10-139

FALL OF WICKETS
1-10, 2-34, 3-45, 4-105

Umpires: B.L.Aldridge (29) and D.B.Cowie (2).

INDIA v ENGLAND 1992-93

At Sawai Mansingh Stadium, Jaipur on 18 January 1993.   Result: **ENGLAND** won by 4 wickets.   Toss: England.
Award: V.G.Kambli.   LOI debuts: None.

England won off the last ball when Chris Lewis jabbed a single to gully. Former schoolmates Vinod Kambli and Sachin Tendulkar shared an unbroken partnership of 164 which remains India's highest for the fourth wicket against all countries.

INDIA		Runs	Balls	4/6
M.Prabhakar	b Jarvis	25	29	4
N.S.Sidhu	b Jarvis	0	2	–
V.G.Kambli	not out	100	149	9/1
* M.Azharuddin	lbw b Lewis	6	28	–
S.R.Tendulkar	not out	82	81	6/1
P.K.Amre				
Kapil Dev				
† V.Yadav				
A.Kumble				
S.L.V.Raju				
J.Srinath				
Extras	(b 2, lb 7, w 1)	10		
Total	(48 overs; 3 wickets)	**223**		

ENGLAND		Runs	Balls	4/6
* G.A.Gooch	lbw b Kapil Dev	4	25	–
† A.J.Stewart	c Yadav b Kapil Dev	91	126	6/2
R.A.Smith	c and b Prabhakar	16	39	–
M.W.Gatting	b Kumble	30	39	2
N.H.Fairbrother	not out	46	38	5/1
G.A.Hick	run out	13	14	1
D.A.Reeve	b Prabhakar	2	3	–
C.C.Lewis	not out	8	7	–
J.E.Emburey				
P.A.J.DeFreitas				
P.W.Jarvis				
Extras	(b 1, lb 8, w 3, nb 2)	14		
Total	(48 overs; 6 wickets)	**224**		

ENGLAND	O	M	R	W
DeFreitas	9	3	40	0
Jarvis	10	0	49	2
Reeve	10	0	37	0
Lewis	9	0	26	1
Emburey	8	0	49	0
Gooch	2	0	13	0

INDIA	O	M	R	W
Kapil Dev	10	1	36	2
Prabhakar	10	0	43	2
Srinath	10	0	47	0
Raju	8	1	35	0
Kumble	10	0	54	1

FALL OF WICKETS
1-0, 2-31, 3-59

FALL OF WICKETS
1-29, 2-85, 3-145, 4-161, 5-200, 6-203

Umpires: S.K.Bansal (3) and S.Venkataraghavan (1).

Referee: C.W.Smith (West Indies).

398

INDIA v ENGLAND 1992-93

At Sector 16 Stadium, Chandigarh on 21 January 1993.   Result: **INDIA** won by 5 wickets.   Toss: India.
Award: N.S.Sidhu.   LOI debuts: England – I.D.K.Salisbury.

Kapil Dev delighted his local crowd by produced an opening spell of 6-2-9-1, only to concede 31 runs from his last four overs.

ENGLAND		Runs	Balls	4/6	INDIA		Runs	Balls	4/6
* G.A.Gooch	c Tendulkar b Srinath	7	27	–	N.S.Sidhu	c Reeve b DeFreitas	76	107	5/2
† A.J.Stewart	c Azharuddin b Kapil Dev	7	21	1	M.Prabhakar	c Reeve b Lewis	36	59	4
R.A.Smith	lbw b Kumble	42	106	4	V.G.Kambli	c and b Jarvis	9	24	–
M.W.Gatting	c and b Srinath	0	12	–	* M.Azharuddin	lbw b Reeve	36	44	3
N.H.Fairbrother	lbw b Raju	7	17	1	S.R.Tendulkar	lbw b DeFreitas	1	5	–
G.A.Hick	b Kapil Dev	56	73	4	P.K.Amre	not out	24	32	4
D.A.Reeve	not out	33	33	4	Kapil Dev	not out	5	4	1
C.C.Lewis	not out	16	16	–	† V.Yadav				
P.A.J.DeFreitas					A.Kumble				
P.W.Jarvis					S.L.V.Raju				
I.D.K.Salisbury					J.Srinath				
Extras	(lb 13, w 13, nb 4)	30			Extras	(lb 3, w 5, nb 6)	14		
Total	(50 overs; 6 wickets)	198			Total	(45.1 overs; 5 wickets)	201		

INDIA	O	M	R	W	ENGLAND	O	M	R	W
Kapil Dev	10	2	40	2	DeFreitas	10	1	31	2
Prabhakar	8	0	30	0	Jarvis	10	1	43	1
Srinath	10	2	34	2	Reeve	6.1	0	33	1
Tendulkar	3	0	16	0	Lewis	10	0	47	1
Raju	9	0	28	1	Salisbury	8	1	42	0
Kumble	10	0	37	1	Gatting	1	0	2	0

FALL OF WICKETS
1-19, 2-20, 3-22, 4-49, 5-132, 6-153

FALL OF WICKETS
1-79, 2-99, 3-148, 4-161, 5-195

Umpires: R.V.Ramani (9) and V.K.Ramaswamy (25).

Referee: C.W.Smith (*West Indies*).

INDIA v ENGLAND 1992-93

At Chinnaswamy Stadium, Bangalore on 26 February 1993.   Result: **ENGLAND** won by 48 runs.
Toss: India.   Award: P.W.Jarvis.   LOI debuts: None.

Javagal Srinath returned India's only five-wicket analysis against England, a feat which Paul Jarvis subsequently reciprocated for the touring team.

ENGLAND		Runs	Balls	4/6	INDIA		Runs	Balls	4/6
R.A.Smith	c More b Srinath	29	50	4	M.Prabhakar	run out	0	10	–
† A.J.Stewart	lbw b Srinath	14	32	2	N.S.Sidhu	c Gooch b DeFreitas	40	57	4
G.A.Hick	c Amre b Prabhakar	56	81	3	V.G.Kambli	c Stewart b Jarvis	33	60	4
M.W.Gatting	b Srinath	7	13	1	S.R.Tendulkar	c Hick b Lewis	3	6	–
N.H.Fairbrother	run out	5	15	–	* M.Azharuddin	lbw b Jarvis	1	3	–
* G.A.Gooch	b Prabhakar	45	61	2	P.K.Amre	c Hick b Jarvis	16	24	2
C.C.Lewis	c Tendulkar b Srinath	19	19	1	Kapil Dev	c Gooch b Malcolm	32	44	3
D.A.Reeve	not out	13	11	1	† K.S.More	lbw b Jarvis	0	2	–
P.A.J.DeFreitas	c Prabhakar b Srinath	2	3	–	A.Kumble	b Jarvis	24	39	3
P.W.Jarvis	c Azharuddin b Kapil Dev	1	3	–	J.Srinath	c Hick b Malcolm	2	7	–
D.E.Malcolm	not out	0	3	–	S.L.V.Raju	not out	1	3	–
Extras	(lb 15, w 4, nb 8)	27			Extras	(lb 4, w 11, nb 3)	18		
Total	(47 overs; 9 wickets)	218			Total	(41.4 overs)	170		

INDIA	O	M	R	W	ENGLAND	O	M	R	W
Kapil Dev	8	1	27	1	Malcolm	9	1	47	2
Prabhakar	10	0	50	2	DeFreitas	8	0	27	1
Srinath	9	1	41	5	Lewis	10	0	32	1
Raju	10	0	46	0	Jarvis	8.4	1	35	5
Kumble	10	1	39	0	Reeve	6	0	25	0

FALL OF WICKETS
1-42, 2-65, 3-79, 4-102, 5-157, 6-185, 7-209, 8-212, 9-218

FALL OF WICKETS
1-3, 2-61, 3-66, 4-67, 5-100, 6-114, 7-115, 8-160, 9-166, 10-170

Umpires: V.K.Ramaswamy (26) and M.R.Singh (1).

Referee: C.W.Smith (*West Indies*).

INDIA v ENGLAND 1992-93

At Keenan Stadium, Jamshedpur on 1 March 1993.   Result: **ENGLAND** won by 6 wickets.   Toss: England.
Award: N.H.Fairbrother.   LOI debuts: None.

England failed to bowl their 28 overs in the allotted time after rain had delayed the start by 3½ hours. Neil Fairbrother completed his match-winning innings with a runner after being struck on the knee. A six-inch metal bolt narrowly missed boundary fielder Devon Malcolm.

INDIA		Runs	Balls	4/6
N.S.Sidhu	c DeFreitas b Malcolm	18	28	1
M.Prabhakar	c Blakey b DeFreitas	2	7	–
V.G.Kambli	run out	23	37	1
S.R.Tendulkar	b Jarvis	24	32	1
* M.Azharuddin	c Fairbrother b Lewis	23	22	1
Kapil Dev	not out	15	13	1
P.K.Amre	c Gooch b Jarvis	19	13	3
S.A.Ankola	run out	2	3	–
† K.S.More	not out	1	2	–
A.Kumble				
J.Srinath				
Extras	(lb 6, w 3, nb 1)	10		
Total	(26 overs; 7 wickets)	**137**		

ENGLAND		Runs	Balls	4/6
* G.A.Gooch	c More b Kapil Dev	15	19	1
R.A.Smith	run out	17	27	1
G.A.Hick	c Azharuddin b Ankola	1	8	–
N.H.Fairbrother	not out	53	52	4
C.C.Lewis	lbw b Prabhakar	25	30	1
D.A.Reeve	not out	17	20	2
M.W.Gatting				
† R.J.Blakey				
P.A.J.DeFreitas				
P.W.Jarvis				
D.E.Malcolm				
Extras	(lb 8, w 5)	13		
Total	(25.4 overs; 4 wickets)	**141**		

ENGLAND	O	M	R	W
DeFreitas	4	0	17	1
Malcolm	6	0	17	1
Lewis	5	0	25	1
Reeve	6	0	32	0
Jarvis	5	0	40	2

INDIA	O	M	R	W
Kapil Dev	4	1	10	1
Prabhakar	5.4	0	34	1
Srinath	6	0	38	0
Ankola	6	0	28	1
Kumble	4	0	23	0

FALL OF WICKETS
1-11, 2-46, 3-51, 4-96, 5-99, 6-122, 7-127

FALL OF WICKETS
1-27, 2-33, 3-43, 4-93

Umpires: L.Narasimhan (4) and C.K.Sathe (1).

Referee: C.W.Smith (*West Indies*).

INDIA v ENGLAND 1992-93

At Roop Singh Stadium, Gwalior on 4 March 1993.   Result: **INDIA** won by 3 wickets.   Toss: India.
Award: N.S.Sidhu.   LOI debuts: None.

England contrived to lose their last seven wickets for 10 runs in 20 balls. The stand of 175 between Navjot Sidhu and Mohammed Azharuddin remains India's highest for the third wicket against England. Alec Stewart was struck on the head by a concrete missile.

ENGLAND		Runs	Balls	4/6
R.A.Smith	lbw b Srinath	129	145	12/4
A.J.Stewart	b Kumble	33	68	2
G.A.Hick	c More b Prabhakar	18	25	1
N.H.Fairbrother	c Maninder b Srinath	37	39	3/1
C.C.Lewis	lbw b Prabhakar	4	9	–
* G.A.Gooch	run out	1	3	–
D.A.Reeve	run out	3	6	–
† R.J.Blakey	lbw b Srinath	0	1	–
P.A.J.DeFreitas	not out	2	5	–
P.W.Jarvis	b Prabhakar	0	2	–
D.E.Malcolm	b Prabhakar	0	1	–
Extras	(b 1, lb 16, w 8, nb 4)	29		
Total	(50 overs)	**256**		

INDIA		Runs	Balls	4/6
N.S.Sidhu	not out	134	160	15
M.Prabhakar	lbw b DeFreitas	0	1	–
V.G.Kambli	c Gooch b Malcolm	2	7	–
* M.Azharuddin	c Stewart b Malcolm	74	72	6/1
S.R.Tendulkar	b Jarvis	5	6	1
A.K.Sharma	run out	0	1	–
Kapil Dev	c Hick b Jarvis	2	9	–
† K.S.More	c Hick b Malcolm	1	3	–
A.Kumble	not out	19	33	–
Maninder Singh				
J.Srinath				
Extras	(b 2, lb 9, w 8, nb 1)	20		
Total	(48 overs; 7 wickets)	**257**		

INDIA	O	M	R	W
Kapil Dev	9	0	39	0
Prabhakar	10	0	54	4
Srinath	10	0	41	3
Kumble	10	0	41	1
Maninder Singh	8	0	46	0
Sharma	3	0	18	0

ENGLAND	O	M	R	W
DeFreitas	10	0	52	1
Malcolm	10	0	40	3
Lewis	10	0	56	0
Jarvis	10	0	43	2
Reeve	6	0	37	0
Hick	2	0	18	0

FALL OF WICKETS
1-101, 2-154, 3-227, 4-246, 5-246, 6-251, 7-251, 8-256, 9-256, 10-256

FALL OF WICKETS
1-1, 2-4, 3-179, 4-189, 5-190, 6-202, 7-205

Umpires: A.V.Jayaprakash (1) and P.D.Reporter (20).

Referee: C.W.Smith (*West Indies*).

INDIA v ENGLAND 1992-93

At Roop Singh Stadium, Gwalior on 5 March 1993. Result: **INDIA** won by 4 wickets. Toss: India.
Award: M.Azharuddin.   LOI debuts: None.

This match was added to the itinerary after the cancellation of the first scheduled international at Ahmedabad on 16 January. A brilliant exhibition of batting by Mohammed Azharuddin (50 off 34 balls) carried India to a series-levelling victory.

ENGLAND		Runs	Balls	4/6
R.A.Smith	c Sharma b Maninder	72	106	7/1
† A.J.Stewart	c More b Srinath	11	28	1
G.A.Hick	not out	105	109	7/2
N.H.Fairbrother	c Kapil Dev b Srinath	41	39	3
M.W.Gatting	c Sidhu b Srinath	6	7	1
C.C.Lewis	not out	3	2	–
* G.A.Gooch				
D.A.Reeve				
P.A.J.DeFreitas				
P.W.Jarvis				
D.E.Malcolm				
Extras	(lb 8, w 17, nb 2)	27		
Total	(48 overs; 4 wickets)	265		

INDIA		Runs	Balls	4/6
M.Prabhakar	b Jarvis	73	112	5
N.S.Sidhu	c Hick b Lewis	19	27	3
V.G.Kambli	c Reeve b DeFreitas	22	40	1
* M.Azharuddin	not out	95	63	12/1
S.R.Tendulkar	c sub (J.P.Taylor) b Lewis	34	30	2/1
Kapil Dev	c Reeve b Jarvis	2	3	–
A.K.Sharma	c Gooch b Jarvis	2	2	–
† K.S.More	not out	10	6	2
A.Kumble				
Maninder Singh				
J.Srinath				
Extras	(lb 1, w 7, nb 2)	10		
Total	(46.4 overs; 6 wickets)	267		

INDIA	O	M	R	W
Kapil Dev	10	2	48	0
Prabhakar	9	0	52	0
Srinath	9	0	37	3
Maninder Singh	10	0	62	1
Kumble	10	0	58	0

ENGLAND	O	M	R	W
Malcolm	8	0	56	0
Lewis	10	1	51	2
Jarvis	10	0	39	3
Reeve	8.4	0	64	0
DeFreitas	10	0	56	1

FALL OF WICKETS
1-42, 2-158, 3-246, 4-258

FALL OF WICKETS
1-41, 2-99, 3-166, 4-245, 5-251, 6-253

Umpires: S.K.Bansal (4) and S.Venkataraghavan (2).

Referee: C.W.Smith (*West Indies*).

PAKISTAN v ZIMBABWE 1992-93

At Sharjah CA Stadium, UAE on 1 February 1993. Result: **PAKISTAN** won by 49 runs. Toss: Zimbabwe.
Award: Inzamam-ul-Haq.   LOI debuts: Pakistan – Arshad Khan; Zimbabwe – G.A.Briant.

India absented themselves from this tournament in protest against biased umpiring in its predecessor. The Flower brethren celebrated Zimbabwe's first appearance at Sharjah with their country's highest LOI opening stand outside Harare. Waqar Younis took his 100th wicket in 59 internationals.

PAKISTAN		Runs	Balls	4/6
Saeed Anwar	c and b Shah	26	41	3
Ramiz Raja	c A.Flower b Brandes	5	8	1
Inzamam-ul-Haq	c Ranchod b Brandes	90	133	11
Javed Miandad	c A.Flower b Shah	14	26	1
Salim Malik	c A.Flower b Shah	0	3	–
† Rashid Latif	c Dekker b Brain	39	41	4
* Wasim Akram	c Shah b Brain	38	30	4/1
Waqar Younis	c G.W.Flower b Brain	26	15	1/3
Mushtaq Ahmed	not out	4	2	1
Arshad Khan	not out	0	–	–
Aqib Javed				
Extras	(b 4, lb 6, w 10)	20		
Total	(50 overs; 8 wickets)	262		

ZIMBABWE		Runs	Balls	4/6
† A.Flower	run out	49	71	5
G.W.Flower	c Waqar b Mushtaq	57	109	4/1
K.J.Arnott	c Rashid b Salim	7	19	–
* D.L.Houghton	b Waqar	36	32	2/2
M.H.Dekker	run out	7	19	–
G.A.Briant	not out	14	28	1
A.H.Shah	b Waqar	0	3	–
S.G.Peall	not out	12	22	1
D.H.Brain				
E.A.Brandes				
U.Ranchod				
Extras	(lb 16, w 13, nb 2)	31		
Total	(50 overs; 6 wickets)	213		

ZIMBABWE	O	M	R	W
Brandes	10	0	66	2
Brain	10	0	51	3
Ranchod	10	1	40	0
Peall	10	0	62	0
Shah	10	2	33	3

PAKISTAN	O	M	R	W
Wasim Akram	10	0	34	0
Aqib Javed	7	1	11	0
Arshad Khan	6	0	43	0
Waqar Younis	10	3	26	2
Mushtaq Ahmed	10	0	42	1
Salim Malik	7	0	41	1

FALL OF WICKETS
1-18, 2-47, 3-88, 4-88, 5-163, 6-199, 7-252, 8-258

FALL OF WICKETS
1-121, 2-127, 3-138, 4-178, 5-188, 6-189

Umpires: R.V.Ramani (*India*) (10) and R.C.Sharma (*India*) (1).

PAKISTAN v SRI LANKA 1992-93

At Sharjah CA Stadium, UAE on 2 February 1993.   Result: **PAKISTAN** won by 8 wickets.   Toss: Pakistan.
Award: Wasim Akram.   LOI debuts: None.

Asanka Gurusinha's defiant innings, which accounted for exactly half of Sri Lanka's total, could not prevent Pakistan from reaching the final.

SRI LANKA		Runs	Balls	4/6
R.S.Mahanama	lbw b Wasim	1	6	–
U.C.Hathurusinghe	c Saeed b Salim	36	82	3
A.P.Gurusinha	c sub (Zahid Fazal) b Wasim	90	112	5/3
P.A.de Silva	c Asif b Waqar	7	10	–
* A.Ranatunga	c Rashid b Aqib	8	15	–
H.P.Tillekeratne	lbw b Aqib	2	5	–
R.S.Kalpage	c Asif b Wasim	6	18	–
† A.G.D.Wickremasinghe	b Wasim	2	10	–
C.P.H.Ramanayake	b Waqar	15	19	2
G.P.Wickremasinghe	not out	1	5	–
S.D.Anurasiri				
Extras	(lb 7, w 3, nb 2)	12		
Total	(46 overs; 9 wickets)	**180**		

PAKISTAN		Runs	Balls	4/6
Saeed Anwar	c Tillekeratne b De Silva	55	92	5
Ramiz Raja	c Gurusinha b De Silva	73	104	8
Inzamam-ul-Haq	not out	27	24	3
Asif Mujtaba	not out	15	26	1
Javed Miandad				
Salim Malik				
* Wasim Akram				
† Rashid Latif				
Waqar Younis				
Mushtaq Ahmed				
Aqib Javed				
Extras	(b 2, lb 1, w 7, nb 1)	11		
Total	(40.2 overs; 2 wickets)	**181**		

PAKISTAN	O	M	R	W
Wasim Akram	10	1	24	4
Aqib Javed	10	1	31	2
Waqar Younis	10	0	37	2
Mushtaq Ahmed	10	1	41	0
Asif Mujtaba	2	0	16	0
Salim Malik	4	0	24	1

SRI LANKA	O	M	R	W
Ramanayake	8.2	1	19	0
G.P.Wickremasinghe	7	0	30	0
Kalpage	7	0	29	0
Hathurusinghe	3	0	19	0
Anurasiri	7	0	39	0
De Silva	5	0	24	2
Ranatunga	3	0	18	0

FALL OF WICKETS
1-2, 2-98, 3-119, 4-141, 5-147, 6-160, 7-160, 8-164, 9-180

FALL OF WICKETS
1-132, 2-137

Umpires: R.V.Ramani (India) (11) and R.C.Sharma (India) (2).

SRI LANKA v ZIMBABWE 1992-93

At Sharjah CA Stadium, UAE on 3 February 1993.   Result: **SRI LANKA** won by 30 runs.   Toss: Sri Lanka.
Award: E.A.Brandes.   LOI debuts: Sri Lanka – N.Ranatunga.

Zimbabwe's valiant effort failed to unseat Sri Lanka, whose innings had been terminated prematurely by rain. Nisantha Ranatunga's appearance provided the first instance of three brothers representing their country at this level; a fourth was to follow (*LOI No. 916*). The second eldest, Arjuna, scored his 3000th run in 115 matches.

SRI LANKA		Runs	Balls	4/6
R.S.Mahanama	c Arnott b Crocker	62	70	9
U.C.Hathurusinghe	lbw b Brandes	66	91	7
A.P.Gurusinha	run out	20	12	3
P.A.de Silva	b Brain	46	38	4
* A.Ranatunga	c Campbell b Brandes	39	31	2
† H.P.Tillekeratne	not out	13	10	1
R.S.Kalpage	not out	8	8	1
N.Ranatunga				
C.P.H.Ramanayake				
G.P.Wickremasinghe				
S.D.Anurasiri				
Extras	(lb 3, w 8, nb 1)	12		
Total	(43 overs; 5 wickets)	**266**		

ZIMBABWE		Runs	Balls	4/6
† A.Flower	b Gurusinha	26	36	–
G.W.Flower	c Tillekeratne b Ramanayake	0	3	–
K.J.Arnott	c Kalpage b Ramanayake	7	23	–
* D.L.Houghton	run out	31	57	1
G.A.Briant	run out	3	8	–
A.D.R.Campbell	c Mahanama b N.Ranatunga	8	15	–
E.A.Brandes	c A.Ranatunga b Ramanayake	55	35	4/3
A.H.Shah	b Wickremasinghe	25	38	–/1
G.J.Crocker	not out	36	29	5
D.H.Brain	b Wickremasinghe	12	10	2
U.Ranchod	not out	3	6	–
Extras	(lb 18, w 11, nb 1)	30		
Total	(43 overs; 9 wickets)	**236**		

ZIMBABWE	O	M	R	W
Brandes	9	1	57	2
Brain	7	0	41	1
Ranchod	9	1	46	0
Shah	6	0	37	0
G.W.Flower	7	0	45	0
Crocker	5	0	37	1

SRI LANKA	O	M	R	W
Ramanayake	9	0	28	3
Wickremasinghe	9	0	50	2
De Silva	3	0	26	0
Gurusinha	8	1	34	1
Anurasiri	2	0	24	0
N.Ranatunga	9	0	33	1
A.Ranatunga	3	0	23	0

FALL OF WICKETS
1-112, 2-154, 3-165, 4-243, 5-246

FALL OF WICKETS
1-2, 2-20, 3-54, 4-65, 5-85, 6-85, 7-154, 8-194, 9-219

Umpires: R.V.Raman (India) (12) and R.C.Sharma (India) (3).

PAKISTAN v SRI LANKA 1992-93

At Sharjah CA Stadium, UAE on 4 February 1993.　Result: **PAKISTAN** won by 114 runs.　Toss: Sri Lanka.
Award: Saeed Anwar.　LOI debuts: None.

Saeed Anwar and Ramiz Raja shared an opening stand of 204 in 34 overs to surpass their own national LOI record; it remains the second-highest start in internationals. Wasim Akram's tenth four-wicket haul in 140 matches, his second in successive matches, equalled the (then) record tally of Waqar Younis.

PAKISTAN		Runs	Balls	4/6
Saeed Anwar	c Ramanayake b Gurusinha	110	105	9/1
Ramiz Raja	not out	109	115	8
Inzamam-ul-Haq	c Wickremasinghe b Ramanayake	20	11	3
* Wasim Akram	b Gurusinha	22	11	4
Javed Miandad	not out	12	5	–/1
Salim Malik				
Asif Mujtaba				
† Rashid Latif				
Waqar Younis				
Mushtaq Ahmed				
Aqib Javed				
Extras	(lb 6, w 2)	8		
Total	(41 overs; 3 wickets)	281		

SRI LANKA		Runs	Balls	4/6
R.S.Mahanama	lbw b Wasim	0	6	–
U.C.Hathurusinghe	c Mushtaq b Aqib	42	72	4
P.A.de Silva	lbw b Aqib	9	17	–
A.P.Gurusinha	run out	36	59	2
* A.Ranatunga	lbw b Wasim	25	34	3
† H.P.Tillekeratne	lbw b Wasim	11	26	–
R.S.Kalpage	not out	19	25	3
N.Ranatunga	lbw b Wasim	0	3	–
C.P.H.Ramanayake	not out	1	7	–
G.P.Wickremasinghe				
K.P.J.Warnaweera				
Extras	(b 4, lb 6, w 11, nb 3)	24		
Total	(41 overs; 7 wickets)	167		

SRI LANKA	O	M	R	W
Ramanayake	10	1	62	1
Wickremasinghe	5	0	38	0
Gurusinha	7	0	63	2
N.Ranatunga	8	0	49	0
Warnaweera	7	0	39	0
Kalpage	4	0	24	0

PAKISTAN	O	M	R	W
Wasim Akram	10	3	24	4
Aqib Javed	10	2	30	2
Mushtaq Ahmed	10	0	59	0
Waqar Younis	10	0	36	0
Salim Malik	1	0	8	0

FALL OF WICKETS
1-204, 2-231, 3-267

FALL OF WICKETS
1-4, 2-15, 3-105, 4-105, 5-139, 6-162, 7-162

Umpires: R.V.Ramani (India) (13) and R.C.Sharma (India) (4).

SOUTH AFRICA v PAKISTAN 1992-93

At Kingsmead, Durban on 9 February 1993.　Result: **PAKISTAN** won by 10 runs.　Toss: South Africa.
Award: Waqar Younis.　LOI debuts: South Africa – D.J.Cullinan.

Waqar Younis swiftly reclaimed the outright four-wicket record and extended his five-wicket one, this sixth instance in 62 matches precipitating a collapse in which eight wickets fell for 33 runs.

PAKISTAN		Runs	Balls	4/6
Saeed Anwar	b Donald	0	4	–
Ramiz Raja	c Richardson b Matthews	29	45	5
Inzamam-ul-Haq	run out	47	68	4
Javed Miandad	c Richardson b McMillan	22	54	2
Salim Malik	c McMillan b Cronje	14	26	1
Asif Mujtaba	not out	49	66	4
† Rashid Latif	c Richardson b McMillan	15	19	1
* Wasim Akram	not out	20	19	–/1
Waqar Younis				
Mushtaq Ahmed				
Aqib Javed				
Extras	(lb 10, w 2)	12		
Total	(50 overs; 6 wickets)	208		

SOUTH AFRICA		Runs	Balls	4/6
A.C.Hudson	b Waqar	93	124	10/1
* K.C.Wessels	lbw b Wasim	42	84	3
P.N.Kirsten	b Asif	18	42	2
W.J.Cronje	b Waqar	11	17	–
D.J.Cullinan	b Waqar	0	2	–
J.N.Rhodes	run out	5	8	–
B.M.McMillan	run out	2	8	–
† D.J.Richardson	run out	11	10	2
C.R.Matthews	b Waqar	3	6	–
P.S.de Villiers	b Waqar	1	2	–
A.A.Donald	not out	1	2	–
Extras	(lb 7, w 1, nb 3)	11		
Total	(50 overs)	198		

SOUTH AFRICA	O	M	R	W
Donald	10	2	32	1
De Villiers	10	0	41	0
Matthews	10	0	54	1
McMillan	10	1	35	2
Cronje	10	0	36	1

PAKISTAN	O	M	R	W
Wasim Akram	10	1	36	1
Aqib Javed	10	1	38	0
Mushtaq Ahmed	10	0	46	0
Waqar Younis	10	0	25	5
Asif Mujtaba	10	1	46	1

FALL OF WICKETS
1-0, 2-46, 3-93, 4-107, 5-132, 6-166

FALL OF WICKETS
1-101, 2-159, 3-165, 4-165, 5-180, 6-181, 7-182, 8-195, 9-197, 10-198

Umpires: K.E.Liebenberg (10) and C.J.Mitchley (4).

SOUTH AFRICA v WEST INDIES 1992-93

At St George's Park, Port Elizabeth on 11 February 1993.   Result: **SOUTH AFRICA** won by 6 wickets.
Toss: South Africa.   Award: J.N.Rhodes.   LOI debuts: None.

No batsman managed to score 50 on a slow pitch with uneven bounce.

WEST INDIES		Runs	Balls	4/6
D.L.Haynes	b De Villiers	43	104	1
B.C.Lara	lbw b Pringle	13	30	1
P.V.Simmons	lbw b Pringle	0	3	–
* R.B.Richardson	b McMillan	3	12	–
C.L.Hooper	c Richardson b Callaghan	17	32	1
A.L.Logie	c Richardson b Donald	8	16	1
† J.R.Murray	not out	30	53	1
I.R.Bishop	lbw b De Villiers	7	11	1
C.E.L.Ambrose	c Wessels b McMillan	9	12	1
C.A.Walsh	c Cronje b Donald	12	17	2
B.P.Patterson	b Donald	1	6	–
Extras	(lb 4, nb 2)	6		
Total	(49 overs)	**149**		

SOUTH AFRICA		Runs	Balls	4/6
* K.C.Wessels	c Murray b Patterson	8	43	1
A.C.Hudson	c Murray b Patterson	10	40	1
W.J.Cronje	c Simmons b Walsh	1	4	–
P.N.Kirsten	not out	45	93	5
D.J.Callaghan	c Hooper b Bishop	10	40	1
J.N.Rhodes	not out	46	77	4
B.M.McMillan				
† D.J.Richardson				
M.W.Pringle				
P.S.de Villiers				
A.A.Donald				
Extras	(lb 4, w 10, nb 16)	30		
Total	(46.5 overs; 4 wickets)	**150**		

SOUTH AFRICA	O	M	R	W
Donald	10	1	27	3
De Villiers	9	2	21	2
Pringle	10	1	25	2
McMillan	10	0	32	2
Cronje	7	0	23	0
Callaghan	3	0	17	1

WEST INDIES	O	M	R	W
Ambrose	10	3	17	0
Bishop	9	1	23	1
Patterson	8.5	0	46	2
Walsh	10	1	32	1
Hooper	7	1	21	0
Simmons	2	0	7	0

FALL OF WICKETS
1-27, 2-27, 3-42, 4-77, 5-89, 6-91, 7-103, 8-125, 9-144, 10-149

FALL OF WICKETS
1-29, 2-32, 3-33, 4-65

Umpires: R.E.Koertzen (4) and S.B.Lambson (4).

WEST INDIES v PAKISTAN 1992-93

At The Wanderers, Johannesburg on 13 February 1993.   Result: **WEST INDIES** won by 8 wickets (revised target).
Toss: Pakistan.   Award: D.L.Haynes.   LOI debuts: None.

The first international between two visiting teams in South Africa attracted a capacity crowd of 30,000. A break for rain
when West Indies were 73 for 2 after 18 overs reduced their target to 106 from 27 overs.

PAKISTAN		Runs	Balls	4/6
Ramiz Raja	c Logie b Patterson	13	18	2
Shoaib Mohammed	c Lara b Bishop	49	69	8
Inzamam-ul-Haq	c and b Simmons	23	54	2
Javed Miandad	c Hooper b Ambrose	13	37	1
Salim Malik	lbw b Walsh	1	3	–
Asif Mujtaba	c Richardson b Ambrose	5	19	1
† Rashid Latif	b Patterson	9	20	1
* Wasim Akram	c Logie b Bishop	11	19	1
Waqar Younis	not out	3	10	–
Mushtaq Ahmed	lbw b Bishop	5	6	1
Aqib Javed	c Hooper b Bishop	0	3	–
Extras	(lb 4, w 6, nb 8)	18		
Total	(41.5 overs)	**150**		

WEST INDIES		Runs	Balls	4/6
D.L.Haynes	not out	50	76	5
P.V.Simmons	lbw b Waqar	17	43	3
B.C.Lara	b Waqar	0	1	–
C.L.Hooper	not out	22	39	2
* R.B.Richardson				
A.L.Logie				
† J.R.Murray				
I.R.Bishop				
C.E.L.Ambrose				
C.A.Walsh				
B.P.Patterson				
Extras	(lb 8, w 5, nb 7)	20		
Total	(25.1 overs; 2 wickets)	**109**		

WEST INDIES	O	M	R	W
Bishop	9.5	0	25	4
Patterson	8	1	33	2
Ambrose	8	0	31	2
Simmons	7	0	35	1
Walsh	9	2	22	1

PAKISTAN	O	M	R	W
Wasim Akram	6	0	24	0
Aqib Javed	6	0	16	0
Waqar Younis	5	0	19	2
Mushtaq Ahmed	5	0	25	0
Salim Malik	1	0	8	0
Shoaib Mohammed	1.1	0	6	0
Asif Mujtaba	1	0	3	0

FALL OF WICKETS
1-21, 2-74, 3-100, 4-103, 5-111, 6-127, 7-135, 8-143, 9-150, 10-150

FALL OF WICKETS
1-62, 2-62

Umpires: S.B.Lambson (5) and C.J.Mitchley (5).

SOUTH AFRICA v PAKISTAN 1992-93

At Buffalo Park, East London on 15 February 1993.　Result: **PAKISTAN** won by 9 runs (revised target).
Toss: Pakistan.　Award: Javed Miandad.　LOI debuts: South Africa – E.L.R.Stewart.

Javed Miandad scored the last of his eight hundreds. Rain extended the interval and revised South Africa's target to 172 from 31 overs. Wasim Akram recorded his best LOI analysis, taking four wickets in 13 balls as the hosts lost seven wickets for 11 runs.

PAKISTAN		Runs	Balls	4/6
Ramiz Raja	c Callaghan b De Villiers	5	13	1
Shoaib Mohammed	b De Villiers	0	1	–
Salim Malik	c Callaghan b Pringle	13	45	–
Javed Miandad	run out	107	144	9/2
Asif Mujtaba	c Wessels b De Villiers	74	96	6/1
* Wasim Akram	c Stewart b De Villiers	2	3	–
Saeed Anwar	not out	1	1	–
† Rashid Latif				
Waqar Younis				
Mushtaq Ahmed				
Aqib Javed				
Extras	(lb 4, w 6, nb 2)	12		
Total	(50 overs; 6 wickets)	**214**		

SOUTH AFRICA		Runs	Balls	4/6
A.C.Hudson	b Wasim	4	16	–
* K.C.Wessels	run out	27	45	1
W.J.Cronje	run out	81	70	3/2
P.N.Kirsten	c Shoaib b Salim	1	5	–
J.N.Rhodes	b Wasim	35	34	2/1
D.J.Callaghan	b Waqar	0	1	–
† E.L.R.Stewart	c Rashid b Wasim	1	3	–
B.M.McMillan	lbw b Wasim	1	3	–
M.W.Pringle	run out	2	5	–
P.S.de Villiers	not out	0		–
A.A.Donald	b Wasim	0	1	–
Extras	(b 3, lb 6, nb 1)	10		
Total	(30.1 overs)	**162**		

SOUTH AFRICA	O	M	R	W
Donald	10	2	38	0
De Villiers	10	2	27	4
Pringle	10	1	41	1
McMillan	10	0	62	0
Cronje	8	0	30	0
Callaghan	2	0	12	0

PAKISTAN	O	M	R	W
Wasim Akram	6.1	0	16	5
Aqib Javed	6	0	29	0
Mushtaq Ahmed	6	0	37	0
Waqar Younis	6	0	30	1
Shoaib Mohammed	1	0	11	0
Salim Malik	5	0	30	1

FALL OF WICKETS
1-0, 2-7, 3-29, 4-194, 5-206, 6-214

FALL OF WICKETS
1-8, 2-80, 3-82, 4-151, 5-154, 6-155, 7-157, 8-160, 9-162, 10-162

Umpires: W.A.Diedricks (3) and K.E.Liebenberg (11).

SOUTH AFRICA v WEST INDIES 1992-93

At Newlands, Cape Town on 17 February 1993.　Result: **SOUTH AFRICA** won by 4 runs.　Toss: West Indies.
Award: W.J.Cronje.　LOI debuts: None.

Another close scrape on a poor pitch with erratic bounce enabled South Africa to remain in contention.

SOUTH AFRICA		Runs	Balls	4/6
A.C.Hudson	c Simmons b Patterson	0	10	–
* K.C.Wessels	b Patterson	1	5	–
W.J.Cronje	c Murray b Simmons	31	80	1
P.N.Kirsten	c Logie b Walsh	30	123	1
D.J.Cullinan	c Haynes b Simmons	40	56	3
J.N.Rhodes	b Walsh	0	3	–
† E.L.R.Stewart	c and b Bishop	1	13	–
C.R.Matthews	c sub (J.C.Adams) b Hooper	9	11	1
M.W.Pringle	not out	8	8	1
P.S.de Villiers	c and b Hooper	0	2	–
A.A.Donald	not out	0	1	–
Extras	(lb 5, w 6, nb 9)	20		
Total	(50 overs; 9 wickets)	**140**		

WEST INDIES		Runs	Balls	4/6
D.L.Haynes	run out	0	5	–
P.V.Simmons	c Cronje b Pringle	20	35	4
* R.B.Richardson	c De Villiers b Donald	2	6	–
B.C.Lara	run out	14	28	2
C.L.Hooper	lbw b Cronje	34	71	4
A.L.Logie	c Hudson b Cronje	15	55	–
† J.R.Murray	run out	1	4	–
I.R.Bishop	c Rhodes b Pringle	6	25	–
C.E.L.Ambrose	not out	19	27	2
C.A.Walsh	c Stewart b Cronje	10	19	1
B.P.Patterson	lbw b Pringle	1	9	–
Extras	(lb 9, w 4, nb 1)	14		
Total	(47 overs)	**136**		

WEST INDIES	O	M	R	W
Patterson	9	2	20	2
Walsh	10	2	24	2
Ambrose	10	3	23	0
Bishop	10	1	31	1
Simmons	10	0	36	2
Hooper	1	0	1	2

SOUTH AFRICA	O	M	R	W
Donald	10	2	20	1
De Villiers	10	3	28	0
Pringle	9	0	27	3
Matthews	10	1	25	0
Cronje	8	0	27	3

FALL OF WICKETS
1-2, 2-5, 3-66, 4-99, 5-100, 6-110, 7-130, 8-139, 9-140

FALL OF WICKETS
1-15, 2-17, 3-30, 4-47, 5-88, 6-91, 7-99, 8-113, 9-134, 10-136

Umpires: R.E.Koertzen (5) and C.J.Mitchley (6).

WEST INDIES v PAKISTAN 1992-93

At Kingsmead, Durban on 19 February 1993.   Result: **WEST INDIES** won by 124 runs.   Toss: Pakistan.
Award: B.C.Lara.   LOI debuts: None.

An outstanding exhibition of strokeplay brought Brian Lara his first LOI hundred; his tally of 20 fours remains the record for internationals in South Africa. Pakistan emulated their hosts' capacity for startling collapses.

WEST INDIES		Runs	Balls	4/6
D.L.Haynes	lbw b Wasim	6	20	1
B.C.Lara	c Shoaib b Waqar	128	125	20
P.V.Simmons	c Ramiz b Aamir	70	103	7/1
* R.B.Richardson	c Rashid b Waqar	7	12	–
C.L.Hooper	not out	20	23	1
A.L.Logie	c Rashid b Waqar	5	7	–
J.C.Adams	not out	12	17	1
† J.R.Murray				
I.R.Bishop				
C.E.L.Ambrose				
C.A.Walsh				
Extras	(lb 8, w 6, nb 6)	20		
Total	(50 overs; 5 wickets)	**268**		

PAKISTAN	O	M	R	W
Wasim Akram	10	0	41	1
Aqib Javed	10	2	40	0
Ata-ur-Rehman	10	1	57	0
Waqar Younis	10	0	53	3
Aamir Sohail	4	0	27	1
Asif Mujtaba	3	0	19	0
Shoaib Mohammed	3	0	23	0

FALL OF WICKETS
1-12, 2-209, 3-229, 4-230, 5-238

PAKISTAN		Runs	Balls	4/6
Aamir Sohail	c Hooper b Bishop	14	41	1
Ramiz Raja	run out	34	76	1
Shoaib Mohammed	c Hooper b Bishop	0	3	–
Javed Miandad	c and b Hooper	67	94	7
Zahid Fazal	c Haynes b Ambrose	8	19	1
Asif Mujtaba	b Hooper	3	12	–
† Rashid Latif	c Hooper b Bishop	0	3	–
* Wasim Akram	c Ambrose b Bishop	6	17	1
Waqar Younis	c Simmons b Hooper	2	12	–
Ata-ur-Rehman	c Murray b Walsh	0	3	–
Aqib Javed	not out	3	6	–
Extras	(lb 3, nb 4)	7		
Total	(46.5 overs)	**144**		

WEST INDIES	O	M	R	W
Ambrose	8	2	18	1
Walsh	10	1	21	1
Simmons	9	0	43	0
Bishop	10	1	32	4
Hooper	9.5	1	27	3

FALL OF WICKETS
1-20, 2-20, 3-95, 4-108, 5-113, 6-114, 7-125, 8-133, 9-133, 10-144

Umpires: W.A.Diedricks (4) and S.B.Lambson (6).

SOUTH AFRICA v PAKISTAN 1992-93

At Centurion Park, Verwoerdburg, Pretoria on 21 February 1993.   Result: **PAKISTAN** won by 22 runs.   Toss: Pakistan.
Award: Ramiz Raja.   LOI debuts: None.

A capacity crowd of 18,000, including many local Muslims, saw Pakistan gain their third tournament victory over the hosts.

PAKISTAN		Runs	Balls	4/6
Aamir Sohail	c Wessels b Donald	62	92	6
Ramiz Raja	c Wessels b De Villiers	53	79	4/1
Javed Miandad	c Richardson b Pringle	16	30	–
Zahid Fazal	c Kirsten b Pringle	16	28	–
Salim Malik	run out	9	10	1
Asif Mujtaba	c Wessels b Pringle	8	23	–
† Rashid Latif	c Richardson b Donald	3	10	–
* Wasim Akram	run out	16	15	–
Waqar Younis	not out	20	15	2
Mushtaq Ahmed	not out	1	1	–
Aqib Javed				
Extras	(lb 5, w 9, nb 2)	16		
Total	(50 overs; 8 wickets)	**220**		

SOUTH AFRICA	O	M	R	W
Donald	10	0	61	2
De Villiers	10	2	27	1
Pringle	10	0	52	3
Snell	10	0	31	0
Cronje	10	0	44	0

FALL OF WICKETS
1-121, 2-131, 3-147, 4-167, 5-169, 6-174, 7-192, 8-218

SOUTH AFRICA		Runs	Balls	4/6
A.C.Hudson	c Rashid b Aqib	7	22	–
* K.C.Wessels	run out	39	76	1
W.J.Cronje	c Waqar b Mushtaq	17	31	2
P.N.Kirsten	st Rashid b Mushtaq	35	62	1/1
D.J.Cullinan	run out	15	23	1
J.N.Rhodes	c Miandad b Wasim	25	30	1
R.P.Snell	lbw b Waqar	19	28	1
† D.J.Richardson	run out	10	12	–
M.W.Pringle	b Waqar	10	8	1
P.S.de Villiers	not out	6	10	–
A.A.Donald	not out	5	5	–
Extras	(lb 2, w 2, nb 6)	10		
Total	(50 overs; 9 wickets)	**198**		

PAKISTAN	O	M	R	W
Wasim Akram	10	0	34	1
Aqib Javed	10	0	31	1
Waqar Younis	10	0	50	2
Mushtaq Ahmed	10	0	29	2
Aamir Sohail	7	0	32	0
Asif Mujtaba	3	0	20	0

FALL OF WICKETS
1-18, 2-52, 3-84, 4-117, 5-130, 6-163, 7-167, 8-185, 9-188

Umpires: R.E.Koertzen (6) and C.J.Mitchley (7).

SOUTH AFRICA v WEST INDIES 1992-93

At Springbok Park, Bloemfontein on 23 February 1993.   Result: **WEST INDIES** won by 9 wickets.
Toss: South Africa.   Award: B.C.Lara.   LOI debuts: None.

Another sublime hundred from Brian Lara, his second in successive innings, extinguished South Africa's hopes of reaching the final. His stand of 152 with Desmond Haynes was the best start in any LOI in South Africa until 1995-96 (*No. 1040*).

SOUTH AFRICA		Runs	Balls	4/6
* K.C.Wessels	b Simmons	49	89	3
A.C.Hudson	lbw b Simmons	17	46	1
W.J.Cronje	b Bishop	5	9	–
P.N.Kirsten	b Ambrose	10	29	–
D.J.Cullinan	c Richardson b Bishop	45	66	1
J.N.Rhodes	run out	22	39	1
† E.L.R.Stewart	not out	23	28	2
R.P.Snell	not out	0	–	–
M.W.Pringle				
P.S.de Villiers				
A.A.Donald				
Extras	(b 4, lb 5, w 2, nb 3)	14		
Total	(50 overs; 6 wickets)	185		

WEST INDIES		Runs	Balls	4/6
D.L.Haynes	c Stewart b Snell	57	105	2/1
B.C.Lara	not out	111	140	14/1
P.V.Simmons	not out	6	23	1
* R.B.Richardson				
C.L.Hooper				
A.L.Logie				
J.C.Adams				
† J.R.Murray				
I.R.Bishop				
C.E.L.Ambrose				
C.A.Walsh				
Extras	(b 6, lb 5, w 2, nb 1)	14		
Total	(44.3 overs; 1 wicket)	188		

WEST INDIES	O	M	R	W
Ambrose	10	1	31	1
Walsh	10	2	26	0
Simmons	10	0	36	2
Bishop	10	0	52	2
Hooper	10	0	31	0

SOUTH AFRICA	O	M	R	W
Donald	10	1	24	0
de Villiers	10	0	38	0
Pringle	10	0	50	0
Snell	10	1	36	1
Cronje	4	0	25	0
Kirsten	0.3	0	4	0

FALL OF WICKETS
1-52, 2-60, 3-84, 4-92, 5-138, 6-183

FALL OF WICKETS
1-152

Umpires: S.B.Lambson (7) and K.E.Liebenberg (12).

WEST INDIES v PAKISTAN 1992-93

At Newlands, Cape Town on 25 February 1993.   Result: **WEST INDIES** won by 7 wickets.   Toss: West Indies.
Award: C.A.Walsh.   LOI debuts: Pakistan – Ghulam Ali.

A disgraceful pitch, over-grassed and uneven in bounce, threatened the international status of Newlands and produced the lowest innings total (43) and match aggregate (88), as well as the shortest completed innings (19.5 overs) and the briefest match (32.2 overs). Uniquely, the first ball of each innings produced a wicket.

PAKISTAN		Runs	Balls	4/6
Ramiz Raja	c Lara b Patterson	0	1	–
Ghulam Ali	c Hooper b Patterson	2	19	–
Saeed Anwar	c Murray b Walsh	5	19	–
Zahid Fazal	c Lara b Simmons	21	44	2
Salim Malik	c Haynes b Walsh	1	7	–
Asif Mujtaba	c Lara b Walsh	0	3	–
* Wasim Akram	c Hooper b Walsh	0	2	–
† Rashid Latif	c Logie b Cummins	0	9	–
Waqar Younis	b Cummins	0	1	–
Mushtaq Ahmed	c Simmons b Cummins	0	5	–
Aqib Javed	not out	4	16	1
Extras	(b 1, lb 1, w 2, nb 6)	10		
Total	(19.5 overs)	43		

WEST INDIES		Runs	Balls	4/6
D.L.Haynes	lbw b Waqar	0	1	–
B.C.Lara	not out	26	34	3
P.V.Simmons	c Salim b Wasim	2	4	–
C.L.Hooper	c Mushtaq b Wasim	1	9	–
* R.B.Richardson	not out	7	29	1
A.L.Logie				
J.C.Adams				
† J.R.Murray				
A.C.Cummins				
C.A.Walsh				
B.P.Patterson				
Extras	(lb 7, nb 2)	9		
Total	(12.3 overs; 3 wickets)	45		

WEST INDIES	O	M	R	W
Patterson	6	0	14	2
Walsh	9	2	16	4
Cummins	4	0	11	3
Simmons	0.5	0	0	1

PAKISTAN	O	M	R	W
Waqar Younis	5	1	7	1
Wasim Akram	6	0	22	2
Aqib Javed	1.3	0	9	0

FALL OF WICKETS
1-0, 2-9, 3-11

FALL OF WICKETS
1-10, 2-10, 3-11, 4-14, 5-14, 6-14, 7-25, 8-25, 9-26, 10-43

Umpires: W.A.Diedricks (5) and K.E.Liebenberg (13).

WEST INDIES v PAKISTAN 1992-93

At The Wanderers, Johannesburg on 27 February 1993.　　Result: **WEST INDIES** won by 5 wickets.
Toss: West Indies.　　Award: Aamir Sohail.　　LOI debuts: None.

West Indies confirmed their supremacy with their seventh consecutive victory against the World Cup holders. In his 220th international, Desmond Haynes became the first to score 8000 runs. Brian Lara's aggregate of 341, average 68.20, won the tournament award.

PAKISTAN		Runs	Balls	4/6
Aamir Sohail	c Hooper b Ambrose	57	95	3
Ramiz Raja	lbw b Simmons	11	35	1
Shoaib Mohammed	b Bishop	0	4	–
Javed Miandad	lbw b Bishop	0	7	–
Zahid Fazal	c Murray b Simmons	7	21	–
Asif Mujtaba	run out	25	62	–
* Wasim Akram	run out	34	42	3/1
† Rashid Latif	run out	1	1	–
Waqar Younis	b Ambrose	37	35	1/2
Mushtaq Ahmed	not out	0	1	–
Aqib Javed	b Ambrose	0	1	–
Extras	(lb 7, w 5, nb 3)	15		
Total	(50 overs)	187		

WEST INDIES		Runs	Balls	4/6
D.L.Haynes	b Waqar	59	77	7
B.C.Lara	b Aamir	49	68	4/1
P.V.Simmons	b Waqar	5	9	1
C.L.Hooper	b Aqib	12	16	1
* R.B.Richardson	c Ramiz b Aamir	11	32	–
A.L.Logie	not out	41	33	6
J.C.Adams	not out	5	9	–
† J.R.Murray				
I.R.Bishop				
C.E.L.Ambrose				
C.A.Walsh				
Extras	(lb 4, w 1, nb 3)	8		
Total	(39.4 overs; 5 wickets)	190		

WEST INDIES	O	M	R	W
Ambrose	10	2	33	3
Walsh	10	3	28	0
Simmons	10	1	23	2
Bishop	10	0	46	2
Hooper	10	0	50	0

PAKISTAN	O	M	R	W
Wasim Akram	8	0	32	0
Aqib Javed	7	0	32	1
Mushtaq Ahmed	5	0	27	0
Waqar Younis	9.4	1	63	2
Aamir Sohail	10	0	32	2

FALL OF WICKETS
1-46, 2-48, 3-55, 4-73, 5-87, 6-141, 7-142, 8-187, 9-187, 10-187

FALL OF WICKETS
1-112, 2-114, 3-124, 4-142, 5-158

Umpires: S.B.Lambson (8) and K.E.Liebenberg (14).

ZIMBABWE v PAKISTAN 1992-93

At Harare Sports Club on 2 March 1993.　　Result: **PAKISTAN** won by 7 wickets.　　Toss: Pakistan.
Award: Javed Miandad.　　LOI debuts: None.

Victory in this one-off match played en route for home brought Pakistan some compensation. Gavin Briant kept wicket throughout the innings after Andy Flower had damaged a finger while batting.

ZIMBABWE		Runs	Balls	4/6
† A.Flower	c and b Mushtaq	10	23	–
G.W.Flower	c Aamir b Mushtaq	35	108	1
K.J.Arnott	run out	17	30	1
* D.L.Houghton	lbw b Waqar	51	74	3
G.A.Briant	c Rashid b Mushtaq	0	1	–
M.H.Dekker	c Rashid b Aqib	16	34	–/1
A.H.Shah	c Shoaib b Wasim	0	6	–
S.G.Peall	c Rashid b Waqar	3	10	–
E.A.Brandes	b Waqar	5	10	–
D.H.Brain	b Wasim	1	4	–
A.J.Traicos	not out	0	–	–
Extras	(b 2, lb 7, w 13, nb 4)	26		
Total	(49.1 overs)	164		

PAKISTAN		Runs	Balls	4/6
Aamir Sohail	c Brandes b Shah	15	18	2
Ramiz Raja	c G.W.Flower b Brandes	0	3	–
Shoaib Mohammed	c Traicos b Brain	43	118	2
Javed Miandad	not out	86	132	4/2
Zahid Fazal	not out	8	13	–
Asif Mujtaba				
* Wasim Akram				
† Rashid Latif				
Waqar Younis				
Mushtaq Ahmed				
Aqib Javed				
Extras	(b 2, lb 3, w 8)	13		
Total	(47.2 overs; 3 wickets)	165		

PAKISTAN	O	M	R	W
Wasim Akram	10	0	35	2
Aqib Javed	10	1	32	1
Waqar Younis	8.1	1	31	3
Mushtaq Ahmed	10	2	22	3
Aamir Sohail	10	0	30	0
Asif Mujtaba	1	0	5	0

ZIMBABWE	O	M	R	W
Brandes	8.2	1	33	1
Brain	10	3	29	1
Shah	10	0	26	1
Traicos	10	1	29	0
Peall	9	0	43	0

FALL OF WICKETS
1-55, 2-60, 3-92, 4-92, 5-139, 6-140, 7-152, 8-159, 9-164, 10-164

FALL OF WICKETS
1-1, 2-27, 3-142

Umpires: K.Kanjee (3) and I.D.Robinson (10).

SRI LANKA v ENGLAND 1992-93

At Khettarama Stadium, Colombo on 10 March 1993.   Result: **SRI LANKA** won by 32 runs (revised target).
Toss: Sri Lanka.   Award: H.P.Tillekeratne.   LOI debuts: None.

With Graham Gooch opting out of the Sri Lanka leg of their tour, Alec Stewart captained these two internationals and the Test match they sandwiched. Heavy rain, when England were 67 for 3 in the 20th over, reduced their target to 203 from 38 overs.

SRI LANKA		Runs	Balls	4/6
R.S.Mahanama	c Hick b Malcolm	7	20	–
U.C.Hathurusinghe	lbw b Emburey	43	80	4
A.P.Gurusinha	c DeFreitas b Jarvis	5	24	–
P.A.de Silva	c and b Reeve	34	48	1/1
* A.Ranatunga	c Stewart b Lewis	36	41	1
H.P.Tillekeratne	not out	66	65	6
S.T.Jayasuriya	not out	34	22	1/2
† A.M.de Silva				
R.S.Kalpage				
C.P.H.Ramanayake				
G.P.Wickremasinghe				
Extras	(b 3, lb 4, w 10, nb 8)	25		
Total	(47 overs; 5 wickets)	**250**		

ENGLAND		Runs	Balls	4/6
R.A.Smith	c and b Wickremasinghe	3	21	–
*†A.J.Stewart	lbw b Ramanayake	5	12	–
G.A.Hick	c Mahanama b Hathurusinghe	31	42	5
N.H.Fairbrother	lbw b Jayasuriya	24	55	1
M.W.Gatting	b Kalpage	1	8	–
C.C.Lewis	b Kalpage	16	17	–/1
D.A.Reeve	c Ranatunga b Kalpage	16	18	1
P.A.J.DeFreitas	c Ranatunga b Wickremasinghe	21	27	1/1
J.E.Emburey	st A.M.de Silva b Jayasuriya	10	8	1
P.W.Jarvis	not out	16	9	1/1
D.E.Malcolm	run out	2	2	–
Extras	(lb 10, w 4, nb 1)	15		
Total	(36.1 overs)	**170**		

ENGLAND	O	M	R	W
Malcolm	7	1	32	1
Lewis	9	0	40	1
Jarvis	9	0	57	1
DeFreitas	3	0	25	0
Emburey	10	1	42	1
Reeve	9	1	47	1

SRI LANKA	O	M	R	W
Ramanayake	7	0	25	1
Wickremasinghe	6.1	1	21	2
Hathurusinghe	6	0	28	1
Gurusinha	2	0	7	0
Kalpage	8	0	34	3
Jayasuriya	7	0	45	2

FALL OF WICKETS
1-16, 2-33, 3-101, 4-109, 5-180

FALL OF WICKETS
1-7, 2-9, 3-67, 4-71, 5-99, 6-103, 7-120, 8-137, 9-152, 10-170

Umpires: K.T.Francis (15) and S.Ponnadurai (8).

SRI LANKA v ENGLAND 1992-93

At Tyronne Fernando Stadium, Moratuwa on 20 March 1993.   Result: **SRI LANKA** won by 8 wickets.
Toss: Sri Lanka.   Award: S.T.Jayasuriya.   LOI debuts: England – J.P.Taylor.

England's disastrous tour ended in a comprehensive defeat with 14.4 overs to spare. Sanath Jayasuriya's left-arm tweakers were rewarded with Sri Lanka's only six-wicket LOI analysis.

ENGLAND		Runs	Balls	4/6
C.C.Lewis	c Ramanayake b Wickremasinghe	8	17	2
R.A.Smith	st A.M.de Silva b Jayasuriya	31	48	3/1
G.A.Hick	lbw b Kalpage	36	44	6
N.H.Fairbrother	c A.M.de Silva b Jayasuriya	21	47	1/1
*†A.J.Stewart	lbw b Tillekeratne	14	32	1
M.W.Gatting	lbw b P.A.de Silva	2	8	–
D.A.Reeve	b Jayasuriya	21	44	–
J.E.Emburey	c Ramanayake b Jayasuriya	20	41	–
I.D.K.Salisbury	not out	2	6	–
P.W.Jarvis	c A.M.de Silva b Jayasuriya	4	4	–
J.P.Taylor	b Jayasuriya	1	8	–
Extras	(b 2, lb 9, w 3, nb 6)	20		
Total	(48.5 overs)	**180**		

SRI LANKA		Runs	Balls	4/6
R.S.Mahanama	c Stewart b Salisbury	29	48	5
U.C.Hathurusinghe	c and b Salisbury	33	48	5
A.P.Gurusinha	not out	35	54	2
P.A.de Silva	not out	75	68	7/4
* A.Ranatunga				
H.P.Tillekeratne				
S.T.Jayasuriya				
† A.M.de Silva				
R.S.Kalpage				
C.P.H.Ramanayake				
G.P.Wickremasinghe				
Extras	(b 1, lb 2, w 2, nb 6)	11		
Total	(35.2 overs; 2 wickets)	**183**		

SRI LANKA	O	M	R	W
Ramanayake	4	0	20	0
Wickremasinghe	8	0	23	1
Gurusinha	4	0	21	0
Hathurusinghe	2	0	13	0
Kalpage	10	0	27	1
Jayasuriya	9.5	0	29	6
P.A.de Silva	7	1	22	1
Tillekeratne	4	0	14	1

ENGLAND	O	M	R	W
Lewis	7	1	13	0
Jarvis	4	0	22	0
Taylor	3	0	20	0
Emburey	6	0	29	0
Salisbury	4	0	36	2
Hick	6.2	1	36	0
Reeve	5	0	24	0

FALL OF WICKETS
1-23, 2-77, 3-85, 4-111, 5-114, 6-125, 7-168, 8-172, 9-177, 10-180

FALL OF WICKETS
1-66, 2-68

Umpires: B.C.Cooray (9) and T.M.Samarasinghe (2).

NEW ZEALAND v AUSTRALIA 1992-93

At Carisbrook, Dunedin on 19 March 1993.　　Result: **AUSTRALIA** won by 129 runs.　　Toss: New Zealand.
Award: A.I.C.Dodemaide.　　LOI debuts: New Zealand – J.W.Wilson.

All-rounder Jeff Wilson was subsequently to represent New Zealand at rugby. Martin Crowe 'walked' after being given not out by umpire King.

AUSTRALIA		Runs	Balls	4/6
M.E.Waugh	c Crowe b Watson	60	75	4/2
M.A.Taylor	run out	78	122	5/3
D.M.Jones	c Greatbatch b Larsen	52	56	2/2
S.R.Waugh	not out	23	26	1
D.R.Martyn	b Wilson	22	16	–/1
* A.R.Border	not out	14	8	–/1
† I.A.Healy				
M.G.Hughes				
A.I.C.Dodemaide				
P.R.Reiffel				
T.B.A.May				
Extras	(lb 7, nb 2)	9		
Total	(50 overs; 4 wickets)	**258**		

NEW ZEALAND	O	M	R	W
Morrison	10	0	36	0
Wilson	10	0	58	1
Patel	8	0	40	0
Watson	10	0	58	1
Larsen	10	0	44	1
Latham	2	0	15	0

FALL OF WICKETS
1-95, 2-199, 3-200, 4-236

Umpires: R.S.Dunne (12) and C.E.King (2).

NEW ZEALAND		Runs	Balls	4/6
M.J.Greatbatch	c Jones b Hughes	0	3	–
R.T.Latham	c Healy b Dodemaide	1	3	–
A.H.Jones	b Reiffel	24	60	1
* M.D.Crowe	c Healy b Dodemaide	1	8	–
K.R.Rutherford	b Dodemaide	21	33	3
† T.E.Blain	b Dodemaide	0	2	–
J.W.Wilson	b Reiffel	0	4	–
D.N.Patel	c Martyn b May	11	28	–
G.R.Larsen	st Healy b May	22	47	1/1
D.K.Morrison	not out	20	40	1/1
W.Watson	c Martyn b May	21	28	1/1
Extras	(lb 3, w 3, nb 2)	8		
Total	(42.2 overs)	**129**		

AUSTRALIA	O	M	R	W
Hughes	7	0	23	1
Dodemaide	10	4	20	4
Reiffel	9	2	17	2
S.R.Waugh	7	0	15	0
May	9.2	0	51	3

FALL OF WICKETS
1-0, 2-2, 3-10, 4-46, 5-46, 6-49, 7-52, 8-72, 9-97, 10-129

Referee: Javed Burki (*Pakistan*).

NEW ZEALAND v AUSTRALIA 1992-93

At Lancaster Park, Christchurch on 21, 22 March 1993.　　Result: **AUSTRALIA** won by 1 wicket.　　Toss: New Zealand.
Award: P.R.Reiffel.　　LOI debuts: None.

The first international in New Zealand to be taken into a second day had been reduced by earlier rain to a 45-over game. David Boon was the first Australian to be given out by a video-armed spare umpire, while Ian Healy uniquely incurred separate run out appeals at each end off the same ball. Australia were 51 for 2 after 13.3 overs at stumps on the first day.

NEW ZEALAND		Runs	Balls	4/6
R.T.Latham	c S.R.Waugh b Hughes	13	21	2
M.J.Greatbatch	c Jones b Reiffel	32	63	4/1
A.H.Jones	c Healy b Reiffel	22	44	2
* M.D.Crowe	b Reiffel	1	7	–
K.R.Rutherford	b S.R.Waugh	35	35	3/1
C.Z.Harris	b Reiffel	0	1	–
† T.E.Blain	c Jones b M.E.Waugh	41	65	1
D.N.Patel	run out	13	13	2
G.R.Larsen	not out	23	19	–/1
C.Pringle	not out	2	3	–
D.K.Morrison				
Extras	(b 5, lb 7, w 1, nb 1)	14		
Total	(45 overs; 8 wickets)	**196**		

AUSTRALIA	O	M	R	W
Hughes	9	3	27	1
Dodemaide	10	4	27	0
Reiffel	10	2	38	4
May	9	0	52	0
S.R.Waugh	6	0	35	1
M.E.Waugh	1	0	5	1

FALL OF WICKETS
1-22, 2-65, 3-74, 4-75, 5-75, 6-139, 7-163, 8-191

Umpires: R.S.Dunne (13) and D.M.Quested (2).

AUSTRALIA		Runs	Balls	4/6
* M.A.Taylor	c Crowe b Patel	3	12	–
M.E.Waugh	st Blain b Harris	57	80	4/1
D.M.Jones	b Morrison	6	10	1
D.C.Boon	run out	55	66	6
S.R.Waugh	b Morrison	30	54	–
D.R.Martyn	c Jones b Harris	1	8	–
† I.A.Healy	run out	15	24	–
M.G.Hughes	c and b Pringle	0	1	–
A.I.C.Dodemaide	run out	8	11	–
P.R.Reiffel	not out	1	4	–
T.B.A.May	not out	0	–	–
Extras	(b 1, lb 13, w 4, nb 3)	21		
Total	(44.3 overs; 9 wickets)	**197**		

NEW ZEALAND	O	M	R	W
Morrison	9	0	45	2
Patel	9	0	33	1
Larsen	9	2	28	0
Pringle	8.3	0	41	1
Harris	9	1	36	2

FALL OF WICKETS
1-7, 2-19, 3-122, 4-130, 5-142, 6-179, 7-179, 8-196, 9-196

Referee: Javed Burki (*Pakistan*).

NEW ZEALAND v AUSTRALIA 1992-93

At Basin Reserve, Wellington on 24 March 1993.　Result: **NEW ZEALAND** won by 88 runs.　Toss: New Zealand.
Award: G.R.Larsen.　LOI debuts: Australia – S.K.Warne.

Shane Warne's debut in limited-overs internationals gave scant indication of the deeds which were to follow. He bruised his right thumb fielding and missed the rest of this series.

NEW ZEALAND		Runs	Balls	4/6
M.J.Greatbatch	c S.R.Waugh b Dodemaide	8	19	1
R.T.Latham	lbw b Reiffel	21	47	3
A.H.Jones	st Healy b Warne	29	54	1
* M.D.Crowe	not out	91	105	4/2
C.Z.Harris	run out	18	29	1
† T.E.Blain	c and b Border	9	10	1
J.W.Wilson	c S.R.Waugh b Warne	15	23	–
D.N.Patel	c M.E.Waugh b Border	7	9	–
G.R.Larsen	run out	4	9	–
C.Pringle	run out	1	1	–
D.K.Morrison	c Boon b Dodemaide	0	1	–
Extras	(lb 3, w 8)	11		
Total	(50 overs)	**214**		

AUSTRALIA		Runs	Balls	4/6
M.E.Waugh	b Morrison	0	3	–
M.A.Taylor	c Latham b Patel	50	94	5
D.M.Jones	c Blain b Larsen	25	36	4
D.C.Boon	b Wilson	2	14	–
S.R.Waugh	b Harris	9	20	–
* A.R.Border	run out	0	5	–
† I.A.Healy	c Wilson b Larsen	1	3	–
M.G.Hughes	b Larsen	2	14	–
A.I.C.Dodemaide	c Greatbatch b Patel	7	24	–
P.R.Reiffel	not out	8	15	–
S.K.Warne	b Wilson	3	3	–
Extras	(b 4, lb 5, w 7, nb 3)	19		
Total	(37.2 overs)	**126**		

AUSTRALIA	O	M	R	W
Hughes	4	0	21	0
Dodemaide	9	1	38	2
Reiffel	10	1	21	1
Warne	10	0	40	2
S.R.Waugh	7	0	37	0
Border	10	0	54	2

NEW ZEALAND	O	M	R	W
Morrison	4	1	21	1
Pringle	5	1	11	0
Wilson	5.2	0	21	2
Larsen	10	3	17	3
Harris	8	1	33	1
Patel	5	0	14	2

FALL OF WICKETS
1-26, 2-49, 3-95, 4-127, 5-140, 6-168, 7-178, 8-205, 9-213, 10-214

FALL OF WICKETS
1-0, 2-42, 3-55, 4-71, 5-71, 6-77, 7-93, 8-108, 9-122, 10-126

Umpires: C.E.King (3) and D.M.Quested (3).

Referee: Javed Burki (*Pakistan*).

NEW ZEALAND v AUSTRALIA 1992-93

At Seddon (Trust Bank) Park, Hamilton on 27 March 1993.　Result: **NEW ZEALAND** won by 3 wickets.
Toss: Australia.　Award: M.D.Crowe.　LOI debuts: None.

Mark Waugh's maiden LOI hundred was overshadowed by a series-levelling epic from 19-year-old Jeff Wilson. He was to play only one more international before devoting himself to rugby.

AUSTRALIA		Runs	Balls	4/6
* M.A.Taylor	c Blain b Morrison	13	37	2
M.E.Waugh	b Morrison	108	131	7/1
D.M.Jones	run out	64	84	4
D.C.Boon	c Morrison b Harris	2	5	–
S.R.Waugh	b Pringle	19	21	2
D.R.Martyn	c Blain b Morrison	17	17	2
† I.A.Healy	lbw b Pringle	1	3	–
A.I.C.Dodemaide	not out	1	2	–
M.G.Hughes	not out	10	5	1/1
P.R.Reiffel				
T.B.A.May				
Extras	(b 1, lb 6, w 5)	12		
Total	(50 overs; 7 wickets)	**247**		

NEW ZEALAND		Runs	Balls	4/6
M.J.Greatbatch	c Healy b Hughes	13	42	2
A.H.Jones	run out	18	50	1
* M.D.Crowe	run out	91	101	8/1
K.R.Rutherford	c Healy b Reiffel	9	16	–
C.Z.Harris	c Healy b Reiffel	0	4	–
† T.E.Blain	b Dodemaide	41	43	3/1
J.W.Wilson	not out	44	28	3/1
D.N.Patel	run out	4	5	–
G.R.Larsen	not out	12	14	–
C.Pringle				
D.K.Morrison				
Extras	(b 2, lb 11, w 5)	18		
Total	(49.4 overs; 7 wickets)	**250**		

NEW ZEALAND	O	M	R	W
Morrison	9	0	35	3
Pringle	8	1	41	2
Larsen	10	0	42	0
Wilson	3	0	20	0
Patel	10	0	47	0
Harris	7	0	37	1
Jones	3	0	18	0

AUSTRALIA	O	M	R	W
Hughes	10	3	28	1
Dodemaide	10	1	39	1
Reiffel	10	2	46	2
May	10	0	45	0
S.R.Waugh	7.4	0	59	0
M.E.Waugh	2	0	20	0

FALL OF WICKETS
1-29, 2-172, 3-178, 4-215, 5-217, 6-227, 7-235

FALL OF WICKETS
1-24, 2-59, 3-88, 4-94, 5-172, 6-196, 7-210

Umpires: B.L.Aldridge (30) and D.B.Cowie (3).

Referee: Javed Burki (*Pakistan*).

NEW ZEALAND v AUSTRALIA 1992-93

At Eden Park, Auckland on 28 March 1993.   Result: **AUSTRALIA** won by 3 runs.   Toss: New Zealand.
Award: M.E.Waugh.   LOI debuts: None.

This closely fought series went to the wire, enthralling a crowd of 31,942 to the very last ball. New Zealand needed 14 from the final over, bowled by Merv Hughes and six from the last ball. When Chris Pringle managed only a scambled two, the Bank of New Zealand Trophy went to Australia.

AUSTRALIA		Runs	Balls	4/6
M.E.Waugh	c Greatbatch b Latham	83	83	8/1
M.A.Taylor	c and b Morrison	1	12	–
D.M.Jones	run out	25	38	3
D.C.Boon	c Patel b Latham	40	77	1
S.R.Waugh	b Latham	39	53	1
* A.R.Border	c Patel b Latham	1	9	–
† I.A.Healy	c Crowe b Pringle	17	19	1
A.I.C.Dodemaide	c Crowe b Latham	0	2	–
M.G.Hughes	not out	12	8	–/1
P.R.Reiffel	not out	2	5	–
T.B.A.May				
Extras	(b 1, lb 5, w 5, nb 1)	12		
Total	(50 overs; 8 wickets)	**232**		

NEW ZEALAND		Runs	Balls	4/6
R.T.Latham	c M.E.Waugh b Hughes	22	48	3
M.J.Greatbatch	c Border b S.R.Waugh	68	100	7/1
A.H.Jones	st Healy b May	2	18	–
* M.D.Crowe	lbw b May	11	29	–
K.R.Rutherford	run out	6	12	–
† T.E.Blain	run out	8	15	–
J.W.Wilson	c Border b Dodemaide	21	28	3
D.N.Patel	c M.E.Waugh b S.R.Waugh	8	12	–/1
G.R.Larsen	not out	33	28	1/1
C.Pringle	not out	22	18	2
D.K.Morrison				
Extras	(lb 19, w 8, nb 1)	28		
Total	(50 overs; 8 wickets)	**229**		

NEW ZEALAND	O	M	R	W
Morrison	8	0	41	1
Wilson	7	0	36	0
Pringle	9	0	52	1
Larsen	10	1	32	0
Patel	6	0	33	0
Latham	10	1	32	5

AUSTRALIA	O	M	R	W
Hughes	10	0	46	1
Dodemaide	10	1	39	1
Reiffel	10	0	49	0
May	10	0	40	2
S.R.Waugh	8	1	27	2
M.E.Waugh	2	0	9	0

FALL OF WICKETS
1-7, 2-71, 3-145, 4-178, 5-183, 6-213, 7-213, 8-215

FALL OF WICKETS
1-50, 2-67, 3-97, 4-114, 5-136, 6-139, 7-166, 8-175

Umpires: B.L.Aldridge (31) and D.B.Cowie (4).

Referee: Javed Burki (*Pakistan*).

INDIA v ZIMBABWE 1992-93

At Nahar Singh Stadium, Faridabad on 19 March 1993.   Result: **INDIA** won by 67 runs.   Toss: Zimbabwe.
Award: V.G.Kambli.   LOI debuts: None.

Making their first tour overseas as a Test-playing nation, Zimbabwe followed a one-off Test with this three-match series. Vinod Kambli's blazing innings took the contest out of the touring team's reach.

INDIA		Runs	Balls	4/6
M.Prabhakar	c Houghton b Traicos	56	80	5
N.S.Sidhu	c Brain b Crocker	56	83	2
V.G.Kambli	b Brain	80	75	8/1
* M.Azharuddin	c and b G.W.Flower	8	13	–
S.R.Tendulkar	c and b G.W.Flower	3	9	–
P.K.Amre	c James b Brandes	2	5	–
† V.Yadav	not out	19	23	1
A.Kumble	c James b Brain	0	1	–
S.A.Ankola	not out	1	2	–
J.Srinath				
S.L.V.Raju				
Extras	(b 7, lb 8, w 8, nb 1)	24		
Total	(48 overs; 7 wickets)	**249**		

ZIMBABWE		Runs	Balls	4/6
† A.Flower	b Prabhakar	9	21	1
G.W.Flower	c Kumble b Raju	42	67	2
A.D.R.Campbell	c Prabhakar b Raju	12	52	–
* D.L.Houghton	run out	23	29	2
M.H.Dekker	c Azharuddin b Srinath	22	49	2
W.R.James	run out	0	2	–
A.H.Shah	c Raju b Kumble	2	8	–
E.A.Brandes	lbw b Srinath	7	5	1
G.J.Crocker	c Yadav b Srinath	2	6	–
D.H.Brain	st Yadav b Tendulkar	27	20	2/2
A.J.Traicos	not out	7	20	–
Extras	(b 8, lb 14, w 6, nb 1)	29		
Total	(46.2 overs)	**182**		

ZIMBABWE	O	M	R	W
Brandes	10	0	32	1
Brain	9	0	36	2
Shah	4	0	26	0
Crocker	10	0	54	1
Traicos	10	0	61	1
G.W.Flower	5	0	25	2

INDIA	O	M	R	W
Prabhakar	9	1	33	1
Srinath	10	1	38	3
Ankola	7	1	20	0
Raju	10	0	26	2
Kumble	10	0	37	1
Tendulkar	0.2	0	6	1

FALL OF WICKETS
1-114, 2-149, 3-183, 4-204, 5-207, 6-245, 7-245

FALL OF WICKETS
1-20, 2-71, 3-85, 4-105, 5-115, 6-126, 7-135, 8-141, 9-147, 10-182

Umpires: N.Menon (1) and R.C.Sharma (5).

Referee: Asif Iqbal (*Pakistan*).

INDIA v ZIMBABWE 1992-93

At Nehru Stadium, Gauhati on 22 March 1993.   Result: **INDIA** won by 7 wickets.   Toss: India.
Award: G.W.Flower.   LOI debuts: None.

Overnight rain leaked on to the pitch, delayed the start by three hours and reduced the contest to a 28-over affair. Needing 16 from the last two overs, India romped home with three balls to spare.

ZIMBABWE		Runs	Balls	4/6
†A.Flower	c Kumble b Ankola	26	43	2
G.W.Flower	c Kambli b Kumble	57	65	6
A.D.R.Campbell	run out	29	34	2
*D.L.Houghton	lbw b Kumble	8	12	1
M.H.Dekker	b Prabhakar	2	5	–
G.A.Briant	not out	6	5	–
E.A.Brandes	b Srinath	2	2	–
K.J.Arnott	not out	1	3	–
D.H.Brain				
G.J.Crocker				
A.J.Traicos				
Extras	(b 1, lb 12, w 3, nb 2)	18		
Total	(28 overs; 6 wickets)	149		

INDIA		Runs	Balls	4/6
M.Prabhakar	c Houghton b Brandes	51	80	2
N.S.Sidhu	b Crocker	25	30	3
V.G.Kambli	b G.W.Flower	32	43	2
*M.Azharuddin	not out	15	10	–/1
S.R.Tendulkar	not out	8	6	–
P.K.Amre				
Kapil Dev				
†V.Yadav				
A.Kumble				
S.A.Ankola				
J.Srinath				
Extras	(b 1, lb 6, w 10, nb 2)	19		
Total	(27.3 overs; 3 wickets)	150		

INDIA	O	M	R	W
Kapil Dev	6	0	21	0
Prabhakar	5	0	31	1
Srinath	5	0	19	1
Ankola	6	0	33	1
Kumble	6	0	32	2

ZIMBABWE	O	M	R	W
Brain	6	0	39	0
Brandes	6	0	14	1
Traicos	6	0	32	0
Crocker	6	0	35	1
G.W.Flower	3.3	0	23	1

FALL OF WICKETS
1-56, 2-112, 3-137, 4-137, 5-145, 6-148

FALL OF WICKETS
1-67, 2-122, 3-128

Umpires: S.Choudhury (1) and R.T.Ramachandran (1).

Referee: Asif Iqbal (*Pakistan*).

INDIA v ZIMBABWE 1992-93

At Nehru Stadium, Poona on 25 March 1993.   Result: **INDIA** won by 8 wickets.   Toss: India.
Award: V.G.Kambli.   LOI debuts: None.

Zimbabwe's best batting performance of the series could not avert their ninth consecutive defeat against India.

ZIMBABWE		Runs	Balls	4/6
†A.Flower	run out	32	36	5
G.W.Flower	c Yadav b Kumble	50	86	5
A.D.R.Campbell	st Yadav b Kumble	22	39	1
*D.L.Houghton	b Kapil Dev	46	57	3
M.H.Dekker	run out	8	21	–
G.A.Briant	run out	16	27	1
A.H.Shah	c Yadav b Kapil Dev	1	11	–
E.A.Brandes	c Kumble b Srinath	5	8	1
G.J.Crocker	b Kapil Dev	1	3	–
D.H.Brain	not out	12	11	1
A.J.Traicos	c Ankola b Srinath	4	6	–
Extras	(b 2, lb 14, w 17, nb 4)	37		
Total	(49.5 overs)	234		

INDIA		Runs	Balls	4/6
W.V.Raman	c G.W.Flower b Traicos	66	86	7/2
N.S.Sidhu	run out	45	74	5
V.G.Kambli	not out	47	62	5
A.K.Sharma	not out	59	55	8
*M.Azharuddin				
S.R.Tendulkar				
Kapil Dev				
†V.Yadav				
A.Kumble				
S.A.Ankola				
J.Srinath				
Extras	(lb 8, w 10, nb 3)	21		
Total	(45.3 overs; 2 wickets)	238		

INDIA	O	M	R	W
Kapil Dev	10	1	54	3
Srinath	9.5	1	34	2
Ankola	6	0	32	0
Tendulkar	4	0	30	0
Sharma	10	0	34	0
Kumble	10	0	34	2

ZIMBABWE	O	M	R	W
Brandes	10	0	31	0
Brain	9.3	0	47	0
G.W.Flower	5	0	39	0
Crocker	8	1	39	0
Shah	3	0	24	0
Traicos	10	0	50	1

FALL OF WICKETS
1-58, 2-122, 3-129, 4-154, 5-196, 6-199, 7-212, 8-215, 9-217, 10-234

FALL OF WICKETS
1-114, 2-134

Umpires: K.Parthasarathy (1) and S.Shastri (1).

Referee: Asif Iqbal (*Pakistan*).

WEST INDIES v PAKISTAN 1992-93

At Sabina Park, Kingston, Jamaica on 23 March 1993.　　Result: **WEST INDIES** won by 4 wickets.　　Toss: West Indies.
Award: B.C.Lara.　　LOI debuts: Pakistan – Basit Ali.

A record Sabina Park crowd, varying in estimate between 18,000 and 20,000, thousands of whom gained entry illegally, was treated to a breathtaking innings by Brian Lara, his third hundred of the 1992-93 programme.

PAKISTAN		Runs	Balls	4/6
Aamir Sohail	c sub (K.L.T.Arthurton) b Ambrose	87	167	6
Ramiz Raja	b Simmons	22	57	2
Inzamam-ul-Haq	lbw b Bishop	50	50	2/2
* Wasim Akram	c Hooper b Bishop	0	3	–
Javed Miandad	c Simmons b Hooper	16	17	1
Basit Ali	st Murray b Hooper	17	19	–
† Rashid Latif	not out	1	1	–
Asif Mujtaba				
Waqar Younis				
Mushtaq Ahmed				
Aqib Javed				
Extras	(b 4, lb 7, w 11, nb 8)	30		
Total	(50 overs; 6 wickets)	**223**		

WEST INDIES		Runs	Balls	4/6
B.C.Lara	b Aamir	114	116	11/1
D.L.Haynes	c Ramiz b Wasim	7	16	1
P.V.Simmons	b Mushtaq	28	42	2
* R.B.Richardson	b Wasim	17	38	–
C.L.Hooper	c and b Aamir	21	36	–
A.L.Logie	c Mushtaq b Aamir	7	9	–
J.C.Adams	not out	11	13	–
† J.R.Murray	not out	1	2	–
C.E.L.Ambrose				
I.R.Bishop				
C.A.Walsh				
Extras	(lb 6, w 5, nb 7)	18		
Total	(44 overs; 6 wickets)	**224**		

WEST INDIES	O	M	R	W
Ambrose	10	2	31	1
Walsh	10	2	40	0
Simmons	10	2	26	1
Bishop	9	1	54	2
Hooper	8	0	28	2
Adams	3	0	33	0

PAKISTAN	O	M	R	W
Wasim Akram	9	0	47	2
Aqib Javed	6	1	18	0
Waqar Younis	10	1	46	0
Mushtaq Ahmed	10	0	64	1
Aamir Sohail	9	0	43	3

FALL OF WICKETS
1-67, 2-185, 3-185, 4-187, 5-221, 6-223

FALL OF WICKETS
1-21, 2-101, 3-180, 4-184, 5-197, 6-223

Referee: R.Subba Row (*England*).

Umpires: L.H.Barker (20) and S.A.Bucknor (14).

WEST INDIES v PAKISTAN 1992-93

At Queen's Park Oval, Port-of-Spain, Trinidad on 26 March 1993.　　Result: **WEST INDIES** won by 5 wickets.
Toss: West Indies.　　Award: B.C.Lara.　　LOI debuts: Pakistan – Aamir Nazir.

West Indies gained their ninth successive win against the World Cup champions. Pakistan's innings, begun in heavy, overcast conditions, was crucially reduced after being interrupted by rain at 96 for 2 from 26 overs.

PAKISTAN		Runs	Balls	4/6
Aamir Sohail	c Richardson b Simmons	47	86	5
Ramiz Raja	c Richardson b Bishop	15	33	1
Inzamam-ul-Haq	run out	11	33	–
Javed Miandad	c Simmons b Hooper	41	66	2
Basit Ali	c Hooper b Walsh	34	43	2
* Wasim Akram	run out	0	–	–
† Rashid Latif	run out	10	5	2
Waqar Younis	not out	4	8	–
Mushtaq Ahmed	not out	0	2	–
Ata-ur-Rehman				
Aamir Nazir				
Extras	(b 1, lb 6, w 20, nb 5)	32		
Total	(45 overs; 7 wickets)	**194**		

WEST INDIES		Runs	Balls	4/6
B.C.Lara	not out	95	106	10
D.L.Haynes	c sub ‡ b Aamir Nazir	11	40	2
P.V.Simmons	c Rashid b Waqar	13	26	2
* R.B.Richardson	b Aamir Nazir	32	46	3
C.L.Hooper	lbw b Aamir Nazir	0	1	–
A.L.Logie	c Rashid b Wasim	1	5	–
J.C.Adams	not out	15	36	1
† J.R.Murray				
C.E.L.Ambrose				
I.R.Bishop				
C.A.Walsh				
Extras	(lb 11, w 9, nb 9)	29		
Total	(41 overs; 5 wickets)	**196**		

WEST INDIES	O	M	R	W
Ambrose	10	0	40	0
Walsh	8	2	30	1
Bishop	7	0	42	1
Simmons	10	1	34	1
Hooper	10	0	41	1

PAKISTAN	O	M	R	W
Wasim Akram	9	0	36	1
Waqar Younis	8	1	39	1
Aamir Nazir	9	0	43	3
Ata-ur-Rehman	10	0	42	0
Mushtaq Ahmed	5	0	25	0

FALL OF WICKETS
1-56, 2-85, 3-108, 4-170, 5-170, 6-187, 7-188

FALL OF WICKETS
1-35, 2-69, 3-133, 4-133, 5-137　　　　　　‡ (Asif Mujtaba)

Umpires: S.A.Bucknor (15) and C.E.Cumberbatch (17).

Referee: R.Subba Row (*England*).

WEST INDIES v PAKISTAN 1992-93

At Queen's Park Oval, Port-of-Spain, Trinidad on 27 March 1993.   Result: **PAKISTAN** won by 7 wickets.
Toss: West Indies.   Award: Inzamam-ul-Haq.   LOI debuts: Pakistan – Nadeem Khan.

Another packed crowd (c 28,000) was rewarded with a batting bonanza, 520 runs coming from 88.1 overs, including 54
boundaries. Pakistan's long-awaited win came at the expense of a hefty fine for a shortfall of five overs.

WEST INDIES		Runs	Balls	4/6
B.C.Lara	c Rashid b Aamir Nazir	5	19	–
D.L.Haynes	c Basit b Aamir Nazir	68	92	9
P.V.Simmons	not out	80	112	7
* R.B.Richardson	c Inzamam b Aamir Sohail	46	28	8
C.L.Hooper	c Wasim b Waqar	34	28	3/1
A.L.Logie	not out	1	1	–
J.C.Adams				
† J.R.Murray				
C.E.L.Ambrose				
I.R.Bishop				
C.A.Walsh				
Extras	(lb 15, w 4, nb 6)	25		
Total	(45 overs; 4 wickets)	**259**		

PAKISTAN		Runs	Balls	4/6
Aamir Sohail	c Ambrose b Bishop	42	41	7
Ramiz Raja	run out	43	56	6
Inzamam-ul-Haq	not out	90	104	8
Basit Ali	run out	17	21	1
Asif Mujtaba	not out	45	40	4
* Wasim Akram				
† Rashid Latif				
Waqar Younis				
Nadeem Khan				
Ata-ur-Rehman				
Aamir Nazir				
Extras	(lb 11, w 10, nb 3)	24		
Total	(43.1 overs; 3 wickets)	**261**		

PAKISTAN	O	M	R	W
Wasim Akram	10	0	62	0
Waqar Younis	10	3	50	1
Aamir Nazir	8	0	52	2
Ata-ur-Rehman	10	0	31	0
Nadeem Khan	6	0	39	0
Aamir Sohail	1	0	10	1

WEST INDIES	O	M	R	W
Ambrose	9	1	49	0
Walsh	10	0	63	0
Bishop	10	0	49	1
Simmons	7	0	44	0
Hooper	7.1	0	45	0

FALL OF WICKETS
1-33, 2-115, 3-182, 4-249

FALL OF WICKETS
1-71, 2-100, 3-130

Umpires: S.A.Bucknor (16) and C.E.Cumberbatch (18).

Referee: R.Subba Row (*England*).

WEST INDIES v PAKISTAN 1992-93

At Arnos Vale, Kingstown, StVincent on 30 March 1993.   Result: **PAKISTAN** won by 38 runs.
Toss: West Indies.   Award: Basit Ali.   LOI debuts: None.

Richie Richardson's fourth success with the toss led to his side's downfall when he condemned them to batting second
on a slow, uneven surface. Wasim Akram's record 12th four-wicket haul levelled the series.

PAKISTAN		Runs	Balls	4/6
Aamir Sohail	c Richardson b Simmons	29	67	3
Ramiz Raja	lbw b Bishop	2	7	–
Inzamam-ul-Haq	c Murray b Hooper	17	44	–
Javed Miandad	b Ambrose	19	42	–
Basit Ali	b Walsh	60	86	4
Asif Mujtaba	c and b Hooper	23	35	–
* Wasim Akram	b Walsh	1	3	–
† Rashid Latif	not out	18	16	1
Waqar Younis	run out	1	3	–
Ata-ur-Rehman	run out	2	5	–
Aamir Nazir	not out	1	1	–
Extras	(lb 3, w 5, nb 5)	13		
Total	(50 overs; 9 wickets)	**186**		

WEST INDIES		Runs	Balls	4/6
B.C.Lara	c Rashid b Waqar	5	21	1
D.L.Haynes	lbw b Wasim	6	18	1
P.V.Simmons	c Rashid b Rehman	20	44	3
* R.B.Richardson	c Rashid b Rehman	2	9	–
C.L.Hooper	b Aamir Sohail	16	43	–
J.C.Adams	c Miandad b Wasim	27	71	–
A.L.Logie	c Wasim b Asif	8	16	–
† J.R.Murray	b Waqar	14	22	–/1
I.R.Bishop	not out	20	29	1
C.E.L.Ambrose	b Wasim	4	4	–
C.A.Walsh	lbw b Wasim	1	5	–
Extras	(b 3, lb 3, w 4, nb 15)	25		
Total	(44.3 overs)	**148**		

WEST INDIES	O	M	R	W
Bishop	10	0	44	1
Walsh	10	0	34	2
Ambrose	10	2	31	1
Hooper	10	1	35	2
Simmons	10	0	39	1

PAKISTAN	O	M	R	W
Wasim Akram	7.3	2	18	4
Waqar Younis	8	0	27	2
Ata-ur-Rehman	10	0	38	2
Aamir Nazir	6	1	17	0
Aamir Sohail	6	1	23	1
Asif Mujtaba	7	0	19	1

FALL OF WICKETS
1-9, 2-52, 3-54, 4-111, 5-159, 6-161, 7-166, 8-169, 9-180

FALL OF WICKETS
1-14, 2-14, 3-19, 4-48, 5-75, 6-87, 7-108, 8-125, 9-134, 10-148

Umpires: L.H.Barker (21) and G.T.Johnson (3).

Referee: R.Subba Row (*England*).

WEST INDIES v PAKISTAN 1992-93

At Bourda, Georgetown, Guyana on 3 April 1993.   Result: **MATCH TIED.**   Toss: Pakistan.
Award: C.L.Hooper.   LOI debuts: None.

The series ended in splendid chaos when hordes of spectators surged on to the ground as Ian Bishop on-drove Wasim
Akram's final ball for two runs to tie the match. When Pakistan protested that their fielders had been 'visually impeded',
referee Raman Subba Row overruled the 'fewer wickets lost' playing condition which would have awarded victory to the
hosts.

PAKISTAN		Runs	Balls	4/6	WEST INDIES		Runs	Balls	4/6
Aamir Sohail	c and b Ambrose	33	51	5	D.L.Haynes	lbw b Waqar	82	131	7
Ramiz Raja	c and b Hooper	26	50	4	B.C.Lara	b Aamir Nazir	15	35	2
Inzamam-ul-Haq	lbw b Walsh	53	91	3	P.V.Simmons	run out	12	24	1
Javed Miandad	lbw b Cummins	2	13	–	* R.B.Richardson	st Rashid b Aamir Sohail	41	37	4/3
Basit Ali	c Murray b Walsh	57	69	5	C.L.Hooper	not out	69	70	5/1
* Wasim Akram	not out	39	27	4	A.L.Logie	b Wasim	1	4	–
† Rashid Latif	c sub b Bishop	15	13	1	I.R.Bishop	not out	3	3	–
Asif Mujtaba					† J.R.Murray				
Waqar Younis					C.E.L.Ambrose				
Ata-ur-Rehman					A.C.Cummins				
Aamir Nazir					C.A.Walsh				
Extras	(b 1, lb 6, w 6, nb 6)	19			Extras	(lb 13, w 5, nb 3)	21		
Total	(50 overs; 6 wickets)	244			Total	(50 overs; 5 wickets)	244		

WEST INDIES	O	M	R	W	PAKISTAN	O	M	R	W
Bishop	10	0	62	1	Wasim Akram	10	1	50	1
Simmons	2	0	19	0	Waqar Younis	10	0	54	1
Walsh	10	0	48	2	Ata-ur-Rehman	8	0	39	0
Ambrose	10	1	44	1	Aamir Nazir	8	0	28	1
Hooper	10	0	27	1	Aamir Sohail	10	1	42	1
Cummins	8	0	37	1	Asif Mujtaba	4	0	18	0

FALL OF WICKETS
1-66, 2-76, 3-85, 4-188, 5-189, 6-244

FALL OF WICKETS
1-24, 2-54, 3-117, 4-223, 5-228

Umpires: L.H.Barker (22) and C.R.Duncan (6).

Referee: R.Subba Row (*England*).

ENGLAND v AUSTRALIA 1993

At Old Trafford, Manchester on 19 May 1993.   Result: **AUSTRALIA** won by 4 runs.   Toss: England.
Award: C.J.McDermott.   LOI debuts: England – A.R.Caddick, G.P.Thorpe; Australia – M.L.Hayden.

Craig McDermott became the first Australian to take 150 LOI wickets. Top-scorer Graeme Hick (50 off 60 balls)
completed his 1000th run in 30 internationals. Merv Hughes conceded just a single and a leg bye when England needed
seven runs from the final over.

AUSTRALIA		Runs	Balls	4/6	ENGLAND		Runs	Balls	4/6
M.L.Hayden	c Stewart b Lewis	29	55	4	* G.A.Gooch	c M.E.Waugh b McDermott	4	14	–
M.A.Taylor	c Fairbrother b Illingworth	79	126	6	† A.J.Stewart	b Hughes	22	20	2
M.E.Waugh	c Fairbrother b Jarvis	56	63	5	R.A.Smith	c and b McDermott	9	26	–
D.C.Boon	c Fairbrother b Illingworth	2	6	–	G.A.Hick	b Reiffel	85	102	8/1
* A.R.Border	c Lewis b Illingworth	4	14	–	N.H.Fairbrother	c Reiffel b S.R.Waugh	59	89	5/1
S.R.Waugh	c and b Lewis	27	30	4	G.P.Thorpe	c Taylor b McDermott	31	38	3
† I.A.Healy	c Thorpe b Caddick	20	21	3	C.C.Lewis	run out	4	12	–
M.G.Hughes	b Lewis	20	13	1/1	D.R.Pringle	c Taylor b S.R.Waugh	6	10	1
P.R.Reiffel	run out	2	3	–	R.K.Illingworth	run out	12	14	–
C.J.McDermott	not out	3	2	–	P.W.Jarvis	c Reiffel b S.R.Waugh	2	4	–
T.B.A.May	not out	1	1	–	A.R.Caddick	not out	1	4	–
Extras	(b 1, lb 8, w 2, nb 4)	15			Extras	(lb 8, w 9, nb 2)	19		
Total	(55 overs; 9 wickets)	258			Total	(54.5 overs)	254		

ENGLAND	O	M	R	W	AUSTRALIA	O	M	R	W
Caddick	11	1	50	1	McDermott	11	2	38	3
Pringle	10	3	36	0	Hughes	9.5	1	40	1
Lewis	11	1	54	3	May	11	2	40	0
Jarvis	11	0	55	1	Reiffel	11	0	63	1
Illingworth	11	0	48	3	M.E.Waugh	2	0	12	0
Hick	1	0	6	0	S.R.Waugh	10	0	53	3

FALL OF WICKETS
1-60, 2-168, 3-171, 4-178, 5-186, 6-219, 7-237, 8-254, 9-255

FALL OF WICKETS
1-11, 2-38, 3-44, 4-171, 5-194, 6-211, 7-227, 8-240, 9-247, 10-254

Umpires: B.J.Meyer (23) and D.R.Shepherd (51).

ENGLAND v AUSTRALIA 1993

At Edgbaston, Birmingham on 21 May 1993   Result: **AUSTRALIA** won by 6 wickets.   Toss: Australia.
Award: R.A.Smith.   LOI debuts: None.

Robin Smith passed 2000 runs during the highest LOI innings for England; he went from 50 to 150 in 65 balls, his third fifty taking just 20. With Graham Thorpe he shared a national record fifth-wicket stand of 142 from 130 balls. Mark Waugh and Allan Border's stand of 168 is the highest for the fourth wicket against England.

ENGLAND		Runs	Balls	4/6
* G.A.Gooch	c Healy b McDermott	17	49	2
† A.J.Stewart	b McDermott	0	5	–
R.A.Smith	not out	167	163	17/3
G.A.Hick	c Healy b Reiffel	2	9	–
N.H.Fairbrother	c Taylor b S.R.Waugh	23	45	3
G.P.Thorpe	c Border b McDermott	36	63	1
C.C.Lewis	not out	13	9	1/1
D.R.Pringle				
D.G.Cork				
P.W.Jarvis				
A.R.Caddick				
Extras	(b 2, lb 4, w 2, nb 11)	19		
Total	(55 overs; 5 wickets)	**277**		

AUSTRALIA		Runs	Balls	4/6
M.A.Taylor	b Lewis	26	47	2
M.L.Hayden	b Jarvis	14	30	2
M.E.Waugh	c Fairbrother b Lewis	113	122	8
D.C.Boon	c Stewart b Pringle	21	29	3
* A.R.Border	not out	86	97	9
S.R.Waugh	not out	6	3	1
† I.A.Healy				
M.G.Hughes				
P.R.Reiffel				
C.J.McDermott				
T.B.A.May				
Extras	(lb 5, w 3, nb 6)	14		
Total	(53.3 overs; 4 wickets)	**280**		

AUSTRALIA	O	M	R	W
McDermott	11	1	29	3
Hughes	11	2	51	0
Reiffel	11	1	70	1
May	11	0	45	0
S.R.Waugh	8	0	55	1
M.E.Waugh	3	0	21	0

ENGLAND	O	M	R	W
Caddick	11	1	43	0
Jarvis	10	1	51	1
Lewis	10.3	0	61	2
Pringle	11	0	63	1
Cork	11	1	57	0

FALL OF WICKETS
1-3, 2-40, 3-55, 4-105, 5-247

FALL OF WICKETS
1-28, 2-55, 3-95, 4-263

Umpires: M.J.Kitchen (10) and K.E.Palmer (18).

ENGLAND v AUSTRALIA 1993

At Lord's, London on 23 May 1993.   Result: **AUSTRALIA** won by 19 runs.   Toss: England.
Award: B.P.Julian.   LOI debuts: Australia – B.P.Julian.

Denis Compton's 75th birthday was saluted by the Band of the Coldstream Guards before England subsided to their seventh consecutive limited-overs defeat. Australia held every chance during this three-match series.

AUSTRALIA		Runs	Balls	4/6
M.L.Hayden	c Stewart b Caddick	4	19	–
* M.A.Taylor	c Stewart b Reeve	57	104	3
M.E.Waugh	c Stewart b Caddick	14	23	2
D.C.Boon	b Illingworth	73	125	8
D.R.Martyn	not out	51	43	5
S.R.Waugh	c Gooch b Caddick	8	9	1
† I.A.Healy	not out	12	10	–
M.G.Hughes				
B.P.Julian				
C.J.McDermott				
T.B.A.May				
Extras	(lb 3, w 6, nb 2)	11		
Total	(55 overs; 5 wickets)	**230**		

ENGLAND		Runs	Balls	4/6
* G.A.Gooch	c Hughes b May	42	77	4
† A.J.Stewart	c M.E.Waugh b Julian	74	119	10
R.A.Smith	st Healy b May	6	22	–
G.A.Hick	b Julian	7	13	1
N.H.Fairbrother	c Boon b Julian	18	25	1
G.P.Thorpe	c Healy b S.R.Waugh	22	24	2
D.A.Reeve	run out	2	8	–
D.G.Cork	b Hughes	11	16	–
R.K.Illingworth	c Healy b Hughes	9	10	1
P.W.Jarvis	c Hayden b McDermott	3	5	–
A.R.Caddick	not out	2	1	–
Extras	(lb 6, w 8, nb 1)	15		
Total	(53.1 overs)	**211**		

ENGLAND	O	M	R	W
Jarvis	11	1	51	0
Caddick	11	3	39	3
Cork	9	2	24	0
Illingworth	10	0	46	1
Reeve	11	1	50	1
Hick	3	0	17	0

AUSTRALIA	O	M	R	W
McDermott	10	1	35	1
Hughes	10.1	0	41	2
Julian	11	1	50	3
May	11	1	36	2
S.R.Waugh	11	0	43	1

FALL OF WICKETS
1-12, 2-31, 3-139, 4-193, 5-208

FALL OF WICKETS
1-96, 2-115, 3-129, 4-159, 5-160, 6-169, 7-195, 8-201, 9-208, 10-211

Umpires: H.D.Bird (62) and R.Palmer (6).

SRI LANKA v INDIA 1993-94

At Khettarama Stadium, Colombo on 25 July 1993.   Result: **INDIA** won by 1 run.   Toss: Sri Lanka.
Award: M.Azharuddin.   LOI debuts: India – R.K.Chauhan.

An inswinging yorker from Manoj Prabhakar completed a dramatic collapse in which the hosts, seemingly coasting to victory, lost eight wickets for 50 runs.

INDIA		Runs	Balls	4/6
M.Prabhakar	c and b Gurusinha	39	77	2
N.S.Sidhu	b Kalpage	39	69	3
V.G.Kambli	b Kalpage	9	22	–
* M.Azharuddin	c Hathurusinghe b Ramanayake	53	57	2/1
S.R.Tendulkar	c Gurusinha b Jayasuriya	21	39	1
P.K.Amre	b Kalpage	7	5	1
Kapil Dev	c Tillekeratne b Wickremasinghe	27	31	2/1
† V.Yadav	c Kalpage b Ramanayake	6	5	1
A.Kumble	not out	0	1	–
R.K.Chauhan				
J.Srinath				
Extras	(lb 1, w 5, nb 5)	11		
Total	(50 overs; 8 wickets)	**212**		

SRI LANKA		Runs	Balls	4/6
R.S.Mahanama	st Yadav b Kumble	24	49	4
U.C.Hathurusinghe	lbw b Chauhan	64	121	2
A.P.Gurusinha	c Kapil Dev b Kumble	0	1	–
P.A.de Silva	c Amre b Srinath	62	79	1/2
* A.Ranatunga	lbw b Chauhan	2	11	–
H.P.Tillekeratne	c Kambli b Prabhakar	5	9	–
S.T.Jayasuriya	c Amre b Kapil Dev	17	17	1
R.S.Kalpage	not out	9	6	–
† A.M.de Silva	run out	4	6	–
C.P.H.Ramanayake	b Srinath	0	1	–
G.P.Wickremasinghe	b Prabhakar	0	1	–
Extras	(lb 5, w 15, nb 4)	24		
Total	(49.2 overs)	**211**		

SRI LANKA	O	M	R	W
Ramanayake	10	0	50	2
Wickremasinghe	9	0	41	1
Hathurusinghe	4	0	24	0
Gurusinha	7	0	21	1
Jayasuriya	10	0	33	1
Kalpage	10	0	42	3

INDIA	O	M	R	W
Kapil Dev	10	3	29	1
Prabhakar	9.2	0	50	2
Srinath	10	0	64	2
Kumble	10	2	22	2
Chauhan	10	0	41	2

FALL OF WICKETS
1-77, 2-92, 3-97, 4-139, 5-148, 6-200, 7-210, 8-212

FALL OF WICKETS
1-46, 2-46, 3-161, 4-172, 5-173, 6-186, 7-196, 8-207, 9-208, 10-211

Umpires: K.T.Francis (16) and T.M.Samarasinghe (3).

SRI LANKA v INDIA 1993-94

At Khettarama Stadium, Colombo on 11 August 1993.   Result: **SRI LANKA** won by 8 runs.   Toss: India.
Award: A. Ranatunga.   LOI debuts: Sri Lanka – M.Muralitharan.

The first floodlit contest between these countries attracted a crowd estimated at 40,000 and produced another sensational collapse. This time it was India's turn to snatch defeat from victory; needing 30 off eight overs, they lost their last seven wickets for 21 runs in 46 balls.

SRI LANKA		Runs	Balls	4/6
A.P.Gurusinha	c Chauhan b Prabhakar	9	22	1
U.C.Hathurusinghe	run out	38	91	1
H.P.Tillekeratne	lbw b Chauhan	23	62	1
P.A.de Silva	c Azharuddin b Kapil Dev	16	24	1
* A.Ranatunga	c Tendulkar b Prabhakar	50	52	2
S.T.Jayasuriya	lbw b Chauhan	17	22	1
† R.S.Kaluwitharana	run out	9	10	–
R.S.Kalpage	not out	17	20	–
G.P.Wickremasinghe	not out	1	1	–
C.P.H.Ramanayake				
M.Muralitharan				
Extras	(b 1, lb 8, w 13, nb 2)	24		
Total	(50 overs; 7 wickets)	**204**		

INDIA		Runs	Balls	4/6
M.Prabhakar	c Kalpage b Jayasuriya	86	123	4
N.S.Sidhu	c Tillekeratne b Wickremasinghe	0	2	–
V.G.Kambli	lbw b Wickremasinghe	7	16	–
* M.Azharuddin	c Gurusinha b Wickremasinghe	62	89	2/2
S.R.Tendulkar	run out	15	30	–
P.K.Amre	b Muralitharan	1	5	–
Kapil Dev	lbw b Jayasuriya	0	2	–
† V.Yadav	b Kalpage	1	2	–
A.Kumble	lbw b De Silva	10	18	–
R.K.Chauhan	c and b Kalpage	4	7	–
J.Srinath	not out	0	2	–
Extras	(lb 6, w 4)	10		
Total	(49.2 overs)	**196**		

INDIA	O	M	R	W
Kapil Dev	10	1	36	1
Prabhakar	8	1	33	2
Srinath	8	1	34	0
Tendulkar	6	1	20	0
Chauhan	9	0	37	2
Kumble	9	0	35	0

SRI LANKA	O	M	R	W
Ramanayake	7	2	23	0
Wickremasinghe	8	0	34	3
Gurusinha	2	0	10	0
Hathurusinghe	5	0	14	0
Muralitharan	10	0	38	1
Jayasuriya	10	0	45	2
Kalpage	6	0	22	2
De Silva	1.2	0	4	1

FALL OF WICKETS
1-27, 2-82, 3-103, 4-109, 5-142, 6-158, 7-202

FALL OF WICKETS
1-0, 2-16, 3-152, 4-175, 5-178, 6-179, 7-180, 8-189, 9-196, 10-196

Umpires: B.C.Cooray (10) and D.N.Pathirana (1).

SRI LANKA v INDIA 1993-94

At Tyronne Fernando Stadium, Moratuwa on 14 August 1993.   Result: **SRI LANKA** won by 4 wickets.   Toss: India.
Award: R.S.Mahanama.   LOI debuts: None.

Mohammed Azharuddin's third fifty of the series took his LOI aggregate beyond Krish Srikkanth's Indian record of 4092 runs. Roshan Mahanama, suffering from cramp and an inflamed toe, battled heroically until collapsing and being stretchered off at 213 for 4.

INDIA		Runs	Balls	4/6
M.Prabhakar	c Gurusinha b Wickremasinghe	17	34	2
N.S.Sidhu	c Kalpage b Wickremasinghe	7	8	-
V.G.Kambli	c Mahanama b Muralitharan	19	44	1
* M.Azharuddin	c Jayasuriya b Ramanayake	85	103	5/2
S.R.Tendulkar	c Muralitharan b Jayasuriya	25	39	1
A.K.Sharma	st Kaluwitharana b Jayasuriya	20	39	-
Kapil Dev	c De Silva b Ramanayake	4	16	-
† V.Yadav	run out	27	15	1/2
A.Kumble	not out	4	3	-
R.K.Chauhan	b Wickremasinghe	0	1	-
J.Srinath	not out	5	2	1
Extras	(lb 8, w 3, nb 3)	14		
Total	(50 overs; 9 wickets)	227		

SRI LANKA		Runs	Balls	4/6
R.S.Mahanama	retired hurt	92	143	8
U.C.Hathurusinghe	c Kambli b Prabhakar	12	11	2
A.P.Gurusinha	run out	43	65	4/1
P.A.de Silva	b Chauhan	30	41	3
* A.Ranatunga	c Kumble b Prabhakar	22	23	2
S.T.Jayasuriya	lbw b Prabhakar	2	5	-
† R.S.Kaluwitharana	c Kapil Dev b Srinath	1	5	-
R.S.Kalpage	not out	5	3	-
C.P.H.Ramanayake	not out	4	4	-
G.P.Wickremasinghe				
M.Muralitharan				
Extras	(lb 15, w 5)	20		
Total	(49.3 overs; 6 wickets)	231		

SRI LANKA	O	M	R	W
Ramanayake	10	1	42	2
Wickremasinghe	10	1	54	3
Hathurusinghe	3	0	12	0
Gurusinha	2	0	7	0
Muralitharan	5	1	21	1
Jayasuriya	10	1	38	2
Kalpage	10	0	45	0

INDIA	O	M	R	W
Kapil Dev	7	1	22	0
Prabhakar	9	1	38	3
Srinath	9.3	1	46	1
Tendulkar	4	0	15	0
Chauhan	10	0	39	1
Kumble	7	0	37	0
Sharma	3	0	19	0

FALL OF WICKETS
1-22, 2-43, 3-65, 4-112, 5-165, 6-181, 7-217, 8-218, 9-219

FALL OF WICKETS
1-27, 2-112, 3-178, 4-216, 5-217, 6-222

Umpires: B.C.Cooray (11) and P.Manuel (3).

SRI LANKA v SOUTH AFRICA 1993-94

At Asgiriya Stadium, Kandy on 22 August 1993.   No result.   Toss: South Africa.
LOI debuts: South Africa – P.L.Symcox.

Initially delayed and reduced to a 46-over match, this contest was repeatedly interrupted and revised. South Africa's eventual target was 107 from 25 overs but rain had the final say. Roshan Mahanama scored his 2000th run in internationals.

SRI LANKA		Runs	Balls	4/6
R.S.Mahanama	run out	49	95	3
U.C.Hathurusinghe	c Cullinan b Symcox	51	85	5
P.A.de Silva	c Rhodes b Symcox	2	7	-
* A.Ranatunga	c Snell b Donald	29	32	2/1
S.T.Jayasuriya	run out	3	14	-
A.P.Gurusinha	not out	22	24	3
† R.S.Kaluwitharana	not out	1	3	-
H.P.Tillekeratne				
R.S.Kalpage				
G.P.Wickremasinghe				
M.Muralitharan				
Extras	(lb 7, w 15)	22		
Total	(41.3 overs; 5 wickets)	179		

SOUTH AFRICA		Runs	Balls	4/6
A.C.Hudson	b De Silva	6	16	1
* K.C.Wessels	c Ranatunga b De Silva	4	13	-
W.J.Cronje	c Mahanama b Muralitharan	22	33	3
D.J.Cullinan	b Muralitharan	0	4	-
J.N.Rhodes	not out	8	14	1
B.M.McMillan	not out	3	3	-
† D.J.Richardson				
R.P.Snell				
P.S.de Villiers				
P.L.Symcox				
A.A.Donald				
Extras	(lb 5, w 4)	9		
Total	(14 overs; 4 wickets)	52		

SOUTH AFRICA	O	M	R	W
Donald	7	0	23	1
De Villiers	5	0	23	0
Snell	6.3	0	33	0
McMillan	5	0	33	0
Symcox	9	1	28	2
Cronje	9	0	32	0

SRI LANKA	O	M	R	W
Wickremasinghe	3	1	6	0
De Silva	5	0	23	2
Kalpage	1	0	3	0
Muralitharan	3	0	6	2
Jayasuriya	2	0	9	0

FALL OF WICKETS
1-9, 2-26, 3-39, 4-40

FALL OF WICKETS
1-110, 2-116, 3-121, 4-127, 5-171

Umpires: B.C.Cooray (12) and P.Manuel (4).

SRI LANKA v SOUTH AFRICA 1993-94

At Khettarama Stadium, Colombo on 2 September 1993.　　Result: **SOUTH AFRICA** won by 124 runs.
Toss: South Africa.　　Award: B.M.McMillan.　　LOI debuts: Sri Lanka – P.B.Dassanayake.

Victims of the white ball's exceptional movement in the humid and dewy early evening conditions (note the 16 wides), Sri Lanka were dismissed for their lowest total in a home international.

SOUTH AFRICA		Runs	Balls	4/6
* K.C.Wessels	c Tillekeratne b Jayasuriya	28	76	–
A.C.Hudson	c Mahanama b Ranatunga	48	80	3
D.J.Cullinan	st Dassanayake b Jayasuriya	5	16	–
J.N.Rhodes	c Mahanama b Kalpage	43	63	–/1
S.J.Cook	c Dassanayake b Wickremasinghe	15	20	1
B.M.McMillan	c Tillekeratne b Jayasuriya	35	43	1
P.L.Symcox	c Mahanama b Jayasuriya	12	6	1/1
R.P.Snell	not out	12	8	1
† D.J.Richardson	not out	1	1	–
P.S.de Villiers				
A.A.Donald				
Extras	(lb 12, w 8, nb 3)	23		
Total	(50 overs; 7 wickets)	**222**		

SRI LANKA		Runs	Balls	4/6
R.S.Mahanama	c Richardson b De Villiers	11	22	–
U.C.Hathurusinghe	c McMillan b Donald	10	33	–
S.T.Jayasuriya	lbw b McMillan	3	18	–
P.A.de Silva	c Richardson b McMillan	8	22	1
* A.Ranatunga	c De Villiers b McMillan	6	17	–
A.P.Gurusinha	c McMillan b Snell	1	4	–
H.P.Tillekeratne	c Richardson b De Villiers	20	52	1
R.S.Kalpage	c Richardson b Symcox	0	5	–
† P.B.Dassanayake	c McMillan b Donald	11	25	–
G.P.Wickremasinghe	b De Villiers	4	13	–
M.Muralitharan	not out	0	10	–
Extras	(lb 7, w 16, nb 1)	24		
Total	(34 overs)	**98**		

SRI LANKA	O	M	R	W
Wickremasinghe	7	0	28	1
Hathurusinghe	3	0	14	0
De Silva	4	1	14	0
Kalpage	10	1	42	1
Muralitharan	6	0	28	0
Jayasuriya	10	0	53	4
Ranatunga	10	1	31	1

SOUTH AFRICA	O	M	R	W
Donald	7	1	18	2
De Villiers	10	4	15	3
Snell	5	0	15	1
McMillan	5	1	12	3
Symcox	5	0	20	1
Wessels	2	0	11	0

FALL OF WICKETS
1-90, 2-92, 3-102, 4-138, 5-174, 6-198, 7-214

FALL OF WICKETS
1-24, 2-24, 3-34, 4-39, 5-43, 6-52, 7-60, 8-92, 9-92, 10-98

Umpires: D.N.Pathirana (2) and T.M.Samarasinghe (4).

SRI LANKA v SOUTH AFRICA 1993-94

At Khettarama Stadium, Colombo on 4 September 1993.　　Result: **SRI LANKA** won by 44 runs.　　Toss: Sri Lanka.
Award: P.A.de Silva.　　LOI debuts: Sri Lanka – R.P.A.H.Wickremaratne.

The toss again virtually decided the outcome as the ball swung and seamed extravagantly under the lights. Richard Snell and 'Fanie' de Villiers inspired dreams of the improbable during their record South African tenth-wicket partnership of 51.

SRI LANKA		Runs	Balls	4/6
R.S.Mahanama	st Richardson b Symcox	41	59	2
U.C.Hathurusinghe	c Richardson b Donald	2	20	–
H.P.Tillekeratne	c Richardson b McMillan	15	48	1
P.A.de Silva	not out	61	89	1
* A.Ranatunga	c Donald b Snell	30	32	1
S.T.Jayasuriya	b Donald	5	13	–
R.P.A.H.Wickremaratne	st Richardson b Symcox	1	3	–
R.S.Kalpage	c and b Snell	9	24	–
† P.B.Dassanayake	run out	14	37	–
G.P.Wickremasinghe	b De Villiers	0	1	–
C.P.H.Ramanayake				
Extras	(b 1, lb 5, w 14)	20		
Total	(50 overs; 9 wickets)	**198**		

SOUTH AFRICA		Runs	Balls	4/6
A.C.Hudson	c Dassanayake b Wickremasinghe	1	6	–
* K.C.Wessels	lbw b Ramanayake	16	54	2
W.J.Cronje	c Dassanayake b Ramanayake	2	13	–
D.J.Cullinan	b Ramanayake	3	9	–
J.N.Rhodes	b Kalpage	27	64	–
B.M.McMillan	c Mahanama b Hathurusinghe	7	31	–
† D.J.Richardson	run out	5	21	–
P.L.Symcox	c Kalpage b Hathurusinghe	3	9	–
R.P.Snell	c Kalpage b Ramanayake	51	61	3
A.A.Donald	b Kalpage	0	8	–
P.S.de Villiers	not out	12	24	–
Extras	(lb 3, w 19, nb 5)	27		
Total	(46.1 overs)	**154**		

SOUTH AFRICA	O	M	R	W
Donald	10	0	35	2
De Villiers	10	1	31	1
Snell	10	0	52	2
McMillan	10	0	41	1
Symcox	10	1	33	2

SRI LANKA	O	M	R	W
Ramanayake	8.1	0	17	4
Wickremasinghe	6	2	24	1
Hathurusinghe	10	2	18	2
Ranatunga	6	0	24	0
Kalpage	10	0	36	2
Jayasuriya	6	0	32	0

FALL OF WICKETS
1-7, 2-53, 3-73, 4-127, 5-136, 6-141, 7-156, 8-191, 9-198

FALL OF WICKETS
1-2, 2-10, 3-18, 4-38, 5-56, 6-72, 7-77, 8-101, 9-103, 10-154

Umpires: K.T.Francis (17) and P.Manuel (5).

WEST INDIES v SRI LANKA 1993-94

At Sharjah CA Stadium, UAE on 28 October 1993.   Result: **WEST INDIES** won by 8 wickets.   Toss: West Indies.
Award: P.V.Simmons.   LOI debuts: None.

India continued to harbour grievances about pro-Pakistani bias in earlier Sharjah tournaments and were replaced by Sri Lanka. The Cricketer's Benefit Fund awarded $US35,000 apiece to Desmond Haynes (West Indies) and Pakistanis Nazir Mohammad and Shoaib Mohammed.

SRI LANKA		Runs	Balls	4/6
R.S.Mahanama	c Lara b Cummins	27	85	–
U.C.Hathurusinghe	run out	2	14	–
A.P.Gurusinha	b Cummins	8	21	1
P.A.de Silva	c Lara b Benjamin	1	8	–
H.P.Tillekeratne	c Murray b Benjamin	1	2	–
* A.Ranatunga	not out	83	93	6/3
S.T.Jayasuriya	c Ambrose b Benjamin	23	32	2
† R.S.Kaluwitharana	c Simmons b Hooper	0	1	–
R.S.Kalpage	c Murray b Cummins	7	15	1
C.P.H.Ramanayake	c Richardson b Ambrose	9	21	–
G.P.Wickremasinghe	c and b Ambrose	0	2	–
Extras	(b 1, lb 6, w 3, nb 1)	11		
Total	(48.5 overs)	**172**		

WEST INDIES		O	M	R	W
Ambrose		7.5	1	20	2
Walsh		7	4	10	0
Benjamin		9	1	34	3
Cummins		10	1	32	3
Simmons		5	0	17	0
Hooper		10	1	52	1

FALL OF WICKETS
1-6, 2-24, 3-27, 4-29, 5-71, 6-117, 7-119, 8-138, 9-171, 10-172

Umpires: H.D.Bird (*England*) (63) and D.R.Shepherd (*England*) (52).

WEST INDIES		Runs	Balls	4/6
P.V.Simmons	b Jayasuriya	92	161	8
B.C.Lara	c Ranatunga b Gurusinha	5	24	–
* R.B.Richardson	not out	69	90	6/1
K.L.T.Arthurton	not out	1	4	–
C.L.Hooper				
J.C.Adams				
† J.R.Murray				
A.C.Cummins				
C.E.L.Ambrose				
C.A.Walsh				
K.C.G.Benjamin				
Extras	(w 4, nb 2)	6		
Total	(46 overs; 2 wickets)	**173**		

SRI LANKA		O	M	R	W
Wickremasinghe		7	1	27	0
Ramanayake		8	2	22	0
Gurusinha		3	0	14	1
Kalpage		10	0	25	0
Jayasuriya		9	0	41	1
De Silva		6	0	34	0
Hathurusinghe		2	0	10	0
Tillekeratne		1	1	0	0

FALL OF WICKETS
1-34, 2-171

WEST INDIES v PAKISTAN 1993-94

At Sharjah CA Stadium, UAE on 29 October 1993.   Result: **WEST INDIES** won by 39 runs.   Toss: Pakistan.
Award: J.C.Adams.   LOI debuts: None.

West Indies gained their second victory in successive days, Keith Arthurton and Jimmy Adams sharing their record fifth-wicket stand against Pakistan (119). Waqar Younis sustained a calf muscle strain while bowling and missed the next three games.

WEST INDIES		Runs	Balls	4/6
P.V.Simmons	c Rashid b Waqar	25	38	3
B.C.Lara	c Rashid b Wasim	14	30	1
* R.B.Richardson	c Saeed b Aqib	2	4	–
K.L.T.Arthurton	c Aamir b Mushtaq	84	100	10/1
C.L.Hooper	c Rashid b Mushtaq	6	13	1
J.C.Adams	not out	81	94	6/1
† J.R.Murray	lbw b Wasim	6	10	–
A.C.Cummins	b Wasim	18	12	3
W.K.M.Benjamin	not out	2	3	–
K.C.G.Benjamin				
C.E.L.Ambrose				
Extras	(b 1, lb 19, w 7, nb 2)	29		
Total	(50 overs; 7 wickets)	**267**		

PAKISTAN		O	M	R	W
Wasim Akram		10	0	36	3
Aqib Javed		10	0	38	1
Waqar Younis		7.1	0	57	1
Mushtaq Ahmed		10	1	44	2
Aamir Sohail		4.5	0	31	0
Asif Mujtaba		8	0	41	0

FALL OF WICKETS
1-32, 2-35, 3-57, 4-82, 5-201, 6-225, 7-263

Umpires: J.W.Holder (*England*) (9) and D.R.Shepherd (*England*) (53).

PAKISTAN		Runs	Balls	4/6
Aamir Sohail	lbw b K.C.G.Benjamin	3	7	–
Saeed Anwar	c Lara b Cummins	22	42	3
Inzamam-ul-Haq	c K.C.G.Benjamin b Hooper	25	56	4
Javed Miandad	b K.C.G.Benjamin	0	3	–
Basit Ali	run out	46	58	4
Asif Mujtaba	not out	60	91	4
* Wasim Akram	c Adams b Ambrose	28	21	4
† Rashid Latif	c Lara b Ambrose	0	2	–
Mushtaq Ahmed	c Murray b Hooper	2	7	–
Waqar Younis	c Lara b Hooper	15	8	2
Aqib Javed	not out	6	6	–
Extras	(lb 6, w 14, nb 1)	21		
Total	(50 overs; 9 wickets)	**228**		

WEST INDIES		O	M	R	W
Ambrose		9	1	29	2
K.C.G.Benjamin		9	1	37	2
W.K.M.Benjamin		6	0	40	0
Cummins		10	1	44	1
Hooper		10	0	33	3
Simmons		6	0	39	0

FALL OF WICKETS
1-4, 2-47, 3-48, 4-59, 5-147, 6-185, 7-190, 8-194, 9-213

PAKISTAN v SRI LANKA 1993-94

At Sharjah CA Stadium, UAE on 30 October 1993.　　Result: **PAKISTAN** won by 114 runs.　　Toss: Sri Lanka.
Award: Asif Mujtaba.　　LOI debuts: None.

Saeed Anwar, who hit his fourth hundred, and Asif Mujtaba, who batted throughout the innings, shared the highest opening stand by a pair of left-handers until 1994-95 (*LOI No. 970*).

PAKISTAN		Runs	Balls	4/6
Saeed Anwar	c Muralitharan b Ranatunga	107	108	11/2
Asif Mujtaba	not out	113	134	5
Inzamam-ul-Haq	b Ramanayake	37	35	4
* Wasim Akram	b Ramanayake	15	11	2
Basit Ali	not out	29	16	3/1
Javed Miandad				
Salim Malik				
† Rashid Latif				
Mushtaq Ahmed				
Aqib Javed				
Ata-ur-Rehman				
Extras	(lb 4, w 4, nb 4)	12		
Total	(50 overs; 3 wickets)	**313**		

SRI LANKA		Runs	Balls	4/6
R.S.Mahanama	lbw b Wasim	1	10	–
A.P.Gurusinha	lbw b Wasim	6	13	1
S.T.Jayasuriya	c Inzamam b Mushtaq	58	70	7/1
P.A.de Silva	run out	14	24	2
H.P.Tillekeratne	c Saeed b Salim	20	31	1
* A.Ranatunga	c Rashid b Mushtaq	24	24	1/1
† R.S.Kaluwitharana	c Wasim b Asif	31	40	–/1
R.S.Kalpage	not out	16	49	–
C.P.H.Ramanayake	not out	14	41	1
G.P.Wickremasinghe				
M.Muralitharan				
Extras	(b 2, lb 5, w 7, nb 1)	15		
Total	(50 overs; 7 wickets)	**199**		

SRI LANKA	O	M	R	W
Wickremasinghe	10	2	59	0
Ramanayake	10	1	54	2
Gurusinha	4	1	22	0
Kalpage	10	0	63	0
Muralitharan	6	0	42	0
Jayasuriya	3	0	31	0
Ranatunga	7	0	38	1

PAKISTAN	O	M	R	W
Wasim Akram	8	1	21	2
Aqib Javed	3	0	15	0
Ata-ur-Rehman	8	0	35	0
Salim Malik	10	0	44	1
Mushtaq Ahmed	10	1	45	2
Asif Mujtaba	9	0	28	1
Basit Ali	2	0	4	0

FALL OF WICKETS
1-171, 2-247, 3-270

FALL OF WICKETS
1-4, 2-26, 3-53, 4-103, 5-114, 6-145, 7-173

Umpires: H.D.Bird (*England*) (64) and J.W.Holder (*England*) (10).

WEST INDIES v PAKISTAN 1993-94

At Sharjah CA Stadium, UAE on 1 November 1993.　　Result: **PAKISTAN** won by 5 wickets.　　Toss: West Indies.
Award: Saeed Anwar.　　LOI debuts: None.

Saeed Anwar's second consecutive hundred was Pakistan's highest individual score in internationals for five months (until *LOI No. 911*).

WEST INDIES		Runs	Balls	4/6
B.C.Lara	c Rashid b Mushtaq	14	39	2
D.L.Haynes	c Mushtaq b Wasim	6	25	–
P.V.Simmons	b Rehman	81	94	6/2
K.L.T.Arthurton	c Saeed b Mushtaq	63	81	6
* R.B.Richardson	c Salim b Mushtaq	7	8	1
C.L.Hooper	c Asif b Wasim	18	13	1/1
† J.C.Adams	not out	18	20	1
R.A.Harper	b Wasim	2	5	–
A.C.Cummins	st Rashid Latif b Qadir	10	12	–
K.C.G.Benjamin	b Wasim	4	4	1
C.A.Walsh	not out	2	2	–
Extras	(b 3, lb 10, w 20, nb 2)	35		
Total	(50 overs; 9 wickets)	**260**		

PAKISTAN		Runs	Balls	4/6
Saeed Anwar	c Lara b Hooper	131	141	12/3
Asif Mujtaba	c Arthurton b Cummins	15	32	2
Inzamam-ul-Haq	run out	20	36	1
Javed Miandad	c Adams b Benjamin	20	29	–/1
Basit Ali	run out	16	17	1/1
Salim Malik	not out	34	37	2
* Wasim Akram	not out	5	4	1
† Rashid Latif				
Mushtaq Ahmed				
Abdul Qadir				
Ata-ur-Rehman				
Extras	(b 1, lb 9, w 9, nb 1)	20		
Total	(49 overs; 5 wickets)	**261**		

PAKISTAN	O	M	R	W
Wasim Akram	10	1	40	4
Ata-ur-Rehman	10	1	59	1
Mushtaq Ahmed	10	1	46	3
Abdul Qadir	10	0	43	1
Salim Malik	7	0	35	0
Asif Mujtaba	3	0	24	0

WEST INDIES	O	M	R	W
Walsh	10	1	39	0
Benjamin	10	1	54	1
Cummins	10	0	69	1
Simmons	2	0	10	0
Harper	8	0	36	0
Hooper	9	0	43	1

FALL OF WICKETS
1-26, 2-57, 3-189, 4-201, 5-204, 6-222, 7-234, 8-251, 9-256

FALL OF WICKETS
1-42, 2-86, 3-143, 4-186, 5-251

Umpires: J.W.Holder (*England*) (11) and D.R.Shepherd (*England*) (54).

PAKISTAN v SRI LANKA 1993-94

At Sharjah CA Stadium, UAE on 2 November 1993.   Result: **PAKISTAN** won by 2 wickets.   Toss: Sri Lanka.
Award: Saeed Anwar.   LOI debuts: Pakistan – Aamer Hanif.

Sanath Jayasuriya's 27-ball fifty was Sri Lanka's fastest until 1995-96. Saeed Anwar scored his third hundred in successive innings to emulate the feat of his fellow Pakistani, Zaheer Abbas, in 1982-83. Wasim Akram fractured a finger while batting and was out of action for six weeks.

SRI LANKA		Runs	Balls	4/6
R.S.Mahanama	st Rashid b Mushtaq	59	101	3
A.P.Gurusinha	lbw b Hanif	7	32	1
S.T.Jayasuriya	c Mushtaq b Salim	65	56	6/1
* A.Ranatunga	st Rashid b Salim	35	37	–/2
P.A.de Silva	run out	62	52	5/1
† R.S.Kaluwitharana	c Inzamam b Rehman	23	25	3
R.S.Kalpage	not out	1	2	–
H.P.Tillekeratne				
C.P.H.Ramanayake				
G.P.Wickremasinghe				
D.K.Liyanage				
Extras	(lb 5, w 10, nb 3)	18		
Total	(50 overs; 6 wickets)	**270**		

PAKISTAN		Runs	Balls	4/6
Saeed Anwar	c Mahanama b Liyanage	111	104	11/2
Asif Mujtaba	c Kaluwitharana b Liyanage	34	54	5
Inzamam-ul-Haq	c Wickremasinghe b Liyanage	53	76	3/1
Basit Ali	run out	13	17	1
Salim Malik	c and b Ramanayake	14	15	1
Aamer Hanif	not out	17	24	1
* Wasim Akram	run out	5	4	1
† Rashid Latif	c Mahanama b Wickremasinghe	2	3	–
Mushtaq Ahmed	run out	6	3	–
Abdul Qadir	not out	7	7	–/1
Ata-ur-Rehman				
Extras	(lb 1, w 1, nb 7)	9		
Total	(49.4 overs; 8 wickets)	**271**		

PAKISTAN	O	M	R	W
Wasim Akram	10	1	42	0
Ata-ur-Rehman	10	1	53	1
Aamer Hanif	3.4	0	27	1
Mushtaq Ahmed	10	1	56	1
Abdul Qadir	7.2	0	35	0
Salim Malik	9	0	52	2

SRI LANKA	O	M	R	W
Wickremasinghe	9.4	0	35	1
Ramanayake	8	0	62	1
Liyanage	10	0	49	3
Kalpage	10	0	37	0
Jayasuriya	5	0	37	0
Ranatunga	2	0	17	0
De Silva	5	1	33	0

FALL OF WICKETS
1-26, 2-131, 3-153, 4-197, 5-263, 6-270

FALL OF WICKETS
1-86, 2-195, 3-209, 4-225, 5-233, 6-244, 7-254, 8-260

Umpires: H.D.Bird (*England*) (65) and J.W.Holder (*England*) (12).

WEST INDIES v SRI LANKA 1993-94

At Sharjah CA Stadium, UAE on 3 November 1993.   Result: **WEST INDIES** won by 8 wickets.   Toss: Sri Lanka.
Award: P.V.Simmons.   LOI debuts: West Indies – R.I.C.Holder; Sri Lanka – D.P.Samaraweera.

Pakistan's victory in the previous match determined that they would meet West Indies in the final and thus made this match irrelevant.

SRI LANKA		Runs	Balls	4/6
R.S.Mahanama	c Murray b Simmons	23	46	1
D.P.Samaraweera	c Hooper b Walsh	3	15	–
S.T.Jayasuriya	c Murray b W.K.M.Benjamin	27	32	5
P.A.de Silva	c and b Harper	14	27	–
H.P.Tillekeratne	c Walsh b Hooper	26	59	2
* A.Ranatunga	c Haynes b Harper	17	36	–
† R.S.Kaluwitharana	c Holder b Harper	0	3	–
R.S.Kalpage	c W.K.M.Benjamin b K.C.G.Benjamin	30	47	2
D.K.Liyanage	c Harper b K.C.G.Benjamin	14	27	1
C.P.H.Ramanayake	not out	9	7	2
G.P.Wickremasinghe	not out	6	3	1
Extras	(lb 9, w 2, nb 2)	13		
Total	(50 overs; 9 wickets)	**182**		

WEST INDIES		Runs	Balls	4/6
B.C.Lara	c Kaluwitharana b Kalpage	42	63	5/1
* D.L.Haynes	b Wickremasinghe	0	2	–
P.V.Simmons	not out	90	109	9
C.L.Hooper	not out	47	65	1/1
R.I.C.Holder				
J.C.Adams				
R.A.Harper				
W.K.M.Benjamin				
K.C.G.Benjamin				
† J.R.Murray				
C.A.Walsh				
Extras	(nb 4)	4		
Total	(38.4 overs; 2 wickets)	**183**		

WEST INDIES	O	M	R	W
Walsh	10	2	34	1
K.C.G.Benjamin	8	0	30	2
Simmons	4	0	19	1
W.K.M.Benjamin	8	0	32	1
Harper	10	1	31	3
Hooper	10	0	27	1

SRI LANKA	O	M	R	W
Wickremasinghe	8	1	37	1
Ramanayake	7	0	33	0
Liyanage	5	0	30	0
Kalpage	7.4	1	32	1
Jayasuriya	10	0	48	0
Tillekeratne	1	0	3	0

FALL OF WICKETS
1-16, 2-50, 3-62, 4-74, 5-110, 6-110, 7-132, 8-167, 9-167

FALL OF WICKETS
1-1, 2-87

Umpires: J.W.Holder (*England*) (13) and D.R.Shepherd (*England*) (55).

WEST INDIES v PAKISTAN 1993-94

At Sharjah CA Stadium, UAE on 5 November 1993.   Result: **WEST INDIES** won by 6 wickets.   Toss: West Indies.
Award: B.C.Lara.   Series Award: P.V.Simmons.   LOI debuts: None.

Basit Ali scored his maiden international hundred off only 67 balls, then the second-fastest in all LOIs and still the record for Pakistan. Brian Lara's 153 was the record score at Sharjah until he himself exceeded it in 1995-96; his tally of 21 boundaries equalled Viv Richards's world record.

PAKISTAN		Runs	Balls	4/6
Saeed Anwar	b Cummins	16	36	2
Aamir Sohail	c Lara b Benjamin	10	40	–
Inzamam-ul-Haq	c Haynes b Walsh	30	51	1/1
Salim Malik	c Walsh b Ambrose	84	96	6/1
Basit Ali	not out	127	79	12/5
† Rashid Latif	not out	2	3	–
Asif Mujtaba				
Mushtaq Ahmed				
* Waqar Younis				
Aamir Nazir				
Ata-ur-Rehman				
Extras	(b 1, lb 5, w 4, nb 5)	15		
Total	(50 overs; 4 wickets)	284		

WEST INDIES		Runs	Balls	4/6
B.C.Lara	c Rashid b Mushtaq	153	143	21
D.L.Haynes	c Rashid b Rehman	3	7	–
P.V.Simmons	c and b Salim Malik	42	38	7
K.L.T.Arthurton	c sub (Aamer Hanif) b Rehman	44	30	5/1
* R.B.Richardson	not out	15	50	1
C.L.Hooper	not out	5	11	–
† J.C.Adams				
C.E.L.Ambrose				
A.C.Cummins				
K.C.G.Benjamin				
C.A.Walsh				
Extras	(lb 10, w 8, nb 5)	23		
Total	(45.3 overs; 4 wickets)	285		

WEST INDIES	O	M	R	W
Ambrose	10	2	64	1
Walsh	10	4	33	1
Cummins	9	0	57	1
Benjamin	8	0	37	1
Hooper	10	1	65	0
Simmons	3	0	22	0

PAKISTAN	O	M	R	W
Waqar Younis	8	0	65	0
Ata-ur-Rehman	8	0	43	2
Aamir Nazir	8.3	0	54	0
Mushtaq Ahmed	10	1	46	1
Aamir Sohail	2	0	20	0
Salim Malik	9	1	47	1

FALL OF WICKETS
1-28, 2-30, 3-87, 4-259

FALL OF WICKETS
1-29, 2-140, 3-213, 4-273

Umpires: H.D.Bird (*England*) (66) and D.R.Shepherd (*England*) (56).

INDIA v SRI LANKA 1993-94

At Green Park, Kanpur on 7 November 1993.   Result: **INDIA** won by 7 wickets.   Toss: India.
Award: J.Srinath.   LOI debuts: None.

Pakistan, fearful of Hindu militants, were notable absentees from this five-nation tournament to celebrate the diamond jubilee of the Bengal Cricket Association. Javagal Srinath returned his second five-wicket analysis.

SRI LANKA		Runs	Balls	4/6
R.S.Mahanama	lbw b Chauhan	73	124	4/1
A.P.Gurusinha	c Yadav b Srinath	11	38	1
S.T.Jayasuriya	c Sharma b Srinath	7	9	1
P.A.de Silva	run out	33	47	1/1
* A.Ranatunga	c and b Tendulkar	1	4	–
H.P.Tillekeratne	c Srinath b Prabhakar	35	44	2
† R.S.Kaluwitharana	c Sharma b Chauhan	20	20	1
D.K.Liyanage	c Kapil Dev b Srinath	4	8	–
R.S.Kalpage	c Kumble b Srinath	3	3	–
C.P.H.Ramanayake	not out	3	4	–
G.P.Wickremasinghe	c Kapil Dev b Srinath	0	1	–
Extras	(lb 5, w 8)	13		
Total	(49.4 overs)	203		

INDIA		Runs	Balls	4/6
M.Prabhakar	c Kalpage b Wickremasinghe	20	33	3
W.V.Raman	lbw b Wickremasinghe	0	1	–
V.G.Kambli	c Ramanayake b Liyanage	78	100	9
* M.Azharuddin	not out	75	105	4/2
S.R.Tendulkar	not out	26	30	4
Kapil Dev				
A.K.Sharma				
A.Kumble				
† V.Yadav				
J.Srinath				
R.K.Chauhan				
Extras	(lb 4, w 2)	6		
Total	(44.4 overs; 3 wickets)	205		

INDIA	O	M	R	W
Prabhakar	7	2	27	1
Kapil Dev	7	0	30	0
Srinath	6.4	1	24	5
Tendulkar	10	2	27	1
Kumble	10	0	46	0
Chauhan	6	0	28	2
Sharma	3	0	16	0

SRI LANKA	O	M	R	W
Wickremasinghe	6	1	13	2
Ramanayake	5.4	0	31	0
Liyanage	7	0	40	1
Ranatunga	3	0	19	0
Kalpage	8	0	27	0
Jayasuriya	6	0	32	0
Tillekeratne	9	0	39	0

FALL OF WICKETS
1-43, 2-53, 3-116, 4-117, 5-147, 6-175, 7-188, 8-200, 9-202, 10-203

FALL OF WICKETS
1-1, 2-46, 3-146

Umpires: S.A.Bucknor (*West Indies*) (17) and I.D.Robinson (*Zimbabwe*) (11).

WEST INDIES v SRI LANKA 1993-94

At Wankhede Stadium, Bombay on 9 November 1993.   Result: **WEST INDIES** won by 46 runs.   Toss: Sri Lanka.
Awards: W.K.M.Benjamin and H.P.Tillekeratne.   LOI debuts: None.

Hashan Tillekeratne scored Sri Lanka's first hundred against West Indies; it was the only one in this 13-match
tournament. Winston Benjamin converted an opening spell of 6-3-4-3 into the sole five-wicket analysis of his entire
international career.

WEST INDIES		Runs	Balls	4/6
B.C.Lara	c Muralitharan b Ranatunga	67	109	11
* D.L.Haynes	c Mahanama b Wickremasinghe	0	7	–
P.V.Simmons	c Mahanama b Liyanage	3	23	–
C.L.Hooper	b Ranatunga	38	37	3
K.L.T.Arthurton	st Kaluwitharana b Muralitharan	6	7	1
J.C.Adams	st Kaluwitharana b Kalpage	55	55	6
R.A.Harper	lbw b Kalpage	20	22	–
† J.R.Murray	not out	11	16	1
A.C.Cummins	c sub (C.P.H. Ramanayake) b Kalpage	41	19	4/2
W.K.M.Benjamin	not out	0	1	–
C.A.Walsh				
Extras	(b 1, lb 18, w 8)	27		
Total	(50 overs; 8 wickets)	**268**		

SRI LANKA		Runs	Balls	4/6
R.S.Mahanama	lbw b Benjamin	11	29	1
U.C.Hathurusinghe	b Benjamin	1	16	–
S.T.Jayasuriya	c Haynes b Benjamin	2	11	–
H.P.Tillekeratne	b Benjamin	104	116	7
D.P.Samaraweera	c and b Harper	25	45	2
* A.Ranatunga	st Murray b Hooper	14	31	–
† R.S.Kaluwitharana	c Arthurton b Hooper	10	14	–
R.S.Kalpage	not out	29	27	–
D.K.Liyanage	b Benjamin	3	5	–
M.Muralitharan	not out	4	9	–
G.P.Wickremasinghe				
Extras	(b 1, lb 14, w 2, nb 2)	19		
Total	(50 overs; 8 wickets)	**222**		

SRI LANKA	O	M	R	W
Wickremasinghe	10	2	54	1
Liyanage	8	0	24	1
Hathurusinghe	2	0	22	0
Ranatunga	10	1	44	2
Kalpage	10	0	64	3
Muralitharan	10	1	41	1

WEST INDIES	O	M	R	W
Walsh	8	2	25	0
Benjamin	10	3	22	5
Cummins	8	2	37	0
Harper	5	0	36	1
Simmons	10	0	38	0
Hooper	9	0	49	2

FALL OF WICKETS
1-10, 2-26, 3-104, 4-111, 5-172, 6-211, 7-220, 8-268

FALL OF WICKETS
1-10, 2-16, 3-21, 4-72, 5-118, 6-143, 7-204, 8-214

Umpires: S.K.Bansal (5) and R.T.Ramachandran (2).

SOUTH AFRICA v ZIMBABWE 1993-94

At Chinnaswamy Stadium, Bangalore on 10 November 1993.   No result.   Toss: Zimbabwe.
LOI debuts: Zimbabwe – J.A.Rennie, H.H.Streak.

A contest delayed by two hours and reduced to a 37-over affair was terminated by torrential rain after 40 minutes.

SOUTH AFRICA		Runs	Balls	4/6
* K.C.Wessels	not out	10	33	2
A.C.Hudson	lbw b Brain	5	19	–
W.J.Cronje	not out	4	1	1
D.J.Cullinan				
J.N.Rhodes				
D.J.Callaghan				
B.M.McMillan				
† D.J.Richardson				
P.S.de Villiers				
A.A.Donald				
C.R.Matthews				
Extras	(w 3)	3		
Total	(9 overs; 1 wicket)	**22**		

ZIMBABWE
*† A.Flower
G.W.Flower
A.D.R.Campbell
D.L.Houghton
A.C.Waller
S.G.Peall
H.H.Streak
M.H.Dekker
J.A.Rennie
D.H.Brain
I.P.Butchart

ZIMBABWE	O	M	R	W
Brain	5	0	12	1
Streak	4	1	10	0

FALL OF WICKETS
1-18

Umpires: P.D.Reporter (21) and S.K.Sharma (1).

SOUTH AFRICA v WEST INDIES 1993-94

At Brabourne Stadium, Bombay on 14 November 1993.   Result: **SOUTH AFRICA** won by 41 runs.
Toss: West Indies.   Award: J.N.Rhodes.   LOI debuts: None.

Leaking covers had delayed the start by 80 minutes. The exceptionally nimble and fleet-footed 'Jonty' Rhodes dominated this match with his world fielding record of five catches, three of them quite outstanding. Daryll Cullinan retired with heat exhaustion at 136. Desmond Haynes (7) retired at 15 and resumed at 87.

SOUTH AFRICA		Runs	Balls	4/6
A.C.Hudson	c Simmons b K.C.G.Benjamin	5	18	1
* K.C.Wessels	c Lara b Ambrose	3	17	–
W.J.Cronje	lbw b Hooper	12	27	1
D.J.Cullinan	retired ill	70	81	5
J.N.Rhodes	b W.K.M.Benjamin	40	42	4
B.M.McMillan	b W.K.M.Benjamin	24	31	1
† D.J.Richardson	not out	17	23	–
P.L.Symcox	not out	3	3	–
P.S.de Villiers				
R.P.Snell				
A.A.Donald				
Extras	(lb 2, w 3, nb 1)	6		
Total	(40 overs; 5 wickets)	**180**		

WEST INDIES		Runs	Balls	4/6
B.C.Lara	c Rhodes b Snell	7	20	1
D.L.Haynes	c Rhodes b Snell	28	73	1
P.V.Simmons	c Rhodes b Symcox	29	39	4
K.L.T.Arthurton	st Richardson b Symcox	16	14	2
C.L.Hooper	lbw b Cronje	17	29	–
* R.B.Richardson	c and b Cronje	1	3	–
† J.C.Adams	c Rhodes b Symcox	4	7	–
A.C.Cummins	c Rhodes b Donald	17	21	3
W.K.M.Benjamin	c Cronje b McMillan	0	4	–
C.E.L.Ambrose	c Snell b McMillan	0	4	–
K.C.G.Benjamin	not out	7	8	1
Extras	(b 4, lb 7, w 2)	13		
Total	(37 overs)	**139**		

WEST INDIES	O	M	R	W
Ambrose	8	1	23	1
K.C.G.Benjamin	8	0	41	1
W.K.M.Benjamin	8	0	40	2
Cummins	8	1	43	0
Hooper	8	0	31	1

SOUTH AFRICA	O	M	R	W
Donald	5	0	15	1
De Villiers	5	2	5	0
Snell	6	0	30	2
McMillan	5	0	25	2
Symcox	8	1	20	3
Cronje	8	1	33	2

FALL OF WICKETS
1-9, 2-11, 3-52, 4-117, 5-176

FALL OF WICKETS
1-14, 2-50, 3-73, 4-78, 5-87, 6-95, 7-120, 8-124, 9-131, 10-139

Umpires: V.K.Ramaswamy (27) and R.C.Sharma (6).

SRI LANKA v ZIMBABWE 1993-94

At Moin-ul-Haq Stadium, Patna on 15 November 1993.   Result: **SRI LANKA** won by 55 runs.   Toss: Zimbabwe.
Award: A.Ranatunga.   LOI debuts: Zimbabwe – G.J.Whittall.

Patna, the 28th Indian city/town to stage an international, became the 107th LOI venue. Sanath Jayasuriya needed only four overs to produce his third analysis of four or more wickets.

SRI LANKA		Runs	Balls	4/6
R.S.Mahanama	c Dekker b Brain	16	35	2
S.T.Jayasuriya	c Waller b Brain	23	27	4
H.P.Tillekeratne	lbw b Shah	24	56	1
P.A.de Silva	c and b Shah	68	94	4
* A.Ranatunga	c Rennie b Dekker	59	64	7
D.K.Liyanage	b Rennie	8	6	–
R.J.Ratnayake	not out	32	15	3/1
† R.S.Kaluwitharana	not out	4	6	–
R.S.Kalpage				
G.P.Wickremasinghe				
M.Muralitharan				
Extras	(b 8, lb 5, w 15, nb 1)	29		
Total	(50 overs; 6 wickets)	**263**		

ZIMBABWE		Runs	Balls	4/6
*†A.Flower	run out	11	31	1
D.H.Brain	lbw b Ratnayake	2	8	–
A.D.R.Campbell	c Ratnayake b Jayasuriya	37	88	2
D.L.Houghton	b Liyanage	12	33	2
A.C.Waller	c Tillekeratne b Ranatunga	55	46	7/1
M.H.Dekker	lbw b Ranatunga	1	3	–
G.J.Whittall	b Jayasuriya	36	33	2
A.H.Shah	b Jayasuriya	14	32	–
S.G.Peall	c Tillekeratne b Kalpage	12	9	–
H.H.Streak	st Kaluwitharana b Jayasuriya	5	7	–
J.A.Rennie	not out	3	8	–
Extras	(b 5, lb 4, w 9, nb 2)	20		
Total	(49 overs)	**208**		

ZIMBABWE	O	M	R	W
Brain	10	1	45	2
Streak	8	0	67	0
Rennie	9	0	37	1
Peall	10	0	35	0
Shah	10	0	50	2
Dekker	3	0	16	1

SRI LANKA	O	M	R	W
Wickremasinghe	6	1	13	0
Ratnayake	7	0	12	1
Liyanage	10	1	36	1
Muralitharan	10	0	43	0
Kalpage	6	0	46	1
Jayasuriya	4	0	19	4
Ranatunga	5	0	24	2
Tillekeratne	1	0	6	0

FALL OF WICKETS
1-38, 2-53, 3-114, 4-210, 5-221, 6-225

FALL OF WICKETS
1-6, 2-22, 3-53, 4-130, 5-132, 6-133, 7-188, 8-189, 9-202, 10-208

Umpires: S.Choudhury (2) and K.Parthasarthy (2).

INDIA v WEST INDIES 1993-94

At Gujarat Stadium, Motera, Ahmedabad on 16 November 1993.   Result: **WEST INDIES** won by 69 runs (revised target).   Toss: West Indies.   Award: W.K.M.Benjamin.   LOI debuts: None.

The match was halted for 48 minutes when some of the 50,000 spectators grew disenchanted with India's score of 57 for 6 (16.1 overs) and forced the fielders into mid-pitch safety with a fusillade of stones, firecrackers and assorted debris. Facing a revised challenge of 170 from 38 overs, India notched their lowest total against West Indies.

WEST INDIES		Runs	Balls	4/6
B.C.Lara	b Kumble	23	37	2
P.V.Simmons	run out	9	36	1
* R.B.Richardson	c Kambli b Kumble	41	80	3/1
K.L.T.Arthurton	b Kumble	41	80	–/1
C.L.Hooper	c Yadav b Srinath	8	10	–
† J.C.Adams	not out	26	33	–
R.I.C.Holder	c Chauhan b Srinath	10	16	–
R.A.Harper	run out	2	5	–
W.K.M.Benjamin	not out	14	14	1
C.E.L.Ambrose				
C.A.Walsh				
Extras	(b 1, lb 21, w 6)	28		
Total	(50 overs; 7 wickets)	**202**		

INDIA		Runs	Balls	4/6
M.Prabhakar	c Adams b Walsh	11	14	2
Kapil Dev	lbw b Ambrose	1	2	–
V.G.Kambli	c Lara b Benjamin	10	18	1
* M.Azharuddin	c Ambrose b Simmons	23	44	2
S.R.Tendulkar	lbw b Walsh	2	8	–
W.V.Raman	c Lara b Benjamin	4	14	–
A.K.Sharma	b Benjamin	0	1	–
† V.Yadav	st Adams b Hooper	20	26	2
A.Kumble	c Benjamin b Hooper	14	27	1
R.K.Chauhan	not out	3	10	–
J.Srinath	c Harper b Hooper	2	8	–
Extras	(lb 2, w 8)	10		
Total	(28.3 overs)	**100**		

INDIA	O	M	R	W
Prabhakar	10	1	50	0
Srinath	10	1	33	2
Kumble	10	1	24	3
Kapil Dev	8	0	21	0
Chauhan	10	2	41	0
Tendulkar	2	0	11	0

WEST INDIES	O	M	R	W
Ambrose	6	0	18	1
Walsh	7	2	25	2
Simmons	5	0	19	1
Benjamin	6	0	27	3
Hooper	4.3	1	9	3

FALL OF WICKETS
1-34, 2-36, 3-114, 4-128, 5-157, 6-177, 7-186

FALL OF WICKETS
1-12, 2-18, 3-37, 4-40, 5-55, 6-55, 7-77, 8-85, 9-96, 10-100

Umpires: K.E.Liebenberg (SA) (15) and I.D.Robinson (*Zimbabwe*) (12).

INDIA v ZIMBABWE 1993-94

At Nehru Stadium, Indore on 18 November 1993.   Result: **MATCH TIED.**   Toss: Zimbabwe.
Award: M.Prabhakar.   LOI debuts: None.

Zimbabwe's last pair needed ten from Manoj Prabhakar's final over to register their first win of the tournament. With two needed from the last ball, Heath Streak, attempting a second leg-bye, was run out by the keeper. The 'fewer wickets lost' regulation did not apply to this competition.

INDIA		Runs	Balls	4/6
M.Prabhakar	st A.Flower b Peall	91	126	4
W.V.Raman	c Houghton b Brain	0	7	–
V.G.Kambli	c Rennie b Peall	55	96	1
† V.Yadav	c G.W.Flower b Peall	0	2	–
* M.Azharuddin	not out	54	56	4/1
S.R.Tendulkar	c and b Streak	24	16	1/1
P.K.Amre	not out	1	1	–
Kapil Dev				
A.Kumble				
J.Srinath				
R.K.Chauhan				
Extras	(b 4, lb 8, w 8, nb 3)	23		
Total	(50 overs; 5 wickets)	**248**		

ZIMBABWE		Runs	Balls	4/6
*† A.Flower	st Yadav b Chauhan	56	82	6
G.W.Flower	b Prabhakar	2	14	–
A.D.R.Campbell	b Srinath	7	17	1
D.L.Houghton	lbw b Kapil Dev	22	32	3/1
A.C.Waller	c Azharuddin b Tendulkar	32	50	3
G.J.Whittall	run out	33	43	3
A.H.Shah	c Chauhan b Srinath	37	31	4
S.G.Peall	c Yadav b Srinath	17	15	2
D.H.Brain	c Azharuddin b Prabhakar	1	2	–
H.H.Streak	run out	11	9	1
J.A.Rennie	not out	9	6	1
Extras	(lb 10, w 11)	21		
Total	(50 overs)	**248**		

ZIMBABWE	O	M	R	W
Brain	10	0	37	1
Streak	10	2	44	1
Rennie	9	0	36	0
Shah	5	0	31	0
Peall	10	0	54	3
G.W.Flower	6	0	34	0

INDIA	O	M	R	W
Prabhakar	10	0	41	2
Srinath	10	0	44	3
Tendulkar	8	0	48	1
Kapil Dev	6	0	31	1
Kumble	8	0	42	0
Chauhan	8	0	32	1

FALL OF WICKETS
1-6, 2-128, 3-128, 4-197, 5-239

FALL OF WICKETS
1-10, 2-23, 3-67, 4-131, 5-143, 6-207, 7-208, 8-212, 9-237, 10-248

Umpires: S.A.Bucknor (*West Indies*) (18) and K.E.Liebenberg (SA) (16).

SOUTH AFRICA v SRI LANKA 1993-94

At Nehru Stadium, Gauhati on 19 November 1993.   Result: **SOUTH AFRICA** won by 78 runs.   Toss: Sri Lanka.
Award: R.P.Snell.   LOI debuts: None.

Playing in his 90th international, Roshan Mahanama became the first Sri Lankan to hold 50 catches in the field. Richard Snell removed three key batsmen for eight runs in his opening six-over spell.

SOUTH AFRICA		Runs	Balls	4/6
A.C.Hudson	c Kaluwitharana b Ratnayake	5	19	-
* K.C.Wessels	st Kaluwitharana b Muralitharan	53	91	5
W.J.Cronje	b Muralitharan	28	48	2
D.J.Cullinan	b Jayasuriya	41	59	1/2
J.N.Rhodes	c Mahanama b Jayasuriya	16	27	1
B.M.McMillan	not out	31	39	1
P.L.Symcox	b Jayasuriya	4	8	-
R.P.Snell	b Ratnayake	20	11	1/1
† D.J.Richardson	not out	1	1	-
P.S.de Villiers				
A.A.Donald				
Extras	(lb 7, w 6, nb 2)	15		
Total	(50 overs; 7 wickets)	**214**		

SRI LANKA		Runs	Balls	4/6
R.S.Mahanama	c Richardson b Donald	10	21	1
S.T.Jayasuriya	c Richardson b Snell	27	59	2
H.P.Tillekeratne	lbw b Snell	4	24	-
P.A.de Silva	lbw b Snell	2	10	-
* A.Ranatunga	lbw b Symcox	6	31	-
† R.S.Kaluwitharana	c Rhodes b Cronje	17	24	2
R.S.Kalpage	c De Villiers b Cronje	1	8	-
R.J.Ratnayake	run out	21	16	-/2
D.K.Liyanage	c Cronje b De Villiers	16	29	1
G.P.Wickremasinghe	b Snell	17	21	1
M.Muralitharan	not out	0	6	-
Extras	(lb 5, w 4, nb 6)	15		
Total	(40.1 overs)	**136**		

SRI LANKA	O	M	R	W
Wickremasinghe	6	0	29	0
Ratnayake	8	2	24	2
Liyanage	5	1	27	0
Muralitharan	10	1	36	2
Kalpage	10	1	40	0
Jayasuriya	7	0	30	3
De Silva	4	0	21	0

SOUTH AFRICA	O	M	R	W
Donald	8	0	33	1
De Villiers	9	1	29	1
Snell	7.1	2	12	4
McMillan	5	0	16	0
Cronje	6	1	21	2
Symcox	5	0	20	1

FALL OF WICKETS
1-25, 2-48, 3-50, 4-59, 5-78, 6-80, 7-81, 8-109, 9-135, 10-136

FALL OF WICKETS
1-18, 2-81, 3-101, 4-132, 5-163, 6-171, 7-212

Umpires: S.Choudhury (3) and V.K.Ramaswamy (20).

WEST INDIES v ZIMBABWE 1993-94

At Lal Bahadur Stadium, Hyderabad on 21 November 1993.   Result: **WEST INDIES** won by 134 runs.
Toss: West Indies.   Award: D.L.Haynes.   LOI debuts: None.

Zimbabwe, with Eddo Brandes, who damaged his hand attempting a fierce return catch from Winston Benjamin, unable to bat, were dismissed for their only double-figure total in limited-over internationals.

WEST INDIES		Runs	Balls	4/6
B.C.Lara	c Streak b Brain	4	18	-
D.L.Haynes	run out	75	90	11
P.V.Simmons	lbw b Streak	0	13	-
* R.B.Richardson	c A.Flower b Streak	5	8	1
R.I.C.Holder	c Brandes b Peall	50	87	4
K.L.T.Arthurton	run out	16	38	1
R.A.Harper	b Rennie	26	17	2
A.C.Cummins	c Brain b Rennie	26	17	4
W.K.M.Benjamin	run out	8	8	-/1
K.C.G.Benjamin	not out	1	1	-
† J.R.Murray				
Extras	(b 2, lb 9, w 9, nb 2)	22		
Total	(50 overs; 9 wickets)	**233**		

ZIMBABWE		Runs	Balls	4/6
*† A.Flower	c Haynes b K.C.G.Benjamin	22	47	3
G.W.Flower	c Simmons b W.K.M.Benjamin	7	27	-
A.D.R.Campbell	lbw b W.K.M.Benjamin	0	2	-
D.L.Houghton	c Murray b Simmons	22	48	1
A.C.Waller	b Simmons	9	20	-/1
G.J.Whittall	c Cummins b Harper	9	22	1
S.G.Peall	b Cummins	10	34	1
D.H.Brain	c Harper b Simmons	1	5	-
H.H.Streak	not out	0	7	-
J.A.Rennie	lbw b Cummins	0	1	-
E.A.Brandes	absent hurt	-	-	-
Extras	(lb 9, w 5, nb 5)	19		
Total	(36.3 overs)	**99**		

ZIMBABWE	O	M	R	W
Brain	6	1	24	1
Streak	10	2	44	2
Rennie	9	0	42	2
Brandes	9.3	0	56	0
Peall	10	0	34	1
Campbell	5	0	16	0
Whittall	0.3	0	6	0

WEST INDIES	O	M	R	W
K.C.G.Benjamin	7	1	19	1
W.K.M.Benjamin	6	2	13	2
Cummins	5.3	0	19	2
Simmons	10	0	23	3
Harper	8	2	16	1

FALL OF WICKETS
1-23, 2-23, 3-43, 4-67, 5-80, 6-88, 7-91, 8-98, 9-99

FALL OF WICKETS
1-10, 2-24, 3-38, 4-130, 5-156, 6-169, 7-212, 8-231, 9-233

Umpires: S.K.Bansal (6) and R.C.Sharma (7).

INDIA v SOUTH AFRICA 1993-94

At Punjab CA Stadium, Mohali, Chandigarh on 22 November 1993.　　Result: **INDIA** won by 43 runs.
Toss: South Africa.　　Award: V.G.Kambli.　　LOI debuts: None.

This was the inaugural cricket match at the Punjab Cricket Association's new ground which superseded Chandigarh's romantically named Sector 16 Stadium seven miles away. Appropriately it provided the setting for India's 100th LOI victory.

INDIA		Runs	Balls	4/6
M.Prabhakar	lbw b De Villiers	1	8	–
A.Jadeja	run out	39	62	6
V.G.Kambli	b Cronje	86	116	10
S.R.Tendulkar	c Richardson b Cronje	3	25	–
* M.Azharuddin	run out	31	50	3
P.K.Amre	c Donald b Cronje	2	6	–
Kapil Dev	c Wessels b De Villiers	22	17	3
† V.Yadav	b Snell	2	6	–
A.Kumble	run out	2	2	–
J.Srinath	c Hudson b Snell	1	4	–
S.A.Ankola	not out	2	3	–
Extras	(b 1, lb 10, w 16, nb 3)	30		
Total	(49.2 overs)	**221**		

SOUTH AFRICA		Runs	Balls	4/6
A.C.Hudson	lbw b Kapil Dev	27	47	5
* K.C.Wessels	c Yadav b Srinath	1	9	–
W.J.Cronje	b Jadeja	39	70	4
J.N.Rhodes	lbw b Ankola	56	72	1
D.J.Callaghan	c Kapil Dev b Jadeja	6	22	–
B.M.McMillan	lbw b Kumble	2	7	–
† D.J.Richardson	not out	23	36	–
P.L.Symcox	b Prabhakar	2	7	–
R.P.Snell	c Kumble b Ankola	2	3	–
P.S.de Villiers	c Yadav b Ankola	1	6	–
A.A.Donald	not out	5	24	–
Extras	(lb 4, w 7, nb 3)	14		
Total	(50 overs; 9 wickets)	**178**		

SOUTH AFRICA	O	M	R	W
Donald	8	0	39	0
De Villiers	8.2	0	27	2
Snell	10	0	54	2
McMillan	10	0	45	0
Cronje	10	0	29	3
Symcox	3	0	16	0

INDIA	O	M	R	W
Prabhakar	10	0	36	1
Srinath	7	1	22	1
Ankola	10	1	33	3
Kapil Dev	8	1	32	1
Kumble	10	0	35	1
Jadeja	5	1	16	2

FALL OF WICKETS
1-6, 2-94, 3-129, 4-180, 5-188, 6-192, 7-196, 8-199, 9-211, 10-221

FALL OF WICKETS
1-7, 2-40, 3-108, 4-124, 5-127, 6-144, 7-147, 8-150, 9-157

Umpires: S.A.Bucknor (*WI*) (19) and I.D.Robinson (*Zimbabwe*) (13).

INDIA v SOUTH AFRICA 1993-94

At Eden Gardens, Calcutta on 24 November 1993.　　Result: **INDIA** won by 2 runs.　　Toss: India.
Award: M.Azharuddin.　　LOI debuts: None.

Calcutta's first floodlit match attracted a crowd of around 90,000, vast swarms of insects which were dispersed by smoke bombs, and one mongoose. Vinod Kambli was the first to be despatched by a video-assisted third umpire, S.K.Bansal. South Africa failed to score six off Sachin Tendulkar's final over.

INDIA		Runs	Balls	4/6
M.Prabhakar	run out	3	19	1
A.Jadeja	lbw b De Villiers	6	11	1
V.G.Kambli	run out	4	6	1
* M.Azharuddin	c Richardson b Snell	90	118	7/1
S.R.Tendulkar	c Richardson b Snell	15	31	3
P.K.Amre	run out	48	90	2
Kapil Dev	run out	7	10	1
† V.Yadav	c Rhodes b De Villiers	3	7	–
A.Kumble	c McMillan b Snell	0	2	–
J.Srinath	b De Villiers	4	6	–
S.A.Ankola	not out	2	3	–
Extras	(lb 5, w 5, nb 3)	13		
Total	(50 overs)	**195**		

SOUTH AFRICA		Runs	Balls	4/6
* K.C.Wessels	lbw b Srinath	5	23	1
A.C.Hudson	b Kumble	62	112	5
W.J.Cronje	run out	13	30	1
D.J.Cullinan	lbw b Kapil Dev	10	23	1
J.N.Rhodes	c Azharuddin b Jadeja	16	31	1
B.M.McMillan	not out	48	57	4
P.L.Symcox	c Amre b Jadeja	6	11	–
R.P.Snell	st Yadav b Kumble	1	3	–
† D.J.Richardson	run out	15	16	1
P.S.de Villiers	run out	0	1	–
A.A.Donald	not out	1	4	–
Extras	(lb 9, w 4, nb 3)	16		
Total	(50 overs; 9 wickets)	**193**		

SOUTH AFRICA	O	M	R	W
Donald	8	0	44	0
De Villiers	10	1	19	3
Snell	8	0	33	3
McMillan	9	0	41	0
Cronje	9	0	25	0
Symcox	6	0	28	0

INDIA	O	M	R	W
Prabhakar	8	1	30	0
Srinath	8	0	39	1
Kapil Dev	8	0	31	1
Ankola	6	0	21	0
Kumble	10	0	29	2
Jadeja	9	0	31	2
Tendulkar	1	0	3	0

FALL OF WICKETS
1-12, 2-18, 3-18, 4-53, 5-148, 6-173, 7-184, 8-189, 9-192, 10-195

FALL OF WICKETS
1-10, 2-45, 3-65, 4-106, 5-130, 6-141, 7-145, 8-189, 9-191

Umpires: S.A.Bucknor (*WI*) (20) and I.D.Robinson (*Zimbabwe*) (14).

WEST INDIES v SRI LANKA 1993-94

At Eden Gardens, Calcutta on 25 November 1993.   Result: **WEST INDIES** won by 7 wickets.   Toss: West Indies.
Award: B.C.Lara.   LOI debuts: None.

The mongoose returned with the illuminations as West Indies coasted into the final with a third-wicket stand of 163 in 35.1 overs between Brian Lara and Keith Arthurton.

SRI LANKA		Runs	Balls	4/6
R.S.Mahanama	lbw b Cummins	31	81	2
S.T.Jayasuriya	c Simmons b Benjamin	18	27	3
H.P.Tillekeratne	lbw b Cummins	11	27	–
P.A.de Silva	run out	68	79	4/1
* A.Ranatunga	c Lara b Hooper	2	5	–
† R.S.Kaluwitharana	b Hooper	1	17	–
R.S.Kalpage	not out	41	65	3
R.J.Ratnayake	not out	2	1	–
G.P.Wickremasinghe				
C.P.H.Ramanayake				
M.Muralitharan				
Extras	(lb 11, w 3)	14		
Total	(50 overs; 6 wickets)	**188**		

WEST INDIES		O	M	R	W
Ambrose		10	0	59	0
Walsh		10	3	33	0
Benjamin		10	2	29	1
Cummins		10	0	38	2
Hooper		10	3	18	2

FALL OF WICKETS
1-33, 2-65, 3-68, 4-73, 5-77, 6-186

Umpires: S.K.Bansal (7) and S.Choudhury (4).

WEST INDIES		Runs	Balls	4/6
B.C.Lara	b Muralitharan	82	121	8
D.L.Haynes	lbw b Wickremasinghe	0	1	–
P.V.Simmons	c Mahanama b Wickremasinghe	0	6	–
K.L.T.Arthurton	not out	72	117	6/1
* R.B.Richardson	not out	15	21	3
C.L.Hooper				
† J.C.Adams				
A.C.Cummins				
C.E.L.Ambrose				
W.K.M.Benjamin				
C.A.Walsh				
Extras	(lb 2, w 12, nb 7)	21		
Total	(41.5 overs; 3 wickets)	**190**		

SRI LANKA	O	M	R	W
Wickremasinghe	6	0	27	2
Ramanayake	3	0	18	0
Ratnayake	4	0	11	0
Kalpage	9.5	0	47	0
Muralitharan	10	0	37	1
De Silva	3	0	16	0
Jayasuriya	2	0	14	0
Ranatunga	4	0	18	0

FALL OF WICKETS
1-1, 2-3, 3-166

INDIA v WEST INDIES 1993-94

At Eden Gardens, Calcutta on 27 November 1993.   Result: **INDIA** won by 102 runs.   Toss: West Indies.
Award: A.Kumble.   Tournament Award: M.Azharuddin.   LOI debuts: None.

West Indies' decision to bat second on the pitch used for both semi-finals back-fired when they were dismissed for their lowest total against India, Anil Kumble taking the last six wickets for four runs in 26 balls to return the third-best LOI analysis. The estimated attendance of 100,000, plus mongoose, set a world record for any day's cricket.

INDIA		Runs	Balls	4/6
M.Prabhakar	c Adams b Ambrose	11	23	1
A.Jadeja	c Richardson b W.K.M.Benjamin	30	63	2/1
V.G.Kambli	run out	68	90	6
* M.Azharuddin	c Adams b Cummins	38	43	3
S.R.Tendulkar	not out	28	43	2
P.K.Amre	lbw b Cummins	0	4	–
Kapil Dev	c Hooper b Cummins	24	28	2
† V.Yadav	b Ambrose	3	4	–
A.Kumble	not out	5	3	1
S.L.V.Raju				
J.Srinath				
Extras	(b 2, lb 12, w 2, nb 2)	18		
Total	(50 overs; 7 wickets)	**225**		

WEST INDIES	O	M	R	W
Ambrose	10	1	35	2
K.C.G.Benjamin	10	1	35	0
W.K.M.Benjamin	10	1	47	1
Cummins	10	1	38	3
Hooper	8	0	42	0
Simmons	2	0	14	0

FALL OF WICKETS
1-25, 2-81, 3-161, 4-161, 5-161, 6-207, 7-218

Umpires: K.E.Liebenberg (SA) (17) and I.D.Robinson (Zimbabwe) (15).

WEST INDIES		Runs	Balls	4/6
B.C.Lara	b Tendulkar	33	47	6
P.V.Simmons	b Prabhakar	0	5	–
* R.B.Richardson	c and b Kapil Dev	18	43	3
K.L.T.Arthurton	lbw b Kapil Dev	5	11	1
C.L.Hooper	lbw b Kumble	23	57	–
R.I.C.Holder	b Kumble	15	38	1
† J.C.Adams	c Azharuddin b Kumble	4	7	–
A.C.Cummins	b Kumble	1	16	–
W.K.M.Benjamin	b Kumble	3	7	–
C.E.L.Ambrose	b Kumble	0	2	–
K.C.G.Benjamin	not out	0	6	–
Extras	(lb 12, w 8, nb 1)	21		
Total	(40.1 overs)	**123**		

INDIA	O	M	R	W
Prabhakar	6	0	21	1
Srinath	6	0	12	0
Jadeja	1	0	18	0
Kapil Dev	10	3	18	2
Tendulkar	7	1	24	1
Kumble	6.1	2	12	6
Raju	4	0	6	0

FALL OF WICKETS
1-1, 2-57, 3-57, 4-63, 5-101, 6-113, 7-118, 8-122, 9-122, 10-123

SRI LANKA v WEST INDIES 1993-94

At P.Saravanamuttu Stadium, Colombo on 1 December 1993.　　No result.　　Toss: West Indies.
LOI debuts: None.

The first of 17 meetings between these sides not to be played on a neutral ground was delayed two hours by overnight rain, reduced to 40 overs each, and terminated by a massive thunderstorm. Sanath Jayasuriya was carried off with cramp with the total 13.

WEST INDIES		Runs	Balls	4/6
B.C.Lara	c and b Jayasuriya	89	118	8
P.V.Simmons	c Kalpage b Ratnayake	11	24	2
* R.B.Richardson	b Anurasiri	21	48	2
K.L.T.Arthurton	not out	37	31	1/2
C.L.Hooper	not out	13	15	1
J.C.Adams				
R.A.Harper				
† J.R.Murray				
C.E.L.Ambrose				
K.C.G.Benjamin				
C.A.Walsh				
Extras	(lb 15, w 9, nb 2)	26		
Total	(39 overs; 3 wickets)	197		

SRI LANKA		Runs	Balls	4/6
R.S.Mahanama	not out	10	31	1
S.T.Jayasuriya	retired hurt	4	25	–
P.A.de Silva	c Simmons b Walsh	2	5	–
* A.Ranatunga	not out	11	14	1/1
H.P.Tillekeratne				
R.P.A.H.Wickremaratne				
R.S.Kalpage				
† R.S.Kaluwitharana				
R.J.Ratnayake				
G.P.Wickremasinghe				
S.D.Anurasiri				
Extras	(lb 6, w 1, nb 1)	8		
Total	(12.1 overs; 1 wicket)	35		

SRI LANKA	O	M	R	W
Wickremasinghe	7	1	22	0
Ratnayake	7	1	37	1
Kalpage	8	0	37	0
Ranatunga	1	0	10	0
Anurasiri	8	1	26	1
Jayasuriya	7	1	40	1
De Silva	1	0	10	0

WEST INDIES	O	M	R	W
Ambrose	5	2	4	0
Walsh	5	1	10	1
Benjamin	1.1	0	5	0
Hooper	1	0	10	0

FALL OF WICKETS
1-33, 2-121, 3-154

FALL OF WICKETS
1-16

Umpires: B.C.Cooray (13) and P.Manuel (6).

Referee: Zaheer Abbas (*Pakistan*).

SRI LANKA v WEST INDIES 1993-94

At Khettarama Stadium, Colombo on 16 December 1993.　　Result: **SRI LANKA** won by 3 wickets.　　Toss: West Indies.
Award: A.Ranatunga.　　LOI debuts: None.

Sri Lanka gained only their second win in 18 matches against West Indies and became the first team to win batting second under the Khettarama lights.

WEST INDIES		Runs	Balls	4/6
D.L.Haynes	c and b Anurasiri	51	83	4/1
B.C.Lara	c Mahanama b Jayasuriya	65	77	5
P.V.Simmons	c Wickremasinghe b Kalpage	10	32	1
K.L.T.Arthurton	not out	50	60	1
* R.B.Richardson	b Kalpage	15	18	–
C.L.Hooper	c Tillekeratne b Kalpage	4	7	–
A.C.Cummins	run out	1	1	–
† J.C.Adams	lbw b Kalpage	0	1	–
W.K.M.Benjamin	b Liyanage	11	16	–
C.E.L.Ambrose	not out	2	2	–
C.A.Walsh				
Extras	(lb 9, w 9, nb 2)	20		
Total	(49 overs; 8 wickets)	229		

SRI LANKA		Runs	Balls	4/6
R.S.Mahanama	c Lara b Cummins	18	45	–
S.T.Jayasuriya	c Adams b Walsh	11	17	–
H.P.Tillekeratne	b Hooper	26	64	2
P.A.de Silva	c Hooper b Cummins	51	75	2
* A.Ranatunga	not out	66	78	3
R.S.Kalpage	lbw b Cummins	1	4	–
† R.S.Kaluwitharana	lbw b Cummins	2	3	–
R.P.A.H.Wickremaratne	b Ambrose	3	3	–
D.K.Liyanage	not out	11	11	1
S.D.Anurasiri				
G.P.Wickremasinghe				
Extras	(b 4, lb 9, w 18, nb 10)	41		
Total	(48.1 overs; 7 wickets)	230		

SRI LANKA	O	M	R	W
Wickremasinghe	8	0	40	0
Liyanage	8	0	36	1
Kalpage	10	0	45	4
Anurasiri	10	0	32	1
Ranatunga	2	0	16	0
Jayasuriya	10	0	41	1
De Silva	1	0	10	0

WEST INDIES	O	M	R	W
Ambrose	9	0	49	1
Walsh	8.1	0	31	1
Cummins	10	0	33	4
Benjamin	10	0	50	0
Hooper	7	0	33	1
Arthurton	4	0	21	0

FALL OF WICKETS
1-128, 2-136, 3-155, 4-184, 5-194, 6-195, 7-195, 8-223

FALL OF WICKETS
1-26, 2-40, 3-120, 4-180, 5-187, 6-189, 7-208

Umpires: B.C.Cooray (14) and K.T.Francis (18).

Referee: Zaheer Abbas (*Pakistan*).

SRI LANKA v WEST INDIES 1993-94

At Sinhalese Sports Club, Colombo on 18 December 1993.   Result: **WEST INDIES** won by 6 wickets.
Toss: West Indies.   Award: K.L.T.Arthurton.   Series Award: B.C.Lara.   LOI debuts: None.

Reduced to 25 overs apiece after overnight rain had delayed the start, this encounter was further truncated by West Indies' slow over rate. The touring team scored 38 off the last 25 balls to square the series.

SRI LANKA		Runs	Balls	4/6
R.S.Mahanama	c Richardson b Walsh	10	21	1
S.T.Jayasuriya	c Arthurton b Walsh	1	3	–
H.P.Tillekeratne	b Walsh	6	17	1
P.A.de Silva	c Ambrose b Simmons	34	49	1
* A.Ranatunga	c Adams b Simmons	7	14	–
R.S.Kalpage	not out	26	28	2
† R.S.Kaluwitharana	not out	6	8	–
D.P.Samaraweera				
D.K.Liyanage				
S.D.Anurasiri				
G.P.Wickremasinghe				
Extras	(b 1, lb 6, w 5, nb 1)	13		
Total	(23 overs; 5 wickets)	**103**		

WEST INDIES		Runs	Balls	4/6
D.L.Haynes	c Jayasuriya b Anurasiri	23	30	2
B.C.Lara	b Jayasuriya	29	54	1
* R.B.Richardson	c Samaraweera b Jayasuriya	2	8	–
C.L.Hooper	run out	4	11	–
P.V.Simmons	not out	15	14	1
K.L.T.Arthurton	not out	24	17	1/1
† J.C.Adams				
A.C.Cummins				
W.K.M.Benjamin				
C.E.L.Ambrose				
C.A.Walsh				
Extras	(lb 5, w 4, nb 1)	10		
Total	(22.1 overs; 4 wickets)	**107**		

WEST INDIES	O	M	R	W
Ambrose	5	2	12	0
Walsh	5	0	24	3
Benjamin	4	0	21	0
Cummins	4	0	15	0
Simmons	5	0	24	2

SRI LANKA	O	M	R	W
Wickremasinghe	4.1	0	20	0
Liyanage	3	1	16	0
Anurasiri	5	0	17	1
Kalpage	5	0	21	0
Jayasuriya	5	0	28	2

FALL OF WICKETS
1-2, 2-14, 3-25, 4-49, 5-82

FALL OF WICKETS
1-42, 2-58, 3-65, 4-67

Umpires: D.N.Pathirana (3) and T.M.Samarasinghe (5).

Referee: Zaheer Abbas (*Pakistan*).

AUSTRALIA v SOUTH AFRICA 1993-94

At Melbourne Cricket Ground on 9 December 1993.   Result: **SOUTH AFRICA** won by 7 wickets.   Toss: Australia.
Award: W.J.Cronje.   LOI debuts: Australia – G.D.McGrath, M.J.Slater.

The first LOI pairing of two former Wagga Wagga schoolboys realised 105 runs from 20 overs, Michael Slater scoring a 45-ball fifty on his debut. Glenn McGrath repeated the start to his Test match career by being out first ball. Kepler Wessels's two-nation runs tally reached 3000.

AUSTRALIA		Runs	Balls	4/6
M.A.Taylor	b Cronje	30	58	1
M.J.Slater	c and b Symcox	73	69	8/1
D.C.Boon	run out	1	1	–
M.E.Waugh	c Symcox b Cronje	8	18	–
S.R.Waugh	run out	33	54	1
* A.R.Border	b Snell	11	21	–
† I.A.Healy	not out	21	37	–
S.K.Warne	run out	3	12	–
P.R.Reiffel	lbw b De Villiers	0	1	–
C.J.McDermott	c Richardson b De Villiers	5	7	–
G.D.McGrath	b De Villiers	0	1	–
Extras	(lb 2, w 2)	4		
Total	(45.5 overs)	**189**		

SOUTH AFRICA		Runs	Balls	4/6
A.C.Hudson	c Taylor b McDermott	4	12	–
* K.C.Wessels	b McDermott	70	118	4
W.J.Cronje	not out	91	147	5
D.J.Cullinan	b Warne	0	4	–
J.N.Rhodes	not out	20	16	1
D.J.Callaghan				
† D.J.Richardson				
R.P.Snell				
P.L.Symcox				
A.A.Donald				
P.S.de Villiers				
Extras	(lb 2, w 1, nb 2)	5		
Total	(48.4 overs; 3 wickets)	**190**		

SOUTH AFRICA	O	M	R	W
Donald	10	1	32	0
De Villiers	7.5	0	30	3
Snell	8	0	43	1
Cronje	10	0	42	2
Symcox	10	0	40	1

AUSTRALIA	O	M	R	W
McDermott	10	1	31	2
McGrath	8.4	1	28	0
Reiffel	4	0	19	0
S.R.Waugh	10	0	37	0
Border	3	0	15	0
Warne	10	0	43	1
M.E.Waugh	3	0	15	0

FALL OF WICKETS
1-105, 2-106, 3-106, 4-119, 5-151, 6-166, 7-180, 8-181, 9-189, 10-189

FALL OF WICKETS
1-4, 2-144, 3-149

Umpires: T.A.Prue (20) and W.P.Sheahan (1).

AUSTRALIA v NEW ZEALAND 1993-94

At Adelaide Oval on 12 December 1993.　Result: **AUSTRALIA** won by 8 wickets.　Toss: New Zealand.
Award: S.K.Warne.　LOI debuts: None.

Rain had forced the second match of this tournament, between South Africa and New Zealand at Adelaide the previous day, to be abandoned without a ball bowled. Shane Warne took the first of his four-wicket hauls as New Zealand's last seven wickets fell for 31 runs.

NEW ZEALAND		Runs	Balls	4/6
B.A.Young	b Reiffel	18	54	1
R.T.Latham	c M.E.Waugh b McGrath	1	21	–
* K.R.Rutherford	c Reiffel b McGrath	15	15	3
M.J.Greatbatch	lbw b Warne	28	60	1
C.L.Cairns	c Border b Warne	31	70	–
C.Z.Harris	c and b Warne	4	13	–
† T.E.Blain	not out	9	28	–
D.N.Patel	c Healy b McDermott	1	6	–
G.R.Larsen	c Reiffel b Warne	8	17	–
C.Pringle	c Border b McGrath	4	3	–
D.K.Morrison	c Healy b McGrath	3	8	–
Extras	(lb 8, w 3, nb 2)	13		
Total	(48.2 overs)	**135**		

AUSTRALIA		Runs	Balls	4/6
M.J.Slater	lbw b Pringle	8	23	1
M.L.Hayden	not out	50	99	4
M.E.Waugh	run out	21	23	2
D.C.Boon	not out	51	90	2
* A.R.Border				
S.R.Waugh				
† I.A.Healy				
P.R.Reiffel				
S.K.Warne				
C.J.McDermott				
G.D.McGrath				
Extras	(lb 4, w 1, nb 1)	6		
Total	(38.5 overs; 2 wickets)	**136**		

AUSTRALIA	O	M	R	W
McDermott	10	2	15	1
McGrath	8.2	2	32	4
Reiffel	8	2	20	1
S.R.Waugh	7	0	16	0
M.E.Waugh	5	0	19	0
Warne	10	1	25	4

NEW ZEALAND	O	M	R	W
Morrison	8	2	31	0
Pringle	8	3	18	1
Cairns	9.5	0	27	0
Larsen	9	0	37	0
Patel	4	0	19	0

FALL OF WICKETS
1-6, 2-33, 3-79, 4-104, 5-109, 6-112, 7-113, 8-124, 9-132, 10-135

FALL OF WICKETS
1-16, 2-42

Umpires: A.J.McQuillan (1) and W.P.Sheahan (2).

AUSTRALIA v SOUTH AFRICA 1993-94

At Sydney Cricket Ground on 14 December 1993.　Result: **AUSTRALIA** won by 103 runs.　Toss: South Africa.
Award: P.R.Reiffel.　LOI debuts: South Africa – G.Kirsten.

On a pitch rated as 'disgraceful' by their captain, Australia gained their first victory against South Africa, dismissing them for their only double-figure total. Paul Reiffel shared in a key stand of 68, returned his best LOI bowling figures, held two catches and effected the only run out. 'Jonty' Rhodes fractured his left hand fielding.

AUSTRALIA		Runs	Balls	4/6
M.A.Taylor	run out	11	32	–
M.J.Slater	c Rhodes b De Villiers	10	27	1
M.E.Waugh	c Kirsten b Matthews	36	75	2
D.C.Boon	c Richardson b Matthews	4	14	–
S.R.Waugh	c Richardson b Cronje	13	31	–
* A.R.Border	c De Villiers b Matthews	8	34	1
† I.A.Healy	c Cronje b Donald	38	60	2
P.R.Reiffel	not out	29	41	3
S.K.Warne	c Cullinan b De Villiers	0	1	–
C.J.McDermott	c Cronje b De Villiers	3	3	–
G.D.McGrath				
Extras	(b 1, lb 4, w 7, nb 8)	20		
Total	(50 overs; 9 wickets)	**172**		

SOUTH AFRICA		Runs	Balls	4/6
A.C.Hudson	c Reiffel b McDermott	0	4	–
G.Kirsten	c Healy b McGrath	4	27	–
* K.C.Wessels	lbw b Reiffel	19	43	3
W.J.Cronje	c Healy b Reiffel	20	47	2
D.J.Cullinan	c S.R.Waugh b McGrath	1	10	–
† D.J.Richardson	c Healy b Reiffel	1	4	–
R.P.Snell	b Reiffel	0	3	–
C.R.Matthews	c Reiffel b S.R.Waugh	7	14	–
J.N.Rhodes	not out	4	19	–
P.S.de Villiers	run out	0	6	–
A.A.Donald	b S.R.Waugh	0	1	–
Extras	(lb 3, w 8, nb 2)	13		
Total	(28 overs)	**69**		

SOUTH AFRICA	O	M	R	W
Donald	10	1	49	1
De Villiers	10	0	37	3
Matthews	10	0	23	3
Snell	10	0	44	0
Cronje	10	4	14	1

AUSTRALIA	O	M	R	W
McDermott	6	2	8	1
McGrath	8	0	25	2
Reiffel	8	4	13	4
S.R.Waugh	6	0	20	2

FALL OF WICKETS
1-28, 2-30, 3-44, 4-76, 5-95, 6-96, 7-164, 8-164, 9-172

FALL OF WICKETS
1-0, 2-23, 3-34, 4-38, 5-47, 6-48, 7-59, 8-65, 9-69, 10-69

Umpires: D.B.Hair (8) and P.D.Parker (1).

433

AUSTRALIA v NEW ZEALAND 1993-94

At Melbourne Cricket Ground on 16 December 1993.   Result: **AUSTRALIA** won by 3 runs.   Toss: Australia.
Award: S.K.Warne.   LOI debuts: New Zealand – R.P.de Groen.

This game provided the only cliffhanging finish of the tournament, Danny Morrison failing to hit Craig McDermott's final ball for six. Shane Warne achieved his second four-wicket analysis in successive innings. Steve Waugh (torn hamstring) retired at 188.

AUSTRALIA		Runs	Balls	4/6
M.L.Hayden	c Cairns b Pringle	5	18	–
M.A.Taylor	c Blain b Cairns	81	130	1
M.E.Waugh	c Rutherford b De Groen	53	80	1
D.C.Boon	c Morrison b De Groen	14	30	–
S.R.Waugh	retired hurt	25	28	3
* A.R.Border	run out	9	10	–
† I.A.Healy	not out	5	7	–
P.R.Reiffel				
S.K.Warne				
T.B.A.May				
C.J.McDermott				
Extras	(lb 7, w 3)	10		
Total	(50 overs; 5 wickets)	**202**		

NEW ZEALAND		Runs	Balls	4/6
B.A.Young	lbw b McDermott	0	3	–
R.T.Latham	st Healy b Warne	39	94	2
* K.R.Rutherford	b M.E.Waugh	39	67	5
M.J.Greatbatch	lbw b Warne	41	51	2/1
C.L.Cairns	c Healy b Warne	5	16	–
S.A.Thomson	c Border b McDermott	42	41	4
† T.E.Blain	c Border b Warne	1	6	–
G.R.Larsen	b M.E.Waugh	17	16	1
C.Pringle	run out	4	4	–
D.K.Morrison	not out	2	1	–
R.P.de Groen	not out	2	2	–
Extras	(b 1, lb 5, w 1)	7		
Total	(50 overs; 9 wickets)	**199**		

NEW ZEALAND	O	M	R	W
Pringle	9	1	26	1
Morrison	7	2	17	0
Cairns	7	0	33	1
Larsen	10	0	57	0
De Groen	10	0	40	2
Thomson	7	0	22	0

AUSTRALIA	O	M	R	W
McDermott	9	1	40	2
Reiffel	10	1	44	0
M.E.Waugh	9	0	42	2
May	10	0	35	0
Warne	10	1	19	4
Border	2	0	13	0

FALL OF WICKETS
1-8, 2-97, 3-131, 4-183, 5-202

FALL OF WICKETS
1-0, 2-66, 3-99, 4-109, 5-146, 6-154, 7-187, 8-193, 9-194

Umpires: L.J.King (23) and A.J.McQuillan (2).

SOUTH AFRICA v NEW ZEALAND 1993-94

At Bellerive Oval, Hobart on 18 December 1993.   Result: **NEW ZEALAND** won by 4 wickets.   Toss: South Africa.
Award: G.R.Larsen.   LOI debuts: None.

Gavin Larsen returned his country's fourth most economical analysis as New Zealand gained their first win of the tournament.

SOUTH AFRICA		Runs	Balls	4/6
A.C.Hudson	c Blain b Pringle	8	21	1
G.Kirsten	c Young b Pringle	7	23	–
* K.C.Wessels	c Blain b Larsen	15	43	–
W.J.Cronje	c Morrison b Larsen	18	35	–
D.J.Cullinan	c Blain b Thomson	8	28	–
D.J.Callaghan	b Pringle	25	60	2
† D.J.Richardson	not out	38	65	1
P.L.Symcox	c Blain b Cairns	8	18	1
R.P.Snell	not out	13	10	1
C.R.Matthews				
P.S.de Villiers				
Extras	(lb 4, w 3)	7		
Total	(50 overs; 7 wickets)	**147**		

NEW ZEALAND		Runs	Balls	4/6
B.A.Young	lbw b Matthews	74	115	7
R.T.Latham	c Wessels b Matthews	7	20	–
* K.R.Rutherford	run out	9	31	1
M.J.Greatbatch	run out	8	15	1
C.L.Cairns	not out	30	53	1
S.A.Thomson	b Matthews	9	18	1
† T.E.Blain	c Richardson b Matthews	5	11	–
G.R.Larsen	not out	4	4	–
D.N.Patel				
C.Pringle				
D.K.Morrison				
Extras	(w 1, nb 1)	2		
Total	(44.1 overs; 6 wickets)	**148**		

NEW ZEALAND	O	M	R	W
Pringle	10	1	28	3
Morrison	8	1	32	0
Larsen	10	5	12	2
Cairns	7	0	27	1
Patel	10	2	25	0
Thomson	5	0	19	1

SOUTH AFRICA	O	M	R	W
De Villiers	9.1	1	23	0
Matthews	10	1	38	4
Snell	10	2	29	0
Cronje	5	0	33	0
Symcox	10	0	25	0

FALL OF WICKETS
1-15, 2-22, 3-50, 4-53, 5-66, 6-101, 7-119

FALL OF WICKETS
1-22, 2-54, 3-66, 4-112, 5-132, 6-142

Umpires: S.J.Davis (3) and S.G.Randell (56).

SOUTH AFRICA v NEW ZEALAND 1993-94

At Woolloongabba, Brisbane on 8 January 1994.　　Result: **NEW ZEALAND** won by 9 runs (revised target).
Toss: South Africa.　　Award: P.N.Kirsten.　　LOI debuts: None.

A tropical downpour halted play for 66 minutes with South Africa 19 for 0 after 5 overs. The revised version of the 'fastest scoring overs' formula set a target of 229 from 39 overs. Peter Kirsten scored his last 78 runs with a runner after straining a thigh muscle.

NEW ZEALAND		Runs	Balls	4/6
B.A.Young	c Cullinan b McMillan	28	48	2
R.T.Latham	c McMillan b Donald	11	20	1
A.H.Jones	c Kirsten b Matthews	9	24	1
* K.R.Rutherford	b McMillan	1	3	–
M.J.Greatbatch	c Rhodes b Donald	21	35	–
S.A.Thomson	c Donald b Cronje	68	90	3/1
C.L.Cairns	run out	70	54	4/3
† T.E.Blain	not out	36	23	1/2
G.R.Larsen	not out	6	7	–
C.Pringle				
R.P.de Groen				
Extras	(lb 2, w 2, nb 2)	6		
Total	(50 overs; 7 wickets)	**256**		

SOUTH AFRICA		Runs	Balls	4/6
A.C.Hudson	c Thomson b Pringle	14	19	–
P.N.Kirsten	c Jones b Cairns	97	108	6/1
† E.L.R.Stewart	c and b Thomson	19	36	2
* W.J.Cronje	c Greatbatch b Thomson	19	23	1
D.J.Cullinan	c Greatbatch b De Groen	37	32	4
J.N.Rhodes	c Blain b Cairns	21	13	1
B.M.McMillan	b Pringle	0	1	–
P.L.Symcox	not out	4	3	–
C.R.Matthews	c Latham b Pringle	1	2	–
P.S.de Villiers	not out	0	1	–
A.A.Donald				
Extras	(lb 4, w 2, nb 1)	7		
Total	(39 overs; 8 wickets)	**219**		

SOUTH AFRICA	O	M	R	W
Donald	8	0	38	2
De Villiers	10	2	40	0
Matthews	10	2	52	1
McMillan	10	0	59	2
Symcox	7	1	26	0
Cronje	5	0	39	1

NEW ZEALAND	O	M	R	W
Pringle	8	1	38	3
Cairns	8	1	44	2
Larsen	8	0	42	0
De Groen	7	0	41	1
Thomson	6	0	38	2
Latham	2	0	12	0

FALL OF WICKETS
1-33, 2-47, 3-52, 4-55, 5-86, 6-197, 7-221

FALL OF WICKETS
1-24, 2-62, 3-96, 4-181, 5-207, 6-213, 7-215, 8-217

Umpires: I.S.Thomas (8) and C.D.Timmins (18).

AUSTRALIA v SOUTH AFRICA 1993-94

At Woolloongabba, Brisbane on 9 January 1994.　　Result: **AUSTRALIA** won by 48 runs.　　Toss: South Africa.
Award: D.M.Jones.　　LOI debuts: South Africa – D.B.Rundle.

Off-spinner Dave Rundle commemorated his debut with a four-wicket analysis which included three wickets in five balls. Ian Healy overtook Rod Marsh's Australian record of 124 dismissals.

AUSTRALIA		Runs	Balls	4/6
D.C.Boon	c Rundle b McMillan	45	61	5
M.A.Taylor	b De Villiers	12	22	1
D.M.Jones	b Rundle	98	124	3/1
M.E.Waugh	c Cullinan b Symcox	10	19	1
D.R.Martyn	c Cronje b Rundle	23	37	2
* A.R.Border	c Kirsten b Rundle	15	10	1
† I.A.Healy	c and b Rundle	0	1	–
P.R.Reiffel	run out	9	18	–
C.J.McDermott	run out	2	3	–
T.B.A.May	not out	5	11	–
G.D.McGrath				
Extras	(lb 4, w 6, nb 1)	11		
Total	(50 overs; 9 wickets)	**230**		

SOUTH AFRICA		Runs	Balls	4/6
* W.J.Cronje	c Healy b Reiffel	17	32	3
G.Kirsten	c Healy b Waugh	51	88	4
D.J.Cullinan	c Reiffel b Border	27	56	–
J.N.Rhodes	c Healy b May	46	63	–
D.J.Callaghan	run out	1	1	–
B.M.McMillan	c and b Border	6	9	–
† D.J.Richardson	lbw b McGrath	15	23	–
P.L.Symcox	lbw b McGrath	0	1	–
R.P.Snell	c Martyn b McGrath	9	8	–/1
D.B.Rundle	c Border b McGrath	0	1	–
P.S.de Villiers	not out	1	2	–
Extras	(lb 6, w 2, nb 1)	9		
Total	(46.5 overs)	**182**		

SOUTH AFRICA	O	M	R	W
De Villiers	10	0	28	1
Snell	8	0	36	0
McMillan	10	2	42	1
Cronje	5	0	31	0
Symcox	8	0	47	1
Rundle	9	0	42	4

AUSTRALIA	O	M	R	W
McDermott	5	1	14	0
McGrath	8.5	0	24	4
Reiffel	7	0	24	1
May	9	0	45	1
Waugh	7	0	29	1
Border	10	0	40	2

FALL OF WICKETS
1-20, 2-108, 3-127, 4-180, 5-205, 6-208, 7-211, 8-214, 9-230

FALL OF WICKETS
1-33, 2-88, 3-118, 4-119, 5-138, 6-168, 7-168, 8-178, 9-181, 10-182

Umpires: D.B.Hair (9) and A.J.McQuillan (3).

AUSTRALIA v NEW ZEALAND 1993-94

At Sydney Cricket Ground on 11 January 1994.   Result: **NEW ZEALAND** won by 13 runs.   Toss: New Zealand.
Award: C.Pringle.   LOI debuts: None.

Ian Healy completed his last 26 runs with a runner after being struck on the ankle by a return. New Zealand's place in the finals was assured ... provided they did not lose their last two games and South Africa did not win theirs by substantial margins.

NEW ZEALAND		Runs	Balls	4/6
B.A.Young	b Waugh	19	39	3
R.T.Latham	c Taylor b Reiffel	0	3	–
A.H.Jones	lbw b McGrath	6	20	–
* K.R.Rutherford	c Healy b Border	65	90	1
M.J.Greatbatch	lbw b Warne	50	58	2
S.A.Thomson	st Healy b Warne	1	9	–
C.L.Cairns	c Healy b McGrath	16	24	–/1
† T.E.Blain	c and b Border	0	4	–
G.R.Larsen	not out	29	34	2/1
C.Pringle	b McGrath	1	7	–
R.P.de Groen	not out	7	13	–
Extras	(b 3, lb 1)	4		
Total	(50 overs; 9 wickets)	**198**		

AUSTRALIA		Runs	Balls	4/6
M.A.Taylor	run out	1	2	–
D.C.Boon	b Pringle	67	121	4
D.M.Jones	c Pringle b De Groen	21	41	3
M.E.Waugh	b Pringle	15	34	1
D.R.Martyn	run out	7	18	–
* A.R.Border	b Thomson	1	2	–
† I.A.Healy	c Blain b De Groen	48	48	2
P.R.Reiffel	lbw b Pringle	3	5	–
S.K.Warne	b Cairns	9	13	1
T.B.A.May	not out	4	6	–
G.D.McGrath	b Pringle	4	6	–
Extras	(w 4, nb 1)	5		
Total	(48.3 overs)	**185**		

AUSTRALIA	O	M	R	W
McGrath	10	3	29	3
Reiffel	9	0	33	1
Waugh	7	0	38	1
May	10	1	43	0
Warne	10	1	27	2
Border	4	0	24	2

NEW ZEALAND	O	M	R	W
De Groen	10	0	34	2
Pringle	9.3	0	40	4
Cairns	9	2	18	1
Larsen	9	0	43	0
Thomson	9	0	40	1
Latham	2	0	10	0

FALL OF WICKETS
1-4, 2-13, 3-40, 4-129, 5-131, 6-152, 7-152, 8-164, 9-168

FALL OF WICKETS
1-1, 2-38, 3-76, 4-86, 5-87, 6-164, 7-166, 8-171, 9-180, 10-185

Umpires: S.J.Davis (4) and S.G.Randell (57).

SOUTH AFRICA v NEW ZEALAND 1993-94

At WACA Ground, Perth on 14 January 1994.   Result: **SOUTH AFRICA** won by 5 wickets.   Toss: New Zealand.
Award: A.A.Donald.   LOI debuts: None.

A wide completed South Africa's first victory against New Zealand. Achieved with 19½ overs in hand, it significantly improved their 'net' run rate.

NEW ZEALAND		Runs	Balls	4/6
B.A.Young	c Richardson b De Villiers	2	10	–
A.H.Jones	lbw b Donald	0	3	–
* K.R.Rutherford	b McMillan	25	48	3
M.J.Greatbatch	c Richardson b Matthews	16	32	–/1
S.A.Thomson	c Richardson b McMillan	0	7	–
C.L.Cairns	c Richardson b Callaghan	29	29	5
C.Z.Harris	not out	29	68	1
† T.E.Blain	run out	32	48	2
G.R.Larsen	c Matthews b McMillan	2	14	–
C.Pringle	b Donald	1	4	–
R.P.de Groen	c Cullinan b Donald	0	7	–
Extras	(lb 7, w 6, nb 1)	14		
Total	(44.2 overs)	**150**		

SOUTH AFRICA		Runs	Balls	4/6
P.N.Kirsten	run out	50	85	2
G.Kirsten	c Blain b Pringle	31	54	4
* W.J.Cronje	c sub (R.T.Latham) b Thomson	40	35	6
J.N.Rhodes	c De Groen b Pringle	3	6	–
D.J.Cullinan	not out	5	7	–
D.J.Callaghan	c Rutherford b Pringle	2	4	–
B.M.McMillan	not out	1	1	–
† D.J.Richardson				
C.R.Matthews				
A.A.Donald				
P.S.de Villiers				
Extras	(lb 10, w 8, nb 1)	19		
Total	(30.3 overs; 5 wickets)	**151**		

SOUTH AFRICA	O	M	R	W
Donald	8.2	3	15	3
De Villiers	8	0	15	1
Matthews	10	1	46	1
McMillan	10	2	39	3
Callaghan	5	1	15	1
Cronje	3	0	13	0

NEW ZEALAND	O	M	R	W
Pringle	8.3	0	24	3
De Groen	5	0	30	0
Cairns	7	0	32	0
Larsen	8	0	36	0
Thomson	2	0	19	1

FALL OF WICKETS
1-1, 2-3, 3-45, 4-46, 5-58, 6-84, 7-133, 8-145, 9-148, 10-150

FALL OF WICKETS
1-80, 2-117, 3-139, 4-141, 5-148

Umpires: R.J.Evans (17) and D.J.Harper (1).

AUSTRALIA v SOUTH AFRICA 1993-94

At WACA Ground, Perth on 16 January 1994.   Result: **SOUTH AFRICA** won by 82 runs.   Toss: Australia.
Award: D.J.Callaghan.   LOI debuts: Australia – D.W.Fleming.

South African coach Mike Procter lost his hotel key testing gaping cracks in the pitch. Peter Kirsten sustained multiple fractures of the cheekbone after ducking into a ball from Glenn McGrath with the total 6. His substitute held three catches at slip. Tim Zoehrer represented Australia for the first time since April 1987.

SOUTH AFRICA		Runs	Balls	4/6
P.N.Kirsten	retired hurt	5	11	1
G.Kirsten	c Zoehrer b M.E.Waugh	55	102	5
* W.J.Cronje	c Warne b Reiffel	11	28	1
J.N.Rhodes	run out	14	28	2
D.J.Cullinan	c Warne b M.E.Waugh	34	42	3
D.J.Callaghan	lbw b Warne	26	43	2
† D.J.Richardson	run out	25	35	1
R.P.Snell	not out	20	14	2
C.R.Matthews	st Zoehrer b Warne	0	2	–
P.S.de Villiers	not out	0	1	–
A.A.Donald				
Extras	(b 1, lb 8, w 9)	18		
Total	(50 overs; 7 wickets)	**208**		

AUSTRALIA		Runs	Balls	4/6
D.C.Boon	c sub (B.M.McMillan) b Snell	11	30	1
* M.A.Taylor	c Richardson b Snell	29	56	3
D.M.Jones	c sub (B.M.McMillan) b Matthews	10	22	1
M.E.Waugh	c sub (B.M.McMillan) b Callaghan	14	26	–
S.R.Waugh	c Richardson b Callaghan	25	39	3
D.R.Martyn	c Richardson b Cronje	0	7	–
† T.J.Zoehrer	lbw b De Villiers	9	18	1
P.R.Reiffel	not out	10	27	–
S.K.Warne	run out	1	3	–
D.W.Fleming	lbw b Matthews	2	12	–
G.D.McGrath	b Snell	4	8	1
Extras	(lb 9, w 1, nb 1)	11		
Total	(41 overs)	**126**		

AUSTRALIA	O	M	R	W
McGrath	10	1	38	0
Reiffel	10	2	25	1
Fleming	7	0	42	0
S.R.Waugh	6	0	32	0
Warne	10	0	36	2
M.E.Waugh	7	0	26	2

SOUTH AFRICA	O	M	R	W
Donald	8	0	20	0
De Villiers	8	2	19	1
Snell	7	0	26	3
Matthews	7	1	20	2
Cronje	6	1	17	1
Callaghan	5	1	15	2

FALL OF WICKETS
1-27, 2-69, 3-133, 4-133, 5-176, 6-196, 7-196

FALL OF WICKETS
1-22, 2-49, 3-57, 4-92, 5-93, 6-93, 7-109, 8-110, 9-121, 10-126

Umpires: T.A.Prue (21) and W.P.Sheahan (3).

AUSTRALIA v NEW ZEALAND 1993-94

At Melbourne Cricket Ground on 19 January 1994.   Result: **AUSTRALIA** won by 51 runs.   Toss: Australia.
Award: D.M.Jones.   LOI debuts: None.

A record Australian crowd for a match against New Zealand (61,788) saw the Kiwis eliminated on 'net' run rate (batting run rate minus opponents' batting run rate). Final points: Australia 10, South Africa 7 (-0.059), New Zealand 7 (-0.409).

AUSTRALIA		Runs	Balls	4/6
M.L.Hayden	c Blain b Watson	13	17	2
D.C.Boon	c Rutherford b Cairns	65	109	1
D.M.Jones	c Cairns b Pringle	82	120	3
M.E.Waugh	not out	45	53	1
S.R.Waugh	not out	0	1	–
* A.R.Border				
† I.A.Healy				
P.R.Reiffel				
S.K.Warne				
D.W.Fleming				
G.D.McGrath				
Extras	(lb 12)	12		
Total	(50 overs; 3 wickets)	**217**		

NEW ZEALAND		Runs	Balls	4/6
B.A.Young	b Warne	43	98	2
R.T.Latham	c Warne b Reiffel	10	37	1
A.H.Jones	lbw b Fleming	9	26	–
* K.R.Rutherford	run out	0	1	–
M.J.Greatbatch	c Reiffel b Warne	13	25	2
S.A.Thomson	lbw b McGrath	12	27	–
C.L.Cairns	lbw b Fleming	39	41	2
† T.E.Blain	c Hayden b Warne	4	10	–
G.R.Larsen	not out	17	18	–
C.Pringle	b Reiffel	6	11	–
W.Watson	c Healy b Reiffel	0	1	–
Extras	(lb 4, w 8, nb 1)	13		
Total	(47.5 overs)	**166**		

NEW ZEALAND	O	M	R	W
Pringle	10	0	45	1
Watson	10	2	33	1
Cairns	10	0	53	1
Larsen	10	1	23	0
Thomson	4	0	27	0
Latham	6	0	24	0

AUSTRALIA	O	M	R	W
McGrath	9	1	48	1
Reiffel	9.5	2	35	3
Fleming	9	2	15	2
S.R.Waugh	10	0	36	0
Warne	10	1	28	3

FALL OF WICKETS
1-15, 2-136, 3-214

FALL OF WICKETS
1-37, 2-60, 3-64, 4-80, 5-82, 6-107, 7-124, 8-147, 9-166, 10-166

Umpires: P.D.Parker (2) and S.G.Randell (58).

437

AUSTRALIA v SOUTH AFRICA 1993-94

At Melbourne Cricket Ground on 21 January 1994.   Result: **SOUTH AFRICA** won by 28 runs.   Toss: South Africa.
LOI debuts: None.

Gary Kirsten's maiden international hundred was the first of this tournament and only the second for South Africa in LOIs. Richard Snell's yorker featured prominently in his only five-wicket return in Tests or internationals.

SOUTH AFRICA		Runs	Balls	4/6
P.N.Kirsten	c Healy b S.R.Waugh	28	51	4
G.Kirsten	not out	112	137	8
* W.J.Cronje	c Jones b Warne	40	65	2
J.N.Rhodes	c Healy b McGrath	31	37	1
D.J.Cullinan	c Hayden b McDermott	7	8	–
R.P.Snell	c Jones b McGrath	3	3	–
D.J.Callaghan	not out	3	3	–
B.M.McMillan				
† D.J.Richardson				
A.A.Donald				
P.S.de Villiers				
Extras	(lb 2, w 3, nb 1)	6		
Total	(50 overs; 5 wickets)	230		

AUSTRALIA		Runs	Balls	4/6
D.C.Boon	run out	45	78	3
M.L.Hayden	b Snell	20	46	1
D.M.Jones	c Cronje b McMillan	3	7	–
M.E.Waugh	c Richardson b Donald	36	51	–
S.R.Waugh	c P.N.Kirsten b Snell	27	36	1
* A.R.Border	b Snell	42	44	1
† I.A.Healy	c P.N.Kirsten b De Villiers	0	2	–
P.R.Reiffel	b Snell	18	22	–
S.K.Warne	c McMillan b De Villiers	1	5	–
C.J.McDermott	b Snell	1	2	–
G.D.McGrath	not out	5	3	–
Extras	(lb 1, w 3)	4		
Total	(48.5 overs)	202		

AUSTRALIA	O	M	R	W
McDermott	10	1	40	1
McGrath	9	0	52	2
Reiffel	7	2	23	0
S.R.Waugh	7	0	27	1
Warne	10	1	45	1
Border	4	0	26	0
M.E.Waugh	3	0	15	0

SOUTH AFRICA	O	M	R	W
Donald	10	0	48	1
De Villiers	9	1	26	2
Snell	9.5	0	40	5
McMillan	10	2	38	1
Callaghan	5	0	27	0
Cronje	5	0	22	0

FALL OF WICKETS
1-53, 2-143, 3-196, 4-217, 5-223

FALL OF WICKETS
1-41, 2-53, 3-84, 4-128, 5-150, 6-150, 7-192, 8-195, 9-197, 10-202

Umpires: T.A.Prue (22) and W.P.Sheahan (4).

AUSTRALIA v SOUTH AFRICA 1993-94

At Sydney Cricket Ground on 23 January 1994.   Result: **AUSTRALIA** won by 69 runs.   Toss: Australia.
LOI debuts: None.

Mark Waugh's 104-ball hundred was his first in Australia, while his partnership of 175 with Dean Jones is a national record for any wicket against South Africa. Ian Healy, appearing in his 100th international, stumped 'Hansie' Cronje by two yards as Shane Warne took 3 for 4 in 15 balls.

AUSTRALIA		Runs	Balls	4/6
M.L.Hayden	c Snell b Donald	16	25	2
D.C.Boon	c Rhodes b Donald	14	36	–
D.M.Jones	c Cronje b Donald	79	113	5
M.E.Waugh	c G.Kirsten b De Villiers	107	111	8
S.R.Waugh	b Donald	1	2	–
* A.R.Border	c Richardson b De Villiers	6	8	–
† I.A.Healy	not out	10	6	1
P.R.Reiffel	not out	5	3	–
S.K.Warne				
C.J.McDermott				
T.B.A.May				
Extras	(lb 5, w 3, nb 1)	9		
Total	(50 overs; 6 wickets)	247		

SOUTH AFRICA		Runs	Balls	4/6
P.N.Kirsten	run out	11	37	–
G.Kirsten	c Boon b May	42	51	3
* W.J.Cronje	st Healy b Warne	28	61	1
J.N.Rhodes	b McDermott	52	59	2/1
D.J.Cullinan	c S.R.Waugh b Warne	3	13	–
B.M.McMillan	lbw b Warne	0	8	–
† D.J.Richardson	b Border	16	34	–
R.P.Snell	b McDermott	6	5	1
P.L.Symcox	run out	12	6	2
P.S.de Villiers	not out	0	–	–
A.A.Donald	c and b McDermott	0	2	–
Extras	(lb 7, nb 1)	8		
Total	(45.5 overs)	178		

SOUTH AFRICA	O	M	R	W
Donald	10	0	40	4
De Villiers	10	2	39	2
Snell	10	0	59	0
McMillan	7	0	40	0
Symcox	6	0	26	0
Cronje	7	0	38	0

AUSTRALIA	O	M	R	W
McDermott	8.5	0	39	3
Reiffel	8	0	23	0
S.R.Waugh	5	0	11	0
May	10	1	35	0
Warne	10	0	42	3
Border	4	0	21	1

FALL OF WICKETS
1-33, 2-35, 3-210, 4-221, 5-227, 6-241

FALL OF WICKETS
1-50, 2-74, 3-102, 4-106, 5-107, 6-156, 7-160, 8-174, 9-176, 10-178

Umpires: D.B.Hair (10) and S.G.Randell (59).

AUSTRALIA v SOUTH AFRICA 1993-94

At Sydney Cricket Ground on 25 January 1994.　Result: **AUSTRALIA** won by 35 runs.　Toss: Australia.
Finals Award: M.E.Waugh.　LOI debuts: None.

Australia marked Allan Border's final international appearance on home soil by winning this tournament for the fourth time in five seasons. It was his 100th World Series match as captain, his final record being 64 wins, 34 defeats and two no results.

AUSTRALIA		Runs	Balls	4/6	SOUTH AFRICA		Runs	Balls	4/6
D.C.Boon	c Rhodes b De Villiers	64	98	5	P.N.Kirsten	run out	14	13	–
M.L.Hayden	st Richardson b Rundle	20	70	1	G.Kirsten	c M.E.Waugh b Reiffel	10	27	–
D.M.Jones	c Rundle b Donald	25	29	–	* W.J.Cronje	run out	0	13	–
M.E.Waugh	run out	60	53	7	J.N.Rhodes	c Healy b Warne	43	68	1
S.R.Waugh	b Cronje	17	22	2	E.L.R.Stewart	b Warne	13	31	1
* A.R.Border	b De Villiers	30	26	1	D.J.Callaghan	c Healy b McDermott	30	47	1
† I.A.Healy	run out	0	–	–	† D.J.Richardson	not out	38	61	–
P.R.Reiffel	run out	2	2	–	R.P.Snell	run out	6	7	–
S.K.Warne	not out	1	2	–	D.B.Rundle	lbw b May	6	10	1
T.B.A.May					P.S.de Villiers	b S.R.Waugh	15	18	1
C.J.McDermott					A.A.Donald	not out	7	9	–
Extras	(lb 3, w 1)	4			Extras	(b 1, lb 2, w 3)	6		
Total	(50 overs; 8 wickets)	223			Total	(50 overs; 9 wickets)	188		

SOUTH AFRICA	O	M	R	W	AUSTRALIA	O	M	R	W
Donald	10	1	40	1	McDermott	10	1	41	1
De Villiers	10	2	41	2	Warne	10	0	36	2
Snell	10	1	34	0	Reiffel	9	0	32	1
Cronje	10	0	35	1	S.R.Waugh	10	2	39	1
Rundle	7	0	53	1	May	10	0	31	1
Callaghan	3	0	17	0	Border	1	0	6	0

FALL OF WICKETS
1-62, 2-112, 3-114, 4-150, 5-218, 6-220, 7-221, 8-223

FALL OF WICKETS
1-21, 2-23, 3-26, 4-51, 5-110, 6-117, 7-124, 8-136, 9-166

Umpires: D.B.Hair (11) and S.G.Randell (60).

PAKISTAN v ZIMBABWE 1993-94

At National Stadium, Karachi on 24 December 1993.　Result: **PAKISTAN** won by 7 wickets.　Toss: Pakistan.
Award: Wasim Akram.　LOI debuts: None.

Wasim Akram's best LOI analysis included the wicket of Andy Flower to the first ball of the match and it extended his world record tally of five-wicket analyses to 14.

ZIMBABWE		Runs	Balls	4/6	PAKISTAN		Runs	Balls	4/6
*† A.Flower	c Rashid b Wasim	0	1	–	Saeed Anwar	b Streak	68	84	7
G.W.Flower	b Aqib	6	24	1	Asif Mujtaba	b Brain	11	15	2
A.D.R.Campbell	b Wasim	8	18	2	Inzamam-ul-Haq	b Streak	12	28	1
D.L.Houghton	c Basit b Salim	52	75	3	Basit Ali	not out	41	65	3
M.H.Dekker	run out	33	47	2	† Rashid Latif	not out	10	11	–/1
G.J.Whittall	run out	18	37	–	Javed Miandad				
D.H.Brain	b Aqib	4	11	–	Salim Malik				
E.A.Brandes	lbw b Wasim	2	7	–	* Wasim Akram				
S.G.Peall	b Wasim	0	1	–	Waqar Younis				
H.H.Streak	c Miandad b Wasim	2	7	–	Mushtaq Ahmed				
J.A.Rennie	not out	3	4	–	Aqib Javed				
Extras	(b 1, lb 9, w 3, nb 2)	15			Extras	(lb 2, w 2, nb 1)	5		
Total	(38 overs)	143			Total	(33.5 overs; 3 wickets)	147		

PAKISTAN	O	M	R	W	ZIMBABWE	O	M	R	W
Wasim Akram	7	1	15	5	Brandes	5	0	31	0
Aqib Javed	8	1	21	2	Brain	7	0	30	1
Waqar Younis	7	0	43	0	Peall	7	1	30	0
Mushtaq Ahmed	8	1	21	0	Streak	8	2	15	2
Salim Malik	5	0	19	1	Rennie	6	0	32	0
Asif Mujtaba	3	0	14	0	Dekker	0.5	0	7	0

FALL OF WICKETS
1-0, 2-19, 3-22, 4-92, 5-117, 6-128, 7-131, 8-131, 9-139, 10-143

FALL OF WICKETS
1-18, 2-48, 3-126

Umpires: Amanullah Khan (13) and Feroz Butt (3).

Referee: R.S.Madugalle (*Sri Lanka*).

PAKISTAN v ZIMBABWE 1993-94

At Rawalpindi Cricket Stadium on 25 December 1993.   Result: **PAKISTAN** won by 6 wickets.   Toss: Pakistan.
Award: Asif Mujtaba.   LOI debuts: None.

Pakistan won the series with their second victory in two days. David Houghton scored 57 off 49 balls and became the first to score 1000 LOI runs for Zimbabwe.

ZIMBABWE		Runs	Balls	4/6
* A.Flower	lbw b Wasim	14	22	2
M.H.Dekker	b Aamir	23	63	–
A.D.R.Campbell	b Wasim	74	106	5
D.L.Houghton	c Basit b Waqar	57	49	7
D.H.Brain	c Asif b Waqar	0	1	–
G.J.Whittall	not out	3	3	–
G.W.Flower				
E.A.Brandes				
† W.R.James				
H.H.Streak				
J.A.Rennie				
Extras	(lb 12, w 9, nb 3)	24		
Total	(40 overs; 5 wickets)	195		

PAKISTAN		Runs	Balls	4/6
Saeed Anwar	b Dekker	45	66	4/1
Asif Mujtaba	c Whittall b Streak	61	102	2
Basit Ali	b Dekker	5	6	–
Javed Miandad	c Rennie b Brandes	19	13	3
Inzamam-ul-Haq	not out	44	45	3
* Wasim Akram	not out	6	4	–
Salim Malik				
† Rashid Latif				
Waqar Younis				
Aamir Nazir				
Aqib Javed				
Extras	(b 1, lb 7, w 8)	16		
Total	(39.4 overs; 4 wickets)	196		

PAKISTAN	O	M	R	W
Wasim Akram	8	0	32	2
Aamir Nazir	8	0	30	1
Aqib Javed	8	0	31	0
Waqar Younis	8	0	46	2
Salim Malik	7	0	37	0
Asif Mujtaba	1	0	7	0

ZIMBABWE	O	M	R	W
Brandes	8	1	40	1
Brain	7	1	30	0
Rennie	7.4	0	38	0
Streak	7	0	31	1
G.W.Flower	3	0	15	0
Dekker	4	0	16	2
Campbell	2	0	9	0
A.Flower	1	0	9	0

FALL OF WICKETS
1-30, 2-87, 3-189, 4-190, 5-195

Umpires: Khalid Aziz (7) and Siddiq Khan (1).

FALL OF WICKETS
1-88, 2-98, 3-121, 4-188

Referee: R.S.Madugalle (*Sri Lanka*).

PAKISTAN v ZIMBABWE 1993-94

At Gaddafi Stadium, Lahore on 27 December 1993.   Result: **PAKISTAN** won by 75 runs.   Toss: Pakistan.
Award: Inzamam-ul-Haq.   LOI debuts: Pakistan – Irfan Bhatti; Zimbabwe – G.K.Bruk-Jackson.

Pakistan completed a whitewash of this, the first three-match series to span only four days.

PAKISTAN		Runs	Balls	4/6
Saeed Anwar	c James b Brandes	25	22	5
Asif Mujtaba	c James b Rennie	12	23	1
Inzamam-ul-Haq	not out	80	94	9
Basit Ali	b Streak	9	18	1
Javed Miandad	lbw b Streak	55	78	3
* Wasim Akram	not out	17	11	1/1
Salim Malik				
† Rashid Latif				
Mushtaq Ahmed				
Aqib Javed				
Irfan Bhatti				
Extras	(b 1, lb 3, w 10, nb 4)	18		
Total	(40 overs; 4 wickets)	216		

ZIMBABWE		Runs	Balls	4/6
* A.Flower	c Aqib b Irfan	15	11	3
M.H.Dekker	c Mushtaq b Irfan	4	11	–
A.D.R.Campbell	st Rashid b Mushtaq	26	50	2
D.L.Houghton	lbw b Mushtaq	9	35	–
G.J.Whittall	c Rashid b Mushtaq	7	28	–
G.K.Bruk-Jackson	st Rashid b Salim	12	33	2
† W.R.James	not out	14	42	–
D.H.Brain	c and b Salim	1	5	–
E.A.Brandes	c Irfan b Salim	7	4	1
H.H.Streak	c Asif b Basit	7	10	–
J.A.Rennie	not out	12	16	2
Extras	(b 4, lb 9, w 11, nb 3)	27		
Total	(40 overs; 9 wickets)	141		

ZIMBABWE	O	M	R	W
Brandes	8	0	44	1
Brain	6	0	33	0
Rennie	8	0	53	1
Streak	8	1	32	2
Dekker	5	0	27	0
Whittall	4	0	18	0
Campbell	1	0	5	0

PAKISTAN	O	M	R	W
Wasim Akram	5	0	29	0
Irfan Bhatti	8	0	22	2
Aqib Javed	4	0	8	0
Mushtaq Ahmed	8	1	19	3
Salim Malik	8	1	22	3
Asif Mujtaba	4	0	11	0
Basit Ali	3	0	17	1

FALL OF WICKETS
1-41, 2-42, 3-61, 4-188

Umpires: Iftikhar Malik (1) and Ikram Rabbani (5).

FALL OF WICKETS
1-21, 2-21, 3-61, 4-66, 5-79, 6-88, 7-91, 8-101, 9-117

Referee: R.S.Madugalle (*Sri Lanka*).

INDIA v SRI LANKA 1993-94

At Racecourse Ground, Rajkot on 15 February 1994.   Result: INDIA won by 8 runs.   Toss: Sri Lanka.
Award: N.S.Sidhu.   LOI debuts: India – N.R.Mongia; Sri Lanka – U.N.K.Fernando, W.P.U.C.J.Vaas.

With Sri Lanka requiring 16 from his final over, Javagal Srinath scored two direct hits on the middle stump and conceded only seven runs.

INDIA		Runs	Balls	4/6
M.Prabhakar	run out	67	87	9
N.S.Sidhu	c Mahanama b Vaas	108	132	8
V.G.Kambli	run out	25	41	–
* M.Azharuddin	run out	14	17	1
S.R.Tendulkar	c Ranatunga b Kalpage	1	5	–
P.K.Amre	not out	16	17	–
Kapil Dev	not out	4	3	–
† N.R.Mongia				
A.Kumble				
J.Srinath				
R.K.Chauhan				
Extras	(b 1, lb 1, w 8, nb 1)	11		
Total	(50 overs; 5 wickets)	246		

SRI LANKA		Runs	Balls	4/6
R.S.Mahanama	c and b Tendulkar	35	47	4
D.P.Samaraweera	st Mongia b Tendulkar	14	44	1
H.P.Tillekeratne	c Mongia b Kumble	35	46	2
P.A.de Silva	b Kumble	67	85	2/1
* A.Ranatunga	c Mongia b Tendulkar	8	13	–
S.T.Jayasuriya	c Kambli b Kumble	31	42	2
R.S.Kalpage	b Srinath	25	25	1/1
† U.N.K.Fernando	not out	2	3	–
G.P.Wickremasinghe	b Srinath	1	2	–
S.D.Anurasiri	not out	0	1	–
W.P.U.C.J.Vaas				
Extras	(lb 6, w 5, nb 9)	20		
Total	(50 overs; 8 wickets)	238		

SRI LANKA	O	M	R	W
Vaas	8	2	40	1
Wickremasinghe	10	2	41	0
Ranatunga	2	0	18	0
Anurasiri	7	0	43	0
Kalpage	10	0	37	1
Jayasuriya	10	0	47	0
De Silva	3	0	18	0

INDIA	O	M	R	W
Prabhakar	10	0	53	0
Srinath	7	0	37	2
Kapil Dev	6	0	25	0
Tendulkar	8	0	43	3
Kumble	10	0	41	3
Chauhan	9	0	33	0

FALL OF WICKETS
1-122, 2-181, 3-211, 4-214, 5-236

FALL OF WICKETS
1-46, 2-66, 3-119, 4-137, 5-200, 6-218, 7-235, 8-238

Referee: E.de C.Weekes (West Indies).

Umpires: J.Kurishinkal (1) and P.D.Reporter (22).

INDIA v SRI LANKA 1993-94

At Lal Bahadur Stadium, Hyderabad on 18 February 1994.   Result: INDIA won by 7 wickets.   Toss: India.
Award: M.Prabhakar.   LOI debuts: Sri Lanka – A.A.W.Gunawardene, K.R.Pushpakumara.

Arjuna Ranatunga and Kalpage added 132 in 27.4 overs, still Sri Lanka's highest sixth-wicket LOI partnership, after Manoj Prabhakar had taken the first four wickets for 16 runs in 27 balls.

SRI LANKA		Runs	Balls	4/6
R.S.Mahanama	c Tendulkar b Prabhakar	15	25	1
A.A.W.Gunawardene	c Mongia b Prabhakar	2	10	–
H.P.Tillekeratne	c Mongia b Prabhakar	0	5	–
P.A.de Silva	c Chauhan b Prabhakar	0	2	–
* A.Ranatunga	c Mongia b Prabhakar	98	115	10
S.T.Jayasuriya	c Mongia b Tendulkar	9	22	–
R.S.Kalpage	c and b Srinath	51	104	2
† U.N.K.Fernando	not out	20	22	2
K.R.Pushpakumara	not out	3	6	–
W.P.U.C.J.Vaas				
M.Muralitharan				
Extras	(b 3, lb 10, w 9, nb 6)	28		
Total	(50 overs; 7 wickets)	226		

INDIA		Runs	Balls	4/6
M.Prabhakar	c Jayasuriya b Muralitharan	39	68	5
N.S.Sidhu	run out	79	113	8/1
V.G.Kambli	not out	56	84	2
* M.Azharuddin	c Pushpakumara b Jayasuriya	16	13	2
S.R.Tendulkar	not out	11	18	–
P.K.Amre				
Kapil Dev				
† N.R.Mongia				
A.Kumble				
J.Srinath				
R.K.Chauhan				
Extras	(b 10, lb 7, w 6, nb 3)	26		
Total	(48.2 overs; 3 wickets)	227		

INDIA	O	M	R	W
Prabhakar	10	0	35	5
Srinath	10	1	44	1
Kapil Dev	6	1	19	0
Tendulkar	8	0	36	1
Chauhan	9	0	40	0
Kumble	7	0	39	0

SRI LANKA	O	M	R	W
Pushpakumara	7.2	0	30	0
Vaas	7	1	22	0
De Silva	6	0	34	0
Muralitharan	10	0	39	1
Jayasuriya	8	0	38	1
Kalpage	10	0	47	0

FALL OF WICKETS
1-3, 2-11, 3-17, 4-31, 5-65, 6-197, 7-217

FALL OF WICKETS
1-98, 2-161, 3-197

Umpires: S.Choudhury (5) and S.K.Sharma (2).

Referee: E.de C.Weekes (West Indies).

INDIA v SRI LANKA 1993-94

At Burlton Park, Jullundur on 20 February 1994.   Result: **SRI LANKA** won by 4 wickets (revised target).
Toss: Sri Lanka.   Award: P.A.de Silva.   Series Award: N.S.Sidhu.   LOI debuts: None.

Three rain interruptions totalling 68 minutes reduced Sri Lanka's target to 141 from 33 overs. With the aid of two wides they scored 15 off the last over to avoid a whitewash in this series sponsored by Pepsi Foods.

INDIA		Runs	Balls	4/6
A.Jadeja	b Kalpage	37	62	4
N.S.Sidhu	b Muralitharan	46	79	4/1
V.G.Kambli	c Tillekeratne b Muralitharan	12	22	–
P.K.Amre	b Jayasuriya	3	12	–
S.R.Tendulkar	run out	52	63	3
* M.Azharuddin	c Samaraweera b De Silva	11	13	–
† N.R.Mongia	run out	3	11	–
J.Srinath	c Samaraweera b De Silva	7	14	–
R.K.Chauhan	not out	26	27	2
S.A.Ankola	b Vaas	0	1	–
S.L.V.Raju	not out	1	1	–
Extras	(b 2, lb 1, w 8, nb 4)	15		
Total	(50 overs; 9 wickets)	**213**		

SRI LANKA	O	M	R	W
Vaas	10	2	43	1
Wickremasinghe	9	0	34	0
Kalpage	10	0	36	1
Muralitharan	10	2	40	2
Jayasuriya	4	0	27	1
De Silva	7	0	30	2

FALL OF WICKETS
1-83, 2-102, 3-112, 4-112, 5-136, 6-142, 7-161, 8-209, 9-209

Umpires: K.S.Giridharan (1) and M.R.Singh (2).

SRI LANKA		Runs	Balls	4/6
R.S.Mahanama	lbw b Srinath	6	7	–
D.P.Samaraweera	run out	49	65	5
H.P.Tillekeratne	lbw b Raju	23	41	–
P.A.de Silva	not out	32	49	4
S.T.Jayasuriya	b Raju	0	2	–
* A.Ranatunga	c Mongia b Raju	0	1	–
R.S.Kalpage	st Mongia b Tendulkar	4	14	–
† P.B.Dassanayake	not out	20	18	2
G.P.Wickremasinghe				
W.P.U.C.J.Vaas				
M.Muralitharan				
Extras	(b 2, lb 3, w 2)	7		
Total	(32.5 overs; 6 wickets)	**141**		

INDIA	O	M	R	W
Srinath	7.5	0	53	1
Ankola	5	0	23	0
Raju	8	0	19	3
Chauhan	8	2	18	0
Tendulkar	4	0	23	1

FALL OF WICKETS
1-8, 2-72, 3-88, 4-88, 5-88, 6-99

Referee: E.de C.Weekes (West Indies).

WEST INDIES v ENGLAND 1993-94

At Kensington Oval, Bridgetown, Barbados on 16 February 1994.   Result: **ENGLAND** won by 61 runs.
Toss: England.   Award: M.A.Atherton.   LOI debuts: England – A.P.Igglesden, M.P.Maynard, S.L.Watkin.

Michael Atherton dominated his first LOI since May 1991, and his initial one as captain, as England became the first team to defeat the West Indies in Bridgetown since January 1935. It ended a sequence of seven defeats since beating India in March 1993.

ENGLAND		Runs	Balls	4/6
* M.A.Atherton	c Richardson b Cummins	86	146	6
† A.J.Stewart	c Lara b Benjamin	11	34	2
G.P.Thorpe	c Adams b Benjamin	4	14	–
R.A.Smith	c and b Harper	12	23	–
G.A.Hick	c Simmons b Cummins	47	63	4
M.P.Maynard	not out	22	16	1
C.C.Lewis	not out	6	7	–
S.L.Watkin				
A.P.Igglesden				
P.C.R.Tufnell				
D.E.Malcolm				
Extras	(b 4, lb 7, nb 3)	14		
Total	(50 overs; 5 wickets)	**202**		

WEST INDIES	O	M	R	W
Ambrose	10	2	35	0
Walsh	10	0	42	0
Benjamin	10	2	38	2
Cummins	10	1	28	2
Harper	10	0	48	1

FALL OF WICKETS
1-35, 2-45, 3-73, 4-166, 5-176

Umpires: L.H.Barker (23) and C.R.Duncan (7).

WEST INDIES		Runs	Balls	4/6
D.L.Haynes	c Malcolm b Igglesden	17	38	3
B.C.Lara	c Igglesden b Malcolm	9	16	2
* R.B.Richardson	c Maynard b Lewis	12	28	1
K.L.T.Arthurton	b Lewis	6	23	1
P.V.Simmons	b Lewis	0	1	–
† J.C.Adams	c Thorpe b Igglesden	29	54	3
R.A.Harper	lbw b Watkin	11	23	1
A.C.Cummins	c Thorpe b Malcolm	24	38	3
W.K.M.Benjamin	c Thorpe b Tufnell	0	5	–
C.E.L.Ambrose	c Smith b Malcolm	10	18	1
C.A.Walsh	not out	1	1	–
Extras	(b 1, lb 10, w 11)	22		
Total	(40.4 overs)	**141**		

ENGLAND	O	M	R	W
Malcolm	8.4	1	41	3
Watkin	8	1	27	1
Lewis	8	2	18	3
Igglesden	8	2	12	2
Tufnell	8	0	32	1

FALL OF WICKETS
1-17, 2-43, 3-48, 4-48, 5-55, 6-82, 7-121, 8-122, 9-136, 10-141

Referee: S.M.Gavaskar (India).

WEST INDIES v ENGLAND 1993-94

At Sabina Park, Kingston, Jamaica on 26 February 1994.   Result: **WEST INDIES** won by 3 wickets (revised target).
Toss: West Indies.   Award: J.C.Adams.   LOI debuts: None.

England converted their first century opening partnership in the Caribbean into their highest total there. Interrupted by a 12-minute shower when they were 158 for 4 after 36 overs, West Indies were set a reduced target of 238 off 47.

ENGLAND		Runs	Balls	4/6
* M.A.Atherton	c Arthurton b Harper	46	74	4
† A.J.Stewart	run out	66	88	9/1
R.A.Smith	c Harper b K.C.G.Benjamin	56	64	1/2
G.A.Hick	c Cummins b Arthurton	31	36	1/1
M.P.Maynard	b Cummins	22	19	3
N.Hussain	c Richardson b Cummins	10	14	–
C.C.Lewis	b K.C.G.Benjamin	0	3	–
S.L.Watkin	b K.C.G.Benjamin	0	1	–
A.P.Igglesden	not out	2	3	–
P.C.R.Tufnell	not out	2	2	–
A.R.C.Fraser				
Extras	(lb 9, w 7, nb 2)	18		
Total	(50 overs; 8 wickets)	**253**		

WEST INDIES		Runs	Balls	4/6
D.L.Haynes	c and b Hick	53	83	6
B.C.Lara	lbw b Watkin	8	21	1
P.V.Simmons	b Fraser	39	65	4
K.L.T.Arthurton	st Stewart b Hick	12	9	2
* R.B.Richardson	c Fraser b Watkin	32	39	2
† J.C.Adams	not out	52	46	5
R.A.Harper	lbw b Watkin	0	2	–
A.C.Cummins	c Smith b Watkin	16	10	1
W.K.M.Benjamin	not out	9	5	1
K.C.G.Benjamin				
C.A.Walsh				
Extras	(b 3, lb 7, w 6, nb 3)	19		
Total	(45.5 overs; 7 wickets)	**240**		

WEST INDIES	O	M	R	W
Walsh	5	1	26	0
K.C.G.Benjamin	10	1	44	3
Cummins	8	1	42	2
W.K.M.Benjamin	8	0	33	0
Harper	8	0	45	1
Simmons	7	0	32	0
Arthurton	4	0	22	1

ENGLAND	O	M	R	W
Igglesden	7	1	29	0
Watkin	9.5	1	49	4
Fraser	9	0	50	1
Lewis	9	0	48	0
Tufnell	4	0	22	0
Hick	7	0	32	2

FALL OF WICKETS
1-112, 2-128, 3-209, 4-214, 5-247, 6-248, 7-248, 8-249

FALL OF WICKETS
1-13, 2-111, 3-128, 4-130, 5-186, 6-186, 7-223

Umpires: L.H.Barker (24) and S.A.Bucknor (21).

Referee: S.M.Gavaskar (*India*).

WEST INDIES v ENGLAND 1993-94

At Arnos Vale, Kingstown, St Vincent on 2 March 1994.   Result: **WEST INDIES** won by 165 runs.   Toss: England.
Award: D.L.Haynes.   LOI debuts: None.

England conceded their highest total and sustained their biggest defeat by a runs margin. Desmond Haynes shared in the last of his 26 century partnerships. Brian Lara and Richie Richardson (200th LOI) completed their fifties off 31 and 25 balls respectively.

WEST INDIES		Runs	Balls	4/6
D.L.Haynes	c Lewis b Tufnell	83	95	8/2
P.V.Simmons	c Hussain b Tufnell	63	99	7/1
B.C.Lara	c Stewart b Fraser	60	41	5
K.L.T.Arthurton	c Smith b Watkin	28	25	–/1
* R.B.Richardson	not out	52	26	6/2
† J.C.Adams	c Smith b Watkin	6	4	1
R.A.Harper	run out	15	12	1
A.C.Cummins	not out	0	–	–
W.K.M.Benjamin				
C.E.L.Ambrose				
K.C.G.Benjamin				
Extras	(lb 4, w 2)	6		
Total	(50 overs; 6 wickets)	**313**		

ENGLAND		Runs	Balls	4/6
C.C.Lewis	lbw b Cummins	2	10	–
† A.J.Stewart	c Adams b K.C.G.Benjamin	13	20	1
R.A.Smith	b Ambrose	18	35	3
G.A.Hick	c Cummins b Harper	32	85	2
M.P.Maynard	c Simmons b Cummins	6	19	1
N.Hussain	c and b Harper	16	28	–
* M.A.Atherton	not out	19	41	1
S.L.Watkin	c Lara b Arthurton	4	22	–
A.P.Igglesden	c Ambrose b Lara	18	28	2
A.R.C.Fraser	st Adams b Lara	1	8	–
P.C.R.Tufnell	not out	0	4	–
Extras	(b 1, lb 12, w 6)	19		
Total	(50 overs; 9 wickets)	**148**		

ENGLAND	O	M	R	W
Igglesden	10	1	65	0
Watkin	9	0	61	2
Lewis	9	0	67	0
Fraser	10	1	46	1
Hick	3	0	18	0
Tufnell	9	0	52	2

WEST INDIES	O	M	R	W
K.C.G.Benjamin	6	0	21	1
Cummins	8	1	22	2
W.K.M.Benjamin	5	1	15	0
Ambrose	6	2	13	1
Simmons	7	1	18	0
Harper	10	0	29	2
Arthurton	6	1	12	1
Lara	2	0	5	2

FALL OF WICKETS
1-145, 2-156, 3-230, 4-242, 5-256, 6-300

FALL OF WICKETS
1-7, 2-24, 3-41, 4-64, 5-98, 6-105, 7-119, 8-144, 9-148

Umpires: L.H.Barker (25) and G.T.Johnson (4).

Referee: S.M.Gavaskar (*India*).

WEST INDIES v ENGLAND 1993-94

At Queen's Park Oval, Port-of-Spain, Trinidad on 5 March 1994.   Result: **WEST INDIES** won by 15 runs (revised target).
Toss: England.   Award: D.L.Haynes.   LOI debuts: None.

Desmond Haynes, who had scored 148 on debut, celebrated the last of his 238 LOI appearances by extending his record tallies of runs and hundreds to 8648 and 17 respectively. Rain terminated the hosts' innings and reduced England's target to 209 from 36 overs.

WEST INDIES		Runs	Balls	4/6
D.L.Haynes	b Lewis	115	112	14
P.V.Simmons	c Hick b Lewis	16	19	3
B.C.Lara	lbw b Fraser	19	25	4
K.L.T.Arthurton	c Stewart b Fraser	0	2	–
* R.B.Richardson	c Ramprakash b Caddick	13	34	2
† J.C.Adams	c Caddick b Fraser	40	68	2
R.A.Harper	b Lewis	23	12	5
A.C.Cummins	not out	13	7	–/1
W.K.M.Benjamin	not out	0	–	–
C.E.L.Ambrose				
K.C.G.Benjamin				
Extras	(b 4, lb 4, w 13, nb 5)	26		
Total	(45.4 overs; 7 wickets)	**265**		

ENGLAND		Runs	Balls	4/6
* M.A.Atherton	b K.C.G.Benjamin	41	56	5
† A.J.Stewart	b K.C.G.Benjamin	2	15	–
R.A.Smith	b Harper	45	59	5
G.A.Hick	c and b Harper	10	21	–
M.P.Maynard	b Harper	8	9	–
M.R.Ramprakash	b Ambrose	31	25	3
C.C.Lewis	c Lara b Harper	4	8	–
A.R.Caddick	not out	20	17	2
I.D.K.Salisbury	b Cummins	5	6	–
A.P.Igglesden	run out	0	–	–
A.R.C.Fraser	not out	4	3	1
Extras	(b 1, lb 9, w 11, nb 2)	23		
Total	(36 overs; 9 wickets)	**193**		

ENGLAND	O	M	R	W
Igglesden	3	0	16	0
Caddick	10	0	60	1
Fraser	10	0	31	3
Lewis	9.4	1	59	3
Salisbury	9	0	58	0
Hick	4	0	33	0

WEST INDIES	O	M	R	W
K.C.G.Benjamin	8	0	37	2
Cummins	6	0	34	1
Ambrose	8	0	34	1
W.K.M.Benjamin	7	0	38	0
Harper	7	0	40	4

FALL OF WICKETS
1-45, 2-75, 3-75, 4-98, 5-222, 6-238, 7-265

FALL OF WICKETS
1-23, 2-86, 3-110, 4-121, 5-130, 6-145, 7-177, 8-184, 9-184

Referee: S.M.Gavaskar (India).

Umpires: S.A.Bucknor (22) and C.E.Cumberbatch (19).

WEST INDIES v ENGLAND 1993-94

At Queen's Park Oval, Port-of-Spain, Trinidad on 6 March 1994.   Result: **ENGLAND** won by 5 wickets (revised target).
Toss: West Indies.   Award: A.J.Stewart.   LOI debuts: None.

A 55-minute break for rain when England were 3 for 0 after 2.4 overs reduced their target to 201 from 40 overs. Alec Stewart reached 50 off 34 balls.

WEST INDIES		Runs	Balls	4/6
P.V.Simmons	b Salisbury	84	104	12/1
† J.C.Adams	c Atherton b Salisbury	23	61	1
B.C.Lara	c Stewart b Caddick	16	29	–
K.L.T.Arthurton	c Ramprakash b Lewis	17	19	3
* R.B.Richardson	c Stewart b Salisbury	15	23	1/1
R.I.C.Holder	run out	26	16	1
R.A.Harper	c and b Lewis	37	33	4
A.C.Cummins	c Smith b Lewis	11	10	–
W.K.M.Benjamin	c Ramprakash b Lewis	8	6	–
K.C.G.Benjamin	not out	0	–	–
C.A.Walsh				
Extras	(b 1, lb 10, w 1, nb 1)	13		
Total	(50 overs; 9 wickets)	**250**		

ENGLAND		Runs	Balls	4/6
* M.A.Atherton	b K.C.G.Benjamin	51	79	4
† A.J.Stewart	b Cummins	53	38	9/1
R.A.Smith	lbw b Cummins	4	16	–
G.A.Hick	not out	47	60	3
M.P.Maynard	c Adams b K.C.G.Benjamin	1	6	–
M.R.Ramprakash	c Adams b Walsh	10	11	1
C.C.Lewis	not out	16	19	2
A.R.Caddick				
I.D.K.Salisbury				
S.L.Watkin				
A.R.C.Fraser				
Extras	(b 2, lb 9, w 4, nb 4)	19		
Total	(36.4 overs; 5 wickets)	**201**		

ENGLAND	O	M	R	W
Fraser	10	2	41	0
Watkin	10	0	56	0
Lewis	10	0	35	4
Caddick	10	2	66	1
Salisbury	10	0	41	3

WEST INDIES	O	M	R	W
W.K.M.Benjamin	8	1	33	0
Walsh	10	0	58	1
Cummins	7.4	0	36	2
K.C.G.Benjamin	9	0	55	2
Harper	2	0	8	0

FALL OF WICKETS
1-89, 2-126, 3-135, 4-164, 5-164, 6-230, 7-232, 8-248, 9-250

FALL OF WICKETS
1-62, 2-83, 3-151, 4-156, 5-174

Referee: S.M.Gavaskar (India).

Umpires: S.A.Bucknor (23) and C.E.Cumberbatch (20).

SOUTH AFRICA v AUSTRALIA 1993-94

At The Wanderers, Johannesburg on 19 February 1994.　Result: **SOUTH AFRICA** won by 5 runs.　Toss: South Africa.
Award: W.J.Cronje.　LOI debuts: South Africa – E.O.Simons.

Australia's first limited-overs campaign in South Africa involved the longest series of matches between two countries.
The penultimate over, bowled by 'Fanie' de Villiers, consisted entirely of yorkers and produced only a single run.

SOUTH AFRICA		Runs	Balls	4/6
P.N.Kirsten	c Reiffel b McGrath	47	114	3
G.Kirsten	c Healy b Reiffel	12	31	1
W.J.Cronje	c Reiffel b McDermott	112	120	7/3
J.N.Rhodes	not out	47	40	4
A.P.Kuiper	not out	2	1	–
* K.C.Wessels				
† D.J.Richardson				
E.O.Simons				
R.P.Snell				
P.S.de Villiers				
A.A.Donald				
Extras	(lb 5, w 2, nb 5)	12		
Total	(50 overs; 3 wickets)	**232**		

AUSTRALIA		Runs	Balls	4/6
M.A.Taylor	b Snell	30	48	3
D.C.Boon	c Rhodes b Kuiper	58	81	7
D.M.Jones	c Cronje b Simons	42	62	3
M.E.Waugh	c Richardson b Simons	14	20	–/1
S.R.Waugh	not out	46	59	3
* A.R.Border	b De Villiers	25	27	2
† I.A.Healy	not out	4	4	–
P.R.Reiffel				
S.K.Warne				
C.J.McDermott				
G.D.McGrath				
Extras	(lb 4, w 3, nb 1)	8		
Total	(50 overs; 5 wickets)	**227**		

AUSTRALIA	O	M	R	W
McDermott	10	0	52	1
Reiffel	10	1	36	1
McGrath	10	1	29	1
S.R.Waugh	10	0	54	0
Warne	10	0	56	0

SOUTH AFRICA	O	M	R	W
Donald	9	1	46	0
De Villiers	10	0	43	1
Snell	10	0	55	1
Simons	10	0	29	2
Kuiper	7	0	30	1
Cronje	4	0	20	0

FALL OF WICKETS
1-39, 2-123, 3-229

FALL OF WICKETS
1-61, 2-108, 3-143, 4-155, 5-209

Umpires: S.B.Lambson (9) and C.J.Mitchley (8).

Referee: D.B.Carr (*England*).

SOUTH AFRICA v AUSTRALIA 1993-94

At Centurion Park, Verwoerdburg, Pretoria on 20 February 1994.　Result: **SOUTH AFRICA** won by 56 runs.
Toss: South Africa.　Award: W.J.Cronje.　LOI debuts: None.

Adrian Kuiper struck 26 runs, including three successive sixes, off the final over of South Africa's innings, bowled by
Craig McDermott: 2042666, the sixth offering being a no-ball.

SOUTH AFRICA		Runs	Balls	4/6
P.N.Kirsten	b M.E.Waugh	22	50	2
G.Kirsten	c S.R.Waugh b McGrath	18	35	2
W.J.Cronje	run out	97	102	8/3
J.N.Rhodes	lbw b Warne	44	63	3
* K.C.Wessels	c Healy b McGrath	22	32	3
A.P.Kuiper	not out	47	22	2/4
E.O.Simons	not out	2	3	–
† D.J.Richardson				
R.P.Snell				
P.S.de Villiers				
C.R.Matthews				
Extras	(lb 6, w 3, nb 4)	13		
Total	(50 overs; 5 wickets)	**265**		

AUSTRALIA		Runs	Balls	4/6
D.C.Boon	c Cronje b Matthews	2	12	–
M.A.Taylor	run out	21	49	2
D.M.Jones	b Matthews	5	14	–
M.E.Waugh	lbw b Matthews	0	2	–
S.R.Waugh	b Simons	86	91	4/3
* A.R.Border	run out	41	49	2/1
† I.A.Healy	c G.Kirsten b Kuiper	4	3	1
P.R.Reiffel	c Simons b De Villiers	10	15	–
S.K.Warne	c Wessels b Cronje	9	10	1
C.J.McDermott	run out	16	12	1/1
G.D.McGrath	not out	0	0	–
Extras	(lb 12, w 3)	15		
Total	(42.4 overs)	**209**		

AUSTRALIA	O	M	R	W
McDermott	10	3	46	0
Reiffel	8	0	50	0
M.E.Waugh	9	1	52	1
McGrath	10	1	42	2
S.R.Waugh	5	0	28	0
Warne	8	1	41	1

SOUTH AFRICA	O	M	R	W
De Villiers	8	2	20	1
Matthews	8	2	26	3
Simons	7.4	0	39	1
Snell	8	0	38	0
Kuiper	6	0	38	1
Cronje	5	0	36	1

FALL OF WICKETS
1-45, 2-58, 3-152, 4-203, 5-229

FALL OF WICKETS
1-11, 2-19, 3-19, 4-34, 5-141, 6-145, 7-174, 8-189, 9-209, 10-209

Umpires: W.A.Diedricks (6) and K.E.Liebenberg (18).

Referee: D.B.Carr (*England*).

SOUTH AFRICA v AUSTRALIA 1993-94

At St George's Park, Port Elizabeth on 22 February 1994.　　Result: **AUSTRALIA** won by 88 runs.　　Toss: Australia.
Award: M.E.Waugh.　　LOI debuts: None.

Australia's total was the highest for internationals in South Africa until the following season. Dean Jones, David Boon and 'Jonty' Rhodes completed 6000, 5000 and 1000 LOI runs respectively.

AUSTRALIA		Runs	Balls	4/6
M.A.Taylor	c Richardson b De Villiers	2	9	
D.C.Boon	b De Villiers	76	105	7
D.M.Jones	run out	67	92	7
M.E.Waugh	c Rhodes b Matthews	60	55	4/2
C.J.McDermott	run out	15	9	1
S.R.Waugh	c Matthews b Donald	18	15	3
* A.R.Border	not out	40	17	4/3
† I.A.Healy	not out	1	1	–
P.R.Reiffel				
S.K.Warne				
G.D.McGrath				
Extras	(lb 1, w 1)	2		
Total	(50 overs; 6 wickets)	**281**		

SOUTH AFRICA		Runs	Balls	4/6
P.N.Kirsten	c McGrath b Warne	27	66	3
G.Kirsten	b McDermott	6	15	1
W.J.Cronje	c McDermott b S.R.Waugh	45	58	1/1
J.N.Rhodes	c Healy b M.E.Waugh	36	45	1
* K.C.Wessels	run out	5	5	1
A.P.Kuiper	b McDermott	33	17	3/2
† D.J.Richardson	not out	23	32	1
P.L.Symcox	c Boon b Warne	4	12	–
C.R.Matthews	b Warne	0	5	–
P.S.de Villiers	b Warne	4	8	–
A.A.Donald	b McDermott	0	2	–
Extras	(lb 6, nb 4)	10		
Total	(43 overs)	**193**		

SOUTH AFRICA	O	M	R	W
De Villiers	10	1	55	2
Matthews	10	1	46	1
Donald	10	0	60	1
Cronje	10	1	62	0
Symcox	4	0	25	0
Kuiper	6	0	32	0

AUSTRALIA	O	M	R	W
McDermott	10	1	35	3
McGrath	7	2	17	0
Reiffel	8	0	40	0
Warne	10	0	36	4
S.R.Waugh	4	0	33	1
M.E.Waugh	4	0	26	1

FALL OF WICKETS
1-12, 2-135, 3-180, 4-198, 5-233, 6-276

FALL OF WICKETS
1-8, 2-49, 3-115, 4-125, 5-127, 6-165, 7-178, 8-181, 9-188, 10-193

Umpires: R.E.Koertzen (7) and C.J.Mitchley (9).

Referee: D.B.Carr (*England*).

SOUTH AFRICA v AUSTRALIA 1993-94

At Kingsmead, Durban on 24 February 1994.　　Result: **SOUTH AFRICA** won by 7 wickets.　　Toss: Australia.
Award: C.R.Matthews.　　LOI debuts: None.

South Africa's victory ended a sequence of results between these two countries in which the side batting first had won nine games in succession. This was the hosts' 50th international in just over two years, their inaugural one having being played on 10 November 1991.

AUSTRALIA		Runs	Balls	4/6
D.C.Boon	c De Villiers b Simons	34	90	4
M.J.Slater	c Richardson b De Villiers	1	2	–
D.M.Jones	lbw b Matthews	8	13	1
M.E.Waugh	c Hudson b Matthews	3	17	–
S.R.Waugh	lbw b Simons	2	5	–
* A.R.Border	not out	69	84	9/1
† I.A.Healy	c Richardson b Kuiper	0	3	–
P.R.Reiffel	c Wessels b Kuiper	0	7	–
S.K.Warne	b Matthews	23	30	2/1
C.J.McDermott	b Matthews	0	2	–
G.D.McGrath	c Richardson b Cronje	0	9	–
Extras	(lb 7, w 4, nb 3)	14		
Total	(43.2 overs)	**154**		

SOUTH AFRICA		Runs	Balls	4/6
A.C.Hudson	lbw b Reiffel	37	52	5
P.N.Kirsten	c Healy b Reiffel	15	47	2
W.J.Cronje	not out	50	78	7
J.N.Rhodes	c M.E.Waugh b Warne	3	19	–
* K.C.Wessels	not out	40	79	4
A.P.Kuiper				
E.O.Simons				
† D.J.Richardson				
R.P.Snell				
C.R.Matthews				
P.S.de Villiers				
Extras	(lb 1, w 8, nb 3)	12		
Total	(45 overs; 3 wickets)	**157**		

SOUTH AFRICA	O	M	R	W
De Villiers	8	0	30	1
Matthews	8	5	10	4
Simons	10	4	22	2
Snell	9	1	42	0
Cronje	3.2	0	19	1
Kuiper	5	0	24	2

AUSTRALIA	O	M	R	W
McDermott	10	0	35	0
McGrath	10	4	20	0
S.R.Waugh	4	0	24	0
Reiffel	10	1	31	2
Warne	8	2	32	1
M.E.Waugh	3	0	14	0

FALL OF WICKETS
1-3, 2-12, 3-18, 4-23, 5-91, 6-93, 7-100, 8-138, 9-138, 10-154

FALL OF WICKETS
1-51, 2-55, 3-69

Umpires: W.A.Diedricks (7) and K.E.Liebenberg (19).

Referee: D.B.Carr (*England*).

SOUTH AFRICA v AUSTRALIA 1993-94

At Buffalo Park, East London on 2 April 1994.　　Result: **AUSTRALIA** won by 7 wickets.　　Toss: South Africa.
Award: A.R.Border.　　LOI debuts: None.

After a break of five weeks, during which the teams contested three Test matches, the series began its illuminated stage with South Africa leading 3-1. Steve Waugh was a shade unlucky to miss the match award.

SOUTH AFRICA		Runs	Balls	4/6
A.C.Hudson	c Warne b Reiffel	14	38	2
P.N.Kirsten	c M.E.Waugh b Warne	53	105	3/1
W.J.Cronje	c Warne b May	10	36	–
J.N.Rhodes	st Healy b May	16	30	1
A.P.Kuiper	run out	12	21	1
* K.C.Wessels	run out	15	26	–
E.O.Simons	st Healy b Border	6	18	–
B.M.McMillan	b S.R.Waugh	17	19	1
† D.J.Richardson	not out	7	8	–
C.R.Matthews	c Healy b Border	0	1	–
P.S.de Villiers	st Healy b Border	0	1	–
Extras	(lb 4, w 1, nb 3)	8		
Total	(49.5 overs)	**158**		

AUSTRALIA		Runs	Balls	4/6
M.J.Slater	c Kirsten b Simons	31	56	4
D.C.Boon	run out	30	57	3
D.M.Jones	lbw b Simons	8	23	–
M.E.Waugh	not out	21	45	1
S.R.Waugh	not out	67	60	11
* A.R.Border				
† I.A.Healy				
P.R.Reiffel				
S.K.Warne				
T.B.A.May				
G.D.McGrath				
Extras	(lb 2)	2		
Total	(40 overs; 3 wickets)	**159**		

AUSTRALIA	O	M	R	W
McGrath	6	1	20	0
Reiffel	7	1	13	1
S.R.Waugh	9	1	25	1
May	10	0	35	2
Warne	10	0	34	1
Border	7.5	0	27	3

SOUTH AFRICA	O	M	R	W
De Villiers	8	0	31	0
Matthews	8	0	34	0
Simons	10	2	32	2
McMillan	6	0	21	0
Cronje	7	0	32	0
Kuiper	1	0	7	0

FALL OF WICKETS
1-35, 2-62, 3-87, 4-109, 5-118, 6-129, 7-139, 8-155, 9-158, 10-158

FALL OF WICKETS
1-57, 2-66, 3-71

Umpires: R.E.Koertzen (8) and K.E.Liebenberg (20).

Referee: D.B.Carr (*England*).

SOUTH AFRICA v AUSTRALIA 1993-94

At St George's Park, Port Elizabeth on 4 April 1994.　　Result: **SOUTH AFRICA** won by 26 runs.　　Toss: South Africa.
Award: J.N.Rhodes.　　LOI debuts: None.

Paul Reiffel and Shane Warne shared an LOI record eighth-wicket partnership of 119 from 116 balls. Mark Waugh completed 2000 runs in 67 LOI innings. Floodlighting problems delayed the start of Australia's innings and they were compelled to bat with two of the towers on reduced power.

SOUTH AFRICA		Runs	Balls	4/6
A.C.Hudson	c Warne b May	63	110	4
P.N.Kirsten	b Reiffel	10	19	2
W.J.Cronje	c Healy b M.E.Waugh	11	21	1
J.N.Rhodes	c Jones b S.R.Waugh	66	90	5/1
* K.C.Wessels	b Reiffel	27	36	1
E.O.Simons	run out	23	22	3
B.M.McMillan	not out	2	2	–
† D.J.Richardson	not out	2	3	–
T.G.Shaw				
C.R.Matthews				
P.S.de Villiers				
Extras	(b 1, lb 15, w 5, nb 2)	23		
Total	(50 overs; 6 wickets)	**227**		

AUSTRALIA		Runs	Balls	4/6
D.C.Boon	c Wessels b De Villiers	4	11	–
M.J.Slater	c Richardson b Matthews	16	41	2
D.M.Jones	b Simons	13	29	1
M.E.Waugh	b Simons	17	26	2
S.R.Waugh	lbw b McMillan	7	19	1
* A.R.Border	lbw b Shaw	5	16	1
† I.A.Healy	c Wessels b Shaw	5	21	–
P.R.Reiffel	c Simons b Matthews	58	68	4/1
S.K.Warne	run out	55	58	8
T.B.A.May	c and b De Villiers	4	7	–
G.D.McGrath	not out	0	–	–
Extras	(lb 13, w 4)	17		
Total	(49.1 overs)	**201**		

AUSTRALIA	O	M	R	W
McGrath	10	1	41	0
Reiffel	10	1	33	2
M.E.Waugh	7	0	26	1
S.R.Waugh	10	1	48	1
May	10	0	45	1
Warne	3	0	18	0

SOUTH AFRICA	O	M	R	W
De Villiers	9	1	42	2
Matthews	9.1	1	35	2
McMillan	8	0	38	1
Simons	10	3	24	2
Shaw	8	2	19	2
Cronje	5	1	30	0

FALL OF WICKETS
1-18, 2-48, 3-153, 4-175, 5-216, 6-223

FALL OF WICKETS
1-4, 2-35, 3-50, 4-59, 5-65, 6-68, 7-77, 8-196, 9-201, 10-201

Umpires: W.A.Diedricks (8) and S.B.Lambson (10).

Referee: D.B.Carr (*England*).

SOUTH AFRICA v AUSTRALIA 1993-94

At Newlands, Cape Town on 6 April 1994.   Result: **AUSTRALIA** won by 36 runs.   Toss: Australia.
Award: M.E.Waugh.   LOI debuts: None.

A high class spell of leg-spin bowling by Shane Warne kept the series alive. Kepler Wessels appeared in his 100th international, the first 54 having been in Australia's colours.

AUSTRALIA		Runs	Balls	4/6	SOUTH AFRICA		Runs	Balls	4/6
M.A.Taylor	run out	63	100	4	A.C.Hudson	lbw b Warne	62	92	6
M.L.Hayden	lbw b Matthews	0	3	–	G.Kirsten	c M.E.Waugh b Reiffel	3	23	–
D.M.Jones	c Richardson b Matthews	8	12	1	W.J.Cronje	c Taylor b Warne	37	64	2
M.E.Waugh	b Matthews	71	99	5	J.N.Rhodes	st Healy b Warne	35	46	1/1
S.R.Waugh	b Simons	23	22	3	A.P.Kuiper	not out	38	45	3
* A.R.Border	not out	40	47	4	* K.C.Wessels	c Border b M.E.Waugh	12	22	–
† I.A.Healy	c Wessels b Matthews	26	22	1	E.O.Simons	not out	9	10	1
P.R.Reiffel					B.M.McMillan				
S.K.Warne					† D.J.Richardson				
T.B.A.May					C.R.Matthews				
G.D.McGrath					P.S.de Villiers				
Extras	(lb 8, w 1, nb 2)	11			Extras	(b 1, lb 8, nb 1)	10		
Total	(50 overs; 6 wickets)	**242**			**Total**	(50 overs; 5 wickets)	**206**		

SOUTH AFRICA	O	M	R	W	AUSTRALIA	O	M	R	W
De Villiers	10	1	52	0	McGrath	10	1	38	0
Matthews	10	0	47	4	Reiffel	7	2	18	1
McMillan	10	0	46	0	May	10	1	38	0
Simons	10	0	31	1	S.R.Waugh	4	0	22	0
Cronje	5	0	40	0	Warne	10	0	31	3
Kuiper	5	0	18	0	M.E.Waugh	9	1	50	1

FALL OF WICKETS
1-0, 2-10, 3-133, 4-163, 5-180, 6-242

FALL OF WICKETS
1-22, 2-101, 3-114, 4-163, 5-186

Umpires: R.E.Koertzen (9) and C.J.Mitchley (10).

Referee: D.B.Carr (*England*).

SOUTH AFRICA v AUSTRALIA 1993-94

At Springbok Park, Bloemfontein on 8 April 1994.   Result: **AUSTRALIA** won by 1 run.   Toss: Australia.
Award: A.C.Hudson.   Series Award: S.R.Waugh.   LOI debuts: None.

The only series to involve eight matches was decided off the last scheduled ball by the closest margin possible, Dave Richardson being run out to tie the rubber 4-4. It was a fitting finale to the longest LOI individual career, Allan Border retiring after 273 matches, including a record 178 as captain.

AUSTRALIA		Runs	Balls	4/6	SOUTH AFRICA		Runs	Balls	4/6
M.J.Slater	st Richardson b Shaw	34	76	2	A.C.Hudson	c Border b Reiffel	84	132	8
M.A.Taylor	c Wessels b Matthews	1	6	–	* K.C.Wessels	b S.R.Waugh	28	63	1
M.E.Waugh	c Wessels b Simons	13	36	–	W.J.Cronje	b McGrath	18	31	1
D.C.Boon	c Wessels b Matthews	45	79	4	J.N.Rhodes	c S.R.Waugh b Reiffel	13	21	–
S.R.Waugh	c McMillan b De Villiers	42	51	2	A.P.Kuiper	c M.E.Waugh b Warne	6	13	–
* A.R.Border	c McMillan b Matthews	11	16	–	B.M.McMillan	run out	4	6	–
† I.A.Healy	not out	41	30	3	† D.J.Richardson	run out	18	18	2
P.R.Reiffel	not out	8	8	–	E.O.Simons	b S.R.Waugh	18	14	1/1
S.K.Warne					T.G.Shaw	not out	2	3	–
D.W.Fleming					C.R.Matthews				
G.D.McGrath					P.S.de Villiers				
Extras	(lb 6, w 1, nb 1)	8			Extras	(lb 6, w 4, nb 1)	11		
Total	(50 overs; 6 wickets)	**203**			**Total**	(50 overs; 8 wickets)	**202**		

SOUTH AFRICA	O	M	R	W	AUSTRALIA	O	M	R	W
De Villiers	10	1	44	1	McGrath	10	0	44	1
Matthews	10	0	40	3	Fleming	10	2	33	0
Simons	10	2	36	1	Reiffel	10	0	34	2
Shaw	10	0	30	1	Warne	10	0	37	1
McMillan	7	0	34	0	S.R.Waugh	10	0	48	2
Kuiper	3	0	13	0					

FALL OF WICKETS
1-7, 2-31, 3-69, 4-140, 5-143, 6-184

FALL OF WICKETS
1-82, 2-111, 3-143, 4-158, 5-162, 6-164, 7-196, 8-202

Umpires: S.B.Lambson (11) and K.E.Liebenberg (21).

Referee: D.B.Carr (*England*).

NEW ZEALAND v PAKISTAN 1993-94

At Carisbrook, Dunedin on 3 March 1994.　　Result: **PAKISTAN** won by 5 wickets.　　Toss: New Zealand.
Award: Saeed Anwar.　　LOI debuts: None.

New Zealand's decision to bat first backfired when two breaks for rain totalling 192 minutes reduced their innings to 30 overs after they had reached 32 for 1 in the tenth.

NEW ZEALAND		Runs	Balls	4/6
M.J.Greatbatch	run out	14	20	–/1
B.A.Young	c Salim b Akram Raza	20	46	1
A.H.Jones	c Wasim b Akram Raza	15	32	2
C.L.Cairns	c Asif b Akram Raza	13	22	–/1
* K.R.Rutherford	st Rashid b Aamir	3	10	–
S.A.Thomson	st Rashid b Aamir	8	12	–
C.Z.Harris	c and b Salim	19	14	1/1
† T.E.Blain	c Asif b Salim	5	6	–
G.R.Larsen	not out	9	12	–
D.K.Morrison	c Asif b Salim	1	8	–
C.Pringle	not out	6	3	1
Extras	(lb 5, w 1, nb 3)	9		
Total	(30 overs; 9 wickets)	**122**		

PAKISTAN		Runs	Balls	4/6
Saeed Anwar	not out	60	72	5
Aamir Sohail	c Blain b Pringle	5	13	1
Inzamam-ul-Haq	c Jones b Pringle	1	8	–
* Salim Malik	lbw b Cairns	2	8	–
Basit Ali	lbw b Cairns	4	7	–
Asif Mujtaba	c Cairns b Morrison	14	32	–
† Rashid Latif	not out	32	18	1/3
Wasim Akram				
Akram Raza				
Waqar Younis				
Ata-ur-Rehman				
Extras	(lb 2, w 3)	5		
Total	(26.1 overs; 5 wickets)	**123**		

PAKISTAN	O	M	R	W
Wasim Akram	6	2	18	0
Waqar Younis	4	1	14	0
Ata-ur-Rehman	4	0	17	0
Akram Raza	6	1	18	3
Aamir Sohail	6	0	33	2
Salim Malik	4	0	17	3

NEW ZEALAND	O	M	R	W
Pringle	5	0	20	2
Thomson	4	1	21	0
Larsen	5	1	15	0
Cairns	6	1	33	2
Harris	3	0	17	0
Morrison	3.1	0	15	1

FALL OF WICKETS
1-18, 2-54, 3-58, 4-72, 5-74, 6-99, 7-105, 8-109, 9-114

FALL OF WICKETS
1-17, 2-24, 3-27, 4-35, 5-74

Umpires: R.S.Dunne (14) and C.E.King (4).

Referee: R.Subba Row (*England*).

NEW ZEALAND v PAKISTAN 1993-94

At Eden Park, Auckland on 6 March 1994.　　Result: **PAKISTAN** won by 36 runs.　　Toss: New Zealand.
Award: Wasim Akram.　　LOI debuts: None.

Play was suspended for 11 minutes when Pakistan left the field after Ata-ur-Rehman had been wounded on the side of his head by a missile. Wasim Akram extended his record tally of four-wicket analyses to 15.

PAKISTAN		Runs	Balls	4/6
Saeed Anwar	c Blain b Morrison	9	18	2
Aamir Sohail	c Rutherford b Thomson	48	92	4
Inzamam-ul-Haq	lbw b Pringle	14	31	–
* Salim Malik	c Blain b Larsen	5	9	1
Basit Ali	c Blain b Larsen	16	12	2
Asif Mujtaba	lbw b Morrison	1	10	–
† Rashid Latif	c Greatbatch b Harris	3	9	–
Wasim Akram	c Greatbatch b Thomson	33	55	3
Akram Raza	run out	3	9	–
Waqar Younis	b Thomson	7	13	–/1
Ata-ur-Rehman	not out	0	1	–
Extras	(b 1, lb 4, w 8, nb 2)	15		
Total	(43.3 overs)	**146**		

NEW ZEALAND		Runs	Balls	4/6
M.J.Greatbatch	c Akram Raza b Rehman	23	47	2
B.A.Young	lbw b Wasim	0	2	–
A.H.Jones	c Aamir b Wasim	1	4	–
* K.R.Rutherford	run out	37	88	2
S.A.Thomson	c Salim b Akram Raza	6	38	–
C.L.Cairns	b Aamir	3	15	–
C.Z.Harris	c Rashid b Waqar	18	38	–
† T.E.Blain	st Rashid b Akram Raza	2	8	–
G.R.Larsen	b Wasim	5	17	–
D.K.Morrison	c Rashid b Wasim	0	5	–
C.Pringle	not out	4	6	–
Extras	(lb 2, w 8, nb 1)	11		
Total	(44.3 overs)	**110**		

NEW ZEALAND	O	M	R	W
Morrison	8	2	16	2
Pringle	8	0	31	1
Cairns	7	1	24	0
Larsen	10	0	27	2
Harris	7	0	29	1
Thomson	3.3	1	14	3

PAKISTAN	O	M	R	W
Wasim Akram	7.3	0	23	4
Waqar Younis	8	0	18	1
Ata-ur-Rehman	9	2	25	1
Salim Malik	2	0	4	0
Akram Raza	10	1	21	2
Aamir Sohail	8	0	17	1

FALL OF WICKETS
1-10, 2-33, 3-41, 4-60, 5-61, 6-65, 7-127, 8-139, 9-139, 10-146

FALL OF WICKETS
1-3, 2-8, 3-45, 4-62, 5-71, 6-86, 7-90, 8-104, 9-105, 10-110

Umpires: D.B.Cowie (5) and D.M.Quested (4).

Referee: R.Subba Row (*England*).

NEW ZEALAND v PAKISTAN 1993-94

At Basin Reserve, Wellington on 9 March 1994.   Result: **PAKISTAN** won by 11 runs.   Toss: New Zealand.
Award: Inzamam-ul-Haq.   LOI debuts: None.

Drizzle delayed the start and reduced the contest by two overs per innings. Although Danny Morrison took three key wickets in seven balls, Pakistan secured an unbeatable lead in the five-match series.

PAKISTAN		Runs	Balls	4/6
Saeed Anwar	b Cairns	16	33	2
Aamir Sohail	c Young b Morrison	76	103	8
Inzamam-ul-Haq	c Cairns b Pringle	88	131	8/1
Basit Ali	b Morrison	1	3	–
Wasim Akram	b Morrison	0	2	–
* Salim Malik	not out	10	13	–
† Rashid Latif	b Larsen	3	4	–
Asif Mujtaba	not out	1	1	–
Akram Raza				
Waqar Younis				
Ata-ur-Rehman				
Extras	(b 4, lb 9, w 3, nb 2)	18		
Total	**(48 overs; 6 wickets)**	**213**		

NEW ZEALAND		Runs	Balls	4/6
B.A.Young	run out	37	62	3
M.J.Greatbatch	c Aamir b Rehman	9	17	–
A.H.Jones	run out	38	67	1
* K.R.Rutherford	c Salim b Waqar	46	75	1
S.A.Thomson	b Wasim	38	40	3
C.L.Cairns	b Wasim	2	6	–
C.Z.Harris	not out	8	4	1
† T.E.Blain	run out	3	4	–
G.R.Larsen	b Waqar	6	9	–
D.K.Morrison	not out	4	4	1
C.Pringle				
Extras	(b 3, lb 5, w 3)	11		
Total	**(48 overs; 8 wickets)**	**202**		

NEW ZEALAND	O	M	R	W
Pringle	9	0	52	1
Morrison	10	1	32	3
Larsen	10	1	42	1
Cairns	10	0	26	1
Thomson	2	0	14	0
Harris	7	0	34	0

PAKISTAN	O	M	R	W
Wasim Akram	10	1	41	2
Waqar Younis	10	0	43	2
Ata-ur-Rehman	6	0	15	1
Aamir Sohail	6	0	29	0
Salim Malik	10	0	37	0
Akram Raza	6	0	29	0

FALL OF WICKETS
1-29, 2-171, 3-174, 4-174, 5-206, 6-209

FALL OF WICKETS
1-32, 2-76, 3-106, 4-168, 5-176, 6-177, 7-181, 8-193

Umpires: B.L.Aldridge (32) and D.M.Quested (5).

Referee: R.Subba Row (*England*).

NEW ZEALAND v PAKISTAN 1993-94

At Eden Park, Auckland on 13 March 1994.   Result: **MATCH TIED**.   Toss: Pakistan.
Award: Waqar Younis.   LOI debuts: New Zealand – M.N.Hart.

The hosts, who lost their last six wickets for 19 runs, required just three runs off the final over with two wickets in hand. Their destroyer, Waqar Younis, returned the best LOI analysis against New Zealand and extended his record number of five-wicket hauls to seven.

PAKISTAN		Runs	Balls	4/6
Saeed Anwar	c Blain b Larsen	25	54	3
Aamir Sohail	c Blain b Larsen	24	28	3
Inzamam-ul-Haq	c Young b Larsen	7	28	–
* Salim Malik	b Thomson	7	23	1
Basit Ali	run out	34	60	2
Asif Mujtaba	c Rutherford b Hart	5	7	1
† Rashid Latif	b Thomson	5	18	–
Wasim Akram	b Larsen	15	30	2
Akram Raza	not out	11	23	–
Waqar Younis	c Hartland b Pringle	2	11	–
Ata-ur-Rehman	not out	11	13	2
Extras	(b 2, lb 8, w 5)	15		
Total	**(50 overs; 9 wickets)**	**161**		

NEW ZEALAND		Runs	Balls	4/6
B.A.Young	b Waqar	5	11	–
B.R.Hartland	b Waqar	3	24	–
A.H.Jones	c Basit b Akram Raza	21	68	2
* K.R.Rutherford	c Waqar b Salim	47	76	3
C.L.Cairns	run out	39	62	1/1
S.A.Thomson	c Rashid b Waqar	24	37	2
† T.E.Blain	c Rashid b Wasim	0	4	–
G.R.Larsen	lbw b Waqar	1	7	–
M.N.Hart	b Waqar	6	5	1
C.Pringle	not out	1	4	–
R.P.de Groen	lbw b Waqar	2	3	–
Extras	(lb 5, w 7)	12		
Total	**(49.4 overs)**	**161**		

NEW ZEALAND	O	M	R	W
Pringle	10	0	29	1
De Groen	6	2	26	0
Cairns	7	1	21	0
Larsen	10	0	24	4
Hart	10	1	29	1
Thomson	7	1	22	2

PAKISTAN	O	M	R	W
Wasim Akram	10	1	24	1
Waqar Younis	9.4	1	30	6
Ata-ur-Rehman	4	0	22	0
Akram Raza	10	1	21	1
Aamir Sohail	9	0	29	0
Salim Malik	7	0	30	1

FALL OF WICKETS
1-38, 2-59, 3-60, 4-80, 5-85, 6-101, 7-126, 8-139, 9-146

FALL OF WICKETS
1-8, 2-9, 3-65, 4-85, 5-142, 6-144, 7-152, 8-152, 9-159, 10-161

Umpires: D.B.Cowie (6) and R.S.Dunne (15).

Referee: R.Subba Row (*England*).

NEW ZEALAND v PAKISTAN 1993-94

At Lancaster Park, Christchurch on 16 March 1994.   Result: **NEW ZEALAND** won by 7 wickets.
Toss: New Zealand.   Award: B.R.Hartland.   LOI debuts: None.

Pakistan fielded an unchanged eleven throughout the five-match series.

PAKISTAN		Runs	Balls	4/6
Saeed Anwar	c Hart b Pringle	2	21	–
Aamir Sohail	c Rutherford b Morrison	1	8	–
Inzamam-ul-Haq	c Young b Pringle	4	24	–
Asif Mujtaba	b Cairns	3	21	–
* Salim Malik	c Young b Cairns	15	34	2
Basit Ali	c Young b Pringle	57	85	3/1
† Rashid Latif	c Parore b Morrison	9	21	–
Wasim Akram	c Parore b Larsen	7	23	1
Akram Raza	not out	23	46	1
Waqar Younis	c Cairns b Morrison	4	14	–
Ata-ur-Rehman	not out	3	7	–
Extras	(lb 6, w 8, nb 3)	17		
Total	**(50 overs; 9 wickets)**	**145**		

NEW ZEALAND		Runs	Balls	4/6
B.A.Young	c Rashid b Waqar	3	19	–
B.R.Hartland	not out	68	109	4
A.H.Jones	c Rashid b Waqar	1	3	–
* K.R.Rutherford	c Akram Raza b Rehman	1	10	–
S.A.Thomson	not out	48	67	4
C.L.Cairns				
M.N.Hart				
† A.C.Parore				
G.R.Larsen				
D.K.Morrison				
C.Pringle				
Extras	(lb 8, w 14, nb 3)	25		
Total	**(34.1 overs; 3 wickets)**	**146**		

NEW ZEALAND	O	M	R	W
Morrison	10	2	20	3
Pringle	10	1	21	3
Cairns	10	0	36	2
Larsen	10	1	21	1
Hart	4	0	17	0
Thomson	6	0	24	0

PAKISTAN	O	M	R	W
Wasim Akram	6.3	0	17	0
Waqar Younis	8.1	1	33	2
Ata-ur-Rehman	9	0	44	1
Aamir Sohail	4	0	18	0
Akram Raza	3.3	0	14	0
Salim Malik	3	0	12	0

FALL OF WICKETS
1-3, 2-8, 3-17, 4-19, 5-45, 6-65, 7-86, 8-121, 9-136

Umpires: B.L.Aldridge (33) and C.E.King (5).

Referee: R.Subba Row (*England*).

NEW ZEALAND v INDIA 1993-94

At McLean Park, Napier on 25 March 1994.   Result: **NEW ZEALAND** won by 28 runs.   Toss: India.
Award: S.A.Thomson.   LOI debuts: New Zealand – S.P.Fleming.

Stephen Fleming, who scored 92 in his first Test, made his country's highest score on LOI debut. Danny Morrison achieved New Zealand's first hat-trick in internationals when he bowled Kapil Dev and Ankola with the last two balls of his eighth over, followed by Mongia with the first of his ninth.

NEW ZEALAND		Runs	Balls	4/6
B.R.Hartland	c Mongia b Srinath	8	24	–
B.A.Young	c Mongia b Srinath	11	23	2
* K.R.Rutherford	c Mongia b Ankola	23	36	3
S.P.Fleming	run out	90	107	8
S.A.Thomson	c Jadeja b Kumble	83	97	7/1
C.Z.Harris	not out	18	13	1/1
D.J.Nash	not out	1	2	–
† A.C.Parore				
G.R.Larsen				
D.K.Morrison				
C.Pringle				
Extras	(lb 2, w 3, nb 1)	6		
Total	**(50 overs; 5 wickets)**	**240**		

INDIA		Runs	Balls	4/6
A.Jadeja	c Pringle b Harris	59	93	4
N.S.Sidhu	c Parore b Larsen	34	42	4
V.G.Kambli	st Parore b Thomson	37	59	1
* M.Azharuddin	b Harris	9	20	–
S.R.Tendulkar	c Rutherford b Nash	15	19	1
S.V.Manjrekar	not out	22	29	–
Kapil Dev	b Morrison	17	16	2
S.A.Ankola	b Morrison	0	1	–
J.Srinath	c Hartland b Pringle	4	5	1
† N.R.Mongia	b Morrison	0	1	–
A.Kumble	not out	1	2	–
Extras	(b 2, lb 6, w 5, nb 1)	14		
Total	**(50 overs; 9 wickets)**	**212**		

INDIA	O	M	R	W
Kapil Dev	10	0	36	0
Srinath	10	1	59	2
Ankola	7	0	24	1
Jadeja	8	0	41	0
Kumble	10	0	41	1
Tendulkar	5	0	37	0

NEW ZEALAND	O	M	R	W
Pringle	10	1	37	1
Morrison	9	1	35	3
Nash	9	0	34	1
Larsen	9	1	40	1
Harris	8	0	32	2
Thomson	5	0	26	1

FALL OF WICKETS
1-17, 2-26, 3-60, 4-204, 5-230

FALL OF WICKETS
1-66, 2-123, 3-150, 4-152, 5-176, 6-206, 7-206, 8-211, 9-211

Umpires: R.S.Dunne (6) and D.M.Quested (16).

Referee: R.Subba Row (*England*).

NEW ZEALAND v INDIA 1993-94

At Eden Park, Auckland on 27 March 1994.   Result: **INDIA** won by 7 wickets.   Toss: New Zealand.
Award: S.R.Tendulkar.   LOI debuts: None.

Opening at international level for the first time, Sachin Tendulkar hit 2 sixes, 15 fours, a three, 3 twos and just one single – his final scoring stroke; his 50 took 34 balls. Nayan Mongia became the fourth Indian to make five dismissals in an innings. Kapil Dev extended his record tally of wickets to 250 in 218 matches.

NEW ZEALAND		Runs	Balls	4/6
B.A.Young	c Mongia b Ankola	16	48	2
B.R.Hartland	c Azharuddin b Kapil Dev	0	2	–
* K.R.Rutherford	c Azharuddin b Srinath	6	22	–
S.P.Fleming	c Mongia b Kapil Dev	6	28	–
S.A.Thomson	c Mongia b Ankola	1	8	–
C.Z.Harris	not out	50	71	3/1
† A.C.Parore	run out	23	77	1
M.N.Hart	b Chauhan	10	21	–
G.R.Larsen	st Mongia b Chauhan	5	8	1
D.K.Morrison	st Mongia b Chauhan	2	3	–
C.Pringle	b Srinath	17	11	2/1
Extras	(lb 2, w 3, nb 1)	6		
Total	(49.4 overs)	**142**		

INDIA		Runs	Balls	4/6
A.Jadeja	c Rutherford b Pringle	18	25	3
S.R.Tendulkar	c and b Hart	82	49	15/2
V.G.Kambli	c Hart b Harris	21	30	3
* M.Azharuddin	not out	12	17	–
S.V.Manjrekar	not out	7	20	–
Kapil Dev				
† N.R.Mongia				
S.A.Ankola				
J.Srinath				
A.Kumble				
R.K.Chauhan				
Extras	(w 2, nb 1)	3		
Total	(23.2 overs; 3 wickets)	**143**		

INDIA	O	M	R	W
Kapil Dev	10	1	18	2
Srinath	7.4	2	17	2
Ankola	8	0	27	2
Jadeja	4	0	6	0
Kumble	10	2	29	0
Chauhan	10	1	43	3

NEW ZEALAND	O	M	R	W
Morrison	6	0	46	0
Pringle	6	1	41	1
Larsen	2	0	24	0
Hart	5.2	0	19	1
Harris	4	1	13	1

FALL OF WICKETS
1-1, 2-11, 3-31, 4-33, 5-34, 6-86, 7-105, 8-111, 9-115, 10-142

FALL OF WICKETS
1-61, 2-117, 3-126

Umpires: B.L.Aldridge (34) and C.E.King (6).

Referee: R.Subba Row (*England*).

NEW ZEALAND v INDIA 1993-94

At Basin Reserve, Wellington on 30 March 1994.   Result: **INDIA** won by 12 runs.   Toss: New Zealand.
Award: A.Kumble.   LOI debuts: None.

Gavin Larsen was the first to appear in 50 internationals before playing Test cricket. Anil Kumble returned India's first five-wicket analysis in New Zealand.

INDIA		Runs	Balls	4/6
A.Jadeja	b Morrison	56	90	2/1
S.R.Tendulkar	lbw b Larsen	63	75	9
N.S.Sidhu	not out	71	77	3/1
V.G.Kambli	c Pringle b Nash	23	33	–
* M.Azharuddin	b Morrison	24	20	3
Kapil Dev	c Thomson b Pringle	4	4	–
† N.R.Mongia	not out	3	3	–
S.A.Ankola				
J.Srinath				
A.Kumble				
R.K.Chauhan				
Extras	(b 1, lb 4, w 6)	11		
Total	(50 overs; 5 wickets)	**255**		

NEW ZEALAND		Runs	Balls	4/6
B.A.Young	b Srinath	2	11	–
C.Z.Harris	c Jadeja b Kumble	44	52	7
B.R.Hartland	st Mongia b Kumble	21	45	2
* K.R.Rutherford	c Kapil Dev b Srinath	35	41	2
S.P.Fleming	run out	2	8	–
S.A.Thomson	st Mongia b Kumble	60	61	4/1
† A.C.Parore	b Kumble	47	61	1
G.R.Larsen	b Srinath	2	5	–
D.J.Nash	c Kapil Dev b Kumble	6	8	–
C.Pringle	not out	8	6	–
D.K.Morrison	not out	4	3	–
Extras	(b 1, lb 6, w 4, nb 1)	12		
Total	(50 overs; 9 wickets)	**243**		

NEW ZEALAND	O	M	R	W
Pringle	7	0	36	1
Morrison	10	0	57	2
Nash	9	0	55	1
Larsen	10	0	33	1
Harris	5	0	30	0
Thomson	9	0	39	0

INDIA	O	M	R	W
Kapil Dev	8	0	40	0
Srinath	10	3	31	3
Ankola	10	0	55	0
Kumble	10	0	33	5
Chauhan	5	0	30	0
Jadeja	5	0	35	0
Tendulkar	2	0	12	0

FALL OF WICKETS
1-105, 2-154, 3-199, 4-237, 5-248

FALL OF WICKETS
1-5, 2-65, 3-70, 4-76, 5-131, 6-216, 7-221, 8-231, 9-232

Umpires: R.S.Dunne (17) and C.E.King (7).

Referee: R.Subba Row (*England*).

NEW ZEALAND v INDIA 1993-94

At Lancaster Park, Christchurch on 2 April 1994.　　Result: **NEW ZEALAND** won by 6 wickets.　　Toss: India.
Award: A.C.Parore.　　LOI debuts: India – B.K.V.Prasad.

An unbroken fifth-wicket partnership of 88 from 89 balls between Shane Thomson and Adam Parore took New Zealand to a series-levelling win with one ball to spare. They had needed 40 from the last five overs and ten from the final one.

INDIA		Runs	Balls	4/6
A.Jadeja	c Rutherford b Pringle	68	132	3
S.R.Tendulkar	b Larsen	40	26	8
N.S.Sidhu	c Nash b Harris	9	11	1
V.G.Kambli	run out	19	32	2
* M.Azharuddin	c Larsen b Hart	1	8	–
Kapil Dev	b Morrison	15	38	–
† N.R.Mongia	not out	40	39	5
A.Kumble	not out	18	14	1/1
S.A.Ankola				
J.Srinath				
B.K.V.Prasad				
Extras	(lb 7, w 5)	12		
Total	(50 overs; 6 wickets)	**222**		

NEW ZEALAND		Runs	Balls	4/6
B.A.Young	b Kumble	43	79	5
C.Z.Harris	lbw b Kapil Dev	0	11	–
* K.R.Rutherford	c and b Kumble	61	90	5/1
S.P.Fleming	c Prasad b Kumble	25	33	3
S.A.Thomson	not out	40	43	2
† A.C.Parore	not out	47	46	4
D.J.Nash				
G.R.Larsen				
M.N.Hart				
D.K.Morrison				
C.Pringle				
Extras	(lb 2, w 4, nb 1)	7		
Total	(49.5 overs; 4 wickets)	**223**		

NEW ZEALAND	O	M	R	W
Morrison	10	1	47	1
Pringle	6	0	43	1
Nash	5	0	33	0
Larsen	9	1	37	1
Harris	10	1	25	1
Hart	10	1	30	1

INDIA	O	M	R	W
Kapil Dev	8	3	20	1
Srinath	9.5	0	46	0
Prasad	9	0	49	0
Ankola	8	0	37	0
Kumble	10	0	47	3
Tendulkar	5	0	22	0

FALL OF WICKETS
1-61, 2-80, 3-114, 4-118, 5-150, 6-183

FALL OF WICKETS
1-7, 2-89, 3-135, 4-135

Umpires: B.L.Aldridge (35) and D.B.Cowie (7).

Referee: R.Subba Row (*England*).

UNITED ARAB EMIRATES v INDIA 1993-94

At Sharjah CA Stadium, UAE on 13 April 1994.　　Result: **INDIA** won by 71 runs.　　Toss: United Arab Emirates.
Award: V.G.Kambli.　　LOI debuts: UAE – all; India – A.C.Bedade, Bhupinder Singh.

Sponsored by Pepsi Foods, the third Austral-Asia Cup introduced the UAE to official international status. Winners of the ICC Trophy, the Emirates team included ten recent immigrants from the Indian subcontinent. Sachin Tendulkar (20 years, 356 days) became the youngest to score 2000 LOI runs.

INDIA		Runs	Balls	4/6
A.Jadeja	c Arshad b Sohail	25	37	2
S.R.Tendulkar	c Imtiaz b Zarawani	63	77	7/1
N.S.Sidhu	b Sohail	0	7	–
* M.Azharuddin	c Samarasekera b Salim	81	99	4/2
V.G.Kambli	not out	82	66	4/3
A.C.Bedade	c Imtiaz b Samarasekera	7	10	1
† N.R.Mongia	not out	4	7	–
A.Kumble				
Bhupinder Singh				
J.Srinath				
S.L.V.Raju				
Extras	(b 1, lb 2, w 6, nb 2)	11		
Total	(50 overs; 5 wickets)	**273**		

UNITED ARAB EMIRATES		Runs	Balls	4/6
R.H.Poonawalla	c Mongia b Bhupinder Singh	22	14	5
Azhar Saeed	c Mongia b Srinath	3	10	–
Mazhar Hussain	c Jadeja b Bhupinder Singh	70	112	5
V.Mehra	c Mongia b Bhupinder Singh	43	83	6
Mohammad Ishaq	c Jadeja b Srinath	23	29	2
Salim Raza	c Mongia b Srinath	6	8	1
J.A.Samarasekera	c Tendulkar b Raju	3	8	–
Arshad Laiq	b Kumble	4	7	–
* Sultan M.Zarawani	b Kumble	4	13	–
† Imtiaz Abbasi	not out	6	11	1
Sohail Butt	not out	6	9	1
Extras	(lb 4, w 5, nb 3)	12		
Total	(50 overs; 9 wickets)	**202**		

UNITED ARAB EMIRATES	O	M	R	W
Samarasekera	10	0	48	1
Sohail Butt	10	0	52	2
Arshad Laiq	10	0	56	0
Azhar Saeed	10	1	38	0
Zarawani	3	0	22	1
Salim Raza	7	0	54	1

INDIA	O	M	R	W
Srinath	10	1	49	3
Bhupinder Singh	10	1	34	3
Jadeja	5	0	32	0
Tendulkar	5	0	22	0
Raju	10	0	31	1
Kumble	10	0	30	2

FALL OF WICKETS
1-49, 2-55, 3-130, 4-230, 5-254

FALL OF WICKETS
1-26, 2-26, 3-120, 4-161, 5-169, 6-182, 7-183, 8-189, 9-192

Umpires: K.Kanjee (*Zimbabwe*) (4) and S.B.Lambson (*South Africa*) (12).

Referee: A.M.Ibrahim (*Zimbabwe*).

AUSTRALIA v SRI LANKA 1993-94

At Sharjah CA Stadium, UAE on 14 April 1994.   Result: **AUSTRALIA** won by 9 wickets.   Toss: Sri Lanka.
Award: M.E.Waugh.   LOI debuts: Australia – M.G.Bevan, J.L.Langer; Sri Lanka – U.U.Chandana, A.M.N.Munasinghe.

Led by Roshan Mahanama for the first time, following a players' revolt prior to this tournament, Sri Lanka were easily defeated by an equally depleted Australian side lacking a specialist wicket-keeper.

SRI LANKA		Runs	Balls	4/6
* R.S.Mahanama	lbw b Reiffel	10	19	1
M.A.R.Samarasekera	c Langer b S.R.Waugh	24	40	3
A.P.Gurusinha	run out	1	16	–
S.T.Jayasuriya	run out	8	30	1
H.P.Tillekeratne	c Taylor b S.R.Waugh	64	97	4
R.S.Kalpage	c Bevan b Warne	4	28	–
U.U.Chandana	c Bevan b Reiffel	18	37	1
† P.B.Dassanayake	lbw b Warne	7	7	–
C.P.H.Ramanayake	lbw b Warne	2	7	–
A.M.N.Munasinghe	b Fleming	2	19	–
W.P.U.C.J.Vaas	not out	0	3	–
Extras	(lb 10, w 1, nb 3)	14		
Total	(49.3 overs)	**154**		

AUSTRALIA	O	M	R	W
Reiffel	10	1	28	2
Fleming	9.3	1	27	1
S.R.Waugh	6	0	17	2
May	10	0	25	0
Warne	10	1	29	3
M.E.Waugh	4	0	18	0

FALL OF WICKETS
1-30, 2-38, 3-40, 4-61, 5-91, 6-124, 7-136, 8-142, 9-153, 10-154

Umpires: K.Kanjee (Zimbabwe) (5) and K.E.Liebenberg (SA) (22).

AUSTRALIA		Runs	Balls	4/6
* M.A.Taylor	not out	68	106	4
M.J.Slater	b Vaas	15	33	1
M.E.Waugh	not out	64	83	6
M.L.Hayden				
M.G.Bevan				
S.R.Waugh				
† J.L.Langer				
P.R.Reiffel				
S.K.Warne				
T.B.A.May				
D.W.Fleming				
Extras	(b 1, lb 7, w 3)	11		
Total	(36.5 overs; 1 wicket)	**158**		

SRI LANKA	O	M	R	W
Ramanayake	8	1	15	0
Vaas	10	1	35	1
Munasinghe	6.5	0	28	0
Jayasuriya	4	0	22	0
Kalpage	5	0	29	0
Chandana	3	0	21	0

FALL OF WICKETS
1-25

Referee: A.M.Ibrahim (Zimbabwe).

INDIA v PAKISTAN 1993-94

At Sharjah CA Stadium, UAE on 15 April 1994.   Result: **PAKISTAN** won by 6 wickets.   Toss: Pakistan.
Award: Saeed Anwar.   LOI debuts: None.

India, overcoming their objections of bias to return to Sharjah after a 2½-year interlude, met Pakistan for the first time since March 1992. Sachin Tendulkar and Saeed Anwar scored fifties off 42 and 40 balls respectively.

INDIA		Runs	Balls	4/6
A.Jadeja	c Rashid b Aqib	19	45	2
S.R.Tendulkar	c Basit b Akram Raza	73	64	10/3
N.S.Sidhu	c Rashid b Rehman	47	68	3
* M.Azharuddin	c Inzamam b Salim	29	34	2/1
A.C.Bedade	st Rashid b Salim	1	3	–
V.G.Kambli	c Akram Raza b Rehman	4	13	–
† N.R.Mongia	run out	5	9	–
A.Kumble	b Wasim	6	13	–
Bhupinder Singh	run out	6	13	–
R.K.Chauhan	c Saeed b Aqib	13	18	1/1
J.Srinath	not out	1	2	–
Extras	(lb 2, w 10, nb 3)	15		
Total	(46.3 overs)	**219**		

PAKISTAN	O	M	R	W
Wasim Akram	8.3	1	36	1
Aqib Javed	9	1	41	2
Ata-ur-Rehman	9	0	50	2
Salim Malik	10	0	49	2
Akram Raza	10	0	41	1

FALL OF WICKETS
1-62, 2-111, 3-156, 4-164, 5-179, 6-187, 7-187, 8-197, 9-218, 10-219

Umpires: S.B.Lambson (SA) (13) and K.E.Liebenberg (SA) (23).

PAKISTAN		Runs	Balls	4/6
Saeed Anwar	lbw b Chauhan	71	69	9/2
Aamir Sohail	b Chauhan	20	39	3
Inzamam-ul-Haq	c Mongia b Chauhan	1	11	–
* Salim Malik	c Azharuddin b Srinath	25	51	–
Basit Ali	not out	75	77	6/1
Asif Mujtaba	not out	16	25	2
Wasim Akram				
† Rashid Latif				
Akram Raza				
Aqib Javed				
Ata-ur-Rehman				
Extras	(lb 4, w 7, nb 4)	15		
Total	(44.3 overs; 4 wickets)	**223**		

INDIA	O	M	R	W
Srinath	9.3	0	59	1
Bhupinder Singh	7	0	44	0
Kumble	9	0	26	0
Chauhan	10	0	47	3
Tendulkar	8	0	34	0
Jadeja	1	0	9	0

FALL OF WICKETS
1-77, 2-89, 3-106, 4-171

Referee: A.M.Ibrahim (Zimbabwe).

AUSTRALIA v NEW ZEALAND 1993-94

At Sharjah CA Stadium, UAE on 16 April 1994.   Result: **AUSTRALIA** won by 7 wickets.   Toss: New Zealand.
Award: S.K.Warne.   LOI debuts: New Zealand – M.W.Douglas.

Gavin Larsen, playing in his 52nd LOI but still awaiting his Test match call-up, led New Zealand for the first time.

NEW ZEALAND		Runs	Balls	4/6
B.A.Young	c and b Fleming	63	97	8
B.R.Hartland	lbw b Warne	23	49	3
M.W.Douglas	lbw b Warne	0	2	–
S.P.Fleming	c Taylor b Fleming	35	47	3
S.A.Thomson	c Taylor b Fleming	32	42	3
A.C.Parore	c and b Warne	12	27	–
* G.R.Larsen	not out	9	11	–
M.N.Hart	c Hayden b Fleming	2	5	–
D.K.Morrison	b McGrath	2	3	–
C.Pringle	not out	2	2	–
Extras	(b 1, lb 6, w 2, nb 4)	13		
Total	(50 overs; 9 wickets)	**207**		

AUSTRALIA		Runs	Balls	4/6
M.J.Slater	b Morrison	0	2	–
M.L.Hayden	c Harris b Pringle	67	106	10
D.C.Boon	c sub (D.J.Nash) b Thomson	68	98	10/1
M.G.Bevan	not out	39	63	1
† J.L.Langer	not out	20	18	3
* M.A.Taylor				
S.R.Waugh				
P.R.Reiffel				
S.K.Warne				
G.D.McGrath				
D.W.Fleming				
Extras	(lb 11, w 3)	14		
Total	(47.5 overs; 3 wickets)	**208**		

AUSTRALIA	O	M	R	W
Reiffel	10	0	35	0
McGrath	10	0	44	1
Waugh	10	1	48	0
Warne	10	0	34	4
Fleming	10	0	39	4

NEW ZEALAND	O	M	R	W
Morrison	6	2	22	1
Pringle	9.5	1	43	1
Larsen	9	0	42	0
Harris	6	0	25	0
Hart	7	0	26	0
Thomson	10	2	39	1

FALL OF WICKETS
1-75, 2-75, 3-126, 4-135, 5-170, 6-184, 7-192, 8-202, 9-204

FALL OF WICKETS
1-0, 2-123, 3-166

Umpires: K.Kanjee (*Zimbabwe*) (6) and S.B.Lambson (*South Africa*) (14).

Referee: A.M.Ibrahim (*Zimbabwe*).

UNITED ARAB EMIRATES v PAKISTAN 1993-94

At Sharjah CA Stadium, UAE on 17 April 1994.   Result: **PAKISTAN** won by 9 wickets.   Toss: United Arab Emirates.
Award: Ata-ur-Rehman.   LOI debuts: None.

The Emirates, 68 for 6 after 25 overs, were rescued from total disaster by a seventh-wicket partnership of 57 in 19.2 overs between Johanne Samarasekera, younger brother of Sri Lanka's Athula, and Arshad Laiq.

UNITED ARAB EMIRATES		Runs	Balls	4/6
R.H.Poonawalla	c Rashid b Rehman	22	42	3
Azhar Saeed	c Akram Raza b Wasim	0	10	–
Mazhar Hussain	c Rashid b Rehman	10	33	1
V.Mehra	c Aamir b Salim	5	7	1
Mohammad Ishaq	c Rashid b Salim	4	17	–
Salim Raza	c Akram Raza b Wasim	16	29	1
J.A.Samarasekera	not out	31	75	–
Arshad Laiq	c Wasim b Salim	31	68	2/2
* Sultan M.Zarawani	run out	6	13	–
† Imtiaz Abbasi	b Wasim	2	5	–
Sohail Butt	b Rehman	2	5	–
Extras	(lb 2, w 10, nb 4)	16		
Total	(49.5 overs)	**145**		

PAKISTAN		Runs	Balls	4/6
Saeed Anwar	c Poonawalla b Salim	39	28	6/1
Aamir Sohail	not out	51	67	7
Inzamam-ul-Haq	not out	50	47	9
* Salim Malik				
Basit Ali				
Asif Mujtaba				
Wasim Akram				
† Rashid Latif				
Akram Raza				
Aqib Javed				
Ata-ur-Rehman				
Extras	(lb 2, w 4)	6		
Total	(23.1 overs; 1 wicket)	**146**		

PAKISTAN	O	M	R	W
Wasim Akram	10	1	19	3
Aqib Javed	10	2	29	0
Ata-ur-Rehman	9.5	0	32	3
Salim Malik	10	1	42	3
Akram Raza	10	3	21	0

UNITED ARAB EMIRATES	O	M	R	W
Samarasekera	5	0	31	0
Sohail Butt	3	0	27	0
Arshad Laiq	4	0	25	0
Salim Raza	3	1	17	1
Azhar Saeed	4.1	0	18	0
Zarawani	4	0	26	0

FALL OF WICKETS
1-7, 2-40, 3-45, 4-45, 5-65, 6-68, 7-125, 8-138, 9-141, 10-145

FALL OF WICKETS
1-76

Umpires: K.Kanjee (*Zimbabwe*) (7) and K.E.Liebenberg (*SA*) (24).

Referee: A.M.Ibrahim (*Zimbabwe*).

NEW ZEALAND v SRI LANKA 1993-94

At Sharjah CA Stadium, UAE on 18 April 1994.　　Result: **NEW ZEALAND** won by 2 runs.　　Toss: Sri Lanka.
Award: A.P.Gurusinha.　　LOI debuts: New Zealand – H.T.Davis; Sri Lanka – A.P.Weerakkody.

Asanka Gurusinha's first hundred in 91 internationals was the first by a Sri Lankan in Sharjah. The closest finish of the tournament culminated in his needing ten off Dion Nash's last two balls; he managed a six and a single. Shane Thomson reached his 50 off 41 balls.

NEW ZEALAND		Runs	Balls	4/6
B.R.Hartland	run out	5	9	1
B.A.Young	c Jayasuriya b Gurusinha	34	59	3
† A.C.Parore	c Dassanayake b Jayasuriya	37	72	3
M.W.Douglas	run out	30	54	1/1
S.P.Fleming	c Tillekeratne b Kalpage	14	16	–/1
S.A.Thomson	c Chandana b Vaas	50	42	3/2
C.Z.Harris	c Chandana b Ramanayake	22	35	–
D.J.Nash	run out	2	4	–
* G.R.Larsen	not out	14	9	–/1
C.Pringle	not out	0	–	–
H.T.Davis				
Extras	(b 1, lb 5, w 3)	9		
Total	(50 overs; 8 wickets)	**217**		

SRI LANKA		O	M	R	W
Ramanayake		10	1	41	1
Vaas		10	1	31	1
Weerakkody		6	0	41	0
Gurusinha		10	1	30	1
Jayasuriya		7	0	37	1
Kalpage		7	0	31	1

SRI LANKA		Runs	Balls	4/6
* R.S.Mahanama	lbw b Pringle	18	23	3
M.A.R.Samarasekera	c Fleming b Nash	4	11	–
A.P.Gurusinha	not out	117	140	9/1
S.T.Jayasuriya	c Davis b Nash	5	7	1
H.P.Tillekeratne	run out	0	11	–
U.U.Chandana	c Young b Nash	26	69	1
R.S.Kalpage	c Harris b Thomson	6	11	–
† P.B.Dassanayake	c Parore b Larsen	5	3	1
C.P.H.Ramanayake	b Pringle	21	21	1
A.P.Weerakkody	c Nash b Pringle	2	4	–
W.P.U.C.J.Vaas	not out	1	2	–
Extras	(b 1, lb 6, w 3)	10		
Total	(50 overs; 9 wickets)	**215**		

NEW ZEALAND	O	M	R	W
Pringle	10	1	46	3
Davis	2	0	14	0
Nash	10	1	43	3
Larsen	10	1	34	1
Harris	9	0	33	0
Thomson	9	0	38	1

FALL OF WICKETS
1-12, 2-68, 3-94, 4-121, 5-135, 6-194, 7-198, 8-206

FALL OF WICKETS
1-24, 2-24, 3-30, 4-41, 5-129, 6-147, 7-152, 8-189, 9-202

Umpires: S.B.Lambson (SA) (15) and K.E.Liebenberg (SA) (25).　　　　**Referee:** A.M.Ibrahim (Zimbabwe).

AUSTRALIA v INDIA 1993-94

At Sharjah CA Stadium, UAE on 19 April 1994.　　Result: **INDIA** won by 7 wickets.　　Toss: Australia.
Award: A.Jadeja.　　LOI debuts: None.

Shane Warne conceded 22 off his ninth over, including two sixes and two fours to Vinod Kambli, after bowling his first eight for only 18 runs. Justice Ahmed Ibrahim, the first ICC referee not to have played first-class cricket, fined Nayan Mongia $US750 for excessive appealing.

AUSTRALIA		Runs	Balls	4/6
* M.A.Taylor	b Srinath	11	33	1
D.C.Boon	b Kumble	21	45	2
M.E.Waugh	run out	16	26	2
S.R.Waugh	c Mongia b Srinath	53	72	2
M.G.Bevan	c Jadeja b Kumble	25	30	1
M.L.Hayden	c Jadeja b Kumble	48	46	4
† J.L.Langer	run out	36	22	1/3
P.R.Reiffel	c Tendulkar b Srinath	7	12	–
S.K.Warne	run out	4	13	–
D.W.Fleming	not out	2	3	–
G.D.McGrath	not out	0	1	–
Extras	(lb 14, w 6, nb 1)	21		
Total	(50 overs; 9 wickets)	**244**		

INDIA		O	M	R	W
Srinath		9	1	32	3
Prasad		8	1	39	0
Kumble		10	1	50	3
Chauhan		10	2	37	0
Tendulkar		8	0	39	0
Jadeja		5	0	33	0

INDIA		Runs	Balls	4/6
A.Jadeja	c Boon b Warne	87	106	12/1
S.R.Tendulkar	c Taylor b McGrath	6	7	1
N.S.Sidhu	st Langer b Warne	80	110	5
* M.Azharuddin	not out	36	37	2
V.G.Kambli	not out	28	17	3/2
A.C.Bedade				
† N.R.Mongia				
A.Kumble				
B.K.V.Prasad				
R.K.Chauhan				
J.Srinath				
Extras	(lb 4, w 2, nb 2)	8		
Total	(45.4 overs; 3 wickets)	**245**		

AUSTRALIA	O	M	R	W
McGrath	8	0	35	1
Reiffel	8	0	32	0
S.R.Waugh	8	0	52	0
Fleming	9.4	0	59	0
Warne	8	0	40	2
M.E.Waugh	3	0	23	0

FALL OF WICKETS
1-29, 2-53, 3-62, 4-115, 5-158, 6-222, 7-227, 8-241, 9-244

FALL OF WICKETS
1-11, 2-141, 3-210

Umpires: K.Kanjee (Zimbabwe) (8) and S.B.Lambson (South Africa) (16).　　　**Referee:** A.M.Ibrahim (Zimbabwe).

NEW ZEALAND v PAKISTAN 1993-94

At Sharjah CA Stadium, UAE on 20 April 1994.   Result: **PAKISTAN** won by 62 runs.   Toss: New Zealand.
Award: Inzamam-ul-Haq.   LOI debuts: None.

Aamir Sohail and Inzamam-ul-Haq, who registered Pakistan's highest score and completed 2000 runs, shared a world-record LOI partnership for any wicket, adding 263 from 251 balls to eclipse the previous highest stand by 39 runs. Pakistan's total remains the highest scored against New Zealand. Dion Nash was fined $US350 for swearing at Saeed Anwar.

PAKISTAN		Runs	Balls	4/6
Saeed Anwar	c Parore b Nash	37	23	6/1
Aamir Sohail	c Douglas b Pringle	134	146	13
Inzamam-ul-Haq	not out	137	129	15
Wasim Akram	not out	7	4	–/1
* Salim Malik				
Basit Ali				
Asif Mujtaba				
† Rashid Latif				
Akram Raza				
Ata-ur-Rehman				
Aqib Javed				
Extras	(b 1, lb 2, w 8, nb 2)	13		
Total	(50 overs; 2 wickets)	**328**		

NEW ZEALAND		Runs	Balls	4/6
B.A.Young	c Saeed b Rehman	36	35	6
B.R.Hartland	c Rashid b Wasim	11	19	2
† A.C.Parore	c sub (Ijaz Ahmed) b Salim	82	102	5
S.A.Thomson	run out	62	89	3
S.P.Fleming	b Aamir	1	2	–
M.W.Douglas	b Salim	3	5	–
C.Z.Harris	not out	34	27	3
D.J.Nash	b Wasim	2	5	–
* G.R.Larsen	not out	18	22	1
C.Pringle				
H.T.Davis				
Extras	(lb 6, w 7, nb 4)	17		
Total	(50 overs; 7 wickets)	**266**		

NEW ZEALAND	O	M	R	W
Pringle	10	0	57	1
Davis	4	0	37	0
Nash	9	0	60	1
Larsen	10	0	71	0
Thomson	7	0	44	0
Harris	10	0	56	0

PAKISTAN	O	M	R	W
Wasim Akram	10	0	50	2
Aqib Javed	10	0	56	0
Ata-ur-Rehman	5	0	35	1
Akram Raza	10	0	42	0
Salim Malik	10	0	55	2
Aamir Sohail	5	0	22	1

FALL OF WICKETS
1-57, 2-320

FALL OF WICKETS
1-19, 2-66, 3-199, 4-202, 5-204, 6-207, 7-218

Umpires: K.Kanjee (*Zimbabwe*) (9) and K.E.Liebenberg (*SA*) (26).   **Referee:** A.M.Ibrahim (*Zimbabwe*).

INDIA v PAKISTAN 1993-94

At Sharjah CA Stadium, UAE on 22 April 1994.   Result: **PAKISTAN** won by 39 runs.   Toss: India.
Award: Aamir Sohail.   LOI debuts: None.

Pakistan gained their 12th victory against India in 15 internationals at Sharjah to complete a hat-trick of Austral-Asia Cup titles; they are its only holders.

PAKISTAN		Runs	Balls	4/6
Saeed Anwar	c Prasad b Chauhan	47	63	7/1
Aamir Sohail	b Srinath	69	87	6
Inzamam-ul-Haq	st Mongia b Chauhan	12	26	–
* Salim Malik	c Azharuddin b Chauhan	1	3	–
Basit Ali	b Srinath	57	58	3/2
Asif Mujtaba	not out	34	52	1
Wasim Akram	c Azharuddin b Srinath	2	5	–
† Rashid Latif	not out	17	12	3
Akram Raza				
Aqib Javed				
Ata-ur-Rehman				
Extras	(lb 3, w 3, nb 5)	11		
Total	(50 overs; 6 wickets)	**250**		

INDIA		Runs	Balls	4/6
A.Jadeja	c Basit b Wasim	0	3	–
S.R.Tendulkar	c Aamir b Rehman	24	26	4
N.S.Sidhu	c and b Akram Raza	36	61	5
* M.Azharuddin	c Rashid b Aqib	3	3	–
V.G.Kambli	c Akram Raza b Salim	56	99	1
A.C.Bedade	c Asif b Aamir	44	45	1/4
† N.R.Mongia	c and b Aamir	3	10	–
A.Kumble	c Rashid b Salim	12	18	1
R.K.Chauhan	run out	5	17	–
J.Srinath	not out	6	9	–
B.K.V.Prasad	lbw b Wasim	0	4	–
Extras	(lb 4, w 10, nb 8)	22		
Total	(47.4 overs)	**211**		

INDIA	O	M	R	W
Srinath	10	0	56	3
Prasad	9	1	44	0
Kumble	10	0	56	0
Chauhan	9	0	29	3
Tendulkar	8	0	45	0
Jadeja	4	0	17	0

PAKISTAN	O	M	R	W
Wasim Akram	8.4	0	39	2
Aqib Javed	7	1	27	1
Ata-ur-Rehman	8	0	27	1
Akram Raza	10	0	47	1
Salim Malik	9	0	45	2
Aamir Sohail	5	0	22	2

FALL OF WICKETS
1-96, 2-125, 3-127, 4-149, 5-215, 6-219

FALL OF WICKETS
1-1, 2-60, 3-63, 4-83, 5-163, 6-180, 7-182, 8-203, 9-209, 10-211

Umpires: S.B.Lambson (*SA*) (17) and K.E.Liebenberg (*SA*) (27).   **Referee:** A.M.Ibrahim (*Zimbabwe*).

ENGLAND v NEW ZEALAND 1994

At Edgbaston, Birmingham on 19 May 1994.   Result: **ENGLAND** won by 42 runs.   Toss: New Zealand.
Award: M.A.Atherton.   LOI debuts: England – D.Gough, S.D.Udal.

Chris Pringle remains the only bowler to take five wickets in the 47 matches under the Texaco Trophy banner. Darren Gough took a wicket with his sixth ball. The second match, at Lord's on 21-22 May, was abandoned without a ball bowled, the first such instance involving England at home.

ENGLAND		Runs	Balls	4/6	NEW ZEALAND		Runs	Balls	4/6
* M.A.Atherton	run out	81	137	8	B.A.Young	b Gough	65	114	4
A.J.Stewart	c Nash b Pringle	24	30	2	M.D.Crowe	c Stewart b Gough	0	3	–
R.A.Smith	c Parore b Thomson	15	38	1	† A.C.Parore	b Udal	42	65	4
G.A.Gooch	b Thomson	23	40	1	* K.R.Rutherford	lbw b Udal	0	5	–
G.A.Hick	b Pringle	18	32	1	S.P.Fleming	c and b Hick	17	28	2
D.A.Reeve	c Fleming b Pringle	16	26	–	S.A.Thomson	c Lewis b Hick	7	25	–
† S.J.Rhodes	c Thomson b Pringle	12	13	–/1	G.R.Larsen	c and b Lewis	13	20	1/1
C.C.Lewis	b Pringle	19	10	3	D.J.Nash	b Lewis	0	2	–
S.D.Udal	not out	3	4	–	M.N.Hart	c Stewart b Lewis	13	28	1
D.Gough					C.Pringle	c Hick b Fraser	3	3	–
A.R.C.Fraser					D.K.Morrison	not out	17	24	1
Extras	(b 1, lb 5, w 7)	13			Extras	(lb 4, w 1)	5		
Total	(55 overs; 8 wickets)	**224**			**Total**	(52.5 overs)	**182**		

NEW ZEALAND	O	M	R	W	ENGLAND	O	M	R	W
Morrison	6	0	31	0	Fraser	10	0	37	1
Pringle	11	1	45	5	Gough	11	1	36	2
Nash	6	1	20	0	Udal	11	0	39	2
Larsen	10	1	43	0	Reeve	4	0	15	0
Hart	11	0	45	0	Lewis	9.5	2	20	3
Thomson	11	0	34	2	Hick	7	0	31	2

FALL OF WICKETS
1-33, 2-84, 3-140, 4-161, 5-180, 6-199, 7-199, 8-224

FALL OF WICKETS
1-2, 2-78, 3-81, 4-110, 5-134, 6-136, 7-136, 8-149, 9-152, 10-182

Umpires: R.Palmer (7) and N.T.Plews (5).

Referee: C.H.Lloyd (*West Indies*).

ENGLAND v SOUTH AFRICA 1994

At Edgbaston, Birmingham on 25 August 1994.   Result: **ENGLAND** won by 6 wickets.   Toss: South Africa.
Award: G.A.Hick.   LOI debuts: None.

The highlight of this contest was the announcement that Michael Atherton would captain the imminent tour to Australia and become England's youngest Ashes captain since the Honourable Ivo Bligh in 1882-83.

SOUTH AFRICA		Runs	Balls	4/6	ENGLAND		Runs	Balls	4/6
* K.C.Wessels	b DeFreitas	4	8	1	* M.A.Atherton	run out	49	80	7
G.Kirsten	c DeFreitas b Lewis	30	48	5	A.J.Stewart	c De Villiers b Shaw	32	70	4
P.N.Kirsten	c Rhodes b DeFreitas	8	27	–	G.A.Hick	c Shaw b Snell	81	116	5/1
J.N.Rhodes	c Thorpe b Cork	35	52	3	G.P.Thorpe	run out	26	41	1
D.J.Cullinan	b DeFreitas	45	87	4	N.H.Fairbrother	not out	19	19	3
W.J.Cronje	b Lewis	36	66	2/1	† S.J.Rhodes	not out	0	–	–
† D.J.Richardson	not out	20	18	1	C.C.Lewis				
R.P.Snell	c Gough b Lewis	2	4	–	P.A.J.DeFreitas				
T.G.Shaw	not out	17	22	–	D.G.Cork				
C.R.Matthews					D.Gough				
P.S.de Villiers					S.D.Udal				
Extras	(lb 6, w 10, nb 2)	18			Extras	(lb 9, w 2, nb 1)	12		
Total	(55 overs; 7 wickets)	**215**			**Total**	(54 overs; 4 wickets)	**219**		

ENGLAND	O	M	R	W	SOUTH AFRICA	O	M	R	W
DeFreitas	9	1	38	3	De Villiers	11	2	27	0
Gough	11	2	40	0	Matthews	11	1	42	0
Lewis	8	0	32	3	Shaw	11	0	34	1
Udal	11	0	34	0	Cronje	9	0	50	0
Cork	11	0	46	1	Snell	11	0	49	1
Hick	5	1	19	0	G.Kirsten	1	0	8	0

FALL OF WICKETS
1-5, 2-30, 3-58, 4-103, 5-174, 6-176, 7-182

FALL OF WICKETS
1-57, 2-126, 3-181, 4-215

Umpires: J.C.Balderstone (1) and H.D.Bird (67).

Referee: P.J.P.Burge (*Australia*).

ENGLAND v SOUTH AFRICA 1994

At Old Trafford, Manchester on 27, 28 August 1994.   Result: **ENGLAND** won by 4 wickets.   Toss: England.
Award: S.J.Rhodes.   LOI debuts: None.

The hosts gained their fourth win in as many meetings with South Africa. Playing in his 87th international, Phillip DeFreitas became the second bowler after Ian Botham to take 100 wickets for England, the latter being 80 for 4 after 26.5 overs when rain brought a premature close to the first day.

SOUTH AFRICA		Runs	Balls	4/6
G.Kirsten	c Lewis b Cork	30	78	3
* K.C.Wessels	lbw b DeFreitas	21	39	3
W.J.Cronje	run out	0	12	–
J.N.Rhodes	lbw b Cork	0	1	–
D.J.Cullinan	run out	54	92	4
B.M.McMillan	st Rhodes b Udal	0	7	–
† D.J.Richardson	c Lewis b Gough	14	54	–
T.G.Shaw	b Gough	6	7	1
C.R.Matthews	b Cork	26	29	2
P.S.de Villiers	not out	14	9	–/1
A.A.Donald	not out	2	7	–
Extras	(lb 6, w 4, nb 4)	14		
Total	(55 overs; 9 wickets)	181		

ENGLAND		Runs	Balls	4/6
* M.A.Atherton	c Wessels b Matthews	19	50	2
A.J.Stewart	c Cullinan b Donald	11	18	2
G.A.Hick	lbw b Donald	0	1	–
G.P.Thorpe	c Cullinan b Shaw	55	116	6
N.H.Fairbrother	run out	3	10	–
† S.J.Rhodes	run out	56	75	7
C.C.Lewis	not out	17	30	1
P.A.J.DeFreitas	not out	7	2	1
D.G.Cork				
D.Gough				
S.D.Udal				
Extras	(w 4, nb 10)	14		
Total	(48.2 overs; 6 wickets)	182		

ENGLAND	O	M	R	W
DeFreitas	11	4	12	1
Gough	10	1	39	2
Lewis	9	0	44	0
Udal	11	2	17	1
Cork	11	1	49	3
Hick	3	0	14	0

SOUTH AFRICA	O	M	R	W
Donald	10.2	1	47	2
De Villiers	8	1	29	0
McMillan	10	1	53	0
Matthews	9	2	20	1
Shaw	11	0	33	1

FALL OF WICKETS
1-43, 2-47, 3-47, 4-64, 5-68, 6-113, 7-121, 8-163, 9-163

FALL OF WICKETS
1-27, 2-28, 3-42, 4-60, 5-130, 6-171

Umpires: M.J.Kitchen (11) and K.E.Palmer (19).

Referee: P.J.P.Burge (*Australia*).

SRI LANKA v PAKISTAN 1994-95

At R.Premadasa Stadium, Khettarama, Colombo on 3 August 1994.   Result: **PAKISTAN** won by 9 wickets (revised target).
Toss: Sri Lanka.   Award: Saeed Anwar.   LOI debuts: Sri Lanka – S.Ranatunga; Pakistan – Ashfaq Ahmed.

Sanjeeva's first appearance, before a crowd of 40,000, took the tally of Ranatunga brethren to represent Sri Lanka at this level to four. A brief deluge reduced Pakistan's target to 169 from 42 overs. The Khetterama stadium had recently been renamed after Sri Lanka's assassinated president, Ranasinghe Premadasa.

SRI LANKA		Runs	Balls	4/6
S.T.Jayasuriya	c Akram Raza b Salim	77	106	4/1
S.Ranatunga	st Rashid b Salim	31	84	–
A.P.Gurusinha	b Akram Raza	5	15	–
P.A.de Silva	run out	15	24	–
* A.Ranatunga	run out	33	38	2
H.P.Tillekeratne	run out	13	25	–
R.S.Kalpage	not out	7	7	–
† P.B.Dassanayake	not out	5	4	–
C.P.H.Ramanayake				
G.P.Wickremasinghe				
M.Muralitharan				
Extras	(lb 4, w 6, nb 4)	14		
Total	(50 overs; 6 wickets)	200		

PAKISTAN		Runs	Balls	4/6
Saeed Anwar	not out	70	83	8
Aamir Sohail	c Tillekeratne b Muralitharan	38	42	5
Inzamam-ul-Haq	not out	53	53	6/1
* Salim Malik				
Asif Mujtaba				
Zahid Fazal				
† Rashid Latif				
Wasim Akram				
Akram Raza				
Waqar Younis				
Ashfaq Ahmed				
Extras	(b 3, lb 5)	8		
Total	(30.2 overs; 1 wicket)	169		

PAKISTAN	O	M	R	W
Wasim Akram	10	0	38	0
Waqar Younis	8	2	38	0
Ashfaq Ahmed	8	1	33	0
Akram Raza	10	1	27	1
Salim Malik	10	0	44	2
Aamir Sohail	4	0	16	0

SRI LANKA	O	M	R	W
Wickremasinghe	7	0	43	0
Ramanayake	7.2	0	38	0
Kalpage	9	1	34	0
Gurusinha	1	0	10	0
Muralitharan	4	1	21	1
Jayasuriya	2	0	15	0

FALL OF WICKETS
1-86, 2-97, 3-133, 4-143, 5-186, 6-194

FALL OF WICKETS
1-71

Umpires: K.T.Francis (10) and W.A.U.Wickremasinghe (8).

Referee: C.W.Smith (*West Indies*).

SRI LANKA v PAKISTAN 1994-95

At R.Premadasa Stadium, Khettarama, Colombo on 6 August 1994.　　Result: **SRI LANKA** won by 7 wickets.
Toss: Sri Lanka.　　Award: S.Ranatunga.　　LOI debuts: None.

Sanath Jayasuriya and Sanjeeva Ranatunga contributed Sri Lanka's first three-figure opening partnership against Pakistan.

PAKISTAN		Runs	Balls	4/6
Saeed Anwar	c and b Wickremasinghe	0	2	–
Aamir Sohail	b Vaas	11	19	1
Inzamam-ul-Haq	c De Silva b A.Ranatunga	14	42	2
* Salim Malik	c Wickremasinghe b Kalpage	61	111	3
Basit Ali	b Kalpage	40	69	1/1
† Rashid Latif	c Jayasuriya b Kalpage	27	31	1
Wasim Akram	c Dassanayake b Muralitharan	0	5	–
Asif Mujtaba	not out	12	15	–
Waqar Younis	c and b Kalpage	0	1	–
Akram Raza	not out	9	6	1
Ashfaq Ahmed				
Extras	(lb 2, w 3, nb 1)	6		
Total	(50 overs; 8 wickets)	**180**		

SRI LANKA		Runs	Balls	4/6
S.T.Jayasuriya	st Rashid b Akram Raza	54	92	5
S.Ranatunga	lbw b Aamir	70	116	4
P.A.de Silva	c Rashid b Waqar	22	35	–
* A.Ranatunga	not out	15	23	–
A.P.Gurusinha	not out	10	17	–
H.P.Tillekeratne				
R.S.Kalpage				
† P.B.Dassanayake				
G.P.Wickremasinghe				
M.Muralitharan				
W.P.U.C.J.Vaas				
Extras	(lb 5, w 3, nb 2)	10		
Total	(47.2 overs; 3 wickets)	**181**		

SRI LANKA	O	M	R	W
Wickremasinghe	7	1	25	1
Vaas	7	0	20	1
A.Ranatunga	10	0	35	1
Muralitharan	10	1	36	1
Kalpage	10	1	36	4
Jayasuriya	6	0	26	0

PAKISTAN	O	M	R	W
Wasim Akram	10	2	34	0
Waqar Younis	9	0	43	1
Ashfaq Ahmed	5	1	20	0
Akram Raza	10	0	27	1
Salim Malik	6	0	26	0
Aamir Sohail	7.2	0	26	1

FALL OF WICKETS
1-0, 2-21, 3-39, 4-113, 5-142, 6-145, 7-163, 8-163

FALL OF WICKETS
1-104, 2-153, 3-153

Umpires: I.Anandappa (3) and T.M.Samarasinghe (6).

Referee: C.W.Smith (*West Indies*).

SRI LANKA v PAKISTAN 1994-95

At Sinhalese Sports Club, Colombo on 7 August 1994.　　Result: **PAKISTAN** won by 19 runs.　　Toss: Sri Lanka.
Award: Salim Malik.　　LOI debuts: None.

Muthiah Muralitharan conceded a record 27 off one over (Salim Malik 22, Asif Mujtaba 5). Ruwan Kalpage and Chaminda Vaas shared Sri Lanka's highest ninth-wicket partnership (76).

PAKISTAN		Runs	Balls	4/6
Saeed Anwar	c Dassanayake b A.Ranatunga	33	60	5
Aamir Sohail	c Jayasuriya b Wickremasinghe	4	8	–
Inzamam-ul-Haq	c Mahanama b Kalpage	10	36	–
* Salim Malik	not out	93	94	6/3
Basit Ali	c Gurusinha b Jayasuriya	50	79	2/2
† Rashid Latif	c Gurusinha b Jayasuriya	2	5	–
Wasim Akram	st Dassanayake b Kalpage	23	11	–/3
Asif Mujtaba	c Mahanama b Wickremasinghe	6	4	1
Waqar Younis	not out	4	4	–
Akram Raza				
Ashfaq Ahmed				
Extras	(lb 6, w 5, nb 1)	12		
Total	(50 overs; 7 wickets)	**237**		

SRI LANKA		Runs	Balls	4/6
S.T.Jayasuriya	c Inzamam b Akram Raza	50	63	3/1
S.Ranatunga	c Rashid b Wasim	2	11	–
A.P.Gurusinha	lbw b Wasim	0	2	–
P.A.de Silva	c Salim b Waqar	21	29	3
R.S.Mahanama	lbw b Salim	32	44	1
* A.Ranatunga	b Aamir	19	19	2
† P.B.Dassanayake	st Rashid b Aamir Sohail	1	4	–
R.S.Kalpage	not out	44	52	2/1
G.P.Wickremasinghe	c Saeed b Salim	0	3	–
W.P.U.C.J.Vaas	b Wasim	33	65	2
M.Muralitharan	b Waqar	1	2	–
Extras	(lb 6, w 7, nb 2)	15		
Total	(49 overs)	**218**		

SRI LANKA	O	M	R	W
Wickremasinghe	8	1	26	2
Vaas	7	1	22	0
A.Ranatunga	10	0	44	1
Muralitharan	8	1	53	0
Kalpage	10	0	48	2
Jayasuriya	7	0	38	2

PAKISTAN	O	M	R	W
Wasim Akram	9	0	24	3
Waqar Younis	10	0	57	2
Ashfaq Ahmed	4	0	31	0
Akram Raza	10	2	31	1
Salim Malik	10	1	45	2
Aamir Sohail	6	0	24	2

FALL OF WICKETS
1-7, 2-50, 3-58, 4-154, 5-161, 6-193, 7-222

FALL OF WICKETS
1-13, 2-13, 3-51, 4-97, 5-118, 6-121, 7-132, 8-133, 9-209, 10-218

Umpires: B.C.Cooray (15) and P.Manuel (7).

Referee: C.W.Smith (*West Indies*).

SRI LANKA v PAKISTAN 1994-95

At Sinhalese Sports Club, Colombo on 22 August 1994.   Result: **PAKISTAN** won by 5 wickets.   Toss: Pakistan.
Award: Akram Raza.   LOI debuts: None.

Two additional internationals replaced the second Test match, scheduled for 19-24 August but cancelled because of the curfew which followed a general election. In his 173rd international, Wasim Akram equalled Kapil Dev's world record tally of 251 wickets from 220 matches.

SRI LANKA		Runs	Balls	4/6
R.S.Mahanama	c Akram Raza b Waqar	11	29	1
S.T.Jayasuriya	lbw b Wasim	2	7	–
S.Ranatunga	c and b Akram Raza	14	48	–
P.A.de Silva	c Aamir b Akram Raza	5	3	1
* A.Ranatunga	run out	74	102	2/1
H.P.Tillekeratne	run out	0	4	–
R.S.Kalpage	c Salim b Aamir	24	59	1
† P.B.Dassanayake	b Wasim	13	25	–
W.P.U.C.J.Vaas	not out	7	10	–
G.P.Wickremasinghe	b Waqar	11	12	–
K.R.Pushpakumara				
Extras	(lb 5, w 6, nb 2)	13		
Total	(50 overs; 9 wickets)	**174**		

PAKISTAN		Runs	Balls	4/6
Saeed Anwar	c Dassanayake b Pushpakumara	9	16	2
Aamir Sohail	c S.Ranatunga b Kalpage	35	47	6
Inzamam-ul-Haq	c and b Jayasuriya	33	51	5/1
* Salim Malik	not out	50	74	4
Basit Ali	st Dassanayake b Jayasuriya	26	46	2
Asif Mujtaba	b De Silva	3	3	–
Akram Raza	not out	8	12	1
† Rashid Latif				
Wasim Akram				
Waqar Younis				
Mushtaq Ahmed				
Extras	(lb 2, w 3, nb 6)	11		
Total	(41.4 overs; 5 wickets)	**175**		

PAKISTAN	O	M	R	W
Wasim Akram	10	1	35	2
Waqar Younis	10	1	35	2
Akram Raza	10	1	26	2
Mushtaq Ahmed	10	1	28	0
Aamir Sohail	5	0	17	1
Salim Malik	5	0	28	0

SRI LANKA	O	M	R	W
Vaas	6	1	23	0
Pushpakumara	7	0	50	1
Wickremasinghe	5.4	1	26	0
Kalpage	10	0	39	1
Jayasuriya	10	0	28	2
De Silva	3	0	7	1

FALL OF WICKETS
1-5, 2-23, 3-29, 4-55, 5-55, 6-102, 7-155, 8-157, 9-174

FALL OF WICKETS
1-20, 2-61, 3-114, 4-160, 5-165

Umpires: I.Anandappa (4) and T.M.Samarasinghe (7).

Referee: C.W.Smith (*West Indies*).

SRI LANKA v PAKISTAN 1994-95

At R.Premadasa Stadium, Khettarama, Colombo on 24 August 1994.   Result: **PAKISTAN** won by 27 runs.
Toss: Sri Lanka.   Award: Waqar Younis.   LOI debuts: Sri Lanka – H.D.P.K.Dharmasena.

Wasim Akram became the leading wicket-taker in limited-overs internationals when he dismissed Sanath Jayasuriya with his fourth ball. Roshan Mahanama (44) retired with cramp at 93 and resumed with a runner at 139.

SRI LANKA		Runs	Balls	4/6
Saeed Anwar	c and b Wickremasinghe	0	4	–
Aamir Sohail	run out	25	45	1
Inzamam-ul-Haq	lbw b A.Ranatunga	25	61	1
* Salim Malik	run out	19	31	–
Basit Ali	c Vaas b Dharmasena	31	61	–
Asif Mujtaba	c Mahanama b Dharmasena	28	52	1
Wasim Akram	run out	0	1	–
Akram Raza	not out	33	37	–/1
† Rashid Latif	b Kalpage	0	1	–
Waqar Younis	b Kalpage	13	9	2
Mushtaq Ahmed	b Vaas	1	3	–
Extras	(lb 5, w 3, nb 4)	12		
Total	(49.5 overs)	**187**		

SRI LANKA		Runs	Balls	4/6
R.S.Mahanama	c Asif b Waqar	52	89	1
S.T.Jayasuriya	lbw b Wasim	0	1	–
S.Ranatunga	run out	23	63	1
P.A.de Silva	c Rashid b Aamir	6	26	–
* A.Ranatunga	b Waqar	32	53	1
† R.S.Kaluwitharana	lbw b Akram Raza	4	8	–
H.P.Tillekeratne	b Waqar	15	34	–
R.S.Kalpage	c Salim b Wasim	4	5	–
H.D.P.K.Dharmasena	not out	3	6	–
W.P.U.C.J.Vaas	run out	1	4	–
G.P.Wickremasinghe	c Rashid b Wasim	1	2	–
Extras	(b 2, lb 6, w 10, nb 1)	19		
Total	(48.1 overs)	**160**		

SRI LANKA	O	M	R	W
Wickremasinghe	3	0	9	1
Vaas	7.5	1	39	1
A.Ranatunga	10	0	23	1
Kalpage	10	1	38	2
Jayasuriya	10	0	39	0
Dharmasena	9	0	34	2

PAKISTAN	O	M	R	W
Wasim Akram	9.1	2	20	3
Waqar Younis	8	0	33	3
Akram Raza	10	0	25	1
Mushtaq Ahmed	10	0	27	0
Aamir Sohail	10	0	41	2
Salim Malik	1	0	6	0

FALL OF WICKETS
1-1, 2-54, 3-59, 4-92, 5-130, 6-130, 7-160, 8-162, 9-184, 10-187

FALL OF WICKETS
1-4, 2-58, 3-73, 4-102, 5-139, 6-140, 7-151, 8-151, 9-157, 10-160

Umpires: P.Manuel (8) and W.A.U.Wickremasinghe (9).

Referee: C.W.Smith (*West Indies*).

SRI LANKA v INDIA 1994-95

At R.Premadasa Stadium, Khettarama, Colombo on 4 (*void*), 5 September 1994.   Result: **SRI LANKA** won by 7 wickets.
Toss: Sri Lanka.   Award: G.P.Wickremasinghe.   LOI debuts: None.

Rain bedevilled this four-nation tournament from the start, washing out the opening match on 4 September with India
16 for 0 after 4 overs. The ICC declared it void for record purposes (see *Preface*) when it was replaced by a 'half' match
begun at 6.25pm following drying operations led by a helicopter.

INDIA		Runs	Balls	4/6	SRI LANKA		Runs	Balls	4/6
M.Prabhakar	c Jayasuriya b Wickremasinghe	14	18	–	R.S.Mahanama	not out	50	78	–
S.R.Tendulkar	c Dharmasena b Wickremasinghe	6	5	–	S.T.Jayasuriya	run out	3	3	–
N.S.Sidhu	c Mahanama b Jayasuriya	17	31	–	P.A.de Silva	c Mongia b Kumble	14	18	1
* M.Azharuddin	c Chandana b Dharmasena	25	35	1	* A.Ranatunga	run out	41	48	2
V.G.Kambli	not out	30	39	–	R.S.Kalpage	not out	3	3	–
A.C.Bedade	b Wickremasinghe	21	21	–/1	H.P.Tillekeratne				
Kapil Dev	not out	1	1	–	U.U.Chandana				
† N.R.Mongia					† P.B.Dassanayake				
J.Srinath					H.D.P.K.Dharmasena				
A.Kumble					W.P.U.C.J.Vaas				
R.K.Chauhan					G.P.Wickremasinghe				
Extras	(b 3, lb 7, w 1)	11			Extras	(lb 12, w 2, nb 1)	15		
Total	(25 overs; 5 wickets)	125			Total	(24.2 overs; 3 wickets)	126		

SRI LANKA	O	M	R	W	INDIA	O	M	R	W
Wickremasinghe	5	0	28	3	Prabhakar	4.2	0	17	0
Vaas	4	0	20	0	Srinath	5	0	21	0
Dharmasena	5	0	22	1	Kumble	5	0	17	1
Ranatunga	2	0	11	0	Tendulkar	4	0	21	0
Jayasuriya	5	0	17	1	Kapil Dev	2	0	15	0
Kalpage	4	0	17	0	Chauhan	4	0	23	0

FALL OF WICKETS
1-20, 2-23, 3-55, 4-87, 5-122

FALL OF WICKETS
1-7, 2-31, 3-119

Umpires: B.L.Aldridge (*New Zealand*) (36) and K.T.Francis (20).

Referee: C.W.Smith (*West Indies*).

AUSTRALIA v PAKISTAN 1994-95

At Sinhalese Sports Club, Colombo on 7 September 1994.   Result: **AUSTRALIA** won by 28 runs.   Toss: Pakistan.
Award: S.K.Warne.   LOI debuts: None.

Playing their first international since April, Australia were led by their newly appointed captain, Allan Border having
reigned since January 1985. Asif Mujtaba fractured two fingers on his left hand when catching Michael Slater. Saeed
Anwar (43) retired with cramp at 80 and resumed at 124 with a runner.

AUSTRALIA		Runs	Balls	4/6	PAKISTAN		Runs	Balls	4/6
* M.A.Taylor	lbw b Wasim	8	26	–	Saeed Anwar	c McGrath b S.R.Waugh	46	78	5/1
M.J.Slater	c Asif b Wasim	4	12	–	Aamir Sohail	b McGrath	0	4	–
D.C.Boon	b Akram Raza	19	48	3	Inzamam-ul-Haq	st Healy b Warne	29	69	4
M.E.Waugh	st Rashid b Mushtaq	23	36	1	Basit Ali	c and b Warne	0	13	–
S.R.Waugh	c Rashid b Mushtaq	1	8	–	* Salim Malik	c Taylor b S.R.Waugh	22	51	1
M.G.Bevan	c Mushtaq b Salim	37	73	1	† Rashid Latif	c Taylor b S.R.Waugh	7	19	–
† I.A.Healy	not out	30	55	–	Wasim Akram	b McGrath	16	33	1
S.K.Warne	b Wasim	30	40	–	Akram Raza	c Healy b McDermott	10	19	–
C.J.McDermott	not out	2	3	–	Waqar Younis	c Slater b Warne	2	9	–
G.D.McGrath					Mushtaq Ahmed	not out	2	3	–
T.B.A.May					Asif Mujtaba	not out	1	7	–
Extras	(b 7, lb 9, w 9)	25			Extras	(b 2, lb 5, w 6, nb 3)	16		
Total	(50 overs; 7 wickets)	179			Total	(50 overs; 9 wickets)	151		

PAKISTAN	O	M	R	W	AUSTRALIA	O	M	R	W
Wasim Akram	10	2	24	3	McDermott	10	2	21	1
Waqar Younis	8	2	43	0	McGrath	10	3	25	2
Mushtaq Ahmed	10	1	34	2	May	10	0	53	0
Akram Raza	10	1	26	1	Warne	10	1	29	3
Aamir Sohail	7	0	17	0	S.R.Waugh	10	1	16	3
Salim Malik	5	0	19	1					

FALL OF WICKETS
1-11, 2-34, 3-48, 4-49, 5-85, 6-128, 7-174

FALL OF WICKETS
1-2, 2-77, 3-83, 4-94, 5-124, 6-129, 7-129, 8-147, 9-150

Umpires: B.C.Cooray (16) and W.A.U.Wickremasinghe (10).

Referee: C.W.Smith (*West Indies*).

AUSTRALIA v INDIA 1994-95

At R.Premadasa Stadium, Khettarama, Colombo on 9 September 1994.   Result: **INDIA** won by 31 runs.   Toss: India.
Award: S.R.Tendulkar.   LOI debuts: None.

Playing in his 78th international (his ninth as an opener), Sachin Tendulkar scored his first hundred. Ian Healy became the second wicket-keeper after Jeff Dujon to make 150 LOI dismissals.

INDIA		Runs	Balls	4/6
M.Prabhakar	c Slater b Warne	20	41	2
S.R.Tendulkar	b McDermott	110	130	8/2
N.S.Sidhu	c Boon b May	24	32	1/1
* M.Azharuddin	c Healy b McDermott	31	30	2
V.G.Kambli	not out	43	47	–/1
Kapil Dev	run out	4	4	1
A.C.Bedade	run out	1	5	–
† N.R.Mongia	c Healy b Warne	3	5	–
A.Kumble	b S.R.Waugh	1	3	–
R.K.Chauhan	not out	2	3	–
S.L.V.Raju				
Extras	(lb 2, w 5)	7		
Total	(50 overs; 8 wickets)	**246**		

AUSTRALIA		Runs	Balls	4/6
M.J.Slater	c Prabhakar b Kapil Dev	26	36	3
* M.A.Taylor	c and b Prabhakar	4	11	–
M.E.Waugh	b Chauhan	61	81	3
D.C.Boon	b Chauhan	40	55	2
S.R.Waugh	b Prabhakar	22	42	–
M.G.Bevan	c Sidhu b Kumble	26	40	–
C.J.McDermott	c Kumble b Prabhakar	2	3	–
† I.A.Healy	run out	15	14	–
S.K.Warne	b Raju	1	5	–
T.B.A.May	not out	1	1	–
G.D.McGrath	run out	1	2	–
Extras	(b 2, lb 10, w 2, nb 2)	16		
Total	(47.4 overs)	**215**		

AUSTRALIA	O	M	R	W
McDermott	10	1	46	2
McGrath	6	0	41	0
Warne	10	0	53	2
May	10	0	35	1
S.R.Waugh	8	1	33	1
Bevan	2	0	17	0
M.E.Waugh	4	0	19	0

INDIA	O	M	R	W
Prabhakar	8	0	34	3
Kapil Dev	8	1	44	1
Raju	9.4	0	38	1
Kumble	9	0	31	1
Chauhan	10	0	41	2
Tendulkar	3	0	15	0

FALL OF WICKETS
1-87, 2-129, 3-173, 4-211, 5-216, 6-218, 7-226, 8-237

FALL OF WICKETS
1-22, 2-56, 3-123, 4-143, 5-181, 6-183, 7-209, 8-212, 9-213, 10-215

Umpires: I.Anandappa (5) and T.M.Samarasinghe (8).

Referee: C.W.Smith (*West Indies*).

SRI LANKA v PAKISTAN 1994-95

At Sinhalese Sports Club, Colombo on 11 September 1994.   Result: **SRI LANKA** won by 7 wickets.   Toss: Sri Lanka.
Award: A.Ranatunga.   LOI debuts: Pakistan – Kabir Khan.

After Roshan Mahanama had retired with cramp at 97 for 3, Arjuna Ranatunga and Hashan Tillekeratne added an unbroken 116 which remains Sri Lanka's highest fourth-wicket stand in a home international.

PAKISTAN		Runs	Balls	4/6
Saeed Anwar	c Jayasuriya b Vaas	24	24	4/1
Aamir Sohail	run out	32	54	1
Inzamam-ul-Haq	run out	2	5	–
* Salim Malik	c Tillekeratne b Kalpage	53	85	3
Basit Ali	c Mahanama b Jayasuriya	39	63	–
Zahid Fazal	run out	15	24	1
† Rashid Latif	not out	28	34	2
Akram Raza	not out	9	13	–
Waqar Younis				
Mushtaq Ahmed				
Kabir Khan				
Extras	(lb 2, w 4, nb 2)	8		
Total	(50 overs; 6 wickets)	**210**		

SRI LANKA		Runs	Balls	4/6
R.S.Mahanama	retired hurt	39	88	1
S.T.Jayasuriya	c Salim b Kabir	4	8	–
S.Ranatunga	c Inzamam b Akram Raza	16	33	1
P.A.de Silva	c and b Mushtaq	11	17	–
* A.Ranatunga	not out	82	76	6
H.P.Tillekeratne	not out	39	62	3
R.S.Kalpage				
† P.B.Dassanayake				
H.D.P.K.Dharmasena				
W.P.U.C.J.Vaas				
G.P.Wickremasinghe				
Extras	(b 5, lb 10, w 6, nb 1)	22		
Total	(47.2 overs; 3 wickets)	**213**		

SRI LANKA	O	M	R	W
Wickremasinghe	8	0	37	0
Vaas	8	0	38	1
A.Ranatunga	8	0	29	0
Dharmasena	8	0	39	0
Jayasuriya	10	0	33	1
Kalpage	8	0	32	1

PAKISTAN	O	M	R	W
Waqar Younis	9	1	42	0
Kabir Khan	9.2	1	34	1
Akram Raza	10	0	49	1
Aamir Sohail	8	0	28	0
Mushtaq Ahmed	8	0	31	1
Salim Malik	3	0	14	0

FALL OF WICKETS
1-28, 2-31, 3-82, 4-136, 5-169, 6-171

FALL OF WICKETS
1-9, 2-44, 3-65

Umpires: B.L.Aldridge (*New Zealand*) (37) and P.Manuel (9).

Referee: C.W.Smith (*West Indies*).

SRI LANKA v AUSTRALIA 1994-95

At P.Saravanamuttu Stadium, Colombo on 13 September 1994.　Result: **SRI LANKA** won by 6 wickets (revised target).
Toss: Sri Lanka.　Award: A.Ranatunga.　LOI debuts: Australia – J.Angel, G.R.Robertson.

Rain during the interval caused an 80-minute delay and reduced Sri Lanka's target (based on basic run rate) to 163 from 36 overs. Heavy rain waterlogged the R.Premadasa Stadium, causing the India-Pakistan match, scheduled for 15-16 September, to be abandoned without a ball bowled.

AUSTRALIA		Runs	Balls	4/6
* M.A.Taylor	c De Silva b Kalpage	41	63	3
M.J.Slater	run out	24	70	1
M.E.Waugh	st Dassanayake b Jayasuriya	24	39	–/1
J.L.Langer	c Wickremasinghe b Kalpage	9	10	–/1
S.R.Waugh	c Dassanayake b Jayasuriya	30	33	3
M.G.Bevan	not out	47	54	1
† I.A.Healy	run out	28	27	1
G.R.Robertson	not out	5	6	–
S.K.Warne				
D.W.Fleming				
J.Angel				
Extras	(lb 11, w 5, nb 1)	17		
Total	(50 overs; 6 wickets)	**225**		

SRI LANKA		Runs	Balls	4/6
R.S.Mahanama	b Warne	20	20	3
S.T.Jayasuriya	c Taylor b Angel	0	14	–
P.A.de Silva	st Healy b Warne	33	60	3
* A.Ranatunga	lbw b S.R.Waugh	59	71	2/1
H.P.Tillekeratne	not out	29	34	2
R.S.Kalpage	not out	9	8	1
U.U.Chandana				
† P.B.Dassanayake				
H.D.P.K.Dharmasena				
W.P.U.C.J.Vaas				
G.P.Wickremasinghe				
Extras	(lb 10, w 3, nb 1)	14		
Total	(34.4 overs; 4 wickets)	**164**		

SRI LANKA	O	M	R	W
Wickremasinghe	7	0	29	0
Vaas	9	2	26	0
Ranatunga	2	0	14	0
Kalpage	9	0	42	2
Dharmasena	10	1	45	0
Jayasuriya	10	0	42	2
De Silva	3	0	16	0

AUSTRALIA	O	M	R	W
Angel	7	1	29	1
Fleming	6.4	0	42	0
Warne	8	0	27	2
S.R.Waugh	6	0	32	1
Robertson	7	0	24	0

FALL OF WICKETS
1-61, 2-90, 3-100, 4-116, 5-144, 6-204

FALL OF WICKETS
1-4, 2-48, 3-102, 4-141

Umpires: B.L.Aldridge (*New Zealand*) (38) and T.M.Samarasinghe (9).

Referee: C.W.Smith (*West Indies*).

SRI LANKA v INDIA 1994-95

At Sinhalese Sports Club, Colombo on 17 September 1994.　Result: **INDIA** won by 6 wickets.　Toss: India.
Award: M.Azharuddin.　Series Award: A.Ranatunga.　LOI debuts: None.

With the R.Premadasa Stadium still waterlogged, this final, originally scheduled as a floodlit match, was transferred to the saturated SSC ground. A 25-over thrash began at 2pm in slippery conditions on a wet, slow pitch and ended in dire light.

SRI LANKA		Runs	Balls	4/6
R.S.Mahanama	run out	2	11	–
S.T.Jayasuriya	c Bedade b Prabhakar	1	4	–
P.A.de Silva	c Prasad b Chauhan	10	14	1
H.P.Tillekeratne	c Kambli b Kapil Dev	7	21	–
* A.Ranatunga	c Chauhan b Kumble	13	22	–
R.S.Kalpage	c Mongia b Prasad	39	57	2
U.U.Chandana	run out	2	7	–
† P.B.Dassanayake	run out	1	1	–
H.D.P.K.Dharmasena	b Prabhakar	8	12	–
W.P.U.C.J.Vaas	not out	2	4	–
G.P.Wickremasinghe	not out	3	2	–
Extras	(lb 2, w 5, nb 3)	10		
Total	(25 overs; 9 wickets)	**98**		

INDIA		Runs	Balls	4/6
M.Prabhakar	c Jayasuriya b Wickremasinghe	10	17	1
S.R.Tendulkar	c De Silva b Vaas	0	2	–
N.S.Sidhu	lbw b Wickremasinghe	24	46	–
* M.Azharuddin	c Mahanama b Vaas	45	51	1/1
V.G.Kambli	not out	8	18	–
A.C.Bedade	not out	4	8	–
Kapil Dev				
† N.R.Mongia				
A.Kumble				
R.K.Chauhan				
B.K.V.Prasad				
Extras	(b 4, lb 1, w 3)	8		
Total	(23.4 overs; 4 wickets)	**99**		

INDIA	O	M	R	W
Prabhakar	5	0	19	2
Prasad	5	0	17	1
Kumble	5	0	22	1
Chauhan	5	0	21	1
Kapil Dev	5	0	17	1

SRI LANKA	O	M	R	W
Wickremasinghe	5	0	13	2
Vaas	5	0	16	2
Dharmasena	5	0	22	0
Kalpage	5	1	23	0
Jayasuriya	3	0	15	0
De Silva	0.4	0	5	0

FALL OF WICKETS
1-5, 2-5, 3-24, 4-28, 5-64, 6-74, 7-76, 8-91, 9-95

FALL OF WICKETS
1-6, 2-15, 3-86, 4-88

Umpires: B.L.Aldridge (*New Zealand*) (39) and K.T.Francis (21).

Referee: C.W.Smith (*West Indies*).

AUSTRALIA v SOUTH AFRICA 1994-95

At Gaddafi Stadium, Lahore on 12 October 1994.   Result: **AUSTRALIA** won by 6 runs.   Toss: Australia.
Award: S.R.Waugh.   LOI debuts: None.

The first triangular tournament to be played in Pakistan was staged in traditional clothing and employed a red ball. Both teams were confined to their hotels on the eve of the match when rioting was anticipated following the calling of a national strike. South Africa needed 14 from Craig McDermott's final over.

AUSTRALIA		Runs	Balls	4/6
* M.A.Taylor	st Richardson b Shaw	56	72	6
M.J.Slater	st Richardson b Shaw	44	88	2
M.E.Waugh	c and b Cronje	3	10	–
D.C.Boon	run out	8	24	–
S.R.Waugh	c Kirsten b Matthews	56	71	5
M.G.Bevan	run out	15	17	1
† I.A.Healy	not out	18	22	–
G.R.Robertson	not out	1	2	–
S.K.Warne				
C.J.McDermott				
D.W.Fleming				
Extras	(lb 1, nb 5)	6		
Total	(50 overs; 6 wickets)	**207**		

SOUTH AFRICA		Runs	Balls	4/6
* K.C.Wessels	c Healy b Fleming	6	29	–
G.Kirsten	c Healy b Fleming	4	12	1
W.J.Cronje	not out	98	130	7/1
D.J.Cullinan	c Slater b S.R.Waugh	12	30	–
J.N.Rhodes	lbw b S.R.Waugh	42	59	1
B.M.McMillan	b M.E.Waugh	3	6	–
E.O.Simons	b McDermott	19	29	–
† D.J.Richardson	b McDermott	4	5	–
C.R.Matthews	b McDermott	1	2	–
T.G.Shaw	not out	1	1	–
P.S.de Villiers				
Extras	(b 4, lb 7)	11		
Total	(50 overs; 8 wickets)	**201**		

SOUTH AFRICA	O	M	R	W
De Villiers	9	1	38	0
Matthews	10	1	41	1
McMillan	3	0	24	0
Simons	8	0	37	0
Shaw	10	0	34	2
Cronje	10	1	32	1

AUSTRALIA	O	M	R	W
McDermott	10	2	32	3
Fleming	10	3	29	2
S.R.Waugh	10	0	35	2
Warne	10	0	39	0
Robertson	7	0	41	0
M.E.Waugh	3	0	14	1

FALL OF WICKETS
1-98, 2-107, 3-107, 4-128, 5-160, 6-202

FALL OF WICKETS
1-8, 2-15, 3-50, 4-126, 5-143, 6-182, 7-194, 8-200

Umpires: Athar Zaidi (5) and Mian Mohammad Aslam (9).

Referee: J.R.Reid (New Zealand).

PAKISTAN v AUSTRALIA 1994-95

At Ibn-e-Qasim Bagh Stadium, Multan on 14 October 1994.   Result: **AUSTRALIA** won by 7 wickets.   Toss: Pakistan.
Award: D.C.Boon.   LOI debuts: None.

Saeed Anwar completed 2000 runs in his 62nd international.

PAKISTAN		Runs	Balls	4/6
Saeed Anwar	b Fleming	22	31	3
Aamir Sohail	b Fleming	5	9	–
Inzamam-ul-Haq	run out	59	86	7
* Salim Malik	c Healy b Warne	32	66	3
Ijaz Ahmed	c Healy b McDermott	21	45	1
Aamer Malik	c Healy b McDermott	20	34	1
Wasim Akram	b Fleming	9	12	–
† Rashid Latif	b Fleming	16	13	1
Akram Raza	not out	5	6	–
Waqar Younis	not out	0	1	–
Mushtaq Ahmed				
Extras	(b 6, lb 1, w 3, nb 1)	11		
Total	(50 overs; 8 wickets)	**200**		

AUSTRALIA		Runs	Balls	4/6
M.J.Slater	lbw b Wasim	0	10	–
* M.A.Taylor	b Akram Raza	46	62	5
M.E.Waugh	c Rashid b Waqar	0	4	–
D.C.Boon	not out	84	134	5
S.R.Waugh	not out	59	70	7
M.G.Bevan				
† I.A.Healy				
G.R.Robertson				
S.K.Warne				
C.J.McDermott				
D.W.Fleming				
Extras	(b 1, lb 6, w 4, nb 1)	12		
Total	(46 overs; 3 wickets)	**201**		

AUSTRALIA	O	M	R	W
McDermott	10	1	34	2
Fleming	10	0	49	4
S.R.Waugh	10	1	37	0
Warne	10	1	29	1
Robertson	5	0	24	0
M.E.Waugh	5	0	20	0

PAKISTAN	O	M	R	W
Wasim Akram	8	3	26	1
Waqar Younis	9	0	39	1
Akram Raza	10	0	35	1
Mushtaq Ahmed	9	0	48	0
Aamir Sohail	6	0	26	0
Salim Malik	4	0	20	0

FALL OF WICKETS
1-9, 2-32, 3-113, 4-132, 5-164, 6-166, 7-184, 8-199

FALL OF WICKETS
1-10, 2-11, 3-81

Umpires: Riazuddin (5) and Saqib Qureshi (1).

Referee: J.R.Reid (New Zealand).

PAKISTAN v SOUTH AFRICA 1994-95

At National Stadium, Karachi on 16 October 1994.   Result: **PAKISTAN** won by 8 wickets.   Toss: South Africa.
Award: Salim Malik.   LOI debuts: South Africa – D.N.Crookes.

Dave Richardson was run out in bizarre circumstances. The red and green dismissal lights operated by reserve umpire
Atiq Khan had been wrongly wired so that his signal for 'not out' illuminated the red bulb. Aqib Javed took his 100th
wicket in 93 internationals.

SOUTH AFRICA		Runs	Balls	4/6	PAKISTAN		Runs	Balls	4/6
A.C.Hudson	lbw b Akram Raza	23	49	2	Saeed Anwar	st Richardson b Cronje	20	51	2
* K.C.Wessels	c Salim b Akram Raza	33	66	1	Aamir Sohail	c and b Simons	22	51	1
W.J.Cronje	run out	21	35	–	Inzamam-ul-Haq	not out	51	86	5
D.J.Cullinan	c Ijaz b Aamir	10	18	–	* Salim Malik	not out	62	85	3
J.N.Rhodes	c Salim b Aqib	16	40	2	Asif Mujtaba				
E.O.Simons	c Salim b Wasim	14	36	–	Ijaz Ahmed				
† D.J.Richardson	run out	7	15	1	Wasim Akram				
D.N.Crookes	b Wasim	10	18	1	† Rashid Latif				
T.G.Shaw	run out	0	2	–	Akram Raza				
M.W.Pringle	not out	13	16	–	Waqar Younis				
P.S.de Villiers	not out	7	7	–	Aqib Javed				
Extras	(lb 4, w 4, nb 1)	9			Extras	(lb 2, w 4, nb 5)	11		
Total	(50 overs; 9 wickets)	163			Total	(44.4 overs; 2 wickets)	166		

PAKISTAN	O	M	R	W	SOUTH AFRICA	O	M	R	W
Wasim Akram	10	0	28	2	De Villiers	9.4	1	38	0
Aqib Javed	10	2	25	1	Pringle	8	0	35	0
Waqar Younis	10	2	40	0	Simons	10	2	39	1
Akram Raza	10	0	30	2	Cronje	6	1	12	1
Salim Malik	3	0	14	0	Shaw	7	1	23	0
Aamir Sohail	7	1	22	1	Crookes	4	0	17	0

FALL OF WICKETS   FALL OF WICKETS
1-49, 2-70, 3-90, 4-90, 5-121, 6-131, 7-137, 8-137, 9-145   1-41, 2-51

Umpires: Feroz Butt (4) and Salim Badar (5).   **Referee:** J.R.Reid (New Zealand).

AUSTRALIA v SOUTH AFRICA 1994-95

At Iqbal Stadium, Faisalabad on 18 October 1994.   Result: **AUSTRALIA** won by 22 runs.   Toss: Australia.
Award: W.J.Cronje.   LOI debuts: None.

Shane Warne snared four wickets for one run in six balls, three to stumpings, to conclude a drab match played on a
slow, low pitch of rolled mud. Lunchtime entertainment featured a police lathi attack on 40 spectators.

AUSTRALIA		Runs	Balls	4/6	SOUTH AFRICA		Runs	Balls	4/6
* M.A.Taylor	c Richardson b de Villiers	4	13	–	* K.C.Wessels	c Bevan b May	30	69	4
M.J.Slater	b Eksteen	38	73	3	A.C.Hudson	run out	5	12	1
M.E.Waugh	c Richardson b Cronje	38	57	4	W.J.Cronje	c S.R.Waugh b McDermott	64	94	5
D.C.Boon	c Wessels b Pringle	43	73	3	J.N.Rhodes	c Boon b May	11	18	1
S.R.Waugh	b Simons	23	37	1	G.Kirsten	b McGrath	24	44	1
M.G.Bevan	not out	36	31	3	† D.J.Richardson	lbw b McGrath	10	13	1
† I.A.Healy	c De Villiers b Simons	4	5	–	E.O.Simons	st Healy b Warne	11	18	–
S.K.Warne	not out	15	15	–	D.N.Crookes	not out	20	19	2
C.J.McDermott					M.W.Pringle	lbw b Warne	0	1	–
T.B.A.May					C.E.Eksteen	st Healy b Warne	0	2	–
G.D.McGrath					P.S.de Villiers	st Healy b Warne	0	1	–
Extras	(b 1, lb 2, w 3, nb 1)	7			Extras	(lb 7, w 3, nb 1)	11		
Total	(50 overs; 6 wickets)	208			Total	(48.2 overs)	186		

SOUTH AFRICA	O	M	R	W	AUSTRALIA	O	M	R	W
De Villiers	9	2	41	1	McDermott	9	2	34	1
Pringle	9	1	49	1	McGrath	10	2	31	2
Simons	10	0	41	2	Warne	9.2	0	40	4
Cronje	10	1	31	1	May	10	0	34	2
Eksteen	8	0	26	1	S.R.Waugh	10	1	40	0
Crookes	4	0	17	0					

FALL OF WICKETS   FALL OF WICKETS
1-6, 2-69, 3-95, 4-143, 5-160, 6-167   1-7, 2-64, 3-86, 4-124, 5-138, 6-156, 7-176, 8-176, 9-185, 10-186

Umpires: Islam Khan (1) and Khizer Hayat (45).

Referee: J.R.Reid (New Zealand).

PAKISTAN v SOUTH AFRICA 1994-95

At Rawalpindi Cricket Stadium on 20 October 1994.   Result: **PAKISTAN** won by 39 runs.   Toss: South Africa.
Award: Ijaz Ahmed.   LOI debuts: None.

Ijaz Ahmed's third hundred was his first on home soil; his last 60 came off 39 balls. South Africa, strangled by their captain's 19-over reconnaissance for as many runs, capitulated in a hat-trick of run outs.

PAKISTAN		Runs	Balls	4/6
Saeed Anwar	c Cullinan b Simons	42	53	9
Aamir Sohail	c Richardson b Matthews	1	10	–
Inzamam-ul-Haq	run out	10	18	2
* Salim Malik	c Wessels b Eksteen	56	82	2
Ijaz Ahmed	b Matthews	110	110	13/1
Wasim Akram	b Matthews	12	25	–
† Rashid Latif	not out	3	3	–
Akram Raza	not out	4	1	1
Asif Mujtaba				
Waqar Younis				
Aqib Javed				
Extras	(b 4, lb 4, w 1, nb 2)	11		
Total	(50 overs; 6 wickets)	**249**		

SOUTH AFRICA		Runs	Balls	4/6
A.C.Hudson	c Rashid b Waqar	20	39	2
* K.C.Wessels	lbw b Waqar	19	46	1
W.J.Cronje	run out	53	80	1
D.J.Cullinan	run out	36	50	2
J.N.Rhodes	run out	33	35	2
G.Kirsten	not out	20	36	1
† D.J.Richardson	not out	10	15	–
E.O.Simons				
C.R.Matthews				
P.S.de Villiers				
C.E.Eksteen				
Extras	(b 2, lb 12, w 3, nb 2)	19		
Total	(50 overs; 5 wickets)	**210**		

SOUTH AFRICA	O	M	R	W
De Villiers	10	0	41	0
Matthews	10	2	50	3
Cronje	10	0	45	0
Simons	10	1	56	1
Eksteen	10	1	49	1

PAKISTAN	O	M	R	W
Wasim Akram	10	1	40	0
Aqib Javed	10	0	36	0
Waqar Younis	10	0	35	2
Akram Raza	10	0	41	0
Salim Malik	5	0	24	0
Aamir Sohail	5	0	20	0

FALL OF WICKETS
1-2, 2-39, 3-61, 4-186, 5-232, 6-245

FALL OF WICKETS
1-35, 2-61, 3-130, 4-159, 5-189

Umpires: Javed Akhtar (12) and Said Ahmed Shah (3).

Referee: J.R.Reid (New Zealand).

PAKISTAN v AUSTRALIA 1994-95

At Rawalpindi Cricket Stadium on 22 October 1994.   Result: **PAKISTAN** won by 9 wickets.   Toss: Pakistan.
Award: Saeed Anwar.   LOI debuts: None.

Saeed Anwar shared an unbroken stand of 160 off 154 balls, Pakistan's record for the second wicket against Australia, as the hosts raced home with 11 overs in hand. Justin Langer kept wicket after Ian Healy fractured a thumb taking a leg-side ball.

AUSTRALIA		Runs	Balls	4/6
M.J.Slater	b Aqib	4	6	1
* M.A.Taylor	c Akram Raza b Aqib	14	35	–
M.E.Waugh	not out	121	132	9
J.L.Langer	c Saeed b Wasim	27	58	2
S.R.Waugh	lbw b Salim	14	15	2
M.G.Bevan	b Waqar	22	36	1
† I.A.Healy	run out	16	13	2
S.K.Warne	not out	11	8	1
C.J.McDermott				
G.D.McGrath				
T.B.A.May				
Extras	(b 1, lb 13, w 5, nb 2)	21		
Total	(50 overs; 6 wickets)	**250**		

PAKISTAN		Runs	Balls	4/6
Saeed Anwar	not out	104	119	13/1
Aamir Sohail	c Bevan b May	45	37	7/1
Inzamam-ul-Haq	not out	91	80	11/3
* Salim Malik				
Ijaz Ahmed				
Basit Ali				
Wasim Akram				
† Rashid Latif				
Akram Raza				
Waqar Younis				
Aqib Javed				
Extras	(b 3, lb 4, w 2, nb 2)	11		
Total	(39 overs; 1 wicket)	**251**		

PAKISTAN	O	M	R	W
Wasim Akram	10	0	47	1
Aqib Javed	10	0	44	2
Waqar Younis	10	0	50	1
Aamir Sohail	5	0	25	0
Akram Raza	10	0	36	0
Salim Malik	5	0	34	1

AUSTRALIA	O	M	R	W
McDermott	8	1	54	0
McGrath	6	1	37	0
May	9	0	65	1
Warne	9	1	47	0
S.R.Waugh	5	0	26	0
M.E.Waugh	2	0	15	0

FALL OF WICKETS
1-14, 2-50, 3-114, 4-140, 5-206, 6-234

FALL OF WICKETS
1-91

Umpires: Mahboob Shah (26) and Javed Akhtar (13).

Referee: J.R.Reid (New Zealand).

AUSTRALIA v SOUTH AFRICA 1994-95

At Shahi Bagh Stadium, Peshawar on 24 October 1994.　　Result: **AUSTRALIA** won by 3 wickets.　　Toss: South Africa.
Award: W.J.Cronje.　　LOI debuts: None.

Appalling crowd behaviour overshadowed a close contest, Slater and Warne being struck by missiles, while firecrackers exploded near Boon and Cullinan. Needing 17 off the last two overs, Justin Langer took 16 (three fours and boundary leg-byes) off the 49th.

SOUTH AFRICA		Runs	Balls	4/6
* K.C.Wessels	c Bevan b McDermott	4	14	1
G.Kirsten	b McGrath	45	61	5
W.J.Cronje	not out	100	124	4/3
D.J.Cullinan	b Warne	36	35	4/1
J.N.Rhodes	c Taylor b Angel	3	10	–
† D.J.Richardson	c Slater b Waugh	25	38	2
D.N.Crookes	lbw b McGrath	0	1	–
E.O.Simons	not out	10	22	–
C.R.Matthews				
T.G.Shaw				
P.S.de Villiers				
Extras	(b 12, lb 9, w 3, nb 4)	28		
Total	(50 overs; 6 wickets)	**251**		

AUSTRALIA		Runs	Balls	4/6
* M.A.Taylor	c Richardson b De Villiers	17	26	2
M.J.Slater	run out	54	82	5
M.E.Waugh	c Rhodes b Shaw	43	54	3/1
D.C.Boon	run out	39	44	4
M.G.Bevan	c Shaw b De Villiers	45	56	5
† J.L.Langer	not out	33	20	4
S.K.Warne	run out	13	11	1
J.Angel	b Matthews	0	3	–
C.J.McDermott	not out	1	1	–
T.B.A.May				
G.D.McGrath				
Extras	(lb 5, w 2)	7		
Total	(49.4 overs; 7 wickets)	**252**		

AUSTRALIA	O	M	R	W
McDermott	9	0	48	1
Angel	10	1	37	1
McGrath	10	2	22	2
Waugh	6	0	39	1
May	5	0	33	0
Warne	10	0	51	1

SOUTH AFRICA	O	M	R	W
De Villiers	10	2	49	2
Matthews	9.4	1	43	1
Simons	8	0	46	0
Cronje	10	0	46	0
Shaw	10	0	49	1
Crookes	2	0	14	0

FALL OF WICKETS
1-7, 2-92, 3-157, 4-167, 5-207, 6-207

FALL OF WICKETS
1-38, 2-105, 3-119, 4-186, 5-223, 6-239, 7-251

Umpires: Mohammad Nazir, jr (1) and Shakil Khan (13).　　　　**Referee:** J.R.Reid (*New Zealand*).

PAKISTAN v SOUTH AFRICA 1994-95

At Iqbal Stadium, Faisalabad on 28 October 1994.　　Result: **PAKISTAN** won by 6 wickets.　　Toss: South Africa.
Award: Ijaz Ahmed.　　LOI debuts: None.

The 8th Match, between Pakistan and Australia at Jinnah Stadium, Gujranwala on 26 October 1994, was abandoned without a ball bowled. South Africa's defeat was their tenth in succession. The match ended with a no-ball which 'bowled' Ijaz Ahmed.

SOUTH AFRICA		Runs	Balls	4/6
G.Kirsten	run out	69	97	6
* K.C.Wessels	c and b Wasim	51	97	4
W.J.Cronje	b Salim	18	28	–
D.J.Cullinan	c Akram Raza b Waqar	4	8	–
J.N.Rhodes	not out	45	46	1/1
† D.J.Richardson	not out	27	28	1
C.R.Matthews				
E.O.Simons				
T.G.Shaw				
P.S.de Villiers				
C.E.Eksteen				
Extras	(b 1, lb 2, w 2, nb 3)	8		
Total	(50 overs; 4 wickets)	**222**		

PAKISTAN		Runs	Balls	4/6
Saeed Anwar	c Cullinan b Matthews	14	29	1
Aamir Sohail	c Cullinan b Simons	25	43	4
Inzamam-ul-Haq	c Eksteen b Simons	19	39	1
* Salim Malik	b Simons	7	11	–
Ijaz Ahmed	not out	98	87	11/1
Basit Ali	not out	52	60	7
† Rashid Latif				
Wasim Akram				
Akram Raza				
Waqar Younis				
Aqib Javed				
Extras	(b 1, lb 4, w 1, nb 2)	8		
Total	(44.3 overs; 4 wickets)	**223**		

PAKISTAN	O	M	R	W
Wasim Akram	10	0	36	1
Aqib Javed	10	0	35	0
Waqar Younis	10	0	55	1
Akram Raza	10	0	46	0
Salim Malik	8	0	37	1
Aamir Sohail	2	0	10	0

SOUTH AFRICA	O	M	R	W
De Villiers	8	0	46	0
Matthews	9	3	31	1
Cronje	2	1	10	0
Simons	8.3	0	49	3
Eksteen	10	1	52	0
Shaw	7	0	30	0

FALL OF WICKETS
1-125, 2-130, 3-138, 4-166

FALL OF WICKETS
1-26, 2-47, 3-66, 4-76

Umpires: Afzal Ahmed (1) and Salim Badar (6).　　　　**Referee:** J.R.Reid (*New Zealand*).

PAKISTAN v AUSTRALIA 1994-95

At Gaddafi Stadium, Lahore on 30 October 1994.   Result: **AUSTRALIA** won by 64 runs.   Toss: Australia.
Award: G.D.McGrath.   LOI debuts: Australia – P.A.Emery.

Michael Bevan's 41-ball fifty included 13 from the 50th over bowled by Wasim Akram. Salim Malik completed 5000 runs in 199 internationals. Glenn McGrath returned his best LOI analysis.

AUSTRALIA		Runs	Balls	4/6
* M.A.Taylor	c and b Salim	56	71	6
M.J.Slater	st Rashid b Salim	66	76	9
M.E.Waugh	b Salim	38	50	4
D.C.Boon	c Salim b Waqar	21	42	–
S.R.Waugh	b Aamir	1	10	–
M.G.Bevan	not out	53	42	5
† P.A.Emery	not out	11	13	1
S.K.Warne				
C.J.McDermott				
D.W.Fleming				
G.D.McGrath				
Extras	(b 1, lb 16, w 4, nb 2)	23		
Total	(50 overs; 5 wickets)	**269**		

PAKISTAN		Runs	Balls	4/6
Saeed Anwar	c Taylor b Fleming	0	9	–
Aamir Sohail	c S.R.Waugh b Fleming	21	28	2/1
Inzamam-ul-Haq	c Emery b McGrath	10	21	2
* Salim Malik	b Fleming	35	44	3
Ijaz Ahmed	c Emery b McGrath	4	17	–
Basit Ali	lbw b McGrath	63	64	5/2
Wasim Akram	b McGrath	26	30	3
Akram Raza	c Emery b M.E.Waugh	0	2	–
† Rashid Latif	not out	10	41	–
Waqar Younis	b McGrath	2	5	–
Aqib Javed	b M.E.Waugh	17	22	1/1
Extras	(lb 8, w 7, nb 2)	17		
Total	(46.5 overs)	**205**		

PAKISTAN	O	M	R	W
Wasim Akram	10	1	63	0
Aqib Javed	7	0	30	0
Waqar Younis	8	0	48	1
Akram Raza	10	0	45	0
Aamir Sohail	5	0	35	1
Salim Malik	10	0	31	3

AUSTRALIA	O	M	R	W
McDermott	9	0	32	0
Fleming	8	2	32	3
McGrath	10	0	52	5
Warne	10	2	32	0
S.R.Waugh	2	0	6	0
M.E.Waugh	7.5	0	43	2

FALL OF WICKETS
1-121, 2-146, 3-188, 4-191, 5-226

FALL OF WICKETS
1-17, 2-26, 3-43, 4-64, 5-112, 6-173, 7-174, 8-176, 9-178, 10-205

Umpires: Khizer Hayat (46) and Mian Mohammad Aslam (10).

Referee: J.R.Reid (*New Zealand*).

INDIA v WEST INDIES 1994-95

At Nahar Singh Stadium, Faridabad on 17 October 1994.   Result: **WEST INDIES** won by 96 runs.
Toss: West Indies.   Award: P.V.Simmons.   LOI debuts: West Indies – S.Chanderpaul, C.E.Cuffy, S.C.Williams.

Kapil Dev (3783 runs and 253 wickets) made the last of his 224 LOI appearances. Keith Arthurton provided the first instance in international cricket of a batsman being adjudged by a third umpire to have hit his wicket.

WEST INDIES		Runs	Balls	4/6
P.V.Simmons	c Mongia b Chauhan	76	100	3/4
S.C.Williams	c Kumble b Srinath	61	109	8/2
B.C.Lara	c Azharuddin b Kumble	10	16	1
C.L.Hooper	not out	61	50	6/1
K.L.T.Arthurton	hit wicket b Srinath	39	48	2
A.C.Cummins	c Bedade b Srinath	0	1	–
† J.C.Adams	not out	1	4	–
S.Chanderpaul				
K.C.G.Benjamin				
* C.A.Walsh				
C.E.Cuffy				
Extras	(b 6, lb 12, w 5, nb 2)	25		
Total	(50 overs; 5 wickets)	**273**		

INDIA		Runs	Balls	4/6
M.Prabhakar	b Walsh	3	11	–
S.R.Tendulkar	c Lara b Walsh	0	4	–
N.S.Sidhu	c Cummins b Benjamin	52	87	7
* M.Azharuddin	c Lara b Cuffy	1	6	–
V.G.Kambli	c Adams b Cuffy	5	21	1
A.C.Bedade	c Adams b Benjamin	51	55	7
Kapil Dev	c Walsh b Simmons	12	18	1
† N.R.Mongia	not out	16	42	1
A.Kumble	c Simmons b Hooper	4	12	–
R.K.Chauhan	c Adams b Arthurton	20	22	2
J.Srinath	c Simmons b Hooper	0	3	–
Extras	(lb 2, w 2, nb 9)	13		
Total	(45 overs)	**177**		

INDIA	O	M	R	W
Prabhakar	10	1	45	0
Srinath	10	2	42	3
Kapil Dev	5	0	37	0
Kumble	10	0	54	1
Tendulkar	5	0	32	0
Chauhan	10	0	45	1

WEST INDIES	O	M	R	W
Walsh	5	0	11	2
Cuffy	7	2	19	2
Cummins	7	0	27	0
Benjamin	8	0	48	2
Hooper	6	0	23	2
Simmons	10	1	38	1
Arthurton	2	0	9	1

FALL OF WICKETS
1-132, 2-148, 3-164, 4-254, 5-254

FALL OF WICKETS
1-2, 2-5, 3-12, 4-21, 5-117, 6-129, 7-135, 8-149, 9-176, 10-177

Umpires: S.K.Sharma (3) and I.Shivram (1).

Referee: R.Subba Row (*England*).

INDIA v WEST INDIES 1994-95

At Wankhede Stadium, Bombay on 20 October 1994.   Result: **INDIA** won on faster scoring rate.   Toss: India.
Award: N.S.Sidhu.   LOI debuts: West Indies – B.St A.Browne.

Navjot Sidhu's six, struck just before rain terminated play, elevated India's run rate to 4.09, compared with 3.84 by West Indies. Sachin Tendulkar was dismissed for his third successive LOI duck. This series continued on 7 November after the Wills World Series.

WEST INDIES		Runs	Balls	4/6	INDIA		Runs	Balls	4/6
P.V.Simmons	lbw b Prasad	24	52	3	M.Prabhakar	c Lara b Walsh	0	1	–
S.C.Williams	c Kambli b Srinath	0	6	–	S.R.Tendulkar	c Hooper b Cuffy	0	4	–
B.C.Lara	c Prasad b Srinath	6	18	–	N.S.Sidhu	not out	65	102	4/2
C.L.Hooper	c Mongia b Srinath	70	86	7	* M.Azharuddin	c Chanderpaul b Cuffy	34	37	3
K.L.T.Arthurton	c Mongia b Kumble	2	7	–	V.G.Kambli	c Arthurton b Cummins	17	38	3
† J.C.Adams	c Mongia b Prasad	2	7	–	A.C.Bedade	not out	11	12	1
S.Chanderpaul	run out	22	39	2	† N.R.Mongia				
A.C.Cummins	c Tendulkar b Prabhakar	34	49	1	B.K.V.Prasad				
* C.A.Walsh	c Bedade b Prasad	3	11	–	J.Srinath				
B.St A.Browne	not out	8	22	–	A.Kumble				
C.E.Cuffy	not out	1	5	–	R.K.Chauhan				
Extras	(lb 3, w 13, nb 4)	20			Extras	(lb 1, w 4, nb 3)	8		
Total	(50 overs; 9 wickets)	**192**			**Total**	(33.1 overs; 4 wickets)	**135**		

INDIA	O	M	R	W	WEST INDIES	O	M	R	W
Prabhakar	10	1	34	1	Walsh	7	1	15	1
Srinath	10	2	34	3	Cuffy	8.1	1	29	2
Prasad	10	1	36	3	Cummins	6	0	34	1
Kumble	10	0	42	1	Browne	7	0	27	0
Chauhan	10	1	43	0	Hooper	5	0	29	0

FALL OF WICKETS
1-3, 2-17, 3-33, 4-48, 5-57, 6-111, 7-154, 8-167, 9-182

FALL OF WICKETS
1-0, 2-2, 3-63, 4-111

Umpires: N.Menon (2) and R.T.Ramachandran (3).

Referee: R.Subba Row (*England*).

INDIA v WEST INDIES 1994-95

At M.A.Chidambaram Stadium, Madras on 23 October 1994.   Result: **INDIA** won by 4 wickets.   Toss: India.
Award: M.Azharuddin.   LOI debuts: West Indies – S.L.Campbell

The opening contest of this seven-match triangular tournament, unlike the Pepsi Series played in coloured clothing, attracted a crowd of more than 50,000.

WEST INDIES		Runs	Balls	4/6	INDIA		Runs	Balls	4/6
P.V.Simmons	b Srinath	2	13	–	M.Prabhakar	lbw b Walsh	38	62	6
S.C.Williams	c Mongia b Prasad	39	64	5	N.S.Sidhu	c Lara b Walsh	3	17	–
B.C.Lara	lbw b Tendulkar	74	83	5	S.R.Tendulkar	c Hooper b Cummins	8	24	–
C.L.Hooper	c and b Kumble	58	80	6	* M.Azharuddin	c Walsh b Cummins	81	84	7/1
† J.C.Adams	c and b Tendulkar	0	6	–	V.G.Kambli	c Hooper b Benjamin	22	34	1
S.L.Campbell	st Mongia b Tendulkar	3	14	–	A.Jadeja	c Campbell b Benjamin	21	42	1
S.Chanderpaul	b Prabhakar	19	32	1	† N.R.Mongia	not out	24	31	3
A.C.Cummins	run out	16	13	1	A.Kumble	not out	9	11	1
K.C.G.Benjamin	b Prasad	2	3	–	J.Srinath				
* C.A.Walsh	not out	0	2	–	R.K.Chauhan				
B.St A.Browne	run out	0	1	–	B.K.V.Prasad				
Extras	(lb 5, w 1, nb 2)	8			Extras	(lb 1, w 4, nb 14)	19		
Total	(49.2 overs)	**221**			**Total**	(48.2 overs; 6 wickets)	**225**		

INDIA	O	M	R	W	WEST INDIES	O	M	R	W
Prabhakar	8	0	37	1	Walsh	10	1	33	2
Srinath	7	0	24	1	Benjamin	10	0	42	2
Prasad	8.2	1	38	2	Cummins	9.2	0	50	2
Chauhan	6	0	46	0	Browne	8	0	38	0
Kumble	10	0	35	1	Simmons	6	0	29	0
Tendulkar	10	0	36	3	Hooper	5	0	32	0

FALL OF WICKETS
1-29, 2-64, 3-176, 4-178, 5-178, 6-202, 7-204, 8-209, 9-221, 10-221

FALL OF WICKETS
1-17, 2-42, 3-80, 4-136, 5-178, 6-195

Umpires: K.S.Giridharan (2) and K.Parathasarathy (3).

Referee: R.Subba Row (*England*).

WEST INDIES v NEW ZEALAND 1994-95

At Fatorda Stadium, Margao on 26 October 1994.   No result.   Toss: West Indies.
LOI debuts: West Indies – R.Dhanraj.

A lunchtime deluge rescued West Indies after left-arm spinner Matthew Hart had returned New Zealand's best LOI analysis and Adam Parore had set a national record with five dismissals. Brian Lara was fined half his match fee and suspended for one game for showing dissent.

WEST INDIES		Runs	Balls	4/6
S.C.Williams	run out	24	42	2
S.L.Campbell	c Parore b Pringle	0	2	–
B.C.Lara	st Parore b Hart	32	38	5
C.L.Hooper	b Hart	22	18	1/2
P.V.Simmons	c Young b Hart	0	23	–
K.L.T.Arthurton	run out	1	8	–
†J.C.Adams	st Parore b Hart	5	23	–
A.C.Cummins	c Parore b Harris	11	44	1
*C.A.Walsh	c Parore b Hart	0	2	–
R.Dhanraj	b Pringle	8	30	–
C.E.Cuffy	not out	0	1	–
Extras	(b 4, lb 7, w 9)	20		
Total	(39.1 overs)	**123**		

NEW ZEALAND		Runs	Balls	4/6
B.A.Young	not out	13	22	2
B.R.Hartland	hit wicket b Walsh	6	20	–
†A.C.Parore	not out	3	12	–
*K.R.Rutherford				
S.P.Fleming				
S.A.Thomson				
C.Z.Harris				
D.J.Nash				
M.N.Hart				
C.Pringle				
R.P.de Groen				
Extras	(w 2, nb 1)	3		
Total	(9 overs; 1 wicket)	**25**		

NEW ZEALAND	O	M	R	W
Pringle	4.1	0	19	2
Nash	8	1	25	0
De Groen	4	0	19	0
Hart	10	2	22	5
Thomson	10	5	19	0
Harris	3	0	8	1

WEST INDIES	O	M	R	W
Walsh	5	1	17	1
Cuffy	4	1	8	0

FALL OF WICKETS
1-14

Referee: R.Subba Row (*England*).

FALL OF WICKETS
1-4, 2-71, 3-92, 4-94, 5-95, 6-97, 7-102, 8-102, 9-123, 10-123

Umpires: B.A.Jamula (2) and K.Murali (1).

INDIA v NEW ZEALAND 1994-95

At IPCL Sports Complex, Baroda on 28 October 1994.   Result: **INDIA** won by 7 wickets.   Toss: New Zealand.
Award: S.R.Tendulkar.   LOI debuts: None.

Indian Petrochemicals Corporation Limited provided the 109th LOI venue and the 33rd in India. Adam Parore, whose 96 is the highest LOI score without a boundary, and Ken Rutherford, first hundred in his 103rd match, shared New Zealand's record partnership for any wicket (180).

NEW ZEALAND		Runs	Balls	4/6
B.A.Young	c Mongia b Srinath	5	11	1
B.R.Hartland	c Kumble b Prabhakar	8	25	1
†A.C.Parore	c Kumble b Prabhakar	96	138	–
*K.R.Rutherford	run out	108	102	13
S.P.Fleming	not out	33	25	1/1
S.A.Thomson	not out	0	–	–
C.Z.Harris				
D.J.Nash				
M.N.Hart				
C.Pringle				
R.P.de Groen				
Extras	(b 5, lb 7, w 2, nb 5)	19		
Total	(50 overs; 4 wickets)	**269**		

INDIA		Runs	Balls	4/6
M.Prabhakar	c and b Hart	74	95	7
S.R.Tendulkar	run out	115	136	9
N.S.Sidhu	c De Groen b Hart	11	10	1
*M.Azharuddin	not out	47	39	5
V.G.Kambli	not out	12	6	2
A.Jadeja				
†N.R.Mongia				
A.Kumble				
J.Srinath				
S.L.V.Raju				
B.K.V.Prasad				
Extras	(lb 3, w 9)	12		
Total	(48.1 overs; 3 wickets)	**271**		

INDIA	O	M	R	W
Prabhakar	10	0	49	2
Srinath	10	1	41	1
Prasad	10	0	49	0
Raju	7	1	38	0
Kumble	10	0	53	0
Tendulkar	3	0	27	0

NEW ZEALAND	O	M	R	W
Pringle	9.1	0	53	0
Nash	10	0	51	0
De Groen	9	0	52	0
Hart	10	0	56	2
Harris	5	0	31	0
Thomson	5	0	25	0

FALL OF WICKETS
1-7, 2-27, 3-207, 4-268

Umpires: S.K.Bansal (8) and S.Shastri (2).

FALL OF WICKETS
1-144, 2-162, 3-247

Referee: R.Subba Row (*England*).

INDIA v WEST INDIES 1994-95

At Green Park, Kanpur on 30 October 1994.   Result: **WEST INDIES** won by 46 runs.   Toss: India.
Award: K.L.T.Arthurton.   LOI debuts: None.

Suspecting chicanery when India's sixth-wicket pair scored 16 runs from the last 43 balls when 63 were needed for victory, the referee fined the hosts two points. These were restored by the ICC, who rescinded his decision on appeal.

WEST INDIES		Runs	Balls	4/6
P.V.Simmons	c Srinath b Tendulkar	65	96	6/2
S.C.Williams	c and b Tendulkar	45	86	4
C.L.Hooper	lbw b Raju	1	2	–
K.L.T.Arthurton	run out	72	62	4/1
R.I.C.Holder	b Srinath	32	49	1
A.C.Cummins	run out	14	12	–
K.C.G.Benjamin	not out	1	2	–
† J.C.Adams				
S.Chanderpaul				
* C.A.Walsh				
C.E.Cuffy				
Extras	(lb 18, w 3, nb 6)	27		
Total	**(50 overs; 6 wickets)**	**257**		

INDIA		Runs	Balls	4/6
M.Prabhakar	not out	102	154	9
S.R.Tendulkar	b Cummins	34	47	7
N.S.Sidhu	run out	2	5	–
* M.Azharuddin	c Cummins b Cuffy	26	34	2
V.G.Kambli	run out	16	28	1
A.Jadeja	run out	9	11	–
† N.R.Mongia	not out	4	21	–
A.Kumble				
J.Srinath				
S.L.V.Raju				
B.K.V.Prasad				
Extras	(lb 9, w 5, nb 4)	18		
Total	**(50 overs; 5 wickets)**	**211**		

INDIA	O	M	R	W
Prabhakar	6	0	50	0
Srinath	9	0	31	1
Prasad	7	0	36	0
Kumble	10	0	50	0
Raju	10	1	41	1
Tendulkar	8	0	31	2

WEST INDIES	O	M	R	W
Walsh	9	2	20	0
Cuffy	10	0	49	1
Simmons	2	0	19	0
Benjamin	10	1	39	0
Cummins	10	1	39	1
Hooper	8	0	36	0
Arthurton	1	1	0	0

FALL OF WICKETS
1-115, 2-120, 3-130, 4-219, 5-250, 6-257

Umpires: Jasbir Singh (1) and C.K.Sathe (2).

FALL OF WICKETS
1-56, 2-78, 3-119, 4-169, 5-195

Referee: R.Subba Row (*England*).

WEST INDIES v NEW ZEALAND 1994-95

At Nehru Stadium, Gauhati on 1 November 1994.   Result: **WEST INDIES** won by 135 runs.   Toss: West Indies.
Award: C.L.Hooper.   LOI debuts: None.

West Indies posted their highest total against New Zealand. Chris Pringle's 34 not out is the highest LOI score batting at number 11. Leg-spinner Rajindra Dhanraj took 4 for 2 in his first four overs in internationals.

WEST INDIES		Runs	Balls	4/6
P.V.Simmons	b Nash	0	5	–
S.C.Williams	lbw b Doull	25	28	4
B.C.Lara	c Hart b Nash	69	75	7
C.L.Hooper	c Hartland b Pringle	111	114	11
K.L.T.Arthurton	b Nash	45	47	2/1
A.C.Cummins	not out	29	17	1/1
R.I.C.Holder	b Pringle	4	5	–
† J.C.Adams	not out	5	4	1
* C.A.Walsh				
R.Dhanraj				
C.E.Cuffy				
Extras	(b 5, lb 6, w 7)	18		
Total	**(50 overs; 6 wickets)**	**306**		

NEW ZEALAND		Runs	Balls	4/6
B.R.Hartland	b Walsh	9	26	–
B.A.Young	c Williams b Dhanraj	33	72	1
† A.C.Parore	run out	9	27	–
* K.R.Rutherford	b Hooper	13	27	1
S.P.Fleming	c Simmons b Dhanraj	18	42	–
S.A.Thomson	st Adams b Dhanraj	2	9	–
C.Z.Harris	lbw b Arthurton	12	23	–/1
M.N.Hart	b Dhanraj	2	4	–
D.J.Nash	not out	20	34	1
S.B.Doull	b Arthurton	4	4	1
C.Pringle	not out	34	22	2/2
Extras	(b 4, lb 8, w 1, nb 2)	15		
Total	**(50 overs; 9 wickets)**	**171**		

NEW ZEALAND	O	M	R	W
Nash	10	1	48	3
Pringle	9	1	71	2
Doull	9	0	65	1
Hart	5	0	34	0
Harris	10	0	43	0
Thomson	7	0	34	0

WEST INDIES	O	M	R	W
Walsh	6	1	18	1
Cuffy	6	0	13	0
Simmons	7	1	13	0
Cummins	4	0	18	0
Dhanraj	10	2	26	4
Hooper	10	1	28	1
Arthurton	5	0	26	2
Lara	2	0	17	0

FALL OF WICKETS
1-1, 2-45, 3-156, 4-259, 5-272, 6-281

Umpires: S.Banerjee (11) and M.R.Singh (3).

FALL OF WICKETS
1-15, 2-33, 3-60, 4-92, 5-95, 6-95, 7-101, 8-119, 9-123

Referee: R.Subba Row (*England*).

INDIA v NEW ZEALAND 1994-95

At Feroz Shah Kotla Ground, Delhi on 3 November 1994.   Result: **INDIA** won by 107 runs.   Toss: India.
Award: S.R.Tendulkar.   LOI debuts: New Zealand – D.J.Murray.

Playing in his 183rd international, Mohammed Azharuddin became the first Indian to score 5000 runs, his fifty requiring only 38 balls. Vinod Kambli took a wicket with his fourth ball in limited-overs internationals – in his 48th match.

INDIA		Runs	Balls	4/6	NEW ZEALAND		Runs	Balls	4/6
A.Jadeja	c Hart b Nash	90	127	7	B.A.Young	c Yadav b Srinath	0	3	–
S.R.Tendulkar	b Hart	62	54	13	D.J.Murray	run out	3	17	–
N.S.Sidhu	c Hart b De Groen	35	52	1/1	†A.C.Parore	lbw b Raju	51	105	1
*M.Azharuddin	not out	58	45	6	*K.R.Rutherford	c Srinath b Prasad	8	12	1
V.G.Kambli	not out	36	22	2/2	S.P.Fleming	lbw b Tendulkar	56	48	8
†V.Yadav					S.A.Thomson	c Raju b Tendulkar	9	27	–
C.Sharma					C.Z.Harris	c Srinath b Raju	16	27	–
J.Srinath					M.N.Hart	run out	16	16	1/1
A.Kumble					D.J.Nash	b Kumble	3	7	–
S.L.V.Raju					S.B.Doull	st Yadav b Kambli	8	10	–/1
B.K.V.Prasad					R.P.de Groen	not out	1	7	–
Extras	(lb 3, w 5)	8			Extras	(lb 4, w 5, nb 2)	11		
Total	(50 overs; 3 wickets)	**289**			**Total**	(45.4 overs)	**182**		

NEW ZEALAND	O	M	R	W	INDIA	O	M	R	W
Nash	10	0	50	1	Srinath	7	1	22	1
Doull	10	1	58	0	Prasad	7	0	26	1
De Groen	9	0	67	1	Sharma	1	0	23	0
Hart	9	0	36	1	Kumble	10	1	41	1
Harris	2	0	24	0	Tendulkar	10	2	29	2
Thomson	10	0	51	0	Raju	10	0	30	2
					Kambli	0.4	0	7	1

FALL OF WICKETS
1-100, 2-175, 3-222

FALL OF WICKETS
1-0, 2-12, 3-27, 4-106, 5-132, 6-142, 7-168, 8-172, 9-173, 10-182

Umpires: T.K.Handoo (1) and R.C.Sharma (8).

Referee: R.Subba Row (*England*).

INDIA v WEST INDIES 1994-95

At Eden Gardens, Calcutta on 5 November 1994.   Result: **INDIA** won by 72 runs.   Toss: West Indies.
Award: S.R.Tendulkar.   Series Award: S.R.Tendulkar.   LOI debuts: None.

Supported by a capacity crowd (c 100,000), India achieved their first hundred opening partnership against West Indies. Navjot Sidhu completed 3000 runs in 82 internationals, Vinod Kambli contributed a 36-ball fifty, and Javagal Srinath took his 100th wicket in 67 matches.

INDIA		Runs	Balls	4/6	WEST INDIES		Runs	Balls	4/6
A.Jadeja	c Lara b Dhanraj	58	100	–/1	P.V.Simmons	run out	21	53	2
S.R.Tendulkar	c Williams b Cuffy	66	68	8	S.C.Williams	c Azharuddin b Srinath	29	34	6
N.S.Sidhu	c Adams b Cummins	28	51	–/1	B.C.Lara	b Prasad	1	11	–
*M.Azharuddin	c Holder b Hooper	41	38	3	C.L.Hooper	c Azharuddin b Raju	30	43	2
V.G.Kambli	not out	58	40	4/2	K.L.T.Arthurton	b Raju	42	59	3
A.C.Bedade	c Arthurton b Dhanraj	3	5	–	R.I.C.Holder	c Jadeja b Tendulkar	5	9	–
†V.Yadav	lbw b Walsh	0	1	–	†J.C.Adams	c Kumble b Jadeja	1	5	–
A.Kumble	not out	1	2	–	A.C.Cummins	b Kumble	21	36	1/1
J.Srinath					*C.A.Walsh	c Tendulkar b Raju	30	14	1/3
S.L.V.Raju					R.Dhanraj	not out	0	2	–
B.K.V.Prasad					C.E.Cuffy	c Kumble b Raju	0	1	–
Extras	(b 10, lb 5, nb 4)	19			Extras	(b 2, lb 14, w 5, nb 1)	22		
Total	(50 overs; 6 wickets)	**274**			**Total**	(44 overs)	**202**		

WEST INDIES	O	M	R	W	INDIA	O	M	R	W
Walsh	10	0	46	1	Srinath	7	0	25	1
Cuffy	10	1	53	1	Prasad	7	3	23	1
Cummins	10	0	50	1	Kumble	7	0	27	1
Hooper	10	0	55	1	Raju	10	0	58	4
Dhanraj	10	0	55	2	Tendulkar	8	2	35	1
					Jadeja	5	0	18	1

FALL OF WICKETS
1-108, 2-147, 3-175, 4-237, 5-266, 6-267

FALL OF WICKETS
1-46, 2-49, 3-68, 4-101, 5-116, 6-121, 7-162, 8-182, 9-202, 10-202

Umpires: V.K.Ramaswamy (29) and S.Venkataraghavan (3).

Referee: R.Subba Row (*England*).

INDIA v WEST INDIES 1994-95

At Indira Priyadarshani Stadium, Vishakhapatnam on 7 November 1994.   Result: **INDIA** won by 4 runs.
Toss: West Indies.   Award: N.S.Sidhu.   LOI debuts: None.

This series resumed 90 minutes (six overs) late because the tourists' luggage had been flown to Madras. West Indies were penalised a vital over for their tardy bowling rate. Navjot Sidhu became the first Indian to score five LOI hundreds. Vinod Kambli registered his first duck in international or first-class matches. Carl Hooper scored 50 off 31 balls.

INDIA		Runs	Balls	4/6
A.Jadeja	c Murray b Cummins	38	54	5
S.R.Tendulkar	c Cummins b Hooper	54	64	5
N.S.Sidhu	not out	114	103	9/2
* M.Azharuddin	c Walsh b Arthurton	45	42	4
V.G.Kambli	c Arthurton b Walsh	0	1	–
M.Prabhakar	not out	1	1	–
† N.R.Mongia				
J.Srinath				
A.Kumble				
S.L.V.Raju				
B.K.V.Prasad				
Extras	(lb 2, w 4, nb 2)	8		
Total	(44 overs; 4 wickets)	**260**		

WEST INDIES		Runs	Balls	4/6
P.V.Simmons	b Tendulkar	51	77	4/1
S.C.Williams	run out	49	60	7/1
B.C.Lara	c Raju b Prabhakar	39	55	2
C.L.Hooper	not out	74	47	7/2
K.L.T.Arthurton	c Azharuddin b Kumble	13	8	1
A.C.Cummins	run out	2	1	–
R.I.C.Holder	c Azharuddin b Prabhakar	0	1	–
* C.A.Walsh	b Kumble	3	4	–
† J.R.Murray	not out	3	4	–
C.E.Cuffy				
B.St A.Browne				
Extras	(b 2, lb 15, w 5)	22		
Total	(43 overs; 7 wickets)	**256**		

WEST INDIES	O	M	R	W
Browne	5	0	41	0
Walsh	9	0	50	1
Cuffy	9	0	41	0
Cummins	7	0	43	1
Simmons	5	0	23	0
Hooper	7	0	46	1
Arthurton	2	0	14	1

INDIA	O	M	R	W
Prabhakar	9	1	61	2
Srinath	8	0	31	0
Prasad	3	0	26	0
Kumble	7	0	41	2
Tendulkar	9	0	39	1
Raju	7	0	41	0

FALL OF WICKETS
1-64, 2-137, 3-250, 4-258

FALL OF WICKETS
1-86, 2-145, 3-178, 4-202, 5-215, 6-220, 7-230

Umpires: H.S.Shekon (1) and R.C.Sharma (9).

Referee: R.Subba Row (*England*).

INDIA v WEST INDIES 1994-95

At Barabati Stadium, Cuttack on 9 November 1994.   Result: **INDIA** won by 8 wickets.   Toss: West Indies.
Award: A.Jadeja.   LOI debuts: None.

India posted their highest opening partnership against West Indies and achieved their first series victory against those opponents.

WEST INDIES		Runs	Balls	4/6
P.V.Simmons	run out	32	50	3
S.C.Williams	c Prabhakar b Sharma	15	33	2
B.C.Lara	st Mongia b Kumble	89	106	8/1
C.L.Hooper	run out	2	11	–
K.L.T.Arthurton	c Mongia b Raju	27	37	2
R.I.C.Holder	not out	36	37	1/1
S.Chanderpaul	lbw b Jadeja	0	2	–
† J.R.Murray	c Prabhakar b Jadeja	3	6	–
A.C.Cummins	lbw b Kumble	8	13	–
* C.A.Walsh	b Kumble	0	2	–
C.E.Cuffy	not out	17	15	2
Extras	(lb 3, w 7, nb 12)	22		
Total	(50 overs; 9 wickets)	**251**		

INDIA		Runs	Balls	4/6
A.Jadeja	c Cuffy b Walsh	104	126	4/3
S.R.Tendulkar	b Simmons	88	112	10
V.G.Kambli	not out	40	35	2
* M.Azharuddin	not out	17	18	1
A.C.Bedade				
M.Prabhakar				
† N.R.Mongia				
C.Sharma				
J.Srinath				
A.Kumble				
S.L.V.Raju				
Extras	(lb 1, w 5, nb 1)	7		
Total	(49.2 overs; 2 wickets)	**256**		

INDIA	O	M	R	W
Prabhakar	8	0	36	0
Srinath	7	0	32	0
Sharma	7	1	31	1
Kumble	10	0	43	3
Tendulkar	2	0	20	0
Raju	6	0	31	1
Jadeja	10	0	55	2

WEST INDIES	O	M	R	W
Walsh	10	1	29	1
Cuffy	10	1	36	0
Cummins	9.2	0	58	0
Hooper	4	0	34	0
Arthurton	3	0	28	0
Simmons	8	0	46	1
Chanderpaul	5	0	24	0

FALL OF WICKETS
1-47, 2-67, 3-77, 4-168, 5-191, 6-192, 7-202, 8-228, 9-228

FALL OF WICKETS
1-176, 2-222

Umpires: A.V.Jayaprakash (2) and J.Kurishinkal (2).

Referee: R.Subba Row (*England*).

INDIA v WEST INDIES 1994-95

At Sawai Mansingh Stadium, Jaipur on 11 November 1994.   Result: **INDIA** won by 5 runs.   Toss: India.
Award: C.L.Hooper.   Series Award: S.R.Tendulkar.   LOI debuts: None.

At 25 years 193 days, Brian Lara became the youngest to lead West Indies in a limited-overs international. Needing 23 runs off 24 balls, West Indies lost their last five wickets for 16 in three overs.

INDIA		Runs	Balls	4/6
A.Jadeja	c and b Hooper	31	63	4
S.R.Tendulkar	c Adams b Browne	105	134	10
V.G.Kambli	c Lara b Cummins	66	64	4/1
A.C.Bedade	not out	15	19	1
* M.Azharuddin	c Simmons b Cummins	2	5	–
C.Sharma	c Cuffy b Browne	1	3	–
M.Prabhakar	not out	4	1	1
† N.R.Mongia				
A.Kumble				
J.Srinath				
S.L.V.Raju				
Extras	(b 6, lb 11, w 9, nb 9)	35		
Total	(50 overs; 5 wickets)	**259**		

WEST INDIES		Runs	Balls	4/6
P.V.Simmons	c Azharuddin b Srinath	2	6	–
S.C.Williams	c Mongia b Sharma	13	32	–
* B.C.Lara	lbw b Raju	47	59	8
C.L.Hooper	lbw b Raju	84	88	6/2
† J.C.Adams	c Kambli b Kumble	50	55	5
K.L.T.Arthurton	c Azharuddin b Kumble	14	8	1/1
R.I.C.Holder	run out	8	12	–
S.Chanderpaul	c Bedade b Prabhakar	8	6	2
A.C.Cummins	b Raju	1	2	–
C.E.Cuffy	b Raju	2	3	–
B.St A.Browne	not out	0	1	–
Extras	(b 1, lb 16, w 5, nb 3)	25		
Total	(49 overs)	**254**		

WEST INDIES	O	M	R	W
Cummins	10	0	49	2
Cuffy	10	0	40	0
Browne	10	0	50	2
Hooper	10	1	35	1
Simmons	5	0	25	0
Chanderpaul	5	0	43	0

INDIA	O	M	R	W
Prabhakar	9	1	35	1
Srinath	7	0	42	1
Sharma	10	0	39	1
Kumble	10	1	44	2
Raju	9	0	46	4
Tendulkar	4	0	31	0

FALL OF WICKETS
1-95, 2-212, 3-239, 4-245, 5-252

FALL OF WICKETS
1-3, 2-50, 3-90, 4-216, 5-218, 6-238, 7-247, 8-251, 9-252, 10-254

Umpires: S.Choudhury (6) and S.K.Porel (1).

Referee: R.Subba Row (*England*).

ZIMBABWE v SRI LANKA 1994-95

At Harare Sports Club on 3 November 1994.   Result: **SRI LANKA** won by 56 runs.   Toss: Zimbabwe.
Award: R.S.Mahanama.   LOI debuts: Zimbabwe – G.C.Martin.

In stark contrast to his form in the three Tests preceding this series (37 runs in five innings), Roshan Mahanama batted throughout the innings for his second LOI hundred. Aravinda de Silva contributed a brilliant cameo. Chaminda Vaas returned his best analysis.

SRI LANKA		Runs	Balls	4/6
R.S.Mahanama	not out	119	142	8
A.P.Gurusinha	c Dekker b Whittall	20	33	3
S.Ranatunga	c Houghton b Dekker	51	79	1
* A.Ranatunga	b Peall	14	20	–
P.A.de Silva	c Waller b Whittall	35	24	4/1
S.T.Jayasuriya	c Waller b Whittall	1	2	–
R.S.Kalpage	not out	0	–	–
† H.P.Tillekeratne				
G.P.Wickremasinghe				
W.P.U.C.J.Vaas				
K.R.Pushpakumara				
Extras	(lb 6, w 10)	16		
Total	(50 overs; 5 wickets)	**256**		

ZIMBABWE		Runs	Balls	4/6
G.W.Flower	c Tillekeratne b Pushpakumara	0	2	–
A.C.Waller	c sub b Wickremasinghe	40	46	5
A.D.R.Campbell	c A.Ranatunga b Vaas	5	16	1
D.L.Houghton	c Jayasuriya b Vaas	1	11	–
*† A.Flower	b Vaas	61	81	4
G.J.Whittall	c Tillekeratne b Wickremasinghe	0	4	–
M.H.Dekker	c Vaas b Kalpage	20	45	1
G.C.Martin	c De Silva b Kalpage	7	16	–
D.H.Brain	b Pushpakumara	10	19	–
H.H.Streak	not out	18	33	–
S.G.Peall	b Vaas	21	18	4
Extras	(b 1, lb 8, w 7, nb 1)	17		
Total	(48.1 overs)	**200**		

ZIMBABWE	O	M	R	W
Streak	9	1	50	0
Brain	7	1	31	0
Whittall	10	1	58	3
Martin	10	1	39	0
Peall	7	0	36	1
G.W.Flower	2	0	12	0
Dekker	5	0	24	1

SRI LANKA	O	M	R	W
Pushpakumara	10	0	51	2
Vaas	9.1	1	20	4
Wickremasinghe	8	0	42	2
A.Ranatunga	10	1	38	0
Kalpage	10	1	27	2
Jayasuriya	1	0	13	0

FALL OF WICKETS
1-40, 2-159, 3-198, 4-252, 5-255

FALL OF WICKETS
1-0, 2-12, 3-20, 4-66, 5-71, 6-129, 7-145, 8-149, 9-167, 10-200

Umpires: Q.J.Goosen (1) and I.D.Robinson (16).

Referee: P.L.van der Merwe (*South Africa*).

ZIMBABWE v SRI LANKA 1994-95

At Harare Sports Club on 5 November 1994.　　Result: **ZIMBABWE** won by 2 runs.　　Toss: Zimbabwe.
Award: A.D.R.Campbell.　　LOI debuts: None.

Andrew Campbell's first LOI hundred, completed off 96 balls, was rewarded by Zimbabwe's first win on home soil
despite Roshan Mahanama's second successive century. Non-striker Aravinda de Silva survived an appeal for
obstruction when he collided with the bowler attempting a return catch.

ZIMBABWE		Runs	Balls	4/6
*†A.Flower	b Vaas	76	98	8
G.W.Flower	run out	21	37	2
A.D.R.Campbell	not out	131	115	11/4
D.L.Houghton	c Kalpage b Pushpakumara	22	27	2
A.C.Waller	c Tillekeratne b Vaas	3	5	–
M.H.Dekker	b Vaas	9	10	1
G.J.Whittall	not out	15	9	1
G.C.Martin				
H.H.Streak				
S.G.Peall				
J.A.Rennie				
Extras	(b 1, lb 8, w 3, nb 1)	13		
Total	(50 overs; 5 wickets)	290		

SRI LANKA		Runs	Balls	4/6
R.S.Mahanama	c G.W.Flower b Streak	108	149	6/1
S.T.Jayasuriya	c Waller b Streak	37	24	4/2
S.Ranatunga	run out	15	19	1
P.A.de Silva	not out	97	89	5/1
* A.Ranatunga	c Waller b Whittall	1	3	–
A.P.Gurusinha	c G.W.Flower b Streak	4	6	–
R.S.Kalpage	lbw b Streak	0	1	–
† H.P.Tillekeratne	run out	7	11	–
G.P.Wickremasinghe	b Whittall	1	2	–
W.P.U.C.J.Vaas	not out	0	–	–
K.R.Pushpakumara				
Extras	(b 3, lb 3, w 10, nb 2)	18		
Total	(50 overs; 8 wickets)	288		

SRI LANKA	O	M	R	W
Vaas	10	0	59	3
Pushpakumara	10	1	43	1
Wickremasinghe	10	0	55	0
A.Ranatunga	5	0	38	0
Kalpage	10	0	53	0
Gurusinha	5	0	33	0

ZIMBABWE	O	M	R	W
Streak	10	0	44	4
Rennie	8	0	54	0
Whittall	8	0	57	2
Martin	2	0	24	0
Peall	10	0	52	0
G.W.Flower	7	0	28	0
Dekker	5	0	23	0

FALL OF WICKETS
1-60, 2-152, 3-228, 4-235, 5-250

FALL OF WICKETS
1-66, 2-111, 3-233, 4-234, 5-245, 6-245, 7-276, 8-278

Umpires: Q.J.Goosen (2) and I.D.Robinson (17).　　　　Referee: P.L.van der Merwe (*South Africa*).

ZIMBABWE v SRI LANKA 1994-95

At Harare Sports Club on 6 November 1994.　　Result: **SRI LANKA** won by 191 runs.　　Toss: Sri Lanka.
Award: P.A.de Silva.　　LOI debuts: None.

Aravinda de Silva, who completed his hundred with a six, and Arjuna Ranatunga added 143 in 24 overs to record Sri
Lanka's highest fourth-wicket partnership. Zimbabwe were dismissed for their lowest LOI total, Mark Dekker (18)
having retired at 51 with a split finger, resumed at 93 and retreated finally at 105.

SRI LANKA		Runs	Balls	4/6
R.S.Mahanama	lbw b Brain	40	57	5
S.T.Jayasuriya	c A.Flower b Brain	11	10	1/1
A.P.Gurusinha	c A.Flower b Whittall	25	45	2
P.A.de Silva	not out	107	100	9/1
* A.Ranatunga	c G.W.Flower b Brain	85	83	6
R.S.Kalpage	not out	12	9	–/1
† H.P.Tillekeratne				
G.P.Wickremasinghe				
M.Muralitharan				
W.P.U.C.J.Vaas				
K.R.Pushpakumara				
Extras	(lb 6, w 10)	16		
Total	(50 overs; 4 wickets)	296		

ZIMBABWE		Runs	Balls	4/6
* A.Flower	c Muralitharan b Pushpakumara	8	9	2
G.W.Flower	c Tillekeratne b Vaas	0	2	–
A.D.R.Campbell	c Mahanama b Vaas	2	8	–
D.L.Houghton	lbw b Pushpakumara	0	1	–
M.H.Dekker	retired hurt	23	109	–
G.J.Whittall	c Gurusinha b Pushpakumara	7	18	1
† W.R.James	run out	29	62	–
H.H.Streak	run out	8	8	–
D.H.Brain	b Muralitharan	0	10	–
J.A.Rennie	not out	20	49	–
S.G.Peall	b Wickremasinghe	2	8	–
Extras	(lb 3, w 1, nb 2)	6		
Total	(48.1 overs)	105		

ZIMBABWE	O	M	R	W
Streak	10	1	40	0
Brain	10	0	67	3
Rennie	7	0	60	0
Whittall	7	0	43	1
Peall	8	0	41	0
G.W.Flower	3	0	13	0
Campbell	3	0	14	0
Dekker	2	0	12	0

SRI LANKA	O	M	R	W
Vaas	7	2	12	2
Pushpakumara	9	1	25	3
Wickremasinghe	9	1	17	1
Muralitharan	10	0	21	1
Kalpage	10	1	21	0
Jayasuriya	2	1	2	0
Tillekeratne	1	0	1	0
Mahanama	0.1	0	3	0

FALL OF WICKETS
1-18, 2-76, 3-106, 4-249

FALL OF WICKETS
1-1, 2-9, 3-9 4-11, 5-22, 6-69, 7-70, 8-86, 9-93

Umpires: S.N.Fleming (1) and K.Kanjee (10).　　　　Referee: P.L.van der Merwe (*South Africa*).

AUSTRALIA v ZIMBABWE 1994-95

At WACA Ground, Perth on 2 December 1994.   Result: **AUSTRALIA** won by 2 wickets.   Toss: Australia.
Award: S.K.Warne.   LOI debuts: Australia – S.G.Law; Zimbabwe – P.A.Strang.

The inclusion of a second Australian team, with players shuffling between the two host teams, rendered much of this tournament superfluous, particularly when the ICC, quite rightly, decreed that matches involving Australia 'A' did not qualify for official LOI status. Craig McDermott took his 100th World Series wicket.

ZIMBABWE		Runs	Balls	4/6	AUSTRALIA		Runs	Balls	4/6
* A.Flower	c Warne b Fleming	29	32	3	M.J.Slater	c A.Flower b Streak	18	44	3
G.W.Flower	b McGrath	20	48	2	* M.A.Taylor	c G.W.Flower b Brandes	45	45	5
A.D.R.Campbell	hit wicket b Warne	22	33	2	D.C.Boon	c Houghton b Strang	8	30	–
D.L.Houghton	run out	13	29	1	M.G.Bevan	c James b Streak	30	81	1
M.H.Dekker	lbw b McGrath	16	51	1	S.G.Law	c Houghton b Martin	7	19	–
† W.R.James	run out	8	21	–	† I.A.Healy	c Campbell b G.W.Flower	40	43	3
G.C.Martin	b Law	16	29	–	S.K.Warne	c and b G.W.Flower	5	5	1
P.A.Strang	not out	17	37	–	C.J.McDermott	c Dekker b G.W.Flower	0	2	–
E.A.Brandes	c Healy b McDermott	5	12	–	M.E.Waugh	not out	6	9	–
H.H.Streak	c Fleming b Warne	7	10	–	D.W.Fleming	not out	0	8	–
D.H.Brain	not out	1	1	–	G.D.McGrath				
Extras	(lb 9, w 3)	12			Extras	(lb 6, w 1, nb 1)	8		
Total	(50 overs; 9 wickets)	**166**			**Total**	(47.2 overs; 8 wickets)	**167**		

AUSTRALIA	O	M	R	W	ZIMBABWE	O	M	R	W
McDermott	10	0	32	1	Brain	8.2	2	39	0
Fleming	10	0	45	1	Streak	10	1	31	2
McGrath	10	1	23	2	Brandes	10	1	29	1
Waugh	1	0	3	0	Strang	10	1	30	1
Law	9	0	27	1	Martin	5	0	17	1
Warne	10	1	27	2	G.W.Flower	4	0	15	3

FALL OF WICKETS
1-49, 2-56, 3-83, 4-88, 5-109, 6-117, 7-144, 8-151, 9-164

FALL OF WICKETS
1-69, 2-69, 3-87, 4-96, 5-156, 6-161, 7-161, 8-164

Umpires: T.A.Prue (23) and W.P.Sheahan (5).

Referee: J.R.Reid (*New Zealand*).

AUSTRALIA v ENGLAND 1994-95

At Sydney Cricket Ground on 6 December 1994.   Result: **AUSTRALIA** won by 28 runs.   Toss: Australia.
Award: D.C.Boon.   LOI debuts: England – J.E.Benjamin, C.White.

Australia's 100th win in 170 World Series matches (64 lost) was only their third in ten games against England at the SCG.

AUSTRALIA		Runs	Balls	4/6	ENGLAND		Runs	Balls	4/6
* M.A.Taylor	c and b Hick	57	96	2	* M.A.Atherton	lbw b Law	60	101	4
M.J.Slater	c Hick b Udal	50	66	5	A.J.Stewart	c Law b May	48	73	5
M.E.Waugh	b Udal	4	15	–	G.A.Hick	c Boon b May	6	16	–
D.C.Boon	not out	64	64	4	G.P.Thorpe	c Bevan b McDermott	21	34	–
M.G.Bevan	c Gooch b Gough	46	59	1	G.A.Gooch	c McDermott b Warne	21	23	1
S.G.Law	not out	0	–	–	C.White	b McDermott	0	1	–
† I.A.Healy					† S.J.Rhodes	c Warne b Law	8	12	–
S.K.Warne					P.A.J.DeFreitas	run out	6	6	–
C.J.McDermott					D.Gough	not out	8	10	–
T.B.A.May					S.D.Udal	b McGrath	4	10	–
G.D.McGrath					J.E.Benjamin	b McDermott	0	6	–
Extras	(lb 2, w 1)	3			Extras	(lb 7, w 6, nb 1)	14		
Total	(50 overs; 4 wickets)	**224**			**Total**	(48.3 overs)	**196**		

ENGLAND	O	M	R	W	AUSTRALIA	O	M	R	W
Benjamin	6	0	25	0	McDermott	9.3	0	34	3
DeFreitas	9	1	43	0	McGrath	9	4	22	1
Gough	10	0	51	1	Warne	10	0	46	1
White	5	0	22	0	Law	10	0	52	2
Udal	10	1	37	2	May	10	1	35	2
Hick	10	0	44	1					

FALL OF WICKETS
1-96, 2-105, 3-126, 4-218

FALL OF WICKETS
1-100, 2-112, 3-133, 4-147, 5-149, 6-164, 7-180, 8-187, 9-195, 10-196

Umpires: D.B.Hair (12) and P.D.Parker (3).

Referee: J.R.Reid (*New Zealand*).

AUSTRALIA v ZIMBABWE 1994-95

At Bellerive Oval, Hobart on 8 December 1994.   Result: **AUSTRALIA** won by 84 runs.   Toss: Australia.
Award: S.G.Law.   LOI debuts: None.

Given a rare opportunity to open the innings, Stuart Law responded with a hundred in his third international. David Boon completed 1000 runs in a calendar year but failed to hit his final ball for the six which would have brought up his hundred.

AUSTRALIA		Runs	Balls	4/6
M.J.Slater	c Whittall b Brain	10	10	1
S.G.Law	c G.W.Flower b Dekker	110	135	6/1
M.E.Waugh	c G.W.Flower b Whittall	12	28	2
D.C.Boon	not out	98	119	5/1
M.G.Bevan	not out	11	15	–
* M.A.Taylor				
† I.A.Healy				
S.K.Warne				
D.W.Fleming				
T.B.A.May				
G.D.McGrath				
Extras	(b 5, lb 2, w 5, nb 1)	13		
Total	(50 overs; 3 wickets)	**254**		

ZIMBABWE		Runs	Balls	4/6
* A.Flower	c Healy b May	39	56	4
G.W.Flower	c Healy b McGrath	8	14	–
A.D.R.Campbell	b McGrath	1	10	–
D.L.Houghton	b May	4	13	–
M.H.Dekker	run out	11	32	–
G.J.Whittall	c Healy b Fleming	35	78	3
† W.R.James	c Healy b Warne	15	49	–
I.P.Butchart	b Fleming	10	22	–
P.A.Strang	not out	21	23	2
H.H.Streak	not out	12	10	2
D.H.Brain				
Extras	(lb 6, w 7, nb 1)	14		
Total	(50 overs; 8 wickets)	**170**		

ZIMBABWE	O	M	R	W
Brain	10	1	51	1
Streak	9	0	55	0
Whittall	7	1	22	1
Dekker	10	0	42	1
Strang	9	0	51	0
G.W.Flower	5	0	26	0

AUSTRALIA	O	M	R	W
McGrath	8	2	18	2
Fleming	10	0	42	2
May	10	2	34	2
Law	10	1	25	0
Warne	9	0	23	1
Boon	2	0	11	0
Slater	1	0	11	0

FALL OF WICKETS
1-12, 2-55, 3-214

FALL OF WICKETS
1-15, 2-24, 3-47, 4-64, 5-73, 6-117, 7-129, 8-136

Umpires: A.J.McQuillan (4) and S.G.Randell (61).

Referee: J.R.Reid (New Zealand).

ENGLAND v ZIMBABWE 1994-95

At Sydney Cricket Ground on 15 December 1994.   Result: **ZIMBABWE** won by 13 runs.   Toss: Zimbabwe.
Award: G.W.Flower.   LOI debuts: England – J.P.Crawley.

Zimbabwe's fourth LOI victory was their second in two encounters with England, both being in New South Wales (see LOI No. 748). Grant Flower became the first to bat throughout a completed innings and, with David Houghton, he also shared Zimbabwe's first fourth-wicket century partnership.

ZIMBABWE		Runs	Balls	4/6
*†A.Flower	c Stewart b Fraser	12	15	–
G.W.Flower	not out	84	143	6
A.D.R.Campbell	b Gough	23	30	3/1
G.J.Whittall	c Stewart b Gough	0	2	–
D.L.Houghton	c Stewart b Gough	57	74	3
M.H.Dekker	c DeFreitas b Fraser	5	8	–
G.C.Martin	b DeFreitas	7	11	–
P.A.Strang	run out	0	2	–
H.H.Streak	run out	1	3	–
S.G.Peall	c Stewart b Gough	0	2	–
D.H.Brain	b Gough	7	8	1
Extras	(lb 7, w 1, nb 1)	9		
Total	(49.3 overs)	**205**		

ENGLAND		Runs	Balls	4/6
G.A.Gooch	c and b Strang	38	54	3
* M.A.Atherton	c A.Flower b Whittall	14	38	–
G.A.Hick	run out	64	88	1
G.P.Thorpe	lbw b Strang	0	3	–
J.P.Crawley	lbw b Dekker	18	55	–
† A.J.Stewart	b Streak	29	38	2
P.A.J.DeFreitas	run out	5	3	–
D.Gough	b Streak	2	4	–
S.D.Udal	run out	10	9	1
A.R.C.Fraser	b Dekker	2	3	–
P.C.R.Tufnell	not out	0		–
Extras	(lb 5, w 5)	10		
Total	(49.1 overs)	**192**		

ENGLAND	O	M	R	W
DeFreitas	10	2	27	1
Fraser	10	0	45	2
Gough	9.3	0	44	5
Tufnell	10	0	43	0
Udal	8	0	31	0
Hick	2	0	8	0

ZIMBABWE	O	M	R	W
Brain	8	1	27	0
Streak	8.1	1	36	2
Whittall	4	1	21	1
Strang	10	2	30	2
Peall	10	2	29	0
Dekker	9	0	44	2

FALL OF WICKETS
1-24, 2-61, 3-61, 4-171, 5-179, 6-192, 7-192, 8-198, 9-198, 10-205

FALL OF WICKETS
1-49, 2-60, 3-60, 4-105, 5-169, 6-178, 7-179, 8-181, 9-192, 10-192

Umpires: D.B.Hair (13) and C.D.Timmins (19).

Referee: J.R.Reid (New Zealand).

ENGLAND v ZIMBABWE 1994-95

At Woolloongabba, Brisbane on 7 January 1995.   Result: ENGLAND won by 26 runs.   Toss: England.
Award: G.P.Thorpe.   LOI debuts: None.

Graham Thorpe's doughty innings enabled England to beat Zimbabwe at their third attempt but batting for 155 minutes in 100°F heat and 85% humidity resulted in him being hospitalised for dehydration.

ENGLAND		Runs	Balls	4/6
G.A.Gooch	b Brain	0	4	–
* M.A.Atherton	lbw b Martin	26	64	2
G.A.Hick	c A.Flower b Streak	8	19	1
G.P.Thorpe	c Brain b Strang	89	119	7
N.H.Fairbrother	run out	7	8	1
J.P.Crawley	lbw b G.W.Flower	14	22	1
† S.J.Rhodes	st A.Flower b Dekker	20	28	–
D.Gough	c Campbell b Dekker	4	6	–
P.A.J.DeFreitas	not out	12	17	–
S.D.Udal	not out	11	13	–
J.E.Benjamin				
Extras	(b 4, lb 2, w 3)	9		
Total	(50 overs; 8 wickets)	200		

ZIMBABWE		Runs	Balls	4/6
G.W.Flower	c Rhodes b Udal	19	48	1
A.D.R.Campbell	c Fairbrother b DeFreitas	3	23	–
M.H.Dekker	b Benjamin	5	12	–
*†A.Flower	c Rhodes b Gough	52	60	4
G.J.Whittall	c Rhodes b DeFreitas	53	74	4
I.P.Butchart	run out	2	12	–
G.C.Martin	st Rhodes b Hick	1	10	–
P.A.Strang	b Gough	16	29	1
D.H.Brain	c Hick b Udal	2	4	–
H.H.Streak	not out	9	12	–
S.G.Peall	run out	3	5	–
Extras	(lb 7, w 2)	9		
Total	(48.1 overs)	174		

ZIMBABWE	O	M	R	W
Brain	8	0	27	1
Streak	7	1	26	1
Whittall	5	0	19	0
Martin	5	1	15	1
Peall	5	0	19	0
Strang	10	0	42	1
G.W.Flower	3	0	16	1
Dekker	7	0	30	2

ENGLAND	O	M	R	W
Gough	9.1	3	17	2
DeFreitas	10	0	28	2
Benjamin	6	0	22	1
Udal	8	0	41	2
Hick	7	1	29	1
Gooch	8	0	30	0

FALL OF WICKETS
1-8, 2-16, 3-56, 4-103, 5-123, 6-124, 7-149, 8-156, 9-169, 10-174

FALL OF WICKETS
1-0, 2-20, 3-72, 4-82, 5-107, 6-164, 7-170, 8-182

Referee: J.R.Reid (New Zealand).

Umpires: A.J.McQuillan (5) and C.D.Timmins (20).

AUSTRALIA v ENGLAND 1994-95

At Melbourne Cricket Ground on 10 January 1995.   Result: ENGLAND won by 37 runs.   Toss: England.
Award: G.A.Hick.   LOI debuts: None.

England's joy at inflicting Australia's sole defeat of the tournament was clouded by an injury to Darren Gough. Having rescued the innings with his highest LOI score, he collapsed with a stress fracture of his left foot (third metatarsal) as he ran in to bowl. England's subsequent defeat by the 'A' team left the hosts to play among themselves in the finals.

ENGLAND		Runs	Balls	4/6
G.A.Gooch	c Taylor b McGrath	2	14	–
* M.A.Atherton	c S.R.Waugh b M.E.Waugh	14	30	–
G.A.Hick	c Fleming b Warne	91	120	2/1
G.P.Thorpe	c Healy b M.E.Waugh	8	14	1
N.H.Fairbrother	c Healy b Warne	35	58	2
J.P.Crawley	c Healy b McGrath	2	7	–
† S.J.Rhodes	lbw b McGrath	2	5	–
D.Gough	b McGrath	45	49	4
P.A.J.DeFreitas	not out	2	4	–
S.D.Udal	not out	2	1	–
A.R.C.Fraser				
Extras	(b 4, lb 10, w 6, nb 2)	22		
Total	(50 overs; 8 wickets)	225		

AUSTRALIA		Runs	Balls	4/6
* M.A.Taylor	c Rhodes b Fraser	6	13	–
M.J.Slater	b Fraser	2	12	–
M.E.Waugh	b Hick	41	66	3
S.R.Waugh	c Rhodes b Fraser	0	3	–
S.G.Law	c and b Udal	17	28	–
D.C.Boon	b Hick	26	47	–
† I.A.Healy	c Atherton b Hick	56	63	1
G.R.Robertson	run out	1	7	–
S.K.Warne	b Fraser	21	25	–
D.W.Fleming	not out	5	12	–
G.D.McGrath	b DeFreitas	10	12	–
Extras	(w 3)	3		
Total	(48 overs)	188		

AUSTRALIA	O	M	R	W
Fleming	10	1	36	0
McGrath	10	1	25	4
M.E.Waugh	10	1	43	2
Warne	10	0	37	2
Robertson	5	0	38	0
Law	5	0	32	0

ENGLAND	O	M	R	W
Fraser	10	2	22	4
DeFreitas	9	0	32	1
Gooch	10	0	50	0
Udal	9	1	43	1
Hick	10	1	41	3

FALL OF WICKETS
1-3, 2-16, 3-19, 4-62, 5-76, 6-125, 7-131, 8-173, 9-173, 10-188

FALL OF WICKETS
1-11, 2-31, 3-44, 4-133, 5-136, 6-142, 7-216, 8-223

Referee: J.R.Reid (New Zealand).

Umpires: P.D.Parker (4) and S.G.Randell (62).

PAKISTAN v SRI LANKA 1994-95

At Kingsmead, Durban on 2 December 1994.   Result: **PAKISTAN** won by 6 wickets.   Toss: Sri Lanka.
Award: A.Ranatunga.   LOI debuts: None.

Arjuna Ranatunga's maiden hundred came in his 152nd international. Salim Malik, making his 200th LOI appearance, required six stitches in his shin after colliding with his brother-in-law, Ijaz Ahmed. Hashan Tillekeratne retired at 88.

SRI LANKA		Runs	Balls	4/6
R.S.Mahanama	b Waqar	24	29	3/1
S.T.Jayasuriya	c Akram Raza b Aqib	26	34	3/1
A.P.Gurusinha	lbw b Akram Raza	11	46	–
P.A.de Silva	b Aqib	10	8	1/1
* A.Ranatunga	not out	101	108	8
† H.P.Tillekeratne	retired hurt	1	4	–
R.S.Kalpage	st Rashid b Salim	29	50	1
H.D.P.K.Dharmasena	not out	23	24	1
W.P.U.C.J.Vaas				
G.P.Wickremasinghe				
K.R.Pushpakumara				
Extras	(b 1, lb 2, w 7, nb 3)	13		
Total	(50 overs; 5 wickets)	**238**		

PAKISTAN		Runs	Balls	4/6
Saeed Anwar	b Vaas	5	21	
Aamir Sohail	c De Silva b Kalpage	100	118	
Inzamam-ul-Haq	c Gurusinha b Dharmasena	32	49	
* Salim Malik	not out	65	66	
Ijaz Ahmed	c Mahanama b Jayasuriya	7	9	
Basit Ali	not out	22	29	
† Rashid Latif				
Akram Raza				
Waqar Younis				
Ata-ur-Rehman				
Aqib Javed				
Extras	(lb 5, w 3)	8		
Total	(47.5 overs; 4 wickets)	**239**		

PAKISTAN	O	M	R	W
Waqar Younis	10	0	50	1
Aqib Javed	10	0	44	2
Ata-ur-Rehman	8	1	38	0
Akram Raza	10	1	26	1
Aamir Sohail	6	0	30	0
Salim Malik	6	0	47	1

SRI LANKA	O	M	R	W
Vaas	8	0	32	1
Pushpakumara	8	0	47	0
Wickremasinghe	6	0	28	0
Kalpage	10	0	40	1
Dharmasena	9.5	0	56	1
Jayasuriya	6	0	31	1

FALL OF WICKETS
1-44, 2-57, 3-68, 4-86, 5-172

FALL OF WICKETS
1-22, 2-110, 3-177, 4-191

Umpires: K.E.Liebenberg (28) and D.L.Orchard (1).

Referee: P.J.P.Burge (Australia).

PAKISTAN v SRI LANKA 1994-95

At Centurion Park, Verwoerdburg, Pretoria on 4 December 1994.   Result: **PAKISTAN** won by 12 runs.   Toss: Sri Lanka.
Award: Aamir Sohail.   LOI debuts: None.

South Africa's first quadrangular tournament, sponsored by Benson and Hedges and named after their president, Nelson Mandela, continued with a closer encounter. Aravinda de Silva scored his last 45 runs off 28 balls.

PAKISTAN		Runs	Balls	4/6
Saeed Anwar	c Muralitharan b Kalpage	57	74	4/1
Aamir Sohail	c and b Muralitharan	67	94	6/1
Inzamam-ul-Haq	c Dassanayake b Vaas	62	68	4/1
* Salim Malik	run out	20	23	1
Ijaz Ahmed	run out	1	3	–
Basit Ali	c De Silva b Kalpage	7	10	1
† Rashid Latif	c Pushpakumara b Vaas	7	19	–
Akram Raza	not out	8	8	–
Waqar Younis	c Mahanama b Vaas	1	2	–
Ata-ur-Rehman	c Mahanama b Wickremasinghe	3	4	–
Aqib Javed				
Extras	(b 1, lb 7, w 3, nb 1)	12		
Total	(50 overs; 9 wickets)	**245**		

SRI LANKA		Runs	Balls	4/6
R.S.Mahanama	run out	8	25	–
S.T.Jayasuriya	c Aamir b Waqar	8	16	1
A.P.Gurusinha	c and b Aamir	43	62	4/1
P.A.de Silva	c and b Waqar	95	105	7/3
* A.Ranatunga	b Aamir	24	27	4
R.S.Kalpage	c Rashid b Aamir	4	9	–
† P.B.Dassanayake	run out	8	18	–
W.P.U.C.J.Vaas	run out	3	10	–
G.P.Wickremasinghe	not out	13	17	–
M.Muralitharan	c sub (Manzoor Elahi) b Aqib	1	3	–
K.R.Pushpakumara	not out	14	10	1
Extras	(lb 8, w 3, nb 1)	12		
Total	(50 overs; 9 wickets)	**233**		

SRI LANKA	O	M	R	W
Vaas	8	0	46	3
Pushpakumara	10	0	39	0
Wickremasinghe	10	0	39	1
Muralitharan	8	0	49	1
Kalpage	10	0	41	2
Jayasuriya	4	0	23	0

PAKISTAN	O	M	R	W
Waqar Younis	10	0	73	2
Aqib Javed	10	2	31	1
Ata-ur-Rehman	10	0	53	0
Akram Raza	10	2	22	0
Aamir Sohail	10	0	46	3

FALL OF WICKETS
1-130, 2-130, 3-175, 4-184, 5-198, 6-229, 7-237, 8-239, 9-245

FALL OF WICKETS
1-16, 2-36, 3-95, 4-140, 5-146, 6-167, 7-177, 8-210, 9-214

Umpires: W.A.Diedricks (9) and R.E.Koertzen (10).

Referee: P.J.P.Burge (Australia).

SOUTH AFRICA v NEW ZEALAND 1994-95

At Newlands, Cape Town on 6 December 1994.   Result: **SOUTH AFRICA** won by 69 runs.   Toss: South Africa.
Award: M.J.R.Rindel.   LOI debuts: South Africa – M.J.R.Rindel.

Debutant Mike Rindel gained the match award for his fine all-round contribution in ending his country's sequence of ten LOI defeats. Mark Priest had arrived from New Zealand as a replacement for the injured Matthew Hart earlier that day.

SOUTH AFRICA		Runs	Balls	4/6
A.C.Hudson	lbw b Pringle	9	19	1
G.Kirsten	lbw b De Groen	19	34	2
*W.J.Cronje	c Young b Priest	38	63	1
D.J.Cullinan	c Young b Doull	25	49	2
M.J.R.Rindel	run out	32	51	–
J.N.Rhodes	b Pringle	21	26	2
†D.J.Richardson	run out	23	24	1
E.O.Simons	run out	24	30	–/1
C.R.Matthews	not out	4	4	–
P.S.de Villiers	not out	0	–	–
C.E.Eksteen				
Extras	(b 1, lb 5, w 1, nb 1)	8		
Total	(50 overs; 8 wickets)	**203**		

NEW ZEALAND		O	M	R	W
Doull		7	0	35	1
De Groen		10	1	34	1
Pringle		10	3	29	2
Priest		10	0	42	1
Harris		10	0	45	0
Su'a		3	0	12	0

NEW ZEALAND		Runs	Balls	4/6
B.A.Young	c Rindel b Matthews	25	24	6
S.P.Fleming	c Cronje b De Villiers	12	37	1
M.D.Crowe	c Richardson b Cronje	9	31	–
*K.R.Rutherford	c Cronje b De Villiers	40	73	4
†A.C.Parore	run out	13	15	1
C.Z.Harris	c Richardson b Rindel	10	23	1
M.L.Su'a	run out	1	3	–
M.W.Priest	lbw b Rindel	1	6	–
S.B.Doull	not out	19	15	1/1
C.Pringle	b Simons	1	11	–
R.P.de Groen	b Simons	0	1	–
Extras	(lb 3)	3		
Total	(39.5 overs)	**134**		

SOUTH AFRICA		O	M	R	W
De Villiers		8	2	36	2
Matthews		8	3	22	1
Cronje		5	1	10	1
Simons		8.5	1	28	2
Eksteen		5	1	20	0
Rindel		5	0	15	2

FALL OF WICKETS
1-23, 2-35, 3-83, 4-104, 5-145, 6-153, 7-199, 8-200

FALL OF WICKETS
1-39, 2-39, 3-52, 4-75, 5-101, 6-103, 7-106, 8-124, 9-134, 10-134

Umpires: S.B.Lambson (18) and C.J.Mitchley (11).

Referee: P.J.P.Burge (*Australia*).

NEW ZEALAND v SRI LANKA 1994-95

At Springbok Park, Bloemfontein on 8 December 1994.   No result.   Toss: Sri Lanka.
LOI debuts: New Zealand – L.K.Germon.

Left-handed Sanath Jayasuriya amassed his country's highest individual score until 1995-96 (*LOI No. 1073*) and was the first Sri Lankan to hit six sixes in an innings. His fifty took 66 balls and his hundred another 55. New Zealand were rescued by a torrential thunderstorm.

SRI LANKA		Runs	Balls	4/6
R.S.Mahanama	c Germon b Pringle	0	1	–
S.T.Jayasuriya	c Crowe b Pringle	140	143	9/6
A.P.Gurusinha	c and b Harris	53	91	5
P.A.de Silva	c Harris b Pringle	55	45	2/2
*A.Ranatunga	not out	20	17	1
R.S.Kalpage	not out	4	4	–
†P.B.Dassanayake				
H.D.P.K.Dharmasena				
W.P.U.C.J.Vaas				
G.P.Wickremasinghe				
K.R.Pushpakumara				
Extras	(b 4, lb 6, w 5, nb 1)	16		
Total	(50 overs; 4 wickets)	**288**		

NEW ZEALAND		O	M	R	W
Pringle		10	0	29	3
De Groen		10	0	75	0
Doull		10	1	66	0
Harris		10	0	54	1
Priest		10	0	54	0

NEW ZEALAND		Runs	Balls	4/6
B.A.Young	not out	22	31	2
S.P.Fleming	b Pushpakumara	11	10	2
A.C.Parore	not out	31	48	4
M.D.Crowe				
*K.R.Rutherford				
C.Z.Harris				
†L.K.Germon				
M.W.Priest				
S.B.Doull				
C.Pringle				
R.P.de Groen				
Extras	(lb 1, nb 1)	2		
Total	(14.3 overs; 1 wicket)	**66**		

SRI LANKA		O	M	R	W
Pushpakumara		5	0	18	1
Vaas		7	1	33	0
Wickremasinghe		2.3	0	14	0

FALL OF WICKETS
1-1, 2-133, 3-235, 4-278

FALL OF WICKETS
1-15

Umpires: W.A.Diedricks (10) and R.E.Koertzen (11).

Referee: P.J.P.Burge (*Australia*).

SOUTH AFRICA v PAKISTAN 1994-95

At The Wanderers, Johannesburg on 10 December 1994.　Result: **SOUTH AFRICA** won by 7 wickets.　Toss: Pakistan.
Award: W.J.Cronje.　LOI debuts: None.

The stand of 145 between Andrew Hudson and 'Hansie' Cronje, the first South African to reach 1000 LOI runs, was the hosts' highest for the second wicket until the following match.

PAKISTAN		Runs	Balls	4/6
Saeed Anwar	c Rindel b Snell	26	54	1/1
Aamir Sohail	run out	23	32	2/1
Inzamam-ul-Haq	st Richardson b Cronje	55	74	6
* Salim Malik	c McMillan b Snell	5	12	–
Ijaz Ahmed	c De Villiers b Snell	73	86	10
Basit Ali	run out	2	2	–
† Rashid Latif	c Snell b Cronje	13	9	2
Akram Raza	c Richardson b Matthews	1	4	–
Waqar Younis	b Snell	6	12	–
Ata-ur-Rehman	run out	2	4	–
Aqib Javed	not out	1	7	–
Extras	(lb 3, w 4)	7		
Total	(49.1 overs)	**214**		

SOUTH AFRICA		Runs	Balls	4/6
A.C.Hudson	lbw b Rehman	74	111	10
G.Kirsten	b Waqar	9	22	1
* W.J.Cronje	c Rashid b Waqar	81	104	6/1
D.J.Cullinan	not out	18	25	–
M.J.R.Rindel	not out	13	19	1
J.N.Rhodes				
B.M.McMillan				
† D.J.Richardson				
R.P.Snell				
C.R.Matthews				
P.S.de Villiers				
Extras	(lb 11, w 3, nb 6)	20		
Total	(45.4 overs; 3 wickets)	**215**		

SOUTH AFRICA	O	M	R	W
De Villiers	10	1	25	0
Matthews	10	1	45	1
Snell	9.1	1	37	4
McMillan	10	0	51	0
Rindel	3	0	16	0
Cronje	7	0	37	2

PAKISTAN	O	M	R	W
Waqar Younis	9.4	1	38	2
Aqib Javed	10	0	39	0
Ata-ur-Rehman	10	0	57	1
Akram Raza	10	0	40	0
Aamir Sohail	2	0	13	0
Salim Malik	4	0	17	0

FALL OF WICKETS
1-46, 2-61, 3-70, 4-165, 5-176, 6-196, 7-199, 8-205, 9-211, 10-214

FALL OF WICKETS
1-18, 2-163, 3-185

Umpires: S.B.Lambson (19) and C.J.Mitchley (12).

Referee: P.J.P.Burge (*Australia*).

SOUTH AFRICA v NEW ZEALAND 1994-95

At Centurion Park, Verwoerdburg, Pretoria on 11 December 1994.　Result: **SOUTH AFRICA** won by 81 runs.
Toss: South Africa.　Award: D.J.Callaghan.　LOI debuts: None.

Dave Callaghan posted national records for their highest score (until *LOI No. 1048*) and most fours, in addition to sharing a record second-wicket stand of 149 with his captain. The hosts' total was their highest until 1995-96 and remains the record in South Africa. Adam Parore completed his maiden hundred off 87 balls.

SOUTH AFRICA		Runs	Balls	4/6
A.C.Hudson	c Priest b Doull	3	13	–
D.J.Callaghan	not out	169	143	19/4
* W.J.Cronje	c Young b Thomson	68	79	6/1
D.J.Cullinan	c Thomson b Su'a	38	41	3/1
M.J.R.Rindel	c Parore b Su'a	1	6	–
J.N.Rhodes	c Parore b Su'a	2	4	–
† D.J.Richardson	run out	4	6	–
E.O.Simons	c Rutherford b Su'a	10	10	–
R.P.Snell	not out	1	1	–
C.R.Matthews				
P.S.de Villiers				
Extras	(lb 14, w 1, nb 3)	18		
Total	(50 overs; 7 wickets)	**314**		

NEW ZEALAND		Runs	Balls	4/6
B.A.Young	c Hudson b Matthews	27	34	4/1
S.P.Fleming	c Rindel b Matthews	0	5	–
† A.C.Parore	c Cullinan b Callaghan	108	95	8/3
* K.R.Rutherford	c Matthews b Simons	14	10	3
M.D.Crowe	run out	6	10	1
S.A.Thomson	c Richardson b Callaghan	39	47	2
C.Z.Harris	c Cronje b Rindel	3	12	–
M.W.Priest	c and b Simons	13	18	–
M.L.Su'a	lbw b Callaghan	1	6	–
S.B.Doull	c Richardson b Simons	13	8	1/1
C.Pringle	not out	1	1	–
Extras	(lb 2, w 4, nb 2)	8		
Total	(40.3 overs)	**233**		

NEW ZEALAND	O	M	R	W
Pringle	10	0	40	0
Doull	9	0	70	1
Su'a	10	1	59	4
Harris	10	0	64	0
Priest	5	0	35	0
Thomson	6	0	32	1

SOUTH AFRICA	O	M	R	W
De Villiers	8	1	29	0
Matthews	6	1	28	2
Simons	6.3	0	46	3
Snell	4	0	32	0
Cronje	3	0	30	0
Rindel	7	0	34	1
Callaghan	6	0	32	3

FALL OF WICKETS
1-10, 2-159, 3-239, 4-261, 5-263, 6-282, 7-294

FALL OF WICKETS
1-0, 2-37, 3-60, 4-82, 5-188, 6-195, 7-215, 8-216, 9-232, 10-233

Umpires: K.E.Liebenberg (29) and D.L.Orchard (2).

Referee: P.J.P.Burge (*Australia*).

NEW ZEALAND v PAKISTAN 1994-95

At St. George's Park, Port Elizabeth on 13 December 1994. Result: **PAKISTAN** won by 5 wickets. Toss: Pakistan.
Award: Waqar Younis. LOI debuts: None.

New Zealand lost their last eight wickets for 28 runs as Waqar Younis claimed his 13th four-wicket haul.

NEW ZEALAND		Runs	Balls	4/6	PAKISTAN		Runs	Balls	4/6
B.A.Young	lbw b Aqib	13	43	1	Saeed Anwar	c Fleming b De Groen	17	29	3
M.D.Crowe	c and b Salim	83	99	8/1	Aamir Sohail	b Pringle	75	95	10
† A.C.Parore	c Ijaz b Salim	59	86	1	Inzamam-ul-Haq	c Rutherford b Su'a	17	33	3
* K.R.Rutherford	c Saeed b Akram	16	21	1	* Salim Malik	not out	53	82	3/1
C.Z.Harris	c Moin b Waqar	6	4	–	Ijaz Ahmed	c Parore b Pringle	23	23	–
S.P.Fleming	lbw b Waqar	4	14	–	Basit Ali	c Parore b Pringle	0	2	–
S.A.Thomson	b Waqar	8	12	–	Manzoor Elahi	not out	8	16	1
M.L.Su'a	b Waqar	3	11	–	† Moin Khan				
M.W.Priest	not out	4	5	–	Akram Raza				
C.Pringle	b Aqib	0	2	–	Waqar Younis				
R.P.de Groen	b Aqib	0	2	–	Aqib Javed				
Extras	(b 1, lb 4)	5			Extras	(lb 5, w 7, nb 1)	13		
Total	(49.4 overs)	**201**			**Total**	(46.2 overs; 5 wickets)	**206**		

PAKISTAN	O	M	R	W	NEW ZEALAND	O	M	R	W
Waqar Younis	10	0	32	4	Pringle	10	0	43	3
Aqib Javed	9.4	1	25	3	Thomson	6	0	31	0
Manzoor Elahi	10	0	40	0	De Groen	7.3	1	30	1
Akram Raza	8	0	36	1	Su'a	10	2	30	1
Aamir Sohail	4	0	30	0	Priest	6.3	1	26	0
Salim Malik	8	0	33	2	Harris	6.2	0	41	0

FALL OF WICKETS
1-41, 2-142, 3-173, 4-180, 5-181, 6-194, 7-195, 8-200, 9-201, 10-201

FALL OF WICKETS
1-51, 2-86, 3-142, 4-182, 5-182

Umpires: R.E.Koertzen (12) and C.J.Mitchley (13).

Referee: P.J.P.Burge (*Australia*).

SOUTH AFRICA v SRI LANKA 1994-95

At Springbok Park, Bloemfontein on 15 December 1994. Result: **SRI LANKA** won by 35 runs. Toss: Sri Lanka.
Award: A.Ranatunga. LOI debuts: South Africa – S.D.Jack.

Sri Lanka's first win of the tournament owed much to a fourth-wicket stand of 91 from 92 balls between Aravinda de
Silva and Arjuna Ranatunga.

SRI LANKA		Runs	Balls	4/6	SOUTH AFRICA		Runs	Balls	4/6
R.S.Mahanama	c Hudson b Jack	10	41	–	A.C.Hudson	run out	44	75	7
S.T.Jayasuriya	c Rhodes b Jack	23	45	2/1	D.J.Callaghan	c Ranatunga b Vaas	9	22	1
A.P.Gurusinha	c Rindel b Simons	14	35	1	* W.J.Cronje	c Mahanama b Muralitharan	14	27	–
P.A.de Silva	c Hudson b De Villiers	73	95	4	D.J.Cullinan	b Kalpage	16	39	–
* A.Ranatunga	run out	60	52	7	M.J.R.Rindel	run out	8	20	–
† H.P.Tillekeratne	b De Villiers	21	30	2	J.N.Rhodes	b Muralitharan	27	28	–
R.S.Kalpage	c Jack b Simons	4	5	–	† D.J.Richardson	c Muralitharan b De Silva	1	8	–
G.P.Wickremasinghe	b Simons	11	7	–/1	S.D.Jack	run out	1	3	–
M.Muralitharan	not out	0	–	–	E.O.Simons	c Ranatunga b Kalpage	21	26	1/1
W.P.U.C.J.Vaas					C.R.Matthews	not out	15	23	–
K.R.Pushpakumara					P.S.de Villiers	c Mahanama b Jayasuriya	20	15	3
Extras	(lb 3, w 3, nb 4)	10			Extras	(b 3, lb 12)	15		
Total	(50 overs; 8 wickets)	**226**			**Total**	(47.5 overs)	**191**		

SOUTH AFRICA	O	M	R	W	SRI LANKA	O	M	R	W
De Villiers	10	1	31	2	Pushpakumara	3	0	20	0
Matthews	10	2	37	0	Vaas	7	1	20	1
Jack	10	0	41	2	Wickremasinghe	6	0	16	0
Simons	10	1	51	3	Kalpage	10	0	42	2
Callaghan	3	0	16	0	Muralitharan	10	0	23	2
Rindel	4	0	24	0	Jayasuriya	8.5	0	42	1
Cronje	3	0	23	0	De Silva	3	0	13	1

FALL OF WICKETS
1-33, 2-44, 3-70, 4-161, 5-201, 6-214, 7-226, 8-226

FALL OF WICKETS
1-48, 2-68, 3-81, 4-96, 5-109, 6-113, 7-115, 8-152, 9-154, 10-191

Umpires: S.B.Lambson (20) and D.L.Orchard (3).

Referee: P.J.P.Burge (*Australia*).

SOUTH AFRICA v PAKISTAN 1994-95

At Kingsmead, Durban on 17 December 1994.   Result: **PAKISTAN** won by 8 wickets.   Toss: Pakistan.
Award: Ijaz Ahmed.   LOI debuts: None.

After Waqar Younis had returned his second four-wicket analysis in successive matches, Ijaz Ahmed sped to an 87-ball hundred, his fourth successive score of fifty or more against South Africa (395 runs for twice out). His tally of 17 fours remains the Pakistan record.

SOUTH AFRICA		Runs	Balls	4/6
A.C.Hudson	c Inzamam b Waqar	1	14	–
D.J.Callaghan	c Inzamam b Aqib	9	28	2
* W.J.Cronje	c Basit b Waqar	2	9	–
D.J.Cullinan	c Rashid b Aqib	5	25	–
M.J.R.Rindel	run out	10	30	–
J.N.Rhodes	lbw b Aamir	61	77	2
† D.J.Richardson	c Ijaz b Waqar	53	83	3
E.O.Simons	b Waqar	19	20	2
R.P.Snell	not out	27	16	3/1
C.R.Matthews	not out	3	5	–
P.S.de Villiers				
Extras	(lb 4, w 8, nb 4)	16		
Total	(50 overs; 8 wickets)	**206**		

PAKISTAN		Runs	Balls	4/6
Saeed Anwar	c Richardson b De Villiers	10	13	2
Aamir Sohail	c Richardson b Snell	44	52	8
Ijaz Ahmed	not out	114	90	17/3
* Salim Malik	not out	36	58	4
Inzamam-ul-Haq				
Basit Ali				
† Rashid Latif				
Waqar Younis				
Akram Raza				
Manzoor Elahi				
Aqib Javed				
Extras	(w 3, nb 1)	4		
Total	(35 overs; 2 wickets)	**208**		

PAKISTAN	O	M	R	W
Waqar Younis	10	0	52	4
Aqib Javed	10	3	37	2
Manzoor Elahi	10	1	27	0
Akram Raza	10	0	39	0
Salim Malik	3	0	13	0
Aamir Sohail	7	0	34	1

SOUTH AFRICA	O	M	R	W
Matthews	9	1	54	0
De Villiers	10	0	46	1
Simons	6	0	31	0
Snell	7	0	49	1
Callaghan	3	0	28	0

FALL OF WICKETS
1-2, 2-10, 3-20, 4-27, 5-44, 6-132, 7-174, 8-178

FALL OF WICKETS
1-13, 2-72

Umpires: W.A.Diedricks (11) and K.E.Liebenberg (30).

Referee: P.J.P.Burge (*Australia*).

NEW ZEALAND v SRI LANKA 1994-95

At Buffalo Park, East London on 18 December 1994.   Result: **SRI LANKA** won by 5 wickets.   Toss: New Zealand.
Award: K.R.Rutherford.   LOI debuts: None.

ICC's coffers feasted at the expense of the captains, Ken Rutherford, who scored a 96-ball hundred, being fined half his match fee for 'attempting to intimidate the umpire into making a favourable decision', while Arjuna Ranatunga lost a quarter of his for 'obvious dissent' on dismissal. Sanath Jayasuriya's fifty took 30 balls.

NEW ZEALAND		Runs	Balls	4/6
B.A.Young	c Tillekeratne b Wickremasinghe	24	56	–
B.R.Hartland	b Kalpage	32	49	4
† A.C.Parore	c Tillekeratne b Pushpakumara	67	83	3/1
* K.R.Rutherford	not out	102	98	7/2
S.P.Fleming	c Wickremasinghe b Vaas	5	10	–
S.A.Thomson	not out	11	10	–
C.Z.Harris				
D.J.Nash				
M.L.Su'a				
M.W.Priest				
C.Pringle				
Extras	(lb 11, w 3)	14		
Total	(50 overs; 4 wickets)	**255**		

SRI LANKA		Runs	Balls	4/6
S.T.Jayasuriya	c Parore b Pringle	52	31	5/3
R.S.Mahanama	c Fleming b Nash	1	2	–
A.P.Gurusinha	c and b Thomson	47	59	4
P.A.de Silva	c Hartland b Harris	4	10	1
* A.Ranatunga	c Parore b Nash	32	45	4
† H.P.Tillekeratne	not out	68	86	6
R.S.Kalpage	not out	43	53	2
K.R.Pushpakumara				
W.P.U.C.J.Vaas				
G.P.Wickremasinghe				
M.Muralitharan				
Extras	(b 2, lb 5, w 3)	10		
Total	(47.1 overs; 5 wickets)	**257**		

SRI LANKA	O	M	R	W
Pushpakumara	10	1	50	1
Vaas	10	1	33	1
Wickremasinghe	9	1	42	1
Kalpage	7	1	42	1
Muralitharan	9	1	50	0
Jayasuriya	5	0	27	0

NEW ZEALAND	O	M	R	W
Pringle	8	1	73	1
Nash	10	0	52	2
Su'a	3.1	0	23	0
Thomson	10	1	37	1
Harris	10	0	40	1
Priest	6	0	25	0

FALL OF WICKETS
1-63, 2-63, 3-199, 4-220

FALL OF WICKETS
1-15, 2-102, 3-110, 4-110, 5-166

Umpires: C.J.Mitchley (14) and D.L.Orchard (4).

Referee: P.J.P.Burge (*Australia*).

NEW ZEALAND v PAKISTAN

At Buffalo Park, East London on 19 December 1994.   Result: **PAKISTAN** won by 5 wickets.   Toss: New Zealand.
Award: Waqar Younis.   LOI debuts: None.

Waqar Younis ended New Zealand's innings with an all-bowled hat-trick, inswinging yorkers accounting for Harris, Pringle and De Groen. It was his third sequence of four-wicket analyses in three successive matches; no other bowler has exceeded two matches in succession.

NEW ZEALAND		Runs	Balls	4/6
B.A.Young	c Akram b Kabir	17	24	3
B.R.Hartland	b Akram	44	69	5
† A.C.Parore	b Aqib	1	8	–
* K.R.Rutherford	c Rashid b Aamir	30	46	3
S.P.Fleming	b Aamir	19	31	–
S.A.Thomson	c Rashid b Kabir	15	38	–
C.Z.Harris	b Waqar	18	38	–
M.L.Su'a	b Waqar	2	12	–
M.W.Priest	not out	17	27	1
C.Pringle	b Waqar	0	1	–
R.P.de Groen	b Waqar	0	1	–
Extras	(lb 1, w 7, nb 1)	9		
Total	**(47.4 overs)**	**172**		

PAKISTAN		Runs	Balls	4/6
Saeed Anwar	c Parore b Thomson	41	76	4
Aamir Sohail	c Parore b Harris	52	62	9
Basit Ali	c Hartland b Priest	12	14	1
Inzamam-ul-Haq	run out	15	19	1/1
* Salim Malik	c Su'a b Priest	14	17	1
Ijaz Ahmed	not out	25	30	3
† Rashid Latif	not out	8	17	1
Akram Raza				
Waqar Younis				
Kabir Khan				
Aqib Javed				
Extras	(lb 2, w 5, nb 1)	8		
Total	**(38.5 overs; 5 wickets)**	**175**		

PAKISTAN	O	M	R	W
Waqar Younis	8.4	1	33	4
Aqib Javed	10	2	31	1
Kabir Khan	10	1	32	2
Akram Raza	7	0	25	1
Salim Malik	5	0	30	0
Aamir Sohail	7	0	20	2

NEW ZEALAND	O	M	R	W
Pringle	8	0	36	0
Su'a	6	1	26	0
De Groen	4	0	30	0
Thomson	10	0	34	1
Harris	4	0	15	1
Priest	6	0	27	2
Fleming	0.5	0	5	0

FALL OF WICKETS
1-36, 2-38, 3-83, 4-108, 5-132, 6-136, 7-145, 8-172, 9-172, 10-172

FALL OF WICKETS
1-97, 2-102, 3-122, 4-126, 5-151

Umpires: W.A.Diedricks (12) and S.B.Lambson (21).

Referee: P.J.P.Burge (*Australia*).

SOUTH AFRICA v SRI LANKA 1994-95

At St George's Park, Port Elizabeth on 21 December 1994.   Result: **SOUTH AFRICA** won by 44 runs (revised target).
Toss: South Africa.   Award: C.R.Matthews.   LOI debuts: None.

Daryll Cullinan (62) retired at 160 for stitches, after top-edging a reverse sweep into his mouth, and resumed at 198. Rain disrupted Sri Lanka's innings when they were 101 for 5 in the 29th over and left them with an unattainable revised target of 184 from 34 overs.

SOUTH AFRICA		Runs	Balls	4/6
A.C.Hudson	lbw b Wickremasinghe	27	31	4/1
G.Kirsten	b Dharmasena	20	44	1
D.J.Cullinan	c Gurusinha b Dharmasena	63	75	4/1
* W.J.Cronje	c De Silva b Kalpage	5	19	–
J.N.Rhodes	c Mahanama b Dharmasena	53	80	4
D.J.Callaghan	c Jayasuriya b Dharmasena	23	25	2
† D.J.Richardson	c Ranatunga b Vaas	7	7	–
E.O.Simons	c Kalpage b Vaas	11	7	2
C.R.Matthews	not out	11	8	1
P.S.de Villiers	not out	7	2	–/1
C.E.Eksteen				
Extras	(b 3, lb 7)	10		
Total	**(50 overs; 8 wickets)**	**237**		

SRI LANKA		Runs	Balls	4/6
R.S.Mahanama	c Eksteen b Matthews	3	12	–
S.T.Jayasuriya	c sub (M.J.R.Rindel) b Matthews	20	26	2/1
A.P.Gurusinha	lbw b Cronje	23	52	3
P.A.de Silva	c Callaghan b Matthews	0	4	–
* A.Ranatunga	c and b Cronje	29	38	2/1
† H.P.Tillekeratne	not out	36	52	2
R.S.Kalpage	b Callaghan	9	11	–
H.D.P.K.Dharmasena	not out	12	11	–
W.P.U.C.J.Vaas				
G.P.Wickremasinghe				
M.Muralitharan				
Extras	(b 2, lb 4, nb 1)	7		
Total	**(34 overs; 6 wickets)**	**139**		

SRI LANKA	O	M	R	W
Wickremasinghe	8	0	44	1
Vaas	9	0	42	2
Dharmasena	10	0	37	4
Muralitharan	10	0	32	0
Kalpage	10	0	51	1
Jayasuriya	3	0	21	0

SOUTH AFRICA	O	M	R	W
De Villiers	7	1	24	0
Matthews	7	0	22	3
Simons	7	0	25	0
Cronje	8	0	27	2
Callaghan	3	0	19	1
Eksteen	2	0	16	0

FALL OF WICKETS
1-30, 2-53, 3-79, 4-198, 5-200, 6-200, 7-210, 8-229

FALL OF WICKETS
1-5, 2-34, 3-34, 4-55, 5-84, 6-112

Umpires: R.E.Koertzen (13) and K.E.Liebenberg (31).

Referee: P.J.P.Burge (*Australia*).

SOUTH AFRICA v PAKISTAN 1994-95

At Newlands, Cape Town on 10 January 1995.   Result: **SOUTH AFRICA** won by 37 runs.   Toss: Pakistan.
Award: E.O.Simons.   LOI debuts: None.

Aamir Sohail reached 50 off 41 balls after extracting 28 from Steve Jack's first two overs. Dave Richardson was fined 20% of his match fee for abusing the stumps after being given run out, one of six such victims in the game.

SOUTH AFRICA		Runs	Balls	4/6
G.Kirsten	lbw b Akram Raza	43	68	3
D.J.Callaghan	c Ijaz b Aqib	4	5	1
* W.J.Cronje	c Aamir b Aqib	21	43	3
D.J.Cullinan	run out	64	90	1
J.N.Rhodes	c Aamir b Akram Raza	21	25	2
M.J.R.Rindel	run out	31	47	–
† D.J.Richardson	run out	4	3	1
E.O.Simons	c Inzamam b Waqar	6	11	–
P.L.Symcox	c sub (Asif Mujtaba) b Waqar	3	5	–
S.D.Jack	b Waqar	6	5	–
P.S.de Villiers	not out	0	–	–
Extras	(lb 4, w 3, nb 5)	12		
Total	**(49.3 overs)**	**215**		

PAKISTAN		O	M	R	W
Wasim Akram		10	0	43	0
Aqib Javed		10	1	51	2
Waqar Younis		9.3	0	32	3
Akram Raza		10	0	38	2
Salim Malik		4	0	22	0
Aamir Sohail		6	0	25	0

FALL OF WICKETS
1-6, 2-54, 3-89, 4-121, 5-193, 6-198, 7-200, 8-207, 9-215, 10-215

Umpires: C.J.Mitchley (15) and D.L.Orchard (5).

PAKISTAN		Runs	Balls	4/6
Aamir Sohail	run out	71	74	11
Saeed Anwar	b Simons	5	15	–
Inzamam-ul-Haq	lbw b Simons	4	25	–
* Salim Malik	run out	19	25	1
Ijaz Ahmed	c Callaghan b Jack	5	15	1
Basit Ali	c Simons b Cronje	6	8	–
† Rashid Latif	run out	17	31	1
Wasim Akram	c Jack b Simons	12	29	1
Akram Raza	c Jack b Simons	12	25	1
Waqar Younis	c De Villiers b Cronje	14	11	–/2
Aqib Javed	not out	6	1	–/1
Extras	(b 5, lb 2)	7		
Total	**(42.5 overs)**	**178**		

SOUTH AFRICA	O	M	R	W
De Villiers	8	0	23	0
Jack	8	0	45	1
Simons	8	0	42	4
Cronje	8.5	0	31	2
Symcox	10	0	30	0

FALL OF WICKETS
1-48, 2-58, 3-101, 4-105, 5-111, 6-122, 7-133, 8-149, 9-159, 10-178

Referee: P.J.P.Burge (*Australia*).

SOUTH AFRICA v PAKISTAN 1994-95

At The Wanderers, Johannesburg on 12 January 1995.   Result: **SOUTH AFRICA** won by 157 runs.   Toss: Pakistan.
Award: M.J.R.Rindel.   LOI debuts: None.

The partnership of 190 between Gary Kirsten and Mike Rindel remains the South African record for any wicket and the highest LOI opening stand featuring a left-handed pair. Dave Richardson became the first South African to make five dismissals in an innings.

SOUTH AFRICA		Runs	Balls	4/6
G.Kirsten	st Rashid b Salim	87	111	8/1
M.J.R.Rindel	run out	106	139	9
* W.J.Cronje	c Aqib b Wasim	37	36	3/1
D.J.Cullinan	b Waqar	5	7	–
J.N.Rhodes	run out	6	3	1
D.J.Callaghan	not out	7	5	1
† D.J.Richardson	not out	1	1	–
B.M.McMillan				
E.O.Simons				
P.S.de Villiers				
A.A.Donald				
Extras	(lb 9, w 6, nb 2)	17		
Total	**(50 overs; 5 wickets)**	**266**		

PAKISTAN		O	M	R	W
Wasim Akram		10	1	47	1
Aqib Javed		9	1	33	0
Waqar Younis		9	0	57	1
Akram Raza		8	0	44	0
Aamir Sohail		10	0	52	0
Salim Malik		4	0	24	1

FALL OF WICKETS
1-190, 2-243, 3-251, 4-257, 5-260

Umpires: K.E.Liebenberg (32) and C.J.Mitchley (16).

PAKISTAN		Runs	Balls	4/6
Aamir Sohail	lbw b De Villiers	0	3	–
Saeed Anwar	c Richardson b De Villiers	3	14	–
Ijaz Ahmed	c Richardson b De Villiers	4	4	1
Inzamam-ul-Haq	c Richardson b Donald	19	20	3/1
* Salim Malik	c Richardson b Donald	12	20	2
Asif Mujtaba	c Richardson b Cronje	24	57	1
† Rashid Latif	c McMillan b Donald	0	4	–
Wasim Akram	run out	26	43	1
Akram Raza	c McMillan b Simons	0	3	–
Waqar Younis	c Cronje b Simons	6	14	–
Aqib Javed	not out	4	18	–
Extras	(lb 3, w 6, nb 2)	11		
Total	**(32.3 overs)**	**109**		

SOUTH AFRICA	O	M	R	W
De Villiers	7	1	21	3
Donald	8	2	25	3
Simons	9.3	1	26	2
McMillan	5	0	25	0
Cronje	3	0	9	1

FALL OF WICKETS
1-1, 2-7, 3-14, 4-37, 5-42, 6-42, 7-97, 8-98, 9-98, 10-109

Referee: P.J.P.Burge (*Australia*).

NEW ZEALAND v WEST INDIES 1994-95

At Eden Park, Auckland on 22 January 1995.　Result: **WEST INDIES** won on faster scoring rate.　Toss: New Zealand.
Award: B.C.Lara.　LOI debuts: New Zealand – N.J.Astle.

Rain interruptions of 71 and 63 minutes reduced New Zealand's innings to 37 overs. Brian Lara's 30-ball fifty proved crucial to the final equation.

NEW ZEALAND		Runs	Balls	4/6	WEST INDIES		Runs	Balls	4/6
B.A.Young	b Arthurton	42	73	5	S.C.Williams	not out	73	80	7/1
A.H.Jones	c Lara b Walsh	10	22	–	S.L.Campbell	b Larsen	17	55	1
†A.C.Parore	c Adams b Walsh	1	12	–	B.C.Lara	not out	55	32	8/1
*K.R.Rutherford	c Adams b Arthurton	17	32	2	K.L.T.Arthurton				
S.A.Thomson	run out	37	38	3/1	†J.C.Adams				
N.J.Astle	c Cummins b Dhanraj	25	23	2	R.I.C.Holder				
J.T.C.Vaughan	not out	21	19	2	A.C.Cummins				
S.B.Doull	not out	6	8	–	C.E.L.Ambrose				
D.N.Patel					*C.A.Walsh				
G.R.Larsen					K.C.G.Benjamin				
D.K.Morrison					R.Dhanraj				
Extras	(lb 4, w 1, nb 3)	8			Extras	(lb 3, nb 1)	4		
Total	(37 overs; 6 wickets)	**167**			**Total**	(27.4 overs; 1 wicket)	**149**		

WEST INDIES	O	M	R	W	NEW ZEALAND	O	M	R	W
Ambrose	8	1	34	0	Morrison	5	0	19	0
Walsh	8	1	26	2	Doull	6.4	1	32	0
Cummins	7	1	25	0	Vaughan	4	0	14	0
Benjamin	6	0	32	0	Larsen	7	0	35	1
Arthurton	4	0	25	2	Patel	1	0	8	0
Dhanraj	4	0	21	1	Astle	3	0	27	0
					Thomson	1	0	11	0

FALL OF WICKETS
1-31, 2-35, 3-67, 4-80, 5-123, 6-146

FALL OF WICKETS
1-61

Umpires: B.L.Aldridge (40) and D.B.Cowie (8).

Referee: P.L.van der Merwe (*South Africa*).

NEW ZEALAND v WEST INDIES 1994-95

At Basin Reserve, Wellington on 25 January 1995.　Result: **WEST INDIES** won by 41 runs.　Toss: New Zealand.
Award: B.C.Lara.　LOI debuts: None.

Brian Lara completed 3000 runs in 79 internationals. The match began on time despite the Basin Reserve square being vandalised the previous day, an incident allegedly not unrelated to Maori protests about cricket telecasts being given precedence over Maori news bulletins.

WEST INDIES		Runs	Balls	4/6	NEW ZEALAND		Runs	Balls	4/6
S.C.Williams	b Doull	8	17	1	B.A.Young	c Benjamin b Cummins	39	43	5
S.L.Campbell	b Morrison	7	8	1	A.H.Jones	c and b Dhanraj	26	53	4
B.C.Lara	run out	72	85	7	†A.C.Parore	lbw b Walsh	18	34	1
K.L.T.Arthurton	run out	30	66	2	*K.R.Rutherford	c Adams b Dhanraj	16	38	1
R.I.C.Holder	c Morrison b Thomson	35	59	3	S.A.Thomson	c Adams b Ambrose	22	31	3
W.K.M.Benjamin	b Astle	5	10	–	N.J.Astle	c Adams b Benjamin	11	32	–
A.C.Cummins	not out	44	38	5	J.T.C.Vaughan	run out	9	11	–
†J.C.Adams	c Parore b Morrison	8	9	–	D.N.Patel	b Walsh	25	25	2
C.E.L.Ambrose	not out	8	8	1	G.R.Larsen	c Ambrose b Arthurton	15	25	2
*C.A.Walsh					S.B.Doull	not out	9	6	1
R.Dhanraj					D.K.Morrison	st Adams b Arthurton	2	4	–
Extras	(lb 22, w 7)	29			Extras	(lb 3, w 5, nb 5)	13		
Total	(50 overs; 7 wickets)	**246**			**Total**	(48.5 overs)	**205**		

NEW ZEALAND	O	M	R	W	WEST INDIES	O	M	R	W
Morrison	8	1	32	2	Walsh	9	1	42	2
Doull	7	0	37	1	Ambrose	8	0	29	1
Larsen	10	1	30	0	Cummins	5	0	34	1
Vaughan	6	0	30	0	Benjamin	9	2	29	1
Patel	5	0	28	0	Dhanraj	10	0	31	2
Astle	8	0	46	1	Arthurton	7.5	0	37	2
Thomson	6	0	21	1					

FALL OF WICKETS
1-15, 2-15, 3-95, 4-163, 5-173, 6-187, 7-223

FALL OF WICKETS
1-54, 2-81, 3-103, 4-109, 5-137, 6-151, 7-151, 8-193, 9-194, 10-205

Umpires: R.S.Dunne (18) and C.E.King (8).

Referee: P.L.van der Merwe (*South Africa*).

NEW ZEALAND v WEST INDIES 1994-95

At Lancaster Park, Christchurch on 28 January 1995.   Result: **WEST INDIES** won by 9 wickets.   Toss: West Indies.
Award: W.K.M.Benjamin.   LOI debuts: New Zealand – R.L.Hayes.

Roydon Hayes was an intriguing selection; he had just been omitted from his Northern Districts limited-overs team because of his wayward fast bowling. New Zealand's defeat extended their run of non-success to 13 losses and two 'no results' since their last victory.

NEW ZEALAND		Runs	Balls	4/6
B.A.Young	c Adams b Arthurton	13	27	1
A.H.Jones	c Murray b Arthurton	9	37	1
† A.C.Parore	c Holder b Dhanraj	9	18	–
* K.R.Rutherford	b Benjamin	30	54	4
M.W.Douglas	c Ambrose b Benjamin	12	24	1
S.A.Thomson	c Murray b Benjamin	3	10	–
N.J.Astle	c Holder b Cummins	9	26	1
J.T.C.Vaughan	run out	9	29	–
G.R.Larsen	b Adams	12	16	1
D.K.Morrison	not out	14	31	–
R.L.Hayes	c Holder b Arthurton	13	25	1
Extras	(b 1, lb 3, w 6, nb 3)	13		
Total	(49 overs)	**146**		

WEST INDIES		Runs	Balls	4/6
S.C.Williams	not out	69	107	6/1
S.L.Campbell	b Larsen	36	79	6
* B.C.Lara	not out	34	48	4
K.L.T.Arthurton				
J.C.Adams				
R.I.C.Holder				
† J.R.Murray				
W.K.M.Benjamin				
C.E.L.Ambrose				
A.C.Cummins				
R.Dhanraj				
Extras	(lb 1, w 1, nb 8)	10		
Total	(37.4 overs; 1 wicket)	**149**		

WEST INDIES	O	M	R	W
Ambrose	7	2	15	0
Benjamin	8	1	12	3
Arthurton	10	0	31	3
Cummins	8	1	23	1
Dhanraj	10	0	37	1
Adams	6	0	24	1

NEW ZEALAND	O	M	R	W
Morrison	10	1	29	0
Hayes	7	0	31	0
Larsen	10	4	39	1
Vaughan	3	0	16	0
Thomson	5	1	19	0
Astle	2.4	0	14	0

FALL OF WICKETS
1-17, 2-24, 3-53, 4-69, 5-73, 6-85, 7-99, 8-109, 9-123, 10-146

FALL OF WICKETS
1-98

Umpires: C.E.King (9) and D.M.Quested (7).

Referee: P.L.van der Merwe (*South Africa*).

AUSTRALIA v SOUTH AFRICA 1994-95

At Basin Reserve, Wellington on 15 February 1995.   Result: **AUSTRALIA** won by 3 wickets.   Toss: South Africa.
Award: S.R.Waugh.   LOI debuts: Australia – G.S.Blewett, R.T.Ponting.

This quadrangular tournament, staged in coloured clothing, commemorated the centenary of the New Zealand Cricket Council. Surprisingly, it was launched on a recently used Test pitch of low, slow and uneven bounce.

SOUTH AFRICA		Runs	Balls	4/6
G.Kirsten	c Healy b Reiffel	15	35	1
M.J.R.Rindel	c Taylor b Reiffel	14	27	1
* W.J.Cronje	c Taylor b Blewett	22	41	2
D.J.Cullinan	st Healy b Warne	0	7	–
J.N.Rhodes	b McGrath	25	61	1
D.J.Callaghan	c S.R.Waugh b Warne	1	7	–
† D.J.Richardson	not out	22	56	–
E.O.Simons	lbw b McGrath	0	2	–
P.L.Symcox	c M.E.Waugh b May	10	31	1
P.S.de Villiers	b Reiffel	8	6	1
A.A.Donald	b Reiffel	0	10	–
Extras	(lb 3, nb 3)	6		
Total	(46.2 overs)	**123**		

AUSTRALIA		Runs	Balls	4/6
* M.A.Taylor	c Cullinan b De Villiers	24	33	3
G.S.Blewett	run out	14	21	2
M.E.Waugh	b Symcox	11	23	1
D.C.Boon	lbw b De Villiers	1	2	–
S.R.Waugh	not out	44	92	3
R.T.Ponting	b Simons	1	6	–
† I.A.Healy	lbw b Cronje	18	57	1
P.R.Reiffel	c Rhodes b Cronje	8	24	2
S.K.Warne	not out	2	4	–
T.B.A.May				
G.D.McGrath				
Extras	(b 1)	1		
Total	(43.2 overs; 7 wickets)	**124**		

AUSTRALIA	O	M	R	W
McGrath	10	1	25	2
Reiffel	8.2	1	27	4
Blewett	10	0	30	1
Warne	10	3	18	2
May	8	0	20	1

SOUTH AFRICA	O	M	R	W
Donald	7	0	32	0
De Villiers	10	2	34	2
Simons	10	3	19	1
Symcox	10	1	23	1
Cronje	6.2	1	15	2

FALL OF WICKETS
1-20, 2-48, 3-52, 4-54, 5-55, 6-95, 7-95, 8-111, 9-121, 10-123

FALL OF WICKETS
1-38, 2-39, 3-39, 4-55, 5-56, 6-103, 7-115

Umpires: B.L.Aldridge (41) and R.S.Dunne (19).

Referee: F.J.Cameron (*New Zealand*).

NEW ZEALAND v INDIA 1994-95

At McLean Park, Napier on 16 February 1995.   Result: **NEW ZEALAND** won by 4 wickets.   Toss: New Zealand.
Award: S.P.Fleming.   LOI debuts: None.

New Zealand's eighth win in as many internationals at Napier ended a barren run dating back to April 1994. Ken Rutherford set a New Zealand record with four catches in the field, although John Bracewell had held four as a substitute in *LOI No. 96*.

INDIA		Runs	Balls	4/6
A.Jadeja	run out	7	21	I
S.R.Tendulkar	c Thomson b Morrison	13	15	3
N.S.Sidhu	c Rutherford b Su'a	73	111	6
* M.Azharuddin	c Rutherford b Thomson	28	66	2
V.G.Kambli	c Rutherford b Vaughan	17	26	2
M.Prabhakar	c Rutherford b Cairns	2	12	–
† N.R.Mongia	c Greatbatch b Larsen	4	10	–
A.Kumble	not out	6	13	I
J.Srinath	run out	2	2	–
B.K.V.Prasad	lbw b Morrison	0	I	–
S.L.V.Raju	b Morrison	0	3	–
Extras	(b 1, lb 4, w 3)	8		
Total	(45.5 overs)	**160**		

NEW ZEALAND		Runs	Balls	4/6
M.J.Greatbatch	b Prabhakar	32	35	4/I
M.D.Crowe	c and b Srinath	7	23	–
* K.R.Rutherford	c Kambli b Raju	25	43	I/I
S.P.Fleming	not out	59	60	5/I
C.L.Cairns	c Azharuddin b Srinath	25	24	2/I
S.A.Thomson	c Azharuddin b Srinath	0	2	–
† A.C.Parore	c Mongia b Srinath	0	2	–
J.T.C.Vaughan	not out	5	10	–
G.R.Larsen				
M.L.Su'a				
D.K.Morrison				
Extras	(lb 2, w 3, nb 4)	9		
Total	(32.2 overs; 6 wickets)	**162**		

NEW ZEALAND	O	M	R	W
Morrison	7.5	I	22	3
Thomson	5	0	29	I
Su'a	10	I	35	I
Cairns	8	I	17	I
Larsen	10	2	28	I
Vaughan	5	0	24	I

INDIA	O	M	R	W
Prabhakar	7	I	28	I
Srinath	9.2	I	52	4
Kumble	9	0	34	0
Prasad	2	0	11	0
Raju	5	0	35	I

FALL OF WICKETS
1-20, 2-22, 3-79, 4-104, 5-127, 6-138, 7-157, 8-160, 9-160, 10-160

FALL OF WICKETS
1-42, 2-42, 3-103, 4-144, 5-144, 6-144

Referee: B.N.Jarman (*Australia*).

Umpires: D.B.Cowie (9) and C.E.King (10).

SOUTH AFRICA v INDIA 1994-95

At Seddon (Trust Bank) Park, Hamilton on 18 February 1995.   Result: **SOUTH AFRICA** won by 14 runs.
Toss: South Africa.   Award: G.Kirsten.   LOI debuts: None.

The stand of 120 between Gary Kirsten and Daryll Cullinan remains South Africa's only century partnership in New Zealand.

SOUTH AFRICA		Runs	Balls	4/6
A.C.Hudson	b Srinath	24	33	4
G.Kirsten	run out	80	127	I
D.J.Cullinan	c Prasad b Kumble	65	94	4
* W.J.Cronje	c and b Kumble	3	6	–
J.N.Rhodes	lbw b Kumble	0	2	–
D.J.Callaghan	lbw b Kumble	16	26	2
† D.J.Richardson	not out	11	14	I
E.O.Simons	not out	7	8	–
P.L.Symcox				
A.A.Donald				
P.S.de Villiers				
Extras	(b 1, lb 7, w 4, nb 5)	17		
Total	(50 overs; 6 wickets)	**223**		

INDIA		Runs	Balls	4/6
A.Jadeja	c Kirsten b Symcox	29	91	3
S.R.Tendulkar	c Symcox b Cronje	37	51	3/I
N.S.Sidhu	c Callaghan b Cronje	5	12	–
* M.Azharuddin	run out	20	37	I
V.G.Kambli	c Richardson b Donald	30	49	–/I
J.Srinath	c Simons b Donald	37	25	I/2
M.Prabhakar	run out	6	7	–
† N.R.Mongia	run out	24	20	I
A.Kumble	lbw b De Villiers	I	3	–
B.K.V.Prasad	not out	5	5	–
S.L.V.Raju				
Extras	(b 2, lb 3, w 10)	15		
Total	(50 overs; 9 wickets)	**209**		

INDIA	O	M	R	W
Prabhakar	6	0	24	0
Srinath	8	0	30	I
Prasad	7	0	32	0
Kumble	10	0	40	4
Raju	9	0	46	0
Tendulkar	10	0	43	0

SOUTH AFRICA	O	M	R	W
Donald	9	I	43	2
De Villiers	10	I	56	I
Simons	8	I	28	0
Cronje	10	0	34	2
Symcox	10	0	20	I
Callaghan	3	0	23	0

FALL OF WICKETS
1-47, 2-167, 3-174, 4-174, 5-201, 6-201

FALL OF WICKETS
1-61, 2-73, 3-76, 4-118, 5-148, 6-159, 7-196, 8-200, 9-209

Umpires: D.B.Cowie (10) and E.A.Watkin (1).

Referee: B.N.Jarman (*Australia*).

NEW ZEALAND v AUSTRALIA 1994-95

At Eden Park, Auckland on 19 February 1995.   Result: **AUSTRALIA** won by 27 runs.   Toss: Australia.
Award: M.A.Taylor.   LOI debuts: None.

Mark Taylor's highest score in 72 internationals provided the base for a win which put Australia through to the final.

AUSTRALIA		Runs	Balls	4/6
G.S.Blewett	c Fleming b Thomson	3	6	–
* M.A.Taylor	c and b Pringle	97	128	8
M.E.Waugh	c and b Vaughan	74	97	4
D.C.Boon	c Larsen b Morrison	44	42	3
S.R.Waugh	b Pringle	13	15	–
R.T.Ponting	not out	10	8	1
† I.A.Healy	not out	4	6	–
S.K.Warne				
P.R.Reiffel				
T.B.A.May				
G.D.McGrath				
Extras	(b 1, lb 5, w 2, nb 1)	9		
Total	(50 overs; 5 wickets)	**254**		

NEW ZEALAND		Runs	Balls	4/6
B.A.Young	b Reiffel	4	8	–
M.J.Greatbatch	c Healy b Reiffel	74	93	2/2
* K.R.Rutherford	st Healy b Warne	7	19	–
S.P.Fleming	c Warne b May	53	71	7
C.L.Cairns	lbw b McGrath	22	26	2
S.A.Thomson	run out	9	12	1
† A.C.Parore	not out	27	44	1
J.T.C.Vaughan	c Healy b Reiffel	3	7	–
G.R.Larsen	c Reiffel b M.E.Waugh	3	9	–
C.Pringle	b McGrath	4	11	–
D.K.Morrison	not out	3	4	–
Extras	(lb 12, w 4, nb 2)	18		
Total	(50 overs; 9 wickets)	**227**		

NEW ZEALAND	O	M	R	W
Morrison	10	1	40	1
Thomson	10	1	43	1
Pringle	10	0	54	2
Cairns	3	0	21	0
Larsen	10	0	49	0
Vaughan	7	0	41	1

AUSTRALIA	O	M	R	W
McGrath	10	0	40	2
Reiffel	10	4	35	3
Warne	10	1	40	1
May	10	0	43	1
Blewett	2	0	18	0
Boon	4	0	20	0
M.E.Waugh	4	0	19	1

FALL OF WICKETS
1-3, 2-150, 3-214, 4-238, 5-241

FALL OF WICKETS
1-19, 2-42, 3-124, 4-169, 5-181, 6-187, 7-193, 8-199, 9-217

Umpires: D.B.Cowie (11) and D.M.Quested (8).

Referee: P.L.van der Merwe (*South Africa*).

AUSTRALIA v INDIA 1994-95

At Carisbrook, Dunedin on 22 February 1995.   Result: **INDIA** won by 5 wickets.   Toss: Australia.
Award: N.S.Sidhu.   LOI debuts: India – A.R.Kapoor, P.S.Vaidya.

A day unlikely to appear in the Shane Warne scrapbook: having conceded 61 runs, including 19 off his first over, he was
fined $500 for wearing a wristband with an unauthorised sponsor's name on it.

AUSTRALIA		Runs	Balls	4/6
D.C.Boon	c Kambli b Vaidya	32	54	5
G.S.Blewett	c and b Tendulkar	46	70	4/1
R.T.Ponting	c Vaidya b Prabhakar	62	92	1/1
S.R.Waugh	c and b Kumble	23	37	1
M.E.Waugh	c Azharuddin b Srinath	48	32	4/1
† I.A.Healy	not out	21	12	2/1
* M.A.Taylor	b Srinath	0	2	–
S.K.Warne	not out	5	7	–
T.B.A.May				
G.D.McGrath				
J.Angel				
Extras	(b 2, lb 3, w 2, nb 6)	13		
Total	(50 overs; 6 wickets)	**250**		

INDIA		Runs	Balls	4/6
M.Prabhakar	b Angel	50	68	7
S.R.Tendulkar	c Taylor b Angel	47	40	7
N.S.Sidhu	run out	54	70	4/1
* M.Azharuddin	c Healy b Blewett	25	24	–/2
V.G.Kambli	not out	51	55	5
S.V.Manjrekar	c Healy b May	14	21	1
† N.R.Mongia	not out	6	10	–
J.Srinath				
P.S.Vaidya				
A.Kumble				
A.R.Kapoor				
Extras	(lb 1, w 3, nb 1)	5		
Total	(47.5 overs; 5 wickets)	**252**		

INDIA	O	M	R	W
Prabhakar	10	0	61	1
Srinath	9	0	49	2
Vaidya	7	0	36	1
Kumble	7	0	28	1
Kapoor	9	0	38	0
Tendulkar	8	0	33	1

AUSTRALIA	O	M	R	W
McGrath	9	1	45	0
Angel	10	1	47	2
Warne	10	0	61	0
May	10	0	51	1
Blewett	8.5	0	47	1

FALL OF WICKETS
1-56, 2-103, 3-158, 4-207, 5-226, 6-226

FALL OF WICKETS
1-97, 2-100, 3-144, 4-213, 5-233

Umpires: R.S.Dunne (20) and C.E.King (11).

Referee: P.L.van der Merwe (*South Africa*).

NEW ZEALAND v SOUTH AFRICA 1994-95

At Lancaster Park, Christchurch on 23 (*no play*), 24 February 1995.   Result: **NEW ZEALAND** won by 46 runs.
Toss: South Africa.   Award: M.J. Greatbatch.   LOI debuts: None.

Postponed until the reserve day because of heavy rain, this contest decided who would meet Australia in the final. Gary Kirsten took an astonishing right-handed catch on the extra-cover boundary, diving full length to hold a skimming drive.

NEW ZEALAND		Runs	Balls	4/6
M.J.Greatbatch	c and b Cronje	76	85	7/2
M.W.Douglas	lbw b Matthews	8	27	–
* K.R.Rutherford	c Callaghan b Cronje	61	94	3
S.P.Fleming	c Cullinan b Matthews	21	26	2
C.L.Cairns	c Kirsten b Matthews	33	30	4
S.A.Thomson	c Richardson b De Villiers	6	16	–
† A.C.Parore	not out	30	17	2
J.T.C.Vaughan	run out	7	7	1
G.R.Larsen	not out	2	1	–
C.Pringle				
D.K.Morrison				
Extras	(lb 2, w 1, nb 2)	5		
Total	(50 overs; 7 wickets)	**249**		

SOUTH AFRICA		Runs	Balls	4/6
A.C.Hudson	c Douglas b Morrison	10	28	1
G.Kirsten	c Fleming b Thomson	63	92	5
D.J.Cullinan	c Vaughan b Larsen	13	22	2
* W.J.Cronje	st Parore b Vaughan	34	44	–/1
J.N.Rhodes	c Greatbatch b Morrison	14	23	–/1
D.J.Callaghan	lbw b Larsen	23	37	–
† D.J.Richardson	c Thomson b Vaughan	7	9	–
E.O.Simons	c Greatbatch b Vaughan	7	9	–
C.R.Matthews	b Larsen	16	11	–/2
P.S.de Villiers	c Thomson b Pringle	7	7	1
A.A.Donald	not out	0	1	–
Extras	(b 1, lb 4, w 4)	9		
Total	(47 overs)	**203**		

SOUTH AFRICA	O	M	R	W
De Villiers	10	0	39	1
Matthews	10	1	49	3
Donald	10	0	50	0
Simons	6	0	33	0
Callaghan	4	0	26	0
Cronje	10	0	50	2

NEW ZEALAND	O	M	R	W
Pringle	8	0	35	1
Morrison	8	1	30	2
Vaughan	10	0	37	3
Cairns	4	0	24	0
Larsen	10	0	39	3
Thomson	7	0	33	1

FALL OF WICKETS
1-28, 2-126, 3-167, 4-172, 5-190, 6-227, 7-245

FALL OF WICKETS
1-28, 2-67, 3-117, 4-138, 5-143, 6-162, 7-173, 8-190, 9-197, 10-203

Umpires: B.L.Aldridge (42) and D.M.Quested (9).

Referee: B.N.Jarman (*Australia*).

NEW ZEALAND v AUSTRALIA 1994-95

At Eden Park, Auckland on 26 February 1995.   Result: **AUSTRALIA** won by 6 wickets.   Toss: New Zealand.
Award: T.B.A.May.   LOI debuts: None.

With 18.5 overs to spare, Australia gained an emphatic victory to win their third limited-overs tournament of the season, following the Wills Triangular in Pakistan and the World Series at home.

NEW ZEALAND		Runs	Balls	4/6
M.J.Greatbatch	c McGrath b Reiffel	8	34	1
M.W.Douglas	c Healy b Reiffel	2	11	–
* K.R.Rutherford	c Boon b May	46	92	3
S.P.Fleming	c Healy b M.E.Waugh	0	3	–
C.L.Cairns	c Taylor b May	17	49	1
S.A.Thomson	c and b Warne	9	29	–
† A.C.Parore	c Taylor b Warne	2	4	–
J.T.C.Vaughan	not out	20	41	1
G.R.Larsen	run out	0	4	–
C.Pringle	b May	1	10	–
D.K.Morrison	not out	4	27	–
Extras	(b 1, lb 10, w 13, nb 4)	28		
Total	(50 overs; 9 wickets)	**137**		

AUSTRALIA		Runs	Balls	4/6
G.S.Blewett	c and b Pringle	7	13	1
* M.A.Taylor	st Parore b Vaughan	44	75	5
M.E.Waugh	c Parore b Morrison	46	47	8
D.C.Boon	not out	24	42	1
S.R.Waugh	c Rutherford b Thomson	1	9	–
R.T.Ponting	not out	7	6	–
† I.A.Healy				
P.R.Reiffel				
S.K.Warne				
T.B.A.May				
G.D.McGrath				
Extras	(lb 3, w 3, nb 3)	9		
Total	(31.1 overs; 4 wickets)	**138**		

AUSTRALIA	O	M	R	W
McGrath	9	1	25	0
Reiffel	10	3	14	2
M.E.Waugh	10	1	38	1
Warne	10	2	21	2
May	10	2	19	3
Blewett	1	0	9	0

NEW ZEALAND	O	M	R	W
Morrison	9	1	31	1
Pringle	9.1	1	52	1
Thomson	5	0	22	1
Vaughan	6	1	18	1
Larsen	2	0	12	0

FALL OF WICKETS
1-8, 2-29, 3-35, 4-81, 5-102, 6-106, 7-106, 8-106, 9-112

FALL OF WICKETS
1-15, 2-93, 3-116, 4-121

Umpires: B.L.Aldridge (43) and R.S.Dunne (21).

Referee: P.L.van der Merwe (*South Africa*).

ZIMBABWE v PAKISTAN 1994-95

At Harare Sports Club on 22 February 1995.   Result: **MATCH TIED**.   Toss: Zimbabwe.
Award: Saeed Anwar and B.C.Strang.   LOI debuts: Zimbabwe – S.V.Carlisle, B.C.Strang; Pakistan – Shakil Ahmed.

Guy Whittall took the final wicket with the penultimate ball as Wasim Akram, batting last and one-handed because of six stitches in its gashed partner, could only spoon a simple return catch. Saeed Anwar was the second to carry his bat through a completed innings.

ZIMBABWE		Runs	Balls	4/6
* A.Flower	b Aamir Nazir	25	38	2
G.W.Flower	c Rashid b Aamir Sohail	41	83	–
M.G.Burmester	b Aamir Sohail	25	40	2
† A.D.R.Campbell	c Ijaz b Aamir Sohail	21	44	–/1
D.L.Houghton	c Rashid b Wasim	32	40	1
G.J.Whittall	c Inzamam b Aqib	33	33	4
S.V.Carlisle	run out	0	6	–
P.A.Strang	c Rashid b Wasim	9	14	1
S.G.Peall	b Aqib	1	4	–
B.C.Strang	not out	4	6	–
M.P.Jarvis				
Extras	(lb 19, w 4, nb 5)	28		
Total	(50 overs; 9 wickets)	**219**		

PAKISTAN		Runs	Balls	4/6
Aamir Sohail	c and b B.C.Strang	7	8	1
Saeed Anwar	not out	103	131	6
Inzamam-ul-Haq	c Campbell b B.C.Strang	0	8	–
* Salim Malik	c Campbell b Whittall	22	50	–
Ijaz Ahmed	c B.C.Strang b Peall	25	20	4
Shakil Ahmed	run out	25	48	1
† Rashid Latif	run out	1	2	–
Manzoor Elahi	c P.A.Strang b B.C.Strang	21	27	–/1
Aqib Javed	c A.Flower b B.C.Strang	0	2	–
Aamir Nazir	c Carlisle b Whittall	3	3	–
Wasim Akram	c and b Whittall	0	1	–
Extras	(b 4, lb 5, w 3)	12		
Total	(49.5 overs)	**219**		

PAKISTAN	O	M	R	W
Wasim Akram	8.5	0	24	2
Aqib Javed	10	1	43	2
Aamir Nazir	10	0	52	1
Manzoor Elahi	8	0	36	0
Aamir Sohail	10	0	33	3
Salim Malik	3.1	0	12	0

ZIMBABWE	O	M	R	W
Jarvis	7	0	30	0
B.C.Strang	10	1	36	4
Whittall	9.5	0	46	3
Burmester	3	0	16	0
Peall	6	0	27	1
P.A.Strang	10	0	41	0
A.Flower	4	0	14	0

FALL OF WICKETS
1-45, 2-105, 3-108, 4-159, 5-168, 6-170, 7-188, 8-189, 9-219

FALL OF WICKETS
1-9, 2-13, 3-68, 4-107, 5-172, 6-175, 7-209, 8-210, 9-213, 10-219

Umpires: M.Esat (1) and I.D.Robinson (18).

Referee: J.L.Hendriks (*West Indies*).

ZIMBABWE v PAKISTAN 1994-95

At Harare Sports Club on 25 February 1995.   Result: **PAKISTAN** won by 4 wickets.   Toss: Pakistan.
Award: Inzamam-ul-Haq.   LOI debuts: None.

The stand of 152 between Inzamam-ul-Haq and Ijaz Ahmed remains Pakistan's highest for the fifth wicket in internationals.

ZIMBABWE		Runs	Balls	4/6
*† A.Flower	c Moin b Wasim	9	23	1
G.W.Flower	c Moin b Manzoor	32	64	1
M.G.Burmester	c Aamir b Manzoor	17	48	1
A.D.R.Campbell	c Inzamam b Salim	27	53	–
D.L.Houghton	not out	73	77	7/1
G.J.Whittall	c Ijaz b Wasim	13	29	–
S.V.Carlisle	not out	9	13	–
S.G.Peall				
H.H.Streak				
P.A.Strang				
B.C.Strang				
Extras	(b 13, w 11, nb 5)	29		
Total	(50 overs; 5 wickets)	**209**		

PAKISTAN		Runs	Balls	4/6
Aamir Sohail	c Whittall b Streak	7	17	–
Saeed Anwar	c Burmester b B.C.Strang	0	8	–
Inzamam-ul-Haq	not out	116	138	9/1
Asif Mujtaba	c A.Flower b B.C.Strang	0	8	–
* Salim Malik	c A.Flower b Streak	0	5	–
Ijaz Ahmed	b B.C.Strang	54	96	2
† Moin Khan	c Houghton b P.A.Strang	19	15	2
Manzoor Elahi	not out	3	6	–
Wasim Akram				
Akram Raza				
Aqib Javed				
Extras	(lb 2, w 8, nb 1)	11		
Total	(48.3 overs; 6 wickets)	**210**		

PAKISTAN	O	M	R	W
Wasim Akram	10	0	40	2
Aqib Javed	10	1	41	0
Manzoor Elahi	10	0	36	2
Akram Raza	10	0	27	0
Aamir Sohail	6	0	30	0
Salim Malik	4	0	22	1

ZIMBABWE	O	M	R	W
Streak	9	1	50	2
B.C.Strang	10	0	22	3
Whittall	7	0	33	0
Burmester	4	0	21	0
P.A.Strang	8	0	33	1
Peall	8	0	35	0
G.W.Flower	2	0	13	0
Campbell	0.3	0	1	0

FALL OF WICKETS
1-26, 2-70, 3-74, 4-130, 5-185

FALL OF WICKETS
1-9, 2-17, 3-19, 4-23, 5-175, 6-206

Umpires: M.Esat (2) and Q.J.Goosen (3).

Referee: J.L.Hendriks (*West Indies*).

ZIMBABWE v PAKISTAN 1994-95

At Harare Sports Club on 26 February 1995.   Result: **ZIMBABWE** won by 74 runs.   Toss: Pakistan.
Award: A.Flower.   LOI debuts: None.

Zimbabwe gained their first victory in nine encounters with Pakistan. A back injury sustained while bowling prevented Aamir Sohail from batting. Moin Khan was the first Pakistan wicket-keeper to hold five catches in an innings.

ZIMBABWE		Runs	Balls	4/6
*†A.Flower	c Moin b Manzoor	73	104	3
G.W.Flower	c Moin b Wasim	6	11	–
M.G.Burmester	c Ijaz b Akram Raza	39	75	2
D.L.Houghton	c Aqib b Salim	34	33	3
A.D.R.Campbell	c Inzamam b Aqib	18	34	–
G.J.Whittall	c Moin b Manzoor	1	3	–
S.V.Carlisle	c Moin b Wasim	4	15	–
P.A.Strang	c Moin b Aqib	4	10	–
H.H.Streak	c Manzoor b Aqib	18	15	3
B.C.Strang	not out	0	–	–
M.P.Jarvis				
Extras	(lb 16, w 9)	25		
Total	(50 overs; 9 wickets)	**222**		

PAKISTAN		Runs	Balls	4/6
Shakil Ahmed	c A.Flower b Jarvis	36	80	2
† Moin Khan	c Whittall b Jarvis	8	32	–
Inzamam-ul-Haq	c sub (D.N.Erasmus) b P.A.Strang	45	54	3/1
* Salim Malik	c Whittall b P.A.Strang	3	9	–
Ijaz Ahmed	c B.C.Strang b P.A.Strang	12	25	1
Asif Mujtaba	run out	20	32	–
Manzoor Elahi	c Carlisle b Whittall	10	16	–
Akram Raza	c A.Flower b Whittall	2	5	–
Aqib Javed	not out	2	5	–
Wasim Akram	st A.Flower b G.W.Flower	3	3	–
Aamir Sohail	absent hurt			
Extras	(lb 3, w 4)	7		
Total	(43.3 overs)	**148**		

PAKISTAN	O	M	R	W
Wasim Akram	10	1	33	2
Aqib Javed	10	1	46	3
Manzoor Elahi	10	0	41	2
Akram Raza	10	0	45	1
Aamir Sohail	6.5	0	31	0
Salim Malik	3.1	0	10	1

ZIMBABWE	O	M	R	W
Streak	6	2	7	0
B.C.Strang	6	1	15	0
Whittall	6	0	24	2
Jarvis	10	1	37	2
P.A.Strang	10	0	42	3
G.W.Flower	5.3	0	20	1

FALL OF WICKETS
1-15, 2-119, 3-171, 4-171, 5-175, 6-187, 7-194, 8-222, 9-222

FALL OF WICKETS
1-26, 2-73, 3-80, 4-106, 5-112, 6-138, 7-143, 8-143, 9-148

Umpires: Q.J.Goosen (4) and I.D.Robinson (19).

Referee: J.L.Hendriks (*West Indies*).

WEST INDIES v AUSTRALIA 1994-95

At Kensington Oval, Bridgetown, Barbados on 8 March 1995.   Result: **WEST INDIES** won by 6 runs.
Toss: West Indies.   Award: C.L.Hooper.   LOI debuts: West Indies – V.C.Drakes.

Richie Richardson injured his shoulder diving in vain to avoid being run out and missed the remainder of the series, Courtney Walsh deputising as captain. A third (video) umpire was used in the Caribbean for the first time.

WEST INDIES		Runs	Balls	4/6
P.V.Simmons	c Taylor b Warne	37	40	8
S.C.Williams	c Healy b Reiffel	11	24	2
B.C.Lara	c Taylor b Blewett	55	72	7
* R.B.Richardson	run out	9	16	2
C.L.Hooper	c May b McDermott	84	84	8/1
J.C.Adams	c M.E.Waugh b McDermott	2	4	–
† J.R.Murray	c Healy b M.E.Waugh	12	20	–/1
W.K.M.Benjamin	c May b McDermott	22	25	1/1
V.C.Drakes	c Warne b M.E.Waugh	9	12	–
C.E.L.Ambrose	c Taylor b M.E.Waugh	0	1	–
C.A.Walsh	not out	6	8	–
Extras	(b 1, lb 3, w 1, nb 5)	10		
Total	(49.4 overs)	**257**		

AUSTRALIA		Runs	Balls	4/6
* M.A.Taylor	c Simmons b Walsh	41	69	7
M.J.Slater	c Adams b Benjamin	21	40	1
M.E.Waugh	c Murray b Walsh	29	32	2/1
D.C.Boon	not out	85	85	7
S.R.Waugh	b Drakes	26	34	2
G.S.Blewett	c Walsh b Ambrose	33	36	3
† I.A.Healy	run out	0	–	–
P.R.Reiffel	not out	10	9	1
S.K.Warne				
C.J.McDermott				
T.B.A.May				
Extras	(lb 1, w 5)	6		
Total	(50 overs; 6 wickets)	**251**		

AUSTRALIA	O	M	R	W
McDermott	10	0	25	3
Reiffel	10	1	50	1
M.E.Waugh	6.4	0	42	3
Warne	10	1	56	1
Blewett	8	0	44	1
May	5	0	36	0

WEST INDIES	O	M	R	W
Ambrose	10	1	43	1
Walsh	10	1	52	2
Benjamin	6.1	0	24	1
Drakes	9.5	0	39	1
Hooper	5	0	46	0
Simmons	9	0	46	0

FALL OF WICKETS
1-26, 2-69, 3-87, 4-155, 5-158, 6-191, 7-241, 8-242, 9-246, 10-257

FALL OF WICKETS
1-50, 2-94, 3-94, 4-156, 5-235, 6-236

Umpires: L.H.Barker (26) and D.Holder (1).

Referee: Hanumant Singh (*India*).

WEST INDIES v AUSTRALIA 1994-95

At Queen's Park Oval, Port-of-Spain, Trinidad on 11 March 1995.   Result: **AUSTRALIA** won by 26 runs.
Toss: Australia.   Award: I.A.Healy.   LOI debuts: None.

Greg Blewett was the first batsman to be adjudged out in the Caribbean by the video umpire. Brian Lara batted in front of his home crowd for the first time since breaking the world Test and first-class highest score records.

AUSTRALIA		Runs	Balls	4/6	WEST INDIES		Runs	Balls	4/6
M.J.Slater	c and b Hooper	55	73	6	P.V.Simmons	b McGrath	34	50	6
* M.A.Taylor	c Walsh b Ambrose	16	25	1	S.C.Williams	lbw b Reiffel	0	3	–
M.E.Waugh	b Benjamin	0	3	–	B.C.Lara	c Healy b Blewett	62	72	8
D.C.Boon	c Benjamin b Simmons	48	76	4	C.L.Hooper	c Blewett b Warne	55	58	4/1
S.R.Waugh	b Walsh	58	59	5/1	J.C.Adams	run out	15	29	–
G.S.Blewett	run out	4	7	–	K.L.T.Arthurton	c Boon b McDermott	35	43	1/1
† I.A.Healy	run out	51	45	3/1	† J.R.Murray	lbw b Reiffel	0	6	–
P.R.Reiffel	b Benjamin	14	19	–	W.K.M.Benjamin	b Reiffel	3	8	–
S.K.Warne	not out	4	2	–	V.C.Drakes	c Reiffel b McDermott	16	23	2
C.J.McDermott					C.E.L.Ambrose	b McDermott	1	2	–
G.D.McGrath					* C.A.Walsh	not out	0	–	–
Extras	(lb 3, w 6, nb 1)	10			Extras	(lb 8, w 4, nb 1)	13		
Total	(50 overs; 8 wickets)	**260**			**Total**	(47.5 overs)	**234**		

WEST INDIES	O	M	R	W	AUSTRALIA	O	M	R	W
Ambrose	10	0	47	1	McDermott	6.5	0	37	3
Walsh	8	0	59	1	Reiffel	10	2	32	3
Benjamin	10	0	49	2	McGrath	9	1	36	1
Drakes	10	0	47	0	Warne	10	0	63	1
Hooper	7	0	33	1	Blewett	8	0	43	1
Simmons	5	0	22	1	S.R.Waugh	4	0	15	0

FALL OF WICKETS
1-37, 2-39, 3-93, 4-153, 5-162, 6-207, 7-252, 8-260

FALL OF WICKETS
1-5, 2-79, 3-121, 4-175, 5-182, 6-185, 7-191, 8-232, 9-234, 10-234

Umpires: S.A.Bucknor (24) and C.E.Cumberbatch (21).

Referee: Hanumant Singh (India).

WEST INDIES v AUSTRALIA 1994-95

At Queen's Park Oval, Port-of-Spain, Trinidad on 12 March 1995.   Result: **WEST INDIES** won by 133 runs.
Toss: West Indies.   Award: B.C.Lara.   LOI debuts: None.

Cheered on by his seven brothers and four sisters, Brian Lara completed his first international hundred in his native Trinidad off 105 balls. Damien Fleming damaged his shoulder bowling his eighth over and was flown home. Australia's last seven wickets fell for 31 runs in 40 balls.

WEST INDIES		Runs	Balls	4/6	AUSTRALIA		Runs	Balls	4/6
P.V.Simmons	c Healy b Fleming	6	29	–	* M.A.Taylor	run out	26	44	3
S.C.Williams	run out	6	25	1	M.J.Slater	run out	1	13	–
B.C.Lara	c Reiffel b Waugh	139	125	15/3	R.T.Ponting	c Drakes b Simmons	43	68	3
C.L.Hooper	c Slater b Reiffel	41	55	2/2	D.C.Boon	b Benjamin	4	12	1
J.C.Adams	not out	51	59	6	S.R.Waugh	c Hooper b Simmons	44	45	5/1
K.L.T.Arthurton	c Boon b Waugh	12	9	–/1	G.S.Blewett	st Murray b Hooper	0	1	–
† J.R.Murray	not out	4	4	–	† I.A.Healy	c Williams b Hooper	3	5	–
W.K.M.Benjamin					P.R.Reiffel	run out	1	1	–
V.C.Drakes					S.K.Warne	b Simmons	12	12	–/1
C.E.L.Ambrose					D.W.Fleming	not out	5	10	–
* C.A.Walsh					G.D.McGrath	b Simmons	0	4	–
Extras	(b 6, lb 11, w 5, nb 1)	23			Extras	(lb 4, w 4, nb 2)	10		
Total	(50 overs; 5 wickets)	**282**			**Total**	(34.5 overs)	**149**		

AUSTRALIA	O	M	R	W	WEST INDIES	O	M	R	W
Reiffel	10	0	36	1	Ambrose	6	1	8	0
Fleming	7.3	1	27	1	Walsh	4	1	14	0
McGrath	10	0	57	0	Benjamin	7	1	31	1
Warne	10	1	52	0	Drakes	7	0	36	0
Blewett	3	0	32	0	Hooper	6	0	38	2
Waugh	9.3	1	61	2	Simmons	4.5	0	18	4

FALL OF WICKETS
1-17, 2-26, 3-125, 4-260, 5-276

FALL OF WICKETS
1-12, 2-50, 3-59, 4-118, 5-124, 6-126, 7-127, 8-129, 9-147, 10-149

Umpires: S.A.Bucknor (25) and C.E.Cumberbatch (22).

Referee: Hanumant Singh (India).

WEST INDIES v AUSTRALIA 1994-95

At Arnos Vale, Kingstown, St Vincent on 15 March 1995.   Result: **WEST INDIES** won by 7 wickets (revised target).
Toss: Australia.   Award: P.V.Simmons.   LOI debuts: None.

A 50-minute rain break when Australia were 160 for 5 after 39.2 overs reduced the innings by two overs. A combination of the hosts' tardy over rate and the groundstaff forgetting to roll the pitch revised their target to 206 from 46 overs. Lara (injured hip) fielded for only the first 30 minutes.

AUSTRALIA		Runs	Balls	4/6
M.J.Slater	b Arthurton	68	108	6
* M.A.Taylor	c Simmons b Walsh	3	10	–
M.E.Waugh	c Murray b Benjamin	26	37	2
D.C.Boon	b Arthurton	33	45	1
S.R.Waugh	c Arthurton b Simmons	25	29	1
G.S.Blewett	b Drakes	4	14	–
† I.A.Healy	c Simmons b Walsh	12	19	–
P.R.Reiffel	c Murray b Walsh	9	16	1
S.K.Warne	not out	6	10	–
C.J.McDermott	run out	11	9	1
G.D.McGrath	not out	1	1	–
Extras	(lb 5, w 6, nb 1)	12		
Total	(48 overs; 9 wickets)	**210**		

WEST INDIES		Runs	Balls	4/6
P.V.Simmons	c Healy b Warne	86	110	12/1
S.L.Campbell	st Healy b Warne	20	54	2
J.C.Adams	b McGrath	3	9	–
C.L.Hooper	not out	60	65	5/1
K.L.T.Arthurton	not out	22	28	3
† J.R.Murray				
B.C.Lara				
W.K.M.Benjamin				
V.C.Drakes				
C.E.L.Ambrose				
* C.A.Walsh				
Extras	(b 2, lb 10, w 4, nb 1)	17		
Total	(43.1 overs; 3 wickets)	**208**		

WEST INDIES	O	M	R	W
Ambrose	8	0	22	0
Walsh	9	0	30	3
Benjamin	7	0	32	1
Drakes	7	0	36	1
Arthurton	10	0	45	2
Simmons	7	0	40	1

AUSTRALIA	O	M	R	W
McDermott	9	1	46	0
Reiffel	9	1	37	0
McGrath	10	1	40	1
Warne	9.1	3	33	2
Blewett	3	0	26	0
Boon	3	0	14	0

FALL OF WICKETS
1-6, 2-57, 3-130, 4-137, 5-152, 6-171, 7-190, 8-190, 9-209

FALL OF WICKETS
1-47, 2-56, 3-152

Umpires: L.H.Barker (27) and G.T.Johnson (5).

Referee: Hanumant Singh (*India*).

WEST INDIES v AUSTRALIA 1994-95

At Bourda, Georgetown, Guyana on 18 March 1995.   Result: **WEST INDIES** won by 5 wickets.   Toss: Australia.
Award: C.L.Hooper.   LOI debuts: None.

Australia scored their highest total against West Indies. Broken glass featured heavily in this contest. Mark Waugh's six caused facial cuts to a spectator behind a window, Carl Hooper's six bounced off a roof through the back window of a Mercedes, and sections of the crowd indulged in sporadic bottle throwing.

AUSTRALIA		Runs	Balls	4/6
* M.A.Taylor	c Adams b Hooper	66	98	6
M.J.Slater	c Holder b Drakes	41	60	5
M.E.Waugh	run out	70	58	5/1
S.R.Waugh	c Benjamin b Hooper	11	14	–
R.T.Ponting	b Hooper	0	2	–
J.L.Langer	run out	6	9	–
† I.A.Healy	c Williams b Simmons	36	35	4
P.R.Reiffel	c Campbell b Benjamin	22	22	4
B.P.Julian	b Walsh	11	11	1
T.B.A.May	not out	3	4	–
G.D.McGrath				
Extras	(b 2, lb 11, w 4, nb 3)	20		
Total	(50 overs; 9 wickets)	**286**		

WEST INDIES		Runs	Balls	4/6
S.C.Williams	c and b M.E.Waugh	45	54	8/1
S.L.Campbell	b Reiffel	9	10	2
P.V.Simmons	c Slater b S.R.Waugh	70	63	9/2
C.L.Hooper	c Slater b Reiffel	50	54	6/1
J.C.Adams	not out	60	60	7
K.L.T.Arthurton	c M.E.Waugh b McGrath	0	1	–
R.I.C.Holder	not out	34	51	3
† J.R.Murray				
W.K.M.Benjamin				
V.C.Drakes				
* C.A.Walsh				
Extras	(lb 10, w 3, nb 6)	19		
Total	(47.2 overs; 5 wickets)	**287**		

WEST INDIES	O	M	R	W
Simmons	10	0	54	1
Walsh	8	2	38	1
Benjamin	9	0	51	1
Drakes	6	0	46	1
Arthurton	7	0	48	0
Hooper	10	0	36	3

AUSTRALIA	O	M	R	W
Reiffel	10	1	48	2
Julian	10	1	66	0
May	7	0	42	0
McGrath	8.2	0	51	1
M.E.Waugh	3	0	23	0
S.R.Waugh	9	0	47	1

FALL OF WICKETS
1-78, 2-166, 3-203, 4-203, 5-205, 6-229, 7-259, 8-276, 9-286

FALL OF WICKETS
1-17, 2-108, 3-172, 4-192, 5-193

Umpires: C.R.Duncan (8) and E.Nicholls (1).

Referee: Hanumant Singh (*India*).

NEW ZEALAND v SRI LANKA 1994-95

At Lancaster Park, Christchurch on 26 March 1995.   Result: **NEW ZEALAND** won by 33 runs.   Toss: Sri Lanka.
Award: K.R.Rutherford.   LOI debuts: Sri Lanka – K.J.Silva.

New Zealand successfully defended their highest total for 51 internationals, and their highest at Lancaster Park, despite
Sri Lanka's opening pair bludgeoning 83 from the first ten overs.

NEW ZEALAND		Runs	Balls	4/6
M.J.Greatbatch	b Pushpakumara	17	26	2
B.A.Young	run out	3	6	–
* K.R.Rutherford	c Gurusinha b Muralitharan	65	75	7/1
S.P.Fleming	run out	46	72	2
C.L.Cairns	c S.Ranatunga b Pushpakumara	72	72	3/3
† A.C.Parore	b Vaas	31	36	1
D.N.Patel	not out	23	14	3
J.T.C.Vaughan	not out	1	1	–
G.R.Larsen				
M.L.Su'a				
C.Pringle				
Extras	(b 2, lb 5, w 5, nb 1)	13		
Total	(50 overs; 6 wickets)	271		

SRI LANKA		Runs	Balls	4/6
A.P.Gurusinha	c Greatbatch b Vaughan	33	36	3/1
S.T.Jayasuriya	c Greatbatch b Vaughan	46	35	6/1
S.Ranatunga	run out	11	18	1
P.A.de Silva	c and b Vaughan	54	78	3
* A.Ranatunga	run out	2	10	–
† H.P.Tillekeratne	c Young b Pringle	10	27	–
R.S.Kalpage	c Fleming b Vaughan	35	50	1
W.P.U.C.J.Vaas	run out	27	20	1
M.Muralitharan	c Parore b Cairns	8	9	1
K.R.Pushpakumara	c Patel b Cairns	3	6	–
K.J.Silva	not out	1	1	–
Extras	(lb 3, w 4, nb 1)	8		
Total	(47.5 overs)	238		

SRI LANKA	O	M	R	W
Pushpakumara	10	0	53	2
Vaas	10	1	41	1
Gurusinha	4	0	19	0
Kalpage	8	0	54	0
Muralitharan	10	0	42	1
Silva	8	0	55	0

NEW ZEALAND	O	M	R	W
Pringle	9	1	47	1
Su'a	3	0	35	0
Cairns	7.5	0	49	2
Vaughan	10	1	33	4
Larsen	10	1	38	0
Patel	8	0	33	0

FALL OF WICKETS
1-5, 2-28, 3-122, 4-177, 5-235, 6-265

FALL OF WICKETS
1-83, 2-96, 3-98, 4-105, 5-132, 6-193, 7-208, 8-228, 9-236, 10-238

Umpires: B.L.Aldridge (44) and D.M.Quested (10).

Referee: B.N.Jarman (*Australia*).

NEW ZEALAND v SRI LANKA 1994-95

At Seddon (Trust Bank) Park, Hamilton on 29 March 1995.   Result: **NEW ZEALAND** won on faster scoring rate.
Toss: Sri Lanka.   Award: N.J.Astle.   LOI debuts: Sri Lanka – J.C.Gamage.

Promoted to open in his fourth international, Nathan Astle led the hosts to an even higher total, Adam Parore
contributing a 37-ball fifty. The second of two heavy showers confirmed New Zealand's first series win at any level since
December 1992.

NEW ZEALAND		Runs	Balls	4/6
B.A.Young	c Tillekeratne b Vaas	4	20	–
N.J.Astle	b Vaas	95	137	9/1
* K.R.Rutherford	c Kalpage b Muralitharan	34	33	3/1
S.P.Fleming	c Pushpakumara b Kalpage	6	14	–
C.L.Cairns	c Gamage b Vaas	42	37	–/4
† A.C.Parore	not out	61	45	4/2
S.A.Thomson	b Jayasuriya	1	4	–
D.N.Patel	not out	22	11	1/1
J.T.C.Vaughan				
G.R.Larsen				
C.Pringle				
Extras	(lb 9, w 6)	15		
Total	(50 overs; 6 wickets)	280		

SRI LANKA		Runs	Balls	4/6
A.P.Gurusinha	c Larsen b Pringle	7	12	1
S.T.Jayasuriya	c Young b Patel	6	5	1
S.Ranatunga	run out	15	33	1
P.A.de Silva	run out	7	10	1
* A.Ranatunga	c Parore b Larsen	27	44	3
† H.P.Tillekeratne	not out	39	52	1/1
R.S.Kalpage	c Patel b Larsen	11	23	–
W.P.U.C.J.Vaas	not out	1	4	–
M.Muralitharan				
K.R.Pushpakumara				
J.C.Gamage				
Extras	(b 1, lb 2, w 1)	4		
Total	(31 overs; 6 wickets)	117		

SRI LANKA	O	M	R	W
Pushpakumara	5	0	32	0
Vaas	10	1	36	3
Gamage	5	0	37	0
Kalpage	7	0	35	1
Muralitharan	10	1	62	1
Jayasuriya	10	0	47	1
A.Ranatunga	3	0	22	0

NEW ZEALAND	O	M	R	W
Pringle	7	1	22	1
Patel	10	1	31	1
Vaughan	3	0	18	0
Larsen	6	0	20	2
Thomson	5	0	23	0

FALL OF WICKETS
1-23, 2-83, 3-94, 4-173, 5-242, 6-245

FALL OF WICKETS
1-8, 2-16, 3-30, 4-46, 5-80, 6-111

Umpires: B.F.Bowden (1) and C.E.King (12).

Referee: B.N.Jarman (*Australia*).

NEW ZEALAND v SRI LANKA 1994-95

At Eden Park, Auckland on 1 April 1995.   Result: **SRI LANKA** won by 51 runs.   Toss: Sri Lanka.
Award: S.T.Jayasuriya.   LOI debuts: Sri Lanka – M.C.Mendis.

Sri Lanka gave a foretaste of the form that was to win the World Cup a year later, their batsmen building on Asanka
Gurusinha's 143-ball hundred to average five an over before the spinners applied the brake on a slow surface.

SRI LANKA		Runs	Balls	4/6	NEW ZEALAND		Runs	Balls	4/6
A.P.Gurusinha	b Cairns	108	149	10/1	B.A.Young	b Gamage	6	15	1
S.T.Jayasuriya	c and b Patel	49	63	4/1	M.J.Greatbatch	c De Silva b Muralitharan	43	53	2/2
P.A.de Silva	c and b Patel	9	17	–	N.J.Astle	b Jayasuriya	35	61	1
* A.Ranatunga	b Pringle	39	50	2	* K.R.Rutherford	c Jayasuriya b De Silva	30	59	1
R.S.Kalpage	c Rutherford b Cairns	9	11	–	C.L.Cairns	c Gamage b Jayasuriya	15	21	1
† H.P.Tillekeratne	c Fleming b Pringle	16	11	1/1	S.P.Fleming	b Jayasuriya	18	21	–/1
M.C.Mendis	not out	3	2	–	† A.C.Parore	c Mendis b Kalpage	19	21	2
W.P.U.C.J.Vaas	not out	1	1	–	D.N.Patel	c Mendis b Kalpage	11	11	1
S.Ranatunga					J.T.C.Vaughan	run out	5	11	–
M.Muralitharan					G.R.Larsen	not out	2	4	–
J.C.Gamage					C.Pringle	lbw b Kalpage	4	5	–
Extras	(b 3, lb 7, w 3, nb 3)	16			Extras	(b 1, lb 5, w 4, nb 1)	11		
Total	(50 overs; 6 wickets)	**250**			**Total**	(46.3 overs)	**199**		

NEW ZEALAND	O	M	R	W	SRI LANKA	O	M	R	W
Pringle	10	0	56	2	Vaas	8	0	34	0
Patel	10	1	28	2	Gamage	7	0	27	1
Cairns	10	0	45	2	Muralitharan	10	0	32	1
Vaughan	4	0	30	0	Kalpage	9.3	0	47	3
Larsen	10	0	49	0	Jayasuriya	10	0	35	3
Astle	6	1	32	0	De Silva	2	0	18	1

FALL OF WICKETS   FALL OF WICKETS
1-91, 2-106, 3-218, 4-224, 5-238, 6-246   1-13, 2-80, 3-104, 4-135, 5-139, 6-173, 7-178, 8-192, 9-192, 10-199

Umpires: D.B.Cowie (12) and R.S.Dunne (22).   **Referee:** B.N.Jarman (*Australia*).

INDIA v BANGLADESH 1994-95

At Sharjah CA Stadium, UAE on 5 April 1995.   Result: **INDIA** won by 9 wickets.   Toss: Bangladesh.
Award: M.Prabhakar.   LOI debuts: India – U.Chatterjee; Bangladesh – Anis-ur-Rehman, Javed Omar, Khalid Masud,
Mohammad Rafiq, Sajjad Ahmed.

Sponsored by Pepsi, the fifth Asia Cup began with Bangladesh sustaining their tenth defeat in as many matches, the
three at the hands of India all being by the margin of nine wickets.

BANGLADESH		Runs	Balls	4/6	INDIA		Runs	Balls	4/6
Athar Ali Khan	c Mongia b Srinath	17	19	3	M.Prabhakar	not out	53	87	5
Javed Omar	run out	18	43	2	S.R.Tendulkar	b Rafiq	48	30	9/1
Sajjad Ahmed	c Mongia b Prabhakar	4	6	–	N.S.Sidhu	not out	56	51	7
Amin-ul-Islam	c Vaidya b Chatterjee	30	53	2/1	* M.Azharuddin				
Minhaz-ul-Abedin	run out	21	39	1	V.G.Kambli				
* Akram Khan	c Chatterjee b Vaidya	24	42	1	S.V.Manjrekar				
Inam-ul-Haq	lbw b Prabhakar	8	21	–	† N.R.Mongia				
Mohammad Rafiq	b Kumble	2	6	–	A.Kumble				
† Khalid Masud	lbw b Kumble	4	1	1	J.Srinath				
Saif-ul-Islam	not out	22	28	2	P.S.Vaidya				
Anis-ur-Rehman	c Sidhu b Vaidya	2	10	–	U.Chatterjee				
Extras	(lb 7, w 1, nb 3)	11			Extras	(lb 1, w 5, nb 1)	7		
Total	(44.4 overs)	**163**			**Total**	(27.5 overs; 1 wicket)	**164**		

INDIA	O	M	R	W	BANGLADESH	O	M	R	W
Prabhakar	10	0	43	2	Anis-ur-Rehman	5	0	42	0
Srinath	8	3	21	1	Saif-ul-Islam	5	0	31	0
Chatterjee	10	0	28	1	Inam-ul-Haq	6	0	25	0
Vaidya	8.4	1	41	2	Mohammad Rafiq	5	0	15	1
Kumble	8	0	23	2	Athar Ali Khan	3	0	22	0
					Minhaz-ul-Abedin	3	0	19	0
					Amin-ul-Islam	0.5	0	9	0

FALL OF WICKETS   FALL OF WICKETS
1-30, 2-40, 3-51, 4-93, 5-99, 6-114, 7-119, 8-125, 9-138, 10-163   1-72

Umpires: N.T.Plews (*England*) (6) and I.D.Robinson (*Zimbabwe*) (20).   **Referee:** C.H.Lloyd (*West Indies*).

SRI LANKA v BANGLADESH 1994-95

At Sharjah CA Stadium, UAE on 6 April 1995.   Result: **SRI LANKA** won by 107 runs.   Toss: Bangladesh.
Award: A.Ranatunga.   LOI debuts: Sri Lanka – C.I.Dunusinghe; Bangladesh – Habib-ul-Bashar, Hasib-ul-Hassan.

Playing their 11th official international, Bangladesh dismissed their opponents for the first time, Saif-ul-Islam returning their first four-wicket analysis. Sanath Jayasuriya (51) retired at 79 with dehydration and resumed at 194.

SRI LANKA		Runs	Balls	4/6
A.P.Gurusinha	c Amin b Saif	0	1	–
S.T.Jayasuriya	c Khalid Masud b Saif	51	72	8
R.S.Mahanama	b Hasib	2	11	–
P.A.de Silva	c Khalid Masud b Minhaz	36	69	2
* A.Ranatunga	b Saif	71	72	2/1
H.P.Tillekeratne	c Habib b Rafiq	37	41	2
R.S.Kalpage	run out	1	1	–
† C.I.Dunusinghe	run out	1	1	–
W.P.U.C.J.Vaas	c Akram Khan b Saif	11	12	1
M.Muralitharan	c Akram Khan b Rafiq	6	11	–
J.C.Gamage	not out	7	7	–
Extras	(lb 5, w 5)	10		
Total	**(49.4 overs)**	**233**		

BANGLADESH	O	M	R	W
Saif-ul-Islam	10	2	36	4
Hasib-ul-Hassan	6	2	29	1
Athar Ali Khan	7	0	28	0
Inam-ul-Haq	10	0	38	0
Minhaz-ul-Abedin	6	0	30	1
Mohammad Rafiq	8.4	0	50	2
Amin-ul-Islam	2	0	17	0

FALL OF WICKETS
1-0, 2-8, 3-101, 4-194, 5-197, 6-198, 7-203, 8-203, 9-220, 10-233

Umpires: C.J.Mitchley (*South Africa*) (17) and N.T.Plews (*England*) (7).

BANGLADESH		Runs	Balls	4/6
Athar Ali Khan	run out	2	14	–
Sajjad Ahmed	c Jayasuriya b Muralitharan	11	40	–
Habib-ul-Bashar	c De Silva b Gamage	16	35	3
Amin-ul-Islam	lbw b Gamage	0	1	–
Minhaz-ul-Abedin	c Dunusinghe b Kalpage	26	37	1
* Akram Khan	c Ranatunga b Vaas	24	62	–
Inam-ul-Haq	c Vaas b Jayasuriya	1	16	–
† Khalid Masud	c and b Muralitharan	15	23	2
Mohammad Rafiq	st Dunusinghe b Muralitharan	13	28	1
Saif-ul-Islam	c Vaas b Muralitharan	5	10	1
Hasib-ul-Hassan	not out	1	3	–
Extras	(b 8, w 4)	12		
Total	**(44.2 overs)**	**126**		

SRI LANKA	O	M	R	W
Vaas	7	4	9	1
Gamage	7	2	17	2
Muralitharan	8.2	1	23	4
Ranatunga	5	0	24	0
Jayasuriya	7	0	19	1
Kalpage	10	1	26	1

FALL OF WICKETS
1-4, 2-32, 3-32, 4-42, 5-76, 6-85, 7-100, 8-111, 9-123, 10-126

Referee: C.H.Lloyd (*West Indies*).

INDIA v PAKISTAN 1994-95

At Sharjah CA Stadium, UAE on 7 April 1995.   Result: **PAKISTAN** won by 97 runs.   Toss: Pakistan.
Award: Aqib Javed.   LOI debuts: Pakistan – Zafar Iqbal.

Pakistan, led for the first time by Moin Khan, celebrated their 300th international by securing their biggest victory against India by a runs margin in 41 encounters. Aqib Javed returned the record analysis for Asia Cup matches.

PAKISTAN		Runs	Balls	4/6
Aamir Sohail	c Tendulkar b Srinath	40	40	6/1
Saeed Anwar	c Azharuddin b Kumble	25	40	2/1
Ghulam Ali	c Tendulkar b Chatterjee	13	49	–
Inzamam-ul-Haq	b Prasad	88	100	7
Asif Mujtaba	run out	4	7	–
*† Moin Khan	b Chatterjee	2	5	–
Wasim Akram	run out	50	46	4/2
Zafar Iqbal	b Kumble	18	10	1/1
Naeem Ashraf	not out	8	4	1
Nadeem Khan	run out	2	3	–
Aqib Javed				
Extras	(lb 8, w 7, nb 1)	16		
Total	**(50 overs; 9 wickets)**	**266**		

INDIA	O	M	R	W
Prabhakar	10	0	64	0
Srinath	9	0	60	1
Prasad	8	0	43	1
Kumble	8	0	29	2
Tendulkar	7	0	27	0
Chatterjee	8	0	35	2

FALL OF WICKETS
1-58, 2-73, 3-104, 4-122, 5-133, 6-214, 7-255, 8-255, 9-266

Umpires: C.J.Mitchley (*SA*) (18) and I.D.Robinson (*Zimbabwe*) (21).

INDIA		Runs	Balls	4/6
M.Prabhakar	c Moin b Aqib	0	5	–
S.R.Tendulkar	c Moin b Aqib	4	9	1
N.S.Sidhu	lbw b Zafar	54	81	7
* M.Azharuddin	c Asif b Aqib	11	24	1
V.G.Kambli	b Aqib	0	2	–
S.V.Manjrekar	c Asif b Aamir	50	73	1/2
† N.R.Mongia	hit wicket b Wasim	18	29	1
J.Srinath	c and b Aqib	0	3	–
A.Kumble	run out	0	2	–
U.Chatterjee	not out	3	25	–
B.K.V.Prasad	c Moin b Aamir	3	16	–
Extras	(lb 8, w 7, nb 11)	26		
Total	**(42.4 overs)**	**169**		

PAKISTAN	O	M	R	W
Wasim Akram	8	0	23	1
Aqib Javed	9	1	19	5
Zafar Iqbal	8	0	34	1
Naeem Ashraf	6	0	40	0
Nadeem Khan	10	0	42	0
Aamir Sohail	1.4	0	3	2

FALL OF WICKETS
1-2, 2-11, 3-37, 4-37, 5-106, 6-144, 7-151, 8-151, 9-152, 10-169

Referee: C.H.Lloyd (*West Indies*).

PAKISTAN v BANGLADESH 1994-95

At Sharjah CA Stadium, UAE on 8 April 1995.　Result: **PAKISTAN** won by 6 wickets.　Toss: Bangladesh.
Award: Wasim Akram.　LOI debuts: Bangladesh – Naim-ur-Rehman.

Pakistan's comprehensive victory was achieved with 20.2 overs in hand. Wasim Akram completed the rout with successive sixes and, because the scoreboard was a run short, added another boundary which was subsequently expunged from the records.

BANGLADESH		Runs	Balls	4/6
Athar Ali Khan	c Moin b Wasim	2	16	–
Javed Omar	b Aamir Nazir	9	26	–
Habib-ul-Bashar	b Wasim	0	2	–
Amin-ul-Islam	c and b Arshad	42	81	4
Minhaz-ul-Abedin	c Moin b Aamir Nazir	0	2	–
* Akram Khan	run out	44	82	2
Naim-ur-Rehman	run out	3	7	–
† Khalid Masud	not out	27	52	1
Inam-ul-Haq	run out	7	26	–
Saif-ul-Islam	not out	3	12	–
Hasib-ul-Hassan				
Extras	(lb 1, w 9, nb 4)	14		
Total	(50 overs; 8 wickets)	**151**		

PAKISTAN		Runs	Balls	4/6
Aamir Sohail	c Naim b Saif	30	29	6
Saeed Anwar	c Khalid Masud b Hasib	18	34	2
Ghulam Ali	c and b Naim	38	53	2
Inzamam-ul-Haq	not out	29	23	2
Asif Mujtaba	b Athar	0	5	–
Wasim Akram	not out	30	25	2/2
*† Moin Khan				
Zafar Iqbal				
Aqib Javed				
Aamir Nazir				
Arshad Khan				
Extras	(lb 1, w 6)	7		
Total	(29.4 overs; 4 wickets)	**152**		

PAKISTAN	O	M	R	W
Wasim Akram	10	0	25	2
Aqib Javed	10	0	29	0
Zafar Iqbal	5	1	8	0
Aamir Nazir	7	0	23	2
Arshad Khan	10	0	29	1
Aamir Sohail	8	1	36	0

BANGLADESH	O	M	R	W
Saif-ul-Islam	7	0	33	1
Hasib-ul-Hassan	8	0	43	1
Inam-ul-Haq	4	0	20	0
Naim-ur-Rehman	6.4	0	29	1
Athar Ali Khan	2	0	10	1
Minhaz-ul-Abedin	2	0	16	0

FALL OF WICKETS
1-12, 2-16, 3-19, 4-19, 5-91, 6-97, 7-119, 8-133

FALL OF WICKETS
1-35, 2-68, 3-106, 4-107

Umpires: N.T.Plews (*England*) (8) and I.D.Robinson (*Zimbabwe*) (22).

Referee: C.H.Lloyd (*West Indies*).

INDIA v SRI LANKA 1994-95

At Sharjah CA Stadium, UAE on 9 April 1995.　Result: **INDIA** won by 8 wickets.　Toss: Sri Lanka.
Award: S.R.Tendulkar.　LOI debuts: None.

At 21 years 350 days, Sachin Tendulkar became the youngest to score 3000 runs in internationals. His stand of 161 with Manoj Prabhakar is India's highest opening partnership at Sharjah and against Sri Lanka anywhere.

SRI LANKA		Runs	Balls	4/6
A.P.Gurusinha	c Mongia b Srinath	15	32	1/1
S.T.Jayasuriya	b Kumble	31	39	5
R.S.Mahanama	c Azharuddin b Prasad	11	27	2
P.A.de Silva	c Tendulkar b Prasad	21	30	1/1
* A.Ranatunga	lbw b Srinath	5	13	1
H.P.Tillekeratne	run out	48	78	2
† R.S.Kaluwitharana	c Jadeja b Prasad	1	3	–
H.D.P.K.Dharmasena	run out	30	71	2
W.P.U.C.J.Vaas	not out	10	12	1
C.P.H.Ramanayake	b Prabhakar	0	1	–
J.C.Gamage	not out	1	2	–
Extras	(lb 12, w 12, nb 5)	29		
Total	(50 overs; 9 wickets)	**202**		

INDIA		Runs	Balls	4/6
M.Prabhakar	c Tillekeratne b Jayasuriya	60	79	7
S.R.Tendulkar	not out	112	107	15/1
N.S.Sidhu	c and b Jayasuriya	3	7	–
J.Srinath	not out	14	12	2
* M.Azharuddin				
A.Jadeja				
S.V.Manjrekar				
† N.R.Mongia				
A.Kumble				
B.K.V.Prasad				
A.R.Kapoor				
Extras	(lb 3, w 13, nb 1)	17		
Total	(33.1 overs; 2 wickets)	**206**		

INDIA	O	M	R	W
Prabhakar	10	1	51	1
Srinath	10	1	35	2
Prasad	10	0	37	3
Kumble	10	0	37	1
Kapoor	10	0	30	0

SRI LANKA	O	M	R	W
Vaas	9	0	67	0
Gamage	3	0	23	0
Ramanayake	4.1	0	38	0
Dharmasena	5	0	16	0
Jayasuriya	10	0	42	2
De Silva	2	0	17	0

FALL OF WICKETS
1-25, 2-60, 3-70, 4-76, 5-105, 6-113, 7-184, 8-196, 9-199

FALL OF WICKETS
1-161, 2-167

Umpires: C.J.Mitchley (*South Africa*) (19) and N.T.Plews (*England*) (9).

Referee: C.H.Lloyd (*West Indies*).

PAKISTAN v SRI LANKA 1994-95

At Sharjah CA Stadium, UAE on 11 April 1995.   Result: **SRI LANKA** won by 5 wickets.   Toss: Sri Lanka.
Award: S.T.Jayasuriya.   LOI debuts: Pakistan – Javed Qadir, Mahmood Hamid.

Saeed Anwar led Pakistan for the first time, in the absence of Moin Khan with smallpox. Romesh Kaluwitharana was the 11th wicket-keeper (third Sri Lankan) to make five dismissals in an innings. Roshan Mahanama completed 3000 runs in his 118th international. Sri Lanka won with 19.1 overs to spare and qualified for the final ahead of Pakistan on run rate.

PAKISTAN		Runs	Balls	4/6
Aamir Sohail	c Kaluwitharana b Vaas	0	3	–
* Saeed Anwar	c Gurusinha b Ramanayake	4	23	–
Asif Mujtaba	c Kaluwitharana b Ramanayake	13	33	1
Inzamam-ul-Haq	c Kaluwitharana b Vaas	73	96	2/3
Mahmood Hamid	run out	1	6	–
Wasim Akram	st Kaluwitharana b Jayasuriya	6	23	–
Naeem Ashraf	c Kaluwitharana b Muralitharan	16	39	1
Zafar Iqbal	run out	13	27	–
† Javed Qadir	c Jayasuriya b Ramanayake	12	23	1
Arshad Khan	not out	9	12	–
Aamir Nazir	not out	9	16	–
Extras	(lb 4, w 17, nb 1)	22		
Total	(50 overs; 9 wickets)	**178**		

SRI LANKA		Runs	Balls	4/6
R.S.Mahanama	c Arshad b Aamir Sohail	48	74	3
S.T.Jayasuriya	c Arshad b Aamir Nazir	30	15	4/1
A.P.Gurusinha	run out	14	20	1
P.A.de Silva	c Qadir b Aamir Sohail	23	27	4
* A.Ranatunga	not out	23	24	1
† R.S.Kaluwitharana	b Wasim	17	12	3
H.P.Tillekeratne	not out	8	15	–/1
R.S.Kalpage				
W.P.U.C.J.Vaas				
C.P.H.Ramanayake				
M.Muralitharan				
Extras	(lb 9, w 7, nb 1)	17		
Total	(30.5 overs; 5 wickets)	**180**		

SRI LANKA	O	M	R	W
Vaas	10	3	30	2
Ramanayake	10	1	25	3
Jayasuriya	10	1	31	1
Muralitharan	10	0	42	1
Kalpage	10	2	46	0

PAKISTAN	O	M	R	W
Wasim Akram	9	0	37	1
Aamir Nazir	5	0	47	1
Zafar Iqbal	5	0	25	0
Arshad Khan	5.5	0	29	0
Naeem Ashraf	1	0	12	0
Aamir Sohail	5	0	21	2

FALL OF WICKETS
1-0, 2-19, 3-22, 4-25, 5-38, 6-74, 7-137, 8-156, 9-158

Umpires: C.J.Mitchley (SA) (2) and I.D.Robinson (Zimbabwe) (23).

FALL OF WICKETS
1-34, 2-65, 3-118, 4-137, 5-165

Referee: C.H.Lloyd (West Indies).

INDIA v SRI LANKA 1994-95

At Sharjah CA Stadium, UAE on 14 April 1995.   Result: **INDIA** won by 8 wickets.   Toss: India.
Award: M.Azharuddin.   Series Award: N.S.Sidhu.   LOI debuts: None.

India won the Asia Cup for the fourth time in as many attempts, having withdrawn from the 1985-86 tournament. Mohammed Azharuddin, who became the third batsman after Pakistanis Salim Malik and Javed Miandad to score 1000 LOI runs at Sharjah, shared in a national record unbroken third-wicket stand of 175 with Navjot Sidhu.

SRI LANKA		Runs	Balls	4/6
R.S.Mahanama	b Kumble	15	37	1
S.T.Jayasuriya	c Mongia b Prasad	22	28	3
A.P.Gurusinha	run out	85	122	2/3
P.A.de Silva	c Mongia b Prabhakar	13	24	2
* A.Ranatunga	run out	3	7	–
H.P.Tillekeratne	c Mongia b Prasad	22	55	1
† R.S.Kaluwitharana	b Kumble	18	19	3
R.S.Kalpage	not out	7	10	–
W.P.U.C.J.Vaas	not out	8	5	–
C.P.H.Ramanayake				
M.Muralitharan				
Extras	(lb 23, w 10, nb 4)	37		
Total	(50 overs; 7 wickets)	**230**		

INDIA		Runs	Balls	4/6
M.Prabhakar	c Kaluwitharana b Vaas	9	17	–
S.R.Tendulkar	c Jayasuriya b Ramanayake	41	41	5
N.S.Sidhu	not out	84	106	5
* M.Azharuddin	not out	90	89	5/2
A.Jadeja				
S.V.Manjrekar				
† N.R.Mongia				
J.Srinath				
A.Kumble				
A.R.Kapoor				
B.K.V.Prasad				
Extras	(lb 1, w 7, nb 1)	9		
Total	(41.5 overs; 2 wickets)	**233**		

INDIA	O	M	R	W
Prabhakar	10	0	45	1
Srinath	9	2	38	0
Prasad	10	1	32	2
Kumble	10	1	50	2
Kapoor	10	0	32	0
Tendulkar	1	0	10	0

SRI LANKA	O	M	R	W
Vaas	9	0	52	1
Ramanayake	8.5	0	52	1
Jayasuriya	6	0	38	0
Muralitharan	10	0	46	0
Kalpage	8	0	44	0

FALL OF WICKETS
1-46, 2-46, 3-81, 4-89, 5-150, 6-192, 7-218

Umpires: C.J.Mitchley (South Africa) (21) and N.T.Plews (England) (10).

FALL OF WICKETS
1-48, 2-58

Referee: C.H.Lloyd (West Indies).

ENGLAND v WEST INDIES 1995

At Trent Bridge, Nottingham on 24, 25 May 1995.   Result: **WEST INDIES** won by 5 wickets.   Toss: West Indies.
Award: C.A.Walsh.   LOI debuts: None.

West Indies gained their first LOI victory in England since 1984. Rain ended play when they were 76 for 1 after 19.5 overs (one ball short of the number needed for a result if no further play had been possible), but a prompt start on the reserve day enabled the game to be concluded before lunch.

ENGLAND		Runs	Balls	4/6	WEST INDIES		Runs	Balls	4/6
* M.A.Atherton	c Lara b Walsh	8	33	–	C.L.Hooper	b Cork	34	57	6
† A.J.Stewart	b Hooper	74	127	11	S.L.Campbell	run out	80	137	8
G.A.Hick	c Murray b Benjamin	8	27	–	B.C.Lara	c Atherton b Gough	70	95	7/1
G.P.Thorpe	c Murray b Walsh	7	10	–	* R.B.Richardson	c DeFreitas b Gough	1	7	–
N.H.Fairbrother	b Bishop	12	23	–	J.C.Adams	lbw b Cork	2	12	–
M.R.Ramprakash	b Walsh	32	36	1/1	K.L.T.Arthurton	not out	1	3	–
P.A.J.DeFreitas	run out	15	29	–	† J.R.Murray	not out	7	6	1
D.G.Cork	b Arthurton	14	27	–	W.K.M.Benjamin				
D.Gough	run out	3	4	–	I.R.Bishop				
S.D.Udal	not out	5	7	–	C.E.L.Ambrose				
A.R.C.Fraser	not out	4	8	–	C.A.Walsh				
Extras	(lb 11, w 5, nb 1)	17			Extras	(lb 1, w 4, nb 1)	6		
Total	(55 overs; 9 wickets)	**199**			**Total**	(52.4 overs; 5 wickets)	**201**		

WEST INDIES	O	M	R	W	ENGLAND	O	M	R	W
Ambrose	8	1	33	0	DeFreitas	10.4	1	44	0
Walsh	10	1	28	3	Fraser	10	2	29	0
Bishop	11	2	30	1	Gough	11	1	30	2
Benjamin	8	1	22	1	Cork	11	0	48	2
Hooper	10	0	45	1	Udal	8	0	37	0
Arthurton	8	0	30	1	Hick	2	0	12	0

FALL OF WICKETS
1-25, 2-60, 3-85, 4-121, 5-125, 6-157, 7-186, 8-190, 9-191

FALL OF WICKETS
1-66, 2-180, 3-183, 4-191, 5-194

Umpires: N.T.Plews (11) and D.R.Shepherd (57).

Referee: J.R.Reid (*New Zealand*).

ENGLAND v WEST INDIES 1995

At Kennington Oval, London on 26 May 1995.   Result: **ENGLAND** won by 25 runs.   Toss: West Indies.
Award: P.J.Martin.   LOI debuts: England – P.J.Martin.

The Kennington Oval, scene of the first Test staged in England in 1880, had the honour of staging the 1000th limited-overs international. The hosts celebrated the event by becoming the first country to total 300 against West Indies. Peter Martin took four wickets on debut, the first with his fifth ball.

ENGLAND		Runs	Balls	4/6	WEST INDIES		Runs	Balls	4/6
* M.A.Atherton	b Benjamin	92	118	10	C.L.Hooper	c Atherton b Gough	17	21	4
† A.J.Stewart	c Murray b Bishop	16	37	3	S.L.Campbell	c Thorpe b Martin	20	35	2/1
G.A.Hick	run out	66	81	6	B.C.Lara	b Martin	39	36	6
G.P.Thorpe	run out	26	28	2	J.C.Adams	lbw b Martin	2	8	–
N.H.Fairbrother	not out	61	52	5/1	* R.B.Richardson	c and b Cork	15	27	1
M.R.Ramprakash	c Adams b Hooper	16	16	–/1	K.L.T.Arthurton	run out	39	66	4
D.Gough	not out	8	6	1	† J.R.Murray	run out	86	77	6/2
P.A.J.DeFreitas					W.K.M.Benjamin	c Ramprakash b DeFreitas	17	15	–/1
D.G.Cork					I.R.Bishop	run out	18	16	1
P.J.Martin					C.E.L.Ambrose	b Martin	10	13	1
S.D.Udal					C.A.Walsh	not out	5	4	1
Extras	(b 6, lb 5, w 6, nb 4)	21			Extras	(lb 6, w 7)	13		
Total	(55 overs; 5 wickets)	**306**			**Total**	(53 overs)	**281**		

WEST INDIES	O	M	R	W	ENGLAND	O	M	R	W
Ambrose	10	1	47	0	Gough	11	0	62	1
Walsh	5.2	0	17	0	DeFreitas	10	0	73	1
Bishop	11	0	60	1	Cork	11	0	56	1
Benjamin	10.4	0	55	1	Udal	11	0	40	0
Arthurton	8	0	48	0	Martin	10	1	44	4
Hooper	10	0	68	1					

FALL OF WICKETS
1-33, 2-177, 3-188, 4-243, 5-295

FALL OF WICKETS
1-25, 2-69, 3-77, 4-88, 5-114, 6-166, 7-213, 8-261, 9-275, 10-281

Umpires: H.D.Bird (68) and R.Palmer (8).

Referee: J.R.Reid (*New Zealand*).

501

ENGLAND v WEST INDIES 1995

At Lord's, London on 28 May 1995.   Result: **ENGLAND** won by 73 runs.   Toss: West Indies.
Award: M.A.Atherton.   LOI debuts: England – A.P.Wells; West Indies – O.D.Gibson.

Michael Atherton's first LOI hundred took his aggregate in 25 matches beyond 1000 and ensured that England would win their third successive Texaco Trophy against West Indies.

ENGLAND		Runs	Balls	4/6
* M.A.Atherton	c Adams b Gibson	127	160	14/1
† A.J.Stewart	c Lara b Bishop	8	16	2
G.A.Hick	b Hooper	24	55	3
G.P.Thorpe	c Hooper b Gibson	28	49	1
M.R.Ramprakash	not out	29	43	1
A.P.Wells	b Gibson	15	10	2
D.Gough	b Benjamin	8	5	–/1
D.G.Cork	lbw b Benjamin	0	1	–
P.J.Martin	not out	4	1	1
S.D.Udal				
A.R.C.Fraser				
Extras	(b 4, lb 13, w 9, nb 7)	33		
Total	(55 overs; 7 wickets)	**276**		

WEST INDIES		O	M	R	W
Ambrose		11	1	45	0
Bishop		11	2	53	1
Benjamin		10	0	61	2
Gibson		11	0	51	3
Hooper		11	0	38	1
Arthurton		1	0	11	0

FALL OF WICKETS
1-12, 2-79, 3-152, 4-244, 5-263, 6-272, 7-272

Umpires: J.H.Hampshire (6) and M.J.Kitchen (12).

WEST INDIES		Runs	Balls	4/6
S.C.Williams	c Atherton b Cork	21	30	5
C.L.Hooper	c Gough b Cork	40	89	2
B.C.Lara	c Stewart b Cork	11	10	2
J.C.Adams	c Stewart b Martin	29	46	2
K.L.T.Arthurton	c Stewart b Gough	35	49	6
* R.B.Richardson	lbw b Gough	23	33	1/1
† J.R.Murray	b Fraser	5	7	–
O.D.Gibson	c Atherton b Fraser	7	8	–
W.K.M.Benjamin	b Fraser	6	9	–
I.R.Bishop	not out	1	5	–
C.E.L.Ambrose	b Martin	1	4	–
Extras	(lb 13, w 11)	24		
Total	(48.2 overs)	**203**		

ENGLAND	O	M	R	W
Fraser	11	3	34	3
Martin	9.2	1	36	2
Cork	9	2	27	3
Gough	10	0	31	2
Udal	8	0	52	0
Hick	1	0	10	0

FALL OF WICKETS
1-29, 2-44, 3-94, 4-128, 5-171, 6-184, 7-190, 8-198, 9-201, 10-203

Referee: J.R.Reid (New Zealand).

PAKISTAN v SRI LANKA 1995-96

At Municipal Stadium, Gujranwala on 29 September 1995.   Result: **PAKISTAN** won by 9 wickets.
Toss: Pakistan.   Award: Salim Elahi.   LOI debuts: Pakistan – Mohammad Akram, Salim Elahi, Saqlain Mushtaq.

Salim Elahi, brother of Manzoor Elahi, became the fourth batsman (first Pakistani) to score a hundred on LOI debut; at 18 years 312 days he remains the youngest to do so and he completed it with a straight six.

SRI LANKA		Runs	Balls	4/6
R.S.Mahanama	run out	12	31	1
S.T.Jayasuriya	c Basit b Rehman	25	31	3/1
A.P.Gurusinha	c Saqlain b Akram	57	104	3
P.A.de Silva	c Saqlain b Rehman	1	5	–
* A.Ranatunga	not out	102	112	9
R.S.Kaluwitharana	run out	6	11	1
† H.P.Tillekeratne	not out	11	10	–
R.S.Kalpage				
H.D.P.K.Dharmasena				
G.P.Wickremasinghe				
K.R.Pushpakumara				
Extras	(b 1, lb 8, w 6, nb 4)	19		
Total	(50 overs; 5 wickets)	**233**		

PAKISTAN		O	M	R	W
Aqib Javed		9	1	43	0
Mohammad Akram		10	1	43	1
Ata-ur-Rehman		10	0	46	2
Aamer Hanif		10	0	38	0
Saqlain		5	0	27	0
Aamir Sohail		6	0	27	0

FALL OF WICKETS
1-32, 2-39, 3-48, 4-185, 5-206

Umpires: Mian Mohammad Aslam (11) and Ikram Rabbani (6).

PAKISTAN		Runs	Balls	4/6
Aamir Sohail	c sub ‡ b Jayasuriya	77	97	8
Salim Elahi	not out	102	133	7/1
* Ramiz Raja	not out	44	37	4/1
Inzamam-ul-Haq				
Basit Ali				
† Moin Khan				
Aamer Hanif				
Saqlain Mushtaq				
Aqib Javed				
Mohammad Akram				
Ata-ur-Rehman				
Extras	(b 1, lb 1, w 7, nb 2)	11		
Total	(44 overs; 1 wicket)	**234**		

SRI LANKA	O	M	R	W
Wickremasinghe	7	0	41	0
Pushpakumara	7	0	47	0
Dharmasena	7	1	35	0
Ranatunga	2	0	14	0
Kalpage	6	0	32	0
Jayasuriya	10	0	43	1
De Silva	5	0	20	0

FALL OF WICKETS
1-156

‡ (M.Muralitharan)

Referee: P.L.van der Merwe (South Africa).

PAKISTAN v SRI LANKA 1995-96

At Iqbal Stadium, Faisalabad on 1 October 1995.   Result: **SRI LANKA** won by 49 runs.   Toss: Pakistan.
Award: S.T.Jayasuriya.   LOI debuts: None.

Asanka Gurusinha's 20th score of fifty or more took him beyond 3000 runs in 112 internationals.

SRI LANKA		Runs	Balls	4/6
R.S.Mahanama	lbw b Rehman	30	57	2
S.T.Jayasuriya	c Aqib b Rehman	51	72	4
A.P.Gurusinha	st Moin b Arshad	66	73	5/1
P.A.de Silva	run out	47	54	4
* A.Ranatunga	b Akram	15	16	–
† H.P.Tillekeratne	b Akram	14	18	1
R.S.Kaluwitharana	run out	11	12	1
H.D.P.K.Dharmasena	not out	1	1	–
W.P.U.C.J.Vaas	not out	0	1	–
G.P.Wickremasinghe				
M.Muralitharan				
Extras	(lb 14, w 5, nb 3)	22		
Total	(50 overs; 7 wickets)	**257**		

PAKISTAN		Runs	Balls	4/6
Aamir Sohail	c Muralitharan b Vaas	9	9	2
Salim Elahi	run out	47	61	6
* Ramiz Raja	c Jayasuriya b Dharmasena	33	50	3
Inzamam-ul-Haq	c Gurusinha b Jayasuriya	14	32	1
† Moin Khan	c sub b Muralitharan	31	41	2
Basit Ali	b Jayasuriya	16	40	–
Aamer Hanif	b De Silva	19	23	1
Aqib Javed	b De Silva	21	32	1
Ata-ur-Rehman	not out	6	7	–
Arshad Khan	not out	4	7	–
Mohammad Akram				
Extras	(lb 5, w 1, nb 2)	8		
Total	(50 overs; 8 wickets)	**208**		

PAKISTAN	O	M	R	W
Aqib Javed	8	1	34	0
Mohammad Akram	10	0	48	2
Ata-ur-Rehman	10	0	46	2
Aamer Hanif	2	0	21	0
Arshad Khan	10	0	32	1
Aamir Sohail	10	0	62	0

SRI LANKA	O	M	R	W
Wickremasinghe	7	0	36	0
Vaas	2	0	17	1
De Silva	10	0	33	2
Dharmasena	10	0	38	1
Muralitharan	10	2	37	1
Jayasuriya	10	0	38	2
Ranatunga	1	0	4	0

FALL OF WICKETS
1-75, 2-100, 3-209, 4-222, 5-232, 6-256, 7-256

Umpires: Salim Badar (7) and Siddiq Khan (4).

FALL OF WICKETS
1-10, 2-89, 3-92, 4-116, 5-154, 6-160, 7-195, 8-200

Referee: P.L.van der Merwe (*South Africa*).

PAKISTAN v SRI LANKA 1995-96

At Rawalpindi Cricket Stadium on 3 October 1995.   Result: **SRI LANKA** won by 4 wickets.
Toss: Sri Lanka.   Award: A.Ranatunga.   LOI debuts: Pakistan – Saeed Azad; Sri Lanka – K.E.A.Upashanta.

A week after winning their first Test series against Pakistan having lost the opening match, Sri Lanka repeated the formula in this limited-over rubber. Overnight rain delayed the start by three hours and reduced the match to 38 overs each. Inzamam-ul-Haq reached 3000 runs in his 90th international.

PAKISTAN		Runs	Balls	4/6
Aamir Sohail	st Kaluwitharana b Dharmasena	26	55	2
Salim Elahi	c Kalpage b Dharmasena	30	33	3/1
* Ramiz Raja	st Kaluwitharana b Dharmasena	4	8	–
Inzamam-ul-Haq	c Jayasuriya b De Silva	25	28	1/1
Saeed Azad	c Wickremasinghe b De Silva	19	35	1
Aamer Hanif	not out	36	44	2
† Moin Khan	c Kaluwitharana b De Silva	0	1	–
Zafar Iqbal	run out	13	14	1
Aqib Javed	c Gurusinha b Kalpage	11	11	–/1
Arshad Khan	run out	2	2	–
Mohammad Akram	not out	0	1	–
Extras	(lb 7, w 6, nb 4)	17		
Total	(38 overs; 9 wickets)	**183**		

SRI LANKA		Runs	Balls	4/6
R.S.Mahanama	b Zafar	23	45	–
S.T.Jayasuriya	c Inzamam b Aqib	19	25	1/1
A.P.Gurusinha	b Zafar	10	13	1
P.A.de Silva	lbw b Hanif	32	53	–
* A.Ranatunga	lbw b Hanif	42	53	3
† R.S.Kaluwitharana	c Saeed b Hanif	12	10	1
H.P.Tillekeratne	not out	13	15	–
R.S.Kalpage	not out	10	11	–
H.D.P.K.Dharmasena				
G.P.Wickremasinghe				
K.E.A.Upashanta				
Extras	(lb 12, w 11)	23		
Total	(37.4 overs; 6 wickets)	**184**		

SRI LANKA	O	M	R	W
Wickremasinghe	5	0	11	0
Upashanta	5	0	36	0
Dharmasena	8	0	30	3
Gurusinha	1	0	6	0
Kalpage	4	0	26	1
Jayasuriya	8	0	31	0
De Silva	7	0	36	3

PAKISTAN	O	M	R	W
Mohammad Akram	8	0	38	0
Aqib Javed	7.4	0	28	1
Arshad Khan	7	1	26	0
Aamir Sohail	1	0	7	0
Aamer Hanif	6	0	36	3
Zafar Iqbal	8	0	37	2

FALL OF WICKETS
1-55, 2-65, 3-80, 4-104, 5-134, 6-134, 7-158, 8-176, 9-180

Umpires: Islam Khan (2) and Shakil Khan (14).

FALL OF WICKETS
1-42, 2-60, 3-63, 4-138, 5-151, 6-165

Referee: P.L.van der Merwe (*South Africa*).

WEST INDIES v SRI LANKA 1995-96

At Sharjah CA Stadium, UAE on 11 October 1995.   Result: **SRI LANKA** won by 6 runs.   Toss: West Indies.
Award: R.S.Mahanama.   LOI debuts: West Indies – H.A.G.Anthony, C.O.Browne.

Roshan Mahanama developed his customary cramp and completed his hundred, in the final over, with the aid of a runner. Phil Simmons equalled the fielding records for West Indies and at Sharjah by holding four catches.

SRI LANKA		Runs	Balls	4/6
R.S.Mahanama	c Simmons b Bishop	101	153	5/1
S.T.Jayasuriya	c Simmons b Bishop	1	2	–
A.P.Gurusinha	c Harper b Simmons	18	56	2
P.A.de Silva	c Simmons b Chanderpaul	9	24	–
* A.Ranatunga	c Browne b Gibson	58	54	3/2
† R.S.Kaluwitharana	run out	11	5	–
H.P.Tillekeratne	c Simmons b Bishop	7	7	–
R.S.Kalpage	not out	1	1	–
H.D.P.K.Dharmasena	not out	1	1	–
M.Muralitharan				
G.P.Wickremasinghe				
Extras	(lb 7, w 20)	27		
Total	(50 overs; 7 wickets)	**234**		

WEST INDIES		Runs	Balls	4/6
P.V.Simmons	c De Silva b Wickremasinghe	5	10	1
S.L.Campbell	c Dharmasena b Muralitharan	86	119	5/1
B.C.Lara	run out	19	40	–
* R.B.Richardson	st Kaluwitharana b Jayasuriya	67	83	3/2
R.I.C.Holder	not out	26	31	1
R.A.Harper	c and b Jayasuriya	1	2	–
S.Chanderpaul	c De Silva b Dharmasena	11	10	–/1
O.D.Gibson	lbw b Dharmasena	0	1	–
H.A.G.Anthony	c Muralitharan b De Silva	2	3	–
† C.O.Browne	st Kaluwitharana b Dharmasena	2	2	–
I.R.Bishop	not out	1	1	–
Extras	(lb 6, w 1, nb 1)	8		
Total	(50 overs; 9 wickets)	**228**		

WEST INDIES	O	M	R	W
Bishop	10	1	42	3
Gibson	10	1	40	1
Anthony	8	0	49	0
Simmons	8	1	29	1
Harper	10	0	49	0
Chanderpaul	4	0	18	1

SRI LANKA	O	M	R	W
Wickremasinghe	7	0	27	1
De Silva	10	0	38	1
Dharmasena	9	0	49	3
Muralitharan	10	1	35	1
Jayasuriya	10	0	48	2
Kalpage	4	0	25	0

FALL OF WICKETS
1-8, 2-59, 3-84, 4-210, 5-222, 6-228, 7-233

FALL OF WICKETS
1-13, 2-69, 3-165, 4-192, 5-194, 6-211, 7-211, 8-218, 9-226

Umpires: R.S.Dunne (*New Zealand*) (23) and D.B.Hair (*Australia*) (14).

Referee: R.Subba Row (*England*).

PAKISTAN v SRI LANKA 1995-96

At Sharjah CA Stadium, UAE on 12 October 1995.   Result: **PAKISTAN** won by 82 runs.   Toss: Pakistan.
Award: Aamir Sohail.   LOI debuts: None.

Pakistan avenged their recent humiliations at the hands of Sri Lanka with this decisive win. Salim Elahi took his batting aggregate after four internationals to 229, average 76.33.

PAKISTAN		Runs	Balls	4/6
Aamir Sohail	c Kaluwitharana b Muralitharan	85	110	4
Salim Elahi	c Wickremasinghe b De Silva	50	74	2/1
* Ramiz Raja	c Hathurusinghe b Muralitharan	12	19	–
Inzamam-ul-Haq	c Jayasuriya b Dharmasena	69	59	1/3
Saeed Anwar	st Kaluwitharana b Jayasuriya	14	20	1
† Moin Khan	c Ranatunga b Wickremasinghe	5	8	–
Zafar Iqbal	c Gurusinha b Dharmasena	2	2	–
Mushtaq Ahmed	not out	9	3	2
Waqar Younis	not out	9	5	1
Aqib Javed				
Saqlain Mushtaq				
Extras	(b 2, lb 1, w 6)	9		
Total	(50 overs; 7 wickets)	**264**		

SRI LANKA		Runs	Balls	4/6
U.C.Hathurusinghe	lbw b Aqib	11	28	1
S.T.Jayasuriya	c sub (Basit Ali) b Saqlain	24	34	3
A.P.Gurusinha	b Aamir	19	37	1
P.A.de Silva	c and b Saqlain	3	5	–
* A.Ranatunga	c Ramiz b Aamir	14	24	–
H.P.Tillekeratne	c Moin b Aamir	15	28	–
† R.S.Kaluwitharana	b Aamir	19	25	1
R.S.Kalpage	b Saeed	22	58	–
H.D.P.K.Dharmasena	not out	30	64	1
M.Muralitharan	not out	7	5	–/1
G.P.Wickremasinghe				
Extras	(lb 10, w 3, nb 5)	18		
Total	(50 overs; 8 wickets)	**182**		

SRI LANKA	O	M	R	W
Wickremasinghe	7	1	54	1
Hathurusinghe	10	0	39	0
Dharmasena	10	0	43	2
Muralitharan	10	0	51	2
Jayasuriya	8	0	51	1
De Silva	5	0	23	1

PAKISTAN	O	M	R	W
Waqar Younis	7	0	29	0
Aqib Javed	8	1	31	1
Zafar Iqbal	5	1	12	0
Saqlain Mushtaq	10	1	30	2
Aamir Sohail	8	0	22	4
Mushtaq Ahmed	10	0	39	0
Saeed Anwar	2	1	9	1

FALL OF WICKETS
1-107, 2-138, 3-162, 4-213, 5-232, 6-244, 7-246

FALL OF WICKETS
1-33, 2-44, 3-51, 4-67, 5-82, 6-107, 7-114, 8-174

Umpires: R.S.Dunne (*New Zealand*) (24) and N.T.Plews (*England*) (12).

Referee: R.Subba Row (*England*).

WEST INDIES v PAKISTAN 1995-96

At Sharjah CA Stadium, UAE on 13 October 1995.   Result: **PAKISTAN** won by 15 runs.   Toss: Pakistan.
Award: Ramiz Raja.   LOI debuts: None.

Moin Khan hit the last three balls of Pakistan's innings for six, Ian Bishop conceding 27 runs off the over to equal the record created by Muthiah Muralitharan (*LOI No. 918*).

PAKISTAN		Runs	Balls	4/6
Aamir Sohail	c Browne b Bishop	10	20	2
Salim Elahi	c Harper b Cummins	9	25	–
* Ramiz Raja	not out	104	134	7/1
Saeed Anwar	c Browne b Anthony	18	25	3
Basit Ali	c Harper b Cummins	64	87	1/1
† Moin Khan	not out	27	10	1/3
Zafar Iqbal				
Waqar Younis				
Mushtaq Ahmed				
Saqlain Mushtaq				
Aqib Javed				
Extras	(lb 1, w 8, nb 1)	10		
Total	(50 overs; 4 wickets)	**242**		

WEST INDIES		O	M	R	W
Bishop		10	0	78	1
Cummins		10	0	31	2
Anthony		10	0	47	1
Simmons		9	0	40	0
Harper		10	0	38	0
Chanderpaul		1	0	7	0

FALL OF WICKETS
1-16, 2-24, 3-49, 4-190

WEST INDIES		Runs	Balls	4/6
P.V.Simmons	lbw b Waqar	4	8	1
S.L.Campbell	lbw b Aamir	42	46	6
B.C.Lara	c Aqib b Saqlain	21	15	2/1
* R.B.Richardson	b Aqib	34	50	1/1
S.Chanderpaul	c Salim b Waqar	36	57	2/1
R.I.C.Holder	st Moin b Saqlain	11	22	1
R.A.Harper	not out	43	57	2/1
† C.O.Browne	st Moin b Saqlain	12	26	–
A.C.Cummins	c Moin b Saqlain	4	7	–
H.A.G.Anthony	run out	0	1	–
I.R.Bishop	st Moin b Mushtaq Ahmed	7	9	–
Extras	(lb 8, w 3, nb 2)	13		
Total	(49 overs)	**227**		

PAKISTAN	O	M	R	W
Aqib Javed	9	0	30	1
Waqar Younis	9	0	51	2
Zafar Iqbal	1	0	13	0
Saqlain Mushtaq	10	1	47	4
Aamir Sohail	10	1	40	1
Mushtaq Ahmed	10	1	38	1

FALL OF WICKETS
1-5, 2-51, 3-74, 4-124, 5-154, 6-156, 7-189, 8-197, 9-198, 10-227

Umpires: D.B.Hair (*Australia*) (15) and N.T.Plews (*England*) (13).

Referee: R.Subba Row (*England*).

WEST INDIES v PAKISTAN 1995-96

At Sharjah CA Stadium, UAE on 15 October 1995.   Result: **WEST INDIES** won by 4 wickets.   Toss: West Indies.
Award: S.C.Williams.   LOI debuts: None.

Mindful of the likely importance of scoring rates in qualifying for the final, West Indies sped to victory with 10.5 overs to spare.

PAKISTAN		Runs	Balls	4/6
Salim Elahi	run out	66	109	5
* Ramiz Raja	b Simmons	20	50	1
Inzamam-ul-Haq	c sub (R.I.C.Holder) b Harper	34	51	2
Basit Ali	c Lara b Bishop	25	41	1
† Moin Khan	run out	1	3	–
Zafar Iqbal	run out	0	4	–
Mushtaq Ahmed	c Browne b Gibson	4	8	–
Waqar Younis	lbw b Gibson	6	12	–
Aqib Javed	not out	8	9	–
Saqlain Mushtaq	run out	0	6	–
Mohammad Akram	not out	7	9	1
Extras	(lb 5, w 17, nb 1)	23		
Total	(50 overs; 9 wickets)	**194**		

WEST INDIES	O	M	R	W
Bishop	8	0	29	1
Cummins	9	0	31	0
Gibson	9	1	47	2
Simmons	10	1	31	1
Chanderpaul	5	0	25	0
Harper	9	1	26	1

FALL OF WICKETS
1-74, 2-139, 3-148, 4-150, 5-150, 6-168, 7-177, 8-180, 9-181

WEST INDIES		Runs	Balls	4/6
S.C.Williams	c Zafar b Saqlain	57	63	7/1
S.L.Campbell	c Basit b Akram	20	13	4
B.C.Lara	c Basit b Mushtaq Ahmed	52	58	5/2
* R.B.Richardson	b Saqlain	34	50	2/1
P.V.Simmons	lbw b Akram	1	5	–
S.Chanderpaul	c Moin b Aqib	11	30	–
R.A.Harper	not out	5	11	–
† C.O.Browne	not out	2	7	–
A.C.Cummins				
O.D.Gibson				
I.R.Bishop				
Extras	(lb 3, w 9, nb 1)	13		
Total	(39.1 overs; 6 wickets)	**195**		

PAKISTAN	O	M	R	W
Aqib Javed	8.1	0	41	1
Waqar Younis	4	0	30	0
Mushtaq Ahmed	10	1	43	1
Mohammad Akram	7	0	36	2
Saqlain Mushtaq	10	1	42	2

FALL OF WICKETS
1-44, 2-109, 3-147, 4-151, 5-183, 6-189

Referee: R.Subba Row (*England*).

Umpires: R.S.Dunne (*New Zealand*) (25) and D.B.Hair (*Australia*) (16).

WEST INDIES v SRI LANKA 1995-96

At Sharjah CA Stadium, UAE on 16 October 1995.   Result: **WEST INDIES** won by 4 runs.   Toss: West Indies.
Award: B.C.Lara.   LOI debuts: None.

Sri Lanka contributed the highest second innings LOI total to the (then) record match aggregate, narrowly failing to gain a miraculous victory when Hashan Tillekeratne's attempted six was held at deep mid-wicket. Brian Lara converted a 90-ball hundred into the fastest 150 (111 balls).

WEST INDIES		Runs	Balls	4/6
S.C.Williams	lbw b Wickremasinghe	2	6	–
S.L.Campbell	c De Silva b Wickremasinghe	10	20	1
B.C.Lara	b Dharmasena	169	129	15/4
* R.B.Richardson	b Muralitharan	29	53	1/1
P.V.Simmons	b Hathurusinghe	30	41	2
S.Chanderpaul	not out	62	45	2/3
O.D.Gibson	c Mahanama b Hathurusinghe	10	13	–
R.A.Harper	run out	1	1	–
A.C.Cummins	not out	0	–	–
† C.O.Browne				
I.R.Bishop				
Extras	(lb 3, w 12, nb 5)	20		
Total	(50 overs; 7 wickets)	**333**		

SRI LANKA	O	M	R	W
Wickremasinghe	10	0	58	2
Hathurusinghe	10	0	67	2
De Silva	6	0	51	0
Dharmasena	10	0	72	1
Muralitharan	10	0	52	1
Jayasuriya	4	0	30	0

SRI LANKA		Runs	Balls	4/6
R.S.Mahanama	c and b Simmons	76	78	5/1
S.T.Jayasuriya	c Richardson b Gibson	5	3	1
P.A.de Silva	lbw b Bishop	20	12	3
† R.S.Kaluwitharana	c Simmons b Cummins	31	20	3/2
A.P.Gurusinha	b Harper	1	5	–
* A.Ranatunga	run out	0	2	–
H.P.Tillekeratne	c Williams b Cummins	100	106	4/1
U.C.Hathurusinghe	c Chanderpaul b Gibson	45	43	4
H.D.P.K.Dharmasena	run out	24	18	2
M.Muralitharan	run out	2	6	–
G.P.Wickremasinghe	not out	5	6	–
Extras	(lb 4, w 1, nb 15)	20		
Total	(49.3 overs)	**329**		

WEST INDIES	O	M	R	W
Cummins	9.3	0	61	2
Gibson	8	0	74	2
Bishop	8	0	63	1
Harper	10	0	38	1
Simmons	10	0	53	1
Chanderpaul	4	0	36	0

FALL OF WICKETS
1-6, 2-37, 3-133, 4-193, 5-282, 6-315, 7-319

FALL OF WICKETS
1-21, 2-46, 3-101, 4-103, 5-103, 6-171, 7-257, 8-306, 9-316, 10-329

Umpires: R.S.Dunne (*New Zealand*) (26) and N.T.Plews (*England*) (14).   **Referee:** R.Subba Row (*England*).

PAKISTAN v SRI LANKA 1995-96

At Sharjah CA Stadium, UAE on 17 October 1995.   Result: **SRI LANKA** won by 8 wickets.   Toss: Pakistan.
Award: A.Ranatunga.   LOI debuts: None.

Set a target some 190 runs fewer than the previous day's, Sri Lanka had little difficulty in boosting their scoring rate above that of Pakistan. Final run rates (each team finishing with two wins and two losses): West Indies 5.19, Sri Lanka 5.05, Pakistan 4.21.

PAKISTAN		Runs	Balls	4/6
Salim Elahi	c Kaluwitharana b Hathurusinghe	0	9	–
* Ramiz Raja	c Kaluwitharana b Wickremasinghe	9	20	1
Basit Ali	c Mahanama b Ranatunga	21	46	1/1
Aamer Hanif	run out	17	37	2
† Moin Khan	c and b Dharmasena	16	36	–
Zafar Iqbal	c Mahanama b Ranatunga	2	5	–
Mushtaq Ahmed	b Jayasuriya	26	74	1
Saqlain Mushtaq	c Wickremasinghe b Dharmasena	30	52	1/1
Waqar Younis	lbw b Dharmasena	3	6	–
Aqib Javed	not out	3	4	–
Mohammad Akram	c Ranatunga b Jayasuriya	1	5	–
Extras	(lb 1, w 11, nb 3)	15		
Total	(48.3 overs)	**143**		

SRI LANKA	O	M	R	W
Wickremasinghe	7	1	19	1
Hathurusinghe	10	1	33	1
Muralitharan	9	0	43	0
Ranatunga	10	1	21	2
Dharmasena	10	3	16	3
Jayasuriya	2.3	0	10	2

SRI LANKA		Runs	Balls	4/6
R.S.Mahanama	not out	45	73	5
S.T.Jayasuriya	c Moin b Akram	25	23	2/1
A.P.Gurusinha	c Salim b Mushtaq Ahmed	31	38	3
P.A.de Silva	not out	35	33	1/2
* A.Ranatunga				
U.C.Hathurusinghe				
H.P.Tillekeratne				
† R.S.Kaluwitharana				
H.D.P.K.Dharmasena				
M.Muralitharan				
G.P.Wickremasinghe				
Extras	(lb 7, w 2, nb 4)	13		
Total	(26.5 overs; 2 wickets)	**149**		

PAKISTAN	O	M	R	W
Aqib Javed	5	0	25	0
Mohammad Akram	5	0	24	1
Saqlain Mushtaq	4.5	0	27	0
Zafar Iqbal	1	0	8	0
Mushtaq Ahmed	8	0	35	1
Waqar Younis	3	0	23	0

FALL OF WICKETS
1-11, 2-25, 3-52, 4-63, 5-68, 6-82, 7-134, 8-137, 9-140, 10-143

FALL OF WICKETS
1-35, 2-94

Umpires: D.B.Hair (*Australia*) (17) and N.T.Plews (*England*) (15).   **Referee:** R.Subba Row (*England*).

WEST INDIES v SRI LANKA 1995-96

At Sharjah CA Stadium, UAE on 20 October 1995.　Result: **SRI LANKA** won by 50 runs.　Toss: West Indies.
Award: P.A.de Silva.　Series Award: R.S.Mahanama.　LOI debuts: None.

Put in, Sri Lanka dominated the match through their aggressive batting and won their first tournament involving more than two teams. Although he missed one match, Roshan Mahanama was an outstanding candidate for the series award with 288 runs @ 96.00.

SRI LANKA		Runs	Balls	4/6
R.S.Mahanama	b Cummins	66	103	6
S.T.Jayasuriya	c Gibson b Simmons	57	82	5/3
P.A.de Silva	c Chanderpaul b Anthony	50	35	4/2
* A.Ranatunga	c Cummins b Anthony	17	26	–
H.P.Tillekeratne	c Browne b Gibson	32	30	1
† R.S.Kaluwitharana	b Cummins	15	6	3
A.P.Gurusinha	c Browne b Gibson	12	8	2
U.C.Hathurusinghe	b Gibson	0	4	–
H.D.P.K.Dharmasena	c Campbell b Gibson	4	6	–
K.E.A.Upashanta	run out	3	2	–
M.Muralitharan	not out	0	–	–
Extras	(lb 8, w 7, nb 2)	17		
Total	(49.5 overs)	**273**		

WEST INDIES		Runs	Balls	4/6
S.C.Williams	c Muralitharan b Upashanta	5	12	–
S.L.Campbell	b Muralitharan	38	78	2/1
B.C.Lara	c and b Upashanta	8	25	–
* R.B.Richardson	run out	10	14	1
P.V.Simmons	run out	7	15	–
S.Chanderpaul	c Muralitharan b Dharmasena	27	32	1
R.A.Harper	c sub (R.S.Kalpage) b Muralitharan	31	47	2
† C.O.Browne	c and b Jayasuriya	18	21	–
A.C.Cummins	c Ranatunga b Muralitharan	0	1	–
O.D.Gibson	not out	33	25	3/1
H.A.G.Anthony	c De Silva b Dharmasena	21	18	–/2
Extras	(lb 15, w 7, nb 3)	25		
Total	(47.3 overs)	**223**		

WEST INDIES	O	M	R	W
Cummins	9	1	50	2
Gibson	5.5	0	35	4
Anthony	8	0	47	2
Simmons	7	1	44	1
Harper	10	1	36	0
Chanderpaul	10	0	53	0

SRI LANKA	O	M	R	W
Upashanta	8	1	24	2
Hathurusinghe	8	0	30	0
Muralitharan	10	0	31	3
Ranatunga	7	0	25	0
Dharmasena	8.3	1	58	2
Jayasuriya	6	0	40	1

FALL OF WICKETS
1-111, 2-157, 3-196, 4-215, 5-234, 6-259, 7-259, 8-269, 9-273, 10-273

FALL OF WICKETS
1-28, 2-41, 3-59, 4-74, 5-88, 6-141, 7-156, 8-157, 9-177, 10-223

Umpires: R.S.Dunne (*New Zealand*) (27) and D.B.Hair (*Australia*) (18).　　Referee: R.Subba Row (*England*).

ZIMBABWE v SOUTH AFRICA (1st Match)　　　　　　　　　　　　LOI No: 1012/3

ZIMBABWE v SOUTH AFRICA 1995-96

At Harare Sports Club on 21 October 1995.　Result: **SOUTH AFRICA** won by 134 runs.　Toss: South Africa.
Award: B.M.McMillan.　LOI debuts: Zimbabwe – H.K.Olonga; South Africa – N.Boje.

Brian McMillan, promoted above number six for the first time in 42 internationals, responded with a maiden hundred off 107 balls. Dave Richardson completed 100 dismissals and became the first to make five in an innings twice.

SOUTH AFRICA		Runs	Balls	4/6
A.C.Hudson	run out	36	43	5/1
† D.J.Richardson	c A.Flower b Olonga	5	14	1
B.M.McMillan	c A.Flower b Streak	127	120	14/3
* W.J.Cronje	c Campbell b P.A.Strang	33	48	5
J.N.Rhodes	c A.Flower b Streak	25	28	1/1
G.Kirsten	not out	36	41	1
A.P.Kuiper	not out	14	9	–/1
N.Boje				
C.R.Matthews				
P.S.de Villiers				
A.A.Donald				
Extras	(b 4, lb 15, w 6, nb 2)	27		
Total	(50 overs; 5 wickets)	**303**		

ZIMBABWE		Runs	Balls	4/6
*†A.Flower	c Richardson b Matthews	2	14	–
G.W.Flower	c Richardson b McMillan	19	40	2
A.C.Waller	run out	0	3	–
D.L.Houghton	c Cronje b Matthews	9	18	–/1
A.D.R.Campbell	not out	68	110	3
G.J.Whittall	c Richardson b McMillan	6	15	1
C.N.Evans	c Richardson b Donald	8	21	1
P.A.Strang	c Richardson b Cronje	24	56	–/1
H.H.Streak	not out	23	23	1/1
B.C.Strang				
H.K.Olonga				
Extras	(lb 6, w 4)	10		
Total	(50 overs; 7 wickets)	**169**		

ZIMBABWE	O	M	R	W
Streak	10	2	54	2
Olonga	10	1	59	1
B.C.Strang	9	0	51	0
Whittall	7	0	48	0
P.A.Strang	10	0	51	1
G.W.Flower	4	0	21	0

SOUTH AFRICA	O	M	R	W
De Villiers	10	2	34	0
Matthews	10	1	42	2
McMillan	5	0	13	2
Donald	10	2	28	1
Boje	10	1	29	0
Cronje	5	0	17	1

FALL OF WICKETS
1-7, 2-66, 3-152, 4-192, 5-284

FALL OF WICKETS
1-11, 2-14, 3-30, 4-30, 5-44, 6-68, 7-119

Umpires: Q.J.Goosen (5) and I.D.Robinson (24).　　Referee: B.N.Jarman (*Australia*).

ZIMBABWE v SOUTH AFRICA 1995-96

At Harare Sports Club on 22 October 1995.   Result: **SOUTH AFRICA** won by 112 runs.   Toss: South Africa.
Award: H.H.Streak.   LOI debuts: South Africa – G.F.J.Liebenberg, P.J.R.Steyn.

South Africa achieved a 100% record on their four-match tour. 'Fanie' de Villiers began what transpired to be the final over by bowling a paper cup.

SOUTH AFRICA		Runs	Balls	4/6
† D.J.Richardson	hit wicket b Streak	0	4	–
G.F.J.Liebenberg	c A.Flower b Streak	12	19	2
P.J.R.Steyn	c A.Flower b Streak	4	14	–
A.P.Kuiper	lbw b Campbell	50	72	3
G.Kirsten	run out	38	51	5
J.N.Rhodes	c Houghton b Campbell	53	47	2/2
* W.J.Cronje	c A.Flower b Whittall	7	18	–
P.L.Symcox	c Houghton b Brandes	35	42	5
C.R.Matthews	c A.Flower b Streak	6	15	–
P.S.de Villiers	c A.Flower b Whittall	5	8	–
A.A.Donald	not out	5	11	–
Extras	(lb 7, w 14, nb 3)	24		
Total	(49.2 overs)	**239**		

ZIMBABWE		Runs	Balls	4/6
*†A.Flower	c Richardson b Matthews	2	5	–
G.W.Flower	c Richardson b Donald	21	66	1
A.C.Waller	c Richardson b Cronje	15	32	2
D.L.Houghton	c De Villiers b Symcox	25	40	1
A.D.R.Campbell	c Liebenberg b Cronje	5	10	1
G.J.Whittall	run out	0	–	–
P.A.Strang	b Matthews	15	39	1
H.H.Streak	c Richardson b Cronje	13	29	1
D.H.Brain	not out	12	26	2
E.A.Brandes	c Matthews b Cronje	5	6	1
H.K.Olonga	c Symcox b De Villiers	6	5	1
Extras	(lb 6, w 1, nb 1)	8		
Total	(42.5 overs)	**127**		

ZIMBABWE	O	M	R	W
Streak	10	1	25	4
Olonga	4	0	32	0
Brain	5	1	28	0
Brandes	4.2	0	23	1
Strang	5	0	30	0
G.W.Flower	5	0	25	0
Whittall	10	0	47	2
Campbell	6	1	22	2

FALL OF WICKETS
1-1, 2-18, 3-28, 4-87, 5-171, 6-180, 7-184, 8-203, 9-217, 10-239

Umpires: I.D.Robinson (25) and R.B.Tiffin (2).

SOUTH AFRICA	O	M	R	W
De Villiers	8.5	2	30	1
Matthews	8	2	19	2
Cronje	10	0	33	4
Donald	8	0	21	0
Symcox	8	1	18	1

FALL OF WICKETS
1-3, 2-35, 3-48, 4-53, 5-55, 6-82, 7-92, 8-113, 9-119, 10-127

Referee: B.N.Jarman (*Australia*).

INDIA v NEW ZEALAND 1995-96

At Keenan Stadium, Jamshedpur on 15 November 1995.   Result: **NEW ZEALAND** won by 8 wickets.
Toss: New Zealand.   Award: M.D.Crowe.   LOI debuts: New Zealand – R.G.Twose.

Martin Crowe's fourth and highest LOI hundred, completed off 128 balls, was to be the last of his international career. New Zealand achieved their first victory against their hosts on Indian soil.

INDIA		Runs	Balls	4/6
M.Prabhakar	c Astle b Larsen	83	120	6
S.R.Tendulkar	c Greatbatch b Morrison	30	19	5
N.S.Sidhu	c Nash b Larsen	12	21	–
* M.Azharuddin	b Cairns	32	48	3
V.G.Kambli	b Nash	15	28	–
A.Jadeja	c and b Thomson	0	2	–
† N.R.Mongia	b Morrison	26	28	2
A.Kumble	b Nash	4	6	–
J.Srinath	not out	17	15	2
U.Chatterjee	run out	3	3	–
B.K.V.Prasad	c Cairns	1	3	–
Extras	(lb 6, w 7)	13		
Total	(49.1 overs)	**236**		

NEW ZEALAND		Runs	Balls	4/6
M.J.Greatbatch	b Prasad	31	42	4
N.J.Astle	lbw b Prabhakar	7	9	1
M.D.Crowe	not out	107	134	8/2
S.P.Fleming	not out	78	96	5
S.A.Thomson				
R.G.Twose				
C.L.Cairns				
*†L.K.Germon				
G.R.Larsen				
D.J.Nash				
D.K.Morrison				
Extras	(lb 9, w 3, nb 2)	14		
Total	(47 overs; 2 wickets)	**237**		

NEW ZEALAND	O	M	R	W
Morrison	9	0	49	2
Nash	10	0	56	2
Cairns	9.1	1	33	2
Larsen	10	0	40	2
Astle	3	0	17	0
Thomson	8	1	35	1

FALL OF WICKETS
1-45, 2-94, 3-159, 4-177, 5-178, 6-194, 7-204, 8-222, 9-234, 10-236

Umpires: K.S.Giridharan (3) and C.K.Sathe (3).

INDIA	O	M	R	W
Prabhakar	7	0	37	1
Srinath	8	1	30	1
Prasad	10	0	50	1
Kumble	10	0	40	0
Chatterjee	9	0	54	0
Tendulkar	3	0	17	0

FALL OF WICKETS
1-18, 2-66

Referee: P.J.P.Burge (*Australia*).

INDIA v NEW ZEALAND 1995-96

At Gandhi Sports Complex, Amritsar on 18 November 1995.   Result: **INDIA** won by 6 wickets.   Toss: India.
Award: M.Prabhakar.   LOI debuts: None.

Manoj Prabhakar's best analysis included his 150th wicket in 122 internationals. The Third International, scheduled for the Fatorda Stadium at Margao in Goa on 21 November, was abandoned without a ball bowled because of heavy rain.

NEW ZEALAND		Runs	Balls	4/6	INDIA		Runs	Balls	4/6
M.J.Greatbatch	c Tendulkar b Prabhakar	2	4	–	M.Prabhakar	lbw b Nash	1	12	–
N.J.Astle	lbw b Tendulkar	59	86	5	S.R.Tendulkar	c Germon b Thomson	39	51	4
M.D.Crowe	lbw b Prabhakar	2	12	–	N.S.Sidhu	c Fleming b Cairns	8	22	1
S.P.Fleming	c Mongia b Srinath	3	12	–	* M.Azharuddin	run out	17	37	–
R.G.Twose	b Prasad	5	22	–	S.V.Manjrekar	not out	44	78	5
C.L.Cairns	b Kumble	4	12	–	A.Jadeja	not out	26	66	2
S.A.Thomson	c Srinath b Prabhakar	14	59	–	† N.R.Mongia				
*†L.K.Germon	c Mongia b Prabhakar	9	26	–	J.Srinath				
G.R.Larsen	c Mongia b Srinath	20	28	–/2	A.Kumble				
D.J.Nash	lbw b Prabhakar	0	1	–	A.R.Kapoor				
D.K.Morrison	not out	2	7	–	B.K.V.Prasad				
Extras	(b 2, lb 12, w 8, nb 3)	25			Extras	(b 2, lb 1, w 4, nb 4)	11		
Total	(44.1 overs)	**145**			**Total**	(43.4 overs; 4 wickets)	**146**		

INDIA	O	M	R	W	NEW ZEALAND	O	M	R	W
Prabhakar	10	0	33	5	Morrison	6	0	20	0
Srinath	8.1	1	26	2	Nash	6	1	17	1
Prasad	6	0	14	1	Cairns	7	0	33	1
Kumble	6	0	16	1	Larsen	10	3	23	0
Kapoor	10	1	27	0	Thomson	10	1	38	1
Tendulkar	4	0	15	1	Astle	4	0	9	0
					Twose	0.4	0	3	0

FALL OF WICKETS
1-12, 2-22, 3-37, 4-57, 5-69, 6-96, 7-112, 8-123, 9-123, 10-145

Umpires: S.K.Porel (2) and S.K.Sharma (4).

FALL OF WICKETS
1-2, 2-25, 3-65, 4-72

Referee: P.J.P.Burge (*Australia*).

INDIA v NEW ZEALAND 1995-96

At Nehru Stadium, Poona on 24 November 1995.   Result: **INDIA** won by 5 wickets.   Toss: India.
Award: C.L.Cairns.   LOI debuts: None.

Chris Cairns completed his maiden international hundred from 84 balls, the fastest on record for New Zealand. His partnership of 147 from 133 balls with Roger Twose remains a national fifth-wicket record.

NEW ZEALAND		Runs	Balls	4/6	INDIA		Runs	Balls	4/6
M.J.Greatbatch	c Mongia b Srinath	13	43	2	M.Prabhakar	c Twose b Cairns	20	31	3
N.J.Astle	run out	11	34	1	S.R.Tendulkar	c Larsen b Morrison	7	11	1
M.D.Crowe	lbw b Kapoor	15	36	–	V.G.Kambli	run out	42	65	3
S.P.Fleming	c and b Tendulkar	26	39	2	* M.Azharuddin	lbw b Cairns	58	68	5
R.G.Twose	c Mongia b Prasad	46	57	2	S.V.Manjrekar	not out	47	56	3
C.L.Cairns	st Mongia b Tendulkar	103	87	10/4	A.Jadeja	b Cairns	12	17	1
S.A.Thomson	not out	7	6	1	† N.R.Mongia	not out	36	30	7
*†L.K.Germon					A.Kumble				
G.R.Larsen					J.Srinath				
D.J.Nash					A.R.Kapoor				
D.K.Morrison					B.K.V.Prasad				
Extras	(lb 7, w 5, nb 2)	14			Extras	(lb 3, w 8, nb 3)	14		
Total	(50 overs; 6 wickets)	**235**			**Total**	(45.5 overs; 5 wickets)	**236**		

INDIA	O	M	R	W	NEW ZEALAND	O	M	R	W
Prabhakar	8	0	31	0	Morrison	9	0	62	1
Srinath	10	1	42	1	Nash	8	0	48	0
Prasad	8	1	45	1	Cairns	10	1	37	3
Kumble	8	0	35	0	Larsen	8.5	0	42	0
Kapoor	7	0	26	1	Thomson	4	0	17	0
Tendulkar	9	0	49	2	Twose	3	0	16	0
					Astle	3	0	11	0

FALL OF WICKETS
1-27, 2-31, 3-68, 4-75, 5-222, 6-235

Umpires: S.Chowdhury (7) and K.Parthasarathy (4).

FALL OF WICKETS
1-20, 2-56, 3-127, 4-158, 5-179

Referee: P.J.P.Burge (*Australia*).

INDIA v NEW ZEALAND 1995-96

At Vidarbha CA Ground, Nagpur on 26 November 1995.　　Result: NEW ZEALAND won by 99 runs.　　Toss: India.
Award: N.J.Astle.　　LOI debuts: None.

Sadly for New Zealand, who amassed their record total, this fixture produced the greatest tragedy involving an international cricket match. During the lunch interval a newly built unreinforced staircase wall collapsed resulting in 12 deaths and 61 serious injuries. The players were not informed. The architect and contractor were charged with negligence.

NEW ZEALAND		Runs	Balls	4/6
M.J.Greatbatch	b Kapoor	38	40	8
N.J.Astle	c Azharuddin b Prasad	114	128	12/1
M.D.Crowe	st Mongia b Kapoor	63	62	7/1
S.P.Fleming	c Azharuddin b Prasad	60	40	4/1
C.L.Cairns	c Manjrekar b Kumble	14	8	2
R.G.Twose	run out	9	10	–
S.A.Thomson	lbw b Kumble	15	9	2/1
*†L.K.Germon	b Srinath	1	2	–
G.R.Larsen	not out	5	5	1
D.J.Nash	not out	4	3	–
D.K.Morrison				
Extras	(lb 20, w 3, nb 2)	25		
Total	(50 overs; 8 wickets)	**348**		

INDIA		Runs	Balls	4/6
M.Prabhakar	run out	9	10	2
S.R.Tendulkar	run out	65	60	9/1
V.G.Kambli	c Crowe b Cairns	16	25	3
* M.Azharuddin	b Cairns	1	6	–
S.V.Manjrekar	c sub (B.A.Young) b Astle	44	46	6
A.Jadeja	st Germon b Larsen	61	44	5/2
† N.R.Mongia	c sub b Thomson	20	28	–
J.Srinath	c Nash b Thomson	6	8	1
A.R.Kapoor	lbw b Larsen	6	6	1
A.Kumble	c sub b Thomson	12	9	2
B.K.V.Prasad	not out	0	1	–
Extras	(lb 5, nb 4)	9		
Total	(39.3 overs)	**249**		

INDIA	O	M	R	W
Prabhakar	8	0	55	0
Srinath	9	0	42	1
Kapoor	7	0	48	2
Kumble	10	0	48	2
Prasad	8	0	62	2
Tendulkar	6	0	54	0
Jadeja	2	0	19	0

NEW ZEALAND	O	M	R	W
Morrison	4	0	25	0
Nash	5	0	35	0
Cairns	7	0	32	2
Larsen	9	0	58	2
Astle	5	0	31	1
Thomson	9.3	0	63	3

FALL OF WICKETS
1-62, 2-190, 3-288, 4-306, 5-317, 6-323, 7-337, 8-343

FALL OF WICKETS
1-23, 2-71, 3-77, 4-123, 5-150, 6-202, 7-211, 8-218, 9-241, 10-249

Umpires: N.Menon (3) and S.Shastri (3).

Referee: P.J.P.Burge (*Australia*).

INDIA v NEW ZEALAND 1995-96

At Brabourne Stadium, Bombay on 29 November 1995.　　Result: INDIA won by 6 wickets.　　Toss: India.
Award: J.Srinath.　　LOI debuts: None.

New Zealand, dismissed for their lowest total against India, lost the series 3-2 and extended Mohammed Azharuddin's unbeaten home record in Tests and LOIs since he became captain in 1990. Watched by 35,000, this match was awarded as a benefit to India's former wicket-keeper, Syed Kirmani.

NEW ZEALAND		Runs	Balls	4/6
M.J.Greatbatch	c Manjrekar b Srinath	4	5	1
N.J.Astle	c Prasad b Prabhakar	9	9	1
S.P.Fleming	c and b Srinath	8	17	1
† A.C.Parore	run out	14	13	1
R.G.Twose	st Mongia b Kapoor	14	29	1
S.A.Thomson	run out	20	40	3
* L.K.Germon	b Kumble	29	47	2
G.R.Larsen	c Srinath b Kapoor	6	22	–
D.J.Nash	c Prasad b Kumble	11	13	–
S.B.Doull	c Prasad b Kumble	2	12	–
D.K.Morrison	not out	1	4	–
Extras	(lb 3, w 2, nb 3)	8		
Total	(35 overs)	**126**		

INDIA		Runs	Balls	4/6
M.Prabhakar	not out	32	93	3
S.R.Tendulkar	b Morrison	1	4	–
V.G.Kambli	c Greatbatch b Doull	48	32	8
* M.Azharuddin	c Germon b Doull	4	4	–
S.V.Manjrekar	c Thomson b Doull	0	2	–
A.Jadeja	not out	35	54	5
† N.R.Mongia				
A.Kumble				
A.R.Kapoor				
J.Srinath				
B.K.V.Prasad				
Extras	(lb 2, w 6)	8		
Total	(32 overs; 4 wickets)	**128**		

INDIA	O	M	R	W
Prabhakar	5	0	29	1
Srinath	6	0	22	2
Prasad	6	0	22	0
Kapoor	10	0	33	2
Kumble	8	0	17	3

NEW ZEALAND	O	M	R	W
Morrison	9	2	32	1
Nash	8	1	25	0
Doull	6	0	42	3
Larsen	9	1	27	0

FALL OF WICKETS
1-7, 2-20, 3-38, 4-38, 5-64, 6-89, 7-97, 8-113, 9-125, 10-126

FALL OF WICKETS
1-7, 2-71, 3-75, 4-75

Umpires: A.V.Jayaprakash (3) and I.Shivram (2).

Referee: P.J.P.Burge (*Australia*).

NEW ZEALAND v PAKISTAN 1995-96

At Carisbrook, Dunedin on 15 December 1995.　Result: **PAKISTAN** won by 20 runs.　Toss: Pakistan.
Award: Waqar Younis.　LOI debuts: New Zealand – C.M.Spearman.

Pakistan defended a below-par total with ease after Waqar Younis had swept away three key batsmen in nine balls.
Battling to the end, Warwickshire's emigre, Roger Twose, contributed a dogged maiden fifty.

PAKISTAN		Runs	Balls	4/6
Ramiz Raja	b Cairns	35	75	2
Aamir Sohail	c Spearman b Patel	17	20	2/1
Ijaz Ahmed	lbw b Larsen	9	14	–
Inzamam-ul-Haq	c Patel b Astle	32	49	–/1
Salim Malik	c Twose b Astle	13	18	1
Basit Ali	run out	19	45	–
* Wasim Akram	run out	16	26	1
† Rashid Latif	not out	26	33	1
Mushtaq Ahmed	c Twose b Cairns	5	12	–
Waqar Younis	b Morrison	0	3	–
Aqib Javed	not out	8	5	1
Extras	(lb 6, w 3)	9		
Total	(50 overs; 9 wickets)	**189**		

NEW ZEALAND	O	M	R	W
Patel	7	0	21	1
Morrison	9	0	39	1
Larsen	10	0	29	1
Cairns	9	1	42	2
Astle	10	0	34	2
Twose	5	0	18	0

FALL OF WICKETS
1-31, 2-52, 3-82, 4-101, 5-123, 6-138, 7-158, 8-173, 9-175

Umpires: R.S.Dunne (28) and C.E.King (13).

NEW ZEALAND		Runs	Balls	4/6
C.M.Spearman	c Ijaz b Aqib	5	10	1
N.J.Astle	c and b Wasim	5	7	–
B.A.Young	b Waqar	17	38	–
S.P.Fleming	lbw b Waqar	15	15	2
A.C.Parore	b Waqar	2	11	–
R.G.Twose	b Wasim	59	93	3
C.L.Cairns	c Rashid b Mushtaq	18	31	–
*†L.K.Germon	c Wasim b Mushtaq	1	2	–
D.N.Patel	c Basit b Salim	9	23	–
G.R.Larsen	c Ijaz b Wasim	23	55	–
D.K.Morrison	not out	0	2	–
Extras	(lb 9, w 5, nb 1)	15		
Total	(47.4 overs)	**169**		

PAKISTAN	O	M	R	W
Wasim Akram	9.4	1	18	3
Aqib Javed	9	0	38	1
Waqar Younis	9	0	38	3
Mushtaq Ahmed	10	1	31	2
Aamir Sohail	9	0	30	0
Salim Malik	1	0	5	1

FALL OF WICKETS
1-5, 2-16, 3-43, 4-46, 5-50, 6-92, 7-94, 8-114, 9-164, 10-169

Referee: R.S.Madugalle (*Sri Lanka*).

NEW ZEALAND v PAKISTAN 1995-96

At Lancaster Park, Christchurch on 17 December 1995.　Result: **NEW ZEALAND** won by 1 wicket.　Toss: Pakistan.
Award: Inzamam-ul-Haq.　LOI debuts: None.

Needing ten off the final over, New Zealand's last pair scraped home with a ball to spare. One of them, Danny Morrison,
had earlier produced his best analysis, including his 100th wicket in 81 internationals.

PAKISTAN		Runs	Balls	4/6
Ramiz Raja	b Morrison	14	25	1
Aamir Sohail	c Spearman b Patel	10	17	1
Ijaz Ahmed	lbw b Cairns	14	40	1
Inzamam-ul-Haq	b Larsen	80	95	6/1
Salim Malik	c sub (G.R.Loveridge) b Twose	58	82	6
* Wasim Akram	b Morrison	10	12	1
Basit Ali	b Morrison	23	19	3
† Rashid Latif	c Astle b Morrison	11	9	1
Waqar Younis	b Morrison	0	1	–
Mushtaq Ahmed	not out	0	1	–
Aqib Javed				
Extras	(b 5, lb 5, w 2)	12		
Total	(50 overs; 9 wickets)	**232**		

NEW ZEALAND	O	M	R	W
Patel	10	0	41	1
Morrison	10	0	46	5
Cairns	10	1	42	1
Larsen	10	0	49	1
Astle	8	0	32	0
Twose	2	0	12	1

FALL OF WICKETS
1-25, 2-27, 3-61, 4-175, 5-185, 6-202, 7-230, 8-231, 9-232

Umpires: C.E.King (14) and D.M.Quested (11).

NEW ZEALAND		Runs	Balls	4/6
C.M.Spearman	c Rashid b Aqib	8	17	1
N.J.Astle	c Rashid b Aqib	5	14	–
B.A.Young	c Wasim b Aamir	34	69	3
S.P.Fleming	b Aamir	48	62	5
A.C.Parore	c Basit b Wasim	45	58	–
C.L.Cairns	c Ramiz b Wasim	54	63	2
R.G.Twose	c Mushtaq b Waqar	10	10	1
*†L.K.Germon	c Basit b Waqar	5	3	1
D.N.Patel	c Ijaz b Waqar	0	1	–
G.R.Larsen	not out	14	7	2
D.K.Morrison	not out	0	1	–
Extras	(lb 5, w 5, nb 3)	13		
Total	(49.5 overs; 9 wickets)	**236**		

PAKISTAN	O	M	R	W
Aqib Javed	10	0	53	2
Wasim Akram	9.5	0	41	2
Waqar Younis	10	0	55	3
Mushtaq Ahmed	6	0	30	0
Aamir Sohail	10	0	39	2
Salim Malik	4	0	13	0

FALL OF WICKETS
1-13, 2-21, 3-98, 4-107, 5-204, 6-214, 7-220, 8-221, 9-221

Referee: R.S.Madugalle (*Sri Lanka*).

NEW ZEALAND v PAKISTAN 1995-96

At Basin Reserve, Wellington on 20 December 1995.   Result: **PAKISTAN** won by 54 runs.   Toss: New Zealand.
Award: Wasim Akram.   LOI debuts: None.

A decisive all-round performance by Wasim Akram was overshadowed by the misbehaviour of two of his players. Both were fined part of their match fees, Aqib Javed (half) for abusing Adam Parore after dismissing him, and Mushtaq Ahmed (10%) for dissent following an unrewarded caught and bowled appeal.

PAKISTAN		Runs	Balls	4/6
Aamir Sohail	b Larsen	58	82	6
Ramiz Raja	run out	21	37	2/1
Ijaz Ahmed	c Cairns b Twose	42	55	1/1
Inzamam-ul-Haq	b Twose	54	66	6
Salim Malik	not out	42	48	2
* Wasim Akram	not out	36	15	3/2
Basit Ali				
† Rashid Latif				
Mushtaq Ahmed				
Waqar Younis				
Aqib Javed				
Extras	(b 2, lb 5, w 1)	8		
Total	(50 overs; 4 wickets)	**261**		

NEW ZEALAND		Runs	Balls	4/6
C.M.Spearman	c Aamir b Wasim	33	31	5
N.J.Astle	c Ramiz b Aqib	9	19	1
B.A.Young	lbw b Wasim	0	1	–
S.P.Fleming	c Basit b Mushtaq	35	40	4
A.C.Parore	lbw b Aqib	4	15	1
R.G.Twose	b Aamir	37	55	3
C.L.Cairns	run out	7	13	–
*†L.K.Germon	b Wasim	40	59	3
D.N.Patel	run out	13	15	1
G.R.Larsen	c sub (Moin Khan) b Aqib	2	5	–
D.K.Morrison	not out	11	18	1
Extras	(lb 13, w 3)	16		
Total	(44.5 overs)	**207**		

NEW ZEALAND	O	M	R	W
Morrison	10	0	59	0
Patel	10	2	43	0
Cairns	10	1	62	0
Larsen	10	0	37	1
Twose	7	0	31	2
Astle	3	0	22	0

PAKISTAN	O	M	R	W
Aqib Javed	10	1	51	3
Wasim Akram	7.5	0	31	3
Waqar Younis	4	0	22	0
Mushtaq Ahmed	10	2	26	1
Salim Malik	3	0	17	0
Aamir Sohail	10	0	47	0

FALL OF WICKETS
1-51, 2-107, 3-138, 4-217

FALL OF WICKETS
1-48, 2-48, 3-48, 4-60, 5-107, 6-119, 7-143, 8-166, 9-174, 10-207

Umpires: R.S.Dunne (29) and E.A.Watkin (2).

Referee: R.S.Madugalle (*Sri Lanka*).

NEW ZEALAND v PAKISTAN 1995-96

At Eden Park, Auckland on 23 December 1995.   Result: **NEW ZEALAND** won by 32 runs.   Toss: Pakistan.
Award: N.J.Astle.   LOI debuts: None.

New Zealand squared the series, amassing the biggest total of this rubber despite their innings being reduced by five overs when the start was delayed by rain.

NEW ZEALAND		Runs	Balls	4/6
C.M.Spearman	c Basit b Mushtaq	48	62	6
B.A.Young	c Rashid b Aqib	15	23	1
S.P.Fleming	c Wasim b Aamir	38	45	4
† A.C.Parore	b Waqar	42	65	2
C.L.Cairns	c Wasim b Aamir	11	14	1
R.G.Twose	b Waqar	41	33	5
N.J.Astle	not out	20	14	4
* L.K.Germon	b Wasim	5	8	1
D.N.Patel	lbw b Waqar	1	2	–
G.R.Larsen	not out	3	8	–
D.K.Morrison				
Extras	(lb 11, w 6, nb 3)	20		
Total	(45 overs; 8 wickets)	**244**		

PAKISTAN		Runs	Balls	4/6
Aamir Sohail	c Patel b Cairns	37	43	6/1
Ramiz Raja	c Cairns b Astle	46	54	4
Salim Elahi	run out	7	17	–
Inzamam-ul-Haq	c sub (G.R.Loveridge) b Astle	17	23	2
Salim Malik	b Astle	58	52	4/3
Basit Ali	run out	0	3	–
* Wasim Akram	c Astle b Morrison	4	8	–
† Rashid Latif	b Larsen	3	14	–
Mushtaq Ahmed	b Larsen	16	17	2
Waqar Younis	c Young b Twose	5	10	–
Aqib Javed	not out	12	10	2
Extras	(lb 5, w 2)	7		
Total	(41.4 overs)	**212**		

PAKISTAN	O	M	R	W
Wasim Akram	9	0	27	1
Aqib Javed	6	0	28	1
Waqar Younis	9	0	70	3
Mushtaq Ahmed	7	0	39	1
Aamir Sohail	9	0	42	2
Salim Malik	5	0	27	0

NEW ZEALAND	O	M	R	W
Morrison	6	0	22	1
Patel	4	0	26	0
Cairns	7	0	38	1
Larsen	9	0	42	2
Twose	7.4	0	37	1
Astle	8	0	42	3

FALL OF WICKETS
1-28, 2-88, 3-132, 4-148, 5-207, 6-214, 7-222, 8-223

FALL OF WICKETS
1-56, 2-89, 3-109, 4-117, 5-118, 6-125, 7-146, 8-188, 9-196, 10-212

Umpires: B.F.Bowden (2) and D.B.Cowie (13).

Referee: R.S.Madugalle (*Sri Lanka*).

WEST INDIES v SRI LANKA 1995-96

At Adelaide Oval on 15 December 1995. Result: **SRI LANKA** won by 4 wickets. Toss: Sri Lanka.
Award: A.Ranatunga. LOI debuts: None.

The World Series tournament returned to normal with the teams reduced to three and the Australian entry to one. For the first time players wore numbers on their backs, not always the designated ones. Engineering problems concerning its innovative retractable towers prevented Adelaide from staging its first floodlit games.

WEST INDIES		Runs	Balls	4/6
P.V.Simmons	c Mahanama b Ranatunga	18	51	2
S.L.Campbell	lbw b Muralitharan	47	106	1
* R.B.Richardson	c Kaluwitharana b Ranatunga	5	13	–
S.Chanderpaul	run out	1	10	–
C.L.Hooper	c Tillekeratne b Muralitharan	23	48	1
J.C.Adams	c Muralitharan b Dharmasena	11	22	–
R.A.Harper	c Jayasuriya b Vaas	23	29	1
† C.O.Browne	run out	6	12	–
I.R.Bishop	not out	8	16	–
C.E.L.Ambrose	not out	0	–	–
C.A.Walsh				
Extras	(lb 10, w 6, nb 2)	18		
Total	(50 overs; 8 wickets)	**160**		

SRI LANKA		Runs	Balls	4/6
R.S.Mahanama	c Campbell b Ambrose	0	1	–
S.T.Jayasuriya	c Bishop b Walsh	28	59	1
A.P.Gurusinha	b Bishop	15	30	1
P.A.de Silva	c Browne b Hooper	46	61	3
* A.Ranatunga	c Campbell b Bishop	27	37	2
H.P.Tillekeratne	not out	17	61	–
† R.S.Kaluwitharana	c Browne b Bishop	8	21	–
H.D.P.K.Dharmasena	not out	5	12	–
W.P.U.C.J.Vaas				
G.P.Wickremasinghe				
M.Muralitharan				
Extras	(b 1, lb 5, w 2, nb 7)	15		
Total	(45 overs; 6 wickets)	**161**		

SRI LANKA	O	M	R	W
Wickremasinghe	7	0	22	0
Vaas	7	1	17	1
Gurusinha	8	0	25	0
Ranatunga	10	1	24	2
Muralitharan	10	0	35	2
Dharmasena	8	0	27	1

WEST INDIES	O	M	R	W
Ambrose	7	0	29	1
Walsh	10	5	23	1
Bishop	10	1	38	3
Simmons	3	0	17	0
Harper	5	0	25	0
Hooper	10	1	23	1

FALL OF WICKETS
1-40, 2-50, 3-56, 4-101, 5-122, 6-122, 7-136, 8-160

FALL OF WICKETS
1-0, 2-24, 3-54, 4-113, 5-130, 6-152

Umpires: D.J.Harper (2) and T.A.Prue (24).

Referee: G.T.Dowling (*New Zealand*).

AUSTRALIA v WEST INDIES 1995-96

At Adelaide Oval on 17 December 1995. Result: **AUSTRALIA** won by 121 runs. Toss: West Indies.
Award: M.E.Waugh. LOI debuts: Australia – S.Lee.

Rain delayed the start by 90 minutes, reducing the match to 47 overs each. Shane Lee made a feisty start to his international career, adding 63 off 47 balls in 29 minutes with Michael Bevan. West Indies sustained their heaviest defeat by a runs margin.

AUSTRALIA		Runs	Balls	4/6
* M.A.Taylor	b Harper	47	91	4
M.J.Slater	b Bishop	32	40	4/1
M.E.Waugh	c Hooper b Harper	53	65	3
R.T.Ponting	st Browne b Harper	11	21	–
S.G.Law	c Hooper b Harper	13	19	–
M.G.Bevan	not out	32	27	4
S.Lee	st Browne b Hooper	39	27	3
† I.A.Healy	not out	0	1	–
S.K.Warne				
C.J.McDermott				
G.D.McGrath				
Extras	(b 1, lb 7, w 7)	15		
Total	(47 overs; 6 wickets)	**242**		

WEST INDIES		Runs	Balls	4/6
P.V.Simmons	c Waugh b McGrath	7	20	1
S.L.Campbell	run out	4	10	1
* R.B.Richardson	c Healy b McDermott	4	5	–
C.L.Hooper	lbw b McDermott	0	10	–
S.Chanderpaul	c Taylor b Waugh	39	83	4
J.C.Adams	c Law b Lee	20	46	1
R.A.Harper	not out	31	82	1
† C.O.Browne	not out	11	30	–
I.R.Bishop				
C.E.L.Ambrose				
C.A.Walsh				
Extras	(lb 2, w 3)	5		
Total	(47 overs; 6 wickets)	**121**		

WEST INDIES	O	M	R	W
Ambrose	9	0	43	0
Walsh	10	1	46	0
Bishop	8	0	33	1
Simmons	2	0	17	0
Hooper	8	0	49	1
Harper	10	0	46	4

AUSTRALIA	O	M	R	W
McDermott	7	2	8	2
McGrath	5	1	13	1
Law	7	1	23	0
Lee	7	0	20	1
Waugh	10	0	26	1
Warne	7	1	22	0
Bevan	3	0	7	0
Slater	1	1	0	0

FALL OF WICKETS
1-60, 2-108, 3-142, 4-166, 5-169, 6-232

FALL OF WICKETS
1-8, 2-16, 3-16, 4-17, 5-54, 6-97

Umpires: A.J.McQuillan (6) and T.A.Prue (25).

Referee: G.T.Dowling (*New Zealand*).

AUSTRALIA v WEST INDIES 1995-96

At Melbourne Cricket Ground on 19 December 1995.   Result: **AUSTRALIA** won by 24 runs.   Toss: Australia.
Award: M.G.Bevan.   LOI debuts: Australia – M.S.Kasprowicz.

West Indies continued to display their batting frailty in the aftermath of Brian Lara's late withdrawal from this tour. The match was played on a bitterly cold evening featuring 30-knot gusts which blew the covers off the pitch prior to the start.

AUSTRALIA		Runs	Balls	4/6
M.J.Slater	c Richardson b Ambrose	2	7	–
* M.A.Taylor	c Hooper b Simmons	63	90	2
M.E.Waugh	run out	15	38	1
R.T.Ponting	c Browne b Walsh	6	11	1
S.G.Law	st Browne b Hooper	74	86	5
M.G.Bevan	not out	44	41	2
S.Lee	c Chanderpaul b Ambrose	3	4	–
† I.A.Healy	not out	34	27	2
S.K.Warne				
C.J.McDermott				
M.S.Kasprowicz				
Extras	(lb 4, w 2, nb 2)	8		
Total	(50 overs; 6 wickets)	**249**		

WEST INDIES		Runs	Balls	4/6
S.C.Williams	lbw b Lee	44	56	6
S.L.Campbell	c Ponting b Kasprowicz	2	5	–
S.Chanderpaul	c and b Bevan	73	116	4/2
P.V.Simmons	c McDermott b Waugh	24	39	1
C.L.Hooper	c Healy b Bevan	10	15	1
* R.B.Richardson	c Law b McDermott	15	20	1
R.A.Harper	st Healy b Warne	15	12	1/1
A.C.Cummins	not out	26	25	–
† C.O.Browne	run out	2	3	–
C.E.L.Ambrose	b McDermott	1	4	–
C.A.Walsh	c Healy b Warne	1	3	–
Extras	(lb 9, w 1, nb 2)	12		
Total	(49.1 overs)	**225**		

WEST INDIES	O	M	R	W
Ambrose	10	1	36	2
Walsh	9	0	32	1
Cummins	6	0	40	0
Harper	10	1	46	0
Hooper	9	0	60	1
Simmons	6	0	31	1

AUSTRALIA	O	M	R	W
McDermott	10	0	40	2
Kasprowicz	6	0	32	1
Lee	10	1	40	1
Warne	9.1	1	41	2
Waugh	6	0	32	1
Bevan	8	0	31	2

FALL OF WICKETS
1-6, 2-39, 3-46, 4-164, 5-172, 6-181

FALL OF WICKETS
1-5, 2-84, 3-125, 4-147, 5-166, 6-177, 7-209, 8-213, 9-224, 10-225

Umpires: P.D.Parker (5) and S.G.Randell (63).   **Referee:** G.T.Dowling (*New Zealand*).

AUSTRALIA v SRI LANKA 1995-96

At Sydney Cricket Ground on 21 December 1995.   Result: **AUSTRALIA** won by 5 wickets.   Toss: Sri Lanka.
Award: M.A.Taylor.   LOI debuts: None.

Michael Bevan scored the winning boundary with two balls to spare. Half the 14 wickets fell to run outs.

SRI LANKA		Runs	Balls	4/6
R.S.Mahanama	run out	5	11	1
S.T.Jayasuriya	c Healy b McGrath	24	26	4
A.P.Gurusinha	c Waugh b Bevan	38	58	4
P.A.de Silva	c and b Lee	75	94	7
* A.Ranatunga	run out	7	14	–
H.P.Tillekeratne	c Lee b McGrath	62	67	6
† R.S.Kaluwitharana	b Kasprowicz	0	4	–
H.D.P.K.Dharmasena	run out	7	17	–
W.P.U.C.J.Vaas	run out	14	14	–
G.P.Wickremasinghe	not out	4	3	–
M.Muralitharan	not out	0	–	–
Extras	(b 2, lb 11, w 5, nb 1)	19		
Total	(50 overs; 9 wickets)	**255**		

AUSTRALIA		Runs	Balls	4/6
* M.A.Taylor	run out	90	115	6
M.J.Slater	c Kaluwitharana b Vaas	10	13	1
M.E.Waugh	run out	55	70	2
R.T.Ponting	c Muralitharan b Dharmasena	56	71	1
S.G.Law	run out	7	10	1
M.G.Bevan	not out	18	16	1
S.Lee	not out	4	7	–
† I.A.Healy				
S.K.Warne				
M.S.Kasprowicz				
G.D.McGrath				
Extras	(lb 13, w 4)	17		
Total	(49.4 overs; 5 wickets)	**257**		

AUSTRALIA	O	M	R	W
McGrath	10	1	47	2
Kasprowicz	10	0	51	1
Lee	10	0	40	1
Warne	10	1	53	0
Waugh	6	0	31	0
Bevan	4	0	20	1

SRI LANKA	O	M	R	W
Wickremasinghe	7	0	24	0
Vaas	9	0	50	1
Gurusinha	2	0	12	0
Ranatunga	1	0	12	0
Muralitharan	10	0	52	0
Dharmasena	8.4	0	41	1
Jayasuriya	8	0	35	0
De Silva	4	0	18	0

FALL OF WICKETS
1-7, 2-32, 3-111, 4-134, 5-173, 6-175, 7-203, 8-239, 9-253

FALL OF WICKETS
1-23, 2-131, 3-192, 4-212 5-239

Umpires: D.B.Hair (19) and D.J.Harper (3).

Referee: G.T.Dowling (*New Zealand*).

AUSTRALIA v WEST INDIES 1995-96

At Sydney Cricket Ground on 1 January 1996.   Result: **AUSTRALIA** won by 1 wicket.   Toss: Australia.
Award: P.R.Reiffel.   LOI debuts: None.

After a Christmas hiatus, Michael Bevan repeated his winning boundary party piece, this time off the last ball and with number 11 in attendance.

WEST INDIES		Runs	Balls	4/6
S.C.Williams	c Healy b Reiffel	5	17	–
S.L.Campbell	lbw b Warne	15	46	2
P.V.Simmons	c Warne b Reiffel	4	11	1
S.Chanderpaul	c Taylor b Reiffel	3	11	–
C.L.Hooper	not out	93	99	8
J.C.Adams	c Waugh b Warne	0	2	–
R.A.Harper	run out	28	64	1
O.D.Gibson	b McGrath	4	9	–
† C.O.Browne	c Warne b Reiffel	2	6	–
C.E.L.Ambrose	b Warne	0	1	–
* C.A.Walsh	not out	3	2	–
Extras	(lb 6, w 7, nb 2)	15		
Total	(43 overs; 9 wickets)	**172**		

AUSTRALIA		Runs	Balls	4/6
M.J.Slater	c Simmons b Ambrose	5	26	–
* M.A.Taylor	run out	1	4	–
M.E.Waugh	c Harper b Gibson	16	38	1
R.T.Ponting	b Ambrose	0	1	–
S.G.Law	c Browne b Ambrose	10	14	2
M.G.Bevan	not out	78	89	6
S.Lee	c Browne b Gibson	0	2	–
† I.A.Healy	b Harper	16	37	–
P.R.Reiffel	c Hooper b Simmons	34	49	2
S.K.Warne	run out	3	5	–
G.D.McGrath	not out	1	1	–
Extras	(lb 2, w 3, nb 4)	9		
Total	(43 overs; 9 wickets)	**173**		

AUSTRALIA	O	M	R	W
McGrath	9	2	22	1
Reiffel	9	2	29	4
Law	6	0	34	0
Lee	6	0	20	0
Warne	9	2	30	3
Bevan	4	0	31	0

WEST INDIES	O	M	R	W
Ambrose	9	3	20	3
Walsh	9	2	22	0
Gibson	9	2	40	2
Harper	8	0	38	1
Simmons	5	0	31	1
Hooper	3	0	20	0

FALL OF WICKETS
1-13, 2-21, 3-28, 4-54, 5-54, 6-135, 7-150, 8-164, 9-168

FALL OF WICKETS
1-4, 2-15, 3-15, 4-32, 5-38, 6-38, 7-74, 8-157, 9-167

Umpires: A.J.McQuillan (7) and P.D.Parker (6).

Referee: G.T.Dowling (*New Zealand*).

WEST INDIES v SRI LANKA 1995-96

At Bellerive Oval, Hobart on 3 January 1996.   Result: **WEST INDIES** won by 70 runs.   Toss: Sri Lanka.
Award: S.Chanderpaul.   LOI debuts: None.

West Indies gained their first win of the tournament. Off-spinner Muthiah Muralitharan, controversially no-balled for throwing in a Test match eight days earlier, escaped further censure on this occasion. Chanderpaul and Gurusinha completed their innings with runners.

WEST INDIES		Runs	Balls	4/6
P.V.Simmons	c Kaluwitharana b Vaas	0	2	–
S.L.Campbell	c Kaluwitharana b Hathurusinghe	38	76	3
S.Chanderpaul	c Vaas b Muralitharan	77	122	4
* R.B.Richardson	c Gurusinha b Dharmasena	18	25	–
C.L.Hooper	c De Silva b Vaas	36	34	2
R.A.Harper	b Muralitharan	1	3	–
O.D.Gibson	c De Silva b Hathurusinghe	6	7	–
† C.O.Browne	not out	4	14	–
I.R.Bishop	run out	3	10	–
C.E.L.Ambrose	c Tillekeratne b Vaas	0	1	–
C.A.Walsh	b Munasinghe	1	4	–
Extras	(lb 3, w 7)	10		
Total	(48.2 overs)	**194**		

SRI LANKA		Runs	Balls	4/6
R.S.Mahanama	c Campbell b Gibson	10	43	–
S.T.Jayasuriya	c Ambrose b Walsh	3	4	–
A.P.Gurusinha	run out	48	84	3
* P.A.de Silva	c Campbell b Gibson	6	8	1
H.P.Tillekeratne	c Browne b Gibson	5	28	–
† R.S.Kaluwitharana	run out	8	15	2
U.C.Hathurusinghe	c Richardson b Bishop	3	11	–
H.D.P.K.Dharmasena	c Browne b Gibson	12	17	1
W.P.U.C.J.Vaas	c Campbell b Harper	10	21	–
A.M.N.Munasinghe	c Simmons b Gibson	0	6	–
M.Muralitharan	not out	2	4	–
Extras	(lb 2, w 5, nb 10)	17		
Total	(37.5 overs)	**124**		

SRI LANKA	O	M	R	W
Vaas	9	2	21	3
Munasinghe	8.2	1	21	1
Hathurusinghe	10	1	50	2
Gurusinha	3	0	14	0
Muralitharan	10	0	46	2
Dharmasena	6	0	30	1
Jayasuriya	2	0	9	0

WEST INDIES	O	M	R	W
Ambrose	6	0	13	0
Walsh	8	1	22	1
Bishop	8	1	28	1
Gibson	8.5	0	42	5
Harper	7	0	17	1

FALL OF WICKETS
1-0, 2-83, 3-125, 4-161, 5-168, 6-179, 7-187, 8-193, 9-193, 10-194

FALL OF WICKETS
1-4, 2-39, 3-47, 4-74, 5-89, 6-94, 7-100, 8-121, 9-121, 10-124

Umpires: S.J.Davis (5) and T.A.Prue (26).

Referee: G.T.Dowling (*New Zealand*).

WEST INDIES v SRI LANKA 1995-96

At Woolloongabba, Brisbane on 5 January 1996.   Result: **WEST INDIES** won by 7 wickets.   Toss: Sri Lanka.
Award: C.E.L.Ambrose.   LOI debuts: None.

Brisbane staged its first floodlit international on the 25th anniversary of the inaugural one in Melbourne. Muthiah Muralitharan was no-balled for throwing seven times in three overs by umpire Ross Emerson officiating at the bowler's end, once in tandem with his square-leg partner. Courtney Browne was the first West Indian to make five dismissals in an innings.

SRI LANKA		Runs	Balls	4/6
U.C.Hathurusinghe	c Browne b Ambrose	0	6	–
S.T.Jayasuriya	c Browne b Walsh	3	30	–
A.P.Gurusinha	c Hooper b Ambrose	3	12	–
* P.A.de Silva	c Gibson b Bishop	10	17	1
R.S.Mahanama	c Browne b Ambrose	0	4	–
H.P.Tillekeratne	not out	37	124	2
† R.S.Kaluwitharana	run out	0	1	–
W.P.U.C.J.Vaas	c Browne b Gibson	14	70	1
A.M.N.Munasinghe	c Browne b Simmons	8	23	–
G.P.Wickremasinghe	c Harper b Walsh	2	6	–
M.Muralitharan	b Gibson	0	2	–
Extras	(lb 2, w 18, nb 5)	25		
Total	(45.2 overs)	**102**		

WEST INDIES		Runs	Balls	4/6
P.V.Simmons	lbw b Vaas	6	4	1
S.L.Campbell	c Muralitharan b Vaas	34	39	2
S.Chanderpaul	run out	10	44	1
* R.B.Richardson	not out	19	47	2
C.L.Hooper	not out	18	42	–
R.A.Harper				
O.D.Gibson				
† C.O.Browne				
I.R.Bishop				
C.E.L.Ambrose				
C.A.Walsh				
Extras	(lb 2, w 8, nb 7)	17		
Total	(26.1 overs; 3 wickets)	**104**		

WEST INDIES	O	M	R	W
Ambrose	10	3	20	3
Walsh	9	2	19	2
Gibson	8.2	2	15	2
Bishop	7	1	18	1
Simmons	9	2	19	1
Harper	2	0	9	0

SRI LANKA	O	M	R	W
Vaas	10	2	24	2
Munasinghe	7	1	34	0
Wickremasinghe	6	0	24	0
Muralitharan	3	0	16	0
Tillekeratne	0.1	0	4	0

FALL OF WICKETS
1-0, 2-12, 3-17, 4-19, 5-33, 6-34, 7-77, 8-95, 9-98, 10-102

FALL OF WICKETS
1-10, 2-46, 3-68

Umpires: R.A.Emerson (1) and A.J.McQuillan (8).

Referee: G.T.Dowling (*New Zealand*).

AUSTRALIA v WEST INDIES 1995-96

At Woolloongabba, Brisbane on 7 January 1996.   Result: **WEST INDIES** won by 14 runs.   Toss: Australia.
Award: O.D.Gibson.   LOI debuts: None.

Before a capacity crowd of 21,632, West Indies gained a third successive victory, leaving Sri Lanka to win three of their last four matches to reach the finals. Ottis Gibson's 34-ball fifty included a hook off Craig McDermott that soared over the Queensland Cricketers Club.

WEST INDIES		Runs	Balls	4/6
S.C.Williams	c Healy b McGrath	0	2	–
S.L.Campbell	b McGrath	5	19	–
P.V.Simmons	c Lee b Waugh	42	64	2/1
* R.B.Richardson	c Bevan b Law	81	111	5/2
C.L.Hooper	c Slater b Reiffel	18	19	3
R.A.Harper	b Waugh	10	22	–
† C.O.Browne	run out	1	4	–
O.D.Gibson	b Lee	52	40	4/2
I.R.Bishop	run out	5	16	–
C.E.L.Ambrose	not out	3	8	–
C.A.Walsh	b McGrath	0	4	–
Extras	(lb 3, w 6, nb 5)	14		
Total	(49.3 overs)	**231**		

AUSTRALIA		Runs	Balls	4/6
* M.A.Taylor	c Browne b Bishop	14	20	2
M.J.Slater	c Campbell b Ambrose	0	4	–
M.E.Waugh	c Browne b Walsh	5	11	–
R.T.Ponting	c Harper b Bishop	61	86	4/1
S.G.Law	c and b Simmons	62	99	3
M.G.Bevan	run out	17	32	–
S.Lee	c Simmons b Walsh	6	11	1
† I.A.Healy	c Walsh b Gibson	15	24	1
P.R.Reiffel	run out	14	12	1
C.J.McDermott	b Gibson	1	2	–
G.D.McGrath	not out	0	–	–
Extras	(lb 6, w 7, nb 9)	22		
Total	(47.4 overs)	**217**		

AUSTRALIA	O	M	R	W
McGrath	9.3	1	47	3
Reiffel	7	1	50	1
McDermott	8	0	43	0
Waugh	10	0	30	2
Bevan	3	0	16	0
Lee	8	1	30	1
Law	4	1	12	1

WEST INDIES	O	M	R	W
Ambrose	9	2	20	1
Walsh	9	0	56	2
Bishop	10	0	49	2
Gibson	5.4	0	38	2
Harper	4	1	9	0
Simmons	10	0	39	1

FALL OF WICKETS
1-2, 2-27, 3-101, 4-131, 5-165, 6-167, 7-171, 8-218, 9-228, 10-231

FALL OF WICKETS
1-1, 2-10, 3-27, 4-142, 5-179, 6-180, 7-187, 8-216, 9-217, 10-217

Umpires: D.B.Hair (20) and P.D.Parker (7).

Referee: G.T.Dowling (*New Zealand*).

AUSTRALIA v SRI LANKA 1995-96

At Melbourne Cricket Ground on 9 January 1996.   Result: **SRI LANKA** won by 3 wickets.   Toss: Australia.
Award: R.S.Kaluwitharana.   LOI debuts: None.

Ricky Ponting scored Australia's first LOI hundred for more than a year and, with Michael Bevan, shared a world record fifth-wicket partnership of 159 from 183 balls. Romesh Kaluwitharana's blazing innings paved the way for Sri Lanka's World Cup batting plan.

AUSTRALIA		Runs	Balls	4/6
M.J.Slater	c Kaluwitharana b Munasinghe	2	17	–
*M.A.Taylor	c Kaluwitharana b Munasinghe	9	38	–
M.E.Waugh	b Munasinghe	0	4	–
R.T.Ponting	run out	123	142	7/1
S.G.Law	c Tillekeratne b Wickremasinghe	8	17	–
M.G.Bevan	not out	65	86	5
S.Lee				
†I.A.Healy				
P.R.Reiffel				
S.K.Warne				
C.J.McDermott				
Extras	(lb 2, w 2, nb 2)	6		
Total	(50 overs; 5 wickets)	**213**		

SRI LANKA		Runs	Balls	4/6
S.T.Jayasuriya	c Lee b Reiffel	8	14	2
†R.S.Kaluwitharana	run out	77	79	12
A.P.Gurusinha	run out	0	2	–
*P.A.de Silva	lbw b McDermott	35	53	1
R.S.Mahanama	lbw b Bevan	51	70	4
H.P.Tillekeratne	lbw b McDermott	0	1	–
R.S.Kalpage	b Warne	1	6	–
H.D.P.K.Dharmasena	not out	28	62	1
W.P.U.C.J.Vaas	not out	0	4	–
A.M.N.Munasinghe				
G.P.Wickremasinghe				
Extras	(lb 7, w 5, nb 2)	14		
Total	(47.3 overs; 7 wickets)	**214**		

SRI LANKA	O	M	R	W
Vaas	10	3	41	0
Munasinghe	10	1	30	3
Wickremasinghe	6	0	29	1
Dharmasena	10	0	31	0
Jayasuriya	10	0	56	0
Kalpage	4	0	24	0

AUSTRALIA	O	M	R	W
McDermott	10	0	42	2
Reiffel	10	0	47	1
Lee	6	2	26	0
Warne	10	1	37	1
Waugh	6	0	31	0
Bevan	5.3	0	24	1

FALL OF WICKETS
1-8, 2-10, 3-33, 4-54, 5-213

FALL OF WICKETS
1-17, 2-39, 3-127, 4-144, 5-144, 6-147, 7-209

Umpires: D.J.Harper (4) and A.J.McQuillan (9).

Referee: G.T.Dowling (*New Zealand*).

AUSTRALIA v SRI LANKA 1995-96

At WACA Ground, Perth on 12 January 1996.   Result: **AUSTRALIA** won by 83 runs.   Toss: Australia.
Award: M.E.Waugh.   LOI debuts: None.

Promoted to open after Michael Slater had contributed 19 runs in five innings, Mark Waugh scored the highest of his five hundreds to date. The partnership of 189 from 217 balls with his captain remains Australia's best start in a home international.

AUSTRALIA		Runs	Balls	4/6
*M.A.Taylor	c sub ‡ b Jayasuriya	85	111	5
M.E.Waugh	run out	130	151	7/3
R.T.Ponting	b Jayasuriya	11	19	–
S.R.Waugh	b Vaas	11	17	–
S.G.Law	run out	9	11	1
M.G.Bevan	not out	1	2	–
†I.A.Healy	c Jayasuriya b Vaas	0	1	–
P.R.Reiffel				
S.K.Warne				
C.J.McDermott				
G.D.McGrath				
Extras	(lb 8, w 9, nb 2)	19		
Total	(50 overs; 6 wickets)	**266**		

SRI LANKA		Runs	Balls	4/6
S.T.Jayasuriya	c Healy b Law	27	43	2
†R.S.Kaluwitharana	c Ponting b McGrath	20	29	3
A.P.Gurusinha	b McDermott	45	78	5
*P.A.de Silva	lbw b Law	0	1	–
R.S.Mahanama	c Healy b Reiffel	3	8	–
H.P.Tillekeratne	not out	58	104	3
R.S.Kalpage	c Bevan b McDermott	1	6	–
H.D.P.K.Dharmasena	run out	2	6	–
W.P.U.C.J.Vaas	st Healy b Warne	10	23	–
G.P.Wickremasinghe	run out	2	8	–
K.R.Pushpakumara	not out	1	2	–
Extras	(lb 8, w 5, nb 1)	14		
Total	(50 overs; 9 wickets)	**183**		

SRI LANKA	O	M	R	W
Vaas	10	1	33	2
Pushpakumara	8	0	41	0
Wickremasinghe	9	0	60	0
Dharmasena	10	0	51	0
De Silva	1	0	7	0
Kalpage	2	0	18	0
Jayasuriya	10	0	48	2

AUSTRALIA	O	M	R	W
McDermott	10	0	39	2
McGrath	8	1	22	1
Law	10	0	30	2
Reiffel	9	2	25	1
Warne	10	0	45	1
S.R.Waugh	3	0	14	0

FALL OF WICKETS
1-189, 2-209, 3-251, 4-259, 5-266, 6-266

FALL OF WICKETS
1-56, 2-56, 3-56, 4-67, 5-138, 6-142, 7-151, 8-172, 9-175

Umpires: D.B.Hair (21) and P.D.Parker (8).

Referee: G.T.Dowling (*New Zealand*).   ‡ (M.Muralitharan).

WEST INDIES v SRI LANKA 1995-96

At WACA Ground, Perth on 14 January 1996.　Result: **SRI LANKA** won by 16 runs.　Toss: West Indies.
Award: R.S.Kaluwitharana.　LOI debuts: None.

Ottis Gibson returned his second five-wicket analysis of the tournament; it included a sequence of 4 for 3 in 21 balls. Thwarted by spin on a pitch favouring pace, West Indies were unable to reach the target which would have secured them a place in the finals.

SRI LANKA		Runs	Balls	4/6
S.T.Jayasuriya	lbw b Gibson	28	44	2
† R.S.Kaluwitharana	b Gibson	50	55	5/1
A.P.Gurusinha	c Browne b Gibson	5	11	1
* P.A.de Silva	run out	1	1	–
H.P.Tillekeratne	c Browne b Gibson	0	14	–
R.S.Mahanama	b Bishop	50	81	4
S.Ranatunga	b Hooper	5	23	–
H.D.P.K.Dharmasena	hit wicket b Walsh	16	36	–
W.P.U.C.J.Vaas	c Ambrose b Gibson	21	28	1
K.E.A.Upashanta	not out	8	14	–
K.R.Pushpakumara	run out	5	5	1
Extras	(lb 4, w 4, nb 5)	13		
Total	(50 overs)	**202**		

WEST INDIES		Runs	Balls	4/6
P.V.Simmons	b Upashanta	5	20	–
S.L.Campbell	c Vaas b De Silva	20	52	1
S.Chanderpaul	c Gurusinha b De Silva	44	90	3
* R.B.Richardson	run out	7	18	1
C.L.Hooper	c Gurusinha b Dharmasena	1	5	–
R.I.C.Holder	c Kaluwitharana b Jayasuriya	38	51	2
† C.O.Browne	c Pushpakumara b Vaas	22	34	1
O.D.Gibson	st Kaluwitharana b De Silva	19	23	2
I.R.Bishop	run out	4	4	–
C.E.L.Ambrose	not out	8	10	–
C.A.Walsh	not out	3	8	–
Extras	(lb 3, w 4, nb 8)	15		
Total	(50 overs; 9 wickets)	**186**		

WEST INDIES	O	M	R	W
Ambrose	8	2	32	0
Walsh	9	0	34	1
Bishop	10	2	46	1
Gibson	10	1	40	5
Hooper	10	0	33	1
Simmons	3	0	13	0

SRI LANKA	O	M	R	W
Vaas	9	0	27	1
Pushpakumara	8	2	21	0
Upashanta	6	0	31	1
Dharmasena	7	2	22	1
De Silva	10	0	43	3
Jayasuriya	10	1	39	1

FALL OF WICKETS
1-80, 2-89, 3-90, 4-91, 5-92, 6-121, 7-161, 8-176, 9-193, 10-102

FALL OF WICKETS
1-18, 2-51, 3-65, 4-67, 5-114, 6-131, 7-160, 8-171, 9-176

Umpires: D.J.Harper (5) and T.A.Prue (27).

Referee: G.T.Dowling (*New Zealand*).

AUSTRALIA v SRI LANKA 1995-96

At Melbourne Cricket Ground on 16 January 1996.　Result: **SRI LANKA** won by 3 wickets.　Toss: Australia.
Award: R.S.Kaluwitharana.　LOI debuts: None.

Romesh Kaluwitharana's 32-ball fifty, the third-fastest in WS matches, provided the impetus for the victory, with two balls to spare, which took Sri Lanka into the finals for the first time. Final points: Australia 10, Sri Lanka 8, West Indies 6. Steve Waugh waited a record 187 internationals for his maiden hundred.

AUSTRALIA		Runs	Balls	4/6
M.E.Waugh	c Mahanama b Vaas	6	17	1
* M.A.Taylor	c Kaluwitharana b Wickremasinghe	32	55	5
R.T.Ponting	c Kaluwitharana b Wickremasinghe	5	12	1
S.R.Waugh	not out	102	116	6/1
S.G.Law	c Ranatunga b Pushpakumara	47	69	4
M.G.Bevan	not out	43	38	3
† I.A.Healy				
P.R.Reiffel				
S.K.Warne				
C.J.McDermott				
G.D.McGrath				
Extras	(lb 3, w 2, nb 2)	7		
Total	(50 overs; 4 wickets)	**242**		

SRI LANKA		Runs	Balls	4/6
S.T.Jayasuriya	c Healy b McGrath	3	18	–
† R.S.Kaluwitharana	c M.E.Waugh b Warne	74	69	8
A.P.Gurusinha	c Healy b Reiffel	17	50	2
H.P.Tillekeratne	c Healy b Warne	0	5	–
P.A.de Silva	lbw b Bevan	45	61	1
R.S.Mahanama	b Warne	31	41	2
* A.Ranatunga	run out	18	25	1
H.D.P.K.Dharmasena	not out	24	24	1
W.P.U.C.J.Vaas	not out	13	8	2
G.P.Wickremasinghe				
K.R.Pushpakumara				
Extras	(b 1, lb 18, w 2)	21		
Total	(49.4 overs; 7 wickets)	**246**		

SRI LANKA	O	M	R	W
Vaas	10	2	43	1
Pushpakumara	10	0	47	1
Wickremasinghe	8	0	33	2
Dharmasena	8	0	42	0
De Silva	6	0	30	0
Jayasuriya	8	0	44	0

AUSTRALIA	O	M	R	W
McDermott	10	3	27	0
McGrath	9.4	0	76	1
Reiffel	10	1	36	1
Warne	10	0	40	3
Law	6	0	28	0
M.E.Waugh	2	0	11	0
Bevan	2	0	9	1

FALL OF WICKETS
1-12, 2-28, 3-54, 4-156

FALL OF WICKETS
1-35, 2-96, 3-107, 4-108, 5-180, 6-196, 7-222

Umpires: D.B.Hair (22) and S.G.Randell (64).

Referee: G.T.Dowling (*New Zealand*).

AUSTRALIA v SRI LANKA 1995-96

At Melbourne Cricket Ground on 18 January 1996.   Result: **AUSTRALIA** won by 18 runs.   Toss: Sri Lanka.
LOI debuts: None.

Australia's largest crowd of the season (72,614) saw their team win a tense battle after losing four key wickets cheaply. In his 136th international, Craig McDermott became the third bowler after Kapil Dev (166 matches) and Wasim Akram (143) to take 200 wickets. Roshan Mahanama (4) retired (more leg trouble) at 124 and returned with his runner at 132.

AUSTRALIA		Runs	Balls	4/6
* M.A.Taylor	c Kaluwitharana b Vaas	0	3	–
M.E.Waugh	b Vaas	4	10	–
R.T.Ponting	run out	51	75	4
S.R.Waugh	c Gurusinha b Wickremasinghe	13	33	2
S.G.Law	c Kaluwitharana b Pushpakumara	0	1	–
M.G.Bevan	c Mahanama b Pushpakumara	59	102	5
† I.A.Healy	not out	50	55	–
P.R.Reiffel	b Vaas	15	21	1
S.K.Warne	not out	3	3	–
C.J.McDermott				
G.D.McGrath				
Extras	(lb 3, w 2, nb 1)	6		
Total	(50 overs; 7 wickets)	**201**		

SRI LANKA		Runs	Balls	4/6
S.T.Jayasuriya	c S.R.Waugh b McGrath	19	25	1
† R.S.Kaluwitharana	lbw b McGrath	13	9	3
A.P.Gurusinha	c Bevan b McDermott	47	82	4
P.A.de Silva	c Taylor b Warne	34	47	3
H.P.Tillekeratne	c Healy b Warne	1	4	–
R.S.Mahanama	b M.E.Waugh	16	34	1
* A.Ranatunga	b McGrath	31	57	1
H.D.P.K.Dharmasena	b McDermott	4	5	1
W.P.U.C.J.Vaas	c Healy b McDermott	2	12	–
G.P.Wickremasinghe	c Taylor b Reiffel	0	5	–
K.R.Pushpakumara	not out	8	13	–
Extras	(lb 5, w 2, nb 1)	8		
Total	(48.1 overs)	**183**		

SRI LANKA	O	M	R	W
Vaas	10	1	42	3
Pushpakumara	10	1	34	2
Wickremasinghe	8	0	30	1
Dharmasena	10	1	31	0
De Silva	5	0	24	0
Jayasuriya	7	0	37	0

AUSTRALIA	O	M	R	W
McGrath	9.1	0	28	3
Reiffel	10	2	44	1
M.E.Waugh	6	0	23	1
McDermott	10	1	41	3
Warne	10	1	29	2
Law	3	0	13	0

FALL OF WICKETS
1-0, 2-9, 3-39, 4-39, 5-100, 6-155, 7-192

FALL OF WICKETS
1-17, 2-46, 3-107, 4-110, 5-120, 6-129, 7-131, 8-132, 9-152, 10-183

Umpires: D.B.Hair (23) and S.G.Randell (65).

Referee: G.T.Dowling (*New Zealand*).

AUSTRALIA v SRI LANKA 1995-96

At Sydney Cricket Ground on 20 January 1996.   Result: **AUSTRALIA** won by 8 runs (revised target).
Toss: Sri Lanka.   Finals Awards: M.A.Taylor and S.K.Warne.   LOI debuts: None.

A thunderstorm during the interval delayed the start of Sri Lanka's innings by 125 minutes and reduced their target under the complex 'highest scoring overs minus 0.5% per over' formula to 168 from 25 overs. The match ended at the exceptionally late hour of 10.56pm, Australia winning their third successive WS title.

AUSTRALIA		Runs	Balls	4/6
M.E.Waugh	c and b Kalpage	73	82	8
* M.A.Taylor	c Kaluwitharana b Kalpage	82	96	6
R.T.Ponting	c Vaas b Dharmasena	17	26	1
S.R.Waugh	c Kalpage b Dharmasena	2	7	–
S.G.Law	b Vaas	21	28	1
M.G.Bevan	not out	32	35	1
† I.A.Healy	not out	40	28	1
P.R.Reiffel				
S.K.Warne				
C.J.McDermott				
G.D.McGrath				
Extras	(lb 5, w 1)	6		
Total	(50 overs; 5 wickets)	**273**		

SRI LANKA		Runs	Balls	4/6
S.T.Jayasuriya	c McGrath b Warne	30	26	5
† R.S.Kaluwitharana	lbw b McGrath	0	1	–
P.A.de Silva	c Reiffel b M.E.Waugh	6	7	–
A.P.Gurusinha	c Warne b Reiffel	24	15	2
* A.Ranatunga	c Law b Warne	41	44	2
R.S.Kalpage	c Taylor b McDermott	9	10	1
H.P.Tillekeratne	run out	25	26	1
H.D.P.K.Dharmasena	c S.R.Waugh b Warne	7	11	–
A.M.N.Munasinghe	not out	3	6	–
W.P.U.C.J.Vaas	not out	8	8	–
K.R.Pushpakumara				
Extras	(lb 3, w 3)	6		
Total	(25 overs; 8 wickets)	**159**		

SRI LANKA	O	M	R	W
Vaas	10	1	47	1
Pushpakumara	8	1	39	0
Munasinghe	4	0	33	0
Dharmasena	10	0	45	2
Kalpage	10	0	47	2
Jayasuriya	8	0	57	0

AUSTRALIA	O	M	R	W
McGrath	5	0	36	1
M.E.Waugh	5	0	31	1
Warne	5	0	20	3
S.R.Waugh	1	0	14	0
Reiffel	4	0	22	1
McDermott	5	0	33	1

FALL OF WICKETS
1-135, 2-170, 3-176, 4-184, 5-210

FALL OF WICKETS
1-1, 2-22, 3-49, 4-66, 5-87, 6-135, 7-146, 8-146

Umpires: P.D.Parker (9) and S.G.Randell (66).

Referee: G.T.Dowling (*New Zealand*).

SOUTH AFRICA v ENGLAND 1995-96

At Newlands, Cape Town on 9 January 1996.   Result: **SOUTH AFRICA** won by 6 runs.   Toss: South Africa.
Award: S.M.Pollock.   LOI debuts: South Africa – P.R.Adams, J.H.Kallis, S.M.Pollock; England – N.M.K.Smith.

At their fifth attempt South Africa gained their first win against England. Shaun Pollock enjoyed a remarkable LOI
debut, scoring a 58-ball fifty and taking four wickets as England's last seven fell for 50 runs.

SOUTH AFRICA		Runs	Balls	4/6		ENGLAND		Runs	Balls	4/6
G.Kirsten	lbw b Cork	8	12	2		* M.A.Atherton	b Donald	35	56	6
† D.J.Richardson	c Stewart b Martin	11	28	–		† A.J.Stewart	lbw b Donald	23	40	2
B.M.McMillan	c Stewart b Martin	4	9	–		G.A.Hick	lbw b Donald	21	18	3
D.J.Cullinan	c Stewart b Reeve	17	33	3		G.P.Thorpe	c Matthews b McMillan	62	96	2
J.N.Rhodes	c Stewart b White	16	32	–		N.H.Fairbrother	c Adams b Pollock	28	40	2
* W.J.Cronje	run out	24	44	–		C.White	c and b Pollock	5	7	–
J.H.Kallis	c Thorpe b White	38	65	3		D.A.Reeve	c Richardson b Matthews	2	4	–
S.M.Pollock	not out	66	66	6		D.G.Cork	run out	7	12	1
C.R.Matthews	c Reeve b Cork	10	19	1		N.M.K.Smith	c McMillan b Pollock	3	6	–
A.A.Donald						D.Gough	b Pollock	3	18	–
P.R.Adams						P.J.Martin	not out	4	6	–
Extras	(b 1, lb 6, w 4, nb 6)	17				Extras	(lb 6, w 4, nb 2)	12		
Total	(50 overs; 8 wickets)	**211**				**Total**	(49.5 overs)	**205**		

ENGLAND	O	M	R	W		SOUTH AFRICA	O	M	R	W
Cork	10	0	51	2		Matthews	10	1	39	1
Martin	10	1	34	2		Pollock	9.5	0	34	4
Gough	9	0	39	0		Donald	10	0	38	3
Reeve	9	1	40	1		McMillan	10	0	38	1
White	10	1	31	2		Adams	2	0	18	0
Smith	2	0	9	0		Cronje	5	0	18	0
						Kallis	3	0	14	0

FALL OF WICKETS
1-12, 2-20, 3-44, 4-57, 5-77, 6-107, 7-152, 8-211

Umpires: K.E.Liebenberg (33) and D.L.Orchard (6).

FALL OF WICKETS
1-59, 2-65, 3-95, 4-155, 5-161, 6-166, 7-177, 8-189, 9-199, 10-205

Referee: C.W.Smith (West Indies).

SOUTH AFRICA v ENGLAND 1995-96

At Springbok Park, Bloemfontein on 11 January 1996.   Result: **ENGLAND** won by 5 wickets.   Toss: South Africa.
Award: M.A.Atherton.   LOI debuts: None.

Accelerated by Graeme Hick's 33-ball fifty, England squared the series with ten balls to spare. Although a power failure
stopped play for 41 minutes when England were 129 for 2 after 23.4 overs, there was no revision of their target.

SOUTH AFRICA		Runs	Balls	4/6		ENGLAND		Runs	Balls	4/6
A.C.Hudson	c Stewart b Hick	64	97	5		P.A.J.DeFreitas	c Rhodes b Pollock	17	19	2
R.P.Snell	c Fairbrother b Hick	63	65	4/1		* M.A.Atherton	c Cronje b Pollock	85	110	5
B.M.McMillan	b Martin	44	54	4		G.A.Hick	lbw b Cronje	55	42	9/1
J.H.Kallis	c Hick b Smith	29	35	2/1		G.P.Thorpe	not out	72	85	5
* W.J.Cronje	b Cork	19	18	1/1		M.R.Ramprakash	run out	1	4	–
J.N.Rhodes	b Cork	4	6	–		N.H.Fairbrother	c Rhodes b McMillan	12	16	1
G.Kirsten	c Fairbrother b Cork	2	3	–		† A.J.Stewart	not out	13	16	1
S.M.Pollock	c Ramprakash b Smith	5	5	–		C.White				
† D.J.Richardson	not out	13	10	–		D.G.Cork				
N.Boje	not out	2	7	–		N.M.K.Smith				
A.A.Donald						P.J.Martin				
Extras	(b 6, lb 4, w 7)	17				Extras	(lb 4, w 5, nb 1)	10		
Total	(50 overs; 8 wickets)	**262**				**Total**	(48.2 overs; 5 wickets)	**265**		

ENGLAND	O	M	R	W		SOUTH AFRICA	O	M	R	W
Cork	10	0	44	3		Pollock	9.2	0	48	2
DeFreitas	6	0	30	0		Snell	6	0	39	0
White	6	0	37	0		McMillan	7	0	46	1
Martin	6	0	43	1		Donald	10	1	44	0
Smith	10	0	46	2		Cronje	7	0	32	1
Hick	10	0	38	2		Kallis	5	0	27	0
Ramprakash	2	0	14	0		Boje	4	0	25	0

FALL OF WICKETS
1-116, 2-164, 3-197, 4-226, 5-228, 6-236, 7-237, 8-248

Umpires: R.E.Koertzen (14) and W.A.Diedricks (13).

FALL OF WICKETS
1-37, 2-108, 3-198, 4-200, 5-223

Referee: C.W.Smith (West Indies).

SOUTH AFRICA v ENGLAND 1995-96

At The Wanderers, Johannesburg on 13 January 1996.　Result: **SOUTH AFRICA** won by 3 wickets.　Toss: England.
Award: S.M.Pollock.　LOI debuts: England – M.Watkinson.

Returning to the scene of his epic match-saving Test innings of 185 not out, Michael Atherton was caught first ball.
England's specialist wicket-keeper, 'Jack' Russell, was given his first limited-overs international outing since May 1991
(*LOI No. 678*).

ENGLAND		Runs	Balls	4/6
P.A.J.DeFreitas	c Donald b Pollock	13	23	2
* M.A.Atherton	c McMillan b Pollock	0	1	–
R.A.Smith	lbw b Pollock	9	25	1
G.A.Hick	b Donald	14	29	1
M.R.Ramprakash	c Richardson b Cronje	27	68	2
N.H.Fairbrother	not out	57	92	2/1
C.White	c Cronje b McMillan	34	38	5
D.A.Reeve	c Richardson b Donald	10	15	1
† R.C.Russell	c Cronje b Snell	18	12	2/1
M.Watkinson				
D.Gough				
Extras	(lb 7, w 7, nb 2)	16		
Total	(50 overs; 8 wickets)	**198**		

SOUTH AFRICA		Runs	Balls	4/6
A.C.Hudson	b Gough	17	33	–
R.P.Snell	c Fairbrother b DeFreitas	8	12	–
* W.J.Cronje	c Russell b DeFreitas	7	10	1
D.J.Cullinan	c Russell b Gough	25	30	4
J.H.Kallis	run out	16	49	–
J.N.Rhodes	c Russell b Gough	44	65	1
B.M.McMillan	c Smith b White	35	49	3
S.M.Pollock	not out	18	29	1
† D.J.Richardson	not out	10	15	–
C.R.Matthews				
A.A.Donald				
Extras	(b 1, lb 7, w 8, nb 3)	19		
Total	(48.1 overs; 7 wickets)	**199**		

SOUTH AFRICA	O	M	R	W
Pollock	10	2	31	3
Matthews	8	0	34	0
Donald	10	0	53	2
McMillan	10	0	27	0
Snell	6	1	29	1
Cronje	6	0	17	1

ENGLAND	O	M	R	W
Gough	10	2	31	3
DeFreitas	8	0	35	2
Reeve	10	0	43	0
Hick	3	0	13	0
Watkinson	9	0	43	0
White	8.1	1	26	1

FALL OF WICKETS
1-1, 2-23, 3-25, 4-53, 5-88, 6-139, 7-168, 8-198

FALL OF WICKETS
1-19, 2-29, 3-63, 4-73, 5-114, 6-157, 7-180

Umpires: R.E.Koertzen (15) and D.L.Orchard (7).

Referee: C.W.Smith (*West Indies*).

SOUTH AFRICA v ENGLAND 1995-96

At Centurion Park, Centurion (Verwoerdburg), Pretoria on 14 January 1996.　Result: **SOUTH AFRICA** won by 7 wickets.
Toss: England.　Award: G.Kirsten.　LOI debuts: None.

In a reversal of an incident involving the same players in the recent Cape Town Test, fielder Graham Thorpe
successfully appealed for a third umpire's decision when he held a legitimate boundary catch off 'Hansie' Cronje, only to
see umpire Wilf Diedricks signal a six. Verwoerdburg was renamed 'Centurion' in November 1995.

ENGLAND		Runs	Balls	4/6
* A.J.Stewart	c Cullinan b Symcox	64	78	8/1
R.A.Smith	c Symcox b Donald	63	90	6
G.A.Hick	b Cronje	21	17	–
G.P.Thorpe	c Pollock b Symcox	15	18	2
M.R.Ramprakash	c Kallis b Donald	32	44	–
C.White	c Donald b Cronje	19	30	1
† R.C.Russell	not out	39	19	6
D.G.Cork	c Richardson b Matthews	0	2	–
P.A.J.DeFreitas	c Cullinan b Donald	2	3	–
D.Gough	not out	1	1	–
R.K.Illingworth				
Extras	(lb 5, w 10, nb 1)	16		
Total	(50 overs; 8 wickets)	**272**		

SOUTH AFRICA		Runs	Balls	4/6
A.C.Hudson	lbw b Gough	72	85	7/2
G.Kirsten	b Cork	116	125	11
* W.J.Cronje	c Thorpe b Illingworth	47	46	3/2
D.J.Cullinan	not out	25	21	2
J.H.Kallis	not out	14	13	2
J.N.Rhodes				
† D.J.Richardson				
S.M.Pollock				
C.R.Matthews				
P.L.Symcox				
A.A.Donald				
Extras	(w 2)	2		
Total	(48 overs; 3 wickets)	**276**		

SOUTH AFRICA	O	M	R	W
Matthews	10	0	48	1
Pollock	10	1	36	0
Cronje	10	0	57	2
Donald	9	0	72	3
Symcox	10	1	48	2
Kirsten	1	0	6	0

ENGLAND	O	M	R	W
Cork	10	0	65	1
DeFreitas	10	0	46	0
Gough	10	1	41	1
Hick	3	0	17	0
Illingworth	9	0	65	1
White	6	1	42	0

FALL OF WICKETS
1-103, 2-139, 3-168, 4-174, 5-216, 6-245, 7-249, 8-260

FALL OF WICKETS
1-156, 2-223, 3-247

Umpires: W.A.Diedricks (14) and K.E.Liebenberg (34).

Referee: C.W.Smith (*West Indies*).

SOUTH AFRICA v ENGLAND 1995-96

At Kingsmead, Durban on 17 January 1996.   Result: **SOUTH AFRICA** won by 5 wickets.   Toss: South Africa.
Award: A.A.Donald.   LOI debuts: None.

Allan Donald extracted England's first four batsmen for 19 runs in 27 balls. 'Hansie' Cronje and Jacques Kallis added 118, sharing South Africa's highest third-wicket stand in a home international, as South Africa won the seven-match series with two games in hand.

ENGLAND		Runs	Balls	4/6
* M.A.Atherton	c Richardson b Donald	17	45	1
A.J.Stewart	b Donald	31	44	6
R.A.Smith	c Richardson b Donald	8	24	–
G.A.Hick	c Richardson b Donald	6	11	–
G.P.Thorpe	b Matthews	63	74	4
C.White	b Pollock	16	41	1
† R.C.Russell	run out	21	36	–
D.G.Cork	b Matthews	1	7	–
P.A.J.DeFreitas	b Pollock	3	8	–
D.Gough	b De Villiers	3	6	–
P.J.Martin	not out	2	3	–
Extras	(b 1, lb 6, w 6)	13		
Total	(49.5 overs)	**184**		

SOUTH AFRICA		Runs	Balls	4/6
A.C.Hudson	lbw b Cork	5	17	1
G.Kirsten	c Russell b Cork	0	2	–
* W.J.Cronje	b White	78	133	4/1
J.H.Kallis	c Hick b DeFreitas	67	107	6
B.M.McMillan	c Hick b DeFreitas	13	19	2
J.N.Rhodes	not out	12	9	1
S.M.Pollock	not out	1	6	–
† D.J.Richardson				
P.S.de Villiers				
C.R.Matthews				
A.A.Donald				
Extras	(lb 2, w 3, nb 4)	9		
Total	(48.2 overs; 5 wickets)	**185**		

SOUTH AFRICA	O	M	R	W
Pollock	10	1	31	2
Matthews	10	1	37	2
De Villiers	9.5	0	35	1
Donald	10	0	41	4
McMillan	8	0	25	0
Cronje	2	0	8	0

ENGLAND	O	M	R	W
Martin	10	2	34	0
Cork	9.2	3	29	2
DeFreitas	9	0	41	2
Gough	10	0	32	0
White	8	1	39	1
Hick	2	0	8	0

FALL OF WICKETS
1-51, 2-52, 3-61, 4-78, 5-132, 6-164, 7-170, 8-177, 9-178, 10-184

FALL OF WICKETS
1-1, 2-9, 3-127, 4-150, 5-183

Umpires: W.A.Diedricks (15) and D.L.Orchard (8).

Referee: C.W.Smith (*West Indies*).

SOUTH AFRICA v ENGLAND 1995-96

At Buffalo Park, East London on 19 January 1996.   Result: **SOUTH AFRICA** won by 14 runs.   Toss: South Africa.
Award: P.R.Adams.   LOI debuts: South Africa – L.Klusener.

Border were fined R5000 (£914) by the United Cricket Board for producing a 'pitch that fell a long way short of the standard required for international cricket'. Dave Richardson fractured his left index finger diving to take a wide ball from Jacques Kallis and missed the World Cup.

SOUTH AFRICA		Runs	Balls	4/6
G.Kirsten	c Smith b Cork	17	37	2
R.P.Snell	c Atherton b Martin	8	19	–
* W.J.Cronje	b White	13	28	1
J.H.Kallis	lbw b Martin	0	3	–
B.M.McMillan	not out	45	92	3
J.N.Rhodes	c Gough b Illingworth	10	36	1
L.Klusener	lbw b Gough	0	3	–
S.M.Pollock	b Gough	6	10	–
† D.J.Richardson	lbw b Gough	0	2	–
P.S.de Villiers	b White	15	20	2
P.R.Adams	b Cork	0	3	–
Extras	(b 1, lb 11, w 1, nb 2)	15		
Total	(41.4 overs)	**129**		

ENGLAND		Runs	Balls	4/6
* M.A.Atherton	c Richardson b De Villiers	6	27	–
C.White	c Richardson b De Villiers	6	11	1
R.A.Smith	b Pollock	0	4	–
G.A.Hick	c Kirsten b Adams	39	65	3
† R.C.Russell	run out	12	68	–
G.P.Thorpe	b Adams	0	1	–
N.H.Fairbrother	b Snell	13	45	1
D.G.Cork	b Adams	2	15	–
R.K.Illingworth	run out	1	7	–
D.Gough	lbw b Snell	4	11	1
P.J.Martin	not out	5	9	1
Extras	(b 1, lb 13, w 12, nb 1)	27		
Total	(43.4 overs)	**115**		

ENGLAND	O	M	R	W
Cork	8.4	1	22	2
Martin	7	0	23	2
Gough	10	1	25	3
White	7	1	18	2
Illingworth	9	1	29	1

SOUTH AFRICA	O	M	R	W
Pollock	10	3	15	1
De Villiers	8	1	10	2
Klusener	4	0	19	0
Snell	9.4	2	22	2
Kallis	3	0	9	0
Adams	9	1	26	3

FALL OF WICKETS
1-25, 2-29, 3-29, 4-54, 5-89, 6-89, 7-98, 8-98, 9-128, 10-129

FALL OF WICKETS
1-10, 2-11, 3-19, 4-75, 5-76, 6-78, 7-88, 8-95, 9-104, 10-115

Umpires: C.J.Mitchley (22) and D.L.Orchard (9).

Referee: C.W.Smith (*West Indies*).

SOUTH AFRICA v ENGLAND 1995-96

At St George's Park, Port Elizabeth on 21 January 1996.　Result: **SOUTH AFRICA** won by 64 runs.
Toss: South Africa.　Award: A.P.Kuiper.　Series Award: S.M.Pollock.　LOI debuts: South Africa – S.J.Palframan.

Adrian Kuiper, who batted with a runner after straining a hamstring when he had made 16, won the match award for scoring a 61-ball fifty in what proved to be his final international appearance. South Africa won the series by a resounding 6-1 margin.

SOUTH AFRICA		Runs	Balls	4/6
A.C.Hudson	c Thorpe b White	44	77	4
† S.J.Palframan	c Russell b Martin	10	16	2
G.Kirsten	c Russell b Gough	17	29	2
* W.J.Cronje	c Hick b Martin	60	74	4
A.P.Kuiper	not out	61	66	5
J.H.Kallis	run out	2	9	–
B.M.McMillan	b White	4	13	–
S.M.Pollock	c Thorpe b Gough	0	3	–
P.L.Symcox	b Gough	7	10	1
P.S.de Villiers	b Gough	0	1	–
P.R.Adams	not out	0	2	–
Extras	(b 1, lb 7, w 5)	13		
Total	(50 overs; 9 wickets)	**218**		

ENGLAND		Runs	Balls	4/6
* M.A.Atherton	c McMillan b Pollock	3	7	–
C.White	c sub (A.A.Donald) b De Villiers	20	34	–/1
R.A.Smith	c Palframan b McMillan	21	44	1
G.A.Hick	b Symcox	43	64	2
N.H.Fairbrother	b McMillan	0	1	–
G.P.Thorpe	b Adams	21	53	1
† R.C.Russell	c McMillan b Symcox	3	16	–
D.G.Cork	lbw b De Villiers	21	37	1
P.J.Martin	c Symcox b De Villiers	6	9	–
D.Gough	b De Villiers	4	8	–
R.K.Illingworth	not out	2	6	–
Extras	(b 1, lb 5, w 2, nb 2)	10		
Total	(46.1 overs)	**154**		

ENGLAND	O	M	R	W
Cork	10	0	53	0
Martin	9	0	47	2
Gough	10	0	33	4
Illingworth	10	1	31	0
Hick	4	0	19	0
White	7	0	27	2

SOUTH AFRICA	O	M	R	W
De Villiers	9.1	1	32	4
Pollock	6	1	17	1
Cronje	4	0	17	0
McMillan	8	0	29	2
Symcox	10	0	31	2
Adams	9	1	22	1

FALL OF WICKETS
1-30, 2-61, 3-123, 4-167, 5-172, 6-195, 7-196, 8-206, 9-206

FALL OF WICKETS
1-5, 2-35, 3-70, 4-70, 5-113, 6-118, 7-124, 8-147, 9-151, 10-154

Umpires: R.E.Koertzen (16) and C.J.Mitchley (23).

Referee: C.W.Smith (*West Indies*).

NEW ZEALAND v ZIMBABWE 1995-96

At Eden Park, Auckland on 28 January 1996.　Result: **NEW ZEALAND** won by 74 runs.　Toss: New Zealand.
Award: N.J.Astle.　LOI debuts: Zimbabwe – S.G.Davies.

This match attracted the biggest crowd of their season, despite the efforts of 'New Zealand Cricket', the new name for their revamped board, who advertised the contest for the previous day and then opened so few turnstiles that many queuing spectators missed most of Nathan Astle's 121-ball hundred.

NEW ZEALAND		Runs	Balls	4/6
C.M.Spearman	c Whittall b Streak	22	23	3/1
N.J.Astle	c Campbell b Peall	120	137	13/1
S.P.Fleming	run out	2	20	–
R.G.Twose	c Brandes b P.A.Strang	53	69	5/1
C.L.Cairns	run out	23	25	–/1
A.C.Parore	not out	26	18	1
S.A.Thomson	not out	11	11	1
*† L.K.Germon				
D.N.Patel				
G.R.Larsen				
D.K.Morrison				
Extras	(lb 6, w 14, nb 1)	21		
Total	(50 overs; 5 wickets)	**278**		

ZIMBABWE		Runs	Balls	4/6
G.W.Flower	c Parore b Larsen	46	48	6
C.N.Evans	lbw b Morrison	1	11	–
G.J.Whittall	run out	70	73	9
*† A.Flower	c Larsen b Thomson	21	17	2
A.D.R.Campbell	c sub (D.J.Nash) b Thomson	23	47	2
S.G.Davies	c Fleming b Thomson	3	12	–
H.H.Streak	c Spearman b Larsen	17	31	1
P.A.Strang	c Thomson b Larsen	11	16	–
E.A.Brandes	b Morrison	1	9	–
S.G.Peall	c Patel b Morrison	0	1	–
B.C.Strang	not out	0	–	–
Extras	(lb 2, w 4, nb 5)	11		
Total	(43.5 overs)	**204**		

ZIMBABWE	O	M	R	W
Streak	10	0	32	1
Brandes	6	0	58	0
B.C.Strang	7	0	34	0
Whittall	10	0	58	0
Peall	7	0	48	1
P.A.Strang	10	0	42	0

NEW ZEALAND	O	M	R	W
Morrison	6.5	0	34	3
Patel	10	0	44	0
Larsen	8	0	42	3
Astle	5	0	28	0
Thomson	10	1	32	3
Twose	4	0	22	0

FALL OF WICKETS
1-40, 2-61, 3-196, 4-232, 5-251

FALL OF WICKETS
1-6, 2-91, 3-117, 4-158, 5-170, 6-171, 7-193, 8-200, 9-200, 10-204

Umpires: B.F.Bowden (3) and R.S.Dunne (30),

Referee: Nasim-ul-Ghani (*Pakistan*).

NEW ZEALAND v ZIMBABWE 1995-96

At Basin Reserve, Wellington on 31 January 1996.   Result: **NEW ZEALAND** won by 6 wickets.   Toss: Zimbabwe.
Award: S.P.Fleming.   LOI debuts: New Zealand – R.J.Kennedy; Zimbabwe – A.C.I.Lock.

The hosts clinched the series through accurate bowling, Gavin Larsen's medium-paced swing proving exceptionally economical, and throwing, with direct hits securing four run outs.

ZIMBABWE		Runs	Balls	4/6
G.W.Flower	run out	48	90	6
C.N.Evans	c Fleming b Morrison	2	5	–
G.J.Whittall	run out	9	12	1
*†A.Flower	lbw b Nash	10	24	1
A.D.R.Campbell	lbw b Nash	2	4	–
S.G.Davies	b Larsen	10	46	1
S.V.Carlisle	run out	28	61	2
H.H.Streak	b Nash	15	37	1
P.A.Strang	not out	28	23	4
B.C.Strang	run out	3	3	–
A.C.I.Lock				
Extras	(b 1, lb 14, w 8, nb 3)	26		
Total	(50 overs; 9 wickets)	**181**		

NEW ZEALAND		Runs	Balls	4/6
C.M.Spearman	c G.W.Flower b Streak	1	6	–
N.J.Astle	b Whittall	18	27	1
S.P.Fleming	b Streak	70	101	10
R.G.Twose	c G.W.Flower b Evans	41	77	4
A.C.Parore	not out	25	19	3/1
S.A.Thomson	not out	4	11	1
*†L.K.Germon				
G.R.Larsen				
D.J.Nash				
D.K.Morrison				
R.J.Kennedy				
Extras	(b 1, lb 7, w 15, nb 2)	25		
Total	(39.3 overs; 4 wickets)	**184**		

NEW ZEALAND	O	M	R	W
Morrison	10	2	37	1
Kennedy	10	0	57	0
Nash	10	0	30	3
Larsen	10	5	14	1
Astle	10	0	28	0

ZIMBABWE	O	M	R	W
Streak	10	0	44	2
Lock	8	1	34	0
Whittall	5	0	22	1
B.C.Strang	9.3	0	50	0
P.A.Strang	5	0	20	0
Evans	2	1	6	1

FALL OF WICKETS
1-10, 2-33, 3-55, 4-65, 5-98, 6-98, 7-132, 8-171, 9-181

Umpires: D.B.Cowie (14) and C.E.King (15).

FALL OF WICKETS
1-6, 2-56, 3-143, 4-169

Referee: Nasim-ul-Ghani (*Pakistan*).

NEW ZEALAND v ZIMBABWE 1995-96

At McLean Park, Napier on 3 February 1996.   Result: **ZIMBABWE** won by 21 runs.   Toss: New Zealand.
Award: A.Flower.   LOI debuts: None.

Attracting a capacity crowd, the first floodlit international to be staged in New Zealand was played between 2.30 and 10.36pm. Charlie Lock returned Zimbabwe's first five-wicket LOI analysis, single-handedly taking 5 for 5 in 11 balls to snatch his country's first win in eight matches against New Zealand.

ZIMBABWE		Runs	Balls	4/6
G.W.Flower	c Astle b Morrison	7	19	1
C.N.Evans	c Fleming b Morrison	0	4	–
G.J.Whittall	c Harris b Morrison	12	21	1
*†A.Flower	lbw b Patel	57	67	5
A.D.R.Campbell	c Germon b Nash	26	33	2/1
S.G.Davies	run out	45	80	3/1
S.V.Carlisle	run out	25	35	1
H.H.Streak	not out	36	28	4
P.A.Strang	not out	24	17	2
A.C.I.Lock				
E.A.Brandes				
Extras	(b 1, lb 11, w 19, nb 4)	35		
Total	(50 overs; 7 wickets)	**267**		

NEW ZEALAND		Runs	Balls	4/6
C.M.Spearman	lbw b Brandes	28	26	2/1
N.J.Astle	c A.Flower b Brandes	30	37	1/2
S.P.Fleming	lbw b Strang	50	64	6
R.G.Twose	lbw b Lock	60	95	2
A.C.Parore	c Streak b G.W.Flower	3	7	–
C.Z.Harris	c A.Flower b Strang	22	28	3
*†L.K.Germon	b Lock	7	15	–
D.N.Patel	c and b Lock	4	6	–
D.J.Nash	b Lock	4	8	–
D.K.Morrison	lbw b Lock	1	2	–
R.J.Kennedy	not out	8	5	1
Extras	(lb 11, w 14, nb 4)	29		
Total	(48.1 overs)	**246**		

NEW ZEALAND	O	M	R	W
Morrison	10	2	39	3
Kennedy	9	0	67	0
Patel	10	0	49	1
Nash	10	2	39	1
Astle	6	1	36	0
Harris	5	0	25	0

ZIMBABWE	O	M	R	W
Streak	9	0	45	0
Lock	8.1	0	44	5
Brandes	8	1	37	2
Strang	10	0	44	2
Whittall	9	0	49	0
G.W.Flower	4	0	16	1

FALL OF WICKETS
1-6, 2-18, 3-38, 4-93, 5-133, 6-199, 7-213

Umpires: R.S.Dunne (31) and D.M.Quested (12).

FALL OF WICKETS
1-65, 2-72, 3-164, 4-169, 5-201, 6-228, 7-229, 8-233, 9-235, 10-246

Referee: Nasim-ul-Ghani (*Pakistan*).

ENGLAND v NEW ZEALAND 1995-96

At Gujarat Stadium, Motera, Ahmedabad, India on 14 February 1996.   Result: **NEW ZEALAND** won by 11 runs.
Toss: England.   Award: N.J.Astle.   LOI debuts: None.

Sponsored by Wills and played in coloured clothing, the sixth World Cup was the biggest cricketing bonanza yet
conceived. It involved more teams (12), more host countries (3) and more grounds (26) than any of its predecessors.
Nathan Astle's 126-ball hundred founded the highest total in eight internationals in Ahmedabad.

NEW ZEALAND		Runs	Balls	4/6
C.M.Spearman	c and b Cork	5	16	–
N.J.Astle	c Hick b Martin	101	132	8/2
S.P.Fleming	c Thorpe b Hick	28	47	3
R.G.Twose	c Thorpe b Hick	17	26	1
C.L.Cairns	c Cork b Illingworth	36	30	4/1
C.Z.Harris	run out	10	16	1
S.A.Thomson	not out	17	23	1
*†L.K.Germon	not out	13	12	–
G.R.Larsen				
D.J.Nash				
D.K.Morrison				
Extras	(b 4, lb 2, w 4, nb 2)	12		
Total	(50 overs; 6 wickets)	**239**		

ENGLAND		Runs	Balls	4/6
* M.A.Atherton	b Nash	1	3	–
A.J.Stewart	c and b Harris	34	72	3
G.A.Hick	run out	85	101	9
G.P.Thorpe	b Larsen	9	21	–
N.H.Fairbrother	b Morrison	36	46	1
† R.C.Russell	c Morrison b Larsen	2	9	–
C.White	c Cairns b Thomson	13	12	–/1
D.G.Cork	c Germon b Nash	19	11	2/1
D.Gough	not out	15	17	–
P.J.Martin	c Cairns b Nash	3	7	–
R.K.Illingworth	not out	3	4	–
Extras	(b 1, lb 4, w 1, nb 2)	8		
Total	(50 overs; 9 wickets)	**228**		

ENGLAND	O	M	R	W
Cork	10	1	36	1
Martin	6	0	37	1
Gough	10	0	63	0
Illingworth	10	1	31	1
Hick	9	0	45	2
White	5	0	21	0

NEW ZEALAND	O	M	R	W
Morrison	8	0	38	1
Nash	7	1	27	3
Cairns	4	0	24	0
Larsen	10	1	32	2
Thomson	10	0	51	1
Harris	9	0	45	1
Astle	2	0	6	0

FALL OF WICKETS
1-12, 2-108, 3-141, 4-196, 5-204, 6-212

FALL OF WICKETS
1-1, 2-100, 3-123, 4-144, 5-151, 6-180, 7-185, 8-210, 9-222

Umpires: B.C.Cooray (*Sri Lanka*) (17) and S.G.Randell (*Australia*) (67).   **Referee:** M.A.K.Pataudi (*India*).

SOUTH AFRICA v UNITED ARAB EMIRATES 1995-96

At Rawalpindi Cricket Stadium, Pakistan on 15 (*no play*), 16 February 1996.   Result: **SOUTH AFRICA** won by 169 runs.
Toss: United Arab Emirates.   Award: G.Kirsten.   LOI debuts: UAE – S.F.Dukanwala, Mohammad Aslam,
G.Mylvaganam, Shahzad Altaf.

The Emirates, consisting of ten immigrants from the sub-continent led by a denizen sultan, were swiftly introduced to the
harsh realities of World Cup cricket. Gary Kirsten, the eighth to score a hundred on WC debut, fell one short of the world
record LOI score. Sultan Zarawani, declining protective headgear, was predictably 'skulled' first ball by Allan Donald.

SOUTH AFRICA		Runs	Balls	4/6
A.C.Hudson	b Samarasekera	27	33	5
G.Kirsten	not out	188	159	13/4
* W.J.Cronje	st Imtiaz b Zarawani	57	62	1/1
D.J.Cullinan	not out	41	51	2
J.H.Kallis				
J.N.Rhodes				
B.M.McMillan				
S.M.Pollock				
† S.J.Palframan				
C.R.Matthews				
A.A.Donald				
Extras	(b 1, lb 1, w 3, nb 3)	8		
Total	(50 overs; 2 wickets)	**321**		

UNITED ARAB EMIRATES		Runs	Balls	4/6
Azhar Saeed	c McMillan b Pollock	11	24	2
G.Mylvaganam	c Palframan b Donald	23	35	3
Mazhar Hussain	b Donald	14	42	–
V.Mehra	run out	2	11	–
Mohammad Aslam	b McMillan	9	9	1
Arshad Laiq	not out	43	79	4
J.A.Samarasekera	c Hudson b Donald	4	12	–
* Sultan M.Zarawani	c Cronje b McMillan	0	7	–
† Imtiaz Abbasi	c Palframan b McMillan	1	7	–
S.F.Dukanwala	not out	40	77	4
Shahzad Altaf				
Extras	(w 3, nb 2)	5		
Total	(50 overs; 8 wickets)	**152**		

UNITED ARAB EMIRATES	O	M	R	W
Samarasekera	9	2	39	1
Shahzad Altaf	3	0	22	0
Arshad Laiq	6	0	52	0
Dukanwala	10	0	64	0
Azhar Saeed	7	0	41	0
Zarawani	10	0	69	1
Mazhar Hussain	5	0	32	0

SOUTH AFRICA	O	M	R	W
Pollock	9	2	28	1
Matthews	10	0	39	0
Donald	10	0	21	3
Cronje	4	0	17	0
McMillan	8	1	11	3
Kallis	6	0	27	0
Kirsten	3	1	9	0

FALL OF WICKETS
1-60, 2-176

FALL OF WICKETS
1-24, 2-42, 3-46, 4-60, 5-62, 6-68, 7-70, 8-72

Umpires: S.A.Bucknor (*WI*) (26) and V.K.Ramaswamy (*India*) (30).   **Referee:** R.S.Madugalle (*Sri Lanka*).

WEST INDIES v ZIMBABWE 1995-96

At Lal Bahadur Stadium, Hyderabad, India on 16 February 1996.   Result: **WEST INDIES** won by 6 wickets.
Toss: Zimbabwe.   Award: C.E.L.Ambrose.   LOI debuts: None.

The tournament's first floodlit match attracted a capacity crowd of 30,000. Leg-spinner Paul Strang claimed all four West Indies wickets to fall, three of them in seven balls. Brian Lara, returning to the fold after going AWOL earlier in the season, concluded the formalities with a six.

ZIMBABWE		Runs	Balls	4/6
*†A.Flower	c Browne b Ambrose	3	4	–
G.W.Flower	c and b Gibson	31	54	6
G.J.Whittall	run out	14	62	–
A.D.R.Campbell	run out	0	8	–
A.C.Waller	st Browne b Harper	21	44	2
C.N.Evans	c Browne b Ambrose	21	31	2
S.G.Davies	run out	9	35	–
H.H.Streak	lbw b Walsh	7	18	–
P.A.Strang	not out	22	29	2
E.A.Brandes	c Chanderpaul b Ambrose	7	13	1
A.C.I.Lock	not out	1	4	–
Extras	(lb 10, w 4, nb 1)	15		
Total	(50 overs; 9 wickets)	**151**		

WEST INDIES		O	M	R	W
Ambrose		10	2	28	3
Walsh		10	3	27	1
Gibson		9	1	27	1
Bishop		10	3	18	0
Harper		10	1	30	1
Arthurton		1	0	11	0

FALL OF WICKETS
1-11, 2-53, 3-56, 4-59, 5-91, 6-103, 7-115, 8-125, 9-142

Umpires: R.S.Dunne (*New Zealand*) (32) and S.Venkataraghavan (4).

WEST INDIES		Runs	Balls	4/6
S.L.Campbell	b Strang	47	88	5
* R.B.Richardson	c Campbell b Strang	32	47	3
B.C.Lara	not out	43	31	5/2
S.Chanderpaul	b Strang	8	4	2
K.L.T.Arthurton	c Campbell b Strang	1	3	–
R.A.Harper	not out	5	6	1
† C.O.Browne				
O.D.Gibson				
I.R.Bishop				
C.E.L.Ambrose				
C.A.Walsh				
Extras	(b 5, lb 3, w 10, nb 1)	19		
Total	(29.3 overs; 4 wickets)	**155**		

ZIMBABWE		O	M	R	W
Streak		7	0	34	0
Lock		6	0	23	0
Brandes		7	0	42	0
Whittall		2	0	8	0
Strang		7.3	1	40	4

FALL OF WICKETS
1-78, 2-115, 3-123, 4-136

Referee: R.Subba Row (*England*).

NEW ZEALAND v HOLLAND 1995-96

At IPCL Sports Complex, Baroda, India on 17 February 1996.   Result: **NEW ZEALAND** won by 129 runs.
Toss: New Zealand.   Award: C.M.Spearman.   LOI debuts: Holland – All.

Holland's introduction to official international cricket began well when the dangerous Nathan Astle perished to the game's eighth ball. Umpire Ian Robinson miscounted the number of overs and, applying the fielding regulations for the first 15 overs, initially ruled the first ball of the 16th, which dismissed Flavian Aponso, as a 'no-ball'.

NEW ZEALAND		Runs	Balls	4/6
C.M.Spearman	c Zuiderent b Lubbers	68	59	8
N.J.Astle	run out	0	5	–
S.P.Fleming	c Zuiderent b Lubbers	66	79	4
R.G.Twose	st Schewe b Lubbers	25	32	1
C.L.Cairns	b Cantrell	52	38	4/2
A.C.Parore	c Clarke b Aponso	55	54	–/3
C.Z.Harris	c Schewe b Bakker	8	12	–
*†L.K.Germon	not out	14	11	1
D.N.Patel	c Schewe b Bakker	11	10	1
D.K.Morrison	not out	0	–	–
R.J.Kennedy				
Extras	(lb 7, w 1)	8		
Total	(50 overs; 8 wickets)	**307**		

HOLLAND		O	M	R	W
Lefebvre		10	0	48	0
Bakker		10	0	51	2
De Leede		7	0	58	0
Aponso		10	0	60	1
Lubbers		9	0	48	3
Cantrell		4	0	35	1

FALL OF WICKETS
1-1, 2-117, 3-155, 4-165, 5-253, 6-279, 7-292, 8-306

Umpires: Khizer Hayat (*Pakistan*) (47) and I.D.Robinson (*Zim*) (26).

HOLLAND		Runs	Balls	4/6
N.E.Clarke	b Kennedy	14	21	2
P.E.Cantrell	c Astle b Harris	45	86	5
G.J.A.F.Aponso	c Astle b Harris	11	31	2
* S.W.Lubbers	run out	5	19	–
R.P.Lefebvre	b Kennedy	45	64	4
T.B.M.de Leede	lbw b Harris	1	4	–
K-J.J.van Noortwijk	not out	36	55	3
† M.M.C.Schewe	st Germon b Fleming	12	16	1
B.Zuiderent	not out	1	6	–
P-J.Bakker				
E.L.Gouka				
Extras	(b 4, lb 4, w 8, nb 2)	18		
Total	(50 overs; 7 wickets)	**188**		

NEW ZEALAND		O	M	R	W
Morrison		4	1	11	0
Kennedy		10	2	36	2
Cairns		7	1	24	0
Harris		10	1	24	3
Patel		10	0	42	0
Astle		5	0	19	0
Fleming		2	0	8	1
Twose		2	0	16	0

FALL OF WICKETS
1-18, 2-52, 3-65, 4-100, 5-102, 6-147, 7-182

Referee: M.A.K.Pataudi (*India*).

INDIA v KENYA 1995-96

At Barabati Stadium, Cuttack, India on 18 February 1996.　　Result: **INDIA** won by 7 wickets.　　Toss: India.
Award: S.R.Tendulkar.　　LOI debuts: Kenya – All.

The Fifth Match, between Sri Lanka and Australia, scheduled on 17 February at Colombo's R.Premadasa Stadium, became the first LOI to be awarded to the home side on forfeit when Australia, fearful about security following terrorist bombings, declined to appear. At Cuttack, Mohammed Azharuddin became the eighth player to appear in 200 LOIs.

KENYA		Runs	Balls	4/6
D.Chudasama	c Mongia b Prasad	29	49	5
† K.Otieno	c Mongia b Raju	27	60	3
S.O.Tikolo	c Kumble b Raju	65	80	4/1
* M.Odumbe	st Mongia b Kumble	26	52	–
H.Modi	c Jadeja b Kumble	2	4	–
T.Odoyo	c Prabhakar b Kumble	8	14	–
E.T.Odumbe	not out	15	22	–
Asif Karim	not out	6	13	–
D.L.Tikolo				
M.Suji				
R.Ali				
Extras	(b 2, lb 11, w 7, nb 1)	21		
Total	(50 overs; 6 wickets)	**199**		

INDIA		Runs	Balls	4/6
A.Jadeja	c Ali b Asif Karim	53	88	4/1
S.R.Tendulkar	not out	127	136	15/1
N.S.Sidhu	c Suji b S.O.Tikolo	1	11	–
V.G.Kambli	c D.L.Tikolo b M.Odumbe	2	11	–
† N.R.Mongia	not out	8	6	1
* M.Azharuddin				
M.Prabhakar				
J.Srinath				
A.Kumble				
B.K.V.Prasad				
S.L.V.Raju				
Extras	(lb 5, w 6, nb 1)	12		
Total	(41.5 overs; 3 wickets)	**203**		

INDIA	O	M	R	W
Prabhakar	5	1	19	0
Srinath	10	0	38	0
Prasad	10	0	41	1
Kumble	10	0	28	3
Raju	10	2	34	2
Tendulkar	5	0	26	0

KENYA	O	M	R	W
Ali	5	0	25	0
E.T.Odumbe	3	0	18	0
Suji	5	0	20	0
Odoyo	3	0	22	0
Asif Karim	10	1	27	1
D.L.Tikolo	3	0	21	0
M.Odumbe	9.5	1	39	1
S.O.Tikolo	3	0	26	1

FALL OF WICKETS
1-41, 2-65, 3-161, 4-161, 5-165, 6-184

FALL OF WICKETS
1-165, 2-167, 3-182

Umpires: K.T.Francis (*Sri Lanka*) (22) and D.R.Shepherd (*England*) (58).

Referee: C.H.Lloyd (*West Indies*).

ENGLAND v UNITED ARAB EMIRATES 1995-96

At Shahi Bagh Stadium, Peshawar, Pakistan on 18 February 1996.　　Result: **ENGLAND** won by 8 wickets.
Toss: United Arab Emirates.　　Award: N.M.K.Smith.　　LOI debuts: None.

Neil Smith retired with gastric problems at 57. Sultan Zarawani again eschewed a helmet. During the early matches of this tournament, which coincided with Ramadan, the players left the field for drinks to avoid offending fasting observers.

UNITED ARAB EMIRATES		Runs	Balls	4/6
Azhar Saeed	lbw b DeFreitas	9	36	1
G.Mylvaganam	c Fairbrother b DeFreitas	0	6	–
Mazhar Hussain	b Smith	33	59	6
V.Mehra	c Russell b Smith	1	34	–
Mohammad Aslam	b Gough	23	47	1
Arshad Laiq	b Smith	0	6	–
Salim Raza	b Cork	10	31	–
J.A.Samarasekera	run out	29	39	3
* Sultan M.Zarawani	b Cork	2	8	–
S.F.Dukanwala	lbw b Illingworth	15	21	1
† Imtiaz Abbasi	not out	1	5	–
Extras	(b 4, lb 4, w 4, nb 1)	13		
Total	(48.3 overs)	**136**		

ENGLAND		Runs	Balls	4/6
A.J.Stewart	c Mylvaganam b Arshad	23	52	3
N.M.K.Smith	retired ill	27	31	4
G.P.Thorpe	not out	44	66	5
* M.A.Atherton	b Azhar	20	40	1
N.H.Fairbrother	not out	12	29	1
† R.C.Russell				
C.White				
D.G.Cork				
P.A.J.DeFreitas				
D.Gough				
R.K.Illingworth				
Extras	(b 4, lb 2, w 2, nb 6)	14		
Total	(35 overs; 2 wickets)	**140**		

ENGLAND	O	M	R	W
Cork	10	1	33	2
DeFreitas	9.3	3	16	2
Gough	8	3	23	1
White	1.3	1	2	0
Smith	9.3	2	29	3
Illingworth	10	2	25	1

UNITED ARAB EMIRATES	O	M	R	W
Samarasekera	7	1	35	0
Arshad Laiq	7	0	25	1
Salim Raza	5	1	20	0
Azhar Saeed	10	1	26	1
Zarawani	6	0	28	0

FALL OF WICKETS
1-3, 2-32, 3-48, 4-49, 5-49, 6-80, 7-88, 8-100, 9-135, 10-136

FALL OF WICKETS
1-52, 2-109

Umpires: B.C.Cooray (*Sri Lanka*) (18) and V.K.Ramaswamy (*India*) (31).

Referee: J.R.Reid (*New Zealand*).

SOUTH AFRICA v NEW ZEALAND 1995-96

At Iqbal Stadium, Faisalabad, Pakistan on 20 February 1996.　　Result: **SOUTH AFRICA** won by 5 wickets.
Toss: New Zealand.　　Award: W.J.Cronje.　　LOI debuts: None.

South Africa's superb fielding was the dominant feature of a match which attracted only 2,000 spectators, the smallest audience of the tournament. 'Jonty' Rhodes provided the highlight with his dive and direct hit to run out Adam Parore. 'Hansie' Cronje scored 50 off 36 balls.

NEW ZEALAND		Runs	Balls	4/6
C.M.Spearman	c Palframan b Matthews	14	14	3
N.J.Astle	run out	1	4	–
S.P.Fleming	b McMillan	33	79	2
R.G.Twose	c McMillan b Pollock	13	17	2
C.L.Cairns	b Donald	9	20	2
A.C.Parore	run out	27	48	–
C.Z.Harris	run out	8	21	–
S.A.Thomson	c Cronje b Donald	29	55	4
*†L.K.Germon	not out	31	32	2
G.R.Larsen	c Cullinan b Donald	1	7	–
D.K.Morrison	not out	5	6	–
Extras	(lb 4, nb 2)	6		
Total	(50 overs; 9 wickets)	**177**		

SOUTH AFRICA		Runs	Balls	4/6
G.Kirsten	lbw b Harris	35	46	5
† S.J.Palframan	b Morrison	16	26	3
* W.J.Cronje	c Fleming b Astle	78	64	11/3
D.J.Cullinan	c Thomson b Astle	27	42	2
J.H.Kallis	not out	11	26	1
J.N.Rhodes	c and b Larsen	9	12	1
B.M.McMillan	not out	2	10	–
S.M.Pollock				
P.L.Symcox				
C.R.Matthews				
A.A.Donald				
Extras		0		
Total	(37.3 overs; 5 wickets)	**178**		

SOUTH AFRICA	O	M	R	W
Pollock	10	1	45	1
Matthews	10	2	30	1
Donald	10	0	34	3
Cronje	3	0	13	0
Symcox	10	1	25	0
McMillan	7	1	26	1

NEW ZEALAND	O	M	R	W
Morrison	8	0	44	1
Cairns	6	0	24	0
Larsen	8	1	41	1
Harris	4	0	25	1
Thomson	8.3	0	34	0
Astle	3	1	10	2

FALL OF WICKETS
1-7, 2-17, 3-36, 4-54, 5-85, 6-103, 7-116, 8-158, 9-165

FALL OF WICKETS
1-41, 2-87, 3-146, 4-159, 5-170

Umpires: S.G.Randell (*Australia*) (68) and S.Venkataraghavan (*India*) (5).

Referee: R.S.Madugalle (*Sri Lanka*).

SRI LANKA v ZIMBABWE 1995-96

At Sinhalese Sports Club, Colombo, Sri Lanka on 21 February 1996.　　Result: **SRI LANKA** won by 6 wickets.
Toss: Zimbabwe.　　Award: P.A.de Silva.　　LOI debuts: None.

Zimbabwe received a royal welcome for braving security fears to appear in Sri Lanka's first home international for 15 months. The partnership of 172 in 27 overs between Asanka Gurusinha and Aravinda de Silva was Sri Lanka's highest for any wicket in LOIs until a fortnight later.

ZIMBABWE		Runs	Balls	4/6
*†A.Flower	run out	8	17	1
G.W.Flower	run out	15	32	–
G.J.Whittall	c Jayasuriya b Muralitharan	35	64	5
A.D.R.Campbell	c Muralitharan b Vaas	75	102	7
A.C.Waller	b Jayasuriya	19	37	–/1
C.N.Evans	not out	39	35	5
H.H.Streak	c De Silva b Vaas	15	13	–
P.A.Strang	not out	0	1	–
A.C.I.Lock				
E.A.Brandes				
S.G.Peall				
Extras	(b 1, lb 16, w 4, nb 1)	22		
Total	(50 overs; 6 wickets)	**228**		

SRI LANKA		Runs	Balls	4/6
S.T.Jayasuriya	b Streak	6	11	1
† R.S.Kaluwitharana	c Peall b Streak	0	1	–
A.P.Gurusinha	run out	87	100	5/6
P.A.de Silva	lbw b Streak	91	86	10/2
* A.Ranatunga	not out	13	11	1
H.P.Tillekeratne	not out	7	16	1
R.S.Mahanama				
W.P.U.C.J.Vaas				
H.D.P.K.Dharmasena				
G.P.Wickremasinghe				
M.Muralitharan				
Extras	(lb 5, w 17, nb 3)	25		
Total	(37 overs; 4 wickets)	**229**		

SRI LANKA	O	M	R	W
Vaas	10	0	30	2
Wickremasinghe	8	0	36	0
Ranatunga	2	0	14	0
Muralitharan	10	0	37	0
Dharmasena	10	1	50	0
Jayasuriya	10	0	44	1

ZIMBABWE	O	M	R	W
Streak	10	0	60	3
Lock	4	0	17	0
Brandes	8	0	35	0
Peall	3	0	23	0
Strang	5	0	43	0
Whittall	2	0	20	0
G.W.Flower	5	1	26	0

FALL OF WICKETS
1-19, 2-51, 3-92, 4-160, 5-194, 6-227

FALL OF WICKETS
1-5, 2-23, 3-195, 4-209

Umpires: R.S.Dunne (*NZ*) (33) and Mahboob Shah (*Pakistan*) (27).

Referee: Nasim-ul-Ghani (*Pakistan*).

INDIA v WEST INDIES 1995-96

At Roop Singh Stadium, Gwalior, India on 21 February 1996.   Result: **INDIA** won by 5 wickets.   Toss: West Indies.
Award: S.R.Tendulkar.   LOI debuts: None.

The inaugural floodlit match to be staged in Gwalior produced the first real contest of the tournament. Named after an Indian hockey international, the ground is set beneath a fort, whose two miles of perimeter wall protects six palaces and two temples.

WEST INDIES		Runs	Balls	4/6
S.L.Campbell	b Srinath	5	14	1
* R.B.Richardson	c Kambli b Prabhakar	47	70	4
B.C.Lara	c Mongia b Srinath	2	5	–
S.Chanderpaul	c Azharuddin b Kapoor	38	66	6
R.I.C.Holder	b Kumble	0	3	–
R.A.Harper	b Kumble	23	42	1/1
† C.O.Browne	b Prabhakar	18	43	–
O.D.Gibson	b Kumble	6	5	–/1
I.R.Bishop	run out	9	26	–
C.E.L.Ambrose	c Kumble b Prabhakar	8	17	1
C.A.Walsh	not out	9	11	2
Extras	(lb 2, w 5, nb 1)	8		
Total	(41 overs)	**173**		

INDIA		Runs	Balls	4/6
A.Jadeja	b Ambrose	1	3	–
S.R.Tendulkar	run out	70	91	8
N.S.Sidhu	b Ambrose	1	5	–
* M.Azharuddin	c Walsh b Harper	32	59	4
V.G.Kambli	not out	33	48	4/1
M.Prabhakar	c and b Harper	1	12	–
† N.R.Mongia	not out	24	33	3
A.R.Kapoor				
A.Kumble				
J.Srinath				
B.K.V.Prasad				
Extras	(lb 3, w 1, nb 8)	12		
Total	(39.4 overs; 5 wickets)	**174**		

INDIA	O	M	R	W
Prabhakar	10	0	39	3
Srinath	10	0	22	2
Kumble	10	0	35	3
Prasad	10	0	34	0
Kapoor	10	2	41	1

WEST INDIES	O	M	R	W
Ambrose	8	1	41	2
Walsh	9	3	18	0
Bishop	5	0	28	0
Gibson	8.4	0	50	0
Harper	9	1	34	2

FALL OF WICKETS
1-16, 2-24, 3-91, 4-99, 5-99, 6-141, 7-141, 8-149, 9-162, 10-173

FALL OF WICKETS
1-2, 2-15, 3-94, 4-125, 5-127

Umpires: Khizer Hayat (*Pakistan*) (48) and I.D.Robinson (*Zim*) (27).   **Referee:** R.Subba Row (*England*).

ENGLAND v HOLLAND 1995-96

At Shahi Bagh Stadium, Peshawar, Pakistan on 22 February 1996.   Result: **ENGLAND** won by 49 runs.
Toss: England.   Award: G.A.Hick.   LOI debuts: Holland – F.Jansen.

During their first three-figure partnership (111 between Klaas van Noortwijk and Bas Zuiderent), Holland threatened an epic victory. Zuiderent (18) was the second-youngest after Sachin Tendulkar to score a World Cup fifty. Opener Flavian Aponso was taken ill and unable to bat.

ENGLAND		Runs	Balls	4/6
A.J.Stewart	b Bakker	5	13	–
N.M.K.Smith	c Clarke b Jansen	31	33	5
G.A.Hick	not out	104	133	6/2
G.P.Thorpe	lbw b Lefebvre	89	82	7/1
* M.A.Atherton	b Lubbers	10	10	–
N.H.Fairbrother	not out	24	29	1
† R.C.Russell				
D.G.Cork				
P.A.J.DeFreitas				
D.Gough				
P.J.Martin				
Extras	(lb 12, w 4)	16		
Total	(50 overs; 4 wickets)	**279**		

HOLLAND		Runs	Balls	4/6
N.E.Clarke	lbw b Cork	0	8	–
P.E.Cantrell	lbw b DeFreitas	28	44	4
T.B.M.de Leede	lbw b DeFreitas	41	42	7
* S.W.Lubbers	c Russell b DeFreitas	9	8	1
K-J.J.van Noortwijk	c Gough b Martin	64	82	3/2
B.Zuiderent	c Thorpe b Martin	54	93	2
R.P.Lefebvre	not out	11	14	–
† M.M.C.Schewe	not out	11	13	1
G.J.A.F.Aponso				
F.Jansen				
P-J.Bakker				
Extras	(lb 4, w 6, nb 2)	12		
Total	(50 overs; 6 wickets)	**230**		

HOLLAND	O	M	R	W
Lefebvre	10	1	40	1
Bakker	8	0	46	1
Jansen	7	0	40	1
Aponso	8	0	55	0
Lubbers	10	0	51	1
De Leede	2	0	9	0
Cantrell	5	0	26	0

ENGLAND	O	M	R	W
Cork	8	0	52	1
DeFreitas	10	3	31	3
Smith	8	0	27	0
Gough	3	0	23	0
Martin	10	1	42	2
Hick	5	0	23	0
Thorpe	6	0	28	0

FALL OF WICKETS
1-11, 2-42, 3-185, 4-212

FALL OF WICKETS
1-1, 2-46, 3-70, 4-84, 5-195, 6-210

Umpires: S.A.Bucknor (*WI*) (27) and K.T.Francis (*Sri Lanka*) (23).   **Referee:** J.R.Reid (*New Zealand*).

AUSTRALIA v KENYA 1995-96

At Indira Priyadarshani Stadium, Vishakhapatnam, India on 23 February 1996.   Result: **AUSTRALIA** won by 97 runs.
Toss: Kenya.   Award: M.E.Waugh.   LOI debuts: None.

The Waugh twins, one of three sets of brothers on view, shared a third-wicket stand of 207 off 198 balls, the highest for any wicket in World Cup matches. Mark's sixth LOI hundred took 109 balls. Steve completed 4000 runs in his 190th international. Kennedy Otieno (82) retired with cramp at 166 and returned with a runner at 188.

AUSTRALIA		Runs	Balls	4/6
* M.A.Taylor	c Modi b Suji	6	20	–
M.E.Waugh	c Suji b Ali	130	130	14/1
R.T.Ponting	c Otieno b Ali	6	14	I
S.R.Waugh	c and b Suji	82	92	5/1
S.G.Law	run out	35	32	3
M.G.Bevan	b Rajab Ali	12	13	–
† I.A.Healy	c E.T.Odumbe b Asif Karim	17	11	2
P.R.Reiffel	not out	3	2	–
S.K.Warne	not out	0	2	–
C.J.McDermott				
G.D.McGrath				
Extras	(b I, w 10, nb 2)	13		
Total	(50 overs; 7 wickets)	**304**		

KENYA		Runs	Balls	4/6
† K.Otieno	b McGrath	85	141	8/1
D.Chudasama	c Healy b McDermott	5	8	I
S.O.Tikolo	c Ponting b Reiffel	6	8	I
* M.Odumbe	c Reiffel b Bevan	50	53	7
H.Modi	b Bevan	10	21	I
E.T.Odumbe	c Bevan b Reiffel	14	34	–
D.L.Tikolo	not out	11	34	–
T.Odoyo	st Healy b Warne	10	6	2
M.Suji	not out	I	4	–
Asif Karim				
R.Ali				
Extras	(lb 7, w 6, nb 2)	15		
Total	(50 overs; 7 wickets)	**207**		

KENYA	O	M	R	W
Suji	10	I	55	2
Ali	10	0	45	3
Odoyo	8	0	58	0
E.T.Odumbe	4	0	21	0
Asif Karim	10	I	54	I
M.Odumbe	4	0	35	0
D.L.Tikolo	3	0	21	0
S.O.Tikolo	I	0	14	0

AUSTRALIA	O	M	R	W
McDermott	3	0	12	I
Reiffel	7	I	18	2
McGrath	10	0	44	I
S.R.Waugh	7	0	43	0
Warne	10	0	25	I
Bevan	8	0	35	2
M.E.Waugh	5	0	23	0

FALL OF WICKETS
1-10, 2-26, 3-233, 4-237, 5-261, 6-301, 7-301

FALL OF WICKETS
1-12, 2-30, 3-132, 4-167, 5-188, 6-195, 7-206

Umpires: C.J.Mitchley (SA) (24) and D.R.Shepherd (England) (59).

Referee: C.H.Lloyd (West Indies).

PAKISTAN v UNITED ARAB EMIRATES 1995-96

At Municipal Stadium, Gujranwala, Pakistan on 24 February 1996.   Result: **PAKISTAN** won by 9 wickets.
Toss: Pakistan.   Award: Mushtaq Ahmed.   LOI debuts: None.

Pakistan's Ramadan-enforced late entry was further delayed by early morning rain. Led by an Air Force helicopter, drying operations were completed in time for a 33-over match. Javed Miandad established a unique record by appearing in his sixth World Cup tournament. Mushtaq Ahmed took his 100th wicket in 91 internationals.

UNITED ARAB EMIRATES		Runs	Balls	4/6
G.Mylvaganam	b Mushtaq	13	50	I
Salim Raza	c Miandad b Aqib	22	20	2/1
Azhar Saeed	run out	I	13	–
Mazhar Hussain	c Waqar b Mushtaq	7	22	–
Mohammad Aslam	b Mushtaq	5	9	I
Mohammad Ishaq	b Wasim	12	20	I
Arshad Laiq	c Ijaz b Aqib	9	19	2
J.A.Samarasekera	b Waqar	10	21	–
S.F.Dukanwala	not out	21	19	1/1
* Sultan M.Zarawani	b Wasim	I	3	–
† Imtiaz Abbasi	not out	0	4	–
Extras	(lb I, w 5, nb 2)	8		
Total	(33 overs; 9 wickets)	**109**		

PAKISTAN		Runs	Balls	4/6
Aamir Sohail	b Samarasekera	5	5	I
Saeed Anwar	not out	40	49	4
Ijaz Ahmed	not out	50	58	4/1
Inzamam-ul-Haq				
Javed Miandad				
Salim Malik				
* Wasim Akram				
† Rashid Latif				
Mushtaq Ahmed				
Aqib Javed				
Waqar Younis				
Extras	(lb I, w 12, nb 4)	17		
Total	(18 overs; I wicket)	**112**		

PAKISTAN	O	M	R	W
Wasim Akram	7	I	25	2
Waqar Younis	7	I	33	I
Aqib Javed	6	0	18	2
Mushtaq Ahmed	7	0	16	3
Aamir Sohail	6	I	16	0

UNITED ARAB EMIRATES	O	M	R	W
Samarasekera	3	0	17	I
Arshad Laiq	4	0	24	0
Dukanwala	3	I	14	0
Salim Raza	3	0	17	0
Zarawani	3	0	23	0
Azhar Saeed	2	0	16	0

FALL OF WICKETS
1-27, 2-40, 3-47, 4-53, 5-54, 6-70, 7-80, 8-108, 9-109

FALL OF WICKETS
1-7

Umpires: B.C.Cooray (SL) (19) and S.Venkataraghavan (India) (6).

Referee: R.S.Madugalle (Sri Lanka).

ENGLAND v SOUTH AFRICA 1995-96

At Rawalpindi Cricket Stadium, Pakistan on 25 February 1996.   Result: **SOUTH AFRICA** won by 78 runs.
Toss: South Africa.   Award: J.N.Rhodes.   LOI debuts: None.

South Africa inflicted their sixth successive defeat on England. Phillip DeFreitas celebrated his 100th international by hitting the only six of the contest. The 15th Match, between Sri Lanka and West Indies, scheduled on 26 February at Colombo's R.Premadasa Stadium, was awarded to the hosts on forfeit when the visitors declined to appear.

SOUTH AFRICA		Runs	Balls	4/6
G.Kirsten	run out	38	60	4
† S.J.Palframan	c Russell b Martin	28	36	3
* W.J.Cronje	c Russell b Gough	15	31	1
D.J.Cullinan	b DeFreitas	34	42	2
J.H.Kallis	c Russell b Cork	26	42	2
J.N.Rhodes	b Martin	37	32	3
B.M.McMillan	b Smith	11	17	–
S.M.Pollock	c Fairbrother b Cork	12	13	–
P.L.Symcox	c Thorpe b Martin	1	4	–
C.R.Matthews	not out	9	13	–
P.S.de Villiers	c Smith b Gough	12	11	1
Extras	(lb 1, w 5, nb 1)	7		
Total	(50 overs)	**230**		

ENGLAND		Runs	Balls	4/6
* M.A.Atherton	c Palframan b Pollock	0	4	–
N.M.K.Smith	b De Villiers	11	24	1
G.A.Hick	c McMillan b De Villiers	14	27	1
G.P.Thorpe	c Palframan b Symcox	46	69	3
A.J.Stewart	run out	7	29	–
N.H.Fairbrother	c Palframan b Symcox	3	10	–
† R.C.Russell	c Rhodes b Pollock	12	32	–
D.G.Cork	b Matthews	17	32	1
P.A.J.DeFreitas	run out	22	24	1/1
D.Gough	b Matthews	11	13	2
P.J.Martin	not out	1	3	–
Extras	(lb 7, w 1)	8		
Total	(44.3 overs)	**152**		

ENGLAND	O	M	R	W
Cork	10	0	36	2
DeFreitas	10	0	55	1
Gough	10	0	48	2
Martin	10	0	33	3
Smith	8	0	40	1
Thorpe	2	0	17	0

SOUTH AFRICA	O	M	R	W
Pollock	8	1	16	2
De Villiers	7	1	27	2
Matthews	9.3	0	30	2
McMillan	6	0	17	0
Symcox	10	0	38	2
Cronje	4	0	17	0

FALL OF WICKETS
1-56, 2-85, 3-88, 4-137, 5-163, 6-195, 7-199, 8-202, 9-213, 10-230

Umpires: S.G.Randell (*Australia*) (69) and I.D.Robinson (*Zim*) (28).

FALL OF WICKETS
1-0, 2-22, 3-33, 4-52, 5-62, 6-97, 7-97, 8-139, 9-141, 10-152

Referee: J.R.Reid (*New Zealand*).

PAKISTAN v HOLLAND 1995-96

At Gaddafi Stadium, Lahore, Pakistan on 26 February 1996.   Result: **PAKISTAN** won by 8 wickets.   Toss: Holland.
Award: Waqar Younis.   LOI debuts: None.

Two of Pakistan's key players confirmed their full recovery from recent injury and illness problems: Waqar Younis (back) became the first to take four wickets in an innings on 16 occasions, while Saeed Anwar (typhoid) ended a commanding innings with a match-winning six.

HOLLAND		Runs	Balls	4/6
N.E.Clarke	c Rashid b Aqib	4	27	–
P.E.Cantrell	c Ijaz b Waqar	17	33	1
T.B.M.de Leede	c Rashid b Waqar	0	18	–
K-J.J.van Noortwijk	c Mushtaq b Aqib	33	89	2/1
G.J.A.F.Aponso	b Waqar	58	106	3/1
* R.P.Lefebvre	b Waqar	10	26	–
B.Zuiderent	run out	6	6	1
E.L.Gouka	not out	0	1	–
† M.M.C.Schewe				
F.Jansen				
P-J.Bakker				
Extras	(lb 7, w 4, nb 6)	17		
Total	(50 overs; 7 wickets)	**145**		

PAKISTAN		Runs	Balls	4/6
Aamir Sohail	c Jansen b Lefebvre	9	24	1
Saeed Anwar	not out	83	93	9/3
Ijaz Ahmed	c Lefebvre b Cantrell	39	54	2/1
Inzamam-ul-Haq	not out	18	14	–/1
Javed Miandad				
Salim Malik				
* Wasim Akram				
† Rashid Latif				
Mushtaq Ahmed				
Aqib Javed				
Waqar Younis				
Extras	(lb 1, w 1)	2		
Total	(30.4 overs; 2 wickets)	**151**		

PAKISTAN	O	M	R	W
Wasim Akram	10	1	30	0
Waqar Younis	10	0	26	4
Aqib Javed	9	2	25	2
Mushtaq Ahmed	10	2	27	0
Aamir Sohail	9	0	21	0
Salim Malik	2	0	9	0

HOLLAND	O	M	R	W
Lefebvre	7	1	20	1
Bakker	7	1	13	0
Jansen	2	0	22	0
De Leede	4	0	20	0
Aponso	5	0	38	0
Cantrell	4	0	18	1
Gouka	1.4	0	19	0

FALL OF WICKETS
1-16, 2-28, 3-29, 4-102, 5-130, 6-142, 7-145

Umpires: S.A.Bucknor (*West Indies*) (28) and K.T.Francis (*SL*) (24).

FALL OF WICKETS
1-10, 2-104

Referee: R.Subba Row (*England*).

ZIMBABWE v KENYA 1995-96

At Moin-ul-Haq Stadium, Patna, India on 26 (*void*), 27 February 1996.   Result: **ZIMBABWE** won by 5 wickets.
Toss: Zimbabwe.   Award: P.A.Strang.   LOI debuts: Kenya – Tariq Iqbal.

The original match was terminated by rain after 15.5 overs when Zimbabwe were 45 for 3. Under the tournament regulations, play was abandoned, the match and its statistics declared void and a new match begun on the reserve day. Leg-spinner Paul Strang took three wickets in four balls and finished with Zimbabwe's record LOI analysis.

KENYA		Runs	Balls	4/6		ZIMBABWE		Runs	Balls	4/6
D.Chudasama	run out	34	66	5		A.C.Waller	c Tikolo b M.Odumbe	30	32	3
† Tariq Iqbal	b Lock	1	20	–		G.W.Flower	b Ali	45	112	4
K.Otieno	b Peall	19	51	1		A.D.R.Campbell	c Tikolo b M.Odumbe	6	26	1
S.O.Tikolo	st A.Flower b B.C.Strang	0	6	–		G.J.Whittall	c E.T.Odumbe b Ali	6	36	–
* M.Odumbe	c B.C.Strang b P.A.Strang	30	64	1		*†A.Flower	lbw b Ali	5	8	1
H.Modi	b B.C.Strang	3	10	–		C.N.Evans	not out	8	18	1
E.T.Odumbe	c Campbell b P.A.Strang	20	55	–		H.H.Streak	not out	15	27	1
T.Odoyo	c G.W.Flower b P.A.Strang	0	2	–		P.A.Strang				
Asif Karim	lbw b P.A.Strang	0	1	–		S.G.Peall				
M.Suji	c G.W.Flower b P.A.Strang	15	24	1		B.C.Strang				
R.Ali	not out	0	–	–		A.C.I.Lock				
Extras	(lb 3, w 8, nb 1)	12				Extras	(b 3, lb 4, w 12, nb 3)	22		
Total	(49.4 overs)	**134**				**Total**	(42.2 overs; 5 wickets)	**137**		

ZIMBABWE	O	M	R	W		KENYA	O	M	R	W
Streak	7	2	23	0		Suji	9.2	0	37	0
Lock	8	2	19	1		Ali	8	1	22	3
Whittall	5	0	21	0		E.T.Odumbe	2	0	14	0
Peall	10	1	23	1		Odoyo	2	0	7	0
B.C.Strang	10	0	24	2		Asif Karim	10	1	21	0
P.A.Strang	9.4	1	21	5		M.Odumbe	10	2	24	2
						Tikolo	1	0	5	0

FALL OF WICKETS
1-7, 2-60, 3-61, 4-63, 5-67, 6-109, 7-109, 8-109, 9-134, 10-134

Umpires: Khizer Hayat (*Pakistan*) (49) and C.J.Mitchley (*SA*) (25).

FALL OF WICKETS
1-59, 2-79, 3-104, 4-108, 5-113

Referee: M.A.K.Pataudi (*India*).

NEW ZEALAND v UNITED ARAB EMIRATES 1995-96

At Iqbal Stadium, Faisalabad, Pakistan on 27 February 1996.   Result: **NEW ZEALAND** won by 109 runs.
Toss: United Arab Emirates.   Award: R.G.Twose.   LOI debuts: None.

Fog delayed the start by an hour and reduced the match to 47 overs apiece. Some scores erroneously showed Chris Cairns catching Mohammad Ishaq to equal the New Zealand fielding record of four catches.

NEW ZEALAND		Runs	Balls	4/6		UNITED ARAB EMIRATES		Runs	Balls	4/6
C.M.Spearman	b Salim Raza	78	77	10		Azhar Saeed	c Fleming b Nash	5	22	–
N.J.Astle	b Samarasekera	2	2	–		Salim Raza	c Kennedy b Morrison	21	17	3/1
S.P.Fleming	c and b Dukanwala	16	11	4		Mazhar Hussain	c Cairns b Thomson	29	54	5
R.G.Twose	c Mazhar b Azhar Saeed	92	112	8		V.Mehra	c Cairns b Thomson	12	31	1
C.L.Cairns	c Abbasi b Zarawani	6	11	–		Mohammad Ishaq	c Fleming b Kennedy	8	11	1
A.C.Parore	c Azhar Saeed b Zarawani	15	18	–		Mohammad Aslam	c Twose b Thomson	1	13	–
S.A.Thomson	not out	31	36	2		S.F.Dukanwala	c and b Cairns	8	18	–
*†L.K.Germon	b Azhar Saeed	3	6	–		Arshad Laiq	run out	14	37	2
D.J.Nash	lbw b Azhar Saeed	8	12	–		J.A.Samarasekera	not out	47	59	7
D.K.Morrison	not out	10	2	1/1		* Sultan M.Zarawani	c Thomson b Nash	13	18	1
R.J.Kennedy						† Imtiaz Abbasi	not out	2	6	–
Extras	(b 2, lb 12, nb 1)	15				Extras	(lb 2, w 3, nb 2)	7		
Total	(47 overs; 8 wickets)	**276**				**Total**	(47 overs; 9 wickets)	**167**		

UNITED ARAB EMIRATES	O	M	R	W		NEW ZEALAND	O	M	R	W
Samarasekera	6	0	30	1		Morrison	7	0	37	1
Arshad Laiq	2	0	16	0		Nash	9	1	34	2
Dukanwala	10	0	46	1		Cairns	10	2	31	1
Mazhar Hussain	3	0	28	0		Kennedy	6	0	20	1
Azhar Saeed	7	0	45	3		Thomson	10	2	20	3
Salim Raza	9	0	48	1		Astle	5	0	23	0
Zarawani	10	0	49	2						

FALL OF WICKETS
1-11, 2-42, 3-162, 4-173, 5-210, 6-228, 7-239, 8-266

Umpires: B.C.Cooray (*SL*) (20) and S.Venkataraghavan (*India*) (7).

FALL OF WICKETS
1-23, 2-29, 3-65, 4-70, 5-81, 6-88, 7-92, 8-124, 9-162

Referee: R.S.Madugalle (*Sri Lanka*).

INDIA v AUSTRALIA 1995-96

At Wankhede Stadium, Bombay, India on 27 February 1996.   Result: **AUSTRALIA** won by 16 runs.
Toss: Australia.   Award: M.E.Waugh.   LOI debuts: None.

Bombay's inaugural floodlit international saw Mark Waugh become the first to score consecutive World Cup hundreds.
Australia lost four wickets in the 50th over, two to run outs during an innings which featured five. Ian Healy became the
second wicket-keeper after Jeff Dujon to make 200 LOI dismissals.

AUSTRALIA		Runs	Balls	4/6	INDIA		Runs	Balls	4/6
M.E.Waugh	run out	126	135	8/3	A.Jadeja	lbw b Fleming	1	17	–
* M.A.Taylor	c Srinath b Raju	59	75	8/1	S.R.Tendulkar	st Healy b M.E.Waugh	90	88	14/1
R.T.Ponting	c Manjrekar b Raju	12	21	–	V.G.Kambli	b Fleming	0	2	–
S.R.Waugh	run out	7	15	–	* M.Azharuddin	b Fleming	10	17	1
S.G.Law	c and b Kumble	21	31	1	S.V.Manjrekar	c Healy b S.R.Waugh	62	93	7
M.G.Bevan	run out	6	5	–	M.Prabhakar	run out	3	6	–
S.Lee	run out	9	10	–	† N.R.Mongia	c Taylor b Warne	27	32	3
† I.A.Healy	c Kumble b Prasad	6	9	–	A.Kumble	b Fleming	17	23	3
S.K.Warne	c Azharuddin b Prasad	0	1	–	J.Srinath	c Lee b Fleming	7	12	1
D.W.Fleming	run out	0	1	–	B.K.V.Prasad	c Bevan b S.R.Waugh	0	3	–
G.D.McGrath	not out	0	–	–	S.L.V.Raju	not out	3	4	–
Extras	(lb 8, w 2, nb 2)	12			Extras	(b 5, lb 8, w 8, nb 1)	22		
Total	(50 overs)	258			Total	(48 overs)	242		

INDIA	O	M	R	W	AUSTRALIA	O	M	R	W
Prabhakar	10	0	55	0	McGrath	8	3	48	0
Srinath	10	1	51	0	Fleming	9	0	36	5
Prasad	10	0	49	2	Warne	10	1	28	1
Kumble	10	1	47	1	Lee	3	0	23	0
Raju	10	0	48	2	M.E.Waugh	10	0	44	1
					Bevan	5	0	28	0
					S.R.Waugh	3	0	22	2

FALL OF WICKETS
1-103, 2-140, 3-157, 4-232, 5-237, 6-244, 7-258, 8-258, 9-258, 10-258

Umpires: R.S.Dunne (NZ) (34) and D.R.Shepherd (England) (60).

FALL OF WICKETS
1-7, 2-7, 3-70, 4-143, 5-147, 6-201, 7-205, 8-224, 9-231, 10-242

Referee: C.H.Lloyd (West Indies).

WEST INDIES v KENYA 1995-96

At Nehru Stadium, Poona, India on 29 February 1996.   Result: **KENYA** won by 73 runs.   Toss: West Indies.
Award: M.Odumbe.   LOI debuts: None.

Kenya celebrated their extraordinary victory, one of international cricket's greatest reversals, with a lap of honour.
Defending a modest total, they dismissed West Indies for their lowest WC total and their second-lowest in all
internationals. Jimmy Adams equalled the LOI and WC records with five dismissals in an innings.

KENYA		Runs	Balls	4/6	WEST INDIES		Runs	Balls	4/6
D.Chudasama	c Lara b Walsh	8	7	2	S.L.Campbell	b Suji	4	21	1
† Tariq Iqbal	c Cuffy b Walsh	16	32	2	* R.B.Richardson	b Ali	5	11	1
K.Otieno	c Adams b Walsh	2	5	–	B.C.Lara	c Tariq Iqbal b Ali	8	11	1
S.O.Tikolo	c Adams b Harper	29	51	3/1	S.Chanderpaul	c Tikolo b M.Odumbe	19	47	3
* M.Odumbe	hit wicket b Bishop	6	30	–	K.L.T.Arthurton	run out	0	6	–
H.Modi	c Adams b Ambrose	28	74	1	† J.C.Adams	c Modi b M.Odumbe	9	37	–
M.Suji	c Lara b Harper	0	4	–	R.A.Harper	c Tariq Iqbal b M.Odumbe	17	18	2
T.Odoyo	st Adams b Harper	24	59	3	I.R.Bishop	not out	6	42	–
E.T.Odumbe	b Cuffy	1	4	–	C.E.L.Ambrose	run out	3	13	–
Asif Karim	c Adams b Ambrose	11	26	1	C.A.Walsh	c Chudasama b Asif Karim	4	8	1
R.Ali	not out	6	19	–	C.E.Cuffy	b Ali	1	8	–
Extras	(lb 8, w 14, nb 13)	35			Extras	(b 5, lb 6, w 4, nb 2)	17		
Total	(49.3 overs)	166			Total	(35.2 overs)	93		

WEST INDIES	O	M	R	W	KENYA	O	M	R	W
Ambrose	8.3	3	21	2	Suji	7	2	16	1
Walsh	9	0	46	3	Ali	7.2	2	17	3
Bishop	10	2	30	1	Asif Karim	8	1	19	1
Cuffy	8	0	31	1	M.Odumbe	10	3	15	3
Harper	10	4	15	3	Odoyo	3	0	15	0
Arthurton	4	0	15	0					

FALL OF WICKETS
1-15, 2-19, 3-45, 4-72, 5-77, 6-81, 7-125, 8-126, 9-155, 10-166

Umpires: Khizer Hayat (Pakistan) (50) and V.K.Ramaswamy (32).

FALL OF WICKETS
1-18, 2-22, 3-33, 4-35, 5-55, 6-65, 7-78, 8-83, 9-89, 10-93

Referee: M.A.K.Pataudi (India).

PAKISTAN v SOUTH AFRICA 1995-96

At National Stadium, Karachi, Pakistan on 29 February 1996.   Result: **SOUTH AFRICA** won by 5 wickets.
Toss: Pakistan.   Award: W.J.Cronje.   LOI debuts: None.

South Africa stunned a capacity crowd of about 33,000 by comfortably maintaining their unbeaten run. Their fourth win of the tournament guaranteed them top place in Group B. Aamir Sohail strained a groin muscle late in his innings and batted with a runner for his last three overs.

PAKISTAN		Runs	Balls	4/6	SOUTH AFRICA		Runs	Balls	4/6
Aamir Sohail	c Cronje b Pollock	111	139	8	A.C.Hudson	b Waqar	33	26	6
Saeed Anwar	c McMillan b Cronje	25	30	3	G.Kirsten	b Saqlain	44	57	5
Ijaz Ahmed	lbw b Cronje	0	2	–	B.M.McMillan	lbw b Waqar	1	4	–
Inzamam-ul-Haq	run out	23	39	3	D.J.Cullinan	b Waqar	65	76	6
Salim Malik	c Palframan b Adams	40	66	3	J.H.Kallis	c and b Saqlain	9	14	–
* Wasim Akram	not out	32	25	3	* W.J.Cronje	not out	45	72	2
† Rashid Latif	lbw b Matthews	0	1	–	S.M.Pollock	not out	20	27	1
Ramiz Raja	not out	2	2	–	† S.J.Palframan				
Mushtaq Ahmed					C.R.Matthews				
Saqlain Mushtaq					A.A.Donald				
Waqar Younis					P.R.Adams				
Extras	(b 1, lb 2, w 4, nb 2)	9			Extras	(b 8, lb 4, w 6, nb 8)	26		
Total	(50 overs; 6 wickets)	242			Total	(44.2 overs; 5 wickets)	243		

SOUTH AFRICA	O	M	R	W	PAKISTAN	O	M	R	W
Pollock	9	0	49	1	Wasim Akram	9.2	0	49	0
Matthews	10	0	47	1	Waqar Younis	8	0	50	3
Cronje	5	0	20	2	Mushtaq Ahmed	10	0	54	0
Donald	8	0	50	0	Aamir Sohail	6	0	35	0
Adams	10	0	42	1	Saqlain Mushtaq	10	1	38	2
McMillan	8	0	31	0	Salim Malik	1	0	5	0

FALL OF WICKETS   FALL OF WICKETS
1-52, 2-52, 3-112, 4-189, 5-233, 6-235   1-51, 2-53, 3-111, 4-125, 5-203

Umpires: S.A.Bucknor (*West Indies*) (29) and K.T.Francis (*SL*) (25).   **Referee:** R.Subba Row (*England*).

AUSTRALIA v ZIMBABWE 1995-96

At Vidarbha CA Ground, Nagpur, India on 1 March 1996.   Result: **AUSTRALIA** won by 8 wickets.
Toss: Zimbabwe.   Award: S.K.Warne.   LOI debuts: None.

Had Zimbabwe thrown off the shackles imposed by some high quality fielding on a small ground and achieved a bigger total, Mark Waugh would have had an excellent chance of scoring his third hundred in succession.

ZIMBABWE		Runs	Balls	4/6	AUSTRALIA		Runs	Balls	4/6
A.C.Waller	run out	67	102	10	* M.A.Taylor	c B.C.Strang b P.A.Strang	34	51	5
G.W.Flower	b McGrath	4	16	–	M.E.Waugh	not out	76	109	10
G.J.Whittall	c and b S.R.Waugh	6	22	1	R.T.Ponting	c and b P.A.Strang	33	51	4
A.D.R.Campbell	c M.E.Waugh b S.R.Waugh	5	10	1	S.R.Waugh	not out	5	7	1
*† A.Flower	st Healy b Warne	7	15	1	S.G.Law				
C.N.Evans	c Healy b Warne	18	25	2/1	M.G.Bevan				
H.H.Streak	c S.R.Waugh b Fleming	13	42	–	S.Lee				
P.A.Strang	not out	16	29	1	† I.A.Healy				
B.C.Strang	b Fleming	0	2	–	S.K.Warne				
S.G.Peall	c Healy b Warne	0	4	–	D.W.Fleming				
A.C.I.Lock	b Warne	5	11	1	G.D.McGrath				
Extras	(lb 8, w 3, nb 2)	13			Extras	(b 6, lb 2, w 1, nb 1)	10		
Total	(45.3 overs)	154			Total	(36 overs; 2 wickets)	158		

AUSTRALIA	O	M	R	W	ZIMBABWE	O	M	R	W
McGrath	8	2	12	1	Streak	10	3	29	0
Fleming	9	1	30	2	Lock	4	0	25	0
Lee	4	2	8	0	B.C.Strang	3	0	20	0
S.R.Waugh	7	2	22	2	Whittall	2	0	11	0
Warne	9.3	1	34	4	P.A.Strang	10	2	33	2
M.E.Waugh	5	0	30	0	Peall	4	0	20	0
Law	3	0	10	0	G.W.Flower	3	0	12	0

FALL OF WICKETS   FALL OF WICKETS
1-21, 2-41, 3-55, 4-68, 5-106, 6-126, 7-140, 8-140, 9-145, 10-154   1-92, 2-150

Umpires: R.S.Dunne (*NZ*) (35) and D.R.Shepherd (*England*) (61).   **Referee:** C.H.Lloyd (*West Indies*).

HOLLAND v UNITED ARAB EMIRATES 1995-96

At Gaddafi Stadium, Lahore, Pakistan on 1 March 1996.   Result: **UNITED ARAB EMIRATES** won by 7 wickets.
Toss: United Arab Emirates.   Awards: S.F.Dukanwala and Salim Raza.   LOI debuts: Holland – R.F.van Oosterom;
UAE – Saeed-al-Saffar.

The first official international between two ICC Associate Members produced the Emirates' first win in seven matches,
first century partnership, record total, highest individual score and best bowling analysis. Salim Raza scored a 41-ball
fifty and perished trying to equal Viv Richards's WC record of seven sixes.

HOLLAND		Runs	Balls	4/6
N.E.Clarke	c Mehra b Shahzad	0	11	–
P.E.Cantrell	c Abbasi b Azhar Saeed	47	106	1
G.J.A.F.Aponso	c and b Dukanwala	45	80	7
T.B.M.de Leede	c and b Azhar Saeed	36	47	3
K-J.J.van Noortwijk	c Zarawani b Dukanwala	26	19	3
* S.W.Lubbers	c Saeed-al-Saffar b Zarawani	8	8	1
R.P.Lefebvre	c Ishaq b Dukanwala	12	9	–/1
B.Zuiderent	st Abbasi b Dukanwala	3	5	–
† M.M.C.Schewe	b Dukanwala	6	6	–
R.F.van Oosterom	not out	2	5	–
P-J.Bakker	not out	0	4	–
Extras	(b 5, lb 15, w 11)	31		
Total	(50 overs; 9 wickets)	**216**		

UNITED ARAB EMIRATES		Runs	Balls	4/6
Azhar Saeed	run out	32	82	3
Salim Raza	c Zuiderent b Lubbers	84	68	7/6
Mazhar Hussain	c Clarke b Lefebvre	16	15	3
V.Mehra	not out	29	48	2
Mohammad Ishaq	not out	51	53	8
J.A.Samarasekera				
S.F.Dukanwala				
* Sultan M.Zarawani				
Saeed-al-Saffar				
Imtiaz Abbasi				
† Shahzad Altaf				
Extras	(lb 7, w 1)	8		
Total	(44.2 overs; 3 wickets)	**220**		

UNITED ARAB EMIRATES	O	M	R	W
Shahzad Altaf	10	3	15	1
Samarasekera	9	1	35	0
Saeed-al-Saffar	3	0	25	0
Dukanwala	10	0	29	5
Zarawani	8	0	40	1
Salim Raza	5	0	23	0
Azhar Saeed	5	0	29	2

HOLLAND	O	M	R	W
Bakker	8	0	41	0
Lefebvre	8	0	24	1
Lubbers	9	0	38	1
Cantrell	8	0	30	0
Aponso	7.2	0	47	0
De Leede	4	0	33	0

FALL OF WICKETS
1-3, 2-77, 3-148, 4-153, 5-168, 6-200, 7-200, 8-209, 9-210

FALL OF WICKETS
1-117, 2-135, 3-138

Umpires: Mahboob Shah (28) and S.G.Randell (*Australia*) (70).

Referee: Nasim-ul-Ghani (*Pakistan*).

INDIA v SRI LANKA 1995-96

At Feroz Shah Kotla, Delhi, India on 2 March 1996.   Result: **SRI LANKA** won by 6 wickets.   Toss: Sri Lanka.
Award: S.T.Jayasuriya.   LOI debuts: None.

Sachin Tendulkar became the first Indian to score six LOI hundreds and added 175 off 156 balls with his captain, a
national WC record for any wicket. Sanath Jayasuriya savaged 22 runs from Manoj Prabhakar's second over. The latter
bowled off-spin in his second spell, was dropped and swiftly retired from international cricket.

INDIA		Runs	Balls	4/6
M.Prabhakar	c Gurusinha b Pushpakumara	7	36	1
S.R.Tendulkar	run out	137	137	8/5
S.V.Manjrekar	c Kaluwitharana b Dharmasena	32	46	2/1
* M.Azharuddin	not out	72	80	4
V.G.Kambli	not out	1	1	–
A.Jadeja				
† N.R.Mongia				
J.Srinath				
A.Kumble				
S.A.Ankola				
B.K.V.Prasad				
Extras	(b 4, lb 7, w 11)	22		
Total	(50 overs; 3 wickets)	**271**		

SRI LANKA		Runs	Balls	4/6
S.T.Jayasuriya	c Prabhakar b Kumble	79	76	9/2
† R.S.Kaluwitharana	c Kumble b Prasad	26	16	6
A.P.Gurusinha	run out	25	27	2/1
P.A.de Silva	st Mongia b Kumble	8	14	1
* A.Ranatunga	not out	46	63	2
H.P.Tillekeratne	not out	70	98	6
R.S.Mahanama				
H.D.P.K.Dharmasena				
W.P.U.C.J.Vaas				
K.R.Pushpakumara				
M.Muralitharan				
Extras	(b 4, lb 9, w 2, nb 3)	18		
Total	(48.4 overs; 4 wickets)	**272**		

SRI LANKA	O	M	R	W
Vaas	9	3	37	0
Pushpakumara	8	0	53	1
Muralitharan	10	1	42	0
Dharmasena	9	0	53	1
Jayasuriya	10	0	52	0
Ranatunga	4	0	23	0

INDIA	O	M	R	W
Prabhakar	4	0	47	0
Srinath	9.4	0	51	0
Prasad	10	1	53	1
Ankola	5	0	28	0
Kumble	10	1	39	2
Tendulkar	10	0	41	0

FALL OF WICKETS
1-27, 2-93, 3-268

FALL OF WICKETS
1-53, 2-129, 3-137, 4-141

Umpires: C.J.Mitchley (*SA*) (26) and I.D.Robinson (*Zimbabwe*) (29).

Referee: J.R.Reid (*New Zealand*).

PAKISTAN v ENGLAND 1995-96

At National Stadium, Karachi, Pakistan on 3 March 1996.   Result: **PAKISTAN** won by 7 wickets.   Toss: England.
Award: Aamir Sohail.   LOI debuts: None.

Robin Smith and Mike Atherton put on 147 from 172 balls to record England's highest LOI opening stand against a Test-playing country and the best for any wicket against Pakistan. Inzamam-ul-Haq celebrated his 100th international and his 26th birthday by scoring 50 off 54 balls.

ENGLAND		Runs	Balls	4/6
R.A.Smith	c Waqar b Salim	75	92	8/1
* M.A.Atherton	b Aamir	66	91	6
G.A.Hick	st Rashid b Aamir	1	2	–
G.P.Thorpe	not out	52	64	3
N.H.Fairbrother	c Wasim b Mushtaq	13	21	1
† R.C.Russell	c and b Mushtaq	4	7	–
D.A.Reeve	b Mushtaq	3	5	–
D.G.Cork	lbw b Waqar	0	2	–
D.Gough	b Wasim	14	15	1
P.J.Martin	run out	2	4	–
R.K.Illingworth	not out	1	1	–
Extras	(lb 11, w 4, nb 3)	18		
Total	(50 overs; 9 wickets)	**249**		

PAKISTAN	O	M	R	W
Wasim Akram	7	1	31	1
Waqar Younis	10	1	45	1
Aqib Javed	7	0	34	0
Mushtaq Ahmed	10	0	53	3
Aamir Sohail	10	0	48	2
Salim Malik	6	1	27	1

FALL OF WICKETS
1-147, 2-151, 3-156, 4-194, 5-204, 6-212, 7-217, 8-241, 9-247

Umpires: B.C.Cooray (SL) (21) and S.Venkataraghavan (India) (8).

PAKISTAN		Runs	Balls	4/6
Aamir Sohail	c Thorpe b Illingworth	42	56	6
Saeed Anwar	c Russell b Cork	71	72	8
Ijaz Ahmed	c Russell b Cork	70	83	6
Inzamam-ul-Haq	not out	53	54	6
Javed Miandad	not out	11	21	–
Salim Malik				
* Wasim Akram				
† Rashid Latif				
Mushtaq Ahmed				
Waqar Younis				
Aqib Javed				
Extras	(lb 1, w 2)	3		
Total	(47.4 overs; 3 wickets)	**250**		

ENGLAND	O	M	R	W
Cork	10	0	59	2
Martin	9	0	45	0
Gough	10	0	45	0
Illingworth	10	0	46	1
Reeve	6.4	0	37	0
Hick	2	0	17	0

FALL OF WICKETS
1-81, 2-139, 3-214

Referee: R.S.Madugalle (Sri Lanka).

AUSTRALIA v WEST INDIES 1995-96

At Sawai Mansingh Stadium, Jaipur, India on 4 March 1996.   Result: **WEST INDIES** won by 4 wickets.
Toss: Australia.   Award: R.B.Richardson.   LOI debuts: None.

Recovering impressively from their dramatic reversal at the hands of Kenya, West Indies inflicted Australia's first defeat of the tournament. Ricky Ponting completed his second LOI hundred from 110 balls.

AUSTRALIA		Runs	Balls	4/6
M.E.Waugh	st Browne b Harper	30	62	1
* M.A.Taylor	c Browne b Walsh	9	38	–
R.T.Ponting	run out	102	112	5/1
S.R.Waugh	b Walsh	57	64	3/1
M.G.Bevan	run out	2	3	–
S.G.Law	not out	12	12	–
† I.A.Healy	run out	3	5	–
P.R.Reiffel	not out	4	6	–
S.K.Warne				
D.W.Fleming				
G.D.McGrath				
Extras	(lb 3, w 6, nb 1)	10		
Total	(50 overs; 6 wickets)	**229**		

WEST INDIES	O	M	R	W
Ambrose	10	4	25	0
Walsh	9	2	35	2
Bishop	9	0	52	0
Harper	10	0	46	1
Arthurton	9	0	53	0
Adams	3	0	15	0

FALL OF WICKETS
1-22, 2-84, 3-194, 4-200, 5-216, 6-224

Umpires: Mahboob Shah (Pak) (29) and D.R.Shepherd (England) (62).

WEST INDIES		Runs	Balls	4/6
S.L.Campbell	c Healy b Fleming	1	5	–
† C.O.Browne	run out	10	18	2
B.C.Lara	c McGrath b M.E.Waugh	60	70	7
* R.B.Richardson	not out	93	132	10/1
S.Chanderpaul	b M.E.Waugh	10	17	–
R.A.Harper	lbw b Reiffel	22	28	2
K.L.T.Arthurton	lbw b M.E.Waugh	0	3	–
J.C.Adams	not out	17	22	3
I.R.Bishop				
C.E.L.Ambrose				
C.A.Walsh				
Extras	(lb 12, w 5, nb 2)	19		
Total	(48.5 overs; 6 wickets)	**232**		

AUSTRALIA	O	M	R	W
Reiffel	10	3	45	1
Fleming	7.5	1	44	1
McGrath	9	0	46	0
Warne	10	1	30	0
M.E.Waugh	10	0	38	3
Bevan	2	0	17	0

FALL OF WICKETS
1-1, 2-26, 3-113, 4-146, 5-194, 6-196

Referee: R.Subba Row (England).

SOUTH AFRICA v HOLLAND 1995-96

At Rawalpindi Cricket Stadium, Pakistan on 5 March 1996.　Result: **SOUTH AFRICA** won by 160 runs.
Toss: South Africa.　Award: A.C.Hudson.　LOI debuts: None.

South Africa easily defended their highest total in internationals to register their tenth consecutive victory. Gary Kirsten and Andrew Hudson (whose second LOI hundred took 104 balls) shared a World Cup opening partnership record of 186. The 47-year-old former Barbados batsman, Nolan Clarke, produced an exuberant cameo.

SOUTH AFRICA		Runs	Balls	4/6
G.Kirsten	c Zuiderent b Aponso	83	98	6
A.C.Hudson	c Van Oosterom b Gouka	161	133	13/4
* W.J.Cronje	c Lubbers b Cantrell	41	38	3
D.J.Cullinan	not out	19	17	1
J.H.Kallis	not out	17	16	–
B.M.McMillan				
S.M.Pollock				
† S.J.Palframan				
P.L.Symcox				
C.R.Matthews				
A.A.Donald				
Extras	(lb 5, w 2)	7		
Total	(50 overs; 3 wickets)	**328**		

HOLLAND		Runs	Balls	4/6
N.E.Clarke	c Pollock b Donald	32	46	4/2
P.E.Cantrell	c and b Matthews	23	39	4
T.B.M.de Leede	b Donald	12	26	2
K-J.J.van Noortwijk	c Palframan b Symcox	9	24	1
G.J.A.F.Aponso	c Kirsten b Symcox	6	31	–
B.Zuiderent	run out	27	50	2
† M.M.C.Schewe	b Matthews	20	34	1
E.L.Gouka	c Kallis b Pollock	19	35	2
R.F.van Oosterom	not out	5	15	–
* S.W.Lubbers	not out	2	2	–
P-J.Bakker				
Extras	(lb 7, w 5, nb 1)	13		
Total	(50 overs; 8 wickets)	**168**		

HOLLAND	O	M	R	W
Bakker	10	1	64	0
Lubbers	8	0	50	0
De Leede	10	0	59	0
Aponso	10	0	57	1
Cantrell	10	0	61	1
Gouka	2	0	32	1

SOUTH AFRICA	O	M	R	W
Pollock	8	0	35	1
Matthews	10	0	38	2
Donald	6	0	21	2
Cronje	3	1	3	0
Symcox	10	2	22	2
McMillan	4	2	5	0
Kallis	7	1	30	0
Cullinan	2	0	7	0

FALL OF WICKETS
1-186, 2-274, 3-301

FALL OF WICKETS
1-56, 2-70, 3-81, 4-86, 5-97, 6-126, 7-158, 8-163

Umpires: Khizer Hayat (51) and S.G.Randell (*Australia*) (71).

Referee: Nasim-ul-Ghani (*Pakistan*).

INDIA v ZIMBABWE 1995-96

At Green Park, Kanpur, India on 6 March 1996.　Result: **INDIA** won by 40 runs.　Toss: Zimbabwe.
Award: A.Jadeja.　LOI debuts: None.

Zimbabwe's defeat ended their World Cup campaign. They gave Vinod Kambli three lives before he had completed his second LOI hundred off 107 balls and added 142 off 174 balls with Navjot Sidhu.

INDIA		Runs	Balls	4/6
S.R.Tendulkar	b Streak	3	12	–
N.S.Sidhu	c Streak b P.A.Strang	80	116	5
S.V.Manjrekar	c Campbell b Lock	2	18	–
* M.Azharuddin	c Campbell b B.C.Strang	2	10	–
V.G.Kambli	c G.W.Flower b Lock	106	110	11
A.Jadeja	not out	44	27	3/2
† N.R.Mongia	not out	6	9	–
A.Kumble				
J.Srinath				
B.K.V.Prasad				
S.L.V.Raju				
Extras	(lb 1, w 3)	4		
Total	(50 overs; 5 wickets)	**247**		

ZIMBABWE		Runs	Balls	4/6
A.C.Waller	c Tendulkar b Kumble	22	36	1
G.W.Flower	c Azharuddin b Raju	30	42	1
G.J.Whittall	run out	10	28	–
A.D.R.Campbell	c and b Jadeja	28	56	4
*†A.Flower	b Raju	28	40	1
C.N.Evans	c Srinath b Jadeja	6	6	1
H.H.Streak	lbw b Raju	30	38	3
P.A.Strang	b Srinath	14	22	1
B.C.Strang	lbw b Srinath	3	13	–
S.G.Peall	c Raju b Kumble	9	14	2
A.C.I.Lock	not out	2	4	–
Extras	(b 4, lb 9, w 11, nb 1)	25		
Total	(49.4 overs)	**207**		

ZIMBABWE	O	M	R	W
Streak	10	4	29	1
Lock	10	1	57	2
B.C.Strang	5	1	22	1
P.A.Strang	10	0	55	1
Peall	6	0	35	0
Whittall	3	0	19	0
G.W.Flower	3	1	16	0
Campbell	3	0	13	0

INDIA	O	M	R	W
Srinath	10	1	36	2
Prasad	7	0	40	0
Kumble	9.4	1	33	2
Raju	10	2	30	3
Tendulkar	6	0	23	0
Jadeja	7	0	32	2

FALL OF WICKETS
1-5, 2-25, 3-32, 4-174, 5-219

FALL OF WICKETS
1-59, 2-59, 3-96, 4-99, 5-106, 6-165, 7-173, 8-193, 9-195, 10-207

Referee: J.R.Reid (*New Zealand*).

Umpires: S.A.Bucknor (*WI*) (30) and C.J.Mitchley (*South Africa*) (27).

SRI LANKA v KENYA 1995-96

At Asgiriya Stadium, Kandy, Sri Lanka on 6 March 1996.   Result: **SRI LANKA** won by 144 runs.   Toss: Kenya.
Award: P.A.de Silva.   LOI debuts: Kenya – L.Onyango.

This batting extravaganza began with Sri Lanka posting 102 for 2 in the opening ten overs and produced a world record LOI total and the highest WC match aggregate. Aravinda de Silva converted Sri Lanka's first WC hundred (off 92 balls) into a national record score. Both he and Arjuna Ranatunga, who scored a WC record 29-ball fifty, passed 5000 runs.

SRI LANKA		Runs	Balls	4/6
S.T.Jayasuriya	c D.L.Tikolo b E.T.Odumbe	44	27	5/3
† R.S.Kaluwitharana	b E.T.Odumbe	33	18	4/2
A.P.Gurusinha	c Onyango b Asif Karim	84	103	7/3
P.A.de Silva	c Modi b Suji	145	115	14/5
* A.Ranatunga	not out	75	40	13/1
H.P.Tillekeratne	run out	0	1	–
R.S.Mahanama	not out	0	–	–
W.P.U.C.J.Vaas				
H.D.P.K.Dharmasena				
K.R.Pushpakumara				
M.Muralitharan				
Extras	(lb 6, w 11)	17		
Total	(50 overs; 5 wickets)	**398**		

KENYA		Runs	Balls	4/6
D.Chudasama	b Muralitharan	27	23	5
† K.Otieno	b Vaas	14	28	1/1
S.O.Tikolo	b Dharmasena	96	95	8/4
* M.Odumbe	st Kaluwitharana b Muralitharan	0	2	–
H.Modi	run out	41	82	2
D.L.Tikolo	not out	25	40	2/1
E.T.Odumbe	c Muralitharan b Ranatunga	4	13	–
L.Onyango	c sub b Ranatunga	23	18	2/1
M.Suji	not out	2	4	–
Asif Karim				
R.Ali				
Extras	(b 1, lb 9, w 7, nb 5)	22		
Total	(50 overs; 7 wickets)	**254**		

KENYA	O	M	R	W
Suji	9	0	85	1
Ali	6	0	67	0
Onyango	4	0	31	0
E.T.Odumbe	5	0	34	2
Asif Karim	10	0	50	1
D.L.Tikolo	2	0	13	0
M.Odumbe	9	0	74	0
S.O.Tikolo	5	0	38	0

SRI LANKA	O	M	R	W
Vaas	10	0	44	1
Pushpakumara	7	0	46	0
Muralitharan	10	1	40	2
Dharmasena	10	0	45	1
Jayasuriya	7	0	34	0
Ranatunga	5	0	31	2
Tillekeratne	1	0	4	0

FALL OF WICKETS
1-83, 2-88, 3-272, 4-378, 5-384

FALL OF WICKETS
1-47, 2-51, 3-51, 4-188, 5-196, 6-215, 7-246

Referee: M.A.K.Pataudi (India).

Umpires: R.S.Dunne (NZ) (36) and V.K.Ramaswamy (India) (33).

PAKISTAN v NEW ZEALAND 1995-96

At Gaddafi Stadium, Lahore, Pakistan on 6 March 1996.   Result: **PAKISTAN** won by 46 runs.   Toss: New Zealand.
Award: Salim Malik.   LOI debuts: None.

Aamir Sohail deputised as captain in this match and the quarter-final after Wasim Akram ruptured a side muscle during his innings. Rashid Latif was the first Pakistan wicket-keeper to make five dismissals in a WC innings.

PAKISTAN		Runs	Balls	4/6
Aamir Sohail	c Thomson b Kennedy	50	62	10
Saeed Anwar	run out	62	67	6/1
Ijaz Ahmed	c Spearman b Cairns	26	46	–
Inzamam-ul-Haq	run out	39	41	4/1
Javed Miandad	run out	5	19	–
Salim Malik	not out	55	47	6
* Wasim Akram	not out	28	26	3
† Rashid Latif				
Waqar Younis				
Mushtaq Ahmed				
Aqib Javed				
Extras	(lb 5, w 5, nb 6)	16		
Total	(50 overs; 5 wickets)	**281**		

NEW ZEALAND		Runs	Balls	4/6
C.M.Spearman	c Rashid b Aqib	14	13	2
N.J.Astle	c Rashid b Waqar	6	17	1
*†L.K.Germon	c sub (Ata-ur-Rehman) b Mushtaq	41	67	1
S.P.Fleming	st Rashid b Salim	42	43	7
R.G.Twose	c Salim b Mushtaq	24	38	–
C.L.Cairns	c Rashid b Aamir	32	34	1/2
A.C.Parore	c Mushtaq b Salim	36	34	3
S.A.Thomson	c Rashid b Waqar	13	25	–
D.J.Nash	not out	5	13	–
R.J.Kennedy	b Aqib	2	3	–
D.K.Morrison	absent hurt			
Extras	(b 4, lb 9, w 6, nb 1)	20		
Total	(47.3 overs)	**235**		

NEW ZEALAND	O	M	R	W
Morrison	2	0	17	0
Nash	10	1	49	0
Cairns	10	1	53	1
Kennedy	5	0	32	1
Astle	9	0	50	0
Thomson	6	0	35	0
Twose	8	0	40	0

PAKISTAN	O	M	R	W
Waqar Younis	9	2	32	2
Aqib Javed	7.3	0	45	2
Mushtaq Ahmed	10	0	32	2
Salim Malik	7	0	41	2
Ijaz Ahmed	4	0	21	0
Aamir Sohail	10	0	51	1

FALL OF WICKETS
1-70, 2-139, 3-155, 4-173, 5-200

FALL OF WICKETS
1-23, 2-23, 3-83, 4-132, 5-132, 6-182, 7-221, 8-228, 9-235

Referee: C.H.Lloyd (West Indies).

Umpires: K.T.Francis (SL) (26) and I.D.Robinson (Zimbabwe) (30).

ENGLAND v SRI LANKA 1995-96

At Iqbal Stadium, Faisalabad, Pakistan on 9 March 1996.   Result: **SRI LANKA** won by 5 wickets.   Toss: England.
Award: S.T.Jayasuriya.   LOI debuts: None.

After what amounted to a practice period of three weeks and 30 matches, the tournament proper began. Another onslaught by Sri Lanka's left-handed whirlwind, Sanath Jayasuriya, ended England's World Cup trail. He scored 50 off 30 balls, hit boundaries off four successive balls from Richard Illingworth and took 22 off an over from Phillip DeFreitas.

ENGLAND		Runs	Balls	4/6
R.A.Smith	run out	25	41	3
* M.A.Atherton	c Kaluwitharana b Vaas	22	27	2
G.A.Hick	c Ranatunga b Muralitharan	8	21	–
G.P.Thorpe	b Dharmasena	14	31	1
P.A.J.DeFreitas	lbw b Jayasuriya	67	64	5/2
A.J.Stewart	b Muralitharan	17	38	1
† R.C.Russell	b Dharmasena	9	17	–
D.A.Reeve	b Jayasuriya	35	34	5
D.Gough	not out	26	26	2
P.J.Martin	not out	0	1	–
R.K.Illingworth				
Extras	(lb 8, w 4)	12		
Total	(50 overs; 8 wickets)	**235**		

SRI LANKA		Runs	Balls	4/6
S.T.Jayasuriya	st Russell b Reeve	82	44	13/3
† R.S.Kaluwitharana	b Illingworth	8	3	2
A.P.Gurusinha	run out	45	63	5
P.A.de Silva	c Smith b Hick	31	30	5
* A.Ranatunga	lbw b Gough	25	17	5
H.P.Tillekeratne	not out	19	50	1
R.S.Mahanama	not out	22	38	2
H.D.P.K.Dharmasena				
W.P.U.C.J.Vaas				
M.Muralitharan				
G.P.Wickremasinghe				
Extras	(lb 1, w 2, nb 1)	4		
Total	(40.4 overs; 5 wickets)	**236**		

SRI LANKA	O	M	R	W
Wickremasinghe	7	0	43	0
Vaas	8	1	29	1
Muralitharan	10	1	37	2
Dharmasena	10	0	30	2
Jayasuriya	9	0	46	2
De Silva	6	0	42	0

ENGLAND	O	M	R	W
Martin	9	0	41	0
Illingworth	10	1	72	1
Gough	10	1	36	1
DeFreitas	3.4	0	38	0
Reeve	4	1	14	1
Hick	4	0	34	1

FALL OF WICKETS
1-31, 2-58, 3-66, 4-94, 5-145, 6-171, 7-173, 8-235

FALL OF WICKETS
1-12, 2-113, 3-165, 4-194, 5-198

Umpires: Mahboob Shah (30) and I.D.Robinson (*Zimbabwe*) (31).

Referee: Nasim-ul-Ghani (*Pakistan*).

INDIA v PAKISTAN 1995-96

At Chinnaswamy Stadium, Bangalore, India on 9 March 1996.   Result: **INDIA** won by 39 runs.   Toss: India.
Award: N.S.Sidhu.   LOI debuts: None.

Bangalore's inaugural floodlit international coincided with the first meeting of these teams on Indian soil for 6½ years. Waqar Younis became the fourth bowler to take 200 LOI wickets when he dismissed Ajay Jadeja after he had plundered 22 off one over. Pakistan were docked an over for their tardy bowling rate. Javed Miandad announced his final retirement.

INDIA		Runs	Balls	4/6
N.S.Sidhu	b Mushtaq	93	115	11
S.R.Tendulkar	b Rehman	31	59	3
S.V.Manjrekar	c Miandad b Aamir Sohail	20	43	–
* M.Azharuddin	c Rashid b Waqar	27	23	1/1
V.G.Kambli	b Mushtaq	24	26	1
A.Jadeja	c Aamir b Waqar	45	26	4/2
† N.R.Mongia	run out	3	3	–
A.Kumble	c Miandad b Aqib	10	6	2
J.Srinath	not out	12	4	2
B.K.V.Prasad	not out	0	–	–
S.L.V.Raju				
Extras	(lb 3, w 15, nb 4)	22		
Total	(50 overs; 8 wickets)	**287**		

PAKISTAN		Runs	Balls	4/6
* Aamir Sohail	b Prasad	55	46	9/1
Saeed Anwar	c Kumble b Srinath	48	32	5/2
Ijaz Ahmed	c Srinath b Prasad	12	16	1
Inzamam-ul-Haq	c Mongia b Prasad	12	22	1
Salim Malik	lbw b Kumble	38	50	4
Javed Miandad	run out	38	68	2
† Rashid Latif	st Mongia b Raju	26	25	1/2
Mushtaq Ahmed	c and b Kumble	0	2	–
Waqar Younis	not out	4	19	–
Ata-ur-Rehman	lbw b Kumble	0	1	–
Aqib Javed	not out	6	10	–
Extras	(b 1, lb 3, w 5)	9		
Total	(49 overs; 9 wickets)	**248**		

PAKISTAN	O	M	R	W
Waqar Younis	10	1	67	2
Aqib Javed	10	0	67	1
Ata-ur-Rehman	10	0	40	1
Mushtaq Ahmed	10	0	56	2
Aamir Sohail	5	0	29	1
Salim Malik	5	0	25	0

INDIA	O	M	R	W
Srinath	9	0	61	1
Prasad	10	0	45	3
Kumble	10	0	48	3
Raju	10	0	46	1
Tendulkar	5	0	25	0
Jadeja	5	0	19	0

FALL OF WICKETS
1-90, 2-138, 3-168, 4-200, 5-226, 6-236, 7-260, 8-279

FALL OF WICKETS
1-84, 2-113, 3-122, 4-132, 5-184, 6-231, 7-232, 8-239, 9-239

Umpires: S.A.Bucknor (*WI*) (31) and D.R.Shepherd (*England*) (63).

Referee: R.Subba Row (*England*).

539

SOUTH AFRICA v WEST INDIES 1995-96

At National Stadium, Karachi, Pakistan on 11 March 1996.   Result: **WEST INDIES** won by 19 runs.
Toss: West Indies.   Award: B.C.Lara.   LOI debuts: None.

South Africa's attempt to equal the record sequence of 11 limited-overs wins was thwarted by their lack of technique against spin, the unlikely trio of Harper, Adams and Arthurton sharing eight wickets. Brian Lara's seventh LOI hundred was his first in 13 World Cup innings.

WEST INDIES		Runs	Balls	4/6
S.Chanderpaul	c Cullinan b McMillan	56	93	4
† C.O.Browne	c Cullinan b Matthews	26	18	3
B.C.Lara	c Pollock b Symcox	111	94	16
* R.B.Richardson	c Hudson b Symcox	10	27	–
R.A.Harper	lbw b McMillan	9	15	1
R.I.C.Holder	run out	5	9	–
K.L.T.Arthurton	c Kirsten b Adams	1	5	–
J.C.Adams	not out	13	17	1
I.R.Bishop	b Adams	17	22	1/1
C.E.L.Ambrose	not out	0	1	–
C.A.Walsh				
Extras	(b 2, lb 11, w 2, nb 1)	16		
Total	(50 overs; 8 wickets)	**264**		

SOUTH AFRICA	O	M	R	W
Pollock	9	0	46	0
Matthews	10	0	42	1
Cronje	3	0	17	0
McMillan	10	1	37	2
Symcox	10	0	64	2
Adams	8	0	45	2

SOUTH AFRICA		Runs	Balls	4/6
A.C.Hudson	c Walsh b Adams	54	79	8
G.Kirsten	hit wicket b Ambrose	3	14	–
D.J.Cullinan	c Bishop b Adams	69	78	3/3
* W.J.Cronje	c Arthurton b Adams	40	47	2/2
J.N.Rhodes	c Adams b Harper	13	24	–
B.M.McMillan	lbw b Harper	6	7	–
† S.J.Palframan	c and b Harper	1	7	–
S.M.Pollock	c Adams b Harper	6	2	–
P.L.Symcox	c Harper b Arthurton	24	20	1/2
C.R.Matthews	not out	8	12	–
P.R.Adams	b Walsh	10	14	–
Extras	(b 1, lb 4, w 2, nb 4)	11		
Total	(49.3 overs)	**245**		

WEST INDIES	O	M	R	W
Ambrose	10	0	29	1
Walsh	8.3	1	51	1
Bishop	5	1	31	0
Harper	10	0	47	4
Adams	10	0	53	3
Arthurton	6	0	29	1

FALL OF WICKETS
1-42, 2-180, 3-210, 4-214, 5-227, 6-230, 7-230, 8-254

FALL OF WICKETS
1-21, 2-119, 3-140, 4-186, 5-196, 6-196, 7-198, 8-227, 9-228, 10-245

Umpires: K.T.Francis (*Sri Lanka*) (27) and S.G.Randell (*Australia*) (72).   **Referee:** R.S.Madugalle (*Sri Lanka*).

AUSTRALIA v NEW ZEALAND 1995-96

At M.A.Chidambaram Stadium, Madras, India on 11 March 1996.   Result: **AUSTRALIA** won by 6 wickets.
Toss: New Zealand.   Award: M.E.Waugh.   LOI debuts: None.

The first floodlit international in Madras produced Australia's highest total to win an LOI batting second. Mark Waugh became the first to score three hundreds in a WC tournament and overtook Graham Gooch's record campaign aggregate of 471 runs. Lee Germon and Chris Harris posted a WC and national record fourth-wicket stand of 168 from 166 balls.

NEW ZEALAND		Runs	Balls	4/6
C.M.Spearman	c Healy b Reiffel	12	12	3
N.J.Astle	c Healy b Fleming	1	6	–
*† L.K.Germon	c Fleming b McGrath	89	96	9/1
S.P.Fleming	c S.R.Waugh b McGrath	8	18	1
C.Z.Harris	c Reiffel b Warne	130	124	13/4
R.G.Twose	b Bevan	4	12	–
C.L.Cairns	c Reiffel b M.E.Waugh	4	9	–
A.C.Parore	lbw b Warne	11	13	–
S.A.Thomson	run out	11	10	1
D.N.Patel	not out	3	4	–
D.J.Nash				
Extras	(lb 6, w 3, nb 4)	13		
Total	(50 overs; 9 wickets)	**286**		

AUSTRALIA	O	M	R	W
Reiffel	4	0	38	1
Fleming	5	1	20	1
McGrath	9	2	50	2
M.E.Waugh	8	0	43	1
Warne	10	0	52	2
Bevan	10	0	52	1
S.R.Waugh	4	0	25	0

AUSTRALIA		Runs	Balls	4/6
* M.A.Taylor	c Germon b Patel	10	24	1
M.E.Waugh	c Parore b Nash	110	112	6/2
R.T.Ponting	c sub (R.J.Kennedy) b Thomson	31	43	4
S.K.Warne	lbw b Astle	24	14	1/2
S.R.Waugh	not out	59	71	4
S.G.Law	not out	42	28	4/1
M.G.Bevan				
† I.A.Healy				
P.R.Reiffel				
D.W.Fleming				
G.D.McGrath				
Extras	(b 1, lb 6, w 3, nb 3)	13		
Total	(47.5 overs; 4 wickets)	**289**		

NEW ZEALAND	O	M	R	W
Nash	9	1	44	1
Patel	8	0	45	1
Cairns	6.5	0	51	0
Harris	10	0	41	0
Thomson	8	0	57	1
Astle	3	0	21	1
Twose	3	0	23	0

FALL OF WICKETS
1-15, 2-16, 3-44, 4-212, 5-227, 6-240, 7-259, 8-282, 9-286

FALL OF WICKETS
1-19, 2-84, 3-126, 4-213

Umpires: C.J.Mitchley (*South Africa*) (28) and S.Venkataraghavan (9).   **Referee:** M.A.K.Pataudi (*India*).

INDIA v SRI LANKA 1995-96

At Eden Gardens, Calcutta, India on 13 March 1996.　Result: **SRI LANKA** won by default.　Toss: India.
Award: P.A.de Silva　LOI debuts: None.

Aravinda de Silva counter-attacked with a 32-ball fifty after both openers fell in the first over. Roshan Mahanama's undercarriage failed yet again and he was carried off by his runner at 182. As India lost seven wickets for 22, sections of a crowd estimated at 100,000 lit fires and hurled missiles at the Sri Lankan fielders. It was the first major cricket match to be awarded by default.

SRI LANKA		Runs	Balls	4/6
S.T.Jayasuriya	c Prasad b Srinath	1	3	–
† R.S.Kaluwitharana	c Manjrekar b Srinath	0	1	–
A.P.Gurusinha	c Kumble b Srinath	1	16	–
P.A.de Silva	b Kumble	66	47	14
R.S.Mahanama	retired ill	58	101	6
* A.Ranatunga	lbw b Tendulkar	35	42	4
H.P.Tillekeratne	c Tendulkar b Prasad	32	43	2
H.D.P.K.Dharmasena	b Tendulkar	9	20	–
W.P.U.C.J.Vaas	run out	23	16	3
G.P.Wickremasinghe	not out	4	9	–
M.Muralitharan	not out	5	4	–
Extras	(b 1, lb 10, w 4, nb 2)	17		
Total	(50 overs; 8 wickets)	**251**		

INDIA		Runs	Balls	4/6
S.R.Tendulkar	st Kaluwitharana b Jayasuriya	65	88	9
N.S.Sidhu	c Jayasuriya b Vaas	3	8	–
S.V.Manjrekar	b Jayasuriya	25	48	1
* M.Azharuddin	c and b Dharmasena	0	6	–
V.G.Kambli	not out	10	29	–
J.Srinath	run out	6	6	1
A.Jadeja	b Jayasuriya	0	11	–
† N.R.Mongia	c Jayasuriya b De Silva	1	8	–
A.R.Kapoor	c De Silva b Muralitharan	0	1	–
A.Kumble	not out	0	–	–
B.K.V.Prasad				
Extras	(b 1, lb 4, w 5)	10		
Total	(34.1 overs; 8 wickets)	**120**		

INDIA	O	M	R	W
Srinath	7	1	34	3
Kumble	10	0	51	1
Prasad	8	0	50	1
Kapoor	10	0	40	0
Jadeja	5	0	31	0
Tendulkar	10	1	34	2

SRI LANKA	O	M	R	W
Wickremasinghe	5	0	24	0
Vaas	6	1	23	1
Muralitharan	7.1	0	29	1
Dharmasena	7	0	24	1
Jayasuriya	7	1	11	3
De Silva	2	1	4	1

FALL OF WICKETS
1-1, 2-1, 3-35, 4-85, 5-168, 6-206, 7-236, 8-244

FALL OF WICKETS
1-8, 2-98, 3-99, 4-101, 5-110, 6-115, 7-120, 8-120

Umpires: R.S.Dunne (*NZ*) (37) and C.J.Mitchley (*South Africa*) (29).　　**Referee:** C.H.Lloyd (*West Indies*).

AUSTRALIA v WEST INDIES 1995-96

At Punjab CA Stadium, Mohali, Chandigarh, India on 14 March 1996.　Result: **AUSTRALIA** won by 5 runs.
Toss: Australia.　Award: S.K.Warne.　LOI debuts: None.

Yet another Indian venue staged its first illuminated international, this Chandigarh suburb producing the best contest of the tournament. Australia recovered from desperate positions in both innings, finally seizing eight wickets for 37 runs in 50 balls with Shane Warne taking 3 for 6 in three overs.

AUSTRALIA		Runs	Balls	4/6
M.E.Waugh	lbw b Ambrose	0	2	–
* M.A.Taylor	b Bishop	1	11	–
R.T.Ponting	lbw b Ambrose	0	15	–
S.R.Waugh	b Bishop	3	18	–
S.G.Law	run out	72	105	5
M.G.Bevan	c Richardson b Harper	69	110	4/1
† I.A.Healy	run out	31	28	2
P.R.Reiffel	run out	7	11	–
S.K.Warne	not out	6	6	–
D.W.Fleming				
G.D.McGrath				
Extras	(lb 11, w 5, nb 2)	18		
Total	(50 overs; 8 wickets)	**207**		

WEST INDIES		Runs	Balls	4/6
S.Chanderpaul	c Fleming b McGrath	80	126	7
† C.O.Browne	c and b Warne	10	18	–
B.C.Lara	b S.R.Waugh	45	45	5
* R.B.Richardson	not out	49	83	4
R.A.Harper	lbw b McGrath	2	5	–
O.D.Gibson	c Healy b Warne	1	2	–
J.C.Adams	lbw b Warne	2	11	–
K.L.T.Arthurton	c Healy b Fleming	0	4	–
I.R.Bishop	lbw b Warne	3	3	–
C.E.L.Ambrose	run out	2	2	–
C.A.Walsh	b Fleming	0	1	–
Extras	(lb 4, w 2, nb 2)	8		
Total	(49.3 overs)	**202**		

WEST INDIES	O	M	R	W
Ambrose	10	1	26	2
Bishop	10	1	35	2
Walsh	10	1	33	0
Gibson	2	0	13	0
Harper	9	0	47	1
Adams	9	0	42	0

AUSTRALIA	O	M	R	W
McGrath	10	2	30	2
Fleming	8.3	0	48	2
Warne	9	0	36	4
M.E.Waugh	4	0	16	0
S.R.Waugh	7	0	30	1
Reiffel	5	0	13	0
Bevan	4	1	12	0
Law	2	0	13	0

FALL OF WICKETS
1-0, 2-7, 3-8, 4-15, 5-153, 6-171, 7-186, 8-207

FALL OF WICKETS
1-25, 2-93, 3-165, 4-173, 5-178, 6-183, 7-187, 8-194, 9-202, 10-202

Umpires: B.C.Cooray (*Sri Lanka*) (22) and S.Venkataraghavan (10).　　**Referee:** J.R.Reid (*New Zealand*).

AUSTRALIA v SRI LANKA 1995-96

At Gaddafi Stadium, Lahore, Pakistan on 17 March 1996.   Result: **SRI LANKA** won by 7 wickets.   Toss: Sri Lanka.
Award: P.A.de Silva.   Tournament Award: S.T.Jayasuriya.   LOI debuts: None.

Sri Lanka became the first team to win a World Cup final either batting second or under lights (the first such international in Pakistan). Intriguingly they were the fifth different country to win it in successive tournaments. Aravinda de Silva scored 50 off 50 balls and 100 off 119, took three wickets and held two catches. Prime Minister Benazir Bhutto presented the Wills World Cup.

AUSTRALIA		Runs	Balls	4/6
* M.A.Taylor	c Jayasuriya b De Silva	74	83	8/1
M.E.Waugh	c Jayasuriya b Vaas	12	15	1
R.T.Ponting	b De Silva	45	73	2
S.R.Waugh	c De Silva b Dharmasena	13	25	–
S.K.Warne	st Kaluwitharana b Muralitharan	2	5	–
S.G.Law	c De Silva b Jayasuriya	22	30	–/1
M.G.Bevan	not out	36	49	2
† I.A.Healy	b De Silva	2	3	–
P.R.Reiffel	not out	13	18	–
D.W.Fleming				
G.D.McGrath				
Extras	(lb 10, w 11, nb 1)	22		
Total	(50 overs; 7 wickets)	**241**		

SRI LANKA		Runs	Balls	4/6
S.T.Jayasuriya	run out	9	7	1
† R.S.Kaluwitharana	c Bevan b Fleming	6	13	–
A.P.Gurusinha	b Reiffel	65	99	6/1
P.A.de Silva	not out	107	124	13
* A.Ranatunga	not out	47	37	4/1
H.P.Tillekeratne				
R.S.Mahanama				
H.D.P.K.Dharmasena				
W.P.U.C.J.Vaas				
G.P.Wickremasinghe				
M.Muralitharan				
Extras	(b 1, lb 4, w 5, nb 1)	11		
Total	(46.2 overs; 3 wickets)	**245**		

SRI LANKA	O	M	R	W
Wickremasinghe	7	0	38	0
Vaas	6	1	30	1
Muralitharan	10	0	31	1
Dharmasena	10	0	47	1
Jayasuriya	8	0	43	1
De Silva	9	0	42	3

AUSTRALIA	O	M	R	W
McGrath	8.2	1	28	0
Fleming	6	0	43	1
Warne	10	0	58	0
Reiffel	10	0	49	1
M.E.Waugh	6	0	35	0
S.R.Waugh	3	0	15	0
Bevan	3	0	12	0

FALL OF WICKETS
1-36, 2-137, 3-152, 4-156, 5-170, 6-202, 7-205

FALL OF WICKETS
1-12, 2-23, 3-148

Umpires: S.A.Bucknor (*WI*) (32) and D.R.Shepherd (*England*) (64).

Referee: C.H.Lloyd (*West Indies*).

WEST INDIES v NEW ZEALAND (1st Match)   LOI No: 1082/20

WEST INDIES v NEW ZEALAND 1995-96

At Sabina Park, Kingston, Jamaica on 26 March 1996.   Result: **WEST INDIES** won by 1 wicket.   Toss: West Indies.
Award: D.N.Patel.   LOI debuts: West Indies – R.D.Jacobs.

Their highest seventh-wicket partnership in internationals, 111 between Adam Parore and Dipak Patel, carried New Zealand to their record total against West Indies. Courtney Walsh's winning hit was intercepted by the crowd and awarded four runs by umpire Lloyd Barker.

NEW ZEALAND		Runs	Balls	4/6
C.M.Spearman	c Holder b Ambrose	11	15	1
N.J.Astle	c Adams b Ambrose	41	46	4
*† L.K.Germon	run out	0	2	–
S.P.Fleming	b Walsh	8	11	1
C.Z.Harris	c Lara b Ambrose	2	7	–
C.L.Cairns	c and b Harper	21	37	2
A.C.Parore	c Harper b Walsh	61	106	1/1
D.N.Patel	c and b Simmons	71	58	5/3
G.R.Larsen	b Ambrose	9	12	–
D.J.Nash	b Walsh	2	4	–
D.K.Morrison	not out	1	2	–
Extras	(lb 4, w 8, nb 4)	16		
Total	(49.1 overs)	**243**		

WEST INDIES		Runs	Balls	4/6
S.C.Williams	b Harris	62	90	8
S.Chanderpaul	c and b Harris	61	75	5
B.C.Lara	lbw b Harris	12	13	2
P.V.Simmons	b Larsen	28	46	2
J.C.Adams	c Fleming b Morrison	2	9	–
R.I.C.Holder	c Germon b Cairns	16	22	–
† R.D.Jacobs	c Spearman b Astle	3	5	–
R.A.Harper	not out	26	26	2/1
I.R.Bishop	lbw b Larsen	0	1	–
C.E.L.Ambrose	b Morrison	17	10	1/1
* C.A.Walsh	not out	5	3	1
Extras	(b 1, lb 6, w 5, nb 3)	15		
Total	(49.1 overs; 9 wickets)	**247**		

WEST INDIES	O	M	R	W
Ambrose	10	0	36	4
Bishop	10	0	56	0
Walsh	9.1	1	30	3
Harper	10	0	63	1
Simmons	7	0	38	1
Adams	3	0	16	0

NEW ZEALAND	O	M	R	W
Nash	6	0	46	0
Morrison	5.1	0	38	2
Harris	10	0	45	3
Patel	5	0	28	0
Astle	6	1	28	1
Cairns	7	1	26	1
Larsen	10	3	29	2

FALL OF WICKETS
1-22, 2-24, 3-51, 4-70, 5-70, 6-113, 7-224, 8-238, 9-241, 10-243

FALL OF WICKETS
1-126, 2-133, 3-142, 4-147, 5-179, 6-184, 7-197, 8-197, 9-221

Umpires: L.H.Barker (28) and S.A.Bucknor (33).

Referee: M.H.Denness (*England*).

WEST INDIES v NEW ZEALAND 1995-96

At Queen's Park Oval, Port-of-Spain, Trinidad on 29 March 1996.   Result: **NEW ZEALAND** won by 4 wickets.
Toss: New Zealand.   Award: S.P.Fleming.   LOI debuts: None.

With a ball to spare, New Zealand gained their first victory against West Indies in three tours of the Caribbean. Stephen Fleming scored his first international hundred. By a happy coincidence, it was on his home ground that Brian Lara made his 100th LOI appearance.

WEST INDIES		Runs	Balls	4/6
S.C.Williams	c Cairns b Patel	20	33	3
S.Chanderpaul	b Nash	6	16	1
B.C.Lara	c Astle b Harris	11	20	1
P.V.Simmons	c Fleming b Larsen	45	75	3/1
J.C.Adams	not out	59	93	–/1
R.I.C.Holder	b Astle	65	48	6/1
R.A.Harper	c and b Astle	2	3	–
† R.D.Jacobs	c Thomson b Larsen	10	10	1
I.R.Bishop	not out	12	4	–/1
C.E.L.Ambrose				
* C.A.Walsh				
Extras	(b 1, lb 2, w 3, nb 2)	8		
Total	(50 overs; 7 wickets)	**238**		

NEW ZEALAND		Runs	Balls	4/6
C.M.Spearman	c Simmons b Harper	37	47	6
N.J.Astle	c Harper b Ambrose	2	12	–
*†L.K.Germon	c Simmons b Walsh	6	14	–
S.P.Fleming	not out	106	108	7/1
A.C.Parore	c Adams b Walsh	0	4	–
C.L.Cairns	b Adams	41	69	3
C.Z.Harris	b Ambrose	32	40	1/1
D.N.Patel	not out	4	7	–
S.A.Thomson				
G.R.Larsen				
D.J.Nash				
Extras	(lb 7, w 3, nb 1)	11		
Total	(49.5 overs; 6 wickets)	**239**		

NEW ZEALAND	O	M	R	W
Nash	6	0	29	1
Larsen	10	1	42	2
Harris	10	3	45	1
Patel	8	0	30	1
Astle	9	1	32	2
Thomson	5	0	36	0
Cairns	2	0	21	0

WEST INDIES	O	M	R	W
Ambrose	9.5	1	42	2
Bishop	5	0	37	0
Walsh	10	0	51	2
Harper	10	2	28	1
Simmons	10	0	50	0
Adams	5	0	24	1

FALL OF WICKETS
1-15, 2-32, 3-42, 4-119, 5-210, 6-212, 7-225

FALL OF WICKETS
1-16, 2-35, 3-71, 4-71, 5-163, 6-230

Umpires: L.H.Barker (29) and S.A.Bucknor (34).

Referee: M.H.Denness (*England*).

WEST INDIES v NEW ZEALAND 1995-96

At Queen's Park Oval, Port-of-Spain, Trinidad on 30 March 1996.   Result: **WEST INDIES** won by 7 wickets.
Toss: New Zealand.   Award: B.C.Lara.   LOI debuts: West Indies – L.R.Williams.

Brian Lara treated his home crowd to a spectacular exhibition of strokeplay, winning the match with his third six. Coming to the crease at 6 for 2, he took 72 balls for his first fifty and just 40 more to complete his eighth LOI hundred.

NEW ZEALAND		Runs	Balls	4/6
C.M.Spearman	b Ambrose	7	11	1
R.G.Twose	c and b Harper	48	70	4
N.J.Astle	run out	43	85	4
S.P.Fleming	c Walsh b Simmons	4	10	–
C.L.Cairns	st Jacobs b Harper	38	51	–/2
A.C.Parore	c Harper b Adams	33	42	1
C.Z.Harris	run out	10	14	–
*†L.K.Germon	not out	13	11	–
S.A.Thomson	run out	6	5	–
D.N.Patel	not out	3	2	–
G.R.Larsen				
Extras	(b 1, lb 6, w 6, nb 1)	14		
Total	(50 overs; 8 wickets)	**219**		

WEST INDIES		Runs	Balls	4/6
S.C.Williams	c Fleming b Larsen	4	12	–
S.Chanderpaul	lbw b Larsen	1	10	–
B.C.Lara	not out	146	134	12/3
P.V.Simmons	lbw b Larsen	47	67	4
J.C.Adams	not out	24	51	2
R.I.C.Holder				
R.A.Harper				
L.R.Williams				
† R.D.Jacobs				
C.E.L.Ambrose				
* C.A.Walsh				
Extras	(lb 3)	3		
Total	(45.4 overs; 3 wickets)	**225**		

WEST INDIES	O	M	R	W
Ambrose	10	0	33	1
Walsh	9	2	37	0
Simmons	10	1	35	1
L.R.Williams	2	0	18	0
Adams	9	0	44	1
Harper	10	0	45	2

NEW ZEALAND	O	M	R	W
Patel	10	0	45	0
Larsen	8.4	3	26	3
Astle	8	0	43	0
Harris	8	1	37	0
Thomson	4	0	24	0
Twose	3	0	19	0
Cairns	4	0	28	0

FALL OF WICKETS
1-10, 2-104, 3-105, 4-113, 5-178, 6-197, 7-205, 8-215

FALL OF WICKETS
1-5, 2-6, 3-116

Umpires: L.H.Barker (30) and S.A.Bucknor (35).

Referee: M.H.Denness (*England*).

WEST INDIES v NEW ZEALAND 1995-96

At Bourda, Georgetown, Guyana on 3 April 1996.　　Result: **NEW ZEALAND** won by 4 runs.　　Toss: West Indies.
Award: New Zealand team.　　LOI debuts: None.

A dazzling fielding display, with Chris Harris quite outstanding, enabled New Zealand to defend a modest total on an ultra-slow surface and square the rubber in a tense finish. Adjudicator Basil Butcher decided the match award should go to the touring side *en bloc* for a sterling team effort.

NEW ZEALAND		Runs	Balls	4/6
C.M.Spearman	b Ambrose	41	39	8
N.J.Astle	lbw b Ambrose	20	16	3
*†L.K.Germon	run out	19	32	–
S.P.Fleming	c Harper b Simmons	9	8	2
C.Z.Harris	c Harper b Simmons	8	21	1
R.G.Twose	run out	8	12	–
C.L.Cairns	c and b L.R.Williams	29	36	4
S.A.Thomson	c Harper b L.R.Williams	6	20	–
D.N.Patel	c Jacobs b Walsh	2	17	–
J.T.C.Vaughan	not out	4	10	–
G.R.Larsen	hit wicket b L.R.Williams	1	5	–
Extras	(lb 7, w 3, nb 1)	11		
Total	(35.5 overs)	**158**		

WEST INDIES		Runs	Balls	4/6
S.C.Williams	lbw b Larsen	6	17	–
S.Chanderpaul	c Harris b Patel	11	26	2
B.C.Lara	c Astle b Larsen	17	13	4
P.V.Simmons	c Harris b Vaughan	11	36	1
J.C.Adams	run out	23	75	–
R.I.C.Holder	not out	49	86	2
†R.D.Jacobs	c Germon b Cairns	0	5	–
R.A.Harper	b Harris	5	6	1
L.R.Williams	c Twose b Astle	1	4	–
C.E.L.Ambrose	lbw b Vaughan	16	21	2
*C.A.Walsh	b Cairns	1	6	–
Extras	(b 1, lb 8, w 5)	14		
Total	(49.1 overs)	**154**		

WEST INDIES	O	M	R	W
Ambrose	7	1	33	2
Walsh	6	0	38	1
Simmons	10	0	42	2
Harper	8	1	22	0
L.R.Williams	4.5	0	16	3

NEW ZEALAND	O	M	R	W
Patel	10	1	35	1
Larsen	10	1	18	2
Harris	10	1	23	1
Vaughan	7	0	26	2
Astle	7	1	26	1
Cairns	5.1	0	17	2

FALL OF WICKETS
1-55, 2-77, 3-90, 4-100, 5-113, 6-113, 7-138, 8-145, 9-155, 10-158

FALL OF WICKETS
1-21, 2-35, 3-39, 4-68, 5-104, 6-111, 7-116, 8-120, 9-152, 10-154

Umpires: C.R.Duncan (9) and E.Nicholls (2).

Referee: M.H.Denness (*England*).

WEST INDIES v NEW ZEALAND 1995-96

At Arnos Vale, Kingstown, St Vincent on 6 April 1996.　　Result: **WEST INDIES** won by 7 wickets.　　Toss: West Indies.
Award: P.V.Simmons.　　LOI debuts: None.

Brian Lara, whose ninth hundred took 98 balls, and Phil Simmons added 186 off 31 overs for the third wicket, Simmons completing his fifth hundred and winning the match and a closely fought series with his tenth four.

NEW ZEALAND		Runs	Balls	4/6
C.M.Spearman	c Browne b Walsh	4	6	–
N.J.Astle	c Simmons b Ambrose	4	13	1
*†L.K.Germon	c and b Adams	50	66	3
S.P.Fleming	c Simmons b Adams	75	102	6
R.G.Twose	c Browne b Chanderpaul	6	5	1
C.L.Cairns	c and b Adams	11	10	–/1
A.C.Parore	b Williams	23	29	2
C.Z.Harris	not out	42	49	2
D.N.Patel	run out	2	2	–
J.T.C.Vaughan	not out	13	20	–
G.R.Larsen				
Extras	(b 2, lb 2, w 6, nb 1)	11		
Total	(50 overs; 8 wickets)	**241**		

WEST INDIES		Runs	Balls	4/6
P.A.Wallace	c Fleming b Patel	0	6	–
S.Chanderpaul	c Twose b Harris	13	37	–
B.C.Lara	c Patel b Cairns	104	103	10/1
P.V.Simmons	not out	103	124	10/2
R.I.C.Holder	not out	13	23	2
J.C.Adams				
†C.O.Browne				
R.A.Harper				
L.R.Williams				
C.E.L.Ambrose				
*C.A.Walsh				
Extras	(lb 2, w 6, nb 1)	9		
Total	(48.3 overs; 3 wickets)	**242**		

WEST INDIES	O	M	R	W
Ambrose	7	0	32	1
Walsh	9	0	38	1
Simmons	3	0	25	0
Harper	10	0	48	0
Adams	10	0	50	3
Chanderpaul	8	0	35	0
Williams	3	0	9	1

NEW ZEALAND	O	M	R	W
Patel	10	1	46	1
Larsen	8	2	31	0
Harris	8	0	48	1
Vaughan	10	0	37	0
Cairns	8.3	0	49	1
Astle	2	0	14	0
Fleming	2	0	15	0

FALL OF WICKETS
1-10, 2-10, 3-131, 4-137, 5-154, 6-167, 7-189, 8-197

FALL OF WICKETS
1-0, 2-31, 3-217

Umpires: L.H.Barker (31) and B.Morgan (1).

Referee: M.H.Denness (*England*).

PAKISTAN v SRI LANKA 1995-96

At Singapore Cricket Club on 1 (*void*), 2 April 1996.　　Result: **SRI LANKA** won by 34 runs.　Toss: Pakistan.
Award: S.T.Jayasuriya. First match abandoned on 1 April – Pakistan 54-3 (10 overs), made void.　　LOI debuts: None.

Singapore Cricket Club's historic Padang, the 110th LOI venue, staged a record-breaking assault by Sanath Jayasuriya.
He scored the fastest hundred (48 balls, 14 fewer than the previous record), most sixes (11, an increase of three,
including four in succession), and most runs (29) off one over. The match aggregate of 664 was another record.

SRI LANKA		Runs	Balls	4/6	PAKISTAN		Runs	Balls	4/6
S.T.Jayasuriya	c Akram b Saqlain	134	65	11/11	* Aamir Sohail	lbw b Dharmasena	46	46	5
† R.S.Kaluwitharana	c Saqlain b Waqar	24	10	2/2	Saeed Anwar	c Kaluwitharana b Vaas	32	32	3
A.P.Gurusinha	c Aamir b Saqlain	29	50	3	Ramiz Raja	c and b De Silva	27	32	2
P.A.de Silva	c and b Salim	7	4	–/1	Salim Malik	c Dharmasena b Muralitharan	68	77	4/1
* A.Ranatunga	c Inzamam b Waqar	14	19	1	Inzamam-ul-Haq	b Vaas	67	54	6
H.P.Tillekeratne	b Akram	25	40	1	Ijaz Ahmed	st Kaluwitharana b Jayasuriya	32	22	1/2
R.S.Mahanama	c Waqar b Akram	35	52	1	Waqar Younis	c Muralitharan b Dharmasena	1	4	–
H.D.P.K.Dharmasena	b Waqar	51	49	4	† Rashid Latif	c Dharmasena b Muralitharan	7	8	–
W.P.U.C.J.Vaas	c Aamir b Waqar	6	5	1	Saqlain Mushtaq	run out	0	4	–
G.P.Wickremasinghe	not out	7	6	–	Aqib Javed	c Muralitharan b Tillekeratne	20	15	1/2
M.Muralitharan	not out	2	2	–	Mohammad Akram	not out	3	6	–
Extras	(b 1, lb 3, w 9, nb 2)	15			Extras	(b 3, lb 6, w 1, nb 2)	12		
Total	(50 overs; 9 wickets)	349			Total	(49.4 overs)	315		

PAKISTAN	O	M	R	W	SRI LANKA	O	M	R	W
Waqar Younis	10	0	62	4	Wickremasinghe	5	0	46	0
Mohammad Akram	7	0	66	2	Vaas	10	0	50	2
Saqlain Mushtaq	10	0	45	2	Muralitharan	10	0	59	2
Aqib Javed	10	0	65	0	Dharmasena	8	0	51	2
Aamir Sohail	8	0	73	0	De Silva	4	0	22	1
Salim Malik	5	0	34	1	Jayasuriya	10	0	45	1
					Ranatunga	2	0	20	0
					Tillekeratne	0.4	0	13	1

FALL OF WICKETS
1-40, 2-196, 3-197, 4-203, 5-238, 6-245, 7-318, 8-328, 9-346

FALL OF WICKETS
1-77, 2-96, 3-120, 4-247, 5-253, 6-257, 7-281, 8-291, 9-291, 10-315

Umpires: D.L.Orchard (*SA*) (10) and R.B.Tiffin (*Zimbabwe*) (3).

Referee: H.Gardiner (*Zimbabwe*).

INDIA v SRI LANKA 1995-96

At Singapore Cricket Club on 3 April 1996.　　Result: **INDIA** won by 12 runs.　　Toss: India.
Award: N.S.Sidhu.　LOI debuts: India – R.Dravid.

A day later the same pitch had lost its bounce and batsmen struggled to score runs. Navjot Sidhu was hospitalised with
heatstroke after his painstaking innings. Javagal Srinath effectively decided the match when he removed Sri Lanka's
dangerous openers.

INDIA		Runs	Balls	4/6	SRI LANKA		Runs	Balls	4/6
S.R.Tendulkar	c Jayasuriya b Wickremasinghe	28	31	3/1	S.T.Jayasuriya	c Manjrekar b Srinath	7	9	1
N.S.Sidhu	b Vaas	94	116	4	† R.S.Kaluwitharana	c Azharuddin b Srinath	4	3	1
* M.Azharuddin	run out	9	11	1	M.S.Atapattu	lbw b Srinath	10	17	1
R.Dravid	c Kaluwitharana b Muralitharan	3	4	–	P.A.de Silva	c Dravid b Prasad	1	6	–
S.V.Manjrekar	lbw b Muralitharan	7	16	–	R.S.Mahanama	c Dravid b Raju	59	124	3
A.Jadeja	c Chandana b Jayasuriya	7	31	–	* A.Ranatunga	c Azharuddin b Raju	13	22	2
† N.R.Mongia	c and b De Silva	4	14	–	H.P.Tillekeratne	c Prasad b Raju	42	66	1
A.Kumble	c Atapattu b De Silva	4	10	–	U.U.Chandana	run out	11	17	2
J.Srinath	not out	28	32	1/1	W.P.U.C.J.Vaas	b Srinath	6	6	1
B.K.V.Prasad	c Jayasuriya b Vaas	7	11	–/1	M.Muralitharan	not out	7	8	–
S.L.V.Raju	c Kaluwitharana b Vaas	0	2	–	G.P.Wickremasinghe	run out	11	13	1
Extras	(lb 2, w 2, nb 4)	8			Extras	(lb 8, w 7, nb 1)	16		
Total	(45.4 overs)	199			Total	(48.1 overs)	187		

SRI LANKA	O	M	R	W	INDIA	O	M	R	W
Wickremasinghe	8	0	39	1	Srinath	10	0	35	4
Vaas	7.4	0	35	3	Prasad	10	2	39	1
Muralitharan	8	0	25	2	Kumble	10	1	46	0
Chandana	10	0	52	0	Raju	10	1	26	3
Jayasuriya	8	0	31	1	Tendulkar	5.1	0	19	0
De Silva	4	0	15	2	Jadeja	3	0	14	0

FALL OF WICKETS
1-33, 2-58, 3-62, 4-82, 5-114, 6-130, 7-136, 8-191, 9-199, 10-199

FALL OF WICKETS
1-5, 2-12, 3-13, 4-23, 5-53, 6-145, 7-163, 8-169, 9-169, 10-187

Umpires: G.Sharp (*England*) (1) and R.B.Tiffin (*Zimbabwe*) (4).

Referee: H.Gardiner (*Zimbabwe*).

INDIA v PAKISTAN 1995-96

At Singapore Cricket Club on 5 April 1996.　　Result: **PAKISTAN** won by 8 wickets (revised target).　　Toss: Pakistan.
Award: Aamir Sohail.　　LOI debuts: None.

Heavy rain terminated India's innings and caused Pakistan's target to be revised to 187 from 33 overs. This result left the three teams with equal points, the finalists being determined by net run rate: Pakistan 0.56, Sri Lanka 0.22, India -0.46.

INDIA		Runs	Balls	4/6
N.S.Sidhu	c Rashid b Aqib Javed	14	35	1
S.R.Tendulkar	st Rashid b Saqlain	100	111	9/1
* M.Azharuddin	c Rashid b Aamir	29	51	–
R.Dravid	run out	4	7	–
S.V.Manjrekar	c Aqib b Saqlain	41	56	2
A.Jadeja	run out	5	5	–
† N.R.Mongia	run out	3	9	–
A.Kumble	not out	14	10	1/1
J.Srinath	st Rashid b Saqlain	0	1	–
B.K.V.Prasad	not out	1	4	–
S.L.V.Raju				
Extras	(lb 3, w 9, nb 3)	15		
Total	(47.1 overs; 8 wickets)	**226**		

PAKISTAN		Runs	Balls	4/6
* Aamir Sohail	not out	76	89	7
Saeed Anwar	c Dravid b Raju	74	49	8/3
Ramiz Raja	lbw b Kumble	5	10	–
Salim Malik	not out	25	24	5
Inzamam-ul-Haq				
Ijaz Ahmed				
† Rashid Latif				
Waqar Younis				
Mushtaq Ahmed				
Saqlain Mushtaq				
Aqib Javed				
Extras	(lb 3, w 4, nb 3)	10		
Total	(28 overs; 2 wickets)	**190**		

PAKISTAN	O	M	R	W
Waqar Younis	8	1	42	0
Aqib Javed	7.1	0	12	1
Inzamam-ul-Haq	1	0	10	0
Mushtaq Ahmed	9	0	58	0
Saqlain Mushtaq	10	0	38	3
Salim Malik	3	0	17	0
Aamir Sohail	9	0	46	1

INDIA	O	M	R	W
Srinath	7	0	34	0
Prasad	7	0	45	0
Kumble	7	1	39	1
Raju	5	0	51	1
Tendulkar	2	0	18	0

FALL OF WICKETS
1-44, 2-110, 3-127, 4-181, 5-195, 6-205, 7-223, 8-224

FALL OF WICKETS
1-144, 2-162

Umpires: D.L.Orchard (South Africa) (11) and G.Sharp (England) (2).

Referee: H.Gardiner (Zimbabwe).

PAKISTAN v SRI LANKA 1995-96

At Singapore Cricket Club on 7 April 1996.　　Result: **PAKISTAN** won by 43 runs.　　Toss: Sri Lanka.
Award: Saqlain Mushtaq.　　Series award: S.T.Jayasuriya.　　LOI debuts: None.

Pakistan withstood another memorable assault from Sanath Jayasuriya to win the Singer Cup. This time he struck the fastest LOI fifty, completed with a six off his 17th ball. He had scored all but four of an opening stand of 70 when his partner was bowled for a duck in the sixth over. Ata-ur-Rehman took three wickets in five balls.

PAKISTAN		Runs	Balls	4/6
* Aamir Sohail	b Vaas	18	26	3
Saeed Anwar	c Muralitharan b Wickremasinghe	17	18	–
Ramiz Raja	run out	37	55	2
Salim Malik	c and b Muralitharan	27	49	–/1
Inzamam-ul-Haq	c Tillekeratne b De Silva	24	29	–
Ijaz Ahmed	b Jayasuriya	51	75	2/2
† Rashid Latif	b Dharmasena	2	6	–
Aqib Javed	c Mahanama b Muralitharan	11	21	–
Saqlain Mushtaq	c Tillekeratne b Vaas	8	14	1
Waqar Younis	run out	0	1	–
Ata-ur-Rehman	not out	1	3	–
Extras	(b 6, lb 4, w 6, nb 3)	19		
Total	(48.3 overs)	**215**		

SRI LANKA		Runs	Balls	4/6
S.T.Jayasuriya	c Aamir b Waqar	76	28	8/5
† R.S.Kaluwitharana	b Aqib	0	11	–
A.P.Gurusinha	lbw b Aqib	20	16	4
P.A.de Silva	c Rashid b Saqlain	4	11	1
R.S.Mahanama	lbw b Waqar	14	33	–
* A.Ranatunga	c Rashid b Saqlain	0	2	–
H.P.Tillekeratne	lbw b Rehman	33	65	3
H.D.P.K.Dharmasena	c Inzamam b Saqlain	5	27	–
W.P.U.C.J.Vaas	not out	5	4	1
G.P.Wickremasinghe	b Rehman	0	1	–
M.Muralitharan	c Ramiz b Rehman	0	3	–
Extras	(lb 5, w 7, nb 3)	15		
Total	(32.5 overs)	**172**		

SRI LANKA	O	M	R	W
Wickremasinghe	8	1	30	1
Vaas	8	0	35	2
Muralitharan	10	0	42	2
Dharmasena	10	1	39	1
Jayasuriya	8.3	0	39	1
De Silva	4	0	20	1

PAKISTAN	O	M	R	W
Waqar Younis	7	0	38	2
Aqib Javed	7	0	32	2
Ata-ur-Rehman	3.5	0	27	3
Saqlain Mushtaq	7	0	46	3
Aamir Sohail	6	0	21	0
Salim Malik	2	0	3	0

FALL OF WICKETS
1-29, 2-41, 3-102, 4-106, 5-140, 6-143, 7-175, 8-199, 9-199, 10-215

FALL OF WICKETS
1-70, 2-96, 3-100, 4-106, 5-106, 6-146, 7-164, 8-172, 9-172, 10-172

Umpires: G.Sharp (England) (3) and R.B.Tiffin (Zimbabwe) (5).

Referee: H.Gardiner (Zimbabwe).

INDIA v PAKISTAN 1995-96

At Sharjah CA Stadium, UAE on 12 April 1996.   Result: **PAKISTAN** won by 38 runs.   Toss: India.
Award: Aamir Sohail.   LOI debuts: None.

Five days after competing in Singapore's inaugural tournament, India and Pakistan were in action in the Gulf, this time with South Africa as the third party. Aamir Sohail's fifth LOI hundred was completed from 122 balls.

PAKISTAN		Runs	Balls	4/6
* Aamir Sohail	c and b Kumble	105	127	8
Saeed Anwar	b Vaidya	44	43	5
Ramiz Raja	run out	17	33	1
Salim Malik	run out	22	22	2
Inzamam-ul-Haq	c Mongia b Tendulkar	9	7	2
Ijaz Ahmed	not out	43	53	1/1
† Rashid Latif	not out	21	15	–/1
Waqar Younis				
Aqib Javed				
Mushtaq Ahmed				
Saqlain Mushtaq				
Extras	(lb 6, w 4)	10		
Total	(50 overs; 5 wickets)	**271**		

INDIA		Runs	Balls	4/6
A.Jadeja	c Saeed b Saqlain	43	35	4/1
S.R.Tendulkar	c Saeed b Aqib	1	5	–
N.S.Sidhu	c and b Saqlain	31	43	3
* M.Azharuddin	c Aqib b Mushtaq Ahmed	7	25	–
R.Dravid	c Rashid b Mushtaq Ahmed	3	5	–
S.V.Manjrekar	c Saeed b Waqar	59	84	2/1
† N.R.Mongia	b Mushtaq Ahmed	69	78	5/1
J.Srinath	run out	0	1	–
A.Kumble	c sub ‡ b Mushtaq Ahmed	3	4	–
P.S.Vaidya	b Waqar	3	3	–
S.L.V.Raju	not out	0	2	–
Extras	(lb 4, w 10)	14		
Total	(47.2 overs)	**233**		

INDIA	O	M	R	W
Srinath	10	1	46	0
Vaidya	9	0	55	1
Kumble	10	0	50	1
Raju	9	0	57	0
Tendulkar	10	0	46	1
Azharuddin	2	0	11	0

PAKISTAN	O	M	R	W
Waqar Younis	9	1	44	2
Aqib Javed	7	0	33	1
Saqlain Mushtaq	9	0	42	2
Mushtaq Ahmed	9.2	0	47	4
Aamir Sohail	6	0	28	0
Salim Malik	7	0	35	0

FALL OF WICKETS
1-77, 2-115, 3-156, 4-167, 5-235

FALL OF WICKETS
1-8, 2-76, 3-89, 4-91, 5-95, 6-211, 7-212, 8-219, 9-229, 10-233

Umpires: D.B.Cowie (*NZ*) (15) and M.J.Kitchen (*England*) (13).

Referee: R.S.Madugalle (*Sri Lanka*).   ‡ (Ata-ur-Rehman)

PAKISTAN v SOUTH AFRICA 1995-96

At Sharjah CA Stadium, UAE on 13 April 1996.   Result: **SOUTH AFRICA** won by 143 runs.   Toss: South Africa.
Award: D.J.Cullinan.   LOI debuts: None.

South Africa began their first international in Sharjah on a high note when they equalled their highest total against a Test-playing country. An opening partnership of 115 in 17 overs was followed by Daryll Cullinan's 98-ball hundred, his first in 48 internationals.

SOUTH AFRICA		Runs	Balls	4/6
A.C.Hudson	c Aqib b Waqar	57	51	6/1
G.Kirsten	b Aqib	64	70	4/2
D.J.Cullinan	not out	110	109	6/3
* W.J.Cronje	c Inzamam b Mushtaq Ahmed	26	32	2
J.N.Rhodes	not out	47	39	4
B.M.McMillan				
S.M.Pollock				
† D.J.Richardson				
P.L.Symcox				
C.R.Matthews				
P.S.de Villiers				
Extras	(lb 7, w 3)	10		
Total	(50 overs; 3 wickets)	**314**		

PAKISTAN		Runs	Balls	4/6
* Aamir Sohail	c Hudson b De Villiers	11	12	1
Saeed Anwar	c Cronje b De Villiers	33	29	3
Ramiz Raja	c McMillan b Pollock	1	11	–
Salim Malik	not out	64	115	2
Inzamam-ul-Haq	run out	1	5	–
Ijaz Ahmed	c Richardson b McMillan	1	9	–
† Rashid Latif	c McMillan b Matthews	2	5	–
Saqlain Mushtaq	lbw b Cronje	7	44	–
Aqib Javed	not out	45	70	2/1
Waqar Younis				
Mushtaq Ahmed				
Extras	(lb 2, w 4)	6		
Total	(50 overs; 7 wickets)	**171**		

PAKISTAN	O	M	R	W
Waqar Younis	10	1	56	1
Aqib Javed	9	0	59	1
Mushtaq Ahmed	10	0	63	1
Saqlain Mushtaq	9	1	55	0
Aamir Sohail	10	0	56	0
Salim Malik	2	0	18	0

SOUTH AFRICA	O	M	R	W
Pollock	10	1	44	1
De Villiers	10	0	40	2
McMillan	7	0	20	1
Matthews	8	1	21	1
Symcox	10	1	21	0
Cronje	5	0	23	1

FALL OF WICKETS
1-115, 2-157, 3-222

FALL OF WICKETS
1-24, 2-45, 3-49, 4-50, 5-58, 6-62, 7-90

Umpires: B.C.Cooray (*Sri Lanka*) (23) and D.B.Cowie (*NZ*) (16).

Referee: R.S.Madugalle (*Sri Lanka*).

INDIA v SOUTH AFRICA 1995-96

At Sharjah CA Stadium, UAE on 14 April 1996.   Result: **SOUTH AFRICA** won by 80 runs.   Toss: South Africa.
Award: W.J.Cronje.   LOI debuts: None.

Sharjah became the first venue to stage 100 internationals. Faced with another high total based on a national record fourth-wicket stand of 154 in 25 overs between Gary Kirsten and 'Hansie' Cronje, India eventually decided to bat out their overs in order to boost their net run rate.

SOUTH AFRICA		Runs	Balls	4/6
G.Kirsten	b Raju	106	116	9
A.C.Hudson	c Tendulkar b Srinath	0	1	–
D.J.Cullinan	c Dravid b Kumble	28	33	6
P.L.Symcox	b Kumble	0	1	–
* W.J.Cronje	run out	90	82	4/3
J.N.Rhodes	c Dravid b Raju	23	33	1
B.M.McMillan	not out	14	24	–
S.M.Pollock	not out	15	11	1/1
† D.J.Richardson				
C.R.Matthews				
P.S.de Villiers				
Extras	(lb 7, w 4, nb 1)	12		
Total	(50 overs; 6 wickets)	**288**		

INDIA		Runs	Balls	4/6
A.Jadeja	c Richardson b Matthews	42	48	3/1
S.R.Tendulkar	c Kirsten b De Villiers	2	15	–
P.S.Vaidya	lbw b Pollock	12	9	2
N.S.Sidhu	c Kirsten b Pollock	1	5	–
S.V.Manjrekar	c Cronje b Symcox	53	80	3/1
* M.Azharuddin	c Hudson b Symcox	28	62	1
J.Srinath	b De Villiers	35	31	1/2
R.Dravid	c Rhodes b Pollock	11	22	–
† N.R.Mongia	not out	9	16	–
A.Kumble	not out	9	14	–
S.L.V.Raju				
Extras	(b 1, lb 1, w 3, nb 1)	6		
Total	(50 overs; 8 wickets)	**208**		

INDIA	O	M	R	W
Srinath	9	0	43	1
Vaidya	6	0	42	0
Kumble	10	0	45	2
Raju	10	0	67	2
Tendulkar	7	0	40	0
Jadeja	8	0	44	0

SOUTH AFRICA	O	M	R	W
Pollock	10	0	42	3
De Villiers	10	0	54	2
McMillan	7	0	18	0
Matthews	10	0	26	1
Symcox	7	0	43	2
Cronje	6	0	23	0

FALL OF WICKETS
1-1, 2-56, 3-56, 4-210, 5-249, 6-266

FALL OF WICKETS
1-20, 2-41, 3-45, 4-62, 5-143, 6-148, 7-188, 8-194

Umpires: B.C.Cooray (*Sri Lanka*) (24) and M.J.Kitchen (*England*) (14).

Referee: R.S.Madugalle (*Sri Lanka*).

INDIA v PAKISTAN 1995-96

At Sharjah CA Stadium, UAE on 15 April 1996.   Result: **INDIA** won by 28 runs.   Toss: India.
Award: S.R.Tendulkar.   LOI debuts: India – V.Rathore.

India's highest LOI total was founded upon their record all-wicket partnership. Sachin Tendulkar and Navjot Sidhu, who added 231 for the second wicket, scored their eighth and sixth hundreds respectively. Pakistan were penalised two overs for a sluggish bowling rate.

INDIA		Runs	Balls	4/6
V.Rathore	c Inzamam b Waqar	2	12	–
S.R.Tendulkar	c Aamir b Waqar	118	140	8/2
N.S.Sidhu	run out	101	117	3/3
A.Jadeja	c Rashid b Waqar	17	14	–/1
J.Srinath	c Aamir b Rehman	16	10	2
* M.Azharuddin	not out	29	10	2/2
S.V.Manjrekar	not out	0	–	–
† N.R.Mongia				
A.R.Kapoor				
A.Kumble				
B.K.V.Prasad				
Extras	(b 2, lb 7, w 12, nb 1)	22		
Total	(50 overs; 5 wickets)	**305**		

PAKISTAN		Runs	Balls	4/6
* Aamir Sohail	run out	78	76	6
Saeed Anwar	c Mongia b Prasad	2	4	–
† Rashid Latif	c Azharuddin b Kumble	50	31	6/1
Ijaz Ahmed	b Srinath	42	51	3
Salim Malik	c Kapoor b Kumble	42	52	1/1
Inzamam-ul-Haq	c Azharuddin b Prasad	6	11	–
Basit Ali	c Rathore b Tendulkar	32	34	3
Aqib Javed	c Rathore b Srinath	5	7	–
Waqar Younis	not out	8	6	1
Ata-ur-Rehman	c sub (R.Dravid) b Srinath	4	4	–
Saqlain Mushtaq	lbw b Tendulkar	0	1	–
Extras	(lb 4, w 4)	8		
Total	(46.1 overs)	**277**		

PAKISTAN	O	M	R	W
Waqar Younis	10	2	44	3
Aqib Javed	10	0	58	0
Ata-ur-Rehman	10	0	85	1
Saqlain Mushtaq	10	1	60	0
Aamir Sohail	10	0	49	0

INDIA	O	M	R	W
Srinath	10	0	65	3
Prasad	9	0	64	2
Kumble	9	1	38	2
Kapoor	9	0	52	0
Tendulkar	7.1	0	40	2
Jadeja	2	0	14	0

FALL OF WICKETS
1-9, 2-240, 3-245, 4-264, 5-281

FALL OF WICKETS
1-16, 2-88, 3-172, 4-190, 5-199, 6-248, 7-260, 8-271, 9-277, 10-277

Umpires: D.B.Cowie (*NZ*) (17) and M.J.Kitchen (*England*) (15).

Referee: R.S.Madugalle (*Sri Lanka*).

PAKISTAN v SOUTH AFRICA 1995-96

At Sharjah CA Stadium, UAE on 16 April 1996.   Result: **SOUTH AFRICA** won by 8 wickets.   Toss: Pakistan.
Award: C.R.Matthews.   LOI debuts: None.

South Africa maintained their unbeaten record and booked their place in the final by crushing Pakistan with 16.5 overs to spare.

PAKISTAN		Runs	Balls	4/6
* Aamir Sohail	c Cronje b Matthews	46	73	6
Saeed Anwar	c Kirsten b Pollock	10	20	2
Ramiz Raja	c Matthews b De Villiers	40	69	3/1
Inzamam-ul-Haq	c Richardson b Kallis	41	42	1/2
† Rashid Latif	lbw b De Villiers	7	11	–
Salim Malik	c Crookes b Matthews	10	13	–
Basit Ali	c Crookes b Kallis	8	14	–
Aqib Javed	c Richardson b Matthews	6	8	1
Waqar Younis	not out	8	14	–
Mushtaq Ahmed	c Richardson b Kallis	0	1	–
Mohammad Akram	lbw b De Villiers	0	5	–
Extras	(b 2, lb 4, w 6)	12		
Total	(45 overs)	**188**		

SOUTH AFRICA		Runs	Balls	4/6
A.C.Hudson	not out	94	86	11/2
G.Kirsten	c Akram b Waqar	32	40	3/1
P.L.Symcox	lbw b Akram	35	35	3/2
J.H.Kallis	not out	24	38	2
* W.J.Cronje				
J.N.Rhodes				
D.N.Crookes				
S.M.Pollock				
† D.J.Richardson				
C.R.Matthews				
P.S.de Villiers				
Extras	(w 4)	4		
Total	(33.1 overs; 2 wickets)	**189**		

SOUTH AFRICA	O	M	R	W
De Villiers	10	1	28	3
Pollock	8	1	34	1
Matthews	8	1	19	3
Cronje	1	0	4	0
Symcox	7	0	38	0
Crookes	5	0	38	0
Kallis	6	1	21	3

PAKISTAN	O	M	R	W
Mohammad Akram	10	0	52	1
Aqib Javed	4	0	27	0
Mushtaq Ahmed	10	1	50	0
Aamir Sohail	1	0	12	0
Waqar Younis	7	0	44	1
Salim Malik	1.1	0	4	0

FALL OF WICKETS
1-22, 2-84, 3-145, 4-151, 5-162, 6-169, 7-177, 8-185, 9-185, 10-188

FALL OF WICKETS
1-73, 2-132

Referee: R.S.Madugalle (*Sri Lanka*).

Umpires: B.C.Cooray (*Sri Lanka*) (25) and D.B.Cowie (NZ) (18).

INDIA v SOUTH AFRICA 1995-96

At Sharjah CA Stadium, UAE on 17 April 1996.   Result: **SOUTH AFRICA** won by 5 wickets.   Toss: India.
Award: P.R.Adams.   LOI debuts: None.

Although comfortably beaten, India qualified for the final on net run rate, the product of subtracting runs conceded per over from runs scored per over. Final points and rates: South Africa 8 (1.68); India 2 (0.64); Pakistan 2 (-1.15).

INDIA		Runs	Balls	4/6
V.Rathore	c Cronje b Adams	50	91	5
S.R.Tendulkar	c Kirsten b De Villiers	17	26	2
N.S.Sidhu	lbw b De Villiers	1	10	–
S.V.Manjrekar	c Kirsten b Kallis	14	33	–
* M.Azharuddin	st Richardson b Adams	4	8	–
A.Jadeja	not out	71	69	2/2
† N.R.Mongia	c Kirsten b Adams	13	35	–
A.Kumble	run out	16	21	1
J.Srinath	c sub (C.R.Matthews) b Pollock	15	8	2
B.K.V.Prasad	not out	1	1	–
S.L.V.Raju				
Extras	(lb 4, w 7, nb 2)	13		
Total	(50 overs; 8 wicktes)	**215**		

SOUTH AFRICA		Runs	Balls	4/6
G.Kirsten	c Mongia b Kumble	39	57	2
J.H.Kallis	run out	22	32	2
D.J.Cullinan	c Prasad b Raju	64	100	3
* W.J.Cronje	b Raju	1	4	–
D.N.Crookes	b Raju	54	61	2/2
S.M.Pollock	not out	11	15	1
J.N.Rhodes	not out	12	14	–/1
B.M.McMillan				
† D.J.Richardson				
P.S.de Villiers				
P.R.Adams				
Extras	(b 3, lb 2, w 8)	13		
Total	(47.1 overs; 5 wickets)	**216**		

SOUTH AFRICA	O	M	R	W
Pollock	8	0	39	1
De Villiers	10	2	28	2
McMillan	5	0	25	0
Kallis	7	0	34	1
Adams	10	0	30	3
Crookes	10	0	55	0

INDIA	O	M	R	W
Srinath	10	0	55	0
Prasad	10	0	43	0
Kumble	10	0	37	1
Raju	10	0	38	3
Jadeja	7	0	37	0
Sidhu	0.1	0	1	0

FALL OF WICKETS
1-23, 2-26, 3-72, 4-89, 5-100, 6-140, 7-177, 8-199

FALL OF WICKETS
1-53, 2-85, 3-98, 4-192, 5-193

Umpires: B.C.Cooray (*Sri Lanka*) (26) and M.J.Kitchen (*England*) (16).

Referee: R.S.Madugalle (*Sri Lanka*).

INDIA v SOUTH AFRICA 1995-96

At Sharjah CA Stadium, UAE on 19 April 1996.   Result: **SOUTH AFRICA** won by 38 runs.   Toss: South Africa.
Award: G.Kirsten.   Series award: G.Kirsten.   LOI debuts: None.

The final produced the best contest of the tournament, South Africa's tenacious fielding defending a par total for Sharjah. Gary Kirsten's second hundred of this campaign was his fourth in 15 innings within six months. South Africa took their tally of wins in the 1995-96 season to 18 out of 20.

SOUTH AFRICA		Runs	Balls	4/6
G.Kirsten	not out	115	142	4/1
A.C.Hudson	c Azharuddin b Srinath	0	1	–
D.J.Cullinan	b Prasad	2	19	–
P.L.Symcox	c Jadeja b Raju	61	49	5/2
* W.J.Cronje	c Rathore b Kumble	25	34	1
D.N.Crookes	c Rathore b Kumble	26	30	1
B.M.McMillan	not out	37	25	2/3
S.M.Pollock				
† D.J.Richardson				
C.R.Matthews				
P.S.de Villiers				
Extras	(lb 5, w 16)	21		
Total	(50 overs; 5 wickets)	287		

INDIA		Runs	Balls	4/6
V.Rathore	c Richardson b Matthews	23	35	1/1
S.R.Tendulkar	run out	57	71	6
A.Kumble	run out	10	9	1
N.S.Sidhu	c Matthews b Cronje	26	44	2
S.V.Manjrekar	run out	41	47	1
* M.Azharuddin	run out	39	43	3
A.Jadeja	c Cullinan b McMillan	2	3	–
J.Srinath	c Richardson b De Villiers	10	22	–
† N.R.Mongia	c and b Pollock	23	24	1
B.K.V.Prasad	not out	5	4	1
S.L.V.Raju	not out	0	1	–
Extras	(lb 10, w 1, nb 2)	13		
Total	(50 overs; 9 wickets)	249		

INDIA	O	M	R	W
Srinath	10	1	51	1
Prasad	10	0	50	1
Tendulkar	7	0	51	0
Kumble	10	1	42	2
Raju	9	0	70	1
Jadeja	4	0	18	0

SOUTH AFRICA	O	M	R	W
De Villiers	10	0	42	1
Pollock	10	0	57	1
McMillan	10	0	48	1
Matthews	10	1	46	1
Symcox	6	0	23	0
Cronje	4	0	23	1

FALL OF WICKETS
1-5, 2-20, 3-115, 4-175, 5-227

FALL OF WICKETS
1-59, 2-78, 3-112, 4-130, 5-204, 6-206, 7-209, 8-243, 9-249

Umpires: B.C.Cooray (*Sri Lanka*) (27) and M.J.Kitchen (*England*) (17).

Referee: R.S.Madugalle (*Sri Lanka*).

WEST INDIES v SRI LANKA 1995-96

At Queen's Park Oval, Port-of-Spain, Trinidad on 13 April 1996.   Result: **SRI LANKA** won by 35 runs.
Toss: Sri Lanka.   Award: H.D.P.K.Dharmasena.   LOI debuts: None.

Less than a fortnight after winning the World Cup, Sri Lanka made their first visit to the Caribbean, a lightning affair which formed part of the celebrations of the centenary of Trinidad's Queen's Park Oval. Watched by a crowd of around 20,000, the visiting openers scored 67 off 6.2 overs.

SRI LANKA		Runs	Balls	4/6
S.T.Jayasuriya	c Wallace b Walsh	46	33	8
† R.S.Kaluwitharana	c Adams b Harper	25	22	2/1
A.P.Gurusinha	c Lara b Adams	59	107	2
P.A.de Silva	c and b Williams	25	33	2
* A.Ranatunga	c Wallace b Adams	15	15	1
H.P.Tillekeratne	c and b Chanderpaul	22	34	–
W.P.U.C.J.Vaas	b Bishop	12	12	–
R.S.Mahanama	c Chanderpaul b Walsh	14	17	1
U.U.Chandana	c Adams b Harper	7	13	–
H.D.P.K.Dharmasena	not out	3	4	–
M.Muralitharan	c Adams b Harper	4	6	–
Extras	(lb 8, w 8, nb 3)	19		
Total	(48.3 overs)	251		

WEST INDIES		Runs	Balls	4/6
S.Chanderpaul	run out	3	8	–
P.A.Wallace	c Muralitharan b Vaas	3	15	–
B.C.Lara	c Jayasuriya b Dharmasena	71	93	6/1
P.V.Simmons	c Dharmasena b Muralitharan	45	63	5
J.C.Adams	not out	37	55	1
R.I.C.Holder	b Dharmasena	1	14	–
R.A.Harper	c Kaluwitharana b Chandana	0	4	–
L.R.Williams	b Muralitharan	5	14	–
† C.O.Browne	c and b Jayasuriya	9	19	–
I.R.Bishop	c Ranatunga b Tillekeratne	22	17	1/1
* C.A.Walsh				
Extras	(lb 8, w 10, nb 2)	20		
Total	(50 overs; 9 wickets)	216		

WEST INDIES	O	M	R	W
Bishop	5	0	49	1
Walsh	8	1	40	2
Harper	9.3	1	34	3
Williams	8	0	42	1
Adams	10	0	42	2
Chanderpaul	8	0	36	1

SRI LANKA	O	M	R	W
Vaas	6	1	19	1
De Silva	9	1	42	0
Muralitharan	10	1	37	2
Dharmasena	9	1	33	2
Chandana	10	0	40	2
Jayasuriya	5	0	32	1
Tillekeratne	1	0	5	1

FALL OF WICKETS
1-67, 2-88, 3-137, 4-168, 5-200, 6-217, 7-219, 8-243, 9-246, 10-251

FALL OF WICKETS
1-8, 2-15, 3-131, 4-134, 5-140, 6-141, 7-156, 8-180, 9-216

Umpires: C.E.Cumberbatch (23) and E.Nicholls (3).

Referee: M.H.Denness (*England*).

ENGLAND v INDIA 1996

At Kennington Oval, London on 23, 24 (*no play*) May 1996. No result. Toss: England.
Award: C.C.Lewis. LOI debuts: England – A.D.Brown, M.A.Ealham, R.C.Irani; India – P.L.Mhambrey.

The first 50-over LOI in England with just one interval. Paras Mhambrey took a wicket with his fifth ball in international cricket. Graeme Hick completed 2000 runs in 60 matches. Rain brought a halt for two hours (India 73 for 5 after 13 overs), bad light ended play after another 20 minutes and the reserve day was washed out.

ENGLAND		Runs	Balls	4/6	INDIA		Runs	Balls	4/6
* M.A.Atherton	c Mongia b Prasad	13	31	–	V.Rathore	lbw b Lewis	23	19	3
A.D.Brown	b Mhambrey	37	52	4	S.R.Tendulkar	lbw b Martin	30	19	5/1
N.M.K.Smith	c Tendulkar b Mhambrey	17	11	4	A.Kumble	c Hick b Lewis	0	2	–
G.A.Hick	c Manjrekar b Srinath	91	102	4/1	N.S.Sidhu	b Lewis	3	13	–
G.P.Thorpe	c Mongia b Jadeja	26	31	2	* M.Azharuddin	not out	15	25	1
† A.J.Stewart	run out	3	6	–	S.V.Manjrekar	b Lewis	3	8	–
R.C.Irani	c Prasad b Kumble	11	13	–	A.Jadeja	not out	11	18	2
M.A.Ealham	b Kumble	40	34	3/2	† N.R.Mongia				
C.C.Lewis	not out	29	21	2/1	J.Srinath				
D.G.Cork	not out	0	1	–	P.L.Mhambrey				
P.J.Martin					B.K.V.Prasad				
Extras	(b 1, lb 11, w 11, nb 1)	24			Extras	(b 4, lb 2, w 4, nb 1)	11		
Total	(50 overs; 8 wickets)	291			Total	(17.1 overs; 5 wickets)	96		

INDIA	O	M	R	W	ENGLAND	O	M	R	W
Srinath	10	1	45	1	Cork	3	0	21	0
Prasad	10	1	63	1	Lewis	8.1	0	40	4
Mhambrey	9	0	69	2	Martin	6	0	29	1
Kumble	10	1	29	2					
Tendulkar	6	0	44	0	FALL OF WICKETS				
Jadeja	5	0	29	1	1-54, 2-54, 3-56, 4-62, 5-68				

FALL OF WICKETS
1-31, 2-57, 3-85, 4-141, 5-147, 6-176, 7-252, 8-276

Referee: C.W.Smith (*West Indies*).

Umpires: R.Julian (1) and P.Willey (1).

ENGLAND v INDIA 1996

At Headingley, Leeds on 25 May 1996. Result: **ENGLAND** won by 6 wickets. Toss: England.
Award: G.P.Thorpe. LOI debuts: None.

Rain delayed the start and, there being no reserve day, the match was reduced to 42 overs each. An all-Surrey partnership rescued England from a disastrous start in a low-scoring match on a drab day.

INDIA		Runs	Balls	4/6	ENGLAND		Runs	Balls	4/6
V.Rathore	c Thorpe b Cork	7	26	–	* M.A.Atherton	c Tendulkar b Prasad	7	36	–
S.R.Tendulkar	run out	6	19	1	A.D.Brown	lbw b Srinath	0	2	–
N.S.Sidhu	run out	20	41	2	G.A.Hick	lbw b Prasad	0	1	–
* M.Azharuddin	c Brown b Martin	40	68	2/1	G.P.Thorpe	not out	79	118	10
S.V.Manjrekar	run out	24	33	1	M.P.Maynard	run out	14	23	2
A.Jadeja	c Martin b Cork	33	27	3	† A.J.Stewart	not out	47	59	4
† N.R.Mongia	c Atherton b Cork	9	13	1	M.A.Ealham				
A.Kumble	c Stewart b Martin	0	2	–	C.C.Lewis				
J.Srinath	c Cork b Gough	5	4	1	D.Gough				
P.L.Mhambrey	not out	7	5	1	D.G.Cork				
B.K.V.Prasad	c Stewart b Martin	1	5	–	P.J.Martin				
Extras	(lb 1, w 5)	6			Extras	(lb 5, w 8, nb 2)	15		
Total	(40.2 overs)	158			Total	(39.3 overs; 4 wickets)	162		

ENGLAND	O	M	R	W	INDIA	O	M	R	W
Cork	9	1	46	3	Srinath	9	4	18	1
Lewis	9	1	30	0	Prasad	9	2	33	2
Martin	8.2	1	34	3	Kumble	9	0	36	0
Gough	8	1	24	1	Mhambrey	6	0	29	0
Ealham	6	0	23	0	Tendulkar	3	0	15	0
					Jadeja	3	0	22	0
					Manjrekar	0.3	0	4	0

FALL OF WICKETS
1-16, 2-17, 3-58, 4-94, 5-113, 6-145, 7-145, 8-149, 9-155, 10-158

Umpires: M.J.Kitchen (18) and A.G.T.Whitehead (13).

FALL OF WICKETS
1-1, 2-2, 3-23, 4-68

Referee: C.W.Smith (*West Indies*).

ENGLAND v INDIA 1996

At Old Trafford, Manchester on 26, 27 May 1996.   Result: **ENGLAND** won by 4 wickets.   Toss: India.
Award: A.D.Brown.   LOI debuts: None.

An outstanding innings by Alistair Brown brought England a convincing victory, and the Texaco Trophy, in their 250th international. Navjot Sidhu abandoned the tour after being dropped for this match. Rain terminated the first day's play when England were 2 for 1 after one over.

INDIA		Runs	Balls	4/6
V.Rathore	c Cork b Thorpe	54	95	4
S.R.Tendulkar	c Hick b Cork	1	11	–
S.C.Ganguly	st Stewart b Thorpe	46	83	3
* M.Azharuddin	not out	73	64	3/1
A.Jadeja	c Stewart b Cork	29	32	1/1
R.David	not out	22	15	3
A.Kumble				
† N.R.Mongia				
J.Srinath				
S.L.V.Raju				
B.K.V.Prasad				
Extras	(b 1, lb 4, w 6)	11		
Total	(50 overs; 4 wickets)	**236**		

ENGLAND		Runs	Balls	4/6
* M.A.Atherton	lbw b Srinath	0	2	–
A.D.Brown	c Dravid b Srinath	118	137	10/2
N.M.K.Smith	c and b Prasad	11	27	1
G.A.Hick	c Dravid b Prasad	32	45	2/1
G.P.Thorpe	run out	29	33	3
M.P.Maynard	lbw b Kumble	14	28	1
† A.J.Stewart	not out	13	19	2
C.C.Lewis	not out	4	2	1
D.Gough				
D.G.Cork				
P.J.Martin				
Extras	(lb 10, w 8)	18		
Total	(48.5 overs; 6 wickets)	**239**		

ENGLAND	O	M	R	W
Cork	10	3	35	2
Lewis	10	1	49	0
Gough	10	1	43	0
Martin	10	0	50	0
Smith	6	0	39	0
Thorpe	4	0	15	2

INDIA	O	M	R	W
Srinath	10	1	35	2
Prasad	10	1	26	2
Kumble	10	0	52	1
Raju	9.5	1	50	0
Ganguly	2	0	14	0
Tendulkar	2	0	22	0
Jadeja	5	0	30	0

FALL OF WICKETS
1-11, 2-103, 3-118, 4-190

FALL OF WICKETS
1-2, 2-32, 3-117, 4-186, 5-217, 6-226

Umpires: D.J.Constant (30) and A.A.Jones (1).

Referee: C.W.Smith (*West Indies*).

AUSTRALIA v ZIMBABWE 1996-97

At R.Premadasa Stadium, Colombo on 26 August 1996.   Result: **AUSTRALIA** won by 125 runs.   Toss: Australia.
Award: S.R.Waugh.   LOI debuts: Australia – G.B.Hogg; Zimbabwe – C.B.Wishart.

Both teams employed new captains, Alistair Campbell succeeding Andrew Flower (abdicated) while Ian Healy deputised for Mark Taylor (recovering from back surgery). Although rain halted play for 55 minutes during Australia's innings, there was no reduction of overs.

AUSTRALIA		Runs	Balls	4/6
M.J.Slater	c Strang b Whittall	50	69	4
M.E.Waugh	b Strang	18	27	2
R.T.Ponting	c and b Whittall	53	82	–
S.R.Waugh	c Campbell b Whittall	82	70	5/3
S.G.Law	b Streak	20	24	1
M.G.Bevan	c Campbell b Brandes	9	8	1
*† I.A.Healy	b Brandes	5	10	–
G.B.Hogg	not out	11	14	–
P.R.Reiffel				
D.W.Fleming				
G.D.McGrath				
Extras	(b 1, lb 8, w 3, nb 3)	15		
Total	(50 overs; 7 wickets)	**263**		

ZIMBABWE		Runs	Balls	4/6
G.W.Flower	c Ponting b Fleming	7	23	–
A.H.Shah	c M.E.Waugh b Hogg	41	76	–/1
† A.Flower	lbw b Fleming	0	2	–
* A.D.R.Campbell	lbw b McGrath	9	11	1
C.B.Wishart	c Healy b Reiffel	0	7	–
G.J.Whittall	b Reiffel	11	27	1
C.N.Evans	c Healy b S.R.Waugh	15	29	2
M.H.Dekker	not out	8	43	–
P.A.Strang	b M.E.Waugh	9	26	–
H.H.Streak	b M.E.Waugh	0	1	–
E.A.Brandes	c Hogg b M.E.Waugh	17	12	2/1
Extras	(lb 4, w 10, nb 7)	21		
Total	(41 overs)	**138**		

ZIMBABWE	O	M	R	W
Streak	10	1	50	1
Brandes	10	1	47	2
Strang	9	0	41	1
G.W.Flower	6	0	28	0
Whittall	10	0	53	3
Dekker	3	0	17	0
Shah	2	0	18	0

AUSTRALIA	O	M	R	W
McGrath	7	2	13	1
Fleming	7	0	24	2
Reiffel	6	1	23	2
S.R.Waugh	7	2	24	1
Hogg	9	2	26	1
M.E.Waugh	5	0	24	3

FALL OF WICKETS
1-48, 2-92, 3-167, 4-230, 5-240, 6-242, 7-263

FALL OF WICKETS
1-16, 2-16, 3-33, 4-35, 5-56, 6-98, 7-100, 8-120, 9-120, 10-138

Umpires: K.T.Francis (28) and W.A.U.Wickremasinghe (11).

Referee: J.R.Reid (*New Zealand*).

SRI LANKA v INDIA 1996-97

At R.Premadasa Stadium, Colombo on 28 August 1996.   Result: **SRI LANKA** won by 9 wickets.   Toss: India.
Award: S.T.Jayasuriya.   LOI debuts: None.

Sachin Tendulkar celebrated his debut as India's captain with his ninth hundred. Exhorted by a crowd of 35,000, Sanath Jayasuriya scored his third hundred off 103 balls. His stand of 129 with Roshan Kaluwitharana was Sri Lanka's highest for the first wicket.

INDIA		Runs	Balls	4/6
A.Jadeja	run out	0	9	–
* S.R.Tendulkar	run out	110	138	5/1
S.C.Ganguly	c De Silva b Dharmasena	16	41	3
M.Azharuddin	st Kaluwitharana b Jayasuriya	58	99	1
V.G.Kambli	run out	18	14	1/1
R.Dravid	not out	7	4	–
J.Srinath	not out	1	1	–
† N.R.Mongia				
A.Kumble				
A.R.Kapoor				
B.K.V.Prasad				
Extras	(b 1, lb 3, w 9, nb 3)	16		
Total	(50 overs; 5 wickets)	226		

SRI LANKA		Runs	Balls	4/6
S.T.Jayasuriya	not out	120	128	8/3
† R.S.Kaluwitharana	b Tendulkar	53	65	3
P.A.de Silva	not out	49	76	4
A.P.Gurusinha				
* A.Ranatunga				
H.P.Tillekeratne				
R.S.Mahanama				
H.D.P.K.Dharmasena				
W.P.U.C.J.Vaas				
M.Muralitharan				
K.R.Pushpakumara				
Extras	(lb 3, w 2, nb 3)	8		
Total	(44.2 overs; 1 wicket)	230		

SRI LANKA	O	M	R	W
Vaas	9	2	35	0
Pushpakumara	6	0	23	0
Dharmasena	10	0	59	1
Muralitharan	10	0	42	0
Jayasuriya	10	1	39	1
De Silva	5	0	24	0

INDIA	O	M	R	W
Srinath	8	0	33	0
Prasad	6	0	47	0
Kapoor	10	2	51	0
Kumble	10	1	40	0
Tendulkar	6	0	29	1
Jadeja	2.2	0	13	0
Ganguly	2	0	14	0

FALL OF WICKETS
1-4, 2-57, 3-186, 4-217, 5-218

FALL OF WICKETS
1-129

Umpires: S.A.Bucknor (WI) (36) and C.J.Mitchley (South Africa) (30).

Referee: J.R.Reid (New Zealand).

SRI LANKA v AUSTRALIA 1996-97

At R.Premadasa Stadium, Colombo on 30 August 1996.   Result: **SRI LANKA** won by 4 wickets.   Toss: Australia.
Award: P.A.de Silva.   LOI debuts: Australia – J.N.Gillespie, D.S.Lehmann.

A sixth-wicket stand of 115 between Aravinda de Silva and Roshan Mahanama carried Sri Lanka into the final.

AUSTRALIA		Runs	Balls	4/6
M.E.Waugh	c and b Jayasuriya	50	55	7
M.J.Slater	run out	9	19	–
S.G.Law	c Tillekeratne b Dharmasena	13	8	1
M.G.Bevan	c Vaas b Chandana	56	78	2
S.R.Waugh	b Muralitharan	22	36	–
R.T.Ponting	not out	46	57	1/1
D.S.Lehmann	st Kaluwitharana b Chandana	2	4	–
*†I.A.Healy	c Ranatunga b Muralitharan	8	16	–
J.N.Gillespie	st Kaluwitharana b Chandana	6	13	–
D.W.Fleming	c Chandana b Jayasuriya	3	6	–
G.D.McGrath	not out	8	12	–
Extras	(lb 3, nb 2)	5		
Total	(50 overs; 9 wickets)	228		

SRI LANKA		Runs	Balls	4/6
S.T.Jayasuriya	c Healy b Fleming	44	28	8/1
† R.S.Kaluwitharana	b S.R.Waugh	8	13	1
A.P.Gurusinha	run out	16	30	2
P.A.de Silva	not out	83	95	11
* A.Ranatunga	lbw b Fleming	0	3	–
H.P.Tillekeratne	lbw b Fleming	1	10	–
R.S.Mahanama	b McGrath	50	78	3
U.U.Chandana	not out	14	25	2
H.D.P.K.Dharmasena				
W.P.U.C.J.Vaas				
M.Muralitharan				
Extras	(lb 3, w 7, nb 6)	16		
Total	(45.5 overs; 6 wickets)	232		

SRI LANKA	O	M	R	W
Vaas	7	0	29	0
De Silva	4	0	25	0
Dharmasena	9	0	49	1
Muralitharan	10	0	41	2
Jayasuriya	10	0	43	2
Chandana	10	0	38	3

AUSTRALIA	O	M	R	W
S.R.Waugh	5	1	36	1
Law	2	0	23	0
McGrath	9.5	0	44	1
Fleming	8	1	26	3
Gillespie	6	0	27	0
M.E.Waugh	5	0	29	0
Lehmann	6	0	26	0
Bevan	4	0	18	0

FALL OF WICKETS
1-21, 2-52, 3-97, 4-149, 5-157, 6-163, 7-178, 8-198, 9-203

FALL OF WICKETS
1-22, 2-78, 3-78, 4-78, 5-81, 6-196

Umpires: S.A.Bucknor (WI) (37) and C.J.Mitchley (South Africa) (31).

Referee: J.R.Reid (New Zealand).

INDIA v ZIMBABWE 1996-97

At Sinhalese Sports Club, Colombo on 1 September 1996.　　Result: **INDIA** won by 7 wickets.　　Toss: India.
Award: A.Jadeja.　　LOI debuts: India – S.B.Joshi.

Mid-way through India's innings the total was reduced by one run at the request of match referee John Reid, because his video replays did not show umpire Samarasinghe signalling a wide bowled by Prasad. Signalled late, the TV cameras missed it. As both scorers witnessed and acknowledged the signal, their official score is published here.

ZIMBABWE		Runs	Balls	4/6
* A.D.R.Campbell	c Tendulkar b Prasad	10	20	2
P.A.Strang	st Mongia b Joshi	19	35	3
† A.Flower	c Prasad b Kumble	78	115	3
C.N.Evans	c Mongia b Joshi	4	15	–
G.W.Flower	b Kumble	26	44	–
C.B.Wishart	c Joshi b Kumble	53	41	3/3
G.J.Whittall	run out	1	4	–
M.H.Dekker	c Kumble b Srinath	3	13	–
H.H.Streak	b Kumble	2	7	–
A.H.Shah	c Azharuddin b Prasad	6	5	1
B.C.Strang	not out	1	3	–
Extras	(lb 12, w 9, nb 2)	23		
Total	**(49.4 overs)**	**226**		

INDIA		Runs	Balls	4/6
A.Jadeja	c A.Flower b Evans	68	80	6/2
* S.R.Tendulkar	c B.C.Strang b Streak	40	46	8
S.C.Ganguly	c B.C.Strang b P.A.Strang	36	52	3/1
M.Azharuddin	not out	40	54	5
V.G.Kambli	not out	29	36	4
R.Dravid				
† N.R.Mongia				
S.B.Joshi				
A.Kumble				
J.Srinath				
B.K.V.Prasad				
Extras	(lb 1, w 9, nb 6)	16		
Total	**(43.5 overs; 3 wickets)**	**229**		

INDIA	O	M	R	W
Srinath	10	2	42	1
Prasad	7.4	0	42	2
Joshi	10	1	37	2
Jadeja	5	0	20	0
Tendulkar	4	0	20	0
Kumble	10	2	33	4
Ganguly	3	0	20	0

ZIMBABWE	O	M	R	W
Streak	10	1	46	1
B.C.Strang	7.5	0	52	0
P.A.Strang	10	0	73	1
Whittall	9	0	28	0
G.W.Flower	2	0	10	0
Evans	5	0	19	1

FALL OF WICKETS
1-22, 2-50, 3-61, 4-117, 5-201, 6-204, 7-217, 8-218, 9-220, 10-226

FALL OF WICKETS
1-91, 2-148, 3-161

Umpires: B.C.Cooray (28) and T.M.Samarasinghe (10).

Referee: J.R.Reid (*New Zealand*).

SRI LANKA v ZIMBABWE 1996-97

At Sinhalese Sports Club, Colombo on 3 September 1996.　　Result: **SRI LANKA** won by 6 wickets.　　Toss: Sri Lanka.
Award: P.A.de Silva.　　LOI debuts: Zimbabwe – A.R.Whittall.

Craig Evans scored his first fifty in 15 LOIs and was only a boundary short of Zimbabwe's fourth hundred in 59 matches. Aravinda de Silva's match-winning innings was his sixth hundred at this level.

ZIMBABWE		Runs	Balls	4/6
G.W.Flower	c Kaluwitharana b Pushpakumara	0	8	–
P.A.Strang	c Kaluwitharana b Pushpakumara	24	33	3
A.Flower	c Kaluwitharana b Wickremasinghe	11	22	–
* A.D.R.Campbell	st Kaluwitharana b Muralitharan	54	94	3
C.B.Wishart	c Chandana b Ranatunga	7	13	1
C.N.Evans	not out	96	105	6/3
G.J.Whittall	not out	15	28	1
† W.R.James				
H.H.Streak				
A.R.Whittall				
H.K.Olonga				
Extras	(lb 7, w 13)	20		
Total	**(50 overs; 5 wickets)**	**227**		

SRI LANKA		Runs	Balls	4/6
S.T.Jayasuriya	b Olonga	5	17	–
† R.S.Kaluwitharana	c Wishart b Olonga	12	14	2
A.P.Gurusinha	run out	15	47	–
P.A.de Silva	not out	127	123	13/1
* A.Ranatunga	c Olonga b A.R.Whittall	20	24	4
H.P.Tillekeratne	not out	34	64	2
M.S.Atapattu				
U.U.Chandana				
G.P.Wickremasinghe				
K.R.Pushpakumara				
M.Muralitharan				
Extras	(b 1, lb 2, w 8, nb 4)	15		
Total	**(47 overs; 4 wickets)**	**228**		

SRI LANKA	O	M	R	W
Wickremasinghe	9	1	32	1
Pushpakumara	6	0	28	2
Muralitharan	10	1	36	1
Ranatunga	5	0	22	1
Chandana	10	0	48	0
Jayasuriya	10	0	54	0

ZIMBABWE	O	M	R	W
Streak	8	0	24	0
Olonga	6	0	47	2
G.J.Whittall	5	0	26	0
A.R.Whittall	10	1	30	1
Strang	10	0	50	0
Campbell	4	0	24	0
G.W.Flower	1	0	10	0
Evans	3	0	14	0

FALL OF WICKETS
1-13, 2-48, 3-48, 4-66, 5-180

FALL OF WICKETS
1-18, 2-25, 3-100, 4-129

Umpires: S.A.Bucknor (*West Indies*) (38) and C.J.Mitchley (*SA*) (32).

Referee: J.R.Reid (*New Zealand*).

AUSTRALIA v INDIA 1996-97

At Sinhalese Sports Club, Colombo on 5 (*no play*), 6 September 1996.   Result: **AUSTRALIA** won by 3 wickets.
Toss: Australia.   Award: S.R.Waugh.   LOI debuts: None.

Match reduced to 45 overs each by rain. Steve Waugh was reprimanded and fined 30% of his match fee (suspended for three months) for challenging umpire Cooray's decisions regarding wide deliveries. Sourav Ganguly and Sunil Joshi shared India's first hundred partnership for the seventh wicket.

INDIA		Runs	Balls	4/6
† N.R.Mongia	c Bevan b McGrath	38	30	8
* S.R.Tendulkar	c S.R.Waugh b McGrath	7	11	1
R.Dravid	b Reiffel	13	25	1
M.Azharuddin	c M.E.Waugh b Reiffel	3	6	–
V.G.Kambli	c Healy b McGrath	1	7	–
A.Jadeja	c and b S.R.Waugh	6	17	1
S.C.Ganguly	lbw b Bevan	59	75	7
S.B.Joshi	b Bevan	48	67	5
J.Srinath	run out	2	5	–
A.Kumble	c S.R.Waugh b M.E.Waugh	0	3	–
B.K.V.Prasad	not out	6	7	–
Extras	(lb 4, w 11, nb 3)	18		
Total	(41 overs)	**201**		

AUSTRALIA		Runs	Balls	4/6
M.J.Slater	c Azharuddin b Prasad	29	56	4
M.E.Waugh	c Tendulkar b Joshi	23	33	3
R.T.Ponting	lbw b Joshi	0	3	–
S.R.Waugh	st Mongia b Kumble	55	83	2
S.G.Law	c Dravid b Prasad	67	70	3/2
M.G.Bevan	not out	12	9	1
*†I.A.Healy	run out	4	13	–
G.B.Hogg	b Kumble	2	4	–
P.R.Reiffel	not out	1	1	–
D.W.Fleming				
G.D.McGrath				
Extras	(lb 2, w 4, nb 3)	9		
Total	(44.3 overs; 7 wickets)	**202**		

AUSTRALIA	O	M	R	W
McGrath	9	1	33	3
Fleming	6	0	25	0
Reiffel	5	0	37	2
S.R.Waugh	6	0	20	1
Hogg	5	0	33	0
M.E.Waugh	7	0	35	1
Bevan	3	0	14	2

INDIA	O	M	R	W
Srinath	6	0	32	0
Prasad	9	0	53	2
Joshi	9	1	23	2
Kumble	8.3	1	36	2
Tendulkar	8	0	38	0
Jadeja	4	0	18	0

FALL OF WICKETS
1-32, 2-64, 3-67, 4-68, 5-72, 6-89, 7-189, 8-191, 9-194, 10-201

FALL OF WICKETS
1-50, 2-50, 3-69, 4-182, 5-185, 6-194, 7-197

Umpires: B.C.Cooray (29) and K.T.Francis (29).

Referee: J.R.Reid (*New Zealand*).

SRI LANKA v AUSTRALIA 1996-97

At R.Premadasa Stadium, Colombo on 7 September 1996.   Result: **SRI LANKA** won by 50 runs.   Toss: Australia.
Award: P.A.de Silva.   Series Award: P.A.de Silva.   LOI debuts: None.

Sri Lanka were again convincing winners of this repeat of the World Cup final. Aravinda de Silva was again the batting star and he deservedly picked up the awards for this match and for a series in which he had scored 334 runs without being dismissed.

SRI LANKA		Runs	Balls	4/6
S.T.Jayasuriya	c Law b McGrath	27	20	5
† R.S.Kaluwitharana	c and b Lehmann	58	45	5
A.P.Gurusinha	c Bevan b McGrath	29	46	1
P.A.de Silva	not out	75	64	2/3
* A.Ranatunga	not out	39	40	1/1
H.P.Tillekeratne				
R.S.Mahanama				
U.U.Chandana				
H.D.P.K.Dharmasena				
W.P.U.C.J.Vaas				
M.Muralitharan				
Extras	(b 1, lb 1, w 2, nb 2)	6		
Total	(35 overs; 3 wickets)	**234**		

AUSTRALIA		Runs	Balls	4/6
M.E.Waugh	run out	9	12	–
M.J.Slater	c Chandana b Vaas	8	6	1
R.T.Ponting	c Jayasuriya b Vaas	17	26	2
S.R.Waugh	c and b Chandana	55	53	2/1
S.G.Law	c Muralitharan b Dharmasena	31	37	2
M.G.Bevan	b Dharmasena	7	11	–
D.S.Lehmann	st Kaluwitharana b Muralitharan	15	12	2
*†I.A.Healy	c Muralitharan b Chandana	20	19	–
P.R.Reiffel	c Mahanama b Chandana	15	20	–
D.W.Fleming	not out	1	1	–
G.D.McGrath	c Mahanama b Chandana	0	3	–
Extras	(w 4, nb 2)	6		
Total	(33 overs)	**184**		

AUSTRALIA	O	M	R	W
McGrath	7	0	35	2
Fleming	7	0	53	0
Reiffel	4	0	43	0
Lehmann	5	0	29	1
S.R.Waugh	7	0	31	0
M.E.Waugh	5	0	41	0

SRI LANKA	O	M	R	W
Vaas	5	0	23	2
Gurusinha	2	0	17	0
De Silva	3	0	18	0
Muralitharan	7	0	31	1
Jayasuriya	5	0	27	0
Dharmasena	5	0	33	2
Chandana	6	0	35	4

FALL OF WICKETS
1-42, 2-104, 3-131

FALL OF WICKETS
1-17, 2-26, 3-48, 4-104, 5-129, 6-145, 7-151, 8-183, 9-183, 10-184

Umpires: S.A.Bucknor (*West Indies*) (39) and C.J.Mitchley (*SA*) (33).

Referee: J.R.Reid (*New Zealand*).

ENGLAND v PAKISTAN 1996

At Old Trafford, Manchester on 29 August 1996.   Result: **ENGLAND** won by 5 wickets.   Toss: Pakistan.
Award: M.A.Atherton.   LOI debuts: England – R.D.B.Croft, D.W.Headley, N.V.Knight, G.D.Lloyd, A.D.Mullally.

England gained some revenge for their defeat in The Oval Test three days earlier. Dean Headley provided the first instance of three generations of a family appearing at international level.

PAKISTAN		Runs	Balls	4/6
Saeed Anwar	c Mullally b Irani	57	75	7
Aamir Sohail	b Croft	48	117	2
Ijaz Ahmed	c Irani b Mullally	48	56	4
* Wasim Akram	b Croft	6	6	1
Inzamam-ul-Haq	not out	37	28	4
† Moin Khan	b Gough	10	9	2
Salim Malik	not out	6	9	–
Mushtaq Ahmed				
Saqlain Mushtaq				
Waqar Younis				
Ata-ur-Rehman				
Extras	(b 2, lb 4, w 7)	13		
Total	(50 overs; 5 wickets)	**225**		

ENGLAND		Runs	Balls	4/6
N.V.Knight	c Moin b Wasim	26	34	2
† A.J.Stewart	lbw b Waqar	48	58	5
* M.A.Atherton	b Wasim	65	93	5
G.P.Thorpe	st Moin b Aamir	23	32	–
M.P.Maynard	b Wasim	41	53	1/1
G.D.Lloyd	not out	2	15	–
R.C.Irani	not out	6	2	1
R.D.B.Croft				
D.Gough				
D.W.Headley				
A.D.Mullally				
Extras	(lb 4, w 7, nb 4)	15		
Total	(46.4 overs; 5 wickets)	**226**		

ENGLAND	O	M	R	W
Gough	10	0	44	1
Mullally	10	3	31	1
Headley	10	0	52	0
Irani	10	0	56	1
Croft	10	1	36	2

PAKISTAN	O	M	R	W
Wasim Akram	9.4	1	45	3
Waqar Younis	7	0	28	1
Saqlain Mushtaq	10	1	54	0
Ata-ur-Rehman	3	0	14	0
Mushtaq Ahmed	10	0	52	0
Aamir Sohail	7	1	29	1

FALL OF WICKETS
1-82, 2-141, 3-160, 4-174, 5-203

Umpires: N.T.Plews (16) and G.Sharp (4).

FALL OF WICKETS
1-57, 2-98, 3-146, 4-200, 5-220

Referee: P.L.van der Merwe (*South Africa*).

ENGLAND v PAKISTAN 1996

At Edgbaston, Birmingham on 31 August 1996.   Result: **ENGLAND** won by 107 runs.   Toss: Pakistan.
Award: N.V.Knight.   LOI debuts: England – A.J.Hollioake.

Nick Knight scored a hundred on his home ground limited-overs international debut. Alec Stewart completed 2000 runs in 78 matches.

ENGLAND		Runs	Balls	4/6
N.V.Knight	st Moin b Saqlain	113	132	11
† A.J.Stewart	b Mushtaq Ahmed	46	32	4/2
* M.A.Atherton	lbw b Mushtaq Ahmed	1	2	–
G.P.Thorpe	lbw b Rehman	21	28	2
M.P.Maynard	run out	1	3	–
R.C.Irani	not out	45	63	1/1
A.J.Hollioake	run out	15	27	1
D.Gough	run out	0	1	–
R.D.B.Croft	b Waqar	15	13	1
D.W.Headley	not out	3	4	–
A.D.Mullally				
Extras	(lb 25, w 4, nb 3)	32		
Total	(50 overs; 8 wickets)	**292**		

PAKISTAN		Runs	Balls	4/6
Saeed Anwar	c Stewart b Gough	33	25	4/1
Aamir Sohail	c Croft b Gough	0	3	–
† Moin Khan	lbw b Mullally	0	5	–
Ijaz Ahmed	b Croft	79	80	10
Inzamam-ul-Haq	c Thorpe b Croft	6	16	–
Salim Malik	c Stewart b Hollioake	23	29	1
* Wasim Akram	c Knight b Hollioake	21	21	1
Mushtaq Ahmed	not out	14	19	1
Saqlain Mushtaq	b Hollioake	0	5	–
Waqar Younis	lbw b Gough	4	11	–
Ata-ur-Rehman	c Knight b Hollioake	2	15	–
Extras	(lb 2, nb 1)	3		
Total	(37.5 overs)	**185**		

PAKISTAN	O	M	R	W
Wasim Akram	10	0	50	0
Waqar Younis	9	0	54	1
Ata-ur-Rehman	6	0	40	1
Saqlain Mushtaq	10	0	59	1
Mushtaq Ahmed	10	0	33	2
Aamir Sohail	5	0	31	0

ENGLAND	O	M	R	W
Gough	8	0	39	3
Mullally	6	0	30	1
Headley	7	0	32	0
Irani	2	0	22	0
Croft	8	0	37	2
Hollioake	6.5	1	23	4

FALL OF WICKETS
1-103, 2-105, 3-163, 4-168, 5-221, 6-257, 7-257, 8-286

Umpires: M.J.Kitchen (19) and P.Willey (2).

FALL OF WICKETS
1-1, 2-6, 3-54, 4-104, 5-137, 6-164, 7-164, 8-168, 9-177, 10-185

Referee: P.L.van der Merwe (*South Africa*).

ENGLAND v PAKISTAN 1996

At Trent Bridge, Nottingham on 1 September 1996.   Result: **PAKISTAN** won by 2 wickets.   Toss: England.
Award: Pakistan team.   LOI debuts: Pakistan – Shadab Kabir, Shahid Anwar, Shahid Nazir.

Nick Knight emulated David Gower and Graham Gooch by scoring hundreds for England in consecutive internationals.
Remarkably he did so on consecutive days and completed each from 120 balls. Michael Atherton (14) retired with a
damaged thumb at 55 and returned at 178.

ENGLAND		Runs	Balls	4/6
N.V.Knight	not out	125	145	9
† A.J.Stewart	c and b Wasim	3	7	–
* M.A.Atherton	c Shahid Nazir b Wasim	30	48	1
M.P.Maynard	b Shahid Nazir	24	35	1
G.D.Lloyd	c Shadab b Saqlain	15	25	–
R.C.Irani	b Shahid Nazir	0	3	–
A.J.Hollioake	c Ijaz b Saqlain	13	23	–
D.Gough	b Wasim	5	11	–
R.D.B.Croft	b Waqar	0	1	–
P.J.Martin	run out	6	4	1
A.D.Mullally	b Waqar	2	3	–
Extras	(b 2, lb 8, w 9, nb 4)	23		
Total	(50 overs)	**246**		

PAKISTAN		Runs	Balls	4/6
Saeed Anwar	b Martin	61	59	9
Shahid Anwar	lbw b Martin	37	44	6
Ijaz Ahmed	c Lloyd b Gough	59	88	3
Aamir Sohail	b Croft	29	46	2
Shadab Kabir	c Irani b Hollioake	0	2	–
Asif Mujtaba	b Hollioake	2	7	–
* Wasim Akram	lbw b Hollioake	5	7	–
† Rashid Latif	not out	31	28	2
Saqlain Mushtaq	c Maynard b Hollioake	12	17	–
Waqar Younis	not out	0	–	–
Shahid Nazir				
Extras	(lb 5, w 6)	11		
Total	(49.4 overs; 8 wickets)	**247**		

PAKISTAN	O	M	R	W
Wasim Akram	10	1	45	3
Waqar Younis	10	1	49	2
Shahid Nazir	10	0	47	2
Asif Mujtaba	5	0	27	0
Saqlain Mushtaq	10	0	35	2
Aamir Sohail	5	0	33	0

ENGLAND	O	M	R	W
Gough	10	1	43	1
Mullally	9	0	66	0
Martin	10	0	38	2
Croft	10	0	38	1
Irani	2	0	12	0
Hollioake	8.4	0	45	4

FALL OF WICKETS
1-10, 2-108, 3-137, 4-139, 5-178, 6-216, 7-226, 8-231, 9-240, 10-246

FALL OF WICKETS
1-93, 2-114, 3-177, 4-182, 5-187, 6-199, 7-219, 8-240

Umpires: J.W.Holder (14) and D.R.Shepherd (65).

Referee: P.L.van der Merwe (*South Africa*).

INDIA v PAKISTAN 1996

At Toronto Cricket, Skating and Curling Club on 16 September 1996.   Result: **INDIA** won by 8 wickets.   Toss: India.
Award: S.R.Tendulkar.   LOI debuts: Pakistan – Azhar Mahmood.

Canada, the fourth non-Test-playing country to stage official internationals, provided the 111th venue. Following three
days of heavy rain, the ground required a delay of 4½ hours to recover before a 33-over match could begin.

PAKISTAN		Runs	Balls	4/6
Saeed Anwar	c and b Kumble	46	34	7
Aamir Sohail	c Dravid b Srinath	12	31	1
Ijaz Ahmed	lbw b Srinath	35	50	2
Inzamam-ul-Haq	c Kumble b Prasad	5	6	–
Salim Malik	c Joshi b Kumble	3	11	–
Shadab Kabir	c Azharuddin b Kumble	0	1	–
* Wasim Akram	run out	9	19	–
† Moin Khan	c Tendulkar b Srinath	2	5	–
Azhar Mahmood	c Joshi b Prasad	6	1	1
Saqlain Mushtaq	not out	22	11	1
Waqar Younis	not out	6	23	–
Extras	(lb 13, w 9, nb 2)	24		
Total	(33 overs; 9 wickets)	**170**		

INDIA		Runs	Balls	4/6
† N.R.Mongia	b Waqar	9	13	1
* S.R.Tendulkar	not out	89	89	9/3
R.Dravid	c Aamir b Salim	39	50	3
M.Azharuddin	not out	30	29	1/2
V.G.Kambli				
A.Jadeja				
S.C.Ganguly				
S.B.Joshi				
A.Kumble				
J.Srinath				
B.K.V.Prasad				
Extras	(lb 2, w 3, nb 1)	6		
Total	(29.5 overs; 2 wickets)	**173**		

INDIA	O	M	R	W
Srinath	7	0	23	3
Prasad	7	0	38	2
Jadeja	4	0	30	0
Joshi	6	0	22	0
Kumble	7	0	32	3
Tendulkar	2	0	12	0

PAKISTAN	O	M	R	W
Waqar Younis	6	0	30	1
Wasim Akram	6.5	0	37	0
Azhar Mahmood	4	0	19	0
Aamir Sohail	3	0	25	0
Saqlain Mushtaq	6	0	39	0
Salim Malik	4	0	21	1

FALL OF WICKETS
1-44, 2-80, 3-91, 4-98, 5-108, 6-123, 7-131, 8-135, 9-148

FALL OF WICKETS
1-18, 2-108

Umpires: L.H.Barker (*WI*) (32) and D.R.Shepherd (*England*) (66).

Referee: C.W.Smith (*West Indies*).

INDIA v PAKISTAN 1996

At Toronto Cricket, Skating and Curling Club on 17 September 1996.   Result: **PAKISTAN** won by 2 wickets.
Toss: Pakistan.   Award: Salim Malik.   LOI debuts: None.

An unbroken record ninth-wicket partnership of 45 between Salim Malik and Saqlain Mushtaq enabled Pakistan to draw level, Salim hitting the penultimate ball for four to take his team to the highest total of the tournament. Mohammed Azharuddin became the first Indian to score 6000 runs.

INDIA		Runs	Balls	4/6
† N.R.Mongia	c Wasim b Azhar	18	35	2
* S.R.Tendulkar	c Wasim b Azhar	20	23	3
R.Dravid	b Saqlain	90	114	6
M.Azharuddin	c Azhar b Mushtaq Ahmed	88	99	9
V.G.Kambli	c Aamir b Mushtaq Ahmed	3	5	–
A.Jadeja	not out	21	17	3
J.Srinath	c Wasim b Saqlain	0	1	–
S.C.Ganguly	not out	11	8	1
A.Kumble				
S.B.Joshi				
B.K.V.Prasad				
Extras	(b 4, lb 5, w 3, nb 1)	13		
TOTAL	(50 overs; 6 wickets)	**264**		

PAKISTAN		Runs	Balls	4/6
Saeed Anwar	c Joshi b Tendulkar	80	78	6/3
Aamir Sohail	c Mongia b Prasad	0	2	–
Ijaz Ahmed	c Mongia b Prasad	13	19	2
Inzamam-ul-Haq	c Dravid b Kumble	29	48	1/2
Salim Malik	not out	70	81	6
† Moin Khan	c Azharuddin b Joshi	14	16	2
* Wasim Akram	c Ganguly b Srinath	20	24	1/1
Azhar Mahmood	run out	1	2	–
Mushtaq Ahmed	c and b Srinath	4	8	–
Saqlain Mushtaq	not out	11	21	–
Waqar Younis				
Extras	(b 4, lb 11, w 9)	24		
TOTAL	(49.5 overs; 8 wickets)	**266**		

PAKISTAN	O	M	R	W
Wasim Akram	10	1	52	0
Waqar Younis	6	0	37	0
Azhar Mahmood	9	2	38	2
Mushtaq Ahmed	9	0	47	2
Saqlain Mushtaq	10	0	39	2
Aamir Sohail	5	0	33	0
Salim Malik	1	0	9	0

INDIA	O	M	R	W
Srinath	10	0	53	2
Prasad	10	0	54	2
Jadeja	3	0	20	0
Joshi	9.5	1	57	1
Kumble	10	0	32	1
Tendulkar	7	0	35	1

FALL OF WICKETS
1-32, 2-44, 3-205, 4-214, 5-245, 6-245

FALL OF WICKETS
1-10, 2-44, 3-115, 4-144, 5-169, 6-213, 7-215, 8-221

Umpires: L.H.Barker (*West Indies*) (33) and D.L.Orchard (*SA*) (12).   **Referee:** C.W.Smith (*West Indies*).

INDIA v PAKISTAN 1996

At Toronto Cricket, Skating and Curling Club on 18 September 1996.   Result: **INDIA** won by 55 runs.   Toss: India.
Award: R.S.Dravid.   LOI debuts: None.

This was a contest of collapses, India losing their last five wickets for 12 runs before Pakistan's first six fell for 66.

INDIA		Runs	Balls	4/6
† N.R.Mongia	lbw b Wasim	2	5	–
* S.R.Tendulkar	c Aamir b Wasim	2	13	–
R.Dravid	c Salim Elahi b Saqlain	46	93	3
M.Azharuddin	st Moin b Aamir	38	68	3
V.G.Kambli	st Moin b Mushtaq Ahmed	29	43	2/1
A.Jadeja	b Wasim	23	37	2
S.B.Joshi	run out	31	32	1/2
J.Srinath	c Saqlain b Wasim	3	5	–
A.R.Kapoor	c Mushtaq Ahmed b Saqlain	0	3	–
A.Kumble	run out	2	1	–
B.K.V.Prasad	not out	0	–	–
Extras	(lb 8, w 7)	15		
TOTAL	(50 overs)	**191**		

PAKISTAN		Runs	Balls	4/6
Saeed Anwar	c Tendulkar b Kumble	28	52	2
Salim Elahi	c Kambli b Srinath	4	9	1
Aamir Sohail	c Mongia b Prasad	1	3	–
Ijaz Ahmed	c Mongia b Prasad	0	7	–
Salim Malik	lbw b Kumble	27	51	1/1
Azhar Mahmood	b Kumble	10	34	–
* Wasim Akram	st Mongia b Kumble	0	1	–
† Moin Khan	c Mongia b Srinath	42	67	2/3
Saqlain Mushtaq	c Tendulkar b Prasad	9	24	–
Mushtaq Ahmed	st Mongia b Joshi	1	3	–
Waqar Younis	not out	0	5	–
Extras	(b 1, lb 10, w 3)	14		
TOTAL	(42.4 overs)	**136**		

PAKISTAN	O	M	R	W
Wasim Akram	9	0	35	4
Waqar Younis	7	1	15	0
Azhar Mahmood	5	1	28	0
Mushtaq Ahmed	10	2	29	1
Aamir Sohail	9	1	31	1
Saqlain Mushtaq	10	0	45	2

INDIA	O	M	R	W
Srinath	7.4	0	20	2
Prasad	9	3	22	3
Kapoor	6	0	27	0
Joshi	9	1	27	1
Kumble	7	2	12	4
Tendulkar	4	0	17	0

FALL OF WICKETS
1-5, 2-14, 3-88, 4-103, 5-133, 6-179, 7-187, 8-189, 9-189, 10-191

FALL OF WICKETS
1-9, 2-12, 3-16, 4-63, 5-66, 6-66, 7-91, 8-124, 9-131, 10-136

Umpires: D.L.Orchard (*SA*) (13) and D.R.Shepherd (*England*) (67).   **Referee:** C.W.Smith (*West Indies*).

INDIA v PAKISTAN 1996

At Toronto Cricket, Skating and Curling Club on 21 September 1996.　Result: **PAKISTAN** won by 97 runs.
Toss: India.　Award: Ijaz Ahmed.　LOI debuts: None.

Pakistan again drew level thanks to Ijaz Ahmed's innings of 90 which equalled Rahul Dravid's highest score of the tournament. Saqlain Mushtaq's off-breaks returned the remarkable analysis of 7-1-9-3.

PAKISTAN		Runs	Balls	4/6
Aamir Sohail	c Srinath b Joshi	23	54	1/1
Saeed Anwar	b Prasad	35	26	4/1
Salim Elahi	lbw b Srinath	1	3	–
Ijaz Ahmed	b Kumble	90	110	7/1
Salim Malik	run out	1	1	–
Inzamam-ul-Haq	run out	40	67	4/1
† Moin Khan	st Mongia b Tendulkar	33	21	1/2
* Wasim Akram	c Prasad b Kumble	10	8	2
Saqlain Mushtaq	not out	10	9	1
Waqar Younis	not out	0	1	–
Mushtaq Ahmed				
Extras	(b 3, lb 8, w 4)	15		
TOTAL	(50 overs; 8 wickets)	**258**		

INDIA		Runs	Balls	4/6
† N.R.Mongia	c Ijaz b Wasim	0	9	–
* S.R.Tendulkar	c Salim Malik b Wasim	3	9	–
R.Dravid	c Moin b Saqlain	25	25	3/1
M.Azharuddin	c Salim Elahi b Saqlain	16	31	2
V.G.Kambli	run out	6	15	–
A.Jadeja	st Moin b Salim Malik	47	84	3
S.B.Joshi	c Moin b Saqlain	1	5	–
A.R.Kapoor	c Moin b Waqar	19	33	1
A.Kumble	c Aamir b Salim Malik	16	20	1
J.Srinath	c Saqlain b Waqar	10	5	2
B.K.V.Prasad	not out	0	–	–
Extras	(b 8, lb 7, w 3)	18		
TOTAL	(39.2 overs)	**161**		

INDIA	O	M	R	W
Srinath	9	0	51	1
Prasad	10	0	50	1
Jadeja	1	0	8	0
Kapoor	8	0	34	0
Joshi	9	1	45	1
Kumble	10	0	37	2
Tendulkar	3	0	22	1

PAKISTAN	O	M	R	W
Wasim Akram	6	2	11	2
Waqar Younis	8	0	51	2
Saqlain Mushtaq	7	1	9	3
Aamir Sohail	10	0	36	0
Mushtaq Ahmed	7	0	33	0
Salim Malik	1.2	0	6	2

FALL OF WICKETS
1-42, 2-43, 3-84, 4-91, 5-177, 6-214, 7-235, 8-248

FALL OF WICKETS
1-4, 2-9, 3-41, 4-58, 5-63, 6-64, 7-118, 8-148, 9-160, 10-161

Umpires: L.H.Barker (*WI*) (34) and D.R.Shepherd (*England*) (68).

Referee: C.W.Smith (*West Indies*).

INDIA v PAKISTAN 1996

At Toronto Cricket, Skating and Curling Club on 23 September 1996.　Result: **PAKISTAN** won by 52 runs.
Toss: Pakistan.　Award: Mushtaq Ahmed.　Series Award: A.Kumble.　LOI debuts: None.

Spin accounted for all but one of the 14 wickets to fall to bowlers as Pakistan won the series 3-2. Mushtaq secured the first five-wicket analysis in Canada and the first match award by a bowler. Anil Kumble gained the second for his series tally of 13 wickets for 160 runs. Salim Malik completed 6000 runs.

PAKISTAN		Runs	Balls	4/6
Aamir Sohail	c Jadeja b Kumble	44	96	2
Saeed Anwar	c Dravid b Kapoor	14	30	1
Ijaz Ahmed	c and b Kumble	27	53	1
Shadab Kabir	c Dravid b Kumble	0	2	–
Salim Malik	b Prasad	43	47	7
Inzamam-ul-Haq	c Prasad b Kapoor	9	19	–
† Moin Khan	run out	15	29	–
* Wasim Akram	run out	17	10	–/2
Saqlain Mushtaq	run out	0	–	–
Waqar Younis	not out	12	10	–/1
Mushtaq Ahmed	not out	5	5	–
Extras	(b 1, lb 21, w 4, nb 1)	27		
TOTAL	(50 overs; 9 wickets)	**213**		

INDIA		Runs	Balls	4/6
A.Jadeja	b Mushtaq Ahmed	20	80	–
* S.R.Tendulkar	run out	23	44	–/1
R.Dravid	c sub (Shahid Nazir) b Mushtaq	20	39	–
S.B.Joshi	c Salim b Mushtaq Ahmed	2	3	–
M.Azharuddin	c Inzamam b Mushtaq Ahmed	2	13	–
S.C.Ganguly	lbw b Aamir	12	21	1
J.Srinath	run out	2	4	–
† N.R.Mongia	c Wasim b Saqlain	10	25	–
A.R.Kapoor	c Ijaz b Mushtaq Ahmed	18	19	–/1
A.Kumble	not out	8	8	–/1
B.K.V.Prasad	c Saeed b Saqlain	19	19	–/2
Extras	(b 7, lb 3, w 15)	25		
TOTAL	(45.5 overs)	**161**		

INDIA	O	M	R	W
Srinath	10	0	40	0
Prasad	10	0	32	1
Kapoor	10	0	36	2
Joshi	10	1	36	0
Kumble	10	0	47	3

PAKISTAN	O	M	R	W
Wasim Akram	8	1	16	0
Waqar Younis	8	0	27	0
Saqlain Mushtaq	7.5	0	34	2
Aamir Sohail	10	1	27	1
Mushtaq Ahmed	10	0	36	5
Salim Malik	2	0	11	0

FALL OF WICKETS
1-44, 2-95, 3-99, 4-108, 5-135, 6-174, 7-195, 8-195, 9-197

FALL OF WICKETS
1-46, 2-62, 3-66, 4-70, 5-92, 6-96, 7-99, 8-127, 9-128, 10-161

Umpires: L.H.Barker (*West Indies*) (35) and D.L.Orchard (*SA*) (14).

Referee: C.W.Smith (*West Indies*).

Limited-Overs Internationals
Records

LIMITED-OVERS INTERNATIONALS RECORDS

These records include all official Limited-Overs Internationals played before 28 September 1996. They exclude any matches which were curtailed by rain before being aborted and replaced by another contest on the reserve day. Throughout this section an asterisk (*) denotes a not out innings or an unfinished partnership. The key to the abbreviations for Colombo's grounds is as follows:

PSS   P.Saravanamuttu Stadium
RPS   R.Premadasa Stadium (formerly Khettarama Stadium)
SSC   Sinhalese Sports Club

LIMITED-OVERS INTERNATIONAL GROUNDS

Limited-overs internationals have been staged on 111 different grounds up to 28 September 1996, India creating the highest number of venues with 33. There would have been another, at Jammu's Molana Azad Stadium in December 1988, had rain not prevented play. The Emirates ground at Sharjah has staged the most with an astonishing 104 matches since April 1984. Next come the oldest Australian Test match arenas in Melbourne and Sydney with 89 and 88 respectively. Of the 111 venues, 21 have staged just a solitary international. They are listed chronologically by countries (counting the 'West Indies' as one).

Venue	Ground	First LOI	Total
AUSTRALIA (308)			
Adelaide	Adelaide Oval	20.12.75	39
Albury	Lavington Sports Club	18.3.92	1
Ballarat	Eastern Oval	9.3.92	1
Berri	Berri Oval	13.3.92	1
Brisbane	Woolloongabba	23.12.79	35
Canberra	Manuka Oval	10.3.92	1
Devonport	Devonport Oval	3.2.87	1
Hobart	Tasmania CA Ground	10.1.85	1
	Bellerive Oval	12.1.88	11
Launceston	North Tasmania CA Ground	2.2.86	1
Mackay	Harrup Park	28.2.92	1
Melbourne	Melbourne Cricket Ground	5.1.71	89
Perth	Western Australia CA Ground	9.12.80	38
Sydney	Sydney (*No. 1*) Cricket Ground	13.1.79	88
ENGLAND and WALES (135)			
Birmingham	Edgbaston	28.8.72	22
Bristol	County Ground	13.6.83	1
Chelmsford	County Ground	20.6.83	1
Derby	County Ground	18.6.83	1
Leeds	Headingley	5.9.73	19
Leicester	Grace Road	11.6.83	1
London	Lord's Cricket Ground	26.8.72	20
	Kennington Oval	7.9.73	20
Manchester	Old Trafford	24.8.72	25
Nottingham	Trent Bridge	31.8.74	17
Scarborough	North Marine Road	26.8.76	2
Southampton	County Ground	16.6.83	1
Swansea	St Helen's	18.7.73	2
Taunton	County Ground	11.6.83	1
Tunbridge Wells	Nevill Ground	18.6.83	1
Worcester	New Road	13.6.83	1
NEW ZEALAND (109)			
Auckland	Eden Park (*No. 1*)	22.2.76	31
Christchurch	Lancaster Park	11.2.73	24
Dunedin	Carisbrook	30.4.74	16
Hamilton	Seddon (Trust Bank) Park	15.2.81	9
Napier	McLean Park	19.3.83	9
New Plymouth	Pukekura Park	23.2.92	1
Wellington	Basin Reserve	9.3.75	19

Venue	Ground	First LOI	Total
PAKISTAN (104)			
Faisalabad	Iqbal Stadium	23.11.84	9
Gujranwala	Municipal Stadium	3.12.82	8
Hyderabad	Niaz Stadium	20.9.82	5
Karachi	National Stadium	21.11.80	20
Lahore	Gaddafi Stadium	13.1.78	23
Multan	Ibn-e-Qasim Bagh Stadium	17.12.82	6
Peshawar	Shahi Bagh Stadium	12.11.84	10
Quetta	Ayub National Stadium	1.10.78	2
Rawalpindi	Pindi Club Ground	4.12.85	2
	Cricket Stadium	19.1.92	8
Sahiwal	Zafar Ali Stadium	23.12.77	2
Sargodha	Sargodha Stadium	10.1.92	1
Sialkot	Jinnah Park	16.10.76	8
WEST INDIES (66)			
Berbice, Guyana	Albion Sports Complex	16.3.77	5
Bridgetown, Barbados	Kensington Oval	23.4.85	7
Castries, St Lucia	Mindoo Phillip Park	12.4.78	2
Georgetown, Guyana	Bourda	30.3.88	8
Kingston, Jamaica	Sabina Park	26.4.84	9
Kingstown, St Vincent	Arnos Vale	4.2.81	5
Port-of-Spain, Trinidad	Queen's Park Oval	9.3.83	25
St George's, Grenada	Queen's Park	7.4.83	1
St John's, Antigua	Recreation Ground	22.2.78	4
INDIA (156)			
Ahmedabad	Sardar Patel Stadium	25.11.81	2
	Gujarat Stadium, Motera	5.10.86	6
Amritsar	Gandhi Sports Complex	12.9.82	2
Bangalore	Karnataka State CA (Chinnaswamy) Stadium	26.9.82	7
Baroda	Moti Bagh Stadium	9.11.83	3
	IPCL Sports Complex	28.10.94	2
Bombay	Wankhede Stadium	17.1.87	7
	Brabourne Stadium	23.10.89	3
Calcutta	Eden Gardens	18.2.87	14
Chandigarh	Sector 16 Stadium	27.1.85	4
	Punjab CA Stadium, Mohali	22.11.93	2
Cuttack	Barabati Stadium	27.1.82	8
Delhi	Feroz Shah Kotla	15.9.82	8
	Jawaharlal Nehru Stadium, New Delhi	28.9.84	2
Faridabad	Nahar Singh Stadium	19.1.88	3
Gauhati	Nehru Stadium	17.12.83	6
Gwalior	Roop Singh Stadium	22.1.88	6
Hyderabad	Lal Bahadur Stadium	10.9.83	8
Indore	Nehru Stadium	1.12.83	6
Jaipur	Sawai Mansingh Stadium	2.10.83	6
Jamshedpur	Keenan Stadium	7.12.83	5
Jullundur	Burlton Park	20.12.81	3
Kanpur	Green Park	24.12.86	6
Lucknow	K.D. 'Babu' Singh Stadium	27.10.89	1
Madras	M.A.Chidambaram Stadium, Chepauk	9.10.87	5
Margao	Fatorda Stadium	25.10.89	3
Nagpur	Vidarbha CA Ground	23.1.85	8
Patna	Moin-ul-Haq Stadium	15.11.93	2
Poona (Pune)	Nehru Stadium	5.12.84	7
Rajkot	Racecourse Ground	7.10.86	4
Srinigar	Sher-i-Kashmir Stadium	13.10.83	2
Trivandrum	University Stadium	1.10.84	2
Vishakhapatnam	Indira Priyadarshani Stadium	10.12.88	3
SRI LANKA (60)			
Colombo	Sinhalese Sports Club (SSC)	13.2.82	19
	P.Saravanamuttu Stadium (PSS)	13.4.83	11
	R.Premadasa Stadium, Khettarama (RPS)	5.4.86	20
Kandy	Asgiriya Stadium	2.3.86	4
Moratuwa	Tyronne Fernando Stadium	31.3.84	6

Venue	Ground	First LOI	Total
UNITED ARAB EMIRATES (104)			
Sharjah	Sharjah CA Stadium	6.4.84	104
BANGLADESH (7)			
Chittagong	Chittagong Stadium	27.10.88	2
Dacca (Dhaka)	National Stadium	27.10.88	5
ZIMBABWE (12)			
Bulawayo	Bulawayo Athletic Club	31.10.92	1
Harare	Harare Sports Club	25.10.92	11
SOUTH AFRICA (46)			
Bloemfontein	Springbok Park	15.12.92	6
Cape Town	Newlands	7.12.92	7
Durban	Kingsmead	17.12.92	7
East London	Buffalo Park	19.12.92	6
Johannesburg	The Wanderers	†13.12.92	7
Port Elizabeth	St George's Park	9.12.92	7
Pretoria	Centurion Park, Verwoerdburg (Centurion)	11.12.92	6
SINGAPORE (4)			
Singapore	Singapore Cricket Club	††2.4.96	4
CANADA (5)			
Toronto	Toronto Cricket, Skating and Curling Club	16.9.96	5

† Scheduled to start 12.12.92. †† Void match played 1.4.96.

MERIT TABLE OF ALL L-O INTERNATIONALS
1970-71 to 23 September 1996 (1116 matches)

	Matches	Won	Lost	Tied	No Result	Won (exc NR)
West Indies	323	204	109	4	6	64.35
Australia	354	196	144	3	11	57.14
South Africa	93	49	42	–	2	53.84
England	253	130	114	1	8	53.06
Pakistan	334	171	151	5	7	52.29
India	295	134	151	2	8	46.68
New Zealand	263	110	142	1	10	43.47
Sri Lanka	223	73	141	–	9	34.11
Kenya	5	1	4	–	–	20.00
United Arab Emirates	7	1	6	–	–	14.28
Zimbabwe	59	7	49	2	1	12.06
Canada	3	–	3	–	–	–
East Africa	3	–	3	–	–	–
Holland	5	–	5	–	–	–
Bangladesh	12	–	12	–	–	–

LIMITED-OVERS INTERNATIONALS RESULTS SUMMARY
1970-71 to 23 September 1996

	Opponents	Matches	E	A	SA	WI	NZ	I	P	SL	Z	B	C	EA	H	K	UAE	Tied	NR
England	Australia	57	26	29	–	–	–	–	–	–	–	–	–	–	–	–	–	1	1
	South Africa	12	5	–	7	–	–	–	–	–	–	–	–	–	–	–	–	–	–
	West Indies	51	22	–	–	27	–	–	–	–	–	–	–	–	–	–	–	–	2
	New Zealand	42	21	–	–	–	18	–	–	–	–	–	–	–	–	–	–	–	3
	India	32	18	–	–	–	–	13	–	–	–	–	–	–	–	–	–	–	1
	Pakistan	40	25	–	–	–	–	–	14	–	–	–	–	–	–	–	–	–	1
	Sri Lanka	12	8	–	–	–	–	–	–	4	–	–	–	–	–	–	–	–	–
	Zimbabwe	3	1	–	–	–	–	–	–	–	2	–	–	–	–	–	–	–	–
	Canada	1	1	–	–	–	–	–	–	–	–	–	0	–	–	–	–	–	–
	East Africa	1	1	–	–	–	–	–	–	–	–	–	–	0	–	–	–	–	–
	Holland	1	1	–	–	–	–	–	–	–	–	–	–	–	0	–	–	–	–
	U A Emirates	1	1	–	–	–	–	–	–	–	–	–	–	–	–	–	0	–	–

	Opponents	Matches	Won by															Tied	NR
			E	A	SA	WI	NZ	I	P	SL	Z	B	C	EA	H	K	UAE		
Australia	South Africa	20	–	12	8	–	–	–	–	–	–	–	–	–	–	–	–	–	–
	West Indies	80	–	31	–	47	–	–	–	–	–	–	–	–	–	–	–	1	1
	New Zealand	63	–	44	–	–	17	–	–	–	–	–	–	–	–	–	–	–	2
	India	45	–	26	–	–	–	16	–	–	–	–	–	–	–	–	–	–	3
	Pakistan	42	–	21	–	–	–	–	18	–	–	–	–	–	–	–	–	1	2
	Sri Lanka	35	–	22	–	–	–	–	–	11	–	–	–	–	–	–	–	–	2
	Zimbabwe	9	–	8	–	–	–	–	–	–	1	–	–	–	–	–	–	–	–
	Bangladesh	1	–	1	–	–	–	–	–	–	–	0	–	–	–	–	–	–	–
	Canada	1	–	1	–	–	–	–	–	–	–	–	0	–	–	–	–	–	–
	Kenya	1	–	1	–	–	–	–	–	–	–	–	–	–	–	0	–	–	–
S Africa	West Indies	9	–	–	4	5	–	–	–	–	–	–	–	–	–	–	–	–	–
	New Zealand	8	–	–	4	–	4	–	–	–	–	–	–	–	–	–	–	–	–
	India	17	–	–	11	–	–	6	–	–	–	–	–	–	–	–	–	–	–
	Pakistan	14	–	–	7	–	–	–	7	–	–	–	–	–	–	–	–	–	–
	Sri Lanka	7	–	–	3	–	–	–	–	3	–	–	–	–	–	–	–	–	1
	Zimbabwe	4	–	–	3	–	–	–	–	–	0	–	–	–	–	–	–	–	1
	Holland	1	–	–	1	–	–	–	–	–	–	–	–	–	0	–	–	–	–
	U A Emirates	1	–	–	1	–	–	–	–	–	–	–	–	–	–	–	0	–	–
W Indies	New Zealand	24	–	–	–	18	4	–	–	–	–	–	–	–	–	–	–	–	2
	India	51	–	–	–	32	–	18	–	–	–	–	–	–	–	–	–	1	–
	Pakistan	75	–	–	–	51	–	–	22	–	–	–	–	–	–	–	–	2	–
	Sri Lanka	27	–	–	–	19	–	–	–	7	–	–	–	–	–	–	–	–	1
	Zimbabwe	5	–	–	–	5	–	–	–	–	0	–	–	–	–	–	–	–	–
	Kenya	1	–	–	–	0	–	–	–	–	–	–	–	–	–	1	–	–	–
N Zealand	India	41	–	–	–	–	18	23	–	–	–	–	–	–	–	–	–	–	–
	Pakistan	41	–	–	–	–	16	–	23	–	–	–	–	–	–	–	–	1	1
	Sri Lanka	32	–	–	–	–	22	–	–	8	–	–	–	–	–	–	–	–	2
	Zimbabwe	8	–	–	–	–	7	–	–	–	1	–	–	–	–	–	–	–	–
	Bangladesh	1	–	–	–	–	1	–	–	–	–	0	–	–	–	–	–	–	–
	East Africa	1	–	–	–	–	1	–	–	–	–	–	–	0	–	–	–	–	–
	Holland	1	–	–	–	–	1	–	–	–	–	–	–	–	0	–	–	–	–
	U A Emirates	1	–	–	–	–	1	–	–	–	–	–	–	–	–	–	0	–	–
India	Pakistan	50	–	–	–	–	–	16	32	–	–	–	–	–	–	–	–	–	2
	Sri Lanka	41	–	–	–	–	–	25	–	14	–	–	–	–	–	–	–	–	2
	Zimbabwe	12	–	–	–	–	–	11	–	–	0	–	–	–	–	–	–	1	–
	Bangladesh	3	–	–	–	–	–	3	–	–	–	0	–	–	–	–	–	–	–
	East Africa	1	–	–	–	–	–	1	–	–	–	–	–	0	–	–	–	–	–
	Kenya	1	–	–	–	–	–	1	–	–	–	–	–	–	–	0	–	–	–
	U A Emirates	1	–	–	–	–	–	1	–	–	–	–	–	–	–	–	0	–	–
Pakistan	Sri Lanka	56	–	–	–	–	–	–	41	14	–	–	–	–	–	–	–	–	1
	Zimbabwe	9	–	–	–	–	–	–	7	–	1	–	–	–	–	–	–	1	–
	Bangladesh	3	–	–	–	–	–	–	3	–	–	0	–	–	–	–	–	–	–
	Canada	1	–	–	–	–	–	–	1	–	–	–	0	–	–	–	–	–	–
	Holland	1	–	–	–	–	–	–	1	–	–	–	–	–	0	–	–	–	–
	U A Emirates	2	–	–	–	–	–	–	2	–	–	–	–	–	–	–	0	–	–
Sri Lanka	Zimbabwe	8	–	–	–	–	–	–	–	7	1	–	–	–	–	–	–	–	–
	Bangladesh	4	–	–	–	–	–	–	–	4	–	0	–	–	–	–	–	–	–
	Kenya	1	–	–	–	–	–	–	–	1	–	–	–	–	–	0	–	–	–
Zimbabwe	Kenya	1	–	–	–	–	–	–	–	–	1	–	–	–	–	0	–	–	–
Holland	U A Emirates	1	–	–	–	–	–	–	–	–	–	–	–	–	0	–	1	–	–
		1116	130	196	49	204	110	134	171	73	7	0	0	0	0	1	1	9	31

TEAM RECORDS

HIGHEST INNINGS TOTALS

398-5	(50 overs)	Sri Lanka v Kenya	Kandy	1995-96
363-7	(55 overs)	England v Pakistan	Nottingham	1992
360-4	(50 overs)	West Indies v Sri Lanka	Karachi	1987-88
349-9	(50 overs)	Sri Lanka v Pakistan	Singapore	1995-96
348-8	(50 overs)	New Zealand v India	Nagpur	1995-96
338-4	(50 overs)	New Zealand v Bangladesh	Sharjah	1989-90
338-5	(60 overs)	Pakistan v Sri Lanka	Swansea	1983
334-4	(60 overs)	England v India	Lord's	1975
333-7	(50 overs)	West Indies v Sri Lanka	Sharjah	1995-96
333-8	(45 overs)	West Indies v India	Jamshedpur	1983-84
333-9	(60 overs)	England v Sri Lanka	Taunton	1983
332-3	(50 overs)	Australia v Sri Lanka	Sharjah	1989-90
330-6	(60 overs)	Pakistan v Sri Lanka	Nottingham	1975
329	(49.3 overs)	Sri Lanka v West Indies	Sharjah	1995-96
328-2	(50 overs)	Pakistan v New Zealand	Sharjah	1993-94
328-3	(50 overs)	South Africa v Holland	Rawalpindi	1995-96
328-5	(60 overs)	Australia v Sri Lanka	The Oval	1975
323-2	(50 overs)	Australia v Sri Lanka	Adelaide	1984-85
322-6	(60 overs)	England v New Zealand	The Oval	1983
321-2	(50 overs)	South Africa v UAE	Rawalpindi	1995-96
320-8	(55 overs)	England v Australia	Birmingham	1980
320-9	(60 overs)	Australia v India	Nottingham	1983
315-3	(50 overs)	Pakistan v Sri Lanka	Adelaide	1989-90
315-4	(47 overs)	West Indies v Pakistan	Port-of-Spain	1987-88
315	(49.4 overs)	Pakistan v Sri Lanka	Singapore	1995-96
314-3	(50 overs)	South Africa v Pakistan	Sharjah	1995-96
314-7	(50 overs)	South Africa v New Zealand	Pretoria	1994-95
313-3	(50 overs)	Pakistan v Sri Lanka	Sharjah	1993-94
313-6	(50 overs)	West Indies v England	Kingstown	1993-94
313-7	(49.2 overs)	Sri Lanka v Zimbabwe	New Plymouth	1991-92
313-9	(50 overs)	West Indies v Australia	St John's	1977-78
312-4	(50 overs)	Zimbabwe v Sri Lanka	New Plymouth	1991-92
311-8	(50 overs)	Pakistan v Sri Lanka	Sharjah	1989-90
309-5	(60 overs)	New Zealand v East Africa	Birmingham	1975
309-6	(50 overs)	West Indies v Sri Lanka	Perth	1984-85
307-8	(50 overs)	New Zealand v Holland	Baroda	1995-96
306-5	(55 overs)	England v West Indies	The Oval	1995
306-6	(50 overs)	West Indies v New Zealand	Gauhati	1994-95
305-5	(50 overs)	India v Pakistan	Sharjah	1995-96
304-5	(50 overs)	New Zealand v Sri Lanka	Auckland	1982-83
304-7	(50 overs)	Australia v Kenya	Vishakhapatnam	1995-96
303-5	(50 overs)	South Africa v Zimbabwe	Harare	1995-96
302-5	(55 overs)	England v Pakistan	The Oval	1992
302-8	(50 overs)	Australia v New Zealand	Melbourne	1982-83
300-5	(50 overs)	Australia v Pakistan	Brisbane	1989-90

HIGHEST TOTALS BATTING SECOND

329	(49.3 overs)	Sri Lanka v West Indies (Lost by 4 runs)	Sharjah	1995-96
315	(49.4 overs)	Pakistan v Sri Lanka (Lost by 34 runs)	Singapore	1995-96
313-7	(49.2 overs)	Sri Lanka v Zimbabwe (Won by 3 wickets)	New Plymouth	1991-92

HIGHEST MATCH AGGREGATES

664-19	(99.4 overs)	Pakistan v Sri Lanka	Singapore	1995-96
662-17	(99.3 overs)	Sri Lanka v West Indies	Sharjah	1995-96
652-12	(91 overs)	Sri Lanka v Kenya	Kandy	1995-96
626-14	(120 overs)	Pakistan v Sri Lanka	Swansea	1983
625-11	(99.2 overs)	Sri Lanka v Zimbabwe	New Plymouth	1991-92

LOWEST INNINGS TOTALS *(Excluding abbreviated matches)*

43	(19.5 overs)	Pakistan v West Indies	Cape Town	1992-93
45	(40.3 overs)	Canada v England	Manchester	1979
55	(28.3 overs)	Sri Lanka v West Indies	Sharjah	1986-87
63	(25.5 overs)	India v Australia	Sydney	1980-81
64	(35.5 overs)	New Zealand v Pakistan	Sharjah	1985-86
69	(28 overs)	South Africa v Australia	Sydney	1993-94
70	(25.2 overs)	Australia v England	Birmingham	1977
70	(26.3 overs)	Australia v New Zealand	Adelaide	1985-86
71	(23.4 overs)	Pakistan v West Indies	Brisbane	1992-93
74	(29 overs)	New Zealand v Australia	Wellington	1981-82
74	(31.1 overs)	New Zealand v Pakistan	Sharjah	1989-90
74	(44.2 overs)	Pakistan v England	Adelaide	1991-92
78	(24.1 overs)	India v Sri Lanka	Kanpur	1986-87
79	(34.2 overs)	India v Pakistan	Sialkot	1978-79
81	(48 overs)	Pakistan v West Indies	Sydney	1992-93
85	(47 overs)	Pakistan v England	Manchester	1978
86	(37.2 overs)	Sri Lanka v West Indies	Manchester	1975
87	(32.5 overs)	Pakistan v India	Sharjah	1984-85
87	(29.3 overs)	West Indies v Australia	Sydney	1992-93
91	(35.5 overs)	Sri Lanka v Australia	Adelaide	1984-85
91	(35.4 overs)	Australia v West Indies	Perth	1986-87
93	(35.2 overs)	England v Australia	Leeds	1975
93	(36.2 overs)	West Indies v Kenya	Poona	1995-96
94	(52.3 overs)	East Africa v England	Birmingham	1975
94	(31.7 overs)	England v Australia	Melbourne	1978-79
94	(35.3 overs)	Bangladesh v Pakistan	Moratuwa	1985-86
94	(25.2 overs)	New Zealand v Australia	Christchurch	1989-90
96	(41 overs)	Sri Lanka v India	Sharjah	1983-84
98	(34 overs)	Sri Lanka v South Africa	Colombo (RPS)	1993-94
99	(36.3 overs)	Zimbabwe v West Indies	Hyderabad, India	1993-94

LOWEST MATCH AGGREGATES

88-13	(32.2 overs)	Pakistan v West Indies	Cape Town	1992-93
91-12	(54.2 overs)	England v Canada	Manchester	1979
127-11	(46.5 overs)	Australia v India	Sydney	1980-81
130-10	(58.3 overs)	New Zealand v Pakistan	Sharjah	1985-86
143-11	(43 overs)	Pakistan v West Indies	Brisbane	1992-93
149-12	(49.3 overs)	New Zealand v Australia	Wellington	1981-82

LARGEST MARGINS OF VICTORY (RUNS)

232 runs	Australia beat Sri Lanka	Adelaide	1984-85
206 runs	New Zealand beat Australia	Adelaide	1985-86
202 runs	England beat India	Lord's	1975
198 runs	England beat Pakistan	Nottingham	1992
196 runs	England beat East Africa	Birmingham	1975

LARGEST MARGINS OF VICTORY (WICKETS)

10 wickets	India beat East Africa	Leeds	1975
10 wickets	New Zealand beat India	Melbourne	1980-81
10 wickets	West Indies beat Zimbabwe	Birmingham	1983
10 wickets	India beat Sri Lanka	Sharjah	1983-84
10 wickets	West Indies beat New Zealand	Port-of-Spain	1984-85
10 wickets	Pakistan beat New Zealand	Sharjah	1985-86
10 wickets	West Indies beat New Zealand	Christchurch	1986-87
10 wickets	West Indies beat Pakistan	Melbourne	1991-92
10 wickets	West Indies beat South Africa	Port-of-Spain	1991-92

TIED MATCHES *(Overs in brackets)*

West Indies	222-5 (50)	Australia	222-9 (50)	Melbourne	1983-84
England	226-5 (55)	Australia	226-8 (55)	Nottingham	1989
West Indies	186-5 (39)	Pakistan	186-9 (39)	Lahore	1991-92
India	126 (47.4)	West Indies	126 (41)	Perth	1991-92
Australia	228-7 (50)	Pakistan	228-9 (50)	Hobart	1992-93
Pakistan	244-6 (50)	West Indies	244-5 (50)	Georgetown	1992-93
India	248-5 (50)	Zimbabwe	248 (50)	Indore	1993-94
Pakistan	161-9 (50)	New Zealand	161 (49.4)	Auckland	1993-94
Zimbabwe	219-9 (50)	Pakistan	219 (49.5)	Harare	1994-95

SMALLEST MARGINS OF VICTORY *(Excluding abbreviated matches)*

1 run	New Zealand beat Pakistan	Sialkot	1976-77
1 run	New Zealand beat Australia	Sydney	1980-81
1 run	Australia beat India	Madras	1987-88
1 run	New Zealand beat Australia	Perth	1987-88
1 run	West Indies beat Australia	Sydney	1988-89
1 run	India beat New Zealand	Wellington	1989-90
1 run	New Zealand beat Australia	Hobart	1990-91
1 run	Pakistan beat West Indies	Sharjah	1991-92
1 run	India beat Sri Lanka	Colombo (RPS)	1993-94
1 run	Australia beat South Africa	Bloemfontein	1993-94
1 wicket	England beat West Indies	Leeds	1973
1 wicket	West Indies beat Pakistan	Birmingham	1975
1 wicket	New Zealand beat West Indies	Christchurch	1979-80
1 wicket	West Indies beat Pakistan	Adelaide	1983-84
1 wicket	Pakistan beat New Zealand	Multan	1984-85
1 wicket	Pakistan beat India	Sharjah	1985-86
1 wicket	Pakistan beat Australia	Perth	1986-87
1 wicket	England beat Pakistan	Birmingham	1986-87
1 wicket	Pakistan beat West Indies	Lahore	1987-88
1 wicket	England beat West Indies	Birmingham	1990-91
1 wicket	West Indies beat Pakistan	Sharjah	1991-92
1 wicket	Australia beat New Zealand	Christchurch	1992-93
1 wicket	New Zealand beat Pakistan	Christchurch	1995-96
1 wicket	Australia beat West Indies	Sydney	1995-96

INDIVIDUAL RECORDS – BATTING

HIGHEST INDIVIDUAL INNINGS

189*	I.V.A.Richards	West Indies v England	Manchester	1984
188*	G.Kirsten	South Africa v UAE	Rawalpindi	1995-96
181	I.V.A.Richards	West Indies v Sri Lanka	Karachi	1987-88
175*	Kapil Dev	India v Zimbabwe	Tunbridge Wells	1983
171*	G.M.Turner	New Zealand v East Africa	Birmingham	1975
169*	D.J.Callaghan	South Africa v New Zealand	Pretoria	1994-95
169	B.C.Lara	West Indies v Sri Lanka	Sharjah	1995-96
167*	R.A.Smith	England v Australia	Birmingham	1993
161	A.C.Hudson	South Africa v Holland	Rawalpindi	1995-96
158	D.I.Gower	England v New Zealand	Brisbane	1982-83
153*	I.V.A.Richards	West Indies v Australia	Melbourne	1979-80
153	B.C.Lara	West Indies v Pakistan	Sharjah	1993-94
152*	D.L.Haynes	West Indies v India	Georgetown	1988-89

Highest individual innings for other Test-playing countries:

145	D.M.Jones	Australia v England	Brisbane	1990-91
145	P.A.de Silva	Sri Lanka v Kenya	Kandy	1995-96
142	D.L.Houghton	Zimbabwe v New Zealand	Hyderabad, India	1987-88
137*	Inzamam-ul-Haq	Pakistan v New Zealand	Sharjah	1993-94

568

HUNDREDS

ENGLAND (44)

Amiss, D.L.	(4)	103	Australia	Manchester	1972
		100	New Zealand	Swansea	1973
		137	India	Lord's	1975
		108	Australia	The Oval	1977
Atherton, M.A.		127	West Indies	Lord's	1995
Athey, C.W.J.	(2)	142*	New Zealand	Manchester	1986
		111	Australia	Brisbane	1986-87
Boycott, G.		105	Australia	Sydney	1979-80
Brown, A.D.		118	India	Manchester	1996
Broad, B.C.		106	New Zealand	Napier	1987-88
Fairbrother, N.H.		113	West Indies	Lord's	1991
Fletcher, K.W.R.		131	New Zealand	Nottingham	1975
Gatting, M.W.		115*	India	Poona	1984-85
Gooch, G.A.	(8)	108	Australia	Birmingham	1980
		115	Australia	Birmingham	1985
		117*	Australia	Lord's	1985
		129*	West Indies	Port-of-Spain	1985-86
		115	India	Bombay	1987-88
		142	Pakistan	Karachi	1987-88
		136	Australia	Lord's	1989
		112*	New Zealand	The Oval	1990
Gower, D.I.	(7)	114*	Pakistan	The Oval	1978
		101*	Australia	Melbourne	1978-79
		122	New Zealand	Melbourne	1982-83
		158	New Zealand	Brisbane	1982-83
		109	New Zealand	Adelaide	1982-83
		130	Sri Lanka	Taunton	1983
		102	Australia	Lord's	1985
Hick, G.A.	(2)	105*	India	Gwalior	1992-93
		104*	Holland	Peshawar	1995-96
Knight, N.V.	(2)	113	Pakistan	Birmingham	1996
		125*	Pakistan	Nottingham	1996
Lamb, A.J.	(4)	118	Pakistan	Nottingham	1982
		108*	New Zealand	Sydney	1982-83
		102	New Zealand	The Oval	1983
		100*	Australia	Nottingham	1989
Larkins, W.		124	Australia	Hyderabad, India	1989-90
Lloyd, D.		116*	Pakistan	Nottingham	1974
Radley, C.T.		117*	New Zealand	Manchester	1978
Smith R.A.	(4)	128	New Zealand	Leeds	1990
		103	India	Nottingham	1990
		129	India	Gwalior	1992-93
		167*	Australia	Birmingham	1993
Stewart, A.J.		103	Pakistan	The Oval	1992

AUSTRALIA (48)

Boon, D.C.	(5)	111	India	Jaipur	1986-87
		122	Sri Lanka	Adelaide	1987-88
		102*	India	Hobart	1991-92
		100	New Zealand	Auckland	1991-92
		100	West Indies	Melbourne	1991-92
Border, A.R.	(3)	105*	India	Sydney	1980-81
		118*	Sri Lanka	Adelaide	1984-85
		127*	West Indies	Sydney	1984-85
Chappell, G.S.	(3)	125*	England	The Oval	1977
		138*	New Zealand	Sydney	1980-81
		108	New Zealand	Auckland	1981-82
Chappell, T.M.		110	India	Nottingham	1983
Jones, D.M.	(7)	104	England	Perth	1986-87
		121	Pakistan	Perth	1986-87
		101	England	Brisbane	1986-87
		107	New Zealand	Christchurch	1989-90
		102*	New Zealand	Auckland	1989-90
		117*	Sri Lanka	Sharjah	1989-90
		145	England	Brisbane	1990-91
Laird, B.M.		117*	West Indies	Sydney	1981-82

Law, S.G.		110	Zimbabwe	Hobart	1994-95
Marsh, G.R.	(9)	125	India	Sydney	1985-86
		104	India	Jaipur	1986-87
		110	India	Madras	1987-88
		126*	New Zealand	Chandigarh	1987-88
		101	New Zealand	Sydney	1987-88
		125*	Pakistan	Melbourne	1988-89
		111*	England	Lord's	1989
		113	West Indies	Bridgetown	1990-91
		106*	West Indies	Georgetown	1990-91
Ponting, R.T.	(2)	123	Sri Lanka	Melbourne	1995-96
		102	West Indies	Jaipur	1995-96
Smith, S.B.	(2)	117	New Zealand	Melbourne	1982-83
		106	Pakistan	Sydney	1983-84
Turner, A.		101	Sri Lanka	The Oval	1975
Waugh, M.E.	(8)	108	New Zealand	Hamilton	1992-93
		113	England	Birmingham	1993
		107	South Africa	Sydney	1993-94
		121*	Pakistan	Rawalpindi	1994-95
		130	Sri Lanka	Perth	1995-96
		130	Kenya	Vishakhapatnam	1995-96
		126	India	Bombay	1995-96
		110	New Zealand	Madras	1995-96
Waugh, S.R.		102*	Sri Lanka	Melbourne	1995-96
Wessels, K.C.		107	India	Delhi	1984-85
Wood, G.M.	(3)	108	England	Leeds	1981
		104*	West Indies	Adelaide	1984-85
		114*	England	Lord's	1985

SOUTH AFRICA (13)

Callaghan, D.J.		169*	New Zealand	Pretoria	1994-95
Cronje, W.J.	(2)	112	Australia	Johannesburg	1993-94
		100*	Australia	Peshawar	1994-95
Cullinan, D.J.		110*	Pakistan	Sharjah	1995-96
Hudson, A.C.	(2)	108	India	Bloemfontein	1992-93
		161	Holland	Rawalpindi	1995-96
Kirsten, G.	(5)	112*	Australia	Melbourne	1993-94
		116	England	Pretoria	1995-96
		188*	UAE	Rawalpindi	1995-96
		106	India	Sharjah	1995-96
		115*	India	Sharjah	1995-96
McMillan, B.M.		127	Zimbabwe	Harare	1995-96
Rindel, M.J.R.		106	Pakistan	Johannesburg	1994-95

WEST INDIES (65)

Best, C.A.		100	England	Georgetown	1989-90
Fredericks, R.C.		105	England	The Oval	1973
Gomes, H.A.		101	Sri Lanka	Perth	1984-85
Greenidge, C.G.	(11)	106*	India	Birmingham	1979
		103	New Zealand	Christchurch	1979-80
		103	Pakistan	Melbourne	1981-82
		105*	Zimbabwe	Worcester	1983
		115	India	Jamshedpur	1983-84
		110*	Sri Lanka	Adelaide	1984-85
		100	Australia	Perth	1986-87
		104	New Zealand	Auckland	1986-87
		133*	New Zealand	Christchurch	1986-87
		102*	Pakistan	Sharjah	1988-89
		117	India	St John's	1988-89
Haynes, D.L.	(17)	148	Australia	St John's	1977-78
		108*	Australia	Sydney	1983-84
		133*	Australia	Berbice	1983-84
		102*	Australia	Castries	1983-84
		104*	Australia	Kingston	1983-84
		123*	Australia	Melbourne	1984-85
		145*	New Zealand	Berbice	1984-85
		116	New Zealand	Bridgetown	1984-85
		105	Sri Lanka	Karachi	1987-88
		142*	Pakistan	Port-of-Spain	1987-88

Player	(No.)	Score	Opponent	Venue	Season
		111	Pakistan	Adelaide	1988-89
		101	Pakistan	Hobart	1988-89
		117*	India	Bridgetown	1988-89
		152*	India	Georgetown	1988-89
		138*	England	Gwalior	1989-90
		107*	Pakistan	Calcutta	1989-90
		115	England	Port-of-Spain	1993-94
Hooper, C.L.	(2)	113*	India	Gwalior	1987-88
		111	New Zealand	Gauhati	1994-95
Lara, B.C.	(9)	128	Pakistan	Durban	1992-93
		111*	South Africa	Bloemfontein	1992-93
		114	Pakistan	Kingston	1992-93
		153	Pakistan	Sharjah	1993-94
		139	Australia	Port-of-Spain	1994-95
		169	Sri Lanka	Sharjah	1995-96
		111	South Africa	Karachi	1995-96
		146*	New Zealand	Port-of-Spain	1995-96
		104	New Zealand	St Vincent	1995-96
Lloyd, C.H.		102	Australia	Lord's	1975
Logie, A.L.		109*	Pakistan	Kingston	1987-88
Richards, I.V.A.	(11)	119*	England	Scarborough	1976
		138*	England	Lord's	1979
		153*	Australia	Melbourne	1979-80
		119	India	The Oval	1983
		149	India	Jamshedpur	1983-84
		103*	Australia	Sydney	1983-84
		106	Australia	Melbourne	1983-84
		189*	England	Manchester	1984
		119	New Zealand	Dunedin	1986-87
		181	Sri Lanka	Karachi	1987-88
		110*	India	Rajkot	1987-88
Richardson, R.B.	(5)	109	Sri Lanka	Sharjah	1986-87
		110	Pakistan	Karachi	1987-88
		108*	England	Kingston	1989-90
		106*	Pakistan	Sharjah	1991-92
		122	Pakistan	Sharjah	1991-92
Simmons, P.V.	(5)	104*	India	Trivandrum	1987-88
		110	Sri Lanka	Berri	1991-92
		122	South Africa	Kingston	1991-92
		104	South Africa	Port-of-Spain	1991-92
		103*	New Zealand	St Vincent	1995-96

NEW ZEALAND (22)

Player	(No.)	Score	Opponent	Venue	Season
Astle, N.J.	(3)	114	India	Nagpur	1995-96
		120	Zimbabwe	Auckland	1995-96
		101	England	Ahmedabad	1995-96
Cairns, C.L.		103	India	Poona	1995-96
Congdon, B.E.		101	England	Wellington	1974-75
Crowe, M.D.	(4)	105*	England	Auckland	1983-84
		104	India	Dunedin	1989-90
		100*	Australia	Auckland	1991-92
		107*	India	Jamshedpur	1995-96
Edgar, B.A.		102*	Australia	Melbourne	1980-81
Fleming, S.P.		106*	West Indies	Port-of-Spain	1995-96
Greatbatch, M.J.	(2)	102*	England	Leeds	1990
		111	England	The Oval	1990
Harris, C.Z.		130	Australia	Madras	1995-96
Parore, A.C.		108	South Africa	Pretoria	1994-95
Rutherford, K.R.	(2)	108	India	Baroda	1994-95
		102*	Sri Lanka	East London	1994-95
Turner, G.M.	(3)	171*	East Africa	Birmingham	1975
		114*	India	Manchester	1975
		140	Sri Lanka	Auckland	1982-83
Wadsworth, K.J.		104	Australia	Christchurch	1973-74
Wright, J.G.		101	England	Napier	1987-88

INDIA (40)

Player	(No.)	Score	Opponent	Venue	Season
Amarnath, M.	(2)	100*	West Indies	Faridabad	1987-88
		102*	New Zealand	Sharjah	1987-88

Azharuddin, M.	(3)	108*	Sri Lanka	Bombay	1986-87
		108*	New Zealand	Baroda	1988-89
		108	Sri Lanka	Sharjah	1989-90
Gavaskar, S.M.		103*	New Zealand	Nagpur	1987-88
Jadeja, A.		104	West Indies	Cuttack	1994-95
Kambli, V.G.	(2)	100*	England	Jaipur	1992-93
		106	Zimbabwe	Kanpur	1995-96
Kapil Dev		175*	Zimbabwe	Tunbridge Wells	1983
Lamba, R.		102	Australia	Rajkot	1986-87
Manjrekar, S.V.		105	South Africa	Chandigarh	1991-92
Prabhakar, M.	(2)	106	Pakistan	Jamshedpur	1986-87
		102*	West Indies	Kanpur	1994-95
Raman, W.V.		114	South Africa	Pretoria	1992-93
Sharma, C.		101*	England	Kanpur	1989-90
Shastri, R.J.	(4)	102	Australia	Indore	1984-85
		102	England	Cuttack	1984-85
		101*	Sri Lanka	Nagpur	1990-91
		109	South Africa	Chandigarh	1990-91
Sidhu, N.S.	(6)	108	Pakistan	Sharjah	1989-90
		104*	Bangladesh	Chandigarh	1990-91
		134*	England	Gwalior	1992-93
		108	Sri Lanka	Rajkot	1993-94
		114*	West Indies	Vishakhapatnam	1994-95
		101	Pakistan	Sharjah	1995-96
Srikkanth, K.	(4)	102	Australia	Jaipur	1986-87
		123	Pakistan	Calcutta	1986-87
		101	West Indies	Trivandrum	1987-88
		112	West Indies	Sharjah	1988-89
Tendulkar, S.R.	(9)	110	Australia	Colombo (RPS)	1994-95
		115	New Zealand	Baroda	1994-95
		105	West Indies	Jaipur	1994-95
		112*	Sri Lanka	Sharjah	1994-95
		127*	Kenya	Cuttack	1995-96
		137	Sri Lanka	Delhi	1995-96
		100	Pakistan	Singapore	1995-96
		118	Pakistan	Sharjah	1995-96
		110	Sri Lanka	Colombo (RPS)	1996-97
Vengsarkar, D.B.		105	England	Poona	1984-95

PAKISTAN (59)

Aamir Sohail	(5)	114	Zimbabwe	Hobart	1991-92
		134	New Zealand	Sharjah	1993-94
		100	Sri Lanka	Durban	1994-95
		111	South Africa	Karachi	1995-96
		105	India	Sharjah	1995-96
Asif Mujtaba		113*	Sri Lanka	Sharjah	1993-94
Basit Ali		127*	West Indies	Sharjah	1993-94
Ijaz Ahmed	(4)	124*	Bangladesh	Chittagong	1988-89
		102*	Sri Lanka	Brisbane	1989-90
		110	South Africa	Rawalpindi	1994-95
		114*	South Africa	Durban	1994-95
Imran Khan		102*	Sri Lanka	Leeds	1983
Inzamam-ul-Haq	(4)	101	Sri Lanka	Multan	1991-92
		117	Sri Lanka	Rawalpindi	1991-92
		137*	New Zealand	Sharjah	1993-94
		116*	Zimbabwe	Harare	1994-95
Javed Miandad	(8)	106*	India	Gujranwala	1982-83
		119*	India	Lahore	1982-83
		116*	India	Sharjah	1985-86
		113	England	The Oval	1987
		103	Sri Lanka	Hyderabad, Pakistan	1987-88
		100*	West Indies	Georgetown	1987-88
		115*	Sri Lanka	Hyderabad, Pakistan	1991-92
		107	South Africa	East London	1992-93
Majid Khan		109	England	Nottingham	1974
Mohsin Khan	(2)	104	Australia	Hyderabad, Pakistan	1982-83
		117*	India	Multan	1982-83
Moin-ul-Atiq		105	Bangladesh	Chittagong	1988-89

572

Ramiz Raja	(9)	113	England	Karachi	1987-88
		101	New Zealand	Auckland	1988-89
		116*	Sri Lanka	Hobart	1989-90
		107*	Sri Lanka	Adelaide	1989-90
		114	New Zealand	Sialkot	1990-91
		102*	West Indies	Melbourne	1991-92
		119*	New Zealand	Christchurch	1991-92
		109*	Sri Lanka	Sharjah	1992-93
		104*	West Indies	Sharjah	1995-96
Saeed Anwar	(8)	126	Sri Lanka	Adelaide	1989-90
		101	New Zealand	Lahore	1989-90
		110	Sri Lanka	Sharjah	1992-93
		107	Sri Lanka	Sharjah	1993-94
		131	West Indies	Sharjah	1993-94
		111	Sri Lanka	Sharjah	1993-94
		104*	Australia	Rawalpindi	1994-95
		103*	Zimbabwe	Harare	1994-95
Salim Elahi		102*	Sri Lanka	Gujranwala	1995-96
Salim Malik	(5)	100	Sri Lanka	Faisalabad	1987-88
		101	India	Sharjah	1988-89
		100*	Sri Lanka	Sharjah	1988-89
		102	India	Sharjah	1989-90
		102	Sri Lanka	Rawalpindi	1991-92
Shoaib Mohammed		126*	New Zealand	Wellington	1988-89
Zaheer Abbas	(7)	108	Australia	Sydney	1981-82
		123	Sri Lanka	Lahore	1981-82
		109	Australia	Lahore	1982-83
		118	India	Multan	1982-83
		105	India	Lahore	1982-83
		113	India	Karachi	1982-83
		103*	New Zealand	Nottingham	1983

SRI LANKA (21)

De Silva, P.A.	(6)	104	India	Nagpur	1990-91
		105	Australia	Colombo (PSS)	1992-93
		107*	Zimbabwe	Harare	1994-95
		145	Kenya	Kandy	1995-96
		107*	Australia	Lahore	1995-96
		127*	Zimbabwe	Colombo (SSC)	1996-97
Dias, R.L.	(2)	102	India	Delhi	1982-83
		121	India	Bangalore	1982-83
Gurusinha, A.P.	(2)	117*	New Zealand	Sharjah	1993-94
		108	New Zealand	Auckland	1994-95
Jayasuriya, S.T.	(3)	140	New Zealand	Bloemfontein	1994-95
		134	Pakistan	Singapore	1995-96
		120*	India	Colombo (RPS)	1996-97
Mahanama, R.S.	(4)	107	New Zealand	Colombo (RPS)	1992-93
		119*	Zimbabwe	Harare	1994-95
		108	Zimbabwe	Harare	1994-95
		101	West Indies	Sharjah	1995-96
Ranatunga, A.	(2)	101*	Pakistan	Durban	1994-95
		102*	Pakistan	Gujranwala	1995-96
Tillekeratne, H.P.	(2)	104	West Indies	Bombay	1993-94
		100	West Indies	Sharjah	1995-96

ZIMBABWE (3)

Campbell, A.D.R.		131*	Sri Lanka	Harare	1994-95
Flower, A.		115*	Sri Lanka	New Plymouth	1991-92
Houghton, D.L.		142	New Zealand	Hyderabad, India	1987-88

ASSOCIATE MEMBER COUNTRIES – No instance – highest scores

S.O.Tikolo	96	Kenya v Sri Lanka	Kandy	1995-96
Salim Raza	84	UAE v Holland	Lahore	1995-96
Athar Ali Khan	78*	Bangladesh v Sri Lanka	Calcutta	1990-91
K-J.J.Van Noortwijk	64	Holland v England	Peshawar	1995-96
Frasat Ali	45	East Africa v New Zealand	Birmingham	1975
G.R.Sealy	45	Canada v Pakistan	Leeds	1979

MOST HUNDREDS

		E	A	SA	WI	NZ	I	P	SL	Z	Ass
17	D.L.Haynes (WI)	2	6	–	–	2	2	4	1	–	–
11	C.G.Greenidge (WI)	–	1	–	–	3	3	2	1	1	–
11	I.V.A.Richards (WI)	3	3	–	–	1	3	–	1	–	–
9	B.C.Lara (WI)	–	1	2	–	2	–	3	1	–	–
9	G.R.Marsh (A)	1	–	–	2	2	3	1	–	–	–
9	Ramiz Raja (P)	1	–	–	2	3	–	–	3	–	–
9	S.R.Tendulkar (I)	–	1	–	1	1	–	2	3	–	1
9	G.A.Gooch (E)	–	4	–	1	1	1	1	–	–	–
8	Javed Miandad (P)	1	–	1	1	–	3	–	2	–	–
8	Saeed Anwar (P)	–	1	–	1	1	–	–	4	1	–
8	M.E.Waugh (A)	1	–	1	–	2	1	1	1	–	1

HUNDREDS IN CONSECUTIVE INNINGS

THREE

Zaheer Abbas (Pakistan)	118	India	Multan	1982-83
	105	India	Lahore	1982-83
	113	India	Karachi	1982-83
Saeed Anwar (Pakistan)	107	Sri Lanka	Sharjah	1993-94
	131	West Indies	Sharjah	1993-94
	111	Sri Lanka	Sharjah	1993-94

TWO

R.L.Dias (Sri Lanka)	102	India	Delhi	1982-83
	121	India	Bangalore	1982-83
D.I.Gower (England)	122	New Zealand	Melbourne	1982-83
	158	New Zealand	Brisbane	1982-83
D.L.Haynes (West Indies)	102*	Australia	Castries	1983-84
	104*	Australia	Kingston	1983-84
A.R.Border (Australia)	118*	Sri Lanka	Adelaide	1984-85
	127*	West Indies	Sydney	1984-85
G.A.Gooch (England)	115	Australia	Birmingham	1985
	117*	Australia	Lord's	1985
D.M.Jones (Australia)	104	England	Perth	1986-87
	121	Pakistan	Perth	1986-87
C.G.Greenidge (West Indies)	104	New Zealand	Auckland	1986-87
	133*	New Zealand	Christchurch	1986-87
Ramiz Raja (Pakistan)	116*	Sri Lanka	Hobart	1989-90
	107*	Sri Lanka	Adelaide	1989-90
M.J.Greatbatch (New Zealand)	102*	England	Leeds	1990
	111	England	The Oval	1990
G.R.Marsh (Australia)	113	West Indies	Bridgetown	1990-91
	106*	West Indies	Georgetown	1990-91
Inzamam-ul-Haq (Pakistan)	101	Sri Lanka	Multan	1991-92
	117	Sri Lanka	Rawalpindi	1991-92
P.V.Simmons (West Indies)	122	South Africa	Kingston	1991-92
	104	South Africa	Port-of-Spain	1991-92
B.C.Lara (West Indies)	128	Pakistan	Durban	1992-93
	111*	South Africa	Bloemfontein	1992-93
R.S.Mahanama (Sri Lanka)	119*	Zimbabwe	Harare	1994-95
	108	Zimbabwe	Harare	1994-95

M.E.Waugh (Australia)		130	Kenya	Vishakhapatnam	1995-96
		126	India	Bombay	1995-96
N.V.Knight (England)		113	Pakistan	Birmingham	1996
		125*	Pakistan	Nottingham	1996

HUNDRED ON DEBUT

D.L.Amiss	103	England v Australia	Manchester	1972
D.L.Haynes	148	West Indies v Australia	St John's	1977-78
A.Flower	115*	Zimbabwe v Sri Lanka	New Plymouth	1991-92
Salim Elahi	102*	Pakistan v Sri Lanka	Gujranwala	1995-96

CARRYING BAT THROUGH COMPLETED INNINGS

G.W.Flower	84*	Zimbabwe (205) v England	Sydney	1994-95
Saeed Anwar	103*	Pakistan (219) v Zimbabwe	Harare	1994-95
N.V.Knight	125*	England (246) v Pakistan	Nottingham	1996

MOST FOURS IN AN INNINGS

21	I.V.A.Richards (189*)	WI v E	Manchester	1984
21	B.C.Lara (153)	WI v P	Sharjah	1993-94
20	I.V.A.Richards (119*)	WI v E	Scarborough	1976
20	I.V.A.Richards (149)	WI v I	Jamshedpur	1983-84
20	B.C.Lara (128)	WI v P	Durban	1992-93
19	D.J.Callaghan (169*)	SA v NZ	Pretoria	1994-95
18	D.L.Amiss (137)	E v I	Lord's	1975
18	D.I.Gower (158)	E v NZ	Brisbane	1982-83
18	W.Larkins (124)	E v A	Hyderabad, India	1989-90
17	G.A.Gooch (129*)	E v WI	Port-of-Spain	1985-86
17	R.A.Smith (167*)	E v A	Birmingham	1993
17	Ijaz Ahmed (114*)	P v SA	Durban	1994-95
16	K.J.Wadsworth (104)	NZ v A	Christchurch	1973-74
16	Majid Khan (109)	P v E	Nottingham	1974
16	G.M.Turner (171*)	NZ v EA	Birmingham	1975
16	D.L.Haynes (148)	WI v A	St John's	1977-78
16	I.V.A.Richards (153*)	WI v A	Melbourne	1979-80
16	Kapil Dev (175*)	I v Z	Tunbridge Wells	1983
16	D.L.Haynes (145*)	WI v NZ	Berbice	1984-85
16	C.G.Greenidge (133*)	WI v NZ	Christchurch	1986-87
16	I.V.A.Richards (181)	WI v SL	Karachi	1987-88
16	R.A.Smith (128)	E v NZ	Leeds	1990
16	Ramiz Raja (119*)	P v NZ	Christchurch	1991-92
16	B.C.Lara (111)	WI v SA	Karachi	1995-96
15	G.S.Chappell (108)	A v NZ	Auckland	1981-82
15	Zaheer Abbas (123)	P v SL	Lahore	1981-82
15	Mohsin Khan (104)	P v A	Hyderabad, Pakistan	1982-83
15	C.L.Smith (70)	E v NZ	Wellington	1983-84
15	D.L.Haynes (123*)	WI v A	Melbourne	1984-85
15	C.G.Greenidge (110*)	WI v SL	Adelaide	1984-85
15	D.C.Boon (122)	A v SL	Adelaide	1987-88
15	J.G.Wright (101)	NZ v E	Napier	1987-88
15	G.A.Gooch (112*)	E v NZ	The Oval	1990
15	N.S.Sidhu (134*)	I v E	Gwalior	1992-93
15	S.R.Tendulkar (82)	I v NZ	Auckland	1993-94
15	Inzamam-ul-Haq (137*)	P v NZ	Sharjah	1993-94
15	B.C.Lara (139)	WI v A	Port-of-Spain	1994-95
15	S.R.Tendulkar (112*)	I v SL	Sharjah	1994-95
15	B.C.Lara (169)	WI v SL	Sharjah	1995-96
15	S.R.Tendulkar (127*)	I v K	Cuttack	1995-96

MOST SIXES IN AN INNINGS

11	S.T.Jayasuriya (134)	SL v P	Singapore	1995-96
8	C.G.Greenidge (117)	WI v I	St John's	1988-89
7	I.V.A.Richards (181)	WI v SL	Karachi	1987-88
7	I.V.A.Richards (110*)	WI v I	Rajkot	1987-88
6	B.L.Cairns (52)	NZ v A	Melbourne	1982-83

6	Kapil Dev (175*)	I v Z	Tunbridge Wells	1983
6	D.L.Houghton (142)	Z v NZ	Hyderabad, India	1987-88
6	D.L.Haynes (152*)	WI v I	Georgetown	1988-89
6	Saeed Anwar (126)	P v SL	Adelaide	1989-90
6	S.P.O'Donnell (74)	A v SL	Sharjah	1989-90
6	S.T.Jayasuriya (140)	SL v NZ	Bloemfontein	1994-95
6	A.P.Gurusinha (87)	SL v Z	Colombo (SSC)	1995-96
6	Salim Raza (84)	UAE v H	Lahore	1995-96
5	Javed Miandad (119*)	P v I	Lahore	1982-83
5	D.I.Gower (130)	E v SL	Taunton	1983
5	C.G.Greenidge (115)	WI v I	Jamshedpur	1983-84
5	I.V.A.Richards (189*)	WI v E	Manchester	1984
5	N.S.Sidhu (73)	I v A	Madras	1987-88
5	C.G.Greenidge (84)	WI v I	Trivandrum	1987-88
5	K.Srikkanth (112)	I v WI	Sharjah	1988-89
5	D.L.Haynes (117*)	WI v I	Bridgetown	1988-89
5	A.R.Border (84*)	A v E	Hyderabad, India	1989-90
5	D.M.Jones (102*)	A v NZ	Auckland	1989-90
5	P.V.Simmons (122)	WI v SA	Kingston	1992-93
5	Basit Ali (127*)	P v WI	Sharjah	1993-94
5	S.R.Tendulkar (137)	I v SL	Delhi	1995-96
5	P.A.de Silva (145)	SL v K	Kandy	1995-96
5	S.T.Jayasuriya (76)	SL v P	Singapore	1995-96

FASTEST INNINGS
(In terms of fewest balls received)

FASTEST FIFTIES

17	S.T.Jayasuriya (134)	SL v P	Singapore	1995-96
18	S.P.O'Donnell (74)	A v SL	Sharjah	1989-90
21	B.L.Cairns (52)	NZ v A	Melbourne	1982-83
22	Kapil Dev (72)	I v WI	Berbice	1982-83
23	Salim Malik (72*)	P v I	Calcutta	1986-87
23	R.S.Kaluwitharana (74)	SL v A	Melbourne	1995-96
25	I.V.A.Richards (82)	WI v E	Port-of-Spain	1985-86
25	R.B.Richardson (52*)	WI v E	Kingstown	1993-94
26	W.B.Phillips (53)	A v NZ	Wellington	1985-86
26	Kapil Dev (58)	I v A	Rajkot	1986-87
27	S.T.Jayasuriya (65)	SL v P	Sharjah	1993-94
28	S.M.Patil (51)	I v P	Jaipur	1983-84
28	C.H.Lloyd (54*)	WI v SL	Perth	1984-85
29	I.D.S.Smith (51*)	NZ v E	Auckland	1990-91
29	S.P.Fleming (60)	NZ v I	Nagpur	1995-96
29	A.Ranatunga (75*)	SL v K	Kandy	1995-96
30	C.M.Old (51*)	E v I	Lord's	1975
30	Imran Khan (56*)	P v SL	Swansea	1983
30	M.D.Crowe (74*)	NZ v Z	Napier	1991-92
30	S.T.Jayasuriya (52)	SL v NZ	East London	1994-95

FASTEST HUNDREDS

48	S.T.Jayasuriya (134)	SL v P	Singapore	1995-96
62	M.A.Azharuddin (108*)	I v NZ	Baroda	1988-89
67	Basit Ali (127*)	P v WI	Sharjah	1993-94
72	Zaheer Abbas (118)	P v I	Multan	1982-83
72	Kapil Dev (175*)	I v Z	Tunbridge Wells	1983
72	I.V.A.Richards (149)	WI v I	Jamshedpur	1983-84
73	Javed Miandad (119*)	P v I	Lahore	1982-83
75	I.V.A.Richards (110*)	WI v I	Rajkot	1987-88
78	A.R.Border (118*)	A v SL	Adelaide	1984-85
79	Zaheer Abbas (105)	P v I	Lahore	1982-83
80	Zaheer Abbas (123)	P v SL	Lahore	1981-82
81†	S.V.Manjrekar (105)	I v SA	Delhi	1991-92
82	C.H.Lloyd (102)	WI v A	Lord's	1975
82	G.S.Chappell (108)	A v NZ	Auckland	1981-82
82	D.I.Gower (109)	E v NZ	Adelaide	1982-83
83†	Ijaz Ahmed (124*)	P v B	Chittagong	1988-89

83	B.C.Lara (111)	WI v SA	Faisalabad	1995-96
84	C.L.Cairns (103)	NZ v I	Poona	1995-96
85	D.I.Gower (158)	E v NZ	Brisbane	1982-83
85	S.M.Gavaskar (103*)	I v NZ	Nagpur	1987-88
87	Saeed Anwar (126)	P v SL	Adelaide	1989-90
87	A.C.Parore (108)	NZ v SA	Pretoria	1994-95
87	Ijaz Ahmed (114*)	P v SA	Durban	1994-95
88	Majid Khan (109)	P v E	Nottingham	1974
88†	H.A.Gomes (101)	WI v SL	Perth	1984-85
89	K.Srikkanth (123)	I v P	Calcutta	1986-87
90	B.C.Lara (169)	WI v Sl	Sharjah	1995-96

† or fewer – exact number not known.

FASTEST 150s

111	B.C.Lara (169)	WI v SL	Sharjah	1995-96
112	I.V.A.Richards (181)	WI v SL	Karachi	1987-88
114	D.I.Gower (158)	E v NZ	Brisbane	1982-83
126	D.L.Haynes (152*)	WI v I	Georgetown	1988-89

PARTNERSHIP RECORDS

HIGHEST PARTNERSHIP FOR EACH WICKET

1st	212	G.R.Marsh (104), D.C.Boon (111)	A v I	Jaipur	1986-87
2nd	263	Aamir Sohail (134), Inzamam-ul-Haq (137*)	P v NZ	Sharjah	1993-94
3rd	224*	D.M.Jones (99*), A.R.Border (118*)	A v SL	Adelaide	1984-85
4th	173	D.M.Jones (121), S.R.Waugh (82)	A v P	Perth	1986-87
5th	159	R.T.Ponting (123), M.G.Bevan (65*)	A v SL	Melbourne	1995-96
6th	154	R.B.Richardson (122), P.J.L.Dujon (53)	WI v P	Sharjah	1991-92
7th	115	P.J.L.Dujon (57*), M.D.Marshall (66)	WI v P	Gujranwala	1986-87
8th	119	P.R.Reiffel (58), S.K.Warne (55)	A v SA	Port Elizabeth	1993-94
9th	126*	Kapil Dev (175*), S.M.H.Kirmani (24*)	I v Z	Tunbridge Wells	1983
10th	106*	I.V.A.Richards (189*), M.A.Holding (12*)	WI v E	Manchester	1984

PARTNERSHIPS OF 200 AND OVER

263	2nd	Aamir Sohail (134), Inzamam-ul-Haq (137*)	P v NZ	Sharjah	1993-94
231	2nd	S.R.Tendulkar (118), N.S.Sidhu (101)	I v P	Sharjah	1995-96
224*	3rd	D.M.Jones (99*), A.R.Border (118*)	A v SL	Adelaide	1984-85
221	2nd	C.G.Greenidge (115), I.V.A.Richards (149)	WI v I	Jamshedpur	1983-84
213	3rd	G.A.Hick (86*), N.H.Fairbrother (113)	E v WI	Lord's	1991
212	1st	G.R.Marsh (104), D.C.Boon (111)	A v I	Jaipur	1986-87
207	3rd	M.E.Waugh (130), S.R.Waugh (82)	A v Ken	Vishakhapatnam	1995-96
206	3rd	Moin-ul-Atiq (105), Ijaz Ahmed (124*)	P v Ban	Chittagong	1988-89
205	2nd	D.L.Haynes (80), I.V.A.Richards (153*)	WI v A	Melbourne	1979-80
205	2nd	Mohsin Khan (117*), Zaheer Abbas (118)	P v I	Multan	1982-83
204	2nd	Inzamam-ul-Haq (117), Salim Malik (102)	P v SL	Rawalpindi	1991-92
204	1st	Saeed Anwar (110), Ramiz Raja (109*)	P v SL	Sharjah	1992-93
202	2nd	G.A.Gooch (117*), D.I.Gower (102)	E v A	Lord's	1985
202	1st	Ramiz Raja (107*), Saeed Anwar (126)	P v SL	Adelaide	1989-90

HUNDRED PARTNERSHIPS

ENGLAND – 1st Wicket

			A	SA	WI	NZ	I	P	SL	Z
G.A.Gooch, C.W.J.Athey	Manchester	1986	–	–	–	193	–	–	–	–
G.A.Gooch, W.Larkins	Hyderabad, India	1989-90	185	–	–	–	–	–	–	–
D.L.Amiss, J.M.Brearley	The Oval	1977	161	–	–	–	–	–	–	EA
B.Wood, D.L.Amiss	Birmingham	1975	–	–	–	–	–	–	–	158
G.A.Gooch, M.A.Atherton	Manchester	1991	–	–	156	–	–	–	–	–
G.A.Gooch, G.Boycott	Birmingham	1980	154	–	–	–	–	–	–	–
R.A.Smith, M.A.Atherton	Karachi	1995-96	–	–	–	–	–	147	–	–
P.Willey, G.Boycott	Lord's	1980	–	–	135	–	–	–	–	–
B.Wood, C.J.Tavaré	Leeds	1982	–	–	–	133	–	–	–	–
J.M.Brearley, G.Boycott	Lord's	1979	–	–	129	–	–	–	–	–
G.A.Gooch, R.T.Robinson	Poona	1987-88	–	–	–	–	–	–	123	–
G.A.Gooch, D.I.Gower	Lord's	1989	123	–	–	–	–	–	–	–
B.C.Broad, C.W.J.Athey	Adelaide	1986-87	–	–	121	–	–	–	–	–

ENGLAND – 1st Wicket – *continued*

			A	SA	WI	NZ	I	P	SL	Z
G.A.Gooch, B.C.Broad	Sharjah	1986-87	118	–	–	–	–	–	–	–
G.Fowler, C.J.Tavaré	Manchester	1983	–	–	–	–	–	115	–	–
M.A.Atherton, A.J.Stewart	Kingston	1993-94	–	–	112	–	–	–	–	–
G.A.Gooch, G.Cook	Colombo (SSC)	1981-82	–	–	–	–	–	–	109	–
G.A.Gooch, G.Boycott	The Oval	1980	108	–	–	–	–	–	–	–
G.A.Gooch, I.T.Botham	Sydney	1991-92	107	–	–	–	–	–	–	–
B.C.Broad, C.W.J.Athey	Perth	1986-87	–	–	–	–	–	104	–	–
A.J.Stewart, R.A.Smith	Pretoria	1995-96	–	103	–	–	–	–	–	–
N.V.Knight, A.J.Stewart	Birmingham	1996	–	–	–	–	–	103	–	–
G.A.Gooch, B.C.Broad	Peshawar	1987-88	–	–	–	–	–	101	–	–
R.A.Smith, A.J.Stewart	Gwalior	1992-93	–	–	–	–	101	–	–	–
M.A.Atherton, A.J.Stewart	Sydney	1994-95	100	–	–	–	–	–	–	–

ENGLAND – 2nd Wicket

			A	SA	WI	NZ	I	P	SL	Z
G.A.Gooch, D.I.Gower	Lord's	1985	202	–	–	–	–	–	–	–
D.L.Amiss, K.W.R.Fletcher	Lord's	1975	–	–	–	–	176	–	–	–
M.A.Atherton, G.A.Hick	The Oval	1995	–	–	144	–	–	–	–	–
B.C.Broad, R.T.Robinson	Sharjah	1986-87	–	–	–	–	–	140	–	–
D.L.Amiss, K.W.R.Fletcher	Manchester	1972	125	–	–	–	–	–	–	–
G.Boycott, P.Willey	Sydney	1979-80	118	–	–	–	–	–	–	–
B.C.Broad, A.J.Lamb	The Oval	1987	–	–	–	–	–	116	–	–
R.A.Smith, G.A.Hick	Gwalior	1992-93	–	–	–	–	116	–	–	–
G.A.Gooch, R.A.Smith	Leeds	1990	–	–	–	113	–	–	–	–
G.A.Gooch, C.T.Radley	Scarborough	1978	–	–	–	111	–	–	–	–
G.Boycott, P.Willey	Sydney	1979-80	111	–	–	–	–	–	–	–
G.A.Gooch, R.A.Smith	Perth	1991-92	–	–	–	–	–	110	–	–
C.J.Tavaré, A.J.Lamb	Nottingham	1982	–	–	–	–	107	–	–	–

ENGLAND – 3rd Wicket

			A	SA	WI	NZ	I	P	SL	Z	H
G.A.Hick, N.H.Fairbrother	Lord's	1991	–	–	213	–	–	–	–	–	
C.J.Tavaré, A.J.Lamb	Sydney	1982-83	–	–	–	190*	–	–	–	–	
A.J.Lamb, D.I.Gower	The Oval	1982	–	–	–	–	159	–	–	–	
G.A.Hick, G.P.Thorpe	Peshawar	1995-96	–	–	–	–	–	–	–	–	143
C.W.J.Athey, M.W.Gatting	Karachi	1987-88	–	–	–	–	–	135	–	–	
R.A.Smith, N.H.Fairbrother	Nottingham	1992	–	–	–	–	–	129	–	–	
K.J.Barnett, A.J.Lamb	The Oval	1988	–	–	–	–	–	–	118	–	
G.A.Gooch, M.W.Gatting	Bombay	1987-88	–	–	–	–	117	–	–	–	
D.I.Gower, A.J.Lamb	Manchester	1986	–	–	–	–	115	–	–	–	
G.Fowler, A.J.Lamb	Lord's	1983	–	–	–	–	–	106*	–	–	
C.T.Radley, D.I.Gower	Manchester	1978	–	–	–	105	–	–	–	–	
D.Lloyd, M.H.Denness	Nottingham	1974	–	–	–	–	–	103	–	–	
R.A.Smith, A.J.Lamb	Delhi	1989-90	–	–	–	–	–	–	103	–	
A.J.Lamb, M.W.Gatting	Nottingham	1982	–	–	–	–	–	102	–	–	
M.A.Atherton, A.J.Lamb	Manchester	1991	–	–	102	–	–	–	–	–	

ENGLAND – 4th Wicket

			A	SA	WI	NZ	I	P	SL	Z
A.J.Lamb, D.W.Randall	Melbourne	1982-83	139	–	–	–	–	–	–	–
A.J.Lamb, A.J.Stewart	Kanpur	1989-90	–	–	–	–	130	–	–	–
G.A.Hick, N.H.Fairbrother	Manchester	1993	127	–	–	–	–	–	–	–
G.A.Gooch, I.T.Botham	Manchester	1985	116	–	–	–	–	–	–	–
A.J.Lamb, M.W.Gatting	The Oval	1983	–	–	115	–	–	–	–	–
R.A.Smith, R.C.Russell	Nottingham	1990	–	–	–	–	111	–	–	–
G.A.Gooch, D.J.Capel	Karachi	1987-88	–	–	–	–	–	109	–	–
D.I.Gower, D.W.Randall	Adelaide	1982-83	106	–	–	–	–	–	–	–
A.J.Lamb, I.T.Botham	Perth	1986-87	106	–	–	–	–	–	–	–
D.I.Gower, G.R.J.Roope	The Oval	1978	–	–	–	–	–	105	–	–

ENGLAND – 5th Wicket

			A	SA	WI	NZ	I	P	SL	Z
R.A.Smith, G.P.Thorpe	Birmingham	1993	142	–	–	–	–	–	–	–
D.I.Gower, D.W.Randall	Brisbane	1982-83	–	–	–	113	–	–	–	–
D.I.Gower, M.W.Gatting	Jullundur	1981-82	–	–	–	–	110	–	–	–
G.A.Gooch, R.C.Russell	The Oval	1990	–	–	109*	–	–	–	–	–

England – 6th Wicket – No instance – highest partnership

			A	SA	WI	NZ	I	P	SL	Z
D.I.Gower, I.J.Gould	Taunton	1983	–	–	–	–	–	–	98	–

England – 7th Wicket – No instance – highest partnership

			A	SA	WI	NZ	I	P	SL	Z
M.W.Gatting, P.R.Downton	Poona	1984-85	–	–	–	–	86*	–	–	–

England – 8th Wicket – No instance – highest partnership

			A	SA	WI	NZ	I	P	SL	Z
D.A.Reeve, D.Gough	Faisalabad	1995-96	–	–	–	–	–	–	62	–

England – 9th Wicket – No instance – highest partnership

			A	SA	WI	NZ	I	P	SL	Z
A.J.Lamb, N.A.Foster	Manchester	1984	–	–	47	–	–	–	–	–

England – 10th Wicket – No instance – highest partnership

			A	SA	WI	NZ	I	P	SL	Z
A.R.C.Fraser, P.C.R.Tufnell	Melbourne	1990-91	43*	–	–	–	–	–	–	–

AUSTRALIA – 1st Wicket

			E	SA	WI	NZ	I	P	SL	Z
G.R.Marsh, D.C.Boon	Jaipur	1986-87	–	–	–	–	212	–	–	–
M.A.Taylor, M.E.Waugh	Perth	1995-96	–	–	–	–	–	–	189	–
R.B.McCosker, A.Turner	The Oval	1975	–	–	–	–	–	–	182	–
K.C.Wessels, J.Dyson	Melbourne	1982-83	–	–	154	–	–	–	–	–
M.A.Taylor, T.M.Moody	Brisbane	1989-90	–	–	–	–	–	154	–	–
G.R.Marsh, D.C.Boon	Sydney	1985-86	–	–	–	–	152	–	–	–
G.R.Marsh, D.C.Boon	Melbourne	1985-86	–	–	–	–	146	–	–	–
G.M.Wood, S.B.Smith	Melbourne	1982-83	–	–	–	140	–	–	–	–
S.B.Smith, G.M.Wood	Melbourne	1984-85	–	–	135	–	–	–	–	–
M.E.Waugh, M.A.Taylor	Sydney	1995-96	–	–	–	–	–	–	135	–
G.R.Marsh, D.C.Boon	Sydney	1991-92	–	–	128	–	–	–	–	–
M.A.Taylor, M.J.Slater	Lahore	1994-95	–	–	–	–	–	121	–	–
T.M.Moody, G.R.Marsh	Adelaide	1991-92	–	–	–	–	–	–	120	–
G.R.Marsh, D.C.Boon	Adelaide	1987-88	–	–	–	–	–	–	115	–
G.R.Marsh, M.A.Taylor	Hamilton	1989-90	–	–	–	112	–	–	–	–
T.M.Moody, M.A.Taylor	Sydney	1992-93	–	–	–	–	–	112	–	–
D.C.Boon, G.R.Marsh	Madras	1987-88	–	–	–	–	110	–	–	–
G.R.Marsh, D.M.Wellham	Sydney	1986-87	109	–	–	–	–	–	–	–
T.M.Moody, M.A.Taylor	Colombo (PSS)	1992-93	–	–	–	–	–	–	109	–
T.M.Moody, D.C.Boon	Melbourne	1991-92	–	–	107	–	–	–	–	–
K.C.Wessels, S.B.Smith	Berbice	1983-84	–	–	106	–	–	–	–	–
M.A.Taylor, M.J.Slater	Melbourne	1993-94	–	105	–	–	–	–	–	–
B.M.Laird, G.M.Wood	Hyderabad, Pakistan	1982-83	–	–	–	–	–	104	–	–
R.B.McCosker, J.M.Weiner	Sydney	1979-80	–	–	103	–	–	–	–	–
M.E.Waugh, M.A.Taylor	Bombay	1995-96	–	–	–	–	–	103	–	–
D.C.Boon, G.R.Marsh	Brisbane	1988-89	–	–	–	–	–	100	–	–

AUSTRALIA – 2nd Wicket

			E	SA	WI	NZ	I	P	SL	Z
G.R.Marsh, D.M.Jones	Brisbane	1990-91	185	–	–	–	–	–	–	–
G.R.Marsh, D.M.Jones	Brisbane	1986-87	178	–	–	–	–	–	–	–
D.C.Boon, T.M.Moody	Sydney	1991-92	–	–	–	–	167*	–	–	–
S.B.Smith, W.B.Phillips	Perth	1984-85	–	–	–	–	–	–	157*	–
J.Dyson, G.S.Chappell	Sydney	1980-81	–	–	151	–	–	–	–	–
R.D.Robinson, G.S.Chappell	The Oval	1977	148	–	–	–	–	–	–	–
M.A.Taylor, M.E.Waugh	Auckland	1994-95	–	–	–	147	–	–	–	–
G.M.Wood, G.S.Chappell	Melbourne	1980-81	–	–	–	145	–	–	–	–
D.C.Boon, D.M.Jones	Christchurch	1989-90	–	–	–	145	–	–	–	–
T.M.Chappell, K.J.Hughes	Nottingham	1983	–	–	–	144	–	–	–	–
M.E.Waugh, D.M.Jones	Hamilton	1992-93	–	–	–	143	–	–	–	–
G.R.Marsh, D.M.Jones	Sharjah	1989-90	–	–	–	–	–	–	137	–
K.R.Stackpole, I.M.Chappell	Dunedin	1973-74	–	–	–	136	–	–	–	–
M.A.Taylor, M.E.Waugh	Sharjah	1993-94	–	–	–	–	–	–	133*	–
G.M.Wood, G.N.Yallop	Leeds	1981	130	–	–	–	–	–	–	–
D.C.Boon, D.M.Jones	Hobart	1991-92	–	–	–	–	129	–	–	–
K.C.Wessels, K.J.Hughes	Delhi	1984-85	–	–	–	–	128	–	–	–
A.R.Border, G.S.Chappell	Sydney	1980-81	–	–	–	–	127*	–	–	–
G.R.Marsh, D.M.Jones	Adelaide	1988-89	–	–	–	–	–	–	126*	–
G.R.Marsh, D.M.Jones	Chandigarh	1987-88	–	–	–	–	126	–	–	–
D.C.Boon, D.M.Jones	Melbourne	1992-93	–	–	–	–	–	124	–	–
D.C.Boon, D.M.Jones	Port Elizabeth	1993-94	–	123	–	–	–	–	–	–
M.L.Hayden, D.C.Boon	Sharjah	1993-94	–	–	–	123	–	–	–	–
G.R.Marsh, A.R.Border	Sydney	1985-86	–	–	–	–	121	–	–	–
D.C.Boon, D.M.Jones	Melbourne	1993-94	–	–	–	121	–	–	–	–
M.A.Taylor, D.M.Jones	Melbourne	1990-91	–	–	–	118	–	–	–	–
G.R.Marsh, D.C.Boon	Perth	1989-90	–	–	–	–	–	–	117*	–
D.C.Boon, D.M.Jones	Indore	1987-88	–	–	117	–	–	–	–	–
G.R.Marsh, A.R.Border	Melbourne	1988-89	–	–	–	–	–	114	–	–
K.C.Wessels, K.J.Hughes	Melbourne	1983-84	–	–	109	–	–	–	–	–
G.R.Marsh, D.M.Jones	Hyderabad, India	1989-90	108	–	–	–	–	–	–	–

AUSTRALIA – 2nd Wicket – *continued*

			E	SA	WI	NZ	I	P	SL	Z
M.A.Taylor, M.E.Waugh	Manchester	1993	108	–	–	–	–	–	–	–
M.A.Taylor, M.E.Waugh	Sydney	1995-96	–	–	–	–	–	–	108	–
M.A.Taylor, D.M.Jones	Dunedin	1992-93	–	–	–	104	–	–	–	–
M.A.Taylor, D.M.Jones	Adelaide	1992-93	–	–	–	–	–	101	–	–
M.A.Taylor, R.T.Ponting	Lahore	1995-96	–	–	–	–	–	–	101	–
G.R.Marsh, D.M.Jones	Sydney	1990-91	–	–	–	100	–	–	–	–

AUSTRALIA – 3rd Wicket

			E	SA	WI	NZ	I	P	SL	Z	K
D.M.Jones, A.R.Border	Adelaide	1984-85	–	–	–	–	–	–	224*	–	
M.E.Waugh, S.R.Waugh	Vishakhapatnam	1995-96	–	–	–	–	–	–	–	–	207
D.M.Jones, M.E.Waugh	Sydney	1993-94	–	175	–	–	–	–	–	–	
S.G.Law, D.C.Boon	Hobart	1994-95	–	–	–	–	–	–	159	–	
D.C.Boon, A.R.Border	Sharjah	1986-87	159	–	–	–	–	–	–	–	
G.R.Marsh, A.R.Border	Bridgetown	1990-91	–	–	146	–	–	–	–	–	
K.C.Wessels, A.R.Border	Sydney	1983-84	–	–	–	–	–	140	–	–	
D.M.Jones, A.R.Border	Adelaide	1991-92	–	–	–	–	137	–	–	–	
M.A.Taylor, M.E.Waugh	Georgetown	1990-91	–	123	–	–	–	–	–	–	
M.A.Taylor, M.E.Waugh	Cape Town	1993-94	–	123	–	–	–	–	–	–	
K.C.Wessels, K.J.Hughes	Perth	1983-84	–	–	119	–	–	–	–	–	
G.R.Marsh, A.R.Border	Madras	1987-88	–	–	–	–	–	–	–	113	
G.R.Marsh, A.R.Border	Lord's	1989	113	–	–	–	–	–	–	–	
G.N.Yallop, D.W.Hookes	Colombo (SSC)	1982-83	–	–	–	–	–	–	112	–	
G.R.Marsh, A.R.Border	Madras	1989-90	–	–	112	–	–	–	–	–	
R.T.Ponting, S.R.Waugh	Jaipur	1995-96	–	–	110	–	–	–	–	–	
M.A.Taylor, D.C.Boon	Lord's	1993	108	–	–	–	–	–	–	–	
D.M.Jones, M.R.J.Veletta	Melbourne	1987-88	–	–	–	107*	–	–	–	–	
D.M.Jones, S.P.O'Donnell	Sharjah	1989-90	–	–	–	–	–	–	106	–	
M.E.Waugh, D.C.Boon	Christchurch	1992-93	–	–	–	103	–	–	–	–	
D.M.Jones, A.R.Border	Melbourne	1986-87	103	–	–	–	–	–	–	–	
K.J.Hughes, D.W.Hookes	Lord's	1983	–	–	101	–	–	–	–	–	
A.R.Border, K.J.Hughes	Sydney	1980-81	–	–	–	–	100	–	–	–	
D.C.Boon, K.J.Hughes	Melbourne	1983-84	–	–	100	–	–	–	–	–	

AUSTRALIA – 4th Wicket

			E	SA	WI	NZ	I	P	SL	Z
D.M.Jones, S.R.Waugh	Perth	1986-87	–	–	–	–	–	173	–	–
M.E.Waugh, A.R.Border	Birmingham	1993	168	–	–	–	–	–	–	–
A.R.Border, S.R.Waugh	Adelaide	1986-87	164	–	–	–	–	–	–	–
R.B.Kerr, D.M.Jones	Melbourne	1984-85	157*	–	–	–	–	–	–	–
A.R.Border, K.J.Hughes	Castries	1983-84	–	–	150	–	–	–	–	–
B.M.Laird, K.J.Hughes	Sydney	1981-82	–	–	147*	–	–	–	–	–
D.M.Jones, M.E.Waugh	Kingston	1990-91	–	–	136	–	–	–	–	–
P.L.Taylor, A.R.Border	Hyderabad, India	1989-90	120*	–	–	–	–	–	–	–
D.C.Boon, S.R.Waugh	Multan	1994-95	–	–	–	–	–	120*	–	–
M.A.Taylor, S.G.Law	Melbourne	1995-96	–	–	118	–	–	–	–	–
G.S.Chappell, K.D.Walters	The Oval	1975	–	–	–	–	–	–	117	–
B.M.Laird, K.J.Hughes	Lahore	1982-83	–	–	–	–	–	117	–	–
K.C.Wessels, D.W.Hookes	Sydney	1982-83	–	–	116	–	–	–	–	–
A.R.Border, D.C.Boon	Melbourne	1984-85	–	–	115	–	–	–	–	–
R.T.Ponting, S.G.Law	Brisbane	1995-96	–	–	115	–	–	–	–	–
D.C.Boon, S.P.O'Donnell	Sharjah	1986-87	–	–	–	–	–	114	–	–
S.R.Waugh, S.G.Law	Colombo (SSC)	1996-97	–	–	–	–	113	–	–	–
D.M.Jones, A.R.Border	Melbourne	1989-90	–	–	–	–	–	109*	–	–
G.S.Chappell, A.P.Sheahan	Lord's	1972	103	–	–	–	–	–	–	–
K.J.Hughes, G.N.Yallop	Birmingham	1980	103	–	–	–	–	–	–	–
S.R.Waugh, S.G.Law	Melbourne	1995-96	–	–	–	–	–	–	102	–

AUSTRALIA – 5th Wicket

			E	SA	WI	NZ	I	P	SL	Z
R.T.Ponting, M.G.Bevan	Melbourne	1995-96	–	–	–	–	–	–	159	–
S.G.Law, M.G.Bevan	Chandigarh	1995-96	–	–	138	–	–	–	–	–
B.M.Laird, A.R.Border	Dunedin	1981-82	–	–	–	115*	–	–	–	–
M.E.Waugh, S.R.Waugh	Hobart	1991-92	–	–	–	–	–	–	113	–
S.R.Waugh, A.R.Border	Pretoria	1993-94	–	107	–	–	–	–	–	–
A.R.Border, W.B.Phillips	Sydney	1984-85	–	105	–	–	–	–	–	–
G.M.Ritchie, G.R.J.Matthews	Auckland	1985-86	–	–	–	100	–	–	–	–

AUSTRALIA – 6th Wicket

			E	SA	WI	NZ	I	P	SL	Z
M.E.Waugh, S.P.O'Donnell	Sydney	1990-91	112	–	–	–	–	–	–	–
D.M.Jones, S.P.O'Donnell	Melbourne	1989-90	–	–	–	–	–	–	108*	–

AUSTRALIA – 7th Wicket

	Venue	Season	E	SA	WI	NZ	I	P	SL	Z
S.R.Waugh, G.C.Dyer	Delhi	1986-87					102*			

AUSTRALIA – 8th Wicket

	Venue	Season	E	SA	WI	NZ	I	P	SL	Z
P.R.Reiffel, S.K.Warne	Port Elizabeth	1993-94		119						

Australia – 9th Wicket – No instance – highest partnership

	Venue	Season	E	SA	WI	NZ	I	P	SL	Z
S.P.O'Donnell, G.M.Wood	Sydney	1984-85			52					

Australia – 10th Wicket – No instance – highest partnership

	Venue	Season	E	SA	WI	NZ	I	P	SL	Z
T.J.Laughlin, M.H.N.Walker	Sydney	1979-80	45							

SOUTH AFRICA – 1st Wicket

	Venue	Season	E	A	WI	NZ	I	P	SL	Z	H
G.Kirsten, M.J.R.Rindel	Johannesburg	1994-95						190			
G.Kirsten, A.C.Hudson	Rawalpindi	1995-96									186
A.C.Hudson, G.Kirsten	Pretoria	1995-96	156								
K.C.Wessels, A.C.Hudson	Melbourne	1991-92	151								
A.C.Hudson, P.N.Kirsten	Adelaide	1991-92					128				
K.C.Wessels, A.C.Hudson	Bloemfontein	1992-93					125				
K.C.Wessels, G.Kirsten	Faisalabad	1994-95					125				
A.C.Hudson, R.P.Snell	Bloemfontein	1995-96	116								
A.C.Hudson, G.Kirsten	Sharjah	1995-96							115		
A.C.Hudson, K.C.Wessels	Durban	1992-93							101		

SOUTH AFRICA – 2nd Wicket

	Venue	Season	E	A	WI	NZ	I	P	SL	Z	UAE
D.J.Callaghan, W.J.Cronje	Pretoria	1994-95				149					
A.C.Hudson, W.J.Cronje	Johannesburg	1994-95						145			
K.C.Wessels, W.J.Cronje	Melbourne	1993-94		140							
G.Kirsten, D.J.Cullinan	Hamilton	1994-95					120				
G.Kirsten, W.J.Cronje	Rawalpindi	1995-96									116
K.C.Wessels, P.N.Kirsten	Canberra	1991-92								112	
K.C.Wessels, P.N.Kirsten	Chandigarh	1991-92					111				

SOUTH AFRICA – 3rd Wicket

	Venue	Season	E	A	WI	NZ	I	P	SL	Z	UAE
G.Kirsten, D.J.Cullinan	Rawalpindi	1995-96									145*
W.J.Cronje, J.H.Kallis	Durban	1995-96	118								
W.J.Cronje, J.N.Rhodes	Johannesburg	1993-94		106							
P.N.Kirsten, A.P.Kuiper	Chandigarh	1991-92					105*				
A.C.Hudson, J.N.Rhodes	Port Elizabeth	1993-94		105							

SOUTH AFRICA – 4th Wicket

	Venue	Season	E	A	WI	NZ	I	P	SL	Z
A.C.Hudson, W.J.Cronje	Sharjah	1995-96					154			
D.J.Cullinan, J.N.Rhodes	Port Elizabeth	1994-95							119	

South Africa – 5th Wicket – No instance – highest partnership

	Venue	Season	E	A	WI	NZ	I	P	SL	Z
B.M.McMillan, G.Kirsten	Harare	1995-96								92

South Africa – 6th Wicket – No instance – highest partnership

	Venue	Season	E	A	WI	NZ	I	P	SL	Z
J.N.Rhodes, D.J.Richardson	Durban	1994-95						88		

South Africa – 7th Wicket – No instance – highest partnership

	Venue	Season	E	A	WI	NZ	I	P	SL	Z
D.J.Richardson, E.O.Simons	Cape Town	1994-95				46				

South Africa – 8th Wicket – No instance – highest partnership

	Venue	Season	E	A	WI	NZ	I	P	SL	Z
S.M.Pollock, C.R.Matthews	Cape Town	1995-96	59							

South Africa – 9th Wicket – No instance – highest partnerships

	Venue	Season	E	A	WI	NZ	I	P	SL	Z
D.J.Richardson, P.S.de Villiers	Sydney	1993-94		30						
B.M.McMillan, P.S.de Villiers	East London	1995-96	30							

South Africa – 10th Wicket – No instance – highest partnership

	Venue	Season	E	A	WI	NZ	I	P	SL	Z
R.P.Snell, P.S.de Villiers	Colombo (RPS)	1993-94							51	

WEST INDIES – 1st Wicket

	Venue	Season	E	A	SA	NZ	I	P	SL	Z
C.G.Greenidge, D.L.Haynes	Christchurch	1986-87				192*				
C.G.Greenidge, D.L.Haynes	Georgetown	1988-89					185			
C.G.Greenidge, D.L.Haynes	Melbourne	1981-82						182		
D.L.Haynes, B.C.Lara	Melbourne	1991-92						175*		
D.L.Haynes, S.F.A.F.Bacchus	Birmingham	1983								172*
D.L.Haynes, C.G.Greenidge	Adelaide	1988-89						169		

WEST INDIES – 1st Wicket – *continued*

			E	A	SA	NZ	I	P	SL	Z
C.G.Greenidge, D.L.Haynes	Sharjah	1988-89	–	–	–	–	165	–	–	–
C.G.Greenidge, P.V.Simmons	Trivandrum	1987-88	–	–	–	–	164	–	–	–
D.L.Haynes, B.C.Lara	Port-of-Spain	1991-92	–	154*	–	–	–	–	–	–
D.L.Haynes, B.C.Lara	Bloemfontein	1992-93	–	152	–	–	–	–	–	–
C.G.Greenidge, D.L.Haynes	Indore	1983-84	–	–	–	–	149	–	–	–
D.L.Haynes, P.V.Simmons	Kingstown	1993-94	145	–	–	–	–	–	–	–
C.G.Greenidge, D.L.Haynes	Birmingham	1979	–	–	–	–	138	–	–	–
C.G.Greenidge, D.L.Haynes	Auckland	1986-87	–	–	–	134	–	–	–	–
C.G.Greenidge, D.L.Haynes	Adelaide	1984-85	–	–	–	–	–	–	133	–
C.G.Greenidge, D.L.Haynes	The Oval	1979	–	–	–	–	–	132	–	–
C.G.Greenidge, R.B.Richardson	Sharjah	1986-87	–	–	–	–	–	–	132	–
P.V.Simmons, S.C.Williams	Faridabad	1994-95	–	–	–	–	–	132	–	–
C.G.Greenidge, D.L.Haynes	Sydney	1984-85	–	–	–	–	–	–	128	–
D.L.Haynes, B.C.Lara	Colombo (RPS)	1993-94	–	–	–	–	–	–	128	–
D.L.Haynes, C.G.Greenidge	Sharjah	1986-87	–	–	–	–	–	126	–	–
C.G.Greenidge, D.L.Haynes	Port-of-Spain	1982-83	–	–	–	–	125	–	–	–
S.C.Williams, S.Chanderpaul	Kingston	1995-96	–	–	–	125	–	–	–	–
D.L.Haynes, P.A.Wallace	Adelaide	1991-92	–	–	–	–	124	–	–	–
D.L.Haynes, R.B.Richardson	Port-of-Spain	1984-85	–	–	117*	–	–	–	–	–
P.V.Simmons, S.C.Williams	Kanpur	1994-95	–	–	–	–	115	–	–	–
D.L.Haynes, R.B.Richardson	Sharjah	1985-86	–	–	–	–	114	–	–	–
D.L.Haynes, C.A.Best	Georgetown	1989-90	113	–	–	–	–	–	–	–
C.G.Greenidge, P.V.Simmons	Port-of-Spain	1987-88	–	–	–	–	–	112	–	–
D.L.Haynes, B.C.Lara	Johannesburg	1992-93	–	–	–	–	–	112	–	–
C.G.Greenidge, D.L.Haynes	Brisbane	1979-80	109	–	–	–	–	–	–	–
C.G.Greenidge, D.L.Haynes	Srinagar	1983-84	–	–	–	–	108*	–	–	–

WEST INDIES – 2nd Wicket

			E	A	SA	NZ	I	P	SL	Z
C.G.Greenidge, I.V.A.Richards	Jamshedpur	1983-84	–	–	–	–	221	–	–	–
D.L.Haynes, I.V.A.Richards	Melbourne	1979-80	–	205	–	–	–	–	–	–
B.C.Lara, P.V.Simmons	Durban	1992-93	–	–	–	–	–	197	–	–
D.L.Haynes, H.A.Gomes	Bridgetown	1984-85	–	–	–	184	–	–	–	–
S.F.A.F.Bacchus, I.V.A.Richards	Sialkot	1980-81	–	–	–	–	–	176	–	–
D.L.Haynes, R.B.Richardson	Berbice	1983-84	–	167	–	–	–	–	–	–
P.V.Simmons, R.B.Richardson	Georgetown	1987-88	–	–	–	–	–	157	–	–
D.L.Haynes, R.B.Richardson	Port-of-Spain	1987-88	–	–	–	–	–	152	–	–
D.L.Haynes, P.J.L.Dujon	Hobart	1988-89	–	–	–	–	–	145	–	–
R.C.Fredericks, A.I.Kallicharran	The Oval	1973	143	–	–	–	–	–	–	–
C.G.Greenidge, I.V.A.Richards	Sydney	1981-82	–	138	–	–	–	–	–	–
D.L.Haynes, R.B.Richardson	Karachi	1990-91	–	–	–	–	–	138	–	–
S.Chanderpaul, B.C.Lara	Karachi	1995-96	–	–	138	–	–	–	–	–
P.V.Simmons, R.B.Richardson	Sharjah	1993-94	–	–	–	–	–	–	137	–
R.B.Richardson, H.A.Gomes	Sydney	1983-84	–	132*	–	–	–	–	–	–
D.L.Haynes, R.B.Richardson	Kingston	1983-84	–	131*	–	–	–	–	–	–
C.G.Greenidge, R.B.Richardson	St John's	1988-89	–	–	–	–	130	–	–	–
C.G.Greenidge, A.I.Kallicharran	The Oval	1975	–	–	–	125	–	–	–	–
D.L.Haynes, R.B.Richardson	Gwalior	1989-90	124	–	–	–	–	–	–	–
R.C.Fredericks, A.I.Kallicharran	The Oval	1975	–	124	–	–	–	–	–	–
C.G.Greenidge, I.V.A.Richards	Lord's	1983	–	124	–	–	–	–	–	–
C.G.Greenidge, I.V.A.Richards	Sydney	1979-80	119	–	–	–	–	–	–	–
D.L.Haynes, R.B.Richardson	Bombay	1989-90	–	–	–	–	117	–	–	–
S.L.Campbell, B.C.Lara	Nottingham	1995	114	–	–	–	–	–	–	–
C.G.Greenidge, I.V.A.Richards	Melbourne	1981-82	–	112	–	–	–	–	–	–
D.L.Haynes, P.V.Simmons	Perth	1992-93	–	111*	–	–	–	–	–	–
B.C.Lara, P.V.Simmons	Sharjah	1993-94	–	–	–	–	–	111	–	–
C.G.Greenidge, I.V.A.Richards	Brisbane	1979-80	109*	–	–	–	–	–	–	–
P.V.Simmons, R.B.Richardson	Faridabad	1987-88	–	–	–	–	108	–	–	–
D.L.Haynes, I.V.A.Richards	The Oval	1983	–	–	–	–	101	–	–	–

WEST INDIES – 3rd Wicket

			E	A	SA	NZ	I	P	SL	Z
C.G.Greenidge, H.A.Gomes	Worcester	1983	–	–	–	–	–	–	–	195*
R.B.Richardson, A.L.Logie	Kingston	1987-88	–	–	–	–	–	187	–	–
B.C.Lara, P.V.Simmons	St Vincent	1995-96	–	–	–	186	–	–	–	–
D.L.Haynes, I.V.A.Richards	Karachi	1987-88	–	–	–	–	–	182	–	–
B.C.Lara, K.L.T.Arthurton	Calcutta	1993-94	–	–	–	–	–	163	–	–
I.V.A.Richards, C.H.Lloyd	Perth	1981-82	–	153*	–	–	–	–	–	–
R.B.Richardson, I.V.A.Richards	Karachi	1987-88	–	–	–	–	–	137	–	–
H.A.Gomes, I.V.A.Richards	Lord's	1984	134*	–	–	–	–	–	–	–

WEST INDIES – 3rd Wicket – *continued*

			E	A	SA	NZ	I	P	SL	Z
I.V.A.Richards, H.A.Gomes	The Oval	1983	–	–	–	–	–	132*	–	–
P.V.Simmons, B.C.Lara	Sharjah	1993-94	–	–	–	–	–	132	–	–
D.L.Haynes, I.V.A.Richards	Sydney	1984-85	–	128	–	–	–	–	–	–
D.L.Haynes, I.V.A.Richards	St John's	1984-85	–	–	–	127	–	–	–	–
D.L.Haynes, I.V.A.Richards	Berbice	1984-85	–	–	–	125	–	–	–	–
A.L.Logie, I.V.A.Richards	Gujranwala	1985-86	–	–	–	–	–	119*	–	–
H.A.Gomes, I.V.A.Richards	Perth	1984-85	–	–	–	–	–	–	117	–
R.B.Richardson, I.V.A.Richards	Port-of-Spain	1985-86	117	–	–	–	–	–	–	–
R.B.Richardson, I.V.A.Richards	Bridgetown	1985-86	117	–	–	–	–	–	–	–
R.B.Richardson, C.L.Hooper	Brisbane	1991-92	–	–	–	–	–	–	–	117
B.C.Lara, P.V.Simmons	Port-of-Spain	1995-96	–	–	–	–	–	–	116	–
R.B.Richardson, C.A.Best	Bridgetown	1989-90	112	–	–	–	–	–	–	–
B.C.Lara, C.L.Hooper	Madras	1994-95	–	–	–	–	112	–	–	–
B.C.Lara, C.L.Hooper	Gauhati	1994-95	–	–	–	111	–	–	–	–
C.G.Greenidge, I.V.A.Richards	Port-of-Spain	1983-84	–	110	–	–	–	–	–	–
B.C.Lara, R.B.Richardson	Brisbane	1991-92	–	110	–	–	–	–	–	–
B.C.Lara, P.V.Simmons	Port-of-Spain	1995-96	–	–	–	110	–	–	–	–
I.V.A.Richards, A.I.Kallicharran	Adelaide	1979-80	109	–	–	–	–	–	–	–
D.L.Haynes, R.B.Richardson	Brisbane	1991-92	–	–	–	–	109	–	–	–
D.L.Haynes, I.V.A.Richards	Sydney	1988-89	–	107*	–	–	–	–	–	–
R.B.Richardson, I.V.A.Richards	Sharjah	1985-86	–	–	–	–	–	–	105	–
P.V.Simmons, R.B.Richardson	Kingston	1991-92	–	–	105	–	–	–	–	–
P.V.Simmons, R.B.Richardson	Port-of-Spain	1991-92	–	–	104	–	–	–	–	–
I.V.A.Richards, C.H.Lloyd	Melbourne	1983-84	–	103	–	–	–	–	–	–

WEST INDIES – 4th Wicket

			E	A	SA	NZ	I	P	SL	Z
R.B.Kanhai, C.H.Lloyd	Lord's	1975	–	149	–	–	–	–	–	–
B.C.Lara, J.C.Adams	Port-of-Spain	1994-95	–	135	–	–	–	–	–	–
C.L.Hooper, J.C.Adams	Jaipur	1994-95	–	–	–	–	126	–	–	–
A.L.Logie, P.J.L.Dujon	Melbourne	1983-84	–	124	–	–	–	–	–	–
C.L.Hooper, I.V.A.Richards	Manchester	1991	121	–	–	–	–	–	–	–
C.L.Hooper, I.V.A.Richards	Dunedin	1986-87	–	–	–	120	–	–	–	–
I.V.A.Richards, A.L.Logie	Karachi	1986-87	–	–	–	–	–	–	116	–
B.C.Lara, J.C.Adams	Port-of-Spain	1995-96	–	–	–	109*	–	–	–	–
R.B.Richardson, C.L.Hooper	Georgetown	1992-93	–	–	–	–	–	106	–	–
C.L.Hooper, K.L.T.Arthurton	Gauhati	1994-95	–	–	–	103	–	–	–	–

WEST INDIES – 5th Wicket

			E	A	SA	NZ	I	P	SL	Z
I.V.A.Richards, C.H.Lloyd	Brisbane	1984-85	–	–	–	–	–	–	152	–
I.V.A.Richards, C.L.King	Lord's	1979	139	–	–	–	–	–	–	–
D.L.Haynes, J.C.Adams	Port-of-Spain	1993-94	124	–	–	–	–	–	–	–
K.L.T.Arthurton, J.C.Adams	Sharjah	1993-94	–	–	–	–	–	119	–	–
A.L.Logie, C.L.Hooper	Gwalior	1987-88	–	–	–	–	108	–	–	–

WEST INDIES – 6th Wicket

			E	A	SA	NZ	I	P	SL	Z
R.B.Richardson, P.J.L.Dujon	Sharjah	1991-92	–	–	–	–	–	154	–	–
D.L.Haynes, D.L.Murray	St John's	1977-78	–	126	–	–	–	–	–	–

WEST INDIES – 7th Wicket

			E	A	SA	NZ	I	P	SL	Z
P.J.L.Dujon, M.D.Marshall	Gujranwala	1986-87	–	–	–	–	–	115	–	–

West Indies – 8th Wicket – No instance – highest partnership

			E	A	SA	NZ	I	P	SL	Z
C.L.Hooper, W.K.M.Benjamin	Nagpur	1987-88	–	–	–	–	65	–	–	–

West Indies – 9th Wicket – No instance – highest partnership

			E	A	SA	NZ	I	P	SL	Z
M.D.Marshall, J.Garner	Sydney	1984-85	–	63	–	–	–	–	–	–

WEST INDIES – 10th Wicket

			E	A	SA	NZ	I	P	SL	Z
I.V.A.Richards, M.A.Holding	Manchester	1984	106*	–	–	–	–	–	–	–

NEW ZEALAND – 1st Wicket

			E	A	SA	WI	I	P	SL	Z	B
M.D.Crowe, J.G.Wright	Sharjah	1989-90	–	–	–	–	–	–	–	–	158
G.M.Turner, B.A.Edgar	Wellington	1982-83	152	–	–	–	–	–	–	–	–
J.G.Wright, A.H.Jones	Baroda	1988-89	–	–	–	–	140	–	–	–	–
G.M.Turner, B.A.Edgar	Auckland	1982-83	–	–	–	–	–	–	132	–	–
K.R.Rutherford, B.A.Edgar	Christchurch	1985-86	–	125	–	–	–	–	–	–	–
M.J.Greatbatch, R.T.Latham	Auckland	1991-92	–	–	114	–	–	–	–	–	–
J.G.Wright, B.A.Edgar	Melbourne	1980-81	–	–	–	–	113*	–	–	–	–
M.D.Crowe, J.G.Wright	Brisbane	1990-91	109	–	–	–	–	–	–	–	–

NEW ZEALAND – 1st Wicket – *continued*

			E	A	SA	WI	I	P	SL	Z	
G.M.Turner, B.A.Edgar	Auckland	1982-83	101	–	–	–	–	–	–	–	
J.G.Wright, B.A.Edgar	Leeds	1979	–	–	–	–	100	–	–	–	

NEW ZEALAND – 2nd Wicket

			E	A	SA	WI	I	P	SL	Z	
B.A.Edgar, M.D.Crowe	Brisbane	1985-86	–	–	–	–	130	–	–	–	
N.J.Astle, M.D.Crowe	Nagpur	1995-96	–	–	–	–	128	–	–	–	
G.M.Turner, G.P.Howarth	Nottingham	1979	–	–	–	–	–	–	126*	–	H
C.M.Spearman, S.P.Fleming	Baroda	1995-96	–	–	–	–	–	–	–	–	116
A.H.Jones, K.R.Rutherford	Vishakhapatnam	1988-89	–	–	–	–	114	–	–	–	
A.H.Jones, M.D.Crowe	Perth	1987-88	–	106	–	–	–	–	–	–	
J.G.Wright, M.D.Crowe	Auckland	1986-87	–	–	–	105	–	–	–	–	
J.G.Wright, G.P.Howarth	Sydney	1980-81	–	103	–	–	–	–	–	–	
J.G.Wright, A.H.Jones	Adelaide	1987-88	–	–	–	–	–	–	102	–	
M.D.Crowe, A.C.Parore	Port Elizabeth	1993-94	–	–	–	–	101	–	–	–	

NEW ZEALAND – 3rd Wicket

			E	A	SA	WI	I	P	SL	Z	
A.C.Parore, K.R.Rutherford	Baroda	1994-95	–	–	–	–	180	–	–	–	
M.D.Crowe, S.P.Fleming	Jamshedpur	1995-96	–	–	–	–	171*	–	–	–	
G.P.Howarth, M.D.Crowe	Auckland	1983-84	160	–	–	–	–	–	–	–	EA
G.M.Turner, J.M.Parker	Birmingham	1975	–	–	–	–	–	–	–	–	149
A.C.Parore, K.R.Rutherford	East London	1994-95	–	–	–	–	–	–	136	–	
N.J.Astle, R.G.Twose	Auckland	1995-96	–	–	–	–	–	–	–	135	
A.C.Parore, S.A.Thomson	Sharjah	1993-94	–	–	–	–	–	133	–	–	
A.H.Jones, M.D.Crowe	Napier	1991-92	–	–	–	–	–	–	–	129	
L.K.Germon, S.P.Fleming	St Vincent	1995-96	–	–	–	121	–	–	–	–	UAE
C.M.Spearman, R.G.Twose	Faisalabad	1995-96	–	–	–	–	–	–	–	–	120
B.A.Edgar, J.G.Wright	Adelaide	1985-86	–	120	–	–	–	–	–	–	
M.D.Crowe, M.J.Greatbatch	Leeds	1990	118	–	–	–	–	–	–	–	
J.G.Wright, M.J.Greatbatch	Napier	1987-88	110	–	–	–	–	–	–	–	
A.H.Jones, M.D.Crowe	Wellington	1991-92	109	–	–	–	–	–	–	–	
A.H.Jones, K.R.Rutherford	Sharjah	1987-88	–	–	–	–	–	–	103	–	
A.H.Jones, M.D.Crowe	Christchurch	1988-89	–	–	–	–	103	–	–	–	

NEW ZEALAND – 4th Wicket

			E	A	SA	WI	I	P	SL	Z	
L.K.Germon, C.Z.Harris	Madras	1995-96	–	168	–	–	–	–	–	–	
M.D.Crowe, K.R.Rutherford	Dunedin	1989-90	–	–	–	–	152	–	–	–	
S.P.Fleming, S.A.Thomson	Napier	1993-94	–	–	–	–	144	–	–	–	
M.D.Crowe, K.R.Rutherford	Harare	1992-93	–	–	–	–	–	–	–	130	
M.D.Crowe, K.R.Rutherford	Auckland	1991-92	–	118	–	–	–	–	–	–	
M.D.Crowe, K.R.Rutherford	Auckland	1991-92	–	–	–	–	–	107	–	–	
B.R.Hartland, S.A.Thomson	Christchurch	1993-94	–	–	–	–	101*	–	–	–	

NEW ZEALAND – 5th Wicket

			E	A	SA	WI	I	P	SL	Z	
R.G.Twose, C.L.Cairns	Poona	1995-96	–	–	–	–	147	–	–	–	
M.D.Crowe, J.J.Crowe	Manchester	1986	113	–	–	–	–	–	–	–	
M.D.Crowe, I.D.S.Smith	Wellington	1988-89	–	–	–	–	–	108*	–	–	
A.C.Parore, S.A.Thomson	Pretoria	1994-95	–	–	106	–	–	–	–	–	

NEW ZEALAND – 6th Wicket

			E	A	SA	WI	I	P	SL	Z	
K.J.Wadsworth, B.E.Congdon	Christchurch	1973-74	–	130	–	–	–	–	–	–	
K.R.Rutherford, C.Z.Harris	Christchurch	1990-91	122	–	–	–	–	–	–	–	
J.V.Coney, R.J.Hadlee	Adelaide	1982-83	121	–	–	–	–	–	–	–	
S.A.Thomson, C.L.Cairns	Brisbane	1993-94	–	–	111	–	–	–	–	–	

NEW ZEALAND – 7th Wicket

			E	A	SA	WI	I	P	SL	Z	
A.C.Parore, D.N.Patel	Kingston	1995-96	–	–	–	111	–	–	–	–	

New Zealand – 8th Wicket – No instance – highest partnership

			E	A	SA	WI	I	P	SL	Z	
B.E.Congdon, B.L.Cairns	Scarborough	1978	68	–	–	–	–	–	–	–	

New Zealand – 9th Wicket – No instance – highest partnership

			E	A	SA	WI	I	P	SL	Z	
R.J.Hadlee, G.B.Troup	Brisbane	1982-83	63	–	–	–	–	–	–	–	

New Zealand – 10th Wicket – No instance – highest partnership

			E	A	SA	WI	I	P	SL	Z	
M.C.Snedden, E.J.Chatfield	Derby	1983	–	–	–	–	–	–	65	–	

INDIA – 1st Wicket

			E	A	SA	WI	NZ	P	SL	Z	
K.Srikkanth, R.J.Shastri	Cuttack	1984-85	188	–	–	–	–	–	–	–	
A.Jadeja, S.R.Tendulkar	Cuttack	1994-95	–	–	–	176	–	–	–	–	

INDIA – 1st Wicket – *continued*

			E	A	SA	WI	NZ	P	SL	Z	K
A.Jadeja, S.R.Tendulkar	Cuttack	1995-96	–	–	–	–	–	–	–	–	165
M.Prabhakar, S.R.Tendulkar	Sharjah	1994-95	–	–	–	–	–	–	161	–	
S.M.Gavaskar, M.Prabhakar	Jamshedpur	1986-87	–	–	–	–	–	154	–	–	
M.Prabhakar, S.R.Tendulkar	Baroda	1994-95	–	–	–	–	144	–	–	–	
K.Srikkanth, S.M.Gavaskar	Nagpur	1987-88	–	–	–	–	136	–	–	–	
N.S.Sidhu, R.J.Shastri	Nagpur	1990-91	–	–	–	–	–	–	133	–	
K.Srikkanth, N.S.Sidhu	Gwalior	1991-92	–	–	130	–	–	–	–	–	
R.J.Shastri, K.Srikkanth	Melbourne	1984-85	–	124	–	–	–	–	–	–	
R.J.Shastri, V.G.Kambli	Sharjah	1991-92	–	–	–	–	–	124	–	–	EA
S.M.Gavaskar, F.M.Engineer	Leeds	1975	–	–	–	–	–	–	–	–	123*
M.Prabhakar, N.S.Sidhu	Rajkot	1993-94	–	–	–	–	–	–	122	–	B
W.V.Raman, N.S.Sidhu	Chandigarh	1990-91	–	–	–	–	–	–	–	–	121
K.Srikkanth, R.Lamba	Nagpur	1989-90	–	–	–	–	–	120	–	–	
K.Srikkanth, S.M.Gavaskar	Sharjah	1985-86	–	–	–	–	–	117	–	–	
K.Srikkanth, R.Lamba	Bangalore	1989-90	–	115	–	–	–	–	–	–	
M.Prabhakar, N.S.Sidhu	Faridabad	1992-93	–	–	–	–	–	–	–	114	
N.S.Sidhu, W.V.Raman	Poona	1992-93	–	–	–	–	–	–	–	114	
A.Jadeja, S.R.Tendulkar	Calcutta	1994-95	–	–	–	108	–	–	–	–	
A.Jadeja, S.R.Tendulkar	Wellington	1993-94	–	–	–	–	105	–	–	–	
R.J.Shastri, R.M.H.Binny	Ahmedabad	1984-85	–	104	–	–	–	–	–	–	
R.J.Shastri, K.Srikkanth	Melbourne	1984-85	–	–	–	–	–	–	103	–	
A.Jadeja, S.R.Tendulkar	Delhi	1994-95	–	–	–	–	100	–	–	–	

INDIA – 2nd Wicket

			E	A	SA	WI	NZ	P	SL	Z
S.R.Tendulkar, N.S.Sidhu	Sharjah	1995-96	–	–	–	–	–	231	–	–
R.J.Shastri, S.V.Manjrekar	Delhi	1991-92	–	–	175	–	–	–	–	–
S.M.Gavaskar, M.Azharuddin	Sharjah	1986-87	–	165	–	–	–	–	–	–
S.M.Gavaskar, M.Azharuddin	The Oval	1986	163*	–	–	–	–	–	–	–
N.S.Sidhu, M.Amarnath	Sharjah	1989-90	–	–	–	–	–	161	–	–
M.Azharuddin, S.R.Tendulkar	Dunedin	1991-92	–	–	–	–	145	–	–	–
K.Srikkanth, D.B.Vengsarkar	Delhi	1982-83	–	–	–	–	–	–	134	–
A.Jadeja, N.S.Sidhu	Sharjah	1993-94	–	130	–	–	–	–	–	–
Arun Lal, M.Amarnath	Calcutta	1987-88	–	–	–	128	–	–	–	–
N.S.Sidhu, S.V.Manjrekar	Sharjah	1991-92	–	–	–	128	–	–	–	–
K.Srikkanth, M.Amarnath	Trivandrum	1987-88	–	–	–	127	–	–	–	–
M.Prabhakar, V.G.Kambli	Indore	1993-94	–	–	–	–	–	–	–	122
A.D.Gaekwad, S.Amarnath	Sahiwal	1978-79	–	–	–	–	–	119	–	–
K.Srikkanth, D.B.Vengsarkar	Bangalore	1982-83	–	–	–	–	–	–	119	–
K.Srikkanth, D.B.Vengsarkar	Poona	1984-85	118	–	–	–	–	–	–	–
S.R.Tendulkar, V.G.Kambli	Jaipur	1994-95	–	–	–	117	–	–	–	–
S.M.Gavaskar, S.M.Patil	Lahore	1982-83	–	–	–	–	–	–	115	–
N.S.Sidhu, S.V.Manjrekar	Sharjah	1991-92	–	–	–	108	–	–	–	–
K.Srikkanth, R.Lamba	Jaipur	1986-87	–	102	–	–	–	–	–	–
S.M.Gavaskar, D.B.Vengsarkar	Melbourne	1980-81	–	101	–	–	–	–	–	–

INDIA – 3rd Wicket

			E	A	SA	WI	NZ	P	SL	Z
N.S.Sidhu, M.Azharuddin	Sharjah	1994-95	–	–	–	–	–	–	175*	–
N.S.Sidhu, M.Azharuddin	Gwalior	1992-93	175	–	–	–	–	–	–	–
S.R.Tendulkar, M.Azharuddin	Delhi	1995-96	–	–	–	–	–	–	175	–
R.Dravid, M.Azharuddin	Toronto	1996	–	–	–	–	–	161	–	–
N.S.Sidhu, M.Amarnath	Sharjah	1987-88	–	–	–	–	158	–	–	–
D.B.Vengsarkar, S.M.Patil	Sialkot	1984-85	–	–	–	–	–	143	–	–
M.Prabhakar, M.Azharuddin	Colombo (RPS)	1993-94	–	–	–	–	–	–	136	–
S.R.Tendulkar, M.Azharuddin	Colombo (RPS)	1996-97	–	–	–	–	–	–	129	–
K.Srikkanth, D.B.Vengsarkar	Sharjah	1988-89	–	–	–	120	–	–	–	–
R.J.Shastri, S.M.Gavaskar	Indore	1984-85	–	115	–	–	–	–	–	–
M.Azharuddin, D.B.Vengsarkar	Bombay	1986-87	–	–	–	–	–	–	115	–
N.S.Sidhu, M.Azharuddin	Sharjah	1989-90	–	–	–	–	–	–	114	–
N.S.Sidhu, M.Azharuddin	Vishakhapatnam	1994-95	–	–	–	113	–	–	–	–
K.Srikkanth, M.Azharuddin	Sharjah	1986-87	–	–	–	–	–	–	111	–
S.M.Gavaskar, A.Malhotra	Jamshedpur	1983-84	–	–	–	105	–	–	–	–
N.S.Sidhu, C.Sharma	Kanpur	1989-90	105	–	–	–	–	–	–	–
V.G.Kambli, A.K.Sharma	Poona	1992-93	–	–	–	–	–	–	–	104*
S.M.Gavaskar, D.B.Vengsarkar	Melbourne	1985-86	–	102	–	–	–	–	–	–
R.Lamba, D.B.Vengsarkar	Delhi	1986-87	–	102	–	–	–	–	–	–
S.R.Manjrekar, S.R.Tendulkar	Hobart	1991-92	–	102	–	–	–	–	–	–
V.G.Kambli, M.Azharuddin	Kanpur	1993-94	–	–	–	–	–	–	100	–

INDIA – 4th Wicket

			E	A	SA	WI	NZ	P	SL	Z
V.G.Kambli, S.R.Tendulkar	Jaipur	1992-93	164*	–	–	–	–	–	–	–
K.Srikkanth, M.Azharuddin	Calcutta	1986-87	–	–	–	–	–	145	–	–
N.S.Sidhu, V.G.Kambli	Kanpur	1995-96	–	–	–	–	–	–	–	142
M.Azharuddin, S.M.Gavaskar	Melbourne	1984-85	–	–	–	–	–	132	–	–
A.Malhotra, S.M.Patil	Delhi	1982-83	–	–	–	–	–	–	110	–
D.B.Vengsarkar, S.M.Patil	Multan	1982-83	–	–	–	–	–	109	–	–
D.B.Vengsarkar, R.J.Shastri	St John's	1988-89	–	–	–	107	–	–	–	–
D.B.Vengsarkar, Kapil Dev	Sydney	1984-85	–	–	–	–	105*	–	–	–
S.M.Gavaskar, M.Azharuddin	Sharjah	1985-86	–	–	–	100	–	–	–	–UAE
M.Azharuddin, V.G.Kambli	Sharjah	1993-94	–	–	–	–	–	–	–	100

INDIA – 5th Wicket

			E	A	SA	WI	NZ	P	SL	Z
R.J.Shastri, Kapil Dev	Hyderabad, India	1986-87	–	–	–	–	–	112	–	–

INDIA – 6th Wicket

			E	A	SA	WI	NZ	P	SL	Z
M.Azharuddin, A.Sharma	Baroda	1988-89	–	–	–	–	127	–	–	–
S.V.Manjrekar, N.R.Mongia	Sharjah	1995-96	–	–	–	–	116	–	–	–
Kapil Dev, K.S.More	Nagpur	1987-88	–	–	–	113	–	–	–	–
R.J.Shastri, Kapil Dev	Manchester	1986	104	–	–	–	–	–	–	–

INDIA – 7th Wicket

			E	A	SA	WI	NZ	P	SL	Z
S.C.Ganguly, S.B.Joshi	Colombo (SSC)	1996-97	–	100	–	–	–	–	–	–

India – 8th Wicket – No instance – highest partnership

			E	A	SA	WI	NZ	P	SL	Z
Kapil Dev, K.S.More	Bangalore	1987-88	–	–	–	–	82*	–	–	–

INDIA – 9th Wicket

			E	A	SA	WI	NZ	P	SL	Z
Kapil Dev, S.M.H.Kirmani	Tunbridge Wells	1983	–	–	–	–	–	–	–	126*

India – 10th Wicket – No instance – highest partnership

			E	A	SA	WI	NZ	P	SL	Z
R.J.Shastri, N.Hirwani	Gwalior	1987-88	–	–	53	–	–	–	–	–

PAKISTAN – 1st Wicket

			E	A	SA	WI	NZ	I	SL	Z
Saeed Anwar, Ramiz Raja	Sharjah	1992-93	–	–	–	–	–	–	204	–
Ramiz Raja, Saeed Anwar	Adelaide	1989-90	–	–	–	–	–	–	202	–
Saeed Anwar, Asif Mujtaba	Sharjah	1993-94	–	–	–	–	–	–	171	–
Sadiq Mohammed, Majid Khan	Nottingham	1975	–	–	–	–	–	–	159	–
Aamir Sohail, Salim Elahi	Gujranwala	1995-96	–	–	–	–	–	–	156	–
Ramiz Raja, Inzamam-ul-Haq	Multan	1991-92	–	–	–	–	–	–	149	–
Aamir Sohail, Saeed Anwar	Singapore	1995-96	–	–	–	–	–	144	–	–
Mudassar Nazar, Shoaib Mohammed	Melbourne	1984-85	–	141	–	–	–	–	–	–
Saeed Anwar, Ramiz Raja	Sharjah	1992-93	–	–	–	–	–	–	132	–
Saeed Anwar, Aamir Sohail	Pretoria	1994-95	–	–	–	–	–	–	130	–
Aamir Sohail, Ramiz Raja	Pretoria	1992-93	–	–	121	–	–	–	–	–
Sadiq Mohammed, Majid Khan	Nottingham	1974	113	–	–	–	–	–	–	–
Mudassar Nazar, Shoaib Mohammed	Peshawar	1985-86	–	–	–	–	–	–	113	–
Mudassar Nazar, Ramiz Raja	Sharjah	1988-89	–	–	–	113	–	–	–	–
Ramiz Raja, Moin-ul-Atiq	Sharjah	1987-88	–	–	–	109	–	–	–	–
Aamir Sohail, Salim Raza	Sharjah	1995-96	–	–	–	–	–	–	107	–
Ramiz Raja, Younis Ahmed	Calcutta	1986-87	–	–	–	–	–	106	–	–
Mudassar Nazar, Mohsin Khan	Nottingham	1982	102	–	–	–	–	–	–	–

PAKISTAN – 2nd Wicket

			E	A	SA	WI	NZ	I	SL	Z
Aamir Sohail, Inzamam-ul-Haq	Sharjah	1993-94	–	–	–	–	263	–	–	–
Mohsin Khan, Zaheer Abbas	Multan	1982-83	–	–	–	–	–	205	–	–
Inzamam-ul-Haq, Salim Malik	Rawalpindi	1991-92	–	–	–	–	–	–	204	–
Ramiz Raja, Salim Malik	Karachi	1982-83	–	–	–	–	–	170	–	–
Ramiz Raja, Salim Malik	Karachi	1987-88	167	–	–	–	–	–	–	–
Majid Khan, Zaheer Abbas	The Oval	1979	–	–	–	166	–	–	–	–
Saeed Anwar, Inzamam-ul-Haq	Rawalpindi	1994-95	–	160*	–	–	–	–	–	–
Aamir Sohail, Inzamam-ul-Haq	Wellington	1993-94	–	–	–	–	142	–	–	–
Ramiz Raja, Salim Malik	Sialkot	1990-91	–	–	–	–	139	–	–	–
Shoaib Mohammed, Salim Malik	Sharjah	1988-89	–	–	–	–	–	–	127	–
Aamir Sohail, Inzamam-ul-Haq	Kingston	1992-93	–	–	–	118	–	–	–	–
Mudassar Nazar, Ramiz Raja	Sharjah	1985-86	–	115	–	–	–	–	–	–
Ramiz Raja, Javed Miandad	Sargodha	1991-92	–	–	–	–	–	–	112	–
Inzamam-ul-Haq, Javed Miandad	Hyderabad, Pakistan	1991-92	–	–	–	–	–	–	109	–
Saeed Anwar, Inzamam-ul-Haq	Sharjah	1993-94	–	–	–	–	–	–	109	–

PAKISTAN – 2nd Wicket – *continued*

			E	A	SA	WI	NZ	I	SL	Z	UAE
Saeed Anwar, Ijaz Ahmed	Gujranwala	1995-96	–	–	–	–	–	–	–	–	105*
Mudassar Nazar, Zaheer Abbas	Sydney	1981-82	–	105	–	–	–	–	–	–	
Mohsin Khan, Javed Miandad	Karachi	1981-82	–	–	–	–	–	–	105	–	
Mudassar Nazar, Ramiz Raja	Sharjah	1985-86	–	–	–	–	–	100	–	–	

PAKISTAN – 3rd Wicket

			E	A	SA	WI	NZ	I	SL	Z	B
Moin-ul-Atiq, Ijaz Ahmed	Chittagong	1988-89	–	–	–	–	–	–	–	–	205
Zahid Fazal, Salim Malik	Sharjah	1991-92	–	–	–	–	–	171*	–	–	
Zaheer Abbas, Javed Miandad	Lahore	1982-83	–	–	–	–	–	158	–	–	
Shoaib Mohammed, Ramiz Raja	Wellington	1988-89	–	–	–	–	152	–	–	–	
Aamir Sohail, Javed Miandad	Hobart	1991-92	–	–	–	–	–	–	–	145	
Imran Khan, Javed Miandad	Melbourne	1991-92	139	–	–	–	–	–	–	–	
Ramiz Raja, Imran Khan	Sharjah	1991-92	–	–	–	–	137	–	–	–	
Ijaz Ahmed, Salim Malik	Durban	1994-95	–	–	136*	–	–	–	–	–	
Salim Malik, Javed Miandad	Sharjah	1988-89	–	–	–	–	–	126	–	–	
Ramiz Raja, Javed Miandad	Melbourne	1991-92	–	–	–	123*	–	–	–	–	
Aamer Malik, Javed Miandad	Jullundur	1989-90	–	–	–	–	121	–	–	–	
Zaheer Abbas, Javed Miandad	Lahore	1982-83	–	119	–	–	–	–	–	–	
Mudassar Nazar, Javed Miandad	Sharjah	1986-87	–	116	–	–	–	–	–	–	
Inzamam-ul-Haq, Salim Malik	Karachi	1994-95	–	–	115*	–	–	–	–	–	
Ramiz Raja, Javed Miandad	Christchurch	1991-92	–	–	–	–	115	–	–	–	
Shoaib Mohammed, Javed Miandad	Harare	1992-93	–	–	–	–	–	–	–	115	
Ramiz Raja, Javed Miandad	Hyderabad, Pakistan	1987-88	–	–	–	–	–	113	–	–	
Mudassar Nazar, Javed Miandad	The Oval	1987	110	–	–	–	–	–	–	–	
Aamer Malik, Javed Miandad	Brisbane	1988-89	–	–	–	107	–	–	–	–	
Mudassar Nazar, Javed Miandad	Melbourne	1981-82	–	105	–	–	–	–	–	–	
Ramiz Raja, Javed Miandad	Hobart	1989-90	–	–	–	–	–	105	–	–	
Shoaib Mohammed, Salim Malik	Sharjah	1988-89	–	–	–	–	–	102	–	–	

PAKISTAN – 4th Wicket

			E	A	SA	WI	NZ	I	SL	Z
Salim Malik, Basit Ali	Sharjah	1993-94	–	–	–	172	–	–	–	–
Javed Miandad, Asif Mujtaba	East London	1992-93	–	–	165	–	–	–	–	–
Zaheer Abbas, Imran Khan	Nottingham	1983	–	–	–	–	147*	–	–	–
Ramiz Raja, Basit Ali	Sharjah	1995-96	–	–	–	141	–	–	–	–
Inzamam-ul-Haq, Asif Mujtaba	Port-of-Spain	1992-93	–	–	–	131*	–	–	–	–
Inzamam-ul-Haq, Javed Miandad	Lahore	1993-94	–	–	–	–	–	–	–	127
Salim Malik, Inzamam-ul-Haq	Singapore	1995-96	–	–	–	–	–	–	127	–
Salim Malik, Ijaz Ahmed	Rawalpindi	1994-95	–	–	125	–	–	–	–	–
Zaheer Abbas, Haroon Rashid	Lahore	1981-82	–	–	–	–	–	–	123	–
Ramiz Raja, Salim Malik	Nagpur	1989-90	122	–	–	–	–	–	–	–
Javed Miandad, Salim Malik	Hobart	1988-89	–	–	–	121	–	–	–	–
Inzamam-ul-Haq, Salim Malik	Christchurch	1995-96	–	–	–	–	114	–	–	–
Javed Miandad, Imran Khan	Lahore	1987-88	–	112	–	–	–	–	–	–
Javed Miandad, Imran Khan	Gujranwala	1982-83	–	–	–	–	–	111	–	–
Inzamam-ul-Haq, Basit Ali	Georgetown	1992-93	–	–	–	103	–	–	–	–
Javed Miandad, Salim Malik	Perth	1991-92	–	–	–	–	–	–	101	–
Salim Malik, Imran Khan	Sharjah	1988-89	–	–	–	–	–	–	101*	–

PAKISTAN – 5th Wicket

			E	A	SA	WI	NZ	I	SL	Z
Inzamam-ul-Haq, Ijaz Ahmed	Harare	1994-95	–	–	–	–	–	–	–	152
Ijaz Ahmed, Basit Ali	Faisalabad	1994-95	–	–	147*	–	–	–	–	–
Javed Miandad, Imran Khan	Nagpur	1986-87	–	–	–	–	–	142	–	–
Salim Malik, Imran Khan	Lahore	1989-90	–	–	–	123	–	–	–	–
Zaheer Abbas, Salim Malik	Gujranwala	1985-86	–	–	–	–	–	–	116	–

PAKISTAN – 6th Wicket

			E	A	SA	WI	NZ	I	SL	Z
Imran Khan, Shahid Mahboob	Leeds	1983	–	–	–	–	–	–	144	–

PAKISTAN – 7th Wicket

			E	A	SA	WI	NZ	I	SL	Z
Ramiz Raja, Anil Dalpat	Christchurch	1984-85	–	–	–	–	108	–	–	–

Pakistan – 8th Wicket – No instance – highest partnership

			E	A	SA	WI	NZ	I	SL	Z
Salim Malik, Aqib Javed	Sharjah	1995-96	–	–	81*	–	–	–	–	–

Pakistan – 9th Wicket – No instance – highest partnership

			E	A	SA	WI	NZ	I	SL	Z
Salim Malik, Saqlain Mushtaq	Toronto	1996	–	–	–	–	–	45*	–	–

Pakistan – 10th Wicket – No instance – highest partnerships

			E	A	SA	WI	NZ	I	SL	Z
Javed Miandad, Salim Jaffer	Perth	1986-87	35*	–	–	–	–	–	–	–
Imran Khan, Mohsin Khan	Birmingham	1987	35*	–	–	–	–	–	–	–

SRI LANKA – 1st Wicket			E	A	SA	WI	NZ	I	P	Z	
S.T.Jayasuriya, R.S.Kaluwitharana	Colombo (RPS)	1996-97	–	–	–	–	–	129	–	–	
R.S.Mahanama, M.A.R.Samarasekera	New Plymouth	1991-92	–	–	–	–	–	–	–	128	
R.S.Mahanama, U.C.Hathurusinghe	Sharjah	1992-93	–	–	–	–	–	–	–	112	
R.S.Mahanama, S.T.Jayasuriya	Sharjah	1995-96	–	–	–	111	–	–	–	–	
R.S.Mahanama, U.C.Hathurusinghe	Kandy	1993-94	–	–	110	–	–	–	–	–	
S.T.Jayasuriya, S.Ranatunga	Colombo (RPS)	1994-95	–	–	–	–	–	–	104	–	
S.Wettimuny, E.R.N.S.Fernando	Colombo (RPS)	1982-83	–	101	–	–	–	–	–	–	

SRI LANKA – 2nd Wicket			E	A	SA	WI	NZ	I	P	Z	
S.Wettimuny, R.L.Dias	Delhi	1982-83	–	–	–	–	–	170	–	–	
R.S.Mahanama, A.P.Gurusinha	Colombo (RPS)	1992-93	–	–	–	–	166	–	–	–	
M.A.R.Samarasekera, A.P.Gurusinha	Multan	1991-92	–	–	–	–	–	–	157	–	
S.T.Jayasuriya, R.S.Kaluwitharana	Singapore	1995-96	–	–	–	–	–	–	156	–	
B.Warnapura, A.P.Gurusinha	Karachi	1981-82	–	–	–	–	–	–	139	–	
H.P.Tillekeratne, A.P.Gurusinha	Brisbane	1989-90	–	–	–	–	–	–	138	–	
S.T.Jayasuriya, A.P.Gurusinha	Bloemfontein	1994-95	–	–	–	–	132	–	–	–	
R.S.Mahanama, S.Ranatunga	Harare	1994-95	–	–	–	–	–	–	–	119	
R.S.Mahanama, S.T.Jayasuriya	Sharjah	1993-94	–	–	–	–	–	–	105	–	
S.T.Jayasuriya, P.A.de Silva	Colombo (RPS)	1996-97	–	–	–	–	–	101*	–	–	
U.C.Hathurusinghe, A.P.Gurusinha	Colombo (RPS)	1992-93	–	101	–	–	–	–	–	–	
S.T.Jayasuriya, A.P.Gurusinha	Faisalabad	1995-96	101	–	–	–	–	–	–	–	
R.S.Mahanama, J.R.Ratnayeke	Perth	1984-85	–	–	–	100	–	–	–	–	

SRI LANKA – 3rd Wicket			E	A	SA	WI	NZ	I	P	Z	K
A.P.Gurusinha, P.A.de Silva	Kandy	1995-96	–	–	–	–	–	–	–	–	184
A.P.Gurusinha, P.A.de Silva	Colombo (SSC)	1995-96	–	–	–	–	–	–	–	172	
H.P.Tillekeratne, P.A.de Silva	Lucknow	1989-90	–	–	–	–	–	150	–	–	
A.P.Gurusinha, P.A.de Silva	Colombo (PSS)	1992-93	–	147	–	–	–	–	–	–	
R.S.Mahanama, P.A.de Silva	Sharjah	1987-88	–	–	–	–	–	137	–	–	
M.A.R.Samaresekera, P.A.de Silva	Dacca	1988-89	–	–	–	–	–	126	–	–	
A.P.Gurusinha, P.A.de Silva	Lahore	1995-96	–	125	–	–	–	–	–	–	
R.S.Mahanama, P.A.de Silva	Harare	1994-95	–	–	–	–	–	–	–	122	
A.P.Gurusinha, P.A.de Silva	Moratuwa	1992-93	115*	–	–	–	–	–	–	–	
U.C.Hathurusinghe, P.A.de Silva	Colombo (RPS)	1993-94	–	–	–	–	–	115	–	–	
A.P.Gurusinha, A.Ranatunga	Auckland	1994-95	–	–	–	–	112	–	–	–	
A.P.Gurusinha, P.A.de Silva	Faisalabad	1994-95	–	–	–	–	–	–	109	–	
R.S.Mahanama, P.A.de Silva	Hobart	1987-88	–	–	–	–	103	–	–	–	
S.T.Jayasuriya, P.A.de Silva	Bloemfontein	1994-95	–	–	–	–	102	–	–	–	

SRI LANKA – 4th Wicket			E	A	SA	WI	NZ	I	P	Z	
P.A.de Silva, A.Ranatunga	Harare	1994-95	–	–	–	–	–	–	143	B	
P.A.de Silva, A.Ranatunga	Calcutta	1990-91	–	–	–	–	–	–	–	139	
A.P.Gurusinha, A.Ranatunga	Gujranwala	1995-96	–	–	–	–	–	137	–	–	
R.S.Mahanama, A.Ranatunga	Sharjah	1995-96	–	–	126	–	–	–	–	–	
A.Ranatunga, H.P.Tillekeratne	Colombo (SSC)	1994-95	–	–	–	–	–	116*	–	–	
R.L.Dias, A.Ranatunga	Colombo (SSC)	1985-86	–	–	–	–	–	110	–	–	K
P.A.de Silva, A.Ranatunga	Kandy	1995-96	–	–	–	–	–	–	–	106	
P.A.de Silva, A.Ranatunga	Colombo (RPS)	1996-97	–	103*	–	–	–	–	–	–	

SRI LANKA – 5th Wicket			E	A	SA	WI	NZ	I	P	Z	
L.R.D.Mendis, P.A.de Silva	Sydney	1984-85	–	139	–	–	–	–	–	–	
A.Ranatunga, H.P.Tillekeratne	Delhi	1995-96	–	–	–	–	–	131*	–	–	
A.Ranatunga, R.S.Mahanama	Adelaide	1989-90	–	–	–	–	–	128	–	–	

SRI LANKA – 6th Wicket			E	A	SA	WI	NZ	I	P	Z	
A.Ranatunga, R.S.Kalpage	Hyderabad, India	1993-94	–	–	–	–	–	132	–	–	
P.A.de Silva, R.S.Mahanama	Colombo (RPS)	1996-97	–	115	–	–	–	–	–	–	
P.A.de Silva, R.S.Kalpage	Calcutta	1993-94	–	–	–	109	–	–	–	–	

Sri Lanka – 7th Wicket – No instance – highest partnership			E	A	SA	WI	NZ	I	P	Z	
A.Ranatunga, S.H.U.Karnain	Perth	1984-85	–	–	–	90*	–	–	–	–	

Sri Lanka – 8th Wicket – No instance – highest partnership			E	A	SA	WI	NZ	I	P	Z	
R.S.Kalpage, H.D.P.K.Dharmasena	Sharjah	1995-96	–	–	–	–	–	–	60	–	

Sri Lanka – 9th Wicket – No instance – highest partnership			E	A	SA	WI	NZ	I	P	Z	
R.S.Kalpage, W.P.U.C.J.Vaas	Colombo (SSC)	1994-95	–	–	–	–	–	–	76	–	

Sri Lanka – 10th Wicket – No instance – highest partnership			E	A	SA	WI	NZ	I	P	Z	
R.J.Ratnayake, V.B.John	Leeds	1983	33	–	–	–	–	–	–	–	

ZIMBABWE – 1st Wicket

			E	A	SA	WI	NZ	I	P	SL
A.Flower, G.W.Flower	Harare	1992-93	–	–	–	–	124	–	–	–
A.Flower, G.W.Flower	Sharjah	1992-93	–	–	–	–	–	–	121	–

ZIMBABWE – 2nd Wicket

			E	A	SA	WI	NZ	I	P	SL
A.Flower, M.G.Burmester	Harare	1994-95	–	–	–	–	–	–	104	–

ZIMBABWE – 3rd Wicket

			E	A	SA	WI	NZ	I	P	SL
A.D.R.Campbell, D.L.Houghton	Rawalpindi	1993-94	–	–	–	–	–	–	102	–

ZIMBABWE – 4th Wicket

			E	A	SA	WI	NZ	I	P	SL
G.W.Flower, D.L.Houghton	Sydney	1994-95	110	–	–	–	–	–	–	–

ZIMBABWE – 5th Wicket

			E	A	SA	WI	NZ	I	P	SL
A.Flower, A.C.Waller	New Plymouth	1991-92	–	–	–	–	–	–	–	145*
A.D.R.Campbell, C.N.Evans	Colombo (SSC)	1996-97	–	–	–	–	–	–	–	114

ZIMBABWE – 6th Wicket

			E	A	SA	WI	NZ	I	P	SL
D.L.Houghton, K.M.Curran	Southampton	1983	–	103	–	–	–	–	–	–

Zimbabwe – 7th Wicket – No instance – highest partnership

			E	A	SA	WI	NZ	I	P	SL
D.A.G.Fletcher, I.P.Butchart	Nottingham	1983	–	75*	–	–	–	–	–	–

ZIMBABWE – 8th Wicket

			E	A	SA	WI	NZ	I	P	SL
D.L.Houghton, I.P.Butchart	Hyderabad, India	1987-88	–	–	–	–	117	–	–	–

Zimbabwe – 9th Wicket – No instance – highest partnership

			E	A	SA	WI	NZ	I	P	SL
K.M.Curran, P.W.E.Rawson	Birmingham	1983	–	–	–	55	–	–	–	–

Zimbabwe – 10th Wicket – No instance – highest partnership

			E	A	SA	WI	NZ	I	P	SL
A.J.Pycroft, M.P.Jarvis	Bombay	1987-88	–	–	–	–	–	36	–	–

Bangladesh – 1st Wicket – No instance – highest partnerships

			A	NZ	I	P	SL
Gazi Ashraf, Farooq Ahmed	Chittagong	1988-89	–	–	–	30	–
Athar Ali Khan, Javed Omar	Sharjah	1994-95	–	–	30	–	–

Bangladesh – 2nd Wicket – No instance – highest partnership

			A	NZ	I	P	SL
Sajjad Ahmed, Habib-ul-Bashar	Sharjah	1994-95	–	–	–	–	28

BANGLADESH – 3rd Wicket

			A	NZ	I	P	SL
Farooq Ahmed, Athar Ali Khan	Chandigarh	1990-91	–	–	108	–	–

Bangladesh – 4th Wicket – No instance – highest partnership

			A	NZ	I	P	SL
Azhar Hussain, Minhaz-ul-Abedin	Sharjah	1989-90	–	76	–	–	–

Bangladesh – 5th Wicket – No instance – highest partnership

			A	NZ	I	P	SL
Amin-ul-Islam, Akram Khan	Sharjah	1994-95	–	–	–	72	–

Bangladesh – 6th Wicket – No instance – highest partnership

			A	NZ	I	P	SL
Amin-ul-Islam, Inam-ul-Haq	Sharjah	1989-90	–	40*	–	–	–

Bangladesh – 7th Wicket – No instance – highest partnership

			A	NZ	I	P	SL
Amin-ul-Islam, Inam-ul-Haq	Sharjah	1989-90	48	–	–	–	–

Bangladesh – 8th Wicket – No instance – highest partnership

			A	NZ	I	P	SL
Amin-ul-Islam, Ghulam Farooq	Dacca	1988-89	–	–	–	–	46

Bangladesh – 9th Wicket – No instance – highest partnership

			A	NZ	I	P	SL
Jahangir Shah, Nasir Ahmed	Chittagong	1988-89	–	–	20*	–	–

Bangladesh – 10th Wicket – No instance – highest partnership

			A	NZ	I	P	SL
Saif-ul-Islam, Anis-ur-Rehman	Sharjah	1994-95	–	–	25	–	–

Canada – 1st Wicket – No instance – highest partnership

			E	A	P
C.J.D.Chappell, G.R.Sealy	Leeds	1979	–	–	54

Canada – 2nd Wicket – No instance – highest partnership

			E	A	P
G.R.Sealy, F.A.Dennis	Leeds	1979	–	–	31

Canada – 3rd Wicket – No instance – **highest partnership**			E	A	P	
G.R.Sealy, M.P.Stead	Leeds	1979	–	–	18	

Canada – 4th Wicket – No instance – **highest partnership**			E	A	P	
M.P.Stead, C.A.Marshall	Leeds	1979	–	–	7	

Canada – 5th Wicket – No instance – **highest partnership**			E	A	P	
C.J.D.Chappell, J.C.B.Vaughan	Birmingham	1979	–	27	–	

Canada – 6th Wicket – No instance – **highest partnerships**			E	A	P	
C.A.Marshall, B.M.Mauricette	Leeds	1979	–	–	19	
J.C.B.Vaughan, B.M.Mauricette	Birmingham	1979	–	19	–	

Canada – 7th Wicket – No instance – **highest partnership**			E	A	P	
B.M.Mauricette, J.C.B.Vaughan	Leeds	1979	–	–	5	

Canada – 8th Wicket – No instance – **highest partnership**			E	A	P	
B.M.Mauricette, Tariq Javed	Leeds	1979	–	–	4	

Canada – 9th Wicket – No instance – **highest partnership**			E	A	P	
R.G.Callender, C.C.Henry	Birmingham	1979	–	6	–	

Canada – 10th Wicket – No instance – **highest partnership**			E	A	P	
R.G.Callender, J.N.Valentine	Manchester	1979	3	–	–	

East Africa – 1st Wicket – No instance – **highest partnership**			E	NZ	I	
Frasat Ali, S.Walusimba	Birmingham	1975	–	30	–	

East Africa – 2nd Wicket – No instance – **highest partnership**			E	NZ	I	
S.Walusimba, P.S.Mehta	Leeds	1975	–	–	10	

East Africa – 3rd Wicket – No instance – **highest partnership**			E	NZ	I	
S.Walusimba, Jawahir Shah	Birmingham	1975	8	–	–	

East Africa – 4th Wicket – No instance – **highest partnership**			E	NZ	I	
Frasat Ali, S.Sumar	Birmingham	1975	–	–	23	

East Africa – 5th Wicket – No instance – **highest partnership**			E	NZ	I	
R.K. Sethi, Mehmood Quaraishy	Birmingham	1975	21	–	–	

East Africa – 6th Wicket – No instance – **highest partnership**			E	NZ	I	
Jawahir Shah, R.K.Sethi	Leeds	1975	–	–	42	

East Africa – 7th Wicket – No instance – **highest partnership**			E	NZ	I	
Mehmood Quaraishy, Zulfiqar Ali	Birmingham	1975	–	37	–	

East Africa – 8th Wicket – No instance – **highest partnership**			E	NZ	I	
Zulfiqar Ali, H.McLeod	Birmingham	1975	–	5	–	

East Africa – 9th Wicket – No instance – **highest partnership**			E	NZ	I	
Mehmood Quaraishy, P.G.Nana	Birmingham	1975	9	–	–	

East Africa – 10th Wicket – No instance – **highest partnership**			E	NZ	I	
P.G.Nana, D.J.Pringle	Birmingham	1975	6	–	–	

Holland – 1st Wicket – No instance – **highest partnership**			E	SA	NZ	P UAE
N.E.Clarke, P.E.Cantrell	Rawalpindi	1995-96	–	56	–	– –

Holland – 2nd Wicket – No instance – **highest partnership**			E	SA	NZ	P UAE
P.E.Cantrell, G.J.A.F.Aponso	Lahore	1995-96	–	–	–	– 74

Holland – 3rd Wicket – No instance – **highest partnership**			E	SA	NZ	P UAE
G.J.A.F.Aponso, T.B.M.de Leede	Lahore	1995-96	–	–	–	– 71

Holland – 4th Wicket – No instance – **highest partnership**			E	SA	NZ	P UAE
K-J.J.van Noortwijk, G.J.A.F.Aponso	Lahore	1995-96	–	–	73	– –

HOLLAND – 5th Wicket			E	SA	NZ	P UAE
K-J.J.van Noortwijk, B.Zuiderent	Peshawar	1995-96	111	–	–	– –

590

Holland – 6th Wicket – No instance – highest partnership
R.P.Lefebvre, K-J.J.van Noortwijk — Baroda — 1995-96

E	SA	NZ	P	UAE
–	–	45	–	–

Holland – 7th Wicket – No instance – highest partnership
K-J.J.van Noortwijk, M.M.C.Schewe — Baroda — 1995-96

E	SA	NZ	P	UAE
–	–	35	–	–

Holland – 8th Wicket – No instance – highest partnership
R.P.Lefebvre, M.M.C.Schewe — Lahore — 1995-96

E	SA	NZ	P	UAE
–	–	–	–	9

Holland – 9th Wicket – No instance – highest partnership
R.F.van Oosterom, S.W.Lubbers — Rawalpindi — 1995-96

E	SA	NZ	P	UAE
–	5*	–	–	–

Holland – 10th Wicket – No instance – highest partnership
R.F.van Oosterom, P-J.Bakker — Lahore — 1995-96

E	SA	NZ	P	UAE
–	–	–	–	6*

Kenya – 1st Wicket – No instance – highest partnership
D.Chudasama, K.Otieno — Kandy — 1995-96

A	WI	I	SL	Z
–	–	–	47	–

Kenya – 2nd Wicket – No instance – highest partnership
D.Chudasama, K.Otieno — Patna — 1995-96

A	WI	I	SL	Z
–	–	–	–	53

KENYA – 3rd Wicket
K.Otieno, M.Odumbe — Vishakhapatnam — 1995-96

A	WI	I	SL	Z
102	–	–	–	–

KENYA – 4th Wicket
S.O.Tikolo, H.Modi — Kandy — 1995-96

A	WI	I	SL	Z
–	–	–	137	–

Kenya – 5th Wicket – No instance – highest partnership
M.Odumbe, E.T.Odumbe — Vishakhapatnam — 1995-96

A	WI	I	SL	Z
21	–	–	–	–

Kenya – 6th Wicket – No instance – highest partnership
M.Odumbe, E.T.Odumbe — Patna — 1995-96

A	WI	I	SL	Z
–	–	–	–	42

Kenya – 7th Wicket – No instance – highest partnership
H.Modi, T.Odoyo — Poona — 1995-96

A	WI	I	SL	Z
–	44	–	–	–

Kenya – 8th Wicket – No instance – highest partnership
D.L.Tikolo, M.Suji — Kandy — 1995-96

A	WI	I	SL	Z
–	–	–	8*	–

Kenya – 9th Wicket – No instance – highest partnership
T.Odoyo, Asif Karim — Poona — 1995-96

A	WI	I	SL	Z
–	29	–	–	–

Kenya – 10th Wicket – No instance – highest partnership
Asif Karim, R.Ali — Poona — 1995-96

A	WI	I	SL	Z
–	11	–	–	–

UNITED ARAB EMIRATES – 1st Wicket
Azhar Saeed, Salim Raza — Lahore — 1995-96

E	SA	NZ	I	P	H
–	–	–	–	–	117

United Arab Emirates – 2nd Wicket – No instance – highest partnership
R.H.Poonawalla, Mazhar Hussain — Sharjah — 1993-94

E	SA	NZ	I	P	H
–	–	–	–	33	–

United Arab Emirates – 3rd Wicket – No instance – highest partnership
Mazhar Hussain, V.Mehra — Sharjah — 1993-94

E	SA	NZ	I	P	H
–	–	–	94	–	–

United Arab Emirates – 4th Wicket – No instance – highest partnership
V.Mehra, Mohammad Ishaq — Lahore — 1995-96

E	SA	NZ	I	P	H
–	–	–	–	–	82*

United Arab Emirates – 5th Wicket – No instance – highest partnership
Mazhar Hussain, Salim Raza — Sharjah — 1993-94

E	SA	NZ	I	P	H
–	–	–	–	20	–

United Arab Emirates – 6th Wicket – No instance – highest partnership
Mohammad Aslam, J.A.Samarasekera — Peshawar — 1995-96

E	SA	NZ	I	P	H
31	–	–	–	–	–

United Arab Emirates – 7th Wicket – No instance – highest partnership

			E	SA	NZ	I	P	H
J.A.Samarasekera, Arshad Laiq	Sharjah	1993-94	–	–	–	–	57	–

United Arab Emirates – 8th Wicket – No instance – highest partnership

			E	SA	NZ	I	P	H
Arshad Laiq, J.A.Samarasekera	Faisalabad	1995-96	–	–	32	–	–	–

United Arab Emirates – 9th Wicket – No instance – highest partnership

			E	SA	NZ	I	P	H
Arshad Laiq, S.F.Dukanwala	Rawalpindi	1995-96	–	80*	–	–	–	–

United Arab Emirates – 10th Wicket – No instance – highest partnership

			E	SA	NZ	I	P	H
Imtiaz Abbasi, Sohail Butt	Sharjah	1993-94	–	–	–	10*	–	–

CAREER RECORDS – 3000 RUNS

	LOI	I	Runs	E	A	SA	WI	NZ	I	P	SL	Z	Ass
D.L.Haynes (WI)	238	237	**8648**	1185	2262	226	–	580	1357	2390	483	165	–
Javed Miandad (P)	233	218	**7381**	991	1019	145	1930	702	1175	–	1141	263	15
I.V.A.Richards (WI)	187	167	**6721**	1619	2187	–	–	379	997	1079	444	16	–
A.R.Border (A)	273	252	**6524**	1302	–	343	1546	867	1104	647	537	153	25
R.B.Richardson (WI)	224	217	**6249**	957	1499	84	–	128	971	1988	524	93	5
M.Azharuddin (I)	224	208	**6091**	808	683	558	926	827	–	845	1203	160	81
D.M.Jones (A)	164	161	**6068**	955	–	879	855	1301	723	832	879	114	19
Salim Malik (P)	234	211	**6006**	653	615	359	1033	837	1191	–	1264	39	15
D.C.Boon (A)	181	177	**5964**	602	–	551	832	1305	1212	698	515	249	–
P.A.de Silva (SL)	188	184	**5661**	272	1278	153	416	485	992	1210	–	585	270
Ramiz Raja (P)	177	176	**5386**	687	278	130	1624	900	565	–	1178	14	10
A.Ranatunga (SL)	191	182	**5250**	257	747	224	616	555	963	1318	–	319	251
C.G.Greenidge (WI)	128	127	**5134**	958	1091	–	–	478	1181	974	347	105	–
M.D.Crowe (NZ)	143	141	**4704**	788	1096	18	279	–	596	992	528	338	69
S.R.Waugh (A)	200	180	**4420**	516	–	557	848	676	661	531	352	197	82
S.R.Tendulkar (I)	126	123	**4378**	271	489	356	675	652	–	663	836	198	238
G.R.Marsh (A)	117	115	**4357**	716	–	25	902	819	943	501	352	99	–
B.C.Lara (WI)	104	103	**4332**	255	796	436	–	604	468	999	647	119	8
G.A.Gooch (E)	125	122	**4290**	–	1395	2	881	713	420	517	303	38	23
K.Srikkanth (I)	146	145	**4092**	511	789	121	808	314	–	688	748	89	24
A.J.Lamb (E)	122	118	**4010**	–	710	19	710	921	556	830	247	17	–
N.S.Sidhu (I)	106	103	**3936**	455	283	100	535	554	–	616	921	261	211
J.G.Wright (NZ)	149	148	**3891**	930	1109	–	169	–	560	412	588	30	93
M.E.Waugh (A)	117	113	**3828**	331	–	546	780	747	277	274	546	178	130
A.P.Gurusinha (SL)	141	138	**3820**	146	543	60	296	747	680	1006	–	176	166
R.S.Mahanama (SL)	148	140	**3816**	93	409	192	495	495	759	942	–	404	27
Kapil Dev (I)	224	198	**3783**	449	655	182	842	684	–	382	356	233	–
Inzamam-ul-Haq (P)	115	110	**3725**	256	366	318	523	574	213	–	977	401	97
Imran Khan (P)	175	151	**3709**	377	748	34	1202	279	433	–	636	–	–
D.B.Vengsarkar (I)	129	120	**3508**	526	746	–	493	401	–	643	620	79	–
Aamir Sohail (P)	106	105	**3491**	324	171	439	418	618	677	–	606	143	95
Saeed Anwar (P)	103	102	**3435**	222	350	189	253	475	601	–	898	267	180
K.C.Wessels (A/SA)	109	105	**3367**	328	359	–	675	217	805	479	348	156	–
C.L.Hooper (WI)	141	126	**3270**	348	810	87	–	193	868	699	202	63	–
P.V.Simmons (WI)	117	115	**3242**	300	452	281	–	234	604	807	543	21	–
D.I.Gower (E)	114	111	**3170**	–	794	178	404	874	469	451	178	–	–
K.R.Rutherford (NZ)	121	115	**3143**	381	820	150	106	–	634	365	563	94	30
Ijaz Ahmed (P)	141	126	**3108**	418	275	411	402	209	536	–	553	91	213
R.J.Shastri (I)	150	128	**3108**	485	616	179	589	291	–	510	419	19	–
S.M.Gavaskar (I)	108	102	**3092**	436	840	–	395	258	–	600	401	97	65
M.A.Taylor (A)	96	93	**3027**	225	–	300	395	567	153	569	733	79	6

The highest aggregate for South Africa is 2681 (88 matches) by W.J.Cronje and for Zimbabwe 1279 (47 matches) by D.L.Houghton.

INDIVIDUAL RECORDS – BOWLING

BEST ANALYSES

7-37	Aqib Javed	Pakistan v India	Sharjah	1991-92
7-51	W.W.Davis	West Indies v Australia	Leeds	1983
6-12	A.Kumble	India v West Indies	Calcutta	1993-94
6-14	G.J.Gilmour	Australia v England	Leeds	1975
6-14	Imran Khan	Pakistan v India	Sharjah	1984-85
6-15	C.E.H.Croft	West Indies v England	Kingstown	1980-81
6-26	Waqar Younis	Pakistan v Sri Lanka	Sharjah	1989-90
6-29	B.P.Patterson	West Indies v India	Nagpur	1987-88
6-29	S.T.Jayasuriya	Sri Lanka v England	Moratuwa	1992-93
6-30	Waqar Younis	Pakistan v New Zealand	Auckland	1993-94
6-39	K.H.MacLeay	Australia v India	Nottingham	1983
6-41	I.V.A.Richards	West Indies v India	Delhi	1989-90
6-50	A.H.Gray	West Indies v Australia	Port-of-Spain	1990-91

Best analyses for other countries:

5-20	V.J.Marks	England v New Zealand	Wellington	1983-84
5-21	P.A.Strang	Zimbabwe v Kenya	Patna	1995-96
5-22	M.N.Hart	New Zealand v West Indies	Margao	1994-95
5-29	A.A.Donald	South Africa v India	Calcutta	1991-92
5-29	S.F.Dukanwala	UAE v Holland	Lahore	1995-96
4-36	Saif-ul-Islam	Bangladesh v Sri Lanka	Sharjah	1994-95
3-15	M.Odumbe	Kenya v West Indies	Poona	1995-96
3-48	S.W.Lubbers	Holland v New Zealand	Baroda	1995-96
3-63	Zulfiqar Ali	East Africa v England	Birmingham	1975
2-27	C.C.Henry	Canada v Australia	Birmingham	1979

FIVE WICKETS IN AN INNINGS

ENGLAND (5)

Gough, D.		5-44	Zimbabwe	Sydney	1994-95
Hendrick, M.		5-31	Australia	The Oval	1980
Jarvis, P.W.		5-35	India	Bangalore	1992-93
Marks, V.J.	(2)	5-39	Sri Lanka	Taunton	1983
		5-20	New Zealand	Wellington	1983-84

AUSTRALIA (20)

Alderman, T.M.	(2)	5-17	New Zealand	Wellington	1981-82
		5-32	India	Christchurch	1989-90
Chappell, G.S.	(2)	5-20	England	Birmingham	1977
		5-15	India	Sydney	1980-81
Cosier, G.J.		5-18	England	Birmingham	1977
Dodemaide, A.I.C.		5-21	Sri Lanka	Perth	1987-88
Fleming, D.W.		5-36	India	Bombay	1995-96
Gilbert, D.R.		5-46	New Zealand	Sydney	1985-86
Gilmour, G.J.	(2)	6-14	England	Leeds	1975
		5-48	West Indies	Lord's	1975
Hurst, A.G.		5-21	Canada	Birmingham	1979
Lillee, D.K.		5-34	Pakistan	Leeds	1975
MacLeay, K.H.		6-39	India	Nottingham	1983
McDermott, C.J.		5-44	Pakistan	Lahore	1987-88
McGrath, G.D.		5-52	Pakistan	Lahore	1994-95
O'Donnell, S.P.		5-13	New Zealand	Christchurch	1989-90
Pascoe, L.S.		5-30	New Zealand	Sydney	1980-81
Rackemann, C.G.		5-16	Pakistan	Adelaide	1983-84
Reid, B.A.		5-53	India	Adelaide	1985-86
Waugh, M.E.		5-24	West Indies	Melbourne	1992-93

SOUTH AFRICA (3)

Cronje, W.J.		5-32	India	Cape Town	1992-93
Donald, A.A.		5-29	India	Calcutta	1991-92
Snell, R.P.		5-40	Australia	Melbourne	1993-94

WEST INDIES (23)

Ambrose, C.E.L.	(4)	5-17	Australia	Melbourne	1988-89
		5-26	Australia	Melbourne	1988-89
		5-53	Pakistan	Sharjah	1991-92
		5-32	Australia	Sydney	1992-93
Benjamin, W.K.M.		5-22	Sri Lanka	Bombay	1993-94
Bishop, I.R.	(2)	5-27	Pakistan	Perth	1988-89
		5-25	Pakistan	Brisbane	1992-93
Croft, C.E.H.		6-15	England	Kingstown	1980-81
Cummins, A.C.		5-31	India	Brisbane	1991-92
Davis, W.W.		7-51	Australia	Leeds	1983
Garner, J.	(3)	5-38	England	Lord's	1979
		5-31	Australia	Melbourne	1983-84
		5-47	England	Perth	1986-87
Gibson, O.D.	(2)	5-42	Sri Lanka	Hobart	1995-96
		5-40	Sri Lanka	Perth	1995-96
Gray, A.H.		6-50	Australia	Port-of-Spain	1990-91
Holder, V.A.		5-50	England	Birmingham	1976
Holding, M.A.		5-26	Australia	Sydney	1984-85
Patterson, B.P.		6-29	India	Nagpur	1987-88
Richards, I.V.A.	(2)	5-41	New Zealand	Dunedin	1986-87
		6-41	India	Delhi	1989-90
Roberts, A.M.E.		5-22	England	Adelaide	1979-80
Walsh, C.A.		5- 1	Sri Lanka	Sharjah	1986-87

NEW ZEALAND (12)

Cairns, B.L.		5-28	England	Scarborough	1978
Chatfield, E.J.		5-34	Australia	Adelaide	1980-81
Collinge, R.O.		5-23	India	Christchurch	1975-76
Hadlee, R.J.	(5)	5-32	India	Perth	1980-81
		5-26	Australia	Sydney	1980-81
		5-25	Sri Lanka	Bristol	1983
		5-32	England	Christchurch	1983-84
		5-38	Pakistan	Dunedin	1988-89
Hart, M.N.		5-22	West Indies	Margao	1994-95
Latham, R.T.		5-32	Australia	Auckland	1992-93
Morrison, D.K.		5-46	Pakistan	Christchurch	1995-96
Pringle, C.		5-45	England	Birmingham	1994

INDIA (12)

Arshad Ayub		5-21	Pakistan	Dacca	1988-89
Kapil Dev		5-43	Australia	Nottingham	1983
Kumble, A.	(2)	6-12	West Indies	Calcutta	1993-94
		5-33	New Zealand	Wellington	1993-94
Prabhakar, M.	(2)	5-35	Sri Lanka	Hyderabad, India	1993-94
		5-33	New Zealand	Amritsar	1995-96
Sharma, S.K.		5-26	West Indies	Sharjah	1988-89
Shastri, R.J.		5-15	Australia	Perth	1991-92
Srikkanth, K.	(2)	5-27	New Zealand	Vishakhapatnam	1988-89
		5-32	New Zealand	Indore	1988-89
Srinath, J.	(2)	5-41	England	Bangalore	1992-93
		5-24	Sri Lanka	Kanpur	1993-94

PAKISTAN (20)

Abdul Qadir	(2)	5-44	Sri Lanka	Leeds	1983
		5-53	Australia	Melbourne	1983-84
Aqib Javed	(2)	7-37	India	Sharjah	1991-92
		5-19	India	Sharjah	1994-95
Imran Khan		6-14	India	Sharjah	1984-85
Mudassar Nazar		5-28	West Indies	Melbourne	1984-85
Mushtaq Ahmed		5-36	India	Toronto	1996
Salim Malik		5-35	New Zealand	Lahore	1990-91
Waqar Younis	(7)	6-26	Sri Lanka	Sharjah	1989-90
		5-20	New Zealand	Sharjah	1989-90
		5-11	New Zealand	Peshawar	1990-91
		5-16	New Zealand	Sialkot	1990-91
		5-52	West Indies	Karachi	1990-91
		5-25	South Africa	Durban	1992-93
		6-30	New Zealand	Auckland	1993-94

Wasim Akram	(5)	5-21	Australia	Melbourne	1984-85
		5-38	West Indies	Sharjah	1989-90
		5-19	New Zealand	Wellington	1992-93
		5-16	South Africa	East London	1992-93
		5-15	Zimbabwe	Karachi	1993-94

SRI LANKA (6)

De Mel, A.L.F.	(2)	5-39	Pakistan	Leeds	1983
		5-32	New Zealand	Derby	1983
Jayasuriya, S.T.		6-29	England	Moratuwa	1992-93
Karnain, S.H.U.		5-26	New Zealand	Moratuwa	1983-84
Labrooy, G.F.		5-57	India	Baroda	1986-87
Ratnayake, R.J.		5-32	Pakistan	Sharjah	1990-91

ZIMBABWE (2)

Lock, A.C.I.	5-44	New Zealand	Napier	1995-96
Strang, P.A.	5-21	Kenya	Patna	1995-96

UNITED ARAB EMIRATES (1)

Dukanwala, S.F.	5-29	Holland	Lahore	1995-96

FIVE WICKETS ON DEBUT

S.H.U.Karnain	5-26	New Zealand	Moratuwa	1983-84
A.I.C.Dodemaide	5-21	Sri Lanka	Perth	1987-88

FOUR OR MORE WICKETS IN SUCCESSIVE INNINGS

THREE

Waqar Younis (Pakistan)	4-42	India	Sharjah	1989-90
	6-26	Sri Lanka	Sharjah	1989-90
	5-20	New Zealand	Sharjah	1989-90
Waqar Younis (Pakistan)	5-11	New Zealand	Peshawar	1990-91
	5-16	New Zealand	Sialkot	1990-91
	5-52	West Indies	Karachi	1990-91
Waqar Younis (Pakistan)	4-32	New Zealand	Port Elizabeth	1994-95
	4-52	South Africa	Durban	1994-95
	4-33	New Zealand	East London	1994-95

TWO

G.J.Gilmour (Australia)	6-14	England	Leeds	1975
	5-48	West Indies	Lord's	1975
A.M.E.Roberts (West Indies)	4-32	England	Scarborough	1976
	4-27	England	Lord's	1976
D.K.Lillee (Australia)	4-56	England	Sydney	1979-80
	4-28	West Indies	Sydney	1979-80
A.L.F.de Mel (Sri Lanka)	5-39	Pakistan	Leeds	1983
	5-32	New Zealand	Derby	1983
M.Prabhakar (India)	4-25	Pakistan	Sharjah	1991-92
	4-30	West Indies	Sharjah	1991-92
Wasim Akram (Pakistan)	4-24	Sri Lanka	Sharjah	1992-93
	4-24	Sri Lanka	Sharjah	1992-93
A.J.Hollioake (England)	4-23	Pakistan	Birmingham	1996
	4-45	Pakistan	Nottingham	1996

HAT-TRICKS

Jalaluddin	Pakistan v Australia	Hyderabad, Pakistan	1982-83
B.A.Reid	Australia v New Zealand	Sydney	1985-86
C.Sharma	India v New Zealand	Nagpur	1987-88
Wasim Akram	Pakistan v West Indies	Sharjah	1989-90
Wasim Akram	Pakistan v Australia	Sharjah	1989-90
Kapil Dev	India v Sri Lanka	Calcutta	1990-91
Aqib Javed	Pakistan v India	Sharjah	1991-92
D.K.Morrison	New Zealand v India	Napier	1993-94
Waqar Younis	Pakistan v New Zealand	East London	1994-95

MOST ECONOMICAL ANALYSES

O	M	R	W				
10	8	3	4	P.V.Simmons	West Indies v Pakistan	Sydney	1992-93
12	8	6	1	B.S.Bedi	India v East Africa	Leeds	1975
10	5	8	4	C.M.Old	England v Canada	Manchester	1979
10	4	8	1	E.J.Chatfield	New Zealand v Sri Lanka	Dunedin	1982-83
10	5	9	2	M.F.Malone	Australia v West Indies	Melbourne	1981-82
10	4	9	4	Abdul Qadir	Pakistan v New Zealand	Sharjah	1985-86
12	6	10	0	R.J.Hadlee	New Zealand v East Africa	Birmingham	1975
10	6	10	0	B.L.Cairns	New Zealand v Sri Lanka	Dunedin	1982-83

MOST EXPENSIVE ANALYSES

O	M	R	W				
12	1	105	2	M.C.Snedden	New Zealand v England	The Oval	1983
10	0	97	1	A.L.F.de Mel	Sri Lanka v West Indies	Karachi	1987-88
9	0	91	1	M.Suji	Kenya v Sri Lanka	Kandy	1995-96
10	0	85	1	Ata-ur-Rehman	Pakistan v India	Sharjah	1995-96
11	0	84	0	B.L.Cairns	New Zealand v England	Manchester	1978
11	1	83	0	K.D.Ghavri	India v England	Lord's	1975
10	0	83	0	D.R.Pringle	England v West Indies	Gujranwala	1987-88

CAREER RECORDS – 100 WICKETS

	LOI	Wkts	E	A	SA	WI	NZ	I	P	SL	Z	Ass
Wasim Akram (P)	206	297	29	35	13	68	38	42	–	43	18	11
Kapil Dev (I)	224	253	28	45	12	43	33	–	42	38	9	3
Waqar Younis (P)	133	220	16	14	26	39	48	21	–	44	7	5
C.J.McDermott (A)	138	203	21	–	17	63	26	30	23	17	5	1
C.E.L.Ambrose (WI)	133	184	11	52	8	–	12	26	60	10	3	2
C.A.Walsh (WI)	162	182	21	27	4	–	18	36	48	24	1	3
Imran Khan (P)	175	182	23	28	2	54	8	35	–	29	–	3
S.R.Waugh (A)	200	170	26	–	11	35	28	28	19	15	6	2
R.J.Hadlee (NZ)	115	158	34	46	–	11	–	27	15	25	–	–
M.Prabhakar (I)	129	157	20	20	11	25	20	–	20	28	10	3
M.D.Marshall (WI)	136	157	41	47	2	–	1	19	43	2	2	–
J.Srinath (I)	107	148	19	10	15	23	19	–	22	21	15	4
J.Garner (WI)	98	146	36	54	–	–	20	6	24	4	2	–
Aqib Javed (P)	133	146	10	15	8	20	22	30	–	28	9	4
I.T.Botham (E)	116	145	–	35	1	31	28	12	27	7	3	1
M.A.Holding (WI)	102	142	27	52	–	–	9	17	26	9	2	–
E.J.Chatfield (NZ)	114	140	25	51	–	6	–	22	11	24	1	–
A.Kumble (I)	96	133	8	8	17	27	16	–	23	15	12	7
Abdul Qadir (P)	104	132	23	14	–	29	12	16	–	33	–	5
C.L.Hooper (WI)	141	129	17	30	5	–	4	24	33	14	2	–
R.J.Shastri (I)	150	129	18	27	2	27	14	–	24	14	3	–
Mushtaq Ahmed (P)	106	124	11	16	4	24	15	23	–	21	7	3
I.V.A.Richards (WI)	187	118	8	32	–	–	9	36	20	10	3	–
D.K.Morrison (NZ)	92	117	10	22	3	5	–	23	37	8	8	1
P.A.J.DeFreitas (E)	101	115	–	24	11	24	10	10	21	6	4	5
M.C.Snedden (NZ)	93	114	19	38	–	2	–	26	16	10	2	1
Mudassar Nazar (P)	122	111	16	21	–	28	13	19	–	14	–	–
I.R.Bishop (WI)	75	110	15	16	4	–	–	16	46	12	–	1

	LOI	**Wkts**	E	A	SA	WI	NZ	I	P	SL	Z	Ass
S.P.O'Donnell (A)	87	**108**	23	–	–	18	16	7	18	20	4	2
D.K.Lillee (A)	63	**103**	31	–	–	24	28	10	8	–	2	–
C.Pringle (NZ)	64	**103**	26	24	12	4	–	4	12	21	–	–
W.K.M.Benjamin (WI)	85	**100**	10	14	8	–	6	19	26	12	5	–
R.A.Harper (WI)	105	**100**	19	16	7	–	14	10	16	13	2	3

The most wickets for South Africa is 89 by A.A.Donald (61 matches), for Sri Lanka 85 by J.R.Ratnayeke (78 matches) and by S.T.Jayasuriya (112 matches), and for Zimbabwe 34 by H.H.Streak (29 matches) and E.A.Brandes (30 matches).

INDIVIDUAL RECORDS – WICKET-KEEPING

MOST DISMISSALS IN AN INNINGS

5	(5 ct)	R.W.Marsh	Australia v England	Leeds	1981
5	(5 ct)	R.G.de Alwis	Sri Lanka v Australia	Colombo (PSS)	1982-83
5	(5 ct)	S.M.H.Kirmani	India v Zimbabwe	Leicester	1983
5	(3 ct, 2 st)	S.Viswanath	India v England	Sydney	1984-85
5	(3 ct, 2 st)	K.S.More	India v New Zealand	Sharjah	1987-88
5	(5 ct)	H.P.Tillekeratne	Sri Lanka v Pakistan	Sharjah	1990-91
5	(3 ct, 2 st)	N.R.Mongia	India v New Zealand	Auckland	1993-94
5	(3 ct, 2 st)	A.C.Parore	New Zealand v West Indies	Margao	1994-95
5	(5 ct)	D.J.Richardson	South Africa v Pakistan	Johannesburg	1994-95
5	(5 ct)	Moin Khan	Pakistan v Zimbabwe	Harare	1994-95
5	(4 ct, 1 st)	R.S.Kaluwitharana	Sri Lanka v Pakistan	Sharjah	1994-95
5	(5 ct)	D.J.Richardson	South Africa v Zimbabwe	Harare	1995-96
5	(5 ct)	A.Flower	Zimbabwe v South Africa	Harare	1995-96
5	(5 ct)	C.O.Browne	West Indies v Sri Lanka	Brisbane	1995-96
5	(4 ct, 1 st)	J.C.Adams	West Indies v Kenya	Poona	1995-96
5	(4 ct, 1 st)	Rashid Latif	Pakistan v New Zealand	Lahore	1995-96
5	(3 ct, 2 st)	N.R.Mongia	India v Pakistan	Toronto	1996

MOST STUMPINGS IN AN INNINGS

3	Salim Yousuf	Pakistan v New Zealand	Lahore	1990-91
3	I.A.Healy	Australia v South Africa	East London	1993-94
3	I.A.Healy	Australia v South Africa	Faisalabad	1994-95
3	Moin Khan	Pakistan v West Indies	Sharjah	1995-96

CAREER RECORDS – 100 DISMISSALS

		LOI	**Dis**	Ct	St
I.A.Healy	Australia	150	**213**	181	32
P.J.L.Dujon	West Indies	169	**204**	183	21
R.W.Marsh	Australia	92	**124**	120	4
D.J.Richardson	South Africa	82	**121**	108	13
Rashid Latif	Pakistan	84	**103**	81	22
Salim Yousuf	Pakistan	86	**103**	81	22

INDIVIDUAL RECORDS – FIELDING

MOST CATCHES IN AN INNINGS

5	J.N.Rhodes	South Africa v West Indies	Bombay	1993-94
4	Salim Malik	Pakistan v New Zealand	Sialkot	1984-85
4	S.M.Gavaskar	India v Pakistan	Sharjah	1984-85
4	R.B.Richardson	West Indies v England	Birmingham	1991
4	K.C.Wessels	South Africa v West Indies	Kingston	1991-92
4	M.A.Taylor	Australia v West Indies	Sydney	1992-93
4	C.L.Hooper	West Indies v Pakistan	Durban	1992-93
4	K.R.Rutherford	New Zealand v India	Napier	1994-95
4	P.V.Simmons	West Indies v Sri Lanka	Sharjah	1995-96
4	R.A.Harper	West Indies v New Zealand	Georgetown	1995-96

J.G.Bracewell held 4 catches as substitute while fielding for New Zealand v Australia at Adelaide in 1980-81.

CAREER RECORDS – 70 CATCHES

		LOI	Ct
A.R.Border	Australia	273	127
I.V.A.Richards	West Indies	187	101
M.Azharuddin	India	224	94
R.S.Mahanama	Sri Lanka	148	75
R.B.Richardson	West Indies	224	75
Kapil Dev	India	224	71
S.R.Waugh	Australia	200	70

INDIVIDUAL RECORDS – ALL-ROUND PERFORMANCES

50 RUNS AND 5 WICKETS IN A MATCH

I.V.A.Richards	119	5-41	West Indies v New Zealand	Dunedin	1986-87
K.Srikkanth	70	5-27	India v New Zealand	Vishakhapatnam	1988-89
M.E.Waugh	57	5-24	Australia v West Indies	Melbourne	1992-93

CAREER RECORDS – 1000 RUNS AND 100 WICKETS

		LOI	Runs	Wkts
I.T.Botham	England	116	2113	145
R.J.Hadlee	New Zealand	115	1751	158
C.L.Hooper	West Indies	141	3270	129
Imran Khan	Pakistan	175	3709	182
Kapil Dev	India	224	3783	253
Mudassar Nazar	Pakistan	122	2653	111
S.P.O'Donnell	Australia	87	1242	108
M.Prabhakar	India	129	1855	157
I.V.A.Richards	West Indies	187	6721	118
R.J.Shastri	India	150	3108	129
Wasim Akram	Pakistan	206	1894	297
S.R.Waugh	Australia	200	4420	170

1000 RUNS AND 100 DISMISSALS

		LOI	Runs	Dis
P.J.L.Dujon	West Indies	169	1945	204
I.A.Healy	Australia	150	1593	213
R.W.Marsh	Australia	92	1225	124

INDIVIDUAL RECORDS – GENERAL

MOST APPEARANCES

	LOI	E	A	SA	WI	NZ	I	P	SL	Z	Ass
A.R.Border (A)	273	43	–	15	61	52	38	34	23	5	2
D.L.Haynes (WI)	238	35	64	8	–	13	36	65	14	3	–
Salim Malik (P)	234	24	24	14	45	36	37	–	42	8	4
Javed Miandad (P)	233	27	35	3	64	24	35	–	35	6	4
M.Azharuddin (I)	224	21	33	16	37	29	–	37	36	10	5
Kapil Dev (I)	224	23	41	13	42	29	–	32	33	9	2
R.B.Richardson (WI)	224	35	51	9	–	11	32	61	21	3	1
Wasim Akram (P)	206	24	25	10	46	21	33	–	32	9	6
S.R.Waugh (A)	200	23	–	18	37	40	31	24	20	5	2

The most for other Test-playing countries:

	LOI	E	A	SA	WI	NZ	I	P	SL	Z	Ass
A.Ranatunga (SL)	191	10	28	7	20	27	37	50	–	8	4
J.G.Wright (NZ)	149	30	42	–	11	–	21	18	24	2	1
G.A.Gooch (E)	125	–	32	1	32	16	18	16	6	3	1
W.J.Cronje (SA)	88	12	20	–	8	8	15	13	6	4	2
A.Flower (Z)	47	3	5	4	3	6	8	9	8	–	1
D.L.Houghton (Z)	47	2	7	4	4	5	10	9	6	–	–

MOST MATCHES AS CAPTAIN

178	A.R.Border (A)	74	Kapil Dev (I)
139	Imran Khan (P)	62	Javed Miandad (P)
118	M.Azharuddin (I)	61	L.R.D.Mendis (SL)
115	A.Ranatunga (SL)	60	G.P.Howarth (NZ)
108	I.V.A.Richards (WI)	52	K.C.Wessels (SA)
87	R.B.Richardson (WI)	50	G.A.Gooch (E)
81	C.H.Lloyd (WI)	50	M.A.Taylor (A)

The most for Zimbabwe is 27 by A.Flower.

MOST MATCHES AS UMPIRE

83	A.R.Crafter (A)	68	D.R.Shepherd (E)
72	S.G.Randell (A)	57	R.A.French (A)
68	H.D.Bird (E)	51	Khizer Hayat (P)
68	P.J.McConnell (A)		

The most by umpires based in other Test-playing countries is:

44	B.L.Aldridge (NZ)	33	V.K.Ramaswamy (I)
39	S.A.Bucknor (WI)	31	I.D.Robinson (Z)
34	K.E.Liebenberg (SA)	29	K.T.Francis (SL)

WORLD CUP RECORDS 1975 to 1995-96

RESULTS SUMMARY

	Played	Won	Lost	No Result
West Indies	38	25	12	1
England	40	25	14	1
Australia	37	22	15	–
Pakistan	37	21	15	1
New Zealand	35	19	16	–
India	36	18	17	1
South Africa	15	10	5	–
Sri Lanka	32	10	20	2
Zimbabwe	25	3	22	–
Kenya	5	1	4	–
United Arab Emirates	5	1	4	–
Canada	3	–	3	–
East Africa	3	–	3	–
Holland	5	–	5	–

WORLD CUP FINALS

1975	WEST INDIES (291-8) beat Australia (274) by 17 runs	Lord's
1979	WEST INDIES (286-9) beat England (194) by 92 runs	Lord's
1983	INDIA (183) beat West Indies (140) by 43 runs	Lord's
1987-88	AUSTRALIA (253-5) beat England (246-8) by 7 runs	Calcutta
1991-92	PAKISTAN (249-6) beat England (227) by 22 runs	Melbourne
1995-96	SRI LANKA (245-3) beat Australia (241-7) by 7 wickets	Lahore

TEAM RECORDS

HIGHEST TOTAL
398-5	Sri Lanka v Kenya	Kandy	1995-96

HIGHEST TOTAL – BATTING SECOND
313-7	Sri Lanka v Zimbabwe	New Plymouth	1991-92

LOWEST TOTAL
45	Canada v England	Manchester	1979

HIGHEST MATCH AGGREGATE

652-12	Sri Lanka v Kenya	Kandy	1995-96

LARGEST MARGINS OF VICTORY

10 wkts	India beat East Africa	Leeds	1975
10 wkts	West Indies beat Zimbabwe	Birmingham	1983
10 wkts	West Indies beat Pakistan	Melbourne	1991-92
202 runs	England beat India	Lord's	1975

NARROWEST MARGINS OF VICTORY

1 wkt	West Indies beat Pakistan	Birmingham	1975
1 wkt	Pakistan beat West Indies	Lahore	1987-88
1 run	Australia beat India	Madras	1987-88
1 run	Australia beat India	Brisbane	1991-92

INDIVIDUAL RECORDS – BATTING

MOST RUNS

		M	I	NO	HS	Runs	Avge	100
Javed Miandad	P	33	30	5	103	1083	43.32	1
I.V.A.Richards	WI	23	21	5	181	1013	63.31	3
G.A.Gooch	E	21	21	1	115	897	44.85	1
M.D.Crowe	NZ	21	21	5	100*	880	55.00	1
D.L.Haynes	WI	25	25	2	105	854	37.13	1
A.Ranatunga	SL	25	24	8	88*	835	52.18	–
D.C.Boon	A	16	16	1	100	815	54.33	2
S.R.Tendulkar	I	15	14	2	137	806	67.16	2

HIGHEST INDIVIDUAL SCORE

188*	G.Kirsten	South Africa v UAE	Rawalpindi	1995-96

HUNDRED BEFORE LUNCH

101	A.Turner	Australia v Sri Lanka	The Oval	1975

MOST HUNDREDS

3   I.V.A.Richards (West Indies), Ramiz Raja (Pakistan), M.E.Waugh (Australia)

HIGHEST PARTNERSHIP FOR EACH WICKET

1st	186	G.Kirsten/A.C.Hudson	SA v H	Rawalpindi	1995-96
2nd	176	D.L.Amiss/K.W.R.Fletcher	E v I	Lord's	1975
3rd	207	M.E.Waugh/S.R.Waugh	A v K	Vishakhapatnam	1995-96
4th	168	L.K.Germon/C.Z.Harris	NZ v A	Madras	1995-96
5th	145*	A.Flower/A.C.Waller	Z v SL	New Plymouth	1991-92
6th	144	Imran Khan/Shahid Mahboob	P v SL	Leeds	1983
7th	75*	D.A.G.Fletcher/I.P.Butchart	Z v A	Nottingham	1983
8th	117	D.L.Houghton/I.P.Butchart	Z v NZ	Hyderabad	1987-88
9th	126*	Kapil Dev/S.M.H.Kirmani	I v Z	Tunbridge Wells	1983
10th	71	A.M.E.Roberts/J.Garner	WI v I	Manchester	1983

INDIVIDUAL RECORDS – BOWLING

MOST WICKETS

		Balls	Runs	Wkts	Avge	Best	4w
Imran Khan	P	1017	655	34	19.26	4-37	2
I.T.Botham	E	1332	762	30	25.40	4-31	1
Kapil Dev	I	1422	892	28	31.85	5-43	1
Wasim Akram	P	1118	768	28	27.42	4-32	1
C.J.McDermott	A	894	599	27	22.18	5-44	2
Mushtaq Ahmed	P	810	549	26	21.11	3-16	–
A.M.E.Roberts	WI	1021	552	26	21.23	3-32	–

BEST ANALYSIS

7-51	W.W.Davis	West Indies v Australia	Leeds	1983

HAT-TRICK

	C.Sharma	India v New Zealand	Nagpur	1987-88

MOST ECONOMICAL BOWLING

12-8-6-1	B.S.Bedi	India v East Africa	Leeds	1975

MOST EXPENSIVE BOWLING

12-1-105-2	M.C.Snedden	New Zealand v England	The Oval	1983

INDIVIDUAL RECORDS – WICKET-KEEPING

MOST DISMISSALS

22	(18ct, 4st)	Wasim Bari	Pakistan
20	(19ct, 1st)	P.J.L.Dujon	West Indies
20	(17ct, 3st)	I.A.Healy	Australia
18	(17ct, 1st)	R.W.Marsh	Australia
18	(12ct, 6st)	K.S.More	India
16	(16ct)	D.L.Murray	West Indies
15	(14ct, 1st)	D.J.Richardson	South Africa

MOST DISMISSALS IN AN INNINGS

5 (5ct)	S.M.H.Kirmani	India v Zimbabwe	Leicester	1983
5 (4ct, 1st)	J.C.Adams	West Indies v Kenya	Poona	1995-96
5 (4ct, 1st)	Rashid Latif	Pakistan v New Zealand	Lahore	1995-96

INDIVIDUAL RECORDS – FIELDING

MOST CATCHES

12	C.H.Lloyd	West Indies
12	Kapil Dev	India
12	D.L.Haynes	West Indies
11	C.L.Cairns	New Zealand
10	I.T.Botham	England
10	A.R.Border	Australia

MOST CATCHES IN AN INNINGS

3	C.H.Lloyd	West Indies v Sri Lanka	Manchester	1975
3	D.A.Reeve	England v Pakistan	Adelaide	1991-92
3	Ijaz Ahmed, sr	Pakistan v Australia	Perth	1991-92
3	A.R.Border	Australia v Zimbabwe	Hobart	1991-92
3	C.L.Cairns	New Zealand v UAE	Faisalabad	1995-96

INDIVIDUAL RECORDS – GENERAL

MOST APPEARANCES

33	Javed Miandad (Pakistan)
28	Imran Khan (Pakistan)
26	Kapil Dev (India)
25	A.R.Border (Australia), D.L.Haynes (West Indies), A.Ranatunga (Sri Lanka)

Individual Career Records
1970-71 to 1996

INDIVIDUAL CAREER RECORDS

These career records are for all players appearing in official Limited-Overs Internationals before 28 September 1996. * denotes not out.

ENGLAND (143 players)

		BATTING AND FIELDING								BOWLING					
	M	I	NO	HS	Runs	Avge	100	50	Ct/St	Balls	Runs	Wkts	Avge	Best	4w
Agnew, J.P.	3	1	1	2*	2	–	–	–	1	126	120	3	40.00	3-38	–
Allott, P.J.W.	13	6	1	8	15	3.00	–	–	2	819	552	15	36.80	3-41	–
Amiss, D.L.	18	18	–	137	859	47.72	4	1	2						
Arnold, G.G.	14	6	3	18*	48	16.00	–	–	2	714	339	19	17.84	4-27	1
Atherton, M.A.	43	43	2	127	1449	35.34	1	11	11						
Athey, C.W.J.	31	30	3	142*	848	31.40	2	4	16						
Bailey, R.J.	4	4	2	43*	137	68.50	–	–	1						
Bairstow, D.L.	21	20	6	23*	206	14.71	–	–	17/4						
Barlow, G.D.	6	6	1	80*	149	29.80	–	1	4						
Barnett, K.J.	1	1	–	84	84	84.00	–	1	–						
Benjamin, J.E.	2	1	1	0*	0	0.00	–	–	–	72	47	1	47.00	1-22	–
Benson, M.R.	1	1	–	24	24	24.00	–	–	–						
Bicknell, M.P.	7	6	2	31*	96	24.00	–	–	2	413	347	13	26.69	3-55	–
Blakey, R.J.	3	2	–	25	25	12.50	–	–	2/1						
Botham, I.T.	116	106	15	79	2113	23.21	–	9	36	6271	4139	145	28.54	4-31	3
Boycott, G.	36	34	4	105	1082	36.06	1	9	5	168	105	5	21.00	2-14	–
Brearley, J.M.	25	24	3	78	510	24.28	–	3	12						
Broad, B.C.	34	34	–	106	1361	40.02	1	11	10	6	6	0	–		
Brown, A.D.	3	3	–	118	155	51.66	1	–	1	6	6	0	–		
Butcher, A.R.	1	1	–	14	14	14.00	–	–	–						
Butcher, R.O.	3	3	–	52	58	19.33	–	1	1						
Caddick, A.R.	5	3	3	20*	23	–	–	–	1	318	258	6	43.00	3-39	–
Capel, D.J.	23	19	3	50*	327	19.23	–	1	6	1038	805	17	47.35	3-38	–
Close, D.B.	3	3	–	43	49	16.33	–	–	1	18	21	0	–	–	–
Cook, G.	6	6	–	32	106	17.66	–	–	2						
Cook, N.G.B.	3	1	1	1*	1	–	–	–	2	144	95	5	19.00	2-18	–
Cope, G.A.	2	1	1	1*	1	–	–	–	–	112	35	2	17.50	1-16	–
Cork, D.G.	22	12	1	21	92	8.36	–	–	5	1272	926	34	27.23	3-27	–
Cowans, N.G.	23	8	3	4*	13	2.60	–	–	5	1282	913	23	39.69	3-44	–
Cowdrey, C.S.	3	3	1	46*	51	25.50	–	–	–	52	55	2	27.50	1- 3	–
Cowdrey, M.C.	1	1	–	1	1	1.00	–	–	–						
Crawley, J.P.	3	3	–	18	34	11.33	–	–	–						
Croft, R.D.B.	3	2	–	15	15	7.50	–	–	1	168	111	5	22.20	2-36	–
DeFreitas, P.A.J.	101	66	23	67	690	16.04	–	1	26	5610	3693	115	32.11	4-35	1
Denness, M.H.	12	11	2	66	264	29.33	–	1	1						
Dilley, G.R.	36	18	8	31*	114	11.40	–	–	4	2043	1291	48	26.89	4-23	3

ENGLAND (continued)

	BATTING AND FIELDING									BOWLING					
	M	I	NO	HS	Runs	Avge	100	50	Ct/St	Balls	Runs	Wkts	Avge	Best 1-19	4w
D'Oliveira, B.L.	4	4	1	17	30	10.00	–	–	1	204	140	3	46.66	–	–
Downton, P.R.	28	20	5	44*	242	16.13	–	–	26/3						
Ealham, M.A.	2	1	–	40	40	40.00	–	–	–	36	23	0	–	–	–
Edmonds, P.H.	29	18	7	20	116	10.54	–	–	6	1534	965	26	37.11	3-39	–
Edrich, J.H.	7	6	–	90	223	37.16	–	2	–						
Ellison, R.M.	14	12	4	24	86	10.75	–	–	2	696	510	12	42.50	3-42	–
Emburey, J.E.	61	45	10	34	501	14.31	–	–	19	3425	2346	76	30.86	4-37	1
Fairbrother, N.H.	56	54	13	113	1539	37.53	1	11	24	6	9	0	–	–	–
Fletcher, K.W.R.	24	22	3	131	757	39.84	1	5	4						
Foster, N.A.	48	25	12	24	150	11.53	–	–	12	2627	1836	59	31.11	3-20	–
Fowler, G.	26	26	2	81*	744	31.00	–	4	4/2						
Fraser, A.R.C.	33	14	6	38*	80	10.00	–	–	1	1876	1132	38	29.78	4-22	1
French, B.N.	13	8	3	9*	34	6.80	–	–	13/3						
Gatting, M.W.	92	88	17	115*	2095	29.50	1	9	22	392	336	10	33.60	3-32	–
Gifford, N.	2	1	–	0	0	0.00	–	–	1	120	50	4	12.50	4-23	1
Gooch, G.A.	125	122	6	142	4290	36.98	8	23	45	2066	1516	36	42.11	3-19	–
Gough, D.	27	18	5	45	164	12.61	–	–	4	1492	982	38	25.84	5-44	2
Gould, I.J.	18	14	2	42	155	12.91	–	–	15/3						
Gower, D.I.	114	111	8	158	3170	30.77	7	12	44	5	14	0	–	–	–
Greig, A.W.	22	19	3	48	269	16.81	–	–	7	916	619	19	32.57	4-45	1
Hampshire, J.H.	3	3	1	25*	48	24.00	–	–	–						
Hayes, F.C.	6	6	1	52	128	25.60	–	1	–						
Headley, D.W.	2	1	1	3*	3	–	–	–	–	102	84	0	–	–	–
Hemmings, E.E.	33	12	6	8*	30	5.00	–	–	5	1752	1294	37	34.97	4-52	1
Hendrick, M.	22	10	5	2*	6	1.20	–	–	5	1248	681	35	19.45	5-31	3
Hick, G.A.	62	61	7	105*	2105	38.98	2	16	32	840	696	18	38.66	3-41	–
Hollioake, A.J.	2	2	–	15	28	14.00	–	–	–	93	68	8	8.50	4-23	2
Humpage, G.W.	3	2	–	6	11	5.50	–	–	2						
Hussain, N.	4	4	1	16	43	14.33	–	–	2						
Igglesden, A.P.	4	3	1	18	20	10.00	–	–	–	168	122	2	61.00	2-12	–
Illingworth, R.	3	2	–	4	5	2.50	–	–	1	130	84	4	21.00	3-50	–
Illingworth, R.K.	25	11	5	14	68	11.33	–	–	8	1501	1059	30	35.30	3-33	–
Irani, R.C.	4	4	2	45*	62	31.00	–	–	2	84	90	1	90.00	1-56	–
Jackman, R.D.	15	9	1	14	54	6.75	–	–	4	873	598	19	31.47	3-41	–
Jameson, J.A.	3	3	–	28	60	20.00	–	–	–	12	3	0	–	–	–
Jarvis, P.W.	16	8	2	16*	31	5.16	–	–	1	879	672	24	28.00	5-35	2
Jesty, T.E.	10	10	4	52*	127	21.16	–	1	5	108	93	1	93.00	1-23	–
Knight, N.V.	3	3	1	125*	264	132.00	2	–	2						
Knott, A.P.E.	20	14	4	50	200	20.00	–	1	15/1						
Lamb, A.J.	122	118	16	118	4010	39.31	4	26	31	6	3	0	–	–	–

ENGLAND (continued)

			BATTING AND FIELDING							BOWLING					
	M	I	NO	HS	Runs	Avge	100	50	Ct/St	Balls	Runs	Wkts	Avge	Best	4w
Larkins, W.	25	24	–	124	591	24.62	1	–	8	15	22	0	–	–	–
Lawrence, D.V.	1	–	–	–	–	–	–	–	–	66	67	4	16.75	4-67	1
Lever, J.K.	22	11	4	27*	56	8.00	–	–	6	1152	713	24	29.70	4-29	1
Lever, P.	10	3	2	8*	17	17.00	–	–	2	440	261	11	23.72	4-35	1
Lewis, C.C.	51	38	13	33	348	13.92	–	–	20	2513	1854	65	28.52	4-30	4
Lloyd, D.	8	8	1	116*	285	40.71	1	–	3	12	3	1	3.00	1-3	–
Lloyd, G.D.	2	2	1	15	17	17.00	–	–	1						
Lloyd, T.A.	3	3	–	49	101	33.66	–	–	–						
Love, J.D.	3	3	–	43	61	20.33	–	–	1						
Luckhurst, B.W.	3	3	–	14	15	5.00	–	–	1						
Lynch, M.A.	3	3	2	6	8	2.66	–	–	1						
Malcolm, D.E.	10	5	2	4	9	3.00	–	–	1	526	404	16	25.25	3-40	–
Marks, V.J.	34	24	3	44	285	13.57	–	–	8	1838	1135	44	25.79	5-20	2
Martin, P.J.	16	10	6	6	33	8.25	–	–	1	838	610	25	24.40	4-44	1
Maynard, M.P.	10	10	1	41	153	17.00	–	–	3						
Miller, G.	25	18	2	46	136	8.50	–	–	4	1268	813	25	32.52	3-27	–
Morris, J.E.	8	8	1	63*	167	23.85	–	1	2						
Moxon, M.D.	8	8	–	70	174	21.75	–	1	5						
Mullally, A.D.	3	1	–	2	2	2.00	–	–	5	150	127	2	63.50	1-30	–
Old, C.M.	32	25	7	51*	338	18.77	–	1	8	1755	999	45	22.20	4- 8	2
Pocock, P.I.	1	1	–	4	4	4.00	–	–	–	60	20	0	–	–	–
Pringle, D.R.	44	30	12	49*	425	23.61	–	1	11	2379	1677	44	38.11	4-42	1
Radford, N.V.	6	3	2	0*	0	0.00	–	–	2	348	230	2	115.00	1-32	–
Radley, C.T.	4	4	1	117*	250	83.33	1	1	–						
Ramprakash, M.R.	10	10	3	32	184	26.28	–	–	5	12	14	0	–	–	–
Randall, D.W.	49	45	5	88	1067	26.67	–	5	25	2	2	1	2.00	1- 2	–
Reeve, D.A.	29	21	9	35	291	24.25	–	–	12	1147	820	20	41.00	3-20	–
Rhodes, S.J.	9	8	2	56	107	17.83	–	1	9/2						
Richards, C.J.	22	16	3	50	154	11.84	–	1	16/1						
Robinson, R.T.	26	26	–	83	597	22.96	–	3	6						
Roope, G.R.J.	8	8	–	44	173	21.62	–	–	2						
Rose, B.C.	2	2	–	54	99	49.50	–	1	1						
Russell, R.C.	37	28	7	50	381	18.14	–	1	39/6						
Salisbury, I.D.K.	4	2	1	5	7	7.00	–	–	1	186	177	5	35.40	3-41	–
Shuttleworth, K.	1	1	–	7	7	7.00	–	–	1	56	29	1	29.00	1-29	–
Slack, W.N.	2	2	–	34	43	21.50	–	–	–						
Small, G.C.	53	24	9	18*	98	6.53	–	–	7	2793	1942	58	33.48	4-31	1
Smith, C.L.	4	4	–	70	109	27.25	–	1	–	36	28	2	14.00	2- 8	–
Smith, D.M.	2	2	1	10*	15	15.00	–	–	1						
Smith, M.J.	5	5	–	31	70	14.00	–	–	–						

ENGLAND (continued)

Player	M	I	NO	HS	Runs	Avge	100	50	Ct/St	Balls	Runs	Wkts	Avge	Best	4w
			BATTING AND FIELDING							BOWLING					
Smith, N.M.K.	7	6	1	31	100	20.00	-	-	1	261	190	6	31.66	3-29	-
Smith, R.A.	71	70	8	167*	2419	39.01	4	15	26	-	-	-	-	-	-
Snow, J.A.	9	4	2	5*	9	4.50	-	-	1	538	232	14	16.57	4-11	2
Steele, D.S.	1	1	-	8	8	8.00	-	-	-	6	9	0	-	-	-
Stevenson, G.B.	4	4	3	28*	43	43.00	-	-	2	192	125	7	17.85	4-33	1
Stewart, A.J.	79	74	7	103	2042	30.47	1	12	60/5	-	-	-	-	-	-
Tavaré, C.J.	29	28	2	83*	720	27.69	-	4	7	-	-	-	-	-	-
Taylor, J.P.	1	1	1	1*	1	1.00	-	-	-	12	3	0	-	-	-
Taylor, L.B.	2	1	1	1*	1	-	-	-	-	18	20	0	-	-	-
Taylor, R.W.	27	17	7	26*	130	13.00	-	-	26/6	-	-	-	-	-	-
Thomas, J.G.	3	3	2	1*	1	1.00	-	-	-	84	47	0	-	-	-
Thorpe, G.P.	30	30	4	89	1018	39.15	-	8	16	156	144	3	48.00	2-59	-
Titmus, F.J.	2	1	-	11	11	11.00	-	-	1	72	60	2	30.00	2-15	-
Tolchard, R.W.	1	-	-	-	-	-	-	-	1	-	-	-	-	-	-
Tufnell, P.C.R.	19	10	9	5*	15	15.00	-	-	3	960	677	15	45.13	3-40	-
Udal, S.D.	10	6	4	11*	35	17.50	-	-	1	570	371	8	46.37	2-37	-
Underwood, D.L.	26	13	4	17	53	5.88	-	-	6	1278	734	32	22.93	4-44	1
Watkin, S.L.	4	2	-	4	4	2.00	-	-	-	221	193	7	27.57	4-49	1
Watkinson, M.	1	1	-	15	15	15.00	-	-	-	54	43	0	-	-	-
Wells, A.P.	1	1	-	17	17	17.00	-	-	1	-	-	-	-	-	-
Wells, C.M.	2	2	-	17	22	11.00	-	-	-	56	53	3	17.66	3-53	-
Whitaker, J.J.	2	2	1	44*	48	48.00	-	-	-	-	-	-	-	-	-
White, C.	10	8	-	34	113	14.12	-	-	1	382	265	8	33.12	2-18	-
Willey, P.	26	24	1	64	538	23.39	-	5	4	1031	659	13	50.69	3-33	-
Willis, R.G.D.	64	22	14	24	83	10.37	-	-	22	3595	1968	80	24.60	4-11	4
Wood, B.	13	12	2	78*	314	31.40	-	2	6	420	224	9	24.88	2-14	-
Woolmer, R.A.	6	4	-	9	21	5.25	-	-	3	321	260	9	28.88	3-33	-

AUSTRALIA (128 players)

Player	M	I	NO	HS	Runs	Avge	100	50	Ct/St	Balls	Runs	Wkts	Avge	Best	4w
			BATTING AND FIELDING							BOWLING					
Alderman, T.M.	65	18	6	9*	32	2.66	-	-	29	3371	2056	88	23.36	5-17	3
Angel, J.	3	1	-	0	0	0.00	-	-	-	162	113	4	28.25	2-47	-
Beard, G.R.	2	-	-	-	-	-	-	-	1	112	70	4	17.50	2-20	-
Bennett, M.J.	8	4	1	6*	9	3.00	-	-	1	408	275	4	68.75	2-27	-
Bevan, M.G.	36	32	15	78*	1030	60.58	-	6	15	423	343	10	34.30	2-14	-
Bishop, G.A.	2	2	-	7	13	6.50	-	-	1	-	-	-	-	-	-
Blewett, G.S.	8	8	-	46	111	13.87	-	-	1	263	249	4	62.25	1-30	-
Boon, D.C.	181	177	16	122	5964	37.04	5	37	45	82	86	0	-	-	-

AUSTRALIA (continued)

				BATTING AND FIELDING						BOWLING					
	M	I	NO	HS	Runs	Avge	100	50	Ct/St	Balls	Runs	Wkts	Avge	Best	4w
Border, A.R.	273	252	39	127*	6524	30.62	3	39	127	2661	2071	73	28.36	3-20	-
Bright, R.J.	11	8	4	19*	66	16.50	-	-	2	462	350	3	116.66	1-28	-
Callen, I.W.	5	3	2	3*	6	6.00	-	-	2	180	148	5	29.60	3-24	-
Campbell, G.D.	12	3	1	4*	6	3.00	-	-	4	613	404	18	22.44	3-17	-
Carlson, P.H.	4	2	-	11	11	5.50	-	-	-	168	70	2	35.00	1-21	-
Chappell, G.S.	74	72	14	138*	2331	40.18	3	14	23	3108	2097	72	29.12	5-15	2
Chappell, I.M.	16	16	2	86	673	48.07	-	8	5	42	23	2	11.50	2-14	-
Chappell, T.M.	20	13	-	110	229	17.61	1	-	8	736	538	19	28.31	3-31	-
Clark, W.M.	2	-	-	-	-	-	-	-	-	100	61	3	20.33	2-39	-
Colley, D.J.	1	-	-	-	-	-	-	-	-	66	72	0	-	-	-
Connolly, A.N.	1	-	-	-	-	-	-	-	-	64	62	0	-	-	-
Cosier, G.J.	9	7	2	84	154	30.80	-	1	4	409	248	14	17.71	5-18	1
Darling, W.M.	18	18	1	74	363	21.35	-	1	6						
Davis, I.C.	3	3	1	11*	12	6.00	-	-	-						
Davis, S.P.	39	11	7	6	20	5.00	-	-	5	2016	1135	44	25.79	3-10	2
Dodemaide, A.I.C.	24	16	7	30	124	13.77	-	-	7	1327	753	36	20.91	5-21	-
Dyer, G.C.	23	13	2	45*	174	15.81	-	-	24/4						
Dymock, G.	15	7	4	14*	35	11.66	-	-	1	806	412	15	27.46	2-21	-
Dyson, J.	29	27	4	79	755	32.82	-	4	12						
Edwards, R.	9	8	1	80*	255	36.42	-	3	-						
Edwards, W.J.	1	1	-	2	2	2.00	-	-	-						
Emery, P.A.	1	1	1	11*	11	-	-	-	3	1	0	0	-	-	-
Fleming, D.W.	24	8	5	5*	18	6.00	-	-	5	1204	866	37	23.40	5-36	3
Gilbert, D.R.	14	8	3	8	39	7.80	-	-	3	684	552	18	30.66	5-46	1
Gillespie, J.N.	1	1	-	6	6	6.00	-	-	-	36	27	0	-	-	-
Gilmour, G.J.	5	2	1	28*	42	42.00	-	-	2	320	165	16	10.31	6-14	2
Graf, S.F.	11	6	-	8	24	4.00	-	-	1	522	345	8	43.12	2-23	-
Hammond, J.R.	1	1	1	15*	15	-	-	-	-	54	41	1	41.00	1-41	-
Hayden, M.L.	13	12	1	67	286	26.00	-	2	4						
Healy, I.A.	150	105	32	56	1592	21.80	-	4	181/32						
Hilditch, A.M.J.	8	8	-	72	226	28.25	-	1	1						
Hogan, T.G.	16	12	4	27	72	9.00	-	-	10	917	574	23	24.95	4-33	1
Hogg, G.B.	2	2	1	11*	13	13.00	-	-	-	84	59	1	59.00	1-26	-
Hogg, R.M.	71	35	20	22	137	9.13	-	-	8	3677	2418	85	28.44	4-29	5
Holland, R.G.	2	-	-	-	-	-	-	-	-	126	99	2	49.50	2-49	-
Hookes, D.W.	39	36	2	76	826	24.29	-	5	11	29	28	1	28.00	1- 2	-
Hughes, K.J.	97	88	6	98	1968	24.00	-	17	27	1	4	0	-	-	-
Hughes, M.G.	33	17	8	20	100	11.11	-	-	6	1639	1115	38	29.34	4-44	1
Hurst, A.G.	8	4	4	3*	7	-	-	-	1	402	203	12	16.91	5-21	1
Jenner, T.J.	1	1	-	12	12	12.00	-	-	-	64	28	0	-	-	-

AUSTRALIA (continued)

				BATTING AND FIELDING						BOWLING					
	M	I	NO	HS	Runs	Avge	100	50	Ct/St	Balls	Runs	Wkts	Avge	Best	4w
Jones, D.M.	164	161	25	145	6068	44.61	7	46	54	106	81	3	27.00	2-34	–
Julian, B.P.	2	1	–	11	11	11.00	–	–	–	126	116	3	38.66	3-50	–
Kasprowicz, M.S.	2	–	–	–	–	–			–	96	83	2	41.50	1-32	–
Kent, M.F.	5	5	1	33	78	19.50	–	1	4						
Kerr, R.B.	4	4	1	87*	97	32.33	–	1	1						
Laird, B.M.	23	23	3	117*	594	29.70	1	2	5						
Langer, J.L.	7	6	2	36	131	32.75	–	1	1/1						
Laughlin, T.J.	6	5	1	74	105	26.25	–	1	5	308	224	8	28.00	3-54	–
Law, S.G.	25	24	3	110	720	34.28	1	4	5	462	322	6	53.66	2-30	–
Lawry, W.M.	1	1	–	27	27	27.00	–	–	1						
Lawson, G.F.	79	52	18	33*	378	11.11	–	–	18	4259	2592	88	29.45	4-26	1
Lee, S.	8	6	1	39	61	12.20	–	–	5	324	207	4	51.75	1-20	–
Lehmann, D.S.	2	2	–	15	17	8.50	–	–	1	66	55	1	55.00	1-29	–
Lillee, D.K.	63	34	8	42*	240	9.23	–	–	10	3593	2145	103	20.82	5-34	6
McCosker, R.B.	14	14	2	95	320	22.85	–	2	3						
McCurdy, R.J.	11	6	2	13*	33	8.25	–	–	1	515	375	12	31.25	3-19	–
McDermott, C.J.	138	78	17	37	432	7.08	–	–	27	7461	5018	203	24.71	5-44	5
McGrath, G.D.	55	17	9	10	34	4.25	–	–	5	2926	1895	75	25.26	5-52	4
McKenzie, G.D.	1	–	–	–	–	–	–	–	1	60	22	2	11.00	2-22	–
MacLean, J.A.	2	1	–	11	11	11.00	–	–	2						
MacLeay, K.H.	16	13	2	41	139	12.63	–	–	2	857	626	15	41.73	6-39	1
Maguire, J.N.	23	11	5	14*	42	7.00	–	–	2	1009	769	19	40.47	3-61	–
Mallett, A.A.	9	3	1	8	14	7.00	–	–	4	502	341	11	31.00	3-34	–
Malone, M.F.	10	7	3	15*	36	9.00	–	–	1	612	315	11	28.63	2-9	–
Marsh, G.R.	117	115	6	126*	4357	39.97	9	22	31	6	4	0	–	–	–
Marsh, R.W.	92	76	15	66	1225	20.08	–	4	120/4						
Martyn, D.R.	11	10	1	51*	166	18.44	–	1	6						
Massie, R.A.L.	3	1	1	16*	16	–	–	1	1	183	129	3	43.00	2-35	–
Matthews, G.R.J.	59	50	13	54	619	16.72	–	1	23	2808	2004	57	35.15	3-27	–
May, T.B.A.	47	12	8	15	39	9.75	–	–	3	2504	1772	39	45.43	3-19	–
Moody, T.M.	34	32	3	89	751	25.89	–	7	10	894	651	16	40.68	3-56	–
Moss, J.K.	1	1	–	7	7	7.00	–	–	2						
O'Donnell, S.P.	87	64	15	74*	1242	25.34	–	9	22	4350	3102	108	28.72	5-13	6
O'Keeffe, K.J.	2	2	1	16*	16	16.00	–	–	–	132	79	2	39.50	1-36	–
Pascoe, L.S.	29	11	7	15*	39	9.75	–	–	6	1568	1066	53	20.11	5-30	5
Phillips, W.B.	48	41	6	75*	852	24.34	–	6	42/7						
Ponting, R.T.	27	27	3	123	809	33.70	2	5	4						
Porter, G.D.	2	1	1	3	3	3.00	–	–	1	108	33	3	11.00	2-13	–
Rackemann, C.G.	52	18	6	9*	34	2.83	–	–	6	2791	1833	82	22.35	5-16	4
Redpath, I.R.	5	5	–	24	46	9.20	–	–	2						

AUSTRALIA (continued)

	M	I	NO	HS	Runs	Avge	100	50	Ct/St	Balls	Runs	Wkts	Avge	Best	4w
											BATTING AND FIELDING → **BOWLING**				
Reid, B.A.	61	21	8	10	49	3.76	–	–	6	3250	2203	63	34.96	5-53	1
Reiffel, P.R.	63	40	18	58	408	18.54	–	1	21	3241	2080	83	25.06	4-13	4
Ritchie, G.M.	44	42	7	84	959	27.40	–	6	9						
Rixon, S.J.	6	6	3	20*	40	13.33	–	–	9/2						
Robertson, G.R.	4	3	2	5*	7	7.00	–	–	–	144	127	0	–	–	–
Robinson, R.D.	2	2	–	70	82	41.00	–	1	3/1						
Serjeant, C.S.	3	3	–	46	73	24.33	–	–	1						
Sheahan, A.P.	3	3	–	50	75	25.00	–	1	–						
Siddons, J.D.	1	1	–	32	32	32.00	–	–	–						
Simpson, R.B.	2	2	–	23	36	18.00	–	–	–	102	95	2	47.50	2-30	–
Slater, M.J.	37	37	–	73	861	23.27	–	7	4	12	11	0	–	–	–
Smith, S.B.	28	24	2	117	861	39.13	2	8	8	7	5	0	–	–	–
Stackpole, K.R.	6	6	–	61	224	37.33	–	3	1	77	54	3	18.00	3-40	–
Taylor, M.A.	96	93	1	97	3027	32.90	–	27	48						
Taylor, P.L.	83	47	25	54*	437	19.86	–	1	34	3937	2740	97	28.24	4-38	1
Thomson, A.L.	1	–		–	–	–	–	–	–	64	22	1	22.00	1-22	–
Thomson, J.R.	50	30	6	21	181	7.54	–	–	9	2696	1942	55	35.30	4-67	1
Toohey, P.M.	5	4	2	54*	105	52.50	–	1	–						
Trimble, G.S.	2	2	1	4	4	4.00	–	–	1						
Turner, A.	6	6	–	101	247	41.16	1	2	3	24	32	0	–	–	–
Veletta, M.R.J.	20	19	4	68*	484	32.26	–	2	8						
Walker, M.H.N.	17	11	3	20	79	9.87	–	–	6	1006	546	20	27.30	4-19	1
Walters, K.D.	28	24	6	59	513	28.50	–	2	10	314	273	4	68.25	2-24	–
Warne, S.K.	59	30	10	55	272	13.60	–	1	18	3307	2133	99	21.54	4-19	7
Watson, G.D.	2	2	1	11*	11	11.00	–	–	–	48	28	2	14.00	2-28	–
Waugh, M.E.	117	113	9	130	3828	36.80	8	24	46	2403	1939	67	28.94	5-24	2
Waugh, S.R.	200	180	42	102*	4420	32.02	1	25	70	7692	5710	170	33.58	4-33	2
Wellham, D.M.	17	17	2	97	379	25.26	1	1	8						
Wessels, K.C.	54	51	3	107	1740	36.25	1	14	19	737	655	18	36.38	2-16	–
Whatmore, D.F.	1	1	–	2	2	2.00	–	–	–						
Whitney, M.R.	38	13	7	9*	40	6.66	–	–	11	2106	1249	46	27.15	4-34	2
Wiener, J.M.	7	7	–	50	140	20.00	–	1	2	24	34	0	–	–	–
Wood, G.M.	83	77	11	114*	2219	33.62	3	11	17						
Woodcock, A.J.	1	1	–	53	53	53.00	–	1	–						
Woolley, R.D.	4	3	2	16	31	31.00	–	–	1/1						
Wright, K.J.	5	2	–	23	29	14.50	–	–	8						
Yallop, G.N.	30	27	6	66*	823	39.19	–	7	5	138	119	3	39.66	2-28	–
Yardley, B.	7	4	–	28	58	14.50	–	–	1	198	130	7	18.57	3-28	–
Zesers, A.K.	2	2	2	8*	10	–	–	–	1	90	74	1	74.00	1-37	–
Zoehrer, T.J.	22	15	3	50	130	10.83	–	1	21/2						

SOUTH AFRICA (41 players)

				BATTING AND FIELDING						BOWLING					
	M	I	NO	HS	Runs	Avge	100	50	Ct/St	Balls	Runs	Wkts	Avge	Best	4w
Adams, P.R.	6	3	1	10	10	5.00	-	-	1	288	183	10	18.30	3-26	-
Boje, N.	2	1	1	2*	2	-	-	-	-	84	54	0	-	-	-
Bosch, T.	2	-	-	-	-	-	-	-	-	51	66	0	-	-	-
Callaghan, D.J.	27	24	6	169*	478	26.55	1	-	6	444	365	10	36.50	3-32	2
Cook, S.J.	4	4	-	35	67	16.75	-	-	1	-	-	-	-	-	-
Cronje, W.J.	88	84	12	112	2681	37.23	2	15	36	2817	1960	58	33.79	5-32	-
Crookes, D.N.	6	5	1	54	110	27.50	-	1	2	150	141	0	-	-	-
Cullinan, D.J.	51	50	7	110*	1386	32.23	1	8	19	12	7	0	-	-	-
De Villiers, P.S.	68	28	12	20	135	8.43	-	-	12	3666	2137	79	27.05	4-27	2
Donald, A.A.	61	18	10	7*	34	4.25	-	-	7	3266	2195	89	24.66	5-29	3
Eksteen, C.E.	6	2	1	6*	6	6.00	-	-	3	222	181	2	90.50	1-26	-
Henry, O.	3	3	1	11	20	10.00	-	-	1	149	125	2	62.50	1-31	-
Hudson, A.C.	68	67	1	161	2140	32.42	2	16	11	-	-	-	-	-	-
Jack, S.D.	2	2	-	6	7	3.50	-	-	3	108	86	3	28.66	2-41	-
Kallis, J.H.	14	13	4	67	275	30.55	-	1	2	222	162	4	40.50	3-21	-
Kirsten, G.	46	46	5	188*	1890	46.09	5	8	16	30	23	0	-	-	-
Kirsten, P.N.	40	40	6	97	1293	38.02	-	9	11	183	152	6	25.33	3-31	-
Klusener, L.	1	1	-	0	0	0.00	-	-	3	24	19	0	-	-	-
Kuiper, A.P.	25	23	7	63*	539	33.68	-	3	3	588	518	18	28.77	3-33	-
Liebenberg, G.F.J.	1	1	-	12	12	12.00	-	-	-	-	-	-	-	-	-
McMillan, B.M.	58	39	14	127	669	26.76	1	-	34	2705	1890	52	36.34	4-32	1
Matthews, C.R.	53	21	8	26	141	10.84	-	-	10	2936	1896	79	24.00	4-10	3
Palframan, S.J.	7	4	-	28	55	13.75	-	-	9	-	-	-	-	-	-
Pollock, S.M.	18	11	6	66*	160	32.00	-	1	5	985	647	26	24.88	4-34	1
Pringle, M.W.	17	8	3	13*	48	9.60	-	-	2	870	604	22	27.45	4-11	1
Rhodes, J.N.	84	78	12	66	1886	28.57	-	6	29	-	-	-	-	-	-
Rice, C.E.B.	3	2	-	14	26	13.00	-	-	-	138	114	2	57.00	1-46	-
Richardson, D.J.	82	54	21	53	670	20.30	-	1	108/13	-	-	-	-	-	-
Rindel, M.J.R.	8	8	1	106	215	30.71	-	1	4	114	89	3	29.66	2-15	-
Rundle, D.B.	2	2	-	6	6	3.00	-	-	3	96	95	5	19.00	4-42	1
Rushmere, M.W.	4	4	-	35	78	19.50	-	-	1	-	-	-	-	-	-
Schultz, B.N.	1	-	-	-	-	-	-	-	-	54	35	1	35.00	1-35	-
Shaw, T.G.	9	6	4	17*	26	13.00	-	-	2	504	298	9	33.11	2-19	-
Simons, E.O.	23	18	4	24	217	15.50	-	2	6	1212	810	33	24.54	4-42	1
Snell, R.P.	42	28	8	63	322	16.10	-	-	7	2095	1574	44	35.77	5-40	3
Stewart, E.L.R.	5	5	1	23*	57	14.25	-	1	3	-	-	-	-	-	-
Steyn, P.J.R.	1	1	-	4	4	4.00	-	-	-	-	-	-	-	-	-
Symcox, P.L.	27	20	2	61	234	13.00	-	1	6	1314	798	26	30.69	3-20	-
Van Zyl, C.J.P.G.	2	2	1	3*	3	3.00	-	-	-	108	93	0	-	-	-
Wessels, K.C.	55	54	4	90	1627	32.54	-	12	30	12	11	0	-	-	-
Yachad, M.	1	1	-	31	31	31.00	-	-	1	-	-	-	-	-	-

				BATTING AND FIELDING						BOWLING					
	M	I	NO	HS	Runs	Avge	100	50	Ct/St	Balls	Runs	Wkts	Avge	Best	4w
Adams, J.C.	60	46	17	81*	878	30.27	-	7	39/5	432	346	12	28.83	3-50	-
Ambrose, C.E.L.	133	70	29	26*	449	10.95	-	-	33	7105	4129	184	22.44	5-17	9
Anthony, H.A.G.	3	3	-	21	23	7.66	-	-	-	156	143	3	47.66	2-47	-
Arthurton, K.L.T.	86	76	15	84	1652	27.08	-	9	21	797	666	22	30.27	3-31	-
Austin, R.A.	1	1	-	8	8	8.00	-	-	-	6	13	0	-	-	-
Bacchus, S.F.A.F.	29	26	3	80*	612	26.60	-	3	10						
Baptiste, E.A.E.	43	16	4	31	184	15.33	-	-	14	2214	1511	36	41.97	2-10	-
Benjamin, K.C.G.	23	11	7	17	54	13.50	-	-	4	1153	800	31	25.80	3-34	1
Benjamin, W.K.M.	85	52	12	31	298	7.45	-	-	16	4442	3079	100	30.79	5-22	1
Best, C.A.	24	23	4	100	473	24.89	1	2	5	19	12	0	-	-	-
Bishop, I.R.	75	40	16	33*	339	14.12	-	-	12	3919	2777	110	25.24	5-25	8
Boyce, K.D.	8	4	-	34	57	14.25	-	-	-	470	313	13	24.07	4-50	1
Browne, B.St A	4	3	2	8*	8	8.00	-	-	-	180	156	2	78.00	2-50	-
Browne, C.O.	20	16	3	26	155	11.92	-	-	27/5						
Campbell, S.L.	26	26	-	86	610	23.46	-	2	9						
Chanderpaul, S.	30	28	1	80	749	27.74	-	6	7	300	277	3	92.33	1-18	-
Clarke, S.T.	10	8	2	20	60	10.00	-	-	4	524	245	13	18.84	3-22	1
Croft, C.E.H.	19	6	4	8	18	9.00	-	-	1	1070	620	30	20.66	6-15	1
Cuffy, C.E.	10	6	3	17*	21	7.00	-	-	3	493	319	7	45.57	2-19	-
Cummins, A.C.	63	41	11	44*	459	15.30	-	1	11	3143	2246	78	28.79	5-31	3
Daniel, W.W.	18	5	4	16*	49	49.00	-	-	5	912	595	23	25.86	3-27	1
Davis, W.W.	35	5	3	10	28	14.00	-	-	1	1923	1302	39	33.38	7-51	1
Dhanraj, R.	6	2	1	8	8	8.00	-	-	1	264	170	10	17.00	4-26	1
Drakes, V.C.	5	2	-	16	25	12.50	-	-	1	239	204	3	68.00	1-36	-
Dujon, P.J.L.	169	120	36	82*	1945	23.15	-	6	183/21						
Foster, M.L.C.	2	1	-	25	25	25.00	-	-	1	30	22	2	11.00	2-22	-
Fredericks, R.C.	12	12	-	105	311	25.91	1	1	4	10	10	2	5.00	2-10	-
Gabriel, R.S.	11	11	-	41	167	15.18	-	-	1						
Garner, J.	98	41	15	37	239	9.19	-	-	30	5330	2752	146	18.84	5-31	5
Gibbs, L.R.	3	1	1	0*	0	-	-	-	-	156	59	2	29.50	1-12	-
Gibson, O.D.	13	10	1	52	138	15.33	-	1	3	631	512	29	17.65	5-40	3
Gomes, H.A.	83	64	15	101	1415	28.87	1	6	14	1345	1045	41	25.48	4-31	2
Gray, A.H.	25	11	5	10*	51	8.50	-	-	3	1270	835	44	18.97	6-50	3
Greenidge, A.E.	1	1	-	23	23	23.00	-	-	-						
Greenidge, C.G.	128	127	13	133*	5134	45.03	11	31	45	60	45	1	45.00	1-21	-
Harper, R.A.	105	73	20	45*	855	16.13	-	-	55	5175	3431	100	34.31	4-40	3
Haynes, D.L.	238	237	28	152*	8648	41.37	17	57	59	30	24	0	-	-	-
Haynes, R.C.	8	6	1	18	26	5.20	-	-	5	270	224	5	44.80	2-36	-
Headley, R.G.A.	1	1	-	19	19	19.00	-	-	-						
Holder, R.I.C.	26	22	5	65	479	28.17	-	2	7						

WEST INDIES (continued)

				BATTING AND FIELDING						BOWLING					
	M	I	NO	HS	Runs	Avge	100	50	Ct/St	Balls	Runs	Wkts	Avge	Best	4w
Holder, V.A.	12	6	1	30	64	12.80	-	-	6	681	454	19	23.89	5-50	1
Holding, M.A.	102	42	11	64	282	9.09	-	2	30	5473	3034	142	21.36	5-26	6
Hooper, C.L.	141	126	29	113*	3270	33.71	2	19	69	5626	4107	129	31.83	4-34	1
Jacobs, R.D.	4	3	-	10	13	4.33	-	-	1/1						
Julien, B.D.	12	8	2	26*	86	14.33	-	-	4	778	463	18	25.72	4-20	2
Kallicharran, A.I.	31	28	4	78	826	34.41	-	6	8	105	64	3	21.33	2-10	-
Kanhai, R.B.	7	5	2	55	164	54.66	-	2	4						
King, C.L.	18	14	2	86	280	23.33	-	1	6	744	529	11	48.09	4-23	1
Lambert, C.B.	5	5	-	66	132	26.40	-	1	-						
Lara, B.C.	104	103	9	169	4332	46.08	9	29	52	24	22	2	11.00	2-5	-
Lloyd, C.H.	87	69	19	102	1977	39.54	1	11	39	358	210	8	26.25	2-4	-
Logie, A.L.	158	133	36	109*	2809	28.95	1	14	61	24	18	0	-	-	-
Marshall, M.D.	136	83	19	66	955	14.92	-	2	15	7175	4233	157	26.96	4-18	6
Mattis, E.H.	2	2	-	62	86	43.00	-	1	2						
Moseley, E.A.	9	6	2	2*	7	1.75	-	-	-	330	278	7	39.71	2-52	-
Murray, D.A.	10	7	2	35	45	9.00	-	-	16						
Murray, D.L.	26	17	5	61*	294	24.50	-	2	37/1						
Murray, J.R.	38	19	6	86	213	16.38	-	1	35/5						
Parry, D.R.	6	5	1	32	61	15.25	-	-	8	330	259	11	23.54	3-47	-
Patterson, B.P.	59	20	15	13*	44	8.80	-	-	9	3050	2206	90	24.51	6-29	2
Payne, T.R.O.	7	4	-	60	126	31.50	-	1	6						
Phillip, N.	1	1	-	0	0	0.00	-	-	-	42	22	1	22.00	1-22	-
Pydanna, M.R.	3	1	1	2*	2	-	-	-	2/1						
Richards, I.V.A.	187	167	24	189*	6721	47.00	11	45	101	5644	4228	118	35.83	6-41	3
Richardson, R.B.	224	217	30	122	6248	33.41	5	44	74	58	46	1	46.00	1- 4	-
Roberts, A.M.E.	56	32	9	37*	231	10.04	-	1	6	3123	1771	87	20.35	5-22	3
Rowe, L.G.	11	8	-	60	136	17.00	-	1	2						
Shillingford, I.T.	2	2	-	24	30	15.00	-	-	2						
Shivnarine, S.	1	1	1	20*	20	-	-	-	-	18	16	0	-	-	-
Simmons, P.V.	117	115	7	122	3242	30.01	5	17	50	2950	2121	61	34.77	4- 3	2
Small, M.A.	2	-	-	-	-	-	-	-	1	84	54	1	54.00	1-40	-
Sobers, G.St A.	1	1	-	0	0	0.00	-	-	1	63	31	1	31.00	1-31	-
Wallace, P.A.	12	12	-	52	217	18.08	-	1	3						
Walsh, C.A.	162	60	25	30	278	7.94	-	-	24	8554	5484	182	30.13	5- 1	6
Williams, D.	29	17	6	32*	119	10.81	-	-	33/8						
Williams, L.R.	4	2	1	5	6	3.00	-	-	2	107	85	5	17.00	3-16	-
Williams, S.C.	28	28	2	73*	738	28.38	-	5	5						

NEW ZEALAND (97 players)

	BATTING AND FIELDING									BOWLING					
	M	I	NO	HS	Runs	Avge	100	50	Ct/St	Balls	Runs	Wkts	Avge	Best	4w
Anderson, R.W.	2	2	1	12	16	16.00	–	–	1	862	681	14	48.64	3-42	–
Astle, N.J.	28	28	1	120	803	29.74	3	2	9						
Blain, T.E.	38	38	11	49*	442	16.37	–	–	37/1	30	34	1	34.00	1- 7	–
Blair, B.R.	14	14	2	29*	174	14.50	–	–	4	700	513	15	34.20	3-28	–
Boock, S.L.	14	7	4	12	30	10.00	–	–	5	66	41	1	41.00	1-41	–
Bracewell, B.P.	1	1	1	0*	0	–	–	–							
Bracewell, J.G.	53	43	12	43	512	16.51	–	–	19	2247	1884	33	57.09	2- 3	–
Bradburn, G.E.	7	7	1	30	57	9.50	–	–	1	234	195	4	48.75	2-18	–
Brown, V.R.	3	3	–	32	44	14.66	–	–	2	66	75	1	75.00	1-24	–
Burgess, M.G.	26	20	–	47	336	16.80	–	–	8	74	69	1	69.00	1-10	–
Cairns, B.L.	78	65	6	60	987	16.72	–	2	19	4015	2717	89	30.52	5-28	3
Cairns, C.L.	49	45	4	103	1099	26.80	1	4	20	1989	1559	45	34.64	4-55	1
Chatfield, E.J.	114	48	37	19*	118	10.72	–	–	19	6065	3618	140	25.84	5-34	4
Collinge, R.O.	15	9	3	9	34	5.66	–	–	1	859	479	18	26.61	5-23	1
Coman, P.G.	3	3	–	38	62	20.66	–	–	2						
Coney, J.V.	88	80	19	66*	1874	30.72	1	8	40	2931	2039	54	37.75	4-46	1
Congdon, B.E.	11	9	3	101	338	56.33	1	2	–	437	287	7	41.00	2-17	–
Crowe, J.J.	75	71	12	88*	1518	25.72	–	7	28	6	1	0	–	–	–
Crowe, M.D.	143	141	19	107*	4704	38.55	4	34	66	1296	954	29	32.89	2- 9	–
Davis, H.T.	2	–	–	–	–	–	–	–	1	36	51	0	–	–	–
De Groen, R.P.	12	8	3	7*	12	2.40	–	–	2	549	478	8	59.75	2-34	–
Douglas, M.W.	6	6	–	30	55	9.16	–	–	2						
Doull, S.B.	9	8	4	19*	63	15.75	–	–	–	448	447	9	49.66	3-42	–
Edgar, B.A.	64	64	4	102*	1814	30.74	1	10	12						
Edwards, G.N.	6	6	–	41	138	23.00	–	–	5	12	5	0	–	–	–
Fleming, S.P.	48	47	4	106*	1379	32.06	1	10	19	6	5	1	5.00	1- 5	–
Franklin, T.J.	3	3	–	21	27	9.00	–	–	–	29	28	1	28.00	1- 8	–
Germon, L.K.	24	19	4	89	376	25.06	–	2	8/2						
Gillespie, S.R.	19	11	5	18*	70	11.66	–	–	7	963	736	23	32.00	4-30	1
Gray, E.J.	10	7	1	38	98	16.33	–	–	3	386	286	8	35.75	2-26	–
Greatbatch, M.J.	78	78	5	111	2086	28.57	2	12	32	6	5	0	–	–	–
Hadlee, B.G.	2	2	1	19	26	26.00	–	–	–						
Hadlee, D.R.	11	7	2	20	40	8.00	–	–	2	628	364	20	18.20	4-34	4
Hadlee, R.J.	115	98	17	79	1751	21.61	–	4	27	6182	3407	158	21.56	5-25	6
Harris, C.Z.	67	59	15	130	1094	24.86	1	3	18	2918	2220	64	34.68	3-15	–
Hart, M.N.	10	6	–	16	49	8.16	–	–	7	488	314	11	28.54	5-22	1
Hart, R.T.	1	1	–	3	3	3.00	–	–	–						
Hartland, B.R.	16	16	1	68*	311	20.73	–	2	5						
Haslam, M.J.	1	1	–	9	9	9.00	–	–	–	30	28	1	28.00	1-28	–
Hastings, B.F.	11	9	1	37	151	18.87	–	–	4						

NEW ZEALAND (continued)

	BATTING AND FIELDING									BOWLING					
	M	I	NO	HS	Runs	Avge	100	50	Ct/St	Balls	Runs	Wkts	Avge	Best	4w
Hayes, R.L.	1	1	-	13	13	13.00	-	-	-	42	31	0	-	-	-
Horne, P.A.	4	4	1	18	50	12.50	-	-	-	90	68	3	22.66	1-4	-
Howarth, G.P.	70	65	5	76	1384	23.06	-	6	16	492	280	11	25.45	3-29	-
Howarth, H.J.	9	5	2	11	18	6.00	-	-	3	306	216	4	54.00	2-42	-
Jones, A.H.	87	87	9	93	2784	35.69	-	25	23	240	212	4	53.00	2-36	-
Kennedy, R.J.	5	2	1	8*	10	10.00	-	-	1						
Kuggeleijn, C.M.	16	11	2	40	142	15.77	-	-	9	817	604	12	50.33	2-31	-
Larsen, G.R.	83	48	20	37	455	16.25	-	1	13	4480	2772	73	37.97	4-24	1
Latham, R.T.	33	33	4	60	583	20.10	-	1	11	450	386	11	35.09	5-32	1
Lees, W.K.	31	24	5	26	215	11.31	-	-	28/2						
McEwan, P.E.	17	15	-	41	204	13.60	-	-	1	420	353	6	58.83	2-29	-
McKechnie, B.J.	14	8	4	27	54	13.50	-	-	2	818	495	19	26.05	3-23	-
McSweeney, E.B.	16	14	5	18*	73	8.11	-	-	14/3						
Millmow, J.P.	5	1	1	0*	0	-	-	-	1	270	232	4	58.00	2-22	-
Morrison, D.K.	92	41	23	20*	170	9.44	-	-	18	4382	3318	117	28.34	5-46	2
Morrison, J.F.M.	18	15	3	55	252	21.00	-	1	6	283	199	8	24.87	3-24	-
Murray, D.J.	1	1	-	3	3	3.00	-	-	-						
Nash, D.J.	28	18	5	40*	128	9.84	-	-	6	1284	1024	26	39.38	3-27	-
O'Sullivan, D.R.	3	2	1	1*	2	2.00	-	-	-	168	123	2	61.50	1-38	-
Owens, M.B.	1	1	-	0	0	0.00	-	-	-	48	37	0	-	-	-
Parker, J.M.	24	20	-	66	248	12.40	-	1	11/1	16	10	1	10.00	1-10	-
Parker, N.M.	1	1	-	0	0	0.00	-	-	1						
Parore, A.C.	54	50	9	108	1426	34.78	1	8	32/8						
Patel, D.N.	63	51	8	71	550	12.79	-	1	20	2711	1875	39	48.07	3-22	-
Petrie, R.G.	12	8	3	21	65	13.00	-	-	2	660	449	12	37.41	2-25	-
Pollard, V.	3	2	-	55	67	33.50	-	1	1						
Priest, M.W.	12	10	2	24	95	11.87	-	-	2	507	419	4	104.75	2-27	-
Pringle, C.	64	41	19	34*	193	8.77	-	-	7	3314	2459	103	23.87	5-45	3
Redmond, R.E.	2	1	-	3	3	3.00	-	-	-	7	13	1	13.00	1-13	-
Reid, J.F.	25	24	1	88	633	27.52	-	4	5	56	30	1	30.00	1-30	-
Reid, R.B.	9	9	1	64	248	27.55	-	2	3	42	47	0	-	-	-
Roberts, A.D.G.	1	1	-	16	16	16.00	-	-	1						
Roberts, S.J.	2	1	1	1*	1	-	-	-	-						
Robertson, G.K.	10	6	1	17	49	8.16	-	-	2	498	321	6	53.50	2-29	-
Rutherford, K.R.	121	115	9	108	3143	29.65	2	18	41	389	323	10	32.30	2-39	-
Smith, I.D.S.	98	77	16	62*	1055	17.29	-	3	81/5						
Snedden, M.C.	93	54	19	64	535	15.28	-	1	19	4525	3237	114	28.39	4-34	1
Spearman, C.M.	18	18	-	78	436	24.22	-	2	5	234	207	6	34.50	2-29	-
Stirling, D.A.	6	5	2	13*	21	7.00	-	-	3	72	48	3	16.00	3-48	-
Stott, L.W.	1	-	-	-	-	-	-	-	1						

NEW ZEALAND (continued)

			BATTING AND FIELDING							BOWLING					
	M	I	NO	HS	Runs	Avge	100	50	Ct/St	Balls	Runs	Wkts	Avge	Best	4w
Su'a, M.L.	12	7	2	12*	24	4.80	–	–	1	463	367	9	40.77	4-59	1
Taylor, B.R.	2	1	–	22	22	22.00	–	–	1	114	62	4	15.50	3-25	–
Thomson, S.A.	56	52	10	83	964	22.95	–	5	18	2121	1602	42	38.14	3-14	–
Troup, G.B.	22	12	8	39	101	25.25	–	–	2	1180	791	32	24.71	4-19	3
Turner, G.M.	41	40	6	171*	1598	47.00	3	9	13	6	0	0	–	–	–
Twose, R.G.	21	20	–	92	612	30.60	–	4	5	272	237	4	59.25	2-31	–
Vance, R.H.	8	8	–	96	248	31.00	–	1	4						
Vaughan, J.T.C.	15	14	6	33	148	18.50	–	–	3	534	377	12	31.41	4-33	1
Vivian, G.E.	1	1	–	14	14	14.00	–	–	–						
Wadsworth, K.J.	13	10	1	104	258	28.66	1	–	13/2						
Watson, W.	61	24	13	21	86	7.81	–	–	9	3251	2247	74	30.36	4-27	1
Webb, P.N.	5	5	1	10*	38	9.50	–	–	3						
Webb, R.J.	3	1	1	6*	6	–	–	–	–	161	105	4	26.25	2-28	–
White, D.J.	3	3	–	15	37	12.33	–	–	1						
Wilson, J.W.	4	4	1	44*	80	26.66	–	–	1	152	135	3	45.00	2-21	–
Wright, J.G.	149	148	1	101	3891	26.46	1	24	51	24	8	0	–	–	–
Young, B.A.	47	46	4	74	997	23.73	–	3	20						

INDIA (98 players)

			BATTING AND FIELDING							BOWLING					
	M	I	NO	HS	Runs	Avge	100	50	Ct/St	Balls	Runs	Wkts	Avge	Best	4w
Abid Ali, S.	5	3	–	70	93	31.00	–	1	1	336	187	7	26.71	2-22	–
Amarnath, M.	85	75	12	102*	1924	30.53	2	13	23	2730	1971	46	42.84	3-12	–
Amarnath, S.	3	3	–	62	100	33.33	–	1	1						
Amre, P.K.	37	30	5	84*	513	20.52	–	2	12						
Ankola, S.A.	15	8	4	7*	14	3.50	–	–	1	567	414	11	37.63	3-33	–
Arshad Ayub	32	17	7	31*	116	11.60	–	–	5	1769	1216	31	39.22	5-21	1
Arun, B.	4	3	1	8	21	10.50	–	–	–	102	103	1	103.00	1-43	–
Arun Lal	13	13	–	51	122	9.38	–	1	4						
Azad, K.	25	21	2	39*	269	14.15	–	–	7	390	273	7	39.00	2-48	–
Azharuddin, M.	224	208	41	108*	6091	36.47	3	34	94	552	479	12	39.91	3-19	–
Banerjee, S.T.	6	5	3	25*	49	24.50	–	–	3	240	202	5	40.40	3-30	–
Bedade, A.C.	12	10	3	51	158	22.57	–	1	4						
Bedi, B.S.	10	7	2	13	31	6.20	–	–	4	590	340	7	48.57	2-44	–
Bhupinder Singh	2	1	–	6	6	6.00	–	–	–	102	78	3	26.00	3-34	–
Binny, R.M.H.	72	49	10	57	629	16.12	–	1	12	2957	2260	77	29.35	4-29	3
Bose, G.	1	1	–	13	13	13.00	–	–	–	66	39	1	39.00	1-39	–
Chandrasekhar, B.S.	1	1	1	11*	11	–	–	–	–	56	36	3	12.00	3-36	–
Chandrasekhar, V.B.	7	7	–	53	88	12.57	–	1	1						
Chatterjee, U.	3	2	1	3*	6	6.00	–	–	1	161	117	3	39.00	2-35	–

INDIA (continued)

	BATTING AND FIELDING									BOWLING					
	M	I	NO	HS	Runs	Avge	100	50	Ct/St	Balls	Runs	Wkts	Avge	Best	4w
Chauhan, C.P.S.	7	7	–	46	153	21.85	–	–	3	1008	714	21	34.00	3-29	–
Chauhan, R.K.	20	8	3	26*	73	14.60	–	–	5	792	524	22	23.81	4-30	2
Doshi, D.R.	15	5	2	5*	9	3.00	–	–	3						
Dravid, R.	13	12	2	90	283	28.30	–	1	12						
Engineer, F.M.	5	4	1	54*	114	38.00	–	1	3/1						
Gaekwad, A.D.	15	14	1	78*	269	20.69	–	1	6	48	39	1	39.00	1-39	–
Ganguly, S.C.	8	7	1	59	183	30.50	–	1	1	42	48	0	–	–	–
Gavaskar, S.M.	108	102	14	103*	3092	35.13	1	27	22	20	25	1	25.00	1-10	–
Ghai, R.S.	6	1	–	1	1	1.00	–	–	–	275	260	3	86.66	1-38	–
Ghavri, K.D.	19	16	6	20	114	11.40	–	–	2	1033	708	15	47.20	3-40	–
Gursharan Singh	1	1	–	4	4	4.00	–	–	1						
Hirwani, N.D.	18	7	3	4	8	2.00	–	–	2	960	719	23	31.26	4-43	3
Jadeja, A.	67	61	7	104	1759	32.57	1	10	16	974	852	11	77.45	2-16	–
Joshi, S.B.	7	4	–	48	82	20.50	–	–	4	377	247	7	35.28	2-23	–
Kambli, V.G.	75	70	18	106	2003	38.51	2	11	12	4	7	1	7.00	1-7	–
Kapil Dev	224	198	39	175*	3783	23.79	1	14	71	11202	6945	253	27.45	5-43	4
Kapoor, A.R.	14	5	–	19	43	8.60	–	–	1	756	515	8	64.37	2-33	–
Khanna, S.C.	10	10	2	56	176	22.00	–	2	4/4						
Kirmani, S.M.H.	49	31	13	48*	373	20.72	–	2	27/9						
Krishnamurthy, P.	1	1	–	6	6	6.00	–	–	1/1						
Kulkarni, R.R.	10	5	3	15	33	16.50	–	–	2	444	345	10	34.50	3-42	–
Kumble, A.	96	45	15	24	280	9.33	–	–	34	5288	3544	133	26.64	6-12	6
Lamba, R.	32	31	2	102	782	26.96	1	6	10	19	20	1	20.00	1-9	–
Madan Lal	67	35	14	53*	401	19.09	–	1	18	3164	2137	73	29.27	4-20	2
Malhotra, A.	20	19	4	65	457	30.46	–	1	4	6	0	0	–	–	–
Maninder Singh	59	18	14	8*	49	12.25	–	–	18	3133	2067	66	31.31	4-22	1
Manjrekar, S.V.	73	69	10	105	1987	33.67	1	15	23	8	10	1	10.00	1-2	–
Mankad, A.V.	1	1	–	44	44	44.00	–	–	–	35	47	1	47.00	1-47	–
Mhambrey, P.L.	2	1	1	7*	7	–	–	–	2	90	98	2	49.00	2-69	–
Mongia, N.R.	59	37	12	69	515	20.60	–	1	56/20						
More, K.S.	94	65	22	42*	563	13.09	–	1	63/27						
Mukherjee, S.P.	3	1	1	2*	2	–	–	–	1	174	98	2	49.00	1-30	–
Naik, S.S.	2	2	–	20	38	19.00	–	–	1						
Nayak, S.V.	4	1	–	3	3	3.00	–	–	–	222	161	1	161.00	1-51	–
Pandit, C.S.	36	23	9	33*	290	20.71	–	1	15/15						
Parkar, G.A.	10	10	1	42	165	18.33	–	1	4						
Patel, A.K.	8	2	1	6	6	3.00	–	–	1	360	263	7	37.57	3-43	–
Patel, B.P.	10	9	1	82	243	30.37	–	1	1						
Patel, R.	1	1	–	–	–	–	–	–	–	60	58	0	–	–	–
Patil, S.M.	45	42	1	84	1005	24.51	–	9	11	864	589	15	39.26	2-28	–

INDIA (continued)

	BATTING AND FIELDING									BOWLING					
	M	I	NO	HS	Runs	Avge	100	50	Ct/St	Balls	Runs	Wkts	Avge	Best	4w
Prabhakar, M.	129	97	20	106	1855	24.09	2	11	27	6360	4534	157	28.88	5-33	6
Prasad, B.K.V.	44	17	9	19	49	6.12	–	–	16	2202	1744	49	35.59	3-22	–
Rajput, L.S.	4	4	1	8	9	3.00	–	–	2	42	42	0	–	–	–
Raju, S.L.V.	53	16	8	8	32	4.00	–	–	8	2770	2014	63	31.96	4-46	2
Raman, W.V.	26	26	1	114	588	23.52	1	3	1	126	145	2	72.50	1-23	–
Randhir Singh	2	–	–	–	–	–	–	–	–	72	48	1	48.00	1-30	–
Rathore, V.	6	6	–	54	159	26.50	–	2	4						
Razdan, V.	3	3	1	18	23	11.50	–	–	4	84	77	1	77.00	1-37	–
Reddy, B.	3	2	2	8*	11	–	–	–	2						
Sandhu, B.S.	22	7	3	16*	51	12.75	–	–	5	1110	763	16	47.68	3-27	1
Sekhar, T.A.P.	4	–	–	–	–	–	–	–	–	156	128	5	25.60	3-23	3
Sharma, A.K.	31	27	6	59*	424	20.19	–	3	6	1140	875	15	58.33	3-41	–
Sharma, C.	65	35	16	101*	456	24.00	1	–	7	2835	2336	67	34.86	3-22	2
Sharma, G.	11	2	–	7	11	5.50	–	–	2	486	361	10	36.10	3-29	4
Sharma, P.	2	2	–	14	20	10.00	–	–	–						
Sharma, S.K.	23	12	4	28	80	10.00	–	–	7	979	813	22	36.95	5-26	1
Shastri, R.J.	150	128	21	109	3108	29.04	4	18	40	6613	4650	129	36.04	5-15	3
Sidhu, N.S.	106	103	8	134*	3936	41.43	6	31	15	4	3	0	–	–	–
Singh, R.P.	2	–	–	–	–	–	–	–	–	82	77	1	77.00	1-58	–
Singh, R.R.	2	2	1	10*	13	13.00	–	–	–	8	7	0	–	–	–
Sivaramakrishnan, L.	16	4	2	2*	5	2.50	–	–	7	756	538	15	35.86	3-35	–
Solkar, E.D.	7	6	–	13	27	4.50	–	–	2	252	169	4	42.25	2-31	–
Srikkanth, K.	146	145	4	123	4092	29.02	4	27	42	712	641	25	25.64	5-27	2
Srinath, J.	107	51	17	37	328	9.64	–	–	17	5558	3991	148	26.96	5-24	4
Srinivasan, T.E.	2	2	–	6	10	5.00	–	–	–						
Sudhakar Rao, R.	1	1	–	4	4	4.00	–	–	1						
Tendulkar, S.R.	126	123	12	137	4378	39.44	9	27	40	2979	2371	42	56.45	4-34	1
Vaidya, P.S.	4	2	–	12	15	7.50	–	–	2	184	174	4	43.50	2-41	–
Vengsarkar, D.B.	129	120	19	105	3508	34.73	1	23	37	6	4	0	–	–	–
Venkataraghavan, S.	15	9	4	26*	54	10.80	–	–	4	868	542	5	108.40	2-34	–
Venkataramana, M.	1	1	1	0*	0	–	–	–	–	60	36	2	18.00	2-36	–
Viswanath, G.R.	25	23	1	75	439	19.95	–	2	3						
Viswanath, S.	22	12	4	23*	72	9.00	–	–	17/7						
Wadekar, A.L.	2	2	–	67	73	36.50	–	1	1						
Wassan, A.S.	9	6	2	16	33	8.25	–	–	2	426	283	11	25.72	3-28	–
Yadav, N.S.	7	2	2	1*	1	–	–	–	–	330	228	8	28.50	2-18	–
Yadav, V.	19	12	2	34*	118	11.80	–	–	12/7						
Yashpal Sharma	42	40	9	89	883	28.48	–	4	10	201	199	1	199.00	1-27	–
Yograj Singh	6	4	2	1	1	0.50	–	–	2	244	186	4	46.50	2-44	–

PAKISTAN (108 players)

			BATTING AND FIELDING						BOWLING					
	M	I	NO	HS	Runs	Avge	100	50	Ct/St	Balls	Runs	Wkts	Avge	Best	4w
Aamer Hameed	2	-	-	-	-	-	-	-	1	88	38	1	38.00	1-32	-
Aamer Hanif	5	4	2	36*	89	44.50	-	-	-	130	122	4	30.50	3-36	-
Aamer Malik	24	23	1	90	556	25.27	-	5	13/3	120	86	3	28.66	2-35	-
Aamir Nazir	9	3	2	9*	13	13.00	-	-	-	417	346	11	31.45	3-43	-
Aamir Sohail	106	105	2	134	3491	33.89	5	21	32	3769	2809	67	41.92	4-22	1
Abdul Qadir	104	68	26	41*	641	15.26	-	-	21	5100	3453	132	26.15	5-44	6
Akram Raza	49	25	14	33*	193	17.54	-	-	19	2601	1611	38	42.39	3-18	-
Anil Dalpat	15	10	3	37	87	12.42	-	-	13/2						
Aqib Javed	133	42	24	45*	237	13.16	-	-	19	6673	4637	146	31.76	7-37	3
Arshad Khan	5	4	3	9*	15	15.00	-	-	3	233	159	2	79.50	1-29	-
Arshad Pervez	2	2	-	8	11	5.50	-	-	-						
Ashfaq Ahmed	3	-	-	-	-	-	-	-	-	102	84	0	-	-	-
Ashraf Ali	16	9	5	19*	69	17.25	-	-	17/3						
Asif Iqbal	10	8	2	62	330	55.00	-	5	7	592	378	16	23.62	4-56	1
Asif Masood	7	3	1	6	10	5.00	-	-	1	402	234	5	46.80	2-9	-
Asif Mujtaba	66	55	14	113*	1068	26.04	1	6	18	756	658	7	94.00	2-38	-
Ata-ur-Rehman	30	13	6	11*	34	4.85	-	-	-	1492	1186	27	43.92	3-27	1
Azeem Hafeez	15	10	7	15	45	15.00	-	-	3	719	586	15	39.06	4-22	1
Azhar Mahmood	3	3	1	10	17	5.66	-	-	1	108	85	2	42.50	2-38	-
Azmat Rana	2	2	-	22*	42	42.00	-	-	-						
Basit Ali	49	43	6	127*	1265	34.18	1	9	15	30	21	1	21.00	1-17	-
Ghulam Ali	3	3	-	38	53	17.66	-	-	-						
Haafiz Shahid	3	3	2	7*	11	11.00	-	-	-	127	112	3	37.33	2-56	-
Haroon Rashid	12	10	2	63*	166	20.75	-	1	3						
Hasan Jamil	6	5	-	28	111	22.20	-	-	1	232	154	8	19.25	3-18	-
Ijaz Ahmed	141	126	19	124*	3108	29.04	4	16	47	402	293	3	97.66	2-31	-
Ijaz Faqih	27	19	3	42*	197	12.31	-	-	2	1116	819	13	63.00	4-43	1
Imran Khan	175	151	40	102*	3709	33.41	1	19	37	7461	4845	182	26.62	6-14	4
Intikhab Alam	4	2	-	10	17	8.50	-	-	-	158	118	4	29.50	2-36	-
Inzamam-ul-Haq	115	110	16	137*	3725	39.62	4	26	30	40	52	2	26.00	1-4	-
Iqbal Qasim	15	7	1	13	39	6.50	-	-	3	664	500	12	41.66	3-13	-
Iqbal Sikander	4	1	1	1*	1	-	-	-	-	210	147	3	49.00	1-30	-
Irfan Bhatti	1	-	-	-	-	-	-	-	-	48	22	2	11.00	2-22	-
Jalaluddin	8	2	-	5	5	2.50	-	-	1	306	211	14	15.07	4-32	1
Javed Miandad	233	218	41	119*	7381	41.70	8	50	71/2	436	297	7	42.42	2-22	-
Javed Qadir	1	1	-	12	12	12.00	-	-	1						
Kabir Khan	2	-	-	-	-	-	-	-	-	116	66	3	22.00	2-32	-
Liaqat Ali	3	1	-	7	7	7.00	-	-	-	188	111	2	55.50	1-41	-
Mahmood Hamid	1	1	-	7	1	1.00	-	-	-						
Majid Khan	23	22	1	109	786	37.42	1	7	3	658	374	13	28.76	3-27	-

PAKISTAN (continued)

				BATTING AND FIELDING						BOWLING					
	M	I	NO	HS	Runs	Avge	100	50	Ct/St	Balls	Runs	Wkts	Avge	Best	4w
Mansoor Akhtar	41	35	1	47	593	17.44	-	-	14	138	110	2	55.00	1- 7	-
Mansoor Rana	2	2	-	10	15	7.50	-	-	-	6	7	0	-	-	-
Manzoor Elahi	54	46	13	50*	741	22.45	-	1	21	1743	1262	29	43.51	3-22	-
Maqsood Rana	1	1	-	5	5	5.00	-	-	-	12	11	0	-	-	-
Masood Iqbal	1	1	-	2	2	2.00	-	-	-						
Mohammad Akram	7	5	3	7*	11	5.50	-	-	2	342	307	9	34.11	2-36	-
Mohammad Nazir	4	3	3	2*	4	-	-	-	-	222	156	3	52.00	2-37	-
Mohsin Kamal	19	6	3	11*	27	9.00	-	-	4	881	760	21	36.19	4-47	1
Mohsin Khan	75	75	5	117*	1877	26.81	2	8	13	12	5	1	5.00	1- 2	-
Moin Khan	47	33	7	42	393	15.11	-	-	49/17						
Moin-ul-Atiq	5	5	-	105	199	39.80	1	-	-						
Mudassar Nazar	122	115	10	95	2653	25.26	-	16	21	4855	3432	111	30.91	5-28	2
Mushtaq Ahmed	106	53	20	26	287	8.69	-	-	23	5429	3981	124	32.10	5-36	2
Mushtaq Mohammed	10	9	3	55	209	34.83	-	1	3	42	23	0	-	-	-
Nadeem Ghauri	6	3	2	7*	14	14.00	-	-	-	342	230	5	46.00	2-51	-
Nadeem Khan	2	1	-	2	2	2.00	-	-	-	96	81	0	-	-	-
Naeem Ahmed	1	1	1	0*	0	-	-	-	1	60	43	0	-	-	-
Naeem Ashraf	2	2	1	16	24	24.00	-	-	-	42	52	0	-	-	-
Naseer Malik	3	1	1	0*	0	-	-	-	1	180	98	5	19.60	2-37	-
Nasim-ul-Ghani	1	1	-	1	1	1.00	-	-	-						
Naved Anjum	13	12	3	30	113	12.55	-	-	2	472	344	8	43.00	2-27	-
Parvez Mir	3	3	1	18	26	13.00	-	-	3	122	77	3	25.66	1-17	-
Qasim Omar	31	31	3	69	642	22.92	-	4	3						
Ramiz Raja	177	176	14	119*	5386	33.24	9	29	27	6	10	0	-	-	-
Rashid Khan	29	15	7	17	110	13.75	-	-	3	1414	923	20	46.15	3-47	-
Rashid Latif	84	57	16	50	664	16.19	-	1	81/22						
Rizwan-uz-Zaman	3	3	-	14	20	6.66	-	-	2						
Saadat Ali	8	7	1	78*	184	30.66	-	1	1						
Sadiq Mohammed	19	19	1	74	383	21.27	-	2	5	27	29	2	14.50	2-24	-
Saeed Anwar	103	102	8	131	3435	36.54	8	14	24	38	26	2	13.00	2-20	-
Saeed Azad	1	1	-	19	19	19.00	-	-	-	150	130	3	43.33	1- 9	-
Sajid Ali	10	9	-	16	83	9.22	-	-	1						
Sajjad Akbar	2	1	-	5	5	5.00	-	-	1	60	45	2	22.50	2-45	-
Salim Altaf	6	2	1	21	25	25.00	-	-	-	285	151	5	30.20	2- 7	-
Salim Elahi	10	10	1	102*	316	35.11	1	2	4						
Salim Jaffer	39	13	11	10*	36	18.00	-	-	3	1900	1382	40	34.55	3-25	-
Salim Malik	234	211	33	102	6006	33.74	5	39	69	2513	2073	62	33.43	5-35	1
Salim Pervez	1	1	-	18	18	18.00	-	-	-						
Salim Yousuf	86	62	19	62	768	17.86	-	4	80/22						
Saqlain Mushtaq	20	13	3	30	109	10.90	-	-	8	1054	811	32	25.34	4-47	1

PAKISTAN (continued)

	BATTING AND FIELDING									BOWLING					
	M	I	NO	HS	Runs	Avge	100	50	Ct/St	Balls	Runs	Wkts	Avge	Best	4w
Sarfraz Nawaz	45	31	8	34*	221	9.60	–	–	8	2412	1463	63	23.22	4-27	4
Shadab Kabir	3	3	–	0	0	0.00	–	–	1						
Shafiq Ahmed	3	3	–	29	41	13.66	–	–	1						
Shahid Anwar	1	1	–	37	37	37.00	–	–	–						
Shahid Mahboob	10	6	1	77	119	23.80	–	1	1	540	382	7	54.57	1-23	–
Shahid Nazir	1	–	–	–	–	–	–	–	–	60	47	2	23.50	2-47	–
Shahid Saeed	10	10	–	50	141	14.10	–	1	2	222	159	3	53.00	2-20	–
Shakil Ahmed	2	2	–	36	61	30.50	–	–	–						
Shakil Khan	1	1	–	0	0	0.00	–	–	–						
Shoaib Mohammed	63	58	6	126*	1269	24.40	1	8	13	54	50	1	50.00	1-50	–
Sikander Bakht	27	11	7	16*	31	7.75	–	–	4	919	725	20	36.25	3-20	–
Sohail Fazal	2	2	–	32	56	28.00	–	–	–	1277	860	33	26.06	4-34	1
Tahir Naqqash	40	23	9	61	210	15.00	–	1	11	6	4	0	–	–	–
Tanvir Mehdi	1	1	–	0	0	0.00	–	–	–	1596	1240	34	36.47	3-23	–
Taslim Arif	2	2	–	24	28	14.00	–	–	1/1	66	72	1	72.00	1-72	–
Tausif Ahmed	70	25	14	27*	116	10.54	–	–	10	3250	2247	55	40.85	4-38	1
Waqar Younis	133	63	25	37	378	9.94	–	–	13	6618	4992	220	22.69	6-26	17
Wasim Akram	206	158	30	86	1894	14.79	–	2	44	10635	6707	297	22.58	5-15	16
Wasim Bari	51	26	13	34	221	17.00	–	–	52/10						
Wasim Haider	3	2	–	13	26	13.00	–	–	–	114	79	1	79.00	1-36	–
Wasim Raja	54	45	10	60	782	22.34	–	2	24	1036	687	21	32.71	4-25	1
Younis Ahmed	2	2	–	58	84	42.00	–	1	1						
Zafar Iqbal	8	6	–	18	48	8.00	–	–	–	198	137	3	45.66	2-37	–
Zaheer Abbas	62	60	6	123	2572	47.62	7	13	16	280	223	7	31.85	2-26	–
Zahid Ahmed	2	2	1	3*	3	3.00	–	–	–	96	61	3	20.33	2-24	–
Zahid Fazal	19	18	3	98*	348	23.20	–	2	2						
Zakir Khan	17	5	4	11*	27	27.00	–	–	–	646	494	16	30.87	4-19	1
Zulqarnain	16	6	3	11*	18	6.00	–	–	18/5						

SRI LANKA (87 players)

	BATTING AND FIELDING									BOWLING					
	M	I	NO	HS	Runs	Avge	100	50	Ct/St	Balls	Runs	Wkts	Avge	Best	4w
Ahangama, F.S.	1	–	–	–	–	–	–	–	–	18	23	0	–	–	–
Amalean, K.N.	8	3	1	9	15	7.50	–	–	–	318	207	9	23.00	4-46	1
Anurasiri, S.D.	45	18	12	11	62	10.33	–	–	10	2100	1464	32	45.75	3-40	–
Atapattu, M.S.	9	8	3	19*	53	10.60	–	–	2	3	4	0	–	–	–
Chandana, U.U.	10	6	1	26	78	15.60	–	–	8	294	234	8	29.25	4-35	1
Dassanayake, P.B.	15	10	2	20*	85	10.62	–	–	9/4						
De Alwis, R.G.	31	27	8	59*	401	21.10	–	2	27/3						
De Mel, A.L.F.	57	41	9	36	466	14.56	–	–	13	2735	2237	59	37.91	5-32	3

SRI LANKA (continued)

				BATTING AND FIELDING						BOWLING					
	M	I	NO	HS	Runs	Avge	100	50	Ct/St	Balls	Runs	Wkts	Avge	Best	4w
De Silva, A.M.	4	2	-	8	12	6.00	-	-	4/2	120	54	2	27.00	2-36	-
De Silva, D.L.S.	2	1	-	10	10	10.00	-	-	1	2076	1557	32	48.65	3-29	-
De Silva, D.S.	41	29	10	37*	371	19.52	-	-	5	1374	967	17	56.88	3-38	-
De Silva, E.A.R.	28	20	6	19*	138	9.85	-	-	6	194	169	0	-	-	-
De Silva, G.N.	4	2	1	7	9	9.00	-	-	-	305	262	9	29.11	3-41	-
De Silva, G.R.A.	6	4	2	6*	9	4.50	-	-	2						
De Silva, P.A.	188	184	20	145	5661	34.51	6	38	56	2642	2189	53	41.30	3-36	-
Dharmasena, H.D.P.K.	38	23	10	51	309	23.76	-	1	7	1914	1445	44	32.84	4-37	1
Dias, R.L.	58	55	5	121	1573	31.46	2	11	16	56	70	3	23.33	3-25	-
Dunusinghe, C.I.	3	1	-	1	1	1.00	-	-	1/1						
Fernando, E.R.	3	3	-	22	47	15.66	-	-	-						
Fernando, E.R.N.S.	7	5	1	36	101	20.20	-	-	-						
Fernando, T.L.	1	1	-	8	8	8.00	-	-	-						
Fernando, U.N.K.	2	2	2	20*	22	-	-	-	-	18	16	1	16.00	1-16	-
Gamage, J.C.	4	2	2	7*	8	-	-	-	2						
Goonasekera, Y.	3	3	-	35	69	23.00	-	-	-	132	104	3	34.66	2-17	-
Goonatilleke, F.R.M.de S.	1	-	-	-	-	-	-	-	-/4	36	35	1	35.00	1-24	-
Goonatilleke, H.M.	6	4	3	14*	31	31.00	-	-	-						
Gunawardene, A.A.W.	1	1	-	2	2	2.00	-	-	1	54	34	0	-	-	-
Gurusinha, A.P.	141	138	5	117*	3820	28.72	2	22	46	1585	1354	26	52.07	2-25	-
Hathurusinghe, U.C.	32	30	1	66	648	22.34	-	4	5	840	614	14	43.85	4-57	1
Heyn, P.D.	2	2	-	2	3	1.50	-	-	1						
Jayasekera, R.S.A.	2	1	-	17	17	17.00	-	-	-						
Jayasinghe, S.A.	2	1	-	1	1	1.00	-	-	1						
Jayasuriya, S.T.	112	106	3	140	2456	23.84	3	12	48	3759	3004	85	35.34	6-29	3
Jeganathan, S.	5	4	1	20*	25	8.33	-	-	1	276	208	5	41.60	2-45	-
John, V.B.	45	19	10	15	84	9.33	-	-	5	2311	1655	34	48.67	3-28	-
Kalpage, R.S.	74	61	27	51	750	22.05	-	1	24	3456	2548	67	38.02	4-36	2
Kaluperuma, L.W.S.	4	3	3	14*	33	-	-	-	-	208	137	2	68.50	1-35	-
Kaluperuma, S.M.S.	2	2	-	7	11	5.50	-	-	2	6	3	0	-	-	-
Kaluwitharana, R.S.	54	51	3	77	792	16.50	-	5	34/22						
Karnain, S.H.U.	19	17	5	41*	229	19.08	-	-	1	635	505	16	31.56	5-26	1
Kuruppu, D.S.B.P.	54	52	1	72	1022	20.03	-	4	30/8						
Labrooy, G.F.	44	36	7	33	249	8.58	-	-	8	2308	1876	45	41.68	5-57	2
Liyanage, D.K.	9	6	1	16	56	11.20	-	-	1	372	282	7	40.28	3-49	-
Madugalle, R.S.	63	56	5	73	950	18.62	-	3	18	4	1	0	-	-	-
Madurasinghe, M.A.W.R.	12	6	4	8*	21	10.50	-	-	3	480	358	5	71.60	1-11	-
Mahanama, R.S.	148	140	16	119*	3816	30.77	4	26	75	2	7	0	-	-	-
Mendis, L.R.D.	79	74	9	80	1527	23.49	-	7	14						
Mendis, M.C.	1	1	1	3*	3	-	-	-	2						

622

SRI LANKA (continued)

			BATTING AND FIELDING						BOWLING					
	M	I	NO	HS	Runs	Avge	100	50	Ct/St	Balls	Runs	Wkts	Avge	Best	4w
Munasinghe, A.M.N.	5	4	1	8	13	4.33	–	–	–	217	146	4	36.50	3-30	–
Muralitharan, M.	49	19	11	8	49	6.12	–	–	24	2649	1830	56	32.67	4-23	1
Opatha, A.R.M	5	3	–	18	29	9.66	–	–	3	253	180	5	36.00	3-31	–
Pasqual, S.P.	2	2	1	23*	24	24.00	–	–	–	28	20	0	–	–	–
Perera, K.G.	1	–	–	–	–	–	–	–	–	12	15	0	–	–	–
Pieris, H.S.M.	3	3	1	16	19	9.50	–	–	–	132	135	2	67.50	2-68	–
Pushpakumara, K.R.	22	6	4	14*	34	17.00	–	–	4	1034	837	17	49.23	3-25	–
Ramanayake, C.P.H.	62	35	14	26	210	10.00	–	–	11	2864	2049	68	30.13	4-17	1
Ranasinghe, A.N.	9	8	1	51	153	21.85	–	1	1	324	281	2	140.50	1-21	–
Ranasinghe, S.K	4	3	–	41	55	18.33	–	–	–	126	96	3	32.00	1-28	–
Ranatunga, A	191	182	35	102*	5250	35.71	2	33	42	4584	3646	77	47.35	4-14	1
Ranatunga, D.	4	4	1	25	49	12.25	–	–	1	102	82	1	82.00	1-33	–
Ranatunga, N.	2	1	–	0	0	0.00	–	–	–	–	–	–	–	–	–
Ranatunga, S.	12	11	–	70	253	23.00	–	2	2	–	–	–	–	–	–
Ratnayake, N.L.K	2	–	–	–	–	–	–	–	–	101	98	1	49.00	1-39	–
Ratnayake, R.J.	70	55	18	33*	612	16.54	–	–	11	3575	2712	76	35.68	5-32	2
Ratnayeke, J.R.	78	69	14	50	824	14.98	–	1	14	3573	2866	85	33.71	4-23	1
Samarasekera, M.A.R.	39	39	2	76	844	22.81	–	4	5	338	291	0	–	–	–
Samaraweera, D.P.	5	4	–	49	91	22.75	–	–	3	–	–	–	–	–	–
Senanayake, C.P.	7	7	1	27	126	18.00	–	–	2	–	–	–	–	–	–
Silva, K.J.	1	1	1	1*	1	–	–	–	–	48	55	0	–	–	–
Silva, S.A.R.	20	20	–	85	441	22.05	–	3	17/3	–	–	–	–	–	–
Tennekoon, A.P.B.	4	4	–	59	137	34.25	–	1	3	–	–	–	–	–	–
Tillekeratne, H.P.	136	118	30	104	2620	29.77	2	9	60/5	124	92	4	23.00	1- 3	–
Tissera, M.H.	3	3	–	52	78	26.00	–	1	–	–	–	–	–	–	–
Upashanta, K.E.A.	3	2	1	8*	11	11.00	–	–	1	114	91	3	30.33	2-24	–
Vaas, W.P.U.C.J.	53	29	14	33	249	16.60	–	–	8	2608	1722	66	26.09	4-20	1
Vonhagt, D.M.	1	1	–	8	8	8.00	–	–	–	–	–	–	–	–	–
Warnapura, B.	12	12	–	77	180	15.00	–	1	5	414	316	8	39.50	3-42	–
Warnaweera, K.P.J.	6	3	3	1*	2	–	–	–	2	294	200	6	33.33	2-24	–
Weerakkody, A.P.	1	1	–	2	2	2.00	–	–	–	36	41	0	–	–	–
Wettimuny, M.de S.	1	1	–	2	2	2.00	–	–	3	–	–	–	–	–	–
Wettimuny, S.	35	33	1	86*	786	24.56	–	4	–	–	–	–	–	–	–
Wettimuny, S.R.de S.	3	3	1	67	136	68.00	–	2	–	57	70	1	70.00	1-13	–
Wickremaratne, R.P.A.H.	3	2	–	3	4	2.00	–	–	–	–	–	–	–	–	–
Wickremasinghe, A.G.D.	4	1	–	2	2	2.00	–	–	2/4	–	–	–	–	–	–
Wickremasinghe, G.P.	83	31	12	21*	140	7.36	–	–	15	3602	2648	60	44.13	3-28	–
Wijegunawardene, K.I.W.	26	12	5	8*	20	2.85	–	–	3	1186	986	25	39.44	4-49	1
Wijesuriya, R.G.C.E.	8	3	2	12*	18	18.00	–	–	2	312	287	8	35.87	2-25	–

ZIMBABWE (45 players)

					BATTING AND FIELDING					BOWLING					
	M	I	NO	HS	Runs	Avge	100	50	Ct/St	Balls	Runs	Wkts	Avge	Best	4w
Arnott, K.J.	13	12	2	60	238	23.80	–	3	3						
Brain, D.H.	23	18	4	27	117	8.35	–	–	5	1091	849	21	40.42	3-51	–
Brandes, K.A.	30	22	3	55	212	11.15	–	1	7	1495	1258	34	37.00	4-21	1
Briant, G.A.	5	5	–	16	39	13.00	–	–	–						
Brown, R.D.	7	7	–	38	110	15.71	–	–	5						
Bruk-Jackson, G.K	1	1	–	12	12	12.00	–	–	–						
Burmester, M.G.	8	7	1	39	109	18.16	–	–	2	209	213	5	42.60	3-36	–
Butchart, I.P.	20	16	2	54	252	18.00	–	–	4	702	640	12	53.33	3-57	–
Campbell, A.D.R.	39	37	2	131*	800	22.85	1	4	15	147	104	2	52.00	2-22	–
Carlisle, S.V.	5	5	–	28	66	16.50	–	–	2						
Crocker, G.J.	6	5	1	50	98	24.50	–	1	1	238	208	7	29.71	4-26	1
Curran, K.M.	11	11	–	73	287	26.09	–	2	1	506	398	9	44.22	3-65	–
Davies, S.G.	4	4	–	45	67	16.75	–	–	–						
Dekker, M.H.	21	20	–	79	350	19.44	–	2	5	323	258	9	28.66	2-16	–
Duers, K.G.	6	2	1	5	7	7.00	–	–	2	300	256	3	85.33	1-17	–
Essop-Adam, E.A.	1	1	–	14*	14	–	–	–	2						
Evans, C.N.	15	15	3	96*	253	21.08	–	1	1	60	39	2	19.50	1- 6	–
Fletcher, D.A.G.	6	6	2	71*	191	47.75	–	2	–	301	221	7	31.57	4-42	1
Flower, A.	47	46	2	115*	1260	28.63	1	9	35/6	30	23	0	–	–	–
Flower, G.W.	37	35	2	84*	883	25.97	–	5	19	702	608	14	43.42	3-15	–
Heron, J.G.	6	6	–	18	50	8.33	–	–	1						
Hogg, V.R.	2	1	1	7*	7	–	–	–	–	90	49	0	–	–	–
Houghton, D.L.	47	45	1	142	1279	29.06	1	10	24/2	12	19	1	19.00	1-19	–
James, W.R.	11	8	1	29	101	14.42	–	–	6						
Jarvis, M.P.	12	5	3	17	37	18.50	–	–	1	601	451	9	50.11	2-37	–
Lock, A.C.I.	7	3	2	5	8	8.00	–	–	1	289	219	8	27.37	5-44	1
Martin, G.C.	5	4	–	16	31	7.75	–	–	–	132	95	2	47.50	1-15	–
Meman, M.A.	1	1	–	19	19	19.00	–	–	–	41	34	0	–	–	–
Olonga, H.K	3	1	–	6	6	6.00	–	–	1	120	138	3	46.00	2-47	–
Paterson, G.A.	10	10	–	27	123	12.30	–	–	2						
Peall, S.G.	20	15	1	21	91	6.50	–	–	1	900	678	8	84.75	3-54	–
Peckover, G.E.	3	3	–	16*	33	16.50	–	–	–						
Pycroft, A.J.	20	19	2	61	295	17.35	–	2	6						
Ranchod, U.	3	1	1	3*	3	–	–	–	1	174	130	1	130.00	1-44	–
Rawson, P.W.E.	10	8	3	24*	80	16.00	–	–	4	571	427	12	35.58	3-47	–
Rennie, J.A	9	6	5	20*	47	47.00	–	–	3	382	352	4	88.00	2-42	–
Shah, A.H.	28	28	2	60*	437	16.80	–	1	6	1077	812	18	45.11	3-33	–
Strang, B.C.	10	7	4	4*	11	3.66	–	–	7	464	326	10	32.60	4-36	1
Strang, P.A	20	18	7	28*	273	24.81	–	–	4	1069	812	26	31.23	5-21	2
Streak, H.H.	29	24	7	36*	284	16.70	–	–	4	1525	1077	34	31.67	4-25	2

ZIMBABWE (continued)

	M	I	NO	HS	Runs	Avge	100	50	Ct/St	Balls	Runs	Wkts	Avge	Best	4w
											BOWLING				
					BATTING AND FIELDING										
Traicos, A.J.	27	17	9	19	88	11.00	–	–	3	1524	987	19	51.94	3-35	–
Waller, A.C.	29	28	3	83*	662	26.48	–	3	8						
Whittall, A.R.	1	–	–	–	–	–	–	–	–	60	30	1	30.00	1-30	–
Whittall, G.J.	28	28	3	70	458	18.32	–	2	8	884	757	19	39.84	3-46	–
Wishart, C.B.	3	3	–	53	60	20.00	–	1	1						

BANGLADESH (32 players)

	M	I	NO	HS	Runs	Avge	100	50	Ct/St	Balls	Runs	Wkts	Avge	Best	4w
Akram Khan	9	9	1	44	182	22.75	–	–	4	66	59	0	–	–	–
Alam Talukdar	2	1	1	7*	7	–	–	–	1	42	36	0	–	–	–
Amin-ul-Islam	10	10	3	42	184	26.28	–	–	1	110	125	0	–	–	–
Anis-ur-Rehman	1	1	–	2	2	2.00	–	–	–	30	42	0	–	–	–
Athar Ali Khan	8	8	1	78*	211	30.14	–	1	1	222	190	3	63.33	1-10	–
Azhar Hussain	7	7	–	54	96	13.71	–	–	2	263	209	4	52.25	1-20	–
Farooq Ahmed	5	5	1	57	89	17.80	–	1	1	87	35	1	35.00	1-22	–
Farooq Chowdhury	2	2	–	14	17	17.00	–	–	–						
Gazi Ashraf	7	7	1	18	59	8.42	–	–	1	51	33	2	16.50	1- 7	–
Ghulam Farooq	3	2	1	23*	27	27.00	–	–	–	99	81	1	81.00	1-28	–
Ghulam Nousher	9	3	2	4	8	8.00	–	–	1	408	314	5	62.80	1-27	–
Habib-ul-Bashar	2	2	–	16	16	8.00	–	–	–						
Hafiz-ur-Rehman	2	1	–	8	8	8.00	–	–	1						
Harun-ur-Rashid	2	2	–	8	8	8.00	–	–	2	84	72	2	36.00	1-29	–
Hasib-ul-Hassan	2	1	1	0*	0	0.00	–	–	–	228	203	0	–	–	–
Inam-ul-Haq	7	7	2	1*	1	–	–	–	1	234	172	2	86.00	2-23	–
Jahangir Shah	5	4	2	18	55	11.00	–	–	–						
Javed Omar	2	2	–	8*	16	8.00	–	–	3						
Khalid Masud	3	3	1	18	27	13.50	–	–	1						
Minhaz-ul-Abedin	12	12	–	27*	196	16.33	–	–	–	252	248	6	41.33	2-39	–
Mohammad Rafiq	2	2	–	40	46	23.00	–	–	2	82	65	3	21.66	2-50	–
Naim-ur-Rehman	1	1	–	13	15	7.50	–	–	1/1	40	29	1	29.00	1-29	–
Nasir Ahmed	7	4	2	3	3	3.00	–	–	–						
Nur-ul-Abedin	4	4	–	11	25	12.50	–	–	1						
Rafiq Alam	2	2	–	13	15	3.75	–	–	–						
Raquib-ul-Hassan	2	2	–	14	24	12.00	–	–	–	1	4	0	–	–	–
Saif-ul-Islam	4	3	2	12	17	8.50	–	–	1	186	142	5	28.40	4-36	1
Sajjad Ahmed	2	2	–	22*	30	30.00	–	–	–	60	30	0	–	–	–
Sami-ur-Rehman	2	2	–	11	15	7.50	–	–	1						
Shahid-ur-Rehman	2	2	–	4	4	2.00	–	–	–	36	32	0	–	–	–
Wahid-ul-Ghani	1	–	–	37	62	31.00	–	–	–						
Zahid Razzak	3	3	–	6	14	4.66	–	–	–						

625

CANADA (13 players)

	M	I	NO	HS	Runs	Avge	100	50	Ct/St	Balls	Runs	Wkts	Avge	Best	4w
Baksh, S.	1	1	–	0	0	0.00	–	–	–	54	26	1	26.00	1-14	–
Callender, R.G.	2	2	–	0	0	0.00	–	–	–						
Chappell, C.J.D.	3	3	–	19	38	12.66	–	–	–						
Dennis, F.A.	3	3	–	25	47	15.66	–	–	–	90	53	2	26.50	2-27	–
Henry, C.C.	2	2	1	5	6	6.00	–	–	–						
Marshall, C.A.	2	2	–	8	10	5.00	–	–	–						
Mauricette, B.M.	3	3	–	15	20	6.66	–	–	–						
Patel, J.M.	3	3	–	2	3	1.00	–	–	–	91	47	0	–	–	–
Sealy, G.R.	3	3	–	45	73	24.33	–	–	–	36	21	0	–	–	–
Stead, M.P.	2	2	–	10	10	5.00	–	–	–	29	24	0	–	–	–
Tariq Javed	3	3	–	8	15	5.00	–	–	–						
Valentine, J.N.	3	3	2	3*	3	–	–	–	1	114	66	3	22.00	1-18	–
Vaughan, J.C.B.	3	3	–	29	30	10.00	–	–	–	66	36	0	–	–	–

EAST AFRICA (14 players)

	M	I	NO	HS	Runs	Avge	100	50	Ct/St	Balls	Runs	Wkts	Avge	Best	4w
Frasat Ali	3	3	–	45	57	19.00	–	–	–	144	107	0	–	–	–
Harilal Shah	3	3	–	6	6	2.00	–	–	–						
Jawahir Shah	3	3	–	37	46	15.33	–	–	–						
McLeod, H.	2	2	–	5	5	2.50	–	–	–						
Mehmood Quaraishy	3	3	1	19	41	20.50	–	–	–	108	94	3	31.33	2-55	–
Mehta, P.S.	1	1	–	12	12	12.00	–	–	–						
Nagenda, J.	1	–	–	–	–	–	–	–	–	54	50	1	50.00	1-50	–
Nana, P.G.	3	3	2	8*	9	9.00	–	–	2	173	116	1	116.00	1-34	–
Pringle, D.J.	2	2	–	3	5	2.50	–	–	–	90	55	0	–	–	–
Sethi, R.K.	3	3	–	30	54	18.00	–	–	1	120	100	1	100.00	1-51	–
Sumar, S.	1	1	–	4	4	4.00	–	–	–						
Walusimba, S.	3	3	–	16	38	12.66	–	–	–						
Yunus Badat	2	2	–	1	1	0.50	–	–	–						
Zulfiqar Ali	3	3	1	30	39	19.50	–	–	1	210	166	4	41.50	3-63	–

HOLLAND (13 players)

	M	I	NO	HS	Runs	Avge	100	50	Ct/St	Balls	Runs	Wkts	Avge	Best	4w
Aponso, G.J.A.F.	5	4	0	58	120	30.00	–	1	–	242	257	2	128.50	1-57	–
Bakker, P.J.	5	1	1	0*	0	–	–	–	–	258	215	3	71.66	2-51	–
Cantrell, P.E.	5	5	–	47	160	32.00	–	–	–	186	170	3	56.66	1-18	–
Clarke, N.E.	5	5	–	32	50	10.00	–	–	3						
De Leede, T.B.M.	5	5	–	41	90	18.00	–	–	–	162	179	0	–	–	–
Gouka, E.L.	3	2	1	19	19	19.00	–	–	–	22	51	1	51.00	1-32	–
Jansen, F.	2	–		–	–	–	–	–	1	54	62	1	62.00	1-40	–
Lefebvre, R.P.	4	4	1	45	78	26.00	–	–	1	210	132	3	44.00	1-20	–
Lubbers, S.W.	4	4	1	9	24	8.00	–	–	1	216	187	5	37.40	3-48	–
Schewe, M.M.C.	5	4	1	20	49	16.33	–	–	2/1						
Van Noortwijk, K.J.	5	5	1	64	168	42.00	–	1	–						
Van Oosterom, R.F.	2	2	2	5*	7	–	–	–	1						
Zuiderent, B.	5	5	1	54	91	22.75	–	1	4						

KENYA (13 players)

	M	I	NO	HS	Runs	Avge	100	50	Ct/St	Balls	Runs	Wkts	Avge	Best	4w
Ali, R.	5	2	2	6*	6	–	–	–	1	218	176	9	19.55	3-17	–
Asif Karim	5	3	1	11	17	8.50	–	–	–	288	171	4	42.75	1-19	–
Chudasama, D.	5	5	–	34	103	20.60	–	–	1						
Modi, H.	5	5	–	41	84	16.80	–	–	3	96	102	0	–	–	–
Odoyo, T.	4	4	1	24	42	10.50	–	–	–	84	87	2	43.50	2-42	–
Odumbe, E.T.	5	5	–	20	54	13.50	–	1	2	257	187	6	31.16	3-15	–
Odumbe, M.	5	5	–	50	112	22.40	–	–	1	24	31	0	–	–	–
Onyango, L.	1	1	–	23	23	23.00	–	–	1						
Otieno, K.	5	5	–	85	147	29.40	–	1	3						
Suji, M.	5	4	2	15	18	9.00	–	–	2	242	213	4	53.25	2-55	–
Tariq Iqbal	2	2	–	16	17	8.50	–	–	2						
Tikolo, D.L.	3	2	2	25*	36	–	–	–	2	48	55	0	–	–	–
Tikolo, S.O.	5	5	1	96	196	39.20	–	2	3	60	83	1	83.00	1-26	–

UNITED ARAB EMIRATES (16 players)

				BATTING AND FIELDING						BOWLING					
	M	I	NO	HS	Runs	Avge	100	50	Ct/St	Balls	Runs	Wkts	Avge	Best	4w
Arshad Laiq	6	6	1	43*	101	20.20	–	–	1	198	198	1	198.00	1-25	–
Azhar Saeed	7	7	–	32	61	8.71	–	–	2	271	213	6	35.50	3-45	–
Dukanwala, S.F.	5	4	2	40*	84	42.00	–	–	2	198	153	6	25.50	5-29	1
Imtiaz Abbasi	7	6	4	6*	12	6.00	–	–	4/2						
Mazhar Hussain	7	7	–	70	179	25.57	–	1	1	48	60	0	–	–	–
Mehra, V.	6	6	1	43	92	18.40	–	–	1						
Mohammad Aslam	4	4	–	23	38	9.50	–	–	–						
Mohammad Ishaq	5	5	1	51*	98	24.50	–	1	1						
Mylvaganam, G.	3	3	–	23	36	12.00	–	–	1						
Poonawalla, R.H.	2	2	–	22	44	22.00	–	–	1						
Saeed-al-Saffar	1	–	–	–	–	–	–	–	1	18	25	0	–	–	–
Salim Raza	6	6	–	84	159	26.50	–	1	–	192	179	3	59.66	1-17	–
Samarasekera, J.A.	7	6	2	47*	124	31.00	–	–	1	294	235	4	58.75	1-17	–
Shahzad Altaf	2	–	–	–	–	–	–	–	–	78	37	1	37.00	1-15	–
Sohail Butt	2	2	1	6*	8	8.00	–	–	–	78	79	2	39.50	2-52	–
Zarawani, Sultan M.	7	6	–	13	26	4.33	–	–	1	264	257	5	51.40	2-49	–

COMPLETE LOI RECORD FOR PLAYER REPRESENTING TWO COUNTRIES

				BATTING AND FIELDING						BOWLING					
	M	I	NO	HS	Runs	Avge	100	50	Ct/St	Balls	Runs	Wkts	Avge	Best	4w
K.C.Wessels (A/SA)	109	105	7	107	3367	34.35	1	26	49	749	666	18	37.00	2-16	–

Index of Limited-Overs
International Cricketers 1970-71 to 1996

INDEX OF L-O INTERNATIONAL CRICKETERS

Every cricketer who appeared in official Limited-Overs Internationals before 28 September 1996 is listed alphabetically within his country's section of the index. The numbers in brackets show the total number of LOI appearances by the player for that country. The numbers that follow are the reference numbers of the matches in which he played; only the prefix of each match number is listed; e.g. LOI No. 1111/40 is shown as 1111. * Denotes players who had not appeared in official Test matches before 28 September 1996.

ENGLAND (143 players)

AGNEW, Jonathan Philip; b Macclesfield, Cheshire 4 Apr 1960; (3) 283, 284, 307.

ALLOTT, Paul John Walter; b Altrincham, Cheshire 14 Sep 1956; (13) 144, 152, 153, 197, 201, 205, 209, 213, 217, 221, 329, 330, 331.

AMISS, Dennis Leslie; b Harborne, Birmingham 7 Apr 1943; (18) 2, 3, 4, 6, 7, 12, 16, 17, 19, 23, 27, 31, 37, 38, 39, 42, 43, 44.

ARNOLD, Geoffrey Graham; b Earlsfield, Surrey 3 Sep 1944; (14) 2, 3, 4, 6, 7, 9, 12, 13, 15, 16, 17, 19, 23, 31.

ATHERTON, Michael Andrew; b Manchester 23 Mar 1968; (43) 634, 635, 643, 652, 668, 669, 670, 676, 677, 678, 882, 883, 884, 885, 886, 913, 914, 915, 952, 954, 955, 956, 999, 1000, 1001, 1037, 1038, 1039, 1041, 1042, 1043, 1047, 1052, 1056, 1059, 1069, 1075, 1099, 1100, 1101, 1109, 1110, 1111.

ATHEY, Charles William Jeffrey; b Middlesbrough, Yorkshire 27 Sep 1957; (31) 91, 92, 389, 413, 415, 417, 418, 419, 420, 422, 423, 425, 427, 428, 429, 431, 432, 448, 449, 450, 460, 463, 468, 472, 476, 477, 478, 479, 480, 503, 506.

BAILEY, Robert John; b Biddulph, Staffordshire 28 Oct 1963; (4) 327, 446, 521, 614.

BAIRSTOW, David Leslie; b Horton, Bradford, Yorkshire 1 Sep 1951; (21) 58, 59, 60, 76, 77, 79, 81, 82, 83, 84, 86, 87, 89, 90, 91, 92, 115, 116, 264, 265, 266.

BARLOW, Graham Derek; b Folkestone, Kent 26 Mar 1950; (6) 37, 38, 39, 42, 43, 44.

BARNETT, Kim John; b Stoke-on-Trent, Staffordshire 17 Jul 1960; (1) 521.

BENJAMIN, Joseph Emmanuel; b Christ Church, St Kitts 2 Feb 1961; (2) 952, 955.

BENSON, Mark Richard; b Shoreham, Sussex 6 Jul 1958; (1) 388.

BICKNELL, Martin Paul; b Guildford, Surrey 14 Jan 1969; (7) 645, 646, 648, 650, 653, 668, 669.

BLAKEY, Richard John; b Huddersfield, Yorkshire 15 Jan 1967; (3) 759, 797, 798.

BOTHAM, Ian Terence; b Heswall, Cheshire 24 Nov 1955; (116) 37, 39, 45, 46, 47, 50, 51, 52, 53, 57, 58, 59, 60, 63, 67, 71, 72, 74, 76, 77, 79, 81, 82, 83, 84, 86, 87, 89, 90, 91, 92, 115, 116, 119, 120, 121, 141, 142, 143, 144, 145, 152, 153, 154, 155, 167, 168, 169, 170, 172, 174, 175, 176, 177, 179, 183, 184, 185, 197, 201, 205, 209, 213, 217, 221, 249, 250, 251, 259, 264, 265, 266, 329, 330, 331, 365, 366, 367, 413, 415, 417, 418, 419, 420, 422, 423, 425, 427, 428, 429, 431, 432, 448, 449, 450, 566, 567, 568, 676, 712, 713, 715, 721, 726, 731, 736, 741, 744, 748, 751, 752, 756, 757, 758, 759, 760.

BOYCOTT, Geoffrey; b Fitzwilliam, Yorkshire 21 Oct 1940; (36) 1, 2, 3, 4, 6, 7, 8, 46, 47, 50, 57, 58, 59, 60, 63, 67, 71, 72, 74, 77, 79, 81, 82, 86, 87, 89, 90, 91, 92, 115, 116, 119, 120, 121, 141, 142.

BREARLEY, John Michael; b Harrow, Middlesex 28 Apr 1942; (25) 42, 43, 44, 45, 47, 52, 53, 57, 58, 59, 60, 63, 67, 71, 72, 74, 76, 77, 79, 81, 82, 83, 84, 86, 87.

BROAD, Brian Christopher; b Knowle, Bristol 29 Sep 1957; (34) 413, 415, 417, 418, 419, 420, 422, 423, 425, 427, 428, 429, 431, 432, 442, 445, 446, 448, 449, 450, 452, 455, 460, 478, 479, 480, 503, 504, 505, 506, 507, 518, 519, 520.

*BROWN, Alistair Duncan; b Beckenham, Kent 11 Feb 1970; (2) 1099, 1100, 1101.

BUTCHER, Alan Raymond; b Croydon, Surrey 7 Jan 1954; (1) 91.

BUTCHER, Roland Orlando; b East Point, St Philip, Barbados 14 Oct 1953; (3) 92, 115, 116.

CADDICK, Andrew Richard; b Christchurch, New Zealand 21 Nov 1968; (5) 830, 831, 832, 885, 886.

CAPEL, David John; b Northampton 6 Feb 1963; (23) 442, 445, 446, 478, 479, 480, 503, 504, 505, 506, 507, 575, 576, 579, 583, 586, 590, 610, 611, 612, 613, 614, 615.

CLOSE, Dennis Brian; b Rawdon, Leeds, Yorkshire 24 Feb 1931; (3) 2, 3, 4.

COOK, Geoffrey; b Middlesbrough, Yorkshire 9 Oct 1951; (6) 141, 142, 143, 144, 145, 170.

COOK, Nicholas Grant Billson; b Leicester 17 Jun 1956; (3) 260, 480, 579.

COPE, Geoffrey Alan; b Burmantofts, Leeds, Yorkshire 23 Feb 1947; (2) 46, 47.

CORK, Dominic Gerald; b Newcastle-under-Lyme, Staffordshire 7 Aug 1971; (22) 760, 831, 832, 914, 915, 999, 1000, 1001, 1037, 1038, 1040, 1041, 1042, 1043, 1047, 1052, 1056, 1059, 1069, 1099, 1100, 1101.

COWANS, Norman George; b Enfield St Mary, Jamaica 17 Apr 1961; (23) 167, 168, 169, 170, 172, 174, 179, 185, 217, 249, 250, 251, 260, 280, 281, 282, 283, 307, 312, 314, 329, 330, 331.

COWDREY, Christopher Stuart; b Farnborough, Kent 20 Oct 1957; (3) 283, 284, 307.

COWDREY, Michael Colin; b Bangalore, India 24 Dec 1932; (1) 1.

CRAWLEY, John Paul; b Maldon, Essex 21 Sep 1971; (3) 954, 955, 956.

CROFT, Robert Damien Bale; b Morriston, Glamorgan, Wales 25 May 1970; (3) 1109, 1110, 1111.

DeFREITAS, Phillip Anthony Jason; b Scotts Head, Dominica 18 Feb 1966; (101) 413, 417, 418, 419, 420, 422, 423, 425, 427, 428, 429, 431, 432, 442, 445, 446, 448, 449, 450, 452, 455, 460, 463, 468, 472, 476, 477, 478, 479, 480, 503, 504, 505, 506, 507, 518, 519, 520, 566, 567, 568, 575, 583, 586, 590, 612, 613, 615, 632, 633, 634, 635, 649, 650, 652, 653, 668, 669, 670, 676, 677, 678, 711, 715, 721, 726, 731, 736, 741, 744, 748, 751, 752, 756, 757, 758, 759, 760, 794, 795, 796, 797, 798, 799, 815, 914, 915, 952, 954, 955, 956, 999, 1000, 1038, 1039, 1040, 1041, 1052, 1056, 1059, 1075.

DENNESS, Michael Henry; b Bellshill, Lanarkshire, Scotland 1 Dec 1940; (12) 8, 9, 12, 13, 14, 15, 16, 18, 19, 23, 27, 31.

DILLEY, Graham Roy; b Dartford, Kent 18 May 1959; (36) 76, 77, 79, 81, 82, 86, 87, 89, 116, 152, 153, 197, 201, 205, 209, 213, 221, 259, 386, 387, 388, 389, 413, 415, 418, 419, 420, 422, 423, 425, 431, 432, 448, 449, 518, 519.

D'OLIVEIRA, Basil Lewis; b Signal Hill, Cape Town, South Africa 4 Oct 1931; (4) 1, 2, 3, 4.

DOWNTON, Paul Rupert; b Farnborough, Kent 4 Apr 1957; (28) 45, 280, 281, 282, 283, 307, 312, 314, 329, 330, 331, 364, 365, 366, 367, 386, 387, 452, 455, 460, 463, 468, 472, 476, 477, 518, 519, 520.

EALHAM, Mark Alan, b Willesborough, Ashford, Kent 27 Aug 1969; (2) 1099, 1100.

EDMONDS, Phillippe Henri, b Lusaka, Northern Rhodesia 8 Mar 1951; (29) 45, 46, 47, 50, 53, 57, 58, 60, 63, 71, 74, 280, 281, 282, 283, 284, 307, 312, 314, 326, 327, 329, 330, 367, 387, 389, 415, 422, 442.

EDRICH, John Hugh, b Blofield, Norfolk 21 Jun 1937; (7) 1, 12, 13, 14, 15, 17, 18.

ELLISON, Richard Mark; b Willesborough, Ashford, Kent 21 Sep 1959; (14) 280, 281, 282, 284, 307, 312, 314, 326, 327, 365, 367, 386, 387, 388.

EMBUREY, John Ernest; b Peckham, London 20 Aug 1952; (61) 83, 84, 86, 87, 92, 115, 116, 144, 364, 365, 366, 367, 386, 387, 388, 389, 413, 415, 417, 418, 419, 420, 422, 423, 425, 427, 428, 429, 431, 432, 442, 445, 446, 448, 449, 450, 452, 455, 460, 463, 468, 472, 476, 477, 478, 479, 480, 503, 504, 505, 506, 507, 518, 519, 520, 566, 567, 568, 794, 815, 816.

FAIRBROTHER, Neil Harvey; b Warrington, Lancashire 9 Sep 1963; (56) 442, 445, 446, 478, 479, 480, 503, 504, 505, 506, 507, 676, 677, 678, 711, 715, 721, 726, 731, 736, 741, 748, 751, 752, 756, 757, 758, 759, 760, 794, 795, 796, 797, 798, 799, 815, 816, 830, 831, 832, 914, 915, 955, 956, 999, 1000, 1037, 1038, 1039, 1042, 1043, 1047, 1052, 1056, 1059, 1069.

FLETCHER, Keith William Robert; b Worcester 20 May 1944; (24) 1, 2, 3, 4, 6, 7, 8, 9, 12, 13, 14, 15, 16, 17, 18, 19, 23, 27, 31, 141, 142, 143, 144, 145.

FOSTER, Neil Alan; b Colchester, Essex 6 May 1962; (48) 249, 250, 251, 259, 260, 264, 265, 266, 280, 281, 282, 284, 312, 314, 326, 331, 364, 365, 366, 367, 388, 389, 417, 427, 428, 429, 431, 432, 442, 445, 446, 448, 449, 450, 452, 455, 463, 468, 472, 476, 477, 478, 479, 480, 521, 566, 567, 568.

FOWLER, Graeme; b Accrington, Lancashire 20 Apr 1957; (26) 172, 197, 201, 205, 209, 213, 217, 221, 259, 260, 264, 265, 266, 280, 281, 282, 283, 284, 307, 312, 314, 326, 327, 329, 386, 387.

FRASER, Angus Robert Charles; b Billinge, Lancashire 8 Aug 1965; (33) 575, 576, 579, 583, 586, 590, 610, 611, 612, 613, 614, 634, 635, 643, 645, 646, 648, 649, 650, 652, 653, 668, 669, 670, 883, 884, 885, 886, 913, 954, 956, 999, 1001.

FRENCH, Bruce Nicholas; b Warsop, Nottinghamshire 13 Aug 1959; (13) 284, 326, 327, 428, 429, 431, 432, 478, 479, 504, 505, 506, 507.

GATTING, Michael William; b Kingsbury, Middlesex 6 Jun 1957; (92) 45, 46, 47, 91, 92, 115, 116, 119, 120, 121, 141,

142, 143, 144, 145, 154, 155, 197, 201, 205, 209, 213, 217, 221, 249, 250, 251, 259, 260, 264, 265, 280, 281, 282, 283, 284, 307, 312, 314, 329, 330, 331, 364, 386, 387, 388, 389, 413, 415, 417, 418, 419, 420, 422, 423, 425, 427, 428, 429, 431, 432, 448, 450, 452, 455, 460, 463, 468, 472, 476, 477, 478, 479, 480, 503, 504, 505, 506, 507, 518, 519, 520, 566, 567, 568, 794, 795, 796, 797, 799, 815, 816.

GIFFORD, Norman; b Ulverston, Lancashire 30 Mar 1940; (2) 326, 327.

GOOCH, Graham Alan; b Leytonstone, Essex 23 Jul 1953; (125) 37, 38, 39, 52, 53, 57, 58, 59, 60, 63, 67, 71, 72, 74, 76, 77, 79, 81, 82, 83, 84, 86, 87, 89, 90, 91, 92, 115, 116, 119, 120, 121, 141, 142, 143, 144, 145, 329, 330, 331, 364, 365, 366, 367, 386, 387, 388, 389, 442, 445, 446, 449, 452, 455, 460, 463, 468, 472, 476, 477, 478, 479, 480, 518, 519, 520, 521, 566, 567, 568, 575, 576, 579, 583, 586, 590, 610, 611, 612, 613, 614, 632, 633, 634, 635, 648, 649, 650, 652, 653, 668, 669, 670, 676, 677, 678, 711, 712, 713, 715, 721, 726, 731, 736, 748, 751, 752, 756, 757, 758, 760, 794, 795, 796, 797, 798, 799, 830, 831, 832, 913, 952, 954, 955, 956.

GOUGH, Darren; b Barnsley, Yorkshire 18 Sep 1970; (27) 913, 914, 915, 952, 954, 955, 956, 999, 1000, 1001, 1037, 1039, 1040, 1041, 1042, 1043, 1047, 1052, 1056, 1059, 1069, 1075, 1100, 1101, 1109, 1110, 1111.

*GOULD, Ian James; b Taplow, Buckinghamshire 19 Aug 1957; (18) 169, 170, 172, 174, 175, 176, 177, 179, 183, 184, 185, 197, 201, 205, 209, 213, 217, 221.

GOWER, David Ivon; b Tunbridge Wells, Kent 1 Apr 1957; (114) 50, 51, 52, 53, 57, 58, 59, 60, 63, 67, 71, 72, 74, 76, 77, 79, 81, 82, 83, 84, 86, 87, 89, 90, 115, 116, 119, 120, 121, 141, 142, 143, 144, 145, 152, 153, 154, 155, 167, 168, 169, 170, 172, 174, 175, 176, 177, 179, 183, 184, 185, 197, 201, 205, 209, 213, 217, 221, 249, 250, 251, 259, 260, 264, 265, 266, 280, 281, 282, 283, 284, 307, 312, 314, 329, 330, 331, 364, 365, 366, 367, 386, 387, 388, 389, 413, 415, 417, 418, 419, 420, 422, 423, 425, 427, 428, 429, 431, 432, 448, 449, 450, 566, 567, 568, 632, 633, 634, 635, 643, 653, 668, 669, 670.

GREIG, Anthony William; b Queenstown, South Africa 6 Oct 1946; (22) 2, 3, 4, 6, 7, 8, 9, 12, 13, 14, 15, 16, 18, 19, 23, 27, 31, 38, 39, 42, 43, 44.

HAMPSHIRE, John Harry; b Thurnscoe, Yorkshire 10 Feb 1941; (3) 1, 2, 3.

HAYES, Frank Charles; b Preston, Lancashire 6 Dec 1946; (6) 6, 7, 8, 23, 27, 31.

*HEADLEY, Dean Warren; b Norton, Stourbridge, Worcestershire 27 Jan 1970; (2) 1109, 1110.

HEMMINGS, Edward Ernest; b Leamington Spa, Warwickshire 20 Feb 1949; (33) 154, 155, 175, 176, 177, 460, 463, 468, 472, 476, 477, 478, 479, 575, 576, 579, 583, 586, 610, 611, 612, 613, 614, 615, 632, 633, 634, 635, 643, 648, 650, 652, 668.

HENDRICK, Michael; b Darley Dale, Derbyshire 22 Oct 1948; (22) 8, 17, 18, 37, 38, 39, 45, 52, 57, 58, 59, 60, 63, 67, 71, 72, 74, 91, 92, 119, 120, 121.

HICK, Graeme Ashley; b Salisbury, Rhodesia 23 May 1966; (62) 676, 677, 678, 711, 712, 713, 715, 721, 726, 731, 736, 741, 744, 748, 751, 752, 756, 757, 758, 759, 760, 794, 795, 796, 797, 798, 799, 815, 816, 830, 831, 832, 882, 883, 884, 885, 886, 913, 914, 915, 952, 954, 955, 956, 999, 1000, 1001, 1037, 1038, 1039, 1040, 1041, 1042, 1043, 1047, 1056, 1059, 1069, 1075, 1099, 1100, 1101.

*HOLLIOAKE, Adam John; b Melbourne, Australia 5 Sep 1971; (2) 1110, 1111.

*HUMPAGE, Geoffrey William; b Sparkhill, Birmingham 24 Apr 1954; (3) 119, 120, 121.

HUSSAIN, Nasser; b Madras, India 28 Mar 1968; (4) 490, 615, 883, 884.

IGGLESDEN, Alan Paul; b Farnborough, Kent 8 Oct 1964; (4) 882, 883, 884, 885.

ILLINGWORTH, Raymond; b Pudsey, Yorkshire 8 Jun 1932; (3) 1, 6, 7.

ILLINGWORTH, Richard Keith; b Bradford, Yorkshire 23 Aug 1963; (25) 676, 677, 678, 712, 713, 736, 741, 744, 748, 751, 752, 756, 757, 758, 759, 760, 830, 832, 1040, 1042, 1043, 1047, 1052, 1069, 1075.

IRANI, Ronald Charles; b Leigh, Lancashire 26 Oct 1971; (4) 1099, 1109, 1110, 1111.

JACKMAN, Robin David; b Simla, India 13 Aug 1945; (15) 12, 13, 38, 91, 92, 119, 120, 121, 175, 176, 177, 179, 183, 184, 185.

JAMESON, John Alexander; b Byculla, Bombay, India 30 Jun 1941; (3) 9, 19, 23.

JARVIS, Paul William; b Redcar, Yorkshire 29 Jun 1965; (16) 503, 504, 505, 506, 507, 794, 795, 796, 797, 798, 799, 815, 816, 830, 831, 832.

*JESTY, Trevor Edward; b Gosport, Hampshire 2 Jun 1948; (10) 167, 168, 169, 170, 174, 175, 176, 177, 179, 183.

KNIGHT, Nicholas Verity; b Watford, Hertfordshire 28 Nov 1969; (3) 1109, 1110, 1111.

KNOTT, Alan Philip Eric; b Belvedere, Kent 9 Apr 1946; (20) 1, 2, 3, 4, 6, 7, 12, 13, 14, 16, 19, 23, 27, 31, 37, 38, 39, 42, 43, 44.

LAMB, Allan Joseph; b Langebaanweg, Cape Province, South Africa 20 Jun 1954; (122) 152, 153, 154, 155, 167, 168, 169, 170, 172, 174, 175, 176, 177, 179, 183, 184, 185, 197, 201, 205, 209, 213, 217, 221, 249, 250, 251, 259, 260, 264, 265, 266, 280, 281, 282, 283, 284, 307, 312, 314, 329, 330, 331, 364, 365, 366, 367, 386, 387, 388, 389, 413, 415, 417, 418, 419, 420, 422, 423, 425, 427, 428, 429, 431, 432, 448, 449, 450, 452, 455, 460, 463, 468, 472, 476, 477, 518, 519, 520, 521, 566, 567, 568, 575, 576, 579, 583, 586, 590, 610, 611, 612, 613, 614, 615, 632, 633, 634, 635, 643, 645, 646, 648, 649, 650, 668, 669, 670, 676, 677, 711, 712, 713, 744, 748, 751, 752, 756, 757, 758, 759, 760.

LARKINS, Wayne, b Roxton, Bedfordshire 22 Nov 1953; (25) 72, 74, 83, 84, 86, 87, 575, 576, 579, 583, 586, 590, 610, 611, 612, 613, 614, 615, 645, 646, 648, 649, 650, 652, 653.

LAWRENCE, David Valentine; b Gloucester 28 Jan 1964; (1) 678.

LEVER, John Kenneth; b Stepney, London 24 Feb 1949; (22) 37, 39, 42, 43, 44, 46, 47, 51, 52, 53, 57, 58, 59, 60, 83, 84, 89, 90, 141, 142, 143, 145.

LEVER, Peter; b Todmorden, Yorkshire 17 Sep 1940; (10) 1, 7, 14, 15, 16, 18, 19, 23, 27, 31.

LEWIS, Clairmonte Christopher; b Georgetown, Guyana 1 Feb 1968; (51) 610, 611, 615, 632, 633, 634, 635, 643, 645, 646, 648, 649, 676, 677, 711, 712, 713, 715, 721, 726, 731, 736, 741, 744, 751, 752, 756, 757, 758, 759, 794, 795, 796, 797, 798, 799, 815, 816, 830, 831, 882, 883, 884, 885, 886, 913, 914, 915, 1099, 1100, 1101.

LLOYD, David; b Accrington, Lancashire 18 Mar 1947; (8) 9, 12, 13, 14, 15, 16, 51, 89.

*LLOYD, Graham David; b Accrington, Lancashire 1 Jul 1969; (2) 1109, 1111.

LLOYD, Timothy Andrew; b Oswestry, Shropshire 5 Nov 1956; (3) 264, 265, 266.

*LOVE, James Derek; b Headingley, Leeds, Yorkshire 22 Apr 1955; (3) 119, 120, 121.

LUCKHURST, Brian William; b Sittingbourne, Kent 5 Feb 1939; (3) 16, 17, 18.

*LYNCH, Monte Alan; b Georgetown, British Guiana 21 May 1958; (3) 518, 519, 520.

MALCOLM, Devon Eugene; b Kingston, Jamaica 22 Feb 1963; (10) 633, 634, 643, 649, 796, 797, 798, 799, 815, 882.

MARKS, Victor James; b Middle Chinnock, Somerset 25 Jun 1955; (34) 90, 167, 168, 169, 170, 172, 175, 176, 177, 179, 183, 184, 185, 197, 201, 205, 209, 213, 217, 221, 249, 250, 251, 259, 260, 280, 281, 282, 283, 284, 307, 312, 314, 521.

MARTIN, Peter James; b Accrington, Lancashire 15 Nov 1968; (16) 1000, 1001, 1037, 1038, 1041, 1042, 1043, 1047, 1056, 1059, 1069, 1075, 1099, 1100, 1101, 1111.

MAYNARD, Matthew Peter; b Oldham, Lancashire 21 Mar 1966; (10) 882, 883, 884, 885, 886, 1100, 1101, 1109, 1110, 1111.

MILLER, Geoffrey; b Chesterfield, Derbyshire 8 Sep 1952; (25) 44, 45, 46, 50, 51, 52, 53, 67, 76, 152, 153, 154, 155, 167, 168, 169, 170, 172, 174, 183, 184, 185, 264, 265, 266.

MORRIS, John Edward; b Crewe, Cheshire 1 Apr 1964; (8) 643, 645, 646, 648, 649, 650, 652, 653.

MOXON, Martyn Douglas; b Barnsley, Yorkshire 4 May 1960; (10) 283, 312, 314, 326, 327, 504, 505, 507.

MULLALLY, Alan David; b Southend-on-Sea, Essex 12 Jul 1969; (3) 1109, 1110, 1111.

OLD, Christopher Middleton; b Middlesbrough, Yorkshire 22 Dec 1948; (32) 8, 9, 12, 13, 14, 15, 16, 17, 18, 19, 23, 27, 31, 42, 43, 44, 45, 47, 50, 51, 57, 59, 63, 67, 71, 72, 74, 89, 90, 91, 92, 115.

POCOCK, Patrick Ian; b Bangor, Caernarvonshire, Wales 24 Sep 1946; (1) 327.

PRINGLE, Derek Raymond; b Nairobi, Kenya 18 Sep 1958; (44) 154, 155, 174, 184, 264, 265, 266, 326, 327, 386, 387, 388, 389, 452, 455, 460, 518, 519, 520, 521, 566, 567, 568, 576, 590, 632, 676, 677, 678, 711, 712, 713, 715, 721, 726, 731, 736, 741, 744, 752, 756, 757, 830, 831.

RADFORD, Neal Victor; b Luanshya, Northern Rhodesia 7 Jun 1957; (6) 503, 504, 505, 506, 507, 520.

RADLEY, Clive Thornton; b Hertford 13 May 1944; (4) 50, 51, 52, 53.

RAMPRAKASH, Mark Ravin; b Bushey, Hertfordshire 5 Sep 1969; (10) 677, 678, 885, 886, 999, 1000, 1001, 1038, 1039, 1040.

RANDALL, Derek William; b Retford, Nottinghamshire 24 Feb 1951; (49) 38, 39, 42, 43, 44, 45, 46, 47, 53, 57, 58, 59, 60, 63, 67, 71, 72, 74, 76, 77, 79, 81, 82, 83, 84, 152, 153, 154, 155, 167, 168, 169, 170, 172, 174, 175, 176, 177, 179, 183, 184, 185, 249, 250, 251, 259, 260, 266, 326.

REEVE, Dermot Alexander; b Kowloon, Hong Kong 2 Apr 1963; (29) 678, 711, 712, 713, 715, 721, 726, 731, 736, 741, 744, 751, 752, 759, 760, 794, 795, 796, 797, 798, 799, 815, 816, 832, 913, 1037, 1039, 1069, 1075.

RHODES, Steven John; b Bradford, Yorkshire 17 Jun 1964; (9) 566, 567, 568, 913, 914, 915, 952, 955, 956.

RICHARDS, Clifton John; b Penzance, Cornwall 10 Aug 1958; (22) 141, 142, 144, 388, 389, 413, 415, 417, 418, 419, 420, 422, 423, 425, 427, 442, 445, 446, 448, 449, 450, 503.

ROBINSON, Robert Timothy; b Sutton in Ashfield, Nottinghamshire 21 Nov 1958; (26) 280, 281, 282, 326, 327, 330, 331, 364, 366, 367, 442, 445, 446, 452, 455, 463, 468, 472, 476, 477, 503, 504, 505, 506, 507, 521.

ROOPE, Graham Richard James; b Fareham, Hampshire 12 Jul 1946; (8) 6, 7, 45, 46, 47, 50, 51, 52.

ROSE, Brian Charles; b Dartford, Kent 4 Jun 1950; (2) 45, 46.

RUSSELL, Robert Charles; b Stroud, Gloucestershire 15 Aug 1963; (37) 480, 521, 575, 576, 579, 583, 586, 610, 611, 612, 613, 614, 615, 632, 633, 634, 635, 643, 645, 646, 668, 669, 670, 676, 677, 678, 1039, 1040, 1041, 1042, 1043, 1047, 1052, 1056, 1059, 1069, 1075.

SALISBURY, Ian David Kenneth; b Northampton 21 Jan 1970; (4) 795, 816, 885, 886.

SHUTTLEWORTH, Kenneth; b St Helens, Lancashire 13 Nov 1944; (1) 1.

SLACK, Wilfred Norris; b Troumaca, St Vincent 12 Dec 1954; d Banjul, The Gambia 15 Jan 1989; (2) 365, 366.

SMALL, Gladstone Cleophas; b St George, Barbados 18 Oct 1961; (53) 413, 415, 417, 418, 419, 420, 423, 425, 427, 428, 429, 445, 446, 452, 455, 460, 463, 468, 472, 476, 477, 518, 519, 520, 521, 575, 576, 579, 583, 586, 590, 610, 611, 612, 613, 614, 615, 632, 633, 635, 643, 645, 646, 652, 653, 670, 713, 726, 741, 744, 748, 751, 758.

SMITH, Christopher Lyall; b Durban, South Africa 15 Oct 1958; (4) 249, 250, 251, 260.

SMITH, David Mark; b Balham, London 9 Jan 1956; (2) 365, 615.

*SMITH, Michael John; b Enfield, Middlesex 4 Jan 1942; (5) 8, 9, 13, 14, 15,

*SMITH, Neil Michael Knight; b Solihull, Birmingham 27 Jul 1967; (7) 1037, 1038, 1052, 1056, 1059, 1099, 1101.

SMITH, Robin Arnold; b Durban, South Africa 13 Sep 1963; (71) 521, 566, 567, 568, 575, 576, 579, 583, 586, 590, 610, 611, 612, 613, 614, 615, 632, 633, 634, 635, 643, 645, 646, 648, 649, 650, 652, 653, 668, 669, 670, 711, 712, 713, 715, 721, 726, 731, 736, 741, 744, 748, 756, 757, 758, 759, 760, 794, 795, 796, 797, 798, 799, 815, 816, 830, 831, 832, 882, 883, 884, 885, 886, 913, 1039, 1040, 1041, 1042, 1043, 1069, 1075.

SNOW, John Augustine; b Peopleton, Worcestershire 13 Oct 1941; (9) 1, 2, 3, 4, 6, 7, 19, 27, 31.

STEELE, David Stanley; b Bradeley, Staffordshire 29 Sep 1941; (1) 37.

STEVENSON, Graham Barry; b Ackworth, Yorkshire 16 Dec 1955; (4) 83, 84, 115, 116.

STEWART, Alec James; b Merton, Surrey 8 Apr 1963; (79) 575, 576, 579, 583, 586, 590, 610, 611, 612, 613, 614, 632, 633, 645, 646, 648, 649, 650, 652, 653, 668, 669, 670, 711, 712, 713, 715, 721, 726, 731, 736, 741, 744, 748, 751, 752, 756, 757, 758, 759, 760, 794, 795, 796, 798, 799, 815, 816, 830, 831, 832, 882, 883, 884, 885, 886, 913, 914, 915, 952, 954, 999, 1000, 1001, 1037,

1038, 1040, 1041, 1047, 1052, 1056, 1059, 1075, 1099, 1100, 1101, 1109, 1110, 1111.

TAVARÉ, Christopher James; b Orpington, Kent 27 Oct 1954; (29) 89, 90, 143, 145, 152, 153, 154, 155, 167, 168, 169, 172, 174, 175, 176, 177, 179, 183, 184, 185, 197, 201, 205, 209, 213, 217, 221, 259, 260.

TAYLOR, Jonathan Paul; b Ashby-de-la-Zouch, Leicestershire 8 Aug 1964; (1) 816.

TAYLOR, Leslie Brian; b Earl Shilton, Leicestershire 25 Oct 1953; (2) 364, 386.

TAYLOR, Robert William; b Stoke-on-Trent, Staffordshire 17 Jul 1941; (27) 8, 9, 15, 17, 18, 46, 47, 50, 51, 52, 53, 63, 67, 71, 72, 74, 143, 145, 152, 153, 154, 155, 167, 168, 249, 250, 251.

THOMAS, John Gregory; b Trebanos, Glamorgan, Wales 12 Aug 1960; (3) 364, 366, 450.

THORPE, Graham Paul; b Farnham, Surrey 1 Aug 1969; (30) 830, 831, 832, 882, 914, 915, 952, 954, 955, 956, 999, 1000, 1001, 1037, 1038, 1040, 1041, 1042, 1043, 1047, 1052, 1056, 1059, 1069, 1075, 1099, 1100, 1101, 1109, 1110.

TITMUS, Frederick John; b King's Cross, London 24 Nov 1932; (2) 17, 18.

TOLCHARD, Roger William; b Torquay, Devon 15 Jun 1946; (1) 57.

TUFNELL, Philip Clive Roderick; b Barnet, Hertfordshire 29 Apr 1966; (19) 645, 646, 648, 649, 650, 652, 653, 669, 670, 711, 712, 715, 721, 731, 748, 882, 883, 884, 954.

*UDAL, Shaun David; b Cove, Farnborough, Surrey 18 Mar 1969; (10) 913, 914, 915, 952, 954, 955, 956, 999, 1000, 1001.

UNDERWOOD, Derek Leslie; b Bromley, Kent 8 Jun 1945; (26) 6, 8, 9, 13, 14, 15, 16, 17, 23, 27, 37, 38, 39, 42, 43, 44, 76, 77, 79, 81, 82, 141, 142, 143, 144, 145.

WATKIN, Steven Llewellyn; b Maesteg, Glamorgan, Wales 15 Sep 1964; (4) 882, 883, 884, 886.

WATKINSON, Michael; b Westhoughton, Lancashire 1 Aug 1961; (1) 1039.

WELLS, Alan Peter; b Newhaven, Sussex 2 Oct 1961; (1) 1001.

*WELLS, Colin Mark; b Newhaven, Sussex 3 Mar 1960; (2) 326, 327.

WHITAKER, John James; b Skipton, Yorkshire 5 May 1962; (2) 442, 445.

WHITE, Craig; b Morley, Yorkshire 16 Dec 1969; (10) 952, 1037, 1038, 1039, 1040, 1041, 1042, 1043, 1047, 1052.

WILLEY, Peter; b Sedgefield, Co. Durham 6 Dec 1949; (26) 42, 43, 76, 77, 79, 81, 82, 83, 84, 86, 87, 89, 90, 91, 115, 116, 119, 120, 121, 329, 330, 331, 364, 365, 366, 367.

WILLIS, Robert George (Dylan assumed); b Sunderland, Co. Durham 30 May 1949; (64) 8, 9, 14, 42, 43, 44, 50, 51, 52, 53, 58, 59, 60, 63, 67, 71, 72, 76, 77, 79, 81, 82, 86, 87, 90, 119, 120, 121, 141, 142, 143, 144, 145, 152, 153, 154, 155, 167, 168, 169, 170, 172, 174, 175, 176, 177, 179, 183, 184, 185, 197, 201, 205, 209, 213, 217, 221, 249, 250, 251, 259, 264, 265, 266.

WOOD, Barry; b Ossett, Yorkshire 26 Dec 1942; (13) 4, 17, 18, 19, 27, 31, 37, 38, 39, 50, 51, 152, 153.

WOOLMER, Robert Andrew; b Kanpur, India 14 May 1948; (6) 2, 3, 4, 12, 37, 38.

AUSTRALIA (128 players)

* Denotes players who had not appeared in official Test matches before 28 September 1996.

ALDERMAN, Terence Michael; b Subiaco, Perth 12 Jun 1956; (65) 120, 121, 123, 124, 126, 127, 129, 130, 146, 147, 148, 159, 160, 161, 245, 246, 252, 253, 299, 307, 311, 315, 326, 540, 541, 542, 545, 546, 548, 549, 551, 552, 553, 566, 567, 568, 576, 578, 581, 585, 587, 597, 599, 600, 602, 603, 606, 607, 608, 609, 617, 618, 620, 622, 624, 630, 631, 644, 646, 647, 651, 652, 653, 654, 655.

ANGEL, Jo; b Subiaco, Perth 22 Apr 1968; (3) 925, 933, 978.

BEARD, Graeme Robert; b Auburn, New South Wales 19 Aug 1950; (2) 112, 113.

BENNETT, Murray John; b Brisbane 6 Oct 1956; (8) 271, 285, 286, 289, 290, 292, 326, 328.

BEVAN, Michael Gwyl; b Belconnen, ACT 8 May 1970; (36) 905, 907, 910, 922, 923, 925, 927, 928, 930, 932, 933, 935, 951, 952, 953, 1024, 1025, 1026, 1027, 1030, 1031, 1032, 1034, 1035, 1036, 1057, 1063, 1066, 1070, 1078, 1080, 1081, 1102, 1104, 1107, 1108.

*BISHOP, Glenn Andrew; b North Adelaide 25 Feb 1960; (2) 414, 416.

BLEWETT, Gregory Scott; b Adelaide 29 Oct 1971; (8) 974, 977, 978, 980, 984, 985, 986, 987.

BOON, David Clarence; b Launceston, Tasmania 29 Dec 1960; (181) 248, 285, 286, 289, 290, 292, 293, 294, 297, 329, 330, 331, 347, 349, 350, 351, 353, 354, 357, 358, 359, 360, 362, 363, 371, 372, 373, 374, 382, 390, 391, 392, 393, 394, 395, 413, 416, 443, 444, 446, 453, 456, 462, 465, 470, 471, 475, 477, 489, 490, 492, 494, 496, 498, 499, 500, 501, 502, 503, 522, 540, 541, 542, 545, 546, 548, 549, 550, 551, 552, 553, 566, 567, 568, 576, 578, 581, 585, 587, 596, 597, 599, 617, 618, 620, 621, 622, 624, 628, 630, 631, 642, 644, 646, 647, 650, 651, 652, 653, 654, 655, 671, 672, 675, 693, 694, 695, 697, 698, 699, 701, 702, 704, 705, 714, 719, 725, 731, 733, 739, 743, 749, 761, 762, 763, 771, 772, 773, 775, 776, 779, 780, 781, 782, 783, 818, 819, 820, 821, 830, 831, 832, 862, 863, 864, 865, 868, 869, 871, 872, 873, 874, 875, 887, 888, 889, 890, 891, 892, 894, 907, 910, 922, 923, 927, 928, 930, 933, 935, 951, 952, 953, 956, 974, 977, 978, 980, 984, 985, 986, 987.

BORDER, Allan Robert; b Cremorne, Sydney 27 Jul 1955; (273) 57, 58, 63, 66, 70, 75, 77, 78, 79, 80, 82, 83, 91, 92, 96, 97, 98, 99, 101, 104, 106, 107, 108, 110, 111, 112, 113, 114, 119, 120, 121, 123, 124, 126, 127, 129, 130, 131, 133, 135, 136, 137, 138, 139, 140, 146, 147, 148, 159, 160, 161, 166, 167, 170, 171, 173, 174, 175, 177, 178, 180, 181, 182, 192, 193, 194, 195, 196, 199, 203, 207, 212, 215, 219, 231, 232, 235, 236, 238, 239, 240, 242, 243, 245, 246, 247, 248, 252, 253, 254, 255, 267, 268, 269, 270, 285, 286, 289, 290, 292, 293, 294, 296, 297, 299, 300, 301, 302, 307, 311, 315, 326, 328, 329, 330, 331, 347, 349, 350, 351, 353, 354, 357, 358, 359, 360, 362, 363, 371, 372, 373, 374, 390, 391, 392, 393, 394, 395, 413, 414, 416, 420, 421, 422, 424, 425, 426, 428, 430, 431, 432, 443, 446, 453, 456, 462, 465, 470, 471, 475, 477, 489, 490, 492, 494, 496, 498, 499, 500, 501, 502, 503, 522, 540, 541, 542, 545, 546, 548, 549, 550, 551, 552, 553, 566, 567, 568, 576, 578, 581, 585, 587, 596, 597, 599, 600, 602, 603, 606, 607, 608, 609, 617, 618, 620, 622, 624, 628, 630, 631, 642, 644, 646, 647, 650, 651, 652, 653, 671, 672, 673, 674, 675, 693, 694, 695, 697, 698, 699, 701, 702, 704, 705, 714, 719, 725, 731, 733, 739, 743, 749, 761, 762, 763, 771, 779, 780, 781, 782, 783, 817, 819, 821, 830, 831, 862, 863, 864, 865, 868, 869, 872, 873, 874, 875, 887, 888, 889, 890, 891, 892, 893, 894.

BRIGHT, Raymond James; b Footscray, Melbourne 13 Jul 1954; (11) 10, 43, 44, 75, 77, 78, 92, 119, 373, 374, 382.

CALLEN, Ian Wayne; b Alexandra, Victoria 2 May 1955; (5) 48, 49, 159, 160, 161.

CAMPBELL, Gregory Dale; b Launceston, Tasmania 10 Mar 1964; (12) 596, 597, 606, 607, 608, 609, 617, 618, 620, 621, 622, 628.

CARLSON, Phillip Henry; b Kedron, Brisbane 8 Aug 1951; (4) 57, 58, 59, 60.

CHAPPELL, Gregory Stephen; b Unley, Adelaide 7 Aug 1948; (74) 1, 2, 3, 4, 10, 11, 16, 21, 25, 29, 31, 33, 34, 42, 43, 44, 75, 77, 78, 79, 80, 82, 83, 85, 91, 92, 96, 97, 98, 99, 101, 104, 106, 107, 108, 110, 111, 112, 113, 114, 123, 124, 126, 127, 129, 130, 131, 133, 135, 136, 137, 138, 139, 140, 146, 147, 148, 166, 167, 170, 171, 173, 174, 175, 177, 178, 180, 181, 182, 192, 193, 194, 195, 196.

CHAPPELL, Ian Michael; b Unley, Adelaide 26 Sep 1943; (16) 1, 2, 3, 4, 10, 11, 16, 21, 25, 29, 31, 33, 34, 80, 82, 83.

CHAPPELL, Trevor Martin; b Glenelg, Adelaide 21 Oct 1952; (20) 96, 97, 98, 99, 101, 104, 106, 107, 108, 110, 112, 113, 114, 119, 120, 121, 207, 212, 215, 219.

CLARK, Wayne Maxwell; b Perth 19 Sep 1953; (2) 48, 49.

COLLEY, David John; b Mosman, Sydney 15 Mar 1947; (1) 3.

CONNOLLY, Alan Norman; b Skipton, Victoria 29 Jun 1939; (1) 1.

COSIER, Gary John; b Richmond, Melbourne 25 Apr 1953; (9) 34, 43, 48, 57, 59, 60, 63, 66, 70.

DARLING, Warrick Maxwell; b Waikerie, South Australia 1 May 1957; (18) 48, 49, 57, 59, 60, 63, 66, 70, 79, 123, 124, 126, 127, 129, 130, 131, 136, 137.

DAVIS, Ian Charles; b North Sydney 25 Jun 1953; (3) 10, 42, 43.

DAVIS, Simon Peter; b Brighton, Melbourne 8 Nov 1959; (39) 347, 349, 350, 351, 353, 354, 357, 358, 359, 360, 362, 363, 371, 372, 373, 374, 382, 390, 391, 392, 393, 394, 395, 413, 424, 425, 426, 428, 430, 431, 432, 443, 444, 446, 498, 500, 501, 502, 503.

DODEMAIDE, Anthony Ian Christopher; b Williamstown, Melbourne 5 Oct 1963; (24) 489, 490, 492, 494, 496, 498, 499, 500, 501, 502, 503, 522, 761, 762, 763, 780, 781, 782, 783, 817, 818, 819, 820, 821.

DYER, Gregory Charles; b Parramatta, Sydney 16 Mar 1959; (23) 392, 393, 394, 395, 453, 456, 462, 465, 470, 471, 475, 477, 489, 490, 492, 494, 496, 498, 499, 500, 501, 502, 503.

DYMOCK, Geoffrey; b Maryborough, Queensland 21 Jul 1945; (15) 10, 11, 44, 57, 58, 59, 60, 63, 66, 70, 80, 82, 83, 85, 91.

DYSON, John; b Kogarah, Sydney 11 Jun 1954; (29) 92, 96, 97, 98, 99, 101, 104, 106, 119, 121, 130, 136, 137, 138, 146, 147, 148, 159, 160, 161, 166, 167, 170, 171, 173, 174, 175, 177, 178.

EDWARDS, Ross; b Cottesloe, Perth 1 Dec 1942; (9) 2, 3, 4, 16, 21, 25, 29, 31, 33.
EDWARDS, Walter John; b Subiaco, Perth 23 Dec 1949; (1) 16.
EMERY, Phillip Allen; b St Ives, New South Wales 25 Jun 1964; (1) 935.

FLEMING, Damien William; b Bentley, Western Australia 24 Apr 1970; (24) 871, 872, 894, 905, 907, 910, 925, 927, 928, 935, 951, 953, 956, 986, 1063, 1066, 1070, 1078, 1080, 1081, 1102, 1104, 1107, 1108.

GILBERT, David Robert; b Darlinghurst, Sydney 29 Dec 1960; (14) 347, 349, 350, 351, 354, 357, 358, 359, 360, 371, 372, 392, 393, 394.
*GILLESPIE, Jason Neil; b Darlinghurst, Sydney 19 Apr 1975; (1) 1104.
GILMOUR, Gary John; b Waratah, New South Wales 26 Jun 1951; (5) 10, 11, 31, 33, 34.
*GRAF, Shaun Francis; b Somerville, Melbourne 19 May 1957; (11) 96, 97, 98, 99, 101, 106, 107, 108, 110, 123, 124.

HAMMOND, Jeffrey Roy; b North Adelaide 19 Apr 1950; (1) 4.
HAYDEN, Matthew Lawrence; b Kingaroy, Queensland 29 Oct 1971; (13) 830, 831, 832, 863, 865, 872, 873, 874, 875, 893, 905, 907, 910.
HEALY, Ian Andrew; b Spring Hill, Brisbane 30 Apr 1964; (150) 522, 540, 541, 542, 545, 546, 548, 549, 550, 551, 552, 553, 566, 567, 576, 578, 581, 585, 587, 596, 597, 599, 600, 602, 603, 606, 607, 608, 609, 617, 618, 620, 621, 622, 624, 628, 630, 631, 642, 644, 646, 647, 650, 651, 652, 653, 654, 655, 671, 672, 673, 674, 675, 693, 694, 695, 697, 698, 699, 701, 702, 704, 705, 714, 719, 731, 733, 739, 743, 749, 761, 762, 763, 771, 772, 773, 775, 776, 779, 780, 781, 782, 783, 817, 818, 819, 820, 821, 830, 831, 832, 862, 863, 864, 865, 868, 869, 872, 873, 874, 875, 887, 888, 889, 890, 891, 892, 893, 894, 922, 923, 925, 927, 928, 930, 932, 951, 952, 953, 956, 974, 977, 978, 980, 984, 985, 986, 987, 988, 1024, 1025, 1026, 1027, 1030, 1031, 1032, 1034, 1035, 1036, 1057, 1063, 1066, 1070, 1078, 1080, 1081, 1102, 1104, 1107, 1108.
HILDITCH, Andrew Mark Jefferson; b North Adelaide 20 May 1956; (8) 58, 63, 66, 70, 285, 286, 289, 331.
HOGAN, Thomas George; b Merredin, Western Australia 23 Sep 1956; (16) 178, 193, 194, 195, 207, 212, 215, 219, 243, 247, 248, 254, 255, 267, 268, 270.
*HOGG, George Bradley; b Narrogin, Western Australia 6 Feb 1971; (2) 1102, 1107.
HOGG, Rodney Malcolm; b Richmond, Melbourne 5 Mar 1951; (71) 58, 63, 70, 75, 77, 78, 80, 82, 101, 104, 107, 108, 110, 111, 114, 119, 120, 121, 166, 167, 170, 171, 173, 174, 175, 177, 178, 180, 181, 182, 193, 194, 195, 196, 199, 203, 207, 212, 215, 219, 231, 232, 235, 236, 238, 239, 240, 242, 243, 245, 246, 247, 248, 252, 253, 255, 267, 269, 285, 286, 289, 292, 293, 294, 296, 297, 299, 300, 301, 302, 315.

HOLLAND, Robert George; b Camperdown, Sydney 19 Oct 1946; (2) 290, 329.
HOOKES, David William; b Mile End, Adelaide 3 May 1955; (39) 42, 44, 75, 78, 139, 140, 166, 167, 170, 171, 173, 174, 175, 177, 178, 180, 181, 182, 192, 193, 194, 195, 196, 199, 203, 207, 212, 215, 219, 232, 235, 236, 238, 239, 253, 254, 255, 347, 349.
HUGHES, Kimberley John; b Margaret River, Western Australia 26 Jan 1954; (97) 43, 44, 57, 58, 59, 60, 63, 66, 70, 75, 77, 78, 79, 80, 82, 83, 85, 91, 92, 96, 97, 98, 99, 101, 104, 106, 107, 108, 110, 111, 112, 113, 114, 119, 120, 121, 123, 124, 126, 129, 133, 135, 136, 137, 138, 139, 140, 146, 147, 148, 159, 160, 161, 166, 167, 170, 171, 173, 174, 175, 177, 178, 180, 181, 182, 192, 199, 203, 207, 212, 215, 231, 232, 235, 236, 238, 239, 240, 242, 243, 245, 246, 247, 248, 252, 253, 254, 255, 267, 268, 269, 270, 271, 307, 311, 326, 328.
HUGHES, Mervyn Gregory; b Euroa, Victoria 23 Nov 1961; (33) 540, 541, 542, 545, 549, 550, 551, 552, 553, 578, 581, 585, 587, 596, 597, 599, 600, 602, 620, 621, 628, 631, 647, 675, 725, 817, 818, 819, 820, 821, 830, 831, 832.
HURST, Alan George; b Altona, Melbourne 15 Jul 1950; (8) 16, 57, 58, 59, 60, 63, 66, 70.

JENNER, Terrence James; b Mount Lawley, Perth 8 Sep 1944; (1) 16.
JONES, Dean Mervyn, b Coburg, Victoria 24 Mar 1961; (164) 243, 245, 246, 247, 248, 252, 253, 254, 293, 294, 296, 297, 299, 300, 301, 302, 307, 311, 315, 326, 328, 359, 360, 362, 363, 382, 390, 391, 392, 393, 394, 395, 413, 414, 416, 420, 421, 422, 424, 425, 426, 428, 430, 431, 432, 453, 456, 462, 465, 470, 471, 475, 477, 489, 490, 492, 494, 496, 498, 499, 500, 501, 502, 503, 540, 541, 542, 545, 546, 548, 550, 551, 552, 553, 566, 567, 568, 576, 578, 581, 585, 587, 596, 597, 599, 600, 602, 603, 606, 607, 608, 609, 617, 618, 621, 622, 624, 628, 630, 631, 642, 644, 646, 647, 650, 651, 652, 653, 654, 655, 671, 672, 673, 674, 675, 693, 694, 695, 697, 698, 699, 701, 704, 705, 714, 719, 725, 731, 733, 739, 743, 749, 761, 762, 763, 771, 772, 773, 775, 776, 779, 780, 781, 782, 783, 817, 818, 819, 820, 821, 868, 869, 871, 872, 873, 874, 875, 887, 888, 889, 890, 891, 892, 893.
JULIAN, Brendon Paul; b Hamilton, New Zealand 10 Aug 1970; (2) 832, 988.

*KASPROWICZ, Michael Scott; b South Brisbane 10 Feb 1972; (2) 1025, 1026.
KENT, Martin Francis; b Mossman, Queensland 23 Nov 1953; (5) 111, 113, 114, 119, 120.
KERR, Robert Byers; b Aspley, Queensland 16 Jun 1961; (4) 302, 307, 311, 315.

LAIRD, Bruce Malcolm; b Mount Lawley, Perth 21 Nov 1950; (23) 75, 77, 78, 80, 82, 91, 92, 124, 126, 127, 129, 130, 131, 133, 135, 138, 139, 140, 146, 147, 148, 159, 160.
LANGER, Justin Lee; b Perth 21 Nov 1970; (7) 905, 907, 910, 925, 932, 933, 988.
LAUGHLIN, Trevor John; b Nyah West, Victoria 30 Jan 1951; (6) 48, 58, 59, 60, 63, 79.
LAW, Stuart Grant; b Herston, Brisbane 18 Oct 1968; (25) 951, 952, 953, 956, 1024, 1025, 1026, 1027, 1030, 1031, 1032, 1034, 1035, 1036, 1057, 1063, 1066, 1070, 1078, 1080, 1081, 1102, 1104, 1107, 1108.

LAWRY, William Morris; b Thornbury, Melbourne 11 Feb 1937; (1) 1.

LAWSON, Geoffrey Francis; b Wagga Wagga, New South Wales 7 Dec 1957; (79) 96, 97, 98, 119, 120, 121, 123, 124, 126, 127, 129, 130, 131, 133, 135, 159, 160, 161, 166, 167, 170, 171, 173, 177, 178, 180, 181, 182, 199, 203, 207, 219, 231, 232, 235, 236, 238, 239, 240, 242, 245, 246, 247, 248, 252, 253, 254, 255, 267, 268, 269, 270, 271, 285, 289, 290, 292, 293, 294, 296, 297, 299, 300, 301, 302, 307, 311, 315, 329, 330, 331, 566, 567, 568, 576, 578, 581, 585, 587.

*LEE, Shane; b Wollongong, New South Wales 8 Aug 1973; (8) 1024, 1025, 1026, 1027, 1030, 1031, 1063, 1066.

*LEHMANN, Darren Scott; b Gawler, South Australia 5 Feb 1970; (2) 1104, 1108.

LILLEE, Dennis Keith; b Subiaco, Perth 18 Jul 1949; (63) 2, 3, 4, 21, 25, 29, 31, 33, 34, 75, 77, 78, 79, 80, 82, 83, 85, 91, 92, 96, 97, 98, 99, 101, 104, 106, 107, 108, 110, 111, 112, 113, 114, 119, 120, 121, 126, 127, 129, 130, 131, 133, 135, 136, 137, 138, 139, 140, 146, 147, 148, 174, 175, 177, 180, 181, 182, 193, 194, 199, 203, 212, 215.

McCOSKER, Richard Bede; b Inverell, New South Wales 11 Dec 1946; (14) 21, 25, 29, 31, 33, 34, 42, 44, 75, 83, 85, 131, 133, 135.

*McCURDY, Rodney John; b Melbourne 30 Dec 1959; (11) 296, 297, 299, 300, 301, 302, 307, 311, 315, 326, 328.

McDERMOTT, Craig John; b Ipswich, Queensland 14 Apr 1965; (138) 285, 286, 289, 290, 292, 293, 294, 296, 300, 301, 302, 307, 311, 328, 329, 330, 331, 347, 349, 350, 351, 353, 354, 357, 358, 359, 360, 362, 363, 371, 372, 373, 374, 382, 390, 391, 394, 395, 416, 453, 456, 462, 465, 470, 471, 475, 477, 489, 490, 492, 494, 496, 498, 500, 501, 502, 522, 540, 541, 542, 545, 546, 548, 550, 603, 671, 672, 673, 674, 675, 693, 694, 695, 697, 698, 699, 701, 702, 704, 705, 714, 719, 725, 731, 733, 739, 743, 749, 761, 762, 763, 771, 772, 773, 775, 776, 779, 780, 781, 782, 783, 830, 831, 832, 862, 863, 864, 865, 868, 873, 874, 875, 887, 888, 889, 890, 922, 923, 927, 928, 930, 932, 933, 935, 951, 952, 984, 985, 987, 1024, 1025, 1030, 1031, 1032, 1034, 1035, 1036, 1057.

McGRATH, Glenn Donald; b Dubbo, New South Wales; 9 Feb 1970; (55) 862, 863, 864, 868, 869, 871, 872, 873, 887, 888, 889, 890, 891, 892, 893, 894, 907, 910, 922, 923, 930, 932, 933, 935, 951, 952, 953, 956, 974, 977, 978, 980, 985, 986, 987, 988, 1024, 1026, 1027, 1030, 1032, 1034, 1035, 1036, 1057, 1063, 1066, 1070, 1078, 1080, 1081, 1102, 1104, 1107, 1108.

McKENZIE, Graham Douglas; b Cottesloe, Perth 24 Jun 1941; (1) 1.

MACLEAN, John Alexander; b Brisbane 27 Apr 1946; (2) 57, 58.

*MacLEAY, Kenneth Harvey, b Bradford-on-Avon, Wiltshire, England 2 Apr 1959; (16) 178, 182, 192, 203, 207, 212, 219, 235, 236, 413, 414, 416, 420, 421, 422, 425.

MAGUIRE, John Norman; b Murwillumbah, New South Wales 15 Sep 1956; (23) 174, 175, 192, 193, 195, 196, 231, 232, 235, 236, 238, 239, 240, 242, 243, 253, 254, 255, 267, 268, 269, 270, 271.

MALLETT, Ashley Alexander; b Chatswood, Sydney 13 Jul 1945; (9) 1, 2, 3, 4, 11, 21, 25, 29, 34.

MALONE, Michael Francis; b Perth 9 Oct 1950; (10) 42,
43, 131, 133, 135, 136, 137, 138, 139, 140.

MARSH, Geoffrey Robert; b Northam, Western Australia 31 Dec 1958; (117) 350, 351, 353, 354, 357, 358, 359, 360, 362, 363, 371, 372, 373, 374, 382, 390, 391, 392, 393, 394, 395, 413, 414, 416, 420, 421, 422, 424, 425, 426, 428, 430, 431, 432, 443, 444, 446, 453, 456, 462, 465, 470, 471, 475, 477, 489, 490, 492, 494, 496, 498, 499, 500, 501, 502, 503, 522, 540, 541, 542, 545, 546, 548, 549, 550, 551, 552, 553, 566, 567, 568, 576, 578, 581, 585, 587, 596, 597, 599, 600, 618, 620, 621, 622, 624, 628, 630, 642, 644, 646, 647, 650, 651, 652, 653, 654, 655, 671, 672, 673, 674, 675, 693, 694, 695, 697, 698, 699, 701, 702, 704, 705, 714, 719, 725, 733, 739.

MARSH, Rodney William; b Armadale, Western Australia 11 Nov 1947; (92) 1, 2, 3, 4, 10, 11, 16, 21, 25, 29, 31, 33, 34, 42, 43, 75, 77, 78, 79, 80, 82, 83, 85, 91, 92, 96, 97, 98, 99, 101, 104, 106, 107, 108, 110, 111, 112, 113, 114, 119, 120, 121, 123, 124, 126, 127, 129, 130, 131, 133, 135, 136, 137, 138, 139, 140, 146, 147, 148, 159, 160, 161, 166, 167, 170, 171, 173, 174, 175, 177, 178, 180, 181, 182, 192, 199, 203, 207, 212, 215, 219, 231, 232, 235, 236, 238, 240, 242, 245, 246, 247, 248.

MARTYN, Damien Richard; b Darwin 21 Oct 1971; (11) 772, 773, 775, 776, 817, 818, 820, 832, 868, 869, 871.

MASSIE, Robert Arnold Lockyer; b Subiaco, Perth 14 Apr 1947; (3) 2, 3, 4.

MATTHEWS, Gregory Richard John; b Newcastle, New South Wales 15 Dec 1959; (59) 231, 232, 255, 326, 328, 329, 330, 331, 347, 349, 350, 351, 353, 354, 357, 358, 359, 362, 363, 371, 372, 373, 374, 382, 390, 391, 392, 393, 394, 395, 414, 420, 421, 422, 424, 425, 426, 428, 430, 431, 432, 443, 444, 446, 552, 587, 646, 647, 650, 651, 761, 762, 763, 771, 772, 776, 781, 782, 783.

MAY, Timothy Brian Alexander; b North Adelaide 26 Jan 1962; (47) 456, 462, 470, 471, 475, 477, 489, 496, 499, 522, 567, 568, 576, 578, 773, 775, 779, 780, 817, 818, 820, 821, 830, 831, 832, 865, 868, 869, 874, 875, 891, 892, 893, 905, 922, 923, 930, 932, 933, 952, 953, 974, 977, 978, 980, 984, 988.

MOODY, Thomas Massoon; b Adelaide 2 Oct 1965; (34) 453, 462, 465, 566, 567, 568, 585, 602, 603, 606, 607, 608, 609, 693, 694, 695, 697, 698, 699, 701, 702, 704, 705, 714, 719, 725, 731, 733, 739, 743, 749, 761, 762, 763.

MOSS, Jeffrey Kenneth; b Melbourne 29 Jun 1947; (1) 66.

O'DONNELL, Simon Patrick; b Deniliquin, New South Wales 26 Jan 1963; (87) 285, 286, 289, 290, 292, 293, 294, 296, 297, 299, 300, 301, 302, 307, 311, 315, 326, 328, 329, 330, 331, 413, 414, 416, 420, 421, 422, 424, 425, 426, 428, 430, 431, 432, 443, 444, 446, 453, 456, 462, 465, 471, 475, 477, 545, 546, 548, 549, 550, 551, 553, 576, 578, 581, 585, 587, 596, 597, 599, 600, 602, 603, 606, 607, 608, 609, 617, 618, 620, 621, 622, 624, 628, 630, 631, 642, 644, 646, 647, 650, 651, 652, 653, 654, 655, 693, 694.

O'KEEFFE, Kerry James; b Hurstville, Sydney 25 Nov 1949; (2) 42, 44.

PASCOE, Leonard Stephen (*formerly* DURTANOVICH); b Bridgetown, Western Australia 13 Feb 1950; (29) 42, 44, 75, 80, 82, 83, 85, 91, 92, 96, 97, 98, 99, 101, 104, 106, 107, 108, 111, 112, 114, 136, 137, 138, 139, 140, 146, 147, 148.

PHILLIPS, Wayne Bentley; b Adelaide 1 Mar 1958; (48) 161, 231, 232, 239, 240, 242, 243, 248, 252, 253, 254, 255, 267, 268, 269, 270, 271, 285, 286, 292, 293, 294, 296, 297, 299, 300, 301, 302, 307, 311, 315, 329, 330, 331, 347, 349, 350, 351, 353, 354, 357, 358, 359, 360, 371, 372, 373, 374.

PONTING, Ricky Thomas; b Launceston, Tasmania 19 Dec 1974; (27) 974, 977, 978, 980, 986, 988, 1024, 1025, 1026, 1027, 1030, 1031, 1032, 1034, 1035, 1036, 1057, 1063, 1066, 1070, 1078, 1080, 1081, 1102, 1104, 1107, 1108.

*PORTER, Graham David; b Middle Swan, Western Australia 18 Mar 1955; (2) 66, 70.

RACKEMANN, Carl Gray; b Wondai, Queensland 3 Jun 1960; (52) 166, 167, 170, 171, 173, 174, 192, 231, 232, 235, 236, 238, 239, 240, 242, 243, 245, 246, 247, 248, 252, 254, 267, 268, 269, 270, 271, 286, 566, 567, 568, 599, 600, 602, 603, 606, 607, 608, 609, 617, 618, 621, 622, 624, 630, 631, 642, 644, 646, 650, 652, 653.

REDPATH, Ian Ritchie; b Geelong, Victoria 11 May 1941; (5) 1, 10, 11, 16, 34.

REID, Bruce Anthony; b Osborne Park, Perth 14 Mar 1963; (61) 347, 349, 350, 351, 353, 354, 357, 358, 359, 360, 362, 363, 371, 372, 373, 374, 382, 390, 391, 392, 393, 395, 413, 414, 416, 420, 421, 422, 424, 431, 443, 444, 446, 453, 456, 462, 465, 470, 471, 475, 477, 642, 650, 651, 654, 655, 671, 672, 673, 674, 693, 694, 695, 697, 698, 714, 719, 731, 739, 743, 749.

REIFFEL, Paul Ronald; b Box Hill, Victoria 19 Apr 1966; (63) 702, 771, 772, 773, 775, 776, 779, 780, 781, 782, 783, 817, 818, 819, 820, 821, 830, 831, 862, 863, 864, 865, 868, 869, 871, 872, 873, 874, 875, 887, 888, 889, 890, 891, 892, 893, 894, 905, 907, 910, 974, 977, 980, 984, 985, 986, 987, 988, 1027, 1030, 1031, 1032, 1034, 1035, 1036, 1057, 1070, 1078, 1080, 1081, 1102, 1107, 1108.

RITCHIE, Gregory Michael; b Stanthorpe, Queensland 23 Jan 1960; (44) 160, 161, 235, 236, 238, 239, 240, 242, 243, 245, 246, 247, 252, 254, 255, 271, 290, 292, 293, 331, 347, 349, 350, 351, 353, 354, 357, 371, 372, 373, 374, 382, 390, 391, 392, 393, 394, 395, 426, 428, 430, 431, 432, 444.

RIXON, Stephen John; b Albury, New South Wales 25 Feb 1954; (6) 48, 49, 289, 290, 326, 328.

*ROBERTSON, Gavin Ron; b Sydney 28 May 1966; (4) 925, 927, 928, 956.

ROBINSON, Richard Daryl; b East Melbourne 8 Jun 1946; (2) 43, 44.

SERJEANT, Craig Stanton; b Nedlands, Perth 1 Nov 1951; (3) 42, 43, 49.

SHEAHAN, Andrew Paul; b Werribee, Victoria 30 Sep 1946; (3) 2, 3, 4.

*SIDDONS, James Darren; b Robinvale, Victoria 25 Apr 1964; (1) 522.

SIMPSON, Robert Baddeley; b Marrickville, Sydney 3 Feb 1936; (2) 48, 49.

SLATER, Michael Jonathon; b Wagga Wagga, New South Wales 21 Feb 1970; (37) 862, 863, 864, 890, 891, 892, 894, 905, 907, 922, 923, 925, 927, 928, 930, 932, 933, 935, 951, 952, 953, 956, 984, 985, 986, 987, 988, 1024, 1025, 1026, 1027, 1030, 1031, 1102, 1104, 1107, 1108.

SMITH, Stephen Barry; b Sydney 18 Oct 1961; (28) 180, 181, 182, 192, 193, 196, 238, 239, 240, 242, 243, 245, 246, 247, 252, 253, 254, 255, 268, 269, 270, 271, 294, 296, 297, 299, 300, 301.

STACKPOLE, Keith Raymond; b Collingwood, Melbourne 10 Jul 1940; (6) 1, 2, 3, 4, 10, 11.

TAYLOR, Mark Anthony; b Leeton, New South Wales 27 Oct 1964; (96) 596, 597, 600, 602, 603, 606, 607, 608, 609, 617, 620, 621, 624, 628, 630, 631, 654, 655, 673, 674, 725, 731, 761, 762, 763, 771, 772, 773, 775, 776, 779, 780, 781, 782, 783, 817, 818, 819, 820, 821, 830, 831, 832, 862, 864, 865, 868, 869, 871, 887, 888, 889, 893, 894, 905, 907, 910, 922, 923, 925, 927, 928, 930, 932, 933, 935, 951, 952, 953, 956, 974, 977, 978, 980, 984, 985, 986, 987, 988, 1024, 1025, 1026, 1027, 1030, 1031, 1032, 1034, 1035, 1036, 1057, 1063, 1066, 1070, 1078, 1080, 1081.

TAYLOR, Peter Laurence; b North Sydney 22 Aug 1956; (83) 420, 421, 422, 424, 425, 426, 428, 430, 431, 432, 443, 446, 453, 456, 490, 492, 494, 496, 498, 499, 500, 501, 502, 503, 522, 540, 541, 542, 546, 548, 549, 550, 551, 552, 553, 576, 581, 596, 599, 600, 602, 603, 606, 607, 608, 609, 617, 618, 620, 621, 622, 624, 628, 630, 631, 642, 644, 652, 653, 654, 655, 671, 672, 673, 674, 675, 693, 694, 695, 697, 698, 699, 701, 702, 704, 705, 714, 719, 725, 731, 733, 743, 749.

THOMSON, Alan Lloyd; b Reservoir, Melbourne 2 Dec 1945; (1) 1.

THOMSON, Jeffrey Robert; b Greenacre, Sydney 16 Aug 1950; (50) 16, 21, 25, 29, 31, 33, 43, 44, 48, 49, 77, 78, 79, 83, 91, 92, 123, 124, 126, 127, 129, 130, 133, 135, 136, 137, 138, 139, 140, 146, 147, 148, 159, 160, 161, 166, 167, 170, 171, 173, 175, 177, 178, 180, 181, 199, 215, 219, 330, 331.

TOOHEY, Peter Michael; b Blayney, New South Wales 20 Apr 1954; (5) 48, 49, 57, 59, 60.

*TRIMBLE, Glenn Samuel; b Herston, Brisbane 1 Jan 1963; (2) 535, 358.

TURNER, Alan; b Camperdown, Sydney 23 Jul 1950; (6) 21, 25, 29, 31, 33, 34.

VELETTA, Michael Robert John; b Subiaco, Perth 30 Oct 1963; (20) 443, 444, 470, 471, 475, 477, 489, 490, 492, 494, 496, 498, 499, 500, 501, 502, 503, 522, 566, 568.

WALKER, Maxwell Henry Norman; b West Hobart 12 Sep 1948; (17) 10, 11, 16, 21, 25, 29, 31, 33, 34, 42, 43, 79, 85, 110, 111, 112, 113.

WALTERS, Kevin Douglas; b Dungog, New South Wales 21 Dec 1945; (28) 1, 2, 4, 10, 11, 16, 21, 25, 29, 31, 33, 42, 44, 77, 79, 97, 98, 99, 101, 104, 106, 107, 108, 110, 111, 112, 113, 114.

WARNE, Shane Keith; b Ferntree Gully, Melbourne 13 Sep 1969; (59) 819, 862, 863, 864, 865, 869, 871, 872, 873, 874, 875, 887, 888, 889, 890, 891, 892, 893, 894, 905, 907, 910, 922, 923, 925, 927, 928, 930, 932, 933, 935, 951, 952, 953, 956, 974, 977, 978, 980, 984, 985, 986, 987, 1024, 1025, 1026, 1027, 1031, 1032, 1034, 1035, 1036, 1057, 1063, 1066, 1070, 1078, 1080, 1081.

WATSON, Graeme Donald; b Kew, Melbourne 8 Mar 1945; (2) 2, 3.

WAUGH, Mark Edward; b Canterbury, Sydney 2 Jun 1965; (117) 540, 541, 542, 549, 550, 552, 553, 609, 642, 644, 646, 647, 650, 651, 652, 653, 654, 655, 671, 672, 673, 674, 675, 699, 701, 702, 704, 705, 714, 733, 739, 743, 749, 761, 762, 763, 771, 772, 773, 775, 776, 779, 780, 781, 782, 783, 817, 818, 819, 820, 821, 830, 831, 832, 862, 863, 864, 865, 868, 869, 871, 872, 873, 874, 875, 887, 888, 889, 890, 891, 892, 893, 894, 905, 910, 922, 923, 925, 927, 928, 930, 932, 933, 935, 951, 952, 953, 956, 974, 977, 978, 980, 984, 985, 987, 988, 1024, 1025, 1026, 1027, 1030, 1031, 1032, 1034, 1035, 1036, 1057, 1063, 1066, 1070, 1078, 1080, 1081, 1102, 1104, 1107, 1108.

WAUGH, Stephen Rodger; b Canterbury, Sydney 2 Jun 1965; (200) 347, 349, 350, 351, 353, 354, 357, 358, 359, 360, 362, 363, 371, 372, 373, 374, 382, 390, 391, 392, 393, 394, 395, 413, 414, 416, 420, 421, 422, 424, 425, 426, 428, 430, 431, 432, 443, 444, 446, 453, 456, 462, 465, 470, 471, 475, 477, 489, 490, 492, 494, 496, 498, 499, 500, 501, 502, 503, 522, 540, 541, 542, 545, 546, 548, 549, 550, 551, 552, 553, 566, 567, 568, 576, 578, 581, 585, 587, 596, 597, 599, 600, 602, 603, 606, 607, 608, 617, 618, 620, 621, 622, 624, 628, 630, 631, 642, 644, 646, 647, 650, 651, 652, 653, 654, 655, 671, 672, 673, 674, 675, 693, 694, 695, 697, 698, 699, 701, 702, 704, 705, 714, 719, 725, 731, 733, 739, 743, 749, 771, 772, 773, 775, 776, 779, 780, 781, 782, 783, 817, 818, 819, 820, 821, 830, 831, 832, 862, 863, 864, 865, 871, 872, 873, 874, 875, 887, 888, 889, 890, 891, 892, 893, 894, 905, 907, 910, 922, 923, 925, 927, 928, 930, 932, 935, 956, 974, 977, 978, 980, 984, 985, 986, 987, 988, 1032, 1034, 1035, 1036, 1057, 1063, 1066, 1070, 1078, 1080, 1081, 1102, 1104, 1107, 1108.

WELLHAM, Dirk MacDonald; b Marrickville, Sydney 13 Mar 1959; (17) 127, 329, 330, 360, 362, 363, 420, 421, 422, 424, 425, 426, 428, 430, 432, 444, 446.

WESSELS, Kepler Christoffel; b Bloemfontein, South Africa 14 Sep 1957; (54) 166, 167, 170, 171, 173, 174, 175, 177, 194, 195, 196, 199, 203, 207, 231, 232, 235, 236, 238, 239, 240, 242, 243, 245, 246, 247, 248, 252, 253, 267, 268, 269, 270, 271, 285, 286, 289, 290, 292, 293, 294, 296, 297, 299, 300, 301, 302, 307, 311, 315, 326, 328, 329, 330. *(Also 55 LOIs for South Africa:*

686, 687, 688, 719, 723, 727, 730, 735, 738, 741, 745, 751, 753, 754, 755, 784, 785, 786, 787, 788, 789, 790, 804, 805, 807, 808, 810, 811, 836, 837, 838, 848, 849, 853, 855, 856, 862, 864, 866, 887, 888, 889, 890, 891, 892, 893, 894, 914, 915, 927, 929, 930, 931, 933, 934).

WHATMORE, Davenell Frederick; b Colombo, Ceylon 16 Mar 1954; (1) 85.

WHITNEY, Michael Roy; b Surry Hills, Sydney 24 Feb 1959; (38) 192, 413, 414, 489, 490, 492, 494, 499, 503, 671, 672, 673, 674, 675, 695, 697, 698, 699, 701, 702, 704, 705, 719, 725, 731, 733, 739, 743, 749, 761, 762, 763, 771, 772, 773, 775, 776, 779.

WIENER, Julien Mark; b Melbourne 1 May 1955; (7) 77, 78, 79, 80, 82, 83, 85.

WOOD, Graeme Malcolm; b East Fremantle, Western Australia 6 Nov 1956; (83) 48, 49, 57, 58, 59, 60, 91, 96, 99, 104, 106, 107, 108, 110, 111, 112, 113, 114, 119, 120, 121, 123, 124, 126, 127, 129, 130, 131, 133, 135, 136, 137, 138, 139, 140, 146, 147, 148, 159, 160, 161, 180, 181, 182, 192, 193, 194, 195, 196, 199, 203, 212, 215, 219, 267, 268, 269, 270, 271, 285, 286, 289, 290, 292, 293, 294, 296, 297, 299, 300, 301, 302, 315, 326, 328, 329, 330, 331, 545, 546, 548, 549, 551.

WOODCOCK, Ashley John; b Adelaide 27 Feb 1947; (1) 11.

WOOLLEY, Roger Douglas; b Hobart 16 Sep 1954; (4) 193, 194, 195, 196.

WRIGHT, Kevin John; b North Fremantle, Western Australia 27 Dec 1953; (5) 59, 60, 63, 66, 70.

YALLOP, Graham Neil; b Balwyn, Melbourne 7 Oct 1952; (30) 48, 49, 57, 58, 59, 60, 63, 66, 70, 85, 91, 92, 120, 121, 193, 194, 195, 196, 199, 203, 207, 212, 215, 219, 231, 267, 268, 269, 270, 271.

YARDLEY, Bruce; b Midland, Western Australia 5 Sep 1947; (7) 49, 123, 131, 159, 194, 195, 196.

*ZESERS, Andris Karlis; b Medindie, South Australia 11 Mar 1967; (2) 465, 470.

ZOEHRER, Timothy Joseph; b Armadale, Western Australia 25 Sep 1961; (22) 362, 363, 382, 390, 391, 413, 414, 416, 420, 421, 422, 424, 425, 426, 428, 430, 431, 432, 443, 444, 446, 871.

SOUTH AFRICA (41 players)

* Denotes players who had not appeared in official Test matches before 28 September 1996.

ADAMS, Paul Regan; b Cape Town 20 Jan 1977; (6) 1037, 1042, 1043, 1065, 1077, 1096.

*BOJE, Nico; b Bloemfontein 20 Mar 1973; (2) 1012, 1038.

BOSCH, Tertius; b Vereeniging, Transvaal 14 Mar 1966; (2) 723, 755.

*CALLAGHAN, David John; b Queenstown, Cape Province 1 Feb 1965; (27) 784, 785, 786, 787, 788, 789, 790, 805, 807, 848, 855, 862, 866, 868, 870, 871, 873, 875, 962, 964, 965, 968, 969, 970, 974, 976, 979.

COOK, Stephen James; b Johannesburg 31 Jul 1953; (4) 686, 687, 688, 837.

CRONJE, Wessel Johannes; b Bloemfontein 25 Sep 1969; (88) 719, 723, 727, 735, 738, 741, 745, 751, 753, 754, 755, 784, 785, 786, 787, 788, 789, 790, 804, 805, 807, 808, 810, 811, 836, 838, 848, 849, 853, 855, 856, 862, 864, 866, 867, 868, 870, 871, 873, 874, 875, 887, 888, 889, 890, 891, 892, 893, 894, 914, 915, 927, 929, 930, 931, 933, 934, 959, 961, 962, 964, 965, 968, 969, 970, 974, 976, 979, 1012, 1013, 1037, 1038, 1039, 1040, 1041, 1042, 1043, 1048, 1053, 1059, 1065, 1071, 1077, 1092, 1093, 1095, 1096, 1097.

*CROOKES, Derek Norman; b Mariannhill, Natal 5 Mar 1969; (6) 929, 930, 933, 1095, 1096, 1097.

CULLINAN, Daryll John; b Kimberley 4 Mar 1967; (51) 804, 808, 810, 811, 836, 837, 838, 848, 849, 853, 856, 862, 864, 866, 867, 868, 870, 871, 873, 874, 914, 915, 927, 929, 931, 933, 934, 959, 961, 962, 964, 965, 968, 969, 970, 974, 976, 979, 1037, 1039, 1040, 1048, 1053, 1059, 1065, 1071, 1077, 1092, 1093, 1096, 1097.

De VILLIERS, Petrus Stephanus; b Vereeniging, Transvaal 13 Oct 1964; (68) 784, 786, 787, 788, 789, 790, 804, 805, 807, 808, 810, 811, 836, 837, 838, 848, 849, 853, 855, 856, 862, 864, 866, 867, 868, 870, 871, 873, 874, 875, 887, 888, 889, 890, 891, 892, 893, 894, 914, 915, 927, 929, 930, 931, 933, 934, 959, 961, 962, 964, 965, 968, 969, 970, 974, 976, 979, 1012, 1013, 1041, 1042, 1043, 1059, 1092, 1093, 1095, 1096, 1097.

DONALD, Allan Anthony; b Bloemfontein 20 Oct 1966; (61) 686, 687, 688, 719, 723, 727, 730, 735, 738, 741, 745, 751, 753, 754, 784, 785, 786, 787, 788, 789, 790, 804, 805, 807, 808, 810, 811, 836, 837, 838, 848, 849, 853, 855, 856, 862, 864, 867, 870, 871, 873, 874, 875, 887, 889, 915, 970, 974, 976, 979, 1012, 1013, 1037, 1038, 1039, 1040, 1041, 1048, 1053, 1065, 1071.

EKSTEEN, Clive Edward; b Johannesburg 2 Dec 1966; (6) 687, 930, 931, 934, 959, 968.

HENRY, Omar; b Stellenbosch, Cape Province 23 Jan 1952; (3) 727, 753, 754.

HUDSON, Andrew Charles; b Eshowe, Natal (Zululand) 17 Mar 1965; (68) 686, 688, 719, 723, 730, 735, 738, 741, 745, 751, 753, 754, 755, 784, 785, 786, 787, 788, 789, 790, 804, 805, 807, 808, 810, 811, 836, 837, 838, 848, 849, 853, 855, 856, 862, 864, 866, 867, 890, 891, 892, 893, 894, 929, 930, 931, 959, 961, 962, 964, 965, 968, 976, 979, 1012, 1038, 1039, 1040, 1041, 1043, 1048, 1065, 1071, 1077, 1092, 1093, 1095, 1097.

JACK, Steven Douglas; b Durban 4 Aug 1970; (2) 964, 969.

KALLIS, Jacques Henry; b Pinelands, Cape Town 16 Oct 1975; (14) 1037, 1038, 1039, 1040, 1041, 1042, 1043, 1048, 1053, 1059, 1065, 1071, 1095, 1096.

KIRSTEN, Gary; b Cape Town 23 Nov 1967; (46) 864, 866, 868, 870, 871, 873, 874, 875, 887, 888, 889, 893, 914, 915, 927, 930, 931, 933, 934, 959, 961, 968, 969, 970, 974, 976, 979, 1012, 1013, 1037, 1038, 1040, 1041, 1042, 1043, 1048, 1053, 1059, 1065, 1071, 1077, 1092, 1093, 1095, 1096, 1097.

KIRSTEN, Peter Noel, b Pietermaritzburg 14 May 1955; (40) 686, 687, 688, 719, 723, 727, 730, 738, 741, 745, 751, 753, 754, 755, 784, 785, 786, 787, 788, 789, 790, 804, 805, 807, 808, 810, 811, 867, 870, 871, 873, 874, 875, 887, 888, 889, 890, 891, 892, 914.

*KLUSENER, Lance; b Durban 4 Sep 1971; (1) 1042.

KUIPER, Adrian Paul; b Johannesburg 24 Aug 1959; (25) 686, 687, 688, 719, 723, 727, 730, 735, 738, 741, 745, 751, 753, 754, 755, 887, 888, 889, 890, 891, 893, 894, 1012, 1013, 1043.

*LIEBENBERG, Gerhardus Frederick Johannes; b Upington, Cape Province 7 Apr 1972: (1) 1013.

McMILLAN, Brian Mervin; b Welcom, Orange Free State 22 Dec 1963; (58) 686, 688, 719, 723, 727, 730, 735, 738, 741, 745, 751, 784, 785, 786, 787, 788, 790, 804, 805, 807, 836, 837, 838, 848, 849, 853, 855, 856, 867, 868, 870, 873, 874, 891, 892, 893, 894, 915, 927, 961, 970, 1012, 1037, 1038, 1039, 1041, 1042, 1043, 1048, 1053, 1059, 1065, 1071, 1077, 1092, 1093, 1096, 1097.

MATTHEWS, Craig Russell; b Cape Town 15 Feb 1965; (53) 687, 688, 784, 785, 786, 787, 788, 789, 790, 804, 808, 848, 864, 866, 867, 870, 871, 888, 889, 890, 891, 892, 893, 894, 914, 915, 927, 931, 933, 934, 959, 961, 962, 964, 965, 968, 979, 1012, 1013, 1037, 1039, 1040, 1041, 1048, 1053, 1059, 1065, 1071, 1077, 1092, 1093, 1095, 1097.

*PALFRAMAN, Steven John; b East London 12 May 1970; (7) 1043, 1048, 1053, 1059, 1065, 1071, 1077.

POLLOCK, Shaun Maclean; b Port Elizabeth 16 Jul 1973; (18) 1037, 1038, 1039, 1040, 1041, 1042, 1043, 1048, 1053, 1059, 1065, 1071, 1077, 1092, 1093, 1095, 1096, 1097.

PRINGLE, Meyrick Wayne; b Adelaide, Cape Province 22 Jun 1966; (17) 719, 730, 735, 738, 741, 745, 751, 754, 755, 789, 805, 807, 808, 810, 811, 929, 930.

RHODES, Jonathan Neil; b Pietermaritzburg 27 Jul 1969; (84) 719, 723, 727, 730, 735, 738, 741, 745, 751, 753, 754, 784, 785, 786, 787, 788, 789, 790, 804, 805, 807, 808, 810, 811, 836, 837, 838, 848, 849, 853, 855, 856, 862, 864, 867, 868, 870, 871, 873, 874, 875, 887, 888, 889, 890, 891, 892, 893, 894, 914, 915, 927, 929, 930, 931, 933, 934, 959, 961, 962, 964, 965, 968, 969, 970, 974, 976, 979, 1012, 1013, 1037, 1038, 1039, 1040, 1041, 1042, 1048, 1053, 1059, 1077, 1092, 1093, 1095, 1096.

*RICE, Clive Edward Butler; b Johannesburg 23 Jul 1949; (3) 686, 687, 688.

RICHARDSON, David John; b Johannesburg 16 Sep 1959; (82) 686, 687, 688, 719, 723, 727, 730, 735, 738, 741, 745, 751, 753, 754, 755, 784, 785, 786, 787, 788, 789, 790, 804, 805, 810, 836, 837, 838, 848, 849, 853, 855, 856, 862, 864, 866, 868, 870, 871, 873, 874, 875, 887, 888, 889, 890, 891, 892, 893, 894, 914, 915, 927, 929, 930, 931, 933, 934, 959, 961, 962, 964, 965, 968, 969, 970, 974, 976, 979, 1012, 1013, 1037, 1038, 1039, 1040, 1041, 1042, 1092, 1093, 1095, 1096, 1097.

*RINDEL, Michael John Raymond; b Durban 9 Feb 1963; (8) 959, 961, 962, 964, 965, 969, 970, 974.

*RUNDLE, David Bryan; b Cape Town 25 Sep 1965: (2) 868, 875.

RUSHMERE, Mark Weir; b Port Elizabeth 7 Jan 1965; (4) 727, 730, 735, 755

SCHULTZ, Brett Nolan; b East London 26 Aug 1970; (1) 785.

*SHAW, Timothy Gower; b Empangeni, Natal (Zululand) 5 Jul 1959: (9) 686, 892, 894, 914, 915, 927, 929, 933, 934.

*SIMONS, Eric Owen; b Cape Town 9 Mar 1962; (23) 887, 888, 890, 891, 892, 893, 894, 927, 929, 930, 931, 933, 934, 959, 962, 964, 965, 968, 969, 970, 974, 976, 979.

SNELL, Richard Peter; b Durban 12 Sep 1968; (42) 686, 687, 688, 719, 723, 727, 730, 735, 738, 741, 745, 751, 753, 754, 755, 810, 811, 836, 837, 838, 849, 853, 855, 856, 862, 864, 866, 868, 871, 873, 874, 875, 887, 888, 890, 914, 961, 962, 965, 1038, 1039, 1042.

*STEWART, Errol Leslie Rae; b Durban 30 Jul 1969; (5) 807, 808, 811, 867, 875.

STEYN, Philippus Jeremia Rudolf; b Kimberley 30 Jun 1967; (1) 1013.

SYMCOX, Patrick Leonard; b Kimberley 14 Apr 1960; (27) 836, 837, 838, 849, 853, 855, 856, 862, 866, 867, 868, 874, 889, 969, 974, 976, 1013, 1040, 1043, 1053, 1059, 1071, 1077, 1092, 1093, 1095, 1097.

*VAN ZYL, Cornelius Johannes Petrus Gerthardus; b Bloemfontein 1 Oct 1961; (2) 753, 755.

WESSELS, Kepler Christoffel; b Bloemfontein 14 Sep 1957; (55) 686, 687, 688, 719, 723, 727, 730, 735, 738, 741, 745, 751, 753, 754, 755, 784, 785, 786, 787, 788, 789, 790, 804, 805, 807, 808, 810, 811, 836, 837, 838, 848, 849, 853, 855, 856, 862, 864, 866, 887, 888, 889, 890, 891, 892, 893, 894, 914, 915, 927, 929, 930, 931,

933, 934. (*Also 54 LOIs for Australia: 166, 167, 170, 171, 173, 174, 175, 177, 194, 195, 196, 199, 203, 207, 231, 232, 235, 236, 238, 239, 240, 242, 243, 245, 246, 247, 248, 252, 253, 267, 268, 269, 270, 271, 285, 286, 289, 290, 292, 293, 294, 296, 297, 299, 300, 301, 302, 307, 311, 315, 326, 328, 329, 330*).

*YACHAD, Mandy; b Johannesburg 17 Nov 1960; (1) 687.

WEST INDIES (77 players)

* Denotes players who had not appeared in official Test matches before 28 September 1996.

ADAMS, James Clive; b Port Maria, Jamaica 9 Jan 1968; (60) 777, 778, 809, 811, 812, 813, 825, 826, 827, 828, 839, 840, 842, 844, 845, 847, 849, 851, 857, 858, 859, 860, 861, 882, 883, 884, 885, 886, 936, 937, 938, 939, 941, 942, 944, 947, 971, 972, 973, 984, 985, 986, 987, 988, 999, 1000, 1001, 1023, 1024, 1027, 1064, 1070, 1077, 1080, 1082, 1083, 1084, 1085, 1086, 1098.

AMBROSE, Curtly Elconn Lynwall; b Swetes Village, Antigua 21 Sep 1963; (133) 508, 509, 510, 518, 519, 523, 524, 526, 527, 539, 541, 542, 543, 546, 547, 550, 551, 552, 553, 559, 560, 561, 562, 563, 569, 570, 572, 573, 577, 578, 582, 584, 586, 591, 592, 614, 615, 639, 640, 671, 672, 673, 674, 676, 677, 678, 679, 681, 682, 683, 689, 690, 691, 692, 695, 696, 698, 699, 700, 701, 703, 717, 721, 730, 734, 737, 742, 749, 753, 754, 755, 770, 771, 772, 774, 776, 777, 778, 782, 783, 805, 806, 808, 809, 811, 813, 825, 826, 827, 828, 829, 839, 840, 845, 849, 851, 857, 858, 859, 860, 861, 882, 884, 885, 971, 972, 973, 984, 985, 986, 987, 999, 1000, 1001, 1023, 1024, 1025, 1027, 1028, 1029, 1030, 1033, 1049, 1055, 1064, 1070, 1077, 1080, 1082, 1083, 1084, 1085, 1086.

*ANTHONY, Hamish Aubrey Gervais; b Urlings Village, Antigua 16 Jan 1971; (3) 1005, 1007, 1011.

ARTHURTON, Keith Lloyd Thomas; b Charlestown, Nevis 21 Feb 1965; (86) 527, 550, 559, 560, 561, 562, 563, 569, 570, 572, 573, 584, 591, 612, 613, 614, 681, 683, 689, 690, 691, 692, 695, 696, 698, 699, 717, 721, 724, 730, 734, 737, 742, 749, 753, 754, 755, 770, 771, 772, 774, 776, 778, 779, 839, 840, 842, 845, 847, 849, 851, 854, 857, 858, 859, 860, 861, 882, 883, 884, 885, 886, 936, 937, 939, 941, 942, 944, 945, 946, 947, 971, 972, 973, 985, 986, 987, 988, 999, 1000, 1001, 1049, 1064, 1070, 1077, 1080.

AUSTIN, Richard Arkwright; b Kingston, Jamaica 5 Sep 1954; (1) 48.

BACCHUS, Sheik Faoud Ahamul Fasiel; b Georgetown, British Guiana 31 Jan 1954; (29) 48, 49, 89, 90, 93, 94, 115, 122, 124, 125, 128, 129, 134, 135, 136, 137, 138, 139, 140, 190, 191, 200, 203, 208, 210, 215, 220, 222, 223.

BAPTISTE, Eldine Ashworth Elderfield; b Liberta, Antigua 12 Mar 1960; (43) 226, 227, 228, 229, 230, 231, 233, 234, 236, 237, 239, 241, 242, 244, 245, 246, 247, 248, 254, 255, 264, 265, 266, 285, 320, 321, 322, 323, 324, 459, 483, 484, 485, 486, 487, 488, 559, 560, 561, 562, 563, 613, 614.

BENJAMIN, Kenneth Charlie Griffith; b St John's, Antigua 8 Apr 1967; (23) 770, 777, 778, 779, 782, 783, 839, 840, 842, 844, 845, 849, 854, 858, 859, 883, 884, 885, 886, 936, 938, 941, 971.

BENJAMIN, Winston Keithroy Matthew; b St John's, Antigua 31 Dec 1964; (85) 396, 397, 398, 399, 400, 402, 403, 405, 412, 426, 430, 452, 457, 464, 468, 473, 481, 482, 483, 484, 485, 486, 487, 488, 508, 509, 510, 511, 512, 520, 523, 539, 541, 542, 543, 544, 546, 547, 572, 573, 577, 578, 582, 584, 586, 591, 592, 679, 683, 717, 721, 724, 730, 734, 737, 742, 749, 753, 754, 755, 840, 844, 847, 849, 851, 854, 857, 858, 860, 861, 882, 883, 884, 885, 886, 972, 973, 984, 985, 986, 987, 988, 999, 1000, 1001.

BEST, Carlisle Alonza; b Richmond Gap, St Michael, Barbados 14 May 1959; (24) 365, 452, 457, 509, 511, 570, 572, 573, 577, 578, 582, 610, 611, 612, 613, 614, 615, 639, 640, 641, 695, 700, 701, 703.

BISHOP, Ian Raphael; b Port-of-Spain, Trinidad 24 Oct 1967; (75) 519, 520, 524, 526, 527, 544, 546, 547, 550, 551, 552, 553, 559, 560, 561, 562, 563, 569, 570, 573, 577, 610, 611, 612, 613, 614, 639, 640, 641, 679, 681, 682, 683, 689, 690, 770, 771, 772, 774, 778, 782, 783, 805, 806, 808, 809, 811, 813, 825, 826, 827, 828, 829, 999, 1000, 1001, 1005, 1007, 1008, 1009, 1023, 1024, 1028, 1029, 1030, 1033, 1049, 1055, 1064, 1070, 1077, 1080, 1082, 1083, 1098.

BOYCE, Keith David; b Castle, St Peter, Barbados 11 Oct 1943; d Barbados 11 Oct 1996; (8) 8, 9, 22, 26, 29, 32, 33, 34.

*BROWNE, Barrington St Aubyn; b Georgetown, Guyana 16 Sep 1967; (4) 937, 938, 945, 947.

BROWNE, Courtney Oswald; b Lambeth, London, England 7 Dec 1970; (20) 1005, 1007, 1008, 1009, 1011, 1023, 1024, 1025, 1027, 1028, 1029, 1030, 1033, 1049, 1055, 1070, 1077, 1080, 1086, 1098.

CAMPBELL, Sherwin Legay; b Belle Plaine, St Andrew, Barbados 1 Nov 1970; (26) 938, 939, 971, 972, 973, 987, 988, 999, 1000, 1005, 1007, 1008, 1009, 1011, 1023, 1024, 1025, 1027, 1028, 1029, 1030, 1033, 1049, 1055, 1064, 1070.

CHANDERPAUL, Shivnarine; b Unity Village, Guyana 18 Aug 1974; (30) 936, 937, 938, 941, 946, 947, 1005, 1007, 1008, 1009, 1011, 1023, 1024, 1025, 1027, 1028, 1029, 1033, 1049, 1055, 1064, 1070, 1077, 1080, 1082, 1083, 1084, 1085, 1086, 1098.

CLARKE, Sylvester Theophilus; b Lead Vale, Christ Church, Barbados 11 Dec 1954; (10) 49, 94, 95, 134, 135, 136, 137, 138, 139, 140.

CROFT, Colin Everton Hunte; b Lancaster Village, Demerara, British Guiana 15 Mar 1953; (19) 41, 48, 61, 69, 73, 74, 75, 76, 85, 86, 87, 88, 93, 94, 95, 115, 116, 122, 124.

CUFFY, Cameron Eustace; b South Rivers, St Vincent 8 Feb 1970; (10) 936, 937, 939, 941, 942, 944, 945, 946, 947, 1064.

CUMMINS, Anderson Cleophas; b Packer's Valley, Christ Church, Barbados 7 May 1966; (63) 689, 691, 692, 695, 696, 698, 699, 700, 701, 703, 724, 730, 734, 737, 742, 749, 753, 754, 755, 770, 771, 772, 774, 776, 779, 782, 783, 812, 829, 839, 840, 842, 845, 847, 849, 854, 857, 858, 860, 861, 882, 883, 884, 885, 886, 936, 937, 938, 939, 941, 942, 944, 945, 946, 947, 971, 972, 973, 1007, 1008, 1009, 1011, 1025.

DANIEL, Wayne Wendell; b Brereton Village, St Philip, Barbados 16 Jan 1956; (18) 48, 203, 208, 220, 227, 230, 231, 233, 234, 236, 237, 239, 241, 242, 245, 246, 252, 253.

DAVIS, Winston Walter; b Kingstown, St Vincent 18 Sep 1958; (35) 190, 203, 208, 210, 215, 220, 234, 236, 237, 244, 248, 252, 288, 289, 290, 291, 293, 295, 296, 298, 300, 301, 302, 309, 313, 317, 318, 320, 321, 322, 323, 324, 485, 486, 488.

DHANRAJ, Rajindra; b Port-of-Spain, Trinidad 6 Feb 1969; (6) 939, 942, 944, 971, 972, 973.

*DRAKES, Vasbert Conneil; b St James, Barbados 5 Aug 1969; (5) 984, 985, 986, 987, 988.

DUJON, Peter Jeffrey Leroy; b Lyndhurst Town, Kingston, Jamaica 28 May 1956; (169) 125, 128, 129, 131, 132, 134, 135, 136, 137, 138, 139, 140, 189, 190, 191, 200, 203, 208, 210, 215, 220, 222, 223, 226, 227, 228, 229, 231, 233, 234, 236, 237, 239, 241, 242, 244, 245, 246, 247, 248, 252, 253, 254, 255, 264, 265, 266, 285, 287, 288, 289, 290, 291, 293, 295, 296, 298, 300, 301, 302, 309, 313, 317, 318, 320, 321, 322, 323, 324, 339, 341, 342, 343, 344, 345, 346, 364, 366, 367, 396, 397, 398, 399, 400, 402, 403, 405, 412, 415, 416, 419, 421, 423, 424, 426, 427, 429, 430, 439, 440, 452, 457, 459, 464, 468, 473, 481, 482, 483, 485, 486, 487, 508, 509, 510, 511, 512, 518, 519, 520, 523, 524, 526, 527, 541, 542, 543, 544, 546, 547, 550, 551, 552, 559, 560, 561, 562, 563, 569, 570, 572, 573, 577, 578, 582, 584, 586, 591, 592, 610, 611, 612, 613, 614, 615, 639, 640, 671, 672, 673, 674, 675, 676, 677, 678, 679, 681, 682, 683.

FOSTER, Maurice Linton Churchill; b Retreat, St Mary, Jamaica 9 May 1943; (2) 8, 9.

FREDERICKS, Roy Clifton; b Blairmont, Berbice, British Guiana 11 Nov 1942; (12) 8, 9, 22, 26, 29, 32, 33, 34, 37, 38, 39, 41.

*GABRIEL, Richard Simeon; b Point Fortin, Trinidad 5 Jun 1952; (11) 231, 233, 234, 236, 237, 239, 241, 242, 244, 245, 247.

GARNER, Joel; b Enterprise, Christ Church, Barbados 16 Dec 1952; (98) 41, 48, 61, 69, 73, 74, 75, 76, 78, 80, 81, 84, 86, 87, 88, 89, 90, 93, 94, 95, 115, 116, 122, 124, 125, 128, 129, 131, 132, 134, 135, 136, 137, 138, 139, 140, 189, 191, 200, 220, 222, 223, 231, 233, 244, 246, 247, 248, 252, 253, 254, 255, 264, 265, 266, 285, 287, 288, 289, 290, 293, 295, 296, 298, 300, 301, 302, 309, 313, 317, 318, 320, 321, 322, 323, 324, 339, 341, 342, 344, 345, 364, 365, 366, 367, 415, 416, 419, 421, 423, 424, 426, 427, 429, 430, 439, 440, 441.

GIBBS, Lancelot Richard; b Georgetown, British Guiana 29 Sep 1934; (3) 8, 9, 22.

GIBSON, Ottis Delroy; b Sion Hill, St James, Barbados 16

Mar 1969; (13) 1001, 1005, 1008, 1009, 1011, 1027, 1028, 1029, 1030, 1033, 1049, 1055, 1080.

GOMES, Hilary Angelo; Arima, Trinidad 13 Jul 1953; (83) 49, 85, 94, 95, 115, 116, 122, 128, 129, 131, 132, 134, 135, 136, 137, 138, 139, 140, 189, 190, 191, 200, 203, 208, 210, 215, 220, 222, 223, 226, 227, 228, 229, 230, 231, 233, 239, 241, 242, 246, 247, 248, 252, 253, 264, 265, 266, 285, 287, 288, 289, 290, 295, 298, 300, 301, 302, 309, 313, 321, 322, 323, 324, 339, 341, 343, 344, 345, 346, 364, 365, 366, 367, 396, 399, 400, 405, 416, 424, 426, 427, 429, 430.

GRAY, Anthony Hollis; b Port-of-Spain, Trinidad 23 May 1963; (25) 339, 342, 343, 346, 396, 398, 399, 402, 403, 405, 412, 416, 423, 424, 429, 430, 439, 440, 441, 511, 512, 671, 672, 673, 675.

GREENIDGE, Alvin Ethelbert; b Bath Village, Christ Church, Barbados 20 Aug 1956; (1) 49.

GREENIDGE, Cuthbert Gordon; b Black Bess, St Peter, Barbados 1 May 1951; (128) 26, 29, 32, 33, 34, 37, 38, 39, 41, 61, 69, 73, 74, 75, 76, 78, 80, 81, 84, 86, 87, 88, 89, 90, 93, 116, 122, 124, 125, 131, 132, 134, 135, 136, 137, 138, 139, 140, 189, 190, 191, 200, 203, 208, 210, 215, 222, 223, 226, 227, 228, 229, 230, 252, 253, 254, 255, 264, 265, 266, 285, 287, 291, 293, 295, 296, 298, 320, 364, 366, 367, 396, 397, 398, 400, 402, 403, 405, 412, 415, 416, 419, 421, 423, 439, 440, 441, 481, 483, 484, 488, 509, 510, 511, 512, 518, 519, 520, 523, 524, 526, 527, 539, 541, 542, 544, 546, 547, 551, 552, 553, 559, 560, 561, 562, 563, 610, 611, 614, 615, 640, 641, 671, 673, 674, 675, 676, 677.

HARPER, Roger Andrew; b Georgetown, British Guiana 17 Mar 1963; (105) 226, 227, 228, 229, 230, 244, 248, 254, 255, 266, 291, 317, 318, 320, 321, 322, 323, 324, 339, 341, 342, 343, 344, 345, 346, 364, 365, 366, 367, 396, 397, 398, 399, 400, 402, 403, 405, 412, 415, 416, 419, 421, 423, 424, 426, 427, 429, 430, 452, 457, 459, 464, 468, 473, 481, 482, 518, 523, 524, 526, 527, 543, 544, 546, 547, 550, 717, 721, 754, 755, 842, 844, 847, 851, 854, 859, 882, 883, 884, 885, 886, 1005, 1007, 1008, 1009, 1011, 1023, 1024, 1025, 1027, 1028, 1029, 1030, 1049, 1055, 1064, 1070, 1077, 1080, 1082, 1083, 1084, 1085, 1086, 1098.

HAYNES, Desmond Leo; b Holder's Hill, St James, Barbados 15 Feb 1956; (238) 48, 61, 69, 73, 74, 75, 76, 78, 80, 81, 84, 85, 86, 87, 88, 89, 90, 93, 94, 95, 115, 116, 122, 124, 125, 128, 129, 131, 132, 134, 135, 136, 137, 138, 139, 140, 189, 190, 191, 200, 203, 208, 210, 215, 220, 222, 223, 226, 227, 228, 229, 230, 231, 233, 234, 236, 237, 239, 241, 242, 244, 245, 246, 247, 248, 252, 253, 254, 255, 264, 265, 266, 285, 287, 289, 290, 291, 293, 295, 296, 298, 300, 301, 302, 309, 313, 317, 318, 320, 321, 322, 323, 324, 339, 341, 342, 343, 344, 345, 346, 364, 365, 366, 367, 397, 398, 399, 400, 402, 403, 412, 415, 416, 419, 421, 423, 424, 426, 427, 439, 440, 441, 452, 457, 459, 464, 468, 473, 481, 482, 483, 484, 486, 487, 508, 510, 512, 520, 523, 524, 526, 527, 539, 541, 542, 543, 544, 546, 547, 550, 551, 552, 553, 559, 560, 561, 562, 563, 569, 570, 572, 573, 577, 578, 582, 584, 586, 591, 592, 610, 611, 612, 613, 615, 639, 640, 641, 671, 672, 673, 674, 675, 689, 690, 691, 692, 695, 696, 698, 699, 700, 701, 703, 717, 721, 730, 734, 737, 742, 749, 753, 754, 755, 770, 771, 772, 774, 776, 777, 778, 779, 782, 783, 805, 806, 808, 809, 811, 812, 813, 825, 826, 827, 828, 829, 842, 844, 845, 847, 849, 854, 857, 860, 861, 882, 883, 884, 885.

*HAYNES, Robert Christopher; b Kingston, Jamaica 2 Nov 1964; (8) 573, 578, 582, 586, 592, 641, 691, 698.

HEADLEY, Ronald George Alphonso; b Vineyard Town, Kingston, Jamaica 29 Jun 1939; (1) 9.

*HOLDER, Roland Irwin Christopher; b Port-of-Spain, Trinidad 22 Dec 1967; (26) 844, 851, 854, 858, 886, 941, 942, 944, 945, 946, 947, 971, 972, 973, 988, 1005, 1007, 1033, 1055, 1077, 1082, 1083, 1084, 1085, 1086, 1098.

HOLDER, Vanburn Alonza; b Dean's Village, St Michael, Barbados 8 Oct 1945; (12) 8, 9, 22, 26, 29, 32, 33, 34, 37, 38, 39, 49.

HOLDING, Michael Anthony; b Half Way Tree, Kingston, Jamaica 16 Feb 1954; (102) 37, 38, 39, 61, 69, 73, 74, 75, 76, 78, 80, 81, 84, 85, 86, 87, 88, 89, 90, 93, 115, 116, 124, 125, 128, 129, 131, 132, 134, 135, 136, 137, 138, 139, 140, 189, 190, 191, 200, 203, 208, 210, 215, 222, 223, 226, 228, 229, 230, 231, 233, 234, 236, 237, 239, 241, 242, 245, 246, 247, 248, 254, 255, 264, 265, 266, 285, 287, 288, 289, 290, 291, 293, 295, 296, 300, 301, 302, 309, 313, 317, 318, 320, 321, 322, 323, 324, 339, 341, 342, 343, 344, 345, 346, 366, 367, 412, 415, 416, 419, 421, 427.

HOOPER, Carl Llewellyn; b Georgetown, Guyana 15 Dec 1966; (141) 439, 440, 441, 452, 457, 459, 464, 468, 473, 481, 482, 483, 484, 485, 486, 487, 488, 508, 509, 510, 511, 512, 518, 519, 520, 523, 524, 526, 527, 539, 541, 542, 543, 544, 546, 547, 551, 552, 553, 610, 611, 612, 613, 614, 615, 639, 640, 641, 671, 672, 673, 674, 675, 676, 677, 678, 679, 681, 682, 683, 689, 690, 691, 692, 695, 696, 698, 699, 700, 701, 703, 717, 721, 724, 730, 734, 737, 742, 749, 753, 770, 771, 772, 774, 776, 777, 778, 779, 782, 783, 805, 806, 808, 809, 811, 812, 813, 825, 826, 827, 828, 829, 839, 840, 842, 844, 845, 847, 849, 851, 857, 858, 859, 860, 861, 936, 937, 938, 939, 941, 942, 944, 945, 946, 947, 984, 985, 986, 987, 988, 999, 1000, 1001, 1023, 1024, 1025, 1027, 1028, 1029, 1030, 1033.

*JACOBS, Ridley Detamore; b Antigua 26 Nov 1967; (4) 1082, 1083, 1084, 1085.

JULIEN, Bernard Denis; b Carenage, Trinidad 13 Mar 1950; (12) 8, 9, 22, 26, 29, 32, 33, 34, 37, 38, 39, 41.

KALLICHARRAN, Alvin Isaac; b Port Mourant, Berbice, British Guiana 21 Mar 1949; (31) 8, 9, 22, 26, 29, 32, 33, 34, 41, 48, 49, 61, 69, 73, 74, 75, 76, 78, 80, 81, 84, 85, 86, 87, 88, 89, 90, 93, 94, 95, 115.

KANHAI, Rohan Bholalall; b Port Mourant, Berbice, British Guiana 26 Dec 1935; (7) 8, 9, 22, 26, 29, 32, 33.

KING, Collis Llewellyn; b Fairview, Christ Church, Barbados 11 Jun 1951; (18) 37, 38, 39, 41, 61, 69, 73, 74, 75, 78, 80, 81, 84, 85, 86, 87, 88, 90.

LAMBERT, Clayton Benjamin; b New Amsterdam, Berbice, Guyana 10 Feb 1962; (5) 614, 679, 681, 682, 683.

LARA, Brian Charles; b Santa Cruz, Trinidad 2 May 1969; (104) 639, 678, 679, 681, 682, 689, 690, 691, 692, 695, 696, 698, 699, 700, 701, 703, 717, 721, 724, 730, 734, 737, 742, 749, 753, 754, 755, 770, 771, 772, 774, 776, 777, 778, 779, 782, 783, 805, 806, 808, 809, 811, 812, 813, 825, 826, 827, 828, 829, 839, 840, 842, 844, 845, 847, 849, 851, 854, 857, 858, 859, 860, 861, 882,

883, 884, 885, 886, 936, 937, 938, 939, 942, 944, 945, 946, 947, 971, 972, 973, 984, 985, 986, 987, 999, 1000, 1001, 1005, 1007, 1008, 1009, 1011, 1049, 1055, 1064, 1070, 1077, 1080, 1082, 1083, 1084, 1085, 1086, 1098.

LLOYD, Clive Hubert; b Queenstown, Georgetown, British Guiana 31 Aug 1944; (87) 8, 9, 22, 26, 29, 32, 33, 34, 37, 38, 39, 41, 61, 69, 73, 74, 75, 76, 80, 81, 84, 85, 86, 87, 88, 89, 93, 94, 95, 115, 116, 122, 124, 125, 128, 129, 131, 132, 134, 135, 137, 138, 139, 140, 189, 190, 191, 200, 203, 208, 210, 215, 220, 222, 223, 226, 227, 228, 229, 231, 233, 234, 236, 239, 241, 242, 245, 246, 247, 253, 264, 265, 266, 285, 288, 289, 290, 293, 295, 296, 298, 300, 301, 302, 309, 313, 317.

LOGIE, Augustine Lawrence; b Sobo Village, La Brea, Trinidad 28 Sep 1960; (158) 128, 129, 131, 132, 189, 220, 234, 236, 237, 239, 241, 242, 244, 245, 248, 252, 254, 255, 287, 288, 289, 290, 291, 293, 295, 296, 298, 300, 301, 302, 309, 313, 317, 318, 320, 321, 322, 323, 324, 339, 341, 342, 343, 344, 345, 346, 396, 397, 398, 399, 400, 402, 403, 405, 412, 415, 416, 419, 421, 423, 424, 426, 427, 429, 430, 439, 440, 441, 452, 457, 459, 464, 468, 473, 481, 482, 483, 484, 485, 486, 487, 488, 508, 509, 510, 511, 512, 518, 519, 520, 523, 524, 526, 539, 541, 542, 543, 550, 551, 552, 553, 559, 560, 561, 562, 563, 569, 577, 578, 582, 584, 586, 591, 592, 615, 639, 640, 641, 671, 672, 673, 674, 675, 676, 677, 678, 679, 681, 682, 683, 717, 721, 724, 730, 734, 737, 742, 749, 771, 772, 774, 776, 777, 779, 782, 783, 805, 806, 808, 809, 811, 812, 813, 825, 826, 827, 828, 829.

MARSHALL, Malcolm Denzil; b Bridgetown, Barbados 18 Apr 1958; (136) 89, 90, 93, 94, 95, 122, 124, 125, 128, 129, 131, 132, 136, 189, 190, 191, 200, 210, 215, 220, 222, 223, 226, 227, 228, 229, 230, 231, 233, 237, 239, 241, 242, 244, 245, 246, 247, 248, 253, 254, 255, 264, 265, 266, 285, 287, 288, 289, 290, 291, 293, 296, 298, 300, 301, 302, 309, 313, 317, 318, 339, 341, 342, 343, 344, 345, 346, 364, 365, 366, 367, 396, 397, 398, 399, 402, 403, 405, 415, 419, 421, 423, 424, 426, 427, 429, 512, 518, 519, 520, 539, 541, 542, 543, 544, 547, 550, 551, 552, 553, 569, 570, 572, 578, 582, 584, 586, 591, 592, 610, 611, 612, 615, 639, 640, 671, 672, 674, 676, 677, 678, 690, 691, 692, 695, 696, 698, 699, 700, 701, 703, 717, 721, 724, 730, 734.

MATTHIS, Everton Hugh; b Kingston, Jamaica 11 Apr 1957; (2) 115, 116.

MOSELEY, Ezra Alphonsa; b Waldrons Village, Christ Church, Barbados 5 Jan 1958; (9) 610, 611, 612, 613, 614, 615, 640, 641, 672.

MURRAY, David Anthony; b Bridgetown, Barbados 29 Sep 1950; (10) 9, 49, 85, 90, 95, 115, 116, 122, 124, 125.

MURRAY, Deryck Lance; b Port-of-Spain, Trinidad 20 May 1943; (26) 8, 22, 26, 29, 32, 33, 34, 37, 38, 39, 41, 48, 61, 69, 73, 74, 75, 76, 78, 80, 81, 84, 86, 87, 88, 89.

MURRAY, Junior Randalph; b St George's, Grenada 20 Jan 1968; (38) 770, 771, 772, 774, 776, 777, 778, 782, 783, 805, 806, 808, 809, 811, 812, 813, 825, 826, 827, 828, 829, 839, 840, 844, 847, 854, 859, 945, 946, 973, 984, 985, 986, 987, 988, 999, 1000, 1001.

PARRY, Derick Ricaldo; b Charlestown, Nevis 22 Dec 1954; (6) 49, 76, 78, 85, 88, 95.

PATTERSON, Balfour Patrick; b Portland, Jamaica 15 Sep 1961; (59) 364, 365, 366, 396, 397, 400, 439, 440, 441, 452, 457, 459, 464, 468, 473, 481, 482, 483, 484, 485, 487, 488, 508, 509, 510, 511, 523, 524, 526, 527, 550, 673, 675, 676, 677, 678, 679, 681, 682, 683, 689, 690, 692, 695, 696, 699, 700, 701, 703, 724, 753, 754, 755, 777, 779, 805, 806, 808, 812.

PAYNE, Thelston Rodney O'Neale; b Foul Bay, St Philip, Barbados 13 Feb 1957; (7) 254, 288, 318, 365, 429, 430, 441.

PHILLIP, Norbert; b Bioche, Dominica 12 Jun 1948; (1) 49.

*PYDANNA, Milton Robert; b Berbice, British Guiana 27 Jan 1950; (3) 93, 94, 230.

RICHARDS, Isaac Vivian Alexander; b St John's, Antigua 7 Mar 1952; (187) 22, 26, 29, 32, 33, 34, 37, 38, 39, 41, 48, 61, 69, 73, 74, 75, 78, 80, 81, 84, 86, 87, 89, 90, 93, 94, 95, 116, 122, 124, 125, 128, 129, 131, 132, 134, 135, 136, 137, 138, 139, 140, 189, 190, 191, 200, 203, 208, 210, 215, 220, 222, 223, 226, 227, 228, 229, 230, 231, 233, 234, 236, 237, 239, 241, 242, 244, 245, 246, 247, 252, 253, 255, 264, 265, 266, 285, 287, 288, 289, 290, 291, 293, 295, 296, 298, 300, 301, 302, 309, 313, 317, 318, 320, 321, 322, 323, 324, 339, 341, 342, 343, 344, 345, 346, 364, 365, 366, 367, 396, 397, 398, 399, 400, 402, 403, 405, 412, 415, 416, 419, 421, 423, 424, 426, 427, 429, 430, 439, 440, 441, 452, 457, 459, 464, 468, 473, 481, 482, 483, 484, 485, 486, 487, 488, 508, 518, 519, 520, 539, 541, 542, 543, 544, 546, 547, 550, 551, 552, 553, 559, 560, 561, 562, 563, 569, 570, 572, 577, 578, 582, 584, 586, 591, 592, 610, 611, 612, 613, 671, 672, 673, 674, 675, 676, 677, 678.

RICHARDSON, Richard Benjamin; b Five Islands, Antigua 12 Jan 1962; (224) 230, 234, 236, 237, 244, 245, 246, 247, 248, 252, 253, 254, 255, 264, 265, 285, 287, 288, 289, 290, 291, 293, 296, 300, 301, 302, 309, 313, 317, 318, 320, 321, 322, 323, 324, 339, 341, 342, 343, 344, 345, 346, 364, 365, 366, 367, 396, 397, 398, 399, 400, 402, 403, 405, 412, 415, 419, 421, 423, 424, 426, 427, 429, 430, 439, 440, 441, 452, 457, 459, 464, 468, 473, 481, 482, 483, 484, 485, 486, 487, 488, 508, 509, 510, 511, 512, 518, 519, 520, 523, 524, 526, 527, 539, 541, 542, 543, 544, 546, 547, 550, 551, 552, 553, 559, 560, 561, 562, 563, 569, 570, 572, 573, 577, 578, 582, 584, 586, 591, 592, 610, 611, 612, 613, 614, 615, 639, 640, 641, 671, 672, 673, 674, 675, 676, 677, 678, 679, 681, 682, 683, 689, 690, 691, 692, 695, 696, 698, 699, 700, 701, 703, 717, 721, 724, 730, 734, 737, 742, 749, 753, 754, 755, 770, 771, 772, 774, 776, 777, 778, 779, 782, 783, 805, 806, 808, 809, 811, 812, 813, 825, 826, 827, 828, 829, 839, 840, 842, 845, 849, 851, 854, 857, 858, 859, 860, 861, 882, 883, 884, 885, 886, 984, 999, 1000, 1001, 1005, 1007, 1008, 1009, 1011, 1023, 1024, 1025, 1028, 1029, 1030, 1033, 1049, 1055, 1064, 1070, 1077, 1080.

ROBERTS, Anderson Montgomery Everton; b Urlings Village, Antigua 29 Jan 1951; (56) 22, 26, 29, 32, 33, 34, 37, 38, 39, 41, 48, 61, 69, 73, 74, 75, 76, 78, 80, 81, 84, 85, 86, 87, 89, 90, 115, 116, 122, 124, 125, 128,

129, 131, 132, 134, 135, 136, 137, 138, 139, 140, 189, 190, 191, 200, 203, 208, 210, 215, 222, 223, 226, 227, 228, 229.

ROWE, Lawrence George; b Whitfield Town, Kingston, Jamaica 8 Jan 1949; (11) 34, 37, 38, 39, 76, 78, 80, 81, 84, 85, 88.

SHILLINGFORD, Irvine Theodore; b Dublanc, Dominica 18 Apr 1944; (2) 48, 49.

SHIVNARINE, Sew; b British Guiana 13 May 1952; (1) 49.

SIMMONS, Phillip Verant; b Arima, Trinidad 18 Apr 1963; (117) 459, 464, 468, 473, 482, 485, 486, 487, 488, 508, 509, 510, 511, 512, 518, 519, 569, 570, 572, 573, 577, 584, 586, 591, 592, 672, 673, 674, 675, 676, 677, 678, 679, 681, 682, 683, 724, 737, 742, 749, 753, 754, 755, 770, 771, 772, 774, 776, 777, 778, 782, 783, 805, 806, 808, 809, 811, 812, 813, 825, 826, 827, 828, 829, 839, 840, 842, 844, 845, 847, 849, 851, 854, 857, 858, 859, 860, 861, 882, 883, 884, 885, 886, 936, 937, 938, 939, 941, 942, 944, 945, 946, 947, 984, 985, 986, 987, 988, 1005, 1007, 1008, 1009, 1011, 1023, 1024, 1025, 1027, 1028, 1029, 1030, 1033, 1082, 1083, 1084, 1085, 1086, 1098.

SMALL, Milton Aster; b Blades Point, St Philip, Barbados 12 Feb 1964; (2) 252, 253.

SOBERS, Garfield St Aubrun; b Bay Land, Bridgetown, Barbados 28 Jul 1936; knighted for services to cricket 1975; (1) 8.

*WALLACE, Philo Alphonzo; b Around-The-Town, St Peter, Barbados 2 Aug 1970; (12) 689, 690, 691, 692, 696, 698, 699, 700, 701, 703, 1086, 1098.

WALSH, Courtney Andrew; b Kingston, Jamaica 30 Oct 1962; (162) 287, 291, 295, 298, 341, 342, 343, 344, 345, 346, 364, 365, 367, 397, 398, 399, 400, 402, 403, 405, 412, 415, 416, 419, 421, 423, 424, 426, 427, 429, 430, 439, 440, 441, 452, 457, 459, 464, 468, 473, 481, 482, 483, 484, 486, 487, 508, 509, 510, 511, 512, 518, 519, 520, 523, 524, 526, 527, 539, 541, 542, 543, 544, 546, 551, 552, 553, 559, 560, 561, 562, 563, 569, 570, 572, 573, 577, 578, 582, 584, 586, 591, 592, 610, 611, 612, 613, 615, 639, 641, 671, 674, 675, 676, 677, 678, 682, 776, 779, 805, 806, 808, 809, 811, 812, 813, 825, 826, 827, 828, 829, 839, 842, 844, 845, 847, 851, 857, 859, 860, 861, 882, 883, 886, 936, 937, 938, 939, 941, 942, 944, 945, 946, 971, 972, 984, 985, 986, 987, 988, 999, 1000, 1023, 1024, 1025, 1027, 1028, 1029, 1030, 1033, 1049, 1055, 1064, 1070, 1077, 1080, 1082, 1083, 1084, 1085, 1086, 1098.

WILLIAMS, David; b San Fernando, Trinidad 4 Nov 1963; (29) 484, 485, 488, 539, 553, 641, 689, 690, 691, 692, 695, 696, 698, 699, 700, 701, 703, 717, 721, 724, 730, 734, 737, 742, 749, 753, 754, 755, 779.

*WILLIAMS, Laurie Rohan; b Jamaica 12 Dec 1968; (4) 1084, 1085, 1086, 1098.

WILLIAMS, Stuart Clayton; b Charlestown, Nevis 12 Aug 1969; (28) 936, 937, 938, 939, 941, 942, 944, 945, 946, 947, 971, 972, 973, 984, 985, 986, 988, 1001, 1008, 1009, 1011, 1025, 1027, 1030, 1082, 1083, 1084, 1085.

NEW ZEALAND (97 players)

* Denotes players who had not appeared in official Test matches before 28 September 1996.

ANDERSON, Robert Wickham; b Christchurch 2 Oct 1948; (2) 40, 52.

ASTLE, Nathan John; b Christchurch 15 Sep 1971; (28) 971, 972, 973, 990, 991, 1014, 1015, 1016, 1017, 1018, 1019, 1020, 1021, 1022, 1044, 1045, 1046, 1047, 1050, 1053, 1062, 1074, 1078, 1082, 1083, 1084, 1085, 1086.

BLAIN, Tony Elston; b Nelson 17 Feb 1962; (38) 371, 372, 373, 374, 378, 380, 381, 384, 490, 491, 492, 493, 495, 497, 498, 500, 501, 502, 515, 516, 537, 538, 817, 818, 819, 820, 821, 863, 865, 866, 867, 869, 870, 872, 895, 896, 897, 898.

*BLAIR, Bruce Robert; b Dunedin 27 Dec 1957; (14) 147, 148, 347, 348, 358, 359, 361, 371, 372, 373, 374, 380, 381, 384.

BOOCK, Stephen Lewis; b Dunedin 20 Sep 1951; (14) 52, 99, 251, 256, 258, 274, 347, 348, 355, 440, 454, 458, 466, 470.

BRACEWELL, Brendon Paul; b Auckland 14 Sep 1959; (1) 53.

BRACEWELL, John Garry; b Auckland 15 Apr 1958; (53) 202, 209, 218, 277, 278, 279, 303, 304, 305, 306, 318, 322, 323, 347, 350, 355, 356, 358, 359, 371, 372, 373, 374, 378, 380, 381, 384, 388, 389, 439, 440, 441, 454, 458, 462, 470, 490, 491, 492, 500, 501, 502, 504, 505, 535, 536, 537, 538, 618, 622, 624, 626, 629.

BRADBURN, Grant Eric; b Hamilton 26 May 1966; (7) 637, 638, 647, 648, 767, 768, 769.

BROWN, Vaughan Raymond; b Christchurch 3 Nov 1959; (3) 498, 500, 501.

BURGESS, Mark Gordon; b Auckland 17 Jul 1944; (26) 5, 6, 7, 10, 11, 35, 36, 52, 53, 62, 65, 69, 72, 97, 99, 100, 102, 103, 105, 107, 109, 110, 111, 112, 113, 114.

CAIRNS, Bernard Lance; b Picton 10 Oct 1949; (78) 10, 11, 32, 35, 36, 40, 52, 53, 62, 65, 69, 72, 88, 96, 97, 100, 102, 103, 105, 107, 109, 110, 111, 112, 113, 114, 117, 146, 147, 148, 166, 168, 169, 171, 172, 173, 176, 178, 179, 180, 181, 182, 183, 184, 185, 186, 187, 188, 192, 197, 202, 206, 209, 214, 218, 249, 250, 251, 256, 257, 258, 274, 276, 277, 278, 279, 303, 304, 305, 309, 310, 316, 318, 320, 321, 322, 323, 324.

CAIRNS, Christopher Lance; b Picton 13 Jun 1970; (49) 669, 670, 711, 712, 713, 714, 723, 728, 740, 744, 863, 865, 866, 867, 869, 870, 872, 895, 896, 897, 898, 899, 975, 977, 979, 980, 989, 990, 991, 1014, 1015, 1016, 1017, 1019, 1020, 1021, 1022, 1044, 1047, 1050, 1053, 1062, 1074, 1078, 1082, 1083, 1084, 1085, 1086.

CHATFIELD, Ewen John; b Dannevirke 3 Jul 1950; (114) 69, 96, 97, 99, 100, 103, 105, 107, 109, 110, 111, 112, 114, 117, 118, 147, 166, 168, 169, 171, 172, 173, 176, 178, 179, 180, 181, 182, 183, 184, 185, 186, 187, 188, 192, 197, 202, 206, 209, 214, 218, 249, 250, 251, 256, 257, 258, 274, 275, 276, 277, 303, 304, 305, 306, 309, 310, 316, 318, 320, 321, 322, 323, 324, 347, 348, 350, 352, 353, 355, 356, 358, 359, 361, 371, 372, 373, 374, 380, 381, 384, 388, 439, 440, 441, 454, 458, 462, 466, 470, 474, 490, 491, 492, 493, 495, 497, 498, 500, 501, 502, 504, 505, 506, 507, 514, 515, 516, 517, 535, 536, 537, 538, 554.

COLLINGE, Richard Owen; b Wellington 2 Apr 1946; (15) 5, 6, 7, 11, 17, 18, 20, 23, 28, 32, 35, 36, 40, 52, 53.

*COMAN, Peter George; b Christchurch 13 Apr 1943; (3) 5, 10, 11.

CONEY, Jeremy Vernon; b Wellington 21 Jun 1952; (88) 62, 65, 69, 72, 88, 96, 99, 100, 102, 103, 105, 107, 109, 110, 111, 112, 117, 118, 146, 147, 148, 166, 168, 169, 171, 172, 176, 178, 179, 180, 181, 182, 183, 184, 185, 186, 187, 192, 197, 202, 206, 209, 214, 218, 249, 250, 251, 256, 257, 258, 274, 275, 276, 277, 278, 279, 303, 304, 305, 306, 309, 310, 316, 318, 320, 321, 322, 323, 324, 347, 348, 350, 352, 353, 355, 356, 358, 359, 361, 371, 372, 373, 374, 388, 389, 439, 440, 441.

CONGDON, Bevan Ernest; b Motueka 11 Feb 1938; (11) 5, 6, 7, 10, 11, 17, 18, 35, 36, 52, 53.

CROWE, Jeffrey John; b Cornwall Park, Auckland 14 Sep 1958; (75) 166, 171, 172, 173, 176, 178, 179, 180, 182, 183, 185, 186, 187, 188, 206, 209, 249, 250, 251, 256, 257, 258, 274, 275, 276, 277, 278, 279, 303, 304, 305, 306, 309, 318, 320, 321, 322, 323, 324, 350, 352, 353, 355, 356, 358, 359, 361, 373, 378, 380, 381, 384, 388, 389, 439, 441, 454, 458, 462, 466, 470, 474, 490, 491, 492, 495, 498, 500, 501, 502, 554, 557, 558, 619, 622.

CROWE, Martin David; b Henderson, Auckland 22 Sep 1962; (143) 146, 147, 148, 187, 188, 192, 197, 202, 206, 209, 214, 218, 249, 250, 251, 256, 257, 258, 274, 275, 276, 277, 278, 279, 303, 304, 305, 309, 310, 316, 318, 320, 321, 322, 323, 324, 347, 348, 350, 352, 353, 355, 356, 358, 359, 361, 371, 372, 373, 374, 378, 380, 381, 384, 388, 389, 439, 440, 441, 454, 458, 462, 466, 470, 474, 490, 491, 492, 493, 495, 497, 498, 501, 502, 504, 505, 507, 554, 555, 556, 557, 558, 616, 618, 619, 621, 624, 626, 629, 632, 633, 636, 637, 638, 642, 643, 644, 645, 647, 648, 649, 651, 654, 655, 665, 666, 667, 668, 669, 670, 711, 712, 713, 714, 718, 723, 728, 734, 740, 744, 747, 750, 765, 766, 767, 791, 792, 793, 817, 818, 819, 820, 821, 913, 959, 960, 962, 963, 975, 1014, 1015, 1016, 1017.

DAVIS, Heath Te-Ihi-O-Te-Rangi; b Lower Hutt 30 Nov 1971; (2) 909, 911.

De GROEN, Richard Paul; b Otorohanga 5 Aug 1962; (12) 865, 867, 869, 870, 898, 939, 940, 943, 959, 960, 963, 967.

*DOUGLAS, Mark William; b Nelson 20 Oct 1968; (6) 907, 909, 911, 973, 979, 980.

DOULL, Simon Blair; b Pukekohe 6 Aug 1969; (9) 765, 942, 943, 959, 960, 962, 971, 972, 1018.

EDGAR, Bruce Adrian; b Wellington 23 Nov 1956; (64) 52, 65, 69, 72, 88, 96, 97, 99, 100, 102, 105, 107, 109, 110, 111, 112, 113, 114, 117, 118, 146, 147, 148, 166, 168, 169, 171, 172, 173, 178, 181, 183, 184, 185, 186, 187, 188, 192, 197, 202, 209, 214, 218, 249, 250, 257, 258, 274, 347, 348, 350, 352, 353, 355, 356, 358, 359, 361, 371, 372, 373, 374, 388, 389.

EDWARDS, Graham Neil; b Nelson 27 May 1955; (6) 35, 36, 52, 53, 117, 118.

FLEMING, Stephen Paul; b Christchurch 1 Apr 1973; (48) 900, 901, 902, 903, 907, 909, 911, 913, 939, 940, 942, 943, 959, 960, 962, 963, 966, 967, 975, 977, 979, 980, 989, 990, 991, 1014, 1015, 1016, 1017, 1018, 1019, 1020, 1021, 1022, 1044, 1045, 1046, 1047, 1050, 1053, 1062, 1074, 1078, 1082, 1083, 1084, 1085, 1086.

FRANKLIN, Trevor John; b Mt Eden, Auckland 18 Mar 1962; (3) 192, 250, 535.

GERMON, Lee Kenneth; b Christchurch 4 Nov 1968; (24) 960, 1014, 1015, 1016, 1017, 1018, 1019, 1020, 1021, 1022, 1044, 1045, 1046, 1047, 1050, 1053, 1062, 1074, 1078, 1082, 1083, 1084, 1085, 1086.

GILLESPIE, Stuart Ross; b Wanganui 2 Mar 1957; (19) 348, 350, 352, 353, 356, 358, 359, 361, 371, 372, 373, 374, 490, 492, 493, 495, 497, 498, 500.

GRAY, Evan John; b Wellington 18 Nov 1954; (10) 275, 374, 378, 380, 381, 384, 388, 389, 536, 537.

GREATBATCH, Mark John; b Auckland 11 Dec 1963; (78) 504, 505, 506, 507, 514, 515, 516, 517, 535, 536, 537, 538, 555, 556, 557, 558, 616, 618, 619, 621, 622, 624, 626, 629, 632, 633, 636, 637, 638, 642, 645, 647, 665, 666, 667, 668, 670, 711, 712, 713, 723, 728, 734, 740, 744, 747, 750, 765, 766, 791, 792, 793, 817, 818, 819, 820, 821, 863, 865, 866, 867, 869, 870, 872, 895, 896, 897, 975, 977, 979, 980, 989, 991, 1014, 1015, 1016, 1017, 1018.

*HADLEE, Barry George; b Christchurch 14 Dec 1941; (2) 17, 23.

HADLEE, Dayle Robert; b Christchurch 6 Jan 1948; (11) 5, 10, 11, 17, 18, 20, 23, 28, 32, 35, 36.

HADLEE, Richard John; b Christchurch 3 Jul 1951; knighted for services to cricket 1990; (115) 5, 6, 7, 10, 17, 18, 20, 23, 28, 35, 36, 52, 53, 62, 65, 69, 72, 88, 96, 97, 99, 100, 102, 103, 105, 107, 109, 110, 111, 112, 113, 114, 117, 118, 146, 147, 148, 166, 168, 169, 171, 172, 173, 176, 178, 179, 180, 186, 187, 188, 192, 197, 202, 206, 209, 214, 218, 249, 250, 251, 256, 257, 258, 303, 304, 305, 306, 309, 310, 316, 318, 320, 321, 322, 323, 324, 347, 348, 350, 352, 353, 355, 356, 358, 359, 361, 371, 372, 373, 374, 388, 389, 439, 440, 441, 490, 491, 492, 493, 495, 497, 498, 501, 502, 507, 514, 516, 517, 554, 618, 619, 621, 622, 632, 633.

HARRIS, Chris Zinzan; b Christchurch 20 Nov 1969; (67) 642, 643, 644, 645, 648, 649, 651, 665, 666, 667, 668, 669, 670, 711, 712, 713, 714, 718, 723, 728, 734, 740, 744, 747, 750, 766, 767, 768, 769, 791, 792, 793, 818, 819, 820, 863, 870, 895, 896, 897, 900, 901, 902, 903, 907, 909, 911, 939, 940, 942, 943, 959, 960, 962, 963, 966, 967, 1046, 1047, 1050, 1053, 1078, 1082, 1083, 1084, 1085, 1086.

HART, Matthew Norman; b Hamilton 16 May 1972; (10) 898, 899, 901, 903, 907, 913, 939, 940, 942, 943.

*HART, Ronald Terence; b Lower Hutt 7 Nov 1961; (1) 320.

HARTLAND, Blair Robert; b Christchurch 22 Oct 1966; (16) 766, 768, 769, 898, 899, 900, 901, 902, 907, 909, 911, 939, 940, 942, 966, 967.

HASLAM, Mark James; b Bury, Lancashire, England; 26 Sep 1972; (1) 769.

HASTINGS, Brian Frederick; b Wellington 23 Mar 1940; (11) 5, 6, 7, 10, 11, 17, 18, 20, 23, 28, 32.

*HAYES, Roydon Leslie; b Paeroa 9 May 1971; (1) 973.

HORNE, Philip Andrew; b Upper Hutt 21 Jan 1960; (4) 439, 440, 441, 474.

HOWARTH, Geoffrey Philip; b Auckland 29 Mar 1951; (70) 17, 18, 20, 28, 32, 40, 52, 53, 62, 72, 88, 96, 97, 102, 103, 105, 107, 109, 110, 111, 112, 113, 114, 117, 118, 146, 147, 148, 166, 168, 169, 171, 172, 173, 176, 178, 179, 180, 181, 182, 183, 184, 185, 186, 188, 192,

197, 202, 206, 209, 214, 218, 249, 250, 251, 256, 257, 303, 304, 305, 306, 309, 310, 316, 318, 320, 321, 322, 323, 324.

HOWARTH, Hedley John; b Auckland 25 Dec 1943; (9) 5, 6, 7, 17, 18, 20, 23, 28, 32.

JONES, Andrew Howard; b Wellington 9 May 1959; (87) 454, 458, 462, 466, 490, 491, 492, 493, 497, 498, 500, 501, 502, 506, 507, 514, 515, 516, 517, 535, 536, 537, 538, 554, 555, 556, 557, 558, 616, 618, 619, 621, 622, 624, 626, 629, 632, 633, 642, 643, 644, 645, 649, 651, 654, 655, 665, 666, 667, 668, 669, 670, 711, 712, 714, 718, 723, 728, 734, 740, 744, 747, 750, 765, 767, 768, 769, 791, 792, 793, 817, 818, 819, 820, 821, 867, 869, 870, 872, 895, 896, 897, 898, 899, 971, 972, 973.

KENNEDY, Robert John; b Dunedin 3 Jun 1972; (5) 1045, 1046, 1050, 1062, 1074.

KUGGELEIJN, Christopher Mary; b Auckland 10 May 1956; (16) 504, 505, 506, 507, 514, 515, 516, 517, 535, 536, 537, 538, 555, 556, 557, 558.

LARSEN, Gavin Rolf; b Wellington 27 Sep 1962; (83) 616, 618, 619, 621, 622, 654, 655, 665, 666, 667, 668, 669, 670, 711, 712, 713, 714, 718, 723, 728, 734, 740, 744, 747, 750, 765, 766, 791, 792, 793, 817, 818, 819, 820, 821, 863, 865, 866, 867, 869, 870, 872, 895, 896, 897, 898, 899, 900, 901, 902, 903, 907, 909, 911, 913, 971, 972, 973, 975, 977, 979, 980, 989, 990, 991, 1014, 1015, 1016, 1017, 1018, 1019, 1020, 1021, 1022, 1044, 1045, 1047, 1053, 1082, 1083, 1084, 1085, 1086.

LATHAM, Rodney Terry; b Christchurch 12 Jun 1961; (33) 643, 644, 647, 648, 649, 651, 654, 655, 711, 712, 713, 714, 718, 723, 728, 734, 740, 747, 765, 766, 791, 792, 793, 817, 818, 819, 821, 863, 865, 866, 867, 869, 872.

LEES, Warren Kenneth; b Dunedin 19 Mar 1952; (31) 62, 65, 69, 72, 88, 96, 97, 99, 100, 102, 103, 105, 168, 172, 173, 176, 178, 179, 181, 182, 183, 184, 185, 186, 187, 188, 192, 197, 202, 214, 218.

McEWAN, Paul Ernest; b Christchurch 19 Dec 1953; (17) 88, 96, 97, 99, 100, 110, 112, 113, 114, 275, 276, 277, 278, 279, 306, 310, 316.

*McKECHNIE, Brian John; b Gore 6 Nov 1953; (14) 20, 23, 28, 32, 35, 36, 62, 65, 69, 72, 110, 111, 112, 113.

*McSWEENEY, Ervin Bruce; b Wellington 8 Mar 1957; (16) 347, 348, 350, 352, 353, 355, 356, 358, 359, 361, 378, 381, 384, 439, 440, 441.

*MILLMOW, Jonathan Paul; b Wellington 22 Sep 1967; (5) 624, 626, 629, 632, 633.

MORRISON, Daniel Kyle; b Auckland 3 Feb 1966; (92) 474, 491, 493, 495, 497, 506, 514, 515, 517, 538, 555, 556, 557, 558, 616, 618, 619, 621, 622, 624, 626, 629, 632, 633, 636, 637, 638, 642, 643, 644, 645, 647, 648, 649, 651, 654, 655, 665, 667, 711, 712, 718, 728, 734, 747, 750, 791, 792, 793, 817, 818, 819, 820, 821, 863, 865, 866, 895, 896, 897, 899, 900, 901, 902, 903, 907, 913, 971, 972, 973, 975, 977, 979, 980, 1014, 1015, 1016, 1017, 1018, 1019, 1020, 1021, 1022, 1044, 1045, 1046, 1047, 1050, 1053, 1062, 1074, 1082.

MORRISON, John Francis Maclean; b Wellington 27 Aug 1947; (18) 18, 20, 23, 28, 32, 40, 65, 69, 166, 168, 179, 180, 181, 182, 183, 184, 185, 192.

MURRAY, Darrin James; b Christchurch 4 Sep 1967; (1) 943.

NASH, Dion Joseph; b Auckland 20 Nov 1971; (28) 765, 767, 768, 769, 900, 902, 903, 909, 911, 913, 939, 940, 942, 943, 966, 1014, 1015, 1016, 1017, 1018, 1045, 1046, 1047, 1062, 1074, 1078, 1082, 1083.

O'SULLIVAN, David Robert; b Palmerston North 16 Nov 1944; (3) 10, 11, 40.

OWENS, Michael Barry; b Christchurch 11 Nov 1969; (1) 769.

PARKER, John Morton; b Dannevirke 21 Feb 1951; (24) 11, 17, 18, 20, 23, 28, 32, 35, 36, 40, 52, 53, 88, 96, 97, 99, 100, 102, 103, 105, 107, 109, 113, 114.

PARKER, Norman Murray; b Dannevirke 28 Aug 1948; (1) 40.

PARORE, Adam Craig; b Auckland 23 Jan 1971; (54) 765, 766, 767, 768, 769, 791, 792, 793, 899, 900, 901, 902, 903, 907, 909, 911, 913, 939, 940, 942, 943, 959, 960, 962, 963, 966, 967, 971, 972, 973, 975, 977, 979, 980, 989, 990, 991, 1018, 1019, 1020, 1021, 1022, 1044, 1045, 1046, 1050, 1053, 1062, 1074, 1078, 1082, 1083, 1084, 1086.

PATEL, Dipak Narshibhai; b Nairobi, Kenya 25 Oct 1958; (63) 439, 440, 441, 454, 458, 462, 466, 470, 474, 490, 491, 492, 493, 495, 497, 500, 502, 515, 516, 517, 554, 636, 637, 638, 714, 718, 723, 728, 734, 740, 744, 747, 750, 765, 766, 791, 792, 793, 817, 818, 819, 820, 821, 863, 866, 971, 972, 989, 990, 991, 1019, 1020, 1021, 1022, 1044, 1046, 1050, 1078, 1082, 1083, 1084, 1085, 1086.

*PETRIE, Richard George; b Christchurch 23 Aug 1967; (12) 642, 643, 644, 645, 647, 648, 649, 651, 654, 655, 666, 668.

POLLARD, Victor; b Burnley, Lancashire, England 7 Sep 1945; (3) 6, 7, 10.

PRIEST, Mark Wellings; b Greymouth 12 Aug 1961; (12) 624, 632, 633, 636, 637, 638, 959, 960, 962, 963, 966, 967.

PRINGLE, Christopher; b Auckland 26 Jan 1968; (64) 632, 633, 636, 637, 638, 642, 643, 644, 645, 647, 648, 649, 651, 654, 655, 665, 666, 667, 668, 669, 670, 711, 767, 768, 769, 818, 819, 820, 821, 863, 865, 866, 867, 869, 870, 872, 895, 896, 897, 898, 899, 900, 901, 902, 903, 907, 909, 911, 913, 939, 940, 942, 959, 960, 962, 963, 966, 967, 977, 979, 980, 989, 990, 991.

REDMOND, Rodney Ernest; b Whangarei 29 Dec 1944; (2) 6, 7.

REID, John Fulton; b Auckland 3 Mar 1956; (25) 88, 146, 256, 258, 274, 275, 276, 278, 279, 303, 304, 305, 306, 309, 310, 316, 318, 347, 348, 350, 352, 353, 355, 356, 361.

*REID, Richard Bruce; b Lower Hutt 3 Dec 1958; (9) 504, 505, 654, 655, 665, 666, 667, 669, 670.

ROBERTS, Andrew Duncan Glenn; b Te Aroha 6 May 1947; d Wellington 26 Oct 1989; (1) 40.

*ROBERTS, Stuart James; b Christchurch 22 Mar 1965; (2) 616, 636.

ROBERTSON, Gary Keith; b New Plymouth 15 Jul 1960; (10) 118, 249, 250, 378, 380, 381, 555, 556, 557, 558.

RUTHERFORD, Kenneth Robert; b Dunedin 26 Oct 1965;

(121) 321, 324, 371, 372, 373, 374, 378, 380, 381, 384, 388, 389, 441, 458, 462, 466, 470, 474, 493, 495, 497, 498, 500, 504, 505, 506, 507, 514, 515, 516, 535, 536, 537, 538, 616, 618, 619, 621, 622, 624, 626, 629, 632, 633, 636, 637, 638, 642, 643, 644, 645, 647, 648, 649, 651, 654, 655, 667, 668, 669, 670, 712, 713, 714, 718, 723, 728, 734, 740, 744, 747, 750, 765, 766, 767, 768, 769, 791, 792, 793, 817, 818, 820, 821, 863, 865, 866, 867, 869, 870, 872, 895, 896, 897, 898, 899, 900, 901, 902, 903, 913, 939, 940, 942, 943, 959, 960, 962, 963, 966, 967, 971, 972, 973, 975, 977, 979, 980, 989, 990, 991.

SMITH, Ian David Stockley; b Nelson 28 Feb 1957; (98) 97, 107, 109, 110, 111, 112, 113, 114, 117, 118, 146, 147, 148, 206, 209, 249, 250, 251, 256, 257, 258, 274, 275, 276, 277, 278, 279, 303, 304, 305, 306, 309, 310, 316, 318, 320, 321, 322, 323, 324, 388, 389, 454, 458, 462, 466, 470, 474, 495, 504, 505, 506, 507, 514, 517, 535, 536, 538, 554, 555, 556, 557, 558, 616, 618, 619, 621, 622, 624, 626, 629, 632, 633, 636, 637, 638, 642, 643, 644, 645, 665, 666, 667, 668, 669, 670, 711, 712, 713, 714, 718, 723, 728, 734, 740, 744, 747, 750.

SNEDDEN, Martin Colin; b Mt Eden, Auckland 23 Nov 1958; (93) 96, 97, 102, 103, 105, 107, 109, 111, 113, 114, 117, 118, 146, 147, 148, 166, 168, 169, 171, 172, 173, 176, 178, 179, 180, 181, 182, 183, 184, 185, 186, 187, 188, 192, 197, 206, 214, 274, 275, 276, 277, 278, 279, 306, 309, 310, 316, 352, 353, 361, 378, 380, 381, 384, 439, 440, 441, 454, 458, 462, 466, 470, 474, 490, 491, 492, 493, 497, 498, 500, 501, 502, 504, 505, 506, 507, 535, 536, 537, 538, 554, 555, 556, 557, 558, 616, 618, 619, 621, 622, 624, 626, 629.

SPEARMAN, Craig Murray; b Auckland 4 Jul 1972; (18) 1019, 1020, 1021, 1022, 1044, 1045, 1046, 1047, 1050, 1053, 1062, 1074, 1078, 1082, 1083, 1084, 1085, 1086.

STIRLING, Derek Alexander; b Upper Hutt 5 Oct 1961; (6) 257, 275, 276, 277, 278, 279.

*STOTT, Leslie Warren; b Rochdale, Lancashire, England 8 Dec 1946; (1) 62.

SU'A, Murphy Logo; b Wanganui 7 Nov 1966; (12) 712, 713, 766, 767, 768, 959, 962, 963, 966, 967, 975, 989.

TAYLOR, Bruce Richard; b Timaru 12 Jul 1943; (2) 6, 7.

THOMSON, Shane Alexander; b Hamilton 27 Jan 1969; (56) 616, 618, 619, 621, 626, 629, 865, 866, 867, 869, 870, 872, 895, 896, 897, 898, 899, 900, 901, 902, 903, 907, 909, 911, 913, 939, 940, 942, 943, 962, 963, 966, 967, 971, 972, 973, 975, 977, 979, 980, 990, 1014, 1015, 1016, 1017, 1018, 1044, 1045, 1047, 1053, 1062, 1074, 1078, 1083, 1084, 1085,

TROUP, Gary Bertram; b Taumarunui 3 Oct 1952; (22) 40, 62, 65, 72, 88, 99, 100, 102, 103, 117, 118, 146, 148, 169, 173, 176, 181, 320, 321, 322, 323, 324.

TURNER, Glenn Maitland; b Dunedin 26 May 1947; (41) 5, 6, 7, 10, 11, 17, 18, 20, 23, 28, 32, 35, 36, 40, 62, 65, 69, 72, 168, 169, 171, 172, 173, 176, 178, 179, 180, 181, 182, 183, 184, 185, 186, 187, 188, 197, 202, 206, 209, 214, 218.

TWOSE, Roger Graham; b Torquay, Devon, England 17 Apr 1968; (21) 1014, 1015, 1016, 1017, 1018, 1019, 1020, 1021, 1022, 1044, 1045, 1046, 1047, 1050, 1053, 1062, 1074, 1078, 1084, 1085, 1086.

VANCE, Robert Howard; b Wellington 31 Mar 1955; (8) 506, 514, 515, 516, 517, 554, 555, 556.

VAUGHAN, Justin Thomas Caldwell; b Hereford, England 30 Aug 1967; (15) 767, 768, 769, 971, 972, 973, 975, 977, 979, 980, 989, 990, 991, 1085, 1086.

VIVIAN, Graham Ellery; b Auckland 28 Feb 1946; (1) 5.

WADSWORTH, Kenneth John; b Nelson 30 Nov 1946; d Nelson 19 Aug 1976; (13) 5, 6, 7, 10, 11, 17, 18, 20, 23, 28, 32, 35, 36.

WATSON, William; b Auckland 31 Aug 1965; (61) 378, 384, 389, 454, 458, 462, 466, 470, 474, 500, 501, 502, 504, 505, 506, 507, 514, 515, 516, 517, 535, 536, 537, 554, 555, 556, 557, 558, 636, 637, 638, 642, 643, 644, 645, 647, 648, 649, 651, 665, 666, 667, 668, 669, 670, 713, 714, 718, 723, 734, 740, 744, 747, 750, 765, 766, 791, 792, 793, 817, 872.

WEBB, Peter Neil; b Auckland 14 Jul 1957; (5) 166, 169, 171, 180, 251.

*WEBB, Richard John; b Invercargill 15 Sep 1952; (3) 182, 183, 184.

WHITE, David John; b Gisborne 26 Jun 1961; (3) 636, 637, 638.

*WILSON, Jeffrey William; b Invercargill 24 Oct 1973; (4) 817, 819, 820, 821.

WRIGHT, John Geoffrey; b Darfield, Canterbury 5 Jul 1954; (149) 52, 53, 62, 65, 69, 72, 88, 96, 99, 100, 102, 103, 105, 107, 109, 110, 111, 112, 113, 114, 117, 118, 146, 147, 148, 166, 168, 169, 171, 172, 173, 176, 178, 179, 180, 181, 182, 184, 185, 186, 187, 188, 197, 202, 206, 214, 218, 249, 251, 256, 257, 258, 274, 275, 276, 277, 278, 279, 303, 304, 305, 306, 309, 310, 316, 318, 320, 321, 322, 323, 324, 347, 348, 350, 352, 353, 355, 356, 358, 359, 371, 372, 378, 380, 388, 389, 439, 440, 454, 462, 466, 470, 474, 490, 491, 492, 493, 495, 497, 498, 501, 502, 504, 505, 506, 507, 514, 515, 516, 517, 535, 536, 537, 538, 554, 555, 556, 557, 558, 616, 621, 622, 624, 626, 629, 632, 633, 642, 643, 644, 645, 647, 648, 649, 651, 654, 655, 665, 666, 668, 669, 711, 713, 714, 718, 744, 750, 767, 768.

YOUNG, Bryan Andrew; b Whangarei 3 Nov 1964; (47) 647, 648, 649, 651, 654, 655, 863, 865, 866, 867, 869, 870, 872, 895, 896, 897, 898, 899, 900, 901, 902, 903, 907, 909, 911, 913, 939, 940, 942, 943, 959, 960, 962, 963, 966, 967, 971, 972, 973, 977, 989, 990, 991, 1019, 1020, 1021, 1022.

INDIA (98 players)

* Denotes players who had not appeared in official Test matches before 28 September 1996.

ABID ALI, Syed; b Hyderabad 9 Sep 1941; (5) 12, 13, 19, 24, 28.

AMARNATH, Mohinder; b Patiala 24 Sep 1950; (85) 19, 24, 28, 35, 36, 54, 55, 56, 61, 65, 68, 156, 157, 158, 162, 163, 164, 165, 189, 190, 191, 200, 204, 207, 210, 216, 219, 221, 223, 224, 225, 228, 229, 230, 272, 273, 281, 308, 312, 315, 316, 319, 325, 328, 332, 333, 334, 340, 341, 348, 349, 351, 352, 354, 355, 356, 357, 361, 362, 363, 482, 483, 485, 486, 487, 488, 513, 514, 517, 523, 525, 526, 529, 530, 532, 534, 569, 571, 572, 574, 580, 582, 587, 589, 591.

AMARNATH, Surinder; b Kanpur 30 Dec 1948; (3) 54, 55, 56.

AMRE, Pravin Kalyan; b Bombay 14 Aug 1968; (37) 686, 687, 688, 692, 693, 694, 696, 697, 703, 704, 705, 715, 722, 737, 745, 764, 784, 785, 786, 787, 788, 790, 794, 795, 796, 797, 822, 823, 833, 834, 852, 855, 856, 858, 879, 880, 881.

ANKOLA, Salil Ashok; b Sholapur 1 Mar 1968; (15) 593, 594, 595, 797, 822, 823, 824, 855, 856, 881, 900, 901, 902, 903, 1068.

ARSHAD AYUB; b Hyderabad 2 Aug 1958; (32) 481, 482, 484, 485, 486, 487, 513, 514, 517, 529, 530, 532, 534, 535, 536, 537, 587, 589, 591, 656, 657, 658.

ARUN, Bharathi; b Vijayawada 14 Dec 1962; (4) 407, 442, 444, 447.

ARUN LAL; b Moradabad, Uttar Pradesh 1 Aug 1955; (13) 143, 163, 165, 228, 229, 481, 483, 484, 485, 486, 487, 562, 563.

AZAD, Kirtivardhan; b Purnea, Bihar 2 Jan 1959; (25) 98, 100, 101, 108, 109, 118, 141, 142, 219, 221, 223, 224, 225, 226, 227, 262, 263, 267, 268, 269, 270, 271, 381, 383, 385.

AZHARUDDIN, Mohammed; b Hyderabad 8 Feb 1963; (224) 282, 283, 284, 308, 312, 315, 316, 319, 325, 328, 332, 333, 334, 340, 341, 348, 349, 351, 352, 354, 355, 356, 357, 360,

361, 362, 363, 381, 383, 385, 386, 387, 390, 391, 392, 393, 394, 395, 401, 403, 406, 408, 409, 410, 411, 433, 434, 435, 436, 437, 438, 442, 444, 447, 453, 458, 461, 465, 469, 474, 476, 482, 483, 484, 486, 487, 488, 513, 514, 517, 523, 525, 526, 529, 530, 532, 534, 535, 536, 537, 538, 559, 560, 561, 562, 563, 569, 571, 572, 574, 580, 582, 583, 587, 591, 593, 594, 595, 616, 617, 619, 620, 623, 625, 634, 635, 656, 657, 658, 661, 662, 664, 680, 681, 683, 684, 685, 686, 687, 692, 693, 694, 696, 697, 700, 702, 703, 704, 705, 715, 722, 725, 729, 732, 737, 740, 745, 764, 784, 785, 786, 787, 788, 789, 790, 794, 795, 796, 797, 798, 799, 822, 823, 824, 833, 834, 835, 846, 851, 852, 855, 856, 858, 879, 880, 881, 900, 901, 902, 903, 904, 906, 910, 912, 921, 923, 926, 936, 937, 938, 940, 941, 943, 944, 945, 946, 947, 975, 976, 978, 992, 994, 996, 998, 1014, 1015, 1016, 1017, 1018, 1051, 1055, 1063, 1068, 1072, 1076, 1079, 1088, 1089, 1091, 1093, 1094, 1096, 1097, 1099, 1100, 1101, 1103, 1105, 1107, 1112, 1113, 1114, 1115, 1116.

BANERJEE, Subroto Tata; b Patna 13 Feb 1969; (6) 692, 693, 694, 715, 740, 790.

*BEDADE, Atul Chandrakant; b Bombay 24 Jun 1966; (12) 904, 906, 910, 912, 921, 923, 926, 936, 937, 944, 946, 947.

BEDI, Bishan Singh; b Amritsar 25 Sep 1946; (10) 12, 24, 28, 35, 54, 55, 56, 61, 65, 68.

*BHUPINDER SINGH; b Hoshiarpur 1 Apr 1965; (2) 904, 906.

BINNY, Roger Michael Humphrey; b Bangalore 19 Jul 1955; (72) 98, 100, 101, 103, 104, 105, 106, 108, 109, 117, 118, 141, 156, 157, 158, 200, 204, 207, 210, 216, 219, 221, 223, 224, 225, 226, 227, 228, 229, 230, 262, 263, 269, 270, 271, 272, 273, 280, 281, 308, 312, 315, 316, 325, 328, 333, 334, 340, 341, 348, 349, 351, 352, 354, 355, 356, 360, 361, 362, 363, 381, 386, 387, 390, 391, 393, 394, 401, 403, 406, 434, 453.

*BOSE, Gopal; b Calcutta 20 May 1947; (1) 13.

CHANDRASEKHAR, Bhagwat Subramanya; b Mysore 17 May 1945; (1) 36.
*CHANDRASEKHAR, Vakkadai Biksheswaran; b Madras 21 Aug 1961; (7) 535, 536, 537, 538, 616, 617, 620.
*CHATTERJEE, Utpal; b Calcutta 13 Jul 1964; (3) 992, 994, 1014.
CHAUHAN, Chetendra Pratap Singh; b Bareilly, Uttar Pradesh 21 Jul 1947; (7) 54, 56, 102, 103, 104, 117, 118.
CHAUHAN, Rajesh Kumar; b Ranchi, Bihar 19 Dec 1966; (20) 833, 834, 835, 846, 851, 852, 879, 880, 881, 901, 902, 906, 910, 912, 921, 923, 926, 936, 937, 938.

DOSHI, Dilip Rasiklal; b Rajkot 22 Dec 1947; (15) 98, 100, 101, 102, 103, 104, 105, 106, 108, 109, 141, 156, 157, 158, 163.
DRAVID, Rahul; b Indore 11 Jan 1973; (13) 1088, 1089, 1091, 1093, 1101, 1103, 1105, 1107, 1112, 1113, 1114, 1115, 1116.

ENGINEER, Farokh Maneksha; b Bombay 25 Feb 1938; (5) 12, 13, 19, 24, 28.

GAEKWAD, Anshuman Dattajirao; b Bombay 23 Sep 1952; (15) 19, 24, 28, 35, 36, 54, 56, 61, 65, 68, 189, 227, 273, 481, 482.
GANGULY, Sourav Chandidas; b Calcutta 8 Jul 1973; (8) 700, 1101, 1103, 1105, 1107, 1112, 1113, 1116.
GAVASKAR, Sunil Manohar; b Bombay 10 Jul 1949; (108) 12, 13, 19, 24, 28, 55, 61, 65, 68, 98, 100, 101, 102, 103, 104, 105, 106, 108, 109, 117, 141, 142, 143, 152, 153, 162, 164, 165, 189, 190, 191, 200, 204, 216, 219, 221, 223, 224, 225, 226, 228, 229, 262, 263, 267, 268, 269, 270, 271, 272, 280, 281, 282, 283, 284, 308, 312, 315, 316, 319, 325, 328, 332, 333, 334, 340, 341, 348, 349, 351, 352, 354, 357, 360, 361, 362, 363, 381, 383, 385, 386, 387, 390, 391, 393, 394, 401, 403, 406, 407, 408, 409, 410, 411, 433, 435, 436, 437, 438, 444, 447, 453, 458, 461, 465, 469, 474, 476.
*GHAI, Rajinder Singh; b Jullundur 12 Jun 1960; (6) 280, 281, 282, 341, 357, 395.
GHAVRI, Karsan Devji; b Rajkot 28 Feb 1951; (19) 19, 54, 55, 56, 61, 65, 68, 98, 100, 101, 102, 103, 104, 105, 106, 108, 109, 117, 118.
GURSHARAN SINGH; b Amritsar 8 Mar 1963; (1) 620.

HIRWANI, Narendra Deepchand; b Gorakhpur 18 Oct 1968; (18) 487, 488, 513, 514, 517, 523, 525, 526, 529, 530, 560, 561, 617, 619, 620, 696, 703, 704.

JADEJA, Ajaysinhji; b Jamnagar 1 Feb 1971; (67) 722, 725, 729, 732, 737, 740, 764, 784, 785, 786, 787, 788, 789, 855, 856, 858, 881, 900, 901, 902, 903, 904, 906, 910, 912, 938, 940, 941, 943, 944, 945, 946, 947, 975, 976, 996, 998, 1014, 1015, 1016, 1017, 1018, 1051, 1055, 1063, 1068, 1072, 1076, 1079, 1088, 1089, 1091, 1093, 1094, 1096, 1097, 1099, 1100, 1101, 1103, 1105, 1107, 1112, 1113, 1114, 1115, 1116.
JOSHI, Sunil Bandacharya; b Gadag, Karnataka 6 Oct 1979; (7) 1105, 1107, 1112, 1113, 1114, 1115, 1116.

KAMBLI, Vinod Ganpat; b Bombay 18 Jan 1972; (75) 680, 681, 683, 684, 685, 715, 722, 729, 732, 745, 794, 795, 796, 797, 798, 799, 822, 823, 824, 833, 834, 835, 846, 851, 852, 855, 856, 858, 879, 880, 881, 900, 901, 902, 903, 904, 906, 910, 912, 921, 923, 926, 936, 937, 938, 940, 941, 943, 944, 945, 946, 947, 975, 976, 978, 992, 994, 1014, 1016, 1017, 1018, 1051, 1055, 1063, 1068, 1072, 1076, 1079, 1103, 1105, 1107, 1112, 1113, 1114, 1115.
KAPIL DEV, Nikhanj; b Chandigarh 6 Jan 1959; (224) 54, 55, 56, 61, 65, 68, 98, 100, 101, 102, 103, 104, 105, 106, 108, 109, 117, 118, 142, 143, 152, 153, 156, 157, 158, 162, 163, 164, 165, 189, 190, 191, 200, 204, 207, 210, 216, 219, 221, 223, 224, 225, 226, 227, 228, 229, 267, 268, 269, 270, 271, 272, 282, 283, 284, 308, 312, 315, 316, 319, 325, 328, 332, 333, 334, 340, 341, 348, 349, 351, 352, 354, 355, 356, 357, 360, 361, 362, 363, 381, 383, 385, 386, 387, 390, 391, 392, 393, 394, 395, 401, 403, 406, 407, 408, 409, 410, 411, 434, 435, 436, 437, 438, 442, 444, 447, 453, 458, 461, 465, 469, 474, 476, 481, 482, 483, 484, 485, 486, 487, 488, 513, 514, 517, 523, 525, 526, 529, 530, 532, 534, 535, 536, 537, 559, 560, 561, 562, 563, 569, 571, 572, 580, 582, 583, 587, 589, 591, 594, 616, 617, 619, 620, 623, 625, 634, 635, 656, 657, 658, 661, 662, 664, 680, 681, 683, 684, 685, 686, 687, 688, 692, 693, 694, 696, 697, 700, 702, 703, 704, 705, 715, 722, 725, 729, 732, 737, 740, 745, 764, 784, 785, 786, 787, 788, 789, 790, 794, 795, 796, 797, 798, 799, 823, 824, 833, 834, 835, 846, 851, 852, 855, 856, 858, 879, 880, 900, 901, 902, 903, 921, 923, 926, 936.
KAPOOR, Aashish Rakesh; b Madras 25 Mar 1971; (14) 978, 996, 998, 1015, 1016, 1017, 1018, 1055, 1079, 1094, 1103, 1114, 1115, 1116.
*KHANNA, Surinder Chamanlal; b Delhi 3 Jun 1956; (10) 61, 65, 68, 262, 263, 267, 268, 269, 271, 272.
KIRMANI, Syed Mujtaba Hussain; b Madras 29 Dec 1949; (49) 35, 54, 55, 98, 100, 101, 102, 103, 104, 105, 106, 117, 118, 141, 142, 143, 152, 153, 156, 157, 158, 162, 163, 164, 165, 189, 190, 191, 200, 204, 207, 210, 216, 219, 221, 223, 224, 225, 226, 227, 228, 229, 230, 270, 273, 340, 341, 348, 349.
KRISHNAMURTHY, Pallemoni; b Hyderabad 12 Jul 1947; (1) 36.
KULKARNI, Rajiv Ramesh; b Bombay 25 Sep 1962; (10) 230, 356, 357, 361, 409, 410, 411, 433, 436, 438.
KUMBLE, Anil; b Bangalore 17 Oct 1970; (96) 623, 625, 634, 635, 656, 657, 658, 681, 683, 684, 764, 784, 785, 786, 787, 788, 789, 790, 794, 795, 796, 797, 798, 799, 822, 823, 824, 833, 834, 835, 846, 851, 852, 855, 856, 858, 879, 880, 900, 901, 902, 903, 904, 906, 910, 912, 921, 923, 926, 936, 937, 938, 940, 941, 943, 944, 945, 946, 947, 975, 976, 978, 992, 994, 996, 998, 1014, 1015, 1016, 1017, 1018, 1051, 1055, 1063, 1068, 1072, 1076, 1079, 1088, 1089, 1091, 1093, 1094, 1096, 1097, 1099, 1100, 1101, 1103, 1105, 1107, 1112, 1113, 1114, 1115, 1116.

LAMBA, Raman; b Meerut, Uttar Pradesh 2 Jan 1960; (32) 390, 391, 392, 393, 394, 395, 401, 403, 406, 407, 408, 409, 410, 411, 433, 434, 435, 436, 437, 438, 442, 488, 572, 580, 582, 583, 587, 589, 591, 593, 594, 595.

MADAN LAL Sharma; b Amritsar 20 Mar 1951; (67) 12, 13, 19, 24, 28, 35, 36, 141, 142, 143, 152, 153, 156, 157, 158, 162, 164, 189, 190, 191, 200, 204, 207, 210, 216, 219, 221, 223, 224, 225, 226, 227, 228, 229, 262, 263, 267, 268, 269, 270, 271, 272, 273, 308, 312, 315, 316, 319, 325, 328, 381, 383, 385, 392, 393, 394, 395, 401, 403, 406, 407, 408, 409, 411, 433, 434, 435.

MALHOTRA, Ashok; b Amritsar 26 Jan 1957; (20) 143, 153, 156, 157, 158, 189, 190, 191, 227, 228, 229, 230, 351, 352, 354, 355, 356, 360, 361, 362.

MANINDER SINGH; b Poona 13 Jun 1965; (59) 165, 189, 272, 273, 381, 383, 385, 386, 387, 390, 391, 392, 393, 394, 395, 401, 403, 406, 407, 408, 409, 410, 411, 433, 434, 435, 436, 437, 438, 442, 444, 447, 453, 458, 461, 465, 469, 474, 476, 481, 482, 483, 486, 488, 523, 525, 526, 529, 530, 532, 534, 535, 536, 537, 593, 594, 595, 798, 799.

MANJREKAR, Sanjay Vijay; b Mangalore 12 Jul 1965; (73) 484, 485, 488, 538, 589, 594, 595, 617, 619, 620, 625, 634, 635, 656, 657, 658, 661, 662, 664, 680, 681, 683, 684, 685, 686, 687, 688, 692, 693, 694, 696, 697, 700, 702, 703, 704, 705, 725, 729, 732, 737, 740, 745, 764, 784, 785, 789, 790, 900, 901, 978, 992, 994, 996, 998, 1015, 1016, 1017, 1018, 1063, 1068, 1072, 1076, 1079, 1088, 1089, 1091, 1093, 1094, 1096, 1097, 1099, 1100.

MANKAD, Ashok Vinoo; b Bombay 12 Oct 1946; (1) 13.

MHAMBREY, Paras Laxmikant; b Bombay 20 Jun 1972; (2) 1099, 1100.

MONGIA, Nayan Ramlal; b Baroda 19 Dec 1969; (59) 879, 880, 881, 900, 901, 902, 903, 904, 906, 910, 912, 921, 923, 926, 936, 937, 938, 940, 941, 945, 946, 947, 975, 976, 978, 992, 994, 996, 998, 1014, 1015, 1016, 1017, 1018, 1051, 1055, 1063, 1068, 1072, 1076, 1079, 1088, 1089, 1091, 1093, 1094, 1096, 1097, 1099, 1100, 1101, 1103, 1105, 1107, 1112, 1113, 1114, 1115, 1116.

MORE, Kiran Shankar; b Baroda 4 Sep 1961; (94) 280, 281, 351, 352, 354, 355, 356, 357, 360, 361, 362, 363, 453, 458, 461, 465, 469, 476, 481, 482, 483, 486, 487, 488, 513, 514, 517, 523, 525, 526, 529, 530, 559, 560, 561, 562, 563, 569, 571, 572, 574, 580, 582, 583, 587, 589, 591, 593, 594, 595, 616, 617, 619, 620, 623, 625, 634, 635, 656, 657, 658, 661, 662, 664, 680, 681, 683, 684, 685, 686, 687, 692, 693, 694, 696, 697, 700, 715, 722, 725, 729, 732, 737, 740, 745, 764, 784, 785, 786, 787, 796, 797, 798, 799.

*MUKHERJEE, Saradindu Purnendu; b Calcutta 5 Oct 1964; (3) 661, 662, 664.

NAIK, Sudhir Sakharam; b Bombay 21 Feb 1945; (2) 12, 13.

NAYAK, Surendra Vithal; b Bombay 20 Oct 1954; (4) 142, 143, 152, 153.

PANDIT, Chandrakant Sitaram; b Bombay 30 Sep 1961; (36) 381, 383, 385, 386, 387, 390, 391, 392, 393, 394, 395, 401, 403, 406, 407, 408, 409, 410, 411, 433, 434, 474, 476, 481, 526, 532, 534, 535, 536, 537, 538, 688, 702, 703, 704, 705.

PARKAR, Ghulam Ahmed; b Kalusta, Maharashtra 24 Oct 1955; (10) 152, 153, 230, 262, 263, 267, 268, 269, 271, 273.

*PATEL, Ashok Kurjibhai; b Bhavnagar, Gujarat 6 Mar 1957; (8) 267, 268, 269, 270, 271, 281, 282, 283.

PATEL, Brijesh Parsuram; b Baroda 24 Nov 1952; (10) 12, 13, 19, 24, 28, 35, 36, 61, 65, 68.

PATEL, Rashid; b Sabarkantha 1 Jun 1964; (1) 538.

PATIL, Sandeep Madhusudan; b Bombay 18 Aug 1956; (45) 98, 100, 101, 102, 103, 105, 106, 108, 109, 117, 118, 142, 143, 152, 153, 156, 157, 158, 162, 163, 164, 200, 204, 207, 210, 216, 219, 221, 223, 224, 225, 226, 227, 262, 263, 267, 268, 270, 272, 273, 280, 381, 383, 386, 387.

PRABHAKAR, Manoj; b Ghaziabad, Uttar Pradesh 15 Apr 1963; (129) 262, 263, 271, 280, 281, 283, 284, 435, 436, 437, 438, 442, 444, 447, 453, 458, 461, 465, 469, 474, 476, 482, 569, 571, 572, 574, 580, 582, 583, 587, 589, 591, 593, 594, 595, 616, 617, 619, 620, 623, 625, 634, 635, 656, 657, 658, 661, 662, 664, 680, 681, 683, 684, 685, 686, 687, 688, 692, 693, 694, 696, 697, 700, 702, 703, 704, 705, 715, 722, 725, 729, 732, 737, 740, 745, 764, 784, 785, 786, 787, 788, 789, 790, 794, 795, 796, 797, 798, 799, 822, 823, 833, 834, 835, 846, 851, 852, 855, 856, 858, 879, 880, 921, 923, 926, 936, 937, 938, 940, 941, 945, 946, 947, 975, 976, 978, 992, 994, 996, 998, 1014, 1015, 1016, 1017, 1018, 1051, 1055, 1063, 1068.

PRASAD, Bapu Krishnarao Venkatesh; b Bangalore 5 Aug 1969; (44) 903, 910, 912, 926, 937, 938, 940, 941, 943, 944, 945, 975, 976, 994, 996, 998, 1014, 1015, 1016, 1017, 1018, 1051, 1055, 1063, 1068, 1072, 1076, 1079, 1088, 1089, 1094, 1096, 1097, 1099, 1100, 1101, 1103, 1105, 1107, 1112, 1113, 1114, 1115, 1116.

RAJPUT, Lalchand Sitaram; b Bombay 18 Dec 1961; (4) 283, 284, 434, 437.

RAJU, Sagi Laksmi Venkatapathy; b Hyderabad 9 Jul 1969; (53) 616, 661, 662, 664, 680, 681, 683, 684, 685, 686, 687, 688, 697, 700, 702, 705, 722, 725, 729, 732, 737, 740, 745, 789, 790, 794, 795, 796, 822, 858, 881, 904, 923, 940, 941, 943, 944, 945, 946, 947, 975, 976, 1051, 1063, 1072, 1076, 1088, 1089, 1091, 1093, 1096, 1097, 1101.

RAMAN, Woorkeri Venkat; b Madras 23 May 1965; (26) 483, 484, 485, 486, 487, 513, 514, 517, 538, 616, 617, 619, 620, 623, 634, 661, 683, 784, 785, 786, 787, 788, 824, 846, 851, 852.

*RANDHIR SINGH; b Delhi 16 Aug 1957; (2) 141, 230.

RATHORE, Vikram; b Jullundur 26 Mar 1969; (6) 1094, 1096, 1097, 1099, 1100, 1101.

RAZDAN, Vivek; b Delhi 25 Aug 1969; (3) 593, 595, 656.

REDDY, Bharath; b Madras 12 Nov 1954; (3) 56, 108, 109.

SANDHU, Balwinder Singh; b Bombay 3 Aug 1956; (22) 162, 163, 164, 165, 190, 191, 200, 204, 207, 210, 216, 219, 221, 223, 224, 225, 226, 227, 228, 271, 272, 273.

SEKAR, Thirumalai Ananthan Pillai; b Madras 28 Mar 1956; (4) 165, 282, 283, 284.

SHARMA, Ajay Kumar; b Alwar, Rajasthan 3 Apr 1964; (31) 483, 484, 532, 534, 535, 536, 537, 538, 559, 560, 561, 562, 563, 569, 572, 574, 580, 583, 587, 589, 591, 616, 617, 619, 620, 798, 799, 824, 835, 846, 851.

SHARMA, Chetan; b Ludhiana, Punjab b 3 Jan 1966; (65) 229, 230, 262, 263, 267, 268, 269, 270, 272, 280, 284, 319, 332, 333, 334, 340, 348, 349, 351, 352, 354, 355, 356, 357, 360, 361, 362, 363, 383, 385, 386, 387, 390, 391, 401, 407, 433, 437, 465, 469, 474, 476, 481, 485, 486, 513, 514, 538, 559, 560, 561, 562, 563, 571, 574, 582, 583, 587, 589, 591, 789, 790, 943, 946, 947.

SHARMA, Gopal; b Kanpur 3 Aug 1960; (11) 332, 333, 334, 392, 394, 435, 436, 438, 442, 444, 447.

SHARMA, Parthasarthi; b Alwar, Rajasthan 5 Jan 1948; (2) 35, 36.

SHARMA, Sanjeev Kumar; b Delhi 25 Aug 1965; (23) 483, 484, 485, 487, 488, 517, 523, 525, 526, 529, 530, 532, 534, 535, 536, 537, 538, 559, 560, 623, 625, 634, 635.

SHASTRI, Ravishankar Jayadritha; b Bombay 27 May 1962; (150) 141, 142, 143, 152, 153, 162, 163, 164, 190, 191, 200, 204, 207, 210, 216, 227, 228, 229, 230, 262, 263, 267, 268, 269, 270, 271, 272, 273, 280, 281, 282, 283, 284, 308, 312, 315, 316, 319, 325, 328, 332, 333, 334, 340, 341, 348, 349, 351, 352, 354, 355, 356, 357, 360, 361, 362, 363, 381, 383, 385, 386, 387, 390, 391, 392, 393, 394, 395, 401, 403, 406, 407, 408, 409, 410, 433, 434, 435, 436, 437, 438, 442, 444, 447, 453, 458, 461, 465, 469, 474, 476, 481, 482, 483, 484, 485, 486, 487, 488, 513, 514, 517, 523, 525, 526, 559, 560, 561, 562, 563, 569, 571, 572, 574, 580, 582, 593, 594, 595, 623, 625, 634, 635, 656, 657, 658, 662, 664, 680, 681, 684, 685, 686, 688, 692, 693, 694, 696, 697, 702, 703, 704, 705, 715, 725, 764, 786, 787, 788, 789.

SIDHU, Navjot Singh; b Patiala, Punjab 20 Oct 1963; (106) 453, 458, 461, 465, 469, 474, 476, 513, 514, 517, 523, 525, 529, 530, 532, 534, 535, 536, 537, 559, 560, 561, 563, 569, 571, 574, 580, 582, 583, 593, 594, 595, 623, 625, 634, 635, 656, 657, 658, 661, 662, 664, 680, 681, 683, 685, 686, 687, 700, 702, 794, 795, 796, 797, 798, 799, 822, 823, 824, 833, 834, 835, 879, 880, 881, 900, 902, 903, 904, 906, 910, 912, 921, 923, 926, 936, 937, 938, 940, 941, 943, 944, 945, 975, 976, 978, 992, 994, 996, 998, 1014, 1015, 1051, 1055, 1072, 1076, 1079, 1088, 1089, 1091, 1093, 1094, 1096, 1097, 1099, 1100.

*SINGH, Rudra Pratap; b Lucknow 6 Jan 1963; (2) 392, 395.

*SINGH, Rabindra Ramanarayan; b Princes Town, Trinidad 14 Sep 1963; (2) 561, 562.

SIVARAMAKRISHNAN, Laxman; b Madras 31 Dec 1965; (16) 308, 312, 315, 316, 319, 325, 328, 332, 340, 341, 351, 352, 354, 360, 458, 461.

SOLKAR, Eknath Dhondu; b Bombay 18 Mar 1948; (7) 12, 13, 19, 24, 28, 35, 36.

SRIKKANTH, Krishnamachari; b Madras 21 Dec 1959; (146) 141, 142, 156, 157, 158, 162, 163, 164, 165, 200, 204, 207, 210, 216, 219, 221, 223, 224, 225, 226, 227, 228, 229, 230, 280, 281, 282, 283, 284, 308, 312, 315, 316, 319, 325, 328, 332, 333, 334, 340, 341, 348, 349, 351, 352, 354, 355, 356, 357, 360, 361, 362, 363, 381, 383, 385, 386, 387, 390, 391, 392, 393, 394, 395, 401, 403, 406, 407, 408, 409, 410, 411, 433, 434, 435, 442, 444, 447, 453, 458, 461, 465, 469, 474, 476, 481, 482, 483, 484, 485, 486, 487, 488, 513, 514, 517, 523, 525, 526, 529, 530, 532, 534, 535, 536, 537, 559, 560, 561, 562, 563, 569, 571, 572, 574, 580, 582, 583, 587, 589, 591, 593, 594, 595, 623, 625, 687, 688, 692, 693, 694, 696, 697, 700, 702, 703, 704, 705, 715, 722, 725, 729, 732, 737, 740, 745.

SRINATH, Javagal; b Mysore 31 Aug 1969; (107) 680, 684, 685, 686, 687, 688, 692, 693, 694, 696, 697, 700, 702, 703, 704, 705, 715, 722, 725, 729, 732, 737, 740, 745, 764, 784, 785, 786, 787, 788, 794, 795, 796, 797, 798, 799, 822, 823, 824, 833, 834, 835, 846, 851, 852, 855, 856, 858, 879, 880, 881, 900, 901, 902, 903, 904, 906, 910, 912, 921, 936, 937, 938, 940, 941, 943, 944, 945, 946, 947, 975, 976, 978, 992, 994, 996, 998, 1014, 1015, 1016, 1017, 1018, 1051, 1055, 1063, 1068, 1072, 1076, 1079, 1088, 1089, 1091, 1093, 1094, 1096, 1097, 1099, 1100, 1101, 1103, 1105, 1107, 1112, 1113, 1114, 1115, 1116.

SRINIVASAN, Tirumalai Echambadi; b Madras 26 Oct 1950; (2) 98, 105.

*SUDHAKAR RAO, Ramchandra; b Bangalore 8 Aug 1952; (1) 36.

TENDULKAR, Sachin Ramesh; b Bombay 24 Apr 1973; (126) 593, 616, 619, 623, 625, 634, 635, 656, 657, 658, 661, 662, 664, 680, 681, 683, 684, 685, 686, 687, 688, 692, 693, 694, 696, 697, 700, 702, 703, 704, 705, 715, 722, 725, 729, 732, 737, 740, 745, 764, 784, 785, 786, 787, 788, 789, 790, 794, 795, 796, 797, 798, 799, 822, 823, 824, 833, 834, 835, 846, 851, 852, 855, 856, 858, 879, 880, 881, 900, 901, 902, 903, 904, 906, 910, 912, 921, 923, 926, 936, 937, 938, 940, 941, 943, 944, 945, 946, 947, 975, 976, 978, 992, 994, 996, 998, 1014, 1015, 1016, 1017, 1018, 1051, 1055, 1063, 1068, 1072, 1076, 1079, 1088, 1089, 1091, 1093, 1094, 1096, 1097, 1099, 1100, 1101, 1103, 1105, 1107, 1112, 1113, 1114, 1115, 1116.

*VAIDYA, Prashant Sridhar; b Nagpur 23 Sep 1967; (4) 978, 992, 1091, 1093.

VENGSARKAR, Dilip Balwant; b Rajapur, Maharashtra 6 Apr 1956; (129) 35, 36, 54, 55, 61, 65, 68, 98, 100, 101, 102, 103, 104, 105, 106, 108, 109, 117, 118, 141, 142, 143, 152, 153, 156, 157, 158, 162, 163, 164, 165, 189, 190, 191, 207, 210, 226, 230, 262, 263, 267, 268, 269, 270, 273, 280, 281, 282, 283, 308, 312, 315, 316, 319, 325, 328, 332, 333, 334, 340, 341, 348, 349, 355, 356, 357, 360, 362, 363, 385, 386, 387, 390, 391, 392, 393, 395, 403, 406, 407, 408, 409, 410, 411, 433, 434, 436, 437, 438, 442, 444, 447, 453, 458, 461, 465, 469, 474, 481, 482, 523, 525, 526, 529, 530, 532, 534, 535, 536, 537, 538, 559, 560, 561, 562, 563, 569, 571, 572, 574, 583, 587, 589, 591, 616, 617, 619, 635, 688.

VENKATARAGHAVAN, Srinivasaraghavan; b Madras 21 Apr 1946; (15) 12, 19, 24, 28, 35, 36, 54, 55, 56, 61, 65, 68, 189, 190, 191.

VENKATARAMANA, Margasaghayam; b Secunderabad 24 Apr 1966; (1) 538.

VISWANATH, Gundappa Ranganath; b Bhadravati, Mysore 12 Feb 1949; (25) 12, 13, 19, 24, 28, 35, 54, 55, 56, 61, 65, 68, 98, 100, 101, 102, 104, 105, 106, 108, 109, 117, 118, 141, 152.

VISWANATH, Sadanand; b Bangalore 29 Nov 1962; (22) 282, 283, 284, 308, 312, 315, 316, 319, 325, 328, 332, 333, 334, 435, 436, 437, 438, 442, 444, 447, 484, 485.

WADEKAR, Ajit Laxman; b Bombay 1 Apr 1941; (2) 12, 13.

WASSAN, Atil Satish; b Delhi 23 Mar 1968; (9) 616, 617, 619, 620, 657, 658, 661, 662, 664.

YADAV, Nandlal Shivlal; b Hyderabad 26 Jan 1957; (7) 348, 349, 355, 363, 408, 410, 411.

YADAV, Vijay; b Gonda 14 Mar 1967; (19) 788, 789, 790, 794, 795, 822, 823, 824, 833, 834, 835, 846, 851, 852, 855, 856, 858, 943, 944.

YASHPAL SHARMA; b Ludhiana, Punjab 11 Aug 1954; (42) 55, 56, 100, 101, 102, 103, 104, 105, 106, 108, 109, 117, 118, 142, 143, 152, 153, 156, 157, 158, 162, 163, 164, 165, 189, 190, 191, 200, 204, 207, 210, 216, 219, 221, 223, 224, 225, 226, 280, 281, 282, 284.

YOGRAJ SINGH; b Chandigarh 25 Mar 1958; (6) 102, 103, 104, 106, 117, 118.

PAKISTAN (108 players)

* Denotes players who had not appeared in official Test matches before 28 September 1996.

*AAMER HAMEED; b Lahore 18 Oct 1954; (2) 45, 47.

*AAMER HANIF; b Karachi 4 Oct 1971; (5) 843, 1002, 1003, 1004, 1010.

AAMER MALIK; b Mandi Bahauddin 3 Jan 1963; (24) 510, 512, 528, 532, 545, 547, 548, 549, 554, 555, 556, 557, 558, 564, 565, 584, 588, 589, 590, 592, 598, 599, 607, 928.

AAMIR NAZIR; b Lahore 2 Jan 1971; (9) 826, 827, 828, 829, 845, 877, 981, 995, 997.

AAMIR SOHAIL; b Lahore 14 Sep 1966; (106) 660, 684, 685, 689, 690, 717, 720, 726, 729, 735, 739, 746, 747, 750, 752, 756, 757, 758, 759, 760, 770, 773, 774, 775, 777, 780, 781, 791, 792, 809, 810, 813, 814, 825, 826, 827, 828, 829, 840, 845, 895, 896, 897, 898, 899, 906, 908, 911, 912, 916, 917, 918, 919, 920, 922, 924, 928, 929, 931, 932, 934, 935, 957, 958, 961, 963, 965, 967, 969, 970, 981, 982, 983, 994, 995, 997, 1002, 1003, 1004, 1006, 1007, 1019, 1020, 1021, 1022, 1058, 1060, 1065, 1069, 1074, 1076, 1087, 1089, 1090, 1091, 1092, 1094, 1095, 1109, 1110, 1111, 1112, 1113, 1114, 1115, 1116.

ABDUL QADIR Khan; b Lahore 15 Sep 1955; (104) 202, 205, 211, 213, 218, 222, 233, 234, 237, 238, 240, 241, 243, 244, 260, 261, 263, 335, 336, 337, 338, 339, 340, 342, 343, 344, 345, 346, 368, 369, 370, 375, 376, 379, 380, 382, 384, 385, 396, 397, 398, 399, 400, 433, 434, 435, 436, 437, 438, 443, 445, 447, 451, 455, 459, 463, 467, 473, 475, 478, 479, 480, 510, 511, 512, 522, 524, 525, 527, 528, 531, 532, 539, 540, 543, 547, 548, 549, 554, 555, 556, 557, 558, 564, 570, 571, 573, 574, 579, 581, 584, 588, 589, 590, 592, 593, 594, 595, 598, 599, 625, 641, 842, 843.

AKRAM RAZA; b Lahore 22 Nov 1964; (49) 581, 588, 589, 590, 592, 636, 637, 638, 639, 640, 641, 660, 680, 682, 684, 685, 706, 895, 896, 897, 898, 899, 906, 908, 911, 912, 916, 917, 918, 919, 920, 922, 924, 928, 929, 931, 932, 934, 935, 957, 958, 961, 963, 965, 967, 969, 970, 982, 983.

ANIL DALPAT Sonavaria; b Karachi 20 Sep 1963; (15) 260, 261, 263, 276, 277, 303, 304, 305, 306, 308, 311, 314, 317, 319, 396.

AQIB JAVED; b Sheikhupura 5 Aug 1972; (133) 539, 540, 543, 544, 545, 547, 548, 549, 554, 555, 556, 557, 558, 564, 565, 571, 574, 589, 592, 593, 594, 595, 598, 599, 601, 602, 603, 604, 605, 607, 625, 627, 629, 631, 659, 679, 680, 682, 684, 685, 689, 690, 691, 706, 707, 708, 709, 710, 717, 720, 726, 729, 735, 739, 746, 747, 750, 752, 756, 757, 758, 759, 760, 773, 774, 775, 778, 780, 781, 791, 792, 800, 801, 803, 804, 806, 807, 809, 810, 812, 813, 814, 825, 840, 841, 876, 877, 878, 906, 908, 911, 912, 929, 931, 932, 934, 935, 957, 958, 961, 963, 965, 967, 969, 970, 981, 982, 983, 994, 995, 1002, 1003, 1004, 1006, 1007, 1008, 1010, 1019, 1020, 1021, 1022, 1058, 1060, 1069, 1074, 1076, 1087, 1089, 1090, 1091, 1092, 1094, 1095.

*ARSHAD KHAN; b Peshawar 22 Mar 1971; (5) 800, 995, 997, 1003, 1004.

*ARSHAD PERVEZ; b Sargodha 1 Oct 1952; (2) 47, 51.

ASHFAQ AHMED; b Lyallpur 6 Jun 1973; (3) 916, 917, 918.

ASHRAF ALI; b Lahore 22 Apr 1958; (16) 94, 122, 123, 125, 126, 127, 134, 150, 240, 244, 259, 272, 273, 325, 327, 335.

ASIF IQBAL Razvi; b Hyderabad, India 6 Jun 1943; (10) 5, 14, 15, 21, 41, 56, 64, 66, 71, 73.

ASIF MASOOD; b Lahore 23 Jan 1946; (7) 5, 14, 15, 21, 26, 30, 40.

ASIF MUJTABA, Mohammad; b Karachi 4 Nov 1967; (66) 397, 402, 406, 414, 417, 418, 479, 756, 757, 758, 760, 770, 773, 774, 775, 777, 778, 780, 781, 791, 801, 803, 804, 806, 807, 809, 810, 812, 813, 814, 825, 827, 828, 829, 840, 841, 842, 843, 845, 876, 877, 878, 895, 896, 897, 898, 899, 906, 908, 911, 912, 916, 917, 918, 919, 920, 922, 929, 931, 970, 982, 983, 994, 995, 997, 1111.

ATA-UR-REHMAN; b Lahore 28 Mar 1975; (30) 770, 777, 809, 826, 827, 828, 829, 841, 842, 843, 845, 895, 896, 897, 898, 899, 906, 908, 911, 912, 957, 958, 961, 1002, 1003, 1076, 1090, 1094, 1109, 1110.

AZEEM HAFEEZ; b Karachi 29 Jul 1963; (15) 224, 225, 232, 233, 234, 235, 237, 238, 244, 263, 303, 304, 305, 314, 319.

AZHAR MAHMOOD; b Rawalpindi 28 Feb 1975; (3) 1112, 1113, 1114.

AZMAT RANA; b Lahore 3 Nov 1951; (2) 55, 56.

BASIT ALI; b Karachi 13 Dec 1970; (49) 825, 826, 827, 828, 829, 840, 841, 842, 843, 845, 876, 877, 878, 895, 896, 897, 898, 899, 906, 908, 911, 912, 917, 918, 919, 920, 922, 924, 932, 934, 935, 957, 958, 961, 963, 965, 967, 969, 1002, 1003, 1007, 1008, 1010, 1019, 1020, 1021, 1022, 1094, 1095.

*GHULAM ALI; b Karachi 8 Sep 1966; (3) 812, 994, 995.

*HAAFIZ SHAHID; b Lahore 10 May 1963; (3) 509, 511, 532.

HAROON RASHID Dar; b Karachi 25 Mar 1953; (12) 46, 50, 51, 64, 66, 71, 73, 149, 150, 151, 159, 160.

*HASAN JAMIL Alvi; b Lahore 25 Jul 1952; (6) 45, 46, 47, 54, 55, 56.

IJAZ AHMED; b Sialkot 20 Sep 1968; (141) 398, 399, 400, 402, 404, 406, 412, 433, 437, 438, 443, 445, 447, 448, 451, 455, 459, 463, 467, 473, 475, 478, 479, 480, 508, 509, 510, 511, 512, 522, 524, 525, 527, 528, 531, 532, 539, 540, 543, 544, 545, 547, 548, 549, 554, 555, 556, 557, 558, 564, 565, 571, 573, 574, 579, 581, 584, 588, 589, 590, 592, 598, 599, 601, 602, 603, 604, 605, 607, 608, 609, 625, 627, 629, 631, 636, 637, 638, 641, 659, 660, 679, 680, 682, 684, 685, 690, 691, 707, 708, 709, 710, 717, 726, 735, 739, 746, 747, 752, 758, 928, 929, 931, 932, 934, 935, 957, 958, 961, 963, 965, 967, 969, 970, 981, 982, 983, 1019, 1020, 1021, 1058, 1060, 1065, 1069, 1074, 1076, 1087, 1089, 1090, 1091, 1092, 1094, 1109, 1110, 1111, 1112, 1113, 1114, 1115, 1116.

IJAZ FAQIH; b Karachi 24 Mar 1956; (27) 95, 123, 125, 126, 128, 130, 132, 133, 162, 163, 164, 165, 198, 202, 211, 213, 218, 222, 238, 240, 241, 243, 244, 435, 436, 443, 512.

IMRAN KHAN Niazi; b Lahore 25 Nov 1952; (175) 14, 15, 21, 30, 40, 41, 54, 56, 64, 66, 71, 73, 93, 94, 122, 123, 125, 126, 127, 128, 130, 132, 133, 134, 150, 151, 154, 155, 160, 161, 162, 163, 164, 165, 198, 202, 205, 211, 213, 218, 222, 232, 233, 234, 235, 237, 238, 240, 308, 311, 314, 317, 319, 325, 327, 335, 336, 337, 339, 340, 342, 343, 344, 345, 346, 368, 369, 370, 375, 376, 379, 384, 385, 396, 398, 399, 400, 402, 404, 406, 412, 414, 417, 418, 433, 434, 435, 436, 437, 438, 445, 447, 448, 449, 450, 451, 455, 459, 463, 467, 473, 475, 508, 509, 510, 511, 512, 539, 540, 543, 544, 545, 547, 548, 549, 554, 555, 556, 557, 558, 564, 565, 570, 571, 573, 579, 581, 584, 588, 589, 590, 592, 593, 594, 595, 598, 599, 601, 602, 603, 604, 605, 607, 608, 609, 625, 627, 629, 631, 639, 640, 641, 659, 660, 679, 680, 682, 684, 685, 689, 690, 691, 706, 707, 708, 709, 710, 720, 729, 735, 739, 746, 747, 750, 752.

INTIKHAB ALAM Khan; b Hoshiarpur, Punjab, India 28 Dec 1941; (4) 5, 14, 15, 40.

INZAMAM-UL-HAQ; b Multan 3 Mar 1970; (115) 690, 691, 706, 707, 708, 709, 710, 717, 720, 726, 729, 735, 739, 746, 747, 750, 752, 756, 757, 758, 759, 760, 770, 773, 774, 775, 777, 778, 780, 781, 791, 792, 793, 800, 801, 803, 804, 806, 825, 826, 827, 828, 829, 840, 841, 842, 843, 845, 876, 877, 878, 895, 896, 897, 898, 899, 906, 908, 911, 912, 916, 917, 918, 919, 920, 922, 924, 928, 929, 931, 932, 934, 935, 957, 958, 961, 963, 965, 967, 969, 970, 981, 982, 983, 994, 995, 997, 1002, 1003, 1004, 1006, 1008, 1019, 1020, 1021, 1022, 1058, 1060, 1065, 1069, 1074, 1076, 1087, 1089, 1090, 1091, 1092, 1094, 1095, 1109, 1110, 1112, 1113, 1115, 1116.

IQBAL QASIM, Mohammad; b Karachi 6 Aug 1953; (15) 46, 47, 50, 54, 93, 94, 122, 134, 149, 154, 155, 303, 304, 305, 531.

*IQBAL SIKANDER; b Karachi 19 Dec 1958; (4) 717, 720, 735, 750.

*IRFAN BHATTI; b Peshawar 28 Sep 1964; (1) 878.

JALALUDDIN; b Karachi 12 Jun 1959; (8) 149, 159, 160, 161, 162, 163, 224, 225.

JAVED MIANDAD Khan; b Karachi 12 Jun 1957; (233) 26, 30, 40, 41, 45, 46, 47, 50, 51, 54, 55, 56, 64, 66, 71, 73, 93, 94, 95, 122, 123, 125, 126, 127, 128, 130, 132, 133, 134, 149, 150, 154, 159, 160, 161, 162, 163, 164, 165, 198, 202, 205, 211, 213, 218, 224, 225, 232, 233, 234, 235, 237, 238, 240, 241, 243, 244, 261, 272, 273, 276, 277, 278, 279, 303, 304, 305, 306, 308, 311, 314, 317, 319, 325, 327, 335, 336, 337, 338, 339, 340, 342, 343, 344, 345, 346, 368, 369, 370, 375, 376, 379, 380, 382, 384, 385, 396, 397, 398, 399, 400, 402, 404, 406, 412, 414, 417, 418, 433, 434, 435, 436, 437, 438, 443, 445, 447, 448, 449, 450, 451, 455, 459, 463, 467, 473, 475, 508, 509, 510, 511, 512, 522, 524, 525, 527, 528, 539, 540, 543, 544, 545, 547, 548, 549, 554, 571, 574, 579, 581, 584, 589, 590, 592, 593, 594, 595, 598, 601, 602, 603, 604, 605, 608, 609, 625, 627, 629, 631, 636, 637, 638, 639, 640, 659, 660, 679, 680, 682, 689, 706, 707, 708, 709, 710, 717, 720, 726, 729, 739, 746, 747, 750, 752, 756, 757, 759, 770, 773, 774, 775, 777, 778, 780, 781, 791, 792, 793, 800, 801, 803, 804, 806, 807, 809, 810, 813, 814, 825, 826, 828, 829, 840, 841, 842, 876, 877, 878, 1058, 1060, 1069, 1074, 1076.

*JAVED QADIR; b Karachi 25 Aug 1976; (1) 997.

KABIR KHAN; b Peshawar 12 Apr 1974; (2) 924, 967.

LIAQAT ALI Khan; b Karachi 21 May 1955; (3) 45, 50, 51.

*MAHMOOD HAMID; b Karachi 19 Jan 1969; (1) 997.

MAJID Jahangir KHAN; b Ludhiana, Punjab, India 28 Sep 1946; (23) 5, 14, 15, 21, 26, 30, 40, 41, 54, 56, 64, 66, 71, 73, 93, 94, 95, 122, 127, 128, 134, 154, 155.

MANSOOR AKHTAR; b Karachi 25 Dec 1957; (41) 93, 122, 123, 130, 132, 133, 134, 149, 150, 151, 155, 159, 160, 161, 162, 163, 164, 165, 205, 211, 232, 233, 234, 235, 237, 238, 241, 243, 244, 448, 449, 450, 451, 455, 459, 463, 467, 475, 593, 598, 599.

*MANSOOR RANA; b Lahore 27 Dec 1962; (2) 627, 631.

MANZOOR ELAHI; b Sahiwal 15 Apr 1963; (54) 272, 273, 276, 277, 278, 279, 325, 375, 376, 379, 380, 382, 384, 385, 397, 398, 400, 402, 404, 406, 412, 414, 417, 418, 433, 434, 435, 436, 437, 438, 443, 445, 447, 448, 449, 450, 467, 478, 479, 480, 522, 524, 525, 527, 528, 531, 636, 637, 638, 963, 965, 981, 982, 983.

*MAQSOOD RANA; b Lahore 1 Aug 1972; (1) 599.

*MASOOD IQBAL Qureshi; b Lahore 17 Apr 1952; (1) 279.

MOHAMMAD AKRAM; b Islamabad 10 Sep 1972; (7) 1002, 1003, 1004, 1008, 1010, 1087, 1095.

MOHAMMAD NAZIR (*also known as* NAZIR JUNIOR); b Rawalpindi 8 Mar 1946; (4) 93, 224, 225, 232.

MOHSIN KAMAL; b Faisalabad 15 Jun 1963; (19) 278, 279, 303, 337, 338, 340, 342, 342, 344, 345, 346, 380, 382, 449, 450, 479, 480, 522, 544.

MOHSIN Hasan KHAN; b Karachi 15 Mar 1955; (75) 41, 47, 50, 54, 125, 126, 127, 128, 132, 149, 150, 151, 154, 155, 159, 160, 161, 162, 163, 164, 165, 198, 202, 205, 211, 213, 218, 222, 224, 225, 232, 233, 234, 235, 237, 238, 240, 243, 244, 259, 260, 261, 263, 272, 277, 278, 303, 304, 308, 311, 314, 317, 319, 325, 327, 338, 339, 340, 342, 343, 344, 346, 368, 369, 370, 375, 376, 379, 380, 382, 384, 385, 396, 397, 404.

MOIN KHAN; b Rawalpindi 23 Sep 1971; (47) 641, 679, 680, 682, 684, 685, 689, 690, 691, 706, 707, 708, 709, 710, 717, 720, 726, 729, 735, 739, 746, 747, 750, 752, 756, 757, 759, 760, 963, 982, 983, 994, 995, 1002, 1003, 1004, 1006, 1007, 1008, 1010, 1109, 1110, 1112, 1113, 1114, 1115, 1116.

*MOIN-UL-ATIQ; b Karachi 5 Aug 1964; (5) 511, 531, 532, 545, 547.

MUDASSAR NAZAR; b Lahore 6 Apr 1956; (122) 45, 46, 47, 50, 51, 54, 64, 66, 71, 73, 93, 94, 122, 123, 125, 126, 127, 128, 130, 133, 134, 150, 151, 154, 155, 159, 160, 161, 162, 163, 164, 165, 198, 202, 205, 213, 218, 222, 224, 225, 232, 233, 234, 235, 237, 238, 240, 241, 243, 244, 259, 260, 261, 263, 272, 273, 276, 277, 278, 279, 303, 304, 305, 306, 308, 311, 314, 317, 319, 325, 327, 335, 336, 337, 338, 339, 340, 342, 343, 344, 368, 369, 370, 375, 376, 379, 380, 382, 384, 385, 396, 402, 404, 406, 412, 414, 417, 418, 433, 434, 443, 445, 447, 448, 449, 450, 451, 473, 478, 480, 509, 510, 522, 524, 525, 527, 543, 554, 555, 556, 557, 558.

MUSHTAQ AHMED; b Sahiwal 28 Jun 1970; (106) 564, 565, 570, 571, 573, 574, 579, 584, 588, 589, 590, 592, 601, 602, 607, 609, 627, 629, 631, 636, 637, 639, 640, 641, 659, 660, 679, 689, 690, 691, 707, 708, 709, 710, 720, 726, 729, 735, 739, 746, 747, 750, 752, 756, 757, 758, 759, 760, 770, 773, 774, 775, 777, 778, 781, 791, 792, 793, 800, 801, 803, 804, 806, 807, 810, 812, 813, 814, 825, 826, 840, 841, 842, 843, 845, 876, 878, 919, 920, 922, 924, 928, 1006, 1007, 1008, 1010, 1019, 1020, 1021, 1022, 1058, 1060, 1065, 1069, 1074, 1076, 1089, 1091, 1092, 1095, 1109, 1110, 1113, 1114, 1115, 1116.

MUSHTAQ MOHAMMED; b Junagadh, Gujarat, India 22 Nov 1943; (10) 5, 14, 15, 21, 26, 30, 40, 54, 55, 56.

NADEEM GHAURI; b Lahore 12 Oct 1962; (6) 599, 603, 604, 605, 608, 609.
NADEEM KHAN; b Rawalpindi 10 Dec 1969; (2) 827, 994.
*NAEEM AHMED; b Karachi 20 Sep 1952; (1) 51.
*NAEEM ASHRAF; b Lahore 10 Nov 1972; (2) 994, 997.
*NASEER MALIK; b Lyallpur 1 Feb 1950; (3) 21, 26, 30.
NASIM-UL-GHANI; b Delhi, India 14 May 1941; (1) 5.
NAVED ANJUM; b Lahore 27 Jul 1963; (13) 260, 272, 273, 276, 508, 509, 510, 532, 756, 757, 759, 760, 793.

*PARVEZ Jamil MIR; b Sutrapur, Dacca 24 Sep 1953; (3) 26, 30, 45.

QASIM Ali OMAR; b Nairobi, Kenya 9 Feb 1957; (31) 224, 232, 233, 234, 235, 237, 238, 240, 241, 243, 244, 259, 260, 263, 303, 304, 305, 306, 308, 311, 314, 317, 319, 339, 345, 375, 376, 412, 414, 417, 418.

RAMIZ Hasan RAJA; b Lyallpur 14 Jul 1962; (177) 305, 306, 308, 311, 314, 317, 319, 325, 327, 335, 336, 337, 338, 339, 340, 342, 343, 344, 345, 346, 368, 369, 370, 375, 376, 379, 380, 382, 384, 385, 396, 397, 398, 399, 400, 402, 404, 406, 412, 414, 417, 418, 434, 435, 436, 437, 438, 443, 445, 447, 448, 449, 450, 451, 455, 459, 463, 467, 473, 475, 478, 479, 480, 508, 509, 510, 511, 512, 522, 524, 525, 527, 528, 531, 532, 539, 540, 543, 544, 547, 548, 555, 556, 557, 558, 564, 565, 570, 573, 581, 584, 588, 589, 590, 592, 593, 594, 595, 601, 602, 604, 605, 607, 608, 609, 637, 638, 639, 640, 679, 680, 682, 689, 690, 691, 706, 707, 708, 709, 710, 717, 720, 726, 739, 746, 747, 750, 752, 756, 757, 758, 759, 760, 770, 773, 774, 775, 777, 780, 781, 791, 792, 793, 800, 801, 803, 804, 806, 807, 809, 810, 812, 813, 814, 825, 826, 827, 828, 829, 1002, 1003, 1004, 1006, 1007, 1008, 1010, 1019, 1020, 1021, 1022, 1065, 1087, 1089, 1090, 1091, 1092, 1095.
RASHID KHAN; b Karachi 15 Dec 1959; (29) 95, 149, 150, 151, 198, 202, 205, 211, 213, 218, 222, 232, 233, 234, 235, 237, 238, 240, 241, 243, 244, 259, 260, 261, 272, 273, 306, 308, 311.
RASHID LATIF; b Karachi 14 Oct 1968; (84) 758, 770, 773, 774, 775, 777, 778, 780, 781, 791, 792, 793, 800, 801, 803, 804, 806, 807, 809, 810, 812, 813, 814, 825, 826, 827, 828, 829, 840, 841, 842, 843, 845, 876, 877, 878, 895, 896, 897, 898, 899, 906, 908, 911, 912, 916, 917, 918, 919, 920, 922, 924, 928, 929, 931, 932, 934, 935, 957, 958, 961, 965, 967, 969, 970, 981, 1019, 1020, 1021, 1022, 1058, 1060, 1065, 1069, 1074, 1076, 1087, 1089, 1090, 1091, 1092, 1094, 1095, 1111.
RIZWAN-UZ-ZAMAN; b Karachi 4 Sep 1962; (3) 122, 398, 433.

*SAADAT ALI; b Lahore 3 Feb 1955; (8) 259, 260, 261, 263, 272, 273, 276, 279.
SADIQ MOHAMMED; b Junagadh, Gujarat, India 3 May 1945; (19) 5, 14, 15, 21, 26, 30, 40, 41, 45, 46, 50, 51, 55, 64, 66, 71, 73, 93, 94.
SAEED ANWAR; b Karachi 6 Sep 1968; (103) 544, 545, 549, 593, 594, 595, 598, 599, 602, 603, 604, 605, 607, 608, 609, 625, 627, 629, 631, 636, 637, 638, 639, 640, 641, 659, 660, 684, 775, 778, 793, 800, 801, 803, 804,

807, 812, 840, 841, 842, 843, 845, 876, 877, 878, 895, 896, 897, 898, 899, 906, 908, 911, 912, 916, 917, 918, 919, 920, 922, 924, 928, 929, 931, 932, 934, 935, 957, 958, 961, 963, 965, 967, 969, 970, 981, 982, 994, 995, 997, 1006, 1007, 1058, 1060, 1065, 1069, 1074, 1076, 1087, 1089, 1090, 1091, 1092, 1094, 1095, 1109, 1110, 1111, 1112, 1113, 1114, 1115, 1116.
*SAEED AZAD; b Karachi 14 Aug 1966; (1) 1004.
*SAJID ALI; b Karachi 1 Jul 1963; (10) 273, 276, 399, 400, 539, 540, 679, 680, 682, 685.
*SAJJAD AKBAR; b Lahore 1 Mar 1961; (2) 625, 629.
SALIM ALTAF Bokhari; b Lahore 19 Apr 1944; (6) 5, 41, 45, 46, 55, 56.
SALIM ELAHI; b Sahiwal 21 Nov 1976; (10) 1002, 1003, 1004, 1006, 1007, 1008, 1010, 1022, 1114, 1115.
SALIM JAFFER; b Karachi 19 Nov 1962; (39) 396, 397, 398, 399, 400, 402, 404, 406, 412, 414, 417, 418, 433, 434, 435, 436, 437, 438, 447, 455, 459, 463, 473, 475, 478, 508, 509, 510, 512, 525, 555, 556, 557, 558, 564, 565, 636, 639, 640.
SALIM MALIK; b Lahore 16 Apr 1963; (234) 132, 149, 225, 241, 243, 244, 259, 260, 261, 263, 277, 278, 279, 303, 304, 305, 306, 314, 317, 319, 325, 327, 335, 336, 337, 338, 339, 340, 342, 343, 344, 345, 346, 368, 369, 370, 379, 380, 382, 384, 385, 396, 433, 434, 435, 436, 437, 438, 443, 445, 447, 448, 449, 450, 451, 455, 459, 463, 467, 473, 475, 478, 479, 480, 508, 509, 510, 511, 512, 522, 524, 525, 527, 528, 531, 532, 539, 540, 543, 544, 545, 547, 548, 549, 554, 555, 556, 557, 558, 564, 565, 570, 571, 573, 574, 579, 581, 584, 588, 589, 590, 592, 593, 594, 595, 601, 602, 603, 604, 605, 607, 608, 609, 625, 627, 629, 631, 636, 637, 638, 639, 640, 641, 659, 660, 679, 680, 682, 684, 685, 689, 690, 691, 706, 707, 708, 709, 710, 717, 720, 726, 729, 735, 739, 746, 747, 750, 752, 756, 757, 758, 759, 770, 773, 774, 777, 778, 780, 781, 791, 792, 793, 800, 801, 803, 804, 806, 807, 810, 812, 841, 842, 843, 845, 876, 877, 878, 895, 896, 897, 898, 899, 906, 908, 911, 912, 916, 917, 918, 919, 920, 922, 924, 928, 929, 931, 932, 934, 935, 957, 958, 961, 963, 965, 967, 969, 970, 981, 982, 983, 1019, 1020, 1021, 1022, 1058, 1060, 1065, 1069, 1074, 1076, 1087, 1089, 1090, 1091, 1092, 1094, 1095, 1109, 1110, 1112, 1113, 1114, 1115, 1116.
*SALIM PERVEZ; b Lahore 7 Nov 1972; (1) 95.
SALIM YOUSUF; b Karachi 7 Dec 1959; (86) 149, 151, 278, 336, 337, 338, 339, 340, 342, 343, 344, 397, 398, 399, 400, 402, 404, 406, 412, 414, 417, 418, 433, 434, 435, 436, 437, 438, 443, 445, 447, 448, 449, 450, 451, 455, 459, 463, 467, 473, 475, 478, 508, 509, 510, 511, 522, 524, 525, 527, 528, 531, 539, 540, 543, 544, 545, 547, 548, 554, 565, 570, 571, 573, 574, 579, 595, 601, 602, 603, 604, 605, 607, 608, 609, 625, 627, 629, 631, 636, 637, 638, 639, 640, 659, 660.
SAQLAIN MUSHTAQ; b Lahore 29 Dec 1976; (20) 1002, 1006, 1007, 1008, 1010, 1065, 1087, 1089, 1090, 1091, 1092, 1094, 1109, 1110, 1111, 1112, 1113, 1114, 1115, 1116.
SARFRAZ NAWAZ Malik; b Lahore 1 Dec 1948; (45) 5, 14, 15, 21, 26, 40, 41, 47, 50, 51, 54, 55, 56, 64, 73, 93, 94, 122, 123, 125, 126, 127, 128, 130, 133, 134, 154, 165, 198, 202, 205, 211, 213, 218, 222, 232, 233, 234, 235, 237, 259, 260, 261, 263, 276.
SHADAB KABIR, Mohammad; b Karachi 12 Nov 1977; (3) 1111, 1112, 1116.

SHAFIQ AHMED; b Lahore 28 Mar 1949; (3) 45, 46, 47.
SHAHID ANWAR; b Multan 5 Jul 1968; (1) 1111.
SHAHID MAHBOOB; b Karachi 25 Aug 1962; (10) 164, 198, 202, 211, 218, 222, 259, 261, 263, 279.
SHAHID NAZIR; b Faisalabad 4 Dec 1977; (1) 1111.
SHAHID SAEED; b Lahore 6 Jan 1966; (10) 570, 571, 573, 574, 579, 581, 778, 780, 792, 793.
SHAKIL AHMED; b Daska 12 Nov 1971; (2) 981, 983.
*SHAKIL KHAN; b Lahore 28 May 1968; (1) 480.
SHOAIB MOHAMMED; b Karachi 8 Jan 1962; (63) 277, 278, 279, 304, 327, 335, 336, 337, 345, 346, 397, 398, 399, 400, 404, 406, 412, 414, 417, 418, 473, 478, 479, 480, 508, 511, 512, 522, 524, 527, 528, 531, 532, 548, 549, 554, 555, 556, 557, 558, 564, 565, 570, 571, 573, 574, 579, 581, 584, 588, 594, 595, 598, 599, 603, 636, 641, 760, 806, 807, 809, 813, 814.
SIKANDER BAKHT; b Karachi 25 Aug 1957; (27) 46, 50, 51, 55, 64, 66, 71, 73, 94, 95, 122, 123, 125, 126, 127, 128, 130, 132, 133, 134, 150, 151, 154, 155, 159, 163, 554.
*SOHAIL FAZAL; b Lahore 11 Nov 1967; (2) 573, 574.

TAHIR NAQQASH; b Lahore 6 Jul 1959; (40) 95, 123, 125, 126, 127, 130, 132, 133, 149, 150, 155, 159, 160, 161, 162, 164, 165, 198, 224, 225, 235, 240, 241, 272, 273, 303, 304, 305, 306, 308, 311, 314, 317, 319, 325, 327, 335, 336, 337, 338.
*TANVIR MEHDI; b Lahore 15 Jun 1971; (1) 757.
*TASLIM ARIF; b Karachi 1 May 1954; (2) 93, 95.
TAUSIF AHMED; b Karachi 10 May 1958; (70) 151, 159, 160, 161, 272, 273, 276, 277, 278, 279, 325, 327, 338, 339, 340, 342, 344, 345, 346, 368, 369, 370, 380, 382, 384, 385, 396, 397, 398, 399, 400, 402, 436, 437, 438, 443, 445, 448, 449, 450, 451, 455, 459, 463, 467, 475, 480, 508, 524, 525, 527, 528, 531, 532, 539, 540, 543, 544, 545, 549, 555, 556, 557, 558, 564, 565, 601, 602, 607, 608.

WAQAR YOUNIS; b Vehari 16 Nov 1969; (133) 570, 573, 574, 579, 581, 584, 588, 590, 593, 594, 595, 598, 601, 603, 604, 605, 607, 608, 609, 625, 627, 629, 631, 636, 637, 638, 639, 640, 641, 659, 660, 679, 680, 682, 684, 685, 689, 690, 691, 706, 707, 708, 709, 710, 758, 759, 760, 770, 773, 774, 775, 777, 778, 780, 781, 791, 792, 793, 800, 801, 803, 804, 806, 807, 809, 810, 812, 813, 814, 825, 826, 827, 828, 829, 840, 845, 876, 877, 895, 896, 897, 898, 899, 916, 917, 918, 919, 920, 922, 924, 928, 929, 931, 932, 934, 935, 957, 958, 961, 963, 965, 967, 969, 970, 1006, 1007, 1008, 1010, 1019, 1020, 1021, 1022, 1058, 1060, 1065, 1069, 1074, 1076, 1087, 1089, 1090, 1091, 1092, 1094, 1095, 1109, 1110, 1111, 1112, 1113, 1114, 1115, 1116.
WASIM AKRAM; b Lahore 3 Jun 1966; (206) 277, 306, 308, 311, 314, 317, 325, 327, 339, 340, 342, 343, 344, 345,

346, 368, 369, 370, 375, 376, 379, 380, 382, 384, 385, 396, 397, 399, 402, 404, 406, 412, 414, 417, 418, 433, 434, 435, 436, 437, 438, 443, 445, 447, 448, 449, 450, 451, 455, 459, 463, 467, 473, 475, 478, 479, 509, 512, 522, 524, 525, 527, 528, 531, 532, 539, 540, 543, 544, 545, 547, 548, 549, 570, 571, 579, 581, 584, 588, 589, 590, 592, 593, 594, 595, 598, 599, 601, 602, 603, 604, 605, 608, 609, 625, 629, 631, 659, 660, 679, 680, 682, 684, 685, 689, 690, 691, 706, 707, 708, 709, 710, 717, 720, 726, 729, 735, 739, 746, 747, 750, 752, 756, 758, 759, 760, 770, 773, 774, 775, 777, 778, 780, 781, 791, 792, 793, 800, 801, 803, 804, 806, 807, 809, 810, 812, 813, 814, 825, 826, 827, 828, 829, 840, 841, 842, 843, 876, 877, 878, 895, 896, 897, 898, 899, 906, 908, 911, 912, 916, 917, 918, 919, 920, 922, 928, 929, 931, 932, 934, 935, 969, 970, 981, 982, 983, 994, 995, 997, 1019, 1020, 1021, 1022, 1058, 1060, 1065, 1069, 1074, 1109, 1110, 1111, 1112, 1113, 1114, 1115, 1116.
WASIM BARI; b Karachi 23 Mar 1948; (51) 5, 14, 15, 21, 26, 30, 40, 41, 45, 46, 47, 50, 51, 54, 55, 56, 64, 66, 71, 73, 95, 128, 130, 132, 133, 154, 155, 159, 160, 161, 162, 163, 164, 165, 198, 202, 205, 211, 213, 218, 222, 224, 225, 232, 233, 234, 235, 237, 238, 241, 243.
*WASIM HAIDER; b Lyallpur 6 Jun 1967; (3) 717, 726, 729.
WASIM Hasan RAJA; b Multan 3 Jul 1952; (54) 5, 14, 15, 21, 26, 30, 40, 41, 45, 46, 47, 50, 51, 55, 66, 71, 93, 94, 95, 122, 123, 125, 126, 127, 128, 130, 132, 133, 134, 149, 151, 154, 155, 161, 162, 163, 164, 165, 205, 213, 222, 224, 225, 240, 241, 243, 259, 260, 303, 304, 305, 306, 317, 319.

YOUNIS AHMED, Mohammad; b Jullundur, Punjab, India 20 Oct 1947; (2) 434, 435.

*ZAFAR IQBAL; b Lahore 23 Mar 1970; (8) 994, 995, 997, 1004, 1006, 1007, 1008, 1010.
ZAHEER ABBAS, Syed; b Sialkot 24 Jul 1947; (62) 14, 15, 21, 26, 30, 40, 41, 54, 55, 56, 64, 66, 71, 73, 94, 95, 123, 125, 126, 127, 128, 130, 132, 133, 134, 150, 151, 154, 155, 159, 160, 161, 162, 163, 164, 165, 198, 202, 205, 211, 213, 218, 222, 224, 225, 259, 261, 263, 272, 273, 276, 277, 278, 279, 305, 306, 308, 311, 335, 336, 337, 338.
*ZAHID AHMED; b Karachi 15 Nov 1961; (2) 478, 479.
ZAHID FAZAL; b Sialkot 10 Nov 1973; (19) 638, 639, 640, 641, 659, 684, 685, 689, 691, 706, 729, 735, 809, 810, 812, 813, 814, 916, 924.
ZAKIR KHAN; b Bannu 3 Apr 1963; (17) 276, 277, 278, 335, 336, 343, 368, 369, 370, 375, 376, 379, 508, 511, 627, 637, 638.
ZULQARNAIN; b Lahore 25 May 1962; (16) 345, 346, 368, 369, 370, 375, 376, 379, 380, 382, 384, 385, 479, 480, 593, 594.

SRI LANKA (87 players)

* Denotes players who had not appeared in official Test matches before 28 September 1996.

AHANGAMA, Franklyn Saliya; b Colombo 14 Sep 1959; (1) 337.
AMALEAN, Kaushik Naginda; b Colombo 7 Apr 1965; (8) 369, 370, 375, 377, 378, 379, 489, 515.
ANURASIRI, Sangarange Don; b Panadura 25 Feb 1966; (45) 368, 369, 370, 375, 377, 378, 379, 383, 401, 410, 411, 451, 457, 460, 464, 467, 472, 513, 515, 516, 521, 528, 533, 575, 657, 658, 662, 663, 709, 718, 727, 733, 736, 742, 761, 762, 767, 768, 769, 801, 802, 859, 860, 861, 879.
ATAPATTU, Marvan Samson; b Kalutara 22 Nov 1970; (9) 656, 657, 706, 708, 709, 710, 761, 1088, 1106.

*CHANDANA, Umagiliyedurage Upul; b Galle 3 Sep 1972; (10) 905, 909, 921, 925, 926, 1088, 1098, 1104, 1106, 1108.

DASSANAYAKE, Pubudu Bathiya; b Kandy 11 Jul 1970; (15) 837, 838, 881, 905, 909, 916, 917, 918, 919, 921, 924, 925, 926, 958, 960.

De ALWIS, Ronald Guy; b Colombo 15 Feb 1959; (31) 186, 187, 188, 193, 194, 195, 198, 201, 206, 211, 214, 217, 256, 257, 258, 383, 401, 404, 407, 408, 409, 410, 489, 491, 494, 495, 496, 497, 499, 513, 516.

De MEL, Ashantha Lakdasa Francis; b Colombo 9 May 1959; (57) 144, 145, 149, 150, 151, 156, 157, 158, 186, 187, 188, 193, 194, 195, 196, 198, 201, 206, 211, 214, 217, 256, 274, 275, 286, 291, 292, 294, 295, 298, 299, 310, 313, 332, 333, 334, 335, 336, 337, 338, 368, 369, 370, 375, 377, 379, 383, 401, 404, 405, 407, 408, 409, 411, 457, 467, 472.

De SILVA, Ashley Matthew; b Colombo 3 Dec 1963; (4) 368, 815, 816, 833.

*De SILVA, Deva Lokesh Stanley; b Ambalangoda 17 Nov 1956; d Balapitiya 12 Apr 1980; (2) 62, 68.

De SILVA, Dandeniyage Somachandra; b Galle 11 Jun 1942; (41) 22, 25, 30, 62, 68, 144, 145, 149, 150, 151, 156, 158, 186, 187, 188, 193, 194, 195, 198, 201, 206, 211, 214, 217, 256, 257, 258, 261, 262, 274, 275, 286, 287, 288, 291, 292, 294, 295, 297, 310, 313.

De SILVA, Ellawalakankanamage Asoka Ranjith; b Kalutara 28 Mar 1956; (28) 407, 408, 491, 493, 494, 495, 515, 516, 564, 565, 575, 577, 580, 585, 588, 596, 600, 601, 604, 605, 606, 623, 627, 630, 665, 666, 667, 763.

*De SILVA, Granville Nissaura; b Colombo 12 Mar 1955; (4) 196, 288, 295, 297.

De SILVA, Ginigalgodage Ramba Ajith; b Ambalangoda 12 Dec 1952; (6) 30, 62, 144, 145, 151, 157.

De SILVA, Pinnaduwage Aravinda; b Colombo 17 Oct 1965; (188) 257, 258, 261, 262, 274, 275, 286, 287, 288, 291, 292, 294, 297, 298, 299, 332, 333, 334, 335, 336, 337, 338, 368, 369, 370, 375, 377, 378, 379, 383, 401, 404, 405, 407, 408, 409, 451, 457, 460, 464, 467, 472, 489, 491, 493, 494, 495, 496, 497, 499, 513, 515, 516, 521, 528, 530, 533, 534, 564, 565, 575, 577, 580, 585, 588, 596, 597, 598, 600, 601, 604, 605, 606, 623, 627, 630, 656, 657, 658, 659, 660, 662, 663, 664, 665, 666, 667, 706, 707, 708, 709, 710, 716, 718, 722, 727, 733, 736, 742, 746, 761, 762, 763, 767, 768, 769, 801, 802, 803, 815, 816, 833, 834, 835, 836, 837, 838, 839, 841, 843, 844, 846, 850, 853, 857, 859, 860, 861, 879, 880, 881, 916, 917, 918, 919, 920, 921, 924, 925, 926, 948, 949, 950, 957, 958, 960, 964, 966, 968, 989, 990, 991, 993, 996, 997, 998, 1002, 1003, 1004, 1005, 1006, 1009, 1010, 1011, 1023, 1026, 1028, 1029, 1031, 1032, 1033, 1034, 1035, 1036, 1054, 1068, 1073, 1075, 1079, 1081, 1087, 1088, 1090, 1098, 1103, 1104, 1106, 1108.

DHARMASENA, Handunettige Deepthi Priyantha Kumara; b Colombo 24 Apr 1971; (38) 920, 921, 924, 925, 926, 957, 960, 968, 996, 1002, 1003, 1004, 1005, 1006, 1009, 1010, 1011, 1023, 1026, 1028, 1031, 1032, 1033, 1034, 1035, 1036, 1054, 1068, 1073, 1075, 1079, 1081, 1087, 1090, 1098, 1103, 1104, 1108.

DIAS, Roy Luke; b Colombo 18 Oct 1952; (58) 62, 68, 144, 145, 149, 150, 151, 156, 157, 158, 193, 194, 195, 196, 198, 201, 206, 211, 214, 217, 256, 261, 262, 274, 275, 286, 287, 288, 291, 292, 294, 295, 297, 298, 299, 310, 313, 332, 333, 334, 335, 336, 337, 338, 368, 369, 370, 375, 377, 378, 383, 407, 408, 409, 410, 411, 451, 472.

DUNUSINGHE, Chamara Iroshan; b Colombo 19 Oct 1970; (1) 993.

*FERNANDO, Edward Ranjit; b Colombo 22 Feb 1944; (3) 22, 25, 30.

FERNANDO, Ellekutige Rufus Nemesion Susil; b Colombo 19 Dec 1955; (7) 186, 187, 188, 193, 194, 195, 196.

*FERNANDO, Thewarathantrige Lalithamana; b ? 27 Dec 1962; (1) 585.

*FERNANDO, Ungamandadige Nisal Kumudusiri; b Colombo 10 Mar 1970; (2) 879, 880.

*GAMAGE, Janak Champika; b Matara 17 Apr 1964; (4) 990, 991, 993, 996.

GOONASEKERA, Yohan; b Colombo 8 Nov 1957; (3) 186, 187, 188.

*GOONATILLEKE, Frederick Ranjan Manilal de Silva; b Colombo 15 Aug 1951; (1) 68.

GOONATILLEKE, Hettiarachige Mahes; b Kandy 16 Aug 1952; (6) 145, 150, 151, 156, 157, 158.

*GUNAWARDENE, Aruna Alwis Wijesiri; b Colombo 31 Mar 1969; (1) 880.

GURUSINHA, Asanka Pradeep; b Colombo 16 Sep 1966; (141) 338, 375, 377, 378, 379, 383, 401, 404, 405, 407, 408, 409, 410, 411, 451, 457, 460, 472, 489, 491, 493, 494, 495, 496, 497, 499, 513, 515, 516, 575, 577, 580, 585, 588, 596, 597, 598, 600, 601, 604, 605, 606, 623, 627, 630, 656, 657, 658, 659, 660, 662, 663, 664, 665, 666, 667, 706, 707, 708, 709, 710, 716, 718, 722, 727, 733, 736, 742, 746, 761, 762, 763, 767, 768, 769, 801, 802, 803, 815, 816, 833, 834, 835, 836, 837, 839, 841, 843, 846, 905, 909, 916, 917, 918, 948, 949, 950, 957, 958, 960, 964, 966, 968, 989, 990, 991, 993, 996, 997, 998, 1002, 1003, 1004, 1005, 1006, 1009, 1010, 1011, 1023, 1026, 1028, 1029, 1031, 1032, 1033, 1034, 1035, 1036, 1054, 1068, 1073, 1075, 1079, 1081, 1087, 1090, 1098, 1103, 1104, 1106, 1108.

HATHURUSINGHE, Upul Chandika; b Colombo 13 Sep 1968; (32) 706, 707, 708, 709, 722, 727, 742, 746, 762, 763, 767, 768, 769, 801, 802, 803, 815, 816, 833, 834, 835, 836, 837, 838, 839, 847, 1006, 1009, 1010, 1011, 1028, 1029.

*HEYN, Peter David; b Colombo 26 Jun 1945; (2) 22, 30.

JAYASEKERA, Rohan Stanley Amarasiriwardena; b Colombo 7 Dec 1957; (2) 144, 149.

*JAYASINGHE, Sunil Asoka; b Matugama 15 Jul 1955; d 20 Apr 1995; (2) 62, 68.

JAYASURIYA, Sanath Teran; b Matara 30 Jun 1969; (112) 596, 597, 598, 600, 601, 606, 623, 659, 660, 662, 663, 664, 665, 666, 667, 706, 707, 708, 709, 710, 716, 718, 722, 727, 733, 736, 762, 763, 768, 769, 815, 816, 833, 834, 835, 836, 837, 838, 839, 841, 843, 844, 846, 847, 850, 853, 857, 859, 860, 861, 879, 880, 881, 905, 909, 916, 917, 918, 919, 920, 921, 924, 925, 926, 948, 949, 950, 957, 958, 960, 964, 966, 968, 989, 990, 991, 993, 996, 997, 998, 1002, 1003, 1004, 1005, 1006, 1009, 1010, 1011, 1023, 1026, 1028, 1029, 1031, 1032, 1033, 1034, 1035, 1036, 1054, 1068, 1073, 1075, 1079, 1081, 1087, 1088, 1090, 1098, 1103, 1104, 1106, 1108.

JEGANATHAN, Sridharan; b Colombo 11 Jul 1951; d 14 May 1996; (5) 188, 464, 467, 472, 496.
JOHN, Vinothen Bede *(formerly* J.V.B.JEYARAJASING-HAM); b Colombo 27 May 1960; (45) 156, 157, 158, 186, 187, 193, 194, 195, 196, 198, 201, 206, 211, 217, 256, 257, 258, 261, 262, 274, 275, 286, 287, 288, 291, 292, 294, 297, 298, 299, 310, 313, 332, 333, 334, 335, 336, 337, 338, 451, 457, 460, 464, 467, 472.

KALPAGE, Ruwan Senani; b Kandy 19 Feb 1970; (74) 706, 707, 716, 718, 722, 727, 733, 742, 746, 761, 762, 763, 767, 768, 769, 801, 802, 803, 815, 816, 833, 834, 835, 836, 837, 838, 839, 841, 843, 844, 846, 847, 850, 853, 857, 859, 860, 861, 879, 880, 881, 905, 909, 916, 917, 918, 919, 920, 921, 924, 925, 926, 948, 949, 950, 957, 958, 960, 964, 966, 968, 989, 990, 991, 993, 997, 998, 1002, 1004, 1005, 1006, 1031, 1032, 1036.
KALUPERUMA, Lalith Wasantha Silva; b Colombo 25 May 1949; (4) 22, 25, 30, 144.
KALUPERUMA, Sanath Mohan Silva; b Colombo 22 Oct 1961; (2) 499, 515.
KALUWITHARANA, Romesh Shantha; b Colombo 24 Nov 1969; (54) 658, 667, 761, 834, 835, 836, 839, 841, 843, 844, 846, 847, 850, 853, 857, 859, 860, 861, 920, 996, 997, 998, 1002, 1003, 1004, 1005, 1006, 1009, 1010, 1011, 1023, 1026, 1028, 1029, 1031, 1032, 1033, 1034, 1035, 1036, 1054, 1068, 1073, 1075, 1079, 1081, 1087, 1088, 1090, 1098, 1103, 1104, 1106, 1108.
*KARNAIN, Shaul Hameed Uvais; b Colombo 11 Aug 1962; (19) 257, 258, 261, 262, 287, 288, 291, 292, 294, 295, 297, 298, 299, 310, 313, 533, 534, 623, 627.
KURUPPU, Don Sardha Brendon Priyantha; b Colombo 5 Jan 1962; (54) 196, 198, 201, 206, 211, 214, 217, 256, 257, 258, 261, 262, 286, 287, 288, 295, 369, 370, 375, 377, 378, 379, 405, 451, 457, 460, 464, 467, 493, 494, 495, 496, 497, 499, 513, 515, 516, 521, 528, 530, 533, 534, 564, 565, 575, 577, 580, 585, 588, 604, 605, 606, 627, 630.

LABROOY, Graeme Fredrick; b Colombo 9 Jun 1964; (44) 401, 404, 405, 409, 410, 411, 489, 491, 493, 494, 495, 496, 497, 499, 513, 515, 516, 521, 528, 534, 564, 565, 575, 577, 580, 585, 588, 596, 597, 598, 600, 604, 605, 656, 657, 659, 660, 663, 664, 665, 666, 707, 708, 736.
LIYANAGE, Dulip Kapila; b Kalutara 6 Jun 1972; (9) 767, 843, 844, 846, 847, 850, 853, 860, 861.

MADUGALLE, Ranjan Senerath; b Kandy 22 Apr 1959; (63) 68, 144, 145, 149, 150, 151, 156, 157, 158, 186, 187, 188, 193, 194, 195, 196, 201, 206, 211, 214, 217, 256, 257, 258, 261, 262, 274, 275, 291, 292, 294, 295, 297, 310, 313, 332, 333, 334, 335, 336, 337, 338, 408, 409, 410, 457, 460, 464, 467, 472, 489, 491, 493, 494, 495, 496, 497, 499, 513, 515, 516, 521, 528.
MADURASINGHE, Madurasinghe Arachchige Wijayasiri Ranjith; b Kurunegala 30 Jan 1961; (12) 521, 530, 533, 534, 606, 623, 627, 630, 656, 708, 709, 710.
MAHANAMA, Roshan Siriwardene; b Colombo 31 May 1966; (148) 368, 369, 370, 377, 378, 379, 383, 401, 404, 405, 407, 410, 411, 451, 457, 460, 464, 467, 472, 489, 491, 493, 494, 495, 496, 497, 499, 513, 516, 528, 530, 534, 564, 565, 575, 577, 580, 585, 588, 596, 597, 598, 600, 601, 604, 605, 656, 657, 658, 659, 662, 663, 664, 665, 666, 706, 707, 710, 716, 718, 722, 727, 733,

736, 742, 746, 761, 762, 763, 767, 768, 769, 801, 802, 803, 815, 816, 833, 835, 836, 837, 838, 839, 841, 843, 844, 846, 847, 850, 853, 857, 859, 860, 861, 879, 880, 881, 905, 909, 918, 919, 920, 921, 924, 925, 926, 948, 949, 950, 957, 958, 960, 964, 966, 968, 993, 996, 997, 998, 1002, 1003, 1004, 1005, 1009, 1010, 1011, 1023, 1026, 1028, 1029, 1031, 1032, 1033, 1034, 1035, 1054, 1068, 1073, 1075, 1079, 1081, 1087, 1088, 1090, 1098, 1103, 1104, 1108.
MENDIS, Louis Rohan Duleep; b Colombo 25 Aug 1952; (79) 22, 25, 62, 68, 144, 145, 149, 150, 151, 156, 157, 158, 187, 188, 193, 194, 195, 196, 198, 201, 206, 211, 214, 217, 256, 257, 258, 261, 262, 274, 275, 286, 287, 288, 291, 292, 294, 295, 297, 298, 299, 310, 313, 332, 333, 334, 335, 336, 337, 338, 368, 369, 370, 375, 377, 378, 379, 383, 401, 404, 405, 407, 408, 409, 410, 411, 451, 457, 460, 464, 467, 472, 521, 528, 530, 533, 534, 564, 565.
*MENDIS, Manimeldura Chaminda; b Galle 28 Dec 1968; (1) 991.
*MUNASINGHE, Arachchige Manjula Nishantha; b Colombo 10 Dec 1971; (5) 905, 1028, 1029, 1031, 1036.
MURALITHARAN, Muthiah; b Kandy 17 Apr 1972; (49) 834, 835, 836, 837, 841, 847, 850, 853, 857, 880, 881, 916, 917, 918, 950, 958, 964, 966, 968, 989, 990, 991, 993, 997, 998, 1003, 1005, 1006, 1009, 1010, 1011, 1023, 1026, 1028, 1029, 1054, 1068, 1073, 1075, 1079, 1081, 1087, 1088, 1090, 1098, 1103, 1104, 1106, 1108.

*OPATHA, Antony Ralph Marinon; b Colombo 5 Aug 1947; (5) 22, 25, 30, 62, 68.

*PASQUAL, Sudath Prajiv; b Colombo 15 Oct 1961; (2) 62, 68.
*PERERA, Kahawelage Gamini; b Colombo 22 May 1964; (1) 368.
*PIERIS, Henry Sri Mevan; b Colombo 16 Feb 1946; (3) 22, 25, 30.
PUSHPAKUMARA, Karuppiahyage Ravindra; b Panadura 21 Jul 1975; (22) 880, 919, 948, 949, 950, 957, 958, 960, 964, 966, 989, 990, 1002, 1032, 1033, 1034, 1035, 1036, 1068, 1073, 1103, 1106.

RAMANAYAKE, Champaka Priyadarshi Hewage; b Colombo 8 Jan 1965; (62) 369, 370, 379, 489, 491, 493, 494, 495, 496, 497, 499, 513, 530, 533, 601, 630, 658, 659, 660, 662, 663, 664, 665, 666, 667, 706, 707, 708, 709, 710, 716, 718, 722, 727, 733, 736, 742, 746, 761, 762, 763, 801, 802, 803, 815, 816, 833, 834, 835, 838, 839, 841, 843, 844, 846, 857, 905, 909, 916, 996, 997, 998.
RANASINGHE, Anura Nandana; b Colombo 13 Oct 1956; (9) 22, 25, 30, 144, 145, 150, 151, 156, 157.
*RANASINGHE, Sirimewan Keerthi; b 4 Jul 1962; (4) 368, 369, 370, 378.
RANATUNGA, Arjuna; b Colombo 1 Dec 1963; (191) 145, 149, 150, 151, 193, 194, 195, 196, 198, 201, 206, 211, 214, 217, 256, 257, 258, 261, 262, 274, 275, 295, 297, 298, 299, 310, 313, 332, 333, 334, 335, 336, 337, 338, 368, 369, 370, 375, 377, 378, 379, 383, 401, 404, 405, 407, 408, 409, 410, 411, 451, 457, 460, 464, 467, 489, 491, 493, 494, 495, 496, 497, 499, 513, 515, 516, 521, 528, 530, 534, 564, 565, 575, 577, 580, 585, 588, 596,

RANATUNGA, A. (continued)
597, 598, 600, 601, 604, 605, 606, 623, 627, 630, 656,
657, 658, 659, 660, 662, 663, 664, 665, 666, 667, 716,
718, 722, 727, 733, 736, 742, 746, 761, 762, 763, 767,
768, 769, 801, 802, 803, 815, 816, 833, 834, 835, 836,
837, 838, 839, 841, 843, 844, 846, 847, 850, 853, 857,
859, 860, 861, 879, 880, 881, 916, 917, 918, 919, 920,
921, 924, 925, 926, 948, 949, 950, 957, 958, 960, 964,
966, 968, 989, 990, 991, 993, 996, 997, 998, 1002,
1003, 1004, 1005, 1006, 1009, 1010, 1011, 1023, 1026,
1034, 1035, 1036, 1054, 1068, 1073, 1075, 1079, 1081,
1087, 1088, 1090, 1098, 1103, 1104, 1106, 1108.

RANATUNGA, Dammika; b Colombo 12 Oct 1962; (4) 657,
658, 659, 660.

*RANATUNGA, Nishantha; b Gampaha 22 Jan 1966; (2)
802, 803.

RANATUNGA, Sanjeeva; b Colombo 25 Apr 1969; (12)
916, 917, 918, 919, 920, 924, 948, 949, 989, 990, 991,
1033.

*RATNAYAKE, Nilantha Lakshitha Kithsiri; b Colombo 22
Nov 1968; (2) 565, 601.

RATNAYAKE, Rumesh Joseph; b Colombo 2 Jan 1964;
(70) 158, 186, 187, 188, 193, 194, 195, 198, 201, 206,
211, 214, 217, 286, 287, 288, 291, 292, 294, 295, 297,
298, 299, 310, 313, 332, 333, 334, 335, 336, 337, 338,
368, 383, 401, 404, 405, 407, 408, 409, 410, 411, 451,
460, 464, 596, 597, 598, 600, 601, 604, 605, 606, 623,
627, 630, 656, 657, 658, 659, 660, 662, 664, 665, 666,
667, 850, 853, 857, 859.

RATNAYEKE, Joseph Ravindran; b Colombo 2 May 1960;
(78) 149, 150, 151, 156, 157, 158, 186, 187, 188, 196,
256, 257, 258, 261, 262, 274, 275, 286, 287, 291, 298,
299, 310, 313, 332, 333, 334, 335, 336, 338, 375, 377,
378, 379, 383, 404, 405, 407, 408, 409, 410, 411, 451,
457, 460, 464, 467, 472, 489, 491, 493, 494, 495, 496,
497, 499, 513, 515, 516, 521, 528, 530, 533, 534, 564,
565, 575, 577, 580, 585, 588, 596, 597, 598, 600, 623,
627, 630.

SAMARASEKERA, Maitipage Athula Rohitha; b Colombo
4 Aug 1961; (39) 198, 214, 375, 493, 497, 521, 528,
530, 533, 534, 564, 565, 575, 577, 580, 588, 596, 597,
598, 600, 601, 604, 605, 606, 623, 627, 630, 656, 708,
709, 710, 716, 718, 733, 736, 742, 746, 905, 909.

SAMARAWEERA, Dulip Prasanna; b Colombo 12 Feb
1972; (5) 844, 847, 861, 879, 881.

SENANAYAKE, Charith Panduka; b Colombo 19 Dec
1962; (7) 660, 662, 663, 664, 665, 666, 667.

SILVA, Kelaniyage Jayantha; b ?, Sri Lanka 2 Jun 1973; (1)
989.

SILVA, Sampathawaduge Amal Rohitha; b Moratuwa 12
Dec 1960; (20) 274, 275, 286, 287, 288, 291, 292, 294,
295, 297, 298, 299, 310, 313, 332, 333, 334, 335, 336,
337.

*TENNEKOON, Anura Punchi Banda; b Anuradhapura 29
Oct 1946; (4) 22, 25, 30, 62.

TILLEKERATNE, Hashan Prasantha; b Colombo 14 Jul
1967; (136) 401, 404, 405, 489, 491, 521, 530, 533,
564, 565, 577, 580, 585, 588, 596, 597, 598, 600, 601,
604, 605, 606, 623, 627, 630, 656, 657, 658, 659, 660,
662, 663, 664, 665, 666, 667, 706, 707, 708, 709, 710,
716, 718, 722, 727, 733, 736, 742, 746, 761, 762, 763,
767, 768, 769, 801, 802, 803, 815, 816, 833, 834, 836,

837, 838, 839, 841, 843, 844, 846, 847, 850, 853, 857,
859, 860, 861, 879, 880, 881, 905, 909, 916, 917, 919,
920, 921, 924, 925, 926, 948, 949, 950, 957, 964, 966,
968, 989, 990, 991, 993, 996, 997, 998, 1002, 1003,
1004, 1005, 1006, 1009, 1010, 1011, 1023, 1026, 1028,
1029, 1031, 1032, 1033, 1034, 1035, 1036, 1054, 1068,
1073, 1075, 1079, 1081, 1087, 1088, 1090, 1098, 1103,
1104, 1106, 1108.

*TISSERA, Michael Hugh; b Colombo 23 Mar 1939; (3) 22,
25, 30.

*UPASHANTA, Kalutarage Eric Amila; b Kurunegala 10
Jun 1972; (3) 1004, 1011, 1033.

VAAS, Warnakulasuriya Patabendige Ushantha Chaminda Joseph; b Colombo 27 Jan 1974; (53) 879,
880, 881, 905, 909, 917, 918, 919, 920, 921, 924,
925, 926, 948, 949, 950, 957, 958, 960, 964, 966,
968, 989, 990, 991, 993, 996, 997, 998, 1003, 1023,
1026, 1028, 1029, 1031, 1032, 1033, 1034, 1035,
1036, 1054, 1068, 1073, 1075, 1079, 1081, 1087,
1088, 1090, 1098, 1103, 1104, 1108.

*VONHAGT, Dudley Marlon; b Kalutara 31 Mar 1965; (1)
299.

WARNAPURA, Bandula; b Rambukkana, Colombo 1 Mar
1953; (12) 22, 25, 30, 62, 68, 144, 145, 149, 150, 156,
157, 158.

WARNAWEERA, Khahakachchi Patabandige Jayananda;
b Matara 23 Nov 1960; (6) 658, 659, 660, 662, 664,
803.

*WEERAKKODY, Ajith Priyantha; b Colombo 1 Oct 1970;
(1) 909.

WETTIMUNY, Mithra de Silva; b Colombo 11 Jun 1951;
(1) 186.

WETTIMUNY, Sidath; b Colombo 12 Aug 1956; (35) 144,
145, 149, 150, 151, 156, 157, 158, 186, 187, 188, 193,
194, 195, 196, 198, 201, 206, 211, 214, 217, 256, 257,
258, 261, 262, 274, 275, 286, 287, 288, 292, 294, 298,
411.

*WETTIMUNY, Sunil Ramsay de Silva; b Colombo 2 Feb
1949; (3) 25, 62, 68.

*WICKREMARATNE, Ranasinghe Pattikirikoralalage
Aruna Hemantha; b Colombo 21 Feb 1971; (3) 838,
859, 860.

WICKREMASINGHE, Anguppulige Gamini Dayantha; b
Colombo 27 Dec 1965; (4) 767, 768, 769, 801.

WICKREMASINGHE, Gallage Pramoda; b Matara 14 Aug
1971; (83) 663, 706, 707, 710, 716, 718, 722, 727, 733,
736, 742, 746, 761, 762, 763, 767, 768, 769, 801, 802,
803, 815, 816, 833, 834, 835, 836, 837, 838, 839, 841,
843, 844, 846, 847, 850, 853, 857, 859, 860, 861, 879,
881, 916, 917, 918, 919, 920, 921, 924, 925, 926, 948,
949, 950, 957, 958, 960, 964, 966, 968, 1002, 1003,
1004, 1005, 1006, 1009, 1010, 1023, 1026, 1029, 1031,
1032, 1034, 1035, 1054, 1075, 1079, 1081, 1087, 1088,
1090, 1106.

WIJEGUNAWARDENE, Kapila Indaka Weerakkody; b
Colombo 23 Nov 1964; (26) 528, 530, 533, 534, 564,
575, 577, 580, 585, 588, 597, 598, 604, 605, 606, 656,
657, 667, 706, 707, 708, 709, 710, 716, 722, 746.

WIJESURIYA, Roger Garrad Christopher Ediriweera; b
Moratuwa 18 Feb 1960; (8) 149, 332, 333, 334, 335,
336, 337, 338.

ZIMBABWE (45 players)

* Denotes players who had not appeared in official Test matches before 28 September 1996.

ARNOTT, Kevin John; b Salisbury 8 Mar 1961; (13) 461, 466, 469, 471, 716, 720, 724, 743, 748, 800, 802, 814, 823.

BRAIN, David Hayden; b Salisbury 4 Oct 1964; (23) 764, 765, 766, 800, 802, 814, 822, 823, 824, 848, 850, 852, 854, 876, 877, 878, 948, 950, 951, 953, 954, 955, 1013.

BRANDES, Eddo Andre; b Port Shepstone, Natal, South Africa 5 Mar 1963; (30) 454, 466, 469, 471, 716, 720, 724, 728, 732, 738, 743, 748, 766, 800, 802, 814, 822, 823, 824, 854, 876, 877, 878, 951, 1013, 1044, 1046, 1049, 1054, 1102.

BRIANT, Gavin Aubrey; b Salisbury 11 Apr 1969; (5) 800, 802, 814, 823, 824.

*BROWN, Robin David; b Gatooma 11 Mar 1951; (7) 204, 212, 216, 220, 454, 456, 469.

BRUK-JACKSON, Glen Keith; b Salisbury 25 Apr 1969; (1) 878.

BURMESTER, Mark Greville; b Durban, South Africa 24 Jan 1968; (8) 728, 732, 738, 743, 764, 981, 982, 983.

BUTCHART, Iain Peter; b Bulawayo 9 May 1960; (20) 199, 204, 208, 212, 216, 220, 454, 456, 461, 466, 469, 471, 716, 720, 728, 732, 748, 848, 953, 955.

CAMPBELL, Alistair Douglas Ross; b Salisbury 23 Sep 1972; (39) 724, 728, 732, 743, 764, 802, 822, 823, 824, 848, 850, 852, 854, 876, 877, 878, 948, 949, 950, 951, 953, 954, 955, 981, 982, 983, 1012, 1013, 1044, 1045, 1046, 1049, 1054, 1061, 1066, 1072, 1102, 1105, 1106.

CARLISLE, Stuart Vance; b Salisbury 10 May 1972; (5) 981, 982, 983, 1045, 1046.

CROCKER, Gary John; b Bulawayo 16 May 1962; (6) 764, 765, 802, 822, 823, 824.

*CURRAN, Kevin Malcolm; b Rusape 7 Sep 1959; (11) 199, 204, 208, 212, 216, 220, 454, 456, 461, 466, 471.

*DAVIES, Sean Gerard; b Salisbury 15 Oct 1973; (4) 1044, 1045, 1046, 1049.

DEKKER, Mark Hamilton; b Gatooma 5 Dec 1969; (21) 765, 766, 800, 814, 822, 823, 824, 848, 850, 876, 877, 878, 948, 949, 950, 951, 953, 954, 955, 1102, 1105.

*DUERS, Kevin Gary; b Lusaka, Northern Rhodesia 30 Jun 1960; (6) 716, 724, 728, 732, 738, 743.

*ESSOP-ADAM, Ebrahim Ali; b Salisbury 16 Nov 1968; (1) 766.

*EVANS, Craig Neil; b Salisbury 29 Nov 1969; (15) 764, 765, 766, 1012, 1044, 1045, 1046, 1049, 1054, 1061, 1066, 1072, 1102, 1105, 1106.

*FLETCHER, Duncan Andrew Gwynne; b Salisbury 27 Sep 1948; (6) 199, 204, 208, 212, 216, 220.

FLOWER, Andrew; b Cape Town, South Africa 28 Apr 1968; (47) 716, 720, 724, 728, 732, 738, 743, 748, 764, 765, 766, 800, 802, 814, 822, 823, 824, 848, 850, 852, 854, 876, 877, 878, 948, 949, 950, 951, 953, 954, 955, 981, 982, 983, 1012, 1013, 1044, 1045, 1046, 1049, 1054, 1061, 1066, 1072, 1102, 1105, 1106.

FLOWER, Grant William; b Salisbury 20 Dec 1970; (37) 764, 765, 766, 800, 802, 814, 822, 823, 824, 848, 852, 854, 876, 877, 948, 949, 950, 951, 953, 954, 955, 981, 982, 983, 1012, 1013, 1044, 1045, 1046, 1049, 1054, 1061, 1066, 1072, 1102, 1105, 1106.

*HERON, Jack Gunner; b Salisbury 8 Nov 1948; (6) 199, 204, 208, 212, 216, 220.

*HOGG, Vincent Richard; b Salisbury 3 Jul 1952; (2) 199, 212.

HOUGHTON, David Laud; b Bulawayo 23 Jun 1957; (47) 199, 204, 208, 212, 216, 220, 454, 456, 461, 466, 469, 471, 716, 720, 724, 728, 732, 738, 743, 748, 764, 765, 766, 800, 802, 814, 822, 823, 824, 848, 850, 852, 854, 876, 877, 878, 948, 949, 950, 951, 953, 954, 981, 982, 983, 1012, 1013.

JAMES, Wayne Robert; b Bulawayo 27 Aug 1965; (11) 716, 720, 738, 748, 822, 877, 878, 950, 951, 953, 1106.

JARVIS, Malcolm Peter; b Fort Victoria 6 Dec 1955; (12) 456, 461, 466, 469, 471, 716, 720, 724, 738, 748, 981, 983.

LOCK, Alan Charles Ingram; b Marandellas 10 Sep 1962; (7) 1045, 1046, 1049, 1054, 1061, 1066, 1072.

*MARTIN, Gary Charles; b Marandellas 30 May 1966; (5) 948, 949, 951, 954, 955.

*MEMAN, Mohamed Ahmed; b Lundazi, Northern Rhodesia 26 Jun 1952; (1) 461.

OLONGA, Henry Khaaba; b Lusaka, Zambia 3 Jul 1976; (3) 1012, 1013, 1106.

*PATERSON, Grant Andrew; b Salisbury 9 Jun 1960; (10) 199, 204, 208, 212, 216, 220, 454, 456, 461, 466.

PEALL, Stephen Guy; b Salisbury 2 Sep 1970; (20) 765, 800, 814, 848, 850, 852, 854, 876, 948, 949, 950, 954, 955, 981, 982, 1044, 1054, 1061, 1066, 1072.

*PECKOVER, Gerald Edward; b Salisbury 2 Jun 1955; (3) 208, 216, 220.

PYCROFT, Andrew John; b Salisbury 6 Jun 1956; (20) 199, 204, 208, 212, 216, 220, 454, 456, 461, 466, 469, 471, 716, 720, 724, 728, 732, 738, 743, 748.

RANCHOD, Ujesh; b Salisbury 17 May 1969; (3) 766, 800, 802.

*RAWSON, Peter Walter Edward; b Salisbury 25 May 1957; (10) 199, 204, 208, 212, 216, 220, 454, 456, 469, 471.

RENNIE, John Alexander; b Fort Victoria 29 Jul 1970; (9) 848, 850, 852, 854, 876, 877, 878, 949, 950.

SHAH (*registered as* OMARSHAH), Ali Hassimshah; b Salisbury 7 Aug 1959; (28) 199, 204, 208, 454, 456, 461, 466, 469, 471, 720, 724, 728, 732, 738, 743, 748, 764, 765, 766, 800, 802, 814, 822, 824, 850, 852, 1102, 1105.

STRANG, Bryan Colin; b Bulawayo 9 Jun 1972; (10) 981, 982, 983, 1012, 1044, 1045, 1061, 1066, 1072, 1105.

STRANG, Paul Andrew; b Bulawayo 28 Jul 1970; (20) 951, 953, 954, 955, 981, 982, 983, 1012, 1013, 1044, 1045, 1046, 1049, 1054, 1061, 1066, 1072, 1102, 1105, 1106.

STREAK, Heath Hilton; b Bulawayo 16 Mar 1974; (29) 848, 850, 852, 854, 876, 877, 878, 948, 949, 950, 951, 953, 954, 955, 982, 983, 1012, 1013, 1044, 1045, 1046, 1049, 1054, 1061, 1066, 1072, 1102, 1105, 1106.

TRAICOS, Athanasios John; b Zagazig, Egypt 17 May 1947; (27) 199, 204, 208, 212, 216, 220, 454, 456, 461, 466, 469, 471, 716, 720, 724, 728, 732, 738, 743, 748, 764, 765, 766, 814, 822, 823, 824.

*WALLER, Andrew Christopher; b Salisbury 25 Sep 1959; (29) 454, 456, 461, 466, 469, 471, 716, 720, 724, 728, 732, 738, 743, 748, 764, 765, 848, 850, 852, 854, 948, 949, 1012, 1013, 1049, 1054, 1061, 1066, 1072.

*WHITTALL, Andrew Richard; b Umtali 28 Mar 1973; (1) 1106.

WHITTALL, Guy James; b Chipinga 5 Sep 1972; (28) 850, 852, 854, 876, 877, 878, 948, 949, 950, 953, 954, 955, 981, 982, 983, 1012, 1013, 1044, 1045, 1046, 1049, 1054, 1061, 1066, 1072, 1102, 1105, 1106.

WISHART, Craig Brian; b Salisbury 9 Jan 1974; (3) 1102, 1105, 1106.

BANGLADESH (32 players)

AKRAM Hussain KHAN; b Chittagong 1 Nov 1968; (9) 531, 533, 626, 628, 661, 663, 992, 993, 995.

ALAM TALUKDAR, Jahangir; b Dacca 19 Apr 1968; (2) 628, 661.

AMIN-UL-ISLAM Bulbul; b Dacca 2 Feb 1968; (10) 529, 531, 533, 626, 628, 661, 663, 992, 993, 995.

ANIS-UR-REHMAN; (1) 992.

ATHAR ALI KHAN; b Dacca 10 Feb 1962; (8) 529, 531, 533, 661, 663, 992, 993, 995.

AZHAR HUSSAIN Shantu; b Dacca 15 Mar 1964; (7) 529, 531, 533, 626, 628, 661, 663.

FAROOQ AHMED, b Dacca 24 Jul 1966; (5) 531, 533, 628, 661, 663.

FAROOQ CHOWDHURY; (2) 376, 377.

GAZI ASHRAF Hussain; (7) 376, 377, 529, 531, 533, 626, 628.

GHULAM FAROOQ Suru; (3) 529, 533, 626.

GHULAM Mohammad NOUSHER; b Dacca 6 Oct 1964; (9) 376, 377, 529, 531, 533, 626, 628, 661, 663.

HABIB-UL-BASHAR; (2) 993, 995.

HAFIZ-UR-REHMAN; (2) 376, 377.

HARUN-UR-RASHID Liton; (2) 529, 533.

HASIB-UL-HASSAN; (2) 993, 995.

INAM-UL-HAQ; b Comilla 27 Feb 1967; (7) 626, 628, 661, 663, 992, 993, 995.

JAHANGIR SHAH Badshah; (5) 376, 377, 529, 531, 626.

JAVED OMAR, Mohammad; (2) 992, 995.

KHALID MASUD; (3) 992, 993, 995.

MINHAZ-UL-ABEDIN Mannu; b Chittagong 25 Sep 1965; (12) 376, 377, 529, 531, 533, 626, 628, 661, 663, 992, 993, 995.

MOHAMMAD RAFIQ; (2) 992, 993.

NAIM-UR-REHMAN; (1) 995.

NASIR AHMED Nasu; b Dacca 1 Jan 1964; (7) 529, 531, 533, 626, 628, 661, 663.

NUR-UL-ABEDIN; b Chittagong 7 Sep 1964; (4) 376, 377, 661, 663.

RAFIQ ALAM; (2) 376, 377.

RAQUIB-UL-HASSAN; (2) 376, 377.

SAIF-UL-ISLAM; b Mymensingh 1 Apr 1969; (4) 663, 992, 993, 995.

SAJJAD AHMED; (2) 992, 993.

SAMI-UR-REHMAN; (2) 376, 377.

SHAHID-UR-REHMAN; (2) 376, 377.

WAHID-UL-GHANI; (1) 531.

ZAHID RAZZAK; (3) 529, 626, 628.

CANADA (13 players)

BAKSH, Shaukat; b Preysal, Trinidad 15 Mar 1940; (1) 70.

CALLENDER, Robert Grantley; b Christ Church, Barbados 2 Nov 1950; (2) 67, 70.

CHAPPELL, Christopher James David; b Toronto 12 Jul 1955; (3) 64, 67, 70.

DENNIS, Franklyn Anthony; b Kingston, Jamaica 26 Sep 1947; (3) 64, 67, 70.

HENRY, Cornelius Cyprian; b Vieux Fort, St Lucia 16 Sep 1956; (2) 64, 70.

MARSHALL, Cecil Alphonso; b Rio Claro, Trinidad 13 Sep 1939; (2) 64, 67.

MAURICETTE, Bryan Michael; b St Lucia 4 Sep 1946; (3) 64, 67, 70.

PATEL, Jitendra Motibhai; b Mbale, Uganda 26 Nov 1945; (3) 64, 67, 70.

SEALY, Glenroy Ricardo; b Barbados 11 Jun 1940; (3) 64, 67, 70.

STEAD, Martin Peter; b Vancouver 1 Jun 1958; (2) 64, 67.

TARIQ JAVED; b Sheikhupura, Pakistan 12 Jun 1949; (3) 64, 67, 70.

VALENTINE, John Nugent; b Montreal 20 Sep 1954; (3) 64, 67, 70.

VAUGHAN, John Cecil Beaumont; b St Andrew, Barbados 8 Jun 1945; (3) 64, 67, 70.

EAST AFRICA (14 players)

FRASAT ALI Mughal; (*Kenya*); b Lahore, Pakistan 31 Jul 1949; (3) 20, 24, 27.

HARILAL Raishi SHAH; (*Kenya*); b Nairobi, Kenya 14 Apr 1943; (3) 20, 24, 27.

JAWAHIR SHAH; (*Kenya*); b Nairobi, Kenya 1942; (3) 20, 24, 27.

McLEOD, Hamish; (*Zambia*); (2) 20, 27.

MEHMOOD QUARAISHY; (*Kenya*); b Kenya 4 Feb 1942; (3) 20, 24, 27.

MEHTA, Praful Swantilal; (*Tanzania*); b Dar-es-Salaam, Tanganyika 1941; (1) 24.

NAGENDA, John; (*Uganda*); b Gahim, Ruanda-Urundi 25 Apr 1938; (1) 20.

NANA, P.G.; (*Zambia*); b Northern Rhodesia 1933; (3) 20, 24, 27.

PRINGLE, Donald James; (*Kenya*); b Prestwich, Lancashire, England 1 May 1932; d near Nairobi, Kenya 4 Oct 1975; (2) 24, 27.

SETHI, Ramesh Kumar; (*Kenya*); b Kenya 4 Sep 1941; (3) 20, 24, 27.

SUMAR, Shiraz; (*Tanzania*); b Tanganyika 1950; (1) 20.

WALUSIMBA, Samuel; (*Uganda*); b Uganda 1948; (3) 20, 24, 27.

YUNUS BADAT; (*Zambia*); b Northern Rhodesia 1943; (2) 24, 27.

ZULFIQAR ALI; (*Kenya*); b Mombasa, Kenya 1947; (3) 20, 24, 27.

HOLLAND (13 players)

APONSO, Goniamalimage John Anthony Flavian; b Moratuwa, Ceylon 28 Oct 1952; (5) 1050, 1056, 1060, 1067, 1071.

BAKKER, Paul-Jan; b Vlaardingen 19 Aug 1957; (5) 1050, 1056, 1060, 1067, 1071.

CANTRELL, Peter Edward; b Gunnedah, New South Wales, Australia 28 Oct 1962; (5) 1050, 1056, 1060, 1067, 1071.

CLARKE, Nolan Ewatt; b St Michael, Barbados 22 Jun 1948; (5) 1050, 1056, 1060, 1067, 1071.

De LEEDE, Timotheus Bernardus Maria; b Leidschendam 25 Jan 1968; (5) 1050, 1056, 1060, 1067, 1071.

GOUKA, Erik Laurentius; b Schiedam 29 Jan 1970; (3) 1050, 1060, 1071.

JANSEN, Floris; b Voorburg 10 Jun 1962; (2) 1056, 1060.

LEFEVBRE, Roland Philippe; b Rotterdam 7 Feb 1963; (4) 1050, 1056, 1060, 1067.

LUBBERS, Steven William; b Curacao, West Indies 24 Mar 1953; (4) 1050, 1056, 1067, 1071.

SCHEWE, Marcelis Michaël Catharinus; b Wateringen 10 May 1969; (5) 1050, 1056, 1060, 1067, 1071.

Van NOORTWIJK, Klaas-Jan Jeroen; b Rotterdam 10 Jul 1970; (5) 1050, 1056, 1060, 1067, 1071.

Van OOSTEROM, Robert Frank; b The Hague, 16 Oct 1968; (2) 1067, 1071.

ZUIDERENT, Bastiaan; b Rotterdam 3 Mar 1977; (5) 1050, 1056, 1060, 1067, 1071.

KENYA (13 players)

ALI, Rajab; b Nairobi 19 Nov 1965; (5) 1051, 1057, 1061, 1064, 1073.

ASIF KARIM; b Mombasa 15 Dec 1963; (5) 1051, 1057, 1061, 1064, 1073.

CHUDASAMA, Dipak; b Mombasa 20 May 1963; (5) 1051, 1057, 1061, 1064, 1073.

MODI, Hitesh; b Kisumu 13 Oct 1971; (5) 1051, 1057, 1061, 1064, 1073.

ODOYO, Thomas; b Nairobi 12 May 1978; (4) 1051, 1057, 1061, 1064.

ODUMBE Edward Tito; b Kendub 19 May 1965; (5) 1051, 1057, 1061, 1064, 1073.

ODUMBE, Maurice; b Nairobi 15 Jun 1969; (5) 1051, 1057, 1061, 1064, 1073.

ONYANGO, Lameck; b Nairobi 22 Sep 1973; (1) 1073.

OTIENO, Kennedy; b Nairobi 11 Mar 1972; (5) 1051, 1057, 1061, 1064, 1073.

SUJI, Martin; b Nairobi 2 Jun 1971; (5) 1051, 1057, 1061, 1064, 1073.

TARIQ IQBAL; b Nairobi 3 Apr 1964; (2) 1061, 1064.

TIKOLO, David Lazaro; b Nairobi 27 Dec 1964; (3) 1051, 1057, 1073.

TIKOLO, Stephen Ogomji; b Nairobi 25 Jun 1971; (5) 1051, 1057, 1061, 1064, 1073.

UNITED ARAB EMIRATES (16 players)

ARSHAD LAIQ; b Karachi, Pakistan 28 Nov 1970; (6) 904, 908, 1048, 1052, 1058, 1062.

AZHAR SAEED, Syed; b Lahore, Pakistan 25 Dec 1968; (7) 904, 908, 1048, 1052, 1058, 1062, 1067.

DUKANWALA, Shaukat Fakirbhai; b Bombay, India 21 Jan 1957; (5) 1048, 1052, 1058, 1062, 1067.

IMTIAZ ABBASI; b Karachi, Pakistan 6 Feb 1968; (7) 904, 908, 1048, 1052, 1058, 1062, 1067.

MAZHAR HUSSAIN; b Lahore, Pakistan 25 Oct 1967; (7) 904, 908, 1048, 1052, 1058, 1062, 1067.

MEHRA, Vijay; b New York, USA , 17 Oct 1963; (6) 904, 908, 1048, 1052, 1062, 1067.

MOHAMMAD ASLAM; b Karachi, Pakistan 7 Sep 1961 (4) 1048, 1052, 1058, 1062.

MOHAMMAD ISHAQ; b Lahore, Pakistan 7 Mar 1963; (5) 904, 908, 1058, 1062, 1067.

MYLVAGANAM, Ganesh; b Colombo, Ceylon 1 Aug 1966; (3) 1048, 1052, 1058.

POONAWALLA, Riaz Husein; b Poona, India 8 May 1961; (2) 904, 908.

SAEED-AL-SAFFAR; b Dubai 31 Jul 1968; (1) 1067.

SALIM RAZA; b Lahore, Pakistan 5 Jul 1964; (6) 904, 908, 1052, 1058, 1062, 1067.

SAMARASEKERA, Johanne Abeyratne; b Colombo, Ceylon 22 Feb 1968; (7) 904, 908, 1048, 1052, 1058, 1062, 1067.

SHAHZAD ALTAF; b Lahore, Pakistan 6 Oct 1957; (2) 1048, 1067.

SOHAIL BUTT; b Lahore, Pakistan 6 Jun 1966; (2) 904, 908.

ZARAWANI, *Sultan* Mohammed; b Dubai 24 Jan 1961; (7) 904, 908, 1048, 1052, 1058, 1062, 1067.

VOID MATCHES

The following three matches were abandoned, declared void and replaced by matches begun and completed on the reserve day which followed immediately. They have not been included in the match or individual career records sections of this compendium (see *Preface*).

SINGER WORLD SERIES (1st Match – floodlit)

SRI LANKA v INDIA 1994-95

At R.Premadasa Stadium, Khettarama, Colombo on 4 September 1994.   No Result – match declared void and replayed (*LOI No. 921*).   Toss: Sri Lanka.

INDIA		Runs	Balls	4/6	SRI LANKA
M.Prabhakar	not out	3			S.Ranatunga
S.R.Tendulkar	not out	11			R.S.Mahanama
N.S.Sidhu					S.T.Jayasuriya
* M.Azharuddin					P.A.de Silva
V.G.Kambli					* A.Ranatunga
A.C.Bedade					H.P.Tillekeratne
Kapil Dev					R.S.Kalpage
† N.R.Mongia					† P.B.Dassanayake
J.Srinath					H.D.P.K.Dharmasena
A.Kumble					W.P.U.C.J.Vaas
R.K.Chauhan					G.P.Wickremasinghe
Extras	(lb 1, w 1)	2			
Total	(4 overs; 0 wickets)	16			

SRI LANKA	O	M	R	W
Wickremasinghe	2	0	9	0
Vaas	2	0	6	0

Umpires: B.L.Aldridge (*New Zealand*) and K.T.Francis.

SIXTH (WILLS) WORLD CUP (17th Match)

ZIMBABWE v KENYA 1995-96

At Moin-ul-Haq Stadium, Patna, India on 26 February 1996.   No Result – match declared void and replayed (*LOI No. 1061*).   Toss: Zimbabwe.

ZIMBABWE		Runs	Balls	4/6	KENYA
G.W.Flower	not out	25			D.Chudasama
A.C.Waller	c E.T.Odumbe b Ali	3			† Tariq Iqbal
G.J.Whittall	c M.Odumbe b E.T.Odumbe	12			K.Otieno
A.D.R.Campbell	lbw b E.T.Odumbe	0			S.O.Tikolo
*†A.Flower	not out	0			* M.Odumbe
C.N.Evans					H.Modi
H.H.Streak					E.T.Odumbe
P.A.Strang					T.Odoyo
S.G.Peall					Asif Karim
B.C.Strang					M.Suji
A.C.I.Lock					R.Ali
Extras	(lb 1, w 4)	5			
Total	(15.5 overs; 3 wickets)	45			

KENYA	O	M	R	W
Suji	5	1	11	0
Ali	5	0	14	1
E.T.Odumbe	2.5	0	8	2

FALL OF WICKETS
1-8, 2-44, 3-45.

Umpires: Khizer Hayat (*Pakistan*) and C.J.Mitchley (*South Africa*).

PAKISTAN v SRI LANKA 1995-96

At Singapore Cricket Club on 1 April 1996.   No Result – match declared void and replayed (*LOI No. 1087*).
Toss: Sri Lanka.

PAKISTAN		Runs	Balls	4/6	SRI LANKA
* Aamir Sohail	c Kaluwitharana b Vaas	22			S.T.Jayasuriya
Saeed Anwar	c Dharmasena b Vaas	3			† R.S.Kaluwitharana
Inzamam-ul-Haq	c Vaas b Ranatunga	15			A.P.Gurusinha
Ijaz Ahmed	not out	6			P.A.de Silva
Salim Malik	not out	6			* A.Ranatunga
Basit Ali					R.S.Mahanama
† Rashid Latif					H.P.Tillekeratne
Waqar Younis					H.D.P.K.Dharmasena
Saqlain Mushtaq					W.P.U.C.J.Vaas
Aqib Javed					G.P.Wickremasinghe
Mohammad Akram					M.Muralitharan
Extras	(w 2)	2			
Total	(10 overs; 3 wickets)	**54**			

SRI LANKA	O	M	R	W
Wickremasinghe	4	0	31	0
Vaas	3	1	11	2
Ranatunga	2	0	8	1
Dharmasena	1	0	4	0

FALL OF WICKETS
1-9, 2-32, 3-43.

Umpires: D.L.Orchard (*South Africa*) and R.B.Tiffin (*Zimbabwe*).